# The
# Bare Facts
# Video Guide

## Fifth Edition

Craig Hosoda

Additional copies of this book (volume purchases also available)
can be purchased from:

    The Bare Facts
    P.O. Box 3255
    Santa Clara, CA 95055-3255
    (408) 249-2021

    Internet e-mail: chosoda@aol.com

Cover Design:  Robert Steven Pawlak Design
               San Francisco, California.

ISBN 0-9625474-5-X

# HOW TO USE THIS BOOK

The book is divided into three sections: Actresses, Actors and Titles. In the People sections, everyone is listed alphabetically by last name. If a • appears in front of someone's name, it means they are new to this edition. Under each name are films, TV shows and magazines that a person has appeared in. The non-nudity titles are listed to help you remember who a particular person is. If they have appeared nude in a film or magazine, the title is in bold face. Following the title is the year the film was released, then the character name or article title. "n.a." for the character name is an abbreviation for "not available." Under the title is a • to ••• rating and the time or the page number the nudity occurs. Lastly, is a brief description of how the person appears in the scene.

In the Title section, Films or Made for Cable TV Movies that have nude scenes (of someone in the People section) are listed. Under each entry, are the cast and character names. All the nude scenes for each cast member are listed under their names. If a person is listed in the Title section, they have a listing in the Actor or Actress section. Note that a film can have more nude scenes than are listed—I only list nude scenes of people who are in the Actress or Actor section.

Time definitions:
| | |
|---|---|
| Very, very brief: | Need to use PAUSE to see one frame |
| Very brief: | Use SLOW MOTION to see under 1 second |
| Brief: | About 1 second |
| No comment: | 2 to 15 seconds |
| Long scene: | Longer than 15 seconds |

Rating definitions:
| | |
|---|---|
| • | Yawn. Usually too brief or hard to see for some reason. |
| •• | Okay. Check it out if you are interested in the person. |
| ••• | Wow! Don't miss it. The scene usually lasts for a while. |

The ratings are approximate guides to how much nudity an actor or actress has in a scene. More weight is given on how famous a person is, how well lit and clear the scene is, if it's a close shot and the length of time they stay still so you can see clearly. So if someone has an erotic love scene but they don't show any skin or they are topless but their backs are toward the camera, it won't get rated.

To help you find the nude scenes quickly and accurately, the location on video tape is specified in hours and minutes rather than counter numbers since different VCR's have different counters. The time starts at 0:00 after the last film company logo disappears (Universal, Paramount, etc.). It's easier to locate the scenes if you have a VCR that has a real-time counter.

In the descriptions, "breasts" means you see both breasts, "full frontal nudity" means you see both breasts and the pubic area, "lower frontal nudity" means you see the pubic area and "nude" means you see both breasts, the pubic area and the buns.

Actresses that have appeared nude in only one film and are never seen anywhere else are not included because this book helps you locate someone unclothed that you've seen somewhere else before. "One timer" actors are listed though, because without them, the Actors section would be woefully thin!

Some film titles have bold type with no descriptions and others have bold type with descriptions and no time. These are video tapes that readers have sent as additions that aren't on video tape or I haven't had time to verify. These titles are listed so as not to waste people's time sending me duplicate additions.

# INTRODUCTION

It used to be that people did nude scenes in films at the beginning of their careers trying to get their "big break." Once they established themselves, they announced they would not be doing any more nudity and hoped everyone would forget their earlier performances. Phoebe Cates for example. But more and more actors and actresses are surprising us by doing nude scenes later in their careers (Sigourney Weaver and Julie Andrews). Fortunately, there are a few who do nudity in just about every film they are in. Sylvia Kristel and Marilyn Chambers for example. This book compiles all of these unbashful actors and actresses into one reference to help you locate their nude scenes on video tape to save you time and money. I have listed a few close calls like Janine Turner in *Monkey Shines* and Christina Applegate in *Streets*.

Some actresses who have done *Playboy* and *Penthouse* pictorials are included because not all actresses do nude scenes in films. Unrevealing pictorials that would be rated PG are not listed (Janet Jones and Jayne Kennedy for example). I also include *Playboy* Special Edition magazines, like the *Book of Lingerie*, because there are some actresses who appear nude in them who are also in films. I haven't finished reviewing all of the magazine back issues in this edition but I will in future editions. I'm slow on the magazines because this is a guide for nude scenes on video tape, so magazines are not really supposed to be the focus.

Actresses that *look* like they have done nudity in films, but have used body doubles instead, are also noted. A body double is another person who is used for nude scenes when an actor or actress is too modest. You can usually spot a body double in a movie when there is a nude body without seeing a face.

Some filmographies (Marilyn Monroe, Elizabeth Taylor) are incomplete. Everyone knows who there actress are, so I try to save space by just listing the important things for them. For everyone else, I try to list all of their most recent work. Older, less well known films might get left off a person's filmography. If you need complete filmographies for people, please consult *The Motion Picture Guide* or some of the other reference books listed in the back of this book.

I have spent my time concentrating on getting the greatest *number* of people into this book as possible. Therefore, you'll find the entries for some people like Laura Gemser or Claudia Jennings, incomplete since it's relatively easy to locate films they have nude scenes in. Obviously, I haven't been able to view all the movies ever made (yet), so there will be films with nude scenes that I have missed. (I still haven't even started looking at Russ Meyers' films!)

I realize that I don't always use the best English in my descriptions, "Right breast making love." Please try not to laugh out loud too much! I'd rather be succinct and to the point, because I know this book isn't going to win a Pulitzer Prize.

If you find any mistakes or have additions, please write to me and they will be corrected in the next edition. I have a long list of nude scenes compiled from reader's letters which I need to verify because occasionally, scenes have been incorrectly remembered or have been cut from the film on the video release. There is no need to send *Playboy* and *Penthouse* magazine information, I have a friend who has back issues and I'll eventually include them.

I only review video tapes, not the theatrical release in movie theaters, so you won't see times for *Sirens* or *Color of Night* in this edition because they weren't on video tape when this book was being prepared. But you can be assured that they will be in the next edition!

Enjoy!

# THANKS, THANKS AND MORE THANKS!

First of all, I need to thank my wife, Marie, for her help and patience putting up with all my video tape viewing. I also need to thank my children, Christopher and Melanie, for taking their naps so I can watch video tapes. Thanks also to my parents and parents in-laws and the rest of my family for all their help and support.

Thank you to Dave Dell'Aquila of Rae Technology, Inc. who is my 4th Dimension Consultant. Without his help, I couldn't have set up the database, imported the data or generated the Title cross reference section of this book. Also thank you to Ron Dell'Aquila of Protron D.C. who programmed the export from 4th Dimension into FrameMaker. Thank you to both Dave and Ron for their continued support.

Thanks to Nelson and Nona Si of Videoscope in Palo Alto. They have been in the video rental business since 1982 and are an excellent local source for renting hard-to-find video tapes. Thanks to Seema and Pankaj Shah from American Video Center in Santa Clara and Bill Siep from American Video Center in San Jose. Thanks to Irv Slifkin and Greg Romankiw/Roman Video for letting me borrow some of their hard-to-find video tapes.

Thanks to all my friends who have helped:
Jim Chase, Deanna Dean, Amir Ferdowsali, Heather King, Holly King, David Muscara, Huu-Quyen Ngo, Emily Nguyen, Mike Santomauro and Monica Zadworski.

Thanks to the personalities who have provided information or answered questions:
Avalon Anders, Michelle Bauer, Venus De Light, Deborah Dutch, Leslie Glass, Ellen Greene, Lauren Hays, Lené Hefner, Amelia Kinkade, Shawn Lusader, Pia Reyes, Suzi Simpson, Brinke Stevens, Julie Strain, Jennifer Tilly, Wally Anne Wharton, Frank and Ona Zee.

Thanks to all the business relations who have helped:
Ari Bass, Rick Bitzelberger/General Media Entertainment, Tony Borg/Playboy Video, Ken Boxer, Scott Brastow/Pacific Media Entertainment, Thomas Burford/Celebrity Access, Tony Chiu/People Magazine, John Cross/Hot Body International, S. C. Dacy, David DeCoteau/Cinema Home Video, Lynn Donahue/Playboy Entertainment Group, Inc, Robert Dyke/Magic Lantern Productions, James Erlich/ICFX Inc., Donald Farmer, John Fitzwater/Blockbuster Catalog Divison, Dean Goldfarb/DG Distributors Inc., Bruce Kluger/Playboy Enterprises, Inc., Barry A. Leshtz/Playboy Video, Laura Malek/Playboy Enterprises, David and Svetlana Marsh/Marsh Entertainment Group, Dan O'Day, Mark Ouimet/Publishers Group West, Robb Pawlak, Jim Pehling/Consolidated Printers, Stephanie Ponce/Imperial Entertainment, Stephanie Pressman/Frog On The Moon, Ed Rasen/ERI, Fred Olen Ray/American Independent Productions, Neil Reshen/Media Management, Dawn Reshen-Doty/Media Management, Bert Rhine/Bert Rhine Productions, Bill Saunders/Beachball Entertainment Productions, Norman Scherer/Video Oyster, James E. Singer/Lone Wolf Ink, Deborah Sleezer/Playboy Video, Rick Sloane/Rick Sloane Productions, Susan Theriot/Time Warner Viewer's Edge, Stuart Wall, Jim Wynorski, and Bernadette Zaborski/Time Warner Viewer's Edge

Thanks to all the media people who have enabled me to spread word about *The Bare Facts* through newspapers, magazines, radio and television:
Marty Burden/New York Post, Paul Donnelley/Dataday Productions, Mark Dylan/The Home Front, Liam Fay/Hot Press, LeeAnn Goodwin/Les Publications Condé Nast S.A., Steve Hirano/Transpacific Magazine, Richard Kadrey/Future Sex Magazine, Gersh Kuntzman/New York Post, Thomas Lenthal/French Glamour, Jeff Rosen/Gay Chicago Magazine, Dave Saltonstall/New York Daily News, and Michael J. Weldon/Psychotronic Video.

# THANKS TO MY CONTRIBUTORS

Thanks to all the people who have sent me additions and corrections:

A very special thank you to Erich Mees who has provided a lot of hard to find information for the book.

These individuals have gone beyond the call of duty:
Raj Bahanda, Nicolas Barbano, Matt Bear, Herbert S. Block, José X. Bonastre, Robert F. Bradford, Wallace C. Clopton, Edward Dolan, Samuel K. Drew, Anders Engstrom, Matthew Goodman, Tim Greaves, Dave Grubka, Kevin K., Donald C. R. Lort, Phil Penne, H. C. Roth, George M. St. George, David Stephens, Ed Sutton, Jesse Thurber, Leonard Van Horne and Francis Verwerft.

A big thank you also to:
Mario Ableitner, Paul A. Alter, Milwaukee Bart, Robert Bell, Jim Bigg, L. Ray Black, Bobby-Joe, Larry Booty, James H. Buffington, Joe Burns, Daniel Cantey, Tom Cipullo, Kris Clark, "Cowtown" Charlie, Earl G. Daggett, John Daniels, Alfonso del Grando, Jr., Don Douglas, Peter Downes, Steve Draper, Todd Dudek, Daniel J. Dudych, Scott Dunham, Alvin Easter, Joseph P. Falco, Curtis D. Farley, Fred Floreth, Fred From Mars, David Furr, Ward Gambrell, Robert C. Gilleo, J. D. Green, Rodney Eric Griffith, W. H. Groenheijde, C. P. Hall II, Mike Hamilton, Christopher Hobbs, Daniel Hutter, John W. Johnson, Joe Paul Jones, Rex Joyner, Jodie M. Kingsley, Wayne A. Kingsley, Victor J. Lejarde, Joseph Lobosco, Philip Long, Jay Lounsbury, Michael Lutz, James W. Marcel, Jr., James Marshall, Gary McClellan, Raymond L. McDonald, John McDougall, Paul Mewborn, Mike Minnich, Fritz Moore, Bryan F. Moose, Marc Moris, Tom Neet, Jr., J. Nelson, Otomo, Gordon Panei, Dennis Parish, Robin Phillips, John Reeks, Fred Reischl, Dan Rontello, Erick "Ricky" Donald Rosenholm, Jay Runge, T. L. Ruppe, Jake Satre, Mike Sawyers, Terry Scoggin, F. F. Scott, Norman Sean, Freeman Seyler, Jr., John Thomas Smith, Philip Smith, Allen Stenhouse, Scot W. Stevenson, Richard A. Stoll, Jr., John Tompkins, Chuck Torbyn, M. Rory Waite, John Weimer, Brian A. White, Richard A. White, Robbie White and Gary Whitehead.

Note: If you send additions and/or corrections and don't want your name printed in the next edition, please use a pseudonym like "Cowtown" Charlie above.

# RANDOM NOTES

We are still planning on making a CD-ROM version of *The Bare Facts Video Guide*. It will include all the data you see in this book in addition to all the "one timer", close call and body double actresses who are currently not published in the book. You'll be able to do keyword searches on descriptions to quickly locate scenes with your favorite diversions (for example: find all scene descriptions with the word "stockings" in them). The PC version of the CD-ROM will depend on how quickly ACI makes the Windows version of 4th Dimension available.

If you are interested in the CD-ROM, please write to The Bare Facts at the address in the front of this book and let us know what type of computer you have (Macintosh or PC). We'll put your name on our confidential mailing list and notify you when it's ready.

# Actresses

## Aames, Angela
*Films:*
**Fairytales** (1979). . . . . . . . . . . . . . . . . . Little Bo Peep
••• 0:14—Nude with The Prince in the woods.
**H.O.T.S.** (1979) . . . . . . . . . . . . . . .Boom-Boom Bangs
*a.k.a. T & A Academy*
• 0:21—Breasts parachuting into pool.
• 0:39—Breasts in bathtub playing with a seal.
• 1:33—Breasts while playing football.
**...All the Marbles** (1981). . . . . . . . . . . . . . . . .Louise
*a.k.a. The California Dolls*
•• 0:20—Breasts in Peter Falk's motel room talking with
Iris, then sitting on the bed.
**The Best of Sex and Violence** (1981). . Little Bo Peep
• 0:18—Brief breasts in scene from *Fairytales*.
• 0:20—Brief right breast in scene from *Fairytales*.
**Famous T & A** (1982) . . . . . . . . . . . . . . Little Bo Peep
(No longer available for purchase, check your video
store for rental.)
•• 0:50—Breasts scene from *Fairytales*.
**The Lost Empire** (1983) . . . . . . . . . Heather McClure
••• 0:31—Breasts and buns taking a shower while Angel
and White Star talk to her.
Scarface (1983). . . . . . . . . .Woman at the Babylon Club
Bachelor Party (1984) . . . . . . . . . . . . . . . .Mrs. Klupner
**Basic Training** (1984). . . . . . . . . . . . . . . . . Cheryl
• 0:19—Brief breasts in bathtub.
Chopping Mall (1986) . . . . . . . . . . . . . . .Miss Vanders
*a.k.a. Killbots*

## Abigail
*Films:*
Alvin Purple (1973; Australian) . . . . Girl in See-Through
0:01—On bus in see-through top. Hard to see any-
thing.
**Alvin Rides Again** (1974; Australian) . . . . . . . . . Mae
••• 0:12—Breasts in store with Alvin.
**The Adventures of Eliza Fraser** (1976; Australian)
. . . . . . . . . . . . . . . . . . . . . . . . . . . . . . . .Buxom Girl
• 0:01—Breasts when Martin pulls the sheets off her.
Breaking Loose (1988; Australian) . . . . . . . . . . . . Helen

## Able, Sheri
*Films:*
**The Evil Below** (1991) . . . . . . . . . . . . . . . . . . . . Tracy
• 0:10—Buns, in two piece swimsuit on boat.
0:16—In wet T-shirt getting on boat after diving.
• 0:21—Right breast, with Max behind curtain. Hard
to see.
Ultimate Desires (1991). . . . . . . . . . . . .Carlos' Girlfriend
*a.k.a. Silhouette*

## Abril, Victoria
*Films:*
Comin' At Ya! (1982) . . . . . . . . . . . . . . . . . . . . Abilene
**The Moon in the Gutter** (1983; French/Italian)
. . . . . . . . . . . . . . . . . . . . . . . . . . . . . . . . . . . . . Bella
*a.k.a. La Lune dans Le Caniveau*
• 0:28—Left breast, while riding on swing and getting
felt by Gérard Depardieu.
•• 1:26—Breasts, while lying in bed. Dark.
••• 1:27—Nude, getting out of bed and arguing with
Depardieu. Long scene. Subtitles get in the way
sometimes.
• 1:50—Upper half of right breast, popping out of the
top of her dress when Depardieu leans her back on
the counter.
**On the Line** (1984; Spanish) . . . . . . . . . . . . Engracia
••• 0:16—Breasts getting undressed to make love with
Mitch.
• 0:29—Very brief breasts, making love in bed with
Mitch.
0:54—In white lingerie getting dressed.
L'Addition (1985; French). . . . . . . . . . . . . . . . . . Patty
**Padre Nuestro** (1985) . . . . . . . . . . . . . . . . Cardenala
**Tie Me Up! Tie Me Down!** (1990; Spanish)
. . . . . . . . . . . . . . . . . . . . . . . . . . . . Marina Osorio
••• 0:24—Full frontal nudity playing with a frogman toy
in the bathtub.
• 0:34—Buns and brief side of right breast, getting
dressed.
•• 0:44—Breasts while changing clothes, then on TV
while Maximo watches.
•• 1:09—Breasts while changing clothes.
••• 1:16—Right breast, then breasts while making love
in bed with Ricky.
**High Heels** (1991; Spanish) . . . . . . . . . Rebecca Giner
• 0:31—Breasts, when her dress falls down slightly
while hanging on a pole and making love with Lethal.
**Lovers** (1992; Spanish) . . . . . . . . . . . . . . . . . . . Luisa
*a.k.a. Amantes*
Jimmy Hollywood (1993) . . . . . . . . . . . . . . . . . . . n.a.
Kika (1994; Spanish) . . . . . . . . . . . . . .Andrea Scarface
*Magazines:*
**Playboy** (Nov 1987) . . . . . . . . . . Sex in Cinema 1987
• 143—Breasts in bed from *Padre Nuestro*.
**Playboy** (Nov 1992) . . . . . . . . . . Sex in Cinema 1992
• 147—Buns, from *Amantes (Lovers)*.

## Ackerman, Leslie
*Films:*
The First Nudie Musical (1979) . . . . . . . . . . . . . Susie
**Hardcore** (1979) . . . . . . . . . . . . . . . . . . . . . . .Felice
• 0:44—Breasts in porno house with George C. Scott.
Blame It on the Night (1984). . . . . . . . . . . . . . Shelly
*TV:*
Skag (1980) . . . . . . . . . . . . . . . . . . . .Barbara Skagska

## Adams, Brooke

*Films:*
Shock Wave (1977) . . . . . . . . . . . . . . . . . . . . . . . Rose
Days of Heaven (1978) . . . . . . . . . . . . . . . . . . . . Abby
**Invasion of the Body Snatchers** (1978)
. . . . . . . . . . . . . . . . . . . . . . . . . . Elizabeth Driscoll
    0:49—All covered in pod gunk in her bedroom
    when Donald Sutherland discovers her. Don't really
    see anything.
  •• 1:43—Brief breasts behind plants when Sutherland
    sees her change into a pod person. Hard to see be-
    cause plants are in the way.
  • 1:48—Breasts walking through the pod factory
    pointing out Sutherland to everybody. Long shot,
    hard to see.
Cuba (1979) . . . . . . . . . . . . . . . . . . . . .Alexandra Pulido
Tell Me a Riddle (1980) . . . . . . . . . . . . . . . . . . .Jeannie
The Dead Zone (1983) . . . . . . . . . . . . . Sarah Bracknell
Utilities (1983) . . . . . . . . . . . . . . . . . . . . . . . Marion
Almost You (1984) . . . . . . . . . . . . . . . . . Erica Boyer
**Key Exchange** (1985) . . . . . . . . . . . . . . . . . . . . .Lisa
    0:10—Nude on bicycle with her boyfriend, but you
    can't see anything because of his strategically placed
    arms.
  • 0:45—Very brief right breast getting into the shower
    with her boyfriend, then hard to see behind the
    shower curtain.
**The Unborn** (1991). . . . . . . . . . . . . . .Virginia Marshall
  • 1:12—Right breast, while breast feeding her baby
    creature.
Gas Food Lodging (1992) . . . . . . . . . . . . . . . . . . .Nora
*Made for Cable Movies:*
The Last Hit (1993; USA) . . . . . . . . . . . . . . . . .Anna
*Miniseries:*
Lace (1984) . . . . . . . . . . . . . . . . . . . . . . . . . . .Pagan
Lace II (1985) . . . . . . . . . . . . . . . . . . . . . . . . .Pagan
*Made for TV Movies:*
Bridesmaids (1989) . . . . . . . . . . . . . . . . . . . . . Pat
Stephen King's "Sometimes They Come Back" (1991)
. . . . . . . . . . . . . . . . . . . . . . . . . . . . . . . . . . Sally
*TV:*
O.K. Crackerby (1965-66) . . . . . . . . . Cynthia Crackerby

## Adams, Maud

*Films:*
The Christian Licorice Store (1971) . . . Cynthia Vicstrom
**The Girl in Blue** (1973; Canadian) . . . . . . .Paula/Tracy
  *a.k.a. U-turn*
  • 1:16—Side view of right breast, while sitting on bed
    with Scott.
    1:19—In two piece swimsuit getting out of lake.
The Man with the Golden Gun (1974; British)
. . . . . . . . . . . . . . . . . . . . . . . . . . . . Andrea Anders
Killer Force (1975; Swiss/Irish) . . . . . . .Claire Chambers
Rollerball (1975) . . . . . . . . . . . . . . . . . . . . . . . . Ella
Laura (1979) . . . . . . . . . . . . . . . . . . . . . . . . . Sarah
  *a.k.a. Shattered Innocence*

**Tattoo** (1981) . . . . . . . . . . . . . . . . . . . . . . . . . .Maddy
  • 0:22—Very brief breasts taking off clothes and put-
    ting a bathrobe on.
  •• 0:23—Breasts opening bathrobe so Bruce Dern can
    start painting.
  •• 0:25—Brief breasts getting into the shower to take
    off body paint.
  •• 0:58—Brief breasts and buns getting out of bed.
  •• 1:04—Breasts, knocked out on table before Dern
    starts tattooing her.
  ••• 1:07—Breasts looking at herself in the mirror with a
    few tattoos on.
  •• 1:24—Breasts lying on table masturbating while
    Dern watches through peep hole in the door.
  ••• 1:36—Full frontal nudity taking off robe then mak-
    ing love with Dern (her body is covered with tat-
    toos).
Target Eagle (1982) . . . . . . . . . . . . . . . . . . . . .Carmen
Octopussy (1983; British) . . . . . . . . . . . . . . . Octopussy
    1:06—Very brief nude getting out of swimming pool
    while Bond watches. Long, long shot.
Hell Hunters (1985) . . . . . . . . . . . . . Amanda Hoffman
Nairobi Affair (1986) . . . . . . . . . . . . . . . . .Anne Malone
Jane and the Lost City (1987; British) . . . . . . Lola Pagola
The Women's Club (1987) . . . . . . . . . . . . . . Angie Blake
    0:17—In black panties, garter belt and stockings
    making out with Michael Paré.
Angel III: The Final Chapter (1988). . . . . . . . . . Nadine
Intimate Power (1989) . . . . . . . . . . . . . . . . . Sineperver
The Kill Reflex (1990) . . . . . . . . . . . . . . .Crystal Tarver
Silent Night, Deadly Night 4: Initiation (1990) . . . . Fima
*Made for TV Movies:*
Playing for Time (1980) . . . . . . . . . . . . . . . . . . . Mala
*TV:*
Chicago Story (1982). . . . . . . . . . . Dr. Judith Bergstrom
Emerald Point N.A.S. (1983-84) . . . . . . . . Maggie Farrell
*Magazines:*
**Playboy** (Oct 1981) . . . . . . . . . . . . . Tattooed Woman
  ••• 100-107—Breasts photos from *Tattoo.*
**Playboy** (Dec 1981) . . . . . . . . . . . . . Sex Stars of 1981
    238—Right breast, holding pink robe against her-
    self.
**Playboy** (Aug 1983) . . . . . .The Spy They Love To Love
    92—Breasts on pier.
**Playboy** (Sep 1987) . . . . . . . . .25 Years of James Bond
  •• 131—Left breast.

## Adams, Stephanie

*Video Tapes:*
**Playboy Video Calendar 1994** (1993) . . . . . . . . April
  ••• 0:15—Nude with brightly colored props in studio.
  ••• 0:17—Nude (down to stockings and garter belt) in
    hot office fantasy.
**Playboy's Playmate Review 1993** (1993)
. . . . . . . . . . . . . . . . . . . . . . . . . . . . Miss November
  ••• 0:12—Nude in house and in bed.
*Magazines:*
**Playboy** (Nov 1992) . . . . . . . . . . . . . . . . . . Playmate
  ••• 114-125—Nude.

**Playboy's Playmate Review** (Jun 1993) . . November
••• 92-99—Nude.
**Playboy's Book of Lingerie** (Jul 1993) . . . . . . Herself
•• 18—Buns.
**Playboy's Wet & Wild Women** (Aug 1993) . . Herself
••• 64-65—Nude.
**Playboy's Blondes, Brunettes & Redheads**
(Sep 1993) . . . . . . . . . . . . . . . . . . . . . . . . . . Herself
•• 62—Right breast.
**Playboy's Book of Lingerie** (Sep 1993) . . . . . Herself
• 97—Inner half of breasts.
**Playboy's Book of Lingerie** (Nov 1993) . . . . . Herself
8—Right breast under sheer material.
• 34—In sheer white bodysuit.
• 96—Buns.
**Playboy's Book of Lingerie** (Jan 1994) . . . . . . Herself
• 9—Partial left breast.
Playboy's Book of Lingerie (Mar 1994) . . . . . . . . Herself

# •Adams, Stephanie
*Adult Films:*
Centerfold Strippers (1994). . . . . . . . . . . . . . . . . .n.a.
*Magazines:*
**Penthouse** (Jan 1988) . . . . . . . . . . . . . . . . . . . . . . Pet

# Adams, Tracey
See: Blaisdell, Deborah.

# •Adell, Traci
*Video Tapes:*
**Playboy Video Centerfold: Anna-Marie Goddard**
(1994). . . . . . . . . . . . . . . . . . . . .Runner-Up Playmate
••• 0:43—Nude in lingerie in sequence with a small
pool and chair.
*Magazines:*
**Playboy** (Jul 1994). . . . . . . . . . . . . . . . . . . . Playmate
••• 94-105—Nude.

# Adjani, Isabelle
*Films:*
Story of Adele H. (1975; French). . . . . . . . . Adele Hugo
The Tenant (1976; French) . . . . . . . . . . . . . . . . Stella
The Driver (1978) . . . . . . . . . . . . . . . . . . . . .The Player
The Bronte Sisters (1979; French) . . . . . . . . . . . Emily
Nosferatu, The Vampire (1979; French/German)
. . . . . . . . . . . . . . . . . . . . . . . . . . . . . . Lucy Harker
**Possession** (1981; French/German). . . . . . Anna/Helen
• 0:04—Breasts in bed.
• 0:16—Breasts lying in bed when Sam Neill pulls the
covers over her.
••• 0:47—Right breast, then breasts lying in bed with
Neill.
• 1:08—Right breast, while lying on the floor with
Neill, then sitting up.
**Quartet** (1981; British/French) . . . . . . . . . Marya Zelli
•• 1:06—Breasts in bed with Alan Bates.
**Next Year if All Goes Well** (1983; French) . . .Isabelle
• 0:27—Brief right breast, lying in bed with Maxime.

**One Deadly Summer** (1984; French) . . . . . . . . .Eliane
•• 0:21—Brief breasts changing in the window for Florimond.
••• 0:32—Nude, walking in and out of the barn.
• 0:36—Brief left breast lying in bed when Florimond
gets up.
• 0:40—Buns and breasts taking a bath.
• 1:41—Part of right breast, getting felt up by an old
guy, then right breast then brief breasts.
•• 1:47—Breasts in bedroom with Florimond.
1:49—In white bra and panties talking with Florimond.
Subway (1985; French) . . . . . . . . . . . . . . . . . . . .Helena
**Ishtar** (1987) . . . . . . . . . . . . . . . . . . . . . . Shirra Assel
• 0:27—Very brief left breast flashing herself to Dustin
Hoffman at the airport while wearing sunglasses.
Camille Claudel (1989; French) . . . . . . . Camille Claudel

# Agbayani, Tetchie
*Films:*
**The Dolls** . . . . . . . . . . . . . . . . . . . . . . . . . . . . . Lee
*a.k.a. The Story of the Dolls*
• 0:12—Brief right breast, several times, while fighting
with Pedro on the beach.
••• 0:24—Breasts and buns, while undressing and taking a bubble bath with the other models.
••• 0:39—Buns and right breast, then full fronal nudity
while posing on beach for Tom.
••• 0:41—Full frontal nudity, while making love on the
beach with Tom.
•• 0:57—Buns, while making love with Tom.
• 0:58—Breasts in magazine photos.
• 1:01—Brief breasts in magazine photos.
• 1:03—Nude in magazine photos.
•• 1:04—Nude, while running on beach in flashback.
• 1:10—Very brief right breast, during tribal ceremony.
••• 1:12—Breasts, getting paint taken off her in bed,
then sitting up.
• 1:24—Brief buns, while on the ground with Tom.
**The Emerald Forest** (1985). . . . . . . . . . . . . . . Caya
• 1:48—Breasts in the river when Kachiri is match
making all the couples together.
Gymkata (1985). . . . . . . . . . . . . . . . . .Princess Rubali
The Money Pit (1986) . . . . . . . . . . . . . . . . . . . .Florinda
**Rikky & Pete** (1988; Australian). . . . . . . . . . . . Flossie
• 0:58—Brief upper half of left breast in bed with Pete
when Rikky accidentally sees them in bed.
••• 1:30—Breasts in black panties dancing outside the
jail while Pete watches from inside.
Mission Manila (1989) . . . . . . . . . . . . . . . . . . . . .Maria
Indio 2: The Revolt (1990) . . . . . . . . . . . . .Mrs. Morrell
Deathfight (1993) . . . . . . . . . . . . . . . . . . . . . . . . . n.a.

# Ager, Suzanne
a.k.a. Amy Page.
*Films:*
Crocodile Dundee II (1988) . . . . . . . . . . . . . . . Hooker

The Alien Within (1990) . . . . . . . . . . . . . . . . Erin West
Contains footage from *The Evil Spawn* woven together
with new material.

Mob Boss (1990). . . . . . . . . . . . . . . . . . . . . . . Pool Girl

Shock 'Em Dead (1990) . . . . . . . . . . . . . . . . Groupie 3

**Smooth Talker** (1990) . . . . . . . Candy (The 976-GIRL)
- 0:23—Left breast and partial buns, while lying on
  the floor dead.
- 0:24—More left breast, while lying dead on the
  floor. Lit with red light.
- 0:35—Left breast, while lying dead on the floor. Very
  brief buns in G-string.

**Angel Eyes** (1991). . . . . . . . . . . . . . . . . .Nurse Stewart

Camp Fear (1991). . . . . . . . . . . . . . . . . . . . . . . . . .n.a.
*a.k.a. Millenium Countdown*

**Evil Toons** (1991) . . . . . . . . . . . . . . . . . . . . . . . Terry
- •• 0:31—Breasts and buns in G-string, taking off
  clothes to put on her pajamas.
- •• 1:09—Right breast, while on the floor getting her
  pajamas ripped open by Roxanne.
- •• 1:10—Brief breasts when Roxanne rips the pajamas
  all the way down.

Inner Sanctum (1991). . . . . . . . . . . . . . . . . .Maureen

**Little Devils** (1991). . . . . . . . . . . . . . . . . . . . . . . .n.a.

**The Bikini Carwash Company** (1992) . . . . . . . . Foxy
(Unrated version reviewed.)
- 0:59—Buns in G-string, doing strip routine.

**Buford's Beach Bunnies** (1992) . . . .Boopsie Underall
- •• 0:19—Breasts in the shower.
- 0:20—Brief breasts when her towel falls off in front
  of telegram guy.
- 0:36—Buns, in red two piece swimsuit at the beach.
- 0:37—Buns, while walking up the stairs.
- 0:38—In white lingerie in her bedroom with Jeeter.

**Fatal Justice** (1992) . . . . . . . . . . . . . . . . . . . . . Diana
- ••• 0:12—In black body suit, then breasts and buns in
  G-string while making love with her boyfriend.
- 0:36—Breasts while changing clothes behind room
  divider. Hard to see.

# • *Aguilar, Orietta*

*Films:*

La Ruletera (1987; Mexican) . . . . . . . . . . . . . . . . . . . .n.a.

**Barbarian Queen II: The Empress Strikes Back**
(1989). . . . . . . . . . . . . . . . . . . . . . . . . . . . . . Erigina
- •• 0:14—Breasts during fight in mud with Lana Clark-
  son.

# *Agutter, Jenny*

*Films:*

East of Sudan (1964; British) . . . . . . . . . . . . . . . . . Asua

Gates to Paradise (1968; British/German) . . . . . . . Maud

I Started Counting (1970; British) . . . . . . . . . . . Wynne

The Railway Children (1971; British) . . . . . . . . . . Bobbie

**Walkabout** (1971; Australian/U.S.) . . . . . . . . . . . . .Girl
(Hard to find this video tape.)
Nude several times.

Logan's Run (1976). . . . . . . . . . . . . . . . . . . . . . Jessica
- 1:05—Very brief breasts and buns changing into fur
  coat in ice cave with Michael York.

The Eagle Has Landed (1977; British) . . . . . . .Molly Prior

**Equus** (1977) . . . . . . . . . . . . . . . . . . . . . . . . .Jill Mason
- ••• 2:00—Nude in loft above the horses in orange light,
  then making love with Alan.

**China 9, Liberty 37** (1978; Italian) . . . . . . . Catherine
*a.k.a. Gunfire*
(Hard to find this video tape.)
*Gunfire* has the nude scenes cut out.

Dominique is Dead (1978; British) . . . . . . . .Miss Ballard
*a.k.a. Dominique*

Survivor (1980; Australian). . . . . . . . . . . . . . . . . Hobbs

**Sweet William** (1980; British) . . . . . . . . . . . . . . . Ann
0:27—Buns, while standing on balcony with Sam
Waterston.
- •• 0:28—Breasts sitting on edge of the bed while talking with Waterston.
- 0:44—Brief left breast when Waterston takes her
  blouse off in the living room.

**An American Werewolf in London** (1981)
. . . . . . . . . . . . . . . . . . . . . . . . . . . . . . . . .Alex Price
- 0:41—Brief right breast in bed with David Naugh-
  ton. Dark, hard to see.

Riddle of the Sands (1984; British) . . . . . . Clara Dollman

Secret Places (1984; British) . . . . . . . . . . . . Miss Lowrie

Dark Tower (1987). . . . . . . . . . . . . . . . . . .Carolyn Page
0:05—In black teddy in her office while a window
washer watches from outside.

Child's Play 2 (1990) . . . . . . . . . . . . . . .Joanne Simpson

Darkman (1990) . . . . . . . . . . . . . . . .Uncredited Doctor

*Made for Cable TV:*

Dream On: No Deposit, No Return (1992; HBO) . . Ellen

*Made for TV Movies:*

The Man in the Iron Mask (1977). . . Louise de la Valliere

Beulah Land (1980) . . . . . . . . . . . . . . . . . Lizzie Corlay

Silas Marner (1985; British) . . . . . . . . .Nancy Lammeter

# *Aimee, Anouk*

*Films:*

La Dolce Vita (1960; Italian/French) . . . . . . . Maddalena

Lola (1961; French/Italian) . . . . . . . . . . . . . . . . . . . Lola

A Man and a Woman (1966; French) . . . . Anne Gauthier

**Justine** (1969; Italian/Spanish) . . . . . . . . . . . . . Justine
- •• 0:36—Nude, while frolicking in the ocean.

The Model Shop (1969). . . . . . . . . . . . . . . . . . . . . Lola

The Tragedy of a Ridiculous Man (1981; Italian)
. . . . . . . . . . . . . . . . . . . . . . . . . Barbara Spaggiari

Success is the Best Revenge (1984; British)
. . . . . . . . . . . . . . . . . . . . . . Monique de Fontaine

A Man and a Woman: 20 Years Later (1986; French)
. . . . . . . . . . . . . . . . . . . . . . . . . . .Anne Gauthier

Dr. Bethune (1993; Canadian/French)
. . . . . . . . . . . . . . . . . . . .Marie-Frances Coudaire

# Aiton, Lisa Bradford

See: Bradford-Aiton, Lisa.

# Akesson, Monica

*Films:*

**Novel Desires** (1991) . . . . . . . . . . . . . . . . . . .Model
••• 0:17—Buns, then breasts while making love outside
during story.
••• 0:18—Breasts making love on picnic table with Eric.

**The Swindle** (1991) . . . . . . . . . . . . .Tom's Last Hurrah
••• 1:17—Breasts, then full frontal nudity, posing on
couch for Tom.

Last Dance (1992). . . . . . . . . . . . . . . . . . Body Double

# • Akkemay

*Films:*

**Army Brats** (1984; Dutch) . . . . . . . .Madeline Gisberts
•• 0:22—Breasts in the shower with her boyfriend.
• 0:26—Brief breasts, taking off towel and putting on
robe while arguing with her mother.
• 0:32—Brief breasts while changing tops.
• 0:47—Brief breasts while sunbathing outside (seen
through binoculars).
• 1:24—Breasts in bed with her boyfriend.

The Assault (1986; Dutch). . . . . . . . . . . . . . . . Sandra

# • Alard, Nelly

*Films:*

**Eating** (1990) . . . . . . . . . . . . . . . . . . . . . . . . . .n.a.
••• 0:06—Breasts, several times while sunbathing, then
getting up and walking by pool, sitting down and
tying a blouse around her waist.

Venice/Venice (1992) . . . . . . . . . . . . . . . . . . . . Jeanne

# Albert, Laura

*Films:*

**Angel III: The Final Chapter** (1988). . . Nude Dancer
• 0:00—Brief breasts dancing in a casino. Wearing red
G-string.
• 0:01—Brief breasts dancing in background.
• 0:06—Side view of left breast and buns, while yelling at Molly for taking her picture.

**Bloodstone** (1988) . . . . . . . . . . . . . . . . . Kim Chi
• 0:05—Very brief side view of left breast turning
around in pool to look at a guy.

**Glitch** (1988). . . . . . . . . . . . . . . . . . . . . . . . . Topless
• 0:35—Brief breasts auditioning for two guys by tak-
ing off her top.

**The Jigsaw Murders** (1988). . . . . . . . .Blonde Stripper
••• 0:19—Breasts and buns in black G-string, stripping
during bachelor party in front of a group of policemen.

**Party Plane** (1988). . . Uncredited Auditioning Woman
•• 0:30—Breasts, taking off blue dress during audition.
She's wearing a white ribbon in her ponytail.

**The Unnameable** (1988) . . . . . . . . . . .Wendy Barnes
•• 0:46—Left breast while lying on floor kissing John,
then brief buns when he pulls her panties down.

**Blood Games** (1989) . . . . . . . . . . . . . . . . . . . . . . Babe
0:03—Pitching in baseball game in braless T-shirt.
0:16—In white bra and black shorts in locker room.

**Dr. Alien** (1989). . . . . . . . . . . . . . . .Rocker Chick #3
*a.k.a. I Was a Teenage Sex Mutant*
••• 0:21—Breasts in black outfit during dream sequence
with two other rocker chicks.

**Dr. Caligari** (1989). . . . . . . . . . . . . . Mrs. Van Houten
••• 0:05—Breasts taking off yellow towel, then sitting in
bathtub.
•• 0:07—Lying down, making love with guy wearing a
mask.
••• 0:10—Breasts taking orange bra off, then lying back
and playing with herself.
•• 0:11—More breasts, lying on the floor.
•• 0:12—More breasts, lying on the floor again.
• 0:30—Brief left breast with big tongue.

**Roadhouse** (1989) . . . . . . . . . . . . . . . Strip Joint Girl
•• 0:45—Breasts and buns dancing on stage, wearing
a hat.

**Stone Cold** (1991) . . . . . . . . . . . . . . . .Joe's Girlfriend
• 0:11—Buns, in bed when waking up. Very brief right
breast.

Live By the Fist (1992) . . . . . . . . . . . . . . . Helen Ferris

*Made for Cable TV:*

**Tales From the Crypt: The Man Who was Death**
(1989; HBO). . . . . . . . . . . . . . . . . . . . . Go-Go Dancer
• 0:20—Brief breasts a couple of times dancing in a
cage in a nightclub.

Dream On: The First Episode (1990; HBO)
. . . . . . . . . . . . . . . . . . . . . . . . . Whipped Cream Girl
0:22—Covered with whipped cream in bed with
Martin.

**Dream On: Pants on Fire** (1991; HBO) . . . . . . .Tanya
•• 0:16—Breasts sitting up on the couch, talking to
Martin.

*Magazines:*

**Playboy** (Nov 1989) . . . . . . . . . . . Sex in Cinema 1989
•• 136—Right breast in still from *Roadhouse.*

# Alda, Rutanya

*Films:*

The Long Goodbye (1973). . . . . . . . .Marloe's Neighbor

**Pat Garrett and Billy the Kid** (1973) . . . . Ruthie Lee
(Uncut Director's version reviewed.)
•• 1:35—Breasts, while sitting on bed with James
Coburn. (She's the only girl wearing a necklace.)

Scarecrow (1973). . . . . . . . . . . . . . Woman in Camper

Swashbuckler (1976) . . . . . . . . . . . . . Bath Attendant

The Deer Hunter (1978). . . . . . . . . . . . . . . . .Angela

The Fury (1978) . . . . . . . . . . . . . . . . . . . . . . .Kristen

When a Stranger Calls (1979). . . . . . . . Mrs. Mandrakis

Mommie Dearest (1981) . . . . . . . . . . . . . . Carol Ann

Amityville II: The Possession (1982) . . . .Deloris Montelli

Girls Nite Out (1982). . . . . . . . . . . . . . . . . . . . .Barney
*a.k.a. Scared to Death*

Vigilante (1983) . . . . . . . . . . . . . . . . . . . . . . . .Vickie

Racing with the Moon (1984) . . . . . . . . . . . Mrs. Nash

Rappin' (1985). . . . . . . . . . . . . . . . . . . . . . . .Cecilia

The Stuff (1985) . . . . . . . . . . . . . . . . . . . . . Psychologist
Hot Shot (1986) . . . . . . . . . . . . . . . Georgia Kristidis
Apprentice to Murder (1987) . . . . . . . . . . . .Elma Kelly
Black Widow (1987) . . . . . . . . . . . . . . . . . . . . . .Irene
Gross Anatomy (1989) . . . . . . . . . . . . . Mama Slovak
Prancer (1990) . . . . . . . . . . . . . . . . . . . . . Aunt Sarah
Article 99 (1992) . . . . . . . . . . . . . . . . . . . .Ann Travis
Leaving Normal (1992). . . . . . . . . Palmer House Nurse
The Dark Half (1993). . . . . . . . . . . . . . .Miriam Cowley
*Made for Cable Movies:*
Laguna Heat (1987; HBO). . . . . . . . . . . . . . . .n.a.
They (1993; Showtime). . . . . . . . . . . . Sue Madehurst

## Alden, Stacey

*Films:*
Grotesque (1987) . . . . . . . . . . . . . . . . . . . . . . . . .n.a.
**A Nightmare on Elm Street 3: The Dream Warriors**
(1987). . . . . . . . . . . . . . . . . . . . . . . . . . . . . . . Marcie
••• 0:49—Breasts and buns in white G-string, taking off
nurse's uniform and seducing Joey in hospital room.
Then giving him the tongue before turning into
Freddy Kruger.
*Magazines:*
**Playboy's Girls of Summer '86** (Aug 1986) . . Herself
• 85—Lower frontal nudity.

## Alessandrini, Toni

*Films:*
Bachelor Party (1984)
. . . . . . . . . . . . .Desiree, Woman Dancing with Donkey
1:24—Buns, in G-string, while dancing with donkey
during party.
Hell Squad (1986). . . . . . . . . . . . . Night Club Waitress
**Vice Academy, Part 2** (1990) . . . . . . . . . . Aphrodisia
• 0:33—Breasts in dressing room.
••• 0:34—Breasts and buns in G-string, dancing in club.
**Vice Academy, Part 3** (1991) . . . . . . . . . . . Stripper
•• 0:26—Breasts taking off dress on stage.
•• 0:27—More breasts on stage (about five times).
•• 0:28—More breasts giving her money to the robbers.
• 0:34—Buns in G-string, while dancing on stage.
**Mind, Body & Soul** (1992). . . . . . . . . . Priestess Tura
•• 1:05—Breasts under fishnet body stocking during
occult dance in a house.
**Pleasure in Paradise** (1992) . . . . . . Lingerie Girl/First
•• 0:51—In black lingerie, then breasts and buns in G-
string, while dancing in bar.

## • Alexander, Annastasia

a.k.a. Raven Alexander.
*Films:*
**Anthony's Desire** (1993) . . . . . . . . . . . . . . . . Dancer
••• 0:04—Nude, on stage stripping out of black dress.
Wearing gloves.
•• 0:22—Full frontal nudity, while stretching in the
background on the left.
•• 0:54—Breasts while lying on her back in the middle
of the group of women.

• 1:02—Breasts, while sitting in the background on
the left.
**Witchcraft V: Dance with the Devil** (1993). Sacrifice
••• 1:15—Nude, undressing and getting sacrificed on
table. Long scene.

## • Alexander, Barbara Lee

*Films:*
Hired to Kill (1990) . . . . . . . . . . . . . . . . . . . . . Sheila
0:19—In white bra, spraying on perfume.
**Illegal Entry** (1992). . . . . . . . . . . . . . . . Pamela Raby
••• 1:02—Breasts, while making out with her boyfriend.
•• 1:15—Breasts, while making love on piano with her
boyfriend.
Psycho Cop 2 (1992) . . . . . . . . . . . . . . . . . . . .Sharon

## Alexander, Jane

Appointed Chairperson of the National Endowment for
the Arts in 1993.
*Films:*
A Gunfight (1971) . . . . . . . . . . . . . . . . . .Nora Tenneray
The New Centurions (1972). . . . . . . . . . . . . .Dorothy
The Betsy (1978) . . . . . . . . . . . . . . . . . Alicia Hardeman
Kramer vs. Kramer (1979) . . . . . . . . . . Margaret Phelps
Brubaker (1980). . . . . . . . . . . . . . . . . . . . . . . .Lillian
Night Crossing (1981) . . . . . . . . . . . . . Doris Strelzyks
Testament (1983). . . . . . . . . . . . . . . . .Carol Wetherly
City Heat (1984) . . . . . . . . . . . . . . . . . . . . . . . . Addy
**Sweet Country** (1985). . . . . . . . . . . . . . . . . . . .Anna
• 1:39—Brief side view of left breast after getting out
of bed.
Square Dance (1987) . . . . . . . . . . . . . . . . . . . .Juanelle
*a.k.a. Home is Where the Heart Is*
*Made for TV Movies:*
Playing for Time (1980) . . . . . . . . . . . . . . . . Alma Rose
Stay the Night (1992) . . . . . . . . . . Blanche Kettmann

## • Alexander, Khandi

*Films:*
A Chorus Line (1985) . . . . . . . . . . . . . . . . . . . . Dancer
Streetwalkin' (1985). . . . . . . . . . . . . . . . . . . . . . . Star
Army of One (1993). . . . . . . . . . . . . . . . . . .Maralena
**CB4** (1993) . . . . . . . . . . . . . . . . . . . . . . . . . . . . Sissy
• 0:51—In bra and brief partial buns in panties on bed
on top of Chris Rock. Side view of right breast, twice,
while letting Allen Payne and Chris Rock poke it
(Don't see her face, probably a body double).
Greedy (1993) . . . . . . . . . . . . . . . . . . . . . . . . . .Laura
Menace II Society (1993) . . . . . . . . . . . . Karen Lawson
Poetic Justice (1993) . . . . . . . . . . . . . . . . . . . Simone
Sugar Hill (1993) . . . . . . . . . . . . . . . . . . . Ella Scuggs
What's Love Got to Do With It (1993) . . . . . . . . Darlene
*Made for TV Movies:*
Shameful Secrets (1993) . . . . . . . . . . . . . . . . .Rosalie
To My Daughter with Love (1994) . . . . . . . . . . . Harriet

# Alexander, Nina

See: Parton, Julie.

# • Alexander, Raven

See: Alexander, Annastasia.

# • Alfred, Rebekah

*Films:*
**Bikini Summer** (1991) . . . . . . . . . D.A. Rachel Green
•• 1:20—In bra, then breasts and buns in dressing
room, trying on swimsuit after everyone has left.
*Video Tapes:*
Score with Chicks (1992) . . . . . . . . . . . . Cast Member

# Alhanti, Iris

*Films:*
Kramer vs. Kramer (1979) . . . . . . . . . . . . . . . . . . . .n.a.
**Partners** (1982) . . . . . . . . . . . . . . . . . . . . . Jogger
•• 0:21—Breasts in the shower when Ryan O'Neal
opens the shower curtain.

# Aliff, Lisa

*Films:*
Dragnet (1987) . . . . . . . . . . . . . . . . . . . . . . . . . . April
Remote Control (1987) . . . . . . . . . . . . . . . . Heroine
Trained to Kill (1988) . . . . . . . . . . . . . . . Jessie Revels
**Playroom** (1989) . . . . . . . . . . . . . . . . . . . . . . . . Jenny
*a.k.a. Schizo*
•• 0:23—Breasts making love on top of Christopher.
**Damned River** (1990) . . . . . . . . . . . . . . . . . . . .Anne
0:28—Silhouette of breasts while undressing in tent.
• 0:32—Very, very brief top of right breast in open
blouse, then half of right breast in wet blouse washing her hair.
• 0:50—Very brief breasts struggling with Ray when
he rips her top open. Don't see her face.

# Alise, Esther

a.k.a. Esther Elise.
*Films:*
**Deathrow Game Show** (1988) . . . . . . . . . . . Groupie
•• 0:08—Breasts in bed with Chuck.
**Hollywood Chainsaw Hookers** (1988) . . . . . . . .Lisa
••• 0:25—Breasts playing with a baseball bat while a
John photographs her.
Midnight Cabaret (1988) . . . . . . . . . . . . . . . . . Dancer
**Vampire at Midnight** (1988) . . . . . . . .Lucia Giannini
••• 1:01—In black lingerie, then breasts and buns while
taking off clothes to wish Roger a happy birthday.

# Allen, Ashley

*Video Tapes:*
**Playboy Video Calendar 1994** (1993) . . . . . . .March
••• 0:10—Nude on bed and in various lingerie outfits.
••• 0:12—Nude, lit with different lights.
**Playboy's Playmate Review 1993** (1993)
. . . . . . . . . . . . . . . . . . . . . . . . . . . . . . Miss August
••• 0:32—Nude in a field and on horseback.
••• 0:33—Nude outside posing by freeway.

*Magazines:*
**Playboy** (Aug 1992) . . . . . . . . . . . . . . . . . . . Playmate
••• 90-10—Nude.
**Playboy's Playmate Review** (Jun 1993) . . . . . .August
••• 68-75—Nude.
**Playboy's Book of Lingerie** (Sep 1993) . . . . . .Herself
•• 59—Left breast and buns.
••• 71-73—Full frontal nudity.
**Playboy's Book of Lingerie** (Nov 1993) . . . . .Herself
••• 24—Buns and side of right breast.
**Playboy's Bathing Beauties** (Mar 1994) . . . . .Herself
• 8—Left breast.
**Playboy Presents Playmates in Paradise**
(Mar 1994). . . . . . . . . . . . . . . . . . . . . . . . . Playmate
••• 80-85—Breasts and buns.
**Playboy's Book of Lingerie** (Mar 1994). . . . . .Herself
•• 62-63—Nude.
**Playboy's Book of Lingerie** (May 1994) . . . . .Herself
••• 99—Full frontal nudity.
**Playboy's Book of Lingerie** (Sep 1994) . . . . . .Herself
••• 98-99—Full frontal nudity.

# Allen, Ginger Lynn

Former adult film actress.
*Films:*
Vice Academy (1988) . . . . . . . . . . . . . . . . . . . . . . Holly
1:20—Buns, in white lingerie outfit when gradua-
tion robe gets torn off.
**Wild Man** (1988) . . . . . . . . . . . . . . . . . . . . . Dawn Hall
•• 0:24—Breasts taking off her dress in front of Eric,
then making love with him.
**Cleo/Leo** (1989) . . . . . . . . . . . . . . . . . . . . . . . .Karen
••• 0:39—Full frontal nudity getting out of the shower,
getting dried with a towel by Jane Hamilton, then in
nightgown.
••• 0:57—Full frontal nudity getting out of the shower
and dried off again.
**Dr. Alien** (1989) . . . . . . . . . . . . . . . . . .Rocker Chick #1
*a.k.a. I Was a Teenage Sex Mutant*
••• 0:21—Breasts in red panties during dream sequence
with two other rocker chicks.
**Edgar Allan Poe's "Buried Alive"** (1989) . . . Debbie
• 0:12—Very, very brief left breast, while struggling
with the other girls in the kitchen.
**Hollywood Boulevard II** (1989) . . . . Candy Chandler
•• 0:33—Breasts in screening room with Woody, the
writer.
**Vice Academy, Part 2** (1990) . . . . . . . . . . . . . . Holly
• 0:44—Buns in black bra, panties, garter belt and
stockings.
•• 1:04—Buns in G-string, then breasts dancing with
Linnea Quigley on stage at club.
Young Guns II (1990) . . . . . . . . . . . . . . . . . . . . . .Dove
**Leather Jackets** (1991) . . . . . . . . . . . . . . . . . . . .Bree
•• 0:39—Breasts on stage for Mickey's bachelor party.
Buns, in G-string. Made up to look like Geisha Girls.
Vice Academy, Part 3 (1991) . . . . . . . . . . . . . . . Holly
Whore (1991) . . . . . . . . . . . . . . . . . . . . . Wounded Girl
*a.k.a. If you're afraid to say it... Just see it*

**Mind, Body & Soul** (1992). . . . . . . . . . . . . . . Brenda
•• 0:13—Breasts in open blouse while getting raped in jail by a guard.
••• 0:17—Breasts while talking with her boyfriend in open blouse and dripping candle wax on him.
••• 1:10—Breasts while lying in bed with her boyfriend, Sean.

**Trouble Bound** (1992) . . Uncredited Adult Film Actress
•• 0:22—Breasts on TV in motel room that Kit and Harry are watching.

**Bound and Gagged: A Love Story** (1993) . . . . Leslie
••• 0:13—Breasts, while making love on kitchen counter with Chris Mulkey, then on the floor.
0:43—Very, very brief inner half of right breast, when her blouse is opened by Elizabeth.
• 0:48—Breasts, in back seat of car when a guy tries to "help" her.

*TV:*
SuperForce (1991-92) . . . . . . . . . . . . . . . . . . . . Crystal
**NYPD Blue: Tempest In a C-Cup** (Nov 16, 1993)
. . . . . . . . . . . . . . . . . . . . . . . . . . . . . . . . . . . .Monique
• 0:22—Brief buns in G-string, while dancing in front Sipowicz at his table.
• 0:23—Brief buns in G-string, while closing door in backstage room with Sipowicz.

*Video Tapes:*
Ginger Lynn Allen's Lingerie Gallery . . . . . . . . . . . . .n.a.
**B-Movie Queens Revealed: The Making of "Vice Academy"** (1993) . . . . . . . . . . . . . . . . . . . . . . . .Holly
• 0:35—Buns in T-back, dancing on stage with Linnea from *Vice Academy 2.*
•• 0:38—Breasts, dancing on stage with Linnea Quigley from *Vice Academy 2.*

*Magazines:*
**Playboy** (Nov 1985) . . . . . . . . . . . Sex in Cinema 1985
• 131—Buns in still from *New Wave Hookers.*
**Playboy** (Jul 1989). . . . . . . . . . . . . . . B-Movie Bimbos
••• 137—Full frontal nudity, standing in a car.

# Allen, India

Ex-wife of TV sportscaster Bill Macatee.
*Films:*
Round Numbers (1990) . . . . . . . . . . . Swimsuit Model
**Wild Cactus** (1992). . . . . . . . . . . . . . . . . . . . . . Alex
(Unrated version reviewed.)
0:02—In white body suit, in bedroom with David Naughton.
••• 0:21—Buns and breasts, making love in bed on top of Naughton.
••• 0:34—Breasts, while pouring maple syrup on herself and making love with Naughton in the kitchen. Yummy!
1:07—In beige bra and panties, trying to escape.
••• 1:10—Nude, getting into and out of the shower.
••• 1:13—Nude, getting lotion rubbed on her by Maggie.
•• 1:18—Breasts, while making love in bed with Randall.

•• 1:20—Lower frontal nudity when Randall gets out of bed.
1:21—In beige bra and panties.
**Seduce Me: Pamela Principle 2** (1994). . . . . . .Elaine
•• 0:19—Breasts when Charles opens her pajamas in bed to try to make love with her.
••• 0:27—Breasts and buns, while taking a shower.
•• 1:13—Nude, walking outside and getting into spa, then in spa. Medium long shots.
••• 1:25—Nude, while making love with her lover in shower while Charles watches from outside.
**Silk Degrees** (1994). . . . . . . . . . . . . . . . . . . . . Sheila
•• 0:02—Breasts, while making love in bed with Degrillo.

*Video Tapes:*
**Playboy Video Calendar 1989** (1988). . . . . . January
••• 0:01—Nude.
**Playboy Video Centerfold: India Allen** (1988)
. . . . . . . . . . . . . . . . . . . . .Playmate of the Year 1988
••• 0:05—Nude in still photos.
•• 0:06—Nude in a field and by the side of a motel.
••• 0:09—Nude in and outside of house during the day and at night.
••• 0:12—Breasts and buns while exercising. Nice and sweaty.
••• 0:13—Nude posing on chair in house. Quick cuts.
••• 0:15—Nude and in lingerie, while dancing. Color and B&W.
•• 0:18—Nude while dancing in a sheer dress.
••• 0:19—Nude in bed. Lit with a swinging lamp, then continuous light.
**Playboy's Playmates of the Year: The '80s** (1989)
. . . . . . . . . . . . . . . . . . . . .Playmate of the Year 1988
••• 0:03—Nude, posing in chair.
••• 0:04—Nude, exercising and dancing around the house.
••• 0:06—Nude in bed.
• 0:52—Breasts in chair. Full frontal nudity in bed.
**Playmates at Play** (1990). . . . . . . Hoops, Hardbodies
**The Best of Video Playmate Calendars** (1992)
. . . . . . . . . . . . . . . . . . . . . . . . . . . . . . . . . . Playmate
•• 0:39—Breasts and buns in B&W music video.
••• 0:40—Nude in bed.
••• 0:41—Nude in more B&W and color music video segments.
••• 0:42—Nude in bed.
*Magazines:*
**Playboy** (Dec 1987) . . . . . . . . . . . . . . . . . . Playmate
**Playboy's Nudes** (Oct 1990) . . . . . . . . . . . . . . Herself
••• 98-99—Full frontal nudity.
**Playboy's Calendar Playmates** (Nov 1992). . .Herself
••• 69—Full frontal nudity.
**Playboy's Video Playmates** (Sep 1993). . . . . .Herself
••• 6-9—Nude.

## Allen, Karen

*Films:*

Animal House (1978) . . . . . . . . . Katherine "Katy" Fuller
    1:21—Brief buns putting on shirt when Boone visits
    her at her house.
Manhattan (1979). . . . . . . . . . . . . . . . . . . . . . . . TV Actor
The Wanderers (1979). . . . . . . . . . . . . . . . . . . . . . Nina
Cruising (1980). . . . . . . . . . . . . . . . . . . . . . . . . . . Nancy
**A Small Circle of Friends** (1980). . . . . . . . . . .Jessica
    • 0:47—Brief breasts in bathroom with Brad Davis.
    Don't see her face.
    • 0:48—Very brief breasts, pushing Davis off her. Then
    very, very brief half of left breast turning around to
    walk to the mirror.
Raiders of the Lost Ark (1981) . . . . . Marion Ravenwood
Shoot the Moon (1982) . . . . . . . . . . . . . . . . . . . . Sandy
Split Image (1982) . . . . . . . . . . . . . . . . . . . . . . Rebecca
Starman (1984). . . . . . . . . . . . . . . . . . . . . Jenny Hayden
**Until September** (1984). . . . . . . . . . . . .Mo Alexander
    •• 0:41—Breasts in bed making love with Thierry Lher-
    mitte.
    •• 1:13—Breasts and buns walking from bed to Lher-
    mitte.
    • 1:25—Brief breasts jumping out of bathtub.
**Backfire** (1987). . . . . . . . . . . . . . . . . . . . . . . . . . .Mara
    • 0:48—Lots of buns, then brief breasts with Keith
    Carradine in the bedroom.
    • 1:00—Brief breasts in the shower.
The Glass Menagerie (1987) . . . . . . . . . . . . . . . . Laura
Scrooged (1988). . . . . . . . . . . . . . . . . . . Claire Phillips
Sweet Talker (1991; Australian) . . . . . . . . . . . . . . . Julie
Malcolm X (1992). . . . . . . . . . . . . . . . . . . . Miss Dunne
Ghost in the Machine (1993) . . . . . . . . . . . . . . . .n.a.
King of the Hill (1993). . . . . . . . . . . . . . . .Miss Mathey
The Sandlot (1993). . . . . . . . . . . . . . . . . . . . . . . . Mom
*Made for Cable Movies:*
Secret Weapon (1990) . . . . . . . . . . . . . . . . . . . . Ruth
*Made for Cable TV:*
Voyage (1993; USA) . . . . . . . . . . . . . . . . . . . . . . . Kit
*Made for TV Movies:*
Challenger (1990). . . . . . . . . . . . . . . . Christa McAuliffe
*TV:*
East of Eden (1981). . . . . . . . . . . . . . . . . . . . . . . Abra
The Road Home (1994- ). . . . . . . . . . . . .Alison Matson

## Allen, Nancy

*Films:*

The Last Detail (1973). . . . . . . . . . . . . . . . . . . .Nancy
Forced Entry (1975) . . . . . . . . . . . . . . . . . . .Hitchhiker
**Carrie** (1976). . . . . . . . . . . . . . . . . . .Chris Hargenson
    •• 0:01—Nude, in slow motion in girls' locker room be-
    hind Amy Irving.
I Wanna Hold Your Hand (1978) . . . . . . . . . . . . . . Pam
1941 (1979) . . . . . . . . . . . . . . . . . . . . . . . . . . . Donna
    0:17—Wearing red bra in cockpit of airplane with
    Tim Matheson.
    1:12—In red bra again with Matheson in the air-
    plane.

**Dressed to Kill** (1980). . . . . . . . . . . . . . . . . . Liz Blake
    1:21—In black bra, panties and stockings in Michael
    Caine's office.
    • 1:36—Breasts (from above), buns and brief right
    breast in shower.
**Home Movies** (1980). . . . . . . . . . . . . . . . . . . . Kristina
    • 1:14—Very brief left breast when bending over
    while sitting on bed and again when reaching up to
    touch Keith Gordon's face.
**Blow Out** (1981) . . . . . . . . . . . . . . . . . . . . . . . . .Sally
    • 0:58—Brief upper half of right breast with the sheet
    pulled up in B&W photograph that John Travolta ex-
    amines.
Strange Invaders (1983). . . . . . . . . . . . . . . Betty Walker
The Buddy System (1984) . . . . . . . . . . . . . . . . . Carrie
Not for Publication (1984) . . . . . . . . . . . Lois Thorndyke
The Philadelphia Experiment (1984). . . . . . . . . . Allison
Terror in the Aisles (1984) . . . . . . . . . . . . . . . . Hostess
Robocop (1987). . . . . . . . . . . . . . . . . . . . . Anne Lewis
Sweet Revenge (1987). . . . . . . . . . . . . . . . . Jillian Grey
Poltergeist III (1988). . . . . . . . . . . . . . .Patricia Gardner
Limit Up (1989) . . . . . . . . . . . . . . . . . . . . . .Casey Falls
Robocop 2 (1990) . . . . . . . . . . . . . . . . . . . Anne Lewis
Robocop 3 (1993) . . . . . . . . . . . . . . . . . . . Anne Lewis
*Made for Cable Movies:*
Memories of Murder (1990; Lifetime). . . . . . . . . . . n.a.
Acting on Impulse (1993; Showtime) . . . . . Cathy Tomas

## Allen, Rosalind

*Films:*

Three Men and a Little Lady (1990) . . . . . . . . Pretty Girl
**To Die For 2** (1991) . . . . . . . . . . . . . . . . . . . . . . . Nina
*a.k.a. Son of Darkness: To Die For II*
    • 0:37—Breasts a few times in bed, while making love
    with Max.
Children of the Corn II: The Final Sacrifice (1992)
. . . . . . . . . . . . . . . . . . . . . . . . . . . . . . . . . . . .Angela
Naked Gun 33 1/3: The Final Insult (1993) . . . . . .Bobbi
Ticks (1993) . . . . . . . . . . . . . . . . . . . . . . Holly Lambert
*Made for Cable TV:*
Dream On: Trojan War (1990; HBO). . . . . . . . . .Lauren
*Made for TV Movies:*
Ray Alexander: A Taste for Justice (1994) Patricia Radcliff
*TV:*
Seaquest DSV (1994- ). . . . . . . . . . . . . . . . . . . . . n.a.

## Alley, Kirstie

Wife of actor Parker Stevenson.
*Films:*
Star Trek II: The Wrath of Kahn (1982) . . . . . . .Lt. Saavik
**Blind Date** (1984) . . . . . . . . . . . . . . . . . . Claire Parker
*a.k.a. Deadly Seduction*
(Not the same 1987 *Blind Date* with Bruce Willis.)
*Deadly Seduction* has Kirstie Alley's nude scene cut out.)
    • 0:12—Brief breasts making love in bed with Joseph
    Bottoms. Dark, hard to see anything.
Runaway (1984). . . . . . . . . . . . . . . . . . . . . . . . . .Jackie
    1:04—Briefly in white bra getting scanned at the po-
    lice station for bugging devices.

Summer School (1987) . . . . . . . . . . . . . . Robin Bishop
Shoot to Kill (1988) . . . . . . . . . . . . . . . . . . . . . . Sarah
Look Who's Talking (1989) . . . . . . . . . . . . . . . . Mollie
Loverboy (1989) . . . . . . . . . . . . . . . . . . . . Joyce Palmer
Look Who's Talking Too (1990) . . . . . . . . . . . . . Mollie
Madhouse (1990) . . . . . . . . . . . . . . . . . . . . . . . . Jessie
>    0:02—In white slip in bedroom with John Laro-
>    quette.
>    0:18—Brief bra shots while doing a sexy strip tease
>    for Laroquette.
>    1:16—In bra under blazer throwing everybody out
>    of her house.

Sibling Rivalry (1990) . . . . . . . . . . . . . . Marjorie Turner
Look Who's Talking Now! (1993) . . . . . Mollie Ubriacco
*Made for Cable TV:*
The Hitchhiker: Out of the Night (1985; HBO)
. . . . . . . . . . . . . . . . . . . . . . . . . . . . . . . . . . . Angelica
*Miniseries:*
North and South (1985) . . . . . . . . . . . . Virgilia Hazard
North and South, Book II (1986) . . . . . . Virgilia Hazard
*Made for TV Movies:*
Sins of the Past (1984) . . . . . . . . . . . . . . . . . . Patrice
A Bunny's Tale (1985) . . . . . . . . . . . . . . Gloria Steinem
Stark: Mirror Images (1986) . . . . . . . . . . . . . . Maggie
David's Mother (1994) . . . . . . . . . . . . . . Sally Goodson
*TV:*
Masquerade (1983-84) . . . . . . . . . . . . . . Casey Collins
Cheers (1987-93) . . . . . . . . . . . . . . . . . Rebecca Howe

## • Allman, Cie
*Films:*
**Renegade: Fighting Cage** (1993) . . . . . . . . Cheetah
(Nudity added for video release.)
>  •• 0:46—Breasts in bed, while making love with a guy.

Trapped (1993) . . . . . . . . . . . . . . . . . . . Buxom Blonde
*a.k.a. The Killing Jar*

## Almgren, Susan
*Films:*
**Separate Vacations** (1985) . . . . . . . . . Helene Gilbert
>  •• 1:05—Breasts and buns in G-string before getting
>    into bed and then in bed with David Naughton.
>  • 1:07—Breasts and buns in bed, then in bathroom
>    with Naughton.

Shades of Love: Lilac Dream (1987) . . . . . . . . . . . . n.a.
*Made for Cable Movies:*
**Deadly Surveillance** (1991; Showtime) . . . . . . Rachel
>    0:00—Very, very brief right breast, while getting
>    dressed. Don't see her face. B&W.
>  • 0:12—Breasts in the shower. Long shot.
>  •• 0:34—Breasts in the shower with Nickels.
>  ••• 0:54—Buns, in black panties and bra, then breasts in
>    room with Michael Ironside.

**Twin Sisters** (1992) . . . . . . . . . . . . . . . . . . . Sophie
>  •• 0:06—Breasts and buns, while making love in bed
>    with a guy.

## Alonso, Maria Conchita
Miss Teen World 1975.
Miss Venezuela 1981.
*Films:*
Fear City (1984) . . . . . . . . . . . . . . . . . . . . Silver Chavez
**Moscow on the Hudson** (1984) . . . . . Lucia Lombardo
>  •• 1:17—Breasts in bathtub with Robin Williams.

Touch and Go (1984) . . . . . . . . . . . . . . . . . . . . . Denise
A Fine Mess (1986) . . . . . . . . . . . . . . . . Claudia Pazzo
**Extreme Prejudice** (1987) . . . . . . . . . . Sarita Cisneros
>  •• 0:27—Brief breasts in the shower while Nick Nolte is
>    in the bathroom talking to her.

The Running Man (1987) . . . . . . . . . . . . Amber Mendez
>    0:16—In black body suit, exercising in her apart-
>    ment.
>    0:20—In black body suit, tied up to weight machine
>    in her apartment, talking to Arnold Schwarzeneg-
>    ger.

**Colors** (1988) . . . . . . . . . . . . . . . . . . . . Louisa Gomez
>  ••• 0:48—Breasts making love in bed with Sean Penn.

**Con el Corazón en la Mano** (1988; Mexican) . . . n.a.
>  • 0:38—Very, very brief right breast, while turning
>    over in bed with her husband.
>  • 0:39—Breasts several times, taking a bath.
>  •• 1:15—Breasts while ripping off her dress. Long shot,
>    side view, standing while kissing a guy.

Vampire's Kiss (1989) . . . . . . . . . . . . . . . . . . . . . Alva
>    0:47—In white bra, ironing her clothes in her living
>    room.
>    0:59—In white bra getting attacked by Nicolas
>    Cage.

Predator 2 (1990) . . . . . . . . . . . . . . . . . . . . . . Leona
McBain (1991) . . . . . . . . . . . . . . . . . . . . . . . Christine
Teamster Boss (1992) . . . . . . . . . . . . . . . . . . . Carmen
*Made for Cable Movies:*
**Blood Ties** (1986; Italian; Showtime) . . . . . . . Caterina
>  •• 0:35—Brief breasts when Vincent Spano rips her
>    dress off.

*Made for TV Movies:*
MacShayne: The Final Roll of the Dice (1994)
. . . . . . . . . . . . . . . . . . . . . . . . . . . . . . . Cindy Evans
*Video Tapes:*
Dance It Up: Hot Fitness (1991) . . . . . . . . . . . . Herself

## Alphen, Corinne
a.k.a. Corinne Wahl.
Ex-wife of actor Ken Wahl.
*Films:*
**Hot T-Shirts** (1980) . . . . . . . . . . . . . . . . . . . . . Judy
>    0:55—In braless T-shirt as a car hop.
>  • 1:10—In yellow outfit dancing in wet T-shirt contest.
>    Brief breasts while flashing the crowd.

**New York Nights** (1981) . . . . . . . . . . . The Debutante
>  •• 0:10—Breasts, making love in the back seat of a lim-
>    ousine with the rock star.
>  ••• 1:38—Breasts dancing in the bedroom while the
>    Financier watches from the bed.

**Brainwaves** (1983) . . . . . . . . . . . . . . . . . Lelia Adams
- 0:03—Brief side of right breast, reaching out to turn off the water faucets in the bathtub.
- 0:05—Full frontal nudity, getting electrocuted in the bubble bath.
- 0:50—Brief right breast, during Kaylie's vision.

**C.O.D.** (1983). . . . . . . . . . . . . . . . . Cheryl Westwood
- 0:21—Brief breasts changing clothes in dressing room while talking to Zacks.
- 1:25—Brief breasts taking off her blouse in dressing room scene.
  1:26—In green bra, talking to Albert.
  1:28—In green bra during fashion show.

Spring Break (1983; Canadian) . . . . . . . . . . . . . . Joan
  0:32—Taking a shower in a two piece bathing suit in an outdoor shower at the beach.

Equalizer 2000 (1986). . . . . . . . . . . . . . . . . . . Karen

**Amazon Women on the Moon** (1987) . . . . . . . Shari
- ••• 1:13—In black bra, then breasts on TV while Ray watches.

**Screwball Hotel** (1988) . . . . . . . . . . . . . Cherry Amour
- 0:46—Buns, in black outfit on bed with Norman.

*Magazines:*
**Penthouse** (Jun 1978). . . . . . . . . . . . . . . . . . . . . Pet
**Penthouse** (Aug 1981) . . . . . . . . . . . . . . . . . . . . Pet
**Penthouse** (Nov 1982) . . . . . . . . . . . . Pet of the Year
- ••• 123-139—Nude.
**Penthouse** (Sep 1983) . . . . . . . Pet of the Year Play-Off
- ••• 60-61—Breasts and buns.

## Alt, Carol
Supermodel.
*Films:*
**Portfolio** (1983) . . . . . . . . . . . . . . . . . . . . . . Herself
- 0:28—Brief right breast, while adjusting black, see-through blouse.
  0:31—Brief side view of a little bit of right breast while changing clothes backstage at a fashion show.

Bye Bye Baby (1989; Italian) . . . . . . . . . . . . . . Sandra
  0:09—Part of right breast, while in the shower.
  0:22—Wearing a white bra, while taking off her blouse in the doctor's office.

My Wonderful Life (1989; Italian) . . . . . . . . . . . Marina
  0:50—In wet, green dress.

**A Family Matter** (1990) . . . . . . . . . . . . . . . . . . Nancy
- •• 1:08—Buns, in panties. Brief side view of left breast with Eric Roberts.

Millions (1990) . . . . . . . . . . . . . . . . . . . . . . . . . Beta
Beyond Justice (1992) . . . . . . . . . . . . Christine Sanders
*TV:*
Thunder in Paradise (1994- ) . . . . . . . . . . . . . . . . n.a.
*Video Tapes:*
Sports Illustrated's 25th Anniversary Swimsuit Video (1989). . . . . . . . . . . . . . . . . . . . . . . . . . . Herself
  (The version shown on HBO left out two music video segments at the end. If you like buns, definitely watch the video tape!)
  0:40—Briefly in wet white swimsuit.

## Always, Julie
*Films:*
**Hardbodies** (1984) . . . . . . . . Photo Session Hardbody
- •• 0:40—Breasts with other girls posing breasts getting pictures taken by Rounder. She's wearing blue dress with a white belt.

**The Rosebud Beach Hotel** (1985) . . . . . . . . . Bellhop
- •• 0:22—Breasts, in open blouse, undressing with two other bellhops. She's the blonde on the left.
- •• 0:44—Breasts, playing spin the grenade, with two guys and the two other bellhops. She's on the left.

## Ames, Denise
*Films:*
Slash Dance (1989) . . . . . . . . . . . . . . . . . . . . Dancer
Danger Zone III: Steel Horse War (1991) . . . . . . . . n.a.
**The Last Boy Scout** (1991) . . . . . . . Jacuzzi Party Girl
- 0:11—Brief breasts getting out of the Jacuzzi.
*Magazines:*
Playboy (Apr 1993) . . . . . . . . . . . . . . . . . . Grapevine

## • Amick, Mädchen
*Films:*
The Borrower (1989) . . . . . . . . . . . . . . . . . . . Megan
Don't Tell Her It's Me (1990) . . . . . . . . . . . . . . Mandy
I'm Dangerous Tonight (1990). . . . . . . . . . Amy O'Neil
Stephen King's Sleepwalkers (1992) . . . Tanya Robertson
Twin Peaks: Fire Walk With Me (1992) . . . Shelly Johnson
**Dreamlover** (1994) . . . . . . . . . . . . . . . . . . . . . Lena
*Made for Cable Movies:*
**Love, Cheat & Steal** (1993; Showtime)
. . . . . . . . . . . . . . . . . . . . . . . . Lauren Harrington
  0:01—Silhouette of side view of a breast, while kneeling above Eric Roberts. Don't see her face.
  0:14—Almost buns, while in bedroom with John Lithgow.
- 0:26—Buns, when Roberts rips her pants off. Don't see her face.
- 0:47—Brief back side of right breast, twice, getting out of bed and putting on robe.
*TV:*
Twin Peaks (1990-91) . . . . . . . . . . . . . . Shelly Johnson

## • Amidou, Souad
*Films:*
A Man and a Woman (1966; French)
. . . . . . . . . . . . . . . . . . . . . . . Francoise Gauthier
Life Love Death (1969; French/Italian) . . Francois Toledo
**Petit Con** (1986; French) . . . . . . . . . . . . . . . . Salima
- •• 0:42—Breasts, after taking off her top and getting into bed, while Michel watches her.
- 0:50—Breasts, while lying in bed, then making love with Michel. Dark.
- 0:53—Breasts, getting out of bed and getting back in.
Levy and Goliath (1987; French) . . . . . . . . . . . . . n.a.

## Amis, Suzy

*Films:*
Fandango (1985) . . . . . . . . . . . . . . . . . . . . . . . The Girl
The Big Town (1987) . . . . . . . . . . . . . Aggie Donaldson
Plain Clothes (1988) . . . . . . . . . . . . . . . Robin Torrence
Rocket Gibraltar (1988). . . . . . . . . . . . . . . . . . . . Aggie
Twister (1989). . . . . . . . . . . . . . . . . . . . . . .Maureen
**Where the Heart Is** (1990) . . . . . . . . .Chloe McBain
- • 0:08—Breasts during her art film. Artfully covered with paint, with a bird. Breasts again in the third segment.
- • 0:09—Breasts during the film again. Hard to see because of the paint. Last segment while she narrates.
Rich in Love (1992). . . . . . . . . . . . . . . . . . . . Rae Odom
**The Ballad of Little Jo** (1993) . . . . . . . . Jo Monaghan
- • 0:12—Buns and left breast in reflection in mirror. Hard to see her face clearly.
- ••• 1:16—Breasts, while on bed with Tinman.
Watch It (1993). . . . . . . . . . . . . . . . . . . . . . . . . .Anne
Blown Away (1994). . . . . . . . . . . . . . . . . . . . . . . .n.a.
*Magazines:*
**Playboy** (Sep 1993). . . . . . . . . . . . . . . . . . . .Grapevine
- • 175—Right breast, under sheer black dress. B&W.

## Amore, Gianna

*Films:*
Screwball Hotel (1988) . . . . . . . . . . . . . . . . .Mary Beth
Nothing But Trouble (1991) . . . . . . . . . . . . . Party Girl
*Video Tapes:*
**Wet and Wild** (1989). . . . . . . . . . . . . . . . . . . .Model
**Playmates at Play** (1990)
. . . . . . . . . . . . . . . . . . . . . .Free Wheeling, Gotta Dance
**Playboy Video Calendar 1992** (1991) . . . . . .January
- ••• 0:01—Nude in Italian restaurant fantasy.
- ••• 0:02—Nude in classical music fantasy in warehouse.
*Magazines:*
**Playboy** (Aug 1989) . . . . . . . . . . . . . . . . . . Playmate
**Playboy's Nudes** (Oct 1990). . . . . . . . . . . . . . Herself
- •• 71—Side of left breast and buns.
**Playboy's Book of Lingerie** (Jan 1991) . . . . . . Herself
- •• 52—Right breast.
**Playboy's Book of Lingerie** (Mar 1991) . . . . . Herself
- •• 92—Breasts and lower frontal nudity.
**Playboy's Book of Lingerie** (Jul 1991) . . . . . . Herself
- ••• 69—Breasts and lower frontal nudity.
**Playboy's Book of Lingerie** (Mar 1992) . . . . . Herself
- ••• 14-15—Left breast and lower frontal nudity.
**Playboy's Bathing Beauties** (Apr 1992) . . . . . Herself
- ••• 23—Breasts.
**Playboy's Girls of Summer '92** (Jun 1992). . . Herself
- •• 9—Buns and side of right breast.
- ••• 14—Breasts.
- ••• 99—Full frontal nudity.
**Playboy's Book of Lingerie** (Jul 1992) . . . . . . Herself
- •• 36-37—Side of right breast and buns.
**Playboy's Calendar Playmates** (Nov 1992) . . Herself
- •• 99—Lower frontal nudity and right breast.
**Playboy's Book of Lingerie** (Jan 1993) . . . . . . Herself
- ••• 61—Full frontal nudity.

**Playboy's Book of Lingerie** (Nov 1993) . . . . .Herself
- ••• 78-79—Full frontal nudity.
**Playboy Presents Playmates in Paradise**
(Mar 1994). . . . . . . . . . . . . . . . . . . . . . . . . .Playmate
- ••• 62-67—Nude.
**Playboy's Book of Lingerie** (May 1994) . . . . .Herself
- ••• 48-49—Nude.
**Playboy's Book of Lingerie** (Jul 1994). . . . . . .Herself
- ••• 84-85—Buns, right breast and partial lower frontal nudity.

## Amy-Rochelle

See: Weiss, Amy-Rochelle.

## Anders, Avalon

a.k.a. Sheila Stronegger.
*Films:*
**Bikini Summer 2** (1992) . . . . . . . . . . . . . . . . . .Clarice
- ••• 0:11—Breasts in sexy outfit, acting as a dominatrix with Harry in his office.
- • 0:13—More breasts in Harry's office.
- • 0:33—Buns and brief left breast, teasing Harry.
- ••• 0:37—In black body stocking then breasts with Harry in his office.
- ••• 0:41—More breasts in white corset with Harry.
Buford's Beach Bunnies (1992). . . . . . . . . Santa's Helper
**Sorority House Party** (1992) . . . . . . . . . . . . .Miranda
- • 1:05—Breasts and buns under sheer purple body suit.
  1:18—Briefly hanging out of car to flash her bra to distract bad guys.
**Die Watching** (1993) . . . . . . . . . . . . . . . . . . . .Marie
- ••• 0:40—In pink outfit doing strip tease while getting videotaped by Christopher Atkins, then breasts. Long scene.
- • 0:52—Brief breasts, seen on TV monitor.
**The Great Bikini Off-Road Adventure** (1994)
. . . . . . . . . . . . . . . . . . . . . . . . . . . . Paulina Smalls
- •• 0:01—Breasts, while sunbathing and lying on ground and spraying herself with water.
- •• 0:16—Breasts, while sunbathing outside on the rocks with Tisha.
- ••• 0:21—Breasts, while undoing her swimsuit top in front of two guys out in the desert.
- • 0:31—Brief buns, while in swimsuit.
- ••• 0:44—Breasts, while posing on a jeep for a customer with a camera.
- ••• 0:50—Breasts and buns, while posing outside for a customer.
- ••• 1:02—Breasts and buns during water fight.
*Made for Cable TV:*
**Red Shoe Diaries: Burning Up** (1994; Showtime)
. . . . . . . . . . . . . . . . . . . . . . . . . . . . . . . . . . Ruby
- •• 0:15—Breasts and buns in G-string, while dancing on stage in club.
- •• 0:18—Breasts and buns in G-string, while making love with the fireman in restroom stall.

*Video Tapes:*

**California Girl Fox Hunt Bikini Competition #6**
. . . . . . . . . . . . . . . . . . . . . . . . . . . . . . . . . . . Avalon
••• 0:02—Buns in sexy one piece swimsuit.
0:47—Buns during review.
**Hot Body Video Magazine #1** (1992) . . . . . . .Model
••• 0:41—Buns and breasts modeling, sunbathing and
dancing. Great, long scenes.
**Hot Body Video Magazine: The Best Of** (1994)
. . . . . . . . . . . . . . . . . . . . . . . . . . . . . . . . . . . Herself

*Magazines:*

**Playboy** (Jan 1992) . . . . . . . . .The Swedish Bikini Team
Uma Thorensen.
••• 78-85—Right breast, while holding squirt gun.
Breasts lying in inflatable lounge in pool. Buns, while
holding up surfboard (first one on the left). Right
breast in green bikini bottoms. Breasts, kneeling and
holding suspender with her left hand. Buns and side
of right breast, while climbing cliff. Partial left breast,
while holding swimsuit string with both hands.

# • *Anders, Lola*

*Video Tapes:*

**Penthouse Paradise Revisited** (1992) . . . . . . . . Pet

*Magazines:*

**Penthouse** (Feb 1989) . . . . . . . . . . . . . . . . . . . . Pet
**Penthouse** (Apr 1991). . . . . . . . . . . . . . . . . . . . Lola
••• 87-97—Nude. 1991 Pet of the Year Runner-Up.

# Anderson, Erika

*Films:*

Nightmare on Elm Street 5: The Dream Child (1989)
. . . . . . . . . . . . . . . . . . . . . . . . . . . . . . . . . . . Greta
**Zandalee** (1991) . . . . . . . . . . . . . . . .Zandalee Martin
••• 0:02—Nude, taking off robe and dancing around
the room.
••• 0:21—Nude, undressing, then in bed with Judge Reinhold. Long scene.
•• 0:30—Right breast, then breasts making love in bed
with Nicolas Cage.
•• 0:32—Breasts as Cage paints on her with his finger.
••• 0:45—Left breast, then breasts and lower frontal nudity on floor with Cage.
•• 0:47—Nude, getting massaged by Cage with an oil
and cocaine mixture.
• 0:48—Brief breasts getting into bed with Reinhold.
Slightly out of focus.
•• 1:09—Breasts opening her dress for Reinhold while
lying on a river bank, then making love with him at
night in bed.
**Quake** (1992) . . . . . . . . . . . . . . . . . . . . . .Jenny Sutton
• 0:05—Breasts, getting out of the shower and drying
herself off. More breasts, putting on bra.
• 0:40—Breasts in photos from 0:05 in darkroom.
•• 0:50—Breasts on table when Steve Railsback rips her
bra off.
•• 0:51—Breasts, in drugged sleep while Railsback
takes pictures of her.
• 0:52—More breasts asleep, then awake.

*Made for Cable TV:*

Dream On: B.S. Elliot (1992; HBO). . . . . . . . . . .Marina
**Red Shoe Diaries: Liar's Tale** (1994; Showtime)
. . . . . . . . . . . . . . . . . . . . . . . . . . . . .Joanna Dunston
••• 0:19—In bra, then breasts and partial lower frontal
nudity while making love with Jack at his house. Intercut with Audie England's nude scenes.

*TV:*

Twin Peaks (1990-91). . . . . . . . . . . . . . . .Emerald/Jade

*Magazines:*

**Playboy** (Nov 1991) . . . . . . . . . . . Sex in Cinema 1991
• 144—Full frontal nudity in mirror. From *Zandalee*.
**Playboy** (Dec 1991) . . . . . . . . . . . . . . . .Sex Stars 1991
• 185—Right breast in B&W photo.

# Anderson, Kim

*Films:*

**Fatal Skies** (1989) . . . . . . . . . . . . . . . . . . . . . . . Cindy
• 0:48—Buns in lingerie, while posing for Lance in his
office.
Hot Times at Montclair High (1989). . . . . . . . . Bridgette
Small Time (1991) . . . . . . . . . . . . . . Woman on Street

*Video Tapes:*

Swimwear Illustrated: On Location (1986)
. . . . . . . . . . . . . . . . . . . . . . . . . . . . . .Swimsuit Model
(Blonde hair.)
**Rock Video Girls** (1991) . . . . . . . . . . . . . . . . .Herself
(Brunette hair.)
• 0:02—Dancing in wet T-shirt. Buns and brief breasts
on the beach (some in B&W).

*Magazines:*

**Inside Sports** (Apr 1992) . . . . . . . . .Journey to St. John
39—Buns, while sitting in two piece swimsuit.
• 46-47—Buns, while lying in the surf in a two piece
swimsuit.
**Playboy** (Aug 1993) . . . . . . . . . . . . . . . . . . . Grapevine
• 159—Buns in swimsuit. B&W.

# Anderson, Melody

*Films:*

Flash Gordon (1980) . . . . . . . . . . . . . . . . . . Dale Arden
Dead and Buried (1981). . . . . . . . . . . . . . . . . . . Janet
**The Boy in Blue** (1986; Canadian). . . . . . . . . . . Dulcie
• 0:07—Brief cleavage while making love with Nicolas
Cage, then very brief top half of right breast when a
policeman scares her.
Firewalker (1986) . . . . . . . . . . . . . . . . Patricia Goodwyn
Final Notice (1989) . . . . . . . . . . . . . . . . . . . . Kate Davis
Landslide (1992) . . . . . . . . . . . . . . . . . . Claire Trinavant

*Made for Cable Movies:*

Hitler's Daughter (1990). . . . . . . . . . . . . . . . . . . . n.a.
Marilyn & Bobby: Her Final Affair (1993; USA)
. . . . . . . . . . . . . . . . . . . . . . . . . . . . . .Marilyn Monroe

*Made for TV Movies:*

Policewoman Centerfold (1983). . . . . . . . . . . . Jan Oaks
0:51—Very brief partial side of right breast kneeling
on bed during photo shoot.

*TV:*

Manimal (1983). . . . . . . . . . . . . . . . .Brooke McKenzie

## Anderson, Pamela

*Films:*
The Taking of Beverly Hills (1991) . . . . . . . . Cheerleader
**Snapdragon** (1993) . . . . . . . . . . . . . . . . . . . . . Felicity
• 0:06—Brief side view of right breast, while making
love on top of a guy in bed before killing him.
• 0:26—Right breast, while making love on top of another guy in bed before killing him.
••• 0:55—Breasts and buns, while making love in bed
on top of Steven Bauer in his dream.
• 1:06—In white bra and panties, then left breast and
buns while making love on top of Bauer on the floor.
••• 1:22—Breasts and buns, while making love with
Bauer.
**Raw Justice** (1994) . . . . . . . . . . . . . . . . . . . . . . Sarah
*a.k.a. Good Cop, Bad Cop*
••• 0:40—Breasts, while making out with David Keith in
building while standing up.
•• 0:58—Breasts, while making love with Robert Hayes
in hotel room.
*TV:*
Home Improvement (1991-93)
. . . . . . . . . . . . . . . . . . . . . Lisa the "Tool Time" Girl
Baywatch (1992- ) . . . . . . . . . . . . . . . . . . . . C. J. Parker
*Video Tapes:*
**Playboy Video Calendar 1991** (1990) . . . . . . . . July
••• 0:26—Nude.
**Sexy Lingerie II** (1990) . . . . . . . . . . . . . . . . . . . .Model
**Sexy Lingerie III** (1991) . . . . . . . . . . . . . . . . . .Model
**Wet and Wild III** (1991) . . . . . . . . . . . . . . . . . .Model
**The Best of Video Playmate Calendars** (1992)
. . . . . . . . . . . . . . . . . . . . . . . . . . . . . . . . . . Playmate
••• 0:34—Nude on spiral staircase, then on floor.
••• 0:36—In lingerie, then nude during modeling session with lots of sheets.
**Playboy Video Centerfold: Pamela Anderson**
(1992) . . . . . . . . . . . . . . . . . . . . . . . . . . . . . Playmate
••• 0:00—Nude throughout.
*Magazines:*
**Playboy** (Feb 1990) . . . . . . . . . . . . . . . . . . . . Playmate
••• 102-113—Nude.
**Playboy's Book of Lingerie** (Jul 1991) . . . . . . Herself
••• 68—Breasts.
••• 82-83—Full frontal nudity.
•• 109—Right breast and lower frontal nudity.
**Playboy's Book of Lingerie** (Sep 1991) . . . . . Herself
••• 44-45—Nude.
••• 57—Full frontal nudity.
**Playboy's Book of Lingerie** (Nov 1991) . . . . . Herself
• 26-27—Right breast.
**Playboy Presents International Playmates**
(Feb 1992) . . . . . . . . . . . . . . . . . . . . . . . . . . . Herself
••• 68-71—Nude.
**Playboy's Book of Lingerie** (Mar 1992) . . . . . Herself
••• 80-81—Full frontal nudity.
•• 93—Buns and partial right breast.
**Playboy's Book of Lingerie** (May 1992) . . . . . Herself
••• 79—Full frontal nudity.
**Playboy's Girls of Summer '92** (Jun 1992) . . . Herself

••• 11-13—Buns and breasts.
••• 22—Full frontal nudity.
**Playboy's Book of Lingerie** (Jul 1992) . . . . . . .Herself
••• 38—Breasts.
**Playboy** (Jul 1992) . . . . . . . . Getting Kicks on Route 66
••• 67-73—Nude.
**Playboy's Career Girls** (Aug 1992)
. . . . . . . . . . . . . . . . . . . . . . . . . . Baywatch Playmates
••• 5—Full frontal nudity.
**Playboy's Calendar Playmates** (Nov 1992). . . Herself
••• 93—Full frontal nudity.
**Playboy** (Dec 1992) . . . . . . . . . . . . . . . .Sex Stars 1992
••• 188—Breasts.
**Playboy's Girls of Summer '93** (Jun 1993) . . . Herself
••• 6-7—Full frontal nudity.
••• 44—Full frontal nudity.
**Playboy's Wet & Wild Women** (Aug 1993). . . Herself
• 60—Breasts in wet slip.
• 78-79—Buns under wet sheet.
**Playboy's Book of Lingerie** (Sep 1993) . . . . . .Herself
••• 47—Full frontal nudity.
**Playboy's Video Playmates** (Sep 1993) . . . . . .Herself
•• 10-11—Breasts.
**Playboy's Book of Lingerie** (Nov 1993) . . . . .Herself
••• 98-99—Full frontal nudity.
**Playboy** (Dec 1993) . . . . . . . . . . . . . . . .Sex Stars 1993
••• 176—Breasts and partial lower frontal nudity.
**Playboy's Book of Lingerie** (Jan 1994) . . . . . .Herself
••• 99—Full frontal nudity.
**Playboy Presents Playmates in Paradise**
(Mar 1994). . . . . . . . . . . . . . . . . . . . . . . . . . Playmate
••• 38-43—Full frontal nudity.
**Playboy's Book of Lingerie** (Mar 1994). . . . . .Herself
•• 94—Buns and side of right breast.
**Playboy's Book of Lingerie** (May 1994) . . . . .Herself
••• 47—Breasts.
**Playboy's Girls of Summer '94** (Jul 1994). . . .Herself
•• 86—Buns and right breast.
**Playboy's Book of Lingerie** (Jul 1994) . . . . . . .Herself
••• 32—Full frontal nudity.
••• 96—Breasts.
**Playboy** (Nov 1994) . . . . . . . . . . . . . . . . . .Pamwatch
••• 82-89—Nude.

## Anderson, Pat

*Films:*
Dirty O'Neil (1974) . . . . . . . . . . . . . . . . . . . . . . . . Lisa
Newman's Law (1974) . . . . . . . . . . . . . . . . . . . .Sharon
Cover Girl Models (1975) . . . . . . . . . . . . . . . . . Barbara
**Summer School Teachers** (1975). . . . . . . . . . . .Sally
•• 0:52—Breasts and buns, posing for photos, then in
bed with Bob.
• 1:05—Side view of right breast in photo in magazine.
**TNT Jackson** (1975) . . . . . . . . . . . . . . . . . . . . . .Elaine
•• 0:58—Buns and breasts, getting out of the shower
and putting robe on.

**Bloodfist III: Forced to Fight** (1991) . . . . . . . . Elaine
 • 0:55—Buns and breasts in clip from movie *TNT Jackson* that the inmates watch while Diddler gets stabbed to death.
*Magazines:*
**Playboy** (Nov 1974) . . . . . . . . . . Sex in Cinema 1974
 •• 152—Breasts sitting in bed from *Newman's Law*.

# • Anderson, Stephanie

*Films:*
Buford's Beach Bunnies (1992) . . . . . . . . . . . . . .Marilyn
Death Becomes Her (1992) . . . . . . . . . Marilyn Monroe
**Calendar Girl** (1993) . . . . . . . . . . . . Marilyn Monroe
 • 0:44—Buns and long shot of left breast at the nude beach while wearing a wig.
 • 0:46—Buns, standing up at the beach, taking off her wig while the bad guys talk to the boys in the water.

# Andersson, Bibi

*Films:*
The Seventh Seal (1956; Swedish) . . . . . . . . . . . . . .Mia
Brink of Life (1957; Swedish) . . . . . . . . . . . . . . . Hjordis
Wild Strawberries (1957; Swedish) . . . . . . . . . . . . Sara
The Magician (1959) . . . . . . . . . . . . . . . . . . . . . . . Sara
Duel at Diablo (1966) . . . . . . . . . . . . . . . . .Ellen Grange
Persona (1966; Swedish) . . . . . . . . . . . . . . .Nurse Alma
**The Touch** (1971; U.S./Swedish) . . . . . Karen Vergerus
 • 0:31—Breasts in bed with Elliott Gould.
 ••• 0:56—Breasts kissing Gould.
    1:13—Very, very brief right breast washing Gould's hair in the sink.
Scenes from a Marriage (1973; Swedish) . . . . . . Katarina
I Never Promised You a Rose Garden (1977) . . . Dr. Fried
Quintet (1979) . . . . . . . . . . . . . . . . . . . . . . . Ambrosia
**Twice a Woman** (1979) . . . . . . . . . . . . . . . . . . Laura
 • 0:05—Breasts taking off her bra and putting a blouse on.
 • 0:06—Brief side view of left breast, getting into bed, brief left breast lying back in bed.
Exposed (1983) . . . . . . . . . . . . . . . . . . . . . . . Margaret
Babette's Feast (1987; Danish)
 . . . . . . . . . . . . . . . . . . . . Swedish Court Lady-in-Waiting
*a.k.a. Babettes Gaestebud*
*Made for TV Movies:*
Wallenberg: A Hero's Story (1985) . . . . . . . . . . . . .Maj

# • Andersson, Harriet

*Films:*
**Monika** (1952; Swedish) . . . . . . . . . . . . . . . . .Monika
*a.k.a. Sommaren Med Monika*
 • 0:42—Brief back side of left breast, while sitting down next to water. Buns while getting up to run to water.
 • 1:33—Buns and long shot of right breast in Harry's flashback. This scene lasts longer than the 0:42 one.
Sawdust and Tinsel (1955; Swedish) . . . . . . . . . . .Anne
*a.k.a. The Naked Night*
Smiles of a Summer Night (1957; Swedish)
 . . . . . . . . . . . . . . . . . . . . . . . . . . . . Petra the Maid

Dreams (1960; Swedish) . . . . . . . . . . . . . . . . . . . Doris
A Lesson in Love (1960; Swedish) . . . . . . . . . . . . . . Nix
Through a Glass Darkly (1962; Swedish) . . . . . . . Karin
Cries and Whispers (1972; Swedish) . . . . . . . . . . Agnes
 *a.k.a. Viskingar Och Rop*
Fanny and Alexander (1983; Swedish/French/German)
 . . . . . . . . . . . . . . . . . . . . . . . . . . . . . . . . . . . . . n.a.

# Andreeff, Starr

*Films:*
Skullduggery (1983; Canadian) . . . . . . . . . . . . . . Irene
**Dance of the Damned** (1988) . . . . . . . . . . . . . . Jodi
 •• 0:03—Breasts dancing in black bikini bottoms on stage in a club.
    1:06—In black bra, panties, garter belt and stockings dancing in bar just for the vampire.
 •• 1:08—Breasts in the bar with the vampire.
Ghoulies II (1988) . . . . . . . . . . . . . . . . . . . . . . . . Alice
Out of the Dark (1988) . . . . . . . . . . . . . . . . . . Camille
The Terror Within (1988) . . . . . . . . . . . . . . . . . . . Sue
Streets (1989) . . . . . . . . . . . . . Policewoman on Horse
Syngenor (1990) . . . . . . . . . . . . . . . . . . . . . . . .Susan
Driving Me Crazy (1991) . . . . . . . . . . . . . . . . . . .Legs
Scanner Cop (1993) . . . . . . . . . . . . . . . . . . . . . Glenda

# Andress, Ursula

*Films:*
Dr. No (1962; British) . . . . . . . . . . . . . . . . . . . . .Honey
    1:19—Almost very, very brief breasts after going through shower to remove radioactivity.
Four for Texas (1963) . . . . . . . . . . . . . . Maxine Richter
Fun in Acapulco (1963) . . . . . . . . . Margarita Douphine
Nightmare in the Sun (1964) . . . . . . . . . .Marsha Wilson
What's New, Pussycat? (1965; U.S./French) . . . . . . . Rita
**The Blue Max** (1966) . . . . . . . . . . . . . . .Countess Kasti
 • 1:26—Very, very brief half of left breast, lying on her back in bed.
 • 1:47—(0:04 into tape 2) Very brief half of right breast, while kneeling down in front of Peppard in hotel room. Very, very brief breasts under towel around her neck when she stands up.
 • 1:48—(0:05 into tape 2) Very, very brief silhouette of right breast, while lying back down in bed with George Peppard in bedroom.
Casino Royale (1967; British) . . . . . . . . . . .Vesper Lynd
Anyone Can Play (1968; Italian) . . . . . . . . . . . . .Norma
**The Southern Star** (1969; French/British)
 . . . . . . . . . . . . . . . . . . . . . . . . . . . . . Erica Kramer
 • 1:07—Buns, walking into lake to wash herself. Long shot.
 • 1:08—Breasts seen through water while she talks to George Segal.
**Perfect Friday** (1970; British) . . . . . .Lady Britt Dorsett
Red Sun (1972; French/Italian/Spanish) . . . . . . . Cristina
    1:12—Almost side view of right breast, then left breast while changing tops in room while Charles Bronson watches.
**Loaded Guns** (1975) . . . . . . . . . . . . . . . . . . . . .Laura
    0:32—Buns, lying in bed with a guy.

••• 0:33—Breasts and buns getting out of bed. Full frontal nudity in elevator.

•• 0:40—Nude getting out of bed and putting dress on.

••• 0:48—Nude getting into bathtub, breasts in tub, nude getting out and drying herself off.
1:00—Buns while getting undressed and hopping in to bed.

• 1:02—Brief side view of right breast while getting dressed.

**The Sensuous Nurse** (1975; Italian) . . . . . . . . . .Anna

•• 0:16—Breasts and buns in bed after making love with Benito.

•• 0:22—Nude swimming in pool while Adonais watches.

••• 0:50—Nude slowly stripping and getting in bed with Adonais.

••• 1:10—Nude getting into bed.

**Stateline Motel** (1975; Italian) . . . . . . Michelle Nolton
*a.k.a. Last Chance for a Born Loser*

••• 0:34—Left breast, then breasts on bed with Oleg.

The Loves and Times of Scaramouche (1976; Italian)
. . . . . . . . . . . . . . . . . . . . . . . . . . . . . . . . . . Josephine

**Slave of the Cannibal God** (1979; Italian) . . . . . .n.a.

•• 0:33—Breasts taking off shirt and putting on a T-shirt.

••• 1:07—Nude getting tied to a pole by the Cannibal People and covered with red paint.
1:20—Brief peek at buns under her skirt when running away from the Cannibal People.

**Tigers in Lipstick** (1979)
. . . . . . . . . . . . . . . . . . . . The Stroller and The Widow
0:02—In black bra, panties and garter belt and stockings opening her fur coat to cause an accident.
0:48—In slip posing for photographer.

• 0:50—Very brief breasts when top of slip accidentally falls down.

• 0:51—More breasts with the photographer.

Clash of the Titans (1981) . . . . . . . . . . . . . . .Aphrodite

**Famous T & A** (1982) . . . . . . . . . . . . . . . . . . . Herself
(No longer available for purchase, check your video store for rental.)

••• 0:15—Full frontal nudity scenes from *Slave of the Cannibal God.*

The Chinatown Murders: Man Against the Mob (1989)
. . . . . . . . . . . . . . . . . . . . . . . . . . . . . . . Betty Starr

*Video Tapes:*

**Playboy Video Magazine, Volume 1** (1982)
. . . . . . . . . . . . . . . . . . . . . . . . . . . . . . . . . . Herself

•• 0:58—Breasts in still photos from *Playboy* pictorial.

*Magazines:*

**Playboy** (Nov 1973) . . . . . . . . . . . . . . . . . . . Encore
••• 102-109—Breasts and buns.

**Playboy** (Jan 1974) . . . . . . . . Twenty Years of Playboy
••• 206—Breasts in water from *She is Ursula Andress* pictorial.

**Playboy** (Nov 1974) . . . . . . . . . . Sex in Cinema 1974
•• 145—Breasts from *Last Chance For a Born Loser.*

**Playboy** (Jan 1975) . . . . . . . . . .Playboy Mansion West
•• 100—Breasts in pool, looking at goose.

**Playboy** (Apr 1976) . . . . . . . . . . Incomparably Ursula
••• 91-95—Photos from the film *The Loves and Times of Scaramouche.* Full frontal nudity.

**Playboy** (Nov 1976) . . . . . . . . . . Sex in Cinema 1976
• 151—Upper half of breasts.

**Playboy** (Nov 1977) . . . . . . . . . . Sex in Cinema 1977
••• 157—Breasts.

**Playboy** (Jan 1979) . . . . . . . . . . . . 25 Beautiful Years
•• 158—Breasts in a stream.

**Playboy** (Jan 1989) . . . . . . . . . . . .Women of the Sixties
••• 163—Breasts running her fingers through her hair sitting by a pond.

**Playboy's Nudes** (Oct 1990)
. . . . . . . . . . . . . . . . . . . . . . . . . . . . . . . . . . . Herself
••• 18-19—Breasts.

**Playboy** (Jan 1994) . . . . . . . . . . . . . . Remember Ursula
••• 162-163—Breasts.

## Andrews, Julie

Wife of dirctor Blake Edwards.

*Films:*

Americanization of Emily (1964). . . . . . . . . . . . . .Emily

Mary Poppins (1964) . . . . . . . . . . . . . . . Mary Poppins
(Academy Award for Best Actress.)

The Sound of Music (1965) . . . . . . . . . . . . . . . . . .Maria

Hawaii (1966) . . . . . . . . . . . . . . . . . . .Jerusha Bromley

Thoroughly Modern Millie (1967) . . . . .Millie Dillmount

**Darling Lili** (1970) . . . . . . . . . . . . . . . . . . . Lili Smith

• 1:12—Very, very brief left breast, when doing strip tease and tossing aside yellow outfit to duck behind curtain.

The Tamarind Seed (1974; British) . . . . . . .Judith Farrow

10 (1979). . . . . . . . . . . . . . . . . . . . . . . . . . . . . .Sam

Little Miss Marker (1980) . . . . . . . . . . . . . . . . .Amanda

**S.O.B.** (1981) . . . . . . . . . . . . . . . . . . . . . . . Sally Miles

•• 1:19—Breasts pulling the top off her red dress during the filming of a movie.

Victor/Victoria (1982). . . . . . . . . . . . . . Victor/Victoria

The Man Who Loved Women (1983) . . . . . . . .Marianna

That's Life! (1986) . . . . . . . . . . . . . . . . Gillian Fairchild

**Duet for One** (1987) . . . . . . . . . . .Stephanie Anderson

• 0:28—Very brief left breast in gaping blouse in bathroom splashing water on her face because she feels sick, then wet T-shirt.

••• 1:06—Breasts stretching, lying in bed.

• 1:07—Very brief buns and very brief right breast, when she rolls off the bed onto the floor.
1:30—In wet white blouse from perspiring after taking an overdose of pills.

A Fine Romance (1992; Italian). . . . . . . Pamela Picquet

*Made for TV Movies:*

Our Sons (1991) . . . . . . . . . . . . . . . . . . .Audrey Grant

*TV:*

The Julie Andrews Hour (1972-73) . . . . . . . . . . Hostess

Julie (1992) . . . . . . . . . . . . . . . . . . . . . .Julie Carlisle

# Angel, Vanessa

*Films:*

Spies Like Us (1985) . . . . . Russian Rocket Crewmember
1:31—In bra, putting on her snow outfit, coming out of tent after Dan Aykroyd.
**Another Chance** (1989). . . . . . . . . . . Jacky Johanssen
• 0:26—Sort of breasts under water in spa. Hard to see because of the bubbles.
King of New York (1990). . . . . . . . . . . . . British Female
**Homicidal Impulse** (1992). . . . . . . . . . . . . . Deborah
*a.k.a. Killer Instinct*
(Unrated version reviewed.)
•• 0:13—In bra, then breasts making love with Scott Valentine in his office on top of the photocopier (Don't see her face).
•• 0:24—Breasts and buns, while making love in bed (you can see her face a little bit).
••• 0:30—In black bra, then breasts while making love (don't see her face).
• 0:39—Very brief breasts in flashes during Valentine's drug induced visions.
Stop! Or My Mom Will Shoot (1992) . . . . . . Stewardess
*TV:*
Baywatch (1992- ). . . . . . . . . . . . . . . . . . . . . . . Megan
Reasonable Doubts (1992-93). . . . . . Officer Peggy Eliot
Weird Science (1994- ) . . . . . . . . . . . . . . . . . . . . . Lisa

# Ann, Tiffany

*Video Tapes:*

**Hot Body International: #2 Miss Puerto Vallarta**
(1990). . . . . . . . . . . . . . . . . . . . . . . . . . . . Contestant
•• 0:29—Breasts wearing pasties and buns, in G-string.
•• 0:57—1st place.
•• 0:58—Buns, posing in wet, green two piece swim-suit.
**Hot Body International: #4 Spring Break** (1992)
. . . . . . . . . . . . . . . . . . . . . . . . . . . . . . . Contestant
0:07—Dancing in two piece swimsuit on stage.
0:15—5th place winner.
• 0:36—Barely there wet T-shirt. Brief right breast, when bending over.
0:58—Winning 4th place in wet T-shirt contest.
**Hot Body: The Best of Hot Body** (1994) . . . . Herself
••• 0:58—Buns in swimsuits. Breasts under pasties.

# Ann-Margret

Wife of actor Roger Smith.
*Films:*

Pocketful of Miracles (1961) . . . . . . . . . . . . . . .Louise
State Fair (1962) . . . . . . . . . . . . . . . . . . . . Emily Porter
Bye Bye Birdie (1963) . . . . . . . . . . . . . . . . . Kim McAfee
The Pleasure Seekers (1964) . . . . . . . . . . . .Fran Hobson
Viva Las Vegas (1964) . . . . . . . . . . . . . . . .Rusty Martin
Bus Riley's Back in Town (1965). . . . . . . . . . . . . Laurel
The Cincinnati Kid (1965) . . . . . . . . . . . . . . . . . Melba
Murderer's Row (1966) . . . . . . . . . . . . . . . Suzie Solaris
The Swinger (1966) . . . . . . . . . . . . . . . . . Kelly Olsson
Tiger and the Pussycat (1967; U.S./Italian) . . . . Carolina
C. C. & Company (1970) . . . . . . . . . . . . . . . . . . . Ann

**R.P.M.** (1970) . . . . . . . . . . . . . . . . . . . . . . . . . . Rhoda
•• 0:07—Brief left breast and buns getting out of bed talking with Anthony Quinn.
0:30—In fishnet top.
**Carnal Knowledge** (1971) . . . . . . . . . . . . . . .Bobbie
•• 0:48—Breasts and buns making love in bed with Jack Nicholson, then getting out of bed and into shower with Jack.
• 1:07—Brief side view of left breast putting a bra on in the bedroom.
The Outside Man (1973; U.S./French) . . . . . . . . Nancy
The Train Robbers (1973) . . . . . . . . . . . . . . . Mrs. Lowe
Tommy (1975; British) . . . . . . . . . . . . . . . Nora Walker
**The Twist** (1976) . . . . . . . . . . . . . . . . . .Charlie Minerva
0:24—Left breast when Claire daydreams someone is sticking a pin into Ann-Margret's breast. A little bloody. Body double.
1:24—Very, very brief left breast during Bruce Dern's daydream. Seen from above, body double again.
Joseph Andrews (1977; British/French). . . . . Lady Boaby
0:19—Standing in pool in wet dress.
0:23—Upper half of breasts in black outfit in bed. Hard to see because of the shadows.
The Last Remake of Beau Geste (1977)
. . . . . . . . . . . . . . . . . . . . . . . . . Lady Flavia Geste
The Cheap Detective (1978) . . . . . . . . . Jezebel Desire
**Magic** (1978) . . . . . . . . . . . . . . . . . . . Peggy Ann Snow
••• 0:44—Right breast, lying on her side in bed talking to Anthony Hopkins.
The Villain (1979). . . . . . . . . . . . . . . . .Charming Jones
Middle Age Crazy (1980; Canadian). . . . . . . . .Sue Ann
I Ought to Be in Pictures (1982). . . . . . . . . . Stephanie
Return of the Soldier (1983; British) . . . . . . . . . .Jenny
Twice in a Lifetime (1985) . . . . . . . . . . . . . . . .Audrey
52 Pick-Up (1986) . . . . . . . . . . . . . . . Barbara Mitchell
A New Life (1988) . . . . . . . . . . . . . . . . . . . . . . . .Jackie
**A Tiger's Tale** (1988). . . . . . . . . . . . . . . . . . . . Rose
• 0:45—Side view of left breast in bra, then breasts jumping up after fire ants start biting her. Brief buns running along a hill. Long shot, probably a body double.
Newsies (1992) . . . . . . . . . . . . . . . . . . . Medda Larkson
Grumpy Old Men (1993). . . . . . . . . . . . . . . . . . .Ariel
*Made for Cable Movies:*
Nobody's Children (1994; USA) . . . . . . . . .Carol Stevens
*Miniseries:*
Queen (1993) . . . . . . . . . . . . . . . . . . . . Sally Jackson
*Made for TV Movies:*
Our Sons (1991) . . . . . . . . . . . . . . . . . .Luanne Barnes
*Magazines:*
**Playboy** (Feb 1981) . . . . . . . . . . . . . . The Year in Sex
•• 146—Left breast in still from *Magic*.

# •Annabi, Amina

*Films:*

**The Sheltering Sky** (1990) . . . . . . . . . . . . . .Mahrnia
•• 0:20—Left breast, then breasts in tent with John Malkovich.

•• 0:22—Right breast while lying down with Malkovich, breasts when he gets up.

The Hour of the Pig (1993; British/French) . . . . . Samira

## Annen, Glory

*Films:*

**Felicity** (1978; Australian) . . . . . . . . . . . . . . . . Felicity

•• 0:02—Breasts taking off leotard in girl's shower room, then nude taking a shower.

• 0:05—Buns, then left breast, then right breast undressing to go skinny dipping.

•• 0:10—Breasts and buns at night at the girl's dormitory with Jenny.

•• 0:15—Breasts undressing in room in front of Christine.

• 0:16—Left breast, while touching herself in bed.

••• 0:20—Lots of lower frontal nudity trying on clothes, bras and panties in dressing room. Brief breasts and buns.

••• 0:25—Buns and breasts taking a bath. Full frontal nudity when Steve peeks in at her.

• 0:31—Brief full frontal nudity losing her virginity on car with Andrew.

••• 0:38—Full frontal nudity in bath with Mei Ling and two other girls, then getting massaged. Long scene.

••• 0:58—Full frontal nudity in bed with Miles.

••• 1:13—Full frontal nudity with Mei Ling making love on bed. Long scene.

• 1:20—Left breast, while making love standing up.

•• 1:21—Breasts and buns making love with Miles.

•• 1:27—Nude making love again with Miles.

1:29—Buns, in the water with Miles.

**Spaced Out** (1980; British) . . . . . . . . . . . . . . . . Cosia

*a.k.a. Outer Touch*

••• 0:23—Breasts talking to the other two space women. Long scene.

• 0:31—Very brief breasts changing clothes while dancing.

•• 0:43—Breasts in bed with Willy.

••• 1:08—Breasts lying down.

**The Lonely Lady** (1983) . . . . . . . . . . . . . . . . . Marion

• 0:07—Brief left breast in back seat of car with Ray Liotta. Dark, hard to see.

**Alien Prey** (1984; British) . . . . . . . . . . . . . . . . . Jessica

• 0:22—Breasts unbuttoning blouse to sunbathe.

•• 0:34—Breasts taking off top, getting into bed with Josephine, then making love with her.

0:36—Buns, rolling on top of Josephine.

••• 0:38—More breasts when Josephine is playing with her.

0:39—More buns in bed. Long shot.

• 0:46—Left breast and buns standing up in bathtub.

•• 1:05—Breasts getting out of bed and putting a dress on.

•• 1:19—Breasts in bed with Anders. Brief buns when he rips her panties off.

Supergirl (1984; British) . . . . . . . . . . Midvale Protestor

## Annesley, Imogen

*Films:*

Playing Beatie Bow (1986; Australian) . . . . . . . . Abigail

**Howling III: The Marsupials** (1987) . . . . . . . . Jerboa

• 0:42—Very brief breasts taking off dress in barn to give birth. Breasts are covered with makeup.

Kiss the Night (1988; Australian) . . . . . . . . . . . . Sacha

Strapless (1990) . . . . . . . . . . . . . . . . . . . . . . . . Imogen

## Annis, Francesca

*Films:*

Saturday Night Out (1963; British) . . . . . . . . . . . . . Jean

**Macbeth** (1972) . . . . . . . . . . . . . . . . . . Lady Macbeth

• 1:41—Buns, while walking around after the bad guys have attacked and looted the castle. Side view of left breast, hard to see because it's covered by her hair.

Dune (1984) . . . . . . . . . . . . . . . . . . . . . . Lady Jessica

Under the Cherry Moon (1986) . . . . . . . Mrs. Wellington

*Made for Cable Movies:*

Doomsday Gun (1994; HBO) . . . . . . . . . . . . . . Sophie

*Miniseries:*

Masterpiece Theatre: Lilli (1979) . . . . . . . . Lilli Langtree

*Made for TV Movies:*

The Richest Man in the World: The Story of Aristotle Onassis (1988) . . . . . . . . . Jacqueline Kennedy Onassis

Parnell & The Englishwoman (1991) . . Katharine O'Shea

*Magazines:*

Playboy (Feb 1972) . . . . . . . . The Making of "Macbeth"

**Playboy** (Nov 1972) . . . . . . . . . . Sex in Cinema 1972

• 167—Right breast, sticking out of hair. Photo from *MacBeth*.

## Anspach, Susan

*Films:*

Five Easy Pieces (1970) . . . . . . . . . . Catherine Van Oost

The Landlord (1970) . . . . . . . . . . . . . . . Susan Enders

Play It Again, Sam (1972) . . . . . . . . . . . . . . . . Nancy

Blume in Love (1973) . . . . . . . . . . . . . . . . Nina Blume

The Big Fix (1978) . . . . . . . . . . . . . . . . . . . . . . Lila

Running (1979) . . . . . . . . . . . . . . . Janet Andropolis

Gas (1981; Canadian) . . . . . . . . . . . . . . Jane Beardsley

**Montenegro** (1981; British/Swedish) . . . Marilyn Jordan

•• 1:08—Full frontal nudity taking a shower.

• 1:28—Right breast making love with Montenegro.

Blood Red (1988) . . . . . . . . . . . . . . . . . . . . . . Widow

**Into the Fire** (1988) . . . . . . . . . . . . . Rosalind Winfield

*a.k.a. Legend of Lone Wolf*

•• 0:22—Left breast, under trench coat when she first comes into the house, briefly again in the kitchen.

•• 0:31—Breasts in bedroom standing up with Wade.

Back to Back (1990) . . . . . . . . . . . . . . . . Madeline Hix

The Rutanga Tapes (1991) . . . . . . . . . . . Kate Simpson

*Made for Cable Movies:*

Gone Are the Dayes (1984; Disney) . . . . . . . . . . . n.a.

*Made for Cable TV:*
The Hitchhiker: Dead Man's Curve . . . . . . . . . .Claudia
(Available on *The Hitchhiker, Volume 2.*)
>0:14—Buns (probably a body double) in a hotel room with a guy.

*TV:*
The Yellow Rose (1983). . . . . . . . . . . . Grace McKenzie

# Anthony, Lysette
*Films:*
Krull (1983). . . . . . . . . . . . . . . . . . . . . . . . . . . .Lyssa
**Looking for Eileen** (1988; Dutch)
. . . . . . . . . . . . . . . . . . . . . .Marjan/Eileen/Karnen
(Not available on video tape.)
Breasts.
Without a Clue (1988) . . . . . . . . . . . . . . . . . Fake Leslie
The Pleasure Principal (1991; British). . . . . . . Charlotte
**Switch** (1991) . . . . . . . . . . . . . . . . . . . . . . . . . . . Liz
> • 0:05—Brief breasts in spa with JoBeth Williams and Felicia, trying to kill Steve.

Husbands and Wives (1992) . . . . . . . . . . . . . . . . . Sam
The Hour of the Pig (1993; British/French)
. . . . . . . . . . . . . . . . . . . . . . . . . Filette d'Auferre
Look Who's Talking Now! (1993) . . . . . . . . . .Samantha
**Save Me** (1993). . . . . . . . . . . . . . . . . . . . . . . . . .Ellie
(Unrated version reviewed.)
> 0:22—Brief buns in body suit, when Harry Hamlin picks her up in back room of lingerie store.
> 0:31—Upper half of right breast in bra, while making love in convertible Mustang with Hamlin.
> • • • 0:39—Nude, while sleeping then making love in bed with Hamlin.
> • • 0:49—Breasts in spa with Hamlin. Long shot of buns, when getting out. Breasts again while putting on swimsuit.
> • • • 0:52—In bra, then breasts while making love with Hamlin in front of fireplace.
> • 1:05—Breasts, when Hamlin forces himself on her in stairway of parking garage.

**A Brilliant Disguise** (1994) . . . . . . . . Michele Ramsey
> • • 0:44—Breasts and buns, while making love with Andy.

**The Hard Truth** (1994) . . . . . . . . . . . . . Lisa Kantrell
> 0:04—In black bra and panties.
> 0:22—In black bra in office with Jonah.
> • • • 0:39—In black bra, then breasts, while making love with Jonah.

*Made for Cable Movies:*
A Ghost in Monte Carlo (1990). . . . . . . . . . . . . . .n.a.
*Made for Cable TV:*
**Tales From the Crypt: Forever Ambergris** (1993; HBO) . . . . . . . . . . . . . . . . . . . . . . . . . Bobbi
> • • • 0:08—Right breast in mirror, then breasts while making love with Ike when Roger Daltrey peeks in.
> • • • 0:24—Breasts, while making love with Daltrey in bed.

*Made for TV Movies:*
Ivanhoe (1982) . . . . . . . . . . . . . . . . . . . . Lady Rowena
Jack the Ripper (1988). . . . . . . . . . . . . .Mary Jane Kelly

The Lady and the Highwayman (1989)
. . . . . . . . . . . . . . . . . . . . . . . . Lady Panthea Vyne
*TV:*
Dark Shadows (1991). . . . . . . . . . . . . . . . . . Angelique
*Magazines:*
**Playboy** (Dec 1988) . . . . . . . . . . . . . . . . . . . . . .Lysette
> • 166-173—Breasts B&W photos.

**Playboy's Nudes** (Oct 1990) . . . . . . . . . . . . . . .Herself
> • • 9—Breasts.

# Antonelli, Laura
*Films:*
Dr. Goldfoot and the Girl Bombs (1966; Italian)
. . . . . . . . . . . . . . . . . . . . . . . . . . . . . . . .Rosanna
Man Called Sledge (1971; Italian) . . . . . . . . . . . . . .Ria
Docteur Popaul (1972; French) . . . . . . . . . . . . Martine
**High Heels** (1972; French) . . . . . . . . . . . . . . . Martine
*a.k.a. Docteur Popaul*
> 0:35—Breasts undressing while Jean-Paul Belmondo watches. Long, long shot.
> • 0:36—Briefly nude when Belmondo watches through opera glasses.
> • • • 0:53—Breasts and buns, getting out of bed and walking around.
> • 0:55—Buns, getting a shot while lying on examination table.
> • • 0:56—Breasts, twice, sitting naked on examination table.
> • 1:30—Brief side of right breast during flashback of 0:56 scene.
> 1:31—Brief full frontal nudity, running around her house while Mia Farrow watches. Long shot.

Without Apparent Motive (1972; French)
. . . . . . . . . . . . . . . . . . . . . . . . . Juliette Vaudreuil
**How Funny Can Sex Be?** (1973)
. . . . . . . . . . . . . . . . . . . Miscellaneous Personalities
> • 0:01—Brief breasts taking off swimsuit.
> • 0:04—Brief breasts in bathtub covered with bubbles.
> 0:13—Lying in bed in sheer nightgown.
> 0:18—Lying in bed again.
> • 0:26—Breasts getting into bed.
> • 0:36—Breasts making love in elevator behind frosted glass. Shot at fast speed.
> • 1:08—In sheer white nun's outfit during fantasy sequence. Brief breasts and buns. Nice slow motion.
> 1:16—In black nightie.
> • 1:24—In black bra and panties, then breasts while changing clothes.

**Malicious** (1974; Italian). . . . . . . . . . . . . . . . . .Angela
> • 1:14—Breasts after undressing while two boys watch from above.
> • • 1:27—Breasts, undressing under flashlight. Hard to see because the light is moving around a lot.
> • 1:29—Breasts and buns running around the house.

**Till Marriage Do Us Part** (1974; Italian). . . . . Eugenia
> • • 0:58—Breasts in the barn lying on hay after guy takes off her clothes.

•• 1:02—Full frontal nudity standing up in bathtub while maid washes her.
•• 1:07—Right breast with chauffeur in barn.
•• 1:36—Breasts surrounded by feathers on the bed while priest is talking.

**The Innocent** (1976; Italian) . . . . . . . . . . . . . Julianna
••• 0:41—Breasts in bed with her husband.
••• 0:53—Full frontal nudity in bed when her husband lifts her dress up.

**The Divine Nymph** (1977; Italian)
. . . . . . . . . . . . . . . . . . . . . . . . . . Manoela Roderighi
•• 0:10—Full frontal nudity reclining in chair.
• 0:18—Right breast in open blouse sitting in bed. Lower frontal nudity while getting up.

Wifemistress (1977; Italian) . . . . . . . . Antonia De Angelis
0:50—In lacy nightgown in her bedroom.
1:22—Brief upper half of left breast in bed with Clara and her husband.
1:25—In sheer lacy nightgown leaning out the window.
1:29—Almost right breast making love with a guy in bed.

Tigers in Lipstick (1979) . . . . . . . . . . . . . . The Pick Up
0:24—In brown lingerie lying in bed, then getting dressed.
0:34—In same lingerie, getting undressed, then in bed.

**Secret Fantasy** (1981) . . . . . . . . . . . . Costanza Vivaldi
(Breasts a lot. Only the best are listed.)
••• 0:16—In black bra in Doctor's office, then left breast, then breasts getting examined.
•• 0:18—In black bra and panties in another Doctor's office. Breasts and buns.
•• 0:19—Breasts getting X-rayed. Brief breasts lying down.
•• 0:32—Breasts and buns when Nicolo drugs her and takes Polaroid photos of her.
•• 0:49—Breasts and buns posing around the house for Nicolo while he takes Polaroid photos.
•• 0:53—Breasts and buns during Nicolo's dream.
••• 1:12—Breasts in Doctor's office.
•• 1:14—Breasts and buns in room with another guy.
•• 1:16—Breasts on train while workers "accidentally" see her.
•• 1:20—Breasts on bed after being carried from bathtub.
•• 1:25—Breasts dropping dress during opera.
•• 1:27—More breasts scenes from 0:49.

Passion of Love (1982) . . . . . . . . . . . . . . . . . . . . .Clara
*a.k.a. Passion D'Amor*
0:05—Brief side of right breast, undressing by the fire. Long shot.

La Venexiana (1986) . . . . . . . . . . . . . . . . . . . . Angela

**Collector's Item** (1988) . . . . . . . . . . . .Marie Colbert
*a.k.a. The Trap*
0:18—In white lingerie with Tony Musante.
• 0:20—Lower frontal nudity, then right breast making love with Musante. Dark.

0:37—In black bra, garter belt and stockings in open robe undressing for Musante.
0:41—In the same lingerie again dropping robe and getting dressed.

*Magazines:*
**Playboy** (Dec 1974) . . . . . . . . . . . . .Sex Stars of 1974
••• 209—Breasts.
**Playboy** (Dec 1979) . . . . . . . . . . . . .Sex Stars of 1979
••• 250—Breasts.
**Playboy** (Nov 1980) . . . . . . . . . . Sex in Cinema 1980
••• 179—Full frontal nudity.

# *Antonia*
See: Dorian, Antonia.

# *Anulka*
See: Dziubinska, Anulka.

# • *Anwar, Gabrielle*
*Films:*
Manifesto (1988) . . . . . . . . . . . . . . . . . . . . . . . . .Tina
If Looks Could Kill (1991) . . . . . . . . . . . . . . . . Mariska
*a.k.a. Teen Agent*
Wild Hearts Can't Be Broken (1991) . . . . Sonora Webster
Scent of a Woman (1992) . . . . . . . . . . . . . . . . .Donna
The Concierge (1993) . . . . . . . . . . . . . . . . Andy Hart
For Love or Money (1993) . . . . . . . . . . . . . . . . . . n.a.
The Three Musketeers (1993). . . . . . . . . . . Queen Anne
**Body Snatchers** (1994) . . . . . . . . . . . . . .Marti Malone
• 0:49—Very, very brief breast while in bathtub when pod creature falls on top of her.
••• 1:13—Several brief breast shots, while sitting up, looking at Tim and writhing around on bed in infirmary.
*Made for Cable TV:*
Fallen Angels: Dead-End for Delia (1993; Showtime)
. . . . . . . . . . . . . . . . . . . . . . . . . . . . . . . . . . . Delia
(Available on video tape on *Fallen Angels Two*.)

# *Apollonia*
Real name is Patty Kotero.
Singer.
*Films:*
**Amor Ciego** (1980; Mexican). . . . . . . . . . . . . . . Patty
• 0:32—Breasts getting out of hammock.
••• 0:52—Right breast, standing up, then breasts kissing Daniel. More breasts in bed.
••• 0:59—Buns, making love in bed, then breasts afterwards.
•• 1:11—Breasts, taking off her towel and putting Daniel's hand on her left breast.
•• 1:15—Breasts, turning over, then lying in bed.
Heartbreaker (1983). . . . . . . . . . . . . . . . . . . . . Rose
**Purple Rain** (1984) . . . . . . . . . . . . . . . . . . . .Apollonia
•• 0:20—Brief breasts taking off jacket before jumping into lake.
0:41—In lingerie making love with Prince.
1:06—In black lingerie and stockings singing on stage.

Ministry of Vengeance (1989) . . . . . . . . . . . . . . . Zarah
Back to Back (1990) . . . . . . . . . . . . . . . . . . . .Jesse Duro
Black Magic Woman (1990) . . . . . . . . Cassandra Perry
   0:18—Brief side of left breast with Mark Hamill.
   Don't see her face.
   0:25—Very brief upper half of left breast, while in
   shower with Hamill.
*TV:*
Falcon Crest (1985-86) . . . . . . . . . . . . . . . . Apollonia
*Magazines:*
Playboy (Jan 1985) . . . . . . . . . The Girls of Rock 'n' Roll
   98—In leather bikini, rated PG.

## Applegate, Christina

*Films:*
Streets (1989) . . . . . . . . . . . . . . . . . . . . . . . . . . Dawn
   1:09—Very, very brief almost side view of left breast,
   while kissing her boyfriend. His hand is over her
   breast. Not really a nude scene, but I'm including it
   because people might send this in as an addition.
Don't Tell Mom the Babysitter's Dead (1991) . . . . .Swell
*TV:*
Heart of the City (1986-87) . . . . . . . . . .Robin Kennedy
Married ...with Children (1987- ) . . . . . . . . Kelly Bundy

## Applegate, Colleen

a.k.a. Adult film actress Shauna Grant.
*Video Tapes:*
Nudes in Limbo (1983) . . . . . . . . . . . . . . . . . . . .Model
**Penthouse Love Stories** (1986)
. . . . . . . . . . . . . . . . . . . . . . . Service Station Woman
••• 0:10—Nude, making love in a bedroom. Long
   scene.
**Penthouse: On the Wild Side** (1988) . . . . . . .Colleen
••• 0:39—Breasts in lingerie on bed. Nude on the floor.

## Archer, Anne

Daughter of actor John Archer and actress Marjorie Lord.
*Films:*
Cancel My Reservation (1972) . . . . . . . . . . . . . . Crazy
The Honkers (1972) . . . . . . . . . . . . . . . .Deborah Moon
The All-American Boy (1973) . . . . . . . Drenna Valentine
**Lifeguard** (1975) . . . . . . . . . . . . . . . . . . . . . . Cathy
  • 1:04—Very brief nipple while kissing Sam Elliott.
   Need to crank the brightness on your TV to the max-
   imum. It appears in the lower right corner of the
   screen as the camera pans from right to left.
Trackdown (1976) . . . . . . . . . . . . . . . . . . . . .Barbara
Paradise Alley (1978) . . . . . . . . . . . . . . . . . . . . Annie
Good Guys Wear Black (1979) . . . . . . . . . Margaret
Hero at Large (1980) . . . . . . . . . . . . . . . . . . J. Marsh
Raise the Titanic (1980; British) . . . . . . .Dana Archibald
Green Ice (1981; British) . . . . . . . . . . . . . . . Holbrook
The Naked Face (1984) . . . . . . . . . . . . . . . .Ann Blake
Too Scared to Scream (1985) . . . . . . . . . . . . . . . Kate
The Check is in the Mail (1986) . . . . . . . .Peggy Jackson
Fatal Attraction (1987) . . . . . . . . . . . . Ellen Gallagher
  0:51—In white bra, sitting in front of mirror, getting
   ready for a party.

Love at Large (1990) . . . . . . . . . . . . . . . . . .Miss Dolan
Narrow Margin (1990) . . . . . . . . . . . . . . . . . . Hunnicut
Eminent Domain (1991) . . . . . . . . . . . . . . . . . . . . Mita
Body of Evidence (1992) . . . . . . . . . . Joanne Braslow
   (Unrated version reviewed.)
   1:12—Nude scene on video playback is body double
   Shawn Lusader.
Patriot Games (1992) . . . . . . . . . . . . . . Dr. Cathy Ryan
Family Prayers (1993) . . . . . . . . . . . . . . . . . . . . . n.a.
Short Cuts (1993) . . . . . . . . . . . . . . . . . . . Claire Kane
   1:49—(0:6 into Part 2) Very brief side view of buns,
   while hiking up nightgown and sitting on edge of
   tub.
Clear and Present Danger (1994) . . . . . . . . . . . . . n.a.
*Made for Cable Movies:*
The Last of His Tribe (1992; HBO) . . . Henriette Kroeber
Nails (1992; Showtime) . . . . . . . . . . . . . . . .Mary Niles
   0:16—Breasts and buns belong to body double
   Shelley Michelle.
*Miniseries:*
Seventh Avenue (1977) . . . . . . . . . . . . . . .Myrna Gold
*Made for TV Movies:*
Jane's House (1994) . . . . . . . . . . . . . . . . . . . . . . n.a.
*TV:*
Bob & Carol & Ted & Alice (1973) . . . . . . Carol Sanders
The Family Tree (1983) . . . . . . .Annie Benjamin Nichols
Falcon Crest (1985) . . . . . . . . . . . . . .Cassandra Wilder

## • Argento, Asia

Daughter of Italian director Dario Argento and actress
  Daria Nicolodi.
*Films:*
The Church (1991; Italian) . . . . . . . . . . . . . . . . . Lotte
  *a.k.a. La Chiesa*
**Trauma** (1992) . . . . . . . . . . . . . . . . . . . . .Aura Petrescu
•• 0:27—Breasts, after taking off bra in bathroom.

## Argo, Allison

*Films:*
**Between the Lines** (1977) . . . . . . . . . . . . . . Dancer
  • 0:28—Breasts dancing on stage.
Cry From the Mountain (1986) . . . . . . Laurie Matthews
*TV:*
Ladies' Man (1980-81) . . . . . . . . . . . . . . . . . . . .Susan

## Ariane

Model.
Full name is Ariane Koizumi.
*Films:*
**The Year of the Dragon** (1985) . . . . . . . . .Tracy Tzu
  • 0:59—Very brief breasts when Mickey Rourke rips
   her blouse off in her apartment.
  •• 1:14—Nude, taking a shower in her apartment.
  •• 1:18—Breasts straddling Rourke, while making love
   on the bed.
King of New York (1990) . . . . . . . . . . . . . Dinner Guest
**Skin Art** (1993) . . . . . . . . . . . . . . . . . . . . . . . . .Lin
  • 1:00—Left breast when Will pulls her lingerie top
   down and kisses her.

*Made for Cable Movies:*
  Women & Men 2: Three Short Stories (1991; HBO)
  . . . . . . . . . . . . . . . . . . . . . . . . . . . . . . . . . . . . . Alice

# Ariel, Brigitte

*Films:*
  Rosebud (1975) . . . . . . . . . . . . . . . . . . . . . . . Sabine
  Piaf—The Early Years (1982) . . . . . . . . . . . . . Edith Piaf
*Magazines:*
  **Playboy** (Jun 1975) . . . . . . . Sex in Cinema French Style
  ••• 86—Full frontal nudity.
  **Playboy** (Dec 1975). . . . . . . . . . . . . Sex Stars of 1975
  ••• 183—Full frontal nudity.

# Aries, Anna

*Films:*
  The Omega Man (1971) . . . . Woman in Cemetary Crypt
  Rage (1972) . . . . . . . . . . . . . . . . . . . . . . . . . . . . . .n.a.
  **Invasion of the Bee Girls** (1973) . . . . . . . .Cora Kline
  •• 0:55—Buns and breasts getting transformed into a
    Bee Girl.
  ••• 1:00—Breasts getting out of the bee transformer.

# •Armitage, Alison

  See: York, Brittany.

# Armstrong, Bess

*Films:*
  **Four Seasons** (1981). . . . . . . . . . . . . . .Ginny Newley
    0:26—In two piece swimsuit on boat putting lotion
      on herself.
    • 0:38—Brief buns twice skinny dipping in the water
      with Nick.
    0:40—In one piece swimsuit.
  Jekyll & Hyde... Together Again (1982). . . . . . . . .Mary
  High Road to China (1983) . . . . . . . . . . . . . . . . . . Eve
  Jaws 3 (1983) . . . . . . . . . . . . . . . . . . . . Kathryn Morgan
  **The House of God** (1984) . . . . . . . . . Dr. Worthington
    (Not available on video tape.)
    Breasts.
  Nothing in Common (1986) . . . . Donna Mildred Martin
  Second Sight (1989) . . . . . . . . . . . . . . . Sister Elizabeth
  The Skateboard Kid (1993) . . . . . . . . . . . . . . . .Maggie
*Made for Cable TV:*
  Tales From the Crypt: What's Cookin' (1992; HBO)
  . . . . . . . . . . . . . . . . . . . . . . . . . . . . . . . . . . . . . .Erma
*Miniseries:*
  Lace (1984). . . . . . . . . . . . . . . . . . . . . . . . Judy Hale
*Made for TV Movies:*
  The Lakeside Killer (1979) . . . . . . . . . . . . . . . . . . .n.a.
*TV:*
  On Our Own (1977-78) . . . . . . . . . . . . . . . Julia Peters
  All Is Forgiven (1986) . . . . . . . . . . . . . . Paula Russell
  Married People (1990-91) . . . . . . . .Elizabeth Meyers
  My So-Called Life (1994- ) . . . . . . . . . . . . . . . . . .Patty

# Armstrong, Katherine

*Films:*
  The Arrival (1990). . . . . . . . . . . . . . . . . . . . . . . . .n.a.

**Crash and Burn** (1990) . . . . . . . . . . . . . . . . Christine
  ••• 1:00—Breasts taking a shower before being killed.
**Ambition** (1991) . . . . . . . . . . . . . . . . . . . . .Roseanne
  ••• 1:13—Buns in G-string, then breasts in Clancy
    Brown's apartment.
Street Soldiers (1991). . . . . . . . . . . . . . . . . . . . . .Julie
**Silk Degrees** (1994). . . . . . . . . . . . . . . . . . . . Nicole
  • 1:05—Very, very brief breast, while in water, while
    killing Mark Hamill.

# Armstrong, Kerry

*Films:*
  Key Exchange (1985) . . . . . . . . . . . . . . . . . . The Beauty
  **Hunting** (1990; Australian). . . . . . . . . . .Michelle Harris
    • 0:29—Side view of left breast in steamy shower.
    •• 0:35—Breasts, making love with John Savage in bed.
      Seen on video monitors.
    • 1:00—Breasts and upper half of buns, making love
      with Savage.
    • 1:02—Brief buns, turning over in bed.
    • 1:26—Very, very brief breasts, getting her dress top
      yanked down. Breasts, long shot, getting raped on
      dining table. Left breast, lying on the floor after-
      wards.

# Armstrong, Melinda

*Films:*
  In the Cold of the Night (1989) . . . . . . . . Laser Model 2
  **Bikini Summer** (1991). . . . . . . . . . . . . . . . . . . Cheryl
    • 0:07—Very brief breasts and partial buns, in bath-
      room when Chet interrupts her.
    0:25—Close-up of buns, bending over while wear-
      ing a swimsuit.
    ••• 0:35—Nude in swimming pool and talking to Burt.
      Nice, long scene.
    •• 0:49—Breasts and buns, trying on swimsuits, then
      having a water fight with Shelley Michelle.
    0:51—Buns, in swimsuit at the beach.
    ••• 1:17—Full frontal nudity in swimming pool flash-
      back.
  **Alien Intruder** (1992) . . . . . . . . . . . . . . . . . . . Tammy
    •• 0:29—In two piece swimsuit, then nude in shower
      during Maxwell Caulfield's virtual reality experience.
    • 0:30—Very, very brief right breast, while putting on
      robe while walking on balcony.
    • 0:54—Breasts, while lying dead on beach.
  **Bikini Summer 2** (1992) . . . . . . . . . . . . . . . . Venessa
    ••• 0:05—Breasts and buns, taking a shower.
    ••• 0:52—Breasts, taking off swimsuit top in bedroom.
      Breasts and buns, taking a shower.
    ••• 0:54—Breasts and buns in T-back panties, taking off
      robe and getting into bed, then sitting up to eat
      breakfast.
  Encino Man (1992) . . . . . . . . . . . . . . . . .Mountain Nug
  **Jailbait** (1993) . . . . . . . . . . . . . . . . . . . . . . . . . . Dawn
    • 0:43—Brief buns in G-string, then breasts, while
      talking to C. Thomas Howell in room in sex club.

*Video Tapes:*

**Hot Body Video Magazine #2** (1992) . . . . . . .Model
•• 0:00—Breasts during opening credits.
••• 0:03—In white bra, then breasts, buns in panties, posing outside.
••• 0:25—Breasts and buns (on the left), changing swimsuits.
**Hot Body: The Best of Hot Body** (1994) . . . . Herself
••• 0:11—Buns in swimsuits. Breasts while trying on lingerie.

*Magazines:*

**Playboy** (May 1992) . . . . . . . . . . . . . . . . . .Grapevine
•• 167—Buns in G-string. Lower half of right breast.
**Playboy** (Feb 1993) . . . . . . . . . . Being in Nothingness
• 126—Lower frontal nudity.
**Playboy's Girls of Summer '93** (Jun 1993). . . Herself
•• 39—Buns.
Playboy's Wet & Wild Women (Aug 1993) . . . . . Herself

## Armstrong, Rebekka

*Films:*

Mortuary Academy (1988) . . . . . . . . . . . . . . . . . Nurse
**Hider in the House** (1989). . . . . . . .Attractive Woman
• 0:47—Brief breasts in bed with Mimi Roger's husband when she surprises them.
**Immortalizer** (1990) . . . . . . . . . . . . . . . . . . . . June
• 0:16—Breasts getting blouse taken off by nurse.
••• 0:29—Breasts when a worker fondles her while she's asleep.
Instant Karma (1990) . . . . . . . . . . . . . . . . . . . . Jamie
**Angel 4: Undercover** (1993) . . . . . . .Catfight Groupie
• 0:41—Brief breasts, while with a band member and another woman in dressing room.

*Music Videos:*

Give Me the Keys/Huey Lewis & the News . . . . . . . .n.a.

*Video Tapes:*

**Playboy Video Centerfold: Rebekka Armstrong**
. . . . . . . . . . . . . . . . . . . . . . . . . . . . . . . . Playmate
**Playboy Video Calendar 1987** (1986) . . . . Playmate
**Playboy Video Magazine, Volume 10** (1986)
. . . . . . . . . . . . . . . . . . . . . . . . . . . . . . . Playmate
••• 0:40—Nude in song and dance number in car repair shop.
**Sexy Lingerie** (1988) . . . . . . . . . . . . . . . . . .Model
**Wet and Wild** (1989). . . . . . . . . . . . . . . . . . .Model
**Playboy Video Centerfold: Kerri Kendall** (1990)
. . . . . . . . . . . . . . . . . . . . . . . . . . . . . . Playmate
••• 0:33—Nude.
**Playmates at Play** (1990) . . . . . . . . . . . .Gotta Dance
**Wet and Wild II** (1990) . . . . . . . . . . . . . . . . .Model
**Sexy Lingerie III** (1991) . . . . . . . . . . . . . . . .Model
**Ultimate Sensual Massage** (1991) . . . . . . . Seduction
••• 0:39—Nude, during massage session in surreal outdoor setting.
**Wet and Wild III** (1991). . . . . . . . . . . . . . . . .Model
**The Best of Wet and Wild** (1992) . . . . . . . . .Model

**Intimate Workout For Lovers** (1992)
. . . . . . . . . . . . . . . . . . . . . . . . . .Sensual Exercise
••• 0:11—Nude, exercising in living room and exercise room.

*Magazines:*

**Playboy's Girls of Summer '86** (Aug 1986). . . Herself
••• 50-51—Full frontal nudity.
**Playboy** (Sep 1986) . . . . . . . . . . . . . . . . . . . Playmate
**Playboy's Book of Lingerie** (Jan 1991) . . . . . .Herself
••• 32—Full frontal nudity.
**Playboy's Book of Lingerie** (Jul 1991). . . . . .Herself
••• 37-39—Breasts.
**Playboy's Book of Lingerie** (May 1992) . . . . .Herself
•• 43—Breasts.
**Playboy's Calendar Playmates** (Nov 1992). . .Herself
••• 55—Full frontal nudity.
**Playboy's Girls of Summer '93** (Jun 1993) . . .Herself
••• 21—Full frontal nudity.
**Playboy's Video Playmates** (Sep 1993) . . . . . .Herself
••• 12-15—Buns and right breast.
**Playboy's Book of Lingerie** (Jan 1994) . . . . . .Herself
••• 94—Full frontal nudity.
**Playmates at Play** (Jul 1994) . . . . . . . . . . . .Herself
••• 45—Full frontal nudity.
••• 52-55—Breasts and buns.

## Arnett, Sherry

*Video Tapes:*

**Playboy Video Centerfold: Sherry Arnett**
. . . . . . . . . . . . . . . . . . . . . . . . . . . . . . . . Playmate
**Playboy Video Calendar 1987** (1986). . . . . Playmate
**Playboy Video Calendar 1988** (1987). . . . . Playmate

*Magazines:*

**Playboy** (Jan 1986). . . . . . . . . . . . . . . . . . . . Playmate
**Playboy's Girls of Summer '86** (Aug 1986). . . Herself
••• 21—Full frontal nudity.
••• 46—Right breast and lower frontal nudity.
••• 47—Full frontal nudity.
••• 88-89—Full frontal nudity.
• 104—Back side of left breast and buns.
•• 110—Right breast.
**Playboy's Calendar Playmates** (Nov 1992). . .Herself
••• 51—Full frontal nudity.
••• 63—Full frontal nudity.
**Playboy's Nudes** (Dec 1992) . . . . . . . . . . . . . .Herself
• 50-51—Buns.

## Arnold, Caroline

*Films:*

**Vindicator** (1986; Canadian) . . . . . . . . . . . . . . . .Lisa
*a.k.a. Frankenstein '88*
•• 0:40—Breasts in bed with a jerk, then putting her blouse on.
Meatballs III (1987) . . . . . . . . . . .Ida (Girl in VW Bug)

## Aronson, Judie

*Films:*

**Friday the 13th, Part IV—The Final Chapter**
(1984) . . . . . . . . . . . . . . . . . . . . . . . . . . . . Samantha
- • 0:26—Brief breasts and very brief buns taking
  clothes off to go skinny dipping.
- • 0:29—Brief breasts under water pretending to be
  dead.
- •• 0:39—Breasts and brief buns taking off her T-shirt to
  go skinny dipping at night.

American Ninja (1985) . . . . . . . . . . . . . . . . . . . Patricia
Weird Science (1985) . . . . . . . . . . . . . . . . . . . . . Hilly
After Midnight (1989). . . . . . . . . . . . . . . . . . . . Jennifer
**Cool Blue** (1990). . . . . . . . . . . . . . . . . . . . . . . . Cathy
- •• 1:03—Breasts in bed on top of Woody Harrelson.

**The Sleeping Car** (1990) . . . . . . . . . . . . . . . . . . Kim
- •• 0:42—Brief breasts on top of David Naughton making love. Brief breasts three times after he hallucinates.

Desert Kickboxer (1991) . . . . . . . . . . . . . . . . . .Claudia
*TV:*
Pursuit of Happiness (1987-88) . . . . . . . . .Sara Duncan

## • Arquette, Patricia

Sister of actress Rosanna Arquette.
Granddaughter of actor Cliff Arquette a.k.a. Charlie
  Weaver.
Daughter of actor/director Lewis Arquette.
*Films:*

Pretty Smart (1986) . . . . . . . . . . . . . . . . . . . . . . . Zero
A Nightmare on Elm Street 3: The Dream Warriors
  (1987). . . . . . . . . . . . . . . . . . . . . . . . . Kristen Parker
Far North (1988). . . . . . . . . . . . . . . . . . . . . . . . . . Jilly
Prayer of the Rollerboys (1990) . . . . . . . . . . . . . Casey
The Indian Runner (1991) . . . . . . . . . . . . . . . Dorothy
Trouble Bound (1992). . . . . . . . . . . . . . . . . . . . . . Kit
Ethan Frome (1993) . . . . . . . . . . . . . . . . . . . . . .n.a.
Inside Monkey Zetterland (1993) . . . . .Grace Zetterland
**True Romance** (1993) . . . . . . . . . . Alabama Whitman
  (Unrated version reviewed.)
- • 0:11—Brief breasts, while lying in bed with Christian
  Slater. Wide screen laser disc version only: Right
  breast two more times and partial left breast (••).

*Made for Cable Movies:*
Wildflower (1991; Lifetime). . . . . . . . . . . .Alice Guthrie
  0:42—Very brief side view of right breast, while
  splashing in the water at night. Long shot. (In later
  close-up shots, you can see top of swimsuit top.)

*Made for Cable TV:*
Tales From the Crypt: Four Sided Triangle (1990; HBO)
  . . . . . . . . . . . . . . . . . . . . . . . . . . . . . . . . .Mary Jo

*Made for TV Movies:*
Dillinger (1991). . . . . . . . . . . . . . . . . . . . . . . . . Polly
Betrayed by Love (1994) . . . . . . . . . . . . . . . . .Deanne

## Arquette, Rosanna

Sister of actress Patricia Arquette.
Granddaughter of actor Cliff Arquette a.k.a. Charlie
  Weaver.
Daughter of actor/director Lewis Arquette.
*Films:*

Gorp (1980). . . . . . . . . . . . . . . . . . . . . . . . . . . . .Judy
**S.O.B.** (1981) . . . . . . . . . . . . . . . . . . . . . . . . . . Babs
- • 0:21—Brief breasts taking off white T-shirt on the
  deck of the house. Long shot, hard to see.

**The Executioner's Song** (1982) . . . . . . . Nicole Baker
  (European Version reviewed.)
- ••• 0:30—Brief breasts in bed, then getting out of bed.
  Buns, walking to kitchen.
- ••• 0:41—Breasts in bed with Tommy Lee Jones.
- ••• 0:48—Breasts on top of Jones making love.
- •• 1:36—Right breast and buns, standing up getting
  strip searched before visiting Jones in prison.

Off the Wall (1982) . . . . . . . . . . . . . . . . . . . . . . .Pam
**Baby, It's You** (1983). . . . . . . . . . . . . . . . . . . . . . . Jill
- •• 1:17—Left breast, making love in bed with Vincent
  Spano.

The Aviator (1984). . . . . . . . . . . . . . . . . . . Tilly Hansen
After Hours (1985) . . . . . . . . . . . . . . . . . . . . . . Marcy
  0:48—In bed, dead, in panties. Arm covers breasts.
**Desperately Seeking Susan** (1985) . . . .Roberta Glass
- • 0:46—Breasts getting dressed when Aidan Quinn
  sees her through the fish tank. Long shot, hard to
  see.

Silverado (1985). . . . . . . . . . . . . . . . . . . . . . Hannah
8 Million Ways to Die (1986) . . . . . . . . . . . . . . .Sarah
  1:00—In a bra in Jeff Bridges' apartment.
Nobody's Fool (1986) . . . . . . . . . . . . . . . . . . . Cassie
Amazon Women on the Moon (1987) . . . . . . . . .Karen
The Big Blue (1988). . . . . . . . . . . . . . . . . . . . .Johana
  1:00—Brief right breast in bra in water when Jacques
  helps her out of the dolphin tank and her sweater
  gets pulled up.
**Black Rainbow** (1989; British) . . . . . . . . .Martha Travis
  0:48—In black bra, panties, garter belt and stockings in while talking to Tom Hulce.
- ••• 0:50—Breasts in bed with Hulce, then walking to
  bathroom.

New York Stories (1989). . . . . . . . . . . . . . . . .Paulette
...Almost (1990; Australian) . . . . . . . . . . . . . . . .Wendy
Flight of the Intruder (1991) . . . . . . . . . . . . . . .Callie
The Linguini Incident (1991) . . . . . . . . . . . . . . . Lucy
Fathers and Sons (1992) . . . . . . . . . . . . . .Miss Athena
Don't Hang Up (1993) . . . . . . . . . . . . . . . Sarah Weiss
**Nowhere to Run** (1993) . . . . . . . . . . . . . . . . . Clydie
- ••• 0:11—In white bra and panties, undressing in bath-
  room, then nude, getting into the shower while
  Jean-Claude Van Damme peeks in through the win-
  dow.
- ••• 1:01—In bra, then breasts while making love in bed
  with Van Damme.

*Made for Cable Movies:*
Sweet Revenge (1990) . . . . . . . . . . . . . . . . . . . .Kate

**The Wrong Man** (1993; Showtime) . . . . . . . . . Missy
- •• 0:34—Buns in black panties, then breasts, taking off her dress at the beach and going into the water. Medium long shot.
  1:08—In red bra and panties in hotel room with John Lithgow and Kevin Anderson.
- ••• 1:15—Breasts after taking off bra and dancing on table in room, then putting on dress afterwards. Very nice, long scene.
- • 1:23—Very, very brief part of right breast in open robe and very brief side view of buns while in bed on top of Anderson.
  1:26—Brief squished left breast, while lying in bed.

*Miniseries:*
Son of Morning Star (1991) . . . . . . . . . . Libbie Custer
*Made for TV Movies:*
In the Deep Woods (1992) . . . . . . . . . . . . . . . Joanna
*TV:*
Shirley (1979-80) . . . . . . . . . . . . . . . . . . . Debra Miller
*Magazines:*
**Playboy** (Sep 1990) . . . . . . . . . . . . . . . . . . . . Rosanna
- ••• 126-137—B&W and color photos nude in the surf. Some are out of focus.

# Arth, Emily

*Video Tapes:*
**Playboy Video Calendar 1990** (1989) . . . . . . . . May
- ••• 0:23—Nude.
**Playboy Video Playmate Six-Pack 1992** (1992)
. . . . . . . . . . . . . . . . . . . . . . . . . . . . . . . . Playmate
*Magazines:*
**Playboy** (Jun 1988) . . . . . . . . . . . . . . . . . . . . Playmate
**Playboy's Nudes** (Dec 1992) . . . . . . . . . . . . . . Herself
- •• 63—Lower frontal nudity and left breast.

# Arthur, Sean'a

a.k.a. Shana Arthur.
*Films:*
**Body Waves** (1991) . . . . . . . . . . . . . . . . . . . Dream Girl
- •• 0:02—Brief buns in swimsuit, walking into office.
- ••• 0:03—Breasts, taking off her bathing suit top during Rick's dream.
- •• 0:07—Breasts and side view of buns in swimsuit bottom, during Dooner's fantasy.
**Dance with Death** (1991) . . . . . . . . . . . . . . Sherilyn
- • 0:42—Buns, while dancing on stage with Lola.
**Uncaged** (1991) . . . . . . . . . . . . . . . . . . . . . . . Dancer
a.k.a. Angel in Red
- •• 0:44—Buns in lingerie. Breasts dancing on stage.
Black Belt (1992) . . . . . . . . . . . . . . . . . . . . . . Reporter

# Arthur, Stacy

Mrs. Ohio 1990.
*Video Tapes:*
**Playboy Video Calendar 1992** (1991) . . . . . October
- ••• 0:39—Buns in lingerie. Full frontal nudity fantasizing in bed.
- ••• 0:41—Nude in various locations around the house.

**Playboy's Playmate Review 1992** (1992)
. . . . . . . . . . . . . . . . . . . . . . . . . . . . . Miss January
- ••• 0:18—Nude, dancing on back of truck, then using a pottery wheel.
**Sexy Lingerie IV** (1992) . . . . . . . . . . . . . . . . . . Model
*Magazines:*
**Playboy** (Jan 1991) . . . . . . . . . . . . . . . . . . . . Playmate
- ••• 118-129—Nude.
**Playboy's Calendar Playmates** (Nov 1992). . . Herself
- ••• 106—Full frontal nudity.

# Ashbrook, Daphne

*Films:*
Gimme an "F" (1981) . . . . . . . . . . . . . . . Phoebe Willis
a.k.a. T & A Academy 2
**Sunset Heat** (1991) . . . . . . . . . . . . . . . . . . . . . . Julie
(Unrated version reviewed.)
- • 1:06—Brief breasts in silhouette, while making love with Michael Paré. Dark.
- •• 1:07—More breasts, on top of Paré, then lying down.
*Made for TV Movies:*
Daughters of Privilege (1990). . . . . . . . . . . Mary Hope
Intruders (1992). . . . . . . . . . . . . . . . . . . . . Lesley Hahn
Poisoned by Love: The Kern County Murders (1993)
. . . . . . . . . . . . . . . . . . . . . . . . . . . . . . . . . . Dyna
*TV:*
Our Family Honor (1985-86) . . . . . . . Officer Liz McKay
Fortune Dane (1986) . . . . . . . Kathy "Speed" Davenport

# •Ashland, Brittany

*Films:*
**Psycho Cop 2** (1992) . . . . . . . . . . . Go Go Dancer #1
- • 0:21—Breasts on film that the guys are watching at bachelor party. (She's the blonde one.)
- • 1:17—Breasts and buns in panties in film during end credits.
*Video Tapes:*
**Starlet Screen Test III** (1992) . . . . . . Brigitte Williams
- ••• 0:34—Breasts in silhouette during audition, then nude with the lights on and playing with ice.

# Ashley, Elizabeth

*Films:*
The Carpetbaggers (1964) . . . . . . . . . Monica Winthrop
The Marriage of a Young Stockbroker (1971) . . . . . . Nan
**Paperback Hero** (1973; Canadian) . . . . . . . . . Loretta
- ••• 0:37—Nude in shower with Keir Dullea. Long scene.
- ••• 0:39—Breasts, straddling Dullea in the shower.
Rancho Deluxe (1975) . . . . . . . . . . . . . . . . Cora Brown
The Great Scout and Cathouse Thursday (1976)
. . . . . . . . . . . . . . . . . . . . . . . . . . . . . . . Nancy Sue
Coma (1978) . . . . . . . . . . . . . . . . . . . . . Mrs. Emerson
Paternity (1981). . . . . . . . . . . . . . . . . . Sophia Thatcher
Split Image (1982) . . . . . . . . . . . . . . . . . . . . . . . Diana
Dragnet (1987) . . . . Police Commissioner Jane Kilpatrick
Vampire's Kiss (1989) . . . . . . . . . . . . . . . . . . Dr. Glaser

*Made for Cable TV:*
The Hitchhiker: Out of the Night (1985; HBO)
............................................Woman

*Made for TV Movies:*
In the Best Interest of the Children (1992)
.................................... Carla Scott

*TV:*
Evening Shade (1990- ) ................ Frieda Evans

## Ashley, Jennifer

*Films:*
Your Three Minutes Are Up (1973) ..... Teenage Driver
**The Centerfold Girls** (1974) ...............Charly
- • 0:34—Breasts taking off blouse while changing
  clothes.
- •• 0:49—Breasts and buns posing for photographer
  outside with Glory.

**The Pom Pom Girls** (1976) ................ Laurie
- • 1:02—Brief breasts (on the left), taking off her white
  blouse in locker room. Brief buns, taking off panties
  and pulling down her cheerleader body suit.

**Tintorera** (1977)......................... Kelly
- • 0:27—Buns and brief side of left breast, taking off
  her dress to swim to boat. She's the first one to take
  off her dress.
- •• 0:28—Breasts and buns, while on boat deck and
  getting into hammock with Steven.
- •• 0:29—Breasts, while sleeping in hammock and getting out. Brief nude in water, while swimming from
  the boat.
- • 1:11—Breasts, while taking off her yellow top. Dark.
- • 1:12—Brief breasts, while doing backstroke in water
  near Cynthia.
- • 1:14—Brief breasts, while getting pulled out of the
  water by Steven, then lying on her back on beach.

Horror Planet (1980; British) .................Holly
*a.k.a. Inseminoid*
Partners (1982)....................... Secretary
Chained Heat (1983; U.S./German) .........Grinder
The Man Who Loved Women (1983) ...David's Mother

*Magazines:*
**Playboy** (Nov 1978) .......... Sex in Cinema 1978
- • 187—Breasts above the water.

## • Ashley, Kirsten

*Films:*
**The Rain Killer** (1990) ............... Dancer #2
- • 0:32—Nude, dancing on stage in club. Backlit too
  much.
- • 0:49—Buns, then brief nude on stage in club. Slightly out of focus.

Sex Crimes (1991) ..................... Dancer

## Ashley, Susan

*Made for Cable TV:*
**Dream On: What I Did for Lust** (1991; HBO)
.....................................Marsha
- •• 0:01—Breasts in Eddie's dressing room with a sweater over her head.

*Video Tapes:*
Rock Video Girls (1991) ................... Herself

## • Ashton, Vali

*Films:*
Blue Desert (1990).......................... n.a.
**Die Watching** (1993) .............. Nola Carlisle
- 0:41—Very, very briefly in pink bra in Christopher
  Atkins' hallucinations.
- • 1:00—Buns in white panties and right breast while
  making love with Atkins.

Mortal Danger (1993) ................... Couselor

## Assan, Ratna

*Films:*
**Papillon** (1973) .........................Zoraima
- • 1:54—Breasts, first seeing Steve McQueen.
- •• 1:55—Breasts, helping clean up McQueen on the
  beach and in the ocean.
- •• 1:56—Breasts, walking on the beach with Mc-
  Queen.
- •• 1:57—Breasts, getting off boat and watching a guy
  open oysters.
- •• 2:00—Breasts, on beach, walking with McQueen
  while holding a torch.

*Magazines:*
**Playboy** (Feb 1974) ................."Butterfly" Girl
- ••• 151-153—Full frontal nudity.

## Asti, Adrianna

*Films:*
Before the Revolution (1964; Italian) .......... Gina
Ludwig (1973; Italian) ............ Lila Von Buliowski
Down the Ancient Staircase (1975; Italian)......Gianna
The Inheritance (1978; Italian) ........ Teta Ferramonti
**Caligula** (1980) .........................Ennia
(X-rated, 147 minute version.)
- • 0:27—Breasts at side of bed with Malcolm McDow-
  ell when he feels her breasts.
- •• 0:54—Breasts lying down surrounded by slaves.
  Mostly her right breast.

Chimere (1989; French).............. Alice's Mother

## Astley, Pat

*Films:*
**Playbirds** (1978; British)...........Doreen Hamilton
- •• 0:00—Breasts posing for photo session.
**Don't Open Till Christmas** (1984; British) ....Sharon
- ••• 0:19—Breasts in sexy gold outfit while posing for
  photo session. Nice, long scene.
- •• 0:22—Breasts flashing while wearing a Santa outfit
  for Cliff.
- •• 0:24—Breasts in Santa outfit when the killer checks
  her out while holding a razor.
- •• 0:26—Breasts, sitting on bed opening her robe for
  policemen.

## • Atwood, Kathryn

*Films:*
To Die For 2 (1991) . . . . . . . . . . . . . . . . . . . . . . . . .n.a.
*a.k.a. Son of Darkness: To Die For II*
A Woman, Her Men and Her Futon (1992) . .Waitress #2
**Jason Goes to Hell—The Final Friday** (1993)
. . . . . . . . . . . . . . . . . . . . . Alexis, the blonde camper
(Unrated Director's Original Cut reviewed.)
•• 0:26—Breasts, after taking off wet blouse after skinny dipping with her friends.

## • Auger, Claudine

*Films:*
Thunderball (1965; British) . . . . . . . . . . Domino Dervall
**The Head of the Family** (1967; Italian/French)Adriana
• 1:18—Very brief side of right breast, while putting Marco's shirt on.
Black Belly of the Tarantula (1972; Italian) . . . . . . . Laura
Summertime Killer (1973) . . . . . . . . . Michele Dobvien
Lovers and Liars (1979; Italian) . . . . . . . . . . . . . . . Elisa
The Associate (1982; French/German) . . . . . . . . . Agnes
Secret Places (1984; British) . . . . . . . . . Sophy Meister

## Austin, Julie

*Films:*
Elves (1989) . . . . . . . . . . . . . . . . . . . . . . . . . . Kirsten
**Night of the Wilding** (1990) . . . . . . . . . . . . . . .Betty
0:13—In bra and panties, undressing in bedroom.
•• 0:14—Side of left breast, taking off bra in bathroom. Breasts in shower.
• 0:16—More breasts in the shower.
0:17—Breasts behind shower door.
Smooth Talker (1990) . . . . . . . . . . . . . . . Ms. Weston
Twisted Justice (1990) . . . . . . . . . . . . . . Andrea Leyton
*Made for Cable Movies:*
Extreme Justice (1993; HBO) . . . . . . . . . . . . . . . Cindy

## Austin, Lynne

*Video Tapes:*
**Playboy Video Centerfold: Lynne Austin**
. . . . . . . . . . . . . . . . . . . . . . . . . . . . . . . . . Playmate
**Playboy Video Calendar 1989** (1988) . . . . . . . . May
••• 0:17—Nude.
**Sexy Lingerie** (1988) . . . . . . . . . . . . . . . . . . . .Model
**Wet and Wild** (1989) . . . . . . . . . . . . . . . . . . .Model
**Playboy's Fantasies II** (1990) . . . . . . . . . . . . . . .n.a.
*Magazines:*
**Playboy** (Jul 1986) . . . . . . . . . . . . . . . . . . . . Playmate
**Playboy's Book of Lingerie** (Mar 1991) . . . . . Herself
••• 8—Breasts.
**Playboy's Girls of the World** (Oct 1992) . . . . Herself
••• 108—Full frontal nudity.
**Playboy's Calendar Playmates** (Nov 1992) . . Herself
••• 72—Full frontal nudity.
**Playboy's Video Playmates** (Sep 1993) . . . . . Herself
••• 16-17—Full frontal nudity.
**Playboy's Book of Lingerie** (Jul 1994) . . . . . . Herself
•• 36—Left breast.

## Austin, Teri

*Films:*
Terminal Choice (1985; Canadian) . . . . . . . Lylah Crane
0:14—Full frontal nudity, covered with blood on operating table. Long shot.
0:21—Right breast, on table being examined by Ellen Barkin. Dead, covered with dried blood.
0:26—Very brief left breast under plastic on table, hard to see.
**Vindicator** (1986; Canadian) . . . . . . . . Lauren Lehman
*a.k.a. Frankenstein '88*
• 0:30—Very brief left breast and buns in mirror getting out of the bubble bath covered with bubbles. Long shot, hard to see anything.
Dangerous Love (1988) . . . . . . . . . . . . . . . Dominique
Raising Cain (1992) . . . . . . . . . . . . . . . . . . . . . .Karen
*Made for TV Movies:*
Laura Lansing Slept Here (1988). . . . .Melody Gomphers
False Witness (1989) . . . . . . . . . . . . . . . . . . Sandralee
*TV:*
Knots Landing (1985-89) . . . . . . . . . . . . . . .Jill Bennett

## Austine, Nicola

*Films:*
Not Tonight Darling (1971; British)
. . . . . . . . . . . . . . . . . . . .At the West Side Health Club
Suburban Wives (1973; British) . . . . . . . . . . . . . .Jean
**The Adventures of a Private Eye** (1974; British)
. . . . . . . . . . . . . . . . . . . . . . . . . . . . . . Wife in Bed
•• 0:00—Breasts and buns, getting out of bed to take a shower.
Old Dracula (1975; British) . . . . . . . . . . .Playboy Bunny

## Avery, Belle

*Films:*
Repossessed (1990) . . . . . . . . . . . . . . Gym Receptionist
*Made for Cable Movies:*
**Sketch Artist** (1992; Showtime) . . . . . . . . . . . .Krista
• 1:11—Right breast, while making love with Paul by swimming pool. Long shot, don't see her face very well.

## Avery, Margaret

*Films:*
Cool Breeze (1972) . . . . . . . . . . Lark/Mercer's Mistress
Terror House (1972). . . . . . . . . . . . . . . . . . . . Edwina
**Hell Up in Harlem** (1973) . . . . . . . . . . . .Sister Jennifer
••• 0:42—Breasts in bed, while making love with Fred Williamson.
Magnum Force (1973) . . . . . . . . . . . . . . . . . .Prostitute
Which Way Is Up? (1977) . . . . . . . . . . . . . . .Annie Mae
The Fish That Saved Pittsburgh (1979) . . . Toby Millman
The Color Purple (1985). . . . . . . . . . . . . . . Shug Avery
Riverbend (1990) . . . . . . . . . . . . . . . . . . . Bell Coleman
Mardi Gras for the Devil (1993) . . . . . . . . . . Miss Sadie
*Miniseries:*
The Jacksons: An American Dream (1992) . . . . . Martha

# • Aviles, Angel
*Films:*
**Chain of Desire** (1992) . . . . . . . . . . . . . . . . . . . . Isa
• 0:14—In bra in bed with Jesus, then breasts. Dark.
Equinox (1992) . . . . . . . . . . . . . . . . . . . Anna Gutierrez
Jailbait (1993) . . . . . . . . . . . . . . . . . . . . . . . . . Pizza Girl
Mi Vida Loca (1994) . . . . . . . . . . . . . . . . . . . . . . .n.a.

## Axelrod, Lisa
*Films:*
Click: Calendar Girl Killer (1989) . . . . . . . . . . . .Jennifer
Night Angel (1989) . . . . . . . . . . . . . . . . . . . . . Double
Roadhouse (1989). . . . . . . . . . . . . . . . . . Party Girl
**Coldfire** (1990) . . . . . . . . . . . . . . . . . . . . . . Dancer
•• 0:11—Breasts, twice, dancing on stage.
• 0:13—Brief breasts, getting pushed off the stage.

## Axelrod, Nina
*Films:*
Roller Boogie (1979) . . . . . . . . . . . . . . Bobby's Friend
**Motel Hell** (1980) . . . . . . . . . . . . . . . . . . . . . . .Terry
0:58—In wet white T-shirt, tubin' with Ida.
•• 1:01—Breasts sitting up in bed to kiss Vincent.
• 1:04—Very brief breasts in tub when Bruce breaks
the door down, then getting out of tub.
Time Walker (1982). . . . . . . . . . . . . . . . . . . . . .Susie
Brainstorm (1983) . . . . . . . . . . . Simulator Technician
Cross Country (1983; Canadian). . . . . . . . . .Lois Hayes
0:28—Brief buns and sort of breasts, getting fondled
by Richard.
1:05—Very, very brief breasts fighting outside the
motel in the rain with Johnny.
Cobra (1986) . . . . . . . . . . . . . . . . . . . . . . . . Waitress
Critters 3 (1991) . . . . . . . . . . . . . . . . . . . .Mrs. Briggs

## Ayer, Lois
a.k.a. Adult film actress Lois Ayers or Sondra Stilman.
*Films:*
Tougher Than Leather (1988) . . . . . . . . . . . . Charlotte
*Video Tapes:*
**In Search of the Perfect 10** (1986) . . Perfect Girl #2
••• 0:08—In swimsuit, then breasts exercising by the
pool.
**Wet Water T's** (1987) . . . . . . . . . . . . . . . . . Herself
••• 0:55—Breasts during boxing match. Long scene.

## Ayres-Hamilton, Leah
*Films:*
All That Jazz (1979) . . . . . . . . . . . . . Nurse Capobianco
The Burning (1981) . . . . . . . . . . . . . . . . . . . . Michelle
Eddie Macon's Run (1983) . . . . . . . . . . . . . . . . . .Chris
Bloodsport (1987) . . . . . . . . . . . . . . . . . . . . . . .Janice
**Hot Child in the City** (1987) . . . . . . . . . . . . Rachel
0:38—In braless white T-shirt walking out by the
pool and inside her sister's house.
• 1:12—Very brief breasts in the shower with a guy.
Long shot, hard to see anything.
The Player (1992) . . . . . . . . . . . . . . . . . . . . . . Sandy

*TV:*
9 to 5 (1983) . . . . . . . . . . . . . . . . . . . . .Linda Bowman

# Bach, Barbara
Wife of singer/former *Beatles* drummer Ringo Starr.
*Films:*
Black Belly of the Tarantula (1972; Italian) . . . . . . .Jenny
Stateline Motel (1975; Italian) . . . . . . . . . . . . . . .Emily
a.k.a. Last Chance for a Born Loser
The Spy Who Loved Me (1977; British)
. . . . . . . . . . . . . . . . . . . . . . . . . . .Major Anya Amosova
1:21—Brief side view of right breast in shower on
submarine. Don't see her face.
**Force Ten from Navarone** (1978) . . . . . . . . . Maritza
• 0:32—Brief breasts taking a bath in the German of-
ficer's room.
Screamers (1978; Italian) . . . . . . . . . . . . . . . . . .Amanda
a.k.a. The Island of the Fishmen
a.k.a. Something Waits in the Dark
The Humanoid (1979; Italian) . . . . . . . . . . . . . . . n.a.
Jaguar Lives (1979) . . . . . . . . . . . . . . . . . . . . . . Anna
Great Alligator (1980; Italian) . . . . . . . . . . . . . . . n.a.
Caveman (1981) . . . . . . . . . . . . . . . . . . . . . . . . . Lana
The Unseen (1981) . . . . . . . . . . . . . . . . . . . Jennifer
Up the Academy (1981) . . . . . . . . . . . . . . . . . . . .Bliss
Give My Regards to Broad Street (1984; British)
. . . . . . . . . . . . . . . . . . . . . . . . . . . . . . . . Journalist
*Miniseries:*
Princess Daisy (1983) . . . . . . . . . . . . . . Vanessa Valerian
*Magazines:*
**Playboy** (Jun 1977) . . . . . . . . . . . . . . . .Bonded Barbara
•• 106-109—Breasts and buns. Lower frontal nudity in
sheer panties.
**Playboy** (Jan 1981) . . . . . . . . . . . . . . . . . Barbara Bach
••• 120-127—Full frontal nudity.
**Playboy** (Sep 1987) . . . . . . . . 25 Years of James Bond
•• 130—Left breast.
Playboy (Jan 1989) . . . . . . . . . . Women of the Seventies
212-213—Buns.

# Bach, Catherine
*Films:*
**Nicole** (1972) . . . . . . . . . . . . . . . . . . . . . . . . . . Sue
a.k.a. The Widow's Revenge
•• 1:01—Brief breasts, twice, undressing to put on
nightgown on boat. Nice shots, but too brief.
•• 1:10—Very brief side view of breasts, three times,
getting felt by Leslie Caron. Don't see either Bach's
or Caron's face.
The Midnight Man (1974) . . . . . . . . . . . . . . . .Natalie
Thunderbolt and Lightfoot (1974) . . . . . . . . . . Melody
Hustle (1975) . . . . . . . . . . . . . . . . . .Peggy Summers
Cannonball Run II (1984) . . . . . . . . . . . . . . . .Marcie
Street Justice (1988) . . . . . . . . . . . . . . . . . .Tamarra
Driving Force (1990) . . . . . . . . . . . . . . . . . . .Harry
Masters of Menace (1990) . . . . . . . . . . .Kitty Wheeler
Rage and Honor (1992) . . . . . . . . . . Captain Murdoch
*TV:*
The Dukes of Hazzard (1979-85) . . . . . . . . Daisy Duke

African Skies (1992-93) . . . . . . . . . . . . . . . . . . . . Margo
*Magazines:*
**Playboy** (Mar 1980). . . . . . . . . . . . . . . . . .Grapevine
• 259—Right nipple sticking out of dress top. B&W.

## Bach, Pamela

Wife of actor/singer David Hasselhoff.
*Films:*
**Appointment with Fear** (1988) . . . . . . . . Samantha
• 0:56—Breasts getting into the spa. Long shot, hard
to see.
Nudity Required (1989) . . . . . . . . . . . . . . . . . Dee Dee
*TV:*
Baywatch (1991- ). . . . . . . . . . . . . . . . . . . Kay Morgan

## Bachman, Cheryl

*Films:*
Renegade: Fighting Cage (1993). . . . . . . .Ring Card Girl
(Nudity added for video release.)
*Video Tapes:*
**Playboy Video Calendar 1993** (1992) . . . . . . . April
••• 0:14—Nude in studio setting.
••• 0:16—Nude outside on rocks and in bathtub.
**Playboy's Playmate Review 1992** (1992)
. . . . . . . . . . . . . . . . . . . . . . . . . . . . . . . Miss October
••• 0:30—Nude on rooftop and then outside in a field.
*Magazines:*
**Playboy** (Oct 1991). . . . . . . . . . . . . . . . . . . Playmate
••• 110-121—Nude.
**Playboy's Book of Lingerie** (Jul 1992) . . . . . . Herself
• 15—Lower frontal nudity.
**Playboy's Book of Lingerie** (Sep 1992) . . . . . Herself
• 23—In wet bra and panties.
**Playboy's Book of Lingerie** (Nov 1992) . . . . . Herself
••• 44—Breasts.
**Playboy's Nudes** (Dec 1992) . . . . . . . . . . . . . Herself
••• 44—Breasts and partial lower frontal nudity.
••• 95—Buns and side of left breast.
**Playboy's Book of Lingerie** (Jan 1993). . . . . . Herself
••• 107—Breasts.
**Playboy's Book of Lingerie** (May 1993) . . . . . Herself
••• 21—Breasts and side view of buns.
**Playboy** (Jul 1993). . . . . . . . . . . . . . . . . . . .Lucky Stiff
••• 78-83—Nude.
**Playboy's Wet & Wild Women** (Aug 1993) . . Herself
•• 101—Buns.
**Playboy's Book of Lingerie** (Nov 1993) . . . . . Herself
• 3—Upper half of breasts.
**Playboy's Nudes** (Dec 1993) . . . . . . . . . . . . . Herself
••• 22-23—Full frontal nudity.
**Playboy's Book of Lingerie** (Mar 1994) . . . . . Herself
••• 21—Breasts.
**Playboy's Girls of Summer '94** (Jul 1994) . . . Herself
••• 24-25—Full frontal nudity.
••• 99—Left breast.
**Playboy's Book of Lingerie** (Sep 1994) . . . . . Herself
••• 13—Breasts.

## Backlinie, Susan

*Films:*
**Jaws** (1975). . . . . . . . . . . . . . . . . . . . .Chrissie Watkins
• 0:02—Brief back side of right breast, while taking off
her clothes and running on the beach. Seen mostly
in sihouette.
• 0:03—Brief left breast (seen from the shark's point-
of-view from underneath), while swimming in the
water. Dark.
Day of the Animals (1976) . . . . . . . . . . . Mandy Young
**1941** (1979) . . . . . . . . . . . . . . . . . . . . . . Polar Bear Girl
• 0:02—Brief breasts and buns, while taking off robe
and running into the ocean. Dark, hard to see. This
is a parody of her part in *Jaws.*
0:05—Buns, while hanging on submarine periscope.
0:06—Very, very brief left breast when getting back
into the water.
*Magazines:*
**Penthouse** (Jan 1973) . . . . . . . . The Lady and the Lion
••• 80-85—Nude posing with a lion.

## • Badler, Jane

*Films:*
The First Time (1981). . . . . . . . . . . . . . . . . . . . .Karen
*a.k.a. Doin' It*
Black Snow (1989). . . . . . . . . . . . . . . . . . Shelby Collins
**Easy Kill** (1989) . . . . . . . . . . . . . . . . . . . . . . . . . .Jade
• 0:35—Brief breasts, while sitting in spa with slit
wrists. Brief crotch shot when Frank Stallone carries
her out of the spa.
• 0:43—Brief right breast, while making love in bed
with Stallone.
• 1:07—Left breast, while making love in bed with
Stallone. Don't see her face.
*Miniseries:*
V (1983) . . . . . . . . . . . . . . . . . . . . . . . . . . . . . . .Diana
*TV:*
One Life to Live (1977-81) . . . . . . . . . . .Melinda Kramer
The Doctors (1981-82). . . . . . . . . . . . . . . . . Natalie Bell
Falcon Crest (1986-87). . . . . . . . . . . . . Meredith Braxton
Highwayman (1987-88). . . . . . . . . . . . . Tania Winthrop
Mission Impossible (1989-90) . . . . . . . . . Shannon Reed

## Bagdasarian, Carol

*Films:*
The Strawberry Statement (1970) . . . . . . Telephone Girl
Charge of the Model T's (1979) . . . . . . . . . . . . . . n.a.
**The Octagon** (1980) . . . . . . . . . . . . . . . . . . . . . Aura
• 1:18—Brief side view of right breast, while sitting on
bed next to Chuck Norris and taking her blouse off.
The Aurora Encounter (1985). . . . . . . . . . . . . . . Alain

## • Baird, Roxanne

*Films:*
**Open House** (1987) . . . . . . . . . . . . . . . . . . . . Allison
•• 1:12—Buns and brief side view of left breast walking
to swimming pool, then breasts getting out of the
pool before the killer gets her.
Black Belt II: Fatal Force (1988) . . . . . . . Karen Pendleton

## Baker, Alretha

*Films:*
**Dance with Death** (1991) . . . . . . . . . . . . . . . . . Sunny
••• 0:23—Breasts and buns in G-string, dancing on
stage and falling off because she's on drugs.
The Baby Doll Murders (1992) . . . . . . . . . . . . . . . .n.a.

## Baker, Carroll

*Films:*
**You've Got to Have Heart** . . . . . . . . . . . . . . . .Lucia
*a.k.a. At Last, At Last*
•• 1:23—Left breast, while in cabin, consoling Giovan-
ni.
•• 1:24—More left breast, while with Giovanni.
•• 1:25—Right breast while making love.
Baby Doll (1956). . . . . . . . . . . . . . . . . . . . . . . Baby Doll
Giant (1956). . . . . . . . . . . . . . . . . . . . . . Luz Benedict II
How the West was Won (1963). . . . . . . . . . Eve Prescott
The Carpetbaggers (1964) . . . . . . . . . . . . . . . . . Rina
Harlow (1965). . . . . . . . . . . . . . . . . . . . . . Jean Harlow
Sylvia (1965). . . . . . . . . . . . . . . . . . . . . . . Sylvia West
Orgasmo (1968) . . . . . . . . . . . . . . . . . . . . . . . . . .n.a.
**The Sweet Body of Deborah** (1968) . . . . . .Deborah
(Not available on video tape.)
Breasts.
**Paranoia** (1969; Italian/French). . . . . . . . Kathryn West
• 0:13—Buns and partial glimpses of breasts, in shower with Peter.
• 0:16—Very, very brief upper half of right breast
when Peter rips her dress.
•• 0:17—Buns, while lying in bed with Peter.
0:25—Brief buns, under mesh black robe.
**Bloodbath** (1976). . . . . . . . . . . . . . . . . . . . . Treasure
*a.k.a. The Sky is Falling*
• 0:16—Outline of left breast in see-through blouse
when kneeling in the ocean to urinate.
• 0:50—Very brief buns, while mooning her mute lover.
**My Father's Wife** (1976; Italian) . . . . . . . . . . . . Lara
*a.k.a. Confessions of a Frustrated Housewife*
• 0:03—Right breast making love in bed with her husband, Antonio.
•• 0:06—Breasts standing in front of bed talking to Antonio.
••• 0:18—Breasts kneeling in bed, then getting out and
putting a robe on while wearing beige panties.
Andy Warhol's Bad (1977; Italian) . . . . . . . . Mrs. Aiken
**The World Is Full of Married Men** (1979; British)
. . . . . . . . . . . . . . . . . . . . . . . . . . . . . Linda Cooper
• 0:19—Brief left breast, while sitting up in bathtub
covered with bubbles.
The Watcher in the Woods (1981; British) . . Helen Curtis
Star 80 (1983). . . . . . . . . . . . . . . . . Dorothy's Mother
The Secret Diary of Sigmund Freud (1984)
. . . . . . . . . . . . . . . . . . . . . . . . . . . . . . . .Mama Freud
Ironweed (1987). . . . . . . . . . . . . . . . . . . Annie Phelan
Kindergarten Cop (1990) . . . . . . . . . . . . Eleanor Crisp

*Made for Cable TV:*
Tales From the Crypt: The Trap (1991; HBO)
. . . . . . . . . . . . . . . . . . . . . . . . . . . Mother Paloma
*Made for TV Movies:*
Judgment Day: The John List Story (1993) . . . . Alma List
Men Don't Tell (1993) . . . . . . . . . . . . . . . . . . . . . Ruth
*Magazines:*
**Playboy** (Jun 1980). . . . . . . . . . . . . . . . . . Grapevine
• 300—Left breast in bathtub in B&W still from *The
World is Full of Married Men.*

## Baker, Cheryl

*Films:*
Lethal Weapon (1987) . . . . . . . . . . . . .Girl in Shower #1
**Die Hard** (1988). . . . . . . . . . . . . . . Woman with Man
• 0:22—Brief breasts in office with a guy when the ter-
rorists first break into the building.
Roadhouse (1989) . . . . . . . . . . . . . . Well-Endowed Wife
**L.A. Story** (1991) . . . . . . . . . . Changing Room Woman
• 0:18—Brief breasts in dressing room, when Steve
Martin sees her.

## Baker, Cynthia

*Films:*
Risky Business (1983) . . . . . . . . . . . . . . . . . .Test Teacher
**Blood Diner** (1987) . . . . . . . . . . . . . . . . . . . Cindy
••• 0:44—Nude outside by fire with her boyfriend, then
fighting a guy with an axe.
The Fugitive (1993) . . . . . . . . . . . . . . . . .Woman In Car

## Baker, Kai

*Films:*
Armed Response (1986). . . . . . . . . . . . . . . . . . . .Pam
**Stormquest** (1988) . . . . . . . . . . . . . . . . . . . . . .Arr
• 0:37—Very, very brief left breast, while struggling
with Zar in the water.
American Eagle (1990). . . . . . . . . . . . . Angela Argente

## Baker, Kirsten

*Films:*
California Dreaming (1978) . . . . . . . . . . . . . . . .Karen
Gas Pump Girls (1978). . . . . . . . . . . . . . . . . . . .June
**Teen Lust** (1978) . . . . . . . . . . . . . . . . . . . Carol Hill
*a.k.a. Girls Next Door*
• 0:45—Brief side view of left breast, while changing
clothes in her bedroom.
Midnight Madness (1980) . . . . . . . . . . . . . . . Sunshine
**Friday the 13th, Part II** (1981) . . . . . . . . . . . . Terry
•• 0:45—Breasts and buns taking off clothes to go skinny dipping.
• 0:47—Very brief breasts jumping up in the water.
• 0:48—Full frontal nudity and buns getting out of the
water. Long shot.
Sector 13 (1982) . . . . . . . . . . . . . . . . . . . . . . . n.a.
**Terror in the Aisles** (1984). . . . . . . . . . . . . . . Terry
•• 1:03—Breasts and buns, undressing to go skinny
dipping from *Friday the 13th, Part II.*
Weeds (1987). . . . . . . . . . . . . . . . . . . . . . . . . .Kirsten

*Made for TV Movies:*
　The Seduction of Miss Leona (1980) . . . . . . . . . . . . Sue
*TV:*
　James at 15 (1978) . . . . . . . . . . . . . . Christina Kollberg

## Baker, LeeAnne

*Films:*
**Breeders** (1986) . . . . . . . . . . . . . . . . . . . . . . Kathleen
••• 0:28—Nude, undressing from her nurse outfit in the
　　kitchen, then taking a shower.
• 0:59—Brief breasts in alien nest. (She's the blonde in
　　front.)
•• 1:08—Breasts in alien nest.
•• 1:09—Breasts in alien nest again. (Behind Alec.)
• 1:11—Breasts behind Alec again. Then long shot
　　when nest is electrocuted. (On the left.)
Mutant Hunt (1987) . . . . . . . . . . . . . . . Pleasure Droid
**Necropolis** (1987) . . . . . . . . . . . . . . . . . . . . . . . . Eva
• 0:04—Right breast, while dancing in skimpy black
　　outfit during vampire ceremony.
• 0:38—Brief breasts in front of three evil things. (Be-
　　fore she has special make up to make it look like she
　　has six breasts).
**Psychos in Love** (1987) . . . . . . . . . . Heavy Metal Girl
••• 0:25—Breasts, undressing in room in front of Joe.
**Galactic Gigolo** (1988) . . . . . . . . . . . . . . . . . . . . Lucy
*a.k.a. Club Earth*
• 0:08—Breasts in hot tub behind Eoj.

## Baker, Marina

*Films:*
　Casanova (1987) . . . . . . . . . . . . . . . . . . . . . . Lucretia
*Video Tapes:*
**Playboy Video Calendar 1988** (1987) . . . . Playmate
**Wet and Wild** (1989) . . . . . . . . . . . . . . . . . . . Model
**Playboy Video Playmate Six-Pack 1992** (1992)
. . . . . . . . . . . . . . . . . . . . . . . . . . . . . . . . . Playmate
*Magazines:*
**Playboy** (Mar 1987) . . . . . . . . . . . . . . . . . . Playmate
**Playboy Presents International Playmates**
　(Feb 1992) . . . . . . . . . . . . . . . . . . . . . . . . . . Herself
••• 82-85—Nude.
**Playboy's Calendar Playmates** (Nov 1992) . . Herself
••• 59—Full frontal nudity.
••• 90—Full frontal nudity.

## Baker, Penny

*Films:*
　Real Genius (1985) . . . . . . . . . . . . . . . Ick's Girl at Party
**The Men's Club** (1986) . . . . . . . . . . . . . . . . . . . . Lake
•• 1:13—Breasts while lying in bed with Treat Williams.
Million Dollar Mystery (1987) . . . . . . . . . . . . . Charity
*Video Tapes:*
**Playboy Video Magazine, Volume 4** (1983)
. . . . . . . . . . . . . . . . . . . . . . . . . . . . . . . . . Playmate
**Playboy Video Magazine, Volume 5** (1983)
. . . . . . . . . . . . . . . . . . . . . . . . . . . . . . . . . Playmate
••• 1:03—Full frontal nudity, in outdoor bathtub.
•• 1:04—Full frontal nudity on a chair in a field.

•• 1:09—Miscellaneous breasts shots.
••• 1:11—Full frontal nudity in an Asian-theme bed-
　　room set.
**Wet and Wild** (1989) . . . . . . . . . . . . . . . . . . . . Model
**Playboy Video Centerfold: Anna-Marie Goddard**
　(1994) . . . . . . . . . . . . . . . . . . . . . . . . . . . . Playmate
• 0:28—Brief breasts, in still photo during retrospec-
　　tive.
*Magazines:*
**Playboy** (Jan 1984) . . . . . . . . . . . . . . . . . . . Playmate
**Playboy** (Nov 1986) . . . . . . . . . . . Sex in Cinema 1986
• 126—Breasts in bed with Treat Williams.
**Playboy's 1987 Book of Lingerie** (Mar 1987)
. . . . . . . . . . . . . . . . . . . . . . . . . . . . . . . . . . Herself
••• 53—Full frontal nudity.
••• 88—Breasts.
**Playboy** (Jan 1989) . . . . . . . . . . Women of the Eighties
••• 253—Full frontal nudity.
**Playboy's Nudes** (Oct 1990) . . . . . . . . . . . . . Herself
••• 31—Full frontal nudity.
**Playboy's Calendar Playmates** (Nov 1992) . . . Herself
••• 37—Full frontal nudity.
**Playboy** (Jan 1994) . . . . . . . . . . . 40 Memorable Years
••• 95—Full frontal nudity.
**Playboy's Great Playmate Search** (Feb 1994)
. . . . . . . . . . . . . . . . . . . . . . . . . . . . . . . . . . Herself
••• 5—Full frontal nudity in centerfold photo.

## Baker, Sylvia

*Films:*
　Roadhouse (1989) . . . . . . . . . . . . . . . . . . . Table Dancer
*Video Tapes:*
**Centerfold Screen Test, Take 3** (1988) . . . . . . Herself
••• 0:38—Nude after taking off dress during audition.
**Starlet Screen Test II** (1991) . . . . . . . . . . . . . Herself
••• 0:01—Nude on couch (same segment from *Center-
　　fold Screen Test, Take 3*.)

## Bakke, Brenda

*Films:*
**Last Resort** (1985) . . . . . . . . . . . . . . . . . . . Veroneeka
•• 0:36—Breasts in the woods with Charles Grodin.
**Hardbodies 2** (1986) . . . . . . . . . . . . . . . . . . Morgan
•• 0:34—Buns, getting into bathtub, then breasts, tak-
　　ing a bath.
**Death Spa** (1987) . . . . . . . . . . . . . . . . . . . . . . Laura
••• 0:05—Very brief lower frontal nudity, while taking
　　off pants in locker room. Don't see her face. Then
　　nude, in steam room.
Fast Gun (1987) . . . . . . . . . . . . . . . . . . . Julie Comstock
Dangerous Love (1988) . . . . . . . . . . . . . . . . . . . Chris
Scavengers (1988) . . . . . . . . . . . . . . . . Kimberly Blake
Fist Fighter (1989) . . . . . . . . . . . . . . . . . . . . . . Ellen
Nowhere to Run (1989) . . . . . . . . . . . . . . . . . . Joanie
Solar Crisis (1992) . . . . . . . . . . . . . . . . Claire Beeson
Gunmen (1993) . . . . . . . . . . . . . . . . . . . . . . . . Maria
Hot Shots! Part Deux (1993)
. . . . . . . . . . . . . . . . . . Michelle Rodham Huddleston

*Made for TV Movies:*
  Danielle Steel's "Secrets" (1992) . . . . . . . Sandy Warwick
*TV:*
  Brisco County Jr. (1993- ) . . . . . . . . . . . . . . . . . Frances
  Ned Blessing (1993) . . . . . . . . . . . . . . . . . . . . . . Wren
*Magazines:*
  **Playboy** (Nov 1994) . . . . . . . . . . . Sex in Cinema 1994
    • 141—Lower frontal nudity from *Twogether*.

## Bako, Brigitte

*Films:*
  One Good Cop (1991) . . . . . . . . . . . . . . . Mrs. Garrett
  **Dark Tide** (1993) . . . . . . . . . . . . . . . . . . . . . . . Andi
    0:16—In wet white blouse, coming out of the water.
    • 0:26—Very brief tip of left breasts in bathtub. Brief
      breasts, while covering up when Richard Tyson looks
      at her.
    • 0:27—Right breast, under water after Tyson leaves.
    ••• 0:43—Breasts, while making love with Tyson in un-
      derground pool. Great!
    ••• 1:05—Breasts, while sitting in bathtub, with a snake
      crawling up her chest.
*Made for Cable Movies:*
  **Red Shoe Diaries** (1992; Showtime). . . . . . . . . . Alex
  (Unrated video tape version reviewed.)
  (Most of the scenes where you don't see her face are a
  body double.)
    • 0:26—Buns and breasts, getting out of bathtub with
      Jake.
    • 0:35—Very brief buns when Tom rips off her panties.
    •• 0:36—Several brief breasts shots while making love
      with Tom in bed.
    • 0:40—Brief breasts, leaning back on bed with Tom.

## Balaski, Belinda

*Films:*
  **Bobbie Jo and the Outlaw** (1976) . . .Essie Beaumont
    ••• 0:29—Breasts in pond with Marjoe Gortner and Lyn-
      da Carter.
    • 0:43—Very brief breasts, when Gortner pushes her
      into a pond.
  Cannonball (1976; U.S./Hong Kong). . . . . . . .Maryanne
  Food of the Gods (1976). . . . . . . . . . . . . . . . . . . . .Rita
  Piranha (1978) . . . . . . . . . . . . . . . . . . . . . . . . . . Betsy
  Till Death (1978) . . . . . . . . . . . . . . . . . . . . . . . . . .n.a.
  The Howling (1981) . . . . . . . . . . . . . . . . . . .Terry Fisher
  Amazon Women on the Moon (1987). . . . Bernice Pitnik
  Gremlins 2: The New Batch (1990)
    . . . . . . . . . . . . . . . . . . . . . . . . . .Movie Theatre Mom
  Matinee (1993). . . . . . . . . . . . . . . . . . . . . . . Stan's Mom
*Made for Cable TV:*
  Rebel Highway: Runaway Daughters (1994; Showtime)
    . . . . . . . . . . . . . . . . . . . . . . . . . . . . . Mrs. Nicholson
*Made for TV Movies:*
  Deadly Care (1987). . . . . . . . . . . . . . . . . . . . . . . Terry

## • Balding, Rebecca

*Films:*
  **Silent Scream** (1980). . . . . . . . . . . . . . . Scotty Parker
    • 0:50—Brief right breast while making love in bed
      with Jack.
  **The Boogens** (1982) . . . . . . . . . . . . . . . . . . . . . Trish
  (Not available on videotape.)
*Made for TV Movies:*
  Deadly Game (1977) . . . . . . . . . . . . . . . . Amy Franklin
  The Gathering (1977) . . . . . . . . . . . . . . . .Julie Pelham
  The French-Atlantic Affair (1979) . . . . . .Harriet Kleinfeld
  The Gathering, Part II (1979) . . . . . . . . . . . .Julie Pelham
*TV:*
  Lou Grant (1977). . . . . . . . . . . . . . . . . .Carla Mardigian
  Soap (1978-81) . . . . . . . . . . . . . . . . . . . . . Carol David
  Makin' It (1979). . . . . . . . . . . . . . . . . . . .Corky Crandall

## Baldwin, Janit

*Films:*
  **Prime Cut** (1972). . . . . . . . . . . . . . . . . . . . . . . .Violet
    • 0:25—Very brief nude, being swung around when
      Gene Hackman lifts her up to show to Lee Marvin.
    • 0:41—Brief breasts putting on a red dress.
  **Gator Bait** (1973) . . . . . . . . . . . . . . . . . . . . . . . Julie
    •• 0:27—Breasts and buns walking into a pond, then
      getting out and getting dressed.
    • 0:35—Very brief right breast, twice, popping out of
      her dress when the bad guys hold her.
    • 0:40—Brief left breast struggling against two guys
      on the bed.
  Ruby (1977). . . . . . . . . . . . . . . . . . . . . . . . Leslie Claire
  Where the Buffalo Roam (1980). . . . . . . . . . . . . . n.a.
  Humongous (1982; Canadian). . . . . . . . Carla Simmons

## Baldwin, Judy

*Films:*
  The Seven Minutes (1971) . . . . . . . .Fremont's Girlfriend
  Evel Knievel (1972). . . . . . . . . . . . . . . . . . . Sorority Girl
  Talking Walls (1982). . . . . . . . . . . . . . . . . . . . . . . .n.a.
  **No Small Affair** (1984) . . . . . . . . . . . . . . . Stephanie
    ••• 0:36—In white bra, panties and garter belt, then
      breasts in Jon Cryer's bedroom trying to seduce him.
  Made in U.S.A. (1988) . . . . . . . . . . . . . . . . . . . .Dorie
  Pretty Woman (1990). . . . . . . . . . . . . . . . . . . . .Susan
*TV:*
  The Bold and the Beautiful (1987) . . . . . . . . Beth Logan

## • Baltay, Julie

*Films:*
  **Caroline at Midnight** (1993) . . . . . . . . . Dream Lover
    • 0:31—Right breast, while in bed during Jack's
      dream. Don't see her face.
  Dinosaur Island (1993). . . . . . . . . . . . . . . . . Cave Girl

## Baltron, Donna

*Films:*
  **Hide and Go Shriek** (1988). . . . . . . . . . Judy Ramerize
    •• 0:56—In white bra and panties, then breasts after
      undressing seductively in front of her boyfriend.

Shallow Grave (1988) . . . . . . . . . . . . . . . . . . . . . . . Rose
Death Becomes Her (1992) . . . . . Madeline Body Double
Intent to Kill (1992). . . . . . . . . . . . . . . . . . . . Girl in Bar
      0:44—In black bra and panties, caught in bed with
      Al by Traci Lords.
The Naked Truth (1992) . . . . . . . . . . . . . . . . .Miss Cuba
*Made for Cable TV:*
Dream On: Reach Out and Touch Yourself (1993; HBO)
  . . . . . . . . . . . . . . . . . . . . . . . . . . . . . . . . . . . . . . . . Lola
*TV:*
Down the Shore (1993- ) . . . . . . . . . . . . . . . Cheyenne
**NYPD Blue: Tempest In a C-Cup** (Nov 16, 1993)
  . . . . . . . . . . . . . . . . . . . . . . . . . . . . . . . . . . . . . . Ingrid
    • 0:21—Brief buns, several times, while dancing on
      stage.
    • 0:22—Brief buns in G-string, while walking up to ta-
      ble in front of Metavoy.
    • 0:23—Almost left breast, after taking off her top in
      front of Metavoy.
*Video Tapes:*
Morgan Fairchild Stress Management (1991) . . . Herself

## Bang, Joy

*Films:*
**Cisco Pike** (1971) . . . . . . . . . . . . . . . . . . . . . . . . .Lynn
    0:45—Very, very brief right breast, seen under Kris
    Kristofferson's arm at the beginning of the scene in
    bed with Merna.
**Pretty Maids All in a Row** (1971). . . . . . . . . . . .Rita
    • 0:57—Brief breasts in car with Rock Hudson.
    • 1:01—Right breast, in car with Hudson. Dark. More
      right breast, while getting dressed.
Red Sky at Morning (1971) . . . . . . . . . . . . . . . . . Corky
Play It Again, Sam (1972) . . . . . . . . . . . . . . . . . . Julie
Dead People (1974) . . . . . . . . . . . . . . . . . . . . . . . Toni
Night of the Cobra Woman (1974; U.S./Philippines)
  . . . . . . . . . . . . . . . . . . . . . . . . . . . . . . . . . . . . . Joanna

## • Bangert, Lisa

*Video Tapes:*
**Page 3 Girls** (1993) . . . . . . . . . . . . . . . . . . . . Herself
*Magazines:*
**Playboy's Book of Lingerie** (Jul 1992) . . . . . . Herself
  •• 56-57—Right breast and lower frontal nudity.
  •• 69—Left breast and lower frontal nudity.
**Playboy's Book of Lingerie** (Sep 1992) . . . . . Herself
  •• 26—Left breast and lower frontal nudity.
  • 82—Buns.
**Playboy's Book of Lingerie** (Nov 1992) . . . . . Herself
  ••• 88-89—Full frontal nudity.

## Banks, Laura

*Films:*
**Wheels of Fire** (1984) . . . . . . . . . . . . . . . . . . Stinger
*a.k.a. Desert Warrior*
    • 0:49—Brief breasts when Trace rips her top open
      outside.
Demon of Paradise (1987) . . . . . . . . . . . . . . . . . Cahill

Hexed (1993). . . . . . . . . . . . . . . . . . . . . .1st Reporter
*a.k.a. All Shook Up*

## • Barba, Vana

*Films:*
Vios Ke Politia (1988; German). . . . . . . . . . . . . . . . n.a.
**Mediterraneo** (1991; Italian). . . . . . . . . . . . Vassilissa
  •• 1:03—Side of left breast, while in bed with Antonio.

## Barbeau, Adrienne

Ex-wife of director John Carpenter.
*Films:*
The Fog (1980) . . . . . . . . . . . . . . . . . . . . . Stevie Wayne
The Cannonball Run (1981). . . . . . . . . . . . . . . . Marcie
Escape from New York (1981) . . . . . . . . . . . . . Maggie
**Swamp Thing** (1981) . . . . . . . . . . . . . . . Alice Cable
    • 1:03—Side view of left breast washing herself off in
      the swamp. Long shot.
Creepshow (1982). . . . . . . . . . . . . . . . Wilma Northrup
The Next One (1983). . . . . . . . . . . . . . Andrea Johnson
Back to School (1986) . . . . . . . . . . . . . . . . . . Vanessa
**Open House** (1987) . . . . . . . . . . . . . . . . Lisa Grant
    • 0:27—In black lace lingerie, then very brief half of
      left breast making love with Joseph Bottoms on the
      floor.
    •• 1:15—Brief side view of right breast getting out of
      bed at night to look at something in her briefcase.
    ••• 1:16—Brief breasts taking off bathrobe and getting
      back into bed. Kind of dark.
Cannibal Women in the Avocado Jungle of Death (1988)
  . . . . . . . . . . . . . . . . . . . . . . . . . . . . . . . . . . Dr. Kurtz
Two Evil Eyes (1991) . . . . . . . . . . . . . . . . . . . . Jessica
Father Hood (1993) . . . . . . . . . . . . . . . . . . . . Celeste
Silk Degrees (1994) . . . . . . . . . . . . . . . . . . . . .Violet
*Made for Cable Movies:*
Doublecrossed (1991; HBO). . . . . . . . . . . Debbie Seal
Rebel Highway: Jailbreakers (1994; Showtime)
  . . . . . . . . . . . . . . . . . . . . . . . . . . . . . .Mrs. Norton
*Made for Cable TV:*
Dream On: Bad Girls (1992; HBO) . . . . . . . Gloria Gantz
*Miniseries:*
The Burden of Proof (1992) . . . . . . . . . . . .Silvia Hartnell
*TV:*
Maude (1972-78). . . . . . . . . . . . . . . . . . . . . . . . Carol

## Barber, Frances

*Films:*
The Missionary (1982; British) . . . . . . . . . . . Mission Girl
Acceptable Levels (1983; British) . . . . . . . . . . . . . . . Jill
**A Zed and Two Noughts** (1985; British)
  . . . . . . . . . . . . . . . . . . . . . . . . . . . . Venus de Milo
    ••• 0:22—Breasts, sitting in bed, talking to Oliver, then
      nude while getting thrown out of his place.
Castaway (1986) . . . . . . . . . . . . . .Sister Saint Winifred
Prick Up Your Ears (1987; British) . . . . . . . Leonie Orton

**Sammy and Rosie Get Laid** (1987; British)
................................. Rosie Hobbs
- 1:09—Very brief breasts, while bending over to kiss Danny. More brief breasts while making love (short cuts).
  1:21—Partial right breast while sitting in bubble bath with Sammy.
We Think the World of You (1988; British)....... Megan
Young Soul Rebels (1991; British) .............. Ann
Soft Top, Hard Shoulder (1992; British).... Miss Trimble

## Barber, Glynnis
*Films:*
Terror (1979; British)....................... Carol
Yesterday's Hero (1979; British).............. Susan
The Hound of the Baskervilles (1983; British)........n.a.
**The Wicked Lady** (1983; British) ......... Caroline
- ••• 0:58—Breasts and buns making love with Kitt in the living room. Possible body double.
Edge of Sanity (1988) ............... Elisabeth Jekyll
*TV:*
Blake's 7 (1981; British)..................... Soolin
Dempsey and Makepeace (1984-86)
............. Detective Sergeant Harriet Makepeace

## • Barbieri, Paula
*Films:*
The Dangerous (1994) ....................... n.a.
*Made for Cable TV:*
**Red Shoe Diaries: Double or Nothing**
(1993; Showtime) ..................... The Girl
- 0:02—Brief breasts, while making love in bed.
- 0:03—Brief breasts, in open blouse, while fighting with Carl.
- 0:15—Brief breasts and buns, while making love with Tommy.
- •• 0:16—Breasts and very brief partial lower frontal nudity several times while making love with Tommy in bed and outside in the rain.
- •• 0:18—Left breast, while making love with Tommy.
- 0:19—Buns, while getting out of bed and putting on panties.
- 0:29—Left breast while starting to make love with Tommy on pool table. More breasts in long shot.
*Magazines:*
**Playboy** (Oct 1994)................. Paula Barbieri
- ••• 74-79—Nude.

## Bardot, Brigitte
Ex-wife of director Roger Vadim.
*Films:*
Head Over Heels ......................... Cecile
Doctor at Sea (1955; British).......... Helene Colbert
**...and God created woman** (1957; French) .. Juliette
- 0:40—Very brief side view of right breast getting out of bed.
A Very Private Affair (1962; French/Italian) ......... Jill
**Contempt** (1963; French/Italian)........ Camille Javal
- 0:04—Buns.

0:52—Almost buns walking through door after bath.
- 0:54—Buns, while lying on rug.
- 1:30—Buns, while lying on beach. Long shot.
Dear Brigitte (1965) ....................... Herself
Shalako (1968; British) ......... Countess Irini Lazaar
**Ms. Don Juan** (1973) ....................... Joan
- 0:19—Left breast in bathtub.
- •• 1:19—Breasts through fish tank. Buns and left breast, then brief breasts in mirror with Paul.
**Famous T & A** (1982) ..................... Joan
(No longer available for purchase, check your video store for rental.)
- 0:25—Buns, then brief breasts in scene from *Ms. Don Juan.*
*Magazines:*
**Playboy** (Jan 1975)........... Bardot—Incroyable!
- ••• 147-151—Full frontal nudity.
**Playboy** (Jan 1994).............. Remember Brigitte
- 132-133—Partial buns and right breast in color and B&W photos.

## Barkin, Ellen
Wife of actor Gabriel Byrne.
*Films:*
Diner (1982) ............................. Beth
Daniel (1983)..................... Phyllis Isaacson
Eddie and the Cruisers (1983) ............. Maggie
Tender Mercies (1983)..................Sue Anne
The Adventures of Buckaroo Banzai, Across the 8th
 Dimension (1984)................. Penny Priddy
Harry and Son (1984) ..................... Katie
Terminal Choice (1985; Canadian)..... Mary O'Connor
Desert Bloom (1986) ....................... Starr
Down by Law (1986).................... Laurette
The Big Easy (1987) ................ Anne Osborne
 0:21—White panties in lifted up dress in bed with Dennis Quaid.
 0:32—Brief buns jumping up in kitchen after pinching a guy who she thinks is Quaid.
Made in Heaven (1987) ................... Lucille
**Siesta** (1987) ......................... Diane
- ••• 0:03—Brief full frontal nudity long shot taking off red dress, breasts, brief buns standing up, then full frontal nudity lying down.
  1:22—Right nipple sticking out of dress while imagining she's with Gabriel Byrne instead of the reality of getting raped by taxi driver.
- 1:23—Brief lower frontal nudity, very brief silhouette of a breast, then brief buns some more while with Byrne. Dark, hard to see.
- 1:24—Lower frontal nudity, with torn dress while lying in bed after the taxi driver gets up.
  1:26—Very brief lower frontal nudity, while running down road and her dress flies up as police cars pass by.
  1:28—Very brief side view of right breast putting on dress in bed just before Isabella Rossellini comes into the bedroom to attack her. Long distance shot.

Johnny Handsome (1989) . . . . . . . . . . . . . Sunny Boyd
Sea of Love (1989) . . . . . . . . . . . . . . . . . Helen Cruger
    0:56—Side view of left breast of body double, then
    buns standing up making out with Al Pacino in his
    apartment.
    0:59—Back view wearing panties, putting blouse on
    in bathroom.
    1:13—Brief upper half of buns, lying in bed with
    Pacino.
Switch (1991) . . . . . . . . . . . . . . Amanda Brooks/Steve
Mac (1992). . . . . . . . . . . . . . . . . . . . . . . . . . Oona
Man Trouble (1992) . . . . . . . . . . . . . . . . Joan Spruance
Into the West (1993). . . . . . . . . . . . . . . . . . Kathleen
This Boy's Life (1993) . . . . . . . . . . . . . . Caroline Wolff
*Made for Cable Movies:*
Act of Vengeance (1986). . . . . . . . . . . . . . . . Annette
Blood Money: The Story of Clinton and Nadine
(1988; HBO) . . . . . . . . . . . . . . . . . . . . . . . . . . . .n.a.
    Original title: *Clinton and Nadine.*

## Barnes, Priscilla

*Films:*
**Delta Fox** (1977). . . . . . . . . . . . . . . . . . . . . . Karen
    0:36—Left breast undressing in room for David. Very
    dark, hard to see.
    • 0:38—Very brief breasts struggling with a bad guy
    and getting slammed against the wall.
    0:39—Very brief blurry left breast running in front of
    the fireplace.
    • 0:40—Breasts sneaking out of house. Brief breasts
    getting into Porsche.
    • 0:49—Brief right breast reclining onto bed with Dav-
    id. Side view of left breast several times while mak-
    ing love.
    1:29—Very brief side view of left breast in David's
    flashback.
**Texas Detour** (1977) . . . . . . . . . . . . . Claudia Hunter
    ••• 1:03—Breasts, changing clothes and walking
    around in bedroom. Wearing white panties. This is
    her best breasts scene.
    • 1:11—Breasts sitting up in bed with Patrick Wayne.
**Tintorera** (1977). . . . . . . . . . . . . . . . . . Girl from Bar
    • 1:12—Brief breasts, while pouring beer over her
    head. Breasts seen from under water, while she turns
    around while wearing white panties. Breasts, while
    dropping her beer in the water.
    • 1:14—Breasts, while on the beach after the shark at-
    tack (on the left).
**Seniors** (1978). . . . . . . . . . . . . . . . . . . . . . . Sylvia
    •• 0:18—Breasts at the top of the stairs while Arnold
    climbs up the stairs while the rest of the guys watch.
The Last Married Couple in America (1980)
. . . . . . . . . . . . . . . . . . . . . . . . . . . . . Helena Dryden
Sunday Lovers (1980; Italian/French) . . . . . . . . . Donna
Traxx (1988) . . . . . . . . . . . . . . . Mayor Alexandria Cray
License to Kill (1989). . . . . . . . . . . . . . Della Churchill
Lords of the Deep (1989) . . . . . . . . . . . . . . . . Claire
Little Devils (1991) . . . . . . . . . . . . . . . . . . . . . .n.a.

**Stepfather III: Father's Day** (1992) . . .Christine Davis
    • 1:27—Very brief buns, sitting down in bubble bath.
Talons of the Eagle (1992; Canadian)
. . . . . . . . . . . . . . . . . . . . . . . . . . . Cassandra Hubbard
*Made for Cable Movies:*
Attack of the 5' 2" Women (1994; Showtime) . . .Crystal
*Made for TV Movies:*
Perry Mason: The Case of the Reckless Romeo (1992)
. . . . . . . . . . . . . . . . . . . . . . . . . . . . . Brenda Kingsley
*TV:*
The American Girls (1978) . . . . . . . . . Rebecca Tomkins
Three's Company (1981-84) . . . . . . . . . . . . Terri Alden
*Magazines:*
**Penthouse** (Mar 1976). . . . . . . . . . . . . . . . . . . .Pet
    (Used the name Joann Witty.)
    ••• 77-89—Nude. Left breast on cover photo.

## Baron, Carla

*Films:*
**Necromancer** (1988) . . . . . . . . . . . . . . . . . . . . Gail
    • 0:42—Brief breasts getting out of bed with Paul.
    Dark.
Sorority Babes in the Slimeball Bowl-O-Rama (1988)
. . . . . . . . . . . . . . . . . . . . . . . . . . . . . . . . . .Frankie

## Barrault, Marie-Christine

*Films:*
My Night at Maud's (1970; French) . . . . . . . . .Francoise
**Cousin, Cousine** (1975; French) . . . . . . . . . . Marthe
    •• 1:05—Breasts in bed with her lover, cutting his nails.
    • 1:07—Brief side view of right breast, while giving
    him a bath.
    ••• 1:16—Breasts with penciled tattoos all over her
    body.
    1:33—Braless in see-through white blouse saying
    "good bye" to everybody.
The Daydreamer (1975; French) . . . . . . . . . . . . . Lisa
The Medusa Touch (1978; British) . . . . . . . . . . Patricia
Stardust Memories (1980) . . . . . . . . . . . . . . . .Isabel
Table for Five (1983) . . . . . . . . . . . . . . . . . . . .Marie
**A Love in Germany** (1984; French/German)
. . . . . . . . . . . . . . . . . . . . . . . . . . . . . . .Maria Wyler
    • 0:23—Right breast, in bed with her lover when
    Pauline peeks from across the way.
    •• 0:28—Right breast in bedroom with Karl. Very brief
    lower frontal nudity getting back into bed. Long
    scene.
    ••• 0:43—Breasts in bedroom with Karl. Subtitles get in
    the way! Long scene.
Swann in Love (1984; French/German)
. . . . . . . . . . . . . . . . . . . . . . . . . . . Madame Verdunn
    *a.k.a. Un Amour de Swann*
*Magazines:*
**Playboy** (Nov 1977) . . . . . . . . . . . Sex in Cinema 1977
    • 163—Breasts, while in bed from *Cousin, Cousine.*
    Dark.

## Barrese, Katherine

*Films:*
Homer & Eddie (1989) . . . . . . . . . . . . . . . . . Waitress
**Jezebel's Kiss** (1990). . . . . . . . . . . . . . . . . . . . Jezebel
- •• 0:36—Full frontal nudity washing herself off in kitchen after having sex with the sheriff.
- • 0:42—Brief buns, going for a swim in the ocean. Dark.
- ••• 0:48—Breasts taking off her robe in front of Hunt, then making love with him.
- • 0:58—Brief right breast and buns while Malcolm McDowell watches through slit in curtain. Long shot.
- • 1:09—Right breast and buns getting undressed. Long shot. Closer shot of buns, putting robe on.
- ••• 1:12—Breasts making love with McDowell. More breasts after.

## Barrett, Alice

*Films:*
**Incoming Freshman** (1979). . . . . . . . .Boxing Student
- •• 0:43—Breasts answering a question during Professor Bilbo's fantasy.
- • 0:55—Breasts in another of Bilbo's fantasy.
- • 1:18—Breasts during end credits.
Mission Hill (1982) . . . . . . . . . . . . . . . . . . Laura Doyle

## Barrett, Jamie

*Films:*
Club Life (1987) . . . . . . . . . . . . . . . . . . . . . . . . . Sissy
**House of the Rising Sun** (1987) . . . . . . . . . . . .Janet
- • 1:04—Very brief breasts making love with Louis.

## Barrett, Nitchie

*Films:*
**Preppies** (1984) . . . . . . . . . . . . . . . . . . . . . . .Roxanne
- • 0:11—Brief breasts changing into waitress costumes with her two friends.
She-Devil (1989) . . . . . . . . . . . . . . . . . . Bob's Secretary
**A Time to Die** (1991) . . . . . . . . . . . . . . . . . . . . Sheila
- • 0:12—Buns, getting out of bed.
- •• 0:16—Breasts making love in bed with Sam.

## Barrett, Victoria

*Films:*
Hot Resort (1984) . . . . . . . . . . . . . . . . . . . . . . . . . Jane
**Hot Chili** (1985) . . . . . . . . . . . . . . Victoria Stevenson
- • 0:55—Very brief close up shot of right breast when it pops out of her dress. Don't see her face.
Three Kinds of Heat (1987) . . . . . . . . . . . . .Terry O'Shea

## • Barrick, Melissa

*Films:*
**The Pamela Principle** (1992)
. . . . . . . . . . . . . . . . . . . .Uncredited Steve's Girlfriend
(Unrated version reviewed.)
- ••• 0:45—Breasts and buns in red G-string, then lower frontal nudity, while playing strip-card game in living room with Steve.

**The Bikini Carwash Company II** (1993) . . . . . Cyndi
(Unrated version reviewed.)
- ••• 0:38—In black lingerie, then breasts during kitchen commercial.
- ••• 0:42—Breasts and buns under black body stocking in "Rock Me" music video number.
- ••• 0:46—In lingerie, then breasts during repairman commercial.
- • 0:52—Brief breasts, while making out on kitchen table.
- • 1:28—Breasts during music video number at the carwash.

## • Barringer, Pat

*Films:*
Orgy of the Dead (1965) . . . . . . . . . . . . . . Shirley/Gold
**Agony of Love** (1966) . . . . . . . . . . . . .Barbara Thomas
   0:09—Undressing for a customer down to a white bra.
- •• 0:10—Breasts, after taking off bra, then on bed with the customer. Upper half of buns in pulled down panties.
- ••• 0:16—Breasts and buns, standing in front of bathroom mirror, then taking a bath and drying herself off.
- •• 0:19—Breasts, while making love with the Beatnik and his girlfriend.
- • 0:29—Brief breasts several times during nightmare with money.
   0:36—In black bra, undressing in room with two Conventioneers.
- • 0:38—Brief breasts while wearing panties, in bed with a Conventioneer.
- ••• 0:42—Breasts, while lying on bed and getting out of bed after making love with the Conventioneer.
- • 0:43—Breasts, while sitting up after making love with the other Conventioneer.
- • 0:54—In white bra and panties on bed, then breasts several times with a customer.
- •• 1:02—In white bra, taking off her clothes in front of a customer. Then breasts while wearing panties while she poses and he messily eats a lot of food.
- • 1:16—Brief breasts, while turning over in bed before seeing her husband.
**Psychopathia Sexualis** (1966) . . . . . . . . . . . . Dancer
*a.k.a. On Her Bed of Roses*
- ••• 0:34—Breasts, while belly dancing during party (she's the second dancer). Long scene.

## Barrington, Rebecca

*Films:*
Dance or Die (1988) . . . . . . . . . . . . . . . . . . . . . . . n.a.
**The Newlydeads** (1988) . . . . . . . . . . . . . . . . Blanche
- • 0:08—Right breast, while making out with her fiancee, Bull, in the car.
   1:00—In white body suit, while lying on the floor.
- • 1:01—Right breast, peeking out of the top of her body suit.
- • 1:02—Brief buns, while on the floor with Bull.

**Living to Die** (1990) . . . . . . . . . . . . . Married Woman
- 0:23—In red bra, blindfolded and tied to a lounge chair, then breasts while getting photographed.
- 0:27—Breasts in chair when Wings Hauser talks to her.

# Barry, Wendy

*Films:*
**Savage Dawn** (1984) . . . . . . . . . . . . . . . . . Lipservice
- 1:01—Breasts, after taking off top in room in front of Richard Lynch.
- •• 1:03—Breasts and buns after getting up with Lynch, then getting dressed.

3:15—The Moment of Truth (1986) . . . . . . . . . . . Lora
Knights of the City (1986). . . . . . . . . . . . . . . .Jasmine
**Young Lady Chatterley II** (1986)
. . . . . . . . . . . . . . . . . . . . . . Sybil "Maid in Hot House"
- 0:12—Breasts in hot house with the Gardener.

# Barrymore, Drew

Model for *Guess?* jeans.
*Films:*
Altered States (1980) . . . . . . . . . . . . . Margaret Jessup
E.T. The Extraterrestrial (1982) . . . . . . . . . . . . . .Gertie
Firestarter (1984) . . . . . . . . . . . . . . . . . Charlie McGee
Irreconcilable Differences (1984). . . . . . . Casey Brodsky
Cat's Eye (1985) . . . . . . . . . . . . . . . . . . . . . . . . . . .Girl
Far From Home (1989) . . . . . . . . . . . . . . . Joleen Cox
0:40—In wet T-shirt in water with Jimmy.
See You in the Morning (1989) . . . . . . . . . . . . . Cathy
Motorama (1991) . . . . . . . . . . . . . . . . . . . .Fantasy Girl
No Place to Hide (1991) . . . . . . . . . . . . . Tinsel Hanley
Waxwork II: Lost in Time (1991) . . . . . . . Vampire Victim
1:30—Briefly lying in bed in sheer nightgown during B&W vampire segment.
**Doppelganger: The Evil Within** (1992)
. . . . . . . . . . . . . . . . . . . . . . . . . . . Holly Gooding
- •• 0:23—Breasts in shower when water turns blood red. Great shot, but ruined by the red water.
- 0:26—Brief side of left breast in kitchen with Patrick.
Poison Ivy (1992) . . . . . . . . . . . . . . . . . . . . . . . . . Ivy
(Unrated version reviewed.)
(Body double used for nude scenes in European version.)
1:00—In wet bra on hood of car in rain with Tom Skerritt.
Wayne's World 2 (1993) . . . . . . . . . . . . Bjergen Kjergen
Bad Girls (1994) . . . . . . . . . . . . . . . . . . . . . . . . .Lilly
*Made for Cable Movies:*
**Guncrazy** (1992; Showtime) . . . . . . . . . . . . . . . .Anita
1:00—Briefly in wet blouse in shower with her boyfriend. Seen from above.
- 1:24—Brief buns, while in bed on top of her boyfriend. Don't see her face.
Sketch Artist (1992; Showtime). . . . . . . . . . . . . . Daisy
*Made for TV Movies:*
The Amy Fisher Story (1993). . . . . . . . . . . . Amy Fisher
(Body double nude scene added for video tape version.)
0:28—Brief right breast and partial lower frontal nudity in bed with Joey is a body double.

*TV:*
2000 Malibu Road (1992) . . . . . . . . . . . . . . . . . Lindsay
*Magazines:*
**Interview** (Jul 1992). . . . . . . . . . . . . . . . .Darling Drew
- 54-65—Upper half of breasts and side view of buns in B&W and color photos. Posing with other models.
**Vogue** (Jun 1993) . . . . . . . . . . . . . . . . . Crazy for Drew
- 170-177—Two photos in braless, sheer clothing (one in B&W, the other in color). One breasts B&W photo, while sitting in a chair.

# Barton, Diana

*Films:*
Skin Deep (1989). . . . . . . . . . . . . . . . . . . . . . . .Helena
Body of Influence (1992) . . . . . . . . . . . . . . . . Jennifer
(Unrated version reviewed.)
**Sexual Malice** (1993). . . . . . . . . . . . . . . . . . Christine
(Unrated version reviewed.)
- 0:13—Brief buns in panties, taking off robe and getting into bed.
- ••• 0:32—Breasts in shower, then nude getting out and putting on a robe.
- •• 0:33—Left breast in open robe, looking at herself in the mirror.
- ••• 0:36—Breasts and buns in hotel room when takes her robe off and makes love with her in bed.
- ••• 0:42—Breasts while making love in surf under pier at the beach.
- ••• 0:48—In white bra, panties and stockings, then buns and breasts while making love.
- •• 0:55—Breasts and buns while making love in dressing room of clothing store.
- ••• 1:04—Breasts, while in bed with a black girl while Quinn takes photos.
- 1:13—Breasts, while in spa with Edward Albert.
*Video Tapes:*
**Eden** (1992) . . . . . . . . . . . . . . . . . . . . . . . . . .Andrea
- ••• 0:05—Breasts, undressing, making love, then getting dressed in locker room with Ian. Long scene.
- ••• 0:37—Breasts, taking off her swimsuit top to tease Ian. More breasts and buns while making love with him on the sofa.

# Basil, Toni

Singer and Choreographer.
*Films:*
Pajama Party (1964). . . . . . . . . . . . . . . . . . Pajama Girl
**Easy Rider** (1969). . . . . . . . . . . . . . . . . . . . . . . . Mary
- 1:24—Brief right breast (her hair gets in the way) and very, very brief buns, taking off clothes in graveyard during hallucination sequence.
1:26—Very brief buns, climbing on something (seen through fish-eye lens).
- 1:27—Buns, while lying down (seen through fish-eye lens).
Sweet Charity (1969)
. . . . . . . . . . . . . . Dancer in "Rhythm of Life" Number
Five Easy Pieces (1970). . . . . . . . . . . . . . . Terry Grouse

The Last Movie (1971) . . . . . . . . . . . . . . . . . . . . . . Rose
Mother, Jugs & Speed (1976) . . . . . . . . . . . . . . Addict
Angel III: The Final Chapter (1988) . . . . . . . . . . . .Hillary
Slaughterhouse Rock (1988) . . . . . . . . Sammy Mitchell
Eating (1990) . . . . . . . . . . . . . . . . . . . . . . . . . . . Jackie
Rockula (1990) . . . . . . . . . . . . . . . . . . . . . . . . .Phoebe

# Basinger, Kim

Wife of actor Alec Baldwin.
*Films:*
Hard Country (1981) . . . . . . . . . . . . .Jodie Lynn Palmer
Motherlode (1982) . . . . . . . . . . . . . . .Andrea Spalding
The Man Who Loved Women (1983) . . . . Louise "Lulu"
Never Say Never Again (1983) . . . . . . . .Domino Vitale
The Natural (1984) . . . . . . . . . . . . . . . . . . Memo Paris
Fool For Love (1985) . . . . . . . . . . . . . . . . . . . . . . May
**9 1/2 Weeks** (1986) . . . . . . . . . . . . . . . . . . .Elizabeth
  • 0:27—Blindfolded while Mickey Rourke plays with
     an ice cube on her. Brief right breast.
     0:36—Masturbating while watching slides of art.
     0:41—Playing with food at the refrigerator with
     Rourke. Messy, but erotic.
  • 0:54—Very brief left breast, while rolling over in bed.
     0:58—Making love with Rourke in clock tower.
  ••• 1:11—In wet lingerie, then breasts making love in a
     wet stairwell with Rourke.
  • 1:19—Doing a sexy dance for Rourke in a white slip.
  • 1:22—Buns, showing off to Rourke on building.
  • 1:44—Brief buns, putting on pants and getting out
     of bed.
No Mercy (1986) . . . . . . . . . . . . . . . . . . Michel Duval
Blind Date (1987) . . . . . . . . . . . . . . . . . . . Nadia Gates
Nadine (1987) . . . . . . . . . . . . . . . . Nadine Hightower
My Stepmother Is An Alien (1988) . . . . . Celeste Martin
     0:40—Dancing very seductively in a white slip in
     front of Dan Aykroyd while he lies in bed. No nudity,
     but still very exciting.
Batman (1989) . . . . . . . . . . . . . . . . . . . . . . Vicki Vale
The Marrying Man (1991). . . . . . . . . . . Vicki Anderson
  *a.k.a. Too Hot to Handle*
Cool World (1992) . . . . . . . . . . . . . . . . . . .Holli Would
     0:51—In white slip.
     1:05—In white bra under sheer white body suit.
**Final Analysis** (1992) . . . . . . . . . . . . . .Heather Evans
  •• 0:21—Right breast, while making love in bed under
     Richard Gere.
**The Getaway** (1993). . . . . . . . . . . . . . . Carol McCoy
  (Unrated version reviewed.)
  •• 0:18—In bra and panties in bedroom with Alec Bald-
     win, then nude (kind of silhouette).
  • 0:25—Very brief left breast and lower frontal nudity
     while pulling down towel behind steamy shower
     door. Hard to see.
  • 1:29—Side view of buns in the shower.
  ••• 1:30—Breasts and buns, while making love with
     Baldwin. Nice. Very, very brief lower frontal nudity.
     1:32—In white bra and panties in hotel room.
The Real McCoy (1993). . . . . . . . . . . . . . Karen McCoy
Wayne's World 2 (1993) . . . . . . . . . . . . Honey Hornée

*Miniseries:*
From Here to Eternity (1979) . . . . . . . . . Lorene Rogers
*Made for TV Movies:*
Katie: Portrait of a Centerfold (1978) . . . . Katie McEvera
*TV:*
Dog and Cat (1977). . . . . . . . . . . . . . Officer J.Z. Kane
From Here to Eternity (1980) . . . . . . . . . Lorene Rogers
*Music Videos:*
Mary Jane's Last Dance/Tom Petty (1993) . . . . . . . . n.a.
*Video Tapes:*
**Playboy Video Magazine, Volume 10** (1986)
  . . . . . . . . . . . . . . . . . . . . . . . . . . . . . . 9 1/2 Weeks
  • 0:32—Brief right breast in ice cube scene.
  • 0:34—Brief right breast during slide show scene.
  • 0:37—Brief breasts in wet stairwell scene.
*Magazines:*
**Playboy** (Feb 1983) . . . . . . . . . . . . Betting on Kim
  ••• 82-89—Nude.
**Playboy** (Dec 1983) . . . . . . . . . . . . .Sex Stars of 1983
  •• 211—Breasts.
**Playboy** (Dec 1984) . . . . . . . . . . . . .Sex Stars of 1984
  ••• 208—Breasts walking in water.
**Playboy** (Sep 1987) . . . . . . . . . 25 Years of James Bond
  •• 130—Breasts.
**Playboy** (Jan 1988). . . . . . . . . . . . . . . . . . . . . . Kim
  ••• 78-85—Breasts and buns from Feb 1983.
**Playboy** (Jan 1989). . . . . . . . . . .Women of the Eighties
  256—Buns.
**Playboy** (Dec 1990) . . . . . . . . . . . .Sex Stars of 1990
  • 173—Buns, lying in water. B&W.
**Playboy** (Dec 1991) . . . . . . . . . . . . .Sex Stars 1991
  • 180—Left breast under sheer dress top. B&W.
**Playboy** (Jan 1994). . . . . . . . . . . . . . . Remember Kim
  ••• 176-177—Breasts and buns.

# Basler, Marianne

*Films:*
**A Soldier's Tale** (1988; New Zealand) . . . . . . . . . Belle
  • 0:19—Brief breasts, while undressing in bedroom
     for Gabriel Byrne.
  •• 0:21—Breasts in bed with Byrne.
  •• 1:02—Buns and brief breasts while washing herself
     when Byrne sees her.
Softly From Paris III (1990) . . . . . . . . . . . . . . . . . . n.a.
Overseas (1991; French) . . . . . . . . . . . . . . . . . . .Gritte

# Basone, Jeanne

G.L.O.W. wrestler name is Hollywood.
*Video Tapes:*
Thunder and Mud (1989) . . . . . . . . . .Barbie the Bimbo
*Magazines:*
**Playboy** (Dec 1989) . . . . . . . . . . . . . . .Lethal Women
  ••• 149—Full frontal nudity.
**Playboy's Career Girls** (Aug 1992) . . . .Lethal Women
  ••• 107—Full frontal nudity.
**Playboy's Book of Lingerie** (Jan 1993) . . . . . .Herself
  •• 63—Breasts.
**Playboy's Book of Lingerie** (May 1993) . . . . .Herself
  ••• 104—Breasts.

## Bass, Victoria

*Films:*

**Too Scared to Scream** (1985) . . . . . Cynthia Oberman
••• 0:08—Breasts and buns, undressing and hanging up
her dress in closet. More walking to shower.
•• 0:10—Brief breasts, getting out of the shower.
The Bodyguard (1992) . . . . . . . . . . . . Woman in Green
Traces of Red (1992) . . . . . . . . . . . . . . . . Susan Dobson

## Bassett, Angela

*Films:*

F/X (1986) . . . . . . . . . . . . . . . . . . . . . . . TV Reporter
Boyz N the Hood (1991) . . . . . . . . . . . . . . . Reva Styles
**City of Hope** (1991) . . . . . . . . . . . . . . . . . . . . Reesha
•• 1:20—Breasts in bed with Joe Morton.
**Critters 4: They're Invading Your Space** (1992)
. . . . . . . . . . . . . . . . . . . . . . . . . . . . . . . . . . . Fran
0:24—Side view of body in silhouette while taking a
shower.
•• 0:25—Buns in nice, tilt-up shot with partial back side
view of right breast, but you don't see her face.
Innocent Blood (1992) . . . . . . . . . U.S. Attorney Sinclair
Malcolm X (1992) . . . . . . . . . . . . . . . . . . Betty Shabazz
Passion Fish (1993) . . . . . . . . . . . . . . . . Dawn/Rhonda
What's Love Got to Do With It (1993) . . . . . . Tina Turner

*Miniseries:*

The Jacksons: An American Dream (1992)
. . . . . . . . . . . . . . . . . . . . . . . . . . Katherine Jackson

## Bates, Jo Anne

*Films:*

**Perfect Timing** (1984) . . . . . . . . . . . . . . . . . . . Karen
••• 0:21—Nude, getting ready to get her picture taken.
Heavenly Bodies (1985) . . . . . . . . . Girl in Locker Room
Immediate Family (1989) . . . . . . . . . . . . . Home Buyer

## Bates, Kathy

*Films:*

Straight Time (1978) . . . . . . . . . . . . . . . . Selma Darin
Come Back to the Five and Dime, Jimmy Dean, Jimmy
(1982) . . . . . . . . . . . . . . . . . . . . . . . . . . . Stella May
Two of a Kind (1983) . . . . . . . . . . . Furniture Man's Wife
The Morning After (1986) . . . . . Woman on Mateo Street
Summer Heat (1987) . . . . . . . . . . . . . . . Ruth Stanton
Arthur 2 On the Rocks (1988) . . . . . . . . . . . Mrs. Canby
High Stakes (1989) . . . . . . . . . . . . . . . . . . . . . . . . Jill
Men Don't Leave (1989) . . . . . . . . . . . . . Lisa Coleman
Dick Tracy (1990) . . . . . . . . . . . . . . . . . . . Mrs. Green
Misery (1990) . . . . . . . . . . . . . . . . . . . . . Annie Wilkes
(Academy Award for Best Actress.)
White Palace (1990) . . . . . . . . . . . . . Rosemary Powers
**At Play in the Fields of the Lord** (1991)
. . . . . . . . . . . . . . . . . . . . . . . . . . . . Hazel Quarrier
• 2:22—(0:52 into tape 2) Nude, covered with mud
and leaves, going crazy outside after her son dies.
Fried Green Tomatoes (1991) . . . . . . . . . Evelyn Couch
*a.k.a. Fried Green Tomatoes at the Whistle Stop Café*
Shadows and Fog (1991) . . . . . . . . . . . . . . . Prostitute
Prelude to a Kiss (1992) . . . . . . . . . . . . . . . Leah Blier

Used People (1992) . . . . . . . . . . . . . . . . . . . . . . Bibby
A Home of Our Own (1993) . . . . . . . . . . . . . . . . . n.a.

*Made for Cable Movies:*

Hostages (1993; HBO) . . . . . . . . . . . . . . . . Peggy Say

*Miniseries:*

Stephen King's "The Stand" (1994) . . . . . . . Rae Flowers

## Bauer, Belinda

*Films:*

The American Success Company (1979) . . . . . . . . Sarah
**Winter Kills** (1979) . . . . . . . . . . . . . . . Yvette Malone
•• 0:46—Breasts making love in bed with Jeff Bridges,
then getting out of bed.
• 1:25—Breasts, dead as a corpse when sheet uncov-
ers her body.
Flashdance (1983) . . . . . . . . . . . . . . . . . . Katie Hurley
Timerider (1983) . . . . . . . . . . . . . . . . . . . Clair Cygne
The Rosary Murders (1987) . . . . . . . . . . . . Pat Lennon
UHF (1989) . . . . . . . . . . . . . . . . . . . . . . Mud Wrestler
Act of Piracy (1990) . . . . . . . . . . . . . . . Sandy Andrews
Robocop 2 (1990) . . . . . . . . . . . . . . . . . . Juliette Faxx
Servants of Twilight (1991) . . . . . . . . Christine Scavello

*Made for Cable Movies:*

A Case for Murder (1993; USA) . . . . . . . . Joanna Gaines

*Made for Cable TV:*

**The Hitchhiker: Love Sounds** . . . . Veronica Hoffman
• 0:15—Brief breasts, making love in the house with
Kerry.
•• 0:22—Breasts, making love in the boat.

*Made for TV Movies:*

Starcrossed (1985) . . . . . . . . . . . . . . . . . . . . . . Mary

## Bauer, Jaime Lyn

(Yes, her name is spelled Jaime.)

*Films:*

**The Centerfold Girls** (1974) . . . . . . . . . . . . . . Jackie
•• 0:04—Breasts getting out of bed and walking
around the house.
••• 0:14—Breasts getting undressed in the bathroom.
•• 0:15—Brief breasts and buns putting on robe and
getting out of bed, three times.
Young Doctors in Love (1982) . . . . . . . . . . . . . Cameo

*TV:*

The Young and the Restless (1973-82)
. . . . . . . . . . . . . . . . Lauralee (Laurie) Brooks Prentiss
Bare Essence (1983) . . . . . . . . . . . . . . . . Barbara Fisher
The Young and the Restless (1984)
. . . . . . . . . . . . . . . . Lauralee (Laurie) Brooks Prentiss

*Magazines:*

**Penthouse** (May 1974) . . . . . . . . . . . . . . . . . Jessica
(Used the name Jessica Len.)
••• 48-55—Nude.

## Bauer, Michelle

a.k.a. Michelle McClellan briefly when her ex-husband
  threatened to sue for using "Bauer."
a.k.a. Former adult film actress Pia Snow.
The two easiest adult video tapes to find are *Cafe Flesh*
  and *Bad Girls*.

*Films:*

**Homework** (1982) . . . . . . .Uncredited Dream Groupie
  ••• 1:01—Breasts with two other groupies, groping
    Tommy while he sings. (She has a flower in her hair
    and is the only brunette.)
**Cave Girl** (1985) . . . . . . . . . . . . . Locker Room Student
  •• 0:05—Breasts with four other girls in the girls' locker
    room undressing, then running after Rex. She's the
    first to take her top off, wearing white panties, run-
    ning and carrying a tennis racket.
**Tomboy** (1985) . . . . . . . . . .Uncredited Girl in Corvette
  • 1:16—Brief breasts, while opening her dress in Cor-
    vette.
**Armed Response** (1986) . . . . . . . . . . . . . . . . Stripper
  • 0:41—Breasts, dancing on stage.
**Cyclone** (1986) . . . . . . . . . . . Uncredited Shower Girl
  • 0:06—Very brief buns and side of left breast walking
    around in locker room. (Passes several times in front
    of camera.)
**Reform School Girls** (1986). . Uncredited Shower Girl
  •• 0:25—Breasts, then nude in the shower.
**Roller Blade** (1986) . . . . . . . . . . . . . . . . . . .Bod Sister
  • 0:11—Breasts, being held by Satacoy's Devils.
  ••• 0:13—More breasts and buns in G-string during
    fight. Long scene.
  • 0:16—Brief breasts twice, getting saved by the Sis-
    ters.
  •• 0:33—Breasts during ceremony with the other two
    Bod Sisters. Buns also.
  ••• 0:35—Full frontal nudity after dip in hot tub. (Sec-
    ond to leave the tub.)
  •• 0:40—Nude, on skates with the other two Bod Sis-
    ters. (She's on the left.)
**Screen Test** (1986) . . . . . . . . . . . . . Dancer/Ninja Girl
  •• 0:04—Breasts dancing on stage.
  ••• 0:42—Nude, with Monique Gabrielle, making love
    in a boy's dream.
**Nightmare Sisters** (1987) . . . . . . . . . . . . . . . Mickey
  ••• 0:39—Breasts standing in panties with Melody and
    Marci after transforming from nerds to sexy women.
  ••• 0:40—Breasts in the kitchen with Melody and Marci.
  ••• 0:44—Full frontal nudity in the bathtub with Melody
    and Marci. Excellent, long scene.
  ••• 0:47—Breasts in the bathtub. Nice close up.
  •• 0:48—Still more breasts in the bathtub.
  •• 0:53—Breasts in bed with J.J.
**Phantom Empire** (1987) . . . . . . . . . . . . Cave Bunny
    0:32—Running around in the cave a lot in two piece
    loincloth swimsuit.
  •• 1:13—Breasts after losing her top during a fight,
    more breasts until Andrew puts his jacket on her.
The Tomb (1987) . . . . . . . . . . . . . . . . . . . . . .Nefartis
**Demonwarp** (1988) . . . . . . . . . . . . . . . . . . . . Betsy

  •• 0:41—Breasts, taking off her T-shirt to get a tan in
    the woods.
  •• 0:43—Left breast, lying down, then brief breasts
    getting up when the creature attacks.
  •• 0:47—Breasts putting blood-stained T-shirt back on.
  •• 1:19—Breasts, strapped to table, getting ready to be
    sacrificed.
  • 1:22—Breasts on stretcher, dead.
**Hollywood Chainsaw Hookers** (1988) . . . .Mercedes
  ••• 0:09—Nude in motel room with a John just before
    chainsawing him to pieces.
**The Jigsaw Murders** (1988) . . . . . . . . . Cindy Jakulski
    0:20—Brief buns on cover of puzzle box during
    bachelor party.
  • 0:21—Brief breasts in puzzle on underside of glass
    table after the policemen put the puzzle together.
  • 0:29—Very brief breasts when the police officers
    show the photographer the puzzle picture.
  • 0:43—Very brief breasts long shots in some pictures
    that the photographer is watching on a screen.
**Sorority Babes in the Slimeball Bowl-O-Rama**
  (1988) . . . . . . . . . . . . . . . . . . . . . . . . . . . . . . . . . Lisa
    0:07—In panties getting spanked with Brinke
    Stevens.
  ••• 0:12—Breasts brushing herself in the front of mirror
    while Stevens takes a shower.
  • 0:14—Brief full frontal nudity when the three nerds
    fall into the bathroom.
    0:33—In black bra, panties, garter belt and stock-
    ings asking for Keith.
    0:35—Wearing the same lingerie, on top of Keith in
    the locker room.
  ••• 0:40—Breasts taking off her bra.
  ••• 0:43—More breasts undoing garter belt.
  •• 0:46—More breasts in locker room.
  •• 0:47—More breasts taking off stockings.
  • 1:04—Full frontal nudity sitting on the floor by her-
    self.
  • 1:05—Full frontal nudity getting up after the lights
    go out. Kind of dark.
**Warlords** (1988) . . . . . . . . . . . . . . . . . . . . .Harem Girl
  ••• 0:14—Breasts, getting her top ripped off, then shot
    by a bad guy.
**Wild Man** (1988) . . . . . . . . . . . . . . . . . . Trisha Collins
    1:02—In sheer white lingerie with Eric. Buns also.
  ••• 1:06—Breasts on couch making love with Eric. Brief
    lower frontal nudity.
**Assault of the Party Nerds** (1989) . . . . . . . . .Muffin
  • 0:16—Side view of left breast kissing Bud.
  ••• 0:20—Breasts lying in bed seen from Bud's point of
    view, then sitting up by herself.
  • 1:15—Brief right breast, then breasts in bed with
    Scott.
**Beverly Hills Vamp** (1989) . . . . . . . . . . . . . . Kristina
  • 0:12—Buns and brief side view of right breast in bed
    biting a guy.
    0:33—In red slip, with Kyle.
  •• 0:38—Breasts trying to get into Kyle's pants.

1:09—In black lingerie attacking Russell in bed with Debra Lamb and Jillian Kesner.

1:19—In black lingerie enticing Mr. Pendleton into bedroom.

1:22—In black lingerie, getting killed as a vampire by Kyle.

**Deadly Embrace** (1989) . . . . . . . Female Spirit of Sex
- •• 0:22—Breasts caressing herself during fantasy sequence.
- ••• 0:28—Breasts taking off tube top and caressing herself.
- ••• 0:40—Breasts and buns kissing blonde guy. Nice close up of him kissing her breasts.
- • 0:42—Side of left breast lying down with the guy.
- • 1:03—Buns and side of right breast with the guy.

**Dr. Alien** (1989) . . . . . . . . . . . . . . . . . . . . . Coed #1
*a.k.a. I Was a Teenage Sex Mutant*
- ••• 0:53—Breasts taking off her top (she's on the left) in the women's locker room after another coed takes hers off in front of Wesley.

**Murder Weapon** (1989) . . . . . . . .Girl in Shower on TV
- • 1:00—Brief left breast on TV that the guys are watching. Scene from *Nightmare Sisters*.

**Puppet Master III: Toulon's Revenge** (1990) . . . Lili
- • 0:15—Brief breasts bringing the phone to the General while he takes a bath.
- •• 0:43—Breasts, twice, making love on top of the General.

Virgin High (1990) . . . . . . . . . . . . . . . . . . . . . Miss Bush

Camp Fear (1991) . . . . . . . Body Double for Betsy Russell
*a.k.a. Millenium Countdown*

**The Dwelling** (1991) . . . . . . . . . . . . . . . . . . . . . .n.a.

**Evil Toons** (1991) . . . . . . . . . . . . . . . . . . . Mrs. Burt
- •• 0:48—Breasts opening her lingerie for Burt. Buns, while walking away in G-string.

**Inner Sanctum** (1991)
. . . . . . . . . . . . Body Double for Margaux Hemingway
- • 0:09—Left breast, body double in office for Margaux Hemingway.
- •• 0:23—Breasts body double for Hemingway, while in bed with Joseph Bottoms.

**Lady Avenger** (1991) . . . . . . . . . . . . . . . . . . Annalee
- ••• 0:30—Breasts, making love in bed on top of J.C.
- ••• 0:52—Breasts, making love in bed on top of Ray.

**Little Devils** (1991). . . . . . . . . . . . . . . . . . . . .n.a.

**Spirits** (1991) . . . . . . . . . . . . . . . . . . . . Sister Mary
- ••• 0:21—Breasts, taking off nun's habit, trying to seduce Erik Estrada. Brief lower frontal nudity and buns also. Long scene.

**Terror Night** (1991) . . . . . . . . . . . . . . . . . . . . .n.a.

**Chickboxer** (1992) . . . . . . . .Greta "Chickboxer" Holtz
0:39—In sexy pink outfit.
- ••• 0:57—Full frontal nudity, making love with a guy in bed.

**Hellroller** (1992). . . . . . . . . . . . . . . .Michelle Novak
0:26—Undressing in motel room down to white body suit, then exercising.
- ••• 0:30—Breasts taking a bath.

0:35—Dead in bathroom, covered with blood and with her guts hanging out.

**Dinosaur Island** (1993) . . . . . . . . . . . . . . . . . . . .June
- ••• 0:20—Breasts (she has white necklaces on), while bathing in a stream with April and May, then bathing the guys.
- ••• 0:22—More breasts, while bathing the guys.
- • 0:38—Brief upper half of left breast, popping out of bikini top after winning fight with the Queen.
- ••• 1:07—Breasts, while making love outside at night with Turbo.

**Naked Instinct** (1993). . . . . . . . . . . . . . . .Michelle
- ••• 0:10—Full frontal nudity with Virgin Rich Kid after taking off her maid outfit and making love with him on bed. Long scene.
- ••• 0:13—More full frontal nudity with him on top of her.
- ••• 0:43—Full frontal nudity with Frat Bully and making love with him. Long scene.
- ••• 1:07—Breasts and buns in red panties, making love with the Therapist. Long scene.
- ••• 1:10—Full frontal nudity making love on the floor, with her on top.
- ••• 1:11—More full frontal nudity with him on top.
- ••• 1:13—More full frontal nudity making love on her hands and knees.

**One Million Heels B.C.** (1993) . . . . . . . . . . .Cavegirl
- ••• 0:10—Half of right breast, while in skimpy top, under Rose in bed. Nude in the shower with Rose.
- •• 0:12—Breasts, while sitting on bed.
- ••• 0:13—Full frontal nudity while trying on lingerie.
- ••• 0:21—Nude, while soaping Savannah and Rose in the spa.
- • 0:25—Brief full frontal nudity taking off her towel in bedroom.
- ••• 0:26—Breasts and buns, while getting dressed on bed.

*Video Tapes:*

Nudes in Limbo (1983) . . . . . . . . . . . . . . . . . . . Model

**Best Chest in the West** (1984). . . . . . . . . .Michelle
- ••• 0:24—In two piece swimsuit, then breasts and buns.

**Love Skills: A Guide to the Pleasures of Sex** (1984)
. . . . . . . . . . . . . . . . . . . . . . . . . . . . . . . . . . . Model
- ••• 0:34—Full frontal nudity, caressing herself in front of a mirror.

**Candid Candid Camera, Volume 4** (1985). . . Model
- ••• 0:08—Full frontal nudity, undressing while complaining about a bad tan from a tanning salon.
- ••• 0:50—Nude, posing in front of a guy, asking his opinion on her poses. Long scene.

Terror on Tape (1985) Unsatisfied Video Store Customer

**Candid Candid Camera, Volume 5** (1986)
. . . . . . . . . . . . . . . . . . . . . . . . . . . Debbie White
- ••• 0:34—Buns, pulling down her pants while a guy rubs purple paint on her rear.

**Centerfold Screen Test, Take 2** (1986) . . . . . Marsha
- ••• 0:12—Breasts taking off her dress for Mr. Johnson. Then full frontal nudity. Nice, long scene.

**In Search of the Perfect 10** (1986)
. . . . . . . . . . . . . . . . . . . . . . . . . . . . Perfect Girl #10
••• 0:53—In yellow outfit stripping in office. Breasts and buns in G-string bottom.

**Penthouse Love Stories** (1986). . . .Therapist's Patient
••• 0:45—Nude, making love in Therapist's office with his assistant.

**Night of the Living Babes** (1987). . . . . . . . . . . .Sue
•• 0:44—Breasts chained up with Chuck and Buck.
••• 0:46—More breasts chained up.
• 0:50—Breasts getting rescued with Lulu.

**Playboy Video Magazine, Volume 12** (1987)
. . . . . . . . . . . . . . . . . . . . . . . . Candid Candid Camera
•• 0:35—Lower nudity when her skirt falls down whenever she sneezes.

**Penthouse: On the Wild Side** (1988)
. . . . . . . . . . . . . . . . . . . . . . Punk or Bust Hairdresser
• 0:32—Breasts in black leather outfit.
••• 0:34—Nude while wearing black leather outfit, making love with Julie Parton.

**Scream Queen Hot Tub Party** (1991). . . . . . . Herself
•• 0:00—Full frontal nudity during opening credits.
•• 0:07—Breasts taking off pink outfit and putting on red teddy.
• 0:12—Buns, while walking up the stairs.
••• 0:33—Nude, stripping out of blue dress in scene from *Hollywood Chainsaw Hookers*. Long scene.
••• 0:38—In black lingerie, then stripping to breasts to demonstrate the proper Scream Queen use of a chainsaw.
••• 0:44—Breasts taking off her swimsuit top and soaping up with the other girls.
•• 0:46—Breasts in still shot during the end credits.

*Magazines:*
**Penthouse** (Nov 1980) . . . . . . . . . . . . . . Swept Away
••• 142-151—Nude with a blonde woman.
**Penthouse** (Jul 1981) . . . . . . . . . . . . . . . . . . . . . Pet
**Playboy** (Jul 1989). . . . . . . . . . . . . . . B-Movie Bimbos
•• 138—Breasts and buns lying in a car that looks like a shark.
**Playboy** (Nov 1991) . . . . . . . . . . . . . . . . . .Grapevine
••• 183—Breasts, kneeling. B&W.

# Baxter, Amy Lynn

*Films:*
**Summer's Games** (1987) . . Boxer/Girl from Penthouse
•• 0:04—Breasts opening her swimsuit top after contest. (1st place winner.)
•• 0:18—Breasts during boxing match.
Spring Fever USA (1988). . . . . . . . .Amy (Car Wash Girl)
*a.k.a. Lauderdale*
**Summer Job** (1989) . . . . . . . . . . . . . . . . . . . . . Susan
•• 0:10—Breasts changing in room with the other three girls. More breasts sitting on bed.
0:15—In white bra, looking at herself in mirror.
• 0:34—Brief breasts when her swimsuit top pops off after saving a guy in swimming pool.
• 0:45—In white lingerie, brief breasts on stairs, flashing her breasts (wearing curlers).

1:00—Brief buns in two piece swimsuit turning around.
• 1:23—Breasts pulling her top down talking to Mr. Burns.

**Affairs of the Heart** (1992) . . . . . . . . . . . .Josie Hart
•• 0:00—Breasts during opening credits.
•• 0:02—Breasts and buns in G-string, while posing for photos.
••• 1:09—Breasts posing in santa cap during photo session.
•• 1:13—Breasts with Richard during smoky dream scene.

*Video Tapes:*
**Wet Water T's** (1987) . . . . . . . . . . . . . . . . . . .Herself
••• 0:33—Breasts in black lingerie bottoms, then buns in G-string, dancing on stage in a contest.
•• 0:38—Breasts during judging.
•• 0:39—Breasts during semi-finals.
••• 0:40—Breasts dancing with the other women during semi-final judging.
••• 0:43—Breasts during finals.
••• 0:47—Breasts during final judging.
••• 0:48—Breasts dancing after winning first place.

**Penthouse Centerfold—Amy Lynn** (1991) . . . . .Pet
**Penthouse Passport to Paradise/Hawaii** (1991)
. . . . . . . . . . . . . . . . . . . . . . . . . . . . . . . . . . . Model
••• 0:49—Undressing on boat in white swimsuit top and white panties, then full frontal nudity.

**Penthouse Pet of the Year Playoff 1991** (1992)
. . . . . . . . . . . . . . . . . . . . . . . . . . . . . . . . . . . . .Pet
••• 0:02—Full frontal nudity during Hollywood starlet/photographer segment.
••• 0:04—Full frontal nudity on bed during interview.
••• 0:06—Full frontal nudity in still photos.
••• 0:08—Nude, while posing on boat.
••• 0:14—Nude, while posing with large sculptures.
••• 0:19—Nude, while wearing black wig and posing in house and playing with food (including a banana!).

**Penthouse Pet of the Year Winners 1992: Brandy & Amy** (1992). . . . . . . . . . . . . . . . . . . . . . . . . .Pet
**Penthouse Forum Letters: Volume 1** (1993)
. . . . . . . . . . . . . . . . . . . . . Maid to Order/The Maid
0:18—In pink bra and panties.
••• 0:21—Breasts, taking off bra and playing with herself while watching the owners of the house make love. Buns in panties.

**Penthouse The Great Pet Hunt—Part II** (1993)
. . . . . . . . . . . . . . . . . . . . . . . . . . . . . . . . . . . . .Pet
••• 0:34—Breasts and buns in T-back after stripping out of bride outfit on stage. More fun while playing with oil.

*Magazines:*
**Penthouse** (Feb 1992) . . . . . Pet of the Year Runner-Up
••• 111-119—Nude.
**Penthouse** (Dec 1993). . . . . Searching for Bob Fischer
••• 116-127—Nude with Janine Lindemulder with painted and unpainted bodies by artist Robert A. Fischer.

# Baye, Nathalie

*Films:*
Day for Night (1973; French) . . . . . . . . . . . . . Assistant
The Man Who Loved Women (1977; French)
. . . . . . . . . . . . . . . . . . . . . . . . . . . . Martine Desdoit
Beau Pere (1981; French) . . . . . . . . . . . . . . . Charlotte
**The Return of Martin Guerre** (1983; French)
. . . . . . . . . . . . . . . . . . . . . . . . . . . . Bertrande de Rols
   • 0:59—Brief side view of left breast, making love in
     bed on top of Martin. Don't see her face.
Detective (1985; French/Swiss) . . . . . . Francoise Chenal
C'est La Vie (1990; French) . . . . . . . . . . . . . . . . . Lena
The Man Inside (1990) . . . . . . . . . . . . . . . . . . Christine
*Made for Cable Movies:*
And the Band Played On (1992; HBO)
. . . . . . . . . . . . . . . . . . . . . . . . . Dr. Francoise Barre

# Beacham, Stephanie

*Films:*
The Games (1970) . . . . . . . . . . . . . . .Angela Simmonds
**The Nightcomers** (1971; British)
. . . . . . . . . . . . . . . . . . . . . . . . . Miss Margaret Jessel
   • 0:13—Brief left breast lying in bed having her
     breasts fondled.
   ••• 0:30—Breasts in bed with Marlon Brando while a lit-
     tle boy watches through the window.
   •• 0:55—Breasts in bed pulling the sheets down.
The Devil's Widow (1972; British) . . . . . . . . . . . . .Janet
Dracula A.D. 1972 (1972; British) . . . Jessica Van Helsing
   *a.k.a. Dracula Today*
And Now the Screaming Starts (1973; British)
. . . . . . . . . . . . . . . . . . . . . . . . . Catherine Fengrifen
The Confessional (1977; British) . . . . . . . . . . . .Vanessa
   *a.k.a. House of Mortal Sin*
Schizo (1977; British) . . . . . . . . . . . . . . . . . . . . Beth
   *a.k.a. Amok*
   *a.k.a. Blood of the Undead*
Horror Planet (1980; British) . . . . . . . . . . . . . . . Kate
   *a.k.a. Inseminoid*
Troop Beverly Hills (1989) . . . . . . . . . . . . .Vicki Sprantz
*Made for Cable Movies:*
Foreign Affairs (1993; TNT) . . . . . . . . .Rosemary Radley
*Miniseries:*
Napolean and Josephine (1987) . . . . . . . . . . . .Therese
*Made for TV Movies:*
Danielle Steel's "Secrets" (1992) . . . . . . . Sabina Quarles
To Be The Best (1992) . . . . . . . . . . . . . . . . . . Arabella
*TV:*
The Colbys (1985-87) . . . . . . . . . . . . Sable Scott Colby
Dynasty (1988-89) . . . . . . . . . . . . . . . . . Sable Colby
Sister Kate (1989-90) . . . . . . . Sister Katherine Lambert
Seaquest DSV (1993-94) . . . . . . . .Dr. Kristin Westphalen
*Magazines:*
**Playboy** (Nov 1972) . . . . . . . . . . . Sex in Cinema 1972
   •• 160—Right breast, B&W photo from *The Nightcom-
     ers.*
**Playboy** (Feb 1987) . . . . . . . . . . . . . . . . . . . . .n.a.
   •• 112-121—Color photos taken in 1972.

# Beal, Cindy

*Films:*
My Chauffeur (1986) . . . . . . . . . . . . . . . . . . . . Beebop
**Slavegirls from Beyond Infinity** (1987) . . . . . . . Tisa
(Wearing skimpy outfits during most of the movie.)
   0:25—Walking around in white bra and panties.
   ••• 0:36—Breasts on beach wearing white panties.
   • 1:05—Left breast leaning back on table while get-
     ting attacked by Zed.

# Beall, Sandra

*Films:*
Easy Money (1983) . . . . . . . . . . . . . . . .Maid of Honor
**A Night in Heaven** (1983) . . . . . . . . . . . . . . . .Slick
   • 1:09—Brief close up of left breast in shower with
     Christopher Atkins.
The Cotton Club (1984). . . . . . . . . . . . . . . Myrtle Fay
Birdy (1985). . . . . . . . . . . . . . . . . . . . . . . . . Shirley
**Key Exchange** (1985) . . . . . . . . . . . . . . . . . . Marcy
   ••• 1:14—Breasts on bed taking off her clothes and talk-
     ing to Daniel Stern.
Loverboy (1989) . . . . . . . . . . . . . . . . . . . . . . .Robin
State of Grace (1990). . . . . . . . . . . . . . . .Steve's Date

# Beals, Jennifer

*Films:*
Flashdance (1983) . . . . . . . . . . . . . . . . . . . . . . .Alex
The Bride (1985) . . . . . . . . . . . . . . . . . . . . . . . Eva
   0:21—Lower frontal nudity and buns of body dou-
     ble coming down stairs and to kneel down and talk
     to Sting.
   0:53—Standing in wet white nightgown in the rain
     talking to Sting.
Split Decisions (1988) . . . . . . . . . . . . . . . Barbara Uribe
Vampire's Kiss (1989) . . . . . . . . . . . . . . . . . . . .Rachel
   0:14—Almost breasts in bed with Nicolas Cage.
     Squished left breast against Cage while she bites
     him. In one shot, you can see the beige pastie she
     put over her left nipple.
   0:27—In bed again with Cage.
   0:41—In black lingerie taking her dress off for Cage.
**Club Extinction** (1990) . . . . . . . . . . . . . Sonja Vogler
   *a.k.a. Doctor M*
   • 1:16—Brief side of left breast rolling over in bed with
     Hartmann. Don't see her face, but probably her.
   •• 1:17—Brief breasts in bed with Hartmann when he
     kisses her right breast, then brief right breast.
**Blood & Concrete: A Love Story** (1991) . . . . . Mona
   • 0:10—Buns, in pulled up slip on bed with Billy Zane.
     Brief, out-of-focus shot of her left breast. Don't see
     her face.
In the Soup (1992). . . . . . . . . . . . . . . . . . . Angelica
Indecency (1992). . . . . . . . . . . . . . . . . . . . . . . Ellie
Day of Atonement (1993; French) . . . . . . . Joyce Ferratti
*TV:*
2000 Malibu Road (1992) . . . . . . . . . . . . . .Perry Quinn

## Beaman, Lee Anne

*Films:*

**Mirror Images** (1991) . . . . . . . . . . . . . . . . . Rebecca
- ••• 1:11—Buns in G-string, then breasts in conference room, undressing in front of Jeff Conaway and Carter.

**The Other Woman** (1992) . . . . . . . . Jessica Mathews
(Unrated version reviewed.)
- ••• 0:17—Nude, undressing and getting into the shower.
- •• 0:40—Breasts in the bathtub.
- •• 0:51—Buns, while lying in bed in the fetal position.
- ••• 1:09—Nude, on the floor making love with Traci. Interesting camera angles.
- ••• 1:13—Nude, getting up and out of bed, taking a shower, then making love with Carl. Long scene.
- •• 1:23—Breasts on floor with Traci during video playback on TV.
- ••• 1:34—Buns, in long shot, taking off robe to greet Zmed. Breasts and buns in bed with him.

**Sins of the Night** (1993) . . . . . . . . . . . . . . . Sue Ellen
(Unrated version reviewed.)
- •• 0:46—In black bra and G-string panties under sheer robe while drunk in her house, then breasts.

**Tropical Heat** (1993) . . . . . . . . . . . . . . . . . . . Carolyn
- ••• 0:10—Nude, taking her clothes off outside by swimming pool, then getting in and making love with Rick Rossovich. Long scene.
- •• 0:14—Breasts, while sitting at bar in swimming pool with Rossovich.

## Béart, Emmanuelle

Model for *Borghese* cosmetics.

*Films:*

Date with an Angel (1987) . . . . . . . . . . . . . . . . . Angel

**Manon of the Spring** (1987; French) . . . . . . . Manon
- • 0:11—Brief nude dancing around a spring playing a harmonica.

**La Belle Noiseuse** (1992; French) . . . . . . . . Marianne
- •• 1:11—Full frontal nudity, after taking off robe and posing in studio.
- •• 1:24—Left breast and lower frontal nudity while posing.
- •• 1:27—Full frontal nudity after finishing posing and putting on robe.
- •• 1:34—Nude, after taking off robe and getting ready to pose.
- ••• 1:38—Nude, after taking off robe and getting ready to pose while leaning on stool.
- ••• 1:43—Nude, after taking off robe and posing while sitting on chair.
- •• 1:49—Nude, lying on chair after taking off robe.
- •• 1:51—Nude, after taking off robe and posing on floor.
- ••• 1:53—Nude, while kneeling on bench while posing.
- ••• 1:57—Full frontal nudity while posing on stool, then sitting on chairs and sitting on floor. Long scene.
- • 2:03—(0:00 into tape 2) Full frontal nudity while posing on bench.
- •• 2:06—(0:03 into tape 2) Nude, while getting off bench and putting on robe.
- •• 2:10—(0:07 into tape 2) Breasts and buns, after taking off robe and sitting on bench.
- ••• 2:16—(0:13 into tape 2) Breasts, while posing on stool, then full frontal nudity, getting up off stool and putting on robe.
- ••• 2:33—(0:30 into tape 2) Nude, after taking off robe, and posing on mattress on the floor.
- ••• 2:42—(0:39 into tape 2) Nude, while walking around the studio, looking at the paintings, then sitting on mattress on the floor. Long scene.
- ••• 2:57—(0:54 into tape 2) Buns and breasts, while sitting on mattress on the floor. Full frontal nudity while lying down, then getting up, putting on robe and walking away.
- •• 3:17—(1:14 into tape 2) Breasts and buns, while standing and posing.
- •• 3:20—(1:17 into tape 2) Right beast, while standing and posing. Long shot at first, then closer shot.

Un Coeur en Hiver (1993; French) . . . . . . . . . . Camille

*Magazines:*

**Playboy** (Nov 1992) . . . . . . . . . . Sex in Cinema 1992
- •• 146—Left breast and partial buns, lying down from *La Belle Noiseuse.*

## • Beatty, Debra

*Films:*

Sorority House Party (1992) . . . Mennonite Fury Woman

**Animal Instincts 2** (1993) . . . . . . . . . . . . . . . Cindy
- •• 0:24—Full frontal nudity, while posing for Eric in his studio and putting a robe on.

**Anthony's Desire** (1993) . . . . . . . . . . . . . . . . Dancer
- ••• 0:04—Full frontal nudity, while stripping out of green dress on stage with other women.
- •• 0:22—Breasts, while sitting on stage on the right.
- • 1:02—Left breast, while sitting behind Annastasia Alexander on the left side of the stage.

**Hollywood Dreams** (1993) . . . . . . . . . . . . . . . . . Sara
(Unrated version reviewed.)
- ••• 0:11—Breasts after taking off her top in office for audition in front of Lou.
- ••• 0:19—Nude, diving into pool and getting out, then making love at Lou's.
- •• 0:24—Left breast and partial lower frontal nudity while lying on bed on a set.
- •• 0:39—Breasts while making love with Robby on bed in bedroom set.
- • 1:06—Side of right breast while getting made up.

**Strike a Pose** (1993) . . . . . . . . . . . . . . . . . . . . Model

**Witchcraft 6: The Devil's Mistress** (1993) . . . . . Keli
(Unrated version reviewed.)
- ••• 0:50—Breasts, while sitting in bubble bath, then nude, while making love with Will in the tub.
- ••• 1:06—Full frontal nudity getting into the bathtub, then washing herself.
- • 1:11—Brief right breast, while washing herself.

## Beatty, Linda

See: Carpenter, Linda.

## Beck, Kimberly

*Films:*
Yours, Mine and Ours (1968) . . . . . . . . . Janette North
**Massacre at Central High** (1976). . . . . . . . . .Theresa
- 0:32—Nude romping in the ocean with David. Long shot, dark, hard to see anything.
-- 0:42—Breasts on the beach making love with Andrew Stevens after a hang glider crash.

Roller Boogie (1979) . . . . . . . . . . . . . . . . . . . . . . .Lana
Friday the 13th, Part IV—The Final Chapter (1984)
. . . . . . . . . . . . . . . . . . . . . . . . . . . . . . . . . . . . . . Trish
Maid to Order (1987) . . . . . . . . . . . . . . . . . . . . . Kim
Nightmare At Noon (1987). . . . . . . . . . . .Sherry Griffith
*a.k.a. Deathstreet USA*
The Big Blue (1988) . . . . . . . . . . . . . . . . . . . . . Sally
Messenger of Death (1988). . . . . . . . . . . Piety Beecham
Operation: Paratrooper (1988) . . . . . . . . . . . . . . Kim
*a.k.a. Private War*
Adventures in Dinosaur City (1992). . . . . . . . Chanteuse
*Made for Cable TV:*
Sex, Shock and Censorship in the 90's (1993; Showtime)
. . . . . . . . . . . . . . . . . . . . . . . . . . . . . . . Marsha Miller
*Made for TV Movies:*
In the Deep Woods (1992) . . . . . . . . . . . . . . . . Margot
*TV:*
Peyton Place (1965) . . . . . . . . . . . . . . . . . Kim Schuster
Lucas Tanner (1974-75) . . . . . . . . . . . . . .Terry Klitsner
General Hospital (1975) . . . . . . . . . Samantha Chandler
Rich Man, Poor Man—Book II (1976-77) . . Diane Porter
Capitol (1982-83) . . . . . . . . . . . . . . . . . . . . . Julie Clegg

## • Becker, Brooke

*Films:*
Cat Chaser (1988). . . . . . . . . . . . . . . . . . . . . . . Philly
**Deadly Rivals** (1992) . . . . . . . . . . . . . . . . Shallie Kittle
- 0:14—Breasts visible under sheer white blouse while talking to Andrew Stevens in auditorium.

## Becker, Desiree

*Films:*
**Good Morning, Babylon** (1987; Italian/French)
. . . . . . . . . . . . . . . . . . . . . . . . . . . . . . . . . . . . .Mabel
- 1:06—Brief breasts in the woods making love.
*Made for Cable TV:*
**The Hitchhiker: Out of the Night** (1985; HBO)
. . . . . . . . . . . . . . . . . . . . . . . . . . . . . . . . . . . . Kathy
-- 0:12—Brief breasts lying in the steam room talking to Peter, then close up of breasts.

## Bedelia, Bonnie

Aunt of actor Macaulay Culkin.
*Films:*
**The Gypsy Moths** (1969) . . . . . . . . . . . . Annie Burke
- 0:28—Very, very brief right breast, while opening and folding her robe together while walking up the stairs. Partially hidden by shadow.

Lovers and Other Strangers (1970). . . .Susan Henderson
The Big Fix (1978) . . . . . . . . . . . . . . . . . . . . . .Suzanne
Heart Like a Wheel (1983) . . . . . . . Shirley Muldowney
The Boy Who Could Fly (1986) . . . . . . . . . . . Charlene
**The Stranger** (1986) . . . . . . . . . . . . . . . . . Alice Kildee
- 0:15—Brief right breast sticking up from behind her lover's arm making love in bed during flashback sequence (B&W).
- 0:19—Brief left breast turning over in hospital bed when a guy walks in. Long shot, hard to see.
-- 0:38—Right breast again making love (B&W).
Violets Are Blue (1986). . . . . . . . . . . . . . . Ruth Squires
Die Hard (1988). . . . . . . . . . . . . . . . . . . .Holly McClane
The Prince of Pennsylvania (1988) . . . . . Pam Marshetta
0:12—In black bra in open blouse in kitchen. Long scene.
Fat Man and Little Boy (1989) . . . . . Kitty Oppenheimer
Die Hard 2 (1990) . . . . . . . . . . . . . . . . . . .Holly McClane
Presumed Innocent (1990). . . . . . . . . . . .Barbara Sabich
Needful Things (1993). . . . . . . . . . . . . . . .Polly Chalmers
*Made for Cable Movies:*
Somebody Has to Shoot the Picture (1990; HBO)
. . . . . . . . . . . . . . . . . . . . . . . . . . . . . .Hannah McGrath
1:15—Upper half of left breast, lying in bed with Roy Scheider.
*Made for Cable TV:*
Fallen Angels: The Quiet Room (1993; Showtime)
. . . . . . . . . . . . . . . . . . . . . . . . . . . . . Sally Creighton
(Available on video tape on *Fallen Angels Two.*)
*Made for TV Movies:*
Memorial Day (1983). . . . . . . . . . . . . . . . . . . . . . n.a.
Switched at Birth (1991) . . . . . . . . . . . . . .Regina Twigg
A Mother's Right: The Elizabeth Morgan Story (1992)
. . . . . . . . . . . . . . . . . . . . . . . . . .Dr. Elizabeth Morgan
The Fire Next Time (1993) . . . . . . . . . . Suzanne Morgan
*TV:*
The New Land (1974) . . . . . . . . . . . . . . .Anna Larsen

## Bega, Leslie

*Films:*
For Keeps (1988) . . . . . . . . . . . . . . . . . . . . . . Carlita
Mobsters (1991) . . . . . . . . . . . . . . . . . Anna Lansky
*a.k.a. Mobsters—The Evil Empire*
**Uncaged** (1991) . . . . . . . . . . . . . . . . . . . . . . . . Micki
*a.k.a. Angel in Red*
-- 0:02—Breasts on top of a customer, in bed.
-- 0:16—Breasts in bed with Evan.
- 0:42—Brief breasts with Evan on the floor.
0:51—In white lingerie outfit with a customer and Ros.
*TV:*
Head of the Class (1986-89) . . . . . . . . . . . Maria Borges

## • Behr, Jena

*Video Tapes:*
**Playboy Night Dreams** (1993)
. . . . . . . . . . . . . . . . . . . . . . . . Arresting Development
--- 0:47—Nude, after stripping out of police officer uniform then making love.

**Supermodels Go Wild** (1993) . . . . . . . . . . . . .Model
••• 0:00—Nude throughout.

## Beldam, Lia
*Films:*
**The Shining** (1980). . . . . . . . . Young Woman in Bath
••• 1:12—Full frontal nudity getting out of bathtub
while Jack Nicholson watches.
*Magazines:*
**Playboy** (Nov 1980) . . . . . . . . . . . Sex in Cinema 1980
•• 174—Side view of left breast.

## • Bell, Catherine
*Films:*
**Death Becomes Her** (1992) . . . . . . .Lisle Body Double
•• 1:19—Buns, while getting out of swimming pool
and drying herself off. (2 long shots and 1 close-up.)
*Made for Cable TV:*
**Dream On: Those Who Can't, Edit** (1994; HBO)
. . . . . . . . . . . . . . . . . . . . . . . . . . . . . . . . . . . . . .Kay
••• 0:01—Breast, while starting to make love with Mar-
tin in his apartment.

## Bell, Jeannie
*Films:*
Black Gunn (1972) . . . . . . . . . . . . . . . . . . . . . . . .Lisa
**Mean Streets** (1973) . . . . . . . . . . . . . . . . . . . Diane
• 0:07—Breasts dancing on stage with pasties on.
• 1:00—Breasts backstage wearing pasties.
The Klansman (1974) . . . . . . . . . . . . . . . . . . Mary Anne
**Policewomen** (1974) . . . . . . . . . . . . . . . Pam Harris
•• 0:02—Buns and breasts changing clothes during
prison break.
••• 1:28—Brief breasts changing into military clothes
outside next to truck.
Three the Hard Way (1974). . . . . . . . . . . . . . . . . Polly
**TNT Jackson** (1975) . . . . . . . . . . Diana "TNT" Jackson
••• 0:43—Breasts, getting her blouse ripped off by the
bad guys. More breasts during fight (notice her
panties change from black to white to black).
• 0:45—Brief breasts, almost hitting Joe.
••• 0:50—Breasts, while making love with Charlie.
The Choirboys (1977) . . . . . . . . . . . . . . . Fanny Forbes
**Sex on the Run** (1979; German/French/Italian)
. . . . . . . . . . . . . . . . . . . . . . . . . . . . . Slave Girl
*a.k.a. Some Like It Cool*
*a.k.a. Casanova and Co.*
••• 0:01—Breasts, reading book in large bath with
Marisa Berenson.
••• 0:24—Breasts, giving Berenson a back massage.
**Bloodfist III: Forced to Fight** (1991) . . . TNT Jackson
•• 0:55—Breasts several times in movie *TNT Jackson*
that the inmates watch while Diddler gets stabbed
to death.
*Magazines:*
**Playboy** (Oct 1969). . . . . . . . . . . . . . . . . . . Playmate
**Playboy** (Nov 1975) . . . . . . . . . . Sex in Cinema 1975
••• 132—Breasts in still photo from *TNT Jackson.*

**Playboy** (Mar 1977) . . . . . . . . Comeback for Casanova
••• 88—Breasts.
**Playboy** (Dec 1980) . . . . . . . . . . . . . . Bunny Birthday
••• 153—Breasts.

## • Bell, Josie
*Films:*
Bright Lights, Big City (1988) . . . . . . . . . Runway Model
**SnakeEater** (1988). . . . . . . . . . . . . . . . . . . . The Kid
• 0:39—Very brief side view of right breast and buns,
while walking past open doorway while Lorenzo La-
mas watches. Medium long shot.
A Family Matter (1990) . . . . . . . . . . . . . . . . . . . . Cissy

## Beller, Kathleen
*Films:*
The Godfather, Part II (1974) . . . . Girl in "Senza Mama"
**The Betsy** (1978) . . . . . . . . . . . . . . . Betsy Hardeman
••• 0:12—Nude getting into swimming pool.
•• 1:14—Breasts lying under Tommy Lee Jones.
Movie Movie (1978) . . . . . . . . . . . . . . . . Angie Popchik
Promises in the Dark (1979) . . . . . . . . . . . Buffy Koenig
**Surfacing** (1980) . . . . . . . . . . . . . . . . . . . . . . . .Kate
0:22—Very brief buns, pulling down pants to
change. Dark, hard to see.
0:23—Very brief right breast undressing. Dark, hard
to see.
• 0:24—Very, very brief breasts turning over in bed.
0:25—Buns, standing next to bed.
••• 1:23—Breasts washing herself in the water. One
long shot, one side view of right breast.
Fort Apache, The Bronx (1981) . . . . . . . . . . . Theresa
**The Sword and the Sorcerer** (1982) . . . . . . . .Alana
• 0:54—Side view of buns, lying face down getting oil
rubbed all over her.
Touched (1982) . . . . . . . . . . . . . . . . . . . . . . Jennifer
Cloud Waltzing (1986) . . . . . . . . . . . . . . . . . . . . . n.a.
Time Trackers (1989) . . . . . . . . . . . . . . . . . . R. J. Craig
*Miniseries:*
Blue and the Gray (1982) . . . . . . . . . . . Kathy Reynolds
Dynasty: The Reunion (1991) . . . . . . . . . . . . . . . Kirby
*Made for TV Movies:*
Mary White (1977). . . . . . . . . . . . . . . . . . Mary White
Are You in the House Alone? (1978) . . . . . . . . . . . Gail
*TV:*
Search for Tomorrow (1971-74) . . . . . . . . . Liza Walton
Dynasty (1982-84) . . . . . . . . . . . . . . . . . Kirby Anders
Bronx Zoo (1987-88) . . . . . . . . . . . . . . . . . . Callahan

## Belli, Agostina
*Films:*
**Bluebeard** (1972). . . . . . . . . . . . . . . . . . . .Caroline
• 1:31—Brief left breast lying on grass getting a tan.
•• 1:32—Breasts taking off clothes and lying on the
couch.
Blood in the Streets (1974; French/Italian) . . . . . . .Maria
The Seduction of Mimi (1974; Italian) . . . . . . . . .Rosalia
The Purple Taxi (1977; French/Italian/Irish)
. . . . . . . . . . . . . . . . . . . . . . . . . . . . . Anne Taubelman

**Holocaust 2000** (1978) . . . . . . . . . . . . . . Sara Golen
•• 0:50—Breasts in bed making love with Kirk Douglas.

# • *Belliveau, Cynthia*
a.k.a. Cyd Belliveau.
*Films:*
Loose Screws (1986) . . . . . . . . . . . . . . . . . . Mona Lott
Goofballs (1987) . . . . . . . . . . . . . . . . . . . . . . . . .n.a.
Night Friend (1987; Canadian) . . . . . . . . . . . . .Maggie
**The Dark** (1993) . . . . . . . . . . . . . . . . . . . . . . . Tracy
•• 0:29—In slip, then bra, then breasts, while making
love on bed in motel with Hunter.
*Made for Cable Movies:*
The Spider and the Fly (1994; USA). . . . . . . . . . . Blair
*TV:*
E.N.G. (1989-90; Canadian) . . . . . . . . . . . . . . . . .n.a.

# • *Bellomo, Sara*
a.k.a. Adult film actress Roxanne Blaze.
*Films:*
**Beach Babes From Beyond** (1993) . . . . . . . . . . .Xena
••• 0:01—Breasts and very brief lower frontal nudity
while in shower and getting dressed with Luna and
Sola during opening credits.
• 0:32—Buns, in swimsuit at the beach.
• 0:58—Buns, while dancing in swimsuits and boots
on stage at beach during bikini contest.
**Seduce Me: Pamela Principle 2** (1994) . . . . . . Inger
•• 0:33—Breasts, twice, while walking past Charles in
house.
• 0:50—Breasts, while sitting in spa. (She's on the
left.)
•• 1:01—Breasts, while making love (loudly) on bed
when Charles passes by open door. Dark.

# *Bellwood, Pamela*
*Films:*
Two-Minute Warning (1976). . . . . . . . . Peggy Ramsay
Airport '77 (1977). . . . . . . . . . . . . . . . . . . . . . . .Lisa
Hanger 18 (1980) . . . . . . . . . . . . . . . . . . . . . . Sarah
Serial (1980) . . . . . . . . . . . . . . . . . . . . . . . . . . Carol
The Incredible Shrinking Woman (1981)
. . . . . . . . . . . . . . . . . . . . . . . . . . . . . Sandra Dyson
Cellar Dweller (1987) . . . . . . . . . . . . . . . . . . Amanda
*Made for TV Movies:*
Double Standard (1988) . . . . . . . . . . . . . . . . . . Joan
*TV:*
W.E.B. (1978) . . . . . . . . . . . . . . . . . Ellen Cunningham
Dynasty (1981-86) . . . . . . . . . . . . . . Claudia Blaisdel
*Magazines:*
**Playboy** (Apr 1983) . . . . . . . . . . . . . . . . Going Native
• Covered with mud and body paint.

# *Bening, Annette*
Wife of actor Warren Beatty.
*Films:*
The Great Outdoors (1988). . . . . . . . . . . . . Kate Craig

Valmont (1989) . . . . . . . . . . . . . . .Marquise de Merteuil
0:10—Very brief, hard to see right breast, while
reaching up to kiss Jeffrey Jones.
**The Grifters** (1990) . . . . . . . . . . . . . . . . .Myra Langtry
•• 0:36—In bra and panties in her apartment, then
breasts lying in bed "paying" her rent. Kind of dark.
••• 1:06—Nude, walking down the hall to the bedroom
and into bed.
1:30—Very brief right breast, dead in morgue. Long
shot.
Postcards from the Edge (1990). . . . . . . . . Evelyn Ames
Bugsy (1991) . . . . . . . . . . . . . . . . . . . . . . . Virginia Hill
Guilty by Suspicion (1991). . . . . . . . . . . . . Ruth Merrill
1:01—In white bra and slip getting dressed.
Regarding Henry (1991). . . . . . . . . . . . . . . Sarah Turner
*Magazines:*
**Playboy** (Nov 1991) . . . . . . . . . . Sex in Cinema 1991
• 143—Breasts, lying in bed, in scene from *The Grift-
ers*.

# *Bennett, Angela*
*Films:*
**Fatal Games** (1984). . . . . . . . . . . . . . .Sue Allen Baines
•• 0:21—Full frontal nudity in the sauna with Teal Roberts.
• 0:23—Nude, running around the school, trying to
get away from the killer. Dark.
Punchline (1988) . . . . . . . . . . . . . . . . . . . . . . . Nurse

# *Benson, Vickie*
*Films:*
**Private Resort** (1985) . . . . . . . . . . . . . . . . .Bikini Girl
• 0:28—In blue two piece swimsuit, showing her
buns, then brief breasts with Reeves.
1:11—Buns, in locker room, trying to slap Reeves.
**Las Vegas Weekend** (1986) . . . . . . . . . . . . .Amanda
• 1:12—Breasts and buns, while making love in bed
with Percy.
My Chauffeur (1986) . . . . . . . . . . . . . . . . . Party Girl
**The Wraith** (1986). . . . . . . . . . . . . . . . . . . .Waitress
• 0:59—Breasts in bed with Packard when Loomis interrupts them.
**Cheerleader Camp** (1987) . . . . . . . . . . . . Miss Tipton
*a.k.a. Bloody Pom Poms*
• 0:27—Brief breasts undressing in her bedroom.
Blue Movies (1988) . . . . . . . . . . . . . . . . . . . .Andrea
Mortuary Academy (1988). . . . . . . . . . . . . . .Salesgirl

# *Bentley Konkel, Dana*
*Films:*
**Bad Girls from Mars** (1990). . . . . . . . . . . . . Martine
•• 0:28—Breasts taking off her blouse in office.
•• 0:59—Breasts several times wrestling with Edy Williams.
**Death Merchant** (1990) . . . . . . . . . . Jason's Girlfriend
• 0:35—Brief breasts undressing for shower during
dream.
**Invisible Maniac** (1990) . . . . . . . . . . . . . Newscaster
• 1:22—Brief breasts on monitor doing the news.

Repo Jake (1990). . . . . . . . . . . . . . . . . . . . . . . Jenny
**Sorority House Massacre 2** (1990). . . . . . . . . . Janey
••• 0:23—Breasts in bedroom talking to Suzanne and
looking in the mirror. Buns, while getting dressed in
black bodysuit.
0:48—Left breast, sticking out of bodysuit, covered
with blood, when the girls discover her dead.

## Benton, Barbi

*Films:*
**Hospital Massacre** (1982) . . . . . . . . . . Susan Jeremy
*a.k.a. X-Ray*
0:29—Undressing behind a curtain while the Doctor
watches her silhouette.
••• 0:31—Breasts getting examined by the Doctor. First
sitting up, then lying down.
••• 0:34—Great close up shot of breasts while the Doctor uses stethoscope on her.
**Deathstalker** (1983). . . . . . . . . . . . . . . . . . . Codille
•• 0:39—Breasts struggling while chained up and everybody is fighting.
• 0:47—Right breast, struggling on the bed with
Deathstalker.
*TV:*
Hee Haw (1971-76) . . . . . . . . . . . . . . . . . . . . .Regular
Sugar Time! (1977-78) . . . . . . . . . . . . . . . . . . . . Maxx
*Video Tapes:*
Playboy Video Magazine, Volume 9. . . . . . . . . . Herself
*Magazines:*
**Playboy** (Dec 1973). . . . . . . . . . . . . . . . Barbi's Back!
••• 143-149—Nude.
**Playboy** (Jan 1975) . . . . . . . . . . Playboy Mansion West
•• 94-99—Nude.
**Playboy** (Jan 1989) . . . . . . . . .Women of the Seventies
••• 210—Breasts.

## Benton, Suzanne

*Films:*
**That Cold Day in the Park** (1969) . . . . . . . . . . Nina
• 0:38—Side view of left breast putting top on. Long
shot.
• 1:05—Breasts taking off her clothes and getting into
the bathtub. Another long shot.
Catch-22 (1970) . . . . . . . . . . . . . . . . . . Dreedle's WAC
Best Friends (1975). . . . . . . . . . . . . . . . . . . . . Kathy
**A Boy and His Dog** (1976). . . . . . . . . . . . Quilla June
•• 0:29—Nude, getting dressed while Don Johnson
watches.
• 0:45—Right breast lying down with Johnson after
making love with him.

## Bentzen, Jane

*Films:*
Nightmare at Shadow Woods (1983) . . . . . . . . . . Julie
*a.k.a. Blood Rage*
0:38—In red lingerie, black stockings and garter belt
in her apartment with Phil.

*Made for Cable Movies:*
**A Breed Apart** (1984; HBO) . . . . . . . . . . . . Reporter
••• 0:55—Left breast in bed with Powers Booth, then
full frontal nudity getting out of bed and putting her
clothes on.

## • Benussi, Femi

*Films:*
The Hawks and the Sparrows (1967; Italian). . . . . . Luna
The Biggest Bundle of Them All (1968) . . . . . . . . . . . .
Uncle Carlo's Bride
Hatchet for the Honeymoon (1969; Spanish/Italian)
. . . . . . . . . . . . . . . . . . . . . . . . . . . . . . . . . . . n.a.
*a.k.a. Blood Brides*
The Italian Connection (1973; U.S./Italian). . . . . . . Nana
**My Father's Wife** (1976; Italian) . . . . . . . . . . Patricia
*a.k.a. Confessions of a Frustrated Housewife*
• 0:33—Close up view of left breast.
•• 0:51—Right breast, while making love in bed with
Claudio. Breasts after.

## Benz, Donna Kei

*Films:*
Looker (1981) . . . . . . . . . . . . . . . . . . . . . . . . . . Ellen
**The Challenge** (1982) . . . . . . . . . . . . . . . . . .Akiko
• 1:23—Breasts making love with Scott Glenn in mo-
tel room. Could be a body double. Dark, hard to see
anything.
Pray for Death (1986) . . . . . . . . . . . . . . . . . Aiko Saito
Moon in Scorpio (1987). . . . . . . . . . . . .Nurse Mitchell
*Magazines:*
**Playboy** (Nov 1982). . . . . . . . . . Sex in Cinema 1982
• 161—Breasts.

## Berenson, Marisa

*Films:*
Death in Venice (1971; Italian/French)
. . . . . . . . . . . . . . . . . . . . . . . . Frau Von Aschenbach
Cabaret (1972) . . . . . . . . . . . . . . . . .Natalia Landauer
**Barry Lyndon** (1975; British) . . . . . . . . . Lady Lyndon
Breasts in bathtub.
Killer Fish (1979; Italian/Brazilian). . . . . . . . . . . . . .Ann
Sex on the Run (1979; German/French/Italian) . . . . n.a.
*a.k.a. Some Like It Cool*
*a.k.a. Casanova and Co.*
1:23—Almost right breast, while in bed with Tony
Curtis when she rolls over him.
**S.O.B.** (1981) . . . . . . . . . . . . . . . . . . . . . . . . .Mavis
•• 1:20—Breasts in bed with Robert Vaughn.
The Secret Diary of Sigmund Freud (1984)
. . . . . . . . . . . . . . . . . . . . . . . . . . . .Emma Herrmann
Trade Secrets (1989; French) . . . . . . . . . . . . . . Jeanne
Night of the Cyclone (1990) . . . . . . . . . . . . .Francoise
White Hunter Black Heart (1990) . . . . . . . . Kay Gibson
*Made for Cable Movies:*
Notorious (1992; Lifetime). . . . . . . . . . . . . . . .Katarina
*Miniseries:*
Sins (1986). . . . . . . . . . . . . . . . . . . . . . . Luba Tcherina

*Made for TV Movies:*
Playing for Time (1980). . . . . . . . . . . . . . . . . . .Elzvieta
*Magazines:*
**Playboy** (Dec 1973). . . . . . . . . . . . . Sex Stars of 1973
• 210—Right breast.
**Playboy** (Feb 1976). . . . . . . . . . . . . Kubrick's Countess
•• 74-77—Left breast.
**Playboy** (Jul 1976). . . . . . . . . . . . . . . . . . . . . . . .Press
• 34—Breasts in B&W photo that appeared in the November 17, 1975 issue of *Time* magazine.
**Playboy** (Nov 1976) . . . . . . . . . . Sex in Cinema 1976
•• 144—Left breast in a shot that wasn't used in *Barry Lyndon.*
**Playboy** (Dec 1976). . . . . . . . . . . . . . Sex Stars of 1976
• 184—Partial lower frontal nudity.

# Berg, Carmen

*Video Tapes:*
**Playboy Video Calendar 1989** (1988) . . . . . . . . .July
••• 0:25—Nude.
**Sexy Lingerie** (1988) . . . . . . . . . . . . . . . . . . . .Model
**Wet and Wild** (1989). . . . . . . . . . . . . . . . . . . .Model
*Magazines:*
**Playboy** (Jul 1987). . . . . . . . . . . . . . . . . . . . Playmate
**Playboy's Book of Lingerie** (Mar 1991) . . . . . Herself
• 83—Left breast.
**Playboy's Book of Lingerie** (Sep 1991) . . . . . Herself
••• 74—Breasts.
**Playboy's Book of Lingerie** (Mar 1992) . . . . . Herself
• 60—Partial left breast.
**Playboy's Calendar Playmates** (Nov 1992) . . Herself
••• 74—Full frontal nudity.

# Bergen, Candice

Former model.
Wife of French director Louis Malle.
Daughter of ventriloquist Edgar Bergen.
*Films:*
The Group (1966). . . . . . . . . . . . . . . . . .Lakey Eastlake
The Adventurers (1970) . . . . . . . . . . . . . . . . . Sue Ann
Getting Straight (1970). . . . . . . . . . . . . . . . . . . . . . Jan
**Soldier Blue** (1970) . . . . . . . . . . Cresta Marybelle Lee
• 0:57—Close-up of buns, in open skirt while in back of wagon when Peter Strauss tries to cover her up. Don't see her face.
Carnal Knowledge (1971). . . . . . . . . . . . . . . . . Susan
The Hunting Party (1971; British) . . . . . . . Melissa Ruger
T. R. Baskin (1971) . . . . . . . . . . . . . . . . . . T.R. Baskin
Bite the Bullet (1975) . . . . . . . . . . . . . . . . . .Miss Jones
The Wind and the Lion (1975) . . . . . . . . Eden Pedecaris
**A Night Full of Rain** (1978; Italian) . . . . . . . . . .Lizzy
• 1:04—Right breast, while in car with Giancarlo Giannini.
Oliver's Story (1978) . . . . . . . . . . . . . . . Marcie Bonwit
**Starting Over** (1979) . . . . . . . . . . . . . . . .Jessica Potter
1:01—In a sheer blouse sitting on couch talking to Burt Reynolds.

• 1:29—Very, very brief left breast in bed with Reynolds when he undoes her top. You see her breast just before the scene dissolves into the next one. Long shot, hard to see.
Rich and Famous (1981) . . . . . . . . . . .Merry Noel Blake
Gandhi (1982). . . . . . . . . . . . . . Margaret Bourke-White
*Made for TV Movies:*
Mayflower Madam (1987) . . . . . .Sydney Biddle Barrows
*TV:*
Murphy Brown (1988- ) . . . . . . . . . . . . Murphy Brown

# •Berger, Katia

*Films:*
The Moon in the Gutter (1983; French/Italian). . . . . n.a.
  *a.k.a. La Lune dans Le Caniveau*
**Tales of Ordinary Madness** (1983; Italian)
. . . . . . . . . . . . . . . . . . . . . . . . . . . . . . . .Girl on Beach
••• 1:30—Full frontal nudity, taking off her clothes in front of Ben Gazzara at the beach.

# Berger, Senta

*Films:*
Ambushers (1967) . . . . . . . . . . . . . . . . . . . . .Francesca
If It's Tuesday, This Must Be Belgium (1969). . . . . Herself
**When Women Had Tails** (1970; Italian). . . . . . . . Felli
• 0:22—Buns, while lying in pit.
• 1:08—Buns, while getting carried around.
• 1:30—Buns, after her boyfriend gets caught in tree.
**When Women Lost Their Tails** (1971; Italian) . . Felli
• 0:13—Very long shot of buns, while walking into pond.
**Cross of Iron** (1977) . . . . . . . . . . . . . . . . . . . . . Eva
• 0:55—Brief buns, while taking off her nightgown in bedroom.
Killing Cars (1986) . . . . . . . . . . . . . . . . . . . . . . .Marie

# Berger, Sophie

*Films:*
**Emmanuelle IV** (1984) . . . . . . . . . . . . . . . . . . .Maria
•• 0:46—Full frontal nudity putting on robe.
0:49—Buns, taking off robe in front of Mia Nygren.
**Love Circles Around the World** (1984) . . . .Dagmar
••• 0:38—Breasts in women's restroom in casino making love with a guy in a tuxedo.
••• 0:43—Breasts in steam room wearing a towel around her waist, then making love.

# Bergman, Sandahl

*Films:*
**All That Jazz** (1979) . . . . . . . . . . . . . . . . . . . .Sandra
•• 0:51—Breasts and buns in T-back while dancing on scaffolding during a dance routine.
Xanadu (1980). . . . . . . . . . . . . . . . . . . . . . . . A Muse
Airplane II: The Sequel (1982) . . . . . . . . . . . Officer #1
**Conan the Barbarian** (1982) . . . . . . . . . . . . .Valeria
•• 0:49—Brief left breast making love with Arnold Schwarzenegger.

**She** (1983) . . . . . . . . . . . . . . . . . . . . . . . . . . . . . . .She
- •• 0:22—Breasts getting into a pool of water to clean her wounds after sword fight.

Red Sonja (1985) . . . . . . . . . . . . . . . . . Queen Gedren

Hell Comes to Frogtown (1987) . . . . . . . . . . . Spangle

Kandyland (1987) . . . . . . . . . . . . . . . . . .Harlow Divine

**Programmed to Kill** (1987) . . . . . . . . . . . . . . Samira

*a.k.a. The Retaliator*
- • 0:11—Brief side view of right breast taking off T-shirt and leaning over to kiss a guy. Don't see her face.

Stewardess School (1987) . . . . . . . . . . Wanda Polanski

Raw Nerve (1991). . . . . . . . . . . . . . . .Gloria Freedman

Body of Influence (1992). . . . . . . . . . . . . . . . . . .Clarissa

(Unrated version reviewed.)
- 0:32—In white bra, white panties and black stockings in psychiatrist's office.
- 0:41—In bra and panties on TV during video playback.

**Loving Lulu** (1992). . . . . . . . . . . . . . . . . . . . . . . Lulu
- 0:34—In red bra and blue panties with Sam.
- ••• 0:35—Breasts, making love with Sam.
- • 0:42—Brief buns and brief breasts in shower with Sam.
- • 0:57—Brief right breast in bathroom, twice, with Sam.

**Lipstick Camera** (1993) . . . . . . . . . . . . . . .Lilly Miller
- • 0:19—Buns, while in T-back panties, while making love with Flynn in bed.
- • 1:18—Buns on monitor during video playback.

**Possessed by the Night** (1993) . . . . . . .Peggy Hansen
- ••• 0:06—Breasts and buns, while making love with Ted Prior in bed.
- • 0:08—More right breast and buns, while lying in bed after making love.
- 0:26—In white bra and panties in bedroom with Prior.
- 0:58—Briefly in bra in bathroom.
- • 0:59—Breasts, while in bathtub.
- 1:02—In white bra and panties, after undressing while Shannon Tweed hold Prior at gunpoint.
- ••• 1:03—Breasts, while lying in bed after Prior rips her bra and panties off.
- ••• 1:14—Breasts, while changing tops in bedroom.

*Made for TV Movies:*

Getting Physical (1984). . . . . . . . . . . . .Nadine Cawley

In the Arms of a Killer (1992) . . . . . . . Nurse Henninger

*Video Tapes:*

The Firm Aerobic Workout With Weights, Vol. 3
. . . . . . . . . . . . . . . . . . . . . . . . . . . . . . . . . Instructor

*Magazines:*

**Playboy** (Mar 1980). . . . . . . . . . . . . . . . All That Fosse
- ••• 174-175—Breasts stills from *All That Jazz.*

**Playboy** (Dec 1981). . . . . . . . . . . . . . Sex Stars of 1981
- •• 239—Breasts.

# Berland, Terri

*Films:*

The Strangeness (1980) . . . . . . . . . . . . .Cindy Flanders

**Pink Motel** (1982) . . . . . . . . . . . . . . . . . . . . . . .Marlene
- 0:47—In red bra, while in bed with Max.
- 0:56—In red bra and panties, while standing up with Max.
- ••• 1:18—Breasts, dropping her sheet in room in front of Max and Skip.

The Sting II (1983) . . . . . . . . . . . . . . . . . . . . . . . . . n.a.

# Bernard, Sue

Film writer and producer.

*Films:*

Faster Pussycat, Kill! Kill! (1966) . . . . . . . . . . . . . .Linda

**The Killing Kind** (1973) . . . . . . . . . . . . . . . . . . . .Tina
- • 0:00—Breasts during gang rape.
- • 0:19—Breasts again during flashback.
- • 1:12—Brief breasts again several times during flashbacks.

**The Witching** (1983). . . . . . . . . . . . . . . . . . . . Nancy

*a.k.a. Necromancy*

(Originally filmed in 1971 as *Necromancy*, additional scenes were added and re-released in 1983.)
- • 1:03—Brief breasts in bed with Michael Ontkean.

*Magazines:*

**Playboy** (Dec 1966) . . . . . . . . . . . . . . . . . . . Playmate

**Playboy** (May 1977). . . . . . . . . . . . . . . . . . Grapevine
- • 242—Breast in small B&W photo.

# Bernhard, Sandra

Comedienne.

*Films:*

Cheech & Chong's Nice Dreams (1981). . . . . . .Girl Nut

King of Comedy (1983) . . . . . . . . . . . . . . . . . . . Masha

Track 29 (1988; British) . . . . . . . . . . . . . . . Nurse Stein

Heavy Petting (1989). . . . . . . . . . . Herself/Comedienne

**Without You I'm Nothing** (1990)
. . . . . . . . . . . . . . . . . . . . . .Miscellaneous Characters
- ••• 1:20—Dancing in very small pasties on stage. Buns in very small G-string. Long scene.

Hudson Hawk (1991). . . . . . . . . . . Minerva Mayflower

Truth or Dare (1991) . . . . . . . . . . . . . . . . . . . . .Herself

Inside Monkey Zetterland (1993) . . . . . . . . . . Imogene

*Made for Cable TV:*

The Hitchhiker: O. D. Feeling . . . . . . . . . . . . . . . n.a.

Tales From the Crypt: Top Billing (1991; HBO)
. . . . . . . . . . . . . . . . . . . . . . . . . . . . Sheila Winters

**Sandra After Dark** (1992; HBO). . . . . . . . . . Hostess
- ••• 0:47—Breasts and buns, taking off bra and panties and getting into bed.

*TV:*

Roseanne (1992- ) . . . . . . . . . . . . . . . Nancy Thomas

*Magazines:*

**Playboy** (May 1991). . . . . . . . . . . . . . . . . . Grapevine
- • 182—Upper half of right breast in open dress. B&W.

**Playboy** (Aug 1992) . . . . . . . . . . . . . . . . Next Month
- • 166—Partial right breast.

**Playboy** (Sep 1992) . . . . . .Not Just Another Pretty Face
  •• 70-77—Full frontal nudity in B&W and color photos.
**Playboy** (Dec 1992). . . . . . . . . . . . . . . Sex Stars 1992
  •• 183—Full frontal nudity, wearing metallic G-string in
    B&W photo.
**Playboy** (Mar 1994). . . . . . . . . . . .Safe Sex, Great Sex
  ••• 71—Left breast and lower frontal nudity in B&W
    photo.

## • Bernstein, Caron

*Films:*
Who's the Man? (1993). . . . . . . . . . . . . . . . . . . . Kelly
*Made for Cable TV:*
**Red Shoe Diaries: The Game** (1994; Showtime). . Lily
  • 0:04—Left breast in open blouse with John.
  ••• 0:07—Breasts, while doing various things around
    the house, including caressing herself.
  •• 0:08—Breasts, while making love with John while
    blindfolded.
  •• 0:10—Breasts and buns in panties, taking off rain-
    coat outside in the rain.
  •• 0:14—Breasts, while playing game with neighbor
    couple, then making love with John while watching
    the couple also make love.
  •• 0:18—Breasts and brief buns, while making love in
    restroom with a sailor in a fantasy.

## Berridge, Elizabeth

*Films:*
**The Funhouse** (1981) . . . . . . . . . . . . . . . . . . . . . Amy
  •• 0:03—Brief breasts taking off robe to get into the
    shower, then very brief breasts getting out to chase
    Joey.
Amadeus (1984) . . . . . . . . . . . . . . . . . . . . . Constanze
Five Corners (1988). . . . . . . . . . . . . . . . . . . . Melanie
When the Party's Over (1991). . . . . . . . . . . . . Frankie
    0:04—In white bra, while talking to Taylor.
*TV:*
The Powers That Be (1992) . . . . . . . . . . . . . . Charlotte
The John Larroquette Show (1993- ) . . . . . . . . . . . .n.a.

## Bertinelli, Valerie

Wife of singer Eddie Van Halen.
*Films:*
Number One with a Bullet (1987). . . . . . . . . . . . . .n.a.
*Made for TV Movies:*
Young Love, First Love (1979). . . . . . . . . Robin Gibson
The Seduction of Gina (1984). . . . . . . . . . . Gina Breslin
**Ordinary Heroes** (1986). . . . . . . . . . . . . . Maria Pezzo
  • 0:28—Brief silhouette of breast in darkened room
    backlit by window, when she takes off her blouse
    while on top of Richard Dean Anderson in bed.
Pancho Barnes (1988). . . . . . . . . . . . . . Pancho Barnes
    0:10—Very brief silhouette of back side of left breast
    while putting sheet around herself before getting
    into bed with her first husband.
Taken Away (1989) . . . . . . . . . . . . . . . . . . . . . . . .n.a.
In a Child's Name (1991) . . . . . . . . . . . Angela Cimarelli
Murder of Innocence (1993). . . . . . . . . . . . . . . . .n.a.

*TV:*
One Day at a Time (1975-84). . . . Barbara Cooper Royer
Sydney (1990) . . . . . . . . . . . . . . . . . . . . . . . . . Sydney
Café Americain (1993- ) . . . . . . . . . . . . . . . . . . . Holly

## Besch, Bibi

Mother of actress Samantha Mathis.
*Films:*
The Long Dark Night (1977) . . . . . . . . . . . . . . . Marge
  *a.k.a. The Pack*
Hardcore (1979) . . . . . . . . . . . . . . . . . . . . . . . . Mary
**The Beast Within** (1982) . . . . . . . Caroline MacCleary
  •• 0:06—Breasts, getting her blouse torn off by the
    beast while she is unconscious. Dark, hard to see her
    face.
Star Trek II: The Wrath of Kahn (1982)
  . . . . . . . . . . . . . . . . . . . . . . . . . . . Dr. Carol Marcus
The Lonely Lady (1983) . . . . . . . . . . . . . . . . Veronica
Who's That Girl? (1987). . . . . . . . . . . Mrs. Worthington
Kill Me Again (1989) . . . . . . . . . . . . . . Jack's Secretary
Steel Magnolias (1989) . . . . . . . . . . . .Belle Marmillion
Tremors (1989) . . . . . . . . . . Megan, The Doctor's Wife
Betsy's Wedding (1990). . . . . . . . . . . . . . Nancy Lovell
Lonely Hearts (1991) . . . . . . . . . . . . . . . Maria Wilson
    0:05—Almost breasts in bed with Eric Roberts.
*Made for TV Movies:*
Death of a Centerfold: The Dorothy Stratten Story
  (1981) . . . . . . . . . . . . . . . . . . . . . . . . . . . . . . Hilda
Doing Time on Maple Drive (1992) . . . . . . . . . . . Lisa
*TV:*
Secrets of Midland Heights (1980-81)
  . . . . . . . . . . . . . . . . . . . . . . . . . . Dorothy Wheeler
The Hamptons (1983) . . . . .Adrienne Duncan Mortimer
Freshman Dorm (1992-93). . . . . . . . . . . . . Mrs. Flynn

## • Best, Alyson

*Films:*
Pacific Banana (1980). . . . . . . . . . . . . . . . . . . . . n.a.
Brothers (1984; Australian). . . . . . . . . . Janine Williams
**Man of Flowers** (1984; Australian) . . . . . . . . . . . Lisa
  •• 0:04—Undressing out of clothes, in bra, panties and
    stockings in front of Charles, then full frontal nudity,
    then getting dressed.
  •• 0:13—Full frontal nudity after taking off robe and sit-
    ting on chair for art class.
  • 0:36—Brief breasts while in bed with a guy.

## Beswicke, Martine

*Films:*
From Russia with Love (1963; British). . . . . . . . . Zora
Saturday Night Out (1963; British). . . . . . . . . . . . n.a.
Thunderball (1965; British). . . . . . . . . . . Paula Caplan
One Million Years B.C. (1966; U.S./British). . . . Nupondi
Slave Girls (1968). . . . . . . . . . . . . . . . . . . . . . . . Kari
  *a.k.a. Prehistoric Women*
**Dr. Jekyll and Sister Hyde** (1971) . . . . . . Sister Hyde
  • 0:25—Breasts, opening her blouse and examining
    her breasts after transforming from a man.
  • 0:27—Left breast, feeling herself.

• 0:44—Brief buns, taking off coat to put on a dress.
Seizure (1973)...................... The Queen
**The Happy Hooker Goes Hollywood** (1980)
................................ Xaviera Hollander
•• 0:05—Brief breasts in bedroom with Policeman.
••• 0:22—Brief buns, jumping into the swimming pool, then breasts next to the pool with Adam West.
• 0:27—Breasts in bed with West, then breasts waking up.
Melvin and Howard (1980)........ Real Estate Woman
Cyclone (1986)......................... Waters
The Offspring (1986) ............. Katherine White
Evil Spirits (1990) ...................... Vanya
Miami Blues (1990)...................... Noira
Trancers II (1991) ................. Nurse Trotter
Life on the Edge (1992)................ Linda James
Wide Sargasso Sea (1993)............... Aunt Cora
(Unrated version reviewed.)

*TV:*
Aspen (1977) .................... Joan Carolinian

# Betchley, Leigh
*Films:*
**Novel Desires** (1991) .................... Susan
••• 0:13—Breasts in warehouse making love with Sandman. Long scene.
••• 0:15—More breasts while talking to Sandman.
**Knockouts** (1992)...................... Brooke
• 0:04—Brief breasts while putting on white bra in dressing room.
• 0:26—Very brief left breast after winning strip poker game.
••• 0:41—Breasts while taking off lingerie, while wearing blue panties.
••• 0:44—Breasts while posing in space costume for photographs.
• 0:46—Brief right breast while posing in front of blinds.

# • Betzler, Geri
See: Trilling, Zoe.
*Films:*
Fear (1988)...................... Jennifer Haden
The Borrower (1989)..................... Astrid

# Beyer, Tanya
*Video Tapes:*
**The Best of Wet and Wild** (1992) ......... Model
**Playboy Playmates in Paradise** (1992) ... Playmate
**Playboy Video Calendar 1993** (1992) ....... March
•• 0:09—Breasts under sheer dress. Full frontal nudity by pool.
••• 0:11—Nude indoors and outdoors.
**Wet and Wild IV** (1992) .................. Model
**Playboy's Playmate Review 1993** (1993)
............................ Miss February
••• 0:06—Nude, dancing in front of a big screen TV.
••• 0:08—Nude on fountain in front of a house.

*Magazines:*
**Playboy** (Feb 1992) .................. Playmate
••• 90-101—Nude.
**Playboy's Playmate Review** (Jun 1993).... February
••• 14-21—Nude.
**Playboy's Book of Lingerie** (Jul 1993)....... Herself
•• 50-51—Right breast and lower frontal nudity.
**Playboy's Wet & Wild Women** (Aug 1993)... Herself
•• 86—Buns and side of right breast.
••• 105—Full frontal nudity.
**Playboy's Book of Lingerie** (Sep 1993)...... Herself
••• 44—Breasts.
••• 81—Breasts.
**Playboy's Video Playmates** (Sep 1993)...... Herself
••• 18-19—Nude.
**Playboy's Book of Lingerie** (Nov 1993)...... Herself
••• 62—Full frontal nudity.
**Playboy's Book of Lingerie** (Jan 1994) ...... Herself
••• 96-97—Breasts and buns.
**Playboy's Book of Lingerie** (May 1994) ..... Herself
• 14—Lower frontal nudity.
••• 21—Full frontal nudity.
**Playmates at Play** (Jul 1994) .............. Herself
•• 46—Right breast and lower frontal nudity.
**Playboy's Girls of Summer '94** (Jul 1994).... Herself
••• 44—Full frontal nudity.
••• 54—Full frontal nudity.

# Biffignani, Monique
*Video Tapes:*
**Rock Video Girls 2** (1992) ................ Herself
0:00—Brief right breast in gauze during opening credits.
0:47—In pink bra, in dressing room.
• 0:49—Right breast under gauze and buns in G-string after being unwrapped as a mummy.
0:53—Briefly in pink bra and gauze again during end credits.
0:54—Briefly in gauze again during end credits.
**Sexy Lingerie IV** (1992) ................. Model
*Magazines:*
**Playboy's Book of Lingerie** (Sep 1992)...... Herself
••• 3-7—Full frontal nudity.
•• 11—Left breast.
**Playboy's Book of Lingerie** (Nov 1992) ..... Herself
•• 92-93—Buns and lower frontal nudity.
**Playboy's Book of Lingerie** (Mar 1993)...... Herself
•• 23—Buns in T-back.
**Playboy's Girls of Summer '93** (Jun 1993) ... Herself
• 19—Lower frontal nudity.
**Playboy's Book of Lingerie** (Jul 1993)....... Herself
•• 24-25—Buns and lower frontal nudity.
•• 104—Lower frontal nudity and buns.
**Playboy's Wet & Wild Women** (Aug 1993)... Herself
•• 8—Breasts under wet T-shirt and lower frontal nudity.
• 62-63—Breasts under wet shirt and lower frontal nudity.

**Playboy's Blondes, Brunettes & Redheads**
(Sep 1993) . . . . . . . . . . . . . . . . . . . . . . . . . . Herself
• 76—Partial buns.
**Playboy's Book of Lingerie** (Sep 1993) . . . . . Herself
••• 28-29—Full frontal nudity.
• 54—Lower frontal nudity.
**Playboy's Book of Lingerie** (Mar 1994) . . . . . Herself
• 56—Lower half of breasts and buns in panties.
**Playboy's Book of Lingerie** (May 1994) . . . . . Herself
•• 58—Buns.

## • Billings, Dawn Ann
*Films:*
Trancers III (1993) . . . . . . . . . . . . . . . . . . . . . . . Jana
**Warlock: The Armageddon** (1993) . . Amanda Sloan
• 0:10—Very brief side of left breast, walking through
hallway while taking off robe. Brief breasts, while
walking past doorway.
A Brilliant Disguise (1994)
. . . . . . . . . . . . . . . . . . . Brunette in French Restaurant

## Binoche, Juliette
*Films:*
Hail, Mary (1985; French) . . . . . . . . . . . . . . . . . Juliette
*a.k.a. Je Vous Salve, Marie*
**Rendez-Vous** (1986; French) . . . . . Anne "Nina" Larrieu
• 0:07—Brief breasts in dressing room when Paulot
surprises her and Fred.
••• 0:25—Side of left breast, then breasts and buns in
empty apartment with Paulot.
•• 0:32—Full frontal nudity in bed with Quentin.
•• 0:35—Buns, then brief breasts in bed with Paulot
and Quentin. Full frontal nudity getting out.
•• 1:08—Breasts taking off her top in front of Paulot in
the dark, then breasts lying on the floor.
• 1:11—Right breast, making love on the stairs. Dark.
**The Unbearable Lightness of Being** (1988) . . Tereza
0:22—In white bra in Tomas' apartment.
• 1:33—Brief breasts jumping onto couch.
1:36—Buns, sitting in front of fire being photographed, then running around, trying to hide.
• 2:18—Left breast in The Engineer's apartment.
**Damage** (1992; French/British) . . . . . . . . . . . . . . Anna
(Unrated Director's cut reviewed.)
• 0:52—Brief breasts while sitting on floor and making
love with Jeremy Irons.
•• 1:31—Breasts on bed after getting caught with by
Iron's son.
Blue (1993; French/Polish) . . . . . . . . . . . . . . . . . . Julie
*a.k.a. Trois Couleurs Bleu*
*Made for Cable Movies:*
Women & Men 2: Three Short Stories (1991; HBO)
. . . . . . . . . . . . . . . . . . . . . . . . . . . . . . . . . . Mara
*Magazines:*
**Playboy** (Nov 1987) . . . . . . . . . . Sex in Cinema 1987
• 143—Side view of right breast from *Rendez-vous*.

## Bird, Minah
*Films:*
Oh, Alfie! (1975; British) . . . . . . . . . . . . . . . . . . Gloria
*a.k.a. Alfie Darling*
**The Stud** (1978; British) . . . . . . . . . . . . . . . . . . Molly
•• 0:26—Breasts in bed when Tony is talking on the
telephone.

## Birkin, Jane
Mother of actress Charlotte Gainsbourg.
*Films:*
**Blow-Up** (1966; British/Italian) . . . . . . . . . . . Teenager
• 1:06—Breasts, while changing clothes in David
Hemming's studio.
• 1:08—Brief breasts while frolicking with Hemmings
and the other teenage girl in the studio. Very, very
brief lower frontal nudity under Hemmings.
**Ms. Don Juan** (1973) . . . . . . . . . . . . . . . . . . . . Clara
0:58—Lower frontal nudity lying in bed with Brigitte
Bardot.
1:00—Brief breasts in bed with Bardot. Long shot.
•• 1:01—Full frontal nudity getting dressed. Brief
breasts in open blouse.
Dark Places (1974; British) . . . . . . . . . . . . . . . . . . Alta
**Catherine & Co.** (1975; French) . . . . . . . . . Catherine
• 0:07—Breasts, standing up in the bathtub to open
the door for another woman.
•• 0:09—Side view of left breast, while taking off her
blouse in bed.
••• 0:10—Breasts, sitting up and turning the light on,
smoking a cigarette.
•• 0:17—Right breast, while making love in bed.
•• 0:24—Breasts taking off her dress, then buns jumping into bed.
•• 0:36—Buns and left breast posing for a painter.
• 0:45—Breasts taking off dress, walking around the
house. Left breast, inviting the neighbor in.
Stuntwoman (1981) . . . . . . . . . . . . . . . . . . . . . . . n.a.
**Dust** (1985; French/Belgian) . . . . . . . . . . . . . . Magda
1:17—Brief breasts and buns, taking off robe and
pounding the wall. Very dark.
Le Petit Amour (1988; French) . . . . . . . . . . . Mary-Jane
*a.k.a. Kung Fu Master*
Daddy Nostalgie (1991; French) . . . . . . . . . . . Caroline
La Belle Noiseuse (1992; French) . . . . . . . . . . . . . . Liz

## Bishop, Stephanie
a.k.a. Adult film actress Viper.
*Films:*
Vice Academy (1988) . . . . . . . . . . . . . Desiree/Redhead

## Bisignano, Jeannine
*Films:*
Body Rock (1984) . . . . . . . . . . . . . . . . . . . . . . . . . Girl
**My Chauffeur** (1986) . . . . . . . . . . . . . . . . . . Party Girl
• 1:23—Breasts, several times, taking off her white
blouse in the back of the limousine. (She's the only
brunette.)

**Ruthless People** (1986) . . . . . . . . . . . . Hooker in Car
0:17—Breasts, hanging out of the car. Long, long
shot, don't see anything.
• 0:40—Breasts in the same scene three times on TV
while Danny De Vito watches.
• 0:49—Left breast hanging out of the car when the
Chief of Police watches on TV. Closest shot.
1:15—Same scene again in department store TV's.
Long shot, hard to see.
**Stripped to Kill II** (1988) . . . . . . . . . . . . . . . . . Sonny
0:06—Buns, while wearing a black bra in dressing
room.
••• 0:38—Breasts and buns during strip dance routine
in white lingerie.
License to Kill (1989) . . . . . . . . . . . . . . . . . . . . Stripper
*Made for Cable Movies:*
Lies of the Twins (1991; USA) . . . . . . . . . . . . . Biker Girl
*Magazines:*
**Playboy** (Nov 1986) . . . . . . . . . . Sex in Cinema 1986
•• 131—Breasts in a photo from *Ruthless People*, leaning out of the car.

# Bisset, Jacqueline

*Films:*
Cul-de-sac (1966) . . . . . . . . . . . . . . . . . . . . . . Jacqueline
Casino Royale (1967; British) . . . . . . . . Miss Goodthighs
Two for the Road (1967; British) . . . . . . . . . . . . . Jackie
Bullitt (1968) . . . . . . . . . . . . . . . . . . . . . . . . . . . . . Cathy
The Detective (1968) . . . . . . . . . . . . . . . Norma McIver
The Sweet Ride (1968) . . . . . . . . . . . . . Vicki Cartwright
(Not available on video tape.)
Breasts.
The Secret World (1969; French) . . . . . . . . . . . . Wendy
Airport (1970) . . . . . . . . . . . . . . . . . . . . Gwen Meighen
**The Grasshopper** (1970) . . . . . . . . . Christine Adams
*a.k.a. The Passing of Evil*
*a.k.a. Passions*
0:21—In flesh-colored Las Vegas-style showgirl costume. Partial buns.
0:27—More showgirl shots.
1:14—In black two piece swimsuit.
1:16—Brief, almost left breast while squished
against Jay in the shower.
Believe in Me (1971) . . . . . . . . . . . . . . . . . . . Pamela
**The Mephisto Waltz** (1971) . . . . . . . . Paula Clarkson
• 0:48—Very brief right and side view of left breast in
bed with Alan Alda.
1:36—Sort of left breast getting undressed for
witchcraft ceremony. Long shot side views of right
breast, but you can't see her face.
•• 1:45—Very brief breasts twice under bloody water in
blood covered bathtub, dead. Discovered by Kathleen Widdoes.
**Secrets** (1971) . . . . . . . . . . . . . . . . . . . . . . . . . Jenny
0:49—Very brief lower frontal nudity, putting pant-
ies on while wearing a black dress.
••• 1:02—Brief buns and a lot of breasts on bed making
love with Raoul.

The Life and Times of Judge Roy Bean (1972)
. . . . . . . . . . . . . . . . . . . . . . . . . . . . . . . . Rose Bean
The Thief Who Came to Dinner (1973) . . . . . . . . Laura
The Magnificent One (1974; French/Italian)
. . . . . . . . . . . . . . . . . . . . . . . . . Tatiana/Christine
Murder on the Orient Express (1974; British)
. . . . . . . . . . . . . . . . . . . . . . . . Countess Andrenyi
The Spiral Staircase (1975; British) . . . . . . . . . . Helen
End of the Game (1976; Italian/German)
. . . . . . . . . . . . . . . . . . . . . . . . . . . Anna Crawley
St. Ives (1976) . . . . . . . . . . . . . . . . . . . . Janet Whistler
**The Deep** (1977) . . . . . . . . . . . . . . . . . . . . Gail Berke
••• 0:01—Scuba diving underwater in a wet T-shirt.
• 0:08—More wet T-shirt, getting out of water, onto
boat.
The Greek Tycoon (1978) . . . . . . . . . . . . . . Liz Cassidy
Who is Killing the Great Chefs of Europe? (1978)
. . . . . . . . . . . . . . . . . . . . . . . . . . . . . . . . Natasha
When Time Ran Out! (1980) . . . . . . . . . . . . . Kay Kirby
Inchon (1981) . . . . . . . . . . . . . . . . Barbara Hallsworth
Rich and Famous (1981) . . . . . . . . . . . . . Liz Hamilton
**Famous T & A** (1982) . . . . . . . . . . . . . . . . . . . Jenny
(No longer available for purchase, check your video
store for rental.)
••• 0:31—Breasts scene from *Secrets*.
Class (1983) . . . . . . . . . . . . . . . . . . . . . . . . . . . . Ellen
Under the Volcano (1984) . . . . . . . . . . . Yvonne Firmin
**High Season** (1988; British) . . . . . . . . Katherine Shaw
• 0:56—Brief breasts doing the backstroke in the water with Kenneth Branagh, then left breast while lying down. Hard to see, everything is lit with blue
light.
Scenes from the Class Struggle in Beverly Hills (1989)
. . . . . . . . . . . . . . . . . . . . . . . . . . . . . . . . . . Clare
The Maid (1990) . . . . . . . . . . . . . . . . Nicole Chantrelle
0:47—In lingerie, changing clothes in front of Martin Sheen while talking to him.
1:13—Very, very brief side of left breast shadow on
wall, leaping out of bed with Sheen.
Wild Orchid (1990) . . . . . . . . . . . . . . . . . . . . . Claudia
1:21—Dancing in braless white tank top during car-
nival.
*Made for Cable Movies:*
Forbidden (1985) . . . . . . . . . . . . . . . . Nina von Halder
0:25—In bra and slip in villa with her lover.
0:47—Squished breasts against Jurgen Prochnow in
bed making love.
*Miniseries:*
Anna Karenina (1985) . . . . . . . . . . . . . Anna Karenina
Napolean and Josephine (1987)
. . . . . . . . . . . . . . . . Josephine de Beauharnais
Lots of cleavage.
*Made for TV Movies:*
Leave of Absence (1994) . . . . . . . . . . . . . . . . . . . Nell
*Magazines:*
**Playboy** (Jun 1977) . . . . . . . . . . . . . Ad for "The Deep"
•• 18-21—In braless T-shirt while scuba diving under
water in fold-out advertisement for *The Deep*.

**Playboy** (Nov 1977) . . . . . . . . . . Sex in Cinema 1977
• 158—In wet T-shirt, while underwater in photo from *The Deep*.

## Bissett, Josie

Wife of actor Rob Estes.
Model for Soft & Dri deodorant.
*Films:*
**Desire** (1989; Italian) . . . . . . . . . . . . . . Jessica Harrison
••• 0:28—Breasts and buns, while making love in bed with her boyfriend. Long scene.
•• 0:32—Brief breasts, getting out of bed and getting dressed.
••• 0:45—Breasts, while making love with the taxi boy.
••• 0:51—Breasts, playing the piano while getting caressed and kissed.
••• 0:55—Breasts, while lying in bed.
•• 1:16—Breasts in bed with an older man.
• 1:17—Brief breasts in bed while wearing a brunette wig (she's supposed to be her mother).
• 1:20—Side view of left breast on top of a guy in bed in slow motion. (Wearing a wig).
• 1:21—More left breast (still wearing wig).
• 1:27—Left breast, while in bed in flashbacks.
**All-American Murder** (1991) . . . . . . . . . . Tally Fuller
1:01—Brief breasts in Polaroid photographs that Charlie Schlatter looks at. Hard to see.
• 1:07—Very brief breasts several times during B&W flashbacks.
• 1:12—Breasts on top of the Dean during Joanna Cassidy's B&W flashbacks. Quick cuts.
The Book of Love (1991) . . . . . . . . . . . . . . . . . . . . . . Lily
The Doors (1991) . . . . . . . . . Robby Krieger's Girlfriend
**I Posed for Playboy** (1991) . . . . . . . Claire Baywood
*a.k.a. Posing: Inspired by Three Real Stories*
(Shown on network TV without the nudity.)
• 0:09—Close-up of left breast, while on couch with Nick. Don't see her face.
Mikey (1992) . . . . . . . . . . . . . . . . . . . . . . . . . . . Jessie
0:44—In black bra and panties, in bedroom with David.
0:58—In red one piece body leotard while in a spa with David.
*Made for TV Movies:*
Danielle Steel's "Secrets" (1992) . . . . . . . . Gaby Smith
Deadly Vows (1994) . . . . . . . . . . . . . . . . Bobbi Gilbert
*TV:*
Hogan Family (1990-91) . . . . . . . . . . . . . . . . . . . . Cara
Doogie Howser, M.D. (1990) . . . . . . . . . . . . . . . .n.a.
Melrose Place (1992- ) . . . . . . . . . . . . . . .Jane Mancini

## Bittner, Carrie

a.k.a. Adult film actress Alicyn Sterling.
*Films:*
**Bikini Summer 2** (1992) . . . . . . . . . . . . . . . . . Sandra
• 0:15—Buns in two piece swimsuit, while walking with Sandy.
•• 0:38—Breasts (she's the blonde), taking off her T-shirt and jumping into the pool with Sandra.

• 0:40—Very brief breasts, running past some guys.
••• 0:42—More breasts, while running around the backyard.
••• 0:44—More breasts and buns in swimsuits, while running around some more.
**Night Rhythms** (1992) . . . . . . . . . . . . . . . . . . . .Elaine
(Unrated version reviewed.)
••• 0:06—Right breast, then breasts and lower frontal nudity while talking on the phone and playing with herself. Long scene.
*Video Tapes:*
**Penthouse Satin & Lace: An Erotic History of Lingerie** (1992) . . . . . . . . . . . . . . . . . . . . . . . . Model

## Black, Karen

*Films:*
Easy Rider (1969) . . . . . . . . . . . . . . . . . . . . . . . .Karen
Five Easy Pieces (1970) . . . . . . . . . . . . . Rayette Dipesto
0:48—In sheer black nightie in bathroom, then walking to bedroom with Jack Nicholson.
**Cisco Pike** (1971) . . . . . . . . . . . . . . . . . . . . . . . . . Sue
•• 0:47—Breasts, getting dressed in bedroom.
**Drive, He Said** (1972) . . . . . . . . . . . . . . . . . . . . Olive
• 1:05—Brief breasts screaming in the bathtub when she gets scared when a bird flies in.
1:19—Brief lower frontal nudity running out of the house in her bathrobe.
Little Laura and Big John (1972) . . . . . . . . . . . . . .Laura
Portnoy's Complaint (1972) . . . . . . . . . . . The Monkey
Airport 1975 (1974) . . . . . . . . . . . . . . . . . . . . . . Nancy
The Great Gatsby (1974) . . . . . . . . . . . . . Myrtle Wilson
The Day of the Locust (1975) . . . . . . . . . . . . . . . .Faye
Nashville (1975) . . . . . . . . . . . . . . . . . . . Connie White
Burnt Offerings (1976) . . . . . . . . . . . . . . . . . . . Marion
Capricorn One (1978) . . . . . . . . . . . . . . .Judy Drinkwater
**In Praise of Older Women** (1978; Canadian) . .Maya
•• 0:35—Breasts in bed with Tom Berenger.
**Separate Ways** (1979) . . . . . . . . . . . . . Valentine Colby
• 0:04—Breasts and in panties changing while her husband talks on the phone, then in bra. Long shot.
•• 0:18—Breasts in bed, while making love with Tony Lo Bianco.
•• 0:36—Breasts taking a shower, then getting out.
Chanel Solitaire (1981) . . . . . . . . . . Emilienne D'Alencon
**Killing Heat** (1981) . . . . . . . . . . . . . . . . . .Mary Turner
•• 0:41—Full frontal nudity giving herself a shower in the bedroom.
Come Back to the Five and Dime, Jimmy Dean, Jimmy (1982) . . . . . . . . . . . . . . . . . . . . . . . . . . . . . . . .Joanne
**Can She Bake a Cherry Pie?** (1983) . . . . . . . . . . Zee
0:40—Sort of left breast squished against a guy, while kissing him in bed.
• 1:02—Very brief upper half of left breast in bed when she reaches up to touch her hair.
Savage Dawn (1984) . . . . . . . . . . . . . . . . . . . . . Rachel
Cut and Run (1985; Italian) . . . . . . . . . . . . . . . . Karin
Eternal Evil (1985; Canadian) . . . . . . . . . . . . . . . Janus
Invaders from Mars (1986) . . . . . . . . . . . . . . . . .Linda
Dixie Lanes (1987) . . . . . . . . . . . . . . . . . . . . . . Zelma

**Miss Right** (1987; Italian) . . . . . . . . . . . . . . . . . . Amy
- 0:47—Brief breasts jumping out of bed and running to get a bucket of water to put out a fire.

The Invisible Kid (1988) . . . . . . . . . . . . . . . . . . Mom
It's Alive III: Island of the Alive (1988) . . . . . . Ellen Jarvis
Out of the Dark (1988) . . . . . . . . . . . . . . . . . . . . Ruth
Bad Manners (1989) . . . . . . . . . . . . . . Mrs. Fitzpatrick
Homer & Eddie (1989) . . . . . . . . . . . . . . . . . . . Belle
Night Angel (1989) . . . . . . . . . . . . . . . . . . . . . . . Rita
Zapped Again! (1989) . . . . . . . . . . Homeroom Teacher
The Children (1990; British/German) . . . . . Sybil Lollmer
Club Fed (1990) . . . . . . . . . . . . . . . . . . . . Sally Rich
Evil Spirits (1990) . . . . . . . . . . . . . . . . . . . Ella Purdy
Haunting Fear (1990) . . . . . . . . . . . . Dr. Julia Harcourt
Mirror Mirror (1990) . . . . . . . . . . . . . . . . Mrs. Gordon
Overexposed (1990) . . . . . . . . . . . . . . Mrs. Trowbridge
Twisted Justice (1990) . . . . . . . . . . . . . . Mrs. Granger
Auntie Lee's Meat Pies (1991) . . . . . . . . . . Auntie Lee
Blood Money (1991) . . . . . . . . . . . . . . . . . . . Barrett
*a.k.a. The Killer's Edge*
Children of the Night (1991) . . . . . . . Karen Thompson
Caged Fear (1992) . . . . . . . . . . . . . . . . . . . . Blanche
The Double O Kid (1992) . . . . . . . . . . . . . . Mrs. Elliot
Final Judgement (1992) . . . . . . . . . . . . . . Mrs. Sorrel
Hitz (1992) . . . . . . . . . . . . . . . . . . . . Tiffany Powers
*a.k.a. Judgment*
The Player (1992) . . . . . . . . . . . . . . . . . . . . Cameo
Rubin & Ed (1992) . . . . . . . . . . . . . . . . . . . . . Rula
Bound and Gagged: A Love Story (1993) . . . . . . . Carla
*Made for Cable TV:*
The Hitchhiker: Hired Help (1985; HBO)
. . . . . . . . . . . . . . . . . . . . . . . . . . Mrs. Kay Mason
(Available on *The Hitchhiker, Volume 1.*)
*Made for TV Movies:*
Trilogy of Terror (1974)
. . Millicent Larimore/Therese Larimorex/Julie Eldridgex/ Amelia
Tales of the City (1994) . . . . . . . . . . . . . . . . . Herself
*TV:*
The Second Hundred Years (1967-68)
. . . . . . . . . . . . . . . . . . . . . . . . Marcia Garroway
*Magazines:*
**Playboy** (Dec 1973) . . . . . . . . . . . . Sex Stars of 1973
- 207—Half of left breast under gaping blouse.
**Playboy** (Dec 1975) . . . . . . . . . . . . Sex Stars of 1975
- 189—Out of focus left breast.
**Playboy** (Dec 1976) . . . . . . . . . . . . Sex Stars of 1976
- 185—Breasts under pink see-through night gown.

## Black, Nicole
a.k.a. Adult film actress Nicole Noir.
*Films:*
**Simply Irresistible** (1983) . . . . . . . . . . . . Mata Hari
(R-rated version. *Irresistible* is the X-rated version.)
1:07—Pulling up her dress, then stripping in front of two guys in prison.
- 1:14—Full frontal nudity tied to a chair.
*Video Tapes:*
Nudes in Limbo (1983) . . . . . . . . . . . . . . . . . Model

## Blackburn, Greta
*Films:*
**48 Hrs.** (1982) . . . . . . . . . . . . . . . . . . . . . . . . Lisa
- 0:13—Breasts and buns in bathroom in hotel room with James Remar.
The Concrete Jungle (1982) . . . . . . . . . . . . Lady in Bar
Time Walker (1982) . . . . . . . . . . . . . . . . . . . . Sherri
Chained Heat (1983; U.S./German) . . . . . . . . . . . . Lulu
Yellowbeard (1983) . . . . . . . . . . . . . . . Mr. Prostitute
**Party Line** (1988) . . . . . . . . . . . . . . . . . . . Angelina
- 0:01—Partial side of left breast in open dress, while standing and kissing Curtis.
- 0:02—Breasts in bed with Curtis. Brief breasts after rolling off him when Leif Garrett comes in.
0:13—In bra and panties in bed.
Death Feud (1989) . . . . . . . . . . . . . . . . . . . . . Jenny
0:29—In sexy black dress talking to Frank Stallone.
1:04—In black lingerie on couch.
Under the Boardwalk (1989) . . . . . . . . . . Mrs. Vorpin
My Blue Heaven (1990) . . . . . . . . . . . . . Stewardess
Life on the Edge (1992) . . . . . . . . . . . . . Joanie Hardy
*Miniseries:*
V: The Final Battle (1984) . . . . . . . . . . . . . . Lorraine

## Blackman, Joan
*Films:*
Vengeance of Virgo (1972) . . . . . . . . . . . . . . . . n.a.
Macon County Line (1974) . . . . . . . . . . Carol Morgan
**Pets** (1974) . . . . . . . . . . . . . . . . . . . Geraldine Mills
- 0:46—Brief side view of left breast, while getting out of bed after making love with Bonnie.
Moonrunners (1975) . . . . . . . . . . . . . . . . . . . Reba
One Man (1979; Canadian) . . . . . . . . . . . . . . . . n.a.
Return to Waterloo (1986) . . . . . . . . . . . . . . . . n.a.

## Blackwood, Nina
*Films:*
Vice Squad (1982) . . . . . . . . . . . . . . . . . . . . Ginger
*TV:*
Entertainment Tonight . . . . . . . . Music Correspondent
Music Television . . . . . . . . . . . . . . . . . Video Jockey
*Magazines:*
**Playboy** (Aug 1978) . . . . . . . . . . The Girls in the Office
- 142—Full frontal nudity (with brunette hair).

## Blair, Linda
*Films:*
Way We Live Now (1970) . . . . . . . . . . Sara Aldridge
The Exorcist (1973) . . . . . . . . . . . . . . . . . . . Regan
Airport 1975 (1974) . . . . . . . . . . . . . . . Janice Abbott
Exorcist II: The Heretic (1977) . . . . . . . . . . . . Regan
Roller Boogie (1979) . . . . . . . . . . . . . . Terry Barkley
Hell Night (1981) . . . . . . . . . . . . . . . . . . . . . Marti
**Chained Heat** (1983; U.S./German) . . . . . . . . . . Carol
- 0:30—Breasts in the shower.
- 0:56—In bra, then breasts in the Warden's office when he rapes her.

**Night Patrol** (1985) . . . . . . . . . . . . . . . . . . . . . . . Sue
• 1:19—Brief left breast, in bed with The Unknown Comic.
Savage Island (1985) . . . . . . . . . . . . . . . . . . . . . . . Daly
**Savage Streets** (1985) . . . . . . . . . . . . . . . . . . . Brenda
••• 1:05—Breasts sitting in the bathtub thinking.
Nightforce (1986) . . . . . . . . . . . . . . . . . . . . . . . . . Carla
Grotesque (1987) . . . . . . . . . . . . . . . . . . . . . . . . . . . Lisa
**Red Heat** (1987; U.S./German) . . . . . . . . Chris Carlson
0:09—In blue nightgown in the bedroom with her boyfriend, almost breasts.
••• 0:56—Breasts in shower room scene.
••• 1:01—Brief breasts getting raped by Sylvia Kristel while the male guard watches.
Silent Assassins (1988) . . . . . . . . . . . . . . . . . . . . Sara
0:48—Very brief, wearing light blue bra struggling on couch with a masked attacker.
Up Your Alley (1988) . . . . . . . . . . . . . . . . Vickie Adderly
W. B., Blue and the Bean (1988) . . . . . . . . . . . . . Nettie
*a.k.a. Bail Out*
Witchery (1988) . . . . . . . . . . . . . . . . . . . . . . Jane Brooks
**Bedroom Eyes II** (1989) . . . . . . . . . . . Sophie Stevens
0:31—Buns, in bed with Wings Hauser.
• 0:33—Brief left breast under bubbles in the bathtub. Don't see her face.
A Woman Obsessed (1989) . . . . . . . . . . . . . Evie Barnes
Zapped Again! (1989) . . . . . . . . . . . . . . . Miss Mitchell
0:31—Panties and lingerie in raised skirt.
Dead Sleep (1990; Australian) . . . . . . . . Maggie Healey
Repossessed (1990) . . . . . . . . . . . . . . . . . Nancy Aglet
**Fatal Bond** (1991; Australian) . . . . . . . . . . . . . Leonie
•• 0:25—Brief right breast out of her slip, while making love on top of Joe in bed.
1:00—Breasts and buns, while washing herself off in shower. Seen behind textured glass door.
*Made for TV Movies:*
Born Innocent (1974) . . . . . . . . . . . . . . . Chris Parker
Sarah T.: Portrait of a Teenage Alcoholic (1975) . . Sarah
Sweet Hostage (1975) . . . . . . . . . . . . . . . . . . . . . . n.a.
Calendar Girl, Cop, Killer? The Bambi Bembenek Story (1992) . . . . . . . . . . . . . . . . . . . . . . . . . . Jane Mader
Perry Mason: The Case of the Heartbroken Bride (1992) . . . . . . . . . . . . . . . . . . . . . . . . . Hannah Hawkes
*Magazines:*
**Playboy** (Dec 1983) . . . . . . . . . . . . . Sex Stars of 1983
••• 209—Breasts.
**Playboy** (Dec 1984) . . . . . . . . . . . . . Sex Stars of 1984
••• 207—Breasts in the water up to her breasts.

# Blaisdell, Deborah

a.k.a. Adult film actress Tracey Adams.
*Films:*
**The Lost Empire** (1983) . . . . . . . . . . . . . Girl Recruit
• 0:42—Brief buns and breasts, turning over on exam table.
**Screen Test** (1986) . . . . . . . . . . . . . . . . . . . . . Dancer
• 1:20—Brief breasts, twice, dancing on stage. Long shot.

**Student Affairs** (1987) . . . . . . . . . . . . . . . . . . Kelly
••• 0:26—Breasts sitting up in bed talking to a guy.
**Wildest Dreams** (1987) . . . . . . . . . . . . Joan Peabody
• 1:10—Brief breasts during fight on floor with two other women.
**Wimps** (1987) . . . . . . . . . . . . . . . Roxanne Chandless
• 1:22—Brief breasts and buns taking off clothes and getting into bed with Francis in bedroom.
**Enrapture** (1989) . . . . . . . . . . . . . . . . . . . . . . Martha
••• 0:10—Breasts undressing in her apartment with Keith.
•• 0:17—Left breast, in bed with Keith, then brief breasts.

# Blake, Stephanie

a.k.a. Stella Blalack and Cimmaron.
*Films:*
**The Big Bet** (1985) . . . . . . . . . . . . . . . . Mrs. Roberts
••• 0:04—Breasts sitting on bed, then making love with Chris.
•• 0:37—Nude on bed with Chris. Shot at fast speed, he runs between bedrooms.
•• 0:59—Full frontal nudity in bed again. Shot at fast speed.
The Sure Thing (1985) . . . . . . . . . . . . . . . . . . Barmaid
Ferris Bueller's Day Off (1986) . . . . . . . . Singing Nurse
Over the Top (1987) . . . . . . . . . . . . . . . . Ticket Agent
**Danger Zone II: Reaper's Revenge** (1988)
. . . . . . . . . . . . . . . . . . . . . Tattooed Topless Dancer
••• 0:47—Breasts, dancing on stage in bikini bottoms.
**Invisible Maniac** (1990) . . . . . . . . . . . . . . Mrs. Cello
•• 0:42—Breasts opening her blouse for Chet.
•• 0:52—Breasts in her office trying to seduce Dr. Smith. Nice close up of right breast.
**Whore** (1991) . . . . . . . . . . . . . . . . Stripper in Big T's
*a.k.a. If you're afraid to say it... Just see it*
• 0:35—Buns, in G-string on stage.
••• 0:36—Breasts, dancing on stage in a club.
The Mambo Kings (1992) . . . . . . . . . . . . . . . . Stripper

# Blakely, Susan

*Films:*
Savages (1972) . . . . . . . . . . . . . . . . . . . . . . . . . Cecily
The Way We Were (1973) . . . . . . . . . . . . . . . . Judianne
The Lords of Flatbush (1974) . . . . . . . . . Jane Bradshaw
The Towering Inferno (1974) . . . . . . . . Patty Simmons
**Capone** (1975) . . . . . . . . . . . . . . . . . . . . Iris Crawford
•• 1:13—Breasts, taking off her clothes outside in front of Ben Gazzara.
• 1:22—Left breast, while lying in bed with Gazzara.
••• 1:23—Nude, getting out of bed and getting dressed, then more breasts while fooling around with Gazzara.
**Report to the Commissioner** (1975)
. . . . . . . . . . . . . . . . . . . . . . . Patty Butler/Chiclet
Airport '79: The Concorde (1979) . . . . . . . . . . Maggie
Over the Top (1987) . . . . . . . . . . . . . . . Christine Hawk
Blackmail (1991) . . . . . . . . . . . . . . . . Lucinda Sullivan

*Made for Cable Movies:*
Wildflower (1991; Lifetime)............. Ada Guthrie
*Made for Cable TV:*
**The Hitchhiker: Remembering Melody**
(1984; HBO) .........................Melody
••• 0:17—Right breast in shower with Ted and brief breasts in the bathtub.
*Miniseries:*
Rich Man, Poor Man (1976)
...................Julie Prescott Abbott Jordache
*Made for TV Movies:*
Broken Angel (1988).............Catherine Coburn
Ladykillers (1988) ...........................n.a.
The Incident (1989) ........................n.a.
Murder Times Seven (1990) ............ Gert Kiley
And the Sea Will Tell (1991) ........... Gail Bugliosi
Against Her Will: An Incident in Baltimore (1992) .. Billie
Intruders (1992) ....................Leigh Holland
No Child of Mine (1993)............. Peggy Young
Honor Thy Father & Mother (1994) .......Abramson
*Magazines:*
**Playboy** (Mar 1972)................... Savages
• 142—Breasts.
• 145—Breasts.

# Blanchard, Vanessa
*Films:*
**Witchfire** (1986)......................... Liz
•• 0:52—Brief breasts in bed and then the shower.
Uphill All the Way (1987) .................. Velma

# • Blaze, Roxanne
See: Bellomo, Sara.

# Blee, Debra
*Films:*
**The Beach Girls** (1982) ................... Sarah
••• 1:22—Brief breasts opening her swimsuit top on the beach.
**Sloane** (1984) ...................Cynthia Thursby
• 0:15—Very brief breasts during attempted rape.
The Malibu Bikini Shop (1985) ............... Jane
Savage Streets (1985) ................... Rachel
0:20—In a bra in the girls locker room.
Hamburger—The Motion Picture (1986) .... Mia Vunk
0:25—Briefly in wet dress in the swimming pool.

# Blondi
Adult film actress.
a.k.a. Marjorie Miller and Blondi Bee.
*Films:*
**Party Favors** (1987) ...................... Bobbi
•• 0:04—Breasts in dressing room, taking off red top and putting on black one.
• 0:23—Brief breasts when blouse pops off while delivering pizza.
••• 0:27—Breasts and buns in G-string doing a strip routine outside.
• 0:31—Brief breasts flapping her blouse to cool off.

••• 1:04—Breasts doing a strip routine in a little girl outfit. Buns, in G-string. More breasts after.
• 1:16—Nude taking off swimsuit next to pool during final credits.
*Video Tapes:*
**The Girls of Malibu** (1986)..............Marjorie
••• 0:06—In two piece swimsuit. Breasts riding a motorcycle. Full frontal nudity posing on it. Nude outside.
**In Search of the Perfect 10** (1986)... Perfect Girl #3
••• 0:14—Breasts in back of car.
**Best Buns on the Beach** (1987)........... Blondi
••• 0:06—Breasts, stripping on stage during dance routine. Buns, in G-string.
•• 0:52—Breasts and buns with all the contestants during review.
••• 0:53—Breasts and buns in final pose-off.
•• 0:57—Breasts and buns winning the contest.
••• 0:58—More slow motion breasts and bun shots during the final credits.
**Night of the Living Babes** (1987)
................... Mondo Zombie Girl Darlene
••• 0:12—Breasts wearing dark purple wig and long gloves, with the other Mondo Zombie Girls.
••• 0:16—More breasts and buns in bed with Buck.
• 0:50—Breasts on the couch with the other Zombie Girls.
• 0:52—Breasts on the couch again.
**The Perfect Body Contest** (1987) ........ Jennifer
•• 0:46—Buns, in two piece swimsuit, then breasts.
• 0:50—Breasts on stage with the other contestants.
**High Society Centerspread Video #3: Blondi** (1990)
.......................................Herself

# Bloom, Claire
*Films:*
The Illustrated Man (1969)................. Felicia
Three into Two Won't Go (1969; British)
.............................Frances Howard
**A Severed Head** (1971; British) ........ Honor Klein
• 1:10—Breasts leaning up then right beast while sitting up in bed with Richard Attenborough.
A Doll's House (1973; British).......... Nora Helmer
Islands in the Stream (1977)................Audrey
Clash of the Titans (1981) .................. Hera
Deja Vu (1984)...................Eleanor Harvey
Queenie (1987) ..................... Vicky Kelley
Sammy and Rosie Get Laid (1987; British) ....... Alice
*Miniseries:*
Brideshead Revisited (1981; British) ... Lady Marchmain
*Made for TV Movies:*
Promises to Keep (1985) ....................Sally
It's Nothing Personal (1993)......... Evelyn Whitloff

# Bloom, Lindsay
*Films:*
Cover Girl Models (1975)....................Claire
Six Pack Annie (1975) .....................Annie
Texas Detour (1977) ............. Sugar McCarthy

French Quarter (1978)
............. "Big Butt" Annie/Policewoman in Bar
**H.O.T.S.** (1979) .................: Melody Ragmore
*a.k.a. T & A Academy*
- 0:28—Very brief right breast on balcony.
- 1:34—Brief breasts during football game throwing football as quarterback.
The Main Event (1979) ................ Girl in Bed
The Happy Hooker Goes Hollywood (1980) ......Chris
*TV:*
Dallas (1982) .................... Bonnie Robertson
Mike Hammer (1984-87) ................. Velda

## Blount, Lisa
*Films:*
9/30/55 (1977)....................... Billie Jean
**Dead and Buried** (1981) ......... Girl on the Beach
- 0:06—Brief breasts on the beach getting her picture taken by a photographer.
An Officer and a Gentleman (1982) .. Lynette Pomeroy
1:25—In a red bra and tap pants in a motel room with David Keith.
Radioactive Dreams (1984) ............ Miles Archer
Cease Fire (1985) .................... Paula Murphy
Cut and Run (1985; Italian)............Fran Hudson
What Waits Below (1986) ........... Leslie Peterson
Nightflyers (1987)..................... Audrey
Prince of Darkness (1987) .............. Catherine
South of Reno (1987) ............... Anette Clark
1:02—In black bra getting blouse torn open while lying down.
Great Balls of Fire (1989)............... Lois Brown
Out Cold (1989) ......................Phyllis
Blind Fury (1990) ............... Annie Winchester
Femme Fatale (1990) ................... Jenny
*Made for Cable TV:*
The Hitchhiker: One Last Prayer ........... Miranda
0:06—Briefly in a black bra putting a new home-made outfit on.
*Made for TV Movies:*
Unholy Matrimony (1988) ......... Karen Stockwell
In Sickness and in Health (1992) ........... Carmen
Murder Between Friends (1994) ........ Janet Myers
*TV:*
Sons and Daughters (1990-91) .......... Mary Ruth

## Blueberry
*Films:*
One Man Force (1989) ........ Santiago's Girlfriend
*Video Tapes:*
**Rock Video Girls 2** (1992) ............... Herself
- 0:28—Buns in G-string under sheer body stocking.

## Blye, Margaret
*Films:*
Waterhole 3 (1967)................Billie Copperod
**The Sporting Club** (1971) ................ Janey
- 0:31—Breasts, sunbathing on rock when seen by James. Medium long shot.

Ash Wednesday (1973) .....................Kate
The Entity (1983)..................... Cindy Nash
*TV:*
Kodiak (1974) .........................Mandy

## Bockrath, Tina
*Films:*
**Totally Exposed** (1991)............. Lillian Tucker
- • 0:00—Buns and breasts, turning over on tanning table during opening credits.
- 0:01—Brief full frontal nudity, lying on tanning table.
- • 0:03—Brief nude, getting out of bed and putting on towel while talking to Bill.
- ••• 1:01—Full frontal nudity, turning over in tanning table. Full frontal nudity, dropping her towel in reception area.
- ••• 1:02—Buns, walking back to the room. Nude, taking off towel and lying on massage table.
- ••• 1:04—Nude, sitting up on table and standing up with Bill.
*Made for Cable TV:*
**Tales From the Crypt: Abra Cadaver** (1991; HBO)
.................................. Paula/Cadaver
- 0:04—Breasts (in B&W) pretending to be a corpse during practical joke.
*Video Tapes:*
**Playboy Video Calendar 1991** (1990)...... January
- ••• 0:01—Nude.
**Sexy Lingerie II** (1990) ................... Model
*Magazines:*
**Playboy** (May 1990).................... Playmate
**Playboy's Book of Lingerie** (Jul 1991)....... Herself
- 29—Buns.
**Playboy's Book of Lingerie** (Sep 1991)...... Herself
- •• 61—Left breast and lower frontal nudity.
**Playboy's Book of Lingerie** (Nov 1991) .....Herself
- •• 22—Side view of right breast and lower frontal nudity.
Playboy's Book of Lingerie (Mar 1992) .........Herself
**Playboy's Book of Lingerie** (Jul 1992).......Herself
- ••• 69—Breasts.
**Playboy's Career Girls** (Aug 1992)
.................... Baywatch Playmates
- ••• 9—Full frontal nudity.
**Playboy's Book of Lingerie** (Sep 1992)......Herself
- 71—Tip of left breast.
**Playboy's Calendar Playmates** (Nov 1992)...Herself
- ••• 89—Full frontal nudity.
**Playboy's Book of Lingerie** (Nov 1992) .....Herself
- ••• 80—Breasts.
**Playboy's Book of Lingerie** (Jan 1993) ......Herself
- 99—Right breast.
**Playboy's Book of Lingerie** (Mar 1993)......Herself
- ••• 47—Full frontal nudity.
- ••• 87—Breasts.
**Playboy's Book of Lingerie** (May 1993) .....Herself
- 8—Lower frontal nudity.
- 88—Lower frontal nudity.

**Playboy's Girls of Summer '93** (Jun 1993) . . . Herself
••• 14—Breasts.
••• 63—Breasts.
**Playboy's Wet & Wild Women** (Aug 1993) . . Herself
••• 23—Breasts.
••• 76—Full frontal nudity.
**Playboy's Blondes, Brunettes & Redheads**
(Sep 1993) . . . . . . . . . . . . . . . . . . . . . . . . . . . Herself
••• 13—Full frontal nudity.
**Playboy's Book of Lingerie** (Sep 1993) . . . . . Herself
••• 96—Full frontal nudity.
**Playboy's Nudes** (Dec 1993) . . . . . . . . . . . . . Herself
••• 18—Full frontal nudity.
**Playboy's Book of Lingerie** (Jan 1994) . . . . . . Herself
••• 62—Breasts.
**Playboy's Bathing Beauties** (Mar 1994). . . . . Herself
••• 36-37—Breasts.
••• 84—Breasts.
**Playboy's Girls of Summer '94** (Jul 1994) . . . Herself
• 62-63—Lower frontal nudity.
**Playboy's Book of Lingerie** (Jul 1994) . . . . . . Herself
••• 100—Breasts.

# Bohrer, Corinne

*Films:*
The Beach Girls (1982) . . . . . . . . . . . . .Champagne Girl
I, the Jury (1982). . . . . . . . . . . . . . .Soap Opera Actress
My Favorite Year (1982) . . . . . . . . . . . . . . . . . . . . . .n.a.
Zapped! (1982). . . . . . . . . . . . . . . . . . . . . . . . . . Cindy
Joysticks (1983). . . . . . . . . . . . . . . . . . . . . Patsy Rutter
Surf II (1984). . . . . . . . . . . . . . . . . . . . . . . . .Cindy Lou
Police Academy 4: Citizens on Patrol (1987) . . . . . Laura
Stewardess School (1987). . . . . . . . . . . . . Cindy Adams
Vice Versa (1988) . . . . . . . . . . . . . . . . . . . . . . . . . Sam
*Made for Cable Movies:*
**Dead Solid Perfect** (1988; HBO) . . . . . . Janie Rimmer
••• 0:31—Nude, getting out of bed to get some ice for
    Randy Quaid. Nice scene!
*Made for Cable TV:*
Dream On: What I Did for Lust (1991; HBO) . . . . . Chloe
*Made for TV Movies:*
Revenge of the Nerds IV: Nerds in Love (1994) . . . . . . .
    Jeanie Humphrey
*TV:*
E/R (1984-85) . . . . . . . . . . . . . . . . . .Nurse Cory Smith
Free Spirit (1989-90). . . . . . . . . . . . . .Winnie Goodwin
Man of the People (1991) . . . . . . . . . . . . . . Constance

# Boisson, Christine

*Films:*
**Emmanuelle** (1974) . . . . . . . . . . . . . . . . .Marie-Ange
    (R-rated version reviewed.)
•• 0:16—Full frontal nudity diving into swimming
    pool. Also buns, under water.
••• 0:19—Breasts outside in hanging chair with Sylvia
    Kristel.
Identification of a Woman (1983; Italian) . . . . . . . . . Ida
Le Passage (1986; French). . . . . . . . . . . . Catherine Diez
Dreamers (1987). . . . . . . . . . . . . . . . . . . . . . . . . Sima

Sandra (1989; French) . . . . . . . . . . . . . . . . . . . .Sandra
*Magazines:*
**Playboy** (Jun 1975) . . . . . . . Sex in Cinema French Style
••• 90—Breasts with hands in her pants, sitting in chair
    from *Emmanuelle.*

# Bolling, Tiffany

*Films:*
Tony Rome (1967) . . . . . . . . . . . . . . . . . . . . Photo Girl
The Marriage of a Young Stockbroker (1971)
. . . . . . . . . . . . . . . . . . . . . . . . . . . . .Girl in the Rain
**Bonnie's Kids** (1973). . . . . . . . . . . . . . . . . . . . . Ellie
•• 0:21—Breasts, modeling in office.
• 1:16—Brief right breast making love in bed.
Wicked, Wicked (1973) . . . . . . . . . . . . . . . Lisa James
**The Centerfold Girls** (1974). . . . . . . . . . . . . . . .Vera
• 1:02—Brief breasts in photograph.
••• 1:12—Breasts in the shower.
• 1:21—Brief breasts in motel bed getting raped by
    two guys after they drug her beer.
The Wild Party (1975) . . . . . . . . . . . . . . . . . . . . .Kate
Kingdom of the Spiders (1977) . . . . . . . . Diane Ashley
The Vals (1982) . . . . . . . . . . .Valley Attorney and Parent
**Love Scenes** (1984) . . . . . . . . . . . . . . . . . . . . . . .Val
*a.k.a. Ecstacy*
•• 0:01—Side view of left breast in bed with Peter.
••• 0:06—Breasts getting photographed by Britt Ekland
    in the house.
• 0:09—Brief breasts opening her bathrobe to show
    Peter.
• 0:12—Breasts in bathtub with Peter.
••• 0:19—Breasts lying in bed talking with Peter, then
    making love.
•• 0:43—Breasts acting in a movie when Rick opens her
    blouse.
•• 0:57—Nude behind shower door, then breasts get-
    ting out and talking to Peter.
•• 0:59—Breasts making love tied up on bed with Rick
    during filming of movie.
•• 1:07—Breasts, then full frontal nudity acting with
    Elizabeth during filming of movie.
•• 1:17—Full frontal nudity getting out of pool.
•• 1:26—Breasts with Peter on the bed.
Open House (1987) . . . . . . . . . . . . . . . . . Judy Roberts
*Made for TV Movies:*
Key West (1973). . . . . . . . . . . . . . . . . . . . . . . . Ruth
*TV:*
The New People (1969-70) . . . . . . . . . . . Susan Bradley
*Magazines:*
**Playboy** (Apr 1972) . . . . . . . . . . . . . Tiffany's A Gem
**Playboy** (Dec 1972) . . . . . . . . . . . . .Sex Stars of 1972
••• 210—Breasts.
**Playboy** (Nov 1973) . . . . . . . . . . . Sex in Cinema 1973
•• 152—Left breast in red light.
**Playboy** (Dec 1973) . . . . . . . . . . . . .Sex Stars of 1973
•• 208—Left breast.
**Playboy** (Dec 1974) . . . . . . . . . . . . .Sex Stars of 1974
••• 211—Breasts.

# Bonet, Lisa

Ex-wife of singer Lenny Kravitz.
*Films:*
**Angel Heart** (1987) . . . . . . . . . . Epiphany Proudfoot
(Original Unedited Version reviewed.)
    0:53—In wet top, talking with Mickey Rourke outside.
- 1:01—Brief left breast, twice, in open dress during voodoo ceremony.
••• 1:27—Breasts in bed with Rourke. It gets kind of bloody.
- 1:32—Breasts in bathtub.
- 1:48—Breasts in bed, dead. Covered with a bloody sheet.

**Bank Robber** (1993). . . . . . . . . . . . . . . . . . . Priscilla
•• 0:36—Buns, while lying on bed, waiting for Patrick Dempsey.
•• 0:37—Breasts, while making love in bed with Dempsey.
•• 1:05—Brief breasts while making love in bed with Dempsey.

**Dead Connection** (1993) . . . . . . . . . . Catherine Briggs
- 0:58—Breasts, while making love in bed with Michael Madsen.

**New Eden** (1994) . . . . . . . . . . . . . . . . . . . . . . . . Lily
- 1:02—Brief back side of left breast while in bed with Stephen Baldwin.

*TV:*
The Cosby Show (1984-87). . . . . . . . . Denise Huxtable
A Different World (1987-89) . . . . . . . . Denise Huxtable
The Cosby Show (1989-92). . . . Denise Huxtable-Kendall

# Bonet, Nai

*Films:*
The Greatest (1977; U.S./British). . . . . . . Suzie Gomez
**Fairytales** (1979). . . . . . . . . . . . . . . . . . . Sheherazade
- 0:29—Buns and very brief left breast doing a belly dance and rubbing oil on herself.
Nocturna (1979). . . . . . . . . . . . . . . . . . . . . Nocturna

# Bonham Carter, Helena

*Films:*
A Room with a View (1986; British). . Lucy Honeychurch
**Lady Jane** (1987; British) . . . . . . . . . . . Lady Jane Grey
- 1:19—Breasts kneeling on the bed with Guilford.
- 2:09—Side view of right breast and very, very brief breasts sitting by fire with Guilford.
Maurice (1987; British) . . . Young Lady at Cricket Match
**Getting It Right** (1989) . . . . . . . . . . Minerva Munday
•• 0:18—Breasts a couple of times in bed talking to Gavin. It's hard to recognize her because she has lots of makeup on her face.
Hamlet (1990; British/French) . . . . . . . . . . . . . Ophelia
Howards End (1992) . . . . . . . . . . . . . . . Helen Schlegel
Where Angels Fear to Tread (1992) . . . . Caroline Abbott
*Made for TV Movies:*
A Hazard of Hearts (1987). . . . . . . . . . . . . . . . .n.a.
Fatal Deception: Mrs. Lee Harvey Oswald (1993)
. . . . . . . . . . . . . . . . . . . . . . . . . Marina Oswald

# Bonnaire, Sandrine

*Films:*
**A Nos Amours** (1984; French). . . . . . . . . . . .Suzanne
- 0:17—Brief breasts, pulling dress top down to put on nightgown.
•• 0:34—Breasts sitting up in bed talking to Bernard. Brief side view of buns.
- 0:42—Very brief side view of left breast while waking up in bed.
- 0:57—Very brief lower frontal nudity, while getting out of bed with Martine and her boyfriend. Long shot of buns, while hugging Bernard in the background (out of focus).
**Police** (1985; French) . . . . . . . . . . . . . . . . . . . . Lydie
••• 0:49—Full frontal nudity, undressing in front of Gérard Depardieu, then getting out of the shower.
Vagabond (1985; French). . . . . . . . . . . . . . . . . Mona
Monsieur Hire (1990; French) . . . . . . . . . . . . . . Alice
Prague (1991; French/British). . . . . . . . . . . . . . Elena
**The Plague** (1992; French/British) . . . Martine Rambert
••• 0:53—Breasts, while in bathroom, examining herself for the plague.

# Boorman, Katrine

*Films:*
**Excalibur** (1981; British). . . . . . . . . . . . . . . . Igrayne
- 0:14—Right breast, then breasts in front of the fire when Uther tricks her into thinking that he is her husband and makes love to her.
Dream One (1984; British/French)
. . . . . . . . . . . . . . . . . . . . . Duchka/Nemo's Mother
Marche A L'Hombre (1984; French) . . . . . . . . . .Katrina
Hope and Glory (1987; British). . . . . . . . . . . . . Charity
Camille Claudel (1989; French) . . . . . . . . . . . . . Jessie

# Booth, Connie

*Films:*
Monty Python and the Holy Grail (1974; British)
. . . . . . . . . . . . . . . . . . . . . . . . . . . . . . The Witch
**Romance with a Double Bass** (1974; British)
. . . . . . . . . . . . . . . . . . . . . . . . . Princess Costanza
•• 0:10—Very brief buns, going into the water to retrieve her fishing float, then full frontal nudity while yelling at a guy who steals her clothes.
•• 0:11—Full frontal nudity, while walking around, looking for her clothes.
••• 0:18—Breasts, while holding her hand over her eyes.
•• 0:20—Brief left breast, while reaching up to close the bass case.
84 Charring Cross Road (1987) . . . .Lady from Delaware
Hawks (1988; British). . . . . . . . . . . . . . . . Nurse Jarvis
High Spirits (1988). . . . . . . . . . . . . . . . . . . . . . Marge
Leon the Pig Farmer (1993; British) . . Yvonne Chadwick
*Made for TV Movies:*
How to Irritate People (1968; British) . . . . . . . . . . . n.a.
*TV:*
Fawlty Towers (British) . . . . . . . . . . . . . . . . . . . Polly

# Botsford, Sara

*Films:*

**By Design** (1982; Canadian) . . . . . . . . . . . . . . Angie
  • 0:23—Full frontal nudity in the ocean. Long shot,
   hard to see anything.
  • 1:08—Brief side view of left breast making love in
   bed while talking on the phone.
**Deadly Eyes** (1982; Canadian) . . . . . . . Kelly Leonard
  • 0:42—Breasts several times, making love with Paul.
Still of the Night (1982) . . . . . . . . . . . . . . . Gail Phillips
Murder By Phone (1983; Canadian) . . . . . . Ridley Taylor
  *a.k.a. Bells*

*Made for TV Movies:*

Fatal Memories (1992) . . . . . . . . . . . . . . . . . . . . Janice
My Breast (1994) . . . . . . . . . . . . . . . . . . . . . . . . . . Eve

*TV:*

E.N.G. (1989-90; Canadian) . . . . . . . . . . . . . . . . . Ann

# Bouche, Sugar

*Films:*

**Heavenly Bodies** (1985). . . . . . . . . . . . . . . . Stripper
  • 0:16—Breasts doing stripper-gram for Steve.
**Graveyard Shift** (1987) . . . . . . . . . . . Fabulous Frannie
  ••• 0:12—Breasts doing a stripper routine on stage.
  • 0:24—Brief breasts in the shower.

# Bouchet, Barbara

*Films:*

A Global Affair (1964) . . . . . . . . . . . . . . . . . . . . . . Girl
Good Neighbor Sam (1964) . . . . . . . . . . . . Receptionist
Sex and the Single Girl (1964) . . . . . . . . . . . . Frannie
What a Way to Go (1964) . . . . . . . . . . . . . Girl on Plane
**In Harm's Way** (1965) . . . . . . . . . . . . . Liz Eddington
  • 0:05—Very, very brief right breast, while waving to
   Hugh O'Brian from the water (B&W).
Agent for H.A.R.M. (1966) . . . . . . . . . . . . . Ava Vestak
Casino Royale (1967; British). . . . . . . . . . Moneypenny
Danger Route (1968; British). . . . . . . . . . . . . . . Mari
Sweet Charity (1969) . . . . . . . . . . . . . . . . . . . . Ursula
Black Belly of the Tarantula (1972; Italian). . . Maria Zani
**Cry of a Prostitute: Love Kills** (1975; Italian)
. . . . . . . . . . . . . . . . . . . . . . . . . . . . . . . . . . . Margie
  • 0:30—Brief left breast, lying in bed with Rico.
  • 0:31—Brief breasts in bed, with Rico when he starts
   making love with her.
  •• 0:50—Breasts in panties and robe, walking angrily
   around her room.
  0:56—In braless blouse in Bedroom with Tony.
Down the Ancient Staircase (1975; Italian) . . . . . . Carla
Blood Feast (1976; Italian). . . . . . . . . . . . . . . . . . n.a.
Duck in Orange Sauce (1976; Italian) . . . . . . . . . . Patty
**Sex with a Smile** (1976; Italian)
. . . . . . . . . . . . . . . . . . "One for the Money" segment
  ••• 0:50—Breasts sitting up in bed with a guy in bed,
   then lying down, wearing glasses.
Death Rage (1978; Italian) . . . . . . . . . . . . . . . . . n.a.
Maniac Mansion (1978; Italian). . . . . . . . . . . . . . n.a.

*Made for TV Movies:*

The Scarlet and the Black (1983) . . . . . . . Minna Kappler

---

*Magazines:*

**Playboy** (Nov 1972) . . . . . . . . . . . Sex in Cinema 1972
  • 161—Buns.
**Playboy's Nudes** (Dec 1992) . . . . . . . . . . . . . . Herself
  • 38—Buns, while sitting in chair.

# Boulting, Ingrid

*Films:*

**The Last Tycoon** (1976) . . . . . . . . . . . Kathleen Moore
  • 0:56—Buns and side of right breast taking off her
   dress in unfinished beach house in front of Robert
   De Niro.
  •• 0:58—More buns, lying down afterwards.
  • 1:00—Buns, getting up and putting dress on. Very
   brief side of left breast.
  • 1:02—Brief right breast when De Niro takes her
   dress off.
**Deadly Passion** (1985) . . . . . . . . . Martha Greenwood
  • 0:46—Brief buns taking off clothes and jumping into
   pool. Long shot.
  •• 0:47—Breasts getting out of pool and kissing Brent
   Huff. Right breast in bed.
  • 0:54—Breasts in whirlpool bath with Huff.
  ••• 1:02—Breasts, wearing white panties and massaging herself in front of a mirror.
  •• 1:31—Breasts taking off clothes and jumping into
   bed with Huff.

# Bouquet, Carole

Model for *Chanel* cosmetics.

*Films:*

**That Obscure Object of Desire** (1977; French/
  Spanish). . . . . . . . . . . . . . . . . . . . . . . . . . . Conchita
  ••• 0:53—Breasts in bedroom.
  ••• 1:01—Breasts in bed with Fernando Rey.
For Your Eyes Only (1981) . . . . . . . . . . Melina Havelock
Bingo Bongo (1983). . . . . . . . . . . . . . . . . . . . . . Laura
Dream One (1984; British/French) . . . . . . . . Rals-Akrai
Too Beautiful for You (1990; French)
. . . . . . . . . . . . . . . . . . . . . . . . Florence Barthelemy
Tango (1993; French). . . . . . . . . . . . . . . Female Guest

# Boushel, Joy

*Films:*

**Pick-Up Summer** (1979; Canadian). . . . . . . . . . . Sally
  ••• 0:56—Breasts playing pinball, then running around.
**Terror Train** (1980; Canadian). . . . . . . . . . . . . . . Pet
  •• 0:49—Breasts wearing panties in sleeper room on
   train with Mo.
Quest For Fire (1981) . . . . . . . . . . . . . . . Tribe Member
**Humongous** (1982; Canadian). . . . . . . . . Donna Blake
  •• 0:09—Breasts looking out the window. More breasts
   in the room in the mirror.
  • 0:48—Breasts undoing her top to warm up Bert.
Thrillkill (1984). . . . . . . . . . . . . . . . . . . . . . . . Maggie
**The Fly** (1986) . . . . . . . . . . . . . . . . . . . . . . . . Tawny
  • 0:54—Very brief breasts viewed from below when
   Jeff Goldblum pulls her by the arm to get her out of
   bed.

Keeping Track (1988) . . . . . . . . . . . . . . . . . . . . . . Judy
Look Who's Talking (1989) . . . . . . . . . . . . . . . . Melissa

## Bow, Clara

*Films:*
Down to the Sea in Ships (1923) . . . . . . . . Dot Morgan
Dancing Mothers (1926) . . . . . . . . . . .Kitten Westcourt
Mantrap (1926) . . . . . . . . . . . . . . . . . . . . . . . . . . . .n.a.
It (1927) . . . . . . . . . . . . . . . . . . . . . . . . . . . . Betty Lou
**Wings** (1927) . . . . . . . . . . . . . . . . . . . . Mary Preston
   • 1:22—It looks like very, very brief left breast (blurry)
    when military guys walk in on her and she stands up
    straight while in front of a mirror.
The Wild Party (1929) . . . . . . . . . . . . . . . . . Stella Ames

## Bowker, Judi

*Films:*
Brother Sun, Sister Moon (1973) . . . . . . . . . . . . . .Clare
East of Elephant Rock (1976; British) . . . . .Eve Proudfoot
**Clash of the Titans** (1981) . . . . . . . . . . . Andromeda
   • 1:41—Buns and partial side view of right breast get-
    ting out of bath. Don't see her face.
The Shooting Party (1985; British) . . . . . . . Olivia Lilburn
*Miniseries:*
Ellis Island (1984) . . . . . . . . . . . . . Georgiana O'Donnell
Anna Karenina (1985) . . . . . . . . . . . . . . . . . . . . . Kitty
Sins (1986) . . . . . . . . . . . . . . . . . . . . . . . Natalie Junot
*Made for TV Movies:*
In This House of Brede (1975) . . . . . . . . . . . . . . Joanne

## Bowser, Sue

*Films:*
Stripes (1981) . . . . . . . . . . . . . . . . . . . . . Mud Wrestler
Doctor Detroit (1983) . . . . . . . . . . . . . . . . . Dream Girl
**Into the Night** (1985) . . . . . . . . . . . . . . Girl on Boat
  •• 0:24—Breasts taking off blouse with Jake on his boat
    after Michelle Pfeiffer leaves.
*Magazines:*
**Playboy** (Nov 1985) . . . . . . . . . . Sex in Cinema 1985
  ••• 130—Breasts in still from *Into the Night*.

## Boyd, Tanya

*Films:*
Black Shampoo (1976) . . . . . . . . . . . . . . . . . . . Brenda
**Ilsa, Harem Keeper of the Oil Sheiks** (1978) . .Satin
**The Happy Hooker Goes Hollywood** (1980) . . Sylvie
   • 0:39—Brief breasts in jungle room when an older
    customer accidentally comes in.
Wholly Moses (1980) . . . . . . . . . . . . . . . . . . . Princess
Jo Jo Dancer, Your Life Is Calling (1986) . . . . . . . . Alicia
Loving Lulu (1992) . . . . . . . . . . . . . . . . . Background

## •Boyle, Lara Flynn

*Films:*
Poltergeist III (1988) . . . . . . . . . . . . . . . Donna Gardner
How I Got Into College (1989) . . . . . . . . . Jessica Kailo
May Wine (1990; French) . . . . . . . . . . . . . . . Cammie
The Rookie (1990) . . . . . . . . . . . . . . . . . . . . . . Sarah
The Dark Backward (1991) . . . . . . . . . . . . . . Rosarita

Eye of the Storm (1991) . . . . . . . . . . . . . . . . . . Sandra
Mobsters (1991) . . . . . . . . . . . . . . . . . . . Mara Motes
  *a.k.a. Mobsters—The Evil Empire*
Equinox (1992) . . . . . . . . . . . . . . . . . . . .Berverly Franks
Red Rock West (1992) . . . . . . . . . . . . . . . . . . .Suzanne
   0:57—Very brief almost silhouette of left breast,
    while on top of Nicolas Gage in bed, when scooting
    up to kiss him.
Wayne's World (1992) . . . . . . . . . . . . . . . . . . . . Stacy
Where The Day Takes You (1992) . . . . . . . . . . . Heather
The Temp (1993) . . . . . . . . . . . . . . . . . . . . Kris Bolin
**Threesome** (1994) . . . . . . . . . . . . . . . . . . . . . . .Alex
   0:34—Briefly in braless, white blouse while in bed
    with Stephen Baldwin and Josh Charles.
   • 0:52—Buns, while walking and diving into lake to go
    skinny dipping.
   • 0:54—Partial buns, while lying on lake shore with
    Baldwin and Charles.
   • 1:21—Partial buns, while lying in bed between Bald-
    win and Charles.
*Made for Cable Movies:*
**Past Tense** (1994; Showtime) . .Tory Bass/Sabrina James
   • 0:10—In black bra with Scott Glenn. Brief breasts
    two times. You don't see her face very well and one
    is a medium long shot.
   • 0:13—Supposedly her breasts, while making love
    with another guy during video playback on TV.
   • 0:15—Very brief buns in flashback while on top of
    Glenn on the floor. Medium long shot.
   • 0:28—Breasts, several times, during video playback
    on TV. Don't see her face very well.
*Miniseries:*
Amerika . . . . . . . . . . . . . . . . . . . . . . . . . . . . . . . n.a.
*TV:*
Twin Peaks (1990-91) . . . . . . . . . . . . . Donna Hayward

## •Boyle, Lisa

*a.k.a. Cassandra Leigh.*
*Films:*
**Midnight Witness** (1992) . . . . . . . . . . . . . . . . . Heidi
  •• 1:11—Breasts, while getting out of bed. Buns and
    breasts some more, seen in mirror.
**Midnight Tease** (1994) . . . . . . . . . . . . . . . Samantha
  •• 0:02—Breasts in lingerie outfit, walking up to her
    stepfather and slicing his throat.
   • 0:11—Buns in T-back and in bra, while undressing,
    then lying on bed.
  •• 0:12—Breasts in lingerie outfit, while killing her step-
    father in dream.
  •• 0:24—Breasts, after opening her leather jacket on ta-
    ble in front of Dr. Saul.
  ••• 0:37—Breasts, while making love with Dr. Saul in his
    office.
  ••• 0:44—Breasts and buns in T-back while dancing on
    stage with Mantra.
  •• 0:47—Breasts while talking with Mantra in dressing
    room.
  •• 0:50—Breasts in lingerie outfit in dream, while slit-
    ting Mantra's throat.

••• 0:53—Full frontal nudity while taking a shower behind clear plastic curtain.
•• 0:58—In white bra and panties, then breasts and buns after stripping out of schoolgirl outfit. Intercut with flashbacks of her stepfather's suicide.

*Made for Cable TV:*

**Red Shoe Diaries: Emily's Dance** (1993; Showtime) . . . . . . . . . . . . . . . . . . . . . . European Version Dancer
••• 0:25—Breasts and buns, dancing in black G-string for music video.

**Sex, Shock and Censorship in the 90's**
(1993; Showtime) . . . . . . . . Psychiatrist's Receptionist
•• 0:42—Breasts in Robert Hays' daydream when the pixelation effect to censor her breasts has a hard time keeping up with her movements.

**Dream On: The Courtship of Martin's Father**
(1994; HBO) . . . . . . . . . . . . . . . . . . . . . . . . . . . . . Lisa
••• 0:03—Breasts, after taking off her lingerie in Martin's bedroom. Very brief buns, going into bathroom.

*Magazines:*

**Playboy** (Apr 1992) . . . . . . . . . . . . . . . . . . . . Grapevine
••• 175—Breasts.
**Playboy** (Feb 1993) . . . . . . . . . . Being in Nothingness
•• 127—Side of right breast and buns.
•• 128—Buns and side of left breast visible under sheer black top.
**Playboy's Girls of Summer '93** (Jun 1993) . . . Herself
• 73—Left breast and lower frontal nudity.
**Playboy** (Sep 1994) . . . . . . . . . . . . . . . . . . . . Grapevine
• 158—Right breast under sheer bodysuit. B&W.

## Bracci, Teda

*Films:*

C. C. & Company (1970) . . . . . . . . . . . . . . . . . . . . . Pig
R.P.M. (1970) . . . . . . . . . . . . . . . . . . . . . . . . . . . Student
**The Big Bird Cage** (1972) . . . . . . . . . . . . . . Bull Jones
• 0:15—Breasts in front of the guard, Rocco.
• 0:51—Very brief right breast, then left breast during fight with Pam Grier. Brief left breast standing up in rice paddy.
**The Centerfold Girls** (1974) . . . . . . . . . . . . . . . . Rita
• 0:18—Breasts taking off her clothes in the living room in front of everybody.
The Trial of Billy Jack (1974) . . . . . . . . . . . . . . . . Teda
The World's Greatest Lover (1977) . . . . . . . . . . . . n.a.

## Brackett, Sarah

*Films:*

The Third Secret (1964; British) . . . . . . . . . . . . . . Nurse
Battle Beneath the Earth (1968; British) . . . Meg Webson
**Emily** (1976; British) . . . . . . . . . . . . . . . . . Margaret
• 0:09—Buns, while looking out the window at Koo Stark.
Priest of Love (1980) . . . . . . . . . . . . . . . Athsah Brester
The Lords of Discipline (1983) . . . . . . . . . . Mrs. Durrell

## Bradford-Aiton, Lisa

*Films:*

Screwball Hotel (1988) . . . . . . . . . . . . . . . . Punk Singer
*Video Tapes:*
**Penthouse The Great Pet Hunt—Part II** (1993)
. . . . . . . . . . . . . . . . . . . . . . . . . . . . . . . . . . . . . . . . Pet
••• 0:01—Breasts and buns in T-back while dancing on stage. (She's a great dancer.)
*Magazines:*
**Penthouse** (Nov 1987) . . . . . . . . . . . . . . . . . . . . . Pet
**Penthouse** (Aug 1988) . . . . . . . . . . . . . . . . . . . . . Pet

## Brady, Janelle

*Films:*

**Class of Nuke 'Em High** (1986) . . . . . . . . . . . Chrissy
•• 0:26—Breasts sitting on bed in the attic with Warren.
• 0:31—Brief breasts scene from 0:26 superimposed over Warren's nightmare.
Teen Wolf Too (1987) . . . . . . . . . . . . . . History Student

## Braga, Sonia

*Films:*

**Dona Flor and Her Two Husbands** (1978; Brazilian)
. . . . . . . . . . . . . . . . . . . . . . . . . . . . . . . . . . . . . . . Flor
• 0:13—Buns and brief breasts with her husband.
•• 0:15—Breasts lying on the bed.
0:17—Buns, getting out of bed.
••• 0:54—Breasts making love on the bed with her husband.
•• 0:57—Breasts lying on the bed.
••• 1:41—Breasts kissing her first husband.
**Lady on the Bus** (1978; Brazilian) . . . . . . . . . . . . n.a.
• 0:11—Brief left breast.
••• 0:12—Breasts, then buns, then full frontal nudity in bed getting her slip torn off by her newlywed husband. Long struggle scene.
•• 0:39—Right breast standing with half open dress, then breasts lying in bed, then getting into the pool.
••• 0:48—Breasts and buns on the beach after picking up a guy on the bus.
• 0:54—Brief breasts in bed dreaming.
• 1:02—Brief breasts in waterfall with bus driver.
• 1:05—Breasts in cemetery after picking up another guy on the bus.
• 1:13—Breasts on the ground with another guy from a bus.
• 1:16—Left breast sitting on sofa while her husband talks.
**I Love You** (1982; Brazilian) . . . . . . . . . . . . . . . Maria
*a.k.a. Eu Te Amo*
••• 0:34—Full frontal nudity making love with Paulo.
•• 0:36—Breasts sitting on the edge of the bed.
• 0:49—Breasts running around the house teasing Paulo.
•• 0:50—Brief nude in blinking light. Don't see her face.
• 0:53—Breasts eating fruit with Paulo.

••• 0:54—Breasts wearing white panties in front of windows with Paulo. Long scene.
• 1:03—Left breast standing talking to Paulo.
• 1:10—Left breast talking to Paulo.
• 1:15—Very brief full frontal nudity, several times, in Paulo's flashback in blinking light scene.
••• 1:23—Breasts with Paulo during an argument. Dark, but long scene.
•• 1:28—Breasts walking around Paulo's place with a gun. Dark.
•• 1:33—Various breasts scenes.

**Gabriela** (1984; Brazilian) . . . . . . . . . . . . . . Gabriela
•• 0:26—Breasts leaning back out the window making love on a table with Marcello Mastroianni.
••• 0:27—Nude, taking a shower outside and cleaning herself up.
• 0:32—Right breast in bed.
•• 0:38—Nude, making love with Mastroianni on the kitchen table.
•• 0:45—Nude, getting in bed with Mastroianni.
1:13—Full frontal nudity, on bed with another man, then getting beat up by Mastroianni.
••• 1:17—Nude, changing clothes in the bedroom.
•• 1:32—Breasts and buns making love outside with Mastroianni. Lots of passion!
Kiss of the Spider Woman (1985; U.S./Brazilian)
. . . . . . . . . . . . . . . . . . . . Leni/Marta/Spider Woman
The Milagro Beanfield War (1988) . . . . . . Ruby Archuleta
Moon Over Parador (1988) . . . . . . . . Madonna Mendez
The Rookie (1990). . . . . . . . . . . . . . . . . . . . . . . . Liesl
*Made for Cable Movies:*
The Last Prostitute (1991; Lifetime) . . . . . . . . . . . . Loah
The Burning Season (1994; HBO) . . . . . . . . . . . . . .n.a.
*Made for Cable TV:*
Tales From the Crypt: This'll Kill Ya (1992; HBO) . . . .n.a.
*Magazines:*
**Playboy** (May 1979) . . . . . . . . . . . . . Foreign Sex Stars
•• 165—Breasts.
**Playboy** (Nov 1983) . . . . . . . . . . . Sex in Cinema 1983
••• 149—Breasts.
**Playboy** (Oct 1984) . . . . . . . . . . . . The Girls from Brazil
••• 86-91—Nude.
**Playboy** (Dec 1984). . . . . . . . . . . . . . Sex Stars of 1984
••• 205—Full frontal nudity leaning against bed.
**Playboy** (Nov 1985) . . . . . . . . . . . Sex in Cinema 1985
• 132—Side view of right breast in scene not used in *Kiss of the Spider Woman.*
**Playboy** (Dec 1987). . . . . . . . . . . . . . Sex Stars of 1987
••• 153—Full frontal nudity.
**Playboy** (Dec 1988). . . . . . . . . . . . . . Sex Stars of 1988
••• 183—Full frontal nudity leaning against bed.
**Playboy's Nudes** (Oct 1990). . . . . . . . . . . . . . Herself
••• 26-27—Full frontal nudity.
**Playboy** (Sep 1992) . . . . . . . . . . . . . . . . . . Grapevine
• 162—Breasts under sheer blouse. B&W.
**Playboy** (Mar 1994). . . . . . . . . . . . . .Safe Sex, Great Sex
••• 69—Breasts in B&W photo.

## Brahms, Penny
*Films:*
The Wrong Box (1966; British)
. . . . . . . . . . . . . . . . . . . . .Twitering Female on Moor
2001: A Space Odyssey (1968; British/U.S.)
. . . . . . . . . . . . . . . . . . . . . . . . . . Stewardess Girl
Hammerhead (1968) . . . . . . . . . . . . . . . . . . . . Frieda
**Games That Lovers Play** (1970). . . . . . . . . Constance
•• 0:08—Breasts outside with a customer.
•• 0:10—Breasts again putting dress back on.
Dracula A.D. 1972 (1972; British). . . . . . . . . . Hippy Girl
*a.k.a. Dracula Today*

## Brando, Rikki
*Films:*
**The Bikini Carwash Company** (1992). . . . . . . . .Amy
(Unrated version reviewed.)
• 0:15—Brief breasts when Stanley steals her bikini top.
• 0:30—Brief breasts during water fight.
• 0:31—Brief breasts at car wash.
• 0:43—Brief right breast, while making love with Donovan.
•• 0:44—Buns and breasts, making love with Donovan.
•• 0:59—Breasts, making out in car with Donovan.
••• 1:00—More breasts in car with Donovan.
• 1:02—Brief breasts in car wash.
•• 1:12—Breasts posing for photos.
**Buford's Beach Bunnies** (1992) . . . . . . Lauren Beatty
•• 0:54—Breasts in bed with Jeeter.
**The Bikini Carwash Company II** (1993) . . . . . . .Amy
(Unrated version reviewed.)
••• 0:09—Breasts with the other three girls, celebrating in office during music video number.
•• 1:09—Buns in lingerie, then breasts in dressing room with Marshall.

## Brandt, Brandi
Wife of Mötley Crüe band member Nikki Sixx.
*Films:*
Wedding Band (1989) . . . . . . . Serena (Gypsy Wedding)
*Video Tapes:*
**Playboy Video Calendar 1989** (1988). . . . November
••• 0:41—Nude.
Glamour Through Your Lens—Outdoor Techniques
(1989) . . . . . . . . . . . . . . . . . . . . . . . . . . . . . .Herself
0:42—In white lingerie on couch.
**Playmates at Play** (1990) . . . . . . . . . . . . . Easy Rider
*Magazines:*
**Playboy** (Oct 1987) . . . . . . . . . . . . . . . . . . Playmate
**Playboy's Book of Lingerie** (Jan 1991) . . . . . .Herself
•• 74—Side of right breast and buns.
•• 98—Breasts.
Playboy's Bathing Beauties (Apr 1992) . . . . . . . .Herself
**Playboy's Calendar Playmates** (Nov 1992). . .Herself
•• 97—Buns and side of right breast.
**Playboy's Book of Lingerie** (Nov 1992) . . . . .Herself
••• 100-101—Breasts.

**Playboy's Book of Lingerie** (Jan 1993) . . . . . . Herself
• 106—Lower frontal nudity.
**Playboy's Book of Lingerie** (Mar 1993) . . . . . Herself
••• 36—Breasts.
**Playboy** (Apr 1993) . . . . . . . . . . . . . . . . . . Tattoo You
•• 84-85—Buns. Posing with her husband. Tattoos on her ankle and above her right butt cheek.
**Playboy's Book of Lingerie** (May 1993) . . . . . Herself
••• 50—Breasts.
**Playboy's Wet & Wild Women** (Aug 1993) . . Herself
••• 40-41—Full frontal nudity.
**Playboy's Book of Lingerie** (Nov 1993) . . . . . Herself
••• 30—Breasts.
••• 66—Breasts.
**Playboy's Book of Lingerie** (Jan 1994) . . . . . . Herself
••• 92—Breasts.
**Playboy's Bathing Beauties** (Mar 1994) . . . . . Herself
••• 90-91—Breasts.
**Playboy's Book of Lingerie** (Mar 1994) . . . . . Herself
•• 13—Left breast.
**Playboy's Book of Lingerie** (May 1994) . . . . . Herself
•• 53—Right breast and lower frontal nudity.
**Playboy's Book of Lingerie** (Jul 1994) . . . . . . Herself
•• 60—Breasts under sheer bodysuit.
•• 76—Left breast.

## Brandy

a.k.a. Jisél.
*Video Tapes:*
**Penthouse Fast Cars/Fantasy Women** (1992)
. . . . . . . . . . . . . . . . . . . . . . . . . . . . . . . . . . . . .Model
**Penthouse Pet of the Year Playoff 1991** (1992)
. . . . . . . . . . . . . . . . . . . . . . . . . . . . . . . . . . . . Pet
••• 0:32—Nude in bubble bath.
••• 0:34—Nude doing different things in a house in various lingerie outfits, then in bath again, then covered with rose petals.
••• 0:39—Nude in still photos, then in motion while wearing sunglasses while posing in front of a wall.
••• 0:40—Nude in color and B&W while posing in country setting with different lingerie.
••• 0:43—Nude in science-fiction style segment.
••• 0:45—Buns in G-string and bra, then nude while posing on bed. B&W.
••• 0:50—Nude while posing in a field during end credits.
**Penthouse Pet of the Year Winners 1992: Brandy & Amy** (1992) . . . . . . . . . . . . . . . . . . . . . . . . . Pet
Penthouse Satin & Lace II: Hollywood Undercover (1992). . . . . . . . . . . . . . . . . . . . . . . . . . . . . . Pet
**Penthouse Satin & Lace: An Erotic History of Lingerie** (1992). . . . . . . . . . . . . . . . . . . . . . .Model
**Penthouse DreamGirls** (1994) . . . . . . . . . . . Brandy
••• 0:10—Nude in a house, on a piano bench, on a sofa.
*Magazines:*
**Penthouse** (Jan 1992) . . . . . . . . . . . . . Pet of the Year
••• 123-137—Nude.
**Penthouse** (Sep 1992) . . . . . . . . . . . . . . . . . . Brandy
••• 150-159—Nude.

**Penthouse** (Oct 1992) . . . . . . The Seduction of Brandy
••• 99-107—Nude with adult film actress Tori Welles.
**Penthouse** (Sep 1993) . . . . . . . . . . . The Body Electric
••• 151-159—Nude in B&W photos.

## Brannon, Sandi

*Films:*
**A Killing Affair** (1985) . . . . . . . . . . . . . . . . . . . . .Sara
•• 0:08—Breasts, sitting up in bed, then kissing Pink.
**Dead Aim** (1987) . . . . . . . . . . . . . . . . . . . . . . . .Misty
• 0:05—Buns in G-string, while dancing on stage during opening credits.
• 0:09—Breasts, while dancing on stage with the other girls (wearing a white bottom).
••• 1:02—Breasts and buns in G-string doing dance routine.
• 1:14—Very brief right breast, several times, while covered with blood, lying dead on bed.

## Bremmer, Leslee

*Films:*
**Hardbodies** (1984) . . . . . . . . Photo Session Hardbody
• 0:02—Breasts in the surf when her friends take off her swimsuit top during the opening credits.
•• 0:40—Breasts with other topless girls posing for photographs taken by Rounder. She takes off her dress and is wearing a black G-string.
**Paradise Motel** (1985)
. . . . . . . . . . . . . . . . . .Uncredited Girl Leaving Room
• 0:38—Breasts buttoning her pink sweater, leaving motel room.
**School Spirit** (1985) . . . . . . . . . . . . . . . . . . . . Sandy
• 1:18—Breasts on a guy's shoulder in pool. (She's on the right, wearing red swimsuit bottoms.)
**My Chauffeur** (1986) . . . . . . . . . . . . . . . . . .Party Girl
1:19—Dancing in yellow outfit at a club. Most of buns.
• 1:24—Buns and brief breasts in back of the limousine, taking off her yellow outfit.
• 1:25—Breasts sleeping when Penn and Teller leave the limousine.
**Reform School Girls** (1986) . . Uncredited Shower Girl
•• 0:25—Brief breasts in the shower three times. Walking from left to right in the background, full frontal nudity by herself with wet hair, breasts walking from left to right.
Another Chance (1989) . . . Girl in Womanizer's Meeting
*Video Tapes:*
**Best Chest in the West** (1984). . . . . . . . . . . . Leslee
••• 0:29—In black, two piece swimsuit, then breasts and buns.
• 0:32—More breasts during judging and winning the 2nd round.
E. Nick: A Legend in His Own Mind (1984)
. . . . . . . . . . . . . . . . . . . . . . . . .Nymphet/Announcer
**Centerfold Screen Test** (1985). . . . . . . . . . . .Herself
0:22—Breasts under fishnet top. (Practically see-through top.)

•• 0:24—Dancing, wearing the fishnet top and black
    G-string.
••• 0:28—Closer shot, dancing, while wearing the top.
**Best Chest in the West II** (1986) . . . . . . . . . . . . . Herself
    0:49—Dancing in pink top. Buns, in G-string.
**The Girls of Malibu** (1986) . . . . . . . . . . . . . . . Leslie
••• 0:01—In two piece swimsuit, then nude, posing
    outside.
**Starlet Screen Test** (1986). . . . . . . . . . . . . . . Leslie
••• 0:11—Nude, taking off towel in hot tub.
**Best Chest in the U.S.** (1987) . . . . . . . . . Bernadette
• 0:25—Buns in G-string.
**Hot Body International: #1 Miss Cancun** (1990)
    . . . . . . . . . . . . . . . . . . . . . . . . . . . . . Contestant
•• 0:25—Buns in two piece swimsuit.
**Starlet Screen Test II** (1991) . . . . . . . . . . . . . Lauren
••• 0:41—Breasts and buns, in swimsuit bottom, danc-
    ing on stage.
**Starlets Exposed! Volume II** (1991) . . . . . . . . . Leslie
    (Same as *The Girls of Malibu*.)
••• 0:40—Breasts, then nude, taking off two piece
    swimsuit in garden.

## Brennan, Eileen

*Films:*
The Last Picture Show (1971) . . . . . . . . . . . . Genevieve
**Scarecrow** (1973) . . . . . . . . . . . . . . . . . . . .Darlene
• 0:27—Brief breasts in bed when Gene Hackman
    takes off her bra and grabs her breasts.
The Sting (1973) . . . . . . . . . . . . . . . . . . . . . . . . Billie
Daisy Miller (1974) . . . . . . . . . . . . . . . . . . Mrs. Walker
Hustle (1975) . . . . . . . . . . . . . . . . . . . Paula Hollinger
The Great Smokey Roadblock (1976) . . . . . . . Penelope
Murder by Death (1976) . . . . . . . . . . . . Tess Skeffington
The Cheap Detective (1978) . . . . . . . . . . . Betty DeBoop
FM (1978) . . . . . . . . . . . . . . . . . . . . . . . . . . . Mother
Private Benjamin (1980) . . . . . . . .Captain Doreen Lewis
Clue (1985). . . . . . . . . . . . . . . . . . . . . . Mrs. Peacock
The New Adventures of Pippi Longstocking (1988)
    . . . . . . . . . . . . . . . . . . . . . . . . . . . . .Miss Bannister
Rented Lips (1988) . . . . . . . . . . . . . . . Hotel Desk Clerk
Texasville (1990) . . . . . . . . . . . . . . . Genevieve Morgan
White Palace (1990) . . . . . . . . . . . . . . . . . . . . . . Judy
I Don't Buy Kisses Anymore (1992) . . . . . . . . . . . Frieda
*Made for Cable TV:*
Tales From the Crypt: Till Death Do We Part
    (1994; HBO) . . . . . . . . . . . . . . . . . . . . . . . . . Ruth
*Made for TV Movies:*
My Old Man (1979) . . . . . . . . . . . . . . . . . . . . . Marie
Deadly Intentions...Again? (1991). . . . . . . . . Charlotte
Taking Back My Life: The Nancy Ziegenmeyer Story
    (1992). . . . . . . . . . . . . . . . . . . . . . . . . Vicky Martin
Poisoned by Love: The Kern County Murders (1993)
    . . . . . . . . . . . . . . . . . . . . . . . . . . . . Martha Catlin
Precious Victims (1993). . . . . . . . . . . . . . Minnie Gray
My Name is Kate (1994) . . . . . . . . . . . Barbara Mannix
*TV:*
Private Benjamin (1981-83). . . . . .Captain Doreen Lewis

## • Brenneman, Amy

*TV:*
NYPD Blue (1993- ) . . . . . . . . . . . . . . . . .Janice Licalsi
**NYPD Blue: Pilot** (Sep 21, 1993). . . . . . .Janice Licalsi
• 0:41—In white bra and panties in room with Kelly.
    Buns and brief right breast while in bed.
**NYPD Blue: 4B or not 4B** (Sep 28, 1993)
    . . . . . . . . . . . . . . . . . . . . . . . . . . . .Janice Licalsi
• 0:25—Brief breasts, while on top of Kelly in bed.
**NYPD Blue: Ice Follies** (Nov 30, 1993) . . .Janice Licalsi
• 0:38—Most of left breast, while making love in bed
    with John.
• 0:39—Brief buns, while getting out of bed.

## Brentano, Amy

*Films:*
**Blood Sisters** (1986) . . . . . . . . . . . . . . . . . . . . .Linda
••• 0:12—Breasts, getting out of bed.
•• 0:14—Breasts, walking around. Right breast, in bed
    with Russ. Brief upper half of buns.
**Breeders** (1986). . . . . . . . . . . . . . . . . . . . . . . . . Gail
• 0:59—Long shot of buns, getting into the nest.
• 1:07—Breasts in nest, throwing her head back.
•• 1:08—Brief breasts, writhing around in the nest,
    then breasts, arching her back.
• 1:11—Breasts, long shot, just before the nest is de-
    stroyed.
Robot Holocaust (1986) . . . . . . . . . . .Irradiated Female
**Prime Evil** (1987) . . . . . . . . . . . . . . . . . . . . . . . Brett
••• 1:13—Breasts removing her gown (she's in the mid-
    dle) with Cathy and Judy.

## Bresee, Bobbie

*Films:*
**Mausoleum** (1983) . . . . . . . . . . . . . . . . . Susan Farrell
••• 0:25—Breasts and buns wrapping a towel around
    herself in her bedroom.
•• 0:26—Breasts on the balcony showing herself to the
    gardener.
• 0:29—Breasts in the garage with the gardener. Brief,
    dark, hard to see.
• 0:32—Brief left breast, while kissing Marjoe Gortner.
• 1:10—Breasts in the bathtub talking to Gortner.
    Long shot.
Armed Response (1986). . . . . . . . . . . . . . . . . . . Anna
Star Slammer—The Escape (1986). . . . . . . . . . . .Marai
Surf Nazis Must Die (1986) . . . . . . . . . . . Smeg's Mom
**Evil Spawn** (1987) . . . . . . . . . . . . . . . . . . Lynn Roman
• 0:14—Very brief half of right breast in bed with a
    guy.
0:26—In red one piece swimsuit.
••• 0:36—Breasts and side view of buns in bathroom
    looking at herself in the mirror, then taking a show-
    er.
**The Alien Within** (1990). . . . . . . . . . . . Lynn Roman
Contains footage from *The Evil Spawn* woven together
with new material.
• 0:12—Very brief half of right breast in bed with a
    guy.

••• 0:37—Breasts and side view of buns in bathroom looking at herself in the mirror, then taking a shower.

*Magazines:*

**Playboy** (Jul 1989). . . . . . . . . . . . . . . B-Movie Bimbos
••• 133—Full frontal nudity leaning on a car.

# Brighton, Connie

*Video Tapes:*

**Playboy's Playmate Review 3** (1985). . . . . Playmate
**Playboy Video Centerfold: Kerri Kendall** (1990)
. . . . . . . . . . . . . . . . . . . . . . . . . . . . . . . Playmate
••• 0:31—Nude.

*Magazines:*

**Playboy** (Sep 1982). . . . . . . . . . . . . . . . . . . Playmate

# Brimhall, Cynthia

*Films:*

**Hard Ticket to Hawaii** (1987). . . . . . . . . . . . . . . Edy
•• 0:47—Breasts changing out of a dress into a blouse and pants.
• 1:33—Breasts during the end credits.
**Picasso Trigger** (1989). . . . . . . . . . . . . . . . . . . Edy
•• 0:59—Breasts in weight room with a guy.
**Guns** (1990). . . . . . . . . . . . . . . . . . . . . . . . Edy Stark
0:26—Buns, in G-string singing and dancing at club.
•• 0:27—Breasts in dressing room.
0:53—Buns, in black one piece outfit and stockings, singing in club. Nice legs!
**Do or Die** (1991). . . . . . . . . . . . . . . . . Edy Stark
• 0:31—Most of buns, wearing white lingerie outfit, singing and dancing at night.
••• 0:36—Breasts and buns, making love with Lucas on floor in front of fire.
Every Breath (1992) . . . . . . . . . . . . . . . . . . . . . . . Kris
**Fit To Kill** (1993). . . . . . . . . . . . . . . . . . . . Edy Stark
•• 1:00—Breasts under sheer white body suit while posing for her boyfriend while he photographs her.
**Hard Hunted** (1993). . . . . . . . . . . . . . . . . Edy Stark
••• 0:50—Breasts in bedroom while making love with Lucas.
•• 1:18—Left breast, then breasts in bed with Lucas.

*Video Tapes:*

**Playboy Video Calendar 1987** (1986) . . . . Playmate
**Playboy Video Magazine, Volume 10** (1986)
. . . . . . . . . . . . . . . . . . . . . . . . . . . . . . . Playmate
••• 0:53—Nude in still photos, then in the woods after riding motorcycle and then in the desert.
**Sexy Lingerie** (1988) . . . . . . . . . . . . . . . . . . . .Model
**Playmates at Play** (1990) . . . . . . . . . . . . . Easy Rider

*Magazines:*

**Playboy** (Oct 1985). . . . . . . . . . . . . . . . . . . Playmate
**Playboy's 1987 Book of Lingerie** (Mar 1987)
. . . . . . . . . . . . . . . . . . . . . . . . . . . . . . . Herself
••• 18—Full frontal nudity.
• 32-33—Lower frontal nudity.
• 58—Lower frontal nudity.
••• 100—Full frontal nudity.

**Playboy's Nudes** (Oct 1990) . . . . . . . . . . . . . .Herself
••• 22—Full frontal nudity.
**Playboy's Book of Lingerie** (Mar 1991). . . . . .Herself
• 32—Left breast.
**Playboy's Calendar Playmates** (Nov 1992). . .Herself
••• 56—Breasts.
**Playboy** (Nov 1992) . . . . . . . . . . . Sex in Cinema 1992
••• 145—Breasts in bed with Tony Peck from *Hard Hunted.*
**Playboy's Blondes, Brunettes & Redheads**
(Sep 1993). . . . . . . . . . . . . . . . . . . . . . . . . . .Herself
••• 85—Breasts.
**Playboy's Video Playmates** (Sep 1993). . . . . .Herself
••• 20-23—Nude.

# Brin, Michele

a.k.a. Michelle Lamothe.

*Films:*

**Secret Games** (1991). . . . . . . . . . . . . . . . . . .Julianne
(Unrated version reviewed.)
(Nude a lot, only the best are listed.)
•• 0:03—Left breast, while lying in bed with Billy Drago.
••• 0:08—Breasts and buns, while taking a shower.
•• 0:09—Breasts under sheer white robe, trying to entice Drago.
••• 0:34—Breasts, sunbathing with the other girls. (She's wearing brown framed sunglasses.)
••• 0:38—Breasts in bed, making love with Martin Hewitt.
••• 0:43—Buns and breasts making love in bed with Drago.
••• 0:48—Breasts, while tied to the bed.
••• 0:54—In white bra and panties, then nude taking them off and putting new ones on.
••• 1:10—Breasts, while lying in bed with Hewitt.
••• 1:13—Breasts and buns, making love with Hewitt in bathtub.
•• 1:15—Breasts under sheer robe.
• 1:32—Buns in G-string, then breasts, getting into bed and making love with Drago.
**Sins of the Night** (1993). . . . . . . . . . . . .Laura Winters
(Unrated version reviewed.)
• 0:05—In black bra and panties in her house with her lover. Brief buns in G-string while Jack takes photos.
••• 0:06—Breasts, while making love with her lover. Long scene.
• 0:14—Breasts and buns, getting out of bed.
**Strike a Pose** (1993) . . . . . . . . . . . . . . . Miranda Cross
••• 0:06—Breasts, while making love with Nick at night outside by a fire. Long scene.
••• 0:32—In black bra and panties, then breasts while making love with Nick. Long scene.
• 0:40—Buns in panties that are squished against a glass door.
••• 1:06—Brief left breast in bed, then breasts and buns while making love with Nick.

**Sexual Intent** (1994) . . . . . . . . . . . . Barbara Hayden
- 0:28—Breasts, on balcony after John talks to her on cellular phone. Long shot.
- 0:47—Breasts during fantasy with John while she's watching video tape of an interview.
- ••• 0:49—In bra and panties, then breasts and buns while making love with John in her office.
- •• 0:54—Breasts, while sitting in bathtub.

*Made for Cable TV:*
**Dream On: Up All Night** (1992; HBO) . . . . . . . . Ariel
- ••• 0:14—Breasts, taking off her dress and walking down hallway during Martin's dream.

*Video Tapes:*
Eden 6 (1994). . . . . . . . . . . . . . . . . . . . . . Ginny Lynch

# Brisebois, Danielle

*Films:*
The Premonition (1976) . . . . . . . . . . . . . . . . . . . .Janie
King of the Gypsies (1978) . . . . . . . . . . . . . Young Tita
**Big Bad Mama II** (1987). . . . . . . Billy Jean McClatchie
- ••• 0:12—Breasts with Julie McCullough playing in a pond underneath a waterfall.
- 0:36—In a white slip standing at the door talking to McCullough, then talking to Angie Dickinson.

**Kill Crazy** (1989). . . . . . . . . . . . . . . . . . . . . Libby
- •• 0:39—Breasts taking off top to go skinny dipping with Rachel.
- 0:46—Very brief right breast, while lying on ground with a bad guy while getting raped. Buns, getting turned over before being shot.

*TV:*
All In the Family (1978-83) . . . . . . . . . . Stephanie Mills
Knots Landing (1983-84) . . . . . . .Mary-Frances Sumner

# Brittany, Tally

See: Chanel, Tally.

# Broady, Eloise

*Films:*
**Dangerous Love** (1988) . . . . . . . . . . . . . . . . . . Bree
- ••• 0:06—Breasts changing into lingerie in the mirror.
To Die For (1988) . . . . . . . . . . . . . . . . . . . . Girl at Party
Troop Beverly Hills (1989) . . . . . . . . . . Starlet at Party
Weekend at Bernie's (1989). . . . . . . . . . . . . . .Tawny
*a.k.a. Hot and Cold*
- 0:35—Buns in two piece swimsuit, coming into Bernie's house to get the keys to the ski boat.

*Video Tapes:*
**Playboy Video Calendar 1989** (1988) . . . .December
- ••• 0:45—Nude.
**Wet and Wild III** (1991). . . . . . . . . . . . . . . .Model
**The Best of Wet and Wild** (1992) . . . . . . . . .Model
**Playboy Video Playmate Six-Pack 1992** (1992)
. . . . . . . . . . . . . . . . . . . . . . . . . . . . . . Playmate

*Magazines:*
**Playboy** (Apr 1988) . . . . . . . . . . . . . . . . . . . Playmate
**Playboy's Calendar Playmates** (Nov 1992) . . Herself
- ••• 77—Full frontal nudity.

**Playboy's Video Playmates** (Sep 1993) . . . . . .Herself
- ••• 24-27—Full frontal nudity.
**Playboy's Nudes** (Dec 1993) . . . . . . . . . . . . . .Herself
- ••• 20-21—Breasts.
**Playboy's Girls of Summer '94** (Jul 1994) . . . .Herself
- •• 55—Left breast and lower frontal nudity.
- 84-85—Buns.

# • Brochet, Anne

*Films:*
Cyrano De Bergerac (1990; French) . . . . . . . . Roxanne
**All the Mornings of the World** (1992; French)
. . . . . . . . . . . . . . . . . . . . . . . . . . . . Madeleine
*a.k.a. Tout Les Matins Du Monde*
- 0:46—Nude by river bank while running to hide behind tree when seen by Marin. Long shot.
- •• 0:56—Left breast, while opening her dress and letting Marin feel and kiss her breast.
- 1:06—Brief breasts, after opening her blouse for Marin in the hallway.
- 1:08—Brief upper half of right breast while holding Marin's hand.
- •• 1:20—Lower frontal nudity under nightgown, while getting out of bed.
Barjo (1993; French) . . . . . . . . . . . . . . . . . . Fanfan

# • Broderson, Nicole

*Films:*
**Anthony's Desire** (1993). . . . . . . . . . . . . . . . Dancer
- 0:54—Buns, while sitting on her stomach in the middle of the group of women. Tattoo on her right butt cheek.

*Video Tapes:*
**Penthouse Forum Letters: Volume 2** (1994)
. . . . . . . . . . . . . . . . . . . . . The Loving Nurse/Nurse
- ••• 0:01—Nude, while making love in hospital bed with a patient.

# Brooke, Sandy

*Films:*
**Bits and Pieces** (1985) . . . . . . . . . . . . . . Mrs. Talbot
- ••• 1:03—Breasts in bathtub washing herself before the killer drowns her. Very brief right breast when struggling.
- 1:09—Brief breasts under water in bathtub, dead.
**Star Slammer—The Escape** (1986) . . . . . . . . . .Taura
- ••• 0:21—Breasts in jail putting a new top on. In braless white T-shirt for most of the rest of the film.
- •• 1:09—Breasts changing into a clean top.
**The Terror on Alcatraz** (1986). . . . . . . . . . . . Mona
- 0:05—Right breast on bed getting burned with a cigarette by Frank.
Nightmare Sisters (1987) . . . . . . . . . .Amanda Detweiler
Deep Space (1988) . . . . . . . . . . . . . .Woman in House

## Brooks, Elisabeth

*Films:*
**The Howling** (1981) . . . . . . . . . . . . . . . . . . . Marsha
•• 0:46—Full frontal nudity taking off her robe in front
of a campfire.
• 0:48—Breasts sitting on Bill by the fire.
Deep Space (1988) . . . . . . . . . . . . . . . . . . . Mrs. Ridley
The Forgotten One (1989) . . . . . . . . . . . . . . . . . Carla
Jaded (1989). . . . . . . . . . . . . . . . . . . . . . . . . . . . . Rita
*TV:*
Doctors' Hospital (1975-76) . . Nurse Connie Kimbrough
*Magazines:*
**Playboy** (Nov 1980) . . . . . . . . . . . Sex in Cinema 1980
••• 174—Full frontal nudity.

## Brooks, Randi

a.k.a. Randi Brazen.
*Films:*
Looker (1981) . . . . . . . . . . . . . . . . . . . . . Girl in Bikini
Deal of the Century (1983) . . . . . . . . . . Ms. Della Rosa
**The Man with Two Brains** (1983) . . . . . . . . . . . Fran
•• 1:11—Brief breasts showing Steve Martin her
breasts in front of the hotel. Buns, changing in the
hotel room, then wearing black see-through negligee.
**Tightrope** (1984) . . . . . . . . . . . . . . . . . . . Jamie Cory
••• 0:20—Nude, taking off her robe and getting into
the spa.
• 0:24—Buns and side of left breast, dead in the spa
while Clint Eastwood looks at her.
**Hamburger—The Motion Picture** (1986)
. . . . . . . . . . . . . . . . . . . . . . . . . . . . . . . . . Mrs. Vunk
•• 0:52—Brief breasts in helicopter with a guy.
Terrorvision (1986) . . . . . . . . . . . . . . . . . . . . . Cherry
Cop (1988) . . . . . . . . . . . . . . . . . . . . . . . . Jeanie Pratt
0:32—In a bra making love in her kitchen with James
Woods.
*TV:*
Wizards and Warriors (1983) . . . . . . . . . . . Witch Bethel
The Last Precinct (1986) . . . . . . . . Officer Mel Brubaker
Mancuso, FBI (1989-90) . . . . . . . . . . . . . Jean St. John
*Magazines:*
**Playboy** (Nov 1983) . . . . . . . . . . . Sex in Cinema 1983
• 150—See-through negligee.
**Playboy** (Dec 1983) . . . . . . . . . . . . Sex Stars of 1983
• 210—Side view of right breast and buns.
**Playboy's Girls of Summer '86** (Aug 1986) . . Herself
••• 30-31—Breasts.
•• 47—Breasts.

## Brown, Blair

*Films:*
The Choirboys (1977) . . . . . . . . . . . . . . Kimberly Lyles
**Altered States** (1980) . . . . . . . . . . . . . . Emily Jessup
• 0:10—Brief left breast making love with William Hurt
in red light from an electric heater.
•• 0:34—Breasts lying on her stomach during Hurt's
mushroom induced hallucination.

1:39—Buns, sitting in hallway with Hurt after the
transformations go away.
One Trick Pony (1980) . . . . . . . . . . . . . . . . . . Marion
Continental Divide (1981) . . . . . . . . . . . . . . . . . . Nell
**A Flash of Green** (1984) . . . . . Catherine "Kat" Hubble
• 1:30—Very brief right breast moving around in bed
with Ed Harris.
Strapless (1990) . . . . . . . . . . . . . . Dr. Lillian Hempel
Passed Away (1992) . . . . . . . . . . . . . . . . Amy Scanlan
*Made for Cable TV:*
Days and Nights of Molly Dodd
. . . . . . . . . . . . . . . . . . . . . . . . . . . . . . Molly Dodd
*Miniseries:*
Wheels (1978) . . . . . . . . . . . . . . . . . . Barbara Lipton
Space (1987) . . . . . . . . . . . . . . Penny Hardesty Pope
*Made for TV Movies:*
Hands of a Stranger (1987) . . . . . . . . . . . Diane Benton
Extreme Close-Up (1990) . . . . . . . . . . . . . . . . . . n.a.
Those Secrets (1992) . . . . . . . . . . . . . . . . . . . . . n.a.
Rio Shannon (1993) . . . . . . . . . . . . . . . . . . . . . . n.a.
Moment of Truth: To Walk Again (1994) . . . . . . . . n.a.
*TV:*
Captains and the Kings (1976)
. . . . . . . . . . . . . . . . . . . . Elizabeth Healey Hennessey
Days and Nights of Molly Dodd (1987-88)
. . . . . . . . . . . . . . . . . . . . . . . . . . . . . . Molly Dodd

## • Brown, Bobbi

*Films:*
**Betrayal of the Dove** (1992) . . . . . . . . . . . . Dancer
•• 1:03—Buns in outfit, then breasts while dancing on
stage in club.
*Video Tapes:*
**Penthouse Forum Letters: Volume 2** (1994) . . . . . .
The Window Washer/Lover
••• 0:46—Nude, making love with another woman on
sofa, on kitchen counter and on bed.
*Magazines:*
**Penthouse** (Aug 1991) . . . . . . . . . . . . . . Army Brat
••• 86-95—Nude.

## Brown, Juanita

*Films:*
**Caged Heat** (1974) . . . . . . . . . . . . . . . . . . Maggie
a.k.a. Renegade Girls
• 0:25—Breasts in shower scene.
Foxy Brown (1974) . . . . . . . . . . . . . . . . . . . Claudia

## Brown, Julie

Comedienne.
Singer–"The Homecoming Queen's Got a Gun."
Not to be confused with MTV Video Jockey "Downtown"
Julie Brown.
*Films:*
Any Which Way You Can (1980) . . . . . . . . . . . . Candy
**Bloody Birthday** (1980) . . . . . . . . . . . . . . . Beverly
••• 0:13—Dancing in red bra, then breasts while two
boys peek through hole in the wall, then buns. Nice,
long scene.

0:48—In bedroom wearing red bra.
1:03—In bedroom again in the red bra.
Police Academy II: Their First Assignment (1985)
. . . . . . . . . . . . . . . . . . . . . . . . . . . . . . . . . . . . . . Chloe
Earth Girls are Easy (1989). . . . . . . . . . . . . . . . . .Candy
Timebomb (1990). . . . Uncredited Waitress at Al's Diner
Nervous Ticks (1991) . . . . . . . . . . . . . .Nancy Rudman
The Spirit of '76 (1991). . . . . . . . . . . . . . . Ms. Liberty
The Opposite Sex ...and How to Live with Them (1992)
. . . . . . . . . . . . . . . . . . . . . . . . . . . . . . . . . . . . . . .Zoe
Shakes the Clown (1992) . . . . . . . . . . . . . . . . . . . Judy
*Made for Cable Movies:*
Medusa: Dare to be Truthful (1991; Showtime)
. . . . . . . . . . . . . . . . . . . . . . . . . . . . . . . . . . . Medusa
Attack of the 5' 2" Women (1994; Showtime)
. . . . . . . . . . . . . . . . . . . . Tonya Hardly/Lenora Babbitt
*Made for Cable TV:*
Just Say Julie . . . . . . . . . . . . . . . . . . . . . . . . . . .Hostess
*TV:*
The Edge (1992- ) . . . . . . . . . . . . . . . . . . Cast Member

## Brown, Linda

*Films:*
**Pleasure in Paradise** (1992) . . . . . . . . . . . . . Heather
• 0:02—Full frontal nudity, while getting out of the
shower and wrapping a towel around herself.
••• 0:41—Breasts while in bed, making love with Rob.
Long scene.
*Magazines:*
**Playboy's Book of Lingerie** (May 1993) . . . . . Herself
••• 88—Full frontal nudity.

## Brown, Robin

*Video Tapes:*
**Penthouse Satin & Lace II: Hollywood Undercover**
(1992). . . . . . . . . . . . . . . . . . . . . . . . . . . . . . . . . Pet
**Penthouse The Great Pet Hunt—Part I** (1992)
. . . . . . . . . . . . . . . . . . . . . . . . . . . . . . . . . . . . . . Pet
**Making of the "Carousel Girls' Calendar"** (1993)
. . . . . . . . . . . . . . . . . . . . . . . . . . . . . . . Miss January
••• 0:09—Nude during photo shoot.
••• 0:13—Nude during interview segment.
**The Penthouse All-Pet Workout** (1993) . . . . . . . .Pet
• 0:00—Right breast during introduction.
•• 0:03—Brief nude shots while getting undressed and
suited up.
••• 0:21—Nude on sofa inside.
••• 0:43—Nude with the other girls, exercising, working
with equipment, in the pool and spa.
**Penthouse DreamGirls** (1994) . . . . . . . . . . . . Robin
••• 0:14—Nude, in a house in lingerie, by a window, in
a bubble bath.
*Magazines:*
**Penthouse** (Apr 1992). . . . . . . . . . . . . . . . . . . . Pet
••• 67-81—Nude.

## •Brown, Robin Joi

*Films:*
**Test Tube Teens From the Year 2000** (1993)
. . . . . . . . . . . . . . . . . . . . . . . . . . . . . . . . . . Victoria
*a.k.a. Virgin Hunters*
••• 0:31—Breasts, in the showers (she's on the left) with
Annie while Vin and Naldo watch.
Hard Drive (1994) . . . . . . . . . . . . . .Assistant Examiner
(Unrated version reviewed.)

## Brown, Sara Suzanne

*Films:*
**The Last Boy Scout** (1991) . . . . . . . . . . . . . . Dancer
• 0:19—Brief breasts and buns while dancing in club.
**The Bikini Carwash Company** (1992) . . . . . . Sunny
(Unrated version reviewed.)
• 0:15—Brief breasts when Stanley steals her bikini
top.
•• 0:25—Breasts, washing windshield and side window.
••• 0:26—More breasts while window washing.
•• 0:30—Breasts during water fight.
•• 0:31—Breasts at car wash.
•• 0:35—Breasts running after a guy who stole her bikini top.
••• 0:46—Breasts and buns in G-string, hand washing a
customer with Rita.
••• 0:47—Breasts and buns, dancing inside car wash.
•• 0:53—Breasts outside at car wash.
••• 1:02—Nude, soaped up in car wash with Melissa
and Rita.
••• 1:12—Breasts, posing for photos.
•• 1:15—Breasts when Stanley takes her top off.
**The Bikini Carwash Company II** (1993) . . . . . Sunny
(Unrated version reviewed.)
••• 0:09—Breasts with the other three girls, celebrating
in office during music video number.
••• 0:16—Breasts at carwash during music video number. (Wearing yellow bikini bottoms.)
• 0:24—Buns in lingerie in offices of The Miracle Network with Rita.
• 0:27—Brief breasts, twice, while flashing her breasts
in office.
••• 1:16—In black lingerie, then breasts in office fantasy.
•• 1:29—Breasts and buns in bikini bottoms during
music video number at the carwash.
**Mirror Images II** (1993) . . . . . . . . . . . . . . .Prostitute
••• 0:13—In red bra and panties, then breasts and buns
while making love with Clete in motel room. Long
scene.
**Secret Games 2—The Escort** (1993) . . . . . . . . Irene
(Unrated version reviewed.)
••• 0:32—Undressing in bedroom, then nude while
making love with Martin Hewitt in bed.
• 0:53—Breasts, while making love next to dining
room table with Hewitt.
•• 1:00—Breasts, while lying in bed with Hewitt.
••• 1:20—Nude, while making love with Hewitt in bed.

**Test Tube Teens From the Year 2000** (1993)
. . . . . . . . . . . . . . . . . . . . . . . . . . . . . . . . . . . . .Reena
*a.k.a. Virgin Hunters*
- •• 0:03—In black bra and panties, then buns in panties and breasts stripping out of her jumpsuit during Vin's day dream.

**Killer Looks** (1994) . . . . . . . . . . . . . . . . . . . . . Diane
(Unrated version reviewed.)
- • 0:01—Buns, while in two piece swimsuit in pool.
- • 0:02—Buns and breasts after getting out of pool and taking off swimsuit top.
- ••• 0:04—Full frontal nudity while making love with the plumber.
- ••• 0:26—Breasts, while making love in spa with her husband.
- • 0:30—Breasts, while putting bra on in bedroom.
- ••• 0:41—Nude while making love with Mickey in bed.
- • 0:47—Briefly nude, while getting into bed.
- • 0:50—Full frontal nudity in flashbacks while on bed with Mickey.
- • 0:59—Breasts in open dress top, while trying to get back away from Cynthia's advances.
- •• 1:23—In bra and panties, then breasts, while blindfolded and making out with Janine Lindemulder and Lené Hefner on stairway.
- ••• 1:25—Nude, while in the shower.

## Brown, Tricia

*Films:*
**Vamp** (1986) . . . . . . . . . . . . . . . . . . . . . . . . . . . Candi
- • 0:32—Brief breasts doing strip tease.

Phantom Empire (1987) . . . . . . . . . . . . . . . . . . Cavegirl
**Hollywood Chainsaw Hookers** (1988) . . . . . . . . Ilsa
- •• 0:37—Breasts while Jack is tied up in bed.

## Browne, Leslie

*Films:*
**The Turning Point** (1977) . . . . . . . . . . . Emilia Rogers
- • 0:51—Brief side view of right breast, while lying in bed with Mikhail Baryshnikov at the end of the love scene. Don't see her face.

**Nijinsky** (1980; British) . . . . . . . . . . . . . . . . . . Romula
- • 1:34—Very brief breasts, twice, on the floor when Nijinksy rips her dress off. Dark.

Dancers (1987) . . . . . . . . . . . . . . . . . . . . . . . . . Nadine
*Magazines:*
**Playboy** (Nov 1980) . . . . . . . . . . . Sex in Cinema 1980
- • 180—Right breast in still from *Nijinsky*.

## Bruce, Andi

*Films:*
**Summer's Games** (1987) . . . . . . . . . . . News Anchor
0:12—Brief right breast, while turning around to look at monitor.
- • 0:42—Breasts turning around to look at the monitor.

Screwball Hotel (1988) . . . . . . . . . . . . . . . . . Bobbi Jo
*Magazines:*
**Penthouse** (Aug 1987) . . . . . . . . . . . . . . . . . . . . Pet

## Bruinooge, Lucienne

*Films:*
**The Secrets of Love—Three Rakish Tales** (1986)
. . . . . . . . . . . . . . . . . . . . . . . . . . . . . . . . . . .Marietta
- • 0:02—Buns, while getting spanking.
- •• 0:27—Breasts, while lying in bed.

*Magazines:*
**Playboy's Nudes** (Oct 1990) . . . . . . . . . . . . . . Herself
- ••• 80—Full frontal nudity.

**Playboy's Girls of the World** (Oct 1992). . . . . Herself
- ••• 106—Full frontal nudity.

## Brunaux, Olivia

*Films:*
**The Secrets of Love—Three Rakish Tales** (1986)
. . . . . . . . . . . . . . . . . . . . . . . . . . . . . . . . . . . Célestine
- • 1:03—Brief breasts and buns fantasizing.
- ••• 1:14—Breasts and buns in the greenhouse making love.
- ••• 1:18—Breasts while kneeling in the greenhouse and making love.

Grand Guignol (1987; French) . . . . . . . . . . . . . . . Coco
Cayenne Palace (1989; French) . . . . . . . . . . . . . Alice

## Bryant, D'Andrea

*Films:*
Nothing But Trouble (1991) . . . . . . . . . . . . . Party Girl
*Video Tapes:*
**Sexy Lingerie II** (1990) . . . . . . . . . . . . . . . . . . Model
*Magazines:*
**Playboy's Book of Lingerie** (Mar 1991) . . . . . .Herself
- •• 11—Buns.
- ••• 79—Breasts.

**Playboy's Book of Lingerie** (Sep 1991) . . . . . .Herself
- • 20-21—Buns.

**Playboy's Book of Lingerie** (Nov 1991) . . . . .Herself
- ••• 62-63—Breasts.

Playboy's Book of Lingerie (Jan 1992) . . . . . . . . .Herself
**Playboy's Book of Lingerie** (Mar 1992) . . . . . .Herself
- ••• 28—Buns and left breast.

**Playboy's Bathing Beauties** (Apr 1992) . . . . . .Herself
- ••• 95—Breasts.

**Playboy's Book of Lingerie** (May 1992) . . . . .Herself
- ••• 73—Breasts.

**Playboy's Book of Lingerie** (Mar 1993) . . . . . .Herself
- ••• 51—Side view of left breast and buns.

**Playboy's Book of Lingerie** (May 1993) . . . . . .Herself
- • 101—Buns in G-string.

**Playboy's Blondes, Brunettes & Redheads**
(Sep 1993) . . . . . . . . . . . . . . . . . . . . . . . . . . .Herself
- ••• 66—Full frontal nudity.

**Playboy's Book of Lingerie** (Mar 1994) . . . . . .Herself
- ••• 30—Breasts.

## Bryant, Pamela

*Films:*
Lovely But Deadly (1973) . . . . . . . . . . . . . . . . . Gloria
**Don't Answer the Phone** (1979) . . . . . . . . Sue Ellen

•• 0:28—Breasts in the killer's photo studio when he rips her jacket off and kills her.

**H.O.T.S.** (1979) . . . . . . . . . . . . . . . . . . . . . . .Teri Lynn
*a.k.a. T & A Academy*
• 1:33—Breasts during football game.

Separate Ways (1979) . . . . . . . . . . . . .Cocktail Waitress

Looker (1981) . . . . . . . . . . . . . . . . . . . Reston Girl

**Lunch Wagon** (1981) . . . . . . . . . . . . . . . . . . . .Marcy
*a.k.a. Lunch Wagon Girls*
*a.k.a. Come 'N' Get It*
•• 0:04—Breasts while changing tops in room in gas station with Rosanne Katon while a guy watches through key hole.
• 0:55—Left breast, several times, in van with Bif.

**Private Lessons** (1981). . . . . . . . . . . . . . . . . . . Joyce
• 0:03—Very brief right breast, changing in the house while Billy and his friend peep from outside.

Scorpion (1986) . . . . . . . . . . . . . . . . . Flight Attendant

**Trapped** (1993). . . . . . . . . . . . . . . . .Laura Armstrong
*a.k.a. The Killing Jar*
0:03—In white lingerie in house, showing it off to her husband.
• 0:04—Brief breasts on TV monitor.
• 0:05—Brief buns and right breast in mirror while changing clothes in the bathroom.
•• 0:11—Breasts, while starting to make love in backyard with Curtis.
• 0:15—Brief breasts in bathroom with her husband while he fantasizes about Monica.
• 0:24—Breasts, while on TV.
•• 0:27—Breasts, while in shower, getting out and getting dressed.
• 0:29—Brief right breast when it slips out of nightgown while she lies in bed.
• 0:32—Brief left breast when masked guy cuts her nightgown strap open.
• 0:48—Brief side of left breast on TV.
••• 0:50—Nude, getting into bathtub, in bathtub, then getting dragged around house by guy.

*TV:*
B.J. and the Bear . . . . . . . . . . . . . . . . . . . . . . . . . . . .n.a.

*Magazines:*
**Playboy** (Sep 1977) . . . . . . . . . . . . . Girls of the Big Ten
••• 148—Full frontal nudity.
**Playboy** (Dec 1977). . . . . . . . . . . . . . . Dear Playboy
•• 16—Breasts in open jumpsuit.
**Playboy** (Apr 1978) . . . . . . . . . . . . . . . . . . . Playmate
**Playboy** (Nov 1980) . . . . . . . . . . The World of Playboy
••• 12—Full frontal nudity.

## Buchanan, Yvette

*Films:*
**Night Eyes** (1990). . . . . . . . . . . . . . . . . . . . Baby Doll
(Unrated version reviewed.)
• 0:07—Brief left breast, then breasts making love in bathroom with Ronee.
The Malibu Beach Vampires (1991)
. . . . . . . . . . . . . . . . . . . . . . . . . The Rocket Scientist

Roots of Evil (1991) . . . . . . . . . . . . . . . . . . . . . Hooker
(Unrated version reviewed.)

## Buchfellner, Ursula

*a.k.a. Ursula Fellner.*
*Films:*
**Popcorn and Ice Cream** (1978; West German)
. . . . . . . . . . . . . . . . . . . . . . . . . . . . . . . . . . . . Yvonne
*a.k.a. Sex and Ice Cream*
••• 0:30—Nude with the hotel manager, Vivi and Bea.
• 0:40—Breasts in open dress at the disco.
**The Manhunters** (1980; French/Spanish/German)
. . . . . . . . . . . . . . . . . . . . . . . . . Laura Crawford
• 0:06—Buns and side view breasts, walking around the house. Long shot.
• 0:08—Breasts taking a bath.
•• 0:10—Breasts in the bathtub.
• 0:15—Full frontal nudity getting pulled out of the tub unconscious.
• 0:19—Brief right breast when a kidnapper opens her blouse while she's tied up.
0:43—Very brief breasts running through the jungle.
• 0:58—Brief lower frontal nudity, then breasts captured by the natives.
•• 1:04—Breasts, unconscious, while tribe women undress her.
•• 1:05—Full frontal nudity tied to a pole.
•• 1:06—Nude, getting dragged into a hut.
•• 1:10—Full frontal nudity taking a shower under waterfall with three tribe women.
•• 1:12—Full frontal nudity, lying down while three tribe women put flowers on her.
•• 1:23—Breasts and buns, getting carried away by the cannibal creature.
• 1:26—Buns, being carried by the creature.
•• 1:27—Breasts on the ground.
•• 1:29—Buns and right breast, getting carried down the mountain side.
••• 1:30—Breasts on the boat with Peter.
*Magazines:*
**Playboy** (Oct 1979) . . . . . . . . . . . . . . . . . . . . Playmate
**Playboy's Nudes** (Oct 1990) . . . . . . . . . . . . . . Herself
••• 77—Full frontal nudity.

## Buckman, Tara

*Films:*
Rollercoaster (1977) . . . . . . . . . . . . . . Coaster Attendant
Hooper (1978). . . . . . . . . . . . . . . . . . . . . . . . . Debbie
The Cannonball Run (1981) . . . . . . . . . . . . . . . . . . Jill
**Silent Night, Deadly Night** (1984) . . . .Mother (Ellie)
• 0:12—Brief right breast twice when the killer dressed as Santa Claus, rips her blouse open. Breasts lying dead with slit throat.
• 0:18—Very, very brief breasts during Billy's flashback.
• 0:43—Brief breasts a couple of times again in another of Billy's flashbacks.
Never Too Young to Die (1986) . . . . Sacrificed Punkette

**Silent Night, Deadly Night, Part 2** (1986) . . Mother
- 0:09—Very brief right breast, with Santa Claus during flashback.
- 0:14—Very brief breasts on ground during flashback.
- 0:22—Very, very brief blurry breasts during flashback.
- 0:47—Very, very brief breasts during flashback.

Terminal Exposure (1988) . . . . . . . . . . . . . . . . . . . . n.a.

**The Loves of a Wall Street Woman** (1989)
. . . . . . . . . . . . . . . . . . . . . . . . . Brenda Baxter
- 0:00—Breasts taking a shower, opening the door and getting a towel.
- 0:06—Breasts changing clothes in locker room in black panties. Nice legs!
- 0:18—Breasts in bed making love with Alex.
- 0:31—Breasts in bed with Alex making love.
- 0:40—Breasts in black panties dressing in locker room.
- 0:46—Brief breasts lying in bed, talking to her lover, side view of buns. Long shot.
- 1:16—Breasts making love in bed with Alex.

**The Marilyn Diaries** (1990) . . . . . . . . . . . . . . . Jane
- 0:53—Breasts and buns, taking off robe and getting into bathtub. Left breast, in tub reading diary.
- 0:54—Breasts in and getting out of tub. Very brief lower frontal nudity.
- 1:27—Breasts in bathtub talking with John.

**Object of Desire** (1991) . . . . . . . . . . . . . . . . . Angie
- 0:12—Breasts, leaning up on massage table.
- 0:14—Breasts, getting dressed so Derrick can see.
- 0:23—Breasts, making love with Derrick in her dressing room.
- 0:28—Breasts in bathtub with Derrick.
- 0:43—Right breast, while making love in bed with Derrick.
- 0:50—Side view of buns, while lying in bed.
- 0:51—Right breast, while sitting up in bed, then full frontal nudity.
- 0:55—Breasts, opening her blouse in Steve's office in front of him.
- 1:09—Full frontal nudity, posing for photographer in studio. Also side view of his buns.
- 1:12—Brief breasts in magazine photos.
- 1:18—Breasts changing clothes in dressing room.

Xtro 2, The Second Encounter (1991)
. . . . . . . . . . . . . . . . . . . . . . . . Dr. Julie Casserly
Round Trip to Heaven (1992) . . . . . . . . . . . . . . . Phyllis

## • Buick, Denise
*Films:*
**Full Contact** (1992) . . . . . . . . . . . . . . . . . . . . . . Tori
- 0:31—Buns in T-back, then in bra, then breasts, while doing strip routine on stage.
- 0:39—Buns in T-back and breasts while dancing on stage.
- 1:02—Breasts and buns, while making love with Luke.

*Video Tapes:*
**Inside Out 4** (1992) . . . . . Claudia/What Anna Wants...
(Unrated version reviewed.)
- 1:08—Nude in bed with William while Anna takes photos.

## Bujold, Genevieve
*Films:*
King of Hearts (1966; French/Italian) . . . . . . Colombine
(Letterboxed French version with English subtitles.)
The Thief of Paris (1967; French/Italian) . . . . . . Charlotte
Anne of the Thousand Days (1969; British)
. . . . . . . . . . . . . . . . . . . . . . Anne Boleyn
The Trojan Women (1972; British) . . . . . . . . Cassandra
**Kamouraska** (1973; Canadian/French) . . . . . Elisabeth
Nude in long shot.
Earthquake (1974) . . . . . . . . . . . . . . . . . . . . . . Denise
Obsession (1976)
. . . . . . . . . . . . Elizabeth Courtland/Sandra Portinari
**Swashbuckler** (1976) . . . . . . . . . . . . . . . . Jane Barnet
- 1:00—Very brief side view nude, diving from the ship into the water. Long shot, don't really see anything.
- 1:01—Buns and brief side of left breast seen from under water.

Coma (1978) . . . . . . . . . . . . . . . . . . Dr. Susan Wheeler
0:03—Nude behind frosted glass shower door, so you can't see anything.
Murder by Decree (1979). . . . . . . . . . . . . Annie Crook
Last Flight of Noah's Ark (1980) . . . . . Bernadette Lafleur
**Monsignor** (1982) . . . . . . . . . . . . . . . . . . . . . . . Clara
- 1:05—Breasts getting undressed and climbing into bed while talking to Christopher Reeve.

Choose Me (1984) . . . . . . . . . . . . . . . . . . . . . Dr. Love
Tightrope (1984) . . . . . . . . . . . . . . . Beryl Thibodeaux
Trouble in Mind (1986) . . . . . . . . . . . . . . . . . . Wanda
**Dead Ringers** (1988) . . . . . . . . . . . . . . . Claire Niveau
- 0:49—Very brief right breast in bed with Jeremy Irons, then brief breasts reaching for pills and water. Dark, hard to see.

The Moderns (1988) . . . . . . . . . . . . . . Libby Valentin
False Identity (1990) . . . . . . . . . . . . . . . . . . . . . . n.a.
Paper Wedding (1991; Canadian) . . . . . . . . . . . . Claire
Oh, What a Night (1992). . . . . . . . . . . . . . . . . . . Eva
*Made for TV Movies:*
Red Earth, White Earth (1989) . . . . . . . . . . . . Madeline

## • Buono, Cara
*Films:*
Gladiator (1992) . . . . . . . . . . . . . . . . . . . . . . . Dawn
**Waterland** (1992; British/U.S.) . . . . . . . . Jody Dobson
- 0:38—Brief breasts, while sitting in chair in classroom during Jeremy Irons' daydream.

## Burch, Tracey
*Films:*
**Marked for Death** (1990). . . . . . . . . . . . Sexy Girl #1
- 0:39—Brief breasts on bed with Jimmy when Steven Seagal bursts into the room. (She's the blonde.)

**Dance with Death** (1991) . . . . . . . . . . . . . . Whitney
- ••• 0:03—Breasts and buns in G-string, dancing on stage.
- ••• 0:05—More breasts and buns while dancing.

## Burger, Michele

*Films:*
**Emmanuelle 5** (1986). . . . . . . . . . . . . . . Girl No. 3
- ••• 0:42—Breasts, while talking with the two other girls. Wearing a blue head band.
- •• 0:44—Breasts, while drinking champagne with the other harem girls.

The Newlydeads (1988) . . . . . . . . . . . . . . . . Bikini Girl
**Party Plane** (1988) . . . . . . . . . . . . . . . . . . . . Carol
- • 0:31—Breasts, squirting whipped cream on herself for her audition.
- •• 0:38—Breasts doing a strip tease routine on the plane.
- ••• 1:02—Breasts mud wrestling with Renee on the plane.
- • 1:09—Breasts in the cockpit, covered with mud.
- •• 1:17—Breasts in serving cart.

**Payback** (1988) . . . . . . . . . . . . . . . . . . . . . . Laura
- • 0:08—Brief breasts sitting up in bed just before getting shot, then brief breasts twice, dead in bed.

Roadhouse (1989). . . . . . . . . . . . . . . . . Strip Joint Girl
Ninja Academy (1990) . . . . . . . . . . . . . . . . . . . Nudist

## Burgoyne, Victoria

*Films:*
Death Ship (1980; Canadian) . . . . . . . . . . . . . . . . Lori
**Stealing Heaven** (1988; British/Yugoslavian)
. . . . . . . . . . . . . . . . . . . . . . . . . . . . . . . . Prostitute
- • 0:28—Left breast, taking off her top. Side view of right breast and buns.
- •• 0:29—Breasts lying in bed.

## Burkett, Laura

*Films:*
Avenging Angel (1985) . . . . . . . . . . . . . Blonde Hooker
**Daddy's Boys** (1988). . . . . . . . . . . . . . . . . . . Christie
- ••• 0:17—Breasts in room with Jimmy.
- •• 0:20—Left breast, while making love with Jimmy in bed again.
- • 0:21—Brief breasts during Jimmy's nightmare.
- • 0:43—Brief breasts in bed again, then getting dressed.
- • 0:53—Brief breasts in bed consoling Jimmy.
- • 1:11—Left breast, while in bed with Jimmy.

**Rush Week** (1989) . . . . . . . . . . . . . . . Rebecca Winters
- •• 0:43—Breasts in the shower, talking to Jonelle.
- • 0:55—Brief breasts getting dressed after modeling session.

## Burnette, Kim

*Films:*
**Da Vinci's War** (1992) . . . . . . . . . . . . . . . . Monique
- ••• 0:49—Breasts, kneeling by herself, while putting on a show for the bad guy.

*Made for Cable TV:*
Red Shoe Diaries: Talk To Me Baby (1992; Showtime)
. . . . . . . . . . . . . . . . . . . . . . . . . . . . . . . . Regina
(Available on video tape on *Red Shoe Diaries 3: Another Woman's Lipstick*.)
- 0:04—In wet T-shirt, entering the Men's restroom.
- 0:07—Briefly in wet T-shirt in flashback.

## Burns, Bobbi

*Films:*
**New York Nights** (1981) . . . . . . . . . . . The Authoress
- •• 0:16—Breasts on the couch outside with the rock star, then breasts in bed.

**I, the Jury** (1982) . . . . . . . . . . . . . . . . . . Sheila Kyle
- • 0:01—Brief side view of right breast, while in bed with Armand Assante.

**Q** (1982) . . . . . . . . . . . . . . . . . . . . . . . . Sunbather
- •• 0:06—Breasts taking off swimsuit top and rubbing lotion on herself.

## Burns, Catherine

*Films:*
**Last Summer** (1969) . . . . . . . . . . . . . . . . . . . Rhoda
- • 1:31—Very brief breasts struggling with Stacy, Peter and Dan. Long shot.

Me, Natalie (1969). . . . . . . . . . . . . . . . . . . . . Hester
Red Sky at Morning (1971) . . . . . . . . Marcia Davidson

## Burns, Janell

*Video Tapes:*
**Hot Body International: #3 Lingerie Special** (1992) . . . . . . . . . . . . . . . . . . . . . . . . . Contestant
- •• 0:31—Buns in one piece body suit.

**Hot Body International: #5 Miss Acapulco** (1992) . . . . . . . . . . . . . . . . . . . . . . . . . . . . Contestant
- ••• 0:14—Breasts and buns in swimsuit in pool. Breasts applying flowers to her breasts, then taking them off.
- •• 0:16—Breasts taking off bikini top outside next to pool.

**Hot Body: The Best of Hot Body** (1994). . . . . Herself
- ••• 0:08—Breasts and buns in swimsuit.

## Burrell, Gretchen

*Films:*
**Pretty Maids All in a Row** (1971) . . . . . . . . Marjorie
- • 0:05—Partial side of right breast, in office with Rock Hudson.
- • 0:07—Breasts on the couch in Hudson's office.

*Magazines:*
**Playboy** (Apr 1971) . . . . . . . . Vadim's "Pretty Maids"
- ••• 154—Breasts.

## Burstyn, Ellen

*Films:*
Goodbye Charlie (1964). . . . . . . . . . . . . . . . . Franny
**Tropic of Cancer** (1970) . . . . . . . . . . . . . . . . Mona
- ••• 0:02—Full frontal nudity, while lying on bed.
- •• 0:03—Right breast while lying on her back in bed.

•• 0:04—Nude, getting out of bed to get bugs off her.
The Last Picture Show (1971) . . . . . . . . . . . Lois Farrow
**King of Marvin Gardens** (1972) . . . . . . . . . . . . Sally
• 0:50—Brief breasts, while kneeling on the floor and
turning around to shoot squirt guns.
The Exorcist (1973) . . . . . . . . . . . . . . . . . . Chris
Harry and Tonto (1974) . . . . . . . . . . . . . . . Shirley
Alice Doesn't Live Here Anymore (1975) . . . . Alice Hyatt
(Academy Award for Best Actress.)
A Dream of Passion (1978) . . . . . . . . . . . . . . Brenda
Same Time Next Year (1978). . . . . . . . . . . . . . Doris
Resurrection (1980). . . . . . . . . . . . . . . Edna McCauley
**The Ambassador** (1984) . . . . . . . . . . . Alex Hacker
••• 0:06—Breasts opening her robe to greet her lover.
••• 0:07—Brief breasts making love in bed.
••• 0:29—Breasts in a movie while her husband, Robert
Mitchum, watches.
Twice in a Lifetime (1985). . . . . . . . . . . . . . . Kate
Hanna's War (1988) . . . . . . . . . . . . . . Katalin Senesh
Dying Young (1991) . . . . . . . . . . . . . . . . Mrs. O'Neil
Grand Isle (1991) . . . . . . . . . . . . . Mademoiselle Reisa
The Cemetery Club (1993) . . . . . . . . Esther Moskowitz
*Made for Cable Movies:*
Act of Vengeance (1986). . . . . . . . . . Margaret Yablonski
*Made for TV Movies:*
Pack of Lies (1987) . . . . . . . . . . . . . . . . . . . . . n.a.
When You Remember Me (1990) . . . . . . . Nurse Cooder
Taking Back My Life: The Nancy Ziegenmeyer Story
(1992). . . . . . . . . . . . . . . . . . . . . . . . . . . . Wilma
Shattered Trust: The Shari Karney Story (1993)
. . . . . . . . . . . . . . . . . . . . . . . . . . Joan Delvecchio
Getting Gotti (1994). . . . . . . . . . . . . . . Jo Giacalone
Getting Out (1994). . . . . . . . . . . . . . . Arlie's Mother
*TV:*
The Iron Horse (1967-68) . . . . . . . . . . . . Julie Parsons
The Ellen Burstyn Show (1986-88) . . . . . . . Ellen Brewer

## • *Burton, Jennifer Leigh*

*Made for Cable TV:*
Red Shoe Diaries: How I Met My Husband
(1993; Showtime) . . . . . . . . . . . . . Dominatrix #1
Red Shoe Diaries: Burning Up (1994; Showtime)
. . . . . . . . . . . . . . . . . . . . . . . . . . . . Fire Victim
**Red Shoe Diaries: Runway** (1994; Showtime)
. . . . . . . . . . . . . . . . . . . . . . . . . . . . . . . Coco
0:01—In black bra.
0:19—Lower half of buns, while sitting next to
Miguel.
• 0:21—Brief breasts (she's on the right) while watching Alia and Miguel making love.
*Video Tapes:*
**Playboy's Sensual Fantasy for Lovers** (1993)
. . . . . . . . . . . . . . . . . . . . . . . . . . . . Pretending
0:16—In wet, braless white blouse.
••• 0:17—Nude, in stable after undressing and making
love.
• 0:47—Full frontal nudity during review.

## • *Burton, Kate*

*Films:*
Big Trouble in Little China (1986). . . . . . . . . . . Margo
Life With Mikey (1993). . . . . . . . . . . . . . . Mrs. Burns
*Made for Cable Movies:*
**Love Matters** (1993; Showtime) . . . . . . . . . Deborah
(Unrated version reviewed.)
• 0:05—Brief breasts, getting turned over on bed dur-
ing video playback.
• 0:09—Very brief side view of right breast, while mak-
ing love in bed with Tony Goldwyn during video
playback.
*TV:*
Monty (1994- ) . . . . . . . . . . . . . . . . . . . . . . . . n.a.

## *Bush, Jovita*

*Films:*
The Cheerleaders (1973) . . . . . . . . . . . . . . . . Bonnie
**Fox Style** (1974). . . . . . . . . . . . . . . . . . . . . Bonnie
• 1:02—Brief right breast while in dressing room,
changing clothes.

## *Butler, Bridget*

*Films:*
**Sunset Heat** (1991) . . . . . . . . . . . . . Lady in New York
(Unrated version reviewed.)
• 0:00—Buns, lying in bed.
• 0:01—Buns, when Michael Paré takes off her shirt.
Buns and partial left breast lying on him in bed.
Sunset Strip (1992) . . . . . . . . . . . . . . . . . . Candice
Amore! (1993). . . . . . . . . . . . . . . . . . . . . . . Barbie

## *Butler, Cher*

*Video Tapes:*
**Wet and Wild** (1989) . . . . . . . . . . . . . . . . . . Model
**Playmates at Play** (1990). . . . . . . . . . . . . Bareback
*Magazines:*
**Playboy** (Aug 1985) . . . . . . . . . . . . . . . . . Playmate
**Playboy's Girls of Summer '86** (Aug 1986). . . Herself
••• 48—Breasts, while holding fishing pole.
••• 84—Full frontal nudity.
•• 106—Left breast and lower frontal nudity while
soaping car.
**Playboy's 1987 Book of Lingerie** (Mar 1987)
. . . . . . . . . . . . . . . . . . . . . . . . . . . . . . Herself
•• 11—Breasts and partial lower frontal nudity.
•• 46-47—Left breast and lower frontal nudity.
••• 102—Breasts.

## *Buxbaum, Ingrid*

*Films:*
Stars and Bars (1988). . . . . . . . . . . . . . Photographer
*Made for Cable Movies:*
**Traveling Man** (1989; HBO) . . . . . Uncredited Salesgirl
••• 0:05—Breasts and buns while wearing G-string,
dancing during sales meeting.

# Byrd-Nethery, Miriam

*Films:*
Lies (1984; British) . . . . . . . . . . . . . . . . . . . . . . . . .n.a.
**The Offspring** (1986). . . . . . . . . . . . . Eileen Burnside
• 0:26—Breasts in bathtub filled with ice while her husband tries to kill her with an ice pick.
• 0:29—Very brief right breast, dead in bathtub while her husband is downstairs.
Summer Heat (1987) . . . . . . . . . . . . . . . . . Aunt Patty
Walk Like a Man (1987) . . . . . . . . . . . . . Toy Store Clerk
Stepfather 2 (1989). . . . . . . . . . . . . . . . . Sally Jenkins
Leatherface: The Texas Chainsaw Massacre III (1990)
. . . . . . . . . . . . . . . . . . . . . . . . . . . . . . . . . . . . .Mama
The Raven Red Kiss-Off (1990) . . . . . . . .Motel Manager
*TV:*
Mr. T and Tina (1976) . . . . . . . . . . . . . . .Miss Llewellyn

# Byrne, Patti T.

*Films:*
Fuzz (1972). . . . . . . . . . . . . . . . . . . . . . . . Abigail
**Night Call Nurses** (1972). . . . . . . . . . . . . . .Barbara
*a.k.a. Young LA Nurses 2*
•• 0:59—Breasts several times in bed with the Doctor.

# Byrnes, Maureen

*Films:*
**Cry Uncle** (1971). . . . . . . . . . . . . . . . . . . Lena Right
• 0:16—Breasts and buns in bed with two other girls while spanking Dominic. Hard to see because the negative image is projected.
••• 0:46—Brief breasts with Connie when Jake peeks in the window. Full frontal nudity, talking with Jake at the doorway.
• 0:48—Breasts, making love with Jake in bed.
•• 0:49—Nude, getting out of bed after knocking out Jake.
••• 0:50—Full frontal nudity, while interrogating Jake.
•• 0:53—Breasts, in room with gun while covering Jake.
• 0:54—Full frontal nudity, while shooting gun and leaving.
Hurry Up, Or I'll Be 30 (1973) . . . . . . . . . . . . . . . . . Flo
**Sugar Cookies** (1973). . . . . . . . . . . . . . . . . . . . Dola
•• 0:37—Right breast while Gus is on top of her, then breasts and buns.
Goin' South (1978) . . . . . . . . . . . . . . . . . . Mrs. Warren

# Byun, Susan

*Films:*
**Crime Lords** (1990) . . . . . . . . . . . . . . . . . . Monahan
•• 1:06—Left breast, then right breast, while making out with Wayne Crawford on the couch.
**Dead Connection** (1993). . . . . . . . . . . . . . . . . Sarah
• 0:50—Very, very brief left breast while catching shirt that Michael Madsen throws to her.
*Video Tapes:*
**Inside Out 4** (1992) . . . . . Lee Anne/Three on a Match
(Unrated version reviewed.)
••• 0:58—Breasts, changing blouse in the bathroom.

# Cabasa, Lisa Ann

*Films:*
**Wild at Heart** (1990) . . . . . . . . . . . Reindeer Dancer
•• 0:30—Breasts standing while Mr. Reindeer talks on the phone. More breasts dancing in front of him.
*Made for Cable Movies:*
Lies of the Twins (1991; USA). . . . . . . . . . . . . . . Caryn

# Cable, Tawnni

*Made for Cable Movies:*
Marilyn & Bobby: Her Final Affair (1993; USA) . . . . . n.a.
*Video Tapes:*
**Playboy Video Calendar 1990** (1989). . . . . . . March
••• 0:13—Nude.
**Playboy Video Centerfold: Tawnni Cable** (1990)
. . . . . . . . . . . . . . . . . . . . . . . . . . . . . . . . . . . . .Playmate
••• 0:00—Nude throughout.
**Playmates at Play** (1990) . . . . . . . . . . . . Gotta Dance
**Wet and Wild II** (1990). . . . . . . . . . . . . . . . . Model
**Playboy Playmates in Paradise** (1992). . . . Playmate
**Wet and Wild: The Locker Room** (1994)
. . . . . . . . . . . . . . . . . . . . . . . . . . . . . . . . . . . . .Playmate
*Magazines:*
**Playboy** (Jun 1989). . . . . . . . . . . . . . . . . . Playmate
**Playboy's Nudes** (Oct 1990) . . . . . . . . . . . . .Herself
••• 70—Full frontal nudity.
**Playboy's Book of Lingerie** (Jan 1991) . . . . . .Herself
••• 13—Full frontal nudity.
**Playboy's Book of Lingerie** (Mar 1991). . . . . .Herself
••• 12—Full frontal nudity.
**Playboy's Bathing Beauties** (Apr 1992). . . . . .Herself
••• 6—Breasts.
**Playboy's Book of Lingerie** (May 1992) . . . . .Herself
••• 59—Breasts.
**Playboy's Girls of Summer '92** (Jun 1992) . . .Herself
••• 29—Full frontal nudity.
••• 34—Full frontal nudity.
•• 88—Buns.
**Playboy's Book of Lingerie** (Jul 1992). . . . . . .Herself
•• 59—Breasts.
**Playboy's Calendar Playmates** (Nov 1992). . .Herself
••• 81—Full frontal nudity.
**Playboy's Bathing Beauties** (Apr 1993). . . . . .Herself
••• 96—Breasts.
**Playboy's Wet & Wild Women** (Aug 1993). . .Herself
••• 74—Full frontal nudity.
• 106-107—Buns.
**Playboy's Book of Lingerie** (Sep 1993) . . . . . .Herself
••• 11—Full frontal nudity.
••• 50-51—Full frontal nudity.
••• 98-99—Full frontal nudity.
**Playboy's Video Playmates** (Sep 1993) . . . . . .Herself
••• 28-29—Nude.
**Playboy's Nudes** (Dec 1993) . . . . . . . . . . . . .Herself
••• 54—Full frontal nudity.
**Playboy's Book of Lingerie** (Jan 1994) . . . . . .Herself
••• 53—Breasts.
••• 88—Full frontal nudity.

**Playboy's Bathing Beauties** (Mar 1994) . . . . . Herself
••• 19—Breasts.
••• 77—Breasts.
**Playboy's Book of Lingerie** (Mar 1994) . . . . . Herself
••• 103—Breasts.
**Playboy's Book of Lingerie** (May 1994) . . . . . Herself
••• 60-61—Full frontal nudity.
••• 69—Breasts.
••• 96—Breasts.
**Playboy's Girls of Summer '94** (Jul 1994) . . . Herself
••• 94-95—Breasts and buns.
**Playboy's Book of Lingerie** (Jul 1994) . . . . . . Herself
••• 10—Breasts.
••• 49—Breasts.

## Cadell, Ava

*Films:*
**Happy Housewives** . . . . . . . . . . . . . . . . . . Schoolgirl
0:39—Buns, getting caught by the Squire and getting spanked.
**Confessions of a Window Cleaner** (1974; British)
. . . . . . . . . . . . . . . . . . . . . . . . . . . . . . School Girl
Nude in shower scene with other school girls.
The Hound of the Baskervilles (1977) . . . . . . . . . . Maid
**The Golden Lady** (1979; British) . . . . . . . . . . . . . Anita
**Spaced Out** (1980; British) . . . . . . . . . . . . . . . . Partha
*a.k.a. Outer Touch*
•• 0:41—Left breast making love on bed with Cliff.
•• 0:42—Nude wrestling on bed with Cliff.
• 0:43—Brief left breast lying in bed alone.
•• 1:08—Breasts sitting on bed.
Smokey and the Bandit III (1983) . . . . . . . . . . . . Blond
**Commando** (1985) . . . . . . . . . . . . . . . . . . . . Girl in Bed
• 0:46—Very brief breasts three times in bed when Arnold Schwarzenegger knocks a guy through the motel door into her room.
**Jungle Warriors** (1985) . . . . . . . . . . . . . . . Didi Belair
• 0:50—Brief breasts getting yellow top ripped open by Sybil Danning.
**Not of This Earth** (1988) . . . . . . . . . . Second Hooker
•• 0:41—Breasts in cellar with Paul just before getting killed with two other hookers. Wearing a gold dress.
**Do or Die** (1991) . . . . . . . . . . . . . . . . . . . . . . . . Ava
•• 0:20—Buns and brief breasts, getting dressed in motor home. Lots of buns shots, wearing swimsuit.
**Lunch Box** (1991) . . . . . . . . . . . . . . . . . . . . . Maggie
Amorel (1993) . . . . . . . . . . . . . . . . Mrs. Scarborough
**Fit To Kill** (1993) . . . . . . . . . . . . . . . . . . . . . . . . Ava
1:10—In black bra and panties, while talking on the phone.
•• 1:13—Half of right breast, sticking out of bra. Buns in G-string.
•• 1:14—Left breast, while making love with Petrov in radio station while still talking on the air.
••• 1:17—Breasts in spa with Petrov.
**Hard Hunted** (1993) . . . . . . . . . . . . . . . . . . . . . . Ava
0:08—In two piece swimsuit in radio station.
••• 0:38—Breasts in spa with Becky while doing radio show.

1:19—In white fishnet top while talking on the radio.
*Made for Cable TV:*
Pillow Previews . . . . . . . . . . . . . . . . . . . . . . . . Hostess
*Magazines:*
**Playboy** (Jun 1989) . . . . . . . . . . . . . . . . . . . . Grapevine
187—Buns, on bear skin rug in B&W photo.

## Caffaro, Cheri

*Films:*
**Ginger** (1970) . . . . . . . . . . . . . . . . . . . . . . . . . . Ginger
••• 1:06—Breasts, taking off her top in front of Rodney and lying on top of him in bed.
• 1:10—Full frontal nudity, getting up off the bed.
• 1:22—Sort of breasts during recollection of her rape. Hard to see.
• 1:23—Breasts, taking off her towel in front of Jimmy.
••• 1:32—Nude, on bed handcuffed behind her back by Rex, then getting molested by him. Long scene.
The Abductors (1971) . . . . . . . . . . . . . . . . . . . . Ginger
**A Place Called Today** (1972) . . . . . . Cindy Cartwright
•• 0:14—Full frontal nudity covered with oil or something writhing around on the bed.
• 1:21—Brief side view of right breast undressing in the bathroom.
• 1:23—Brief full frontal nudity getting kidnapped by two guys.
• 1:30—Nude when they take off the blanket.
• 1:35—Brief breasts just before getting killed.
**Girls Are For Loving** (1973) . . . . . . . . . . . . . . Ginger
Savage Sisters (1974) . . . . . . . . . . . . . . . . . . . Jo Turner
**Too Hot To Handle** (1975) . . . . . . . . . Samantha Fox
•• 0:06—Breasts wearing a black push-up bra and buns in black G-string.
• 0:13—Full frontal nudity lying on boat.
••• 0:39—Breasts making love in bed with Dominco.
••• 0:55—Full frontal nudity taking off clothes and lying in bed.
• 1:06—Brief left breast in bed with Dominco.
*Magazines:*
**Playboy** (Nov 1972) . . . . . . . . . . . Sex in Cinema 1972
• 168—Left breast, lit with red light in a photo from *A Place Called Today.*
**Playboy** (Dec 1972) . . . . . . . . . . . . . Sex Stars of 1972
••• 216—Frontal nudity.
**Playboy** (Nov 1973) . . . . . . . . . . Sex in Cinema 1973
••• 156-157—Full frontal nudity.

## Cagan, Andrea

*Films:*
Captain Milkshake (1970) . . . . . . . . . . . . . . . Melissa
**The Hot Box** (1972) . . . . . . . . . . . . . . . . . . . . Bunny
•• 0:16—Breasts cleaning herself off in stream behind Ellie and getting out.
• 0:21—Breasts sleeping in hammock. (She's the third girl from the front, stretching.)
••• 0:45—Breasts in stream while bathing with the other three girls.
Teenager (1975) . . . . . . . . . . . . . . . . . . . . . . . . . n.a.

# Cain, Sharon

a.k.a. Adult film actress Sharon Kane.
*Films:*
Preppies (1984). . . . . . . . . . . . . . . . . . . . Exotic Dancer
**Slammer Girls** (1987). . . . . . . . . . . . . . . . . . . . .Rita
  • 0:23—Brief breasts changing clothes under table in the prison cafeteria.
  •• 1:01—Breasts walking around an electric chair trying to distract a prison guard.
Violated (1987). . . . . . . . . . . . . . . . . . . . . .Party Guest
**California Hot Wax** (1992) . . . . . . . . . . . . . . Loretta
  •• 0:55—Breasts, changing in car wash maintenance room in front of Scott.
  •• 0:59—Breasts in and out of swimming pool with Scott.
*Video Tapes:*
**Inside Out 4** (1992) . . . . . . . . . . . . . . . . .Video Mate
(Unrated version reviewed.)
  •• 1:14—Breasts on TV.
  ••• 1:16—Breasts in Dave's living room.
  • 1:17—Nude, making love with Dave in fast speed.
  ••• 1:18—Breasts and buns, on sofa with Dave.
  • 1:19—More breasts in fast speed.
  ••• 1:20—Nude in Dave's living room.
  • 1:22—Nude on TV again.
**Playboy Night Dreams** (1993) . . . . . .Do Not Disturb
  ••• 0:36—Breasts and buns, while in panties, after getting locked out of her hotel room. Nude, while making love with a guy in his hotel room.

# Calabrese, Gina

*Films:*
**Goin' All the Way** (1981) . . . . . . . . . . . . . . . . . .n.a.
  •• 0:12—Left breast, in the girls' locker room shower. Standing on the left.
**The Vals** (1982). . . . . . . . . . . . . . . . . . . . . . . Annie
  • 0:04—Breasts changing clothes in bedroom with three of her friends. Long shot, hard to see.
  • 0:15—Right breast, while making love with a guy. 0:32—In black bra with her friends in a store dressing room.

# Cameron, Cissie

See: Colpitts-Cameron, Cissie.

# Cameron, Joanna

*Films:*
**B.S. I Love You** (1971) . . . . . . . . . . . Marilyn Michele
(Not available on video tape.)
Pretty Maids All in a Row (1971) . . . . . . . . . . . .Yvonne
*TV:*
Isis (1975-78) . . . . . . . . . . . . . . . . . . . . . . . . . . . . Isis

# Camp, Colleen

*Films:*
Smile (1974) . . . . . . . . . . . . . . . . . . Connie Thompson
  0:47—Side profile of right breast and buns in dressing room while Little Bob is outside taking pictures.
The Swinging Cheerleaders (1974) . . . . . . . . Mary Ann

Fox Fire (1976). . . . . . . . . . . . . . . . . . . . . . . . . . . n.a.
  *a.k.a. Fox Force*
**Death Game, The Seducers** (1977) . . . . . . . . .Donna
  *a.k.a. Mrs. Manning's Weekend*
  0:16—Buns, in spa with Sondra Locke trying to get George in with them.
  • 0:47—Brief breasts jumping up and down on the bed while George is tied up.
  •• 1:16—Breasts behind stained glass door taunting George. Hard to see.
**Cat in the Cage** (1978) . . . . . . . . . . . . .Gilda Riener
  • 0:36—Very brief left breast twice, while making love in bed with Bruce.
Apocalypse Now (1979). . . . . . . . . . . . . . . . . Playmate
The Game of Death (1979) . . . . . . . . . . . .Anne Morris
Cloud Dancer (1980) . . . . . . . . . . . . . . . . . . . Cindy
  1:02—In bra, driving a convertible car while Joseph Bottoms flies a plane over her.
The Deadly Games (1980) . . . . . . . . . . . . . . . . Randy
  *a.k.a. The Eliminator*
They All Laughed (1981) . . . . . . . . . . . . . .Christy Miller
The Seduction (1982) . . . . . . . . . . . . . . . . . . . .Robin
Smokey and the Bandit III (1983). . . . . . . . . Dusty Trails
Valley Girl (1983) . . . . . . . . . . . . . . .Sarah Richman
Doin' Time (1984) . . . . . . . . . . . . . . . . . . . . Catlett
The Joy of Sex (1984). . . . . . . . . . . . . . . . Liz Sampson
Clue (1985) . . . . . . . . . . . . . . . . . . . . . . . . . . Yvette
D.A.R.Y.L. (1985) . . . . . . . . . . . . . . . . . . . . . .Elaine
Police Academy II: Their First Assignment (1985)
  . . . . . . . . . . . . . . . . . . . . . . . . . . . . . . . . .Kirkland
The Rosebud Beach Hotel (1985) . . . . . . . . . . . . Tracy
  0:07—In white lingerie in room with Peter Scolari.
  0:28—In black one piece swimsuit on lounge chair, then walking on the beach.
Police Academy 4: Citizens on Patrol (1987)
  . . . . . . . . . . . . . . . . . . . . .Mrs. Kirkland-Tackleberry
Walk Like a Man (1987) . . . . . . . . . . . . . . . . . . Rhonda
Illegally Yours (1988) . . . . . . . . . . . . . . . Molly Gilbert
Track 29 (1988; British) . . . . . . . . . . . . . . . Arlanda
Wicked Stepmother (1989) . . . . . . . . . . . . . . . .Jenny
My Blue Heaven (1990) . . . . . . . . . . . . . Margaret Snow
The Magic Bubble (1992). . . . . . . . . . . . . . . . Deborah
The Vagrant (1992) . . . . . . . . . . . . . . . . . . Judy Dansig
Wayne's World (1992) . . . . . . . . . . . . .Mrs. Vanderhoff
Greedy (1993) . . . . . . . . . . . . . . . . . . . . . . . . . .Patti
Last Action Hero (1993). . . . . . . . . . . . . . . . . . Ratcliff
Sliver (1993) . . . . . . . . . . . . . . . . . . . . . . . .Judy Marks
*Made for Cable TV:*
Tales From the Crypt: Korman's Kalamity (1992; HBO)
  . . . . . . . . . . . . . . . . . . . . . . . . . . . . . . . . . Mildred
*Made for TV Movies:*
Addicted to his Love (1988) . . . . . . . . . . . . Ellie Snyder
Backfield in Motion (1991). . . . . . . . . . . . . . . . Laurie
For Their Own Good (1993). . . . . . . . . . . . . . . . Chris
*Magazines:*
**Playboy** (Oct 1979) . . . . . . . . . . . "Apocalypse" Finally
  ••• 118-119—Breasts.
**Playboy** (Nov 1979) . . . . . . . . . . . Sex in Cinema 1979
  • 175—Side view of right breast.

# Campbell, Nell

*Films:*

**Lisztomania** (1975; British)..................Olga
- ••• 1:04—Breasts in bed several times with Roger Daltrey when Ringo Starr comes in.
- ••• 1:06—Breasts in bed, sitting up and drinking.
- ••• 1:07—More breasts in bed with a gun after Starr leaves.

**The Rocky Horror Picture Show** (1975; British)
.......................................... Columbia
- • 1:17—Top of breasts popping out of her blouse during song and dance on stage.

Journey Among Women (1977; Australian)....... Meg
Pink Floyd The Wall (1982)................ Groupie

# Cannon, Dyan

*Films:*

Such Good Friends (1971)........... Julie Messinger
(Not available on video tape.)
Dyan's head was composited over a different nude body for a close-up of a Polaroid photograph.

# Cantrell, Cady

*Video Tapes:*

**Playboy Video Calendar 1993** (1992)........ May
- ••• 0:19—Nude outside on bridge and in boat.
- ••• 0:21—Nude in studio setting.

**Playboy Video Centerfold: Cady Cantrell** (1992)
.......................................... Playmate

**Playboy Video Playmate Six-Pack 1992** (1992)
.......................................... Playmate

**Wet and Wild IV** (1992)...................Model

**Playboy's Playmate Review 1993** (1993)
.................................... Miss April
- ••• 0:15—Nude while modeling in studio photo session.
- ••• 0:17—Nude, outside in southern belle style segment.

*Magazines:*

**Playboy's Book of Lingerie** (Mar 1991)..... Herself
- ••• 26—Breasts.

**Playboy's Book of Lingerie** (Jul 1991)...... Herself
- • 64—Partial lower frontal nudity.

**Playboy** (Apr 1992)..................... Playmate
- ••• 90-101—Nude.

**Playboy's Playmate Review** (Jun 1993)....... April
- ••• 30-39—Nude.

**Playboy's Girls of Summer '93** (Jun 1993)... Herself
- ••• 15—Breasts.

**Playboy's Wet & Wild Women** (Aug 1993).. Herself
- ••• 6—Full frontal nudity.
- ••• 30-31—Breasts and buns.
- •• 100—Buns.

**Playboy's Blondes, Brunettes & Redheads** (Sep 1993)............................ Herself
- •• 41—Buns and right breast.

**Playboy's Book of Lingerie** (Sep 1993)..... Herself
- • 15—Side of right breast.

**Playboy's Book of Lingerie** (Nov 1993).....Herself
- ••• 12-13—Left breast, buns and lower frontal nudity.
- ••• 18—Full frontal nudity.
- •• 74—Left breast and lower frontal nudity.

**Playboy's Nudes** (Dec 1993)...............Herself
- ••• 97—Full frontal nudity.

**Playboy's Book of Lingerie** (Jan 1994)......Herself
- ••• 24—Right breast and lower frontal nudity.

**Playboy's Book of Lingerie** (Mar 1994)......Herself
- • 52—Left breast.
- • 58-59—Buns.

**Playboy's Book of Lingerie** (May 1994).....Herself
- ••• 102-103—Breasts.

**Playboy's Girls of Summer '94** (Jul 1994)....Herself
- ••• 32—Full frontal nudity.
- ••• 66-67—Breasts.
- ••• 77—Full frontal nudity.

**Playboy's Book of Lingerie** (Sep 1994)......Herself
- ••• 75—Full frontal nudity.

# Capra, Jordana

*Films:*

Pass the Ammo (1988)................Mary Trenton
After Midnight (1989)..................... Vanessa
Hired to Kill (1990)......................Joanna
- 0:18—Very briefly in black bra, putting on lipstick.
- 0:19—In black bra, talking to Sivi, in front of the mirror.

**Watch It** (1993)....................... Call Girl
- • 1:26—Brief partial buns, while making love with Michael in coat room during concert.

# Capri, Ahna

*Films:*

Company of Killers (1970)......... Mary Jane Smythe
Darker than Amber (1970).................... Del
**Payday** (1972)....................... Mayleen
- • 0:20—Left breast in bed sleeping, then right breast with Rip Torn.
- ••• 0:21—Breasts sitting up in bed smoking a cigarette and talking to Torn. Long scene.

**Enter the Dragon** (1973).................. Tania
- • 0:47—Very brief left breast three times in open blouse in bed with John Saxon.

**The Specialist** (1975)...............Londa Wyeth
- ••• 0:10—Breasts, while in bed, talking on the phone.
- ••• 0:28—Breasts on couch, posing for Bert.
- •• 1:09—Breasts, sitting up in bed and putting robe on.

# • Capshaw, Kate

Wife of director Steven Spielberg.

*Films:*

**A Little Sex** (1982)....................Katherine
- • 0:10—Brief buns under T-shirt, when running away from table after stuffing a pancake down Tim Matheson's underwear.
- • 0:29—Breasts, while sitting on bed next to Matheson. Seen through out-of-focus candles.

Best Defense (1984) ..................... Laura
Dreamscape (1984). ................... Jane DeVries
Indiana Jones and the Temple of Doom (1984)
.............................. Willie Scott
Windy City (1984). ...................... Emily
Power (1986) .................. Syndey Betterman
SpaceCamp (1986). ..................... Andie
Black Rain (1989) ....................... Joyce
Love at Large (1990). ............... Ellen McGraw
My Heroes Have Always Been Cowboys (1991)
............................ Jolie Meadows
*Made for Cable Movies:*
Next Door (1994; Showtime) ........... Karen Coler
*Made for TV Movies:*
Code Name: Dancer (1987) ......... Anne Goodwin
*TV:*
Black Tie Affair (1993) ..................... Margo

## Cara, Irene

*Films:*
Aaron Loves Angela (1975) ............... Angela
Sparkle (1976) ......................... Sparkle
**Fame** (1980) ........................... Coco
   1:16—In leotard, dancing and talking to Hillary.
   • 1:57—Brief breasts during "audition" on a B&W TV
   monitor.
Killing 'Em Softly (1981) ................ Jane Flores
D.C. Cab (1983) ........................ Herself
City Heat (1984) ....................... Ginny Lee
**Certain Fury** (1985) ..................... Tracy
   0:32—Getting undressed to take a shower. Very brief
   side views of left breast.
   0:35—Very brief breasts in shower after Tatum
   O'Neal turns on the kitchen faucet. Hard to see because of the shower door.
   •• 0:36—Frontal nudity and side view of buns, behind
   shower door while Sniffer comes into the bathroom.
   •• 0:39—Breasts several times when Sniffer tries to rape
   her and she fights back.
   • 0:41—Buns, kneeling on floor. Overhead view.
Caged in Paradiso (1989) ..................... Eva
   In two piece swimsuit a lot.
*Miniseries:*
Roots: The Next Generation (1979)
..................... Bertha Palmer Haley

## Cardan, Christina

*Films:*
Chained Heat (1983; U.S./German) ........ Miss King
**Glitch** (1988). ........................ Non SAG
   • 0:47—Brief breasts in spa taking off her swimsuit
   top.

## Cardone, Nathalie

*Films:*
Drole D'Endroit Pour Une Recontre (1988; French)
.............................. Sylvie
**The Little Thief** (1989; French). ......... Mauricette
   *a.k.a. La Petite Voleuse*
   •• 1:19—Breasts in convent arguing with a nun, then
   getting a shot.

## Carides, Gia

*Films:*
**Bliss** (1985; Australian) .................. Lucy Joy
   • 1:25—Brief breasts during nightmare. Cockroaches
   crawl out of cut between her breasts. Pretty gross.
   (The cockroaches—not her.)
Backlash (1986; Australian) ............. Nikki Iceton
Strictly Ballroom (1993; Australian) .......... Liz Holt
*TV:*
Ultraman: Towards the Future (1990; Australian/
   Japanese) ........................... Jean Echo

## Carl, Kitty

*Films:*
Your Three Minutes Are Up (1973). ........... Susan
**The Centerfold Girls** (1974). ............... Sandi
   •• 0:45—Breasts taking off her top while sitting on the
   bed with Perry.
   0:51—Breasts on the beach, dead. Long shot, hard
   to see.
Kitty Can't Help It (1975). .................... n.a.
Carhops (1980) ........................... n.a.

## Carlisi, Olimpia

*Films:*
**Catch-22** (1970). ..................... Luciana
   • 1:04—Breasts lying in bed talking with Alan Arkin.
Casanova (1976; Italian). ................. Isabella
The Tragedy of a Ridiculous Man (1981; Italian)
............................. Chiromat
Rendez-Vous (1986; French). ................ n.a.

## Carlisle, Anne

*Films:*
Liquid Sky (1984). ............... Margaret/Jimmy
**Perfect Strangers** (1984) .................. Sally
   • 0:34—Left breast, while making love in bed with
   Johnny.
Desperately Seeking Susan (1985) .......... Victoria
Suicide Club (1988) .................... Catherine
*Magazines:*
**Playboy** (Sep 1984) ................. Cult Queen
   •• 80-85—Nude.
**Playboy** (Dec 1984) ............. Sex Stars of 1984
   • 203—Right breast and lower frontal nudity, stand-
   ing in bra, garter belt and stockings.

# Carlson, Karen

*Films:*
Shame, Shame, Everybody Knows Her Name (1969)
. . . . . . . . . . . . . . . . . . . . . . . . . . . . Susan Barton
**The Student Nurses** (1970) . . . . . . . . . . . . . . . Phred
*a.k.a. Young LA Nurses*
- 0:08—Breasts in bed with the wrong guy.
  0:19—In bra, on sofa with Dr. Jim Casper.
- ••• 0:50—In bed with Jim, breasts and buns getting out, then breasts sitting in chair. Long scene.
- 1:02—Brief breasts in bed.
The Candidate (1972) . . . . . . . . . . . . . . . Nancy McKay
Black Oak Conspiracy (1977) . . . . . . . . . . . . . . . Lucy
Matilda (1978) . . . . . . . . . . . . . . . . . . . Kathleen Smith
The Octagon (1980) . . . . . . . . . . . . . . . . . . . . Justine
Fleshburn (1984) . . . . . . . . . . . . . . . . . . Shirley Pinter
*TV:*
Dallas (1987) . . . . . . . . . . . . . . . . . . . . Mrs. Scottfield

# • Carlson, Linda

*Films:*
Honey, I Blew Up the Kid (1992) . . . . . . Nosey Neighbor
**The Pickle** (1992) . . . . . . . . . . . . . . . . . . . Bernadette
- •• 0:12—In white bra and panties under stockings, after taking off her clothes in hotel room in front of Danny Aiello, then breasts.
The Beverly Hillbillies (1993) . . . . . . . . . . . . . Aunt Pearl
*TV:*
Westside Medical (1977) . . . . . . . . . . . Dr. Janet Cottrell
Kaz (1978-79) . . . . . . . . . . . . . . . . . . . Katie McKenna
Newhart (1984-88) . . . . . . . . . . . . . . . . . . . Bev Dutton

# Carlton, Hope Marie

*Films:*
**Hard Ticket to Hawaii** (1987) . . . . . . . . . . . . . Taryn
- •• 0:07—Breasts taking a shower outside while talking to Dona Speir.
- ••• 0:23—Breasts in the spa with Speir looking at diamonds they found.
- ••• 0:40—Breasts and buns on the beach making love with her boyfriend, Jimmy John.
- •• 1:33—Breasts during the end credits.
**A Nightmare on Elm Street 4: The Dream Master** (1988) . . . . . . . . . . . . . . . . . . . . . . . . Pin-Up Girl
- 0:21—Brief breasts swimming in a waterbed.
**Slaughterhouse Rock** (1988) . . . . . . . . Krista Halpern
- 0:09—Brief right breast, taking off her top in bedroom with her boyfriend.
- •• 0:49—Breasts, getting raped by Richard as he turns into a monster.
**Terminal Exposure** (1988) . . . . . . . . . . . . . . . Christie
- ••• 1:11—Breasts in bathtub licking ice cream off a guy.
How I Got Into College (1989) . . . . Game Show Hostess
**Picasso Trigger** (1989) . . . . . . . . . . . . . . . . . . Taryn
  0:17—In white lingerie on boat with Dona Speir.
- ••• 0:56—Breasts and buns in spa with a guy.
**Savage Beach** (1989) . . . . . . . . . . . . . . . . . . . Taryn
  0:06—Almost breasts in spa with the three other women.

- 0:32—Breasts changing clothes in airplane with Dona Speir.
- •• 0:48—Nude, going for a swim on the beach with Speir.
**Round Numbers** (1990) . . . . . . . . . . . . . . . . . Mitzi
- 0:39—Left breast, twice, while turning around in steam room in Kate Mulgrew's imagination.
Side Out (1990) . . . . . . . . . . . . . . . . . . . . . . . . Vanna
Slumber Party Massacre 3 (1990) . . . . . . . . . . . . Janine
Bloodmatch (1991) . . . . . . . . . . . . . . . . Connie Angel
Ghoulies III, Ghoulies Go To College (1991) . . . . . . . n.a.
*Miniseries:*
Stephen King's "The Stand" (1994) . . . . . Sally Campion
*Video Tapes:*
**Playboy Video Magazine, Volume 9** . . . . . Playmate
Playmate Playoffs . . . . . . . . . . . . . . . . . . . . . Playmate
**Playboy Video Centerfold: Teri Weigel** (1986)
. . . . . . . . . . . . . . . . . . . . . . . . . . . . . . . Playmate
**Sexy Lingerie** (1988) . . . . . . . . . . . . . . . . . . Model
**Playmates at Play** (1990) . . . . . . . . . Flights of Fancy
*Magazines:*
**Playboy** (Jul 1985) . . . . . . . . . . . . . . . . . . . Playmate
**Playboy's Girls of Summer '86** (Aug 1986). . . Herself
- 61—Most of breasts in open white blouse.
- ••• 99—Breasts.
**Playboy's 1987 Book of Lingerie** (Mar 1987)
. . . . . . . . . . . . . . . . . . . . . . . . . . . . . . . . . Herself
- •• 14—Side of left breast and buns.
- ••• 44—Breasts.
- ••• 86—Breasts.
- ••• 102-103—Full frontal nudity.
- ••• 104—Full frontal nudity.
**Playboy's Book of Lingerie** (Mar 1991) . . . . . Herself
- 34—Right breast.
**Playboy's Book of Lingerie** (Sep 1991) . . . . . Herself
- 8—Side of right breast.
**Playboy's Bathing Beauties** (Apr 1992). . . . . Herself
- ••• 37—Breasts.
**Playboy's Book of Lingerie** (Jul 1992) . . . . . . Herself
- •• 32-33—Lower nudity.
**Playboy's Calendar Playmates** (Nov 1992). . . Herself
- ••• 42—Full frontal nudity.
**Playboy's Girls of Summer '93** (Jun 1993) . . . Herself
- ••• 29—Full frontal nudity.
**Playboy's Book of Lingerie** (Jan 1994) . . . . . . Herself
- ••• 89—Full frontal nudity.

# Carmack, Cody

*Films:*
**Affairs of the Heart** (1992) . . . . . . . . . . . . . . . Itchy
- ••• 0:45—Breasts taking off her bikini top with her husband.
*Magazines:*
**Penthouse** (May 1981) . . . . . . . . . . . . . . . . . . . Pet

## Carney, Bridget

*Films:*

**Hard to Die** (1990) . . . . . . . . . . . . . . . Shayne Hobbie
*a.k.a. Tower of Terror*
- ••• 0:24—Breasts and buns while taking a shower. Long scene.

**Sorority House Massacre 2** (1990) . . . . . . . . . Candy
- ••• 0:40—Breasts and buns in G-string, dancing in club.

Night of the Warrior (1991) . . . . . . . . . . . . . . . Sarah
Martial Law II: Undercover (1992) . . . . . . . Flash Dancer
*Video Tapes:*

**Scream Queen Hot Tub Party** (1991) . . . . . . Shayne
- ••• 0:17—Breasts and buns in shower from *Hard to Die.*

## Carnon, Angela

*Films:*

Guess What Happened to Count Dracula (1970)
. . . . . . . . . . . . . . . . . . . . . . . . . . . . . . . . . . Nurse
Innocent Sally (1973) . . . . . . . . . . . . . . . . . . . . .n.a.
*a.k.a. The Dirty Mind of Young Sally*

**Video Vixens** (1973) . . . . . . . . . . . . . . . Mrs. Gordon
- •• 1:13—Full frontal nudity making love with Mr. Gordon in bed in various positions. Shot at fast speed.

**Alice Goodbody** (1975) . . . . . . . . . . . Harmonica Girl
- ••• 1:07—Buns and lower frontal nudity playing a harmonica without her mouth. (Never see her face.)
- • 1:20—Buns, during end credits.

Young and Wild (1975) . . . . . . . . . . . . . . . . . . . . .n.a.

## Carol, Jean

*a.k.a. Jeannie Daly.*
*Films:*

**Payback** (1988) . . . . . . . . . . . . . . . . . . . Donna Nathan
- ••• 0:24—Breasts opening her pink robe for Jason while reclining on couch.

*TV:*

The Guiding Light . . . . . . . . . . . . . . . . . Nadine Cooper

## Carol, Linda

*Films:*

**School Spirit** (1985) . . . . . . . . . . . . . . . . . . . Hogette
**Reform School Girls** (1986) . . . . . . . Jennifer Williams
- •• 0:05—Nude in the shower.
- • 0:56—Breasts in the back of a truck with Norton.
- ••• 1:13—Breasts getting hosed down by Edna.

Back to the Beach (1987) . . . . . . . . . . . . . . Bridgette
Future Hunters (1987) . . . . . . . . . . . . . . . . . . . . .n.a.
No Man's Land (1988) . . . . . . . . . . . . . . . Party Girl
**Carnal Crimes** (1991) . . . . . . . . . . . . . . . . . . . Elise
- • 0:01—Very brief left breast, while rolling over in bed.
- • 0:05—In wet lingerie and very brief side view of right breast in shower fantasy.
- • 0:07—Breasts in B&W photo collage.
- • 0:09—Full frontal nudity under sheer nightie, trying to get Stanley into bed.
- • 0:11—Breasts in B&W photo again.
- • 0:24—Brief right breast outside window opening her top while watching Renny & Mia make out.

- • 0:26—Brief upper half of right breast when bum molests her.
- ••• 0:28—Breasts posing for Renny with Mia.
- ••• 0:29—Full frontal nudity making love with Renny and Mia.
- • 0:30—Brief buns, sleeping in bed.
- ••• 0:38—Breasts making love with the baker. Long scene.
- • 0:49—Breasts in B&W photo again.
- • 1:02—Brief side view of right breast in gaping blouse.
- • 1:33—Side view of buns in dominatrix outfit.

**Fear of Scandal** (1992; Italian) . . . . . . . . . . . . . . Anna
- • 0:21—Brief left breast, while making love with a guy in bed.
- •• 0:42—Left breast, while making love in bed.
- •• 0:43—Breasts, while covering herself with the bed covers.

*Made for Cable Movies:*

**Prey of the Chameleon** (1992; Showtime) . . . . Nurse
- • 0:00—Breasts several times, making love with a guy in restroom. Dark.
- 0:08—Buns, of dead body, lying on ground. Don't see face.

*Video Tapes:*

**Inside Out 2** (1992) . . . . The Hitchhiker/The Hitchhiker
(Unrated version reviewed.)
- ••• 1:17—Breasts undressing in room, while a guy watches from across the way. Long scene. B&W.

## • Caron, Leslie

*Films:*

Daddy Long Legs (1955) . . . . . . . . . . . . . . . . . . . Julie
The Glass Slipper (1955) . . . . . . . . . . . . . . . . . . . Ella
Gigi (1958) . . . . . . . . . . . . . . . . . . . . . . . . . . . . . Gigi
Fanny (1961) . . . . . . . . . . . . . . . . . . . . . . . . . . Fanny
Father Goose (1964) . . . . . . . . . . . . Catherine Freneau
Is Paris Burning? (1966; U.S./French) . . . . . . . Francoise
Promise Her Anything (1966; British) . . . Michele O'Brien
**The Head of the Family** (1967; Italian/French)
. . . . . . . . . . . . . . . . . . . . . . . . . . . . . . . . . . . Paola
- • 0:22—Very brief upper half of left breast while sitting at drafting table and breast feeding her baby.

Madron (1970; U.S./Israeli) . . . . . . . . . . . . Sister Mary
Nicole (1972) . . . . . . . . . . . . . . . . . . . . . . . . . Nicole
*a.k.a. The Widow's Revenge*
The Man Who Loved Women (1977; French) . . . . . Vera
Valentino (1977; British) . . . . . . . . . . . . . . . Nazimova
Goldengirl (1979) . . . . . . . . . . . . . . . . . . . . . Dr. Lee
Dangerous Moves (1985; Swiss) . . . . . . Henia Liebskind
Damage (1992; French/British) . . . . . Elizabeth Prideaux
(Unrated Director's cut reviewed.)
*Miniseries:*
Master of the Game (1984) . . . . . . . . . . . . . . Solange
*Made for TV Movies:*
QB VII (1974) . . . . . . . . . . . . . . . . . . . . . . . . . . .n.a.

## Carothers, Veronica

Films:
Mankillers (1987) . . . . . . . . . . . . . . . . . .Shannon Smith
Phoenix the Warrior (1988). . . . . . . . . . . . . . . . . . .Suga
**Fatal Skies** (1989). . . . . . . . . . . . . . . . . . . . . . . . Toni
•• 0:31—Buns, while putting on swimsuit bottom.
•• 0:32—Breasts, while putting on swimsuit top.
Kinjite (1989) . . . . . . . . . . . . . . . . . . . . Blonde Hostess
Vice Academy, Part 3 (1991) . . . . . . . . . . . . . . . Loretta
**Mind, Body & Soul** (1992). . . . . . . . . . . Sacrifice Girl
••• 0:02—Breasts when her dress is ripped open during
occult ceremony while tied by her wrists.
•• 0:26—Left breast several times and very, very brief
right breast in black outfit (her face is covered with
a hood) during occult ceremony.
Good Girls Don't (1993) . . . . . . . . . . . . . Bimbo Jeannie
Magazines:
Playboy (Jul 1993). . . . . . . . . . . . . . . . . . . . .Grapevine

## Carpenter, Linda

a.k.a. Playboy Playmate Linda Beatty.
Films:
**Apocalypse Now** (1979). . . . . . . . . . . . . . . . Playmate
• 1:01—Breasts in centerfold photo, hung up for dis-
play. Long shot.
**A Different Story** (1979). . . . . . . . . . . . . . . Chastity
(R-rated version reviewed.)
• 1:33—Very brief breasts in shower, shutting the
door when Meg Foster discovers her with Perry
King.
Magazines:
**Playboy** (Aug 1976) . . . . . . . . . . . . . . . . . Playmate
••• 92-101—Nude.
**Playboy** (Jan 1977) . . . . . . . . . . . . . .Playmate Review
••• 162—Full frontal nudity.

## Carr, Judy

a.k.a. Adult film actress Juliet Anderson.
Films:
**It's Called Murder Baby** (1982) . . . . . . . .Adrian Ross
(R-rated version of the adult film Dixie Ray, Hollywood
Star.)
• 1:21—Brief breasts, sitting up on bed in back-
ground.

## Carr, Laurie Ann

Films:
Mortuary Academy (1988) . . . . . . . . . . . . . . . . . Nurse
Video Tapes:
**Wet and Wild** (1989). . . . . . . . . . . . . . . . . . . .Model
Magazines:
**Playboy** (Dec 1986). . . . . . . . . . . . . . . . . . Playmate
**Playboy's Book of Lingerie** (Jan 1991) . . . . . . Herself
••• 16—Full frontal nudity.
• 108—Partial right breast and partial lower frontal
nudity.
**Playboy's Book of Lingerie** (Mar 1991) . . . . . Herself
•• 27—Breasts.
••• 36-37—Breasts.

• 56—Left breast.
**Playboy's Book of Lingerie** (Jul 1991) . . . . . . .Herself
••• 79—Breasts.
**Playboy's Book of Lingerie** (May 1992) . . . . .Herself
• 11—Partial left breast.
**Playboy's Book of Lingerie** (Nov 1992) . . . . .Herself
••• 73—Breasts.
**Playboy's Blondes, Brunettes & Redheads**
(Sep 1993). . . . . . . . . . . . . . . . . . . . . . . . .Herself
•• 78—Right breast.
**Playboy's Book of Lingerie** (Sep 1993) . . . . . .Herself
• 67—Lower frontal nudity.
**Playboy's Book of Lingerie** (Nov 1993) . . . . .Herself
•• 77—Buns.
**Playboy's Nudes** (Dec 1993) . . . . . . . . . . . . . .Herself
• 47—Lower frontal nudity.
**Playboy's Book of Lingerie** (Jan 1994) . . . . . .Herself
• 10—Lower frontal nudity.
**Playboy's Book of Lingerie** (Sep 1994) . . . . . .Herself
• 43—Lower frontal nudity.

## Carr, Tanya

Video Tapes:
**Hot Body International: #2 Miss Puerto Vallarta**
(1990) . . . . . . . . . . . . . . . . . . . . . . . . . . .Contestant
• 0:15—Very, very brief breasts, while flashing.
•• 0:24—Buns, in two piece swimsuit, then breasts
wearing pasties.
•• 0:56—Wearing pasties.
**Hot Body International: #4 Spring Break** (1992)
. . . . . . . . . . . . . . . . . . . . . . . . . . . . . . . .Contestant
0:08—Dancing in two piece swimsuit on stage.
0:15—4th place winner.
••• 0:42—Breasts popping out of wet T-shirt, quite a
few times. Buns in G-string.
0:58—Brief breasts several times winning 3rd place
in wet T-shirt contest.
**Hot Body: The Best of Hot Body** (1994). . . . .Herself
••• 0:42—Buns in swimsuits. Breasts while wearing pasties.

## Carrera, Barbara

Films:
**Embryo** (1976). . . . . . . . . . . . . . . . . . . . . . . Victoria
0:36—Almost breasts meeting Rock Hudson for the
first time. Hair covers breasts.
1:09—In see through top in bedroom with Hudson.
•• 1:10—Brief buns and breasts in the mirror after making love with Hudson.
• 1:11—Left breast sticking out of bathrobe.
The Island of Dr. Moreau (1977) . . . . . . . . . . . . .Maria
When Time Ran Out! (1980) . . . . . . . . . . . . . . . .Iolani
Condorman (1981) . . . . . . . . . . . . . . . . . . . . . .Natalia
**I, the Jury** (1982). . . . . . . . . . . .Dr. Charolette Bennett
••• 1:02—Nude on bed making love with Armand As-
sante. Very sexy.
• 1:45—Brief breasts, while in hallway kissing Assante.
• 1:46—Brief left breast, while falling to the floor.
Breasts while lying on the floor wounded.

Lone Wolf McQuade (1983) . . . . . . . . . . . . . . . . . . Lola
Never Say Never Again (1983) . . . . . . . . . Fatima Blush
Wild Geese II (1985; British) . . . . . . . . . . . . . . . Kathy
The Underachievers (1987) . . . . . . . . . . . . . . Katherine
Love at Stake (1988) . . . . . . . . . . . . . . . . . Faith Stewart
Loverboy (1989) . . . . . . . . . . . . . . . . . . . . Alex Barnett
**Wicked Stepmother** (1989) . . . . . . . . . . . . . Priscilla
- 1:14—Very, very brief upper half of right breast peeking out of the top of her dress when she flips her head back while seducing Steve.
**Point of Impact** (1993) . . . . . . . . . . . . . . . . . . . . Eva
- 0:39—In wet white swimsuit, after getting out of swimming pool.
- 0:40—Very brief breasts, while swimming under water past underwater window.
  0:49—In black lingerie, taking off clothes on bed with Michael Paré.
- •• 0:51—Close up of left breast, while making love with Paré.
- 0:53—Brief left breast, after getting out of bed.
- ••• 0:59—Breasts and buns in T-back, while swimming under water in pool.
- •• 1:00—Breasts, while making love outside with Paré.
- •• 1:02—Breasts in shower with Paré and on bed in wet sheet.

*Miniseries:*
Masada (1981) . . . . . . . . . . . . . . . . . . . . . . . . . . Sheva
*TV:*
Centennial (1978-79) . . . . . . . . . . . . . . . . . . Clay Basket
Dallas (1985-89) . . . . . . . . . . . . . . . . . . . . Angelica Nero
*Video Tapes:*
**Playboy Video Magazine, Volume 1** (1982)
. . . . . . . . . . . . . . . . . . . . . . . . . . . . . . . . . . . . . Herself
- •• 0:01—Nude in still photos. Nude in scenes from *I, the Jury.*
- •• 0:30—Breasts in still photos.
- ••• 0:32—Nude in scenes from *I, the Jury.*
*Magazines:*
**Playboy** (Nov 1975) . . . . . . . . . . . Sex in Cinema 1975
- •• 131—Right breast in still photo from *Embryo.*
**Playboy** (Dec 1976) . . . . . . . . . . . . . Sex Stars of 1976
- 189—Full frontal nudity under sheer dress.
**Playboy** (Jul 1977) . . . . . . . . . . . . . . . . Acting Beastly
- ••• 93-97—Breasts and buns in panties.
**Playboy** (Dec 1977) . . . . . . . . . . . . . Sex Stars of 1977
- •• 219—Left breast.
**Playboy** (Apr 1980) . . . . . . . . . . . . . . . . . . . Grapevine
- 294—Breasts under wet, white blouse in B&W photo.
**Playboy** (Mar 1982) . . . . . . . . . . . . . . . . . Aye, Barbara
- ••• 148-155—Nude, also photos from *I, the Jury.*
**Playboy** (Sep 1987) . . . . . . . . . 25 Years of James Bond
- •• 129—Breasts.

## Carrere, Tia
*Films:*
Aloha Summer (1988) . . . . . . . . . . . . . . . . . Lani Kepoo
**Fatal Mission** (1990) . . . . . . . . . . . . . . . . . Mai Chang
- 0:22—Side view of right breast while changing tops. Dark.
Harley Davidson and The Marlboro Man (1991)
. . . . . . . . . . . . . . . . . . . . . . . . . . . . . . . . . . . . Kimiko
Little Sister (1991) . . . . . . . . . . . . . . . . . . . . . Adrienne
**Showdown in Little Tokyo** (1991) . . . . . . . . Minako
- 0:50—Buns and side view of left breast, taking off robe and getting into outdoor tub with Dolph Lundgren. Don't see her face.
- 0:52—Left breast, while making love in bed with Lundgren. Don't see her face again.
Wayne's World (1992) . . . . . . . . . . . . . . . . . Cassandra
Quick (1993) . . . . . . . . . . . . . . . . . . . . Janet Sakamoto
Rising Sun (1993) . . . . . . . . . . . . . . . . . . Jingo Asakuma
Wayne's World 2 (1993) . . . . . . . . . . . . . . . Cassandra
True Lies (1994) . . . . . . . . . . . . . . . . . . . . Juno Skinner
*Made for Cable Movies:*
**Intimate Strangers** (1991; Showtime) . . . . . . . . Mino
- 0:34—In black lingerie in Nick's apartment. Very brief side of right breast in bed with him.
*Made for Cable TV:*
Tales From the Crypt: On a Dead Man's Chest (1992; HBO) . . . . . . . . . . . . . . . . . . . . . . . . . Scarlett
*TV:*
General Hospital (1986-87) . . . . . . . . . . . . . Jade Sung
*Music Videos:*
Ballroom Blitz/Wayne's World (1992) . . . . . . . . . Herself

## Carrico, Monica
*Films:*
**Lucky 13** (1984) . . . . . . . . . . . . . . . Charlene Andrews
*a.k.a. Running Hot*
*a.k.a. Highway to Hell*
  0:09—Lying on bed in white bra and open dress top.
  0:18—Walking around in panties and a blouse.
- •• 0:49—Breasts sitting on a rock after skinny dipping with Eric Stoltz.
- •• 0:51—Breasts and buns after getting out of water and picking up clothes.
- •• 1:03—Breasts in bed making love with Stoltz.
- ••• 1:15—Breasts lying in bed with Stoltz.
Guilty by Suspicion (1991) . . . . . . . . . . . . . Nelly Lesser

## Carrillo, Elpidia
*Films:*
**The Border** (1982) . . . . . . . . . . . . . . . . . . . . . . . Maria
- 1:19—Half of right breast and half of left breast, after opening her blouse in shack with Jack Nicholson.
**Beyond the Limit** (1983) . . . . . . . . . . . . . . . . . Clara
- •• 0:31—Breasts making love with Richard Gere. Long scene.
- •• 1:08—Breasts talking to Gere. Another long scene.
Under Fire (1983) . . . . . . . . . . . . . . . . Sandanista (Leon)
Let's Get Harry (1986) . . . . . . . . . . . . . . . . . . Veronica

**Salvador** (1986) . . . . . . . . . . . . . . . . . . . . . . Maria
  • 0:21—Very brief right breast, lying in a hammock
    with James Woods.
Predator (1987) . . . . . . . . . . . . . . . . . . . . . . .Anna
The Assassin (1989). . . . . . . . . . . . . . . . . . . . Elena
Predator 2 (1990) . . . . . . . . . . . . . . . . . . . . .Anna
*Made for TV Movies:*
Dangerous Passion (1990). . . . . . . . . . . . . . . Angela

# Carroll, Jill
*Films:*
The Vals (1982). . . . . . . . . . . . . . . . . . . . . . . . . Sam
Heart Like a Wheel (1983). . . . . . . . . . . John's Girlfriend
The Man Who Loved Women (1983)
. . . . . . . . . . . . . . . . . . . . . . . . . . Sue the Baby Sitter
Psycho II (1983) . . . . . . . . . . . . . . . . . . . . . . . . Kim
Something Wicked this Way Comes (1983)
. . . . . . . . . . . . . . . . . . . . . . . . . . . . . Teenage Girl
Funland (1987) . . . . . . . . . . . . . . . . . . Denise Wilson
Snowballing (1987). . . . . . . . . . . . . . . . . . . . Cheryl
**The Unholy** (1988) . . . . . . . . . . . . . . . . . . . . Millie
  • 1:10—Very brief upper half of left breast, while talk-
    ing in the courtyard with Ben Cross.
*Made for TV Movies:*
American Harvest (1987). . . . . . . . . . . Calla Bergstrom

# Carroll, Regina
*Films:*
Brain of Blood (1971; Philippines) . . . . . . . . . . . . . .n.a.
Blazing Stewardesses (1975) . . . . . . . . . . . . . . . .n.a.
**Jessi's Girls** (1976) . . . . . . . . . . . . . . . . . . . . Claire
  •• 0:58—Breasts and buns in hay with Indian guy.
    Don't see her face.

# Carson, Rachelle
*Films:*
**Kill Crazy** (1989). . . . . . . . . . . . . . . . . . . . . Rachel
  •• 0:39—Breasts taking off top to go skinny dipping
    with Libby.
Eating (1990) . . . . . . . . . . . . . . . . . . . . . . . Cathy

# Carter, Lynda
Miss World U.S.A. 1973.
*Films:*
**Bobbie Jo and the Outlaw** (1976) . . Bobbie Jo Baker
  0:10—Partial side of left breast, changing blouses in
    her bedroom.
  ••• 0:17—Left breast, several times, while making love
    with Marjoe Gortner.
  •• 0:27—Brief left breast, making love with Gortner
    again at night.
  • 0:31—Very brief left breast, then very brief breasts in
    pond with Gortner experimenting with mushrooms.
I Posed for Playboy (1991) . . . . . . . Meredith Lanahan
  *a.k.a. Posing: Inspired by Three Real Stories*
  (Shown on network TV without the nudity.)
*Made for TV Movies:*
Rita Hayworth: The Love Goddess (1983)
. . . . . . . . . . . . . . . . . . . . . . . . . . .Rita Hayworth

Mickey Spillane's Mike Hammer: Murder Takes All
  (1989) . . . . . . . . . . . . . . . . . . . . . . . .Helen Durant
Danielle Steel's "Daddy" (1991). . . . Charlotte Sampson
*TV:*
Wonder Woman (1976-79)
. . . . . . . . . . . Yeoman Diana Prince/Wonder Woman
Partners in Crime (1984) . . . . . . . . . . Carole Stanwyck
Hawkeye (1994- ). . . . . . . . . . . . . . . . Elizabeth Shields

# • Cartlidge, Katrin
*Films:*
Sacred Hearts (1984; British) . . . . . . . . . . . . . . Doris
**Naked** (1993; British) . . . . . . . . . . . . . . . . . .Sophie
  •• 0:16—Breasts, while making love around the house
    with Johnny.
  •• 1:17—In black bra and panties in bed with a guy.
    Breasts, while putting on her dress while sitting on
    bed.
  • 1:23—Brief right breast in gaping dress, when get-
    ting up off the floor.
*Made for Cable Movies:*
Nobody's Children (1994; USA) . . . . . . . . . . . . .Viorica
*Magazines:*
**Playboy** (Nov 1994) . . . . . . . . . . Sex in Cinema 1994
  • 143—Right breast in still from *Naked*.

# Cartwright, Nancy
*Films:*
**Flesh + Blood** (1985) . . . . . . . . . . . . . . . . . Kathleen
  • 0:28—Brief breasts showing Jennifer Jason Leigh
    how to make love. Long shot.
Going Undercover (1988; British) . . . . . . . . Stephanie

# Cartwright, Veronica
Sister of actress Angela Cartwright.
*Films:*
The Birds (1963) . . . . . . . . . . . . . . . . Cathy Brenner
**Inserts** (1976). . . . . . . . . . . . . . . . . . . . . Harlene
  •• 0:16—Breasts sitting on bed with Richard Dreyfuss.
  ••• 0:31—Nude on bed with Stephen Davies making a
    porno movie for Dreyfuss. Long scene.
Goin' South (1978) . . . . . . . . . . . . . . . . . . Hermine
Invasion of the Body Snatchers (1978) . . . Nancy Bellicec
Alien (1979). . . . . . . . . . . . . . . . . . . . . . . .Lambert
Nightmares (1983) . . . . . . . . . . . . . . . . . . . .Claire
The Right Stuff (1983) . . . . . . . . . . . . . . Betty Grissom
Flight of the Navigator (1986) . . . . . . . . Helen Freeman
**My Man Adam** (1986). . . . . . . . . . . . . . .Elaine Swit
  • 1:09—Side view of right breast lying on tanning ta-
    ble when Adam steals her car keys. Long shot, hard
    to see.
Wisdom (1986) . . . . . . . . . . . . . . . .Samantha Wisdom
The Witches of Eastwick (1987) . . . . . . . Felicia Alden
**Valentino Returns** (1988). . . . . . . . . . . . .Pat Gibbs
  ••• 0:33—Breasts sitting in bed with Frederic Forrest.
    Fairly long scene.
False Identity (1990) . . . . . . . . . . . . . . . . . . . n.a.
Man Trouble (1992). . . . . . . . . . . . . . Helen Dextra

**Made for Cable Movies:**
Hitler's Daughter (1990) . . . . . . . . . . . . . . . . . . . .n.a.
Dead In the Water (1991) . . . . . . . . . . . Victoria Haines
**Made for TV Movies:**
It's Nothing Personal (1993) . . . . . . . . . . . . . . .Barbara
**TV:**
Daniel Boone (1964-66) . . . . . . . . . . . . . Jenima Boone

## Case, Catherine
**Films:**
**The Jigsaw Murders** (1988). . . . . . . . . . . . Stripper #2
• 0:27—Brief breasts in black peek-a-boo bra posing
for photographer.
Dr. Caligari (1989) . . . . . . Patient with Extra Hormones
Scanner Cop (1993) . . . . . . . .Nurse in Harrigan's Room
**TV:**
NYPD Blue: Jumpin' Jack Fleishman (Jan 18, 1994)
. . . . . . . . . . . . . . . . . . . . . . . Dawn, The Hygienist

## • Caselli, Chiara
**Films:**
**My Own Private Idaho** (1991) . . . . . . . . . . .Carmella
• 1:17—Breasts and buns in very brief, quick cuts with
Keanu Reeves.
Especially on Sunday (1993) . . . . . . . . . . . . . . . .Bride

## Casey, Elana
**Films:**
Candy Stripe Nurses (1974) . . . . . . . . . . . . . . .Zouzou
**The Boob Tube** (1975) . . . . . . . . . . . .Greta Van Allen
• 0:27—Buns, while lying in bed with Dr. Carstens.
••• 0:48—Breasts, taking off her blouse in bed, then
making love with Natalie.
• 1:01—Buns and side of left breast on sofa.
••• 1:11—Nude, opening the door.
••• 1:12—Breasts during orgy on the couch.
• 1:16—Brief breasts in hallway.

## Cash, Rosalind
**Films:**
Klute (1971) . . . . . . . . . . . . . . . . . . . . . . . . . . . Pat
**The Omega Man** (1971). . . . . . . . . . . . . . . . . . .Lisa
•• 1:09—Side view of left breast and upper half of buns
getting out of bed. Buns and breasts sitting in bed.
• 1:21—Side view breasts in beige underwear while
trying on clothes.
Hickey and Boggs (1972) . . . . . . . . . . . . . . . . . Nyona
The New Centurions (1972) . . . . . . . . . . . . . . . Lorrie
The All-American Boy (1973). . . . . . . . . . . . . . .Poppy
Uptown Saturday Night (1974). . . . . . . . Sarah Jackson
Wrong is Right (1982). . . . . . . . . . . . . . . . . Mrs. Ford
The Adventures of Buckaroo Banzai, Across the 8th
Dimension (1984) . . . . . . . . . . . . . . . . . John Emdall
Go Tell It On the Mountain (1984) . . . . . . Aunt Florence
Death Spa (1987) . . . . . . . . . . . . . . . . . . . . .Sgt. Stone

## Casini, Stefania
**Films:**
**1900** (1976; Italian) . . . . . . . . . . . . . . . . Epileptic Girl
(NC-17 version reviewed.)
•• 2:02—Breasts taking off her top, more breasts in bed
with Robert De Niro and Gerard Depardieu.
••• 2:04—Breasts sitting up in bed, then nude while
having a seizure.
Andy Warhol's Bad (1977; Italian) . . . . . . . . . . . . . .PG
Suspiria (1977; Italian) . . . . . . . . . . . . . . . . . . . . .Sara
**The Belly of an Architect** (1987; British/Italian)
. . . . . . . . . . . . . . . . . . . . . . . . . .Flavia Speckler
••• 1:15—Lower frontal nudity, in open robe with Brian
Dennehy. Then buns and breasts on couch. Kind of
a long shot.
**Magazines:**
**Playboy** (Dec 1976) . . . . . . . . . . . . .Sex Stars of 1976
••• 188—Full frontal nudity.

## Cassidy, Joanna
**Films:**
Bank Shot (1974). . . . . . . . . . . . . . . . . . . . . . . . . .El
The Laughing Policeman (1974) . . . . . . . . . . . Monica
The Stepford Wives (1975). . . . . . . . . . . . . . . . . n.a.
Stay Hungry (1976) . . . . . . . . . . . . . . . . . .Joe Mason
The Late Show (1977) . . . . . . . . . . . . . Laura Birdwell
Stunts (1977). . . . . . . . . . . . . . . . . . . . .Patti Johnson
Our Winning Season (1978) . . . . . . . . . . . . . . Sheila
The Glove (1980). . . . . . . . . . . . . . . . Sheila Michaels
**Night Games** (1980) . . . . . . . . . . . . . . . . .Julie Miller
0:44—Buns, skinny dipping in the pool with Cindy
Pickett.
•• 0:45—Brief full frontal nudity sitting up.
**Blade Runner** (1982). . . . . . . . . . . . . . . . . . . Zhora
•• 0:54—Breasts getting dressed after taking a shower
while talking with Harrison Ford.
Under Fire (1983). . . . . . . . . . . . . . . . . . . . . . .Claire
Club Paradise (1986) . . . . . . . . . . . . . . Terry Hamlin
**The Fourth Protocol** (1987; British) . . . . . . . Vassilieva
• 1:39—Brief left breast. She's lying dead in Pierce Bro-
snan's bathtub.
• 1:49—Same thing, different angle.
1969 (1988). . . . . . . . . . . . . . . . . . . . . . . . . . . . Ev
Who Framed Roger Rabbit (1988) . . . . . . . . . . Dolores
May Wine (1990; French). . . . . . . . . . . . . . .Lorraine
Where the Heart Is (1990) . . . . . . . . . . . . Jean McBain
All-American Murder (1991). . . . . . . . . . . Erica Darby
Don't Tell Mom the Babysitter's Dead (1991). . . . . Rose
Lonely Hearts (1991) . . . . . . . . . . . . . . Erin Randall
Landslide (1992) . . . . . . . . . . . . . . . . Lucy Matterson
**Made for Cable Movies:**
Wheels of Terror (1990) . . . . . . . . . . . . . . . . . . .Laura
Perfect Family (1992; USA). . . . . . . . . . . . . . . . Janice
Barbarians at the Gate (1993; HBO) . . . . Linda Robinson
**Miniseries:**
Hollywood Wives (1988) . . . . . . . . . . . . .Maralee Gray
Grass Roots (1992). . . . . . . . . . . . . . . . . . .Ann Heath
**Made for TV Movies:**
Pleasures (1986). . . . . . . . . . . . . . . . . . .Lillian Benton

LIVE! From Death Row (1992) . . . . . . . . . Alana Powers
Taking Back My Life: The Nancy Ziegenmeyer Story
 (1992). . . . . . . . . . . . . . . . . . . . . . Geneva Overholser
The Tommyknockers (1993) . . . . . . . . . . . Sheriff Ruth
TV:
Shields and Yarnell (1977). . . . . . . . . . . . . . . . Regular
The Roller Girls (1978) . . . . . . . . Selma "Books" Cassidy
240 Robert (1979-80) . . . . . Deputy Morgan Wainwright
Buffalo Bill (1983-84) . . . . . . . . . . . . . . . . . . JoJo White
Falcon Crest (1983). . . . . . . . . . . . . . . Katherine Demery
The Family Tree (1983) . . . . . . . . . . . Elizabeth Nichols
Codename: Foxfire (1985) . . . Elizabeth "Foxfire" Towne
Dudley (1993). . . . . . . . . . . . . . . . . . . . . . . . . . . . n.a.
Hotel Malibu (1994- ) . . . . . . . . . . . . . . Ellie Mayfield

## Castel, Martina

Films:
Hollywood Hot Tubs 2—Educating Crystal (1989)
 . . . . . . . . . . . . . . . . . . . . . . . . . . . . . . . . . . Hardie
Death Merchant (1990) . . . . . . . . . . . . . . . . . Martina
Three for One (1991) . . . . . . . . . . . . . . . . . . . . . . n.a.
**Total Exposure** (1991) . . . . . . . . . . . . . . . . . . . . Cissy
 • 1:06—Breasts in spa being questioned by a guy with
  a gun.

## Catala, Muriel

Films:
Verdict (1975; French/Italian) . . . . . . . . Annie Chartier
Magazines:
**Playboy** (Jun 1975) . . . . . . . Sex in Cinema French Style
 •• 88—Buns in small photo.

## Cates, Phoebe

Wife of actor Kevin Kline.
Films:
**Paradise** (1981). . . . . . . . . . . . . . . . . . . . . . . . Sarah
 •• 0:23—Buns and breasts taking a shower in a cave
  while Willie Aames watches.
  0:36—In wet white dress in a pond with Aames.
 • 0:40—Very brief left breast caressing herself while
  looking at her reflection in the water.
 • 0:43—Buns, getting out of bed to check out Aames'
  body while he sleeps.
 • 0:46—Buns, washing herself in a pond at night.
 •• 0:55—Side view of her silhouette at the beach at
  night. Nude swimming in the water, viewed from
  below.
 •• 1:10—Breasts making love with Aames. It looks like
  a body double. Don't see her face.
 ••• 1:12—Nude swimming under water with Aames.
 •• 1:16—Breasts making love with Aames again. It
  looks like the body double again.
**Fast Times at Ridgemont High** (1982)
 . . . . . . . . . . . . . . . . . . . . . . . . . . . . . . Linda Barrett
 ••• 0:50—Breasts getting out of swimming pool during
  Judge Reinhold's fantasy.
Private School (1983) . . . . . . . . . . . . . . . . . . Christine
 1:21—Brief buns lying in sand with Mathew Mod-
  ine.

1:24—Upper half of buns flashing with the rest of
 the girls during graduation ceremony.
Gremlins (1984). . . . . . . . . . . . . . . . . . . . . . . . . Kate
Date with an Angel (1987). . . . . . . . . . . . Patty Winston
Bright Lights, Big City (1988). . . . . . . . . . . . . . Amanda
Heart of Dixie (1989) . . . . . . . . . . . . . . . . . . . . Aiken
Shag (1989). . . . . . . . . . . . . . . . . . . . Carson McBride
Gremlins 2: The New Batch (1990) . . . . . . Kate Beringer
I Love You to Death (1990) . . . . . Uncredited Girl in Bar
Drop Dead Fred (1991) . . . . . . . . . . . . . . . . Elizabeth
Bodies, Rest & Motion (1993) . . . . . . . . . . . . . . Carol
Princess Caraboo (1994) . . . . . . . . . . . . . . . Caraboo
Miniseries:
Lace (1984) . . . . . . . . . . . . . . . . . . . . . . . . . . . . Lili
Lace II (1985). . . . . . . . . . . . . . . . . . . . . . . . . . . Lili

## Cattrall, Kim

Films:
Rosebud (1975) . . . . . . . . . . . . . . . . . . . . . . . . . Joyce
Tribute (1980; Canadian) . . . . . . . . . . . . . Sally Haines
**Porky's** (1981; Canadian) . . . . . . . . . . . . . . Honeywell
 • 0:58—Brief buns, then very brief lower frontal nudi-
  ty after removing skirt to make love in the boy's lock-
  er room.
Ticket to Heaven (1981; Canadian) . . . . . . . . . . Ruthie
**City Limits** (1984) . . . . . . . . . . . . . . . . . . . Wickings
 •• 1:02—Right breast, while sitting up in bed with a
  piece of paper stuck to her.
Police Academy (1984) . . . . . . . . . . . Karen Thompson
Turk 182 (1985) . . . . . . . . . . . . . . . Danny Boudreau
Big Trouble in Little China (1986). . . . . . . . . Gracie Law
Mannequin (1987). . . . . . . . . . . . . . . . . . . . . . Emmy
**Masquerade** (1988). . . . . . . . . . Mrs. Brooke Morrison
 ••• 0:04—Breasts in bed with Rob Lowe.
  0:47—In white teddy after having sex with Lowe.
Midnight Crossing (1988) . . . . . . . . . . . Alexa Schubb
  0:39—In wet white blouse, arguing in the water
  with her husband.
**Smoke Screen** (1988) . . . . . . . . . . . Odessa Muldoon
  0:31—Brief half of right breast sitting in bed with
  sheet pulled up on her.
 •• 1:16—Breasts in bed on top of Gerald.
 ••• 1:17—Breasts lying in bed under Gerald while he
  kisses her breasts.
The Return of the Musketeers (1989) . . . . . . . . . Justine
The Bonfire of the Vanities (1990) . . . . . . . Judy McCoy
Honeymoon Academy (1990) . . . . . . . . . . . . . . Chris
Star Trek VI: The Undiscovered Country (1991)
 . . . . . . . . . . . . . . . . . . . . . . . . . . Lieutenant Valeris
Double Vision (1992; French/Canadian) . . . Lisa/Caroline
**Split Second** (1992) . . . . . . . . . . . . . . . . . . Michelle
 •• 0:43—Breasts in the shower.
 •• 0:45—Breasts in the shower, when Rutger Hauer
  opens the curtains.
Made for Cable Movies:
Miracle in the Wilderness (1991; TNT) . . . . . . . . . Dora
Made for Cable TV:
Dream On: The Homecoming Queen (1994; HBO)
 . . . . . . . . . . . . . . . . . . . . . . . . . . . . . . . . . Jeannie

*Miniseries:*
**The Bastard** (1978) . . . . . . . . . . . . . . . . . . . . . .n.a.
- 2:17—(0:31 into Tape 2) Very brief right breast when the Colonel rips her dress top down. I believe this blooper is even shown on regular broadcast TV!

Scruples (1980) . . . . . . . . . . . . . . . . . . . . . . . . Melanie
Wild Palms (1993) . . . . . . . . . . . . . . . . . . . . .Paige Katz
*Made for TV Movies:*
Sins of the Past (1984) . . . . . . . . . . . . . . . . . . . Paula
Running Delilah (1992) . . . . . . . . . . . . . . . . . . Delilah
*TV:*
Scruples (1980) . . . . . . . . . . . . . . . . . .Melanie Adams
Angel Falls (1993) . . . . . . . . . . . . . . . . . . . . . . Genna
*Magazines:*
**Playboy** (Nov 1987) . . . . . . . . . . Sex in Cinema 1987
- 138—Left breast lying in bed with Rob Lowe.

## • Cavalli, Valeria

*Films:*
A Blade in the Dark (1986; Italian) . . . . . . . . . . . . . .n.a.
**Everybody's Fine** (1991; Italian) . . . . . . . . . . . . Tosca
*a.k.a. Stanno Tutti Bene*
0:49—In white bra and panties during lingerie modeling assignment.
- 0:54—Brief glimpses of left breast, after taking off her dress backstage at fashion show. Left breast, while breast feeding her baby.

## Cayer, Kim

*Films:*
Screwballs (1983) . . . . . . . . . . . . . Brunette Cheerleader
Oddballs (1984) . . . . . . . . . . . . . . . . . . . . . . . . . .n.a.
Loose Screws (1986) . . . . . . . . . . . . . . . . . .Pig Pen Girl
**Graveyard Shift** (1987) . . . . . . . . . . . . . . . . . . . Suzy
•• 0:06—In black bra, then brief left breast when vampire rips the bra off.
- 0:53—Brief breasts in junk yard with garter belt, black panties and stockings.

Psycho Girls (1987) . . . . . . . . . . . . . . . . . . . . . . . .n.a.
Model By Day (1994) . . . . . . . . . . . . . . Young Woman
(Shown on network TV without the nudity.)

## Cayton, Elizabeth

See: Kaitan, Elizabeth.

## Celedonio, Maria

*Films:*
**One Man Force** (1989) . . . . . . . . . . . . . . . . . . . Maria
- 0:30—Brief breasts, twice, hiding John Matuzak in her apartment. Long shot.

Backstreet Dreams (1990) . . . . . . . . . . . . . . . Maria M.
*Made for Cable Movies:*
Rebel Highway: Dragstrip Girl (1994; Showtime) . .Pearl
*Made for Cable TV:*
Red Shoe Diaries: Hotline (1994; Showtime)
. . . . . . . . . . . . . . . . . . . . . . . . . . Phone Sex Operator

## Cellier, Caroline

*Films:*
Life Love Death (1969; French/Italian) . . . . . . . . . . Girl
This Man Must Die (1970) . . . . . . . . . . Helene Lawson
Femmes de Persone (1986; French) . . . . . . . . . Isabelle
Petit Con (1986; French) . . . . . . . . . . . Annie Choupon
**L'Annee Des Meduses** (1987; French)
. . . . . . . . . . . . . . . . . . . . . . . . Claude, Chris' Mother
•• 0:02—Breasts taking off top at the beach.
•• 0:56—Breasts on boat at night with Romain.
•• 1:06—Breasts on the beach with Valerie Kaprisky.
- 1:14—Left breast, lying on beach with Romain at night.

## Chadwick, June

*Films:*
The Golden Lady (1979; British) . . . . . . . . . . . . . . Lucy
**Forbidden World** (1982) . . . . . . . . . Dr. Barbara Glaser
•• 0:29—Breasts in bed making love with Jesse Vint.
•• 0:54—Breasts taking a shower with Dawn Dunlap.
The Last Horror Film (1984) . . . . . . . . . . . . . . Reporter
This is Spinal Tap (1984) . . . . . . . . . .Jeanine Pettibone
Headhunters (1988) . . . . . . . . . . . . . . Denise Giuliani
Rising Storm (1989) . . . . . . . . . . . . . . . . . . . .Mila Hart
Backstab (1990) . . . . . . . . . . . Mrs. Caroline Chambers
**The Evil Below** (1991) . . . . . . . . . . . Sarah Livingston
- 0:08—Very, very brief left breast, while on the floor with Max after he takes off her bra.
0:39—In red, one piece swimsuit on boat.
- 0:45—Very brief left breast, while on the floor with Max. Different angle from 0:08.
*TV:*
V: The Series (1984-85) . . . . . . . . . . . . . . . . . . . . .Lydia
Riptide (1986) . . . . . . . . . . . . . . . . . . . .Lt. Joanna Parisi
Going to Extremes (1992-93) . . . . . . . . . Dr. Alice Davis

## • Chambers, Carol

*Films:*
**Dead Aim** (1987) . . . . . . . . . . . . . . . . . . . . . . . Nicole
- 0:15—Buns in G-string.
Sleepaway Camp II: Unhappy Campers (1988) . .Brooke

## Chambers, Carrie

*Films:*
**The Divine Enforcer** (1991) . . . . . . . . . . . . . . . . Kim
- 1:21—Upper half of right breast in bra, while strapped into a chair by Dan Stroud.
Wild Cactus (1992) . . . . . . . . . . . . . . . . . . . . . .Waitress
(Unrated version reviewed.)
**The Bikini Carwash Company II** (1993)
. . . . . . . . . . . . . . . . . . . . . . . . . . . . . . . . Chairwoman
(Unrated version reviewed.)
- 0:26—Brief back side of left breast in her office with Derek.

# Chambers, Marie

*Films:*

**Street Asylum** (1989) . . . . . . . . . . . . . . . . . . . .Dr. Cane

*Video Tapes:*

**Inside Out** (1992) . . Terry's Female Half/My Better Half
- •• 1:20—Breasts, while lying on couch with open robe.
- • 1:21—Brief left breast in open robe, while standing up.
- • 1:22—Brief right breast.
- ••• 1:24—Breasts, while kissing Terry and rolling around on the couch and on the floor.

# Chambers, Marilyn

Former adult film actress.

*Films:*

**Rabid** (1977; Canadian). . . . . . . . . . . . . . . . . . . . Rose
- •• 0:14—Breasts in bed.
- •• 1:04—Breasts in closet selecting clothes.
- •• 1:16—Breasts in white panties getting out of bed.

**Angel of H.E.A.T.** (1981) . . . . . . . . . . Angel Harmony
*a.k.a. The Protectors, Book I*
- •• 0:15—Full frontal nudity making love with an intruder on the bed.
- • 0:17—Breasts in a bathtub.
- •• 0:40—Breasts in a hotel room with a short guy.
- • 0:52—Breasts getting out of a wet suit.
- •• 1:01—Breasts sitting on floor with some robots.
- • 1:29—Breasts in bed with Mark.

**Deadly Force** (1983). . . . . . . . . . Actress in Video Tape
- • 0:25—Breasts in adult video tape on projection TV.

**My Therapist** (1983) . . . . . . . . . . . . . . . . Kelly Carson
- •• 0:01—Breasts in sex therapy class.
- •• 0:07—Breasts, then full frontal nudity undressing for Rip. Long scene.
- ••• 0:10—Breasts undressing at home, then full frontal nudity making love on couch. Long scene. Nice. Then brief side view of right breast in shower.
- • 0:18—Breasts on sofa with Mike.
- •• 0:21—Breasts taking off and putting red blouse on at home.
- ••• 0:26—Nude in bedroom by herself masturbating on bed.
- ••• 0:32—Breasts exercising on the floor, buns in bed with Mike, breasts in bed getting covered with whipped cream.
- •• 0:41—Left breast and lower frontal nudity fighting with Don while he rips off her clothes.
- •• 1:08—Breasts and brief buns in bed.
- 1:12—In braless pink T-shirt at the beach.

**Up 'n' Coming** (1987) . . . . . . . . . . . . . . . . . . .Cassie
(R-rated version reviewed, X-rated version available.)
- ••• 0:01—Nude, getting out of bed and taking a shower.
- •• 0:08—Breasts making love in bed with the record producer.
- • 0:30—Brief breasts in bed with two guys.
- •• 0:47—Full frontal nudity getting suntan lotion rubbed on her by another woman.
- •• 0:55—Breasts taking off her top at radio station.

**Party Incorporated** (1989). . . . . . . . .Marilyn Sanders
*a.k.a. Party Girls*
- ••• 0:56—In lingerie, then breasts in bedroom with Weston. Nice!
- • 1:11—Brief breasts on the beach when Peter takes her swimsuit top off.

**Breakfast in Bed** (1990) . . . . . . . . .Marilyn Valentine
- •• 0:04—Full frontal nudity, getting out of bubble bath and drying herself off while talking to her manager.
- ••• 0:21—Breasts, taking off swimsuit top and sunbathing. Nude, swimming underwater.
- •• 0:53—In bra, then breasts making love.
- 1:01—In black bra and panties, undressing in her room.
- •• 1:16—Full frontal nudity, getting out of bed, putting on robe, then getting back in with Jonathan.

**The Marilyn Diaries** (1990) . . . . . . . . . . . . . Marilyn
- •• 0:02—Breasts in bathroom with a guy during party.
- •• 0:26—In bra and panties in Istvan's studio, then breasts.
- ••• 0:27—Breasts in panties when Istvan opens her blouse.
- •• 0:45—Breasts in trench coat, opening it up to give the Iranian secret documents.
- • 0:47—Breasts when the Rebel Leader opens her trench coat.
- • 0:48—Breasts with Colonel South.
- •• 0:57—Breasts opening her top for Hollywood producer.
- • 1:10—In swimsuit, then breasts with Roger.
- ••• 1:13—In black lingerie, then breasts making love with Chet.
- • 1:19—Left breast, in flashback with Roger.
- • 1:25—In slip, then right breast, then breasts with Chet.

**Marilyn Chambers' Bedtime Stories** (1993)
. . . . . . . . . . . . . . . . . . . . . . . . . . . .Marilyn Chambers
- •• 0:02—Breasts, after taking off towel, then opening and adjusting robe.
- • 0:04—Brief breasts in bedroom, taking off robe.
- • 1:02—Brief right breast on TV.
- •• 1:14—Breasts while making love with Bob on bed.
- •• 1:15—Breasts while making love with Bob on bed.

*Video Tapes:*

**Playboy Video Magazine, Volume 4** (1983)
. . . . . . . . . . . . . . . . . . . . . . . . . . . . . . . . . . .Herself
- •• 0:48—Breasts in scenes from miscellaneous films.

*Magazines:*

**Playboy** (Aug 1973) . . . . . . . . . . . . . . . . . Porno Chic
- ••• 141—Full frontal nudity.

**Playboy** (Dec 1973) . . . . . . . . . . . . . .Sex Stars of 1973
- ••• 210—Full frontal nudity.

**Playboy** (Apr 1974) . . . . . . . . . .Sex, Soap and Success
- ••• 147-155—Nude.

**Playboy** (Dec 1974) . . . . . . . . . . . . .Sex Stars of 1974
- ••• 208—Breasts standing in bubble bath.

**Playboy** (Jan 1976). . . Photography By: Richard Fegley
- ••• 93—Full frontal nudity.

**Playboy** (Jul 1976). . . . . . . . . . . . . . . . . . . . . . . .Press
•• 34—Right breast in B&W photo that appeared in the March 26, 1976 issue of *Time* magazine.
**Playboy** (Dec 1976). . . . . . . . . . . . . Sex Stars of 1976
••• 187—Full frontal nudity.
**Playboy** (Feb 1977). . . . . . . . . . . . . . . .The Year in Sex
• 139—Left breast and lower frontal nudity.
**Playboy** (Nov 1977) . . . . . . . . . . Sex in Cinema 1977
••• 162—Breasts in a photo from *Rabid*.
**Playboy** (Feb 1980). . . . . . . . . . . . . . . .The Year in Sex
• 159—Lower frontal nudity.
**Playboy** (Jul 1980). . . . . . . . . . . . . . . . . . .Grapevine
•• 263—Breasts with her body painted.
**Playboy** (Nov 1980) . . . . . . . . . . . . . . Sex in Cinema
••• 180—Left breast.
**Playboy** (Dec 1980). . . . . . . . . . . . Sex Stars of 1980
••• 245—Full frontal nudity.
**Playboy** (Jan 1989) . . . . . . . . Women of the Seventies
••• 214—Breasts.
**Playboy** (Nov 1989) . . . . . . . . . . Sex in Cinema 1989
••• 134—Breasts still from *Party Incorporated*.

## Chambers, Patti

*Films:*
**Psychos in Love** (1987) . . . . . . . . . . . . . . Girl in Bed
•• 0:02—Breasts, sitting in bed and stretching, just before getting killed.
My New Gun (1992). . . . . . . . . . . . . . . . . .Janice Phee

## • Champa, Jo

*Films:*
**Salomé** (1986; Italian) . . . . . . . . . . . . . . . . . . . Salomé
•• 1:12—Nude under blue dress while dancing around.
• 1:20—Full frontal nudity under sheer blue dress while in jail cell.
• 1:27—Full frontal nudity in sheer dress while walking around.
Out for Justice (1991) . . . . . . . . . . . . . . . . Vicky Felino
Beretta's Island (1993). . . . . . . . . . . . . . . . . . . Celeste
Little Buddha (1993). . . . . . . . . . . . . . . . . . . . . Maria

## Chanel, Tally

a.k.a. Tally Brittany.
*Films:*
**Alien Warrior** (1985) . . . . . . . . . . . . . . . . . . . .Barbara
•• 0:46—In white lingerie, then breasts and buns while undressing in room with the Police Captain.
• 1:03—Brief breasts and buns in flashback of 0:46 scene.
Bits and Pieces (1985). . . . . . . . . . . . . . . . . . .Jennifer
0:58—In the woods with the killer, seen briefly in bra and panties before and after being killed.
**Free Ride** (1986) . . . . . . . . . . . . . . . . . . . . . . . .Candy
• 0:53—Brief buns, wearing G-string, taking off her clothes on porch. Long shot.
• 0:57—Brief breasts in bedroom with Dan.
**Sex Appeal** (1986) . . . . . . . . . . . . . . . . . . . . Corinne
• 1:22—Brief breasts at the door of Tony's apartment when he opens the door while fantasizing about her.

**The Nightstalker** (1987). . . . . . . . . . . . . . . . . .Brenda
• 0:54—Brief frontal nudity lying dead in bed covered with paint. Long shot, hard to see anything.
Run If You Can (1987) . . . . . . . . . . . . . . . . . . . . . . . n.a.
**Slammer Girls** (1987) . . . . . . . . . . . . . . . .Candy Treat
• 0:56—Buns, in G-string, doing a dance routine wearing feathery pasties for the Governor in the hospital.
**Warrior Queen** (1987) . . . . . . . . . . . . . . . . . . . .Vespa
••• 0:09—Breasts hanging on a rope, being auctioned.
••• 0:20—Breasts and buns with Chloe.
•• 0:37—Nude, before attempted rape by Goliath.
•• 0:58—Breasts during rape by Goliath.
Hollywood Hot Tubs 2—Educating Crystal (1989)
. . . . . . . . . . . . . . . . . . . . . . . . . . . . . Mindy Wright
**Knockouts** (1992) . . . . . . . . . . . . . . Samantha Peters
•• 0:15—Breasts taking off swimsuit top and getting ready for a bath.
••• 0:16—Breasts and buns, while undressing and getting into bathtub while Garth peeks in.
••• 0:25—Breasts during strip poker game.
•• 0:26—Breasts and buns in G-string while walking to her bedroom.
• 0:29—Breasts while sitting on the bed.
••• 0:39—In white lingerie, then breasts while posing for photographs.
•• 0:42—Breasts while Wesley helps put her top on.
•• 0:43—Breasts while taking a shower (seen on TV monitor).
••• 0:47—Breasts while making love with Wesley.
• 0:59—Brief breasts while punching a bag (seen in mostly silhouette).
• 1:16—Breasts in shower in video playback.
**L.A. Goddess** (1992) . . . . . . . . . . . . . . . . . . . Beverly
•• 0:08—Breasts, while getting dressed in bathroom with Kathy.
•• 0:17—Breasts and buns, while getting out of the shower.
0:37—In two piece swimsuit.
••• 1:07—Buns (nice crotch shot) and breasts in bed while making love with Jeff Conaway and talking on the phone.
*Magazines:*
**Penthouse** (May 1990) . . . . . . . . . . . . . . Dry as Dust
**Playboy's Book of Lingerie** (Jan 1992) . . . . . .Herself
••• 8—Breasts.
**Playboy's Book of Lingerie** (Mar 1992). . . . . .Herself
••• 16—Breasts.
**Playboy's Book of Lingerie** (May 1992) . . . . .Herself
••• 65—Breasts.
**Playboy's Book of Lingerie** (Sep 1992). . . . . .Herself
•• 63—Left breast.
**Playboy's Book of Lingerie** (Nov 1992) . . . . .Herself
••• 53—Breasts.
**Playboy's Blondes, Brunettes & Redheads**
(Sep 1993). . . . . . . . . . . . . . . . . . . . . . . . . .Herself
••• 20—Breasts and buns.
Playboy's Book of Lingerie (Mar 1994) . . . . . . . .Herself

## Chang, Lia

Films:

**Frankenhooker** (1990). . . . . . . . . . . . . . . . . Crystal
- 0:38—Buns, when Jeffrey draws a check mark on her.
- 0:40—Brief buns, fighting with the other girls over the drugs.

A Kiss Before Dying (1991) . . . . . . . . . . Shoe Saleslady

## Chaplin, Geraldine

Daughter of actor Charlie Chaplin.
Granddaughter of Eugene O'Neill.
Films:

Doctor Zhivago (1965) . . . . . . . . . . . . . . . . . . . . . Tonya
The Three Musketeers (1973) . . . . . . . . . Anne of Austria
Nashville (1975) . . . . . . . . . . . . . . . . . . . . . . . . . . . Opal
Buffalo Bill and the Indians (1976). . . . . . . Annie Oakley
Roseland (1977) . . . . . . . . . . . . . . . . . . . . . . . . . Marilyn
**Welcome to L.A.** (1977). . . . . . . . . . . . . Karen Hood
- • 1:28—Full frontal nudity standing in Keith Carradine's living room.

**Remember My Name** (1978). . . . . . . . . . . . . . Emily
- 1:23—Very brief left breast, lying in bed, then right breast, with Anthony Perkins.

A Wedding (1978) . . . . . . . . . . . . . . . . . . Rita Billingsley
Bolero (1982; French) . . . . . . . . . . . . Suzan/Sara Glenn
The Moderns (1988) . . . . . . . . . . . . . . Nathalie de Ville
White Mischief (1988). . . . . . . . . . . . . . . . . . . . . . Nina
The Return of the Musketeers (1989) . . . . . Queen Anne
Barbara Cartland's "Duel of Hearts" (1990; British)
. . . . . . . . . . . . . . . . . . . . . . . . . . . . . . . . . Mrs. Miller
The Children (1990; British/German) . . . Joyce Wheater
Chaplin (1992; British/U.S.). . . . . . . . . Hannah Chaplin
The Age of Innocence (1993) . . . . . . . . . Mrs. Welland

## Charbonneau, Patricia

Films:

**Desert Hearts** (1986) . . . . . . . . . . . . . . . . Cay Rivvers
- • • 1:09—Brief breasts making love in bed with Helen Shaver.

Manhunter (1986) . . . . . . . . . . . . . . . . . Mrs. Sherman
**Call Me** (1988) . . . . . . . . . . . . . . . . . . . . . . . . . . Anna
- • • 1:18—Brief left breast making love in bed with a guy, then breasts putting blouse on and getting out of bed.

Shakedown (1988) . . . . . . . . . . . . . . . . . Susan Cantrell
Brain Dead (1989). . . . . . . . . . . . . . . . . . . Dana Martin
0:43—Buns, on table with Bill Paxton. Briefly almost see side of left breast.

Robocop 2 (1990). . . . . . . . . . . . . Uncredited Engineer
K2 (1991) . . . . . . . . . . . . . . . . . . . . . . . Jacki Metcalfe
Made for Cable TV:
Tales From the Crypt: Strung Along (1992; HBO) . . Ellen
Made for TV Movies:
C.A.T. Squad: Stalking Danger (1986) . . . . . Nikki Pappas
TV:
Wiseguy (1988-89) . . . . . . . . . . . . . . Carole Sternberg

## Charlie

See: Spradling, Charlie.

## Chase, Lynn

See: De Light, Venus.

## Chen, Joan

Films:

**Tai-Pan** (1986) . . . . . . . . . . . . . . . . . . . . . . . May May
0:55—In sheer top sitting on bed talking to Bryan Brown.
- 0:56—Brief left breast washing herself, hard to see anything.
1:14—Sheer top again.
1:30—Sheer top again.

The Last Emperor (1987) . . . . . . . . . . . . . . . . Wan Jung
The Nightstalker (1987) . . . . . . . . . . . . . . . . Mai Wong
The Blood of Heroes (1989) . . . . . . . . . . . . . . . . Kidda
a.k.a. Salute of the Jugger
**Turtle Beach** (1992; Australian) . . . . . . . . . . . . Minou
a.k.a. The Killing Beach
- • • • 0:07—Brief buns, dropping robe and leaving room while talking to Greta Scacchi.
Heaven and Earth (1993) . . . . . . . . . . . . . . . . . Mama
On Deadly Ground (1993) . . . . . . . . . . . . . . . . . Masu
Made for Cable Movies:
Dead Lock (1991; HBO) . . . . . . . . . . . . . . . . . Noelle
Made for Cable TV:
**Strangers: Small Sounds and Tilting Shadows**
(1992) . . . . . . . . . . . . . . . . . . . . . . . . . . . . The Girl
(Available on video tape on Strangers.)
- 0:04—Brief left breast, while making love with Lambert Wilson. Dark.
- 0:05—Inner half of right breast, afterwards.
0:08—Very, very brief partial left breast a couple of times while washing herself.
Tales From the Crypt: Food For Thought (1993; HBO)
. . . . . . . . . . . . . . . . . . . . . . . . . . . . . . . . . Connie
Made for TV Movies:
Shadow of a Stranger (1992) . . . . . . . . . . . . . Vanessa
Steel Justice (1992) . . . . . . . . . . . . . . . . . . . . Nicole
TV:
Twin Peaks (1990-91). . . . . . . . . . . . . Jocelyn Packard
Magazines:
**Playboy** (May 1994). . . . . . . . . . . . . . . . . Grapevine
- 164—Breasts under sheer blouse in B&W photo.

## • Chester, Holly

Films:

Ultimate Desires (1991) . . . . . . . . . . . . . . . . Streetgirl
a.k.a. Silhouette
Knight Moves (1992) . . . . . . . . . . . . . . . . Officer No. 2
**SnakeEater III ...His Law** (1992) . . . . . . . . . . . . Fran
- • • • 0:30—Breasts and buns in G-string while dancing on stage in club.

## Cheung, Daphne

*Films:*
**Rich Girl** (1991) . . . . . . . . . . . . . . Oriental Temptress
• 1:14—Breasts, taking off her jacket in back room trying to get Rick to do drugs.
**Roots of Evil** (1991) . . . . . . . . . . . . . . . . . . . . . . Tina
(Unrated version reviewed.)
••• 0:09—Breasts in alley with a customer.
A Time to Die (1991) . . . . . . . . . . . . . . . . . . . . Sunshine
Mortal Danger (1993) . . . . . . . . . . . . . . . . . . . . . . Jan

## Chevalier, Catherine

*Films:*
Hellraiser II—Hellbound (1988) . . . . . . . Tiffany's Mother
Riders of the Storm (1988) . . . . . . . . . . . . . . . . . Rosita
Stormy Monday (1988) . . . . . . . . . . . Cosmo's Secretary
**Night Breed** (1990) . . . . . . . . . . . . . . . . . . . . . Rachel
• 1:12—Breasts in police jail, going through a door and killing a cop.

## Chiesa, Chana Jael

*Video Tapes:*
**Inside Out** (1992) . . . . . . . . . . . . My Secret Moments
••• 0:42—Breasts, rubbing lotion on them, then joined by a large cast of people during her fantasy as the camera pulls back.
•• 0:44—Full frontal nudity, still in bed. Long shot.
**Inside Out 4** (1992) . . . . . . . . . . . Actress/Motivation
(Unrated version reviewed.)
• 0:13—Lower frontal nudity, dropping her shorts to show Dick her haircut.
••• 0:14—Nude, out in the desert with Dick, shooting a scene.
• 0:16—Breasts, while opening her blouse to show Dick her breasts, brief full frontal nudity, running to get into truck.
•• 0:17—Brief full frontal nudity, out in the desert with Dick again.

## Chiles, Lois

*Films:*
The Way We Were (1973) . . . . . . . . . . . . . . . Carol Ann
Coma (1978) . . . . . . . . . . . . . . . . . . . . Nancy Greenly
Moonraker (1979) . . . . . . . . . . . . . . Dr. Holly Goodhead
Raw Courage (1983) . . . . . . . . . . . . . . . . . . . . . . Ruth
Sweet Liberty (1986) . . . . . . . . . . . . . . . . . . . . Leslie
Broadcast News (1987) . . . . . . . . . . . . . . Jennifer Mack
**Creepshow 2** (1987) . . . . . . . . . . . . . . . Annie Lansing
•• 0:59—Brief breasts getting out of boyfriend's bed, then getting dressed.
Until the End of the World (1991) . . . . . . . . Elsa Farber
Diary of a Hitman (1992) . . . . . . . . . . . . . . . . . Sheila
*Made for Cable Movies:*
Lush Life (1993; Showtime) . . . . . . . . . . . . . . . . Lucy
*Made for TV Movies:*
Burning Bridges (1990) . . . . . . . . . . . . . Claire Morgan
Obsessed (1992) . . . . . . . . . . . . . . . . . . . . . . . Louise
*TV:*
Dallas (1982-84) . . . . . . . . . . . . . . . . Holly Harwood

## Chin, Lonnie

*Films:*
Star 80 (1983) . . . . . . . . . . . . . Playboy Mansion Guest
*Video Tapes:*
**Playboy Video Magazine, Volume 1** (1982)
. . . . . . . . . . . . . . . . . . . . . . . . . . . . . . . . . Playmate
•• 0:00—Full frontal nudity during introduction.
••• 0:15—Nude outside by pool.
••• 0:19—Nude posing in various clothes in clothes store.
••• 0:21—In bra and panties, then nude in garter belt and stockings in a house.
**Playboy's Playmate Review 3** (1985) . . . . . Playmate
*Magazines:*
**Playboy** (Jan 1983) . . . . . . . . . . . . . . . . . . . . Playmate
**Playboy's 1987 Book of Lingerie** (Mar 1987)
. . . . . . . . . . . . . . . . . . . . . . . . . . . . . . . . . . Herself
••• 54-55—Full frontal nudity.
• 82-83—Buns.
**Playboy's Calendar Playmates** (Nov 1992) . . . Herself
••• 35—Full frontal nudity.

## Chong, Rae Dawn

Daughter of comedian/actor Tommy Chong.
Ex-wife of actor C. Thomas Howell.
*Films:*
**Quest For Fire** (1981) . . . . . . . . . . . . . . . . . . . . . Ika
0:37—Breasts and buns, running away from the bad tribe.
0:40—Breasts and buns, following the three guys.
0:41—Brief breasts behind rocks.
• 0:43—Brief side view of left breast, healing Noah's wound.
• 0:50—Right breast, while sleeping by the fire.
0:53—Long shot, side view of left breast after making love.
• 0:54—Breasts shouting to the three guys.
• 1:07—Breasts standing with her tribe.
• 1:10—Breasts and buns, walking through camp at night.
• 1:18—Breasts in a field.
• 1:20—Left breast, turning over to demonstrate the missionary position. Long shot.
• 1:25—Buns and brief left breast running out of bear cave.
Beat Street (1984) . . . . . . . . . . . . . . . . . . . . . . . Tracy
Cheech & Chong's The Corsican Brothers (1984)
. . . . . . . . . . . . . . . . . . . . . . . . . . . . . . . The Gypsy
City Limits (1984) . . . . . . . . . . . . . . . . . . . . . . . Yogi
**Fear City** (1984) . . . . . . . . . . . . . . . . . . . . . . . . Leila
••• 0:26—Breasts and buns, dancing on stage.
• 0:50—Brief breasts in the hospital getting a shock to get her heart started.
American Flyers (1985) . . . . . . . . . . . . . . . . . . . Sarah
The Color Purple (1985) . . . . . . . . . . . . . . . . . Squeak
Commando (1985) . . . . . . . . . . . . . . . . . . . . . . Cindy
**Running Out of Luck** (1986) . . . . . . . . . . . Slave Girl
•• 0:42—Left breast, while hugging Mick Jagger, then again while lying in bed with him.

•• 1:12—Left breast painting some kind of drug laced solution on herself.

•• 1:14—Right breast, while in prison office offering her breast to the warden.

• 1:21—Buns and left breast, in bed with Jagger during a flashback.

Soul Man (1986). . . . . . . . . . . . . . . . . . . . . . . Sarah
The Squeeze (1987) . . . . . . . . . . . . . . . . Rachel Dobs
The Borrower (1989). . . . . . . . . . . . . . . Diana Pierce
Curiosity Kills (1990) . . . . . . . . . . . . . . . . . . . . Jane
Far Out Man (1990) . . . . . . . . . . . . . Rae Dawn Chong
**Tales From the Darkside, The Movie** (1990). .Carola

• 1:09—Left breast in blue light, twice, with James Remar. Don't see her face.

Amazon (1991). . . . . . . . . . . . . . . . . . . . . . . . Paola
Common Bonds (1991) . . . . . . . . . . . . . . Ilene Curtis
Denial (1991) . . . . . . . . . . . . . . . . . . . . . . . . . Julie
**When the Party's Over** (1991) . . . . . . . . . . . . . . MJ

• 0:03—Brief buns, while getting out of bed.

0:27—In bra, while getting caught with Taylor by Will.

0:45—In black bra, while getting dressed.

1:23—Brief partial left breast, while taking off her dress and walking into closet.

Time Runner (1992) . . . . . . . . . . . . . .Karen McDonald
*Made for Cable Movies:*
**Prison Stories, Women on the Inside** (1990; HBO)
. . . . . . . . . . . . . . . . . . . . . . . . . . . . . . . . . .Rhonda

• 0:26—Very brief right breast several times in prison shower with Annabella Sciorra.

*Made for TV Movies:*
Father & Son: Dangerous Relations (1993) . . . . .Yvonne
*Magazines:*
Playboy (Apr 1982). . . . . . . . . . . . . . . . .Quest For Fire

## Chong, Shelby

*Films:*
Cheech & Chong's Nice Dreams (1981) . . .Body Builder
**Far Out Man** (1990) . . . . . . . . . . . . . . . . . . . . . . Tree

• 0:11—Very brief side view of left breast, in gaping blouse when she leans over to light a joint.

Relentless 2: Dead On (1991) . . . . . . . . . . . . Waitress
The Spirit of '76 (1991). . . . . . . . . . . . . . . . . Waitress

## • Chorak, Karen

See: Naples, Toni.

## • Choudhury, Sarita

*Films:*
**Mississippi Masala** (1992). . . . . . . . . . . . . . . . .Mina

• 1:11—Right breast when Denzel Washington sucks on it.

Wild West (1992; British). . . . . . . . . . . . . . . . . Rifat

## Christensen, Tonja

*Video Tapes:*
**Playboy Video Calendar 1993** (1992) . . . .December

••• 0:49—Nude in barn.

••• 0:50—Nude in house.

**Playboy's Playmate Review 1992** (1992)
. . . . . . . . . . . . . . . . . . . . . . . . . . . Miss November

••• 0:02—Nude in hat and chair scenes in a house.

*Magazines:*
**Playboy** (Nov 1991) . . . . . . . . . . . . . . . . . . Playmate
**Playboy's Book of Lingerie** (Jan 1993) . . . . . .Herself

•• 13—Breasts.

**Playboy's Girls of Summer '93** (Jun 1993) . . .Herself

•• 42-43—Buns.

••• 59—Breasts.

**Playboy's Wet & Wild Women** (Aug 1993). . .Herself

••• 16-17—Nude.

**Playboy's Blondes, Brunettes & Redheads**
(Sep 1993). . . . . . . . . . . . . . . . . . . . . . . .Herself

••• 74-75—Full frontal nudity.

**Playboy's Book of Lingerie** (Sep 1993) . . . . . .Herself

••• 58—Breasts.

**Playboy's Book of Lingerie** (Nov 1993) . . . . .Herself

••• 9—Full frontal nudity.

**Playmates at Play** (Jul 1994) . . . . . . . . . . . .Herself

••• 68-69—Full frontal nudity.

## Christian, Claudia

*Films:*
The Hidden (1987). . . . . . . . . . . . . . . . . Brenda Lee
Arena (1988) . . . . . . . . . . . . . . . . . . . . . . . . . Quinn
Clean and Sober (1988). . . . . . . . . . . . . . . . . . . . Iris
**Never on Tuesday** (1988) . . . . . . . . . . . . . . .Tuesday
(There are a lot of braless T-shirt shots of her throughout the film.)

• 0:43—Brief side view of right breast in the shower with Eddie during his fantasy.

Mom (1989) . . . . . . . . . . . . . . . . . . . . . . . Virginia
0:03—Briefly in red bra, when Brion James rips her blouse open.

Mad About You (1990) . . . . . . . . . . . . . . . . .Casey
0:56—On boat in a white, fairly transparent one piece swimsuit.

Maniac Cop 2 (1990). . . . . . . . . . . . . . . . Susan Riley
Think Big (1990) . . . . . . . . . . . . . . . . . . Dr. Marsh
The Dark Backward (1991). . . . . . . . . . . . . . . . Kitty
A Gnome Named Gnorm (1993) . . . . . . . . . Samantha
**Hexed** (1993). . . . . . . . . . . . . . . . . . . . . . . .Hexina
*a.k.a. All Shook Up*

• 0:30—Tip of right breast, several times, while lying on her back in bed. (You can tell when the body double is used because of the bad wig.)

•• 0:31—Brief right breast, several times, while making love in bed.

• 0:34—Very brief inside of right breast in gaping coat, while raising knife. Brief buns, while getting pushed off bed.

*Made for Cable Movies:*
Lies of the Twins (1991; USA). . . . . . . . . . . . . .Felice
Strays (1991; USA). . . . . . . . . . . . . . . . Claire Lederer
*Made for TV Movies:*
Danielle Steel's "Kaleidoscope" (1990). . . . . . .Meagan
Columbo: It's All in the Game (1993). . . . . . . . . . Lisa
Relentless: Mind of a Killer (1993) . . . . . . Leeann Hardy

*TV:*
Berrengers (1985)................. Melody Hughes
Babylon 5 (1994- )
............Lieutenant Commander Susan Ivanova

# • Christie, Julianne

*Films:*
Encino Man (1992)..................... Fresh Nug
*TV:*
**NYPD Blue: NYPD Lou** (Oct 2, 1993)......... Patty
  • 0:39—Buns, a couple of times, getting out of bed
  with Kevin after getting caught by Andy's dad. Very
  brief breasts while getting dressed.

# Christie, Julie

*Films:*
Billy Liar (1963)............................. Liz
Darling (1965) ......................Diana Scott
Doctor Zhivago (1965)..................... Lara
Fahrenheit 451 (1967) ............... Linda/Clarisse
Petulia (1968; U.S./British).......... Petulia Danner
McCabe and Mrs. Miller (1971) .......... Mrs. Miller
**Don't Look Now** (1973)............. Laura Baxter
  • 0:27—Brief breasts in bathroom with Donald Suth-
  erland.
  •• 0:30—Breasts making love with Sutherland in bed.
Shampoo (1975)......................... Jackie
**Demon Seed** (1977) ................. Susan Harris
  • 0:25—Side view of left breast, getting out of bed.
  •• 0:30—Breasts and buns getting out of the shower
  while the computer watches with its camera.
Heaven Can Wait (1978).............. Betty Logan
Heat and Dust (1982) .......................Anne
Return of the Soldier (1983; British) ........... Kitty
Power (1986) ..................... Ellen Freeman
Miss Mary (1987) ............. Miss Mary Mulligan
Fools of Fortune (1990)............. Mrs. Quinton
*Made for Cable Movies:*
**The Railway Station Man** (1992; TNT).. Helen Cuffe
  • 0:35—Buns, undressing to go skinny dipping. Brief
  side of left breast, running into the ocean. Long
  shot.
  • 0:37—Buns, while walking out of the surf. Long
  shot.
*Made for TV Movies:*
Dadah is Death (1988) ...................Barbara
*Magazines:*
**Playboy** (Nov 1974) ........... Sex in Cinema 1974
  •• 147—Breasts from *Don't Look Now.*
**Playboy** (Nov 1975) .......... Sex in Cinema 1975
  • 141—Upper half of right breast from *Shampoo.*

# • Cialini, Julie Lynn

*TV:*
The New Price is Right (1994- ) ...... Showcase Model
*Video Tapes:*
**Playboy Video Centerfold: Anna-Marie Goddard**
(1994) ..................... Runner-Up Playmate
  ••• 0:39—Nude in beach front (shot in a studio) sequence.
**Playboy Video Centerfold: Jenny McCarthy** (1994)
.................................... Playmate
  • 0:35—Buns while dancing in T-back.
  ••• 0:36—Nude in country setting segment.
  •• 0:40—Breasts and buns in T-back while dancing
  around in city settings.
  ••• 0:42—Nude in still photos.
  ••• 0:43—Nude in fashion show fantasy.
  ••• 0:45—Nude, while posing in house while thinking
  about her lover.
**Wet and Wild: The Locker Room** (1994).. Playmate
*Magazines:*
**Playboy** (Sep 1993) ................... Miami Heat
  ••• 138—Breasts in push-up bra.
**Playboy** (Jan 1994)
  ........The Great 40th Anniversary Playmate Search
  ••• 142—Full frontal nudity.
**Playboy** (Feb 1994) ..................... Playmate
  ••• 90-101—Nude.
**Playboy's Great Playmate Search** (Feb 1994)
.....................................Herself
  ••• 58—Full frontal nudity.

# Cicciolina

See: Staller, Ilona.

# • Ciesar, Jennifer

*Films:*
**Lovers' Lovers** (1993) ....................Blaire
(Body double used whenever you don't see her face.
Body double has red fingernail polish.)
  •• 0:29—Breasts and buns while in the shower.
  • 1:07—In white bra and brief breasts while making
  love with Michael on bed.
  1:13—In white bra and panties in bedroom.
*Made for Cable TV:*
**Red Shoe Diaries: Kidnap** (1994; Showtime)
.............................. Sara McCleod
  ••• 0:17—Breasts, while making love outside with Tom
  at night.
  •• 0:24—Nude, while making love in board room and
  in flashbacks with Tom.

# Clark, Anna

*Video Tapes:*
**Playboy Video Calendar 1988** (1987)..... Playmate
**Wet and Wild** (1989) ................... Model
*Magazines:*
**Playboy** (Apr 1987) ..................... Playmate
**Playboy's Calendar Playmates** (Nov 1992)... Herself
  ••• 62—Full frontal nudity.

# Clark, Candy

*Films:*

Fat City (1972) . . . . . . . . . . . . . . . . . . . . . . . . . . . Faye
American Graffiti (1973) . . . . . . . . . . . . . . . . . Debbie
**The Man Who Fell to Earth** (1976; British)
. . . . . . . . . . . . . . . . . . . . . . . . . . . . . . . . . Mary-Lou
(Uncensored version reviewed.)
•• 0:42—Breasts in the bathtub, washing her hair and
talking to David Bowie.
•• 0:55—Breasts sitting on bed and blowing out a candle.
••• 0:56—Breasts in bed with Bowie.
••• 1:26—Full frontal nudity climbing into bed with
Bowie after he reveals his true alien self.
1:56—Nude with Bowie making love and shooting a
gun.
Citizen's Band (1977) . . . . . . . . . . . . . . . . . Electra/Pam
**The Big Sleep** (1978; British) . . . . . Camilla Sternwood
••• 0:18—Breasts, sitting in a chair when Robert
Mitchum comes in after a guy is murdered.
• 0:30—Brief breasts in a photograph that Mitchum is
looking at.
0:38—Breasts in the photos again. Out of focus.
•• 0:39—Breasts sitting in chair during recollection of
the murder.
•• 1:03—Very brief full frontal nudity in bed, throwing
open the sheets for Mitchum.
1:05—Very, very brief buns, getting up out of bed.
When Ya Comin' Back Red Ryder (1979) . . . . . . . Cheryl
(Not available on video tape.)
National Lampoon Goes to the Movies (1982)
. . . . . . . . . . . . . . . . . . . . . . . . . . . . . Susan Cooper
*a.k.a. Movie Madness*
Q (1982) . . . . . . . . . . . . . . . . . . . . . . . . . . . . . . . Joan
Blue Thunder (1983) . . . . . . . . . . . . . . . . . . . . . . Kate
Hambone and Hillie (1984) . . . . . . . . . . . . . . . . Nancy
Cat's Eye (1985) . . . . . . . . . . . . . . . . . . . . . . Sally Ann
At Close Range (1986) . . . . . . . . . . . . . . . . Mary Sue
The Blob (1988) . . . . . . . . . . . . . . . . . . . . Fran Hewitt
Cool As Ice (1991) . . . . . . . . . . . . . . . . . . . . . . Grace
Buffy The Vampire Slayer (1992) . . . . . . . . Buffy's Mom
Original Intent (1992) . . . . . . . . . . . . . Jessica Cameron
*Magazines:*
**Playboy** (Nov 1978) . . . . . . . . . . . Sex in Cinema 1978
• 181—Breasts.

# Clark, Dawn

*Films:*

**The Happy Hooker Goes to Washington** (1977)
. . . . . . . . . . . . . . . . . . . . . . . . . . . . . . . . . . . Candy
• 1:18—Breasts, covered with spaghetti.
**The Hollywood Knights** (1980) . . . . . . Pom Pom Girl
•• 0:01—Breasts sunbathing outside with Fran
Drescher and another Pom Pom Girl.
• 0:11—In bra, then brief breasts, changing clothes at
night.
• 0:20—Breasts in B&W Polaroid photograph. Long
shot.
Stripes (1981) . . . . . . . . . . . . . . . . . . . . . Mud Wrestler

# • Clark, Kerrie

*Films:*

Miami Blues (1990) . . . . . . . . . . . . . . . . . . . . . Hooker
Sunset Heat (1991) . . . . . . . . . . . . . . Brandon's Model
(Unrated version reviewed.)
**Angel 4: Undercover** (1993) . . . . . . . . . . . . . . Paula
••• 0:26—Breasts, while making love with Piston in bed-
room.
•• 0:28—Very briefly nude, getting up out of bed.
Breasts, while taking a shower.

# Clark, Marlene

*Films:*

The Landlord (1970) . . . . . . . . . . . . . . . . . . . . Marlene
**Slaughter** (1972) . . . . . . . . . . . . . . . . . . . . Kim Walker
• 0:11—Very brief buns and right breast, getting
thrown out of room by Jim Brown.
Night of the Cobra Woman (1974; U.S./Philippines)
. . . . . . . . . . . . . . . . . . . . . . . . . . . . . . . . . . . . Lena
Switchblade Sisters (1975) . . . . . . . . . . . . . . . . . Muff

# Clark, Sharon

a.k.a. Sharon Weber or Sharon Clark Weber.
*Films:*
**Lifeguard** (1975) . . . . . . . . . . . . . . . . . . . . . . . . . Tina
• 0:07—Brief side view of right breast undressing and
getting into the shower.
• 0:08—Buns and brief breasts wrestling with Sam El-
liott on the bed.
Lisa (1989) . . . . . . . . . . . . . . . . . . . . Porsche Passenger
*Magazines:*
**Playboy** (Aug 1970) . . . . . . . . . . . . . . . . . . . Playmate
**Playboy** (Jan 1974) . . . . . . . . Twenty Years of Playmates
• 110—Left breast.
**Playboy** (Nov 1976) . . . . . . . . . . . Sex in Cinema 1976
• 145—Partial buns.
**Playboy** (Dec 1976) . . . . . . . . . . . . . Sex Stars of 1976
••• 190—Breasts.

# Clark, Susan

*Films:*

Coogan's Bluff (1968) . . . . . . . . . . . . . . . . . . . . . Julie
Colossus: 'The Forbin' Project (1969) . . . . . . . . . . . Cleo
1:12—After taking off her dress, she's seen through
a wine glass, so it's very distorted. It looks like she's
wearing a body suit.
Tell Them Willie Boy is Here (1969) . . . . . . . . . . . . Liz
0:21—Very brief buns when Robert Redford turns
her over in bed.
0:57—In slip, after taking off dress for Redford.
Skin Game (1971) . . . . . . . . . . . . . . . . . . . . . . Ginger
Valdez is Coming (1971) . . . . . . . . . . . . . . . . Gay Erin
The Apple Dumpling Gang (1975)
. . . . . . . . . . . . . . . . . . Magnolia Dusty Clydesdale
**Night Moves** (1975) . . . . . . . . . . . . . . . . . . . . . Ellen
• 1:09—Brief breasts in bed with Gene Hackman.
French Quarter (1978) . . . . . . . . . . . . . Bag Stealer/Sue

**Deadly Companion** (1979) . . . . . . . . . . . . Paula West
- 0:19—Brief left breast, while consoling Michael Sarrazin in bed, then brief side view of left breast.
- 0:20—Brief breasts sitting up in bed.

The North Avenue Irregulars (1979) . . . . . . . . . . . .Anne
Promises in the Dark (1979) . . . . . . . . . . . . Fran Koenig
Nobody's Perfekt (1981) . . . . . . . . . . . . . . . . . . . Carol
Porky's (1981; Canadian) . . . . . . . . . . . . Cherry Forever
*Made for TV Movies:*
Babe (1975) . . . . . . . . . . . . . . Babe Didrickson Zaharias
(Emmy Award for Best Actress in a Special.)
Snowbound: The Jim and Jennifer Stolpa Story (1994)
. . . . . . . . . . . . . . . . . . . . . . . . . . . Muriel Mulligan
Tonya & Nancy: The Inside Story (1994)
. . . . . . . . . . . . . . . . . . . . . . . . . . . LaVona Harding
*TV:*
Webster (1983-89)
. . . . . . . . . . . . . . .Katherine Calder Young Papadapolis
*Magazines:*
**Playboy** (Feb 1973) . . . . . . . . . . . . . . The Ziegfeld Girls
••• 75-79—Breasts and buns in various poses.

# Clarke, Caitlin

*Films:*
Dragonslayer (1981) . . . . . . . . . . . . . . . . . . . . Valerian
0:27—Body double's very brief side of left breast from under water.
Penn & Teller Get Killed (1989) . . . . . . . . . . . . Carlotta
*Made for TV Movies:*
Mayflower Madam (1987) . . . . . . . . . . . . . . . .Virginia
Love, Lies and Murder (1991) . . . . . . . . . . Sandra Eden
*TV:*
Once a Hero (1979) . . . . . . . . . . . . . . . . Emma Greely

# Clarke, Julie

*Video Tapes:*
**Playboy Video Centerfold: Julie Clarke** . . Playmate
**Playboy Video Calendar 1992** (1991) . . . . . February
••• 0:05—Breasts on stairs. Nude in warehouse, painting on the floor and on herself.
••• 0:07—Nude, putting oil on herself.
**Playboy Playmates in Paradise** (1992) . . . Playmate
**Playboy's Playmate Review 1992** (1992)
. . . . . . . . . . . . . . . . . . . . . . . . . . . . . .Miss March
••• 0:10—Nude in indoor pool, then in art studio and then on horseback.
**Wet and Wild IV** (1992) . . . . . . . . . . . . . . . . .Model
*Magazines:*
**Playboy** (Mar 1991). . . . . . . . . . . . . . . . . . Playmate
••• 86-97—Nude.
**Playboy's Calendar Playmates** (Nov 1992) . . Herself
••• 100—Full frontal nudity.
**Playboy's Book of Lingerie** (Nov 1992) . . . . . Herself
••• 85—Full frontal nudity.
**Playboy** (Jul 1993). . . . . . . . . . . . . . . . . . .Lucky Stiff
••• 78-83—Nude.
**Playboy's Book of Lingerie** (Sep 1993) . . . . . Herself
••• 66-67—Full frontal nudity.
•• 76—Left breast.

**Playboy's Video Playmates** (Sep 1993) . . . . . .Herself
••• 30-31—Full frontal nudity.
**Playboy's Nudes** (Dec 1993) . . . . . . . . . . . . . .Herself
•• 22-23—Side of left breast and buns.
**Playboy's Book of Lingerie** (Jul 1994) . . . . . . .Herself
••• 20—Full frontal nudity.

# • Clarke, Melinda

*Films:*
Hot Under the Collar (1991) . . . . . . . . . . . . . . Monica
Out for Blood (1992) . . . . . . . . . . . . . . . . . . . . . .Laura
**Return of the Living Dead 3** (1993) . . . . Julie Walker
•• 0:16—Breasts, while in bed talking with her boyfriend, Curt.
• 0:17—More breasts, while getting out of bed when Curt's dad comes home.
• 1:07—Breasts under skimpy outfit after doing some severe body piercing.
•• 1:25—Brief breasts when getting rescued by Curt.
**Return to Two Moon Junction** (1993)
. . . . . . . . . . . . . . . . . . . . . . . . Savannah Delongpre
• 0:37—Lying in bed in wet white lingerie, then left breast (close-up shot) while fantasizing about Jake.
• 0:44—Upper half of buns, while in bed with Jake.
•• 0:45—Buns and back half of right breast, while standing up and putting on dress.
••• 0:59—Breasts and very brief lower frontal nudity while making love with Jake.
•• 1:01—Buns, while getting out of bed and putting a shirt on.
• 1:09—Breasts, with Jake in bed.
*TV:*
Heaven Help Us (1994- ) . . . . . . . . . . . . . .Lexy Monroe

# Clarkson, Lana

*Films:*
Fast Times at Ridgemont High (1982) . . . . . Mrs. Vargas
**Deathstalker** (1983) . . . . . . . . . . . . . . . . . . . . . Kaira
•• 0:26—Breasts when her cape opens, while talking to Deathstalker and Oghris.
••• 0:29—Breasts lying down by the fire when Deathstalker comes to make love with her.
• 0:49—Brief breasts with gaping cape, sword fighting with a guard.
Scarface (1983) . . . . . . . . Woman at the Babylon Club
**Blind Date** (1984) . . . . . . . . . . . . . . . . . . . . . . Rachel
*a.k.a. Deadly Seduction*
(Not the same 1987 *Blind Date* with Bruce Willis.)
• 0:52—Brief breasts rolling over in bed when Joseph Bottoms sneaks in. Dark, hard to see.
1:11—In two piece swimsuit during a modeling assignment.
1:18—In two piece swimsuit by pool.
**Barbarian Queen** (1985). . . . . . . . . . . . . . . Amethea
•• 0:38—Brief breasts during attempted rape.
••• 0:48—Breasts being tortured with metal hand then raped by torturer.
Amazon Women on the Moon (1987) . . . . . .Alpha Beta

**Barbarian Queen II: The Empress Strikes Back**
(1989). . . . . . . . . . . . . . . . . . . . . . . . . . . Athelia
- ••• 0:14—Breasts during fight with Erigina in mud. More breasts afterwards.
- ••• 0:31—Left breast, while making love with Aurion outside.
- ••• 0:43—Breasts, tied up to torture rack.
- ••• 0:49—More breasts, tied up to torture rack.
- •• 0:51—Brief right breast then breasts several times, while lying down, tied to the rack.
- • 0:54—Very brief breasts when Aurion covers her up.

**The Haunting of Morella** (1989) . . . . Coel Deveroux
- ••• 0:17—Breasts, taking a bath, then getting out and wrapping a towel around herself.
- ••• 1:00—Breasts in white panties, standing under a waterfall.

Wizards of the Lost Kingdom, Part 2 (1991) . . . . . . .n.a.
*Magazines:*
**Playboy** (Nov 1985) . . . . . . . . . . Sex in Cinema 1985
- •• 134—Breasts, getting her breasts fondled in still from *Barbarian Queen*.

## Clatterbuck, Tamara

*Films:*
The Borrower (1989). . . . . . . . . . . . . . Michele Chodiss
*Made for Cable Movies:*
**Blind Side** (1993; HBO). . . . . . . . . . . . . Barbara Hall
- •• 1:13—In bra and panties, outside with Rutger Hauer by the spa. Then breasts several times.

Rebel Highway: Girls in Prison (1994; Showtime)
. . . . . . . . . . . . . . . . . . . . . . . . . Actress on Newsreel

## Clayburgh, Jill

*Films:*
The Wedding Party (1969) . . . . . . . . . . .Josephine Fish
Portnoy's Complaint (1972) . . . . . . . . . . . . . . . Naomi
The Thief Who Came to Dinner (1973). . . . . . . . . Jackie
The Terminal Man (1974) . . . . . . . . . . . . . .Angela Black
Silver Streak (1976). . . . . . . . . . . . . . . . . . Hilly Burns
Semi-Tough (1977). . . . . . . . . . . Barbara Jane Bookman
**An Unmarried Woman** (1978) . . . . . . . . . . . . . . Erica
0:05—Dancing around the apartment in white long sleeve T-shirt and white panties.
- •• 0:12—Brief breasts getting dressed for bed, kind of dark and hard to see.
- •• 1:10—In bra and panties in guy's apartment, then brief breasts lying on bed.

Luna (1979) . . . . . . . . . . . . . . . . . . . . Caterina Silveri
**Starting Over** (1979) . . . . . . . . . . . Marilyn Holmberg
- • 0:45—Very brief upper half of breasts taking a shower while Burt Reynolds waits outside.

**It's My Turn** (1980). . . . . . . . . . . . . .Kate Gunzinger
- • 1:10—Brief upper half of left breast in bed with Michael Douglas after making love.

First Monday in October (1981) . . . . . . . . Ruth Loomis
1:29—Nude behind shower door, but you can't see anything. Only part of her left breast (seen from the back) when she gets out and puts on her robe.
I'm Dancing as Fast as I Can (1981) . . . Barbara Gordon

Where Are the Children? (1986). . . . . . Nancy Eldgridge
Shy People (1988) . . . . . . . . . . . . . . . . . . . . . .Diana
Rich in Love (1992) . . . . . . . . . . . . . . . . Helen Odom
Whispers in the Dark (1992). . . . . . . . . . . .Sarah Green
Day of Atonement (1993; French) . . . . . . . . Sally White
Naked in New York (1993). . . . . . . . . . . . . . . . . n.a.
*Made for TV Movies:*
Hustling (1975) . . . . . . . . . . . . . . . . . . . . . .Wanda
Female Instinct (1985) . . . . . . . . . . . . . . . . . Mary
Reason for Living: The Jill Ireland Story (1991)
. . . . . . . . . . . . . . . . . . . . . . . . . . . . . . . Jill Ireland
Trial: The Price of Passion (1992) . . . Judge Louise Parker
Firestorm: 72 Hours in Oakland (1993)
. . . . . . . . . . . . . . . . . . . . . . . . . Anneliese Osborn
Honor Thy Father & Mother (1994). . . . . . . . . . . . n.a.

## Clearbranch, Deborah

*Films:*
Caged Heat (1974) . . . . . . . . . . . . . . . . . . . . Debbie
*a.k.a. Renegade Girls*
*Magazines:*
**Penthouse** (Jun 1974) . . . . . . . . . . . . . . . .Georgia Girl
- ••• 82-87—Nude.

## Clément, Aurore

*Films:*
Lovers and Liars (1979; Italian). . . . . . . . . . . . . . Cora
Paris, Texas (1984; French/German). . . . . . . . . . . Anne
Mosca Addio (1987; Italian) . . . . . . . . Elena, Ida's Sister
El Sur (1988; Spanish) . . . . . . . . . . . . . Irene Rios/Laura
Gemini: The Twin Stars (1988; U.S./Swiss)
. . . . . . . . . . . . . . . . . . . . . . . . . . Mrs. Buffington
*Magazines:*
**Playboy** (Jun 1975). . . . . . . Sex in Cinema French Style
- • 86—Half of right breast and partial lower frontal nudity.
**Playboy** (Nov 1975) . . . . . . . . . . Sex in Cinema 1975
- • 136—Buns, lying on sofa from *Lacombe, Lucien*.

## Clery, Corrine

*Films:*
**Kleinhoff Hotel** (1973) . . . . . . . . . . . . . . . . . . . . n.a.
**The Story of "O"** (1975; French). . . . . . . . . . . . . .O
(Nude a lot, only the best are listed.)
- •• 0:04—Breasts in the back of car when her boyfriend pulls her blouse down and rips her bra off.
- ••• 0:08—Breasts, getting made up by two women.
- •• 0:10—Left breast, while getting checked out.
- •• 0:13—Frontal nudity, chained to chandelier and whipped.
- •• 0:14—Breasts on couch.
- •• 0:16—Breasts getting out of tub and sitting on bed.
- ••• 0:18—Breasts and brief buns, getting out of bed and whipped. Frontal nudity, getting up.
- ••• 0:20—Frontal nudity with two guys.
- ••• 0:22—Breasts, sitting in front of a mirror.
- •• 0:24—Breasts, watching another woman have sex in library.
- ••• 0:27—Breasts sitting at table and eating.

•• 0:29—Breasts getting a bath.

•• 0:30—Breasts being led around blindfolded.

•• 0:33—Brief breasts, getting whipped and eating.

•• 0:42—Buns, while bent over sofa.

••• 0:43—Breasts with older man on sofa.

••• 0:44—Nude, taking off her skirt.

••• 0:59—Frontal nudity, reclining on bed, then sitting up.

•• 1:02—Breasts in room with older man when he opens her blouse.

••• 1:05—Breasts and buns in bedroom.

••• 1:06—Nude with other women, getting dressed in a corset.

••• 1:08—Breasts, getting chained to posts and whipped.

••• 1:13—Breasts in bed with another woman.

•• 1:14—Breasts before getting branded.

••• 1:17—Frontal nudity, getting out of tub and putting on robe.

•• 1:19—Breasts getting her blouse opened and breast sucked.

••• 1:21—Nude, making love in bed. Slightly overexposed.

••• 1:26—Tied up to posts by wrists.

•• 1:32—Breasts in open cape, while wearing a mask. Frontal nudity getting cape removed.

**Covert Action** (1978) . . . . . . . . . . . . . . . . . Anne Florio
*a.k.a. Sono Stato Un Agente Cia*

The Switch (1978). . . . . . . . . . . . . . . . . . . . . Charlotte
*a.k.a. The Con Artists*

The Humanoid (1979; Italian) . . . . . . . . . . . . . . . . . .n.a.

Moonraker (1979). . . . . . . . . . . . . . . . Corinne Dufour

**I Hate Blondes** (1981; Italian). . . . . . . . . . . . Angelica
• 1:17—Left breast and upper half of buns, in bedroom with a guy when he tries to seduce her.

Yor: The Hunter from the Future (1983) . . . . . . . Ka-Laa

**Dangerous Obsession** (1990; Italian). . Carol Simpson
• 0:14—Right breast sticking out of lingerie while lying in bed.
•• 0:36—Full frontal nudity lying in bed waiting for her husband, then with him, then getting out of bed.

*Magazines:*

**Playboy** (Nov 1975) . . . . . . . . . . . Sex in Cinema 1975
• 139—Buns, while tied by wrists from *Story of O*.

**Playboy** (Dec 1975). . . . . . . . . . . . . . . . . . . .Story of O
••• 127-131—Nude.

**Playboy** (Sep 1987) . . . . . . . . .25 Years of James Bond
•• 131—Breasts.

# Cleveland, Amanda

*Films:*

**Blow Out** (1981). . . . . . . . . . . . . . . . . . . . .Coed Lover
• 0:01—Left breast in room while someone watches from the outside.

True Confessions (1981) . . . . . . . . . . . . . . . . . . . .Lois

# Cleveland, Missy

*Films:*

**Blow Out** (1981) . . . . . . . . . . . . . . . . . Shower Victim
•• 0:02—Breasts in shower and on TV monitor while killer stalks outside.

*Video Tapes:*

Playboy Video Magazine, Volume 2 (1983)
. . . . . . . . . . . . . . . . . . . . . . . .Herself/Playboy Playoffs

*Magazines:*

**Playboy** (Apr 1979) . . . . . . . . . . . . . . . . . . . Playmate

# Clive, Teagan

a.k.a. Teagan.
Former body guard for David Lee Roth.

*Films:*

Armed and Dangerous (1986) . . . . . . . . . Staff Member

Jumpin' Jack Flash (1986). . . . . Russian Exercise Woman

**Obsession: A Taste For Fear** (1987)
. . . . . . . . . . . . . . . . . . . . . . . . . . . Teagan Morrison
• 0:15—Brief upper half of right breast, when she lies back down in bed.
• 0:29—Buns, while lying dead, covered with plastic wrap.
• 0:37—Very brief buns in flashback to 0:29 scene.

Alienator (1989). . . . . . . . . . . . . . . . . . . . Alienator

Interzone (1989) . . . . . . . . . . . . . . . . . . . . . . Mantis

Mob Boss (1990) . . . . . . . . . . . . . . . . . . . . . . Noelle

Sinbad and the Seven Seas (1990). . . . . . . . . . . . n.a.

Vice Academy, Part 2 (1990) . . . . . . . . . . . Bimbo Cop

*Music Videos:*

California Girls/David Lee Roth . . . . . . Muscular Woman

# Close, Glenn

*Films:*

World According to Garp (1982) . . . . . . . . Jenny Fields

**The Big Chill** (1983) . . . . . . . . . . . . . . . . . . . . . .Sara
• 0:27—Breasts sitting down in the shower crying.

The Natural (1984) . . . . . . . . . . . . . . . . . . . . Iris Gaines

The Stone Boy (1984) . . . . . . . . . . . . . . Ruth Hillerman

Jagged Edge (1985) . . . . . . . . . . . . . . . . . .Teddy Barnes
0:46—Side view of left breast, making love in bed with Jeff Bridges.
1:38—Very brief side view of right breast running down the hall taking off her blouse. Back is toward camera. Blurry shot.

Maxie (1985) . . . . . . . . . . . . . . . . . . . Jan/Maxie Malone
0:37—Very brief back half of left breast, while sitting up in bed.

**Fatal Attraction** (1987) . . . . . . . . . . . . . . Alex Forrest
•• 0:17—Left breast when she opens her top to let Michael Douglas kiss her. Then very brief buns, falling into bed with him.
• 0:20—Brief right breast in freight elevator with Douglas.
••• 0:32—Breasts in bed talking to Douglas. Long scene, sheet keeps changing positions between cuts.

Dangerous Liaisons (1988). . . . . . .Marquise de Merteuil

Immediate Family (1989) . . . . . . . . . . . . Linda Spector

Hamlet (1990; British/French) . . . . . . . Queen Gertrude

Meeting Venus (1990; British) . . . . . . . . Karin Anderson
Reversal of Fortune (1990) . . . . . . . . . Sunny von Bülow
Hook (1991) . . . . . . . . . . . . . . . . . . . . . . . . . . . . Gutless
The House of Spirits (1993). . . . . . . . . . . . . . . . . Ferula
The Paper (1993) . . . . . . . . . . . . . . . . . . . . Alicia Clark
*Made for TV Movies:*
Sarah Plain and Tall (1991) . . . . . . . . . . Sarah Wheaton
Skylark (1993). . . . . . . . . . . . . . . . . . . . . Sarah Witting

## • Clunie, Michelle

*Films:*
**Sunset Strip** (1992) . . . . . . . . . . . . . . . . . . . . . . Jonesy
••• 0:23—In black skirt and bra, then breasts and buns
  in G-string, doing routine on stage.
• 1:16—Breasts in music video.
**Jason Goes to Hell—The Final Friday** (1993)
. . . . . . . . . . . . . . . . Deborah, the dark-haired camper
(Unrated Director's Original Cut reviewed.)
• 0:29—Brief right breast, while on top of Luke in tent.
••• 0:31—Breasts, while making love with Luke in tent
  before getting killed.

## • Cochran, Shannon

*Films:*
The Babe (1992) . . . . . . . . . . . . . . . . . . . . . . . . Flapper
*TV:*
**NYPD Blue: Pilot** (Sep 21, 1993) . . . . . . . Lois Snyder
• 0:25—Very brief buns in panties and blurry breasts,
  while getting dressed after helping to set up Sipow-
  icz.
NYPD Blue (1993- ) . . . . . . . . . . . . . . . . . . . Lois Snyder

## Cochrane, Talie

*Films:*
The Centerfold Girls (1974). . . . . . . . . . . . . . . Donna
**I Spit on Your Corpse** (1974) . . . . . . . . . . Hitchhiker
*a.k.a. Girls for Rent*
• 0:47—Brief right breast, then breasts getting shot.
  More breasts, dead, covered with blood.
Fugitive Girls (1975) . . . . . . . . . . . . . . . . . . . . . . . n.a.
If You Don't Stop It You'll Go Blind (1979) . . . . . . . . n.a.

## Cochrell, Elizabeth

*a.k.a. Liza Cochrell.*
*Films:*
**The Big Bet** (1985) . . . . . . . . . . . . . Sister in Stag Film
••• 1:05—Breasts and buns, undressing and getting
  into bathtub in a video tape that Chris is watching.
•• 1:08—Breasts again on video tape, when Chris
  watches it on TV at home.
**Free Ride** (1986) . . . . . . . . . . . . . . . . Nude Girl #1
• 0:25—Brief buns taking a shower with another girl.
Sunset Strip (1986) . . . . . . . . . . . . . . . . . . . . Stripper

## • Coffey, Elizabeth

*Films:*
Pink Flamingos (1972) . . . . . . . . . . . . . . . . . . . . . n.a.
**Female Trouble** (1974) . . . . . . . . . . . . . . . . Ernestine
• 1:24—Right breast, while lying on cot in jail cell with
  Divine.
• 1:25—More right breast.
• 1:26—Brief lower frontal nudity when kissing Divine.

## Cole, Debra

*Films:*
Crossing Delancey (1988) . . . . . . . . . . . . . . . . Waitress
**The Hot Spot** (1990) . . . . . . . . . . . . . . . . Irene Davey
• 1:26—Breasts sunbathing next to Jennifer Connelly
  at side of lake. Long shot.
•• 1:27—Breasts talking with Connelly some more.

## Coleman, Renee

*Films:*
**After School** (1987). . . . . . . . . . . . . . September Lane
•• 0:35—Breasts and buns getting into bathtub. Al-
  most lower frontal nudity.
Rocket Gibraltar (1988) . . . . . . . . . . . . . . . . . . Waitress
Who's Harry Crumb? (1989) . . . . . . . . Jennifer Downing
A League of Their Own (1992) . . . . . . . . . Alice Gaspers

## Collings, Jeannie

*Films:*
**Happy Housewives** . . . . . . . . . . . . . . . . . . Mrs. Wain
• 0:16—Very, very brief right breast with the News-
  agent's Daughter and Bob in the bathtub.
Confessions of a Window Cleaner (1974; British)
. . . . . . . . . . . . . . . . . . . . . . . . . . . . . . . . Baby Doll
Carry on England (1976; British) . . . . . . Private Edwards
**Emily** (1976; British) . . . . . . . . . . . . . . . . . . . Rosalind
• 1:05—Brief breasts on the couch with Gerald while
  Richard watches.

## Collins, Alana

*a.k.a. Alana Hamilton or Alana Stewart.*
Ex-wife of singer Rod Stewart.
Ex-wife of actor George Hamilton.
*Films:*
Evel Knievel (1972). . . . . . . . . . . . . . . . . . . . . . Nurse
**Night Call Nurses** (1972) . . . . . . . . . . . . . . . . . Janis
*a.k.a. Young LA Nurses 2*
•• 0:12—Breasts in bed with Zach.
0:24—In white two piece swimsuit on boat.
•• 0:28—Breasts and buns on bed with Kyle.
• 0:52—Brief right breast twice in shower with Kyle.
The Ravagers (1979) . . . . . . . . . . . . . . . . . . . . Miriam
**Swing Shift** (1984) . . . . . . . . . . . . . . . Frankie Parker
0:11—Buns in B&W photo that Christine Lahti
  shows to Fred Ward. Possible photo composite.
Where the Boys Are '84 (1984) . . . . . . . . . . . . Maggie
*Magazines:*
**Playboy** (Mar 1993) . . . . . . . . . . . . . . . . . Grapevine
• 167—Half of right breast, under sheer black blouse.

## Collins, Candace

*Films:*

Class (1983) . . . . . . . . . . . . . . . . . . . . . . . .Buxom Girl
Risky Business (1983) . . . . . . . . . . . . . . . . . . . Call Girl
Smokey and the Bandit III (1983) . . . . . . . . . . . . .Maid

*Magazines:*

**Playboy** (Oct 1974). . . . . . . . . . . . . . Bunnies of 1974
• 132—Lower frontal nudity.
**Playboy** (Nov 1975) . . . . . . . . . . . . . . Bunnies of '75
•• 93—Buns and lower frontal nudity.
**Playboy** (Dec 1979). . . . . . . . . . . . . . . . . . Playmate
**Playboy** (Dec 1980). . . . . . . . . . . . . . .Bunny Birthday
•• 156—Right breast and lower frontal nudity.

## Collins, Jo

*Video Tapes:*

**Playboy Video Centerfold: Donna Edmondson**
(1987). . . . . . . . . . . . . . . . . . . . . . . Playmate Update
••• 0:21—Breasts and buns in still photos.

*Magazines:*

**Playboy** (Dec 1964). . . . . . . . . . . . . . . . . . Playmate
**Playboy** (Jan 1974) . . . . . . . Twenty Years of Playmates
•• 107—Buns and side of left breast.
Playboy (Jan 1994) . . . . . . . . . . . . .40 Memorable Years
88—Right breast in wet white blouse.

## Collins, Joan

*Films:*

Decameron Nights (1953) . . . . . . . . . . . . . . . . . Maria
Stopover Tokyo (1957) . . . . . . . . . . . . . . . . . . . . Tina
Subterfuge (1969). . . . . . . . . . . . . . . . . . Anne Langley
The Executioner (1970; British) . . . . . . . . . Sarah Booth
Quest for Love (1971). . . . . . . . . . . . . . . . . . . .Ottilie
Fear in the Night (1972; British) . . . . Molly Charmichael
*a.k.a. Dynasty of Fear*
Tales From the Crypt (1972) . . . . . . . . . .Joanne Clayton
Dark Places (1974; British). . . . . . . . . . . . . . . . Sarah
**Oh, Alfie!** (1975; British) . . . . . . . . . . . . . . . . . . Fay
*a.k.a. Alfie Darling*
0:28—In white bra and panties, running to answer
the phone, then talking to Alfie.
••• 1:00—Breasts lying in bed after Alfie rolls off her.
Bawdy Adventures of Tom Jones (1976; British)
. . . . . . . . . . . . . . . . . . . . . . . . . . . . . . . . Black Bess
Empire of the Ants (1977). . . . . . . . . . . .Marilyn Fryser
The Big Sleep (1978; British) . . . . . . . . . . . Agnes Lozelle
**Fearless** (1978) . . . . . . . . . . . . . . . . . . . . . . Bridgitte
• 0:01—In bra and panties, then brief right breast dur-
ing opening credits.
•• 0:41—Breasts after doing a strip tease routine on
stage.
• 1:17—Undressing in front of Wally in white bra and
panties, then right breast.
• 1:20—Brief right breast lying dead on couch.
**The Stud** (1978; British) . . . . . . . . . . . . . . . .Fontaine
• 0:10—Brief left breast making love with Tony in the
elevator.
0:27—Brief buns in panties, stockings and garter
belt in Tony's apartment.

0:58—Brief black bra and panties under fur coat in
back of limousine with Tony.
• 1:03—Brief breasts taking off dress to get in pool.
• 1:04—Nude in the pool with Tony.
**The Bitch** (1979; British) . . . . . . . . . . .Fontaine Khaled
0:01—In long slip getting out of bed and putting a
bathrobe on.
• 0:03—Brief breasts in the shower with a guy.
•• 0:24—Brief breasts taking black corset off for the
chauffeur in the bedroom, then buns getting out of
bed and walking to the bathroom.
0:39—Making love in bed wearing a blue slip.
• 1:01—Left breast after making love in bed.
Sunburn (1979) . . . . . . . . . . . . . . . . . . . . . . . . Nera
Homework (1982) . . . . . . . . . . . . . . . . . . . . .Diane
Body double used for Joan's nude scene.

*Miniseries:*

Sins (1986). . . . . . . . . . . . . . . . . . . . . . Helene Junot
Dynasty: The Reunion (1991)
. . . . . . . Alexis Morell Carrington Colby Dexter Rowan

*Made for TV Movies:*

Her Life as a Man (1984) . . . . . . . . . . . . . . Pam Dugan
The Cartier Affair (1985) . . . . . . . . . . . . . Cartier Rand
Monte Carlo (1986). . . . . . . . . . . . . . Katrina Petrovna

*TV:*

Dynasty (1981-89) . . . . . . . . . . Alexis Carrington Colby

*Magazines:*

**Playboy** (Nov 1978) . . . . . . . . . . . Sex in Cinema 1978
• 185—Left breast and lower frontal nudity.
**Playboy** (Dec 1983) . . . . . . . . . . . . . . . . . . . . . n.a.
**Playboy** (Dec 1984) . . . . . . . . . . . . . .Sex Stars of 1984
••• 209—Breasts in bed.
**Playboy** (Jan 1989) . . . . . . . . . . .Women of the Eighties
•• 250—Buns and side view of right breast in B&W
photo.

## Collins, Pamela

*Films:*

**Sweet Sugar** (1972). . . . . . . . . . . . . . . . . . . . Dolores
*a.k.a. Hellfire on Ice*
• 0:26—Brief breasts when doctor tears her bra off.
••• 0:50—Breasts in the shower with Phyllis Davis.
So Long, Blue Boy (1973). . . . . . . . . . . . . . . . Cathy
**Famous T & A** (1982) . . . . . . . . . . . . . . . . . . Dolores
(No longer available for purchase, check your video
store for rental.)
••• 1:05—Breasts in scenes and outtakes from *Sweet
Sugar.*

## Collins, Pauline

*Films:*

Secrets of a Windmill Girl (1966; British) . . . . . .Pat Lord
**Shirley Valentine** (1989; British) . . . . Shirley Valentine
(If you like older women, check this out.)
• 0:13—Brief left breast giving Joe a shampoo in the
bathtub.
•• 1:17—Breasts jumping from the boat into the water
in slow motion. Very brief breasts in the water.

•• 1:19—Buns, hugging Tom Conti, left breast several times kissing him.

City of Joy (1992) . . . . . . . . . . . . . . . . . . . . . Joan Bethel

## Collins, Roberta

*Films:*

**The Big Doll House** (1971) . . . . . . . . . . . . . . Alcott
  ••• 0:33—Breasts in shower. Seen through blurry window by prison worker, Fred. Blurry, but nice.
  • 0:34—Brief left breast, while opening her blouse for Fred.

Unholy Rollers (1972) . . . . . . . . . . . . . . . . . . . . Jennifer
  *a.k.a. Leader of the Pack*

The Arousers (1973) . . . . . . . . . . . . . . . . . . . . Call Girl

The Roommates (1973). . . . . . . . . . . . . . . . . . . . Beth

**Caged Heat** (1974). . . . . . . . . . . . . . . . . . . . . . Belle
  *a.k.a. Renegade Girls*
  • 0:11—Very brief breasts getting blouse ripped open by Juanita.
  ••• 1:01—Breasts while the prison doctor has her drugged so he can take pictures of her.

**Death Race 2000** (1975) . . . . . . . . . . Matilda the Hun
  •• 0:27—Breasts being interviewed and arguing with Calamity Jane.

Train Ride to Hollywood (1975). . . . . . . . . Jean Harlow

Death Wish II (1982). . . . . . . . . . . . . . Woman at Party

Hardbodies (1984) . . . . . . . . . . . . . . . . . . . . . . . Lana

School Spirit (1985) . . . . . . . . . . . . . Helen Grimshaw

Hardbodies 2 (1986). . . . . . . . . . . . . . . . . Lana Logan

Vendetta (1986) . . . . . . . . . . . . . . . . . . . . . Miss Dice

## Collins, Ruth Corrine

*Films:*

Blood Sisters (1986) . . . . . . . . . . . . . . . . . . Prostitute

**Sexpot** (1986) . . . . . . . . . . . . . . . . . . . . Ivy Barrington
  •• 0:09—Breasts on table, taking her dress off for Phillip.
  • 0:41—Buns, in Damon's arms.
  •• 0:51—Left breast, while in shower talking to Boopsie.

**Doom Asylum** (1987). . . . . . . . . . . . . . . . . . . . Tina
  •• 0:19—Breasts pulling up her top while yelling at kids below.

Firehouse (1987). . . . . . . . . . . . . . . . . . . . . Bubbles

**Lurkers** (1987) . . . . . . . . . . . . . . . . . . . Jane (Model)
  0:12—Undressing in white bra (on the right) with another model.
  •• 0:13—Breasts, changing clothes with the other model.

**Prime Evil** (1987) . . . . . . . . . . . . . . . . . . . . . . Cathy
  ••• 0:15—Breasts making love with her boyfriend in bed.
  • 0:16—More breasts sitting up and getting out of bed.
  ••• 0:27—Breasts, sitting up while the priest talks to her.
  •• 1:13—Left breast, while removing her gown (she's on the left) with Brett and Judy.

Psychos in Love (1987) . . . . . . . . . . . . . . . . . . Susan
  ••• 0:42—Breasts, dancing and undressing in living room in front of Joe when caught by Kate.

**Wildest Dreams** (1987). . . . . . . . . . . . . . . . . . Stella
  ••• 0:22—Breasts wearing panties in bedroom on bed with Bobby.
  • 1:10—Brief breasts fighting on floor with two other women.

**Alexa** (1988). . . . . . . . . . . . . . . . . . . . . . . Marshall
  • 0:01—Breasts a couple of times taking blue dress off and putting it on again. Long shot.

**Galactic Gigolo** (1988) . . . . . . . . . . . Dr. Ruth Pepper
  *a.k.a. Club Earth*
  •• 0:47—Breasts, while stripping in front of Eoj.
  • 0:49—Breasts, while getting tied up by Sammy.
  • 0:53—Breasts in open cape while in the Goldberg's family room.
  •• 0:55—Breasts, while getting rescued.

**New York's Finest** (1988) . . . . . . . . . . . Joy Sugarman
  • 0:04—Brief breasts with a bunch of hookers.
  • 0:36—Breasts with her two friends doing push-ups on the floor.
  •• 1:02—Breasts making love on top of a guy talking about diamonds.

**Cleo/Leo** (1989). . . . . . . . . . . . . . . . . . . . . . . . Sally
  ••• 0:08—Breasts getting dress pulled off by Leo.

Deadly Embrace (1989) . . . . . . . . . . . . Dede Magnolia

**Party Incorporated** (1989). . . . . . . . . . . . . . . . Betty
  *a.k.a. Party Girls*
  • 0:07—Breasts on desk with Dickie. Long shot.
  •• 1:08—Breasts in bed with Weston when Marilyn Chambers comes in.

Death Collector (1990) . . . . . . . . . . . Annie Northbride

**Eleven Days, Eleven Nights 2** (1990)
  . . . . . . . . . . . . . . . . . . . . . . . . . Dana Durrington
  ••• 0:14—Breasts while wearing stockings and making out with George on bed.

**Little Devils** (1991) . . . . . . . . . . . . . . . . . . . . . n.a.

**Dead Boyz Can't Fly** (1992) . . . . . . . . Myra Kandinsky
  • 0:14—Brief breasts while getting raped by Buzz in elevator.

Hellroller (1992). . . . . . . . . . . . . . . . Eugene's Mother

## • Collins, Tai

Miss Virginia-U.S.A. 1983.

*Films:*

**Enemy Gold** (1993) . . . . . . . . . . . . . . . . . . Ava Noble
  ••• 0:20—Breasts and very brief lower frontal nudity in sauna. Breasts and buns, getting out of the sauna and into the shower.
  ••• 1:26—Breasts, while making love with Mark.

*TV:*

Baywatch (1992-93). . . . . . . . . . . . . . . . . . . . . . n.a.

*Video Tapes:*

**Playboy's Sensual Fantasy for Lovers** (1993) Games
  ••• 0:05—In white bra and panties, then full frontal nudity while in house, in bathtub, then making love in bed.
  • 0:46—Nude during review.

• 0:49—Brief right breast during review.
*Magazines:*
**Playboy** (Oct 1991) . . . . . The Governor and the Beauty
••• 90-97—Nude.
**Playboy** (Dec 1991). . . . . . . . . . . . . . Sex Stars 1991
••• 187—Full frontal nudity.
**Playboy's Nudes** (Dec 1992) . . . . . . . . . . . . . Herself
••• 10—Full frontal nudity.
**Playboy's Blondes, Brunettes & Redheads**
(Sep 1993) . . . . . . . . . . . . . . . . . . . . . . . . . Herself
••• 14-15—Full frontal nudity.

## Collinson, Madeleine

Identical twin sister of Mary Collinson.
*Films:*
Come Back Peter (1971; British) . . . . . . . . . . . . . . . .n.a.
**The Love Machine** (1971) . . . . . . . . . . . . . . . . Sandy
•• 1:22—Breasts in shower with Robin and her sister
when Dyan Cannon discovers them all together.
Can't tell who is who.
**Twins of Evil** (1971) . . . . . . . . . . . . . . Freida Gelhorn
•• 1:07—Right breast, then brief breasts undoing
dress, then full frontal nudity after turning into a
vampire in bedroom.
**Up In Smoke** (1978) . . . . . . . . . . . . . . . . . . . . Pinup
• 0:44—Brief breasts in centerfold photo on inside of
restroom stall door.
*Magazines:*
**Playboy** (Oct 1970) . . . . . . . . . . . . . . . . . . . Playmate
**Playboy** (Dec 1972). . . . . . . . . . . . . Sex Stars of 1972
•• 211—Breasts.
**Playboy** (Jan 1974) . . . . . . . Twenty Years of Playmates
••• 110—Breasts on bed.
**Playboy** (Jan 1979) . . . . . . . . . . . . . 25 Beautiful Years
••• 161—Breasts lying on bed.
**Playboy** (Jan 1994) . . . . . . . . . . . .40 Memorable Years
89—Breasts.

## Collinson, Mary

Identical twin sister of Madeleine Collinson.
*Films:*
Come Back Peter (1971; British) . . . . . . . . . . . . . . . .n.a.
**The Love Machine** (1971) . . . . . . . . . . . . . . . . Debbie
•• 1:22—Breasts in shower with Robin and her sister
when Dyan Cannon discovers them all together.
Can't tell who is who.
Twins of Evil (1971). . . . . . . . . . . . . . . . Maria Gelhorn
**Up In Smoke** (1978) . . . . . . . . . . . . . . . . . . . . Pinup
• 0:44—Brief breasts in centerfold photo on inside of
restroom stall door.
*Magazines:*
**Playboy** (Oct 1970) . . . . . . . . . . . . . . . . . . . Playmate
**Playboy** (Dec 1972). . . . . . . . . . . . . Sex Stars of 1972
•• 211—Breasts.
**Playboy** (Jan 1974) . . . . . . . Twenty Years of Playmates
••• 110—Breasts on bed.
**Playboy** (Jan 1979) . . . . . . . . . . . . . 25 Beautiful Years
••• 161—Breasts lying on bed.

**Playboy** (Jan 1994) . . . . . . . . . . . 40 Memorable Years
••• 89—Breasts.

## Colpitts-Cameron, Cissie

a.k.a. Cisse Cameron.
*Films:*
Beyond the Valley of the Dolls (1970). . . . . . . . . . . . n.a.
Billy Jack (1971) . . . . . . . . . . . . . . . . . . Miss Eyelashes
**The Happy Hooker Goes to Washington** (1977)
. . . . . . . . . . . . . . . . . . . . . . . . . . . . Miss Goodbody
• 0:29—Very brief breasts when her top pops open
during the senate hearing.
**The Baltimore Bullet** (1980) . . . . . . . . . . . . . .Sugar
• 0:09—Breasts behind shower door after James
Coburn gets out.
**Porky's II: The Next Day** (1983; Canadian)
. . . . . . . . . . . . . . . . . . . .Graveyard Gloria/Sandy Le Toi
0:26—Buns in G-string at carnival.
•• 0:39—Breasts and buns in G-string, stripping for Pee
Wee at cemetery.
•• 0:40—More breasts, pretending to die.
•• 0:42—Breasts, being carried by Meat.
*TV:*
The Ted Knight Show (1978) . . . . . . . . . . . . . Graziella

## Colton, Diane

*Films:*
**Pleasure In Paradise** (1992). . . . . . . . . . . . . . Tiffany
••• 0:27—In black bra, then breasts while making love
with Hansen. Long scene.
*Magazines:*
Playboy (Dec 1992) . . . . . . . . . . . . . . . . . . Grapevine

## Comshaw, Lisa

*Films:*
Almost Pregnant (1992). . . . . . . . . . . . . . Body Double
(Unrated version reviewed.)
**Housewife From Hell** (1993) . . . . . . . . . . . . Melissa
•• 0:03—Nude, after taking off robe in front of bathroom mirror (while wearing glasses), then getting
into shower.
•• 0:04—Breasts, while sitting in bathtub and talking to
John.
••• 0:36—Breasts, while sitting in bubble bath and talking to John.
• 0:48—In bra, buns in T-back while dancing in garage in between two other dancers.
• 1:00—Breasts under white bodysuit.
Scanner Cop (1993) . . . . . . . . Nurse in Operating Room
*Video Tapes:*
**Buck Naked Line Dancing** (1993) . . . . . . . . Dancer
••• 0:00—Breasts throughout. She's usually in the front
in the left, wearing a choker.
**Penthouse Forum Letters: Volume 1** (1993)
. . . . . . . . . . . . . . . . . . . . . . . . Mystery Caller/Vicky
••• 0:40—In black bra, then breasts in her cubicle,
squishing her breasts against the window.
••• 0:41—Nude, dancing in front of a different window.

••• 0:42—Breasts, while making love with Brad by the
window.
•• 0:45—Breasts, taking off her clothes in the office
with Tanya and Cindy in front of Brad.
**Playboy Night Dreams** (1993) . . . . . . . .Night Watch
••• 0:21—In bra, panties, garter belt and stockings in
parking structure. Nude, while making love on car.
**Playboy's Erotic Fantasies III** (1993)
. . . . . . . . . . . . . . . . . . . .Midnight Madness/Vampiress
••• 0:00—Nude, while making love with a guy and the
other vampiress. (She's wearing snake arm bands.)
**Playboy's Secret Confessions** (1993)
. . . . . . . . . . . . . . . . . . Here Comes the Judge/The Girl
0:45—In black bra and panties in courtroom with
Spike.
••• 0:47—Full frontal nudity, while taking off the judge's
robe and making love with Spike on the judge's
bench.
Single Alien Seeks Horny Earth Girl (1994) . . . . . . Tracy

# • Conaway, Cristi
*Films:*
Doc Hollywood (1991) . . . . . . . . . . . . . . . Receptionist
Batman Returns (1992) . . . . . . . . . . . . . . . .Ice Princess
Husbands and Wives (1992) . . . . . . . . Shawn Grainger
*Made for Cable Movies:*
**Attack of the 50 ft. Woman** (1993; HBO) . . . .Honey
0:12—In black bra and panties while getting dressed
in motel room with Daniel Baldwin.
• 0:16—Very brief buns and back side of left breast, af-
ter getting out of bed and walking to the bathroom.
1:07—In black bra, while dancing in front of Baldwin
in beauty shop.
*Miniseries:*
Grass Roots (1992) . . . . . . . . . . . . . . . .Charlene Joiner

# Condon, Iris
*Films:*
**Party Plane** (1988) . . . . . . . . . . . . . . . . . . . . . .Renee
• 0:29—Buns, in white lingerie during audition.
••• 0:48—Breasts plane doing a strip tease routine.
••• 1:02—Breasts on plane mud wrestling with Carol.
• 1:12—Left breast, covered with mud, holding the
Mad Bomber.
• 1:17—Left breast, then breasts in trunk with the
Doctor.
**Pucker Up and Bark Like a Dog** (1989)
. . . . . . . . . . . . . . . . . . . . . . . . . . .Stretch Woman
*Video Tapes:*
**In Search of the Perfect 10** (1986)
. . . . . . . . . . . . . . . . . . . . . . . Perfect Girl #6/Jackie
••• 0:37—Breasts (she's the blonde) playing Twister
with Rebecca Lynn. Buns in G-string.

# Congie, Terry
*Films:*
**Malibu Hot Summer** (1981). . . . . . . . .Janice Johnson
*a.k.a. Sizzle Beach*
(*Sizzle Beach* is the re-released version with Kevin Costner featured on the cover. It is missing all the nude
scenes during the opening credits before 0:06.)
0:09—Buns in the shower. Hard to see through the
door.
••• 0:29—Breasts taking off her top and getting into
bed with Steve, then making love.
0:54—In blue bikini top talking on the phone.
• 1:09—Side view of left breast kissing Gary during
the party.
•• 1:11—Breasts making love with Gary the next morning after the party.
**Shadows Run Black** (1981) . . . . . . . . . . Lee Faulkner
•• 0:22—Breasts, going for a swim in pool at night.
• 0:23—Breasts under water.

# Connelly, Jennifer
*Films:*
Once Upon a Time in America (1984) . . Young Deborah
(Long version reviewed.)
Creepers (1985; Italian) . . . . . . . . . . . .Jennifer Corvino
Labyrinth (1986) . . . . . . . . . . . . . . . . . . . . . . . . .Sarah
Some Girls (1988) . . . . . . . . . . . . . . . . . . . . . Gabriella
*a.k.a. Sisters*
**The Hot Spot** (1990) . . . . . . . . . . . . . . .Gloria Harper
1:01—In black bra and panties walking out of lake
with Don Johnson.
1:26—Buns, lying next to Irene next to lake. Long
shot.
••• 1:27—Breasts, talking to Irene next to lake. Wow!
Career Opportunities (1991) . . . . . . . . . Josie McClellan
The Rocketeer (1991). . . . . . . . . . . . . . . . . Jenny Blake
*Made for Cable Movies:*
The Heart of Justice (1993; TNT) . . . . . . .Emma Burgess

# Conrad, Kimberley
Wife of *Playboy* magazine publisher Hugh Hefner.
*Video Tapes:*
**Playboy Video Calendar 1989** (1988). . . . . .October
••• 0:38—Nude.
**Playboy Video Calendar 1990** (1989). . . . December
••• 1:03—Nude.
**Playboy Video Centerfold: Kimberley Conrad**
(1989) . . . . . . . . . . . . . . . . .Playmate of the Year 1989
••• 0:00—Nude throughout.
**Playboy's Playmates of the Year: The '80s** (1989)
. . . . . . . . . . . . . . . . . . . . . . .Playmate of the Year 1989
••• 0:44—Nude in still photos.
••• 0:49—Full frontal nudity in bathtub and in various
scenes around the house.
• 0:53—In lingerie.
**The Best of Video Playmate Calendars** (1992)
. . . . . . . . . . . . . . . . . . . . . . . . . . . . . . . . . Playmate
••• 0:43—Breasts and buns in over exposed music video
segment. Breasts while dancing in silk pajamas.

•• 0:44—In lingerie.
••• 0:45—Nude in outdoor fountain in slow motion.
•• 0:46—Nude in house, lit with a sliver of light.
*Magazines:*
**Playboy** (Jan 1988) . . . . . . . . . . . . . . . . . . . Playmate
**Playboy's Nudes** (Oct 1990). . . . . . . . . . . . . . Herself
••• 110—Full frontal nudity.
**Playboy's Calendar Playmates** (Nov 1992) . . Herself
••• 76—Full frontal nudity.
••• 87—Full frontal nudity.
**Playboy** (Jan 1994) . . . . . . . . . . . 40 Memorable Years
••• 94—Full frontal nudity.

## Contouri, Chantal

*Films:*
**Alvin Rides Again** (1974; Australian)
. . . . . . . . . . . . . . . . . . . . . . . . . . Boobs La Touche
• 1:15—Very brief lower frontal nudity, putting pant-
ies on in the car. Brief breasts, putting red dress on.
The Day After Halloween (1978; Australian) . . Madeline
*a.k.a. Snapshot*
*Made for Cable Movies:*
All the Rivers Run (1984; HBO) . . . . . . . . . . . . . . . Julie

## • Cook, Kelly

See: Jackson, Kelly.

## • Cook, Tracy

*Films:*
**SnakeEater III ...His Law** (1992) . . . . . Hildy Gardener
••• 0:27—Breasts, while making love with Lorenzo La-
mas in bedroom.
*Made for TV Movies:*
Bermuda Grace (1994) . . . . . . . . . . . . . . Lady Harding

## Cooke, Jennifer

*Films:*
Gimme an "F" (1981) . . . . . . . . . . . . . . Pam Bethlehem
*a.k.a. T & A Academy 2*
1:10—Wearing United States flag pasties frolicking
with Dr. Spirit. Nice bouncing action.
1:38—Still of pasties scene during end credits.
Friday the 13th, Part VI: Jason Lives (1986) . . . . . Megan
*Made for Cable TV:*
**The Hitchhiker: Man's Best Friend** (1985; HBO)
. . . . . . . . . . . . . . . . . . . . . . . . . . . . . . . . Elanor
(Available on *The Hitchhiker, Volume 4.*)
• 0:19—Brief side view breasts getting undressed to
take a shower.
*Miniseries:*
A Year in the Life (1986) . . . . . . . . . . . . Debbie Nesbit
*TV:*
The Guiding Light (1981-83) . . . . . . . . Morgan Nelson
V: The Series (1984-85) . . . . . . . . . . . . . . . . . Elizabeth

## Cooke, Victoria

*Video Tapes:*
Playboy Video Magazine, Volume 2 (1983)
. . . . . . . . . . . . . . . . . . . . Herself/Playboy Playoffs

*Magazines:*
**Playboy** (Jan 1980) . . . . . . . . . Playboy's Pajama Parties
••• 126—Full frontal nudity.
**Playboy** (Aug 1980) . . . . . . . . . . . . . . . . . . . . Playmate
•• 12—Full frontal nudity, posing as an artist's model.
••• 124-135—Nude.
**Playboy** (Dec 1980) . . . . . . . . . . . . . Sex Stars of 1980
• 243—Left breast.

## Coolidge, Rita

Singer.
*Films:*
**Pat Garrett and Billy the Kid** (1973) . . . . . . . . Maria
(Uncut Director's version reviewed.)
•• 1:48—Brief right breast, while sitting on bed and
getting undressed with Kris Kristofferson.
*Magazines:*
**Playboy** (Nov 1973) . . . . . . . . . . . Sex in Cinema 1973
• 151—Breasts in photo from *Pat Garrett and Billy the
Kid.*

## Cooper, Jeanne

Mother of actors Corbin and Collin Bernsen.
*Films:*
The Redhead from Wyoming (1952) . . . . . . . . . . . Myra
The Man from the Alamo (1953) . . . . . . . . Kate Lamar
Let No Man Write My Epitaph (1960) . . . . . . . . . . Fran
The Boston Strangler (1968) . . . . . . . . . . . . . . . . Cloe
**There Was a Crooked Man** (1970) . . . . . . . Prostitute
• 0:18—Brief left breast trying to seduce the sheriff,
Henry Fonda, in a room.
Kansas City Bomber (1972) . . . . . . . . . . . . . . . . Vivien
The All-American Boy (1973) . . . . . . . . . . . Nola Bealer
Frozen Assets (1992) . . . . . . . . . . . . . . . Zach's Mother
*Made for TV Movies:*
Beyond Suspicion (1993) . . . . . . . . . . . . . . . . . Renata
*TV:*
Bracken's World (1970) . . . . . . . . . . . . . Grace Douglas
The Young and the Restless (1973- )
. . . . . . . . . . . . . . . . . . Katherine Chancellor-Sterling

## Copley, Teri

*Films:*
**New Year's Evil** (1981) . . . . . . . . . . . . . . Teenage Girl
• 0:49—Brief right breast in the back of the car with
her boyfriend at a drive-in movie. Breast is half sticking out of her white bra. Dark, hard to see anything.
**Down the Drain** (1989) . . . . . . . . . . . . . . Kathy Miller
0:04—Full frontal nudity making love on couch with
Andrew Stevens. Looks like a body double.
0:31—In two piece swimsuit, then body double
nude doing strip tease for Stevens. Notice body
double isn't wearing earrings.
0:33—Buns, (probably the body double) on top of
Stevens.
1:21—In black bra in motel room when bad guy
opens her blouse.
Masters of Menace (1990) . . . . . . . . . . . . . . . . Sunny
Transylvania Twist (1990) . . . . . . . . . . . . . . . . Marisa

Brain Donors (1992) . . . . . . . . . . . . . . . . . . . . . . . Tina
Frozen Assets (1992) . . . . . . . . . . . . . . . . . . . . Peaches
*Made for TV Movies:*
I Married a Centerfold (1984) . . . . . . . . . . . . . . . . . .n.a.
In the Line of Duty: The F.B.I. Murders (1988). . . . Vickie
*TV:*
We Got It Made (1983-84) . . . . . . . . Mickey McKenzie
I Had Three Wives (1985) . . . . . . . . . . . . . . Samantha
*Magazines:*
**Playboy** (Nov 1990) . . . . . . . . . . . . . . . . . Teri Copley
••• 90-99—Nude. Very nice!
**Playboy** (Dec 1990). . . . . . . . . . . . . Sex Stars of 1990
•• 173—Right breast, while leaning against wall.
**Playboy's Blondes, Brunettes & Redheads**
(Sep 1993) . . . . . . . . . . . . . . . . . . . . . . . . . Herself
••• 43—Breasts.

# • Cornell, Angela

*Films:*
**Beach Babes From Beyond** (1993) . . . . . Sally's Model
••• 0:20—Breasts, while posing in spa outside (she's on
the left) during catalog photo session with two other models.
• 1:02—Brief breasts, when swimsuit top flies off while
dancing on stage during bikini contest (she's the
second one).
*Magazines:*
**Playboy** (Sep 1994). . . . . . . . . . . A Walk on the Bi Side
•• 77—Right breast and lower frontal nudity.

# Corri, Adrienne

*Films:*
Corridors of Blood (1957; British) . . . . . . . . . . . . Rachel
Three Men in a Boat (1958) . . . . . . . . . . . . . Clara Willis
Doctor Zhivago (1965) . . . . . . . . . . . . . . . . . . . Amelia
**A Clockwork Orange** (1971) . . . . . . . . Mrs. Alexander
•• 0:11—Breasts through cut-outs in her top, then full
frontal nudity getting raped by Malcolm McDowell
and his friends.
Revenge of the Pink Panther (1978) . . . Therese Douvier

# Corwin, Morena

*Video Tapes:*
**Playboy Video Calendar 1994** (1993) . . . November
••• 0:42—Breasts and buns, while walking around a
house at night. Nude while painting in a field.
••• 0:45—Nude in B&W on sofa during dream, then in
color when getting up out of bed.
**Playboy's Playmate Review 1993** (1993)
. . . . . . . . . . . . . . . . . . . . . . . . . . . Miss September
••• 0:27—Nude in bed and dancing out in a field with a
guy.
••• 0:30—Nude in pool and under water.
*Magazines:*
**Playboy** (Sep 1992). . . . . . . . . . . . . . . . . . . Playmate
**Playboy's Playmate Review** (Jun 1993) .. September
••• 76-83—Nude.
**Playboy** (Jul 1993). . . . . . . . . . . . . . . . . . . .Lucky Stiff
••• 78-83—Nude.

**Playboy's Book of Lingerie** (Nov 1993) . . . . .Herself
• 80—Lower frontal nudity.
••• 103—Breasts.
**Playboy's Nudes** (Dec 1993) . . . . . . . . . . . . . .Herself
••• 22-23—Full frontal nudity.
••• 28—Breasts.
**Playboy's Book of Lingerie** (Mar 1994). . . . . .Herself
••• 95—Full frontal nudity.

# Costa, Sara

*Films:*
**Weekend Pass** (1984) . . . . . . . . . .Tuesday Del Mundo
••• 0:07—Buns in G-string, then breasts during strip
dance routine on stage.
**Stripper** (1985) . . . . . . . . . . . . . . . . . . . . . . . .Herself
••• 0:16—Breasts doing strip dance routine.
••• 0:46—Breasts and buns dancing on stage in a G-
string.
••• 1:12—Breasts doing another strip routine.
*Video Tapes:*
**Hot Bodies** (1988) . . . . . . . . . . . . . . . . . . . . . .Herself
••• 0:00—Nude, dancing on stage. Long scene. Danc-
ing with a big boa snake.
••• 0:04—Breasts and buns in G-string.
**Hot Body Video Magazine #1** (1992)
. . . . . . . . . . . . . . . . . . . . . . . . . .Lingerie Model/Sara
••• 0:26—Breasts and buns in room with three other
models, trying on lingerie.
*Magazines:*
**Playboy** (Nov 1985) . . . . . . . . . . . Sex in Cinema 1985
••• 130—Breasts, doing dance routine in still from *Stripper*.

# • Courau, Clotilde

*Films:*
Map of the Human Heart (1992; Australian/Canadian)
. . . . . . . . . . . . . . . . . . . . . . . . . . . . . . . . . . Rainee
**The Pickle** (1992) . . . . . . . . . . . . . . . . . . . . Francoise
0:54—In white bra in hotel room with Danny Aiello.
• 0:58—Brief half of right breast in gaping bra when
she helps Aiello back onto bed.

# Courtney, Dori

*Films:*
**Hollywood Hot Tubs 2—Educating Crystal** (1989)
. . . . . . . . . . . . . . . . . . . . . . . . . . . . . . .Hot Tub Girl
•• 1:00—Breasts stuck in the spa and getting her hair
freed.
**Tango & Cash** (1989) . . . . . . . . . . Dressing Room Girl
• 1:06—Breasts, sitting in chair looking in the mirror
in the background. Long shot.
Evil Spirits (1990) . . . . . . . . . . . . . . . . . . . . . Bank Teller
**Mob Boss** (1990) . . . . . . . . . . . . . . . . . . . . . Kathryn
••• 0:31—In black bra, talking with Eddie Deezen, then
breasts. Nice close-up. Long scene.
**Sorority Girls and the Creature from Hell** (1990)
. . . . . . . . . . . . . . . . . . . . . . . . . . . . . . . . . . Belinda
•• 0:06—Breasts, drying herself off after shower. (Wear-
ing panties.)

••• 0:08—More breasts, still drying herself off.
• 0:12—Brief right breast, while in car with J.J.
••• 0:35—Breasts in spa with J.J.
•• 0:37—Buns, then left breast, while in spa during Gerald's fantasy.
••• 0:41—Breasts taking off her top by stream while J.J. gets killed.
•• 0:43—Breasts, running around at night getting chased by the creature.
Camp Fear (1991)........................n.a.
*a.k.a. Millenium Countdown*
**Whore** (1991)..............Topless woman on TV
*a.k.a. If you're afraid to say it... Just see it*
• 0:14—Brief breasts on TV in old folks home in a scene from *Mob Boss.*

## Courtney, Lorna

*Films:*
Ghoul School (1990).......................Mary
**Affairs of the Heart** (1992).................Jane
••• 1:04—Breasts, making love in front of a fire in sleeping bag with Dick.
Comrades in Arms (1992)..................Anka

## Cox, Ashley

*Films:*
Drive-In (1976).....................Mary-Louise
King of the Mountain (1981)..............Elaine
Looker (1981)...........................Candy
Night Shift (1982)....................Jenny Lynn
*Magazines:*
**Playboy** (Dec 1977)..................Playmate
••• 178-189—Nude.

## Cox, Courteney

*Films:*
Down Twisted (1987).....................Farah
Masters of the Universe (1987).........Julie Winston
Cocoon, The Return (1988)..................Sara
**Blue Desert** (1990)..................Lisa Roberts
0:52—Silhouette of right breast, standing up with Steve. Probably a body double. Very, very brief right nipple between Steve's arms lying in bed. Dark, hard to see.
•• 0:53—Left breast, lying in bed under Steve. A little hard to see her face, but it sure looks like her to me!
1:14—Buns and part of left breast getting towel. Looks like a body double.
Curiosity Kills (1990).....................Gwen
Mr. Destiny (1990)..................Jewel Jagger
Shaking the Tree (1991)................Kathleen
The Opposite Sex ...and How to Live with Them (1992)
...........................................Carrie
Ace Ventura: Pet Detective (1993)...........Melissa
*Made for Cable TV:*
Dream On: Come and Knock On Our Door... (1992; HBO)....................Alisha Littleton
*Miniseries:*
Till We Meet Again (1989)................Freddy

*Made for TV Movies:*
Roxanne: The Prize Pulitzer (1989)....Jacquie Kimberly
Battling for Baby (1992).................Katherine
*TV:*
Misfits of Science (1985-86)...........Gloria Dinallo
Family Ties (1987-89)................Lauren Miller
Trouble with Larry (1993).................Gabriella
Friends (1994- )............................n.a.
*Music Videos:*
Dancing in the Dark/Bruce Springsteen
.....................Girl Who Goes Up on Stage

## Coyne, Ria

*Films:*
Dolls (1987)................................n.a.
American Born (1989)......................Lupe
**Corporate Affairs** (1990)................Mistress
•• 0:10—Left breast several times in back of car with Arthur.
**Naked Obsession** (1990).................Cynthia
•• 0:11—Breasts on stage, dancing in black lingerie.
• 0:13—Buns in G-string while dancing.
•• 0:14—More breasts and buns while dancing.
*Magazines:*
**Playboy's Book of Lingerie** (Jan 1992)......Herself
••• 17—Full frontal nudity.
**Playboy's Book of Lingerie** (Mar 1992)......Herself
••• 8—Breasts.
**Playboy's Career Girls** (Aug 1992)...... Funny Girls
••• 28—Breasts.
**Playboy's Book of Lingerie** (Jul 1993).......Herself
••• 22—Breasts.
**Playboy's Nudes** (Dec 1993)..............Herself
••• 24—Full frontal nudity.

## Crampton, Barbara

*Films:*
**Body Double** (1984)................Carol Sculley
•• 0:04—Brief right breast, while making love in bed with another man when her husband walks in.
**Fraternity Vacation** (1985)..............Chrissie
••• 0:16—Breasts and buns in bedroom with two guys taking off her swimsuit.
**Re-Animator** (1985)..............Megan Halsey
(Unrated version reviewed.)
•• 0:10—Brief buns putting panties on, then breasts, putting bra on after making love with Dan.
•• 1:09—Full frontal nudity, lying unconscious on table getting strapped down.
• 1:10—Breasts getting her breasts fondled by a headless body.
• 1:19—Breasts on the table.
**Chopping Mall** (1986).....................Suzie
*a.k.a. Killbots*
•• 0:22—Brief breasts taking off top in furniture store in front of her boyfriend on the couch.
**From Beyond** (1986)......Dr. Katherine McMichaels
•• 0:44—Brief breasts after getting blouse torn off by the creature in the laboratory.

0:51—Buns getting on top of Jeffrey Combs in black leather outfit.

**Kidnapped** (1986) ....................... Bonnie

0:35—In white bra and panties in hotel room.

••• 0:37—Breasts getting tormented by a bad guy in bed.

•• 1:12—Breasts opening her pajamas for David Naughton.

•• 1:14—Breasts in white panties getting dressed.

Puppet Master (1989)............Woman at Carnival

Trancers II (1991) .....................Sadie Brady

Robot Wars (1992) ........................ Leda

*TV:*

The Young and the Restless

.....................Leanna Randolph Newman

Days of Our Lives (1983)...............Trista Evans

*Magazines:*

**Playboy** (Dec 1986)........................n.a.

## Craven, Mimi

*Films:*

Servants of Twilight (1991) ........... Ms. Lindstrom

**Mikey** (1992)..................... Rachel Trenton

•• 0:52—Breasts, sitting in bathtub when Mikey comes into the bathroom to talk.

*Made for Cable Movies:*

Disaster in Time (1992; Showtime) ..........Carolyn

*a.k.a. Timescape*

*Made for Cable TV:*

**Dream On: The Thirty-Seven Year Itch** (1991; HBO)

.......................................Monica

••• 0:22—Breasts several times with Martin in his office.

*Video Tapes:*

**Inside Out 4** (1992) ...........Dolores/Put Asunder

(Unrated version reviewed.)

• 0:18—Left breast in bed with her husband.

••• 0:22—Breasts, lying in bed after making love with her husband.

**Eden 5** (1993) ..................... Marla Burke

•• 0:06—Breasts and brief buns in bubble bath with Douglas.

## Crawford, Cindy

Supermodel and pin-up calendar girl.

Wife of actor Richard Gere.

Model for *Revlon* cosmetics.

Model for *Diet Pepsi.*

*TV:*

House of Style (1992- ) .....................Hostess

*Video Tapes:*

Cindy Crawford: Shape Your Body Workout (1992)

........................................ Herself

Cindy Crawford: The Next Challenge (1993) ... Herself

*Magazines:*

**Playboy** (Jul 1988)..................... Skin Suits

•• Breasts B&W photos.

**Playboy** (Dec 1990)........... Sex Stars of 1990

• 176—Buns, while holding a sheet. B&W.

Playboy's Nudes (Dec 1993) ............... Herself

**Playboy** (Jan 1994)...............Remember Cindy

•• 210-211—Breasts under sheer bodysuit in B&W photo.

## Crespo, Teresa

*Films:*

Out of the Dark (1988) ................... Debbie

*Made for Cable Movies:*

**Nails** (1992; Showtime)........... Elena Hernandez

•• 0:44—Breasts, taking off her top in room with Dennis Hopper.

## • Cristal, Raquel

See: Drew, Raquel.

## Cristiani, Tina

*Films:*

Badge 373 (1972) ................... Mrs. Caputo

*a.k.a. The Police Connection*

*Magazines:*

**Playboy** (Jun 1973)................... Next Month

• 254—Full frontal nudity in B&W photo.

**Playboy** (Jul 1973) ............. Tina of the Tanbark

••• 135-141—Full frontal nudity.

## Crockett, Karlene

*Films:*

Charlie Chan & the Curse of the Dragon Queen (1981)

.................... Brenda Lupowitz

**Eyes of Fire** (1983)........................ Leah

• 0:44—Brief breasts sitting up in the water and scaring Mr. Dalton.

• 1:16—Breasts talking to Dalton who is trapped in a tree. Brief breasts again when he pulls the creature out of the tree.

Massive Retaliation (1984) .........Marianne Briscoe

**Return** (1985) ........................Diana

• 0:46—Breasts sitting up and getting out of bed. Long shot.

*Made for TV Movies:*

Diary of a Hitchhiker (1979)................. Dana

The Promise of Love (1980) ................. Tracy

Death of a Centerfold: The Dorothy Stratten Story

(1981) ........................... Anna

Return to Mayberry (1986) ...........Eunice Taylor

## Crosby, Cathy Lee

*Films:*

The Laughing Policeman (1974) .......... Kay Butler

**Coach** (1978)........................ Randy

• 0:31—Very brief side view of left breast when Michael Biehn opens the door while she's putting on her top.

0:52—In wet white T-shirt at the beach and in her house with Biehn.

1:11—Very, very brief breasts in shower room with Biehn. Blurry, hard to see anything.

The Dark (1979)........................... Zoe

The Player (1992)........................ Cameo

*Made for Cable Movies:*
Untamed Love (1994; Lifetime). . . . . . . Maggie Bernard
*TV:*
That's Incredible (1980-84) . . . . . . . . . . . . . . . . . Host

## Crosby, Denise

Granddaughter of actor/singer Bing Crosby.
*Films:*
**48 Hrs.** (1982). . . . . . . . . . . . . . . . . . . . . . . . . . Sally
   0:47—Very, very brief side view of half of left breast,
   while swinging baseball bat at Eddie Murphy.
  • 1:24—Very brief side view of right breast when
   James Remar pushes her onto bed.
  • 1:25—Very brief breasts then very brief side view of
   right breast attacking Nick Nolte.
The Trail of the Pink Panther (1982) . . . . . . . . . . . . .n.a.
Curse of the Pink Panther (1983). . . . . . . . Bruno's Moll
The Man Who Loved Women (1983) . . . . . . . . . . Enid
Desert Hearts (1986). . . . . . . . . . . . . . . . . . . . . . . Pat
Eliminators (1986). . . . . . . . . . . . . . . . . . . Nora Hunter
   0:47—In wet white tank top inside an airplane cock-
   pit that has crashed in the water.
   0:50—Wet tank top getting out of the plane.
**Arizona Heat** (1988) . . . . . . . . . . . . . . . .Jill Andrews
  • 1:13—Brief upper half of left breast in shower with
   Larry.
Blackwater (1989). . . . . . . . . . . . . . . . . . . . . . . . Sally
Miracle Mile (1989). . . . . . . . . . . . . . . . . . . . . . Landa
Pet Sematary (1989) . . . . . . . . . . . . . . . . Rachel Creed
Skin Deep (1989) . . . . . . . . . . . . . . . . . Angie Smith
Desperate Crimes (1991; Italian). . . . . . . . . . . Bella Blu
Dolly Dearest (1992). . . . . . . . . . . . . . . Marilyn Reed
*Made for Cable TV:*
**Red Shoe Diaries: You Have the Right to Remain
Silent** (1992; Showtime)
 . . . . . . . . . . . . . . . . . . . Officer Lynn/Mona McCabe
(Available on video tape on *Red Shoe Diaries 2: Double
Dare.*)
   0:14—In black bra and panties, changing clothes in
   front of Nick.
 ••• 0:22—Breasts, taking off her bra and making love
   with Nick on barber's chair.
  • 0:26—Brief buns, while sitting on Nick's lap in the
   chair.
 ••• 0:28—In black bra and panties, then breasts and
   buns. (Additional footage added for video tape.)
*Made for TV Movies:*
My Wicked Ways... The Legend of Errol Flynn (1985)
 . . . . . . . . . . . . . . . . . . . . . . . . . Diana Dyrenforth
*TV:*
Star Trek: The Next Generation (1987-88)
 . . . . . . . . . . . . . . . . . . . . . . . . . . . Lt. Tasha Yar
Star Trek: The Next Generation (1991) . . . . . . . . .Seela
Key West (1993) . . . . . . . . . . . . . . . . . . . . . . .Chaucy
*Magazines:*
**Playboy** (Mar 1979). . . . . . . A Different Kind of Crosby
 ••• 99-103—Full frontal nudity.
**Playboy** (Feb 1980) . . . . . . . . . . . . . . .The Year in Sex
 •• 160—Full frontal nudity.

**Playboy** (May 1988). . . . . . . . . . . . . . . . . . . .Star Treat
 ••• 74-79—Nude, photos from the 1979 pictorial.

## Crosby, Katja

*Films:*
It's Alive III: Island of the Alive (1988). . . . . Girl in Court
**A Return to Salem's Lot** (1988). . . . . . . . . . . Cathy
 •• 0:36—Breasts making love in bed with Joey.
 • 0:48—Side view of right breast kissing Joey outside
   next to a stream.

## Crosby, Lucinda

*Films:*
Blue Thunder (1983) . . . . . . . . . . . . . . .Bel-Air Woman
The Naked Cage (1985). . . . . . . . . . . . . . . . . . Rhonda
Stitches (1985). . . . . . . . . . . . . . . . . . . . . . . Nurse #5
**Blue Movies** (1988) . . . . . . . . . . . . . . . Randy Moon
 • 0:10—Breasts in a spa, in a movie.
 •• 0:11—Breasts, kneeling on a table, shooting a porno
   movie.
 ••• 0:32—Breasts auditioning for Buzz.
 • 1:02—Breasts on desk in a movie.
Pretty Woman (1990). . . . . . . . . . . . . . . . . Olsen Sister
Frankie & Johnny (1991) . . . . . . . The Abused Neighbor

## Crosby, Mary

Daughter of actor/singer Bing Crosby.
*Films:*
Ice Pirates (1984). . . . . . . . . . . . . . . .Princess Karina
**Deadly Innocents** (1988) . . . . . . . . . . . . Beth/Cathy
 • 0:00—Very, very brief right breast in gaping night-
   gown when her husband grabs her wrist.
 • 0:38—Brief upper back half of left breast in bath-
   room mirror after taking off her nightgown.
Tapeheads (1988) . . . . . . . . . . . . . . . . . . . . Samantha
Body Chemistry (1990) . . . . . . . . . . . . . . . . . . .Marlee
Corporate Affairs (1990). . . . . . . . . . . . Jessica Pierce
   0:27—In bra while sitting in Arthur's lap in chair.
   1:04—In pink bra with Peter Scolari.
Eating (1990). . . . . . . . . . . . . . . . . . . . . . . . . . .Kate
The Berlin Conspiracy (1991). . . . . . . . Ursula Schneider
Desperate Motive (1992) . . . . . . . . . . . . . . . . .Marcie
*Miniseries:*
North and South, Book II (1986) . . . . . . . .Isabel Hazard
*TV:*
Brothers & Sisters (1979) . . . . . . . . . . . . . .Suzi Cooper
Dallas (1979-81) . . . . . . . . . . . . . . . . Kristin Shepard

## • Crouse, Lindsay

*Films:*
**Between the Lines** (1977) . . . . . . . . . . . . . . . .Abbie
 • 0:52—Brief side view of right breast, lying in bed
   with John Heard.
Slap Shot (1977) . . . . . . . . . . . . . . . . . . . . .Lily Braden
Prince of the City (1981) . . . . . . . . . . . . . . Carla Ciello
The Verdict (1982). . . . . . . . . . . Kaitlin Costello Price
Daniel (1983). . . . . . . . . . . . . . . . . . . . . . . . .Rochelle
Iceman (1984) . . . . . . . . . . . . . . . . . . . . Dr. Diane Brady
Places in the Heart (1984) . . . . . . . . . Margaret Lomax

House of Games (1987) . . . . . . . . . . . . Margaret Ford
Communion (1989) . . . . . . . . . . . . . . . . Anne Strieber
Desperate Hours (1990) . . . . . . . . . . . . . . . Chandler
*Made for Cable Movies:*
Chantilly Lace (1993; Showtime). . . . . . . . . . . . Rheza
**Parallel Lives** (1994; Showtime). . . . . . . . . Una Pace
• 0:12—Very brief right breast in gaping dress, while
bending over to make her bed on the sofa.
*Made for TV Movies:*
Final Appeal (1993). . . . . . . . . . . . . . . . . . Dana Cartier
Out of Darkness (1994). . . . . . . . . . . . . Kim Donaldson

## Crow, Emilia

a.k.a. Emilia Lesniak.
*Films:*
Scarface (1983). . . . . . . . . . . . . . . . . . . . . . .Echevera
**Fear City** (1984) . . . . . . . . . . . . . . . . . . . . . . . . .Bibi
•• 0:16—Breasts, dancing at the Metropole club.
•• 1:00—Breasts, dancing on the stage.
9 Deaths of the Ninja (1985). . . . . . . . . Jennifer Barnes
Hollywood Vice Squad (1986). . . . . . . . . . . . . . Linda
**Hitz** (1992) . . . . . . . . . . . . . . . . . . . . . Chelsea Walker
*a.k.a. Judgment*
••• 0:27—Breasts and very brief upper half of lower
frontal nudity, making love in bed with Jimmy. Lit
with red light.
*Made for Cable Movies:*
**Disaster in Time** (1992; Showtime) . . . . . . . . . Reeve
*a.k.a. Timescape*
• 0:18—Side view of left breast, sitting in front of vanity while Jeff Daniels watches. Long shot.

## Crowley, Jeananne

*Films:*
Educating Rita (1983; British) . . . . . . . . . . . . . . . Julia
**Reilly: Ace of Spies** (1984) . . . . . . . . . . . . . Margaret
•• 0:52—Brief breasts, opening her blouse for her invalid husband.

## Cruikshank, Laura

*Films:*
Ruthless People (1986) . . . . . . . . . . . . . . . . . . . . .n.a.
**Buying Time** (1987) . . . . . . . . . . . . . . . . . . . . .Jessica
•• 0:52—Breasts several times making love with Ron on
pool table.

## • Cruz, Penelope

*Films:*
Softly From Paris: Her & Him. . . .Daphné/Javatte/Juliette
**Jamón, Jamón** (1992; Spanish). . . . . . . . . . . . . .Silvia
••• 0:11—Right breast, then breasts, while making out
with José Luis.
• 0:46—Breasts, while kneeling on ground in dream
sequence.
• 1:02—Left breast sticking out of dress while José Luis
has a temper tantrum.
1:03—In braless, wet white dress.
1:05—Partial buns, while kissing Raul.
••• 1:09—Breasts, while making love with Raul.

Belle Epoque (1993; Spanish). . . . . . . . . . . . . . . . . Luz
*Magazines:*
**Playboy** (Nov 1993) . . . . . . . . . . Sex in Cinema 1993
•• 136—Left breast in still from *Jamón Jamón.*

## • Cruzat, Liza

*Films:*
**Sweet Perfection** (1988) . . . . . . . . . . . Linda Johnson
*a.k.a. The Perfect Model*
• 0:31—Left breast, in bed with Mario. Don't see her
face. Probably a body double.
Excessive Force (1993) . . . . . . . . . . . . . . . . . . . Hooker

## Cser, Nancy

*Films:*
Joy (1983; French/Canadian) . . . . . . . . . . . .Unidentified
**Perfect Timing** (1984) . . . . . . . . . . . . . . . . . . . .Lacy
0:54—In white lingerie, taking off clothes for Harry
and posing.
••• 0:56—Breasts getting photographed by Harry.
• 0:58—Breasts, making love with Harry.
• 1:01—Breasts.
Separate Vacations (1985) . . . . . . . . . . . . . Stewardess
Head Office (1986) . . . . . . . . . . . . . Dantley's Secretary
Deceived (1991) . . . . . . . . . . . . . . . Harvey's Girlfriend

## • Cuevas, Diana

*Films:*
**Invasion of Privacy** (1992) . . . . . . . . . . Alex's Mother
(Unrated version reviewed.)
•• 0:01—Left breast, while in bedroom with her lover,
while young Alex watches from closet.
Strike a Pose (1993) . . . . . . . . . . . . . . . . . . . . . . Model
Money to Burn (1994) . . . . . . . . . . . . . . . . . Beach Girl

## • Culliver Pierce, Katheryn

*Films:*
**Traces of Red** (1992). . . . . . . . . . . . . . .Kimberly Davis
•• 0:11—Breasts in bed, dead with blood on her during
James Belushi's recollection.
*Magazines:*
**Playboy** (Jan 1994)
. . . . . . . . The Great 40th Anniversary Playmate Search
••• 143—Full frontal nudity.
**Playboy's Great Playmate Search** (Feb 1994)
. . . . . . . . . . . . . . . . . . . . . . . . . . . . . . . . . . . . . .Herself
••• 33—Full frontal nudity.

## Cummins, Juliette

*Films:*
Lucky 13 (1984) . . . . . . . . . . . . . . . . . . . . . . . . . .Jenny
*a.k.a. Running Hot*
*a.k.a. Highway to Hell*
**Friday the 13th, Part V—A New Beginning** (1985)
. . . . . . . . . . . . . . . . . . . . . . . . . . . . . . . . . . . . . . .Robin
••• 1:01—Breasts, wearing panties getting undressed
and climbing into bed just before getting killed.
1:05—Very brief breasts, covered with blood when
Reggie discovers her dead.

**Psycho III** (1986) . . . . . . . . . . . . . . . . . . . . . . . . . .Red
••• 0:39—Breasts making love with Duke in his motel
    room, then getting thrown out.
**Slumber Party Massacre II** (1987) . . . . . . . . . Sheila
•• 0:24—In black bra, then breasts in living room dur-
    ing a party with her girlfriends.
**Deadly Dreams** (1988) . . . . . . . . . . . . . Maggie Kallir
• 0:25—Breasts on bed, taking off her blouse and kiss-
    ing Alex.
••• 0:55—Breasts and brief buns, making love with Jack
    in bed.
*Magazines:*
**Playboy** (Nov 1986) . . . . . . . . . . Sex in Cinema 1986
•• 129—Breasts in a photo from *Psycho III*.

# • Cupisti, Barbara
*Films:*
The Key (1985; Italian) . . . . . . . . . . . . . . . . . . . . . .n.a.
*a.k.a. La Chiave*
Terror at the Opera (1989; Italian). . . . . . . . . . . . . .n.a.
**The Church** (1991; Italian) . . . . . . . . . . . . . . . . .Lisa
*a.k.a. La Chiesa*
• 0:28—Very brief back side of right breast, while sit-
    ting up in bed. Side of right breast, while scooting
    over on bed while talking to Evald.
• 0:48—Very brief left breast in gaping nightgown,
    while scrambling for the phone. Very brief right
    breast in gaping nightgown when getting up off
    ground after jumping through window.
• 1:25—Breasts, while lying on slab and getting paint-
    ed.
• 1:31—Breasts, while getting raped by beast.

# Curran, Lynette
*Films:*
**Alvin Purple** (1973; Australian). . . . . . First Sugar Girl
•• 0:02—Brief full frontal nudity when Alvin opens the
    door.
Heatwave (1983; Australian) . . . . . . . . . . . . . . . Evonne
Bliss (1985; Australian) . . . . . . . . . . . . . . . . Bettina Joy
The Year My Voice Broke (1987; Australian)
. . . . . . . . . . . . . . . . . . . . . . . . . . . . . . . .Anne Olson

# Currie, Cherie
Singer.
Identical twin sister of singer/actress Marie Currie
Lukather.
*Films:*
Foxes (1980). . . . . . . . . . . . . . . . . . . . . . . . . . . . Annie
Parasite (1982) . . . . . . . . . . . . . . . . . . . . . . . . . Dana
Wavelength (1982) . . . . . . . . . . . . . . . . . .Iris Longacre
0:09—Brief side view of right breast and buns get-
    ting out of bed. Dark, don't really see anything.
The Rosebud Beach Hotel (1985) . . . . . . . . . . . Cherie
1:13—Singing with her twin sister in braless pink T-
    shirt on the beach.
Rich Girl (1991). . . . . . . . . . . . . . . . . . . . . . Michelle

# • Currie, Sandee
See: Warren, Sandra.

# Currie, Sondra
*Films:*
**Teenage Seductress** . . . . . . . . . . . . . . . . . . . . . Terry
••• 0:14—Buns, while taking off robe in bedroom.
    Breasts, while looking at herself in bathroom mirror.
••• 0:16—Breasts, while in front of mirror again. More
    breasts while taking a shower.
• 0:24—Breasts, while in bed, trying to get Preston to
    join her.
• 1:14—Brief partial right breast, while lying on bed
    with Preston.
Mama's Dirty Girls (1974) . . . . . . . . . . . . . . . . . . . n.a.
**Policewomen** (1974). . . . . . . . . . . . . . . . . Lacy Bond
••• 0:50—Breasts and buns taking off sheer robe and
    getting into bed, then making love with Frank.
**Jessi's Girls** (1976) . . . . . . . . . . . . . . . . . . . . . Jessica
• 0:02—Nude in water cleaning up, then brief left
    breast getting dressed.
• 0:07—Breasts getting raped by four guys. Fairly long
    scene.
• 0:37—Breasts kissing Clay under a tree. Hard to see
    because of the shadows.
**The Last Married Couple in America** (1980). . Lainy
•• 1:32—Breasts taking off her clothes in bedroom in
    front of Natalie Wood, George Segal and her hus-
    band.
The Concrete Jungle (1982) . . . . . . . . . . . . . .Katherine
Street Justice (1988). . . . . . . . . . . . . . . . . . . . .Mandy
Illicit Behavior (1991) . . . . . . . . . . . . . . . . . . . .Yolanda
(Unrated version reviewed.)
*Magazines:*
**Playboy** (Nov 1980) . . . . . . . . . . . Sex in Cinema 1980
• 174—Side view of right breast.

# Curtin, Jane
*Films:*
**How to Beat the High Cost of Living** (1980)
. . . . . . . . . . . . . . . . . . . . . . . . . . . . . . . . . .Elaine
1:28—In pink bra, distracting everybody in the mall
    so her friends can steal money.
• 1:29—Close up breasts, taking off her bra. Probably
    a body double.
O.C. and Stiggs (1987) . . . . . . . . . . . . . Elinore Schwab
Coneheads (1993) . . . . . . . . . . . . . . . . . . . . . .Prymaat
*Made for TV Movies:*
Common Ground (1990) . . . . . . . . . . . . . . Alice McGoff
*TV:*
Saturday Night Live (1975-80)
. . . . . . . . . . . . . . . . . .Not Ready For Primetime Player
Kate and Allie (1984-90) . . . . . . . . . . . . . . Allie Lowell
Working It Out (1990) . . . . . . . . . . . . . . Sarah Marshall

## Curtis, Allegra

Daughter of actor Tony Curtis and his second wife, actress Christine Kaufmann.

*Films:*
Midnight Cop (1988; Italian) . . . . . . . . Monika Carstens
Guns (1990) . . . . . . . . . . . . . . . . . . . . . . . . . . . Robyn

*Magazines:*
**Playboy** (Apr 1990) . . . . . . . . . . . . . . . Brava, Allegra!
••• 92-97—Full frontal nudity.

## Curtis, Jamie Lee

Daughter of actor Tony Curtis and actress Janet Leigh. Wife of actor/writer/director Christopher Guest.

*Films:*
Halloween (1978) . . . . . . . . . . . . . . . . . . . . . . . . Laurie
The Fog (1980) . . . . . . . . . . . . . . . . . . . Elizabeth Solley
Prom Night (1980) . . . . . . . . . . . . . . . . . . . . . . . . Kim
Terror Train (1980; Canadian) . . . . . . . . . . . . . . Alena
Halloween II (1981) . . . . . . . . . . . . . . . . . . . . . . Laurie
Road Games (1981; Australian) . . . . . . . . Hitch/Pamela
**Trading Places** (1983) . . . . . . . . . . . . . . . . . . Ophelia
••• 1:00—Breasts in black panties after taking red dress off in bathroom while Dan Aykroyd watches.
••• 1:09—Breasts and black panties taking off halter top and pants getting into bed with a sick Aykroyd.
The Adventures of Buckaroo Banzai, Across the 8th Dimension (1984) . . . . . . . . . . . . . . Dr. Sandra Banzai
**Grandview, U.S.A.** (1984) . . . . Michelle "Mike" Cody
••• 1:00—Left breast, lying in bed with C. Thomas Howell.
**Love Letters** (1984) . . . . . . . . . . . . . . . . Anna Winter
*a.k.a. Passion Play*
••• 0:31—Breasts in bathtub reading a letter, then breasts in bed making love with James Keach.
• 0:36—Brief breasts in lifeguard station with Keach.
••• 0:44—Brief breasts admiring a picture taken of her by Keach.
••• 0:46—Breasts and buns in bedroom undressing with Keach.
• 0:49—Breasts in black and white Polaroid photographs that Keach is taking.
1:02—In white slip in her house with Keach.
• 1:07—Right breast, sticking out of slip, then right breast, while sleeping in bed with Keach.
Perfect (1985) . . . . . . . . . . . . . . . . . . . . . . Jessie Wilson
0:14—No nudity, but doing aerobics in leotards.
0:26—More aerobics in leotards.
0:40—More aerobics, mentally making love with John Travolta while leading the class.
1:19—More aerobics when photographer is shooting pictures.
1:32—In red leotard after the article comes out in *Rolling Stone.*
Tall Tales and Legends: Annie Oakley (1985)
. . . . . . . . . . . . . . . . . . . . . . . . . . . . . . Annie Oakley
A Man in Love (1987) . . . . . . . . . . . . . . . . . Susan Elliot
Dominick and Eugene (1988) . . . . . . . . . Jennifer Reston

A Fish Called Wanda (1988) . . . . . . . . . . . . . . . . Wanda
0:21—In black bra and panties changing in the bedroom talking to Kevin Kline.
0:35—In black bra sitting on bed getting undressed.
Blue Steel (1989) . . . . . . . . . . . . . . . . . . . Megan Turner
1:27—Very, very brief buns twice when rolling out of bed, trying to get her gun. Dark.
My Girl (1991) . . . . . . . . . . . . . . . . . . . . Shelly DeVoto
Queens Logic (1991) . . . . . . . . . . . . . . . . . . . . . Grace
Forever Young (1992) . . . . . . . . . . . . . . . . . . . . Claire
1:00—In bra, while getting dressed.
My Girl 2 (1994) . . . . . . . . . . . . . . . . Shelly Sultenfuss
True Lies (1994) . . . . . . . . . . . . . . . . . . . . Helen Tasher
*Made for TV Movies:*
Death of a Centerfold: The Dorothy Stratten Story (1981) . . . . . . . . . . . . . . . . . . . . . Dorothy Stratten
Breasts in European version.
She's in the Army Now (1981) . . . . . . . . . Rita Jennings
*TV:*
Operation Petticoat (1977-78) . . . . . . Lt. Barbara Duran
Anything but Love (1989-92) . . . . . . . . . Hannah Miller
*Magazines:*
**Playboy** (Nov 1983) . . . . . . . . . . Sex in Cinema 1983
••• 151—Breasts and right breast photo from *Trading Places.*

## Cutter, Lise

*Films:*
Buy and Cell (1988) . . . . . . . . . . . . . . . . Dr. Ellen Scott
**Havana** (1990) . . . . . . . . . . . . . . . . . . . . . . . . . Patty
• 0:44—Most of side of left breast with Robert Redford. Very, very brief part of right breast while he turns her around. Very brief left breast when Redford puts a cold glass on her chest. Dark, hard to see.
Nickel & Dime (1992) . . . . . . . . . . . . Cathleen Markson
Shadowforce (1992) . . . . . . . . . . . . . . . . . . . . . . Mary
*Made for TV Movies:*
Desperado: The Outlaw Wars (1989) . . . . . . . . . . Nora
*TV:*
Equal Justice (1991) . . . . . . . . . . . . . . . . Andrea Kanin
Dangerous Curves (1992-93) . . . . . . . . . . . . . . . Gina

## Cyr, Myriam

*Films:*
**Gothic** (1986; British) . . . . . . . . . . . . . . . . . . . Claire
•• 0:53—Left breast, then breasts while lying in bed with Gabriel Byrne.
• 0:55—Brief left breast lying in bed. Long shot.
• 1:02—Breasts, while sitting on pool table opening her top for Julian Sands. Special effect with eyes in her nipples.
• 1:12—Buns and brief breasts covered with mud.
Frankenstein Unbound (1990) . . . . . Information Officer

# D'Abo, Maryam

Cousin of actress Olivia d'Abo.

*Films:*

**Xtro** (1982) . . . . . . . . . . . . . . . . . . . . . . . . . Analise
- ••• 0:25—Breasts making love with her boyfriend on the floor in her bedroom.
- •• 0:56—Brief breasts with her boyfriend again.

Until September (1984) . . . . . . . . . . . . . . . . . Nathalie
White Nights (1985) . . . . . . . . . . . . . French Girl Friend
The Living Daylights (1987) . . . . . . . . . . . Kara Milovy
**Double Obsession** (1992) . . . . . . . . . . . Claire Burke
- • 0:34—Breasts, while taking a shower. Seen behind plastic shower curtain.

Immortal Sins (1992; Spanish) . . . . . . . . . . . . . . Susan
Shootfighter: Fight to the Death (1992) . . . . . . . Cheryl
Leon the Pig Farmer (1993; British) . . . . . . . . Madeline
**Tomcat: Dangerous Desires** (1993) . . . . . . . . . . Jacki
- ••• 0:07—Breasts in bathroom mirror with Richard Grieco.

**Tropical Heat** (1993) . . . . . . . . . . . . . . . . . . . . Beverly
- •• 0:36—Breasts, several times, while in waterfall with Rick Rossovich.
- ••• 0:47—Breasts in bathtub, giving Rossovich a shave.
- • 0:49—Partial left breast, while lying in bed and making love with Rossovich.
- • 0:50—Brief breasts in bed, while under Rossovich.
- ••• 0:51—Breasts while in bed with Rossovich.

*Made for Cable TV:*

**Red Shoe Diaries: Another Woman's Lipstick**
(1993; Showtime) . . . . . . . . . . . . . . . . . . . . . . . .Zoe
(Available on video tape on *Red Shoe Diaries 3: Another Woman's Lipstick*.)
- •• 0:19—Nude, during fantasy. Don't see her face.
- • 0:28—Brief left nipple in room with the Other Woman.
- ••• 0:29—Breasts in room with the Other Woman.

Tales From the Crypt: Well Cooked Hams (1993; HBO)
. . . . . . . . . . . . . . . . . . . . . . . . . . . . . . . . . . . . . . Greta

*Miniseries:*

Master of the Game (1984) . . . . . . . . . . . . . Dominique

*Made for TV Movies:*

Something Is Out There (1988) . . . . . . . . . . . . . . Ta'ra

*Magazines:*

**Playboy** (Sep 1987) . . . . . . . . . . . . . . . . . . . . . .D'Abo
**Playboy** (Dec 1987) . . . . . . . . . . . . . Sex Stars of 1987
- ••• 154—Right breast, sitting behind cello.

**Playboy's Nudes** (Oct 1990) . . . . . . . . . . . . . . Herself
- •• 12—Breasts, covered with gold paint.

# D'Abo, Olivia

Cousin of actress Maryam d'Abo.

*Films:*

**Bolero** (1984) . . . . . . . . . . . . . . . . . . . . . . . . . Paloma
- • 0:38—Nude covered with bubbles taking a bath.
- • 1:05—Brief breasts in the steam room with Bo.
- • 1:32—Breasts in the steam room talking with Bo. Hard to see because it's so steamy.

Conan the Destroyer (1984) . . . . . . . . . Princess Jehnna

**Bullies** (1985) . . . . . . . . . . . . . . . . . . . . Becky Cullen
- •• 0:39—In wet white T-shirt swimming in river while Matt watches.

Dream to Believe (1985; Canadian) . . . . . . . Robin Crew
0:29—Working out in training room wearing a sexy cotton tank top.

**Into the Fire** (1988). . . . . . . . . . . . . . . . . . . . .Liette
*a.k.a. Legend of Lone Wolf*
0:07—Very, very brief silhouette of left breast in bed with Wade.
- •• 0:32—Breasts on bed with Wade. A little bit dark and hard to see.
- •• 1:10—Breasts in the bathtub. (Note her panties when she gets up.)

The Spirit of '76 (1991) . . . . . . . . . . . . . . . . . Chanel-6
**Bank Robber** (1993) . . . . . . . . . . . . . . . . . . . . Selina
- • 0:03—Very, very brief right breast, while pulling the sheets over herself in bed. Brief breasts, while getting out of bed.
- • 0:04—Brief, upper half of left breast at doorway, then brief partial left breast in mirror.
- • 0:21—Brief side of right breast, while making love in bed with Chris.
- • 1:10—Brief breasts, while turning over in bed after making love with Andy.

Greedy (1993) . . . . . . . . . . . . . . . . . . . . . . . . . .Molly
Point of No Return (1993) . . . . . . . . . . . . . . . .Angela
Wayne's World 2 (1993). . . . . . . . . . . . . . . . . Betty Jo

*Made for Cable Movies:*

Midnight's Child (1992; Lifetime). . . . . . . Anna/Kirsten

*Made for TV Movies:*

For Love and Glory (1993) . . . . . . . . . . . . . . . . . n.a.

*TV:*

The Wonder Years (1987-93) . . . . . . . . . . Karen Arnold

# D'Angelo, Beverly

*Films:*

Annie Hall (1977) . . . . . . . . . . . Actress in Rob's TV Show
**First Love** (1977) . . . . . . . . . . . . . . . . . . . . . .Shelley
0:05—Very, very brief half of left breast when her jacket opens up while talking to William Katt.
0:11—In white bra and black panties in Katt's bedroom.
- • 1:10—Brief breasts taking off her top in bedroom with Katt.

**The Sentinel** (1977). . . . . . . . . . . . . . . . . . . . Sandra
0:25—Masturbating in red leotard and tights on couch in front of Cristina Raines.
- • 0:33—Brief breasts playing cymbals during Raines' nightmare (in B&W).
1:24—Brief breasts long shot with zombie make up, munching on a dead Chris Sarandon.

**Hair** (1979). . . . . . . . . . . . . . . . . . . . . . . . . . . Sheila
- • 0:59—In white bra and panties, then breasts on rock near pond. Medium long shot.
- ••• 1:01—Breasts in panties getting out of the pond.
- • 1:38—Side view of right breast changing clothes in car with George.

Coal Miner's Daughter (1980) . . . . . . . . . . .Patsy Cline

Honky Tonk Freeway (1981) . . . . . . . . . . . . . . Carmen
Paternity (1981) . . . . . . . . . . . . . . . . . . . . . . . . Maggie
Finders Keepers (1983) . . . . . . . . . . . . . Standish Logan
**National Lampoon's Vacation** (1983)
. . . . . . . . . . . . . . . . . . . . . . . . . . . . . . Ellen Griswold
•• 0:18—Brief breasts taking a shower in the motel.
• 1:19—Brief breasts taking off shirt and jumping into
the swimming pool.
Highpoint (1984; Canadian) . . . . . . . . . . . Lise Hatcher
National Lampoon's European Vacation (1985)
. . . . . . . . . . . . . . . . . . . . . . . . . . . . . Ellen Griswold
Big Trouble (1986) . . . . . . . . . . . . . . . Blanche Ricky
**Slow Burn** (1986) . . . . . . . . . . . . . . . Laine Fleischer
• 1:01—Breasts making love with Eric Roberts. Don't
see her face. Part of lower frontal nudity showing
tattoo.
Aria (1987; U.S./British) . . . . . . . . . . . . . . . . . . . Gilda
In the Mood (1987) . . . . . . . . . . . . . . . . Francine Glatt
Maid to Order (1987) . . . . . . . . . . . . . . . . . . . . Stella
High Spirits (1988) . . . . . . . . . . . . . . . . . . . . Sharon
Cold Front (1989; Canadian) . . . . . . . Amanda O'Rourke
National Lampoon's Christmas Vacation (1989)
. . . . . . . . . . . . . . . . . . . . . . . . . . . . . . Ellen Griswold
Daddy's Dyin'... Who's Got the Will? (1990) . . . . . Evalita
**Pacific Heights** (1990) . . . . . . . . . . . . . . . . . . . . Ann
• 0:01—Sort of breasts in reflection on TV screen, then
right breast, in bed with Michael Keaton.
0:03—Very brief buns, turning over on bed when
two guys burst in to the house.
**Lonely Hearts** (1991) . . . . . . . . . . . . . . . . . . . . . Alma
0:33—Most of left breast, while making love in bed
with Eric Roberts.
• 0:57—Brief side view of right breast, while getting
into shower with Roberts.
• 0:58—Very brief left breast in shower after Roberts
gets pushed by Louise.
• 0:59—Very brief buns, when Roberts punches Louise
through the shower door.
The Miracle (1991; British) . . . . . . . . . . . . . . . . Renee
The Pope Must Die (1991) . . . . . . . . . . Veronica Dante
*a.k.a. The Pope Must Diet*
Man Trouble (1992) . . . . . . . . . . . . . . . Andy Ellerman
Lightning Jack (1993; Australian) . . . . . . . . . . . . . . n.a.
*Made for Cable TV:*
Tales From the Crypt: Werewolf Concerto (1992; HBO)
. . . . . . . . . . . . . . . . . . . . . . . . . . . . . . Janice Baird
*Made for TV Movies:*
A Child Lost Forever (1992) . . . . . . . . . . Jerry Sherwood
Trial: The Price of Passion (1992)
. . . . . . . . . . . . . . . . . . . . Johnnie Faye Boudreau
Judgment Day: The John List Story (1993)
. . . . . . . . . . . . . . . . . . . . . . . . . . . . . . . Helen List
The Switch (1993) . . . . . . . . . . . . . . . . . . . . Dee Fine
Jonathan Stone: Threat of Innocence (1994) Annie Hayes
Menendez: A Killing in Beverly Hills (1994) . . . . . . . Kitty
*TV:*
Captains and the Kings (1976) . . . . . . . . . . Miss Emmy

*Video Tapes:*
The Kathy Kaehler Fitness System (1992)
. . . . . . . . . . . . . . . . . . . . . . . . . . . Exercise Student
*Magazines:*
**Playboy** (Nov 1977) . . . . . . . . . . . Sex in Cinema 1977
•• 162—Left breast and most of right breast from *The
Sentinel*. Sort of B&W.
**Playboy** (Jul 1994) . . . . . . . . . . . . . . . . . . Grapevine
••• 166—Breasts after pulling open her bra and T-shirt
in B&W photo.

# D'Angelo, Mirella

*Films:*
**Caligula** (1980) . . . . . . . . . . . . . . . . . . . . . . . . . Livia
(X-rated, 147 minute version.)
•• 1:08—Buns and breasts in kitchen with Malcolm
McDowell. Full frontal nudity on table when he
rapes her in front of her husband-to-be.
Hercules (1983) . . . . . . . . . . . . . . . . . . . . . . . . . Circe
*Magazines:*
**Penthouse** (May 1980) . . . . . . . . . . . . . . . . . Caligula
83—Buns, after rape.
•• 84—Full frontal nudity.
**Playboy** (Jun 1980) . . . . . . . . . Fellini's Feminist Fantasy
•• 132—Right breast and lower frontal nudity.

# D'Arbanville, Patti

Ex-significant other of actor Don Johnson.
*Films:*
**Rancho Deluxe** (1975) . . . . . . . . . . . . . . Betty Fargo
**Bilitis** (1977; French) . . . . . . . . . . . . . . . . . . . . Bilitis
••• 0:25—Breasts copying Melissa undressing.
•• 0:27—Breasts on tree.
••• 0:31—Full frontal nudity taking off swimsuit with
Melissa.
0:36—Buns, cleaning herself in the bathroom.
•• 0:59—Breasts and buns making love with Melissa.
Big Wednesday (1978) . . . . . . . . . . . . . . . . . . . . Sally
The Fifth Floor (1978) . . . . . . . . . . . . . . . . Cathy Burke
The Main Event (1979) . . . . . . . . . . . . . . . . . . . Donna
Time After Time (1979; British) . . . . . . . . . . . . . Shirley
Hog Wild (1980; Canadian) . . . . . . . . . . . . . . . . Angie
**Modern Problems** (1981) . . . . . . . . . . . . . . . . . Darcy
• 0:48—Very brief right breast in bed after Chevy
Chase has telekinetic sex with her.
The Boys Next Door (1985) . . . . . . . . . . . . . . . . Angie
Real Genius (1985) . . . . . . . . . . . . . . . . . Sherry Nugil
Call Me (1988) . . . . . . . . . . . . . . . . . . . . . . . . . Coni
Fresh Horses (1988) . . . . . . . . . . . . . . . . . . . . . . Jean
Frame Up II (1991) . . . . . . . . . . . . . . . . . Babs Griffith
*a.k.a. Deadly Conspiracy*
*Made for Cable Movies:*
Snow Kill (1990; USA) . . . . . . . . . . . . . . . . Lauren Crane
*Made for TV Movies:*
Crossing the Mob (1988) . . . . . . . . . . . . . . Lucy Conte
*TV:*
Wiseguy (1989-90) . . . . . . . . . . . . . . . . . Amber Twine
Another World (1992-93) . . . . . . . . . . . . Christy Carson
South Beach (1993) . . . . . . . . . . . . . . . . . . . . Roxanne

New York Undercover (1994- ) . . . . . . . . . . . . . . . . .n.a.
*Magazines:*
**Playboy** (Aug 1974). . . . . . . . . . . . . . . Instant Warhol
• 83-85—Full frontal nudity in Polaroid photo collages.
**Playboy** (Nov 1974) . . . . . . . . . . Sex in Cinema 1974
•• 145—Breasts on top of Jeff Bridges from *Rancho Deluxe*.
**Playboy** (May 1977) . . . . . . . . . .Our Lady D'Arbanville
••• 98-103—Full frontal nudity in *Bilitis* photos taken by David Hamilton.
**Playboy** (Jun 1980) . . . . . . . . . . . . . . . . . . . .Grapevine
• 301—Breasts under black fishnet top. B&W.

## D'Ortez, Cristobel

*Films:*
Outlaw of Gor (1987) . . . . . . . . . . . . . . . . . . . . . Alicia
Edgar Allan Poe's "The Masque of the Red Death" (1989). . . . . . . . . . . . . . . . . . . . . . . . . . . . Dr. Karen
**Wild Zone** (1989) . . . . . . . . . . . . . . . . . . . . . . . .Mary
•• 1:19—Breasts in the brush, getting molested by a bad guy.

## D'Pella, Pamella

*Films:*
Internal Affairs (1990) . . . . . . . . . . . . . . . . . . . . Cheryl
Illicit Behavior (1991) . . . . . . . . . . . . . . . . . . . .Marilyn
(Unrated version reviewed.)
**Ted & Venus** (1991) . . . . . . . . . . . . . . . . . . . . . Gloria
••• 0:17—Breasts while undressing in locker room while talking to Linda.
Uncaged (1991) . . . . . . . . . . . . . . . . . . . . . . . . . . Ros
*a.k.a. Angel in Red*
**Caged Heat 2: Stripped of Freedom** (1993). . Paula
••• 0:13—Breasts, while making love with the warden on sofa in his office.
••• 0:42—Brief buns in T-back and breasts, while dancing for the warden in his office.
Josh and S.A.M. (1993) . . . . . . . . . . . .Daughter on Bus
*Made for Cable TV:*
Tales From the Crypt: Only Sin Deep (1989; HBO)
. . . . . . . . . . . . . . . . . . . . . . . . . . . . . . . . . . . Raven

## Dahms, Gail

*Films:*
**The Silent Partner** (1978) . . . . . . . . . . . . . . . .Louise
• 0:31—Right breast in bathroom with another guy when Elliott Gould surprises them.
The Tomorrow Man (1979). . . . . . . . . . . . . . . . .n.a.

## Daily, Elizabeth

*a.k.a. E. G. Daily.*
Singer.
*Films:*
The Escape Artist (1982) . . . . . . . . . . . . . . . . . . Sandra
Funny Money (1982) . . . . . . . . . . . . . . . . . . . . . . Cass

**Street Music** (1982). . . . . . . . . . . . . . . . . . . . . Sadie
• 0:00—Nude behind shower door (can't see anything), then brief right breast while reaching for towel.
•• 0:24—Partial lower frontal nudity and left breast with Eddie.
• 1:07—Brief breasts while on top of Eddie on the floor.
•• 1:08—Brief breasts while getting dressed.
One Dark Night (1983) . . . . . . . . . . . . . . . . . . . .Leslie
**Valley Girl** (1983). . . . . . . . . . . . . . . . . . . . . . .Loryn
•• 0:16—In bra through open jumpsuit, then brief breasts on bed with Tommy.
Wacko (1983) . . . . . . . . . . . . . . . . . . . . . . . . . . Bambi
No Small Affair (1984) . . . . . . . . . . . . . . . . . . . . .Susan
Streets of Fire (1984) . . . . . . . . . . . . . . . . . . . .Baby Doll
Fandango (1985). . . . . . . . . . . . . . . . . . . . . . . . . .Judy
Pee Wee's Big Adventure (1985). . . . . . . . . . . . . . Dottie
Bad Dreams (1988) . . . . . . . . . . . . . . . . . . . . . . Lana
Loverboy (1989) . . . . . . . . . . . . . . . . . . . . . . . .Linda
Dogfight (1991). . . . . . . . . . . . . . . . . . . . . . . .Marcie
Dutch (1991) . . . . . . . . . . . . . . . . . . . . . . . . . Halley
*a.k.a. Driving Me Crazy*
*Magazines:*
**Playboy** (Nov 1983) . . . . . . . . . . . Sex in Cinema 1983
•• 146—Breasts.

## Dale, Cynthia

Sister of actress Jennifer Dale.
*Films:*
My Bloody Valentine (1981; Canadian) . . . . . . . . Patty
**Heavenly Bodies** (1985) . . . . . . . . . . Samantha Blair
• 0:30—Brief breasts fantasizing about making love with Steve while doing aerobic exercises.
**The Boy in Blue** (1986; Canadian). . . . . . . . Margaret
••• 1:15—Breasts standing in a loft kissing Nicolas Cage.
Moonstruck (1987) . . . . . . . . . . . . . . . . . . . . . Sheila
*Made for Cable Movies:*
The Liberators (1987; Disney) . . . . . .Elizabeth Giddings
*Made for TV Movies:*
Sadie and Son (1987). . . . . . . . . . . . . . . Paula Melvin
In the Eyes of a Stranger (1992). . . . . . . . . . . . . Nancy

## Dale, Jennifer

Sister of actress Cynthia Dale.
*Films:*
**Stone Cold Dead** (1979; Canadian). . Claudia Grissom
••• 0:05—Breasts, dancing on stage.
**Suzanne** (1980; Canadian) . . . . . . . . . . . . . . .Suzanne
•• 0:29—Breasts when boyfriend lifts her sweatshirt up when she's sitting on couch doing homework.
•• 0:53—Breasts with Nicky on the floor.
**Your Ticket Is No Longer Valid** (1982) . . . . . . .Laura
•• 0:27—In black panties, then breasts when her husband fantasizes, then makes love with her.
1:23—Left breast in bed with Montoya, then sitting, waiting for Richard Harris.
Of Unknown Origin (1983; Canadian) . . . . . Lorrie Wells

**Separate Vacations** (1985) . . . . . . . . . .Sarah Moore
- 0:17—Brief right breast in bed with her husband after son accidentally comes into their bedroom.
  0:20—In a bra and slip showing the baby sitter the house before leaving.
- •• 1:14—Breasts on bed with Jeff after having a fight with her husband.
- 1:19—Brief right breast, in bed with her husband.

**The Adjuster** (1991; Canadian) . . . . . . . . . . .Arianne
- ••• 0:46—Breasts, while making love on top of Elias Koteas and discussing her insurance adjustments. Dark but nice.

**Cadillac Girls** (1993; Canadian) . . . . . . . . . . . . . Sally
- ••• 0:41—In bra, then breasts while making love in bedroom with Gregory Harrison.

*Magazines:*
**Playboy** (Nov 1980) . . . . . . . . . . Sex in Cinema 1980
- •• 181—Right breast.

# Dali, Tracy

*Films:*
Click: Calendar Girl Killer (1989) . . . . . . . . . . . . . June
**Virgin High** (1990) . . . . . . . . . . . . . . . . . . . . . Christy
- •• 0:04—Brief breasts several times when her blouse and bra pop open while talking to her parents.

**Sunset Heat** (1991) . . . . . . . . . . . . . . Carl's Pool Girl
(Unrated version reviewed.)
- •• 1:08—Breasts in pool with Dennis Hopper. Breasts and buns, getting out of pool while wearing a G-string.

**Bikini Summer 2** (1992) . . . . . . . . . . . . . . . . . .Anita
- 0:49—Buns, in black lingerie after taking off her maid outfit in front of Harry.
- ••• 0:51—Breasts in back seat of limousine, while making love with Harry.
- ••• 0:55—Brief buns, while bending over in maid outfit.

*Made for Cable Movies:*
**Fatal Charm** (1992; Showtime). . . . . . . . . Dream Girl
- •• 0:11—Breasts in van with Christopher Atkins. Lots of diffusion.
- 0:20—Brief breasts in van during Amanda Peterson's fantasy.

*Video Tapes:*
Score with Chicks (1992) . . . . . . . . . . . . Cast Member
**Hot Body Video Magazine: The Best Of** (1994)
. . . . . . . . . . . . . . . . . . . . . . . . . . . . . . . . . . . Herself
**Hot Body: The Best of Hot Body** (1994) . . . . Herself
- ••• 0:33—Buns in lingerie and swimsuits. Breasts while trying on lingerie.

*Magazines:*
**Playboy's Book of Lingerie** (Jan 1991) . . . . . . Herself
- ••• 72-73—Full frontal nudity.
- ••• 78—Full frontal nudity.

**Playboy's Book of Lingerie** (Mar 1991) . . . . . Herself
- •• 82—Right breast.

**Playboy's Book of Lingerie** (Sep 1991) . . . . . Herself
- ••• 25—Full frontal nudity.
- ••• 80—Full frontal nudity.

**Playboy's Book of Lingerie** (Nov 1991) . . . . .Herself
- ••• 96—Breasts.

**Playboy's Book of Lingerie** (Mar 1992). . . . . .Herself
- 16—Lower frontal nudity and partial left breast.
- ••• 32-33—Full frontal nudity.

**Playboy's Bathing Beauties** (Apr 1992). . . . . .Herself
- 8-9—Half of right breast and buns.

**Playboy's Book of Lingerie** (May 1992) . . . . .Herself
- •• 9—Left breast.

**Playboy's Girls of Summer '92** (Jun 1992) . . .Herself
- ••• 80-81—Full frontal nudity.

**Playboy's Book of Lingerie** (Jan 1993) . . . . . .Herself
- •• 33—Left breast and lower frontal nudity. Buns, in the mirror.

**Playboy's Book of Lingerie** (May 1993) . . . . .Herself
- 100-101—Left breast.

**Playboy's Book of Lingerie** (Mar 1994). . . . . .Herself
- •• 83—Left breast and lower frontal nudity.

# Dalle, Béatrice

*Films:*
**Betty Blue** (1986; French) . . . . . . . . . . . . . . . . . Betty
- ••• 0:01—Breasts making love in bed with Zorg. Long sequence.
- ••• 0:30—Nude on bed having sex with boyfriend.
- ••• 1:03—Nude trying to sleep in living room.
- ••• 1:21—Breasts in white tap pants in hallway.
- ••• 1:29—Breasts lying down with Zorg.
- ••• 1:39—Breasts sitting on bathtub crying & talking.
On a Vole Charlie Spencer! (1987) . . . . . . . . .Movie Star
Night on Earth (1992) . . . . . . . . . . .The Blind Passenger
*a.k.a. Une Nuit Sur Terre*

*Magazines:*
**Playboy** (Nov 1987) . . . . . . . . . . Sex in Cinema 1987
- •• 141—Breasts in blue light from *Betty Blue.*

# Daly, Jeannie

See: Carol, Jean.

# Daly, Tyne

Daughter of actor James Daly and actress Hope Newell.
Sister of actor Tim Daly.
Ex-wife of actor/director Georg Stanford Brown.
*Films:*
John and Mary (1969) . . . . . . . . . . . . . . . . . . . . .Hilary
**The Adultress** (1973) . . . . . . . . . . . . . . . . . . . . .Inez
- 0:21—Brief side view of right breast in room with Carl. Brief out of focus breasts in bed.
- •• 0:51—Breasts outside with Hank.
- ••• 0:53—Breasts on a horse with Hank.
The Enforcer (1976) . . . . . . . . . . . . . . . . . . . Kate Moore
Telefon (1977) . . . . . . . . . . . . . . . . Dorothy Putterman
Zoot Suit (1981) . . . . . . . . . . . . . . . . . . . . . . . . . Alice
The Aviator (1984) . . . . . . . . . . . . . . . . . . Evelyn Stiller
Movers and Shakers (1985) . . . . . . . . . . Nancy Derman
*Made for TV Movies:*
Intimate Strangers (1977) . . . . . . . . . . . Karen Renshaw
Face of a Stranger (1991) . . . . . . . . . . . Dollie Madison
The Last to Go (1991) . . . . . . . . . . . . . . . . . . . . . n.a.

Scattered Dreams: The Kathryn Messenger Story (1993)
. . . . . . . . . . . . . . . . . . . . . . . . . . . . . Kitty Messenger
*TV:*
Cagney & Lacey (1982-88) . . . . . . . . . Mary Beth Lacey
(Won four Emmy Awards.)
Christy (1994- ) . . . . . . . . . . . . . . . . . . Alice Henderson

# ● *Damiani, Donatella*

*Films:*
**Honey** (1980; Italian) . . . . . . . . . . . . . . . The Landlady
 • 0:24—Very, very brief right breast dodging Clio
  Goldsmith's hand while playfully drying her off with
  a towel.
 0:34—Showing lots of cleavage while massaging a
  guy.
*Magazines:*
**Playboy** (Jun 1980) . . . . . . . . Fellini's Feminist Fantasy
 ••• 129—Full frontal nudity and buns in G-string.

# *Danielson, Lynn*

*Films:*
Mortuary Academy (1988) . . . . . . . . . . . . Valerie Levitt
**Out of the Dark** (1988) . . . . . . . . . . . . . . . . . . . Kristi
 • 0:09—Brief breasts getting out of bed. More breasts
  outside getting photographed.
 •• 1:01—Breasts in motel room making love with
  Kevin.
 • 1:06—Left breast, while getting out of bed.
Nickel & Dime (1992) . . . . . . . . . . . . . . Destiny Charm
Ghoulies IV (1993) . . . . . . . . . . . . . . . . . Female Victim

# *Danner, Blythe*

*Films:*
**To Kill a Clown** (1971) . . . . . . . . . . . . . . . Lily Frischer
 • 1:10—Side view of left breast sitting on bed talking
  to Alan Alda. Hair covers breast, hard to see. Buns,
  getting up and running out of the house.
1776 (1972) . . . . . . . . . . . . . . . . . . . . Martha Jefferson
Hearts of the West (1975) . . . . . . . . . . . . . . . Miss Trout
Futureworld (1976) . . . . . . . . . . . . . . . . . . Tracy Ballard
The Great Santini (1980) . . . . . . . . . . . Lillian Meechum
Man, Woman and Child (1983) . . . . . . . Sheila Beckwith
Brighton Beach Memoirs (1986) . . . . . . . . . . . . . . Kate
Another Woman (1988) . . . . . . . . . . . . . . . . . . . Lydia
Alice (1990) . . . . . . . . . . . . . . . . . . . . . . . . . Dorothy
Mr. & Mrs. Bridge (1990) . . . . . . . . . . . . . . . . . Grace
The Prince of Tides (1991) . . . . . . . . . . . . Sallie Wingo
Husbands and Wives (1992) . . . . . . . . . . . Rain's Mother
*Made for Cable Movies:*
Judgement (1990; HBO) . . . . . . . . . . . . Emmeline Guitry
*Made for TV Movies:*
Are You in the House Alone? (1978) . . . . . . . . . . . Ann
Money, Power, Murder (1989) . . . . . . . . . . . . . Jeannie
Cruel Doubt (1992) . . . . . . . . . . . . . . Bonnie Von Stein
Leave of Absence (1994) . . . . . . . . . . . . . . . . . . Eliza
Oldest Living Confederate Widow Tells All (1994)
. . . . . . . . . . . . . . . . . . . . . . . . . . . . . . . . . . Bianca
*TV:*
Adam's Rib (1973) . . . . . . . . . . . . . . . . Amanda Bonner

# *Danning, Sybil*

a.k.a. Sybille Danninger.
*Films:*
**Bluebeard** (1972) . . . . . . . . . . . . . . . . . The Prostitute
 • 1:08—Brief breasts kissing Nathalie Delon showing
  her how to make love to her husband.
 • 1:09—Brief left breast, lying on the floor with Delon
  just before Richard Burton kills both of them.
**Maiden Quest** (1972) . . . . . . . . . . . . . . . . . . Kriemhild
*a.k.a. The Long Swift Sword of Siegfried*
 • 0:02—Breasts in bath, surrounded by topless blonde
  servants.
 • 0:04—Breasts in the bath again.
 ••• 0:10—Nude in tub surrounded by breasts servant
  girls.
 ••• 0:12—Breasts on bed, getting rubbed with oint-
  ment by the servant girls.
 •• 0:35—Breasts while in bed with Siegfried.
 • 1:00—Breasts in bed with Siegfried.
 ••• 1:19—Breasts in bed with Siegfried.
**Naughty Nymphs** (1972; German) . . . . . . . . Elizabeth
*a.k.a. Passion Pill Swingers*
*a.k.a. Don't Tell Daddy*
 ••• 0:21—Nude taking a bath while yelling at her two
  sisters.
 • 0:30—Breasts and buns throwing Nicholas out of
  her bedroom.
 •• 0:38—Full frontal nudity running away from Burt.
**Albino** (1976) . . . . . . . . . . . . . . . . . . . . . . . . . . Sally
*a.k.a. Night of the Askari*
 • 0:19—Breasts, then full frontal nudity getting raped
  by the Albino and his buddies.
**The Loves of a French Pussycat** (1976) . . . . . Andrea
 ••• 0:18—Breasts dancing with her boss, then in bed.
 •• 0:24—Breasts and buns in swimming pool.
 0:40—In sheer white bra and panties doing things
  around the house. Long sequence.
 • 0:46—Breasts in bathtub with a guy.
 • 1:03—Left breast sticking out of bra, then breasts.
**The Twist** (1976) . . . . . . . . . . . . . . . Jacques' Secretary
 •• 1:24—Brief breasts sitting next to Bruce Dern during
  his daydream.
**God's Gun** (1977) . . . . . . . . . . . . . . . . . . . . . . . Jenny
*a.k.a. A Bullet from God*
 • 1:09—Right breast popping out of dress with a guy
  in the barn during flashback.
**Cat in the Cage** (1978) . . . . . . . . . . . . . . Susan Khan
 • 0:24—Brief breasts getting slapped around by Ralph.
 • 0:25—Brief left breast several times smoking and
  talking to Ralph, brief left breast getting up.
 •• 0:30—Full frontal nudity getting out of the pool.
 • 0:52—Black bra and panties undressing and getting
  into bed with Ralph. Brief left breast and buns.
 1:02—In white lingerie in bedroom.
 1:10—In white slip looking out window.
 1:15—In black slip.
 • 1:18—Very brief right breast several times, struggling with an attacker on the floor.

Kill Castro (1978) . . . . . . . . . . . . . . . . . . . . . . . Veronica
  a.k.a. Cuba Crossing
Separate Ways (1979) . . . . . . . . . . . . . . . . . . . . . .Mary
Battle Beyond the Stars (1980) . . . . . . . . . . . . St. Exmin
**The Day of the Cobra** (1980) . . . . . . . . . . . . . Brenda
  • 0:41—Buns and side view of right breast getting out
    of bed and putting robe on with Lou. Long shot.
How to Beat the High Cost of Living (1980) . . Charlotte
The Man with Bogart's Face (1980). . . . . . . . . .Cynthia
Nightkill (1981). . . . . . . . . . . . . . . . . . . Monika Childs
**Daughter of Death** (1982) . . . . . . . . . . . . . . . . Susan
  a.k.a. Julie Darling
  •• 0:36—Breasts in bed with Anthony Franciosa.
  • 0:38—Brief right breast under Franciosa.
**Famous T & A** (1982) . . . . . . . . . . . . . . . . . . .Hostess
(No longer available for purchase, check your video
store for rental.)
  • 0:00—Brief side view of buns and partial left breast,
    getting dressed.
**S.A.S. San Salvador** (1982) . . . . . Countess Alexandra
  • 0:07—Brief left breast, while lying on the couch and
    kissing Malko.
Talking Walls (1982) . . . . . . . . . . . . . . . Bathing Beauty
**Chained Heat** (1983; U.S./German) . . . . . . . . . . Erika
  ••• 0:30—Breasts in the shower with Linda Blair.
Hercules (1983). . . . . . . . . . . . . . . . . . . . . . . .Arianna
Private Passions (1983) . . . . . . . . . . . . . . . . Katherine
**Howling II: Your Sister is a Werewolf** (1984)
. . . . . . . . . . . . . . . . . . . . . . . . . . . . . . . . . . . . . Stirba
  • 0:35—Left breast, then breasts with Mariana in bed-
    room about to have sex with a guy.
  • 1:20—Very brief breasts during short clips during
    the end credits. Same shot repeated about 10 times.
**Malibu Express** (1984) . . . . . . . . . . Countess Luciana
  • 0:13—Brief breasts making love in bed with Cody.
**They're Playing with Fire** (1984) . . . . .Diane Stevens
  0:04—In two piece swimsuit on boat. Long scene.
  ••• 0:08—Breasts and buns making love on top of Jay in
    bed on boat. Nice!
  •• 0:10—Breasts and buns getting out of shower, then
    brief side view of right breast.
  0:43—In black bra and slip, in boat with Jay.
  •• 0:47—In black bra and slip, at home with Michael,
    then panties, then breasts and buns getting into
    shower.
  ••• 1:12—In white bra and panties in room with Jay
    then breasts.
Jungle Warriors (1985) . . . . . . . . . . . . . . . . . . . . Angel
  0:53—Buns, getting a massage while lying face
    down.
Panther Squad (1986; French/Belgian) . . . . . . . . .Ilona
Reform School Girls (1986) . . . . . . . . . . Warden Sutter
**Young Lady Chatterley II** (1986) . . . .Judith Grimmer
  ••• 1:02—Breasts in the hut on the table with the Gar-
    dener.
Amazon Women on the Moon (1987). . . . . .Queen Lara
Phantom Empire (1987) . . . . . . . . . . . .The Alien Queen
The Tomb (1987) . . . . . . . . . . . . . . . . . . . . . . . . . Jade
Warrior Queen (1987). . . . . . . . . . . . . . . . . . Berenice

L.A. Bounty (1989). . . . . . . . . . . . . . . . . . . . . . Ruger
*Made for Cable TV:*
  **The Hitchhiker: Face to Face** (1984; HBO)
  . . . . . . . . . . . . . . . . . . . . . . . . . . . . . . Gloria Loring
  (Available on *The Hitchhiker, Volume 4.*)
  •• 0:10—In red bra and panties, then right breast mak-
    ing love with Robert Vaughn.
*Magazines:*
  **Playboy** (Dec 1980) . . . . . . . . . . . . . .Sex Stars of 1980
  •• 246—Right breast and buns.
  **Playboy** (Aug 1983) . . . . . . . . . . . . . . . . . . . . . . n.a.
  **Playboy** (Nov 1983) . . . . . . . . . . Sex in Cinema 1983
  •• 145—Breasts.
  **Playboy** (Dec 1983) . . . . . . . . . . . . . . . .Sex Stars of 1983
  ••• 210—Full frontal nudity.
  **Playboy** (Dec 1984) . . . . . . . . . . . . . . . .Sex Stars of 1984
  • 202—Half of right breast and lower frontal nudity.
  **Playboy** (Dec 1986) . . . . . . . . . . . . . . .Sex Stars of 86
  **Playboy's Nudes** (Oct 1990) . . . . . . . . . . . . . .Herself
  •• 20—Left breast and partial lower frontal nudity.

## Danon, Leslie

*Films:*
  **Beach Balls** (1988). . . . . . . . . . . . . . . . . . . . Kathleen
  • 1:06—In bra, then brief breasts in car with Doug.
Marked for Death (1990) . . . . . . . . . . . . . . . . . .Girl #1
The Double O Kid (1992). . . . . . . . . . . . . . .French Girl
Illusions (1992) . . . . . . . . . . . . . . . . . . . . . Young Laura

## Dante, Crisstyn

*Films:*
  **Midnight Crossing** (1988)
  . . . . . . . . . . . . . . . . . . . . . .Body Double for Kim Cattrall
  • 0:29—Brief left breast making love on small boat,
    body double for Kim Cattrall.
  **Phantom of the Mall: Eric's Revenge** (1988)
  . . . . . . . . . . . . . . . . . . Body Double for Ms. Whitman
  •• 0:25—Breasts in bed about five times with Peter.
  **State Park** (1988; Canadian) . . . . . . . . . . Blond in Net
  • 0:45—Very, very brief left breast putting swimsuit
    top back on after being rescued from net by the guy
    in the bear costume.
Nightmare on Elm Street 5: The Dream Child (1989)
  . . . . . . . . . . . . . . . . . . . . . . Body Double for Alice
Last Call (1990) . . . . . . . . . . . . . . . . . . . . . . . Hooker

## Danziger, Maia

*Films:*
The Magician of Lublin (1979) . . . . . . . . . . . . . .Magda
High Stakes (1989). . . . . . . . . . . . . . . . . . . . Veronica
**Last Exit to Brooklyn** (1990) . . . . . . . . . .Mary Black
  0:10—Out of focus buns and right breast taking off
    her slip.
  • 0:12—Very brief breasts making love with Harry.
    Breasts after.

## Darc, Mireille

*Films:*
Tall Blond Man with One Black Shoe (1973; French)
. . . . . . . . . . . . . . . . . . . . . . . . . . . . . . . . .Christine
   0:55—Upper half of buns in low, low cut back of
   dress.
   1:03—Almost left breast, in bed with a guy.
Return of the Tall Blond Man with One Black Shoe
(1974; French) . . . . . . . . . . . . . . . . . . . . . .Christine
*Magazines:*
**Playboy** (Jun 1975) . . . . . . .Sex in Cinema French Style
•• 87—Left breast in small photo.

## Dare, Barbara

Adult film actress.
a.k.a. Stacey Nix.
*Films:*
**Valet Girls** (1987) . . . . . . . . . . . Uncredited Party Girl
  • 1:10—Brief breasts, getting photographed while sitting on railing.
  • 1:14—Brief breasts, popping out of birthday cake
   and putting a pie in Dirk's face.
**Evil Toons** (1991) . . . . . . . . . . . . . . . . . . . . . . Jan
 ••• 0:30—Breasts, taking off robe and putting on red
  nightgown.
 •• 1:06—Breasts when her top is pulled down by Roxanne.
*Video Tapes:*
**High Society Centerspread Video #10: Barbara
Dare** (1990) . . . . . . . . . . . . . . . . . . . . . Herself
 •• 0:01—Breasts undressing.
 ••• 0:03—Nude on bed with a guy video taping, then
  making love with her. Nice, long scene.
 ••• 0:08—Full frontal nudity during photo shoot and interview.
 ••• 0:13—Nude, on lounge chair, masturbating.
 •• 0:18—Breasts, sitting in chair during interview.

## Dare, Debra

See: Dutch, Deborah.

## Darnell, Vicki

*Films:*
**Senior Week** (1987) . . . . . . . Everett's Dream Teacher
 •• 0:03—Breasts during classroom fantasy.
Alien Space Avenger (1988) . . . . . . . . . . . Bordello Lady
Brain Damage (1988) . . . . . . . . . . . .Blonde in Hell Club
**Frankenhooker** (1990). . . . . . . . . . . . . . . . . . . Sugar
 • 0:36—Brief middle part of each breast through slit
  bra during introduction to Jeffrey.
 •• 0:37—Breasts, sticking out of black lingerie while
  getting legs measured.
 • 0:38—Right breast, while sitting in chair.
 • 0:39—Breasts through slit lingerie three times while
  folding clothes.
   0:40—Buns, fighting over drugs.
 ••• 0:41—Very brief right breast, sitting on bed (on the
  right) enjoying drugs. Breasts dancing with the other girls.

**Sorority Girls and the Creature from Hell** (1990)
. . . . . . . . . . . . . . . . . . . . . . . . . . . . . . . Dancer
   0:17—Breasts in bar in open blouse, dancing on
  stage. Lit with red light.
 • 0:24—More breasts dancing on stage.

## • Darrian, Racquel

Adult film actress.
Used the name Kelly Jackson for her *Penthouse* pictorial.
*Video Tapes:*
**High Society Centerspread Video #14: Racquel
Darrian** (1990) . . . . . . . . . . . . . . . . . . . . . . .Herself
**Penthouse Passport to Paradise/Hawaii** (1991)
. . . . . . . . . . . . . . . . . . . . . . . . . . . . . . . . Model
 ••• 0:17—Undressing outside by a spa. In lingerie, then
  nude on a lounge chair and in the spa.
*Magazines:*
**Penthouse** (Oct 1990) . . . . . . . . . . . . . . . . . . . . . .Pet
 ••• 67-81—Nude.

## Das, Alisha

*Films:*
The Slugger's Wife (1985) . . . . . . . . . . . . . . . . . . Lola
Danger Zone II: Reaper's Revenge (1988). . . . . Francine
**Nightwish** (1988) . . . . . . . . . . . . . . . . . . . . . . . . Kim
(Unedited version reviewed.)
 •• 1:09—Brief breasts, then left breast in open dress ca-
  ressing herself while lying on the ground.

## • Dash, Stacey

*Films:*
Enemy Territory (1987) . . . . . . . . . . . . . . . Toni Briggs
Moving (1988). . . . . . . . . . . . . . . . . . . . .Casey Pear
**Blackwater** (1989). . . . . . . . . . . . . . . . . . . . .Minnie
 • 0:37—Upper half of buns and back side of right
  breast, while walking to and sitting on edge of bed.
 • 0:44—Very brief side view of left breast, while prop-
  ping herself up while lying on couch.
 • 0:59—Brief right breast, while in bed on top of Julian
  Sands.
Mo' Money (1992). . . . . . . . . . . . . . . . . . Amber Evans
*Made for TV Movies:*
Farrell for the People . . . . . . . . . . . . . . . . . . . . . . n.a.
*TV:*
TV 101 (1988-89) . . . . . . . . . . . . . . . . . . . . . Monique

## Datcher, Alex

*Films:*
Netherworld (1991) . . . . . . . . . . . . . . Mary Magdalene
Passenger 57 (1992) . . . . . . . . . . . . . . . .Marti Slayton
Rage and Honor (1992) . . . . . . . . . . . . Hannah the Hun
*Made for Cable TV:*
John Carpenter's Body Bags (1993; Showtime)
. . . . . . . . . . . . . . . . . . . . . . . . The Gas Station/Anne
*Made for TV Movies:*
Perry Mason: The Case of the Telltale Talk Show Host
(1993) . . . . . . . . . . . . . . . . . . . . . . . . . . .Cathy Paxton

*Video Tapes:*
**Inside Out 3** (1992) . . . . . . . . Annie/The Wet Dream
- ••• 1:24—Breasts, taking off her blouse in front of the fish tank.
- •• 1:25—Breasts, getting up when Dennis leaves.
- • 1:26—Breasts, getting into bathtub. Long shot.
- • 1:28—Breasts in bathtub.
- • 1:29—Breasts in bathtub with Greg Louganis.

## Davidovich, Lolita
a.k.a. Lolita David.
*Films:*
Class (1983) . . . . . . . . . . . . . . . . . . . . . . 1st Girl (motel)
**Recruits** (1986; Canadian). . . . . . . . . . . . . . . . . Susan
- • 0:19—Very brief breasts when Steve bumps into her in the shower room.
- •• 0:54—Right breast, then breasts while making out with Steve in car.
- •• 0:56—Breasts, twice, while driving around in car with Steve, the Governor and his wife.
- •• 0:58—Breasts, while getting out of the car.
The Big Town (1987) . . . . . . . . . . Black Lace Stripper
**Blindside** (1988; Canadian). . . . . . . . . . . . . . Adele
- •• 0:32—Breasts dancing on stage.
- 0:39—Sort of buns bending over and pointing a gun through her legs in front of mirror.
A New Life (1988). . . . . . . . . . . . . . . . . . . . . . . . . . n.a.
**Blaze** (1989) . . . . . . . . . . . . . . . . . . . . . . Blaze Starr
- 0:09—In bra doing her first strip routine. Very brief side views of left breast under hat.
- 0:15—Strip tease routine in front of Paul Newman. At the end, she takes off bra to reveal pasties.
- 0:42—In black bra and panties with Newman.
- •• 0:48—Breasts on top of Newman, then side view of left breast.
The Inner Circle (1991; Italian) . . . . . . . . . . . Anastasia
The Object of Beauty (1991). . . . . . . . . . . . . . . . . Joan
Boiling Point (1992; U.S./French) . . . . . . . . . . . . Vikki
Leap of Faith (1992) . . . . . . . . . . . . . . . . . . . . . Marva
Raising Cain (1992). . . . . . . . . . . . . . . . . . . . . . Jenny
**Intersection** (1993) . . . . . . . . . . . . . . Olivia Marshak
- • 0:01—Breasts during Richard Gere's flashback. Don't see her face.
- • 0:04—Very brief right breast while rolling over in bed.
- •• 1:15—Brief breasts while pulling up her pajama tops during game of charades.
*Made for Cable Movies:*
Prison Stories, Women on the Inside (1990; HBO)
. . . . . . . . . . . . . . . . . . . . . . . . . . . . . . . . . . . Lorretta
Keep the Change (1992; TNT) . . . . . . . . . . . . . . Ellen

## Davidson, Eileen
*Films:*
**Goin' All the Way** (1981) . . . . . . . . . . . . . . . . . . . BJ
- ••• 0:12—Breasts in the girls' locker room shower. Standing next to Monica.
- ••• 0:22—Exercising in her bedroom in braless pink T-shirt, then breasts talking on the phone to Monica.

**House on Sorority Row** (1983) . . . . . . . . . . . . . Vicki
- •• 0:16—Breasts and buns in room making love with her boyfriend.
- 0:19—In white bikini top by the pool.
Easy Wheels (1989) . . . . . . . . . . . . . . . . . . . . . She Wolf
**Eternity** (1989) . . . . . . . . . . . . . . . . . . . Dahlia/Valerie
- 0:33—In black bra and panties in dressing room. Brief buns standing in bathtub during Jon Voight's flashback.
- • 0:52—Brief left breast, then breasts, in bed with Voight. Don't see face.
*TV:*
Days of Our Lives . . . . . . . . . . . . . . . . . . . . . . Kristen
The Young and the Restless . . . . . . . . . . . Ashley Abbott
Broken Badges (1990-91). . . . . . . . . . . . . . . . . . Bullet

## Davidtz, Embeth
*Films:*
Mutator (1989) . . . . . . . . . . . . . . . . . . . . . . . . Jennifer
**Sweet Murder** (1990) . . . . . . . . . . . . . Laurie Shannon
- 0:22—In white bra and panties in bedroom with Lisa.
- • 0:40—Brief breasts behind wet shower door. Can't really see anything.
Till Death Do Us Part (1991). . . . . . . . . . . . . . . . . Cat
- 0:10—In white bra in front of mirror with Treat Williams.
Army of Darkness (1992) . . . . . . . . . . . . . . . . . Sheila
Schindler's List (1993) . . . . . . . . . . . . . Helen Hirsch
*Made for TV Movies:*
Deadly Matrimony (1992) . . . . . . . . . . Dianne Masters

## Davis, Carole
Singer.
Used the name Tamara Kapitas for her *Penthouse* pictorial.
*Films:*
Piranha II: The Spawning (1981; Italian/U.S.) . . . . . . n.a.
**C.O.D.** (1983) . . . . . . . . . . . . . . . . . . . . Contessa Bazzini
- • 1:25—Brief breasts in dressing room scene in black panties, garter belt and stockings when she takes off her robe.
- 1:29—In black top during fashion show.
The Princess Academy (1986; U.S./Yugoslavian/French)
. . . . . . . . . . . . . . . . . . . . . . . . . . . . . . . . . . . . Sonia
Mannequin (1987). . . . . . . . . . . . . . . . . . . . . . . Roxie
The Shrimp on the Barbie (1990). . . . . . . . . Domonique
- 0:58—Buns, in pool that is visible from inside restaurant. Don't see her face.
- 0:58—In black bra and panties, then breasts doing strip tease in front of Bruce. Very dark.
If Looks Could Kill (1991) . . . . . . . . . . . . Areola Canasta
*a.k.a. Teen Agent*
**The Rapture** (1991). . . . . . . . . . . . . . . . . . . . . . Angie
- • 0:20—Buns, on top of Vic in bed. Most of side of her right breast.
- • 0:21—Very brief right breast, then very brief breasts while turning around to talk.

*Magazines:*
**Playboy** (Feb 1977) . . . . . . .Playboy's Playmate Preview
•• 126—Left breast and lower frontal nudity.
**Penthouse** (Jan 1980) . . . . . . . . . . . . . . . . . . . . . Pet
••• 99-133—Nude.

## Davis, Geena

Wife of director Renny Harlin.
Ex-wife of actor Jeff Goldblum.
*Films:*
Tootsie (1982). . . . . . . . . . . . . . . . . . . . . . . . . . April
   0:34—In white bra and panties in dressing room
   with Dustin Hoffman.
   0:44—In white bra and panties exercising in dress-
   ing room while Hoffman reads his script.
Transylvania 6-5000 (1985). . . . . . . . . . . . . . . . Odette
The Fly (1986). . . . . . . . . . . . . . . . . . Veronica Quaife
   0:40—Brief almost side view of left breast getting
   out of bed.
The Accidental Tourist (1988) . . . . . . . . . . . . . . .Muriel
   (Academy Award for Best Supporting Actress.)
Beetlejuice (1988) . . . . . . . . . . . . . . . . . . . . . . .Barbara
Earth Girls are Easy (1989). . . . . . . . . . . . . . . . Valerie
   0:11—In yellow two piece swimsuit during song and
   dance number in beauty salon.
   0:12—In frilly pink lingerie waiting at home for her
   fiance to return.
   0:22—In pink two piece swimsuit doing a lot of dif-
   ferent things for a long time. This is probably the
   greatest swimsuit scene in a PG movie!
Quick Change (1990) . . . . . . . . . . . . . . . . . . . . .Phyllis
Thelma and Louise (1991). . . . . . . . . . . . . . . Thelma
Hero (1992) . . . . . . . . . . . . . . . . . . . . . . Gale Gayley
A League of Their Own (1992) . . . . . . . . Dottie Hinson
Angie (1993). . . . . . . . . . . . . . . Angie Scacciapensieri
*TV:*
Sara . . . . . . . . . . . . . . . . . . . . . . . Sara McKenna
Buffalo Bill (1983-84) . . . . . . . . . . . . . . Wendy Killian

## Davis, Judy

Wife of actor Colin Friels.
*Films:*
High Rolling (1977; Australian) . . . . . . . . . . . . . . .Lynn
My Brilliant Career (1979; Australian) . . . . Syblla Melvyn
**Winter of Our Dreams** (1981) . . . . . . . . . . . . . . .Lou
   • 0:19—Brief left breast sticking out of yellow robe in
   bed with Pete.
   • 0:26—Very brief side view of left breast taking off
   top to change. Long shot.
   •• 0:48—Breasts taking off top and getting into bed
   with Bryan Brown, then brief right breast lying
   down with him.
The Final Option (1982; British) . . . . . . . . . . . . Frankie
Heatwave (1983; Australian) . . . . . . . . . . . . . . . . Kate
A Passage to India (1984; British) . . . . . . Adela Quested
Kangaroo (1986; Australian) . . . . . . Harriet Somers
High Tide (1987; Australian) . . . . . . . . . . . . . . . . Lilli
Alice (1990) . . . . . . . . . . . . . . . . . . . . . . . . . . . Vicki
Barton Fink (1991) . . . . . . . . . . . . . . . Audrey Taylor

Impromptu (1991). . . . . . . . . . . . . . . . . . George Sand
Naked Lunch (1991) . . . . . . . . . . . Joan Frost/Joan Lee
Husbands and Wives (1992). . . . . . . . . . . . . . . .Sally
Where Angels Fear to Tread (1992) . . . . Harriet Herriton
The Ref (1993) . . . . . . . . . . . . . . . . . Caroline Chasseur
*Made for TV Movies:*
A Woman Called Golda (1982). . . . . . . . . Young Golda
One Against the Wind (1991). . . . . . . . . . Mary Lindell

## Davis, Neriah

a.k.a. Neriah Napaul.
*Films:*
**The Bikini Carwash Company** (1992). . . . . . . . . Rita
   (Unrated version reviewed.)
   ••• 0:15—Breasts taking off her bikini top so Stanley can
   "catch some fish" with it.
   ••• 0:18—Breasts and buns, making love with Big
   Bruce.
   •• 0:43—Breasts and buns, making love with Big
   Bruce. (same as 0:18)
   ••• 0:45—Brief left breast, getting dressed. Then buns,
   after forgetting to put on her bikini bottoms.
   ••• 0:46—Breasts and buns in G-string, hand washing a
   customer with Sunny.
   ••• 0:47—Buns, bending over while wearing a cowboy
   outfit.
   ••• 0:48—Breasts and buns, dancing inside car wash
   with Sunny and Melissa.
   ••• 1:02—Nude, soaped up in car wash with Sunny and
   Melissa.
   •• 1:11—Buns, posing while wearing cowboy outfit.
   ••• 1:13—Breasts and buns.
**Meatballs 4** (1992) . . . . . . . . . . . . . . . . . . . . .Neriah
   • 0:05—Very brief buns, while getting her red towel
   pulled up by another girl while walking to the showers.
**The Bikini Carwash Company II** (1993) . . . . . . . Rita
   (Unrated version reviewed.)
   ••• 0:09—Breasts with the other three girls, celebrating
   in office during music video number.
   ••• 0:16—Breasts at carwash during music video number. (Wearing pink bikini bottoms.)
   • 0:24—Buns in lingerie in offices of The Miracle Network with Sunny.
   • 0:27—Brief breasts while flashing her breasts in office.
   ••• 0:35—Breasts and buns in studio when she's caught
   without her clothes on.
   • 1:15—Brief breasts and buns during clean up at the
   studio.
   •• 1:29—Breasts and buns in swimsuit during music
   video number at the carwash.
*Video Tapes:*
**Playboy Celebrity Centerfold: La Toya Jackson**
   (1994) . . . . . . . . . . . . . . . . . . . . . . . . . . . . . Playmate
   ••• 0:36—Nude, during music video number out in the
   country.
   ••• 0:39—Nude in starry music video number. Sometimes in lingerie.

••• 0:42—Nude in still photos.

••• 0:43—In red bra and panties, then nude in music segment with artwork.

••• 0:47—Nude in farm music video segment.

*Magazines:*

**Playboy's Book of Lingerie** (Nov 1992) . . . . . Herself

••• 65—Breasts.

**Playboy's Book of Lingerie** (Jan 1993) . . . . . . Herself

••• 42-43—Side view of right breast and buns.

**Playboy's Book of Lingerie** (Mar 1993) . . . . . Herself

••• 106—Breasts and buns.

**Playboy's Bathing Beauties** (Apr 1993) . . . . . Herself

••• 84-85—Breasts.

**Playboy's Book of Lingerie** (Jul 1993) . . . . . . Herself

••• 3-7—Breasts and buns.

**Playboy's Wet & Wild Women** (Aug 1993) . . Herself

••• 82—Breasts.

**Playboy's Blondes, Brunettes & Redheads**
(Sep 1993) . . . . . . . . . . . . . . . . . . . . . . . . . . . Herself

••• 18—Breasts.

**Playboy's Book of Lingerie** (Sep 1993) . . . . . Herself

••• 82-83—Breasts.

**Playboy's Book of Lingerie** (Nov 1993) . . . . . Herself

••• 52-53—Breasts.

**Playboy** (Jan 1994)
. . . . . . . . The Great 40th Anniversary Playmate Search

••• 141—Full frontal nudity.

**Playboy's Book of Lingerie** (Jan 1994) . . . . . . Herself

••• 73—Breasts.

**Playboy's Great Playmate Search** (Feb 1994)
. . . . . . . . . . . . . . . . . . . . . . . . . . . . . . . . . . Herself

••• 95—Full frontal nudity.

**Playboy** (Mar 1994). . . . . . . . . . . . . . . . . . . Playmate

••• 86-97—Nude.

## Davis, Phyllis

*Films:*

The Last of the Secret Agents? (1966) . . . . . Beautiful Girl

The Swinger (1966) . . . . . . . . . . . . . . . . . . . . . . . . .n.a.

Live a Little, Love a Little (1968) . . . . . . . . 2nd Secretary

Beyond the Valley of the Dolls (1970) . . . . . . Susan Lake

**Sweet Sugar** (1972) . . . . . . . . . . . . . . . . . . . . . Sugar

*a.k.a. Hellfire on Ice*

(With brown hair.)

••• 0:34—Breasts in bed with a guard.

••• 0:50—Breasts in the shower with Dolores.

•• 0:57—Brief breasts in the bathroom.

The Day of the Dolphin (1973) . . . . . . . . . . . Secretary

**Terminal Island** (1973) . . . . . . . . . . . . . . . Joy Lange

••• 0:39—Breasts and buns in a pond, full frontal nudity getting out, then more breasts putting blouse on while a guy watches.

Train Ride to Hollywood (1975). . . . . . . . Scarlett O'Hara

**The Choirboys** (1977) . . . . . . . . . . . . . . . . .Foxy/Gina

•• 0:29—Breasts wearing pasties, under sheer pink robe.

1:24—In black bra, panties, garter belt and stockings.

**The Best of Sex and Violence** (1981) . . . . . Sugar/Joy

•• 0:56—Breasts after bath and in bed in scenes from *Sweet Sugar*.

••• 0:59—Breasts and buns walking out of lake in scene from *Terminal Island*.

**Famous T & A** (1982) . . . . . . . . . . . . . . . . . Sugar/Joy

(No longer available for purchase, check your video store for rental.)

••• 0:02—Nude in lots of great out-takes from *Terminal Island*. Check this out if you are a Phyllis Davis fan!

••• 0:51—Breasts in scenes from *Sweet Sugar*. Includes more out-takes.

••• 1:04—More out-takes from *Sweet Sugar*.

Guns (1990). . . . . . . . . . . . . . . . . . . . Kathryn Hamilton

*TV:*

Love, American Style (1970-74) . . . . . . Repertory Player

Vega$ (1978-81) . . . . . . . . . . . . . . . . . . . Beatrice Travis

## Davis-Voss, Sammi

No relation to the late entertainer Sammy Davis, Jr.

*Films:*

Hope and Glory (1987; British). . . . . . . . . Dawn Rohan

A Prayer for the Dying (1987) . . . . . . . . . . . . . . . Anna

Consuming Passions (1988; U.S./British) . . . . . . . Felicity

The Lair of the White Worm (1988; British) . .Mary Trent

**The Rainbow** (1989) . . . . . . . . . . . . . Ursula Brangwen

••• 0:21—Breasts and buns with Amanda Donohoe undressing, running outside in the rain, jumping into the water, then talking by the fireplace.

•• 0:30—Breasts and buns posing for a painter.

• 1:33—Brief right breast and buns getting out of bed.

••• 1:44—Nude running outside with Donohoe.

Horseplayer (1991) . . . . . . . . . . . . . . . . . . . . . . .Randi

Shadow of China (1991; U.S./Japanese) . . . . . .Katherine

Indecency (1992). . . . . . . . . . . . . . . . . . . . . . . . . . Nia

*Made for Cable Movies:*

Chernobyl: The Final Warning (1991). . .Elena Mashenko

The Perfect Bride (1991) . . . . . . . . . . . . . . . Stephanie

*Made for TV Movies:*

Pack of Lies (1987). . . . . . . . . . . . . . . . . . . . . . .Julie

*TV:*

Homefront (1991-93). . . . . . . . . . . . . . . Caroline Hailey

## Dawn, Angela

*Video Tapes:*

**Hot Body International: #3 Lingerie Special**
(1992) . . . . . . . . . . . . . . . . . . . . . . . . . . . . .Contestant

•• 0:13—Buns in body suit.

**Hot Body International: #5 Miss Acapulco** (1992)
. . . . . . . . . . . . . . . . . . . . . . . . . . . . . . . . . .Contestant

0:42—In orange two piece swimsuit during modeling session.

•• 0:46—Buns, while dancing in orange two piece swimsuit.

**Hot Body Video Magazine #1** (1992)
. . . . . . . . . . . . . . . . . . . . . . . . . . . Street Scene/Model

••• 0:34—Buns in G-string and breasts during photo session on a Harley.

**Hot Body Video Magazine #2** (1992)

. . . . . . . . . . . . . . . . . . . . . . . . Feature Girl/Model
- •• 0:01—Breasts during opening credits.
- ••• 0:28—Nude, taking off a red swimsuit and putting on a hot pink one.
- ••• 0:30—Outside on hay, in white bra and panties, then breasts and buns.

**Hot Body Video Magazine #4: Extra Sexy** (1993)

. . . . . . . . . . . . . . . . . . . . . . . . . . . . Street Scene
- •• 0:01—Breasts and buns during introduction.
- ••• 0:38—In two piece swimsuit, then breasts and buns while posing on a Harley-Davidson motorcycle.

**Hot Body: The Best of Hot Body** (1994) . . . . Herself
- •• 0:50—Buns in swimsuits.

# • Dawn, Kimberly

See: Dawson, Kim.

# • Dawson, Kim

a.k.a. Kimberly Dawn.
*Films:*
Not of This Earth (1988) . . . . . . . . . . . . . .Girl in House
The Arrival (1990) . . . . . . . . . . . . . . . . . . . . . . Leslie
**Sexual Outlaws** (1993) . . . . . . . . . . . . . . . .Jeannie
- ••• 0:05—Breasts and buns in panties, then nude while changing lingerie, then posing on bed.
- ••• 0:07—Breasts and buns, while posing on bed.
- ••• 0:09—Breasts, while in bed with Rita.
*Made for Cable TV:*
**Love Street: Hope's Creek** (1993; Showtime) . .Jessica
0:18—Running through woods in slip, then in bra and panties.
- ••• 0:19—Breasts, while making love outside with Tucker.
- • 0:22—Very brief buns, while putting on panties.
*Video Tapes:*
**Buck Naked Line Dancing** (1993) . . . . . . . . . Dancer
- ••• 0:00—Breasts throughout. She's in the back in the left.

# Dax, Danielle

British alternative pop singer. Originally with the group the *Lemon Kittens*.
*Films:*
**The Company of Wolves** (1985) . . . . . . . . . .Wolfgirl
- • 1:26—Brief buns and breasts running around outside. Her hair is in the way a lot.

# Day, Alexandra

*Films:*
**Erotic Images** (1983) . . . . . . . . . . . Logan's Girlfriend
- •• 0:37—Breasts getting out of bed while Logan talks on the phone to Britt Ekland.
Boarding House (1984) . . . . . . . . . . . . .Girl in Bathroom
Body Double (1984) . . . . . . . . . . Girl in Bathroom #1
**Young Lady Chatterley II** (1986) Jenny "Maid in Hut"
- ••• 0:06—Breasts and buns in hut on the bed with the Gardener.
- ••• 0:28—Breasts taking bath with Harlee McBride.

*Video Tapes:*
**The Girls of Penthouse** (1984)

. . . . . . . . . . . . . . Tattoo Woman & Use Me Woman
- ••• 0:34—Nude, getting tattooed by another woman, then making love with her.
- ••• 0:40—Nude, dancing and stripping off her clothes down to stockings and garter belt, then on bed. Quick cuts and strobe light make it hard to see.
**Penthouse: On the Wild Side** (1988) . . . . Honey Pot
- ••• 0:43—Breasts, getting honey dribbled on her, then getting it licked off by her lover.

# Day, Catlyn

*Films:*
**Kandyland** (1987) . . . . . . . . . . . . . . . . . . . . . .Diva
- ••• 0:50—Breasts wearing pasties doing strip routine.
- • 1:06—Brief breasts talking on the telephone in dressing room.
- • 1:12—Brief breasts during dance routine with the other girls.
Rented Lips (1988) . . . . . . . . . . . . . . . . . . . . . Dancer
Wilding, The Children of Violence (1990)

. . . . . . . . . . . . . . . . . . . . . . . . Officer Breedlove
Indecent Proposal (1993) . . . . . . . . . . . . .Wine Goddess

# De La Croix, Raven

*Films:*
Jokes My Folks Never Told Me (1976) . . . . . . . . . . . n.a.
**Up!** (1976) . . . . . . . . . . . . . . . . . .Margo Winchester
Breasts.
**The Happy Hooker Goes to Washington** (1977)

. . . . . . . . . . . . . . . . . . . Uncredited Ice Cream Girl
- • 0:31—Brief breasts, while lying on table, getting her rear end covered with ice cream.
**The Lost Empire** (1983) . . . . . . . . . . . . . . White Star
- ••• 1:05—Breasts with a snake after being drugged by the bad guy.
- •• 1:07—Breasts lying on a table.
- •• 1:08—Breasts, getting up off table and punching a guy.
**Screwballs** (1983) . . . . . . . . . . . . . .Miss Anna Tomical
- ••• 1:08—Breasts during strip routine in nightclub.
*Video Tapes:*
**Best Chest in the West** (1984) . . . . . . . . . . . .Herself
- ••• 0:34—Breasts doing strip tease routine on stage.
*Magazines:*
**Playboy** (Nov 1976) . . . . . . . . . . . Sex in Cinema 1976
- •• 153—Breasts in a photo from *Up*.
**Playboy** (Mar 1977) . . . . . . . . . . . . . . . .Dear Playboy
- ••• 17—Breasts in small photo.

# De Leeuw, Lisa

Adult film actress.
*Films:*
**It's Called Murder Baby** (1982) . . . . . . . . . .Dixie Ray
(R-rated version of the adult film *Dixie Ray, Hollywood Star*.)
- • 0:26—Lower frontal nudity, raising her dress at the beach to prove to Nick that she never wears panties.

••• 0:42—Nude on table, getting massaged by Adrian.
•• 0:49—Full frontal nudity when Nick leaves the room.
•• 1:21—Breasts, getting up to get dressed.
• 1:22—Brief lower frontal nudity in open robe, while walking around the house.
••• 1:24—Breasts, opening her nightgown in front of Nick.

**Up 'n' Coming** (1987) . . . . . . . . . . Altheah Anderson
(R-rated version reviewed, X-rated version available.)
• 0:33—Very brief breasts by the pool when her robe opens.
• 0:48—Brief breasts walking around the house when her robe open.
•• 0:49—Left breast talking with a guy, then breasts while walking into the bedroom.

## De Light, Venus

a.k.a. Lynn Chase.
*Films:*
**Stripper** (1985) . . . . . . . . . . . . . . . . . . . . . . Herself
• 0:59—Brief breasts, on stage, blowing fire.
••• 1:07—Breasts and buns in black G-string, doing routine on stage, using fire.

**Angel of Passion** (1991) . . . . . . . . . . . . . . . . . Carol
•• 0:15—Breasts taking a shower.
••• 0:19—Breasts and buns in G-string dancing outside next to pool at a birthday party.
••• 0:23—Breasts and buns in red lingerie in camper, then breasts while making love on top of Will.

*Made for Cable TV:*
**Real Sex 5** (1993; HBO) . . . Introducing Venus de Light
• 0:00—Brief breasts during opening credits.
• 0:01—Brief breasts during opening credits.
••• 0:02—Breasts and buns in T-back, dancing on stage with a dummy, a snake and feather fans.
••• 0:06—Breasts and buns, dancing on stage with a monkey, a bird and fire.

*Video Tapes:*
**In Search of the Perfect 10** (1986) . . Perfect Girl #4
••• 0:18—Breasts talking on the phone and buns in G-string seen through the Nude-Cam.
••• 0:21—In two piece swimsuit, then breasts taking it off in the doorway.

**The Stripper of the Year** (1986) . . . . . Venus De Light
••• 0:37—Nude, doing strip routine that includes fire tricks.
•• 0:53—Breasts on stage with the other contestants.
••• 0:55—Breasts as a finalist, then dance-off.
0:56—Breasts as the winner.

**Hot Bodies** (1988) . . . . . . . . . . . . . . . . . . . . Herself
•• 0:22—Breasts, dancing and taking off dress.
••• 0:24—Nude in large champagne glass prop.
••• 0:27—Nude dancing on stage.
••• 0:47—Breasts and buns in G-string stripping in nurse uniform.
••• 0:49—Breasts and buns on hospital gurney.
••• 0:52—Breasts and buns dancing with a life-size dummy prop.

**Starlets Exposed! Volume II** (1991) . . . . . . . . Venus
••• 0:43—Buns in G-string, then breasts dancing on stage with a life-size dummy and in a giant champagne glass.
*CD-ROM:*
**Venus' Playhouse** (1994) . . . . . . . . . . . . . . . . Herself

## De Liso, Debra

*Films:*
**The Slumber Party Massacre** (1982) . . . . . . . . . Kim
• 0:08—Very brief breasts getting soap from Trish in the shower.
•• 0:29—In beige bra and panties, then breasts putting on a U.S.A. shirt while changing with the other girls.
Outrageous Fortune (1987) . . . Ballet Double for Lauren
**Iced** (1988) . . . . . . . . . . . . . . . . . . . . . . . . . . . . Trina
• 0:11—In a bra, then brief nude making love with Cory in hotel room.
Dr. Caligari (1989) . . . . . . . . . . . . . . . . . . . Grace Butter

## De Medeiros, Maria

*Films:*
1871 (1989; British) . . . . . . . . . . . . . . . . . . . . . . .Maria
La Lectrice (1989; French) . . . . . . . . . . . . . Silent Nurse
a.k.a. The Reader
**Henry & June** (1990) . . . . . . . . . . . . . . . . . . .Anais Nin
• 0:50—Brief right breast, popping out of dress top.
•• 0:52—Breasts lying in bed with Richard E. Grant.
•• 1:13—Breasts in bed with Fred Ward, buns getting out. Right breast standing by the window.
••• 1:31—Breasts in bed with Brigitte Lahaie.
1:37—Nude under sheer black patterned dress.
•• 1:43—Close up of right breast as Ward plays with her.
•• 2:01—Left breast, then breasts after taking off her top in bed with Uma Thurman.
Meeting Venus (1990; British) . . . . . . . . . . . . . Yvonne
*Magazines:*
**Playboy** (Nov 1991) . . . . . . . . . . Sex in Cinema 1991
•• 145—Breasts, lying in bed with Richard E. Grant. From *Henry & June.*

## De Mornay, Rebecca

*Films:*
**Risky Business** (1983) . . . . . . . . . . . . . . . . . . . . Lana
• 0:28—Brief nude standing by the window with Tom Cruise.
Runaway Train (1985) . . . . . . . . . . . . . . . . . . . . . .Sara
The Slugger's Wife (1985) . . . . . . . . . . . . Debby Palmer
The Trip to Bountiful (1986) . . . . . . . . . . . . . . . Thelma
**And God Created Woman** (1988) . . . . . . . . . . .Robin
(Unrated version.)
•• 0:06—Brief Left breast and buns in gymnasium with Vincent Spano. Brief right breast making love.
• 0:53—Brief buns and breasts in the shower when Spano sees her.
•• 1:02—Brief left breast with Langella on the floor.
••• 1:12—Breasts making love with Spano in a museum.
Feds (1988) . . . . . . . . . . . . . . . . . . . . . Elizabeth De Witt

Dealers (1989) . . . . . . . . . . . . . . . . . . Anna Schuman
   0:59—In black bra, making love with Daniel.
Backdraft (1991) . . . . . . . . . . . . . . . . Helen McCaffrey
**The Hand That Rocks the Cradle** (1992). . . . Peyton
  • 0:29—Upper half of right breast, breast feeding
   Claire's baby.
   0:36—Partial right breast, breast feeding the baby
   again.
   1:25—Briefly in wet nightgown in the kitchen with
   Michael.
Guilty as Sin (1993). . . . . . . . . . . . . . . . Jennifer Haines
The Three Musketeers (1993) . . . . . . . . . . . . . Milady
*Made for Cable Movies:*
By Dawn's Early Light (1990; HBO) . . . . . Cindy Moreau
Blind Side (1993; HBO). . . . . . . . . . . . . . . Lynn Kaines
*Made for TV Movies:*
An Inconvenient Woman (1991) . . . . . . . . . . Flo March
Getting Out (1994). . . . . . . . . . . . . . . . . Arlie Holsclaw

# De Moss, Darcy

*Films:*
Gimme an "F" (1981) . . . . . . . . . . One of the "Ducks"
*a.k.a. T & A Academy 2*
**Hardbodies** (1984) . . . . . . . . . . . . . . . . . . . . . . Dede
  ••• 0:55—Breasts in the back seat of the limousine with
   Rounder.
Friday the 13th, Part VI: Jason Lives (1986) . . . . . . . Nikki
Reform School Girls (1986) . . . . . . . . . . . . . . . . . . Knox
Can't Buy Me Love (1987) . . . . . . . . . . . . . . . . . . Patty
   0:46—In black bra and patterned panties in locker
   room.
**Return to Horror High** (1987) . . . . . . . . Sheri Haines
  • 0:21—Very brief left breast when her sweater gets
   lifted up while she's on some guy's back.
For Keeps (1988). . . . . . . . . . . . . . . . . . . . . . . Elaine
Night Life (1989) . . . . . . . . . . . . . . . . . . Roberta Woods
**Coldfire** (1990) . . . . . . . . . . . . . . . . . . . . . . . Maria
  ••• 0:27—Partial right breast and buns, lying in bed
   with Nick. Left breast, then breasts making love with
   him.
  •• 0:30—Breasts in bathtub with Nick.
**Living to Die** (1990). . . . . . . . . . . . . . Maggie Sams
   0:11—Taking off clothes to white bra, panties, garter
   belt and stockings in hotel room with a customer.
  • 0:32—Buns, getting out of spa while Wings Hauser
   watches without her knowing.
   0:33—Buns, in long shot when Hauser fantasizes
   about dancing with her.
  ••• 0:56—In black bra, then breasts and buns making
   love with Hauser.
  • 1:20—Breasts in mirror taking off black top for the
   bad guy.
**Pale Blood** (1990). . . . . . . . . . . . . . . . . . . Cherry
  • 0:33—Very, very brief left breast, while opening her
   robe while posing on couch.
Vice Academy, Part 3 (1991) . . . . . Uncredited Samantha
*Video Tapes:*
Aerobicise: The Ultimate Workout (1982) . . . . . . Herself

Eden (1992) . . . . . . . . . . . . . . . . . . . . . . . . . Randi
  •• 1:21—Breasts, getting out of the water and putting
   on T-shirt.
  ••• 1:22—Breasts on beach, while making love with
   Abe.
  •• 1:30—Brief breasts in bathroom.
**Eden 2** (1992). . . . . . . . . . . . . . . . . . . . . . Randi
  ••• 0:06—Breasts in sauna, while talking with Celine.
  ••• 0:25—Breasts, after waking up in bed with Celine.
  ••• 0:28—Breasts, taking off robe and putting on dress.
  • 1:00—Brief breast, while making love with Celine.
  ••• 1:11—Breasts, in black panties, taking off her dress
   and diving into pool.
  • 1:16—Breasts while frolicking in the ocean with Celine.
**Eden 3** (1993). . . . . . . . . . . . . . . . . . . . . . Randi
  ••• 1:36—In white bra and panties, then breasts while
   making love in bed with Josh.
**Eden 4** (1993). . . . . . . . . . . . . . . . . . . . . . Randi
  • 0:27—Right breast, while in bed talking to Josh.
   0:44—Half of left breast, while making out with Josh
   in workout room.
**Eden 5** (1993). . . . . . . . . . . . . . . . . . . . . . Randi
  • 0:02—Brief left breast, while in bed with Josh.
  • 0:20—Very brief tip of breast, while lying in bed with
   Josh.
  • 0:44—Very brief left breast when Gabe tries to put
   the moves on her.
  •• 1:03—In white bra, then breasts in bedroom with
   Gabe.
  ••• 1:15—Breasts, while making love on bed with Josh.
**Eden 6** (1994). . . . . . . . . . . . . . . . . . . . . . Randi
  •• 0:06—Breasts and buns while making love in bed
   with Josh.
  ••• 1:09—Breasts, while taking off her top in front of
   mirror, then making love with Josh in bed. Nice
   close-up of Josh putting lotion on her breast.
   1:15—Half of right breast in gaping lingerie while lying on bed.
  ••• 1:40—Breasts, with Josh. Seen in mirror.
  • 2:00—Very, very brief side of right breast when Josh
   takes her dress off.
  ••• 2:01—Breasts and buns with Josh.
  ••• 2:14—Breast, while in bed with George.
*Magazines:*
**Playboy** (Jun 1993). . . . . . . . . . . . . . All About "Eden"
  ••• 82-83—Full frontal nudity.
**Playboy's Nudes** (Dec 1993) . . . . . . . . . . . . . Herself
  ••• 12—Full frontal nudity.

# De Prume, Cathryn

*Films:*
**Deadtime Stories** (1985) . . . . . . . . . . . . . Goldi-lox
  •• 1:08—Breasts taking a shower, quick cuts.
Five Corners (1988) . . . . . . . . . . . . . . . . . . . . . Brita
Bloodhounds of Broadway (1989) . . . . . . . . . Showgirl
Navy SEALS (1990) . . . . . . . . . . . . . . . . . . . Bartender
Criss Cross (1992) . . . . . . . . . . . . . . . . . . . . . Oakley

*Made for TV Movies:*
Love, Lies and Murder (1991) . . . . . . Linda Bailey Brown
*TV:*
Down the Shore (1992-93) . . . . . . . . . . . . . . . . Donna

# De Rossi, Barbara

*Films:*
Stay As You Are (1978; Italian) . . . . . . . . . . . . . . .n.a.
English language version.
**Hearts and Armour** (1983) . . . . . . . . . . Bradamante
•• 1:05—Breasts while sleeping with Ruggero.
**La Cicala (The Cricket)** (1983) . . . . . . . . . . . Saveria
•• 0:39—Nude swimming under waterfall with Clio
Goldsmith.
•• 0:43—Breasts undressing in room with Goldsmith.
• 0:57—Brief right breast changing into dress in
room.
• 1:05—In wet white lingerie in waterfall with a guy,
then in a wet dress.
1:26—Very brief buns in bed with Anthony Franciosa.
•• 1:28—Breasts in bathroom with Franciosa.
• 1:36—Brief right breast making love with trucker.
*Made for Cable Movies:*
Mussolini and I (1985; HBO) . . . . . . . . . . . . . . . . . .n.a.
**Blood Ties** (1986; Italian; Showtime) . . . . . . . . . .Luisa
• 0:58—Brief breasts on couch when bad guy rips her
clothes off.

# de Sade, Ana

*Films:*
Return of a Man Called Horse (1976) . . . . . . . Moonstar
Caveman (1981) . . . . . . . . . . . . . . . . . . . . . Grot's Mate
High Risk (1981) . . . . . . . . . . . . . . . . . . . . . . . . . Nude
**Cabo Blanco** (1982) . . . . . . . . . . . . . . . . . . . . . . Rosa
• 0:34—Brief breasts, lying in bed and talking to a
guy.
• 0:36—Brief right breast, twice, when he gets out of
bed to look out the window.
Sorceress (1982) . . . . . . . . . . . . . . . . . . . . . . . . .Delisia
Triumphs of a Man Called Horse (1983; U.S./Mexican)
. . . . . . . . . . . . . . . . . . . . . . . . . . . . . . . . . . . .Redwing

# De Vasquez, Devin

*Star Search* Winner 1986—Spokesmodel.
*Films:*
Can't Buy Me Love (1987) . . . . . . . . . . . . . . . . . . . Iris
House II: The Second Story (1987) . . . . . . . . .The Virgin
**Society** (1989) . . . . . . . . . . . . . . . . . . . . . . . . . Clarisa
••• 0:37—Breasts, making love in bed with Billy.
• 0:40—Left breast, while on sofa with Billy when her
mother comes home.
**Guns** (1990) . . . . . . . . . . . . . . . . . . . . . . . . . . . .Cash
• 1:12—Brief side of right breast and buns undressing
for bath.
A Brilliant Disguise (1994) . . . . . . . . . . . . . . . . Gianna
*Video Tapes:*
**Playboy Video Magazine, Volume 8** . . . . . Playmate
Playmate Playoffs . . . . . . . . . . . . . . . . . . . . . Playmate

**Playboy Video Calendar 1988** (1987) . . . . . Playmate
**The Best of Video Playmate Calendars** (1992)
. . . . . . . . . . . . . . . . . . . . . . . . . . . . . . . . . . . Playmate
••• 0:02—Nude during fantasy photo session.
*Magazines:*
**Playboy** (Oct 1981)
. . . . . . . . Girls of the Southeastern Conference, Part II
144—Breasts. She was attending Louisiana State
University.
**Playboy** (Jun 1985) . . . . . . . . . . . . . . . . . . . . Playmate
**Playboy** (Nov 1986) . . . . . . . . . . . . . . . .Revvin' Devin
••• 80-87—Nude.
**Playboy's 1987 Book of Lingerie** (Mar 1987)
. . . . . . . . . . . . . . . . . . . . . . . . . . . . . . . . . . . . Herself
•• 15—Breasts.
• 34—Partial lower frontal nudity.
••• 72-73—Breasts and partial lower frontal.
•• 86—Breasts.
••• 111—Breasts and partial lower frontal nudity.
**Playboy's Calendar Playmates** (Nov 1992) . . .Herself
••• 44—Full frontal nudity.
••• 66—Full frontal nudity.
**Playboy's Nudes** (Dec 1992) . . . . . . . . . . . . . .Herself
••• 8-9—Full frontal nudity.
**Playboy's Book of Lingerie** (Mar 1994) . . . . .Herself
••• 51—Breasts.
**Playmates at Play** (Jul 1994) . . . . . . . . . . . . .Herself
••• 48—Full frontal nudity.

# Dean, Felicity

*Films:*
Crossed Swords (1978) . . . . . . . . . . . . . . . . .Lady Jane
Success is the Best Revenge (1984; British) . . . . . . . . n.a.
**Steaming** (1985; British) . . . . . . . . . . . . . . . . . Dawn
•• 1:12—Breasts painting on herself.
The Whistle Blower (1987; British) . . .Cynthia Goodburn

# Deane, Lezlie

*Films:*
**976-EVIL** (1988) . . . . . . . . . . . . . . . . . . . . . . . . Suzie
• 0:34—Brief right breast in open leather jacket, mak-
ing love on top of Spike. Brief breasts several times
getting off him.
•• 0:37—Brief breasts opening jacket after putting on
underwear.
Girlfriend from Hell (1989) . . . . . . . . . . . . . . . .Diane
Freddy's Dead: The Final Nightmare (1991) . . . . . . Tracy
Almost Pregnant (1992) . . . . . . . . . . . . . . . . Party Girl
(Unrated version reviewed.)
**To Protect and Serve** (1992) . . . . . . . . . . . . .Harriet
• 0:47—Brief breasts in front of fireplace with C. Thomas Howell. Hard to see because candles get in the
way.
• 0:51—Brief breasts, getting up off the floor.
• 1:18—Brief side view of left breast in mirror in bathroom. Long shot.
*Magazines:*
Playboy (Dec 1993) . . . . . . . . . . . . . . . . . Fem 2 Fem

## Deats, Danyi

*Films:*

The Allnighter (1987) . . . . . . . . . . . . . . . . . . . . . Junkie

**River's Edge** (1987) . . . . . . . . . . . . . . . . . . . . . Jamie

- 0:03—Breasts, dead lying next to river with her killer. (All the shots of her breasts in this film aren't exciting unless you like looking at dead bodies).
- 0:15—Close up breasts, then full frontal nudity when Crispin Glover pokes her with a stick.
  0:16—Full frontal nudity when the three boys leave.
  0:22—Full frontal nudity when all the kids come to see her body. (She's starting to look very discolored).
  0:24—Right breast when everybody leaves.
  0:30—Right breast when they come to dump her body in the river.

## DeBell, Kristine

*Films:*

**Alice in Wonderland** (1977) . . . . . . . . . . . . . . . Alice
(R-rated version reviewed.)

- 0:10—Brief left breast, several times after shrinking.
- 0:12—In braless wet sheet, after getting out of the water.
- 0:14—Brief lower frontal nudity in open sheet during song and dance number.
- •• 0:16—Lower frontal nudity and breasts while getting licked by her new friends.
- •• 0:18—Full frontal nudity while putting new dress on.
- 0:19—Left breast in gaping dress when sitting down on rock.
- ••• 0:22—Breasts, after taking off dress and playing with herself.
- 0:40—Brief right breast, while lying on the ground with Tweedledum and Tweedledee.
- 0:42—Brief breasts under dress while singing and dancing.
- •• 0:51—Full frontal nudity on bed with the king.
- ••• 0:59—Full frontal nudity getting bathed and primped by two women, then making love with them, then with the Queen. Brief buns, when getting up.
- 1:05—Right breast in dress, while running from the Queen.
- •• 1:07—Nude while making love with her boyfriend after returning from Wonderland.
- ••• 1:10—Breasts, while running around in field in white dress, then riding a horse. Full frontal nudity in waterfall.
- •• 1:15—Nude during end credits.

Meatballs (1979; Canadian) . . . . . . . . . . . . . . . . . . .A.L.

The Big Brawl (1980) . . . . . . . . . . . . . . . . . . . . .Nancy

**Willie and Phil** (1980) . . . . . . . . . . . . . . . . . . . . .Rena

- 1:36—Breasts on the beach (mostly silhouette). Brief side of left breast.

T.A.G.: The Assassination Game (1982) . . . . . . . .Nancy

Cheerleaders Wild Weekend (1985). . . . . .Debbie/Pierce

Club Life (1987) . . . . . . . . . . . . . . . . . . . . . . . . . . . Fern

*Magazines:*

**Playboy** (Apr 1976) . . . . . . . . . . . . . . . . . . . . . Cover
•• Right breast on cover photo.

**Playboy** (Aug 1976)
. . . 200 Motels, or, How I Spent My Summer Vacation
••• 77-81—Nude in B&W photos taken by Helmut Newton.

**Playboy** (Nov 1976)
. . . . . . . . . . . . . .Dear Playboy/Sex in Cinema 1976

- 12—Partial right breast and partial lower frontal nudity in small photo.
- 152—Left breast.

## Del Sol, Laura

*Films:*

**Carmen** (1983; Spanish). . . . . . . . . . . . . . . . .Carmen

- 1:14—Left breast, while lying in bed with Antonio.
- 1:27—Brief partial left breast, standing up when Antonio catches her in wardrobe room with another dancer.

The Hit (1984) . . . . . . . . . . . . . . . . . . . . . . . . . Maggie

The Stilts (Los Zancos) (1984; Spanish) . . . . . . . Teresa

## Delaney, Cassandra

Ex-wife of Country music singer John Denver.
*Films:*

**Fair Game** (1985; Australian) . . . . . . . . . . . . . . Jessica

- 0:15—Buns and brief side of left breast, taking off her outfit and lying on bed.
- 0:16—Breasts rolling over in bed.
  0:19—Brief, out of focus buns, in Polaroid photograph taped to inside of the refrigerator.
- 0:32—Brief left breast, taking off outfit to take a shower.
- •• 0:48—Brief breasts when the bad guys cut her blouse open. Breasts several times, while tied to front of truck.
- 0:49—Brief left breast while getting up off the ground.
  0:50—Half of right breast, while sitting in the shower. Dark.

Rebel (1985; Australian) . . . . . . . . All-Girl Band Member

**Hurricane Smith** (1990) . . . . . . . . . . . . . . . . . . .Julie

- •• 0:45—Breasts, while making love with Carl Weathers in bed.

## Delaney, Kim

*Films:*

That Was Then... This Is Now (1985) . . . . Cathy Carlson

Campus Man (1987) . . . . . . . . . . . . . . . Dayna Thomas

Hunter's Blood (1987) . . . . . . . . . . . . . . . . . . . Melanie

**The Drifter** (1988). . . . . . . . . . . . . . . . . . Julia Robbins

- 0:11—Brief breasts making love with Miles O'Keeffe on motel floor.
- •• 0:21—Breasts in bed talking with Timothy Bottoms.

Hangfire (1990) . . . . . . . . . . . . . . . . . . . Maria Slayton

Body Parts (1991) . . . . . . . . . . . . . . . . Karen Crushank
*Made for Cable Movies:*

The Disappearance of Christina (1993). . . . . . . . . . n.a.

Made for Cable TV:
Tales From the Crypt: The Sacrifice (1992; HBO)
. . . . . . . . . . . . . . . . . . . . . . . . . . . . Gloria Fielding
Made for TV Movies:
Cracked Up (1987) . . . . . . . . . . . . . . . . . . . . . . Jackie
Something Is Out There (1988). . . . . . . . . . . . . Mandy
The Broken Cord (1992) . . . . . . . . . . . . . . . . Suzanne
Jackie Collins' Lady Boss (1992). . . . . . Lucky Santangelo
TV:
All My Children . . . . . . . . . . . . . . . . . . Jenny Gardner
Tour of Duty (1988-89). . . . . . . . . . . . . . . Alex Devilin
Fifth Corner (1992-93) . . . . . . . . . . . . . . Erica Fontaine

## Delany, Dana

Films:
The Fan (1981) . . . . . . . . . . . . . . . . . . . . Sales Woman
Almost You (1984) . . . . . . . . . . . . . . . . . Susan McCall
Where the River Runs Black (1986) . . . . . . . . Sister Ana
Masquerade (1988). . . . . . . . . . . . . . . . . .Anne Briscoe
Moon Over Parador (1988). . . . . . . . . . . . . . . . Jenny
Patty Hearst (1989) . . . . . . . . . . . . . . . . . . . . .Gelina
Housesitter (1992) . . . . . . . . . . . . . . . . . . . . . Becky
**Light Sleeper** (1992) . . . . . . . . . . . . . . . . Marianne
••• 0:46—Right breast, while lying on the floor with
Willem Dafoe. Brief left breast when getting up. Lit
with green light. (If this was anyone else, it would
only get one •.)
Tombstone (1993) . . . . . . . . . . . . . . Josephine Marcus
Miniseries:
Wild Palms (1993). . . . . . . . . . . . . . . . . Grace Wyckoff
Made for TV Movies:
Donato and Daughter (1993) . . . . . . . . . . . . . . . .n.a.
TV:
Love of Life (1979-80). . . . . . . . . . . . . . . . . . . . .n.a.
As the World Turns (1981). . . . . . . . . . . . . . . . . .n.a.
China Beach (1988-91) . . . . . .Nurse Colleen McMurphy
(Emmy Award in 1989.)

## Delon, Nathalie

Films:
When Eight Bells Toll (1971; British) . . . . . . . . Charlotte
**Bluebeard** (1972) . . . . . . . . . . . . . . . . . . . . . . Erika
• 1:03—Breasts in bed, showing Richard Burton her
breasts.
• 1:09—Brief right breast lying on the floor with Sybil
Danning just before Richard Burton kills both of
them.
The Godson (1972; Italian/French) . . . . . . Jan Lagrange
The Romantic Englishwoman (1975; British/French)
. . . . . . . . . . . . . . . . . . . . . . . . . . . . . . . . . Miranda

## Delora, Jennifer

Films:
Robot Holocaust (1986) . . . . . . . . . . . . . . . . . . . Nyla
**Sexpot** (1986) . . . . . . . . . . . . . . . . . . . . . . . .Barbara
••• 0:28—In bra, then breasts with her two sisters when
their bras pop off. (She's in the middle.)
•• 0:36—Breasts on bed with Gorilla.
• 1:32—Breasts during outtakes of 0:28 scene.

**Deranged** (1987) . . . . . . . . . . . . . . . . . . . . . Maryann
• 1:09—Breasts in bed with Frank. Long shot.
Young Nurses in Love (1987) . . . . . . . . . . . . . . . Bunny
**New York's Finest** (1988) . . . . . . . . Loretta Michaels
• 0:02—Brief breasts pretending to be a black hooker.
• 0:04—Brief breasts with a bunch of hookers.
• 0:36—Breasts with her two friends doing push-ups
on the floor.
**Sensations** (1988) . . . . . . . . . . . . . . . . . . Della Randall
• 0:11—Brief breasts talking to Jenny to wake her up.
• 0:13—Brief breasts a couple of times in open robe.
•• 0:38—Breasts making love with a guy on bed.
**Bedroom Eyes II** (1989) . . . . . . . . . . . . . Gwendolyn
•• 0:04—Undressing in hotel room with Vinnie.
Breasts, then making love.
Cleo/Leo (1989). . . . . . . . . . . . . . . . . . . . . . Bernice
Savage Lust (1989) . . . . . . . . . . . . . . . . . . . . .Amanda
a.k.a. Deadly Manor
Club Fed (1990). . . . . . . . . . . . . Uncredited Girl at Pool
**Frankenhooker** (1990) . . . . . . . . . . . . . . . . . .Angel
• 0:36—Brief breasts during introduction to Jeffrey.
••• 0:41—Breasts dancing in room with the other hook-
ers. (Nice tattoos!)
Fright House (1990). . . . . . . . . . .Dr. Victoria Sedgewick
Bad Girls Dormitory (1991) . . . . . . . . . . . . . . . . . Lisa
Deadly Manor (1991). . . . . . . . . . . . . . . . . .Amanda
Phantasy (1991). . . . . . . . . . . . . . . . . . . . . . Fantasy
Suburban Commando (1991) . . . . . . . . . . . . Hooker
Dead Boyz Can't Fly (1992) . . . . . . . . . . . . . . .Helen

## Delpy, Julie

Films:
Detective (1985; French/Swiss)
. . . . . . . . . . . . . . . . . . . . . Wise Young Girl Groupie
Bad Blood (1987; French) . . . . . . . . . . . . . . . . . . Lise
**The Passion of Beatrice** (1988; French). . . . . Béatrice
• 0:58—Left breast, then breasts getting out of bed.
••• 1:11—Side view of right breast, holding dress after
getting raped by her father. Nude, running to the
door and barricading it with furniture.
•• 1:12—More nude, arranging furniture.
••• 1:13—Full frontal nudity, wiping her crotch and
burning her clothes.
• 1:36—More of right breast, when her father puts
soot on her face.
•• 1:37—Brief left breast, then breasts and brief buns
standing with soot on her face. Long shot.
••• 1:44—Breasts taking a bath. Subtitles get in the way
a bit.
La Noche Oscura (1989; Spanish)
. . . . . . . . . . . . . . . . . . . . . .Anna de Jesus/Virgin Mary
Europa Europa (1991; German) . . . . . . . . . . . . . . Leni
Voyager (1991; German/French) . . . . . . . . . . . . Sabeth
The Three Musketeers (1993). . . . . . . . . . . . Constance

# • Delvaux, Claudine

*Films:*

**Petit Con** (1986; French)................Maryse
•• 0:28—Right breast, while getting felt up by her husband in front of Michel.
Camille Claudel (1989; French)...........Concierge

# Demitro, Papusha

*Films:*

**Perfect Timing** (1984)...........Bonnie O. Bendix
•• 0:26—Nude, taking off dress in photo studio and kissing Joe.
• 0:29—Breasts walking with Joe through the living room, then brief nude on the roof.
•• 0:32—Nude, walking into the kitchen and getting chocolate out of the refrigerator.
•• 0:34—Nude in bed with Joe.
••• 0:45—Nude in bedroom with Joe.
•• 1:03—Nude on bed with Joe.
Breaking All the Rules (1985; Canadian).........Patty

# Dempsey, Sandra

*Films:*

**Video Vixens** (1973)....................Actress
•• 0:05—Full frontal nudity, lying down getting make up put on.
The Swinging Cheerleaders (1974)....1st Girl at Tryout
If You Don't Stop It You'll Go Blind (1979).........n.a.

# Deneuve, Catherine

*Films:*

The Umbrellas of Cherbourg (1964)..Genevieve Emery
Repulsion (1965).........................Carol
The April Fool's (1969)...........Catherine Gunther
**Mississippi Mermaid** (1969; French)
.....................Julie Roussel/Marion Vergano
•• 1:04—Breasts, changing from a blouse to a sweater while standing up in parked car.
•• 1:26—Brief breasts, taking off her blouse in bedroom.
La Grande Bourgeoise (1974; Italian)......Linda Murri
Hustle (1975).......................Nicole Britton
**Lovers Like Us** (1975).....................Nelly
*a.k.a. The Savage*
• 1:06—Brief left upper half of left breast in bed with Yves Montand. Dark.
••• 1:09—Breasts sitting up in bed.
The Last Metro (1980)....................Marion
Je Vous Aime (1981).......................Alice
*a.k.a. I Love You All*
A Choice of Arms (1983; French).............Nicole
**The Hunger** (1983).....................Miriam
• 0:08—Brief breasts taking a shower with David Bowie. Probably a body double, you don't see her face.
Love Song (1985).......................Margaux
Scene of the Crime (1987; French).............Lili
Indochine (1992; French)..................Eliane
*Magazines:*
**Playboy** (Sep 1963).........Europe's New Sex Sirens

**Playboy** (Oct 1965).........France's Deneuve Wave
**Playboy** (Jan 1989)............Women of the Sixties
• 159—Breasts sitting by the window.

# Denier, Lydie

*Films:*

**The Nightstalker** (1987)..............First Victim
••• 0:03—Breasts making love with big guy.
**Bulletproof** (1988)......................Tracy
•• 0:14—Breasts in Gary Busey's bathtub.
0:20—Brief buns, putting on shirt after getting out of bed. Very, very brief side view of left breast.
Midnight Cabaret (1988)..........Woman in White
Paramedics (1988).........................Liette
**Red Blooded American Girl** (1988)
.........................Rebecca Murrin
••• 0:00—Breasts in bed wearing panties, garter belt and stockings. Buns, rolling over. Long scene.
**Blood Relations** (1989)...................Marie
•• 0:07—Left breast making love with Thomas on stairway.
• 0:44—Brief left breast in bed with Thomas' father. Very brief cuts of her breasts in B&W.
0:47—Getting out of swimming pool in a one piece swimsuit.
••• 0:54—Full frontal nudity undressing for the Grandfather.
**Satan's Princess** (1989)...........Nicole St. James
• 0:27—Full frontal nudity, getting out of pool.
••• 0:28—Full frontal nudity, next to bed and in bed with Karen.
••• 0:45—Breasts and buns, making love in bed with Robert Forster.
**No Place to Hide** (1991)...........Pamela Hanley
• 0:03—Breasts, after opening her ballet costume in the wings backstage before getting sliced up with a knife.
**Invasion of Privacy** (1992)................Vicky
(Unrated version reviewed.)
• 0:54—Brief breasts in her apartment dancing in front of Robby Benson while he video tapes her.
••• 1:19—Breasts on top of Benson in bed.
**Wild Orchid II: Two Shades of Blue** (1992)
.........................Dominique
••• 0:28—Breasts, undressing from lingerie while Blue and Elle watch.
**Mardi Gras for the Devil** (1993)...........Valerie
••• 0:50—Breasts, while making love in bed with Robert Davi.
*Made for Cable TV:*
**Red Shoe Diaries: Talk To Me Baby**
(1992; Showtime).......................Elaine
(Available on video tape on *Red Shoe Diaries 3: Another Woman's Lipstick*.)
• 0:13—Brief left breast several times, making love in bed with Richard Tyson.
•• 0:14—Breasts and buns, taking off robe to shower with Rita.

*TV:*
Tarzan (1991-93) . . . . . . . . . . . . . . . . . . . . . . . . Jane

# Denise, Denise

*Films:*
Lady Sings the Blues (1972) . . . . . . . . . . . . . . . . . .n.a.
**Fox Style** (1974) . . . . . . . . . . . . . . . . . . . . . . . Cindy
• 0:42—Brief breasts rolling over on her stomach on river bank with A. J.
1:21—Most of right breast, in bed with A. J.
Doctor Death: Seeker of Souls (1975) . Girl with Flat Tire

# Derek, Bo

Real name is Cathleen Collins.
Wife of director John Derek.
*Films:*
**Fantasies** (1974) . . . . . . . . . . . . . . . . . . . . . Anastasia
*a.k.a. Once Upon a Love*
• 0:03—Left breast, in bathtub.
•• 0:15—Breasts taking off top, then right breast, in bathtub.
• 0:43—Breasts getting her dress top pulled down.
• 0:59—Brief breasts in the water. Very brief full frontal nudity walking back into the house.
• 1:00—Buns and left breast several times outside the window.
• 1:17—Upper left breast, in bathtub again.
Orca, The Killer Whale (1977) . . . . . . . . . . . . . . . Annie
**10** (1979) . . . . . . . . . . . . . . . . . . . . . . . Jennifer Hanley
1:19—In yellow swimsuit running in slow motion towards Dudley Moore in his daydream.
• 1:29—Brief buns and breasts taking off towel and putting on robe when Moore visits her. Long shot, hard to see.
• 1:36—Brief breasts taking off dress trying to seduce Moore. Dark, hard to see.
• 1:37—Breasts, lying in bed. Dark, hard to see.
•• 1:41—Breasts, going to fix the skipping record. Long shot, hard to see. Buns, while jumping back into bed.
• 1:43—Breasts and buns, while sitting up in bed.
• 1:44—Breasts and buns in bed when Moore gets out.
**A Change of Seasons** (1980) . . . . . Lindsey Routledge
•• 0:00—Breasts in hot tub during the opening credits.
• 0:25—Side view of left breast in the shower talking to Anthony Hopkins.
**Tarzan, The Ape Man** (1981) . . . . . . . . . . . . . Jane
••• 0:43—Nude taking a bath in the ocean, then in a wet white dress.
• 1:35—Brief breasts painted all white.
• 1:45—Breasts washing all the white paint off in the river with Tarzan.
•• 1:47—Breasts during the ending credits playing with Tarzan and the orangutan. (When I saw this film in a movie theater, the entire audience actually stayed to watch the credits!)

**Bolero** (1984) . . . . . . . . . . . . . . . . . . . . Ayre McGillvary
• 0:04—Brief breasts, stripping to panties, outside after graduating from school.
••• 0:19—Breasts making love with Arabian guy covered with honey, messy.
••• 0:58—Breasts making love in bed with Angel.
••• 1:38—Breasts during fantasy love making session with Angel in fog.
**Ghosts Can't Do It** (1989) . . . . . . . . . . . . . . . . .Kate
••• 0:26—In one piece swimsuit on beach, then full frontal nudity taking it off. Brief buns covered with sand on her back. Long scene.
••• 0:32—Breasts, sitting and washing herself. Very brief buns, jumping into tub.
•• 0:48—Full frontal nudity taking a shower.
• 0:49—Very, very brief breasts and buns jumping into pool. Long shot. Full frontal nudity under water.
0:52—Very, very brief partial breasts pulling a guy into the pool
1:00—In wet dress, dancing sexily in the rain.
•• 1:12—Breasts behind mosquito net with her boyfriend.
**Hot Chocolate** (1992) . . . . . . . . . . . . . . . B.J. Cassidy
• 0:30—Brief side view of right breast, while pulling sheets up on herself in bed.
**Woman of Desire** (1993) . . . . . . . . . . . Christina Ford
• 0:07—Very brief right breast, while turning over in bed with Steven Bauer.
• 0:14—Breasts, in photo that a detective finds on boat.
••• 0:19—Breasts, while sunbathing on boat, then nude after taking off bikini bottoms and diving into the water.
0:33—Breasts, while getting out of bed. Seen in "flashback-vision."
•• 0:40—Breasts, while taking off blouse and putting on leather jacket in front of Jeff Fahey.
••• 0:41—Breasts and buns while making love with Fahey on a motorcycle inside. Great!
•• 0:51—Breasts, in shower with Fahey.
• 0:57—Breasts on floor, while making love with Fahey.
1:07—Sort of breasts on boat while sunbathing. Seen in "flashback-vision."
*Video Tapes:*
**Playboy Video Magazine, Volume 1** (1982)
. . . . . . . . . . . . . . . . . . . . . . . . . . . . . . . . . . . . . . Herself
• 0:02—Breasts in still photos.
•• 0:56—Breasts in still photos.
•• 0:57—Breasts with brunette hair in scenes from *Fantasies.*
•• 0:58—Breasts in still photos.
*Magazines:*
**Playboy** (Mar 1980) . . . . . . . . . . . . . . . . . . . . . . . Bo
••• 146-157—Nude.
**Playboy** (Aug 1980) . . . . . . . . . . . . . . . . . . Bo Is Back
••• 108-119—Nude in Japanese bath with a Japanese woman.

**Playboy** (Nov 1980) . . . . . . . . . . Sex in Cinema 1980
- 173—Right breast and lower frontal nudity behind shower door.

**Playboy** (Sep 1981) . . . . . . . . . . . . . . . . . . . . . Tarzan

**Playboy** (Dec 1984) . . . . . . . . . . . . . Sex Stars of 1984
- • • 209—Breasts lying in water.

**Playboy** (Jan 1989) . . . . . . . . . . Women of the Eighties
- • • 255—Full frontal nudity.

**Playboy** (Nov 1989) . . . . . . . . . Sex in Cinema 1989
- • • 133—Breasts in still from *Ghosts Can't Do It.*

**Playboy's Nudes** (Oct 1990) . . . . . . . . . . . . . . Herself
- • • 16-17—Full frontal nudity.

**Playboy** (Jan 1994) . . . . . . . . . . . . . . . .Remember Bo
- • • 170-171—Full frontal nudity.

## Dern, Laura

Daughter of actor Bruce Dern and actress Diane Ladd.
*Films:*
Foxes (1980) . . . . . . . . . . . . . . . . . . . . . . . . . . Debbie
Ladies and Gentlemen, The Fabulous Stains (1982)
. . . . . . . . . . . . . . . . . . . . . . . . . . . .Jessica McNeil
(Not available on video tape.)
Teachers (1984) . . . . . . . . . . . . . . . . . . . . . . . Diane
Mask (1985) . . . . . . . . . . . . . . . . . . . . . . . . . Diana
Smooth Talk (1985) . . . . . . . . . . . . . . . . . . . Connie
Blue Velvet (1986) . . . . . . . . . . . . . . . Sandy Williams
Fat Man and Little Boy (1989) . . . . . . Kathleen Robinson
**Wild at Heart** (1990) . . . . . . . . . . . . . . . . . . . . Lula
- • • 0:07—Breasts putting on black halter top.
- • • 0:26—Left breast, then breasts sitting on Nicolas Cage's lap in bed.
- • • 0:35—Breasts wriggling around in bed with Cage.
- • 0:41—Brief breasts several times making love with Cage. Hard to see because it keeps going overexposed. Great moaning, though.

**Rambling Rose** (1991) . . . . . . . . . . . . . . . . . . . Rose
- • • 0:23—Right breast several times, while lying on bench with Robert Duvall while Lucas Haas peeks in.
Jurassic Park (1993) . . . . . . . . . . . . . . . . Ellie Sattler
A Perfect World (1993) . . . . . . . . . . . . . . . Sally Gerber
*Made for Cable Movies:*
Afterburn (1992; HBO) . . . . . . . . . . . . . . Janet Harduvel
*Made for Cable TV:*
Fallen Angels: Murder, Obliquely (1993; Showtime)
. . . . . . . . . . . . . . . . . . . . . . . . . . . . Annie Ainsley
(Available on video tape on *Fallen Angels One.*)

## Derval, Lamya

*Films:*
The Lonely Guy (1983)
. . . . . . . . . . . . . . . .One of "The Seven Deadly Sins"
**Hellhole** (1985) . . . . . . . . . . . . . . . . . . . . Jacuzzi Girl
- • • 1:08—Breasts (she's on the right) sniffing glue in closet with another woman.
- • • 1:12—Full frontal nudity in Jacuzzi room with Mary Woronov.

**Howling IV: The Original Nightmare** (1988)
. . . . . . . . . . . . . . . . . . . . . . . . . . . . . . . . Elanor
- • • 0:32—Brief left breast, then breasts making love with Richard. Nice silhouette on the wall.

## Desmond, Donna

*Films:*
**Tender Loving Care** (1974) . . . . . . . . . . Karen Jordan
- • • • 0:26—Breasts on waterbed with Reno, brief lower frontal nudity, making love. Long scene.
- • 0:39—Breasts and very brief buns getting out of bed.
- • • 0:55—Brief buns and breasts on bed with Dr. Traynor.
The Black Gestapo (1975) . . . . . . . . . . . . . White Whore
Fugitive Girls (1975) . . . . . . . . . . . . . . . . . . . . . n.a.
**The Naughty Stewardesses** (1978) . . . . . . . . .Margie
*a.k.a. Fresh Air*
- • • 0:12—Breasts leaning out of the shower.

## Detmers, Maruschka

*Films:*
**First Name: Carmen** (1983; French) . . . . . . . .Carmen
- • • • 0:36—Breasts while standing by window with a guy.
- • • 0:40—Breasts several times while in bedroom with Joseph.
- • 0:42—Lower frontal nudity (out of focus) while talking to Joseph. Long scene.
- • 0:44—Brief lower frontal nudity with Joseph.
- • 0:46—More lower frontal nudity.
- • • 0:58—Nude, after Joseph takes off her robe.
- • • 1:07—Breasts while undressing in bedroom.
- • • • 1:08—Breasts in red panties, getting out of bed and walking through the house, sitting on couch and lying on bed. Long scene.
- • • 1:13—Brief full frontal nudity in bathroom and in shower.

**Devil in the Flesh** (1986; French/Italian)
. . . . . . . . . . . . . . . . . . . . . . . . . . . . Giulia Dozza
- • 0:20—Very brief side view of left breast and buns going past open door way to get a robe.
- • • • 0:27—Nude, talking to Andrea's dad in his office.
- • 0:55—Breasts putting a robe on. Dark.
- • 0:57—Breasts and buns in bedroom with Andrea.
- • • 1:09—Breasts in hallway with Andrea.
  1:19—Performing fellatio on Andrea. Dark, hard to see.
- • • • 1:22—Full frontal nudity holding keys for Andrea to see, brief buns.
  1:42—Lower frontal nudity dancing in living room in red robe.
Hanna's War (1988) . . . . . . . . . . . . . . . . Hanna Senesh
**The Mambo Kings** (1992) . . . . . . . . . .Dolores Fuentes
- • • 0:47—Breasts several times, making love in bed with Antonio Banderas.
*Magazines:*
**Playboy** (Nov 1986) . . . . . . . . . . Sex in Cinema 1986
- • • • 128—Breasts in a photo from *Devil in the Flesh* with Federico Pitzalis.

## Devine, Loretta

*Films:*
**Little Nikita** (1988) . . . . . . . . . . . . .Verna McLaughlin
- 1:03—Very brief left breast in bed after Sidney Poitier jumps out of bed when River Phoenix bursts into their bedroom.

Sticky Fingers (1988). . . . . . . . . . . . . . . . . . . Diane
Livin' Large (1991) . . . . . . . . . . . . . . . . Nadine Biggs
Caged Fear (1992) . . . . . . . . . . . . . . . . . . . . . . Judy
Class Act (1992) . . . . . . . . . . . . . . . . . . . .Blade's Mom
Amos & Andrew (1993) . . . . . . . . . . . . . . . . . . . . Ula
The Hard Truth (1994) . . . . . . . . . . . .Nichols' Secretary

## Dey, Neela

*Films:*
My First Wife (1985; Australian) . . . . . . Migrant Teacher
**Naked Country** (1985; Australian) . . . . . . . . . Menyan
- 0:27—Breasts when meeting Mary and Lance.
- 0:28—Breasts during wedding ceremony.
- 1:03—Brief left breast, while on top of cliff.
  1:11—Very, very brief breasts during struggle in cave.

## Dey, Susan

*Films:*
Skyjacked (1972). . . . . . . . . . . . . . . . . . . Elly Brewster
**First Love** (1977). . . . . . . . . . . . . . . . Caroline Hedges
- 0:31—Breasts making love in bed with William Katt. Long scene.
- 0:51—Breasts taking off her top in her bedroom with Katt.

**Looker** (1981) . . . . . . . . . . . . . . . . . . . . . . . . Cindy
  0:28—In white one piece swimsuit shooting a commercial at the beach.
- 0:36—Buns, then brief breasts in computer imaging device. Breasts in computer monitor.

**Echo Park** (1986) . . . . . . . . . . . . . . Meg "May" Greer
- 1:17—Brief glimpse of right breast, while doing a strip tease at a party.

The Trouble with Dick (1986) . . . . . . . . . . . . . . Diane
*Made for TV Movies:*
Cage Without a Key (1975). . . . . . . . . . . . . . . . .n.a.
The Gift of Life (1982). . . . . . . . . . . . . . . Jolee Sutton
Sunset Limousine (1983). . . . . . . . . . . . . . . . . . Julie
Lies and Lullabies (1993). . . . . . . . . . . . . . . . . .n.a.
Whose Child Is This? The War for Baby Jessica (1993)
. . . . . . . . . . . . . . . . . . . . . . . . . . Roberta DeBoer
*TV:*
The Partridge Family (1970-74). . . . . . . Laurie Partridge
Loves Me, Loves Me Not (1977) . . . . . . . . . . . . . Jane
Emerald Point N.A.S. (1983-84) . . Celia Mallory Warren
L.A. Law (1986-92) . . . . . . . Dep. D.A. Grace Van Owen
Love & War (1992-93) . . . . . . . . . .Wallis "Wally" Porter
*Magazines:*
**Playboy** (Dec 1977). . . . . . . . . . . . Sex Stars of 1977
- 215—Left breast under sheer white gown in a photo from *First Love*.

## di Lorenzo, Anneka

Real name is Marjorie Thoreson.
*Films:*
**Act of Vengeance** (1974) . . . . . . . . . . . . . . . . . Chris
*a.k.a. The Rape Squad*
(Not to be confused with the film with the same name starring Charles Bronson.)
- ••• 1:07—Buns and breasts, getting dressed in house. Seen from outside through simulated camera viewfinder.

The Centerfold Girls (1974) . . . . . . . . . . . . . . . . .Pam
**Caligula** (1980) . . . . . . . . . . . . . . . . . . . . . .Messalina
(X-rated, 147 minute version.)
- ••• 1:16—Nude, making love with Lori Wagner. Long scene.

*Video Tapes:*
**Penthouse: On the Wild Side** (1988) . . . . .Messalina
- 0:54—Nude with Lori Wagner during scenes from *The Making of Caligula*.

*Magazines:*
**Penthouse** (Sep 1973) . . . . . . . . . . . . . . . . . . . . . .Pet
- ••• 73-85—Nude.

**Penthouse** (Jun 1975) . . . . . . . Pet of the Year Play-Off
- ••• 58-59—Full frontal nudity.

**Penthouse** (Oct 1975) . . . . . . . . . . . . . Pet of the Year
- ••• 59-69—Nude.

**Penthouse** (May 1980) . . . . . . . . . . . . . . . . Caligula
- ••• 74—Breasts.
- ••• 86—Breasts.

**Penthouse** (Jun 1980) . . . . . . . . . . . . .Anneka and Lori
- ••• 142-153—Nude (she has darker hair) with Lori Wagner.

## Di'Lazzaro, Dalila

*Films:*
**Andy Warhol's Frankenstein** (1974; Italian/German/French). . . . . . . . . . . . . . . . . . . . . . . . . . . . . . The Girl
- •• 0:09—Breasts lying on platform in the lab.
- 0:37—Close up of left breast while the Count cuts her stitches. (Pretty bloody.)
  0:43—Breasts, covered with blood, strapped to table
- 0:49—Breasts on table, all wired up.
- 1:03—Right breast lying on table. Long shot.
- 1:05—More right breast, long shot.
- •• 1:06—More breasts on table, then standing in the lab.
- •• 1:20—Brief right breast when Otto pulls her top down.
- •• 1:23—Breasts on table again, then walking around. (Scar on chest.) Lower frontal nudity when Otto pulls her bandage down, then more gross breasts when he removes her guts.

The Last Romantic Lover (1978). . . . . . . . . . . . . n.a.
Creepers (1985; Italian) . . . . . . . . . . . . . . . . . . . n.a.
Miss Right (1987; Italian) . . . . . . . . . . . . . Art Student
*Magazines:*
**Playboy** (Aug 1974) . . . . . . . . . . . . . . .Instant Warhol
- 84-85—Breasts in Polaroid photo collage.

**Playboy** (Nov 1974) . . . . . . . . . . . Sex in Cinema 1974
•• 146—Breasts from *Andy Warhol's Frankenstein*.
**Playboy** (Jan 1990) . . . . . . . . . . . . . . . . . . . . . . . . .n.a.
••• 104—Polaroid collage taken by Andy Worhol.

# Dial, Nikki

See: Greiner, Nicole.

# Dickinson, Angie

Ex-wife of songwriter Burt Bacharach.
*Films:*
Rio Bravo (1959) . . . . . . . . . . . . . . . . . . . . . . . Feathers
Ocean's Eleven (1960). . . . . . . . . . . . . . . Beatrice Ocean
Cast a Giant Shadow (1966) . . . . . . . . . . .Emma Marcus
The Chase (1966) . . . . . . . . . . . . . . . . . . . . Ruby Calder
**Point Blank** (1967). . . . . . . . . . . . . . . . . . . . . . .Chris
    0:46—In white slip when John Vernon opens her
    dress.
    • 0:51—Breasts in background putting dress on. Kind
    of a long shot.
**Pretty Maids All in a Row** (1971). . . . . . . Miss Smith
    • 1:04—Buns, in long shot, while lying on bed with
    Ponce.
**Big Bad Mama** (1974) . . . . . . . . . Wilma McClatchie
    • 0:38—Buns, getting into bed with Tom Skerritt. Brief
    right breast, while on top of him.
    ••• 0:48—Breasts in bed with William Shatner.
    • 1:00—Very brief breasts, pulling the sheets up while
    lying in bed with Shatner.
    ••• 1:18—Breasts and brief full frontal nudity putting a
    shawl and then a dress on.
**Dressed to Kill** (1980) . . . . . . . . . . . . . . Kate Miller
    • 0:01—Brief side view behind shower door. Long
    shot, hard to see.
    0:02—Frontal nude scene in shower is a body dou-
    ble, Victoria Lynn Johnson.
    0:24—Brief buns getting out of bed after coming
    home from museum with a stranger.
Klondike Fever (1980) . . . . . . . . . . . . . .Belinda McNair
Charlie Chan & the Curse of the Dragon Queen (1981)
. . . . . . . . . . . . . . . . . . . . . . . . . . . . Dragon Queen
Death Hunt (1981) . . . . . . . . . . . . . . . . . . . . .Vanessa
**Big Bad Mama II** (1987). . . . . . . . . Wilma McClatchie
    • 0:48—Very brief full frontal nudity putting on her
    shawl scene from *Big Bad Mama* superimposed over
    a car chase scene.
    •• 0:52—Breasts and brief buns (probably a body dou-
    ble) in bed with Robert Culp. You don't see her face
    with the body.
*Made for Cable Movies:*
Treacherous Crossing (1992; USA). . . . . . . . . . . Beverly
*Miniseries:*
Pearl (1978) . . . . . . . . . . . . . . . . . . . . . . . . . .Midge
Hollywood Wives (1988) . . . . . . . . . . . . . Sadie La Salle
Wild Palms (1993). . . . . . . . . . . . . . . . . . . . Josie Ito
*Made for TV Movies:*
A Touch of Scandal (1984) . . . . . . . . . Katherine Gilvey
Once Upon a Texas Train (1988) . . . . . . . . . . . .Maggie

*TV:*
Police Woman (1974-78)
    . . . . . . . . . . . . . . . .Sgt. Suzanne "Pepper" Anderson
Cassie and Company (1982) . . . . . . . . .Cassie Holland
*Magazines:*
**Playboy** (Apr 1971) . . . . . . . . Vadim's "Pretty Maids"
    • 156—Buns, while lying in bed with John David Car-
    son.

# Dickinson, Janice

Model.
*Films:*
Exposed (1983) . . . . . . . . . . . . . . . . . . . . . . . . Model
*Magazines:*
**Playboy** (Mar 1988) . . . . . . . .Going Wild with a Model
••• 70-77—Full frontal nudity.

# Dietrich, Cindi

*Films:*
The Man Who Loved Women (1983) . . . . . . . . . . Darla
**Out of Control** (1984). . . . . . . . . . . . . . . . . .Robin
    • 0:29—Breasts taking off her red top. Long shot.
St. Elmo's Fire (1985) . . . . . . . . . . . . . . . . . . . . Flirt
Death Spa (1987). . . . . . . . . . . . . . . . . . . . . .Linda
Made in U.S.A. (1988) . . . . . . . . . . . . . . . . . . . n.a.
*Made for TV Movies:*
Mistress (1987) . . . . . . . . . . . . . . . . . . . . . . Rachel

# Digard, Uschi

*Films:*
Cherry, Harry & Raquel (1969). . . . . . . . . . . . . . .Soul
The Scavengers (1969). . . . . . . . . . . . . . . . . . . .n.a.
The Beauties and the Beast (1973) . . . . . . . . . . . .Mary
    Nude by lake.
Supervixens (1973) . . . . . . . . . . . . . . . . . . SuperSoul
**Truck Stop Women** (1974). . . . . . . Truck Stop Woman
    •• 0:18—Breasts getting arrested in the parking lot by
    the police officer, then buns and breasts getting
    frisked in a room.
Chesty Anderson, U.S. Navy (1975)
    . . . . . . . . . . . . . . . . . . . . . . . . . Baron's Girlfriend #1
**The Killer Elite** (1975). . . . . . . . . Uncredited Party Girl
    • 0:00—Brief right breast, while sitting in front of Rob-
    ert Duvall at a party. Long shot. Continuity error:
    Note the next time you see her, the blouse is closed!
Fantasm (1976; Australian). . . . . . . . . . . . . . . . n.a.
**Kentucky Fried Movie** (1977) . . . .Woman in Shower
    •• 0:09—Breasts getting them massaged in the show-
    er, then squished breasts against the shower door.
**Superchick** (1978) . . . . . . . . . . . . . . . . . . .Mayday
    ••• 0:42—Buns and breasts getting whipped acting dur-
    ing the making of a film, then talking to three peo-
    ple.
Beneath the Valley of the Ultravixens (1979)
    . . . . . . . . . . . . . . . . . . . . . . . . . . . . . . SuperSoul
**If You Don't Stop It You'll Go Blind** (1979)
    . . . . . . . . . . . . . . . . . . . . . . . . . . Various Characters
    •• 0:02—Breasts in bed and closets during opening
    credits.

- 0:03—Breasts, pulling up her T-shirt during beginning credits.
- 0:23—Brief breasts raising her hand in classroom.
  0:25—In braless, wet tank top, washing her car.
- ••• 0:26—Breasts, while showing them to a guy and letting him feel them.
- 0:36—Brief upper half of left breast, when it sticks out of her dress.
- ••• 0:52—Full frontal nudity (Contestant #1) on bed, waiting for Omar.
- •• 1:17—Breasts in class during end credits.

**The Best of Sex and Violence** (1981)

. . . . . . . . . . . . . . . . . . . . . . . . . . . Truck Stop Woman

- 0:47—Breasts getting chased by policeman in parking lot in scene from *Truck Stop Women*.

**Famous T & A** (1982) . . . . . . . . . . . Truck Stop Woman
(No longer available for purchase, check your video store for rental.)

- •• 0:44—Breasts scenes from *Harry, Cherry & Raquel* and *Truck Stop Women*.

*Magazines:*

**Playboy** (Nov 1975) . . . . . . . . . . Sex in Cinema 1975
- ••• 132—Breasts with Robert Duvall in still photo from *The Killer Elite*.

**Playboy** (May 1977) . . . . . Bewitched by Older Women
- ••• 147—Full frontal nudity. She's 32 years old.

**Playboy** (Aug 1977) . . . . . . . . . . . . . . . Dear Playboy
- ••• 14—Full frontal nudity in small photo.

# Dillard, Victoria

*Films:*

**Coming to America** (1988) . . . . . . . . . . . . . . .Bather
- •• 0:04—Breasts, standing up in royal bathtub to announce "The royal penis is clean, Your Highness."

Internal Affairs (1990) . . . . . . . . . . . . . . . . . . . . . .Kee
Ricochet (1991) . . . . . . . . . . . . . . . . . . . . . . . . . .Alice
**Deep Cover** (1992) . . . . . . . . . . . . . . . . . . . . .Betty
- 0:52—Brief breasts, taking off her blouse to make love with Larry Fishburne.

Killing Obsession (1994) . . . . . . . . . . . . . . .Jean Wilson

*Magazines:*

**Playboy** (Nov 1988) . . . . . . . . . . . Sex in Cinema 1988
- •• 133—Breasts in bathtub with Eddie Murphy.

# Dillon, Melinda

*Films:*

Bound For Glory (1976) . . . . . . . . . . . . . Mary Guthrie
Close Encounters of the Third Kind (1977)

. . . . . . . . . . . . . . . . . . . . . . . . . . . . . . Jillian Guiler

**Slap Shot** (1977). . . . . . . . . . . . . . . . . . . . . Suzanne
- ••• 0:30—Right breast, lying in bed with Paul Newman, then breasts sitting up and talking. Nice, long scene.

F.I.S.T. (1978) . . . . . . . . . . . . . . . . . . . . .Anna Zerinkas
Absence of Malice (1981) . . . . . . . . . . . . . . . . . .Teresa
A Christmas Story (1983) . . . . . . . . . . . . . .Mrs. Parker
Songwriter (1984). . . . . . . . . . . . . . . . . .Honey Carder
Harry and the Hendersons (1987) . . . .Nancy Henderson
Spontaneous Combustion (1989) . . . . . . . . . . . . .Nina
Staying Together (1989) . . . . . . . . . .Eileen McDermott

Captain America (1990) . . . . . . . . . . . . . . . Mrs. Rogers
The Prince of Tides (1991) . . . . . . . . . . Savannah Wingo
*Made for Cable Movies:*
State of Emergency (1993; HBO) . . . . . . .Mrs. Anderson
*Miniseries:*
Space (1987) . . . . . . . . . . . . . . . . . . . . . . . .Rachel Mott
*Made for TV Movies:*
Shattered Spirits (1986) . . . . . . . . . . .Joyce Mollencamp
Judgment Day: The John List Story (1993) . . . . . Eleanor

# Dion, Jami

*Adult Films:*

**Hidden Obsessions** (1993) . . . . . . . . . . . . Bodyscapes
*Video Tapes:*

**Penthouse Satin & Lace II: Hollywood Undercover** (1992)

. . . . . . . . . . . . . . . . . . . . . . . . . . . . . . . . . . . . .Pet

**The Penthouse All-Pet Workout** (1993). . . . . . . .Pet
- •• 0:00—Nude during introduction.
- •• 0:03—Brief nude shots while getting undressed and suited up.
- ••• 0:28—Nude outside on sculpture and next to fence.
- ••• 0:43—Nude with the other girls, exercising, working with equipment, in the pool and spa.

**Penthouse Pet of the Year Playoff 1993** (1993)

. . . . . . . . . . . . . . . . . . . . . . . . . . . . . . . . . . . . .Pet

- ••• 0:01—Nude in house, on the beach, on bed, with an old T-bird.

**Penthouse Pet of the Year Winners 1993: Mahalia & Julie** (1994)

. . . . . . . . . . . Sneak Preview of Pet of the Year Playoff
- ••• 0:30—Nude while posing around a house.

*CD-ROM:*

**Penthouse Interactive Virtual Photo Shoot, Disc 3** (1993) . . . . . . . . . . . . . . . . . . . . . . . . . . . . . .Pet

*Magazines:*

**Penthouse** (Mar 1992). . . . . . . . . . . . . . . . . . . .Pet
- ••• 67-81—Nude.

**Penthouse** (Jun 1993) . . . . . . . Pet of the Year Play-Off
- ••• 116-117—Nude.

# Ditmar, Marita

*Films:*

**Auditions** (1978) . . . . . . . . . . . . . . . . . . . Frieda Volker
- •• 1:05—Breasts and partial buns with another woman and a guy.

**Fairytales** (1979) . . . . . . . . . . . . . . . . . . S & M Dancer
- 0:38—Breasts wearing masks with two other S&M Dancers.

# Dockery, Erika

*Films:*

**Basic Training** (1984) . . . . . . . . . . . . . . . . . Salesgirl 2
- 0:00—Brief breasts standing behind the desk.

Hardbodies (1984). . . . . . . . . . . . . . . Hardbody in Car

# Doda, Carol

*Films:*
Head (1968) . . . . . . . . . . . . . . . . . . . . . . .Sally Silicone
**Honky Tonk Nights** (1978) . . . . . . . . . Belle Barnette
••• 0:17—Breasts changing blouses in bedroom with Doris Ann.
• 0:28—Left breast several times while making out with a guy.
••• 1:11—Breasts in bedroom with Doris Ann during flashback. (Different camera angle than 0:17.)
*Video Tapes:*
**Playboy Video Magazine, Volume 3** (1983)
. . . . . . . . . . . . Carol Doda A San Francisco Monument
• 0:22—Breasts in B&W before-silicone-injection photo (35 1/2-inch bust).
•• 0:23—Breasts in B&W after-silicone-injection photo. (44-inch bust). Breasts while dancing on stage.2
• 0:24—Brief breasts and buns, on stage in The Condor Club during her act.
••• 0:25—Breasts and buns in G-string. Lit with red light.
••• 0:26—Nude, taking off her clothes and running outside in a park. More breasts, on piano in The Condor Club.

# • Doherty, Shannen

Ex-wife of actor/singer Ashley Hamilton (Son of actor George Hamilton and former wife Alana).
*Films:*
Night Shift (1982) . . . . . . . . . . . . . . . . . . . . . . Bluebird
Girls Just Want to Have Fun (1985) . . . . Maggie Malene
Heathers (1989) . . . . . . . . . . . . . . . . . . Heather Duke
**Blindfold: Acts of Obsession** (1993)
. . . . . . . . . . . . . . . . . . . . . . . . . . . .Madeleine Dalton
(The close-up shots of breasts where you don't see her face are body double shots.)
••• 0:07—Breasts, while making love.
•• 0:08—Breasts while making love in the shower with Mike.
••• 0:21—Breasts, in bed, while making love with Mike.
•• 0:39—Breasts, during photo session with pillows while posing for Mike. More breast flashes while in bed.
1:06—In black bra on desk in Judd Nelson's office. Brief, partial right breast, when he caresses it.
*Made for Cable Movies:*
Rebel Highway: Jailbreakers (1994; Showtime) . . . Angel
*Made for TV Movies:*
Obsessed (1992) . . . . . . . . . . . . . . . . . . . . . . . . . .n.a.
*TV:*
Little House: A New Begining (1982-83) . . . Jenny Wilder
Our House (1986-88) . . . . . . . . . . . . Kris Witherspoon
Beverly Hills, 90210 (1990-94) . . . . . . . . Brenda Walsh
*Magazines:*
**Playboy** (Mar 1994) . . . . . . . . . . . . Safe Sex, Great Sex
••• 76-77—Breasts in two color photos.

# Dollarhide, April Dawn

*Films:*
Party Favors (1987) . . . . . . . . . . . . . . . . . . . . . . . n.a.
**Caged Fury** (1989) . . . . . . . . . . . . . . .Rhonda Wallace
• 0:54—Briefly nude, after dropping towel and joining Kat in the showers.
**Warlords 3000** (1992) . . . . . . . . . . . . . .Terrified Girl
• 0:11—Breasts, while struggling in room with bad guys who are trying to rape her.

# Dombasle, Arielle

*Films:*
Tess (1979; French/British) . . . . . . . . . . . . Mercy Chant
**The Story of "O" Continues** (1981; French)
. . . . . . . . . . . . . . . . . . . . . . . . . . . . . . . . .Nathalie
*a.k.a. Les Fruits de la Passion*
• 0:17—Brief left breast, lying on her stomach in bed with Klaus Kinski.
••• 0:40—Full frontal nudity on bed, making love in front of O.
• 1:00—Very, very brief left breast, while grabbing her blouse out of Kinski's hands.
Le Beau Mariage (1982; French) . . . . . . . . . . . Clarisse
**Pauline at the Beach** (1983; French) . . . . . . . Marion
• 0:24—Brief breasts lying in bed with a guy when her cousin looks in the window.
•• 0:43—Brief breasts in house kissing Henri, while he takes her white dress off.
•• 0:59—Breasts walking down the stairs in a white bikini bottom while putting a white blouse on.
**The Boss' Wife** (1986) . . . . . . . . Mrs. Louise Roalvang
• 1:01—Brief breasts getting a massage by the swimming pool.
••• 1:07—Breasts trying to seduce Daniel Stern at her place.
•• 1:14—Brief breasts in Stern's shower.
Trade Secrets (1989; French) . . . . . . . . . . . Marguerite
Twisted Obsession (1990) . . . . . . . . . . . Marion Derain
*Miniseries:*
Lace II (1985) . . . . . . . . . . . . . . . . . . . . . . . . Maxine
*Magazines:*
**Playboy** (Dec 1983) . . . . . . . . . . . . .Sex Stars of 1983
•• 209—Breasts.

# Dommartin, Solveig

*Films:*
**Wings of Desire** (1987) . . . . . . . . . . . . . . . . . Marion
*a.k.a. Der Himmel Uber Berlin*
• 0:34—Brief side of left breast, while putting robe on. (The film changes from B&W to color.)
**Until the End of the World** (1991) . . Claire Tourneur
••• 0:34—Left breast, then breasts, then full frontal nudity in bedroom with William Hurt and Winter.
Faraway, So Close (1993; German) . . . . . . . . . . Marion

## Doná, Linda

*Films:*
Worth Winning (1989) . . . . . . . . . Lady at the Paddock
**Summer Dreams: The Story of the Beach Boys**
(1990) . . . . . . . . . . . . . . . . . . . . . . . . . . . . . . . n.a.
(Originally a made for TV movie.)
• 1:06—Silhouette of breasts while making love with
Dennis Wilson.
Final Embrace (1991) . . . . . . . . . . . . . . . . . . . . . . Jeri
Future Kick (1991) . . . . . . . . . . . . . . . . . . . . . . . . Tye
**Ricochet** (1991) . . . . . . . . . . . . . . . . . . . . . . Wanda
•• 1:03—Breasts, undoing her dress, then buns, get-
ting on bed to make love with Denzel Washington
while he's drugged.
• 1:16—Buns, on top of Washington during video
playback.
Switch (1991) . . . . . . . . . . . . . . . . . . Gay Club Patron
Delta Heat (1992) . . . . . . . . . . . . . . . . . . . . Tine Tulane
Showdown (1993) . . . . . . . . . . . . . . . . . . . . . . . . n.a.
*Made for Cable TV:*
**Dream On: One Ball, Two Strikes** (1993; HBO)
. . . . . . . . . . . . . . . . . . . . . . . . . . . . . . . . . Alannah
• 0:05—Very brief breasts in utility closet while mak-
ing love with Martin.
•• 0:18—Breasts with Martin in his apartment.
••• 0:23—Breasts, while lying in bed with Martin.
*Made for TV Movies:*
In the Arms of a Killer (1992) . . . . . . . . . . . . . Chrissy

## Donahoe, Terry

*TV:*
Sonny Spoon (1988) . . . . . . . . Asst. D.A. Carolyn Gilder
*Video Tapes:*
**Eden 2** (1992) . . . . . . . . . . . . . . . . . . . . . . . . . Juliet
••• 0:57—Breasts in bed making love with Paul and after
getting interrupted.

## • Donatacci, Camille

*Films:*
**Marilyn Chambers' Bedtime Stories** (1993)
. . . . . . . . . . . . . . . . . . . . . . . . . . . . . . . Angelique
••• 0:34—Breasts and buns while changing lingerie in
bedroom.
••• 0:42—Breasts, while making love with Chris on sofa.
••• 0:55—In pink bra and panties then right breast and
buns in Chris' bedroom.
*Made for Cable TV:*
Club MTV . . . . . . . . . . . . . . . . . . . . . . . . . . Dancer
*Magazines:*
**Playboy's Book of Lingerie** (Nov 1993) . . . . . Herself
••• 82—Breasts.
**Playboy's Nudes** (Dec 1993) . . . . . . . . . . . . . Herself
••• 36—Full frontal nudity.
**Playboy's Book of Lingerie** (Jan 1994) . . . . . . Herself
•• 40—Breasts.
**Playboy's Great Playmate Search** (Feb 1994)
. . . . . . . . . . . . . . . . . . . . . . . . . . . . . . . . . Herself
•• 85—Left breast.

**Playboy's Book of Lingerie** (Mar 1994) . . . . . Herself
••• 67—Breasts.
**Playboy's Book of Lingerie** (Sep 1994) . . . . . . Herself
••• 24—Breasts.

## Donley, Kimberly

*Video Tapes:*
**Playboy Video Calendar 1994** (1993) . . . . December
••• 0:47—Nude, while dancing in a studio with a black
and white color theme.
••• 0:49—Nude, while on bed.
*Magazines:*
**Playboy** (Mar 1993) . . . . . . . . . . . . . . . . . . Playmate
••• 94-105—Nude.
**Playboy** (Jan 1994) . . . . . . . . Playboy's Playmate Review
••• 204—Left breast and lower frontal nudity.
**Playboy's Playmate Review** (May 1994)
. . . . . . . . . . . . . . . . . . . . . . . . . . . . . . Miss March
••• 22-31—Nude.
**Playmates at Play** (Jul 1994) . . . . . . . . . . . . . Herself
••• 30-33—Nude.
**Playboy's Book of Lingerie** (Jul 1994) . . . . . . . Herself
••• 26—Full frontal nudity.
**Playboy's Book of Lingerie** (Sep 1994) . . . . . . Herself
••• 3-6—Nude.

## Donnelly, Patrice

*Films:*
**Personal Best** (1982) . . . . . . . . . . . . . . . Tory Skinner
•• 0:16—Full frontal nudity after making love with Mariel Hemingway.
•• 0:30—Full frontal nudity in steam room.
1:06—Breasts in shower.
American Anthem (1987) . . . . . . . . . . . . . . . . Danielle

## Donohoe, Amanda

Wife of director Nicholas Broomfield.
*Films:*
**Castaway** (1986) . . . . . . . . . . . . . . . . . . . . Lucy Irvine
(Nude a lot, only the best are listed.)
••• 0:22—Breasts talking to Reed.
• 0:32—Nude on beach after helicopter leaves.
•• 0:48—Full frontal nudity lying on her back on the
rocks at the beach.
••• 0:51—Breasts on rock when Reed takes a blue sheet
off her, then catching a shark.
••• 0:54—Nude yelling at Reed at the campsite, then
walking around looking for him.
••• 1:01—Breasts getting seafood out of a tide pool.
•• 1:03—Breasts lying down at night talking with Reed
in the moonlight.
••• 1:18—Breasts taking off bathing suit top after the
visitors leave, then arguing with Reed.
**Foreign Body** (1986; British) . . . . . . . . . . . . . . Susan
0:37—Undressing in her bedroom down to lingerie.
Very brief side view of right breast, then brief left
breast putting blouse on.
•• 0:40—Breasts opening her blouse for Ram.

**The Lair of the White Worm** (1988; British)
........................... Lady Sylvia Marsh
(Wears short black hair in this film.)
- • 0:52—Nude, opening a tanning table and turning over.
- • 0:57—Brief left breast licking the blood off a phallic-looking thing.
- • 1:19—Brief breasts jumping out to attack Angus, then walking around her underground lair (her body is painted for the rest of the film).
- • 1:22—Breasts walking up steps with a large phallic thing strapped to her body.

**Dark Obsession** (1989; British) ............. Ginny
*a.k.a. Diamond Skulls*
- •• 0:01—Breasts getting felt by a pair of hands.
- ••• 0:41—Left breast, breasts, brief lower frontal nudity while making love with Gabriel Byrne.
- • 0:47—In black bra and panties, then full frontal nudity getting into tub. Right breast while sitting in the tub.

Double Cross (1989)........................n.a.

**The Rainbow** (1989) ..............Winifred Inger
- ••• 0:21—Nude with Sammi Davis undressing, running outside in the rain, jumping into the water, then talking by the fireplace.
- ••• 0:43—Full frontal nudity taking off nightgown and getting into bed with Davis, then right breast.
- ••• 1:44—Nude running outside with Davis.

**Paper Mask** (1991; British) ......... Christine Taylor
0:53—Breasts in bed under Matthew then on top of him.

*Made for Cable Movies:*
Shame (1992; Lifetime)................Diana Cadell
The Substitute (1993; USA)....................n.a.

*Made for TV Movies:*
It's Nothing Personal (1993) ...................n.a.

*TV:*
L.A. Law (1991-92) ...................... C.J. Lamb

*Magazines:*
**Playboy** (Nov 1987) ........... Sex in Cinema 1987
- •• 144-145—Full frontal nudity from *Castaway.*

**Playboy** (Feb 1993)....................Grapevine
- • 167—Half of right breast, when it pops out of her blouse, while she bends over backward on a stool. B&W.

## Doody, Alison
*Films:*
A View to a Kill (1985)..................Jenny Flex
A Prayer for the Dying (1987) ............. Siobhan
**Taffin** (1988; U.S./British) .............. Charlotte
- • 0:14—Very, very brief side view of right breast when Pierce Brosnan rips her blouse open. Long shot, hard to see.

Indiana Jones and the Last Crusade (1989)
........................Dr. Elsa Schneider
Barbara Cartland's "Duel of Hearts" (1990; British)
........................... Lady Caroline Faye

## Dorado, Lorraine
*Video Tapes:*
**Becky Bubbles** (1987) ....................Herself
- ••• 0:09—Brief right breast and buns in black and white swimsuit, then breasts in pool.
- ••• 0:12—Breasts while playing on pool float with Becky and Brandi.
- ••• 0:14—Breasts getting in and out of pool, then rubbing lotion on herself.
- ••• 0:18—Breasts while playing on the grass in open swimsuit top.

**Wild Bikinis** (1987) .....................Herself
- ••• 0:10—Breasts in pool and buns in swimsuit from *Becky Bubbles.*
- •• 0:35—Breasts playing with a ball on the grass with Jasaé.

**Thunder and Mud** (1989)......... Quisha/Sex Toy
- • 1:02—Buns, while mud wrestling in white top and pink bikini bottoms.
- ••• 1:06—Breasts, covered with mud after Leslie rips her top off.

**L.A. Strippers** (1992)................Quisha Cori
- ••• 0:00—Breasts dancing on stage during introduction.
- ••• 0:05—In bra, then nude dancing on stage. Long scene.
- ••• 0:12—Breasts, then nude dancing.

## Dorian, Antonia
*Films:*
Tough Cookies (1992) ......................n.a.
**Body Chemistry 3: Point of Seduction** (1993)
........................................Krissy
**Dinosaur Island** (1993) .................... April
- ••• 0:20—Breasts (she has white head band on), while bathing in a stream with May and June, then bathing the guys.
- ••• 0:22—More breasts, while bathing the guys.
- ••• 0:53—Breasts, while making love outside with Skeemer.

Ghoulies IV (1993) ..................... Lady in Red
Munchie Strikes Back (1994) ..............Cleopatra

*Video Tapes:*
**Soft Bodies: Party Favors** (1992)...........Herself
- ••• 0:03—In black bra and panties in bed, then breasts and buns during photo session.
- ••• 0:08—Breasts on hammock outside.
- ••• 0:11—In white lace dress in living room by piano. Breasts and buns in G-string.
- ••• 0:18—Breasts and buns outside by pool with Becky LeBeau.

## Dorman, Samantha
*Video Tapes:*
**The Best of Sexy Lingerie** (1992) .......... Model
**Playboy Playmates in Paradise** (1992).... Playmate
**Playboy Video Calendar 1993** (1992).......August
- ••• 0:33—Full frontal nudity outside in a field and on swing.

••• 0:35—Nude in house in front of fire and on bed.
**Playboy's Erotic Fantasies** (1992) . . . . Cast Member
**Playboy's Playmate Review 1992** (1992)
. . . . . . . . . . . . . . . . . . . . . . . . . . . . . Miss September
••• 0:06—Nude on boat, then in laboratory and then in
surreal artistic setting.
**Sexy Lingerie IV** (1992) . . . . . . . . . . . . . . . . . .Model
**Sexy Lingerie V** (1992) . . . . . . . . . . . . . . . . . .Model
**Wet and Wild IV** (1992) . . . . . . . . . . . . . . . .Model
**Playboy's Erotic Fantasies II** (1993) . . . . . . . .Model
*Magazines:*
**Playboy** (Sep 1991) . . . . . . . . . . . . . . . . . . . Playmate
••• 110-121—Nude.
**Playboy's Book of Lingerie** (Jul 1992) . . . . . . Herself
••• 24—Right breast and lower frontal nudity.
••• 79—Breasts.
**Playboy's Book of Lingerie** (Sep 1992) . . . . . Herself
• 30—Lower frontal nudity.
••• 87—Breasts.
**Playboy's Book of Lingerie** (Nov 1992) . . . . . Herself
•• 66-67—Buns.
**Playboy's Book of Lingerie** (Jan 1993) . . . . . . Herself
••• 25—Right breast and lower frontal nudity.
••• 26-27—Full frontal nudity.
**Playboy's Book of Lingerie** (May 1993) . . . . . Herself
••• 25—Breasts.
**Playboy** (Jul 1993) . . . . . . . . . . . . . . . . . . . . .Lucky Stiff
••• 78-83—Nude.
**Playboy's Wet & Wild Women** (Aug 1993) . . Herself
••• 2-4—Full frontal nudity.
••• 9—Full frontal nudity.
•• 22—Buns.
**Playboy's Blondes, Brunettes & Redheads**
(Sep 1993) . . . . . . . . . . . . . . . . . . . . . . . . . Herself
••• 52—Full frontal nudity.
**Playboy's Book of Lingerie** (Sep 1993) . . . . . Herself
••• 3-7—Full frontal nudity.
**Playboy's Video Playmates** (Sep 1993) . . . . . Herself
••• 32-35—Nude.
**Playboy's Nudes** (Dec 1993) . . . . . . . . . . . . . Herself
••• 22-23—Full frontal nudity.
••• 28—Breasts.
**Playboy Presents Playmates in Paradise**
(Mar 1994) . . . . . . . . . . . . . . . . . . . . . . . . Playmate
••• 68-71—Full frontal nudity.
**Playboy's Book of Lingerie** (Mar 1994) . . . . . Herself
••• 70-71—Breasts.
**Playboy's Book of Lingerie** (May 1994) . . . . . Herself
••• 86—Breasts.
**Playboy's Book of Lingerie** (Jul 1994) . . . . . . Herself
•• 35—Right breast and lower frontal nudity.
**Playboy** (Aug 1994) . . . . . . . . . . . . . . . . . .Viva Milan
••• 128-135—Full frontal nudity.

## Dorsey, Fern
*Films:*
**Love Crimes** (1991) . . . . . . . . . . . . . . . . . Colleen Dells
(Unrated version reviewed.)
••• 0:03—Breasts, getting photographed by Patrick Ber-
gin.
**McBain** (1991) . . . . . . . . . . . . . . . . . . . . . . . . . Dr. Elliott

## Doss, Terri Lynn
*Films:*
Lethal Weapon (1987) . . . . . . . . . . . . .Girl in Shower #2
Die Hard (1988) . . . . . . . . . . . . . . . . . . . . . Girl at Airport
Roadhouse (1989) . . . . . . . . . . . . . . . . Cody's Girlfriend
*Video Tapes:*
Swimwear Illustrated: On Location (1986)
. . . . . . . . . . . . . . . . . . . . . . . . . . . . . .Swimsuit Model
**Playboy Video Calendar 1989** (1988) . . . . . . . March
••• 0:09—Nude.
**Sexy Lingerie** (1988) . . . . . . . . . . . . . . . . . . . . . Model
Glamour Through Your Lens—Outdoor Techniques
(1989) . . . . . . . . . . . . . . . . . . . . . . . . . . . . . . Herself
0:07—Buns in blue swimsuit bottom in wet yellow
top in the pool.
0:47—In black bra, panties, garter belt and stock-
ings standing outside. Most of her buns.
**Sexy Lingerie II** (1990) . . . . . . . . . . . . . . . . . . Model
*Magazines:*
**Playboy** (Jul 1988) . . . . . . . . . . . . . . . . . . . . . Playmate
**Playboy's Book of Lingerie** (Jan 1991) . . . . . .Herself
•• 86-87—Full frontal nudity.
**Playboy's Book of Lingerie** (Mar 1991) . . . . . .Herself
•• 98—Right breast and lower frontal nudity.
**Playboy's Book of Lingerie** (Mar 1992) . . . . . .Herself
••• 90—Full frontal nudity.
**Playboy's Bathing Beauties** (Apr 1992) . . . . . .Herself
••• 101—Breasts.
**Playboy's Book of Lingerie** (May 1992) . . . . . Herself
••• 50—Full frontal nudity.
••• 92—Full frontal nudity.
**Playboy's Calendar Playmates** (Nov 1992) . . .Herself
••• 70—Full frontal nudity.
•• 104—Buns and side of left breast.
Playboy's Book of Lingerie (Nov 1992) . . . . . . . .Herself
**Playboy's Nudes** (Dec 1992) . . . . . . . . . . . . . .Herself
••• 7—Full frontal nudity.
**Playboy's Bathing Beauties** (Apr 1993) . . . . . .Herself
••• 96—Breasts.
**Playboy's Blondes, Brunettes & Redheads**
(Sep 1993) . . . . . . . . . . . . . . . . . . . . . . . . . .Herself
• 10—Lower frontal nudity.
**Playboy's Bathing Beauties** (Mar 1994) . . . . . Herself
••• 86-87—Lower frontal nudity and breasts.
**Playboy's Book of Lingerie** (May 1994) . . . . . Herself
•• 50-51—Lower frontal nudity. Breasts under sheer
black top.
**Playmates at Play** (Jul 1994) . . . . . . . . . . . . . Herself
••• 82-83—Nude.
**Playboy's Girls of Summer '94** (Jul 1994) . . . . Herself
••• 85—Breasts.

**Playboy's Book of Lingerie** (Jul 1994) . . . . . . Herself
••• 67—Full frontal nudity.

## Doucett, Linda
Fiancée of actor/comedian Gary Shandling.
*TV:*
The Larry Sanders Show (1992- ) . . . . Darlene Schepini
*Magazines:*
**Playboy** (Sep 1993) . . . . . . . . . . . . . . . Showstopper
••• 82-87—Breasts and partial buns in G-string panties.
**Playboy's Nudes** (Dec 1993) . . . . . . . . . . . . Herself
••• 13—Breasts.

## Douglass, Robyn
*Films:*
Breaking Away (1979) . . . . . . . . . . . . . . . . . . Katherine
**Partners** (1982) . . . . . . . . . . . . . . . . . . . . . . . . . Jill
•• 1:00—Brief breasts taking off her top and getting
into bed with Ryan O'Neal.
**The Lonely Guy** (1983) . . . . . . . . . . . . . . . . Danielle
• 0:05—Upper half of right breast in sheer nightgown
in bed with Raoul while talking to Steve Martin.
Great nightgown!
0:33—In sheer beige negligee lying on couch talk-
ing to Martin on the phone.
• 1:03—Very, very brief peek at left nipple when she
flashes it for Martin so he'll let her into his party.
Romantic Comedy (1983) . . . . . . . . . . . . . . . . . . Kate
*Made for TV Movies:*
Her Life as a Man (1984) . . . . . . . . . . . . . . Carly Perkins
*TV:*
Battlestar Galactica (1980) . . . . . . . . . . . Jamie Hamilton
Houston Knights (1987-88) . . . . . . Lt. Joanne Beaumont
*Magazines:*
**Playboy** (Dec 1974) . . . . . . . . . . . . . . . . . . Cover Girl
• Half of left breast.
Playboy (Jul 1975) . . . . . . . . . . . . . A Long Look At Legs
**Playboy** (Jan 1980) . . . . . . . . . . . The World of Playboy
• 11—Right breast and lower frontal nudity while
wearing corset and white stockings. Small photo
with lots of diffusion.

## Down, Lesley-Anne
*Films:*
From Beyond the Grave (1973) . . . . . . Rosemary Seaton
The Pink Panther Strikes Again (1976) . . . . . . . . . . . Olga
**The Betsy** (1978) . . . . . . . . . . . . . . Lady Bobby Ayres
• 0:38—Brief left breast and upper half of buns, while
with Tommy Lee Jones.
• 0:57—Very brief left breast in bed with Jones.
A Little Night Music (1978) . . . . . . . . . . Anne Egerman
The Great Train Robbery (1979; British) . . . . . . . . Miriam
**Hanover Street** (1979) . . . . . . . . . Margaret Sallinger
• 0:22—In bra and slip, then brief breasts in bedroom
with Harrison Ford.
Rough Cut (1980; British) . . . . . . . . . . . Gillian Bramley
Sphinx (1981) . . . . . . . . . . . . . . . . . . . . . . . Erica Baron
Nomads (1986) . . . . . . . . . . . . . . . . . . . . . . . . . . Flax
Scenes from the Goldmine (1987) . . . . . . . . . . Herself

Death Wish V: The Face of Death (1993) . . Olivia Regent
Mardi Gras for the Devil (1993) . . . . . . . . . . . Christine
Munchie Strikes Back (1994) . . . . . . . Linda McClelland
*Miniseries:*
North and South (1985) . . . . . . . . . . . Madeline Fabray
North and South, Book II (1986) . . . . . Madeline Fabray
North and South, Book III: Heaven and Hell (1994)
. . . . . . . . . . . . . . . . . . . . . . . . . . . . Madeline Main
*TV:*
Upstairs, Downstairs (1974-77) . . . . . Georgina Worsley
Dallas (1990) . . . . . . . . . . . . . . . . . . Stephanie Rogers
*Magazines:*
**Playboy** (Dec 1979) . . . . . . . . . . . . . Sex Stars of 1979
•• 254—Breasts.
Playboy (May 1985) . . . . . . . . . . . . . . . . . . . Grapevine
217—B&W.

## Downes, Cathy
*Films:*
**Winter of Our Dreams** (1981) . . . . . . . . . . . . . Gretel
• 0:41—Brief right breast putting top on while talking
to Judy Davis.
•• 1:04—Breasts sitting up in bed at night.
• 1:11—Breasts sitting up in bed while Bryan Brown
and Davis talk.
Monkey Grip (1983; Australian) . . . . . . . . . . . . . . Eve

## Downs, Brandi
*Video Tapes:*
**Becky Bubbles** (1987) . . . . . . . . . . . . . . . . . . Herself
•• 0:11—Breasts in pool after Lorraine pushes her off
the pool float.
••• 0:12—Breasts while playing on pool float with Lorraine and Becky.
••• 0:14—Breasts sunbathing on chair and putting her
swimsuit back on.
**Best Chest in the U.S.** (1987) . . . . . . . . . . . Charlene
••• 0:48—Breasts and buns, dancing in two piece swimsuit.
••• 0:54—Breasts on stage with the other finalists.
••• 0:57—Breasts winning.
**The Perfect Body Contest** (1987) . . . . . . . . Charlene
•• 0:18—Buns, in pink, two piece swimsuit, then
breasts.
• 0:50—Breasts on stage with the other contestants.
**Wild Bikinis** (1987) . . . . . . . . . . . . . . . . . . . . Herself
• 0:09—Brief side of right breast, lying next to pool
from *Becky Bubbles.*
**Starlets Exposed! Volume II** (1991) . . . . . . Charlene
(Same as *The Perfect Body Contest.*)
••• 0:21—Buns in pink two piece swimsuit, then breasts
on stage doing strip routine.
*Magazines:*
**Playboy's Book of Lingerie** (Mar 1991) . . . . . . Herself
••• 44-45—Breasts and lower frontal nudity.
•• 76—Left breast and lower frontal nudity.
**Playboy's Book of Lingerie** (Jul 1991) . . . . . . Herself
••• 42-43—Breasts and buns.

**Playboy's Book of Lingerie** (Jan 1992) . . . . . . Herself
••• 20—Breasts.
••• 80-81—Breasts and buns.
**Playboy's Book of Lingerie** (Mar 1992) . . . . . Herself
•• 99—Left breast and lower frontal nudity.
**Playboy's Bathing Beauties** (Apr 1992) . . . . . Herself
•• 32—Buns and side of right breast.
••• 98-99—Breasts.
**Inside Sports** (Apr 1992) . . . . . . . . Journey to St. John
• 61—Buns, while leaning over on a rock.
**Playboy's Book of Lingerie** (May 1992) . . . . . Herself
••• 30-31—Breasts and buns.
**Playboy's Book of Lingerie** (Jul 1992) . . . . . . Herself
•• 28—Left breast.
**Playboy's Book of Lingerie** (Sep 1992) . . . . . Herself
••• 92—Breasts.
**Playboy's Book of Lingerie** (Jan 1993) . . . . . . Herself
•• 48—Buns.
**Playboy's Bathing Beauties** (Apr 1993) . . . . . Herself
••• 93—Breasts.
**Playboy's Girls of Summer '93** (Jun 1993) . . . Herself
• 104—Left breast and partial lower frontal nudity.
**Playboy's Book of Lingerie** (Jul 1993) . . . . . . Herself
••• 88—Breasts.
**Playboy's Book of Lingerie** (Jan 1994) . . . . . . Herself
••• 60—Breasts.
**Playboy's Bathing Beauties** (Mar 1994) . . . . . Herself
••• 48—Breasts.
••• 76—Left breast and buns in T-back.
**Playboy's Book of Lingerie** (Jul 1994) . . . . . . Herself
••• 98—Breasts.

## Drake, Gabrielle

*Films:*
**The Au Pair Girls** . . . . . . . . . . . . . . . . . . . . . . . . . n.a.
The Man Outside (1968; British) . . . . . . . . . . B.E.A. Girl
**There's a Girl in My Soup** (1970)
. . . . . . . . . . . . . . . . . . . . . . . . . Julia Halford-Smythe
• 0:09—In beige bra with Peter Sellers, brief left breast
in bed with him. Don't see her face well, but it is her.
Connecting Rooms (1971; British) . . . . . . . . . . . . . Jean
*TV:*
UFO (1970) . . . . . . . . . . . . . . . . . . . Lieutenant Gay Ellis

## • Drake, Judith

*Films:*
**Tales of Ordinary Madness** (1983; Italian)
. . . . . . . . . . . . . . . . . . . . . . . . . . . . . . Fat Woman
• 0:49—Buns, in bra and panties in her bedroom with
Ben Gazzara, then left breast when he fondles her.
The Sex O'Clock News (1986) . . . . . . . . . . Mary Ferrdip
Angel Heart (1987) . . . . . . . . . . . . . . . . . . . . Izzy's Wife
(Original Unedited Version reviewed.)

## Drake, Marciee

*Films:*
**Jackson County Jail** (1976)
. . . . . . . . . . . . . . . . . . . . . Candy (David's Girlfriend)
• 0:04—Brief breasts wrapping towel around herself,
in front of Howard Hesseman. Long shot.
Jokes My Folks Never Told Me (1976) . . . . . . . . . . . n.a.
**The Toolbox Murders** (1978) . . . . . . . . . . . . Debbie
•• 0:09—In wet blouse, then breasts taking it off and
putting a dry one on.

## Drake, Michele

*Films:*
**American Gigolo** (1980) . . . . . . . . 1st Girl on Balcony
• 0:03—Breasts on the balcony while Richard Gere
and Lauren Hutton talk.
**The Hollywood Knights** (1980) . . . . . . . . Cheerleader
• 0:28—Brief lower nudity in raised cheerleader outfit
doing cheers in front of school assembly.
History of the World, Part I (1981) . . . . . . . . Vestal Virgin
*Magazines:*
**Playboy** (May 1979) . . . . . . . . . . . . . . . . . . . . Playmate
**Playboy's Girls of Summer '86** (Aug 1986) . . . Herself
••• 60—Breasts.
••• 102—Breasts in open blouse.

## Drescher, Fran

*Films:*
The Hollywood Knights (1980) . . . . . . . . . . . . . . . . Sally
Doctor Detroit (1983) . . . . . . . . . . . . . Karen Blittstein
This is Spinal Tap (1984) . . . . . . . . . . . . . Bobbi Flekman
The Rosebud Beach Hotel (1985) . . . . . . . . . . . . . Linda
The Big Picture (1989) . . . . . . . . . . . . . . . . Polo Habel
UHF (1989) . . . . . . . . . . . . . . . . . . Pamela Finklestein
**Cadillac Man** (1990) . . . . . . . . . . . . . . . Joy Munchack
• 0:07—Very brief right breast several times while in
bed with Robin Williams.
We're Talkin' Serious Money (1991) . . . . . . . . . . Valerie
Car 54, Where are You? (1993) . . . . . . . . . . . . . . . n.a.
*Made for Cable TV:*
Dream On: The Second Greatest Story Ever Told
(1991; HBO) . . . . . . . . . . . . . . . . . . . . . . . . Kathleen
*TV:*
Princesses (1991) . . . . . . . . . . . . . . . . . . . . . . Melissa
The Nanny (1993- ) . . . . . . . . . . . . . . . . . . . . . . Fran

## • Drew, Griffin

a.k.a. Raquel Cristal.
*Films:*
**Dinosaur Island** (1993) . . . . . . . . . . . . . . . . . . . . May
••• 0:20—Breasts (she has dark necklaces on), while
bathing in a stream with April and June, then bathing the guys.
••• 0:22—More breasts, while bathing the guys.
••• 0:30—Breasts, while helping Wayne's arm feel better
in prehistoric spa.
••• 0:31—Breasts and buns, while making love with
Wayne in spa.
• 1:15—Side of left breast during end credits.

*Video Tapes:*
Playboy's Erotic Fantasies II (1993) . . . . . . Cast Member
*Magazines:*
**Playboy's Book of Lingerie** (Mar 1991) . . . . . Herself
 •• 68-69—Left breast and buns.
 • 89—Lower frontal nudity.
**Playboy's Book of Lingerie** (Sep 1991) . . . . . Herself
 ••• 86—Full frontal nudity.
**Playboy's Book of Lingerie** (Nov 1991) . . . . . Herself
 ••• 30-31—Nude.
**Playboy's Book of Lingerie** (Jan 1992) . . . . . . Herself
 ••• 46-47—Nude.
**Playboy's Book of Lingerie** (May 1992) . . . . . Herself
 •• 36-37—Left breast and lower frontal nudity.
**Playboy's Girls of Summer '92** (Jun 1992) . . . Herself
 ••• 20—Full frontal nudity.

# Drew, Linzi
Former Editor of the British edition of *Penthouse* maga-
zine.
*Films:*
**An American Werewolf in London** (1981)
. . . . . . . . . . . . . . . . . . . . . . . . . . . . . Brenda Bristols
 • 1:26—Side view of left breast in porno movie while
   David Naughton talks to his friend, Jack.
 • 1:27—Brief breasts in movie talking on the phone.
**Emmanuelle in Soho** (1981) . . . . . . . . . . . . . Showgirl
Breasts on stage.
**Aria** (1987; U.S./British) . . . . . . . . . . . . . . . . . . . . Girl
 • 1:09—Breasts on operating table after car accident.
   Hair is all covered with bandages.
 •• 1:10—Breasts getting shocked to start her heart.
**Salome's Last Dance** (1987) . . . . . . . . . . . . . 1st Slave
(Appears with 2 other slaves—can't tell who is who.)
 •• 0:08—Breasts in black costume around a cage.
 •• 0:52—Breasts during dance number.
The Lair of the White Worm (1988; British) . . . Maid/Nun

# Driggs, Deborah
*Films:*
**Total Exposure** (1991) . . . . . . . . . . . . . . . . . . . . Kathy
 ••• 0:08—Breasts dancing in front of Jeff Conaway, then
   making love in bed with him. Long scene.
 • 0:22—Brief side view breasts in B&W photos that
   Conaway looks at.
 • 0:24—Brief buns in black G-string and side of right
   breast changing clothes in locker room.
 •• 0:25—Breasts and buns, trying to beat up Season
   Hubley.
**Martial Law II: Undercover** (1992). . . . . . . . . Tiffany
 • 0:59—Side of left breast, while taking off lingerie
   and getting into bed with Billy Drago.
 • 1:00—Breasts, rolling off Drago after he passes out.
**Night Rhythms** (1992) . . . . . . . . . . . . . . . . Cinnamon
(Unrated version reviewed.)
 ••• 1:15—Left breast, then breasts and lower frontal nudity, making love with Martin Hewitt in bed.
 ••• 1:19—Breasts, sitting on bed and talking to Hewitt.

*Video Tapes:*
**Playboy Video Calendar 1991** (1990) . . . . . . October
 ••• 0:40—Nude.
**Playboy Video Centerfold: Deborah Driggs &
 Karen Foster** (1990) . . . . . . . . . . . . . . . . . Playmate
 ••• 0:02—Doing a strip tease, other dancing, some in
   bed. Nude.
**Sexy Lingerie II** (1990) . . . . . . . . . . . . . . . . . . Model
**Wet and Wild II** (1990) . . . . . . . . . . . . . . . . . Model
**Sexy Lingerie III** (1991) . . . . . . . . . . . . . . . . . Model
**Wet and Wild III** (1991) . . . . . . . . . . . . . . . . Model
**The Best of Sexy Lingerie** (1992) . . . . . . . . . . Model
**The Best of Wet and Wild** (1992) . . . . . . . . . . Model
**Playboy Playmates in Paradise** (1992) . . . . Playmate
**Sexy Lingerie IV** (1992) . . . . . . . . . . . . . . . . . Model
*Magazines:*
**Playboy** (Mar 1990) . . . . . . . . . . . . . . . . . . Playmate
**Playboy's Book of Lingerie** (Jul 1991) . . . . . . . Herself
 • 86—Side view of left breast.
**Playboy's Book of Lingerie** (Nov 1991) . . . . . Herself
 • 76—Buns.
**Playboy's Book of Lingerie** (Jan 1992) . . . . . . Herself
 • 12—Buns.
**Playboy's Book of Lingerie** (Mar 1992) . . . . . Herself
 ••• 22—Full frontal nudity.
 ••• 74—Full frontal nudity.
**Playboy's Book of Lingerie** (May 1992) . . . . . Herself
 •• 13—Right breast and lower frontal nudity.
**Playboy's Book of Lingerie** (Sep 1992) . . . . . . Herself
 ••• 10—Breasts.
**Playboy's Calendar Playmates** (Nov 1992) . . . Herself
 •• 96—Right breast and lower frontal nudity.
**Playboy's Book of Lingerie** (Nov 1992) . . . . . Herself
 •• 16-17—Half of right breast and lower frontal nudity.
**Playboy's Book of Lingerie** (Jan 1993) . . . . . . Herself
 ••• 11—Full frontal nudity.
**Playboy's Book of Lingerie** (Mar 1993) . . . . . Herself
 ••• 22—Full frontal nudity.
**Playboy's Book of Lingerie** (May 1993) . . . . . Herself
 ••• 32-33—Nude.
**Playboy's Wet & Wild Women** (Aug 1993) . . . Herself
 ••• 15—Breasts.
**Playboy's Video Playmates** (Sep 1993) . . . . . . Herself
 ••• 36-37—Full frontal nudity.
**Playboy's Nudes** (Dec 1993) . . . . . . . . . . . . . Herself
 •• 78—Half of right breast and buns.
**Playboy's Book of Lingerie** (Jan 1994) . . . . . . Herself
 • 60—Buns.
**Playboy's Bathing Beauties** (Mar 1994) . . . . . Herself
 ••• 53—Breasts.
**Playboy's Book of Lingerie** (Mar 1994) . . . . . . Herself
 ••• 11—Full frontal nudity.
 •• 96—Breasts under sheer black bodysuit.
**Playboy's Book of Lingerie** (May 1994) . . . . . Herself
 ••• 3-7—Buns, left breast and lower frontal nudity.
**Playmates at Play** (Jul 1994) . . . . . . . . . . . . . Herself
 • 43—Left breast and lower frontal nudity under sheer
   dress.

# • Dubin, Alexis

See: Ross, Gaylen.

# Ducati, Kristie

a.k.a. Kristi Scott.
*Films:*
**The Bikini Carwash Company** (1992) . . . . . . Melissa
(Unrated version reviewed.)
- • 0:13—Buns in G-string, while at the beach.
- ••• 0:20—Breasts, taking off her bikini top in shack with Jack.
- •• 0:26—Nude, changing clothes in car wash.
- • 0:30—Breasts during water fight.
- • 0:32—Brief breasts in Jack's fantasy.
- • 0:45—Brief left breast and buns, dressing.
- ••• 0:47—Breasts and buns, dancing inside car wash.
- ••• 1:02—Nude, soaped up in car wash with Rita and Sunny.
- ••• 1:07—Breasts and buns, making love in shack with Jack. Wow!
- ••• 1:12—Breasts, posing for photos.

**Intimate Obsession** (1992) . . . . . . . . . . . . . . . Laura
(Unrated version reviewed.)
- ••• 0:15—Breasts while making love with Rick while Rachel watches from outside. Long scene.
- ••• 0:17—More breasts, while making love with Rick.
- ••• 0:18—Buns and more breasts while making love.
- ••• 0:19—Brief partial lower frontal nudity and more breasts while making love with Rick.
- •• 0:21—Breasts during Rachel's recollections.

**Meatballs 4** (1992) . . . . . . . . . . . . . . . . . . . . . . . Kristi
- • 0:05—Very, very brief buns, getting her light blue robe pulled up by Neriah while walking to the showers. Long shot.
- • 0:06—Brief side of left breast, while taking a shower with three other girls. (She's on the far right in the first shot.)
- •• 0:37—Breasts, four times, while playing strip charades.
- • 0:54—Left breast, while riding behind a guy on a four wheel motorcycle. (She's the one closest to the camera.)

**The Bikini Carwash Company II** (1993) . . . . Melissa
(Unrated version reviewed.)
- •• 0:00—Breasts in back of limousine with a guy.
- ••• 0:09—Breasts with the other three girls, celebrating in office during music video number.
- •• 0:16—Breasts at carwash during music video number. (Wearing orange bikini bottoms.)
- ••• 1:20—Breasts and buns while making love with Derek in the TV studio.
- •• 1:29—Breasts and buns in bikini bottoms during music video number at the carwash.

*Magazines:*
**Playboy's Book of Lingerie** (Sep 1993) . . . . . Herself
- •• 79—Left breast.

**Playboy's Book of Lingerie** (Jan 1994) . . . . . . Herself
- •• 29—Right breast.

Playboy's Great Playmate Search (Feb 1994) . . . . Herself

# Duce, Sharon

*Films:*
The Tamarind Seed (1974; British) . . . . . . Sandy Mitchell
Absolution (1978; British) . . . . . . . . . . . . . . . . . . Louella
**Outland** (1981) . . . . . . . . . . . . . . . . . . . . . . . . Prostitute
- • 0:30—Right breast, lying down in room with drug crazed guy.
- • 0:32—Breasts going into medical scanning device.

# Duff, Denice

*Films:*
**Bloodstone: Subspecies II** (1992) . . Michelle Morgan
- • 0:10—Very, very brief left breast under sheer part of dress while taking it off. Back side of right breast while putting on sweater.
- •• 0:16—Breasts, while crying in the shower.

Martial Law II: Undercover (1992) . . . . . . . Nancy Borelli
Return to Frogtown (1992) . . . . . . . . . . . . . Dr. Spangle
*a.k.a. Frogtown II*
**Warlords 3000** (1992) . . . . . . . . . . . . . . . . . . . Anani
- ••• 0:50—Breasts, after taking off blouse in front of Nova, then making love and sleeping after.

Bloodfist V: Human Target (1993) . . . . . Candy/Michelle
Bloodlust: Subspecies III (1993) . . . . . . Michelle Morgan
*Made for Cable TV:*
**Dream On: The Second Greatest Story Ever Told**
(1991; HBO). . . . . . . . . . . . . . . . . . . . . . . Sorority Girl
- •• 0:20—Breasts in bed taking her sweater off, in bed with her boyfriend.

# Duffek, Patty

*Films:*
**Hard Ticket to Hawaii** (1987) . . . . . . . . . . Patticakes
- •• 0:48—Breasts talking to Michelle after swimming.

**Picasso Trigger** (1989) . . . . . . . . . . . . . . . Patticakes
- •• 1:04—Breasts taking a Jacuzzi bath.

**Savage Beach** (1989). . . . . . . . . . . . . . . . . Patticakes
- • 0:06—Breasts in spa with Lisa London, Dona Speir and Hope Marie Carlton.
- •• 0:50—Breasts changing clothes.

*Video Tapes:*
Playmate Playoffs . . . . . . . . . . . . . . . . . . . . . . Playmate
*Magazines:*
**Playboy** (May 1984). . . . . . . . . . . . . . . . . . . Playmate
**Playboy's Girls of Summer '86** (Aug 1986). . . Herself
- ••• 102—Breasts in open white dress.
- •• 112—Buns.

**Playboy's 1987 Book of Lingerie** (Mar 1987)
. . . . . . . . . . . . . . . . . . . . . . . . . . . . . . . . . . . . . . Herself
- ••• 40—Breasts and upper half of lower frontal nudity.
- • 94-95—Right breast.

**Playboy's Calendar Playmates** (Nov 1992). . . Herself
- ••• 45—Full frontal nudity.

# Duffy, Julia

*Films:*
Battle Beyond the Stars (1980) . . . . . . . . . . . . . . . . Mol
Cutter's Way (1981) . . . . . . . . . . . . . . . . . . . Young Girl
*a.k.a. Cutter and Bone*

**Night Warning** (1982)...............Julie Linden
 0:44—Upper half of left breast.
 • 0:46—Brief breasts when her boyfriend pulls the
 sheets down.
 •• 0:47—Brief breasts when Susan Tyrrell opens the
 bedroom door.
Wacko (1983)......................Mary Graves
*Made for Cable TV:*
Sex, Shock and Censorship in the 90's (1993; Showtime)
 ........................ Politically-Correct Mom
*Miniseries:*
Blue and the Gray (1982)...............Mary Hale
*Made for TV Movies:*
Menu for Murder (1990)........... Susan Henshaw
*TV:*
Love of Life (1972).........................n.a.
The Doctors (1973-77).....................n.a.
Newhart (1983-90)..........Stephanie Vanderkellen
Wizards and Warriors (1983)...........Princess Ariel
Baby Talk (1991).................Maggie Campbell
Designing Women (1991-92)...... Allison Sugarbaker
The Mommies (1993-94)................... Barb

# Dukakis, Olympia

Cousin of politician Michael Dukakis.
*Films:*
Lilith (1964)........................... Patient
Twice a Man (1964).....Young Woman/Commentator
John and Mary (1969)...............John's Mother
Made For Each Other (1971)........... Gig's Mother
Rich Kids (1979)........................ Lawyer
The Wanderers (1979)..................Joey's Mom
The Idolmaker (1980)................ Mrs. Vacarri
National Lampoon Goes to the Movies (1982).. Helena
 *a.k.a. Movie Madness*
Flanagan (1985).........................Mary
Moonstruck (1987)................Rose Castorini
 (Academy Award for Best Supporting Actress.)
Dad (1989).......................Bette Tremont
Look Who's Talking (1989)..................Rosie
Steel Magnolias (1989).............. Clairee Belcher
Working Girl (1989)........... Personnel Director
In the Spirit (1990).........................Sue
Look Who's Talking Too (1990)..............Rosie
**Over the Hill** (1991; Australian).............Alma
 •• 0:56—Breasts, while getting them breasts painted
 for tribal ceremony.
The Cemetery Club (1993).......... Doris Silverman
Look Who's Talking Now! (1993).............Rosie
*Made for Cable Movies:*
A Century of Women (1994; TBS)..............n.a.
*Made for TV Movies:*
Sinatra (1992)......................Dolly Sinatra
Tales of the City (1994).............. Anna Madrigal

# Duke, Patty

a.k.a. Patty Duke Astin.
Ex-wife of actor John Astin.
Mother of actors Sean and Mackenzie Astin.
*Films:*
4D Man (1959)................... Marjorie Sullivan
The Miracle Worker (1962)..............Helen Keller
 (Academy Award for Best Supporting Actress.)
Valley of the Dolls (1967)..............Neely O'Hara
**By Design** (1982; Canadian).................Helen
 •• 0:49—Left breast, lying in bed.
 •• 1:05—Brief left breast sitting on bed.
 • 1:06—Brief left breast, then brief right breast lying in
 bed with the photographer.
Something Special (1987)........Mrs. Doris Niceman
Prelude to a Kiss (1992)..................Mrs. Boyle
*Miniseries:*
Captains and the Kings (1976)
 ................... Bernadette Hennessey Armagh
*Made for TV Movies:*
My Sweet Charlie (1970)......... Marlene Chambers
The Miracle Worker (1979)............Anne Sullivan
Everybody's Baby: The Rescue of Jessica McClure (1989)
 ......................................n.a.
Always Remember I Love You (1990)..... Ruth Monroe
Call Me Anna (1990)...................Patty Duke
Absolute Strangers (1991)............... Judge Ray
Grave Secrets: The Legacy of Hilltop Drive (1992)
 ...............................Jean Williams
Last Wish (1992)..................... Betty Rollin
Family of Strangers (1993).................. Beth
A Matter of Justice (1993).............Mary Brown
No Child of Mine (1993).....................n.a.
One Woman's Courage (1994)................n.a.
*TV:*
The Patty Duke Show (1963-66)... Patty & Cathy Lane
It Takes Two (1982-83)................ Molly Quinn
Hail to the Chief (1985)...... President Julia Mansfield

# • Dulany, Caitlin

*Films:*
**Class of 1999 II: The Substitute** (1993)
 ...........................Jenna McKensie
 •• 1:01—Breasts, while making love in bed with Em-
 mett.
 ••• 1:02—More breasts while making love. Intercut with
 John shooting a machine gun.
Maniac Cop 3: Badge of Silence (1993)
 .........................Dr. Susan Fowler
*Made for Cable TV:*
**Red Shoe Diaries: Auto Erotica** (1993; Showtime)
 ............................... Claudia
 (Available on video tape on *Red Shoe Diaries 4: Auto Erotica.*)
 • 0:10—Very brief breasts in clips during car race.
 • 0:12—Very brief right breast.
 • 0:18—Very brief lower frontal nudity.
 • 0:20—Very brief nipple.
 • 0:22—Brief breasts.

- 0:24—Very brief nude several times in quick cuts.

*Made for TV Movies:*

Trouble Shooters: Trapped Beneath the Earth (1993) . . . . . . . . . . . . . . . . . . . . . . . . . . . . . . . . .Claudia

## Dumas, Sandrine

a.k.a. Sandra Dumas.

*Films:*

**Twice a Woman** (1979) . . . . . . . . . . . . . . . . . Sylvia
- 0:06—Breasts, kneeling on the bed, then more brief breasts in bed with Bibi Andersson.
- •• 0:47—Brief right breast, then breasts in bed with Andersson. Long scene.
- 1:15—Left breast, lying in bed with Anthony Perkins. Long shot.
- •• 1:23—Breasts with Andersson.

Aria (1987; U.S./British). . . . . . . . . . . . . . . . . . .n.a.

Beyond Therapy (1987) . . . . . . . . . . . . . . . . . . Cindy

Valmont (1989). . . . . . . . . . . . . . . . . . . . . . . Martine

The Double Life of Veronique (1991; French)

. . . . . . . . . . . . . . . . . . . . . . . . . . . . . . . Catherine

## Dunaway, Faye

*Films:*

Bonnie and Clyde (1967) . . . . . . . . . . . . . Bonnie Parker

The Thomas Crown Affair (1968) . . . . . . Vicki Anderson

**The Arrangement** (1969) . . . . . . . . . . . . . . . . Gwen
- 0:25—Brief buns in various scenes while at the beach with Kirk Douglas.

Little Big Man (1970) . . . . . . . . . . . . . . .Mrs. Pendrake

The Three Musketeers (1973) . . . . . . . . . . . . . . Milady

**Chinatown** (1974) . . . . . . . . . . . . . . . . . . . . .Evelyn
- 1:26—Very brief right breast, in bed talking to Jack Nicholson.
- 1:28—Very brief right breast in bed talking to Nicholson. Very brief flash of right breast under robe when she gets up to leave the bedroom.

The Towering Inferno (1974) . . . . . . . . . .Susan Franklin

The Four Musketeers (1975) . . . . . . . . . . . . . . Milady

Three Days of the Condor (1975) . . . . . . . . Kathy Hale

**Network** (1976) . . . . . . . . . . . . . . . .Diana Christensen

(Academy Award for Best Actress.)
- 1:10—Brief left breast twice, taking off clothes in room with William Holden.

Voyage of the Damned (1976; British). . . Denise Kreisler

Eyes of Laura Mars (1978). . . . . . . . . . . . . . Laura Mars

The Champ (1979) . . . . . . . . . . . . . . . . . . . . . Annie

The First Deadly Sin (1980) . . . . . . . . . Barbara Delaney

Mommie Dearest (1981). . . . . . . . . . . . . . Joan Crawford

The Wicked Lady (1983; British) . . . . . . Barbara Skelton

Ordeal by Innocence (1984) . . . . . . . . . Rachel Argyle

Supergirl (1984; British) . . . . . . . . . . . . . . . . . .Selena

**Barfly** (1987) . . . . . . . . . . . . . . . . . . . .Wanda Wilcox
- 0:58—Brief upper half of breasts in bathtub talking to Mickey Rourke.

Casanova (1987). . . . . . . . . . . . . . . . . . . . . Countess

Midnight Crossing (1988). . . . . . . . . . . . . Helen Barton

A Handmaid's Tale (1990) . . . . . . . . . . . . . Serena Joy

The Two Jakes (1990) . . . . . . . . . . . . . Evelyn Mulwray

Scorchers (1992) . . . . . . . . . . . . . . . . . . . . . . . Thais

The Temp (1993) . . . . . . . . . . . . . . . . . Charlene Towne

*Miniseries:*

Christopher Columbus (1985) . . . . . . . . .Queen Isabella

*Made for TV Movies:*

Columbo: It's All in the Game (1993) . . . . Lauren Staton

*TV:*

Ladies of the Night (1986) . . . . . . . . . . . . . Lil Hutton

It Had To Be You (1993) . . . . . . . . . . . . . . . . . . . n.a.

## Dunlap, Dawn

*Films:*

**Laura** (1979). . . . . . . . . . . . . . . . . . . . . . . . .Laura

a.k.a. Shattered Innocence.
- 0:20—Brief side view of left breast and buns talking to Maud Adams, then brief side view of right breast putting on robe.
- •• 0:23—Nude, dancing while being photographed.
- •• 1:15—Nude, letting Paul feel her so he can sculpt her, then making love with him.
- 1:22—Buns, putting on panties talking to Maud Adams.

**Forbidden World** (1982) . . . . . . . . . . . .Tracy Baxter
- 0:27—Brief breasts getting ready for bed.
- •• 0:37—Nude in steam bath.
- •• 0:54—Breasts in shower with June Chadwick.

Night Shift (1982) . . . . . . . . . . . . . . . . . . . . Maxine

**Heartbreaker** (1983). . . . . . . . . . . . . . . . . . . . Kim
- 0:49—Breasts putting on dress in bedroom.
- 0:51—Very, very brief right breast in open dress during rape attempt. Dark.
- •• 1:02—Left breast, lying on bed with her boyfriend. Long scene.

**Barbarian Queen** (1985). . . . . . . . . . . . . . . Taramis
- 0:00—Breasts, in the woods getting raped.

## Dunsheath, Lisa

*Films:*

**The Prowler** (1981). . . . . . . . . . . . . . . . . . . . Sherry
- 0:20—Very brief breasts in the shower (overhead view).
- •• 0:21—More breasts and buns in shower, then breasts when Carl opens the door.
- 0:22—More breasts from overhead.
- •• 0:23—Breasts, getting killed by the prowler with a pitchfork.
- 1:23—Breasts, dead in the bathtub when Pam discovers her.

They All Laughed (1981) . . . . . . . . . . . . . . . . .Tulips

A Little Sex (1982) . . . . . . . . . . . . Lucy (Down-On Girl)

Eddie Macon's Run (1983) . . . . . . . . . . . . . . . . . Kay

*Made for Cable TV:*

The Hitchhiker: O. D. Feeling . . . . . . . . . . . . . . n.a.

## Dupree, Christine

*Films:*

**Armed and Dangerous** (1986). . . . . . Peep Show Girl
- 0:58—Very, very brief breasts shots behind glass dancing in front of John Candy and Eugene Levy.

**Deathstalker II** (1987)
.......... Uncredited Body Double for Toni Naples
• 0:55—Brief breasts in strobe lights making love with the bad guy. Hard to see because of blinking lights.
*Magazines:*
**Penthouse** (Sep 1985) ..................... Pet

# • Durkin, Shevonne

*Films:*
Rage and Honor (1992) ................. Groupie
Ghost in the Machine (1993) ............... Carol
**The Liars' Club** (1993) ................... Marla
• 0:13—Very, very brief tip of right breast when standing up when Pat sees her. Left breast when he opens her dress top. Brief lower frontal nudity (dark) when he undoes her panties. Very, very brief left breast when she starts to fall backward.
•• 0:15—Right breast, then both breasts, when getting raped. (Don't see her face in close-ups.)
Leprechaun 2 (1994) ...... Bridget/William's Daughter
0:31—Breasts while in garage luring Ian to his death. Obvious body double.

# Dusenberry, Ann

*Films:*
Goodbye Franklin High (1978) ................. n.a.
Jaws II (1978) ..................... Tina Wilcox
**Heart Beat** (1979) ....................... Stevie
•• 0:41—Full frontal nudity frolicking in bathtub with Nick Nolte.
Cutter's Way (1981) ................. Valerie Duran
*a.k.a. Cutter and Bone*
**National Lampoon Goes to the Movies** (1982)
.................................. Dominique
*a.k.a. Movie Madness*
**Basic Training** (1984) ............. Melinda Griffin
••• 1:13—Breasts in Russian guy's bedroom.
**Lies** (1984; British) ................. Robyn Wallace
•• 0:10—Breasts opening the shower curtain in front of her boyfriend.
• 0:11—Right breast while kissing her boyfriend.
**The Men's Club** (1986) ................... Page
•• 1:04—Breasts while lying in bed after making love with Roy Scheider.
Play Nice (1992) ................... Pam Crichmore
(Unrated version reviewed.)
*Made for TV Movies:*
The Secret War of Jackie's Girls (1980) ........ Donna
*TV:*
Little Women (1979) ........... Amy March Laurence
The Family Tree (1983) ........ Molly Nichols Tanner
Life with Lucy (1986-87) ......... Margo McGibbon

# Dutch, Deborah
a.k.a. Debra Dare.
*Films:*
**Jokes My Folks Never Told Me** (1976)
.................... Girl on Bed/Confessional Girl
•• 0:33—Left breast, while sitting on bed (on the right) talking to the sweater girl.
Bruce Lee Fights Back From the Grave (1981) .. Debbie
D.C. Cab (1983) ............................. n.a.
The Man Who Wasn't There (1983) ...... Miss Dawson
Protocol (1984) ........................ Safari Girl
Torchlight (1984) .............. Sydney's Girlfriend
Action Jackson (1988) ....................... n.a.
**The Haunting of Morella** (1989) ....... Serving Girl
••• 0:14—Breasts and buns, taking off pink tap pants and getting into bath.
• 0:15—Buns, lying dead on the floor, covered with blood.
**Hard to Die** (1990) ............... Jackie Webster
*a.k.a. Tower of Terror*
•• 0:25—Breasts and buns, while taking a shower.
**Sorority Girls and the Creature from Hell** (1990)
................................ Mary Anne
0:08—Very brief, side of left breast changing clothes in background.
• 0:32—Lower half of left breast, dancing in cabin.
976-EVIL II: The Astral Factor (1991) .. Commerical Wife
**Death Dancers** (1992) ................... Shannon
**Mind Twister** (1992) .............. Sheila Harrison
(Unrated version reviewed.)
•• 0:01—Brief breasts, after smashing her head through window to scream for help. Left breast, while dead on the floor.
•• 0:04—Breasts, while dead on the floor when photographed by police.
•• 0:05—More brief left breast shots while on the floor. Breasts, while getting put in body bag.
• 1:22—In bra, then breasts on TV monitor during video playback that Heather watches.
**Roadside Justice** (1992) ................... Mom
Swingers (1992) .......................... Debra
Dinosaur Island (1993) ................... Cave Girl
*TV:*
Capitol (1985) ............................. n.a.
The Young and the Restless (1987) .............. n.a.
General Hospital (1988) ...................... n.a.
*Video Tapes:*
**Scream Queen Hot Tub Party** (1991)
.............................. Jackie Webster
•• 0:19—Breasts, taking off towel and getting into shower from *Hard to Die*.

# • Duvall, Shelley

Producer.
*Films:*
Brewster McCloud (1970). . . . . . . . . . . . . . . . Suzanne
McCabe and Mrs. Miller (1971) . . . . . . . . . . Ida Coyle
**Thieves Like Us** (1974). . . . . . . . . . . . . . . . .Keechie
  • 1:16—Brief upper half of left breast, several times,
    while in bathtub.
  •• 1:17—Brief breasts and partial lower frontal nudity,
    then buns, standing up, getting out of tub and dry-
    ing herself off.
  •• 1:18—Brief back side of right breast, while putting
    on nightgown.
Nashville (1975) . . . . . . . . . . . . . . . . . . . . . . . . L.A. Jane
Buffalo Bill and the Indians (1976). . . . . . Mrs. Cleveland
Annie Hall (1977) . . . . . . . . . . . . . . . . . . . . . . . Pam
Three Women (1977) . . . . . . . . . . . . . . . . . . . . Millie
Popeye (1980) . . . . . . . . . . . . . . . . . . . . . . . Olive Oyl
The Shining (1980). . . . . . . . . . . . . . . Wendy Torrance
Time Bandits (1981; British) . . . . . . . . . . . . . . . Pansy
Frankenweenie (1984). . . . . . . . . . . . Susan Frankenstein
Roxanne (1987) . . . . . . . . . . . . . . . . . . . . . . . .Dixie
Suburban Commando (1991) . . . . . . . . . .Jenny Wilcox
*Magazines:*
**Playboy** (Dec 1975). . . . . . . . . . . . . Sex Stars of 1975
  ••• 188—Breasts.

## Dziubinska, Anulka

a.k.a. Anulka.
*Films:*
**Vampyres** (1974; British). . . . . . . . . . . . . . . . Miriam
  • 0:00—Brief full frontal nudity in bed with Fran, kiss-
    ing each other before getting shot.
  • 0:43—Breasts taking a shower with Fran.
  ••• 0:58—Breasts and buns in bed with Fran, drinking
    Ted's blood. Brief lower frontal nudity.
**Lisztomania** (1975; British). . . . . . . . . . . Lola Montez
  •• 0:08—Breasts sitting on Roger Daltrey's lap, kissing
    him. Nice close up.
  • 0:21—Breasts, backstage with Daltrey after the con-
    cert.
  • 0:39—Breasts, wearing pasties, during Daltrey's
    nightmare/song and dance number.
*Magazines:*
**Playboy** (May 1973) . . . . . . . . . . . . . . . . . . Playmate
  ••• 122-129—Full frontal nudity.
**Playboy** (Oct 1975). . . . . . . . . . . . . . . . . Lisztomania
  ••• 84—Breasts.
Playboy (Dec 1976). . . . . . . . . . Portfolio: Pompeo Posar
  115—Left breast in wet white top.

## Easterbrook, Leslie

*Films:*
Just Tell Me What You Want (1980). . . . . Hospital Nurse
Police Academy (1984) . . . . . . . . . . . . . . . . . .Callahan
**Private Resort** (1985) . . . . . . . . . . . . . . Bobbie Sue
  •• 0:14—Very brief buns taking off swimsuit, then
    breasts under sheer white nightgown.
Police Academy III: Back in Training (1986) . . . .Callahan

Police Academy 4: Citizens on Patrol (1987) . . Callahan
  0:35—In wet T-shirt in swimming pool pretending
    to be a drowning victim for the class.
Police Academy 5: Assignment Miami Beach (1988)
  . . . . . . . . . . . . . . . . . . . . . . . . . . . . . . . . . . Callahan
Police Academy 6: City Under Siege (1989) . . . Callahan
*Made for TV Movies:*
The Taking of Flight 847: The Uli Derickson Story (1988)
  . . . . . . . . . . . . . . . . . . . . . . . . . . . . . . . . . . .Audrey
*TV:*
Laverne & Shirley (1980-83) . . . . . . . . . . . Rhonda Lee

## Easton, Jackie

*Films:*
**Hardbodies** (1984) . . . . . . . . . . Girl in Dressing Room
  •• 0:27—Breasts taking off dress to try on swimsuit.
  •• 0:40—Breasts with other topless girls posing for
    photographs taken by Rounder. She's wearing a
    white skirt.
School Spirit (1985) . . . . . . . . . . . . . . . . . . . . .Hogette

## Eastwood, Jayne

*Films:*
**My Pleasure Is My Business** (1974) . . . . . . . . Isabella
  • 1:16—Breasts in bed trying to get His Excellency's
    attention.
  •• 1:28—Breasts sitting up in bed with blonde guy.
One Man (1979; Canadian) . . . . . . . . . . . . Alicia Brady
Finders Keepers (1983). . . . . . . . . Anna-Marie Biddlecoff
Night Friend (1987; Canadian) . . . . . .Rita the Bag Lady
Candy Mountain (1988; Swiss/Canadian/French)
  . . . . . . . . . . . . . . . . . . . . . . . . . . . . . . . . . . Lucille
Cold Comfort (1988) . . . . . . . . . . . . . . . . Mrs. Brocket
Hostile Takeover (1988; Canadian). . . . . . .Mrs. Talmage
  *a.k.a. Office Party*
*Made for TV Movies:*
Anne of Green Gables (1985; Canadian)
  . . . . . . . . . . . . . . . . . . . . . . . . . . . .Mrs. Hammond

## Eccles, Aimée

*Films:*
Little Big Man (1970) . . . . . . . . . . . . . . . . . . . Sunshine
**Pretty Maids All in a Row** (1971) . . . . . . . . . . Hilda
  • 1:06—Partial buns while sitting on desk in Rock
    Hudson's office. Her hair covers most of her right
    breast.
**Group Marriage** (1972) . . . . . . . . . . . . . . . . . . Chris
  0:15—Buns, getting into bed.
  • 1:15—Brief side view of left breast and buns getting
    into the shower.
Ulzana's Raid (1972). . . . . . . . McIntosh's Indian Woman
Paradise Alley (1978) . . . . . . . . . . . . . . . . . . . .Susan
The Concrete Jungle (1982). . . . . . . . . . . . . . . Spider
Lovelines (1984). . . . . . . . . . . . . . . . . . . . . . . . Nisei
*Magazines:*
**Playboy** (Apr 1971) . . . . . . . . . Vadim's "Pretty Maids"
  •• 160—Breasts under gold top.

## Eden, Simone

*Video Tapes:*

**Playboy Video Calendar 1990** (1989) . . . . . . August
••• 0:40—Nude.

**Wet and Wild** (1989) . . . . . . . . . . . . . . . . . . . .Model

**Playmates at Play** (1990) . . . . . . . . . . . .Gotta Dance

*Magazines:*

**Playboy** (Feb 1989) . . . . . . . . . . . . . . . . . . . Playmate

**Playboy's Book of Lingerie** (Jan 1991) . . . . . . Herself
• 26—Lower frontal nudity.

**Playboy's Book of Lingerie** (Mar 1991) . . . . . Herself
•• 46-47—Right breast and lower frontal nudity.

**Playboy's Book of Lingerie** (Mar 1992) . . . . . Herself
• 30—Buns.
••• 31—Full frontal nudity.

**Playboy's Book of Lingerie** (May 1992) . . . . . Herself
• 103—Right breast.

**Playboy's Career Girls** (Aug 1992)
. . . . . . . . . . . . . . . . . . . . . . . . . . Baywatch Playmates
• 10—Left breast.

**Playboy's Book of Lingerie** (Sep 1992) . . . . . Herself
••• 50-51—Breasts.

**Playboy's Calendar Playmates** (Nov 1992) . . Herself
• 84—Full frontal nudity.

**Playboy's Book of Lingerie** (Nov 1993) . . . . . Herself
••• 56-57—Breasts.

## Edmondson, Donna

*Video Tapes:*

**Playboy Video Centerfold: Lynne Austin**. . . . . .n.a.

**Playboy Video Calendar 1988** (1987) . . . . Playmate

**Playboy Video Centerfold: Donna Edmondson**
(1987) . . . . . . . . . . . . . . . . Playmate of the Year 1987
••• 0:00—Nude, behind shower door, in photo session, on sofa in house, in empty house and in the rain.

**Playboy Video Magazine, Volume 12** (1987)
. . . . . . . . . . . . . . . . . . . . . . . . . . . . . . . . Playmate
••• 0:08—Nude in clips from her Playmate video.

**Playboy's Playmates of the Year: The '80s** (1989)
. . . . . . . . . . . . . . . . . . . . Playmate of the Year 1987
••• 0:21—Modeling swimsuits and lingerie. Nude on couch.
••• 0:22—In bra, garter belt and stockings, dancing in strobe light. Lower frontal nudity. Nude seen through open window.
••• 0:23—Nude, taking off her clothes in empty house. Nude in bed.
•• 0:26—Breasts, in the rain.
•• 0:52—Full frontal nudity in bed.

**Wet and Wild** (1989) . . . . . . . . . . . . . . . . . . . .Model

**Playmates at Play** (1990) . . . . . . . . . . . .Gotta Dance

**The Best of Video Playmate Calendars** (1992)
. . . . . . . . . . . . . . . . . . . . . . . . . . . . . . . . Playmate
••• 0:30—In lingerie, then nude during music video segment with a chair.
••• 0:32—In lingerie, then nude in bed and in still photos.

*Magazines:*

**Playboy** (Nov 1986) . . . . . . . . . . . . . . . . . . Playmate

**Playboy's Nudes** (Oct 1990) . . . . . . . . . . . . . .Herself
••• 105—Full frontal nudity.

**Playboy's Calendar Playmates** (Nov 1992). . .Herself
••• 67—Full frontal nudity.

**Playboy's Video Playmates** (Sep 1993) . . . . .Herself
••• 38-39—Full frontal nudity.

## Edwards, Barbara

*Films:*

**Malibu Express** (1984) . . . . . . . . . . . . . . . . . . . .May
•• 0:10—Breasts taking a shower with Kimberly McArthur on the boat.
•• 1:05—Breasts serving Cody coffee while he talks on the telephone.

**Terminal Entry** (1986) . . . . . . . . . . . . . . Lady Electric
••• 0:05—Breasts taking a shower and getting a towel during video game scene.

**Another Chance** (1989) . . . . . . . Diana the Temptress
••• 0:38—Breasts in trailer with Johnny.

*Video Tapes:*

**Playboy Video Magazine, Volume 4** (1983)
. . . . . . . . . . . . . . . . . . . . . . . . . . . . . . . . Playmate
•• 0:20—Breasts on sailboat.
••• 0:22—Nude, posing for centerfold photograph.
••• 0:24—Full frontal nudity on bed by herself.
••• 0:29—Nude, dancing in laser light show.

**Playboy's Playmate Review 3** (1985) . . . . . Playmate

**Playboy Video Calendar 1987** (1986) . . . . . Playmate

**Playboy's Fantasies** (1987) . . . . . . . . . . . . . . Fashion
0:00—Full frontal nudity during modeling session.

**Sexy Lingerie** (1988) . . . . . . . . . . . . . . . . . . . . Model

**Playboy's Playmates of the Year: The '80s** (1989)
. . . . . . . . . . . . . . . . . . . . Playmate of the Year 1984
••• 0:13—Nude in still photos.
••• 0:14—Full frontal nudity in centerfold photo session. More in bed.
•• 0:52—Full frontal nudity in bed.

**Wet and Wild** (1989) . . . . . . . . . . . . . . . . . . . . Model

**Playboy Video Centerfold: Kerri Kendall** (1990)
. . . . . . . . . . . . . . . . . . . . . . . . . . . . . . . . Playmate
••• 0:37—Nude.

**Playboy's Fantasies II** (1990)
. . . . . . . . . . . . . . . . . . The Game/The Secret Garden
••• 0:07—Nude, walking around in garden while a guy watches her.
••• 0:30—Full frontal nudity while trying on different clothes for her lover.

*Magazines:*

**Playboy** (Sep 1983) . . . . . . . . . . . . . . . . . . . Playmate

**Playboy** (Jun 1984) . . . . . . . . . . . Playmate of the Year

**Playboy's 1987 Book of Lingerie** (Mar 1987)
. . . . . . . . . . . . . . . . . . . . . . . . . . . . . . . . .Herself
• 2-4—Buns, right breast and partial lower frontal nudity.
•• 10—Right breast and lower frontal nudity.
• 20-21—Partial right breast and lower frontal nudity under sheer panties.
• 41—Lower frontal nudity and partial right breast.
••• 50-51—Nude.

••• 52—Full frontal nudity.
••• 79—Full frontal nudity.
••• 84-85—Nude.
• 101—Partial left breast and lower frontal nudity.
**Playboy's Nudes** (Oct 1990). . . . . . . . . . . . . . . Herself
••• 104—Full frontal nudity.
**Playboy's Book of Lingerie** (Jan 1991). . . . . . Herself
••• 24-25—Full frontal nudity.
**Playboy's Book of Lingerie** (Mar 1991). . . . . Herself
••• 40-41—Nude.
**Playboy's Book of Lingerie** (Sep 1991). . . . . Herself
••• 91—Full frontal nudity.
**Playboy's Book of Lingerie** (May 1992). . . . . Herself
•• 108—Buns and side view of left breast.
**Playboy's Calendar Playmates** (Nov 1992) . . Herself
••• 29—Full frontal nudity.
••• 42—Full frontal nudity.
•• 55—Buns.
**Playboy's Video Playmates** (Sep 1993) . . . . . Herself
••• 40-41—Nude.
**Playboy Presents Playmates in Paradise**
(Mar 1994) . . . . . . . . . . . . . . . . . . . . . . . . . Playmate
••• 48-53—Nude.
**Playboy's Book of Lingerie** (Mar 1994) . . . . . Herself
••• 96-97—Breasts.
**Playboy's Book of Lingerie** (May 1994). . . . . Herself
••• 70-71—Full frontal nudity.
**Playboy's Girls of Summer '94** (Jul 1994) . . . Herself
••• 4—Breasts.
**Playboy's Book of Lingerie** (Jul 1994) . . . . . . Herself
•• 107—Right breast.

## • *Edwards, Elaine*

*Films:*
Dancing in the Dark (1949). . . . . . . . . . . . . . . . .Girl
Old Oklahoma Plains (1952) . . . . . . . . . . Terry Ramsey
The Harder They Fall (1956) . . . . . . . . .Vince's Girlfriend
Curse of the Faceless Man (1958) . . . . . . . . Tina Enright
The Bat (1959) . . . . . . . . . . . . . . . . . . . . . Dale Dailey
The Purple Gang (1960) . . . . . . . . . . . . . Gladys Harley
You Have to Run Fast (1961) . . . . . . . . .Laurie Maitland
**The Curious Female** (1969). . . . . . . . . . . Mrs. Wilde
• 0:56—Breasts in bed with a young man before Joan walks in the room.
Fiddler on the Roof (1971) . . . . . . . . . . . . . . Shprintze

## *Edwards, Ella*

*Films:*
**Sweet Sugar** (1972) . . . . . . . . . . . . . . . . . . . .Simone
*a.k.a. Hellfire on Ice*
• 0:58—Breasts in bed with Mojo.
Detroit 9000 (1973) . . . . . . . . . . . . . . . . . . . . . Helen
Mr. Ricco (1975). . . . . . . . . . . . . . . . . . . . . . . . Sally
**Famous T & A** (1982) . . . . . . . . . . . . . . . . . .Simone
(No longer available for purchase, check your video store for rental.)
•• 1:07—Buns and breasts in outtakes from *Sweet Sugar.*

## *Ege, Julie*

*Films:*
**Think Dirty** . . . . . . . . . . . . . . . . . . . . . . . . . .Inga
*a.k.a. Every Home Should Have One*
• 0:43—Brief full frontal nudity, twice, in photo that Marty Feldman looks at.
•• 0:44—Brief breasts in another photo. Breasts and buns, while running around in a "documentary" about Sweden with Marty Feldman, then in a "Swedish" film.
On Her Majesty's Secret Sevice (1969; British)
. . . . . . . . . . . . . . . . . . . . . . . . . Scandanavian Girl
**Creatures the World Forgot** (1971; British)
. . . . . . . . . . . . . . . . . . . . . . . . . Nala, The Girl
0:56—Very brief breasts several times (it looks like a stunt double) fighting in cave with The Dumb Girl. Hard to see.
• 1:32—Very, very brief half of right breast when fighting a snake that is wrapped around her face.
**Up Pompeii** (1971; British). . . . . . . . . . . . . . Voluptus
**The Mutations** (1973; British) . . . . . . . . . . . . . . Hedi
*a.k.a. Freakmaker*
Breasts in bathtub.
The Legend of the 7 Golden Vampires (1974; British/Chinese). . . . . . . . . . . . . . . . . . . . . . . . Vanessa Buren

## *Eggar, Samantha*

*Films:*
The Collector (1965) . . . . . . . . . . . . . . . Miranda Grey
Doctor Dolittle (1967) . . . . . . . . . . . . . . . . . . . Emma
**A Name for Evil** (1973) . . . . . . . . . . . . . Joanna Blake
• 0:42—Very brief breasts turning over in bed with Robert Culp. Dark, hard to see.
Battle Force (1976). . . . . . . . . . . . . . . . . . . . . . n.a.
The Uncanny (1977; British). . . . . . . . . . . . . . . .Edina
The Brood (1979; Canadian) . . . . . . . . . . .Nola Carveth
The Executioner (1980) . . . . . . . . . . Dr. Megan Stewart
1:23—In body suit, briefly sitting up in hospital bed with Christopher George.
Curtains (1983; Canadian) . . . . . . . Samantha Sherwood
Round Numbers (1990) . . . . . . . . . . . . . . . . . . Anne
Dark Horse (1992) . . . . . . . . . . . . . . . . . .Mrs. Curtis
*Made for Cable Movies:*
A Ghost in Monte Carlo (1990) . . . . . . . . . . . . . . n.a.
*Miniseries:*
Secrets of Lake Success (1993) . . . . . . . . . . . . .Diana
*Made for TV Movies:*
All the Kind Strangers (1974) . . . . . . . . . . . . . . . n.a.
*TV:*
Anna and the King (1972) . . . . . . . . . . . . Anna Owens

## *Egger, Jolanda*

*Video Tapes:*
**Playmates at Play** (1990) . . . Bareback, Making Waves
*Magazines:*
**Playboy** (Jun 1983). . . . . . . . . . . . . . . . . . Playmate
**Playboy's Girls of Summer '86** (Aug 1986) . . .Herself
••• 28—Breasts.

# Eggert, Nicole

*Films:*

Clan of the Cave Bear (1985) . . . . . . . . . . Middle Ayla
Omega Syndrome (1986) . . . . . . . . . . . . Jessie Corbett
The Haunting of Morella (1989) . . . . . . . Morella/Lenora
(Nude scenes are an obvious body double. Note different color hair and skin.)
Kinjite (1989) . . . . . . . . . . . . . . . . . . . . . . . Dee Dee
**Blown Away** (1992) . . . . . . . . . . . . . . . . . . . . . Megan
(Unrated version reviewed.)
•• 0:15—Breasts and buns, getting out of bed with Haim.
••• 0:21—Right breast then breasts and buns, while standing in bedroom, making out with Corey Haim.
•• 0:24—Breasts, while making love in bed with Haim.
• 0:26—Left breast, while in shower with Haim.
••• 0:46—Breasts, while making love, sitting on Haim's lap in front of fire.
• 1:00—Upper half of buns, in bed with Haim.
• 1:10—Brief breasts and buns, while getting out of bed.
• 1:26—Very brief half of right breast and buns in T-back under sheer nightgown, while making love in bed on top of Corey Feldman.
• 1:28—Very brief right breast, while getting shot by policeman.
The Double O Kid (1992) . . . . . . . . . . . . . . . Melinda
Just One of the Girls (1992). . . . . . . . . . . . Marie Stark
*TV:*
T.J. Hooker (1982-87) . . . . . . . . . . . . . . . . . . Chrissie
Charles in Charge (1987-90). . . . . . . . . . . Jamie Powell
Baywatch (1992- ). . . . . . . . . . . . . . . . . . . . . Summer

# Eichhorn, Lisa

*Films:*

The Europeans (1979; British) . . . . Gertrude Wentworth
**Yanks** (1979) . . . . . . . . . . . . . . . . . . . . . Jean Moreton
• 1:48—Brief breasts in bed when Richard Gere rolls off her.
Why Would I Lie? (1980). . . . . . . . . . . . . . . . . . . Kay
**Cutter's Way** (1981) . . . . . . . . . Maureen "Mo" Cutter
*a.k.a. Cutter and Bone*
• 1:07—Brief right breast, wearing bathrobe, lying on lounge chair while Jeff Bridges looks at her.
The Weather in the Streets (1983; British) . . . . . . . Olivia
Wild Rose (1984). . . . . . . . . . . . . . . . . . . . June Lorich
**Opposing Force** (1986) . . . . . . . . . Lieutenant Casey
*a.k.a. Hell Camp*
• 0:17—Wet T-shirt after going through river.
••• 0:33—Breasts getting sprayed with water and dusted with white powder.
•• 1:03—Breasts after getting raped by Anthony Zerbe in his office, while another officer watches.
••• 1:05—Breasts and buns, getting dressed.
Grim Prairie Tales (1990). . . . . . . . . . . . . . . . Maureen
Moon 44 (1990; West German) . . . . . . . . Terry Morgan
King of the Hill (1993). . . . . . . . . . . . . . Mrs. Kurlander
The Vanishing (1993) . . . . . . . . . . . . . . . . . . Helene

*Made for Cable Movies:*
Devlin (1991; Showtime) . . . . . . . . . . . . Anita Brennan
*Made for TV Movies:*
A Woman Named Jackie (1991) . . . . . . . . . . Dr. Jordan

# Eilbacher, Lisa

*Films:*

An Officer and a Gentleman (1982) . . . . . . Casey Seeger
10 to Midnight (1983) . . . . . . . . . . . . . . Laurie Kessler
Beverly Hills Cop (1984). . . . . . . . . . . . . Jenny Summers
**Live Wire** (1992) . . . . . . . . . . . . . . . . Terry O'Neill
(Unrated version on video tape reviewed, not the R-rated version shown on HBO. )
••• 1:01—Brief breasts several times and partial buns, in bath tub and in bed with Pierce Brosnan. Some of the love making scenes in bed were cut for the R-rated version.
*Made for Cable Movies:*
Blind Man's Bluff (1992; USA) . . . . . . . . . . . . . . . n.a.
*Miniseries:*
Wheels (1978) . . . . . . . . . . . . . . . . . . . . Jody Horton
The Winds of War (1983) . . . . . . . . . . . Madeline Henry
*Made for TV Movies:*
Ordeal of Patty Hearst (1979). . . . . . . . . . Patty Hearst
Manhunt: Search for the Night Stalker (1989) . . . . . Ann
Joshua's Heart (1990). . . . . . . . . . . . . . . . . . . . . Kit
*TV:*
The Texas Wheelers (1974-75) . . . . . . . . . . . . . . Sally
The Hardy Boys Mysteries (1977) . . . . . . . . Callie Shaw
Ryan's Four (1983) . . . . . . . . . . . . . Dr. Ingrid Sorenson
Me and Mom (1985) . . . . . . . . . . . . . . . Kate Morgan

# Eilber, Janet

*Films:*

**Whose Life Is It, Anyway?** (1981) . . . . . . . . . . Patty
•• 0:30—Nude, ballet dancing during B&W dream sequence.
• 1:13—Very brief side of left breast when her back is turned while changing clothes.
Romantic Comedy (1983) . . . . . . . . . . . . . . . Allison
Hard to Hold (1984). . . . . . . . . . . . . . Diana Lawson
*TV:*
Two Marriages (1983-84). . . . . . . . . Nancy Armstrong
The Best Times (1985) . . . . . . . . . . . Joanne Braithwaite

# Ekberg, Anita

*Films:*

Back from Eternity (1956) . . . . . . . . . . . . . . . . Rena
Hollywood or Bust (1956) . . . . . . . . . . . . . . . Herself
War and Peace (1956; U.S./Italian). . . . . . . . . . Helene
Paris Holiday (1957). . . . . . . . . . . . . . . . . . . . Zara
La Dolce Vita (1960; Italian/French) . . . . . . . . . Sylvia
Boccaccio 70 (1962; Italian). . . . . . . . . . . . . . Anita
Four for Texas (1963). . . . . . . . . . . . . . Elya Carlson
Woman Times Seven (1967). . . . . . . . . . . . . Claudie
Northeast of Seoul (1972) . . . . . . . . . . . . . . . n.a.
*Made for TV Movies:*
S.H.E. (1979) . . . . . . . . . . . . . . . . . Dr. Else Biebling

## Magazines:

**Playboy** (Jan 1974) . . . . . . . . Twenty Years of Playboy
••• 199—Full frontal nudity in classic B&W photo.
**Playboy** (Jan 1989) . . . . . . . . . . .Women of the Fifties
•• 118—B&W photo sitting on the floor.
**Playboy's Nudes** (Oct 1990). . . . . . . . . . . . . . Herself
••• 8—Full frontal nudity in B&W photo.

# Ekland, Britt

Ex-wife of the late actor Peter Sellers.
Ex-wife of Stray Cats drummer Jim McDonnell.

## Films:

After the Fox (1966) . . . . . . . . . . . . . . Gina Romantiea
The Bobo (1967). . . . . . . . . . . . . . . . .Olimpia Segura
**The Night They Raided Minsky's** (1968)
. . . . . . . . . . . . . . . . . . . . . . . . Rachel Schpitendavel
• 1:34—Brief breasts, when her dress accidentally falls
down during strip tease routine on stage. Probably
a body double because you don't see her face. (A
reader has a letter from the director who says it's a
body double.)
The Cannibals (1969) . . . . . . . . . . . . . . . . . Antigone
Stiletto (1969). . . . . . . . . . . . . . . . . . . . . . .Illeana
**What the Peeper Saw** (1971; British) . . . . . . . . Elise
a.k.a. Night Hair Child
• 0:38—Sort of side view of left breast in bed. Don't
really see anything.
**The Wicker Man** (1973; British) . . . . . . . . . . . Willow
••• 0:58—Breasts in bed knocking on the wall, then
more breasts and buns getting up and walking
around the bedroom. Long scene. Body double
used when you don't see her face when pounding
on the wall. (Britt's hair is shorter than the body double's.)
The Man with the Golden Gun (1974; British)
. . . . . . . . . . . . . . . . . . . . . . . . . . .Mary Goodnight
The Ultimate Thrill (1974). . . . . . . . . . . . . . Michele
**Endless Night** (1977) . . . . . . . . . . . . . . . . . . Greta
• 1:21—Brief breasts several times with Michael.
**Slavers** (1977). . . . . . . . . . . . . . . . . . . . . . .Anna
• 0:40—Breasts undressing in front of Ron Ely.
**Sex on the Run** (1979; German/French/Italian)
. . . . . . . . . . . . . . . . . . . . . . . . .Countess Trivulsi
a.k.a. Some Like It Cool
a.k.a. Casanova and Co.
• 0:44—Left breast while making love in bed with
Tony Curtis (don't see her face).
Demon Rage (1981) . . . . . . . . . . . . . . . . Ann-Marie
a.k.a. Dark Eyes
a.k.a. Demon Seed
The Monster Club (1981) . . . . . . . . . . .Lintom's Mother
**Erotic Images** (1983) . . . . . . . . . . . . . . . .Julie Todd
• 0:16—Brief side view of left breast in bed with
Glenn.
••• 0:29—In bra, then breasts in bed with Glenn.
0:33—In bra, in open robe looking at herself in the
mirror.
1:27—In black bra, talking to Sonny.

Love Scenes (1984) . . . . . . . . . . . . . . . . . . . .Annie
a.k.a. Ecstacy
Moon in Scorpio (1987). . . . . . . . . . . . . . . . .Linda
Beverly Hills Vamp (1989) . . . . . . . . .Madam Cassandra
**Scandal** (1989). . . . . . . . . . . . . . .Mariella Novotny
(Unrated version reviewed.)
•• 0:31—Breasts lying on table with John Hurt.
• 0:51—Right breast talking with Hurt and Christine.
The Children (1990; British/German) . . . .Zinnia Wrench
Cold Heat (1991). . . . . . . . . . . . . . . . .Jackie Mallon

## Magazines:

**Playboy** (May 1989) . . . . . . . . . . . . . . . . Scandal
• 87-88—Left and right breasts.

# Eleniak, Erika

## Films:

E.T. The Extraterrestrial (1982) . . . . . . . . . . . . Pretty Girl
The Blob (1988). . . . . . . . . . . . . . . . . . Vicki De Soto
**Under Seige** (1992) . . . . . . . . . . . . . . . . . Jordan Tate
•• 0:43—Buns in T-back, then brief breasts in open
coat, while popping out of cake.
The Beverly Hillbillies (1993) . . . . . . . . . . . . .Elly May
**Chasers** (1994). . . . . . . . . . . . . . . . . . Toni Johnson
0:47—Buns in white bra and panties, while climbing
out of hole in ground.
••• 1:03—In bra, then breasts and buns, while making
love in bed with William McNamara.

## Made for TV Movies:

Baywatch (1989) . . . . . . . . . . . . . . . . . . . . .Shauni

## TV:

Charles in Charge (1988-89) . . . . . . . . Stephanie Curtis
Baywatch (1989-90). . . . . . . . . . . . . . .Shauni McLain
Baywatch (1991- ) . . . . . . . . . . . . . . .Shauni McLain

## Video Tapes:

**Playboy Video Centerfold: Fawna MacLaren**
(1988) . . . . . . . . . . . . . . . . . . . . . . . . . . .Playmate
••• 0:07—In studio, nude.
**Playboy Video Calendar 1991** (1990). . . . . . . . .May
••• 0:18—Nude.

## Magazines:

**Playboy** (Jul 1989) . . . . . . . . . . . . . . . . . . . Playmate
**Playboy** (Dec 1989) . . . . . . . . . Holy Sex Stars of 1989!
••• 181—Breasts, reclining.
**Playboy** (Aug 1990) . . . . . . . . . . . Beauty on the Beach
••• 68-75—Nude.
**Playboy's Nudes** (Oct 1990) . . . . . . . . . . . . . .Herself
••• 10—Full frontal nudity.
**Playboy** (Dec 1990) . . . . . . . . . . . . .Sex Stars of 1990
••• 173—Full frontal nudity, leaning back against wall.
**Playboy** (Dec 1991) . . . . . . . . . . . . .Sex Stars 1991
••• 182—Breasts under sheer, wet, white swimsuit.
**Playboy's Book of Lingerie** (Mar 1992). . . . . .Herself
• 9—Lower frontal nudity.
**Playboy's Book of Lingerie** (May 1992) . . . . .Herself
••• 44-45—Breasts.
**Playboy's Girls of Summer '92** (Jun 1992) . . .Herself
••• 5—Full frontal nudity.
••• 92—Full frontal nudity.

**Playboy's Book of Lingerie** (Jul 1992) . . . . . . Herself
•• 66-67—Right breast and upper half of left breast.
**Playboy's Career Girls** (Aug 1992)
. . . . . . . . . . . . . . . . . . . . . . . . . . Baywatch Playmates
• 5—Lower frontal nudity.
**Playboy's Calendar Playmates** (Nov 1992) . . Herself
••• 83—Full frontal nudity.
••• 92—Full frontal nudity.
••• 102—Full frontal nudity.
**Playboy** (Dec 1992). . . . . . . . . . . . . . Sex Stars 1992
••• 188—Full frontal nudity.
**Playboy's Girls of Summer '93** (Jun 1993). . . Herself
•• 54-55—Right breast and lower frontal nudity.
••• 93—Full frontal nudity.
**Playboy's Blondes, Brunettes & Redheads**
(Sep 1993) . . . . . . . . . . . . . . . . . . . . . . . . . Herself
••• 11—Full frontal nudity.
**Playboy's Book of Lingerie** (Sep 1993) . . . . . Herself
••• 10—Breasts.
**Playboy** (Nov 1993) . . . . . . . . . . . Sex in Cinema 1993
•• 134—Breasts in video still from *Under Siege.*
••• 182—Left breast in *Next Month* photo.
**Playboy's Nudes** (Dec 1993) . . . . . . . . . . . . . Herself
••• 9—Breasts and buns.
**Playboy** (Dec 1993). . . . . . . . . . . . . . Beverly Hills Hot
••• 90-99—Nude.
**Playboy Presents Playmates in Paradise**
(Mar 1994) . . . . . . . . . . . . . . . . . . . . . . . . Playmate
••• 24-29—Nude.
**Playboy's Girls of Summer '94** (Jul 1994) . . . Herself
••• 6—Breasts.

# Elian, Yona

*Films:*
The Jerusalem File (1972; U.S./Israel). . . . . . . . . Raschel
**The Last Winter** (1983; Israeli). . . . . . . . . . Maya
•• 0:48—Breasts taking off her robe to get into pool.
0:49—Buns, lying on marble slab with Kathleen
Quinlan.

# Elise, Esther

See: Alise, Esther.

# Elvira

a.k.a. Cassandra Peterson.
*Films:*
**The Working Girls** (1973) . . . . . . . . . . . . . . . . . Katya
0:18—Dancing in a G-string on stage in a club.
•• 0:20—Breasts, dancing on stage.
**The Best of Sex and Violence** (1981). . . . . . . . Katya
•• 0:40—Brief breasts dancing on stage in scene from
*Working Girls.*
**Famous T & A** (1982) . . . . . . . . . . . . . . . . . . . . Katya
(No longer available for purchase, check your video
store for rental.)
••• 0:28—Breasts scene from *Working Girls.*

**Jekyll & Hyde... Together Again** (1982)
. . . . . . . . . . . . . . . . . . . . . . . . . . . . . . . Busty Nurse
• 0:56—Brief right breast, peeking out from smock in
operating room. (She's wearing a surgical mask.)
Stroker Ace (1983). . . . . . . . . . . . . . Woman with Lugs
Pee Wee's Big Adventure (1985). . . . . . . . . Biker Mama
Echo Park (1986) . . . . . . . . . . . . . . . . . . . . . . . Sheri
Allan Quatermain and the Lost City of Gold (1987)
. . . . . . . . . . . . . . . . . . . . . . . . . . . . . . . . . . .Sorais
Elvira, Mistress of the Dark (1988) . . . . . . . . . . Elvira
0:31—Getting undressed into black lingerie in her
bedroom while being watched from outside the
window.
1:31—*Very* skillfully twirling two tassels on the tips of
her bra.
Ted & Venus (1991) . . . . . . . . . . . . . . . . . . . . . . Lisa
*Made for Cable Movies:*
Acting on Impulse (1993; Showtime). . . . . . . . . . Roxy

# • England, Audie

*Made for Cable TV:*
Red Shoe Diaries: Jake's Story (1993; Showtime)
. . . . . . . . . . . . . . . . . . . . . . . . . . . . . . . .Waitress
(Available on video tape on *Red Shoe Diaries 4: Auto Erotica.*)
**Red Shoe Diaries: Hotline** (1994; Showtime)
. . . . . . . . . . . . . . . . . . . . . . . . . . . . Tess Thomas
••• 0:09—Breasts and brief buns, after taking off dress
and making love with Adam on kitchen table.
•• 0:13—Breasts under sheer blouse, while pretending
to be a hooker for Adam. Lower half of buns, under
leather jacket.
• 0:15—Breasts under sheer blouse and partial buns,
after taking off jacket.
• 0:28—Buns and breasts, while making love with
Adam on bed.
**Red Shoe Diaries: Liar's Tale** (1994; Showtime)
. . . . . . . . . . . . . . . . . . . . . . . . . . . . . . . . . . Paula
••• 0:04—In lingerie while dancing in room, then
breasts, then making love with Jack while Erika
Anderson takes photos from outside.
• 0:08—Breasts and buns in still photos.
•• 0:10—Breasts in flashbacks after Anderson gets into
car accident.
• 0:12—Breasts in B&W photos and in flashbacks.
••• 0:18—Breasts in flashbacks intercut with Anderson's
nude scenes.

# Errickson, Krista

*Films:*
Little Darlings (1980) . . . . . . . . . . . . . . . . . . . . Cinder
The First Time (1981). . . . . . . . . . . . . . . . . . . . . Dana
a.k.a. *Doin' It*
Jekyll & Hyde... Together Again (1982) . . . . . . . . . . Ivy
0:31—In red bra and panties in bedroom with Mark
Blankfield.
**Mortal Passions** (1989). . . . . . . . . . . . . . . . . . Emily
•• 0:08—Brief breasts in bed with Darcy, while tied to
the bed. Breasts getting untied and rolling over.

- 0:11—Very brief right breast, rolling back on top of Darcy.
- ••• 0:40—Breasts after dropping her sheet for Burke, then making love with him.
- •• 0:46—Breasts getting into bed with her husband.
Killer Image (1991) . . . . . . . . . . . . . . . . . . . . . . . Shelley
**Jailbait** (1993) . . . . . . . . . . . . . . . . . . . Merci Cooper
0:11—In black bra, panties, garter belt and stockings in room with Tommy.
- •• 0:12—Breasts, while in bed handcuffing Tommy to the bed.
0:19—In black bra in motel room.
1:11—Back half of left breast, while making love with a guy.
Martial Outlaw (1993) . . . . . . . . . . . . . . . . . .Lori White
*TV:*
Hello, Larry (1979-80) . . . . . . . . . . . . . . . . .Diane Adler

## Estores, Lourdes

*Video Tapes:*
Playmate Playoffs . . . . . . . . . . . . . . . . . . . . . Playmate
**Playboy's Playmate Review** (1982) . . . . . . Playmate
- ••• 0:56—Nude at the beach, then under water, then outside near river.
*Magazines:*
**Playboy** (Aug 1980) . . . . . . . . . . . . . . Girls of Hawaii
- ••• 159—Full frontal nudity.
**Playboy** (Jun 1982) . . . . . . . . . . . . . . . . . . . Playmate
**Playboy's Girls of Summer '86** (Aug 1986) . . Herself
- ••• 20—Breasts.
- ••• 22—Full frontal nudity.
- ••• 52-53—Full frontal nudity.
- ••• 94—Breasts and buns.
**Playboy Presents Playmates in Paradise**
(Mar 1994) . . . . . . . . . . . . . . . . . . . . . . . . . Playmate
- ••• 44-47—Full frontal nudity.

## Estrin, Patricia

*Films:*
**Act of Vengeance** (1974). . . . . . . . . . . . . . . . . . Angie
*a.k.a. The Rape Squad*
(Not to be confused with the film with the same name starring Charles Bronson.)
- 0:37—Brief full frontal nudity, several times, under water in spa. (She's third from the right.)
Baby Boom (1987) . . . . . . . . . . . . . . . . . . . . . . . . .n.a.

## Eubank, Shari

*Films:*
Supervixens (1973) . . . . . . . . . SuperAngel/SuperVixen
**Chesty Anderson, U.S. Navy** (1975) . . . . . . . . Chesty
0:03—In bra sitting on bed, talking to Baby.
0:41—In bra and panties during fight in barracks.
- 0:58—Brief right breast, while making love with Fred Willard.
*Magazines:*
**Playboy** (Dec 1975). . . . . . . . . . . . . Sex Stars of 1975
- ••• 186—Breasts.

## Evans, Linda

*Films:*
Beach Blanket Bingo (1965) . . . . . . . . . . . . Sugar Kane
Those Calloways (1965) . . . . . . . . . . . . . . Bridie Mellot
The Klansman (1974). . . . . . . . . . . . . . . .Nancy Poteet
Mitchell (1975) . . . . . . . . . . . . . . . . . . . . . . . . .Greta
The Avalanche Express (1979) . . . . . . . . . . . . .Elsa Lang
Tom Horn (1980) . . . . . . . . . . . . . . Glendoline Kimmel
*Miniseries:*
North and South, Book II (1986) . . . . . . . Rose Sinclair
Dynasty: The Reunion (1991)
. . . . . . . . . . . . . . . . . . . . Krystle Jennings Carrington
*Made for TV Movies:*
The Last Frontier (1986). . . . . . . . . . . . . . . . . . .Kate
The Gambler Returns: The Luck of the Draw (1991)
. . . . . . . . . . . . . . . . . . . . . . . . . . . . . Kate Muldoon
*TV:*
Big Valley (1965-69). . . . . . . . . . . . . . . Audra Barkley
Hunter (1977) . . . . . . . . . . . . . . . . . . . . .Marty Shaw
Dynasty (1981-89) . . . . . . . . Krystle Jennings Carrington
*Video Tapes:*
**Playboy Video Magazine, Volume 1** (1982)
. . . . . . . . . . . . . . . . . . . . . . . . . . . . . . . . . .Herself
- •• 0:58—Breasts and side view of buns, in still photos from *Playboy* layout.
*Magazines:*
**Playboy** (Jul 1971) . . . . . . . . . . . . . . Blooming Beauty
**Playboy** (Dec 1981) . . . . . . . . . . . . .Sex Stars of 1981
- ••• 241—Breasts.
**Playboy** (Jan 1989) . . . . . . . . . Women of the Seventies
- ••• 216—Breasts sitting in water.

## Evens, Candie

See: Poremba, Jean.

## Evenson, Kim

*Films:*
**The Big Bet** (1985) . . . . . . . . . . . . . . . . . . . . . . . Beth
- •• 0:36—Right breast, sitting on couch with Chris.
- •• 0:45—Brief breasts, twice, taking off swimsuit top.
- •• 0:54—Brief breasts three times in elevator when Chris pulls her sweater up.
- •• 1:06—Nude when Chris fantasizes about her being in the video tape that he's watching. Long shot.
- ••• 1:19—In white bra and panties, then nude while undressing for Chris.
**Porky's Revenge** (1985; Canadian) . . . . . . . . . . .Inga
- •• 0:02—Right breast, while opening her graduation gown during Pee Wee's dream.
- •• 1:27—Breasts showing Pee Wee that she doesn't have any clothes under her graduation gown.
**Kidnapped** (1986) . . . . . . . . . . . . . . . . . . . . . Debbie
- 0:25—Right breast in bed talking on the phone. Long shot, hard to see.
0:30—In blue nightgown in room.
- ••• 1:28—Breasts getting her arm prepared for a drug injection. Long scene.
- ••• 1:30—Breasts acting in a movie. Long shot, then close up. Wearing a G-string.

**Kandyland** (1987) . . . . . . . . . . . . . . . . . . . . . . . . .Joni
  0:26—In purple bra and white panties practicing
  dancing on stage.
  ••• 0:31—Breasts doing first dance routine.
  •• 0:45—Brief breasts during another routine with
  bubbles floating around.

*Video Tapes:*
Playmate Playoffs . . . . . . . . . . . . . . . . . . . . . Playmate
**Wet and Wild** (1989) . . . . . . . . . . . . . . . . . . . .Model
**Playboy Video Centerfold: Kerri Kendall** (1990)
. . . . . . . . . . . . . . . . . . . . . . . . . . . . . . . . . . . Playmate
  ••• 0:35—Nude.
**Playmates at Play** (1990) . . . . . . . . . .Flights of Fancy

*Magazines:*
**Playboy** (Sep 1984) . . . . . . . . . . . . . . . . . . . Playmate
**Playboy** (Nov 1985) . . . . . . . . . . . Sex in Cinema 1985
  ••• 128—Breasts in graduation gown in still from *Porky's Revenge*.
**Playboy's Girls of Summer '86** (Aug 1986) . . Herself
  ••• 87—Full frontal nudity.
**Playboy's 1987 Book of Lingerie** (Mar 1987)
. . . . . . . . . . . . . . . . . . . . . . . . . . . . . . . . . . . Herself
  28—Lower half of breasts.
  • 74-75—Left breast and partial lower frontal nudity.

## • Everhard, Nancy

*Films:*
Double Revenge (1988) . . . . . . . . . . . . . . .Susie Taylor
Deepstar Six (1989) . . . . . . . . . . . . . . . . .Joyce Collins
The Punisher (1989) . . . . . . . . . . . . . . . . . . .Sam Leary
Another 48 Hrs. (1990) . . . . . . . . . . . . . Female Doctor
**Demonstone** (1990) . . . . . . . . . . . . . . . . . Sharon Gale
  • 0:47—Very, very brief backside view of tip of left
  breast after bending over to pick up robe off the
  floor.

*Made for Cable Movies:*
This Gun for Hire (1990; USA) . . . . . . . . . . . . . .Anne
*Made for TV Movies:*
An Eight is Enough Wedding (1989) . . . . . . . . . . .Mike
*TV:*
Houston Knights (1987-88) . . . . . . . . . . . . . . . . Carol
The Family Man (1991) . . . . . . . . . . . . . . . .Jill Nichols
Reasonable Doubts (1991-93) . . . . . . . . . . Kay Lockman

## Evridge, Melissa

*Video Tapes:*
**Playboy Video Calendar 1992** (1991) . . . . . . . .April
  ••• 0:13—Nude outside in garden.
  ••• 0:15—Nude in action-movie fantasy in the desert.
*Magazines:*
**Playboy** (Aug 1990) . . . . . . . . . . . . . . . . . . . Playmate
**Playboy's Book of Lingerie** (Sep 1991) . . . . . Herself
  ••• 64-65—Full frontal nudity.
**Playboy's Book of Lingerie** (May 1992) . . . . . Herself
  ••• 39—Breasts in sheer white panties.
**Playboy's Calendar Playmates** (Nov 1992) . . Herself
  ••• 101—Full frontal nudity.
**Playboy's Book of Lingerie** (Jan 1993) . . . . . . Herself
  ••• 93—Full frontal nudity.

**Playboy's Girls of Summer '93** (Jun 1993) . . .Herself
  ••• 89—Breasts.
**Playboy's Book of Lingerie** (Sep 1993) . . . . . Herself
  •• 96—Buns.
**Playboy's Book of Lingerie** (Nov 1993) . . . . .Herself
  •• 60—Right breast and lower frontal nudity.
**Playboy's Book of Lingerie** (Jan 1994) . . . . . Herself
  •• 34-35—Upper half of right breast and lower frontal
  nudity.
  •• 107—Left breast and lower frontal nudity.
**Playboy's Book of Lingerie** (Mar 1994) . . . . .Herself
  ••• 16-17—Full frontal nudity.
**Playboy's Book of Lingerie** (May 1994) . . . . .Herself
  ••• 77—Breasts.
**Playboy's Girls of Summer '94** (Jul 1994) . . . .Herself
  ••• 33—Full frontal nudity.
  ••• 46-47—Breasts.

## Fabian, Ava

*Films:*
Dragnet (1987) . . . . . . . . . . . . . . . . . . . . . . . . Baitmate
Terminal Exposure (1988) . . . . . . . . . . . . . Bruce's Girl
To Die For (1988) . . . . . . . . . . . . . . . . . . . . . . .Franny
Limit Up (1989) . . . . . . . . . . . . . . . . . . . . . . . . .Sasha
**Ski School** (1990) . . . . . . . . . . . . . . . . . . . . . Victoria
  ••• 0:53—In white bra and panties, then breasts making
  love with Johnny.
**Welcome Home Roxy Carmichael** (1990)
. . . . . . . . . . . . . . . . . . . . . . . . . . . Roxy Carmichael
  • 0:10—Buns in water in swimming pool, then more
  while getting out.
Auntie Lee's Meat Pies (1991) . . . . . . . . . . . .Magnolia
  1:29—Buns, while swimming in one piece swimsuit
  under water.
Mobsters (1991) . . . . . . . . . . . . . . . . . . . . . Cute Girl
*a.k.a. Mobsters—The Evil Empire*
*Video Tapes:*
Playmate Playoffs . . . . . . . . . . . . . . . . . . . . . Playmate
**Playboy Video Magazine, Volume 12** (1987)
. . . . . . . . . . . . . . . . . . . . . . . . . . . . . . . . . . . Playmate
  ••• 1:08—Nude, in bed, in still photos, in rainy scene,
  dancing like Kim Basinger in *9 1/2 Weeks*.
**Sexy Lingerie** (1988) . . . . . . . . . . . . . . . . . . . . Model
**Playboy Video Calendar 1990** (1989) . . . . . . . . July
  ••• 0:34—Nude.
**Wet and Wild** (1989) . . . . . . . . . . . . . . . . . . . Model
**Playmates at Play** (1990) . . . . . . . . . . . Gotta Dance
**Sexy Lingerie II** (1990) . . . . . . . . . . . . . . . . . . Model
**Wet and Wild II** (1990) . . . . . . . . . . . . . . . . . . Model
**Sexy Lingerie III** (1991) . . . . . . . . . . . . . . . . . . Model
**Wet and Wild III** (1991) . . . . . . . . . . . . . . . . . Model
**The Best of Sexy Lingerie** (1992) . . . . . . . . . . Model
**The Best of Wet and Wild** (1992) . . . . . . . . . . Model
**Playboy Playmates in Paradise** (1992) . . . . Playmate
*Magazines:*
**Playboy** (Aug 1986) . . . . . . . . . . . . . . . . . . . Playmate
**Playboy's Book of Lingerie** (Jan 1991) . . . . . . Herself
  ••• 60—Breasts.

**Playboy's Book of Lingerie** (Mar 1991) . . . . . Herself
••• 33—Full frontal nudity.
**Playboy's Book of Lingerie** (Jul 1991) . . . . . . Herself
••• 18—Breasts.
**Playboy's Book of Lingerie** (Sep 1991) . . . . . Herself
•• 22—Left breast.
**Playboy's Book of Lingerie** (Nov 1991) . . . . . Herself
••• 78-81—Nude.
**Playboy's Book of Lingerie** (Mar 1992) . . . . . Herself
•• 11—Left breast and lower frontal nudity.
••• 77—Breasts.
**Playboy's Bathing Beauties** (Apr 1992) . . . . . Herself
• 5—Half of right breast.
**Playboy's Book of Lingerie** (May 1992) . . . . . Herself
••• 91—Full frontal nudity.
••• 94-95—Breasts.
• 98—Buns.
**Playboy's Girls of Summer '92** (Jun 1992) . . . Herself
•• 40—Breasts under sheer black blouse and lower
frontal nudity.
**Playboy's Book of Lingerie** (Jul 1992) . . . . . . Herself
••• 35—Full frontal nudity.
••• 61—Breasts.
**Playboy's Book of Lingerie** (May 1993) . . . . . Herself
• 64-65—Partial lower frontal nudity.
**Playboy's Video Playmates** (Sep 1993) . . . . . Herself
••• 42-45—Breasts.
**Playboy's Nudes** (Dec 1993) . . . . . . . . . . . . . Herself
• 34—Half of left breast and lower frontal nudity.
**Playboy's Book of Lingerie** (Jan 1994) . . . . . . Herself
••• 55—Breasts.
**Playboy's Book of Lingerie** (Mar 1994) . . . . . Herself
••• 91-92—Breasts and partial lower frontal nudity.

## Fairchild, June

*Films:*
**Pretty Maids All in a Row** (1971)
. . . . . . . . . . . . . . . . . . . . . . . Sonya "Sonny" Swingle
• 1:10—Brief breasts and lower frontal nudity, taking
Polaroid photos of herself in Rock Hudson's office.
**Drive, He Said** (1972) . . . . . . . . . . . . . . . . . . . . Sylvie
• 0:16—Buns and brief breasts walking around in the
dark while Gabriel shines a flashlight on her.
• 1:01—Breasts, then brief nude getting dressed while
Gabriel goes crazy and starts trashing a house.
Top of the Heap (1972) . . . . . . . . . . . . Balloon Thrower
Detroit 9000 (1973) . . . . . . . . . . . . . . . . . . . . . . Barbara
Your Three Minutes Are Up (1973) . . . . . . . . . . . Sandi
**Thunderbolt and Lightfoot** (1974) . . . . . . . . . Gloria
• 0:20—Very brief right breast and buns, while getting
dressed in the bathroom after making love with
Clint Eastwood.
**The Student Body** (1975) . . . . . . . . . . . Mitzi Mashall
• 0:15—Brief breasts and buns, running and jumping
into the pool during party. Brief long shot breasts,
while in the pool.
•• 0:21—Breasts getting into bed.
Up in Smoke (1978) . . . . . . . . . . . . . . . . . . . Ajax Lady

*Magazines:*
**Playboy** (Apr 1971) . . . . . . . . . Vadim's "Pretty Maids"
•• 160—Left breast.
**Playboy** (Nov 1974) . . . . . . . . . . . Sex in Cinema 1974
••• 145—Full frontal nudity from *Thunderbolt and Lightfoot.*

## Fairchild, Morgan

*Films:*
**The Seduction** (1982) . . . . . . . . . . . . . . . . . . . . . Jamie
• 0:02—Brief breasts under water, swimming in pool.
• 0:05—Very brief left breast, getting out of the pool
to answer the telephone.
0:13—In white bra changing clothes while listening
to telephone answering machine.
0:50—In white lingerie in her bathroom while Andrew Stevens watches from inside the closet.
•• 0:51—Breasts pinning her hair up for her bath, then
brief left breast in bathtub covered with bubbles.
• 1:21—Breasts getting into bed. Kind of dark, hard to
see anything.
**Terror in the Aisles** (1984) . . . . . . . . . . . . . . . . Jamie
•• 1:06—Breasts in mirror in scene from *The Seduction.*
• 1:08—Brief left breast, getting out of pool from *The
Seduction.*
Pee Wee's Big Adventure (1985) . . . . . . . . . . . . "Dottie"
**Red-Headed Stranger** (1986) . . . . . . . . . . . . . Kaysha
• 0:03—Bathing in stream in wet white dress. Long
shot, then closer shot.
Campus Man (1987) . . . . . . . . . . Katherine Van Buren
Deadly Illusion (1987) . . . . . Jane Mallory/Sharon Burton
Midnight Cop (1988; Italian) . . . . . . . . . . . . . . . . . Lisa
0:23—In white panties with her dress pulled up in
restroom with Alex.
Phantom of the Mall: Eric's Revenge (1988)
. . . . . . . . . . . . . . . . . . . . . . . . . . . . . Karen Wilton
Mob Boss (1990) . . . . . . . . . . . . . . . . . . . . . . . . . Gina
Body Chemistry 3: Point of Seduction (1993)
. . . . . . . . . . . . . . . . . . . . . . . . . . . . . Beth Clancey
Test Tube Teens From the Year 2000 (1993)
. . . . . . . . . . . . . . . . . . . . . . . . . . Camella Swales
*a.k.a. Virgin Hunters*
*Made for Cable Movies:*
The Haunting of Sarah Hardy (1989; USA) . . . . . . . . n.a.
*Miniseries:*
North and South (1985) . . . . . . . . . Burdetta Halloran
North and South, Book II (1986) . . . . Burdetta Halloran
*Made for TV Movies:*
The Initiation of Sarah (1978) . . . . . . . . . . . . . Jennifer
How to Murder a Millionaire (1990) . . . . . . . . . Loretta
Menu for Murder (1990) . . . . . . . . . . Paula Preston
Based on an Untrue Story (1993) . . . . . . . . . Satin Chau
*TV:*
Search for Tomorrow (1973-77) . . . Jennifer Pace Phillips
Dallas (1978) . . . . . . . . . . . . . . . . . . . . . . Jenna Wade
Flamingo Road (1981-82) . . . Constance Weldon Carlyle
Paper Dolls (1984) . . . . . . . . . . . . . . . . . . . . . . Racine
Falcon Crest (1985-86) . . . . . . . . . . . . . . Jordan Roberts

Video Tapes:

**Playboy Video Magazine, Volume 5** (1983)
. . . . . . . . . . . . . . . . . . . . . . . . . . . The Seduction
- • 0:43—Brief breasts in scenes from *The Seduction* in pool and bubble bath.

Morgan Fairchild Stress Management (1991) . . . Herself
Magazines:

**Playboy** (Oct 1980) . . . . . . . . . . . . . . . . . . . .Grapevine
- • 246—Left nipple peeking out of top. B&W.

**Playboy** (Apr 1982) . . . . . . . . . . . . . . . . . . . .Grapevine
- • 254—B&W photo, in bathtub. Upper half of right breast.

# Faithfull, Marianne

Singer.
Former girlfriend of *Rolling Stones* singer Mick Jagger.
Films:

**Girl on a Motorcycle** (1968; French/British)
. . . . . . . . . . . . . . . . . . . . . . . . . . . . . . . Rebecca
*a.k.a. Naked Under Leather*
- •• 0:05—Nude, getting out of bed and walking to the door.
- • 0:38—Brief side view of left breast putting nightgown on.
- • 1:23—Brief breasts while lying down and talking with Alain Delon.
- • 1:30—Very brief right breast a couple of times making love with Delon.

Hamlet (1969; British) . . . . . . . . . . . . . . . . . . Ophelia
Madhouse Mansion (1974; British) . . . . . . . . . . .Sophy
Assault on Agathon (1976) . . . . . . . . . Helen Rochefort
The Turn of the Screw (1992; British) . . . . . . . Narrator

# Falana, Lola

Singer.
Films:

The Liberation of L. B. Jones (1970) . . . . . . Emma Jones
0:19—Very brief breasts walking by the doorway in the bathroom. Very long shot, don't really see anything.
The Klansman (1974) . . . . . . . . . . . . . . Loretta Sykes
**Lady Cocoa** (1974) . . . . . . . . . . . . . . . . . . . . . . Coco
- • 0:45—Left breast lying on bed, pulling up yellow towel. Long shot, hard to see.
- ••• 1:23—Breasts on boat with a guy.

Mad About You (1990) . . . . . . . . . . . Casey's Secretary
TV:
The New Bill Cosby Show (1972-73) . . . . . . . . .Regular
Ben Vereen... Comin' At Ya (1975) . . . . . . . . . .Regular

# • Fallace, Mimi

Video Tapes:

**Penthouse Forum Letters: Volume 1** (1993)
. . . . . . . . . . . . . . . . . . . . . . . The Paint Job/Gina
- ••• 0:01—Full frontal nudity in bedroom, rubbing lotion on herself and masturbating.
- ••• 0:05—Nude while making love in kitchen with Mario.

- •• 0:09—Left breast, while making love with Mario on the sofa.
- ••• 0:13—Breasts and buns, while making love in bed with the painter.

Magazines:
Playboy's Girls of the World (Oct 1992) . . . . . . .Herself
87—In braless, white, wet top.

# Fallender, Deborah

Films:

**Monty Python's Jabberwocky** (1977). . .The Princess
- • 0:56—Buns and brief full frontal nudity in bath when Michael Palin accidentally enters the room.
0:57—Breasts under sheer white robe.
Best Defense (1984) . . . . . . . . . . . . . . . . . . . . . Tony
Stitches (1985) . . . . . . . . . . . . . . . . . . . . . . Nurse #1

# • Farentino, Debrah

Ex-wife of actor James Farentino.
Films:

**The Capone** (1989) . . . . . . . . . . . . . . . . . . . . Jennie
*a.k.a. Revenge of Al Capone*
(Originally a Made for TV Movie.)
- • 1:01—Breasts, while making love in bed with Keith Carradine.
Bugsy (1991) . . . . . . . . . . . . . . . . . . . . Girl in Elevator
**Malice** (1993) . . . . . . . . . . . . . . . . . . . . . . . . . .Tanya
- • 0:25—Very brief upper half of right breast, while in bed with Alec Baldwin.
- • 0:26—Brief buns and breasts, while running into the bathroom. Medium long shot.
Son of the Pink Panther (1993) . . . . . . . Princess Yasmin
Made for TV Movies:
The Whereabouts of Jenny (1991) . . . . . . . . . . . . . .Liz
Back to the Streets of San Francisco (1992)
. . . . . . . . . . . . . . . . . . . . . . . . . . . . .Sarah Burns
TV:
Capitol . . . . . . . . . . . . . . . . . . . . . . . . . . . . . n.a.
Hooperman . . . . . . . . . . . . . . . . . . . . . . . . . . n.a.
Equal Justice (1990-91) . . . . . . . . . . . . . .Julie Janovich
Earth 2 (1994- ) . . . . . . . . . . . . . . . . . . . . . . . . n.a.
NYPD Blue (1994) . . . . . . . . . . . . . . . . . . Robin Wirkus
XXX's & OOO's (1994- ) . . . . . . . . . . . . .Pam Randall
**NYPD Blue: Rockin' Robin** (May 17, 1994)
. . . . . . . . . . . . . . . . . . . . . . . . . . . . Robin Wirkus
- • 0:56—Partial breast and partial buns, while making love with Kelly in bed.

# Faria, Betty

Films:

**Bye Bye Brazil** (1980; Brazilian) . . . . . . . . . . . Salomé
- •• 0:28—Breasts, wearing red panties, backstage with Cigano.
- • 0:29—Left breast while sitting in a chair.
- •• 0:38—Breasts backstage with Ciço.
- • 1:24—Buns, under a mosquito net with a customer.
**The Story of Fausta** (1988; Brazilian) . . . . . . . Fausta
- • 1:10—Left breast, while leaning out of the shower to talk to Lourdes.

## Farinelli, Patty

*Video Tapes:*
**Playboy's Playmate Review** (1982) . . . . . . Playmate
••• 0:11—Full frontal nudity during library photo shoot
and then by swimming pool.
*Magazines:*
**Playboy** (Dec 1981). . . . . . . . . . . . . . . . . . Playmate

## Farmer, Marva

*Films:*
**Video Vixens** (1973). . . . . . . . . . . . . . . . . . . . . .Girl
•• 0:59—Full frontal nudity in the swimming pool with
three other women during commercial.
The Candy Tangerine Man (1975). . . . . . . . . . . . . .n.a.

## Farmer, Mimsy

*Films:*
More (1969; Luxemburg) . . . . . . . . . . . . . . . . . .Estelle
**Road to Salina** (1969; French/Italian). . . . . . . . . Billie
••• 0:23—Breasts and buns, undressing and running to
beach with Jonas. Nude, while swimming under water.
•• 0:24—Buns and breasts, while lying on the beach
with Jonas.
• 0:40—Buns and brief right breast while taking a
shower. Seen through lattice work.
•• 0:41—Nude in bed with Jonas.
• 0:42—Breasts, while making love with Jonas in tent.
• 0:44—Breasts and buns, while running out of the
tent into the water. Nude in the water.
0:56—Brief right breast in bed with Jonas.
• 1:28—Buns and brief breasts after taking a shower
outside and wrapping a towel around herself.
• 1:29—Brief nude, while rolling over in bed.
**Allonsanfan** (1974; Italian). . . . . . . . . . . . . . . Mirella
Italian with English subtitles.
•• 1:14—Buns, while lying in bed with Marcello Mastroianni. Breasts, sitting up in bed. (Subtitles get in
the way.)
1:15—Buns, while standing up with Mastroianni.
1:34—Very brief part of right breast, under her arm
while kneeling on bed.
The Black Cat (1984). . . . . . . . . . . . . . . . . . . . . . .Jill
Codename Wildgeese (1985; Italian/German). . . . Kathy
The Death of Mario Ricci (1985; French/Swiss)
. . . . . . . . . . . . . . . . . . . . . . . . . . . . . . Cathy Burns
Poisons (1987; French/Swiss) . . . . . . . . . . . . . . . . Ann

## Faro, Caroline

*Films:*
**Rendez-Vous** (1986; French). . . . . . . . . . . . . . Juliette
• 0:22—Buns, walking up stairs, then full frontal nudi-
ty on second floor during play. Buns, while hugging
Romeo and falling back into a net.
Sincerely Charlotte (1986; French)
. . . . . . . . . . . . . . . . . . . . . . . . . Irene the Baby Sitter

## • Farr, La Joy

*Made for Cable Movies:*
The Hit List (1993; Showtime) . . . . . . . . . . . . . . . Linda
*Made for Cable TV:*
**Dream On: I'm With Stupid** (1994; HBO). . . . Laylee
•• 0:01—Breasts, while doing puzzle in bed while talk-
ing to Martin.

## Farrell, Belinda

*Films:*
**Cabin Fever** (1992) . . . . . . . . . . . . . .Lenore Hoffman
• 0:00—Brief right breast in gaping nightie when
bending over.
••• 0:07—Breasts on the floor with Jack during her fantasy. Long scene.
••• 0:16—Breasts, sitting on floor, while playing with
herself and fantasizing about Jack.
••• 0:20—Breasts and buns, undressing and getting
into bathtub.
• 0:23—Brief lower frontal nudity and right breast in
open robe.
•• 0:27—Nude in bed with Jack and rolling over and
getting out of bed.
• 0:30—Brief breasts opening her blouse in front of
Jack.
••• 0:32—Nude, making love in bed with Jack. Nice,
long scene.
• 0:41—Right breast, while sitting in bed and putting
on a blouse.
0:43—In white lingerie in the house.
*Made for TV Movies:*
It Takes a Thief (1987) . . . . . . . . . . . . . . . . Opera Guest

## Farrell, Sharon

*Films:*
It's Alive (1974) . . . . . . . . . . . . . . . . . . . . Lenore Davies
The Premonition (1976). . . . . . . . . . . . . . .Sheri Bennett
The Fifth Floor (1978) . . . . . . . . . . . . . . . . . . . . Melanie
**Out of the Blue** (1982) . . . . . . . . . . . . . . . . . . . .Kathy
• 1:18—Left breast, when Don Gordon pulls it out of
her nightgown and fondles it.
Sweet Sixteen (1982). . . . . . . . . . . . . . . . . . . . . .Kathy
Can't Buy Me Love (1987) . . . . . . . . . . . . . Mrs. Mancini
One Man Force (1989). . . . . . . . . . . . . . . . . . . . Shirley
**Lonely Hearts** (1991) . . . . . . . . . . . . . . . . . . . Louise
•• 0:52—Breasts, while lying back on bed in room with
Eric Roberts.
*Made for TV Movies:*
Sworn to Vengeance (1993). . . . . . . . . . . . Sylvia Haskell
*TV:*
The Young and the Restless . . . . . . . . . . . . . . . . . .n.a.
Saints & Sinners (1962-63). . . . . . . . . . . . . . . . . Polly
Hawaii Five-O (1979-80) . . . . . . . . . . . . . .Lori Wilson
Rituals (1984-85) . . . . . . . . . . . . . . . . . . . . .Cherry Lane

# Farrow, Mia

Sister of actress Tisa Farrow.
Daughter of actress Maureen O'Sullivan.
Ex-wife of actor/singer Frank Sinatra.
*Films:*
A Dandy in Aspic (1968) . . . . . . . . . . . . . . . . Caroline
**Rosemary's Baby** (1968) . . . . . Rosemary Woodhouse
 • 0:10—Brief left breast in room in new apartment on
  floor with John Cassavetes. Hard to see anything.
 • 0:43—Brief close up of her breasts while she's sitting
  on a boat during a nightmare.
 •• 0:44—Buns walking on boat, then breasts during
  impregnation scene with the devil.
See No Evil (1971) . . . . . . . . . . . . . . . . . . . . . . . Sarah
High Heels (1972; French). . . . . . . . . Christine Du Pont
 a.k.a. Docteur Popaul
The Great Gatsby (1974). . . . . . . . . . . . Daisy Buchanan
Avalanche (1978) . . . . . . . . . . . . . . . . . Caroline Brace
Death on the Nile (1978; British)
. . . . . . . . . . . . . . . . . . . . . . Jacqueline de Bellefort
**A Wedding** (1978) . . . . . . . . . . . . . . . . . Buffy Brenner
 ••• 1:10—Breasts posing in front of a painting, while
  wearing a wedding veil.
**Hurricane** (1979) . . . . . . . . . . . . . . Charlotte Bruckner
 • 0:39—Brief left breast in open dress top while crawl-
  ing under bushes at the beach.
A Midsummer Night's Sex Comedy (1982) . . . . . . . Ariel
Broadway Danny Rose (1984) . . . . . . . . . . . . . Tina Vitale
Supergirl (1984; British) . . . . . . . . . . . . . . . . . . . .Alura
Zelig (1984) . . . . . . . . . . . . . . . . . . . . . . .Dr. Fletcher
The Purple Rose of Cairo (1985) . . . . . . . . . . . . Cecelia
Hannah and Her Sisters (1986) . . . . . . . . . . . . Hannah
Radio Days (1987). . . . . . . . . . . . . . . . . . . . Sally White
September (1987). . . . . . . . . . . . . . . . . . . . . . . . . Lane
Crimes and Misdemeanors (1989). . . . . . . . .Halley Reed
New York Stories (1989) . . . . . . . . . . . . . . . . . . . . .Lisa
Alice (1990) . . . . . . . . . . . . . . . . . . . . . . . . . . . . Alice
Shadows and Fog (1991) . . . . . . . . . . . . . . . . . . . Irmy
Husbands and Wives (1992) . . . . . . . . . . . . . Judy Roth
Widow's Peak (1994). . . . . . . . . . . . . . . . . . Miss O'Hare
*TV:*
Peyton Place (1964-66). . .Allison MacKenzie/Harrington

# Farrow, Tisa

Sister of actress Mia Farrow.
Daughter of actress Maureen O'Sullivan.
*Films:*
**Some Call It Loving** (1972) . . . . . . . . . . . . . .Jennifer
 ••• 1:17—Breasts in bed with Troy.
Strange Shadows in an Empty Room (1976) . . . . . . .n.a.
Fingers (1978). . . . . . . . . . . . . . . . . . . . . . . . . Carol
Winter Kills (1979) . . . . . . . . . . . . . . . . . . . Nurse Two
Zombie (1980) . . . . . . . . . . . . . . . . . . . . .Anne Bolles
Search and Destroy (1981) . . . . . . . . . . . . . . . . Kate.
*Magazines:*
**Playboy** (Jul 1973). . . . . . . . . . . . . . . . . . . . . .Tisa
 ••• 83-87—Breasts.
**Playboy** (Jan 1975) . . . . . . . . . Playboy Mansion West
 •• 131—Left breast, while in waterfall.

# Faulkner, Sally

*Films:*
**Vampyres** (1974; British) . . . . . . . . . . . . . . . .Harriet
 • 1:14—Side of left breast, partial buns, then right
  breast while making love with John in the trailer.
 •• 1:22—Full frontal nudity getting her clothes ripped
  off by Fran and Miriam in the wine cellar before being killed.
**Alien Prey** (1984; British). . . . . . . . . . . . . . .Josephine
 • 0:32—Very, very brief left breast taking off top.
  0:36—Buns, in bed with Glory Annen.
 • 0:37—Breasts on her back in bed with Annen.
*Magazines:*
**Playboy** (Nov 1975) . . . . . . . . . . Sex in Cinema 1975
 ••• 134—Breasts in still photo from *Vampyres... Daughters of Death.*

# Favier, Sophie

*Films:*
**Frank and I** (1983). . . . . . . . . . . . . . . . . . . . . Maud
 • 0:16—Nude, undressing then breasts lying in bed
  with Charles.
 • 0:40—Brief breasts in bed with Charles.
Cheech & Chong's The Corsican Brothers (1984)
. . . . . . . . . . . . . . . . . . . . . . . . . . . . . . . .Lovely II

# Fawcett, Farrah

Ex-wife of actor Lee Majors.
Significant Other of actor Ryan O'Neal.
*Films:*
Myra Breckinridge (1970) . . . . . . . . . . . . . Mary Ann
Logan's Run (1976) . . . . . . . . . . . . . . . . . . . . . . Holly
Sunburn (1979) . . . . . . . . . . . . . . . . . . . . . . . . . Ellie
**Saturn 3** (1980) . . . . . . . . . . . . . . . . . . . . . . . . Alex
 •• 0:17—Brief right breast taking off towel and running
  to Kirk Douglas after taking a shower.
The Cannonball Run (1981) . . . . . . . . . . . . . . Pamela
**Extremities** (1986) . . . . . . . . . . . . . . . . . . . .Marjorie
 • 0:37—Brief side view of right breast when Joe pulls
  down her top in the kitchen. Can't see her face, but
  reportedly her.
Double Exposure: The Story of Margaret Bourke-White
 (1989) . . . . . . . . . . . . . . . . . . Margaret Bourke-White
  0:39—Most of side of left breast, while sitting in bed
  giving Frederic Forrest a shave.
See You in the Morning (1989) . . . . . . . . . Jo Livingston
*Made for TV Movies:*
The Burning Bed (1984). . . . . . . . . . . . Francine Hughes
The Red Light Sting (1984) . . . . . . . . . . . Kathy Dunne
Between Two Women (1986). . . . . . . . . . .Val Petherton
Poor Little Rich Girl: The Barbara Hutton Story (1987)
. . . . . . . . . . . . . . . . . . . . . . . . . . . . . Barbara Hutton
Small Sacrifices (1989) . . . . . . . . . . . . . . .Diane Downs
Criminal Behavior (1992) . . . . . . . . . . . Jessie Lee Stubbs
The Substitute Wife (1994). . . . . . . . . . . . . . . . . . n.a.
*TV:*
Harry-O (1974-76). . . . . . . . . . . . . .Next door neighbor
Charlie's Angels (1976-77). . . . . . . . . . . . . .Jill Munroe
Good Sports (1991) . . . . . . . . . . . . . . . . Gayle Roberts

## Fellner, Ursulla

See: Buchfellner, Ursula.

## Fenech, Edwige

*Films:*

**You've Got to Have Heart** . . . . . . . . . . . . Valentina
*a.k.a. At Last, At Last*
- ••• 0:10—Breasts and buns, while taking off nightgown for Giovanni.
- • 0:11—Brief side view of left breast, while sitting up on the floor with Giovanni.
- ••• 0:20—Nude in bedroom with Giovanni.
- ••• 0:26—Right breast, when Giovanni gets out of bed.
- •• 0:43—Left breast, while entertaining herself and fantasizing.
- ••• 0:47—Breasts, while on boat getting lotion rubbed on her by Brigitte.
- ••• 0:53—Breasts and buns in G-string when Giovanni takes off her body suit.
- • 0:58—Right breast, while getting molested by Uncle Frederico.
- • 1:20—Breasts while getting out of her wet dress in tent.
- •• 1:24—Breasts in tent while making love with another man.
- •• 1:25—Right breast while making love.
- • 1:32—Brief full frontal nudity in bedroom during argument.

**The Seducers** (1970) . . . . . . . . . . . . . . . . . . . . .Ulla
*a.k.a. Sensation*
*a.k.a. Top Sensation*
- • 0:10—Very brief side of right breast, after Tony pulls her top down.
- • 0:11—Brief buns, under towel while walking in hallway.
- ••• 0:13—Breasts, after taking off her top and rubbing suntan lotion on Paula.
- • 0:22—Brief left breast, after opening her robe to let a goat lick her while Aldo takes pictures.
- •• 1:10—Breasts, while on boat deck with Andrew.
- •• 1:12—Breasts, a couple of more times with Andrew.

**Sex with a Smile** (1976; Italian) . . . . . . . . Dream Girl
- •• 0:03—Breasts tied to bed with two holes cut in her red dress top.
- 0:09—Buns, in jail cell in court when the guy pulls her panties down with his sword.
- •• 0:13—Brief breasts in bed with Dracula taking off her top and hugging him.
- • 0:16—Breasts in bathtub. Long shot.

Phantom of Death (1987; Italian) . . . . . . . . . . . Helene

## Fenn, Sherilyn

*Films:*

Out of Control (1984). . . . . . . . . . . . . . . . . . . . .Katie
  0:19—In wet white T-shirt in pond with the other girls.
The Wild Life (1984) . . . . . . . . . . . . . . . . . Penny Hallin
Just One of the Guys (1986) . . . . . . . . . . . . . . . Sandy
Thrashin' (1986) . . . . . . . . . . . . . . . . . . . . . . . . Velvet

**The Wraith** (1986). . . . . . . . . . . . . . . . . . . . . . . . Keri
- • 0:13—Very brief breasts when Packard's gang catches her in bed with Jamie.
- • 1:02—Brief breasts during flashback when caught in bed by Packard's gang.
- • 1:03—Very brief right breast, pulling her swimsuit top off in pond with Charlie Sheen.

Zombie High (1987) . . . . . . . . . . . . . . . . . . . . . . Suzi
*a.k.a. The School That Ate My Brain*

**Two Moon Junction** (1988) . . . . . . . . . . . . . . . April
(Blonde hair throughout the film.)
- ••• 0:07—Breasts and brief buns, while taking a shower in the country club shower room.
- • 0:27—Brief breasts on the floor kissing Perry.
- •• 0:42—Breasts in gas station restroom changing camisole tops with Kristy McNichol.
- • 0:54—Brief breasts making love with Perry in a motel room.
- ••• 1:24—Nude at Two Moon Junction making love with Perry. Very hot!
- • 1:40—Brief left breast, brief lower frontal nudity and buns in the shower with Perry.

**Crime Zone** (1989) . . . . . . . . . . . . . . . . . . . . . . .Helen
  0:16—In black lingerie and stockings in bedroom.
- •• 0:23—Breasts wearing black panties making love with Bone. Dark, long shot.

**Meridian** (1989). . . . . . . . . . . . . . . . . . . . . . Catherine
*a.k.a. Kiss of the Beast*
*a.k.a. Phantoms*
- •• 0:23—White bra and panties, getting clothes taken off by Lawrence, then breasts.
- ••• 0:28—Breasts in bed with Oliver.
- •• 0:51—Breasts getting her blouse ripped open lying in bed.
  1:11—Briefly in white panties and bra putting red dress on.

**True Blood** (1989) . . . . . . . . . . . . . . . . . .Jennifer Scott
- • 1:22—Very brief right breast in closet trying to stab Spider with a piece of mirror.

**Backstreet Dreams** (1990) . . . . . . . . . . . . . . . . Lucy
- • 0:00—Right breast while sleeping in bed with Dean. Medium long shot.

Desire and Hell at Sunset Motel (1990) . . . . . . . . Bridey
Wild at Heart (1990) . . . . . . . . . . . . . . Girl in Accident
Diary of a Hitman (1992) . . . . . . . . . . . . . . . . . . . . Jain
Of Mice and Men (1992) . . . . . . . . . . . . . . Curley's Wife
Ruby (1992). . . . . . . . . . . . . . . . . . . . . . . . .Candy Cane
  0:37—Outer half of breasts after finishing strip tease routine on stage in bar.

**Boxing Helena** (1993). . . . . . . . . . . . . . . . . . . .Helena
  0:11—In bra, undressing in bedroom while Julian Sands watches from outside in tree.
- ••• 0:13—Right breast, then breasts, while making love.
- • 0:17—Very, very brief left breast when rolling over in bed.
- • 0:18—Breasts, while getting out of bed after getting interrupted by a phone call.
  1:39—Briefly in bra in flashback.

Fatal Instinct (1993). . . . . . . . . . . . . . . . . . . . . . .Laura

Three of Hearts (1993) . . . . . . . . . . . . . . . . . . . . . Ellen
*Made for TV Movies:*
Dillinger (1991). . . . . . . . . . . . . . . . . . Billie Frechette
*TV:*
TV 101 (1988-89) . . . . . . . . . . . . . . . . . . . . . . . .n.a.
Twin Peaks (1990-91) . . . . . . . . . . . . . . Audrey Horne
*Magazines:*
**Playboy** (Dec 1990). . . . . . . . . . . . . . . . .Fenn-tastic!
••• 82-91—Breasts photos, some are B&W.

## Ferguson, Kate

*Films:*
Break of Day (1977; Australian) . . . . . . . . . . . . . . . Jean
**Spaced Out** (1980; British) . . . . . . . . . . . . . . . Skipper
*a.k.a. Outer Touch*
• 1:07—Brief breasts making love with Willy in bed. Lit with red light.
The Pirate Movie (1982; Australian). . . . . . . . . . . .Edith

## Ferrare, Ashley

*Films:*
**Revenge of the Ninja** (1983). . . . . . . . . . . . . . Cathy
0:33—In white lingerie sitting on couch with Dave.
• 0:48—Brief breasts getting attacked by the Sumo Servant in the bedroom.
1:13—In wet white tank top talking on the phone.
Cyclone (1986) . . . . . . . . . . . . . . . . . . . . . .Carla Hastings
0:04—Working out at health club with Heather Thomas.

## Ferrare, Cristina

Former model.
Ex-wife of ex-car maker John De Lorean.
Spokeswoman for *Ultra Slim-Fast.*
*Films:*
**Mary, Mary, Bloody Mary** (1975) . . . . . . . . . . . .Mary
•• 0:07—Brief breasts making love with some guy on the couch just before she kills him.
••• 0:41—Breasts when Greta helps pull down Ferrare's top to take a bath.
1:12—Bun and brief silhouette of left breast getting out of bed and getting dressed.
*Made for Cable TV:*
Dream On: Nightmare on Bleecker Street (1992; HBO)
. . . . . . . . . . . . . . . . . . . . . . . . . . . . . . . . . . . . . . Laura
*Made for TV Movies:*
Perry Mason: The Case of the Telltale Talk Show Host (1993). . . . . . . . . . . . . . . . . . . . . . . . . . .Judith Jansen
*TV:*
Incredible Sunday (1988-89). . . . . . . . . . . . . . Co-Host
Shame On You! (1993- ) . . . . . . . . . . . . . . . . . .Hostess

## Ferratti, Rebecca

*Films:*
Three Amigos (1986) . . . . . . . . . . . . . . . . . Hot Señorita
Beverly Hills Cop II (1987). . . . . . . . . . Playboy Playmate
Cheerleader Camp (1987). . . . . . . . . . . .Theresa Salazar
*a.k.a. Bloody Pom Poms*
Outlaw of Gor (1987) . . . . . . . . . . . . . . . . . . . . .Talena

Silent Assassins (1988) . . . . . . . . . . . . . . . . . .Miss Amy
Gor (1989). . . . . . . . . . . . . . . . . . . . . . . . . . . . . Talena
How I Got Into College (1989). . . . Game Show Hostess
Small Kill (1991). . . . . . . . . . . . . . . . . . . . . Diana Conti
Ace Ventura: Pet Detective (1993) . . . . . . . Sexy Woman
**Hard Vice** (1994) . . . . . . . . . . . . . . . . . . . . . . . Christine
••• 0:02—Buns and breasts, getting out of bubble bath and making love on top of a customer in bed. Breasts while taking a shower.
••• 0:21—Breasts, while making love in bed with another customer.
•• 0:22—Breasts and buns, while taking a shower.
1:04—Buns in panties, while standing in bedroom. Long shot.
1:06—Upper half of buns in the shower.
*Video Tapes:*
**Playboy Video Calendar 1989** (1988). . . . . . . . .June
••• 0:21—Nude.
**Wet and Wild** (1989) . . . . . . . . . . . . . . . . . . . . Model
**Playmates at Play** (1990) . . . . . . . . . . . Gotta Dance
**Wet and Wild III** (1991) . . . . . . . . . . . . . . . . . Model
**The Best of Video Playmate Calendars** (1992)
. . . . . . . . . . . . . . . . . . . . . . . . . . . . . . . . . Playmate
•• 0:15—Brief breasts and buns during dancing segment.
••• 0:16—Breasts and buns in B&W segment.
••• 0:17—Full frontal nudity in bathtub in warehouse.
••• 0:18—Nude, doing more dancing.
**The Best of Wet and Wild** (1992). . . . . . . . . . Model
**Wet and Wild IV** (1992) . . . . . . . . . . . . . . . . Model
*Magazines:*
**Playboy** (Jun 1986). . . . . . . . . . . . . . . . . . Playmate
**Playboy's Book of Lingerie** (Jul 1991) . . . . . . .Herself
• 47—Right breast under sheer top.
**Playboy's Book of Lingerie** (Sep 1991) . . . . . .Herself
•• 24—Right breast.
**Playboy's Bathing Beauties** (Apr 1992). . . . . .Herself
••• 15—Breasts.
**Playboy's Book of Lingerie** (May 1992) . . . . .Herself
•• 61—Left breast.
••• 64—Breasts.
**Playboy's Book of Lingerie** (Jul 1992) . . . . . . .Herself
••• 34—Breasts.
**Playboy's Calendar Playmates** (Nov 1992). . .Herself
• 73—Buns.
**Playboy's Book of Lingerie** (Nov 1992) . . . . .Herself
••• 104-105—Breasts.
**Playboy's Nudes** (Dec 1992) . . . . . . . . . . . . . .Herself
••• 5—Breasts.
**Playboy's Book of Lingerie** (Jan 1993) . . . . . .Herself
•• 14-15—Upper half of breasts and partial lower frontal nudity.
Playboy (Feb 1993) . . . . . . . . . . . Being in Nothingness
**Playboy's Book of Lingerie** (May 1993) . . . . .Herself
•• 46—Breasts under sheer red bodysuit.
**Playboy's Wet & Wild Women** (Aug 1993). . .Herself
• 43—Lower frontal nudity.
••• 63—Breasts.

**Playboy's Blondes, Brunettes & Redheads**
(Sep 1993) . . . . . . . . . . . . . . . . . . . . . . . Herself
•• 58—Half of left breast.
**Playboy's Book of Lingerie** (Sep 1993) . . . . . Herself
•• 36—Buns and side of right breast.
**Playboy's Video Playmates** (Sep 1993) . . . . . Herself
••• 46-47—Right breast and partial lower frontal nudity.
**Playboy's Book of Lingerie** (Nov 1993) . . . . . Herself
••• 32—Breasts.
**Playboy's Nudes** (Dec 1993) . . . . . . . . . . . . . Herself
• 93—Buns.
**Playboy's Book of Lingerie** (Jan 1994) . . . . . . Herself
••• 8—Breasts.
**Playboy's Bathing Beauties** (Mar 1994) . . . . . Herself
••• 3—Breasts.
•• 46-47—Side of left breast and buns in T-back.
**Playboy's Book of Lingerie** (Mar 1994) . . . . . Herself
••• 50—Full frontal nudity.
**Playboy's Book of Lingerie** (May 1994) . . . . . Herself
••• 27—Breasts.
**Playboy's Book of Lingerie** (Sep 1994) . . . . . Herself
••• 24—Breasts.
•• 61—Side of left breast and buns.

## Ferréol, Andrea

*Films:*
**Submission** (1976; Italian) . . . . . . . . . . . . . . . . . Juliet
•• 0:43—Breasts in room with Franco Nero and Elaine.
**Despair** (1978; German/French) . . . . . . . . . . . . . Lydia
• 0:07—Long shot of right breast and very brief lower
frontal nudity and buns, while crawling into bed.
Left breast in closer shot, while lying in bed with Dirk
Bogarde.
•• 0:24—Long shot of right breast and buns, while
crawling into bed again. Breasts and buns in closer
shot in bed.
•• 1:21—Nude, when Bogarde takes off her clothes in
the hallway.
• 1:24—Brief breasts when Bogarde walks by her.
••• 1:25—Nude in hall and bedroom while talking to
Bogarde. Long shot of buns. Full frontal nudity while
sitting on bed, then following Bogarde around until
he leaves.
Sex on the Run (1979; German/French/Italian)
. . . . . . . . . . . . . . . . . . . . . . . . . . . . . . . . Beatrice
*a.k.a. Some Like It Cool*
*a.k.a. Casanova and Co.*
The Tin Drum (1979; German) . . . . . . . . . . . Lina Greff
La Nuit de Varennes (1983; French/Italian)
. . . . . . . . . . . . . . . . . . Madame Adelaide Gagnon
Letters to an Unknown Lover (1985) . . . . . . . . . . . Julia
A Zed and Two Noughts (1985; British) . . . Alba Bewick
The Sleazy Uncle (1991; Italian) . . . . . . . . . . . . . Teresa
Street of No Return (1991; U.S./French) . . . . . . . Rhoda
Stroke of Midnight (1991; U.S./French). . . . . . . . Wanda
*a.k.a. If the Shoe Fits*
Sweet Killing (1992; Canadian/French) . . . . Louise Cross

## Ferrer, Leilani
See: Sarelle, Leilani.

## Ferris, Irena
*Films:*
**Covergirl** (1982; Canadian) . . . . . . . . . . . . . . Kit Paget
•• 0:19—Brief breasts taking off robe and getting into
bathtub with Dee.
• 0:43—Very brief right breast sticking out of nightgown.
• 0:46—Upper half of left breast during modeling session.
• 0:47—Breasts in mirror in dressing room.
0:49—Brief breasts getting attacked by Joel.
• 0:53—Brief left breast, putting another blouse on.
• 0:53—Brief left breast, putting on blouse.
*TV:*
Cover Up (1984-85). . . . . . . . . . . . . . . . . . . . . . . Billie

## Feuer, Debra
*Films:*
Moment by Moment (1978) . . . . . . . . . . . . . . . Stacie
The Hollywood Knights (1980). . . . . . . . . . . . .Cheetah
**To Live and Die in L.A.** (1985) . . . . . . . Bianca Torres
0:58—Side view of buns, lying on bed while watching Willem Dafoe burn the counterfeit money. Long
shot.
• 1:47—Brief breasts on video tape being played back
on TV in empty house, hard to see anything.
Homeboy (1988) . . . . . . . . . . . . . . . . . . . . . . . . Ruby
**Night Angel** (1989) . . . . . . . . . . . . . . . . . . . . . . Kirstie
• 0:46—Brief side of left breast. Dark.

## Ficatier, Carol
*Video Tapes:*
**Playboy Video Calendar 1987** (1986). . . . . Playmate
**Playmates at Play** (1990). . . . . . . . . . . .Making Waves
*Magazines:*
**Playboy** (Dec 1985) . . . . . . . . . . . . . . . . . . . Playmate
**Playboy's 1987 Book of Lingerie** (Mar 1987)
. . . . . . . . . . . . . . . . . . . . . . . . . . . . . . . . . . .Herself
••• 106—Nude.
••• 108-109—Full frontal nudity.
**Playboy's Nudes** (Oct 1990) . . . . . . . . . . . . . .Herself
••• 74—Full frontal nudity.
**Playboy's Book of Lingerie** (Sep 1991) . . . . . .Herself
••• 10—Breasts.
•• 92—Breasts.
**Playboy's Book of Lingerie** (Mar 1992). . . . . .Herself
•• 17—Buns and side of left breast in sheer black bodysuit.
**Playboy's Girls of Summer '92** (Jun 1992) . . .Herself
••• 74-75—Breasts.
**Playboy's Book of Lingerie** (Jul 1992) . . . . . . .Herself
••• 82—Breasts.
**Playboy's Calendar Playmates** (Nov 1992). . .Herself
••• 53—Full frontal nudity.
**Playboy's Book of Lingerie** (Mar 1993). . . . . .Herself
••• 69—Breasts.

**Playboy's Blondes, Brunettes & Redheads**
(Sep 1993) . . . . . . . . . . . . . . . . . . . . . . . . . . . Herself
•• 82-83—Lower frontal nudity and breasts under
sheer dress.
**Playboy's Book of Lingerie** (Sep 1993) . . . . . Herself
••• 86—Breasts.
**Playboy's Book of Lingerie** (Nov 1993) . . . . . Herself
••• 8—Breasts.
**Playboy's Nudes** (Dec 1993) . . . . . . . . . . . . . Herself
•• 53—Right breast and lower frontal nudity.
**Playboy's Bathing Beauties** (Mar 1994). . . . . Herself
••• 90—Breasts.
**Playboy's Book of Lingerie** (Mar 1994) . . . . . Herself
••• 66—Breasts.
**Playboy's Book of Lingerie** (May 1994) . . . . . Herself
••• 80—Breasts.
••• 97—Breasts.
**Playmates at Play** (Jul 1994) . . . . . . . . . . . . . Herself
•• 60-61—Buns and left breast.

## Fiedler, Bea

*Films:*
**Island of 1000 Delights** . . . . . . . . . . . . . . . . . . Julia
•• 0:25—Full frontal nudity washing herself in bathtub,
then nude taking off her towel for Michael.
•• 0:27—Breasts lying on floor after making love, then
buns walking to chair.
•• 0:46—Full frontal nudity taking off her dress and
kissing Howard.
•• 0:50—Breasts in white bikini bottoms coming out of
the water to greet Howard.
••• 1:06—Breasts sitting in the sand near the beach,
then nude talking with Sylvia.
••• 1:17—Right breast (great close up) making love
with Sylvia.
••• 1:18—Breasts above Sylvia.
**Popcorn and Ice Cream** (1978; West German)
. . . . . . . . . . . . . . . . . . . . . . . . . . . . . . Policewoman
*a.k.a. Sex and Ice Cream*
••• 0:47—Full frontal nudity getting dressed.
••• 1:13—Right breast, then breasts in bed with a lover.
••• 1:14—Full frontal nudity in bed some more.
**Private Popsicle** (1982) . . . . . . . . . . . . . . . . . . . . Eva
•• 0:04—In black bra with Bobby. Upper half of left
breast, very brief side of right breast, then breasts.
••• 0:06—Full frontal nudity with Bobby in bed.
•• 0:07—More breasts with Bobby.
••• 0:08—Breasts on bed with Hughie.
•• 0:09—More breasts when her husband gets into
bed.
**Hot Chili** (1985) . . . . . . . . . . . . . . The Music Teacher
•• 0:08—Breasts, while playing the cello and being
fondled by Ricky.
0:29—Buns, while playing the violin.
•• 0:34—Nude during fight in restaurant with Chi Chi.
Hard to see because of the flashing light.
••• 0:36—Breasts lying on inflatable lounge in pool,
playing a flute.
••• 0:43—Left breast, while playing a tuba.

••• 1:01—Breasts and buns, while dancing in front of
Mr. Lieberman.
• 1:07—Buns, then right breast while dancing with
Stanley.
Up Your Anchor (1985) . . . . . . . . . . . . . . . . . . . . . n.a.
*Magazines:*
**Playboy** (Nov 1985) . . . . . . . . . . . Sex in Cinema 1985
•• 129—Right breast and lower frontal nudity, while ly-
ing on air mattress in still from *Hot Chili*.

## • Field, Angela

*Films:*
**Psycho From Texas** (1981) . . . . . . . Wheeler's Mother
•• 0:09—Breasts and buns, while making love in bed
with the salesman.
Hollywood High Part II (1984) . . . . . . . . . . . . . . . n.a.

## Field, Chelsea

*Films:*
Commando (1985) . . . . . . . . . . . . . . . . . . :. Stewardess
Perfect (1985) . . . . . . . . . . . . . . . . . . . . . . . . . . Randy
Death Spa (1987). . . . . . . . . . . . . . . . . . . . . . . . . Darla
Masters of the Universe (1987). . . . . . . . . . . . . . Teela
Prison (1987) . . . . . . . . . . . . . . . . . . Katherine Walker
Skin Deep (1989) . . . . . . . . . . . . . . . . . . . . . . . . . .Amy
**Harley Davidson and The Marlboro Man** (1991)
. . . . . . . . . . . . . . . . . . . . . . . . . . . . . . . . Virginia Slim
• 0:40—Side of left breast, sitting up in bed. Very brief
buns standing up. Don't see her face very well.
The Last Boy Scout (1991) . . . . . . . . . .Sarah Hollenbeck
**Dust Devil** (1992; British) . . . . . . . . . . Wendy Robinson
• 0:22—Very, very brief partial left breast, when stand-
ing up in bathtub.
0:50—Putting on bra, while sitting on bed.
The Dark Half (1993) . . . . . . . . . . . . . .Annie Pangburn
Snapdragon (1993) . . . . . . . . . . . . . . . . . . . . Peckham
0:11—In black bra, while making love on top of
Steven Bauer in bed.
*Made for Cable Movies:*
**Extreme Justice** (1993; HBO) . . . . . . . . . Kelly Daniels
• 0:18—In white bra, then brief left breast on sofa
with Lou Diamond Phillips.
The Birds II: Land's End (1994; Showtime) . . . . . . . .May
1:00—Coming out of the ocean in a wet, braless
white nightgown.
Royce (1994; Showtime) . . . . . . . . . . . Marnie Paymer
*Made for Cable TV:*
Dream On: A Midsummer Night's Dream On
(1993; HBO). . . . . . . . . . . . . . . . . . .Allison Knowland
*Made for TV Movies:*
Murder C.O.D. (1990) . . . . . . . . . . . . . . . . . . . . . Ellie
An Inconvenient Woman (1991) . . . . . . . Camilla Ebury
Complex of Fear (1993) . . . . . . . . . . . . '. Michelle Dolan
*TV:*
Bronx Zoo (1988) . . . . . . . . . . . . . . . . . . .Chris Barnes
Nightingales (1989) . . . . . . . . Samantha "Sam" Sullivan
Capital News (1990) . . . . . . . . . . . . . . . . Cassy Swann
Angel Falls (1993) . . . . . . . . . . . . . . . Rae Dawn Snow

# Field, Sally

*Films:*

**Stay Hungry** (1976) . . . . . . . . . . Mary Kay Farnsworth
- 0:27—Buns, then very, very brief side view of left breast jumping back into bed. Very fast, everything is a blur, hard to see anything.

Heroes (1977). . . . . . . . . . . . . . . . . . . . . . . . . . Carol
Smokey and the Bandit (1977) . . . . . . . . . . . . . . Carrie
The End (1978). . . . . . . . . . . . . . . . . . . . . . Mary Ellen
   0:26—Most of right breast, while wearing night-gown while lying in bed with Burt Reynolds.
Hooper (1978) . . . . . . . . . . . . . . . . . . . . . . . . . Gwen
Beyond the Poseidon Adventure (1979)
   . . . . . . . . . . . . . . . . . . . . . . . . . Celeste Whitman
Norma Rae (1979) . . . . . . . . . . . . . . . . . Norma Rae
   (Academy Award for Best Actress.)
   0:11—In white bra in motel room with George.
Absence of Malice (1981) . . . . . . . . . . . . . Megan Carter
Back Roads (1981) . . . . . . . . . . . . . . . . . . . . Amy Post
Kiss Me Goodbye (1982). . . . . . . . . . . . . . . Kay Villano
Places in the Heart (1984). . . . . . . . . . . Edna Spalding
   (Academy Award for Best Actress.)
Murphy's Romance (1985) . . . . . . . . . Emma Moriarity
Punchline (1988) . . . . . . . . . . . . . . . . . . Lilah Krytsick
Surrender (1988) . . . . . . . . . . . . . . . . . . Daisy Morgan
   0:06—In black slip getting up out of bed and wash-ing up in the bathroom.
Steel Magnolias (1989) . . . . . . . . . . . M'Lynn Eatenton
Not Without My Daughter (1991). . . . Betty Mahmoody
Soapdish (1991) . . . . . . . . . . . . . . . . . . . Celeste Talbert
Mrs. Doubtfire (1993). . . . . . . . . . . . . . Miranda Hillard
Forrest Gump (1994) . . . . . . . . . . . . . . . . . . . . . . n.a.

*Made for TV Movies:*

Sybil (1976) . . . . . . . . . . . . . . . . . . . . . . . . . . . Sybil
   (Emmy Award for Best Actress in a Drama Special.)

*TV:*

Gidget (1965-66) . . . . . . . . Francine "Gidget" Lawrence
The Flying Nun (1967-70). . . . . . . . . . . . Sister Bertrille
Alias Smith and Jones (1971-73) . . . . . . Clementine Hale
Girl with Something Extra (1973-74). . . . . . Sally Burton

# Finzi, Lydia

*Films:*

Alien Warrior (1985) . . . . . . . . . . . . . . . . . . . . Beverly
**My Man Adam** (1986) . . . . . . . . . . . . . . . . Sunbather
- 0:32—Brief breasts sunbathing by the swimming pool when Adam jumps into the pool and angers her.

# Fiorentino, Linda

*Films:*

**After Hours** (1985). . . . . . . . . . . . . . . . . . . . . . Kiki
   0:11—In black bra and skirt doing paper maché.
- 0:19—Breasts taking off bra in doorway while Griffin Dunne watches.
**Gotcha!** (1985) . . . . . . . . . . . . . . . . . . . . . . . Sasha
- 0:53—Brief breasts getting searched at customs.
Visionquest (1985) . . . . . . . . . . . . . . . . . . . . . . Carla

The Moderns (1988) . . . . . . . . . . . . . . . Rachel Stone
- 0:40—Breasts sitting in bathtub while John Lone shaves her armpits.
- 0:41—Right breast while turning over onto stomach in bathtub.
- 1:18—Breasts getting out of tub while covered with bubbles to kiss Keith Carradine.
Wildfire (1988). . . . . . . . . . . . . . . . . . . . . . . . . . . Kay
Queens Logic (1991) . . . . . . . . . . . . . . . . . . . . . Carla
Shout (1991) . . . . . . . . . . . . . . . . . . . . . . . . . . Molly
**Chain of Desire** (1992) . . . . . . . . . . . . Alma D'Angeli
- 0:09—Very brief left breast, while rolling over in bed.
**The Last Seduction** (1994). . . . . . . . . Bridget Gregory
- 0:31—Breasts, while walking around the house, gathering her clothes and getting dressed.
- 0:37—Brief side view of buns during pan shot from her feet to her head, while she's lying in bed.
- 0:50—Very brief breasts, buns, then left breast while making love in bed with Peter Berg.
   1:41—Breasts under sheer white blouse.

*Made for Cable Movies:*

The Neon Empire (1989) . . . . . . . . . . . . . . . . . . Lucy
**Beyond the Law** (1992; HBO). . . . . . . . . . . . . Renee
- 0:52—Breasts while making love with Charlie Sheen. Brief buns in T-back panties.
Acting on Impulse (1993; Showtime) . . . . . Susan Gittes

*Made for Cable TV:*

**Strangers: The Last Game** (1992; HBO) . . . . . . Helen
   (Available on video tape on *Strangers*.)
- 0:07—Left breast, three times, making love with James Remar when Etienne walks by. Dark.

# Fischer, Vera

*Films:*

**I Love You** (1982; Brazilian) . . . . . . . . Barbara Bergman
*a.k.a. Eu Te Amo*
- 0:31—Left breast while in front of TV and in chair with Paulo.
- 0:46—Left breast sticking out of nightgown. Silhou-ette of breasts while getting up. Full frontal nudity after taking off nightgown.
- 0:47—Nude in bed with Paulo.
- 1:05—Breasts on couch with Paulo.
- 1:09—Breasts on TV while opening her dress.
**Love Strange Love** (1982; Brazilian) . . . . . . . . . Anna
- 0:23—Brief breasts and lower frontal nudity in bath-tub. Breasts and buns, getting out.
- 0:38—Breasts making love with Dr. Osmar.
- 0:39—Brief buns, while lying in bed.
- 1:19—Breasts in bed with Dr. Osmar when Hugo watches.
The Fifth Monkey (1990) . . . . . . . . . . . . . . Mrs. Watts

# Fisher, Frances

*Films:*

Can She Bake a Cherry Pie? (1983) . . . . . . . . . . Louise
Tough Guys Don't Dance (1987) . . . . . . . . Jessica Pond
Lost Angels (1989). . . . . . . . . . . . . . . . . . Judith Loftis
Patty Hearst (1989) . . . . . . . . . . . . . . . . . . . Yolanda

Pink Cadillac (1989) . . . . . . . . . . . . . . . . . . . . . . . . n.a.
**Frame Up** (1990). . . . . . . . . . . . . . . . . . . . Jo Westlake
•• 0:52—Breasts, lying back in bed with Wings Hauser.
•• 0:54—Left breast, while lying in bed with Hauser.
Welcome Home Roxy Carmichael (1990)
. . . . . . . . . . . . . . . . . . . . . . . . . . . Rochelle Bossetti
Frame Up II (1991) . . . . . . . . . . . . . . . . . . . . . . . . Jo
*a.k.a. Deadly Conspiracy*
L.A. Story (1991). . . . . . . . . . . . . . . . . . . . . . . . June
Unforgiven (1992) . . . . . . . . . . . . . . Strawberry Alice
Molly & Gina (1993). . . . . . . . . . . . . . . . . . . . . . n.a.
*Made for Cable Movies:*
Devlin (1991; Showtime) . . . . . . . . . . . . . . . Maryellen
Attack of the 50 ft. Woman (1993; HBO) . . Dr. Cushing

## FitzGerald, Helen
*Films:*
Nuns on the Run (1990; British) . . . . . . . . . . . . . Tracey
**Close My Eyes** (1991; British) . . . . . . . . . Scottish Girl
•• 0:08—Nude, lying down, then getting up in room
with Richard.
*Magazines:*
**Playboy** (Nov 1992) . . . . . . . . . . Sex in Cinema 1992
•• 146—Left breast and lower frontal nudity, lying on
the floor with Clive Owen from *Close My Eyes*.

## • Fitzgerald, Tara
*Films:*
**Hear My Song** (1991; British) . . . . . . . . . Nancy Doyle
•• 0:07—Brief breasts in bed, then nude, getting out of
bed and getting dressed while angry at Micky.
**Sirens** (1993; Australian) . . . . . . . . . . Estella Campion
*Made for TV Movies:*
Fall From Grace (1994) . . . . . . . . . . . Catherine Pradler

## Flaherty, Maureen
*Films:*
**Shadowzone** (1989). . . . . . . . . . . . . . . . . . . Jenna
•• 0:13—Breasts lying under plastic cover.
• 0:18—Breasts on table getting operated on.
•• 1:11—Breasts again under plastic cover several
times.
•• 1:17—Brief breasts again, then full frontal nudity.
• 1:24—Breasts alive under the plastic cover.
Rich Girl (1991). . . . . . . . . . . . . . . Girl in Restroom #1
**Bikini Summer 2** (1992) . . . . . . . . . . . . . . . . Bridget
•• 0:04—Breasts, waking up in bed in the morning
with William.
••• 0:29—Breasts in bed with William.
The Naked Truth (1992) . . . . . . . . . . . . . Miss Romania
0:24—In sexy red swimsuit in the boy's hotel room
with the other contestants.

## Flanagan, Fionnula
*Films:*
Ulysses (1967; U.S./British) . . . . . . . . Gerty MacDowell
Sinful Davey (1969; British). . . . . . . . . . . . . Penelope

Crossover (1980; Canadian). . . . . . . . . . . . . Abadaba
*a.k.a. Mr. Patman*
• 0:27—Brief breasts opening her robe and flashing
James Coburn.
**James Joyce's Women** (1983). . . . . . . . . Molly Bloom
• 0:48—Brief breasts getting out of bed.
••• 0:56—Breasts getting back into bed.
••• 1:02—Full frontal nudity masturbating in bed talk-
ing to herself. Very long scene—9 minutes!
Reflections (1984; British). . . . . . . . . . Charlotte Lawless
Youngblood (1986) . . . . . . . . . . . . . . . . . . Miss McGill
P.K. and the Kid (1987) . . . . . . . . . . . . . . . . . . . Flo
Mad at the Moon (1993) . . . . . . . . . . . . . . . Mrs. Hill
Money for Nothing (1993). . . . . . . . . . . . . Mrs. Coyle
*Made for Cable Movies:*
While Mile (1994; HBO) . . . . . . . . . . . . . Gena Karns
*Miniseries:*
Rich Man, Poor Man (1976). . . . . . . . . . . . . . Clothilde
*Made for TV Movies:*
Nightmare in Badham County (1976) . . . . . . . . . Dulce
(Nudity added for video tape.)
Mary White (1977). . . . . . . . . . . . . . . . . Sallie White
Young Love, First Love (1979) . . . . . . . . . . . . Audrey
The Ewok Adventure (1984). . . . . . . . . . . . . Catarine
A Winner Never Quits (1986). . . . . . . . . Mrs. Wyshner
*TV:*
How the West was Won (1978-79)
. . . . . . . . . . . . . . . . . . . . . . . . Aunt Molly Culhane

## • Flannigan, Maureen
*Films:*
**Teenage Bonnie and Klepto Clyde** (1993). . . Bonnie
• 0:26—Very brief breasts, while climbing into back
seat of car.
••• 0:34—In black bra and panties, lying on bed when
Clyde pours money all over her. Right breast after
taking off bra. Breasts while making love.
*TV:*
Out of This World (1987-91) . . . . . . . . . . . . . . . Evie

## Floria, Holly
*Films:*
**Presumed Guilty** (1990). . . . . . . . . . . . . Mary Austin
• 1:02—Side view of left breast, very brief lower frontal nudity and buns, while making love with Jessie.
**Bikini Island** (1991). . . . . . . . . . . . . . . . Annie Kelly
• 0:03—Buns in panties, then breasts in shower (seen
through plastic shower curtain). Don't see her face.
0:28—Buns in one piece white swimsuit at the
beach.
• 0:35—Buns in the shower. Don't see her face.
Dark Rider (1991). . . . . . . . . . . . . . . . . . . . . . Dani
Netherworld (1991). . . . . . . . . . . . . . . . Diane Palmer
Private Wars (1993) . . . . . . . . . . . . . . . . . . . Ronnie
*TV:*
Acapulco H.E.A.T. (1993- ) . . . . . . . . . . . . . . . . n.a.

# Fluegel, Darlanne

*Films:*

Eyes of Laura Mars (1978). . . . . . . . . . . . . . . . . . . Lulu
Battle Beyond the Stars (1980) . . . . . . . . . . . . Nanelia
The Last Fight (1983) . . . . . . . . . . . . . . . . . . . . . . Sally
Once Upon a Time in America (1984). . . . . . . . . . . Eve
(Long version reviewed.)
**To Live and Die in L.A.** (1985) . . . . . . . . . Ruth Lanier
  •• 0:44—Brief breasts and buns, in bed when William
  Petersen comes home.
  1:29—In stockings on couch with Petersen.
  • 1:50—Very brief breasts on bed with Petersen in a
  flashback.
Running Scared (1986) . . . . . . . . . . . . . . Anna Costanzo
**Tough Guys** (1986). . . . . . . . . . . . . . . . . . . Skye Foster
  • 0:47—Very brief side view of right breast, leaning
  over to kiss Kirk Douglas.
Border Heat (1988) . . . . . . . . . . . . . . . . . . Peggy Martin
  0:23—In black bra straddling Ryan in the bedroom.
Bulletproof (1988). . . . . . . . . . . . . . . . . .Devon Shepard
**Freeway** (1988). . . . . . . . . . . . . Sarah "Sunny" Harper
  • 0:27—In bra in bathroom taking a pill, then very,
  very brief right breast, getting into bed.
  • 0:28—Brief left breast putting on robe and getting
  out of bed.
Lock Up (1989). . . . . . . . . . . . . . . . . . . . . . . . . Melissa
**Project: Alien** (1990) . . . . . . . . . . . . ."Bird" McNamara
  • 0:18—Buns, getting out of bed and putting on a ki-
  mono.
Pet Sematary II (1992) . . . . . . . . . . . . . . Renee Hallow
  • 1:04—Probably a body double wearing a dog mask,
  breasts on top of Anthony Edwards during night-
  mare, lit with blue light.
Scanner Cop (1993) . . . . . . . . . . . . . . Dr. Joan Alden
*Made for Cable Movies:*
Slaughter of the Innocents (1993; HBO)
. . . . . . . . . . . . . . . . . . . . . . . . . . . Susan Broderick
*TV:*
Crime Story (1986-89) . . . . . . . . . . . . . . . .Julie Torello
Wiseguy (1989). . . . . . . . . . . . . . . . . . . . . . . . . . Lacey
Hunter (1990-91) . . . . . . . . . . . . . . . . . Joanne Malinski
*Magazines:*
**Playboy** (Aug 1978) . . . . . . . . . . . . . . . ."Eyes" Has It
  •• 96—Left breast.
  • 99—Breasts in bed.

# • Flynn, Joni

*Films:*

**Felicity** (1978; Australian) . . . . . . . . . . . . . . . Mei Ling
  ••• 0:38—Nude in bath with Glory Annen and two oth-
  er girls, then getting massaged. Long scene.
  ••• 0:43—Breasts and buns, making love on boat with a
  guy.
  ••• 1:13—Nude, making love in bed with Glory. Long
  scene.
Octopussy (1983; British) . . . . . . . . . . . Octopussy Girl
*Magazines:*
**Penthouse** (Oct 1976) . . . . . . . . . . . . . . . . Joni Flynn
  ••• 108-113—Nude.

# Fonda, Bridget

Daughter of actor Peter Fonda.
Granddaughter of actor Henry Fonda.
*Films:*

You Can't Hurry Love (1984) . . . . . . . . . . . . . . . Peggy
**Aria** (1987; U.S./British) . . . . . . . . . . . . . . . .Girl Lover
  ••• 0:59—Brief right breast, then buns and breasts lying
  down on bed in hotel room in Las Vegas.
  •• 1:02—Breasts in the bathtub with her boyfriend.
**Scandal** (1989). . . . . . . . . . . . . . . Mandy Rice-Davis
(Unrated version reviewed.)
  • 0:20—Brief breasts dressed as an Indian dancing
  while Christine tries to upstage her.
  0:54—In white lingerie, then lower frontal nudity in
  sheer nightgown in room with a guy.
  1:05—Brief buns walking back into bedroom. Long
  shot.
Shag (1989). . . . . . . . . . . . . . . . . . . . . Melaina Buller
Frankenstein Unbound (1990) . . . . . . . . . . . . . . . Mary
The Godfather, Part III (1990). . . . . . . . Grace Hamilton
Out of the Rain (1990). . . . . . . . . . . . . . . . . . . . . . .Jo
Strapless (1990). . . . . . . . . . . . . . . . . . . . Amy Hempel
Doc Hollywood (1991). . . . . . . . . . . . . . . . Nancy Lee
Drop Dead Fred (1991) . . . . . . . . . . . . . . Annabella
Iron Maze (1991). . . . . . . . . . . . . . . . . . . . . . . . Chris
**Leather Jackets** (1991) . . . . . . . . . . . . . . . . . . Claudi
  • 0:15—Brief breasts on bed with Mickey.
Army of Darkness (1992) . . . . . . . . . . . . . . . . . .Linda
**Single White Female** (1992) . . . . . . . . . . . . . . .Allie
  • 0:04—Very, very brief right breast, while getting out
  of bed with Sam. Very brief side view of right breast,
  then buns, while walking to turn off answering machine.
  • 0:05—Brief breasts, grabbing her clothes.
  • 0:34—Buns and brief breasts, getting out of bed.
  Dark.
  • 1:18—Brief right breast, in gaping nightgown while
  kneeling on bathroom floor after throwing up in the
  toilet.
  1:20—Brief silhouette of left breast, while changing
  clothes.
singles (1992) . . . . . . . . . . . . . . . . . . . Janet Livermore
Bodies, Rest & Motion (1993) . . . . . . . . . . . . . . . Beth
Little Buddha (1993) . . . . . . . . . . . . . . . . . Lisa Conrad
**Point of No Return** (1993). . . . . . . . . . . . . . Maggie
  • 0:49—Brief right breast, while making love with J.P.
It Could Happen to You (1994) . . . . . . . . . Yvonne Biasi

# Fonda, Jane

Daughter of actor Henry Fonda.
Sister of actor Peter Fonda.
Has done a lot of exercise video tapes.
Wife of Television Tychoon Ted Turner.
*Films:*

Period of Adjustment (1962) . . . . . . . . Isabel Haverstick
Joy House (1964) . . . . . . . . . . . . . . . . . . . . .Melinda
Cat Ballou (1965). . . . . . . . . . . . . . . . . . . . Cat Ballou
The Chase (1966). . . . . . . . . . . . . . . . . . Anna Reeves

**The Game is Over** (1966). . . . . . . . . . Renee Saccard
- 0:15—Very brief left breast, getting out of bed. Breasts in mirror when running to the door.
- 0:16—Brief breasts, several times, while behind sheer white curtain.
- 0:17—Very brief breasts, while falling onto bed.
- • 0:18—Breasts, while lying in bed with the guy.

Barefoot in the Park (1967). . . . . . . . . . . Corrie Bratter

**Barbarella** (1968; French/Italian) . . . . . . . . Barbarella
- • 0:04—Breasts getting out of space suit during opening credits in zero gravity. Hard to see because the frame is squeezed so the lettering will fit.

They Shoot Horses, Don't They? (1969) . . . . . . . . Gloria

**Klute** (1971) . . . . . . . . . . . . . . . . . . . . . . Bree Daniel
(Academy Award for Best Actress.)
- 0:27—Side view of left and right breasts stripping in the old man's office.

A Doll's House (1973; British) . . . . . . . . . . . . . . . .Nora

Steelyard Blues (1973) . . . . . . . . . . . . . . . Iris Caine

The Blue Bird (1976). . . . . . . . . . . . . . . . . . . . . Night

Fun with Dick and Jane (1977) . . . . . . . . . .Jane Harper

Julia (1977). . . . . . . . . . . . . . . . . . . . . . Lillian Hellman

California Suite (1978) . . . . . . . . . . . Hannah Warren

Comes a Horseman (1978) . . . . . . . . . . . . . . . . Ella

**Coming Home** (1978) . . . . . . . . . . . . . . .Sally Hyde
(Academy Award for Best Actress.)
- • 1:26—Making love in bed with Jon Voight. Breasts only when her face is visible. Buns and brief left breast when you don't see a face is a body double.

The China Syndrome (1979). . . . . . . . . . Kimberly Wells

The Electric Horseman (1979). . . . . . . . . . . . . . Hallie

9 to 5 (1980) . . . . . . . . . . . . . . . . . . . . . . .Judy Bernly

On Golden Pond (1981) . . . . . . . Chelsea Thayer Wayne

Rollover (1981). . . . . . . . . . . . . . . . . . . . . .Lee Winters

Agnes of God (1985). . . . . . . . . . .Dr. Martha Livingston

**The Morning After** (1986) . . . . . . . Alex Sternbergen
- 1:08—Brief breasts making love with Jeff Bridges.

**Old Gringo** (1989) . . . . . . . . . . . . . . Harriet Winslow
- 1:24—Side of left breast, while undressing in front of Jimmy Smits. Sort of brief right breast, while lying in bed and hugging him.

Stanley and Iris (1990) . . . . . . . . . . . . . . . . . Iris King

*Made for TV Movies:*

The Dollmaker (1984). . . . . . . . . . . . . . . Gertie Nevels
(Emmy Award for Best Actress.)

## Fondren, Debra Jo

*Video Tapes:*

**Playboy Playmates in Paradise** (1992) . . . Playmate

**Sexy Lingerie V** (1992) . . . . . . . . . . . . . . . . .Model

*Magazines:*

**Playboy** (Feb 1977) . . . . . . .Playboy's Playmate Preview
- • 125—Right breast and lower frontal nudity.

**Playboy** (Sep 1977). . . . . . . . . . . . . . . . . . Playmate

**Playboy** (Dec 1977). . . . . . . . . . . . . . . Dear Playboy
- 18—Partial right breast.

**Playboy's Girls of Summer '86** (Aug 1986) . . Herself
- • • 8—Full frontal nudity.

- 103—Upper half of breasts while wearing swimsuit bottom.

**Playboy's Nudes** (Oct 1990) . . . . . . . . . . . . . .Herself
- • • 100—Buns.

**Playboy's Book of Lingerie** (Sep 1992) . . . . . .Herself
- • • • 81—Full frontal nudity.

**Playboy's Nudes** (Dec 1992) . . . . . . . . . . . . . .Herself
- • • • 93—Left breast and most of right breast.

**Playboy's Book of Lingerie** (Jan 1993) . . . . . .Herself
- • • • 80—Full frontal nudity.

**Playboy's Blondes, Brunettes & Redheads** (Sep 1993) . . . . . . . . . . . . . . . . . . . . . . . . . . . . .Herself
- • • • 6—Full frontal nudity.

**Playboy** (Jan 1994). . . . . . . . . . . 40 Memorable Years
- • • • 92—Breasts.

**Playboy's Book of Lingerie** (Jan 1994) . . . . . .Herself
- • • • 50—Left breast and lower frontal nudity.

**Playboy's Book of Lingerie** (Jul 1994). . . . . . .Herself
- • • • 21—Full frontal nudity.

## Fontaine, Alisha

*Films:*

The Gang that Couldn't Shoot Straight (1971) . . . . . . . . . . . . . . . . . . . . . . . . . . . . . . . . . .Jelly's Girl

The Gambler (1974) . . . . . . . . . . . . . . . . .Howie's Girl

**French Quarter** (1978)
. . . . . . . . . .Gertrude "Trudy" Dix/Christine Delaplane
- 0:12—Dancing on stage for the first time. Buns in G-string. Breasts in large black pasties.
- 0:47—Brief left breast several times, posing for Mr. Beloq.
- 0:49—Left breast again.
- • 1:13—Breasts during auction.
- • 1:18—Brief breasts, then buns making love with Tom, then breasts again.
- 1:26—Brief breasts getting her top pulled down during party.
- 1:31—Brief breasts getting tied down during voodoo ceremony.
- • 1:32—More breasts tied down during ceremony.

## • Forbes, Michelle

*Films:*

The Playboys (1992) . . . . . . . . . . . . . .Maggie Rudden

**Kalifornia** (1993). . . . . . . . . . . . . . . Carrie Loughlin
(Unrated version reviewed.)
- 0:34—Very, very brief upper half of lower frontal nudity while in bed with David Duchovny.

*TV:*

Star Trek: The Next Generation (1991-93) . . . . . . . . . . . . . . . . . . . . . . . . . . . . .Ensign Laren Ro

## Ford, Anitra

*Films:*

**The Big Bird Cage** (1972). . . . . . . . . . . . . . . . Terry
- 0:15—Left breast and buns taking shower. Brief lower frontal nudity after putting shirt on when leaving.
0:19—Brief lower frontal nudity turing around.
- 0:44—Brief left breast during gang rape.

1:14—Brief left breast in gaping dress. Dark.

**Invasion of the Bee Girls** (1973) ... Dr. Susan Harris
••• 0:47—Breasts and buns undressing in front of a guy in front of a fire.

**Stacey!** (1973)................... Tish Chambers
a.k.a. *Stacey and Her Gangbusters*
•• 0:13—Breasts in bed making love with Frank.

Dead People (1974) ...................... Laura

The Longest Yard (1974).................. Melissa
0:01—Breasts under see-though red nightgown with Burt Reynolds.

# Ford, Maria

*Films:*

**Dance of the Damned** (1988)............Teacher
• 0:11—Brief breasts during dance routine in club wearing black panties, garter belt and stockings.

**Stripped to Kill II** (1988)................. Shady
•• 0:21—Breasts, dancing on table in front of the detective. Buns, walking away.
• 0:40—Brief upper half of left breast in the alley with the detective.
•• 0:52—Breasts and buns during dance routine.

**The Haunting of Morella** (1989) .......... Diane
••• 1:00—Breasts taking off nightgown and swimming in pond, then walking to waterfall.

**The Turn-On** (1989) ..................... Maria
a.k.a. *Le Clic*
••• 0:21—Breasts, then nude while dancing on stage after getting turned on by the black box.

**Deathstalker IV: Match of Titans** (1990) .. Dionara
•• 0:13—Brief buns, then breasts, getting dressed in cave.
• 0:19—Left breast, while kissing Deathstalker in bed.

**Masque of the Red Death** (1990)......... Isabella

**Naked Obsession** (1990) ........... Lynne Hauser
0:16—Dancing on stage doing strip tease. Wearing bra, panties, garter belt and stockings.
••• 0:18—Buns in G-string.
••• 0:20—Breasts and buns in G-string, dancing on stage in front of William Katt. Long scene.
••• 0:23—Nude, dancing with Katt's necktie.
••• 0:34—Nude, on stage at end of another dance routine.
••• 0:44—Breasts in her apartment with Katt.
••• 0:45—Breasts and buns on top of Katt in bed while he gently strangles her with his necktie for oxygen deprivation.
•• 0:47—Breasts in bed after making love with Katt.

**The Rain Killer** (1990) ..................... Satin
•• 0:29—Nude, dancing on stage in club. Backlit too much.
••• 0:37—Breasts in bedroom with Jordan, taking off her clothes, getting tied to bed. Long scene.
• 0:41—Breasts lying on her back on bed, dead.
• 0:48—Same scene from 0:41 when Rosewall looks at B&W police photo.

**Slumber Party Massacre 3** (1990) .......... Maria

**Body Chemistry 2: Voice of a Stranger** (1991)
............................. Uncredited Victim
•• 0:37—Breasts in bed during flashback. (This scene is from *Naked Obsession*.)

Future Kick (1991) ....................... Dancer

**Ring of Fire** (1991) ......................... Julie
•• 1:12—In black lingerie, then breasts, making love with Don Wilson.
• 1:14—Brief left breast, lying in bed, while he undresses her.
••• 1:15—Breasts, several, lying on her back in bed while making love.
• 1:17—Brief breasts, sitting up in bed afterward.

**Final Judgement** (1992) .................. Nicole
••• 0:20—Breasts and buns in G-string while stripping and dancing on stage. Nice bending over action.
••• 0:39—In red bra and panties, then breasts and buns while dancing on stage.
••• 0:52—Breasts and buns in G-string while dancing on stage.
• 0:56—Very, very brief breast, while putting a towel around herself after getting out of the shower.
•• 0:58—Breasts while making love with Brad Dourif in bed during daydream.

Mind Twister (1992) ............. Melanie Duncan
(Unrated version reviewed.)

Ring of Fire II: Blood and Steel (1992) ........... Julie

**The Unnameable II** (1992) ......... Alyda Winthrop
•• 0:52—Buns, when her long hair moves out of the way. Partial tip of right breast when looking at the telephone.
• 0:53—Brief buns and side of right breast in bedroom.
•• 0:54—Buns and breasts while checking out the bed.
• 0:57—Brief buns, while getting out of bed.
•• 0:58—Buns and brief breasts in bedroom with Mary.
• 1:01—Right breast in gaping nightgown while kneeling on elevator floor.
• 1:22—Brief glimpses of right breast in gaping nightgown.
• 1:32—Very brief right breast in gaping nightgown while crawling on the floor.

**Angel of Destruction** (1994) ........... Jo Alwood
••• 0:41—Breast and buns in panties while using martial arts on the bad guys!
••• 0:45—Breasts, while making love with Aaron in bed.
••• 0:59—Breasts and buns in G-string after stripping and dancing on stage.

**Saturday Night Special** (1994) ........... Darlene
(Unrated version reviewed.)
••• 0:37—Breasts, while making love with Travis in the woods.
••• 0:50—Breasts, while making love with Travis on bed. Buns, when lying down afterwards. Great!

*Magazines:*

**Playboy** (Nov 1988).......... Sex in Cinema 1988
••• 137—Full frontal nudity standing in front of a pole.

# • *Ford, Patricia*

*Video Tapes:*

**Playboy's How to Reawaken Your Sexual Powers** (1992). . . . . . . . . . . . . . . . . . . . . . . . . . Cast Member
- 0:01—Buns in one piece swimsuit while on the beach.
- ••• 0:04—Nude, while swimming under water, working out on rock and on beach, and massaging her lover.

*Magazines:*

**Playboy's Book of Lingerie** (Jan 1993). . . . . . Herself
- •• 94-95—Left breast, buns and lower frontal nudity.

**Playboy's Book of Lingerie** (Mar 1993) . . . . . Herself
- • 34-35—Cleavage and buns.

**Playboy's Bathing Beauties** (Apr 1993) . . . . . Herself
- •• 21—Partial breasts and partial lower frontal nudity.
- ••• 75-77—Breasts and lower frontal nudity.

**Playboy's Book of Lingerie** (May 1993) . . . . . Herself
- ••• 3-7—Nude.

**Playboy's Girls of Summer '93** (Jun 1993) . . . Herself
- ••• 60-61—Nude.
- • 100—Lower frontal nudity.

**Playboy's Book of Lingerie** (Jul 1993) . . . . . . Herself
- ••• 8—Full frontal nudity.
- • 49—Lower frontal nudity.
- • 72-73—Breasts under sheer body suit.

**Playboy's Wet & Wild Women** (Aug 1993) . . Herself
- •• 18—Side of left breast.
- ••• 29—Breasts.
- ••• 59—Full frontal nudity.
- • 96—Breasts under wet body suit.

**Playboy's Blondes, Brunettes & Redheads** (Sep 1993) . . . . . . . . . . . . . . . . . . . . . . . . . . Herself
- ••• 61—Breasts.

**Playboy's Book of Lingerie** (Sep 1993) . . . . . Herself
- ••• 78—Breasts.
- • 93—Buns.

**Playboy's Nudes** (Dec 1993) . . . . . . . . . . . . . Herself
- ••• 38—Full frontal nudity.
- ••• 53—Full frontal nudity.

**Playboy's Book of Lingerie** (Jan 1994). . . . . . Herself
- • 25—Upper half of left breast.
- • 63—Buns in G-string.

**Playboy's Bathing Beauties** (Mar 1994). . . . . Herself
- ••• 12-13—Breasts.
- ••• 55—Breasts.
- • 63—Right breast.
- ••• 97—Breasts.

**Playboy's Book of Lingerie** (Mar 1994) . . . . . Herself
- • 57—Lower frontal nudity.
- ••• 83—Full frontal nudity.

**Playboy's Book of Lingerie** (May 1994) . . . . . Herself
- • 34—Lower frontal nudity.
- • 45—Breasts.

**Playboy's Girls of Summer '94** (Jul 1994) . . . Herself
- •• 82—Left breast.
- ••• 92—Breasts.

# *Foreman, Deborah*

a.k.a. Debby Lynn Foreman.

*Films:*

I'm Dancing as Fast as I Can (1981) . . . . . . . . . . Cindy
Valley Girl (1983) . . . . . . . . . . . . . . . . . . . . . . . . . Julie
Real Genius (1985). . . . . . . . . . . . . . . . . . . . . . .Susan

**3:15—The Moment of Truth** (1986)
. . . . . . . . . . . . . . . . . . . . . . . . . . . Sherry Havilland
- 0:26—Very brief blurry buns and side view of left breast jumping out of bed when her parents come home. Long shot, hard to see anything.

April Fool's Day (1986). . . . . . . . . . . . . . . . .Muffy/Buffy
Destroyer (1988) . . . . . . . . . . . . . . . . . . . Susan Malone
Waxwork (1988) . . . . . . . . . . . . . . . . . . . . . . . . . .Sarah
Friends, Lovers & Lunatics (1989). . . . . . . . . . . . .Annie
Sundown: The Vampire in Retreat (1989). . . . . . . Sandy
Lunatics: A Love Story (1991). . . . . . . . . . . . . . . Nancy

# *Foreman, Michelle*

*Films:*

**Stripped to Kill** (1987) . . . . . . . . . . . . . . . . . . . .Angel
- ••• 0:02—Breasts dancing on stage for Norman Fell.

**Sunset Strip** (1992) . . . . . . . . . . . . . . . . . . . . Heather
- •• 0:29—In black bra and G-string, practicing her dance routine in her living room.
- 0:42—Brief back side of left breast, while in the shower.
- 0:46—In black bra and G-string, practicing some more.
- •• 1:24—Buns in G-string, while dancing during contest.
- •• 1:28—Breasts in the shower with Jeff Conaway. Don't see her face well, but it looks like her.
- ••• 1:30—Buns in G-string dancing on stage and breasts (finally!) at the end.

*Made for Cable Movies:*

**Fear** (1991; Showtime) . . . . . . . . . . . Gale the Stripper
- • 0:50—Breasts and buns dancing in bar. Hard to see because seen through the killer's eyes.

# *Forte, Valentina*

*Films:*

**Cut and Run** (1985; Italian) . . . . . . . . . . . . . . . . . Ana
- ••• 0:29—Brief left breast being made love to in bed. Then breasts sitting up in bed and left side view and buns taking a shower.

Inferno in Diretta (1985; Italian). . . . . . . . . . . . . . n.a.

# *Fortea, Isabelle*

*Films:*

**Affairs of the Heart** (1992) . . . . . . . . . . . . . . .Karen
- ••• 1:06—Breasts making love in cabin with Tom.

**Marilyn Chambers' Bedtime Stories** (1993) Tatiana
- ••• 0:18—Breasts and buns in red G-string, after taking off dress with Bart's help.
- ••• 0:25—Breasts and buns with Bart, then in shower. Squished breasts against the glass.
- • 0:33—Breasts in open solid color robe in bathroom.
- • 1:17—Breasts in out take with Bart.

*Magazines:*
**Playboy's Girls of Summer '92** (Jun 1992)... Herself
•• 46-47—Left breast.
**Playboy's Book of Lingerie** (Jul 1992) ...... Herself
•• 46-47—Right breast and buns.
**Playboy's Book of Lingerie** (Sep 1992) ..... Herself
•• 107—Breasts.
**Playboy's Girls of the World** (Oct 1992) .... Herself
••• 3-7—Nude.
**Playboy's Book of Lingerie** (Nov 1992) ..... Herself
••• 26-27—Side view of left breast and buns.
**Playboy's Book of Lingerie** (Jan 1993)...... Herself
• 20-21—Side view of right breast.
**Playboy's Book of Lingerie** (Mar 1993) ..... Herself
••• 20—Full frontal nudity.
••• 58—Breasts.
**Playboy's Bathing Beauties** (Apr 1993) ..... Herself
••• 34-35—Breasts.
••• 101—Breasts.
**Playboy's Book of Lingerie** (May 1993) ..... Herself
• 54—Partial lower frontal nudity.
**Playboy's Girls of Summer '93** (Jun 1993)... Herself
•• 50—Left breast.
•• 66—Right breast.
**Playboy's Wet & Wild Women** (Aug 1993) .. Herself
••• 33—Breasts.
**Playboy's Blondes, Brunettes & Redheads**
(Sep 1993) ........................... Herself
••• 99—Full frontal nudity.
**Playboy's Book of Lingerie** (Sep 1993) ..... Herself
• 38—Partial lower frontal nudity.
**Playboy's Book of Lingerie** (Nov 1993) ..... Herself
••• 21—Breasts.
•• 32-33—Buns and side of right breast.
**Playboy's Nudes** (Dec 1993) .............. Herself
••• 37—Full frontal nudity.
••• 86-87—Breasts.
**Playboy's Book of Lingerie** (Jan 1994)...... Herself
••• 22—Breasts.
••• 72—Breasts.
**Playboy's Girls of Summer '94** (Jul 1994) ... Herself
••• 75—Breasts.

## • Foss, Shirlene

*Films:*
Impure Thoughts (1986)......................n.a.
**Dead Aim** (1987) ........................... B.J.
• 0:14—Buns in G-string and white top.
• 0:55—Brief buns in G-string while dancing on stage
in bridal outfit.
Funland (1987)...............................n.a.

## Fossey, Brigitte

*Films:*
Forbidden Games (1953; French) ........... Paulette
**Going Places** (1974; French)......... Young Mother
••• 0:32—In bra, then breasts in open blouse on the
train when she lets Pierrot suck the milk out of her
breasts.

Blue Country (1977; French) ................ Louise
The Man Who Loved Women (1977; French)
.............................. Benevieve Bigey
Quintet (1979)............................ Vivia
La Boum (1980; French)................. Francoise
Chanel Solitaire (1981)................. Adrienne
**Enigma** (1982)............................Karen
• 0:39—Brief breasts after undressing in jail cell. Very
brief lower frontal nudity and buns, shielding herself
from the light.
•• 0:40—Breasts getting interrogated.
Cinema Paradiso (1988; Italian/French) ........ Elena

## Foster, Jodie

*Films:*
Kansas City Bomber (1972) ................... Rita
Napolean and Samantha (1972) .......... Samantha
One Little Indian (1973)................... Martha
Tom Sawyer (1973) ................ Becky Thatcher
Alice Doesn't Live Here Anymore (1975) ...... Audrey
Bugsy Malone (1976)...................... Tallulah
Echoes of Summer (1976) ......... Deirdre Striden
The Little Girl Who Lives Down the Lane
(1976; Canadian)....................... Rynn
Taxi Driver (1976) ................ Iris Steensman
Candleshoe (1977)........................ Casey
Freaky Friday (1977)............. Annabel Andrews
Carny (1980) ............................ Donna
Foxes (1980) ............................ Jeanie
O'Hara's Wife (1982) ............. Barbara O'Hara
The Hotel New Hampshire (1984) ........... Franny
Siesta (1987) ............................ Nancy
0:47—In a black slip combing Ellen Barkin's hair.
0:50—In a slip again in bedroom with Barkin.
**The Accused** (1988)............... Sarah Tobias
(Academy Award for Best Actress.)
• 1:27—Brief breasts a few times during rape scene on
pinball machine by Dan and Bob.
Five Corners (1988) ........................ Linda
**Backtrack** (1989)................... Anne Benton
*a.k.a. Catch Fire*
• 0:50—Breasts behind textured shower door.
••• 0:51—Breasts, leaning out of the shower to get her
towel. Very, very brief side of left breast and buns,
while drying herself off in bedroom. Side of left
breast and buns, while putting on slip.
Silence of the Lambs (1990)......... Clarice Starling
(Academy Award for Best Actress 1992.)
Little Man Tate (1991) ................. Dede Tate
Shadows and Fog (1991)................. Prostitute
Sommersby (1993) ............. Laurel Sommersby
Maverick (1994)............... Annabelle Bransford
*Made for Cable Movies:*
The Blood of Others (1984; HBO) .....Helene Bertrand
*TV:*
Bob & Carol & Ted & Alice (1973)
....................... Elizabeth Henderson
Paper Moon (1974-75) ................. Addie Pray

# Foster, Karen

*Video Tapes:*
**Playboy Video Calendar 1991** (1990) . . . . . . .March
**Playboy Video Centerfold: Deborah Driggs &
Karen Foster** (1990) . . . . . . . . . . . . . . . . . Playmate
••• 0:24—Baton twirling, outside on bed, other miscel-
laneous things. Nude.
**Sexy Lingerie II** (1990) . . . . . . . . . . . . . . . . . .Model
**Wet and Wild II** (1990) . . . . . . . . . . . . . . . . .Model
**Sexy Lingerie III** (1991) . . . . . . . . . . . . . . . . .Model
**Wet and Wild III** (1991) . . . . . . . . . . . . . . . . .Model
**The Best of Sexy Lingerie** (1992) . . . . . . . . . .Model
**The Best of Wet and Wild** (1992) . . . . . . . . .Model

*Magazines:*
**Playboy** (Oct 1989) . . . . . . . . . . . . . . . . . . Playmate
**Playboy's Nudes** (Oct 1990) . . . . . . . . . . . . . Herself
••• 23—Full frontal nudity.
**Playboy's Book of Lingerie** (Jan 1991) . . . . . . Herself
••• 101—Breasts.
**Playboy's Book of Lingerie** (Mar 1991) . . . . . Herself
••• 71—Full frontal nudity.
••• 95—Breasts.
**Playboy's Book of Lingerie** (Jul 1991) . . . . . . Herself
• 62—Right breast and partial lower frontal nudity.
**Playboy's Book of Lingerie** (Sep 1991) . . . . . Herself
• 18—Partial lower frontal nudity.
**Playboy's Book of Lingerie** (Nov 1991) . . . . . Herself
••• 10-11—Breasts and upper half of buns.
**Playboy's Book of Lingerie** (Jan 1992) . . . . . . Herself
••• 9—Breasts and partial lower frontal nudity.
**Playboy's Book of Lingerie** (Mar 1992) . . . . . Herself
•• 68—Full frontal nudity.
**Playboy's Book of Lingerie** (May 1992) . . . . . Herself
••• 20—Full frontal nudity.
**Playboy's Book of Lingerie** (Jul 1992) . . . . . . Herself
•• 31—Breasts under necklace.
••• 76-77—Breasts.
**Playboy's Career Girls** (Aug 1992)
. . . . . . . . . . . . . . . . . . . . . . . . . Baywatch Playmates
•• 6—Right breast and partial lower frontal nudity.
**Playboy's Book of Lingerie** (Sep 1992) . . . . . Herself
••• 90—Full frontal nudity.
**Playboy's Calendar Playmates** (Nov 1992) . . Herself
••• 90—Full frontal nudity.
••• 106—Full frontal nudity.
**Playboy's Book of Lingerie** (Nov 1992) . . . . . Herself
••• 21—Breasts and partial lower frontal nudity.
**Playboy's Book of Lingerie** (Jan 1993) . . . . . . Herself
•• 99—Partial side view of left breast and buns.
**Playboy's Wet & Wild Women** (Aug 1993) . . Herself
••• 45—Full frontal nudity.
**Playboy's Blondes, Brunettes & Redheads**
(Sep 1993) . . . . . . . . . . . . . . . . . . . . . . . . . . Herself
••• 16—Buns and left breast.
**Playboy's Video Playmates** (Sep 1993) . . . . . Herself
••• 48-49—Breasts and buns.
**Playboy's Book of Lingerie** (Nov 1993) . . . . . Herself
•• 105—Upper half of breasts and lower frontal nudity.

**Playboy's Nudes** (Dec 1993) . . . . . . . . . . . . . .Herself
••• 51—Full frontal nudity.
**Playboy's Book of Lingerie** (Jan 1994) . . . . . .Herself
•• 100—Side of left breast and buns.
**Playboy's Book of Lingerie** (Mar 1994) . . . . . .Herself
•• 25—Full frontal nudity.
**Playmates at Play** (Jul 1994) . . . . . . . . . . . . .Herself
••• 70-71—Full frontal nudity.
**Playboy's Book of Lingerie** (Jul 1994) . . . . . . .Herself
••• 101—Full frontal nudity.

# Foster, Lisa Raines

a.k.a. Lisa Foster or Lisa Raines.
*Films:*
**Fanny Hill** (1981; British) . . . . . . . . . . . . . . Fanny Hill
•• 0:09—Nude, getting into bathtub, then drying her-
self off.
• 0:10—Full frontal nudity getting into bed.
••• 0:12—Full frontal nudity making love with Phoebe
in bed.
••• 0:30—Nude, making love in bed with Charles.
•• 0:49—Breasts, whipping her lover, Mr. H., in bed.
•• 0:53—Nude getting into bed with William while
Hannah watches through the keyhole.
••• 1:26—Nude, getting out of bed, then running down
the stairs to open the door for Charles.
Spring Fever (1983; Canadian) . . . . . . . . . . . . . . . . Lena
The Blade Master (1984) . . . . . . . . . . . . . . . . . . . . .Mila
*a.k.a. Ator, The Invincible*
*Made for Cable TV:*
**The Hitchhiker: Killer** . . . . . . . . . . . . . . . . . . . . Patty
• 0:02—Very brief breasts standing in the bathtub just
before getting shot.
• 0:23—Very brief breasts again in Jenny Seagrove's
flashback.
*Magazines:*
**Playboy** (Nov 1983) . . . . . . . . . . . Sex in Cinema 1983
•• 145—Breasts.

# Foster, Meg

*Films:*
**Thumb Tripping** (1972) . . . . . . . . . . . . . . . . . . Shay
• 1:19—Very, very brief breasts leaning back in field
with Jack. Long shot.
• 1:20—Breasts at night. Face is turned away from the
camera.
**Welcome to Arrow Beach** (1973) . . . Robbin Stanley
*a.k.a. Tender Flesh*
0:12—Buns and brief side view of right breast getting undressed to skinny dip in the ocean. Don't see
her face.
•• 0:40—Breasts getting out of bed.
**A Different Story** (1979) . . . . . . . . . . . . . . . . . Stella
(R-rated version reviewed.)
0:12—In white bra and panties exercising and
changing clothes in her bedroom.
•• 0:53—Breasts sitting on Perry King, rubbing cake all
over each other on bed.

• 0:59—Brief buns and side view of right breast, while getting into bed with King.

Carny (1980) ............................ Greta
Ticket to Heaven (1981; Canadian) ........... Ingrid
The Osterman Weekend (1983) .......... Ali Tanner
   0:14—Very, very brief tip of right breast after getting nightgown out of closet.
The Emerald Forest (1985) ........... Jean Markham
Masters of the Universe (1987) ............ Evil-Lyn
The Wind (1987).................... Sian Anderson
They Live (1988)......................... Holly
Leviathan (1989)....................... Martin
Relentless (1989)..................... Carol Dietz
Stepfather 2 (1989)................. Carol Grayland
Tripwire (1989)......................... Julia
Backstab (1990) .................... Sara Rudnick
Blind Fury (1990) .................. Lynn Devereaux
Jezebel's Kiss (1990) .............. Amanda Faberson
Diplomatic Immunity (1991)......... Gerta Hermann
Future Kick (1991) ................. Nancy Morgan
Relentless 2: Dead On (1991) ........... Carol Dietz
Best of the Best 2 (1992)........... Sue MacCauley
Hidden Fears (1992) ............... Maureen Dietz
Project: Shadowchaser (1992)............... Sarah
Immortal Combat (1993) .................. Quinn
*Made for Cable TV:*
The Hitchhiker: The Martyr (1989; USA) ......... n.a.
*Made for TV Movies:*
To Catch a Killer (1992; Canadian)
   ....................... City Attorney Carlson
*TV:*
Sunshine (1975) ....................... Nora
Cagney & Lacey (1982) ............. Chris Cagney

# • Fox, Jerica

*Adult Films:*
**Bobby Hollander's The Girls from Hootersville-Volume 2** (1993)..................... Herself
*Films:*
**Housewife From Hell** (1993)........... Party Girl
  ••• 0:53—In red bra and panties, then breasts while dancing beside spa, then getting into spa and sitting in spa.
**One Million Heels B.C.** (1993).......... Savannah
  ••• 0:16—In lingerie, then nude while dancing in living room with Rose.
  ••• 0:21—Full frontal nudity, while soaping Rose and Bauer in the spa.
  • 0:25—Brief full frontal nudity taking off her towel in bedroom.
  ••• 0:26—Full frontal nudity, while getting dressed.

# • Fox, Kerry

*Films:*
**An Angel at My Table** (1990; Australian/New Zealand) ............................ Janet
  • 1:45—Brief breasts and partial lower frontal nudity while in bathtub.

•• 2:06—Left breast while sitting on bed with her boyfriend.
• 2:07—Nude, while swimming in the water.
•• 2:09—Long shot of right breast, while lying on rock outside, then breasts in a closer shot.
The Last Days of Chez Nous (1991; Australian). .... Vicki
  1:03—Upper half of buns, while standing on balcony with a sheet wrapped around herself.

# Fox, Marcia

*Films:*
Doctor in Trouble (1970; British) .............. Jean
**Creatures the World Forgot** (1971; British)
  ..........................The Dumb Girl
  • 0:51—Right breast, then brief breasts turning around by the pool.
  • 0:58—Brief breasts fighting with Julie Ege.
  • 1:20—Very brief right breast when The Dark Boy gets his leg cut.

# Fox, Morgan

*Films:*
**Flesh Gordon 2** (1990; Canadian) ...Robunda Hooters
  •• 0:12—Breasts, while opening her top to get Flesh Gordon excited.
  • 1:07—Brief breasts when her top is opened by the Evil Presence to get Flesh aroused.
*Video Tapes:*
**Playboy Video Calendar 1992** (1991).... December
  ••• 0:48—Nude in aqueduct shoot.
  ••• 0:49—Breasts and buns in G-string while singing and dancing on stage.
**Playboy Video Centerfold: Morgan Fox** (1991)
  .......................... Playmate
  ••• 0:02—Nude in aqueduct shoot.
  ••• 0:06—Nude in bedroom/factory fantasy.
  • 0:15—Brief silhouette of breasts and buns, several times while dancing.
  ••• 0:18—Nude, taking a bath.
  ••• 0:20—Breasts and buns in still photos.
  ••• 0:22—Breasts and buns in G-string, garter belt and stockings, dancing on stage.
**Playboy's Erotic Fantasies** (1992) .....Cast Member
**Sexy Lingerie IV** (1992) .................. Model
**Sexy Lingerie V** (1992) .................. Model
**Wet and Wild IV** (1992) .................. Model
**Playboy's Erotic Fantasies II** (1993) ........ Model
*Magazines:*
**Playboy** (Dec 1990) .................... Playmate
**Playboy's Book of Lingerie** (Mar 1992)...... Herself
  • 50—Lower frontal nudity.
**Playboy's Bathing Beauties** (Apr 1992)...... Herself
  ••• 4—Breasts.
**Playboy's Book of Lingerie** (May 1992) ..... Herself
  ••• 16-17—Full frontal nudity.
**Playboy's Girls of Summer '92** (Jun 1992) ...Herself
  ••• 35-37—Nude.
  ••• 66-67—Nude.

**Playboy's Girls of the World** (Oct 1992) .... Herself
•• 10—Right breast and partial lower frontal nudity.
**Playboy's Calendar Playmates** (Nov 1992) .. Herself
••• 107—Full frontal nudity.
**Playboy** (Feb 1993) . . . . . . . . . . Being in Nothingness
•• 128—Lower half of right breast.
**Playboy's Book of Lingerie** (Mar 1993) . . . . . Herself
••• 10—Breasts.
**Playboy's Wet & Wild Women** (Aug 1993) .. Herself
••• 56-57—Buns and side of left breast.
**Playboy's Video Playmates** (Sep 1993) . . . . . Herself
••• 50-51—Full frontal nudity.
**Playboy's Nudes** (Dec 1993) . . . . . . . . . . . . . Herself
••• 89-91—Full frontal nudity.
**Playboy Presents Girl of the World** (May 1994)
. . . . . . . . . . . . . . . . . . . . . . . . . . . . . . . . . . . Herself
••• 24-27—Breasts.
**Playboy's Girls of Summer '94** (Jul 1994) . . . Herself
• 65—Nude under fishnet dress.
••• 90-91—Full frontal nudity.

# Fox, Samantha

Adult film actress.
Not to be confused with the British singer with the same name.
a.k.a. Stacia Micula, Stasha Bergoff.
*Adult Films:*
Babylon Pink (1979) . . . . . . . . . . . . . . . . . . . . . . . . n.a.
*Films:*
I, the Jury (1982). . . . . . . . . . . Uncredited Orgy Woman
**It's Called Murder Baby** (1982) . . . . . . . .Lisa Benson
(R-rated version of the adult film *Dixie Ray, Hollywood Star*.)
••• 1:10—In bra, then breasts in bedroom in front of Nick and Sherry.
•• 1:11—Breasts, sleeping on bed, then waking up and getting out.
• 1:18—Brief breasts in B&W flashback.
C.O.D. (1983). . . . . . . . . . . . . . . . . . Female Reporter
In Love (1983) . . . . . . . . . . . . . . . . . . . . . . . . . . n.a.
**Simply Irresistible** (1983) . . . . . . . . . . Arlene Brooks
(R-rated version. *Irresistible* is the X-rated version.)
• 1:20—In see-through white nightgown, then brief peeks at right breast when nightgown gapes open.
Delivery Boys (1984) . . . . . . . . . . . . Woman in Tuxedo
**Streetwalkin'** (1985) . . . . . . . . . . . . . Topless Dancer
• 0:22—Breasts, dancing on stage in nightclub (She's the one wearing a head band).
• 0:27—More breasts, dancing on stage.
• 0:29—More breasts, dancing on stage.
• 0:56—Breasts, giving Antonio Fargas a massage at the bar.
**Sex Appeal** (1986) . . . . . . . . . . . . . . . . . . . . . Sheila
••• 1:14—In black lingerie, then breasts and buns in black G-string with Rhonda. Long scene.
**Slammer Girls** (1987). . . . . . . . . . . . . . . . . Mosquito
•• 0:17—Breasts in the shower hassling Melody with Tank.

**Violated** (1987) . . . . . . . . . . . . . . . . . . . . . . . . . .Joan
• 0:52—Breasts, while in bed with Marilyn on video playback.
**Warrior Queen** (1987) . . . . . . . . . Philomena/Augusta
••• 0:31—Nude, doing a dance with a snake during orgy scene.
• 1:03—Brief right breast after unsuccessfully trying to seduce Marcus.

# Fox, Samantha

Former British "Page 3 Girl."
Singer - "Touch Me."
Not to be confused with the adult film actress with the same name.
*Magazines:*
**Penthouse** (Jun 1987) . . . . . . . . . . . . . . . . . . . . . n.a.
**Playboy** (Dec 1988) . . . . . . . . . . . . . .Sex Stars of 1988
••• 185—Breasts.
**Playboy** (Feb 1989) . . . . . . . . . . . . . . The Year in Sex
••• 142—Breasts.

# Fox, Vivica

*Films:*
**Born on the Fourth of July** (1989) . . . . . . . . Hooker
• 0:50—Brief right breast, while taking off bra on top of patient in hospital. Dark.
*TV:*
Generations (1990- ) . . . . . . . . . . . . . . . .Maya Daniels
Out All Night (1992-93). . . . . . . . Charisse Chamberlain

# Frank, Diana

*Films:*
Not Since Casanova (1988) . . . . . . . . . . . . . . . . . Gina
Monster High (1990) . . . . . . . . . . . . . . . .Candice Cain
**Pale Blood** (1990) . . . . . . . . . . . . . . . . . . . . . . . .Jenny
•• 0:21—Breasts lying on the bed with Michael when he bites her.
• 0:36—Close up of left breast on TV monitor that Wings Hauser is editing with. Don't see face.
• 0:42—Brief left breast on TV monitor several times while Hauser examines the bite marks.
• 1:03—Very brief breasts when Hauser pulls her dress top down to look at her bite mark.
**Eyes of the Serpent** (1992) . . . . . . . . . . . . . . .Fiona
•• 1:05—Buns and breasts, several times while making love in bed with Galen.

# Franklin, Diane

*Films:*
**Amityville II: The Possession** (1982)
. . . . . . . . . . . . . . . . . . . . . . . . . . . . .Patricia Montelli
• 0:41—Half of right breast, while sitting on bed talking to her brother.
**The Last American Virgin** (1982) . . . . . . . . . .Karen
••• 1:06—Breasts in room above the bleachers with Jason.
•• 1:17—Breasts and almost lower frontal nudity taking off her panties in the clinic.
Better Off Dead (1985) . . . . . . . . . . . . . .Monique Junet

**Second Time Lucky** (1986) . . . . . . . . . . . . . . . . . . Eve
　0:07—In white bra and panties in frat house bedroom taking off her wet dress.
　•• 0:13—Breasts a lot during first sequence in the Garden of Eden with Adam.
　••• 0:28—Brief full frontal nudity running to Adam after trying an apple.
　• 0:41—Left breast, while taking top of dress down.
　••• 1:01—Breasts, opening her blouse in defiance, while standing in front of a firing squad.
Terrorvision (1986) . . . . . . . . . . . . . . . . Suzy Putterman
Bill and Ted's Excellent Adventure (1989)
. . . . . . . . . . . . . . . . . . . . . . . . . . Princess Joanna
How I Got Into College (1989) . . . . . . . . Sharon Browne
*Made for TV Movies:*
Deadly Lessons (1983) . . . . . . . . . . . . . . . . Stephanie

## Franklin, Pamela
*Films:*
The Innocents (1961) . . . . . . . . . . . . . . . . . . . . . Flora
The Lion (1962; British) . . . . . . . . . . . . . . . . . . . Tina
The Nanny (1965; British) . . . . . . . . . . . . . . . . Bobby
**The Prime of Miss Jean Brodie** (1969) . . . . . . Sandy
　•• 1:21—Breasts posing as a model for Teddy's painting. Brief right breast, while kissing him. Long shot of buns, while getting dressed.
**The Legend of Hell House** (1973; British)
. . . . . . . . . . . . . . . . . . . . . . . . . Florence Tanner
　• 1:03—Silhouette of breasts while taking off nightgown and getting into bed.
Food of the Gods (1976) . . . . . . . . . . . . . . . . . Lorna
**The Witching** (1983) . . . . . . . . . . . . . . . . . . . . . . Lori
　*a.k.a. Necromancy*
　(Originally filmed in 1971 as *Necromancy*, additional scenes were added and re-released in 1983.)
　•• 0:38—Breasts lying in bed during nightmare.
　0:46—Partial right breast, tied to a stake. Flames from fire are in the way.
　• 1:07—Brief breasts putting on black robe.
　• 1:17—Brief breasts in several quick cuts.
*Made for TV Movies:*
Flipper's New Adventure (1964) . . . . . . . . . . . . Penny
See How They Run (1964) . . . . . . . . . . . . Tirza Green
David Copperfield (1970) . . . . . . . . . . . Dora Spentow
The Letters (1973) . . . . . . . . . . . . . . . . Karen Foster
Satan's School for Girls (1973) . . . . . . . Elizabeth Sayres
Eleanor and Franklin (1976) . . . . . . . . . . . . . Anna Hall

## Frazier, Sheila
*Films:*
**Superfly** (1972) . . . . . . . . . . . . . . . . . . . . . Georgia
　•• 0:40—Breasts and buns, making love in the bathtub with Superfly.
Three the Hard Way (1974) . . . . . . . . . . . . Wendy Kane
California Suite (1978) . . . . . . . . . . . . . Bettina Panama
Two of a Kind (1983) . . . . . . . . . . . . . . . . . . Reporter
*Made for TV Movies:*
The Lazarus Syndrome (1976) . . . . . . . . Gloria St. Clair

## • Frederick, Lynne
*Films:*
No Blade of Grass (1970; British) . . . . . . Mary Custance
Nicholas and Alexandra (1971; British) . . . . . . . Tatiana
Henry VIII and His Six Wives (1972; British)
. . . . . . . . . . . . . . . . . . . . . . . . Catherine Howard
Voyage of the Damned (1976; British) . . . . . Anna Rosen
**Schizo** (1977; British) . . . . . . . . . . . . . . . . . Samantha
　*a.k.a. Amok*
　*a.k.a. Blood of the Undead*
　0:26—In white bra and panties, while changing clothes in bedroom.
　•• 0:29—Breasts and buns, while walking to and taking a shower.
　• 0:56—Brief frontal nudity, while getting into bed.
The Prisoner of Zenda (1979) . . . . . . . . . Princess Flavia

## Frederick, Vicki
*Films:*
All That Jazz (1979) . . . . . . . . . . . . . . . Menage Partner
**...All the Marbles** (1981) . . . . . . . . . . . . . . . . . . . . Iris
　*a.k.a. The California Dolls*
　• 1:03—Brief side view of left breast, while crying in the shower after fighting with Peter Falk.
Body Rock (1984) . . . . . . . . . . . . . . . . . . . . . . Claire
A Chorus Line (1985) . . . . . . . . . . . . . . . . . . . Sheila
Stewardess School (1987) . . . . . . . . . . . Miss Grummet
Chopper Chicks in Zombietown (1989) . . . . . . . . Jewel
Scissors (1990) . . . . . . . . . . . . . . . . . . Nancy Leahy
Chaplin (1992; British/U.S.) . . . . . . . . . . . . Party Guest
*Made for Cable TV:*
Dream On: Doing the Bossa Nova (1990; HBO)
. . . . . . . . . . . . . . . . . . . . . . . . . . . . . . Valerie

## Freeman, Lindsay
*Films:*
**Young Lady Chatterley** (1977)
. . . . . . . . . . . . . . . . . . . . Sybil (light-duty maid)
　• 1:35—Brief left breast, while on the floor, covered with cake.
**Fairytales** (1979) . . . . . . . . . . . . . . . . . . . . . . . . Jill
　•• 0:24—Nude on hill with Jack.

## French, Paige
*Films:*
**Meatballs 4** (1992) . . . . . . . . . . . . . . . Jennifer Lipton
　•• 0:27—Breasts outside with Wes.
　• 0:29—Brief breasts getting up when splashed with water.
*Made for Cable Movies:*
Intimate Strangers (1991; Showtime) . . . . . Meg Wheeler
*TV:*
George Carlin (1994- ) . . . . . . . . . . . . . . . . . . Sydney

# •Fritz, Nikki

Films:

**Beach Babes From Beyond** (1993) . . . . . Sally's Model
- ••• 0:20—Breasts, while posing in spa outside (she's on the right) during catalog photo session with two other models.
- ••• 0:22—Nude, in bedroom during Hassler's fantasy.
- • 1:02—Brief breasts, twice, when swimsuit top flies off while dancing on stage during bikini contest (she's the last one).

**Dinosaur Island** (1993) . . . . . . . . . . . . High Priestess
- •• 0:00—Breasts (painted blue) and buns in G-string, while dancing during sacrifice ceremony.

# Frost, Sadie

Films:

Empire State (1987; British). . . . . . . . . . . . . . . . . Tracy

**Dark Obsession** (1989; British) . . . . . . . . . . . Rebecca
a.k.a. Diamond Skulls
- • 0:22—Very brief right breast in bed after she rolls off Jamie.
- ••• 0:33—Breasts several times while making love with Jamie when Gabriel Byrne interrupts them.

**Bram Stoker's Dracula** (1992) . . . . . . . . . . . . . Lucy
- • 0:41—Left breast, while making love with Dracula on bench outside at night during the rain.
- •• 0:58—Breasts in bed, quite a few times, after getting bit by Dracula and getting a blood transfusion.
- • 1:12—Brief right breast in gaping nightgown.
- • 1:19—Left breast, while lying in bed when Dracula pays a return visit.
- • 1:20—Brief left breast, when the wolf Dracula jumps on the bed.

Paper Marriage (1993)
. . . . . . . . . . . . . . . . Employment Agency Interviewer

Splitting Heirs (1993) . . . . . . . . . . . . . . . . . . . . Angela

Made for Cable Movies:
The Cisco Kid (1994; TNT) . . . . . . . . . . . . . . . . . .n.a.

# Fulton, Christina

Films:

**The Doors** (1991) . . . . . . . . . . . . . . . . . . . . . . . .Nico
- •• 0:56—Breasts, after taking off her top in elevator with Val Kilmer.

Dangerous Game (1993). . . . . . . . . . . . . . . . . Blonde
(Unrated version reviewed.)

A Brilliant Disguise (1994) . . . . . . . . . . . . . . . Marlene

**Hard Drive** (1994) . . . . . . . . . . . . . . . . Dana/Delilah
(Unrated version reviewed.)
- • 0:23—Brief lower frontal nudity, brief left breast and brief buns while getting attacked on bed by Will.
- • 0:25—Buns, while lying on bed after getting shot.
- • 0:26—Brief buns and left breast in Will's flashback.
- •• 1:15—Left breast, while making love with Will on kitchen counter.

Made for Cable TV:

**Red Shoe Diaries: Another Woman's Lipstick**
(1993; Showtime) . . . . . . . . . . . . . .The Other Woman
(Available on video tape on *Red Shoe Diaries 3: Another Woman's Lipstick*.)
- 0:13—In black bra, panties, garter belt and stockings with Robert.
- ••• 0:16—Breasts in corner of the room and crawling on the floor.
- •• 0:28—Brief right breast, then breasts, while stripping in front of Maryam D'Abo.
- •• 0:29—Left breast, while in room with D'Abo.

# Gabrielle, Monique

Adult Films:

**Bad Girls IV** . . . . . . . . . . . . . . . . . . . . . . . . . . Sandy
(Credits have her listed as Luana Chass.)
- ••• 0:15—Left breast, then breasts in bed masturbating while Ron Jeremy peeks from window.
- ••• 1:24—Nude, making love (non-explicitly) with Jerry Butler.

Films:

**Night Shift** (1982). . . . . . . . . . . . . . . . . . . . . .Tessie
- • 0:55—Brief breasts on college guy's shoulders during party in the morgue.

**Black Venus** (1983) . . . . . . . . . . . . . . . . . . . . Ingrid
- ••• 0:03—Nude in Sailor Room at the bordello.
- ••• 1:01—Breasts and buns, taking off clothes for Madame Lilli's customers.

**Chained Heat** (1983; U.S./German). . . . . . . . Debbie
- ••• 0:08—Nude, stripping for the Warden in his office.
- ••• 0:09—Nude, getting into the spa with the Warden.

**Flashdance** (1983) . . . . . . . . . . . . . Uncredited Stripper
- •• 1:27—Buns, in G-string, walking down walkway of stage in club. Brief breasts, accepting a bill in her red G-string.

**Bachelor Party** (1984). . . . . . . . . . . . . . . . . . Tracey
- •• 1:11—Full frontal nudity in the hotel bedroom with Tom Hanks as his bachelor party gift.

Hard to Hold (1984). . . . . . . . . . . . . . . . . . . . Wife #1

**Hot Moves** (1984) . . . . . . . . . . . . . . . . . . . . . . Babs
- • 0:29—Nude on the nude beach.
- • 1:07—Breasts on and behind the sofa with Barry trying to get her top off.

**Love Scenes** (1984) . . . . . . . . . . . . . . . . . Uncredited
a.k.a. Ecstacy
- ••• 1:11—Full frontal nudity making love with Rick on bed.

**The Big Bet** (1985) . . . . . . . . . Fantasy Girl in Elevator
- ••• 0:51—In purple bra, then eventually nude in elevator with Chris.

**The Rosebud Beach Hotel** (1985) . . . . . . . . . . . Lisa
- •• 0:22—Breasts and buns undressing in hotel room with two other girls. She's on the right.
- •• 0:44—Breasts taking off her red top in basement with two other girls and two guys.
- • 0:56—In black see-through nightie in hotel room with Peter Scolari.

**Emmanuelle 5** (1986). . . . . . . . . . . . . . . Emmanuelle
- ••• 0:01—Breasts and buns with a guy on rocks near the ocean in a film.
- ••• 0:05—Nude on boat after escaping from the crowd at Cannes who rip her clothes off.
- •• 0:09—Brief breasts taking off her jacket in restaurant. Breasts on boat with Charles.
- ••• 0:10—Full frontal nudity, making love on boat with Charles.
- ••• 0:17—In black lingerie, then full frontal nudity while posing for Phillip.
- •• 0:26—Full frontal nudity while changing clothes in her room.
- ••• 0:38—Full frontal nudity while undressing in room with other harem girls.
- •• 0:40—Breasts, getting fixed up by three harem girls.
- ••• 0:52—Buns and breasts while making love with Phillip outside.
- ••• 1:07—Breasts in bed with Charles.
- • 1:09—Very brief right breast, in airplane cockpit with Charles.

**Screen Test** (1986) . . . . . . . . . . . . . . . . . . . . Roxanne
- •• 0:06—Breasts taking off clothes in back room in front of a young boy.
- ••• 0:42—Nude, with Michelle Bauer, seducing a boy in his day dream.
- •• 1:20—Breasts taking off her top for a guy.

**Weekend Warriors** (1986) . . . . . . Showgirl on plane
- •• 0:51—Brief breasts taking off top with other showgirls.

**Young Lady Chatterley II** (1986)
. . . . . . . . . . . . . . . . . . . . . . .Eunice "Maid in Woods"
- •• 0:15—Breasts in the woods with the Gardener.
- ••• 0:43—Breasts in bed with Virgil.

**Amazon Women on the Moon** (1987)
. . . . . . . . . . . . . . . . . . . . . . . . . . . . . . . Taryn Steele
- ••• 0:05—Nude during Penthouse Video sketch. Long sequence of her nude in unlikely places.

**Deathstalker II** (1987) . . . Reena the Seer/Princess Evie
- • 0:57—Brief breasts getting dress torn off by guards.
- ••• 1:01—Breasts making love with Deathstalker.
- • 1:24—Breasts, laughing during the blooper scenes during the end credits.

**Up 'n' Coming** (1987) . . . . . . . . . . . . . . Boat Girl #1
(R-rated version reviewed, X-rated version available.)
- • 0:39—Breasts wearing white shorts on boat. Long shot.
- • 0:40—More brief nude shots on the boat.

Not of This Earth (1988) . . . . . . . . . . . . . . . . . . . .Agnes
The Return of the Swamp Thing (1988)
. . . . . . . . . . . . . . . . . . . . . . . . . . . . Miss Poinsettia
**Silk 2** (1989) . . . . . . . . . . . . . . .Jenny "Silk" Sleighton
- ••• 0:27—Breasts, then full frontal nudity taking a shower while killer stalks around outside.
- 0:28—Very, very brief blurry right breast in open robe when she's on the sofa during fight.
- • 0:29—Brief breasts doing a round house kick on the bad guy. Right breast several times during the fight.

- ••• 0:55—Breasts taking off her blouse and making love on bed. Too much diffusion!

Hard to Die (1990). . . . . . . . . . . . . . . . . . . . Fifi Latour
*a.k.a. Tower of Terror*
Transylvania Twist (1990) . . . . . . . . . . . . Patty (Patricia)
976-EVIL II: The Astral Factor (1991) . . . . . . Miss Lawlor
**Angel Eyes** (1991) . . . . . . . . . . . . . . . . . . . . . . .Angel
- ••• 0:18—Nude, in shower with Michelle.
- • 0:32—Brief breasts in robe in her bedroom.
- ••• 0:45—Left breast and lower frontal nudity, while caressing herself while watching Steven and Michelle make love in bed.
- ••• 0:47—Right breast, then breasts in bed while fantasizing Steven is making love with her. Then breasts in open robe.
- ••• 0:54—Breasts and buns, while making love in bed with Michelle. Very nice!
- ••• 1:10—Nude, while making love with Nick on the floor. (This scene was really worn down on the video tape that I rented—I think I know why!)

**Body Chemistry 2: Voice of a Stranger** (1991)
. . . . . . . . . . . . . . . . . . . . . . . . .Brunette in Flashback
- • 0:19—Very brief buns and left breast in bed.

**Evil Toons** (1991). . . . . . . . . . . . . . . . . . . . . .Megan
- 0:21—In bra in open blouse when Roxanne tries to get her to do a strip tease.
- ••• 0:25—In bra, then breasts undressing in front of mirror.

**Miracle Beach** (1991) . . . . . . . . . . . . . . Cindy Beatty
- •• 0:03—Breasts in bed with a guy when Scotty comes home. Breasts getting out of bed and getting dressed. (Note in first shot when she's lying in bed, she doesn't have a dress around her waist, then in the next shot when she stands up, she does.)

Uncaged (1991). . . . . . . . . . . . . . . . . Beautiful Hooker
*a.k.a. Angel in Red*
Munchie (1992). . . . . . . . . . . . . . . . . . . . . . Miss Laurel
*Made for Cable TV:*
**Dream On: 555-HELL** (1990; HBO) . . . . . . Scuba Lady
- •• 0:07—Breasts wearing a scuba mask and bikini bottom when she opens the door.

*Video Tapes:*
**E. Nick: A Legend in His Own Mind** (1984)
. . . . . . . . . . . . . . . . . . . . . . . . . . . . . . . .Charmaine
- • 0:08—Brief breasts, while stretching in video. Brief side of right breast while sunbathing.
- •• 0:30—Buns and breasts in shower, breasts while coughing on steam. Buns, while trying on clothes in mirror.
- ••• 0:35—Buns in G-string in front of mirror again. Breasts while sunbathing and playing with teddy bear.
- ••• 0:39—Breasts and buns in G-string while sunbathing outside with her family.

**Red Hot Rock** (1984). . . . . . . . . . . . . . . . . . .Lab Girl
*a.k.a. Sexy Shorts (on laser disc)*
- ••• 0:06—Breasts and brief buns dancing after throwing off lab coat during "Lovelite" by O'Bryan.

**Penthouse Love Stories** (1986)
. . . . . . . . . . . . . . . . . . . . . .Monique and AC/DC Lover
••• 0:01—Nude in bedroom entertaining herself. A
   must for Monique fans!
••• 0:18—Nude making love with another woman.
**Playboy's Fantasies** (1987) . . . . . . . . . . Grand Theft
••• 0:25—Nude, in house after stealing jewelry.
**Scream Queen Hot Tub Party** (1991). . . . . . . Herself
•• 0:07—Breasts, taking off blue outfit and putting on
   white teddy.
• 0:12—Buns, while walking up the stairs.
••• 0:21—Breasts and buns making love with a guy
   from *Emmanuelle 5.*
••• 0:23—Breasts taking off bra in front of mirror from
   *Evil Toons.*
••• 0:25—Breasts in black panties demonstrating the
   Dance of the Vampires.
••• 0:44—Breasts taking off her swimsuit·top and soaping up with the other girls.
• 0:46—Breasts in still shot during the end credits.
**Penthouse Ready to Ride** (1992) . . . . . . . . . .Model
**Penthouse Satin & Lace: An Erotic History of
Lingerie** (1992) . . . . . . . . . . . . . . . . . . . . . .Model
••• 0:06—Breasts and buns with a blonde woman.
••• 0:33—Nude in blonde wig, with lover.
••• 0:47—Nude in bed with another blonde.
**Penthouse Forum Letters: Volume 1** (1993)
. . . . . . . . . . . . . . . . . . . . . . . Mystery Caller/Cindy
••• 0:27—Breasts and buns while making love with Brad
   on the floor in the office.
•• 0:45—Full frontal nudity, taking off her clothes in
   the office with Tanya and Vicky in front of Brad.
*Magazines:*
**Playboy** (Nov 1982) . . . . . . . . . . Sex in Cinema 1982
••• 163—Breasts still from *Night Shift.*
**Penthouse** (Dec 1982) . . . . . . . . . . . . . . . . . . . . Pet
••• 105-123—Nude.
**Playboy** (Jul 1989). . . . . . . . . . . . . . B-Movie Bimbos
••• 131—Full frontal nudity sitting on a car/helicopter.
**Playboy** (Apr 1993) . . . . . . . . . . . . . . . . . .Grapevine
••• 179—Breasts. B&W.

# Gainsbourg, Charlotte

Daughter of actress Jane Birkin.
*Films:*
Le Petit Amour (1988; French) . . . . . . . . . . . . . . .Lucy
*a.k.a. Kung Fu Master*
**The Little Thief** (1989; French) . . . . . . Janine Castang
*a.k.a. La Petite Voleuse*
•• 0:41—Breasts twice, taking off blouse in bedroom
   with Michel.

# Gajewskia, Barbara

*Films:*
**Killer Image** (1991) . . . . . . . . . . . . . . . . . . . . .Stacey
• 0:22—Very, very brief left breast, taking off bra at
   window with M. Emmet Walsh.

*Magazines:*
**Playboy's Girls of the World** (Oct 1992). . . . . Herself
•• 16-17—Left breast and lower frontal nudity.

# •Galiena, Anna

*Films:*
Nothing Underneath (1985; Italian). . . . . . . . . . . . n.a.
   *a.k.a. Sotto Il Vestito Niente*
Hotel Colonial (1988). . . . . . . . . . . . . . . . . . . . . . n.a.
The Hairdresser's Husband (1990; French) . . . . Mathilde
   *a.k.a. Le Mari de la Coiffeuse*
**Jamón, Jamón** (1992; Spanish) . . . . . . . . . . . Carmen
•• 0:35—Breasts out of the top of her dress, while in
   the back of the restaurant with José Luis.

# Galik, Denise

*Films:*
The Happy Hooker (1975) . . . . . . . . . . . . . . . . Cynthia
California Suite (1978) . . . . . . . . . . . . . . . . . . . . Bunny
Don't Answer the Phone (1979). . . . . . . . . . . . . . Lisa
**The Deadly Games** (1980) . . . . . . . . . . . . . . . . Mary
   *a.k.a. The Eliminator*
• 1:13—Left breast, twice, making love on top of Rog-
   er in bed.
Humanoids from the Deep (1980) . . . . . . . . Linda Beale
Melvin and Howard (1980) . . . . . . . . . . . . . . . . Lucy
Partners (1982) . . . . . . . . . . . . . . . . . . . . . . . . Clara
Get Crazy (1983) . . . . . . . . . . . . . . . . . Nurse Gwen
Eye of the Tiger (1986). . . . . . . . . . . . . . . . . . Christie
Career Opportunities (1991) . . . . . . . . . . . . . .Lorraine
*Made for Cable TV:*
**The Hitchhiker: Dead Heat** (1987; HBO) . . . . Arielle
•• 0:20—Breasts taking off blouse and standing up
   with Cal in the barn, then right breast lying down in
   the hay with him.
*TV:*
Knots Landing (1980-81) . . . . . . . . . . . . . . Linda Stiker
Flamingo Road (1981-82) . . . . . . . . . . . Christie Kovacs

# Gallardo, Silvana

*Films:*
**Death Wish II** (1982). . . . . . . . . . . . . . . . . . . Rosario
• 0:11—Buns, on bed getting raped by gang. Brief
   breasts on bed and floor.
• 0:13—Nude, trying to get to the phone. Very brief
   full frontal nudity, lying on her back on the floor af-
   ter getting hit.
Out of the Dark (1988) . . . . . . . . . . . . . . . McDonald
Solar Crisis (1992) . . . . . . . . . . . . . . . . . . . . . . .T.C.
*Made for Cable Movies:*
Prison Stories, Women on the Inside (1990; HBO)
. . . . . . . . . . . . . . . . . . . . . . . . . . . . . . .Mercedes

# Gallego, Gina

*Films:*
The Champ (1979) . . . . . . . . . . . . . . . . . . . .Cuban Girl
Deadly Force (1983). . . . . . . . . . . . . . . . . . . . . .Maria
Lust in the Dust (1985) . . . . . . . . . . . . . . . . . . .Ninta
The Men's Club (1986) . . . . . . . . . . . . . . . . . . Felicia

My Demon Lover (1987)................... Sonia
*Made for Cable Movies:*
**Keeper of the City** (1991; Showtime) ........ Elena
  • 0:19—Brief half of left breast, getting out of bed and
    putting on black bra. Wearing black panties.
*TV:*
Flamingo Road (1981-82)............Alicia Sanchez

## Gamba, Veronica

*Films:*
A Night in Heaven (1983)................Tammy
*Video Tapes:*
**Playboy's Playmate Review 2** (1984)..... Playmate
*Magazines:*
**Playboy** (Nov 1983) ................... Playmate
**Playboy's Calendar Playmates** (Nov 1992) .. Herself
  ••• 36—Breasts.

## Gannes, Gayle

*Films:*
**The Prey** (1980) ...........................Gail
  • 0:36—Brief breasts putting T-shirt on before the
    creature attacks her.
**Hot Moves** (1984)...................... Jamie
  • 1:09—Breasts, taking off her white blouse and get-
    ting in bed with Joey.

## Ganzel, Teresa

*Films:*
**National Lampoon Goes to the Movies** (1982)
.................................... Diana
*a.k.a. Movie Madness*
  ••• 0:19—Breasts, while lying in bed with Peter Riegert.
    Nice, long scene.
The Toy (1982) .......................Fancy Bates
**C.O.D.** (1983)........................Lisa Foster
  • 0:46—Right breast hanging out of dress while danc-
    ing at disco with Zack.
  • 1:25—Brief side view of left breast taking off purple
    robe in dressing room scene. Then in white bra talk-
    ing to Albert.
  1:29—In white bra during fashion show.
Hexed (1993) .......................3rd Reporter
*a.k.a. All Shook Up*
*Made for TV Movies:*
Rest In Peace, Mrs. Columbo (1990)......Dede Perkins
Backfield in Motion (1991) ................ Joanne
*TV:*
Teachers Only (1983) ....... Samantha "Sam" Keating
The Duck Factory (1984).......... Mrs. Shree Winkler

## Garber, Terri

*Films:*
**Toy Soldiers** (1983) ..................... Amy
  • 0:18—Brief right breast taking off her tank top when
    the army guys force her. Her head is down.
Key Exchange (1985) ...................... Amy
*Miniseries:*
North and South (1985) ..............Ashton Main

North and South, Book II (1986) ........ Ashton Main
North and South, Book III: Heaven and Hell (1994)
.............................Ashton Main
*TV:*
Mr. Smith (1983) ...................Dr. Judy Tyson
Dynasty (1987-88)............... Leslie Carrington

## Garcia, Cristina

*Films:*
**Surf Nazis Must Die** (1986) ..............Waitress
  • 0:21—Breasts pulling her top up for Wheels while
    sitting on his lap.
*Magazines:*
**Playboy** (Nov 1988) .......... Sex in Cinema 1988
  • 138—Showing her right breast in still from *Surf Na-
    zis Must Die.*

## • Garcia, Nicole

*Films:*
Mon Oncle d'Amerique (1980; French) .. Janine Garnier
Beau Pere (1981; French).................. Martine
Bolero (1982; French) ..................... Anne
A Man and a Woman: 20 Years Later (1986; French)
.......................................... n.a.
La Lumiere du Lac (1988)................... n.a.
**Overseas** (1991; French)..................... Zon
    0:11—In sparkly bra, while admiring herself in the
      mirror.
  • 0:12—Brief breasts behind mosquito net while in
    bed.
  • 0:13—Brief breasts while playing with Paul in the
    bathroom. Very brief left breast, while reaching for
    towel.

## • Gardner, Ashley

*Films:*
**he said, she said** (1991) ...................Susan
  • 1:05—Brief upper half of right breast, when her
    breast pops out of her dress while talking to Kevin
    Bacon and Elizabeth Perkins at restaurant.
Johnny Suede (1992) ....................... Ellen
*Made for TV Movies:*
Complex of Fear (1993)..............Doreen Wylie

## Garner, Shay

*Films:*
Thumbelina (1970) ........................ n.a.
**Humongous** (1982; Canadian)......... Ida Parsons
  • 0:05—Brief left breast and brief lower frontal nudity
    getting her clothes ripped off by a guy. Don't see her
    face.

## Garnett, Gale

*Films:*
The Children (1980)................ Cathy Freeman
**Tribute** (1980; Canadian)...................Hilary
  ••• 1:39—Breasts, while taking off her nurse outfit in
    front of Jack Lemmon. (Pretty amazing for a PG
    movie!)

• 1:42—Brief half of right breast, while standing up.
Overnight (1986) . . . . . . . . . . . . . . . . . . . . . . . . . Del
Mr. & Mrs. Bridge (1990) . . . . . . . . . . . . . Mabel Ong

## Garr, Teri

*Films:*

Head (1968) . . . . . . . . . . . . . . . . . . . . . . . . Testy True
The Conversation (1974). . . . . . . . . . . . . . . . . . . Amy
Young Frankenstein (1974) . . . . . . . . . . . . . . . . . Inga
Won Ton Ton, The Dog Who Saved Hollywood (1976)
. . . . . . . . . . . . . . . . . . . . . . . . . . . . . Fluffy Peters
Close Encounters of the Third Kind (1977)
. . . . . . . . . . . . . . . . . . . . . . . . . . . . Ronnie Neary
Oh God! (1977) . . . . . . . . . . . . . . . . . . . Bobbie Landers
The Black Stallion (1979). . . . . . . . . . . . . Alec's Mother
Honky Tonk Freeway (1981) . . . . . . . . . . . . . . . Ericka
The Escape Artist (1982) . . . . . . . . . . . . . . . . . . Arlene
**One from the Heart** (1982). . . . . . . . . . . . . . Frannie
  •• 0:09—Brief breasts getting out of the shower.
     0:10—In a bra, getting dressed in bedroom.
  •• 0:40—Side view of right breast changing in. bed-
     room while Frederic Forrest watches.
  ••• 1:20—Brief breasts in bed when standing up after
     Forrest drops in though the roof while she's in bed
     with Raul Julia.
Tootsie (1982). . . . . . . . . . . . . . . . . . . . . . . . . Sandy
The Black Stallion Returns (1983) . . . . . . . Alec's Mother
Mr. Mom (1983). . . . . . . . . . . . . . . . . . . . . Caroline
The Sting II (1983) . . . . . . . . . . . . . . . . . . . Veronica
Firstborn (1984) . . . . . . . . . . . . . . . . . . . . . . Wendy
After Hours (1985) . . . . . . . . . . . . . . . . . . . . . . Julie
Miracles (1986). . . . . . . . . . . . . . . . . . . . Jean Briggs
Full Moon in Blue Water (1988) . . . . . . . . . . . . . Louise
     0:50—Walking around in Gene Hackman's bar in a
     bra while changing blouses and talking to him.
Let It Ride (1989) . . . . . . . . . . . . . . . . . . . . . . . Pam
Out Cold (1989) . . . . . . . . . . . . . . . . . Sunny Cannald
Short Time (1990). . . . . . . . . . . . . . Carolyn Simpson
Waiting for the Light (1991) . . . . . . . . . . . . . . . . n.a.
Mom and Dad Save the World (1992). . . . Marge Nelson
The Player (1992) . . . . . . . . . . . . . . . . . . . . . Cameo
*Made for Cable Movies:*
To Catch a King (1984; HBO) . . . . . . . . . Hannah Winter
*Made for Cable TV:*
Tales From the Crypt: The Trap (1991; HBO)
. . . . . . . . . . . . . . . . . . . . . . . . . . . . Irene Paloma
Dream On: And Bimbo Was His Name-O (1992; HBO)
. . . . . . . . . . . . . . . . . . . . . . . . Sondra McCadden
*Made for TV Movies:*
Fresno (1986) . . . . . . . . . . . . . . . . . . Talon Kensington
Pack of Lies (1987) . . . . . . . . . . . . . . . . . . . . . . n.a.
Deliver Them from Evil: The Taking of Alta View (1992)
. . . . . . . . . . . . . . . . . . . . . . . . . . Susan Woolley
*TV:*
Burns and Schreiber Comedy Hour (1973) . . . . . Regular
Girl with Something Extra (1973-74) . . . . . . . . Amber
The Sonny and Cher Comedy Hour (1973-74) . . Regular
The Sonny Comedy Revue (1974). . . . . . . . . . Regular
Good & Evil (1991) . . . . . . . . . . . . . . . . . . . . Denise

## • Garrick, Barbara

*Films:*

Eight Men Out (1988) . . . . . . . . . . . . . . Helen Weaver
Working Girl (1989) . . . . . . . . . . . . . . . . . Phyllis Trask
Postcards from the Edge (1990). . . . . . . . . . . . . Carol
The Firm (1993) . . . . . . . . . . . . . . . . . . . . Kay Quinn
Sleepless in Seattle (1993) . . . . . . . . . . . . . . Victoria
*Made for TV Movies:*
**Tales of the City** (1994) . . . . . . . . DeDe Halcyon Day
  ••• 0:38—(Into Part 3) Brief breasts and partial buns,
     while changing positions in bed. Then breasts while
     sitting in bed and talking on the phone. Very long
     scene for regular TV!

## Gastoni, Lisa

*Films:*

Female Friends (1958; British) . . . . . . . . . . Marny Friend
Three Men in a Boat (1958) . . . . . . Primrose Porterhouse
Gidget Goes to Rome (1963) . . . . . . . . . Anna Cellini
**Submission** (1976; Italian) . . . . . . . . . . . . . . . . Elaine
     0:28—Lower frontal nudity on the floor behind the
     counter with Franco Nero.
  • 0:30—Left breast, while talking on the phone with
     her husband while Nero fondles her.
  •• 0:32—Breasts and buns, making love on bed with
     Nero. Slightly out of focus.
  •• 0:33—Breasts getting out of bed to talk to her
     daughter.
  ••• 0:43—Breasts in room with Juliet and Nero. Long
     scene.
  ••• 0:45—More breasts on the floor yelling at Nero.
     0:54—Brief lower frontal nudity in slip, sitting on
     floor with Nero.
  ••• 0:57—Left breast, while wearing slip, walking in
     front of pharmacy. Then full frontal nudity while
     wearing only stockings. Long scene.
  •• 1:00—Breasts in pharmacy with Nero, singing and
     dancing.
  •• 1:28—Breasts when Nero cuts her slip open. Nice
     close up.
  •• 1:29—Breasts getting up out of bed.

## • Gatti, Jennifer

*Films:*

Mobsters (1991) . . . . . . . . . . . . . . . . . . . . . Secretary
  *a.k.a. Mobsters—The Evil Empire*
We're Talkin' Serious Money (1991) . . . . . . . . . . Sophia
Nemesis (1992) . . . . . . . . . . . . Rosaria/German National
Street Knight (1992) . . . . . . . . . . . . . . . . . . Rebecca
**Double Exposure** (1993). . . . . . . . . . . Maria Putnam
  •• 0:06—Breasts in B&W, while making love with a
     guy.
  • 0:25—In bra, then brief lower frontal nudity and
     brief buns in B&W.
  •• 0:39—Breasts, while making love on top of a guy in
     B&W.
  •• 0:40—Breasts again while on top of and below the
     guy in B&W.

- 1:22—Brief left breast in bed with Dedee Pfeiffer (in color).
- 1:23—Brief right breast while in bed with Pfeiffer.

## Gauthier, Connie

*Films:*
**18 Again!** (1988) . . . . . . . . . . . . . . . . Artist's Model
•• 0:29—Very brief breasts, then buns taking her robe off during art class.
*Magazines:*
**Penthouse** (Jun 1987). . . . . . . . . . . . . . . . . . . . Pet

## • Gava, Cassandra

*Films:*
Night Shift (1982). . . . . . . . . . . . . . . . . . . . . . . . .J.J.
High Road to China (1983) . . . . . . . . . . . . . . . .Alessa
**Dead Aim** (1987) . . . . . . . . . . . . . . . . . . . . . Amber
- 0:14—Buns, while sitting on chair on stage.
- 0:52—Very brief breasts, while making love with Ed Marinaro in bed. Very dark, hard to see.
Mortal Passions (1989) . . . . . . . . . . . . . . . . . . . Cinda
*Made for Cable Movies:*
State of Emergency (1993; HBO) . . . . . . . Paramedic #5

## Gavin, Erica

*Films:*
Vixen. (1968) . . . . . . . . . . . . . . . . . . . . .Vixen Palmer
**Caged Heat** (1974). . . . . . . . . . . . . . Jacqueline Wilson
*a.k.a. Renegade Girls*
- 0:08—Buns, getting strip searched before entering prison.
•• 0:25—Breasts in shower scene.
- 0:30—Brief side view of left breast in another shower scene.

## Gavin, Mary

See: Samples, Candy.

## Gaybis, Annie

*Films:*
**Fairytales** (1979). . . . . . . . . . . . . . . . . . . Snow White
••• 0:21—Nude in room with the seven little dwarfs singing and dancing.
Beyond Evil (1980) . . . . . . . . . . . . . . . . . . . . . .Harlot
10 Violent Women (1982). . . . . . . . . . . . . . . . . Vickie
**The Best Little Whorehouse in Texas** (1982)
. . . . . . . . . . . . . . . . . . . Uncredited Chicken Ranch Girl
- 1:12—Brief breasts, twice, smoking a joint in bed with a football player when Dom DeLuise busts in with his news crew.
Friday the 13th, Part III (1982) . . . . . . . . . . . . . Cashier
**The Lost Empire** (1983). . . . . . . . . . . . .Prison Referee
- 0:30—Breasts when her top gets ripped off by Angelique Pettyjohn during cat fight.
**Scarred** (1983) . . . . . . . . . . . . . . . . . . . . . .Movie Girl
•• 0:32—Breasts, straddling a guy in bed during filming of a movie.

The Witching (1983) . . . . . . . . . . . . . . . . . . . . . . Spirit
*a.k.a. Necromancy*
(Originally filmed in 1971 as *Necromancy*, additional scenes were added and re-released in 1983.)
Bachelor Party (1984). . . . . . . . . . . . . . . . . . . Hooker
**Hollywood Zap!** (1986). . . . . . . . . . . . . . . . Debbie
Bugsy (1991) . . . . . . . . . . . Uncredited Mambo Dancer
**Death Dancers** (1992). . . . . . . . . . . . . . . . .Michelle
Distinguished Gentleman (1992)
. . . . . . . . . . . . . . . . Uncredited 900 Phone Girl, Maria
**Twin Peaks: Fire Walk With Me** (1992)
. . . . . . . . . . . . . . . . . . Uncredited Dancer on Stage
- 1:15—Breasts, dancing on stage. Lit with red light.
- 1:16—More breasts and very brief buns, while on stage.
- 1:18—More breasts while on stage.
*Magazines:*
**Playboy** (Mar 1992) . . . . . . . . . . . . . . . . Grapevine
- 170—Breasts through holes in her T-shirt. B&W.

## • Gazelle, Wendy

*Films:*
Remo Williams: The Adventure Begins (1985)
. . . . . . . . . . . . . . . . . . . . . . . . Linda/Soap Opera
Hot Pursuit (1987) . . . . . . . . . . . . . . . Lori Cronenberg
**Sammy and Rosie Get Laid** (1987; British) . . . . Anna
•• 0:03—Buns, while lying in bed with Sammy.
- 1:10—Breasts, while lying under Sammy. Seen on the top of a three segment split screen. Don't see her face.
The Understudy: Graveyard Shift II (1988)
. . . . . . . . . . . . . . . . . .Camilla Turner/Patti Venus
0:22—Side view of right breast straddling Mathew on bed. Don't see her face or nipple.
Triumph of the Spirit (1989). . . . . . . . . . . . . . .Allegra
Crooked Hearts (1991). . . . . . . . . . . . . . . . . . .Eileen
Queens Logic (1991) . . . . . . . . . . . . . . . . . . . .Kate

## Geeson, Judy

*Films:*
Berserk (1967; British) . . . . . . . . . . . . . . .Angela Rivers
To Sir, with Love (1967; British) . . . . . . . . Pamela Dare
Hammerhead (1968) . . . . . . . . . . . . . . . .Sue Trenton
**Here We Go Round the Mulberry Bush**
(1968; British) . . . . . . . . . . . . . . . . Mary Gloucester
Nude, swimming.
The Executioner (1970; British) . . . . . . . . . .Polly Bendel
10 Rillington Place (1971; British). . . . . . . . . Beryl Evans
Fear in the Night (1972; British). . . . . . . . . Peggy Heller
*a.k.a. Dynasty of Fear*
Brannigan (1975; British) . . . . . . . . . .Jennifer Thatcher
Carry on England (1976; British) . . . . . .Sgt. Tilly Willing
The Eagle Has Landed (1977; British) . . Pamela Verecker
**Horror Planet** (1980; British). . . . . . . . . . . . . Sandy
*a.k.a. Inseminoid*
•• 0:31—Brief breasts on the operating table.
- 0:32—Brief full frontal nudity on table.
- 0:37—Brief full frontal nudity during flashbacks.

## Geffner, Deborah

*Films:*
**All That Jazz** (1979) . . . . . . . . . . . . . . . . . . . . Victoria
  • 0:16—Brief breasts taking off her blouse and walking
    up the stairs while Roy Scheider watches. A little out
    of focus.
Star 80 (1983). . . . . . . . . . . . . . . . . . . . . . . . . . . Billie
Exterminator 2 (1984). . . . . . . . . . . . . . . . . . Caroline
*Magazines:*
**Playboy** (Mar 1980). . . . . . . . . . . . . . . All That Fosse
  ••• 177—Breasts sitting on couch.

## Gemser, Laura

a.k.a. Moira Chen.
*Films:*
Emmanuelle, The Joys of a Woman (1975)
. . . . . . . . . . . . . . . . . . . . . . . . . . . Massage Woman
**Black Emanuelle** (1976). . . . . . . . . . . . . . . Emanuelle
  • 0:00—Brief breasts daydreaming on airplane.
  • 0:19—Left breast in car kissing a guy at night.
  •• 0:27—Breasts in shower with a guy.
  ••• 0:30—Full frontal nudity making love with a guy in
    bed.
  ••• 0:37—Breasts taking pictures with Karin Schubert.
  •• 0:41—Full frontal nudity lying on bed dreaming
    about the day's events while masturbating, then full
    frontal nudity walking around.
  •• 0:49—Breasts in studio with Johnny.
  ••• 0:52—Brief right breast making love on the side of
    the road. Full frontal nudity by the pool kissing Glo-
    ria.
  •• 1:00—Nude, taking a shower, then answering the
    phone.
  •• 1:04—Breasts on boat after almost drowning.
  •• 1:08—Full frontal nudity dancing with African tribe,
    then making love with the leader.
  •• 1:14—Full frontal nudity taking off clothes by water-
    fall with Johnny.
  •• 1:23—Breasts making love with the field hockey
    team on a train.
Emanuelle Around the World (1977; Italian) . .Emanuelle
**Emanuelle in Bangkok** (1977) . . . . . . . . . .Emanuelle
  •• 0:07—Breasts making love with a guy.
  •• 0:12—Full frontal nudity changing in hotel room.
  ••• 0:17—Full frontal nudity getting a bath, then mas-
    saged by another woman.
  •• 0:35—Breasts during orgy scene.
  •• 0:53—Breasts in room with a woman, then taking a
    shower.
  •• 1:01—Breasts in tent with a guy and woman.
  •• 1:08—Full frontal nudity dancing in a group of guys.
  •• 1:16—Full frontal nudity taking a bath with a wom-
    an.
  •• 1:18—Breasts on bed making love with a guy.
Emanuelle in Egypt (1977) . . . . . . . . . . . . . . . . Laura
**Emanuelle's Amazon Adventure** (1977)
. . . . . . . . . . . . . . . . . . . . . . . . . . . . . . . . .Emanuelle
  • 0:17—Brief left breast in flashback sequence in bed
    with a man.

  • 0:21—Brief breasts making love in bed.
  • 0:25—Brief breasts in the water with a blonde wom-
    an.
  •• 1:10—Full frontal nudity painting her body.
  • 1:11—Brief breasts in boat.
  • 1:13—Nude walking out of the water trying to save
    Isabelle.
  • 1:14—Brief breasts getting into the boat with Isa-
    belle.
Two Super Cops (1978; Italian) . . . . . . . . . . . Susy Lee
**Bushido Blade** (1979; British/U.S.) . . . . . . . . .Tomoe
  • 1:08—Brief right breast taking off her top in bed-
    room with Captain Hawk.
**Emanuelle the Seductress** (1979; Greek)
. . . . . . . . . . . . . . . . . . . . . . . . . . . . . . . . Emanuelle
  • 0:01—Full frontal nudity lying in bed with Mario.
  • 0:02—Brief breasts riding horse on the beach.
  •• 0:42—Breasts making love then full frontal nudity
    getting dressed with Tommy.
  ••• 0:48—Breasts undressing in bedroom, then in white
    panties, then nude talking to Alona.
  •• 0:54—Breasts walking around in a skirt.
  •• 1:02—Breasts outside taking a shower, then on
    lounge chair making love with Tommy.
**The Best of Sex and Violence** (1981) . . . . Emanuelle
  • 0:23—Side of left breast while getting clothes taken
    off by a guy. Long shot. Scene from *Emanuelle
    Around the World.*
Ator, The Fighting Eagle (1982) . . . . . . . . . . . . . Indun
**Famous T & A** (1982) . . . . . . . . . . . . . . . . Emanuelle
(No longer available for purchase, check your video
store for rental.)
  ••• 0:55—Breasts scenes from *Emanuelle Around the
    World.*
**Endgame** (1983) . . . . . . . . . . . . . . . . . . . . . . . . Lilith
  • 1:10—Brief breasts a couple of times getting blouse
    ripped open by a gross looking guy.
Caged Women (1984; French/Italian) . Emanuelle/Laura
*a.k.a. Emanuelle in Hell*
**Metamorphosis** (1989). . . . . . . . . . . . . . . .Prostitute
  • 0:37—Very brief breasts several times in Peter's flash-
    back.
  • 0:43—Very brief breasts in flashback again.
Passionate Pleasures (1989) . . . . . . . . . . . . . .Haunani
Quest for the Mighty Sword (1989; Italian) . . . Grimilde
**Top Model** (1989; Italian). . . . . . . . . . . . . Dorothy/Eve
  • 0:44—Brief right breast and buns, frolicking with the
    cowboy.
Eleven Days, Eleven Nights 2 (1990) . . . . . Jackie Forrest
Object of Desire (1991) . . . . . Uncredited Photographer
*Magazines:*
**Playboy** (May 1979). . . . . . . . . . . . . Foreign Sex Stars
  •• 170-171—Nude.

## Gentry, Jaki

*Video Tapes:*
**Hot Body International: #3 Lingerie Special**
(1992) . . . . . . . . . . . . . . . . . . . . . . . . . . . .Contestant
  •• 0:46—Buns, in G-string and bra.

••• 0:53—Breasts, posing for photo shoot.
Hot Body International: #5 Miss Acapulco (1992)
............................................ Contestant

# George, Susan

*Films:*
The Looking Glass War (1970; British) ......... Susan
Die Screaming Marianne (1972) ........... Marianne
**Straw Dogs** (1972) ........................ Amy
•• 0:32—Breasts taking off sweater, tossing it down to Dustin Hoffman, then looking out the door at the workers.
••• 1:00—Breasts on couch getting raped by one of the construction workers.
Dirty Mary, Crazy Larry (1974) ............... Mary
**Mandingo** (1975) ....................... Blanche
• 1:36—Brief breasts in bed with Ken Norton.
**Out of Season** (1975; British) ............. Joanna
• 1:24—Nude, while walking in front of Cliff Robertson. Long shot.
Small Town in Texas (1976)............... Mary Lee
**Tintorera** (1977)........................Gabriella
• 0:42—Brief breasts waking up Steven in hammock.
Enter the Ninja (1981) ........... Mary-Ann Landers
**House Where Evil Dwells** (1982) ........... Laura
••• 0:21—Breasts in bed making love with Edward Albert.
•• 0:59—Breasts making love again.
Venom (1982; British) .....................Louise
The Jigsaw Man (1984).....................Penny
Lightning, The White Stallion (1986).... Madame Rene
*Made for TV Movies:*
Jack the Ripper (1988)................... Catherine
*Magazines:*
**Playboy** (Nov 1972) ........... Sex in Cinema 1972
•• 160—Breasts on couch from *The Straw Dogs.*
**Playboy** (Dec 1972).............. Sex Stars of 1972
•• 208—Breasts.
Playboy (Nov 1976) ........... Sex in Cinema 1976
145—Partial back side of right breast.

# Georges-Picot, Olga

*Films:*
Farewell, Friend (1968; French/Italian) .. Isabelle Manue
Connecting Rooms (1971; British)..... Claudia Fouchet
**Day of the Jackal** (1973) ................. Denise
• 0:55—Brief breasts and buns, getting out of bed to use the phone.
Persecution (1974; British) .......... Monique Kalfon
Love and Death (1975)....... Countess Alexandrovna
Goodbye Emmanuelle (1977).................n.a.
*Magazines:*
Playboy (Nov 1975) ........... Sex in Cinema 1975
131—In lingerie with Woody Allen from *Love and Death.*

# Geraghty, Erin

*Films:*
**Games Girls Play** (1974; British) ............ Ducky
*a.k.a. The Bunny Caper*
*a.k.a. Sex Play*
• 1:11—In bra and panties, then breasts running around outside.
That'll Be the Day (1974; British) ..............Joan

# • Gerardi, Joan

*Films:*
**Affairs of the Heart** (1992) .... Miss Valentine's Day
••• 0:15—Breasts, posing for photos in red bottoms.
Marilyn Chambers' Bedtime Stories (1993) .......Jane

# Gere, Ashlyn

See: McKamy, Kim.

# Gerrish, Flo

*Films:*
Superchick (1978) ......................Funky Jane
**Don't Answer the Phone** (1979)....Dr. Lindsay Gale
• 1:05—Very brief breasts rolling over in bed with McCabe. Brief breasts when he pulls the covers down.
• 1:19—Side view of right breast, several times, while taking off blouse and putting nightgown on.
Schizoid (1980) .............................Pat
Hot Chili (1985)...................... Mrs. Baxter
The Naked Cage (1985)................... Mother
Over the Top (1987) .......... Martha, the Waitress

# Gershon, Gina

*Films:*
3:15—The Moment of Truth (1986)
...............................One of the Cobrettes
**Sweet Revenge** (1987) .....................K.C.
• 0:41—Brief breasts in water under a waterfall with Lee.
**Cocktail** (1988) ......................... Coral
• 0:31—Very, very brief right breast romping around in bed with Tom Cruise.
Red Heat (1988)..................... Cat Manzetti
Voodoo Dawn (1989)........................Tina
City of Hope (1991)........................ Laurie
Out for Justice (1991)................ Patti Modono
The Player (1992).................Whitney Gersh
Joey Breaker (1993).................. Jenny Chaser
*Made for Cable Movies:*
**Love Matters** (1993; Showtime) ............. Heat
(Unrated version reviewed.)
• 0:33—Brief left breast when Tony Goldwyn lays her down.
••• 0:34—Breasts, while on table with Goldwyn. More breasts while making love on kitchen island. Buns when running away.
•• 0:44—Breasts, after turning over and lying under Goldwyn.
• 0:53—Partial left breast, while in shower, talking to Goldwyn.

*Made for TV Movies:*
Miss Rose White (1992). . . . . . . . . . . . . . . . . . . Angie
Sinatra (1992). . . . . . . . . . . . . . Nancy Barbato Sinatra

# Gertz, Jami
*Films:*
Endless Love (1981) . . . . . . . . . . . . . . . . . . . . . .Patty
Alphabet City (1984). . . . . . . . . . . . . . . . . . . . Sophia
Sixteen Candles (1984). . . . . . . . . . . . . . . . . . . Robin
Mischief (1985). . . . . . . . . . . . . . . . . . . . . . . . Rosalie
Crossroads (1986). . . . . . . . . . . . . . . . . . . . .Frances
Quicksilver (1986). . . . . . . . . . . . . . . . . . . . . . . Terri
Solarbabies (1986) . . . . . . . . . . . . . . . . . . . . . .Terra
Less than Zero (1987) . . . . . . . . . . . . . . . . . . . . Blair
The Lost Boys (1987) . . . . . . . . . . . . . . . . . . . . . .Star
Listen to Me (1989) . . . . . . . . . . Monica Tomanski
Renegades (1989). . . . . . . . . . . . . . . . . . . . .Barbara
**Silence Like Glass** (1989). . . . . . . . . . . . . Eva March
1:31—Very brief left breast on operating table, get-
ting defibrillated. Possible body double. The Doc-
tor's arm covers her face.
Don't Tell Her It's Me (1990). . . . . . . . . . . . .Emily Pear
Sibling Rivalry (1990) . . . . . . . . . . . . . . . . . . . Jeanine
*Made for Cable TV:*
Dream On: The Taking of Pablum 1-2-3, Part I
(1994; HBO) . . . . . . . . . . . . . . . . . . . Jane Harnick
Dream On: The Taking of Pablum 1-2-3, Part II
(1994; HBO) . . . . . . . . . . . . . . . . . . . Jane Harnick
*Made for TV Movies:*
Jersey Girl (1993) . . . . . . . . . . . . . . . . . . . . . . . .n.a.
This Can't Be Love (1994). . . . . . . . . . . . . . . . Sarah
*TV:*
Square Pegs (1982-83) . . . . . . . . . . . .Muffy Tepperman
Sibs (1991-92) . . . . . . . . . . . . . . . . . . . . . . . . . . Lily
*Video Tapes:*
The Kathy Kaehler Fitness System (1992)
. . . . . . . . . . . . . . . . . . . . . . . . . . . Exercise Student

# Gianetti, Gina
Adult film actress.
a.k.a. Cassie Blake.
*Films:*
**Simply Irresistible** (1983) . . . . . . . . . . . . . .Sunshine
(R-rated version. *Irresistible* is the X-rated version.)
•• 0:49—Breasts in motel room with Walter and Juliet.

# Gibb, Cynthia
*Films:*
Salvador (1986) . . . . . . . . . . . . . . . . . Cathy Moore
**Youngblood** (1986) . . . . . . . . . . . . . Jessie Chadwick
• 0:50—Brief breasts and buns making love with Rob
Lowe in his room.
Jack's Back (1987) . . . . . . . . . . . . . . . . . . Chris Moscari
1:00—Getting undressed in white camisole and
panties while someone watches her from outside.
1:30—Running around the house in a white slip try-
ing to get away from the killer.
Malone (1987) . . . . . . . . . . . . . . . . . . . . . . . . Jo Barlow
Modern Girls (1987) . . . . . . . . . . . . . . . . . . . . . .Cece

Short Circuit 2 (1988) . . . . . . . . . . . . . . Sandy Banatoni
Death Warrant (1990) . . . . . . . . . . . . Amanda Beckett
0:52—In bra, undressing for prison guards.
*Made for Cable TV:*
Tales From the Crypt: Korman's Kalamity (1992; HBO)
. . . . . . . . . . . . . . . . . . . . . . . . . . . . . . . . . .Lorelai
*Made for TV Movies:*
The Karen Carpenter Story (1989) . . . . Karen Carpenter
When We Were Young (1989) . . . . . . . . . . . . . . Ellen
Gypsy (1993). . . . . . . Gypsy Rose Lee/Rose Louise Hovick
A Twist of the Knife (1993). . . . . . . . . Amanda Bentley
The Woman Who Loved Elvis (1993) . . . . . . . . . . . n.a.
Sin and Redemption (1994). . . . . . . . . . . . Billie Simms
*TV:*
Search for Tomorrow (1981-83). . . . . Suzi Wyatt Martin
Fame (1983-86) . . . . . . . . . . . . . . . . . . . .Holly Laird
Madman of the People (1994- ). . . . . . . . . . . . . . . n.a.

# Giblin, Belinda
*Films:*
**Jock Petersen** (1974; Australian) . . . . . . Moira Winton
*a.k.a. Petersen*
•• 0:21—Left breast several times, under a cover with
Jock, then buns when cover is removed.
End Play (1975; Australian) . . . . . . . . . Margret Gifford
Demolition (1977) . . . . . . . . . . . . . . . . . . . . . . . . n.a.
The Empty Beach (1985) . . . . . . . . . . . . . Marion Singer

# Gibson, Greta
*Films:*
**Warlords** (1988) . . . . . . . . . . . . . . . . . . . . .Harem Girl
•• 1:05—Breasts in tent with the other harem girls.
Holding a snake.
•• 1:09—Breasts again.
**Beverly Hills Vamp** (1989) . . . . . . . Screen Test Starlet
•• 0:53—Breasts and brief buns in G-string lying on Mr.
Pendleton's desk.

# Gidley, Pamela
*Films:*
Thrashin' (1986) . . . . . . . . . . . . . . . . . . . . . . .Chrissy
The Blue Iguana (1988) . . . . . . . . . . . . . . . . . .Dakota
Cherry 2000 (1988) . . . . . . . . . . . . . . . . . . . . .Cherry
Permanent Record (1988) . . . . . . . . . . . . . . . . . . Kim
Disturbed (1990) . . . . . . . . . . . . . . . . Sandy Ramirez
The Last of the Finest (1990) . . . . . . . . . . . . . .Haley
Highway to Hell (1991) . . . . . . . . . . . . . . . . . . Clara
**Liebestraum** (1991). . . . . . . . . . . . . . . . Jane Kessler
(Unrated Director's cut reviewed.)
0:37—Caressing her right breast during dream.
Don't see anything.
• 1:07—Buns, while taking a shower. Almost breasts,
but her arm gets in the way.
Twin Peaks: Fire Walk With Me (1992) . . . . Teresa Banks
**Freefall** (1993) . . . . . . . . . . . . . . . . . . . . . Katy Mazur
• 0:29—Brief back side of left breast and upper half of
buns, while making love with Eric Roberts in bed. Almost breasts when Roberts lies back down. Breasts
later on don't show her face.

- 0:40—Right breast with Roberts in flashback. Don't see her face again.

*TV:*
Angel Street (1992). . . . . . . . . . . . . Dorothy Paretsky

## • Gielser, Regina
a.k.a. Adult film actress Kim Wylde.
*Films:*
**The Other Woman** (1992). . . . . . . . . . . . . Neighbor
(Unrated version reviewed.)
- • 0:49—Breasts and buns, while in bed with Jessica's mother during young Jessica's flashback.

**The Pamela Principle** (1992) . . . . . . . . . . . . . Felicia
(Unrated version reviewed.)
- • • 1:27—Buns in bed with Carl and Pamela, then breasts.

## Giftos, Elaine
*Films:*
Gas-s-s! (1970) . . . . . . . . . . . . . . . . . . . . . . . . . . . Cilla
On a Clear Day You Can See Forever (1970) . . . . . Muriel
**The Student Nurses** (1970). . . . . . . . . . . . . . Sharon
*a.k.a. Young LA Nurses*
- 1:14—Brief breasts undressing and getting into bed with terminally ill boy. Dark, hard to see.

Everything You Wanted to Know About Sex, But Were Afraid to Ask (1972) . . . . . . . . . . . . . . . . . . . Mrs. Ross
The Wrestler (1974) . . . . . . . . . . . . . . . . . . . . Debbie
Paternity (1981) . . . . . . . . . . . . . . . . . . . Woman in Bar
Angel (1983). . . . . . . . . . . . . . . . . . . . . Patricia Allen
The Trouble with Dick (1986) . . . . . . . . . . . . . . . Sheila
*Made for TV Movies:*
The Secret Night Caller (1975) . . . . . . . . . . . . . . Chloe

## Gilbert, Melissa
Sister of actress Sara Gilbert.
Ex-wife of actor/writer Bo Brinkman.
*Films:*
**Sylvester** (1985) . . . . . . . . . . . . . . . . . . . . . . . Charlie
- 0:23—Very, very brief breasts struggling with a guy in truck cab. Seen through a dirty windshield.
- • 0:24—Very brief left breast after Richard Farnsworth runs down the stairs to help her. Seen from the open door of the truck.

Ice House (1988). . . . . . . . . . . . . . . . . . . . . . . . . . Kay
0:51—Making love with another guy while her real-life husband watches while he's tied up.
Babymaker: The Dr. Cecil Jacobson Story (1994). . . . n.a.
*Made for Cable Movies:*
Dying to Remember (1993; USA) . . . . . . Lynn Matthews
*Made for TV Movies:*
The Miracle Worker (1979) . . . . . . . . . . . . Helen Keller
The Diary of Anne Frank (1980) . . . . . . . . . . Anne Frank
Donor (1990) . . . . . . . . . . . . . . . . . . . . . . . . . . . . n.a.
Joshua's Heart (1990) . . . . . . . . . . . . . . . . . . . Claudia
Family of Strangers (1993) . . . . . . . . . . . . . . . . . . n.a.
House of Secrets (1993) . . . . . . . . . . . . Marion Ravinel
Shattered Trust: The Shari Karney Story (1993)
. . . . . . . . . . . . . . . . . . . . . . . . . . . . . . Shari Karney

With Hostile Intent (1993) . . . . . . . . . . . . . . . . . . . n.a.
*TV:*
Little House on the Prairie (1974-83)
. . . . . . . . . . . . . . . . . . . . . . . . . Laura Ingalls Wilder
Stand by Your Man (1992). . . . . . . . . . . . . . . Rochelle
Sweet Justice (1994- ) . . . . . . . . . . . . . . Kate Delcroy

## Gilbert, Pamela
*Films:*
**Cyclone** (1986). . . . . . . . . . . . Uncredited Shower Girl
0:06—Buns and breasts (she's the brunette) in the showers. Long shot.
**Evil Spawn** (1987) . . . . . . . . . . . . . . . . Elaine Talbot
- • • 0:46—Nude taking off black lingerie and going swimming in pool. Hubba, hubba!
- • • 0:49—Breasts in the pool, then full frontal nudity getting out.

**Demonwarp** (1988). . . . . . . . . . . . . . . . Carrie Austin
- • • 0:20—In bra, then breasts in bed with Jack.
- • • 0:22—Right breast, then breasts lying in bed, making love with Jack.
- • 1:23—Breasts, strapped to table.
- 1:24—Breasts several more times on the table.
- • 1:25—Breasts getting up and getting dressed.

**The Alien Within** (1990). . . . . . . . . . . . . Elaine Talbot
Contains footage from *The Evil Spawn* woven together with new material.
- • • 0:48—Nude taking off black lingerie and going swimming in pool.
- • • 0:55—Breasts in the pool, then full frontal nudity getting out.

## Gildersleeve, Linda
*Films:*
Beach Bunnies (1977) . . . . . . . . . . . . . . . . . . . . . . n.a.
**Cinderella** (1977). . . . . . . . . . . . . Farm Girl (redhead)
- • • 0:21—Breasts and buns with her brunette sister in their house making love with the guy who is looking for Cinderella.
- • 1:24—Full frontal nudity with her sister again when the Prince goes around to try and find Cinderella.

**The Happy Hooker Goes to Washington** (1977)
. . . . . . . . . . . . . . . . . . . . . . . . . . . Honeymoon Wife
- 0:35—Brief breasts in a diner during the filming of a commercial.

## Gillingham, Kim
*Films:*
Valet Girls (1987) . . . . . . . . . . . . . . Madonna Wannabe
Captain America (1990). . . . . . . . Bernice Stewart/Sharon
**Corporate Affairs** (1990) . . . . . . . . . Ginny Malmquist
- 1:09—Breasts, climbing out of cubicle.

## Gilmore-Capps, Teresa
*Films:*
**The Arrogant** (1987). . . . . . . . . . . . . . . . . . Charlotte
- 0:23—Brief breasts, making love in a barn.

The Marrying Man (1991) . . . . . . . . . . Bugsy's Blonde
*a.k.a. Too Hot to Handle*

**Made for Cable Movies:**
Fever (1991; HBO) . . . . . . . . . . . . . . . . . . . . . . Jeanine

# Giorgi, Eleonora

*Films:*
Diary of a Cloistered Nun (1973; Italian/German/French)
. . . . . . . . . . . . . . . . . . . . . . . . . . . . . . . . Carmela
**Appassionata** (1979; Italian) . . . . . . . . . . . . . . Nicola
- • 0:14—Very brief left breast in open blouse with Emilio in his dentist office. Breasts several times.
- •• 0:41—Full frontal nudity in bedroom when Emilio comes in. Dark.
- ••• 0:54—Nude in office with Emilio in stockings and garter belt.
- • 1:35—Brief right breast in bed with Emilio. Dark.

**Beyond Obsession** (1982) . . . . . . . . . . . . . . . . . Nina
- •• 0:01—Breasts, taking off her top and getting into the shower with Tom Berenger.
- • 0:59—Right breast in bed with Marcello Mastroianni, brief right breast after.

**Nudo di Donna** (1984; Italian) . . . . . . . . . . . . Laura
*a.k.a. Portrait of a Woman, Nude*
- • 0:11—Very brief left breast, while taking off robe. Subtitles get in the way.
- • 0:12—Right breast, while in the shower, getting consoled.
- • 0:13—Brief upper half breasts, getting into bed.
- •• 0:14—Breasts in bed.
- •• 0:36—Nude, mostly buns, sleeping in bed when Sandro pulls back the covers.
- • 1:12—Brief right breast, while in bed with Sandro.
  1:13—Right breast under sheer dress.

Il Volpone (1988; Italian) . . . . . . . . . . . . . . . . The Mayor
*Magazines:*
**Playboy** (Nov 1977) . . . . . . . . . . Sex in Cinema 1977
- ••• 161—Left breast and most of right breast from *The Sex Machine.*

# Giosa, Susan

*Films:*
America 3000 (1986) . . . . . . . . . . . . . . . . . . . . Morha
**The First Power** (1990) . . . . . . . . . . . . . . . . . Carmen
  0:12—In bra when the killer opens her blouse.
- • 0:22—Brief right breast, lying dead with a bloody pentagram cut into her stomach.
*TV:*
Reasonable Doubts (1992-93) . . . . . . . . . . . . . . Diedre

# Girling, Cindy

*Films:*
**Left for Dead** (1978) . . . . . . . . . . . . . . Pauline Corte
- •• 0:19—Nude, taking off shirt in bedroom.
**Daughter of Death** (1982) . . . . . . . . . . . . . . . . Irene
*a.k.a. Julie Darling*
- •• 0:12—Breasts in bathtub and getting out.
Hostile Takeover (1988; Canadian) . . . . . . Mrs. Gayford
*a.k.a. Office Party*

# Giroux, Jackie

*Films:*
Cross and the Switchblade (1970) . . . . . . . . . . . . . Rosa
**Sweet Sugar** (1972) . . . . . . . . . . . . . . . . . . . . . . Fara
*a.k.a. Hellfire on Ice*
- •• 0:33—Breasts, skinny dipping in stream with Dolores.
This is a Hijack (1973) . . . . . . . . . . . . . . . . . Scott's Girl
Drive-In Massacre (1974) . . . . . . . . . . . . . . . . . . . n.a.
Slaughter's Big Rip-Off (1975) . . . . . . . . . . Mrs. Duncan
Jokes My Folks Never Told Me (1976). . . . . . . . . . . n.a.
Sex Through a Window (1977) . . . . . . . . . . . . . Barbie
Trick or Treats (1982) . . . . . . . . . . . . . . . . . . . . . n.a.
To Live and Die in L.A. (1985) . . . . . . . . . Claudia Leith

# Givens, Robin

Ex-wife of boxer Mike Tyson.
*Films:*
**A Rage in Harlem** (1991) . . . . . . . . . . . . . . . Imabelle
- ••• 0:32—Buns, while lying in bed with Forest Whitaker.
**Boomerang** (1992) . . . . . . . . . . . . . . . . . . Jacqueline
  0:50—Very brief half of left breast, lying with her back on bed with Eddie Murphy when she first puts her arm under his arm.
- •• 1:02—Very brief side view of right breast, while making love on top of Murphy in bed.
  1:42—In black bra and panties, in bed with Murphy.
Foreign Student (1994) . . . . . . . . . . . . . . . . . . . . n.a.
*Made for TV Movies:*
The Penthouse (1989) . . . . . . . . . . . . . . . . . . . . . n.a.
*TV:*
Head of the Class (1986-91). . . . . . . . Darlene Merriman
Angel Street (1992) . . . . . . . . . . . . . . . . . . Anita King
*Magazines:*
**Playboy** (Sep 1994) . . . So How Do You Like Me Now?
- ••• 120-129—Breasts and buns in B&W and color photographs.

# Glaser, Lisa

*Films:*
**Humanoids from the Deep** (1980) . . . . . . . . . . Becky
(Brunette colored hair.)
- ••• 0:34—Full frontal nudity, undressing in tent with Billy and his ventriloquist dummy.
- • 0:35—Nude, running on the beach at night, trying to escape the humanoids.
**Stripped to Kill II** (1988) . . . . . . . . . . . . . . . Victoria
(Blonde colored hair.)
- •• 0:01—Breasts and buns in G-string doing a strip dance routine during Shadey's nightmare.
**Future Kick** (1991) . . . . . . . . . . . Uncredited Dancer
- • 0:36—Breasts, dancing on stage in white outfit. (Taken from *Stripped to Kill II.*)

# Glass, Leslie

Started doing adult films in 1994.
*Films:*
Mannequin Two: On the Move (1991)
. . . . . . . . . . Uncredited Mannequin in Theater Scene

*Video Tapes:*

**Penthouse Satin & Lace II: Hollywood Undercover**
(1992)...................................... Pet
**The Penthouse All-Pet Workout** (1993) ....... Pet
•• 0:00—Breasts during introduction.
•• 0:03—Brief nude shots while getting undressed and
suited up.
••• 0:38—Nude on chair outside and in pool.
••• 0:43—Nude with the other girls, exercising, working
with equipment, in the pool and spa.
**Penthouse Pet of the Year Playoff 1993** (1993)
.............................................. Pet
••• 0:11—Nude in back seat of limousine, in TV station
(sometimes wearing a blonde wig), in Central Park
on horseback, in the desert.
**Penthouse The Great Pet Hunt—Part II** (1993)
.............................................. Pet
••• 0:25—Nude after stripping out of maid outfit on
stage.
**Penthouse Pet of the Year Winners 1993: Mahalia
& Julie** (1994)
............ Sneak Preview of Pet of the Year Playoff
••• 0:28—Nude in and around Central Park in New York
City.
**Penthouse Pet of the Year Winners 1994: Sasha &
Leslie** (1994) .................... Runner-Up Pet
••• 0:30—Breasts then nude in boxing gloves and
shorts.
••• 0:31—Nude, posing inside and outside a house in
color and B&W segments.
••• 0:36—Nude in still photos.
••• 0:37—Nude while posing in a house.
••• 0:38—In lingerie and nude after playing cards with
a blonde woman and a guy.
••• 0:42—Nude on rooftop in city.
• 0:44—Nude in end credits.

*CD-ROM:*

**Penthouse Interactive Virtual Photo Shoot, Disc 2**
(1993)................................... Pet

*Magazines:*

**Penthouse** (Feb 1992) ...................... Pet
••• 67-81—Nude.
**Penthouse** (Jun 1993)........ Pet of the Year Play-Off
••• 114-115—Nude.
**Penthouse** (Apr 1994)...... Pet of the Year Runner-Up
••• 90-99—Nude.
**Penthouse** (Sep 1994) .............. Sasha & Leslie
••• 208-219—Nude with Sasha Vinni.

## • *Glasser, Isabel*

*Films:*

A Marriage (1983)........................... Nancy
**Death Ring** (1992) ................. Lauren Sadler
•• 0:11—Breasts, after taking off swimsuit top on chair
outside with Mike Norris.
Forever Young (1992) ...................... Helen
Pure Country (1992) ............... Harley Tucker

## *Glazowski, Liz*

*Films:*

The Happy Hooker Goes Hollywood (1980) ....... Liz

*Magazines:*

**Playboy** (Jan 1980)......... Playboy's Pajama Parties
•• 126—Right breast.
**Playboy** (Apr 1980) .................... Playmate
••• 140-151—Nude.

## *Glenn, Carrick*

*Films:*

**The Burning** (1981)....................... Sally
••• 0:19—Breasts, taking a shower in the outdoor showers.
• 0:20—Very brief breasts, putting her T-shirt back on.
Girls Nite Out (1982) ...................... Kathy
*a.k.a. Scared to Death*

## *Glenn, Charisse*

*Films:*

**Bad Influence** (1990) ....... Stylish Eurasian Woman
••• 1:26—Breasts and partial lower frontal nudity making love on Rob Lowe.
• 1:28—Very brief left breast in bed with the blonde
woman.

*Magazines:*

**Playboy** (Nov 1990) ........... Sex in Cinema 1990
• 146—Left breast.

## *Go, Jade*

*Films:*

Model Behavior (1982) ................ Golden Girl
Big Trouble in Little China (1986)
.................... Chinese Girl in White Tiger
**The Last Emperor** (1987) .................. Ar Mo
• 0:10—Right breast in open top after breast feeding
the young Pu Yi.
• 0:20—Right breast in open top telling Pu Yi a story.
• 0:29—Right breast in open top breast feeding an
older Pu Yi. Long shot.

## • *Goddard, Anna-Marie*

*Video Tapes:*

**Playboy Video Centerfold: Anna-Marie Goddard**
(1994) ................. 40th Anniversary Playmate
• 0:00—Full frontal nudity during introduction.
••• 0:02—Nude during studio segment. Sometimes in
fishnet body suit and some in B&W.
••• 0:09—Taking off stockings, then full frontal nudity
while fantasizing about a man and woman. A little
bit of rubbing lotion on herself.
••• 0:14—Nude, in bayou shack.
••• 0:18—Nude in still photos.
••• 0:20—Nude in house in dream wedding sequence.
• 0:27—Nude in end segment.
•• 0:45—Breasts in centerfold still.
•• 0:46—Nude during end credits.

*Magazines:*
**Playboy** (Jan 1994)
.The Great 40th Anniversary Playmate Search/Playmate
••• 139—Full frontal nudity.
••• 144-157—Nude.
**Playboy's Great Playmate Search** (Feb 1994)
••• . . . . . . . . . . . . . . . . . . . . . . . . . . . . . . Herself
••• 6-15—Nude.

# Golden, Shana

*Films:*
**State Park** (1988; Canadian). . . . . . . Blond in Shower
• 0:46—Breasts taking a shower outside while park
ranger watches. Long shot.
The Baby Doll Murders (1992) . . . . . . . . . . . Prostitute
**Molly & Gina** (1993). . . . . . . . . . . . . . . . . . . . .Sherry
•• 1:05—Breasts, while making love on top of Peter
Fonda in bed.
• 1:06—Brief right breast, after rolling over after Fonda leaves the room.
• 1:08—Brief buns in G-string after tossing off her
robe.

# Goldsmith, Clio

*Films:*
**Honey** (1980; Italian) . . . . . . . . . . . . . . . . . . . . . Annie
•• 0:05—Nude kneeling in a room.
•• 0:20—Nude getting into the bathtub.
•• 0:42—Nude getting changed.
••• 0:44—Nude while hiding under the bed.
•• 0:58—Nude getting disciplined, taking off clothes,
then kneeling.
**The Gift** (1982; French). . . . . . . . . . . . . . . . .Barbara
•• 0:39—Brief breasts several times in the bathroom,
then right breast in bathtub.
• 0:49—Breasts lying in bed sleeping.
0:51—Very brief left breast turning over in bed.
• 0:52—Brief right breast then buns, reaching for
phone while lying in bed.
1:16—Very brief left breast getting out of bed. Dark,
hard to see.
**The Heat of Desire** (1982; French) . . . . . . . . . Carol
*a.k.a. Plein Sud*
• 0:09—Breasts and buns, getting out of bed in train
to look out the window. Dark.
• 0:12—Brief breasts in bathroom mirror when Serge
peeks in.
•• 0:19—Full frontal nudity in the bathtub.
•• 0:20—Nude, sitting on the floor with Serge's head in
her lap.
•• 0:21—Buns, lying face down on floor. Very brief
breasts. A little dark. Then breasts sitting up and
drinking out of bottle.
• 0:22—Right breast, in gaping robe sitting on floor
with Serge.
• 0:24—Partial left breast consoling Serge in bed.
• 0:25—Breasts sitting on chair on balcony, then walking inside. Dark.

• 0:56—Breasts walking from bathroom and getting
into bed. Dark.
• 0:57—Brief right breast, while on couch with Guy
Marchand.
•• 0:58—Breasts getting dressed while Serge is yelling.
**La Cicala (The Cricket)** (1983). . . . . . . . . . . . Cicala
•• 0:26—Nude when Wilma brings her in to get Anthony Franciosa excited again.
•• 0:39—Nude swimming under waterfall with Barbara
de Rossi.
••• 0:43—Full frontal nudity undressing in room with de
Rossi.
Miss Right (1987; Italian) . . . . . . . . . . . . . . . . . . . n.a.

# • Goldson, Delia

*Films:*
**The Finishing Touch** (1991) . . . . . . . . Sorvino's Model
•• 1:06—In lingerie outfit, then breasts while hand-
cuffed to bed while getting video taped by Sorvino.
*Magazines:*
Playboy's Book of Lingerie (Jan 1993) . . . . . . . . . Herself
**Playboy's Book of Lingerie** (Mar 1993). . . . . .Herself
••• 52—Full frontal nudity.
**Playboy's Book of Lingerie** (May 1993) . . . . .Herself
••• 48—Full frontal nudity.
**Playboy's Girls of Summer '93** (Jun 1993) . . .Herself
•• 94-95—Buns.
**Playboy's Book of Lingerie** (Sep 1993). . . . . .Herself
••• 14—Full frontal nudity.
**Playboy's Book of Lingerie** (Jan 1994) . . . . . .Herself
••• 43—Breasts.
**Playboy's Book of Lingerie** (Mar 1994). . . . . .Herself
• 102—Upper half of left breast and lower frontal nudity in sheer panties.

# Golino, Valeria

*Films:*
Blind Date (1984). . . . . . . . . . . . . . . . . . . . .Girl in Bikini
*a.k.a. Deadly Seduction*
(Not the same 1987 *Blind Date* with Bruce Willis.)
Detective School Dropouts (1986) . . . . . . . . . . .Caterina
Big Top Pee Wee (1988). . . . . . . . . Gina Piccolapupula
**Rain Man** (1988) . . . . . . . . . . . . . . . . . . . . .Suzanna
• 0:35—Very brief left breast four times and very,
brief right breast once with open blouse fighting
with Tom Cruise after getting out of the bathtub.
**The King's Whore** (1990; French/British)
. . . . . . . . . . . . . . . . . . . . . . . . . . . . .Jeanne de Luyes
•• 0:08—Right breast, while making out with Alex-
ander.
• 1:01—Brief upper half of breasts, while lying in bed
with Timothy Dalton.
••• 1:02—Breasts and buns when Dalton beats her up
and throws her out of the room.
• 1:16—Right breast when Dalton helps her with her
skin disease.
• 1:19—Brief right breast when Dalton takes off her
bandages.

- 1:20—Upper half of breasts while in bathtub. (She still has the skin disease.)

Torrents of Spring (1990) ................ Gemma
Hot Shots (1991) ..............Ramada Thompson
The Indian Runner (1991).................. Maria
**Year of the Gun** (1991) .............. Lia Spinelli
- ••• 0:17—Breasts, making love in bed with Andrew Mc-Carthy.
- • 0:25—Half of buns and side of right breast, lying in bed with McCarthy.

Hot Shots! Part Deux (1993)
..................... Ramada Rodham Hayman
Clean Slate (1994) ........................n.a.

## Gonzalez, Cordelia

*Films:*
Homeboy (1988) ..............Cuban Boxer's Wife
**Born on the Fourth of July** (1989)......Maria Elena
- ••• 1:43—Breasts in black panties, then full frontal nudity in bed with Tom Cruise.

## • Good, Melanie

*Films:*
Campus Hustle (1993) ................... Veronica
**Die Watching** (1993) ............... Sheila Walsh
- ••• 0:05—In white bodysuit dancing while Christopher Atkins video tapes her. Then breasts through bodysuit, then breasts after she rips the bodysuit open.
- ••• 0:07—Breasts in ripped bodysuit while taped down in chair before Atkins kills her.

**Money to Burn** (1994) ..................... Ann
- • 0:40—Buns in fishnet body suit, breasts under the suit, while making love with Julie Strain on the floor.

*Video Tapes:*
**Playboy's Secret Confessions** (1993)
..................................... On the Air/D.J.
- ••• 0:11—In bra and panties, then breasts, while making love in radio station.

*Magazines:*
**Playboy's Book of Lingerie** (Sep 1992) ..... Herself
- •• 36—Left breast.

**Playboy's Book of Lingerie** (Nov 1992) ..... Herself
- •• 91—Left breast.

**Playboy's Book of Lingerie** (Mar 1993) ..... Herself
- • 63—Breasts under lace bodysuit.

**Playboy** (Apr 1993) ................... Tattoo You
- •• 84—Right breast. Tattoo on ankle.

## Goodfellow, Joan

*Films:*
Lolly-Madonna XXX (1973)...........Sister Gutshall
**Buster and Billie** (1974) ................... Billie
0:33—Brief breasts in truck with Jan-Michael Vincent. Dark, hard to see.
- • 1:06—Buns, then brief breasts in the woods with Vincent.
- • 1:25—Brief left breast getting raped by jerks.

Sunburn (1979) ........................ Joanna
A Flash of Green (1984) ..................Mitchie

## Gorcey, Elizabeth

*Films:*
Footloose (1984) ......................Wendy Jo
Teen Wolf (1985) ............................ Tina
**The Trouble with Dick** (1986) .............. Haley
- • 0:13—Very brief left breast in gaping T-shirt while she lies on bed, plays with a toy and laughs.
0:26—Lower half of buns under robe on sofa with Dick.
0:27—Half of right breast on top of Dick in bed.

Iced (1988) .............................Diane

## Gracen, Elizabeth

Real name is Elizabeth Ward.
Miss Arkansas and Miss America 1982.

*Films:*
Lisa (1989)................................ Mary
Sundown: The Vampire in Retreat (1989)........ Alice
**Lower Level** (1990) ..................... Hillary
- • 0:11—Breasts in back seat of BMW making love with Craig. Long shot.
0:12—Very, very brief partial left breast afterwards.
- • 0:13—Brief right breast and lower frontal nudity getting dressed. Then in black lingerie.
0:14—In wet black lingerie under fire sprinkler in parking garage.
- •• 0:23—In black lingerie, then brief breasts changing in her office while Sam secretly watches.

Marked for Death (1990) ................. Melissa
0:45—Very brief part of right breast in gaping blouse, while crawling on the floor.

**Discretion Assured** (1993) ..............Miranda
- • 0:28—Brief buns when Michael York removes her panties.
- ••• 0:39—Breasts and buns, while making love with York.
- • 1:09—Back side of right and buns, while rubbing lotion on herself. Brief left breast, while putting on robe. Medium long shots.
- • 1:22—Brief breasts, when York rips her dress open during argument.

**Final Mission** (1993) .................. Caitlin Cole
- ••• 0:28—Breasts, while making out with Billy Wirth.
- • 0:53—Breasts, while making love on bed with Wirth at night.

*Made for TV Movies:*
83 Hours 'til Dawn (1990) ..................Maria

*Magazines:*
**Playboy** (May 1992)................There She Is...
- ••• 70-77—Nude.

**Playboy's Nudes** (Dec 1992) ..............Herself
- ••• 11—Full frontal nudity.

**Playboy** (Dec 1992) ..............Sex Stars 1992
- ••• 182—Full frontal nudity.

**Playboy's Nudes** (Dec 1993) ..............Herself
- • 46—Partial left breast and lower frontal nudity.

# • Graham, Aimee
*Films:*
Amos & Andrew (1993) . . . . . . . . . . . . . . . . . . Stacy
*Made for Cable Movies:*
**Rebel Highway: Reform School Girl**
(1994; Showtime) . . . . . . . . . . . . . .Donna Patterson
0:48—In white bra in shack with Carmen.
• 0:49—Breasts, while making out in shack with Carmen.
• 0:51—Brief breasts while in shower.
*Made for Cable TV:*
**Fallen Angels: Since I Don't Have You**
(1993; Showtime) . . . . . . . . . . . Gretchen Rae Shoftel
(Available on video tape on *Fallen Angels One.*)
• 0:07—Right breast and most of left breast in B&W photo.
• 0:08—Same photo in closer shot.

# Graham, Julie
*Films:*
**Wonderland** (1989; British) . . . . . . . . . . . . . . . Hazel
•• 1:11—Nude, taking off her clothes at the beach while talking to Eddie.
Nuns on the Run (1990; British) . . . . . . .Casino Waitress
**The Big Man** (1991; British) . . . . . . . . . . . . . Melanie
*a.k.a. Crossing the Line*
•• 1:09—Breasts when Liam Neeson undresses her and starts to make love with her.

# • Graham, Juliet
*Films:*
The Serpents of the Pirate Moon (1973) . . . . . . .Woman
**Alice in Wonderland** (1977) . . . . . . . . . . . The Queen
(R-rated version reviewed.)
••• 0:51—Full frontal nudity in garter belt and stockings while walking, then talking with Alice.
••• 0:54—Full frontal nudity during trial.
0:58—Breasts in quick cuts.
•• 1:05—Full frontal nudity, while running after Alice.
•• 1:13—Breasts during the end credits.
*Magazines:*
**Playboy** (Nov 1975) . . . . . . . . . . . Sex in Cinema 1975
• 139—Full frontal nudity on her back, from *The Story of Joanna.*

# Graham, Sherri
*Films:*
**Bad Girls from Mars** (1990) . . . . . . . . . . . Swimmer
•• 0:22—Very brief breasts diving into, then climbing out of pool.
**Haunting Fear** (1990) . . . . . . . . . . . . . Visconti's Girl
• 0:45—Buns in swimming pool. (Breasts seen under water.)
• 0:47—Breasts, giving Visconti a massage while he talks on the phone.
**Mob Boss** (1990) . . . . . . . . . . . . . . . . . . . . . .Bar Girl
•• 0:46—Breasts and buns, dancing on stage. Medium long shot.

Naked Obsession (1990) . . . . . . . . . . . . . . . .Waitress
Carnal Crimes (1991) . . . . . . . . . . . . . . . Party Girl #1

# Grant, Faye
*Films:*
**Internal Affairs** (1990) . . . . . . . . . . . . . . . . . Penny
• 0:50—Right breast, while straddling Richard Gere while she talks on the telephone.
The Gun in Betty Lou's Handbag (1992) . . . . . Charleen
Traces of Red (1992) . . . . . . . . . . . . . . . . . Beth Frayn
0:52—Buns in T-back under sheer dress.
*Made for Cable TV:*
Tales From the Crypt: Spoiled (1991; HBO) . . . . . . Janet
*Miniseries:*
V (1983) . . . . . . . . . . . . . . . . . . . . . . Dr. Julie Parrish
V: The Final Battle (1984) . . . . . . . . . . . Dr. Julie Parrish
*Made for TV Movies:*
Omen IV: The Awakening (1991) . . . . . . . . . .Karen York
*TV:*
Greatest American Hero (1981-83). . . . . . .Rhonda Blake
V: The Series (1984-85) . . . . . . . . . . . . Dr. Julie Parrish

# Grant, Lee
Mother of actress Dinah Manoff.
*Films:*
In the Heat of the Night (1967) . . . . .Mrs. Leslie Colbert
Valley of the Dolls (1967) . . . . . . . . . . . . . . . . .Miriam
Marooned (1969) . . . . . . . . . . . . . . . . . . Celia Pruett
The Landlord (1970) . . . . . . . . . . . . . . . . Mrs. Enders
There Was a Crooked Man (1970) . . . . . . .Mrs. Bullard
Plaza Suite (1971) . . . . . . . . . . . . . . . . .Norma Hubley
Portnoy's Complaint (1972) . . . . . . . . . . Sophie Portnoy
**Shampoo** (1975) . . . . . . . . . . . . . . . . . . . . . . Felicia
(Academy Award for Best Supporting Actress.)
• 0:03—Brief breasts in bed sitting up and putting bra on talking to Warren Beatty. Long shot, hard to see.
Airport '77 (1977) . . . . . . . . . . . . . . . Karen Wallace
Damien, Omen II (1978) . . . . . . . . . . . . ,Ann Thorn
The Mafu Cage (1978). . . . . . . . . . . . . . . . . . . Ellen
*a.k.a. My Sister, My Love*
**When Ya Comin' Back Red Ryder** (1979)
. . . . . . . . . . . . . . . . . . . . . . . Clarisse Ethridge
(Not available on video tape.)
Little Miss Marker (1980) . . . . . . . . . . . . . . The Judge
Charlie Chan & the Curse of the Dragon Queen (1981)
. . . . . . . . . . . . . . . . . . . . . . . . . Mrs. Lupowitz
Visiting Hours (1982; Canadian) . . . . . .Deborah Ballin
Teachers (1984) . . . . . . . . . . . . . . . . . . . . Dr. Burke
The Big Town (1987) . . . . . . . . . . . . Ferguson Edwards
Defending Your Life (1991) . . . . . . . . . . . . Lena Foster
*Made for Cable Movies:*
Citizen Cohn (1992; HBO) . . . . . . . . . . . . . . . . Dora
*Miniseries:*
Backstairs at the White House (1979) . . . Grace Coolidge
*Made for TV Movies:*
The Neon Ceiling (1971) . . . . . . . . . . . . . .Carrie Miller
She Said No (1990) . . . . . . . . . . . . . . . Doris Cantore
Something to Live For: The Alison Gertz Story (1992)
. . . . . . . . . . . . . . . . . . . . . . . . . . . . . . . . n.a.

*TV:*
Peyton Place (1965-66) . . . . . . . . . . . . . Stella Chernak
Fay (1975-76) . . . . . . . . . . . . . . . . . . . . . . .Fay Stewart

# Grassnick, Michelle

*Films:*
Bikini Summer (1991) . . . . . . . . . . . . . . . . . . . . Debbie
**Miracle Beach** (1991). . . . . . . . . . . Miss Great Britain
  • 0:35—Brief buns in swimsuit bottom, then right
    breast, while lying in bed, talking with Lars.
  ••• 1:03—Breasts, while trying on swimsuits backstage.
Final Impact (1992). . . . . . . . . . . . . . . . . . . Foxy Boxer
**Knockouts** (1992) . . . . . . . . . . . . . . . . . . . . . . Margo
  ••• 0:04—Breasts while lifting weights.
  ••• 0:35—Breasts, several times in locker room with her
    girlfriends.
  •• 0:59—Breasts, while putting swimsuit on (she's on
    the left).
    1:10—Buns, in outfit during wrestling match.
  • 1:12—Brief right breast, when it falls out of her top.

# Gravatte, Marianne

*Video Tapes:*
**Playboy Video Magazine, Volume 3** (1983)
  . . . . . . . . . . . . . .Playboy's Playmate of the Year 1983
  ••• 1:04—Nude in still photos.
  ••• 1:08—Full frontal nudity in bed at beach scene.
  ••• 1:09—Nude at the beach during the day.
  ••• 1:16—Nude while sitting at vanity and in bed.
**Playboy Video Magazine, Volume 5** (1983)
  . . . . . . . . . . . . . . . . . . . . . . . . . . . . . . Playmate
  • 0:06—Full frontal nudity outside.
  ••• 0:09—Nude, posing at beach in a bed set.
**Playboy's Playmate Review 2** (1984) . . . . . Playmate
**Playboy's Playmates of the Year: The '80s** (1989)
  . . . . . . . . . . . . . . . . . . . . Playmate of the Year 1983
  ••• 0:32—Nude in still photos.
  ••• 0:33—Nude in bed at the beach during photo ses-
    sion.
  •• 0:51—Breasts in bed scene.
**Playboy Video Centerfold: Reneé Tenison** (1990)
  . . . . . . . . . . Portrait of a Photographer: Richard Fegley
  ••• 0:32—Nude, in photo session at the beach.
*Magazines:*
**Playboy** (Oct 1982) . . . . . . . . . . . . . . . . . Playmate
**Playboy's 1987 Book of Lingerie** (Mar 1987)
  . . . . . . . . . . . . . . . . . . . . . . . . . . . . . . . . Herself
  ••• 62-65—Breasts.
  • 96—Left breast.
**Playboy's Nudes** (Oct 1990) . . . . . . . . . . . . . Herself
  •• 54—Breasts and buns.
  •• 108—Buns and partial left breast.
**Playboy's Calendar Playmates** (Nov 1992) . . Herself
  ••• 27—Full frontal nudity.
  ••• 32—Full frontal nudity.
**Playboy** (Jan 1994) . . . . . . . . . . . .40 Memorable Years
  ••• 92—Full frontal nudity.

**Playboy Presents Playmates in Paradise**
  (Mar 1994). . . . . . . . . . . . . . . . . . . . . . . . Playmate
  ••• 58-61—Nude.
**Playboy** (Apr 1994)
  . . . . . . . . . . . Playmate Revisited: Marianne Gravatte
  ••• 74-77—Nude in new photos.

# Gray, Andee

*Films:*
Sno-Line (1984) . . . . . . . . . . . . . . . . . . . . . . Ruth Lyle
**9 1/2 Ninjas** (1990) . . . . . . . . . . . . . . . . Lisa Thorne
  •• 1:02—Breasts making love with Joe in the rain.
  • 1:19—Brief breasts during flashback.
Dead Men Don't Die (1991) . . . . . . . . . . . . . . Isadora

# Gray, Julie

*Films:*
Gimme an "F" (1981) . . . . . . . . . . . . . .Falcon Marsha
  *a.k.a. T & A Academy 2*
Stryker (1983; Philippines) . . . . . . . . . . . . . . Laurenz
School Spirit (1985) . . . . . . . . . . . . . . . . . . . Kendall
**Dr. Alien** (1989) . . . . . . . . . . . . . . . . . . . . . . . Karla
  *a.k.a. I Was a Teenage Sex Mutant*
  ••• 0:44—In white bra, then breasts in Janitor's room
    with Wesley.
The Naked Truth (1992) . . . . . . . . . . . . . Miss Hungary
*Video Tapes:*
Inside Out 3 (1992) . . . . . . . . . . . .Actress/The Branding

# Grazioli, Irene

*Films:*
Trena Di Panna (1988; Italian) . . . . . . . . . . . . . . .Tina
**Mediterraneo** (1991; Italian) . . . . . . . . . . . .Pastorella
  ••• 0:36—Breasts with the Munaron brothers.
  • 0:52—Brief breasts, swimming in water.
*Magazines:*
**Playboy** (Nov 1992) . . . . . . . . . . . Sex in Cinema 1992
  ••• 146—Breasts with two guys from *Mediterraneo.*

# Green, Marika

*Films:*
Pickpocket (1963; French) . . . . . . . . . . . . . . . . .Jeanne
Singapore, Singapore (1969; French/Italian) . . . Monica
Rider on the Rain (1970; French/Italian)
  . . . . . . . . . . . . . . . . . . . . . . . . . . .Hostess at Tania's
**Emmanuelle** (1974) . . . . . . . . . . . . . . . . . . . . . . Bee
  (R-rated version reviewed.)
  • 0:46—Nude, undressing outside with Sylvia Kristel.
    Brief full frontal nudity, when leaving blanket.
  •• 0:47—Breasts, getting dressed.
  • 0:50—Upper half of buns, while lying down, talking
    to Kristel.
Until September (1984) . . . . . . . . . . . . . . . . . Banker
*Magazines:*
**Playboy** (Jun 1975) . . . . . . . Sex in Cinema French Style
  •• 90—Left breast and lower frontal nudity.

# Greenberg, Sandy

*Video Tapes:*
**Playmates at Play** (1990) . . . . . . . . . . . . . Easy Rider
*Magazines:*
**Playboy's Girls of Summer '86** (Aug 1986) . . Herself
••• 47—Breasts.
**Playboy** (Jun 1987) . . . . . . . . . . . . . . . . . . . Playmate

# Greiner, Nicole

a.k.a. Adult film actress Nikki Dial.
*Video Tapes:*
**Big Bust Casting Call** (1992) . . . . . . . . . . . . Roxanne
••• 0:09—In bra and panties, then nude during her audition.
**The Lover's Guide to Sexual Ecstasy: A Sensual
Guide to Lovemaking** (1992) . . . Advanced Foreplay
••• 0:25—In white bra, then nude, while making love
with her lover.
••• 0:32—Breasts, while making love.
••• 0:36—Nude, while making love in bed in various positions.
••• 0:48—In white bra, then breasts and buns, in female
superior positions.
Penthouse Pet of the Year Playoff 1992 (1992) . . .Model
(Although listed in the credits, her part was cut in the final video tape.)
**Intimate Secrets—How Women Love to be Loved**
(1993). . . . . . . . . . . . . . . . . . . . . . . . . . . . . . . .Nicole
••• 0:13—In white bra and red panties, then full frontal
nudity on couch.
**Penthouse Pet of the Year Winners 1993: Mahalia
& Julie** (1994) . . . . . . . . . . Uncredited Cast Member
••• 0:18—Nude, while acting submissive to Mahalia.
Wearing sunglasses.

# • Grey, Nicole

*Films:*
Wildest Dreams (1987) . . . . . . . . . . . . . . Girl on Street
**Sexual Outlaws** (1993). . . . . . . . . . . . . . . . . . .Rita
••• 0:09—Breasts, after taking off her top with Jeannie,
then making love in hotel room.
**Midnight Tease** (1994) . . . . . . . . . . . . . . . . . Dusty
••• 0:17—Breasts after stripping out of policewoman's
uniform on stage.
*Magazines:*
**Playboy's Book of Lingerie** (Jul 1992) . . . . . . Herself
••• 75—Breasts.
**Playboy's Book of Lingerie** (Jan 1993) . . . . . . Herself
•• 54—Breasts.

# Grier, Pam

Cousin of actor/former football player Rosey Grier.
*Films:*
Beyond the Valley of the Dolls (1970) . . Black Party Goer
**The Big Doll House** (1971) . . . . . . . . . . . . . . . Grear
• 0:28—Very brief most of right breast rolling over in
bed.
•• 0:32—Breasts getting her back washed by Collier.
Arms in the way a little bit.

• 0:44—Left breast covered with mud sticking out of
her top after wrestling with Alcott.
The Big Bird Cage (1972). . . . . . . . . . . . . . . .Blossom
Twilight People (1972). . . . . . . . . . The Panther Woman
**Coffy** (1973). . . . . . . . . . . . . . . . . . . . . . . . . . . Coffy
• 0:05—Upper half of right breast in bed with a guy.
0:19—Buns, walking past the fireplace, seen
through a fish tank.
•• 0:25—Breasts in open dress getting attacked by two
masked burglars.
••• 0:38—Buns and breasts undressing in bedroom.
Wow!
• 0:42—Brief right breast when breast pops out of
dress while she's leaning over. Dark, hard to see.
0:49—In black bra and panties in open dress with a
guy in the bedroom.
**Naked Warriors** (1973). . . . . . . . . . . . . . . . Mamawi
*a.k.a. The Arena*
•• 0:08—Brief left breast, then lower frontal nudity and
side view of right breast getting washed down in
court yard.
••• 0:52—Breasts getting oiled up for a battle. Wow!
Scream, Blacula, Scream (1973). . . . . . . . . . .Lisa Fortier
**Foxy Brown** (1974) . . . . . . . . . . . . . . . . . Foxy Brown
• 0:05—Breasts, getting out of bed and taking off
nightgown.
• 0:40—Brief left breast, while getting dressed.
1:04—Upper half of breasts, while tied to bed.
••• 1:05—Right breast, then breasts rolling over in bed.
**Bucktown** (1975). . . . . . . . . . . . . . . . . . . . . . Aretha
••• 0:29—Left breast, while in bed with Fred William-
son.
**Friday Foster** (1975) . . . . . . . . . . . . . . . Friday Foster
••• 0:29—Breasts, several times, while taking a shower
while Carl Weathers stalks around in her apartment.
••• 1:12—Upper half of breast, while in bubble bath
with Blake. Breasts in bed with him.
**Sheba, Baby** (1975). . . . . . . . . . . . . . . Sheba Shayne
• 0:26—Side view of left breast, while lying in bed
with Brick.
**Drum** (1976). . . . . . . . . . . . . . . . . . . . . . . . . Regine
• 0:58—Very brief breasts getting undressed and into
bed with Maxwell.
Greased Lightning (1977) . . . . . . . . . . . . . Mary Jones
Fort Apache, The Bronx (1981) . . . . . . . . . . .Charlotte
Something Wicked this Way Comes (1983)
. . . . . . . . . . . . . . . . . . . . . . . . . . . . . . . Dust Witch
Tough Enough (1983) . . . . . . . . . . . . . . . . . . . Myra
**On the Edge** (1985). . . . . . . . . . . . . . . . . . . . . Cora
(Unrated version reviewed.)
0:18—In leotards, leading an aerobics dance class.
•• 0:42—Breasts in the mirror, then full frontal nudity
making love with Bruce Dern standing up. Then
brief left breast. A little dark.
Stand Alone (1985) . . . . . . . . . . . . . . . . . Catherine
Vindicator (1986; Canadian) . . . . . . . . . . . . . .Hunter
*a.k.a. Frankenstein '88*
The Allnighter (1987). . . . . . . . . . . . . . . Sgt. MacLeish
Above the Law (1988) . . . . . . . . Delores "Jacks" Jackson

Class of 1999 (1990). . . . . . . . . . . . . . . . .Ms. Connors
1:14—Special effect right breast after getting stabbed in the chest and the boys discover she is a robot.
1:19—More special effect right breast.
Bill and Ted's Bogus Journey (1991) . . . . . .Ms. Wardroe
Posse (1993) . . . . . . . . . . . . . . . . . . . . . . . . . .Phoebe
*Made for TV Movies:*
A Mother's Right: The Elizabeth Morgan Story (1992)
. . . . . . . . . . . . . . . . . . . . . . . . . . . . . .Linda Holman
*Magazines:*
**Playboy** (Nov 1972) . . . . . . . . . . . Sex in Cinema 1972
•• 162—Breasts, sitting on Thalmus Rasulala.
**Playboy** (Nov 1973) . . . . . . . . . . . Sex in Cinema 1973
••• 154—Nude scenes from *Coffy.*
**Playboy** (Dec 1973). . . . . . . . . . . . . Sex Stars of 1973
•• 205—Half of left breast.
Playboy (Dec 1976). . . . . . . . . . . . . . Sex Stars of 1976
188—Partial right breast.

# Griffeth, Simone

*Films:*
**Death Race 2000** (1975) . . . . . . . . . . . . Annie Smith
• 0:32—Side view of left breast, while holding David Carradine. Dark, hard to see.
••• 0:56—Breasts and buns getting undressed and lying on bed with Carradine.
**Hot Target** (1985) . . . . . . . . . . . . . Christine Webber
•• 0:09—Breasts taking off top for shower, then breasts and brief frontal nudity taking shower.
••• 0:19—Breasts in bed after making love with Steve Marachuck.
•• 0:21—Buns, getting out of bed and walking to bathroom.
• 0:23—Breasts in bed with Marachuck again.
• 0:34—Breasts in the woods with Marachuck while cricket match goes on.
**The Patriot** (1986) . . . . . . . . . . . . . . . . . . . . . . Sean
•• 0:49—Brief breasts lying in bed, making love with Ryder.
*TV:*
Ladies' Man (1980-81) . . . . . . . . . . . . . . . . . Gretchen
Bret Maverick (1982). . . . . . . . . . . . . . Jasmine DuBois
Amanda's (1983). . . . . . . . . . . . . . . Arlene Cartwright

# • Griffin, Renee

*Films:*
**Showdown in Little Tokyo** (1991) . . . . . . . . . Angel
•• 0:15—In black bra. Breasts in lingerie and stockings (mostly right breast) just before getting killed.
• 0:34—Right breast, on TV during playback of her execution.
**Cyborg 2: Glass Shadow** (1993) . . . . . . . . . . Dreena
• 0:04—Brief breasts, several times, while making love with a guy before she blows up.

# Griffith, Melanie

Daughter of actress Tippi Hedren.
Wife, ex-wife, wife of actor Don Johnson.
Ex-wife of actor Steven Bauer.
Sister of actress Tracy Griffith.
*Films:*
**Smile** (1974). . . . . . . . . . . . . . . . . . . . . . . .Karen Love
0:07—Brief glimpse at panties, bending over to pick up dropped box.
• 0:34—Very, very brief side view of right breast in dressing room, just before passing behind a rack of clothes.
• 0:47—Very brief side view of right breast, then side view of left breast when Little Bob is outside taking pictures.
• 0:48—Very brief breasts as Polaroid photograph that Little Bob took develops.
• 1:51—Breasts in the same Polaroid in the policeman's sun visor.
**Night Moves** (1975) . . . . . . . . . . . . . . Delly Grastner
• 0:42—Brief breasts changing tops outside while talking with Gene Hackman.
• 0:46—Nude, saying "hi" from under water beneath a glass bottom boat.
• 0:47—Brief side view of right breast getting out of the water.
The Drowning Pool (1976). . . . . . . .Schuuler Devereaux
**Joyride** (1977) . . . . . . . . . . . . . . . . . . . . . . . . . Susie
• 0:05—Breasts in back of station wagon with Robert Carradine, hard to see anything.
•• 0:59—Brief breasts in spa with everybody.
• 1:11—Brief breasts in shower with Desi Arnaz, Jr.
One on One (1977) . . . . . . . . . . . . . . . . . . . Hitchhiker
Roar (1981) . . . . . . . . . . . . . . . . . . . . . . . . . . Melanie
**Body Double** (1984) . . . . . . . . . . . . . . . . . .Holly Body
•• 0:20—Breasts in brunette wig dancing around in bedroom while Craig Wasson watches through a telescope.
• 0:28—Breasts in bedroom again while Wasson and the Indian welding on the satellite dish watch.
•• 1:12—Breasts and buns on TV that Wasson is watching.
•• 1:13—Breasts and buns on TV after Wasson buys the video tape.
• 1:19—Brief buns in black leather outfit in bathroom during filming of movie.
• 1:20—Brief buns again in the black leather outfit.
**Fear City** (1984). . . . . . . . . . . . . . . . . . . . . . .Loretta
0:04—Buns, in blue G-string, dancing on stage.
•• 0:07—Breasts, dancing on stage.
••• 0:23—Breasts dancing on stage wearing a red G-string.
**Something Wild** (1986) . . . . . . "Lulu"/Audrey Hankel
••• 0:16—Strips to breasts in bed with Jeff Daniels.
• 0:24—Buns and brief breasts, while looking out the window.
Cherry 2000 (1988) . . . . . . . . . . . . . . . . . . . E. Johnson
0:19—Breasts in a shadow on the wall while changing clothes.

The Milagro Beanfield War (1988). . . . . . .Flossie Devine

**Stormy Monday** (1988) . . . . . . . . . . . . . . . . . . . Kate
  0:03—Buns and side of right breast, behind shower door. Don't see anything because of the glass.
  • 1:11—Very brief left breast, while making love in bed with Brendan.

**Working Girl** (1989). . . . . . . . . . . . . . . . . Tess McGill
  0:08—In bra, panties, garter belt and stockings in front of a mirror.
  0:32—In black bra, garter belt and stockings trying on clothes.
  0:43—In black bra, garter belt and stockings getting out of bed.
  1:15—In white bra, taking off her blouse with Harrison Ford.
  • 1:18—Very, very brief right breast turning over in bed with Ford.
  • 1:20—Breasts, vacuuming. Long shot seen from the other end of the hall.
The Bonfire of the Vanities (1990) . . . . . . .Maria Ruskin
  0:24—In bra, opening her jacket while on the couch with Tom Hanks.
  0:47—In black bra and panties in apartment with Hanks.
In the Spirit (1990) . . . . . . . . . . . . . . . . . . . . . Lureen
Pacific Heights (1990) . . . . . . . . . . . . . . . . Patty Parker
Paradise (1991). . . . . . . . . . . . . . . . . . . . . . . .Lily Reed
**Shining Through** (1992) . . . . . . . . . . . . . .Linda Voss
  •• 0:22—Breasts, making love in bed on top of Michael Douglas.
Stranger Among Us (1992) . . . . . . . . . . . . . Emily Eden
  *a.k.a. Close to Eden*
Born Yesterday (1993). . . . . . . . . . . . . . . . Billie Dawn
Milk Money (1994) . . . . . . . . . . . . . . . . . . . . . . .n.a.
*Made for Cable Movies:*
Women & Men: Stories of Seduction (1990; HBO)
. . . . . . . . . . . . . . . . . . . . . . . . . . . . . . . . . . Hadley
*Made for TV Movies:*
She's in the Army Now (1981) . . . . . . . . . .Sylvie Knoll
*TV:*
Once an Eagle (1976-77) . . . . . . . . . .Jinny Massengale
Carter Country (1978-79) . . . . . . . . . . . . . Tracy Quinn
*Magazines:*
**Playboy** (Oct 1976). . . . . . . . . . . . . . . . . .Fast Starter
  ••• 100-103—Nude with Don Johnson.
**Playboy** (Nov 1977) . . . . . . . . . . Sex in Cinema 1977
  ••• 160—Breasts, while in pool with her friends from *Joyride.*
**Playboy** (Dec 1977). . . . . . . . . . . . . Sex Stars of 1977
  ••• 216—Full frontal nudity.
**Playboy** (Jan 1986) . . . . . . . . . . . . . . . . Double Take
  •• 94-103—Breasts and buns in photos with Don Johnson in photos that were taken in 1976.

## Griffith, Tracy

Sister of actress Melanie Griffith.
*Films:*
Fear City (1984). . . . . . . . . . . . . . . . . . . Sandra Cook
**The Good Mother** (1988) . . . . . . . . . . . . . . . . . Babe
  • 0:06—Brief breasts opening her blouse to show a young Anna what it's like being pregnant.
Fast Food (1989) . . . . . . . . . . . . . . . . . . . . Samantha
Sleepaway Camp III: Teenage Wasteland (1989)
. . . . . . . . . . . . . . . . . . . . . . . . . . Marcia Holland
The First Power (1990). . . . . . . . . . . . . . . . Tess Seaton
**The Finest Hour** (1991). . . . . . . . . . . . . . . . Barbara
  • 0:21—In wet, braless, white dress, getting out of the water after canoe tips over.
  • 1:02—Swimming with Mazzoli under water in ocean in a wet, braless, white dress.
  • 1:03—Brief side view of right breast, while taking the wet dress off.
All Tied Up (1992) . . . . . . . . . . . . . . . . . Sharon Stevens

## Griffiths, Linda

*Films:*
**Lianna** (1982). . . . . . . . . . . . . . . . . . . . . . . . . . Lianna
  0:22—In sheer white bra while changing blouses.
  •• 0:29—Breasts and buns, making love in bed with Ruth. Dark.
  •• 1:26—Right breast, then breasts while lying in bed with Cindy. Long, dark scene.
  •• 1:42—Left breast while lying in bed with Ruth.
Reno and the Doc (1984; Canadian) . . .Savannah Gates
Samuel Lount (1986; Canadian). . . . . . . Elizabeth Lount
*Made for TV Movies:*
A Town Torn Apart (1992) . . . . . . . . . . . . . . . .Hallie

## Grindlay, Annie

*Films:*
**Lurkers** (1987) . . . . . . . . . . . . . . . . . . . . Lulu (Model)
  • 0:12—Undressing in sheer bra (on the left) with another model.
  •• 0:13—Breasts, changing clothes with the other model.
K2 (1991) . . . . . . . . . . . . . . . . . . . . . . . . . . . . Lisa

## Groff, Nancy

*Films:*
Deranged (1987) . . . . . . . . . . . . . . . . . . . . . . Teacher
**Lurkers** (1987). . . . . . . . . . . . . . . . . . . . . . . . . Rita
  • 1:07—Partial right breast in bathroom with another woman while Cathy talks.

## Grossman, Liora

*Films:*
**I Don't Give a Damn** (1985; Israeli) . . . . . . . . . .Maya
  *a.k.a. Lo Sam Zayin*
  • 1:11—Brief right breast, while posing for Rafi in the kitchen.
Irith, Irith (1985) . . . . . . . . . . . . . . . . . . . . Irith Katz

# Grubel, Ilona

*Films:*
Jonathan (1973; German) . . . . . . . . . . . . . . . . Eleanore
**Target** (1985) . . . . . . . . . . . . . . . . . . . . . . . . . . .Carla
  • 1:12—Brief breasts in bed with Matt Dillon.

# Guerin, Florence

*Films:*
**Black Venus** (1983). . . . . . . . . . . . . . . . . . . . . .Louise
  •• 0:45—Nude talking, then making love with Venus in bed.
  ••• 1:16—Nude frolicking on the beach with Venus.
  ••• 1:18—Nude in bedroom getting out of wet clothes with Venus.
  • 1:21—Buns in bed with Jacques and Venus.
**Bizarre** (1986; Italian) . . . . . . . . . . . . . . . . . . . . .Laurie
  •• 0:03—Breasts on bed with Guido. Lower frontal nudity while he molests her with a pistol.
  ••• 0:18—Nude after taking off her clothes in hotel room with a guy. Nice.
  ••• 0:30—Full frontal nudity making love with Edward in the water.
  • 0:34—Brief side of right breast, taking off robe in bathroom with Edward. (He's made himself up to look like a woman.)
  ••• 0:36—Breasts in white panties making love with Edward.
  •• 0:40—Breasts and brief lower frontal nudity in Guido's office with him.
  ••• 0:45—Nude, playing outside with Edward, then making love with his toe.
  •• 0:47—Breasts getting out of bed and putting a blouse on.
  •• 0:49—Breasts with Edward when Guido comes in.
  • 1:11—Breasts sitting in chair talking to Edward.
  • 1:20—Lower frontal nudity, putting the phone down there.
  • 1:28—Buns and lower frontal nudity on bed when Guido rips her clothes off and rapes her.
**The Turn-On** (1989) . . . . . . . . . . . . . Claudia Christiani
  *a.k.a. Le Clic*
  •• 0:02—Buns and breasts in mirror.
  ••• 0:34—Breasts, while looking at herself in dressing room mirror and caressing herself.
  •• 0:54—Breasts, while walking through the woods and taking off her clothes.
  ••• 0:56—Nude, while playing with herself in the woods, then getting tied up and carried away on a guy's shoulders. Long scene.
  ••• 1:07—Breasts and buns, while on the beach with Dr. Fez. Nude, fighting with her husband and running away into the house.

# Guerra, Blanca

*Films:*
Falcon's Gold (1982). . . . . . . . . . . . . . . . . . . . . . . .n.a.
  *a.k.a. Robbers of the Sacred Mountain*
Erendira (1983; Brazilian) . . . . . . . . . . Ulysses' Mother

Separate Vacations (1985). . . . . . . . . . . . . . . . .Alicia
  • 0:56—Breasts on the bed with David Naughton when she turns out to be a hooker.
Walker (1988) . . . . . . . . . . . . . . . . . . . . . . . . . . . .Yrena
Santa Sangre (1989; Italian/Spanish) . . . . . . . . .Concha
  0:34—Half of buns, in sexy circus outfit.
Danzon (1992; Mexican) . . . . . . . . . . . . . . .La Colorada

# Guerrero, Evelyn

*Films:*
Wild Wheels (1969) . . . . . . . . . . . . . . . . . . . . . . . Sissy
Trackdown (1976) . . . . . . . . . . . . . . . . .Social Worker
The Toolbox Murders (1978) . . . . . . . . . . . . . . .Maria
**Fairytales** (1979) . . . . . . . . . . . . . . . . . . S & M Dancer
  •• 0:38—Breasts wearing masks with two other blonde S&M Dancers.
  •• 0:56—Full frontal nudity dancing with the other S&M Dancers again.
Cheech & Chong's Next Movie (1980)
  . . . . . . . . . . . . . . . . . . . . . . . . . . Welfare Office Worker
**Cheech & Chong's Nice Dreams** (1981) . . . . .Donna
  • 0:43—Brief left breast sticking out of her spandex outfit, sitting down at table in restaurant.
  0:56—In burgundy lingerie in her apartment with Cheech Marin.
Things Are Tough All Over (1982) . . . . . . . . . . .Donna
Blood In, Blood Out: Bound by Honor (1992) . . . . Luisa
  *a.k.a. Bound by Honor*
*TV:*
Dallas (1989-90) . . . . . . . . . . . . . . . . . . . . . . . . Nancy
*Magazines:*
  **Playboy** (Sep 1980) . . . . . . . . . Lights, Camera, Chaos!
  ••• 103-107—Full frontal nudity.

# Guerri, Ruth

*Video Tapes:*
**Playboy's Playmate Review 2** (1984) . . . . . Playmate
**Playmates at Play** (1990) . . . . . Thrill Seeker, Bareback
*Magazines:*
  **Playboy** (Jul 1983) . . . . . . . . . . . . . . . . . . . . . Playmate
  **Playboy's Girls of Summer '86** (Aug 1986). . .Herself
  ••• 92—Full frontal nudity.
  **Playboy's 1987 Book of Lingerie** (Mar 1987)
  . . . . . . . . . . . . . . . . . . . . . . . . . . . . . . . . . . . . . .Herself
  ••• 72—Breasts.
  ••• 110—Breasts.
  **Playboy's Book of Lingerie** (Sep 1991) . . . . . .Herself
  ••• 62—Breasts.
  **Playboy's Calendar Playmates** (Nov 1992). . .Herself
  ••• 33—Full frontal nudity.
  ••• 43—Breasts.
  **Playboy's Book of Lingerie** (Jan 1994) . . . . . .Herself
  ••• 63—Breasts.

# Gunden, Scarlett

*Films:*
**Island of 1000 Delights** . . . . . . . . . . . . . . . Francine
  ••• 0:02—Breasts on beach dancing with Ching. Upper half of buns sitting down.

0:20—Dancing braless in sheer brown dress.
- •• 0:44—Full frontal nudity getting tortured by Ming.
- • 1:16—Breasts on beach after Ching rescues her.

**Melody in Love** (1978) . . . . . . . . . . . . . . . . . . Angela
- ••• 0:17—Full frontal nudity taking off dress and dancing in front of statue.
- ••• 0:50—Nude with a guy on a boat.
- •• 0:53—Breasts on another boat with Octavio.
- •• 0:59—Buns and breasts in bed talking to Rachel.
- •• 1:12—Full frontal nudity getting a tan on boat with Rachel.
- • 1:14—Breasts making love in bed with Rachel and Octavio.

## • Gurnett, Jane

*Films:*

**Drowning by Numbers** (1988; British) . . . . . . .Nancy
- ••• 0:04—Nude, undressing inside and running outside, taking a bath with Jake. Long scene.
- ••• 0:06—More breasts and buns, in the bathtub next to Jake.
- • 0:10—Left breast, passed out in bathtub.
- • 0:11—More left breast in bathtub.
- • 0:15—Left breast, while in wheelbarrow.
- • 0:16—Full frontal nudity when the women pull her onto the bed.

Lorna Doone (1990; British) . . . . . . . . . . . . Annie Ridd

## • Gurwitch, Annabelle

*Films:*

Battle in the Erogenous Zone . . . . . . . . . . . . .Garmento
Delivery Boys (1984) . . . . . . . . . . . Woman with Big Hat
Kiss Daddy Goodnight (1987) . . . . . . . . . . . . . . . . .Sue
Bright Lights, Big City (1988) . . . . . . . . . . . . . Barbara
Life With Mikey (1993) . . . . . . . . . . . . . . . . . . . Debbie

*Made for Cable TV:*

Red Shoe Diaries: Another Woman's Lipstick
(1993; Showtime) . . . . . . . . . . . . . . . . . . . . . . . Annie
(Available on video tape on *Red Shoe Diaries 3: Another Woman's Lipstick.*)

**Dream On: 'Tis a Pity She's a Neighbor**
(1994; HBO) . . . . . . . . . . . . . . . . . . . . . . . . . . . . Jo
- • 0:10—Left breast while sitting on sofa and talking to Jeremy.

*Made for TV Movies:*

Chance of a Lifetime (1991) . . . . . . . . . . . . . . . .Sherry
The Tower (1993) . . . . . . . . . . . . . . . . . . . . . . . . Sally

*TV:*

Eddie Dodd (1991) . . . . . . . . . . . . . . . . . . . . . . . Billie

## Guthrie, Lynne

*Films:*

**Night Call Nurses** (1972) . . . . . . . . . . . . . . . .Cynthia
*a.k.a. Young LA Nurses 2*
- • 0:00—Breasts on hospital roof taking off robe and standing on edge just before jumping off.

**The Working Girls** (1973) . . . . . . . . . . . . . . . . . . .Jill
- ••• 0:43—Breasts, dancing on stage at club.
- •• 0:48—Breasts in swimming pool with Nick.

Tears of Happiness (1974) . . . . . . . . . . . . . . . . . . . Lisa
Chesty Anderson, U.S. Navy (1975) . . . . . . .Lt. Ambrose

## Gutteridge, Lucy

*Films:*

Top Secret (1984) . . . . . . . . . . . . . . . . . . . . . . . Hillary
The Trouble with Spies (1984) . . . . . . . . . Mona Smith
**Tusks** (1990) . . . . . . . . . . . . . . . . . . . . . . . Micah Hill
- •• 0:23—Breasts in tub taking a bath.

*Made for Cable TV:*

**The Hitchhiker: In the Name of Love** (1987; HBO)
. . . . . . . . . . . . . . . . . . . . . . . . . . . . . . . . . . . .Jackie
- •• 0:08—Breasts on bed talking to herself about Billy after unzipping and opening the top of her dress.
- • 0:16—Brief right breast, while pulling down her dress top in car with Greg Evigan.
- •• 0:17—Breasts making love with Evigan in bed.
  0:20—Breasts in black and white photos that accidentally fall out of envelope.

*Miniseries:*

Little Gloria...Happy At Last! (1982)
. . . . . . . . . . . . . . . . . . . . . Gloria Morgan Vanderbilt
Till We Meet Again (1989) . . . . . . . . . . . . . . . . . . Eve

*Made for TV Movies:*

The Woman He Loved (1988) . . . . . . . . . . . . . Thelma

## Hackett, Joan

*Films:*

The Group (1966) . . . . . . . . . . . . . . . . . Dottie Renfrew
Will Penny (1968) . . . . . . . . . . . . . . . . Catherine Allen
Support Your Local Sheriff! (1969) . . . . . . .Prudy Perkins
The Terminal Man (1974). . . . . . . . . . . . . .Dr. Janet Ross
**One Trick Pony** (1980) . . . . . . . . . . . . . . . .Lonnie Fox
- ••• 1:21—Nude getting out of bed and getting dressed while talking to Paul Simon.

Flicks (1981). . . . . . . . . . . . . . . . . . . . . . .Capt. Grace
Only When I Laugh (1981). . . . . . . . . . . . . . . . . Toby
The Escape Artist (1982). . . . . . . . . . . . . . . Aunt Sybil

*Made for TV Movies:*

Paper Dolls (1982) . . . . . . . . . . . . . . . . . . . Julia Blake

*TV:*

The Defenders (1961-62) . . . . . . . . . . . . . . .Joan Miller
Another Day (1978) . . . . . . . . . . . . . . . .Ginny Gardner

## Haddon, Dayle

*Films:*

Paperback Hero (1973; Canadian) . . . . . . . . . . . .Joanna
0:31—Lower half of buns, under T-shirt while standing behind a bar with Keir Dullea.
The World's Greatest Athlete (1973). . . . . . . . . . . .Jane
**Sex with a Smile** (1976; Italian) . . . . . . . . . . The Girl
- •• 0:23—Breasts, covered with bubbles in the bathtub.
- • 0:43—Buns, taking off robe to take a shower, then brief breasts with Marty Feldman.

Spermula (1976) . . . . . . . . . . . . . . . . . . . . . .Spermula
**The Last Romantic Lover** (1978). . . . . . . . . . . . n.a.
0:56—Breasts.

**The French Woman** (1979) . . . . . . . . . . . . .Elizabeth
*a.k.a. Madame Claude*
- 0:15—Very, very brief breasts in dressing room.
- • 0:49—Breasts on bed with Madame Claude.
- 0:55—Breasts kissing Pierre, then buns while lying on the floor.
  1:10—In two piece swimsuit on sailboat.
- 1:11—Left breast, then buns at the beach with Frederick.

North Dallas Forty (1979) . . . . . . . . . . . . . . . Charlotte
Cyborg (1989) . . . . . . . . . . . . . . . . . . . . Pearl Prophet
Silence Like Glass (1989). . . . . . . . . . . . .Darlene Meyers
The Magic Bubble (1992) . . . . . . . . . . . . . . . . . Susan
*Made for Cable Movies:*
Bedroom Eyes (1985; Canadian; HBO) . . . . . . . . . .Alixe
  1:06—Getting undressed in tap pants and white camisole top while Harry watches in the mirror.
*Made for Cable TV:*
**The Hitchhiker: Ghost Writer** (1986; HBO)
. . . . . . . . . . . . . . . . . . . . . . . . . . . . . Debby Hunt
(Available on *The Hitchhiker, Volume 3.*)
  0:05—In black slip kissing Barry Bostwick.
- 0:14—Breasts and buns, getting into hot tub with Willem DaFoe before trying to drown him.
*Magazines:*
**Playboy** (Apr 1973) . . . . . . . . . . . . . .Disney's Latest Hit
- ••• 147-153—Nude.
**Playboy** (Dec 1973). . . . . . . . . . . . . . Sex Stars of 1973
- ••• 209—Breasts.
**Playboy** (Jan 1977) . . . . . . . . . . . . . . . . . . Spermula
- ••• 104—Full frontal nudity.
**Playboy** (Apr 1977) . . . . . . . . . . . . . . . Dear Playboy
- •• 16—Breasts in small photo from April 1973.
**Playboy** (Aug 1977) . . . . . . . . . . . . . .Madame Claude
- •• 130—Buns.

# • *Hagemann, Tracy*
*Films:*
**The Deadly Secret** (1993) . . . . . . . . . . . . . . . . . Sarah
- 0:37—Brief buns in panties.
- 1:22—Very brief right breast, several times, during rape on beach.
*Magazines:*
Playboy (Aug 1994) . . . . . . . . . . . . . . . . . . . Potpourri

# *Hahn, Gisela*
Producer.
*Films:*
They Call Me Trinity (1971; Italian) . . . . . . . . . . . Sarah
**Julia** (1974; German) . . . . . . . . . . . . . . . . . . . Miriam
- •• 0:12—Breasts tanning herself outside.
- 1:14—Brief breasts sitting in the rain.
The Manhunters (1980; French/Spanish/German). . .n.a.

# *Hahn, Jessica*
The woman in the TV evangelist Jim Bakker scandal.
*Films:*
**Bikini Summer 2** (1992) . . . . . . . . . . . . . . . . . Marilyn
- 0:03—In black bra in bed with Harry, then buns in black G-string, climbing on his back.
*Made for Cable TV:*
Dream On: And Bimbo Was His Name-O (1992; HBO)
. . . . . . . . . . . . . . . . . . . . . . . . . . . . . . Reporter
*Music Videos:*
Wild Thing/Sam Kinison . . . . . . . . . . . . . . . . . .The Girl
*Video Tapes:*
Thunder and Mud (1989) . . . . . . . . . . . . . . . Hostess
**Playboy Celebrity Centerfold: Jessica Hahn** (1993)
. . . . . . . . . . . . . . . . . . . . . . . . . . . . . . . . .Herself
- •• 0:02—Breasts and buns in an old church by the beach.
- ••• 0:05—Nude and in lingerie in an old mansion.
- ••• 0:10—Nude outside with a guy.
- •• 0:14—Breasts, in lingerie and swimsuits around town and at a beach.
- ••• 0:17—Nude in bedroom. Very nice!
- ••• 0:20—Nude in still photos.
- •• 0:21—Nude in wigs in studio. Also wearing lingerie and other outfits.
- ••• 0:23—Nude, picking an apple off a tree, lying in bed with a snake.
- ••• 0:26—Nude, checking out different rooms in a hotel, then in a room with a man and a woman.
- ••• 0:32—In bra and panties on a Merry-Go-Round, then nude.
*Magazines:*
**Playboy** (Nov 1987) . . . . . . Jessica, On Her Own Terms
- ••• 90-99—Breasts.
**Playboy** (Dec 1987) . . . . . . . . . . . . .Sex Stars of 1987
- ••• 157—Breasts.
**Playboy** (Feb 1988) . . . . . . . . . . . . . . The Year in Sex
- ••• 128—Breasts wearing a hat.
**Playboy** (Sep 1988) . . . . . . . . . . . . . . . . . . . Jessica
- ••• 118-127— Nude.
**Playboy** (Dec 1988) . . . . . . . . . . . . .Sex Stars of 1988
- ••• 188—Breasts.
**Playboy** (Jan 1989). . . . . . . . . . .Women of the Eighties
- ••• 257—Full frontal nudity.
**Playboy** (Feb 1989) . . . . . . . . . . . . . The Year in Sex
  137—Left breast.
**Playboy's Nudes** (Oct 1990) . . . . . . . . . . . . . .Herself
- ••• 48-49—Full frontal nudity.
**Playboy's Nudes** (Dec 1992) . . . . . . . . . . . . . .Herself
- ••• 22-23—Breasts.
**Playboy** (Dec 1992)
. . . . . . . . . . My Fifteen Minutes of Fame are Up. Not!
- ••• 94-103—Nude. Excellent!
**Playboy's Nudes** (Dec 1993) . . . . . . . . . . . . . .Herself
- ••• 25—Full frontal nudity.
**Playboy** (Dec 1993) . . . . . . . . . . . . . .Sex Stars 1993
- ••• 181—Full frontal nudity.

## Haiduk, Stacy

Films:

**Luther the Geek** (1988) . . . . . . . . . . . . . . . . . . . . Beth
(Hard to find video tape, but worth it when you find it!)
    0:24—In bra and panties after undressing to take a
    shower.
••• 0:26—Breasts with Rob in the shower. Wow!
••• 0:28—Breasts taking off her robe in bed, then mak-
    ing love with Rob.
Steel and Lace (1990) . . . . . . . . . . . . . . . . . . . . . . Alison
Made for Cable Movies:
Sketch Artist (1992; Showtime) . . . . . . . . . . . . . . Claire
Made for TV Movies:
Danielle Steele's "A Perfect Stranger" (1994)
   . . . . . . . . . . . . . . . . . . . . . . . . . . . . Raphaella Phillips
TV:
Superboy (1988-91) . . . . . . . . . . . . . . . . . . . . . Lana Lang
The Round Table (1992) . . . . . . . . . . . Rhea McPherson
Route 66 (1993) . . . . . . . . . . . . . . . . . . . . . . . . . . . . Lilly
Seaquest DSV (1993-94) . . . . . . . Lt. Katherine Hitchcock

## • Hair, Connie

Films:

**Nevada Heat** (1982) . . . . . . . . . . . . . . . . . . . . . Roberta
a.k.a. Fake-Out
  • 0:13—Breasts in the shower scene.
  • 0:14—Brief breasts in the shower again. Brief buns in
    shower (Long shot).
Teenage Bonnie and Klepto Clyde (1993) . . . . . Waitress

## Hajek, Gwendolyn

Films:

Traxx (1988) . . . . . . . . . . . . . . . . . . . . . . . . . Playmate
Magazines:
**Playboy** (Sep 1987) . . . . . . . . . . . . . . . . . . . Playmate
**Playboy's Book of Lingerie** (Mar 1991) . . . . . Herself
••• 106-107—Full frontal nudity.
**Playboy's Calendar Playmates** (Nov 1992) . . Herself
•• 77—Left breast and lower frontal nudity.

## Hale, Georgina

Films:

The Boy Friend (1971; British) . . . . . . . . . . . . . . . . . Fay
**Mahler** (1974; British) . . . . . . . . . . . . . . . Alma Mahler
•• 1:00—Breasts during musical number.
The World is Full of Married Men (1979; British)
 . . . . . . . . . . . . . . . . . . . . . . . . . . . . . . Lori Grossman
McVicar (1980; British) . . . . . . . . . . . . . . . . . . . . . Kate
The Watcher in the Woods (1981; British)
 . . . . . . . . . . . . . . . . . . . . . . . . . Young Mrs. Aylwood
Castaway (1986) . . . . . . . . . . . . . Sister Saint Margaret
Magazines:
**Playboy** (Nov 1974) . . . . . . . . . . . Sex in Cinema 1974
 • 152—Breasts in small photo from Mahler.

## Hall, Jerry

Former model.
Significant Other of singer/actor Mick Jagger.
Films:

Urban Cowboy (1980) . . . | . . . . . . . . . . . . . . . . . . . n.a.
**Willie and Phil** (1980) . . . . . . . . . . . . . . . . . . . . Karen
 • 0:05—Brief breasts getting dressed in bedroom with
  Phil.
Running Out of Luck (1986) . . . . . . . . . . . . . . . . Herself
Batman (1989) . . . . . . . . . . . . . . . . . . . . . . . . . . . Alicia
Freejack (1992) . . . . . . . . . . . . . . . . . . . . Newswoman
Video Tapes:
Jerry Hall Yogasize with Vimla Lalvani (1993) . . . . Herself

## Hall, Leana

Films:

The Linguini Incident (1991) . . . . . . . . . . . . . . . . Tracy
**Witchcraft III: The Kiss of Death** (1991) . . . . . Roxy
•• 1:08—Breasts on bed with William making love
   when Charlotte gets trapped in the room.
Made for Cable Movies:
Red Shoe Diaries (1992; Showtime) . . . . . . . . . . Ingrid
 (Unrated video tape version reviewed.)

## Hall, Susie

Films:

**Forced Vengeance** (1982) . . . . . . . . . . . . . . . Dancer
 • 0:57—Breasts, dancing in club with an Asian dancer.
A Killing Affair (1985) . . . . . . . . . . . . . . . . . . . . Blanche

## Hallaren, Jane

Films:

Hero at Large (1980) . . . . . . . . . . . . . . . Gloria Preston
Body Heat (1981) . . . . . . . . . . . . . . . . . . . . . . . . . Stella
Modern Romance (1981) . . . . . . . . . . . . . . . . . . . Ellen
**Lianna** (1982) . . . . . . . . . . . . . . . . . . . . . . . . . . Ruth
 • 0:29—Brief left breast lying under Lianna during
  love making scene in bed. Dark.
Unfaithfully Yours (1984) . . . . . . . . . . . . . . . . . . Janet
Lost Angels (1989) . . . . . . . . . . . . . . . . . . Grace Willig
My Girl (1991) . . . . . . . . . . . . . . . . . . . . Nurse Randall

## Hallier, Lori

Films:

My Bloody Valentine (1981; Canadian) . . . . . . . . Sarah
Warning Sign (1985) . . . . . . . . . . . . . . . . . . . . Reporter
**Higher Education** (1987; Canadian) . . . Nicole Hubert
 • 0:44—Right breast, twice, while making love with
  Andy in bed.
Blindside (1988; Canadian) . . . . . . . . . . . . . . . . . Julie
Made for TV Movies:
A Woman Scorned: The Betty Broderick Story (1992)
 . . . . . . . . . . . . . . . . . . . . . . . . . . . . . . . . . . . . . Joan
Incident in a Small Town (1994) . . . . . Madeleine Harold

# Halligan, Erin

*Films:*

I'm Dancing as Fast as I Can (1981) . . . . . . . . . Denise

**Joysticks** (1983) . . . . . . . . . . . . . . . . . . . . . . . . . . . Sandy
- •• 1:08—Right breast, then breasts and lower frontal nudity in bed with Jefferson surrounded by candles.

# Halsey, Elizabeth

*Films:*

**Cinderella** (1977) . . . . . . . . . . . . Farm Girl (brunette)
- ••• 0:21—Nude with her redhead sister in their house making love with the guy who is looking for Cinderella.
- •• 1:24—Breasts with her sister again when the Prince goes around to try and find Cinderella.

**Cheerleaders Wild Weekend** (1985) . . . Susan/Pierce
- ••• 0:40—Breasts in red panties, in contest.
- ••• 0:41—Breasts with the other five girls during contest.
- ••• 0:43—Breasts during getting measured with the other two girls.

# Hamilton, Jane

a.k.a. Adult film actress Veronica Hart.

*Films:*

**It's Called Murder Baby** (1982) . . . . . . . . . . . Sherry (R-rated version of the adult film *Dixie Ray, Hollywood Star.*)
- • 0:59—Buns, raising her skirt for Nick.
- • 1:11—Left breast, sleeping in bed, then waking up and getting out.

**Model Behavior** (1982)
. . . . . . . . . . . . . . . . . . . Uncredited Adult Film Actress
- • 0:50—Breasts on TV monitors during playback of adult video.

Deathmask (1983) . . . . . . . . . . . . . . . . . Victoria Howe

Delivery Boys (1984). . . . . . . . . . . . . . . . . . . . Art Snob

R.S.V.P. (1984). . . . . . . . . . . . . . . . Mrs. Ellen Edwards

**Sex Appeal** (1986) . . . . . . . . . . . . . . . . . . . . . . Monica
- ••• 0:58—Breasts dancing on the bed with Tony in his apartment. Long scene.

**Sexpot** (1986) . . . . . . . . . . . . . . . . . . . . . . . . . . . Beth
- ••• 0:28—In bra, then breasts with her two sisters when their bras pop off. (She's on the right.)
- • 1:32—Breasts during outtakes of 0:28 scene.

**Deranged** (1987) . . . . . . . . . . . . . . . . . . . . . . . Joyce
- • 0:29—Buns, getting undressed to take a shower. Side of left breast.
- • 0:37—Side view of left breast, taking off towel and putting blouse on. Long shot.
- • 1:01—Breasts, changing blouses in her bedroom.
- • 1:05—Breasts in bedroom, taking off her blouse with Jamie Gillis.
- • 1:07—Breasts in bed when Jennifer wakes her up.

If Looks Could Kill (1987) . . . . . . . . . . . . . . Mary Beth

Slammer Girls (1987) . . . . . . . . . . . . . Miss Crabapples

**Student Affairs** (1987) . . . . . . . . . . . . . . . . Veronica
- •• 0:48—Breasts changing in dressing room, showing herself off to a guy.

- • 0:51—Brief breasts in a school room during a movie.
- •• 0:56—In black lingerie outfit, then breasts in bedroom while she tape records everything.

Wildest Dreams (1987). . . . . . . . . . . . . . . Ruth Delaney

**Wimps** (1987) . . . . . . . . . . . . . . . . . . . . . . . . . . . Tracy
- • 0:40—Lifting up her sweater and shaking her breasts in the back of the car with Francis. Too dark to see anything.
- •• 0:44—Breasts and buns taking off sweater in a restaurant.

**Young Nurses In Love** (1987). . . . . . . . . . . Franchesca
- •• 1:05—Breasts on top of a guy on a gurney.

New York's Finest (1988) . . . . . . . . . . . . . . . . . . Bunny

Sensations (1988) . . . . . . . . . . . . . . . . . . . . . . . . . Tippy

**Bedroom Eyes II** (1989) . . . . . . . . . JoBeth McKenna
- • 0:50—Breasts knifing Linda Blair, then fighting with Wings Hauser.

Bloodsucking Pharaohs from Pittsburgh (1989) . . .Grace

**Cleo/Leo** (1989). . . . . . . . . . . . . . . . . . . . . Cleo Clock
- •• 0:13—Nude undressing in front of three guys.
- • 0:21—Breasts changing in dressing room.
- ••• 0:22—Breasts changing in dressing room with the Store Clerk.
- 0:40—In bra and panties.
- •• 1:07—Left breast and lower frontal nudity making love with Bob on bed.

Enrapture (1989) . . . . . . . . . . . . . . . . . . . . . . . . .Annie

Party Incorporated (1989)
. . . . . . . . . Uncredited Whipped Cream Wrestling Girl
*a.k.a. Party Girls*

Alien Intruder (1992) . . . . . . . . . . . . . . . . . Turk's Mama

Ruby (1992). . . . . . . . . . . . . . . . . . . Telephone Trixie

**Beauty School** (1993) . . .Countess Sophia Von Spatula
- • 0:18—Left breast while leaning up while lying on massage table.
- • 1:11—Partial left breast while lying in bed. Breasts, when sitting up.
- ••• 1:15—Breasts while lying in bed.

# Hamilton, Linda

Has an identical twin sister.

*Films:*

T.A.G.: The Assassination Game (1982) . . Susan Swayze

Children of the Corn (1984). . . . . . . . . . . .Vicky Baxter

**The Terminator** (1984). . . . . . . . . . . . . Sarah Connor
- •• 1:18—Brief breasts about four times making love on top of Michael Biehn in motel room.

**Black Moon Rising** (1986) . . . . . . . . . . . . . . . . Nina
- • 0:50—Brief left breast, while making love in bed with Tommy Lee Jones.

**King Kong Lives!** (1986). . . . . . . . . . . . Amy Franklin
- • 0:47—Very, very brief right breast getting out of sleeping bag after camping out near King Kong.

Mr. Destiny (1990). . . . . . . . . . . . . . . . . Ellen Burrows

Terminator 2: Judgement Day (1991). . . . Sarah Connor

*Made for TV Movies:*

Rape and Marriage: The Rideout Case (1980)
. . . . . . . . . . . . . . . . . . . . . . . . . . . . . Greta Rideout

Secrets of a Mother and Daughter (1983)
........................ Susan Decker
Secret Weapons (1985). . . . . . . . . . . . . Elena Koslov
Club Med (1986) . . . . . . . . . . . . . . . . . . . Kate
Go Toward the Light (1988) . . . . . . . . Claire Madison
*TV:*
Secrets of Midland Heights (1980-81). . . . . Lisa Rogers
King's Crossing (1982) . . . . . . . . . . . Lauren Hollister
Beauty and the Beast (1987-90) . . . Catherine Chandler

## Hamilton, Suzanna

*Films:*
Tess (1979; French/British) . . . . . . . . . . . . . . . . . Izz
**Brimstone and Treacle** (1982; British)
........................ Patricia Bates
•• 0:47—Breasts in bed when Sting opens her blouse
and fondles her.
•• 1:18—Breasts in bed when Sting fondles her again.
• 1:20—Brief lower frontal nudity writhing around on
the bed after Denholm Elliott comes downstairs.
**1984** (1984). . . . . . . . . . . . . . . . . . . . . . Julia
•• 0:38—Full frontal nudity taking off her clothes in the
woods with John Hurt.
••• 0:52—Nude in secret room standing and drinking
and talking to Hurt. Long scene.
• 1:11—Side view of left breast kneeling down.
•• 1:12—Breasts after picture falls off the view screen
on the wall.
Out of Africa (1985) . . . . . . . . . . . . . . . . Felicity
Wetherby (1985; British). . . . . . . . . . . . Karen Creasy
0:42—In white lingerie top and bottom.
1:03—In white lingerie getting into bed and lying
down.
1:06—In white lingerie, fighting with John.
Barbara Cartland's "Duel of Hearts" (1990; British)
...................... Harriet Wantage
Tale of a Vampire (1993). . . . . . . . . . . . . . . . . . n.a.

## Hamilton, Wendy

*Films:*
Warlock: The Armageddon (1993) . . . . . . . . . . . Model
*Video Tapes:*
**The Best of Sexy Lingerie** (1992). . . . . . . . . . Model
**The Best of Wet and Wild** (1992) . . . . . . . . . Model
**Playboy Video Calendar 1993** (1992) . . . . . October
••• 0:40—Nude, in auto garage setting. Sometimes
covered with grease.
••• 0:42—Nude in fire escape setting.
••• 0:43—Nude with old movies projected on her and
the walls.
**Playboy Video Centerfold: Pamela Anderson**
(1992). . . . . . . . . . . . . . . . . . . . . . . . . . Playmate
••• 0:26—Nude throughout.
**Playboy's Playmate Review 1992** (1992)
.......................... Miss December
••• 0:44—Nude in a house and then dancing next to a
car.
**Sexy Lingerie IV** (1992) . . . . . . . . . . . . . . . . Model
**Sexy Lingerie V** (1992) . . . . . . . . . . . . . . . . Model

**Wet and Wild IV** (1992) . . . . . . . . . . . . . . . . . Model
**Wet and Wild: The Locker Room** (1994)
........................................ Playmate
*Magazines:*
**Playboy** (Dec 1991) . . . . . . . . . . . . . . . . . . . . Playmate
••• 130-141—Nude.
**Playboy's Career Girls** (Aug 1992)
........................ Baywatch Playmates
••• 9—Breasts.
**Playboy's Book of Lingerie** (Nov 1992) . . . . . Herself
••• 36-37—Breasts.
**Playboy's Book of Lingerie** (Jan 1993) . . . . . . Herself
•• 67—Buns.
•• 68-69—Right breast.
**Playboy's Book of Lingerie** (Mar 1993). . . . . . Herself
• 84-85—Lower frontal nudity.
**Playboy's Bathing Beauties** (Apr 1993). . . . . . Herself
•• 93—Right breast and buns.
**Playboy** (Apr 1993) . . . . . . . . . . . . . . . . . . . Tattoo You
••• 84—Breasts. Tattoo on ankle.
**Playboy's Book of Lingerie** (May 1993) . . . . . Herself
••• 44—Full frontal nudity.
**Playboy's Girls of Summer '93** (Jun 1993) . . . Herself
••• 52—Full frontal nudity.
**Playboy's Book of Lingerie** (Jul 1993). . . . . . . Herself
••• 55—Breasts.
**Playboy's Wet & Wild Women** (Aug 1993). . . Herself
••• 77—Full frontal nudity.
• 104—Right breast.
**Playboy's Blondes, Brunettes & Redheads**
(Sep 1993). . . . . . . . . . . . . . . . . . . . . . . . . . Herself
••• 67—Full frontal nudity.
**Playboy's Book of Lingerie** (Sep 1993) . . . . . . Herself
••• 17-19—Full frontal nudity.
**Playboy's Video Playmates** (Sep 1993) . . . . . . Herself
••• 52-53—Right breast and lower frontal nudity.
**Playboy's Book of Lingerie** (Nov 1993) . . . . . Herself
••• 31—Breasts.
**Playboy's Nudes** (Dec 1993) . . . . . . . . . . . . . Herself
••• 30-31—Buns and side of right breast.
••• 83—Full frontal nudity.
**Playboy's Book of Lingerie** (Jan 1994) . . . . . . Herself
••• 58-59—Full frontal nudity.
**Playboy's Book of Lingerie** (Mar 1994). . . . . . Herself
•• 28—Right breast and buns in panties.
**Playboy's Book of Lingerie** (Sep 1994) . . . . . . Herself
•• 26-27—Right breast and lower frontal nudity.

## Hammond, Barbara

*Films:*
**Angel III: The Final Chapter** (1988) . . . Video Girl #2
• 0:34—Breasts (on the right) on video monitor during audition tape talking with her roommate.
**Vampire at Midnight** (1988) . . . . . . . . . . . . . . Kelly
•• 0:07—Breasts and buns, getting out of the shower
and drying herself off.
• 0:16—Left breast, dead, in Victor's car trunk. Blood
on her.

# Hancock, Lynn

*Films:*

**Evilspeak** (1981) . . . . . . . . . . . . . . . . Miss Friedemyer

  •• 0:56—In bra, then breasts taking off bra in front of fireplace. Buns in panties, walking up the stairs.

  ••• 0:57—Breasts and buns in the shower, then getting killed by pigs.

*TV:*

The Nashville Palace (1981-82) . . . . . . . . . . . . . Regular

# Hannah, Daryl

*Films:*

The Final Terror (1981) . . . . . . . . . . . . . . . . . . Wendy

Blade Runner (1982) . . . . . . . . . . . . . . . . . . . . . . Pris

**Summer Lovers** (1982) . . . . . . . . . Cathy Featherstone

  • 0:07—Very brief breasts getting out of bed.

  0:17—In a two piece swimsuit.

  0:54—Buns, lying on rock with Valerie Quennessen watching Michael dive off a rock.

  0:56—In a swimsuit again.

  • 1:03—Brief right breast sweeping the balcony.

The Pope of Greenwich Village (1984) . . . . . . . . Diane

**Reckless** (1984). . . . . . . . . . . . . . . . . Tracey Prescott

  0:48—In a white bra fighting in gymnasium with Johnny then in pool area in bra and panties.

  ••• 0:52—Breasts in furnace room of school making love with Johnny. Lit with red light.

**Splash** (1984) . . . . . . . . . . . . . . . . . . . . . . . Madison

  0:24—Partial buns, while running into the water at the beach. Looks like hair is taped to her buns.

  • 0:27—Brief right breast, swimming under water, entering the sunken ship.

  • 0:28—Buns, while walking around the Statue of Liberty.

  • 1:26—Brief right, then left breast while in tank when Eugene Levy looks at her.

  • 1:44—Brief right breast, under water when frogman grabs her from behind.

Clan of the Cave Bear (1985) . . . . . . . . . . . . . . . . Ayla

Legal Eagles (1986). . . . . . . . . . . . . . Chelsea Deardon

Roxanne (1987) . . . . . . . . . . . . . . Roxanne Kowalski

Wall Street (1987) . . . . . . . . . . . . . . . . . . Darian Taylor

High Spirits (1988) . . . . . . . . . . . . . . . . Mary Plunkett

Steel Magnolias (1989) . . . . . . . . Annelle Dupuy Desoto

Crazy People (1990) . . . . . . . . . . . . . . . . . . . . . Kathy

**At Play in the Fields of the Lord** (1991)

  . . . . . . . . . . . . . . . . . . . . . . . . . . . . . Andy Huben

  2:09—(0:39 into tape 2) Brief buns, swimming in water.

  ••• 2:10—(0:40 into tape 2) Buns, getting out and resting by tree. Long shot, then breasts in (excellent!) closer shot. Very brief top of lower frontal nudity. (Skip tape 1 and fast forward to this!)

  •• 2:11—(0:41 into tape 2) Brief buns, running away after kissing Tom Berenger.

Memoirs of an Invisible Man (1992) . . . . . Alice Monroe

Grumpy Old Men (1993) . . . . . . . . Melanie Gustafson

*Made for Cable Movies:*

Attack of the 50 ft. Woman (1993; HBO)

  . . . . . . . . . . . . . . . . . . . . . . . . . . . . . Nancy Archer

*Made for TV Movies:*

Paper Dolls (1982) . . . . . . . . . . . . . . . . . . Taryn Blake

*Magazines:*

**Playboy** (Nov 1992) . . . . . . . . . . Sex in Cinema 1992

  ••• 147—Breasts while lying against a tree from *At Play in the Fields of the Lord.*

# Hansen, Tammy

*Films:*

In the Cold of the Night (1989) . . . . . . . . . . . . Model 2

Another You (1991) . . . . . . . . . . . . . . . . Hatcheck Girl

Boyz N the Hood (1991) . . . . . . . . . . . . . . . . . . Rosa

*Video Tapes:*

Dream Babies (1989) . . . . . . . . . . . . . . . . . . . Herself

*Magazines:*

**Playboy's Book of Lingerie** (Jan 1991) . . . . . . Herself

  ••• 67—Breasts.

**Playboy's Book of Lingerie** (Mar 1991). . . . . . Herself

  ••• 19—Breasts.

**Playboy's Book of Lingerie** (Jan 1992) . . . . . . Herself

  ••• 58—Breasts.

**Playboy's Book of Lingerie** (Mar 1992). . . . . . Herself

  ••• 47—Full frontal nudity.

**Playboy's Girls of Summer '92** (Jun 1992) . . . Herself

  ••• 57—Breasts.

  •• 71—Left breast.

**Playboy's Book of Lingerie** (Sep 1992) . . . . . . Herself

  •• 28—Right breast.

**Playboy's Book of Lingerie** (Jan 1993) . . . . . . Herself

  •• 81—Side view of left breast and buns.

# Harden, Marcia Gay

*Films:*

Miller's Crossing (1990) . . . . . . . . . . . . . . . . . . Verna

Late for Dinner (1991) . . . . . . . . . . . . . . Joy Husband

Used People (1992) . . . . . . . . . . . . . . . . . . . . . Norma

Crush (1993; New Zealand) . . . . . . . . . . . . . . . . Lane

*Made for Cable Movies:*

**Fever** (1991; HBO) . . . . . . . . . . . . . . . . . . . . . . Lacy

  • 0:18—Brief breasts making love in bed with Sam Neill.

  •• 1:31—In bra in bed with bad guy, then breasts when he opens her bra. Kind of dark.

*Made for TV Movies:*

Sinatra (1992) . . . . . . . . . . . . . . . . . . . . Ava Gardner

# Hardin, Dana

*Films:*

**Beauty School** (1993) . . . . . . . . . . . . . . . . . . Ashley

  • 0:58—Breasts, dancing in cage in club.

*Magazines:*

**Playboy's Book of Lingerie** (Mar 1991). . . . . . Herself

  •• 13—Partial right breast and lower frontal nudity.

  ••• 105—Full frontal nudity.

**Playboy's Book of Lingerie** (Sep 1991) . . . . . . Herself

  •• 46—Breasts.

## Hargitay, Mariska

Daughter of the late actress Jayne Mansfield and Mickey Hargitay.

*Films:*
Jocks (1986) . . . . . . . . . . . . . . . . . . . . . . . . . . .Nicole
**Welcome to 18** (1986) . . . . . . . . . . . . . . . . . . . . Joey
  • 0:26—Buns, taking a shower when video camera is taping her.
  0:43—Watching herself on the videotape playback.
The Perfect Weapon (1991). . . . . . . . . . . . . . . .Jennifer
Bank Robber (1993) . . . . . . . . . . . . . . Marissa Benoit
*Made for Cable Movies:*
Blind Side (1993; HBO). . . . . . . . . . . . . . . . . Melanie
*TV:*
Falcon Crest (1988). . . . . . . . . . . . . . . . . . . Carly Fixx
Tequila and Bonetti (1992) . . . . . . . . . . . . . . . .Garcia
Key West (1993) . . . . . . . . . . . . . . . . . . . . . . . Laurel

## • Harlow, Jean

*Films:*
Platinum Blonde (1931) . . . . . . . . . . . . . Anne Schuyler
The Public Enemy (1931) . . . . . . . . . . . . . .Gwen Allen
Red Dust (1932) . . . . . . . . . . . . . . . . . . . . . . Jantine
**Red-Headed Woman** (1932) . . . . . . . . . . .Lil Andrews
  • 0:17—Very, very brief right breast when Una Merkel passes over a pajama top and Harlow raises it over her head to put it on.
Bombshell (1933) . . . . . . . . . . . . . . . . . . . . . . . . Lola
Hold Your Man (1933) . . . . . . . . . . . . . . . Ruby Adams
The Girl From Missouri (1934). . . . . . . . . . . . . . . Eadie
China Seas (1935). . . . . . . . . . . . . . . . . . . China Doll
Reckless (1935) . . . . . . . . . . . . . . . . . . . . Mona Leslie
Libeled Lady (1936) . . . . . . . . . . . . . . . Gladys Benton
Riff-Raff (1936) . . . . . . . . . . . . . . . . . . . . . . . Hattie
Wife vs. Secretary (1936). . . . . . Helen "Whitney" Wilson
Personal Property (1937). . . . . . . . . . Crystal Wetherby
Saratoga (1937) . . . . . . . . . . . . . . . . . . . Carol Clayton
*Video Tapes:*
**Hollywood Scandals and Tragedies** (1988)
. . . . . . . . . . . . . . . . . . . . . . . . . . . . . . . . . Herself
  • 0:24—Breasts in B&W still photo. Her head is turned toward the side.
  •• 0:26—Breasts in B&W still photos.
*Magazines:*
**Playboy** (Aug 1994). . . . . . . . . . . . . . . . . . . Harlow
  •• 83-85—Left breast in B&W photo.

## Harney, Corinna

*Video Tapes:*
**Wet and Wild III** (1991). . . . . . . . . . . . . . . . .Model
**The Best of Sexy Lingerie** (1992). . . . . . . . . . .Model
**The Best of Wet and Wild** (1992) . . . . . . . . . .Model
**Playboy Video Calendar 1993** (1992) . . . . . . . . June
  ••• 0:23—Nude, dancing in studio setting.
  ••• 0:25—Nude outside in the desert.
**Playboy Video Centerfold: Corrina Harney** (1992)
. . . . . . . . . . . . . . . . . . . . Playmate of the Year 1992
Playboy's Playmate Bloopers & Practical Jokes (1992)
. . . . . . . . . . . . . . . . . . . . . . . . . . . . . . . . . .n.a.

**Playboy's Playmate Review 1992** (1992)
. . . . . . . . . . . . . . . . . . . . . . . . . . . .Miss August
  ••• 0:48—Nude posing in a house and then outside.
**Sexy Lingerie IV** (1992) . . . . . . . . . . . . . . . . . Model
**Sexy Lingerie V** (1992) . . . . . . . . . . . . . . . . . . Model
**Wet and Wild IV** (1992) . . . . . . . . . . . . . . . . . Model
Playboy Video Centerfold: Jenny McCarthy (1994)
. . . . . . . . . . . . . . . . . . . . . . . . . . . . . . . . . .Angel
**Wet and Wild: The Locker Room** (1994) . . Playmate
*Magazines:*
**Playboy** (Aug 1991) . . . . . . . . . . . . . . . . . . Playmate
**Playboy** (Jun 1992). . . . . . . . . . . Playmate of the Year
  ••• 126-135—Nude.
**Playboy's Book of Lingerie** (Sep 1992) . . . . . .Herself
  ••• 13-15—Full frontal nudity.
**Playboy's Book of Lingerie** (Nov 1992) . . . . .Herself
  ••• 15—Full frontal nudity.
**Playboy's Nudes** (Dec 1992) . . . . . . . . . . . . .Herself
  ••• 70-71—Full frontal nudity.
**Playboy's Book of Lingerie** (May 1993) . . . . .Herself
  ••• 12—Full frontal nudity.
**Playboy's Girls of Summer '93** (Jun 1993) . . .Herself
  ••• 22-23—Full frontal nudity.
  ••• 57—Full frontal nudity.
**Playboy's Book of Lingerie** (Jul 1993) . . . . . . .Herself
  ••• 10—Full frontal nudity.
**Playboy's Wet & Wild Women** (Aug 1993). . .Herself
  • 6—Left breast in sheer lingerie.
  ••• 36-37—Full frontal nudity.
  ••• 48—Full frontal nudity.
  •• 71—Right breast, half of left breast and half of lower frontal nudity.
  ••• 90—Full frontal nudity.
**Playboy's Book of Lingerie** (Sep 1993) . . . . . .Herself
  •• 22—Breasts.
**Playboy's Video Playmates** (Sep 1993) . . . . . .Herself
  ••• 3—Full frontal nudity.
  ••• 54-57—Nude.
**Playboy's Nudes** (Dec 1993) . . . . . . . . . . . . .Herself
  •• 28—Left breast.
**Playboy's Bathing Beauties** (Mar 1994) . . . . .Herself
  •• 24-25—Breasts.
  ••• 29—Breasts.
**Playboy Presents Playmates in Paradise**
  (Mar 1994). . . . . . . . . . . . . . . . . . . . . . . Playmate
  ••• 20-23—Nude.
**Playboy's Book of Lingerie** (May 1994) . . . . .Herself
  ••• 68—Breasts.
  ••• 86—Breasts.
  •• 97—Left breast and lower frontal nudity.
**Playmates at Play** (Jul 1994) . . . . . . . . . . . .Herself
  •• 42—Buns.
**Playboy's Girls of Summer '94** (Jul 1994) . . . .Herself
  •• 30—Buns and left breast.
**Playboy's Book of Lingerie** (Jul 1994) . . . . . . .Herself
  ••• 15—Breasts.
  ••• 62-63—Breasts.
**Playboy's Book of Lingerie** (Sep 1994) . . . . . .Herself
  ••• 10—Breasts.

# • *Harnos, Christine*

*Films:*
The Rescue (1988) . . . . . . . . . . . . . . . . . Adrian Phillips
Forbidden Sun (1989). . . . . . . . . . . . . . . . . . . . Steph
Denial (1991) . . . . . . . . . . . . . . . . . . . . . . . . . . . . Sid
Dazed and Confused (1993) . . . . . . . . . . . . . . . . Kaye
Judgement Night (1993). . . . . . . . . . . . . . Linda Wyatt
*Made for Cable Movies:*
**Rebel Highway: Cool and the Crazy**
(1994; Showtime) . . . . . . . . . . . . . . . . . . . Lorraine
•• 0:43—Breasts, several times, while making love in
bed with Michael.

## *Harper, Jessica*

*Films:*
Phantom of the Paradise (1974) . . . . . . . . . . . Phoenix
Love and Death (1975). . . . . . . . . . . . . . . . . . Natasha
**Inserts** (1976) . . . . . . . . . . . . . . . . . . . . . . . Cathy Cake
••• 1:15—Breasts in garter belt and stockings, lying in
bed for Richard Dreyfuss. Long scene.
Suspiria (1977; Italian) . . . . . . . . . . . . . . . Susy Banyon
The Evictors (1979). . . . . . . . . . . . . . . . . . . . . . . Ruth
Stardust Memories (1980). . . . . . . . . . . . . . . . Violinist
**Pennies from Heaven** (1981) . . . . . . . . . . . . . . . Joan
• 0:43—Brief breasts opening her nightgown for
Steve Martin.
Shock Treatment (1981) . . . . . . . . . . . . . . Janet Majors
My Favorite Year (1982) . . . . . . . . . . . . . K.C. Downing
The Imagemaker (1985) . . . . . . . . . . . . . . . . . Cynthia
The Blue Iguana (1988). . . . . . . . . . . . . . . . . . . Cora
Big Man on Campus (1991) . . . . . . . . . . . . . . Dr. Fisk
Mr. Wonderful (1993) . . . . . . . . . . . . . . . Funny Face
*Made for Cable TV:*
Tales From the Crypt: My Brother's Keeper (1990; HBO)
. . . . . . . . . . . . . . . . . . . . . . . . . . . . . Marie Hilton
*TV:*
Aspen (1977) . . . . . . . . . . . . . . . . . . . . . . Kit Pepe
Little Women (1979). . . . . . . . . . . . . . . . . . Jo March
Studs Lonigan (1979) . . . . . . . . . . . . . . . . . . Loretta

## *Harrell, Georgia*

*Films:*
Incoming Freshman (1979). . . . . . . . . . . . . . Student
**The First Turn-On!** (1983) . . . . . . . . Michelle Farmer
••• 1:17—Breasts and brief buns in cave with everybody
during orgy scene.
The Gig (1985) . . . . . . . . . . . . . . . . . . . . The Blonde

# • *Harrington, Laura*

*Films:*
The Adventures of Buckaroo Banzai, Across the 8th
Dimension (1984) . . . . . . . . . . . . . . . . Mrs. Johnson
The City Girl (1984) . . . . . . . . . . . . . . . . . . . . Anne
The Joy of Sex (1984) . . . . . . . . . . . . . . Pretty Girl #2
Maximum Overdrive (1986) . . . . . . . . . . . . . . . . Brett
**Midnight Cabaret** (1988) . . . . . . . . . Tanya Richards
• 0:33—Very, very brief upper half of right breast
while leaning back.

• 0:34—Very, very brief left breast when a guy sticks
his tongue out.
• 0:43—Brief breasts when short guys rip her dress off.
• 0:49—Very brief right breast in gaping nightgown,
while bending over to put pants on.
• 1:08—Brief breasts while making love with a guy.
Verne Miller (1988) . . . . . . . . . . . . . . Judge's Daughter
The Dream Team (1989) . . . . . . . . . . . . . . . . . Nurse
What's Eating Gilbert Grape (1993) . . . . . . . Amy Grape
*Made for Cable Movies:*
Linda (1993; USA) . . . . . . . . . . . . . . . . Stella Jeffries
*Made for TV Movies:*
The Secret (1992) . . . . . . . . . . . . . Meredith Dunmore

## *Harrington, Tabitha*

*Films:*
**Crossover** (1980; Canadian). . . . . . . . . . . Montgomery
*a.k.a. Mr. Patman*
• 0:11—Brief right breast, then brief full frontal nudity
lying in bed, then struggling with James Coburn in
her room. Wearing white makeup on her face.
•• 0:29—Nude walking in to room to talk with Coburn,
then breasts and brief buns leaving.
Star 80 (1983) . . . . . . . . . . . . . . . . . . . . . . . Blonde

## *Harris, Gail*

See: Thackray, Gail.

## *Harris, Jo Ann*

*Films:*
Mary Jane (1968). . . . . . . . . . . . . . . . . . . . . Jo Ann
The Gay Deceivers (1969) . . . . . . . . . . . . Leslie Devlin
**The Beguiled** (1971) . . . . . . . . . . . . . . . . . . . Carol
• 1:09—Right breast, while in bed under Clint Eastwood at night.
• 1:10—Brief left breast and side view of buns on top
of Eastwood in bed. Brief buns, when discovered by
Edwina.
• 1:11—Very brief right breast, covering herself up in
bed. Very brief breasts shadow on the wall, then
very, very brief right breast covering herself with a
sheet and walking out the door.
**The Sporting Club** (1971) . . . . . . . . . . . . . . . . . . Lu
••• 0:55—Breasts (mostly right breast) while in the
woods, talking to James.
**Act of Vengeance** (1974) . . . . . . . . . . . . . . . . Linda
*a.k.a. The Rape Squad*
(Not to be confused with the film with the same name
starring Charles Bronson.)
••• 0:06—Breasts, taking off blouse for rapist, getting
fondled by him, running away, then getting hit.
• 0:09—Brief left breast, while getting her blouse afterwards. Dark.
• 0:37—Breasts under water with other women in
spa. (She's the third from the left.)
**The Deadly Games** (1980) . . . . . . . . . . . . . . Keegan
*a.k.a. The Eliminator*
• 0:48—Breasts in the shower. Hard to see because of
the pattern on the glass.

Caged Fear (1992) . . . . . . . . . . . . . Big As A House #1
Newsies (1992). . . . . . . . . . . . . . . . . Patrick's Mother
*Miniseries:*
Rich Man, Poor Man (1976) . . . . . . . . . . Gloria Bartley
*TV:*
Most Wanted (1976-77) . . . . . . . Officer Kate Manners
B.J. and the Bear . . . . . . . . . . Barbara Sue McCallister
Detective School (1979) . . . . . . . . . . . . Teresa Cleary

## Harris, Lee Anne

Identical twin sister of actress Lynette Harris.
a.k.a. Leigh Harris.
*Films:*
**I, the Jury** (1982) . . . . . . . . . . . . . . . . . . . . . 1st twin
••• 0:48—Breasts on bed talking to Armand Assante.
• 0:52—Full frontal nudity on bed wearing red wig,
talking to the maniac.
• 0:54—Brief breasts, dead on bed when discovered
by Assante.
**Sorceress** (1982). . . . . . . . . . . . . . . . . . . . . . . . Mira
••• 0:11—Breasts (on the left) greeting the creature
with her sister. Upper half of buns, getting dressed.
•• 0:29—Breasts (she's the second one) undressing
with her sister in front of Erlick and Baldar.
*Magazines:*
**Playboy** (Mar 1981). . . . . . . . . . . . . My Sister, My Self
••• 152-155—Breasts and buns.
**Playboy** (Mar 1982). . . . . . . . . . . . . . . . Aye, Barbara
• 152—Breasts in small photos from *I, the Jury.*
**Playboy's Nudes** (Oct 1990). . . . . . . . . . . . . . Herself
••• 36—Full frontal nudity.

## Harris, Lynette

Identical twin sister of actress Leigh Harris.
*Films:*
**I, the Jury** (1982) . . . . . . . . . . . . . . . . . . . . .2nd twin
••• 0:48—Breasts on bed talking to Armand Assante.
• 0:52—Full frontal nudity on bed wearing red wig,
talking to the maniac.
• 0:54—Brief breasts, dead on bed when discovered
by Assante.
**Sorceress** (1982). . . . . . . . . . . . . . . . . . . . . . . .Mara
••• 0:11—Breasts (on the right) greeting the creature
with her sister.
••• 0:29—Breasts (she's the first one) undressing with
her sister in front of Erlick and Baldar.
*Magazines:*
**Playboy** (Mar 1981). . . . . . . . . . . . . My Sister, My Self
••• 152-155—Breasts and buns..
**Playboy** (Mar 1982). . . . . . . . . . . . . . . . Aye, Barbara
• 152—Breasts in small photos from *I, the Jury.*
**Playboy's Nudes** (Oct 1990). . . . . . . . . . . . . . Herself
••• 36—Full frontal nudity.

## Harris, Moira

Wife of actor Gary Sinise.
*Films:*
**The Fanatasist** (1986; Irish). . . . . . . . . Patricia Teeling
• 1:24—Brief breasts and buns climbing onto couch
for the weird photographer.
• 1:28—Brief right breast leaning over to kiss the pho-
tographer.
• 1:31—Very brief side view of left breast in bathtub.
One More Saturday Night (1986) . . . . . . . . . . . Peggy
Of Mice and Men (1992) . . . . . . . . . . Girl in Red Dress
*Made for TV Movies:*
Between Love and Hate (1993) . . . Katherine Templeton

## Harris, Robyn

See: Thackray, Gail.

## Harrison, Cathryn

*Films:*
Images (1972; Irish). . . . . . . . . . . . . . . . . . .Susannah
The Pied Piper (1972; British)
. . . . . . . . . . . . . . . . .Burgermeister's Daughter, Lisa
Black Moon (1975; French) . . . . . . . . . . . . . . . . Lily
The Dresser (1983). . . . . . . . . . . . . . . . . . . . . . Irene
Duet for One (1987) . . . . . . . . . . Penny Smallwood
Empire State (1987; British) . . . . . . . . . . . . . . Marion
A Handful of Dust (1988). . . . . . . . . . . . . . . . . Milly
*Made for TV Movies:*
**Portrait of a Marriage** (1992; British) . .Violet Trefusis
• 0:48—Left breast when Vita admires her.

## Harrison, Jenilee

*Films:*
Tank (1984) . . . . . . . . . . . . . . . . . . . . . . . . . . .Sarah
**Curse III: Blood Sacrifice** (1990)
. . . . . . . . . . . . . . . . . . . . . . . Elizabeth Armstrong
••• 0:43—Breasts sitting in bathtub. Almost side of right
breast when wrapping a towel around herself.
Illicit Behavior (1991) . . . . . . . . . . . . . Charlene Lernoux
(Unrated version reviewed.)
**Prime Target** (1991) . . . . . . . . . . . . Kathy Bloodstone
••• 0:12—Breasts, lying back in bed with David Heaven-
er. Short, but sweet!
• 0:13—Partial right breast, under Heavener's arm.
*TV:*
Three's Company (1980-82) . . . . . . . . . . . .Cindy Snow
Dallas (1984-86) . . . . . . . . . . . . . . Jamie Ewing Barnes

## Harrold, Kathryn

*Films:*
Nightwing (1979) . . . . . . . . . . . . . . . . . . . Anne Dillon
The Hunter (1980). . . . . . . . . . . . . . . . . . . . . .Dotty
**Modern Romance** (1981) . . . . . . . . . . Mary Harvard
• 0:46—Very brief breasts and buns taking off robe
and getting into bed with Albert Brooks.
1:05—In pink lingerie opening her blouse to undo
her skirt while talking to Brooks.
Pursuit of D.B. Cooper (1981) . . . . . . . . . . . . . Hannah
The Sender (1982). . . . . . . . . . . . . . . . . . Gail Farmer

Yes, Giorgio (1982) . . . . . . . . . . . . . . . . . Pamela Taylor
Heartbreakers (1984) . . . . . . . . . . . . . . . . . . . . Cyd
   0:02—In black bra and panties changing clothes in
   Peter Coyote's studio.
Into the Night (1985) . . . . . . . . . . . . . . . . . . . .Christie
Raw Deal (1986) . . . . . . . . . . . . . . . . . . . . . . .Monique
*Made for Cable Movies:*
Best Legs in the 8th Grade (1984; HBO) Leslie Applegate
Dead Solid Perfect (1988; HBO) . . . . . . . . Beverly T. Lee
Rainbow Drive (1990; Showtime) . . . . . . . . . .Christine
Deadly Desire (1991; USA) . . . . . . . . . . . . . . . . .n.a.
*Made for TV Movies:*
Man Against the Mob (1988) . . . . . . . . . .Marilyn Butler
*TV:*
MacGruder & Loud (1985) . . . . . Jenny Loud McGruder
Bronx Zoo (1987-88) . . . . . . . . . . . . . .Sara Newhouse
Capital News (1990) . . . . . . . . . . . . . . . . . Mary Ward
I'll Fly Away (1991-93) . . . . . . . . . . . Christina LeKatzis

# • *Harrow, Lisa*

*Films:*
The Final Conflict (1981) . . . . . . . . . . . . .Kate Reynolds
  *a.k.a. Omen III*
Shaker Run (1985; New Zealand) . . . Dr. Christine Rubin
**The Last Days of Chez Nous** (1991; Australian)
. . . . . . . . . . . . . . . . . . . . . . . . . . . . . . . . . . . Beth
  • 1:10—Brief breasts, while moving around in bed
  with Bruno Ganz.

# *Harry, Deborah*

Lead singer of the rock group *Blondie*.
*Films:*
Union City (1980) . . . . . . . . . . . . . . . . . . . . . Lillian
**Videodrome** (1983; Canadian) . . . . . . . . . .Nicki Brand
  •• 0:16—Breasts rolling over on the floor when James
  Woods is piercing her ear with a pin.
    0:22—In black bra, sitting on couch with James
  Woods.
Forever Lulu (1987) . . . . . . . . . . . . . . . . . . . . Lulu
Hairspray (1988) . . . . . . . . . . . . . . . . . . . . . Velma
Satisfaction (1988) . . . . . . . . . . . . . . . . . . . . Tina
  *a.k.a. Girls of Summer*
  Shown on TV as "Girls of Summer."
Tales From the Darkside, The Movie (1990) . . . . . .Betty
*Made for Cable Movies:*
Intimate Strangers (1991; Showtime) . . . . Cory Wheeler
*Made for Cable TV:*
John Carpenter's Body Bags (1993; Showtime)
. . . . . . . . . . . . . . . . . . . . . . . . . .Hair/The Nurse
*CD-ROM:*
Double Switch (1994) . . . . . . . . . . . . . . . . . . .n.a.

# *Hart, Christina*

*Films:*
Red Sky at Morning (1971) . . . . . . . . . .Velva Mae Cloyd
The Mad Bomber (1973) . . . . . . . . . . . .Fromley's Victim
The Roommates (1973) . . . . . . . . . . . . . . . . . Paula

**Games Girls Play** (1974; British) . . . . . . Bunny O'Hara
  *a.k.a. The Bunny Caper*
  *a.k.a. Sex Play*
  • 0:00—Brief lower frontal nudity and buns when her
  dress blows up from the wind.
  •• 0:01—Full frontal nudity in slow motion, jumping
  into bed. Then nude, twirling around in another
  room.
  ••• 0:18—Nude, undressing with the other girls, then
  walking around the house to the pool, then swimming nude.
  • 1:01—Brief breasts getting dressed.
Charley Varrick (1975) . . . . . . . . . . . . . . . . . . .Jana
**Johnny Firecloud** (1975) . . . . . . . . . . . . . . . . . .June
  •• 0:22—Breasts, lying in bed with Johnny.
  ••• 0:26—Breasts, opening her blouse in barn in front of
  Johnny.
**Mean Dog Blues** (1978) . . . . . . . . . . Gloria Kinsman
  • 1:24—Brief breasts, in house with Gregg Henry.
The Check is in the Mail (1986) . . . . . . . . . . . . . Janet

# *Hart, La Gena*

*Films:*
Million Dollar Mystery (1987) . . . . . . . . . . . . . .Hope
Born to Race (1988) . . . . . . . . . . . . . . . . . . . . .Jenny
*Made for Cable TV:*
**The Hitchhiker: The Last Scene** . . . . . . . . . . . Leda
(Available on *The Hitchhiker, Volume 2*.)
  •• 0:01—Breasts making love with a guy in bed.

# *Hart, Roxanne*

*Films:*
The Bell Jar (1979) . . . . . . . . . . . . . . . . . . . . . n.a.
The Verdict (1982) . . . . . . . . . . . . . . . Sally Doneghy
Oh God, You Devil! (1984) . . . . . . . . . . . Wendy Shelton
Old Enough (1984) . . . . . . . . . . . . . . . . . . . . Carla
The Tender Age (1984) . . . . . . . . . . . . . . . . . .Sara
  1:01—In bed in a camisole and tap pants talking to
  John Savage.
**Highlander** (1986) . . . . . . . . . . . . . . . . .Brenda Wyatt
  • 1:30—Brief breasts making love with Christopher
  Lambert. Dark, hard to see.
The Pulse (1988) . . . . . . . . . . . . . . . . . . . . . Ellen
  1:01—Sort of breasts, while pressed against shower
  door after getting burned by super hot shower wa-
  ter. Don't see her face.
Once Around (1990) . . . . . . . . . . . . . . . . . Gail Bella
*Made for Cable Movies:*
**The Last Innocent Man** (1987; HBO) . . . . . . . . . .n.a.
  ••• 1:06—Breasts in bed making love, then sitting up
  and arguing with Ed Harris in his apartment.
*Made for Cable TV:*
Dream On: Dance Ten, Sex Three (1992; HBO)
. . . . . . . . . . . . . . . . . . . . . . . . . . . . Kate Gower
  0:19—Almost breasts in bed with Martin (you can
  see something covering her breasts).
  0:24—Almost breasts in bed again.
Dream On: The Undergraduate (1992; HBO)
. . . . . . . . . . . . . . . . . . . . . . . . . . . . Kate Gower

*Made for TV Movies:*
Samaritan: The Mitch Snyder Story (1986) Carol Fennelly
*TV:*
Chicago Hope (1994- ) . . . . . . . . . . . . . . . . . . . . . . .n.a.
The Road Home (1994- ). . . . . . . . . . . . . . Dr. Buerring

## Hart, Veronica

See: Hamilton, Jane.

## Hartman Black, Lisa

Wife of Country music singer Clint Black.
*Films:*
Deadly Blessing (1981) . . . . . . . . . . . . . . . . . . . . .Faith
    1:31—It looks like brief left breast after getting hit
    with a rock by Maren Jensen, but it's a special-effect
    appliance over her breasts because she's supposed
    to be a male in the film.
Where the Boys Are '84 (1984) . . . . . . . . . . . . . .Jennie
*Made for Cable Movies:*
Bodily Harm (1989). . . . . . . . . . . . . . . . . . . . . . Laura
Bare Essentials (1991) . . . . . . . . . . . . . . Sydney Wayne
*Made for TV Movies:*
Just Tell Me You Love Me (1978) . . . . . . . . . . . . . .n.a.
Full Exposure: The Sex Tapes Scandal (1989)
. . . . . . . . . . . . . . . . . . . . . . . . . . . . Sarah Dutton
The Return of Eliot Ness (1991). . . . . Madeline Whitfield
Without a Kiss Goodbye (1993). . . . . . . Laurie Samuels
Search for Grace (1994) . . . . . . . . . . . . . . . . . . . . Ivy
*TV:*
Tabitha (1977-78). . . . . . . . . . . . . . . Tabitha Stephens
Knots Landing (1982-83) . . . . . . . . . . . . . Ciji Dunne
High Performance (1983) . . . . . . . . . . . . Kate Flannery
Knots Landing (1983-86) . . . . . . . . . . . . . Cathy Geary
2000 Malibu Road (1992). . . . . . . . . . . . . . . . . Jade

## Hartman, Valerie

*Films:*
**Sleepaway Camp II: Unhappy Campers** (1988)
. . . . . . . . . . . . . . . . . . . . . . . . . . . . . . . . . . . .Ally
••• 0:06—Breasts waking up and stretching in bed, then
    standing next to bathroom.
• 0:33—Breasts in Polaroid photographs that Angela
    confiscates from the boys.
••• 0:39—In beige bra, then breasts in restroom stall
    with Rob.
••• 0:43—Breasts making love in the woods with Rob,
    then getting dressed. Nice!
Intimate Obsession (1992) . . . . . . . . . . . . . . . . Karen
(Unrated version reviewed.)

## Hartt, Cathryn

*Films:*
**Pink Motel** (1982) . . . . . . . . . . . . . . . . . . . . .Charlene
••• 1:18—Breasts, dropping her sheet in room in front
    of Max and Skip.
The Seduction (1982) . . . . . . . . . . . . Teleprompter Girl
Open House (1987) . . . . . . . . . . . . . . . . . . . . . Melody

## • Harvey, Susan

*Films:*
**Caged Heat 2: Stripped of Freedom** (1993) . . Lucy
• 1:00—Brief breasts, while in her cell, flashing to dis-
    tract a guard.
**Caroline at Midnight** (1993) . . . . . . . . . . . . . . Lilli
•• 0:03—Breasts, while being held by Stan, while Judd
    Nelson tries to get information from Miguel.

## • Hassall, Imogen

*Films:*
The Long Duel (1967; British) . . . . . . . . . . . . . . . n.a.
**Bloodsuckers** (1970; British) . . . . . . . . . . . . . Chriseis
• 0:05—Right breast, while standing up at the beach
    and kissing Richard.
Take a Girl Like You (1970; British) . . . . . . . . . Samantha
El Condor (1971) . . . . . . . . . . . . . . . . . . . . . . . . . n.a.
When Dinosaurs Ruled the Earth (1971; British) . . . . n.a.

## Hassett, Marilyn

*Films:*
The Other Side of the Mountain (1975) . . . . Jill Kinmont
Two-Minute Warning (1976) . . . . . . . . . . . . . . . Lucy
The Other Side of the Mountain, Part II (1978)
. . . . . . . . . . . . . . . . . . . . . . . . . . . . Jill Kinmont
**The Bell Jar** (1979) . . . . . . . . . . . . . Esther Greenwood
• 0:10—In bra, then brief breasts in bed with Buddy.
    Dark, hard to see.
•• 1:09—Breasts taking off her clothes and throwing
    them out the window while yelling.
Gypsy Angels (1980) . . . . . . . . . . . . . . . . . . . . . .Jan
Massive Retaliation (1984) . . . . . . . . . . . Louis Fredericks
Messenger of Death (1988) . . . . . . . . . . . . .Josephine
Twenty Dollar Star (1991) . . . . . . . . . . . . . . . . . . n.a.
*Made for Cable TV:*
The Hitchhiker: Man of Her Dreams . . . . . . Jill McGinnis
*Video Tapes:*
Inside Out 3 (1992) . . . . . . . . . . Cindy/The Houseguest

## • Hatcher, Teri

Wife of actor Jon Tenney.
*Films:*
The Big Picture (1989) . . . . . . . . . . . . . . . . . . . .Gretchen
Tango & Cash (1989). . . . . . . . . . . . . . . . . . . . . Kiki
Soapdish (1991). . . . . . . . . . . . . . . . . . . Ariel Maloney
All Tied Up (1992) . . . . . . . . . . . . . . . . . . .Linda Alissio
**The Cool Surface** (1992). . . . . . . . . . . . . .Dani Payson
••• 0:20—Close-up of left breast, while lying in bed with
    Robert Patrick during daydream.
••• 0:27—Breasts, while standing in front of Patrick
    when he takes off her lingerie.
• 0:29—Brief right breast, when Patrick gets out of
    bed.
Straight Talk (1992) . . . . . . . . . . . . . . . . . . . . . . Janice
BrainSmasher... A Love Story (1993) . . .Samantha Crain
*Made for Cable Movies:*
Dead In the Water (1991) . . . . . . . . . . . Laura Stewart

*Made for Cable TV:*
Tales From the Crypt: The Thing From the Grave
(1991; HBO) ............................ Stacy
*TV:*
The Love Boat (1985-86)..................... Amy
Karen's Song (1987) .............. Laura Matthews
Sunday Dinner (1991)................... T.T. Fagori
Lois & Clark: The New Adventures of Superman (1993- )
..................................... Lois Lane

## Hawn, Goldie

Significant Other of actor Kurt Russell.
*Films:*
The One and Only, Genuine, Original Family Band
(1967)........................... Giggly Girl
Cactus Flower (1969) ............... Toni Simmons
(Academy Award for Best Supporting Actress.)
**There's a Girl in My Soup** (1970) .......... Marion
• 0:37—Buns and very brief right side view of her
body getting out of bed and walking to a closet to
get a robe. Long shot.
Butterflies Are Free (1972)..................... Jill
0:02—In white bra and panties, while changing
clothes in her new bedroom.
0:03—Briefly in white bra and panties, after opening
her dress to flash Edward Albert.
0:44—In bra and panties in apartment with Albert.
Very long scene—11 minutes!
Dollars (1972).................... Dawn Divine
The Girl from Petrovka (1974)........... Oktyabrina
1:30—Very, very brief breasts in bed with Hal Hol-
brook. Don't really see anything—it lasts for about
one frame.
The Sugarland Express (1974)........ Lou Jean Poplin
Shampoo (1975)............................ Jill
The Duchess and the Dirtwater Fox (1976)
.............................. Amanda Quaid
Foul Play (1978) .................... Gloria Mundy
Lovers and Liars (1979; Italian) ............... Anita
Private Benjamin (1980) ............. Judy Benjamin
Seems Like Old Times (1980) .............. Glenda
**Best Friends** (1982) .............. Paula McCullen
• 0:18—Very, very brief side view of right breast get-
ting into the shower with Burt Reynolds.
• 1:14—Upper half of left breast in the shower, twice.
Protocol (1984)......................... Sunny
Swing Shift (1984) ..................... Kay Walsh
**Wildcats** (1986) ........................ Molly
• 0:30—Brief breasts in bathtub.
Overboard (1987)............. Joanna Slayton/Annie
0:07—Buns, wearing a revealing swimsuit that
shows most of her derriere to Kurt Russell.
**Bird on a Wire** (1990) ........... Marianne Graves
• 0:31—Buns, in open dress climbing up ladder with
Mel Gibson.
• 1:18—Very brief top of right breast rolling over on
top of Gibson in bed. Don't see her face.
Deceived (1991) ................ Adrienne Saunders

Criss Cross (1992) .................. Tracy Cross
•• 0:23—Buns and breasts in pasties, dancing on stage
in club while her son watches.
Death Becomes Her (1992) ............ Helen Sharp
Housesitter (1992) ....................... Gwen
*TV:*
Good Morning, World (1967-68)....... Sandy Kramer
Rowan And Martin's Laugh-In (1968-70) ...... Regular

## Hay, Alexandra

*Films:*
Guess Who's Coming to Dinner? (1967) ...... Car Hop
How Sweet It Is (1968)..................... Gloria
Skidoo (1968) ................... Darlene Banks
The Model Shop (1969)..................... Gloria
1,000 Convicts and a Woman (1971; British)
.............................. Angela Thorne
**The Love Machine** (1971).......... Tina St. Claire
• 0:34—Brief breasts in bed with Robin.
• 0:38—Brief breasts coming around the corner put-
ting blue bathrobe on.
**How to Seduce a Woman** (1973) .... Nell Brinkman
• 1:05—Brief right breast in mirror taking off black
dress.
••• 1:06—Breasts posing for pictures. Long scene.
• 1:47—Breasts during flashback. Lots of diffusion.
How Come Nobody's on our Side? (1976)..... Brigitte
One Man Jury (1978)...................... Tessie
*Magazines:*
**Playboy** (Feb 1974) ........... Alexandra the Great
••• 81-87—Breasts and side view of buns.
**Playboy** (Nov 1974) ........... Sex in Cinema 1974
•• 151—Breasts from *How to Seduce a Woman.*

## Hayden, Jane

*Films:*
Confessions of a Pop Performer (1975; British)..... n.a.
**Emily** (1976; British) ..................... Rachel
•• 1:09—Breasts in bed with Billy.

## Hayden, Linda

*Films:*
The Barcelona Kill................... n.a.
**Baby Love** (1969)...................... Luci
0:32—Buns, standing in room when Nick sneaks in.
0:34—Very brief right breast, while throwing doll at
Robert.
• 0:39—Breasts in mirror taking a bath. Long shot.
Brief left breast hidden by steam.
• 0:52—Brief breasts taking off her top to show Nick
while sunbathing.
1:25—Brief breasts calling Robert from window.
Long shot.
1:27—Very brief breasts sitting up while talking to
Robert.
• 1:28—Breasts in open robe struggling with Robert.
Taste the Blood of Dracula (1970) ...... Alice Hargood

**Blood on Satan's Claw** (1971; British) . . . .Angel Blake
*a.k.a. Satan's Skin*
•• 0:40—Breasts, while undressing in front of priest to tempt him.
Confessions of a Window Cleaner (1974; British)
. . . . . . . . . . . . . . . . . . . . . . . . . . . . . .Elizabeth
**The House on Straw Hill** (1976; British)
. . . . . . . . . . . . . . . . . . . . . . . .Linda Hindstatt
*a.k.a. Exposé*
• 0:28—Breasts getting undressed in her room.
••• 0:47—Breasts, masturbating in bed.
•• 1:06—Right breast, in bed with Fiona Richmond.
Love Trap (1977). . . . . . . . . . . . . . . . . . . . Gloria
*a.k.a. Let's Get Laid*
**The Boys From Brazil** (1978) . . . . . . . . . . . .Nancy
• 0:44—Very brief right breast, in mirror. Very, very brief left breast, twice, while in bed.
• 0:50—Very brief breasts, gagged, lying dead on bed.

## Hayes, Julia

*Video Tapes:*
**Soft Bodies: Party Favors** (1992) . . . . . . . . . Herself
••• 0:22—Buns in sheer nightie, while posing on bed, then breasts during photo session.
••• 0:29—In bra and panties on couch, then breasts and buns.
••• 0:35—Breasts and buns, on floating bed in pool with Becky LeBeau.
*Magazines:*
**Penthouse** (Oct 1991) . . . . . . . . . . Northern Exposure
••• 104-115—Nude.
**Playboy** (Dec 1993). . . . . . . . . . . . . . . . . .Grapevine
••• 239—Breasts in B&W photo.

## Hayland, Lysa

*Films:*
Novel Desires (1991). . . . . . . . . . . . . . . . . . . . Linda
*Made for Cable TV:*
**Dream On: Here Comes the Bribe** (1992; HBO)
. . . . . . . . . . . . . . . . . . . . . . . . . . . . . . . Amanda
•• 0:01—Breasts on the floor, making love with Martin.

## Haynes, Linda

*Films:*
The Drowning Pool (1976) . . . . . . . . . . . . . . Gretchen
Rolling Thunder (1977). . . . . . . . . . . . . . Linda Forchet
**Brubaker** (1980). . . . . . . . . . . . . . . . . . . . Carol
• 1:03—Breasts getting dressed with Huey in bedroom when Robert Redford comes in.
Human Experiments (1980) . . . . . . . . . . Rachel Foster
*Magazines:*
**Playboy** (Dec 1975). . . . . . . . . . . . . Sex Stars of 1975
••• 185—Full frontal nudity.

## • Hays, Lauren

*Films:*
Alien Intruder (1992) . . . . . . . . . . . . . . . . . . . . .Roni
**Meatballs 4** (1992) . . . . . . . . . . . . . . . . . . . . .Lauren
• 0:05—Brief breasts (she's on the far right), while taking off her black top in cabin with Miche and Hillary.
Ring of Fire II: Blood and Steel (1992)
. . . . . . . . . . . . . . . . . . . . Bad Girl Gang Member
Round Trip to Heaven (1992). . . . . . . . . . . .Contestant
**The Great Bikini Off-Road Adventure** (1994)
. . . . . . . . . . . . . . . . . . . . . . . . . . . . . Lori Baker
• 1:06—Buns in swimsuit while giving a tour.
••• 1:11—In bra in house with her boyfriend, then breasts while making love with him.
*Video Tapes:*
**California Girl Fox Hunt Bikini Competition #6**
. . . . . . . . . . . . . . . . . . . . . . . . . . . . . . Laura
••• 0:03—Buns in two piece swimsuit.
0:48—Buns during review.
0:56—2nd place runner up.
**Hot Body International: #3 Lingerie Special**
(1992) . . . . . . . . . . . . . . . . . . . . . . . . . .Contestant
•• 0:48—Buns in white G-string and bra.
**Hot Body International: #5 Miss Acapulco** (1992)
. . . . . . . . . . . . . . . . . . . . . . . . . . . . . .Contestant
• 0:13—Buns, under mini-skirt.
**Buck Naked Line Dancing** (1993) . . . . . . . . . Dancer
••• 0:00—Breasts and buns throughout. She's in the front on the right, wearing a black wig.
*Magazines:*
Playboy (Nov 1994). . . . . . . . . . . . . . . . . . . Grapevine
178—Lower half of breasts in B&W photo.

## Hayward, Rachel

*Films:*
**Breaking All the Rules** (1985; Canadian). . . . . .Angie
••• 0:16—Breasts changing in the bathroom.
• 0:43—Brief breasts after being felt up on roller coaster.
Xtro 2, The Second Encounter (1991) . . . . . . .Dr. Myers
Just One of the Girls (1992) . . . . . . . . . . . . . Ms. Glatt
**Knight Moves** (1992) . . . . . . . . . . . . . . . . .Last Victim
• 1:05—Very, very brief breasts screaming when the killer pulls the covers on the bed and flashes with a camera.
Time Runner (1992). . . . . . . . . . . . . . . Caroline Raynor

## • Hayward, Susan

*Films:*
Beau Geste (1939) . . . . . . . . . . . . . . . . . . . .Isobel Rivers
Adam Had Four Sons (1941) . . . . . . . . . . . . . . . Hester
Reap the Wild Wind (1942) . . . . . . . . . . Drusilla Alston
Jack London (1943) . . . . . . . . . . . . Charmain Kittredge
Young and Willing (1943) . . . . . . . . . . . . Kate Benson
The Fighting Seebees (1944) . . . . . . Constance Chesley
Deadline at Dawn (1946). . . . . . . . . . . . . . . .June Goff
Smash Up: The Story of a Woman (1947). . .Angie Evans
They Won't Believe Me (1947) . . . . . . . . . Verna Carlson
House of Strangers (1949) . . . . . . . . . . . .Irene Bennett

Tulsa (1949) . . . . . . . . . . . . . . . . . . Cherokee Lansing
David and Bathsheba (1951). . . . . . . . . . . .Bathsheba
Rawhide (1951) . . . . . . . . . . . . . . . . . . . Vinnie Holt
The Lusty Men (1952). . . . . . . . . . . . . . Louise Merritt
The Snows of Kilimanjaro (1952). . . . . . . . . . . . Helen
**With a Song in My Heart** (1952) . . . . . . Jane Froman
    0:48—Very brief upper half of left breast, when it
    pops out of the top of her strapless dress during
    song and dance number when she lifts her right arm
    over her dancing partner's head.
I'll Cry Tomorrow (1955) . . . . . . . . . . . . . Lillian Roth
Soldier of Fortune (1955) . . . . . . . . . . . . . Jane Hoyt
The Conqueror (1956) . . . . . . . . . . . . . . . . . Bortai
I Want to Live! (1958) . . . . . . . . . . . . . Barbara Graham
  (Academy Award for Best Actress.)
Back Street (1961; British). . . . . . . . . . Christine Allison
Stolen Hours (1963) . . . . . . . . . . . . . . . . Laura Pember
Where Love Has Gone (1964) . . . . Valerie Hayden Miller
The Honey Pot (1967; British)
    . . . . . . . . . . . . . . . . . Mrs. Lonestar Crockett Sheridan
Valley of the Dolls (1967) . . . . . . . . . . . . Helen Lawson

## • Headey, Lena

*Films:*
**Waterland** (1992; British/U.S.) . . . . . . . . . Young Mary
  • 0:16—In braless white undershirt, then brief breasts
    while making love with Tom in train.
  ••• 0:20—Breasts, while talking with Tom.
The Remains of the Day (1993; British/U.S.) . . . . . Lizzie

## Healy, Patricia

*Films:*
**Sweet Poison** (1991) . . . . . . . . . . . . . . . . .Charlene
  • 0:01—Breasts and buns, while straddling her hus-
    band in bed.
    0:45—In white bra and panties, taking off her
    clothes and going for a dip in the river.
  ••• 1:05—Breasts, dropping her towel in front of Bauer
    in the bathroom.
  •• 1:08—Side view breasts, straddling Bauer in bed.
The Bodyguard (1992) . . . . . . . . . . . . . .Sound Winner
Public Eye (1992) . . . . . . . . . . . . . . . . . . . . . Vera
**Ultraviolet** (1992). . . . . . . . . . . . . . . . Kristen Halsey
    0:04—In white bra, while changing into "something
    cooler" in motor home.
  • 0:21—Brief breasts, after taking off blouse and pos-
    ing for Esai Morales in motor home.
  ••• 0:50—In wet bra and panties, coming out of the
    pond. Side view of buns, then breasts while posing
    for Morales.
  ••• 0:52—More buns in panties and breasts in pond
    with Morales and struggling with him.

## Heasley, Marla

*Films:*
**Born to Race** (1988). . . . . . . . . . . .Andrea Lombardo
  • 0:52—Buns, outside at night while kissing Joseph
    Bottoms.

The Marrying Man (1991) . . . . . . . . . . . . . . . . . Sheila
  *a.k.a. Too Hot to Handle*
Amore! (1993) . . . . . . . . . . . . . . . . . . . Marge Apple

## • Heatherton, Joey

Singer.
*Films:*
**Bluebeard** (1972). . . . . . . . . . . . . . . . . . . . . . Anne
  • 0:25—Breasts under black see-through nightie while
    Richard Burton photographs her. Very brief right
    breast.
  ••• 1:46—Brief breasts opening her dress top to taunt
    Richard Burton.
The Happy Hooker Goes to Washington (1977)
  . . . . . . . . . . . . . . . . . . . . . . . Xaviera Hollander
Cry Baby (1990). . . . . . . . . . . . . . . . .Milton's Mother
*TV:*
Dean Martin Presents the Golddiggers (1968) . . Regular
Joey & Dad (1975). . . . . . . . . . . . . . . . . .Co-Host
*Magazines:*
**Playboy** (Dec 1972) . . . . . . . . . . . . .Sex Stars of 1972
  •• 214—Breasts.

## • Heche, Anne

*Films:*
The Adventures of Huck Finn (1993) . . Mary Jane Wicks
*Made for Cable Movies:*
**Rebel Highway: Girls in Prison** (1994; Showtime)
  . . . . . . . . . . . . . . . . . . . . . . . . . . . . . . Jennifer
  •• 1:02—Breasts, while walking in showers past the
    other girls, taking a shower and dropping a bar of
    soap.

## • Hefner, Lené

Adult film actress.
*Films:*
**Killer Looks** (1994) . . . . . . . . . . . . . . . Angela's Lover
  (Unrated version reviewed.)
  •• 0:22—In white dress, then breasts, while Janine Lin-
    demulder makes out with her in parking lot of res-
    taurant.
  •• 1:11—In black dress, then breasts and buns, while
    making out with Lindemulder.
  •• 1:18—Breasts, while sunbathing outside by pool
    with Lindemulder.
*Magazines:*
**Playboy** (Sep 1994) . . . . . . . . . .A Walk on the Bi Side
  • 72-77—Buns.

## • Heigl, Katherine

*Films:*
King of the Hill (1993) . . . . . . . . . . . Christina Sebastian
**My Father The Hero** (1993) . . . . . . . . . . . . . . Nicole
  • 0:14—Buns in white, T-back swimsuit, getting up of
    lounge chair and walking while Gérard Depardieu
    tries to cover her up.
That Night (1993) . . . . . . . . . . . . . . . . . . . Kathryn

# Helfer, Britt

*Films:*

Raw Force (1981) . . . . . . . . . . . . . . . . . . . Girl in Cabin

**Surf II** (1984). . . . . . . . . . . . . . . . . . . . Hot Potato #2

•• 0:25—Breasts taking off bikini top with her friend in lifeguard station at beach with Eric Stoltz and his friend.

•• 0:27—Brief breasts with her friend, after dropping towel when she raises her hands for the police.

The Princess Academy (1986; U.S./Yugoslavian/French)
. . . . . . . . . . . . . . . . . . . . . . . . . . . . Lulu Belle

# Helgenberger, Marg

*Films:*

After Midnight (1989). . . . . . . . . . . . . . . . . . . Alex

Always (1989). . . . . . . . . . . . . . . . . . . . . . . Rachel

Blind Vengeance (1990) . . . . . . . . . . . Virginia Whitelaw

Crooked Hearts (1991) . . . . . . . . . . . . . . . . Jennetta

Desperate Motive (1992) . . . . . . . . . . . . . . . . Connie

*Made for Cable Movies:*

Death Dreams (1991; Lifetime) . . . . . . . . Crista Westfield

Lie Down with Lions (1994; Lifetime) . . . . . Kate Neesen

*Made for Cable TV:*

**Tales From the Crypt: Deadline** (1991; HBO) . . Vicki

• 0:08—Brief side of right breast putting on halter top in Richard Jordan's apartment. Don't see her face, but it looks like her.

Fallen Angels: I'll Be Waiting (1993; Showtime)
. . . . . . . . . . . . . . . . . . . . . . . . . . . Eve Cressy

(Available on video tape on *Fallen Angels Two*.)

*Made for TV Movies:*

In Sickness and in Health (1992). . . . . . . . . . . . . .n.a.

Through the Eyes of a Killer (1992) . . . . . . . . . . . .n.a.

The Tommyknockers (1993) . . . . . . . . Bobbi Anderson

When Love Kills: The Seduction of John Hearn (1993)
. . . . . . . . . . . . . . . . . . . . . . . . Debbie Banister

*TV:*

Shell Game (1987) . . . . . . . . . . . . . . . Natalie Thayer

China Beach (1988-91) . . Karen Charlene "K.C." Koloski

# Helmcamp, Charlotte J.

*a.k.a. Charlotte Kemp.*

*Films:*

**Posed for Murder** (1988) . . . . . . . . . . . . Laura Shea

• 0:00—Breasts in photos during opening credits.

••• 0:22—Posing for photos in sheer green teddy, then breasts in sailor's cap, then great breasts shots wearing just a G-string.

0:31—Very brief right breast in photo on desk.

0:44—In black one piece swimsuit.

••• 0:52—Breasts in bed making love with her boyfriend.

**Frankenhooker** (1990). . . . . . . . . . . . . . . . . .Honey

•• 0:26—Breasts yanking down her top outside of Jeffrey's car window.

Repossessed (1990). . . . . . . . . . . . . . . .Incredible Girl

*Video Tapes:*

**Playboy Video Magazine, Volume 3** (1983)
. . . . . . . . . . . . . . . . . . . . . . . . . Video Playmate

••• 0:12—Nude in bubble bath.

• 0:14—Full frontal nudity in centerfold still photo.

••• 0:17—Nude in house and on bed while wearing a girdle.

**Playboy Video Magazine, Volume 5** (1983)
. . . . . . . . . . . . . . . . . . . . . . . . . . . . Playmate

• 0:05—Brief nude in bubble bath.

**Playboy's Playmate Review 3** (1985) . . . . . Playmate

*Magazines:*

**Playboy** (Dec 1982) . . . . . . . . . . . . . . . . Playmate

**Playboy's Calendar Playmates** (Nov 1992). . .Herself

••• 19—Full frontal nudity.

•• 41—Buns and side of left breast.

# Hemingway, Margaux

Model.

Sister of actress Mariel Hemingway.

Granddaughter of writer Ernest Hemingway.

*Films:*

**Lipstick** (1976). . . . . . . . . . . . . . . .Chris McCormick

•• 0:10—Brief breasts opening the shower door to answer the telephone.

•• 0:19—Brief breasts during rape attempt, including close-up of side view of left breast.

0:24—Buns, lying on bed while rapist runs a knife up her leg and back while she's tied to the bed.

•• 0:25—Brief breasts getting out of bed.

Killer Fish (1979; Italian/Brazilian). . . . . . . . . . Gabrielle

They Call Me Bruce? (1982). . . . . . . . . . . . . . Karmen

Over the Brooklyn Bridge (1983) . . . . . . . . . . Elizabeth

Frame Up II (1991). . . . . . . . . . . . . . . . . . . . .Jean

*a.k.a. Deadly Conspiracy*

**Inner Sanctum** (1991). . . . . . . . . . . . .Anna Rawlins

• 0:09—Brief buns and tip of left breast in office with Joseph Bottoms.

••• 0:23—In bra with Bottoms, then breasts, while in bed. (When you don't see her face, it's Michelle Bauer doing the body double work.)

Deadly Rivals (1992) . . . . . . . . . . .Agent Linda Howerton

**Double Obsession** (1992) . . . . . . . . . . Heather Dwyer

•• 0:31—Right breast, while wearing Indian headress and making love on top of Fredric Forrest in bed.

*Magazines:*

**Playboy** (May 1990). . . . . . . . . . . . . . . . . Papa's Girl

••• 126-135—Nude.

**Playboy's Nudes** (Oct 1990) . . . . . . . . . . . . . .Herself

•• 34-35—Right breast.

**Playboy** (Dec 1990) . . . . . . . . . . . . . .Sex Stars of 1990

•• 175—Left breast, lying in bed.

# Hemingway, Mariel

Younger sister of actress Margaux Hemingway.

Granddaughter of writer Ernest Hemingway.

*Films:*

Lipstick (1976) . . . . . . . . . . . . . . . . . Kathy McCormick

Manhattan (1979) . . . . . . . . . . . . . . . . . . . . . . Tracy

**Personal Best** (1982) . . . . . . . . . . . . . . . .Chris Cahill
(Before breast enlargement.)
- •• 0:16—Brief lower frontal nudity getting examined by Patrice Donnelly, then breasts after making love with her.
- •• 0:30—Breasts in the steam room talking with the other women.

**Star 80** (1983) . . . . . . . . . . . . . . . . .Dorothy Stratten
(After breast enlargement.)
- •• 0:00—Breasts in still photos during opening credits.
- • 0:02—Breasts lying on bed in Paul's flashbacks.
- ••• 0:22—Breasts during Polaroid photo session with Paul
- • 0:25—Breasts during professional photography session. Long shot.
- • 0:36—Brief breasts during photo session.
- • 0:57—Right breast, in centerfold photo on wall.
- • 1:04—Upper half of breasts, in bathtub.
- • 1:05—Brief breasts in photo shoot flashback.
- • 1:17—Brief breasts during layout flashbacks.
- • 1:20—Very brief breasts in photos on the wall.
- •• 1:33—Breasts undressing before getting killed by Paul. More brief breasts layout flashbacks.

**Creator** (1985) . . . . . . . . . . . . . . . . . . . . . . . . . Meli
0:38—Brief breasts cooling herself off by pulling up T-shirt in front of a fan.
- • 1:10—Brief breasts flashing David Ogden Stiers during football game to distract him.

**The Mean Season** (1985) . . . . . . . Christine Connelly
- •• 0:15—Breasts taking a shower.

Superman IV: The Quest for Peace (1987)
. . . . . . . . . . . . . . . . . . . . . . . . . . . . . . Lacy Warfield
Suicide Club (1988) . . . . . . . . . . . . . . . Sasha Michaels
Sunset (1988) . . . . . . . . . . . . . . . . . . . . . . Cheryl King
Delirious (1991) . . . . . . . . . . . . . . . . . . . . Janet/Louise
Into the Badlands (1991). . . . . . . . . . . . . . . . . .Alma
Falling From Grace (1992). . . . . . . . . . . . . Alice Parks

*Made for Cable Movies:*
Steal the Sky (1988; HBO). . . . . . . . . . . . Helen Mason
Breasts, but too dark to see anything.

*Made for Cable TV:*
**Tales From the Crypt: Loved to Death** (1991; HBO)
. . . . . . . . . . . . . . . . . . . . . . . . . . . .Miranda Singer
0:03—In black lingerie. Very brief buns.
- •• 0:07—In bra, then side view of left breast several times in laundry room while Andrew McCarthy secretly watches.
0:18—In red lingerie in bedroom with McCarthy.
0:21—More buns in lingerie.

*Made for TV Movies:*
Desperate Rescue: The Cathy Mahone Story (1993)
. . . . . . . . . . . . . . . . . . . . . . . . . . . . . Cathy Mahone

*TV:*
Civil Wars (1991-93) . . . . . . . . . . . . . .Sydney Guilford
On the 9/30/92 show, she had a well-hyped "nude" scene on network TV. You get to see very brief upper half of buns between gaps in some plastic and side view buns, while standing during photo shoot. Side view of buns later when looking at B&W photos. Forget the teasing and watch *Star 80*.

*Magazines:*
**Playboy** (Apr 1982) . . . . . . . . . . . . . . . . . Personal Best
- • 104-109—Breasts in stills from the film, buns doing the splits.
**Playboy** (Jan 1984). . . . . . . . . . . . . . . . . . . . .Star 80
**Playboy** (Jan 1989). . . . . . . . . . .Women of the Eighties
- ••• 248—Breasts.
**Playboy's Nudes** (Oct 1990) . . . . . . . . . . . . . . Herself
- •• 35—Buns and left breast.
Playboy (Mar 1994) . . . . . . . . . . . . Safe Sex, Great Sex

# Hempel, Anouska

*Films:*
**Tiffany Jones**. . . . . . . . . . . . . . . . . . . . . Tiffany Jones
- • 0:02—Brief breasts walking in from the surf in wet white dress.
- •• 0:13—Breasts in bath. Buns also, getting out.
- • 0:18—Brief left breast, taking off her top in front of bright light.
- • 0:23—Breasts, several times, changing clothes in her bedroom.
- •• 0:24—Breasts walking around her apartment in white panties.
- • 0:31—Breasts in bubble bath.
- • 0:32—Brief left breast, wrapping an orange towel around herself.
- ••• 0:39—Lying on table in black and red bra, then breasts. More right breast.
- • 0:41—Side view breasts, covered with sweat.
- •• 0:55—Breasts, partial lower frontal nudity, taking a shower.
- • 1:26—Breasts, running outside in a field when guys rip off her dress.
On Her Majesty's Secret Sevice (1969; British)
. . . . . . . . . . . . . . . . . . . . . . . . . . . . Australian Girl
Scars of Dracula (1970) . . . . . . . . . . . . . . . . . . Tania
Sweet Suzy (1973) . . . . . . . . . . . . . . . . . . Lady Susan
*TV:*
UFO (1970) . . . . . . . . . . . . . . . SHADO Radio Operator

# • Hendrix, Elaine

*Films:*
**Last Dance** (1992) . . . . . . . . . . . . . . . . . . . . . . Kelly
- ••• 0:20—Breasts and buns in bed with Jim. Don't see her face, probably a body double.
- •• 0:52—Buns in white lingerie outfit.
*Made for Cable TV:*
Fallen Angels: Since I Don't Have You (1993; Showtime)
. . . . . . . . . . . . . . . . . . . . . . . Auditioning Blonde #1
(Available on video tape on *Fallen Angels One*.)

# Hendrix, Lori Jo

*Films:*
Bikini Summer (1991) . . . . . . . . . . Smart Girl on Beach
**A Sensuous Summer** (1991) . . . . . . Dream Girl/Beach
- ••• 0:16—Nude on beach with dark haired girl in Jinx's dream.
- •• 0:24—Breasts while kneeling on one knee in Jinx's dream.
- •• 0:39—Breasts again while kneeling on one knee in Jinx's dream.
**Sunset Strip** (1992) . . . . . . . . . . . . . . . . . . Tammy
- •• 0:54—Breasts, taking off her swimsuit top for Crystal's video camera.
- ••• 1:12—Breasts and buns in G-string, doing strip routine on stage.
- • 1:16—Breasts in music video.
**Prison Heat** (1993) . . . . . . . . . . . . . . . . . . . . . . .n.a.
*Video Tapes:*
**Erotic Dreams 2** (1992) . . . . . . . . . . . . . . . . . . .n.a.
**Playboy's Erotic Weekend Getaways** (1992)
. . . . . . . . . . . . . . . . . . . . . . . . . . Escape: The Desert
- •• 0:09—In white bra and panties in moving car. Breasts changing into dress.
- ••• 0:11—Full frontal nudity while making love in the back seat of the convertible.
- ••• 0:12—Nude, outside with her lover by the pool.
- ••• 0:14—Nude, bringing drinks out to the pool.
- ••• 0:15—Nude, swimming in pool. Some are under water shots.
**Playboy's How to Reawaken Your Sexual Powers** (1992). . . . . . . . . . . . . . . . . . . . . . . . . Cast Member
- ••• 0:12—Nude with her lover in the woods, a stream, a pond and under a waterfall.
- ••• 0:45—Nude, outside by beach with her lover. Also on air mattresses and snorkeling under water.
**Starlet Screen Test III** (1992) . . . . . . . . Sherry Miller
- ••• 0:09—In bra, then breasts while kneeling on table.
**Intimate Secrets—How Women Love to be Loved** (1993). . . . . . . . . . . . . . . . . . . . . . . . . . . . . .Lori
- ••• 0:46—In white bra and panties, then nude in bed.
Playboy's Erotic Fantasies II (1993) . . . . . . Cast Member
**Playboy's Secret Confessions** (1993)
. . . . Teacher's Pet/Ruth Ann and Twins/Cindy & Sandy
- ••• 0:25—In green lingerie, then breasts and buns, while making love in bedroom with Jay.
- • 0:36—Breasts and buns in hallway with Stuart.
- ••• 0:38—Nude in bedroom, then making love with Stuart.
*Magazines:*
**Playboy's Book of Lingerie** (Jan 1992) . . . . . . Herself
- ••• 86-87—Breasts and partial lower frontal nudity.
**Playboy's Girls of Summer '92** (Jun 1992). . . Herself
- •• 7—Buns and right breast.
- ••• 61—Full frontal nudity.
- ••• 73—Full frontal nudity.
- •• 74—Buns.
- ••• 107—Breasts.
**Playboy's Career Girls** (Aug 1992) . .Object of Beauty
- ••• 54-57—Nude.

**Playboy's Book of Lingerie** (Sep 1992) . . . . . .Herself
- ••• 43—Breasts and top of lower frontal nudity.
**Playboy's Book of Lingerie** (Nov 1992) . . . . .Herself
- ••• 106—Breasts and partial lower frontal nudity.
**Playboy's Book of Lingerie** (Jan 1993) . . . . . . .Herself
- •• 78—Side view of left breast and buns.
**Playboy's Book of Lingerie** (Mar 1993). . . . . .Herself
- ••• 70-71—Left breast and buns.
**Playboy's Bathing Beauties** (Apr 1993). . . . . .Herself
- • 6—Buns.
- ••• 60—Breasts.
- ••• 74—Breasts.
**Playboy's Book of Lingerie** (May 1993) . . . . .Herself
- •• 66—Right breast and partial lower frontal nudity.
**Playboy's Girls of Summer '93** (Jun 1993) . . .Herself
- ••• 58—Full frontal nudity.
**Playboy's Book of Lingerie** (Jul 1993) . . . . . . .Herself
- • 66—Lower frontal nudity.
- ••• 75—Full frontal nudity.
**Playboy's Blondes, Brunettes & Redheads** (Sep 1993). . . . . . . . . . . . . . . . . . . . . . . . . . . .Herself
- ••• 54-55—Breasts.
**Playboy's Book of Lingerie** (Sep 1993) . . . . . .Herself
- ••• 45—Breasts.
**Playboy's Nudes** (Dec 1993) . . . . . . . . . . . . . .Herself
- ••• 28—Breasts.
**Playboy's Bathing Beauties** (Mar 1994) . . . . .Herself
- ••• 42—Breasts.
- ••• 89—Breasts.
**Playboy's Book of Lingerie** (Mar 1994). . . . . .Herself
- ••• 15—Breasts.
**Playboy's Book of Lingerie** (May 1994) . . . . .Herself
- • 20—Lower frontal nudity.
- ••• 95—Breasts.
**Playboy** (May 1994) . . . . . . . . . . . . . . . . . . . Grapevine
- ••• 165—Left breast in B&W photo.
**Playboy's Girls of Summer '94** (Jul 1994) . . . .Herself
- ••• 82—Breasts.
**Playboy's Book of Lingerie** (Sep 1994) . . . . . .Herself
- ••• 23—Full frontal nudity.

# • Hendry, Beverly

*Films:*
Rad (1986). . . . . . . . . . . . . . . . . . . . . . . . . . . . Tiger
**Hello Mary Lou: Prom Night II** (1987)
. . . . . . . . . . . . . . . . . . . . . . . . . . . . Monica Walters
- • 1:03—Brief side view of buns and breasts, while getting undressed in locker room.
- • 1:04—Nude in shower room with Vicki.
*Made for TV Movies:*
Laura Lansing Slept Here (1988). . . . . . . . . . . . . . . n.a.

# Hendry, Gloria

*Films:*
Black Caesar (1973) . . . . . . . . . . . . . . . . . . . . . .Helen
Hell Up in Harlem (1973) . . . . . . . . . . . . Helen Bradley
Live and Let Die (1973; British) . . . . . . . . . . . . . . Rosie
Black Belt Jones (1974). . . . . . . . . . . . . . . . . . Sidney
Savage Sisters (1974) . . . . . . . . . . . . . . . . Lynn Jackson

Bare Knuckles (1984) . . . . . . . . . . . . . Barbara Darrow
*Magazines:*
**Playboy** (Jul 1973). . . . . . . . . . . . . . . . . Sainted Bond
••• 147-149—Breasts and buns.
**Playboy** (Dec 1973). . . . . . . . . . . . . Sex Stars of 1973
••• 204—Full frontal nudity.

## Henner, Marilu

*Films:*
Between the Lines (1977) . . . . . . . . . . . . . . . . Danielle
    0:27—Dancing on stage wearing pasties.
Bloodbrothers (1978) . . . . . . . . . . . . . . . . . . . Annette
Hammett (1982). . . . . . . . . . . .Kit Conger/Sue Alabama
**The Man Who Loved Women** (1983)
. . . . . . . . . . . . . . . . . . . . . . . . . . . .Agnes Chapman
  •• 0:18—Brief breasts in bed with Burt Reynolds.
Cannonball Run II (1984) . . . . . . . . . . . . . . . . . .Betty
Johnny Dangerously (1984) . . . . . . . . . . . . . . . . . Lil
Perfect (1985). . . . . . . . . . . . . . . . . . . . . . . . . Sally
    0:13—Working out on exercise machine.
Rustler's Rhapsody (1985). . . . . . . . . . . . . .Miss Tracy
L.A. Story (1991). . . . . . . . . . . . . . . . . . . . . . .Trudi
Noises Off (1992) . . . . . . . . Belinda Blair & Flavia Brent
Chasers (1994) . . . . . . . . . . . . . . . . . . . . . . . .Katie
*Made for Cable Movies:*
Love with a Perfect Stranger (1986; Showtime)
. . . . . . . . . . . . . . . . . . . . . . . . . Victoria Ducane
Chains of Gold (1991; Showtime) . . . . . . . . . . . . Jackie
*Made for TV Movies:*
Dream House (1981). . . . . . . . . . . . . . . Laura Griffith
Ladykillers (1988) . . . . . . . . . . . . . . . . . . . . . . .n.a.
*TV:*
Taxi (1978-83) . . . . . . . . . . . . . . . . . .Elaine Nardo
Evening Shade (1990- ). . . . . . . . . . Ava Evans Newton
Marilu (1994- ) . . . . . . . . . . . . . . . . . . . . . . . Host
*Video Tapes:*
Marilu Henner's Dancerobics (1992) . . . . . . . . . Herself

## Henry, Laura

*Films:*
**Heavenly Bodies** (1985). . . . . . . . . . . . . . . . Debbie
  • 0:46—Brief breasts making love while her boyfriend,
    Jack, watches TV.
Separate Vacations (1985). . . . . . . . . . . . . . . .Nancy

## Hensley, Pamela

*Films:*
**There Was a Crooked Man** (1970). . . . . . . . . Edwina
  • 0:12—Very brief left breast lying on pool table with
    a guy.
Making It (1971). . . . . . . . . . . . . . . . . . . . . .Bar Girl
Doc Savage: The Man of Bronze (1975) . . . . . . . . Mona
Rollerball (1975) . . . . . . . . . . . . . . . . . . . . . .Mackie
Buck Rogers in the 25th Century (1979)
. . . . . . . . . . . . . . . . . . . . . . . . . Princess Ardala
Double Exposure (1983) . . . . . . . . . . Sergeant Fontain
*TV:*
Marcus Welby, M.D. (1975-76) . . . . . . . . . . Janet Blake
Kingston: Confidential (1977) . . . . . . . . . . . . Beth Kelly

Buck Rogers (1979-80). . . . . . . . . . . . . . .Princess Ardala
240 Robert (1981) . . . . . . . . . . . Deputy Sandy Harper
Matt Houston (1982-85) . . . . . . . . . . . . . .C. J. Parsons
*Magazines:*
**Playboy** (Sep 1980) . . . . . . . . . . . . . . . . . . Grapevine
  •• 252—Right breast in open blouse. B&W.

## Herd, Carla

*Films:*
**Deathstalker III: The Warriors From Hell** (1988)
. . . . . . . . . . . . . . . . . . . . . . . . . . . Carlisa/Elizena
  • 0:20—Side view of right breast, while making love in
    tent when guard looks in.
  •• 0:46—Breasts taking a bath.
Wild Zone (1989). . . . . . . . . . . . . . . . . .Nicole Laroche

## Herred, Brandy

*Films:*
**Some Call It Loving** (1972) . . . . . . . . . . .Cheerleader
  ••• 1:12—Nude dancing in a club doing a strip tease
    dance in a cheerleader outfit.
The Arousers (1973). . . . . . . . . . . . . . . . . . . . . . n.a.

## Herrin, Kymberly

*Films:*
Ghostbusters (1984) . . . . . . . . . . . . . . . . .Dream Ghost
Romancing the Stone (1984) . . . . . . . . . . . . . . Angelina
    0:00—In wet white blouse in Western setting as
    Kathleen Turner types her story.
Moving Violations (1985). . . . . . . . . . . . . . . . .Queen
Beverly Hills Cop II (1987) . . . . . . . . .Playboy Playmate
Roadhouse (1989) . . . . . . . . . . . . . . . . . . . Party Girl
Money to Burn (1994) . . . . . . . . . . . . . . . . . .Linda
*Music Videos:*
Legs/Z.Z. Top. . . . . . . . . . . . . . . . . . . . . . Legs Girl
*Video Tapes:*
Playmate Playoffs . . . . . . . . . . . . . . . . . . . .Playmate
**Playboy Video Magazine, Volume 2** (1983)
. . . . . . . . . . . . . . . . . . . . .Herself/Playboy Playoffs
  • 0:33—Breasts in tug-of-war game.
**Playboy Video Magazine, Volume 5** (1983)
. . . . . . . . . . . . . . . . . . . . . . . . . . . . . . Playmate
  • 0:05—Brief full frontal nudity next to car.
*Magazines:*
**Playboy** (Mar 1981) . . . . . . . . . . . . . . . . . .Playmate
**Playboy's Girls of Summer '86** (Aug 1986). . .Herself
  •• 16—Side view of left breast.
  ••• 17—Full frontal nudity.
  ••• 44—Breasts.
  •• 96-97—Buns.
**Playboy's Calendar Playmates** (Nov 1992). . .Herself
  • 10—Side of right breast and partial lower frontal nu-
    dity.
  ••• 21—Full frontal nudity.

# Herring, Laura

*Films:*

**Silent Night, Deadly Night III: Better Watch Out!**
(1989)...............................Jerri
••• 0:48—Breasts in bathtub with her boyfriend Chris.
The Forbidden Dance (1990) .................. Nisa
Dead Women In Lingerie (1991)............. Marcia

# Hershey, Barbara

a.k.a. Barbara Seagull.
*Films:*

**Last Summer** (1969).......................Sandy
• 0:19—Breasts after taking off her swimsuit top on
  sailboat with Richard Thomas. Hair is in the way.
• 1:30—Very brief right breast, after taking off her top
  in the woods.
**The Baby Maker** (1970)..................... Tish
• 0:14—Side view of left breast taking off dress and
  diving into the pool. Long shot and dark. Buns in
  water.
0:23—Left breast (out of focus) under sheet in bed.
The Liberation of L. B. Jones (1970)..... Nella Mundine
**Boxcar Bertha** (1972) ........... Bertha Thompson
•• 0:10—Breasts making love with David Carradine in
  a railroad boxcar, then brief buns walking around
  when the train starts moving.
• 0:52—Nude, side view in house with David Carradine.
0:54—Buns, putting on dress after hearing a gun
  shot.
Diamonds (1975) ......................... Sally
**The Stunt Man** (1980) .................... Nina
• 1:29—Buns and side view of left breast in bed in a
  movie within a movie while everybody is watching
  in a screening room.
Americana (1981) .......................... Girl
Take This Job and Shove It (1981)....... J. M. Halstead
**The Entity** (1983) .................... Carla Moran
• 0:33—Breasts and buns getting undressed before
  taking a bath. Don't see her face.
0:59—"Breasts" during special effect when The En-
  tity fondles her breasts with invisible fingers while
  she sleeps.
• 1:32—"Breasts" again getting raped by The Entity
  while Alex Rocco watches helplessly.
The Right Stuff (1983)............... Glennis Yeager
The Natural (1984) .................... Harriet Bird
Hannah and Her Sisters (1986) ................. Lee
Tin Men (1986).......................... Nora
Beaches (1988) .............. Hillary Whitney Essex
**The Last Temptation of Christ** (1988)
...................................... Mary Magdelene
• 0:16—Brief buns behind curtain. Brief right breast
  making love, then brief breasts.
0:17—Buns, while sleeping.
•• 0:20—Breasts, tempting Jesus.
• 2:12—Brief tip of left breast, lying on ground under
  Jesus.
• 2:13—Left breast while caressing her pregnant belly.

Shy People (1988) ........................ Ruth
A World Apart (1988; British) ........... Diana Roth
Tune in Tomorrow (1990) ............... Aunt Julia
  *a.k.a. Aunt Julia and the Scriptwriter*
Defenseless (1991)............... T. K. Katwuller
Public Eye (1992)..................... Kay Levitz
A Dangerous Woman (1993) ........... Frances
Falling Down (1993) ....................... Beth
Splitting Heirs (1993).............. Duchess Lucinda
Swing Kids (1993) ................. Frau Müller
*Made for Cable Movies:*
Paris Trout (1991; Showtime).......... Hanna Trout
*Made for Cable TV:*
Abraham (1994; TNT) .................... Sarah
*Miniseries:*
Return to Lonesome Dove (1993) ........Clara Allen
*Made for TV Movies:*
Flood! (1976)...................... Mary Cutler
My Wicked Ways... The Legend of Errol Flynn (1985)
...................................... Lili Damita
A Killing in a Small Town (1990)...... Candy Morrison
Stay the Night (1992) ........... Jimmie Sue Finger
*TV:*
The Monroes (1966-67)............. Kathy Monroe
From Here to Eternity (1980) ......... Karen Holmes
*Magazines:*
**Playboy** (Aug 1972) ............... Boxcar Bertha
•• 82-85—Nude with David Carradine.
**Playboy** (Nov 1972) ........... Sex in Cinema 1972
161—Buns.
**Playboy** (Dec 1972) ............. Sex Stars of 1972
••• 208—Breasts.

# • Hess, Sandra

*Films:*
Encino Man (1992) ................... Cave Nug
**Endangered** (1994)....................Kate
•• 0:18—Very brief breasts, while jumping up and
  splashing water in the lake. Brief breasts while standing up in lake (closer shot).
• 0:19—Buns, while getting out of the lake and getting blanket.
• 0:20—Brief breasts, while turning around and putting on blouse.
•• 0:38—Buns and back side of left breast while taking
  a bath outside. Breasts in long shot, then closer shot.

# Hetrick, Jennifer

a.k.a. Jenni Hetrick.
*Films:*
**Squeeze Play** (1979) ................ Samantha
a.k.a. Jenni Hetrick.
•• 0:00—Breasts in bed after making love.
• 0:26—Right breast, brief breasts with Wes on the
  floor.
0:37—In bra, in bedroom with Wes.
*Made for Cable Movies:*
And Then There Was One (1994; Lifetime)....... Janet

*Made for TV Movies:*
Absolute Strangers (1991). . . . . . . . . . . . . Nancy Klein
*TV:*
L.A. Law (1989-94) . . . . . . . . . . . . . Connie Hammond
UNSUB (1989) . . . . . . . . . . . . . . . . . . . Ann Madison
Bodies of Evidence (1992-93) . . . . . . . . Det. Haughton

## Hey, Virginia

*Films:*
The Road Warrior (1981). . . . . . . . . . . Warrior Woman
Norman Loves Rose (1982; Australian) . . . The Girlfriend
Castaway (1986). . . . . . . . . . . . . . . . . . . . . . . . Janice
**The Living Daylights** (1987)
. . . . . . . . . . . . Rubavitch (Colonel Pushkin's girlfriend)
  • 1:10—Brief side view of left breast when James Bond
  uses her to distract bodyguard.
**Obsession: A Taste For Fear** (1987) . . . . . . . . Diane
  • 0:02—Breasts, lying in sauna.
  • 0:04—Buns and very brief side view of right breast
  dropping towel to take a shower.
  •• 0:14—Brief right breast in bed when sheet falls
  down.
  • 0:37—Most of left breast, while crying.
  • 0:39—Breasts, lying in bed talking to Kim.
  ••• 1:03—Breasts waking up in bed.
  • 1:05—Breasts, getting ready to get dressed. Long
  shot.
  ••• 1:17—Breasts in hallway with Valerie.
  • 1:19—Brief lower frontal nudity and right breast in
  bed with Valerie, then buns in bed.
  ••• 1:20—Breasts getting dressed, walking and running
  around the house when Valerie gets killed.
  • 1:26—Breasts tied up in chair while Paul torments
  her. Lit with red light.
*Magazines:*
**Playboy** (Sep 1982) . . . . . . . . . . . . . . Warrior Women
  162-163—Nude.

## Heywood, Anne

*Films:*
Checkpoint (1957; British) . . . . . . . . . . . . . . . Gabriela
The Fox (1967) . . . . . . . . . . . . . . . . . . . . . . . . . . March
The Lady of Monza (1970; Italian). . . . Virginia de Leyva
Trader Horn (1973) . . . . . . . . . . . . . . . . . . . . . . .Nicole
**The Shaming** (1979) . . . . . . . . . . . . . Evelyn Wyckoff
  *a.k.a. Good Luck, Miss Wyckoff*
  *a.k.a. The Sin*
  ••• 0:49—Right breast, then breasts in open blouse after
  being raped by Rafe in her classroom.
  0:52—Breasts on classroom floor, making love with
  Rafe.
What Waits Below (1986) . . . . . . . . . . . . Frida Shelley

## Hickey, Marilyn Faith

*Films:*
**Incoming Freshman** (1979)
. . . . . . . . . . . . . . . . . . Sargeant Laverne Finterplay
  • 0:06—Breasts and buns when Professor Bilbo fantasizes about her.

  • 0:56—Breasts and buns during Bilbo's fantasy.
  • 1:18—Breasts during end credits.
The Night the Lights Went Out in Georgia (1981)
. . . . . . . . . . . . . . . . . . . . . . . . . . . . . Woman on Bus

## Hickland, Catherine

Wife of actor Michael Knight.
Ex-wife of actor David Hasselhoff.
*Films:*
The Last Married Couple in America (1980) . . . .Rebecca
Ghost Town (1988) . . . . . . . . . . . . . . . . . . . . . . . .Kate
Witchery (1988). . . . . . . . . . . . . . . . . . Linda Sullivan
**Millions** (1990). . . . . . . . . . . . . . . . . . . . . . . . Connie
  • 0:36—Buns, getting out of bed to open safe. Don't
  see her face, probably a body double because the
  hair is too dark.
  • 1:20—Buns, walking away from John Stockwell. Very
  brief back side of right breast, when she bends over
  to pick up blouse. Don't see her face.
**Sweet Justice** (1991) . . . . . . . . . . . . . . . .Chris Barnes
  • 0:52—Brief buns and left breast, getting into spa.
  (You don't see her face clearly, it looks like a body
  double because her hair is different.)
  •• 0:53—Brief upper half of left breast, while sitting in
  spa. This is definitely her!
*TV:*
Loving . . . . . . . . . . . . . . . . . . . . . . . . . . . . . .Hess

## Hicks, Catherine

*Films:*
Death Valley (1982) . . . . . . . . . . . . . . . . . . . . . . .Sally
Better Late Than Never (1983) . . . . . . . . . . . . . . Sable
Garbo Talks (1984). . . . . . . . . . . . . . . . . . . . . . . .Jane
**The Razor's Edge** (1984). . . . . . . . . . . . . . . . . .Isabel
  • 0:43—Brief upper half of left breast, in bed after see-
  ing a cockroach.
**Fever Pitch** (1985). . . . . . . . . . . . . . . . . . . . . . . .Flo
  • 0:11—Brief left breast, while sitting on bed in hotel
  room talking with Ryan O'Neal.
Peggy Sue Got Married (1986). . . . . . . . . . .Carol Heath
Star Trek IV: The Voyage Home (1986) . . . . Gillian Taylor
Like Father, Like Son (1987) . . . . . . . . . .Dr. Amy Larkin
Child's Play (1988) . . . . . . . . . . . . . . . . . .Karen Barclay
Souvenir (1988; British) . . . . . . . . . . . . . . . Tina Boyer
Daddy's Little Girl (1989) . . . . . . . . . . . . . . . . . . n.a.
Running Against Time (1990). . . . . . . . . . . . . . . . n.a.
Liebestraum (1991) . . . . . . . . . . . . . . . . . Mary Parker
*Made for Cable Movies:*
**Laguna Heat** (1987; HBO). . . . . . . . . . . Jane Algernon
  •• 0:50—Breasts and buns, running around the beach
  with Harry Hamlin.
  •• 1:05—Brief breasts in bed making love with Harry
  Hamlin, having her head hit the headboard.
*Made for TV Movies:*
Hi Honey—I'm Dead (1991) . . . . . . . . . . . . . . . Carol
*TV:*
The Bad News Bears (1979-80) . . . . . Dr. Emily Rappant
Tucker's Witch (1982-83) . . . . . . . . . . . Amanda Tucker
Winnetaka Road (1994) . . . . . . . . . . . . . . . . . Jeannie

## Higgins, Clare

*Films:*

1919 (1984; British) . . . . . . . . . . . . . . . Young Sophie
**Hellraiser** (1987). . . . . . . . . . . . . . . . . . . . . . . Julia
 • 0:17—Very, very brief left breast and buns making love with Frank.
 1:10—In white bra in bedroom putting necklace on.
**Hellraiser II—Hellbound** (1988). . . . . . . . . . . . Julia
 • 0:20—Very, very brief right breast, lying in bed with Frank. Scene from *Hellraiser.*
Wonderland (1989; British) . . . . . . . . . . . . . . . . . . Eve
Bad Behaviour (1992; British) . . . . . . . . Jessica Kennedy

## Higginson, Jane

*Films:*

**Danger Zone II: Reaper's Revenge** (1988) . . Donna
 •• 0:17—Breasts unconscious on sofa while the bad guys take Polaroid photos of her.
 • 0:18—Brief breasts in the photo that Wade looks at.
 • 0:22—Brief left breast adjusting her blouse outside. Long shot.
 • 0:34—Left breast in another Polaroid photograph.
 0:45—In black bra, panties and stockings posing on motorcycle for photograph.
Slaughterhouse (1988) . . . . . . . . . . . . . . . . . . . . Annie
Silent Night, Deadly Night 5: The Toy Maker (1991)
 . . . . . . . . . . . . . . . . . . . . . . . . . . . . . Sarah Quinn

## Hill, Mariana

*Films:*

Paradise, Hawaiian Style (1966). . . . . . . . . . . . . . Lani
**Medium Cool** (1969) . . . . . . . . . . . . . . . . . . . Ruth
 • 0:18—Close-up of breast in bed with John.
 •• 0:36—Nude, running around the house frolicking with John.
El Condor (1971) . . . . . . . . . . . . . . . . . . . . . .Claudine
**Thumb Tripping** (1972). . . . . . . . . . . . . . . . . . Lynn
 • 1:14—In black bra, then very, very brief left breast when Jack comes to cover her up.
 • 1:19—Breasts frolicking in the water with Gary.
 1:20—In white swimsuit, dancing in bar.
High Plains Drifter (1973) . . . . . . . . . . . . . Callie Travers
Dead People (1974) . . . . . . . . . . . . . . . . . . . . Arletty
The Godfather, Part II (1974) . . . . . . . Deanna Corleone
The Last Porno Flick (1974). . . . . . . . . . . . . . . . . .n.a.
Schizoid (1980). . . . . . . . . . . . . . . . . . . . . . . . . Julie
 0:58—Left breast, while making love in bed with Klaus Kinski. Dark, hard to see.
Blood Beach (1981) . . . . . . . . . . . . . . . . . Catherine

## Hilton, Robyn

*Films:*

Bloody Friday (1973). . . . . . . . . . . . . . . . . . . Denise
 *a.k.a. Single Girls*
**Video Vixens** (1973). . . . . . . . . . . . . . . . . . . . Inga
 •• 1:18—Breasts, opening her top in a room full of reporters.
Blazing Saddles (1974) . . . . . . . . . .Governor's Secretary
The Last Porno Flick (1974). . . . . . . . . . . . . . . . . .n.a.

Doc Savage: The Man of Bronze (1975). . . . . . . . . . n.a.
Malibu Express (1984) . . . . . . . . . . . . . . . Maid Marian

## Hippe, Laura

*Films:*

Logan's Run (1976) . . . . . . . . .New You Shop Customer
**Stay Hungry** (1976). . . . . . . . . . . . . . . . . .May Ruth
 • 1:19—Brief buns, hanging upside down in gym.
The Swinging Barmaids (1976) . . . . . . . . . . . . . . . n.a.
Mausoleum (1983). . . . . . . . . . . . . . . . . . . Aunt Cora

## Hoak, Clare

*Films:*

Masque of the Red Death (1990) . . . . . . . . . . . .Julietta
Home Alone 2: Lost in New York (1992)
 . . . . . . . . . . . . . . . . . . . . . . . . . . . Gangster 'Dame'
**The Terror Within II** (1992) . . . . . . . . . . . . . . .Ariel
 • 0:25—Brief side view of right breast, while in front of fire with Andrew Stevens.

## Hodge, Kate

*Films:*

Leatherface: The Texas Chainsaw Massacre III (1990)
 . . . . . . . . . . . . . . . . . . . . . . . . . . . . . .Michelle
Love Kills (1991). . . . . . . . . . . . . . . . . . . . . . . . . Jill
**Rapid Fire** (1992). . . . . . . . . . . . . . . . . Karla Withers
 • 1:06—Brief breasts, taking off her blouse in bed on top of Brandon Lee. Don't see her face well.
*Made for Cable TV:*
Tales From the Crypt: Dead Right (1990; HBO) . . . .Sally
 (Available on *Tales From the Crypt, Volume 3.*)

## Holcomb, Sarah

*Films:*

**Animal House** (1978) . . . . . . . . . . . Clorette DePasto
 •• 0:56—Brief breasts lying on bed after passing out in Tom Hulce's bed during toga party.
Walk Proud (1979). . . . . . . . . . . . . . . . .Sarah Lassiter
Caddyshack (1980) . . . . . . . . . . . . .Maggie O'Hooligan
Happy Birthday, Gemini (1980) . . . . . . . Judith Hastings

## Holden, Marjean

*Films:*

**Stripped to Kill II** (1988) . . . . . . . . . . Something Else
 •• 0:17—Breasts during strip dance routine.
Silent Night, Deadly Night 4: Initiation (1990). . . . .Jane
Sweet Justice (1991). . . . . . . . . . . . . . . . . . . . . . MJ
Nemesis (1992) . . . . . . . . . . . . . . . . . . . . . . . . San
Stop! Or My Mom Will Shoot (1992) . . . . . . Stewardess
The Philadelphia Experiment 2 (1993) . . . . . . . . . . Jess
Renegade: Fighting Cage (1993) . . Tigress/Sharon Miller
 (Nudity added for video release.)

## Hollander, Xaviera

Author of "The Happy Hooker."
*Films:*

**My Pleasure Is My Business** (1974). . . . . . . .Gabriele
 •• 0:14—Full frontal nudity in everybody's daydream.

•• 0:39—Breasts sitting up in bed and putting on a blouse.

•• 0:40—Breasts getting back into bed.

••• 0:59—Breasts and buns taking off clothes to go swimming in the pool, swimming, then getting out.

•• 1:09—Breasts, buns and very brief lower frontal nudity, underwater in indoor pool with Gus.

• 1:31—Buns and very brief side view of right breast, undressing at party.

*Video Tapes:*

Penthouse Love Stories (1986) . . . . . . . . . . . . . Herself

*Magazines:*

**Playboy** (Nov 1975) . . . . . . . . . . Sex in Cinema 1975

•• 138—Breasts in pool from *My Pleasure Is My Business*.

## Hollitt, Raye

*Films:*

Penitentiary III (1987) . . . . . . . . . . . . . . . Female Boxer

**Skin Deep** (1989) . . . . . . . . . . . . . . . . . . . . . . . Lonnie

(Check this out if you like muscular women.)

• 0:26—Brief side view breasts and buns getting undressed and into bed with John Ritter.

Immortalizer (1990) . . . . . . . . . . . . . . . . . . . . Queenie

The Last Hour (1990) . . . . . . . . . . . . . . . . . . . . . Adler

*a.k.a. Concrete War*

## Holloman, Bridget

*Films:*

**Slumber Party '57** (1976) . . . . . . . . . . . Bonnie May

• 0:10—Breasts with her five girl friends during swimming pool scene. Hard to tell who is who.

• 0:26—Left breast in truck with her cousin Cal.

Evils of the Night (1985) . . . . . . . . . . . . . . . . . Heather

Stoogemania (1986) . . . . . . . . . . . . . . . . . Sexy Nurse

## • Holly, Lauren

*Films:*

Band of the Hand (1986) . . . . . . . . . . . . . . . . . . Nikki

Seven Minutes in Heaven (1986). . . . . . . . . . . . . . Lisa

The Adventures of Ford Fairlane (1991). . . . . Julie "Jazz"

**Dragon: The Bruce Lee Story** (1993) . . . . . Linda Lee

• 0:39—Very, very brief tip of left breast when making love with Jason Scott Lee (when she moves her hand from the front of his shoulder to the back).

*Made for Cable Movies:*

Dangerous Heart (1994; USA) . . . . . . . . . . . . . . Carol

0:57—0:52 scene on video playback.

1:05—0:52 scene on video playback again.

*Made for TV Movies:*

Fugitive Among Us (1992) . . . . . . . . . . . Suzie Bryant

*TV:*

All My Children . . . . . . . . . . . . . . . . . . Julie Chandler

The Antagonists (1991). . . . . . . . . . . . . . . . Kate Ward

Picket Fences (1992- ) . . . . . . . . Deputy Maxine Stewart

## • Holman, Clare

*Films:*

Let Him Have It (1991; British) . . . . . . . . . . . Iris Bentley

**Afraid of the Dark** (1992; British/French). . . . . . Rose

••• 0:38—Breasts, while wearing white panties, garter belt and stockings while posing for photographer in studio on a wooden horse. Long scene.

## Holmes, Jennifer

*Films:*

**The Demon** (1981; South African) . . . . . . . . . . . Mary

•• 0:22—Breasts in dressing room.

• 1:18—Brief side of left breast, taking off robe to take a bath.

• 1:26—Breasts, crawling around in the rafters. Dark.

••• 1:29—Breasts climbing through a hole in the roof, then landing on the bed. More breasts in the bathroom.

Raw Force (1981). . . . . . . . . . . . . . . . . . . . Ann Davis

Life on the Edge (1992) . . . . . . . . . . . . . Karen Nelson

*Made for TV Movies:*

Hobson's Choice (1983). . . . . . . . . . . . . Alice Hobson

Sampson and Delilah (1984) . . . . . . . . . . . . . Varinia

*TV:*

Newhart (1982-83) . . . . . . . . . . . . Leslie Vanderkellen

Misfits of Science (1985-86). . . . . . . . . . . . Jane Miller

## Holvöe, Maria

*Films:*

Willow (1988) . . . . . . . . . . . . . . . . . . . . Cherlindrea

**The Last Warrior** (1989). . . . . . . . . . . . . . Katherine

•• 1:24—Right breast, after the Japanese warrior removes her dress.

Worth Winning (1989). . . . . . . . . . . . . . . Erin Cooper

## Hope, Amanda

*Video Tapes:*

**Wet and Wild IV** (1992) . . . . . . . . . . . . . . . . Model

**Playboy Video Calendar 1994** (1993). . . . . . August

••• 0:31—Nude, outside in garden, in gazebo and by a pond.

••• 0:33—Nude in a house with a clarinet.

**Playboy's Playmate Review 1993** (1993) . . Miss July

••• 0:19—Nude in pool and in house.

••• 0:21—Nude in military style segment.

*Magazines:*

**Playboy** (Jul 1992) . . . . . . . . . . . . . . . . . . . . Playmate

••• 90-101—Nude.

**Playboy's Playmate Review** (Jun 1993) . . . . . . . . July

••• 60-67—Nude.

**Playboy's Bathing Beauties** (Mar 1994) . . . . . Herself

• 89—Lower frontal nudity.

**Playboy's Book of Lingerie** (May 1994) . . . . . Herself

••• 37—Breasts.

## Hope, Erica

*Films:*

**Bloody Birthday** (1980) . . . . . . . . . . . . . . . . . . Annie
- 0:04—Brief breasts in cemetery, making out with Duke.

**Graduation Day** (1981) . . . . . . . . . . . . . . . . . . Diane
- 1:02—Brief breasts in open blouse running away from the killer.

*TV:*

The Young and the Restless (1978-79) . . . . . Nikki Reed

## • Hope, Leslie

*Films:*

Prep School (1981; Canadian). . . . . . . . . . . . Penelope
Love Streams (1984) . . . . . . . . . . . . . . . . . . . . . . . Joanie
It Takes Two (1988). . . . . . . . . . . . . . . Stephi Lawrence
Kansas (1988) . . . . . . . . . . . . . . . . . . . . . . . Lori Bayles
Talk Radio (1988) . . . . . . . . . . . . . . . . . . . . . . . Laura
Men at Work (1990) . . . . . . . . . . . . . . . Susan Wilkins
The Big Slice (1991) . . . . . . . . . . . . . . . Jenny Colter
Doppelganger: The Evil Within (1992) . . . . . . Elizabeth
**Sweet Killing** (1992; Canadian/French) . . . Eva Bishop
- • 0:36—Right breast and partial left breast, while making love with Alan.

Caught in the Act (1993) . . . . . . . . . . . . . . . . . Rachel

*Made for TV Movies:*

Working Trash (1990) . . . . . . . . . . . . . Susan Fahnestock

*TV:*

Berrengers (1985) . . . . . . . . . . . . . . . Cammie Springer
Knots Landing (1985-86) . . . . . . . . . . . . . . Linda Martin

## • Hopkins, Kaitlin

Daughter of actress Shirley Knight.

*Films:*

Turk 182 (1985) . . . . . . . . . . . . . . Reporter on Subway
**Spirits** (1991) . . . . . . . . . . . . . . . Succubus/Mrs. Heron
- • 0:36—Breasts, several times, in bed on top of Harry. Then in gross make-up.

## Hopkins, Kim

*Films:*

The Happy Hooker Goes Hollywood (1980)
. . . . . . . . . . . . . . . . . . . . . . . . . . . . Young Xaviera
**The Hollywood Knights** (1980) . . . . . . Pom Pom Girl
- 0:01—Breasts, sunbathing outside with her two girlfriends.

## Hopkins, Rhonda Leigh

*Films:*

Cover Girl Models (1975) . . . . . . . . . . . . . . . . Pamela
**Summer School Teachers** (1975) . . . . . . . . . Denise
- 0:45—Breasts making love with a guy. Close up of a breast.

Tidal Wave (1975; U.S./Japanese) . . . . . . . . . . . . . Fran

## Horan, Barbra

*Films:*

My Favorite Year (1982) . . . . . . . . . . . . . . . . . . . . n.a.
**The Malibu Bikini Shop** (1985) . . . . . . . . . . . Ronnie
- 0:33—In wet tank top during Alan's fantasy.
- 1:13—Most of side of left breast, while kissing Alan in the spa.

Delusion (1990) . . . . . . . . . . . . . . . . . . . . . . . . . . Carly

## Horne, Suzi

*Films:*

Hot Moves (1984) . . . . . . . . . . . . . . . . . . . . . Hooker #1
**Jungle Warriors** (1985). . . . . . . . . . . . . . . Pam Ross
- 0:51—Brief breasts twice during jail scene. Wearing a white blouse, with a yellow shirt underneath. Brief buns. Don't see her face.

## Horrocks, Jane

*Films:*

The Dressmaker (1988; British). . . . . . . . . . . . . . . Rita
Getting It Right (1989) . . . . . . . . . . . . . . . . . . . . Jenny
The Witches (1989) . . . . . . . . . . . . . . . . . . Miss Irvine
Memphis Belle (1990) . . . . . . . . . . . . . . . . . . . . . Faith
**Life is Sweet** (1991; British). . . . . . . . . . . . . . Nicola
- 0:50—Breasts in bed with her boyfriend. Hard to see because she has chocolate all over her chest.

*TV:*

Absolutely Fabulous (1994- ; British) . . . . . . . . . Bubble

## Houlihan, Carolyn

*Films:*

**The Burning** (1981). . . . . . . . . . . . . . . . . . . . . Karen
- • 0:45—Nude, going skinny dipping with Eddy in lake at night.
- • • 0:46—Brief breasts several times in the lake with Eddy, then breasts and buns getting out. Nice buns shot.
- • 0:47—Nude, walking around in the woods, looking for her clothes.

A Little Sex (1982) . . . . . . . . . . . . . Bathing Suit Model

## • House, Joey

*Films:*

**Fist of Honor** (1993) . . . . . . . . . . . . . . . . . . . . . Gina
- 0:19—Side of right breast and buns, after undressing in front of Sam Jones.

*Made for Cable TV:*

**Dream On: Attack of the 59-Inch Woman**
(1994; HBO). . . . . . . . . . . . . . . . . . . . . . . . . . . Amy
- • 0:03—Breast, while trying different sexual positions from a sex manual book with Martin.

## Howard, Barbara

*Films:*

**Friday the 13th, Part IV—The Final Chapter**
(1984) . . . . . . . . . . . . . . . . . . . . . . . . . . . . . . . . Sara
0:52—In white bra and panties putting on a robe in the bedroom getting ready for her boyfriend.
- 1:01—Buns, through shower door.

Racing with the Moon (1984) . . . . . . . . . . . Gatsby Girl
Running Mates (1985) . . . . . . . . . . . . . . . . . . . . . .n.a.
Lucky Stiff (1988) . . . . . . . . . . . . . . . . . . . . . . .Frances
White Palace (1990) . . . . . . . . . . . . . . .Sherri Klugman
Amityville: A New Generation (1993) . . . . . . Jane Cutler
*Made for TV Movies:*
Those Secrets (1992). . . . . . . . . . . . . . . . . . . . . Beth
*TV:*
Falcon Crest (1985-86) . . . . . . . . . . . . . . Robin Agretti

# Howard, Brie

*Films:*
**Android** (1982) . . . . . . . . . . . . . . . . . . . . . . . . .Maggie
- 0:25—Buns, then breasts in bedroom when Klaus Kinski watches her on video monitor.
- 0:54—Brief side of right breast, while sitting on Max's lap and kissing him.
   0:59—Partial left breast, while lying dead in bed.
   1:09—Brief side view of left breast while lying dead in bed.
The Runnin' Kind (1988) . . . . . . . . . . . . . . . . . .Thunder

# Howell, Chéri

*Films:*
**Bloody Friday** (1973) . . . . . . . . . . . . . . . . . .Shannon
*a.k.a. Single Girls*
- 1:01—Breasts and buns after "accidentally" dropping her towel in front of Bud.
Soylent Green (1973) . . . . . . . . . . . . . . . Furniture Girl
Sisters of Death (1976) . . . . . . . . . . . . . . . . . . . . .n.a.

# Howell, Margaret

*Films:*
**Tightrope** (1984) . . . . . . . . . . . . . . . . . . . . Judy Harper
- 0:44—Brief left breast viewed from above in a room with Clint Eastwood.
Girls Just Want to Have Fun (1985) . . . . . . . . Mrs. Glenn
Messenger of Death (1988). . . . . . . . . .Naomi Beecham
*Made for Cable TV:*
**Tales From the Crypt: Food For Thought** (1993; HBO). . . . . . . . . . . . . . . . . . . . . . . . . . . .Twin
- • 0:15—One breast, while joined with a special-effect breast to her twin sister, while standing in shower.

# Hubley, Season

Ex-wife of actor Kurt Russell.
*Films:*
**Hardcore** (1979). . . . . . . . . . . . . . . . . . . . . . . . Niki
- 0:27—Breasts acting in a porno movie.
- • • 1:05—Full frontal nudity talking to George C. Scott in a booth. Panties mysteriously appear later on.
Escape from New York (1981)
. . . . . . . . . . . . . . . . . . . . . . Girl in Chock Full O'Nuts
**Vice Squad** (1982) . . . . . . . . . . . . . . . . . . . . Princess
   0:34—In black bra in Ramrod's apartment.
- • 0:57—Brief left breast and buns, wearing garter belt and stockings, getting out of bed after making love with a John.

- 0:58—More buns, under sheer panties while fighting with the John.
   1:25—In black bra, panties and garter belt, while tied up by Ramrod.
Pretty Kill (1987) . . . . . . . . . . . . . . . . . . . . Heather Todd
Total Exposure (1991) . . . . . . . . . . . . . . .Andi Robinson
   0:07—Buns, getting into hot tub. Probably a body double.
Stepfather III: Father's Day (1992) . . . . . .Jennifer Ashley
*Made for Cable TV:*
The Hitchhiker: Cabin Fever (1987; HBO). . . . .Miranda
   0:12—In white bra, under cabin with Rick.
*Made for TV Movies:*
She Lives (1973). . . . . . . . . . . . . . . . . . . . Pam Rainey
The Three Wishes of Billy Grier (1984) . . . . . . . . Phyllis
Shakedown on Sunset Strip (1988)
. . . . . . . . . . . . . . . . . . . . . . . . . Officer Audre Davis
Child in the Night (1990). . . . . . . . . . . . Valerie Winfield
Vestige of Honor (1990). . . . . . . . . . . . . . . . . . Marilyn
Steel Justice (1992) . . . . . . . . . . . . . . . . . .Gina Morelli
*TV:*
All My Children . . . . . . . . . . . . . . . Angelique Marrick
Kung Fu (1974-75). . . . . . . . . . . . . . Margit McLean
Family (1976-77) . . . . . . . . . . . . . . . . . .Salina Magee

# Hughes, Ann Margaret

*Films:*
**Transformations** (1988) . . . . . . . . . . . . . . . . . . Myra
- 0:42—Right breast, then breasts under Rex Smith in bed.
- 0:43—More breasts, dead in bed.
Blue Tornado (1990) . . . . . . . . . . . . . . . . . . . . . . n.a.
Fatal Temptation (1991; Italian) . . . . . . . . . . . . . . n.a.

# Hughes, Sharon

*Films:*
**Chained Heat** (1983; U.S./German). . . . . . . . . . . .Val
- • 0:30—Brief breasts in the shower with Linda Blair.
- • 0:51—Buns, in lingerie, stripping for a guy.
- • 1:04—Breasts in the spa with the Warden.
The Man Who Loved Women (1983) . . . . . . . . . . Nurse
Hard to Hold (1984). . . . . . . . . . . . . . . . . . . . . . .Wife
The Last Horror Film (1984) . . . . . . . . . . . . . . .Stripper
American Justice (1986) . . . . . . . . . . . . . . . . . Valerie
A Fine Mess (1986) . . . . . . . . . . . . . . . . . . . .Tina
Grotesque (1987). . . . . . . . . . . . . . . . . . . . . . . . n.a.

# Hughes, Wendy

*Films:*
**Jock Petersen** (1974; Australian) . . . . . . . Patricia Kent
*a.k.a. Petersen*
- • • 0:12—Breasts in her office with Tony.
- 0:13—Breasts making love with Tony on the floor.
- • 0:44—Nude running around the beach with Tony.
- • 0:50—Nude in bed making love with Tony.
- 1:24—Full frontal nudity when Tony rapes her in her office.
Newsfront (1978; Australian) . . . . . . . . .Amy McKenzie
My Brilliant Career (1979; Australian) . . . . . . Aunt Helen

**Lonely Hearts** (1983; Australian) . . . . . . . . . . Patricia
- 1:05—Brief breasts getting out of bed and putting a dress on. Dark, hard to see.

Careful, He Might Hear You (1984; Australian) . . Vanessa

**An Indecent Obsession** (1985) . . . . . Honour Langtry
0:32—Possibly Wendy breasts, could be Sue because Luce is fantasizing about Wendy while making love with Sue. Dark, long shot, hard to see.
- •• 1:10—Left breast, making love in bed with Wilson.

**My First Wife** (1985; Australian). . . . . . . . . . . . Helen
1:00—Brief breasts and lower frontal nudity under water during husband's dream. Don't see her face.
- •• 1:08—In bra, then breasts on the floor with her husband.
- •• 1:10—Breasts in bed lying down, then fighting with her husband. A little dark.

Happy New Year (1987) . . . . . . . . . . Carolyn Benedict
Warm Nights on a Slow Moving Train (1987) . . The Girl
1:23—Very, very brief silhouette of right breast getting back into bed after killing a man.

Echoes in Paradise (1989) . . . . . . . . . . . . . . . Maria
Wild Orchid II: Two Shades of Blue (1992) . . . . . . . . Elle
Princess Caraboo (1994) . . . . . . . . . . . . . . . . . . . n.a.

*Made for Cable Movies:*
**The Heist** (1989; HBO) . . . . . . . . . . . . . . . . . . Susan
- 0:52—Very brief side view of right breast making love in bed with Pierce Brosnan.

*Made for TV Movies:*
Donor (1990) . . . . . . . . . . . . . . . . . . . . . . . Dr. Farrell
A Woman Named Jackie (1991) . . . . . Janet Lee Bouvier

## Hull, Dianne

*Films:*
The Arrangement (1969) . . . . . . . . . . . . . . . . . . . Ellen
The Magic Garden of Stanley Sweetheart (1970)
. . . . . . . . . . . . . . . . . . . . . . . . . . . . . . . . . . . . . Cathy
Hot Summer Week (1973; Canadian) . . . . . . . . . . . . n.a.
Man on a Swing (1974) . . . . . . . . . . . Maggie Dawson
Aloha, Bobby and Rose (1975) . . . . . . . . . . . . . . . Rose
**The Fifth Floor** (1978) . . . . . . . . . . . . Kelly McIntyre
- •• 0:29—Breasts and buns in shower while Carl watches, then brief full frontal nudity running out of the shower.
- •• 1:09—Breasts in whirlpool bath getting visited by Carl again, then raped.

You Better Watch Out (1980) . . . . . . . . Jackie Stadling
The New Adventures of Pippi Longstocking (1988)
. . . . . . . . . . . . . . . . . . . . . . . . . . . Mrs. Settigren

## Hunt, Helen

*Films:*
Rollercoaster (1977) . . . . . . . . . . . . . . . . . Tracy Calder
Girls Just Want to Have Fun (1985) . . . . . . . Lynne Stone
Trancers (1985). . . . . . . . . . . . . . . . . . . . . . . . . Lena
Peggy Sue Got Married (1986) . . . . . . . . . . . Beth Bodell
Project X (1987) . . . . . . . . . . . . . . Teresa McDonald
Miles From Home (1988) . . . . . . . . . . . . . . . . Jennifer
Next of Kin (1989) . . . . . . . . . . . . . . . . . . . . . Jessie
Into the Badlands (1991). . . . . . . . . . . . . . . . Blossom

Trancers II (1991) . . . . . . . . . . . . . . . . . . . . Lena Deth
**The Waterdance** (1991) . . . . . . . . . . . . . . . . . . Anna
- ••• 0:51—Breasts in bed, making love with Eric Stoltz.
- •• 0:52—Brief buns and brief right breast, coming back to the bed to clean up.

Bob Roberts (1992; U.S./British) . . Reporter Rose Pondell
Mr. Saturday Night (1992). . . . . . . . . . . . . . . . . Annie
Only You (1992) . . . . . . . . . . . . . . . . . . Clare Enfield
Trancers III (1993) . . . . . . . . . . . . . . . . . . . . . . Lena

*Made for Cable Movies:*
Sexual Healing (1993; Showtime) . . . . . . . . . . . . Rene

*Made for TV Movies:*
Bill: On His Own (1983). . . . . . . . . . . . . . . . . . . Jenny
Quarterback Princess (1983) . . . . . . . . . . . Tami Maida
In the Company of Darkness (1993). . . . . . Gina Pulasky

*TV:*
Amy Prentiss (1974-75) . . . . . . . . . . . . . . . Jill Prentiss
Swiss Family Robinson (1975-76) . . . . . . . Helga Wagner
The Fitzpatricks (1977-78) . . . . . . . . . . . . Kerry Gerardi
It Takes Two (1982-83). . . . . . . . . . . . . . . Lisa Quinn
Mad About You (1992- ) . . . . . . . . . . . . . . . . . Jamie

## Hunt, Marsha A.

*Films:*
The Sender (1982) . . . . . . . . . . . . . . . . . . . . Nurse Jo
**Howling II: Your Sister is a Werewolf** (1984)
. . . . . . . . . . . . . . . . . . . . . . . . . . . . . . . . Mariana
- •• 0:33—Breasts in bedroom with Sybil Danning and a guy.

## Hunter, Heather

Adult film actress.
*Films:*
**Frankenhooker** (1990) . . . . . . . . . . . . . . . . Chartreuse
- 0:36—Brief breasts during introduction to Jeffrey.
- 0:37—Brief breasts bending over behind Sugar.
- ••• 0:41—Brief breasts and buns, running in front of bed. A little blurry. Then breasts and buns dancing with the other girls.
- 0:43—Breasts dodging flying leg with Sugar.
- 0:44—Breasts, crawling on the floor.

*TV:*
Soul Train . . . . . . . . . . . . . . . . . . . . . . . . . . Dancer

## • Hunter, Holly

*Films:*
The Burning (1981) . . . . . . . . . . . . . . . . . . . . . Sophie
Swing Shift (1984). . . . . . . . . . . . . . . . Jeannie Sherman
Broadcast News (1987) . . . . . . . . . . . . . . . Jane Craig
End of the Line (1987) . . . . . . . . . . . . Charlotte Haney
Raising Arizona (1987) . . . . . . . . . . . . . . . . Edwina
Always (1989) . . . . . . . . . . . . . . . . . Dorinda Durston
Miss Firecracker (1989) . . . . . . . . . . . Carnelle Scott
Animal Behavior (1990) . . . . . . . . . . . . . Coral Grable
Once Around (1990) . . . . . . . . . . . . . . Renata Bella
The Firm (1993). . . . . . . . . . . . . . . . Tammy Hemphill

**The Piano** (1993) . . . . . . . . . . . . . . . . . . . . . . . . .Ada
(Academy Award for Best Actress.)
••• 1:02—Nude, while sitting on bed.
••• 1:18—Buns then breasts while lying next to Harvey
Keitel in bed.
• 1:19—Very brief left nipple when kissing. Close-up
shot.
*Made for Cable Movies:*
Crazy in Love (1992; TNT) . . . . .Georgie Swift Symonds
*Magazines:*
**Playboy** (Jul 1994). . . . . . . . . . . . . . . . . . . . .Grapevine
• 167—Right breast under sheer black dress in B&W
photo.

# Hunter, Kaki

*Films:*
Roadie (1980) . . . . . . . . . . . . . . . . . . . . Lola Bouiliabase
Willie and Phil (1980) . . . . . . . . . . . . . Patti Sutherland
**Porky's** (1981; Canadian) . . . . . . . . . . . . . . . . . Wendy
• 1:02—Brief full frontal nudity, then brief breasts in
the shower scene.
Whose Life Is It, Anyway? (1981). . . . . . . . . . . .Mary Jo
Porky's II: The Next Day (1983; Canadian) . . . . . Wendy
Just the Way You Are (1984) . . . . . . . . . . . . . . . . .Lisa
Porky's Revenge (1985; Canadian) . . . . . . . . . . . Wendy
1:22—In white bra and panties taking off her clothes
to jump off a bridge.

# Hunter, Neith

*Films:*
Born in East L.A. (1987). . . . . . . . . . . . . . . . . . Marcie
Less than Zero (1987). . . . . . . . . . . . . . . . . . . . . Alana
Near Dark (1987) . . . . . . . . . . . . . . . . . . . .Lady in Car
Fright Night, Part 2 (1988) . . . . . . . . . . Young Admirer
**Silent Night, Deadly Night 4: Initiation** (1990)
. . . . . . . . . . . . . . . . . . . . . . . . . . . . . . . . . . . . . . . Kim
• 0:03—Brief breasts several times in bed with Hank.
• 0:47—Brief breasts during occult ceremony when a
worm comes out of her mouth.
• 1:05—Right breast, while lying on floor. Long shot.
1:06—Breasts, covered with gunk, transforming into
a worm.
• 1:07—Very brief side of right breast, while sitting up.
Silent Night, Deadly Night 5: The Toy Maker (1991)
. . . . . . . . . . . . . . . . . . . . . . . . . . . . . . . . . . . . . . Kim
*Made for Cable TV:*
**Red Shoe Diaries: How I Met My Husband**
(1993; Showtime). . . . . . . . . . . . . . . . . . . . .Alice/Eve
0:27—On stage in club in sexy outfit with Giuseppe.
0:28—Buns, visible under outfit.
••• 0:29—Breasts and buns, making love with Giuseppe
on the stage.
•• 0:30—Brief breasts again.
*Made for TV Movies:*
Jonathan Stone: Threat of Innocence (1994)
. . . . . . . . . . . . . . . . . . . . . . . . . . . . . . . .Nora Walsh

*Video Tapes:*
**Inside Out** (1992) . . . . . . . . . . . . Angela/The Diaries
1:01—In black bra and panties, modeling lingerie
for Richard and Elliott.
• 1:03—Buns, in swimsuit, while standing up.
•• 1:04—Right breast, then brief breasts in spa with Richard.
••• 1:06—Breasts in bed, getting fondled by David.
•• 1:08—Breasts in the shower.
•• 1:10—Right breast, while in bed with Richard.

# Hunter, Rachel

Wife of singer Rod Stewart.
*Sports Illustrated* swimsuit model.
Spokesmodel for Pantene shampoo.
*Made for Cable TV:*
Body by VH-1. . . . . . . . . . . . . . . . . . . . . . . . . Hostess
*Video Tapes:*
**Sports Illustrated's 25th Anniversary Swimsuit**
**Video** (1989). . . . . . . . . . . . . . . . . . . . . . . . . .Herself
(The version shown on HBO left out two music video
segments at the end. If you like buns, definitely watch
the video tape!)
• 0:03—Right breast in see-through black swimsuit
with white stars on it.
Sports Illustrated Super Shape-Up Program: Body
Sculpting (1990) . . . . . . . . . . . . . . . . . . . . . . .Herself
Sports Illustrated: The 1993 Swimsuit Video (1993)
. . . . . . . . . . . . . . . . . . . . . . . . . . . . . . . . . . . . Model
*Magazines:*
Playboy (Oct 1993) . . . . . . . . . . . . . . . . . . . Grapevine

# Huntly, Leslie

*Films:*
The Naked Cage (1985). . . . . . . . . . . . . . . . . .Peaches
**Back to School** (1986). . . . . . . . . . . . . . . . . Coed #1
•• 0:14—Brief breasts in the shower room when Rod-
ney Dangerfield first arrives on campus.
**Demon of Paradise** (1987). . . . . . . . . . . . . . .Gobby
•• 0:51—Breasts taking off her top on a boat, then
swimming in the ocean.
**Stewardess School** (1987) . . . . . . . . Alison Hanover
•• 0:46—Breasts, doing a strip tease on a table at a party at her house.
**Satan's Princess** (1989). . . . . . . . . . . . Karen Rhodes
••• 0:27—Breasts sitting on bed and in bed with Nicole.

# Huppert, Isabelle

*Films:*
**Going Places** (1974; French) . . . . . . . . . . . Jacqueline
• 1:53—Brief upper half of left breast making love
with Jean-Claude.
**The Lacemaker** (1977; French) . . . . . . . . . . . Beatrice
• 0:50—Briefly nude while getting into bed.
• 0:57—Breasts under shawl, then nude while getting
into bed.
•• 0:58—Breasts, lying in bed.
• 1:04—Nude, in her apartment.
••• 1:22—Nude, in her apartment with François.

**Heaven's Gate** (1980). . . . . . . . . . . . . . . . . . . . . . . Ella
•• 1:10—Nude running around the house and in bed with Kris Kristofferson.
••• 1:18—Nude, taking a bath in the river and getting out.
• 2:24—Very brief left breast getting raped by three guys.

**Loulou** (1980; French). . . . . . . . . . . . . . . . . . . . . Nelly
• 0:06—Very, very brief breasts leaning over in bed.
• 0:18—Brief breasts getting out of bed.
• 0:27—Brief breasts turning over in bed.
•• 0:36—Breasts lying in bed talking on phone. Mostly right breast.
• 0:40—Lower frontal nudity and buns taking off panties and getting into bed.
•• 0:59—Left breast in bed with André, then breasts taking him to the bathroom.

**Clean Slate** (1981; French) . . . . . . . . . . . . . . . Rosalie
*a.k.a. Coup de Torchon.*
•• 0:50—Breasts and buns, after taking off her slip in bedroom in front of Lucien.
••• 1:13—Breasts, after sitting up in bed, then full frontal nudity, after getting out of bed.

**La Truit (The Trout)** (1982; French) . . . . . Frederique

**Entre Nous** (1983; French) . . . . . . . . . . . Helen Webber
*a.k.a. Coup de Foudre.*
• 1:01—Brief breasts in shower room talking about her breasts with Miou-Miou.

**My Best Friend's Girl** (1984; French). . Vivian Arthund
*a.k.a. La Femme du Mon Ami.*
• 0:40—Brief left breast peeking out of bathrobe walking around in living room.
1:00—Buns, making love with Thierry Lhermitte while his friend watches.

**Sincerely Charlotte** (1986; French) . . . . . . . Charlotte
0:20—Brief breasts while in bathtub. Long shot, out of focus.
1:07—Very brief left breast changing into red dress in the back seat of the car.
•• 1:15—Breasts in bed with Mathieu. Kind of dark.

**The Bedroom Window** (1987) . . . . Sylvia Wentworth
•• 0:06—Briefly nude while looking out the window at attempted rape.

Story of Women (1988; French) . . . . . . . . Marie Latour
Madame Bovary (1991; French) . . . . . . . Emma Bovary
Après l'amour (1992; French) . . . . . . . . . . . . . . . Lola
*Magazines:*
**Playboy** (Dec 1980). . . . . . . . . . . . . . . . Grapevine
••• 388—Left breast. B&W.

## • *Hurley, Diane*

*a.k.a. Adult film actress Dyanna Lauren.*
*Films:*
**Killer Looks** (1994). . . . . . . . . . . . . . . . . . . Cynthia
(Unrated version reviewed.)
•• 0:57—Nude, while trying to make out with Sara Suzanne Brown.
••• 0:59—Full frontal nudity while making love with Vince on sofa.

*CD-ROM:*
**Venus' Playhouse** (1994) . . . . . . . . . . . . . . . Herself

## *Hurley, Elizabeth*

*Films:*
**Aria** (1987; U.S./British) . . . . . . . . . . . . . . . Marietta
• 0:46—Brief breasts, turning around while singing to a guy.
• 0:47—Buns while standing and hugging him.
Rowing with the Wind (1988) . . . . . . . Clair Clairmont
**Kill Cruise** (1990; German) . . . . . . . . . . . . . . . . Lou
• 0:15—Very brief breasts during strip tease routine on stage.
• 1:09—Side of right breast, while making love with Jürgen Prochnow.
• 1:15—Very brief right breast in open blouse, several times when Prochnow throws Patsy Kensit overboard.
1:25—Most of side of right breast, while consoling Kensit.
Passenger 57 (1992) . . . . . . . . . . . . . . Sabrina Ritchie

## *Hushaw, Katherine*

*Video Tapes:*
**Playboy Video Calendar 1988** (1987). . . . . Playmate
**Wet and Wild** (1989) . . . . . . . . . . . . . . . . . . Model
*Magazines:*
**Playboy** (Oct 1986) . . . . . . . . . . . . . . . . . Playmate
**Playboy's Calendar Playmates** (Nov 1992). . . Herself
•• 62—Right breast and lower frontal nudity.
**Playboy Presents Playmates in Paradise**
(Mar 1994). . . . . . . . . . . . . . . . . . . . . . . . Playmate
••• 34-37—Nude.

## *Hussey, Olivia*

*Films:*
Battle of the Villa Fiorita (1965; British). . . . . . . . Donna
**Romeo and Juliet** (1968; British/Italian) . . . . . . . Juliet
• 1:37—Very brief breasts rolling over and getting out of bed with Romeo.
The Man with Bogart's Face (1980) . . . . . . . . Elsa Borsht
Virus (1980; Japanese) . . . . . . . . . . . . . . . . . . . . Marit
Escape 2000 (1981). . . . . . . . . . . . . . . . . . . . . . Chris
Undeclared War (1990) . . . . . . . . . . . . . . . . . . . . n.a.
Save Me (1993) . . . . . . . . . . . . . . . . . . . . . . . . . Gail
(Unrated version reviewed.)
*Made for Cable Movies:*
**Psycho IV: The Beginning** (1990; Showtime)
. . . . . . . . . . . . . . . . . . . . . . . . . . . . . . Norma Bates
•• 0:49—Breasts in motel room mirror while young Norman, watches through peephole.
*Miniseries:*
The Bastard (1978) . . . . . . . . . . . . . . . . . . . . . . . n.a.
*Made for TV Movies:*
Jesus of Nazareth (1977) . . . . . . . . . . . . . . Virgin Mary
Ivanhoe (1982) . . . . . . . . . . . . . . . . . . . . . . Rebecca
Stephen King's "It" (1990). . . . . . . . . . . . . . . . Audra

# Huston, Anjelica

Daughter of actor/director John Huston.
*Films:*
Hamlet (1969; British). . . . . . . . . . . . . . . . . Court Lady
A Walk with Love and Death (1969) . . . . . Lady Claudia
The Last Tycoon (1976). . . . . . . . . . . . . . . . . . . Edna
Swashbuckler (1976). . . . . . . . . . Woman of Dark Visage
**The Postman Always Rings Twice** (1981). . . Madge
  • 1:30—Brief side view left breast sitting in trailer with
    Jack Nicholson.
Frances (1982) . . . . . Hospital Sequence: Mental Patient
Ice Pirates (1984) . . . . . . . . . . . . . . . . . . . . . . .Maida
This is Spinal Tap (1984) . . . . . . . . . . . . . Polly Deutsch
Prizzi's Honor (1985). . . . . . . . . . . . . . .Maerose Prizzi
  (Academy Award for Best Supporting Actress.)
The Dead (1987). . . . . . . . . . . . . . . . . . Gretta Conroy
Gardens of Stone (1987). . . . . . . . . . . Samantha Davis
Enemies, A Love Story (1989) . . . . . . . . . . . . Tamara
The Witches (1989). . . . . . . Grand High Witch/Eva Ernst
The Grifters (1990) . . . . . . . . . . . . . . . . . .Lilly Dillon
The Addams Family (1991) . . . . . . . . Morticia Addams
The Player (1992) . . . . . . . . . . . . . . . . . . . . . Cameo
Addams Family Values (1993) . . . . . . . Morticia Addams
Manhattan Murder Mystery (1993). . . . . . . . Marcia Fox
*Made for Cable Movies:*
And the Band Played On (1992; HBO) . . Dr. Betsy Reisz
*Miniseries:*
Lonesome Dove (1989). . . . . . . . . . . . . . . . Clara Allen
Family Pictures (1993). . . . . . . . . . . . . . Lainey Eberlin

# Hutchinson, Tracey E.

*Films:*
**The Wild Life** (1984) . . . . . . . . . . . . . . .Poker Girl #2
  • 1:23—Brief breasts in a room full of guys and girls
    playing strip poker when Lea Thompson looks in.
Into the Night (1985) . . . . . . . . . . . . . . . Federal Agent
**Masterblaster** (1986). . . . . . . . . . . . . . . . . . . . .Lisa
  ••• 0:57—Breasts taking a shower (wearing panties).
**Amazon Women on the Moon** (1987) . . . . . . Floozie
  1:18—Brief right breast, while hitting balloon while
    Carrie Fisher talks to a guy. This sketch is in B&W and
    appears after the first batch of credits.
**Stone Cold** (1991) . . . . . . . . . . . . . Pool Playing Chick
  • 0:25—Brief breasts, playing pool with the guys.

# Hutton, Lauren

Former model.
*Films:*
Little Fauss and Big Halsy (1970). . . . . . . . Rita Nebraska
The Gambler (1974) . . . . . . . . . . . . . . . . . . . . . Billie
Gator (1976). . . . . . . . . . . . . . . . . . . Aggie Maybank
Viva Knievel (1977) . . . . . . . . . . . . . . . . Kate Morgan
**Welcome to L.A.** (1977). . . . . . . . . . . . . .Nora Bruce
  • 0:56—Very brief, obscured glimpse of left breast un-
    der red light in photo darkroom.
A Wedding (1978) . . . . . . . . . . . . . . Florence Farmer
**American Gigolo** (1980) . . . . . . . . . . . . . . Michelle
  • 0:37—Left breast, making love with Richard Gere in
    bed in his apartment.

Paternity (1981). . . . . . . . . . . . . . . . . . . . Jenny Lufton
Zorro, The Gay Blade (1981) . . . . . . . . . . . . .Charlotte
**Lassiter** (1984). . . . . . . . . . . . . . . . . Kari Von Fursten
  • 0:18—Brief breasts over-the-shoulder shot making
    love with a guy on the bed just before killing him.
Once Bitten (1985) . . . . . . . . . . . . . . . . . . . Countess
Malone (1987). . . . . . . . . . . . . . . . . . . . . . . . .Jamie
Trade Secrets (1989; French) . . . . . . . . . . . . .Marléne
Millions (1990). . . . . . . . . . . . . . . . . . . . . Christina
Guilty as Charged (1992). . . . . . . . . . . . . . Liz Stanford
My Father The Hero (1993) . . . . . . . . . . . . . . .Megan
*Made for Cable Movies:*
Fear (1991; Showtime). . . . . . . . . . . . . .Jessica Moreau
*Made for TV Movies:*
Scandal Sheet (1985). . . . . . . . . . . . . . . . Meg North
*TV:*
The Rhinemann Exchange (1977) . . . Leslie Hawkewood
Paper Dolls (1984). . . . . . . . . . . . . . . . . Colette Ferrier
*Magazines:*
**Penthouse** (Sep 1986)
  . . . . . . . . . . . . . . .The Secret Nudes of Lauren Hutton
  ••• 158-169—1962 B&W photos.

# Hyde, Kimberly

*Films:*
**The Last Picture Show** (1971) . . . Annie-Annie Martin
  •• 0:36—Full frontal nudity, getting out of pool to
    meet Randy Quaid and Cybill Shepherd.
  • 0:37—Breasts several times, sitting at edge of pool
    with Bobby.
  • 0:38—More breasts, sitting on edge of pool in back-
    ground.
Video Vixens (1973). . . . . . . . . . . . . . . . . . Claudine
Young Nurses (1973) . . . . . . . . . . . . . . . . Peppermint
Candy Stripe Nurses (1974) . . . . . . . . . . . . . . April
Foxy Brown (1974) . . . . . . . . . . . . . . . . . . . Jennifer

# Hyser, Joyce

Ex-girlfriend of singer Bruce Springsteen.
*Films:*
The Hollywood Knights (1980). . . . . . Brenda Weintraub
They All Laughed (1981) . . . . . . . . . . . . . . . . .Sylvia
Staying Alive (1983). . . . . . . . . . . . . . . . . . . . Linda
Valley Girl (1983) . . . . . . . . . . . . . . . . . . . . . .Joyce
This is Spinal Tap (1984) . . . . . . . . . . . . . . . Belinda
**Just One of the Guys** (1986). . . . . . . . . Terry Griffith
  0:10—In two piece swimsuit by the pool with her
    boyfriend.
  •• 1:27—Brief breasts opening her blouse to prove that
    she is really a girl.
Wedding Band (1989) . . . . . . . . . . . . Karla Thompson
Greedy (1993) . . . . . . . . . . . . . . . . . . . . . . . Muriel
*TV:*
L.A. Law (1988-89) . . . . . . . . . . . . . . . . .Alison Gottlieb

## Illiers, Isabelle

*Films:*

**The Story of "O" Continues** (1981; French)...... O
*a.k.a. Les Fruits de la Passion*
- ••• 0:06—Breasts in chair, getting made up.
- •• 0:08—Breasts and buns, walking up stairs.
- • 0:10—Breasts sitting in bed.
- •• 0:11—Breasts sitting in bed putting up Klaus Kinski's picture on the wall.
- •• 0:12—Breasts and buns getting out of bed and walking around the room.
- • 0:13—Tip of right breast, while looking out the window.
- •• 0:18—Breasts looking out the window.
- • 0:24—Brief left breast, under her dress.
- • 0:26—Tips of breasts, sticking out of dress top.
- •• 0:27—Breasts and buns in chair, more in room with a customer.
- • 0:35—Breasts, sitting while looking at Kinski.
- •• 0:36—Brief left breast, then full frontal nudity lying on bed during fantasy.
  0:40—Full frontal nudity, getting chained up by Kinski.
- •• 0:58—Full frontal nudity running in slow-motion during boy's fantasy.
- •• 1:02—Breasts in room with the boy.
- •• 1:04—Breasts making love with the boy.
Miranda (1985; Italian).......................n.a.
Luci lontane (1988; Italian)...................n.a.

## Iman

Supermodel.
Wife of singer/actor David Bowie.
*Films:*
The Human Factor (1979)................... Sarah
Exposed (1983)............................Model
Out of Africa (1985)................... Mariammo
No Way Out (1987)...................Nina Beka
Surrender (1988)........................ Hedy
House Party 2 (1991)............. Sheila Landreaux
L.A. Story (1991).........................Cynthia
The Linguini Incident (1991).............Dali Guest
Star Trek VI: The Undiscovered Country (1991)...Martia
*Made for Cable Movies:*
Lies of the Twins (1991; USA).............. Elle
Heart of Darkness (1994; TNT)................n.a.
*Made for Cable TV:*
Dream On: oral sex, lies and videotape (1993; HBO)
................................ TV Reporter
*Music Videos:*
Remember the Time/Michael Jackson (1992) ... Queen
*Magazines:*
**Playboy** (Jan 1986)...........Beauty and the Beasts
- ••• 146-155—Breasts.

## Imershein, Deirdre

*Films:*
**Black Belt** (1992)...................... Shanna
- ••• 1:08—Breasts in bed, making love with Don "The Dragon" Wilson.
Scanner Cop (1993)..................Officer Parker
*Made for Cable TV:*
**Dream On: Martin Gets Lucky** (1990; HBO).. Sheila
- ••• 0:06—Breasts in bed making love with Martin. Nice sweaty shot.
*TV:*
Dallas (1991) ............................. Jory
*Video Tapes:*
**Eden 4** (1993)......................... Melissa
- •• 0:04—Breasts and buns, while making love with a guy in front of window in hotel room.
- • 0:07—Breasts again on video playback.
- ••• 0:14—Breasts while making love in bed with a man and a woman.
- •• 0:25—Breasts in bed with B.D.
- • 0:55—Tip of right breast in open dress while in bed with Rod. More left breast seen on TV.
- •• 1:06—Breasts in bed when B.D. helps take her top off.
  1:10—More breasts in video playback.
- • 1:25—Brief left breast twice, while in bed with B.D.

## • Imrie, Kirsten

*Video Tapes:*
**Page 3 Girls** (1993).....................Herself
*Magazines:*
**Playboy's Book of Lingerie** (Sep 1991)......Herself
- •• 30—Partial lower frontal nudity and left breast.
Playboy's Book of Lingerie (Nov 1991)........Herself
  53—Sort of lower frontal nudity and sort of right breast in sheer black body suit.
**Playboy's Book of Lingerie** (May 1994).....Herself
- •• 56-57—Left breast and most of right breast.
**Playboy Presents Girl of the World** (May 1994)
.......................................Herself
- •• 56-57—Breasts under wet top.

## Inch, Jennifer

*Films:*
**Frank and I** (1983)............... Frank/Frances
  0:10—Brief buns, getting pants pulled down for a spanking.
- ••• 0:22—Nude getting undressed and walking to the bed.
- • 0:24—Brief nude when Charles pulls the sheets off her.
  0:32—Brief buns, getting spanked by two older women.
- ••• 0:38—Full frontal nudity getting out of bed and walking to Charles at the piano.
- • 0:45—Full frontal nudity lying on her side by the fireplace. Dark, hard to see.
- •• 1:09—Brief breasts making love with Charles on the floor.

••• 1:11—Nude taking off her clothes and walking toward Charles at the piano.

Higher Education (1987; Canadian) . . . . . Gladys/Glitter

**State Park** (1988; Canadian). . . . . . . . . . . . . . . Linnie
  • 0:34—Brief right breast, undoing swimsuit top while sunbathing.
  • 0:39—Brief breasts, taking off swimsuit top while cutting Raymond's hair.

Physical Evidence (1989). . . . . . . . . . . . . . . . . Waitress

*Made for Cable Movies:*

**Soft Touch** (1987; Playboy). . . . . . . . . Tracy Anderson
(Shown on *The Playboy Channel* as *Birds in Paradise*.)
  • 0:01—Full frontal nudity during the opening credits.
  • 0:02—Breasts with her two girlfriends during the opening credits.
  ••• 0:17—Breasts exercising on the floor, walking around the room, the lying on bed. Long scene.
  • 0:20—Full frontal nudity getting out of bed.
  •• 0:23—Breasts in bed.
  ••• 0:50—Breasts sunbathing on boat with Carrie.
  •• 1:01—Full frontal nudity, sitting on towel, watching Carrie.
  • 1:02—Full frontal nudity, waving to a dolphin.
  •• 1:04—Breasts at night by campfire with Carrie.
  ••• 1:05—Brief left breast, then breasts putting on skirt and walking around the island.
  •• 1:13—Breasts in hut with island guy.
  •• 1:19—Breasts in stills during the end credits.

**Soft Touch II** (1987; Playboy). . . . . . . . Tracy Anderson
(Shown on *The Playboy Channel* as *Birds in Paradise*.)
  • 0:01—Breasts during opening credits.
  • 0:02—Breasts with her two girlfriends during opening credits.
  •• 0:14—Breasts dancing in Harry's bar by herself.
  • 0:27—Full frontal nudity on stage at Harry's after robbers tell her to strip.
  • 0:29—Side of left breast tied to Neill on bed.
  • 0:31—Breasts tied up when Ashley and Carrie discover her.
  • 0:52—Full frontal nudity during strip poker game, then covered with whipped cream.
  • 0:57—Full frontal nudity getting out of bed.

*Made for TV Movies:*

Anne of Green Gables (1985; Canadian) . . . . . Ruby Gillis

## Ingalls, Joyce

*Films:*

The Man Who Would Not Die (1975) . . . . . . Pat Reagan

Paradise Alley (1978). . . . . . . . . . . . . . . . . . . Bunchie

**Deadly Force** (1983) . . . . . . . . . . . . . . . Eddie Cooper
  •• 0:48—Breasts, making out with Wings Hauser on hammock.

## • Ingerman, Randi

*Films:*

Desperate Crimes (1991; Italian) . . . . . . . . . . . . . . Nina

**Deadly Rivals** (1992) . . . . . . . . . . . Rachel Richmond
  ••• 0:18—Breasts, while in bed in open robe with Rudy.
  • 0:20—Right breast in open robe before killing Rudy.

• 0:46—Brief buns in panties, while trying to kill strong bad guy.

## Ingersoll, Amy

*Films:*

**Knightriders** (1981) . . . . . . . . . . . . . . . . . . . . . Linet
  • 0:00—Very brief left breast, while lying down, then sitting up in woods next to Ed Harris.

Splash (1984). . . . . . . . . . . . . . . . . . . . . . . Reporter

## Innes, Alexandra

*Films:*

**Perfect Timing** (1984) . . . . . . . . . . . . . . . . . . Salina
  •• 1:06—Right breast and buns, posing for Harry.

Joshua Then and Now (1985; Canadian) . . . . . . . Joanna

Canvas (1992; Canadian/British) . . . . . . . Anna Maxwell

## • Inouye, Lisa

*Films:*

**Final Judgement** (1992) . . . . . . . . . . . . . . . . . . . Lily
  •• 0:32—Breasts, walking up behind Rob in room, then making love. Brief buns in G-string, getting out of bed. Side view of breasts in mirror.
  • 1:01—Buns in lingerie in mirror.

Death Wish V: The Face of Death (1993) . . Janine Omori

## Irwin, Jennifer

*Films:*

The Gate (1988; Canadian) . . . . . Linda Lee, Lori's Sister

Bikini Summer (1991) . . . . . . . . . . . . . . . . . . . Mindy

**The Bikini Carwash Company** (1992)
  . . . . . . . . . . . . . . . . . . . . . . . Awesome Beach Girl
  (Unrated version reviewed.)
  •• 0:00—Buns, on beach in a very small swimsuit.
  ••• 0:02—Brief right breast, turning over, then breasts while yelling at Jack.

*Made for TV Movies:*

Anne of Green Gables (1985; Canadian) . . . . . . Student

*Video Tapes:*

Big Bust Casting Call (1992). . . . . . . . . . . . . . . . . n.a.

## Isaacs, Susan

*Films:*

**Deadly Passion** (1985) . . . . . . . . . . . . . . . . . Trixie
  •• 0:02—Breasts sitting up in bed talking to Brent Huff.

She's Out of Control (1989) . . . . . . . . . . . . Receptionist

The War of the Roses (1989) . . . . . Auctioneer's Assistant

Delirious (1991) . . . . . . . . . . . . . . . . . . . . . . . . Marie

## Jackson, Glenda

*Films:*

**Negatives** (1968; British) . . . . . . . . . . . . . . . . Vivan
  • 0:27—Brief breasts, putting on fur coat in front of mirror.
  • 0:30—Very brief left breast, while covering herself with fur coat before sitting up.

**The Music Lovers** (1971) . . . . . . . . . . Nina Milyukova
Full frontal nudity after stripping in railway carriage.

Sunday, Bloody Sunday (1971) . . . . . . . . Alex Greville

**Women in Love** (1971) . . . . . . . . . Gudrun Brangwen
(Academy Award for Best Actress.)
••• 1:20—Breasts taking off her blouse on the bed with
Oliver Reed watching her, then making love.
•• 1:49—Brief left breast making love with Reed in bed
again.
A Touch of Class (1972) . . . . . . . . . . . . . Vicki Allessio
(Academy Award for Best Actress.)
The Nelson Affair (1973) . . . . . . . Lady Emma Hamilton
The Triple Echo (1973; British) . . . . . . . . . . . . . . Alice
**The Romantic Englishwoman** (1975; British/French)
. . . . . . . . . . . . . . . . . . . . . . . . . . . . . . . . Elizabeth
• 0:30—Brief full frontal nudity outside, taking robe
off in front of Michael Caine.
• 0:31—Buns, walking back into the house.
• 1:08—Side view of right breast sitting at edge of
pool talking to Thomas.
• 1:45—Very, very brief breasts while in bed talking
with Thomas.
The Incredible Sarah (1976; British). . . . Sarah Bernhardt
Nasty Habits (1977) . . . . . . . . . . . . . . . . . . . Alexandra
House Calls (1978) . . . . . . . . . . . . . . . . . Ann Atkinson
Stevie (1978) . . . . . . . . . . . . . . . . . . . . . Stevie Smith
Lost and Found (1979) . . . . . . . . . . . . . . . . . . . Tricia
Hopscotch (1980) . . . . . . . . . . . . . . Isobel von Schmidt
Return of the Soldier (1983; British) . . . . . . . . Margaret
Turtle Diary (1986; British) . . . . . . . . . Naerea Duncan
Beyond Therapy (1987) . . . . . . . . . . . . . . . . Charlotte
Salome's Last Dance (1987) . . . . . . Herodias/Lady Alice
The Rainbow (1989) . . . . . . . . . . . . . . Anna Brangwen
*Magazines:*
**Playboy** (Dec 1973). . . . . . . . . . . . . Sex Stars of 1973
• 206—Right breast under sheer blouse.
**Playboy** (Nov 1976) . . . . . . . . . . Sex in Cinema 1976
• 146—Side of right breast, while sitting by the pool
in a photo from *The Romantic Englishwoman.*

## Jackson, Jennifer Lyn

*Video Tapes:*
**Playboy Video Calendar 1990** (1989) . . . September
••• 0:46—Nude.
*Magazines:*
**Playboy** (Apr 1989) . . . . . . . . . . . . . . . . . . . Playmate
**Playboy's Book of Lingerie** (Jan 1991) . . . . . . Herself
••• 85—Full frontal nudity.
**Playboy's Book of Lingerie** (Sep 1992) . . . . . Herself
•• 47—Left breast and lower frontal nudity.
**Playboy's Calendar Playmates** (Nov 1992) . . Herself
•• 84—Left breast and lower frontal nudity.
**Playboy's Nudes** (Dec 1992) . . . . . . . . . . . . . Herself
• 100—Left breast.
**Playboy's Blondes, Brunettes & Redheads**
(Sep 1993) . . . . . . . . . . . . . . . . . . . . . . . . . . Herself
• 107—Partial buns.

## •Jackson, Kelly

See: Darrian, Racquel.

## •Jackson, Kelly

a.k.a. Kelly Cook.
a.k.a. Adult film actress Kelly Jaye.
*Films:*
**Anthony's Desire** (1993) . . . . . . . . . . . . . . . . Dancer
•• 0:54—Left breast, while lying on her side in a group
of women. She's near the top of the screen.
•• 1:02—Breasts, while playing the violin on stage.
**Hollywood Dreams** (1993) . . . . . . . . . . . . . Veronica
(Unrated version reviewed.)
•• 0:08—Nude, while making love with Steve on the
floor.
• 0:14—In black lingerie, then left breast after undressing in office for audition in front of Lou.
• 0:25—Buns and breasts while in shower set during
filming.
• 0:52—Breasts, while making love on couch with
Steve.
••• 1:15—Nude, after taking off her dress in bedroom
and making love with Robby.
• 1:19—Brief left breast while hugging Robby.
*Magazines:*
**Playboy's Book of Lingerie** (Mar 1991) . . . . . Herself
•• 79—Right breast and lower frontal nudity.
**Playboy's Book of Lingerie** (Jul 1991) . . . . . . Herself
•• 108—Buns and side view of right breast.
**Playboy's Book of Lingerie** (Sep 1991) . . . . . Herself
••• 90—Breasts.
**Playboy's Book of Lingerie** (Nov 1991) . . . . Herself
• 21—Right breast.
**Playboy's Book of Lingerie** (Jan 1992) . . . . . . Herself
••• 75—Full frontal nudity.
•• 76-77—Left breast and buns.
**Playboy's Bathing Beauties** (Apr 1992). . . . . Herself
••• 16—Breasts.
• 18—Half of left breast.
• 22—Buns.
**Playboy's Girls of Summer '92** (Jun 1992) . . . Herself
• 63—Lower frontal nudity.
**Playboy's Book of Lingerie** (Sep 1992) . . . . . Herself
•• 17—Side of buns and right breast.
••• 22—Full frontal nudity.
**Playboy's Book of Lingerie** (Nov 1992) . . . . Herself
••• 30-31—Breasts.
• 71—Partial lower frontal nudity.
**Playboy's Nudes** (Dec 1992) . . . . . . . . . . . . . Herself
••• 55—Full frontal nudity.
**Playboy's Book of Lingerie** (Mar 1993). . . . . Herself
•• 80—Right breast and lower frontal nudity.
• 89—Right breast.
**Playboy's Bathing Beauties** (Apr 1993). . . . . Herself
••• 104-105—Full frontal nudity.
**Playboy's Book of Lingerie** (May 1993) . . . . Herself
•• 35—Buns and side view of right breast.
**Playboy's Book of Lingerie** (Jul 1993) . . . . . . Herself
• 91—Partial lower frontal nudity.
**Playboy's Wet & Wild Women** (Aug 1993) . . . Herself
•• 33—Side of right breast and buns.

# Jackson, La Toya

Singer.
Member of the singing Jackson clan.
*Video Tapes:*
La Toya Jackson's International Club Tour (1993)
.................................................Hostess
**Playboy Celebrity Centerfold: La Toya Jackson**
(1994)................................. Herself
•• 0:01—Breasts during introduction.
••• 0:04—Breasts and buns during fantasy bedroom segment.
••• 0:09—Breasts and buns in still photos.
••• 0:12—Breasts, while dancing and doing things around the house.
••• 0:15—Breasts and buns in dance number.
••• 0:19—Breasts in recording studio fantasy.
••• 0:29—In red lingerie, then breasts and buns while making love with a guy in vampire fantasy and playing with a snake.
*Magazines:*
**Playboy** (Mar 1989).............Don't Tell Michael
••• 122-133—Breasts and buns.
**Playboy** (Dec 1989).........Holy Sex Stars of 1989!
••• 185—Breasts in bed.
**Playboy's Nudes** (Oct 1990).............. Herself
••• 37—Breasts and buns.
**Playboy** (Nov 1991) ..................Free at Last
••• 82-91—Breasts and buns.
**Playboy** (Dec 1991)................ Sex Stars 1991
••• 186—Breasts.
**Playboy** (Jan 1992) ...............The Year in Sex
••• 149—Breasts under fishnet lingerie.
**Playboy's Nudes** (Dec 1992) .............. Herself
••• 26-27—Breasts and buns.
**Playboy** (Dec 1992)............... Sex Stars 1992
•• 182—Breasts under sheer black net blouse.
**Playboy's Blondes, Brunettes & Redheads**
(Sep 1993) .......................... Herself
••• 70-71—Right breast.

# Jackson, Pamela

*Films:*
Roadhouse (1989)..................Strip Joint Girl
**Angel of Passion** (1991) .................. Eileen
••• 1:13—Breasts and upper half of buns while on bed with Eric making love.

# Jackson, Victoria

*Films:*
Double Exposure (1983) ......... Racetrack Model #1
Baby Boom (1987) .................Eve, the Nanny
**Casual Sex?** (1988)......................Melissa
0:30—Brief buns lying down with Lea Thompson at a nude beach.
0:33—Brief buns wrapping a towel around herself just before getting a massage. Long shot, hard to see.
1:06—Brief buns getting out of bed.

Family Business (1989)..................Christine
UHF (1989) ................................ Teri
I Love You to Death (1990) ..................Lacey
*Made for TV Movies:*
Based on an Untrue Story (1993)...........Corduroy
*TV:*
Half Nelson (1985)...................Annie O'Hara
Saturday Night Live (1986-93).............. Regular

# Jacob, Irène

*Films:*
Au Revoir, Les Enfants (1987; French)...........n.a.
**The Double Life of Veronique** (1991; French)
..........................Veronika/Véronique
•• 0:04—Left breast, then breasts lying in bed with her boyfriend.
0:22—In bra and panties in her bedroom.
••• 0:28—Brief lower frontal nudity, then breasts while making love with her boyfriend.
• 0:41—Brief left breast, while sitting up in bed to answer the phone.
The Secret Garden (1993) . Mary's Mother/Lilias Craven

# Jacobs, Emma

*Films:*
**The Stud** (1978; British) ............... Alexandra
•• 0:44—In bra, then breasts taking bra off in bedroom.
• 0:48—Close up of breasts making love with Tony in his dark apartment.
• 1:14—Breasts in bed with Tony, yelling at him.
Lifeforce (1985) .....................Crew Member

# Jade, Jacqueline

*Films:*
L.A. Heat (1988)...................... Hooker
**Totally Exposed** (1991)................ Eleanor
••• 0:05—Full frontal nudity, taking off towel and lying on tanning table.
•• 0:08—Nude, on massage table, talking with Bill.
•• 0:09—Brief breasts, turning over on table, trying to make the moves on Bill.
•• 0:10—Brief breasts, sitting up.
•• 0:57—Nude, taking off towel and getting on massage table.
••• 0:58—Full frontal nudity, turning over to talk to Bill.
California Hot Wax (1992) ................Bikini Girl
**Pleasure in Paradise** (1992)...............Carol
•• 0:01—Left breast, then breasts while making love in field with a guy at night.

# Jaffe, Chapelle

*Films:*
The Kidnapping of the President (1980; Canadian)
........................................ n.a.
Who Has Seen the Wind? (1980; Canadian).... Maggie
Silence of the North (1981) .........John's Girlfriend

**The Amateur** (1982) . . . . . . . . . . . . . . . . . . Gretchen
• 1:19—Breasts (mostly right breast), while lying on operating table when doctors try to reviver her after John Savage gives her a poison pill.
• 1:20—More right breast again.
The Dead Zone (1983) . . . . . . . . . . . . . . . . . . . . . .n.a.
Terminal Choice (1985; Canadian) . . . . . . .Mrs. Dodson
Confidential (1986). . . . . . . . . . . . . . . . . . . . . Amelia
Millenium (1990) . . . . . . . . . . . . . . . Council Chamber
*Made for TV Movies:*
Sin and Redemption (1994) . . . . . . . . . . . Emma Simms

## Jagger, Bianca
Ex-wife of singer Mick Jagger.
*Films:*
**The American Success Company** (1979) . . . Corinne
• 0:35—Breasts under see-through black top while sitting on bed.
The Cannonball Run (1981) . . . . . . . . . . . . Sheik's Sister
C.H.U.D. II (1989). . . . .'. . . . . . . . . . . . . . . . . . . .n.a.
*Magazines:*
Playboy (Dec 1980). . . . . . . . . . . . . . . . . . .Grapevine
• 389—Breasts under sheer black top.

## Jahan, Marine
*Films:*
Flashdance (1983)
. . . . . . . . . Uncredited Dance Double for Jennifer Beals
**Streets of Fire** (1984) . . . . . . . . . . "Torchie's" Dancer
0:28—Buns in G-string dancing in club.
0:34—More dancing.
• 0:35—Very brief right breast under body stocking, then almost breasts under stocking when taking off T-shirt.
*Video Tapes:*
Freedanse with Marine Jahan . . . . . . . . . . . . . . Herself

## James, Courtney
*Films:*
Galactic Gigolo (1988) . . . . . . . . . . . . . . . . . . . . .Lisa
*a.k.a. Club Earth*
**Breakfast in Bed** (1990) . . . . . . . . . . . . . . . . . .Mitzi
••• 0:36—Breasts, walking into the pool. Also seen from under water.
••• 0:37—Breasts and bun in G-string, getting out of pool.
• 0:39—Breasts on the beach with Mr. Stewart.

## James, Mikel
*Films:*
Hangup (1974). . . . . . . . . . . . . . . . . . . . . . . . . . .n.a.
I Spit on Your Corpse (1974). . . . . . . . . . . . . . . Laura
*a.k.a. Girls for Rent*
**The Naughty Stewardesses** (1978) . . . . . . . . . Diane
*a.k.a. Fresh Air*
•• 0:34—Breasts in bed waiting for Ben then in bed with him.

*Magazines:*
Playboy (Nov 1973) . . . . . . . . . . Sex in Cinema 1973
•• 155—Full frontal nudity in photo from *Hangup* that is incorrectly identifying her as Marki Bey.

## Janisse, Carrie
*Films:*
Ghoulies II (1988) . . . . . . . . . . . . . . . . . . . . . . . Carol
**Desert Passion** (1992). . . . . . . . . . . . . . . . . Heather
•• 0:04—In gold bra and panties, then breasts making love with an actor on bed.
••• 0:17—In white bra, then full frontal nudity, making love in the desert with Nick. Long scene.
•• 0:43—Breasts in S&M outfit during bondage fantasy.
•• 0:54—Nude (near window), while talking to Maggie in the shower room.
••• 1:01—Breasts during cowboy fantasy outside. Long scene.
*Video Tapes:*
**Starlet Screen Test III** (1992) . . . . . . . . . . Alexa Jones
••• 0:14—Breasts, while sitting on table, then full frontal nudity while getting dressed.
**Intimate Secrets—How Women Love to be Loved** (1993) . . . . . . . . . . . . . . . . . . . . . . . . . . . . . . Carrie
••• 0:34—In gold bra and white lingerie, then full frontal nudity posing on and in front of a grand piano.

## Janssen, Marlene
*Films:*
**School Spirit** (1985) . . . . . . . . . . . . . Sleeping Princess
•• 0:16—Breasts in shower room, shaving her legs.
•• 0:42—Breasts and buns, sleeping when old guy goes invisible to peek at her.
*Video Tapes:*
**Playboy Video Magazine, Volume 5** (1983)
. . . . . . . . . . . . . . . . . . . . . . . . . . . . . . . . . . . Playmate
• 0:05—Brief breasts with rose.
**Playboy's Playmate Review 2** (1984) . . . . . Playmate
**Playmates at Play** (1990) . . . . . . . . . . Flights of Fancy
*Magazines:*
Playboy (Nov 1982) . . . . . . . . . . . . . . . . . . . Playmate
**Playboy's 1987 Book of Lingerie** (Mar 1987)
. . . . . . . . . . . . . . . . . . . . . . . . . . . . . . . . . . . Herself
••• 92—Full frontal nudity.
**Playboy's Calendar Playmates** (Nov 1992). . .Herself
• 22—Buns.

## • Janssen, Nicolette
*Films:*
**Angel 4: Undercover** (1993) . . . Music Video Groupie
• 1:00—Breasts, while backstage with the drummer and the other groupie.
*Magazines:*
Playboy (Dec 1993) . . . . . . . . . . . . . . . . . . Grapevine
••• 239—Breasts in B&W photo.

# *Jasaé*

*Films:*

**Cave Girl** (1985) . . . . . . . . . . . . Locker Room Student
•• 0:05—Breasts with four other girls in the girls' locker room undressing, then running after Rex. She's sitting on a bench, wearing red and white panties.
**Unexpected Encounters, Vol. 3** (1988) . . . Neighbor
••• 0:32—Doing strip tease in front of guitar playing neighbor. Buns in G-string and breasts.
**Roadhouse** (1989). . . . . . . . . . . . . . . . . Strip Joint Girl
**Bad Girls from Mars** (1990) . . . . . . . . . . . . . . .Terry
••• 0:03—Breasts taking off her top.
•• 0:05—More breasts going into dressing room.
**Mob Boss** (1990). . . . . . . . . . . . . . . . . . . . . . . . Bar Girl
•• 0:46—Breasts serving drinks to the guys at the table.
**Carnal Crimes** (1991). . . . . . . . . . . . . . . . . . . Christa
••• 0:19—Full frontal nudity in lingerie, making love with a guy while Linda Carol secretly watches.
**Roots of Evil** (1991) . . . . . . . . . . . . . Subway Hooker
(Unrated version reviewed.)
••• 1:05—Breasts taking off her top in subway stairwell, then getting killed by the bad guy.
**The Swindle** (1991) . . . . . . . . . . . . . . . . . . . . . . Nina
••• 0:28—Nude, posing for Tom while he video tapes her. Long scene.
••• 0:31—Nude, making love with Tom.
••• 0:36—Breasts in back of limousine with Dude.
**Teenage Exorcist** (1992) . . . . . . . . . . . Dead Woman
• 0:01—Brief breasts, dead with a slashed throat, on stairway when discovered by the maid.
• 0:16—Brief breasts, several times, during nightmare while Brinke Stevens is sleeping.

*Video Tapes:*

**Candid Candid Camera, Volume 4** (1985) . . .Model
••• 0:03—Full frontal nudity, talking on the phone.
•• 0:18—Buns and lower frontal nudity, when her skirt is blown upwards like Marilyn Monroe.
••• 0:31—Nude, trying to get people to sign a petition against nudity on cable TV.
**Becky Bubbles** (1987) . . . . . . . . . . . . . . . . . . Herself
•• 0:16—Breasts, taking off yellow swimsuit top and getting pushed on swing, then pushing Brandi.
••• 0:17—Breasts, playing with a ball on the grass with Brandi.
••• 0:19—Breasts, drinking wine and sitting on swing.
**Wild Bikinis** (1987) . . . . . . . . . . . . . . . . . . . . Herself
••• 0:32—Breasts on swing, then pushing Brandi on swing from *Becky Bubbles*.
••• 0:35—Breasts playing with ball on the grass.
••• 0:37—Breasts on swing, drinking wine.
• 0:55—Breasts on swing, making a funny face.
**Centerfold Screen Test, Take 3** (1988) . . . . . Herself
••• 0:42—Nude after undressing and posing on sofa. Long scene.
**Starlet Screen Test II** (1991) . . . . . . . . . . . . . .Jasae
••• 0:05—Nude on couch (same segment from *Centerfold Screen Test, Take 3*.)

**Penthouse Forum Letters: Volume 1** (1993)
. . . . . . . . . . .Three is Definitely Not a Crowd/Carmilla
•• 0:00—Nude in the shower during the opening credits.
••• 0:47—Buns in swimsuit, then breasts, getting lotion rubbed on her by Sandy.
••• 0:51—Nude, undressing in bathroom while Chuck peeks through the door, then taking a bath.
••• 0:54—Full frontal nudity in the shower with Sandy and Chuck.

*Magazines:*

**Playboy's Book of Lingerie** (Sep 1991) . . . . . .Herself
••• 75—Breasts.
••• 105—Breasts.
**Playboy's Book of Lingerie** (Nov 1991) . . . . .Herself
••• 12—Breasts.
•• 37—Left breast.
**Playboy** (Jan 1992). . . . . . . . . . . . . . . . . . . Grapevine
•• 208—Buns and side of right breast, wearing G-string and boots. B&W.

# • *Jasmine*

*Video Tapes:*

**The Girls of Penthouse, Volume 2** (1993) . . . . . .Pet
••• 0:00—Nude in pool, outside of house, on the beach, in house covering herself with shaving cream and in front of fireplace.

*Magazines:*

**Penthouse** (May 1992) . . . . . . . . . . . . . . . . . . . . .Pet
••• 67-81—Nude.
**Penthouse** (Jul 1992). . . . . . . . . . . . . . . . .Lustmobile
••• 36-45—Full frontal nudity in limousine with the driver.

# *Jason, Chona*

*Films:*

**Summer Job** (1989) . . . . . . . . . . . . . . . . . Beautiful Lady
**Knockouts** (1992) . . . . . . . . . . . . . . . . . . . . . . . Ninja
••• 0:03—Breasts while doing sit-ups.
• 1:05—Wearing a sheer black body stocking during kick fighting match.

*Video Tapes:*

**Big Bust Casting Call** (1992) . . . . . . . . . . . . . Herself
••• 0:25—Breasts and buns in G-string during audition, undressing and trying on bra and panties in front of mirror.
**Playboy's 101 Ways to Excite Your Lover** (1992)
. . . . . . . . . . . . . . . . . . . . . . . . . . . . . .Touch/Woman
••• 0:15—Nude in bathtub with her lover.
••• 0:35—Nude in shower with her lover, then drying each other off and frolicking in bed.

*Magazines:*

**Playboy's Book of Lingerie** (Jul 1991) . . . . . . .Herself
••• 77—Breasts.
**Playboy's Book of Lingerie** (Sep 1991) . . . . . .Herself
•• 40-41—Left breast.

# Jay, Julie

*Films:*

**Streets** (1989) . . . . . . . . . Dawn's Tattooed Roommate
- 0:20—Brief breasts, twice, pulling her blouse closed when Christina Applegate talks to her.

Poison Ivy (1992) . . . . . . . . . . . . . . . . . . Nurse at Desk

# Jean, Stevie

*Video Tapes:*

**Penthouse Satin & Lace II: Hollywood Undercover** (1992)
. . . . . . . . . . . . . . . . . . . . . . . . . . . . . . . . . . . . . Pet

**Penthouse Satin & Lace: An Erotic History of Lingerie** (1992) . . . . . . . . . . . . . . . . . . . . . . . . Model

**Penthouse Pet of the Year Playoff 1993** (1993)
. . . . . . . . . . . . . . . . . . . . . . . . . . . . . . . . . . . . . Pet
- ••• 0:42—Nude at the beach, in a warehouse, in bathroom while rubbing shaving cream on herself.

**Hot Body Video Magazine: Hot Stuff** (1994) . . . n.a.

**Penthouse Pet of the Year Winners 1993: Mahalia & Julie** (1994)
. . . . . . . . . . . . Sneak Preview of Pet of the Year Playoff
- ••• 0:31—Nude on stairs in empty building.

*Magazines:*

**Penthouse** (Jan 1992) . . . . . . . . . . . . . . . . . . . . . . Pet
- ••• 87-117—Nude.

**Penthouse** (Jun 1993) . . . . . . . . Pet of the Year Play-Off
- ••• 112-113—Nude.

# Jemison, Anna

See: Monticelli, Anna-Maria.

# Jenkin, Devon

*Films:*

**Slammer Girls** (1987) . . . . . . . . . . . Melody Campbell
0:08—In lingerie in her bedroom, then in jail.
- 0:12—Brief breasts getting lingerie ripped off by the prison matron.
- 0:16—Brief breasts getting blouse ripped off by Tank in the shower.

Twisted Nightmare (1987) . . . . . . . . . . . . . . . . . . Julie
Slumber Party Massacre 3 (1990) . . . . . . . . . . . . Sarah

*Music Videos:*

Free Fallin'/Tom Petty . . . . . . . . . . . . . . . . . . . . . . n.a.

*Magazines:*

Playboy (Jun 1992) . . . . . . . . . . . . . . . . . . . . Grapevine

# Jenkins, Rebecca

*Films:*

Cowboys Don't Cry (1988; Canadian) . . . . Lucy Morgan

**Bye Bye Blues** (1989; Canadian) . . . . . . . Daisy Cooper
- 0:01—Brief breasts, getting out of bathtub. Very brief buns, while running outside and putting on robe to get away from snake.
- 0:42—Upper half of breasts, while in bathtub.
- 0:45—Very brief left breast under water in bathtub.

Till Death Do Us Part (1991) . . . . . . . . Sandra Stockton
Bob Roberts (1992; U.S./British) . . . . . Delores Perrigrew
Clearcut (1992; Canadian) . . . . . . . . . Female Reporter

# Jennings, Claudia

*Films:*

Jud (1971) . . . . . . . . . . . . . . . . . . . . . . . . . . . . . n.a.
The Love Machine (1971) . . . . . . . . . . . . . . . . Darlene
The Stepmother (1971) . . . . . . . . . . . . . . . . . . . . n.a.

**Group Marriage** (1972) . . . . . . . . . . . . . . . . . Elaine
- ••• 1:02—Breasts under mosquito net in bed with Phil. Long scene.

**Unholy Rollers** (1972) . . . . . . . . . . . . . . Karen Walker
*a.k.a. Leader of the Pack*
- ••• 0:32—Breasts on pool table, getting gang stripped by the other girls, then walking around and yelling at them.
- 0:38—Buns on top of Nick, on table in the middle of the roller derby rink.
- •• 1:15—Breasts, twice, while changing clothes in locker room, then in bra and panties.

40 Carats (1973) . . . . . . . . . . . . . . . . . . . . Gabriella

**Bloody Friday** (1973) . . . . . . . . . . . . . . . . . . . Allison
*a.k.a. Single Girls*
- 0:40—Breasts, taking off her dress to sunbathe on rock at the beach. Long shot. Side view of right breast, putting dress back on when George talks to her.
- •• 0:57—Breasts, drying herself off after shower.

**Gator Bait** (1973) . . . . . . . . . . . . . . . Desiree Tibidoe
- 0:06—Brief left and right breasts during boat chase sequence.

**Truck Stop Women** (1974) . . . . . . . . . . . . . . . . . Rose
- 0:27—Brief breasts taking off blouse and getting into bed.
  0:48—Brief side view of right breast in mirror, getting dressed.
- 1:10—Brief breasts wrapping and unwrapping a towel around herself.

**The Man Who Fell to Earth** (1976; British)
. . . . . . . . . . . . . . . . . . . . Uncredited Girl by the Pool
(Uncensored version reviewed.)
- 1:42—Breasts, standing by the pool and kissing Bernie Casey.

Sisters of Death (1976) . . . . . . . . . . . . . . . . . . . n.a.
  0:31—Back half of right breast while changing clothes in her room.

The Great Texas Dynamite Chase (1977)
. . . . . . . . . . . . . . . . . . . . . . . . . . . Candy Morgan
Moonshine County Express (1977) . . . . . . Betty Hammer

**Death Sport** (1978) . . . . . . . . . . . . . . . . . . . Deneer

**Impulsion** (1978) . . . . . . . . . . . . . . . . . . . . . . . n.a.

Fast Company (1979; Canadian) . . . . . . . . . . . Sammy

**The Best of Sex and Violence** (1981) . . . . . . . . Rose
- •• 0:46—Breasts taking off her blouse in scene from *Truck Stop Women.*

**Famous T & A** (1982) . . . . . . . . . . . . . . . . . . . Rose
(No longer available for purchase, check your video store for rental.)
- •• 0:26—Breasts scenes from *Single Girls* and *Truck Stop Women.*

## Magazines:

**Playboy** (Nov 1969) . . . . . . . . . . . . . . . . . . Playmate
**Playboy** (Nov 1972) . . . . . . . . . . Sex in Cinema 1972
  • 166—Breasts lying down in a photo from *The Unholy Rollers.*
**Playboy** (Dec 1972). . . . . . . . . . . . . Sex Stars of 1972
  •• 211—Breasts.
**Playboy** (Dec 1973). . . . . . . . . . . . . Sex Stars of 1973
  ••• 208—Full frontal nudity.
**Playboy** (Jan 1974) . . . . . . . Twenty Years of Playmates
  •• 110—Left breast.
**Playboy** (Dec 1974)
  . . . . . . . . . . . . . Claudia Observed & Sex Stars of 1974
  ••• 129-135—Nude.
  •• 206—Breasts in open blouse.
**Playboy** (Dec 1976). . . . . . . . . . . . . Sex Stars of 1976
  ••• 190—Breasts.
**Playboy** (Oct 1977). . . . . . . . . . Having A Masked Ball
  • 116-123—Lower frontal nudity and upper half of breasts.
  • 269—Breasts in small photo.
**Playboy** (Jan 1979) . . . . . . . . . . . . . 25 Beautiful Years
  ••• 162—Breasts.
**Playboy** (Sep 1979). . . . . . . . . . . Claudia Recaptured
  ••• 118-123—Breasts.
**Playboy** (Jan 1989) . . . . . . . . . Women of the Seventies
  ••• 217—Breasts.
**Playboy** (Jan 1994) . . . . . . . . . . 40 Memorable Years
  ••• 89—Breasts.

# Jennings, Julia

*Films:*
**Teachers** (1984) . . . . . . . . . . . . . . . . . . . . The Blonde
  •• 0:05—Brief left breast, while sitting up in bed with Nick Nolte.
Dragnet (1987). . . . . . . . . . . . . . . . . . . . . Sylvia Wiss

# Jenrette, Rita

Ex-wife of former U.S. Representative John Jenrette, who was convicted in 1980 in the FBI's Abscam probe. Now using her maiden name of Rita Carpenter.
*Films:*
**Zombie Island Massacre** (1984). . . . . . . . . . . . Sandy
  ••• 0:01—Breasts taking a shower while Joe sneaks up on her. Breasts in bed with Joe.
  •• 0:10—Brief right breast with open blouse, in boat with Joe. Left breast with him on the couch.
The Malibu Bikini Shop (1985) . . . . . . . . . . . . Aunt Ida
End of the Line (1987) . . . . . . . . . . . . . . . . . . Sharon
*Made for Cable TV:*
Dream On: And Bimbo Was His Name-O (1992; HBO)
  . . . . . . . . . . . . . . . . . . . . . . . . . . . Jennifer Klarik
*Magazines:*
**Playboy** (Apr 1981)
  . . . . . . . . . . . . . The Liberation of a Congressional Wife
  ••• 116-125—Full frontal nudity.
**Playboy** (May 1984) . . . . . . . . . . . Hello, Young Lovers
  •• 128-129—Right breast.

# Jensen, Maren

*Films:*
Beyond the Reef (1981) . . . . . . . . . . . . . . . . . .Diana
  (Not available on video tape.)
**Deadly Blessing** (1981). . . . . . . . . . . . . . . Martha
  •• 0:27—Breasts and buns changing into a nightgown while a creepy guy watches through the window.
  0:52—Buns, getting into the bathtub. Kind of steamy and hard to see.
  • 0:56—Brief breasts in bathtub with snake. (Notice that she gets into the tub naked, but is wearing black panties in the water).
*TV:*
Battlestar Galactica (1978-79) . . . . . . . . . . . . . .Athena

# Jillson, Joyce

Astrologer.
*Films:*
Slumber Party '57 (1976). . . . . . . . . . . . . . . . . .Gladys
The Happy Hooker Goes to Washington (1977) . . Herself
**Superchick** (1978) . . . . . . . . . . Tara B. True/Superchick
  • 0:03—Brief upper half of right breast leaning back in bathtub.
  •• 0:06—Breasts in bed throwing cards up.
  • 0:16—Brief breasts under net on boat with Johnny.
  • 0:29—Brief right breast several times in airplane restroom with a Marine.
  1:12—Buns, frolicking in the ocean with Johnny. Don't see her face.
  • 1:27—Close up of breasts (probably body double) when sweater pops open.

# Jilot, Yolanda

*Films:*
**Diving In** (1990). . . . . . . . . . . . . . . . Amanda Lansky
  0:32—In red, one piece swimsuit, getting out of the pool to talk to Wayne.
  0:54—In blue, one piece swimsuit, getting out of the pool.
  • 0:55—Brief breasts, in open blouse, getting dressed while talking to Burt Young.
Waxwork II: Lost in Time (1991). . . . . Lady of the Night
*Made for TV Movies:*
JFK: Reckless Youth (1993) . . . . . . . . . . . . . .Inga Arvad
*TV:*
Reasonable Doubts (1992-93) . . . . . . . . . . . . . . Marta

# Jisél

See: Brandy.

# Johansen, Linda

*Video Tapes:*
**Penthouse Paradise Revisited** (1992). . . . . . . . .Pet
*Magazines:*
**Penthouse** (Sep 1990) . . . . . . . . . . . . . . . . . . .Pet
  ••• 95-109—Nude.

# Johari, Azizi

*Films:*

**The Killing of a Chinese Bookie** (1976). . . . . Rachel
- 1:14—Brief breasts, while dancing on stage.
- 1:15—Breasts dancing in red light, then coming over to talk to Ben Gazzara.
- 1:26—Brief side view of right breast, while taking a shower.

**Body and Soul** (1981) . . . . . . . . . . . . . . Pussy Willow
- ••• 0:31—Breasts sitting on bed with Leon Isaac Kennedy, then left breast, while lying in bed.

*Magazines:*

**Playboy** (Jun 1975) . . . . . . . . . . . . . . . . . . Playmate
- ••• 104-113—Nude.

**Playboy** (Jan 1976) . . . . . . . . . . . . . . .Playmate Review
- ••• 159—Breasts.

**Playboy** (Dec 1976). . . . . . . . . . . . . Sex Stars of 1976
- ••• 191—Full frontal nudity.

# John, Tylyn

a.k.a. Tylyn.

*Films:*

**Rising Sun** (1993) . . . . . . . . . . . . . . . . . . . . .Redhead
- ••• 0:56—Breasts, while sitting next to Eddie and when he licks sake off her left breast.
- •• 0:58—Breasts and buns, while jumping onto and riding on Wesley Snipes' back.

*Video Tapes:*

**Playboy Video Calendar 1993** (1992) . . . November
- ••• 0:45—Nude on motorcycle in studio and in the rain.
- ••• 0:47—Nude in house and on balcony.

**Playboy Video Centerfold: Corrina Harney** (1992)
. . . . . . . . . . . . . . . . . . . . . . . . . . . . . . . . Playmate

**Playboy's Playmate Review 1993** (1993)
. . . . . . . . . . . . . . . . . . . . . . . . . . . . . .Miss March
- ••• 0:40—Nude, while doing things around a country home.
- ••• 0:42—Nude in white studio fantasy.

*Magazines:*

**Playboy's Book of Lingerie** (Jan 1991) . . . . . . Herself
- ••• 96-97—Breasts.

**Playboy's Book of Lingerie** (Mar 1991) . . . . . Herself
- ••• 57—Breasts.

**Playboy's Book of Lingerie** (Sep 1991) . . . . . Herself
- ••• 47—Breasts.

**Playboy's Book of Lingerie** (Nov 1991) . . . . . Herself
- ••• 59—Breasts.

**Playboy** (Mar 1992). . . . . . . . . . . . . . . . . . Playmate
- ••• 98-109—Nude.

Inside Sports (Apr 1992) . . . . . . . . . Journey to St. John

**Playboy's Playmate Review** (Jun 1993) . . . . . .March
- ••• 22-29—Nude.

**Playboy's Blondes, Brunettes & Redheads**
(Sep 1993) . . . . . . . . . . . . . . . . . . . . . . . . . Herself
- ••• 104-105—Full frontal nudity.

**Playboy's Book of Lingerie** (Sep 1993) . . . . . Herself
- ••• 8—Breasts and buns.
- • 94-95—Breasts under sheer black bodysuit.
- •• 101—Buns and side of right breast.

**Playboy's Book of Lingerie** (Nov 1993) . . . . .Herself
- ••• 15-17—Full frontal nudity.
- ••• 102—Breasts.

**Playboy's Nudes** (Dec 1993) . . . . . . . . . . . . . .Herself
- ••• 19—Full frontal nudity.
- ••• 98-99—Full frontal nudity.

**Playboy's Book of Lingerie** (Mar 1994). . . . . .Herself
- ••• 9—Breasts.

**Playboy's Book of Lingerie** (May 1994) . . . . .Herself
- •• 8—Left breast.

**Playboy's Girls of Summer '94** (Jul 1994). . . .Herself
- •• 45—Right breast.

**Playboy's Book of Lingerie** (Jul 1994) . . . . . .Herself
- ••• 15—Breasts.

# Johns, Tracy Camilla

*Films:*

**She's Gotta Have It** (1987). . . . . . . . . . . Nola Darling
- ••• 0:05—Breasts, making love in bed with Jamie.
- •• 0:25—Brief left breast taking off leotard with Greer. More breasts waiting for him to undress.
- ••• 0:27—Breasts and buns in bed with Greer.
- • 0:38—Breasts, close up of breast, while making love with Spike Lee.
- •• 0:41—Left breast, while lying in bed with Lee.
- •• 1:05—Breasts, twice, in bed masturbating.

Mo' Better Blues (1990) . . . . . . . . . . . . . . .Club Patron

**New Jack City** (1991) . . . . . . . . . . . . . . . . . . Unigua
- • 0:40—Buns, while dancing in red bra, panties, garter belt and stockings.
- • 0:53—Buns and right breast in bed with Wesley Snipes.

*Magazines:*

**Playboy** (Nov 1991) . . . . . . . . . . . Sex in Cinema 1991
- • 141—Buns, in scene from *New Jack City*.

# Johnson, Anne-Marie

*Films:*

Hollywood Shuffle (1987) . . . . . . . . . . . . . . . . . . Lydia

I'm Gonna Git You Sucka (1988) . . . . . . . . . . . . .Cherry

**Robot Jox** (1990) . . . . . . . . . . . . . . . . . . . . . . .Athena
- •• 0:35—Buns, walking to the showers after talking to Achilles and Tex.

The Five Heartbeats (1991) . . . . . . . . . . . Sydney Todd

Strictly Business (1991) . . . . . . . . . . . . . . . . . . Diedre

True Identity (1991) . . . . . . . . . . . . . . . . . . . . . . Kristi

*Miniseries:*

Jackie Collins' Lucky/Chances (1990) . . . . . . . . . . . n.a.

*TV:*

Double Trouble (1984-85) . . . . . . . . . . . . .Aileen Lewis

In the Heat of the Night (1988) . . . . . . . . .Althea Tibbs

# Johnson, Beverly

Model.

*Films:*

**Ashanti, Land of No Mercy** (1979)
. . . . . . . . . . . . . . . . . . . . . . .Dr. Anansa Linderby
- •• 0:07—Buns and brief side view of breasts, taking off clothes to go skinny dipping.

•• 0:08—Briefly nude, running to put her clothes back on.

• 1:15—Right breast in gaping dress while bending over to bury dead bad guy.

Loaded Weapon 1 (1993) . . . . . . . . . . . . . .Doris Luger
0:50—In gold, braless, semi-sheer blouse.

The Meteor Man (1993) . . . . . . . . . . . . . . . . . . Doctor

A Brilliant Disguise (1994). . . . . . . . . . . . . . . .Barbara

## Johnson, Deborah Nicholle

a.k.a. Debi Johnson.
*Video Tapes:*
Playmate Playoffs . . . . . . . . . . . . . . . . . . . . . Playmate
**Playmates at Play** (1990) . . . . . . . . . . . .Hardbodies
*Magazines:*
**Playboy** (Oct 1984). . . . . . . . . . . . . . . . . . . Playmate
**Playboy's 1987 Book of Lingerie** (Mar 1987)
. . . . . . . . . . . . . . . . . . . . . . . . . . . . . . . . . . . Herself
••• 107—Full frontal nudity.
**Playboy's Book of Lingerie** (Jan 1991) . . . . . . Herself
• 53—Buns.
**Playboy's Book of Lingerie** (Jul 1991) . . . . . . Herself
••• 48—Full frontal nudity.
**Playboy's Book of Lingerie** (Nov 1991) . . . . . Herself
•• 86—Full frontal nudity in sheer patterned black bodysuit.
**Playboy's Book of Lingerie** (Jan 1992) . . . . . . Herself
••• 52—Breasts.
••• 68—Breasts.
**Playboy's Book of Lingerie** (Mar 1992) . . . . . Herself
•• 70-71—Right breast and lower frontal nudity.
**Playboy's Book of Lingerie** (Sep 1992) . . . . . Herself
••• 31—Breasts.
**Playboy's Calendar Playmates** (Nov 1992) . . Herself
••• 41—Full frontal nudity.
**Playboy's Blondes, Brunettes & Redheads**
(Sep 1993) . . . . . . . . . . . . . . . . . . . . . . . . . Herself
••• 86—Full frontal nudity.

## Johnson, Echo

*Video Tapes:*
**Sexy Lingerie V** (1992) . . . . . . . . . . . . . . . . .Model
**Playboy Celebrity Centerfold: Jessica Hahn** (1993)
. . . . . . . . . . . . . . . . . . . . . . . . . . . . . . . . . Playmate
••• 0:39—Nude, doing various modeling things.
••• 0:42—Nude in loft fantasy.
••• 0:45—Nude in still photos.
••• 0:46—Nude in a mansion.
**Playboy Video Calendar 1994** (1993) . . . September
••• 0:35—Nude while working out and exercising.
••• 0:37—Nude, undressing from a tuxedo.
*Magazines:*
**Playboy** (Jan 1993) . . . . . . . . . . . . . . . . . . . Playmate
••• 122-133—Nude.
**Playboy** (Jan 1994) . . . . . . . Playboy's Playmate Review
••• 198—Full frontal nudity.
**Playboy's Playmate Review** (May 1994)
. . . . . . . . . . . . . . . . . . . . . . . . . . . . . . . Miss January
••• 4-13—Nude.

**Playboy's Girls of Summer '94** (Jul 1994) . . . .Herself
••• 52-53—Full frontal nudity.
**Playboy's Book of Lingerie** (Jul 1994) . . . . . . .Herself
•• 80-81—Partial lower frontal nudity and buns.
**Playboy's Book of Lingerie** (Sep 1994) . . . . . .Herself
••• 76-77—Breasts.

## Johnson, Jill

*Films:*
**Party Favors** (1987). . . . . . . . . . . . . . . . . . . . .Trixie
•• 0:04—Breasts in dressing room, taking off blue dress and putting on red swimsuit.
••• 0:35—Breasts in doctors office taking off her clothes.
••• 1:03—Breasts doing strip routine in cowgirl costume. More breasts after.
• 1:16—Breasts taking off swimsuit next to pool during final credits.
**Wildest Dreams** (1987). . . . . . . . . . . Rachel Richards
•• 0:51—Breasts on bed underneath Bobby in a net.
• 1:10—Brief breasts during fight with two other women.
**Party Plane** (1988) . . . . . . . . . . . . . . . . . . . . Laurie
••• 0:06—Breasts and buns changing clothes and getting into spa with her two girlfriends. (She's wearing a black swimsuit bottom.)
••• 0:11—Breasts getting out of spa.
•• 0:16—Breasts in pool after being pushed in and her swimsuit top comes off.
•• 0:20—In bra and panties, then breasts on plane doing a strip tease.
Taking Care of Business (1990) . . . . . . . Tennis Court Girl

## Johnson, Kimberly

*Video Tapes:*
**Hot Body International: #2 Miss Puerto Vallarta**
(1990) . . . . . . . . . . . . . . . . . . . . . . . . . . .Contestant
•• 0:43—Buns in two piece swimsuit.
Hot Body International: #4 Spring Break (1992)
. . . . . . . . . . . . . . . . . . . . . . . . . . . . . . . . .Contestant
0:12—Dancing in one piece swimsuit on stage.
0:25—Wet T-shirt contest. Buns in G-string.
*Magazines:*
**Playboy's Book of Lingerie** (Jul 1991) . . . . . . .Herself
• 90—Lower frontal nudity.
**Playboy's Book of Lingerie** (Sep 1991) . . . . . .Herself
••• 23—Full frontal nudity.
**Playboy's Book of Lingerie** (Jan 1992) . . . . . .Herself
••• 31—Full frontal nudity.
**Playboy's Book of Lingerie** (May 1992) . . . . .Herself
•• 40-41—Nude.
**Playboy's Book of Lingerie** (Jul 1992) . . . . . . .Herself
• 88—Side view of left breast.
**Playboy's Book of Lingerie** (Sep 1992) . . . . . .Herself
•• 82—Right breast.

# Johnson, Laura

*Films:*
Opening Night (1977) . . . . . . . . . . . . . . . Nancy Stein
**Fatal Instinct** (1991) . . . . . . . . . . . Catherine Merrims
*a.k.a. To Kill For*
(Unrated version reviewed.)
- • 0:45—Brief left breast in open robe, getting out of bed.
- ••• 0:47—Breasts in bed talking with Michael Madsen, then making love.
- ••• 0:51—Breasts in the bathtub when Bill comes in. Partial lower frontal nudity when standing up.
- •• 0:52—Brief buns and breasts getting dressed in bedroom.
- • 0:59—In wet T-shirt in pool. Brief buns, underwater, more when getting out.
Murderous Vision (1991). . . . . . . . . . . Elizabeth Larwin
**Trauma** (1992) . . . . . . . . . . . . . . . . . Grace Harrington
- • 0:38—Breast, while making love in bed with David and after he leaves.

*Made for Cable TV:*
**Red Shoe Diaries: Double Dare** (1992; Showtime)
. . . . . . . . . . . . . . . . . . . . . . . . . . . . . . . . . . Diane
(Available on video tape on *Red Shoe Diaries 2: Double Dare*.)
0:11—In white bra in her office.
0:14—In black bra in her office.
- ••• 0:16—Breasts, taking off her bra in her office.
- •• 0:17—More breasts, caressing herself.
- • 0:18—Breasts in bed, making love with her husband, Sam.
- •• 0:25—Breasts in the shower.
- •• 1:28—Breasts in bed with her husband. (Additional footage added for video tape.)
*Made for TV Movies:*
Nick Knight (1989) . . . . . . . . . . . . . . . . . . . . . Alyce
*TV:*
Falcon Crest (1983-86) . . . . . . . . Terry Hartford Ranson
Heartbeat (1988-89) . . . . . . . . . . Dr. Eve Autrey/Calvert

# Johnson, Lynn

*Video Tapes:*
**Penthouse Fast Cars/Fantasy Women** (1992)
. . . . . . . . . . . . . . . . . . . . . . . . . . . . . . . . . .Model
**Penthouse Pet of the Year Playoff 1991** (1992)
. . . . . . . . . . . . . . . . . . . . . . . . . . . . . . . . . . . Pet
- ••• 0:23—Nude in African-theme segment with a man and another woman. Muddy.
- • 0:25—Breasts in still photos.
- ••• 0:26—Nude in B&W and color water-theme segment.
- ••• 0:28—Nude in mirrored area.
- ••• 0:30—Nude doing various poses on chair, behind tubular wire screen in studio.
**Penthouse DreamGirls** (1994) . . . . . . . . . . . . .Lynn
- ••• 0:45—Full frontal nudity in house.
*Magazines:*
**Penthouse** (Sep 1989) . . . . . . . . . . . . . . . . . . . Pet

# Johnson, Michelle

*Films:*
**Blame It on Rio** (1984) . . . . . . . . . . . . Jennifer Lyons
- •• 0:19—Breasts on the beach greeting Michael Caine and Joseph Bologna with Demi Moore, then brief breasts in the ocean.
- • 0:26—Breasts taking her clothes off for Caine on the beach. Dark, hard to see.
- • 0:27—Breasts seducing Caine. Dark, hard to see.
- ••• 0:56—Full frontal nudity taking off robe and sitting on bed to take a Polaroid picture of herself.
- • 0:57—Very brief breasts in the Polaroid photo showing it to Caine.
- • 1:02—Brief breasts taking off her top in front of Caine while her dad rests on the sofa.
Gung Ho (1985) . . . . . . . . . . . . . . . . . . . . . Heather
**Beaks The Movie** (1987) . . . . . . . . . . . . . . . Vanessa
- • 0:26—Brief breasts covered with bubbles after taking a bath. Don't see her face.
- • 0:31—Brief breasts covered with bubbles after getting out of bathtub with Christopher Atkins. Don't see her face.
Slipping into Darkness (1987) . . . . . . . . . . . . . . Carlyle
The Jigsaw Murders (1988) . . . . . . . . . . Kathy DaVonzo
0:51—Posing in leotards in dance studio.
1:07—Posing in lingerie on bed.
1:20—In light blue dance outfit.
1:27—Posing in blue swimsuit.
Waxwork (1988) . . . . . . . . . . . . . . . . . . . . . . China
**Genuine Risk** (1989) . . . . . . . . . . . . . . . . . . . . Girl
0:27—In black bra in room with Henry.
0:29—In bra in open top coming out of the bathroom.
- • 0:43—On bed in black bra and panties with Henry. Left breast peeking out of the top of her bra.
Blood Ties (1991). . . . . . . . . . . . . . . . . . . . . . Celia
Driving Me Crazy (1991) . . . . . . . . . . . . . . . . . .Ricki
Death Becomes Her (1992) . . . . . . . . . . . . . . . . Anna
Dr. Giggles (1992) . . . . . . . . . . . . . . . . . . . . Tamara
Far and Away (1992) . . . . . . . . . . . . . . . . . . . .Grace
**Body Shot** (1993). . . . . . . . . . . . . . . . Danielle Wilde
0:23—Brief buns in T-back under fishnet outfit.
- • 0:28—Brief buns, when dropping robe.
*Made for Cable Movies:*
Incident at Deception Ridge (1994; USA) . . . . . . . . n.a.
*Made for Cable TV:*
**Tales From the Crypt: Split Second** (1991; HBO)
. . . . . . . . . . . . . . . . . . . . . . . . . . .Liz Kelly-Dixon
- ••• 0:15—Breasts, offering her towel to Ted for him to dry her off.
0:19—In bra and panties with Ted at night.
*Made for TV Movies:*
A Woman Scorned: The Betty Broderick Story (1992)
. . . . . . . . . . . . . . . . . . . . . . . . . . . . . . . .Linda
*TV:*
Werewolf (1987) . . . . . . . . . . . . . . . . . . . . . . n.a.

# Johnson, Penny

*Films:*

Swing Shift (1984) . . . . . . . . . . . . . . . . . . . Genevieve
**The Hills Have Eyes, Part II** (1989) . . . . . . . . . . . Sue
  • 0:49—Brief breasts in bus, trying to get Foster's attention.
Molly & Gina (1993) . . . . . . . . . . . . . . . . . . . . . . . . n.a.
What's Love Got to Do With It (1993) . . . . . . . Lorraine

*TV:*

Paper Chase (1984-86) . . . . . . . . . . . . . . . . . . . Vivian
Homeroom (1989) . . . . . . . . . . . . . . . . . . . . . . Virginia
The Larry Sanders Show (1992- ) . . . . . . . . . . . Beverly

# Johnson, Sandy

*Films:*

Jokes My Folks Never Told Me (1976) . . . . . . . . . . . n.a.
Two-Minute Warning (1976) . . . . . . . . . . Button's Wife
Gas Pump Girls (1978) . . . . . . . . . . . . . . . . . . . . April
**Halloween** (1978) . . . . . . . . . . . . . . . . . Judith Meyers
  0:06—Very brief breasts covered with blood on floor after Michael stabs her to death.
**H.O.T.S.** (1979) . . . . . . . . . . . . . . . . . . . . . Stephanie
*a.k.a. T & A Academy*
  •• 0:27—Breasts on balcony in red bikini bottoms.
  •• 1:34—Breasts during football game during huddle with all the other girls.
The Best Little Whorehouse in Texas (1982)
  . . . . . . . . . . . . . . . . . . . . . . . Chicken Ranch Girl
**Terror in the Aisles** (1984) . . . . . . . . . . Judith Meyers
  • 0:15—Brief breasts in scene from *Halloween.*

*Magazines:*

**Playboy** (Jun 1974) . . . . . . . . . . . . . . . . . . . Playmate
  ••• 118-127—Full frontal nudity.

# Johnson, Sunny

*Films:*

Animal House (1978) . . . . . . . . . . . . . . . Otter's Co-Ed
Dr. Heckyl and Mr. Hype (1980) . . . . . . . . Coral Careen
Where the Buffalo Roam (1980) . . . . . . . . . . . . . n.a.
The Night the Lights Went Out in Georgia (1981)
  . . . . . . . . . . . . . . . . . . . . . . . . . . . . . . . Wendy
**Flashdance** (1983) . . . . . . . . . . . . . . . . Jennie Szabo
  • 1:28—Breasts, while sitting on stage and moving her legs around.
  • 1:29—Very brief left breast in open rain coat, when Jennifer Beals grabs money outside.

*Made for TV Movies:*

The Red Light Sting (1984) . . . . . . . . . . . . . . . . Sonia

# Johnson, Terri

*Films:*

**Video Vixens** (1973) . . . . . . . . . . . . . . . . . . . . Anita
  •• 0:43—Full frontal nudity, talking with her mother in bedroom during commercial.
The Cocktail Hostess (1976) . . . . . . . . . . . . . . . . n.a.

# Johnson, Victoria Lynn

*Films:*

**Dressed to Kill** (1980)
  . . . . . . . . . . . . . . Body Double for Angie Dickinson
  •• 0:02—Frontal nudity in the shower body doubling for Angie Dickinson.
**Terror in the Aisles** (1984)
  . . . . . . . . . . . . . . Body Double for Angie Dickinson
  • 1:07—Breasts in shower from Angie Dickinson's shower scene in *Dressed to Kill.*

*Video Tapes:*

**The Girls of Penthouse** (1984) . . . . . . . . . Centerfold
  ••• 0:43—Nude during photo session with Bob Guccione.

*Magazines:*

**Penthouse** (Aug 1976) . . . . . . . . . . . . . . . . . . . . Pet
  91-103—Nude.
**Penthouse** (Jun 1977) . . . . . . . Pet of the Year Play-Off
  ••• 66-67—Full frontal nudity.
**Penthouse** (Nov 1977) . . . . . . . . . . . . . Pet of the Year
  ••• 75-89—Nude.

# Johnston, Michelle

*Films:*

A Chorus Line (1985) . . . . . . . . . . . . . . . . . . . . Bebe
Dick Tracy (1990) . . . . . . . . . . . . . . . . . . . . . Dancer
Faith (1990) . . . . . . . . . . . . . . Audition Choreographer
Opportunity Knocks (1990) . . . . . . . . . . . . Club Singer
**California Casanova** (1991) . . . . . . . . . . . . . . . Laura
  0:12—Buns, in black G-string, while dancing on stage.
  • 0:18—Brief breasts under sheer black top, while dancing in front of a guy in pool house.
Shout (1991) . . . . . . . . . . . . . . . . . . . . . . . . Loretta

# • Johnston-Ulrich, Kim

*Films:*

**Blood Ties** (1991) . . . . . . . . . . . . . . . . . . . . . Loren
  • 1:21—Very brief breasts, while rolling over in bed with Harry.
Spellcaster (1992) . . . . . . . . . . . . . . . . . . . . . . Teri

*TV:*

Nightingales (1989) . . . . . . . . . . . . . . . . Allyson Yates

# Joi, Marilyn

*Films:*

**The Happy Hooker Goes to Washington** (1977)
  . . . . . . . . . . . . . . . . . . . . . . . . . . . . . . . Sheila
  • 0:09—Left breast while on a couch.
  • 0:47—Brief breasts during car demonstration.
  •• 1:14—Breasts in military guy's office.
**Kentucky Fried Movie** (1977) . . . . . . . . . . Cleopatra
  • 1:11—Breasts in bed with Schwartz.
**Ilsa, Harem Keeper of the Oil Sheiks** (1978)
  . . . . . . . . . . . . . . . . . . . . . . . . . . . . . . . Velvet
Nurse Sherri (1978) . . . . . . . . . . . . . . . . . . . . . . n.a.
Galaxina (1980) . . . . . . . . . . . . . . . . . . . Winged Girl
**C.O.D.** (1983) . . . . . . . . . . . . . . . . . . . Debbie Winter
  •• 1:16—Breasts during photo session.

• 1:25—Brief breasts taking off robe wearing red garter belt during dressing room scene.
1:26—In red bra, while talking to Albert.
1:30—In red bra during fashion show.
Satan's Princess (1989) . . . . . . . . . . . . . . . . . . Hooker

## Jones, Amanda

*Films:*
**Honky Tonk Nights** (1978) . . . . . . . . . . . . . . .Honey
•• 0:41—Breasts outside by car with Dan.
••• 0:42—Breasts and buns, in the woods with Dan.
Winter Kills (1979) . . . . . . . . . Beautiful Woman Seven

## • Jones, Catherine Zeta

*Films:*
Christopher Columbus: The Discovery (1992; U.S./
Spanish) . . . . . . . . . . . . . . . . . . . . . . . . . . . . . Beatrix
**Splitting Heirs** (1993) . . . . . . . . . . . . . . . . . . . . Kitty
• 0:39—Swimming in lap pool (hard to see anything
because of the water distortion.) Brief buns and back
half of left breast, while getting out of the pool.
Long shot.
0:41—Very, very brief inside half of left breast, while
throwing Eric Idle's second shoe to him.

## Jones, Charlene

*Films:*
**The Curious Female** (1969). . . . Pearl Lucomb/Girl #2
• 0:14—Brief breasts, twice, while taking a shower.
• 0:29—Buns, while running in slow motion to the
pool.
• 0:30—Buns, while lying down.
1:08—Breasts while making love with a guy. Hard to
see because of psychedelic light
•• 1:09—Breasts while turning over on her back with
Andre.
Unholy Rollers (1972) . . . . . . . . . . . . . . . . . . . . Beverly
*a.k.a. Leader of the Pack*
The Woman Hunt (1975; U.S./Philippines) . . . . . . . .n.a.
Hard to Hold (1984) . . . . . . . . . . . . . . . . . . . . . . . Wife
Avenging Angel (1985). . . . . . . . . . . . . . . . . . . Hooker
**Perfect** (1985). . . . . . . . . . . . . . . . . . . . . . . . . Shotsy
• 0:17—Breasts stripping on stage in a club. Buns in
G-string.

## Jones, Grace

*Films:*
Conan the Destroyer (1984) . . . . . . . . . . . . . . . . . Zula
**Deadly Vengeance** (1985). . . . . . . . . Slick's Girlfriend
(Although the copyright on the movie states 1985, it
looks more like the 1970's.)
••• 0:06—Right breast, then breasts in bed with Slick.
•• 0:13—Left breast, when Slick sits up in bed, then full
frontal nudity after he gets up.
A View to a Kill (1985). . . . . . . . . . . . . . . . . . .May Day
Vamp (1986). . . . . . . . . . . . . . . . . . . . . . . . . . Katrina
0:23—Breasts under wire bra, dancing on stage.
Body is painted, so it's difficult to see.
Siesta (1987). . . . . . . . . . . . . . . . . . . . . . . . . .Conchita

Straight to Hell (1987; British) . . . . . . . . . . . . . Sonya
**Boomerang** (1992) . . . . . . . . . . . . . . . . . . . . . Strangé
• 0:35—Brief buns, under stockings during confer-
ence room meeting.
1:19—Brief buns and back side of left breast, several
times on TV monitor during editing of a commercial.
• 1:29—Very brief breasts ripping off dress during a
commercial.
*Magazines:*
**Playboy** (Apr 1979) . . . . . . . . . . . . . . . . . . . . . . n.a.
**Playboy** (Jan 1985). . . . . . . . . . . . . . . . . . . . . . . n.a.
101—Small color photo.
**Playboy** (Jul 1985) . . . . . . . . . . . . . . . Amazing Grace
• 82-87—Breasts and buns in B&W photos of her and
Dolph Lundgren.
**Playboy** (Nov 1992) . . . . . . . . . . . . . . . . . . Grapevine
• 190—Half of left breast in open blouse. B&W.

## Jones, Helen

*Films:*
**Bliss** (1985; Australian) . . . . . . . . . . . . . .Honey Barbara
••• 0:58—Breasts, lying on the floor with Harry. Brief
part of lower frontal nudity. Long scene.
• 1:01—Brief breasts on bed when Adrian runs to the
bathroom.
1:24—Left breast while standing outside with arms
outstretched.
• 1:39—Buns, while swimming. Long shot of buns
while walking up rocks.
The Good Wife (1987; Australian) . . . . . . . . Rosie Gibbs
*a.k.a. The Umbrella Woman*
*Made for TV Movies:*
The Girl From Tomorrow (1990; Australian) . . . . . . . n.a.

## Jones, Josephine Jaqueline

a.k.a. J. J. Jones.
Former Miss Bahamas.
*Films:*
**Black Venus** (1983) . . . . . . . . . . . . . . . . . . . . . . Venus
•• 0:05—Breasts in Jungle Room.
••• 0:11—Nude, in bedroom, posing for Armand while
he sketches.
• 0:14—Breasts and buns making love with Armand in
bed.
•• 0:17—Nude, posing for Armand while he models in
clay, then on the bed, kissing him.
• 0:21—Brief nude getting dressed.
••• 0:38—Nude, making love in bed with Karin Schubert.
0:45—Nude, talking and then making love in bed
with Louise.
•• 0:50—Breasts when Pierre brings everybody in to
see her.
•• 0:57—Breasts in silhouette while Armand fantasizes
about his statue coming to life.
••• 1:04—Nude.
••• 1:07—Nude with the two diplomats on the bed.
••• 1:16—Nude frolicking on the beach with Louise.

••• 1:18—Breasts in bedroom getting out of wet clothes with Louise.
•• 1:21—Breasts in bed with Jacques.
•• 1:24—Full frontal nudity getting out of bed.
**Christina** (1984) . . . . . . . . . . . . . . . . . . . . . . . . . .n.a.
**Love Circles Around the World** (1984) . . . . . . Brigid
•• 0:18—Breasts, then nude running around her apartment chasing Jack.
• 0:30—Breasts, making love with Count Crispa in his hotel room.
**Warrior Queen** (1987) . . . . . . . . . . . . . . . . . . . Chloe
••• 0:20—Breasts making love with Vespa.

## Jones, Marilyn

*Films:*
Support Your Local Sheriff! (1969) . . . . . . . Bordello Girl
The Scenic Route (1978) . . . . . . . . . . . . . . . . . . . . Lena
Meteor (1979) . . . . . . . . . . . . . . . . . . . . . . . . . Stunt
The Love Butcher (1982) . . . . . . . . . . . . . . . . . . Lena
**The Men's Club** (1986) . . . . . . . . . . . . . . . . . . Allison
•• 1:21—Breasts, while in bedroom talking to Harvey Keitel, then putting on dress.
On the Block (1990) . . . . . . . . . . . . . . . . . . . . . . Libby
*Made for TV Movies:*
The Lakeside Killer (1979) . . . . . . . . . . . . . . . Cindy Lee
*TV:*
Secrets of Midland Heights (1980-81) . . . . Holly Wheeler
King's Crossing (1982) . . . . . . . . . . . . . Carey Hollister

## Jones, Rachel

*Films:*
**Dracula's Widow** (1988) . . . . . . . . . . . . . . . . . . Jenny
• 0:54—Brief left breast, then brief breasts, twice, lying in the bathtub, getting stabbed by Sylvia Kristel.
Fresh Horses (1988) . . . . . . . . . . . . . . . . . . . . . Bobo
Lorenzo's Oil (1993) . . . . . . . . . . . . . . . . . Special Child

## Jones, Rebunkah

*Films:*
**Frankenstein General Hospital** (1988)
. . . . . . . . . . . . . . . . . . . . . . . . . . . . Elizabeth Rice
•• 1:05—Breasts in the office letting Mark Blankfield examine her back.
**Hide and Go Shriek** (1988) . . . . . . . . Bonnie Williams
•• 0:27—Breasts taking off her blouse. More breasts sitting in bed.

## •Jones, Samantha

*Films:*
Wait Until Dark (1967) . . . . . . . . . . . . . . . . . . . . .Lisa
Way We Live Now (1970) . . . . . . . . . . . . . . . Samantha
**Get to Know Your Rabbit** (1972) . . . . . . . . . . Susan
•• 0:27—Right breast, after taking the bra off.
0:27—In red bra, in front of Allen Garfield and Tommy Smothers.
• 0:28—Right breast, while dancing with Smothers in the store.

## Jones, Sharon Lee

*Films:*
**9 1/2 Ninjas** (1990) . . . . . . . . . . . . . . . . . . . . . .Zelda
• 0:52—Breasts eating Chinese food in the shower with Joe.
Grand Canyon (1991) . . . . . . . . . . . . . . . . . Studio Girl

## Jones, Susan

*Films:*
**RollerBlade Warriors: Taken By Force** (1988)
. . . . . . . . . . . . . . . . . . . . . . . . . . . . . Slave Girl #2
•• 0:20—Breasts, while getting hassled by two guys.
••• 0:23—Breasts, while walking through the desert.
**Wilding, The Children of Violence** (1990)
. . . . . . . . . . . . . . . . . . . . . . . . . . .Alley Rape Victim
• 1:16—Breasts outside struggling with Jason and Bobby on the ground.

## Jordan, Deanna

*Video Tapes:*
Hot Body International: #2 Miss Puerto Vallarta (1990)
. . . . . . . . . . . . . . . . . . . . . . . . . . . . . .Contestant
**Hot Body International: #4 Spring Break** (1992)
. . . . . . . . . . . . . . . . . . . . . . . . . . . . . .Contestant
• 0:13—Dancing in two piece swimsuit on stage. Brief partial right breast.
• 0:49—Brief breasts several times when she rips her wet T-shirt open. Buns in G-string.

## Jourard, Gina

*Films:*
**Novel Desires** (1991) . . . . . . . . . . . . . . . . . . . . Shari
•• 0:00—Right breast, then breasts in bed with Brian.
•• 0:03—Breasts while taking a shower.
•• 0:04—Brief tip of left breast while putting on a stocking. Breasts while getting dressed.
**A Sensuous Summer** (1991) . . . . . . . . . . . . . . Tracy
••• 0:09—Breasts while making love in bed with Alex.
0:21—In two different bras in bedroom with Alex.
**Pleasure in Paradise** (1992) . . . . . . . . . . . . . Woman
••• 0:06—Breasts, while making in love in bed with Hansen.
• 0:39—Breasts on bed with Hansen.

## Jourdan, Catherine

*Films:*
Girl on a Motorcycle (1968; French/British) . . Catherine
*a.k.a. Naked Under Leather*
The Godson (1972; Italian/French) . . . . . .Hatcheck Girl
**Aphrodite** (1982; German/French) . . . . . . . . . .Valerie
• 0:34—Brief upper half of breasts in bathtub.

## Jovovich, Milla

Model.
Daughter of Soviet actress Galina Jovovich.
*Films:*
Two Moon Junction (1988) . . . . . . . . . . . . . Samantha
**Return to the Blue Lagoon** (1991) . . . . . . . . . . Lilli
• 0:49—Brief upper half breasts in front of mirror.

- 1:07—Very brief breasts under water with Richard. Brief breasts under waterfall with Richard.
- 1:20—Briefly in wet beige blouse, standing up in pond.
- 1:26—Side view of right breast three times, washing make up off her face in the pond.
- • 1:28—Side view of right breast again. Very brief left breast, while picking up her top off rock.
  1:30—Side of left breast, lying on bed while held down.

**Chaplin** (1992; British/U.S.) . . . . . . . . . . .Mildred Harris
- 0:55—Top of left breast peeking over top of lingerie while sitting on bed talking to Chaplin.
- 0:56—Buns, after taking off lingerie and standing in front of Chaplin.

Kuffs (1992) . . . . . . . . . . . . . . . . . . . . . Maya Carlton
  0:00—Dancing, while wearing a braless blue tank top and white panties.

Dazed and Confused (1993) . . . . . . . . . . . . . . Michelle
*Made for Cable Movies:*
Night Train to Kathmandu (1988; Disney). . . . . . . . Lily

## Joyner, Michelle
*Films:*
**Grim Prairie Tales** (1990) . . . . . . . . . . . . . . . . . Jenny
- 0:35—Very brief right breast, then left breast while making love with Marc McClure. Kind of dark.

I Love You to Death (1990) . . . . . . . . . . . . . Donna Joy
**Traces of Red** (1992) . . . . . . . . . . . . . Morgan Cassidy
- 0:08—In black bra, in bedroom with James Belushi. Brief breasts making love.
- • 0:24—Left breast, while lying dead in bed when Belushi sees her.

Cliffhanger (1993). . . . . . . . . . . . . . . . . . . . . . Sarah
*Made for TV Movies:*
Baby of the Bride (1991) . . . . . . . . . . . . . . . . . . Judy
Bonnie and Clyde: The True Story (1992)
. . . . . . . . . . . . . . . . . . . . . . . . . .Blanche Barrow
A Passion for Justice: The Hazel Brannon Smith Story (1994) . . . . . . . . . . . . . . . . . . . . . . . Ann Sinclair
*TV:*
Knots Landing . . . . . . . . . . . . . . . . . . . . . .Lynnette

## • Julia Ann
Adult film actress.
*Video Tapes:*
Ginger Lynn Allen's Lingerie Gallery . . . . . . . . .Julia Ann
**Penthouse's 25th Anniversary Swimsuit Video** (1993). . . . . . . . . . . . . . . . . . . . . . . . . . . . Pet
**Penthouse Forum Letters: Volume 2** (1994)
. . . . . . . . . . . . . . . . . . . . . The Big Switch/Debbie
••• 0:32—Breasts and buns in beige panties while doing strip tease with Cindy in front of their husbands. Nude in hot tub, then nude making love with Dan on bench.
*Magazines:*
**Penthouse** (Sep 1994) . . . . . . . . . . . . . . . .Ice & Easy
••• 91-105—Nude with Janine Lindemulder and ice dildos.

## Julian, Janet
a.k.a. Janet Louise Johnson.
*Films:*
Humongous (1982; Canadian). . . . . . . . . Sandy Ralston
Fear City (1984). . . . . . . . . . . . . . . . . . . . . . . Ruby
Choke Canyon (1986) . . . . . . . . . . . . . Vanessa Pilgrim
**King of New York** (1990) . . . . . . . . . . . . . . . Jennifer
- 0:26—Very brief left breast, standing in subway car kissing Christopher Walken. Don't see her face.
Heaven is a Playground (1991). . . . . . . . . . . .Dalton Ellis
*TV:*
The Nancy Drew Mysteries (1978) . . . . . . . Nancy Drew

## • Justin, Melissa
*Made for Cable TV:*
Dream On: Blinded By the Cheese (1994; HBO). . . .Jolie
**Dream On: Felines... Nothing More than Felines** (1994; HBO). . . . . . . . . . . . . . . . . . . . . . . .Heather
••• 0:17—Breasts, while with Martin in his apartment.
**Dream On: Stone Cold** (1994; HBO) . . . . . . .Heather
••• 0:01—Breasts, while on bed with Martin in his apartment, then getting dressed and leaving.

## Kaelin, Monika
Miss Switzerland.
*Films:*
S.A.S. San Salvador (1982). . . . . . . . . . . . . . . . . n.a.
*Magazines:*
**Penthouse** (May 1980) . . . . . . . . . . . . . . . . . .Pet
••• 95-109—Nude.

## Kafkaloff, Kim
a.k.a Adult film actress Sheri St. Clair or Sheri St. Cloud.
*Films:*
**Sex Appeal** (1986). . . . . . . . . . . . . . . . . . . Stephanie
•• 0:29—Buns, in G-string in Tony's bachelor pad. Breasts dancing and on bed.
**Slammer Girls** (1987) . . . . . . . . . . . . . . . . . . Ginny
- 0:23—Brief breasts changing clothes under table in the prison cafeteria.

## Kaitan, Elizabeth
a.k.a. Elizabeth Cayton.
*Films:*
The Lonely Guy (1983) . . . . . . . . . . . . . . . . . n.a.
The Flamingo Kid (1984) . . . . . . . . . . . . . . . . n.a.
**Savage Dawn** (1984). . . . . . . . . . . . . . . . . Becky Sue
- 0:17—Right breast, while getting mauled by the bad guys.
Silent Madness (1984) . . . . . . . . . . . . . . . . . Barbara
Zelig (1984). . . . . . . . . . . . . . . . . . . . . . .German Girl
Silent Night, Deadly Night, Part 2 (1986). . . . . . Jennifer
  0:58—Most of right breast, then buns, while kissing Ricky.
Thunder Run (1986). . . . . . . . . . . . . . . . . . . . . n.a.

**Slavegirls from Beyond Infinity** (1987)...... Daria
(Wearing skimpy two piece loincloth outfit during most
of the movie.)
••• 0:38—Breasts undressing and jumping into bed
with Rik.
**Violated** (1987).........................Liz Grant
•• 0:03—Breasts and lower frontal nudity while Frank
rapes her in bedroom.
• 0:53—Very brief right breast several times while getting raped by Frank. Seen on video playback.
••• 0:59—Breasts and buns, while in bed with a customer.
**Assault of the Killer Bimbos** (1988).........Lulu
•• 0:41—Brief breasts during desert musical sequence,
opening her blouse, then taking off her shorts, then
putting on a light blue dress. Don't see her face.
**Friday the 13th, Part VII: The New Blood** (1988)
.........................................Robin
• 0:53—Brief left breast in bed making love with a
guy.
• 0:55—Brief breasts sitting up in bed after making
love and the sheet falls down.
•• 1:00—Brief breasts again sitting up in bed and putting a shirt on over her head.
**Necromancer** (1988)................Julie Johnson
•• 0:41—Breasts in the shower with Carl.
• 0:45—Very brief side view of right breast, taking off
dress in front of Paul.
1:01—In red and black lingerie.
**Nightwish** (1988)...................... Donna
(Unedited version reviewed.)
• 0:04—In wet T-shirt, then brief breasts taking it off
during experiment. Long shot.
• 1:10—Briefly in braless, see-through purple dress.
**RollerBlade Warriors: Taken By Force** (1988)
....................................Gretchen Hope
• 0:51—Breasts, while tied to large spool and getting
raped by Marachek.
• 1:03—Very brief breasts, several times, while getting
raped in B&W vision.
Twins (1988)......................... Secretary
Dr. Alien (1989) ...................... Waitress
*a.k.a. I Was a Teenage Sex Mutant*
**Night Club** (1989) ................... Beth/Liza
•• 0:31—Left breast, while pulling down blouse and
caressing herself.
•• 0:33—Left breast in pulled down blouse on stairwell
with Nick.
••• 0:36—Breasts on warehouse floor with Nick.
••• 0:46—Full frontal nudity, taking off her dress in front
of Nick.
••• 1:03—Breasts, making love with another guy in
front of Nick.
Under the Boardwalk (1989)............... Donna
Aftershock (1990)....................... Sabina
**The Girl I Want** (1990) ................... Amy

Lockdown (1990)................... Monica Taylor
**Desperate Crimes** (1991; Italian) .........Jamie Lee
• 0:04—Brief right breast, when getting her jacket
opened by a bad guy, then more right breast after
getting shot.
**Vice Academy, Part 3** (1991) .............. Candy
••• 0:12—Breasts in back of van with her boyfriend.
Hellroller (1992)......................... Lizzy
**Beretta's Island** (1993)...................Linda
•• 1:33—Breasts, while playing with Franco Columbu
in the ocean at the end of the film, during the end
credits and after.
Good Girls Don't (1993) ............. TV Announcer
*Video Tapes:*
B-Movie Queens Revealed: The Making of "Vice
Academy" (1993)........................ Candy

# Kalem, Toni

*Films:*
The Wanderers (1979) ...............Despie Galasso
Private Benjamin (1980)...................... n.a.
I'm Dancing as Fast as I Can (1981).......... Debbie
Paternity (1981)................... Diane Cassabello
**Silent Rage** (1982)................. Alison Halman
•• 0:22—Side view of left breast, then breasts, while in
bed with Chuck Norris.
•• 0:46—Right breast, while lying in bed with Norris.
1:01—Briefly in bra, undressing in bedroom to take
a shower.
Two of a Kind (1983).....................Terri
Reckless (1984) .........................Donna
Billy Galvin (1986) ...................... Nora
Eyes of the Beholder (1992)...........Doctor Gruber
Sister Act (1992) ...............Connie LaRocca
*Made for TV Movies:*
The Odd Couple (1993)..................... Edna
*TV:*
Another World ..................Angie Perini
Arresting Behavior (1992-93).................Wendy

# Kallianiotes, Helena

*Films:*
**The Baby Maker** (1970)...................Wanda
• 1:30—Brief breasts when Barbara Hershey sees her
in bed with Tad.
Five Easy Pieces (1970)............... Palm Apodaca
Kansas City Bomber (1972)...........Jackie Burdette
Shanks (1974) ....................... Mata Hari
The Drowning Pool (1976)............. Elaine Reaves
The Passover Plot (1976; Israeli) ......Visionary Woman
Stay Hungry (1976) ....................... Anita
Backtrack (1989) ................... Grace Carelli
*a.k.a. Catch Fire*

# Kaminsky, Dana

*Films:*
**Hot Resort** (1984) ...................... Melanie
•• 1:02—Breasts taking off her white dress in a boat.
Irreconcilable Differences (1984) . Woman in Dress Shop

## Kane, Carol
*Films:*
Carnal Knowledge (1971) . . . . . . . . . . . . . . . . . Jennifer
Desperate Characters (1971) . . . . . . . . . . . . Young Girl
**The Last Detail** (1973) . . . . . . . . . . . . . Young Whore
   • 1:02—Brief breasts sitting on bed talking with Randy
     Quaid. Her hair is in the way, hard to see.
Dog Day Afternoon (1975) . . . . . . . . . . . . . . . . . . Jenny
Hester Street (1975) . . . . . . . . . . . . . . . . . . . . . . . Gitl
Annie Hall (1977) . . . . . . . . . . . . . . . . . . . . . . . Allison
Valentino (1977; British) . . . . . . . . . . . . . Fatty's Girl
The World's Greatest Lover (1977) . . . . . . . . . . . Annie
The Mafu Cage (1978) . . . . . . . . . . . . . . . . . . . . Cissy
  *a.k.a. My Sister, My Love*
    0:08—Very brief tip of left breast in the bathtub.
When a Stranger Calls (1979) . . . . . . . . . . . Jill Johnson
Norman Loves Rose (1982; Australian) . . . . . . . . . Rose
Over the Brooklyn Bridge (1983) . . . . . . . . . . . . Cheryl
Racing with the Moon (1984) . . . . . . . . . . . . . . Annie
Transylvania 6-5000 (1985) . . . . . . . . . . . . . . . . Lupi
Jumpin' Jack Flash (1986) . . . . . . . . . . . . . . . Cynthia
Ishtar (1987) . . . . . . . . . . . . . . . . . . . . . . . . . . . Carol
The Princess Bride (1987) . . . . . . . . . . . . . . . . Valerie
License to Drive (1988) . . . . . . . . . . . . . . . . . . . . Mom
Scrooged (1988) . . . . . . The Ghost of Christmas Present
Sticky Fingers (1988) . . . . . . . . . . . . . . . . . . . . . Kitty
The Lemon Sisters (1990) . . . . . . . . . . Franki D'Angelo
My Blue Heaven (1990) . . . . . . . . . . . . . . . . Shaldeen
Ted & Venus (1991) . . . . . . Colette/Colette's Twin Sister
Baby On Board (1992) . . . . . . . . . . . . . . . . . . . Maria
In the Soup (1992) . . . . . . . . . . . . . . . . . . . . Barbara
Addams Family Values (1993) . . . . . . . . . . . . . Granny
*Made for Cable Movies:*
When a Stranger Calls Back (1993) . . . . . . . . Jill Johnson
*Made for Cable TV:*
Tales From the Crypt: Judy, You're Not Yourself Today
. . . . . . . . . . . . . . . . . . . . . . . . . . . . . . . . . . . . Judy
*TV:*
Taxi (1981-83) . . . . . . . . . . . . . . . . . . . . Simka Gravas
All Is Forgiven (1986) . . . . . . . . . . Nicolette Bingham
American Dreamer (1990) . . . . . . . . . . Lillian Abernathy

## Kane, Kathleen
*Films:*
Flesh Gordon 2 (1990; Canadian) . . . . . . . . . Girl in Car
Shock 'Em Dead (1990) . . . . . . . . . . . . Pizza Girl 2
**Angel of Passion** (1991) . . . . . . . . . . . . . . . . Suzette
  •• 1:08—Breasts while posing for Marty in the house.

## Kane, Sharon
See: Cain, Sharon.

## • Kaniak, Aleksandra
*Films:*
Blindfold: Acts of Obsession (1993) . . . . . . . . . . Natalie
Three of Hearts (1993) . . . . . . . . . . . . . . . . . . . Bride
*Made for Cable TV:*

Love Street: Much Madness (1993; Showtime)
. . . . . . . . . . . . . . . . . . . . . . . . . . . . . . . . . Maggie
   0:12—In bra by stream after taking off her blouse.
  ••• 0:18—Nude, while making love with Wyatt in front
    of fireplace.
  • 0:24—Brief right breast, while sitting up in bed. Brief
    right breast, while putting on blouse.

## Kaprisky, Valerie
*Films:*
**Aphrodite** (1982; German/French) . . . . . . . . . Pauline
  ••• 0:12—Nude, washing herself off in front of a two-
    way mirror while a man on the other side watches.
**Breathless** (1983) . . . . . . . . . . . . . . Monica Poiccard
   0:23—Brief side view of left breast in her apartment.
    Long shot, hard to see anything.
  ••• 0:47—Breasts in her apartment with Richard Gere
    kissing.
  •• 0:52—Brief full frontal nudity standing in the shower
    when Gere opens the door, afterwards, buns in bed.
  • 0:53—Breasts, holding up two dresses for Gere to
    pick from, then breasts putting the black dress on.
  • 1:23—Breasts behind a movie screen with Gere. Lit
    with red light.
**L'Annee Des Meduses** (1987; French). . . . . . . . . Chris
  •• 0:06—Breasts pulling down swimsuit at the beach.
  ••• 0:24—Full frontal nudity while taking off dress with
    older man.
  ••• 0:42—Breasts walking around the beach talking to
    everybody.
  •• 0:46—Breasts on the beach taking a shower.
  ••• 1:02—Breasts on the beach with her mom.
  ••• 1:37—Nude dancing on the boat for Romain.
  •• 1:42—Breasts walking from the beach to the bar.
  •• 1:43—Breasts in swimming pool.
*Magazines:*
**Playboy** (Dec 1983) . . . . . . . . . . . . . Sex Stars of 1983
  •• 209—Breasts.

## Kapture, Mitzi
*Films:*
**Private Road** (1987) . . . . . . . . . . . . . . Helen Milshaw
   0:50—Wearing a white bra during a strip-spin-the-
    bottle game.
  •• 1:29—Nude, while making love in bed with Greg
    Evigan.
Angel III: The Final Chapter (1988) . . . . . . Molly Stewart
**Lethal Pursuit** (1989) . . . . . . . . . . . . . . . . . Debra J.
  •• 0:32—Breasts in motel shower, then getting out.
    (You can see the top of her swimsuit bottom.)
   0:47—In wet tank top talking with Warren.
Liberty & Bash (1989) . . . . . . . . . . . . . . . . . . . . Sarah
   0:45—Very briefly sitting up in bed in a semi-trans-
    parent yellow sheet.
The Vagrant (1992) . . . . . . . . . . . . . . . . . . Edie Roberts
*TV:*
Silk Stalkings (1991- ) . . . . . . . . . . . . . . Rita Lee Lance

# • *Karasun, May*

*Films:*
**Lake Consequence** (1992) . . . . . . . . . . . . . . . . Grace
(Unrated version reviewed.)
- • 0:24—Brief breasts, coming up for air from under water in lake.
- •• 0:25—Breasts, getting out of the water to get Joan Severance.
- ••• 0:26—Breasts, lying on float in the middle of the lake with Severance.
- ••• 0:28—Full frontal nudity and brief buns, diving into the lake.
- •• 0:29—Buns and breasts, greeting Billy Zane after getting out of the lake.
- • 0:30—Full frontal nudity, drying herself off and getting dressed. Long shot.
- • 0:47—Left breast, while making out with Xiao in bar.
- ••• 0:50—Breasts close-up getting acupuncture.
- •• 0:53—Breasts, walking to spa.
- •• 0:55—Breasts in spa with Severance and Zane.
- •• 0:57—Right breast while making love with Zane in spa.

**Secret Games 3** (1994) . . . . . . . . . . . . . . . . . . . . n.a.

# *Karin, Anna*

*Films:*
Body of Influence (1992) . . . . . . . . . . . . . . . . . . . Beth
**Wild Cactus** (1992) . . . . . . . . . . . . . . . . . . . . . . Inga
(Unrated version reviewed.)
- ••• 0:09—In black lingerie, then breasts and buns after undressing and making love on bed with Randall.
- ••• 0:14—Breasts while tied by her wrists to the bed by Randall.

Martial Outlaw (1993) . . . . . . . . . . . . . . . . . . . Waitress
*Made for Cable Movies:*
**Red Shoe Diaries** (1992; Showtime) . . . . . . . . Heidi #1
(Unrated video tape version reviewed.)
- ••• 1:29—Breasts, three times, making love with Tom.

# *Karina, Anna*

*Films:*
The Oldest Profession (1967) . . . . . . . . . "Anticipation"
**Justine** (1969; Italian/Spanish) . . . . . . . . . . . . . Melissa
- •• 0:13—Half of right breast, while fooling around in bed with Michael York.

Cayenne Palace (1989; French) . . . . . . . . . . . . . . . Lola

# *Kârkkâinen, Kata*

*Video Tapes:*
**Sexy Lingerie** (1988) . . . . . . . . . . . . . . . . . . . . Model
*Magazines:*
**Playboy** (Dec 1988) . . . . . . . . . . . . . . . . . . . Playmate
**Playboy's Nudes** (Oct 1990) . . . . . . . . . . . . . . Herself
- ••• 78-79—Full frontal nudity.

**Playboy Presents International Playmates**
(Feb 1992) . . . . . . . . . . . . . . . . . . . . . . . . . . Herself
- ••• 3-9—Nude.

**Playboy's Wet & Wild Women** (Aug 1993) . . Herself
- • 5—Right breast.

# *Karlatos, Olga*

*Films:*
**Wifemistress** (1977; Italian)
. . . . . . . . . . . . . . . . . . . . . Miss Paula Pagano, M.D.
- •• 0:42—Breasts undressing in room with Laura Antonelli. Right breast and part of left breast lying in bed with Marcello Mastroianni.
- • 0:46—Brief breasts in bed with Mastroianni and Clara.

**Zombie** (1980) . . . . . . . . . . . . . . . . . . . . . Mrs. Menard
- • 0:40—Breasts and buns taking a shower.

**Once Upon a Time in America** (1984)
. . . . . . . . . . . . . . . . . . Woman in the Puppet Theatre
(Long version reviewed.)
- •• 0:11—Right breast twice when bad guy pokes at her nipple with a gun.

*Made for TV Movies:*
The Scarlet and the Black (1983) . . Francesca Lombardo

# *Karman, Janice*

*Films:*
Switchblade Sisters (1975) . . . . . . . . . . . . . . . . . Bunnie
**Slumber Party '57** (1976) . . . . . . . . . . . . . . . . . Hank
- •• 1:06—Breasts, sitting watching Smitty and David make love in the stable.

# *Karr, Marcia*

*Films:*
The Concrete Jungle (1982) . . . . . . . . . . . . . . . . Marcy
**Chained Heat** (1983; U.S./German) . . . . . . . . . Twinks
- ••• 0:30—Breasts, getting soaped up by Edy Williams in the shower.
- • 0:37—Brief breasts, taking off her top in bed with Edy Williams at night.
- •• 0:40—Breasts in cell getting raped by the guard.

Hardbodies (1984) . . . . . . . . . . . . . . Hardbody On Stairs
Real Genius (1985) . . . . . . . . . . . . . Cornell's Girl At Party
Savage Streets (1985) . . . . . . . . . . . . . . . . . . . . Stevie
**Sex Appeal** (1986) . . . . . . . . . . . . . . . . . . . . Christina
- • 1:12—Brief left breast, then in bra and panties on bed with her boyfriend.

**Killer Workout** (1987) . . . . . . . . . . . . . . . . . . Rhonda
*a.k.a. Aerobi-Cide*
1:03—Breasts, opening her jacket to show the policeman her scars. Unappealing.
1:12—Breasts in locker room, killing a guy. Covered with the special effects scars.
The Nightstalker (1987) . . . . . . . . . . . . . . . . . H.J. Salters
Maniac Cop (1988) . . . . . . . . . . . . . . . . . . . . . . Nancy
Night of the Kickfighters (1990) . . . . . . . . . . . . Kedesha

# *Kasdorf, Lenore*

*Films:*
Dark Horse (1984) . . . . . . . . . . . . . . . . . . . . . . Alice
**Missing in Action** (1984) . . . . . . . . . . . . . . . . . Ann
- • 0:41—Very brief breasts when Chuck Norris sneaks back in room and jumps into bed with her.

L.A. Bounty (1989) . . . . . . . . . . . . . . . . . Kelly Rhodes
Kid (1990) . . . . . . . . . . . . . . . . . . . . . . . . . . . Alice

Nervous Ticks (1991) . . . . . . . . . . . . . . . . . . . . . Katie
*Made for Cable Movies:*
Dinner At Eight (1989) . . . . . . . . . . . . . . . . . . . . Lucy
*Made for TV Movies:*
A Murderous Affair: The Carolyn Warmus Story (1992)
. . . . . . . . . . . . . . . . . . . . . . . . . . . . . . . . . . . . .n.a.
*TV:*
The Guiding Light . . . . . . . . . . . . . . . . Rita Stapleton

## Kastner, Daphna

*Films:*
Eating (1990) . . . . . . . . . . . . . . . . . . . . . . . . . . .Jennifer
**Julia Has Two Lovers** (1990) . . . . . . . . . . . . . . . Julia
- 0:11—Brief breasts, changing blouses while talking on the telephone.
- 0:25—Partial left breast, while in bubble bath.
- 0:29—Right breast, while in bubble bath.
- 0:30—Breasts in mirror, getting out of bathtub.
- 0:53—Left breast, while lying in bed with David Duchovny. Long shot.
Venice/Venice (1992) . . . . . . . . . . . . . . . . . . . . . Eve

## • Kates, Kimberly

a.k.a. Kimberly La Belle.
*Films:*
Winners Take All (1987). . . . . . . . . . . . . . . Party Girl #1
Dangerous Love (1988). . . . . . . . . . . . . . . . . . . Susan
**Chained Heat 2** (1993) . . . . . . . . Alexandra Morrison
••• 0:30—Full frontal nudity, while in the shower with Tina.
- 0:56—Buns, in G-string under sheer blue dress during casino party.
•• 1:04—Breasts, while sitting up in bed and getting out. Wearing panties and stockings.

## Kath, Camelia

Ex-wife of actor Kiefer Sutherland.
*Films:*
Nevada Heat (1982) . . . . . . . . . . . . . . . . . . . . . Voice #4
a.k.a. Fake-Out
**The Killing Time** (1987). . . . . . . . . . . . Laura Winslow
- 0:32—Very brief right breast, while making love with Beau Bridges. Hard to see anything. Dark, lit with red light.
- 0:43—Brief breasts lying in bed getting photographed with Beau Bridges to frame Kiefer Sutherland for a murder.

## Katon, Rosanne

*Films:*
**The Swinging Cheerleaders** (1974). . . . . . . . . . .Lisa
•• 0:25—Breasts taking off her blouse in her teacher's office. Half of right breast while he talks on the phone.
**Chesty Anderson, U.S. Navy** (1975). . . . . . . . .Cocoa
0:02—In bra with the other girls in barracks.
•• 0:40—Breasts when bra pops open during fight in barracks.

Fox Fire (1976). . . . . . . . . . . . . . . . . . . . . . . . . . n.a.
a.k.a. Fox Force
**Coach** (1978) . . . . . . . . . . . . . . . . . . . . . . . . . . Sue
- 0:10—Very brief breasts flashing her breasts along with three of her girlfriends for their four boyfriends.
Motel Hell (1980). . . . . . . . . . . . . . . . . . . . . . . . Suzi
**Body and Soul** (1981) . . . . . . . . . . . . . . . . . Melody
- 0:04—Left breast several times making love in restroom with Leon Isaac Kennedy.
**Lunch Wagon** (1981) . . . . . . . . . . . . . . . . Shannon
a.k.a. Lunch Wagon Girls
a.k.a. Come 'N' Get It
- 0:01—Brief breasts getting dressed.
- 0:04—Brief side view of left breast changing tops in room in gas station with Pamela Bryant while a guy watches through key hole.
•• 0:10—Breasts changing again in gas station.
Zapped! (1982) . . . . . . . . . . . . . . . . . . . . . . . . .Donna
Bachelor Party (1984). . . . . . . . . . Bridal Shower Hooker
Harem (1985; French) . . . . . . . . . . . . . . . . . . . . .Judy
*Magazines:*
**Playboy** (Sep 1978) . . . . . . . . . . . . . . . . . . Playmate
**Playboy** (Jan 1980). . . . . . . . . Playboy's Pajama Parties
••• 125—Breasts, standing in a tree.
**Playboy** (Nov 1980) . . . . . . . . . .The World of Playboy
•• 12—Breasts.
**Playboy** (Jul 1981) . . . . . . . . . . . Body and Soulmates
•• 148—Left breast.
**Playboy** (Jun 1991). . . . . . . . . . . . . . . Funny Girls
••• 97—Full frontal nudity in lingerie.
**Playboy's Career Girls** (Aug 1992). . . . . . Funny Girls
••• 28—Full frontal nudity.

## Kaye, Caren

*Films:*
Checkmate (1973) . . . . . . . . . . . . . . . . . . . . . . . .Alex
The Lords of Flatbush (1974) . . . . . . . . . Wedding Guest
Looking for Mr. Goodbar (1977) . . . . . . . . . . . . . Rhoda
Kill Castro (1978) . . . . . . . . . . . . . . . . . . . . . . . . Tracy
a.k.a. Cuba Crossing
Some Kind of Hero (1982) . . . . . . . . . . . . . . . . . Sheila
**My Tutor** (1983) . . . . . . . . . . . . . . . . . . Terry Green
•• 0:25—Breasts walking into swimming pool.
•• 0:52—Breasts in the pool with Matt Lattanzi.
••• 0:55—Right breast, lying in bed making love with Lattanzi.
Satan's Princess (1989). . . . . . . . . . . . . . . . . . . . Leah
Teen Witch (1989) . . . . . . . . . . . . . . . . . . . . .Margaret
*Made for TV Movies:*
Poison Ivy (1985). . . . . . . . . . . . . . . . . . . . . . . .Margo
*TV:*
The Betty White Show (1977-78) . . . . . . . . Tracy Garrett
Blansky's Beauties (1977) . . . . . . . . . . . . . Bambi Benton
Who's Watching the Kids? (1978) . . . . . . . Stacy Turner
Empire (1984) . . . . . . . . . . . . . . . . . . . . . . . . Meredith
It's Your Move (1984-85) . . . . . . . . . . . . .Eileen Burton

# Kaye, Wendy

*Films:*

**Miracle Beach** (1991). . . . . . . . . . . . . . . . Girl in Bed
- 0:14—Breasts, lying in bed next to Scotty, then sitting up. She's on the left.

*Video Tapes:*

**Playboy Video Centerfold: Morgan Fox** (1991)
. . . . . . . . . . . . . . . . . . . . . . . . . . . . . . . . Playmate
- ••• 0:27—Nude in different settings.
- ••• 0:30—Nude in American-theme song and dance number.
- ••• 0:31—Breasts and buns in G-string at the beach.
- ••• 0:33—Full frontal nudity in still photos.
- ••• 0:34—Nude while dancing.

**Wet and Wild III** (1991). . . . . . . . . . . . . . . . .Model
**The Best of Sexy Lingerie** (1992). . . . . . . . . . .Model
**The Best of Wet and Wild** (1992) . . . . . . . . .Model
**Playboy Video Calendar 1993** (1992) . . . . . . . . .July
- ••• 0:28—Nude at the beach.
- ••• 0:30—Nude in building with graffiti on the walls.

**Playboy's Playmate Review 1992** (1992) . . Miss July
- ••• 0:36—Nude in patriotic scene and then in a surreal scene.

**Sexy Lingerie IV** (1992) . . . . . . . . . . . . . . . .Model
**Sexy Lingerie V** (1992) . . . . . . . . . . . . . . . . .Model
**Wet and Wild IV** (1992) . . . . . . . . . . . . . . . .Model

*Magazines:*

**Playboy** (Jul 1991). . . . . . . . . . . . . . . . . . . . Playmate
- ••• 88-110—Nude.

**Playboy's Career Girls** (Aug 1992)
. . . . . . . . . . . . . . . . . . . . . . . . . Baywatch Playmates
- ••• 8—Full frontal nudity.

**Playboy's Book of Lingerie** (Nov 1992) . . . . . Herself
- •• 14—Right breast and lower frontal nudity.

**Playboy's Nudes** (Dec 1992) . . . . . . . . . . . . . Herself
- ••• 48—Breasts.

**Playboy's Book of Lingerie** (Jan 1993) . . . . . . Herself
- •• 10—Left breast and partial lower frontal nudity.

**Playboy** (Feb 1993) . . . . . . . . . . . Being in Nothingness
- ••• 132—Buns.

**Playboy's Girls of Summer '93** (Jun 1993) . . . Herself
- ••• 74-75—Full frontal nudity.
- ••• 88—Full frontal nudity.
- •• 102—Buns.

**Playboy's Book of Lingerie** (Jul 1993) . . . . . . Herself
- ••• 21—Full frontal nudity.

**Playboy's Book of Lingerie** (Sep 1993) . . . . . Herself
- •• 9—Upper half of breasts in push-up bra.

**Playboy's Video Playmates** (Sep 1993) . . . . . Herself
- ••• 58-59—Nude.

**Playboy's Book of Lingerie** (Nov 1993) . . . . . Herself
- ••• 61—Full frontal nudity.

**Playboy's Bathing Beauties** (Mar 1994) . . . . . Herself
- ••• 10—Breasts.
- ••• 50-51—Breasts and buns.

**Playboy Presents Playmates in Paradise**
(Mar 1994) . . . . . . . . . . . . . . . . . . . . . . . . Playmate
- ••• 9-19—Nude.

**Playboy's Book of Lingerie** (May 1994) . . . . . Herself
- ••• 19—Full frontal nudity.
- • 57—Lower frontal nudity. Right breast under black fishnet top.

**Playmates at Play** (Jul 1994) . . . . . . . . . . . . . Herself
- •• 47—Left breast and partial lower frontal nudity.
- ••• 88-91—Nude.

**Playboy's Girls of Summer '94** (Jul 1994) . . . . Herself
- ••• 7—Full frontal nudity.
- ••• 28-29—Nude.
- ••• 68-69—Full frontal nudity.
- ••• 98—Full frontal nudity.

# Kaye-Mason, Clarissa

*Films:*

**Age of Consent** (1969; Australian) . . . . . . . . . . Meg
- 0:05—Brief breasts, crawling on the bed to watch TV.

**Adam's Women** (1972; Australian) . . . . . . . . . . Matron
**The Good Wife** (1987; Australian) . . . . . . . Mrs. Jackson
*a.k.a. The Umbrella Woman*

# Keaton, Camille

*Films:*

**I Spit on Your Grave** (1978) . . . . . . . . . . . . . Jennifer
(Uncut, unrated version reviewed.)
- 0:05—Breasts undressing to go skinny dipping in lake.
- •• 0:23—Left breast sticking out of bathing suit top, then breasts after top is ripped off. Right breast several times.
- 0:25—Breasts, getting raped by the jerks.
- 0:27—Buns and brief full frontal nudity, crawling away from the jerks.
- 0:29—Nude, walking through the woods.
- 0:32—Breasts, getting raped again.
- 0:36—Breasts and buns after rape.
- 0:38—Buns, walking to house.
- 0:40—Buns and lower frontal nudity in the house.
- 0:41—More breasts and buns on the floor.
- 0:45—Nude, very dirty after all she's gone through.
- 0:51—Full frontal nudity while lying on the floor.
- 0:52—Side of left breast while in bathtub.
- •• 1:13—Full frontal nudity seducing Matthew before killing him.
- ••• 1:23—Full frontal nudity in front of mirror, then getting into bathtub. Long scene.

**Raw Force** (1981). . . . . . . . . . . . . . . . . . .Girl in Toilet
- •• 0:28—Breasts in bathroom with a guy.
- •• 0:29—Breasts in bathroom again with the guy.
- •• 0:31—Breasts in bathroom again when he rips her pants off.

**The Concrete Jungle** (1982). . . . . . . . . . . . . . . . Rita
- 0:41—In black bra, then breasts getting raped by Stone. Brief lower frontal nudity sitting up afterwards.

# Keaton, Diane

*Films:*

Lovers and Other Strangers (1970) . . . . . . . . . . . . . Joan
The Godfather (1972) . . . . . . . . . . . . . . . . . Kay Adams
Play It Again, Sam (1972) . . . . . . . . . . . . Linda Christie
Sleeper (1973) . . . . . . . . . . . . . . . . . . . . . . . Luna
The Godfather, Part II (1974) . . . . . . . . . . . Kay Adams
Love and Death (1975) . . . . . . . . . . . . . . . . . . Sonja
Harry and Walter Go to New York (1976)
. . . . . . . . . . . . . . . . . . . . . . . . . . . Lissa Chestnut
I Will, I Will... For Now (1976) . . . . . . . . Katie Bingham
Annie Hall (1977) . . . . . . . . . . . . . . . . . . . Annie Hall
(Academy Award for Best Actress.)
**Looking for Mr. Goodbar** (1977) . . . . . . . . . .Theresa
•• 0:11—Right breast in bed making love with her
teacher, Martin, then putting blouse on.
• 0:31—Brief left breast over the shoulder when the
Doctor playfully kisses her breast.
• 1:04—Brief breasts smoking in bed in the morning,
then more breasts after Richard Gere leaves.
••• 1:17—Breasts making love with Gere after doing a
lot of cocaine.
• 1:31—Brief breasts in the bathtub when James
brings her a glass of wine.
2:00—Getting out of bed in a bra.
•• 2:02—Breasts during rape by Tom Berenger, before
he kills her. Hard to see because of strobe lights.
Interiors (1978) . . . . . . . . . . . . . . . . . . . . . Renata
Manhattan (1979) . . . . . . . . . . . . . . . . . . Mary Wilke
**Reds** (1981) . . . . . . . . . . . . . . . . . . . . . Louise Bryant
• 0:50—Buns, while standing in the water with Jack
Nicholson at night. Very long shot.
Shoot the Moon (1982) . . . . . . . . . . . . . .Faith Dunlap
The Little Drummer Girl (1984) . . . . . . . . . . . . Charlie
Mrs. Soffel (1984) . . . . . . . . . . . . . . . . . . Kate Soffel
Crimes of the Heart (1986) . . . . . . . . . .Lenny Magrath
Baby Boom (1987) . . . . . . . . . . . . . . . . . . J.C. Wiatt
Radio Days (1987) . . . . . . . . . . . . . . New Year's Singer
The Good Mother (1988) . . . . . . . . . . . . . . . . .Anna
The Godfather, Part III (1990) . . . . . . . . . . . Kay Adams
The Lemon Sisters (1990) . . . . . . . . . . . .Eloise Hamer
Father of the Bride (1991) . . . . . . . . . . . . . Nina Banks
Manhattan Murder Mystery (1993) . . . . . . . Carol Lipton
*Made for Cable Movies:*
Running Mates (1992; HBO) . . . . . . . . . . . Aggie Snow
Amelia Earhart: The Final Flight (1994; TNT)
. . . . . . . . . . . . . . . . . . . . . . . . . . . Amelia Earhart

# • Keats, Ele

*Films:*

Frankie & Johnny (1991) . . . . . . . . . . . . . . . .Artemis
Liebestraum (1991) . . . . . . . . . . . Actress on Soap Opera
(Unrated Director's cut reviewed.)
The Rocketeer (1991) . . . . . . . . . . . . . Girl at Newstand
Alive (1992) . . . . . . . . . . . . . . . . . .Susana Parrado
Newsies (1992) . . . . . . . . . . . . . . . . . . Sarah Jacobs
**Lipstick Camera** (1993) . . . . . . . . . . . . . Omy Clark
• 0:57—In bra, while making out with Flynn, then left
breast while lying back with him.

# Kedes, Maureen

*Films:*

**Captive Rage** (1988) . . . . . . . . . . . . . . . . . . . . .Jan
•• 0:31—Breasts, getting chained to bed and raped by
guards.
*Made for Cable TV:*
**Dream On: The Son Also Rises** (1992; HBO). . . Celia
0:01—In black bra, in bed with Martin.
••• 0:03—Breasts in bed while Martin looks for a con-
dom.

# Keisha

Adult film actress.
*Video Tapes:*
**High Society Centerspread Video #11: Keisha**
(1990) . . . . . . . . . . . . . . . . . . . . . . . . . . Herself
**Big Bust Casting Call** (1992) . . . . . . . . . . . . . Keisha
••• 0:40—In sexy swimsuit in spa, then breasts after tak-
ing off her top. (Wearing sunglasses.)
**Penthouse Satin & Lace: An Erotic History of**
**Lingerie** (1992) . . . . . . . . . . . . . . . . . . . . . . Model

# Keller, Marthe

*Films:*

And Now My Love (1974; French)
. . . . . . . . . . . . . Sarah/Her Mother/Her Grandmother
**Marathon Man** (1976) . . . . . . . . . . . . . . . . . . . Elsa
•• 0:42—Breasts lying on the floor after Dustin Hoff-
man rolls off her.
Black Sunday (1977) . . . . . . . . . . . . . . . . . . Dahlia
Bobby Deerfield (1977) . . . . . . . . . . . . . . . . .Lillian
The Formula (1980) . . . . . . . . . . . . . . . . . . . Lisa
The Amateur (1982) . . . . . . . . . . . . . . . . . Elisabeth
Wagner (1983; British) . . . . . . . . . Mathilde Wesedonck
Red Kiss (1985; French) . . . . . . . . . . . . . . .Bronka
Femmes de Persone (1986; French) . . . . . . . . . . Cecile
Dark Eyes (1987; Italian/Russian) . . . . . . . . . . . .Tina
*Made for Cable Movies:*
The Nightmare Years (1989) . . . . . . . . . . . . . . . Tess
Young Catherine (1991) . . . . . . . . . . . . . . . .Johanna

# Kellerman, Sally

*Films:*

The Boston Strangler (1968) . . . . . . . . . . .Dianne Cluny
The April Fool's (1969) . . . . . . . . . . . . . Phyllis Brubaker
**Brewster McCloud** (1970) . . . . . . . . . . . . . . Louise
0:43—Brief back side of right breast giving a boy a
bath.
•• 1:07—Breasts, playing in a fountain.
**M•A•S•H** (1970) . . . . . . . Margaret "Hot Lips" Houlihan
• 0:42—Very, very brief left breast opening her blouse
for Frank in her tent.
• 1:11—Very, very brief buns and side view of right
breast during shower prank. Long shot, hard to see.
• 1:54—Very brief breasts in a slightly different angle
of the shower prank during the credits.
Last of the Red Hot Lovers (1972) . . . . . .Elaine Navazio
Reflection of Fear (1973) . . . . . . . . . . . . . . . . Anne

Rafferty and the Gold Dust Twins (1975)
. . . . . . . . . . . . . . . . . . . . . . . . . . .Mac Beachwood
The Big Bus (1976) . . . . . . . . . . . . . . . . . .Sybil Crane
Welcome to L.A. (1977) . . . . . . . . . . . . . . .Ann Goode
A Little Romance (1979) . . . . . . . . . . . . . . .Kay King
Foxes (1980). . . . . . . . . . . . . . . . . . . . . . . . . .Mary
**Serial** (1980) . . . . . . . . . . . . . . . . . . . . . . .Martha
••• 0:03—Breasts sitting on the floor with a guy.
**Fatal Attraction** (1981; Canadian). . . . . Michelle Keys
*a.k.a. Head On*
   • 0:46—Brief breasts in building making out with a
      guy. Dark, hard to see.
      1:19—Brief half of left breast, after struggling with a
      guy.
You Can't Hurry Love (1984). . . . . . . . . . . . .Kelly Bones
Moving Violations (1985) . . . . . Judge Nedra Henderson
Back to School (1986). . . . . . . . . . . . . . . . . . . . Diane
That's Life! (1986) . . . . . . . . . . . . . . . . . . Holly Parrish
Meatballs III (1987). . . . . . . . . . . . . . . . . Roxy Du Jour
Three for the Road (1987). . . . . . . . . . . . . . . Blanche
Doppelganger: The Evil Within (1992) . . . . . . .Sister Jan
The Player (1992) . . . . . . . . . . . . . . . . . . . . . Cameo
*Made for Cable Movies:*
Boris and Natasha (1992; Showtime) . . . Natasha Fatale
*Made for Cable TV:*
Dream On: Blinded By the Cheese (1994; HBO) . . Tracy
      0:20—Back half of right breast on top of Martin in
      bed.
*Made for TV Movies:*
Secret Weapons (1985). . . . . . . . . . . . . . .Vera Malevich
*TV:*
Centennial (1978-79) . . . . . . . . . . . . . . . .Lise Bockweiss
*Magazines:*
**Playboy** (Dec 1980). . . . . . . . . . . . . Sex Stars of 1980
   •• 243—Breasts still from *Serial*.

## Kelley, Sheila

*Films:*
**Some Girls** (1988). . . . . . . . . . . . . . . . . . . . . . . Irenka
*a.k.a. Sisters*
   • 0:13—Breasts and buns getting something at the
      end of the hall while Michael watches. Long shot,
      hard to see.
   • 1:01—Breasts in window while Michael watches
      from outside. Long shot, hard to see.
      1:17—In black slip seducing Michael after funeral.
Breaking In (1989) . . . . . . . . . . . . . . . . . . . . . . . Carrie
      0:51—In white body suit in bed with Casey Siemasz-
      ko.
Mortal Passions (1989) . . . . . . . . . . . . . . . . . . . . Adele
Staying Together (1989) . . . . . . . . . . . . . . Beth Harper
Where the Heart Is (1990). . . . . . . . . . . . . . . . . Sheryl
Pure Luck (1991). . . . . . . . . . . . . Valerie Highsmith
Soapdish (1991) . . . . . . . . . . . . . . . . . . . . . . . . Fran
singles (1992) . . . . . . . . . . . . . . . . . . . . . . . . Debbie
Passion Fish (1993) . . . . . . . . . . . . . . . . . . . . . . Kim
*Made for Cable Movies:*
Deconstructing Sarah (1994; USA) . . . . . . . . . . . Sarah

*Made for TV Movies:*
The Fulfillment of Mary Gray (1989) . . . . . . . . . . .Kate
*TV:*
L.A. Law (1990-94) . . . . . . . . . . . . . . . . . Gwen Taylor

## Kelly, Moira

*Films:*
Billy Bathgate (1991) . . . . . . . . . . . . . . . . . . .Rebecca
**Chaplin** (1992; British/U.S.) . . Hetty Kelly/Oona O'Neill
   •• 0:20—Brief breasts, while changing in dressing
      room when surprised by Chaplin.
The Cutting Edge (1992) . . . . . . . . . . . . . .Kate Moseley
**Twin Peaks: Fire Walk With Me** (1992)
. . . . . . . . . . . . . . . . . . . . . . . . . . Donna Hayward
   •• 1:22—Breasts, while lying on table in cabin.
With Honors (1994) . . . . . . . . . . . . . . . . . . . . . . n.a.
*Made for Cable Movies:*
**Daybreak** (1993; HBO) . . . . . . . . . . . . . . . . . . . .Blue
   ••• 0:43—Right breast, then breasts while making out
      with Cuba Gooding Jr.
   ••• 1:14—Breasts when Gooding has to take her top off
      in front of a guard.
*Made for TV Movies:*
Love, Lies and Murder (1991) . . . . . . Cinnamon Brown

## Kelly, Paula

*Films:*
**Sweet Charity** (1969) . . . . . . . . . . . . . . . . . . . .Helene
The Andromeda Strain (1971) . . . . . . . . . . . . . . Nurse
Cool Breeze (1972) . . . . . . . . . . . . . . . . . . . .Mrs. Harris
**Top of the Heap** (1972) . . . . . . . . . . . . . . . . . Singer
Trouble Man (1973). . . . . . . . . . . . . . . . . . . . . . .Cleo
Uptown Saturday Night (1974) . . . . . . . . Leggy Peggy
Drum (1976) . . . . . . . . . . . . . . . . . . . . . . . . . . Rachel
Jo Jo Dancer, Your Life Is Calling (1986) . . . . . Satin Doll
      0:26—Doing a strip tease in the night club wearing
      gold pasties and a gold G-string.
Bank Robber (1993) . . . . . . . . . . . . . . . . . . . . Mother
*Miniseries:*
Chiefs (1983). . . . . . . . . . . . . . . . . . . . . . . Liz Watts
*TV:*
Night Court (1984) . . . . . . . . . . . . . . . . . Liz Williams
Room For Two (1992-93). . . . . . . . . . Diahnn Boudreau
South Central (1994- ) . . . . . . . . . . . . . . . . . . . .Sweets
*Magazines:*
**Playboy** (Aug 1969) . . . . . . . . . . . . . . . . . .Sweet Paula
      Debut of pubic hair in *Playboy* magazine.
**Playboy** (Jul 1972) . . . . . . . . . . . . . . . . . . . Too Much
   ••• 138—Breasts.
   ••• 140-141—Breasts.
**Playboy** (Nov 1972) . . . . . . . . . Sex in Cinema 1972
   •• 163—Breasts in photo from *Top of the Heap*.
**Playboy** (Jan 1974). . . . . . . . . Twenty Years of Playboy
   • 208—Nude in strobe light photo.
**Playboy** (Jan 1979). . . . . . . . . . . . . . . 25 Beautiful Years
   •• 160-161—Breasts strobe photo from Aug 1969.
**Playboy** (Jan 1989). . . . . . . . . . .Women of the Sixties
   •• 160-161—Breasts strobe photo from Aug 1969.

# Kelly, Robyn

*Films:*

**Flesh Gordon 2** (1990; Canadian) . . . . . . . Dale Ardor
- •• 0:24—Brief breasts in push-up bra when Dr. Jerkoff rips her jacket open.
- • 0:49—Brief buns, while acting like a dog on all fours on the floor.

Ultimate Desires (1991). . . . . . . . . . . . . . . . . .Streetgirl
*a.k.a. Silhouette*

# Kelly, Sharon

a.k.a. Adult film actress Colleen Brennan.

*Films:*

**The Beauties and the Beast** (1973) . . . . . . . . . . .n.a.
Nude, being carried into a cave by the beast.

**Innocent Sally** (1973). . . . . . . . . . . . . . . . . . . . Sally
*a.k.a. The Dirty Mind of Young Sally*
- ••• 0:35—Breasts, undressing in back of van. Long scene.
- ••• 0:37—Full frontal nudity, on pillow in back of van while caressing herself. Another long scene.
- ••• 0:39—More full frontal nudity in van.
- ••• 0:47—Right breast, then full frontal nudity, making love with Toby in van. Long scene.
- ••• 1:05—Breasts, making love in bed with another guy. Long scene.
- ••• 1:10—Full frontal nudity, making more love. Long scene.
- •• 1:19—Breasts, after making love.
- ••• 1:23—Full frontal nudity, while making love with a guy.

Supervixens (1973). . . . . . . . . . . . . . . . . .SuperCherry

**Delinquent School Girls** (1974) . . . . . . . . . . . Greta
- • 0:05—Left breast in mirror while practicing martial arts.

**Alice Goodbody** (1975) . . . . . . . . . . . Alice Goodbody
- • 0:01—Brief breasts in mirror, getting dressed.
- ••• 0:16—In bra, then full frontal nudity, undressing in Arnold's place. More breasts in the shower with him.
- ••• 0:17—Frontal nudity, while lying in bed and making out with Arnold.
- • 0:27—Breasts with Roger while he eats all sorts of food off her body.
- • 0:28—Breasts, lying in bed with Roger afterwards.
- ••• 0:37—Right breast, then frontal nudity while talking to Rex.
- ••• 0:38—Breasts when Rex carries her to bed and makes love with her, while admiring himself.
- •• 0:47—Breasts with bandages on her face.
- ••• 0:51—Breasts, taking off her robe and getting into bed. (Bandages are still on her face.)
- •• 1:09—Buns, undressing and getting into bed.
- • 1:21—Brief breasts in mirror in bed with Rex during the end credits.

**The Boob Tube** (1975) . . . . . . . . . . . Selma Carpenter
- ••• 0:06—Breasts and buns, trying to seduce Dr. Carstairs.
- ••• 0:10—Breasts and buns, having fun by herself on the bed while Dr. Carstairs watches. Nice close-ups.
- ••• 0:11—More breasts and buns in bed with Dr. Carstairs.
- • 1:03—Breasts under sheer nightie while Harvey checks her sink.
- •• 1:09—Breasts and buns, on sofa, then leaving the room.
- •• 1:11—Breasts and buns, entering the room.
- ••• 1:12—Breasts during orgy on couch.
- • 1:16—Brief breasts in hallway.

Carnal Madness (1975) . . . . . . . . . . . . . . . . . . . . n.a.

**Hustle** (1975) . . . . . . . . . . . . . . . . . . . Gloria Hollinger
- • 0:12—Brief breasts several times getting rolled out of freezer, dead.
- • 1:03—In pasties, dancing behind curtain when Gloria's father imagines the dancer is Gloria.
- • 1:42—In black lingerie, brief buns and side views of breast in bed in film.

**Shampoo** (1975) . . . . . . . . . . . . . . . . . . . Painted Lady
- • 1:17—Brief breasts covered with tattoos all over her body during party. Lit with strobe light.

**Slammer Girls** (1987) . . . . . . . . . . . . . . . . . Professor
- • 0:23—Brief breasts changing clothes under table in the prison cafeteria.
- •• 0:34—Breasts squishing breasts against the window during prison visiting hours.
- •• 0:36—Breasts with an inflatable male doll.

# Kelsey, Tasmin

*Films:*

Who's Harry Crumb? (1989) . . . . . . . . . . . . . . .Marie
Bingo (1991) . . . . . . . . . . . . . . . . . . . . . . . . . . Bunny
**Common Bonds** (1991). . . . . . . . . . . . . . . . . .Ginger
- • 0:04—Breasts in hotel room with the cop when Michael Ironside bursts into the room. Long shot. More out of focus breasts shots in the mirror.

Needful Things (1993) . . . . . . . . . . . . . . . Sheila Ratcliff

# Kemp, Charlotte

See: Helmcamp, Charlotte J.

# Kemp, Elizabeth

*Films:*

**He Knows You're Alone** (1980) . . . . . . . . . . . Nancy
- ••• 1:12—Breasts, taking off robe and taking a shower.

Sticky Fingers (1988) . . . . . . . . . . . . . . . . . . . . Nancy
Eating (1990). . . . . . . . . . . . . . . . . . . . . . . . . . Nancy
Venice/Venice (1992) . . . . . . . . . . . . . . . . Interviewee

# Kendall, Kerri

*Video Tapes:*

**Playboy Video Centerfold: Kerri Kendall** (1990)
. . . . . . . . . . . . . . . . . . . . . . . . . . . . . . . . . Playmate
- ••• 0:00—Nude throughout.

**Wet and Wild II** (1990). . . . . . . . . . . . . . . . . Model
**Playboy Video Calendar 1992** (1991). . . . . . . March
- ••• 0:09—Nude in photo studio.
- ••• 0:10—In bra, then nude in bedroom.

**Sexy Lingerie III** (1991). . . . . . . . . . . . . . . . . Model
**Wet and Wild III** (1991) . . . . . . . . . . . . . . . . Model

**The Best of Sexy Lingerie** (1992) . . . . . . . . . .Model
**The Best of Wet and Wild** (1992) . . . . . . . . .Model
*Magazines:*
**Playboy** (Sep 1990) . . . . . . . . . . . . . . . . . . Playmate
**Playboy's Book of Lingerie** (Jul 1991) . . . . . . Herself
••• 16-17—Full frontal nudity.
**Playboy's Book of Lingerie** (May 1992) . . . . . Herself
••• 34—Full frontal nudity.
**Playboy's Calendar Playmates** (Nov 1992) . . Herself
••• 100—Breasts.
**Playboy's Book of Lingerie** (Nov 1992) . . . . . Herself
••• 10—Full frontal nudity.
**Playboy's Book of Lingerie** (Jan 1993) . . . . . . Herself
••• 63—Breasts.
**Playboy's Book of Lingerie** (Mar 1993) . . . . . Herself
••• 94-95—Full frontal nudity.
**Playboy** (Jul 1993) . . . . . . . . . . . . . . . . . . . .Lucky Stiff
••• 78-83—Nude.
**Playboy's Blondes, Brunettes & Redheads**
(Sep 1993) . . . . . . . . . . . . . . . . . . . . . . . . . . Herself
••• 42—Full frontal nudity.
**Playboy's Book of Lingerie** (Sep 1993) . . . . . Herself
••• 103—Full frontal nudity.
**Playboy's Video Playmates** (Sep 1993) . . . . . Herself
••• 60-63—Full frontal nudity.
**Playboy's Book of Lingerie** (Nov 1993) . . . . . Herself
•• 64—Right breast and buns.
**Playboy's Nudes** (Dec 1993) . . . . . . . . . . . . . Herself
••• 22-23—Full frontal nudity.
**Playboy's Book of Lingerie** (Jan 1994) . . . . . . Herself
••• 33—Breasts.
**Playboy's Bathing Beauties** (Mar 1994) . . . . . Herself
••• 26—Breasts.
•• 32—Left breast.
••• 62—Breasts.
**Playboy Presents Playmates in Paradise**
(Mar 1994) . . . . . . . . . . . . . . . . . . . . . . . . . Playmate
••• 3-7—Nude.
**Playboy's Book of Lingerie** (Mar 1994) . . . . . Herself
••• 54—Full frontal nudity.
••• 64—Left breast and lower frontal nudity.
••• 78-79—Partial left breast in bra, breasts and buns.
**Playboy's Book of Lingerie** (May 1994) . . . . . Herself
••• 15—Breasts.
•• 36—Right breast.
**Playboy's Girls of Summer '94** (Jul 1994) . . . Herself
••• 48—Breasts.
••• 51—Breasts.
**Playboy's Book of Lingerie** (Jul 1994) . . . . . . Herself
•• 8—Lower frontal nudity and breasts under patterned bodysuit.

## • Kennedy, Meredith
*Films:*
**Erotic Images** (1983) . . . . . . . . . . . . . . . . . . . Ginger
•• 1:04—Breasts on the couch with two guys.
**Night Train to Terror** (1985) . . . . . . . Dead Redhead
• 0:16—Right breast, while strapped to gurney, before
getting killed with a saw.

## Kennedy, Sheila
*Films:*
**The First Turn-On!** (1983) . . . . . . . . . . . . . Dreamgirl
• 0:52—In red two piece swimsuit, then breasts when
the top falls down during Danny's daydream.
• 0:59—Right breast, while in bed with Danny.
**Spring Break** (1983; Canadian) . . . . . . . . . . . . . Carla
•• 0:49—Breasts during wet T-shirt contest.
**Ellie** (1984) . . . . . . . . . . . . . . . . . . . . . . . . . Ellie May
•• 0:29—Full frontal nudity posing for Billy while he
takes pictures of her just before he falls over a cliff.
0:38—In white bra and panties, in barn loft with
Frank.
0:58—In white bra and panties struggling to get
away from Edward Albert.
• 1:16—In bra and panties taking off dress with Art.
Breasts taking off bra and throwing them on antlers.
Brief breasts many times while frolicking around.
**Dead Boyz Can't Fly** (1992) . . . . . . . . . . . . . Lorraine
• 0:00—Breasts and buns in G-string, while dancing in
smoke filled club.
•• 0:16—Buns in G-string and breasts, while dancing in
club.
*Magazines:*
**Penthouse** (Dec 1981) . . . . . . . . . . . . . . . . . . . . . .Pet
**Penthouse** (Sep 1983) . . . . . . . Pet of the Year Play-Off
•• 64-65—Nude.
**Penthouse** (Dec 1983) . . . . . . . . . . . . . .Pet of the Year
••• 115-130—Nude.
**Penthouse** (Oct 1987) . . . . . . . . . . . . Sheila Revisited

## Kennell, Kari
See: Whitman, Kari.

## Kensit, Patsy
Was the lead singer in the British group *Eighth Wonder.*
*Films:*
The Great Gatsby (1974) . . . . . . . . . . Daisy's Daughter
Oh, Alfie! (1975; British) . . . . . . . . . . . . . . . . . . . Penny
*a.k.a. Alfie Darling*
Hanover Street (1979) . . . . . . . . . . . . . .Sarah Sallinger
Absolute Beginners (1986; British) . . . . . . Crepe Suzette
Chicago Joe and the Showgirl (1989; British)
. . . . . . . . . . . . . . . . . . . . . . . . . . . . . . . Joyce Cook
**Lethal Weapon 2** (1989) . . . . . . . . .Rika Van Den Haas
•• 1:15—Right breast lying in bed with Mel Gibson.
•• 1:19—Breasts in bed with Gibson.
Blue Tornado (1990) . . . . . . . . . . . . . . . . . . . Christina
Bullseye! (1990) . . . . . . . . . . . . . . . . Sick Lady on Train
Kill Cruise (1990; German) . . . . . . . . . . . . . . . . . . . Su
**Timebomb** (1990) . . . . . . . . . . . . . . Dr. Anna Nolmar
•• 1:15—Breasts, mostly left breast, making love with
Michael Biehn in bed. Partial buns also.
The Skipper (1991) . . . . . . . . . . . . . . . . . . . . . . . n.a.
**Twenty-One** (1991) . . . . . . . . . . . . . . . . . . . . . Katie
••• 1:17—Breasts in reflection in bathroom mirror un-
dressing, then dressing.

Blame It on the Bellboy (1992; British)
. . . . . . . . . . . . . . . . . . . . . . . . . Caroline Wright
0:35—Briefly in black lace body suit.
0:37—More in black lace body suit.
The Turn of the Screw (1992; British) . . . . . . . . . Jenny
**Bitter Harvest** (1993). . . . . . . . . . . . . . . Jolene Leder
••• 0:40—In black bodysuit, then left breast while making love with Stephen Baldwin in bed. Breasts in bathtub.
• 0:41—Left breast, while lying in bathtub with Baldwin.
•• 0:49—Brief breasts in bed with Baldwin and Jennifer Rubin.
*Made for Cable Movies:*
Full Eclipse (1993; HBO) . . . . . . . . . . . . Casey Spencer
0:48—Brief back half of left breast, when starting to make love with Mario Van Peebles.
1:01—Almost breasts on the floor under Adam.
*Made for Cable TV:*
Tales From the Crypt: As Ye Sow (1993; HBO). . . Bridget
*Made for TV Movies:*
Silas Marner (1985; British) . . . . . . . . . . . . . . . . . . Eppie
Masterpiece Theatre: Adam Bede (1992). . . Hetty Sorrel
Fall From Grace (1994) . . . . . . . . . . . . . . . . . . . Deidre

# Kenton, Linda

*Films:*
**Hot Resort** (1984). . . . . . . . . . . . Mrs. Geraldine Miller
• 0:11—Very brief right breast, while in back of car with a guy.
• 0:16—Right breast, while passed out in closet with a bunch of guys.
• 0:24—Brief upper half of right breast, while on boat with a guy.
• 0:46—Brief breasts in Volkswagen.
• 0:51—Brief breasts in bathtub with Bronson Pinchot.
• 1:24—Brief breasts making love on a table while covered with food.
*Magazines:*
**Penthouse** (May 1983). . . . . . . . . . . . . . . . . . . . . . Pet
••• 83-101—Nude.
**Penthouse** (Aug 1983) . . . . . . . . Penthouse Feedback
•• 190—Breasts in small photo.
**Playboy** (Nov 1985) . . . . . . . . . . Sex in Cinema 1985
• 129—Left breast, covered with food in still from *Hot Resort.*

# Kernohan, Roxanne

*Films:*
**Fatal Pulse** (1987). . . . . . . . . . . . . . . . . . . . . . . . Ann
• 0:58—Brief breasts in yellow outfit before getting thrown out of the window.
Angel III: The Final Chapter (1988) . . . . . . White Hooker
**Critters 2: The Main Course** (1988). . . . . . . . . . Lee
•• 0:37—Brief breasts after transforming from an alien into a Playboy Playmate.

**Not of This Earth** (1988) . . . . . . . . . . . Lead Hooker
••• 0:41—Breasts in cellar with Paul just before getting killed with two other hookers. Wearing a blue top.
**Phoenix the Warrior** (1988) . . . . . . . . . . . . . . .Meda
••• 0:15—Breasts in waterfall (she's the white girl).
**Tango & Cash** (1989) . . . . . . . . . Dressing Room Girl
• 1:06—Brief breasts in dressing room with three other girls. She's the second one in the middle.
*Video Tapes:*
**Scream Queen Hot Tub Party** (1991) . . . . . . . Herself
•• 0:07—Breasts, taking off black dress and putting on sheer black robe.
• 0:12—Buns, while walking up the stairs.
•• 0:43—Breasts, struggling with a monster in basement.
••• 0:44—Breasts taking off her swimsuit top and soaping up with the other girls.
•• 0:46—Breasts in still shot during the end credits.
*Magazines:*
**Playboy** (Jul 1989) . . . . . . . . . . . . . . B-Movie Bimbos
••• 136—Breasts straddling a car wearing an open bathing suit.
**Playboy's Book of Lingerie** (Jan 1991) . . . . . .Herself
•• 44—Right breast.

# • Kerns, Joanna

*Films:*
Coma (1978) . . . . . . . . . . . . . . . . . . . . . . . . . . .Diane
Cross My Heart (1987) . . . . . . . . . . . . . . . . . . . Nancy
Street Justice (1988). . . . . . . . . . . . . Katharine Watson
An American Summer (1990). . . . . . . . . . . Aunt Sunny
**The Nightman** (1992). . . . . . . . . . . . . . . Eve Rhodes
0:44—Side view of buns in panties, garter belt and stockings making love with Tom. Don't see her face.
•• 0:47—Buns, while rolling over in bed and sitting up.
••• 0:57—Breasts and buns, while making love with Tom in bed. Don't see her face. Probably a body double.
*Miniseries:*
V (1983) . . . . . . . . . . . . . . . . . . . . . . Marge Donovan
*Made for TV Movies:*
Mistress (1987) . . . . . . . . . . . . . . . . . . . . . Stephanie
Deadly Intentions...Again? (1991) . . . . . . . . . . . . .Sally
Desperate Choices: To Save My Child (1992). . . . . . n.a.
The Man with Three Wives (1993) . . . . . . . . . . . . .Katy
Not in My Family (1993) . . . . . . . . . . . . . . . . . . . . n.a.
Shameful Secrets (1993) . . . . . . . . . . . . . . . . . . . n.a.
*TV:*
Four Seasons (1984). . . . . . . . . . . . . . . . . . Pat Devon
Growing Pains (1985-92). . . . . . . . . . . .Maggie Seaver

# • Kerr, Deborah

*Films:*
Courageous Mr. Penn (1941; British) . . . . . . . .Gugliema
Major Barbara (1941; British) . . . . . . . . . . . . .Jenny Hill
The Life and Death of Colonel Blimp (1945; British)
. . . . . . . . Edith Hunter/Barbara Wynne/Johny Cannon
Love on the Dole (1945; British). . . . . . . Sally Hardcastle
I See a Dark Stranger (1946; British). . . . . . Dridie Quilty

Black Narcissus (1947; British) . . . . . . . . . Sister Clodagh
The Hucksters (1947) . . . . . . . . . . . . . . . Kay Dorrance
Quo Vadis (1951) . . . . . . . . . . . . . . . . . . . . . . . Lygia
The Prisoner of Zenda (1952) . . . . . . . . . Princess Flavia
From Here to Eternity (1953) . . . . . . . . . Karen Holmes
Julius Caesar (1953) . . . . . . . . . . . . . . . . . . . . Portia
The King and I (1956) . . . . . . . . . . . . Anna Leonowens
Tea and Sympathy (1956) . . . . . . . . . . . Laura Reynolds
An Affair to Remember (1958) . . . . . . . . . Terry McKay
Bonjour Tristesse (1958) . . . . . . . . . . . . . Anne Larsen
The Grass Is Greener (1960) . . . . . . . . . . . Hilary Rhyall
The Sundowners (1960) . . . . . . . . . . . . . Ida Carmody
The Naked Edge (1961) . . . . . . . . . Martha Radcliffe
The Chalk Garden (1964) . . . . . . . . . . . . . . . Madrigal
The Night of the Iguana (1964) . . . . . . . Hannah Jelkes
Casino Royale (1967; British)
. . . . . . . . . . . . . . . Agent Mimi/Lady Fiona McTarry
**The Arrangement** (1969) . . . . . . . . . . . . . . Florence
  • 0:36—Buns, behind curtain, while taking off her
    night gown. Brief long shot of left breast, behind
    curtain, getting into bed.
**The Gypsy Moths** (1969) . . . . . . . . Elizabeth Brandon
  ••• 0:52—Buns and left breast, while making love with
    Burt Lancaster on sofa.
*Miniseries:*
A Woman of Substance (1984) . . . . . . . . . . . . . . . n.a.
*Made for TV Movies:*
Witness for the Prosecution (1982) . . . . . . . . . . . . n.a.

## Kerr, E. Katherine

*Films:*
Tattoo (1981) . . . . . . . . . . . . . . . . . . . . . . . . . Wife
**Reuben, Reuben** (1983) . . . . . . . . . . . . Lucille Haxby
  • 0:51—Brief left breast in bedroom, undressing in
    front of Tom Conti.
Silkwood (1984) . . . . . . . . . . . . . . . . . . . Gilda Schultz
Children of a Lesser God (1986) . . . . . . . Mary Lee Ochs

## Kerridge, Linda

*Films:*
**Fade to Black** (1980) . . . . . . . . . . . . . . . . . . . Marilyn
  • 0:44—Breasts in the shower.
Strangers Kiss (1984) . . . . . . . . . . . . . . . . . . . . Shirley
Surf II (1984) . . . . . . . . . . . . . . . . . . . . . . . . . Sparkle
Down Twisted (1987) . . . . . . . . . . . . . . . . . . . Soames
Alien from L.A. (1988) . . . . . . . Roeyis Freki/Auntie Pearl
*Magazines:*
Playboy (Nov 1980) . . . . . . . . . . . . Sex in Cinema 1980
**Playboy** (Dec 1980) . . . . . . . . . . . . . . . . Double Take
  ••• 218-227—Full frontal nudity.
**Playboy's Nudes** (Oct 1990) . . . . . . . . . . . . . Herself
  ••• 6-7—Full frontal nudity.

## Kersh, Kathy

*Films:*
Americanization of Emily (1964) . . . . . . . . . . . . . n.a.
**Gemini Affair** (1974) . . . . . . . . . . . . . . . . . . . Jessica
  0:10—In white bra and black panties changing in
    front of Marta Kristen.

  •• 0:11—Nude getting into bed with Kristen.
  • 0:12—Brief breasts turning over onto her stomach in
    bed.
  •• 0:17—Nude, standing up in bed and jumping off.
  ••• 0:57—Nude in bed with Kristen.
  •• 1:04—Left breast sitting up in bed after Kristen
    leaves.

## Kerwin, Maureen

*Films:*
The Destructors (1974; British) . . . . . . . . . . . . Lucianne
**Laura** (1979) . . . . . . . . . . . . . . . . . . . . . . . Martine
  *a.k.a. Shattered Innocence*
  • 0:03—Brief full frontal nudity getting out of bed and
    putting white bathrobe on.
Reunion (1989; French/German)
. . . . . . . . . . . . . . . . . . . . . . Lisa, Henry's Daughter

## Kesner, Jillian

*Films:*
**The Student Body** (1975) . . . . . . . . . . Carrie Rafferty
  •• 0:29—Left breast, making out with Carter in the car.
Starhops (1978) . . . . . . . . . . . . . . . . . . . . . . . . Angel
**Firecracker** (1981) . . . . . . . . . . . . . . . Susanne Carter
  0:42—In bra and panties, while running around, try-
    ing to get away from bad guys.
  ••• 0:44—Breasts, while fighting bad guys after her bra
    comes off. Nice!
  ••• 0:58—In panties on bed, then buns as Darby Hinton
    cuts her clothes off with a knife. Breasts while mak-
    ing love with him in bed.
Raw Force (1981) . . . . . . . . . . . . . . . . Cookie Winchell
Trick or Treats (1982) . . . . . . . . . . . . . . . . . . . Andrea
**Moon in Scorpio** (1987) . . . . . . . . . . . . . . . . . Claire
  •• 0:39—Breasts sitting on deck of boat with bathing
    suit top down.
Beverly Hills Vamp (1989) . . . . . . . . . . . . . . Claudia
  0:06—In white lingerie riding a guy like a horse.
  0:33—In white slip with Brock.
  0:42—Almost breasts in bed with Brock. Too dark to
    see anything.
  1:09—In white nightgown attacking Russell in bed
    with Debra Lamb and Michelle Bauer.
  1:17—In white nightgown, getting killed as a vam-
    pire by Kyle.
Jaded (1989) . . . . . . . . . . . . . . . . . . . . . . . . . . Sara
**Roots of Evil** (1991) . . . . . . . . . . . . . . . . . . . Brenda
  (Unrated version reviewed.)
  ••• 0:27—Breasts, giving Alex Cord a back massage in
    bed.
  • 0:30—Brief breasts, getting up out of bed.
*TV:*
Co-ed Fever (1979) . . . . . . . . . . . . . . . . . . . . Melba

## Kestelman, Sara

*Films:*
**Zardoz** (1974; British) . . . . . . . . . . . . . . . . . . . May
  • 1:04—Left breast, in open blouse, under sheet with
    Sean Connery.

- 1:05—Very brief breasts grabbing Connery from behind during struggle.

Lisztomania (1975; British) . . . . . . . . . Princess Carolyn
Break of Day (1977; Australian). . . . . . . . . . . . . . . Alice
Lady Jane (1987; British) . . . . . . . . . . . . . . Frances Grey

# Kidder, Margot

*Films:*

Gaily, Gaily (1969) . . . . . . . . . . . . . . . . . . . . . Adeline
**Quackser Fortune has a Cousin in the Bronx**
(1970; Irish) . . . . . . . . . . . . . . . . . . . . . . . . . Zazel
- •• 1:03—Breasts undressing on a chair, then brief right, then breasts when Gene Wilder kisses her.
- • 1:05—Side view of left breast, then buns, getting out of bed.

**Sisters** (1973) . . . . . . . . . . . . . . . . . . Danielle Breton
- • 0:11—Very brief left breast, undressing while walking down hallway. Long shot.
- • 0:14—Breasts opening her robe on couch for her new boyfriend. Shadows make it hard to see.

**Gravey Train** (1974) . . . . . . . . . . . . . . . . . . . . Margie
**The Reincarnation of Peter Proud** (1975)
. . . . . . . . . . . . . . . . . . . . . . . . . . Marcia Curtis
- • 1:29—Brief breasts sitting in bathtub masturbating while remembering getting raped by husband.

Superman (1978) . . . . . . . . . . . . . . . . . . . Lois Lane
**The Amityville Horror** (1979) . . . . . . . Kathleen Lutz
- • 0:21—Brief right breast in reflection in mirror while doing dance stretching exercises in the bedroom. Hard to see because of the pattern on the mirror tiles.
- • 0:22—Cleavage in open blouse while talking to James Brolin.
- • 0:23—Very brief partial right breast, on the floor, kissing Brolin.

Superman II (1980). . . . . . . . . . . . . . . . . . . Lois Lane
**Willie and Phil** (1980) . . . . . . . . Jeanette Sutherland
- • 0:36—Brief breasts in bed when Phil opens up her blouse. Long shot.
- • 0:47—Brief breasts playing in a lake with Willie and Phil.

Heartaches (1981; Canadian) . . . . . . . . . . . . Rita Harris
Some Kind of Hero (1982) . . . . . . . . . . . . . . . . . Toni
0:52—In white corset making love with Richard Pryor on the floor.
0:56—In bra with robe standing outside the door talking to Pryor.
Trenchcoat (1983). . . . . . . . . . . . . . . Mickey Raymond
Little Treasure (1985) . . . . . . . . . . . . . . . . . . Margo
0:53—Stripping in bar, doesn't show anything.
1:13—Nude dancing by swimming pool. Long shot, don't see anything.
Miss Right (1987; Italian) . . . . . . . . . . . . . . . . . Juliet
Superman IV: The Quest for Peace (1987). . . . Lois Lane
Keeping Track (1988) . . . . . . . . . . . . Mickey Tremaine
*Made for Cable Movies:*
The Glitter Dome (1984; HBO) . . . . . . . . . . . . . . Willie

1:04—Breasts on balcony after making love with James Garner the night before. Long shot, hard to see anything.
*Made for Cable TV:*
**The Hitchhiker: Night Shift** (1985; HBO)
. . . . . . . . . . . . . . . . . . . . . . . . . . Jane Reynolds
(Available on *The Hitchhiker, Volume 2*.)
- • 0:13—In a white corset, then brief left breast over the shoulder shot.
Tales From the Crypt: Curiosity Killed (1992; HBO)
. . . . . . . . . . . . . . . . . . . . . . . . . . . . . Cynthia
*Made for TV Movies:*
To Catch a Killer (1992; Canadian). . . . . Rachel Grayson
One Woman's Courage (1994). . . . . . . . . Stella Jenson
*TV:*
Nichols (1971-72) . . . . . . . . . . . . . . . . . . . . . . Ruth
Shell Game (1987) . . . . . . . . . . . . . . . . Jennie Jerome
*Magazines:*
**Playboy** (Dec 1974) . . . . . . . . . . . . . Sex Stars of 1974
- ••• 211—Breasts.
**Playboy** (Mar 1975) . . . . . . . . . . . . . . . . . . Margot
- ••• 86-93—Full frontal nudity in B&W photos.
**Playboy** (Dec 1975) . . . . . . . . . . . . . Sex Stars of 1975
- •• 185—Left breast.
**Playboy** (Nov 1980) . . . . . . . . . . . . . . . . Grapevine
- • 302—Left breast under sheer blouse. B&W.
**Playboy** (Nov 1985) . . . . . . . . . . . Sex in Cinema 1985
- • 131—Buns, in G-string kneeling on stage in still from *Little Treasure*.

# Kidman, Nicole

Wife of actor Tom Cruise.
*Films:*
BMX Bandits (1984; Australian) . . . . . . . . . . . . . . Judy
**Windrider** (1986; Australian) . . . . . . . . . . . . . . . Jade
- • 0:40—Brief breasts in the shower with Tom Burlinson.
- • 0:42—Brief buns and breasts in bed with Burlinson.
- • 0:43—Brief left breast on top of Burlinson in bed. Dark.
- ••• 0:47—Buns and very brief back side of left and right breasts, getting out of bed and putting on robe.
**Dead Calm** (1989) . . . . . . . . . . . . . . . . . Rae Ingram
- • 1:00—Brief buns and breasts on the floor with the Billy Zane.
Days of Thunder (1990). . . . . . . . . . . Dr. Claire Lewicki
**Billy Bathgate** (1991) . . . . . . . . . . . . . . Drew Preston
- •• 0:42—Briefly nude, throwing off towel in front of a vanity with three mirrors.
- •• 0:52—Very brief full frontal nudity underwater. Brief full frontal nudity getting out of water and putting on dress.
Far and Away (1992) . . . . . . . . . . . . . Shannon Christie
1:03—Back half of right breast, seen through sheer room divider when she changes clothes.
Flirting (1992; Australian). . . . . . . . . . . Nicola Radcliffe
**Malice** (1993). . . . . . . . . . . . . . . . . . . . . . . . Tracy
- •• 0:13—Very brief left breast then buns, when leaning over Bill Pullman in bed.

My Life (1993) . . . . . . . . . . . . . . . . . . . . . . . Gail Jones
*Made for Cable Movies:*
Bangkok Hilton (1990) . . . . . . . . . . . . . . . . . . . . . .n.a.

# Kiel, Sue

*Films:*
**Red Heat** (1987; U.S./German) . . . . . . . . . . . . . Hedda
• 0:56—Brief breasts in shower room scene (third girl behind Linda Blair). Long shot, hard to see.
Straight to Hell (1987; British). . . . . . . . . . . . . . .Leticia
**Survivor** (1987). . . . . . . . . . . . . . . . . . . . The Woman
••• 0:33—Right breast, then breasts and buns making love with Survivor in hammock. Long scene.
*Made for Cable TV:*
Red Shoe Diaries: Bounty Hunter (1993; Showtime)
. . . . . . . . . . . . . . . . . . . . . . . . . . . . . . . . . . Francine
Red Shoe Diaries: How I Met My Husband (1993; Showtime) . . . . . . . . . . . . . . Mistress Miranda

# Kiger, Susan Lynn

*Adult Films:*
**Deadly Love** (1974) . . . . . . . . . . . . . . . . . . . . . . .n.a.
*a.k.a. Hot Nasties*
First Playboy Playmate to do an adult film *before* she became a Playmate.
Nude with snake and nude performing fellatio.
*Films:*
**H.O.T.S.** (1979) . . . . . . . . . . . . . . . . . . Honey Shayne
*a.k.a. T & A Academy*
• 0:00—Breasts in shower room with the other girls.
•• 0:33—Breasts in pool making love with Doug.
• 1:33—Breasts in football game.
**Seven** (1979) . . . . . . . . . . . . . . . . . . . . . . . . . . .Jennie
••• 0:58—Breasts, while sitting on bed, then getting up and walking around in the kitchen, making coffee, then putting her swimsuit top on.
• 1:15—Brief breasts, while taking off swimsuit top to change outside by car.
Angels Brigade (1980). . . . . . . . . . . . . . . . . . . . . .n.a.
Galaxina (1980) . . . . . . . . . . . . . . . . . . . . . . Blue Girl
**The Happy Hooker Goes Hollywood** (1980) . . .Susie
• 0:42—Breasts, singing "Happy Birthday" to a guy tied up on the bed.
••• 0:43—Breasts, wearing a red garter belt playing pool with K.C. Winkler.
The Return (1980). . . . . . . . . . . . . . . . . . . . . . . . .n.a.
House of Death (1981) . . . . . . . . . . . . .Lily Carpenter
*Magazines:*
**Playboy** (Dec 1976). . . . . . . . . Portfolio: Pompeo Posar
•• 111—Full frontal nudity in small photo.
**Playboy** (Jan 1977) . . . . . . . . . . . . . . . . . . Playmate
••• 116-127—Nude.
**Playboy** (Oct 1977). . . . . . . . . . . Having A Masked Ball
••• 116-123—Full frontal nudity.
••• 269—Breasts in small photo.
**Playboy** (Dec 1979). . . . . . . . . . . . . Sex Stars of 1979
••• 258—Full frontal nudity.

# • King, Cheryl

*Films:*
**Sex Through a Window** (1977). . . . . . . . . . . Nurse
• 0:19—In bra and panties, under sheer white pantyhose, then breasts after taking off bra, while John watches her through a telephoto lens.
Love Child (1982) . . . . . . . . . . . . . . . . . . . Van Inmate

# • King, Rowena

*Films:*
London Kills Me (1991; British) . . . . . . . . . . . . .Melanie
**Wide Sargasso Sea** (1993) . . . . . . . . . . . . . . .Amelie
(Unrated version reviewed.)
• 0:54—Briefly nude in open window, while showing off for Rochester.
••• 1:16—Breasts, while making love standing up outside with Rochester.
••• 1:17—Full frontal nudity in bed, then getting out and getting dressed.
*Miniseries:*
Masterpiece Theatre: To Play the King (1994) . . . Chloe

# King, Tracey Ann

*Films:*
Hammer (1972). . . . . . . . . . . . The Black Magic Woman
**The Naughty Stewardesses** (1978) . . . . . . . . Barbara
*a.k.a. Fresh Air*
•• 0:56—Breasts dancing by the pool in front of everybody.
**Cheerleaders Wild Weekend** (1985). . . . LaSalle/Polk
• 0:00—Brief breasts while tying her shoelace in locker room.
• 0:33—Brief breasts in catfight with another girl in cabin.
••• 0:39—Breasts, taking off her yellow blouse during contest.
••• 0:41—Breasts with the other five girls during contest.
• 0:42—Breasts, losing contest.

# Kingsley, Danitza

*Films:*
You Can't Hurry Love (1984) . . . . . . . . . . . . . . . Tracey
**Amazons** (1986) . . . . . . . . . . . . . . . . . . . . . . . .Tshingi
••• 0:30—Breasts and buns quite a few times with Colungo out of and in bed.
Jack's Back (1987) . . . . . . . . . . . . . . . . Denise Johnson
South of Reno (1987). . . . . . . . . . . . . . . . . . . . Louise
No Man's Land (1988) . . . . . . . . . . . . . . . . . . . Magot
Verne Miller (1988) . . . . . . . . . . . . . German Drink Girl

# Kingsley, Gretchen

*Films:*
**Blood Sisters** (1986) . . . . . . . . . . . . . . . . . . . . . Ellen
•• 0:32—Breasts, changing clothes to go to sleep in bedroom.
••• 0:50—Breasts in bed with Jim.
If Looks Could Kill (1987). . . . . . . . . . . . . . . Elizabeth
Wimps (1987) . . . . . . . . . . . . . . . . . . . . . . . . . Debbie

## • Kinkade, Amelia
*Films:*
**Night of the Demons** (1987) . . . . . . . . . . . . Angela
(Unrated version reviewed.)
• 0:47—Brief buns in panties, garter belt and stockings under dress while doing sexy dance in living room.
Night of the Demons 2 (1994) . . . . . . . . . . . . Angela

## Kinmont, Kathleen
Wife of actor Lorenzo Lamas.
Daughter of actress Abby Dalton.
*Films:*
Hardbodies (1984) . . . . . . . . . . . . . . . . . . . Pretty Skater
**Fraternity Vacation** (1985) . . . . . . . . . . . . . Marianne
••• 0:16—Breasts and buns taking off her swimsuit in bedroom with two guys.
Nightforce (1986) . . . . . . . . . . . . . . . . . . . . . . . Cindy
Winners Take All (1987) . . . . . . . . . . . . . . Party Girl #5
Halloween 4: The Return of Michael Meyers (1988)
. . . . . . . . . . . . . . . . . . . . . . . . . . . . . . . . . . . Kelly
0:51—In bra and panties in front of the fireplace with Brady.
Phoenix the Warrior (1988) . . . . . . . . . . . . . . . Phoenix
RollerBlade Warriors: Taken By Force (1988)
. . . . . . . . . . . . . . . . . . . . . . . . . . . . Karin Crosse
**Bride of Re-Animator** (1989) . . . . . . Gloria/The Bride
• 0:58—Brief breasts several times with her top pulled down to defibrillate her heart.
1:17—Breasts under gauze. Her body has gruesome looking special effects appliances all over it.
1:22—More breasts under gauze.
1:24—More breasts. Pretty unappealing.
1:27—Brief buns, when turning around after ripping out her own heart.
Midnight (1989) . . . . . . . . . . . . . . . . . . . . . . . . . Party
**Rush Week** (1989) . . . . . . . . . . . . . Julie Ann McGuffin
• 0:07—Brief breasts several times during modeling session. Buns in G-string getting dressed. Long shot.
SnakeEater II: The Drug Buster (1990)
. . . . . . . . . . . . . . . . . . . . . . . . . Detective Lisa Forester
**The Art of Dying** (1991) . . . . . . . . . . . . . . . . . . Holly
• 0:28—Brief left breast, making love with Wings Hauser in the kitchen. Brief breasts when he pours milk on her.
•• 0:33—Breasts in bathtub with Hauser. Intercut with Janet getting stabbed.
**Night of the Warrior** (1991) . . . . . . . Katherine Pierce
0:29—Very brief upper half of right breast, leaning out of the shower to get a towel.
0:46—Very, very brief part of buns, lifting her leg up while kissing Lorenzo Lamas at the art gallery.
• 1:10—Brief right breast, while making love with Lamas on motorcycle.
Sweet Justice (1991) . . . . . . . . . . . . . . . . . . . Heather
**CIA—Code Name: Alexa** (1992) . . . . . . . . . . . Alexa
• 1:04—Very brief buns and very, very brief right breast and brief left breast while making love with Lorenzo Lamas in bed.

Final Impact (1992) . . . . . . . . . . . . . . . . . . . . Maggie
CIA II: Target Alexa (1993) . . . . . . . . . . . . . . . . Alexa
**Final Round** (1993) . . . . . . . . . . . . . . . . . . . . Jordan
0:17—In black bra, panties, garter belt and stockings in room with Lorenzo Lamas.
••• 0:18—Breasts, while making love on the floor with Lamas.
Renegade: Fighting Cage (1993) . . . . . . . . . Cheyenne
(Nudity added for video release.)
Stormswept (1994) . . . . . . . . . . . . . . . . . . . . . . Missy
*TV:*
Renegade (1993- ) . . . . . . . . . . . . . . . . . . . Cheyenne
*Magazines:*
**Playboy** (Nov 1991) . . . . . . . . . . Sex in Cinema 1991
• 144—Breasts under sheer dress, but has the gruesome looking special effects on. From *Bride of Re-Animator.*

## Kinnaman, Melanie
*Films:*
Friday the 13th, Part V—A New Beginning (1985)
. . . . . . . . . . . . . . . . . . . . . . . . . . . . Pam Roberts
1:08—In wet white blouse coming back into the house from the rain.
**Thunder Alley** (1985) . . . . . . . . . . . . . . . . . . . . Star
• 0:52—Brief breasts under water in pool talking to a Richie. Side view of right breast, talking to Donnie.
•• 1:14—Breasts and buns, making love on bed with Richie, then getting out.
Best of the Best (1990) . . . . . . . . . . . . . . . . The Woman

## Kinski, Nastassja
Daughter of the late actor Klaus Kinski.
Real last name is Nakzsynski.
*Films:*
**Boarding School** (1976; German) . . . . Deborah Collins
a.k.a. *Virgin Campus*
a.k.a. *The Passion Flower Hotel*
• 0:15—Brief breasts in the shower with her roommates. Hard to tell who is who.
• 1:11—Left breast, then breasts in the shower (She's the second from the right) consoling Marie-Louise.
• 1:16—Breasts under sheer nightie.
••• 1:32—Breasts making love with Sinclair.
**To the Devil, a Daughter** (1976)
. . . . . . . . . . . . . . . . . . . . . . . . Catherine Beddows
••• 1:24—Full frontal nudity, taking off her robe outside and walking towards Richard Widmark in slow motion.
**Stay As You Are** (1978; Italian) . . . . . . . . . . Francesca
English language version.
• 0:07—Left breast, while sleeping in bed.
• 1:00—Breasts, undressing and sitting in bed. Brief side of left breast, while lying in bed.
••• 1:02—Buns, while lying in bed, then full frontal nudity sitting up and covering herself with a sheet.
••• 1:27—Left breast, then breasts and brief buns in bed with Marcello Mastroianni. Long scene.

••• 1:28—Breasts, sitting up in bed, talking with Mastroianni.

••• 1:30—Nude, fooling around at the table with Mastroianni. Long scene. Nice bun shots.

•• 1:33—Breasts in bedroom at night. Mostly silhouette.

**For Your Love Only** (1979; German) . . . . . . . . . Zena

•• 0:04—Breasts, twice, in the woods with her teacher, Victor, while Michael watches through the bushes.

• 0:15—Brief right breast, in the woods with Michael.

•• 0:58—Partial left breast, sitting up in bed with Victor. Breasts walking around and putting on robe.

**Tess** (1979; French/British) . . . . . . . . . Tess Durbeyfield

• 0:47—Brief left breast, opening blouse in field to feed her baby.

**Cat People** (1982). . . . . . . . . . . . . . . . . Irena Gallier

••• 1:03—Nude at night, walking around outside chasing a rabbit.

••• 1:35—Breasts taking off blouse, walking up the stairs and getting into bed.

• 1:37—Brief right breast, lying in bed with John Heard.

•• 1:38—Breasts getting out of bed and walking to the bathroom.

•• 1:40—Brief buns, getting back into bed. Breasts in bed.

•• 1:47—Full frontal nudity, walking around in the cabin at night.

• 1:49—Breasts, tied to the bed by Heard.

**One from the Heart** (1982). . . . . . . . . . . . . . . Leila

• 1:13—Brief breasts in open blouse when she leans forward after walking on a ball.

**Exposed** (1983). . . . . . . . . . . . . . . . Elizabeth Carlson

•• 0:54—Breasts in bed with Rudolf Nureyev.

The Moon in the Gutter (1983; French/Italian) . . Loretta
a.k.a. La Lune dans Le Caniveau

**Spring Symphony** (1983) . . . . . . . . . . . . . . . . . Clara
0:29—Brief left breast, when it pops out of her corset when she tries on a dress.

The Hotel New Hampshire (1984). . . . . . . Susie the Bear

Paris, Texas (1984; French/German) . . . . . . . . . . . Jane

**Unfaithfully Yours** (1984) . . . . . . . . Daniella Eastman

• 0:37—Breasts and buns in the shower.

**Harem** (1985; French) . . . . . . . . . . . . . . . . . . Diane

• 0:14—Breasts getting into swimming pool.

•• 1:04—Breasts in motel room with Ben Kingsley.

**Maria's Lovers** (1985) . . . . . . . . . . . . . . Maria Bosic
0:59—In a black bra.

• 1:12—Brief right breast, while looking at herself in the mirror.

Revolution (1986). . . . . . . . . . . . . . Daisy McConnahay

Magdalena (1988) . . . . . . . . . . . . . . . . . . Magdalena

Torrents of Spring (1990) . . . . . . . . . . . . . . . . Maria

Faraway, So Close (1993; German) . . . . . . . . . Raphaela

Crackerjack (1994) . . . . . . . . . . . . . . . . . . . . . K.C.

*Magazines:*

**Playboy** (Dec 1980). . . . . . . . . . . . . Sex Stars of 1980

••• 242—Breasts.

**Playboy** (May 1983). . . . . . . . . . . . . . . . . . . Exposed

••• 142-149—Breasts.

**Playboy** (Nov 1985). . . . . . . . . . Sex in Cinema 1985

•• 132—Left breast in still from *Harem*.

**Playboy's Nudes** (Dec 1992) . . . . . . . . . . . . . . Herself

•• 40-41—Half of left breast.

# Kirkland, Sally

*Films:*

Going Home (1971). . . . . . . . . . . . . . . . Ann Graham

Cinderella Liberty (1973) . . . . . . . . . . . . . . Fleet Chick

The Sting (1973) . . . . . . . . . . . . . . . . . . . . Crystal

The Way We Were (1973). . . . . . . . . . . . Pony Dunbar

Young Nurses (1973) . . . . . . . . . . . . . . . . . . Patient

**Big Bad Mama** (1974). . . . . . . . . . . Barney's Woman

•• 0:13—Breasts and buns waiting for Barney then throwing shoe at Billy Jean.

• 1:23—Brief breasts, covering herself up scene from 0:13 during end credits.

Candy Stripe Nurses (1974) . . . . . . . . . Woman in Clinic

Crazy Mama (1975). . . . . . . . . . . . . . . . . . Ella Mae

A Star is Born (1976) . . . . . . . . . . . . . . Photographer

Tracks (1977) . . . . . . . . . . . . . . . . . . . Uncredited

Private Benjamin (1980). . . . . . . . . . . . . . . . . Helga

Talking Walls (1982). . . . . . . . . . . . . . . . . . Hooker

**Double Exposure** (1983). . . . . . . . . . . . . . . Hooker

•• 0:26—Breasts in alley getting killed.

Fatal Games (1984) . . . . . . . . . . . . . . . Diane Paine

Love Letters (1984) . . . . . . . . . . . . . . . . . . Hippie

a.k.a. Passion Play

**Anna** (1987) . . . . . . . . . . . . . . . . . . . . . . Anna

•• 0:28—Breasts in the bathtub talking to Daniel.

White Hot (1988). . . . . . . . . . . . . . . . . . . Harriet

**Cold Feet** (1989) . . . . . . . . . . . Maureen Linoleum

(In tight fitting spandex dresses throughout most of the film.)

• 0:56—In black bra and panties taking off her dress in bedroom with Keith Carradine. Brief right breast pulling bra down.

• 0:58—Brief side view of right breast sitting up in bed talking to Carradine.

**High Stakes** (1989) . . . . . . . . . Melanie "Bambi" Rose

• 0:01—In two piece costume, doing a strip tease routine on stage. Buns in G-string, then very, very brief breasts while flashing.

1:11—In black bra cutting her hair in front of a mirror.

Paint It Black (1989). . . . . . . . . . . . . . Marion Easton
0:05—Most of left breast, while sitting in bed talking to Rick Rossovich.

Best of the Best (1990). . . . . . . . . . . . . Kathevu Wade

Bullseye! (1990) . . . . . . . . . . . . . . . . . . . . Willie

Revenge (1990) . . . . . . . . . . . . . . . . . . . Rock Star

**In the Heat of Passion** (1991) . . . . . . . Dr. Lee Adams

(Unrated version reviewed.)

••• 0:21—In black bra, then breasts making love with Charlie while her husband is downstairs.

• 0:23—Brief breasts in the shower when her husband opens the shower curtain.

•• 0:29—Breasts with Charlie in stall in women's restroom.

•• 0:42—Breasts teasing Charlie from the bathroom.

• 0:45—Right breast, then breasts in bed with Charlie.

• 1:11—Very brief buns, while on the couch with Charlie.

JFK (1991) . . . . . . . . . . . . . . . . . . . . . Rose Cheramie

Two Evil Eyes (1991) . . . . . . . . . . . . . . . . . . . Eleonora

**Double Threat** (1992) . . . . . . . . . . . . Monica Martel

(Unrated version reviewed.)

• 0:13—In lingerie outfit while playing with herself. Partial left breast.

•• 0:51—Brief left breast, then breasts while dressing in bathroom.

Hit the Dutchman (1992) . . . . . . . .Emma Flegenheimer

(Unrated version reviewed.)

The Player (1992) . . . . . . . . . . . . . . . . . . . . . Cameo

Primary Motive (1992) . . . . . . . . . . . . . . .Helen Poulas

Gunmen (1993) . . . . . . . . . . . . . . . . . . . . . . Bennett

*Made for TV Movies:*

The Haunted (1991) . . . . . . . . . . . . . . . . . . . . Janet

The Woman Who Loved Elvis (1993). . . . . . . . . Sandee

*Magazines:*

**Playboy** (Nov 1993) . . . . . . . . . . . Sex in Cinema 1993

•• 135—Right breast while wearing lingerie in still from *Double Threat.*

# • *Kirshner, Mia*

*Films:*

**Cadillac Girls** (1993; Canadian) . . . . . . . . . . . . . Page

• 0:02—Back half of breast in mirror when Miles gets out of bed. Long shot.

*TV:*

Dracula: The Series (1990) . . . . . . . . Sophie Metternich

# *Kitaen, Tawny*

Ex-wife of singer David Coverdale of the rock group *Whitesnake.*

*Films:*

Bachelor Party (1984) . . . . . . . . . . . Debbie Thompson

**The Perils of Gwendoline in the Land of the Yik Yak** (1984; French) . . . . . . . . . . . . . . . . . Gwendoline

••• 0:36—Breasts in the rain in the forest, taking off her top. More breasts with Willard.

•• 0:52—Buns, while walking around with Willard in costumes.

• 0:55—Buns, falling into jail cell, then in jail cell in costume.

• 0:57—Buns, while rescuing Beth in torture chamber.

•• 1:01—Breasts in S&M costume in front of mirrors.

• 1:04—Brief breasts escaping from chains.

• 1:07—Buns, in costume while riding chariot and next to wall.

• 1:09—Buns, while standing up.

•• 1:11—Buns, in costume during fight. Wearing green ribbon.

•• 1:18—Breasts making love with Willard.

**Crystal Heart** (1987) . . . . . . . . . . . . . . . Alley Daniels

•• 0:46—Breasts and buns, while "making love" with Lee Curreri through the glass.

•• 0:50—Nude, crashing through glass shower door, covered with blood during her nightmare.

• 1:14—Brief breasts making love with Curreri in and falling out of bed.

Happy Hour (1987) . . . . . . . . . . . . . . . . . .Misty Roberts

Instant Justice (1987) . . . . . . . . . . . . . . . . . . Virginia

**Witchboard** (1987) . . . . . . . . . . . . . . . . . . . . .Linda

• 1:26—Nude, stuck in the shower and breaking the glass doors to get out.

White Hot (1988). . . . . . . . . . . . . . . . . . . . . Vanessa

1:04—Brief half of lower frontal nudity, while lying in bed.

Three of Hearts (1993) . . . . . . . . . . . . . . Woman in Bar

*Made for Cable Movies:*

The Glory Years (1987; HBO) . . . . . . . . . . . . . . . n.a.

*TV:*

Santa Barbara (1989-90) . . . . . . . . . . . . . . . . . . Lisa

New WKRP in Cincinnati (1991-93) . . . . Mona Loveland

America's Funniest People (1992-94) . . . . . . . . Co-Host

*Video Tapes:*

**Whitesnake—Trilogy** (1987) . . . . . . . . . . . . .The Girl

• 0:10—(2 min., 17 sec. into "Here I Go Again.") Very brief right breast, leaning out of car.

0:18—Most of her buns, while kissing David Coverdale in out-take from "Is This Love."

The Kathy Kaehler Fitness System (1992)

. . . . . . . . . . . . . . . . . . . . . . . . . . . Exercise Student

# *Klarwein, Eleonore*

*Films:*

Peppermint Soda (1979; French) . . . . . . . .Anne Weber

Stroke of Midnight (1991; U.S./French) . . Second Model

*a.k.a. If the Shoe Fits*

**Road to Ruin** (1992) . . . . . . . . . . . . . . . . . Girl Friend

•• 0:03—Breasts and buns, getting out of bed and walking into bathroom.

# *Klein, Barbara Ann*

*Films:*

**Night Eyes** (1990) . . . . . . . . . . . . . . Sleeping Woman

(Unrated version reviewed.)

• 0:02—Brief breasts struggling with burglar/rapist.

Relentless 2: Dead On (1991). . . . . . . . . . . . . .Realtor

Death Becomes Her (1992)

. . . . . . . . . . . . . . . . . . . Goldie Hawn's Stunt Double

Rapid Fire (1992) . . . . . . . . . . . . . . . . . . . . . . Stunts

Straight Talk (1992) . . . . . . . . . . . . . . . . . . . . Stunts

Jason Goes to Hell—The Final Friday (1993). . . . . Stunts

(Unrated Director's Original Cut reviewed.)

Sleepless in Seattle (1993) . . . . . . . . . . . . . . . Stunts

# • *Klemme, Brenda Lynn*

*Films:*

**Cutting Class** (1988) . . . . . . . . . . . . . . . . . . . Colleen

0:32—In bra in locker room. Very, very brief buns cheerleading without any panties on.

- 0:37—More very brief buns, ducking under bleachers.

Stone Cold (1991) . . . . . . . . . . . . . . . . . . . . . . . Marie
Patriot Games (1992) . . . . . . . . . . . . . . . . . Secretary

## Klenck, Margaret

*Films:*

**Hard Choices** (1986) . . . . . . . . . . . . . . . . . . . . . Laura
- •• 1:10—Left breast, then breasts making love with Bobby. Nice close up shot.
- • 1:11—Very brief half of left breast and lower frontal nudity getting back into bed. Long shot.

Loose Cannons (1990) . . . . . . . . . . . . . . . . . Eva Braun

*TV:*

One Life to Live (1977-84) . . . . . . . . . . . Edwina Lewis

## Knight, Shirley

*Films:*

The Couch (1962). . . . . . . . . . . . . . . . . . . . . . . Terry
House of Women (1962). . . . . . . . . . . . . . . . . . . Erica
The Group (1966). . . . . . . . . . . . . . . Polly Andrews
Petulia (1968; U.S./British) . . . . . . . . . . . . . . . . Polo
**The Rain People** (1969) . . . . . . . . . . . . . . . . . Natalie
- • 0:15—Breasts walking around in motel room and getting into bed. Long shot.
- • 1:36—Very brief buns, with sheet wrapped around her, trying to get out of trailer.

Juggernaut (1974; British). . . . . . . . . . . Barbara Banister
Beyond the Poseidon Adventure (1979)
. . . . . . . . . . . . . . . . . . . . . . . . . . . Hannah Meredith
Endless Love (1981) . . . . . . . . . . . . . . . . . . . . . .Anne
The Sender (1982) . . . . . . . . . . . . . . . . . . . . . Jerolyn
Panther Squad (1986; French/Belgian) . . . . . . . . . . .n.a.

*Made for TV Movies:*

The Outsider (1967) . . . . . . . . . . . . . . . . .Peggy Leydon
Billionaire Boys Club (1987) . . . . . . . . . . . . . . . .n.a.
Mother's Revenge (1993) . . . . . . . . . . . . . .Bess Jordan
When Love Kills: The Seduction of John Hearn (1993)
. . . . . . . . . . . . . . . . . . . . . . . . . . . . Edna Larson
Baby Brokers (1994) . . . . . . . . . . . . . . . . . . . . Sylvia

## Knudsen, Bitten

*Films:*

Hollywood Vice Squad (1986). . . . Lucchesi's Girl Friend

*Magazines:*

**Playboy's Nudes** (Oct 1990). . . . . . . . . . . . . . Herself
- • 50—Buns.

## Knudsen, Vibeke

*Films:*

The Story of "O" (1975; French). . . . . . . . . . . . . .n.a.
**The French Woman** (1979) . . . . . . . . . . .Anne-Marie
*a.k.a. Madame Claude*
- • 0:04—Breasts in chair in office with Robert Webber.
- • 0:09—Breasts walking on beach with Japanese Businessman.
- ••• 0:11—Breasts on bed with David while she talks on the telephone. Then hot scene making love with him in the shower.

- 1:19—Breasts in bed with a customer when David comes over.

*Magazines:*

Playboy (Aug 1977) . . . . . . . . . . . . . Madame Claude

## Kober, Marta

*Films:*

Friday the 13th, Part II (1981) . . . . . . . . . . . . . .Sandra
Baby, It's You (1983) . . . . . . . . . . . . . . . . . . . . Debra
Neon Maniacs (1985) . . . . . . . . . . . . . . . . . .Lorraine
School Spirit (1985) . . . . . . . . . . . . . . . . . . . . Ursula
Rad (1986). . . . . . . . . . . . . . . . . . . . . . . . . . .Becky
**Vendetta** (1986) . . . . . . . . . . . . . . . . . . . . . .Sylvia
- • 1:10—Very brief, dark, right breast in open blouse, in her prison cell with the guard.

Slumber Party Massacre 3 (1990). . . . . . . . . . Pizza Girl

*Made for TV Movies:*

Second Sight: A Love Story (1984). . . . . . . . . . .Megan
A Touch of Scandal (1984) . . . . . . . . . . . . . .Toni Allenby
Children of the Night (1985) . . . . . . . . . . . . . . . .Linda

*Video Tapes:*

**Inside Out** (1992) . . . . . . . . . . . . . .The Girl/Doubletalk
- ••• 0:26—Breasts in raised blouse, on top of Jack on sofa.

## Kohnert, Mary

*Films:*

Valet Girls (1987) . . . . . . . . . . . . . . . . . . . . Carnation
**Beyond the Door III** (1989; Yugoslavian) . . . . Beverly
- •• 0:03—Breasts taking a shower.

Mr. Baseball (1992) . . . . . . . . . . . . . . . . . Player's Wife

## Koizumi, Ariane

See: Ariane.

## Komorowska, Liliana

*Films:*

War and Love (1985) . . . . . . . . . . . . . . . . . . . . Esther
Astonished (1988) . . . . . . . . . . . . . . . . . . . . . . Sonia
Her Alibi (1989) . . . . . . . . . . . . . . . . . . . . . . . Laura
**Scanners III: The Takeover** (1992). . . . Helena Monet
- •• 0:32—Breasts in and out of spa, talking with her dad.
- • 0:35—Brief right breast, while sitting up.

Martial Outlaw (1993) . . . . . . . . . . . . . . . . . . .Marina

## Kong, Venice

*Films:*

Beverly Hills Cop II (1987) . . . . . . . . . .Playboy Playmate

*Video Tapes:*

**Wet and Wild** (1989) . . . . . . . . . . . . . . . . . . . Model
**Playboy Video Centerfold: Kerri Kendall** (1990)
. . . . . . . . . . . . . . . . . . . . . . . . . . . . . . . . Playmate
- ••• 0:41—Full frontal nudity.

**Playmates at Play** (1990). . . . . . . . . . . Making Waves

*Magazines:*

**Playboy** (Dec 1980) . . . . . . . . . . . . . . Bunny Birthday
- ••• 156—Full frontal nudity.

**Playboy** (Sep 1985) . . . . . . . . . . . . . . . . . . . Playmate

**Playboy's Girls of Summer '86** (Aug 1986) . . Herself
• 86—Buns.
••• 100-101—Breasts.
**Playboy's 1987 Book of Lingerie** (Mar 1987)
. . . . . . . . . . . . . . . . . . . . . . . . . . . . . . . . Herself
••• 71—Breasts.

## Konop, Kelli

*Films:*
Bikini Summer (1991) . . . . . . . . . . . . . . . . . . . . Rene
**Totally Exposed** (1991) . . . . . . . . . . . . . . . . . . . . Sue
• 0:18—Undressing to take a shower. Brief right
breast, bending over to take off panties. Brief side
view of left breast, while getting into the shower.
• 0:19—Sort of breasts, while washing herself in the
shower. Her arms get in the way.
1:12—In white bra, while making out with Bill on
bed.

## Konopski, Sharry

*Video Tapes:*
**Playboy Video Calendar 1989** (1988) . . . . . . . . April
••• 0:13—Nude.
**Wet and Wild** (1989) . . . . . . . . . . . . . . . . . . . .Model
*Magazines:*
**Playboy** (Aug 1987). . . . . . . . . . . . . . . . . . Playmate
**Playboy's Calendar Playmates** (Nov 1992) . . Herself
••• 71—Full frontal nudity.

## Korn, Sandy

*Films:*
**Possessed by the Night** (1993)
. . . . . . . . Uncredited Body Double for Shannon Tweed
••• 1:05—Breasts and buns in panties, while caressing
herself. Did this because the film makers didn't need
to have Tweed come back to shoot only this one in-
sert scene.
*Video Tapes:*
**Penthouse Passport to Paradise/Hawaii** (1991)
. . . . . . . . . . . . . . . . . . . . . . . . . . . . . . . . . .Model
•• 0:25—Breasts, taking off her top and going down
into an underground cave.
••• 0:27—Nude, taking an outdoor shower to wash the
dirt off herself.
**Penthouse The Great Pet Hunt—Part II** (1993)
. . . . . . . . . . . . . . . . . . . . . . . . . . . . . . . . . . Pet
••• 0:50—Breasts and buns in T-back after stripping out
of motorcycle mama outfit.
*Magazines:*
**Penthouse** (Mar 1991) . . . . . . . . . . . . . . . . . . . . Pet
••• 67-81—Nude.
**Penthouse** (Jun 1992) . . . . . . . . Pet of the Year Playoff
••• 88-89—Nude.

## Korot, Alla

*Films:*
**Night of the Cyclone** (1990) . . . . . . . . . . . Angelique
• 0:21—Right breast, then brief breasts getting out of
the shower.

*TV:*
Another World (1991- ) . . . . . . . . . . . . . . .Jenna Norris

## Koscina, Sylva

*Films:*
Hercules (1959; Italian) . . . . . . . . . . . . . . . . . . . . Iole
The Secret War of Harry Frigg (1969)
. . . . . . . . . . . . . . . . . . . . . Countess di Montefiore
**The House of Exorcism** (1975). . . . . . . . . . . .Sophia
*a.k.a. Lisa and the Devil*
••• 0:24—Breasts, while making love in bed with
George the chauffeur.
**The Slasher** (1975) . . . . . . . . . . . . . . . . . . . . Barbara
•• 0:17—Left breast lying down getting a massage.
•• 1:18—Breasts undressing and putting a robe on at
her lover's house. Left breast after getting stabbed.
**Sex on the Run** (1979; German/French/Italian)
. . . . . . . . . . . . . . . . . . . . . . . . . . . . . . . . Jelsamina
*a.k.a. Some Like It Cool*
*a.k.a. Casanova and Co.*
••• 0:28—Breasts and brief buns dropping her top for
Tony Curtis, then walking around with the "other"
Tony Curtis.
•• 1:20—Breasts talking to her husband.

## Kossack, Christine

*Films:*
Three Men and a Baby (1987) . . . . . . One of Jack's Girls
**The Brain** (1988) . . . . . . . . . . . . . . . . . . . . . . . Vivian
•• 0:24—Breasts on monitor, then breasts in person
during Jim's fantasy.
•• 1:11—Breasts again in the basement during Jim's
hallucination.

## Kotero, Patty

See: Apollonia.

## Kozak, Harley Jane

Sister of actress Heidi Kozak.
*Films:*
House on Sorority Row (1983) . . . . . . . . . . . . . . .Diane
Clean and Sober (1988) . . . . . . . . . .Ralston Receptionist
Parenthood (1989). . . . . . . . . . . . . . . . . . . . . .Susan
When Harry Met Sally... (1989) . . . . . . . . . . . . .Helen
Arachnophobia (1990) . . . . . . . . . . . . . .Molly Jennings
**Side Out** (1990) . . . . . . . . . . . . . . . . . . . Kate Jacobs
• 0:53—Brief left breast, then out of focus left breast,
while in bed with Peter Horton.
All I Want for Christmas (1991) . . . . .Catherine O'Fallon
Necessary Roughness (1991) . . . . . . . . Suzanne Carter
The Taking of Beverly Hills (1991) . . . . . . . .Laura Sage
The Favor (1994) . . . . . . . . . . . . . . . . . . . . . . .Kathy
*Made for Cable TV:*
**Dream On: I'm With Stupid** (1994; HBO)
. . . . . . . . . . . . . . . . . . . . . . . . . . . . Jill Chadfield
• 0:05—Back side of left breast, while undressing Mar-
tin on the sofa. Don't see her face.
*Made for TV Movies:*
The Amy Fisher Story (1993) . . . . . . . . . Amy Pagnozzi

TV:
Santa Barbara . . . . . . . . . . . . . . . . . . . . . . Mary Duvall
Knightwatch (1988-89). . . . . . . . . . . . . . . . . .Barbara
Harts of the West (1993- ). . . . . . . . . . . . . . . . Alison

## Kozak, Heidi

Sister of actress Harley Jane Kozak.

Films:
Slumber Party Massacre II (1987) . . . . . . . . . . . . . Sally
**Friday the 13th, Part VII: The New Blood** (1988)
. . . . . . . . . . . . . . . . . . . . . . . . . . . . . . . Sandra
• 0:36—Buns, while taking off clothes to go skinny
dipping. Brief breasts under water just before get-
ting killed by Jason.
Society (1989). . . . . . . . . . . . . . . . . . . . . . . Shauna

## • Kozlowski, Linda

Wife of actor Paul Hogan.

Films:
**Crocodile Dundee** (1986; Australian) . . . Sue Charlton
•• 0:31—Buns in black one piece swimsuit with thong
back after she takes off her skirt to fill her canteen
with water.
Crocodile Dundee II (1988). . . . . . . . . . . . Sue Charlton
Pass the Ammo (1988) . . . . . . . . . . . . . . . . . . Claire
Target: Favorite Son (1988). . . . . . . . . . . . . . . . .n.a.
Almost an Angel (1990) . . . . . . . . . . . . . . Rose Garner
**Backstreet Justice** (1993) . . . . . . . . . . Kerri Finnegan
••• 0:31—Breasts in open dress and while making love
in bedroom with John Shea.
The Neighbor (1993) . . . . . . . . . . . . . . . Mary Westhill

## Krige, Alice

Films:
Chariots of Fire (1981) . . . . . . . . . . . . . . Sybil Gordon
**Ghost Story** (1981). . . . . . . . . . . . . . . . . . Alma/Eva
• 0:41—Brief breasts making love in bedroom with
Craig Wasson.
•• 0:44—Breasts in bathtub with Wasson.
•• 0:46—Breasts sitting up in bed.
••• 0:49—Buns, then breasts standing on balcony turn-
ing and walking to bedroom talking to Wasson.
**King David** (1985) . . . . . . . . . . . . . . . . . . .Bathsheba
•• 1:16—Full frontal nudity getting a bath outside at
dusk while Richard Gere watches.
Barfly (1987). . . . . . . . . . . . . . . . . . . . . . . . . . Tully
Haunted Summer (1988) . . . . . . . . . . . . Mary Godwin
See You in the Morning (1989). . . . . . . . Beth Goodwin
Code Name: Chaos (1990) . . . . . . . . . . . . . . . Isabelle
Stephen King's Sleepwalkers (1992) . . . . . . .Mary Brady
Made for Cable Movies:
Baja Oklahoma (1988; HBO). . . . . . . . . . . . Patsy Cline
Ladykiller (1992; USA). . . . . . . . . . . . . . .May Packard
Made for Cable TV:
Iran: Days of Crisis (1991; TNT). . . . . . . . . . . . . .n.a.
Made for TV Movies:
Jack Reed: Badge of Honor (1993). . . . . . .Joan Anatole
Judgment Day: The John List Story (1993) . . Jean Syfert

## Krim, Viju

Films:
Bloodsucking Freaks (1982) . . . . . . . . . . . . . .Natasha
**Twelfth Night** (1988; Italian). . . . . . . . . . . . . .Maria
•• 1:09—Breasts, dancing in tavern in open top.

## Kriss, Katherine

Films:
American Flyers (1985) . . . . . . . . . . . . . . . . . . .Vera
**Hot Chili** (1985). . . . . . . . . . . . . . . . . . .Allison Baxter
••• 0:56—Breasts getting out of the pool and talking to
Ricky.
• 1:09—Buns and side view of left breast, while lying
down and kissing Ricky.
Student Confidential (1987). . . . . . . . . . Elaine's Friend

## Kristel, Sylvia

Films:
**Because of the Cats** (1973) . . . . . . . . . . . . . . . . n.a.
• 1:09—Breasts and buns, under water with Case.
**Emmanuelle** (1974). . . . . . . . . . . . . . . . .Emmanuelle
(R-rated version reviewed.)
• 0:00—Very brief left breast in robe, while sitting on
bed.
• 0:02—Breasts in B&W photos.
• 0:10—Breasts and buns, making love in bed with
her husband under a net.
• 0:13—Brief breasts taking off bikini top by swimming pool.
••• 0:14—Breasts getting up from chair, then full frontal
nudity while talking to Ariane.
••• 0:15—Nude, swimming under water. Nice.
• 0:18—Partial left breast, while sleeping in bed.
•• 0:24—Breasts, making love with a stranger on an
airplane.
•• 0:31—Breasts with Ariane in the squash court.
**Julia** (1974; German) . . . . . . . . . . . . . . . . . . . . .Julia
0:23—Brief breasts in the lake.
• 0:25—Breasts on deck in the lake.
• 0:28—Brief breasts changing clothes at night. Long
shot.
•• 0:34—Breasts on boat with two boys.
•• 0:42—Breasts taking off her towel.
• 1:12—Breasts on tennis court with Patrick.
**Emmanuelle, The Joys of a Woman** (1975)
. . . . . . . . . . . . . . . . . . . . . . . . . . . . .Emmanuelle
• 0:18—Breasts making love with her husband in bedroom.
•• 0:22—Breasts, then full frontal nudity, undressing in
bedroom, then making love with her husband.
••• 0:32—Breasts with acupuncture needles stuck in
her. More breasts masturbating while fantasizing
about Christopher.
• 0:53—Right breast, while making love with polo
player in locker room.
••• 0:58—Nude, getting massaged by another woman.
••• 1:14—Right breast in bedroom in open dress, then
breasts with Jean in bed. Flashback of her with three
guys in a bordello.

**Goodbye Emmanuelle** (1977) . . . . . . . . Emmanuelle
•• 0:03—Full frontal nudity in bath and getting out.
•• 0:04—Full frontal nudity taking off dress.
••• 0:06—Full frontal nudity in bed with Angelique.
••• 0:26—Breasts with photographer in old house.
0:42—Brief side view of right breast, in bed with Jean.
••• 1:03—Full frontal nudity on beach with movie director.
•• 1:06—Full frontal nudity lying on beach sleeping.
•• 1:28—Side view of left breast lying on beach with Gregory while dreaming.
Airport '79: The Concorde (1979) . . . . . . . . . . . Isabelle
**Tigers in Lipstick** (1979) . . . . . . . . . . . . . . . The Girl
0:04—Breasts in photograph on the sand.
0:06—Braless in sheer nightgown lying in bed.
•• 0:09—Breasts lying in bed with The Arab.
•• 0:16—Lying in bed in red lingerie, then left breast for awhile.
**Lady Chatterley's Lover** (1981; French/British)
. . . . . . . . . . . . . . . . . . . . . . Constance Chatterley
•• 0:25—Nude in front of mirror.
• 0:59—Brief breasts with the Gardener.
• 1:04—Brief breasts.
••• 1:16—Nude in bedroom with the Gardener.
**Private Lessons** (1981). . . . . . . . . . . . . . . . . Mallow
• 0:20—Very brief breasts sitting up next to the pool when the sprinklers go on.
•• 0:24—Breasts and buns, stripping for Billy. Some shots might be a body double.
•• 0:51—Breasts in bed when she "dies" with Howard Hesseman.
• 1:28—Breasts making love with Billy. Some shots might be a body double.
Private School (1983) . . . . . . . . . . . . . . .Ms. Copuletta
0:57—In wet white dress after falling in the pool.
**Emmanuelle IV** (1984). . . . . . . . . . . . . . . . . . . . Sylvia
•• 0:00—Breasts in photos during opening credits.
**The Big Bet** (1985) . . . . . . . . . . . . . . . . . . . . Michelle
• 0:07—Left breast in open nightgown while Chris tries to fix her sink.
•• 0:20—Breasts dressing while Chris watches through binoculars.
•• 0:28—Breasts undressing while Chris watches through binoculars.
••• 0:40—Breasts getting out of the shower and drying herself off.
• 1:00—Breasts getting into bed while Chris watches through binoculars.
••• 1:13—Breasts in bedroom with Chris, then making love.
**Mata Hari** (1985) . . . . . . . . . . . . . . . . . . . . Mata Hari
••• 0:11—Breasts making love with a guy on a train.
•• 0:31—Breasts standing by window after making love with the soldier.
• 0:35—Breasts making love in empty house by the fireplace.
•• 0:52—Breasts masturbating in bed wearing black stockings.

•• 1:02—Breasts during sword fight with another topless woman.
•• 1:03—Breasts in bed smoking opium and making love with two women.
**The Arrogant** (1987). . . . . . . . . . . . . . . . . . . . .Julie
• 0:14—In wet blouse, in lake.
• 0:22—In wet blouse again, walking out of the lake.
• 0:44—Brief breasts several times, in gaping dress.
Casanova (1987) . . . . . . . . . . . . . . . . . . . . . . . . . . n.a.
**Red Heat** (1987; U.S./German) . . . . . . . . . . . . . Sofia
0:23—In red lingerie.
•• 0:56—Breasts in shower room scene.
• 1:01—Brief breasts raping Linda Blair.
Dracula's Widow (1988). . . . . . . . . . . . . . . . . Vanessa
**Hot Blood** (1989; Spanish). . . . . . . . . . . . . . . . Sylvia
• 0:44—Buns, getting molested by Dom Luis.
**Beauty School** (1993) . . . . . . . . . . . . . . . . . . . Sylvia
• 1:27—Brief breasts in bed with the private investigator.
*Video Tapes:*
**Playboy Video Magazine, Volume 2** (1983)
. . . . . . . . . . . . . . . . . . . . . . . . . . . . . . . . . . . Herself
••• 0:16—Breasts in various scenes from her films.
*Magazines:*
**Playboy** (Jun 1975) . . . . . . Sex in Cinema French Style
•• 90—Breasts in small photo from *Emmanuelle*.
•• 91—Right breast and lower frontal nudity.
**Playboy** (Nov 1975) . . . . . . . . . . . Sex in Cinema 1975
• 136—Buns from *Emmanuelle*.
**Playboy** (Dec 1975) . . . . . . . . . . . .Sex Stars of 1975
••• 182—Full frontal nudity.
**Playboy** (Mar 1976) . . . . . . . . . . . Encore Emmanuelle!
••• 77-81—Breasts.
**Playboy** (May 1976) . . . . . . . . . . . . . .Oui Magazine Ad
• 171—Right breast, twice, in advertisement for *Oui* magazine.
**Playboy** (Dec 1976) . . . . . . . . . . . .Sex Stars of 1976
•• 187—Breasts drinking from champagne bottle.
**Playboy** (Nov 1977) . . . . . . . . . . . Sex in Cinema 1977
•• 164-165—Right breast, while in the surf with Jean-Pierre Bouvier from *Goodbye Emmanuelle*.
**Playboy** (Dec 1977) . . . . . . . . . . . . .Sex Stars of 1977
•• 214—Breasts with Jeff Bridges from *Behind the Iron Mask*.
**Playboy** (Nov 1980) . . . . . . . . . . . Sex in Cinema 1980
• 172—Lower frontal nudity.
••• 182—Breasts in still from *Private Lessons*.
**Playboy** (Dec 1980) . . . . . . . . . . . . .Sex Stars of 1980
••• 245—Breasts.
**Playboy** (Dec 1984) . . . . . . . . . . . . .Sex Stars of 1984
• 205—Left breast, lying on chair.

# Kristen, Marta

*Films:*
Terminal Island (1973) . . . . . . . . . . . . . . . . . .Lee Phillips
**Gemini Affair** (1974). . . . . . . . . . . . . . . . . . . . . .Julie
••• 0:32—Breasts wearing beige panties talking with Jessica in the bathroom.

- 0:56—Very, very brief left breast and lower frontal nudity standing next to bed with a guy. Very brief left breast in bed with him.
- ••• 0:59—Breasts and buns making love in bed with Jessica. Wowzers!

**Once** (1974) . . . . . . . . . . . . . . . . . . . . . . . . . . Humanity
(Not available on video tape.)
Battle Beyond the Stars (1980) . . . . . . . . . . . . . . . . . Lux
*TV:*
Lost in Space (1965-68) . . . . . . . . . . . . . Judy Robinson

## Kruschke, Karman
*Films:*
Under the Gun (1989) . . . . . . . . . . . . . . . . Girl at Pool
Hot Under the Collar (1991) . . . . . . . . . . . . . . . Sherry
**Ironheart** (1991) . . . . . . . . . . . . . . . . . . . . . . . . . . Kristi
- •• 0:55—Buns and brief side of left breast, getting out of bed with John. Brief breasts in bathroom.

Loaded Weapon 1 (1993) . . . . . . . . One of the Cindys

## Kudoh, Youki
*Films:*
The Crazy Family (1986; Japanese) . . . . . . . . Daughter
Typhoon Club (1986; Japanese) . . . . . . . . . . . . . . Rie
**Mystery Train** (1989) . . . . . . . . . . . . . . . . . . Mitzuko
- •• 0:30—In black bra, in bed. Breasts making love with Jun in bed.
  0:37—In black bra, while packing suitcase.

## La Vette, Maureen
*Films:*
**Hardcase and Fist** (1988) . . . . . . . . . . . . . Nora Wilde
- •• 0:24—Breasts, getting out of spa when Tony starts shooting gun in the house.

Virgin High (1990) . . . . . . . . . . . . . . . . . Mrs. Murphy

## • Labdon, Helen
*Video Tapes:*
**Page 3 Girls** (1993) . . . . . . . . . . . . . . . . . . . . Herself
*Magazines:*
**Playboy's Book of Lingerie** (Sep 1992) . . . . . Herself
- • 48—Left breast.
- •• 83—Left breast.

**Playboy's Book of Lingerie** (Jan 1993) . . . . . . Herself
- ••• 34—Breasts.

**Playboy's Book of Lingerie** (May 1993) . . . . . Herself
- ••• 75—Breasts.

## Lace, Vanna
*Video Tapes:*
**Penthouse The Great Pet Hunt—Part I** (1992) . Pet
*CD-ROM:*
**Venus' Playhouse** (1994) . . . . . . . . . . . . . . . . Herself
*Magazines:*
**Penthouse** (Mar 1992) . . . . . . . . . . Miss Nude World
- ••• 38-49—Nude.

## Lahaie, Brigitte
*Films:*
**Come Play with Me** (1977; German) . . . . . . . . . n.a.
**Friendly Favors** (1983) . . . . . . . . . . . . . . . . . . . Greta
*a.k.a. Six Swedes on a Pump*
- •• 0:02—Full frontal nudity riding a guy in bed. (She's wearing a necklace.)
- ••• 0:39—Full frontal nudity having fun on "exercise bike."
- ••• 0:46—Full frontal nudity taking off clothes and running outside with the other girls. Nice slow motion shots.
- •• 0:53—Breasts, making love with Kerstin.
- ••• 1:01—Full frontal nudity in room with the Italian.
- ••• 1:15—Full frontal nudity in room with guy from the band.

**Joy: Chapter II** (1985; French) . . . . . . . . . . . . . . . . Joy
*a.k.a. Joy and Joan*
- • 0:01—Left breast in coat during photo session.
- ••• 0:11—Nude, getting into bubble bath and out with Bruce.
- •• 0:20—Breasts, lying in bed after party.
- •• 0:22—Breasts, talking on the phone.
- ••• 0:27—Nude, getting a massage from Milaka. Nice.
- •• 0:32—Breasts changing clothes.
- ••• 0:45—In bra, then breasts changing clothes with Joanne.
- •• 0:47—Full frontal nudity, masturbating in bed. Medium long shot.
- ••• 0:54—Nude, making love with Joanne on train. Nice, long scene!
- • 1:03—Breasts in the water with Joanne.
- • 1:08—Breasts, getting molested by a bunch of guys in the shower.
- • 1:10—Right breast, lying next to a pool.
- •• 1:17—Nude in bubble bath with Joanne and getting out.
- • 1:23—Buns, dancing with Joanne.
- ••• 1:27—Nude, making love with Joanne and Mark.

**Henry & June** (1990) . . . . . . . . . . . . . . Harry's Whore
- •• 0:23—Brief buns and breasts under sheer white dress going up stairs with Fred Ward.
- •• 1:22—Breasts in sheer white dress again. Nude under dress walking up stairs.
- ••• 1:23—Breasts and buns making love with another woman while Anais and Hugo watch.
- • 1:31—Breasts in bed with Anais. Intercut with Uma Thurman, so hard to tell who is who.

*Magazines:*
Playboy (Nov 1985) . . . . . . . . . . . . . . . . . . . Grapevine

## Laine, Karen
*Films:*
Pretty in Pink (1986) . . . . . . . . . . . . . . . . . Girl at Prom
*Made for Cable Movies:*
**Baja Oklahoma** (1988; HBO) . . . . . . . . Girl at Drive-In
- • 0:04—Left breast, in truck with a jerk guy. Dark, hard to see anything.

## Lala

See: Sloatman, Lala.

## Lamarr, Hedy

First instance of celebrity nudity in film.
*Films:*
**Ecstasy** (1932) . . . . . . . . . . . . . . . . . . . . . . . . The Wife
- 0:25—Brief breasts starting to run after a horse in a field.
- 0:26—Long shot running through the woods, side view naked, then brief breasts hiding behind a tree.
Algiers (1938) . . . . . . . . . . . . . . . . . . . . . . . . . . . Gaby
Ziegfield Girl (1941) . . . . . . . . . . . . . . . . . Sandra Kolter
Dishonored Lady (1947) . . . . . . . . . . Madeleine Damien
Samson and Delilah (1949) . . . . . . . . . . . . . . . . Delilah
Instant Karma (1990) . . . . . . . . . . . . . . . Movie Goddess

## • Lamatsch, Andrea

*Films:*
**Sudden Thunder** (1990) . . . . . . . . . . . Patricia Merrill
- 0:18—Right breast, while getting raped by jerks in the woods and brief breasts after escaping from them.
- ••• 0:27—Nude, while skinny dipping in pond (some body parts are visible under the water).
Blood Ring (1991) . . . . . . . . . . . . . . . . . . Susan Dalton

## Lamb, Debra

*Films:*
Stripped to Kill (1987) . . . . . . . . . . . . . Amateur Dancer
B.O.R.N. (1988) . . . . . . . . . . . . . . . . . . . . . . . . . . . Sue
**Deathrow Game Show** (1988) . . . . . Shanna Shallow
- ••• 0:23—Breasts dancing in white G-string and garter belt during the show.
**Hardcase and Fist** (1988) . . . . . . . . . . . . . . . . Chieko
- 1:08—Buns in G-string while dancing on stage in a club.
- ••• 1:09—Breasts while dancing on stage and doing some fire eating. Nice, long scene.
- •• 1:13—Breasts, three times, while peeking from behind curtain.
Midnight Cabaret (1988) . . . . . . . . . . . . . . . . . . Dancer
**Stripped to Kill II** (1988) . . . . . . . . . . . . . . . . Mantra
- •• 0:04—Breasts during strip dance routine.
- ••• 0:42—Breasts in black lingerie during strip dance routine.
**W. B., Blue and the Bean** (1988) . . . . . . .Motel Clerk
*a.k.a. Bail Out*
- 0:42—Full frontal nudity opening door in motel to talk to David Hasselhoff.
**Warlords** (1988) . . . . . . . . . . . . . . . . . . . Harem Girl
- ••• 0:14—Breasts, getting her blouse ripped off by a bad guy, then kidnapped.
- ••• 0:17—Breasts in harem pants while shackled to another girl.
**Beverly Hills Vamp** (1989) . . . . . . . . . . . . . . . Jessica
0:33—In black slip, with Russell.
- ••• 0:36—Breasts and buns in red G-string posing for Russell while he photographs her.

••• 0:41—More breasts posing on bed.
1:09—In white nightgown attacking Russell in bed with Michelle Bauer and Jillian Kesner.
1:19—In white nightgown, getting killed as a vampire by Kyle.
**Out Cold** (1989) . . . . . . . . . . . . . . . . . Panetti's Dancer
- 1:04—Brief breasts dancing in G-string on stage. Don't see her face.
**Satan's Princess** (1989) . . . . . . . . . . Fire Eater/Dancer
- •• 0:23—Breasts in G-string doing a fire dance in club.
- • 0:25—Breasts, doing more dancing. Long shot.
The Turn-On (1989) . . . . . . . . . . Assistant in White Dress
*a.k.a. Le Clic*
**Evil Spirits** (1990) . . . . . . . . . . . . . . . . . . . . . . . Tina
- ••• 0:22—Breasts, while dancing in her bedroom while Michael Berryman watches through peep hole. Most of her buns in underwear. Long scene.
**Invisible Maniac** (1990) . . . . . . . . . . . . . . . . . . Betty
- • 0:21—Buns and very brief side view of right breast in the shower with the other girls.
- ••• 0:43—In bra, then breasts and buns standing on the left in the locker room with the other girls.
- • 0:44—Buns and brief breasts in the shower with the other girls.
- •• 0:56—In bra, then breasts getting killed by Dr. Smith.
- • 0:58—Brief breasts, dead, discovered by April and Joan.
Mob Boss (1990) . . . . . . . . . . . . . . . . . . . . . . . . Janise
Point Break (1991) . . . Uncredited Flame Blower at Party
*Made for Cable TV:*
Dream On: And Your Little Dog, Too (1991; HBO)
. . . . . . . . . . . . . . . . . . . . . . . . . . . . . . Snake Lady
*Video Tapes:*
**Best Buns on the Beach** (1987) . . . . . . . Buns Model
0:03—In bra and mini skirt, holding model buns.
- ••• 0:04—Buns, in G-string, bending over during "Ideal Buns" demonstration.
**Trashy Ladies Wrestling** (1987) . . . . . . . . . . . . . n.a.
- •• 0:48—In black and silver S&M costume. Buns in G-string.
0:49—In black bra, G-string, stockings and boots, while fire eating.
*Magazines:*
**Playboy** (Jul 1991) . . . . . . . . . . . . . . . . . . . . Grapevine
- ••• 174—In boots, lying on the floor. B&W.

## • Lamothe, Michelle

See: Brin, Michele.

## • Landgrebe, Gudrun

*Films:*
**Woman in Flames** (1984; German) . . . . . . . . . . . Eva
**The Berlin Affair** (1985; Italian/German)
. . . . . . . . . . . . . . . . . . . . . . . . Louise Von Hollendorf
- • 0:23—Very brief inner half of left breast, twice, while making out with Mio.
Colonel Redl (1985; Hungarian) . . . . . . . Katalin Kubinyi

## Landon, Laurene

Girlfriend of Christian Brando (Marlon Brando's son).
*Films:*
...All the Marbles (1981)..................... Molly
  *a.k.a. The California Dolls*
Airplane II: The Sequel (1982)................. Test
I, the Jury (1982)........................... Velda
**Hundra** (1983) ........................Hundra
  • 0:29—Very brief breasts, several times, riding her
  horse in the surf. Partial buns. Blurry.
Yellow Hair and the Fortress of Gold (1984)
  ..................................... Yellow Hair
America 3000 (1986) ....................... Vena
Armed Response (1986) ................... Deborah
It's Alive III: Island of the Alive (1988) ........... Sally
Maniac Cop (1988)...................... Theresa
Wicked Stepmother (1989)................. Vanilla
The Ambulance (1990)..................... Patty
Maniac Cop 2 (1990) ............. Teresa Mallory

## Landry, Karen

*Films:*
The Personals (1982).................... Adrienne
**Patti Rocks** (1988) ....................... Patti
  0:48—Buns, walking from bathroom to bedroom
  and shutting the door. Long shot.
  • 0:48—Very brief right breast in shower with Billy.
  •• 1:04—Breasts in bed with Eddie while Billy is out in
  the living room.
Ambition (1991) ............. Woman in Bookstore

## Landry, Tamara

a.k.a. Shelby Lane.
*Films:*
**R.S.V.P.** (1984)........................... Vicky
  •• 0:43—Breasts sitting in van taking her top off.
  •• 0:48—Breasts making love in the van with two guys.
Las Vegas Weekend (1986) ..................... Lea
Tango & Cash (1989) .................. Girl in Bar
Delusion (1990) ...................... Arabella
Mob Boss (1990)............................. n.a.
**The Pamela Principle** (1992) ....... Anne Breeding
  (Unrated version reviewed.)
  ••• 0:08—Buns, while lying in bed with Carl, then
  breasts and lower frontal nudity.
  ••• 0:28—Breasts, while sitting up in bed.
  ••• 0:48—Breasts, waking up in bed, then buns and
  lower frontal nudity getting out.
  ••• 0:57—Breasts, while making love with Carl in the
  kitchen, then buns in bed.
  ••• 1:03—Buns and breasts while in the shower.
**Beach Babes From Beyond** (1993) ...........Luna
  •• 0:02—Breasts, while taking off pink top, getting
  dressed and talking with Xena and Sola.
  ••• 0:34—Breast, while making love in back of van with
  Jerry.
  •• 0:39—Buns, in swimsuit at the beach.
  • 0:58—Buns, while dancing in swimsuits and boots
  on stage at beach during bikini contest.

**Renegade: Fighting Cage** (1993) ........... Ellen
  (Nudity added for video release.)
  •• 1:06—Breasts and buns in panties, making love with
  a guy and another woman.
**Strike a Pose** (1993) ..................... Candy
  ••• 0:23—In black bra, panties and stockings, then nude
  with Carl. Long scene.
  ••• 1:01—Breasts, while making love on bed.
*Video Tapes:*
**Playboy's Erotic Fantasies III** (1993)
  ........................... Lube Job/Customer
  ••• 0:20—Buns in lingerie in car repair shop, then nude
  while making love with the mechanic.
**Playboy's Secret Confessions** (1993)
  ........................... Jailhouse Rock/Tina
  ••• 0:32—In red lingerie, then nude, while making love
  with the guy in jail cell.

## Lands, Wendy

*Films:*
**One Night Only** (1984; Canadian)............ Jane
  •• 0:36—Breasts taking a bath while Jamie watches
  through keyhole.
  •• 0:38—Brief left breast in open robe.
  • 1:15—Brief breasts in bed with policeman.
Busted Up (1986)................. Drayton's Date

## Lane, Diane

Wife of actor Christopher Lambert.
*Films:*
A Little Romance (1979)................... Lauren
Cattle Annie and Little Britches (1980).......... Jenny
  0:40—Briefly in braless, wet long johns while stand-
  ing in lake.
Touched by Love (1980) ................... Karen
**Ladies and Gentlemen, The Fabulous Stains**
  (1982) ......................... Corinne Burns
  (Not available on video tape.)
National Lampoon Goes to the Movies (1982)..... Lisa
  *a.k.a. Movie Madness*
Six Pack (1982) ........................ Breezy
The Outsiders (1983)............... Cherry Valance
Rumble Fish (1983) ........................ Patty
The Cotton Club (1984)................ Vera Cicero
Streets of Fire (1984) ................... Ellen Aim
**The Big Town** (1987)................. Lorry Dane
  0:51—Doing a strip routine in the club wearing a G-
  string and pasties while Matt Dillon watches.
  ••• 1:17—Breasts making love on bed with Dillon in hotel room.
  1:27—Brief left breast wearing pasties walking into
  dressing room while Dillon plays craps.
**Lady Beware** (1987) ................. Katya Yarno
  0:10—Walking around in her apartment in a red silk
  teddy getting ready for bed.
  0:14—Lying down in white semi-transparent pajamas after fantasizing.
  0:24—In black bra in apartment.

••• 0:46—Breasts in her apartment and in bed making love with Mack.

•• 0:52—Brief breasts during Jack's flashback when he is in the store.

•• 0:59—Brief side view breasts in bed with Mack again during another of Jack's flashbacks.

• 1:02—Very brief breasts in bed with Mack.

1:06—Brief breasts lying in bed behind thin curtain in another of Jack's flashbacks.

**Priceless Beauty** (1989; Italian) . . . . . . . . China/Anna

•• 0:34—Breasts in bed with Christopher Lambert.

• 0:35—Brief left breast, then side of right breast on top of Lambert.

**Vital Signs** (1989). . . . . . . . . . . . . . . . . . . Gina Wyler

••• 1:11—In white bra, then breasts making love with Michael in the basement.

**Chaplin** (1992; British/U.S.) . . . . . . . . Paulette Goddard

• 1:33—Upper half of breasts, while lying in bed.

**Knight Moves** (1992) . . . . . . . . . . . . . Kathy Sheppard

•• 0:45—Breasts while making love with Christopher Lambert in bed.

My New Gun (1992). . . . . . . . . . . . . . . . Debbie Bender

Indian Summer (1993) . . . . . Beth Warden/Claire Everett

*Made for Cable Movies:*

**Descending Angel** (1990; HBO) . . . . . . . . Irina Stroia

• 0:01—Brief right breast, while making love with Eric Roberts on train during opening credits.

•• 0:44—In white camisole top with Roberts, then breasts lying in bed with him.

*Made for Cable TV:*

Fallen Angels: Murder, Obliquely (1993; Showtime)
. . . . . . . . . . . . . . . . . . . . . . . . . . . . Bernette Stone

(Available on video tape on *Fallen Angels One*.)

0:10—In black bustier, girdle and stockings after ripping off her red dress in front of Alan Rickman and Laura Dern.

*Miniseries:*

Lonesome Dove (1989). . . . . . . . . . . . . . Lorena Wood

*Made for TV Movies:*

Oldest Living Confederate Widow Tells All (1994)
. . . . . . . . . . . . . . . . . . . . . . . Lucy Marsden (young)

# Lane, Krista

See: Lynn, Rebecca.

# Lane, Nikki

*Films:*

**Death of a Soldier** (1985; Australian)
. . . . . . . . . . . . . . . . . . . . . . . . . . . . Stripper in Bar

•• 0:49—Nude, dancing on stage.

**The Big Hurt** (1987; Australian) . . . . . . . Tank Girl #1

• 1:26—Possible full frontal nudity standing in water filled tube. Can't recognize her because wearing a swim mask and breathing apparatus.

# • Lane, Shelby

See: Landry, Tamara.

# • Lane, Trisha

*Films:*

Down the Drain (1989) . . . . . . . . . . . . . . . . . . . . . Robin

**Mardi Gras for the Devil** (1993) . . . . . . . . . . . Jackie

•• 0:03—Breasts, while in panties, while simulating sex in front of Michael Ironside.

# • Lang, Helen

*Films:*

**Revenge of the Cheerleaders** (1976) . . . . . . . . Leslie

• 0:00—Left breast, changing in back seat of car.

•• 0:07—Breasts in girl's restroom powdering herself.

••• 0:53—Nude with Gail and hiker guy frolicking in the woods.

•• 0:55—Nude some more making out with the hiker guy with Gail.

••• 0:57—Nude walking down road with Gail when stopped by a policeman.

••• 1:24—Breasts during Hawaiian party. Nice dancing during the end credits.

*Magazines:*

**Penthouse** (Jul 1976). . . . . . . . . . . . . . . . . . . . . . Pet

••• 93-105—Nude.

# • lang, k.d.

Singer.

Real name is Katherine Dawn Lang.

*Films:*

**Salmonberries** (1991; German). . . . . . . . . . Kotzebue

••• 0:13—Brief full frontal nudity while standing in the library.

# Lange, Jessica

*Films:*

King Kong (1976) . . . . . . . . . . . . . . . . . . . . . . . Dwan

1:20—Almost breasts when King Kong is playing with her in his hand. Hand covers nipple of left breast.

All That Jazz (1979) . . . . . . . . . . . . . . . . . . . . Angelique

How to Beat the High Cost of Living (1980). . . . . Louise

**The Postman Always Rings Twice** (1981)
. . . . . . . . . . . . . . . . . . . . . . . . . . Cora Papadakis

0:17—Making love with Jack Nicholson on the kitchen table. No nudity, but still exciting.

0:18—Pubic hair peeking out of right side of her panties when Nicholson grabs her crotch.

• 1:03—Very, very brief breasts, then very, very brief right breast twice, when Nicholson rips her dress down to simulate a car accident.

1:26—Brief lower frontal nudity when Nicholson starts crawling up over her in bed.

**Frances** (1982) . . . . . . . . . . . . . . . . . . . Frances Farmer

• 0:41—Very brief upper half of left breast, while lying on bed and throwing a newspaper.

• 0:50—Brief full frontal nudity covered with bubbles standing up in bathtub and wrapping a towel around herself. Long shot, hard to see.

- 1:01—Brief buns and right breast running into the bathroom when the police bust in. Very, very brief full frontal nudity, then buns closing the bathroom door. Reportedly her, even though you don't see her face clearly.

Tootsie (1982)........................ Julie Nichols
(Academy Award for Best Supporting Actress.)
Country (1984)........................... Jewell Ivy
Sweet Dreams (1985).................. Patsy Kline
Crimes of the Heart (1986)........... Meg Magrath
**Everybody's All-American** (1988)............ Babs
  0:32—Brief breasts under sheer nightgown in bedroom with Dennis Quaid.
- 0:54—Buns and very, very brief side view of left breast by the campfire by the lake with Timothy Hutton at night. Might be a body double.

Far North (1988)........................... Kate
Men Don't Leave (1989)............. Beth Macauley
Blue Skies (1991)..................... Carly Marshall
Cape Fear (1991) ................... Leigh Bowden
Night and the City (1992)........... Helen Nosseros
*Made for Cable Movies:*
Cat on a Hot Tin Roof (1984; HBO)........... Maggie
*Made for TV Movies:*
O Pioneers! (1992)......... Adult Alexandra Bergson

# Langencamp, Heather

*Films:*
**Nickel Mountain** (1985) ................... Callie
••• 0:24—Breasts in bed lying with Willard.
- 0:29—Side view of left breast and brief breasts falling on bed with Willard.
  0:29—In white panties, peeking out the window.

A Nightmare on Elm Street (1985) ... Nancy Thompson
A Nightmare on Elm Street 3: The Dream Warriors (1987).........................Nancy Thompson
Shocker (1989).............................Victim
*Made for TV Movies:*
Tonya & Nancy: The Inside Story (1994)
.................................Nancy Kerrigan
*TV:*
Just the Ten of Us (1989-90) ................. Marie

# Langenfeld, Sarah

*Films:*
**Blood Link** (1983)....................... Christine
•• 1:01—Breasts while taking her top off in bed with Craig.
- 1:04—Breasts in bed with Keith.

The Act (1984) ........................... Leslie

# Langlois, Lisa

*Films:*
Blood Relatives (1978; French/Canadian) ....... Muriel
Violette (1978; French) ................... Maddy
Happy Birthday to Me (1980; Canadian)....... Amelia
Klondike Fever (1980)..................... Gertie
Class of 1984 (1982; Canadian) .............. Patsy
Deadly Eyes (1982; Canadian)............... Trudy

**The Man Who Wasn't There** (1983)... Cindy Worth
•• 0:58—Nude running away from two policemen after turning visible.
••• 1:08—Breasts in white panties dancing in her apartment with an invisible Steve Guttenberg.
  1:47—Very, very brief upper half of left breast, while throwing bouquet at wedding.

The Joy of Sex (1984)...................... Melanie
The Slugger's Wife (1985) ............ Aline Cooper
The Nest (1987)................. Elizabeth Johnson
Transformations (1988) ................... Miranda
Mind Field (1990) ................... Sarah Paradis

# Langrick, Margaret

*Films:*
My American Cousin (1985; Canadian) ........ Sandy
Harry and the Hendersons (1987) .... Sarah Henderson
**Cold Comfort** (1988)................... Dolores
•• 0:16—In tank top and panties, then breasts undressing in front of Stephen.
- 0:19—Very brief side of left breast and buns getting robe.
•• 0:41—Doing strip tease in front of her dad and Stephen. In black bra and panties, then breasts.
- 0:42—Very brief breasts jumping into bed.

Martha, Ruth & Edie (1988; Canadian) .... Young Edie
Thunderground (1989) ..................... Casey
American Boyfriends (1990)........... Sandy Wilcox
*TV:*
Camp Wilder (1992-93).................... Beth

# Lankford, Kim

*Films:*
**Malibu Beach** (1978)...................... Dina
  0:32—Buns, running into the ocean.
- 0:34—Brief right breast getting out of the ocean.
- 1:16—Right breast on beach at night with boyfriend.
- 1:19—Brief breasts at top of the stairs.
•• 1:20—Brief breasts when her parent's come home.
- 1:21—Breasts in bed with her boyfriend.

The Octagon (1980) ...................... Nancy
Cameron's Closet (1989) .............. Dory Lansing
*Made for Cable TV:*
**The Hitchhiker: A Time for Rifles** (1985; HBO)
..................................... Rae Bridgeman
••• 0:03—Breasts on the pool table while making love with a guy.

Dream On: Premarital Ex (1990; HBO)........ Hannah
*TV:*
The Waverly Wonders (1978)......... Connie Rafkin
Knots Landing (1979-83) .............. Ginger Ward

# Lanko, Vivian

*Films:*
**The Rejuvenator** (1988) .......... Elizabeth Warren
- 0:31—Brief breasts in bed with Dr. Ashton while making love. Don't see her face well.

Simple Men (1992; U.S./British)................ Nun

## • Lara, Joanne

*Films:*
**The Baby Doll Murders** (1992) . . . . . . . . Mrs. Jayson
••• 0:44—Breasts, while taking a shower, getting out,
drying herself off, walking to bed and talking on the
phone. Long scene.
•• 0:46—Breasts, on bed while getting killed and afterwards.
**Molly & Gina** (1993). . . . . . . . . . . . . . . . . . . . . . n.a.
••• 0:00—Breasts and buns in G-string while dancing on
stage during opening credits.

## Large, Bonnie

*Films:*
**The Happy Hooker Goes to Washington** (1977)
. . . . . . . . . . . . . . . . . . . . . . . . . . . Carolyn (Model)
• 0:06—Breasts during photo shoot.
*Magazines:*
**Playboy** (Mar 1973). . . . . . . . . . . . . . . . . . Playmate
••• 106-113—Nude.

## Larsen, Annabelle

*Films:*
Hard Rock Zombies (1985) . . . . . . . . . . . . . . . Groupie
**Alligator Eyes** (1990) . . . . . . . . . . . . . . . . . . . Pauline
•• 0:42—Nude, getting up from bed and walking
around.

## Lasseter, Vicki

*Video Tapes:*
**Playboy's Playmate Review** (1982) . . . . . . Playmate
••• 0:43—Full frontal nudity in office, then in the
woods.
*Magazines:*
**Playboy** (Feb 1981) . . . . . . . . . . . . . . . . . . . Playmate

## Laure, Carole

*Films:*
Sweet Movie (1975) . . . . . . . . . . . . . . . . . . Virgin Bride
**Strange Shadows in an Empty Room** (1976)
. . . . . . . . . . . . . . . . . . . . . . . . . . . . . . . . . . . Louise
••• 1:29—Brief breasts, while running around the house
and frolicking with Mrs. Wilkinson and Fred. Breasts
while in slow motion, when beating Mrs. Wilkinson
to death.
**Get Out Your Handkerchiefs** (1978) . . . . . . Solange
•• 0:21—Breasts sitting in bed listening to her boyfriend talk.
•• 0:31—Breasts sitting in bed knitting.
• 0:41—Upper half of left breast in bed.
•• 0:47—Left breast, while sitting in bed and the three
guys talk.
• 1:08—Brief right breast when the little boy peeks at
her while she sleeps.
1:10—Lower frontal nudity while he looks at her
some more.
••• 1:17—Full frontal nudity taking off nightgown while
sitting on bed for the little boy.
Victory (1981). . . . . . . . . . . . . . . . . . . . . . . . . . Renee

Naked Massacre (1983) . . . . . . . . . . . . . . . . . . . . .Amy
**Heartbreakers** (1984) . . . . . . . . . . . . . . . . . . . Liliane
• 0:56—Brief breasts making love in car with Nick
Mancuso. Dark, hard to see.
• 1:25—In sheer black dress, then brief right breast
making love in art gallery with Peter Coyote.
**The Surrogate** (1984; Canadian). . . . Anouk Vanderlin
• 0:48—Very brief breasts when Frank rips her blouse
open in his apartment.
**Sweet Country** (1985). . . . . . . . . . . . . . . . . . . . . Eva
•• 0:31—Breasts changing in apartment while Randy
Quaid watches.
• 0:43—Nude in auditorium with other women prisoners.
••• 1:13—Nude in bed with Quaid.
*Magazines:*
**Playboy** (Nov 1979) . . . . . . . . . . Sex in Cinema 1979
•• 181—Breasts.

## • Lauren, Dyanna

See: Hurley, Diane.

## Lauren, Honey

*Films:*
Bram Stoker's Dracula (1992). . . . . . . . Peep Show Girl
*Made for Cable TV:*
**Dream On: B.S. Elliot** (1992; HBO). . . . . . . . . . . Bibi
•• 0:11—Breasts, dancing on counter in biker bar.

## Laurin, Marie

*Films:*
Talking Walls (1982). . . . . . . . . . . . . . . . . . . . . Jeanne
The Lonely Guy (1983)
. . . . . . . . . . . . . . . . One of "The Seven Deadly Sins"
**Creature** (1985) . . . . . . . . . . . . . . . . Susan Delambre
•• 0:41—Breasts and brief buns with blood on her
shoulders, getting Jon to take his helmet off.
*Made for Cable TV:*
**The Hitchhiker: Petty Thieves** . . . . . . . . . . . . . Pearl
•• 0:09—Breasts making love with Steve Railsback on
the couch.
•• 0:15—Breasts playing with a doll in the bathtub,
then buns, standing up and wrapping herself with a
towel.
0:18—In black bra, then breasts undressing in front
of John Colicos.
*Magazines:*
**Playboy** (Jun 1992). . . . . . . . . . . . . . . . . . Grapevine
• 179—Breasts under sheer blouse with dots on it.
B&W.

## • Lavoie, Jennifer

*Video Tapes:*
**Playboy Celebrity Centerfold: Dian Parkinson**
(1993) . . . . . . . . . . . . . . . . . . . . . . . . . . . . . Playmate
• 0:41—Full frontal nudity in B&W poster, posted on
brick wall.
•• 0:42—Nude, while doing various things outside.
••• 0:44—Nude, while dancing and doing gymnastics.

••• 0:47—Nude in still photos.
••• 0:48—Nude with neighbor in hot night fantasy.
Some food play.
••• 0:55—Nude in hammock in tropical setting.
*Magazines:*
**Playboy's Nudes** (Dec 1992) . . . . . . . . . . . . . Herself
••• 66-67—Full frontal nudity.
**Playboy's Book of Lingerie** (Jan 1993) . . . . . . Herself
•• 32—Right breast.
**Playboy's Book of Lingerie** (Mar 1993) . . . . . Herself
•• 12—Right breast and partial lower frontal nudity
and partial buns.
**Playboy's Bathing Beauties** (Apr 1993) . . . . . Herself
••• 36—Breasts.
• 57—Partial lower frontal nudity.
••• 90-91—Breasts.
• 97—Lower frontal nudity.
**Playboy's Book of Lingerie** (May 1993) . . . . . Herself
• 90—Lower frontal nudity.
**Playboy** (Aug 1993) . . . . . . . . . . . . . . . . . . Playmate
••• 90-101—Nude.
**Playboy** (Jan 1994) . . . . . . . Playboy's Playmate Review
••• 204—Full frontal nudity.
**Playboy's Bathing Beauties** (Mar 1994). . . . . Herself
••• 7—Full frontal nudity.
**Playboy's Playmate Review** (May 1994)
. . . . . . . . . . . . . . . . . . . . . . . . . . . . . . Miss August
••• 66-73—Full frontal nudity.
**Playmates at Play** (Jul 1994) . . . . . . . . . . . . . Herself
••• 8-11—Breasts.
**Playboy's Girls of Summer '94** (Jul 1994) . . . Herself
••• 12-13—Full frontal nudity.
••• 31—Full frontal nudity.
**Playboy's Book of Lingerie** (Sep 1994) . . . . . Herself
• 64—Lower frontal nudity.

# Law, Barbara

*Films:*
The Surrogate (1984; Canadian) . . . . . .Maggie Simpson
*Made for Cable Movies:*
**Bedroom Eyes** (1985; Canadian; HBO) . . . . . . . Jobeth
• 0:02—Breasts taking off clothes while Harry watches
through the window.
•• 0:07—Breasts and buns, kissing a woman.
• 0:14—Breasts during Harry's flashback when he talks
to the psychiatrist.
•• 0:23—Breasts and buns dancing in bedroom.
•• 0:57—Breasts with Mary, kissing on floor.
1:17—In beige bra, panties, garter belt and stockings in bed with Harry.
• 1:23—Brief breasts on top of Harry.

# Lawrence, Mitte

*Films:*
Funny Girl (1968) . . . . . . . . . . . . . . . . . . . . . . . .Emma
The New Centurions (1972) . . . . . . . . . . . . . . . . Gloria
**Night Call Nurses** (1972). . . . . . . . . . . . . . . . Sandra
*a.k.a. Young LA Nurses 2*
•• 0:49—Breasts in bed with a guy.

# • Lawrence, Sharon

*Films:*
Bloodfist V: Human Target (1993) . . .Jewelry Store Clerk
*TV:*
NYPD Blue (1993- ) . . . . . . . . . . . . . . . . . . . Sylvia Costas
**NYPD Blue: Steroid Roy** (Feb 8, 1994). . Sylvia Costas
• 0:56—Back half of left breast, while standing in Sip-
owicz's bedroom.

# Lawrence, Suzanne Remey

*Films:*
Delivery Boys (1984) . . . . . . . . . . . . . . . . . . . . . . Nurse
0:34—In bra and panties after doing a strip tease
with another nurse while dancing in front of a boy
who is lying on an operating table.
**R.S.V.P.** (1984) . . . . . . . . . . . . . . . . . . . . . . . . Stripper
•• 0:56—Breasts dancing in a radio station.

# Layng, Lissa

*Films:*
Whose Life Is It, Anyway? (1981) . . . . . . . . . . .1st Nurse
Night of the Comet (1984) . . . . . . . . . . . . . .Davenport
**Say Yes** (1986) . . . . . . . . . . . . . . . . . . . . . . . . . .Annie
•• 1:06—Breasts, getting her dress ripped off.
• 1:07—More breasts, putting on jacket in restroom.

# Lazar, Ava

*Films:*
Death Wish II (1982) . . . . . . . . . . Girl in TV Soap Opera
Fast Times at Ridgemont High (1982) . . . . . . . Playmate
Night Shift (1982) . . . . . . . . . . . . . . . . . . . . . . .Sharon
**Diamond Run** (1988; Indonesian) . . . . . . . . Samantha
*a.k.a. Java Burn*
•• 0:07—Brief breasts, several times, making love in
bed with Nicky. Hard to see her face.
Forever Young (1992) . . . . . . . . .Waitress at Diner ('92)
*TV:*
Santa Barbara . . . . . . . . . . . . . . . . . . Santana Andrade

# Le Brock, Kelly

Spokeswoman for Pantene cosmetics.
Wife of actor/martial arts expert Steven Seagal.
*Films:*
**The Woman in Red** (1984). . . . . . . . . . . . . .Charlotte
0:02—Wearing the red dress, dancing over the air
vent in the car garage while Gene Wilder watches.
• 1:13—Brief right breast, getting into bed. Too far to
see anything.
1:15—Brief lower frontal nudity getting out of bed
when her husband comes home. Very brief left
breast, but it's blurry and hard to see.
Weird Science (1985). . . . . . . . . . . . . . . . . . . . . . Lisa
0:12—In blue underwear and white top baring her
midriff for the two boys when she is first created.
1:29—In blue leotard and grey tube top gym clothes
to teach boy's gym class.
Hard to Kill (1990) . . . . . . . . . . . . . . . .Andy Stewart
Betrayal of the Dove (1992) . . . . . . . . . . . . . . . . . Una
Hard Bounty (1994) . . . . . . . . . . . . . . . . . . . . . . n.a.

## • Le Priol, Alison

a.k.a. Adult film actress Kascha.
*Films:*
**Caged Fury** (1989) . . . . . . . . . . . . . .Blonde Escapee
  • 0:00—In bra and panties, then buns in G-string.
    Then brief breasts while crawling on the floor.

## • Le Roux, Madeleine

*Films:*
**Behind Locked Doors** (1969) . . . . . . Woman at Party
  • 0:07—Breasts after taking off bra while making out
    with guy in barn.
**Cry Uncle** (1971). . . . . . . . . . . . . . . . . . . Cora Merrill
  ••• 0:22—Breasts and buns, undressing in bathroom
    while talking to Jake.
  ••• 0:27—Nude, taking off her dress in front of Keith
    and making love with him on the sofa. Long scene.
  • 0:42—Brief breasts, sitting up in bed when door is
    slammed in Jake's face.
  • 0:59—Full frontal nudity, while standing in bedroom
    doorway.
  • 1:11—Breasts under sheer red and black nightie,
    then making love with Jake. Long scene.
  • 1:18—Brief buns, while taking off her panties.

## Leachman, Cloris

*Films:*
Kiss Me Deadly (1955) . . . . Christina Dailey/Berga Torn
Butch Cassidy and the Sundance Kid (1969). . . . .Agnes
Lovers and Other Strangers (1970) . . . . . . . . . . Bernice
**The People Next Door** (1970). . . . . . . . . . . . . . Tina
  • 0:59—Buns and very brief side view of right breast,
    while getting up out of bed and putting on a robe.
The Last Picture Show (1971) . . . . . . . . . . Ruth Popper
(Academy Award for Best Supporting Actress.)
The Steagle (1971) . . . . . . . . . . . . . . . . . . . . Rita Weiss
Charley & the Angel (1973) . . . . . . . . . . Nettie Appleby
Daisy Miller (1974) . . . . . . . . . . . . . .Mrs. Ezra B. Miller
Young Frankenstein (1974) . . . . . . . . . . . . Frau Blucher
**Crazy Mama** (1975) . . . . . . . . . . . . . . . . . . . . .Melba
  • 0:53—Brief left breast under clear plastic blouse
    while washing her boyfriend's hair in the sink.
High Anxiety (1977) . . . . . . . . . . . . . . . . . Nurse Diesel
The North Avenue Irregulars (1979) . . . . . . . . . . Claire
Scavenger Hunt (1979) . . . . . . . . . . Mildred Carrothers
Foolin' Around (1980). . . . . . . . . . . . . . . . . Samantha
Herbie Goes Bananas (1980). . . . . . . . . . . .Aunt Louise
History of the World, Part I (1981). . . Madame de Farge
Shadow Play (1986) . . . . . . . . . . . . . . . .Millie Crown
Walk Like a Man (1987). . . . . . . . . . . Margaret Shand
Prancer (1990) . . . . . . . . . . . . . . . . . . Mrs. McFarland
Texasville (1990) . . . . . . . . . . . . . . . . . . Ruth Popper
Love Hurts (1991) . . . . . . . . . . . . . . . . . . Ruth Weaver
The Beverly Hillbillies (1993) . . . . . . . . . . . . . . Granny
My Boyfriend's Back (1993). . . . . . . . . . . . . . .Maggie
*Made for Cable Movies:*
Fade to Black (1993; USA). . . . . . . . . . . . . . . . .Ruth
*Made for TV Movies:*
Danielle Steel's "Fine Things" (1990). . . . . . . . Ruth Fine

In Broad Daylight (1991) . . . . . . . . . . Ruth Westerman
Double, Double, Toil and Trouble (1993) . . . . . . . . n.a.
Miracle Child (1993) . . . . . . . . . . . . . . . . . . . Doc Betty
Without a Kiss Goodbye (1993) . . . . . . . .Mrs. Samuels
*TV:*
Lassie (1957-58). . . . . . . . . . . . . . . . . . . .Ruth Martin
The Mary Tyler Moore Show (1970-75)
. . . . . . . . . . . . . . . . . . . . . . . . . . . Phyllis Lindstrom
Phyllis (1975-77) . . . . . . . . . . . . . . . . Phyllis Lindstrom
The Facts of Life (1986) . . . . . . . . . . Beverly Ann Stickle
Walter and Emily (1991). . . . . . . . . . . . . . Emily Collins

## Leardini, Christina

*Video Tapes:*
**Playboy Video Calendar 1992** (1991). . . . . . .August
  ••• 0:32—Nude trying on various outfits.
  ••• 0:33—Nude in old building.
**Sexy Lingerie III** (1991). . . . . . . . . . . . . . . . . . Model
**The Best of Sexy Lingerie** (1992) . . . . . . . . . . Model
**Playboy Playmates in Paradise** (1992). . . . Playmate
Playboy's Playmate Bloopers & Practical Jokes (1992)
. . . . . . . . . . . . . . . . . . . . . . . . . . . . . . . . . Hostess
**Playboy's Playmate Review 1992** (1992)
. . . . . . . . . . . . . . . . . . . . . . . . . . . . . . . .Miss April
  ••• 0:32—Nude in a car, then in a bed, then inside an
    old building.
**Sexy Lingerie IV** (1992) . . . . . . . . . . . . . . . . . Model
**Sexy Lingerie V** (1992) . . . . . . . . . . . . . . . . . . Model
*Magazines:*
**Playboy** (Apr 1991) . . . . . . . . . . . . . . . . . . Playmate
  ••• 102-113—Nude.
**Playboy's Book of Lingerie** (Jul 1992) . . . . . . .Herself
  ••• 12-13—Breasts.
**Playboy's Book of Lingerie** (Sep 1992) . . . . . .Herself
  •• 72—Left breast.
**Playboy's Book of Lingerie** (Nov 1992) . . . . .Herself
  •• 34—Buns.
**Playboy's Nudes** (Dec 1992) . . . . . . . . . . . . .Herself
  • 49—Side view of left breast.
  •• 52—Buns.
  ••• 90—Full frontal nudity.
**Playboy's Book of Lingerie** (Jan 1993) . . . . . .Herself
  ••• 85—Breasts.
**Playboy's Book of Lingerie** (Mar 1993). . . . . .Herself
  ••• 16—Breasts and lower frontal nudity.
**Playboy's Book of Lingerie** (May 1993) . . . . .Herself
  ••• 10—Breasts.
**Playboy's Girls of Summer '93** (Jun 1993) . . .Herself
  ••• 48—Full frontal nudity.
  ••• 57—Full frontal nudity.
  ••• 86-87—Left breast and buns.
**Playboy's Book of Lingerie** (Jul 1993) . . . . . . .Herself
  ••• 26—Full frontal nudity.
  ••• 106-107—Breasts.
**Playboy's Wet & Wild Women** (Aug 1993). . .Herself
  ••• 27—Breasts.
  ••• 87—Full frontal nudity.
  ••• 88-89—Full frontal nudity.
  ••• 94-95—Full frontal nudity.

**Playboy's Blondes, Brunettes & Redheads**
(Sep 1993) . . . . . . . . . . . . . . . . . . . . . . . . Herself
••• 64-65—Full frontal nudity.
**Playboy's Book of Lingerie** (Sep 1993) . . . . . Herself
• 10—Lower frontal nudity.
• 13—Full frontal nudity.
••• 31—Breasts in push-up bra.
**Playboy's Video Playmates** (Sep 1993) . . . . . Herself
••• 64-65—Full frontal nudity.
**Playboy's Book of Lingerie** (Jan 1994) . . . . . . Herself
•• 80-81—Right breast and lower frontal nudity.
**Playboy's Bathing Beauties** (Mar 1994) . . . . . Herself
••• 6—Breasts.
**Playboy Presents Playmates in Paradise**
(Mar 1994) . . . . . . . . . . . . . . . . . . . . . . . Playmate
••• 9-14—Nude.
**Playboy's Book of Lingerie** (Mar 1994) . . . . . Herself
••• 84-85—Breasts.
**Playboy's Book of Lingerie** (May 1994) . . . . . Herself
••• 66—Breasts.
•• 100—Left breast and partial lower frontal nudity.
**Playmates at Play** (Jul 1994) . . . . . . . . . . . . . Herself
••• 84-87—Nude.
**Playboy's Book of Lingerie** (Jul 1994) . . . . . . Herself
••• 89—Breasts.

# Leary, Laura Jane

*Films:*
**The Best of Sex and Violence** (1981) . . . . Girl Victim
• 0:00—Getting clothes ripped off, then in bra and
panties, then breasts.
**Famous T & A** (1982) . . . . . . . . . . . Motorcycle Rider
(No longer available for purchase, check your video
store for rental.)
• 0:29—Lower nudity, riding a motorcycle with only a
jacket on.

# LeBeau, Becky

*Films:*
Carnival of Love (1983) . . . . . . . . . . . . . . . . . . . .Nancy
*a.k.a. Inside the Love House*
Joysticks (1983) . . . . . . . . . . . . . . . . . . . . . . . . . . .Liza
**Hollywood Hot Tubs** (1984) . . . . . . . . . . . . . Veronica
•• 0:49—Breasts changing in the locker room with other girl soccer players while Jeff watches.
• 0:54—Breasts in hot tub with the other girls and
Shawn.
**School Spirit** (1985) . . . . . . . . . . . . . . . . . . . . Hogette
• 1:07—Breasts sliding down water slide at dance,
wearing black and white swimsuit bottoms.
Back to School (1986) . . . . . . . Bubbles, the Hot Tub Girl
**Off the Mark** (1986) . . . . . . . . Uncredited Shower Girl
• 0:52—Brief breasts, after taking off her pink T-shirt in
locker room. Brief buns, while walking into showers
(2nd to the last girl).
**Takin' It All Off** (1987) . . . . . . . . . . . . . . . . . Becky
••• 0:03—Breasts in pink leotard in dance studio.
••• 0:11—Nude in the showers (she's in the back on the
left).

•• 0:16—Breasts and brief full frontal nudity getting introduced to Allison.
••• 0:23—In black bra and panties, then nude doing a
strip routine outside.
• 0:35—Brief full frontal nudity pushing Elliot into the
pool.
• 0:36—Brief breasts in studio with Allison again.
• 0:36—Brief left breast in dance studio with Allison.
•• 1:23—Nude, dancing with the other girls on stage.
**The Underachievers** (1987) . . . . . . . . Ginger Bronsky
••• 0:40—Breasts in swimming pool playing with an inflatable alligator after her exercise class has left.
**Not of This Earth** (1988) . . . . . . . . .Happy Birthday Girl
••• 0:47—Breasts doing a Happy Birthday stripper-gram
for the old guy.
**Nudity Required** (1989) . . . . . . . . . . . . . . . . .Melanie
•• 0:35—Breasts, taking off pink swimsuit.
•• 0:36—Brief breasts (third girl) standing in line.
• 0:37—Breasts, standing behind Scammer.
• 0:39—Very brief breasts.
•• 0:41—Breasts while sitting next to Scammer by the
pool.
**Ninja Academy** (1990) . . . . . . . . . . . . . . . . . . Nudist
•• 0:26—Nude, carrying plate, then going to swing at
nudist colony. Then playing volleyball (she's the first
one to hit the ball).
Transylvania Twist (1990) . . . . . . . . . . . . . . . . . . . Rita
The Malibu Beach Vampires (1991) . . .The Census Taker
Munchie (1992) . . . . . . . . . . . . . . . . . . . .Pizza Screamer
**Sins of Desire** (1992) . . . . . . . . . . . . . . . . . . . . Sandy
(Unrated version reviewed.)
••• 0:23—Nude, stripping and dancing (she's the
blonde on the left) with Clarise in front of Mr.
O'Connor. Long scene.
**Body Chemistry 3: Point of Seduction** (1993)
. . . . . . . . . . . . . . . . . . . . . . . . . . . . . . . . . . .Margaret
•• 0:04—Full frontal nudity, seen on TV monitor, while
taking her clothes off on bed during call-in show.
**Dinosaur Island** (1993) . . . . . . . . . . . . .Virgin Sacrifice
••• 0:00—Breasts, after getting her bikini top ripped off
while tied by her wrists during sacrifice ceremony.
Munchie Strikes Back (1994) . . . . . . . . Chased Woman
*Music Videos:*
California Girls/David Lee Roth
. . . . . . . . . . . . . . .Girl Squeezing Suntan Lotion Bottle
*Video Tapes:*
Centerfold Screen Test (1985) . . . . . . . . . . . . . . .Herself
0:14—In wet white T-shirt, auditioning in pool.
**Best Chest in the West II** (1986) . . . . . . . . . .Herself
••• 0:46—Dancing in red two piece swimsuit. Buns,
then breasts.
•• 0:55—Buns and breasts after winning semi-finals.
**Becky Bubbles** (1987) . . . . . . . . . . . . . . . . . . . .Herself
••• 0:00—Breasts, when waking up and getting out of
bed.
••• 0:01—Breasts, going outside for a swim in white
panties. Long scene.
••• 0:06—Breasts, while rubbing lotion on herself.

••• 0:08—Breasts outside on chair and in pool with her friends.

••• 0:12—Breasts while playing on pool float with Lorraine and Brandi.

••• 0:22—Breasts drying her hair outside with hair dryer.

••• 0:24—Breasts while putting on makeup and fingernail polish.

•• 0:25—Buns and breasts while taking off swimsuit then getting dressed.

Trashy Ladies Wrestling (1987) . . . . . . . . . . Round Girl

**Soft Bodies** (1988) . . . . . . . . . . . . . . . . . . . . . . Herself

••• 0:01—In two piece swimsuit, then breasts in swimming pool.

•• 0:08—On bed during photo session in various lingerie, then breasts and buns in G-string.

••• 0:16—In bra and panties, then breasts on bed.

**Soft Bodies Invitational** (1990) . . . . . . . . . . Herself

0:00—Buns, under short skirt playing tennis with Nina Alexander.

••• 0:15—Breasts while posing with Alexander in photo session.

•• 0:24—In two piece swimsuit, then breasts arguing with Alexander about who has better breasts.

••• 0:38—In red bra and panties outside on brides, then breasts.

••• 0:44—Breasts and buns in G-string in spa.

**Soft Bodies: Curves Ahead** (1991) . . . . . . . . Herself

0:00—Buns in G-string, playing Frisbee with Kylie Rose.

••• 0:32—Breasts in pool with Tamara. Buns and partial lower frontal nudity. Long scene.

••• 0:36—Breasts while posing for photographs in various outfits.

••• 0:41—On balcony in two piece swimsuit, then breasts and buns taking an outdoor shower. Long scene.

••• 0:45—Breasts and buns in G-string, posing on bed for photo session in various lingerie. Long scene.

••• 0:51—In two piece swimsuit outside at night in spa. Breasts and buns in G-string. Long scene.

**Soft Bodies: Party Favors** (1992) . . . . . . . . . Herself

0:18—In swimsuit by pool with Antonia.

••• 0:35—Breasts and buns, on floating bed in pool with Julia Hayes.

••• 0:39—Breasts and buns posing in bed in various lingerie outfits.

••• 0:46—Breasts and buns on couch.

••• 0:52—On balcony taking off dress, then in white lingerie, then breasts and buns.

**Soft Bodies: Double Exposure** (1994) . . . . . . Herself

*Magazines:*

**Playboy** (Feb 1989) . . . . . . . . . . . . . . . . . . . .Grapevine

• 166—Left breast sticking out from under T-shirt in B&W photo.

**Playboy** (Jul 1989) . . . . . . . . . . . . . . . . B-Movie Bimbos

••• 139—Full frontal nudity, wearing pink stockings and a garter belt, standing in a car filled with bubbles.

## Lee, Adriane

*Films:*

**Breeders** (1986) . . . . . . . . . . . . . . . . . . . . . . . . . . .Alec

•• 0:49—Breasts, undressing while talking on the phone.

• 1:07—Brief breasts, covered with goop, in the alien nest.

• 1:08—Brief breasts in nest behind Frances Raines.

• 1:09—Brief breasts behind Raines again.

• 1:11—Breasts, lying back in the goop, then long shot breasts.

Mutant Hunt (1987) . . . . . . . . . . . . . . . . . .Amber Dawn

Necropolis (1987) . . . . . . . . . . . . . . . . . . .Cult Member

Slammer Girls (1987) . . . . . . . . . . . . . . . Dead Convict

## Lee, Cynthia

*Films:*

**New York Nights** (1981) . . . . . . . . . . . . .The Porn Star

•• 1:15—Breasts in the steam room talking to the prostitute.

••• 1:26—Breasts in office with the financier and making love on his desk.

**Hot Resort** (1984) . . . . . . . . . . . . . . . . . . . . . . . Alice

• 1:08—Breasts in the bathtub.

Hired to Kill (1990) . . . . . . . . . . . . . . . . . . .Armwrestler

## Lee, Hyapatia

Adult film actress.

*Films:*

**Hellroller** (1992) . . . . . . . . . . . . . . . . . . . . . . . Dancer

••• 0:43—Breasts, dancing in room by herself.

••• 0:45—Breasts and buns, while taking a shower.

Swingers (1992) . . . . . . . . . . . . . . . . . . . . . . .Sydney X

**Killing Obsession** (1994) . . . . . . . . . . . . .Annie Smith

••• 0:12—Breasts and buns in G-string, while dancing on bar.

•• 0:15—Breasts, while changing clothes in bathroom, then walking to John Savage.

• 0:18—Brief right breast, while lying dead on floor.

## Lee, Jennifer

*Films:*

**Act of Vengeance** (1974) . . . . . . . . . . . . . . . . . Nancy

*a.k.a. The Rape Squad*

(Not to be confused with the film with the same name starring Charles Bronson.)

• 0:38—Breasts looking up in spa while talking to another woman.

Sunshine Boys (1975). . . . . . . . . . . . . . . . . . . . .Helen

The Wild Party (1975) . . . . . . . . . . . . . . . Madeline Tru

The Duchess and the Dirtwater Fox (1976) . . . . .Trollop

The Believers (1987). . . . . . . . . . . . . . .Calder's Assistant

Slaves of New York (1989) . . . . . . . . . . . . . . . . . . n.a.

## Lee, Joie

Sister of actor/director Spike Lee.

*Films:*

She's Gotta Have It (1987) . . . . . . . . Clorinda Bradford

School Daze (1988) . . . . . . . . . . . . . . . . . . . .Lizzie Life

Bail Jumper (1989) . . . . . . . . . . . . . . . . . . . . . . Athena
Do the Right Thing (1989) . . . . . . . . . . . . . . . . . . Jade
**Mo' Better Blues** (1990) . . . . . . . . . . Indigo Downes
  •• 1:06—Right breast while in bed with Denzel Washington.
  • 1:08—Very, very brief right breast while pounding the bed and yelling at Denzel Washington.
A Kiss Before Dying (1991) . . . . . . . . . . . . . . . . . . Cathy
Fathers and Sons (1992) . . . . . . . . . . . . . . . . . . . . .Lois

## Lee, Kaaren

*Films:*
The Right Stuff (1983) . . . . . . . . . . . . . . .Young Widow
**Roadhouse 66** (1984) . . . . . . . . . . . . . . .Jesse Duran
  •• 1:00—Breasts, taking off her top to go skinny dipping with Willem Dafoe. Dark.
St. Elmo's Fire (1985) . . . . . . . . . . . . . . Welfare Woman
Remote Control (1987) . . . . . . . . . . . . . . . . . . . Patricia

## Lee, Kelli

*Films:*
Slash Dance (1989) . . . . . . . . . . . . . . . . . . . . . . Dancer
**Sorority Girls and the Creature from Hell** (1990) . . . . . . . . . . . . . . . . . . Nude Double for Dori Courtney
  • 0:23—Breasts in bedroom with J.J.
  • 0:36—Breasts getting playfully strangled by Skip in the spa. Buns, getting out.

## Lee, Luann

*Films:*
Beverly Hills Cop II (1987) . . . . . . . . . Playboy Playmate
Terminal Exposure (1988) . . . . . . . . . . . . . . Bruce's Girl
*Video Tapes:*
**Playboy Video Centerfold: Luann Lee** . . . Playmate
**Playboy Video Calendar 1988** (1987) . . . . Playmate
**Wet and Wild** (1989) . . . . . . . . . . . . . . . . . . . .Model
*Magazines:*
**Playboy's Girls of Summer '86** (Aug 1986) . . Herself
  •• 58—Side of right breast and buns.
**Playboy** (Jan 1987) . . . . . . . . . . . . . . . . . . . Playmate
**Playboy's Girls of Summer '92** (Jun 1992) . . . Herself
  • 72—Lower frontal nudity.
**Playboy's Book of Lingerie** (Jul 1992) . . . . . . Herself
  • 73—Left breast.
  •• 106—Left breast and lower frontal nudity.
**Playboy's Calendar Playmates** (Nov 1992) . . Herself
  ••• 61—Full frontal nudity.

## Lee, Margaret

*Films:*
Casanova '70 (1965; Italian) . . . . . . . . Dolly Greenwater
Secret Agent Super Dragon (1966; French/Italian/German) . . . . . . . . . . . . . . . . . . . . . . Cynthia Fulton
Dorian Gray (1970; Italian/British/German) . . . . . . . . . . . . . . . . . . . . . . . . . . Gwendolyn Wotten

**Venus in Furs** (1970) . . . . . . . . . . . . . . . . . . . . Olga
Original version.
  • 0:53—Buns, lying on floor with Maria.
  • 0:54—Buns, while walking and holding candelabra.
The Rogue (1976) . . . . . . . . . . . . . . . . . . . . . . . . n.a.

## Lee, Pat

*Films:*
**Porky's** (1981; Canadian) . . . . . . . . . . . . . . . . Stripper
  • 0:33—Brief breasts dancing on stage at Porky's showing her breasts to Pee Wee.
Starman (1984) . . . . . . . . . . . . . . . . . . . Bracero Wife
And God Created Woman (1988) . . . . . . . . . . .Inmate
(Unrated version.)
Young Guns (1988) . . . . . . . . . . . . . . . . . . . . . . Janey

## Lee, Robin

a.k.a. Robbie Lee.
*Films:*
**Big Bad Mama** (1974) . . . . . . . . . . . Polly McClatchie
  • 0:08—Brief left breast in gaping dress when cops try to pull her car over.
  • 0:22—In see-through dress on stage with her sister and a stripper.
  • 0:32—Brief breasts running around the bedroom chasing her sister.
  • 0:52—Buns, taking off her nightgown and getting into bed with Tom Skerritt.
**Switchblade Sisters** (1975) . . . . . . . . . . . . . . . .Lace
  • 0:48—Breasts sitting up in bed to talk to Dominic. Dark.

## Lee, Sazzy

*Films:*
Angel Eyes (1991) . . . . . . . . . . . . . . . . . . . . . . . .Amy
*Magazines:*
**Playboy** (May 1992) . . . . . . . . . . . . . . . . . . Grapevine
  •• 167—Side view of left breast.

## Lee, Sheryl

*Films:*
Wild at Heart (1990) . . . . . . . . . . . . . . . . . .Good Witch
**Twin Peaks: Fire Walk With Me** (1992)
. . . . . . . . . . . . . . . . . . . . . . . . . . . Laura Palmer
  • 0:37—Very brief breasts, letting her boyfriend feel her breast.
  •• 1:18—Breasts when a guy takes off her dress in cabin.
  ••• 1:19—Breasts, while talking with Ronette at table.
  ••• 1:21—More breasts in cabin and while sitting at the table with Ronette. More breasts when getting up.
  • 1:49—Side view of buns and upper half of right breast (wearing lingerie) while lying in bed and rolling over.
  1:58—Brief upper half of left breast while dancing in lingerie in cabin.
  •• 1:59—Breasts, while struggling on bed with big guy.
  • 2:01—Brief breasts talking with her dad in the cabin.
Backbeat (1994) . . . . . . . . . . . . . . . . . . Astrid Kirchherr

*Made for Cable TV:*
**Red Shoe Diaries: Jake's Story** (1993; Showtime)
. . . . . . . . . . . . . . . . . . . . . . . . . . . . . . . . Kate Lyons
(Available on video tape on *Red Shoe Diaries 4: Auto Erotica*.)
• 0:14—Brief breasts while making love with Jake in and out of truck.
•• 0:20—In black bra, then breasts, while making love with Jake on roof.
• 0:27—Brief left and right breasts, while making love with Jake in bed.
*Made for TV Movies:*
Love, Lies and Murder (1991) . . . . . . . . . . . Patti Bailey
Jersey Girl (1993) . . . . . . . . . . . . . . . . . . . . . . . Tara
*Magazines:*
**Playboy** (Nov 1994) . . . . . . . . . . Sex in Cinema 1994
•• 141—Right breast in still from *Backbeat*.

## Lee, Tamara

Former adult film actress.
*Video Tapes:*
**Soft Bodies: Curves Ahead** (1991) . . . . . . . . Herself
••• 0:23—In lingerie on chair, then breasts during photo session. Brief lower frontal nudity under sheer lingerie. Long scene.
••• 0:31—In chair by pool. Breasts and partial lower frontal nudity.

## Lee-Hsu, Diana

*Films:*
License to Kill (1989). . . . . . . . . . . . . . . . . . . . . . . Loti
Snapdragon (1993). . . . . . . . . . . . . . . . Professor Huan
*Made for Cable Movies:*
Blind Side (1993; HBO). . . . . . . . . . . . . . . .Mrs. Dance
*Video Tapes:*
**Playboy Video Calendar 1989** (1988) . . . . . February
••• 0:05—Nude.
**Playmates at Play** (1990) . . . . . . . . . . . .Gotta Dance
**Wet and Wild III** (1991). . . . . . . . . . . . . . . . . .Model
**The Best of Wet and Wild** (1992) . . . . . . . . .Model
**Playboy Video Playmate Six-Pack 1992** (1992)
. . . . . . . . . . . . . . . . . . . . . . . . . . . . . . . Playmate
*Magazines:*
**Playboy** (May 1988) . . . . . . . . . . . . . . . . . . Playmate
**Playboy** (Aug 1989). . . . . . . . . . . . . . .License to Thrill
••• 126-131—Nude.
**Playboy's Nudes** (Oct 1990). . . . . . . . . . . . . . Herself
••• 13—Full frontal nudity.
**Playboy's Calendar Playmates** (Nov 1992) . . Herself
••• 70—Breasts.
**Playboy's Wet & Wild Women** (Aug 1993) . . Herself
••• 98-99—Full frontal nudity.
**Playboy's Video Playmates** (Sep 1993) . . . . . Herself
••• 66-67—Full frontal nudity.

## Légerè, Phoebe

Singer.
*Films:*
Mondo New York (1987) . . . . . . . . . . . . . . . . . . Singer
0:01—On stage, singing "Marilyn Monroe." Buns and most of lower frontal nudity while writhing on stage in a mini-skirt.
**The Toxic Avenger: Part II** (1988). . . . . . . . . . .Claire
• 0:31—Brief right breast, while caressing herself while making out with the Toxic Avenger.
The Toxic Avenger III: The Last Temptation of Toxie (1989) . . . . . . . . . . . . . . . . . . . . . . . . . . . . . . .Claire
King of New York (1990) . . . . . . . . . . Bordello Woman
*Magazines:*
**Playboy** (Jun 1988). . . . . . . . . . . . . . . Mondo Phoebe
•• 70-77—Nude.
**Playboy** (Nov 1988) . . . . . . . . . . Sex in Cinema 1988
• 138—Left breast, while lying on bed, getting a hug from the Toxic Avenger.
**Playboy** (Dec 1988) . . . . . . . . . . . . . .Sex Stars of 1988
• 184—Right breast, popping out of top.

## Leigh, Barbara

*Films:*
**The Student Nurses** (1970) . . . . . . . . . . . . . . Priscilla
*a.k.a. Young LA Nurses*
••• 0:43—Breasts on the beach with Les. Long scene.
The Christian Licorice Store (1971). . . . . . . . . . . Starlet
**Pretty Maids All in a Row** (1971) . . . . .Jean McDrew
• 0:30—Brief partial side view of right breast when she leans over chess board on bed to touch Rock Hudson.
Junior Bonner (1972) . . . . . . . . . . . . . . . . . . Charmagne
**Terminal Island** (1973) . . . . . . . . . . . Bunny Campbell
••• 0:22—Breasts and buns undressing in room while Bobbie watches from the bed.
Boss (1974) . . . . . . . . . . . . . . . . . . . . . . . . Miss Pruitt
**Mistress of the Apes** (1979; British). . . . . . . . .Laura
••• 0:44—Breasts, washing her blouse in river and putting it on. (Seen through binoculars.)
• 0:46—Breasts, getting her blouse ripped off by jerks.
Seven (1979) . . . . . . . . . . . . . . . . . . . . . . . . . . . .Alexa
0:17—Briefly in braless, semi-sheer yellow blouse.
**Famous T & A** (1982) . . . . . . . . . . Bunny Campbell
(No longer available for purchase, check your video store for rental.)
••• 0:45—Breasts scene from *Terminal Island*. Includes additional takes that weren't used.
*Miniseries:*
The Search for the Nile (1972) . . . Isabel Arundel Burton
*Magazines:*
**Playboy** (Apr 1971) . . . . . . . . . Vadim's "Pretty Maids"
•• 158—Breasts in wet T-shirt.
**Playboy** (May 1973). . . . . . . . . . . . . . . . . . . . . Indian
••• 149-155—Breasts.
**Playboy** (Jan 1977). . . . . . . . . . . . . . . . .Natural Leigh
••• 85-91—B&W photos. Full frontal nudity.
**Playboy** (Apr 1977) . . . . . . . . . . . . . . . . .Dear Playboy
•• 12—Breasts in small photo.

## Leigh, Carrie

Former girlfriend of *Playboy* publisher Hugh Hefner.
*Films:*
A Fine Mess (1986) . . . . . . . . . . . . . . . . . Second Extra
Beverly Hills Cop II (1987) . . . . . . . . . . . . . . . . . Herself
Blood Relations (1989) . . . . . . . . . . Thomas' Girlfriend
*Magazines:*
**Playboy** (Jul 1986) . . . . . . . . . . . . . . . . . Carrie Leigh
••• 114-125—Nude.
**Playboy** (Aug 1988) . . . . . . The Great Palimony Caper
•• 64—Left breast and lower frontal nudity, B&W.
**Playboy** (Dec 1988) . . . . . . . . . . . . . Sex Stars of 1988
••• 188—Full frontal nudity.
**Playboy** (Feb 1989) . . . . . . . . . . . . . . . The Year in Sex
•• 143—Breasts in B&W photo.

## • Leigh, Cassandra

See: Boyle, Lisa.

## Leigh, Jennifer Jason

Daughter of the late actor Vic Morrow.
*Films:*
**Eyes of a Stranger** (1981) . . . . . . . . . . . . . . . . . Tracy
  • 1:15—Very brief breasts lying in bed getting attacked by rapist.
  •• 1:19—Left breast, while cleaning herself in bathroom.
**Fast Times at Ridgemont High** (1982)
. . . . . . . . . . . . . . . . . . . . . . . . . . . Stacy Hamilton
  • 0:18—Left breast, while making out with Ron in a dugout.
  ••• 1:00—Breasts in poolside dressing room.
Wrong is Right (1982) . . . . . . . . . . . . . . . . . Young Girl
Easy Money (1983) . . . . . . . . . . . . . . . Allison Capuletti
Grandview, U.S.A. (1984) . . . . . . . . . . . . Candy Webster
**Flesh + Blood** (1985) . . . . . . . . . . . . . . . . . . . . . Agnes
  • 0:45—Brief right breast, while being held down.
  •• 1:05—Full frontal nudity getting into the bath with Rutger Hauer and making love.
  ••• 1:16—Full frontal nudity getting out of bed with Hauer and walking to the window.
  •• 1:35—Full frontal nudity, while throwing clothes into the fire.
  •• 1:36—Breasts, when Hauer removes sheet that covers her.
  •• 1:37—Buns and long shot brief side view of right breast, while walking to the castle behind Hauer. Brief breasts when stopped on stairs while watching Tom Burlinson throw food into well.
The Hitcher (1986) . . . . . . . . . . . . . . . . . . . . . . .Nash
The Men's Club (1986) . . . . . . . . . . . . . . . . . . . Teensy
**Sister Sister** (1987) . . . . . . . . . . . . . . . . Lucy Bonnard
  •• 0:01—Breasts making love during a dream.
  0:52—In lingerie talking with Eric Stoltz.
  •• 0:53—Left breast, while making love with Stoltz in her bedroom.
  • 0:58—Breasts in bathtub surrounded by candles.
Under Cover (1987) . . . . . . . . . . . . . . . Tanille Lareoux

**Heart of Midnight** (1988) . . . . . . . . . . . . . . . . Carol
  • 0:27—Very brief side view of right breast, while reaching for soap in the shower.
The Big Picture (1989) . . . . . . . . . . . . . . Lydia Johnson
**Last Exit to Brooklyn** (1990) . . . . . . . . . . . . . Tralata
  •• 1:28—Breasts, opening her blouse in bar after getting drunk.
  • 1:33—Breasts getting drug out of car, placed on mattress, then basically raped by a long line of guys. Long, painful-to-watch scene.
  • 1:35—Breasts lying on mattress when Spook comes to save her.
**Miami Blues** (1990) . . . . . . . . . . . . . . Susie Waggoner
  0:07—Very brief upper half of right breast, while changing clothes behind Alec Baldwin.
  ••• 0:10—Breasts in panties, taking off red dress and getting into bed.
  0:24—Very, very brief half of right breast while taking a bath. Long shot.
  • 0:33—Breasts making love with Baldwin in the kitchen.
**Backdraft** (1991) . . . . . . . . . . . . . . . . Jennifer Vaitkus
  • 1:16—Very, very brief left breast on back of fire truck with William Baldwin. (Right after someone knocks open a door with an axe.)
**Crooked Hearts** (1991) . . . . . . . . . . . . . . . . . . Harriet
  •• 1:10—In black bra, then breasts in bathtub with Tom.
**Rush** (1991) . . . . . . . . . . . . . . . . . . . . . . Kristen Cates
  • 1:09—Brief buns, when Jason Patric takes off her pajama bottoms and forces himself on her.
**Single White Female** (1992) . . . . . . . . Hedy Carlson
  ••• 0:18—Breasts, changing clothes in her room in front of Bridget Fonda.
  • 0:29—Upper half of breasts, while in bathtub.
  •• 0:37—Breasts, masturbating in bed while Fonda peeks in bedroom.
  ••• 1:04—Breasts in the shower, then full frontal nudity, getting out.
  •• 1:09—Breasts, getting into bed with Sam.
  1:10—Breasts in bed with Sam.
Short Cuts (1993) . . . . . . . . . . . . . . . . . . . . Lois Kaiser
The Hudsucker Proxy (1994) . . . . . . . . . . . . . . . . . n.a.
*Made for Cable Movies:*
Buried Alive (1990; USA) . . . . . . . . . . . . . . . . Joanna
*Made for TV Movies:*
Girls of the White Orchid (1983) . . . . . . . . Carol Heath
The Killing of Randy Webster (1985) . . . . . . . . . . . n.a.
*Magazines:*
**Playboy** (Nov 1985) . . . . . . . . . . Sex in Cinema 1985
  ••• 135—Breasts in scenes from Flesh + Blood.

## Leigh, Melissa

*Films:*
**Affairs of the Heart** (1992) . . . . . . . . Jealous Woman
  ••• 0:38—Buns, then breasts with the Jealous Man.
*Magazines:*
**Penthouse** (May 1987) . . . . . . . . . . . . . . . . . . . .Pet

# Leigh-Hunt, Barbara
*Films:*
**Frenzy** (1972; British)..............Brenda Blaney
- 0:31—Left breast, while sitting in chair with the necktie killer. Don't see her face.

Henry VIII and His Six Wives (1972; British)
...........................Catherine Parr
The Nelson Affair (1973).........Catherine Matcham
Oh Heavenly Dog! (1980)...............Margaret
Wagner (1983; British)..............Queen Mother
Paper Mask (1991; British)..........Celia Mumford

# Leighton, Roberta
*Films:*
Barracuda (1978)...........................n.a.
**Stripes** (1981)...........................Anita
- 0:07—Breasts, wearing blue panties, while putting her shirt on and talking to Bill Murray.

Covergirl (1982; Canadian)...........Dee Anderson
0:16—Almost breasts, while making love dressed like a nun.
*TV:*
The Young and the Restless (1978-86)..Dr. Casey Reed
Days of Our Lives (1991- )................Ginger

# Lelouch, Christine
*Films:*
The Crook (1971).................... Martine
*Magazines:*
**Playboy** (Jun 1975).......Sex in Cinema French Style
- 88—Breasts.

# LeMay, Dorothy
Adult film actress.
*Films:*
**Simply Irresistible** (1983).............Hitchhiker
(R-rated version. *Irresistible* is the X-rated version.)
- 0:09—Nude in office with Walter.

# Lemmons, Kasi
*Films:*
School Daze (1988).......................Perry
**Vampire's Kiss** (1989)...................Jackie
- 0:05—In black bra and panties, then breasts in living room with Nicolas Cage.

Silence of the Lambs (1990)..........Ardelia Mapp
The Five Heartbeats (1991)...............Cookie
Candyman (1992)..............Bernadette Walsh
Hard Target (1993)....................Carmine
*Made for Cable Movies:*
The Court-Martial of Jackie Robinson (1990)....Rachel
Afterburn (1992; HBO)....................Carol
*Made for TV Movies:*
The Lakeside Killer (1979)................Hostage
*TV:*
Under Cover (1991).................Alex Robbins

# • Lemon, Genevieve
*Films:*
**Sweetie** (1989; Australian)............... Sweetie
- 1:23—Breasts in tree house (she's covered with paint).
- 1:25—Brief buns, mooning her dad.

The Piano (1993)......................... Nessie

# Lennear, Claudia
*Films:*
Thunderbolt and Lightfoot (1974)......... Secretary
*Magazines:*
**Playboy** (Aug 1974)................. Brown Sugar
- 70-73—Breasts.

# Lennox, Lisa
*Video Tapes:*
Hot Body International: #1 Miss Cancun (1990)
.......................................Contestant
Hot Body International: #2 Miss Puerto Vallarta (1990)
.......................................Contestant
**Hot Body International: #4 Spring Break** (1992)
.......................................Contestant
- 0:11—Dancing in one piece swimsuit on stage.
- 0:48—Brief left breast during wet T-shirt contest. Buns in G-string.

# Lennox, Natalie
"Lace" on *American Gladiators*.
*Video Tapes:*
**The Penthouse All-Pet Workout** (1993).......Pet
- 0:00—Full frontal nudity during introduction.
- 0:03—Brief nude shots while getting undressed and suited up.
- 0:35—In sheer white body suit, then nude on rocks and in waterfall.
- 0:43—Nude with the other girls, exercising, working with equipment, in the pool and spa.

*CD-ROM:*
**Penthouse Interactive Virtual Photo Shoot, Disc 1** (1993).....................................Pet
*Magazines:*
**Penthouse** (Jan 1993)......................Pet
- 89-101—Nude.

# Lenska, Rula
*Films:*
Confessions of a Pop Performer (1975; British).....n.a.
**Oh, Alfie!** (1975; British)................. Louise
*a.k.a. Alfie Darling*
- 0:12—Breasts, then left breast in bed after making love with Alfie.

Undercovers Hero (1975)............. Grenier Girl
The Deadly Females (1976).................Luisa

# Lentini, Susan
*Films:*
Action Jackson (1988)................. VW Driver
Roadhouse (1989)................Bandstand Babe

The Runestone (1990)....................Wife #1
Ricochet (1991) ........................Reporter
Demolition Man (1993) ...............TV Reporter
*Made for Cable Movies:*
Love, Cheat & Steal (1993; Showtime) .........Nun
*Made for Cable TV:*
**Dream On: Sex and the Single Parent** (1990; HBO)
.............................. Ms. Susan Brodsky
    0:04—In white bra and panties in front of class while
    Jeremy fantasizes about her.
  •• 0:10—Brief breasts, twice, talking to Martin while he
    fantasizes about her.
·Tales From the Crypt: Dead Right (1990; HBO).. Leanne
  (Available on *Tales From the Crypt, Volume 3.*)

## Lenz, Kay

Ex-wife of actor/singer David Cassidy.
*Films:*
**Breezy** (1974) ......................... Breezy
  Nude.
White Line Fever (1975) .............. Jerri Hummer
The Great Scout and Cathouse Thursday (1976)
.......................................... Thursday
Mean Dog Blues (1978) ..............Linda Ramsey
Moving Violation (1979)..............Cam Johnson
**The Passage** (1979; British)..........Leah Bergson
  Breasts.
**Fast Walking** (1981)..................... Moke
  • 0:26—Brief breasts closing the door after pulling
    James Woods into the room.
    0:42—Caressing herself under her dress while in
    prison visiting room, talking to George.
  ••• 1:27—Right breast in store. Breasts getting hosed
    down and dried off outside by James Woods.
  • 1:32—Brief left breast, making love with Woods.
House (1986) ......................Sandy Sinclair
Death Wish 4: The Crackdown (1987)... Karen Sheldon
**Stripped to Kill** (1987) ............Cody Sheehan
  •• 0:23—Breasts dancing on stage.
  ••• 0:47—Breasts dancing in white lingerie.
Fear (1988).........................Sharon Haden
Headhunters (1988) .................Katherine Hall
Physical Evidence (1989)............Deborah Quinn
Streets (1989)..........................Sergeant
Falling From Grace (1992)..............P.J. Parks
*Made for Cable Movies:*
Hitler's Daughter (1990) .......................n.a.
*Miniseries:*
Rich Man, Poor Man (1976) ..........Kate Jordache
*Made for TV Movies:*
The Initiation of Sarah (1978) ............... Sarah
*TV:*
Rich Man, Poor Man—Book II (1976-77)
..................................... Kate Jordache
Midnight Caller (1988)........................n.a.
Reasonable Doubts (1992-93)........Maggie Zombro
*Magazines:*
**Playboy** (Nov 1982) ..........Sex in Cinema 1982
  ••• 161—Breasts photo from *Fast Walking.*

## Leo, Melissa

*Films:*
**Always** (1984) ...........................Peggy
  • 1:33—Very, brief breasts and buns, jumping over in-
    flatable lounge in pool. Long shot.
**Streetwalkin'** (1985).....................Cookie
  • 0:05—Brief breasts taking off red blouse in front of
    mirror.
  •• 0:15—Breasts, stripping and taking off her top for a
    customer.
  • 0:18—Brief right breast, having sex with her pimp
    on the floor.
  • 0:44—Breasts, taking off her top and sitting on bed
    with a customer (long shot seen in mirror).
    0:53—Buns, in body suit, in hotel room with cus-
    tomer.
A Time of Destiny (1988) ....................Josie
Venice/Venice (1992) ...................... Peggy
The Ballad of Little Jo (1993) .............Mrs. Grey
*Made for TV Movies:*
The Bride in Black (1990)...........Mary Margaret
*TV:*
Young Riders (1989-90) .............Emma Shannon
Homicide: Life on the Street (1993)...Det. Kay Howard

## Leong, Page

*Films:*
White Phantom (1987) ...................Mai Lin
Rented Lips (1988)........................Dancer
The Wizard of Speed & Time (1988) .........Dancer
Ghostbusters II (1989)...........Spengler's Assistant
Angel Town (1990) ..........Mr. Park's Connection
**Another 48 Hrs.** (1990) ...............Angel Lee
  • 1:00—Brief breasts getting out of bed with Willie.

## Leprince, Catherine

*Films:*
**Bilitis** (1977; French) .....................Helene
  •• 0:13—Breasts taking off dress and getting into bed
    with Bilitis.
Vive Les Femmes (1984)....................Viviane
Escalier C (1985; French) ..................Florence
Paulette (1986; French) ............. Joseph, Female

## •Lerman, April

*Films:*
**Sorority House Party** (1992) ................Alex
  0:49—In bra while starting to make love with Jamie
  Z.
  ••• 0:50—Breasts, while making love on bed with Jamie
  Z.
  1:00—Right breast, while in bubble bath with Jamie.
*TV:*
Charles in Charge (1984-85) ..........Zila Pembroke

# LeRoy, Jennifer

*Video Tapes:*

**Sexy Lingerie V** (1992) . . . . . . . . . . . . . . . . .Model
**Playboy Video Calendar 1994** (1993) . . . . . . . June
••• 0:23—Nude in circus setting.
••• 0:23—Nude outside in bathtub by a shack.

*Magazines:*

**Playboy** (Feb 1993) . . . . . . . . . . . . . . . . . . . Playmate
••• 94-105—Nude.
**Playboy** (Apr 1993) . . . . . . . . . . . . . . . . . Tattoo You
•• 81—Right breast. Spider tattoo on her upper right leg.
**Playboy** (Jan 1994) . . . . . . . Playboy's Playmate Review
••• 199—Full frontal nudity.
**Playboy's Playmate Review** (May 1994)
. . . . . . . . . . . . . . . . . . . . . . . . . . . . Miss February
••• 14-21—Nude.
**Playboy's Girls of Summer '94** (Jul 1994) . . . Herself
••• 83—Full frontal nudity.
**Playboy's Book of Lingerie** (Jul 1994) . . . . . . Herself
• 42—Lower frontal nudity.
••• 72-73—Full frontal nudity.

# Lesniak, Emilia

See: Crow, Emilia.

# • Lesseos, Mimi

*Films:*

The American Angels, Baptism of Blood (1989)
. . . . . . . . . . . . . . . . . . . . . . . . . . . .Magnificent Mimi
The Last Riders (1991) . . . . . . . . . . . . . . . . .Feather
0:01—Buns, in yellow two piece swimsuit, walking down the beach.
Pushed to the Limit (1991) . . . . . . . . . . . . . . . . Mimi
Final Impact (1992) . . . . . . . . . . . . . . . . . . . . . . . Roxy
Beyond Fear (1993) . . . . . . . . . . . . . . . . . Tipper Taylor
**Streets of Rage** (1993) . . . . . . . . . . . . . . Melody Sails
• 0:33—Buns and brief side view of breasts after taking off robe and getting into shower. Breasts, sort of visible behind shower door.

*Magazines:*

**Playboy** (Dec 1989) . . . . . . . . . . . . . . . Lethal Women
• 148—Buns and almost side view of right breast.
**Playboy's Career Girls** (Aug 1992) . . . Lethal Women
• 106—Buns in G-string and partial right breast.

# Lester, Eleese

*Films:*

Cloak and Dagger (1984) . . . . . . . . . . Woman on Boat
**Confessions of a Serial Killer** (1987) . . Karen Grimes
• 0:34—Buns, tied and gaged to bed before being raped and killed.

# • Leventon, Annabel

*Films:*

Think Dirty . . . . . . . . . . . . . . . . . . .Chandler's Secretary
*a.k.a. Every Home Should Have One*
Come Back Peter (1971; British) . . . . . . . . . . . . Hippie
Real Life (1984; British) . . . . . . . . . . . . . . . . . . . .Carla

Defense of the Realm (1986; British) . . .Trudy Markham
**M. Butterfly** (1993) . . . . . . . . . . . . . . . . . Frau Baden
•• 0:50—Breasts, while sitting on bed and talking to Jeremy Irons.

# Levin, Rachel

*Films:*

**Gaby, A True Story** (1987) . . . . . . . . . . . . . . . . Gaby
• 0:56—Right breast, then breasts on the floor making love with another handicapped boy, Fernando.
White Palace (1990) . . . . . . . . . . . . . . . . . . . . . . Rachel

# Levine Thomson, Anna

a.k.a. Anna Thomson.

*Films:*

The Pope of Greenwich Village (1984)
. . . . . . . . . . . . . . . . . . . . . . . . Waitress at Country Inn
Desperately Seeking Susan (1985) . . . . . . . . . . . .Crystal
Maria's Lovers (1985) . . . . . . . . . . . . . . . . . . . . . .Kathy
Murphy's Romance (1985) . . . . . . . . . . . . . . . .Wanda
At Close Range (1986) . . . . . . . . . . . . Barroom Dancer
Something Wild (1986) . . . . . . . . . . . . . . .The Girl in 3F
Bird (1988) . . . . . . . . . . . . . . . . . . . . . . . . . .Audrey
Leonard, Part 6 (1988) . . . . . . . . . . . Nurse Carvalho
Talk Radio (1988) . . . . . . . . .Woman at Basketball Game
**White Hot** (1988) . . . . . . . . . . . . . . . . . . . . . . .Heather
••• 0:04—In bra, then breasts undressing for drug dealer in exchange for cocaine.
Warlock (1990) . . . . . . . . . . . . . . . . . . . . Pastor's Wife
Criss Cross (1992) . . . . . . . . . . . . . . . . . . . . Monica
Unforgiven (1992) . . . . . . . . . .Delilah Fitzgerald
The Crow (1993) . . . . . . . . . . . . . . . . . . . . . . . Darla
True Romance (1993) . . . . . . . . . . . . . . . . . . . . Lucy
(Unrated version reviewed.)

*Made for Cable Movies:*

Dead In the Water (1991) . . . . . . . . . . . . .Edie Meyers

# Lewis, Charlotte

*Films:*

The Golden Child (1986) . . . . . . . . . . . . . . . Kee Nang
Pirates (1986; French) . . . . . . . . . . . . . . . . . . . . Dolores
**Dial Help** (1988) . . . . . . . . . . . . . . . . . .Jenny Cooper
1:06—Black panties and bare back dressing in black corset top and stockings. Yowzal
•• 1:09—Brief right breast while rolling around in the bathtub.
Tripwire (1989) . . . . . . . . . . . . . . . . . . . . . . . . .Trudy
**Storyville** (1992) . . . . . . . . . . . . . . . . . . . . . . . . Lee
•• 0:17—Buns, taking off martial arts outfit and getting into hot tub. Brief breasts, sitting down (medium long shot).
• 0:18—Brief upper half of breasts, in hot tub with James Spader.
**Excessive Force** (1993) . . . . . . . . . . . . Anna Gilmour
••• 0:54—Brief right breast, then breasts while in bed with Thomas Ian Griffith.
Lipstick Camera (1993) . . . . . . . . . . . . .Roberta Dailey

*Made for Cable Movies:*
Bare Essentials (1991) . . . . . . . . . . . . . . . . . . . . . . Tarita
   0:55—Upper half of buns, in G-string swimsuit,
   while talking to Mark Linn-Baker.
   0:59—Buns in swimsuit, while giving Linn-Baker a
   massage. Breasts, but her long hair gets in the way.
   1:31—Very brief side view of buns in swimsuit, walking from the ocean onto the beach.
**Sketch Artist** (1992; Showtime) . . . . . . . . . . Leese
••• 0:02—Breasts making love on sofa. Buns in G-string,
   side of right breast, while changing CD. (Does this
   woman have the most awesome waist-to-chest ratio
   or what?)
*Magazines:*
**Playboy** (Jun 1993) . . . . . . . . . . . . . . . . . Next Month
••• 186—Left breast.
**Playboy** (Jul 1993) . . . . . . . . . . . . . . . . . . . Brit Force
•• 132-139—Breasts and buns in color and B&W pho-
   tos.
**Playboy's Nudes** (Dec 1993) . . . . . . . . . . . . . Herself
•• 11—Buns.

## Lewis, Fiona

*Films:*
The Fearless Vampire Killers (1967) . . . . . . . . . . . .Maid
Dr. Phibes Rises Again (1972) . . . . . . . . . . . . . . . Diana
**Lisztomania** (1975; British). . . . . . . . . .Countess Marie
•• 0:00—Breasts in bed getting breasts kissed by Roger
   Daltrey to the beat of a metronome.
• 0:01—Brief breasts swinging a chandelier to Daltrey.
•• 0:03—Brief breasts and buns while running from
   chair (long shot). Brief breasts when catching a candle on the bed.
•• 0:04—Brief left breast when her dress top is cut
   down. Left breast, sitting inside a piano with Daltrey.
**Drum** (1976) . . . . . . . . . . . . . . . . . . Augusta Chauvet
••• 0:57—Breasts taking a bath, getting out, then having Pam Grier dry her off.
**Tintorera** (1977). . . . . . . . . . . . . . . . . . . . . Patricia
• 0:20—Brief side view (silhouette) of left breast while
   in hallway. Breasts and buns, while walking to the
   ocean (long shot).
•• 0:22—Nude, while swimming under water just be-
   fore getting eaten by a shark. Don't see her face.
The Fury (1978) . . . . . . . . . . . . . . . . . Dr. Susan Charles
Dead Kids (1981; Australian/New Zealand)
. . . . . . . . . . . . . . . . . . . . . . . . . . . . Gwen Parkinson
Strange Invaders (1983) . . . . . . . . . .Waitress/Avon Lady
Innerspace (1987). . . . . . . . . . . . . .Dr. Margaret Canker
*Made for TV Movies:*
Dracula (1974) . . . . . . . . . . . . . . . . . . . Lucy Westerna
*Magazines:*
**Playboy** (Oct 1975). . . . . . . . . . . . .Lisztomania/Fiona
• 84—Side of left breast.
••• 89-91—Full frontal nudity.
**Playboy** (Dec 1975). . . . . . . . . . . . . Sex Stars of 1975
••• 182—Breasts.
**Playboy** (Dec 1976). . . . . . . . . . . . . Sex Stars of 1976
••• 187—Full frontal nudity.

## • Lewis, Juliette

Daughter of actor Geoffrey Lewis.
*Films:*
My Stepmother Is An Alien (1988) . . . . . . . . . . . . Lexie
The Runnin' Kind (1988) . . . . . . . . . . . . . .Amy Curtis
Cape Fear (1991). . . . . . . . . . . . . . . . Danny Bowden
Crooked Hearts (1991). . . . . . . . . . . . . . . . . . Cassie
Husbands and Wives (1992). . . . . . . . . . . . . . . .Rain
**Kalifornia** (1993). . . . . . . . . . . . . . . Adele Corners
(Unrated version reviewed.)
•• 0:09—Left breast, after opening robe to say "good-
   bye" to Brad Pitt.
That Night (1993) . . . . . . . . . . . . . . . Sheryl O'Conner
   0:03—In strapless bra and slip in her bedroom.
   0:26—In strapless bra with C. Thomas Howell under
   pier at beach.
What's Eating Gilbert Grape (1993) . . . . . . . . . . .Becky
Natural Born Killers (1994). . . . . . . . . . . . . . Mallory
Romeo Is Bleeding (1994) . . . . . . . . . . . . . . . . Sheri
*TV:*
I Married Dora (1987-88). . . . . . . . . . . . . Kate Farrell
A Family for Joe (1990). . . . . . . . . . . . . .Holly Bankston

## Lightstone, Marilyn

*Films:*
Lies My Father Told Me (1975; Canadian)
. . . . . . . . . . . . . . . . . . . . . . . . . . . . Annie Herman
**In Praise of Older Women** (1978; Canadian) . . .Klari
• 0:45—Left breast, twice, while on floor with Tom Be-
   renger before being discovered by Karen Black.
Spasms (1983; Canadian) . . . . . . . . . . . . . Dr. Rothman
The Surrogate (1984; Canadian) . . . .Dr. Harriet Forman
*Made for Cable Movies:*
Disaster in Time (1992; Showtime). . . . . Madame Iovine
   *a.k.a. Timescape*
*Made for TV Movies:*
Anne of Green Gables (1985; Canadian) . . . Miss Stacey

## Lin, Traci

*Films:*
**Casanova** (1987) . . . . . . . . . . . . . . . . . . . . . . . . Heidi
• 1:56—Very, very brief right breast while bending
   over to help Richard Chamberlain. Long, long shot.
My Little Girl (1987). . . . . . . . . . . . . . . . . . . . . Alice
Fright Night, Part 2 (1988). . . . . . . . . . . . . . . . . . Alex
Moving (1988). . . . . . . . . . . . . . . . . . . . . . . .Natalie
A Tiger's Tale (1988). . . . . . . . . . . . . . . . . . . . Penny
**Survival Quest** (1989) . . . . . . . . . . . . . . . . . .Olivia
• 0:50—Breasts, while bathing in a stream while seen
   by Gray. Long shot.
Class of 1999 (1990) . . . . . . . . . . . .Christine Langford
Spellcaster (1992) . . . . . . . . . . . . . . . . . . . . Yvette

## Lindeland, Liv

*Films:*
Picasso Trigger (1989) . . . . . . . . . . . . . . . . . . .Inga
Guns (1990). . . . . . . . . . . . . . . . . . . . . . . . . . . Ace
*Magazines:*
**Playboy** (Jan 1971). . . . . . . . . . . . . . . . . . . Playmate

Playboy (Dec 1972). . . . . . . . . . . . . . Sex Stars of 1972
**Playboy** (Jan 1974) . . . . . . . Twenty Years of Playmates
••• 110—Breasts and buns, while in bed.
**Playboy's Nudes** (Oct 1990). . . . . . . . . . . . . . Herself
••• 29—Full frontal nudity.
**Playboy** (Jan 1994) . . . . . . . . . . . 40 Memorable Years
••• 90—Breasts and partial lower frontal nudity.

# Lindemulder, Janine

Started doing adult films in 1992. First adult film is *Hidden Obsessions*.
*Adult Films:*
**Hidden Obsessions** (1993). . . . . . . . . . . Various Parts
*Films:*
**Spring Fever USA** (1988) . . . . . . . . . . Heather Lipton
*a.k.a. Lauderdale*
•• 0:14—Taking off her stockings, then brief breasts undressing for bath, then taking a bath.
**Caged Fury** (1989) . . . . . . . . . . . . . . . . . . . . . . Lulu
0:14—Dancing in bar in black bra and G-string.
• 0:15—Brief breasts dancing in front of Erik Estrada.
**Killer Looks** (1994). . . . . . . . . . . . . . . . . . . Angela
(Unrated version reviewed.)
••• 1:12—In white lingerie, then breasts while making out with Lené Hefner and Mickey's lover.
•• 1:18—Breasts, while sunbathing outside by pool with Hefner.
•• 1:23—Breasts while making out on stairway with Hefner and Sara Suzanne Brown.
*Video Tapes:*
**Penthouse Passport to Paradise/Hawaii** (1991)
. . . . . . . . . . . . . . . . . . . . . . . . . . . . . . . . . . . . . .Model
••• 0:37—Stripping out of a dress and lingerie, then nude dancing during her fantasy.
**Penthouse Ready to Ride** (1992) . . . . . . . . . .Model
**Penthouse Satin & Lace II: Hollywood Undercover** (1992). . . . . . . . . . . . . . . . . . . . . . . . . . . . . . . . Pet
**Penthouse Satin & Lace: An Erotic History of Lingerie** (1992). . . . . . . . . . . . . . . . . . . . . .Model
**The Girls of Penthouse, Volume 2** (1993). . . . . . Pet
••• 0:20—Nude in a pool, working out and in bed.
**Penthouse DreamGirls** (1994) . . . . . . . . . . . . .Janine
••• 0:23—Nude, with space/alien style silver body paint and costume.
*CD-ROM:*
**Penthouse Interactive Virtual Photo Shoot, Disc 3** (1993). . . . . . . . . . . . . . . . . . . . . . . . . . . . . . . . Pet
*Magazines:*
**Penthouse** (Dec 1987) . . . . . . . . . . . . . . . . . . . Pet
**Penthouse** (Sep 1990) . . . . . . . . . . . Tony and Janine
•• 82-91—Nude with a guy.
**Penthouse** (Mar 1991) . . . . . . . . . . . . . . . . Robo-Pet
••• 42-51—Nude, partially covered with silver paint.
**Penthouse** (Dec 1993) . . . . . Searching for Bob Fischer
••• 116-127—Nude with Amy Lynn Baxter with painted and unpainted bodies by artist Robert A. Fischer.
**Penthouse** (Sep 1994) . . . . . . . . . . . . . . .Ice & Easy
••• 91-105—Nude with Julia Ann and ice dildos.

# Linden, Jennie

*Films:*
Nightmare (1963; British) . . . . . . . . . . . . . . . . . . . Janet
Dr. Who and the Daleks (1965; British). . . . . . . Barbara
A Severed Head (1971; British). . . . . . . . .Georgie Hands
0:02—Buns, rolling over on the floor with Ian Holm.
**Women in Love** (1971) . . . . . . . . . . . Ursula Bragwen
• 0:38—Brief breasts skinny dipping in the river with Glenda Jackson.
• 1:11—Brief breasts in a field with Alan Bates. Scene is shown sideways.
Hedda (1975; British). . . . . . . . . . . . . . . .Mrs. Elvsted
Old Dracula (1975; British). . . . . . . . . . . . . . .Angela
Valentino (1977; British). . . . . . . . . . . . . . .Agnes Ayres
A Deadly Game (1979; British). . . . . . . . . . . . . . Edith

# Lindley, Gisele

*Films:*
**Forbidden Zone** (1980). . . . . . . . . . . . . . .The Princess
••• 0:21—Breasts in jail cell.
••• 0:39—Breasts turning a table around.
•• 0:45—Breasts bending over, making love with a frog.
•• 0:51—Breasts in a cave.
•• 0:53—More breasts scenes.
•• 1:06—Even more breasts scenes.
S.O.B. (1981). . . . . . . . . . . . . . . . . . . . . . . . . . . n.a.

# Linssen, Saskia

*Video Tapes:*
**Playboy's Playmate Review 1992** (1992) . .Miss June
••• 0:27—Nude doing futuristic dance and then taking a bath.
*Magazines:*
**Playboy** (Jun 1991). . . . . . . . . . . . . . . . . . . Playmate
••• 112-125—Nude.
**Playboy's Book of Lingerie** (Jul 1992). . . . . . .Herself
••• 96—Breasts.
• 98-99—Breasts under fishnet body stocking.
**Playboy's Book of Lingerie** (Sep 1992). . . . . .Herself
••• 94-95—Full frontal nudity.
**Playboy's International Playmates** (Mar 1993)
. . . . . . . . . . . . . . . . . . . . . . . . . . . . . . . . . . . . .Herself
•••• 3-9—Full frontal nudity.
**Playboy's Girls of Summer '93** (Jun 1993) . . .Herself
• 25—Side of left breast.
**Playboy's Blondes, Brunettes & Redheads** (Sep 1993). . . . . . . . . . . . . . . . . . . . . . . . . . . .Herself
••• 84—Full frontal nudity.
**Playboy's Book of Lingerie** (Jan 1994) . . . . . .Herself
••• 82—Breasts.

# •Lippa, Christine

*Films:*
Just One of the Girls (1992) . . . . . . . . . . . . . . Cashier
Intersection (1993). . . . . . . . . . . . . . . .Step Magazine
**Tomcat: Dangerous Desires** (1993). . . . . . . . . .Randi
• 0:56—Buns, while lying on bed and talking to Richard Grieco.

## Little, Michele

*Films:*
Out of the Blue (1982) . . . . . . . . . . . . . . . . . Girl in Car
Radioactive Dreams (1984) . . . . . . . . . . . . . Rusty Mars
My Demon Lover (1987). . . . . . . . . . . . . . . . . Denny
Out of Bounds (1987). . . . . . . . . . . . . . . . . . . Crystal
**Sweet Revenge** (1987). . . . . . . . . . . . . . . . . . . . . Lee
• 0:41—Brief breasts in water under a waterfall with K.C.
Appointment with Fear (1988) . . . . . . . . . . . . . . Carol
Blood Clan (1990). . . . . . . . . . . . . . . . . . . . . Katy Bane
Mystery Date (1991). . . . . . . . . . . . . . . . . . . . . Stella

## Littlefeather, Sacheen

At the 1973 Academy Awards, she announced Marlon Brando's rejection of Best Actor Award.

*Films:*
Freebie and the Bean (1974). . . . . . . . . . . . . . . . . .n.a.
The Laughing Policeman (1974) . . . . . . . . . . . . . . .n.a.
The Trial of Billy Jack (1974) . . . . . . . . . Patsy Littlejohn
**Johnny Firecloud** (1975) . . . . . . . . . . . . . . . . . Nenya
••• 0:55—Breasts, getting raped by jerks on desk in classroom.
Winterhawk (1976). . . . . . . . . . . . . . . . . . . . .Paleflower
Shoot the Sun Down (1981) . . . . . . . . . . . . . . . .n.a.

*Magazines:*
**Playboy** (Sep 1973). . . . . . . . . . . . . . . . . Next Month
•• 270—Breasts B&W.
**Playboy** (Oct 1973). . . . . . . . . . . . . . . . . . . . Sacheen
••• 93-95—Full frontal nudity.

## Liu, Carolyn

*Films:*
**Do or Die** (1991). . . . . . . . . . . . . . . . . . . . . . . . . Silk
••• 0:14—Breasts, getting up off massage table and putting robe on.
•• 1:04—Breasts in bed with Pat Morita.
**Fit To Kill** (1993). . . . . . . . . . . . . . . . . . . . . . . . . Silk
• 0:09—Buns in body suit, while in room with Kane.
•• 0:11—Breasts while making love in bed with Kane.
••• 0:46—Breasts, while taking off lingerie on boat with Kane.
0:49—In two piece swimsuit.
**Hard Hunted** (1993). . . . . . . . . . . . . . . . . . . . . . Silk
• 0:02—Buns, while in lingerie on boat with Mr. Kane.
••• 0:08—Breasts, while taking off her dress top on boat in front of Mr. Kane, then in bed with him.
• 0:10—Brief breasts, while lying in bed with the plastic explosive on the safe blows up.

*Video Tapes:*
**Sexy Lingerie III** (1991) . . . . . . . . . . . . . . . . . .Model
**Penthouse Satin & Lace: An Erotic History of Lingerie** (1992) . . . . . . . . . . . . . . . . . . . . . . . .Model

*Magazines:*
**Playboy** (Mar 1992). . . . . . . . . . . . . . Society Darlings
••• 130-131—Full frontal nudity.

## Lizer, Kari

*Films:*
Smokey Bites the Dust (1981) . . . . . . . . . . . . . . Cindy
**Private School** (1983). . . . . . . . . . . . . . . . . . . . Rita
• 0:30—Very brief left breast popping out of cheerleader's outfit along with the Coach.
Gotchal (1985) . . . . . . . . . . . . . . . . . . . . . . . Muffy
*Made for Cable TV:*
Dream On: A Midsummer Night's Dream On (1993; HBO). . . . . . . . . . . . . . . . . . . . . . . . .Becca
*Made for TV Movies:*
Double Edge (1992). . . . . . . . . . . . . . . Sister Theresa
*TV:*
Sunday Dinner (1991) . . . . . . . . . . . . . . . . . . . .Diana

## Lloyd, Emily

*Films:*
**Wish You Were Here** (1987). . . . . . . . . . . . . . Lynda
• 0:43—Buns, while singing in the alley and lifting up her skirt to moon an older neighbor woman.
Chicago Joe and the Showgirl (1989; British) . . . . . . . . . . . . . . . . . . . . . . . . . . . . . . . Betty Jones
Cookie (1989) . . . . . . . . . . Carmella "Cookie" Voltecki
In Country (1989) . . . . . . . . . . . . . . Samantha Hughes
A River Runs Through It (1992) . . . . . . . . . Jessie Burns
Scorchers (1992) . . . . . . . . . . . . . . . . . . . . . Splendid

## Lloyd, Sue

*Films:*
Happy Housewives. . . . . . . . . . . . . . . . . . The Blonde
Revenge of the Pink Panther (1978)
. . . . . . . . . . . . . . . . Claude Russo/Claudine Russo
**The Stud** (1978; British) . . . . . . . . . . . . . . . . Vanessa
• 1:04—Breasts in the swimming pool with Joan Collins and Tony.
**The Bitch** (1979; British) . . . . . . . . . . . Vanessa Grant
• 1:12—Side view of left breast and breasts in the swimming pool.
Rough Cut (1980; British) . . . . . . . . . . . . . . . . . n.a.

## Locke, Sondra

*Films:*
The Heart is a Lonely Hunter (1968). . . . . . . Mick Kelley
Willard (1971) . . . . . . . . . . . . . . . . . . . . . . . . .Joan
**Suzanne** (1973) . . . . . . . . . . . . . . . . . . . . . .Suzanne
*a.k.a. The Second Coming of Suzanne*
(*Suzanne* has nudity in it, *The Second Coming of Suzanne* has the nudity cut out.)
•• 0:27—Breasts sitting, looking at a guy. Brief left breast several times lying down.
••• 0:29—Breasts lying down.
**The Outlaw Josey Wales** (1976). . . . . . . . . .Laura Lee
•• 1:20—Briefly nude in rape scene.
**Death Game, The Seducers** (1977) . . . . . . . . Jackson
*a.k.a. Mrs. Manning's Weekend*
0:16—Buns and brief right breast in spa with Colleen Camp trying to get George in with them.
• 0:48—Brief breasts running around the room trying to keep George away from the telephone.

**The Gauntlet** (1977) . . . . . . . . . . . . . . . . . Gus Mally
　•• 1:10—Brief right breast, then breasts getting raped
　　by two biker guys in a box car while Clint Eastwood
　　is tied up.
Every Which Way But Loose (1978). . Lynn Halsey Taylor
Any Which Way You Can (1980) . . . . . . . . . . . . Lynne
Bronco Billy (1980) . . . . . . . . . . . . . . . . . . Antoinette
Sudden Impact (1983) . . . . . . . . . . . . Jennifer Spencer
Ratboy (1986) . . . . . . . . . . . . . . . . . . . . Nikki Morrison
*Made for TV Movies:*
Rosie: The Rosemary Clooney Story (1982)
　. . . . . . . . . . . . . . . . . . . . . . . . . Rosemary Clooney

## Lockhart, Anne

Daughter of actress June Lockhart.
*Films:*
**Joyride** (1977) . . . . . . . . . . . . . . . . . . . . . . . . . Cindy
　•• 0:59—Brief breasts in the spa with everybody.
　••• 1:00—Breasts, standing in the kitchen kissing Desi
　　Arnaz Jr.
**The Young Warriors** (1983; U.S./Canadian) . . . . Lucy
　•• 0:42—Breasts and buns making love with Kevin on
　　the bed. Looks like a body double.
Troll (1986) . . . . . . . . . . . . . . . . . Young Eunice St. Clair
Dark Tower (1987) . . . . . . . . . . . . . . . . . . . . . . Elaine
Big Bad John (1989) . . . . . . . . . . . . Lady Police Officer
*Made for TV Movies:*
Just Tell Me You Love Me (1978) . . . . . . . . . . . . . . .n.a.
*TV:*
Battlestar Galactica (1979) . . . . . . . . . . . . . . . Sheeba
*Magazines:*
**Playboy** (Nov 1977) . . . . . . . . . . Sex in Cinema 1977
　•• 160—Breasts, while in pool with her friends from
　　*Joyride.*

## Locklin, Loryn

*Films:*
Catch Me... If You Can (1989) . . . . . . . . . . . . . Melissa
　0:18—In blue one-piece swimsuit by the pool.
　1:32—In bra trying to get policeman's attention.
　Very, very brief side of right breast turing around.
　Looks like she's wearing flesh-colored pasties.
**Taking Care of Business** (1990) . . . . . . . . . . . Jewel
　• 0:42—Buns and very brief side view, twice, seen
　　through door, changing by the pool. Then in black
　　two piece swimsuit.
**Fortress** (1993; U.S./Australian) . . . . . . Karen Brennick
　• 0:18—Lower half of buns, under lingerie while mak-
　　ing love on top of Christopher Lambert in bed.
*Made for TV Movies:*
Shoot First: A Cop's Vengeance (1991) . . . . . . . . . . Lea

## Logan, Phyllis

*Films:*
**Another Time, Another Place** (1983; British) . . Janie
　••• 0:31—Breasts, washing herself off after working in
　　the fields. Nice close-up shot.
　•• 0:53—Full frontal nudity, after undressing then get-
　　ting into bed.

　••• 1:08—Breasts in front of a group of men.
The Chain (1985; British) . . . . . . . . . . . . . . . . . Alison
The Doctor and the Devils (1985) . . . . . . Elizabeth Rock
The McGuffin (1985; British) . . . . . . . . . . . . . . . Anne
The Kitchen Toto (1987; British) . . . . . . Janet Graham
Soft Top, Hard Shoulder (1992; British) . . . . . . . . Karla
*Made for TV Movies:*
Silent Cries (1993) . . . . . . . . . . . . . . . . . . . Nancy Muir

## Lomas, Caroline

*Films:*
**Nudity Required** (1989) . . . . . . . . . . . . . . . .Caroline
　•• 0:36—Brief breasts (fifth girl) standing in line.
　•• 0:37—Breasts doing puppet routine for audition.
　•• 0:38—Breasts while yelling for not having a script.
　• 0:39—Breasts.
　• 0:44—Breasts while sitting on the edge of the pool.
Society (1989) . . . . . . . . . . . . . . . . . . . . . . . . . . n.a.

## • Lombard, Karina

Model.
*Films:*
The Doors (1991). . . . . . . . . . . . . . . . .Warhol Actress
The Firm (1993). . . . . . . . . . . . . . . Woman On Beach
**Wide Sargasso Sea** (1993) . . . . . . . . . . . . .Antoinette
　(Unrated version reviewed.)
　••• 0:31—Buns and breasts, with her new husband,
　　Rochester.
　•• 0:37—Breasts and partial frontal nudity while mak-
　　ing love in bedroom with Rochester.
　•• 0:42—Buns and partial breasts, in wet white clothes.
　　Left breast and buns while in bed with Rochester.
　••• 0:52—Breasts while in bed before making love and
　　after.
　• 0:55—Right breast, while sitting in bed.
　• 1:13—Breasts, while sitting in bed.
*Magazines:*
**Playboy** (Nov 1993) . . . . . . . . . . Sex in Cinema 1993
　•• 138—Full frontal nudity in two video stills from *Wide
　　Sargasso Sea.*

## Lombardi, Leigh

*Films:*
The Wild Life (1984). . . . . . . . . . . . . . . . . . Stewardess
Murphy's Law (1986). . . . . . . . . . . . . . . . . Stewardess
A Tiger's Tale (1988). . . . . . . . . . . . . . . . . . . . Marcia
**Moontrap** (1989). . . . . . . . . . . . . . . . . . . . . . Mera
　•• 1:08—Breasts with Walter Koenig in moon tent.

## Lomez, Céline

*Films:*
The Far Shore (1976) . . . . . . . . . . . . . . Eulalia Turner
Plague (1978; Canadian) . . . . . . . . . . . . . . . . . . n.a.
　*a.k.a. The Gemini Strain*
**The Silent Partner** (1978) . . . . . . . . . . . . . . .Elaine
　• 1:05—Side view of left breast, then breasts, then
　　buns with Elliott Gould.
The Kiss (1988) . . . . . . . . . . . . . . . . . . . . . Aunt Irene

# London, Lisa

*Films:*
**H.O.T.S.** (1979) . . . . . . . . . . . . . . . . . . . . Jennie O'Hara
*a.k.a. T & A Academy*
- • 1:22—Breasts changing clothes by the closet while a crook watches her.
- • 1:33—Breasts playing football.

The Happy Hooker Goes Hollywood (1980) . . . . . Laurie
**Sudden Impact** (1983) . . . . . . . . . . . . . .Young Hooker
- •• 1:04—Breasts in bathroom, walking to Nick in the bed.

**The Naked Cage** (1985) . . . . . . . . . . . . . . . . . .Abbey
- •• 0:22—Breasts in S&M costume with Angel Tompkins.
- •• 0:38—Left breast making out in bed with Angel Tompkins.

Private Resort (1985) . . . . . . . . . . . . . . . . . . . . Alice
0:51—In beige bra and panties several times with Rob Morrow and Johnny Depp while she's drunk.

Black Moon Rising (1986) . . . . . . . . . . . . . . . .Redhead
**Savage Beach** (1989) . . . . . . . . . . . . . . . . . . . Rocky
- • 0:06—Breasts in spa with Patty Duffek, Dona Speir and Hope Marie Carlton.
- •• 0:50—Breasts changing clothes.

Guns (1990) . . . . . . . . . . . . . . . . . . . . . . . . . . Rocky
*Made for Cable Movies:*
Prey of the Chameleon (1992; Showtime) . . . . . . . Alice
*Made for Cable TV:*
**Dream On: The Charlotte Letter** (1991; HBO)
. . . . . . . . . . . . . . . . . . . . . . . . . . . Candy Striper #2
- • 0:06—Breasts several times, acting in adult film that Martin is watching on TV. (She's first to take her outfit off.)

*Video Tapes:*
**Inside Out 2** (1992) . . . . . . . . June/The Right Number
(Unrated version reviewed.)
- •• 1:25—Breasts, lying on the floor having phone sex and in bed.
- •• 1:28—More breasts talking on the phone.

# Long, Nia

*Films:*
Edgar Allan Poe's "Buried Alive" (1989) . . . . . . . Fingers
**Boyz N the Hood** (1991) . . . . . . . . . . . . . . . .Brandi
1:16—In bra, lying in bed with Tre.
- • 1:17—Left breast, while in bed with Tre. Don't see her face, but it is her.

Made in America (1993) . . . . . . . . . . . . Zora Mathews
*TV:*
The Guiding Light . . . . . . . . . . . . . . . . . . Kat Speakes

# Long, Shannon

*Video Tapes:*
**Playboy Video Calendar 1990** (1989) . . . November
- ••• 0:57—Nude.

*Magazines:*
**Playboy** (Oct 1988) . . . . . . . . . . . . . . . . . . . Playmate

**Playboy Presents International Playmates**
(Feb 1992) . . . . . . . . . . . . . . . . . . . . . . . . .Herself
- ••• 102-105—Nude.

**Playboy's Girls of the World** (Oct 1992) . . . . . Herself
- ••• 103—Breasts.

**Playboy's Calendar Playmates** (Nov 1992) . . . Herself
- ••• 86—Full frontal nudity.

**Playboy's Book of Lingerie** (Sep 1993) . . . . . . Herself
- ••• 105—Full frontal nudity.

**Playboy** (Jul 1994) . . . . . . . . . . . . . . Playmate Revisited
- ••• 74-79—Nude.

# Long, Shelley

*Films:*
A Small Circle of Friends (1980) . . . . . . . . . . . . . . Alice
Caveman (1981) . . . . . . . . . . . . . . . . . . . . . . . . . . Tala
Night Shift (1982) . . . . . . . . . . . . . . Belinda Keaton
0:20—In black teddy and robe talking to Henry Winkler in the hallway.
0:37—In panties, socks and tank top cooking breakfast in Winkler's kitchen.

Irreconcilable Differences (1984)
. . . . . . . . . . . . . . . . . . . . . . Lucy Van Patten Brodsky
The Money Pit (1986) . . . . . . . . . . . Anna Crowley
**Hello Again!** (1987) . . . . . . . . . . . . . . Lucy Chadman
- • 0:58—Brief buns, in hospital gown, walking down hallway.

Outrageous Fortune (1987) . . . . . . . . . . Lauren Ames
Troop Beverly Hills (1989) . . . . . . . . . . . . Phyllis Nefler
Don't Tell Her It's Me (1990) . . . . . . . . . . . .Lizzie Potts
Frozen Assets (1992) . . . . . . . . . . . . Dr. Grace Murdock
*Made for Cable TV:*
Sex, Shock and Censorship in the 90's (1993; Showtime)
. . . . . . . . . . . . . . . . . . . . . . . . . Fay Sommerfield
*Made for TV Movies:*
Fatal Memories (1992) . . . . . . . . . . . . . . . . . . . . . n.a.
A Message From Holly (1992) . . . . . . . . . . . Kate Barnes
*TV:*
Cheers (1982-87) . . . . . . . . . . . . . . . . Diane Chambers
Good Advice (1993- ) . . . . . . . . . . . . . . Susan DeRuzza

# Loomis, Deborah

*Films:*
Hercules in New York (1969) . . . . . . . . . . . . . . .Helen
*a.k.a. Hercules Goes Bananas*
Foreplay (1975) . . . . . . . . . . . . . . . . . . . . . . . . . . Doll
*Magazines:*
**Playboy** (Apr 1974)
. . . . . . . . . . . . . . . Foreplay (A Comedy in Three Acts)
- ••• 108-109—Breasts on sofa with Pat Paulsen.

# Lopez, Maria Isabel

*a.k.a. Isabel Lopez.*
*Films:*
**Joy: Chapter II** (1985; French) . . . . . . . . . . . . . Milaka
*a.k.a. Joy and Joan*
- •• 0:10—Breasts, showing Joy her breasts at Bruce's request.

••• 0:27—Breasts, taking off her robe and massaging Joy.

**Silip** (1985; Philippines). . . . . . . . . . . . . . . . . . . Tonya
*a.k.a. Daughters of Eve*

**Mission Manila** (1989). . . . . . . . . . . . . . . . . . Jessie
  • 0:22—Brief right breast several times in bed while Harry threatens her with knife.

**Dune Warriors** (1990). . . . . . . . . . . . . . . . Miranda
  •• 0:25—Breasts in underground lake with Val.
  ••• 0:43—Breasts making love with a guy in bed.

## Lords, Traci

Infamous under age adult film actress. Unfortunately, all of the adult films she was in before she was 18 years old are now illegal. The only legal adult film she did is *Traci, I Love You.*

Real name is Nora Louise Kuzma.

*Films:*

**Not of This Earth** (1988) . . . . . . . . . . . . . . . . Nadine
  •• 0:25—Buns and side view of left breast drying herself off with a towel while talking to Jeremy.
  0:27—In blue swimsuit by swimming pool.
  •• 0:42—Breasts in bed making love with Harry.
  0:46—Walking around the house in white lingerie.

**Fast Food** (1989). . . . . . . . . . . . . . . . . . . . . . .Dixie Love
  1:10—In black bra in storage room with Auggie.

**Cry Baby** (1990) . . . . . . . . . . . . . . . . . . . . . . . Wanda

**Shock 'Em Dead** (1990) . . . . . . . . . . . . Lindsay Roberts

**Desperate Crimes** (1991; Italian). . . . . . . . . . . . Laura

**Raw Nerve** (1991). . . . . . . . . . . . . . . . . . Gina Clayton

**A Time to Die** (1991) . . . . . . . . . . . . . . . . . . . . Jackie

**Intent to Kill** (1992). . . . . . . . . . . . . . Vickie Stewart

**Laser Moon** (1992) . . . . . . . . . . . . . . . Barbara Fleck

**Ice** (1993). . . . . . . . . . . . . . . . . . . . . . . . . .Ellen Reed

**Serial Mom** (1993) . . . . . . . . . . . . . . . . . . Carl's Date

*Made for Cable Movies:*
Rebel Highway: Dragstrip Girl (1994; Showtime)
  . . . . . . . . . . . . . . . . . . . . . . . . . . . . . . . . . Blanche

*Made for Cable TV:*
Tales From the Crypt: Two for the Show (1993; HBO)
  . . . . . . . . . . . . . . . . . . . . . . . . . . . Emma Conway

*Made for TV Movies:*
The Tommyknockers (1993) . . . . . . . . . . . . . . . . Nanci
Bandit: Bandit and the Silver Angel (1994) . . . . . . Angel

*Video Tapes:*

**Red Hot Rock** (1984) . . . . . . . . . . . . . . .Miss Georgia
*a.k.a. Sexy Shorts (on laser disc)*
  •• 0:41—Breasts several times in open-front swimsuit during beauty pageant during "Gimme Gimme Good Lovin'" by Helix.
  •• 0:42—Breasts on stage wearing black outfit with mask, smashing a large avocado during the same song.

Warm Up with Traci Lords (1989) . . . . . . . . . . . Herself

*Magazines:*

**Penthouse** (Sep 1984) . . . . . . . . . . . . . . . . . . . Pet
  ••• 97-115—Nude.

## Loren, Sophia

*Films:*

**Era Lui, Si, Si** (1952) . . . . . . . . . . . . . . . . . . . . . . . n.a.
Two Nights with Cleopatra (1954; Italian)
  . . . . . . . . . . . . . . . . . . . . . . . . . . . .Cleopatra/Nisca
  (It seems that her nude scenes have been cut for the video tape version.)

Boy on a Dolphin (1957) . . . . . . . . . . . . . . . . . .Phaedra
  0:04—Breasts, under yellow wet outfit, coming up out of the water after diving. Not nude, but amazing for 1958!
  0:07—Breasts, under yellow wet outfit, on the boat after getting injured while diving.
  0:55—Brief right breast, under wet orange outfit after scuba diving.

The Pride and the Passion (1957). . . . . . . . . . . . .Juana

Desire Under the Elms (1958). . . . . . . . . . .Anna Cabot

Houseboat (1958) . . . . . . . . . . . . . . . . Cinzia Zaccardi

A Breath of Scandal (1960). . . . . . . . . Princess Olympia

Heller in Pink Tights (1960) . . . . . . . . . . Angela Rossini

Two Women (1960; Italian) . . . . . . . . . . . . . . . . Cesira
  (Academy Award for Best Actress.)

El Cid (1961; U.S./Italian). . . . . . . . . . . . . . . . Chimene

Boccaccio 70 (1962; Italian). . . . . . . . . . . . . . . . . Zoe

The Fall of the Roman Empire (1964) . . . . . . . . . Lucilla

Yesterday, Today and Tomorrow (1964; Italian)
  . . . . . . . . . . . . . . . . . . . . . . . . . . . . . . . . . Adelina

Arabesque (1966) . . . . . . . . . . . . . . . . . Yasmin Azir

Man of La Mancha (1972) . . . . . . . . Dulcinea/Aldonza

Angela (1977; Canadian) . . . . . . . . . . . . . . . . . .Angela

The Cassandra Crossing (1977; British) . . . . . . . Jennifer

A Special Day (1977) . . . . . . . . . . . . . . . . .Antonietta

Brass Target (1978) . . . . . . . . . . . . . . . . . . . . Mara

Firepower (1979) . . . . . . . . . . . . . . . . . . . Adele Tasca

*Magazines:*

**Playboy** (Feb 1980) . . . . . . . . . . . . . . The Year in Sex
  • 157—Sort of breasts under sheer black dress.

Penthouse (May 1982). . . . . . . . . . . . . . . . .Titillation
  • 132—In wet dress. B&W.

**Playboy** (Jan 1989) . . . . . . . . . . . . Women of the Fifties
  • 120—B&W photo from *Era Lui, Si, Si.*

## Loring, Jeana

*Films:*

**The Malibu Bikini Shop** (1985) . . . . . . . . .Margie Hill
  •• 0:43—Breasts, dancing on stage during bikini contest (Contestant #4).

*Magazines:*

**Playboy** (Nov 1985) . . . . . . . . . . . Sex in Cinema 1985
  ••• 128—Breasts in scene from *The Malibu Bikini Shop.*

## Loring, Lisa

Wife of adult film actor Jerry Butler.

*Films:*

Blood Frenzy (1987). . . . . . . . . . . . . . . . . . . . . . Dory
  0:27—In sheer bra, taking off her blouse and dribbling water on herself.

**Iced** (1988). . . . . . . . . . . . . . . . . . . . . . . . . . . .Jeanette
  • 0:46—Brief left breast in bathtub.

- 0:53—Buns and brief right breast in bathtub with Alex.
•• 1:05—Brief lower frontal nudity and buns, while getting into hot tub. Breasts in hot tub just before getting electrocuted.
•• 1:13—Full frontal nudity lying dead in the hot tub.
- 1:18—Brief full frontal nudity lying dead in the hot tub again.
Death Feud (1989) . . . . . . . . . . . . . . . . . . . . . . . Roxey
  0:06—Dancing in club with feathery pasties. Later, wearing the same thing under a sheer negligee.
  0:41—Dancing again with the same pasties.
  1:20—Dancing with red tassel pasties.

*TV:*
As the World Turns . . . . . . . . . . . Cricket Montgomery
The Addams Family (1964-66)
. . . . . . . . . . . . . . . . . . Wednesday Thursday Addams

## Lorraine, Nita

*Films:*
**Happy Housewives** . . . . . . . . . . . . . . . . . Jenny Elgin
- 0:31—Brief side view of left breast and buns in barn chasing after Bob.
- 0:32—Brief breasts in open dress talking to policeman.
The Viking Queen (1967; British). . . . . Nubian Girl-Slave
All Neat in Black Stockings (1969). . . . . . . . . . . .Jolasta

## Louise, Helli

*Films:*
**Happy Housewives** . . . . . . . . Newsagent's Daughter
•• 0:16—Breasts with Mrs. Wain and Bob in the bathtub.
Confessions of a Pop Performer (1975; British) . . . . .n.a.

## Louise, Jeanine

*Made for Cable Movies:*
**Soft Touch** (1987; Playboy). . . . . . . . . Carrie Crawford
(Shown on *The Playboy Channel* as *Birds in Paradise*.)
- 0:00—Breasts during opening credits.
- 0:02—Breasts with her two girlfriends during the opening credits.
- 0:03—Brief breasts getting out of the shower.
- 0:17—Breasts seen in mirror, while taking a shower.
•• 0:19—Full frontal nudity during pillow fight on bed.
- 0:23—Breasts in bed with the other two girls.
- 0:27—Breasts in T-shirt, leaning over to wash car.
- 0:32—Breasts with Neill in open dress.
••• 0:35—Dancing on stage in red lingerie, then breasts and buns in G-string.
•• 0:41—Full frontal nudity walking in water with a guy.
••• 0:50—Breasts sunbathing on the boat with Tracy.
- 1:01—Nude, swinging into water. Long shot.
- 1:02—Buns, waving to a dolphin.
- 1:04—Breasts at night by campfire with Tracy.
- 1:05—Brief left breast, while sleeping.
- 1:06—Breasts when Tracy wakes her up.
- 1:19—Breasts in stills during the end credits.

**Soft Touch II** (1987; Playboy) . . . . . . .Carrie Crawford
(Shown on *The Playboy Channel* as *Birds in Paradise*.)
- 0:00—Breasts during opening credits.
- 0:02—Breasts with her two girlfriends during opening credits.
•• 0:24—Breasts in bed feeling herself.
•• 0:41—Full frontal nudity undressing and putting swimsuit on.
- 0:51—Breasts with her diving instructor.

## • Louise, Tina

*Films:*
God's Little Acre (1958) . . . . . . . . . . . . . . . . . . Griselda
How To Commit Marriage (1969) . . . . . . LaVerne Baker
The Wrecking Crew (1969) . . . . . . . . . . . .Lola Medina
The Stepford Wives (1975). . . . . . . . . . . . . .Charmaine
**Mean Dog Blues** (1978) . . . . . . . . . . . . Donna Lacey
- 1:16—Very brief side view of right breast, while getting up off massage table. Don't see her face very well.
Evils of the Night (1985) . . . . . . . . . . . . . . . . . . . Cora
Dixie Lanes (1987). . . . . . . . . . . . . . . . . . . . . . . .Violet
O.C. and Stiggs (1987) . . . . . . . . Florence Beaugereaux
Johnny Suede (1992). . . . . . . . . . . . . . . Mrs. Fontaine
*Made for TV Movies:*
Nightmare in Badham County (1976) . . . . . . . . . .Greer
(Nudity added for video tape.)
*TV:*
Gilligan's Island (1964-67) . . . . . . . . . . . . Ginger Grant
Dallas (1978) . . . . . . . . . . . . . . . . . . . . . . . . .Julie Grey
Rituals (1984-85) . . . . . . .Taylor Chapin Field Von Platen

## Love, Lucretia

*Films:*
Battle of the Amazons (1973; Italian/Spanish) . . . Eraglia
**Naked Warriors** (1973). . . . . . . . . . . . . . . . . . Deidre
*a.k.a. The Arena*
- 0:07—Brief breasts getting clothes torn off by guards.
•• 0:08—Brief nude getting washed down in court yard.
  1:08—Brief buns, while bent over riding a horse.
The Tormented (1978; Italian) . . . . . . . . . . . . . . . . n.a.
Dr. Heckyl and Mr. Hype (1980). . . . . . . . . . Debra Kate

## Love, Patti

*Films:*
Butley (1974; British) . . . . . . . . . . . . . . Female Student
That'll Be the Day (1974; British) . . . . . . Sandra's Friend
Terror (1979; British) . . . . . . . . . . . . . . . . . . . . . .n.a.
The Long Good Friday (1980; British). . . . . . . . . . Carol
**Steaming** (1985; British) . . . . . . . . . . . . . . . . . .Josie
- 0:08—Frontal nudity, getting undressed.
- 0:45—Brief breasts.
- 1:30—Breasts, jumping around in the pool.
*Made for TV Movies:*
Masterpiece Theatre: Middlemarch (1994; British)
. . . . . . . . . . . . . . . . . . . . . . . . . . . . . Mrs. Plymdale

## Love, Suzanna

*Films:*

Cocaine Cowboys (1979) . . . . . . . . . . . . . . . . . . . Lucy
    1:02—Undressing to see-through bra and panties
    with Herman.
The Boogeyman (1980) . . . . . . . . . . . . . . . . . . Lacey
Boogeyman II (1983) . . . . . . . . . . . . . . . . . . . .n.a.
Brainwaves (1983) . . . . . . . . . . . . . . . Kaylie Bedford
**Devonsville Terror** (1983) . . . . . . . . . . Jessica Scanlon
  •• 0:30—Breasts as an apparition, getting Mr. Gibbs at-
    tention.
  • 0:36—Brief breasts during flashback to 0:30 scene.
  • 0:43—Brief right breast during Ralph's past-life rec-
    ollection.
**Olivia** (1983) . . . . . . . . . . . . . . . . . . . . . . . . . Olivia
*a.k.a. A Taste of Sin*
  •• 0:34—Buns and breasts making love in bed with
    Mike.
  •• 0:58—Breasts and buns making love with Mike in
    the shower.
  • 1:08—Very brief full frontal nudity getting into bed ·
    with Richard. Dark, long shot.
  •• 1:09—Buns, lying in bed. Dark. Full frontal nudity
    getting out of bed and going to the bathroom.

## Lovelace, Linda

Real name is Linda Boreman.

*Adult Films:*

**Deep Throat** (1972) . . . . . . . . . . . . . . . . . . . . . .n.a.
  Nude, etc.

*Films:*

Linda Lovelace for President (1975). . . . . . . . . . . . .n.a.

*Magazines:*

**Playboy** (Mar 1973). . . . . . . . . . . . . . . . Next Month
  • 222—Left breast in B&W photo.
**Playboy** (Apr 1973) . . . . . . . . . . . . . . . . . . . Say "Ah!"
  ••• 95-101—Breasts.
**Playboy** (Aug 1973). . . . . . . . . . . . . . . . . . Porno Chic
  • 132—Partial buns.
  • 141—Partial lower frontal nudity.
**Playboy** (Dec 1973). . . . . . . . . . . . . . Sex Stars of 1973
  • 200—Partial left breast.
**Playboy** (Nov 1974) . . . . . . . . . . . Sex in Cinema 1974
  •• 145—Breasts from *Deep Throat II*.
**Playboy** (Dec 1974). . . . . . . . . . . . . . Sex Stars of 1974
  •• 208—Full frontal nudity in sheer dress.
**Playboy** (Jan 1975) . . . . . . . . . . Playboy Mansion West
  • 105—Right breast under sheer black blouse.
**Playboy** (Feb 1975) . . . . . .Linda Lovelace for President!
  ••• 76-83—Nude.
**Playboy** (Feb 1980) . . . . . . . . . . . . . . . The Year in Sex
  ••• 156—Breasts.
**Playboy** (Jan 1989) . . . . . . . . . Women of the Seventies
  •• 214—Breasts.

## Loving, Candy

*Video Tapes:*

**Playboy Video Magazine, Volume 2** (1983)
  . . . . . . . . . . . . . . . . . . . . . . . . . . . . . . . . Playmate
  ••• 0:14—Full frontal nudity posing for her centerfold
    photograph.
**Dorothy Stratten, The Untold Story** (1985)
  . . . . . . . . . . . . . . . . . . . . . . . . . . . . . . . . . Herself
  • 0:22—Brief left breast in centerfold photo.
**Playboy Video Centerfold: Kimberley Conrad**
  (1989) . . . . . . . . . . . . . . . . . . . . . . . Playboy Update
  ••• 0:42—Nude in old still photos.
**Playboy Video Centerfold: Anna-Marie Goddard**
  (1994) . . . . . . . . . . . . . . . . . . . . . . . . . . Playmate
  • 0:28—Brief breasts in retrospective.

*Magazines:*

**Playboy** (Jan 1979). . . . . . . . . . . . . . . . . . Playmate
**Playboy** (Apr 1980) . . . . . . Playboy's Playmate Reunion
  • 130—Left breast and lower frontal nudity.
**Playboy's Girls of Summer '86** (Aug 1986). . . Herself
  ••• 56-57—Full frontal nudity.
**Playboy's Nudes** (Oct 1990) . . . . . . . . . . . . . Herself
  ••• 30—Full frontal nudity.
**Playboy** (Jan 1994) . . . . . . . . . . . 40 Memorable Years
  ••• 93—Full frontal nudity.
**Playboy's Great Playmate Search** (Feb 1994)
  . . . . . . . . . . . . . . . . . . . . . . . . . . . . . . . . . Herself
  ••• 4—Full frontal nudity in centerfold photo.

## Lowell, Carey

Model for Oil of Olay cosmetics.
Wife of actor Griffin Dunne.

*Films:*

Club Paradise (1986) . . . . . . . . . . . . . . .Fashion Model
Dangerously Close (1986) . . . . . . . . . . . . . . . . . .Julie
Down Twisted (1987). . . . . . . . . . . . . . . . . . Maxine
**Me & Him** (1988; West German) . . . . . Janet Anderson
  • 0:37—Very brief upper half of right breast sticking
    out of nightgown after turning over in bed with Grif-
    fin Dunne.
License to Kill (1989) . . . . . . . . . . . . . . . Pam Bouvier
**The Guardian** (1990). . . . . . . . . . . . . . . . . . . . .Kate
  •• 0:37—Right breast twice, in bed with Phil.
**Road to Ruin** (1992) . . . . . . . . . . . . . . . .Jessie Taylor
  • 0:25—Lower half of buns, while sitting in bed with
    Peter Weller.
    0:26—Very, very brief buns, when Weller pulls her
    onto the bed.
Sleepless in Seattle (1993) . . . . . . . . . .Maggie Baldwin

*TV:*

League of Their Own (1993) . . . . . . . . . Dottie Hinson

## Lowery, Carolyn

*Films:*

Candyman (1992) . . . . . . . . . . . . . . . . . . . . . Stacey

*Made for Cable TV:*

**Dream On: And Your Little Dog, Too** (1991; HBO)
. . . . . . . . . . . . . . . . . . . . . . . . . . . . . . . . . . Ginger
- ••• 0:22—Breasts getting dressed in Eddie's dressing room with Martin and Eddie.

*Made for TV Movies:*

**Tales of the City** (1994) . . . . . . . . . . . . . . . . . . Hillary
- •• 0:25—(Into Part 2) Breast, while sitting on bed and talking to Brian in bathhouse room.

*Video Tapes:*

**Eden 3** (1993) . . . . . . . . . . . . . . . . . . . . . . . . . Amy
- ••• 0:03—Breasts in bed, making love with Lyle. Buns, while getting out.
  0:06—Breasts and buns, making love in bed with Lyle after Eve leaves
- ••• 0:53—Breasts, while making love in bed with Lyle.
- •• 1:16—Breasts while with Lyle in her room.
  1:32—In wet nightgown when Lyle is trying to kill her.

## Lowry, Lynn

*Films:*

**Score** (1973) . . . . . . . . . . . . . . . . . . . . . . . . . Betsy
- • 0:35—Left breast, sticking out of lingerie outfit.
- • 0:38—Brief full frontal nudity, in lingerie outfit while dancing.
- • 0:40—Breasts, in lingerie, while sitting on the floor with Eddie.
- • 1:01—Brief lower frontal nudity while in bed with Elvira.
- • 1:06—Brief left breast in reflection in mirror.
- • 1:07—Breasts in lingerie in bed with Elvira.
- •• 1:15—Brief right breast and lower frontal nudity in bed with Elvira.
- •• 1:22—Full frontal nudity, while in bed, then talking to Eddie.

**Sugar Cookies** (1973) . . . . . . . . . . . . . . . . . . Alta/Julie
- ••• 0:03—Brief breasts falling out of hammock, then breasts on couch with Max, then nude. Long scene. (Brunette wig as Alta.)
  0:13—Brief right breast in B & W photo.
- • 0:14—Left breast while lying on autopsy table.
- •• 0:20—Breasts in movie.
- •• 0:52—Breasts taking off clothes for Mary Woronov. Breasts on bed. (Blonde as Julie.)
- ••• 1:00—Breasts and buns with Woronov in bedroom, nude while wrestling with her.
- • 1:04—Breasts with Woronov in bathtub.
- ••• 1:06—Nude in bed with Woronov. Long scene.
- •• 1:11—Right breast outside displaying herself to Max.
- • 1:16—Right breast, then breasts making love with Woronov.
- ••• 1:20—Nude with Woronov and Max. Long scene.

**They Came From Within** (1975; Canadian) . . . . Forsythe
**Fighting Mad** (1976) . . . . . . . . . . . . . . . . . . . . . Lorene
**Cat People** (1982) . . . . . . . . . . . . . . . . . . . . . . Ruthie
- • 0:16—In black bra in Malcolm McDowell's hotel room, then brief breasts when bra pops open after crawling down the stairs.

*Magazines:*

**Playboy** (Nov 1973) . . . . . . . . . . Sex in Cinema 1973
- • 152—Left breast in photo from *Sugar Cookies*.

**Playboy** (Nov 1976) . . . . . . . . . . Sex in Cinema 1976
- • 146—Breasts in photo from *Fighting Mad*.

## Lukesová, Sárka

*Video Tapes:*

**Playboy International Playmates** (1993) . . . . Sharka
- ••• 0:23—Full frontal nudity in still photos.
- •• 0:24—Full frontal nudity, while posing on the floor.
- ••• 0:25—Full frontal nudity outside in the woods at night.
- ••• 0:44—Full frontal nudity in old mansion and sitting on couch caressing herself.

*Magazines:*

**Playboy Presents International Playmates**
(Feb 1992) . . . . . . . . . . . . . . . . . . . . . . . . . . . . Herself
- ••• 30-33—Full frontal nudity.

## Lumley, Joanna

*Films:*

On Her Majesty's Secret Sevice (1969; British)
. . . . . . . . . . . . . . . . . . . . . . . . . . . . . . . . English Girl

**Games That Lovers Play** (1970) . . . . . . . . . . Fanny
- •• 0:17—Nude, getting out of bed and putting on robe.
- • 0:50—Right breast, while in bed with Jonathan.
- •• 1:18—Breasts sitting in bed, talking on the phone.
- •• 1:29—Brief breasts several times in bed with Constance and a guy. Breasts after and during the end credits.

The Satanic Rites of Dracula (1973) . . Jessica Van Helsing
The Trail of the Pink Panther (1982) . . . . . . . Marie Juvet
Shirley Valentine (1989; British) . . . . . . . . . . . . Marjorie

*TV:*

The New Avengers (1976) . . . . . . . . . . . . . . . . . . Purdy
Absolutely Fabulous (1994- ; British) . . . . . . . . . . Patsy

## Luna, Donyale

Model.

*Films:*

Fellini Satyricon (1969) . . . . . . . . . . . . . . . . . Oenothea

*Magazines:*

**Playboy** (Apr 1975) . . . . . . . . . . . . . . . . . . . . . . Luna
- •• 88-93—Full frontal nudity.

## Lund, Deanna

*Films:*

Dr. Goldfoot and the Bikini Machine (1965) . . . . . Robot
Johnny Tiger (1966) . . . . . . . . . . . . . . . . . . . . . . Louise
Sting of Death (1966) . . . . . . . . . . . . . . . . . . . . Jessica
Tony Rome (1967) . . . . . . . . . . . . . . . . Georgia McKay
Hardly Working (1981) . . . . . . . . . . . . . . . . . . . . Millie
Stick (1985) . . . . . . . . . . . . . . . . . . . . . . . . . . . Diane
Elves (1989) . . . . . . . . . . . . . . . . . . . . Kirsten's Mother
  1:05—Buns and side of right breast getting into bathtub. Body double is Janet Fikany.

1:07—Breasts, getting electrocuted in bathtub. (Body double again.)
The Girl I Want (1990) . . . . . . . . . . . . . . Mrs. Andrews
Transylvania Twist (1990) . . . . . . . . . . . . . . . .Teacher
**Roots of Evil** (1991) . . . . . . . . . . . . . . . . . . . .Marissa
(Unrated version reviewed.)
• 0:19—Most of left breast, then brief right breast, while making love in bed with Johnny.
•• 0:20—More right breast, while making love.
•• 0:21—Still more right breast.
••• 1:33—Right breast, then breasts while lying in bed with Brinke Stevens.
*TV:*
Land of the Giants (1968-70) . . . . . . . . . . Valerie Scott

## Lund, Zoe
See: Tamerlis, Zoe.

## Lunghi, Cherie
*Films:*
**Excalibur** (1981; British) . . . . . . . . . . . . . . Guenevere
• 1:25—Brief breasts in the forest kissing Lancelot.
**King David** (1985) . . . . . . . . . . . . . . . . . . . . Michal
•• 0:28—Breasts lying in bed with Richard Gere. (Her hair is in the way a little bit.)
Letters to an Unknown Lover (1985) . . . . . . . . . Helene
0:40—In white slip in her bedroom.
Parker (1985; British) . . . . . . . . . . . . . . . . Jenny Parker
The Mission (1986; British) . . . . . . . . . . . . . . Carlotta
To Kill a Priest (1988) . . . . . . . . . . . . . . . . . . . .Halina
*Miniseries:*
Master of the Game (1984). . . Margaret Van der Merwe
*Made for TV Movies:*
Silent Cries (1993). . . . . . . . . . . . . . . . . . . . Audrey
*TV:*
Covington Cross (1992-93). . . . . . . . . . . Lady Elizabeth

## Lussier, Sheila
a.k.a. Dusty Rose.
*Films:*
The Big Bet (1985) . . . . . . . . . . . . . . . . . . . . . . .n.a.
**Bits and Pieces** (1985) . . . . . . . . . . . . . . . . . . Tanya
•• 0:07—In bra, tied down by Arthur, then brief breasts as he cuts her bra off before he kills her. Brief right breast several times with blood on her.
**My Chauffeur** (1986) . . . . . . . . . . . . . . . . . . Party Girl
• 1:23—Brief breasts taking off her blue blouse in the back of the limousine.
Reform School Girls (1986) . . . . . . . . . . . . . . . .n.a.
The Nightstalker (1987) . . . . . . . . . . . . . . . . . . .n.a.
Run If You Can (1987). . . . . . . . . . . . . . . . . . . .n.a.
*Video Tapes:*
**Starlet Screen Test II** (1991) . . . . . . . . . . . Dusty Rose
••• 0:31—Breasts, posing on car (same segment from *Centerfold Screen Test*.)

## Lutra, Mara
*Films:*
Fantasm (1976; Australian) . . . . . . . . . . . . . . . . . .n.a.

**Auditions** (1978) . . . . . . . . . . . . . . . . . .Jenny Marino
•• 0:58—Nude during her audition.
•• 1:07—Breasts and buns during orgy scene.

## Luu, Thuy Ann
*Films:*
**Diva** (1982; French) . . . . . . . . . . . . . . . . . . . . .Alba
• 0:13—Breasts in B&W photos when record store clerk asks to see her portfolio.
• 0:15—More of the B&W photos on the wall.
1:27—Very brief upper half of left breast taking off top, seen through window. Long shot.
**Off Limits** (1988). . . . . . . . . . . . . . . . . . . . . . Lanh
•• 0:48—Breasts dancing on stage in a nightclub.

## Lynch, Kelly
*Films:*
Portfolio (1983) . . . . . . . . . . . . . . . . . . . . Elite Model
Light of Day (1987) . . . . . . . . . . . . . . . . . . . .Elaine
Cocktail (1988) . . . . . . . . . . . . . . . . . . . Kerry Coughlin
0:45—Buns, wearing a two piece swimsuit at the beach.
1:01—Buns, in string bikini swimsuit on boat with Tom Cruise and Bryan Brown.
Drugstore Cowboy (1989) . . . . . . . . . . Dianne Hughes
0:17—In black bra and pants in living room with Matt Dillon.
**Roadhouse** (1989) . . . . . . . . . . . . . . . . . . . . . . .Doc
•• 1:04—Breasts and buns getting out of bed with a sheet wrapped around her.
**Warm Summer Rain** (1989). . . . . . . . . . . . . . .Kate
• 0:03—Brief breasts and side view of buns in B&W lying on floor during suicide attempt. Quick cuts breasts getting shocked to start her heart.
•• 0:23—Full frontal nudity when Guy gets off her in bed.
•• 0:24—Side view of right breast in bed, then breasts.
••• 0:58—Buns then breasts, getting washed by Guy on the table.
••• 1:07—Brief buns making love. Quick cuts full frontal nudity spinning around. Side view of left breast with Guy.
••• 1:09—Nude picking up belongings and running out of burning house with Guy.
**Desperate Hours** (1990) . . . . . . . . . . . Nancy Breyers
• 0:10—Brief breasts, walking on sidewalk with Mickey Rourke when her breasts pop out of her suit.
• 1:19—Brief breasts, getting wired with a hidden microphone in bathroom.
Curly Sue (1991) . . . . . . . . . . . . . . . . . . Grey Ellison
Three of Hearts (1993) . . . . . . . . . . . . . . . . . Connie
*Made for Cable TV:*
The Hitchhiker: The Joker (1987; HBO). . Theresa/Melissa
0:11—Very, very brief left breast, while in storage room with Alan getting tied up by Timothy Bottoms.
*Magazines:*
**Playboy** (Nov 1989) . . . . . . . . . Sex in Cinema 1989
• 137—Upper half of left breast from *Roadhouse*.
Playboy (Mar 1994) . . . . . . . . . . . Safe Sex, Great Sex

# Lynley, Carol

*Films:*

**Bad Georgia Road** . . . . . . . . . . . . . . . . Molly Golden
- 1:02—Very brief upper half of right breast, after hitting the water in anger after her clothes are stolen.

The Light in the Forest (1958) . . . . . Shenandoe Hastings
The Poseidon Adventure (1972) . . . . . . . . . Nonny Parry
Son of Blob (1972) . . . . . . . . . . . . . . . . . . . . . . . . .n.a.
  *a.k.a. Beware! The Blob*
The Four Deuces (1975) . . . . . . . . . . . . . . . . . . Wendy
The Cat and The Canary (1978; British). . .Anabelle West
Vigilante (1983) . . . . . . . . . . . . . . . . . . . . .D.A. Fletcher
Dark Tower (1987) . . . . . . . . . . . . . . . . . . . . . . . Tilly
**Blackout** (1989) . . . . . . . . . . . . . . . . . . . Esther Boyle
- • 1:01—Brief breasts leaning against the wall while someone touches her left breast.

Howling VI—The Freaks (1990) . . . . . . .Miss Eddington
Spirits (1991) . . . . . . . . . . . . . . . . . . . . . . . Sister Jillian
*Made for TV Movies:*
Flood! (1976) . . . . . . . . . . . . . . . . . . . . . Abbie Adams
*TV:*
The Immortal (1970-71) . . . . . . . . . . . . . . . . . . Sylvia

# Lynn, Amber

Adult film actress.
*Films:*

**Evils of the Night** (1985). . . . . . . . . . . . . . . . . Joyce
- 0:14—Brief breasts, taking her pink swimsuit top off for Eddie.
- • 0:17—Breasts with Eddie in deserted house. Dark.
- • 0:19—Full frontal nudity when Eddie takes her shorts off. Dark.
- 0:21—Right breast, while in bed with Eddie. Still dark.
- 0:22—More right breast.
- • 0:23—Full frontal nudity in bed when Eddie gets out.
- • 0:24—Nude, while getting out of bed and getting dressed. Dark.

**52 Pick-Up** (1986). . . . . . . . . . . . . . . . . . Party Goer
- 0:23—Breasts opening her blouse while being video taped at party.
- 0:24—Breasts and buns on TV. B&W.
- 0:26—Left breast, then breasts being video taped with another woman.

# Lynn, Amy

See: Baxter, Amy Lynn.

# Lynn, Rebecca

a.k.a. Adult film actress Cameron or Krista Lane.
*Films:*
**Free Ride** (1986). . . . . . . . . . . . . . . . Nude Girl #2
- 0:25—Brief buns taking a shower with another girl.
**Sensations** (1988). . . . . . . . . . . . . . . . . Jenny Hunter
- 0:11—Breasts, sleeping on couch.
- • 0:23—Breasts talking on the telephone.
- • 1:09—Breasts making love in bed with Brian.

**Thrilled to Death** (1988) . . . . . . . . . . . Elaine Jackson
- 0:01—Breasts twice when Baxter opens her blouse.
- • 0:31—Breasts in locker room talking to Nan.
**Sunset Strip** (1992) . . . . . . . . . . . . . . . . . . . . .Crystal
- • 0:17—Breasts and buns in G-string, dancing on stage.
- • 0:38—In red dress, then breasts doing strip routine.
- • 1:03—In dress, then breasts while stripping. Buns in body stocking.
- 1:16—Breasts in music video.
*Video Tapes:*
**In Search of the Perfect 10** (1986)
. . . . . . . . . . . . . . . . . . . . . . . . . .Perfect Girl #7/Ellen
- • • 0:37—Breasts (she's the redhead) playing Twister with Iris Condon. Buns in G-string.
**High Society Centerspread Video #1: Krista Lane**
(1990) . . . . . . . . . . . . . . . . . . . . . . . . . . . . .Krista Lane

# • Lynn, Theresa

*Films:*
Beauty School (1993). . . . . . . . . . . . . . . .Countess's Girl
**Marilyn Chambers' Bedtime Stories** (1993)
. . . . . . . . . . . . . . . . . . . . . . . . . . . . . . . . . . Melissa
- • 0:07—Breasts and buns in G-string, while changing lingerie in bedroom in front of mirror.
- • 0:22—Breasts, while on sofa, practicing her acting with Bart.
- • 0:29—Breasts, while making love with Bart on sofa.
- • 0:33—Breasts, while in bathroom with blue towel.
- • 1:17—Breasts, while on couch with Bart in out take.
*Magazines:*
**Playboy's Book of Lingerie** (May 1993) . . . . .Herself
- • • 20—Breasts.
**Playboy's Blondes, Brunettes & Redheads**
(Sep 1993) . . . . . . . . . . . . . . . . . . . . . . . . . . .Herself
- • 92—Left breast and lower frontal nudity.
**Playboy's Book of Lingerie** (Sep 1993) . . . . . .Herself
- • 38—Buns.
**Playboy's Book of Lingerie** (Nov 1993) . . . . .Herself
- • 49—Buns and side of right breast.
**Playboy's Great Playmate Search** (Feb 1994)
. . . . . . . . . . . . . . . . . . . . . . . . . . . . . . . . . . Herself
- • • 87—Breasts and buns.
**Playboy's Book of Lingerie** (Jul 1994). . . . . . .Herself
- 38—Buns.
**Playboy's Book of Lingerie** (Sep 1994) . . . . . .Herself
- 49—Partial left breast in bra.

# Lyon, Lisa

Bodybuilder.
*Films:*
Vamp (1986) . . . . . . . . . . . . . . . . . . . . . . . .Cimmaron
*Made for TV Movies:*
Getting Physical (1984) . . . . . . . . . . . . . . . Pilar Jones
*Magazines:*
**Playboy** (Oct 1980) . . . . . . . . . . . . . . . Body Beautiful
- • • 103-107—Breasts and buns.

# Lyon, Wendy

*Films:*

**Hello Mary Lou: Prom Night II** (1987)
. . . . . . . . . . . . . . . . . . . . . . . . . . . . .Vicki Carpenter
    0:58—Very, very brief left breast, while turning
    around after getting sucked into the blackboard.
  ••• 1:04—Nude in shower with Monica. Nude a lot
    walking around shower room.
  ••• 1:06—Full frontal nudity, walking in locker room,
    stalking Monica.
*Made for TV Movies:*
Anne of Green Gables (1985; Canadian)
. . . . . . . . . . . . . . . . . . . . . . . . . . . Prissy Andrews

# • Lyons, Laura

*Films:*

**Tintorera** (1977). . . . . . . . . . . . . . . . . . . . . . .Cynthia
  • 0:27—Buns and brief side of left breast, taking off
    her dress to swim to boat. She's the second one to
    take off her dress.
  • 0:28—Full frontal nudity, while dancing on boat
    deck.
  • 0:29—Left breast and brief buns, while getting into
    hammock with Steven.
  • 0:30—Brief buns, while swimming in water.
*Magazines:*
**Playboy** (Nov 1975) . . . . . . . . . . . . . . . Bunnies of '75
  • 93—Partial right breast.
**Playboy** (Feb 1976) . . . . . . . . . . . . . . . . . . . Playmate
  ••• 93-101—Full frontal nudity.
**Playboy** (Jan 1977) . . . . . . . . . . . . . .Playmate Review
  ••• 159—Breasts.
**Playboy** (Dec 1977). . . Playboy's Playmate House Party
  •• 152-161—Buns.

# Lyons, Susan

*Films:*

**The Good Wife** (1987; Australian) . . . . . .Mrs. Fielding
*a.k.a. The Umbrella Woman*
  • 1:22—Very brief breasts coming in from the balco-
    ny.
...Almost (1990; Australian) . . . . . . . . . . . . . .Caroline

# MacDonald, Wendy

*Films:*

Blood Frenzy (1987) . . . . . . . . . . . . . . . . . . . Dr. Shelley
**Dark Side of the Moon** (1989) . . . . . . . . . . . . . Alex
  • 0:54—In bra, then brief breasts having it torn off.
    Don't see her face.
Living to Die (1990) . . . . . . . . . . . .Rookie Policewoman
**Naked Obsession** (1990) . . . . . . . . . Saundra Carlyle
  ••• 0:28—In black bra, panties and stockings on the din-
    ing table during William Katt's fantasy, then breasts.
Sinners! (1990) . . . . . . . . . . . . . . . . . . . . . . . . . . Fran
Blood Money (1991). . . . . . . . . . . . . . . . . . . . . Susan
*a.k.a. The Killer's Edge*
**Legal Tender** (1991) . . . . . . . . . . . . . . Verna Wheeler
  0:22—Brief buns in lingerie in Morton Downey Jr.'s
  office. Don't see her face.

  •• 1:20—Long shot of buns and side of left breast tak-
    ing off robe in front of Downey. Breasts on bed with
    him.
**L.A. Goddess** (1992) . . . . . . . . . . . . . . . . . . . . .Diane
  0:06—In red and black bra and panties in motor
  home.
  •• 0:08—Side of left breast, then breasts while making
    love with the Sheriff actor in motor home.
  • 1:06—Brief buns, while flashing while dancing on
    table during party.
Wild Cactus (1992) . . . . . . . . . . . . . . . . . . . . . . Abby
  (Unrated version reviewed.)
Broken Trust (1993) . . . . . . . . . . . . . . .Dr. Joyce Radley
*Magazines:*
**Playboy** (Oct 1990) . . . . . . . . . . . . . . . . . Grapevine
  • 183—Buns in stocking/garter belt. B&W.

# MacGraw, Ali

Former model.
Ex-wife of the late actor Steve McQueen.
*Films:*

**Goodbye, Columbus** (1969) . . . . . . . . . . . . . .Brenda
  • 0:50—Very brief side view of left breast, taking off
    dress before running and jumping into a swimming
    pool. Brief right breast jumping into pool.
  • 1:11—Very brief side view of right breast in bed with
    Richard Benjamin. Brief buns, getting out of bed and
    walking to the bathroom.
Love Story (1970) . . . . . . . . . . . . . . . . . Jenny Cavilleri
**The Getaway** (1972) . . . . . . . . . . . . . . . .Carol McCoy
  0:16—In wet white blouse after jumping in pond
  with Steve McQueen.
  • 0:19—Very brief left breast lying back in bed kissing
    McQueen.
Convoy (1978). . . . . . . . . . . . . . . . . . . . . . . Melissa
Players (1979) . . . . . . . . . . . . . . . . . . . . . . . . . Nicole
**Just Tell Me What You Want** (1980). . .Bones Burton
  •• 0:16—Breasts getting dressed in her bedroom.
  •• 1:26—Brief breasts in bathroom getting ready to
    take a shower.
*Made for TV Movies:*
Survive the Savage Sea (1992) . . . . . . . Claire Carpenter
Gunsmoke: The Long Ride (1993) . . Uncle Jane Merckel
*TV:*
Dynasty (1985) . . . . . . . . . . . . . . Lady Ashley Mitchell
*Magazines:*
Playboy (May 1980) . . . . . . . . . . . . . . . . . . . Grapevine

# Machart, Maria

*Films:*

**Blood Sisters** (1986) . . . . . . . . . . . . . . . . . . .Marnie
  •• 0:45—In bra, then brief breasts putting on night-
    gown and caressing herself.
**Slammer Girls** (1987) . . . . . . . . . . . . . . . . . . Hooker
  •• 0:06—Breasts, getting fondled by a cop.

# Mack, Kerry

*Films:*

Fair Game (1982; Australian) . . . . . . . . . . . . . .Joanne

**Savage Attraction** (1983; Australian)
.............................Christine Maresch
- ••• 0:10—Breasts, getting out of shower and putting on robe.
- • 0:11—Breasts behind shower door, making love with Walter.
- •• 0:17—Breasts sitting at the end of the bed.
- •• 0:59—Breasts undressing in bedroom, then in bathtub with Walter.
- ••• 1:04—Breasts getting her blouse unbuttoned, then breasts in bed with Walter.
  1:19—On boat, in semi-sheer white blouse.
The Custodian (1993) . . . . . . . . . . . . . . . Policewoman

## MacKenzie, Jan

*Films:*
**Gator Bait II—Cajun Justice** (1988) . . . . . . Angelique
  0:13—Most of right breast while kissing her husband.
  0:29—Most of right breast while in bed.
- •• 0:34—Buns and side view of left breast, taking a bath outside. Brief breasts a couple of times while the bad guys watch.
- • 0:41—Brief side view of left breast taking off towel in front of the bad guys.
  1:05—Brief buns occasionally when her blouse flaps up during boat chase.
**The American Angels, Baptism of Blood** (1989)
. . . . . . . . . . . . . . . . . . . . . . . . . . . . . Luscious Lisa
  0:07—Buns in G-string on stage in club. More buns getting lathered up for wrestling match.
- • 0:11—Breasts and buns when a customer takes her top off. She's covered with shaving cream.
- •• 0:12—Breasts taking a shower when Diamond Dave looks in to talk to her.
- • 0:56—Right breast, while in wrestling ring with Dave.

*Magazines:*
**Playboy** (Dec 1989). . . . . . . . . . . . . . . Lethal Women
- • 151—Buns and not quite side view of right breast.

## Mackenzie, Patch

*Films:*
Goodbye, Norma Jean (1975). . . . . . . . . . .Ruth Latimer
**Serial** (1980) . . . . . . . . . . . . . . . . . . . . . . . . . . . Stella
- • 0:59—Brief breasts in mirror in swinger's club with Martin Mull.
Graduation Day (1981) . . . . . . . . . . . . . .Anne Ramstead
Fighting Back (1982). . . . . . . . . . . . . . . . . .Lilly Morelli
It's Alive III: Island of the Alive (1988) . . . . . . . . Robbins

## MacLaine, Shirley

*Films:*
The Trouble with Harry (1955) . . . . . . . . Jennifer Rogers
Around the World in 80 Days (1956). . . . .Princess Houda
Hot Spell (1958) . . . . . . . . . . . . . . . . . . . . .Virginia Duval
Some Came Running (1958). . . . . . . . Ginny Moorhead
The Apartment (1960) . . . . . . . . . . . . . . . . Fran Kubelik
Can-Can (1960) . . . . . . . . . . . . . . . . . . Simone Pistache

All In a Night's Work (1961) . . . . . . . . . . . .Katie Robbins
Irma La Douce (1963) . . . . . . . . . . . . . . .Irma La Douce
Gambit (1966). . . . . . . . . . . . . . . . . . . . . . . . . . . Nicole
Woman Times Seven (1967). . . . . . . . . . . . . . .Paulette
Sweet Charity (1969) . . . . . . . . . Charity Hope Valentine
Two Mules for Sister Sara (1970) . . . . . . . . . . . . . .Sara
**Desperate Characters** (1971). . . . . Sophie Bentwood
- •• 1:21—Left breast, while standing with Kenneth Mars, when he takes off her blouse.
- ••• 1:22—Breasts, while on bed, reluctantly kissing Kenneth Mars.
The Turning Point (1977) . . . . . . . . . . . . . . . . .DeeDee
Being There (1979) . . . . . . . . . . . . . . . . . . . Eve Rand
A Change of Seasons (1980) . . . . . . . . . . .Karen Evans
Loving Couples (1980). . . . . . . . . . . . . . . . . . . Evelyn
**Terms of Endearment** (1983) . . . . .Aurora Greenway
  (Academy Award for Best Actress.)
  1:00—Very, very brief right breast wrestling with Jack Nicholson in the ocean when she finally frees his hand from her breast. One frame. Hard to see, but for the sake of thoroughness....
Cannonball Run II (1984). . . . . . . . . . . . . . . . Veronica
Madame Sousatzka (1988). . . . . . . Madame Sousatzka
Steel Magnolias (1989) . . . . . . . . . . . Ouiser Boudreaux
Postcards from the Edge (1990) . . . . . . . . . Doris Mann
Defending Your Life (1991) . . . . . . . . . Shirley MacLaine
Waiting for the Light (1991). . . . . . . . . . . . . . . . . . n.a.
Used People (1992) . . . . . . . . . . . . . . . . . . . . . Pearl
Guarding Tess (1993). . . . . . . . . . . . . . . . Tess Carlisle
Wrestling Ernest Hemingway (1993) . . . . . . . . .Helen
*Video Tapes:*
Shirley MacLaine's Inner Workout (1989) . . . . . . .Herself
*Magazines:*
**Playboy** (Nov 1972) . . . . . . . . . . . Sex in Cinema 1972
- • 159—Breasts lying in bed with Kenneth Mars. Small photo, hard to tell it's her.

## MacLaren, Fawna

*Films:*
Dragonfight (1990) . . . . . . . . . . . . . . . . . Dark Servant
Amorel (1993) . . . . . . . . . . . . . . . . . . Cherry Cream Pie
*Video Tapes:*
**Playboy Video Centerfold: Fawna MacLaren**
  (1988) . . . . . . . . . . . . . . . . 35th Anniversary Playmate
- ••• 0:11—In front of brick wall. In studio, in bed. Nude.
**Playboy Video Calendar 1990** (1989). . . . . . January
- ••• 0:01—Nude.
**Playmates at Play** (1990) . . . . . . . . . . . Gotta Dance
**Sexy Lingerie II** (1990) . . . . . . . . . . . . . . . . . Model
**Playboy Video Centerfold: Anna-Marie Goddard**
  (1994) . . . . . . . . . . . . . . . . . . . . . . . . . . . . Playmate
- • 0:29—Brief breasts during retrospective.
**Wet and Wild: The Locker Room** (1994) . . Playmate
*Magazines:*
**Playboy** (Jan 1989). . . . . . . . . . . . . . . . . . . . Playmate
**Playboy's Nudes** (Oct 1990) . . . . . . . . . . . .Herself
- ••• 31—Full frontal nudity.
**Playboy's Book of Lingerie** (Jan 1991) . . . . . .Herself
- • 71—Lower frontal nudity.

••• 108—Full frontal nudity.

**Playboy's Book of Lingerie** (May 1992) . . . . . Herself
•• 48—Half of right breast and lower frontal nudity.

**Playboy's Calendar Playmates** (Nov 1992) . . Herself
••• 79—Full frontal nudity.

**Playboy's Book of Lingerie** (Nov 1992) . . . . . Herself
•• 108—Buns and side of left breast.

**Playboy** (Jan 1994) . . . . . . . . . . . 40 Memorable Years
••• 95—Full frontal nudity.

**Playboy's Great Playmate Search** (Feb 1994)
. . . . . . . . . . . . . . . . . . . . . . . . . . . . . . . . . . . Herself
••• 5—Full frontal nudity in centerfold photo.

# • MacLeod, Mary
*Films:*
**If...** (1969; British) . . . . . . . . . . . . . . . . . . . Mrs. Kemp
•• 1:27—Buns and side of left breast while walking
around deserted boy's dormitory (B&W).
Orlando (1993; British) . . . . . . . . . . . . . . . First Woman

# Macpherson, Elle
*Sports Illustrated* magazine swimsuit model. Cover girl in
1986, 1987 and 1988.
Spokesmodel for *Biotherm* cosmetics.
*Films:*
Alice (1990) . . . . . . . . . . . . . . . . . . . . . . . . . . . .Model
**Sirens** (1993; Australian) . . . . . . . . . . . . . . . . . .Sheela
*Video Tapes:*
**Sports Illustrated's 25th Anniversary Swimsuit
Video** (1989) . . . . . . . . . . . . . . . . . . . . . . . . . Herself
(The version shown on HBO left out two music video
segments at the end. If you like buns, definitely watch
the video tape!)
0:22—In wet yellow tank top and orange bikini bot-
toms at the beach.
• 0:23—Very, very brief lower breasts readjusting the
yellow tank top.
Sports Illustrated Super Shape-Up Program: Stretch and
Strengthen (1990). . . . . . . . . . . . . . . . . . . . . Herself
*Magazines:*
**GQ** (Jan 1991) . . . . . . . .A Man and an Elle of a Woman
• 118-127—Wearing a blue fishnet top, a wet white
swimsuit and just a swimsuit bottom (hair gets in the
way a bit).
**Playboy** (Dec 1991). . . . . . . . . . . . . . . Sex Stars 1991
• 185—Almost breasts. Arm and hands cover most of
her breasts.
**Playboy** (Dec 1993). . . . . . . . . . . . . . . Sex Stars 1993
• 179—Breasts, under sheer black body suit.
Sports Illustrated (Feb 14, 1994)
. . . . . . . . . . . . . . . . . . . . . Everybody Into the Pool
**Playboy** (May 1994) . . . . . . . . . . . . . . . . . . . . . . . Elle
••• 124-133—Breasts and buns in color and B&W pho-
tos. (Also breasts in photo on inside cover.)
**Playboy** (Nov 1994) . . . . . . . . . . . Sex in Cinema 1994
••• 144-145—Full frontal nudity in four stills from *Sirens*.

# MacRae, Elizabeth
*Films:*
Love in a Goldfish Bowl (1961). . . . . . . . . . . . . . .Jackie
The Wild Westerners (1962) . . . . . . . . Crystal Plummer
For Love or Money (1963) . . . . . . . . . . . . . . . Marsha
Wild is My Love (1963) . . . . . . . . . . . . . . . . . .Queenie
**The Conversation** (1974) . . . . . . . . . . . . . Meredith
• 1:14—Breasts and buns, getting undressed in work
area with Gene Hackman. Long shot, dark.

# Madigan, Amy
Wife of actor Ed Harris.
*Films:*
**Love Child** (1982) . . . . . . . . . . . . . . Terry Jean Moore
• 0:08—Brief side view of right breast and buns taking
a shower in jail while the guards watch.
•• 0:53—Brief breasts and buns, making love with Beau
Bridges in a room at the women's prison.
Love Letters (1984) . . . . . . . . . . . . . . . . . . . . . .Wendy
*a.k.a. Passion Play*
Places in the Heart (1984) . . . . . . . . . . . . . Viola Kelsey
Streets of Fire (1984) . . . . . . . . . . . . . . . . . . McCoy
**Alamo Bay** (1985) . . . . . . . . . . . . . . . . . . . . . . . .Glory
•• 0:28—Breasts while lying in motel bed with Ed Har-
ris.
•• 0:30—Breasts while sitting up in the bed.
0:40—Walking in parking lot in a wet T-shirt.
Twice in a Lifetime (1985) . . . . . . . . . . . . Sunny Sobel
**Nowhere to Hide** (1987). . . . . . . . . . . .Barbara Cutter
• 1:04—Brief side view of right breast taking off towel
to get dressed in cabin. Long shot, hard to see.
**The Prince of Pennsylvania** (1988). . . Carla Headlee
• 0:37—Left breast and buns, while getting out of bed
with Keanu Reeves and putting on a robe.
Field of Dreams (1989). . . . . . . . . . . . . . . . . . . .Annie
Uncle Buck (1989) . . . . . . . . . . . . Chanice Kobolowski
The Dark Half (1993) . . . . . . . . . . . . . . . . . .Liz Beaumont
*Made for Cable Movies:*
And Then There Was One (1994; Lifetime)
. . . . . . . . . . . . . . . . . . . . . . . . . . . Roxy Ventola
*Miniseries:*
The Day After (1983) . . . . . . . . . . . . . . . . . . . . Alison
*Made for TV Movies:*
Roe vs. Wade (1989) . . . . . . . . . . . .Sarah Weddington
Lucky Day (1991). . . . . . . . . . . . . . . . Kari Campbell

# Madison
see: Stone, Madison.

# Madison, Lisa
*Films:*
**Beauty School** (1993) . . . . . . . . . . . . . . . . . . . Kristina
•• 0:02—Breasts making out with a guy in bedroom.
••• 1:23—Breasts making out with a guy.
*Magazines:*
**Playboy's Girls of Summer '92** (Jun 1992) . . .Herself
•• 42—Buns and right breast.
**Playboy's Book of Lingerie** (Jul 1992). . . . . . .Herself
•• 48—Buns in G-string and left breast.

**Playboy's Book of Lingerie** (Sep 1992) . . . . . Herself
- 61—Lower frontal nudity.
- ••• 80-81—Breasts and buns.

**Playboy's Book of Lingerie** (Nov 1992) . . . . . Herself
- •• 58—Side of right breast and buns.

**Playboy's Nudes** (Dec 1992) . . . . . . . . . . . . . Herself
- •• 64—Right breast.

**Playboy's Book of Lingerie** (Jan 1993) . . . . . . Herself
- •• 102-103—Buns.

**Playboy's Book of Lingerie** (Mar 1993) . . . . . Herself
- 83—Partial lower frontal nudity.
- ••• 100-101—Breasts and buns.

**Playboy's Bathing Beauties** (Apr 1993) . . . . . Herself
- ••• 14-15—Breasts.
- ••• 38-39—Breasts.
- ••• 60—Breasts.
- •• 66—Buns.

**Playboy's Book of Lingerie** (May 1993) . . . . . Herself
- •• 36-37—Breasts.
- • 49—Sort of right breast under fishnet top.
- ••• 106-107—Breasts.

**Playboy's Girls of Summer '93** (Jun 1993) . . . Herself
- ••• 34—Full frontal nudity.

**Playboy's Book of Lingerie** (Jul 1993) . . . . . . Herself
- ••• 44-45—Right breast and buns.
- ••• 76—Full frontal nudity.
- • 105—Buns.

**Playboy's Book of Lingerie** (Sep 1993) . . . . . Herself
- •• 20—Right breast.
- •• 40-41—Breasts.
- ••• 56-57—Breasts and buns.

**Playboy's Book of Lingerie** (Nov 1993) . . . . . Herself
- •• 86—Buns.

**Playboy's Book of Lingerie** (Jan 1994) . . . . . . Herself
- •• 42—Right breast.
- 98—Partial side of right breast.

**Playboy's Great Playmate Search** (Feb 1994)
. . . . . . . . . . . . . . . . . . . . . . . . . . . . . . . . . . . Herself
- ••• 63—Breasts.

**Playboy's Girls of Summer '94** (Jul 1994) . . . Herself
- ••• 8—Breasts.

## Madonna

Full name is Madonna Louise Cicconi.
Singer.
Ex-wife of actor Sean Penn.
Nude in her book, *Sex* (1992).
*Films:*

**A Certain Sacrifice** (1981) . . . . . . . . . . . . . . . Bruna
(Very grainy film, done before she got famous.)
- ••• 0:22—Breasts during weird rape/love scene with one guy and two girls.
- • 0:40—Brief right breast in open top lying on floor after getting attacked by guy in back of restaurant.
- • 0:57—Brief breasts during love making scene, then getting smeared with blood.

**Desperately Seeking Susan** (1985) . . . . . . . . . . . . Susan
- 0:09—Briefly in black bra taking off her blouse in bus station restroom.
- 1:16—In black bra getting out of pool and lying down on lounge chair.

**Visionquest** (1985) . . . . . . . . . . . . . . . Nightclub Singer

**Shanghai Surprise** (1986) . . . . . . . . . . Gloria Tatlock

**Who's That Girl?** (1987) . . . . . . . . . . . . . . . Nikki Finn

**Bloodhounds of Broadway** (1989) . . Hortense Hathaway

**Dick Tracy** (1990) . . . . . . . . . . . . . . Breathless Mahoney
- 0:20—Breasts under sheer black gown, talking to Warren Beatty.

**Shadows and Fog** (1991) . . . . . . . . . . . . . . . . . . . Marie

**Truth or Dare** (1991) . . . . . . . . . . . . . . . . . . . Herself
- ••• 0:44—Brief breasts changing clothes backstage. B&W.
- 1:16—Wearing a bra, in a store, trying on earrings. B&W.
- 1:35—Very brief half of left breast, while wearing robe and jumping up. B&W.
- 1:43—Sort of breasts in bed with her dancers. Her hands cover her breasts. B&W.

**Body of Evidence** (1992) . . . . . . . . . Rebecca Carlson
(Unrated version reviewed.)
- • 0:01—Breasts, while making love on TV during video playback.
- • 0:03—Breasts and buns some more on TV.
- • 0:20—Upper half of buns, getting acupuncture.
- ••• 0:41—Breasts on stairs and in bed with Willem Dafoe.
- •• 0:42—Breasts on bed behind curtains with Dafoe.
- • 0:43—Brief right breast, while licking champagne off Dafoe's chest.
- ••• 0:45—Full frontal nudity, while climbing on top of Dafoe and making love. Seen through curtains.
- • 0:55—Lower frontal nudity, while making love with Dafoe in parking garage.
- ••• 1:07—Very, very brief left breast when Dafoe grabs her arm. Breasts opening her robe and lying on the floor and playing with herself while Dafoe watches.
- •• 1:10—Buns, while lying on the floor when Dafoe rips her panties off.
- ••• 1:11—Full frontal nudity on TV during video playback.

**A League of Their Own** (1992) . . . . . . . . Mae Mordabito

**Dangerous Game** (1993) . . . . . . . . . . Sarah Jennings
(Unrated version reviewed.)
- 0:13—In braless tank top in room with James Russo.
- • 0:45—Brief buns in G-string, falling over back of sofa on video playback.
- •• 0:53—Nude, while getting out of bed and getting dressed.
- • 1:00—Brief buns, when getting her panties ripped off by Russo.

*Video Tapes:*

**Penthouse: On the Wild Side** (1988) . . . . . Madonna
- ••• 0:14—Full frontal nudity in B&W and color still photographs.

**Madonna: The Immaculate Collection** (1990)
. . . . . . . . . . . . . . . . . . . . . . . . . . . . . . . . . . . . . Herself
- 0:18—(2 min., 10 sec. into "Papa Don't Preach.")
Very, very brief left breast in black strapless outfit
when she throws her head back. (After the daughter
character she plays walks up the subway stairs.)
0:18—(1 min., 36 sec. into "Papa Don't Preach.")
Very, very brief upper half of right breast after first
head throwback in black strapless outfit. Long shot.
0:50—(1 min., 6 sec. into "Vogue.") Wearing sheer
black blouse. (Also at 1:18 and 1:33).

*Magazines:*
**Penthouse** (Sep 1985) . . . . . . . . . . . . . . . . . . Pictorial
- 150-161—B&W photos.
**Playboy** (Sep 1985) . . . . . . . . . . . . . . . . . . . . Pictorial
- 119-131—B&W photos.
**Playboy** (Dec 1986) . . . . . . . . . . . . . . Sex Stars of 86
**Playboy** (Jan 1989) . . . . . . . . . Women of the Eighties
- • 247—Breasts B&W photo.
**Vanity Fair** (Apr 1990) . . . . . . . . . . . . . . White Heat
- • 144—Left breast in B&W photo taken by Helmut
Newton. She's standing on a table, opening her
vest.
**Playboy's Nudes** (Oct 1990) . . . . . . . . . . . . . . Herself
- ••• 39—Full frontal nudity B&W.
**Playboy** (Dec 1990) . . . . . . . . . . . . . Sex Stars of 1990
- •• 171—In sheer top from "Vogue" music video.
**Vanity Fair** (Apr 1991) . . . . . . . . . . . . . . . The Misfit
- •• 167—Breasts under sheer sheet. Other Marilyn
Monroe-like photographs.
**Penthouse** (Sep 1991)
. . . . . . . . . . Truth or Bare, Madonna: The Lost Nudes
- ••• 179-183—B&W photos taken by Jere Threndgill in
spring of 1979.
**Playboy** (Jul 1992) . . . . . . . . . . . . . . Blond Exhibition
- •• 82-85—Full frontal nudity at the beach for her book.
**Vanity Fair** (Oct 1992) . . . . . Madonna in Wonderland
- ••• 204-213—Breasts and buns in color photos.
**Playboy** (Dec 1992) . . . . . . . . . . . . . . Sex Stars 1992
- • 183—Breasts under sheer black bra.
**Playboy** (Jan 1993) . . . . . . . . . . . . . . The Year in Sex
- ••• 145—Breasts, wearing outfit during fashion show.
- ••• 149—Breasts, in open sweater in photo that appeared in the October 1992 issue of *Vanity Fair* magazine. Small photo.
**Playboy** (Apr 1993) . . . . . . . . . . . . . . Mantrack/Forum
- ••• 32—Full frontal nudity, hitchhiking, from *Sex.* B&W.
- •• 50—Side view of right breast, on fish fountain from
*Sex.* B&W.
**Playboy** (Nov 1993) . . . . . . . . . . Sex in Cinema 1993
- ••• 139—Breasts in two stills from *Body of Evidence.*
**Playboy's Nudes** (Dec 1993) . . . . . . . . . . . . . Herself
- ••• 64—Full frontal nudity on beach in grainy telephoto
photo.
**Playboy** (Dec 1993) . . . . . . . . . . . . . . Sex Stars 1993
- • 175—Breasts under jeweled pasties.
**Playboy** (Jan 1994) . . . . . . . . . . Remember Madonna
- ••• 182-183—Full frontal nudity in color and B&W photos.

# Madsen, Virginia

Sister of actor Michael Madsen.
*Films:*
**Class** (1983) . . . . . . . . . . . . . . . . . . . . . . . . . . . Lisa
- •• 0:20—Brief left breast when Andrew McCarthy acci-
dentally rips her blouse open at the girl's school.
Dune (1984) . . . . . . . . . . . . . . . . . . . . . Princess Irulan
Electric Dreams (1984) . . . . . . . . . . . . . . . . . . Madeline
**Creator** (1985) . . . . . . . . . . . . . . . . . . . . . . . . Barbara
0:53—Walking on beach in a blue one piece swim-
suit with Vincent Spano.
- ••• 0:58—Nude in shower with Spano.
Modern Girls (1987) . . . . . . . . . . . . . . . . . . . . . Kelly
Slam Dance (1987) . . . . . . . . . . . . . . Yolanda Caldwell
Zombie High (1987) . . . . . . . . . . . . . . . . . . . .Andrea
*a.k.a. The School That Ate My Brain*
Hot to Trot (1988) . . . . . . . . . . . . . . . . . . Allison Rowe
Heart of Dixie (1989) . . . . . . . . . . . . . . . . . . . . . Delia
**The Hot Spot** (1990) . . . . . . . . . . . . . . Dolly Harshaw
- • 0:41—Side view of left breast while sitting on bed
talking to Don Johnson.
- • 0:47—Tip of right breast when Johnson kisses it.
- •• 1:16—Buns, undressing for a swim outside at night.
Breasts hanging on rope.
- • 1:18—Buns, getting out of water with Johnson.
Long shot.
- •• 1:21—Left breast when robe gapes open while sitting up.
1:23—Brief lower frontal nudity and buns in open
robe after jumping off tower at night.
1:24—Breasts at bottom of hill with Johnson. Long
shot.
1:45—Nude, very, very briefly running out of house.
Very blurry, could be anybody.
Highlander 2: The Quickening (1991) . . . Louise Marcus
Love Kills (1991) . . . . . . . . . . . . . . . . . . Rebecca Bishop
**Becoming Colette** (1992; French/German/U.S.)
. . . . . . . . . . . . . . . . . . . . . . . . . . . . . . . . . . . Polaire
- •• 0:48—Breasts in bed, with Mathilda May.
- •• 0:49—Side view of left breast in bed with May and
Klaus Maria Brandauer.
**Candyman** (1992) . . . . . . . . . . . . . . . . . . . . Helen Lyle
- • 0:47—In bloody bra, while undressing after she was
arrested. Side of right breast, after taking off bra.
Bloody.
- • 0:54—Brief left breast, while in bathtub. Lower half
of right breast, after sitting up.
Caroline at Midnight (1993) . . . . . . . . . . Susan Prince
*Made for Cable Movies:*
Mussolini and I (1985; HBO) . . . . . . . . Claretta Petacci
Fire With Fire (1986; Showtime) . . . . . . . . . . . . . . Lisa
Long Gone (1987; HBO) . . . . . . . . . . . .Dixie Lee Boxx
0:05—Buns, sleeping on bed face down in bedroom
with William L. Petersen and a young kid.
**Gotham** (1988; Showtime) . . . . . . . . . . Rachel Carlyle
*a.k.a. The Dead Can't Lie*
- • 0:50—Brief breasts in the shower when Tommy Lee
Jones comes over to her apartment, then breasts
while lying on the floor.

•• 1:12—Breasts, while dead, in the freezer when Jones comes back to her apartment, then brief breasts on the bed.

• 1:18—Breasts while in the bathtub under water.

Third Degree Burn (1989; HBO) . . . . . . . Anne Scholes
Ironclads (1991) . . . . . . . . . . . . . . . . . . . . Betty Stuart
Linda (1993; USA). . . . . . . . . . . . . . . . . Linda Crowley
Bitter Vengeance (1994; USA) . . . . . . . . . . . . . . . Annie
*Made for Cable TV:*
**The Hitchhiker: Perfect Order** (1987; HBO)
. . . . . . . . . . . . . . . . . . . . . . . . . . . . . . . . . . . .Christina

0:11—In black lingerie being photographed by the photographer in his studio.

•• 0:14—Brief breasts changing clothes while Simon watches her on video monitor.

0:16—Breasts getting into water in Simon's studio. Her body is covered with white makeup.

*Made for TV Movies:*
A Murderous Affair: The Carolyn Warmus Story (1992)
. . . . . . . . . . . . . . . . . . . . . . . . . . . . .Carolyn Warmus

## Magnuson, Ann

*Films:*
Vortex (1982) . . . . . . . . . . . . . . . . . . . Pamela Fleming
**The Hunger** (1983). . . . . . . Young Woman from Disco
• 0:05—Brief breasts in kitchen with David Bowie just before he kills her.
Perfect Strangers (1984) . . . . . . . . . . . . . . . . . .Maida
Desperately Seeking Susan (1985). . . . . . . Cigarette Girl
Making Mr. Right (1987). . . . . . . . . . . . . Frankie Stone
Mondo New York (1987) . . . . . . . . . . . . .Poetry Reader
A Night in the Life of Jimmy Reardon (1987)
. . . . . . . . . . . . . . . . . . . . . . . . . . . . . . Joyce Fickett
1:01—Right leg in stocking and garter belt kissing River Phoenix in the library of her house.
Tequila Sunrise (1988). . . . . . . . . . . . . . . . . . Shaleen
Checking Out (1989) . . . . . . . . . . . . . . . Connie Hagen
Heavy Petting (1989) . . Herself/Television Spokesmodel
Love at Large (1990). . . . . . . . . . . . . . . . . . . . .Doris
*TV:*
Anything but Love (1989-92) . . . . . . .Catherine Hughes
*Magazines:*
**Playboy** (Apr 1992) . . . . . . . . . . . . . . . . . . .Grapevine
• 174—Breasts under fishnet blouse with ribbons tied near the nipple area. B&W.

## Mahalia

See: Maria, Mahalia.

## • Maille, Claudette

*Films:*
**Like Water for Chocolate** (1993; Mexican)  Gertrudis
*a.k.a. Como Agua Para Chocolate*
•• 0:30—Breasts and buns while taking a shower. Nude, running out of shower house after it catches fire, running and jumping on horse with a guy.
• 1:36—Brief side view of left breast in shower flashback.

*Magazines:*
**Playboy** (Nov 1993) . . . . . . . . . . Sex in Cinema 1993
••• 136—Full frontal nudity in still from *Like Water for Chocolate.*

## Maillé, Maïté

*Films:*
A Nos Amours (1984; French) . . . . . . . . . . . . . Martine
**The Passion of Beatrice** (1988; French)
. . . . . . . . . . . . . . . . . . . . . . . . . . . . . .La Noiraude
• 1:24—Brief left breast, showing Béatrice how she was abused.
**Henry & June** (1990) . . . . . . . . . . . . . . Frail Prostitute
• 1:22—In black see-through dress.
••• 1:23—Breasts making love with Brigitte Lahaie in front of Anais and Hugo.

## • Malick, Wendie

*Films:*
**A Little Sex** (1982) . . . . . . . . . . . . . . . . . . . .Philomena
• 0:39—Very, very brief side of left breast in gaping robe when she bends over to put her cigarette down.
Bugsy (1991) . . . . . . . . . . . . . . . . . . . Woman on Train
*TV:*
Trauma Center (1983) . . . . . . . . . . . . .Dr. Brigitte Blaine
Dream On (1990- ) . . . . . . . . . . . . . . . . . . . . . Judith
NYPD Blue: Brown Appetit (Oct 5, 1993)
. . . . . . . . . . . . . . . . . . . . . . . . . . . . . Susan Wagner
NYPD Blue: True Confessions (Oct 12, 1993)
. . . . . . . . . . . . . . . . . . . . . . . . . . . . . Susan Wagner

## Malin, Kym

*Films:*
**Joysticks** (1983) . . . . . . . . . . . . . . . . . . . . . . . . . .Lola
• 0:03—Breasts with Alva showing a nerd their breasts by pulling their blouses open.
••• 0:18—Breasts during strip-video game with Jefferson, then in bed with him.
• 0:57—Breasts during fantasy sequence, lit with red lights, hard to see anything.
• 1:02—Brief breasts in slide show in courtroom.
Mike's Murder (1984) . . . . . . . . . . . . . .Beautiful Girl #1
**Weird Science** (1985) . . . . . . . . . . . Girl Playing Piano
• 0:55—Brief breasts several times as her clothes get torn off by the strong wind and she gets sucked up and out of the chimney.
Die Hard (1988). . . . . . . . . . . . . . . . . . . . . .Hostage
**Picasso Trigger** (1989) . . . . . . . . . . . . . . . . . . .Kym
•• 1:04—Breasts taking a shower.
Roadhouse (1989) . . . . . . . . . . . . . . . . . . . Party Girl
**Guns** (1990) . . . . . . . . . . . . . . . . . . . . . . . . . .Kym
0:27—Oil wrestling with Hugs.
••• 0:28—Showering (in back) while talking to Hugs (in front).
Enemy Gold (1993) . . . . . . . . . . . . . Cowboy's Hostess
*Video Tapes:*
**Playboy's Playmate Review** (1982). . . . . . .Playmate
••• 0:37—Nude in bar, then on empty stage.

Playboy Video Magazine, Volume 2 (1983)
................... Herself/Playboy Playoffs
*Magazines:*
**Playboy** (May 1982) ................. Playmate
**Playboy** (Nov 1983) .......... Sex in Cinema 1983
• 147—Right breast in photo from *Joysticks.*
**Playboy's Girls of Summer '86** (Aug 1986) . . Herself
••• 12—Full frontal nudity.
••• 81—Breasts.
• 96-97—Buns.
**Playboy's Calendar Playmates** (Nov 1992) . . Herself
•• 16—Side of left breast and buns.

## • Maltby, Katrina
*Films:*
**Demon Keeper** (1993) ............. Hilary Jackson
••• 0:27—Breasts, several times, while in black panties, after taking off robe and getting massaged by Dorothy.
*Magazines:*
**Penthouse** (Aug 1993) . . South African Pet of the Year
••• 111-119—Nude.

## • Mandel, Joyce
*Films:*
**Chesty Anderson, U.S. Navy** (1975) ......... Suzi
0:02—In bra with the other girls in barracks.
•• 0:15—Buns and very brief back side of left breast, taking off towel and putting on robe.
The Baltimore Bullet (1980) ............. Waitress

## Mandel, Suzy
*Adult Films:*
**Blonde Ambition** (1980; British) ........ Sugar Kane
Nude in hard core sex scenes.
*Films:*
Confessions of a Driving Instructor (1976; British) . . .n.a.
**Playbirds** (1978; British) ................... Lena
•• 0:12—Nude stripping in Playbird office.
Mistress of the Apes (1979; British) ........ Secretary

## Mani, Karen
*Films:*
**Alley Cat** (1982) ........................ Billie
• 0:01—Brief breasts in panties taking night gown off during opening credits.
0:17—In two piece swimsuit sitting by the pool.
••• 0:38—Brief side view of right breast and buns getting into the shower. Full frontal nudity in the shower.
••• 0:48—Breasts during women's prison shower room scene. Long scene.
**Avenging Angel** (1985) ........... Janie Soon Lee
••• 0:06—Nude taking a shower, right breast in mirror drying herself off, then in bra getting dressed.

## Manion, Cindy
*Films:*
Blow Out (1981) .................. Dancing Coed
**Prepples** (1984) ............................ Jo
• 0:11—Brief breasts changing into waitress costumes with her two friends.
• 0:44—Breasts during party with the three preppie guys.
**The Toxic Avenger** (1985) .................. Julie
0:14—In two piece swimsuit in locker room with Melvin.
••• 0:15—Breasts, after untying her swimsuit top in front of Melvin.

## Mansfield, Jayne
*Films:*
Pete Kelly's Blues (1955). .............. Cigarette Girl
The Girl Can't Help It (1957) ........... Jerri Jordan
**Promises, Promises** (1963). .......... Sandy Brooks
0:02—Bubble bath scene.
••• 0:04—Breasts drying herself off with a towel. Same shot also at 0:48.
••• 0:06—Breasts in bed. Same shot also at 0:08, 0:39 and 0:40.
••• 0:59—Buns, kneeling next to bathtub, right breast in bathtub, then breasts drying herself off.
A Guide for the Married Man (1967) . . Technical Advisor
**The Wild, Wild World of Jayne Mansfield** (1968)
.................................... Herself
Breasts.
*TV:*
Down You Go (1956). .............. Regular Panelist
*Video Tapes:*
**Hollywood Scandals and Tragedies** (1988)
.................................... Herself
• 1:11—Breasts in color still photographs from *Playboy* pictorial.
**Playboy Video Centerfold: Dutch Twins** (1989)
.................................... Herself
••• 0:39—Breasts in color and B&W shots from *Promises, Promises.*
*Magazines:*
**Playboy** (Feb 1955) ................... Playmate
**Playboy** (Jan 1974) ........ Twenty Years of Playmates
• 103—Buns, while lying on cushion.
**Playboy** (Jan 1979). ............. 25 Beautiful Years
•• 154—Breasts while lying on a pink bed.
Playboy's Nudes (Oct 1990). ................ Herself
**Playboy** (Jan 1994). .............. Remember Jayne
• 106-107—Partial buns in color and B&W photos.

## Manson, Jean
*Films:*
Young Nurses (1973) ....................... Kitty
Dirty O'Neil (1974) ....................... Ruby
**10 to Midnight** (1983) ................... Margo
••• 1:25—Breasts in hotel room with killer when he tries to elude Charles Bronson.

- 1:26—Brief right breast, lying in bed, covered with sheet.

*Magazines:*

**Playboy** (Aug 1974) . . . . . . . . . . . . . . . . . . . Playmate
••• 92-101—Nude.
**Playboy** (Aug 1977) . . . . . . . . . . The World of Playboy
•• 8—Full frontal nudity in small photo.
**Playboy** (Sep 1977). . . . . . . . . . . .Playmate's Progress
••• 99-103—Nude.
**Playboy's Girls of Summer '86** (Aug 1986) . . Herself
••• 13—Breasts and partial lower frontal nudity.

## Marceau, Sophie

*Films:*

La Boum (1980; French) . . . . . . . . . . . . . . . . . . . . . Vic
**L'Amour Braque** (1985; French). . . . . . . . . . . . .Mary
**Police** (1985; French). . . . . . . . . . . . . . . . . . . Noria
- 0:10—Brief left breast in window during police strip search.
- 1:36—Right and left breasts several times, while in bed with Gérard Depardieu
Pour Sacha (1992; French) . . . . . . . . . . . . . . . . . Laura

*Magazines:*

**Playboy** (Nov 1985) . . . . . . . . . . . Sex in Cinema 1985
•• 132-133—Breasts, lying in bed in still from *L'Amour Braque.*

## • Marcel, Tammy

*Films:*

**Bikini Summer 2** (1992) . . . . . . . . . . . . . . . . . Sandy
- 0:15—Buns in two piece swimsuit, while walking with Sandra.
•• 0:38—Breasts (she's the brunette), taking off her T-shirt and jumping into the pool with Sandra.
- 0:40—Very brief breasts, running past some guys.
••• 0:42—More breasts, while running around the back-yard.
••• 0:44—More breasts and buns in swimsuits, while running around some more.
Ring of Fire II: Blood and Steel (1992)
. . . . . . . . . . . . . . . . . . . . . .Bad Girl Gang Member

## • March, Jane

*Films:*

**The Lover** (1992) . . . . . . . . . . . . . . . . . . . . The Girl
(Unrated version reviewed.)
(When you don't see her face, it's reportedly a body double.)
•• 0:32—Full frontal nudity in bed with her lover.
••• 0:40—Left breast, while making love under her lov-er.
••• 0:42—Full frontal nudity, while lying in bed. Long shot.
•• 0:43—Buns, while standing in tub, getting washed by her lover.
••• 0:44—Breasts, while lying in bed, talking with her lover. Long scene.
•• 0:47—Left breast, while making love in bed.
•• 0:48—Full frontal nudity, while lying in bed.

•• 0:54—Breasts while making love on the floor with her lover.
••• 0:56—More full frontal nudity on the floor.
••• 0:59—Nude, walking around and watering the plants, getting into bed, then making love.
- 1:02—Brief breasts while making love.
- 1:17—Breasts washing herself with her lover. Hard to see because bars get in the way.
**Color of Night** (1994). . . . . . . . . . . . . . . . . . . . n.a.

*Magazines:*

**Playboy** (Nov 1992) . . . . . . . . . . Sex in Cinema 1992
- 145—Left breast with Tony Leung from *The Lover.*
**Playboy** (Dec 1992) . . . . . . . . . . . . . .Sex Stars 1992
••• 184—Breasts.
**Playboy** (Nov 1994) . . . . . . . . . . Sex in Cinema 1994
•• 137-138—Breasts, while in bathtub with Bruce Willis from *Color of Night.*

## • Marcus, Trula

*Films:*

Man's Best Friend (1993) . . . . . . . . . . . . . . . . .Annie
*Made for Cable TV:*
**Dream On: Depth Be Not Proud** (1993; HBO)
. . . . . . . . . . . . . . . . . . . . . . . . . . . . . . . . . Kelly
•• 0:10—Nude with Eddie Charles after he loses his job and his wife.

## Margolin, Janet

*Films:*

David and Lisa (1962) . . . . . . . . . . . . . . . . . . . . Lisa
Bus Riley's Back in Town (1965) . . . . . . . . . . . . . .Judy
Take the Money and Run (1969) . . . . . . . . . . . . Louise
**The Last Embrace** (1979) . . . . . . . . .Ellie "Eva" Fabian
- 1:10—Brief breasts in bathtub with Bernie, before strangling him.
•• 1:14—Right breast, while reaching for the phone in bed with Roy Scheider.
- 1:20—Left breast in photo that Scheider is looking at with a magnifying glass (it's supposed to be her grandmother).
1:22—Almost breasts in the shower talking to Schei-der.
Distant Thunder (1988) . . . . . . . . . . . Barbara Lambert
Ghostbusters II (1989) . . . . . . . . . . . . . The Prosecutor
*TV:*
Lanigan's Rabbi (1977). . . . . . . . . . . . . . Miriam Small

## Margot, Sandra

a.k.a. Adult film actress Tiffany Million.
Gorgeous Ladies of Wrestling (GLOW) wrestler from 1987-90.

*Films:*

**Caged Fury** (1989). . . . . . . . . . . . . . . . . . Crazy Daisy
1:10—Buns in G-string and bra dancing for some men.
1:11—Breasts after taking off bra.
**Demon Wind** (1990) . . . . . . . . . . . . Beautiful Demon
•• 0:50—Breasts trying to tempt Stacy and Chuck out of the cabin.

**The Sleeping Car** (1990) . . . . . . . . . 19-Year Old Girl
•• 0:00—Brief breasts shots taking off clothes then making love with a guy. Left breast while making love.
**Prime Target** (1991) . . . . . . . . . . . . . .Girl in Shower
••• 0:52—Side view of left breast and buns, taking a shower.
• 0:53—Buns, in hotel room after getting out of the shower.
Spirits (1991) . . . . . . . . . . . . . . . . . . . . . Nun Demon
**Body of Influence** (1992). . . . . . . . . . . . . Margaret
(Unrated version reviewed.)
••• 0:03—Breasts and buns in black G-string panties, while undressing for Jonathon.
*Made for Cable TV:*
**Tales From the Crypt: Dead Right** (1990; HBO)
. . . . . . . . . . . . . . . . . . . . . . . . . . . . . . . . Stripper #2
(Available on *Tales From the Crypt, Volume 3.*)
0:07—Dancing on stage wearing pasties. Long shot.
• 0:13—Dancing on stage wearing pasties.
*Video Tapes:*
Thunder and Mud (1989) . . . . . . . . . . . . . . . . Tiffany

# Maria, Mahalia
*Video Tapes:*
**Penthouse Pet of the Year Playoff 1992** (1992)
. . . . . . . . . . . . . . . . . . . . . . . . . . . . . . . . . . . . . . Pet
••• 0:37—Nude, in the desert, outside around a house, in a wild west theme, in a house and wrestling with another woman, on a bed, in front of a house.
••• 0:57—Nude, outside during the end credits.
**Penthouse Satin & Lace: An Erotic History of Lingerie** (1992) . . . . . . . . . . . . . . . . . . . . . . . .Model
**Penthouse Pet of the Year Winners 1993: Mahalia & Julie** (1994) . . . . . . . . . . . . . . . . . . . . . . . . Pet
• 0:01—Full frontal nudity during introduction.
••• 0:18—Full frontal nudity in dominatrix outfit, while dominating Nikki Dial.
••• 0:20—Nude in pool.
••• 0:22—Nude on grass by some flowers, then inside a house.
••• 0:23—More nude while in house wearing a dark wig.
*Magazines:*
**Penthouse** (Jan 1991) . . . . . . . . . . . . . . . . . . . . . Pet
••• 87-117—Nude.
**Penthouse** (Jun 1992) . . . . . . . . .Pet of the Year Playoff
••• 86-87—Nude.
**Penthouse** (Feb 1993) . . . . .Pet of the Year Runner-Up
••• 111-119—Nude.

# Marie, Jeanne
*Films:*
**If Looks Could Kill** (1987) . . . . . . . . . . . Jeannie Burns
•• 0:06—Breasts taking off her robe and kissing George.
**Prime Evil** (1987) . . . . . . . . . . . . . . . . . . . . . . . Judy
1:13—Breasts after removing her gown (she's on the right) with Cathy and Brett.

**Student Affairs** (1987) . . . . . . . . . . . . . Robin Ready
• 0:35—Brief breasts wearing black panties in bed trying to seduce a guy.
••• 0:41—Breasts making love with another guy, while banging her back against the wall.
• 0:44—Very brief breasts in VW with a nerd.
• 1:09—Very brief breasts falling out of a trailer home filled with water.
**Wildest Dreams** (1987). . . . . . . . . . . . . . . . Isabelle
•• 0:35—Breasts in panties in bedroom with Bobby.
**Wimps** (1987) . . . . . . . . . . . . . . . . . . . . . . . . . Janice
•• 0:20—Breasts in bed taking off top with Charles.
**Young Nurses in Love** (1987) . . . . . . Nurse Ellis Smith
• 0:31—Brief side view of left breast in mirror with Dr. Riley.
•• 1:09—Breasts in panties, getting into bed with Dr. Riley.

# Marino, Bonnie
*Video Tapes:*
**Playboy Video Calendar 1991** (1990). . . . . . . . .June
••• 0:22—Nude.
*Magazines:*
**Playboy** (Jun 1990). . . . . . . . . . . . . . . . . . . . Playmate
**Playboy's Book of Lingerie** (Mar 1992). . . . . .Herself
••• 74-75—Full frontal nudity.
**Playboy's Book of Lingerie** (Jul 1992) . . . . . . .Herself
••• 49—Full frontal nudity.
**Playboy's Book of Lingerie** (Sep 1992) . . . . . .Herself
••• 54-55—Full frontal nudity.
**Playboy's Calendar Playmates** (Nov 1992). . .Herself
••• 92—Full frontal nudity.
**Playboy's Nudes** (Dec 1992) . . . . . . . . . . . . . .Herself
••• 96—Full frontal nudity.
**Playboy's Book of Lingerie** (May 1994) . . . . .Herself
••• 22-23—Full frontal nudity.
••• 64—Full frontal nudity.
• 87—Partial left breast.
••• 98—Full frontal nudity.
**Playboy's Girls of Summer '94** (Jul 1994). . . .Herself
••• 22—Full frontal nudity.

# Markov, Margaret
*Films:*
Pretty Maids All in a Row (1971) . . . . . . . . . . . . . Polly
**The Hot Box** (1972). . . . . . . . . . . . . . . . . .Lynn Forrest
• 0:12—Breasts when bad guy cuts her swimsuit top open.
•• 0:16—Breasts in stream consoling Bunny.
• 0:21—Breasts in the furthest hammock from camera. Long shot.
••• 0:45—Breasts bathing in stream with the other girls.
Black Mama, White Mama (1973; U.S./Philippines)
. . . . . . . . . . . . . . . . . . . . . . . . . . . . . Karen Brent
**Naked Warriors** (1973). . . . . . . . . . . . . . . . . Bodicia
*a.k.a. The Arena*
• 0:07—Brief breasts getting clothes torn off by guards.

- 0:13—Breasts getting her dress ripped off, then raped during party.
- 0:19—Brief left breast, on floor making love, then right breast and buns.
  0:45—In sheer white dress consoling Septimus, then walking around.
- 0:52—Brief breasts sitting down, listening to Cornelia.

*Magazines:*

**Playboy** (Apr 1971) . . . . . . . . . Vadim's "Pretty Maids"
••• 161—Right side view nude.

## •*Marks, Shae*

*Video Tapes:*

**Wet and Wild: The Locker Room** (1994)
. . . . . . . . . . . . . . . . . . . . . . . . . . . . . . . . . . Playmate

*Magazines:*

**Playboy** (May 1994) . . . . . . . . . . . . . . . . . . . Playmate
••• 92-103—Nude.

## *Marlow, Lorrie*

*Films:*

Reform School Girls (1986) . . . . . . . . . . . . . . . . . Shelly
Hollywood Shuffle (1987) . . . . . . . . . . . . . . . . . . . .n.a.
**The Borrower** (1989) . . . . . . . . . . . . . . . Nurse Wilson
- 0:57—Brief left breast and upper half of right breast, while making love with a doctor in operating room.
To Sleep with Anger (1990). . . . . . . . . . . . . Cherry Bell

## *Maroney, Kelli*

*Films:*

Fast Times at Ridgemont High (1982) . . . . . . . . . . Cindy
Night of the Comet (1984) . . . . . . . . . . . . . . Samantha
Slayground (1984; British). . . . . . . . . . . . . . . . . Jolene
The Zero Boys (1985) . . . . . . . . . . . . . . . . . . . . . Jamie
Chopping Mall (1986) . . . . . . . . . . . . . . . . . . . . Alison
  *a.k.a. Killbots*
Big Bad Mama II (1987) . . . . . . . . . . . Willie McClatchie
Not of This Earth (1988) . . . . . . . . . . Nurse Mary Oxford
Jaded (1989). . . . . . . . . . . . . . . . . . . . . . . . . . . Jennifer
Transylvania Twist (1990) . . . . . . . . . . Script Supervisor
Servants of Twilight (1991) . . . . . . . . . . . Sherry Ordway
Midnight Witness (1992). . . . . . . . . . . . . . . . . . Devon

*Miniseries:*

Celebrity (1984) . . . . . . . . . . . . . . . . . . . . . . . . Joanna

*TV:*

Ryan's Hope (1983). . . . . . . . . . . . . . . . . . . . . . . .n.a.

*Video Tapes:*

**Scream Queen Hot Tub Party** (1991). . . . . . . Herself
•• 0:07—Breasts after taking off flower print blouse and putting on pink teddy.
- 0:12—Buns, while walking up the stairs.
••• 0:30—Breasts and buns after stripping out of cheerleader outfit, rubbing lotion on herself and demonstrating the proper Scream Queen way to pump iron.
••• 0:44—Breasts taking off her swimsuit top and soaping up with the other girls.
•• 0:46—Breasts in still shot during the end credits.

## •*Marshall, Paula*

*Films:*

**Hellraiser III: Hell on Earth** (1992) . . . . . . . . . .Terri
  (Unrated version reviewed.)
- 0:47—Very, very brief left breast under gaping blouse, while spinning around to get up off the floor to run to the door.
Warlock: The Armageddon (1993) . . . . Samantha Ellison

*Made for Cable Movies:*

Full Eclipse (1993; HBO). . . . . . . . . . . . . . . . . . . . Liza

*Made for TV Movies:*

Nurses on the Line: The Crash of Flight 7 (1993)
. . . . . . . . . . . . . . . . . . . . . . . . . . . . . . . Jill Houston

*TV:*

Wild Oats (1994- ) . . . . . . . . . . . . . . . . . . . . . . Shelly

## *Marsillach, Blanca*

Sister of actress Christina Marsillach.

*Films:*

**Flesh + Blood** (1985) . . . . . . . . . . . . . . . . . . . . . Clara
•• 0:11—Full frontal nudity on bed having convulsions after getting hit on the head with a sword.
**Collector's Item** (1988). . . . . . . . . . . . . . . Jacqueline
  *a.k.a. The Trap*
•• 0:52—In white bra cleaning up Tony Musante in bed, then breasts.
  1:04—Lower frontal nudity while watching Musante and Laura Antonelli making love in bed.
- 1:18—Breasts getting dressed. A little dark.
•• 1:22—Breasts changing clothes in bedroom while Antonelli talks to her.
**Dangerous Obsession** (1990; Italian) . . . . . . . . Jessica
- 0:02—Left breast, getting fondled by Johnny in recording studio. Lower frontal nudity when he pulls down her panties.
•• 0:05—Breasts while opening her blouse when Johnny plays his saxophone.
- 0:17—Lower frontal nudity on the stairs with Johnny, then brief breasts.
- 0:29—Brief breasts in video tape on T.V.
•• 0:40—Breasts while changing blouses.
••• 0:56—Full frontal nudity masturbating while looking at pictures of Johnny. Buns, then more full frontal nudity getting video taped.
••• 0:58—Breasts in bed with a gun. Nude walking around the house. Long scene.
- 1:05—Brief breasts on beach taking off sweater and burying a dog.
- 1:06—Brief full frontal nudity during video taping session.
•• 1:07—Breasts while cleaning up Dr. Simpson.
••• 1:13—Breasts, taking chains off Dr. Simpson, then lying in bed. Full frontal nudity making love with him.

# Marsillach, Cristina

Sister of actress Blanca Marsillach.

*Films:*

**Every Time We Say Goodbye** (1986) . . . . . . . Sarah
   1:00—In white slip in her bedroom.
   1:03—In white slip again.
  •• 1:09—Right breast, then brief breasts lying in bed
   with Tom Hanks.
**Collector's Item** (1988) . . . . . . . . . . . . . .Young Marie
*a.k.a. The Trap*
  •• 0:12—Right breast in elevator with Tony Musante.
  •• 0:36—Breasts in open blouse, then full frontal nudity in hut with Musante.
**Terror at the Opera** (1989; Italian) . . . . . . . . . .Betty
  • 0:23—Brief left breast during nightmare. Brief
   breasts, sitting up in bed and screaming.

# Martin, Danielle

a.k.a. Adult film actress Danielle.

*Adult Films:*

**The Blond Next Door** . . . . . . . . . . . . . . . . . . . . .n.a.

*Films:*

**My Therapist** (1983) . . . . . . . . . . . . . . . . . . Francine
  •• 0:29—In bra, garter belt, stockings and panties,
   then breasts in room with Rip.

*Video Tapes:*

**The Girls of Penthouse** (1984)
  . . . . . . . . . . . . . . . . . . . . . . .Bad to the Bone Woman
  ••• 0:07—Nude, taking off her leather outfit.

*Magazines:*

**Penthouse** (Feb 1983) . . . . . . . . .Million Dollar Baby
  ••• 107-121—Nude.

# Martin, Pamela Sue

*Films:*

The Poseidon Adventure (1972) . . . . . . . . Susan Shelby
Buster and Billie (1974). . . . . . . . . . . . . . .Margie Hooks
**The Lady in Red** (1979) . . . . . . . . . . . . . Polly Franklin
  • 0:07—Right breast, while in bedroom with a guy
   clutching her clothes.
  ••• 0:20—Breasts in jail with a group of women prisoners waiting to be examined by a nurse.
Flicks (1981) . . . . . . . . . . . . . . . . . . . . . . . . . . . . Liz
Torchlight (1984) . . . . . . . . . . . . . . . . . . Lillian Gregory

*Made for TV Movies:*

Human Feelings (1978). . . . . . . . . . . . . . . . Verna Gold

*TV:*

The Nancy Drew Mysteries (1977-78) . . . . . Nancy Drew
The Hardy Boys Mysteries (1977-78) . . . . . . Nancy Drew
Dynasty (1981-84) . . . . . . . . . . Fallon Carrington Colby

*Magazines:*

**Playboy** (Jul 1978). . . . . . . . . . .Nancy Drew Grows Up
  •• 87-91—Sort of breasts.

# Martin, Sandy

*Films:*

Scalpel (1976). . . . . . . . . . . . . . . . . . . . . . . . . Sandy
48 Hrs. (1982). . . . . . . . . . . . . . . . . . . . . Policewoman
Real Genius (1985) . . . . . . . . . . . . . . . . .Mrs. Meredith

Extremities (1986) . . . . . . . . . . . . . . . . . . Officer Sudow
**Vendetta** (1986) . . . . . . . . . . . . . . . . . . . . Kay Butler
  • 0:34—Brief left breast, while making love with her
   boyfriend. Don't see her face.
Barfly (1987) . . . . . . . . . . . . . . . . . . . . . . . . . . Janice
Defenseless (1991). . . . . . . . . . . . . . . . . . . . . . .Judge

# Mason, Marsha

Ex-wife of playwright Neil Simon.

*Films:*

**Blume in Love** (1973) . . . . . . . . . . . . . . . . . . . Arlene
  • 0:22—Side view of right breast, then brief breasts lying in bed with George Segal.
  • 0:35—Very brief right breast while reaching over the
   bed.
  •• 0:54—Brief breasts twice, reaching over to get a pillow while talking to Segal.
**Cinderella Liberty** (1973). . . . . . . . . . . Maggie Paul
  0:09—Brief panties shot leaning over pool table
   when James Caan watches.
  •• 0:17—Side view of left breast in room with Caan.
   Brief right breast sitting down on bed.
  ••• 0:38—Breasts sitting up in bed, yelling at Caan.
  • 0:54—Very brief left breast turning over in bed and
   sitting up.
Audrey Rose (1977) . . . . . . . . . . . . . . .Janice Templeton
The Goodbye Girl (1977). . . . . . . . . . . Paula McFadden
The Cheap Detective (1978) . . . . . . . . . Georgia Merkle
Chapter Two (1979). . . . . . . . . . . . . . Jennie MacLaine
Promises in the Dark (1979). . . . . . . Dr. Alexandra Kenda
Only When I Laugh (1981). . . . . . . . . . . . . . .Georgia
Max Dugan Returns (1983) . . . . . . . . . . . . . . . Nora
Heartbreak Ridge (1986) . . . . . . . . . . . . . . . .Aggie
Drop Dead Fred (1991) . . . . . . . . . . . . . . . . . . Polly

*Made for Cable Movies:*

Dinner At Eight (1989). . . . . . . . . . . . . Millicent Jordan
**The Image** (1990; HBO). . . . . . . . . . . . .Jean Cromwell
  • 0:08—Two brief side views of left breast standing in
   bathroom after Albert Finney gets out of the shower.

*TV:*

Sibs (1991-92) . . . . . . . . . . . . . . . . . . . . . Nora Rucio

# Massari, Lea

*Films:*

Murmur of the Heart (1971; French/Italian/German)
  . . . . . . . . . . . . . . . . . . . . . . . . . . . Clara Chevalier
Impossible Object (1973; French) . . . . . . . . .Hippolyta
*a.k.a. Story of a Love Story*
**Allonsanfan** (1974; Italian) . . . . . . . . . . . . .Charlotte
Italian with English subtitles.
  • 0:32—Buns, while undressing in bedroom in front of
   Marcello Mastroianni.

# Massey, Anna

Sister of actor Daniel Massey.
Daughter of actor Raymond Massey.

*Films:*

Peeping Tom (1960; British). . . . . . . . . Helen Stephens

**Frenzy** (1972; British). . . . . . . . . . . . . . . Babs Milligan
•• 0:45—Breasts getting out of bed and then buns,
walking to the bathroom. Probably a body double.
Sweet William (1980; British) . . . . . . . . . . . . . . . .Edna
Five Days One Summer (1982) . . . . . . . .Jennifer Pierce
Foreign Body (1986; British) . . . . . . . . . . . Miss Furze
Mountains of the Moon (1989). . . . . . . . Mrs. Arundell
The Tall Guy (1990; British). . . . . . . . . . . . . . . .Mary

## Massey, Edith
*Films:*
Pink Flamingos (1972) . . . . . . . . . . . . . . . . . . . . .n.a.
**Female Trouble** (1974). . . . . . . . . . . . . . . . . . . . Ida
• 0:20—Breasts, massaging her breasts in front of the
mirror.
Polyester (1981) . . . . . . . . . . . . . . . . . . . . . . Cuddles

## • Masterson, Chase
*Films:*
**In a Moment of Passion** (1992) . . . .Tammy Brandon
• 0:36—Very brief side of left breast, when dancing in
a restaurant with Maxwell Caulfield in front of a lot
of people.
• 1:01—Brief left breast, while making love with
Caulfield.
**Married People, Single Sex** (1993) . . . . . . . . . . Beth
• 0:30—Buns in lingerie, while trying on clothes with
her girlfriends.
Robin Hood: Men in Tights (1993)
. . . . . . . . . . . . . . . . . . . . . . . Giggling Court Lady

## Mastrantonio, Mary Elizabeth
Wife of film director Pat O'Connor.
*Films:*
**Scarface** (1983). . . . . . . . . . . . . . . . . . . . . . . .Gina
• 2:36—(0:39 into tape 2) Very, very brief left breast
when she gets shot and her nightgown opens up
when she gets hit.
**The Color of Money** (1986). . . . . . . . . . . . . Carmen
• 0:41—Brief breasts in bathroom mirror drying herself off while Paul Newman talks to Tom Cruise.
Long shot, hard to see.
Slam Dance (1987) . . . . . . . . . . . . . . . .Helen Drood
**The January Man** (1988) . . . . . . . . Bernadette Flynn
• 0:40—Breasts in bed with Kevin Kline. Side view of
left breast squished against Kline.
••• 0:42—Breasts after Kline gets out of bed. Brief shot,
but very nice!
**The Abyss** (1989) . . . . . . . . . . . . . . .Lindsey Brigman
• 1:41—Breasts during C.P.R. scene.
Fools of Fortune (1990). . . . . . . . . . . . . . . Marianne
Class Action (1991). . . . . . . . . . . . . . . .Margaret Ward
Robin Hood: Prince of Thieves (1991) . . . . . . . . Marian
Consenting Adults (1992) . . . . . . . . . . . .Priscilla Parker
**White Sands** (1992) . . . . . . . . . . . . . . . Lane Bodine
• 1:11—Brief left breast in shower with Willem Dafoe.
You see her face, so this shot is really her.
*Made for Cable Movies:*
Mussolini and I (1985; HBO) . . . . . Edda Mussolini Ciano

## Mastrogiacomo, Gina
*Films:*
**Alien Space Avenger** (1988) . . . . . . . . . . . . . Ginny
••• 0:19—Breasts in bed, making love with Matt. Breasts
and buns, getting out and getting dressed.
GoodFellas (1990) . . . . . . . . . . . . . . . . . . . Janice Rossi
Jungle Fever (1991) . . . . . . . . . . . . . . . . . . . . . Louise
The Naked Gun 2 1/2: The Smell of Fear (1991)
. . . . . . . . . . . . . . . . . . . . ."Is this some kind of bust?"
*Made for Cable TV:*
Rebel Highway: Motorcycle Gang (1994; Showtime)
. . . . . . . . . . . . . . . . . . . . . . . . . . . . . . . . .Waitress
*TV:*
NYPD Blue: A Sudden Fish (Feb 15, 1994) . . . . . . . . n.a.

## Mathias, Darian
*Films:*
My Chauffeur (1986) . . . . . . . . . . . . . . . . . . . . Dolly
**Blue Movies** (1988) . . . . . . . . . . . . . . . . . . . .Kathy
• 0:37—Very brief breasts twice acting for the first
time in a porno film.
0:39—Breasts from above during screening of movie. Hard to see.
*Made for TV Movies:*
My Wicked Ways... The Legend of Errol Flynn (1985)
. . . . . . . . . . . . . . . . . . . . . . . . . . . . . . . . . 1st Girl

## Mathis, Samantha
Daughter of actress Bibi Besch.
*Films:*
**Pump Up the Volume** (1990). . . . . . . . . . Nora Diniro
•• 1:13—Breasts taking off sweater on patio with Chris-
tian Slater.
This is My Life (1992). . . . . . . . . . . . . . . . Erica Ingels
Super Mario Bros. (1993). . . . . . . . . . . . . . . . . .Daisy
The Thing Called Love (1993) . . . . . . . .Miranda Presley
*Made for TV Movies:*
83 Hours 'til Dawn (1990) . . . . . . . . . . . . Julie Burdock
Extreme Close-Up (1990). . . . . . . . . . . . . . . . . . n.a.
To My Daughter (1990) . . . . . . . . . . . . . . . . . . . n.a.
*TV:*
Aaron's Way (1988) . . . . . . . . . . . . . . . Roseanne Miller
Knightwatch (1988-89) . . . . . . . . . . . . . . . . . . . Jake

## Matlin, Marlee
*Films:*
**Children of a Lesser God** (1986) . . . . . . . . . . .Sarah
(Academy Award for Best Actress.)
• 0:44—Brief buns under water in swimming pool.
Don't see her face.
0:47—Part of left breast while hugging William Hurt
(seen from under water).
Walker (1988) . . . . . . . . . . . . . . . . . . . . .Ellen Martin
The Linguini Incident (1991) . . . . . . . . . . . . .Jeanette
The Player (1992). . . . . . . . . . . . . . . . . . . . . Cameo
**Hear No Evil** (1993). . . . . . . . . . . . . .Jillian Shananhan
•• 0:30—Brief breasts, getting out of the bathtub.
*Made for TV Movies:*
Bridge to Silence (1988). . . . . . . . . . . . . . . . . . n.a.

TV:
Reasonable Doubts (1991-93) . . . . . . . . . . Tess Kaufman

## Matthews, Lisa

Films:
Hudson Hawk (1991) . . . . . . . . . . . . . . . . . . Girl in Car
Video Tapes:
**Playboy Video Calendar 1991** (1990) . . . September
**Sexy Lingerie II** (1990) . . . . . . . . . . . . . . . . . .Model
**Wet and Wild II** (1990) . . . . . . . . . . . . . . . . . .Model
**Playboy Video Calendar 1992** (1991) . . . . . . . . .July
••• 0:27—Nude in fashion show fantasy.
••• 0:28—Nude in mansion doing various things.
**Playboy Video Centerfold: Lisa Matthews** (1991)
. . . . . . . . . . . . . . . . . . . . . Playmate of the Year 1991
••• 0:00—Nude in front of curtains, then in bed, then in
medical segment, then at the beach and finally in a
fantasy modeling session.
**The Best of Sexy Lingerie** (1992) . . . . . . . . . . .Model
**The Best of Video Playmate Calendars** (1992)
. . . . . . . . . . . . . . . . . . . . . . . . . . . . . . . Playmate
•• 0:19—Breasts and buns, while in the desert.
••• 0:20—Nude in a house.
Magazines:
**Playboy** (Apr 1990) . . . . . . . . . . . . . . . . . . . Playmate
**Playboy** (Jun 1991) . . . . . . . . . . . Playmate of the Year
••• 144-155—Nude.
**Playboy's Girls of Summer '92** (Jun 1992) . . . Herself
•• 15—Breasts.
•• 44—Left breast.
••• 96-97—Side of left breast and buns.
•• 102-103—Left breast.
**Playboy's Book of Lingerie** (Jul 1992) . . . . . . Herself
•• 62—Left breast and lower frontal nudity.
••• 107—Breasts.
**Playboy's Book of Lingerie** (Sep 1992) . . . . . Herself
••• 74-75—Breasts.
**Playboy's Calendar Playmates** (Nov 1992) . . Herself
•• 95—Left breast and buns.
••• 103—Full frontal nudity.
**Playboy's Nudes** (Dec 1992) . . . . . . . . . . . . . Herself
••• 94—Full frontal nudity.
**Playboy's Book of Lingerie** (May 1993) . . . . . Herself
••• 26-27—Nude.
**Playboy's Girls of Summer '93** (Jun 1993) . . . Herself
•• 27—Right breast.
**Playboy's Wet & Wild Women** (Aug 1993) . . Herself
••• 52-53—Full frontal nudity.
**Playboy's Blondes, Brunettes & Redheads**
(Sep 1993) . . . . . . . . . . . . . . . . . . . . . . . . . . Herself
••• 6—Full frontal nudity.
**Playboy's Video Playmates** (Sep 1993) . . . . . Herself
••• 68-71—Breasts and buns.
**Playboy's Book of Lingerie** (Nov 1993) . . . . . Herself
••• 91—Full frontal nudity.
**Playboy's Book of Lingerie** (Mar 1994) . . . . . Herself
••• 69—Breasts.
**Playmates at Play** (Jul 1994) . . . . . . . . . . . . . Herself
••• 24-25—Nude.

**Playboy's Girls of Summer '94** (Jul 1994) . . . . Herself
••• 96-97—Full frontal nudity.
**Playboy's Book of Lingerie** (Jul 1994) . . . . . . Herself
••• 30-31—Breasts.

## Mattson, Robin

Films:
Namu, The Killer Whale (1966) . . . . . . . . . . . . Lisa Rand
**Bonnie's Kids** (1973) . . . . . . . . . . . . . . . . . . . . . Myra
• 0:05—Brief side view of right breast, changing in
bedroom while two men watch from outside.
••• 0:07—Breasts washing herself in the bathroom.
**Candy Stripe Nurses** (1974) . . . . . . . . . . . . . Dianne
•• 0:22—Nude in gym with the basketball player.
••• 0:40—Nude in bed with the basketball player.
Return to Macon County (1975) . . . . . . . . . . . . . Junell
**Wolf Lake** (1978) . . . . . . . . . . . . . . . . . . . . . . . Linda
a.k.a. Survive the Night at Wolf Lake
• 0:54—Brief full frontal nudity during rape in cabin.
Dark.
• 0:55—Brief breasts afterwards.
**Take Two** (1988) . . . . . . . . . . . . . . . . . Susan Bentley
0:21—Exercising in yellow outfit while Frank Stal-
lone plays music.
•• 0:25—Brief breasts taking a shower.
0:26—Showing Grant Goodeve her new two piece
swimsuit.
••• 0:29—Breasts in bed with Goodeve.
••• 0:45—Right breast in shower, then breasts getting
into bed.
• 0:47—Brief breasts getting out of bed and putting
an overcoat on.
0:51—One piece swimsuit by the swimming pool.
1:12—In two piece swimsuit at the beach.
••• 1:28—Breasts taking a shower after shooting Goodeve in bed.
In Between (1991) . . . . . . . . . . . . . . . . . . . . . . . Margo
Made for TV Movies:
The Secret Night Caller (1975) . . . . . . . . . . . Jan Durant
Are You in the House Alone? (1978) . . . Allison Bremmer
False Witness (1989) . . . . . . . . . . . . . . . . . . . . . . Jody
TV:
The Guiding Light (1976-77) . . . . . . . . . . . Hope Bauer
General Hospital (1980-83) . . . . . Heather Grant Webber
Ryan's Hope (1984) . . . . . . . . . . . . . . . . . . . Delia Reid
Santa Barbara (1985-93) . . . . . . Gina Capwell Timmons

## Maur-Thorp, Sarah

Films:
**Edge of Sanity** (1988) . . . . . . . . . . . . . . . . . Susannah
• 0:00—Left breast, while pulling down top to show
the little boy in the barn.
•• 0:09—Breasts, while talking to the two doctors after
they examine her back.
•• 0:50—Breasts in red room with Anthony Perkins and
Johnny.
• 0:56—Very brief breasts in nun outfit.
• 1:10—Brief breasts in Perkins' hallucination at Flora's
whorehouse.

Ten Little Indians (1989) . . . . . . . . . . . Vera Claythorne
**River of Death** (1990) . . . . . . . . . . . . Anna Blakesley
  • 0:14—Very brief left breast while in tent with Micha-
    el Dudikoff.

## Maura, Carmen
*Films:*
Matador (1986; Spanish) . . . . . . . . . . . . . . . . . . Julie
Women on the Verge of a Nervous Breakdown
  (1988; Spanish). . . . . . . . . . . . . . . . . . . Pepa Marcos
**Ay, Carmela!** (1991; Spanish) . . . . . . . . . . . . Carmela
  •• 0:42—Showing her left breast to the Lieutenant to
    explain why she had a Republican flag. Subtitles get
    in the way.
  •• 1:38—Breasts taking off flag on stage during play.
    Subtitles get in the way again.
High Heels (1991; Spanish) . . . . . . . . . . . . . . . . Tina
Pepi, Luci, Bom and Other Girls on the Heap
  (1992; Spanish). . . . . . . . . . . . . . . . . . . . . . . Pepi

## May, Mathilda
a.k.a. Mathilda May Haim.
Daughter of French playwright Victor Haim.
*Films:*
Dream One (1984; British/French) . . . . . . . . . . . . Alice
**Letters to an Unknown Lover** (1985) . . . . . . . Agnes
  • 0:43—Upper half of breasts in bathtub when Gervais
    opens the door.
  ••• 0:58—Buns and breasts taking off her robe in Ger-
    vais' room.
**Lifeforce** (1985) . . . . . . . . . . . . . . . . . . . . . Space Girl
  • 0:08—Full frontal nudity in glass case upside down.
  • 0:13—Breasts, lying down in space shuttle. Lit with
    blue light.
  ••• 0:16—Breasts while sitting up in lab to suck the life
    out of military guard. Brief full frontal nudity.
  •• 0:17—Breasts again in the lab.
  •• 0:19—Breasts while walking around, then buns.
  ••• 0:20—Breasts, while walking down the stairs. Brief
    nude fighting with the guards.
  •• 0:44—Breasts with Steve Railsback during his night-
    mare. Lit with red light.
  • 1:10—Brief breasts in space shuttle with Railsback.
Naked Tango (1990). . . . . . . . . . . . . . . Alba/Stephanie
**Becoming Colette** (1992; French/German/U.S.)
  . . . . . . . . . . . . . . . . . . . . . . . . . . . . Gabrielle Colette
  •• 0:01—Left breast, in open dress top, on stage during
    play.
  •• 0:16—Breasts, sitting up in bed.
  •• 0:48—Left breast, then breasts in bed with Virginia
    Madsen.
  •• 0:49—Side view of right breast in bed with Madsen
    and Klaus Maria Brandauer.
  •• 1:13—Upper half of buns and right breast, while
    making love in bed on top of Brandauer.
The Cry of the Owl (1992; French/Italian) . . . . . . Juliette

## Mayenzet, Maria
*Films:*
**Jagged Edge** (1985). . . . . . . . . . . . . . . . Page Forrester
  • 0:02—Very brief breast, on bed when the killer rips
    her pajamas open. Long shot.
Messenger of Death (1988) . . . . . . . . . Esther Beecham

## Mayne, Belinda
*Films:*
Krull (1983) . . . . . . . . . . . . . . . . . . . . . . . . . . . . Vella
Don't Open Till Christmas (1984; British). . . . . . . . Kate
**Lassiter** (1984). . . . . . . . . . . . . . . . . Helen Boardman
  ••• 0:06—In bra then breasts letting Tom Selleck un-
    dress her while her husband is in the other room.
**White Fire** (1985) . . . . . . . . . . . . . . . . . . . . . Ingrid
  •• 0:33—Nude, while swimming in pool.
  ••• 0:34—Nude, swimming in pool, then getting out
    and taking a shower.
  •• 0:35—Nude, after Robert Ginty steals her towel.
  •• 0:37—Nude, standing up in pool and getting out
    and going up stairs.
  •• 1:16—Breasts, while taking off her dress while on
    boat with Ginty.
Fatal Beauty (1987) . . . . . . . . . . . . . . . . . . . . . . Traci
The Tigress (1992) . . . . . . . . . . . . . . . . . . . . . . . Elsy

## • Mayo, Jennifer
*Films:*
**Scarred** (1983). . . . . . . . . . . . . . . . . . . . . . . . . Ruby
  ••• 0:18—Breasts, undressing in bedroom in front of a
    customer, lying in bed, then making love. Long
    scene.
  • 0:21—Breasts, while lying in bed afterward.
  • 0:27—Breasts in bathtub, getting red paint washed
    off by a friend.
  • 0:29—Left breast, while sitting in bathtub.
Cherry 2000 (1988) . . . . . . . . . . . . . . . . . . . . . Randa

## Mayo-Chandler, Karen
*Films:*
Beverly Hills Cop (1984). . . . . . . . Maitland Receptionist
Explorers (1986). . . . . . . . . . . . . . Starkiller's Girl Friend
**Hamburger—The Motion Picture** (1986)
  . . . . . . . . . . . . . . . . . . . . . . . . . Dr. Victoria Gotbottom
  • 0:03—Brief breasts in her office trying to help, then
    seduce Russell.
**Out of the Dark** (1988). . . . . . . . . . . . . . . . Barbara
  • 0:16—Brief breasts pulling red dress down wearing
    black stocking in Kevin's studio.
  ••• 0:17—Breasts and buns posing during photo shoot.
**Party Line** (1988). . . . . . . . . . . . . . . . . . . Sugar Lips
  0:52—In black bra and panties.
  0:57—Black panties, while hiking up her skirt and
    sitting of Leif Garrett's lap.
  •• 0:58—Breasts, opening her blouse while sitting on
    Garrett's lap.
  1:01—Brief breasts, while lying dead in field, cov-
    ered with blood.

**Stripped to Kill II** (1988) . . . . . . . . . . . . .Cassandra
   0:06—Black bra and panties in dressing room.
 •• 0:18—Breasts taking off her top for a customer.
**Take Two** (1988). . . . . . . . . . . . . . . . . . . . . Dorothy
 •• 1:17—Brief breasts on bed when her gold dress is
   pulled down a bit.
**Death Feud** (1989) . . . . . . . . . . . . . . . . . . . . .Anne
   0:26—In lingerie with a customer.
 •• 0:36—In white lingerie, then breasts several times
   outside taking off robe.
**Hard to Die** (1990) . . . . . . . . . . . . . . . Diana Farrow
  *a.k.a. Tower of Terror*
 •• 0:10—Breasts, putting on her dress in office with Mr.
   Plimpton.
**976-EVIL II: The Astral Factor** (1991) . . . . . . .Laurie
  (With blonde hair.)
 •• 0:00—Breasts in shower room, then putting on wet
   T-shirt.
   0:01—Running around the school hallways wearing
   white panties and wet, white T-shirt.
*Magazines:*
**Playboy** (Dec 1989). . . . . . . . . . . . .The Joker Was Wild
 ••• 94-103—Nude.
**Playboy's Nudes** (Oct 1990). . . . . . . . . . . . . . Herself
 ••• 21—Full frontal nudity.
**Playboy's Blondes, Brunettes & Redheads**
 (Sep 1993) . . . . . . . . . . . . . . . . . . . . . . . . . . Herself
 •• 49—Left breast.

# Mayor, Cari
*Films:*
**Spring Fever USA** (1988). . . . . . . . . . . Girl on Campus
  *a.k.a. Lauderdale*
**Summer Job** (1989) . . . . . . . . . . . . . . . . . . . . Donna
 • 0:10—Brief breasts twice, taking off her top before
  and after Herman comes into the room.

# Mayron, Melanie
*Films:*
**Harry and Tonto** (1974) . . . . . . . . . . . . . . . . Ginger
 (She's a lot heavier in this film than she is now.)
 • 0:57—Very brief breasts in motel room with Art Car-
  ney taking off her towel and putting on blouse.
  Long shot, hard to see.
**Car Wash** (1976). . . . . . . . . . . . . . . . . . . . . . .Marsha
**Gable and Lombard** (1976). . . . . . . . . . . . . . . .Dixie
**The Great Smokey Roadblock** (1976) . . . . . . . . . . Lulu
**You Light Up My Life** (1977). . . . . . . . . . Annie Gerrara
**Girlfriends** (1978). . . . . . . . . . . . . . . Susan Weinblatt
 (She's still a bit overweight.)
 • 0:14—Buns, very brief lower frontal nudity and brief
  left breast getting dressed in bathroom.
**Heartbeeps** (1981) . . . . . . . . . . . . . . . . . . . . . . Susan
**Missing** (1982) . . . . . . . . . . . . . . . . . . . . Terry Simon
**The Boss' Wife** (1986) . . . . . . . . . . . . . . . Janet Keefer
**Sticky Fingers** (1988). . . . . . . . . . . . . . . . . . . . Lolly
**Checking Out** (1989) . . . . . . . . . . . . . . Jenny Macklin
**My Blue Heaven** (1990). . . . . . . . . . . . . . . . . Crystal

*Made for TV Movies:*
**Hustling** (1975) . . . . . . . . . . . . . . . . . . . . . Dee Dee
**Playing for Time** (1980) . . . . . . . . . . . . . . . . . . n.a.
 (Lost a lot of weight.)
   0:11—Brief side view of left breast getting her hair
   cut. She's behind Vanessa Redgrave. You can't really
   see anything.
**Ordeal in the Arctic** (1993). . . . . . . . . . . . . . . . . Sue
*TV:*
**thirtysomething** (1987-91). . . . . . . . Melissa Steadman

# Mays, Melinda
*Video Tapes:*
**Playboy Video Magazine, Volume 5** (1983)
 . . . . . . . . . . . . . . . . . . . . . . . . . . . . . . . . . Playmate
 • 0:05—Brief breasts in hay.
**Playboy's Playmate Review 3** (1985) . . . . . Playmate
*Magazines:*
**Playboy** (Feb 1983) . . . . . . . . . . . . . . . . . . Playmate
**Playboy's Girls of Summer '86** (Aug 1986). . .Herself
 •• 64-65—Side of left breast and buns.
**Playboy's Calendar Playmates** (Nov 1992). . .Herself
 • 20—Buns.

# • Mazar, Debi
*Films:*
**GoodFellas** (1990) . . . . . . . . . . . . . . . . . . . . . Sandy
**The Doors** (1991). . . . . . . . . . . . . . . . . . Whiskey Girl
**Jungle Fever** (1991) . . . . . . . . . . . . . . . . . . . .Denise
**Little Man Tate** (1991) . . . . . . . . . . . . . . . . . . . Gina
**In the Soup** (1992). . . . . . . . . . . . . . . . . . . . . . Suzi
**Malcolm X** (1992) . . . . . . . . . . . . . . . . . . . . . . . Peg
**Toys** (1992). . . . . . . . . . . . . . . . . . . Nurse Debbie
**Beethoven's 2nd** (1993). . . . . . . . . . . . . . . . . . n.a.
**Money for Nothing** (1993). . . . . . . . . . Monica Russo
 •• 0:39—Breasts, while making love in bed with John
  Cusack while covered with money.
   0:42—Brief buns in black panties and bra while get-
   ting dressed.
   1:22—In black bra in bathroom while coloring Cu-
   sack's hair.
**So, I Married an Axe Murderer** (1993)
 . . . . . . . . . . . . . . . . . . . .Tony's Girlfriend Susan
*Made for Cable TV:*
**Musical Shorts** . . . . . . . . . . . . . . . . . . . . . . . . Host
*TV:*
**Civil Wars** (1992-93) . . . . . . . . . . . . . . Denise Iannello
**L.A. Law** (1993-94) . . . . . . . . . . . . . . . Denise Iannello

# McArthur, Kimberly
*Films:*
**Young Doctors in Love** (1982). . . . . . . . . . Jyll Omato
 •• 0:58—Breasts in front of Dabney Coleman after taking off her Santa Claus outfit in his study.
**Easy Money** (1983) . . . . . . . . . . . . . . . . Ginger Jones
 •• 0:47—Breasts sunbathing in the backyard when
  seen by Rodney Dangerfield.

**Malibu Express** (1984) . . . . . . . . . . . . . . . . . . . . Faye
•• 0:10—Breasts taking a shower on the boat with Barbara Edwards.
Slumber Party Massacre II (1987) . . . . . . . . . . . . Amy
*TV:*
Santa Barbara (1988-90) . . . . . . . . . . . . . . . . . . . Kelly
*Video Tapes:*
Playmate Playoffs . . . . . . . . . . . . . . . . . . . . Playmate
**Playboy's Playmate Review** (1982) . . . . . . Playmate
••• 0:19—Nude in sauna, then taking a shower, then in front of fireplace.
Playboy Video Magazine, Volume 2 (1983)
. . . . . . . . . . . . . . . . . . . . . . . Herself/Playboy Playoffs
**Playboy Video Magazine, Volume 5** (1983)
. . . . . . . . . . . . . . . . . . . . . . . . . . . . . . . . . . Playmate
• 0:06—Brief breasts in front of fire.
*Magazines:*
**Playboy** (Jan 1982) . . . . . . . . . . . . . . . . . . . Playmate
**Playboy's 1987 Book of Lingerie** (Mar 1987)
. . . . . . . . . . . . . . . . . . . . . . . . . . . . . . . . . . . Herself
••• 91—Full frontal nudity.
**Playboy's Career Girls** (Aug 1992)
. . . . . . . . . . . . . . . . . . . . . . . . Baywatch Playmates
••• 10—Full frontal nudity.
**Playboy's Calendar Playmates** (Nov 1992) . . Herself
••• 9—Full frontal nudity.
••• 24—Full frontal nudity.
••• 30—Breasts.
**Playmates at Play** (Jul 1994) . . . . . . . . . . . . . Herself
••• 16-19—Breasts, while covered with mud and getting cleaned up.

## McBride, Harlee

Wife of comedian/actor Richard Belzer.
*Films:*
**Young Lady Chatterley** (1977) . . . Cynthia Chatterley
•• 0:19—Nude masturbating in front of mirror.
• 0:28—Brief breasts with young boy.
••• 0:41—Nude in bathtub while maid washes her.
••• 0:52—Nude in back of car with the hitchhiker while the chauffeur is driving.
••• 1:03—Nude in the garden with the sprinklers on making love with the Gardener.
••• 1:31—Breasts and buns in bed with the gardener.
House Calls (1978) . . . . . . . . . . . . . . . . . . . . . . . . .n.a.
**Young Lady Chatterley II** (1986)
. . . . . . . . . . . . . . . . . . . . . . . . Cynthia Chatterley
•• 0:20—Breasts getting a massage with Elanor.
•• 0:22—Full frontal nudity during flashback to the first time she made love with Robert.
••• 0:28—Breasts taking a bath with Jenny.
••• 0:35—Breasts in library seducing Virgil.
••• 0:50—Breasts in back of the car with the Count.
••• 0:58—Breasts in the garden with Robert.
*Magazines:*
**Playboy** (Dec 1977). . . . . . . . . . . . . . Sex Stars of 1977
••• 217—Full frontal nudity lying on bed.

## McBride, Michelle

*Films:*
Edgar Allan Poe's "The Masque of the Red Death" (1989) . . . . . . . . . . . . . . . . . . . . . . . . . . . . . . .Rebecca
**Subspecies** (1990) . . . . . . . . . . . . . . . . . . . . . . .Lillian
• 0:34—Left breast, while sleeping in bed when the vampire comes to get her.
*Made for Cable Movies:*
Prey of the Chameleon (1992; Showtime) . . . . . . .Leslie

## McBroom, Dirga

*Films:*
Flashdance (1983) . . . . . . . . . . . . . . . . . . . . . . . .Heels
**The Rosebud Beach Hotel** (1985) . . . . . . . . . Bellhop
• 0:49—Buns, then breasts, standing with the other bell hops, outfitted with military attire. (She's the one at the far end, furthest from the camera.)
Vendetta (1986). . . . . . . . . . . . . . . . . . . . . . . . .Willow

## • McCarthy, Jenny

*Video Tapes:*
**Playboy Video Centerfold: Jenny McCarthy** (1994)
. . . . . . . . . . . . . . . . . . . . . . . . Playmate of the Year
•• 0:00—Full frontal nudity during introduction.
••• 0:02—Full frontal nudity, while posing around a race track.
••• 0:05—Nude, in pool table/diner fantasy.
••• 0:12—Nude in school girl, cheerleader and graduation gown fantasy.
••• 0:15—Nude while posing around the house.
••• 0:19—Nude in still photos.
••• 0:23—Nude in desert town fantasy with a guy.
••• 0:28—Full frontal nudity in near-death fantasy.
**Wet and Wild: The Locker Room** (1994) . . Playmate
*Magazines:*
**Playboy** (Oct 1993) . . . . . . . . . . . . . . . . . . . Playmate
••• 94-105—Nude.
**Playboy** (Jan 1994). . . . . . . .Playboy's Playmate Review
••• 205—Full frontal nudity.
**Playboy's Playmate Review** (May 1994)
. . . . . . . . . . . . . . . . . . . . . . . . . . . . . .Miss October
••• 82-91—Nude.
**Playboy** (Jun 1994). . . . . . . . . . . Playmate of the Year
••• 132-143—Nude.
**Playmates at Play** (Jul 1994) . . . . . . . . . . . . .Herself
•• 6-7—Left breast.
**Playboy's Girls of Summer '94** (Jul 1994). . . .Herself
••• 7—Full frontal nudity.
**Playboy's Book of Lingerie** (Jul 1994). . . . . . .Herself
••• 29—Left breast and lower frontal nudity.
**Playboy's Book of Lingerie** (Sep 1994). . . . . .Herself
•• 25—Left breast.

## McCartney, Kimberly

*Video Tapes:*
**Hot Body International: #2 Miss Puerto Vallarta** (1990) . . . . . . . . . . . . . . . . . . . . . . . . . . . .Contestant
•• 0:48—Buns in one piece swimsuit. Practically breasts wearing pasties.

0:56—4th runner up.

Hot Body International: #4 Spring Break (1992)

................................. Contestant

**Hot Body: The Best of Hot Body** (1994) .... Herself

••• 0:46—Buns in swimsuits. Breasts while wearing pasties. Brief breasts while flashing.

## McClellan, Michelle

See: Bauer, Michelle.

## McClure, Tané

a.k.a. Tané.

Daughter of actor Doug McClure.

*Films:*

**Crawlspace** (1986) ................ Sophie Fisher

• 0:00—Nipples, sticking out of holes that she cuts in
her red bra. Brief breasts in bed making love with
Hank. Dark.

Commando Squad (1987) .................. Sunny

**Death Spa** (1987) ........................Vicky

•• 1:10—Breasts in sauna with Tom.

• 1:19—Brief breasts during the fire.

**Hot Under the Collar** (1991)............. Rowena

0:28—In red bra and panties in her room, trying to
seduce Max. Almost right breast when she pulls her
bra strap down.

••• 0:32—Breasts in bed with Max.

*Video Tapes:*

**Inside Out 2** (1992)

................ Melanie Moss/Mis-Apprehended
(Unrated version reviewed.)

•• 0:09—Breasts, taking off her blouse outside for Tim.

## McComas, Lorissa

*Films:*

**Can It Be Love** (1992) ................ Montana

*a.k.a. Spring Break Sorority Babes*

••• 0:55—Breasts and buns, changing into lingerie behind two way mirror while David watches.

**Stormswept** (1994) ...................... Kelly

••• 0:53—Breasts, while making love in bed with Brianna.

••• 1:33—Nude, after taking off her robe in room in
front of Eugene.

*Magazines:*

**Playboy's Book of Lingerie** (Sep 1991) ..... Herself

••• 3-7—Breasts and buns.

**Playboy's Book of Lingerie** (Nov 1991) ..... Herself

•• 101—Breasts.

**Playboy's Book of Lingerie** (Jan 1992)...... Herself

•• 49—Right breast.

• 83—Left breast.

**Playboy's Book of Lingerie** (Mar 1992) ..... Herself

••• 58-59—Breasts and buns.

**Playboy's Bathing Beauties** (Apr 1992) ..... Herself

••• 72—Breasts.

**Playboy's Book of Lingerie** (May 1992) ..... Herself

••• 18—Breasts.

**Playboy's Book of Lingerie** (Jul 1992) ....... Herself

••• 21—Breasts.

**Playboy's Book of Lingerie** (Sep 1992) ...... Herself

• 59—Side of left breast.

**Playboy's Book of Lingerie** (Nov 1992) ..... Herself

••• 11—Breasts.

**Playboy's Book of Lingerie** (Jan 1993) ...... Herself

•• 83—Breasts.

**Playboy's Bathing Beauties** (Apr 1993)...... Herself

••• 51—Breasts.

**Playboy's Book of Lingerie** (Jan 1994) ...... Herself

••• 47—Breasts.

**Playboy's Book of Lingerie** (May 1994) ..... Herself

•• 35—Buns.

## McConnell, Denise

*Video Tapes:*

Playboy Video Magazine, Volume 2 (1983)

....................... Herself/Playboy Playoffs

*Magazines:*

**Playboy** (Mar 1979) ................... Playmate

## McCormick, Maureen

*Films:*

Take Down (1978) ................ Brooke Cooper

Skatetown, U.S.A. (1979)................... Susan

The Idolmaker (1980) ................Ellen Fields

**Texas Lightning** (1980) ..................... Fay

1:04—Very brief upper half of right breast popping
out of slip while struggling on bed with two jerks.
Long shot, hard to see.

Return to Horror High (1987)............Officer Tyler

*Made for TV Movies:*

A Very Brady Christmas (1988).......... Marcia Brady

*TV:*

The Brady Bunch (1969-74)........... Marcia Brady

## McCourt, Emer

*Films:*

**London Kills Me** (1991; British)..............Sylvie

• 1:02—Left breast in open blouse, while sleeping.

••• 1:05—Breasts, while sitting in bathtub with Clint.
Long scene.

*Made for TV Movies:*

Parnell & The Englishwoman (1991) ...........Eileen

## • McCrena, Brittany

*Films:*

**A Sensuous Summer** (1991).................. Jill

•• 0:00—Breasts while making love in bed with Bobby
in flashback.

•• 0:11—Breasts while making love with Bobby in
flashback. Buns in swimsuit.

••• 0:59—In black bra then breasts while making love
with Bobby.

**Taxi Dancers** (1993) ...................... Billie

•• 0:16—Breasts, while changing clothes in room with
Star.

••• 0:27—Breasts, while making love on billiard table with Bobby.

••• 0:44—Breasts (mostly left breast) while making love with Bobby in van.

0:45—Partial right breast, when waking up in the morning with Bobby.

*Magazines:*

**Playboy's Book of Lingerie** (Mar 1992) . . . . . Herself
•• 79—Left breast.

**Playboy's Bathing Beauties** (Apr 1992) . . . . . Herself
•• 92—Left breast.

**Playboy's Book of Lingerie** (Jul 1992) . . . . . . Herself
••• 72—Breasts and upper half of lower frontal nudity.

**Playboy's Book of Lingerie** (Mar 1993) . . . . . Herself
••• 102—Breasts.

**Playboy's Book of Lingerie** (Jan 1994) . . . . . . Herself
••• 54—Breasts.

# McCullough, Julie

*Films:*

**Big Bad Mama II** (1987). . . . . . . . . . .Polly McClatchie
•• 0:12—Breasts with Danielle Brisebois playing in a pond underneath a waterfall.
•• 0:36—In lingerie, then breasts sitting on Jordan who is tied up in bed.

The Blob (1988) . . . . . . . . . . . . . . . . . . . . . . .Susie

The Baby Doll Murders (1992) . . . . . . . . . . . . . . .Betty
0:58—In black bra and panties.

Round Trip to Heaven (1992) . . . . . . . . . . . . . . .Lucille

*TV:*

Growing Pains (1989-90) . . . . . . . . . . . . . . . . . . Julie

Robin's Hoods (1994- ) . . . . . . . . . . . . . . . . . . . .n.a.

*Video Tapes:*

**Playboy Video Calendar 1987** (1986) . . . . Playmate

**Playboy Video Calendar 1988** (1987) . . . . Playmate

**Playboy Video Centerfold: Peggy McIntagart**
(1989). . . . . . . . . . . . . . . . . . . . . . . . . . . . Playmate
••• 0:35—Nude in still photos and videos.

*Magazines:*

**Playboy** (Feb 1986). . . . . . . . . . . . . . . . . Playmate

**Playboy's Girls of Summer '86** (Aug 1986) . . Herself
•• 4—Left breast and partial lower frontal nudity.
• 85—Left breast.
• 104—Side of left breast and side of buns.
••• 108—Breasts.
••• 111—Breasts.

**Playboy** (Oct 1989). . . . . . . . . . . . . . Julie McCullough
••• 74-79—Nude.

**Playboy** (Dec 1989). . . . . . . . . .Holy Sex Stars of 1989!
•• 181—Left breast, while sitting in a chair.

**Playboy's Nudes** (Oct 1990). . . . . . . . . . . . . . Herself
••• 11—Full frontal nudity.

**Playboy's Calendar Playmates** (Nov 1992) . . Herself
••• 50—Full frontal nudity.
••• 65—Full frontal nudity.

**Playboy's Nudes** (Dec 1992) . . . . . . . . . . . . . Herself
••• 5—Breasts.

# McCullough, Shanna

Adult film actress.

*Films:*

**Malibu Express** (1984) . . . . . Uncredited Massage Girl
•• 0:33—Breasts, several times while giving a guy a rub down.

# McCurry, Natalie

*Films:*

**Dead-End Drive-In** (1986; Australian) . . . . . . .Carmen
•• 0:19—Breasts in red car with Ned Manning.

*Made for TV Movies:*

Danger Down Under (1988) . . . . .Katherine Dillingham

# McDaniel, Donna

Singer.

*Films:*

**Angel** (1983) . . . . . . . . . . . . . . . . . . . . . . . . . . .Crystal
• 0:19—Brief breasts, dead in bed when the killer pulls the covers down.

Frightmare (1983) . . . . . . . . . . . . . . . . . . . . . . . .Donna

Hollywood Hot Tubs (1984) . . . . . . . . . . Leslie Maynard

# • McDaniel, Sonja

*Video Tapes:*

**The Girls of Penthouse, Volume 2** (1993)
. . . . . . . . . . . . . . . . . . . . . . . . . . . . . . . .Nightstalker
••• 0:41—Nude, while making love in alley.

*Magazines:*

**Penthouse** (May 1994) . . . . . . . . . . . . . . . . . . . . .Pet
••• 73-85—Nude.

# McDermott, Colleen

*Films:*

**Paradise Motel** (1985) . . . . . . . . . . . . . . . . . . Debbie
•• 0:24—Breasts in motel room with Mic, when Sam lets them use a room.

**Demonwarp** (1988). . . . . . . . . . . . . . . . . . . . . Cindy
•• 0:23—Breasts and buns drying herself off after taking a shower.
• 0:24—Very brief lower frontal nudity, under her towel, trying to run up the stairs.

*Video Tapes:*

**Eden 6** (1994). . . . . . . . . . . . . . . . . . . . . . . . .Amanda
• 1:08—Breasts, while in bed after making love with B.D.
••• 1:18—Breasts, when joining B.D. in the shower.

# McDonough, Mary

*Films:*

Lovely But Deadly (1973). . . . . . . . . . . . . . . . . . . .n.a.

Mortuary (1981) . . . . . . . . . . . . . . . . . .Christie Parson
(All scenes with nudity are probably a body double.)
0:45—Buns and very brief breasts making love with her boyfriend on the floor. Long shot, hard to see.
1:06—Full frontal nudity on table in the morgue, dead.

Funland (1987) . . . . . . . . . . . . . . . . . .Kristin Cumming

Snowballing (1987) . . . . . . . . . . . . . . . . . . . . . . .Karen

Mom (1989) . . . . . . . . . . . . . . . . . . . . . . . . . . . . . Alice
*Made for TV Movies:*
A Walton Thanksgiving Reunion (1993). . . . . . . . . . .Erin
*TV:*
The Waltons (1972-81) . . . . . . . . . . . . . . . . .Erin Walton

# • McDormand, Frances
*Films:*
Blood Simple (1984) . . . . . . . . . . . . . . . . . . . . . . . Abby
Crimewave (1986) . . . . . . . . . . . . . . . . . . . . . . . . Nun
Raising Arizona (1987) . . . . . . . . . . . . . . . . . . . . . .Dot
Mississippi Burning (1988) . . . . . . . . . . . . . . . .Mrs. Pell
Chattahoochee (1990) . . . . . . . . . . . . . . . .Mae Foley
Darkman (1990) . . . . . . . . . . . . . . . . . . . Julie Hastings
Hidden Agenda (1990; British) . . . . . . . . . . . . . Ingrid
The Butcher's Wife (1991). . . . . . . . . . . . . . . . . . Grace
Passed Away (1992) . . . . . . . . . . . . . . . . Nora Scanlan
**Short Cuts** (1993). . . . . . . . . . . . . . . . . Betty Weathers
• 0:46—Very brief left breast and partial lower frontal
nudity, while walking past doorway. Brief left breast
and lower frontal nudity, while peeking around
doorway and wrapping a towel around herself.

# McEachin, Bianca
*Films:*
**Coming to America** (1988)
. . . . . . . . . . . . . . . . . Uncredited Miss Black Awareness
• 0:37—Buns, wearing pink sequined, two piece
swimsuit on stage during Black Awareness meeting.
*Video Tapes:*
**Dream Babies** (1989) . . . . . . . . . . . . . . . . . . . Herself
••• 0:06—Dancing in red two-piece swimsuit, then
breasts and buns in G-string. Nice!
•• 0:40—Breasts, introducing her segment.
••• 0:41—More breasts, dancing in red two-piece swimsuit.
Hot Body International: #1 Miss Cancun (1990)
. . . . . . . . . . . . . . . . . . . . . . . . . . . . . . . Contestant

# McEnroe, Annie
*Films:*
**The Hand** (1981). . . . . . . . . . . . . . . . . . . Stella Roche
•• 0:51—Breasts undressing for Michael Caine.
Warlords of the 21st Century (1982) . . . . . . . . . . . Carlie
*a.k.a. Battletruck*
The Survivors (1983) . . . . . . . . . . . . . . . . . . . . Doreen
Howling II: Your Sister is a Werewolf (1984) . . . . . Jenny
**Purple Hearts** (1984) . . . . . . . . . . . . . . . . . . .Hallaway
•• 1:23—Brief breasts coming out of the bathroom sur-
prising Ken Wahl and Cheryl Ladd.
True Stories (1986) . . . . . . . . . . . . . . . . . . . Kay Culver
Wall Street (1987). . . . . . . . . . . . . . . Muffie Livingston
Beetlejuice (1988). . . . . . . . . . . . . . . .Jane Butterfield
Cop (1988). . . . . . . . . . . . . . . . . . . . . .Amy Cranfield
The Doors (1991) . . . . . . . . . . . . . . . . . . . . Secretary
Criss Cross (1992) . . . . . . . . . . . . . . . . . . . . .Mrs. Sivil

Dangerous Game (1993) . . . . . . . . . . . . . . . . . Cameo
(Unrated version reviewed.)
Heaven and Earth (1993) . . . . . . . . . . . Dinner Guest #1
Josh and S.A.M. (1993) . . . . . . . Woman at Laundromat
Mr. Jones (1993) . . . . . . . . . . . . . . . . . Crying Woman
*Magazines:*
**Playboy** (Nov 1981) . . . . . . . . . . Sex in Cinema 1981
•• 172—Breasts.

# McGavin, Graem
*Films:*
**Angel** (1983) . . . . . . . . . . . . . . . . . . . . . . . . . Lana
•• 0:31—Breasts standing in hotel bathroom talking to
her John.
**My Tutor** (1983) . . . . . . . . . . . . . . . . . . . . . . .Sylvia
••• 0:21—In white bra, then breasts in back seat of a car
in a parking lot with Matt Lattanzi.
Weekend Pass (1984) . . . . . . . . . . . . . . . . .Tawny Ryatt

# McGillis, Kelly
*Films:*
Reuben, Reuben (1983) . . . . . . . . . . . Geneva Spofford
**Witness** (1985). . . . . . . . . . . . . . . . . . . . . . . . .Rachel
••• 1:18—Breasts taking off her top to take a bath while
Harrison Ford watches.
Top Gun (1986) . . . . . . . . . . . . . . . . . . . . . . .Charlie
Made in Heaven (1987) . . . .Annie Packert/Ally Chandler
Unsettled Land (1987) . . . . . . . . . . . . . . . . . . . . Anda
The Accused (1988) . . . . . . . . . . . . . . Kathryn Murphy
**Cat Chaser** (1988) . . . . . . . . . . . . . . . . Mary De Boya
••• 0:23—Breasts on the floor with Peter Weller. Long
scene.
••• 1:04—Full frontal nudity taking off her slip and get-
ting raped by her husband's pistol. Kind of dark.
•• 1:06—Brief buns, getting pushed around the house.
Right breast while signing a paper.
**The House on Carroll Street** (1988) . . . . . . . . .Emily
• 0:39—Brief breasts reclining into the water in the
bathtub.
Winter People (1989) . . . . . . . . . . . . . . . Collie Wright
**Grand Isle** (1991). . . . . . . . . . . . . . . . .Edna Pontellier
••• 1:08—Breasts while on the floor making love with
Julian Sands.
••• 1:19—Breasts, twice, in open robe while sketching
while lying on the floor.
••• 1:30—Buns and breasts after taking off clothes at
the beach.
••• 1:31—Nude, quite a few times, while swimming under water. Seen from under water.
•• 1:32—Breasts, while doing the backstroke above
water.
The Babe (1992) . . . . . . . . . . . . Claire Hodgeson-Ruth
*Made for TV Movies:*
Code of Honor (1984) . . . . . . Katherine Dennison Breen
Original title: *Sweet Revenge.*
In the Best of Families, Marriage, Pride and Madness
(1994) . . . . . . . . . . . . . . . . . . . . . . . . . . . .Susie Leary

## McGovern, Elizabeth

*Films:*

Ordinary People (1980). . . . . . . . . . . . . . . . . . .Jeanine
**Ragtime** (1981). . . . . . . . . . . . . . . . . . . Evelyn Nesbit
••• 0:52—Breasts in living room sitting on couch and arguing with a lawyer. Very long scene.
Lovesick (1983). . . . . . . . . . . . . . . . . . . . . .Chloe Allen
**Once Upon a Time in America** (1984). . . . .Deborah
(Long version reviewed.)
• 2:33—(0:32 into tape 2) Brief glimpses of left breast
when Robert De Niro tries to rape her in the back
seat of a car.
**Racing with the Moon** (1984) . . . . . . Caddie Winger
• 0:45—Upper half of breast in pond with Sean Penn.
The Bedroom Window (1987). . . . . . . . . . . . . . Denise
1:25—Silhouette of breasts on shower curtain when
Steve Guttenberg peeks in the bathroom.
She's Having a Baby (1988). . . . . . . . . . . . . . . . Kristy
**Johnny Handsome** (1989) . . . . . . . . . Donna McCarty
•• 0:47—Right breast, while in bed with Mickey
Rourke.
A Handmaid's Tale (1990). . . . . . . . . . . . . . . . . Moira
A Shock to the System (1990). . . . . . . .Stella Anderson
Tune in Tomorrow (1990). . . . . . . . . . . . Elena Quince
*a.k.a. Aunt Julia and the Scriptwriter*
King of the Hill (1993). . . . . . . . . . . . . . . . . . . .Lydia
The Favor (1994) . . . . . . . . . . . . . . . . . . . . . Emily
*Made for Cable Movies:*
**Women & Men: Stories of Seduction** (1990; HBO)
. . . . . . . . . . . . . . . . . . . . . . . . . . . . . . . . . . . . Vicki
0:18—In white lingerie in train car with Beau Bridg-
es.
••• 0:22—Breasts when Bridges takes her top off when
she lies back in bed.

## McGregor, Angela Punch

*Films:*

**The Island** (1980) . . . . . . . . . . . . . . . . . . . . . . . . Beth
•• 0:45—Breasts taking off poncho to make love with
Michael Caine in hut after rubbing stuff on him.
0:50—Braless under poncho walking towards Caine.
We of the Never Never (1983) . . . . . . . . . . . . . .Jeannie
A Test of Love (1984; Australian). . . . . Jessica Hathaway
Spotswood (1991; Australian). . . . . . . . . . . . . Caroline
The Efficiency Expert (1992; Australian). . . . . . Caroline

## McIntaggart, Peggy

*Video Tapes:*

**Playboy Video Centerfold: Peggy McIntagart**
(1989). . . . . . . . . . . . . . . . . . . . . . . . . . . . Playmate
••• 0:00—Nude throughout.
**Playboy Video Calendar 1991** (1990) . . . . .February
••• 0:05—Nude.
**Playmates at Play** (1990) . . . . . . . . . . . Gotta Dance
Rock Video Girls 2 (1992) . . . . . . . . . . . . . . . Herself
*Magazines:*
**Playboy** (Jan 1990) . . . . . . . . . . . . . . . . . . . . Playmate
Playboy's Book of Lingerie (Jul 1991). . . . . . . . . Herself

**Playboy's Book of Lingerie** (Sep 1991) . . . . . .Herself
••• 28-29—Full frontal nudity.
**Playboy's Book of Lingerie** (Jan 1992) . . . . . .Herself
•• 72—Right breast.
**Playboy's Book of Lingerie** (Mar 1992). . . . . .Herself
••• 68—Breasts.
**Playboy's Bathing Beauties** (Apr 1992). . . . . .Herself
••• 28—Breasts.
**Playboy's Book of Lingerie** (May 1992) . . . . .Herself
••• 14—Full frontal nudity.
**Playboy's Career Girls** (Aug 1992)
. . . . . . . . . . . . . . . . . . . . . . . . . . . Baywatch Playmates
••• 6—Full frontal nudity.
**Playboy's International Playmates** (Mar 1993)
. . . . . . . . . . . . . . . . . . . . . . . . . . . . . . . . . . . . .Herself
••• 104-108—Nude.
**Playboy's Bathing Beauties** (Apr 1993). . . . . .Herself
• 5—Left breast and buns.
**Playboy's Book of Lingerie** (Jan 1994) . . . . . .Herself
•• 90-91—Buns.

## • McIntosh, Michelle

*Films:*

**Secret Sins** (1992) . . . . . . . . . . . . . . . . . . . Sara Jenson
• 0:29—Tip of right breast, sticking out of bubbles in
bubble bath, then putting on bra in bedroom while
wearing panties.
•• 0:43—Breasts, while making love with Johnny on
sofa and in living room.
Venice/Venice (1992) . . . . . . . . . . . . . . . . . . . . . . . n.a.

## McIntosh, Valerie

*Films:*

Gimme an "F" (1981) . . . . . . . . . . One of the "Vikings"
*a.k.a. T & A Academy 2*
Weekend Pass (1984) . . . . . . . . . . . . . . . . . . . . . Etta
**The Naked Cage** (1985) . . . . . . . . . . . . . . . . . . Ruby
••• 0:24—Breasts and buns in infirmary, then getting attacked by Smiley. Brief lower frontal nudity.
• 0:28—Breasts, while hanging by rope, dead.
Quicksilver (1986) . . . . . . . . . . . . . . . . . . . . . . Hooker
**The Mambo Kings** (1992). . . . . . . . . . . . . Tracy Blair
•• 1:10—Breasts, getting her bathing suit after Armand
Assante discovers her with Antonio Banderas.

## McIssac, Marianne

*Films:*

**In Praise of Older Women** (1978; Canadian) . . Julika
•• 0:23—Breasts and buns, getting into bed with Tom
Berenger.
*TV:*
The Baxters (1980-81) . . . . . . . . . . . . . . .Allison Baxter

## McIver, Susan

*Films:*
**I Spit on Your Corpse** (1974) ............ Donna
*a.k.a. Girls for Rent*
••• 0:24—Breasts undressing for a guy. More breasts
and buns making love in bed with him, then getting
out of bed.
**Policewomen** (1974) .................... Laura
•• 0:42—Breasts and buns, taking off two piece swimsuit and getting into the shower with Doc.
••• 0:44—Breasts in the shower after Doc leaves.
Shampoo (1975)...................... Customer
Smokey and the Bandit (1977) ........... Hot Pants
Thunder Alley (1985) ................... Redhead

## McKamy, Kim

a.k.a. Adult film actress Ashlyn Gere.
*Films:*
Evil Laugh (1986) ...................... Connie
Creepozoids (1987)...................... Kate
Dreamaniac (1987)......................... Pat
Angel III: The Final Chapter (1988) ...... Video Girl #1
**Fatal Instinct** (1991) ...... Frank Stegner's Girlfriend
*a.k.a. To Kill For*
(Unrated version reviewed.)
•• 0:01—Breasts, opening her towel in front of Frank at
night before he gets shot.
*Video Tapes:*
**High Society Centerspread Video #16: Ashlyn
Gere** (1990) ...................... Ashlyn Gere

## McKee, Lonette

*Films:*
Sparkle (1976) ......................... Sister
Which Way Is Up? (1977) ................. Vanetta
Cuba (1979).................... Therese Mederos
The Cotton Club (1984) ........... Lila Rose Oliver
Brewster's Millions (1985) ......... Angela Drake
Round Midnight (1986; U.S./French) .... Darcey Leigh
Gardens of Stone (1987)................. Betty Rae
**Jungle Fever** (1991) ..................... Drew
•• 0:04—Left breast while making love with Wesley
Snipes in bed.
• 2:03—Brief left breast in bed with Snipes again.
Malcolm X (1992)................... Louise Little
*Miniseries:*
Queen (1993)............................ Alice
*Magazines:*
**Playboy** (Dec 1976)............. Sex Stars of 1976
••• 189—Breasts.

## • McLeod, Shannon

*Films:*
Lightning, The White Stallion (1986)........ Daphne
Necromancer (1988)...................... Edna
The Refrigerator (1992)............. East Village Girl
**Animal Instincts 2** (1993) ........... Miss Geary
•• 0:14—In black bra, then breasts and buns in panties
after taking off her top while trying to tease Steve.

••• 0:20—Breasts, after taking off bra and making love
with a guy in bed.
**Witchcraft 6: The Devil's Mistress** (1993) ..... Cat
(Unrated version reviewed.)
•• 0:17—In bra, then right breast, while making love
with Jonathan in front seat of car.
• 0:42—Brief lower frontal nudity, while cutting a
string off her mini skirt.
• 1:01—Left breast, while making love with Will in his
office.
••• 1:13—Breasts, while making love with Jonathan on
trunk of car.
**Seduce Me: Pamela Principle 2** (1994)..... Melinda
• 0:50—Very brief breasts, while in spa.
*Video Tapes:*
**Playboy's Sensual Fantasy for Lovers** (1993)
.................................. Risk-Taking
• 0:43—In black bra and panties, then buns, while
outside during party with her lover.
••• 0:44—Full frontal nudity while making love outside.

## McNeil, Kate

a.k.a. Kathryn McNeil.
*Films:*
Beach House (1981)....................... Cindy
House on Sorority Row (1983)............ Katherine
**Monkey Shines: An Experiment in Fear** (1988)
.............................. Melanie Parker
• 1:07—Brief upper half of right breast, while making
love with Allan. Dark, hard to see anything.
*Miniseries:*
North and South, Book II (1986) ...... Augusta Barclay
*TV:*
As the World Turns .......... Karen Haines-Stenbeck
WIOU (1990-91) ................... Taylor Young
Bodies of Evidence (1993) .................. Nora

## McNichol, Kristy

*Films:*
The End (1978) ..................... Julie Lawson
Little Darlings (1980) ..................... Angel
The Night the Lights Went Out in Georgia (1981)
............................... Amanda Child
Only When I Laugh (1981)................... Polly
The Pirate Movie (1982; Australian) .......... Mabel
**White Dog** (1982) .................. Julie Sawyer
• 1:25—Most of the inside of breasts in gaping tank
top when bending over to help lift dog off Burl Ives.
**Just the Way You Are** (1984) .............. Susan
• 0:50—Very brief left breast showing her friend that
she's not too hot because there is nothing under her
white coat. Medium long shot.
You Can't Hurry Love (1984) .............. Rhonda
**Dream Lover** (1986) .............. Kathy Gardner
• 0:17—Very, very brief right breast getting out of
bed, then walking around in a white top and underwear.
0:21—Walking around in the white top again. Same
scene used in flashbacks at 0:34, 0:46 and 0:54.

**Two Moon Junction** (1988) . . . . . . . . . . . . Patti Jean
  •• 0:42—Breasts in gas station restroom changing
     camisole tops with Sherilyn Fenn.
The Forgotten One (1989) . . . . . . . . . Barbara Stupple
     0:06—Jogging in braless pink top, then talking to
     Terry O'Quinn.
     1:33—In pink top, lying in bed.
*Made for TV Movies:*
Like Mom, Like Me (1978) . . . . . . . . . . Jennifer Gruen
My Old Man (1979) . . . . . . . . . . . . . . . . . . . . . Jo Butler
Women of Valor (1986) . . . . . . . . . . . . . . . T.J. Nolan
Baby of the Bride (1991) . . . . . . . . . . . . . . . . . . .Mary
Mother of the Bride (1993) . . . . . . . . . . . . . . . . . .Mary
*TV:*
Apple's Way (1974-75) . . . . . . . . . . . . . . Patricia Apple
Family (1976-80) . . . . . . . . . Letitia "Buddy" Lawrence
Empty Nest (1989- ) . . . . . . . . . . . . . . . Barbara Weston

## McQuade, Kris

*Films:*
**Alvin Purple** (1973; Australian). . . . . . . . . . .Samantha
  ••• 0:21—Breasts and buns, while painting Alvin's body.
**Alvin Rides Again** (1974; Australian) . . . . . . . . Mandy
  ••• 0:48—Full frontal nudity, taking off red dress and
     getting into bed with Alvin. More breasts lying in
     bed. Long scene.
Lonely Hearts (1983; Australian) . . . . . . . . . .Rosemarie
The Coca-Cola Kid (1985; Australian) . . . . . . . . Juliana

## • McTague, Heather

*Films:*
Beach Beverly Hills (1992) . . . . . . . . . . . . . . . Michelle
**Intimate Obsession** (1992) . . . . . . . . Beth Thompson
     (Unrated version reviewed.)
  ••• 0:38—Nude, while making love with Tom in bed-
     room. (She's wearing a dark wig and sunglasses.)
     Long scene.
  • 1:04—Breasts on TV in video playback that Rachel
     watches.
  • 1:10—Left breast, while sitting on couch and kissing
     Tom.
*Magazines:*
Sport (Jul 1994) . . . . . . . . . . . . . . . . . . . . . . . Splash!

## McTeer, Janet

*Films:*
Half Moon Street (1986) . . . . . Van Arkady's Ambassador
     *a.k.a. Escort Girl*
Hawks (1988; British) . . . . . . . . . . . . . . . . . . . . . Hazel
*Made for TV Movies:*
**Portrait of a Marriage** (1992; British)
     . . . . . . . . . . . . . . . . . . . . . . . . . Vita Sackville-West
  • 0:47—Brief right breast, while lying in bed with Vio-
     let.
  •• 2:28—(0:04 into Part 3) Left breast and buns, get-
     ting out of bed. Brief breasts and buns, putting robe
     on.

## McVeigh, Rose

a.k.a. Rosemary McVeigh.
*Films:*
A Night in Heaven (1983) . . . . . . . . . . . . . . . . . Alison
**Porky's Revenge** (1985; Canadian) . . . . . Miss Webster
  ••• 0:39—In black bra, panties, garter belt and stock-
     ings then breasts in her apartment with Mr. Dobish
     while Pee Wee and his friends secretly watch.
Casanova (1987) . . . . . . . . . . . . . . . . . . . Captain's Wife

## McWhirter, Jillian

*Films:*
After Midnight (1989) . . . . . . . . . . . . . . . . . . . . Allison
Nowhere to Run (1989) . . . . . . . . . . . . . . . . . . Cynthia
**Dune Warriors** (1990). . . . . . . . . . . . . . . . . . . . . Val
  • 0:25—Brief right breast with Miranda in under-
     ground lake. (Her hair is in the way of her left
     breast.)
Beyond the Call of Duty (1991) . . . . . . . . . Mary Jackson
Servants of Twilight (1991) . . . . . . . . . . Vera Lancaster
Where Sleeping Dogs Lie (1991) . . . . . . . . Dol Whitney

## Medak, Karen

*Films:*
**A Girl to Kill For** (1989) . . . . . . . . . . . . . . . . . . Sue
  ••• 0:17—Breasts showering at the beach after surfing
     with Chuck.
     0:38—In bra lying on desk in office with Chuck.
  •• 1:08—Breasts in spa when Chuck takes her shirt off.
     Then miscellaneous shots making love.
The Marrying Man (1991) . . . . . . . . . . . . . . . . Sherry
     *a.k.a. Too Hot to Handle*
Switch (1991) . . . . . . . . . . . . . . . . . . . . . Saleswoman

## • Meiner, Melissa

*Video Tapes:*
**California Girl Fox Hunt Bikini Competition #6**
     . . . . . . . . . . . . . . . . . . . . . . . . . . . . . . . . .Chanel
  ••• 0:19—Buns in two piece swimsuit.
     0:49—Buns during review.
     0:54—5th place runner up.
*Magazines:*
**Playboy's Great Playmate Search** (Feb 1994)
     . . . . . . . . . . . . . . . . . . . . . . . . . . . . . . . .Herself
  • 61—In bra and lower frontal nudity.

## Mejias, Isabelle

*Films:*
Daughter of Death (1982) . . . . . . . . . . . . . . . . . .Julie
     *a.k.a. Julie Darling*
**Bay Boy** (1985; Canadian) . . . . . . . . . . . . Mary McNeil
  •• 1:28—Brief breasts in her bedroom with Kiefer Suth-
     erland, then brief breasts in bed with him.
Higher Education (1987; Canadian) . . . . . Carrie Hanson
Meatballs III (1987) . . . . . . . . . . . . . . . . . . . . .Wendy
Fall From Innocence (1988) . . . . . . . . Marsa Cummins
State Park (1988; Canadian). . . . . . . . . . . . . . Marsha
Scanners 2: The New Order (1991) . . . . .Alice Leonardo

*Made for TV Movies:*
Special People (1984) . . . . . . . . . . . . . . . . . . . . Julie
*Magazines:*
**Playboy** (Nov 1985) . . . . . . . . . . Sex in Cinema 1985
•• 133—Right breast in still from *The Bay Boy.*

## Melato, Mariangela

*Films:*
Love and Anarchy (1974; Italian). . . . . . . . . . . . Salome
The Nada Gang (1974; French/Italian) . . . . . . . . .Cash
The Seduction of Mimi (1974; Italian). . . . . . . . . .Fiore
**Swept Away** (1975; Italian). . . . . . . . . Raffaela Lenzetti
*a.k.a. Swept Away...by an unusual destiny in the blue sea of august*
•• 1:10—Breasts on the sand when Giancarlo Giannini catches her and makes love with her.
Moses (1976; British/Italian) . . . . . . . . . .Princess Bithia
Flash Gordon (1980). . . . . . . . . . . . . . . . . . . . . . Kala
So Fine (1981) . . . . . . . . . . . . . . . . . . . . . . . . . .Lira
**Summer Night** (1987; Italian) . . . . . . . . . Signora Bolk
•• 0:26—Breasts behind gauze net over bed making love with a German guy.
•• 1:02—Breasts while on the bed making love with the prisoner.
•• 1:09—Breasts again.
••• 1:13—Buns, while walking out of the ocean, then breasts.

## Melini, Angela

*Films:*
Silk Degrees (1994). . . . . . . . . . . . . . . . . . . . Bonnie
*Video Tapes:*
**Playboy Video Calendar 1993** (1992) . . . . .February
• 0:06—Brief full frontal nudity doing various things outdoors.
••• 0:08—Nude outdoors in Japanese garden.
**Wet and Wild IV** (1992) . . . . . . . . . . . . . . . . .Model
**Playboy's Playmate Review 1993** (1993)
. . . . . . . . . . . . . . . . . . . . . . . . . . . . . . . Miss June
••• 0:44—Nude in fashion designer fantasy.
••• 0:46—Nude in bedroom while it rains outside.
*Magazines:*
**Playboy** (Jun 1992) . . . . . . . . . . . . . . . . . . . Playmate
••• 98-109—Nude.
**Playboy's Playmate Review** (Jun 1993) . . . . . . . June
••• 50-59—Nude.
**Playboy's Book of Lingerie** (Jul 1993) . . . . . . Herself
••• 11—Breasts.
**Playboy's Book of Lingerie** (Nov 1993) . . . . . Herself
••• 14—Breasts.
••• 45—Full frontal nudity.
••• 84—Full frontal nudity.
**Playboy's Book of Lingerie** (Jan 1994). . . . . . Herself
••• 24—Full frontal nudity.
**Playboy Presents Girl of the World** (May 1994)
. . . . . . . . . . . . . . . . . . . . . . . . . . . . . . . . . . Herself
••• 58-61—Nude.
**Playmates at Play** (Jul 1994) . . . . . . . . . . . . Herself
••• 56-59—Full frontal nudity.

**Playboy's Girls of Summer '94** (Jul 1994). . . . Herself
••• 64—Full frontal nudity.
••• 80—Full frontal nudity.

## Mell, Marisa

*Films:*
5 Sinners (1961). . . . . . . . . . . . . . . . . . . . . . . Liliane
French Dressing (1964) . . . . . . . . . . . . Francoise Fayol
Casanova '70 (1965; Italian). . . . . . . . . . . . . . Thelma
City of Fear (1965; British) . . . . . . . . . . . . . . . . Ilona
Masquerade (1965) . . . . . . . . . . . . . . . . . . . . .Sophie
Objective 500 Million (1966) . . . . . . . . . . . . . . . . .Yo
Secret Agent Super Dragon (1966; French/Italian/ German). . . . . . . . . . . . . . . . . . . . . Charity Farrell
Anyone Can Play (1968; Italian) . . . . . . . . . . . . . .Paola
Danger: Diabolik (1968). . . . . . . . . . . . . . . Eva Kant
Mahogany (1975) . . . . . . . . . . . . . . . . . .Carlotta Gavin
**Sex on the Run** (1979; German/French/Italian)
. . . . . . . . . . . . . . . . . . . . . . . . . . . . . .Francesca
*a.k.a. Some Like It Cool*
*a.k.a. Casanova and Co.*
• 0:52—Very, very brief left breast, while getting out of bed with Tony Curtis.
1:12—Braless in white nightgown.
Quest for the Mighty Sword (1989; Italian) . . . .Nephele
*Magazines:*
**Playboy** (Mar 1977) . . . . . . . . Comeback for Casanova
••• 89—Breasts and partial lower frontal nudity in water.

## Meneghel, Xuxa

See: Xuxa.

## Menuez, Stephanie

*Films:*
Clean and Sober (1988). . . . . . . . . . . . . . Ticket Agent
Gremlins 2: The New Batch (1990) . . Clamp's Secretary
**The Rapture** (1991). . . . . . . . . . . . . . . . . . . . .Diane
••• 0:06—Breasts in furniture store with Mimi Rogers, Vic and Randy.
*Made for Cable Movies:*
Blindsided (1993; USA) . . . . . . . . . . . . . Racehorse Girl
*Magazines:*
**Playboy** (Nov 1991) . . . . . . . . . . Sex in Cinema 1991
••• 142—Breasts in a scene from *The Rapture.*

## Menzies, Heather

Wife of actor Robert Urich.
*Films:*
The Sound of Music (1965) . . . . . . . . . . . . . . . Louisa
Hawaii (1966) . . . . . . . . . . . . . . . . . . Mercy Bromley
How Sweet It Is (1968). . . . . . . . . . . . . . . . Tour Girl
Hail, Hero! (1969) . . . . . . . . . . . . . . . . . Molly Adams
Outside In (1972). . . . . . . . . . . . . . . . . . . . . . . Chris
Sssssssss (1973). . . . . . . . . . . . . . . . . Kristine Stoner
*a.k.a. Ssssnake*
Piranha (1978). . . . . . . . . . . . . . . Maggie McKeown
Endangered Species (1982) . . . . . . . . . . . . . . .Susan
*TV:*
Logan's Run (1977-78). . . . . . . . . . . . . . . . . . Jessica

*Magazines:*
**Playboy** (Aug 1973) . . . . . . . . . . . . . . . Tender Trapp
••• 81-85—Nude.

## Mercer, Mae

*Films:*
**The Beguiled** (1971). . . . . . . . . . . . . . . . . . . . . Hallie
• 1:28—Very brief breasts in ripped open dress during flashback.
Dirty Harry (1971). . . . . . . . . . . . . . . . . . . Mrs. Russell
Frogs (1972) . . . . . . . . . . . . . . . . . . . . . . . . . . .Maybelle
Pretty Baby (1978) . . . . . . . . . . . . . . Mama Mosebery

## Meredith, Lee

*Films:*
The Producers (1968) . . . . . . . . . . . . . . . . . . . . . . .Ulla
Hello Down There (1969) . . . . . . . . . . . . . . . . Dr. Wells
Welcome to the Club (1971) . . . . . . . . Betsie Wholecloth
The Stoolie (1972) . . . . . . . . . . . . . . . . . . . . . . . . .n.a.
Hail (1973) . . . . . . . . . . . . . . . . . . . . . . . Mrs. Maloney
Sunshine Boys (1975) . . . . . . . . . . . . . Nurse in Sketch
*Magazines:*
**Playboy** (Sep 1973) . . . . . . . . . . . . . . . . A Star is Made
••• 105-111—Nude in different settings.

## Meredith, Penny

*Films:*
**Happy Housewives** . . . . . . . . . . . . . . . . . Margaretta
• 0:02—Brief right breast, while talking on the telephone while Bob makes love with her.
•• 0:19—Breasts while standing up in bathtub and talking to Bob.
• 0:34—In sheer black lingerie.
• 1:05—Brief breasts pulling her top down when interrupted by the policeman at the window.
The Flesh & Blood Show (1974; British) . . . . . . . . . .n.a.

## • Meril, Macha

*Films:*
**The Married Woman** (1964; French). . . . . . . . . . .n.a.
• 0:07—Brief glimpses of breasts while walking around inside house.
• 0:08—Brief side of left breast, when climbing through window from outside.
The Defector (1966; German/French) . . .Frieda Hoffman
Deep Red Hatchet Murders (1976; Italian)
. . . . . . . . . . . . . . . . . . . . . . . . . . . . Helga Ulmann
Beau Pere (1981; French) . . . . . . . . . .Birthday Hostess
Bolero (1982; French) . . . . . . . . . . . . . . . . . . . Magda
**Vagabond** (1985; French) . . . . . . . . . Madame Landier
•• 0:45—Breasts, while sitting in the bathtub and talking on the phone.
Duet for One (1987) . . . . . . . . . . . . . . . . . . . . . .Anya
Meeting Venus (1990; British) . . . . . . . . . Miss Malikoff
Double Vision (1992; French/Canadian) . . . . . . .Jimmy

## Merkle, Tina

*Films:*
The Lost Empire (1983) . . . . . . . . . . . . . . . Girl Recruit

**The Rosebud Beach Hotel** (1985) . . . . . . . . Bellhop
• 0:49—Breasts, standing in line. Closest to the camera.

## Meyer, Bess

*Films:*
**One More Saturday Night** (1986) . . . . . . . . . . . .Tobi
• 1:02—Brief breasts in bed with Tom Davis.
In the Mood (1987) . . . . . . . . . . Teenage Girl (Slapper)
She's Out of Control (1989) . . . . . . . . . . . . . . . .Cheryl
The Inner Circle (1991; Italian). . . . . . . Katya—Age 16
*TV:*
Parenthood (1990). . . . . . . . . . . . . . . . . . . . . . .Julie
Room For Two (1992-93) . . . . . . . . . . . . .Naomi Dillon
The Boys Are Back (1994- ) . . . . . . . . . . . . . . . . n.a.

## Michael, Joy

*Films:*
**Homework** (1982)
. . . . . . . . Diane, Age 16/Body Double for Joan Collins
•• 0:39—In bra, then breasts in car making out with her boyfriend.
•• 1:18—Breasts, taking off her bra and making love with Tommy. (Supposed to be Joan Collins.)
Fear City (1984) . . . . . . . . . . . . . . . . Metropole Dancer
Johnny Dangerously (1984) . . . . . . . . . . . Chorus Girl
**Surf II** (1984) . . . . . . . . . . . . . . . . . . . . Hot Potato #1
•• 0:25—Breasts taking off bikini top with her friend in lifeguard station at beach with Eric Stoltz and his friend.
•• 0:27—Brief breasts with her friend, after dropping towel when she raises her hands for the police.

## Michaels, Julie

*Films:*
**Roadhouse** (1989) . . . . . . . . . . . . . . . . . . . . .Denise
••• 1:18—Breasts dancing on stage in club in front of Patrick Swayze.
**Point Break** (1991) . . . . . . . . . . . . . . . . Freight Train
• 0:53—Brief breasts in the shower.
• 0:54—Nude, beating up Keanu Reeves in the bathroom during shoot-out. Full frontal nudity while stabbing an FBI agent.
**Doctor Mordrid** (1992). . . . . . . . . . . . . . . . . . Irene
••• 0:00—Breasts and buns, while talking with Brian Thompson, then getting picked up and placed on table.
**Jason Goes to Hell—The Final Friday** (1993)
. . . . . . . . . . . . . . . . . . . . . . Elizabeth Marcus F.B.I.
(Unrated Director's Original Cut reviewed.)
•• 0:03—In white bra and panties, then buns and breasts while starting to take a shower. More breasts after grabbing towel.
**Witchboard 2: The Devil's Doorway** (1993) . .Susan
• 1:17—Brief breasts, in B&W photos that Russel looks at.

## Michaels, Lorraine

Films:
Star 80 (1983). . . . . . . . . . . . . . . . . . Paul's Party Guest
**Malibu Express** (1984). . . . . . . . . . . . Liza Chamberlin
••• 0:23—Breasts in the shower making love with
Shane, while getting photographed by a camera.
B.O.R.N. (1988) . . . . . . . . . . . . . . . . . . . . . Dr. Black
Magazines:
**Playboy** (Apr 1981) . . . . . . . . . . . . . . . . . Playmate
**Playmates at Play** (Jul 1994) . . . . . . . . . . . . . Herself
••• 16-19—Nude while covered with mud.

## Michaels, Michele

Films:
**The Slumber Party Massacre** (1982) . . . . . . . . Trish
•• 0:01—Breasts, in white panties, while getting
dressed.
•• 0:08—Buns, then brief breasts while passing the
soap to Kim.
•• 0:29—Breasts, in white panties, while putting shirt
on while two boys watch from outside.
Video Tapes:
**Scream Queen Hot Tub Party** (1991). . . . . . . . Trish
•• 0:14—Breasts and buns in shower scene from *Slumber Party Massacre.*

## Michaels, Roxanna

Films:
**Emmanuelle 5** (1986). . . . . . . . . . . . . . . Girl No. 2
••• 0:42—Breasts, while talking with the two other girls.
••• 0:43—Breasts, talking to Eddie and Monique Gabrielle.
•• 0:48—Breasts, during rescue/escape.
**The Newlydeads** (1988). . . . . . . . . . . . . . . . . Lynda
0:23—In lacy black bra and panties, while in bed.
•• 0:44—Breasts, while in the shower.
• 0:47—Brief breast, while dead on the shower floor
after being stabbed.
**Caged Fury** (1989) . . . . . . . . . Katherine "Kat" Collins
0:32—In white bra in open blouse on couch with
Jack Carter.
• 0:39—Breasts while getting searched upon entering
prison with other topless women.
Video Tapes:
**Inside Out 3** (1992) . . . . . . . Laila/The Perfect Woman
••• 0:38—Breasts and buns in G-string, changing out of
her wet clothes, while Joe watches.
• 0:43—Brief breasts, taking off clothes on talk show
on TV.
Magazines:
**Playboy's Book of Lingerie** (Sep 1991) . . . . . Herself
• 55—Buns.
•• 72—Right breast and lower frontal nudity.
**Playboy's Book of Lingerie** (Nov 1991) . . . . . Herself
••• 18—Breasts.
**Playboy's Girls of Summer '92** (Jun 1992). . . Herself
•• 19—Buns.
Playboy's Book of Lingerie (Jul 1992). . . . . . . . . Herself

**Playboy's Book of Lingerie** (May 1994) . . . . . Herself
•• 84—Buns and side of right breast.
**Playboy's Book of Lingerie** (Jul 1994). . . . . . . Herself
••• 38—Breasts.

## Michaelsen, Helle

Video Tapes:
**Playboy Video Calendar 1991** (1990). . . . . . . . April
••• 0:14—Nude.
Magazines:
**Playboy** (Aug 1988) . . . . . . . . . . . . . . . . . . . Playmate
**Playboy's Nudes** (Oct 1990) . . . . . . . . . . . . . . Herself
••• 76—Full frontal nudity.
**Playboy's Calendar Playmates** (Nov 1992). . . Herself
••• 91—Full frontal nudity.
**Playboy's International Playmates** (Mar 1993)
. . . . . . . . . . . . . . . . . . . . . . . . . . . . . . . . . . . Herself
••• 34-37—Nude.
**Playboy Presents Playmates in Paradise**
(Mar 1994). . . . . . . . . . . . . . . . . . . . . . . . . . Playmate
••• 30-33—Full frontal nudity.

## Michan, Cherie

Films:
Wrong is Right (1982) . . . . . . . . . . . . . . . . . . Erika
Fever Pitch (1985) . . . . . . . . . . . . . . . . . Rose O'Sharon
A Brilliant Disguise (1994) . . . . . . . . . . . . . . . . . Selma
Made for Cable TV:
**Dream On: The Name of the Game is Five-Card
Stud** (1991; HBO). . . . . . . . . . . . . . . . . . . . . . Allison
••• 0:16—In black bra, then breasts, literally losing her
shirt during poker game.
0:17—Very brief nipple seen through her folded
arms.
Dream On: To the Moon, Alex (1992; HBO). . . . . Allison
Dream On: Hack Like Me (1994; HBO). . . . . . . . Allison
Dream On: Where There's Smoke, You're Fired
(1994; HBO). . . . . . . . . . . . . . . . . . . . . . . . . . Allison

## Michelle, Ann

Films:
**Virgin Witch** (1971; British) . . . . . . . . . . . . . Christine
• 0:00—Brief right breast, during opening credits.
••• 0:06—Breasts and lower frontal nudity, after undressing and getting her body measured by Sybil.
•• 0:17—Breasts, undressing and standing by doorway, then prancing around outside for Peter the
photographer.
••• 0:23—Brief breasts, while lying on car, then more
breasts while standing next to it and posing.
••• 0:27—Full frontal nudity, while posing for photographer outside. Buns while making love with him.
•• 0:33—Nude, undressing and taking a shower.
••• 0:47—Nude, while standing, then lying on table
during ceremony.
•• 0:52—Breasts, while getting out of bed with Sybil.
•• 1:20—Breasts, during ceremony.
• 1:23—Breasts, while getting dressed.
House of Whipcord (1974; British) . . . . . . . . . . . . Julia

**The Haunted** (1976) . . . . . . . .Abanaki/Jennifer Baines
- ••• 0:03—Breasts while on horseback as Abanaki.
- •• 0:06—Breasts, while riding on horseback in the desert.
- •• 0:48—Breasts while lying on towel outside with Patrick at night.
- •• 1:19—Breasts while riding the horse again.

Young Lady Chatterley (1977). . . . . . Gwen (roommate)

**French Quarter** (1978)
. . . . . . "Coke Eye" Laura/Policewoman in French Hotel
- • 0:42—Right breast, when Josie wakes her up.
- ••• 0:43—Breasts in bed, caressing Josie's breasts.
- •• 0:58—Breasts during voodoo ceremony. Close ups of breasts with snake.
- • 1:19—Brief breasts, sitting in bed.
- ••• 1:20—More breasts sitting in bed, talking to a customer. Long scene.

## Michelle, Shelley

*Films:*
My Stepmother Is An Alien (1988)
. . . . . . . . . . . . . . . . . . . Body Double for Kim Basinger
0:12—Pulling stocking on her leg in zero gravity.
In the Cold of the Night (1989) . . . . . . . . . . . Model 3

**Overexposed** (1990)
. . . . . . . . . . . . . .Body Double for Catherine Oxenberg
- •• 0:54—Left breast several times, buns when taking off panties, lower frontal nudity while in bed with Hank. Wearing a wig with wavy hair.

Pretty Woman (1990) . . . . Body Double for Julia Roberts
(Body double for Julia Roberts only at the *begining* of the film when she is getting dressed.)
0:04—In black panties and bra, waking up and getting dressed.

**Bikini Summer** (1991) . . . . . . . . . . . . . . . . . . . . .Jazz
- •• 0:33—Breasts and buns in the shower while Max peeks through hole.
- •• 0:49—Breasts and buns, trying on swimsuits, then having a water fight with Cheryl.

Double Impact (1991). . . . . . . . . . Uncredited Student
Final Analysis (1992) . . . . Body Double for Kim Basinger
Body Parts in the begining. One hand with gun and piece of a leg.
The Magic Bubble (1992) . . . . . . . . . . . . Body Double

**The Naked Truth** (1992) . . . . . . . . . . Miss Honduras
- •• 0:18—Nude, changing into "something more comfortable" in front of the two Franks.
- • 0:22—Buns, in pink sequined G-string two piece swimsuit.

Sunset Strip (1992) . . . . . . . . . . . . . . . . . . . . Veronica

**Hexed** (1993). . . . . . Body Double for Claudia Christian
*a.k.a. All Shook Up*
- •• 0:31—Breasts, while making love on top of Matthew in bed.
- • 0:32—Buns and right breast, getting out of bed.
- • 0:57—Buns and brief left breast, while standing up in bed.

**Married People, Single Sex** (1993) . . . . . . . . . Carol
- ••• 0:54—Breasts and buns in G-string, garter belt and stockings while dancing on stage.
- ••• 1:05—Breasts and buns in black G-string, after opening her bathrobe and giving Will a private dance in the kitchen.

**Rising Sun** (1993) . . . . . . . . . . . . . . . . . . . . . .Blonde
- • 0:44—Very, very brief buns in black G-string, when her dress flies up while spinning around during party.
- •• 0:56—Breasts, while lying down on her back with sushi on her front. More breasts when police bust in.

*Made for Cable Movies:*
**Nails** (1992; Showtime). . . . . . . . . . . . . . Body Double
- •• 0:16—Breasts and buns, several times body double for Anne Archer during love scene with Dennis Hopper.

The Hit List (1993; Showtime) . . . . . . . . . . . . . Dancer
*Magazines:*
**Playboy** (Dec 1991) . . . . . . . . . . . . . . . .Sex Stars 1991
- ••• 187—Side view of right breast and partial lower frontal nudity.

**Playboy** (Apr 1992) . . . . . . . . . . . . . . . Double Vision
- ••• 72-77—Nude.

**Playboy's Career Girls** (Aug 1992) . . . .Double Visions
- ••• 30-35—Nude.

**Playboy's Nudes** (Dec 1992) . . . . . . . . . . . . . .Herself
- ••• 61—Full frontal nudity.

**Playboy's Blondes, Brunettes & Redheads**
(Sep 1993). . . . . . . . . . . . . . . . . . . . . . . . . . . .Herself
- ••• 24-25—Full frontal nudity.

## •Michelle, Vicki

*Films:*
**Virgin Witch** (1971; British) . . . . . . . . . . . . . . Betty
- • 0:00—Brief breasts, while sitting up during opening credits.
- •• 0:31—Breasts, while sitting in bathtub. Nude, getting out. Seen through fish-eye lens.
- •• 1:17—Buns, during witches' ceremony. Left breast, then breasts while lying on table.
- • 1:23—Brief left breast, while on the ground with Johnny.
- • 1:25—Left breast, when Johnny gets up off her.

Oh, Alfie! (1975; British). . . . . . . . . . . . . . . . . . . Bird
*a.k.a. Alfie Darling*
The Greek Tycoon (1978). . . . . . . . . . . . . . . . . . n.a.

## Micula, Stacia

See: Fox, Samantha.

## Mierisch, Susan

*Films:*
**Cave Girl** (1985). . . . . . . . . . . . . Locker Room Student
- •• 0:05—Breasts with four other girls in the girls' locker room undressing, then running after Rex. She's blonde, wearing red panties and a necklace.

**Neon Maniacs** (1985) . . . . . . . . . . . . . . Young Lover
• 0:07—Very brief upper half of right breast while kissing her boyfriend at night.

## Miles, Sarah

*Films:*
The Servant (1963) . . . . . . . . . . . . . . . . . . . . . . Vera
Those Magnificent Men in their Flying Machines (1965)
. . . . . . . . . . . . . . . . . . . . . . . . . Patricia Rawnsley
Blow-Up (1966; British/Italian) . . . . . . . . . . . . . Patricia
**Ryan's Daughter** (1970) . . . . . . . . . . . . . . Rosy Ryan
**Lady Caroline Lamb** (1973). . . . . Lady Caroline Lamb
**The Man Who Loved Cat Dancing** (1973)
. . . . . . . . . . . . . . . . . . . . . . . . . Catherine Crocker
•• 1:04—Back of left breast, then breasts, after taking off her blouse, then washing herself in water.
• 1:20—Brief left breast, while in bed with Burt Reynolds.
**The Sailor Who Fell From Grace with the Sea**
(1976). . . . . . . . . . . . . . . . . . . . . . . Anne Osborne
• 0:18—Breasts sitting at the vanity getting dressed while her son watches through peephole.
•• 0:23—Breasts, fantasizing about her husband.
•• 0:42—Breasts, then nude, while making love with Kris Kristofferson.
• 1:15—Brief right breast, while in bed with Kristofferson.
The Big Sleep (1978; British) . . . . . Charlotte Sternwood
Priest of Love (1980) . . . . . . . . . . . . . . . . . . . Film Star
Venom (1982; British) . . . . . . . . . . . . Dr. Marion Stowe
Ordeal by Innocence (1984) . . . . . . . . . . Mary Durrant
**Steaming** (1985; British) . . . . . . . . . . . . . . . . Sarah
•• 0:23—Breasts while getting into pool with Vanessa Redgrave.
•• 0:49—Breasts while getting undressed.
• 1:31—Nude while lying down next to pool.
Hope and Glory (1987; British) . . . . . . . . . Grace Rohan
Queenie (1987). . . . . . . . . . . . . . . . . . . . . Lady Sybil
White Mischief (1988). . . . . . . . . . . . . . . . . . . . Alice
*Made for Cable Movies:*
A Ghost in Monte Carlo (1990). . . . . . . . . . . . . . . n.a.
*Magazines:*
**Playboy** (Jul 1976)
. . . . . . . . . . . . . . . . Kris and Sarah/The Soul of Sarah
••• 122-129—Nude.
**Playboy** (Nov 1976) . . . . . . . . . . Sex in Cinema 1976
• 146—Partial lower frontal nudity.
**Playboy** (Dec 1976). . . . . . . . . . . . . . Sex Stars of 1976
••• 181—Full frontal nudity standing on bed with Kris Kristofferson.
**Playboy** (Feb 1977). . . . . . . . . . . . . . . The Year in Sex
• 141—Right breast with Kris Kristofferson.
**Playboy** (Jan 1989) . . . . . . . . Women of the Seventies
•• 213—Breasts in bed with Kris Kristofferson.

## Miles, Sherry

*Films:*
Making It (1971) . . . . . . . . . . . . . . . . . . . . . . Debbie
**The Velvet Vampire** (1971) . . . . . . . . . . Susan Ritter
• 0:08—Brief breasts in bed with Lee.
••• 0:18—Breasts sitting up in bed, then making love with Lee.
• 0:21—Breasts in bed in desert during dream scene.
••• 0:22—Breasts sitting up in bed and turning on the light.
• 0:42—Breasts in bed during desert dream scene, long shot.
• 0:55—Breasts in bed during desert dream scene.
••• 0:56—Breasts in bed in desert scene, closer shot with Diane.
• 1:19—Brief breasts in desert scene during flashback.
Your Three Minutes Are Up (1973). . . . . . . . . . Debbie
The Harrad Summer (1974) . . . . . . . . . . . . . . . . Dee
*a.k.a. Student Union*
The Long Dark Night (1977) . . . . . . . . . . . . . . . Lois
*a.k.a. The Pack*
*TV:*
Hee Haw (1971-72) . . . . . . . . . . . . . . . . . . . Regular

## Miles, Sylvia

*Films:*
**Midnight Cowboy** (1969). . . . . . . . . . . . . . . . . Cass
• 0:20—Brief buns, running into bedroom and jumping onto bed with Jon Voight. More when changing the TV channel with the remote control. Most of her right breast in bed under Voight.
**The Sentinel** (1977). . . . . . . . . . . . . . . . . . . Gerde
• 0:33—Brief left breast, three times, standing behind Beverly D'Angelo. Right breast, ripping dress of Christina Raines. B&W dream.
1:23—Brief breasts, three times, with D'Angelo made up to look like zombies, munching on a dead Chris Sarandon.
1:27—Very brief right breast during big zombie scene.
• 1:28—Brief breasts when the zombies start dying.
The Funhouse (1981). . . . . . . . . . . . . . . Madame Zena
Wall Street (1987) . . . . . . . . . . . . . . . . . . . . . Realtor
Crossing Delancey (1988) . . . . . . Hannah Mandelbaum
Spike of Bensonhurst (1988) . . . . . . . . Congresswoman
She-Devil (1989) . . . . . . . . . . . . . . . . . . . Mrs. Fisher
*Magazines:*
**Playboy** (Nov 1977) . . . . . . . . . . Sex in Cinema 1977
•• 162—Left breast from *The Sentinel*. Sort of B&W.

## Milford, Penelope

*Films:*
Man on a Swing (1974) . . . . . . . . . . . . . . Evelyn Moore
**Valentino** (1977; British) . . . . . . . . . . . . Lorna Sinclair
••• 1:28—Nude, while making love with Rudolf Nureyev in bedroom. Long scene.

**Coming Home** (1978) . . . . . . . . . . . . . Viola Munson
- 1:19—Doing strip tease in room with Jane Fonda and two guys. Sort of right breast peeking out between her arms when she changes her mind.

The Last Word (1979) . . . . . . . . . . . . . . . . .Denise Travis
Endless Love (1981) . . . . . . . . . . . . . . . . . . . . . .Ingrid
Take This Job and Shove It (1981) . . . . . . Lenore Meade
**Blood Link** (1983). . . . . . . . . . . . . . . . . . . Julie Warren
- • 0:22—Breasts while in bed with Craig. Very brief left breast, when she grabs the pillow.
- • 1:24—In black bra in greenhouse with Keith, then breasts.
- 1:27—Brief buns, while on top of Keith. Long shot.
- • 1:28—Right breast, when Keith tries to strangle her.
- ••• 1:35—Breasts, while in bedroom with Keith.

The Golden Seal (1983) . . . . . . . . . . . . . . . . Tania Lee
Heathers (1989) . . . . . . . . . . . . . . . . Pauline Fleming
Cold Justice (1992; British) . . . . . . . . . . . . . . . . Eileen

*Made for Cable TV:*

**The Hitchhiker: Man at the Window** (1985; HBO)
. . . . . . . . . . . . . . . . . . . . . . . . . . . . . Diane Hampton
- •• 0:09—Breasts in white panties making love with her husband on the couch.

*Made for TV Movies:*

Rosie: The Rosemary Clooney Story (1982) . . . . . . .Betty
The Burning Bed (1984) . . . . . . . . . . . . . . . . . . . Gaby

# Milhench, Ann

*Films:*

Blood Debts (1983). . . . . . . . . . . . . . . . . . . . . . . .Lisa
**Sloane** (1984) . . . . . . . . . . . . . . . . . . . . Janice Thursby
- •• 0:02—Breasts and buns getting out of shower and being held by kidnappers.

# Miller, Ginger

*Films:*

Beach Beverly Hills (1992) . . . . . . .Bikini Audition Girl 14

*Video Tapes:*

**Wild Bikinis** (1987) . . . . . . . . . . . . . . . . . . . Herself
- 0:23—Buns in white two piece swimsuit, while rubbing oil on herself.
- 0:26—Buns on pool float with Beckie Mullen.

Boxing Babes (1991). . . . . . . . . . . . . . . . . . . . Herself
**Made for Man: Intimate Fantasy** (1992)
. . . . . . . . . . . . . . . . . . . . . . . . . . . . Darling Nikki
- 0:03—Buns in G-string, doing strip routine out of black outfit.
- 0:11—Buns, during gelatin wrestling with Baby Driver.
- 0:19—Stripping to two piece swimsuit.
- 0:37—Stripping down to two piece silver swimsuit.
- 0:47—Wrestling with Sugar Ray Rene in lettuce.
- 0:55—Brief left breast, popping out of swimsuit top.

*Magazines:*

**Penthouse** (Sep 1986) . . . . . . . . . . . . . . . . . . . Pet

# Miller, Marjorie

See: Blondi.

# Miller, Mindi

See: Randolph, Ty.

# • Miller, Penelope Ann

*Films:*

Adventures in Babysitting (1987) . . . . . . . . . . . .Brenda
Big Top Pee Wee (1988). . . . . . . . . . . . . . . . . .Winnie
Biloxi Blues (1988) . . . . . . . . . . . . . . . . . . . . . Daisy
Miles From Home (1988) . . . . . . . . . . . . . . . . . .Sally
Dead Bang (1989) . . . . . . . . . . . . . . . . . . . . . .Linda
Downtown (1990) . . . . . . . . . . . . . . . . Lori Mitchell
The Freshman (1990). . . . . . . . . . . . . . . Tina Sabatini
Kindergarten Cop (1990) . . . . . . . . . . . . . . . . .Joyce
Awakenings (1991) . . . . . . . . . . . . . . . . . . . . .Paula
Other People's Money (1991) . . . . . . . . . . Kate Sullivan
Chaplin (1992; British/U.S.) . . . . . . . . Edna Purviance
The Gun in Betty Lou's Handbag (1992) . . . . .Betty Lou
Year of the Comet (1992) . . . . . . Margaret Harwood
**Carlito's Way** (1993) . . . . . . . . . . . . . . . . . . . . Gail
- ••• 0:59—Breasts, while dancing on stage in club in auburn wig.
- ••• 1:18—Breasts, after opening her robe and enticing Al Pacino in her apartment.

*Video Tapes:*

The Kathy Kaehler Fitness System (1992)
. . . . . . . . . . . . . . . . . . . . . . . . . . . Exercise Student

# Miller, Rebecca

*Films:*

Regarding Henry (1991). . . . . . . . . . . . . . . . . .Linda
**Consenting Adults** (1992) . . . . . . . . . . . . . . .Kay Otis
- 0:28—Buns and brief side view of left breast, while getting out of tub. Seen through shutters while Kevin Kline watches through the window.

The Pickle (1992) . . . . . . . . . . . . . . . . . . . . . Carrie
Wind (1992) . . . . . . . . . . . . . . . . . . . . Abigail Weld

# Miller, Sherrie

*Films:*

**Goin' All the Way** (1981) . . . . . . . . . . . . . . . . Candy
  0:47—Brief right breast getting out of bubble bath.
- •• 0:49—Breasts with Artie during his fantasy.

Separate Vacations (1985) . . . . . . . . . . . . . . . . Sandy

# Millian, Andra

*Films:*

Stacy's Knights (1983) . . . . . . . . . . . . . . . . . . . Stacy
**Nightfall** (1988). . . . . . . . . . . . . . . . . . . . . . . .Anna
- 0:12—Very brief breasts making love with David Birney.
- 0:41—Very brief breasts making love in front of a fire.
  0:58—Same scene in a flashback while the guy is talking to another woman.

Love Potion No. 9 (1992). . . . . . . . . . . . . . . Matron

*TV:*

Paper Chase (1984-86) . . . . . . . . . . . . . . . . . .Laura

# • Millington, Mary

*Films:*

**Come Play with Me** (1977; German) . . . . . . . . Nurse
**Playbirds** (1978; British) . . . . . . . . . . . . .Lucy Sheridan
••• 0:55—White bra, black garter belt, panties and
stockings then nude taking off her clothes during
the policewoman audition.
• 1:00—Breasts giving an old man a massage in a
massage parlor.
••• 1:05—Breasts making love with another woman
from the massage parlor.
••• 1:14—Nude doing a photo session for *Playbird* magazine.

# Million, Tiffany

See: Margot, Sandra.

# Mills, Brooke

*Films:*

**The Big Doll House** (1971) . . . . . . . . . . . . . . Harrad
• 0:28—Side of right breast, while lying in bed before
rolling over.
Legacy of Blood (1973). . . . . . . . . . . . . . . .Leslie Dean
The Student Teachers (1973) . . . . . . . . . . . . . . . .n.a.
Walking Tall, Part II (1975) . . . . . . . . . . . . . . Ruby Ann
Two-Minute Warning (1976). . . . . . . . . Tyler's Girlfriend
Freaky Friday (1977) . . . . . . . . . . . . . . . Mrs. Gibbons

# Mills, Donna

*Films:*

The World's Oldest Living Bridesmaid . . . . . . . . . . .n.a.
**Play Misty for Me** (1971). . . . . . . . . . . . . . . Tobie
• 1:10—Brief side view of right breast hugging Clint
Eastwood in a pond near a waterfall. Long shot, hard
to see.
Murph the Surf (1975) . . . . . . . . . . . . . . Ginny Eaton
Firel (1977). . . . . . . . . . . . . . . . . . . . . . . . . . . .n.a.
False Arrest (1991) . . . . . . . . . . . . . . . . Joyce Lukezic
Video tape version is shorter than the miniseries that
aired on TV. It also has nude scenes added.
*Made for Cable TV:*
Dream On: Martin Tupper in "Magnum Farce"
(1994; HBO) . . . . . . . . . . . . . . . . . . . . . . . Ashlyn
*Made for TV Movies:*
Doctor's Private Lives (1978). . . . . . . . .Dr. Beth Demery
The President's Child (1992) . . . . . . Elizabeth Hemming
My Name is Kate (1994) . . . . . . . . . . . . . . . . . . Kate
*TV:*
The Good Life (1971-72). . . . . . . . . . . . . . Jane Miller
Knots Landing (1980-89)
. . . . . . . . . . . . . . Abby Ewing Sumner Cunningham
*Magazines:*
**Playboy** (Nov 1989) . . . . . . . . . . . . . . . . .Oh! Donna
• 82-87—Buns in photos taken around 1966.

# Mills, Hayley

Daughter of actor Sir John Mills.
Sister of actress Juliet Mills.
*Films:*
Tiger Bay (1959; British). . . . . . . . . . . . . . . . . . Gillie
Pollyanna (1960) . . . . . . . . . . . . . . . . . . . . .Pollyanna
Whistle Down the Wind (1961; British) . . Kathy Bostock
In Search of the Castaways (1962) . . . . . . . Mary grant
The Chalk Garden (1964). . . . . . . . . . . . . . . . . Laurel
The Moon-Spinners (1964) . . . . . . . . . . . . Nikky Ferris
The Parent Trap (1964)
. . . . . . . . . . . . . . . . Sharon McKendirck/Susan Evers
That Darn Cat (1965). . . . . . . . . . . . . . . Patti Randall
The Trouble with Angels (1966) . . . . . . . . Mary Clancy
**Deadly Strangers** (1974; British). . . . . . . . . . . . Belle
1:02—Buns in bathtub when her uncle watches her.
1:05—In black bra, garter belt and panties while
Steven fantasizes as he sees her through a keyhole.
••• 1:13—In white bra and panties while Steven watch-
es through keyhole, then breasts after taking off bra
and reading a newspaper.
1:15—In white bra, getting dressed.
Endless Night (1977) . . . . . . . . . . . . . . . . . . . . Ellie
Appointment with Death (1988) . . . . . . . .Miss Quinton
*Miniseries:*
The Flame Trees of Thika (1982). . . . . . . . . . . . . Tilly
*Made for TV Movies:*
The Parent Trap II (1986) . . . . Sharon Ferris/Susan Corey

# Mills, Juliet

Daughter of actor Sir John Mills.
Sister of actress Hayley Mills.
*Films:*
The Rare Breed (1966) . . . . . . . . . . . . . . . Hilary Price
**Avanti!** (1973) . . . . . . . . . . . . . . . . . . Pamela Piggott
(Not available on video tape. Shown on *The Arts and Entertainment Channel* periodically. Scenes are listed as
0:00 since I can't time correctly with the commercials.)
0:00—Buns, climbing out of the water onto a rock.
• 0:00—Side view of right breast while lying on rock
and talking to Jack Lemmon.
••• 0:00—Brief breasts while waving to fishermen on a
passing boat.
0:00—Brief buns putting something up in the closet
in Jack Lemmon's hotel room.
Beyond the Door (1975; Italian/U.S.) . . . . . . . . . Jessica
Waxwork II: Lost in Time (1991). . . .The Defense Lawyer
*Miniseries:*
Till We Meet Again (1989) . . . . . . . . . . . . . . .Vivianne
*Made for TV Movies:*
Columbo: No Time To Die (1992) . . . . . . .Elaine Hacker
*TV:*
Nanny and the Professor (1970-71) . . . . Phoebe Figalilly
*Magazines:*
**Playboy** (Nov 1973) . . . . . . . . . . . Sex in Cinema 1973
••• 153—Breasts in photo from *Avanti*.

# Mimieux, Yvette

*Films:*

The Time Machine (1960)................. Weena
Where the Boys Are (1960) ............... Melanie
Diamond Head (1962) ............. Sloan Howland
The Four Horsemen of the Apocalypse (1962)
.................................. Chi-Chi Desnoyers
Three in the Attic (1968)............. Tobey Clinton
**Jackson County Jail** (1976) .......... Dinah Hunter
• 0:39—Breasts in jail cell getting raped by policeman.
The Black Hole (1979)............. Dr. Kate McGraw
Brainwash (1982) ..................... Bianca Ray
*Made for TV Movies:*
Outside Chance (1978).............. Dinah Hunter
Perry Mason: The Case of the Desperate Deception
(1990)..................... Danielle Altmann
*TV:*
The Most Deadly Game (1970-71) ..... Vanessa Smith
Berrengers (1985)................... Shane Bradley

# Minnick, Dani

*Films:*

Lena's Holiday (1990) ................. Julie Eden
The Sleeping Car (1990).................. Joanne
*Made for Cable TV:*
**Tales From the Crypt: The Man Who was Death**
(1989; HBO) ................... Cynthia Baldwin
• 0:17—Very brief side view of right breast in shower.

# • Minter, Kristin

*Films:*

Cool As Ice (1991) ...................... Kathy
**Flashfire** (1993)....................... Lisa Cates
•• 0:18—In black bra, panties, garter belt and stockings, then breasts while in hotel room with Artie.
•• 0:20—Breasts while making love in bed with Artie.
•• 0:21—Breasts when hit men burst into the room and kill Artie.
• 0:49—Buns in panties and side of right breast while undressing when Billy Zane sees her.
••• 1:11—Breasts, while making love on bed in a boat with Zane.

# Miou-Miou

*Films:*

**Going Places** (1974; French)........... Marie-Ange
••• 0:14—Breasts sitting in bed, filing her nails. Full frontal nudity standing up and getting dressed.
•• 0:48—Breasts in bed with Pierrot and Jean-Claude.
• 0:51—Left breast under Pierrot.
••• 0:52—Buns in bed when Jean-Claude rolls off her. Full frontal nudity sitting up with the two guys in bed.
•• 1:21—Brief breasts opening the door. Breasts and panties walking in after the two guys.
• 1:27—Partial left breast taking off dress and walking into house.
1:28—Very brief breasts while closing the shutters.

•• 1:31—Full frontal nudity in open dress running after the two guys. Long shot. Full frontal nudity putting her wet dress on.
• 1:41—Breasts while in back of car. Dark.
The Genius (1976; Italian/German/French) ...... Lucy
**Jonah—Who Will be 25 in the Year 2000**
(1976; Swiss) ........................... Marie
This Sweet Sickness (1977; French) ........... Juliette
*a.k.a. dites-lui que je l'aime*
1:37—In wet white braless bridal gown, while getting carried out of pool by Gérard Depardieu.
**Memoirs of a French Whore** (1979)......... Marie
My Other Husband (1981; French) ............ Alice
Entre Nous (1983; French) .............. Madeleine
*a.k.a. Coup de Foudre*
Dog Day (1984; French) .................... Jessica
**La Lectrice** (1989; French)........ Constance/Marie
*a.k.a. The Reader*
1:06—Making love with a guy while reading to him in bed.
• 1:18—Full frontal nudity lying in bed. Close-up pan shot from lower frontal nudity, then left breast, then right breast.
• 1:20—Very brief right breast, then lower frontal nudity getting dressed.
Germinal (1993; French) ....................... n.a.
Tango (1993; French)........................ Marie
*Magazines:*
**Playboy** (Nov 1990) .......... Sex in Cinema 1990
•• 144—Breasts in still from *Going Places*.

# Miracle, Irene

*Films:*

**Midnight Express** (1978; British) ........... Susan
•• 1:39—Breasts in prison visiting booth showing her breasts to Brad Davis so he can masturbate.
Inferno (1980; Italian) .................... Rose Elliot
**In the Shadow of Kilimanjaro** (1985) . Lee Ringtree
• 0:18—Brief breasts in bed with Timothy Bottoms. Kind of hard to see anything because it's dark.
The Last Days of Philip Banter (1987)... Elizabeth Banter
Puppet Master (1989) ............... Dana Hadley
**Watchers II** (1990) .............. Sarah Ferguson
0:28—In pink leotard, going into aerobics studio.
••• 0:40—Side view in black bra, then breasts a few times in the bathtub.
*Made for TV Movies:*
Shattered Dreams (1990)................... Elaine
*Magazines:*
**Playboy** (Nov 1978) .......... Sex in Cinema 1978
•• 183—Breasts still from *Midnight Express*.

# Mirren, Helen

*Films:*

A Midsummer Night's Dream (1968)......... Hermia
**Age of Consent** (1969; Australian) .......... Cora
• 0:48—Breasts several times in the mirror. Brief lower frontal nudity, kneeling on the floor.

•• 0:55—Brief breasts and buns quite a few time, snorkeling under water.
••• 1:20—Breasts and half of buns, posing in the water for James Mason. Then getting out.

**Savage Messiah** (1972; British). . . . . Gosh Smith-Boyle
••• 0:39—Full frontal nudity, posing for sketches while walking up and down stairs and around. Nice long scene.
•• 1:15—Brief buns, while covering herself up.

O Lucky Man! (1973; British). . . . . . . . .Patricia Burgess

**Caligula** (1980) . . . . . . . . . . . . . . . . . . . . . .Caesonia
(X-rated, 147 minute version.)
  1:02—Side view of buns with Malcolm McDowell
• 1:13—Brief breasts several times getting out of bed to run after McDowell. Dark.
  1:15—Very brief left breast taking off her dress to dry McDowell off.

The Fiendish Plot of Dr. Fu Manchu (1980) . . .Alice Rage

**Hussy** (1980; British) . . . . . . . . . . . . . . . . . . Beaty
•• 0:22—Left breast, then side of right breast, while lying in bed with John Shea.
••• 0:29—Nude, making love in bed with Shea.
•• 0:31—Full frontal nudity in bathtub.

The Long Good Friday (1980; British) . . . . . . . .Victoria

**Excalibur** (1981; British) . . . . . . . . . . . . . Morgana
• 1:31—Side view of left breast under a fishnet outfit climbing into bed.

2010 (1984) . . . . . . . . . . . . . . . . . . . . .Tanya Kirbuk

**Cal** (1984; Irish) . . . . . . . . . . . . . . . . . . . . Marcella
1:18—In a white bra and slip.
•• 1:20—Brief frontal nudity taking off clothes and getting into bed with Cal in his cottage, then right breast making love.

White Knights (1985) . . . . . . . . . . . . . . Galina Ivanova
The Mosquito Coast (1986) . . . . . . . . . . . . . . Mother

**Pascall's Island** (1988; British) . . . . . . . Lydia Neuman
• 1:00—Left breast, lying in bed with Charles Dance. Long shot.

**The Cook, The Thief, His Wife & Her Lover**
(1989; Dutch/French) . . . . . . . . . . . . . .Georgina Spica
0:22—In black bra in restroom performing fellatio on Michael.
•• 0:32—In lingerie undressing, then lower frontal nudity, buns and left breast in kitchen with Michael.
• 0:42—Buns and right breast, while making love with Michael again.
•• 0:57—Breasts sitting and talking with Michael.
1:01—Buns, kneeling on table.
• 1:05—Brief breasts, while leaning back on table with Michael.
1:07—Lower frontal nudity opening her coat for Michael.
• 1:11—Buns and breasts in kitchen.
••• 1:14—Buns, getting into meat truck. Full frontal nudity in truck and walking around with Michael.

Red King, White Knight (1989) . . . . . . . . . . . . . .Anna
When the Whales Came (1989) . . . . . . Clemmie Jenkins
The Comfort of Strangers (1991) . . . . . . . . . . Caroline
The Hawk (1992; British). . . . . . . . . . . . .Annie Marsh

Where Angels Fear to Tread (1992) . . . . . . Lilia Herriton
Dr. Bethune (1993; Canadian/French)
. . . . . . . . . . . . . . . . . . . . . . . . Frances Penny Bethune
*Made for TV Movies:*
**Mystery! Cause Célèbre** (1991) . . . . Alma Rattenbury
•• 0:27—Breasts in bed when Bowman pulls down the sheets in bed.
• 0:28—Brief breasts and buns putting slip on.
Mystery! Prime Suspect (1992)
. . . . . . . . . . . Detective Chief Inspector Jane Tennison
Mystery! Prime Suspect 2 (1993)
. . . . . . . . . . . Detective Chief Inspector Jane Tennison
Mystery! Prime Suspect 3 (1994)
. . . . . . . . . . . Detective Chief Inspector Jane Tennison
*Magazines:*
**Playboy** (Nov 1990) . . . . . . . . . . Sex in Cinema 1990
• 147—Breasts and buns.

## Misch Owens, Laura
*Films:*
The Great Balloon Race (1975). . . . . . . . . . . . . . . n.a.
**French Quarter** (1978) . . . ."Ice Box" Josie/Girl on Bus
• 0:41—Breasts under sheer white nightgown.
••• 0:43—Full frontal nudity taking off nightgown, wearing garter belt. Getting into bed with Laura.
*Magazines:*
**Playboy** (Oct 1974) . . . . . . . . . . . . . Bunnies of 1974
••• 137—Full frontal nudity.
**Playboy** (Feb 1975) . . . . . . . . . . . . . . . . .Playmate
••• 96-105—Nude.
**Playboy** (Jan 1976). . . . . . . . . . . . . Playmate Review
••• 162—Full frontal nudity.

## • Mitchell, Shareen
*Films:*
Out for Justice (1991). . . . . . . . . . . . . . . Laurie Lupo
**American Heart** (1993). . . . . . . . . . . . . . . . .Diane
•• 1:09—Breasts and buns in sheer black panties while dancing in peep show with three other women.
• 1:10—Breasts, while in dressing room. Seen on B&W monitor.
• 1:11—Breasts under sheer top while in dressing room, putting makeup on and getting a drink.

## Moase, Robyn
*Films:*
Journey Among Women (1977; Australian) . . . . . Moira
**Midnight Dancer** (1987; Australian) . . . . . . . .Brenda
*a.k.a. Belinda*
• 0:43—Brief breasts while putting on black top.

## Moen, Jackie
*Films:*
**Shock 'Em Dead** (1990) . . . . . . . . . . . . . . Groupie 4
•• 1:05—Breasts, taking off her top to tempt Martin.
**Wilding, The Children of Violence** (1990)
. . . . . . . . . . . . . . . . . . . . . . . . . . .Car Rape Victim
• 0:23—Very brief right breast in back of car with her boyfriend when the gang of kids terrorizes them.

Class of Nuke 'Em High Part II: Subhumanoid Meltdown (1991) . . . . . . . . . . . . . . . . .Diane/Bald Subhumanoid
Switch (1991) . . . . . . . . . . . . . . . . . . . .Girl at City Grille

## Moffat, Kitty

a.k.a. Katherine Moffat.
*Films:*
**The Beast Within** (1982) . . . . . . . . . . . Amanda Platt
•• 1:32—Breasts, getting her dress torn off by the beast while she is unconscious. Don't see her face, could be a body double.
*Made for TV Movies:*
The Prince of Bel Air (1986) . . . . . . . . . . . . . . . . . Kelli
*TV:*
Boone (1983-84) . . . . . . . . . . . . . . . Susannah Sawyer

## Moffett, Michelle

*Films:*
Hollywood Boulevard II (1989) . . . . . . . . Mary Randolf
**Deathstalker IV: Match of Titans** (1990) . . . . .Kana
••• 0:52—Very brief left breast, then breasts sitting on bed while trying to seduce Vaniat.
••• 0:59—Breasts on bed, trying to seduce Vaniat. More breasts, getting out of bed and getting dressed.
**Hired to Kill** (1990) . . . . . . . . . . . . . . . . . . . . . . .Ana
• 0:46—Left breast in dress, then breasts when Oliver Reed lowers her top.
•• 0:47—More breasts in open dress top.
•• 1:04—Very, very brief tip of right breast, lying on table when Brian Thompson rips her blouse open. More breasts, lying on the table. Dark.
**Wild Cactus** (1992) . . . . . . . . . . . . . . . . . . . .Maggie
(Unrated version reviewed.)
•• 0:20—Breasts while making love with Randall on truck of car outside at night.
••• 0:58—Nude, taking a shower and getting out to talk to Alex.
• 1:00—Brief buns, while walking into bedroom.
••• 1:14—Breasts, while sitting in bed with Alex, then buns in sheer black panties.
**Indecent Behavior** (1993) . . . . . . . . . . . . .Carol Leiter
(Unrated version reviewed.)
•• 0:07—Breasts, while making love under Frederic behind 2-way glass.
•• 0:10—Breasts and buns, while making love on top of Frederic. The camera move around a lot, so it's kind of hard to see.
•• 0:24—In black bra and panties, then breasts and buns, while making love with Robert while being observed behind 2-way glass.
•• 1:06—Breasts while making love with Brenda and getting video taped.
**Sins of the Night** (1993) . . . . . . . . . . . . . . . . . .Kay
(Unrated version reviewed.)
••• 0:20—In black bra, then breasts and lower frontal nudity while making love in bed with Jack. Long scene.
•• 0:22—Breasts and very brief buns, getting out of bed.

Warlock: The Armageddon (1993) . . . . . . . . . . . Celine
*Made for Cable TV:*
The Hitchhiker: Best Shot (1987; HBO) . . . . . .Lorri Ann
*Video Tapes:*
**Eden 6** (1994) . . . . . . . . . . . . . . . . . . . . . . Sissy Lunch
•• 0:18—Breasts, while making love with Brett outside.
••• 0:20—Breasts, while making love with Brett in bed.
• 0:29—In pink swimsuit, then right breast while making out with Brett on bed.
••• 0:36—Breasts, while sitting on edge and in bathtub.
• 0:39—Breasts while in bed with Brett.
••• 1:06—Breasts and buns while stripping in front of Brett outside, then making love.
•• 1:29—Right breast, while making love on beach with Brett.

## Molina, Angela

*Films:*
**That Obscure Object of Desire** (1977; French/ Spanish) . . . . . . . . . . . . . . . . . . . . . . . . . . . . . Conchita
• 0:53—Brief breasts in bathroom.
•• 1:20—Nude dancing in front of a group of tourists.
• 1:29—Brief breasts behind a gate taunting Fernando Rey.
The Sabina (1979; Spanish/Swedish) . . . . . . . . . . Pepa
The Eyes, The Mouth (1983; Italian/French) . . . . . Vanda
Demons in the Garden (1984; Spanish) . . . . . . . .Angela
**Camorra** (1986; Italian) . . . . . . . . . . . . . . Annunziata
Streets of Gold (1986) . . . . . . . . . . . . . . . . . . . . . Elena
1492: Conquest of Paradise (1992; British/U.S./Spanish/ French) . . . . . . . . . . . . . . . . . . . . . . . . . . . . . . .Beatrix

## • Moncrieff, Karen

*Films:*
**Midnight Witness** (1992) . . . . . . . . . . . . . . . . . .Katy
• 1:08—Very brief buns, while making love with Paul in bed in motel (don't see her face). Very brief part of right nipple. Very brief right breast, when falling back onto bed (medium long shot).
Deathfight (1993) . . . . . . . . . . . . . . . . . . . . . . . . . n.a.

## Moncure, Lisa

*Films:*
Moving (1988) . . . . . . . . . . . . . . . . . . . . . Nina Franklin
Lisa (1989) . . . . . . . . . . . . . . . . . . . . . . . . . . . . . Sarah
**Corporate Affairs** (1990) . . . . . . . . . . . . .Carolyn Bean
• 1:07—Very, very brief left breast, while kicking Douglas out of cubicle.
Carnosaur (1993) . . . . . . . . . . . . . . . . . . . . . . . Mallard
*Made for TV Movies:*
Tales of the City (1994) . . . . . . . . . . . . . Spa Attendant

## Monroe, Marilyn

*Films:*
Love Happy (1949) . . . . . . . . . . . . . . . .Grunion's Client
All About Eve (1950) . . . . . . . . . . . . . . . . .Miss Casswell
Gentlemen Prefer Blondes (1953) . . . . . . . . . . . .Lorelei
How to Marry a Millionaire (1953) . . . . . . . . . . . .Pola
There's no Business like Show Business (1954) . . . . Vicky

Bus Stop (1956) .......................... Cherie
The Prince and the Showgirl (1957) ...... Elsie Marina
The Seven Year Itch (1957) ................ The Girl
Some Like it Hot (1959) .......... Sugar Kane Kowa
The Misfits (1961) ................... Roslyn Taber
    0:33—Almost left breast twice stretching and sitting
    up in bed.
    0:39—In two piece swimsuit running out of the lake.
*Video Tapes:*
**Playboy Video Magazine, Volume 12** (1987)
    .............. A Loving Tribute to Marilyn Monroe
  •• 1:02—Buns and left breast in still photos by swim-
    ming pool from unreleased last film.
  ••• 1:03—Breasts in B&W reference photos for artist Earl
    Moran. Taken around 1946-50.
**Hugh Hefner: Once Upon a Time** (1992) ... Herself
  •• 0:12—Brief breasts in first centerfold.
*Magazines:*
**Playboy** (Dec 1953). ....... Sweetheart of the Month
Premiere issue of *Playboy* magazine.
**Playboy** (Jan 1974) ....... Twenty Years of Playmates
  ••• 102—Breasts in centerfold photo.
**Playboy** (Jan 1979) .............. 25 Beautiful Years
  •• 152—Breasts in pose from premiere issue.
**Playboy** (Jan 1987) ........... Marilyn Remembered
**Playboy** (Jan 1989) ............ Women of the Fifties
  •• 114—Breasts in pose from premiere issue.
**Playboy's Nudes** (Oct 1990). .............. Herself
  ••• 3—Breasts
**Entertainment Weekly** (Jun 26, 1992) ...... Herself
  • 16—Breasts behind sheer fabric. Large red "X"
  drawn by Monroe over the photo.
**Playboy** (Jan 1994) ............ Remember Marilyn
  ••• 100-101—Breasts and buns in photos.

# Monroe, Tami
Adult film actress.
*Video Tapes:*
**Big Bust Casting Call** (1992). .............. Jessica
  ••• 0:00—Nude, during her audition.
**Intimate Secrets—How Women Love to be Loved**
(1993). ................................... Tami
  ••• 0:22—In white bra and panties, then breasts on
  couch.

# Montgomery, Julie
*Films:*
Girls Nite Out (1982) ................ Lynn Connors
*a.k.a. Scared to Death*
**Revenge of the Nerds** (1984) .............. Betty
  •• 0:49—Breasts, after taking off robe to take a shower.
  • 1:10—Breasts in photo in pie pan.
Up the Creek (1984) ....................... Lisa
The Kindred (1987). ................. Cindy Russell
**South of Reno** (1987) ................... Susan
  • 1:22—Brief breasts kissing Martin. Dark, hard to see.
  1:25—In motel room wearing black top and panties,
  then pink spandex top with the panties.
Stewardess School (1987) ............. Pimmie Polk

Black Snow (1989). ............. Lindsey Devereaux
Stop! Or My Mom Will Shoot (1992) ........ Secretary
*Made for TV Movies:*
Earth-Star Voyager (1988) ........... Dr. Sally Arthur
Revenge of the Nerds III: The Next Generation (1992)
  ............................. Betty Skolnick
Revenge of the Nerds IV: Nerds in Love (1994) ... Betty
*TV:*
One Life to Live ......................... n.a.

# • Monti, Mary Elaine
*Films:*
**Is There Sex After Death?** (1975)
  ..................... Stag Film Scene/Sue
  •• 0:53—Buns and right breast, while in bed with a guy
  during filming of stag film.
  •• 1:00—Breasts and buns, while in bed with Fred.
*TV:*
Park Place (1981) ................. Joel "Jo" Keene

# Monticelli, Anna-Maria
a.k.a. Anna Jemison.
*Films:*
**Smash Palace** (1981; New Zealand) ..... Jacqui Shaw
  0:21—Silhouette of right breast changing while sitting on the edge of the bed.
  ••• 0:39—Breasts in bed after arguing, then making up
  with Bruno Lawrence.
Heatwave (1983; Australian) ............... Victoria
My First Wife (1985; Australian) .............. Hillary
**Nomads** (1986) .......................... Niki
  • 0:57—Left breast, making love in bed with Pierce
  Brosnan. Dark, hard to see anything.

# • Montone, Rita
*Films:*
**The Children** (1980) .............. Dee Dee Shore
  •• 0:20—Breasts, lying on chair by pool before talking
  to the Sheriff.
Maniac (1980). .......................... Hooker
Bloodsucking Freaks (1982) ................. n.a.

# Moody, Lynne
*Films:*
The Evil (1977). .......................... Felecia
White Dog (1982) ......................... Molly
*Made for Cable Movies:*
Last Light (1993; Showtime) ........ Hope Whitmore
*Miniseries:*
Roots (1977) .............................. Irene
Roots: The Next Generation (1979) ...... Irene Harvey
*Made for TV Movies:*
**Nightmare in Badham County** (1976)
  .......................... Diane Emery
(Nudity added for video tape.)
  • 0:16—Brief breasts close-up of her breasts when
  Chuck Connors rips her T-shirt off in jail cell. (Don't
  see her face.)
The Atlanta Child Murders (1985) ....... Selena Cobb

*TV:*
That's My Mama (1974-75)........ Tracy Curtis Taylor
Soap (1979-81).................... Polly Dawson
E/R (1984-85) ................. Nurse Julie Williams
Knots Landing (1988-90) .......... Patricia Williams

## Moore, Barbara

*Video Tapes:*
**Sexy Lingerie V** (1992) ...................Model
**Playboy Video Calendar 1994** (1993) .........July
••• 0:27—Nude in diner while dancing and posing.
••• 0:29—Nude on couch and in phone booth during fantasies while waiting at a bar.
**Playboy's Playmate Review 1993** (1993)
................................Miss December
••• 0:02—Nude with children's toys in studio.
••• 0:03—Nude, in a stable with a horse.
**Wet and Wild: The Locker Room** (1994) . Playmate
*Magazines:*
**Playboy** (Dec 1992)................... Playmate
••• 142-153—Nude.
**Playboy's Playmate Review** (Jun 1993) ...December
••• 100-107—Nude.
**Playboy's Blondes, Brunettes & Redheads**
(Sep 1993) ........................... Herself
••• 34-35—Breasts.
**Playboy's Book of Lingerie** (Nov 1993) ..... Herself
••• 38—Full frontal nudity.
**Playboy's Nudes** (Dec 1993) .............. Herself
••• 3—Full frontal nudity.
**Playboy's Book of Lingerie** (Jan 1994)...... Herself
••• 77—Breasts.
**Playboy's Bathing Beauties** (Mar 1994)..... Herself
••• 65—Full frontal nudity.
**Playboy's Book of Lingerie** (Mar 1994) ..... Herself
••• 106-107—Nude.
**Playboy's Book of Lingerie** (May 1994)..... Herself
••• 9—Full frontal nudity.
**Playboy's Girls of Summer '94** (Jul 1994) ... Herself
••• 55—Breasts.
**Playboy's Book of Lingerie** (Jul 1994) ...... Herself
••• 11—Full frontal nudity.
••• 44-45—Breasts.
••• 90-91—Breasts.
**Playboy's Book of Lingerie** (Sep 1994) ..... Herself
••• 55—Full frontal nudity.
••• 88-89—Full frontal nudity.

## Moore, Brooke

*Films:*
Nudity Required (1989) ................. Bikini Girl
*Magazines:*
**Playboy's Book of Lingerie** (Mar 1991) ..... Herself
•• 70—Partial right breast and lower frontal nudity.
•• 72—Partial right breast and lower frontal nudity.
**Playboy's Book of Lingerie** (May 1994)..... Herself
• 73—Upper half of right breast.
**Playboy's Book of Lingerie** (Jul 1994) ...... Herself
•• 92—Right breast and lower frontal nudity.

## Moore, Candy

*Films:*
Tomboy and the Champ (1961).......... Tommy Joe
The Night of the Grizzly (1966) .............. Meg
**Lunch Wagon** (1981) ....................Diedra
*a.k.a. Lunch Wagon Girls*
*a.k.a. Come 'N' Get It*
•• 0:53—Breasts under sheer robe, then breasts on couch with Arnie.

## Moore, Christine

*Films:*
**Lurkers** (1987).......................... Cathy
••• 0:19—Breasts in bed, making love with her boyfriend.
• 0:42—Brief breasts in bubble bath during hallucination scene with her mother.
Prime Evil (1987) .............. Alexandra Parkman
0:09—In white bra in locker room.
**Alexa** (1988)............................Alexa
0:04—In red slip in bedroom.
0:06—In black bra, on bed with Tommy.
0:11—In black lingerie talking on phone in bed.
•• 0:24—Breasts lying in bed with Anthony while reminiscing.
•• 1:08—Breasts in bed with Anthony again.
**Thrilled to Death** (1988) ............ Nan Christie
0:31—In bra in women's locker room.
••• 0:38—Breasts in office with Mr. Dance just before killing him.

## Moore, Demi

Wife of actor Bruce Willis.
*Films:*
Parasite (1982)..................... Patricia Welles
**Blame It on Rio** (1984) ............. Nicole Hollis
• 0:19—Very brief right breast turning around to greet Michael Caine and Joseph Bologna.
**No Small Affair** (1984) ...................Laura
• 1:34—Very, very brief side view of left breast in bed with Jon Cryer.
St. Elmo's Fire (1985)........................Jules
**About Last Night...** (1986).............. Debbie
0:32—In white bra getting dressed.
• 0:34—Brief upper half of right breast in the bathtub with Rob Lowe.
0:35—In white bra getting dressed.
• 0:50—Side view of right breast, then very brief breasts.
••• 0:51—Buns and breasts in bed with Lowe, arching her back, then lying in bed when he rolls off her.
•• 0:52—Breasts and buns in kitchen with Lowe.
One Crazy Summer (1986) .............. Cassandra
Wisdom (1986) ..........................Karen
**The Seventh Sign** (1988) .............Abby Quinn
• 1:03—Brief breasts, taking off bathrobe to take a bath. Her pregnant belly is not real—it's a full body prosthetic. Brief breasts when sitting in bathtub.

- 1:04—Brief tip of left breast, while sitting in bathtub and rubbing her belly.

**We're No Angels** (1989) . . . . . . . . . . . . . . . . . Molly
- 0:18—One long shot, then two brief side views of left breast when Robert De Niro watches from outside. Reflections in the window make it hard to see.

Ghost (1990) . . . . . . . . . . . . . . . . . . . . . Molly Jensen
The Butcher's Wife (1991) . . . . . . . . . . . . . . . . Marina
Mortal Thoughts (1991) . . . . . . . . . . . Cynthia Kellogg
Nothing But Trouble (1991) . . . . . . . . . Diane Lightson
A Few Good Men (1992)
. . . . . . . . . . . . . . . Lt. Commander Jo-Anne Gallaway
**Indecent Proposal** (1993) . . . . . . . . . Diana Murphy
- • 0:05—In black bra, brief buns and breasts while making out with Woody Harrelson on the kitchen floor.
- • 0:37—Upper half of right breast, while lying in bed with Harrelson.
- • 0:40—Upper half of right breast, while lying in bed and talking with Harrelson. Very brief right breast, when lifting sheet over her head.

*Made for Cable TV:*
Tales From the Crypt: Dead Right (1990; HBO)
. . . . . . . . . . . . . . . . . . . . . . . . . Cathy Fitch-Marno
(Available on *Tales From the Crypt, Volume 3.*)
*TV:*
General Hospital (1982-83) . . . . . . . . Jackie Templeton
*Magazines:*
**Vanity Fair** (Aug 1992) . . . . . . . Demi's Body Language
- • • 112-119—Breasts with painted body on the cover. Breasts in B&W photo. Breasts with painted body.
Playboy's Nudes (Dec 1992) . . . . . . . . . . . . . . Herself
72—*Vanity Fair* cover, with painted suit on her body.
**Playboy** (Dec 1992) . . . . . . . . . . . . . . Sex Stars 1992
- • 182—Partial buns, in panties.
**Playboy** (Aug 1993) . . . . . . . . . . . . . . . . . Grapevine
- • 158—Breasts under sheer black blouse. B&W.

# Moore, Glenda

*Video Tapes:*
Nudes in Limbo (1983) . . . . . . . . . . . . . . . . . . . Model
**Hot Bodies** (1988) . . . . . . . . . . . . . . . . . . . . Herself
- • • 0:37—Breasts, dancing with a sword. Sort of buns, under skirt.
- • • 0:40—Dancing without the sword. Buns in G-string.
- • • 0:44—Breasts and buns dancing with sword again.

# Moore, Jeanie

*Films:*
**Vampire at Midnight** (1988) . . . . . . . . . . . . . Amalia
- • 0:32—Breasts getting up to run an errand.
Wild Man (1988). . . . . . . . . . . . . . . . . . . Lady at Pool
Dream Trap (1989) . . . . . . . . . . . . . . . . . . . Blondee
After Dark, My Sweet (1990) . . . . . . . . . . . . . . Nanny
**The Final Alliance** (1990) . . . . . . . . . . . . . . . Carrie
- • 1:03—Brief breasts getting into bed with David Hasselhoff, then brief right breast twice in bed with him. A little dark.
We're Talkin' Serious Money (1991) . . . . . . . . . Amelia

# Moore, Jessica

*Films:*
**Eleven Days, Eleven Nights** (1988; Italian)
. . . . . . . . . . . . . . . . . . . . . . . . . Sarah Asproon
- • 0:03—Breasts opening her raincoat on boat for Michael, then making love.
- • 0:11—Buns, taking off robe in front of Michael.
- • • 0:16—Right breast, on T.V., then side of breast.
- • • 0:29—Breasts with Michael, changing clothes with him in restroom.
- • • • 0:33—Breasts in motel room with Michael, then making love.
- • 0:44—Brief breasts and buns when leaving Michael all tied up.
- • • 0:51—Breasts and buns in recording studio with Michael.
- • 1:17—Breasts during flashbacks.
- • • • 1:19—Nude, making love with Michael on bed.
**Top Model** (1989; Italian) . . . . . . Sarah Asproon/Gloria
- • • • 0:03—Nude, posing for photographer customer in his loft with mannequins, then talking on the phone.
- • 0:08—Breasts in dressing room, when seen by Cliff.
- • • 0:23—Buns and brief side of right breast, undressing in front of a customer.
- • • 0:24—Breasts, rubbing oil on him.
- • • 0:30—Full frontal nudity, in her bedroom when Peter blackmails her.
- • • • 0:35—Nude in photographer customer's loft again.
- • 0:40—Brief buns, turning over in bed.
- • • 0:43—Breasts on couch, making love (disinterestedly) with cowboy.
- • 0:56—Buns and partial right breast, while getting dressed.
- • • • 1:00—Breasts making love with Cliff on sofa, then sleeping afterward.
- • • • 1:04—Nude, undressing and walking down hallway.
- • • • 1:08—Nude, in hotel room, making love with Cliff.
- • • • 1:19—Buns, with Cliff in stairwell. Breasts and buns in bathroom with him.

# Moore, Julianne

Wife of actor John Gould Rubin.
*Films:*
Tales From the Darkside, The Movie (1990) . . . . . . Susan
**Body of Evidence** (1992) . . . . . . . . . . Sharon Dulaney
(Unrated version reviewed.)
- • • • 0:14—Breasts in bed, while making love with Willem Dafoe, then breasts and buns getting out of bed to take a shower.
The Gun in Betty Lou's Handbag (1992) . . . . . . . . Elinor
The Hand That Rocks the Cradle (1992) . . . . . . . Marlene
Benny & Joon (1993) . . . . . . . . . . . . . . . . . . . Ruthie
The Fugitive (1993) . . . . . . . . . . . . . . Dr. Anne Eastman
**Short Cuts** (1993) . . . . . . . . . . . . . . . . Marian Wyman
- • • • 2:22—(0:39 into Part 2) Buns and lower frontal nudity in top part of outfit, after having to take off the skirt to clean it. Long scene.

*Made for Cable Movies:*
Cast a Deadly Spell (1991; HBO). . . . . . . . Connie Stone

# Moore, Lisa

*Films:*
A Dream of Kings (1969). . . . . . . . . . . . . . . . . . Nurse
**Act of Vengeance** (1974). . . . . . . . . . . . . . . . . Karen
*a.k.a. The Rape Squad*
(Not to be confused with the film with the same name
starring Charles Bronson.)
- ••• 0:24—Breasts after rapist cuts her dress open and
  fondles her breasts while she has a cloth stuffed in
  her mouth.
- • 0:37—Buns and breasts, walking into the spa to join
  the other women.
- • 1:27—Brief breasts during fight while tied up in
  cage. Dark.

The Harrad Summer (1974) . . . . . . . . . . . . . . . Arnae
*a.k.a. Student Union*
Slaughter's Big Rip-Off (1975). . . . . . . . . . . . . . .n.a.
Swashbuckler (1976). . . . . . . . . . . . . . . . Pirates' Lady

# Moore, Melissa Anne

*Films:*
Caged Fury (1989) . . . . . . . . . . . . . . . . . . . . . . Gloria
Fatal Skies (1989) . . . . . . . . . . . . . . . . . . . . . . . Suzy
**Scream Dream** (1989) . . . . . . . . . . . . Jamie Summers
- ••• 0:39—Breasts in black panties in room with Derrick.
  Then straddling him.
- •• 0:58—Breasts in dressing room pulling her top
  down during transformation into monster.

**The Alien Within** (1990) . . . . . . . . . . Monica Roarke
Contains footage from *The Evil Spawn* woven together
with new material.
- • 0:52—Left breast, taking off her purple dress.
- ••• 1:18—Breasts, lying on bed when the monster
  strangles her and pulls her top down.
- • 1:19—Left breast, while lying in bed, then getting
  up.

**Hard to Die** (1990). . . . . . . . . . . . . . . . Tess Cochran
*a.k.a. Tower of Terror*
- ••• 0:21—Breasts taking off her top, then more lengthy
  breasts while taking a shower. Long scene.

**Invisible Maniac** (1990). . . . . . . . . . . . . . . . . . Bunny
- • 0:21—Buns in shower with the other girls.
- ••• 0:43—In bra, then breasts sitting with yellow towel
  in locker room with the other girls.
- • 0:44—Breasts in shower with the other girls.
- ••• 1:09—In bra, then breasts making out in Principal's
  Office with Chet. Long scene.

**Repossessed** (1990) . . . . . . . . . . . . . . Bimbo Student
- •• 0:05—Breasts pulling her top down in classroom in
  front of Leslie Nielsen.

**Sorority House Massacre 2** (1990). . . . . . . . . .Jessica
- ••• 0:22—Breasts, talking to Kimberly, then taking a
  shower.
  0:50—In wet lingerie.
- • 0:53—Buns, while going up the stairs.

**Vampire Cop** (1990) . . . . . . . . . . . . .Melanie Roberts
- ••• 0:46—Breasts in bed with the Vampire Cop.
- •• 0:51—Right breast, sitting in bed talking with Hans.
- • 1:21—Right breast, in bed on the phone during end
  credits.

Vice Academy, Part 2 (1990) . . . . . . . . . . . . . . .Glaze
Into the Sun (1991) . . . . . . . . . . . . . . . Female Sergeant
The Killing Zone (1991) . . . . . . . . . . . . . . . . . . Tracy
**Poker Night** (1991) . . . . . . . . . . . . . . . . . . . . . n.a.
Soul Mates (1991) . . . . . . . . . . . . . . . . . . . . . . . n.a.
**Angel Fist** (1992). . . . . . . . . . . . . . . . . . . . . .Lorda
- •• 0:03—Breasts and buns, in the showers.
- • 0:35—Nude, behind Katara in the showers.
- ••• 1:03—Breasts when she gets a bad guy to open her
  blouse and untie her. Very brief breasts during fight
  scenes.

**Consenting Adults** (1992) . . . . . . . . . . . Trudy Seaton
(Melissa is also the reclining model draped with a sheet
used in the advertising artwork. Her name was mis-
spelled as Michelle Moore in the credits.)
- • 0:37—Buns, while lying in bed when Kevin Kline
  takes the place of the husband.

**Da Vinci's War** (1992). . . . . . . . . . . . . . . . . . . .Fred
- ••• 0:14—Breasts and buns, with Michael Nouri in his
  workout room.

**The Other Woman** (1992) . . . . . . . . . . . . . . .Elysse
(Unrated version reviewed.)
- •• 0:58—Breasts, taking off her blouse while taking pictures during photo shoot.

Savage Vengeance: I Will Dance on Your Grave (1992)
. . . . . . . . . . . . . . . . . . . . . . . . . . . . . . . . . Singer
**One Man Army** (1993) . . . . . . . . . . . . . .Natalie Pierce
- ••• 0:26—Breasts, while taking a shower and drying
  herself off.
- ••• 0:29—Breasts, while making love with Jerry Trimble
  in bed.
- •• 0:33—Left breasts, while taking off her blouse to go
  for a swim. Breasts while in water after getting shot
  in the arm.

**Stormswept** (1994). . . . . . . . . . . . . . . . . . . . Dottie
- •• 0:33—Breasts, when her towel falls off while talking
  to Brianna.
- • 0:40—Breasts in open robe, while sitting on bed.
- ••• 1:10—Breasts, while making love on table with Damon.

*Video Tapes:*
**Scream Queen Hot Tub Party** (1991) . . . . . . . Jessica
- • 0:00—Breasts during opening credits.
- ••• 0:17—Breasts opening her towel, then in the shower
  from *Sorority House Massacre 2*.

**Hot Body Video Magazine #1** (1992) . . . . . . .Herself
- • 0:04—Brief breasts on the floor in a robe in front of
  a fireplace.

**Sexy Lingerie IV** (1992) . . . . . . . . . . . . . . . . Model
*Magazines:*
**Playboy** (Jul 1991) . . . . . . . . . . . . . .The Height Report
- ••• 140-141—Full frontal nudity on bed.

Playboy (Nov 1993) . . . . . . . . . . . . . . . . . . . Grapevine

# Moore, Terry

Ex-wife of the late billionaire Howard Hughes.
*Films:*
Mighty Joe Young (1949) . . . . . . . . . . . . . . . Jill Young
Come Back, Little Sheba (1952) . . . . . Marie Buckholder
Daddy Long Legs (1955). . . . . . . . . . . . . . . . . . Linda
Double Exposure (1983) . . . . . . . . . . . Married Woman
Hellhole (1985). . . . . . . . . . . . . . . . . .Sidnee Hammond
Beverly Hills Brats (1989). . . . . . . . . . . . . . . Veronica
*TV:*
Empire (1962-63) . . . . . . . . . . . . . . Constance Garret
*Magazines:*
**Playboy** (Aug 1984). . . . . . . . . . . . The Merriest Widow
••• 130-139—Breasts and buns. 55 years old.
**Playboy** (Dec 1984). . . . . . . . . . . . . . Sex Stars of 1984
••• 208—Breasts.
**Playboy** (Jan 1989) . . . . . . . . . . Women of the Eighties
••• 254—Breasts.

# Moran, Sharon

*Films:*
**If Looks Could Kill** (1987) . . . . . . . . . .Madonna Maid
•• 0:17—Full frontal nudity after Laura leaves the apartment.
Young Nurses in Love (1987) . . . . . . . . . . . Bambi/Bibi

# Morante, Laura

*Films:*
**The Tragedy of a Ridiculous Man** (1981; Italian)
. . . . . . . . . . . . . . . . . . . . . . . . . . . . . . . . . . . . Laura
••• 1:30—Breasts taking off her sweater in front of Primo because she's "uneasy."
Blow to the Heart (1985; Italian). . . . . . . . . . . . . . .n.a.
Distant Lights (1987; Italian) . . . . . . . . . . . . . . . Renata
Man On Fire (1987; Italian/French) . . . Julia, David's Wife
Luci Iontane (1988; Italian) . . . . . . . . . . . . . . . . . .n.a.

# More, Camilla

Identical twin sister of actress Carey More.
*Films:*
**Friday the 13th, Part IV—The Final Chapter**
(1984). . . . . . . . . . . . . . . . . . . . . . . . . . . . . . Tina
• 0:26—Very brief breasts in the lake jumping up with her twin sister to show they are skinny dipping.
• 0:48—Left breast, in bed with Crispin Glover.
Dark Side of the Moon (1989). . . . . . . . . . . . . . . Lesli
**The Serpent of Death** (1989) . . . . . . . . . . . . . .Rene
•• 0:15—Brief breasts in bed with Jeff Fahey.
•• 1:22—Brief left breast while in bed, then breasts and buns, getting out of bed (in mirror).

# More, Carey

Identical twin sister of actress Camilla More.
*Films:*
**Friday the 13th, Part IV—The Final Chapter**
(1984). . . . . . . . . . . . . . . . . . . . . . . . . . . . . . Terri
• 0:26—Very brief breasts in the lake jumping up with her twin sister to show they are skinny dipping.
Once Bitten (1985) . . . . . . . . . . . Moll Flanders Vampire

*TV:*
Days of Our Lives (1987) . . . . . . . . . . . Grace Forrester

# Moreau, Jeanne

*Films:*
The Lovers (1958) . . . . . . . . . . . . . . . . . . . . . .Jeanne
Jules and Jim (1962; French). . . . . . . . . . . . . Catherine
**Mademoiselle** (1966; French/British) . . . Mademoiselle
1:00—Almost breasts, while putting tape over her nipples.
•• 1:17—Right breast, while opening her blouse in field in front of her lover. Don't see her face.
The Oldest Profession (1967) . . . . "Mademoiselle Mimi"
**The Bride Wore Black** (1968; French/Italian)
. . . . . . . . . . . . . . . . . . . . . . . . . . . . . Julie Kohler
0:00—Left breast in B&W photo of a painting, that is coming off a printing press.
0:29—Left breast, in painting on the wall.
• 1:24—Brief breasts, taking of her dress in front of a patterned mirror.
1:37—Breasts in painting when the police photograph it.
Going Places (1974; French) . . . . . . . . . . .Jeanne Pirolle
The Last Tycoon (1976) . . . . . . . . . . . . . . . . . . . . .Didi
La Femme Nikita (1991; French/Italian) . . . . . . .Amande
*a.k.a. Nikita*
Until the End of the World (1991) . . . . . . .Edith Farber
Map of the Human Heart (1992; Australian/Canadian)
. . . . . . . . . . . . . . . . . . . . . . . . . . . . . .Sister Banville

# Morehart, Deborah

See: Tylo, Hunter.

# • Morgan Greene, Kim

*Films:*
Immortal Combat (1993). . . . . . . . . . . . . . . . . . .Karen
**Scorned** (1993) . . . . . . . . . . . . . . . . . Marina Weston
•• 0:42—Brief breasts, while sitting in bubble bath and getting out. Buns, when Shannon Tweed helps dry her off.
••• 1:09—Left breast, then breasts while in bed when Tweed makes love with her.
• 1:28—Breasts, while crying in shower after discovering her birds are dead.

# Morgan, Alexandra

*Films:*
**The First Nudie Musical** (1979) . . . . . . . Mary La Rue
• 0:54—Breasts, singing and dancing during dancing dildo routine.
••• 1:04—Full frontal nudity in bed trying to do a take.
1:07—Breasts in bed with a guy with a continuous erection.
•• 1:17—Breasts in bed in another scene.
**The Deadly Games** (1980) . . . . . . . . . . . . . . . .Linda
*a.k.a. The Eliminator*
•• 0:03—In bra, standing in doorway at night, then breasts. Dark.

- 0:04—Very brief left breast and lots of cleavage in open blouse talking on the phone.
  0:05—Most of right breast, standing up.
The Happy Hooker Goes Hollywood (1980) . . . . . . Max
**Erotic Images** (1983) . . . . . . . . . . . . . . Emily Stewart
- • 0:57—In black lingerie, then breasts on the living room floor with Glenn.
- • 1:05—Breasts in bed, making love with Glenn.
- • • 1:12—Breasts in the kitchen with Glenn.
- • 1:21—Right breast, on couch with Glenn.
Spellbinder (1988) . . . . . . . . . . . . . . . . . . . . . Pamela

## Morgan, Britt

Adult film actress.
*Video Tapes:*
**High Society Centerspread Video #5: Brittany Morgan** (1990) . . . . . . . . . . . . . . . . . . . . Herself
*Magazines:*
**Penthouse** (Mar 1987) . . . . . . . . . . . . . . . . . . . . Pet

## Morgan, Cindy

*Films:*
Up Yours . . . . . . . . . . . . . . . . . . . . . . . . . . . . . Elaine
**Caddyshack** (1980). . . . . . . . . . . . . . . Lacey Underall
  0:50—Very, very brief side view of left breast sliding into the swimming pool. Very blurry.
- • 0:58—Breasts in bed with Danny three times.
Tron (1982). . . . . . . . . . . . . . . . . . . . . . . . . . Lora/Yori
*TV:*
Bring 'Em Back Alive (1982-83) . . . . . . . Gloria Marlowe
Falcon Crest (1987-88) . . . . . . . . . . . . . Gabrielle Short

## Morgan, Debbi

Wife of actor Charles S. Dutton.
*Films:*
**Cry Uncle** (1971). . . . . . . . . . . . . . . . . . Olga Winter
- • • 0:40—Breasts and buns, taking off her blouse and skirt in room with Jake. Long scene.
**Mandingo** (1975) . . . . . . . . . . . . . . . . . . . . . . Dite
- • 0:17—Breasts in bed talking to Perry King.
*Miniseries:*
Roots: The Next Generation (1979). . . . Elizabeth Harvey
*Made for TV Movies:*
The Jesse Owens Story (1984). . . . Ruth Solomon Owens
*TV:*
All My Children . . . . . . . . . . . . . . . . . . Angie Hubbard
Behind the Screen (1981-82) . . . . . . . . . Lynette Porter
Generations (1990-93) . . . . . . . . . . . . Chantal Marshall
Loving (1993- ) . . . . . . . . . . . . . . . . . . . . . . . . . n.a.

## Morgan, Penny

See: Ryan, Rachel.

## Morgan, Shelly Taylor

*Films:*
**The Sword and the Sorcerer** (1982) . . . . . . . Bar-Bra
- • 0:54—Brief breasts when Lee Horsley crashes through the window and almost lands on her.
My Tutor (1983) . . . . . . . . . . . . . . . . . . . . . . . Louisa

Scarface (1983) . . . . . . . . . Woman at the Babylon Club
**Malibu Express** (1984) . . . . . . . . . . Anita Chamberlain
- • 0:22—Breasts doing exercises on the floor.
- • • 0:26—Breasts making love with Shane in bed while being video taped. Then right breast while standing by door.
*Made for Cable TV:*
Tales From the Crypt: The Ventriloquist's Dummy (1990; HBO). . . . . . . . . . . . . . . . . . . . . . . . . . Sally
*TV:*
General Hospital . . . . . . . . . . . . . . . . . Lorena Sharpe

## Moritz, Louisa

*Films:*
**Death Race 2000** (1975). . . . . . . . . . . . . . . . . . Myra
- • 0:28—Breasts and buns getting a massage and talking to David Carradine.
One Flew Over the Cuckoo's Nest (1975). . . . . . . . Rose
**The Happy Hooker Goes to Washington** (1977)
. . . . . . . . . . . . . . . . . . . . . . . Natalie Naussbaum
- • 0:39—Brief breasts and buns, lying down on top of Larry Storch in tennis court.
Loose Shoes (1977) . . . . . . . . . . . . . . . . . . . . . Margie
Up in Smoke (1978). . . . . . . . . . . . . . . . Officer Gloria
Cuba (1979) . . . . . . . . . . . . . . . . . . . . . Miss Wonderly
  0:05—Walking in the street while wearing a plastic blouse with pasties underneath.
  0:55—Dancing on stage in pasties.
  0:57—More dancing on stage with pasties.
  0:58—More.
  1:05—Briefly lying on the floor when shooting starts.
  1:06—Walking around while wearing pasties after the shooting.
**Lunch Wagon** (1981) . . . . . . . . . . . . . . . . . Sunshine
*a.k.a. Lunch Wagon Girls*
*a.k.a. Come 'N' Get It*
- • 0:37—Breasts in spa taking off her swimsuit top.
New Year's Evil (1981) . . . . . . . . . . . . . . . . . . . . Sally
True Confessions (1981). . . . . . . . . . . . . . . . . . Whore
**The Last American Virgin** (1982) . . . . . . . . . Carmela
- • • 0:42—Breasts and buns in her bedroom with Rick.
Chained Heat (1983; U.S./German) . . . . . . . . . Bubbles
**Hot Chili** (1985). . . . . . . . . . . . . . . . . . . . . Chi Chi
  0:06—Brief buns turning around in white apron after talking with the boys.
- • 0:34—Nude during fight in restaurant with the Music Teacher. Hard to see because of the flashing light.
Jungle Warriors (1985) . . . . . . . . . . . . Laura McCashin
*Magazines:*
**Playboy** (Apr 1974)
. . . . . . . . . . . . . . . Foreplay (A Comedy in Three Acts)
- • • 112—Breasts with Jerry Orbach while hanging onto rope.

## • Morley, Grace

*Films:*
**Sex Crimes** (1991) . . . . . . . . . . . . . . . . . . . . . .Cynthia
- 0:13—Buns in swimsuit in club. Very, very brief left breast, while taking off her swimsuit top in dressing room.
- 0:36—Buns in G-string and red pasties while dancing in club. More in dressing room.

American Me (1992) . . . . . . . . . . . . . . . . . . JD's Friend

## Moro, Alicia

*Films:*
The Exterminators of the Year 3000 (1985; Italian)
. . . . . . . . . . . . . . . . . . . . . . . . . . . . . . . . . . . Trash
Slugs (1988; Spanish) . . . . . . . . . . . Maureen Watson
**Hot Blood** (1989; Spanish) . . . . . . . . . . . . . . . Alicia
- 0:00—Buns and lower frontal nudity in stable with Ricardo. Long shot.
- 0:06—In bra and panties with Julio, then buns and breasts. Looks like a body double because hair doesn't match.

Velvet Dreams (1991; Italian) . . . . . . . . . . . . . . .n.a.

## Morrell, Carla

Twin sister of Carmen Morrell.
*Films:*
**Basket Case 3: The Progeny** (1991) . . . . . . . Twin #1
- • 0:41—Breasts in bed with her twin sister and Duane's brother.
- 1:29—Brief breast, lying in bed with her twin sister and Duane's brother after the end credits.

California Hot Wax (1992) . . . . . . . . . . . . . . Bikini Girl
*Made for Cable TV:*
Sessions: Episode 2 (1991; HBO) . . . . . . . . . . . Twin #2
*Magazines:*
**Playboy's Book of Lingerie** (Jul 1991) . . . . . . Herself
  ••• 28—Breasts with her sister.
**Playboy's Book of Lingerie** (Sep 1991) . . . . . Herself
  ••• 25—Breasts.
  ••• 54—Full frontal nudity with her sister.
**Playboy's Book of Lingerie** (Nov 1991) . . . . . Herself
  ••• 28—Breasts with her sister.
**Playboy's Sisters** (Feb 1992) . . . . . . . . . . . . . Herself
  ••• 64-67—Breasts.

## Morrell, Carmen

Twin sister of Carla Morrell.
*Films:*
**Basket Case 3: The Progeny** (1991) . . . . . . . Twin #2
- •• 0:41—Breasts in bed with her twin sister and Duane's brother.
- 1:29—Brief breast, lying in bed with her twin sister and Duane's brother after the end credits.

California Hot Wax (1992) . . . . . . . . . . . . . . Bikini Girl
*Made for Cable TV:*
Sessions: Episode 2 (1991; HBO) . . . . . . . . . . . Twin #1
*Magazines:*
**Playboy's Book of Lingerie** (Jul 1991) . . . . . . Herself
  ••• 28—Breasts with her sister.

**Playboy's Book of Lingerie** (Sep 1991) . . . . . Herself
  ••• 54—Full frontal nudity with her sister.
**Playboy's Book of Lingerie** (Nov 1991) . . . . Herself
  ••• 28—Breasts with her sister.
**Playboy's Sisters** (Feb 1992) . . . . . . . . . . . . . Herself
  ••• 64-67—Breasts.

## Morris, Anita

*Films:*
**The Happy Hooker** (1975) . . . . . Linda Jo/Mary Smith
- 0:59—Breasts lying on table while a customer puts ice cream all over her.
- 1:24—Breasts covered with whipped cream getting it sprayed off with champagne by another customer.

So Fine (1981) . . . . . . . . . . . . . . . . . . . . So Fine Dancer
The Hotel New Hampshire (1984) . . . . . . . . . Ronda Ray
Maria's Lovers (1985) . . . . . . . . . . . . . . . . . . Mrs. Wynic
Absolute Beginners (1986; British) . . . . . . . Dido Lament
Blue City (1986) . . . . . . . . . . . . . . . . . . . Molvina Kerch
Ruthless People (1986) . . . . . . . . . . . . . . . . . . . . . Carol
Aria (1987; U.S./British) . . . . . . . . . . . . . . . . . . Phoebe
18 Again! (1988) . . . . . . . . . . . . . . . . . . . . . . Madeline
Bloodhounds of Broadway (1989) . . . . . Missouri Martin
*Made for Cable TV:*
Tales From the Crypt: Spoiled (1991; HBO) . . . . Fuschia
*TV:*
Berrengers (1985) . . . . . . . . . . . . . . . . . Babs Berrenger
Trade Winds (1993- ) . . . . . . . . . . . . . . . . . . . . Contessa

## Morris, Kim

*Video Tapes:*
E. Nick: A Legend in His Own Mind (1984) . . .Nymphet
**Playboy Video Calendar 1988** (1987) . . . . . Playmate
**Wet and Wild** (1989) . . . . . . . . . . . . . . . . . . . . Model
*Magazines:*
**Playboy** (Mar 1986) . . . . . . . . . . . . . . . . . . . Playmate
**Playboy's Girls of Summer '86** (Aug 1986) . . . Herself
  ••• 29—Breasts and buns.
  ••• 78-79—Full frontal nudity.
  ••• 93—Full frontal nudity.
**Playboy's Calendar Playmates** (Nov 1992) . . . Herself
  •• 60—Buns and side of left breast.

## Morris, Marianne

*Films:*
Percy's Progress (1974; British) . . . . . . Beauty Contestant
**Vampyres** (1974; British) . . . . . . . . . . . . . . . . . .Fran
- •• 0:00—Breasts, then full frontal nudity in bed with Miriam, kissing each other before getting shot.
- ••• 0:20—Side of right breast, then breasts in bed with Ted, drinking wine, then making love.
- 0:23—Buns, lying in bed when Ted gets out.
- ••• 0:39—In black bra, panties, garter belt and stockings, then taking them off in front of Ted. Breasts and buns, then in bed.
- ••• 0:43—Breasts getting kissed by Miriam in the shower.

•• 0:56—Breasts taking off dress in front of Ted and getting into bed. Partial lower frontal nudity getting into bed.

•• 0:58—Breasts and brief lower frontal nudity in bed with Miriam, drinking Ted's blood.

• 1:00—Full frontal nudity getting dragged out of bed by Miriam.

• 1:18—Brief left breast, getting fondled by the Playboy guy in the wine cellar.

# • Morrison, Julie

*Video Tapes:*

**Penthouse Forum Letters: Volume 2** (1994)
. . . . . . . . . . . . . . . . . . . . The Window Washer/Lover
••• 0:46—Nude, making love with another woman on sofa, on kitchen counter and on bed.

*Magazines:*

**Playboy's Book of Lingerie** (Jul 1991) . . . . . . Herself
•• 8—Right breast.

**Playboy's Book of Lingerie** (Jan 1992) . . . . . . Herself
•• 43—Right breast and lower frontal nudity.

**Playboy's Bathing Beauties** (Mar 1994). . . . . Herself
••• 58-59—Right breast and lower frontal nudity.

# Morrow, Deirdre

*Films:*

**Carnal Crimes** (1991). . . . . . . . . . . . . . . . . Leggy Girl
• 1:22—Buns, in G-string, leaning over to talk to Renny and Stanley.

**Mirror Images** (1991) . . . . . . . . . . . . . . . . Slave Girl
••• 0:58—Buns in G-string, then breasts.
••• 1:00—Breasts on bed with masked guy and Julie Strain.

# Morrow, Sue

*Made for Cable Movies:*

**Soft Touch** (1987; Playboy). . . . . . . . . . . Ashley Keyes
(Shown on *The Playboy Channel* as *Birds in Paradise*.)
• 0:01—Breasts during opening credits.
• 0:02—Breasts with her two girlfriends during the opening credits.
•• 0:19—Breasts taking off her T-shirt in bed. More breasts sleeping, then waking up.
• 0:20—Breasts getting out of bed.
•• 0:22—Breasts making love with a guy.
• 0:23—Breasts in bed.
•• 0:53—Breasts on bed with Ensign Landers.
••• 0:59—Breasts and buns in play bowl with Landers.
• 1:19—Breasts in stills during end credits.

**Soft Touch II** (1987; Playboy) . . . . . . . . . Ashley Keyes
(Shown on *The Playboy Channel* as *Birds in Paradise*.)
• 0:01—Breasts during opening credits.
• 0:02—Breasts with her two girlfriends during the opening credits.
•• 0:26—Breasts while sunbathing on boat.
• 0:50—Brief breasts in the water.
• 0:52—Breasts during strip poker game, then covered with whipped cream.
•• 0:56—Full frontal nudity getting out of bed.

# Mosely, Melanie

*Films:*

**Ironheart** (1991) . . . . . . . . . . . . . . . . . . . . . Pretty Girl
•• 0:18—Breasts, while getting her T-shirt ripped off by four jerks. Long shot and closer shots.
My Own Private Idaho (1991) . . . . . . . . Lounge Hostess

# • Mounds, Melissa

Adult film actress.

*Films:*

**Flesh Gordon 2** (1990; Canadian) . . . Bazonga Bomber
••• 0:46—Breasts standing by table with Flesh Gordon and Dr. Jerkoff.
••• 0:48—More breasts with Dr. Jerkoff.

# Mucciante, Christie

*Films:*

**Fatal Pulse** (1987) . . . . . . . . . . . . . . . . . . . . . . Karen
•• 0:52—Breasts, getting dressed for bed.

**Tango & Cash** (1989) . . . . . . . . . . Dressing Room Girl
• 1:06—Brief breasts in dressing room. (She's the first topless blonde.)

# Mulford, Nancy

*Films:*

**Any Man's Death** (1989) . . . . . . . . . . . . . . . . . . . Tara

**Act of Piracy** (1990) . . . . . . . . . . . . . . . Laura Warner
• 0:11—Very brief left breast under Gary Busey in bed. Dark, hard to see.
0:12—In white lingerie, walking around on the boat shooting everybody.
• 0:34—Brief, upper half of left breast, in bed with Ray Sharkey.
0:35—In white nightgown.

# Mullen, Beckie

*Films:*

**Affairs of the Heart** (1992) . . . . . . . . . . . . . Pool Girl
••• 0:52—Breasts, after taking off her bikini top, then diving into pool.
•• 0:53—Breasts, lying on towel on diving board, then turning over.
The Bikini Carwash Company II (1993) . School Teacher
(Unrated version reviewed.)

**Hard Hunted** (1993) . . . . . . . . . . . . . . . . . . . . Becky
0:07—In red, two piece swimsuit in radio station with Shane.
•• 0:38—Breasts and buns in G-string in spa with Ava doing radio show.
••• 0:56—Breasts while getting out of spa and getting coffee.

*Made for Cable Movies:*

Cast a Deadly Spell (1991; HBO) . . . . . Drop Dead Babe

*Made for Cable TV:*

Sessions: Episode 2 (1991; HBO) . . . . . . . . . . . . Vicki

*Video Tapes:*

The Perfect Body Contest (1987) . . . . . . . . . . . . Beckie
Wild Bikinis (1987). . . . . . . . . . . . . . . . . . . . . . Herself
Bikini Blitz (1990). . . . . . . . . . . . . . . . . . . . . . . Model

Rock Video Girls (1991) . . . . . . . . . . . . . . . . . . . . Herself
*Magazines:*
**Playboy's Book of Lingerie** (Jan 1991) . . . . . . Herself
• 15—Buns.
**Playboy's Book of Lingerie** (May 1992) . . . . . Herself
•• 18—Right breast.
**Playboy's Girls of Summer '92** (Jun 1992) . . . Herself
•• 50—Breasts.
**Playboy's Book of Lingerie** (Jul 1992) . . . . . . Herself
••• 20—Breasts.
**Playboy's Book of Lingerie** (Jan 1993) . . . . . . Herself
•• 72—Buns and lower half of right breast.
**Playboy's Book of Lingerie** (May 1993) . . . . . Herself
• 9—Buns in thong.
**Playboy** (Jan 1994)
. . . . . . . . The Great 40th Anniversary Playmate Search
••• 137—Buns and side of left breast.
**Playboy's Great Playmate Search** (Feb 1994)
. . . . . . . . . . . . . . . . . . . . . . . . . . . . . . . . . . . . . Herself
•• 17—Side of left breast and buns.

## Mullen, Patty
*Films:*
**Doom Asylum** (1987) . . . . . . . . . . Judy LaRue/Kiki LaRue
In red two piece swimsuit a lot.
**Frankenhooker** (1990) . . . . . . . . . . . . . . . . .Elizabeth
•• 1:01—Breasts and buns in garter belt and stockings,
in room with a customer.
*Magazines:*
**Penthouse** (Aug 1986) . . . . . . . . . . . . . . . . . . . . . Pet
**Penthouse** (Jan 1988) . . . . . . . . . . . . . . Pet of the Year

## Müller, Lillian
a.k.a. Liliane Mueller or Yulis Ruvaal.
*Films:*
Rosemarie's Daughter (1975; German) . . . . . . . . . . .n.a.
Women's Clinic (1975; German) . . . . . . . . . . . . . . .n.a.
**Sex on the Run** (1979; German/French/Italian)
. . . . . . . . . . . . . . . . . . . . . . . . . . . . . . . . . . . . Angela
a.k.a. Some Like It Cool
a.k.a. Casanova and Co.
••• 0:15—Second woman (blonde) to take off her
clothes with the other two women, nude. Long
scene.
Best Defense (1984) . . . . . . . . . . . . . . . . . French Singer
*Magazines:*
**Playboy** (Aug 1975) . . . . . . . . . . . . . . . . . . . . Playmate
••• 90-101—Nude.
**Playboy** (Dec 1975) . . . . . . . . . . . . . . . . . . . . . . Cover
•• Breasts on the cover.
**Playboy** (Jan 1976) . . . . . . . . . . . . . . .Playmate Review
••• 163—Full frontal nudity.
**Playboy** (Jun 1976) . . . . . . .Playmate of the Year/Cover
• Half of right breast.
••• 132-143—Nude.
**Playboy** (Dec 1976) . . . . . . . . . . . . . Sex Stars of 1976
••• 191—Full frontal nudity.
**Playboy** (Mar 1977) . . . . . . . .Comeback for Casanova
••• 87-93—Full frontal nudity.

**Playboy** (Oct 1977) . . . . . . . . . Having A Masked Ball
•• 116-123—Right breast and lower frontal nudity.
••• 269—Breasts in small photo.
**Playboy** (Nov 1977) . . . . . . . . . . Sex in Cinema 1977
••• 166—Breasts with Tony Curtis from *Sex on the Run*.
**Playboy's Girls of Summer '86** (Aug 1986). . .Herself
••• 9—Full frontal nudity while holding a bottle of baby
oil.
••• 10—Full frontal nudity.
**Playboy's Nudes** (Oct 1990) . . . . . . . . . . . . . . .Herself
•• 101—Right breast and lower frontal nudity.
**Playboy's Nudes** (Dec 1993) . . . . . . . . . . . . . . .Herself
•• 79—Breasts.
**Playboy** (Jan 1994) . . . . . . . . . . . . 40 Memorable Years
••• 91—Right breast and lower frontal nudity.

## Munro, Caroline
*Films:*
Captain Kronos, Vampire Hunter (1972; British) . . . Carla
0:24—"Nude" scene in the barn with Kronos. Dark,
strategically placed shadows hide everything.
0:51—In barn again, but now she has strategically
placed hair hiding everything.
Dracula A.D. 1972 (1972; British) . . . . . . . . . . . . .Laura
*a.k.a. Dracula Today*
**The Golden Voyage of Sinbad** (1974; British)
. . . . . . . . . . . . . . . . . . . . . . . . . . . . . . . . . .Margiana
0:51—Very brief right nipple, sticking out of top
when Sinbad carries her from the boat to the shore.
Long shot.
The Spy Who Loved Me (1977; British) . . . . . . . .Naomi
Starcrash (1979; Italian) . . . . . . . . . . . . . . . . Stella Star
Don't Open Till Christmas (1984; British) . . . . . . .Herself
The Last Horror Film (1984) . . . . . . . . . . . . . Jana Bates
Slaughter High (1986) . . . . . . . . . . . . . . . . . . . . . .Carol
0:19—Walking around her house in lingerie and a
robe.

## Murakoshi, Suzen
*Films:*
**Wall Street** (1987) . . . . . . . . . . . . . . . . . . . . Girl in Bed
• 0:13—Brief full frontal nudity getting out of bed and
walking past the camera in Charlie Sheen's bedroom
(slightly out of focus).
Quick Change (1990) . . . . . . . . . . . . . . . . . . . .Hostage

## Murgia, Antonella
*Films:*
**Reborn** (1978) . . . . . . . . . . . . . . . . . . . . . . . . . .Maria
• 0:35—Breasts in bed with Michael Moriarty.
• 0:37—More breasts in bed with Moriarty.
••• 0:38—Nude, getting out of bed.
••• 0:39—Nude, walking around in bedroom.
Anguish (1987; Spanish) . . . . . . . . . . . . . . . Ticket Girl

# Murray, Beverley

*Films:*
**Cathy's Curse** (1976; Canadian) . . . . . . . . . . . . Vivian
  • 1:13—Very, very brief left breast, while jumping
    around in bathtub, brushing leaches off her body.
The Last Straw (1987; Canadian). . . . . Nurse Thompson
Still Life (1990) . . . . . . . . . . . . Performance Space Lady

# Muscarella, Lynn

Hostess of Manhattan Cable TV "Voyeurvision" live call-in
tele-fantasy show.
*Made for Cable TV:*
**Real Sex 4** (1992; HBO) . . . . . . . . . . . . . . Voyeurvision
  • 0:33—Buns, in lingerie doing her phone-in sex cable
    TV show.
*Magazines:*
**Playboy** (Jun 1992) . . . . . . . . . . . . . . . . . Video Vamp
  ••• 78-83—Breasts and buns.

# Muti, Ornella

*Films:*
**Appassionata** (1979; Italian) . . . . . . . . . . . . . Virginia
  • 0:32—Brief breasts in bathroom when her father rips
    open her T-shirt while looking for hickeys.
    0:57—Partial left breast, leaning over to tempt her
    father.
    1:07—In white bra, changing clothes during party.
    1:21—In white bra, in bathroom, giving herself hick-
    eys.
    1:25—In white bra in bed, showing her father her
    pubic hair.
  • 1:35—Buns, getting out of bed with her father. Brief
    side of left breast when leaving the room.
**Summer Affair** (1979) . . . . . . . . . . . . . . . . . . . . .Lisa
  • 0:44—Silhouette of breasts in cave by the water.
  • 1:00—Brief breasts getting chased around in the
    grass and by the beach.
Flash Gordon (1980). . . . . . . . . . . . . . . . Princess Aura
Love and Money (1980) . . . . . . . . Catherine Stockheinz
    0:31—In bra and panties in bedroom with Ray Shar-
    key getting dressed.
**Famous T & A** (1982) . . . . . . . . . . . . . . . . . . . . . .Lisa
  (No longer available for purchase, check your video
  store for rental.)
  •• 0:07—Breasts in scenes from *Summer Affair*. Nude
    underwater and running around the beach.
**Tales of Ordinary Madness** (1983; Italian) . . . . . Cass
  •• 0:37—Buns, four times, while standing at window in
    room with Ben Gazzara. Medium long shot.
  • 1:06—Buns, while standing at the beach and feed-
    ing the seagulls. One medium long shot and one
    long shot.
**Swann in Love** (1984; French/German)
. . . . . . . . . . . . . . . . . . . . . . . . . . .Odette de Crêcy
  *a.k.a. Un Amour de Swann*
  •• 1:15—Brief left breast, making love with Jeremy
    Irons.
  ••• 1:28—Breasts sitting on bed talking to Irons.
Casanova (1987). . . . . . . . . . . . . . . . . . . . Henriette

Oscar (1991) . . . . . . . . . . . . . . . . . . . . Sofia Provolone
Once Upon A Crime (1992) . . . . . . . . . .Elena Morosco
Especially on Sunday (1993). . . . . . . . . . . . . . . . Anna
*Made for Cable TV:*
The Hitchhiker: True Believer . . . . . . . . . . . . . . . . . . n.a.
  (Available on *The Hitchhiker, Volume 3*.)
*Magazines:*
**Playboy** (Dec 1980) . . . . . . . . . . . . . .Sex Stars of 1980
  •• 245—Right breast.
**Playboy's Nudes** (Dec 1992) . . . . . . . . . . . . . . .Herself
  • 37—Partial left breast and side view of buns.

# Myers, Cynthia

*Films:*
Beyond the Valley of the Dolls (1970). . . Casey Anderson
Molly and Lawless John (1972). . . . . . . . . . . . . . . Dolly
*Magazines:*
**Playboy** (Dec 1968) . . . . . . . . . . . . . . . . . . . Playmate
**Playboy** (Jan 1974). . . . . . . . Twenty Years of Playmates
  ••• 109—Breasts while kneeling on bed.
**Playboy** (Dec 1976) . . . . . . . . Portfolio: Pompeo Posar
  ••• 114—Breasts.
**Playboy** (Dec 1980) . . . . . . . . . . . . . . . Bunny Birthday
  ••• 152—Breasts.

# Nail, Joanne

*Films:*
**Switchblade Sisters** (1975) . . . . . . . . . . . . . Maggie
  • 0:21—Very, very brief right breast in ripped blouse
    when she tries to rip Dominic's shirt off.
The Gumball Rally (1976). . . . . . . . . . . . . . . . .Jane
The Visitor (1980; Italian/U.S.) . . . . . . . . Barbara Collins

# Nankervis, Debbie

*Films:*
**Alvin Purple** (1973; Australian) . . . . Girl in Blue Movie
  •• 1:04—Nude, running after Alvin in bedroom during
    showing of movie.
Libido (1973; Australian) . . . . . . . . . . . . . . . . .First Girl
Alvin Rides Again (1974; Australian) . . .Woman Cricketer

# Nann, Erika

*Films:*
Death Feud (1989). . . . . . . . . . . . . . . . . . . . . Hooker
Camp Fear (1991) . . . . . . . . . . . . . . . . . . . . . . . . n.a.
  *a.k.a. Millenium Countdown*
Animal Instincts (1992) . . . . . . . . . . . . . . . . . Dianne
  (Unrated version reviewed.)
Final Impact (1992) . . . . . . . . . . . . . . . . . . Foxy Boxer
**Mind Twister** (1992) . . . . . . . . . . . . . . . Lisa Strahten
  (Unrated version reviewed.)
  ••• 0:28—Breasts, while making love in candlelit bath-
    tub with a young stud.
    0:33—In black lingerie in bedroom with Daniel.
  • 0:37—Breasts, while in bed with Daniel.
    0:42—In sheer black body suit in bathroom while
    talking to Daniel.
    0:49—In black bra, panties, garter belt and stock-
    ings.

0:54—In black lingerie outfit.

••• 0:56—Breasts and buns, while making love with Heather while getting videotaped by Daniel.

• 1:22—In lingerie on TV monitor during video playback. Buns, while wrestling with Sheila.

**Night Rhythms** (1992) . . . . . . . . . . . . . . . . . . . . Alex

(Unrated version reviewed.)

••• 1:00—Buns in G-string and bra, then breasts, undressing in front of Martin Hewitt and making love with him.

**Die Watching** (1993) . . . . . . . . . . . . . . . . . . Gabrielle

•• 0:51—Right breast, while caressing with herself while Christopher Atkins videotapes her before killing her. Her right hand is handcuffed to shelves.

## Nanty, Isabelle

*Films:*

Red Kiss (1985; French). . . . . . . . . . . . . . . . . . . Jeanine

On a Vole Charlie Spencer! (1987) . . . . . . . . . . Suzette

**The Passion of Beatrice** (1988; French) . . La Nourrice

•• 1:53—Right breast, offering her breast milk to Arnaud.

Tatie Danielle (1991; French). . . . . . . . . . . . . Sandrine

Les Visiteurs (1993; French). . . . . . . . . Fabienne Morlot

## Napaul, Neriah

See: Davis, Neriah.

## Naples, Toni

a.k.a. Karen Chorak.

*Films:*

Doctor Detroit (1983) . . . . . . . . . . . . . . . . . Dream Girl

Chopping Mall (1986) . . . . . . . . . . . . . Bathing Beauty

*a.k.a. Killbots*

Deathstalker II (1987) . . . . . . . . . . . . . . . . . . . Sultana

**The Turn-On** (1989) . . . . . . . . . . . . . . . Harold's Wife

*a.k.a. Le Clic*

••• 0:31—Nude, during ceremony and after getting turned on by the black box.

Hard to Die (1990) . . . . . . . . . . . . . . . . . . . Sgt. Shawlee

*a.k.a. Tower of Terror*

Sorority House Massacre 2 (1990). . . . . . . Sgt. Shawlee

Transylvania Twist (1990) . . . . . . . . . . . . . . . Maxine

**Final Judgement** (1992). . . . . . . . . . . . . . Dancer #2

• 0:51—Breasts, while dancing on stage, wearing sunglasses.

Munchie (1992) . . . . . . . . . . . . . . . . . . . Mrs. Blaylok

American Yakuza (1993) . . . . . . . . . . . Mrs. Campaneia

**Dinosaur Island** (1993) . . . . . . . . . Queen Morganna

• 0:37—Brief left breast, popping out of bikini top when June starts dragging her around by her hair.

Prison Heat (1993) . . . . . . . . . . . . . . . . . . . . . . . . n.a.

Munchie Strikes Back (1994). . . . . . . . . . . . Newscaster

## Napoli, Susan

a.k.a. Stephanie Ryan.

*Films:*

**Wildest Dreams** (1987). . . . . . . . . . . . . . . . . Punk #4

• 0:21—Brief left breast, leaning backwards on couch with her boyfriend.

**Party Incorporated** (1989). . . . . Uncredited Party Girl

*a.k.a. Party Girls*

• 0:05—Brief breasts, while wearing a mask and dancing during party with two other girls.

• 0:08—Brief breasts again.

**Frankenhooker** (1990) . . . . . . . . . . . . . . . . . . . Anise

• 0:42—Brief left breast on bed with Amber, taking off her top. Brief breasts after Angel explodes.

• 0:43—Breasts, kneeling on bed screaming before exploding.

**Street Hunter** (1990) . . . . . . . . . . . . . . . Eddie's Girl

•• 0:40—Breasts in bed with Eddie (she's on the left, wearing white panties).

**Beauty School** (1993) . . . . . . . . . . . . . . . . . Otis' Girl

•• 0:21—Breasts undoing her swimsuit top for Mr. Otis.

*Video Tapes:*

**Penthouse Satin & Lace II: Hollywood Undercover** (1992)

. . . . . . . . . . . . . . . . . . . . . . . . . . . . . . . . . . . . . .Pet

**The Penthouse All-Pet Workout** (1993). . . . . . . .Pet

•• 0:00—Full frontal nudity during introduction.

•• 0:03—Brief nude shots while getting undressed and suited up.

••• 0:14—Nude on couch inside.

••• 0:43—Nude with the other girls, exercising, working with equipment, in the pool and spa.

Penthouse Pet of the Year Winners 1994: Sasha & Leslie (1994) . . . . . . . . . . . . . . . . . . . . . . . . . . . . . . . .Pet

*Magazines:*

**Penthouse** (Feb 1986) . . . . . . . . . . . . . . . . . . . . .Pet

## • Naschak, Andrea

a.k.a. Adult film actress April Rayne.

*Films:*

**Hold Me, Thrill Me, Kiss Me** (1993) . . . . . . . . .Sabra

(Unrated version reviewed.)

• 0:04—Buns in yellow and orange two piece swimsuit while dancing on stage.

• 0:08—Buns in G-string and out of it in trailer with Max.

• 0:09—Very brief left breast under sheer black blouse. 0:25—Buns, while on stage in black outfit.

• 0:46—Buns and most of breast, while dancing on stage in sexy outfit.

## • Nash, Jennifer

*Films:*

The Player (1992). . . . . . . . . . . . . . . . . . . . . . Cameo

**Invisible: The Chronicles of Benjamin Knight** (1993) . . . . . . . . . . . . . . . . . . . . . . . . . . . . . Zanna

• 0:15—Buns, while making love in bed with Wade. Don't see her face well.

## Nassar, Deborah Ann
Films:
**Stripped to Kill** (1987) . . . . . . . . . . . . . . . . . Dazzle
- ••• 0:07—Breasts wearing a G-string dancing on stage with a motorcycle prop.

**Dance of the Damned** (1988). . . . . . . . . . La Donna
- • 0:07—Brief breasts during dance routine in club.

## Natividad, Francesca "Kitten"
Vital statistics: 5' 3" tall, 116 pounds, 44-25-35.
Adult Films:
**Bad Girls IV** . . . . . . . . . . . . . . . . . . . . . . . . .n.a.
- •• 0:26—Breasts in back of pizza truck.

**Bodacious Ta-Tas**. . . . . . . . . . . . . . . . . . . . . .n.a.
**Titillation** (1982) . . . . . . . . . . . . . . . . . . . . . .n.a.
  Breasts.
Films:
Up! (1976) . . . . . . . . . . . . . . . . . . . . . . . Greek Chorus
Beneath the Valley of the Ultravixens (1979)
. . . . . . . . . . . . . . . . . . . . . . . .Lavonia & Lola Langusta
**The Lady in Red** (1979) . . . . . . . Uncredited Partygoer
- • 0:39—Brief breasts outside during party.

**An Evening with Kitten** (1983) . . . . . . . . . . Herself
- •• 0:02—Breasts busting out of her blouse.
- •• 0:09—Breasts while in miniature city scene.
- • 0:11—Brief breasts while on stage.
- • 0:20—Left breast, in bed with a vampire.
- ••• 0:21—Breasts and buns in G-string during dance in large champagne glass prop. Long scene.
- ••• 0:24—Breasts on beach in mermaid costume with little shell pasties.
- ••• 0:25—Breasts while in the glass again.
- •• 0:28—Breasts while in and out of glass.
- •• 0:29—Brief breasts during end credits.

**My Tutor** (1983) . . . . . . . . . . . . . . . . . . . . .Anna Maria
- ••• 0:10—Breasts in room with Matt Lattanzi, then lying in bed.

Doin' Time (1984). . . . . . . . . . . . . . . . . . . . . . Tassle
**Takin' It Off** (1984) . . . . . . . . . . . . . . . Betty Bigones
- •• 0:01—Breasts dancing on stage.
- •• 0:04—Breasts and buns dancing on stage.
- •• 0:29—Breasts in the Doctor's office.
- ••• 0:32—Nude dancing in the Psychiatrists' office.
- ••• 0:39—Nude in bed with a guy during fantasy sequence playing with vegetables and fruits.
- •• 0:49—Breasts in bed covered with popcorn.
- • 0:51—Nude doing a dance routine in the library.
- ••• 1:09—Nude splashing around in a clear plastic bathtub on stage.
- •• 1:20—Nude at a fat farm dancing.
- •• 1:24—Nude running in the woods in slow motion.

**The Wild Life** (1984) . . . . . . . . . . . . . . . . Stripper #2
- ••• 0:50—Breasts doing strip routine in a bar just before a fight breaks out.

**Night Patrol** (1985) . . . . . . . . . . . . . . Hippie Woman
- •• 1:01—Breasts in kitchen with Pat Paulsen, the other police officer and her hippie boyfriend.

**Takin' It All Off** (1987) . . . . . . . . . . . . Betty Bigones
- ••• 0:12—Nude, washing herself in the shower.

- •• 0:39—Nude, on stage in a giant glass, then breasts backstage in her dressing room.
- •• 0:42—Breasts in flashbacks from Takin' It Off.
  0:46—Breasts in group in the studio.
- ••• 0:53—Nude, dancing on the deck outside. Some nice slow motion shots.
- •• 1:16—Breasts on stage in club.
- ••• 1:23—Nude, dancing with the other girls on stage.

**The Tomb** (1987). . . . . . . . . . . . . . . . . . . . . .Stripper
- ••• 0:19—Breasts and buns in G-string dancing on stage.
- • 0:21—Brief breasts again.

**Another 48 Hrs.** (1990) . . . . . . . . . . . . Girl in Movie
- • 1:04—Brief breasts on movie screen when two motorcycles crash through it.

**The Girl I Want** (1990) . . . . . . . . . . . . Miss Langusta
Buford's Beach Bunnies (1992). . . . . . . . . . .Madam #1
Video Tapes:
**The Stripper of the Year** (1986) . . . . . . . . . . . Kitten
- ••• 0:51—Nude, stripping out of black outfit.
- •• 0:53—Breasts on stage with the other contestants.

**Inside Out 2** (1992). . Busty Dusty/Profiles in Cleavage
(Unrated version reviewed.)
- •• 0:56—Bouncing her breasts while wearing pasties.
- • 1:02—Dancing in disco wearing pasties. B&W.
- • 1:03—Brief breasts with pasties.

Magazines:
**Playboy** (Oct 1980) . . . . . . . . . . .The World of Playboy
- • 11—Breasts in small photo.

**Playboy** (Nov 1982) . . . . . . . . . . Sex in Cinema 1982
- ••• 160—Breasts.

**Playboy** (Nov 1990) . . . . . . . . . . Sex in Cinema 1990
- • 138—Breasts in still from Another 48 Hrs.

## Neal, Billie
Films:
**Down by Law** (1986). . . . . . . . . . . . . . . . . . .Bobbie
- •• 0:11—Breasts lying in bed, talking to Jack. Medium long shot. Long scene.
- ••• 0:12—Side view of right breast, partial lower frontal nudity, lying in bed.
- •• 0:13—More breasts, medium long shot again, lying in bed.
- •• 0:14—Right breast when Jack covers her up with sheet.

The January Man (1988) . . . . . . . . . . . . . . . . . . Gwen
Born on the Fourth of July (1989). . . . Nurse Washington
Internal Affairs (1990) . . . . . . . . . . . . . . . Dorian's Wife
Jacob's Ladder (1990) . . . . . . . . . . . . . . . . . . . . Della
A Kiss Before Dying (1991). . . . . . . . . . . . . . . . Nurse
Mortal Thoughts (1991). . . . . . . . . . . . . Linda Nealon
Consenting Adults (1992) . . . . . . . . . .Annie Duttonville
The Gun in Betty Lou's Handbag (1992) . . . . . . . . Gail

## Neal, Christy
Films:
**Coming Together** (1978) . . . . . . . . . . . .Vicky Hughes
a.k.a. A Matter of Love
  0:12—In bra and panties, in bedroom with Frank.

- 0:30—Brief right breast in shower with Angie.
- 0:37—Breasts and buns making love standing up in front of sliding glass door with Frank. Quick cuts.
- 0:49—Brief breasts again during flashbacks.
- •• 0:57—Breasts with Angie and Richard.
- 1:05—Breasts on beach with Angie. Long shot.

Take Down (1978) . . . . . . . . . . . . . . . . . Suzette Smith

# • *Neal, Siri*

*Films:*

The Rachel Papers (1989; British) . . . . . . . . . . . . . Suki
The Children (1990; British/German) . . . . . . . . . Judith
**Waterland** (1992; British/U.S.) . . . . . . . Helen Atkinson
- 0:40—Brief side view of breast in mirror while rubbing her legs. Long shot at far left of TV screen.

# *Negoda, Natalya*

*Films:*

**Little Vera** (1988; U.S.S.R.) . . . . . . . . . . . . . . . . . Vera
0:15—Very brief breasts and buns getting dressed. Dark, hard to see.
- ••• 0:50—Breasts making love with Sergei.
- •• 1:05—Breasts taking off her dress in the kitchen.
**Back In the U.S.S.R.** (1992) . . . . . . . . . . . . . . . . . Lena
- •• 0:46—Side view of left breast, making love with Sloan in the bathtub. Brief right breast when Dimitri comes into the bathroom.
*Made for Cable Movies:*
The Comrades of Summer (1992; HBO) . . . . . . . . Tanya
*Magazines:*
**Playboy** (May 1989) . . . . . . . . . . . . . That Glasnost Girl
- ••• 140-149—Breasts.
**Playboy** (Nov 1989) . . . . . . . . . . Sex in Cinema 1989
- •• 131—Breasts in out-of-focus still from *Little Vera*.
**Playboy** (Dec 1989) . . . . . . . . .Holy Sex Stars of 1989!
- ••• 184—Breasts.
**Playboy** (Dec 1991) . . . . . . . . . . . . . . . Sex Stars 1991
- ••• 183—Left breast.

# *Neidhardt, Elke*

*Films:*

**Alvin Purple** (1973; Australian)
. . . . . . . . . . . . . . . . . . . . . . . . .Woman in Blue Movie
- •• 1:07—In red bra, then full frontal nudity in bedroom with Alvin during showing of film.
Libido (1973; Australian) . . . . . . . . . . . . . . . . . Penelope
Inside Looking Out (1977; Australian) . . . . . . . Marianne

# *Nelkin, Stacey*

*Films:*

California Dreaming (1978) . . . . . . . . . . . . . . . . Marsha
Serial (1980) . . . . . . . . . . . . . . . . . . . . . . . . . . Marlene
Going Apel (1981) . . . . . . . . . . . . . . . . . . . . .Cynthia
Up the Academy (1981) . . . . . . . . . . . . . . . . . . .Candy
Get Crazy (1983) . . . . . . . . . . . . . . . . . . . . . . . . .Susie
**Halloween III: Season of the Witch** (1983)
. . . . . . . . . . . . . . . . . . . . . . . . . . Ellie Grimbridge
- 0:37—Brief right breast, behind shower door, when getting out of the shower.

Yellowbeard (1983) . . . . . . . . . . . . . . . . . . . . . . .Triola
Desperate Motive (1992) . . . . . . . . . . . . . . .Bank Teller
*Made for Cable TV:*
Sex, Shock and Censorship in the 90's (1993; Showtime)
. . . . . . . . . . . . . . . . . . . . . . . . . . . .Patty Turner
*Miniseries:*
The Last Convertible (1979) . . . . . . . . Sheilah Garrigan
*TV:*
The Chisholms (1979) . . . . . . . . . .Bonnie Sue Chisholm

# *Nelligan, Kate*

*Films:*

The Romantic Englishwoman (1975; British/French)
. . . . . . . . . . . . . . . . . . . . . . . . . . . . . . . . . .Isabel
Dracula (1979) . . . . . . . . . . . . . . . . . . . . . . . . . . Lucy
Crossover (1980; Canadian) . . . . . . . . . . . . . . Peabody
*a.k.a. Mr. Patman*
**Eye of the Needle** (1981) . . . . . . . . . . . . . . . . . Lucy
- •• 0:52—Brief left breast, while drying herself off in the bathroom when Donald Sutherland accidentally sees her.
1:15—Top half of buns, making love in bed with Sutherland.
- 1:26—Breasts making love in bed with Sutherland after he killed her husband. Dark, hard to see.
Without a Trace (1983) . . . . . . . . . . . . . . . Susan Selky
Eleni (1985) . . . . . . . . . . . . . . . . . . . . . . . . . . . . Eleni
Frankie & Johnny (1991) . . . . . . . . . . . . . . . . . . Cora
0:34—Upper half of buns, in bed on top of Al Pacino. Don't see her face.
The Prince of Tides (1991) . . . . . . . . . . . . . . Lila Wingo
Shadows and Fog (1991) . . . . . . . . . . . . . . . . . . . Eve
Fatal Instinct (1993) . . . . . . . . . . . . . . . . . Lana Revine
Wolf (1994) . . . . . . . . . . . . . . . . . . . . . . . . . . . . n.a.
*Made for Cable Movies:*
Control (1987; HBO) . . . . . . . . . . . . . . . . . . . . . . n.a.
The Diamond Fleece (1992; USA) . . . . . . . . .Holly Plum
Old Times (1993) . . . . . . . . . . . . . . . . . . . . . . . . .Kate
*Made for TV Movies:*
Therese Raquin (1981) . . . . . . . . . . . . . . . . . . Therese
Kojak: The Price of Justice (1987) . . . . . . . . . . . . Kitty
Liar, Liar (1993) . . . . . . . . . . . . . . . . . . . . . . . . . n.a.
Shattered Trust: The Shari Karney Story (1993)
. . . . . . . . . . . . . . . . . . . . . . . .Stephanie Chadford
Spoils of War (1994) . . . . . . . . . . . . . . . . . . . . . . n.a.

# • *Neri, Rosalba*

*Films:*

Sara Bay . . . . . . . . . . . . . . . . . . . . . . . . . . . . . . n.a.
Johnny Yuma (1967; Italian) . . . . . . . . . Samantha Felton
A Long Ride From Hell (1970; Italian) . . . . . . .Prostitute
**The Seducers** (1970) . . . . . . . . . . . . . . . . . . . . .Paula
*a.k.a. Sensation*
*a.k.a. Top Sensation*
- •• 0:06—Breasts, under lots of necklaces, in cabin with Mudy. Partial buns in panties.
- ••• 0:12—Buns, while sunbathing on boat, then brief left breast.
- •• 0:13—Right breast with Ulla on boat deck.

- 0:35—Brief buns, pulling down her swimsuit bottom to show off her tan.
- 0:54—Brief breasts, while on boat deck with Andrew.
- 1:05—Upper half of buns, when Andrew pulls her swimsuit down.

The Devil's Wedding Night (1971) . . . . . . . . . . . . .n.a.
Slaughter Hotel (1971) . . . . . . . . . . . . . . . . . . . .n.a.
*a.k.a. Asylum Erotica*

## Nero, Toni

*Films:*

**Silent Night, Deadly Night** (1984) . . . . . . . . Pamela

- 0:30—Brief right breast twice just before Billy gets stabbed during fantasy scene.
- 0:42—Breasts in stock room when Andy attacks her.
- 0:44—Breasts while in stock room struggling with Billy, then getting killed by him.

**Silent Night, Deadly Night, Part 2** (1986) . . Pamela

- • 0:22—Breasts in back of toy store in flashback from *Silent Night, Deadly Night.*

Commando Squad (1987) . . . . . . . . . . . . . . . . Putita

## • Nesbitt, Victoria

*Films:*

**Murder Weapon** (1989) . . . . . . . . . . . . . . . . . . Vicki

- • • 0:05—Breasts in bed with a guy after taking off her swimsuit top, then making love on top of him. Long scene.

The Girl I Want (1990) . . . . . . . . . . . . . . . . . . . Cindy
*Video Tapes:*
Linnea Quigley's Horror Workout (1990) . . . . . . . . Missy

## Neumann, Jenny

Writer.
*Films:*

**Mistress of the Apes** (1979; British) . . .Susan Jamison

- 0:23—Brief side of right breast, getting ready for bed in her tent.
- 0:25—Brief half of right breast in open blouse. Very brief right breast, when pushing a guy away.
- 1:08—Back side of left breast and brief breasts while washing her blouse in river and putting it on.

Swim Team (1979) . . . . . . . . . . . . . . . . . . . . . . .Erin
The Last Married Couple in America (1980) . . . . . Nurse
Hell Night (1981) . . . . . . . . . . . . . . . . . . . . . . . . May
My Favorite Year (1982) . . . . . . . . . . . . . . . . . Connie
Off the Wall (1982) . . . . . . . . . . . . . . . . . . . . . Linda
Stagefright (1983; Australian) . . . . . . . . . . Helen Selleck
*a.k.a. Nightmares*
The Delos Adventure (1985) . . . . . . . . . . . . . . . . Deni
Stitches (1985) . . . . . . . . . . . . . . . . . . . . . . . . . Joan
*Miniseries:*
V (1983) . . . . . . . . . . . . . . . . . . . . . . . . . . . .Barbara
*Made for TV Movies:*
The Girl in the Empty Grave (1977) . . . . . . . . . . .Susie

## Newmar, Julie

*Films:*

**Mackenna's Gold** (1969) . . . . . . . . . . . . . . . . .Hesh-ke

1:09—Brief breasts and buns under water. Long shots, hard to see anything. Not clear because of all the dirty water. Brief buns, getting out of the pond.

Love Scenes (1984) . . . . . . . . . . . . . . . . . . . . . Belinda
*a.k.a. Ecstacy*
Evils of the Night (1985) . . . . . . . . . . . . . Doctor Zarma
Streetwalkin' (1985) . . . . . . . . . . . . . . . . . . .Queen Bee
Deep Space (1988) . . . . . . . . . . . . . . . . . . . Lady Elaine
Ghosts Can't Do It (1989) . . . . . . . . . . . . . . . . .Angel
**Nudity Required** (1989) . . . . . . . . . . . . . . . . . .Irina

- 0:57—Side of left breast and side view of buns behind textured shower door with Buddy.

*TV:*
Batman (1966-67) . . . . . . . . . . . . . . . . . The Catwoman

## • Newton, Thandie

*Films:*

**Flirting** (1992; Australian) . . . . . . . . Thandiwe Adjewa

- • 1:30—Brief breasts, getting out of bed and putting a coat on over herself after getting caught with Danny.

The Young Americans (1993; British) . . .Rachael Stevens

## Nicholas, Angela

*Films:*

**Psychos in Love** (1987) . . . . . . . . . . . . . . . . . .Diane

- • 0:04—Breasts while taking a shower, before being killed.

**Wildest Dreams** (1987) . . . . . . . . . . . . . . . . Claudia

- • 1:01—Breasts typing on computer doing Bobby's book keeping.

**Alien Space Avenger** (1988) . . . . . . . . . . . . . Doris

- 0:56—Brief breasts making whoopee with Jaimie Gillis.
- • • 0:57—More breasts making love on top of Gillis while killing him.

**Galactic Gigolo** (1988) . . . . . . . . . . .Peggy Sue Peggy
*a.k.a. Club Earth*

- 0:21—Brief right breast in open blouse leaving room with Eoj.

**Affairs of the Heart** (1992) . . . . . . . . . . . Dreamgirl

- • 0:14—In bra, then left breast while in bed with the Geek.

*Magazines:*
**Penthouse** (Aug 1985) . . . . . . . . . . . . . . . . . . . .Pet

## • Nicholas, Sky

*Films:*

**Fatal Pulse** (1987) . . . . . . . . . . . . . . . . . . . . . Sheila

- • • 0:36—Breasts in bathtub, taking a bath, then getting killed. Long scene.

Campus Hustle (1993) . . . . . . . . . . . . . . . . . . . Ellen

# Nichols, Kelly

Adult film actress.
a.k.a. Marianne Walter.
*Films:*
**The Toolbox Murders** (1978) . . . . . . . . . . . . Dee Ann
••• 0:22—Right breast, then breasts taking a bath and
enjoying herself. Long scene. Nude, running around
trying to get away from the killer.
0:32—Breasts, while dead in her apartment and lat-
er on the coroner's table.
It's Called Murder Baby (1982) . . . . . . . . . . . . . . Leslie
(R-rated version of the adult film *Dixie Ray, Hollywood
Star.*)
**Model Behavior** (1982) . . . . . . . . . . . . . . . . Anne #2
••• 0:40—Breasts, taking off her top first, with the other
Anne in front of Dino.
Deathmask (1983) . . . . . . . . . . . . . . . . . . . Lover Nurse
In Love (1983) . . . . . . . . . . . . . . . . . . . . . . . . . . . . .n.a.
**Delivery Boys** (1984) . . . . . . . . . . . . . . . . . . .Elizabeth
• 0:44—Top half of right breast, while eating rolls with
a young boy.
Sno-Line (1984) . . . . . . . . . . . . . . . . . . . . . . . . . Ellen

# Nickson, Julia

*Films:*
Rambo: First Blood, Part II (1985) . . . . . . . . . . . . . . Co
The Chinatown Murders: Man Against the Mob (1989)
. . . . . . . . . . . . . . . . . . . . . . . . . . . . . . . . . . . Kei Lee
1:15—Breasts, taking off her dress in bedroom in
front of George Peppard. Very dark. It looks like she's
wearing pasties when she gets into bed.
1:18—Very brief breasts getting out of bed. It looks
like she's wearing the pastie things again.
**K2** (1991) . . . . . . . . . . . . . . . . . . . . . . . . . . . . Cindy
• 0:26—Briefly nude, getting up out of bed and put-
ting robe on.
Sidekicks (1992) . . . . . . . . . . . . . . . . . . . Noreen Chan
**Amityville: A New Generation** (1993) . . . . . . . Suki
•• 0:28—Left breast, with David Naughton while taking off her coveralls.
• 0:29—Very brief back side of left breast, putting on
her coverall strap.
*TV:*
Babylon 5 (1994) . . . . . . . . . . . . . . . . . .Catherine Sakai

# Nicolodi, Daria

*Films:*
Deep Red Hatchet Murders (1976; Italian)
. . . . . . . . . . . . . . . . . . . . . . . . . . . . . . . Gianna Brezzi
**Beyond the Door II** (1977; Italian). . . . . . . . . . . .Dora
• 0:30—Buns, in the shower.
• 0:47—Brief left breast in gaping nightgown, sitting
up in bed.
Inferno (1980; Italian). . . . . . . . . . . . . . . .Countess Elise
Creepers (1985; Italian). . . . . School Director's Assistant
Macaroni (1985; Italian) . . . . . . . . . . . . .Laura Di Falco
Terror at the Opera (1989; Italian). . . . . . . . . . . . Mira

# Nielsen, Barbara

*Films:*
**L'Annee Des Meduses** (1987; French). . . . . . Barbara
• 0:37—Brief breasts taking off T-shirt at the beach.
•• 0:40—Breasts at the beach with Valerie Kaprisky.
•• 1:04—Breasts while sitting on Kaprisky at the beach.
•• 1:08—Right breast, lying on the beach with
Kaprisky.
•• 1:41—Breasts on the beach taking off her top.
••• 1:43—Nude, in the swimming pool.
The Light in the Jungle (1990) . . . . . . . . . . . . . .Rachel

# Nielsen, Brigitte

Ex-wife of actor Sylvester Stallone.
*Films:*
**Red Sonja** (1985). . . . . . . . . . . . . . . . . . . . Red Sonja
• 0:01—Half of right nipple through torn outfit, while
sitting up.
Rocky IV (1985) . . . . . . . . . . . . . . . . . . . . . . Ludmilla
Cobra (1986). . . . . . . . . . . . . . . . . . . . . . . . . . Ingrid
Beverly Hills Cop II (1987) . . . . . . . . . . . . . . Karla Fry
**Bye Bye Baby** (1989; Italian) . . . . . . . . . . . . . . Lisa
• 0:20—Brief side view of right breast, while lying on
a guy in bed. Nice buns shot also.
**Domino** (1989). . . . . . . . . . . . . . . . . . . . . . .Domino
• 0:05—Right breast, lying down next to swimming
pool, breasts getting out.
••• 1:04—Right breast, caressing herself in a white lin-
gerie body suit, wearing a black wig.
976-EVIL II: The Astral Factor (1991) . . . . . . . . . Agnes
The Double O Kid (1992). . . . . . . . . . . . . . . . . Rhonda
Mission of Justice (1992) . . . . . . . . . . . . Rachel K. Larkin
Chained Heat 2 (1993). . . . . . . . . . . . . . Magda Kassar
0:36—In black body suit in bedroom with Rosa.
1:00—In lingerie, in bedroom with Alex.
*Made for TV Movies:*
Murder by Moonlight (1989). . . . . . . . . . . . . . . . n.a.
*Magazines:*
**Playboy** (Aug 1986) . . . . . . . . . . . . . . . . . . . Brigitte
•• 70-77—Breasts.
**Playboy** (Dec 1987) . . . . . . . . . . . . . . Gitte the Great
••• 80-93—Nice.
**Playboy** (Feb 1988) . . . . . . . . . . . . . . The Year in Sex
••• 129—Breasts at the beach.
**Playboy** (Dec 1988) . . . . . . . . . . . . . .Sex Stars of 1988
• 187—Buns and side view of right breast.
**Playboy** (Jan 1989). . . . . . . . . . .Women of the Eighties
•• 251—Breasts.

# • Nielsen, Karen

*Films:*
**Wildest Dreams** (1987). . . . . . . . . . . . . . . . . .Punk #2
• 0:21—Left breast, while sitting on couch.
**Galactic Gigolo** (1988) . . . . . . . . . .Kathy/Cheerleader
*a.k.a. Club Earth*
•• 0:27—Breasts (she's on the left) while in hot tub
with Eoj and Sandy.
New York's Finest (1988) . . . . . . . . . . . . . . . Hooker #1
Sensations (1988) . . . . . . . . . . . . . . . . Scared Woman

Thrilled to Death (1988) . . . . . . . . . . . . . . . . . . . . .n.a.
Party Incorporated (1989). . . . . . . . . . . . . . . . . Diane
*a.k.a. Party Girls*
Fright House (1990) . . . . . . . . . . . . . . . . . . . . . . Tracy

## Niemi, Lisa

Wife of actor Patrick Swayze.
*Films:*
**Slam Dance** (1987). . . . . . . . . . . . . . . . . . . .Ms. Schell
••• 0:54—Nude in Tom Hulce's apartment.
• 1:00—Breasts, dead, lying on the floor in Hulce's
apartment.
She's Having a Baby (1988). . . . . . . . . . . . . . . .Model
Steel Dawn (1988) . . . . . . . . . . . . . . . . . . . . . . . Kasha
*TV:*
Super Force (1990) . . . . . . . . . . . . . . . . . . . Carla Frost

## Nirvana, Yana

*Films:*
**Cinderella** (1977) . . . . . . . . . . . . . . . . . . . . . Drucella
• 0:02—Breasts taking off clothes with her sister Mari-
bella to let Cinderella wash.
• 0:06—Brief breasts sitting up in bed with Maribella.
Brewster's Millions (1985). . . . . . . . . . . . . . . . .Louise
Club Life (1987) . . . . . . . . . . . . . . . . . . . . . . . Butchette
He's My Girl (1987). . . . . . . . . . . . . . . . . . . . . . . .Olga
Another 48 Hrs. (1990). . . . . . . . . . . . . . . CHP Officer
*Made for TV Movies:*
Getting Physical (1984). . . . . . . . . . . . . . Astrid Anders
*TV:*
The Last Precinct (1986) . . . . . . . .Sgt. Martha Haggerty

## Nix, Stacey

See: Dare, Barbara.

## • Noel, Magali

*Films:*
**Tropic of Cancer** (1970) . . . . . . . . . . . . . The Princess
••• 0:17—In sheer bra, then breasts after taking off her
bra while sitting in bed in front of a guy.
The Death of Mario Ricci (1985; French/Swiss) . Solange

## Noel, Monique

*Films:*
Bert Rigby, You're a Fool (1989) . .Jim Shirley's Girlfriend
Roadhouse (1989). . . . . . . . . . . . . . . Uncredited Barfly
Mobsters (1991). . . . . . . . . . . . . . . . . . . . . .Showgirl
*a.k.a. Mobsters—The Evil Empire*
Meatballs 4 (1992) . . . . . . . . . . . . . . . . . . . .Lovelie #1
*Video Tapes:*
**Wet and Wild** (1989). . . . . . . . . . . . . . . . . . . .Model
*Magazines:*
**Playboy** (May 1989) . . . . . . . . . . . . . . . . . Playmate
**Playboy's Book of Lingerie** (Jan 1991) . . . . . . Herself
••• 95—Full frontal nudity.
**Playboy's Book of Lingerie** (Mar 1991) . . . . . Herself
•• 35—Full frontal nudity.
**Playboy's Book of Lingerie** (Mar 1992) . . . . . Herself
••• 37—Full frontal nudity.

**Playboy's Girls of Summer '92** (Jun 1992) . . .Herself
••• 23—Full frontal nudity.
••• 39—Full frontal nudity.
**Playboy's Book of Lingerie** (Jul 1992). . . . . . .Herself
•• 82—Side of left breast and buns.
**Playboy's Book of Lingerie** (Sep 1992). . . . . .Herself
•• 73—Left breast and partial lower frontal nudity.
**Playboy's Calendar Playmates** (Nov 1992). . .Herself
••• 82—Full frontal nudity.
**Playboy's Book of Lingerie** (May 1993) . . . . .Herself
••• 45—Full frontal nudity.
**Playboy's Wet & Wild Women** (Aug 1993). . .Herself
•• 42—Side of left breast and buns.
**Playboy's Book of Lingerie** (Sep 1993). . . . . .Herself
•• 102—Left breast.
**Playboy's Book of Lingerie** (Nov 1993) . . . . .Herself
••• 51—Full frontal nudity.
**Playboy's Nudes** (Dec 1993) . . . . . . . . . . . . . .Herself
••• 40-41—Full frontal nudity.
**Playboy's Book of Lingerie** (Mar 1994) . . . . .Herself
••• 48-49—Full frontal nudity.
**Playboy's Book of Lingerie** (May 1994) . . . . .Herself
••• 80—Breasts.
**Playmates at Play** (Jul 1994) . . . . . . . . . . . . .Herself
••• 36-41—Nude.
**Playboy's Girls of Summer '94** (Jul 1994). . . .Herself
••• 104-107—Breasts.

## • North, J. J.

*Films:*
**Beauty School** (1993) . . . . . . . . . . . . . . . . . . . Renee
••• 0:44—Breasts while doing breast exercises, then
buns in G-string going for a swim. (She's on the far
left.)
• 0:46—Brief breasts, while standing in pool.
• 0:57—Breasts and buns in G-string while undressing
in locker room.
*Magazines:*
**Playboy's Book of Lingerie** (May 1994) . . . . .Herself
•• 12—Inner half of breasts.

## North, Noelle

*Films:*
Report to the Commissioner (1975). . . . . . . .Samantha
**Slumber Party '57** (1976). . . . . . . . . . . . . . . .Angie
•• 0:37—Buns, then breasts in bed with a party guest
of her parents.
Sweater Girls (1978). . . . . . . . . . . . . . . . . . . . . n.a.
Blood Song (1982). . . . . . . . . . . . . . . . . . . . . Cathy
*a.k.a. Dreamslayer*
Jekyll & Hyde... Together Again (1982) . . . . . . .Student

## • North, Sheree

*Films:*
Madigan (1968). . . . . . . . . . . . . . . . . . . . . . . .Jonesy
**The Gypsy Moths** (1969) . . . . . . . . . . . . . . .Waitress
•• 0:37—Breasts while dancing on stage in pink pasties
and pink bikini bottoms.

- 0:53—Most of left breast, while lying in bed next to Gene Hackman.

The Trouble with Girls (1969) . . . . . . . . . . . . . Nita Bisk

**Lawman** (1971). . . . . . . . . . . . . . . . . . . .Laura Shelby

(Not available on video tape.)

The Organization (1971). . . . . . . . . . . . Gloria Morgan

Breakout (1975) . . . . . . . . . . . . . . . . . . . . . . . .Myrna

Charley Varrick (1975). . . . . . . . . . . . . . . Jewell Everett

Telefon (1977) . . . . . . . . . . . . . . . . . . . . . Marie Wills

Rabbit Test (1978). . . . . . . . . . . . . . . . Mystery Lady

Only Once in a Lifetime (1979). . . . . . . . . . . . . . Sally

Maniac Cop (1988). . . . . . . . . . . . . . . . Sally Noland

Defenseless (1991) . . . . . . . . . . . . . . . . Mrs. Bodeck

*Made for TV Movies:*

Key West (1973) . . . . . . . . . . . . . . . . . . . . .Brandi

Snatched (1977) . . . . . . . . . . . . . . . . . . Kim Sutter

The Real American Hero (1978). . . . . . . . . . . . . .n.a.

Portrait of a Stripper (1979) . . . . . . . . . . . . . . . .n.a.

*TV:*

I'm a Big Girl Now (1980-81) . . . . . . . .Edie McKendrick

Bay City Blues (1983) . . . . . . . . . . . . . . . . Lynn Holtz

## Norton, Sara

*Video Tapes:*

**Penthouse The Great Pet Hunt—Part I** (1992)

. . . . . . . . . . . . . . . . . . . . . . . . . . . . . . . . . . Pet

*Magazines:*

**Penthouse** (Aug 1989) . . . . . . . . . . . . . . . . . . Pet

**Penthouse** (Apr 1992). . . . . . . . . . . . Born To Be Wild

••• 111-119—Nude.

## • Norton, Terri

*Films:*

**Dust Devil** (1992; British) . . . . . . . . . Saartjie Haarhoff

- 0:06—Breasts and brief side view of buns, while making love in bed with Dust Devil before he breaks her neck.

Freefall (1993). . . . . . . . . . . . . . . . . . . . . . . Susan

## Norton-Taylor, Judy

*Made for TV Movies:*

A Walton Thanksgiving Reunion (1993). . . . . Mary Ellen

*TV:*

The Waltons (1972-81) . . . . . .Mary Ellen Walton Willard

*Video Tapes:*

**Playboy Video Magazine, Volume 10** (1986)

. . . . . . . . . . . . . . . . . . . . . . . . . . . . . . Herself

••• 0:45—Nude in still photos.

*Magazines:*

**Playboy** (Aug 1985). . . . . . . . . . . . .The Punch in Judy

••• 77-81—Frontal nudity.

**Playboy's Nudes** (Oct 1990). . . . . . . . . . . . . Herself

•• 20—Side view of right breast.

## • Nottoli, Elizabeth

Model for Bisou Bisou.

*Films:*

Waxwork II: Lost in Time (1991) . . . . . . . . . Party Babe

**Warlock: The Armageddon** (1993). . . . . . . . . Model

- 0:29—Very brief breasts under sheer black blouse, while backstage during fashion show. (She's blowing a bubble with bubble gum.)

A Brilliant Disguise (1994) . . . . . . . Janet/Fashion Model

*Magazines:*

**Playboy** (Apr 1994) . . . . . . . . . . . Nottoli, Au Naturel

••• 90-93—Full frontal nudity in color and B&W photos.

## Nova

*Video Tapes:*

**Hot Body Video Magazine #3: Blonde Fever**

(1993) . . . . . . . . . . . . . . . . . . . . . . . . . . Fashion

•• 0:00—Breasts during introduction.

••• 0:30—Breasts, while changing clothes with Dottie and Samantha.

**Hot Body Video Magazine #4: Extra Sexy** (1993)

. . . . . . . . . . . . . . . . . . . . . . . . . . . Feature Girl

••• 0:00—Breasts during introduction.

••• 0:26—Breasts under sheer black top, then nude, while posing on balcony.

## Novak, Lenka

*Films:*

**Kentucky Fried Movie** (1977) . . . . . Linda Chambers

- 0:09—Breasts sitting on a couch with two other girls.

**Coach** (1978) . . . . . . . . . . . . . . . . . . . . Marilyn

- 0:10—Very brief breasts flashing her breasts along with her girlfriends for their boyfriends.

**Vampire Hookers** (1979) . . . . . . . . . . . . . . . Suzy

0:22—In sheer green dress getting into coffin.

0:33—In sheer green dress again.

0:45—In sheer green dress again.

•• 0:51—Breasts in bed during the orgy with the guy and the other two Vampire Hookers.

*Video Tapes:*

Terror on Tape (1985) . . . . . . . . . . . . . . . . . . Suzy

0:00—Breasts scene from *Vampire Hookers.*

*Magazines:*

**Playboy** (Aug 1977)

. . . . . . . . . . . . . . . Playboy's Playmate Photo Contest

••• 142—Full frontal nudity.

## Nychols, Darcy

Adult film actress.

*Films:*

Mugsy's Girls (1985) . . . . . . . . . . . .Madame Antoinette

**Slammer Girls** (1987) . . . . . . . . . . . . . . . . . . . Tank

- 0:17—Breasts ripping blouse open while hassling Melody.

## Nygren, Mia

*Films:*

**Emmanuelle IV** (1984) . . . . . . . . . . . . .Emmanuelle IV

0:13—Buns, lying on table after plastic surgery.

••• 0:15—Full frontal nudity walking around looking at her new self in the mirror.

- 0:20—Brief breasts a couple of times making love on top of a guy getting coached by Sylvia Kristel in dream-like sequence.
- 0:22—Full frontal nudity taking off blouse in front of Dona.
  0:25—Almost making love with a guy in bar.
- 0:30—Nude undressing in front of Maria.
- 0:39—Full frontal nudity taking her dress off and getting covered with a white sheet.
- 0:40—Full frontal nudity lying down and then putting dress back on.
- 0:45—Full frontal nudity during levitation trick.
  0:49—Right bra cup reclining on bed.
- 0:52—Brief breasts in stable.
- 0:54—Breasts taking off black dress in chair. Brief lower frontal nudity.
  0:57—Brief lower frontal nudity putting on white panties.
- 1:00—Brief breasts when Susanna takes her dress off.
- 1:03—Brief right breast making love on ground with a boy.
- 1:07—Breasts while walking on beach.
- 1:09—Breasts with Dona. Dark.
Plaza Real (1988)............................n.a.
*Magazines:*
**Playboy** (Dec 1984).............. Sex Stars of 1984
- 204—Right breast.

## O'Brien, Maureen

*Films:*
**She'll be Wearing Pink Pyjamas** (1985; British)
................................................ Joan
- 0:46—Brief breasts making love in bed with Tom. Dark.
Zina (1985; British)..........................n.a.

## •O'Brien, Shauna

*Films:*
**Seduce Me: Pamela Principle 2** (1994) .... Michelle
- 0:15—Breasts and buns in G-string, after taking off lingerie for photo session.
*Video Tapes:*
**Rock Video Girls 2** (1992) ................ Herself
  0:00—Brief, blurry breasts in shower during opening credits.
- 0:33—Breasts in shower during music video.
*Magazines:*
Sport (Mar 1994) ................. Feel the H.E.A.T.

## O'Byrne, Kehli

*Films:*
K2 (1991) ................................. Pam
**Knight Moves** (1992)..............Debi Rutledge
- 0:08—Breasts and partial lower frontal nudity, while making love in bed with Christopher Lambert.
*Made for TV Movies:*
Elvis and the Colonel: The Untold Story (1993)
................................................ Priscilla

## O'Connell, Natalie

*Films:*
**Breeders** (1986).........................Donna
- 0:02—Very brief left breast, getting her blouse ripped by creature.
- 0:44—Breasts, sitting up in hospital bed, then buns, walking down the hall.
- 0:47—More breasts and buns, walking around outside.
- 1:10—Brief breasts, standing up in the alien nest.
I Was a Teenage T.V. Terrorist (1987)
.....................Woman on Audition Line

## O'Connell, Taaffe

*Films:*
**Galaxy of Terror** (1981) ................Damelia
- 0:42—Breasts getting raped by a giant alien slug. Nice and slimy.
  0:46—Buns, covered with slime being discovered by her crew mates.
New Year's Evil (1981) ......................Jane
**Caged Fury** (1984)...................... Honey
- 0:17—Breasts on bed with a guard. Mostly left breast.
  0:40—Very, very brief tip of left breast peeking out between arms in shower.
- 1:06—Very brief breasts getting blouse ripped open by a guard in the train.
**Hot Chili** (1985)........................ Brigitte
- 0:21—Breasts while lying on the bed. Shot with lots of diffusion.
- 0:30—Brief breasts while playing the drums.
- 1:11—Brief breasts in bed while making love with Ernie, next to her drunk husband.
**Not of This Earth** (1988) ................Damelia
- 0:04—Brief breasts and buns from *Galaxy of Terror* during the opening credits.
*TV:*
Blansky's Beauties (1977)........... Hillary S. Prentiss

## O'Connor, Glynnis

*Films:*
Ode to Billy Joe (1976)........... Bobby Lee Hartley
**California Dreaming** (1978).............. Corky
- 0:11—Breasts pulling her top over her head when T.T. is using the bathroom.
  1:12—In white bra, in bed with T.T.
- 1:14—Breasts in bed with T.T.
**Those Lips, Those Eyes** (1980)...........Ramona
- 0:37—Left breast in car with Tom Hulce. Dark, hard to see.
- 1:12—Breasts and buns on bed with Tom Hulce. Dark.
Night Crossing (1981) ............... Petra Wetzel
**Melanie** (1982).........................Melanie
- 0:08—Very brief right breast, while turning over in bed next to Don Johnson.
- 0:09—Breasts, while sitting up and putting on a T-shirt, then getting out of bed.

*Made for TV Movies:*
The Boy in the Plastic Bubble (1976) . . . . . . . . . . . Gina
Why Me? (1984) . . . . . . . . . . . . . . Leola Mae Harmon
*TV:*
Sons and Daughters (1974) . . . . . . . . . . . Anita Cramer

# • O'Grady, Gail

*Films:*
Blackout (1989) . . . . . . . . . . . . . . . . . . Caroline Boyle
Nobody's Perfect (1990) . . . . . . . . . . . . . . . . . Shelly
Spellcaster (1992) . . . . . . . . . . . . . . . . . . . . . Jackie
*Made for TV Movies:*
Parker Kane (1990) . . . . . . . . . . . . . . . . . . Cindy Kane
*TV:*
NYPD Blue (1993- ) . . . . . . . . . . . . . Donna Abandando
**NYPD Blue: Abandando Abandoned** (Jan 11, 1994)
. . . . . . . . . . . . . . . . . . . . . . . . . Donna Abandando
• 0:03—Brief back side of left breast, after dropping
her robe in front of Metavoy.

# O'Grady, Lani

*Films:*
**Massacre at Central High** (1976) . . . . . . . . . . . Jane
••• 1:09—Breasts walking out of a tent and getting back
into it with Rainbeaux Smith and Robert Carradine.
The Campus Corpse (1977) . . . . . . . . . . . Campus Girl
*TV:*
The Headmaster (1970-71) . . . . . . . . . . . . . . . . Judy
Eight is Enough (1977-81) . . . . . . . . . . Mary Bradford

# O'Neal, Tatum

Wife of tennis player John McEnroe.
Daughter of actor Ryan O'Neal and actress Joanna
Moore.
*Films:*
Paper Moon (1973) . . . . . . . . . . . . . . . . . Addie Loggins
(Academy Award for Best Supporting Actress.)
The Bad News Bears (1976) . . . . . . . . Manda Whurlizer
International Velvet (1978; British) . . . . . . . Sarah Brown
**Circle of Two** (1980) . . . . . . . . . . . . . . Sarah Norton
•• 0:56—Breasts standing behind a chair in Richard
Burton's studio talking to him.
**Little Darlings** (1980) . . . . . . . . . . . . . . . . . . Ferris
• 0:35—Very, very brief half of left nipple, sticking out
of swimsuit top when she comes up for air after fall-
ing into the pool to get Armand Assante's attention.
Certain Fury (1985) . . . . . . . . . . . . . . . . . . . . Scarlet
*Made for TV Movies:*
Woman on the Run: The Lawrencia Bembenek Story
(1993) . . . . . . . . . . . . . . Lawrencia "Bambi" Bembenek
*Magazines:*
**Playboy** (Nov 1982) . . . . . . . . . . Sex in Cinema 1982
•• 165—Breasts photo from *Circle of Two*.
Bikini (Apr 1994) . . . . . . . . . . . . . . . . Tatum Verbatim
46-51—Upper 1/4 of right breast in three photos.

# O'Neill, Maggie

*Films:*
Gorillas in the Mist (1988) . . . . . . . . . . . . . . . . . . Kim
**Under Suspicion** (1992) . . . . . . . . . . . . . . . . Hazel
• 0:02—Breasts and lower frontal nudity in shower
with Liam Neeson.
• 0:03—Very brief right breast, while ducking to avoid
shotgun blast.

# O'Neill, Remy

*Films:*
**Angel of H.E.A.T.** (1981) . . . . . . . . . Andrea Shockley
*a.k.a. The Protectors, Book I*
•• 0:43—Breasts, wearing a blue swimsuit, wrestling in
the mud with Mary Woronov.
**Erotic Images** (1983) . . . . . . . . . . . . . Vickie Coleman
••• 0:04—Breasts while sitting in chaise lounge talking
to Britt Ekland about sex survey. Long scene.
• 0:06—Breasts while in bed with Marvin. Brief lower
frontal nudity.
•• 0:07—Brief left breast while in spa with TV repairman, then brief breasts.
**Hollywood Hot Tubs** (1984) . . . . . . . . . Pam Landers
• 1:00—Brief right breast in hot tub with Jeff.
Return to Horror High (1987) . . . . . . . . Esther Molvania
To Die For (1988) . . . . . . . . . . . . . . . . . . . . . . . . Jane
Hollywood Hot Tubs 2—Educating Crystal (1989)
. . . . . . . . . . . . . . . . . . . . . . . . . . . . . Pam Landers
0:57—Swinging tassels on the tips of her belly danc-
ing top.
The Forbidden Dance (1990) . . . . . . . . . . . . . . Robin
To Die For 2 (1991) . . . . . . . . . . . . . . . . . . . . . . Jane
*a.k.a. Son of Darkness: To Die For II*

# O'Reilly, Erin

*Films:*
How Sweet It Is (1968) . . . . . . . . . . . . . . . . . Tour Girl
Little Fauss and Big Halsy (1970) . . . . . . . Sylvene McFall
T. R. Baskin (1971) . . . . . . . . . . . . . . . . . . . . . . Kathy
**Blume in Love** (1973) . . . . . . . . . . . . . . . . . . Cindy
• 0:40—Breasts and buns, getting out of bed with
George Segal.
Busting (1974) . . . . . . . . . . . . . . . . . . . . . . . . Doris

# O'Reilly, Kathryn

*Films:*
Jack's Back (1987) . . . . . . . . . . . . . . . . . . . . Hooker
**Puppet Master** (1989) . . . . . . . . . . Carissa Stamford
• 0:41—Left breast in bathtub, covered with bubbles.
• 0:43—Brief left breast getting out of tub. Nipple
covered with bubbles.
0:50—Riding on Frank in bed. Don't see anything,
but still exciting. Very brief buns under sheer nightgown when she gets off Frank.
1:11—Right breast under sheer black nightgown,
dead sitting at the table. Blood on her face.

# O'Shea, Missy

*Films:*

**Blow Out** (1981). . . . . . . . . . . . . . . . . . Dancing Coed
0:00—Dancing in sheer nightgown while a campus guard watches from outside the window.

**New York Nights** (1981) . . . . . . . . . . . . . The Model
0:30—In white bra in restroom making love with the photographer.

•• 0:37—in black bra, panties, garter belt and stockings then breasts taking off bra and getting into bed.

•• 0:40—Breasts while on the floor when the photographer throws her on the floor and rips her bra off.

••• 0:41—Full frontal nudity putting bathrobe on.

• 0:44—Breasts while standing in front of a mirror with short black hair and a moustache getting dressed to look like a guy.

**Model Behavior** (1982) . . . . . . . . . . . . . . . Anne #1

••• 0:40—Breasts, taking off her top second, with the other Anne in front of Dino.

# O'Toole, Annette

*Films:*

**Smile** (1974). . . . . . . . . . . . . . . . . . . . Doria Houston
0:34—In white bra and panties in dressing room.
1:06—In white bra and slip talking to Joan Prather in bedroom.

One on One (1977) . . . . . . . . . . . . . . . . . . .Janet Hays
King of the Gypsies (1978) . . . . . . . . . . . . . . . Sharon
Foolin' Around (1980). . . . . . . . . . . . . . . . . . . Susan
48 Hrs. (1982). . . . . . . . . . . . . . . . . . . . . . . Elaine

**Cat People** (1982). . . . . . . . . . . . . . . . Alice Perrin

••• 1:30—In a bra, then breasts undressing in locker room.

• 1:31—Some breasts shots of her in the pool. Distorted because of the water.

• 1:33—Brief right breast, after getting out of the pool.

Superman III (1983) . . . . . . . . . . . . . . . . . .Lana Lang

**Cross My Heart** (1987). . . . . . . . . . . . . . . . Kathy
0:44—In pink bra standing in bedroom with Martin Short.

•• 0:46—Left breast, in bed with Short.

•• 0:48—Breasts in bed when Short heads under the covers.

•• 0:49—Brief breasts again getting her purse.

• 1:05—Brief breasts and buns, dressing after Short finds out about her daughter.

Love at Large (1990). . . . . . . . . . . . . . . Mrs. King

*Made for Cable Movies:*

Best Legs in the 8th Grade (1984; HBO)
. . . . . . . . . . . . . . . . . . . . . . . . . Rachel Blackstone
Love Matters (1993; Showtime) . . . . . . . . . . . . . Julie
(Unrated version reviewed.)

*Miniseries:*

The Kennedys of Massachusetts (1990)
. . . . . . . . . . . . . . . . . . . . . . . . . Rose Fitzgerald

*Made for TV Movies:*

Love for Rent (1979). . . . . . . . . . . . . . . Carol Martin

Stand by Your Man (1981). . . . . . . . . . Tammy Wynette
The Dreamer of Oz (1990). . . . . . . . . . . . . . . . Maud
Stephen King's "It" (1990). . . . . . . . . . . Beverly Marsh
Danielle Steel's "Jewels" (1992) . . . . . . . . . . . . .Sarah
Kiss of a Killer (1993) . . . . . . . . . . . . . . . . . . . . . n.a.
Mother's Revenge (1993). . . . . . . . . . . . . . Ellen Wells

*Magazines:*

Playboy (Nov 1982). . . . . . . . . . . Sex in Cinema 1982
166—Buns, in a photo from *48 Hours*, but scene is not on video tape.

# Oberman, Claire

*Films:*

**Goodbye Pork Pie** (1980; New Zealand). . . . . . . .Shirl

•• 0:44—Breasts while in freight car with Gerry.

Patriot Games (1992). . . . . . . . . . . . . . . . Lady Holmes

*Made for TV Movies:*

To Be The Best (1992) . . . . . . . . . . . . . . . . . . .Sarah

# Obregon, Ana

*Films:*

**Bolero** (1984). . . . . . . . . . . . . . . . . . . . Catalina Terry

• 1:32—Brief breasts making love with Robert.

Killing Machine (1986; Spanish/Mexican) . . . . . . . . Liza

# • Oddo, Lynn

*Films:*

Hero (1992). . . . . . . . . . . . . . . . . . . . . . Buxom Woman

**Dead On** (1993). . . . . . . . . . . . . . . . . . . . . . . . . Lisa
(Unrated version reviewed.)

•• 1:00—Breasts, while getting dressed after spending the night in Matt McCoy's bed.

# • Ogle, Natalie

*Films:*

**Joseph Andrews** (1977; British/French). . . . . . . Fanny

• 1:15—Very brief side of left breast, getting her blouse ripped off to get flogged.

•• 1:20—Breasts while hugging Joseph Andrews after he beats up the guy who was attacking her.

•• 1:21—Right breast while walking, then breasts after taking off her blouse in front of Joseph.

•• 1:35—Breasts, after undressing and getting into bed.

The Stud (1978; British). . . . . . . . . . . . . . . . . .Maddy

# Ohana, Claudia

*Films:*

**Erendira** (1983; Brazilian). . . . . . . . . . . . . . . .Erendira

• 0:14—Breasts while getting fondled by a guy against her will.

•• 0:26—Breasts while lying in bed sweating and crying after having to have sex with an army of men.

••• 1:04—Breasts while lying in bed sleeping.
1:08—Brief breasts while getting out of bed. Long shot, hard to see.

•• 1:24—Breasts and buns while on bed with Ulysses.

Priceless Beauty (1989; Italian). . . . . . . . . . . . . . . Lisa

*Magazines:*
**Playboy** (Oct 1984) . . . . . . . . . . . The Girls from Brazil
•• 88-89—Nude.
**Playboy** (Dec 1984) . . . . . . . . . . . . Sex Stars of 1984
•• 205—Left breast, leaning on table.

## Olin, Lena

*Films:*
Fanny and Alexander (1983; Swedish/French/German)
. . . . . . . . . . . . . . . . . . . . . . . . . . . . . . . . . . . .n.a.
After the Rehearsal (1984; Swedish) . . . . Anna Egerman
**The Unbearable Lightness of Being** (1988)
. . . . . . . . . . . . . . . . . . . . . . . . . . . . . Sabina
•• 0:03—Breasts in bed with Tomas looking at themselves in a mirror.
0:17—In black bra and panties looking at herself in
a mirror on the floor.
1:21—In black bra, panties, garter belt and stockings.
•• 1:29—Breasts and buns while Tereza photographs
her. Long shots, hard to see.
• 1:43—Very brief left breast, in bed with Tomas.
2:32—Brief breasts in B&W photo found in a drawer
by Tomas.
**Enemies, A Love Story** (1989) . . . . . . . . . . . . Masha
•• 0:16—In white bra, then brief breasts several times
in bed with Ron Silver. Breasts again after making
love and starting to make love again.
Havana (1990) . . . . . . . . . . . . . . . . . . . . Bobby Duran
Mr. Jones (1993) . . . . . . . . . . . . . . . . . . . . . . . Libbie
**Romeo Is Bleeding** (1994) . . . . . . . . Mona Demakov
•• 1:20—Breasts under leather outfit with fake arm.
•• 1:22—More breasts in the leather outfit.
• 1:29—Buns in sexy black bodysuit.

## Oliver, Anne Marie

*Films:*
**Spring Fever USA** (1988) . . . . . . . . . . . Rita Durango
*a.k.a. Lauderdale*
•• 1:02—Breasts, during wet T-shirt contest.
Summer Job (1989) . . . . . . . . . . . . . . Kathy's Friend #2

## Oliver, Leslie

*Films:*
The Student Teachers (1973) . . . . . . . . . . . . . . . .n.a.
**Thunderbolt and Lightfoot** (1974) . . . . Teenage Girl
•• 1:16—Brief breasts in bed when robbers break in
and George Kennedy watches her.
• 1:31—Brief buns, tied up with her boyfriend in bed.
Venice/Venice (1992) . . . . . . . . . . . . . . . . . .Interviewee

## Oliver, Pita

*Films:*
**Deadly Companion** (1979) . . . . . . . . . . . . . Lorraine
• 0:14—Very brief left breast, then very brief breasts
sitting up in bed during Michael Sarrazin's daydream. Dark.
1:32—Brief full frontal nudity, dead on bed when
Susan Clark comes into the bedroom.

**Prom Night** (1980) . . . . . . . . . . . . . . . . . . . . . . . Vicki
•• 0:35—Brief buns, mooning Mr. Sykes outside of ten-
nis court.

## Olivia, Lorraine

*Video Tapes:*
**Playboy Video Calendar 1992** (1991) . . . . . . . .May
••• 0:18—Full frontal nudity in the desert.
••• 0:19—Nude in Egyptian bed fantasy.
**Playboy Video Centerfold: Lisa Matthews** (1991)
. . . . . . . . . . . . . . . . . . . . . . . . . . . . . . . Playmate
••• 0:28—Nude in the desert, then washing an old car,
then on an airplane, then in Egyptian style bedroom.
*Magazines:*
**Playboy** (Nov 1990) . . . . . . . . . . . . . . . . . . . Playmate
**Playboy's Book of Lingerie** (Jul 1991) . . . . . . Herself
••• 14—Full frontal nudity.
**Playboy's Book of Lingerie** (Nov 1991) . . . . .Herself
•• 105—Side of left breast and partial lower frontal nudity.
**Playboy's Book of Lingerie** (Mar 1992) . . . . .Herself
•• 24-25—Breasts and buns.
**Playboy's Book of Lingerie** (May 1992) . . . .Herself
••• 28—Full frontal nudity.
**Playboy's Girls of Summer '92** (Jun 1992) . . .Herself
••• 56—Breasts.
**Playboy's Book of Lingerie** (Jul 1992) . . . . . .Herself
••• 9—Full frontal nudity.
••• 70-71—Nude.
**Playboy's Book of Lingerie** (Sep 1992) . . . . .Herself
•• 29—Breasts in wet bodysuit.
**Playboy's Book of Lingerie** (Jan 1993) . . . . .Herself
••• 55—Left breast and lower frontal nudity.
**Playboy's Book of Lingerie** (Jul 1993) . . . . . .Herself
••• 71—Breasts under sheer body suit.
**Playboy's Wet & Wild Women** (Aug 1993) . . .Herself
••• 66—Full frontal nudity.
**Playboy's Book of Lingerie** (Nov 1993) . . . . .Herself
••• 48—Full frontal nudity.
**Playboy's Nudes** (Dec 1993) . . . . . . . . . . . . .Herself
••• 20—Full frontal nudity.
**Playboy's Book of Lingerie** (Jan 1994) . . . . . .Herself
•• 99—Side of left breast and buns.
**Playboy's Book of Lingerie** (May 1994) . . . . .Herself
• 31—Right breast under sheer blouse and partial lower frontal nudity.
••• 46—Breasts.
**Playboy's Girls of Summer '94** (Jul 1994) . . . .Herself
••• 57-59—Nude.
**Playboy's Book of Lingerie** (Jul 1994) . . . . . . .Herself
•• 33—Side of left breast.

## Ono, Yoko

Wife of the late singer John Lennon.
*Films:*
**Imagine: John Lennon** (1988) . . . . . . . . . . . . .Herself
• 0:43—Nude in B&W photos from John Lennon's
White Album.

0:57—Brief full frontal nudity from album cover again during an interview.

1:27—Almost breasts in bed with Lennon.

## Oreskovich, Alesha

*Video Tapes:*

**Playboy Video Calendar 1994** (1993) . . . . . February
••• 0:06—Breasts and buns, posing in a big "O" prop.
••• 0:08—Nude, undressing and dancing in an alley.

*Magazines:*

**Playboy** (Jun 1993) . . . . . . . . . . . . . . . . . . . Playmate
••• 98-109—Nude.

**Playboy** (Jan 1994) . . . . . . . Playboy's Playmate Review
••• 201—Full frontal nudity.

**Playboy's Playmate Review** (May 1994) . . Miss June
••• 48-57—Nude.

## Otis, Carré

Model.

Wife of actor Mickey Rourke.

*Films:*

**Wild Orchid** (1990) . . . . . . . . . . . . . . . . Emily Reed
•• 0:51—Left breast in mirror looking at herself while getting dressed.
••• 1:01—Breasts when a guy takes off her dress while Mickey Rourke watches.
••• 1:02—Right breast, then breasts while on the floor with Jerome.
• 1:31—Brief breasts in flashback with Jerome.
• 1:42—Breasts while opening her blouse for Rourke.
••• 1:44—Nude while making love with Rourke. Nice and sweaty.

*Magazines:*

**Playboy** (Jun 1990) . . . . . . . . . . . . . . . . . Wild Orchid
••• 83-87—Nude in photos from *Wild Orchid*.

**Playboy** (Nov 1990) . . . . . . . . . . . Sex in Cinema 1990
•• 146—Breasts in still from *Wild Orchid*.

## • Overbey, Kellie

*Films:*

**Defenseless** (1991) . . . . . . . . . . . . . . . . . Janna Seldes
••• 0:58—Brief breasts, nonchalantly changing into swimsuit at the beach.
•• 1:22—Breasts, posing on bed with her father in video playback.

*Miniseries:*

Stephen King's "The Stand" (1994) . . . . . Dayna Jurgens

## Owens, Susie

*Films:*

**They Bite** (1991) . . . . . . . . . . . . . . . . . . . . . . . Kate
• 1:01—Right breast, while lying on the beach after getting attacked.
••• 1:02—Breasts and buns, while in bed on top of a guy before killing him.

*Video Tapes:*

**Playboy Video Calendar 1989** (1988) . . . . . . August
••• 0:29—Nude.

**Wet and Wild** (1989) . . . . . . . . . . . . . . . . . . . .Model

**Playmates at Play** (1990) . . . . . . . . . . . Gotta Dance

*Magazines:*

**Playboy** (Mar 1988) . . . . . . . . . . . . . . . . . . . . Playmate

**Playboy's Book of Lingerie** (Jan 1991) . . . . . . Herself
•• 20—Breasts.

**Playboy's Calendar Playmates** (Nov 1992). . . Herself
••• 74—Full frontal nudity.

**Playboy's Nudes** (Dec 1992) . . . . . . . . . . . . . . Herself
••• 98—Breasts and partial lower frontal nudity.

**Playboy** (May 1993) . . . . . . . . . . . . . . Super Playmate
••• 82-87—Full frontal nudity.

**Playboy's Blondes, Brunettes & Redheads**
(Sep 1993) . . . . . . . . . . . . . . . . . . . . . . . . . . .Herself
••• 8—Full frontal nudity.

**Playboy's Nudes** (Dec 1993) . . . . . . . . . . . .Herself
••• 17—Full frontal nudity.

**Playboy's Girls of Summer '94** (Jul 1994). . . . Herself
••• 97—Breasts and partial lower frontal nudity.

## Pace, Judy

*Films:*

The Fortune Cookie (1966) . . . . . . . . . . . . . . . . . Elvira

The Thomas Crown Affair (1968) . . . . . . . . . Pretty Girl

Three in the Attic (1968) . . . . . . . . . . . . . . . . . .Eulice

**Cotton Comes to Harlem** (1970). . . . . . . . . . . . .Iris
•• 0:28—Buns and breasts, taking off dress and getting into shower.
••• 0:29—Breasts and buns while getting out of the shower.
• 0:30—Upper half of breasts in mirror while sitting at vanity.
••• 0:31—Brief breasts, unwrapping from towel and lying on bed. Breasts, while lying in bed. Breasts and buns while getting out of bed.

Cool Breeze (1972) . . . . . . . . . . . . . . . . . Obalese Eaton

Frogs (1972) . . . . . . . . . . . . . . . . . . . . . . . . . . . . Bella

*TV:*

The Young Lawyers (1970-71) . . . . . . . . . . . Pat Walters

## Pacula, Joanna

*Films:*

**Gorky Park** (1983). . . . . . . . . . . . . . . . . . . . . . .Irina
•• 1:20—Brief breasts in bed making love with William Hurt.

**Not Quite Paradise** (1986; British) . . . . . . . . . . . Gila
*a.k.a. Not Quite Jerusalem*
• 1:04—Left breast, lying in bed with Sam Robards.

Death Before Dishonor (1987) . . . . . . . . . . . . . . . . Elli

**The Kiss** (1988) . . . . . . . . . . . . . . . . . . . . . . . .Felice
•• 0:49—Side view breasts making love with a guy. Intercut with Meredith Salenger seeing a model of a body spurt blood.
• 0:57—Breasts covered with body paint doing a ceremony in a hotel room.
•• 1:24—Brief right breast, while making love with a guy on bed while Salenger is asleep in the other room.

Sweet Lies (1989). . . . . . . . . . . . . . . . . . . . . . . .Joëlle

Marked for Death (1990) . . . . . . . . . . . . . . . . . . .Leslie

**Husbands and Lovers** (1991; Italian) . . . . . . . Helena
(Unrated version reviewed.)
- ••• 0:03—Breasts, making love on top of Julian Sands in bed. Left breast, while lying in bed after.
- ••• 0:10—Nude, walking around and getting into bed with Sands.
- ••• 0:18—Breasts in bathroom, brushing her teeth, then getting dressed.
- ••• 0:32—Buns and breasts, getting into the shower with Sands.
- • 0:35—Brief breasts getting into bed.
- •• 0:37—Breasts in white panties, putting on stockings.
- • 0:59—Buns, getting spanked by Paolo.
- ••• 1:17—Buns, then breasts making love in bed with Sands. Nude getting out of bed.
- • 1:19—Brief breasts, putting on stockings, then white bra and panties.
- • 1:21—Buns, in greenhouse with Paolo when he beats her.

Black Ice (1992; U.S./Canadian) . . . . . . . . . . . .Vanessa
(Nude scenes are a body double.)
Body Puzzle (1992) . . . . . . . . . . . . . . . . . . . . . . . Tracy
**Every Breath** (1992) . . . . . . . . . . . . . . . . . . . . Lauren
- • 0:21—Very, very brief right breast in jacket while kissing Judd Nelson in bedroom.
- ••• 0:36—Brief back side of right breast, then breasts while kissing Nelson outside by pool.
  0:43—In black bra and panties in bedroom with Bob.
- ••• 1:10—Breasts and buns while in the shower.

Eyes of the Beholder (1992) . . . . . . . . . . . Diana Carlyle
Tombstone (1993) . . . . . . . . . . . . . . . . . . . . . . . . Kate
Warlock: The Armageddon (1993) . . . . . . . . Paula Darc
*Made for Cable Movies:*
36 Hours (1989) . . . . . . . . . . . . . . . . . . . . . . . . . .n.a.
Breaking Point (1989) . . . . . . . . . . . . . . . . . . . Nurse
*Made for TV Movies:*
Condition: Critical (1992) . . . . . . . . . . . . Dr. Lena Poole
*TV:*
E.A.R.T.H. Force (1990) . . . . . . . . . . . . . . Diana Randall

# Paes, Dira

*Films:*
**The Emerald Forest** (1985) . . . . . . . . . . . . . . Kachiri
- •• 0:24—Brief buns while running from waterfall and diving into the pond.
- • 0:33—Breasts while in water talking to Tomme.
- • 0:56—Left breast in courtyard when Tomme proposes marriage to her.
- • 0:57—Left breast in forest with Tomme. Long shot.
- •• 1:01—Breasts, by the river.
- •• 1:04—Breasts and buns during wedding ceremony.
- •• 1:16—Breasts with the other tribe women after being captured by the fierce people.
- • 1:18—Breasts with the other girls being herded into the building.
- •• 1:38—Breasts, in forest taking off clothes.
- • 1:40—Buns, returning to the forest.
- • 1:48—Breasts while in the river.

*Magazines:*
**Playboy** (Nov 1985) . . . . . . . . . . Sex in Cinema 1985
- ••• 127—Breasts while posing with Charley Boorman.

# Page, Amy

See: Ager, Suzanne.

# Pai, Sue Francis

a.k.a. Suzie Pai.
*Films:*
Sharky's Machine (1981) . . . . . . . . . . . . . . . . . .Siakwan
Big Trouble in Little China (1986). . . . . . . . . . . Miao Yin
**Jakarta** (1988) . . . . . . . . . . . . . . . . . . . . . . . . . . .Esha
- • 1:01—Brief right breast, while making love in the courtyard with Falco.
  1:13—Brief side of right breast while kissing Falco.
- •• 1:13—Side view of right breast, then brief breasts twice, making love under a mosquito net with Falco. Hard to see her face clearly.

*Magazines:*
**Penthouse** (Jan 1981) . . . . . . . . . . . . . . . . . . . . . .Pet
**Penthouse** (Jan 1983) . . . . . . . . . Penthouse Feedback
- •• 44—Buns in small photo.

# Paige, Kym

*Films:*
Beverly Hills Cop II (1987) . . . . . . . . . .Playboy Playmate
Mortuary Academy (1988). . . . . . . . . . . . . . . . Nurse
*Video Tapes:*
**Playboy Video Calendar 1988** (1987). . . . . Playmate
**Playboy Video Magazine, Volume 12** (1987)
. . . . . . . . . . . . . . . . . . . . . . . . . . . . . . . .Music Video
- ••• 0:55—Full frontal nudity.
**Playmates at Play** (1990) . . . . . . . . . . . . . . . . Hoops
**The Best of Video Playmate Calendars** (1992)
. . . . . . . . . . . . . . . . . . . . . . . . . . . . . . . . . . Playmate
- •• 0:14—In lingerie during bedroom fantasy, then breasts and buns.
*Magazines:*
**Playboy's Girls of Summer '86** (Aug 1986). . .Herself
- •• 18—Breasts in open baseball jersey.
- •• 19—Breasts in open baseball jersey.
**Playboy** (May 1987) . . . . . . . . . . . . . . . . . . . . Playmate
**Playboy's Calendar Playmates** (Nov 1992). . .Herself
- ••• 64—Full frontal nudity.
**Playboy Presents Playmates in Paradise**
(Mar 1994). . . . . . . . . . . . . . . . . . . . . . . . . . . Playmate
- ••• 72-75—Full frontal nudity.

# Paine, Bonnie

*Films:*
**Ninja Academy** (1990) . . . . . . . . . . . . . . . . . .Nudist
- • 0:26—Brief buns and breasts playing volleyball. (She's the second blonde on the far side of the net who misses the ball.)
**Repo Jake** (1990) . . . . . . . . . . . . . . . . . . . . . R.V. Girl
- •• 0:28—Breasts (mostly left breast) while in R.V. with her boyfriend.
- •• 0:29—More breasts, while making love with him.

**Twisted Justice** (1990) . . . . . . . . . . . . . . . . . Hooker
•• 0:11—Breasts, wearing black panties and stockings, while getting photographed.

# Paine, Heidi

*Films:*
**Emmanuelle 5** (1986). . . . . . . . . . . . . . . . Girl No. 1
••• 0:42—Breasts, while talking with the two other girls. Wearing a red turban.
•• 0:44—Breasts, while drinking champagne with the other harem girls.
**Wildest Dreams** (1987) . . . . . . . . . . . . . . . . .Dancee
• 0:23—Breasts, while being held in the arms of a gladiator in Bobby's bedroom.
**New York's Finest** (1988). . . . . . . . . . .Carley Pointer
• 0:04—Brief breasts with a bunch of hookers.
• 0:36—Breasts with her two friends doing push-ups on the floor.
**Nudity Required** (1989) . . . . . . . . . . . . . . . . . . Jane
**Roadhouse** (1989). . . . . . . . . . . . . . . . . . Party Girl
**Skin Deep** (1989) . . . . . . . . . . . . . . . . . . . . . Tina
• 0:01—Brief side view breasts sitting on John Ritter's lap while Denise Crosby watches.
**Alien Seed** (1991) . . . . . . . . . . . . . . . . . . . . . .n.a.
**Demon Sword** (1991) . . . . . . . . . . . . . . . . . Malina
*a.k.a. Wizards of the Demon Sword*
*Video Tapes:*
**In Search of the Perfect 10** (1986) . . Perfect Girl #8
••• 0:45—Brief breasts pulling down her top outside of car.

# Pallenberg, Anita

*Films:*
A Degree of Murder (1967). . . . . . . . . . . . . . . Marie
Barbarella (1968; French/Italian) . . . . . The Black Queen
Candy (1968) . . . . . . . . . . . . . . . . . . . Nurse Bullock
**Performance** (1970). . . . . . . . . . . . . . . . . .Pherber
• 0:44—Side view of left breast, while in bed with Mick Jagger.
••• 0:47—Breasts and buns, while in bathtub with Lucy and Jagger.
• 0:50—Buns, injecting herself with drugs.
•• 1:20—Right breast, while lying on the floor. Then breasts and buns, in bed with Chas.

# Pallett, Lori Deann

*Films:*
**Summer's Games** (1987) . . . . . . . . . . . . .Torch Carrier
• 0:00—Half breasts running in short T-shirt carrying torch.
•• 0:04—Breasts opening her swimsuit top after contest. (2nd place winner.)
**Screwball Hotel** (1988) . . . . . . . . . . . . . . . .Candy
••• 0:26—Breasts in the shower while Herbie is accidentally in there with her.
*Video Tapes:*
Mermaid's Illustrated. . . . . . . . . . . . . . . . . . . . .n.a.

**How to Fill a Wild Wet T-shirt** (1986)
. . . . . . . . . . . . . . . . . . . . . . . Lori from Dallas
••• 0:16—Breasts while dancing on stage, then being interviewed backstage with two other topless girls.
•• 0:28—Breasts during quiz time.
••• 0:43—Breasts dancing during semi-finals.
••• 0:45—Breasts dancing during finals.
••• 0:46—Breasts dancing as the winner.
•• 0:48—Breasts during final credits "report card."
**Daydreams** (1988). . . . . . . . . . . . . . . . . . . . Lori
••• 0:01—Breasts cleaning sail boat. Long scene.
••• 0:03—Breasts on sail boat during daydream.
• 0:09—Brief breasts, sitting up on lounge chair when beer is spilled on her back.
•• 0:10—Breasts, while sitting on a bar during beer daydream.
••• 0:13—Breasts in kitchen after spilling whipped cream on herself.
••• 0:14—Breasts and buns, getting into bathtub.
••• 0:16—Nude, in bathtub during daydream.
••• 0:20—Breasts in open tuxedo jacket during dance number.
••• 0:21—More breasts during end credits.
**The Best of the Mermaids** (1992)
. . . . . . . . . . . . . . . . . . . . . . .The Snakecharmer
••• 1:05—Breasts while scuba diving, posing on boat and at the beach. Buns in swimsuit.
**Hot Body International: #3 Lingerie Special**
(1992) . . . . . . . . . . . . . . . . . . . . . . . . . . .Contestant
•• 0:21—Buns in G-string and black top.
0:54—5th runner up.
**Hot Body International: #5 Miss Acapulco** (1992)
. . . . . . . . . . . . . . . . . . . . . . . . . . . . .Contestant
•• 0:26—Buns, while dancing in two piece swimsuit.
0:53—4th place winner.
**Mermaids of the Aztec Empire** (1992)
. . . . . . . . . . . . . . . . . . . . . . . . . Carla Monroe
•• 0:01—Breasts scuba diving under water during the opening credits.
••• 0:04—Breasts, wearing swimsuit bottom, posing for photographer outside by pool.
•• 0:06—Breasts outside by pool and under water.
••• 0:13—Breasts on boat.
••• 0:15—Breasts and buns in swimsuit bottom while scuba diving under water.
••• 0:19—Full frontal nudity during disco fantasy.
••• 0:23—Breasts and buns at the beach. Long scene.
••• 0:33—Breasts, while snorkeling under water.
••• 0:37—Breasts and buns at the beach again.
••• 0:41—Breasts, while scuba diving.
••• 0:45—Breasts in spa by herself, then with a girlfriend.
••• 0:49—Breasts and buns, wearing swimsuit bottom, undressing at the beach during the end credits.
*Magazines:*
**Penthouse** (Jun 1989) . . . . . . . . . . . . . . . . . . n.a.

## Palme, Beatrice

*Films:*

**Foxtrap** (1986; U.S./Italian) . . . . . . . . . . . . . Marianna
•• 0:41—Brief breasts and buns in bed with Fred Williamson, then more breasts making love.
Cinema Paradiso (1988; Italian/French) . . . . . . . . . . n.a.
The Sleazy Uncle (1991; Italian) . . . . . . . . . . . . . Singer

## Palmer, Gretchen

One of the three Diet Pepsi Uh-huh! Girls (1992- ).

*Films:*

The Malibu Bikini Shop (1985) . . . . . . . . . . . . . Woman
Crossroads (1986) . . . . . . . . . . . . Beautiful Girl/Dancer
**Red Heat** (1988) . . . . . . . . . . . . . . . . . . . . . . Hooker
• 1:20—Breasts and buns in hotel during shoot out.
Chopper Chicks in Zombietown (1989) . . . . . . . . Rusty
When Harry Met Sally... (1989) . . . . . . . . . . Stewardess

## Palmer, Jacqueline

*Films:*

**Party Plane** (1988) . . . . . . . . . . . . . . . . . . . . . . . Suzie
••• 0:06—Breasts and buns changing clothes and getting into spa with her two girlfriends. (She's the dark haired one.)
••• 0:11—Breasts again, getting out of spa.
••• 0:23—In bra, then breasts doing strip tease routine on plane.
•• 0:35—Breasts doing another routine on the plane.
Sensations (1988) . . . . . . . . . . . . . . . . . . . . . . . . Tess
Roadhouse (1989). . . . . . . . . . . . . . . . . . . . Party Girl
**Repo Jake** (1990) . . . . . . . . . . . . . . . . . . . . . Porn Gal
••• 0:47—Breasts and buns, while on bed, acting in a movie.
Camp Fear (1991). . . . . . . . . . . . . . . . . . . . . . . . . n.a.
*a.k.a. Millenium Countdown*
**Legal Tender** (1991). . . . . . . . . . . . . . . . . . Mal's Girl
• 0:24—Breasts in bubble bath with blonde girl and Morton Downey Jr.
•• 0:31—Breasts outside by the swimming pool.

## • Paltrow, Gwyneth

Daughter of actress Blythe Danner and producer/director Bruce Paltrow.

*Films:*

Hook (1991) . . . . . . . . . . . . . . . . . . . . . . . . . . Wendy
Shout (1991). . . . . . . . . . . . . . . . . . . . . . . . . Rebecca
**Flesh and Bone** (1993) . . . . . . . . . . . . . . . . . Ginnie
•• 1:09—Left breast, while in motel room, talking with Meg Ryan.
Malice (1993) . . . . . . . . . . . . . . . . . . . . . . Paula Bell
*Made for TV Movies:*
Cruel Doubt (1992). . . . . . . . . . . . . . . Angela Pritchard
Deadly Relations (1993) . . . . . . . . . . . . . . . . . . Carol

## Paluzzi, Luciana

*Films:*

Muscle Beach Party (1964) . . . . . . . . . . . . . . . . . Julie
Thunderball (1965; British) . . . . . . . . . . . . . Fiona Volpe
99 Women (1969). . . . . . . . . . . . . . . . . . . . . Nathalie

Black Gunn (1972). . . . . . . . . . . . . . . . . . . . . . . Toni
Manhunt (1973) . . . . . . . . . . . . . . . . . . . . . . . . . Eva
*a.k.a. The Italian Connection.*
The Klansman (1974). . . . . . . . . . . . . . . . . . . . Trixie
**The Sensuous Nurse** (1975; Italian) . . . . . . . . . . . n.a.
•• 0:20—Breasts in room, ripping off her clothes and reluctantly making love with Benito.

## Papanicolas, Tanya

*Films:*

Vamp (1986) . . . . . . . . . . . . . . . . . . . . . . . . Waitress
**Blood Diner** (1987) . . . . . . . . . . . . . . Sheetar & Bitsy
• 0:15—Brief breasts as photographer during topless aerobics photo shoot.
• 0:24—Breasts, dead on operating table, then dead, standing up.

## Papas, Irene

*Films:*

Attila (1958; Italian) . . . . . . . . . . . . . . . . . . . . . Grune
The Guns of Navarone (1961) . . . . . . . . . . . . . . Maria
Electra (1962; German) . . . . . . . . . . . . . . . . . Electra
Zorba the Greek (1963) . . . . . . . . . . . . . . . The Widow
The Brotherhood (1968) . . . . . . . . . . . . . . Ida Ginetta
Anne of the Thousand Days (1969; British). . . . . . . .Ajmi
A Dream of Kings (1969) . . . . . . . . . . . . . . . Caliope
**The Trojan Women** (1972; British) . . . . . . . . . . .Helen
• 1:11—Very brief breasts, kneeling down to bathe in a pan of water. Seen between slats in wall. Long shot.
• 1:12—Brief breasts and very brief side view of buns, standing up and moving away from the slat wall when the women start throwing stones.
Moses (1976; British/Italian). . . . . . . . . . . . . . Zipporah
Bloodline (1979) . . . . . . . . . . . . . . . Simonetta Palazza
Lion of the Desert (1981; Libyan/British) . . . . Mabrouka
Erendira (1983; Brazilian) . . . . . . . . . The Grandmother
The Assisi Underground (1985) . . . . Mother Giuseppina
Into the Night (1985). . . . . . . . . . . . . Shaheen Parvizi
Sweet Country (1985) . . . . . . . . . . . . . . . . Mrs. Araya
High Season (1988; British) . . . . . . . . . . . . . Penelope

## Papusha

See: Demitro, Papusha.

## Parent, Monique

*Films:*

**Secret Games** (1991). . . . . . . . . . . . . . . . . . . .Robin
(Unrated version reviewed.)
• 0:33—Right breast, buns and crotch, while in bed with Julianne.
**Body of Influence** (1992) . . . . . . . . . . . . Chic Woman
(Unrated version reviewed.)
•• 0:57—Buns in lingerie and breasts undressing in front of Jonathan and Lana at gunpoint.
**Buford's Beach Bunnies** (1992) . . . . Amber Dexterous
•• 0:09—Breasts, fooling around with a customer in the restroom.
• 0:11—More breasts, with the customer.

- 0:42—Left breast in gaping vest, trying to get into Jeeter's pants.
- 1:14—Breasts in bedroom with a customer.

**Sins of Desire** (1992) . . . . . . . . . . . . . . . . . . . Clarise
(Unrated version reviewed.)

- 0:23—Nude, stripping and dancing (she's the redhead on the right) with Sandy in front of Mr. O'Connor. Long scene.

**Dangerous Touch** (1993) . . . . . . . . . . . . . . . .Nicole

- 0:47—Full frontal nudity, while in the shower when surprised by Kate Vernon.
- 0:49—Full frontal nudity, after dropping towel to join Lou Diamond Phillips and Vernon in bed.
- 0:51—Breasts, while handcuffed in bed with Vernon.

**Dragon Fire** (1993). . . . . . . . . . . . . . . . . . . . . Dancer

- 0:57—Breasts and buns in T-back, while dancing on stage painted with fluorescent paint. Lit with blacklight.

**Night Eyes 3** (1993) . . . . . . . . . . . . . . . . . . . . Brandy

- 0:09—Breasts and buns in G-string, stripping out of her clothes in Zoe's house in front of Dan.

**Sexual Outlaws** (1993). . . . . . . . . . . Uncredited Annie

- 0:31—In green bra, while sitting on bed and posing for John, then breasts while making love with him.

*Made for Cable TV:*

**Love Street: I Dreamed of Angels Crying**
(1994; Showtime) . . . . . . . . . . . Rebecca Heartstrings

- 0:08—Nude, after taking off dress in her apartment in front of Detective Kowalski.
- 0:09—Breasts and buns, while making love with the Detective on sofa.
- 0:10—Breasts, while bent over back of chair while making love. Buns seen, while on shelf.
- 0:14—Breasts, while in front of closet and the Detective pulls her dress top down.

*Video Tapes:*

**Playboy's Erotic Fantasies** (1992) . . . . Cast Member
**Playboy Night Dreams** (1993) . . . Intimate Strangers

- 0:12—Lower nudity in sheer black nightgown with guy from restaurant. Nude, while making love in hotel room.

**Playboy's Erotic Fantasies III** (1993)
. . . . . . . . . . . . . . . . . . . .Midnight Madness/Vampiress

- 0:00—Nude, while making love with a guy and the other vampiress. (She's wearing solid arm bands.)

**Playboy's Sensual Fantasy for Lovers** (1993)
. . . . . . . . . . . . . . . . . . . . . . . . . . . . . . . Secret Desires

- 0:30—In green bra and panties, while talking on the phone with her lover.
- 0:32—Full frontal nudity after taking off bra and making love in bed.

# Parillaud, Anne

*Films:*

**Patricia** (1984) . . . . . . . . . . . . . . . . . . . Patricia Cook

- 0:25—Breasts, opening her jumpsuit top to get attention while trying to hitchhike.
- 0:30—Breasts in white panties, running around at a seminary, trying to get away from a group of guys.

- 0:31—Breasts in confessional booth.
- 0:32—Running around some more.
- 0:37—Nude making love with Priscilla on bed.
  0:46—Sort of briefly breasts running around in skimpy costume.
- 0:49—Dancing in two piece swimsuit, then breasts.
- 0:50—Breasts while lying on her stomach.
- 0:52—Brief breasts running into the ocean.
- 0:53—Brief breasts under water.
- 0:55—More brief breasts shots under the water.
- 0:56—Nude, getting out of the ocean and lying down on the beach.
- 1:09—Breasts taking off her dress and playing bullfight with Harry.
- 1:10—Nude, dancing in her room. Hard to see because the curtains get in the way.
- 1:24—Brief buns while making love with Harry.
- 1:26—Brief breasts while making love with Harry.
- 1:27—Full frontal nudity making love on top of Harry in bed.

**Juillet en Septembre** (1988; French) . . . . . . . . . . .Marie
**La Femme Nikita** (1991; French/Italian) . . . . . . Nikita
*a.k.a. Nikita*

- 0:59—Very brief right nipple, peeking out of her top when she sits up in bed.

**Innocent Blood** (1992) . . . . . . . . . . . . . . . . . . .Marie

- 0:03—Nude in her apartment.
- 1:17—Brief buns, taking off coat and getting into bed.
  1:21—Very brief partial buns, while sitting up in bed.
- 1:24—Breasts, taking off sheet and kneeling over in bed to get handcuffs put on.
- 1:25—Breasts and buns, while making love in bed with Anthony LaPaglia.

**Map of the Human Heart** (1992; Australian/Canadian) . . . . . . . . . . . . . . . . . . . . . . . . . Albertine

- 1:14—Partial left breast (close-up), then right breast, while making love with Avik on top of blimp.

# Paris, Cheryl

*Films:*

**Liberty & Bash** (1989) . . . . . . . . . . . . . . . . . . . Melissa
**Sweet Justice** (1991) . . . . . . . . . . . . . . . . . . .Suzanne
  0:10—In black bra, outside with Marc Singer.

- 0:12—Brief breasts while making love with Singer standing up by tree.

*Made for TV Movies:*

From the Files of Joseph Wambaugh: A Jury of One
(1992) . . . . . . . . . . . . . . . . . . . . . . . . . . . .Rita Mulick

# Parker, Mary-Louise

*Films:*

Longtime Companion (1990). . . . . . . . . . . . . . . . Lisa
Fried Green Tomatoes (1991). . . . . . . . . . . . . . . Ruth
  *a.k.a. Fried Green Tomatoes at the Whistle Stop Café*
**Grand Canyon** (1991) . . . . . . . . . . . . . . . . . . . . . .Dee

- 1:00—Breasts, pulling sheet down, while lying in bed during dream sequence.

Mr. Wonderful (1993) . . . . . . . . . . . . . . . . . . . . . Rita

Naked in New York (1993) . . . . . . . . . . . . . . . . . . .n.a.
The Client (1994) . . . . . . . . . . . . . . . . . . . . . . . . . .n.a.
*Made for TV Movies:*
A Place for Annie (1994) . . . . . . . . . . . . . . . . . . . Linda

## Parkhurst, Heather

*Films:*
Body of Influence (1992). . . . . . . .Woman in Apartment
(Unrated version reviewed.)
Conflict of Interest (1992). . . . . . . . . . . . . . . Francesca
*Video Tapes:*
**Hot Body International: #1 Miss Cancun** (1990)
. . . . . . . . . . . . . . . . . . . . . . . . . . . . . . . . . Contestant
•• 0:26—Buns, in two piece swimsuit.
•• 0:52—Winner. Buns, in two piece swimsuit during
photo session after the contest.
**Inside Out 2** (1992) . .Woman/I've Got a Crush on You
(Unrated version reviewed.)
•• 0:14—Brief buns, in swimsuit, suntanning. Breasts,
trying to prevent guy from jumping.
• 0:15—More breasts and buns shots when she's flat-
tened during the rest of the segment.
Hot Body: The Best of Hot Body (1994). . . . . . . Herself
*Magazines:*
**Playboy** (Jan 1992) . . . . . . . . .The Swedish Bikini Team
Hilgar Oblief.
••• 78-85—Full frontal nudity with swimmask. Breasts
while reading magazine on boat. Buns, while holding up surfboard (2nd from the left). Breasts while
holding white telephone. Full frontal nudity, lying
down on parachute. Breasts drinking beer from
mug. Breasts while holding sleeping bag with her
left hand.
**Playboy's Girls of Summer '92** (Jun 1992). . . Herself
••• 86—Full frontal nudity.
**Playboy's Nudes** (Dec 1992) . . . . . . . . . . . . . Herself
••• 16—Breasts.

## Parkins, Barbara

*Films:*
**Valley of the Dolls** (1967) . . . . . . . . . . . Anne Welles
• 0:28—Very brief silhouette of a breast, when taking
off nightgown and getting into bed.
**The Mephisto Waltz** (1971) . . . . . . . . . . . . .Roxanne
• 1:26—Left breast, while kissing Alan Alda during
witchcraft sequence.
Asylum (1972; British). . . . . . . . . . . . . . . . . . . Bonnie
Christina (1974) . . . . . . . . . . . . . . . . . . . . . .Christina
Shout at the Devil (1976; British) . . . . . . . . . . . . . Rosa
Bear Island (1980; British/Canadian) . . . . . .Judith Ruben
**Breakfast in Paris** (1981) . . . . . . . . . . . Jackie Wyatt
••• 0:41—Right breast, while rolling over in bed. Breasts
when sitting up in bed.
*Made for Cable Movies:*
To Catch a King (1984; HBO) . . . . .Dutchess of Windsor
*Made for TV Movies:*
Snatched (1977) . . . . . . . . . . . . . . . . . .Barbara Maxvill
Calendar Girl Murders (1984) . . . . . . . . . . . . . . . Cleo

*TV:*
Peyton Place (1964-69)
. . . . . . . . . . . . . . . .Betty Anderson/Harrington/Cord
Captains and the Kings (1976). . . . . . . . . . .Martinique
*Magazines:*
**Playboy** (May 1976). . . . . . . . . . . . . . . .Parkin's Place
••• 86-89—Breasts and side view of buns.
**Playboy** (Dec 1977) . . . . . . . . . . . . .Sex Stars of 1977
•• 215—Left breast and partial lower frontal nudity,
while standing looking out the window.

## Parkinson, Dian

*TV:*
The Price is Right (1975-93) . . . . . . . . . . . . . . . Hostess
*Video Tapes:*
**Playboy Celebrity Centerfold: Dian Parkinson**
(1993) . . . . . . . . . . . . . . . . . . . . . . . . . . . . . .Herself
••• 0:00—Breasts during introduction.
••• 0:05—Nude, after stripping out of a man's business
suit in studio.
••• 0:12—In white, bra, garter belt and stockings, then
nude while making love with a guy in art gallery fantasy.
••• 0:17—Nude in still photos.
••• 0:20—Nude in desert fantasy.
••• 0:23—Nude in dress while dancing in music video.
••• 0:27—In lingerie, then nude in bedroom fantasy.
• 0:32—Brief breasts while changing clothes by car.
••• 0:35—In white bra in hotel room, then nude making
love in robbery fantasy.
*Magazines:*
**Playboy** (Dec 1991)
. . . . . . . . . . . . . . . Dian Parkinson, Come On Down!
••• 94-101—Breasts and buns.
**Playboy's Nudes** (Dec 1992) . . . . . . . . . . . . . .Herself
••• 12-15—Breasts.
**Playboy** (May 1993). . . . . . . . . . . . . . . . .Dian's Back!
••• 130-139—Nude.
**Playboy Presents Dian Parkinson** (Oct 1993)
. . . . . . . . . . . . . . . . . . . . . . . . . . . . . . . . . . .Herself
••• 3-89—Nude throughout.
**Playboy** (Dec 1993) . . . . . . . . . . . . . . .Sex Stars 1993
••• 176—Full frontal nudity.

## Parton, Julia

a.k.a. Adult film actress Nina Alexander.
Cousin of singer/actress Dolly Parton.
*Films:*
**Erotic Images** (1983). . . . . . . . . . . . . Marvin's Nurse
• 0:08—Brief breasts in office with Marvin. Dark, hard
to see.
**The Rosebud Beach Hotel** (1985) . . . . . . . . Bellhop
•• 0:49—Buns, then breasts, standing in line. Second
from the camera.
**Vice Academy, Part 3** (1991) . . . . Melanie/Malathion
•• 0:44—Breasts, opening her blouse after seeing all
the money.
Good Girls Don't (1993) . . . . . . . . . . . . . . . . . . Betina

*Video Tapes:*

**Love Skills: A Guide to the Pleasures of Sex** (1984)
. . . . . . . . . . . . . . . . . . . . . . . . . . . . . . . . . . .Model
••• 0:49—Nude in bed with Barbara Peckinpaugh while
a guy watches.

**Penthouse Love Stories** (1986). . . . Loveboat Woman
••• 0:51—In white bra and panties in bed. Nude masturbating while the other girls watch. Nice, long,
sweaty scene.

**Penthouse: On the Wild Side** (1988)
. . . . . . . . . . . . . . . . . . . . . . . . . Punk or Bust Customer
••• 0:34—Nude while wearing black leather outfit, mak-
ing love with Michelle Bauer.

**High Society Centerspread Video #15: Julia Parton**
(1990). . . . . . . . . . . . . . . . . . . . . . . . . . . . . . Herself
••• 0:01—Breasts and buns taking off her clothes.
••• 0:04—Full frontal nudity in bathtub making love
with a girl friend. Nice, long scene.
••• 0:09—Nude, doing a strip tease dance.
••• 0:17—Nude, relaxing on the floor and masturbating.
••• 0:18—Nude on bed, making love with the maid during fantasy.

**Soft Bodies Invitational** (1990) . . . . .Nina Alexander
0:00—Buns, under short skirt, playing tennis with
Becky LeBeau.
••• 0:03—In lingerie during photo session, then breasts
and buns in G-string. Long scene.
••• 0:15—Breasts posing with LeBeau.
••• 0:18—Outside in dress, then undressing to two
piece swimsuit, then breasts. Long scene.
0:24—In two piece swimsuit, then breasts arguing
with LeBeau about who has better breasts.
••• 0:28—In two piece swimsuit, then breasts by the
pool.

**B-Movie Queens Revealed: The Making of "Vice
Academy"** (1993) . . . . . . . . . . . . . Melanie/Malathion
• 0:00—Brief breasts, opening her blouse from *Vice
Academy 3.*

**Soft Bodies: Double Exposure** (1994) . . . . . . Herself

*CD-ROM:*

**Venus' Playhouse** (1994) . . . . . . . . . . . . . . . . Herself

# Pascal, Olivia

*Films:*

**Island of 1000 Delights** . . . . . . . . . . . . . . . . .Peggy
•• 0:16—Breasts, tied up while being tortured by two
guys. Upper half lower frontal nudity.
•• 0:23—Full frontal nudity lying in bed, then buns
running out the door. Full frontal nudity running up
stairs, nude hiding in bedroom.
0:33—In braless black dress.
••• 0:57—Nude, taking off her clothes in shower with
Michael.
• 1:26—Brief breasts running on the beach with
Michael.

**Vanessa** (1977) . . . . . . . . . . . . . . . . . . . . . . .Vanessa
••• 0:08—Nude undressing, taking a bath and getting
washed by Jackie. Long scene.

•• 0:16—Buns, then full frontal nudity getting a massage.
• 0:26—Breasts, while getting fitted for new clothes.
• 0:47—Full frontal nudity when Adrian rips her
clothes off.
• 0:56—Full frontal nudity on beach with Jackie.
••• 1:05—Nude making love with Jackie in bed. Nice
close up of left breast.
•• 1:19—Full frontal nudity lying on the table.
•• 1:27—Breasts, wearing white panties, garter belt
and stockings shackled up by Kenneth.

**Popcorn and Ice Cream** (1978; West German). . . Vivi
*a.k.a. Sex and Ice Cream*
• 0:26—Full frontal nudity (she's on the right), covered with soap, taking a shower with Bea.

**The Joy of Flying** (1979) . . . . . . . . . . . . . . . . . .Maria
*a.k.a. Erotic Ways*
•• 0:39—Breasts wearing panties, in bedroom with
George, then nude.
• 0:46—Nude with George in bathroom.

**Sex on the Run** (1979; German/French/Italian)
. . . . . . . . . . . . . . . . . . . . . . . . . . . . . . . . Convent Girl
*a.k.a. Some Like It Cool*
*a.k.a. Casanova and Co.*
••• 0:15—First woman (brunette) to take off her clothes
with the other two women, full frontal nudity. Long
scene.

**Bloody Moon** (1980; West German). . . . . . . . . .Angela

**C.O.D.** (1983) . . . . . . . . . . . . . . . . . . . . . . . Holly Fox
1:30—In white top during fashion show.

*Magazines:*

**Playboy** (Mar 1977) . . . . . . . . Comeback for Casanova
••• 88—Breasts.

Playboy (Nov 1977) . . . . . . . . . . . Sex in Cinema 1977

# Pasco, Isabelle

*Films:*

Ave Maria (1984; French). . . . . . . . . . . . . . . . . Ursula

Hors La Loi (1985; French) . . . . . . . . . . . . . . . . . . n.a.

**Prospero's Books** (1991; Dutch/French/Italian)
. . . . . . . . . . . . . . . . . . . . . . . . . . . . . . . . . . .Miranda
• 0:13—Tip of left breast, when it peeks out between
an opening in her blouse, while lying in bed as John
Gielgud sits beside her on the bed.

*Magazines:*

**Playboy** (Dec 1991) . . . . . . . . . . . . . . . . . . . . Isabelle
••• 156-162—Nude in mostly two-tone photos.

# • Pasmore, Kathy

*Films:*

Beach Beverly Hills (1992) . . . . . . . . . . . . . . . . Marilyn

**Hollywood Dreams** (1993) . . . . . . . . . . . . . . . Tiffany
(Unrated version reviewed.)
••• 0:15—Breasts and buns, while sitting on desk in
Lou's office.
••• 0:27—Getting a massage while wearing a sexy suit,
then breasts and buns in T-back while making out
with Natasha.

•• 0:28—Breasts and buns, while making love with Natasha and Robby.
• 1:06—Breasts in background while getting dressed.

# Pass, Cyndi

*Films:*
**Bikini Island** (1991) . . . . . . . . . . . . . . . . . . . . . . .Kari
• 0:47—Brief upper half of right breast, while changing swimsuit tops at the beach.
• 0:55—Side of left breast, while taking off her top on bed with Jack.
   0:59—Buns, in black bra and panties after Max disappears.
Bounty Tracker (1992). . . . . . . . . . . . . . . . . . . . .Jewels
Deadbolt (1992). . . . . . . . . . . . . . . . . . . . . . . . . . Diana
Desperate Motive (1992) . . . . . . . . . . . . . . . Ms. Simms
Mission of Justice (1992) . . . . . . . . . . . . . .Erin Miller
Round Trip to Heaven (1992) . . . . . . . . . . . . . . Cindy
Scanner Cop (1993) . . . . . . . . . . . . . . . . . . Sara Kopek

# • Patitz, Tatjana
Model.
*Films:*
**Rising Sun** (1993) . . . . . . . . . . . . . . Cheryl Lynn Austin
• 0:06—Upper half of buns and side of right breast, while sitting in front of vanity in her apartment.
•• 0:10—Very brief lower frontal nudity and breasts, getting her dress ripped open while on board room table.
• 0:52—Very brief right breast, on video monitor during playback of murder surveillance video.
• 1:44—Brief half of right breast in open dress during Wesley Snipes' daydream after being shot. Out of focus.

# • Patrick, Barbara
*Films:*
Zero Tolerance (1989). . . . . . . . . . . . . . . . . . . Wendy
**Body Shot** (1993) . . . . . . . . . . . . . . . . . . . . . . .Candy
•• 0:06—Breasts, while sitting on couch in Robert Patrick's studio.

# Paul, Alexandra
*Films:*
**American Nightmare** (1981; Canadian)
. . . . . . . . . . . . . . . . . . . . . . Isabelle Blake/Tanya Kelly
••• 0:02—Left breast while smoking in bed. Breasts before getting killed. Long scene.
Christine (1983) . . . . . . . . . . . . . . . . . . . . . . . . . Leigh
Just the Way You Are (1984) . . . . . . . . . . . . . . . Bobbie
**American Flyers** (1985) . . . . . . . . . . . . . . . . . . . Becky
• 0:50—Very brief right breast, then very brief half of left breast changing tops with David Grant. Brief side view of right breast. Dark.
•• 1:13—Brief breasts in white panties getting into bed with David Grant.
**8 Million Ways to Die** (1986) . . . . . . . . . . . . . .'.Sunny
•• 0:24—Full frontal nudity, standing in bathroom while Jeff Bridges watches.

Dragnet (1987) . . . . . . . . . . . . . . . . . . . . . Connie Swail
Harlequin Romance: Out of the Shadows (1988)
. . . . . . . . . . . . . . . . . . . . . . . . . . . . . . . Jan Lindsey
**Millions** (1990). . . . . . . . . . . . . . . . . . . . . . . . . . .Julia
   0:19—In black stockings and body suit, changing clothes.
••• 0:44—Breasts while making love in bed with Billy Zane.
• 0:59—Breasts in bed with Zane.
In Between (1991) . . . . . . . . . . . . . . . . . . . . . . . . .Amy
Kuffs (1992) . . . . . . . . . . Uncredited Police Chief's Wife
**Sunset Grill** (1992) . . . . . . . . . . . . . . . . . . . . . Anita
••• 1:14—Breasts and upper talk of buns, while on top of Peter Weller in bed. Nice.
•• 1:15—Very brief buns, while rolling over on her back, then right breast.
*Made for Cable Movies:*
Prey of the Chameleon (1992; Showtime) . . . . . . Carrie
Death Train (1993; USA) . . . . . . . . . . . . . . . . . . . n.a.
*Made for Cable TV:*
**The Hitchhiker: Minuteman**. . . . . . . . . . . . . . .Julie
•• 0:04—Brief left breast in car with husband, then brief breasts flashing the couple on the motorcycle.
*Made for TV Movies:*
Paper Dolls (1982) . . . . . . . . . . . . . . . . . . . . . Laurie
Getting Physical (1984) . . . . . . . . . . . . . Kendall Gibley
Perry Mason: The Case of the Lethal Lesson (1988)
. . . . . . . . . . . . . . . . . . . . . . . . . . . . . . . . . . . .Amy
The Laker Girls (1990) . . . . . . . . . . . . . . . . Heidi/Jenny
*TV:*
Baywatch (1992- ) . . . . . . . . . . . . Lt. Stephanie Holden

# Paul, Nancy
*Films:*
Sheena (1984) . . . . . . . . . . . . . . . . . . . . . . Betsy Ames
**Gulag** (1985) . . . . . . . . . . . . . . . . . . . . . . . . . . .Susan
•• 0:42—Buns, then breasts taking a shower while David Keith daydreams while he's on a train.
V. I. Warshawski (1991) . . . . . . . . . . . . . . . . . . . .Paige

# Paul, Sue
*Films:*
**All That Jazz** (1979) . . . . . . . . . . . . . . . . . . . . . . Stacy
• 1:18—Brief right breast in bed with Roy Scheider at the hospital.
*Magazines:*
**Playboy** (Mar 1980) . . . . . . . . . . . . . . . . .All That Fosse
• 176—Right breast, while kneeling on her hands and knees.

# Pavis, Bobbi
*Films:*
**The Malibu Bikini Shop** (1985) . . . . . . .Stunning Girl
•• 0:19—Breasts trying on bikini behind two-way glass.
Mortuary Academy (1988). . . . . . . . . . . . Sexy Dancer

# Pavlova, Natasha

*Films:*
The Naked Truth (1992) . . . . . . . . . . . . . . .Miss Bolivia
Martial Outlaw (1993) . . . . . . . . . . . . . . . . . . . . .Mia
Son of the Pink Panther (1993) . . . . . . . . . . . . . . .Rima
*Made for Cable TV:*
**Dream On: The Guilty Party** (1992; HBO) . . . . . . Joy
••• 0:10—In black bra, panties and stockings, stripping
    at Eddie's bachelor party. Breasts and buns in G-
    string.

# Payne, Julie

*Films:*
The Lonely Guy (1983) . . . . . . . . . . . . . . .Rental Agent
**Private School** (1983) . . . . . . . . . . . . . Coach Whelan
  • 0:30—Very, very brief left breast popping out of
    cheerleader's outfit along with Rita.
Fraternity Vacation (1985). . . . . . . . . . . . . Naomi Tvedt
Jumpin' Jack Flash (1986)
  . . . . . . . . . . . . . . . . .Receptionist at Elizabeth Arden
Just Between Friends (1986) . . . . . . . . . . . . . . . Karen
Misery (1990) . . . . . . . . . . . . . . . . . . . . . Reporter #1

# Peabody, Dixie Lee

*Films:*
**Bury Me an Angel** (1972) . . . . . . . . . . . . . . . . . . Dag
    0:11—Very brief silhouette of left breast, while get-
    ting into bed.
  • 0:13—Very brief right breast, while getting back into
    bed.
  ••• 0:41—Nude, skinny dipping in river and getting
    out.
  • 1:16—Breasts making love in bed with Dan Hagger-
    ty. Lit with red light.
**Night Call Nurses** (1972). . . . . . . . . . . . . . . . Robin
*a.k.a. Young LA Nurses 2*
  •• 0:35—Breasts taking off clothes in encounter group.
  • 0:39—Brief breasts in Barbara's flashback.

# • Peace, Jennifer

*a.k.a. Adult film actress Devon Shire.*
*Films:*
Death Dancers (1992). . . . . . . . . . . . . Shower Demon
**Housewife From Hell** (1993). . . . . . . . . . . . . . . .Sue
  •• 0:27—Breasts, while undoing her dress in John's of-
    fice.
**Secret Games 2—The Escort** (1993) . . . . . . . . .Darci
  (Unrated version reviewed.)
  ••• 0:47—Full frontal nudity, while making love with
    Martin Hewitt in bed.
  • 1:05—Breasts, in flashbacks.
**Sexual Outlaws** (1993). . . . . . . . . . . . . . . . . . .Betty
  ••• 0:10—Breasts, in lingerie and after taking it off with
    Frank while acting for a video.
  ••• 0:13—Breasts with Frank and Harriet for video.

# Peake, Teri Lynn

*Films:*
**Boys Night Out** (1987) . . . . . . . . . . . . . . . . . . . Maid
  ••• 0:25—Buns in G-string, then breasts doing a strip
    routine. Long scene.
Summer's Games (1987) . . . . . . . . . . . .Penthouse Girl
*Video Tapes:*
**The Girls of Malibu** (1986). . . . . . . . . . . . . . . Lenee
  ••• 0:51—Nude outside and in a hot tub.
**In Search of the Perfect 10** (1986) . . . Perfect Girl #9
  ••• 0:47—Buns and breasts taking a shower.
**The Stripper of the Year** (1986) . . . . . . . . . . Lenee
  ••• 0:47—Nude, stripping out of red sequined dress.
  •• 0:53—Breasts, on stage with the other contestants.
  •• 0:54—Breasts, as a finalist.
  ••• 0:55—Breasts, as a finalist, then in dance-off.
**Night of the Living Babes** (1987) . . . . . . . . . Vesuvia
  ••• 0:25—Breasts and buns in G-string, dancing in front
    of Chuck and Buck. Long scene.
**Wet Water T's** (1987) . . . . . . . . . . . . . . . . . . .Herself
  ••• 0:13—Breasts and buns, dancing on stage in white
    G-string, in a contest.
  •• 0:36—Breasts again during judging.
  •• 0:39—Breasts during semi-finals.
  •• 0:40—Breasts dancing with the other women.
  ••• 0:43—Breasts dancing during finals.
  •• 0:46—Breasts during final judging.
**Starlets Exposed! Volume II** (1991) . . . . . . . . Lenee
  (Same as *The Girls of Malibu.*)
  ••• 0:52—Nude outside and in a hot tub.
*Magazines:*
**Penthouse** (Oct 1987) . . . . . . . . . . . . . . . . . . . . .Pet

# • Peaker, E.J.

*Films:*
Hello, Dolly! (1969) . . . . . . . . . . . . . . . . . . . .Minnie Fay
**The All-American Boy** (1973) . . . . . . .Janelle Sharkey
  ••• 0:37—Breasts and buns, while in bathroom with Jon
    Voight.
The Four Deuces (1975). . . . . . . . . . . . . . . . . . . .Lory
Graduation Day (1981) . . . . . . . . . . . . . . . . . . Blondie
The Banker (1989) . . . . . . . . . . . . . . . . . . . . . . . Renee
*TV:*
That's Life (1968-69) . . . . . . . . . . Gloria Quigly Dickson

# Pearce, Adrienne

*Films:*
Lethal Woman (1988) . . . . . . . . . . . . . . . . . . . . .Trudy
Out on Bail (1988). . . . . . . . . . . . . . . . . . . . . . Maggie
**Purgatory** (1988). . . . . . . . . . . . . . . . . . . . . . . Janine
  •• 0:51—Brief breasts in shower scene with Kirsten.
American Ninja 3: Blood Hunt (1989)
  . . . . . . . . . . . . . . . . . . . . . . . . Minister's Secretary
Demon Keeper (1993) . . . . . . . . . . . . . . . . .Dia Gregory
    0:51—Very brief right breast under wet nightgown,
    while being carried back into the house.

## Pearce, Jacqueline

*Films:*

The Plague of the Zombies (1966; British)
. . . . . . . . . . . . . . . . . . . . . . . . . . Alice Thompson
The Reptile (1966; British). . . . . . . . . . . .Anna Franklyn
Don't Raise the Bridge, Lower the River (1968)
. . . . . . . . . . . . . . . . . . . . . . . . . . . Pamela Lester
How to Get Ahead in Advertising (1988; British)
. . . . . . . . . . . . . . . . . . . . . . . . . . . . . . . . Maud
**White Mischief** (1988). . . . . . . . . . . . . . . . . .Idina
•• 0:07—Buns, then breasts several times while stand-
ing up in the bathtub and talking with her male and
female friends.

*Made for TV Movies:*

Doctor Who: The Two Doctors (1985; British)
. . . . . . . . . . . . . . . . . . . . . . . . . . . . . Chessene

*TV:*

Blake's 7 (British). . . . . . . . . . . . . . . . . . . . Servalan

## Pease, Patsy

*Films:*

**He Knows You're Alone** (1980). . . . . . . . . . . . Joyce
• 0:42—Very, very brief left breast in open blouse
when she turns around to turn off the lights.
Space Raiders (1983). . . . . . . . . . . . . . . . . . Amanda

## Peckinpaugh, Barbara

a.k.a. Adult film actress Susanna Britton.

*Films:*

**Shadows Run Black** (1981) . . . . . . . . . . . . . . . Sandy
••• 0:57—Full frontal nudity, undressing in bedroom.
•• 0:58—Buns and very, very brief breasts getting into
the shower.
••• 0:59—Full frontal nudity, drying herself off. Nude,
walking around the house. Long scene.
•• 1:01—Nude, in the bathroom, trying to avoid the
killer.
**Homework** (1982) . . . . . .Uncredited Magazine Model
••• 0:01—Brief breasts in magazine layout. In lingerie,
then breasts in Tommy's photo session fantasy.
**Erotic Images** (1983) . . . . . . . . . . . . . . . Cheerleader
• 0:07—Breasts dancing in an office with another
cheerleader.
**The Witching** (1983) . . . . . . . . . . . . . . . . . . . . Jennie
a.k.a. Necromancy
(Originally filmed in 1971 as *Necromancy*, additional
scenes were added and re-released in 1983.)
••• 0:02—Breasts and buns in open gown during occult
ceremony. Brief full frontal nudity holding a doll up.
**Basic Training** (1984). . . . . . . . . . . . . . . . Salesgirl 1
• 0:00—Breasts, while on desk.
**Body Double** (1984) . . Girl #2 (Holly Does Hollywood)
• 1:12—Brief breasts in orgy scene in adult film preview that Craig Wasson watches on TV. (Lettering
gets in the way.)
**Roller Blade** (1986) . . . . . . . . . . . . . . . . . . Bod Sister
•• 0:33—Breasts during ceremony. Cut on her throat is
unappealing.

••• 0:35—Full frontal nudity after dip in hot tub with the
other two Bod Sisters. (She's the first to leave.)
•• 0:40—Nude, on skates with the other two Bod Sisters. (She's in the middle.)

*Video Tapes:*

Nudes in Limbo (1983) . . . . . . . . . . . . . . . . . Model
**Best Chest in the West** (1984). . . . . . . . . . . .Chrissy
••• 0:28—In two piece swimsuit, then breasts and buns.
**Love Skills: A Guide to the Pleasures of Sex** (1984)
. . . . . . . . . . . . . . . . . . . . . . . . . . . . . . . . Model
•• 0:02—Breasts, falling back into bed.
••• 0:09—Nude outside in field, making love with her
lover.
••• 0:36—Nude, making love in bed with her lover.
••• 0:49—Nude in bed with Julie Parton while a guy
watches.
**Penthouse Love Stories** (1986) . . Therapist's Assistant
••• 0:45—Nude, making love in Therapist's office, with
the patient.

## Pedriana, Lesa

*Video Tapes:*

**Playmates at Play** (1990)
. . . . . . . . . . . . . . . . . .Thrill Seeker, Flights of Fancy

*Magazines:*

**Playboy** (Apr 1984) . . . . . . . . . . . . . . . . . . . Playmate
**Playboy's Girls of Summer '86** (Aug 1986). . .Herself
••• 54-55—Full frontal nudity.
**Playboy's 1987 Book of Lingerie** (Mar 1987)
. . . . . . . . . . . . . . . . . . . . . . . . . . . . . .Herself
••• 56-57—Full frontal nudity.
**Playboy's Calendar Playmates** (Nov 1992). . .Herself
••• 35—Full frontal nudity.
••• 40—Full frontal nudity.

## Pelikan, Lisa

*Films:*

Julia (1977) . . . . . . . . . . . . . . . . . . . . . . Young Julia
**Jennifer** (1978). . . . . . . . . . . . . . . . . . . . . . . Jennifer
• 0:45—Back side of right breast, in the showers by
herself.
• 0:49—Full frontal nudity, falling into the pool from
ladder. (Possibly a stunt double.)
The House of God (1984). . . . . . . . . . . . . . . . . . .Jo
(Not available on video tape.)
Swing Shift (1984). . . . . . . . . . . . . . . . Violet Mulligan
Ghoulies (1985). . . . . . . . . . . . . . . . . . . . . .Rebecca
Lionheart (1990) . . . . . . . . . . . . . . . . . . . . .Helena
Into the Badlands (1991) . . . . . . . . . . . . . . . .Sarah
Return to the Blue Lagoon (1991) . . . . . . . . . . .Sarah

*TV:*

Studs Lonigan (1979). . . . . . . . . . . . . . . Lucy Scanlon

## Peluso, Felicia

*Films:*

Enrapture (1989) . . . . . . . . . . . . . . . . . . . . .Ingenue
Lunch Box (1991) . . . . . . . . . . . . . . . . . . . . . n.a.

*Magazines:*
**Playboy's Book of Lingerie** (Jan 1992) . . . . . . Herself
••• 45—Breasts.
•• 67—Buns and right breast.
**Playboy's Sisters** (Feb 1992) . . . . . . . . . . . . . Herself
••• 44-51—Nude.
**Playboy's Bathing Beauties** (Apr 1992) . . . . . Herself
•• 44—Buns and side of left breast.
••• 69—Breasts.

## Peña, Elizabeth
*Films:*
Times Square (1980) . . . . . . . . . . . . . . . . Disco Hostess
They All Laughed (1981) . . . . . . . . . . . . . . . . . . . . Rita
Crossover Dreams (1985) . . . . . . . . . . . . . . . . . . . . Liz
Down and Out in Beverly Hills (1986) . . . . . . . . Carmen
*batteries not included (1987) . . . . . . . . . . . . Marisa
**La Bamba** (1987) . . . . . . . . . . . . . . . . . Rosie Morales
   • 0:06—Brief side view of right breast taking a shower
      outside when two young boys watch her from a wa-
      ter tower. Long shot, hard to see.
Blue Steel (1989) . . . . . . . . . . . . . . . . . . . . . Tracy Perez
**Jacob's Ladder** (1990) . . . . . . . . . . . . . . . . . . . Jezzie
   • 0:14—Side view of right breast taking off robe and
      getting into shower with Tim Robbins.
   ••• 0:16—Breasts several times opening dress and put-
      ting pants on. Then in black bra.
   •• 0:31—Very, very brief breasts in bed with Robbins,
      then left breast a lot. Dark.
The Waterdance (1991) . . . . . . . . . . . . . . . . . . . Rosa
*Made for Cable TV:*
Dream On: Super Freak (1993; HBO) . . . . . . . . . Debra
*Made for TV Movies:*
Shannon's Deal (1989) . . . . . . . . . . . . . . . . . . . Lucy
Fugitive Among Us (1992) . . . . . . . . . . . . . . Flo Martin
Roommates (1994) . . . . . . . . . . . . . . . . . . . . . . . . Lisa
*TV:*
Tough Cookies (1986) . . . . . . . . . . Officer Connie Rivera
I Married Dora (1987-88) . . . . . . . . . . . . . . . . . . Dora
Shannon's Deal (1991) . . . . . . . . . . . . . . . . . . . . Lucy

## Pencheva, Anya
*Films:*
Time of Violence (1988; Bulgarian) . . . . . . . . . . . Sevda
   *a.k.a. Vreme Razdelno*
**Deathstalker IV: Match of Titans** (1990) . . . . Janeris
   • 0:16—Brief left breast in open top, while wrestling
      with Maria Ford in the water.
   • 0:36—Brief left breast, while kissing her lover slave
      girl during brief orgy scene.

## Pendlebury, Anne
*Films:*
**Alvin Purple** (1973; Australian) . . . . . . Woman with Pin
   •• 0:48—Right breast and lower frontal nudity, while
      lying in bed, talking with Alvin.
Jock Petersen (1974; Australian) . . . . . . . . . . . . . Peggy
   *a.k.a. Petersen*

## Penhaligon, Susan
*Films:*
The Land That Time Forgot (1975; British) . . . . . . . . Lisa
**Soldier of Orange** (1977; Dutch) . . . . . . . . . . . Susan
   • 1:34—Brief breasts kissing her boyfriend when Rut-
      ger Hauer sees them through the window. Medium
      long shot.
   ••• 1:36—Breasts in bed with her boyfriend and Hauer.
The Uncanny (1977; British) . . . . . . . . . . . . . . . . Janet

## Pensler Gabrielli, Elisa
*Films:*
Alien Space Avenger (1988) . . . . . . . . Red Riding Hood
Naked Gun 33 1/3: The Final Insult (1993) . . . Mourner
*Made for Cable Movies:*
Rebel Highway: Reform School Girl (1994; Showtime)
   . . . . . . . . . . . . . . . . . . . . . . . . . . . . Velmont Girl
*Video Tapes:*
**Eden 2** (1992) . . . . . . . . . . . . . . . . . . . . . . . . Celine
   ••• 0:06—Breasts in sauna talking with Randi.
   ••• 0:25—Breasts in bed with Randi.
      1:16—Breasts while frolicking in the ocean with Ran-
      di.
   ••• 1:24—Breasts while making love in bed with Greg.
   •• 1:27—Left breast, while lying in bed and talking
      with Greg.

## Perez, Rosie
Dancer/Choreographer.
*Films:*
**Do the Right Thing** (1989) . . . . . . . . . . . . . . . . Tina
   •• 1:22—Breasts when Spike Lee rubs ice all over her.
      Don't see her face, but it's her.
Night on Earth (1992) . . . . . . . . . . . . . . . . . . Angela
   *a.k.a. Une Nuit Sur Terre*
**White Men Can't Jump** (1992) . . . . Gloria Clemente
   •• 0:36—Breasts in shower and making love in bed
      with Woody Harrelson.
   • 0:39—Brief right breast, while sitting up in bed.
   • 0:40—Very brief side of right breast, three times,
      while getting out of bed quickly.
Fearless (1993) . . . . . . . . . . . . . . . . . . . . Carla Rodrigo
Untamed Heart (1993) . . . . . . . . . . . . . . . . . . . Cindy
It Could Happen to You (1994) . . . . . . . . . Muriel Lang

## Perkins, Elizabeth
*Films:*
About Last Night... (1986) . . . . . . . . . . . . . . . . . . Joan
From the Hip (1987) . . . . . . . . . . . . . . . . . . . . Jo Ann
Big (1988) . . . . . . . . . . . . . . . . . . . . . . . . . . . Susan
      1:12—In bra, letting Tom Hanks feel her breast.
Sweet Hearts Dance (1988) . . . . . . . . . . . . . Adie Nims
Avalon (1990) . . . . . . . . . . . . . . . . . . . . . . . . . . . Ann
Love at Large (1990) . . . . . . . . . . . . . Stella Wynkowski
The Doctor (1991) . . . . . . . . . . . . . . . . . . . . June Ellis
**he said, she said** (1991) . . . . . . . . . . . . . Lorie Bryer
   • 1:15—Brief breasts getting into the shower with
      Kevin Bacon.

Over Her Dead Body (1992) . . . . . . . . . . . . . . . . . June
   a.k.a. Enid Is Sleeping
Indian Summer (1993) . . . . . . . . . . . . Jennifer Morton
The Flintstones (1994). . . . . . . . . . . . . Wilma Flintstone
*Made for TV Movies:*
For Their Own Good (1993) . . . . . . . . . . . . . . . . . .n.a.

## Perle, Rebecca

*Films:*
Bachelor Party (1984) . . . . . . . . . . . . Screaming Woman
Tightrope (1984) . . . . . . . . . . . . . . . . . .Becky Jacklin
**Savage Streets** (1985) . . . . . . . . . . . . . . .Cindy Clark
   0:24—In bra and panties, fighting with Brenda in
   the locker room.
  •• 0:53—Brief breasts in biology class getting her top
   torn off by Linda Blair.
**Stitches** (1985) . . . . . . . . . . . . . . . . . .Bambi Belinka
  ••• 0:33—Breasts during female medical student's class
   where they examine each other.
  • 1:00—Brief breasts on bed with Parker Stevenson
   when discovered by Nancy.
**Heartbreak Ridge** (1986) . . . . . . . Student in Shower
  • 1:48—Very brief breasts getting out of shower when
   the Marines rescue the students.
Not of This Earth (1988) . . . . . . . . . . . . . . . Alien Girl
   0:53—In black swimsuit wearing sunglasses.
*Made for TV Movies:*
His Mistress (1984) . . . . . . . . . . . . . . . . . . . . . Megan

## Perrine, Valerie

*Films:*
**Slaughterhouse Five** (1972) . . . . . Montana Wildhack
  • 0:39—Breasts in *Playboy* magazine as a Playmate.
  • 0:43—Breasts getting into the bathtub.
  ••• 1:27—Breasts in a dome with Michael Sacks.
**The Last American Hero** (1973) . . . . . . . . . . Marge
   a.k.a. Hard Driver
**Lenny** (1974) . . . . . . . . . . . . . . . . . . . . . .Honey Bruce
   0:04—Doing a strip tease on stage down to pasties
   and buns in a G-string. No nudity, but still nice.
  ••• 0:14—Breasts in bed when Dustin Hoffman pulls the
   sheet off her then makes love.
  •• 0:17—Breasts sitting on the floor in a room full of
   flowers when Hoffman comes in.
   0:24—Left breast wearing pastie doing dance in
   flashback.
  • 0:43—Right breast with Kathryn Witt.
Mr. Billion (1977) . . . . . . . . . . . . . . . . . . . . Rosi Jones
Superman (1978) . . . . . . . . . . . . . . . . . . . . . . . . .Eve
The Electric Horseman (1979) . . . . . . . . Charlotta Steele
The Magician of Lublin (1979) . . . . . . . . . . . . . . Zeftel
Can't Stop the Music (1980) . . . . . . .Samantha Simpson
Agency (1981; Canadian) . . . . . . . . . . . . Brenda Wilcox
The Border (1982). . . . . . . . . . . . . . . . . . . . . .Marcy
Water (1986; British). . . . . . . . . . . . . . . . . . . Pamela
Maid to Order (1987) . . . . . . . . . . . .Georgette Starkey
Bright Angel (1990) . . . . . . . . . . . . . . . . . . . . .Alleen
Boiling Point (1992; U.S./French) . . . . . . . . . . . . Mona

*Miniseries:*
Secrets of Lake Success (1993) . . . . . .Honey Potts Atkins
*TV:*
Leo and Liz in Beverly Hills (1986) . . . . . . . . .Liz Green
*Magazines:*
**Playboy** (May 1972). . . . . . . . . . . . . . . . . . . .Valerie
  ••• 103-107—Nice.
**Playboy** (Dec 1972) . . . . . . . . . . . . . .Sex Stars of 1972
  •• 210—Breasts.
**Playboy** (Nov 1973) . . . . . . . . . . . Sex in Cinema 1973
  •• 151—Breasts in bed.
**Playboy** (Dec 1973) . . . . . . . . . . . . . .Sex Stars of 1973
  • 208—Half of right breast.
**Playboy** (Dec 1974) . . . . . . . . . . . . . .Sex Stars of 1974
  •• 211—Left breast.
**Playboy** (Apr 1975) . . . . . . . . . . . .Perrine as in Queen
  ••• 99-101—Nude.
**Playboy** (Nov 1975) . . . . . . . . . . . Sex in Cinema 1975
  ••• 131—Right breast in B&W still photo from *Lenny*.
**Playboy** (Dec 1975) . . . . . . . . . . . . . .Sex Stars of 1975
  ••• 179—Breasts.
**Playboy** (Dec 1977) . . . . . . . . . . . . . .Sex Stars of 1977
  •• 211—Left breast.
**Playboy** (Aug 1981) . . . . . . . . . . . . . . . . . Viva Valerie!
  •• 152-159—Breasts.
**Playboy** (Nov 1981) . . . . . . . . . . . Sex in Cinema 1981
  •• 165—Breasts.
**Playboy** (Jan 1989) . . . . . . . . . . .Women of the Eighties
  •• 251—Breasts.

## Persaud, Jenna

*Films:*
**The Other Woman** (1992) . . . . . . . . . . . . Traci Collins
   (Unrated version reviewed.)
  •• 0:21—Breasts under sheer black top in her apartment with her boyfriend.
  ••• 0:22—Breasts taking off her top and getting milk
   poured on her.
  ••• 0:23—Breasts and buns, making love in kitchen
   while Jessica secretly watches.
  ••• 0:31—Breasts posing with Sheila at the beach for
   Elysse.
  ••• 0:32—Full frontal nudity at the beach some more.
  • 0:33—Breasts and buns, running in the surf. Long
   shot.
  •• 0:40—Breasts, during Jessica's flashbacks.
  ••• 0:53—Nude, taking a shower, drying herself off and
   putting on robe.
  ••• 0:57—Breasts posing with Carl during photo shoot.
  •• 0:59—More breasts during photo shoot.
  ••• 1:09—Breasts and buns, on the floor making love
   with Jessica. Interesting camera angles.
   1:23—Breasts, while on the floor with Jessica during
   video playback on TV.
*Video Tapes:*
**Penthouse The Great Pet Hunt—Part I** (1992). .Pet
*Magazines:*
**Penthouse** (Apr 1987) . . . . . . . . . . . . . . . . . . . . .Pet

# Persson, Carina
*Video Tapes:*
**Playboy's Playmate Review 2** (1984) . . . . . Playmate
**Playmates at Play** (1990)
. . . . . . . . . . . . . . . . . . . . . Thrill Seeker, Free Wheeling
*Magazines:*
**Playboy** (Aug 1983) . . . . . . . . . . . . . . . . . Playmate
**Playboy's Calendar Playmates** (Nov 1992) . . Herself
•• 31—Side of left breast and buns.

# Pescia, Lisa
*Films:*
Tough Guys (1986) . . . . . . . . . . . . . . . . . Customer #1
**Body Chemistry** (1990) . . . . . . . . . . . . . . . . . Claire
••• 0:18—Breasts making love with Marc Singer standing up, then at foot of bed.
0:35—In purple bra in van with Singer.
0:55—Buns, standing in hallway. Long shot.
**Body Chemistry 2: Voice of a Stranger** (1991)
. . . . . . . . . . . . . . . . . . . . . . . . . . . . . Claire Archer
• 0:42—Brief buns and side of left breast, making love
on stairs with Dan.
••• 0:52—Breasts and buns, in bathtub, standing up,
sitting back down while talking with Dan.
• 1:07—Buns, in leather outfit in radio control booth
with Morton Downey Jr.
• 1:18—Very brief buns and left breast on the stairs in
flashback.

# Peters, Lorraine
*Films:*
More Deadly than the Male (1961) . . . . . . . . . . . . . Rita
**The Wicker Man** (1973; British) . . . . . . . Girl on Grave
• 0:22—Side view of right breast sitting on grave, cry-
ing. Dark, long shot, hard to see.
The Innocent (1985; British) . . . . . . . . . . . . . . . . . . n.a.

# Peters, Luan
*Films:*
**Freelance** . . . . . . . . . . . . . . . . . . . . . . . . . Rosemary
*a.k.a. Con Man*
• 0:25—Right breast and buns, while making love
with Gary and Mitch.
• 0:26—Left breast, twice, while making love with
Gary and Mitch.
Lust for a Vampire (1970; British) . . . . . . . . . . . . . Trudi
Man of Violence (1970; British) . . . . . . . . . . . . . . Angel
*a.k.a. The Sex Racketeers*
**Not Tonight Darling** (1971; British) . . . . . . . . . Karen
•• 0:04—Breasts and buns, taking off nightie and getting into bathtub.
• 0:05—Most of right breast, while sitting in tub,
wishing her husband would look at her.
•• 0:20—Breasts, while in bathroom, taking off her
nightie while Eddie watches through binoculars.
0:21—In black bra and panties in Eddie's fantasy in
store.
•• 0:26—Right breast, while sitting in bathtub. Brief full
frontal nudity when getting out.

••• 0:38—In white bra, then breasts, while undressing
in room with Alex.
••• 0:39—Right breast, while making love in bed with
Alex. Brief breasts in close-up.
0:42—Breasts under sheer top.
• 0:58—Buns, while getting massaged by Joan at the
health club.
Twins of Evil (1971) . . . . . . . . . . . . . . . . . . . . . . Gerta
The Flesh & Blood Show (1974; British) . . . . . . . . . n.a.
Land of the Minotaur (1976) . . . . . . . . . Laurie Gordon
**Pacific Banana** (1980) . . . . . . . . . . . . Candy Bubbles
•• 1:00—Breasts several times flashing her breasts for
Martin.

# • Peters, Vicki
*Films:*
**Blood Mania** (1970) . . . . . . . . . . . . . . . . . . . . . Gail
•• 1:04—Breasts, while making love with Dr. Cooper in
front of the fire. Seen through flames. Intercut with
a rape scene.
• 1:10—Brief breasts in bathroom. More brief breasts,
while getting beaten to death by Victoria and drug
around on rug.
• 1:15—Very brief breasts, while dead, covered with
blood when discovered by Craig.
• 1:17—Brief breasts while being placed in car. Covered with blood.
*Magazines:*
Playboy (Apr 1972) . . . . . . . . . . . . . . . . . . . Playmate

# Peterson, Cassandra
See: Elvira.

# Peterson, Julie
*Video Tapes:*
**Playboy Video Calendar 1988** (1987) . . . . . Playmate
**Sensual Pleasures of Oriental Massage** (1990)
. . . . . . . . . . . . . . . . . . . . . . . . . . . . . . . . . n.a.
*Magazines:*
**Playboy** (Feb 1987) . . . . . . . . . . . . . . . . . Playmate
**Playboy's Calendar Playmates** (Nov 1992) . . . Herself
••• 67—Full frontal nudity.

# • Petruno, Lisa
*Films:*
**Galactic Gigolo** (1988) . . . . . . . . . . . . . . . . . Sandy
*a.k.a. Club Earth*
•• 0:27—Breasts (she's on the right) while in hot tub
with Eoj and Kathy.
**Angel of Passion** (1991) . . . . . . . . . . Sheryl Diamond
•• 0:00—Making love with the husband on the stairs.

# Pettet, Joanna
*Films:*
The Group (1966) . . . . . . . . . . . . . . . . . . . . Kay Strong
Casino Royale (1967; British) . . . . . . . . . . . Mata Bond
The Night of the Generals (1967; British/French)
. . . . . . . . . . . . . . . . . . . . Ulrike von Seidlitz-Gaber
Robbery (1967; British) . . . . . . . . . . . . . . Kate Clifton

Blue (1968). . . . . . . . . . . . . . . . . . . . . . Joanne Morton
**The Best House in London** (1969; British)
. . . . . . . . . . . . . . . . . . . . . . . . . . Josephine Pacefoot
Welcome to Arrow Beach (1973). . . . . . . . . Grace Henry
*a.k.a. Tender Flesh*
The Evil (1977). . . . . . . . . . . . . . . . . . . . . Caroline
**Double Exposure** (1983) . . . . . . . . . . Mindy Jordache
•• 0:55—Breasts, making love in bed with Adrian.
Sweet Country (1985). . . . . . . . . . . . . . . . . . Monica
*Miniseries:*
Captains and the Kings (1976) . . . .Katherine Hennessey
*TV:*
Knots Landing (1983) . . . . . . . . . . . . . . . Janet Baines

## Petty, Lori

*Films:*
Cadillac Man (1990) . . . . . . . . . . . . . . . . . . . . . Lila
**Point Break** (1991). . . . . . . . . . . . . . . . . . . . Tyler
• 1:14—Very brief buns, running out of Keanu Reeves'
bedroom.
A League of Their Own (1992) . . . . . . . . . . .Kit Keller
Free Willy (1993). . . . . . . . . . . . . . . . . . .Rae Lindley
Poetic Justice (1993) . . . . . . . . . . . . . . . . . . Penelope
*TV:*
The Thorns (1988) . . . . . . . . . . . . . . . . . . Cricket
Booker (1990). . . . . . . . . . . . . . . . . . Suzanne Dunne

## Petty, Rhonda

a.k.a. Adult film actress Rhonda Jo Petty.
*Films:*
**Auditions** (1978) . . . . . . . . . . . . . . . . . . .Patty Rhodes
•• 0:26—Breasts during audition.
•• 0:30—Breasts, standing next to Larry and full frontal
nudity straddling him on the table.

## Pettyjohn, Angelique

a.k.a. Heaven St. John.
*Adult Films:*
**Body Talk** (1982) . . . . . . . . . . . . . . . . . . . . . .Cassie
Breasts and more!
**Titillation** (1982) . . . . . . . . . . . . . . . . . .Brenda Weeks
Breasts and more!
*Films:*
Just Tell Me That You Love Me, Junie Moon. . . . . Melissa
Clambake (1967) . . . . . . . . . . . . . . . . . . . . . . Gloria
Childish Things (1969) . . . . . . . . . . . . . . . .Angelique
**The Curious Female** (1969). . . . . Susan Rome/Girl #1
••• 0:29—Buns, while running in slow motion to the
pool, then putting on towel. Breasts on diving
board.
••• 0:30—Breasts and buns, while on inflatable mattress
in pool.
•• 0:52—Breasts while talking on the phone.
• 0:55—Breasts while making love in bed with a guy.
• 1:01—Brief breasts, while jumping into pool. Long
shot.
Heaven with a Gun (1969) . . . . . . . . . . . . . . . Emily
The Mad Doctor of Blood Island (1969; Philippines/U.S.)
. . . . . . . . . . . . . . . . . . . . . . . . . . . . Sheila Willard

Tell Me That You Love Me, Junie Moon (1970). . Melissa
**The G.I. Executioner** (1971). . . . . . . . . . . . . .Bonnie
*a.k.a. Wit's End*
*a.k.a. Dragon Lady*
•• 0:16—Doing a strip routine on stage. Buns in G-
string, very brief side view of right breast, then
breasts at end.
•• 0:40—Breasts, lying asleep in bed.
••• 0:58—Breasts and buns, undressing in front of Dave,
getting into bed, fighting an attacker and getting
shot. Long scene.
• 1:14—Breasts, lying shot in rope net.
The Lost Empire (1983) . . . . . . . . . . . . . . . . .Whiplash
0:29—In a sexy, black leather outfit fighting in prison with Heather.
**Bio-Hazard** (1984). . . . . . . . . . . . . . . . . . Lisa Martyn
•• 0:30—Partial left breast on couch with Mitchell. In
beige bra and panties talking on telephone, breast
almost falling out of bra.
••• 1:15—Left breast, on couch with Mitchell, in out-
take scene during the end credits.
• 1:16—Upper half of left breast on couch again during a different take.
Repo Man (1984). . . . . . . . . . . . . . . . Repo Wife No. 2
Takin' It Off (1984). . . . . . . . . . . . . . . . . .Anita Little
The Wizard of Speed & Time (1988) . . . . . . .Dora Belair
*TV:*
Star Trek: The Gamesters of Triskelion . . . . . . . . Shahna

## • Pfeiffer, Dedee

Sister of actress Michelle Pfeiffer.
*Films:*
Into the Night (1985). . . . . . . . . . . . . . . . . . . . Hooker
Moving Violations (1985). . . . . . . . . . . . . . . . . . Cissy
Dangerously Close (1986) . . . . . . . . . . . . . . . . . Nicki
Vamp (1986) . . . . . . . . . . . . . . . . . . . . . . . .Amaretto
The Allnighter (1987). . . . . . . . . . . . . . . . . . . . . . Val
The Horror Show (1989) . . . . . . . . . . .Bonnie McCarthy
• 1:06—Brief breasts and buns from above, shampoo-
ing her hair in the shower. Breasts, seen through
shower curtain. Probably a body double.
Red Surf (1989) . . . . . . . . . . . . . . . . . . . . . .Rebecca
A Climate for Killing (1990) . . . . . . . . . . . . . . .Donna
Tune in Tomorrow (1990) . . . . . . . . . . . . . . . . .Nellie
*a.k.a. Aunt Julia and the Scriptwriter*
Frankie & Johnny (1991) . . . . . . . . . . . .Frankie's Cousin
Shoot (1991) . . . . . . . . . . . . . . . . . . . . . . Catherine
**Double Exposure** (1993). . . . . . . . . . . . . Linda Mack
• 1:22—Brief left breast while in bed with Jennifer Gat-
ti.
•• 1:23—Left breast, quite a few times, while lying on
her back.
Falling Down (1993) . . . . . . . . Sheila (Whammyburger)
Running Cool (1993) . . . . . . . . . . . . . . . . . . .Michele
*Made for Cable TV:*
Dream On: ...And Sheep Are Nervous (1990) . . . .Mary
0:15—Very, very brief side view of right breast in bed
on top of Martin.

*Made for TV Movies:*
Toughlove (1985) . . . . . . . . . . . . . . . . . . . Kristen March
Highway Heartbreaker (1992) . . . . . . . . . . . . . . . Emily

## Pfeiffer, Michelle

Sister of actress DeDee Pfeiffer.
Ex-wife of actor Peter Horton.
*Films:*
Falling in Love Again (1980) . . . . . . . . . Sue Wellington
The Hollywood Knights (1980) . . . . . . . . . . . . . Suzi Q.
Charlie Chan & the Curse of the Dragon Queen (1981)
. . . . . . . . . . . . . . . . . . . . . . . Cordella Farrington III
Grease 2 (1982) . . . . . . . . . . . . . . . . . Stephanie Zinone
Scarface (1983) . . . . . . . . . . . . . . . . . . . . . . . Elvira
**Into the Night** (1985) . . . . . . . . . . . . . . . . . . Diana
•• 0:27—Brief buns while in bathroom.
• 0:28—Brief side nudity, twice, walking past door-
way. Medium long shot.
Ladyhawke (1985) . . . . . . . . . . . . . . . . . . . . . . Isabeau
Sweet Liberty (1986) . . . . . . . . . . . . . . . . . Faith Healey
Amazon Women on the Moon (1987) . . . Brenda Landers
The Witches of Eastwick (1987) . . . . . . Sukie Ridgemont
Dangerous Liaisons (1988) . . . . . . . Madame de Tourvel
Married to the Mob (1988) . . . . . . . . . Angela de Marco
Tequila Sunrise (1988) . . . . . . . . . . . . . . . . . . . Jo Ann
1:14—Upside down reflection in water getting on
top of Mel Gibson. Can't tell it's her. Only see silhou-
ette. Probably wearing a body suit. Brief buns, hold-
ing onto Gibson when he pulls a sheet over their
heads. Blurry.
The Fabulous Baker Boys (1989) . . . . . . . Susie Diamond
The Russia House (1990) . . . . . . . . . . . . . . . . . . Katya
Frankie & Johnny (1991) . . . . . . . . . . . . . . . . Frankie
1:06—Most of the top half of her breasts, while lying
in bed with Al Pacino.
Batman Returns (1992) . . . . . . . . Selina Kyle/Catwoman
The Age of Innocence (1993) . . . Countess Ellen Olenska
Love Field (1993) . . . . . . . . . . . . . . . . Lurene Hallett
Wolf (1994) . . . . . . . . . . . . . . . . . . . . . . . . . . . n.a.
*Made for TV Movies:*
Natica Jacks . . . . . . . . . . . . . . . . . . . . Natica Jackson
The Children Nobody Wanted (1980)
. . . . . . . . . . . . . . . . . . . . . . . . . . Jennifer Williams
*TV:*
Delta House (1979) . . . . . . . . . . . . . . . . . . Bombshell

## Pflanzer, Krista

*Films:*
**Cheerleader Camp** (1987) . . . . . . . . . . . . . . . . Suzy
*a.k.a. Bloody Pom Poms*
•• 0:11—Breasts several times sunbathing on the rocks.
• 0:14—Brief breasts in flashback.
• 0:17—Breasts on TV in Timmy's video tape of sunbathing on the rocks.
*Magazines:*
**Penthouse** (Jul 1986) . . . . . . . . . . . . . . . . . . . . Pet
**Penthouse** (Jun 1991) . . . . . . . . . . . . . Krista Revisited
••• 40-45—Nude.

## • Pham, Linh Dan

*Films:*
**Indochine** (1992; French) . . . . . . . . . . . . . . . Camille
•• 0:46—Right breast, when getting blood wiped off
after a prisoner is shot and falls on her.
•• 1:05—Brief breasts, while sitting in front of a mirror.
*Magazines:*
**Playboy** (Nov 1993) . . . . . . . . . . Sex in Cinema 1993
••• 136—Breasts in mirror in still from *Indochine*.

## • Phillips, Michelle

Former singer with the group the Mamas and the Papas.
Mother of actress/singer Chynna Phillips.
Ex-wife of actor Dennis Hopper.
*Films:*
The Last Movie (1971) . . . . . . . . . . . Banker's Daughter
Dillinger (1973) . . . . . . . . . . . . . . . . . Billie Frechette
**Valentino** (1977; British) . . . . . . . . Natasha Rambova
• 0:53—Brief buns, enticing Rudolf Nureyev into tent.
• 0:54—Brief lower frontal nudity, when sitting up in
bed.
••• 0:55—Brief left breast when Nureyev moves her hair
out of the way. Breasts, while getting up and out of
bed.
•• 1:39—Brief right breast, after Nureyev rolls off her.
Bloodline (1979) . . . . . . . . . . . . . . . . . . Vivian Nichols
The Man with Bogart's Face (1980) . . . . . . Gena Anastas
Savage Harvest (1981) . . . . . . . . . . . . . . . . . . Maggie
American Anthem (1987) . . . . . . . . . . . . . Linda Tevere
Let It Ride (1989) . . . . . . . . . . . . . . . . . . Mrs. Davis
Rubdown (1990) . . . . . . . . . . . . . . . . . . . . . . . n.a.
Scissors (1990) . . . . . . . . . . . . . . . . . . . Ann Carter
Army of One (1993) . . . . . . . . . . . . . . . . . . . Esther
*Made for TV Movies:*
The Users (1978) . . . . . . . . . . . . . . . . . Marina Brent
Assault & Matrimony (1987) . . . . . . . . . . . . . . . n.a.
*TV:*
Hotel (1986) . . . . . . . . . . . . Elizabeth Bradshaw Cabot
Knots Landing (1987) . . . . . . . . . . . . . Anne Matheson
Knots Landing (1990-93) . . . . . . . . . . . Anne Matheson
*Magazines:*
**Playboy** (Oct 1977) . . . . . . . . . . . Nureyev's Valentino
• 171-173—Tip of left breast peeking out of her hair.

## Phillips, Sam

*Films:*
**Phantasm II** (1988) . . . . . . . . . . . . . . . . . . Alchemy
•• 1:00—Breasts making love in bed with Lance.
**Deceit** (1989) . . . . . . . . . . . . . . . . . . Eve Bendibuckle
• 0:25—In bra and panties after Bailey forces her to
strip. Buns in panties. Dressed like this until 1:22.
Sonny Boy (1989) . . . . . . . . . . . . . . . . . . . . . . Wife
Dollman (1990) . . . . . . . . . . . . . . . . . . . . . . . . Tina
**Angel 4: Undercover** (1993) . . . . . . . . . . . . . . . Jade
• 0:18—Breasts in open robe, while sitting on dressing
room counter in front of Piston.

**Sexual Malice** (1993) . . . . . . . . . . . . . . . . . . . . Nicole
(Unrated version reviewed.)
••• 1:30—Brief buns in raised skirt, then breasts, while
   making love with Edward Albert on sofa.
Weekend at Bernie's II (1993) . . . . . . Pretty Young Thief
*Video Tapes:*
**Rock Video Girls** (1991). . . . . . . . . . . . . . . . . Herself
•• 0:47—Brief breasts and buns quite a few times,
   while wearing a G-string.
**Playboy's 101 Ways to Excite Your Lover** (1992)
. . . . . . . . . . . . . . . . . . . . . . . . . . . . . Hearing/Woman
•• 0:24—In lingerie, then nude with her lover.
**Playboy's How to Reawaken Your Sexual Powers**
(1992). . . . . . . . . . . . . . . . . . . . . . . . . Cast Member
••• 0:17—Full frontal nudity while making love with her
   lover by lava flow.
••• 0:37—Nude while writing love letter, making love
   by campfire and kissing by waterfall.
**Making of the "Carousel Girls' Calendar"** (1993)
. . . . . . . . . . . . . . . . . . . . . . . . . . . . Miss September
••• 1:00—Breasts and brief buns during photo shoot.
••• 1:03—Nude during interview segment.
**Penthouse's 25th Anniversary Swimsuit Video**
(1993). . . . . . . . . . . . . . . . . . . . . . . . . . . . . . . . Pet
*CD-ROM:*
**Penthouse Interactive Virtual Photo Shoot, Disc 3**
(1993). . . . . . . . . . . . . . . . . . . . . . . . . . . . . . . . Pet
*Magazines:*
**Penthouse** (Jun 1993). . . . . . . . . . . . . . . . . . . . Pet
••• 69-81—Nude.

# Picard, Nicole
*Films:*
**Deadtime Stories** (1985) . . . Rachel (Red Riding Hood)
• 0:48—Very brief right breast in shack with boy-
   friend.
Dangerous Love (1988). . . . . . . . . . . . . . . . . . . . Jane
A Time to Die (1991) . . . . . . . . . . . . . . . . . . . . . Patti

# Picasso, Paloma
Daughter of the late painter Pablo Picasso.
Sells her own perfume.
*Films:*
**Immoral Tales** (1975). . . . . Countess Erzsebet Bathory
••• 0:59—Nude, getting her clothes ripped off by a
   bunch of women in a room.
• 1:00—Brief nude, walking away from the women.
•• 1:02—Nude, bathing in blood.
••• 1:05—Nude, walking down stairs. Then in bed with
   another woman.
••• 1:08—Nude in bed and sitting up.
*Magazines:*
**Playboy** (Jun 1975) . . . . . . . Sex in Cinema French Style
•• 89—Full frontal nudity in small photo from *Contes
   Immoraux (Immoral Tales)*.
**Playboy** (Jul 1976). . . . . . . . . . . . . . . . . . . . . . Press
• 34—Buns from movie in B&W photo that appeared
   in the March 8, 1976 issue of *Time* magazine.

# Pick, Amelie
*Films:*
Souvenir (1988; British) . . . . . . . . . . . . . . . . . . . Janni
**Reunion** (1989; French/German) . . . . . . . Young Lover
• 0:47—Brief breasts, twice, while making out in the
   woods with her boyfriend while two boys watch.

# Pickett, Blake
Former hostess on the Nashville Network game show *Top
Card.*
*Films:*
**Hauntedween** (1991) . . . . . . . . . . . . . . . . . . . . n.a.
**They Bite** (1991) . . . . . . . . . . . . . . . . . . . . . . Model
0:00—Posing for photographer in two piece swim-
   suit.
••• 0:03—Left breast, then breasts and buns, taking off
   swimsuit for the photographer. More breasts in the
   water, struggling with the monster.
Traces of Blood (1991). . . . . . . . . . . . . . . . . . . . n.a.
Vampire Trailer Park (1991) . . . . . . . . . . . . Jana Wisher
Can It Be Love (1992) . . . . . . . . . . . . . . . . . . Dyanne
*a.k.a. Spring Break Sorority Babes*
**Dark Universe** (1993) . . . . . . . . . . . . . . . Kim Masters
••• 0:45—Breasts, in open blouse, while outside in the
   woods with Jack.

# Pickett, Cindy
*Films:*
**Night Games** (1980) . . . . . . . . . . . . . Valerie St. John
•• 0:05—Brief breasts, while getting scared by her husband in the shower.
• 0:45—Buns and breasts by and in the swimming
   pool with Joanna Cassidy.
0:46—Breasts under sheer blue dress during fantasy
   sequence with Cassidy.
•• 0:48—Brief full frontal nudity getting out of the
   pool, then breasts lying down with Cassidy.
1:03—Dancing at night in a see through nightgown.
••• 1:14—Full frontal nudity standing up in bathtub,
   then breasts during fantasy with a guy in gold.
•• 1:18—Breasts, while getting out of pool at night.
••• 1:24—Breasts, while sitting up in bed and stretching.
**Brainwash** (1982) . . . . . . . . . . . . . . . . . . Lyn Nilsson
1:24—In sheer beige bra and panties, while getting
   her clothes taken off in front of group.
Ferris Bueller's Day Off (1986) . . . . . . . . . Katie Bueller
The Men's Club (1986) . . . . . . . . . . . . . . . . . Hannah
Hot to Trot (1988) . . . . . . . . . . . . . . . . Victoria Peyton
Deepstar Six (1989) . . . . . . . . . . . . . . . . . Diane Norris
Crooked Hearts (1991). . . . . . . . . . . . . . . . . . . . . Jill
Original Intent (1992) . . . . . . . . . . . . . . . . Marguerite
Stephen King's Sleepwalkers (1992) . . . . Mrs. Robertson
Son-In-Law (1993) . . . . . . . . . . . . . . . . . . . . Connie
*Made for Cable Movies:*
Wild Card (1992; USA). . . . . . . . . . . . . . . . . . Dana
*Made for TV Movies:*
Into the Homeland (1987) . . . . . . . . . . . . . . . . n.a.

Plymouth (1991). . . . . . . . . . . . . . . . . . . . . . . Addy
TV:
The Guiding Light (1976-80) . . . . . . Jackie Scott Marler
Call to Glory (1984-85). . . . . . . . . . . . . Vanessa Sarnac
St. Elsewhere (1986-88) . . . . . . . . . . . .Dr. Carol Novino
Magazines:
**Playboy** (Nov 1979) . . . . . . . . . . . Sex in Cinema 1979
• 175—Breasts, small photo, hard to see.
**Playboy** (Dec 1980). . . . . . . . . . . . . . . Sex Stars of 1980
•• 244—Breasts and partial lower frontal nudity.

## Pierce, Jill

Films:
**Dance with Death** (1991) . . . . . . . . . . . . . . . . . . Lola
•• 0:07—Breasts and buns, dancing in wedding outfit
on stage.
• 0:11—Breasts and buns in G-string, dancing on
stage. Long shot, seen in mirror. Buns while getting
tips.
0:28—Buns, dancing on stage in the background.
• 0:42—Buns in G-string dancing with Sherilyn on
stage.
• 0:56—Brief breasts on stage when Kelly talks to her.
1:11—Buns, while dancing on stage.
**Kickboxer 4—The Aggressor** (1993) . . . .Darcy Cove
•• 0:44—Breasts, while in room with Lando after taking
off her dress.
• 1:04—Left breast, after sitting up in bed.
• 1:05—Brief breasts while lying back down on bed.
The Unborn II (1993) . . . . . . . . . . . . . . . Young Mother
Video Tapes:
**Eden** (1992). . . . . . . . . . . . . . . . . . . . . . . . . . . Lacey
••• 0:20—In pink bra, then breasts and buns, while
making love with B.D. in bedroom.
••• 1:05—Breasts undressing in bedroom with B.D.
••• 1:06—Breasts and buns, while making love in bed
with B.D.
••• 1:32—Breasts in room with Marnie, while getting
even with B.D.
Magazines:
Sport (Feb 1993). . . . . . . . .Wet & Wild Swimsuit Model

## Pigg, Alexandra

Films:
**Letter to Brezhnev** (1986; British). . . . . . . . . . Elaine
•• 0:57—Brief breasts in bed with a guy.
Chicago Joe and the Showgirl (1989; British) . . . . Violet
Bullseyel (1990) . . . . . . . . . . . . . . . . . . . . . Car Hire Girl

## Pisier, Marie-France

Films:
Love at Twenty (1963; French/Italian/Japan) . . . . Colette
Trans-Europ-Express (1968; French) . . . . . . . . . . . . Eva
Stolen Kisses (1969; French) . . . . . . . . . . . Colette Tazzi
Cousin, Cousine (1975; French) . . . . . . . . . . . . . Karine
**Other Side of Midnight** (1977) . . . . . . . Noëlle Page
• 0:10—Very brief breasts in bed with Lanchon.
0:28—Buns, in bed with John Beck. Medium long
shot.

0:45—In white bra, in dressing room.
0:50—Breasts in bathtub, giving herself an abortion
with a coat hanger. Painful to watch!
•• 1:11—Breasts wearing white slip in room getting
dressed in front of Henri.
••• 1:17—Full frontal nudity in front of fireplace with Armand, rubbing herself with oil, then making love
with ice cubes. Very nice!
• 1:35—Full frontal nudity taking off dress for Constantin in his room.
The Bronte Sisters (1979; French). . . . . . . . . .Charlotte
**French Postcards** (1979). . . . . . . . . . .Madame Tessier
•• 0:16—In white bra, then breasts in dressing room
while a guy watches without her knowing.
Love on the Run (1979) . . . . . . . . . . . . . . . . . . Colette
a.k.a. L'Amour en Fuite
(French version with English subtitles.)
Chanel Solitaire (1981). . . . . . . . . . . . Gabrielle Chanel
**Miss Right** (1987; Italian). . . . . . . . . . . . . . . . . . Bebe
•• 0:07—Breasts in open top dress when the reporter
discovers her in a dressing room behind a curtain.
Miniseries:
Scruples (1980) . . . . . . . . . . . . . . . . . . Valentine O'Neill

## Pitt, Ingrid

Films:
Where Eagles Dare (1969; British) . . . . . . . . . . . . . Heidi
The House That Dripped Blood (1970). . . . . . . . . Carla
**Vampire Lovers** (1970; British) . . . . . Marcilla/Carmilla
•• 0:32—Breasts and buns in the bathtub and reflec-
tion in the mirror talking to Emma.
**The Wicker Man** (1973; British) . . . . . . . . . . Librarian
•• 1:11—Brief breasts in bathtub seen by Edward
Woodward.
Wild Geese II (1985; British) . . . . . . . . . . . . . The Hooker
Transmutations (1986) . . . . . . . . . . . . . . . . . Pepperdine
a.k.a. Underworld
Hanna's War (1988) . . . . . . . . . . . . . . . . . . . . . .Margit

## Place, Mary Kay

Films:
Starting Over (1979) . . . . . . . . . . . . . . . . . . . . . .Marie
The Big Chill (1983) . . . . . . . . . . . . . . . . . . . . . . . Meg
Smooth Talk (1985) . . . . . . . . . . . . . . . . . . . .Katherine
A New Life (1988) . . . . . . . . . . . . . . . . . . . . . . .Donna
Bright Angel (1990) . . . . . . . . . . . . . . . . . . . . . . .Judy
Samantha (1991). . . . . . . . . . . . . . . . . . . . . . Marilyn
**Captain Ron** (1992). . . . . . . . . . . . . Katherine Harvey
• 0:32—Brief right breast, then brief breasts in shower
in boat with Martin Short. Overhead view. Hard to
see her face, but it is her.
0:34—Buns, seen through shower door is a stunt
double.
Made for TV Movies:
Just My Imagination (1992) . . . . . . . . . . . . Sheila Hawk
Telling Secrets (1993). . . . . . . . . . . . . . . . . . .Shelley
In the Line of Duty: The Price of Vengeance (1994)
. . . . . . . . . . . . . . . . . . . . . . . . . . . . .Norma Williams
Tales of the City (1994) . . . . . . . . . . . . . . . Prue Giroux

## Player Jarreau, Susan

*Films:*
Invasion of the Bee Girls (1973). . . . . . . . . . . . . . . .Girl
**The Pom Pom Girls** (1976) . . . . . . . . . . . . . Sue Ann
- 0:14—Breasts, while making out with Jesse in the back of his van while parked at burger joint.
- 0:47—Breasts, while making out with Jesse in the back of his van while parked at school.
- 1:02—Brief buns, taking off her panties in locker room with the other girls.

**Malibu Beach** (1978) . . . . . . . . . . . . . . . . . . . . . Sally
- 0:28—Side view of left breast with boyfriend at night on the beach. Long shot.
0:32—Buns, running into the ocean with her two male friends.
0:33—Brief side view of left breast in water. Long shot.
- 0:34—Brief breasts while in the ocean, then breasts while getting dressed by the fire.

## Plimpton, Shelley

*Films:*
**Alice's Restaurant** (1969) . . . . . . . . . . . . . . . Reenie
- •• 0:21—Breasts, taking off her blouse while sitting on bed and talking to Arlo Guthrie.
Putney Swope (1969) . . . . . . . . . . . . . . . . .Face-Off Girl
**Glen and Randa** (1971) . . . . . . . . . . . . . . . . . . .Randa
- ••• 0:01—Nude in the woods with Glen. Long scene.
- 0:40—Lower nudity, while lying on the ground when Glen tickles her.

## • Plummer, Amanda

Daughter of actor Christopher Plummer.
*Films:*
**Cattle Annie and Little Britches** (1980) . . . . . Annie
- 0:39—Breasts visible under braless, wet long johns while standing in lake.
World According to Garp (1982). . . . . . . . . :. . Ellen James
Daniel (1983) . . . . . . . . . . . . . . . . . . . . . Susan Isaacson
The Hotel New Hampshire (1984). . . . . .Miss Miscarriage
Made in Heaven (1987) . . . . . . . . . . . . . . . Wiley Foxx
Joe vs. the Volcano (1990). . . . . . . . . . . . . . . Dagmar
The Fisher King (1991) . . . . . . . . . . . . . . . . . . . . .Lydia
Freejack (1992). . . . . . . . . . . . . . . . . . . . . . . . . . Nun
Needful Things (1993) . . . . . . . . . . . . . . . . Nettie Cobb
So, I Married an Axe Murderer (1993). . . .Rose Michaels
*Made for Cable Movies:*
Last Light (1993; Showtime) . . . . . . . . . . . Lillian Burke
*Made for TV Movies:*
Miss Rose White (1992). . . . . . . . . . . . . . . . . . .Luisa
Whose Child Is This? The War for Baby Jessica (1993) . .
Cara Clausen Schmidt

## Podewell, Cathy

*Films:*
**Night of the Demons** (1987) . . . . . . . . . . . . . . Judy
(Unrated version reviewed.)
- 0:06—Brief buns, while changing clothes and talking on the phone.

0:07—In white bra after taking off her sweater.
Beverly Hills Brats (1989) . . . . . . . . . . . . . . . . . .Tiffany
*Made for TV Movies:*
Earth Angel (1991). . . . . . . . . . . . . . . . . . . . . .Angela
*TV:*
Dallas (1988-91) . . . . . . . . . . . . . . Cally Harper Ewing

## Polo, Teri

*Films:*
Mystery Date (1991) . . . . . . . . . . . . . . Geena Matthews
Born to Ride (1992) . . . . . . . . . . . . . . . . . . . .Beryl Ann
Passed Away (1992) . . . . . . . . . . . . . . . .Rachel Scanlan
Aspen Extreme (1993) . . . . . . . . . . . . . . . . Robin Hand
**Quick** (1993) . . . . . . . . . . . . . . . . . . . . . . . . . .Quick
- •• 0:42—Breasts, taking off her blouse in front of mirror, then putting on black bra.
- •• 1:06—In black bra, then breasts (mostly right breast) while making love in car with Herschel.

## Pond, Pamela

See: Runo, Pamela.

## Poole, Tonya

*Films:*
**Seduce Me: Pamela Principle 2** (1994). . . . . . . Eve
- ••• 0:58—Breasts, while posing during photo shoot in studio.
*Made for Cable Movies:*
Attack of the 5' 2" Women (1994; Showtime) . . .Cookie
*Video Tapes:*
**Playboy's Erotic Fantasies** (1992) . . . . .Cast Member
**Playboy's Secret Confessions** (1993)
. . . . . . . . . . . . . . . . . . . . . . . . . Wash and Wax/Jogger
- ••• 0:16—In wet leotard top, while washing the car. Full frontal nudity while making love with the guy.
*Magazines:*
**Playboy's Book of Lingerie** (Sep 1991) . . . . . .Herself
- ••• 9—Full frontal nudity.
**Playboy's Book of Lingerie** (Nov 1991) . . . . .Herself
- 19—Left breast.
- 107—Buns and side of right breast.
**Playboy's Book of Lingerie** (Mar 1992). . . . . .Herself
- ••• 29—Breasts.
**Playboy's Bathing Beauties** (Apr 1992). . . . . .Herself
- •• 3—Right breast and partial lower frontal nudity.
- ••• 68—Breasts.
**Playboy's Book of Lingerie** (May 1992) . . . . .Herself
- • 38—Lower frontal nudity.
**Playboy's Girls of Summer '92** (Jun 1992) . . .Herself
- • 17—Partial right breast and partial lower frontal nudity.
- ••• 30-31—Lower frontal nudity, buns and left breast.
- •• 98—Buns.
**Playboy's Book of Lingerie** (Jul 1992). . . . . . .Herself
- •• 105—Right breast.
Sport (Jul 1994) . . . . . . . . . . . . . . . . . . . . . . . .Splash!

# Poremba, Jean

a.k.a. Adult film actress Candie Evens.
*Films:*
**You Can't Hurry Love** (1984) . . . . . . .Model in Back
- 0:05—Breasts posing in the backyard getting photographed.
- •• 0:48—Nude in backyard again getting photographed.

**Takin' It All Off** (1987) . . . . . . . . . . . . . . . . . Allison
- 0:36—Buns in G-string andl in pink bra.
- ••• 0:49—In white lingerie, then breasts, then nude dancing.
- ••• 0:58—Breasts and buns in G-string, dancing outside when she hears the music.
- ••• 0:59—Nude dancing in a park.
- •• 1:01—Nude dancing in a laundromat.
- ••• 1:03—Nude dancing in a restaurant.
- ••• 1:07—Nude in shower with Adam.
- •• 1:13—Breasts dancing for the music in a studio.
- ••• 1:23—Nude, dancing with the other girls on stage.

# Potter, Madeleine

*Films:*
The Bostonians (1984) . . . . . . . . . . . . . Verena Tarrant
Suicide Club (1988) . . . . . . . . . . . . . . . . . . . . .Nancy
Bloodhounds of Broadway (1989). . . . . . . .Widow Mary
**Slaves of New York** (1989) . . . . . . . . . . . . . . . Daria
- 1:14—Breasts making love with Stash on chair. Mostly see left breast. Dark.

Two Evil Eyes (1991) . . . . . . . . . . . . . . . . . . . .Annabelle

# Potts, Annie

*Films:*
**Corvette Summer** (1978) . . . . . . . . . . . . . . .Vanessa
- 0:51—Silhouette of right breast in van with Mark Hamill. Out of focus breasts washing herself in the van while talking to him. Don't really see anything.

King of the Gypsies (1978) . . . . . . . . . . . . . . . . . .Persa
Heartaches (1981; Canadian) . . . . . . . .Bonnie Howard
Crimes of Passion (1984). . . . . . . . . . . . . . . Amy Grady
(Unrated version reviewed.)
Ghostbusters (1984) . . . . . . . . . . . . . . . .Janine Melnitz
Jumpin' Jack Flash (1986) . . . . . . . . . . . . . . Liz Carlson
Pretty in Pink (1986). . . . . . . . . . . . . . . . . . . . . . Iona
Pass the Ammo (1988) . . . . . . . . . . . . . . Darla Potter
Ghostbusters II (1989). . . . . . . . . . . . . . .Janine Melnitz
Who's Harry Crumb? (1989) . . . . . . . . Helen Downing
0:55—In sheer black bra lying in bed with Jeffrey Jones.
1:00—More in the same bra in photograph that Jones is looking at.
Texasville (1990) . . . . . . . . . . . . . . . . . . . . Karla Jackson
1:29—In white bra, getting dressed in bedroom while talking to Jeff Bridges.
Breaking the Rules (1992) . . . . . . . . . . .Mary Klingsmith
*TV:*
Goodtime Girls (1980) . . . . . . . . . . . Edith Bedelmeyer
Designing Women (1986-93) . . . . . . . . .Mary Jo Shively
Love & War (1993- ) . . . . . . . . . . . . . . . . . . . . . .n.a.

# Pouget, Ely

*Films:*
Endless Descent (1989) . . . . . . . . . . . . . . . . Ana Rivera
**Cool Blue** (1990) . . . . . . . . . . . . . . . . . . . . Christiane
- •• 0:18—Side view of right breast, then breasts with Woody Harrelson.

Curly Sue (1991) . . . . . . . . . . . . . . . . . Dinah Tompkins
Silent Victim (1992) . . . . . . . . . . . . . . Lauren McKinley
*Made for Cable TV:*
**Red Shoe Diaries: Weekend Pass** (1993; Showtime)
. . . . . . . . . . . . . . . . . . . . . . .Private Jane Chandler
- ••• 0:07—Breasts while making love in barracks with Eddie. Long scene.
- ••• 0:09—Buns and left breast while playing with camouflage paint.
- ••• 0:11—Breasts, when waking up in the morning and getting dressed.
- 0:12—Breasts in flashbacks.
- ••• 0:23—Breasts in bed with Eddie again.

*TV:*
Dark Shadows (1991). . . . . . . . . . . . . . . Maggie Evans

# • Powell, Brittney

*Films:*
**Round Trip to Heaven** (1992) . . . . . . . . . .Contestant
- 0:36—Brief breasts, while putting on dark gray, one piece swimsuit in dressing room.

Airborne (1993) . . . . . . . . . . . . . . . . . . . . . . . . . Nikki
To Be The Best (1993) . . . . . . . . . . . . . . . . . . . Cheryl
The Unborn II (1993) . . . . . . . . . . . . .Sally Anne Philips
Dragonworld (1994) . . . . . . . . . . . . . .Beth Armstrong
*Magazines:*
**Playboy** (Jun 1993). . . . . . . . . . . . . .All About "Eden"
- 81—Lower half of buns, while in waterfall.

# Power, Deanne

*Films:*
Knockouts (1992). . . . . . . . . . . . . . . Julie the Secretary
**Naked Instinct** (1993). . . . . . . . . . . . . . . . . .Joanne
- ••• 0:19—Breasts, in open robe and red panties, watching the pool man masturbate while she plays with herself.
- ••• 0:28—Nude, taking off robe and getting into tub, then making love with the Hot Tub Repairman.
- ••• 0:32—More nude, while making love with him. Long scene.
- ••• 0:36—Full frontal nudity, standing in tub with him.
- ••• 0:54—Nude, making love with the Military Recruit. Long scene.
- ••• 0:59—Nude, making love with the Football Jock.

**Hard Drive** (1994) . . . . . . . . . . . . . .Candle Dream Girl
(Unrated version reviewed.)
- •• 0:03—Left breast, then breasts, while making love with Will on the floor surrounded by lit candles.
- 0:05—Brief breasts on the floor again.

## Power, Deborah
*Films:*
**Emmanuelle IV** (1984) . . . . . . . . . . . . . . . . . . . Dona
  • 1:09—Buns, while lying down and getting a massage from Mia Nygren.
Glamour (1985; French) . . . . . . . . . . . . . . . . . . . .n.a.

## • Power, Robin
*Films:*
Graffiti Bridge (1990) . . . . . . . . . . . . . . . . . . . . Robin
*Video Tapes:*
**Playboy's Erotic Weekend Getaways** (1992)
. . . . . . . . . . . . . . . . . . . .Anticipation: The Mountains
  ••• 0:03—Breasts in cabin with her lover. Buns in G-string.
  ••• 0:04—Nude in front of fireplace with her lover.
  ••• 0:06—Breasts in bathtub with her lover, playing with honey and other food.
**Playboy's How to Reawaken Your Sexual Powers**
(1992). . . . . . . . . . . . . . . . . . . . . . . . Cast Member
  ••• 0:26—Nude at the beach while standing and touching her lover.
  ••• 0:43—Nude outside by stream and on blanket with her lover.

## Power, Taryn
Daughter of actor Tyrone Power.
*Films:*
Sinbad and the Eye of the Tiger (1977; U.S./British)
. . . . . . . . . . . . . . . . . . . . . . . . . . . . . . . . . Dione
  1:16—Very brief buns, skinny dipping in pond with Jane Seymour. Long shot, but still pretty amazing for a G-rated film.
  1:18—Very brief partial side view of right breast, running away from the troglodyte.
**Tracks** (1977) . . . . . . . . . . . . . . . . . . . . . . . Stephanie
  • 0:32—Brief side view of right breast changing in her room on the train. Don't see her face.
  • 1:15—Brief left breast making love with Dennis Hopper in a field.
Eating (1990) . . . . . . . . . . . . . . . . . . . . . . . . . . .Anita
*Made for TV Movies:*
The Count of Monte Cristo (1975)
. . . . . . . . . . . . . . . . . . . . . . . . Valentine De Villefort

## Powers, Beverly
*Films:*
Kissin' Cousins (1964) . . . . . . . . . . . . . . . . . . . . Trudy
More Dead than Alive (1968) . . . . . . . . . . . . . . Sheree
Angel in My Pocket (1969) . . . . . . . . Charlene de Gaulle
J. W. Coop (1971) . . . . . . . . . . . . . . . . . . . . . .Dora Mae
**Invasion of the Bee Girls** (1973) . . . Harriet Williams
  • 1:14—In white bra and panties, then right breast and buns, taking off her clothes for her husband.

## Powers, Stefanie
*Films:*
**Crescendo** (1972; British) . . . . . . . . . . . . . . . .Susan
(Not available on video tape.)
**Little Moon & Jud McGraw** (1976) . . . . . Little Moon
  *a.k.a. Gone with the West*
  • 0:29—Buns, taking a bath outside. At first, hidden behind a bush, then not. Long shot, Don't see her face. Partial right breast, but her hair gets in the way.

## Prather, Joan
*Films:*
**Bloody Friday** (1973) . . . . . . . . . . . . . . . . . . . Lola
  *a.k.a. Single Girls*
  •• 1:06—Breasts, acting out her fantasy with Blue just before getting killed. Dark.
**Big Bad Mama** (1974) . . . . . . . . . . . . . Jane Kingston
  •• 1:15—Breasts and buns in the bathroom with Tom Skerritt.
**Smile** (1974). . . . . . . . . . . . . . . . . . . . . . . . .Robin
  • 0:47—Brief buns in dressing room, while taking off pants while Little Bob is outside taking pictures. (She's wearing a pink ribbon in her hair.)
The Devil's Rain (1975; U.S./Mexican) . . . . .Julie Preston
Rabbit Test (1978) . . . . . . . . . . . . . . . . . . .:. . . Segoynia
**The Best of Sex and Violence** (1981) . . . . . . .Herself
  •• 0:38—Breasts getting her breasts squeezed by an attacker. Dark.
**Famous T & A** (1982) . . . . . . . . . . . . . . . . . .Herself
  (No longer available for purchase, check your video store for rental.)
  •• 0:49—Brief breasts in scene from *Bloody Friday.*
*Made for TV Movies:*
The Deerslayer (1978) . . .:. . . . . . . . . . . .Judith Hutter
*TV:*
Executive Suite (1976-77) . . . . . . . . . . . Glory Dalessio
Eight is Enough (1979-81) . . . . . . . . . . . Janet Bradford

## Prati, Pamela
*Films:*
**Monsignor** (1982) . . . . . . . . . . . . . . . .1st Roman Girl
  • 1:22—Brief breasts (on the left, wearing necklaces) next to a guy sitting in a chair, with another Roman girl on the right.
Hercules II (1985). . . . . . . . . . . . . . . . . . . . . .Aracne
Man Spricht Deutsh (1988; West German) . . . . . Violetta
**Transformations** (1988) . . . . . . . . . Woman Succubus
  ••• 0:05—Breasts and buns making love on top of Rex Smith in bed. She starts transforming into a creature.
  • 0:21—Brief breasts again during Smith's flashback.
  • 0:24—Brief breasts again, while transforming.
  • 0:26—Brief breasts again, while transforming.

## Prentiss, Paula
*Films:*
Where the Boys Are (1960) . . . . . . . . .Tuggle Carpenter
Man's Favorite Sport? (1964) . . . . . . . . . . .Abigail Page
The World of Henry Orient (1964) . . . . . . . . . . .Stella

In Harm's Way (1965) . . . . . . . . . . . . . . . . . . . . . . . Bev
What's New, Pussycat? (1965; U.S./French) . . . . . . . Liz
**Catch-22** (1970) . . . . . . . . . . . . . . . . . Nurse Duckett
  • 0:22—Full frontal nudity on platform in the water,
    throwing her dress to Alan Arkin during his dream.
    Long shot, over exposed, hard to see.
**Move** (1970) . . . . . . . . . . . . . . . . . . . . . . . . Dolly Jaffe
Last of the Red Hot Lovers (1972) . . . . . . Bobbi Michele
The Parallax View (1974) . . . . . . . . . . . . . . . .Lee Carter
The Stepford Wives (1975) . . . . . . . . . . . . . . . . .Bobby
The Black Marble (1980) . . . . . Sgt. Natalie Zimmerman
Buddy Buddy (1981) . . . . . . . . . . . . . . . . Celia Clooney
Saturday the 14th (1981) . . . . . . . . . . . . . . . . . .Mary
*TV:*
He & She (1967-68) . . . . . . . . . . . . . . . .Paula Hollister

# Presley, Theresa
*Video Tapes:*
**Penthouse Pet of the Year Playoff 1992** (1992)
. . . . . . . . . . . . . . . . . . . . . . . . . . . . . . . . . . . . . . Pet
  ••• 0:01—Nude in helicopter, in office, tearing off her
    clothes in house, fantasy photo shoot, in a car and
    jumping on a trampoline.
**The Girls of Penthouse, Volume 2** (1993) . . . . . . Pet
  ••• 0:11—Nude on bed, in tub, in kitchen, getting
    dressed, in milk bath and in a bar.
  ••• 0:33—Nude on bed, walking and posing in the
    house.
**Penthouse The Great Pet Hunt—Part II** (1993)
. . . . . . . . . . . . . . . . . . . . . . . . . . . . . . . . . . . . . . Pet
  ••• 0:41—Nude after stripping out of red dress with
    white polka dots.
**Penthouse DreamGirls** (1994) . . . . . . . . . . . .Theresa
  ••• 0:01—Nude by waterfall by pool, in a mansion, on
    a bed, in a shower/bath.
*Magazines:*
**Penthouse** (Apr 1991) . . . . . . . . . . . . . . . . . . . . . Pet
  ••• 67-81—Nude.
**Playboy's Book of Lingerie** (Jul 1991) . . . . . . Herself
  ••• 80—Breasts.
**Penthouse** (Jun 1992) . . . . . . . . .Pet of the Year Playoff
  ••• 90-91—Full frontal nudity.

# Preston, Kelly
a.k.a. Kelly Palzis.
Wife of actor John Travolta.
*Films:*
10 to Midnight (1983) . . . . . . . . . . . . . . . . . . . .Doreen
Christine (1983) . . . . . . . . . . . . . . . . . . . . . . Roseanne
Metalstorm: The Destruction of Jared-Syn (1983)
. . . . . . . . . . . . . . . . . . . . . . . . . . . . . . . . . . . .Dhyana
**Mischief** (1985) . . . . . . . . . . . . . . . .Marilyn McCauley
  ••• 0:56—In a bra, then breasts, brief buns and brief
    partial lower frontal nudity, while seducing and
    making love with Doug McKeon in her bedroom.
**Secret Admirer** (1985) . . . . . . .Deborah Anne Fimple
  •• 0:53—Brief breasts in car with C. Thomas Howell.
  • 1:17—Very brief breasts in and out of bed.

**52 Pick-Up** (1986) . . . . . . . . . . . . . . . . . . . . . . . Cini
  • 0:09—Brief buns in video tape made by blackmail-
    ers.
  • 0:36—Breasts, tied to chair on video tape made by
    blackmailers.
    0:39—Very brief breasts covered with blood after
    being shot.
SpaceCamp (1986) . . . . . . . . . . . . . . . . . . . . . . . .Tish
Amazon Women on the Moon (1987) . . . . . . . . .Violet
Love at Stake (1988) . . . . . . . . . . . . . . . . . . .Sara Lee
**Spellbinder** (1988) . . . . . . . . . . . . . . . Miranda Reed
  ••• 0:19—Breasts in bed making love with Timothy Da-
    ly.
    1:26—Dancing around in a sheer white gown with
    nothing underneath during cult ceremony at the
    beach.
**A Tiger's Tale** (1988) . . . . . . . . . . . . . . . . . . . .Shirley
  •• 0:03—Breasts in the car, letting C. Thomas Howell
    open her blouse and look at her breasts.
Twins (1988) . . . . . . . . . . . . . . . . . . . . . . Marnie Mason
The Experts (1989) . . . . . . . . . . . . . . . . . . . . . .Bonnie
Run (1990) . . . . . . . . . . . . . . . . . . . . . . . Karen Landers
Only You (1992) . . . . . . . . . . . . . . . . Amanda Hughes
**Double Cross** (1994) . . . . . . . . . . . . . .Vera Blanchard
  • 0:08—In bra, panties, garter belt and stockings in
    hotel room with Patrick Bergin. Buns and partial left
    breast, when he rips off her panties. Don't see her
    face.
  • 0:24—Buns, while getting into the shower. Don't
    see her face.
*Made for Cable Movies:*
The Perfect Bride (1991) . . . . . . . . . . . . . . . . . . .Laura
*Made for Cable TV:*
Tales From the Crypt: The Switch (1990; HBO) . . .Linda
  (Available on *Tales From the Crypt, Volume 3*.)
    0:19—In red, one piece swimsuit at the beach with
    a young Carlton.
*TV:*
For Love and Honor (1983) . . . . . . . . . . . . . .Mary Lee

# Price, Karen
*Films:*
Swamp Thing (1981) . . . . . . . . . . . . . . . . . .Messenger
Murphy's Law (1986) . . . . . . . . . . . . . . . . . . . .Stunts
The Running Man (1987) . . . . . . . . . . . Amber (Stunts)
*Magazines:*
**Playboy** (Jan 1981) . . . . . . . . . . . . . . . . . . . .Playmate
**Playboy's Calendar Playmates** (Nov 1992) . . .Herself
  ••• 11—Breasts.

# Primeaux, Suzanne
*Films:*
**Stripper** (1985) . . . . . . . . . . . . . . . . . . . . . . .Herself
  •• 0:03—Breasts dancing on stage, kneeling on her left
    knee. Very brief buns in G-string.
**Traxx** (1988) . . . . . . . . . . . . . . . . . . . . . . . Hooker #1
  •• 0:37—Breasts, dancing on stage while wearing a
    mask.

# Principal, Victoria

*Films:*

The Life and Times of Judge Roy Bean (1972)
..........................................Marie Elena

**The Naked Ape** (1972)....................Cathy
(Not available on video tape.)
Breasts.

Earthquake (1974) ........................Rosa

I Will, I Will... For Now (1976)..........Jackie Martin

Vigilante Force (1976).......................Linda

*Miniseries:*

The Burden of Proof (1992)...........Margy Allison

*Made for TV Movies:*

Mistress (1987)......................Rae Colton
        0:09—Briefly in red, one piece swimsuit, getting out
        of swimming pool.

Naked Lie (1989) .................Joanne Dawson

Don't Touch My Daughter (1991)...............n.a.

Seduction: Three Tales from "The Inner Sanctum"
(1992)........................Sylvia/Lisa/Joan

River of Rage: The Taking of Maggie Keene (1993)
.................................... Maggie Keene

Beyond Obsession (1994)....................n.a.

*TV:*

Dallas (1978-89)............. Pamela Barnes Ewing

*Magazines:*

**Playboy** (Dec 1972)............. Sex Stars of 1972
••• 210—Left breast.

**Playboy** (Aug 1973)................. Next Month
• 218—Breasts in B&W photo.

**Playboy** (Sep 1973)..... The Naked Ape & "Ape" Girl
••• 161-167—Breasts and buns.

**Playboy** (Dec 1973)............. Sex Stars of 1973
•• 210—Right breast.

**Playboy** (Dec 1975)............. Sex Stars of 1975
••• 185—Breasts.

**Playboy** (Dec 1976)............. Sex Stars of 1976
••• 183—Breasts and in black panties lying down.

**Playboy** (Dec 1980)............. Sex Stars of 1980
••• 240—Side view of left breast.

# Prophet, Melissa

*Films:*

Players (1979)........................... Ann

Van Nuys Blvd. (1979) ....................Camille

Looker (1981) ........... Commercial Script Girl

**Time Walker** (1982).......................Jennie
        • 0:27—Brief breasts putting bra on while a guy
        watches from outside the window.
        1:17—Very, very brief right breast in shower when
        the mummy comes to get the crystal.

**Fatal Games** (1984) ................ Nancy Wilson
        • 0:14—Buns and side view of left breast in shower
        with other girls. Long shot. (She's wearing a white
        towel on her head.)

Invasion U.S.A. (1985)................... McGuirre

Action Jackson (1988) ...................Newscaster

GoodFellas (1990)......................... Angie

*Magazines:*

**Playboy** (May 1987)..... Diary of a Hollywood Starlet
••• 86-93—Full frontal nudity.

**Playboy's Nudes** (Oct 1990) ...............Herself
• 15—Full frontal nudity.

# Props, Renée

a.k.a. Babette Props.

*Films:*

Weird Science (1985)...........One of The Weenies

**Free Ride** (1986) ..........................Kathy
        • 0:13—Brief breasts in the shower while Dan watch-
        es.

*TV:*

As the World Turns .................. Ellie Snyder

# • Pryor, Gloria

*Films:*

**The Swindle** (1991)................... Claudia
•• 1:15—Breasts with Tom.

Beach Beverly Hills (1992) ................ Roxanne

# Purl, Linda

*Films:*

**Crazy Mama** (1975)...................... Cheryl
        0:05—In pink, two piece swimsuit at the beach.
        • 0:52—Very brief buns, then brief breasts when
        Snake and Donny Most keep opening the door after
        she has taken a shower. Long shot, hard to see.

**The High Country** (1980; Canadian).........Kathy
        • 1:03—Brief buns, while taking a shower in the wa-
        terfall.

Visiting Hours (1982; Canadian)........ Sheila Munroe

Viper (1988)...................... Laura Macalla

Web of Deceit (1991)........................ n.a.

*Made for Cable Movies:*

Body Language (1992; USA) ................Norma

Incident at Deception Ridge (1994; USA)......... n.a.

*Made for TV Movies:*

Outrage! (1986)................... Arlene Robbins

Pleasures (1986).......................Eve Harper

Danielle Steel's "Secrets" (1992) ......... Jane Adams

*TV:*

Happy Days (1974-75)................... Gloria

Happy Days (1982-83)............... Ashley Pfister

Matlock (1986-89)............... Charlene Matlock

Under Cover (1991)............... Kate Del'Amico

Robin's Hoods (1994- )................ Brett Robin

# • Q, Stacey

Real name is Stacey Swain.
Pop singer. Formerly with the group SSQ.

*Films:*

One Man Force (1989)....................... Lea

*Video Tapes:*

**Red Hot Rock** (1984)................... Singer
        a.k.a. Sexy Shorts (on laser disc)
        •• 0:18—Full frontal nudity while in bed with a guy,
        then a woman during "Screaming in My Pillow".

## Quennessen, Valerie

*Films:*
French Postcards (1979) . . . . . . . . . . . . . . . . . . . . Toni
Like a Turtle on Its Back (1981; French) . . . . . . Nietzsche
Conan the Barbarian (1982) . . . . . . . . . . . The Princess
**Summer Lovers** (1982) . . . . . . . . . . . . . . . . . . . Lina
 • 0:12—Breasts, while on balcony.
 ••• 0:19—Nude on the beach with Michael.
 • 0:23—Brief breasts in a cave with Michael.
 •• 0:30—Breasts, while lying on the floor with Michael.
 0:54—Buns, lying on a rock with Daryl Hannah
 watching Michael dive off a rock.
 • 1:03—Left breast, while in bed.
 •• 1:05—Breasts while dancing on the balcony.
 1:09—Breasts while on the beach.

## Quick, Diana

*Films:*
The Big Sleep (1978; British) . . . . . . . . . . . Mona Grant
1919 (1984; British) . . . . . . . . . . . . . . . . . . . . . . .Anna
Ordeal by Innocence (1984) . . . . . . . . .Gwenda Vaughn
The Misadventures of Mr. Wilt (1990) . . . . . . . . . . Sally
*Miniseries:*
**Brideshead Revisited** (1981; British) . . . . . . Julia Flyte
 0:18—(Part 10 on TV or Book 5 on video tape.) Several quick peeks at partial right breast in mirror,
 while lying under Jeremy Irons in bed.
 •• 0:19—Left breast, while lying on top of Jeremy Irons
 after making love with him.

## Quigley, Linnea

*Adult Films:*
Sweethearts (1986) . . . . . . . . . . .Cupid's Corner Hostess
 (Appears fully clothed, only as a hostess to introduce the
 explicit segments.)
*Films:*
**Auditions** (1978) . . . . . . . . . . . . . . . . . Sally Webster
 ••• 0:06—Breasts and buns, undressing and dancing
 during her audition.
 ••• 0:26—Full frontal nudity, acting with two guys.
**Don't Go Near the Park** (1979) . . . . . Bondi's Mother
 0:08—Full frontal nudity, behind shower door.
 • 0:09—Brief left breast, while wrapping a towel
 around herself.
 ••• 0:19—Left breast, while lying in bed with Mark.
**Fairytales** (1979) . . . . . . . . . . . . . . . . . . . Dream Girl
 •• 1:07—Breasts waking up after being kissed by The
 Prince.
Nightstalker (1979) . . . . . . . . . . . . . . . . . . . . . . . . .n.a.
**Stone Cold Dead** (1979; Canadian) . . . . . . First Victim
 • 0:03—Very brief right breast after getting shot
 through shower door. Buns after falling to the floor.
Summer Camp (1979) . . . . . . . . . . . . . . . . . . . . . . .n.a.
Cheech & Chong's Nice Dreams (1981)
 . . . . . . . . . . . . . . . . . . . . . . . . . . .Blondie Group #2
**Graduation Day** (1981) . . . . . . . . . . . . . . . . .Dolores
 •• 0:36—Breasts by the piano in classroom with Mr.
 Roberts unbuttoning her blouse.

**Psycho From Texas** (1981) . . . . . . . . . . . . . .Barmaid
 ••• 1:16—Nude, after taking off her dress and dancing
 in front of Wheeler. (He pours beer on her.) Long
 scene.
**Cheech & Chong's Still Smokin'** (1983)
 . . . . . . . . . . . . . . . . . . . . . . . . . . Uncredited Spa Girl
 •• 0:42—Breasts, looking into two-way mirror. (She's
 the last girl.)
 • 0:53—Breasts, walking in front of Cheech in the
 shower room.
 •• 1:00—Breasts, sitting on the floor with five other naked girls with Cheech.
**The Young Warriors** (1983; U.S./Canadian) . . .Ginger
 • 0:05—Nude in and getting out of bed in bedroom.
The Black Room (1984) . . . . . . . . . . . . . . . . . . . . Milly
Fatal Games (1984) . . . . . . . . . . . . . . . . . . . . .Athelete
**Silent Night, Deadly Night** (1984) . . . . . . . .Denise
 ••• 0:52—Breasts while on pool table with Tommy, then
 putting on shorts and walking around the house.
 More breasts, while impaled on antlers.
**The Return of the Living Dead** (1985) . . . . . . .Trash
 ••• 0:19—Breasts and buns, strip tease and dancing in
 cemetery. (Lower frontal nudity is covered with
 some kind of make-up appliance).
 •• 0:25—Breasts and buns, while in cemetery with her
 boyfriend.
 • 0:37—Breasts and buns, while running around in
 cemetery when it starts to rain.
 • 0:38—Breasts, while running to the car in the rain
 (very long shot). Brief breasts while in back seat of
 car.
 • 0:42—Breasts, while in back seat of car.
 • 0:44—Breasts, while in back seat of car, trying to
 hold the convertible top closed.
 • 0:46—Brief buns, while running up stairs.
 • 0:49—Buns, while running into the cemetery.
 1:04—Brief right breast, while in cemetery after seeing a zombie.
 • 1:05—Brief breasts, while walking from the cemetery on the street to catch a streetperson.
 • 1:21—Brief breasts, while running to munch on a
 policeman in blockade.
 • 1:25—Brief breasts in still photo.
 • 1:27—Breasts, during end credits in cemetery with
 her boyfriend.
**Savage Streets** (1985) . . . . . . . . . . . . . . . . . .Heather
 • 0:28—Breasts getting raped by the jerks.
**Silent Night, Deadly Night, Part 2** (1986) . . .Denise
 ••• 0:26—Breasts on pool table and getting dressed
 flashback from *Silent Night, Deadly Night.*
**Creepozoids** (1987) . . . . . . . . . . . . . . . . . . . . .Blanca
 •• 0:15—Breasts taking off her top to take a shower.
 •• 0:16—Right breast, while standing in shower with
 Butch.
 • 0:24—Right breast several times while sleeping in
 bed with Butch.

**Night of the Demons** (1987) . . . . . . . . . . . Suzanne
(Unrated version reviewed.)

> 0:10—Buns in panties under short skirt, while bending over to distract the convenience store clerks.
> •• 0:52—Breasts twice, opening her dress top while acting weird. Pushes a tube of lipstick into her left breast. (Don't try this at home kids!)
> • 0:56—Lower frontal nudity, lifting her skirt up for Jay.

**Nightmare Sisters** (1987) . . . . . . . . . . . . . . .Melody

> ••• 0:39—Breasts, wearing panties, while standing with Mickey and Marci after transforming from nerds to sexy women.
> ••• 0:40—Breasts in the kitchen with Mickey and Marci.
> ••• 0:44—Breasts in the bathtub with Mickey and Marci. Excellent, long scene.
> ••• 0:46—Breasts, while in the bathtub. Nice close up.
> ••• 0:48—Still more breasts, while in the bathtub.
> ••• 0:55—Breasts, while dancing and singing in front of Kevin. Long scene.
> •• 0:57—Breasts while on the couch with Bud.

Treasure of the Moon Goddess (1987) . . . . . Lu De Belle
American Rampage (1988) . . . . . . . . . . . . . . . . . . .n.a.

**Hollywood Chainsaw Hookers** (1988) . . . . Samantha

> • 0:32—Breasts, dancing on stage.
> • 1:02—Breasts, (but her body is painted) dancing in a ceremony.

**A Nightmare on Elm Street 4: The Dream Master** (1988) . . . . . . . . . . . . . . . . . Soul from Freddy's Chest

> • 1:23—Brief breasts twice, trying to get out of Freddy's body. Don't see her face clearly.

Sorority Babes in the Slimeball Bowl-O-Rama (1988)
. . . . . . . . . . . . . . . . . . . . . . . . . . . . . . . . . . . . .Spider

**Vice Academy** (1988) . . . . . . . . . . . . . . . . . . . . . Didi

> ••• 0:45—Breasts making love with Chuck while he's handcuffed.

**Assault of the Party Nerds** (1989) . . . . . . . . .Bambi

> ••• 0:25—Breasts straddling Cliff in bed.

**Deadly Embrace** (1989) . . . . . . . . . . . . .Michelle Arno

> •• 0:15—In white lingerie, then breasts and buns during Chris' fantasy.
> •• 0:34—Breasts and buns caressing herself.
> •• 0:43—Breasts again.
> 0:46—Brief breasts.
> • 0:50—Breasts and buns undressing.
> ••• 0:58—Breasts in bed on top of Chris, then making love.
> • 1:02—Breasts and buns on top of Chris while Charlotte watches on T.V.
> 1:11—Breasts in Chris' fantasy.
> • 1:12—Breasts and buns in playback of video tape.

**Dr. Alien** (1989) . . . . . . . . . . . . . . . . . Rocker Chick #2
*a.k.a. I Was a Teenage Sex Mutant*

> ••• 0:21—Breasts in white outfit during dream sequence with two other rocker chicks.

**Murder Weapon** (1989) . . . . . . . . . . . . . . . . . . Dawn

> • 0:08—Buns and very brief side of left breast walking into shower. Long shot.
> •• 0:40—Breasts taking off her top in car.

> •• 0:48—Breasts and buns taking off her top in bedroom.
> ••• 0:50—Breasts in bed on top of a guy. Excellent long scene. Brief buns, getting out of bed.

Robot Ninja (1989) . . . . . . . . . . . . . . . . .Miss Barbeau

**Witchtrap** (1989) . . . . . . . . . . . . . . . Ginger Kowoski

> ••• 0:34—Nude taking off robe and getting into the shower.
> •• 0:36—Breasts just before getting killed when the shower head goes into her neck.

The Girl I Want (1990) . . . . . . . . . . . . . . . . . . . . . . Teri

**Vice Academy, Part 2** (1990) . . . . . . . . . . . . . . .Didi

> •• 1:04—Buns in G-string, then breasts dancing with Ginger Lynn Allen on stage at club.

**Virgin High** (1990) . . . . . . . . . . . . . . . . . . . Kathleen

> •• 0:24—Breasts, nonchalantly making love on top of Derrick.
> •• 0:55—Brief breasts several times on top of Derrick, then breasts.
> • 1:21—Breasts in photo during party.

Blood Church (1991) . . . . . . . . . . . . . . . . . . . . . . . n.a.

**Freddy's Dead: The Final Nightmare** (1991)
. . . . . . . . . . . . . . . . . . . . . . Soul from Freddy's Chest

> • 1:25—Brief breasts, struggling in Freddy's stomach during the end credits special-effects review.

The Guyver (1991) . . . . . . . . . . . . . . . . . .Scream Queen
Sex Bomb (1991) . . . . . . . . . . . . . . . . . . . . . . . . . . n.a.
Innocent Blood (1992) . . . . . . . . . . . . . . . . . . . . Nurse
Beach Babes From Beyond (1993) . . . . . . . . . . . . .Sally

*Video Tapes:*

Nudes in Limbo (1983) . . . . . . . . . . . . . . . . . . . Model

**Playboy Video Magazine, Volume 4** (1983)
. . . . . . . . . . . . . . . . . . . . . . . . . . . . . . . . . Flashdancer

> • 0:15—Full frontal nudity.
> •• 0:16—Nude, fighting with Brinke Stevens in the shower.

**Linnea Quigley's Horror Workout** (1990) . . .Herself

> ••• 0:00—Breasts and buns, taking a shower and drying herself off. Nice.
> ••• 0:09—Breasts in scene from *Assault of the Party Nerds*, making love on top of a guy in bed.
> • 0:19—Breasts in still photo from *Return of the Living Dead*.
> •• 0:34—Breasts, singing and dancing in living room, in scene from *Nightmare Sisters*.
> • 0:54—Breasts, screaming.
> • 0:57—Breasts in still photos during end credits.

**Scream Queen Hot Tub Party** (1991) . . . . Samantha

> • 0:01—Breasts during opening credits.
> •• 0:36—Breasts with painted body, doing double chainsaw dance from *Hollywood Chainsaw Hookers*.

**B-Movie Queens Revealed: The Making of "Vice Academy"** (1993) . . . . . . . . . . . . . . . . . . . . . . . .Didi

> • 0:33—Breasts with Chuck while he's handcuffed to sink from *Vice Academy 1*.
> • 0:34—Buns in T-back, dancing on stage with Ginger Lynn Allen from *Vice Academy 2*.
> •• 0:38—Breasts, dancing on stage with Ginger Lynn Allen from *Vice Academy 2*.

*Magazines:*
**Playboy** (Jan 1985) . . . . . . . . The Girls of Rock 'n' Roll
**Playboy** (Nov 1985) . . . . . . . . . . . Sex in Cinema 1985
•• 134—Side view of right breast and buns, in still from *The Return of the Living Dead.*
**Playboy** (Nov 1988) . . . . . . . . . . Sex in Cinema 1988
•• 137—Breasts with tattoos across her breasts holding a chainsaw.
**Playboy** (Jul 1989) . . . . . . . . . . . . . . B-Movie Bimbos
••• 134—Full frontal nudity leaning on a car wearing stockings and an orange garter belt.

## Quinlan, Kathleen

*Films:*
Lifeguard (1975) . . . . . . . . . . . . . . . . . . . . . . . . Wendy
**I Never Promised You a Rose Garden** (1977)
. . . . . . . . . . . . . . . . . . . . . . . . . . . . . . . . . Deborah
• 0:27—Breasts changing in a mental hospital room with the orderly.
• 0:52—Brief breasts riding a horse in a hallucination sequence. Blurry, hard to see. Then close up of left breast (could be anyone's).
The Promise (1979) . . . . . . . . . . . . . . . . Nancy/Marie
The Runner Stumbles (1979) . . . . . . . . . . . . Sister Rita
Hanky Panky (1982) . . . . . . . . . . . . . . . . . Janet Dunn
Independence Day (1983) . . . . . . . . . . Mary Ann Taylor
**The Last Winter** (1983; Israeli) . . . . . . . . . . . . . Joyce
•• 0:48—Brief side view of left breast taking off her robe and diving into pool Very brief buns.
0:49—Buns, lying on marble slab, talking with Maya.
0:50—Very brief right breast sitting up. Long shot, hard to see.
Twilight Zone—The Movie (1983) . . . . . . . . . . . Helen
Warning Sign (1985) . . . . . . . . . . . . . . . . Joanie Morse
Man Outside (1987) . . . . . . . . . . . . . . Grace Freemont
Wild Thing (1987; U.S./Canadian) . . . . . . . . . . . . Jane
Clara's Heart (1988) . . . . . . . . . . . . . . . . . Leona Hart
Sunset (1988) . . . . . . . . . . . . . . . . . Nancy Shoemaker
**The Doors** (1991) . . . . . . . . . . . . . . Patricia Kennealy
••• 1:00—Brief left breast, while in bed with Val Kilmer, breasts (while wearing glasses) out of bed.
• 1:02—Left breast, while crawling on the floor.
••• 1:03—Nude, dancing around her apartment with Kilmer.
*Made for Cable Movies:*
Blackout (1985; HBO) . . . . . . . . . . . . . . . . . . . . Chris
0:26—Brief side view of left breast while making love in bed. Dark, hard to see.
Bodily Harm (1989) . . . . . . . . . . . . Dr. Virginia Betters
Trapped (1989) . . . . . . . . . . . . . . . . . . . . . . . . . n.a.
Strays (1991; USA) . . . . . . . . . . . . . . . . Lindsay Jarrett
Last Light (1993; Showtime) . . . . . . . . . . Kathy Rubicek
Stolen Babies (1993; Lifetime) . . . . . . . . . . . . . . Bekka
*Made for TV Movies:*
She's in the Army Now (1981) . . . . . . . . . . . . . . n.a.
Children of the Night (1985) . . . . . . . . . . . . . Lois Lee
An American Story (1992) . . . . . . . . . . . . . Hope Tyler

## Quinn, Patricia

*Films:*
The Rocky Horror Picture Show (1975; British)
. . . . . . . . . . . . . . . . . . . . . . . . . . . . . . . Magenta
Shock Treatment (1981) . . . . . . . . . . . Nation McKinley
Monty Python's the Meaning of Life (1983; British)
. . . . . . . . . . . . . . . . . . . . . . . . . . . . . . . . . . n.a.
*Miniseries:*
**I, Claudius—Episode 4, What Shall We Do About Claudius?** (1976; British) . . . . . . . . . . . . . . . . . Livilla
(Available on video tape in *I, Claudius—Volume 2.*)
• 1:28—(0:39 into episode 4) Brief right breast, while climbing back onto bed after framing Postumus for rape.
**I, Claudius—Episode 7, Queen of Heaven** (1976; British) . . . . . . . . . . . . . . . . . . . . . . . . . . Livilla
(Available on video tape in *I, Claudius—Volume 4.*)
• 0:20—Very brief tip of right breast under arm of Patrick Stewart in bed.

## Rabett, Catherine

*Films:*
The Living Daylights (1987) . . . . . . . . . . . . . . . . n.a.
Maurice (1987; British) . . . . . . . . . . . . . . Pippa Durham
**Frankenstein Unbound** (1990) . . . . . . . . . Elizabeth
1:10—Very brief left breast, while lying dead after getting shot by Frankenstein. Unappealing looking because of all the gruesome makeup.

## • Racimo, Victoria

*Films:*
The Magic Garden of Stanley Sweetheart (1970)
. . . . . . . . . . . . . . . . . . . . . . . . . . . . . . . . Andrea
**The G.I. Executioner** (1971) . . . . . . . . . Foon Mae Lee
*a.k.a. Wit's End*
*a.k.a. Dragon Lady*
• 0:12—Nude in bathroom mirror getting dressed.
• 0:54—Brief breasts undressing and getting into bed. (See reflection in glass on headboard.)
• 1:15—Sort of buns, lying in Dave's lap. Then left breast.
1:18—Buns, tied up by wrists. Sort of breasts being turned around (hair is in the way).
Red Sky at Morning (1971) . . . . . . . . . . . . . Viola Lopez
The Day of the Dolphin (1973) . . . . . . . . . . . . . . Lana
Prophecy (1979) . . . . . . . . . . . . . . . . . . . . . Ramona
The Mountain Men (1980) . . . . . . . . . . Running Moon
Choke Canyon (1986) . . . . . . . . . . . . . . . . . . Rachel
Ernest Goes to Camp (1987) . . . . . . . . . Nurse St. Cloud
*TV:*
The Chisholms (1979-80) . . . . . . . . . . . . . . Kewedinok
Falcon Crest (1983-84) . . . . . . . . . . . . . Corene Powers

## • Radford, Natalie

*Films:*
**Tomcat: Dangerous Desires** (1993) . . . . . . . . Imogen
••• 1:04—Brief left breast, then breasts and lower frontal nudity in bed with Richard Grieco.
•• 1:08—Brief buns and breasts in bed some more.

•• 1:09—More breasts while sitting in bed and watching video tape on TV.
*Made for TV Movies:*
JFK: Reckless Youth (1993). . . . . . . . . Rosemary Kennedy

# Rae, Taija

Adult film actress.
*Films:*
Delivery Boys (1984). . . . . . . . . . . . . . . . . . . . . . Nurse
   0:34—In bra and panties after doing a strip tease with another nurse while dancing in front of a boy who is lying on an operating table.
**Sex Appeal** (1986) . . . . . . . . . . . . . . . . . . . . .Rhonda
•• 1:14—In black lingerie, then breasts in black push-up teddy with Sheila.

# Ragnarsson, Carina

*Films:*
**Beauty School** (1993). . . . . . . . . . . . . . . . . . Heather
•• 0:40—Breasts, dancing with her top down on stage in club.
*Video Tapes:*
**Penthouse: On the Wild Side** (1988). . . . . Car Wash
••• 0:16—Breasts and buns in car wash with another woman. Nice and wet.
*Magazines:*
**Penthouse** (Nov 1985) . . . . . . . . . . . . . . . . . . . Pet
**Penthouse** (Mar 1993) . . . . . . . . . . . How Swede It Is
••• 96-107—Nude.

# Raines, Cristina

a.k.a. Tina Herazo.
*Films:*
Hex (1973) . . . . . . . . . . . . . . . . . . . . . . . . . . . . .Oriole
Staceyl (1973). . . . . . . . . . . . . . . . . .Pamela Chambers
   *a.k.a. Stacey and Her Gangbusters*
Nashville (1975) . . . . . . . . . . . . . . . . . . . . . . . . . .Mary
Russian Roulette (1975). . . . . . . . . . . . . Bogna Kirchoff
The Duellists (1977; British). . . . . . . . . . . . . . . Adele
**The Sentinel** (1977) . . . . . . . . . . . . . . . .Alison Parker
• 0:18—Briefly in sheer beige bra, putting her blouse on.
• 0:33—Very, very brief left breast immediately after Sylvia Miles rips her dress off. B&W dream sequence.
Touched by Love (1980) . . . . . . . . . . . . . . . . . . . Amy
North Shore (1987). . . . . . . . . . . . . . . . . Rick's Mother
*TV:*
Centennial (1978-79) . . . . . . . . . . . . . . . . Lucinda
Flamingo Road (1981-82) . . . . . . . . . . . . . .Lane Ballou
*Magazines:*
**Playboy** (Dec 1975). . . . . . . . . . . . . . Sex Stars of 1975
••• 188—Full frontal nudity.

# Raines, Frances

*Films:*
Model Behavior (1982) . . . . . . . . . . . . . . .Lily White Girl
**The Mutilator** (1983) . . . . . . . . . . . . . . . . . . . . . Linda
•• 0:35—Breasts, while in swimming pool, just before getting killed.

**Breeders** (1986) . . . . . . . . . . . . . . . . . .Karinsa Marshall
••• 0:12—Nude stretching and exercising in photo studio.
• 0:16—Brief full frontal nudity, getting attacked by the creature.
••• 0:53—Breasts and buns, taking off her blouse and walking down the hall and into the basement. Long scene.
• 1:07—Very brief right breast in the alien nest with the other women.
• 1:10—Brief breasts standing up.

# Raines, Lisa

See: Foster, Lisa Raines.

# Rains, Gianna

*Films:*
**Firehouse** (1987) . . . . . . . . . . . . . . . . . Barrett Hopkins
••• 0:33—Breasts taking a shower, then drying herself just before the fire alarm goes off.
•• 0:56—Breasts making love with the reporter on the roof of a building.
Homeboy (1988) . . . . . . . . . . . . . . . . . . . . . . . Phyllis

# Ramish, Trish

*Made for Cable TV:*
**Dream On: Super Freak** (1993; HBO) . . . . . . .Joanne
••• 0:17—Breasts in shower with Martin and after getting shampoo in their eyes.
*Video Tapes:*
Cher Fitness: Body Confidence (1992) . . . .Cast Member

# Rampling, Charlotte

*Films:*
Rotten to the Core (1965; British) . . . . . . . . . . . . . .Sara
Georgy Girl (1966; British) . . . . . . . . . . . . . . .Meredith
The Long Duel (1967; British) . . . . . . . . . Jane Stafford
The Damned (1969; German) . . . . . Elizabeth Thallman
Three (1969; British) . . . . . . . . . . . . . . . . . . . . Marty
Asylum (1972; British) . . . . . . . . . . . . . . . . . Barbara
Corky (1972) . . . . . . . . . . . . . . . . . . . . . .Corky's Wife
Henry VIII and His Six Wives (1972; British)
. . . . . . . . . . . . . . . . . . . . . . . . . . . . . . Anne Boleyn
**'Tis a Pity She's a Whore** (1972; Italian) . . Annabella
Breasts.
**Caravan to Vaccares** (1974; British/French) . . . . . Lila
Brief buns standing at window, then brief full frontal nudity getting back into bed.
**The Night Porter** (1974; Italian/U.S.) . . . . . . . . . Lucia
•• 0:11—Side nudity being filmed with a movie camera in the concentration camp line.
• 0:13—Nude running around a room while a Nazi taunts her by shooting his gun near her.
••• 1:12—Breasts doing a song and dance number wearing pants, suspenders and a Nazi hat. Long scene.
**Zardoz** (1974; British). . . . . . . . . . . . . . . . . .Consuella
0:29—Breasts under yellow net blouse.

- 1:05—Very brief left breast, when Sean Connery grabs her during struggle.
- 1:26—Wearing yellow blouse, trying to kill Connery.
- 1:44—Very brief right breast feeding her baby in time lapse scene at the end of the film.

**Farewell, My Lovely** (1975; British) . . . . . . . . . Velma
**Foxtrot** (1976; Mexican/Swiss) . . . . . . . . . . . . . . Julia
Orca, The Killer Whale (1977) . . . . . . . . Rachel Bedford
**The Purple Taxi** (1977; French/Italian/Irish) . . . Sharon
Stardust Memories (1980). . . . . . . . . . . . . . . . . .Dorrie
The Verdict (1982) . . . . . . . . . . . . . . . . . . . . . . Laura
**Angel Heart** (1987) . . . . . . . . . . Margaret Krusemark
(Original Unedited Version reviewed.)

- 1:10—Brief left breast, lying dead on the floor, covered with blood.
- 1:46—Very brief left breast during flashback of the dead-on-the-floor-covered-with-blood scene.

**Mascara** (1987; French/Belgian) . . . . . . . . .Gaby Hart

- 1:03—Brief breasts putting on sweater when Michael Sarrazin watches through binoculars.
- 1:18—Right breast, while making love with Chris.

D.O.A. (1988) . . . . . . . . . . . . . . . . . . . .Mrs. Fitzwaring
*Magazines:*
**Playboy** (Nov 1972) . . . . . . . . . . . Sex in Cinema 1972

- 167—Breasts lying down in bed in a photo from *'Tis a Pity She's a Whore*.

**Playboy** (Mar 1974). . . . . . . . . . . . . . . . . . . . Zardoz
•• 144-145—Buns and side view of left breast and partial lower frontal nudity.
**Playboy** (Nov 1974) . . . . . . . . . . Sex in Cinema 1974
••• 148—Breasts from *The Night Porter*.
**Playboy** (Dec 1974). . . . . . . . . . . . . Sex Stars of 1974
••• 209—Full frontal nudity.
**Playboy** (Dec 1975). . . . . . . . . . . . . Sex Stars of 1975
••• 182—Breasts.
**Playboy** (Dec 1976). . . . . . . . . . . . . Sex Stars of 1976

- 186—Right breast.

**Playboy** (Dec 1977). . . . . . . . . . . . . Sex Stars of 1977
•• 215—Right breast and partial lower frontal nudity, while standing next to fireplace.

# Randall, Anne

*Films:*
The Split (1968) . . . . . . . . . . . . . . . . . . . . . Negli's Girl
The Model Shop (1969) . . . . . . . . . . . . . . . . 2nd Model
Hell's Bloody Devils (1970) . . . . . . . . . . . . . . Amanda
The Christian Licorice Store (1971) . . . . . . . . Texas Girl
A Time for Dying (1971) . . . . . . . . . . . . . Nellie Winters
Get to Know Your Rabbit (1972) . . . . . . . . . Stewardess
**Stacey!** (1973). . . . . . . . . . . . . . . . . . . Stacey Hansen
*a.k.a. Stacey and Her Gangbusters*
••• 0:01—Breasts taking off her driving jump suit.
••• 0:12—Breasts changing clothes.
••• 0:39—Breasts in bed with Bob.
Westworld (1973) . . . . . . . . . . . . . . . . . . . .Servant Girl
*TV:*
Hee Haw (1972-73) . . . . . . . . . . . . . . . . . . . .Regular

*Magazines:*
**Playboy** (May 1967). . . . . . . . . . . . . . . . . . . Playmate
**Playboy** (Dec 1973) . . . . . . . . . . . . . .Sex Stars of 1973
•• 208—Left breast.

# Randolph, Ty

a.k.a. Windsor Taylor Randolph.
a.k.a. Mindi Miller.
*Films:*
That Man Bolt (1973). . . . . . . . . . . . . . . . . . . . . n.a.
Westworld (1973) . . . . . . . . . . . . . . . . . . . . . . . n.a.
Airport 1975 (1974). . . . . . . . . . . . . . . . . . . . . . n.a.
Funny Lady (1975). . . . . . . . . . . . . . . . . . Chorus Girl
Take a Hard Ride (1975; U.S./Italian) . . . . . . . . . . . n.a.
1900 (1976; Italian) . . . . . . . . . . . . . . . . . . . . . n.a.
(NC-17 version reviewed.)
The Big Bus (1976). . . . . . . . . . . . . . . . . . . . . . n.a.
Paternity (1981). . . . . . . . . . . . . . . . . . . . . . . . n.a.
**Body Double** (1984) . . . . . . . . . . . . . . . . . . . Mindi
••• 1:50—Breasts in the shower during filming of movie with Craig Wasson made up as a vampire.
Ice Pirates (1984) . . . . . . . . . . . . . . . . . . . . . . n.a.
Sacred Ground (1984) . . . . . . . . . . . . . . . . . . . . n.a.
**Amazons** (1986) . . . . . . . . . . . . . . . . . . . . . .Dyala
•• 0:22—Breasts skinny dipping then getting dressed with Tashi.
•• 0:24—Brief breasts getting her top opened by bad guys then fighting them.
Penitentiary III (1987). . . . . . . . . . . . . . . . . . .Sugar
Turnaround (1987). . . . . . . . . . . . . . . . . . . . . . . n.a.
**Caged Fury** (1989). . . . . . . . . . . . .Warden Sybil Thorn
•• 0:53—Breasts and buns undressing for bath, then in the bathtub.
**Deadly Embrace** (1989) . . . . . . . . . Charlotte Morland
0:19—In yellow one piece swimsuit by the pool with Chris.
0:27—In wet, white T-shirt in the kitchen with Chris.
•• 0:28—Breasts taking off her top. Mostly side view of left breast.

- 0:29—More left breast, while in bed with Chris.

••• 0:30—Breasts, making love in bed with Chris.

- 1:10—Brief right breast, on T.V. when she replays video tape for Linnea Quigley.

Hollywood Boulevard II (1989)
. . . . . . . . . . . . . . . . . Amazon Warrior from Brooklyn
Nudity Required (1989) . . . . . . . . . . . . . . . . . .Brenda
Batman Returns (1992) . . . . Uncredited Penguin Crony
Warlords 3000 (1992) . . . . . . . . . . . . . . . .Bull Woman
*TV:*
Switch (1976-77) . . . . . . . . . . . . . . . . . . . . . . Revel

# Rattray, Heather

*Films:*
Across the Great Divide (1976). . . . . . . . . . . . . Holly
The Further Adventures of the Wilderness Family (1978)
. . . . . . . . . . . . . . . . . . . . . . . . . . Jenny Robinson
The Sea Gypsies (1978) . . . . . . . . . . . . . . . . .Courtney
Mountain Family Robinson (1979) . . . . . . . . . . . .Jenny

**Basket Case 2** (1989) . . . . . . . . . . . . . . . . . . . . Susan
  • 1:20—Brief right breast twice, when white blouse
    gapes open in bedroom with Duane. Special effect
    scar on her stomach makes it a little unappealing
    looking.
Basket Case 3: The Progeny (1991) . . . . . . . . . . . Susan
*TV:*
As the World Turns (1990- ) . . . . . . . . . . . . . Lily Walsh

## Rau, Andrea

*Films:*
**Daughters of Darkness** (1971; Belgian/French/
  German/Italian) . . . . . . . . . . . . . . . . . . . . . . . . Ilona
  • 0:39—Buns and side of right breast, kneeling on
    floor while bending over the toilet.
  • 0:56—Brief breasts on top of Stefan in bed.
  ••• 1:00—Left breast, while standing in bathroom
    watching Stefan take a shower.
  ••• 1:01—Breasts when Stefan tries to drag her into the
    shower.
  • 1:02—Breasts, lying dead on the floor.
  • 1:03—Breasts, lying dead on the floor. Long shot.
**Beyond Erotica** (1979) . . . . . . . . . . . . . . . . . . . . Lola
  • 0:26—Breasts, undressing in her bedroom.
  •• 0:30—Nude, undressing, then lying in bed, then try-
    ing on bunny costume.
  • 0:47—Left breast, while lying on the floor.
  • 0:56—Brief buns, running around in her cell.
  • 0:57—Brief nude, behind wall with holes in it.
  • 0:59—Left breast, seen though hole in the wall.
  •• 1:10—Breasts in her bedroom.
  • 1:23—Left breast, in flashback to 0:47 scene.

## Ray, Ola

*Films:*
**Body and Soul** (1981) . . . . . . . . . . . . . . . Hooker #1
  • 0:54—Brief breasts sitting on top of Leon Isaac
    Kennedy in bed with two other hookers.
48 Hrs. (1982) . . . . . . . . . . . . . . . . . . Vroman's Dancers
Night Shift (1982) . . . . . . . . . . . . . . . . . . . . . . . . Dawn
**10 to Midnight** (1983) . . . . . . . . . . . . . . . . . . . . . Ola
  • 1:30—Very brief buns and very brief left breast, tak-
    ing off robe and getting into the shower.
  •• 1:31—Breasts in the shower.
  •• 1:32—More breasts in the shower.
  • 1:39—Very brief breasts, dead, covered with blood
    in the shower.
Fear City (1984) . . . . . . . . . . . . . . . . . . . . Honey Powers
Beverly Hills Cop II (1987) . . . . . . . . . Playboy Playmate
The Nightstalker (1987) . . . . . . . . . . . . . . . . . Sable Fox
*Music Videos:*
Thriller/Michael Jackson (1983) . . . . . . . . His Girlfriend
*Magazines:*
**Playboy** (Jun 1980) . . . . . . . . . . . . . . . . . . . Playmate
  ••• 144-155—Breasts and buns.
**Playboy** (Jul 1981) . . . . . . . . . . . . . Body and Soulmates
  • 148—Right breast.
**Playboy** (Dec 1984) . . . . . . . . . . . . . Sex Stars of 1984
  ••• 206—Breasts.

## Raymond, Candy
*Films:*
**Alvin Rides Again** (1974; Australian) . . . Girl in Office
  • 0:05—Lower frontal nudity and buns, in office with
    Alvin.
Don's Party (1976; Australian) . . . . . . . . . . . . . . . Kerry
Monkey Grip (1983; Australian) . . . . . . . . . . . . . Lillian

## • Raymond, Cathleen
*Films:*
**Seduce Me: Pamela Principle 2** (1994) . . . . . . Cindy
  • 0:03—Breast, while in background, changing
    clothes. Out of focus.
  ••• 0:04—Breasts and buns in G-string, after taking off
    lingerie during photo session. Long scene.
*Magazines:*
**Penthouse** (Jul 1994) . . . . . . . . . . . . Heavenly Bodies
  ••• 89-95—Nude against outer space backdrops.

## • Rayne, April
See: Naschak, Andrea.

## Redgrave, Lynn
Daughter of actor Sir Michael Redgrave.
Sister of actress Vanessa Redgrave.
Spokeswoman for *Weight Watchers* products.
*Films:*
Georgy Girl (1966; British) . . . . . . . . . . . . . . . . Georgy
The Virgin Soldiers (1969) . . . . . . . . . . . Phillipa Raskin
Everything You Wanted to Know About Sex, But Were
  Afraid to Ask (1972) . . . . . . . . . . . . . . . . . The Queen
The Happy Hooker (1975) . . . . . . . . . Xaviera Hollander
  (Before Weight Watchers.)
      0:43—In black bra and panties doing a strip tease
      routine in a board room while Tom Poston watches.
Morgan Stewart's Coming Home (1987)
  . . . . . . . . . . . . . . . . . . . . . . . . . . . . . Nancy Stewart
**Getting It Right** (1989) . . . . . . . . . . . . . . . . . . . Joan
  •• 0:46—Brief right breast, then brief breasts on couch
    seducing Gavin. More right breast shot when wres-
    tling with him.
Midnight (1989) . . . . . . . . . . . . . . . . . . . . . . Midnight
*Made for TV Movies:*
The Seduction of Miss Leona (1980) . . . . . Leona DeVos
What Ever Happened to Baby Jane? (1991)
  . . . . . . . . . . . . . . . . . . . . . . . . . . . . . . Jane Hudson
*TV:*
Centennial (1978-79)
  . . . . . . . . . . . . . Charlotte Buckland Lloyd Seccombe
House Calls (1979-81) . . . . . . . . . . . . . . Ann Anderson
Teachers Only (1982-83) . . . . . . . . . . . Diana Swanson
Chicken Soup (1989) . . . . . . . . . . . . . . . . . . . . Maddie
*Magazines:*
Playboy (Nov 1975) . . . . . . . . . . . Sex in Cinema 1975
  138—Buns in lingerie on table in front of Tom Pos-
    ton.
**Playboy** (Nov 1989) . . . . . . . . . . . Sex in Cinema 1989
  • 131—Right breast lying in sofa in a still from *Getting
    It Right*.

# Redgrave, Vanessa

Daughter of actor Sir Michael Redgrave.
Sister of actress Lynn Redgrave.
*Films:*
Blow-Up (1966; British/Italian) . . . . . . . . . . . . . . . Jane
Camelot (1967). . . . . . . . . . . . . . . . . . . . . . . Guenevere
**Isadora** (1968; British). . . . . . . . . . . . Isadora Duncan
　　0:47—Brief glimpses of breasts and buns dancing
　　around in her boyfriend's house at night. Hard to see
　　anything.
　　• 2:19—Very brief breasts dancing on stage after com-
　　ing back from Russia.
The Sea Gull (1968) . . . . . . . . . . . . . . . . . . . . . . . . Nina
The Trojan Women (1972; British). . . . . . . .Andromache
Murder on the Orient Express (1974; British) . . . . .Mary
**Out of Season** (1975; British) . . . . . . . . . . . . . . . Ann
　　• 0:35—Breasts, while putting on slip in bedroom.
　　• 0:53—Full frontal nudity, after throwing open bed
　　covers for Cliff Robertson. Don't see her face.
The Seven-Per-Cent Solution (1976) . . . . .Lola Deveraux
Julia (1977). . . . . . . . . . . . . . . . . . . . . . . . . . . . . . Julia
(Academy Award for Best Supporting Actress.)
**Agatha** (1979; British). . . . . . . . . . . . .Agatha Christie
　　• 0:38—Buns, while lying face down and getting a
　　massage. Then wearing a wet gown in bathtub.
**Yanks** (1979) . . . . . . . . . . . . . . . . . . . . . . . . . . Helen
　　• 1:25—Brief side of left breast and buns, taking off
　　robe and getting into bed.
Bear Island (1980; British/Canadian) . . . . Hedi Lindquist
Wagner (1983; British) . . . . . . . . . . . . . . . . . . . .Cosima
The Bostonians (1984) . . . . . . . . . . . . . Olive Chancellor
**Steaming** (1985; British). . . . . . . . . . . . . . . . . .Nancy
　　• 1:32—Buns and brief side view of right breast get-
　　ting into pool.
Wetherby (1985; British). . . . . . . . . . . . . . Jean Travers
Prick Up Your Ears (1987; British) . . . . . . Peggy Ramsay
Consuming Passions (1988; U.S./British) . . . . Mrs. Garza
　　0:40—Almost side view of left breast making love
　　with a guy on her bed.
**Orpheus Descending** (1990) . . . . . . . . .Lady Torrance
　　•• 1:18—Buns, after taking off her robe and opening
　　curtains to see Kevin Anderson. Shadow of left
　　breast on curtain.
The Ballad of the Sad Cafe (1991). . . . . . . Miss Amelia
Howards End (1992). . . . . . . . . . . . . . . . . Ruth Wilcox
The House of Spirits (1993). . . . . . . . . . . . . . . . Nivea
*Made for Cable Movies:*
Young Catherine (1991) . . . . . . . . . . . . . . . . Empress
They (1993; Showtime). . . . . . . . . . . . .Florence Latimer
*Made for TV Movies:*
Playing for Time (1980). . . . . . . . . . . . . .Fania Fenelon
　　0:11—Very brief buns, while sitting down to get her
　　hair cut.
A Man for All Seasons (1988) . . . . . . . . . . . .Lady Alice
What Ever Happened to Baby Jane? (1991)
　　. . . . . . . . . . . . . . . . . . . . . . . . . . . . Blanche Hudson

# Redman, Amanda

*Films:*
**Richard's Things** (1980; British) . . . . . . . . . . . . .Josie
　　•• 0:51—Breasts, while lying in bed talking to Liv Ull-
　　man.
Give My Regards to Broad Street (1984; British)
　　. . . . . . . . . . . . . . . . . . . . . . . . . . .Office Receptionist
For Queen and Country (1989; British) . . . . . . . . Stacey
*Made for TV Movies:*
Masterpiece Theatre: Body & Soul (1994) . . . . . . . Lynn

# Reed, Pamela

*Films:*
**The Long Riders** (1980) . . . . . . . . . . . . . . Belle Starr
　　• 0:18—Buns, while standing up in bathtub to hug
　　David Carradine. (Don't see her face.)
Melvin and Howard (1980) . . . . . . . . . Bonnie Dummar
Eyewitness (1981) . . . . . . . . . . . . . . . . . . . . . . .Linda
Young Doctors in Love (1982) . . . . . . . Norine Sprockett
The Right Stuff (1983) . . . . . . . . . . . . . . Trudy Cooper
Clan of the Cave Bear (1985). . . . . . . . . . . . . . . . .Iza
The Best of Times (1986) . . . . . . . . . . . Gigi Hightower
Rachel River (1989) . . . . . . . . . . . . . . . Mary Graving
Cadillac Man (1990) . . . . . . . . . . . . . . . . . . . . . .Tina
Chattahoochee (1990). . . . . . . . . . . . . . . . . . Earlene
Kindergarten Cop (1990). . . . . . . . . . . . . . . . . Phoebe
Bob Roberts (1992; U.S./British). . . . . . . . .Carol Cruise
Passed Away (1992). . . . . . . . . . . . . . . . .Terry Scanlan
*Made for TV Movies:*
Scandal Sheet (1985). . . . . . . . . . . . . . . . .Helen Grant
Woman with a Past (1992). . . . . . . . . . . . Dee Johnson
Born Too Soon (1993) . . . . . . . . . . . .Elizabeth Mehren
*TV:*
The Andros Targets (1977). . . . . . . . . . . . .Sandi Farrell
Grand (1990). . . . . . . . . . . . . . . . . . . . . Janice Pasetti
Family Album (1993- ) . . . . . . . . . . . . . . . . . . . . n.a.

# Reed, Penelope

*Films:*
**Amazons** (1986) . . . . . . . . . . . . . . . . . . . . . . Tashi
　　•• 0:22—Breasts and buns undressing to go skinny dip-
　　ping. More breasts getting dressed.
　　• 0:24—Brief breasts getting top opened by bad guys.
Hollywood Boulevard II (1989)
　　. . . . . . . . . . . . . . . . . . . Amazon Warrior with Crystal
Far Out Man (1990). . . . . . . . . . . . . . . . . Stewardess
Hired to Kill (1990) . . . . . . . . . . . . . . . . . . . . .Katrina

# Reed, Tracy

*Films:*
...All the Marbles (1981) . . . . . . . . . . . . . . . . . .Diane
*a.k.a. The California Dolls*
**Running Scared** (1986). . . . . . . . . . . . . . . . Maryann
　　• 0:18—Brief buns.
　　• 1:30—Very brief breasts in bed with Gregory Hines.
*Made for TV Movies:*
Death of a Centerfold: The Dorothy Stratten Story
　　(1981) . . . . . . . . . . . . . . . . . . . . . . . . . . . . Mindy

*TV:*
Love, American Style (1969-70) . . . . . . Repertory Player
Barefoot in the Park (1970-71) . . . . . . . . Corie Bratter
Love, American Style (1972-74) . . . . . . Repertory Player
Knots Landing (1990-93) . . . . . . . . Charlotte Anderson

# Reeves, Saskia

*Films:*
**Antonia & Jane** (1991; British) . . . . . . . Antonia McGill
•• 0:42—Brief partial left breast, while lying in bed on top of her lover. Breasts, turning over on her back.
• 0:44—Breasts, leaning over her lover while is tied and blindfolded in bed.
**Close My Eyes** (1991; British) . . . . . . . Natalie Gillespie
•• 0:29—Very brief right breast, twice, then breasts twice in room with Richard.
••• 0:31—Full frontal nudity, getting up and getting dressed.
••• 0:45—In white bra, then breasts standing, then lying on the floor with Richard.
•• 0:46—Buns, while lying in bed with Richard. Nude, getting out of bed and putting on robe.
• 0:56—Right breast, while lying in bed.

# Regan, Linda

*Films:*
**The Adventures of a Private Eye** (1974; British)
. . . . . . . . . . . . . . . . . . . . . . . . . . . . . . . . . . . . Clarissa
• 0:34—Full frontal nudity in boat with Scott.
• 0:36—Very brief side view of left breast, getting up and diving off boat.
Carry on England (1976; British) . . . . . . . . . . .Pvt. Taylor
Fiona (1978; British) . . . . . . . . . . . . . . . . . . . . Secretary

# Regan, Mary

*Films:*
**Heart of the Stag** (1983; New Zealand)
. . . . . . . . . . . . . . . . . . . . . . . . . . . . . .Cathy Jackson
• 0:03—Brief right breast twice, very brief lower frontal nudity in bed with her father.
•• 1:06—Breasts in bed, ripping her blouse open while yelling at her father.
**Midnight Dancer** (1987; Australian) . . . . . . . . Crystal
*a.k.a. Belinda*
•• 0:29—Breasts in dressing room, undressing and rubbing makeup on herself.
•• 0:56—In bra, then breasts in panties, changing clothes and getting into bed.
The Year My Voice Broke (1987; Australian)
. . . . . . . . . . . . . . . . . . . . . . . . . . . . . . . . . . Miss McColl
Out of the Body (1988; Australian) . . . . . . Marry Mason
Fever (1989; Australian) . . . . . . . . . . . . . .Leanne Welles

# Regan, Misty

Adult film actress.
*Films:*
**Nudity Required** (1989). . . . . . . . . . .Featured Dancer
• 0:02—Breasts dancing on stage in club.
• 0:04—Breasts and buns, on stage in G-string.

# Regard, Suzanne M.

*Films:*
48 Hrs. (1982) . . . . . . . . . . . . . . . . . . . Cowgirl Dancer
0:39—Dancer in red-neck bar wearing silver star pasties.
**Malibu Express** (1984) . . . . . . . . . . . . . . . Sexy Sally
• 0:50—Brief breasts, while talking on the telephone.
•• 1:06—Breasts, while talking on the telephone.

# • Register, Meg

*Films:*
Ministry of Vengeance (1989) . . . . . . . . . . . . Gail Miller
Backstreet Dreams (1990) . . . . . . . . . . . . . . . . . . Candy
Lena's Holiday (1990). . . . . . . . . . . . . . . . . . Bridgette
**Boxing Helena** (1993). . . . . . . . . . Marion Cavanaugh
•• 0:06—Right breast in open dress in Julian Sand's flashback.

# Reidy, Gabrielle

*Films:*
Educating Rita (1983; British). . . . . . . . . . . . . . Barbara
**The Fanatasist** (1986; Irish) . . . . . . . . Kathy O'Malley
• 0:03—Breasts getting attacked in a room.
The Baby of Mâcon (1993; British). . . . . . . . . . .Midwife

# Relph, Emma

*Films:*
**Eureka** (1983; British) . . . . . . . . . . . .Mary (blue dress)
• 1:17—Brief breasts during African voodoo ceremony.
The Witches (1989) . . . . . . . . . . . . . . . . . . . . . . . Millie

# • Remberg, Erika

*Films:*
Circus of Horrors (1960; British) . . . . . . . . . . . . . Elissa
Saturday Night Out (1963; British). . . . . . . . . . .Wanda
Cave of the Living Dead (1966; Yugoslavian) . . . . .Maria
**The Lickerish Quartet** (1970; Italian) . . . . . . . . . .Wife
*a.k.a. Erotic Illusion*
•• 1:14—Nude, getting up off sofa and sitting back down, then in B&W film.
•• 1:15—Breasts, while the girl feels her up. Close-up shot.
• 1:26—Right breast, while in bed in film.

# Rene, Sugar Ray

See: Rome, Cindy.

# • Rener, Shawna

*Video Tapes:*
**The Best of the Mermaids** (1992)
. . . . . . . . . . . . . . . . . . . . . . . . .Jus' Catchin' Some Rays
••• 0:20—Breasts and buns, scuba diving.
*Magazines:*
Playboy (Dec 1993) . . . . . . . . . . . . . . . . . . . Grapevine

## Renet, Sinitta

Singer in England.
*Films:*
Shock Treatment (1981) . . . . . . . . . . . . . . . . . . . . . .n.a.
**Foreign Body** (1986; British). . . . . . . Lovely Indian Girl
• 0:06—Buns, then breasts in bedroom.

## • Renney, Janice

*Films:*
**Crimes of Passion** (1984) . . . . . . . . . . . . . . Stripper
(Unrated version reviewed.)
••• 0:06—Breasts and buns dancing while Anthony Perkins watches.
1:00—Buns again.
Savage Dawn (1984). . . . . . . . . . . . . . . . . . . . Susan

## Renshaw, Jeannine

*Films:*
Hook (1991) . . . . . . . . . . . . . . . . . . . . . Drama Teacher
*Made for Cable TV:*
**Dream On: Death Takes a Coffee Break**
(1990; HBO) . . . . . . . . . . . . . . . . . . . . . . . . . . Robin
•• 0:10—Breasts in kitchen after taking off her top with Martin, then on sofa.

## Reuben, Gloria

*Films:*
Immediate Family (1989) . . . . . . . . . . Maternity Nurse
**ShadowHunter** (1992) . . . . . . . . . . . . . . . . . . . . Cayla
• 0:07—Buns, lifting up her skirt to tempt Scott Glenn. Don't see her face and slightly out of focus.
*Made for TV Movies:*
Confessions: Two Faces of Evil (1994) . . Tanya Blackmon

## Reve'e, Paula

*Films:*
**Angel Eyes** (1991). . . . . . . . . . . . . . . . . . . . . . . . Julie
•• 0:13—Breasts, while standing in yellow bikini bottoms and rubbing lotion on herself.
• 0:23—Breasts, while lying on pool float in the pool.
• 0:25—More breasts while on pool float.
**Knockouts** (1992). . . . . . . . . . . . . . . . . . . . . . .Candy
•• 0:04—Breasts, going to look in the guy's locker room.
•• 0:23—Breasts during strip poker game.
•• 0:27—Breasts while sitting on chest of drawers.
••• 0:43—In lingerie, then breasts while posing for photographs.
•• 0:59—Breasts while working out (seen mostly in silhouette).
*Video Tapes:*
**Inside Out 4** (1992) . . . . . Lola/My Cyberian Rhapsody
(Unrated version reviewed.)
1:29—In bra and panties after stripping out of clothes.
••• 1:30—Breasts in cybersex machine.
••• 1:31—Breasts several times when cybersex machine starts malfunctioning.

## Reyes, Pia

*Films:*
**Auntie Lee's Meat Pies** (1991) . . . . . . . . . . . . . . Sky
•• 1:10—Breasts in basement with her rock star boyfriend.
•• 1:15—Breasts in basement with her pot smoking boyfriend.
On Deadly Ground (1993) . . . . . . . . . . . . . . . . . Dancer
Return of the Living Dead 3 (1993) . . . . . . . . . . . Alicia
*Video Tapes:*
**Sexy Lingerie** (1988) . . . . . . . . . . . . . . . . . . . . Model
**Playboy Video Calendar 1990** (1989). . . . . . . . .June
••• 0:28—Nude.
**Sensual Pleasures of Oriental Massage** (1990)
. . . . . . . . . . . . . . . . . . . . . . . . . . . . . . . . . . . . n.a.
*Magazines:*
**Playboy** (Nov 1988) . . . . . . . . . . . . . . . . . . . Playmate
**Playboy's Nudes** (Oct 1990) . . . . . . . . . . . . . Herself
•• 52—Right breast and lower frontal nudity.
**Playboy's Book of Lingerie** (Jan 1991) . . . . . .Herself
••• 42-43—Breasts.
**Playboy's Book of Lingerie** (Mar 1991). . . . . .Herself
••• 52—Breasts.
**Playboy's Book of Lingerie** (Nov 1991) . . . . .Herself
••• 43—Breasts.
**Playboy's Girls of the World** (Oct 1992). . . . .Herself
•• 66—Left breast.
**Playboy's Calendar Playmates** (Nov 1992). . .Herself
••• 82—Full frontal nudity.
**Playboy's Book of Lingerie** (Jan 1994) . . . . . .Herself
••• 9—Left breast and lower frontal nudity.
••• 83—Full frontal nudity.
**Playboy's Book of Lingerie** (May 1994) . . . . .Herself
••• 54—Breasts.
**Playboy's Girls of Summer '94** (Jul 1994) . . . .Herself
••• 48—Breasts.
••• 51—Breasts.

## Rhey, Ashlie

*Films:*
Body of Influence (1992) . . . . . . . . . . . . . . Dominatrix
(Unrated version reviewed.)
Ring of Fire II: Blood and Steel (1992) . . . . . . . . . . . . .
Bad Girl Gang Member
**Anthony's Desire** (1993). . . . . . . . . . . . . . . . Dancer
• 0:22—Breasts, while lying on her back under another woman on stage.
• 0:54—Left breast and brief lower frontal nudity, while lying down with other women. She's at the bottom of the screen.
**Renegade: Fighting Cage** (1993) . . . . . . . . Redhead
(Nudity added for video release.)
••• 1:14—Breasts and buns, while in a room with a guy, then making love with him on a small table.
**Save Me** (1993) . . . . . . . . . . . . . . . . . . . . . Customer
(Unrated version reviewed.)
••• 0:21—Nude, while trying on lingerie after Lysette Anthony shows Harry Hamlin secret one-way mirror in dressing room in lingerie store.

**Midnight Tease** (1994) . . . . . . . . . . . . . . . . . Mantra
- •• 0:00—Breasts and buns during opening credits.
- ••• 0:42—Buns and breasts in black dominatrix outfit while dancing on stage with Samantha.
- •• 0:47—Breasts while talking with Samantha in dressing room.
- • 0:50—Breasts, while whipping Samantha's stepfather in dream while Samantha kills her.

**Money to Burn** (1994) . . . . . . . . . . . . . . . . . . . . . Gina
- • 1:02—Nude in bathtub with Don Swayze.

*Video Tapes:*

**Playboy's Erotic Fantasies III** (1993)
. . . . . . . . . . . . . . . . . . . . . . . . . . . . . Final Exam/Teacher
- 0:37—Briefly in blue lingerie during student's fantasy.
- ••• 0:39—In white bra, panties and stockings, then full frontal nudity while making love with the student.

**Playboy's Sensual Fantasy for Lovers** (1993)
. . . . . . . . . . . . . . . . . . . . . . . . . . . . . . Film Fantasies
- ••• 0:25—In bra and panties, then nude while making love, in "sheik" fantasy with her lover.
- • 0:47—Breasts during review.

*Magazines:*

**Playboy's Book of Lingerie** (Sep 1992) . . . . . Herself
- ••• 42—Breasts.
- ••• 86—Breasts.

**Playboy's Book of Lingerie** (Nov 1992) . . . . . Herself
- • 63—Side of right breast.
- ••• 76—Full frontal nudity.

**Playboy's Nudes** (Dec 1992) . . . . . . . . . . . . . Herself
- ••• 82-85—Full frontal nudity under water in pool.

**Playboy's Book of Lingerie** (Mar 1993) . . . . . Herself
- • 88—Upper half of breasts.
- • 90—Tip of right breast.

**Playboy's Girls of Summer '93** (Jun 1993). . . Herself
- •• 24—Buns and side of right breast.

**Playboy's Book of Lingerie** (Jul 1993) . . . . . . Herself
- ••• 33—Full frontal nudity.
- ••• 46—Side of left breast and buns.

# Rialson, Candice

*Films:*

The Gay Deceivers (1969). . . . . . . . . . . . . . . . . . . . .n.a.

**Candy Stripe Nurses** (1974) . . . . . . . . . . . . . . Sandy
- •• 0:05—Breasts in hospital linen closet with a guy.
- •• 0:08—Breasts smoking and writing in bathtub.
- • 0:14—Breasts in hospital bed.

Mama's Dirty Girls (1974). . . . . . . . . . . . . . . . . . .n.a.

**Pets** (1974) . . . . . . . . . . . . . . . . . . . . . . . . . . Bonnie
- •• 0:26—Breasts dancing in field while Dan is watching her while he's tied up.
- ••• 0:33—Breasts making love on top of Dan while he's still tied up.
- 0:35—Running through woods in braless orange top.
- •• 0:40—Breasts getting into bath at Geraldine's house.
- • 0:45—Breasts posing for Geraldine.

0:54—In black and red lingerie outfit getting ready for bed.
- ••• 1:02—Breasts taking off lingerie in bed with Ron, then making love with him.
- 1:34—Almost breasts, getting whipped by Vincent.

The Eiger Sanction (1975) . . . . . . . . . . . . . . Art Student

**Summer School Teachers** (1975). . . . . . . . Conklin T.
- • 0:14—Breasts and buns when Mr. Lacy fantasizes about what she looks like. Don't see her face, but it looks like her.
- ••• 0:38—Breasts outside with other teacher, kissing on the ground.

**Hollywood Boulevard** (1976). . . . .Candy Wednesday
- •• 0:29—Breasts getting her blouse ripped off by actors during a film.
- ••• 0:32—Breasts sunbathing with Bobbi and Jill.
- •• 0:45—Brief breasts in the films she's watching at the drive-in. Same as 0:29.

Logan's Run (1976)
. . . . . . . . . . . . . . .Uncredited Girl with Richard Jordan

Silent Movie (1976) . . . . . . . . . .Uncredited Club Patron

**Chatterbox** (1977) . . . . . . . . . . . . . . . . . . . . . Penny
- •• 0:01—Left breast, in bed with Ted, then breasts getting out of bed.
- 0:10—In white bra wrestling on couch with another woman.
- ••• 0:15—Side view of right breast then breasts during demonstration on stage.
- ••• 0:26—Breasts in bed talking on phone.
- 0:32—In open dress letting her "chatterbox" sing during talk show. Something covers pubic area.
- •• 0:35—Breasts during photo shoot.
- •• 0:38—Breasts again for more photos while opening a red coat.
- •• 0:43—Breasts in bed with Ted.
- ••• 0:55—Breasts taking off white dress, walking up the stairs and opening the door.
- •• 1:09—Breasts opening her raincoat for Ted.

Moonshine County Express (1977). . . . . . . . . . Mayella

Stunts (1977). . . . . . . . . . . . . . . . . . . . . . . . Judy Blake

Winter Kills (1979) . . . . . . . . . . . . . Second Blonde Girl

# • Riave, Andrea

*Made for Cable TV:*

**Red Shoe Diaries: How I Met My Husband**
(1993; Showtime) . . . . . . . . . . . . . . Wealthy Woman
- •• 0:15—Breasts, while making love with Gusipe in car while Neith Hunter watches.

**Red Shoe Diaries: Runway** (1994; Showtime) . . .Jana
- 0:01—In red bra. Buns in black G-string under body suit.
- •• 0:17—Breasts and buns in panties, several times while posing for photos with Miguel.
- • 0:21—Brief breasts (she's on the left) while watching Alia and Miguel making love.

# Richarde, Tessa

*Films:*
The Beach Girls (1982) . . . . . . . . . . . . . . . . . . . . Doreen
**Cat People** (1982) . . . . . . . . . . . . . . . . . . . . . . . . . Billie
  •• 1:00—Breasts in bed with Malcolm McDowell trying
    to get him excited.
**The Last American Virgin** (1982) . . . . . . . . . . Brenda
  •• 0:15—Brief breasts walking into the living room
    when Gary's parents come home.
Young Doctors in Love (1982) . . . . . . . . . . Rocco's Wife
National Lampoon's Vacation (1983) . . . . . Motel Guest

# Richards, Kim

*Films:*
Escape to Witch Mountain (1975) . . . . . . . . . . . . . Tia
Assault on Precinct 13 (1976) . . . . . . . . . . . . . . . Kathy
No Deposit, No Return (1976) . . . . . . . . . . . . . Tracy
Special Delivery (1976) . . . . . . . . . . . . . . . . . . Juliette
The Car (1977) . . . . . . . . . . . . . . . . . . . . . . . Lynn Marie
Return from Witch Mountain (1978) . . . . . . . . . . . Tia
Meatballs, Part II (1984) . . . . . . . . . . . . . . . . . . Cheryl
**Tuff Turf** (1984) . . . . . . . . . . . . . . . . Frankie Croyden
    1:07—In black lingerie getting dressed.
  • 1:29—Brief breasts supposedly of a body double
    (Fiona Morris) in bedroom with James Spader but I
    have heard from a very reliable source that it really
    was her.
Escape (1988) . . . . . . . . . . . . . . . . . . . . Brooke Howser
*TV:*
Nanny and the Professor (1970-71) . . Prudence Everett
Here We Go Again (1973) . . . . . . . . . . . . . . . . . . . . . Jan
James at 15 (1977-78) . . . . . . . . . . . . . . Sandy Hunter
Hello, Larry (1979-80) . . . . . . . . . . . . . . . Ruthie Adler

# • Richards, Lisa

*Films:*
House of Dark Shadows (1970) . . . . . . . . Daphne Rudd
Rolling Thunder (1977) . . . . . . . . . . . . . . . . . . . . Janet
Heaven Can Wait (1978) . . . . . . . . . . . . . . . . Reporter
Return (1985) . . . . . . . . . . . . . . . . . . . . . Ann Stoving
The Beat (1986) . . . . . . . . . . . . . . . . . . . . . .Amy Kahn
**Eating** (1990) . . . . . . . . . . . . . . . . . . . . . . . . . Helene
    0:12—Brief right breast, while putting a sweater
    over her head.
Venice/Venice (1992) . . . . . . . . . . . . . . . Guest at Party

# Richardson, Joely

Daughter of actress Vanessa Redgrave and director Tony
  Richardson.
Sister of actress Natasha Richardson.
*Films:*
The Hotel New Hampshire (1984) . . . . . . . . . . Waitress
**Wetherby** (1985; British) . . . . . . . . Young Jean Travers
  •• 1:10—Breasts in room with Jim when he takes off
    her coat.
**Drowning by Numbers** (1988; British)
  . . . . . . . . . . . . . . . . . . . . . . . . . . . . . Cisse Colpitts 3
  • 0:28—Breasts, taking off swimsuit and drying herself
    off. Long shot.

  ••• 0:43—Breasts and buns, making love on couch with
    Bellamy.
  • 1:23—Breasts under water in pool with Bellamy.
  •• 1:24—Breasts getting out of pool.
  ••• 1:25—Breasts standing up and putting swimsuit
    back on.
  •• 1:37—Left breast, while in car with Madgett.
King Ralph (1991) . . . . . . . . . . . . . . . . . Princess Anna
Shining Through (1992) . . . . . . Margrete von Eberstien
I'll Do Anything (1994) . . . . . . . . . . . . . . Cathy Breslow
*Magazines:*
**Playboy** (Nov 1991) . . . . . . . . . . Sex in Cinema 1991
  •• 146—Breasts on sofa. From *Drowning by Numbers*.

# Richardson, Miranda

*Films:*
**Dance with a Stranger** (1985; British) . . . . . Ruth Ellis
    0:08—Very brief upper half of left breast, twice,
    while in bed making love with David.
    0:18—Very brief tip of left breast getting into bed
    with David. Dark.
  • 0:20—Very, very brief side view of left breast, put-
    ting robe on in bed.
The Innocent (1985; British) . . . . . . . . . . . .Mary Turner
Underworld (1985; British) . . . . . . . . . . . . . . . . . Oriel
The Death of the Heart (1986; British) . . . . . . . . Daphne
Transmutations (1986) . . . . . . . . . . . . . . . . . . . . Oriel
  *a.k.a. Underworld*
Empire of the Sun (1987) . . . . . . . . . . . . . . .Mrs. Victor
Twisted Obsession (1990) . . . . . . . . . . . . . . . Marilyn
The Bachelor (1991) . . . . . . . . . . . . . . Frederica/Widow
Enchanted April (1991; British) . . . . . . . . . . . . . . Rose
The Crying Game (1992) . . . . . . . . . . . . . . . . . . . .Jude
**Damage** (1992; French/British) . . . . . . . . . . . . . Ingrid
  (Unrated Director's cut reviewed.)
  ••• 1:40—Breasts, while standing in front of Jeremy
    Irons in the bedroom.
*Made for Cable Movies:*
Old Times (1993) . . . . . . . . . . . . . . . . . . . . . . . Anna
*Made for TV Movies:*
Mysteryl Die Kinder (1991) . . . . . . . . . . . Sidonie Reiger

# Richardson, Natasha

Daughter of actress Vanessa Redgrave and director Tony
  Richardson.
Sister of actress Joely Richardson.
Wife of actor Liam Neeson.
*Films:*
Gothic (1986; British) . . . . . . . . . . . . . . . . . . . . . Mary
A Month in the Country (1988; British) . . . . Alice Keach
Fat Man and Little Boy (1989) . . . . . . . . . . . Jean Tatlock
**Patty Hearst** (1989) . . . . . . . . . . . . . . Patricia Hearst
  •• 0:13—Breasts, blindfolded in the bathtub while talk-
    ing to a woman member of the S.L.A.
**A Handmaid's Tale** (1990) . . . . . . . . . . . . . . . . .Kate
  •• 0:30—Breasts twice at the window getting some
    fresh air.
  • 0:59—Breasts making love with Aidan Quinn.
  ••• 1:00—Breasts after Quinn rolls off her.

**The Comfort of Strangers** (1991) . . . . . . . . . .Mary
- ••• 0:45—Breasts sleeping in bed. Long shot. Then closer breasts after waking up. Long scene.
- •• 1:05—Breasts making love with Colin. Lit with blue light.
- •• 1:06—Right breast, lying in bed with Colin. Lit with blue light.

The Favor, the Watch and the Very Big Fish
(1991; French/British) . . . . . . . . . . . . . . . . . . . . . Sybil
*a.k.a. Rue Saint-Sulpice*
Widow's Peak (1994). . . . . . . . . . . . . . Edwina Broome
*Made for Cable Movies:*
**Past Midnight** (1992; USA) . . . . . . . Laura Matthews
- ••• 0:48—Breasts while making love in bed with Rutger Hauer.
- • 1:10—Very brief side of left breast, while getting into the shower.

Hostages (1993; HBO) . . . . . . . . . . . . . . . .Jill Morrell
Zelda (1993; TNT) . . . . . . . . . . .Zelda Sayre-Fitzgerald

# Richardson, Rickey
*Films:*
**Bloody Trail** (1972) . . . . . . . . . . . . . . . . . . . . Miriam
- 1:01—Peek at left breast in torn blouse.
- • 1:05—Right breast while sleeping, dark, hard to see.

**The Hot Box** (1972) . . . . . . . . . . . . . . .Ellie St. George
- •• 0:16—Breasts cleaning herself off in stream and getting out.
- • 0:21—Breasts sleeping in hammocks. (She's the second one from the front.)
- • 0:26—Breasts getting accosted by the People's Army guys.
- ••• 0:43—Full frontal nudity making love with Flavio.
- ••• 0:45—Breasts in stream bathing with the other three girls.
- • 1:01—Breasts taking off top in front of soldiers.

# • Richardson, Salli
*Films:*
Mo' Money (1992) . . . . . . . . . . . . . . . Pretty Customer
Prelude to a Kiss (1992) . . . . . . . . . . . . . Bridesmaid #2
How U Like Me Now (1993) . . . . . . . . . . . . . . . Valerie
**Posse** (1993) . . . . . . . . . . . . . . . . . . . . . . . . . . Lana
- • 1:10—Brief buns, while taking off her dress in front of Mario Van Peebles, then brief breasts (don't see her face).
- •• 1:11—Breasts, while making love with Van Peebles in bed.

*Made for TV Movies:*
I Spy Returns (1994) . . . . . . . . . . . . . . . . . . . . . . .n.a.

# Richmond, Fiona
*Films:*
**The House on Straw Hill** (1976; British) . . . . Suzanne
*a.k.a. Exposé*
- ••• 0:05—Buns and breasts undressing and getting into bed and making love with Udo Kier.
- •• 0:56—In black bra, then breasts undressing in front of Kier.

- ••• 1:00—Breasts in bedroom, then making love with Kier.
- 1:03—Brief buns, lying on Linda's bed.
- 1:05—Buns, lying on Linda's bed.
- •• 1:06—Right breast, in bed with Linda.
- •• 1:07—Breasts in bed with Linda.
- • 1:09—Buns and side of left breast getting up from bed.
- • 1:11—Full frontal nudity, getting stabbed in the bathroom. Covered with blood.

**Love Trap** (1977) . . . . . . . . . . . . . . . Maxine Lupercal
*a.k.a. Let's Get Laid*
- •• 0:10—Nude, while in the shower/tub.
- • 0:21—Brief left breast when her lingerie is torn off in Gordon's hand.
- ••• 0:24—Nude, while doing strip routine on stage (wearing a big blonde wig).
- 0:26—Breasts, with a guy in bedroom.
- • 0:27—Breasts and buns in bed with him.
- •• 0:56—Nude, after stripping out of Nazi uniform, then bra and panties, then making love with two girls.
- •• 1:09—Breasts, while in bubble bath, talking to Gordon, then standing up.
- • 1:34—Brief breasts when Gordon pulls her dress top down during filming.

**Fiona** (1978; British) . . . . . . . . . . . . . Fiona Richmond
- •• 0:23—Breasts on boat with a blonde woman rubbing oil on her.
- •• 0:27—In a bra, then frontal nudity stripping in a guy's office for an audition.
- •• 0:35—Breasts, then frontal nudity lying down during photo session.
- • 0:51—Breasts walking around her apartment in boots.
- •• 1:00—Breasts with old guy ripping each other's clothes off.
- •• 1:08—Frontal nudity taking off clothes for a shower.

History of the World, Part I (1981) . . . . . . . . . . .Queen

# Richmond, Laura
*Video Tapes:*
**Sexy Lingerie** (1988) . . . . . . . . . . . . . . . . . . . . Model
**Playboy Video Calendar 1990** (1989) . . . . . February
- ••• 0:07—Nude.

**Playboy Video Centerfold: Kerri Kendall** (1990)
. . . . . . . . . . . . . . . . . . . . . . . . . . . . . . . . . . Playmate
- ••• 0:39—Nude.

**Playboy Video Playmate Six-Pack 1992** (1992)
. . . . . . . . . . . . . . . . . . . . . . . . . . . . . . . . . . Playmate

*Magazines:*
**Playboy** (Sep 1988) . . . . . . . . . . . . . . . . . . Playmate
**Playboy's Book of Lingerie** (Jan 1991) . . . . . .Herself
- • 79—Left breast.

**Playboy's Calendar Playmates** (Nov 1992). . .Herself
- ••• 80—Full frontal nudity.

**Playboy's Blondes, Brunettes & Redheads**
(Sep 1993). . . . . . . . . . . . . . . . . . . . . . . . . . . .Herself
- ••• 88-89—Full frontal nudity.

## Richter, Debi

Miss California 1975.
*Films:*
Hometown, U.S.A. (1979). . . . . . . . . . . . . . . . .Dolly
Swap Meet (1979) . . . . . . . . . . . . . . . . . . . . . . Susan
Gorp (1980) . . . . . . . . . . . . . . . . . . . . . . .Barbara
**Hot Moves** (1984). . . . . . . . . . . . . . . . . . . . . .Heidi
　　0:06—Brief left bun, pulling pink swimsuit bottom
　　aside for the boys at the beach.
　• 0:29—Breasts on nude beach.
　••• 1:09—Breasts, taking off her red dress in bed.
Square Dance (1987) . . . . . . . . . . . . . . . . . . . . Gwen
*a.k.a. Home is Where the Heart Is*
Winners Take All (1987). . . . . . . . . . . . . . Cindy Wickes
　　0:25—In bra, in bed with motorcycle racer.
Promised Land (1988). . . . . . . . . . . . . . . . . . Pammie
The Banker (1989) . . . . . . . . . . . . . . . . . . . . . Melanie
**Cyborg** (1989). . . . . . . . . . . . . . . . . . . .Nady Simmons
　　0:28—Buns, after taking off clothes and running into
　　the ocean.
　• 0:30—Brief left breast by the fire showing herself to
　　Jean-Claude Van Damme.
*Made for TV Movies:*
My Wicked Ways... The Legend of Errol Flynn (1985)
　. . . . . . . . . . . . . . . . . . . . . . . . . . . . . .Lucille Hartley
*TV:*
Aspen (1977) . . . . . . . . . . . . . . . . . . . . Angela Morelli
All Is Forgiven (1986) . . . . . . . . . . . . . . . .Sherry Levy

## Richters, Christine

*Video Tapes:*
**Playmates at Play** (1990) . . . . . . . . . . Free Wheeling
*Magazines:*
**Playboy** (May 1986) . . . . . . . . . . . . . . . . . . Playmate

## Richwine, Maria

*Films:*
The Buddy Holly Story (1978) . . . . . . . Maria Elena Holly
**Hamburger—The Motion Picture** (1986). .Conchita
　•• 0:49—Breasts trying to seduce Russell in a room.
Ministry of Vengeance (1989) . . . . . . . . . . . . . . Fatima
**Sex Crimes** (1991) . . . . . . . . . . . . . . . . . . . . Rosanna
　• 0:09—Very brief tip of right breast, while sitting in
　　bathtub, covered with bruises and cuts after getting
　　raped.
　• 1:19—Brief breast in mirror, while taking a shower.

## Rief, Tammy

*Video Tapes:*
**Hot Body International: #3 Lingerie Special**
(1992). . . . . . . . . . . . . . . . . . . . . . . . . . . . Contestant
　•• 0:20—Buns in black bra and G-string.
**Hot Body International: #5 Miss Acapulco** (1992)
　. . . . . . . . . . . . . . . . . . . . . . . . . . . . . . . Contestant
　•• 0:52—Buns in one piece swimsuit during photo
　　shoot.
*Magazines:*
**Playboy's Sisters** (Feb 1992) . . . . . . . . . . . . . Herself
　•• 88-91—Buns.

## • Riffel, Rena

*Films:*
**Satan's Princess** (1989). . . . . . . . . . . . . . .Erica Dunn
　•• 0:16—Breasts getting white dress torn open, then
　　killed with a knife.
Gunmen (1993). . . . . . . . . . . . . . . . . . . .Loomis' Bride

## Riley, Colleen

*Films:*
Deadly Blessing (1981). . . . . . . . . . . . . . . . . Melissa
**The Hills Have Eyes, Part II** (1989) . . . . . . . . . .Jane
　• 0:55—Very brief left breast, twice, while taking a
　　shower outside when Foster talks to her.

## Ringstrom, Erica

*Films:*
**Last Dance** (1992) . . . . . . . . . . . . . . . . . . . . . Heather
　•• 0:48—Buns in G-string, dancing on stage during
　　DTV contest.
*Magazines:*
**Playboy's Book of Lingerie** (Jul 1991) . . . . . . Herself
　• 107—Partial lower frontal nudity.
**Playboy's Book of Lingerie** (Nov 1991) . . . . . Herself
　••• 65—Full frontal nudity.
**Playboy's Book of Lingerie** (Jan 1992) . . . . . . Herself
　•• 24—Right breast and lower frontal nudity.
**Playboy's Book of Lingerie** (May 1992) . . . . . Herself
　•• 69—Left breast and lower frontal nudity.
**Playboy's Blondes, Brunettes & Redheads**
(Sep 1993). . . . . . . . . . . . . . . . . . . . . . . . . . .Herself
　• 36—Lower frontal nudity.
**Playboy's Book of Lingerie** (Jan 1994) . . . . . . Herself
　••• 53—Full frontal nudity.

## Rio, Nicole

*Films:*
The Zero Boys (1985). . . . . . . . . . . . . . . . . . . . . Sue
**Sorority House Massacre** (1987) . . . . . . . . . . . Tracy
　•• 0:20—In a sheer bra changing clothes with two oth-
　　er girls in a bedroom.
　•• 0:49—Breasts in a tepee with her boyfriend, Craig,
　　just before getting killed.
The Visitants (1987) . . . . . . . . . . . . . . . . . . . . . n.a.
Terminal Exposure (1988) . . . . . . . . . . . . Hostage Girl

## • Rivet, Catherine

*Films:*
**Emmanuelle, The Joys of a Woman** (1975)
　. . . . . . . . . . . . . . . . . . . . . . . . . . . . . . Anna-Maria
　••• 0:58—Nude, while getting massaged by Laura
　　Gemser.
　••• 1:25—Nude making love with Sylvia Kristel and
　　Jean.
*Magazines:*
**Playboy** (Mar 1976) . . . . . . . . . . . Encore Emmanuelle!
　• 80—Side view of left breast.

# Rixon, Cheryl

*Films:*
Swap Meet (1979) . . . . . . . . . . . . . . . . . . . . . . . Annie
**Used Cars** (1980) . . . . . . . . . . . . . . . . . . . . Margaret
•• 0:29—Breasts after getting her dress torn off during a used car commercial.
*Magazines:*
**Penthouse** (Dec 1977) . . . . . . . . . . . . . . . . . . . . . Pet
••• 127-139—Nude.
**Penthouse** (Nov 1979) . . . . . . . . . . . . . Pet of the Year
**Penthouse** (Jul 1980) . . . . . . . . . . . . . . . . . Used Cars
••• 64-71—Nude.

# • Robbins, Deanna

*Films:*
**Final Exam** (1981) . . . . . . . . . . . . . . . . . . . . . . . . .Lisa
•• 1:13—Buns and breasts, after taking off dress and covering herself with a sheet in studio.
*Made for TV Movies:*
Return of the Rebels (1981). . . . . . . . . . . . . .Amy Allen
A Day for Thanks on Walton's Mountain (1982)
. . . . . . . . . . . . . . . . . . . . . . . . . . . Aimee Godsey
Mother's Day on Walton's Mountain (1982)
. . . . . . . . . . . . . . . . . . . . . . . . . . . Aimee Godsey
A Wedding on Walton's Mountain (1982)
. . . . . . . . . . . . . . . . . . . . . . . . . . . Aimee Godsey
*TV:*
Days of Our Lives . . . . . . . . . . . . . . . . . . .Diane Parker
The Young and the Restless (1982-83) . . . . . Cindy Lake

# Roberts, Julia

Wife of singer/actor Lyle Lovett.
Sister of actor Eric Roberts.
*Films:*
Blood Red (1988) . . . . . . . . . . . . . . . . . Maria Collogero
Mystic Pizza (1988). . . . . . . . . . . . . . . . . . Daisy Araujo
Satisfaction (1988) . . . . . . . . . . . . . . . . . Daryle Shane
*a.k.a. Girls of Summer*
Shown on TV as "Girls of Summer."
Steel Magnolias (1989) . . . . . Shelby Eatenton Latcherio
Flatliners (1990) . . . . . . . . . . . . . . . . . .Rachel Mannus
**Pretty Woman** (1990) . . . . . . . . . . . . . . Vivian Ward
(Shelley Michelle, the body double for Julia Roberts, only did the *opening* scenes when Roberts is supposed to be getting dressed in her sexy outfit—*not* for the nude scene at 1:30.)
• 1:30—Very, very brief tip of left breast, then right breast, then left breast seen through head board, in bed with Gere. It's her—look especially at the vertical vein that pops out in the middle of her forehead whenever her blood pressure goes up.
Dying Young (1991) . . . . . . . . . . . . . . . . .Hilary O'Neil
Hook (1991) . . . . . . . . . . . . . . . . . . . . . . . . Tinkerbell
Sleeping with the Enemy (1991) . . . . .Sara/Laura Burney
The Player (1992) . . . . . . . . . . . . . . . . . . . . . . Cameo
The Pelican Brief (1993) . . . . . . . . . . . . Darby Shaw
I Love Trouble (1994) . . . . . . . . . . . . . . . . . . . . .n.a.
*Made for Cable Movies:*
Baja Oklahoma (1988; HBO) . . . . . . . . . . . . . . .Candy

# Roberts, Luanne

*Films:*
The Dark Side of Tomorrow (1970) . . . . Producer's Wife
Weekend with the Babysitter (1970) . . . . Mona Carlton
Welcome Home, Soldier Boys (1972) . . . . . . . . Charlene
**Thunderbolt and Lightfoot** (1974)
. . . . . . . . . . . . . . . . . . . . . . . Suburban Housewife
• 0:57—Brief full frontal nudity standing behind a sliding glass door tempting Jeff Bridges.

# Roberts, Mariwin

*Films:*
Jokes My Folks Never Told Me (1976). . . . . . . . . . . n.a.
**Cinderella** (1977). . . . . . . . . . . . . . Trapper's Daughter
••• 0:11—Frontal nudity getting a bath outside by her blonde sister. Long scene.
**Jailbait Babysitter** (1978). . . . . . . . . . . . . . . . .Trisha
•• 0:08—Breasts and buns, taking off her dress and getting into van with Cal.
•• 0:18—Breasts and buns in shower with Marion while Mike and Cal help them.
**Fairytales** (1979) . . . . . . . . . . . . . . Elevator Operator
• 0:20—Brief full frontal nudity in the elevator.
•• 0:23—Breasts again, closer shot.
*Magazines:*
**Penthouse** (Apr 1978) . . . . . . . . . . . . . . . . . . . . . .Pet

# Roberts, Tanya

*Films:*
Forced Entry (1975) . . . . . . . . . . . . . . . . . Nancy Ulman
0:57—In white bra and panties while walking around the house.
0:59—Sort of full frontal nudity behind textured glass shower door.
The Yum-Yum Girls (1976) . . . . . . . . . . . . . . . . . . April
California Dreaming (1978) . . . . . . . . . . . . . Stephanie
Fingers (1978) . . . . . . . . . . . . . . . . . . . . . . . . . . .Julie
Racquet (1979) . . . . . . . . . . . . . . . . . . . . . . . . Bambi
The Tourist Trap (1979) . . . . . . . . . . . . . . . . . . .Becky
**The Beastmaster** (1982) . . . . . . . . . . . . . . . . . . .Kiri
••• 0:35—Breasts in a pond while Marc Singer watches, then breasts getting out of the water when his pet ferrets steal her towel.
Hearts and Armour (1983) . . . . . . . . . . . . . . Angelica
**Sheena** (1984) . . . . . . . . . . . . . . . . . . . . . . . Sheena
•• 0:18—Breasts and buns taking a shower under a waterfall. Full frontal nudity (long shot), diving into the water.
••• 0:54—Nude taking a bath in a pond while Ted Wass watches.
A View to a Kill (1985) . . . . . . . . . . . . . . Stacey Sutton
**Purgatory** (1988). . . . . . . . . . . . . . . . . . Carly Arnold
• 0:29—Nude, getting into the shower.
• 0:42—Very brief breasts in bed with the Warden.
0:43—In white lingerie in whorehouse.
•• 0:57—Left breast, then brief breasts in bed talking to Tommy.

**Night Eyes** (1990) . . . . . . . . . . . . . . . . . . . . . . . . Nikki
(Unrated version reviewed.)
    0:18—In white one piece swimsuit by the pool.
  • 0:20—Side view of left breast, while getting dressed
    while sitting on bed.
    0:25—In white lingerie, making love in bed with
    Michael.
    0:30—Repeat of last scene on TV when Andrew
    Stevens brings the video tape home to watch.
    0:55—Making love with Stevens. Don't see any-
    thing, but still steamy. Bubble covered left breast in
    tub with Stevens.
  ••• 1:09—Breasts giving Stevens a massage, then mak-
    ing love. Nice! Buns and left breast, while in the
    shower making love.
  • 1:27—Buns, making love with Stevens in a chair.
Twisted Justice (1990) . . . . . . . . . . . . . . . . . . Secretary
**Inner Sanctum** (1991) . . . . . . . . . . . . . . . Lynn Foster
  • 0:35—Right breast, several times, while looking out
    the window.
  ••• 0:40—Buns in lingerie on sofa with Joseph Bottoms,
    then breasts while making love.
  ••• 0:57—In black lingerie under trench coat, stripping
    for Bret Clark. Buns, then breasts making love.
**Legal Tender** (1991) . . . . . . . . . . . . . . . . Rikki Rennick
  • 0:41—Buns and breasts making love with Robert
    Davi. Don't see her face.
**Almost Pregnant** (1992) . . . . . . . . . . Linda Alderson
(Unrated version reviewed.)
  ••• 0:04—Breasts and buns, in bed with a guy. Long
    scene.
  • 0:10—Brief right breast, while under Conaway in
    bed.
  • 0:18—Brief left breast, while in bed with another
    guy during Conaway's dream.
    0:40—Very brief side view of buns, in lingerie, walk-
    ing down stairs.
  • 1:08—Buns, lying in bed while Gordon writes.
  ••• 1:11—Breasts and buns in bed.
  ••• 1:12—Nude with Conaway.
**Sins of Desire** (1992) . . . . . . . . . . . . . . . . . Kay Egan
(Unrated version reviewed.)
  • 0:50—Buns, while in panties in bed with Barry.
  ••• 0:51—Nude, while making love in bed with Barry.
    Long scene.
  • 1:06—Breasts under patterned black body suit with
    Jessica.
  • 1:10—Brief left breast, under body suit.
*Made for Cable Movies:*
  Body Slam (1989; HBO) . . . . . . . . . . . . . . . . . . . n.a.
*TV:*
  Charlie's Angels (1980-81) . . . . . . . . . . . . . Julie Rogers
*Magazines:*
  **Playboy** (Dec 1980) . . . . . . . . . . . . . Sex Stars of 1980
  • 240—In sheer blue swimsuit.
  **Playboy** (Oct 1982) . . . . . . . . . . . . . . . . . . . . . . . . n.a.
  ••• Nice.
  **Playboy** (Nov 1982) . . . . . . . . . . Sex in Cinema 1982
  ••• 161—Breasts from *The Beastmaster.*

**Playboy** (Jan 1989) . . . . . . . . . . Women of the Eighties
  •• 251—Breasts.
**Playboy** (Nov 1991) . . . . . . . . . . Sex in Cinema 1991
  • 144—Side view of left breast, straddling Andrew
    Stevens. From *Night Eyes.*

## Roberts, Teal

*Films:*
  **Fatal Games** (1984) . . . . . . . . . . . . . . . . . . . . Lynn Fox
  ••• 0:08—Breasts on bed and floor when Frank takes her
    clothes off, more breasts in shower.
  •• 0:21—Breasts in sauna with Sue.
  **Hardbodies** (1984) . . . . . . . . . . . . . . . . . . Kristi Kelly
  •• 0:03—Breasts in bed after making love with Scotty,
    then putting her sweater on.
  ••• 0:47—Breasts standing in front of closet mirrors talk-
    ing about breasts with Kimberly.
  ••• 0:56—Breasts making love with Scotty.
  •• 1:22—Breasts on fancy car bed with Scotty.
  **Beverly Hills Cop II** (1987) . . . . . . . . . . . . . . Stripper
  •• 0:45—Breasts and buns, wearing G-string at the 385
    North Club.
  The Last Boy Scout (1991) . . . . . . . . . . . . . . . . Dancer
  Night of the Warrior (1991) . . . . . . . . . . . . . Still Model
*Video Tapes:*
  The Perfect Body Contest (1987) . . . . . . . . . . . . . Judge

## • Robertson, Jenny

*Films:*
  Bull Durham (1988) . . . . . . . . . . . . . . . . . . . . . . Millie
  Heart of Dixie (1989) . . . . . . . . . . . . . . . . . . . . . Sister
  **The Nightman** (1992) . . . . . . . . . Dr. Margaret Rhodes
  • 1:25—Brief right breast in gaping dress when she
    looks at old things hidden under floor boards.
*Made for Cable Movies:*
  Notorious (1992; Lifetime) . . . . . . . . . . . . . . . . . . . n.a.
*Made for TV Movies:*
  Call Me Anna (1990) . . . . . . . . . Patty (as a young adult)
  Danielle Steel's "Message from Nam" (1993)
    . . . . . . . . . . . . . . . . . . . . . . . . . . . Paxton Andrews

## Robertson, Kimmy

*Films:*
  Battle in the Erogenous Zone . . . . . . . . . . . . . . Tammy
  The Last American Virgin (1982) . . . . . . . . . . . . . Rose
  **Bad Manners** (1989) . . . . . . . . . . . . Sarah Fitzpatrick
  •• 0:38—Breasts and buns taking off robe and getting
    into the shower when Mouse takes a picture of her.
    1:16—In white bra when Piper rips her blouse open
    while she's tied up on the piano.
    1:18—Briefly on piano again.
  Honey, I Shrunk the Kids (1989) . . . . . . Gloria Forrester
  Trust Me (1989) . . . . . . . . . . . . . . . . . . . . . Party Gal
  Don't Tell Mom the Babysitter's Dead (1991) . . . . Cathy
  Leprechaun 2 (1994) . . . . . . . . . . . . Tourist's Girlfriend
*Made for Cable TV:*
  Tales From the Crypt: Top Billing (1991; HBO) . . . . . Lisa
*TV:*
  Twin Peaks (1990-91) . . . . . . . . . . . . . . . . . . . . . Lucy

# Robey

First name is Louise.
Singer.
*Films:*
The Money Pit (1986) . . . . . . . . . . . . . Female Vocalist
Raw Deal (1986) . . . . . . . . . . . . . . . . . . Lamanski's Girl
**Play Nice** (1992) . . . . . . . . . . . . . . . . . . . . Jill/Rapunzel
(Unrated version reviewed.)
• 0:28—Side view of right breast, while sitting on top
of a victim in bed. Don't see her face.
••• 0:35—Breasts, making love in bed with Jack. Nice,
long scene.
•• 0:46—Breasts, making love on the floor with Jack.
••• 1:09—Breasts in bed on top of Jack, then getting out
of bed and getting dressed.
*TV:*
Friday the 13th: The Series (1987-90) . . . . . Micki Foster

# Robinson, Betsy Julia

*Films:*
Return of the Secaucus Seven (1980) . . . . . . . . . . . .n.a.
**Lianna** (1982) . . . . . . . . . . . . . . . . . . . . . . . . . Cindy
•• 1:26—Breasts, getting into bed and in bed with Li-
anna.

# Robinson, Serina

See: Ryan, Rachel.

# Rochelle, Amy

See: Weiss, Amy-Rochelle.
*Films:*
**Possessed by the Night** (1993) . . . Bikini Woman/Tina
••• 0:16—Breasts, while giving Scott a back rub, then
leaving the room.

# Rogers, Mimi

Ex-wife of Tom Cruise.
*Films:*
Gung Ho (1985) . . . . . . . . . . . . . . . . . . . . . . . . Audrey
Someone to Watch Over Me (1987) . . . . Claire Gregory
Street Smart (1987) . . . . . . . . . . . . . . . . .Alison Parker
Hider in the House (1989). . . . . . . . . . . . . .Julie Dreyer
The Mighty Quinn (1989). . . . . . . . . . . . . . . . . Hadley
The Palermo Connection (1989; Italian) . . . . . . . . Carrie
Desperate Hours (1990) . . . . . . . . . . . . . .Nora Cornell
The Doors (1991) . . . . . . . . . . . Magazine Photographer
**The Rapture** (1991) . . . . . . . . . . . . . . . . . . . . Sharon
• 0:08—Most of her left breast, while lying in bed with
Randy
•• 0:36—Very brief side view of right breast, dropping
nightgown and walking into closet.
Dark Horse (1992). . . . . . . . . . . . . . . Dr. Susan Hadley
The Player (1992) . . . . . . . . . . . . . . . . . . . . . . Cameo
Shooting Elizabeth (1992; French) . . . .Elizabeth Pigeon
White Sands (1992) . . . . . . . . Uncredited Molly Dolezal
Monkey Trouble (1993). . . . . . . . . . . . . . . . . . . .n.a.
*Made for Cable Movies:*
The Fourth Story (1990; Showtime)
. . . . . . . . . . . . . . . . . . . . . . . . . Valerie McCoughlin

Dead Lock (1991; HBO) . . . . . . . . . . . . . . . Tracy Riggs
Ladykiller (1992; USA) . . . . . . . . . . . .Michael Madison
*Made for Cable TV:*
Dream On: The Second Greatest Story Ever Told
(1991; HBO). . . . . . . . . . . . . . . . . . . . . . Julia Montana
0:18—In black lingerie on bed with Martin.
Dream On: And Bimbo Was His Name-O (1992; HBO)
. . . . . . . . . . . . . . . . . . . . . . . . . . . Julia Montana
Tales From the Crypt: Beauty Rest (1992; HBO) . . .Helen
0:25—In bra and panties, lying in a chair before get-
ting "made up" after winning beauty contest.
*Miniseries:*
Bloodlines: Murder in the Family (1993). . . . . . . . n.a.
*TV:*
The Rousters (1983-84) . . . . . . . . . . . . . . .Ellen Slade
Paper Dolls (1984) . . . . . . . . . . . . . Blair Harper-Fenton
*Magazines:*
**Playboy** (Mar 1993) . . . . . . . . . . . . . Screaming Mimi!
••• 70-77—Breasts and buns in color and B&W photos.
Playboy (Mar 1994) . . . . . . . . . . . . Safe Sex, Great Sex

# Rohm, Maria

*Films:*
City of Fear (1965; British) . . . . . . . . . . . . . . . . Maid
Against All Odds (1969). . . . . . . . . . . . . . . . . . Ursula
(Breasts in still photo on the back of the video box
cover—not in the film.)
Dorian Gray (1970; Italian/British/German) . . . . . . Alice
**Venus in Furs** (1970) . . . . . . . . . . . . . . . Wanda Reed
Original version.
• 0:05—Breasts on beach, dead, after getting
dragged from the ocean.
• 0:08—Breasts in stockings and panties, getting
whipped by Olga.
•• 0:10—Breasts before getting stabbed by Klaus Kinski.
• 0:11—More breasts on beach, dead.
• 0:17—Brief breasts.
• 0:21—Right breast several times, making love in bed
with a guy.
••• 0:22—Breasts, lying in bed with the guy afterwards.
• 0:23—Brief breasts on beach again.
• 0:32—Breasts, dead on the beach with two cuts.
• 0:43—Breasts on couch when Olga opens her
blouse.
•• 0:45—Breasts in bed.
•• 0:52—Breasts posing for Olga.
• 0:54—Breasts, dead.
•• 0:56—Breasts walking down stairs, wearing panties.
• 0:59—Breasts in bed again.
• 1:02—Brief side view of right breast, hugging Jimmy.
• 1:05—Left breast while acting as a slave girl.
• 1:06—Brief breasts seen through sheer curtain.
1:09—Very brief right breast, dead.
•• 1:10—Left breast, with Klaus Kinski.
1:12—Buns, lying on couch.
Black Beauty (1971; British/German) . . . . . . . . . . Anne
Count Dracula (1971; Spanish/Italian) . . . . . . . . . . n.a.

Treasure Island (1972; British/Spanish) . . . Mrs. Hawkins
Ten Little Indians (1975) . . . . . . . . . . . . . . . . . . . . . .Elsa

## Rohmer, Patrice

*Films:*
**The Harrad Summer** (1974) . . . . . . . . . . . . . Marcia
   *a.k.a. Student Union*
- 0:33—Brief breasts, starting to take off her blouse in motel room with Harry.

**Hustle** (1975) . . . . . . . . . . . . . . . . . . . Linda (Dancer)
- 1:03—In pasties, dancing on stage behind beaded curtain. Buns in G-string.

Jackson County Jail (1976) . . . . . . . . . . . . . Cassie Anne
**Revenge of the Cheerleaders** (1976). . . . . . .Sesame
- 0:28—Brief breasts and buns in the boys shower room.

Small Town in Texas (1976). . . . . . . . . . . . . . . . Trudy

## Rojo, Helena

*Films:*
Aguirre, The Wrath of God (1972; West German) . . Inez
**Mary, Mary, Bloody Mary** (1975) . . . . . . . . . . Greta
- 0:42—Buns and brief breasts getting into bathtub with Cristina Ferrare.

Foxtrot (1976; Mexican/Swiss) . . . . . . . . . . . Alexandra

## Rojo, Maria

*Films:*
**Candy Stripe Nurses** (1974) . . . . . . . . . . . . . Marisa
- •• 0:29—Breasts making love with convict.
- 0:52—Brief breasts during attempted rape in kitchen pantry.

Danzon (1992; Mexican) . . . . . . . . . . . . . . . . . . Julia

## Roman, Candice

*Films:*
**The Big Bird Cage** (1972) . . . . . . . . . . . . . . . .Carla
- 0:16—Buns, while in the shower.

**Unholy Rollers** (1972) . . . . . . . . . . . . . . . . Donna
   *a.k.a. Leader of the Pack*
- ••• 0:06—Breasts in bed with Greg when Karen comes home.
- •• 0:12—Breasts, dancing on stage in club next to a brunette dancer.
- 0:13—More breasts in background.
- 0:14—More breasts in background.

## Romanelli, Carla

*Films:*
**Steppenwolf** (1974). . . . . . . . . . . . . . . . . . . . Maria
- ••• 0:59—Breasts sitting on bed with John Huston. Long scene.

**The Sensuous Nurse** (1975; Italian) . . . . . . . . . Tosca
- •• 0:06—Breasts, then nude standing in the winery, then running around.
- •• 0:41—Nude, in basement, playing army, then making love with bearded guy.

**Sex on the Run** (1979; German/French/Italian)
. . . . . . . . . . . . . . . . . . . . . . . . . . . . . . . . . Dice Girl
   *a.k.a. Some Like It Cool*
   *a.k.a. Casanova and Co.*
- •• 0:58—Breasts and buns with two other women, losing their clothes during dice game.

**The Lonely Lady** (1983) . . . . . . . . .Carla Maria Peroni
- •• 1:10—Brief breasts taking off her top to make love with Pia Zadora while a guy watches.

A Very Moral Night (1985; Hungarian). . . . . . . . . . n.a.
*Magazines:*
**Playboy** (Mar 1977) . . . . . . . . Comeback for Casanova
- ••• 87—Breasts, while standing around table with other unclothed women.

## Romay, Lina

*Films:*
**Erotikill** (1973). . . . . . . . . . . . . . . . . . . . . . . . .Irina
   *a.k.a. La Comtesse Noire*
   *a.k.a. The Loves of Irina*
- •• 0:00—Full frontal nudity, wearing a belt and cape walking towards the camera during the opening credits.
- •• 0:08—Full frontal nudity on bed, then walking around while wearing a cape. Out of focus.
- ••• 0:17—Full frontal nudity, lying in bed and drinking.
- 0:31—Very brief right breast during struggle with another woman on bed.
- •• 0:32—Full frontal nudity, while walking through the woods with a cape and belt.
- 0:33—Breasts, flapping her cape.
- 0:43—Breasts under sheer black nightgown.
- ••• 0:45—Full frontal nudity when the other woman takes her nightgown off.
- ••• 0:47—Full frontal nudity biting another woman and sucking her blood.
- ••• 1:05—Full frontal nudity sitting down in bath filled with red water.
- ••• 1:07—More breasts and brief buns doing pelvic thrusts in bathtub. Out of focus sometimes.
- ••• 1:08—Nude in bathtub.

Demoniac (1974; French/Spanish) . . . . . . . . . . . . Anne
Ilsa, The Wicked Warden (1980). . . . . . . . . . . . . . n.a.
   *a.k.a. Ilsa—Absolute Power*
   *a.k.a. Greta, The Mad Butcher.*
   *Ilsa—Absolute Power* is about 4 minutes shorter.

## Rome, Cindy

   *a.k.a. Sugar Ray Rene.*
*Films:*
Banzai Runner (1986). . . . . . . . . . . Sweet Young Thing
Summer's Games (1987) . . . . . . . . . . . . . . . . . . .Boxer
**Knockouts** (1992) . . . . . . . . . . . . . . . . . . . . . . Vicki
- 0:04—Breasts while putting on makeup in front of mirror. Long shot. Breasts walking in front of Brooke in pink G-string and white tights when Garth peeks in the locker room.
- 0:14—Buns in G-string swimsuit. Brief breasts while lying down in lounge chair.

- 0:25—Brief breasts, after losing her tennis shoe during strip poker game.
- 0:28—Breasts while in bedroom.
- ••• 0:37—In red, white and blue swimsuit, then breasts and buns while posing for photographs.
- ••• 0:45—Breasts and buns in G-string, while posing for October photograph.
- •• 0:59—Breasts while talking on the phone, combing her hair and doing her nails. Seen mostly in silhouette.

*Video Tapes:*
Battling Beauties (1983) . . . . . . . . . . . . . .∴ Foxy Boxer
The Perfect Body Contest (1987) . . . . . .Sugar Ray Rene
**Made for Man: Intimate Fantasy** (1992)
. . . . . . . . . . . . . . . . . . . . . . . . . . . . . . .Sugar Ray Rene
- 0:23—Stripping out of cave girl outfit down to purple two piece swimsuit.
- •• 0:40—Buns, stripping to leopard print two piece swimsuit and wrestling with Ginger Miller.

# Rome, Sydne
*Films:*
**Diary of Forbidden Dreams** (1973; Italian)
. . . . . . . . . . . . . . . . . . . . . . . . . . . . . . . The Girl
- ••• 0:06—Brief breasts taking off torn T-shirt in a room, then breasts sitting on edge of bed.
- ••• 0:09—Nude getting out of shower, drying herself off and getting dressed.
- 0:20—Brief side view of right breast, while talking to Marcello Mastroianni in her room.
- •• 0:22—Brief breasts putting shirt on.
- •• 1:28—Breasts outside on stairs fighting for her shirt.
- 1:30—Brief buns and breasts climbing onto truck.
Sex with a Smile (1976; Italian)
. . . . . . . . . . . . . . . . . . . . . "A Dog's Day" segment
The Twist (1976). . . . . . . . . . . . . . . . . . . . . Nathalie
Just a Gigolo (1979; German) . . . . . . . . . . . . . . Cilly
**Looping** (1981). . . . . . . . . . . . . . . . . . . . . . Tanja
*Magazines:*
**Playboy** (Nov 1980) . . . . . . . . . . . Sex in Cinema 1980
- ••• 178—Breasts.

# Rose, Dusty
See: Lussier, Sheila.

# Rose, Gabrielle
*Films:*
The Journey of Natty Gann (1985) . . . . Exercise Matron
**Family Viewing** (1987; Canadian) . . . . . . . . . . Sandra
- 0:27—Brief left breast, lying down with Stan. Seen on TV that Van watches.
- 0:29—Same 0:27 scene again.
The Stepfather (1987). . . . . . . . . . . . . . . . . . Dorothy
**Speaking Parts** (1989; Canadian) . . . . . . . . . . .Clara
- •• 0:41—Right breast, on TV monitor, masturbating with Lance. Then breasts getting dressed.
The Adjuster (1991; Canadian) . . . . . . . . . . . . . Mimi
*Made for Cable Movies:*
Devlin (1991; Showtime) . . . . . . . .Sister Anne Elizabeth

# Rose, Jamie
*Films:*
**Just Before Dawn** (1980) . . . . . . . . . . . . . . . .Megan
0:33—Breasts in pond. Long shot.
- 0:34—Brief breasts in pond, closer shot.
- •• 0:36—Brief upper half of left breast, then brief breasts several times splashing in the water.
- 0:37—Breasts getting out of the water.
**Heartbreakers** (1984). . . . . . . . . . . . . . . . . . .Libby
- ••• 0:09—Breasts in bed talking with Nick Mancuso and Peter Coyote.
**Tightrope** (1984). . . . . . . . . . . . . . . Melanie Silber
- 0:07—Buns, lying face down on bed, dead.
**Rebel Love** (1985) . . . . . . . . . . .Columbine Cromwell
- 0:43—Very, very brief tip of right breast, while making love in bed under Terence Knox.
Chopper Chicks in Zombietown (1989) . . . . . . . . Dede
Playroom (1989) . . . . . . . . . . . . . . . . . . . . . Marcy
*a.k.a. Schizo*
Crack Down (1990) . . . . . . . . . . . . Constance Bigelow
*Made for TV Movies:*
Voices Within: The Lives of Truddi Chase (1990)
. . . . . . . . . . . . . . . . . . . . . . . . . . .Truddi's Mother
Death Hits the Jackpot (1991) . . . . . . . . . Nancy Brower
*TV:*
Falcon Crest (1981-83). . . . . . . . Victoria Gioberti Hogan
Lady Blue (1985-86). . . . . . . . . Detective Katy Mahoney
St. Elsewhere (1986-88) . . . . . . . . . . . . Dr. Susan Birch

# Rose, Kristine
*Films:*
**Eleven Days, Eleven Nights 2** (1990)
. . . . . . . . . . . . . . . . . . . . . . . . . . Sarah Asproon
- •• 0:18—Breasts, while getting undressed and into bathtub.
- ••• 0:20—Breasts and buns while washing herself in bathtub while being secretly videotaped.
0:32—In lingerie with panties, garter belt and stockings after hopping on stage in club and dancing and stripping, showing off to Sonny.
- •• 0:38—Left breast, while making love in kitchen with Bob, while being watched on video monitor.
0:57—In black bra, panties, garter belt and stockings after taking off dress with George.
- 1:09—Breasts, while pretending Francis with Sonny. Left breast afterwards.
**Auntie Lee's Meat Pies** (1991). . . . . . . . . . . . .Fawn
- •• 1:12—Breasts in Stonehedge bedroom with her rock star boyfriend. More breasts in silhouette.
- 1:28—Buns, in G-string in swimming pool.
**Demonic Toys** (1991) . . . . . . . . . . . . . . . . Miss July
- 0:25—Breasts in centerfold photo in magazine.
- •• 0:59—Breasts in warehouse as a ghost in front of Mark.
Total Exposure (1991) . . . . . . . . . . . . . . . . . . Rita
**Night Rhythms** (1992) . . . . . . . . . . . . . . . . Marilyn
(Unrated version reviewed.)
- ••• 0:17—Taking off her blouse at bar with Martin Hewitt, then nude, making love on the bar with him.

Round Trip to Heaven (1992) . . . . . . . . . . . . . . . . Tina
To Sleep with a Vampire (1992) . . . . . . . . Prom Queen
Save Me (1993). . . . . . . . . . . . . . . . . . . . . . . . Cheryl
(Unrated version reviewed.)
*Video Tapes:*
**Playboy's Erotic Fantasies** (1992) . . . . Cast Member
*Magazines:*
**Playboy's Book of Lingerie** (Jan 1991) . . . . . . Herself
••• 12—Breasts.
••• 46—Full frontal nudity.
• 90—Right breast.
**Playboy's Book of Lingerie** (Mar 1991) . . . . . Herself
••• 3-7—Breasts and buns.
••• 96—Full frontal nudity.
**Playboy's Book of Lingerie** (Jul 1991) . . . . . . Herself
••• 67—Breasts.
**Playboy** (Aug 1991) . . . . . . . . . . . .California Dreamin'
•• 135—Left breast and lower frontal nudity.
**Playboy's Book of Lingerie** (Nov 1991) . . . . . Herself
••• 90-91—Breasts.
**Playboy's Book of Lingerie** (Jan 1992) . . . . . . Herself
••• 28-29—Breasts.
• 74—Right breast.
**Playboy's Bathing Beauties** (Apr 1992) . . . . . Herself
••• 10-11—Breasts.
•• 97—Side of left breast and buns.
**Playboy's Girls of Summer '92** (Jun 1992). . . Herself
•• 39—Left breast and buns.
•• 94—Breasts.
**Playboy's Book of Lingerie** (Sep 1992) . . . . . Herself
•• 24-25—Left breast.
••• 67—Breasts.
**Playboy's Nudes** (Dec 1992) . . . . . . . . . . . . . Herself
••• 78-79—Breasts.
**Playboy's Book of Lingerie** (Jan 1993) . . . . . . Herself
••• 17—Full frontal nudity.
**Playboy** (Feb 1993) . . . . . . . . . . Being in Nothingness
••• 129—Left breast and lower frontal nudity.
••• 130—Full frontal nudity.
•• 132—Left breast and lower frontal nudity.
**Playboy's Book of Lingerie** (Mar 1993) . . . . . Herself
••• 103—Full frontal nudity.
**Playboy's Bathing Beauties** (Apr 1993) . . . . . Herself
••• 58-59—Breasts.
**Playboy** (Apr 1993) . . . . . . . . . . . . . . . . . Tattoo You
••• 80—Breasts. Tattoo on her upper arm.
**Playboy's Book of Lingerie** (May 1993) . . . . . Herself
••• 96-97—Full frontal nudity.
**Playboy's Girls of Summer '93** (Jun 1993). . . Herself
• 72—Side of left breast.
**Playboy's Book of Lingerie** (Jul 1993) . . . . . . Herself
••• 80-81—Breasts.
**Playboy's Wet & Wild Women** (Aug 1993) . . Herself
••• 82—Breasts.
**Playboy's Blondes, Brunettes & Redheads**
(Sep 1993) . . . . . . . . . . . . . . . . . . . . . . . . . . Herself
••• 20-21—Right breast and lower frontal nudity.
**Playboy's Book of Lingerie** (Sep 1993) . . . . . Herself
•• 75—Right breast.

**Playboy's Nudes** (Dec 1993) . . . . . . . . . . . . . .Herself
••• 24—Full frontal nudity.
••• 102-103—Breasts.
**Playboy's Book of Lingerie** (Jan 1994) . . . . . Herself
••• 11—Full frontal nudity.
••• 38-39—Breasts.
**Playboy's Bathing Beauties** (Mar 1994) . . . . . Herself
•• 21—Buns.
**Playboy's Book of Lingerie** (Mar 1994). . . . . . Herself
••• 22-23—Breasts.
••• 46—Full frontal nudity.
**Playboy's Book of Lingerie** (May 1994) . . . . . Herself
••• 28-29—Full frontal nudity.
••• 52—Breasts.

## Rose, Laurie
*Films:*
**The Hot Box** (1972). . . . . . . . . . . . . . . . . . . . . . Sue
•• 0:16—Breasts cleaning herself off in stream and getting out.
•• 0:21—Breasts sleeping in hammocks. (She's the first
one from the front.)
• 0:26—Breasts getting accosted by the People's Army
guys.
••• 0:45—Breasts in stream bathing with the other three
girls.
• 0:58—Full frontal nudity getting raped by Major
Dubay.
The Roommates (1973) . . . . . . . . . . . . . . . . . . . . .Brea
The Working Girls (1973) . . . . . . . . . . . . . . . . . .Denise
**Policewomen** (1974). . . . . . . . . . . . . . . . . . . .Janette
• 0:02—Brief side of left breast, changing clothes during prison break.
The Woman Hunt (1975; U.S./Philippines) . . . . . . . . n.a.
The Wizard of Speed & Time (1988) . . . . . . Bellydancer

## Rose, Sherrie
*Films:*
After School (1987) . . . . . . . . . . . . . First Tribe Member
Cat Chaser (1988) . . . . . . . . . . . . . .Uncredited Waitress
Spring Fever USA (1988) . . . . . . . . . . . . . Vinyl Vixen #1
*a.k.a. Lauderdale*
American Tiger (1989; Italian) . . . . . . . . . . . . . Mary Jo
*a.k.a. American Rickshaw*
**Summer Job** (1989). . . . . . . . . . . . . . . . .Kathy Shields
0:25—In bed wearing white bra and panties talking
to Bruce. Long scene.
0:52—Buns, walking around in swimsuit and jacket.
•• 0:53—Breasts taking off swimsuit top kneeling by
the phone, then brief buns standing up.
1:15—In yellow two piece swimsuit walking on the
beach.
•• 1:24—Brief breasts taking off her yellow top on the
beach talking to Bruce.
**A Climate for Killing** (1990) . . . . . . . . . . . Rita Paris
•• 1:30—Breasts in bed while Wayne recollects his
crime to John Beck.

**King of the Kickboxers** (1990) . . . . . . . . . . . . Molly
- 1:05—Very brief buns in G-string and partial side of left breast, while getting into tub with Jake.

Body Waves (1991) . . . . . . . . . . . . . . . . . . . . Suzanne
In Gold We Trust (1991) . . . . . . . . . . . . . . . . . . n.a.
Deadly Bet (1992) . . . . . . . . . . . . . . . . . . . . . . . Doris
**Double Threat** (1992) . . . . . . . . . . . . . . . Lisa Shane
(Unrated version reviewed.)
- 0:09—Buns in lingerie, while sleeping in bed.
- 0:23—Buns in white lingerie while acting in movie with Andrew Stevens.
- ••• 0:47—Right breast, then breasts while making love with Stevens in bed.

Final Judgement (1992) . . . . . . . . . . Amanda Peterson
Martial Law II: Undercover (1992) . . . . . . . . . . . . Bree
**Maximum Force** (1992) . . . . . . . . . . . . . Cody Randal
- 0:59—Breasts, while in bed with Sam Jones.

**Unlawful Entry** (1992) . . . . . . . . . . . . . . . Girl in Jeep
- •• 0:42—Breasts, making love with Ray Liotta in police car, then getting thrown out.

*Made for Cable TV:*
**Dream On: Terms of Employment** (1992; HBO)
. . . . . . . . . . . . . . . . . . . . . . . . . . . . . . . . . Tasha
- •• 0:03—Breasts, while making love with Martin in his office.

**Tales From the Crypt: On a Dead Man's Chest** (1992; HBO) . . . . . . . . . . . . . . . . . . Danny's Girlfriend
- ••• 0:06—Breasts, opening her blouse to show Danny her new snake tattoo. Breasts, then full frontal nudity, under Danny in bed.
- ••• 0:08—Left breast, then breasts, getting dressed.
- 0:18—Brief buns in G-string, showing Danny her tattoo scar.

*Video Tapes:*
**Wet and Wild II** (1990) . . . . . . . . . . . . . . . . . . Model
**Inside Out** (1992) . . . . . . . . . . . . . . Bethany/The Leda
- 0:35—Right breast, while making love with the other criminal. Dark.
- 0:40—Upper half of right breast while making love with him again after he's connected to the computer.

**Inside Out 2** (1992) . . . . . . . . . . . . Marina/The Freak
(Unrated version reviewed.)
- 0:29—Breasts, getting her clothes and mask taken off in front of other masked people. B&W.
- •• 0:35—Breasts in bed with alien guy. B&W.

**Playboy's Erotic Weekend Getaways** (1992)
. . . . . . . . . . . . . . . . . . . . . . . Adventure: The Beach
- ••• 0:43—Nude, while making love on sofa with her lover.
- ••• 0:46—Nude, taking off swimsuit with him, frolicking at the beach, running home, taking an outdoor shower.
- ••• 0:50—Breasts and very brief buns in pool with her lover.

*Magazines:*
**Playboy** (Apr 1989) . . . . . . . . The Girls of Spring Break
- ••• 74—Breasts lying down, wearing a bikini bottom.

**Playboy's Book of Lingerie** (Jan 1991) . . . . . Herself
- •• 16—Left breast.

**Playboy's Book of Lingerie** (Mar 1991) . . . . . Herself
- •• 64-65—Left breast.

**Playboy's Book of Lingerie** (Sep 1991) . . . . . Herself
- •• 56—Left breast and buns.

**Playboy's Book of Lingerie** (Mar 1994) . . . . . Herself
- ••• 30—Breasts.

**Playboy's Book of Lingerie** (Jul 1994) . . . . . . . Herself
- ••• 27—Breasts.

## Ross, Annie
*Films:*
Straight on Till Morning (1974) . . . . . . . . . . . . . . . Liza
**Oh, Alfie!** (1975; British) . . . . . . . . . . . . . . . . . Claire
*a.k.a. Alfie Darling*
- •• 1:34—Breasts on top of Alfie in open black dress while he's lying injured in bed.

Yanks (1979) . . . . . . . . . . . . . . . . . . . . Red Cross Lady
Superman III (1983) . . . . . . . . . . . . . . . . . Vera Webster
Witchery (1988) . . . . . . . . . . . . . . . . . . . . Rose Brooks
Basket Case 2 (1989) . . . . . . . . . . . . . . . Granny Ruth
Basket Case 3: The Progeny (1991) . . . . . . Granny Ruth
The Player (1992) . . . . . . . . . . . . . . . . . . . . . . Cameo
Short Cuts (1993) . . . . . . . . . . . . . . . . . . Tess Trainer

## • Ross, Gaylen
*a.k.a. Alexis Dubin.*
*Films:*
Dawn of the Dead (1979) . . . . . . . . . . . . . . . Francine
Creepshow (1982) . . . . . . . . . . . . . . . . . . . . . . Becky
**Madman** (1982) . . . . . . . . . . . . . . . . . . . . . . . Betsy
- 0:24—Very brief full frontal nudity, getting into hot tub with T.P.

## Ross, Katharine
Wife of actor Sam Elliott.
*Films:*
The Graduate (1967) . . . . . . . . . . . . . . Elaine Robinson
Butch Cassidy and the Sundance Kid (1969) . . Etta Place
Tell Them Willie Boy is Here (1969) . . . . . . . . . . . . Lola
0:22—Very, very brief breast, while sitting up with Robert Blake. Breasts getting up when guy with rifle disturbs her and Blake. Buns, getting dressed. Long shot, dark, hard to see.

Get to Know Your Rabbit (1972) . . . Terrific-Looking Girl
**They Only Kill Their Masters** (1972) . . . . . . . . . Kate
- 1:00—Very brief upper half of buns and very, very brief back side of right breast, when getting out of bed.

**The Betsy** (1978) . . . . . . . . . . . . . . . . Sally Hardeman
- 1:02—Very brief upper half of left breast, while breast feeding baby in front of Laurence Olivier.

The Legacy (1979; British) . . . . . . . . . . . Maggie Walsh
*a.k.a. The Legacy of Maggie Walsh*
The Final Countdown (1980)
. . . . . . . . . . . . . . . . . . . . Laurel Scott/Mrs. Tideman
Wrong is Right (1982) . . . . . . . . . . . . . . . . Sally Blake
Red-Headed Stranger (1986) . . . . . . . . . . . . . . Laurie

A Climate for Killing (1990). . . . . . . . . . . . Grace Hines
*Made for TV Movies:*
The Shadow Riders (1982) . . . . . . . . . . . Kate Connery
Secrets of a Mother and Daughter (1983). . . . Ava Pryce
*TV:*
The Colbys (1985-87) . . . . . . . . . Francesca Scott Colby
*Magazines:*
**Playboy** (Nov 1975) . . . . . . . . . . . Sex in Cinema 1975
• 137—Breasts under sheer green dress from *The Stepford Wives*.

## • Ross, Mary Ella
*Films:*
Leather Jackets (1991). . . . . . . . . . . . . . Student Girl #2
**Bound and Gagged: A Love Story** (1993) . . . . . Lida
•• 0:05—Partial right breast, when getting caught making love in bed. Breasts, while in bed afterwards.
• 0:54—Right breast, while in bed with Chris Mulkey and Cliff during Cliff's dream.
• 0:58—Brief breasts, while making love with her lover when Cliff looks through skylight.

## Ross, Ruthy
*Films:*
**The Centerfold Girls** (1974) . . . . . . . . . . . . . . Glory
••• 0:49—Breasts and buns posing for photographer outside with Charly.
*Magazines:*
**Playboy** (Jun 1973) . . . . . . . . . . . . . . . . . . . Playmate
•• 120-129—Breasts.
**Playboy** (Oct 1973). . . . . . . . . . . . . . Bunnies of 1973
••• 137—Left breast and lower frontal nudity.
**Playboy's 1987 Book of Lingerie** (Mar 1987)
. . . . . . . . . . . . . . . . . . . . . . . . . . . . . . . . . Herself
•• 67—Buns and lower frontal nudity.

## Ross, Shana
*Video Tapes:*
**Penthouse Love Stories** (1986). . . . . . . AC/DC Lover
••• 0:17—Full frontal nudity in bedroom with Monique Gabrielle.
*Magazines:*
**Penthouse** (Aug 1983) . . . . . . . . . . . . . . . . . . . Pet
••• 83-101—Nude.

## Rossellini, Isabella
Daughter of actress Ingrid Bergman.
Spokesmodel for *Lancôme* cosmetics.
*Films:*
A Matter of Time (1976; Italian/U.S.). . . . . . . . Sister Pia
White Nights (1985) . . . . . . . . . . . . Darya Greenwood
**Blue Velvet** (1986) . . . . . . . . . . . . . . . . . . . . Dorothy
0:34—In black bra and panties, in her apartment while Kyle MacLachlan watches from inside closet.
• 0:36—Buns, after taking off panties in her bathroom. Long shot.
0:45—Partial lower frontal nudity, under robe while lying on the floor after Dennis Hopper pushes her down.

• 1:08—Brief full frontal nudity, while frolicking with MacLachlan in bed.
• 1:27—Very, very brief lower frontal nudity, while rolling over in bed in MacLachlan's flashback.
• 1:40—Nude, standing on porch, bruised.
• 1:41—Briefly, nude, sitting in car. Long shot. Brief right breast, while getting covered up.
•• 1:42—Brief breasts at Laura Dern's house.
Siesta (1987) . . . . . . . . . . . . . . . . . . . . . . . . . Marie
Tough Guys Don't Dance (1987) . . . . . . . . . Madeleine
Cousins (1989). . . . . . . . . . . . . . . . . . . . Maria Hardy
Wild at Heart (1990) . . . . . . . . . . . . . . . . . . . Perdita
Death Becomes Her (1992) . . . . . . . . Lisle Von Rhuman
The Pickle (1992) . . . . . . . . . . . . . . . . Actress in Film
Fearless (1993). . . . . . . . . . . . . . . . . . . . Laura Klein
Wyatt Earp (1994) . . . . . . . . . . . . . . . . . . . . . n.a.
*Made for Cable Movies:*
Lies of the Twins (1991; USA). . . . . . . . . . Rachel Marks
0:33—In bra, on bed with Aidan Quinn.
0:44—Very brief lower half of buns, while putting blouse on.
*Made for Cable TV:*
Fallen Angels: The Frightening Frammis (1993)
. . . . . . . . . . . . . . . . . . . . . . . . . . . . Babe Lonsdale
(Available on video tape on *Fallen Angels One*.)

## Rossini, Bianca
*Films:*
Moon Over Parador (1988) . . . . . . . . . . . . . . . . Tilde
Mobsters (1991) . . . . . . . . . . . . . . . Rosalie Luciano
*a.k.a. Mobsters—The Evil Empire*
*Video Tapes:*
**Inside Out 3** (1992). . . . . . . . . . . Ollala/The Branding
••• 0:23—Breasts, making love in bed with Mike.

## Roth, Andrea
*Films:*
Princess in Exile (1991; Canadian) . . . Marlene Lancaster
Seedpeople (1992). . . . . . . . . . . . . . . . . Heidi Tucker
The Club (1993). . . . . . . . . . . . . . . . . . . . . . . . Amy
*Made for Cable Movies:*
**Psychic** (1992; USA) . . . . . . . . . . . . . . . . . April Morris
• 1:01—Brief buns, partially covered with leaves, lying dead in park.
*Made for TV Movies:*
Spoils of War (1994). . . . . . . . . . . . . . . . . . . . Penny
*TV:*
RoboCop (1994- ) . . . . . . . . . . . . . . . . . . . . . . Diana

## • Roussel, Myriem
*Films:*
First Name: Carmen (1983; French) . . . . . . . . . . . . . n.a.
**Hail, Mary** (1985; French) . . . . . . . . . . . . . . . . . Mary
*a.k.a. Je Vous Salve, Marie*
• 0:56—Brief full frontal nudity in bathroom.
••• 0:57—Full frontal nudity in bathtub, washing herself while kneeling.
••• 1:13—Nude, undressing and putting on nightgown in bedroom.

- 1:17—Brief breasts, while moving around under sheets in bed.
- ••• 1:18—Breasts, while sitting on bed.
- • 1:19—Lower frontal nudity and tops of breasts while undressing and bending over in gaping top.
- •• 1:22—Close-up of lower frontal nudity, while in bedroom with Joseph.
- •• 1:23—Lower frontal nudity and buns, after lifting up her blouse.
- • 1:30—Very, very brief right breast, while rolling around in bed under the sheets.
- ••• 1:31—Lower frontal nudity, then breasts, while in bed. Nice close-ups.
- ••• 1:33—Lower frontal nudity and breasts, while lying in bed on her back.

**Sacrilege** (1986) . . . . . . . . Sister Virginia Maria di Leva
- ••• 0:50—Full frontal nudity, while making love with a guy, while two other sisters watch.

## Routledge, Alison

*Films:*
**The Quiet Earth** (1985; New Zealand) . . . . . . . Joanne
  0:49—Brief buns, after making breakfast for Zac.
- •• 1:24—Breasts in guard tower making love with Api.
Bridge to Nowhere (1986; New Zealand) . . . . . . . . . Lise

## Rowan, Gay

*Films:*
**The Girl in Blue** (1973; Canadian) . . . . . . . . . . Bonnie
*a.k.a. U-turn*
- • 0:06—Left breast, in bed with Scott.
- • 0:31—Brief breasts in bathtub.
- • 0:48—Right breast, while in shower talking to Scott. Brief breasts (long shot) on balcony throwing water down at him.
- • 1:21—Brief right breast and buns getting out of bed and running out of the room.
Sudden Fury (1975) . . . . . . . . . . . . . . . . . . . . . . . Janet
S.O.B. (1981) . . . . . . . . . . . . . . . . . . . . . . . . . . . . . .n.a.
Second Thoughts (1983). . . . . . . . . . . . . . . . . . Annie

## Rowe, Misty

*Films:*
**The Hitchhikers** (1971) . . . . . . . . . . . . . . . . . .Maggie
- • 0:00—Brief side view of left breast getting dressed.
- • 0:17—Very brief breasts getting dress ripped open, then raped in van.
- • 0:48—Brief right breast while getting dressed.
- • 1:09—Left breast, making love with Benson.
- • 1:10—Brief breasts taking a bath in tub.
- • 1:13—Very brief right breast in car with another victim.
**Goodbye, Norma Jean** (1975) . . . . .Norma Jean Baker
  0:02—In white bra putting makeup on.
- •• 0:08—In white bra and panties, then breasts.
- • 0:14—Brief breasts in bed getting raped.
  0:31—Very, very brief silhouette of right breast, in bed with Rob.

- ••• 0:59—Breasts during shooting of stag film, then in B&W when some people watch the film.
  1:14—In white bra and panties undressing.
Loose Shoes (1977) . . . . . . . . . . . . . . . . . . . . . . . Louise
The Man with Bogart's Face (1980) . . . . . . . . . .Duchess
**National Lampoon's Class Reunion** (1982)
  . . . . . . . . . . . . . . . . . . . . . . . . . . . . . . . Cindy Shears
- • 0:37—Very brief breasts running around school stage in Hawaiian hula dance outfit.
Double Exposure (1983) . . . . . . . . . . . . . . . . . . Bambi
Meatballs, Part II (1984). . . . . . . . . . . . . . . . . . . Fanny
*Made for TV Movies:*
When Things Were Rotten (1975) . . . . . . . Maid Marion
*TV:*
Hee Haw (1972-91) . . . . . . . . . . . . . . . . . . . . . . Regular
Happy Days (1974-75). . . . . . . . . . . . . . . . . . . . .Wendy
When Things Were Rotten (1975) . . . . . . . Maid Marion
Hee Haw Honeys (1978-79) . . . . . . . . . . . Misty Honey
Joe's World (1979-80) . . . . . . . . . . . . . . . . Judy Wilson
*Magazines:*
**Playboy** (Nov 1976) . . . . . . . . . . . . . . . . . . . . . . Misty
- ••• 104-107—Nude.
**Playboy** (Dec 1976) . . . . . . . . . . . . . .Sex Stars of 1976
- ••• 188—Breasts.
**Playboy** (Dec 1980) . . . . . . . . . . . . . .Sex Stars of 1980
- •• 246—Breasts.

## Rowland, Leesa

*Films:*
The Book of Love (1991) . . . . . . . . . . . . . . Honeymoon
  0:56—Stripping in tent at carnival, wearing pasties.
**Class of Nuke 'Em High Part II: Subhumanoid Meltdown** (1991). . . . . . . . . . . . . . . . . . . . . . Victoria
- •• 0:24—Breasts in room with Roger. Special effect mouth in her stomach.
  0:25—Most of side of left breast, while making love on top of Roger.

## Royce, Roselyn

*Films:*
**Cheech & Chong's Nice Dreams** (1981)
  . . . . . . . . . . . . . . . . . . . . . . . . . . . . . . .Beach Girl #3
- • 0:29—Brief breasts on the beach with two other girls. Long shot, unsteady, hard to see.
- • 0:32—More brief breasts again.
  0:33—More brief breasts again.
**Malibu Hot Summer** (1981). . . . . . . . . . .Cheryl Rielly
*a.k.a. Sizzle Beach*
(*Sizzle Beach* is the re-released version with Kevin Costner featured on the cover. It is missing all the nude scenes during the opening credits before 0:06.)
- •• 0:15—On exercise bike, then breasts getting into bed.
- ••• 0:16—Breasts sitting up in bed, buns going to closet to get dressed to go jogging.
  0:26—In pink two piece swimsuit running to answer the phone.
- •• 0:52—Breasts on boat with Brent.

**Off the Wall** (1982) . . . . . . . . . . . . . . Buxom Blonde
- 0:35—Left breast, while kissing an inmate in visiting room while the guards watch.
- • 0:51—Left breast again, while kissing inmate through bars while the guards watch.

Stay Tuned (1992). . . . . . . . . . Three's Company Spoof

## Rubanoff, Annie

*Films:*
Breathing Fire (1990) . . . . . . . . . . . . . . . . . . . . . . April
*Video Tapes:*
**Inside Out 4** (1992) . . . Ms. Morely/Save the Wetlands (Unrated version reviewed.)
- • 0:32—Left breast, while playing with herself while being interviewed.
- 0:33—Partial buns, while bending over to pick up photo off the floor.

## Rubens, Mary Beth

*Films:*
**Prom Night** (1980). . . . . . . . . . . . . . . . . . . . . Kelly
- 0:59—Very brief right breast making out with Drew in the locker room.
- 1:02—Brief upper half of breasts, standing up to put dress on. Dark.

Firebird 2015 AD (1981) . . . . . . . . . . . . . . . . . . . . Jill
**Perfect Timing** (1984) . . . . . . . . . . . . . . . . . . . Judy
- 0:04—In a bra, then breasts in bedroom with Joe.
- • 0:05—Nude, walking to kitchen, then talking with Harry.
- 0:08—Left breast seen through the camera's view finder.
- 0:10—Nude, getting dressed in bedroom.
  0:49—In red bra and panties.
- • 0:50—Nude, in bed with Joe.
- • • 1:00—Nude, discovering Joe's hidden video camera, then going downstairs.

*TV:*
E.N.G. (1989-90; Canadian) . . . . . . . . . . . . . . . Bobby

## Rubin, Jennifer

*Films:*
A Nightmare on Elm Street 3: The Dream Warriors (1987). . . . . . . . . . . . . . . . . . . . . . . . . . . . . . Taryn
1969 (1988) . . . . . . . . . . . . . . . . . . . . . . . . . . . . Wife
Bad Dreams (1988). . . . . . . . . . . . . . . . . . . . .Cynthia
Permanent Record (1988). . . . . . . . . . . . . . . . Lauren
**Delusion** (1990) . . . . . . . . . . . . . . . . . . . . . . Patti
- 0:34—Brief buns, pulling her panties down to moon the guys before entering the lake.
  0:37—Walking out of the lake in red bra and panties. More in red bra while playing with her lizard.
  0:46—Very briefly in wet bra, coming up for air from the water. Slow motion.
- • • 1:07—Breasts in motel bathroom, drying her hair. More breasts in the motel room with George.
- 1:12—Right breast, in open blouse, while sitting on the bed, talking with George.

Too Much Sun (1990) . . . . . . . . . . . . . . . . . . .Gracia

The Doors (1991). . . . . . . . . . . . . . . . . . . . . . . . .Edie
**A Woman, Her Men and Her Futon** (1992) . . .Helen
- • 0:22—Breasts, making love in bed with Randy.
- • • 0:31—Breasts, lying in bed with Donald.
- 0:35—Brief breasts, while making love in bed with Randy.
- • 1:04—Breasts, lying in bed and starting to make love with Donald.

**Bitter Harvest** (1993) . . . . . . . . . . . . . .Kelly Ann Walsh
- 0:21—Brief breasts while wearing panties, trying on clothes in front of closet mirror.
- • 0:28—Brief breasts, then left breast while adjusting her robe so Stephen Baldwin can give her a massage.
- • • 0:30—Breasts, after taking off robe, walking to bedroom with Baldwin and making love.
  0:33—Very brief upper half of right breast when she adjusts her position while lying in bed.

The Crush (1993). . . . . . . . . . . . . . . . . . . . . . . . .Amy
**Stranger By Night** (1994). . . . . . . . . .Anne Richmond
- • • 0:57—Breasts, while making love in bed with Steven Bauer.

*Made for Cable Movies:*
**The Fear Inside** (1992; Showtime) . . . . . Jane Caswell
- 0:26—Breasts with Peter. Hard to see because of the strobe light effect.
- 0:53—Buns and partial left breast visible under water while skinny dipping in pool.
  0:55—Full frontal nudity under water. Hard to see because of the distortion.

Full Eclipse (1993; HBO). . . . . . . . . . . . . . . . . .Helen
*Made for Cable TV:*
Tales From the Crypt: Beauty Rest (1992; HBO)
. . . . . . . . . . . . . . . . . . . . . . . . . . . . . . . Druscilla

## Ruddell, Shanae

*Video Tapes:*
**Hot Body International: #2 Miss Puerto Vallarta** (1990) . . . . . . . . . . . . . . . . . . . . . . . . . . . .Contestant
- • 0:33—Buns, in one piece swimsuit.

Hot Body International: #4 Spring Break (1992)
. . . . . . . . . . . . . . . . . . . . . . . . . . . . . . . . .Contestant
  0:07—Dancing in two piece swimsuit on stage.
*Magazines:*
**Playboy** (Apr 1993) . . . . . . . . . . . . . . . . . .Tattoo You
- • 82—Buns. Mermaid tattoo on the back of her neck.

## Ruiz, Mia M.

*Films:*
**Witchcraft II: The Temptress** (1989) . . . . . .Michelle
- 0:27—Brief breasts several times making love with a guy on the floor during William's hallucination.

Demon Wind (1990) . . . . . . . . . . . . . . . . . . . . . Reana
**Wild at Heart** (1990)
. . . . . . . . . . . . . . . . . Mr. Reindeer's Resident Valet #1
- • 0:32—Breasts standing next to Mr. Reindeer on the right, holding a tray. Long scene.

**Black Belt** (1992). . . . . . . . . . . . . . . . . . . . . Hooker
- • • 0:04—Breasts, while sitting on bed.

0:16—Breasts, while dead on bed, covered with blood.

# Runo, Pamela

a.k.a. Pamela Pond.
*Films:*
Munchie (1992) . . . . . . . . . . . . . . . . .Female Celebrity
**Sins of Desire** (1992) . . . . . . . . . . . . . . . . . . . . Rachel
(Unrated version reviewed.)
••• 0:12—Right breast while in bubble bath, covered with bubbles, then rinsed off. Breasts and buns, getting out and walking down hall.
Campus Hustle (1993) . . . . . . . . . . . . . . . . . . . . . Susan
**Dragon Fire** (1993). . . . . . . . . . . . . . . . . . . . . . Marta
••• 0:25—Breasts and buns in T-back, while doing strip routine on stage. Lit with strobe lights.
•• 0:29—Breasts and buns in T-back, while dancing on stage.
••• 0:49—Breasts, while making love in bed with Powers.
Future Shock (1993) . . . . . . . . . . . . . . . . . . . . . .Model
*Magazines:*
Playboy (Jan 1993) . . . . . . . . . . . . . . . . . . . .Grapevine

# Runyon, Jennifer

*Films:*
To All a Goodnight (1980). . . . . . . . . . . . . . . . . . . .n.a.
Ghostbusters (1984) . . . . . . . . . . . . . .Female Student
Up the Creek (1984). . . . . . . . . . .Heather Merriweather
The Falcon and the Snowman (1985) . . . . . . . . .Carole
Flight of the Spruce Goose (1986). . . . . . . . . . . .Terry
18 Again! (1988). . . . . . . . . . . . . . . . . . . . . . . . . Robin
A Man Called Serge (1990) . . . . . . . . . . . . . . . . . Fifi
**Killing Streets** (1991). . . . . . . . . . . . . . . Sandra Ross
• 1:00—In white lingerie then brief breasts taking off lingerie in bed with Michael Paré. Hard to see.
**Till Death Do Us Part** (1991) . . . . . . . . . . . . . . . Judy
• 1:02—Breasts and buns in T-back, undressing in bathroom. Don't see her face.
Carnosaur (1993) . . . . . . . . . . . . . . . . . . . . . . . Thrush
*Miniseries:*
Space (1987) . . . . . . . . . . . . . . . . . . . . . Marcia Grant
*Made for TV Movies:*
A Very Brady Christmas (1988) . . . . . . . . . . Cindy Brady
*TV:*
Charles in Charge (1984-85) . . . . . . . .Gwendolyn Pierce

# Russell, Andaluz

*Films:*
**The Assassin** (1989) . . . . . . . . . . . . .Amanda Portales
• 0:21—Brief breasts while changing clothes in room with the other assassins.
Pure Luck (1991). . . . . . . . . . . . . . Reception Manager
Gunmen (1993) . . . . . . . . . . . . . . . . . . . Guzman's Wife

# Russell, Betsy

*Films:*
**Private School** (1983) . . . . . . . . . .Jordan Leigh-Jensen
(Blonde hair.)
0:02—Taking a shower behind a frosted door.
• 0:04—Very, very brief right breast and buns when Bubba takes her towel off through window.
••• 0:19—Breasts riding a horse after Kathleen Wilhoite steals her blouse.
0:35—In jogging outfit stripping down to black bra and panties, brief upper half of buns.
1:15—In white bra and panties, in room with Bubba.
1:24—Upper half of buns flashing with the rest of the girls during graduation ceremony.
**Out of Control** (1984). . . . . . . . . . . . . . . . . . Chrissie
(Brunette hair.)
0:19—In white corset and panties in the pond.
•• 0:29—Breasts taking off her top while playing Strip Spin the Bottle.
0:30—Buns, taking off her panties.
Avenging Angel (1985) . . . . . . . . . Angel/Molly Stewart
**Tomboy** (1985) . . . . . . . . . Tomasina "Tommy" Boyd
•• 0:44—In wet T-shirt, then brief breasts after landing in the water with her motorcycle.
•• 0:59—Breasts making love with the race car driver in an exercise room.
Cheerleader Camp (1987) . . . . . . . . Alison Wentworth
*a.k.a. Bloody Pom Poms*
Trapper County War (1989) . . . . . . . . Lacey Luddigger
Camp Fear (1991) . . . . . . . . . . . . . . . . . . . . . . . . n.a.
*a.k.a. Millenium Countdown*
**Delta Heat** (1992) . . . . . . . . . . . . . . . . . . . . . . Vicki
0:52—Dancing in front of Anthony Edwards in sexy two piece outfit.
• 0:54—Brief buns and partial side of right breast, walking from bed, past two guys. (More buns seen in mirror.)
Amore! (1993) . . . . . . . . . . . . . . . . . . . .Cheryl Schwartz
*Made for TV Movies:*
Roxanne: The Prize Pulitzer (1989) . . . . . . . . Liza Pulitzer

# Russell, Karen

*Films:*
**Vice Academy** (1988) . . . . . . . . . . . . . . . . . Shawnee
•• 0:09—Breasts exposing herself to Duane to disarm him.
•• 1:13—Breasts pulling her top down to distract a bad guy.
**Dr. Alien** (1989) . . . . . . . . . . . . . . . . . . . . . Coed #2
*a.k.a. I Was a Teenage Sex Mutant*
••• 0:53—Breasts taking off her top (she's on the right) in the women's locker room before another coed takes her's off in front of Wesley.
Easy Wheels (1989) . . . . . . . . . . . . . . . . . . . . . . Candy
**Hell High** (1989) . . . . . . . . . . . . . . . . . . . . Teen Girl
•• 0:04—Breasts in shack with Teen Boy while little girl watches through a hole in the wall.
**Murder Weapon** (1989) . . . . . . . . . . . . . . . . . . .Amy
• 0:34—Brief breasts in shower.

0:58—In black bra and panties in bedroom.
Dick Tracy (1990) . . . . . . . . . . . . . . . . . . . . . . . Dancer
**The Girl I Want** (1990) . . . . . . . . . . . . . . . . . . . .Lisa
Havana (1990) . . . . . . . . . . . . . . . . . . . . . . Dancer #2
Mob Boss (1990). . . . . . . . . . . . . . . . . . . . . . . . .Mary
**Shock 'Em Dead** (1990) . . . . . . . . . . . . . . . Michelle
•• 0:16—In lingerie, then breasts twice with Martin.
**Wilding, The Children of Violence** (1990) . . . Cathy
•• 0:20—Breasts in bedroom when Wings Hauser pulls
   her lingerie down.
Bugsy (1991) . . . . . . . . . . . . . . . . . . . . . . . . . . Dancer
Mobsters (1991) . . . . . . . . . . . . . . . . . . . . . . .Showgirl
   *a.k.a. Mobsters—The Evil Empire*
Murder Blues (1991) . . . . . . . . . . . . . . . . . . . . .Isabella
*Video Tapes:*
**B-Movie Queens Revealed: The Making of "Vice
Academy"** (1993) . . . . . . . . . . . . . . . . . . . .Shawnee
•  0:00—Very brief breasts, pulling down her top from
   *Vice Academy 1.*
•  0:27—Same shot as 0:00.

# Russell, Theresa

Wife of director Nicholas Roeg.
*Films:*
The Last Tycoon (1976). . . . . . . . . . . . . . .Cecilia Brady
**Straight Time** (1978). . . . . . . . . . . . . . Jenny Mercer
••• 1:00—Left breast, while in bed with Dustin Hoffman. Don't see her face.
**Bad Timing: A Sensual Obsession** (1980)
. . . . . . . . . . . . . . . . . . . . . . . . . . . . .Milena Flaherty
   0:14—Buns and breasts under short, sheer blouse.
   0:17—Almost brief right breast in bed during Art
   Garfunkel's flashback. Very brief left breast kneeling
   on bed with him.
•  0:31—Full frontal nudity in bed with Garfunkel. Intercut with tracheotomy footage. Kind of gross.
•• 0:32—Right breast, while sitting in bed talking to
   Garfunkel.
•  0:41—Brief breasts several times on operating table.
•  0:55—Full frontal nudity making love on stairwell
   with Garfunkel. Quick cuts.
•• 0:56—Brief breasts twice after stairwell episode
   while throwing a fit.
•• 1:45—In bra, then breasts passed out on bed while
   Garfunkel cuts her clothes off. Brief full frontal nudity.
•• 1:48—More breasts cuts while Garfunkel makes love
   to her while she's unconscious from an overdose of
   drugs.
**Eureka** (1983; British) . . . . . . . . . . . . . . . . . . . . Tracy
   0:38—In lingerie talking to Rutger Hauer.
•  0:40—Right breast, lying in bed with Hauer.
•  1:04—Very brief left breast in bed with Hauer, then
   brief lower frontal nudity and brief buns when Gene
   Hackman bursts into the room.
•• 1:09—Breasts on a boat with Hauer.
•  1:41—Left breast peeking out from under black top
   while lying in bed.

••• 1:59—Full frontal nudity kicking off sheets in the
   bed.
The Razor's Edge (1984). . . . . . . . . . . . . . . . . . .Sophie
Insignificance (1985) . . . . . . . . . . . . . . . . . . . .Actress
Aria (1987; U.S./British) . . . . . . . . . . . . . . . . . King Zog
**Black Widow** (1987) . . . . . . . . . . . . . . . . . Catherine
•  0:28—Briefly nude, making love in cabin.
•• 1:18—Nude in pool with Paul.
Track 29 (1988; British) . . . . . . . . . . . . . . .Linda Henry
**Impulse** (1989). . . . . . . . . . . . . . . . . . . . . . . .Lottie
•• 0:37—Left breast, while making love with Stan in
   bed.
Physical Evidence (1989) . . . . . . . . . . . . . Jenny Hudson
**Cold Heaven** (1990). . . . . . . . . . . . . . Marie Davenport
•  0:09—Very brief upper half of right breast, when it
   pops out of her swimsuit top when struggling to get
   Mark Harmon onto boat.
•  0:18—Side of left breast while washing herself at the
   sink.
•  1:14—Brief breasts several times, making love in bed
   with James Russo.
**Whore** (1991). . . . . . . . . . . . . . . . . . . . . . . . . . . Liz
   *a.k.a. If you're afraid to say it... Just see it*
•• 0:13—Breasts and buns in G-string outfit, taking off
   her coat.
••• 0:25—In black bra, doing sit-ups. Breasts making
   love in spa with Blake.
•  1:18—Brief buns, in open skirt in back of car with a
   customer.
Kafka (1992; U.S./French) . . . . . . . . . . . . . . . .Gabriela
*Made for TV Movies:*
Thicker Than Water (1993; British) . . . . . . . . Jo/Debbie
*Magazines:*
**Playboy** (Nov 1980) . . . . . . . . . . . Sex in Cinema 1980
•  181—Breasts.
**Playboy** (Nov 1983) . . . . . . . . . . . Sex in Cinema 1983
•  145—Breasts.

# Ruval, Yulis

See: Müller, Lillian.

# Ryan, Meg

Wife of actor Dennis Quaid.
*Films:*
Rich and Famous (1981) . . . . . . . . . . .Debbie at 18 years
Amityville 3-D (1983). . . . . . . . . . . . . . . . . . . . . . Lisa
Armed and Dangerous (1986) . . . . . Maggie Cavanaugh
Top Gun (1986). . . . . . . . . . . . . . . . . . . . . . . . Carole
Innerspace (1987) . . . . . . . . . . . . . . . . . . . . . . . Lydia
D.O.A. (1988) . . . . . . . . . . . . . . . . . . . . Sydney Fuller
The Presidio (1988) . . . . . . . . . . . . . . . . . . . . . Donna
**Promised Land** (1988) . . . . . . . . . . . . . . . . . Beverly
•  0:22—Very brief side view of left breast in bed with
   Kiefer Sutherland.
When Harry Met Sally... (1989) . . . . . . . . Sally Albright
Joe vs. the Volcano (1990) . . . . . DeDe/Angelica/Patricia
**The Doors** (1991). . . . . . . . . . . . . . . Pamela Courson
•• 1:06—Right breast, while lying in bed with Val Kilm-
   er.

Prelude to a Kiss (1992) ................ Rita Boyle
**Flesh and Bone** (1993) .............. Kay Davies
•• 0:59—Right breast, several times, while making love with Dennis Quaid in bed.
Sleepless in Seattle (1993). ............. Annie Reed
When a Man Loves a Woman (1993) ...... Alice Green
*TV:*
As the World Turns .............. Betsy Montgomery
One of the Boys (1982). .................... Jane
Wildside (1985). ...................... Cally Oaks

## Ryan, Rachel

Adult film actress.
a.k.a. Serina Robinson and Penny Morgan.
Ex-wife of actor Richard Mulligan.
*Films:*
**Clean and Sober** (1988). . .Uncredited Dead Girlfriend
• 0:02—Buns, lying dead in Michael Keaton's bed. Don't see her face, but it's her.
*Video Tapes:*
**Secrets of Making Love... To the Same Person Forever** (1991). ................ Blonde Girl/Boat
••• 0:04—Breasts in boat and on river bank with her lover.
•• 0:47—Breasts in boat again.
**Inside Out** (1992) ........ Love the One You're With
•• 1:13—Left breast, in bed with a guy.
•• 1:14—Right breast and buns, climbing on top of him in bed.
•• 1:15—Breasts and buns, making love on top of him. More breasts after making love.

## • Ryan, Seana

*Video Tapes:*
**Penthouse Satin & Lace II: Hollywood Undercover** (1992). ................................... Pet
**Penthouse's 25th Anniversary Swimsuit Video** (1993). ................................... Pet
*Magazines:*
**Penthouse** (Sep 1992) ..................... Pet
••• 95-109—Nude.
**Playboy** (Jan 1994) ................... Grapevine
••• 279—Breasts in B&W photo.
**Penthouse** (Jun 1994). ....... Pet of the Year Play-Off
••• 88-89—Nude.
Sport (Jul 1994) ..................... Splash!

## Ryan, Stephanie

See: Napoli, Susan.

## Ryusaki, Kimberly

*Films:*
Punchline (1988) ............. Gas Station Waitress
Da Vinci's War (1992) .......... Cocktail Waitress #3
*Video Tapes:*
**Inside Out** (1992) ....... Linda/Life Is For the Taking
••• 0:52—Breasts in bedroom, undressing while Charlie has an out of body experience.
•• 0:53—Left breast, while lying on bed.

## Sachs, Adrianne

*Films:*
Cat Chaser (1988) .................. Anita De Boya
**Two to Tango** (1988) ............. Cecilia Lorca
•• 0:29—Side of left breast and buns in bedroom with Lucky Lara. More left breast while Dan Stroud watches through camera.
•• 0:59—Breasts and buns in bed with Dan Stroud.
**In the Cold of the Night** (1989) .... Kimberly Shawn
••• 0:52—Buns and breasts in shower, then making love with Scott. Long, erotic scene.
• 0:59—Brief breasts in outdoor spa.
• 1:06—Breasts making love on Scott's lap in bed.
Best of the Best (1990). ..................... Kelly
Alien Intruder (1992) .................... Yvonne
*Magazines:*
Playboy (Oct 1992) ................... Grapevine

## Sägebrecht, Marianne

*Films:*
Sugarbaby (1985; German) .............. Sugarbaby
**The Bagdad Café** (1988). ................. Jasmin
(Check this out if you like full-figured women.)
•• 1:09—Right breast slowly lowering her top, posing while Jack Palance paints.
•• 1:12—More breasts posing for Palance.
Moon Over Parador (1988) ................. Magor
The War of the Roses (1989) ................. Susan
Rosalie Goes Shopping (1990) ..... Rosalie Greenspace
Dust Devil (1992; British) ............. Dr. Leidzinger
*Magazines:*
**Playboy** (Nov 1988) .......... Sex in Cinema 1988
• 136—Breasts from *Bagdad Café.*

## Sahagun, Elena

*Films:*
**Caged Fury** (1989). ................. Tracy Collins
0:51—In bra when Buck holds her hostage.
•• 0:58—Left breast while taking a shower.
Corporate Affairs (1990). .................... Stacy
**Marked for Death** (1990). ............... Carmen
• 0:06—Breasts in room, shooting Steven Seagal's partner.
**Naked Obsession** (1990). .................. Becky
1:07—Dancing on stage in white outfit (She's got a mask over her face).
••• 1:10—In white bra, panties, garter belt and stockings while wearing the mask. Breasts and buns in G-string.
Sunset Heat (1991) .............. Brandon's Model
(Unrated version reviewed.)
Uncaged (1991). ............................ Joey
*a.k.a. Angel in Red*
Intent to Kill (1992) ...................... Mia
1:08—In lingerie in bed with Salvador.
1:17—In black bra and panties, on bed.
Ring of Fire II: Blood and Steel (1992) .......... Teez

**Teenage Exorcist** (1992) . . . . . . . . . . . . . . . . . . Sally
- 0:09—Brief side view of right breast and buns in panties, while putting robe on.
- 0:31—Buns and brief side of right breast, while getting into the shower.
- 0:32—Buns and right breast, while getting soaped up by creature's hand. Sort of frontal nudity behind fabric shower curtain.

*Magazines:*
**Playboy** (Nov 1991) . . . . . . . . . . Sex in Cinema 1991
- 143—Breasts, wearing white mask, in scene from *Naked Obsession*. (Incorrectly identified as Maria Ford.)

# • *Saint, Bonita*
*Video Tapes:*
**Penthouse Forum Letters: Volume 2** (1994)
. . . . . . . . . . . . . . . . . . . . . . . . The Big Switch/Cindy
- 0:32—Breasts and buns in white panties while doing strip tease with Debbie in front of their husbands. Nude in hot tub, then nude making love with Steve on lounge chair.

*Magazines:*
**Penthouse** (Jan 1994) . . . . . . . . . . . . . . . . . . . . . Pet
- 85-113—Nude.

# *Sal, Jeanne*
*Films:*
**Corporate Affairs** (1990) . . . . . . . . . . . . . . . . Sandy
- 0:38—Left breast in open dress while sneaking around the office with Buster.
**Dead Women In Lingerie** (1991) . . . . . . . . . . . . . Bing

# *Salem, Pamela*
*Films:*
**The Bitch** (1979; British) . . . . . . . . . . . . . . . . . . Lynn
- 0:46—Breasts in bed making love with a guy after playing at a casino.
**Never Say Never Again** (1983) . . . . . Miss Moneypenny
**After Darkness** (1985) . . . . . . . . . . . Elizabeth Huninger
**Salomé** (1986; Italian) . . . . . . . . . . . . . . . . . . . Herodias
- 0:05—Brief left breast, when her top gets ripped off.
- 0:26—Left breast when servant girl helps take her dress off.
- 0:27—Left breast and lower frontal nudity while standing in front of pool. Medium long shot.

# • *Salinger, Diane*
*Films:*
Battle in the Erogenous Zone . . . . . . . Datemaster 2000
Creature (1985) . . . . . . . . . . . . . . . . . . . . Melanie Bryce
Pee Wee's Big Adventure (1985) . . . . . . . . . . . . Simone
The Morning After (1986) . . . . . . . . . . . Isabel Harding
Bird (1988) . . . . . . . . . . . . . . . . . . . . . . . Baroness Nica
Verne Miller (1988) . . . . . . . . . . . . . . . Mortician's Wife
Alice (1990) . . . . . . . . . . . . . . . . . . . . . . . . . . . Carol
The Butcher's Wife (1991) . . . . . . . . . . . . . . . Trendoid
Batman Returns (1992) . . . . . . . . . . . Penguin's Mother

**The Magic Bubble** (1992) . . . . . . . . . . . . . . . . . . Julia
- 0:11—Very, very brief breasts after whipping off towel in front of her husband. Very, very brief buns, walking away. Back side of right breast, while pulling back curtain in front of her husband while he sits on the toilet.
- 1:21—Very brief side of left breast while putting on nightgown.
Venice/Venice (1992) . . . . . . . . . . . . . . . . . . Stephanie
*Made for TV Movies:*
Stormy Weathers (1992) . . . . . . . . . . . . . . . . . . Bogey

# *Salmon, Nancy*
*Films:*
**Cry Uncle** (1971) . . . . . . . . . . . . . . . . . . . . . . Connie
- 0:16—Breasts and buns in bed with two other girls while spanking Dominic. Hard to see because the negative image is projected.
- 0:26—Full frontal nudity in B&W photo that Keith shows Cora.
- 0:45—Brief breasts in the same B&W photo.
- 0:46—Brief right breast with Lena when Jake peeks in the window.
- 0:48—Breasts, fixing drugs while sitting on bed.
- 0:51—Breasts, while sitting on bed, then full frontal nudity getting out of bed.
- 1:04—Buns, while lying on bed.
- 1:06—Full frontal nudity, rolling off bed and onto the floor, when Jake discovers she's dead.
Okay Bill (1971) . . . . . . . . . . . . . . . . . Nancy Thornberry
Injun Fender (1973) . . . . . . . . . . . . . . . . . . . . . . . Girl

# *Salt, Jennifer*
*Films:*
**Midnight Cowboy** (1969) . . . . . . . . . . . . . . . . . Annie
- 0:31—Very brief buns, while running away from some bad guys in flashback.
- 0:42—Brief left breast on bed with Voight in flashback.
- 0:49—Very brief breasts in car in B&W flashback. More brief breasts and buns in car and running on porch.
The Wedding Party (1969) . . . . . . . . . . . . . . . . Phoebe
Brewster McCloud (1970) . . . . . . . . . . . . . . . . . . Hope
Play It Again, Sam (1972) . . . . . . . . . . . . . . . . . . Sharon
Sisters (1973) . . . . . . . . . . . . . . . . . . . . . Grace Collier
It's My Turn (1980) . . . . . . . . . . . . . . . . . . . . . Maisie
*TV:*
Soap (1977-81) . . . . . . . . . . . . . . . . . . . . Eunice Tate
The Marshall Chronicles (1990) . . . . Cynthia Brightman

# • *Salvatore, Donna*
*Films:*
**Marilyn Chambers' Bedtime Stories** (1993) . Letitia
- 0:01—Brief breasts in shower through hole in wall during opening credits.
- 0:11—Breasts, getting out of shower when Bart peeks through hole in wall.

•• 0:32—Buns in T-back and breasts, while dancing with Bart.
• 0:33—Breasts in open polka dot robe.
• 1:17—Brief breasts in shower out take.

*Magazines:*
**Playboy's Book of Lingerie** (Jul 1993) . . . . . . Herself
••• 99—Breasts.
**Playboy's Book of Lingerie** (Nov 1993) . . . . . Herself
• 23—Buns.
**Playboy's Nudes** (Dec 1993) . . . . . . . . . . . . . Herself
••• 42-45—Nude.
**Playboy's Great Playmate Search** (Feb 1994)
. . . . . . . . . . . . . . . . . . . . . . . . . . . . . . . . Herself
••• 36-37—Breasts.
**Playboy's Book of Lingerie** (Mar 1994) . . . . . Herself
••• 104—Breasts.
**Playboy's Book of Lingerie** (Sep 1994) . . . . . Herself
• 85—Back side of left breast.

## Samples, Candy

Adult film actress.
a.k.a. Mary Gavin.
*Films:*
Fantasm (1976; Australian) . . . . . . . . . . . . . . . . . . . .n.a.
Up! (1976) . . . . . . . . . . . . . . . . . . . . . The Headsperson
**Superchick** (1978) . . . . . . . . . . . . . . . . . Lady on Boat
••• 0:08—Breasts in bed with Johnny on boat.
Beneath the Valley of the Ultravixens (1979)
. . . . . . . . . . . . . . . . . . . . . . . . . . The Very Big Blonde
*Video Tapes:*
**Best Chest in the West** (1984) . . . . . . . . . . . . Herself
••• 0:54—Breasts dancing on stripping and dancing on stage with Pat McCormick.

## Sanda, Dominique

*Films:*
**First Love** (1970; German/Swiss). . . . . . . . . . . Sinaida
**The Conformist** (1971; Italian/French). . .Anna Quadri
•• 1:01—Breasts, taking off leotard for Marcello.
**The Garden of the Finzi-Continis** (1971; Italian/ German) . . . . . . . . . . . . . . . . . . . . . . . . . . . . . Micol
0:24—In braless wet white T-shirt after getting caught in a rainstorm.
• 1:12—Breasts sitting on a bed after turning a light on so the guy standing outside can see her.
Without Apparent Motive (1972; French)
. . . . . . . . . . . . . . . . . . . . . . . . . . . . . Sandra Forest
**Impossible Object** (1973; French) . . . . . . . . Nathalie
*a.k.a. Story of a Love Story*
The Makintosh Man (1973; British) . . . . . . . . Mrs. Smith
Conversation Piece (1974; Italian/French) . . . . . .Mother
**Steppenwolf** (1974) . . . . . . . . . . . . . . . . . . . .Hermine
1:40—Brief lower frontal nudity, sleeping with a guy.
• 1:41—Very brief left breast, waking up and rolling over to hug John Huston.

**1900** (1976; Italian) . . . . . . . . . . . . . . . . . . . . . . . Ada
(NC-17 version reviewed.)
••• 2:30—Left breast, then breasts in hay with Robert De Niro. Long shot of full frontal nudity while lying in the hay.
••• 2:48—(0:08 into tape 2.) Nude under thin fabric dancing with De Niro for photographer.
**Beyond Good and Evil** (1977; Italian/German/French)
. . . . . . . . . . . . . . . . . . . . . . . . Lou-Andreas-Salome
Damnation Alley (1977). . . . . . . . . . . . . . . . . . . . Janice
**The Inheritance** (1978; Italian) . . . . . . . . . . . . . Irene
•• 0:18—Full frontal nudity getting undressed and lying on the bed with her new husband.
••• 0:37—Full frontal nudity lying in bed with her lover.
• 1:19—Very brief right breast, while undoing top for Anthony Quinn.
••• 1:22—Left breast, lying in bed. Full frontal nudity jumping out of bed after realizing that Quinn is dead.
**Cabo Blanco** (1982). . . . . . . . . .Marie Claire Allesandri
• 1:27—Buns, swimming in pool. Long shot.
*Made for Cable Movies:*
Nobody's Children (1994; USA) . . . . . Stephanie Vaugier
*Made for TV Movies:*
Voyage of Terror: The Achillie Largo Affair (1990). . . n.a.
*Magazines:*
**Playboy** (Mar 1972) . . . . . . . . . Magnifique Dominique
••• 87-89—Nice.
**Playboy** (Nov 1972) . . . . . . . . . . . Sex in Cinema 1972
• 159—Breasts.
**Playboy** (Dec 1972) . . . . . . . . . . . .Sex Stars of 1972
•• 207—Left breast.
**Playboy** (Jan 1973) . . . . . . . . . . . . . . Impossible Object
• 192—Right breast in open dress top.
**Playboy** (Nov 1973) . . . . . . . . . . . Sex in Cinema 1973
• 158—Partial left breast.
**Playboy** (Dec 1973) . . . . . . . . . . . .Sex Stars of 1973
••• 211—Left breast.
Playboy (Dec 1976) . . . . . . . . . . . . . .Sex Stars of 1976
187—Outline of left breast through sheer blouse.
**Playboy** (Nov 1977) . . . . . . . . . . . Sex in Cinema 1977
• 163—Right breast, while in tub from *Beyond Good and Evil*.
**Playboy** (Nov 1978) . . . . . . . . . . . Sex in Cinema 1978
• 184—Right breast.

## • Sanders, Brandy

*Films:*
**Demolition Man** (1993) . . . . . . . . . . . . . Fiber Op Girl
• 1:13—Very brief breasts, after accidentally calling the wrong number on her video phone.
**Indecent Behavior** (1993) . . . . . . . . . . . . Elaine Croft
(Unrated version reviewed.)
0:31—Half of left breast, while playing with herself while listening in on intercom.
••• 0:59—Breasts and side view of buns, while taking off her clothes in front of Jan-Michael Vincent.
••• 1:10—Breasts, taking off her top in front of Vincent.
National Lampoon's Last Resort (1993) . . . . . . Mermaid

# • Sandifer, Elizabeth

*Films:*

**Animal Instincts 2** (1993) . . . . . . . . . . . . . Catherine
- ••• 0:23—In white bra and panties, then breasts and brief buns, while making love with Steve in bed.
- • 1:16—Brief breasts, while undressing in her room when Steve sees her from outside. Long shot.
- ••• 1:18—Breasts, while in bedroom with Steve, then making love on bed.

**Seduce Me: Pamela Principle 2** (1994) . . . . . . . . Jill
- • 1:13—Buns and breasts, while walking to spa, then in spa. Medium long shot.

# Sandlund, Debra

*Films:*

**Tough Guys Don't Dance** (1987) . . . . . . Patty Lareine
- •• 1:24—Breasts ripping her blouse off to kiss the policeman after they have killed and buried another woman.
- • 1:24—Very brief left breast, twice, in bed with Ryan O'Neal. Long shot.

Murder by Numbers (1990) . . . . . . . . . . . . . . . Leslie
Gladiator (1992) . . . . . . . . . . . . . . . . . . . . . Charlene

*TV:*

Full House (1990) . . . . . . . . . . . . . . . . . . . . . . Cindy

# Sandoval, Christy

*Films:*

Brain Donors (1992) . . . . . . . . . . . Pretty Girl in Jacuzzi

*Magazines:*

**Playboy's Book of Lingerie** (Mar 1993) . . . . . Herself
- •• 63—Right breast.

**Playboy's Girls of Summer '93** (Jun 1993) . . . Herself
- ••• 63—Breasts and buns.

**Playboy's Book of Lingerie** (Jul 1993) . . . . . . Herself
- • 64—Breasts under fishnet top.

# Sandrelli, Stefania

*Films:*

Seduced and Abandoned (1964; Italian)
. . . . . . . . . . . . . . . . . . . . . . . . . . . Agnese Ascalone

**The Conformist** (1971; Italian/French) . . . . . . . Giulia
- • 0:41—Right breast, while in train with her husband.
- • 1:07—Very brief, upper half of buns, while turning around.

1900 (1976; Italian) . . . . . . . . . . . . . . . . . Anita Foschi
(NC-17 version reviewed.)

**The Key** (1985; Italian) . . . . . . . . . . . . . . . . . . Teresa
*a.k.a. La Chiave*
(Nude a lot. Only the best are listed.)
- ••• 0:31—Nude when Nino examines her while she's passed out. Long scene.
- •• 0:42—Full frontal nudity in bathtub while Nino peeks in over the door.
- •• 1:04—In lingerie, then breasts and buns, undressing sexily in front of Nino.
- •• 1:16—Left breast, sticking out of nightgown so Nino can suck on it.

- ••• 1:19—Breasts and buns making love in bed with Laszlo.
- •• 1:21—Breasts and buns getting up and cleaning herself.
- •• 1:28—Breasts sitting in bed talking to Nino.
- ••• 1:30—Nude, getting on top of Nino in bed.

The Sleazy Uncle (1991; Italian) . . . . . . . . . . . Isabella
Jamón, Jamón (1992; Spanish) . . . . . . . . . . . Conchita

# Sands, Peggy

a.k.a. Peggie Sanders.

*Films:*

**Into the Night** (1985) . . . . . . . . . . Shameless Woman
- • 0:43—Breasts putting dress on after coming out of men's restroom stall after a man leaves the stall first.

**Beverly Hills Cop II** (1987) . . . . . . . . . . . . . . Stripper
- • 0:48—Very brief breasts, dancing at the 385 North Club.

Phoenix the Warrior (1988) . . . . . . . . . . . . . . . . Keela
**Far Out Man** (1990). . . . . . . . . . . . . . . . . . . . Misty
- ••• 0:50—Breasts and buns in black G-string, undressing and getting into bathtub with Tommy Chong.

Camp Fear (1991) . . . . . . . . . . . . . . . . . . . . . . . n.a.
*a.k.a. Millenium Countdown*

**Lady Avenger** (1991). . . . . . . . . . . . . . . . . . Maggie
(In braless tank top for most of the film.)
- ••• 0:18—Breasts in bed with Kevin.

# Santangelo, Melody

*Films:*

**Death Wish II** (1982). . . . . . . . . . . . . . . Tourist's Wife
- • 0:37—Breasts, being held as a shield by a gang member in parking garage.

Newsies (1992) . . . . . . . . . . . . . . . . . . . . . . . . . Nun

# Sara, Mia

*Films:*

Ferris Bueller's Day Off (1986) . . . . . . . . . Sloane Peterson
Legend (1986) . . . . . . . . . . . . . . . . . . . . . . . . . . . Lili
**Apprentice to Murder** (1987) . . . . . . . . . . . . . Alice
- • 0:29—Left side view breasts making love with Chad Lowe.

Queenie (1987) . . . . . . . . . . Queenie Keily/Dawn Avalon
Shadows in the Storm (1988). . . . . . . . . . . . . Melanie
0:51—Standing in bathtub all covered with bubbles talking to Ned Beatty.

**Any Man's Death** (1989). . . . . . . . . . . . . . . . Gerlind
- • 0:50—Brief right nipple when John Savage undoes her top. Don't see her face.

A Climate for Killing (1990) . . . . . . . . . . . . . Elise Shipp
Stranger Among Us (1992) . . . . . . . . . . . . . . . . Leah
*a.k.a. Close to Eden*

**Caroline at Midnight** (1993) . . . . . . . . . . . . Victoria
- ••• 0:24—Breasts, while making love with Jack.
- •• 0:30—Left breast, in open robe in bedroom with Tim Daly.
- ••• 0:51—Breasts, while making love on top and under Jack in bed. Nice!

**Timecop** (1994). . . . . . . . . . . . . . . . . . . . . . . . n.a.

**Made for Cable Movies:**
**Blindsided** (1993; USA). . . . . . . . . . Chandler Strange
  • 0:16—Very brief right breast while making love under Jeff Fahey.
*Miniseries:*
Till We Meet Again (1989). . . . . . . . . . . . . . .Delphine
*Made for TV Movies:*
Call of the Wild (1993) . . . . . . . . . . . . . .Jessie Gosselin

# Sarandon, Susan

Significant Other of actor Tim Robbins.
Ex-wife of actor Chris Sarandon.
*Films:*
**Joe** (1970) . . . . . . . . . . . . . . . . . . . . Melissa Compton
  • 0:02—Breasts and very brief lower frontal nudity taking off clothes and getting into bathtub with Frank.
Lady Liberty (1972; Italian/French) . . . . . . . . . . . . Sally
The Front Page (1974) . . . . . . . . . . . . . . . . . . . . .Peggy
The Great Waldo Pepper (1975) . . . . . . . . . .Mary Beth
The Rocky Horror Picture Show (1975; British)
. . . . . . . . . . . . . . . . . . . . . . . . . . . . . . . . Janet Weiss
The Great Smokey Roadblock (1976) . . . . . . . . . .Ginny
**Other Side of Midnight** (1977) . . Catherine Douglas
  • 1:10—Breasts in bedroom with John Beck. Long shot, then right breast while lying in bed.
  2:18—In wet white nightgown running around outside during a storm.
**King of the Gypsies** (1978) . . . . . . . . . . . . . . . Rose
  • 0:49—Brief right breast during fight with Judd Hirsch.
**Pretty Baby** (1978). . . . . . . . . . . . . . . . . . . . .Hattie
  0:12—Feeding a baby with her left breast, while sitting by the window in the kitchen.
  • 0:24—Brief side view, taking a bath.
  ••• 0:39—Breasts on the couch when Keith Carradine photographs her.
Something Short of Paradise (1979) . . . .Madeleine Ross
Loving Couples (1980) . . . . . . . . . . . . . . . . . Stephanie
**Atlantic City** (1981; French/Canadian). . . . . . . . Sally
  •• 0:50—Left breast cleaning herself with lemon juice while Burt Lancaster watches through window.
**The Tempest** (1982). . . . . . . . . . . . . . . . . . . . Aretha
  0:58—In braless white tank top washing clothes with Molly Ringwald in the ocean.
  1:53—In wet white T-shirt on balcony during rainstorm with Jason Robards and Raul Julia.
  1:55—In wet white T-shirt on the beach.
  • 1:57—Brief right, then left breasts in open T-shirt saving someone in the water.
**The Hunger** (1983). . . . . . . . . . . . . . . . Sarah Roberts
  ••• 0:59—In a wine stained white T-shirt, then breasts during love scene with Catherine Deneuve.
The Buddy System (1984). . . . . . . . . . . . . . . . . . Emily
Compromising Positions (1985) . . . . . . . . .Judith Singer
The Witches of Eastwick (1987). . . . . . . . . Jane Spofford

Bull Durham (1988) . . . . . . . . . . . . . . . . . . . .Annie Savoy
  1:39—Brief right breast peeking out from under her dress after crawling on the kitchen floor to get a match.
The January Man (1988) . . . . . . . . . . . Christine Starkey
Sweet Hearts Dance (1988) . . . . . . . . . . . . Sandra Boon
  1:23—Almost a left breast in bathroom mirror changing clothes.
  1:25—Very, very brief left breast under white bathrobe arguing with Don Johnson in the bathroom.
**White Palace** (1990) . . . . . . . . . . . . . . . . Nora Baker
  ••• 0:28—Breasts on top of James Spader. Great shots of right breast.
  • 0:38—Breasts on bed with Spader.
Thelma and Louise (1991) . . . . . . . . . . . . . . . Louise
Bob Roberts (1992; U.S./British). . . . . . . . .Tawna Titan
Light Sleeper (1992). . . . . . . . . . . . . . . . . . . . . . . .Ann
The Player (1992). . . . . . . . . . . . . . . . . . . . . . Cameo
Lorenzo's Oil (1993). . . . . . . . . . . . . . Michaela Odone
The Client (1994). . . . . . . . . . . . . . . . . . . . . . . . n.a.
*Made for Cable Movies:*
Mussolini and I (1985; HBO) . . . . . . . . . . . . Edda Ciano
*Made for TV Movies:*
Women of Valor (1986) . . .Colonel Margaret Ann Jessup

# Sarelle, Leilani

a.k.a. Leilani Ferrer.
Wife of actor Miguel Ferrer.
*Films:*
Neon Maniacs (1985) . . . . . . . . . . . . . . . . . . . .Natalie
Shag (1989). . . . . . . . . . . . . . . . . . . . . . . . . . Suette
Days of Thunder (1990)
. . . . . . . . . . . . . . . . .Female Highway Patrol Officer
  0:35—In bra, while opening her blouse during prank on Tom Cruise.
Little Sister (1991) . . . . . . . . . . . . . . . . . . . . Catherine
Till Death Do Us Part (1991). . . . . . . . . . . . . . . Gloria
Basic Instinct (1992). . . . . . . . . . . . . . . . . . . . . . Roxy
  (Unrated Director's cut reviewed.)
**The Harvest** (1992) . . . . . . . . . . . . . . Natalie Caldwell
  •• 1:13—Side view of buns, then breasts, while in car with Miguel Ferrer. Don't see her face very well.
  ••• 1:19—Full frontal nudity, while making love with Ferrer in bed.
*Made for Cable Movies:*
**Barbarians at the Gate** (1993; HBO)
. . . . . . . . . . . . . . . . . . . . . . . . . . . .Laurie Johnson
  0:57—In black bra and panties after taking off dress.
  • 0:59—Side view of right breast, twice, while taking off bra and putting on T-shirt.

# Sassaman, Nicole

*Films:*
Bikini Summer (1991) . . . . . . . . . . . . . . . Band Member
**Desert Passion** (1992). . . . . . . . . . . . . . . . . . . . .Linda
  •• 0:34—Breasts in spa with Maggie. In the background while Maggie makes love with Mr. Sasso.
  • 0:37—Brief left breast and buns in the spa. Breasts in spa in the background.

••• 0:55—Nude, getting out of the pool.
Knockouts (1992) ........................ Hallie
**Sorority House Party** (1992).... Topless Sorority Girl
•• 0:39—Breasts, opening Alex's bedroom door to ask for a bra.
Hold Me, Thrill Me, Kiss Me (1993)..... Girl on a Leash
(Unrated version reviewed.)
**Witchcraft V: Dance with the Devil** (1993) .. Marta
0:02—In black bra, in hotel room with a customer.
• 0:03—Brief breasts in open bra, just before the customer gets killed.
••• 0:30—Breasts in bed, while making love with Bill while Keli is asleep.
••• 0:51—Breasts under sheer black blouse.
••• 0:55—Breasts with Bill at the top of the stairs.
Money to Burn (1994) ................Rich Girl #1

## Sassoon, Catya
Daughter of hair guy Vidal Sassoon.
*Films:*
Tuff Turf (1984)..........................Feather
**Dance with Death** (1991) ..................Jodie
••• 0:29—Breasts and buns in G-string, while dancing on stage.
••• 0:37—Breasts and buns, dancing on stage. Her body is painted gold.
••• 0:38—More breasts and buns.
**Secret Games** (1991) .................... Sandra
(Unrated version reviewed.)
••• 0:21—Breasts during modeling session with the other girls. (She's the only brunette.)
••• 0:26—Breasts, making love in bed with Emil.
•• 0:34—Breasts in yellow bikini bottoms, sunbathing with the other girls.
••• 0:40—Breasts, getting out of the swimming pool and lying on lounge chair.
**Angel Fist** (1992) ............... Katara/Kat Lang
• 0:19—Brief breasts, dropping towel and putting on shirt in front of Alcatraz.
•• 0:31—Right breast, while in the shower.
••• 0:32—Breasts in red panties, doing martial arts on a couple of bad guys in her apartment.
••• 0:35—Full frontal nudity in the showers.
••• 0:49—Breasts, while making love on bed with Alcatraz. Long scene.
Bloodfist IV: Die Trying (1992).................Lisa
*Video Tapes:*
**Inside Out 4** (1992) ........ Pauline/Natalie Would
(Unrated version reviewed.)
0:07—Doing a strip routine in bra and panties in hotel room for Ted.
••• 0:08—Breasts in bed with Ted, then getting out and getting dressed.
*Magazines:*
**Playboy** (Apr 1993)................... Tattoo You
•• 83—Buns. Tiger tattoo in the small of her back.
**Playboy** (Nov 1993) .......... Sex in Cinema 1993
••• 135—Left breast and buns in G-string still from *Bloodfist IV.*

## Saunders, Loni
Adult film actress.
*Films:*
**Up 'n' Coming** (1987)..................Dixanne
(R-rated version reviewed, X-rated version available.)
• 0:19—Breasts kissing a guy on the bus.
*Magazines:*
**Penthouse** (Apr 1980) ............ Orient Exposed
••• 76-85—Nude.

## Saunders, Pamela
*Video Tapes:*
**Playboy Video Calendar 1987** (1986)..... Playmate
**Playboy Video Magazine, Volume 11** (1986)
.................................... Playmate
••• 0:52—Nude, undressing after party, in still photos and at the beach.
**Playmates at Play** (1990).............. Bareback
*Magazines:*
**Playboy** (Nov 1985) ................... Playmate
**Playboy's Girls of Summer '86** (Aug 1986)... Herself
••• 62—Full frontal nudity.
••• 71—Full frontal nudity.
**Playboy's 1987 Book of Lingerie** (Mar 1987)
....................................Herself
31—Partial left breast.
••• 78—Breasts.
**Playboy's Book of Lingerie** (Jan 1991) ......Herself
•• 36—Breasts.
**Playboy's Calendar Playmates** (Nov 1992)...Herself
•• 51—Full frontal nudity.
**Playboy's Nudes** (Dec 1992) ..............Herself
••• 108—Full frontal nudity.
**Playmates at Play** (Jul 1994) .............Herself
••• 62-65—Nude.

## Saura, Marina
*Films:*
**Flesh + Blood** (1985)...................... Polly
• 0:59—Brief left breast during feast in the castle.
• 1:09—Breasts on balcony of the castle with everybody during the day.
Crystal Heart (1987)......................Justine
The Monk (1990; British/Spanish) ...........Jacinta

## Savage, Tracie
*Films:*
The Devil & Max Devlin (1981) ............... n.a.
**Friday the 13th, Part III** (1982)........... Debbie
0:32—In blue, two piece swimsuit.
• 0:59—Brief breasts, while getting back into the shower after shutting the door.
• 1:00—Very brief right breast, while getting towel.
*Made for TV Movies:*
Hurricane (1974).......................Liz Damon
Friendly Persuasion (1975)........... Mattie Birdwell
*TV:*
Little House on the Prairie (1974-76) .........Christy

# Savannah

See: Wilsey, Shannon.

# Savoy, Teresa Ann

*Films:*

**La Bambina** (1976; Italian) . . . . . . . . . . . . . . . .Clotilde

**Caligula** (1980) . . . . . . . . . . . . . . . . . . . . . . . Druscilla
(X-rated, 147 minute version.)
- •• 0:01—Nude, running around in the forest with Malcolm McDowell.
- • 0:05—Buns, rolling in bed with McDowell. Very brief breasts getting out of bed.
- • 0:26—Left breast several times in bed.
- • 0:46—Brief right breast in bed with McDowell again.
- • 1:15—Left breast with McDowell and Helen Mirren.
- • 1:22—Very brief left breast getting up in open dress.
- •• 1:45—Full frontal nudity, then buns when dead and McDowell tries to revive her.

*Video Tapes:*

**Penthouse: On the Wild Side** (1988) . . . . . . Druscilla
- • 0:51—Breasts in scenes from *Caligula.*

*Magazines:*

**Playboy** (Nov 1976) . . . . . . . . . . Sex in Cinema 1976
- • 147—Lower frontal nudity from *La Bambina.*

**Playboy** (Nov 1977) . . . . . . . . . . Sex in Cinema 1977
- • 159—Buns, while kneeling in front of Helmut Berger.

**Penthouse** (May 1980) . . . . . . . . . . . . . . . . . Caligula
- •• 81—Breasts, carried by Malcolm McDowell.

# Sawyer-Young, Kathi

*Films:*

**Pink Motel** (1982) . . . . . . . . . . . . . . . . . . . . . . . Lola
0:14—In bra, panties, garter belt and stockings in motel room.
0:31—In bra and panties while listening to Mark's football stories.
- • 0:36—Brief breasts, after opening her bra and falling onto bed with Mark.
- ••• 0:41—Breasts and buns in panties, trying to coax Mark out of the bathroom. Long scene.
- •• 1:13—Breasts, while lying in bed with Mark.

Talking Walls (1982) . . . . . . . . . . . . . . . . . . . . . . .n.a.

Life on the Edge (1992). . . . . . . . . . . . .Tovah Torrence

The Unborn II (1993) . . . . . . . . . . . . . . . Mrs. Sanchez

# Saxton, Lisa

*Films:*

**Night Eyes 2** (1991) . . . . . . . . . . . . . . Car Rental Girl
- ••• 0:05—Breasts and buns, making love in bed with Jesse.
- • 0:09—Buns, on TV when video tape is played back.

**Ring of Fire** (1991) . . . . . . . . . . . . . . . . . . . . . Linda
- •• 0:10—Breasts and buns in several times, making love with Brad. Intercut with martial arts fight.
- •• 0:18—Brief buns, in G-string swimsuit, getting into spa with Brad. Breasts in spa.

- ••• 0:22—Breasts and buns in bathroom, while talking to Maria Ford.

*Made for Cable TV:*

**Dream On: The Second Greatest Story Ever Told** (1991; HBO). . . . . . . . . . . . . . . . . . . . . . . Coed #2
- •• 0:08—(She's the brunette one.) Breasts taking off her purple sweater in bedroom set with Coed #1 (redhead). More breasts opening the closet door and falling back onto the bed.
- • 0:34—Brief breasts (on the right) with swamp creature and Coed #1 (on the left) during Martin's daydream.

*Video Tapes:*

Bikini Blitz (1990). . . . . . . . . . . . . . . . . . . . . . Model

**Intimate Workout For Lovers** (1992)
. . . . . . . . . . . . . . . . . . . . . . . . . Intimate Harmony
- ••• 0:39—Nude, in dance studio and in the showers. Excellent!

**Playboy's 101 Ways to Excite Your Lover** (1992)
. . . . . . . . . . . . . . . . . . . . . . . . . . . .Cast Member

*Magazines:*

**Playboy's Book of Lingerie** (Jul 1991) . . . . . . .Herself
- •• 19—Left breast and partial lower frontal nudity.
- ••• 30—Breasts.
- ••• 100-101—Nude.

Playboy (Oct 1991) . . . . . . . . . . . . . . . . . . . Grapevine

**Playboy's Book of Lingerie** (Jan 1992) . . . . . .Herself
- ••• 65—Breasts.

**Playboy's Book of Lingerie** (Mar 1992). . . . . .Herself
- ••• 66—Breasts and buns.
- •• 86—Breasts.

**Playboy's Book of Lingerie** (May 1992) . . . . .Herself
- ••• 12—Breasts.

**Playboy's Book of Lingerie** (Nov 1992) . . . . .Herself
- • 63—Partial lower frontal nudity.
- •• 95—Right breast and lower frontal nudity.

**Playboy's Book of Lingerie** (Jan 1994) . . . . . .Herself
- ••• 75—Breasts.

**Playboy's Book of Lingerie** (May 1994) . . . . .Herself
- ••• 76—Breasts.

**Playboy's Book of Lingerie** (Jul 1994). . . . . . .Herself
- •• 14—Buns and back side of left breast.

# Scacchi, Greta

*Films:*

**Heat and Dust** (1982). . . . . . . . . . . . . . .Olivia Rivers
- •• 1:25—Buns, lying in bed under a mosquito net with Douglas, then breasts rolling over.

Burke and Wills (1985; Australian) . . . . . .Julia Matthews

**The Coca-Cola Kid** (1985; Australian) . . . . . . . . . .Terri
- ••• 0:49—Nude taking a shower with her daughter.
- •• 1:20—Brief breasts wearing a Santa Claus outfit while in bed with Eric Roberts.

**The Ebony Tower** (1985) . . . . . . . . . . . . . . . . .Mouse
- • 0:37—Full frontal nudity, undressing and going skinny dipping in lake. Long shot.
- • 0:41—Brief lower half of left breast, while lying down next to Toyah Wilcox.
- • 0:43—Brief nude walking into the lake.

**Good Morning, Babylon** (1987; Italian/French)
. . . . . . . . . . . . . . . . . . . . . . . . . . . . . . . . .Edna
•• 1:05—Breasts in the woods making love with Vincent Spano.
**A Man in Love** (1987) . . . . . . . . . . . . . . Jane Steiner
••• 0:31—Breasts with Peter Coyote.
•• 1:04—Buns and left breast in bed with Coyote.
1:10—Brief side view breasts, putting black dress on.
• 1:24—Brief breasts in bed.
**White Mischief** (1988). . . . . . . . . . Diana Broughton
•• 0:16—Breasts taking a bath while an old man watches through a peephole in the wall.
•• 0:24—Brief breasts in bedroom with her husband.
•• 0:29—Brief breasts taking off bathing suit top in the ocean in front of Charles Dance.
•• 0:30—Breasts while lying in bed, then talking to Dance.
•• 0:49—Breasts while sitting in bed and talking to Dance.
**Presumed Innocent** (1990) . . . . . . .Carolyn Polhemus
• 0:46—Left breast, while making love on desk with Harrison Ford.
• 0:53—Buns, lying in bed on top of Ford.
**Fires Within** (1991) . . . . . . . . . . . . . . . . . . . . . Isabel
• 0:18—Upper half of buns, very brief breasts in bed.
0:19—In bra, changing clothes.
• 0:38—Very brief breasts in bed.
**Shattered** (1991) . . . . . . . . . . . . . . . . . .Judith Merrick
•• 0:14—Breasts, turning over in bed.
• 0:16—Breasts in a strip of B&W photos that Tom Berenger looks at.
• 0:36—Breasts in B&W photos in Bob Hoskins' office. Brief breasts in flashback.
•• 1:24—Breasts during love-making flashback.
The Player (1992) . . . . . . . . . . . . .June Gudmundsdottir
**Turtle Beach** (1992; Australian) . . . . . . . . . . . . Judith
*a.k.a. The Killing Beach*
• 0:44—Upper half of buns and almost breasts, making love.
*Magazines:*
**Playboy** (Nov 1988) . . . . . . . . . . Sex in Cinema 1988
•• 141—Breasts in bathtub in a photo from *White Mischief.*

## Scarabelli, Michele
*Films:*
Covergirl (1982; Canadian). . . . . . . . . . . . .Snow Queen
**Perfect Timing** (1984) . . . . . . . . . . . . . . . . Charlotte
•• 1:11—Brief buns, then breasts in bed with Harry.
• 1:18—Breasts in bed with Harry during the music video.
SnakeEater II: The Drug Buster (1990). . . . . . . Dr. Pierce
Deadbolt (1992). . . . . . . . . . . . . . . . . . . Theresa Levez
I Don't Buy Kisses Anymore (1992) . . . . . Connie Klinger
*Made for Cable Movies:*
Age-Old Friends (1989; HBO) . . . . . . . . . Nurse Wilson

*Made for Cable TV:*
**The Hitchhiker: Face to Face** (1984; HBO)
. . . . . . . . . . . . . . . . . . . . . . . . . . . . . Dr. Ensman
(Available on *The Hitchhiker, Volume 4.*)
••• 0:07—Breasts in Robert Vaughn's office.
*Made for TV Movies:*
Age-Old Friends (1992) . . . . . . . . . . . . . .Nurse Wilson
*TV:*
Airwolf (1987-88). . . . . . . . . . . . . . . . . . . .Jo Santini
Alien Nation (1989-91) . . . . . . . . . . . Susan Francisco
True Colors (1992). . . . . . . . . . . . . . . . . . . . . . n.a.

## Schick, Stephanie
a.k.a. Stripper Pandora Peaks.
*Films:*
**Do or Die** (1991) . . . . . . . . . . . . . . . . . . . . Atlanta Lee
••• 1:09—Breasts making love with Shane outside at night.
• 1:15—Brief breasts in background, getting dressed. Out of focus.
*Magazines:*
**Playboy** (Nov 1991) . . . . . . . . . . . Sex in Cinema 1991
••• 140—Left breast, standing in front of a guy.

## Schmidtmer, Christiane
*Films:*
The Big Doll House (1971) . . . . . . . . . . . . . Miss Dietrich
**The Specialist** (1975) . . . . . . . . . . . . . . . Nude Model
••• 0:12—Breasts, posing for artist, then buns when she gets up to leave.

## Schneider, Maria
*Films:*
**Last Tango In Paris** (1972). . . . . . . . . . . . . . . .Jeanne
(X-rated, letterbox version.)
• 0:15—Lower frontal nudity and very brief buns, rolling on the floor.
• 0:44—Breasts in jeans, walking around the apartment.
•• 0:53—Left breast, while lying down, then walking to Marlon Brando, then breasts.
••• 0:55—Breasts, kneeling while talking to Brando.
• 0:56—Side of left breast.
• 0:57—Breasts, rolling off the bed, onto the floor.
•• 1:01—Right breast, in bathroom. Breasts in mirror.
• 1:03—Brief breasts in bathroom with Brando while she puts on makeup.
••• 1:04—Nude, in bathroom with Brando, then sitting on counter.
• 1:27—Brief lower frontal nudity, pulling up her dress in elevator.
• 1:30—Breasts in bathtub with Brando.
••• 1:32—Nude, standing up in bathtub while Brando washes her. More breasts, getting out. Long scene.
La Baby Sitter (1975; French/Italian/German). . . Michele
**The Passenger** (1975; Italian) . . . . . . . . . . . . . . Girl
**Memoirs of a French Whore** (1979) . . . . . . . Maloup
**A Woman Called Eva** (1979) . . . . . . . . . . . . . Liliane
*a.k.a. A Woman Like Eve*

Mamma Dracula (1980; Belgian/French). . Nancy Hawaii
Savage Nights (1992; French) . . . . . . . . . . . . . . . Noria
*a.k.a. Les Nuits Fauves*
*Magazines:*
**Playboy** (Feb 1973) . . . . . . . Two to "Tango" & Maria
••• 131-137—Nude.
**Playboy** (Nov 1973) . . . . . . . . . . Sex in Cinema 1973
•• 159—Right breast and lower frontal nudity from *Last Tango in Paris*. Out of focus.
**Playboy** (Dec 1973) . . . . . . . . . . . . . Sex Stars of 1973
•• 211—Half of right breast.
**Playboy** (Dec 1975) . . . . . . . . . . . . . Sex Stars of 1975
•• 183—Side of left breast.

# Schneider, Romy
*Films:*
**Vengeance... One by One** . . . . . . . . . . . . . . . . . .n.a.
0:02—In black slip getting dressed.
• 0:28—Very brief left breast when a soldier rips her bra open during struggle.
1:14—In black lingerie in her husband's flashback.
Boccaccio 70 (1962; Italian) . . . . . . "The Job" Segment
1:18—In white slip talking on the phone.
What's New, Pussycat? (1965; U.S./French)
. . . . . . . . . . . . . . . . . . . . . . . . . . . Carole Werner
**Dirty Hands** (1975; French) . . . . . . . . . . . . . . . Julie
• 0:01—Buns and right breast getting a tan, lying on the grass after a man's kite lands on her.
•• 0:09—Side view of right breast, while lying in bed with a man, then breasts.
• 1:04—Breasts lying on floor, then brief breasts sitting up and looking at something on the table.
Bloodline (1979) . . . . . . . . . . . . . . . . . . .Helene Martin
*Magazines:*
**Playboy** (Dec 1976) . . . . . . . . . . . . . Sex Stars of 1976
•• 186—Breasts lying down, hard to recognize it's her.

# Schoelen, Jill
*Films:*
D.C. Cab (1983) . . . . . . . . . . . . . . . . . . . . . Claudette
Hot Moves (1984) . . . . . . . . . . . . . . . . . . . . .Julie Ann
That Was Then... This Is Now (1985). . . Angela Shepard
**Thunder Alley** (1985) . . . . . . . . . . . . . . . . . . . . Beth
• 0:55—Very, very brief left breast and side view of buns, when Richie sits up while she's lying on her stomach on rocks.
**The Stepfather** (1987) . . . . . . . . . . . .Stephanie Maine
•• 1:16—Buns and brief side of right breast, while getting into the shower. Breasts in the shower.
Curse II: The Bite (1988) . . . . . . . . . . . . . . Lisa Snipes
**Cutting Class** (1988) . . . . . . . . . . . . . . .Paula Carson
0:58—Side view of left breast, while taking off robe. Long shot. Almost breasts turing around.
• 1:00—Very, very brief breasts in mirror when Gary helps put her robe on. (Out of focus.)
Phantom of the Opera (1989) . . . . . . . . . . . . .Christine
Operation Lookout (1991) . . . . . . . . . . . .Julie Converse
Popcorn (1991). . . . . . . . . . . . . . . . . . . . . . . .Maggie
Rich Girl (1991). . . . . . . . . . . . . . . . . . . . . . Courtney

Adventures in Spying (1992) . . . . . . . . . . Julie Converse
*Made for Cable Movies:*
When a Stranger Calls Back (1993) . . . . . . . . . . . .Julia
1:21—Breasts in Polaroid photos, supposedly of her, but it could be anybody.
*Made for TV Movies:*
Shattered Spirits (1986) . . . . . . . . . . . . . . . . . . . Allison

# Schofield, Annabel
*Films:*
Blood Tide (1982) . . . . . . . . . . . . . . . . . . . . . . . Vicki
**Dragonard** (1988) . . . . . . . . . . . . . . . . . . . . . Honore
• 0:26—Brief side view of left breast, brief breasts lying down, then left breast again in stable with Abdee.
**Solar Crisis** (1992) . . . . . . . . . . . . . . . . . . Alex Noffe
•• 0:34—Breasts in the shower.
•• 0:35—Breasts, sitting in chair, getting her mind probed.
•• 0:54—Brief breasts during recollection of shower scene. Slightly distorted and out of focus.
*TV:*
Dallas (1988) . . . . . . . . . . . . . . . . . . . . . Laurel Ellis

# • Schreiner, Alexis
*Films:*
**Scarred** (1983) . . . . . . . . . . . . . . . . . . . . . Movie Girl
• 0:32—Breasts, while dancing during filming of a movie. (She's the auburn hair colored girl wearing a gold necklace.)
**Hollywood Hot Tubs** (1984) . . . . . . . . . . .Soccer Girl

# Schubert, Karin
Has done a lot of adult films in Europe.
*Films:*
**Bluebeard** (1972). . . . . . . . . . . . . . . . . . . . . .Greta
• 1:43—Brief breasts, spinning around, unwrapping herself from a red towel for Richard Burton.
Till Marriage Do Us Part (1974; Italian). . . . . . . . Evelyn
**Black Emanuelle** (1976) . . . . . . . . . . . . .Anne Danielli
• 0:06—Brief breasts adjusting a guy's tie.
••• 0:14—Breasts making love in gas station with the gas station attendant.
••• 0:37—Nude, running in the jungle while Laura Gemser takes pictures of her.
• 0:40—Breasts, kissing Gemser.
• 0:44—Right breast, making love with Johnny in bed.
**Black Venus** (1983) . . . . . . . . . . . . . . . . . . . . .Marie
•• 0:38—Nude in bed with Venus, making love.
Christina (1984). . . . . . . . . . . . . . . . . . . . . . . . n.a.
Panther Squad (1986; French/Belgian) . . . . . . . Barbara

# Schygulla, Hanna
*Films:*
The Bitter Tears of Petra von Kant (1972; German)
. . . . . . . . . . . . . . . . . . . . . . . . . . . Karin Thimm
**The Marriage of Maria Braun** (1979; German)
. . . . . . . . . . . . . . . . . . . . . . . . . . . .Maria Braun
• 0:22—Brief upper half of right breast, when peeking from behind divider in doctor's office.

- 0:33—Buns, while lying in bed with her lover.
- 0:34—Brief buns and left breast, while standing up in doctor's office. Subtitles get in the way.
- •• 1:15—Buns, while dropping sheet in room with her boss.
  1:48—In lingerie and stockings with her husband.
Berlin Alexanderplatz (1983; West German) . . . . . . . Eva
La Nuit de Varennes (1983; French/Italian)
. . . . . . . . . . . . . . . . . . Countess Sophie de la Borde
A Love in Germany (1984; French/German)
. . . . . . . . . . . . . . . . . . . . . . . . . . . . Pauline Kropp
The Delta Force (1986) . . . . . . . . . . . . . . . . . . . . Ingrid
Casanova (1987). . . . . . . . . . . . . . . Casanova's Mother
**Forever Lulu** (1987) . . . . . . . . . . . . . . . . . . . . . Elaine
- 1:03—Brief breasts in and getting out of bubble bath.
Dead Again (1991) . . . . . . . . . . . . . . . . . . . . . . . . Inge

# Sciorra, Annabella

*Films:*
True Love (1989). . . . . . . . . . . . . . . . . . . . . . . . Donna
Cadillac Man (1990) . . . . . . . . . . . . . . . . . . . . . Donna
Reversal of Fortune (1990) . . . . . . . . . . . . . . . . Sarah
The Hard Way (1991) . . . . . . . . . . . . . . . . . . . Susan
Jungle Fever (1991). . . . . . . . . . . . . . . . . . . Angie Tucci
  0:32—In black bra
**The Hand That Rocks the Cradle** (1992)
. . . . . . . . . . . . . . . . . . . . . . . . . . . . Claire Bartel
- 0:08—Brief side of right breast in open gown, while lying on Dr. Mott's examination table.
  0:38—Partial right breast, trying to breast feed her baby.
**Whispers in the Dark** (1992) . . . . . . . . . . Ann Hecker
- 1:25—Buns in mirror in front of closet (don't see her face). Partial left breast.
Mr. Wonderful (1993) . . . . . . . . . . . . . . . . . . . . . Lee
The Night We Never Met (1993). . . . . . . . . Ellen Holder
Romeo Is Bleeding (1994). . . . . . . . . . . . . . . . Natalie
*Made for Cable Movies:*
Prison Stories, Women on the Inside (1990; HBO)
. . . . . . . . . . . . . . . . . . . . . . . . . . . . . . . . . Nicole

# Scoggins, Tracy

*Films:*
Toy Soldiers (1983) . . . . . . . . . . . . . . . . . . . . . Monique
In Dangerous Company (1988). . . . . . . . . . . . . . Evelyn
  0:12—In a white bra, lying on bed making love with a guy.
  0:42—Very, very brief half of left breast in bed with Blake. Then, very, very brief left breast getting out of bed. Blurry, hard to see.
  0:58—Brief upper half of left breast taking a bath. Long shot, hard to see.
**The Gumshoe Kid** (1990). . . . . . . . . . . . . Rita Benson
  0:33—In two piece white swimsuit. Nice bun shot while Jay Underwood hides in the closet.

- ••• 1:10—Side view of left breast in the shower with Underwood. Excellent slow motion breasts shot while turning around. Brief side view of right breast in bed afterwards.
One Last Run (1990) . . . . . . . . . . . . . . . . . . . . . Cindy
The Raven Red Kiss-Off (1990) . . . . . . . . . . Vala Vuvalle
Timebomb (1990) . . . . . . . . . . . . . . . . . . . . . Ms. Blue
Watchers II (1990) . . . . . . . . . . . . . . . . Barbara White
Demonic Toys (1991). . . . . . . . . . . . . . . . . Judith Gray
**Play Murder For Me** (1991) . . . . . . . . . Tricia Merritt
- •• 0:37—Right breast, then breasts when her husband sexually attacks her.
**Ultimate Desires** (1991) . . . . . . . . Samantha Stewart
*a.k.a. Silhouette*
  0:44—In white bra and panties, dancing sexily in her house, while two guys watch from outside.
  0:53—Getting dressed in white bra and panties. Don't see her face.
- 0:59—Very brief buns and side of left breast taking off her dress and walking out of the room.
  1:07—In black bra, panties, garter belt and stockings with Marc Singer.
- ••• 1:10—Breasts, several times, in bed with Singer.
**Alien Intruder** (1992) . . . . . . . . . . . . . . . . . . . Ariel
  0:31—In one piece swimsuit, while walking out of surf at beach in front of Maxwell Caulfield.
- 0:54—Breasts and buns (mostly silhouette) while straddling Caulfield on bed.
**Dead On** (1993) . . . . . . . . . . . . . . . . Marla Beaumont
(Unrated version reviewed.)
- 0:00—Partial breasts in shower during opening credits. Brief breasts when getting out of shower.
- 0:19—Brief left breast while in bathtub when she reaches up to turn off the speaker phone.
Dollman vs. the Demonic Toys (1993) . . . . . Judith Grey
*TV:*
Renegades (1983) . . . . . . . . . . . . . . . . . . . . . . . Tracy
Hawaiian Heat (1984) . . . . . . . . . . . . . . . . Irene Gorley
The Colbys (1985-87) . . . . . . . . . . . . . . . Monica Colby
Dynasty (1989) . . . . . . . . . . . . . . . . . . . Monica Colby
Lois & Clark: The New Adventures of Superman (1993-94) . . . . . . . . . . . . . . . . . . . . . . . . . . . . . . . . . Cat
*Video Tapes:*
Tracy Scoggins: Mind Your Body (1993). . . . . . . Herself

# • Scorsese, Nicolette

*Films:*
Perfect Victims (1988) . . . . . . . . . . . . . . . Melissa Cody
  0:13—In white bra and panties, changing clothes by closet while talking to Carrie.
  0:21—In white bra again when Brandon rips her blouse open while she's drugged out.
National Lampoon's Christmas Vacation (1989) . . . Mary
Aspen Extreme (1993) . . . . . . . . . . . . . . . . . . . . . Tina
**Boxing Helena** (1993). . . . . . . . . Fantasy Lover/Nurse
- ••• 1:22—In black bra, panties and stockings then buns and breasts while making love with Julian Sands while Sherilyn Fenn watches.

*Made for Cable Movies:*
Rebel Highway: Girls in Prison (1994; Showtime) . . Suzy
*Magazines:*
**Playboy** (Nov 1993) . . . . . . . . . . Sex in Cinema 1993
••• 138—Breasts and buns in three stills from *Boxing Helena.*

## • Scott, Kristi
See: Ducati, Kristi.

## • Scott, Leonette
*Films:*
**Boyz N the Hood** (1991) . . . . . . . . . . . . . . . . . .Tisha
• 0:42—Side view of left breast in bed with Tre. Don't see her face.
*TV:*
Soul Train . . . . . . . . . . . . . . . . . . . . . . . . . . . Dancer

## Scott, Susie
*Films:*
**Student Confidential** (1987). . . . . . . . . Susan Bishop
• 0:02—Lying in bed covered with a gold sheet. Sort of right breast through her hair.
•• 1:26—Full frontal nudity standing in front of Greg.
*Video Tapes:*
**Playboy Video Magazine, Volume 5** (1983)
. . . . . . . . . . . . . . . . . . . . . . . . . . . . . . . . Playmate
• 0:05—Brief breasts stroking her hair.
**Playboy's Playmate Review 3** (1985). . . . . Playmate
**Playmates at Play** (1990) . . . . . . . . . . Making Waves
*Magazines:*
**Playboy** (May 1983) . . . . . . . . . . . . . . . . . Playmate
**Playboy's 1987 Book of Lingerie** (Mar 1987)
. . . . . . . . . . . . . . . . . . . . . . . . . . . . . . . . . Herself
••• 101—Breasts.
**Playboy's Nudes** (Oct 1990). . . . . . . . . . . . . Herself
•• 54—Full frontal nudity.
**Playboy's Book of Lingerie** (Mar 1991) . . . . . Herself
•• 18—Left breast.
**Playboy's Calendar Playmates** (Nov 1992) . . Herself
••• 22—Full frontal nudity.
**Playboy's Nudes** (Dec 1992) . . . . . . . . . . . . . Herself
•• 97—Left breast, partial right breast and partial lower frontal nudity.
**Playboy's Book of Lingerie** (Jan 1994). . . . . . Herself
••• 46—Full frontal nudity.
**Playmates at Play** (Jul 1994) . . . . . . . . . . . . . Herself
•• 14-15—Lower frontal nudity and buns.

## • Scott-Thomas, Kristin
*Films:*
Under the Cherry Moon (1986) . . . . . . . . . . . . . .Mary
Four Weddings and a Funeral (1994; British). . . . . Fiona
*Made for Cable Movies:*
The Endless Game (1990; Showtime) . . . . . . . . Caroline

*Made for TV Movies:*
**Masterpiece Theatre: Body & Soul** (1994)
. . . . . . . . . . . . . . . . . . . . . . . . . . . . . Sister Gabriel
••• 1:46—(0:24 into Part 2) Full frontal nudity, taking off nightgown in front of mirror.
• 1:50—(0:28 into Part 2) Full frontal nudity in flashback.
••• 3:42—(0:34 into Part 4) Nude in bedroom with Hal.

## Seagrove, Jenny
*Films:*
Nate and Hayes (1983) . . . . . . . . . . . . . . . . . . . .Sophia
Appointment with Death (1988) . . . . . . . Dr. Sarah King
Harlequin Romance: Magic Moments (1989)
. . . . . . . . . . . . . . . . . . . . . . . . . . . Melanie James
Bullseye! (1990) . . . . . . . . . . . Health Club Receptionist
**The Guardian** (1990). . . . . . . . . . . . . . . . . . Camilla
••• 0:21—Side view of left breast, while in bathtub with the baby. Right breast, then breasts.
0:23—Buns, drying herself off. Long shot.
•• 0:38—Breasts, mostly left breast on top of Phil. Don't see her face, probably a body double.
0:46—Buns, skinny dipping. Long shot.
•• 0:47—Breasts healing her wound by a tree. Side view of right breast.
• 1:18—Very brief breasts under sheer gown in forest just before getting hit by a Jeep.
1:24—Very briefly breasts scaring Carey Lowell. Body is painted all over.
*Made for Cable TV:*
The Hitchhiker: Killer . . . . . . . . . . . . . . . . . . . . . Meg
*Miniseries:*
A Woman of Substance (1984). . . . . . Young Emma Hart
*Made for TV Movies:*
In Like Flynn (1985) . . . . . . . . . . . . . . . . . Terri McLane
Sherlock Holmes and the Incident at Victoria Falls (1991)
. . . . . . . . . . . . . . . . . . . . . . . . . . . . Lillie Langtry

## • Seberg, Jean
*Films:*
Saint Joan (1957). . . . . . . . . . . . . . . . . . . . . . . .Joan
Bonjour Tristesse (1958). . . . . . . . . . . . . . . . . Cecile
Breathless (1959; French). . . . . . . . . . Patricia Franchini
The Mouse That Roared (1959; British) . . . . . . . . .Helen
Lilith (1964). . . . . . . . . . . . . . . . . . . . . . . Lilith Arthur
A Fine Madness (1966). . . . . . . . . . . . . . . . . Lydia West
Paint Your Wagon (1969). . . . . . . . . . . . . . . Elizabeth
Pendulum (1969). . . . . . . . . . . . . . . . .Adele Matthews
Airport (1970) . . . . . . . . . . . . . . . . Tanya Livingston
**Macho Callahan** (1970) . . . . . . . . . . . . . . Alexandra
• 0:36—Brief buns and partial breast in mirror. (Don't see her face clearly.)
• 1:01—Very brief left breast when David Janssen rips her blouse open. Brief breasts during struggle with him before he rapes her. Brief left breast during rape. (Never see face with body.)

**Kill** (1971; French/Spanish/German) . . . . . . . . . . Emily
*a.k.a. Kill! Kill! Kill!*
- 0:42—Side view of right breast and buns. Don't see her face.
- 0:45—More right breast a couple of times. Still don't see her face.

## Sedgwick, Kyra

Wife of actor Kevin Bacon.
*Films:*
War and Love (1985) . . . . . . . . . . . . . . . . . . . . .Halina
Tai-Pan (1986) . . . . . . . . . . . . . . . . . . . . . . . . . . . Tess
Kansas (1988) . . . . . . . . . . . . . . . . . . . .Prostitute Drifter
Born on the Fourth of July (1989) . . . . . . . . . . . Donna
Mr. & Mrs. Bridge (1990) . . . . . . . . . . . . . Ruth Bridge
**Pyrates** (1991) . . . . . . . . . . . . . . . . . . . . . . . . . Sam
- ••• 0:19—In sheer lingerie on top of Kevin Bacon in bed, then breasts.
- 0:21—Partial buns, bouncing in bed with Bacon.
- 0:22—Brief buns, lying on top of Bacon.
- 0:26—Breasts under water in hot tub with Bacon.
singles (1992) . . . . . . . . . . . . . . . . . . . . . . .Linda Powell
Heart and Souls (1993) . . . . . . . . . . . . . . . . . . . . Julia
*Made for Cable Movies:*
Women & Men 2: Three Short Stories (1991; HBO)
. . . . . . . . . . . . . . . . . . . . . . . . . . Arlene Megaffin
*Miniseries:*
Family Pictures (1993). . . . . . . . . . . . . . . . . . , . . Nina
*Made for TV Movies:*
Miss Rose White (1992). . . . . . . Rose White/Reyzel Weiss

## Seigner, Emmanuelle

Wife of director Roman Polanski.
*Films:*
Detective (1985; French/Swiss) . . . . . . . . . . Grace Kelly
**Frantic** (1988) . . . . . . . . . . . . . . . . . . . . . . . . Michelle
- 1:02—Brief side view of right breast, while changing blouses in bedroom.
Bitter Moon (1994) . . . . . . . . . . . . . . . . . . . . . . . Mimi
*Magazines:*
**Playboy** (Nov 1992) . . . . . . . . . . . Sex in Cinema 1992
- ••• 144—Breasts with Peter Coyote from *Bitter Moon.*

## Seka

Adult film actress.
*Films:*
Men Don't Leave (1989). . . . . . . . . . . . Adult Film Star

## • Sellers, Victoria

Daughter of the late actor Peter Sellers.
*Films:*
**Warlords** (1988) . . . . . . . . . . . . . . . . . . . . Desert Girl
0:02—In back of car in sheer white harem girl top.
- 0:06—Getting out of car and running into the desert while wearing the sheer white top.
*Magazines:*
**Playboy** (Apr 1986) . . . . . . . . . . . . . . Victoria Sellers
- ••• 130-139—Nude in B&W and color photos while imitating various personalities.

## Senit, Laurie

*Films:*
**Body and Soul** (1981) . . . . . . . . . . . . . . . . Hooker #3
- 0:54—Brief breasts lying next to Leon Isaac Kennedy in bed with two other hookers.
Doctor Detroit (1983) . . . . . . . . . . . . . . . . . .Dream Girl
The Witching (1983) . . . . . . . . . . . . . . .Witches Coven
*a.k.a. Necromancy*
(Originally filmed in 1971 as *Necromancy*, additional scenes were added and re-released in 1983.)
**R.S.V.P.** (1984) . . . . . . . . . . . . . . . . . . . . . Sherry Worth
- •• 1:00—Breasts in the shower with Harry Reems.
- •• 1:06—Breasts again.

## Sennet, Susan

*Films:*
**Big Bad Mama** (1974). . . . . . . . . . . . . . . . . Billy Jean
- 0:50—Breasts and buns getting onto bed with Tom Skerritt.
- •• 0:51—Breasts and buns, getting out of bed with Skerritt.
- 0:52—Brief buns, getting back into bed with Skerritt along with Polly.
Tidal Wave (1975; U.S./Japanese). . . . . . . . . . . . . n.a.
*TV:*
Ozzie's Girls (1973) . . . . . . . . . . . . . . . .Susie Hamilton

## Serena

Adult film actress.
*Films:*
Fantasm (1976; Australian). . . . . . . . . . . . . . . . n.a.
**Honky Tonk Nights** (1978). . . . . . . . . . . . . .Dolly Pop
- 0:04—Breasts in open blouse, getting restrained after getting in a fight with a guy who tries to molest her.
- ••• 0:10—Breasts in bed with Bobby, then putting on a robe.
- ••• 0:38—Breasts standing in doorway, then in kitchen with Bill.

## Serna, Assumpta

*Films:*
Lola (1986) . . . . . . . . . . . . . . . . . . . . . . . . . . . Silvia
**Matador** (1986; Spanish) . . . . . . . . . . . .Maria Cardinal
- 0:03—Breasts taking off wrap and making love with a guy just before she kills him.
- ••• 1:38—Breasts on floor with Diego. Long shot, hard to see. Breasts in front of the fire.
- 1:41—Brief breasts making love with Diego.
- 1:43—Breasts lying on floor dead.
**Wild Orchid** (1990) . . . . . . . . . . . . . . . . . . . . Hanna
- ••• 0:39—Breasts at the beach and in the limousine. Very erotic.
Chain of Desire (1992). . . . . . . . . . . . . . . . . . . .Cleo
Revolver (1992) . . . . . . . . . . . . Countess Angela Rosetta
*Made for TV Movies:*
Day of Reckoning (1994) . . . . . . . . . . . . . . . . Marissa
*TV:*
Falcon Crest (1989) . . . . . . . . . . . . . . . . . .Anna Cellini

*Magazines:*
**Playboy** (Jun 1990) . . . . . . . . . . . . . . . . . . Wild Orchid
•• 84—Breasts in photos from *Wild Orchid*.

## Severance, Joan
*Films:*
No Holds Barred (1989) . . . . . . . . . . Samantha Moore
**See No Evil, Hear No Evil** (1989) . . . . . . . . . . . . . Eve
•• 1:08—Breasts in and leaning out of the shower while
Gene Wilder tries to get her bag.
Worth Winning (1989) . . . . . . . . . . . . . . . . . . Lizbette
Bird on a Wire (1990) . . . . . . . . . . . . . . . Rachel Varnay
The Runestone (1990). . . . . . . . . . . . . . Marla Stewart
0:50—Very brief upper half of right breast in bed
with her husband.
**Write to Kill** (1990) . . . . . . . . . . . . . Belle Washburn
0:59—Wearing purple bra in house with Scott Valentine.
••• 1:01—Breasts, making love in bed with Valentine.
• 1:04—Very brief, blurry breasts when Valentine tosses her a blouse.
**Illicit Behavior** (1991) . . . . . . . . . . . . . Melissa Yarnell
(Unrated version reviewed.)
(The nude scenes where you don't see faces are body
doubles.)
• 0:12—Buns, while making love standing up in the
kitchen with Jack Scalia. Don't see face.
••• 0:13—Breasts on table making love with Scalia.
Don't see her face.
•• 0:54—Right breast and buns, while taking off stockings, panties and bra in bathtub. Don't see face.
•• 1:10—Breasts and buns in car with Davi. (Sometimes you see her face with her breasts, sometimes
not.)
•• 1:16—Right breast, while lying in bed and talking to
Davi.
**Almost Pregnant** (1992) . . . . . . . . . Maureen Mallory
(Unrated version reviewed.)
••• 0:58—In belly dancer outfit in bedroom with Jeff
Conaway, then breasts.
•• 1:06—In black leather outfit, then breasts and buns
in G-string. Her hair gets in the way a lot.
•• 1:09—Brief breasts and buns in various sexual positions in bed with Conaway.
**Lake Consequence** (1992) . . . . . . . . . . . . . . . . . Irene
(Unrated version reviewed.)
• 0:02—Left breast, while lying in bed.
• 0:41—Brief breasts several times while making love
with Billy Zane.
••• 0:50—Full frontal nudity in spa in bathhouse, while
making love with Zane.
••• 0:54—Breasts in spa making out with Zane and
Grace.
• 1:06—Brief glimpses of right breast in open coat,
while struggling in a field with Zane.
••• 1:07—Breasts in field with Zane. Oh yeah!
•• 1:19—Brief side view breasts and buns in bedroom
with Zane.

*Made for Cable Movies:*
**Another Pair of Aces** (1991) . . . . . . . . . Susan Davis
(Video tape includes nude scenes not shown on cable
TV.)
•• 1:00—Brief breasts several times, making love with
Kris Kristofferson in bed.
*Made for Cable TV:*
**Red Shoe Diaries: Safe Sex** (1992; Showtime)
. . . . . . . . . . . . . . . . . . . . . . . . . . .The Woman
(Available on video tape on *Red Shoe Diaries 2: Double
Dare*.)
• 0:11—Breasts, standing up, then lying on the floor.
Medium long shot.
••• 0:12—Breasts, lying on the floor, then making love
with Steven Bauer.
• 0:13—Brief breasts, gathering her clothes.
•• 0:16—Nude, in front of mirror when Bauer takes her
dress off.
••• 0:17—More nude in bed and in front of mirror.
• 0:19—Breasts during flashback.
••• 0:32—Nude in bed. Nice close-up shots. (Additional
footage added for video tape.)
Tales From the Crypt: The New Arrival (1992; HBO)
. . . . . . . . . . . . . . . . . . . . . . . . . . . . . . . . Rona
*TV:*
Wiseguy (1988) . . . . . . . . . . . . . . . . . . . . Susan Profitt
*Magazines:*
**Playboy** (Jan 1990). . . . . . . . . . . . . . . . . Texas Twister
••• 84-95—Nude.
**Playboy's Nudes** (Oct 1990) . . . . . . . . . . . . . . Herself
••• 14—Full frontal nudity.
**Playboy** (Nov 1992) . . . . . . . . . . . . . . Director's Choice
••• 90-97—Nude. Awesome!
**Playboy's Nudes** (Dec 1992) . . . . . . . . . . . . . . Herself
••• 20-21—Full frontal nudity.
**Playboy** (Dec 1992) . . . . . . . . . . . . . . . Sex Stars 1992
••• 187—Breasts in B&W photo.

## Severeid, Suzanne
*Films:*
**Don't Answer the Phone** (1979) . . . . . . . . . . Hooker
• 0:43—Very brief right breast in open blouse after the
killer strangles her.
**Van Nuys Blvd.** (1979). . . . . . . . . . . . . . . . . . . . . . Jo
0:01—In white bra and panties in trailer with Bobby.
••• 0:02—Breasts and buns, bringing a beer to Bobby,
then sitting and watching TV.
Howling IV: The Original Nightmare (1988) . . . . . Janice

## Seymour, Jane
Her eyes are different colors—left is green and right is
brown.
Wife of actor James Keach.
*Films:*
Young Winston (1972; British) . . . . . . . Pamela Plowden
Live and Let Die (1973; British) . . . . . . . . . . . . Solitaire

Sinbad and the Eye of the Tiger (1977; U.S./British)
. . . . . . . . . . . . . . . . . . . . . . . . . . . . . . . . Farah
    1:16—Very brief buns, skinny dipping in pond with
    Taryn Power. Long shot, but still pretty amazing for
    a G-rated film.
    1:17—Very brief partial right breast (arm covers
    most of it) screaming when scared by the troglo-
    dyte.
Oh Heavenly Dog! (1980). . . . . . . . . . . .Jackie Howard
Somewhere in Time (1980). . . . . . . . . . . Elise McKenna
**Lassiter** (1984) . . . . . . . . . . . . . . . . . . . . . . . . . . Sara
   • 0:10—Buns and brief side view of right breast lying
    on stomach on bed with Tom Selleck.
Head Office (1986) . . . . . . . . . . . . . . . . . . . . . . . . Jane
**The Tunnel** (1987; Spanish) . . . . . . . . . . . . . . . Maria
   • 0:29—Very brief left breast, while in bed with Peter
    Weller when the sheet is pulled down.
  •• 0:44—Brief right beast, while getting dressed,
    throwing off her robe.
Matters of the Heart (1990) . . . . . . . . . . . . . . . . . .n.a.
Sunstroke (1992). . . . . . . . . . . . . . . . . . . . . .Theresa
Praying Mantis (1993). . . . . . . . . . . . . . . . . . . . . .n.a.
*Made for Cable Movies:*
Jamaica Inn (1982) . . . . . . . . . . . . . . . . . . . .Mary Yellan
    1:47—(0:14 into volume 2) Braless under a wet
    white dress changing clothes in a stagecoach.
*Miniseries:*
Captains and the Kings (1976) . . . . . .Chisholm Armagh
Seventh Avenue (1977). . . . . . . . . . . . . . . . Eva Meyers
East of Eden (1981). . . . . . . . . . . . . . Cathy/Kate Ames
War and Remembrance (1988) . . . . . . . Natalie Jastrow
*Made for TV Movies:*
The Story of David (1976). . . . . . . . . . . . . .Bathsheba
Battlestar Gallactica (1978) . . . . . . . . . . . . . . . . Serina
The Dallas Cowboy Cheerleaders (1979). . . . Laura Cole
The Scarlet Pimpernel (1982) . . . . . . Marguerite St. Just
The Sun Also Rises (1984) . . . . . . . . . . . . . . Lady Brett
Jack the Ripper (1988). . . . . . . . . . . . . . . . . . . .Emma
The Richest Man in the World: The Story of Aristotle
   Onassis (1988) . . . . . . . . . . . . . . . . . . . . . Maria Callas
The Woman He Loved (1988) . . . . . . . . . Wallis Simpson
Dr. Quinn, Medicine Woman (1992)
  . . . . . . . . . . . . . . . . . . . . . . . . . Dr. Michaela Quinn
A Passion for Justice: The Hazel Brannon Smith Story
   (1994). . . . . . . . . . . . . . . . . . . . . Hazel Brannon Smith
*TV:*
Dr. Quinn, Medicine Woman (1992- )
  . . . . . . . . . . . . . . . . . . . . . . . . . Dr. Michaela Quinn
*Magazines:*
Playboy (Dec 1973). . . . . . . . . . . . . . Sex Stars of 1973
    204—In wet, braless dress.

## Seymour, Stephanie

*Sports Illustrated* swimsuit model.
*Victoria's Secret* lingerie model.
Ex-fiancée of singer Axl Rose from Guns N' Roses.
*Music Videos:*
Don't Cry/Guns N' Roses. . . . . . . . . . . . . . . . . . . .n.a.
November Rain/Guns N' Roses . . . . . . . . . . . . . . . .n.a.

*Video Tapes:*
Sports Illustrated's 25th Anniversary Swimsuit Video
   (1989) . . . . . . . . . . . . . . . . . . . . . . . . . . . . . .Herself
  (The version shown on HBO left out two music video
  segments at the end. If you like buns, definitely watch
  the video tape!)
*Magazines:*
**Playboy** (Mar 1991) . . . . . . . . . . . . . . . . . . Stephanie
  ••• 112-123—Breasts and buns.
**Playboy** (Feb 1993) . . . . . . . . . . . . . Stephanie's Secret
  ••• 70-77—Full frontal nudity in B&W and color photos.

## Seyrig, Delphine

*Films:*
Muriel (1963). . . . . . . . . . . . . . . . . . . . . . . . . . .Helene
Accident (1967; British) . . . . . . . . . . . . . . . . . .Francesca
Daughters of Darkness (1971; Belgian/French/German/
  Italian) . . . . . . . . . . . . . . . . Countess Elisabeth Bathory
**Day of the Jackal** (1973). . . . . . . . . . . . . . . . Colette
   • 1:25—Side view of right breast while lying in bed
    with the Jackal. Dark.
   • 1:40—Very brief side view of left breast, when she
    rolls on her back. Brief side view of left breast after
    the Jackal kills her.
**The Black Windmill** (1974; British). . . . . Ceil Burrows
  •• 0:34—Right breast and buns, undressing and get-
    ting into bed to pose for a photo taken by John Ver-
    non.
Golden Eighties (1987; French/Belgian) . . . . . . . .Jeanne

## Shaffer, Stacey

*Films:*
**The Naked Cage** (1985) . . . . . . . . . . . . . . . . . . .Amy
  ••• 1:03—Nude in shower room getting hassled by the
    other girls.
Blood Screams (1986; U.S./Mexican) . . . . . . . . . .Karen

## Shannon, Moriah

*Films:*
Alley Cat (1982). . . . . . . . . . . . . . . . . . . . . . . . . . .Sam
**D.C. Cab** (1983) . . . . . . . . . . . . . . Venus Club Passenger
  •• 0:16—In bra, then breasts, undressing in back seat
    of cab.
  •• 0:17—Breasts when Albert tries to get his fare.
   • 0:18—Breasts, then buns when Gary Busey takes her
    money. Buns and very brief lower frontal nudity run-
    ning out of the club after him.

## Shapiro, Hilary

See: Shepard, Hilary.

## Sharkey, Rebecca

See: Wood-Sharkey, Rebecca.

# Sharpe, Becky

*Films:*

**The Boob Tube** (1975) . . . . . . . . . . . . . .Massage Girl
•• 0:20—Right breast, then breasts, while getting massaged by Sid on the table.
If You Don't Stop It You'll Go Blind (1979) . . . . . . . .n.a.

# Sharpe, Cornelia

*Films:*

Kansas City Bomber (1972). . . . . . . . . .Tammy O'Brien
**Serpico** (1973). . . . . . . . . . . . . . . . . . . . . . . . Leslie
•• 0:41—Breasts in bathtub with Al Pacino.
Busting (1974) . . . . . . . . . . . . . . . . . . . . . . . . . Jackie
Open Season (1974; U.S./Spanish) . . . . . . . . . . .Nancy
**The Reincarnation of Peter Proud** (1975)
. . . . . . . . . . . . . . . . . . . . . . . . . . . . . . . .Nora Hayes
•• 0:03—Breasts in bed with Michael Sarrazin, then buns when getting out of bed.
The Next Man (1976) . . . . . . . . . . . . . . . . Nicole Scott
*a.k.a. Double Hit*
Venom (1982; British) . . . . . . . . . . . . . . . Ruth Hopkins
*Made for TV Movies:*
S.H.E. (1979). . . . . . . . . . . . . . . . . . . . . .Lavinia Kean
*Magazines:*
**Playboy** (Nov 1974) . . . . . . . . . . . Sex in Cinema 1974
•• 145—Breasts in tub from *Serpico*.

# Shatner, Melanie

Daughter of actor William Shatner.
*Films:*
Star Trek V: The Final Frontier (1989)
. . . . . . . . . . . . . . . . . . . . . . . . . . . Enterprise Yeoman
The First Power (1990) . . . . . . . . . . . . . . . . . Shopgirl
**Bloodstone: Subspecies II** (1992). . .Rebecca Morgan
• 0:34—Upper half of buns and breasts behind translucent plastic shower door. Hard to see.
**Bloodlust: Subspecies III** (1993). . . .Rebecca Morgan
• 0:04—Very brief left breast and buns, while taking off blood-stained dress and putting on a coat. Long shot.

# Shattuck, Shari

Wife of actor Ronn Moss.
*Films:*
**Tainted** . . . . . . . . . . . . . . . . . . . . . . . . . . . . Cathy
•• 0:09—Buns, while lying on top of Frank.
••• 0:27—Breasts in bubble bath, getting up, drying herself off, then putting on white bra while wearing panties.
0:28—In white bra and panties, masturbating on chair.
0:30—Briefly in white bra and panties, getting attacked by rapist.
••• 0:49—Breasts taking a shower.
• 0:51—Brief side view of left breast in the shower again.
Portfolio (1983). . . . . . . . . . . . . . . . . . . . . Elite Model

**The Naked Cage** (1985) . . . . . . . . . . . . . . . .Michelle
•• 0:42—Buns and breasts in shower, then getting slashed by Rita during a dream.
•• 1:00—Left breast getting attacked by Smiley in jail cell, then fighting back.
1:28—In panties, during fight with Rita.
Death Spa (1987). . . . . . . . . . . . . . . . . . . . . Catherine
Hot Child in the City (1987). . . . . . . . . . . . . . . . Abby
Arena (1988) . . . . . . . . . . . . . . . . . . . . . . . . . . . .Jade
1:06—Upper half of buns sitting up in bed. Brief half of right breast, getting up while wearing robe.
The Uninvited (1988). . . . . . . . . . . . . . . . . . .Suzanne
**The Spring** (1989) . . . . . . . . . . . . . . . . . . . Dyanne
• 0:00—Nude, several times, swimming under the water. Shot from under water.
• 0:50—Breasts and buns, swimming under water.
•• 0:51—Breasts, getting out of the water.
•• 0:59—Brief breasts, turning over in bed with Dack Rambo.
• 1:05—Standing up in wet lingerie, then swimming under water.
Lower Level (1990) . . . . . . . . . . . . . . . . .Dawn Simms
Mad About You (1990) . . . . . . . . . . . . . . . . . . Renee
**Immortal Sins** (1992; Spanish) . . . . . . . . . . . . .Diana
• 0:13—Very brief breasts during Mike's dream.
• 0:32—Breasts several times, while making love with Mike.
•• 0:44—Left breast while making love with Mike.
••• 1:09—Breasts making love with Mike.
••• 1:18—Still more breasts making love with Mike.
1:20—Almost full frontal nudity, while standing in doorway. (Hard to see because of shadows.)
Out for Blood (1992) . . . . . . . . . . . . . Joanna Montague
**Body Chemistry 3: Point of Seduction** (1993)
. . . . . . . . . . . . . . . . . . . . . . . . . . Dr. Claire Archer
•• 0:15—Breasts, while making love on bed with Andrew Stevens at night during storm.
••• 0:28—Side view of buns and breasts, while making love with Stevens on bed.
••• 0:57—Breasts, taking off robe in front of Stevens. More breasts and buns while making love with him.
**Dead On** (1993) . . . . . . . . . . . . . . . . . . Erin Davenport
(Unrated version reviewed.)
••• 0:15—Breasts and buns in panties, while making out with Matt McCoy in doorway, then making love on the floor. Wow!
••• 0:29—Breasts, while making love with McCoy in her studio. Shot almost in silhouette.
• 0:49—Brief breasts, while rolling over in bed to answer the phone.
On Deadly Ground (1993). . . . . . . . . . . . . . . . . .Liles
*Made for TV Movies:*
The Laker Girls (1990) . . . . . . . . . . . . . . . . . . . .Libby
*TV:*
Dallas (1991) . . . . . . . . . . . . . . . . . . . . . . . . . . . Kit

# Shaver, Helen
*Films:*
Shoot (1976; Canadian) . . . . . . . . . . . . .Paula Lissitzen
The Supreme Kid (1976; Canadian) . . . . . . . . . . . .Girl
Outrageous! (1977; Canadian) . . . . . . . . . . . . . . . .Jo
High-Ballin' (1978) . . . . . . . . . . . . . . . . . . . . . Pickup
**In Praise of Older Women** (1978; Canadian)
. . . . . . . . . . . . . . . . . . . . . . . . . . . . . Ann MacDonald
- ••• 1:40—Blue bra and panties, then breasts with Tom Berenger.
- ••• 1:42—Nude lying in bed with Berenger, then getting out and getting dressed.
Starship Invasions (1978; Canadian) . . . . . . . . . . .Betty
The Amityville Horror (1979). . . . . . . . . . . . . . .Carolyn
Gas (1981; Canadian) . . . . . . . . . . . . . . . . . . . . .Rhonda
Harry Tracy (1982; Canadian) . . . . . . . . . . . . Catherine
**The Osterman Weekend** (1983). . .Virginia Tremayne
- •• 0:24—Breasts in an open blouse yelling at her husband in the bedroom.
- • 0:41—Breasts in the swimming pool when everyone watches on the TV.
Best Defense (1984) . . . . . . . . . . . . . . . . . . Claire Lewis
The Color of Money (1986). . . . . . . . . . . . . . . .Janelle
**Desert Hearts** (1986) . . . . . . . . . . . . . . . . . .Vivian Bell
- • 1:05—Brief breasts in bed in hotel room.
- ••• 1:09—Breasts making love in bed with Patricia Charboneau.
**The Men's Club** (1986). . . . . . . . . . Sarah (uncredited)
- •• 0:13—Breasts under Roy Scheider in bed, then breasts again, getting back into bed.
**The Believers** (1987) . . . . . . . . . . . . . Jessica Halliday
- • 0:38—Brief glimpse of right breast while lying in bed with Martin Sheen.
- 1:17—Buns, getting out of bed.
**Innocent Victim** (1988) . . . . . . . . . . . Benet Archdale
- • 1:05—Very brief side of left breast on top of a guy in bed.
Zebrahead (1992). . . . . . . . . . . . . . . . . . . . . . . Diane
Murder So Sweet (1993) . . . . . . . . . . . . . . . . . . .n.a.
That Night (1993). . . . . . . . . . . . . . . . Ann O'Conner
*Made for Cable Movies:*
**The Park is Mine** (1985; HBO). . . . . . . .Valery Weaver
- • 0:46—Very brief breasts undressing then very, very brief left breast, while catching clothes from Tommy Lee Jones.
Survive the Night (1993; USA) . . . . . . . . . . . . . . Stacy
*Made for TV Movies:*
Mothers, Daughters and Lovers (1989). . . . . . . . . . .n.a.
Rest In Peace, Mrs. Columbo (1990) . . . . . Vivian Dimitri
Fatal Memories (1992) . . . . . . . . . . . . . . .Elaine Tipton
Poisoned by Love: The Kern County Murders (1993)
. . . . . . . . . . . . . . . . . . . . . . . . . . . . . . . Edie Ballew
Ride with the Wind (1994) . . . . . . . . .Katherine Barnes
*TV:*
United States (1980). . . . . . . . . . . . . . . . Libby Chapin
Jessica Novak (1981). . . . . . . . . . . . . . . . Jessica Novak
WIOU (1990-91). . . . . . . . . . . . . . . . .Kelby Robinson

*Magazines:*
**Playboy** (Oct 1978) . . . . . . Observing "Older Women"
- •• 193-194—Breasts and buns.
**Playboy** (Nov 1978) . . . . . . . . . . Sex in Cinema 1978
- •• 185—Full frontal nudity on bed.

# Shaw, Alonna
*Films:*
**Double Impact** (1991). . . . . . . . . . . . . Danielle Shaw
- •• 1:09—Breasts, in white panties, changing out of her wet clothes on boat.
- •• 1:10—Breasts and buns several times, making love with Chad during Alex's jealous fantasy.
- • 1:11—More breasts and buns in fantasy.
- • 1:12—More breasts.
**Cyborg Cop** (1993) . . . . . . . . . . . . . . . . . . . . . Cathy
- ••• 0:58—Breasts, while making love with Jack.

# Shaw, Fiona
*Films:*
**Mountains of the Moon** (1989). . . . . . . . . . . .Isabel
- •• 0:33—Breasts and very brief lower frontal nudity letting Patrick Bergin wax the hair off her legs.
- •• 1:43—Breasts in bed after Bergin returns from Africa.
My Left Foot (1989; British) . . . . . . . . . .Dr. Eileen Cole
Three Men and a Little Lady (1990) . . . . . . . Miss Lomax
London Kills Me (1991; British) . . . . . . . . . . . .Headley
Super Mario Bros. (1993). . . . . . . . . . . . . . . . . . . Lena
Undercover Blues (1993) . . . . . . . . . . . . . . . Novacek
*Made for TV Movies:*
Hedda Gabler (1993). . . . . . . . . . . . . . . Hedda Gabler

# Shaw, Linda
Adult film actress.
*Films:*
**Body Double** (1984) . . . . . . . . . . . . . . . . . Linda Shaw
- • 1:11—Left breast on monitor while Craig Wasson watches TV.

# Shaw, Tina
*Films:*
**The Secrets of Love—Three Rakish Tales** (1986)
. . . . . . . . . . . . . . . . . . . . . . . . . . . The Weaver's Wife
- ••• 0:10—Breasts in bed with Luke.
- ••• 0:17—Breasts in the barn.
**Salome's Last Dance** (1987). . . . . . . . . . . . .2nd Slave
(Appears with 2 other slaves–can't tell who is who.)
- •• 0:08—Breasts in black costume around a cage.
- •• 0:52—Breasts during dance number.
The Lair of the White Worm (1988; British) . . Maid/Nun
**Taffin** (1988; U.S./British) . . . . . . . . . . Lola the Stripper
- •• 1:04—Breasts doing routine in a club.
**Split Second** (1992). . . . . . . . . . . . .Nightclub Stripper
- •• 0:07—Breasts, dancing in club in black S&M outfit, wearing a mask over her head.

# Shayne, Linda
*Films:*
Lovely But Deadly (1973) . . . . . . . . . . . . . . . . . . Barb
**Humanoids from the Deep** (1980). . . . . Miss Salmon
  • 1:06—Breasts after getting bathing suit ripped off
  by a humanoid.
Graduation Day (1981) . . . . . . . . . . . Uncredited Paula
The Lost Empire (1983). . . . . . . . . . . . . . . Cindy Blake
**Screwballs** (1983). . . . . . . . . . . . . . Bootsie Goodhead
  ••• 0:43—Right breast, while in back of van at drive-in
  theater, then breasts.
Big Bad Mama II (1987) . . . . . . . . . . . . . . . Bank Teller
Out of Bounds (1987). . . . . . . . . . . . . . . . . Chris Cage
Daddy's Boys (1988) . . . . . . . . . . . . . . . . . . . Nanette
No Man's Land (1988) . . . . . . . . . . . . . . . . . . . Peggy
Munchie (1992) . . . . . . . . . . . . . . . . . Band Member
*Made for TV Movies:*
My Wicked Ways... The Legend of Errol Flynn (1985)
  . . . . . . . . . . . . . . . . . . . . . . . . . . Girl on 1st Train

# Shé, Elizabeth
*Films:*
**Howling V** (1989) . . . . . . . . . . . . Mary Lou Summers
  • 0:33—Buns and side view of right breast getting
  into pool with Donovan.
  • 0:36—Very brief full frontal nudity climbing out of
  pool with Donovan.
Howling VI—The Freaks (1990) . . . Mary Lou Summers

# Shea, Katt
a.k.a. Kathleen M. Shea or Katt Shea Ruben.
Actress turned Director.
*Films:*
The Cannonball Run (1981) . . . . . . . . . . . Starting Girl
**My Tutor** (1983) . . . . . . . . . . . . . . . . . . Mud Wrestler
  • 0:48—Brief breasts when a guy rips her dress off.
Scarface (1983). . . . . . . . . . Woman at the Babylon Club
Cannonball Run II (1984) . . . . . . . . . . . . . . . . . n.a.
**Hollywood Hot Tubs** (1984) . . . . . . . . . . . . Dee-Dee
  • 0:21—Breasts with her boyfriend while Shawn is
  working on the hot tub.
**Preppies** (1984) . . . . . . . . . . . . . . . . . . . . . Margot
  ••• 0:20—Breasts teasing Richard through the glass
  door of her house.
  0:54—In bra and panties with Trini, practicing sexual positions on the bed.
  • 1:07—Brief breasts after taking off bra in bed.
**R.S.V.P.** (1984). . . . . . . . . . . . . . . . . . . Rhonda Rivers
  • 0:31—Side view of left breast, making love in bed
  with Jonathan.
**Barbarian Queen** (1985) . . . . . . . . . . . . . . . . Estrild
  • 0:31—Brief breasts, when her top gets torn off by
  guards.
The Destroyers (1985). . . . . . . . . . . . . . . . . . Audrey
Psycho III (1986) . . . . . . . . . . . . . . . . . . . . . . .Patsy

# Shear, Rhonda
*Films:*
Galaxina (1980) . . . . . . . . . . . . . . . . . . . Mime/Robot
**Basic Training** (1984) . . . . . . . . . . . . . . . . . . Debbie
  •• 0:07—Breasts making love with Mark.
  0:15—In bra, making love on Mark's desk.
Doin' Time (1984) . . . . . . . . . . . . . . . . . . . . Adrianne
Spaceballs (1987). . . . . . . . . . . . . . . Woman in Diner
Return to Frogtown (1992) . . . . . . . . . . . . . . . .Fuzzy
  *a.k.a. Frogtown II*
*Made for Cable TV:*
Up All Night. . . . . . . . . . . . . . . . . . . . . . . . . . Host
*Magazines:*
Playboy (Apr 1977) . . . . . . . The Girls of the New South
**Playboy** (Jun 1991). . . . . . . . . . . . . . . . . Funny Girls
  ••• 92—Full frontal nudity.
**Playboy's Career Girls** (Aug 1992) . . . . . . Funny Girls
  ••• 26—Full frontal nudity.
**Playboy** (Oct 1993) . . . . . . . . . Rhonda Is Up All Night
  ••• 70-75—Nude. Great buns shot while doing splits at
  a bowling alley.
**Playboy's Nudes** (Dec 1993) . . . . . . . . . . . . . .Herself
  ••• 14-15—Full frontal nudity.
**Playboy** (Dec 1993) . . . . . . . . . . . . . . .Sex Stars 1993
  ••• 177—Breasts.

# Sheedy, Ally
Wife of actor David Lansbury.
*Films:*
**Bad Boys** (1983). . . . . . . . . . . . . . . . . . .J. C. Walenski
  • 0:12—Very, very brief left breast, while kneeling on
  floor next to bed when Sean Penn leaves. A little
  blurry and a long shot.
Wargames (1983) . . . . . . . . . . . . . . . . . . . . Jennifer
The Breakfast Club (1985) . . . . . . . . . .Allison Reynolds
St. Elmo's Fire (1985) . . . . . . . . . . . . . . . . . . . Leslie
Blue City (1986). . . . . . . . . . . . . . . . . . Annie Rayford
  0:44—Very very brief left breast, while lying on bed
  reaching her arm around Judd Nelson while kissing
  him. Dark and blurry.
Short Circuit (1986) . . . . . . . . . . . . . Stephanie Speck
Maid to Order (1987) . . . . . . . . . . Jessie Montgomery
  0:40—Buns, taking off dress and diving into the
  pool. Long shot and dark. Don't see her face.
  0:42—Buns, walking with a towel around her hair.
  Another long shot and you don't see her face.
Heart of Dixie (1989) . . . . . . . . . . . . . . . . . . Maggie
Betsy's Wedding (1990) . . . . . . . . . . . Connie Hopper
Only the Lonely (1991) . . . . . . . . . . . . . Theresa Luna
Home Alone 2: Lost in New York (1992)
  . . . . . . . . . . . . . . . . . . . . . . . . . . .NY Ticket Agent
The Pickle (1992) . . . . . . . . . . . . . . . . . . . Molly-Girl
Man's Best Friend (1993) . . . . . . . . . . . . . Lori Tanner
*Made for Cable Movies:*
The Lost Capone (1990) . . . . . . . . . . . . . . Kathleen
Fear (1991; Showtime). . . . . . . . . . . . . . Cayce Bridges
Chantilly Lace (1993; Showtime) . . . . . . . . . . Elizabeth
Parallel Lives (1994; Showtime) . . . . . . . . . . . . Louise

*Made for Cable TV:*
Kurt Vonnegut's Monkey House: Epicac . . . . . . . . . . . Lisa
Red Shoe Diaries: Accidents Happen (1993; Showtime)
. . . . . . . . . . . . . . . . . . . . . . . . . . . . . . . . . . . . . . . Karen
(Available on video tape on *Red Shoe Diaries 4: Auto Erotica*.)
*Made for TV Movies:*
The Best Little Girl in the World (1981) . . . . . . . . . . . n.a.
The Violation of Sarah McDavid (1981) . . . . . . . . . . . n.a.
Deadly Lessons (1983) . . . . . . . . . . . . . . . . . . . . . . . n.a.
Lethal Exposure (1993) . . . . . . . . . . . . . . . Chris Cassidy
Ultimate Betrayal (1994) . . . . . . . . . . . . . . . . . . . . Mary

# Sheen, Jacqueline

*Video Tapes:*
**Playboy Video Calendar 1991** (1990) . . . . December
••• 0:49—Nude.
**Playboy Video Centerfold: Tawnni Cable** (1990)
. . . . . . . . . . . . . . . . . . . . . . . . . . . . . . . . . . . Playmate
••• 0:14—Nude in Hawaii with Tawnni Cable and Pamela Stein.
**Wet and Wild III** (1991) . . . . . . . . . . . . . . . . . Model
**Playboy Playmates in Paradise** (1992) . . . Playmate
*Magazines:*
**Playboy** (Jul 1990) . . . . . . . . . . . . . . . . . . . Playmate
**Playboy's Book of Lingerie** (Jul 1991) . . . . . . Herself
••• 106—Breasts.
••• 106—Breasts.
**Playboy's Book of Lingerie** (Sep 1991) . . . . . Herself
••• 82-83—Nude.
**Playboy's Book of Lingerie** (Nov 1991) . . . . . Herself
••• 89—Full frontal nudity.
**Playboy's Book of Lingerie** (Mar 1992) . . . . . Herself
• 34—Lower frontal nudity.
**Playboy's Bathing Beauties** (Apr 1992) . . . . . Herself
••• 42—Breasts.
••• 52—Breasts.
**Playboy's Book of Lingerie** (May 1992) . . . . . Herself
• 76—Lower frontal nudity and sheer bra.
••• 100-101—Nude.
**Playboy's Girls of Summer '92** (Jun 1992) . . . Herself
•• 8-9—Breasts under fishnet top and lower frontal nudity.
••• 45—Breasts.
••• 51—Full frontal nudity.
••• 70—Full frontal nudity.
••• 89-91—Breasts.
**Playboy's Book of Lingerie** (Jul 1992) . . . . . . Herself
••• 16-17—Full frontal nudity.
**Playboy's Book of Lingerie** (Nov 1992) . . . . . Herself
••• 29—Breasts.
**Playboy's Nudes** (Dec 1992) . . . . . . . . . . . . . Herself
••• 4—Full frontal nudity.
••• 45—Full frontal nudity.
**Playboy's Book of Lingerie** (Mar 1993) . . . . . Herself
••• 43—Breasts.
**Playboy's Girls of Summer '93** (Jun 1993) . . . Herself
••• 105—Breasts.

**Playboy's Book of Lingerie** (Jul 1993) . . . . . . Herself
••• 36—Breasts.
•• 68—Breasts under sheer top.
**Playboy's Wet & Wild Women** (Aug 1993) . . . Herself
••• 7—Full frontal nudity.
**Playboy's Video Playmates** (Sep 1993) . . . . . . Herself
••• 72-73—Full frontal nudity.
**Playboy's Book of Lingerie** (Nov 1993) . . . . . Herself
•• 19—Upper half of right breast and lower frontal nudity.
**Playboy's Bathing Beauties** (Mar 1994) . . . . . Herself
••• 67—Breasts and buns in T-back.
**Playboy's Book of Lingerie** (Mar 1994) . . . . . . Herself
•• 12—Left breast.
••• 32—Breasts.
**Playboy's Book of Lingerie** (May 1994) . . . . . Herself
••• 38-39—Full frontal nudity.
**Playboy's Girls of Summer '94** (Jul 1994) . . . . Herself
••• 99—Full frontal nudity.

# Shelton, Deborah

Miss USA in the 1970-71 Miss Universe Pageant.
*Films:*
Blood Tide (1982) . . . . . . . . . . . . . . . . . . . . . Madeline
0:29—Braless in wet white dress in the ocean.
1:15—Braless in wet white dress sacrificing herself while lying on a rock.
Body Double (1984) . . . . . . . . . . . . . . . . . . . . . . Gloria
Hunk (1987) . . . . . . . . . . . . . . . . . . . . . . . . . . O'Brien
Perfect Victims (1988) . . . . . . . . . . . . . . . . . Liz Winters
0:55—Very brief, upper half of breasts, lying back in bubble bath.
**Blind Vision** (1990) . . . . . . . . . . . . . Leanne Dunaway
••• 0:25—Breasts, making love with her boyfriend on the floor. Some shots are a body double.
**Nemesis** (1992) . . . . . . . . . . . . . . . . . . . . . . . . . Julian
• 0:30—Buns, while lying on bed.
•• 0:31—Buns, while standing up and hugging Billy.
• 0:36—Buns, while standing at window. Side view of left breast.
••• 0:37—Full frontal nudity, punching Billy and getting dressed. Looking good! Very buff—she worked out for three and a half hours a day.
0:53—Special effect left breast, sticking through hole in her bullet-ridden blouse.
**Sins of the Night** (1993) . . . . . . . . . Roxanne Flowers
(Unrated version reviewed.)
0:00—Doing strip tease dance in black bra and panties during the opening credits.
0:39—In white bra and panties when Miles O'Keeffe forces her to dance and strip in front of him.
••• 0:48—Breasts, while making love with Jack. Some nice close-ups! Great, long scene.
0:55—In blonde wig in red bra and red panties in room with Ted.
•• 0:58—Breasts during Jack's recollections.
••• 1:03—Breasts and buns, while making love with Jack. Long scene.

1:13—In blonde wig in red bra and panties on video tape.

**Silk Degrees** (1994) . . . . . . . . . . . . . . . . Alex Ramsey
- 0:49—Full frontal nudity behind plastic shower curtain.
- •• 0:56—Breasts, while making love with Marc Singer in cabin.

*TV:*

The Yellow Rose (1983-84) . . . . . . . . . Juliette Hollister
Dallas (1984-87) . . . . . . . . . . . . . . . . Mandy Winger

*Magazines:*

Playboy (Mar 1974) . . . . . . . . . . . . . . . .Cover Model

## Shepard, Hilary

a.k.a. Hilary Shapiro.
*Films:*

Soup for One (1982). . . . . . . . . . . . . . . . . . . . .n.a.
Radioactive Dreams (1984) . . . . . . . . . . . . Biker Leader
**Weekend Pass** (1984) . . . . . . . . . . . . . Cindy Hazard
- •• 1:05—In red bra, then breasts taking off bra.
- 1:07—Buns and breasts getting into bathtub.

**Private Resort** (1985) . . . . . . . . . . . . . . . . . Shirley
- ••• 0:36—Breasts, then buns, taking off her dress in front of Rob Morrow.

Tough Guys (1986) . . . . . . . . . . . . . . . . . . . . Sandy
Hunk (1987) . . . . . . . . . . . . . . . . . . . . . Alexis Cash
Lucky Stiff (1988) . . . . . . . . . . . . . . . . . . . . . Cissy
**Peace Maker** (1990) . . . . . . . . . . . . . . . Dori Caisson
- 1:08—Brief upper half of buns, taking off shirt and getting into shower. Brief side view of upper half of left breast, twice while making love with Townsend.

I Don't Buy Kisses Anymore (1992) . . . . . . Ada Fishbine
Scanner Cop (1993) . . . . . . . . . . . . . . . . . . . . .Zena

*Made for Cable Movies:*

Attack of the 50 ft. Woman (1993; HBO) . . . . . . . Nurse

*Made for Cable TV:*

Dream On: The First Episode (1990; HBO) . . . . . Date 2

## Shepard, Jewel

*Films:*

**Raw Force** (1981) . . . . . . . . . . . . . . . . Drunk Sexpot
- 0:31—Breasts in black swimsuit, when a guy adjusts her straps and it falls open.

The Junkman (1982) . . . . . . . . . . . . . . . . . . .Credit Girl
**Zapped!** (1982) . . . . . . . . . . . . . .Uncredited Girl in Car
- 0:39—Brief breasts after red and white top pops off when Scott Baio uses his Telekinesis on her.

**My Tutor** (1983) . . . . . . . . . . . . . Girl in Phone Booth
- 0:40—Brief left breast in car when Matt Lattanzi fantasizes about making love with her.

**Christina** (1984) . . . . . . . . . . . . . . . . . . . .Christina
Hollywood Hot Tubs (1984) . . . . . . . . . Crystal Landers
(No breasts, but bouncing around a lot in short, braless T-shirts.)
Operation Overkill (1984) . . . . . . . . . . . . . . . . . .n.a.
The Return of the Living Dead (1985) . . . . . . . . . Casey
**Party Camp** (1987) . . . . . . . . . . . . . . . . Dyanne Stein
- ••• 0:57—In white bra and panties, then breasts playing strip poker with the boys.

Scenes from the Goldmine (1987) . . . . . . . . . . . . Dana
**The Underachievers** (1987) . . . . . . . . .Sci-Fi Teacher
- 0:27—Breasts ripping off her Star Trek uniform when someone enters her classroom. Dark, hard to see.

Going Undercover (1988; British). . . . . . . . . . . Peaches
**Hollywood Hot Tubs 2—Educating Crystal** (1989)
. . . . . . . . . . . . . . . . . . . . . . . . . . Crystal Landers
0:38—In white slip during Gary's fantasy.
- 1:12—Brief left breast, while lying down, kissing Gary.

**Roots of Evil** (1991). . . . . . . . . . . . . . . . . . .Wanda
(Unrated version reviewed.)
- 1:31—Brief right breast, a couple of times, when it pops out of her blouse while she's in police station.

**Caged Heat 2: Stripped of Freedom** (1993)
. . . . . . . . . . . . . . . . . . . . . . . . . . . . . . .Amanda
- •• 0:15—In bra and panties, then breasts, while undressing for strip search in the warden's office.
- •• 0:49—Breasts, after getting her prison shirt ripped open, then whipped in front of the other prisoners.

## Shepherd, Cybill

Former model.
*Films:*

**The Last Picture Show** (1971) . . . . . . . . Jacy Farrow
- •• 0:37—Undressing on diving board. Very brief left breast falling onto diving board. Brief breasts tossing bra aside.
- 0:38—Brief left breast jumping into the water.
- ••• 1:05—Breasts and buns in motel room with Jeff Bridges.

The Heartbreak Kid (1972) . . . . . . . . . . . . Kelly Corcoran
Daisy Miller (1974). . . . . . . . . . . Annie P. "Daisy" Miller
Special Delivery (1976) . . . . . . . . . . . . . . . Mary Jane
Taxi Driver (1976) . . . . . . . . . . . . . . . . . . . . Betsy
The Lady Vanishes (1979; British) . . . . . . . Amanda Kelly
The Return (1980) . . . . . . . . . . . . . . . . . .Daughter
Chances Are (1989) . . . . . . . . . . . . . . . .Corrine Jeffries
1:11—In white bra and tap pants getting dressed.
1:22—In bra with Robert Downey Jr. and Ryan O'Neal in living room.
Alice (1990) . . . . . . . . . . . . . . . . . . . . . .Nancy Brill
Texasville (1990) . . . . . . . . . . . . . . . . . . . Jacy Farrow
Once Upon A Crime (1992) . . . . . . . . Marilyn Schwary
Married to It (1993) . . . . . . . . . . . . . . . Claire Laurent

*Made for Cable Movies:*

Memphis (1991; TNT) . . . . . . . . . . . . . . . . . . . n.a.
Which Way Home (1991). . . . . . . . . . . Karen Parsons

*Made for TV Movies:*

Moonlighting (1985) . . . . . . . . . . . . . . . Maddie Hayes
Stormy Weathers (1992) . . . Samantha "Sam" Weathers
Telling Secrets (1993). . . . . . . . . . . . . . . Faith Kelsey
Baby Brokers (1994). . . . . . . . . . . . . . . . . . . . .n.a.

*TV:*

The Yellow Rose (1983-84). . . . . . . . .Colleen Champion
Moonlighting (1985-89) . . . . . . . . . . . . Maddie Hayes

*Magazines:*

**Playboy** (Nov 1972) . . . . . . . . . . Sex in Cinema 1972
- 170—B&W breasts.

**Playboy** (Dec 1972). . . . . . . . . . . . . Sex Stars of 1972
•• 208—B&W breasts.

# Sheppard, Delia

*Films:*
**Witchcraft II: The Temptress** (1989). . . . . . .Dolores
•• 1:20—Brief breasts several times with William.
**Haunting Fear** (1990) . . . . . . . . . . . . . . . . . . . . .Lisa
••• 0:13—Breasts on desk, making love with Terry.
••• 1:10—Full frontal nudity, making love in bed with Terry. Long scene.
Rocky V (1990) . . . . . . . . . . . . . . . . . . . . . . . . . Karen
The Adventures of Ford Fairlane (1991). . . . . . Pussycat
**Mirror Images** (1991) . . . . . . . . . . . . . Kaitlin/Shauna
•• 0:07—Right breast, while undressing in front of vanity mirror.
•• 0:08—More breasts as Shauna in bed.
0:12—Buns, while dancing on stage with a band, wearing a sexy outfit.
••• 0:14—Breasts in bed with Georgio.
••• 0:27—Breasts and buns in G-string, making love with Joey. Long scene.
••• 0:33—Buns in black bra and panties, walking around her sister's apartment. Long scene.
•• 0:39—Right breast, while with a guy with a mask.
••• 0:41—Nude, taking a shower. Great!
••• 0:43—Breasts in bedroom after her shower.
•• 0:48—Left breast, while making love in bed with Julie Strain.
••• 1:29—Breasts in bed in lingerie with the policeman.
**Roots of Evil** (1991) . . . . . . . . . . . . . . . . . . . .Monica
(Unrated version reviewed.)
••• 0:04—Breasts and buns in G-string, dancing on stage.
• 0:07—Breasts and buns, while on stage when wounded guy disturbs her act.
••• 0:38—Buns in outfit, then breasts dancing on stage.
••• 0:41—More buns and breasts in bed, making love with Johnny. Long scene.
**Secret Games** (1991) . . . . . . . . . . . . . . . . . . . Celeste
(Unrated version reviewed.)
• 0:38—Breasts under sheer black body suit.
0:45—Buns, under sheer robe.
•• 0:48—Breasts with her lover, while watching Julianne and Eric on TV.
Sex Bomb (1991) . . . . . . . . . . . . . . . . . . . . . . . . .n.a.
**Animal Instincts** (1992). . . . . . . . . . . . . . . . . .Ingrid
(Unrated version reviewed.)
•• 0:50—Breasts, while in bed with her lover and Joanne.
••• 0:54—Breasts, while in bed with only Joanne.
**Dead Boyz Can't Fly** (1992). . . . . . . . . . . . . . Angie
•• 1:01—In white bra and panties, then breasts in doctor's office when bad guy pretends to be a doctor and examines her.
**Night Rhythms** (1992). . . . . . . . . . . . . . . . .Bridget
(Unrated version reviewed.)
••• 1:25—Full frontal nudity, making love with Kit in bed. Long scene.

**Sins of Desire** (1992). . . . . . . . . . . . . .Jessica Callister
(Unrated version reviewed.)
••• 0:10—Full frontal nudity, while tied by her wrists in bed with Scott.
••• 0:45—Breasts and buns, while making love on the floor with Scott. Nice close-ups.
Body Chemistry 3: Point of Seduction (1993)
. . . . . . . . . . . . . . . . . . . . . . . . . . . . . .Wilhemina
*Magazines:*
**Penthouse** (Apr 1988) . . . . . . . . . . . . . . . . . . . . .Pet
**Playboy** (Nov 1990) . . . . . . . . . . Sex in Cinema 1990
•• 143—Right breast, in still from *Witchcraft, Part II.*
**Playboy** (Dec 1990) . . . . . . . . . . . . . .Sex Stars of 1990
•• 177—Buns.
**Playboy** (Nov 1993) . . . . . . . . . . Sex in Cinema 1993
••• 135—Breasts in still from *Mirror Images.*

# Sheridan, Nicollette

Ex-wife of actor Harry Hamlin.
*Films:*
The Sure Thing (1985) . . . . . . . . . . . . . The Sure Thing
Noises Off (1992). . . . . . . . . . . . Brooke Ashton & Vicki
0:22—In white bra, panties and stockings for most of the rest of the film.
*Made for Cable Movies:*
**Deceptions** (1990; Showtime) . . . . . Adrienne Erickson
• 0:35—Very, very brief silhouette of breasts, while hugging Harry Hamlin when the camera tilts down from her head to her buns.
*Miniseries:*
Jackie Collins' Lucky/Chances (1990) . .Lucky Santangelo
*Made for TV Movies:*
A Time to Heal (1994) . . . . . . . . . . . . . . . Jenny Barton
*TV:*
Paper Dolls (1984) . . . . . . . . . . . . . . . . . . Taryn Blake
Knots Landing (1986-93) . . . . . . . . . . .Paige Matheson

# Sherman, Geraldine

*Films:*
Interlude (1968; British) . . . . . . . . . . . . . . . . .Natalie
Poor Cow (1968) . . . . . . . . . . . . . . . . . . . . . . . Trixie
Take a Girl Like You (1970; British) . . . . . . . . . . . Anna
**There's a Girl in My Soup** (1970) . . . . . . . .Caroline
•• 0:43—Breasts in bed, then getting out after Goldie Hawn splashes water on her.
Get Carter (1971) . . . . . . . . . . . . . . . . . Girl in Cafe
Cry of the Penguins (1972; British) . . . . . . . . . . Penny

# Sherwood, Robin

*Films:*
Loose Shoes (1977) . . . . . . . . . . . . . . . . Biker Chic #2
The Tourist Trap (1979) . . . . . . . . . . . . . . . . . .Eileen
Hero at Large (1980) . . . . . . . . . . . . . . . . . . . . .n.a.
Serial (1980) . . . . . . . . . . . . . . . . . . . . . . . .Woman
Blow Out (1981) . . . . . . . . . . . . . . . . . . . .Screamer
**Death Wish II** (1982). . . . . . . . . . . . . . Carol Kersey
• 0:15—Breasts after getting raped by gang member in their hideout.

**The Love Butcher** (1982)................. Sheila
- 0:39—Very brief buns, while putting on swimsuit bottom.
- 0:40—Brief breasts several times, while struggling in pool with killer when he kills her with garden hose.
- 0:41—Buns, while getting carried out of pool by killer. Breasts under water in bathtub, dead.
- 0:43—Brief breasts, while throwing bikini top while in pool.

*Made for TV Movies:*
Outside Chance (1978)................... Tootsie

# Shields, Brooke

*Films:*
Alice, Sweet Alice (1977)................... Karen
King of the Gypsies (1978) ................... Tita
**Pretty Baby** (1978)....................... Violet
(She was only 11–12 years old at this time so there isn't really a whole lot to see here!)
- 0:57—Breasts and buns taking a bath.
- 1:26—Breasts posing on couch for Keith Carradine.
- 1:28—Buns, getting thrown out of the room, then trying to get back in.
Tilt (1978).................................. Tilt
**Just You and Me, Kid** (1979)............... Kate
- 0:07—Brief buns, running down stairs after her towel gets caught in fence.
Wanda Nevada (1979) .............. Wanda Nevada
Blue Lagoon (1980) ................... Emmeline
(Nudity is a body double, Kathy Trout.)
0:27—Nude swimming underwater after growing up from little children.
0:43—More underwater swimming.
1:00—Breasts body double lying on a rock.
1:09—Right breast of body double in hammock.
1:24—Body double breast feeding the baby.
Endless Love (1981) ....................... Jade
0:37—Body double, side view of right breast in bed with David.
1:08—Body double very brief left breast, in bed with another guy during David's dream.
Sahara (1984) ........................... Dale
0:51—In a wet T-shirt taking a shower under a water fall.
Brenda Starr (1986)................. Brenda Starr
(Finally released in 1992.)
Speed Zone (1989)................... Stewardess
Backstreet Dreams (1990) .... Stephanie "Stevie" Bloom
Freaked (1993) ...........................n.a.
*Made for Cable TV:*
Tales From the Crypt: Came the Dawn (1993)
.................................... "Norma"
*Made for TV Movies:*
Wet Gold (1984)......................... Laura
I Can Make You Love Me: The Stalking of Laura Black (1993)........................... Laura Black

# Shinas, Sofia

*Films:*
The Crow (1993) ................... Shelly Webster
*Made for Cable TV:*
**Red Shoe Diaries: Borders of Salt** (1994; Showtime)
.................................... n.a.

# Shire, Devon
See: Peace, Jennifer.

# Shirkani, Kym
*Made for Cable TV:*
**Dream On: The Undergraduate** (1992; HBO)... Julie
••• 0:03—In bra, then breasts, while making love with Martin.
Dream On: The French Conception (1993; HBO)... Julie

# Shirley, Aleisa
*Films:*
**Sweet Sixteen** (1982) ............. Melissa Morgan
- 0:16—Side view of body, nude, taking a shower.
- 1:11—Breasts undressing to go skinny dipping with Hank. Dark, hard to see.
- 1:13—Breasts, getting out of the water.
*Made for Cable TV:*
**The Hitchhiker: Shattered Vows** ........ Pamela
- 0:08—Breasts and buns in bathroom with Jeff.
0:12—In bedroom wearing white lingerie.
•• 0:18—In bed wearing black bra, panties, garter belt and stockings, then breasts.
*Video Tapes:*
Rock Video Girls (1991) ................... Herself

# Shoop, Pamela Susan
*Films:*
Empire of the Ants (1977) .......... Coreen Bradford
One Man Jury (1978)..................... Wendy
**Halloween II** (1981)..................... Karen
••• 0:48—Breasts getting into the whirlpool bath with Budd in the hospital.
*Made for TV Movies:*
The Dallas Cowboy Cheerleaders (1979) .. Betty Denton

# Shower, Kathy
*Films:*
Double Exposure (1983) ........... Mudwrestler #1
Commando Squad (1987) ............. Kat Withers
**The Further Adventures of Tennessee Buck** (1987)
.................... Barbara Manchester
0:22—In white lingerie in her hut getting dressed.
••• 0:57—Breasts getting rubbed with oil by the cannibal women. Nice close up shots.
•• 1:02—Breasts in a hut with the Chief of the tribe.
**Frankenstein General Hospital** (1988)
.................... Dr. Alice Singleton
0:35—In white lingerie outfit pacing around in her office.
- 1:15—Brief breasts running out of her office after the monster, putting her lab coat on.

**Out on Bail** (1988) . . . . . . . . . . . . . . . . . . . .Sally Anne
- 1:01—Brief breasts in shower with Robert Ginty.

**Bedroom Eyes II** (1989) . . . . . . . . . . . . . .Carolyn Ross
- •• 0:22—Breasts in the artist's studio fighting with her lover while Wings Hauser watches through the window.

Robo C.H.I.C. (1990) . . . . . . . . . . . . . . . Robo C.H.I.C.

**Velvet Dreams** (1991; Italian) . . . . . . . . . . . . . . Laura
- •• 0:15—Left breast, while making love with Paul in the dressing room.
- • 0:35—Brief buns, while getting a massage.
- •• 0:42—Breasts, tied to a tree during her writing fantasy.

**L.A. Goddess** (1992) . . . . . . . . . . . . . . . . . Lisa Moore
- •• 0:00—Full frontal nudity, getting out of the shower.
- 0:17—In white body suit.
- •• 0:45—Side view of buns and breasts, getting into and in bathtub.
- ••• 0:53—Nude in spa with Damian.
- • 0:56—Left breast, while lying in park with Damian.
- 0:58—Breasts while making love in bed with Damian.
- • 1:20—Brief breasts in spa with Damian in flashback.

**Wild Cactus** (1992) . . . . . . . . . . . . . . . . . . . . . Celeste
(Unrated version reviewed.)
- 0:50—In white bra in bed with Maggie.
- •• 0:52—Breasts, while lying in bed.
- •• 1:16—Breasts in bed with bullet through her head, when discovered by Philip.

**Sexual Malice** (1993) . . . . . . . . . . . . . . . Laura Altman
(Unrated version reviewed.)
- ••• 0:10—Breasts, while making love on pool table with a guy when Christine peeks in room.

A Brilliant Disguise (1994) . . . . . . . . . . . . . . . Lila Foster
*TV:*
Santa Barbara (1987-90) . . . . . . . . . . . . . . . . . . . . .n.a.
*Video Tapes:*
**Playboy Video Magazine, Volume 9** . . . . . Playmate
**Playboy Video Calendar 1987** (1986) . . . . Playmate
**Playboy's Playmates of the Year: The '80s** (1989)
. . . . . . . . . . . . . . . . . . . . . . Playmate of the Year 1986
- ••• 0:17—Full frontal nudity outside by spa.
- ••• 0:19—Breasts in still photos. Full frontal nudity, posing in bed.

**The Best of Sexy Lingerie** (1992) . . . . . . . . . .Model
**The Best of Video Playmate Calendars** (1992)
. . . . . . . . . . . . . . . . . . . . . . . . . . . . . . . . . . . Playmate
- •• 0:04—Full frontal nudity in still photos. In lingerie in bedroom.
- ••• 0:05—Full frontal nudity on bed.

*Magazines:*
**Playboy** (May 1985) . . . . . . . . . . . . . . . . . . Playmate
**Playboy** (Dec 1986) . . . . . . . . . . . . . . Sex Stars of 86
**Playboy's 1987 Book of Lingerie** (Mar 1987)
. . . . . . . . . . . . . . . . . . . . . . . . . . . . . . . . . . . . Herself
- ••• 5-7—Full frontal nudity.
- • 30—Lower frontal nudity.
- ••• 36-37—Full frontal nudity.

**Playboy** (May 1988) . . . . . . . . . Kathy Goes Hollywood
- ••• 130-137—Nude.

**Playboy** (Jan 1989) . . . . . . . . . . .Women of the Eighties
- ••• 254—Full frontal nudity.

**Playboy's Nudes** (Oct 1990) . . . . . . . . . . . . . .Herself
- ••• 109—Full frontal nudity.

**Playboy's Calendar Playmates** (Nov 1992) . . .Herself
- ••• 47—Breasts.
- • 57—Full frontal nudity.

**Playboy's Video Playmates** (Sep 1993) . . . . . .Herself
- ••• 74-77—Nude.

# Shue, Elisabeth
*Films:*
The Karate Kid (1984) . . . . . . . . . . . . . . . . . . . . . . Ali
**Link** (1986) . . . . . . . . . . . . . . . . . . . . . . . . . .Jane Chase
- • 0:50—Brief right breast and buns, side view of a body double, standing in bathroom getting ready to take a bath while Link watches.

Adventures in Babysitting (1987) . . . . . . . . .Chris Parker
Cocktail (1988) . . . . . . . . . . . . . . . . . . . . Jordan Mooney
- 0:52—Side view of left breast while standing up in waterfall with Tom Cruise when she takes off her swimsuit top.

Back to the Future, Part II (1989) . . . . . . . . . . . Jennifer
Back to the Future, Part III (1990) . . . . . . . . . . . Jennifer
The Marrying Man (1991) . . . . . . . . . . . . . Adele Horner
*a.k.a. Too Hot to Handle*
Soapdish (1991) . . . . . . . . . . . . . . . . . . . . . Lori Craven
Heart and Souls (1993) . . . . . . . . . . . . . . . . . . . . Anne
Twenty Bucks (1993) . . . . . . . . . . . . . . . . . . . . Stripper
*Made for Cable Movies:*
**Blind Justice** (1994; HBO) . . . . . . . . . . . . . . .Caroline
- 0:36—Very, very brief right breast in gaping dress after getting up slightly after Armand Assante falls over.
- • 0:39—Brief upper half of right breast with part of nipple sticking out of camisole top while sitting on bed.

*Made for Cable TV:*
Dream On: oral sex, lies and videotape (1993; HBO)
. . . . . . . . . . . . . . . . . . . . . . . . . . . . . . . . . . . . . Maura
*Made for TV Movies:*
Call to Glory (1984) . . . . . . . . . . . . . . . . . Jackie Sarnac
*TV:*
Call to Glory (1984-85) . . . . . . . . . . . . . . . Jackie Sarnac

# Shugart, Reneé
*Films:*
Screwball Hotel (1988) . . . . . . . . . . . . . . . . . . Blue Bell
Spring Fever USA (1988) . . . . . . . . . . . . . Beach Beauty
*a.k.a. Lauderdale*
**Summer Job** (1989) . . . . . . . . . . . . . . . . . . . . . .Karen
- 0:15—In lingerie reading a magazine.
- • 0:42—Breasts taking off her top. Long shot, dark.
- • 0:45—In white lingerie, standing on stairs, then very brief left breast flashing.

# Siani, Sabrina

*Films:*

Ator, The Fighting Eagle (1982). . . . . . . . . . . . . . .Roon
0:44—Breasts bathing in stream. This is such a long
shot, you can't see anything, much less tell it's her.
**2020 Texas Gladiators** (1983; Italian) . . . . . . . .Maida
•• 0:07—Left breast, in open white dress after gang
rape.
• 0:34—Breasts during rape.
The Throne of Fire (1983; Italian) . . . . Princess Belkaren

# Sidney, Ann

*Films:*

Sebastian (1968; British) . . . . . . . . . . . . . . . . . . . Naomi
**Performance** (1970). . . . . . . . . . . . . . . . . . . . . . Dana
• 0:01—Very brief breasts and buns.
• 0:24—Brief breasts with Chas in flashbacks.
The Treasure of the Amazon (1985; Mexican) . . .Barbara

# Siemaszko, Nina

Sister of actor Casey Siemaszko.
*Films:*

One More Saturday Night (1986) . . . . . . Karen Lundahl
Tucker: The Man and His Dream (1988)
. . . . . . . . . . . . . . . . . . . . . . . . Marilyn Lee Tucker
**Lost Angels** (1989) . . . . . . . . . . . . . . . . . . . . .Merilee
• 0:38—Brief breasts and buns, running through
courtyard. Long shot, don't really see anything.
• 0:45—Buns, sitting at table outside, undressing and
rubbing feces (yuck!) on herself.
Bed & Breakfast (1992) . . . . . . . . . . . . . . . . . . . . . .n.a.
**Wild Orchid II: Two Shades of Blue** (1992). . . . Blue
••• 0:27—Breasts and buns, getting undressed in front
of Wendy Hughes.
•• 0:43—Breasts and buns in steam room with a customer.
•• 0:58—Breasts in panties, garter belt and stockings
while undressing for Josh.
••• 1:06—Breasts while humiliating J. J. in front of everyone at a party.
Twenty Bucks (1993). . . . . . . . . . . . . . . . . . Bank Teller
*Made for Cable TV:*
**Red Shoe Diaries: Just Like That** (1993; Showtime)
. . . . . . . . . . . . . . . . . . . . . . . . . . . . . . . . . . . Trudy
(Available on video tape on *Red Shoe Diaries 3: Another
Woman's Lipstick.*)
0:09—In white bra, while making out in the elevator
with Kyle. Very, very brief lower frontal nudity when
he rips her panties off.
••• 0:14—In white bra, then breasts in bed with Phillip.
••• 0:16—Breasts, while making love on top of Phillip in
bed. Full frontal nudity, while lying in bed.
•• 0:17—Briefly in black body suit, then breasts making
love on top of Phillip in bed.
Tales From the Crypt: Creep Course (1993; HBO)
. . . . . . . . . . . . . . . . . . . . . . . . . . . . . . .Stella Bishop
*Made for TV Movies:*
Sinatra (1992) . . . . . . . . . . . . . . . . . . . . . . .Mia Farrow
Baby Brokers (1994) . . . . . . . . . . . . . . . . . . . . Leeanne

# Silver, Cindy

*Films:*

Gimme an "F" (1981) . . . . . . . . . . .One of the "Ducks"
*a.k.a. T & A Academy 2*
**Hardbodies** (1984) . . . . . . . . . . . . . . . . . . . Kimberly
•• 0:07—Brief breasts on beach when a dog steals her
bikini top.
••• 0:47—Breasts standing in front of closet mirrors talking about breasts with Kristi.

# • Silverstone, Alicia

*Films:*

**The Crush** (1993). . . . . . . . . . . . . . . . .Darian Forrester
• 0:31—Buns, after dropping her shirt while Nick is
hiding in her closet. Don't see her face. Brief buns,
when walking into bathroom. Don't see her face.
*Made for Cable Movies:*
**Rebel Highway: Cool and the Crazy**
(1994; Showtime) . . . . . . . . . . . . . . . . . . . . . . Roslyn
• 0:27—Very brief tip of right breast, twice, when Joey
kicks off his shoe and drops his pants. Medium long
shot, don't see her face clearly.
• 0:28—Very brief tip of right breast, twice, when Joey
kneels down and lies back. Once more when she lies
down on him. Medium long shot, don't see her face
well.
*Made for TV Movies:*
Judith Krantz's Torch Song (1993) . . . . . . . . . Delphine
Scattered Dreams: The Kathryn Messenger Story (1993)
. . . . . . . . . . . . . . . . . . . . . . . . . . Phyllis Messenger
*Music Videos:*
Amazing/Aerosmith (1994) . . . . . . . . . . . . . . . . . n.a.
Crazy/Aerosmith (1994). . . . . . . . . . . . . . . . . . . . n.a.
Crying/Aerosmith (1994) . . . . . . . . . . . . . . . . . . . n.a.

# Simmons, Allene

*Films:*

**Porky's** (1981; Canadian) . . . . . . . . . . . . . . . . . .Jackie
• 1:02—Breasts in the shower scene.
Time Walker (1982) . . . . . . . . . . . . . . . . . . . . . . Nurse
**R.S.V.P.** (1984) . . . . . . . . . . . . . . . . . Patty De Fois Gras
•• 0:13—Breasts taking off red top behind the bar with
the bartender.
•• 0:38—Breasts in bed with Mr. Edwards, then buns
running to hide in the closet.
•• 0:41—Frontal nudity in room with Mr. Anderson.
••• 0:51—Breasts talking to Toby in the hallway trying
to get help for the Governor.
The Malibu Bikini Shop (1985). . . . . . . . . . Milinda Riley
Young Lady Chatterley II (1986). . .Marta "Maid in Bed"

# Simonsen, Renee

*Films:*

**Nothing Underneath** (1985; Italian). . . . . . . . Barbara
*a.k.a. Sotto Il Vestito Niente*
• 0:51—Brief side view of left breast, changing backstage during fashion show.
Via Montenapoleone (1987; Italian) . . . . . . . . . . . Elena

# Simpson, Suzi

*Films:*

**Enemy Gold** (1993). . . . . . . . . . . . . . . .Becky Midnite
- ••• 0:09—Breasts, while undressing and changing clothes in bathroom.
- ••• 0:33—Breasts and buns, while making love with Chris.
- ••• 1:05—Breasts and buns while taking a shower out-side.
- • 1:11—Buns in panties, while standing outside when the boys return.

*Video Tapes:*

**Playboy Video Calendar 1993** (1992) . . . September
- ••• 0:37—Nude in cave woman studio setting.
- ••• 0:39—Nude in haunted house setting.

**Playboy's Playmate Review 1993** (1993)
. . . . . . . . . . . . . . . . . . . . . . . . . . . . Miss January
- ••• 0:37—Nude while playing billiards.
- ••• 0:38—Nude in a cabin.

*Magazines:*

**Playboy** (Jan 1992) . . . . . . . . . . . . . . . . . . Playmate
- ••• 116-127—Nude.

**Playboy's Career Girls** (Aug 1992)
. . . . . . . . . . . . . . . . . . . . . . . . Baywatch Playmates
- ••• 7—Breasts.

**Playboy's Playmate Review** (Jun 1993) . . . . .January
- ••• 4-13—Nude.

**Playboy's Book of Lingerie** (Jul 1993) . . . . . . Herself
- ••• 31—Full frontal nudity.

**Playboy's Wet & Wild Women** (Aug 1993) . . Herself
- •• 10—Side of right breast and buns.
- ••• 50—Full frontal nudity.
- • 84—Buns.

**Playboy's Blondes, Brunettes & Redheads**
(Sep 1993) . . . . . . . . . . . . . . . . . . . . . . . . . Herself
- •• 4-5—Breasts under sheer net body suit.

**Playboy's Book of Lingerie** (Sep 1993) . . . . . Herself
- ••• 106-107—Buns and side of right breast.

**Playboy's Book of Lingerie** (Nov 1993) . . . . . Herself
- ••• 76—Breasts.
- •• 104—Left breast.

**Playboy's Nudes** (Dec 1993) . . . . . . . . . . . . . Herself
- • 26—Lower frontal nudity.

**Playboy's Book of Lingerie** (Jan 1994) . . . . . . Herself
- ••• 16-17—Full frontal nudity.

**Playboy's Bathing Beauties** (Mar 1994) . . . . . Herself
- ••• 16-17—Full frontal nudity.
- ••• 82-83—Breasts and partial lower frontal nudity.

**Playboy Presents Playmates in Paradise**
(Mar 1994) . . . . . . . . . . . . . . . . . . . . . . . . Playmate
- ••• 9-19—Nude.

**Playboy's Book of Lingerie** (Mar 1994) . . . . . Herself
- ••• 10—Right breast and lower frontal nudity.

**Playboy's Book of Lingerie** (May 1994) . . . . . Herself
- ••• 32—Breasts.
- ••• 62—Breasts.

**Playboy's Girls of Summer '94** (Jul 1994) . . . Herself
- •• 49—Right breast and lower frontal nudity.
- ••• 51—Full frontal nudity.

••• 87—Breasts and partial lower frontal nudity.

**Playboy's Book of Lingerie** (Jul 1994) . . . . . . Herself
- ••• 2-7—Full frontal nudity.

# Sinclair, Annette

*Films:*

Thief of Hearts (1984) . . . . . . . . . . . . . College Girl #1
(Special Home Video Version reviewed.)

Weekend Pass (1984) . . . . . . . . . . . . . . . . . . . . Maxine

**Hide and Go Shriek** (1988). . . . . . . . . . . Kim Downs
- • 0:51—Brief breasts and buns, undressing and get-ting into bed. Long shot.
- •• 0:57—Breasts, getting up and out of bed, then get-ting dressed.
- • 1:02—Breasts and buns, tied up on top of freight el-evator.
- • 1:05—Breasts on top of elevator.
- • 1:17—Breasts on top of elevator fighting with the killer. Lit with red light.

Listen to Me (1989) . . . . . . . . . . . . . . . . . . Fountain Girl

Instant Karma (1990) . . . . . . . . . . . . . . . . . . . . . . .Amy

Lunatics: A Love Story (1991) . . . . . . . . . . . . . .Blonde

# • Singer, Linda

*Films:*

Zombie Nightmare (1987) . . . . . . . . . . . . . . . . Maggie

Whispers (1989) . . . . . . . . . . . . . . . . . . . . . .Prostitute

**Return to Frogtown** (1992) . . . . . . . . . . .Nurse Cloris
*a.k.a. Frogtown II*
- 0:48—Buns, in sexy outfit in room with Robert D'Zar.
- • 0:50—Brief top of breasts, sticking out of her top while she's on top of D'Zar.

*Video Tapes:*

**Ultimate Sensual Massage** (1991). . . . . . .Awakening
- ••• 0:02—Breasts and buns, during massage session in bed.

# Singer, Lori

Sister of actor Marc Singer.

*Films:*

Footloose (1984) . . . . . . . . . . . . . . . . . . . . Ariel Moore

The Falcon and the Snowman (1985). . . . . . . . . . Lana

The Man With One Red Shoe (1985) . . . . . . . . .Maddy

**Trouble in Mind** (1986) . . . . . . . . . . . . . . . . .Georgia
- • 1:01—Very brief left breast, in bed with Kris Kristof-ferson.

**Summer Heat** (1987) . . . . . . . . . . . . . . . . . . . . Roxy
- •• 0:36—Breasts in bed with Jack. Kind of dark and hard to see.

**Made in U.S.A.** (1988) . . . . . . . . . . . . . . . . . . . .Annie
- • 0:26—Brief left breast and very brief lower frontal nudity in the back of a convertible with Dar at night.
- 0:44—In white, braless tank top talking to a used car salesman.

Warlock (1990) . . . . . . . . . . . . . . . . . . . . . . Kassandra

Equinox (1992) . . . . . . . . . . . . . . . . . . . . . Sharon Ace

**Sunset Grill** (1992) . . . . . . . . . . . . . . . . . . . . .Loren
- •• 0:57—Breasts, taking off bra and putting on robe.

- 0:58—Brief full frontal nudity sitting down in open robe. Left breast, while sitting down in tub.
- ••• 0:59—Breasts and buns, with Peter Weller in bathtub.
- ••• 1:15—Breasts, sitting up in bed after making love with Weller. Covered with sweat.

**Short Cuts** (1993) . . . . . . . . . . . . . . . Zoe Trainer
- •• 0:48—Nude, stripping out of her clothes, then jumping in pool and floating. Seen through a fence.

*Made for TV Movies:*
Storm and Sorrow (1990) . . . . . . . . . . . Molly Higgins
*TV:*
Fame (1982-83) . . . . . . . . . . . . . . . . . Julie Miller

## Sirtis, Marina

*Films:*
**The Wicked Lady** (1983; British) . . . . . . Jackson's Girl
- ••• 1:06—Full frontal nudity in and getting out of bed when Faye Dunaway discovers her in bed with Alan Bates.
- ••• 1:20—Breasts getting whipped by Dunaway during their fight during Bates' hanging.

**Blind Date** (1984) . . . . . . . . . . . . . . . . . . . . Hooker
*a.k.a. Deadly Seduction*
(Not the same 1987 *Blind Date* with Bruce Willis.)
- ••• 0:21—Breasts walking to and lying in bed just before taxi driver kills her.

**Death Wish III** (1985) . . . . . . . . . . . . . . . . . Maria
- • 0:42—Breasts getting blouse ripped open next to a car by the bad guys.
- • 0:43—More breasts on mattress at the bad guy's hangout.

Waxwork II: Lost in Time (1991) . . . . . . . . . . . . Gloria
*TV:*
Star Trek: The Next Generation (1987- )
. . . . . . . . . . . . . . . . . . . . . Counselor Deanna Troi

## Sissons, Kimber

*Films:*
You Can't Hurry Love (1984) . . . . . . . . . . . . . Brenda
0:48—Partial side of right breast in open shirt, bending over to pick up her bra off the coffee table.

**Master of Dragonard Hill** (1987) . . . . . . . Jane Abdee
- •• 0:08—Breasts making love in bed with Richard.

Phantom of the Mall: Eric's Revenge (1988) . . . . . . Suzie
0:14—Briefly in bra, in dressing room on B&W security monitor.

The Adventures of Ford Fairlane (1991) . . . . . . Pussycat
Martial Law II: Undercover (1992) . . . . . . . . . . Celeste
The Opposite Sex ...and How to Live with Them (1992)
. . . . . . . . . . . . . . . . . . . . . . . . . . . . . . . Tracy

*Made for Cable TV:*
**Dream On: The Charlotte Letter** (1991; HBO)
. . . . . . . . . . . . . . . . . . . . Candy Striper #3
- •• 0:06—Breasts several times, getting examined by a doctor while acting in adult film that Martin is watching on TV. (She's the blonde one.)

*TV:*
Sea Hunt (1987-88) . . . . . . . . . . . . . . Jennifer Nelson

## Skinner, Anita

*Films:*
Girlfriends (1978) . . . . . . . . . . . . . . . . . . Anne Munroe
**Sole Survivor** (1982) . . . . . . . . . . . . . . Denise Watson
- • 0:29—Very, very brief right breast in bed with Dr. Richardson. Brief side view of right breast when he jumps out of bed.
1:13—In bra, zipping up pants.

## Skinner, Rainee

*Films:*
**Rebel** (1985; Australian) . . . . . . . . . . Prostitute in bed
- • 0:37—Brief breasts sitting up in bed.
Kiss the Night (1988; Australian) . . . . . . . . . . . . . n.a.
Pandemonium (1988) . . . . . . . . . . . . . . . . . . . . n.a.

## • Skobline, Irene

*Films:*
**Clean Slate** (1981; French) . . . . . . . . . . . . . . . . Anne
*a.k.a. Coup de Torchon*
- •• 1:07—Breasts, while taking a shower and getting spied on by Nono.
Summer (1986; French) . . . . . . . . . . . . . . . . . . . n.a.
*a.k.a. Le Rayon Vert*
*a.k.a. The Green Ray*

## • Skorohodove, Elena

*Films:*
Svidanie Na Mlechnom Puti (1987; U.S.S.R.) . . . . . . n.a.
**Hit the Dutchman** (1992) . . . . . . . . . . . . . Anastasia
(Unrated version reviewed.)
- •• 1:17—Breasts, making love with Arthur in bedroom.
- ••• 1:19—Nude, making love in bed with Arthur and afterwards.
- •• 1:23—Breasts in bed with Arthur.
Killer Instinct (1992) . . . . . . . . . . . . . . . . . . . . Baby
*a.k.a. Mad Dog Coll*

## Skriver, Ina

*Films:*
**Emily** (1976; British) . . . . . . . . . . . . . . . . Augustine
- ••• 0:43—Breasts getting into the shower with Koo Stark to give her a massage.
Victor/Victoria (1982) . . . . . . . . . . . . . Simone Kallisto

## Skye, Ione

a.k.a. Ione Skye Leitch.
Daughter of '60s singer Donovan Leitch.
Wife of Beastie Boy Adam Horovitz.
*Films:*
A Night in the Life of Jimmy Reardon (1987)
. . . . . . . . . . . . . . . . . . . . . . . . Denise Hunter
River's Edge (1987) . . . . . . . . . . . . . . . . . . . Clarissa
Stranded (1987) . . . . . . . . . . . . . . . . . Deirdre Clark
**The Rachel Papers** (1989; British) . . . . . . . . . . Rachel
- •• 0:58—Breasts getting undressed and into bed with Charles. Long shot, then breasts in bed.
- ••• 1:03—Brief breasts in three scenes. From above in bathtub, in bed and in bathtub again.

- •• 1:04—Left breast, making love sitting up with Charles.
- • 1:06—Brief breasts sitting up in bathtub.
- • 1:08—Brief breasts long shot getting dressed in Charles' room.
- • 1:28—Brief breasts kissing Charles in bed during his flashback.

Say Anything (1989) . . . . . . . . . . . . . . . . . Diane Court
Mindwalk (1991) . . . . . . . . . . . . . . . . . . . . . . . . Kit
Samantha (1991) . . . . . . . . . . . . . . . . . . . . . Elaine
**Gas Food Lodging** (1992) . . . . . . . . . . . . . . . . .Trudi
- ••• 0:38—Breasts, taking off her blouse in a cave with her boyfriend, then making love.
- • 0:40—Brief right breast, while sitting up.

Wayne's World (1992). . . . . . . . . . . . . . . . . . . . . Elyse
*Made for Cable Movies:*
Guncrazy (1992; Showtime) . . . . . . . . . . . . . . . . Joy
**Rebel Highway: Girls in Prison** (1994; Showtime)
. . . . . . . . . . . . . . . . . . . . . . . . . . . . . . . . . . . . Carol
- • 0:23—Right breast, while in the showers with Melba.
- • 1:02—Very, very brief breasts, while washing Melba's back in the showers.

*Made for Cable TV:*
Nightmare Classics: Carmilla (1989; HBO) . . . . . . Marie
*TV:*
Covington Cross (1992-93). . . . . . . . . . . . . . . Eleanor

## Slater, Helen

*Films:*
Supergirl (1984; British) . . . . . . . . . .Linda Lee/Supergirl
The Legend of Billie Jean (1985) . . . . . . . . . . Billie Jean
    0:06—Brief wet T-shirt getting out of pond.
Ruthless People (1986) . . . . . . . . . . . . . . Sandy Kessler
The Secret of My Success (1987). . . . . . . . . . . . Christy
**Happy Together** (1988) . . . . . . Alexandra "Alex" Page
- •• 0:17—Brief right breast changing clothes while talking to Patrick Dempsey. Unfortunately, she has a goofy expression on her face.
    0:57—In red lingerie tempting Dempsey. Later, panties under panty hose when Dempsey pulls her dress up while she's on roller skates.
    1:07—Very brief panties under panty hose again straddling Dempsey in the hallway.
    1:14—Panties under white stockings while changing in the closet.

Sticky Fingers (1988). . . . . . . . . . . . . . . . . . . . Hattie
City Slickers (1991) . . . . . . . . . . . . . . . Bonnie Rayburn
**Betrayal of the Dove** (1992) . . . . . . . . . . . . . . . .Ellie
- • 0:29—Brief tip of right breast while in bed with Billy Zane.
- •• 0:30—Brief right breast, while in pool with Zane. Brief breasts in bed, then left breast.
- ••• 0:31—Very, very brief breasts, then more breasts while in bed with Zane.

**A House in the Hills** (1993) . . . . . . . . . . Alex Weaver
- ••• 0:15—Breasts, while in bedroom in front of mirror, trying on various lingerie. Very nice!

0:36—Sort of breasts, in shower when Michael Madsen brings her a dress. Shower door is too fogged up to see anything.
*Made for Cable Movies:*
Chantilly Lace (1993; Showtime) . . . . . . . . . . . Hannah
Parallel Lives (1994; Showtime) . . . . . . . Elsa Freedman
*Made for Cable TV:*
Dream On: Theory of Relativity (1992; HBO) . . . . .Sarah
*Made for TV Movies:*
12:01 (1993) . . . . . . . . . . . . . . . . . . . . . . . . . . Lisa
*TV:*
Capital News (1990) . . . . . . . . . . . . . . . Anne McKenna
The Great Air Race (Australian). . . . Jacqueline Cochrane

## Slater, Suzanne

a.k.a. Suzee Slater.
*Films:*
**Savage Streets** (1985). . . . . . . . . . . . . . . Uncredited
- •• 0:09—Breasts being held by jerks when they yank her tube top down.

**Chopping Mall** (1986). . . . . . . . . . . . . . . . . . .Leslie
*a.k.a. Killbots*
- •• 0:28—Brief breasts in bed showing breasts to Mike.
    0:31—Walking around the mall in panties and a blouse.

**Real Men** (1987) . . . . . . . . . . . . . . . . . .Woman in Bed
- • 0:07—Brief left breast, in bed with James Belushi.

**Take Two** (1988) . . . . . . . . . . . . . . . . . . . . . .Sherrie
- •• 0:11—Breasts in office talking with Grant Goodeve, wearing panties, garter belt and stockings.
- • 1:00—Breasts undressing to get into hot tub wearing black underwear bottom.

The Big Picture (1989) . . . . . . . . . . . . . . . Stewardess
**Cartel** (1990) . . . . . . . . . . . . . . . . . . . . . . . . Nancy
    0:28—In red two piece swimsuit modeling on motorcycle.
    0:35—Brief bra and panties on bed during struggle.
- • 0:36—Breasts during brutal rape/murder scene.

**Mind Twister** (1992) . . . . . . . . . . . . . . Heather Black
(Unrated version reviewed.)
- ••• 0:17—Breasts and partial buns, while making love on sofa with Roy. Long scene.
- • 0:39—Inside half of left breast in open robe when pizza delivery guy sees her.
    0:54—In pink bra and panties in S&M room with Lisa.
- ••• 0:56—Breasts and buns, while in bed with Lisa while getting videotaped by Daniel. A little bit of fluorescent paint added to her breasts for color. Great!

*Magazines:*
**Playboy** (Jul 1989) . . . . . . . . . . . . . . B-Movie Bimbos
- •• 137—Full frontal nudity lying on a car wearing a girdle and stockings.

**Playboy** (Oct 1993) . . . . . . . . . . . . . . . . . . Grapevine
- • 171—Partial left breast in B&W photo.

## • Slavens, Darla

Films:

Class of Nuke 'Em High Part II: Subhumanoid Meltdown (1991)...................... Plain White Rapper
**Married People, Single Sex** (1993) .......... Fran
•• 0:03—In white bra and buns in panties while undressing in bedroom. Full frontal nudity, walking to closet.
•• 0:10—In white bra, then breasts while undressing in bedroom.
••• 0:53—Left breast in mirror, while trying out vibrator.

## Sloan, Tiffany

Video Tapes:

**Playboy Video Centerfold: Tiffany Sloan** (1992)
................................ Playmate
••• 0:00—Nude in the desert.
•• 0:02—Buns, in aqueduct.
••• 0:03—Nude in factory with fire and ice.
••• 0:09—Nude in warehouse gymnastics and dance routine. Nice.
••• 0:12—Nude in still photos.
••• 0:15—Nude in warehouse song and dance routine.
••• 0:18—Nude in bed in fantasy scene with a guy.
••• 0:23—Nude in the desert.
**Sexy Lingerie V** (1992) ...................Model
**Playboy Video Calendar 1994** (1993) ........ May
••• 0:19—Nude in bathtub in the desert.
••• 0:20—Nude in ballet/dance number in warehouse.
**Playboy's Erotic Fantasies II** (1993) ........Model
**Playboy's Playmate Review 1993** (1993)
................................ Miss October
•• 0:48—Lower nudity, while in aqueduct.
••• 0:50—Nude in fire and ice fantasy segment.
Playboy Video Centerfold: Jenny McCarthy (1994)
.............................. Angel/Nurse
**Wet and Wild: The Locker Room** (1994)
.............................. Playmate

Magazines:

**Playboy** (Oct 1992).................... Playmate
••• 102-113—Nude.
**Playboy's Playmate Review** (Jun 1993) .... October
••• 84-91—Nude.
**Playboy's Girls of Summer '93** (Jun 1993)... Herself
••• 4—Full frontal nudity.
**Playboy** (Jul 1993)....................Lucky Stiff
•• 78-83—Nude.
**Playboy's Blondes, Brunettes & Redheads**
(Sep 1993) ......................... Herself
••• 12—Buns and right breast.
**Playboy's Book of Lingerie** (Sep 1993) ..... Herself
••• 77—Full frontal nudity.
••• 85—Breasts.
**Playboy's Book of Lingerie** (Nov 1993) ..... Herself
••• 4-7—Full frontal nudity.
••• 92—Full frontal nudity.
**Playboy's Nudes** (Dec 1993) ............. Herself
••• 22-23—Full frontal nudity.
••• 70-73—Nude.

**Playboy's Book of Lingerie** (Jan 1994) ...... Herself
••• 61—Full frontal nudity.
**Playboy's Bathing Beauties** (Mar 1994) ..... Herself
••• 27—Full frontal nudity.
**Playboy's Book of Lingerie** (Mar 1994)...... Herself
••• 44—Breasts and partial lower frontal nudity.
**Playboy's Girls of Summer '94** (Jul 1994).... Herself
••• 23—Full frontal nudity.
**Playboy's Book of Lingerie** (Jul 1994)....... Herself
••• 70—Breasts.
**Playboy's Book of Lingerie** (Sep 1994) ...... Herself
••• 8—Full frontal nudity.
•• 36-37—Buns.
••• 69—Full frontal nudity.

## Sloatman, Lala

a.k.a. Lala.

Films:

Watchers (1988) ......................... Tracey
Joe vs. the Volcano (1990) ................Waitress
The Adventures of Ford Fairlane (1991) .... Sorority Girl
**Amityville: A New Generation** (1993) .......Lianie
•• 0:14—Breasts, undressing and making love with Keyes.
Dragon: The Bruce Lee Story (1993) .... Sherry Schnell

## Small, Marya

Films:

Sleeper (1973)......................... Dr. Nero
**One Flew Over the Cuckoo's Nest** (1975).... Candy
• 1:00—Very brief side view of left breast, bending over to pick up her clothes on boat.
The Wild Party (1975) ..................... Bertha
The Great Smokey Roadblock (1976)........... Alice
The World's Greatest Lover (1977).............. n.a.
Thank God It's Friday (1978) ................Jackie
Fade to Black (1980) ..................... Doreen
National Lampoon's Class Reunion (1982) ... Iris Augen
Zapped! (1982) ................. Mrs. Springboro

## Smax, Honey

Films:

**Totally Exposed** (1991)....................Linda
•• 0:41—Full frontal nudity, taking off towel in massage room.
**Pleasure in Paradise** (1992)...............Sandra
••• 0:14—Breasts in lingerie, while making love in bed with Hansen. Long scene.
••• 0:57—Nude in pool, while making love with Hansen, then getting out. Long scene.
Good Girls Don't (1993) ....................Lolita

## Smith Bouchér, Savannah

Films:

Five Days from Home (1978) ........ Georgie Haskin
**North Dallas Forty** (1979) ...............Joanne
• 0:27—Very brief breasts in bed tossing around with Nick Nolte.
The Long Riders (1980) ....................... Zee

Meet the Applegates (1989) . . . . . . . . . . . . . . . .Dottie
Eating (1990) . . . . . . . . . . . . . . . . . . . . . . . . . Eloise
**Relentless 3** (1992). . . . . . . . . . . . . . . . . . Marianne
• 0:10—Very brief breast when Walter starts to kiss it.
0:36—In black bra, then in white bra, while sitting in
chair, getting photographed by Walter.
Scanner Cop (1993) . . . . . . . . . . . . Margaret Harrigan

## Smith, Amanda

*Films:*
Dancing In the Dark (1986; Canadian) . . . . . . Neighbor
**Fall From Innocence** (1988) . . . . . . . . Janis Cummins
• 0:05—Brief right breast while lying in bed when Bob
gets out.
• 0:48—Left breast, in open nightie top, while walking
down hallway.
0:52—Very brief side view of right breast standing
up from the bed.
The Freshman (1990) . . . . . . . . . . . . . . . .Mall Patron

## • Smith, Amber

*Made for Cable TV:*
**Red Shoe Diaries: Runway** (1994; Showtime) . . .Alia
•• 0:02—Brief breasts, while sitting in front of mirror
with her lover.
••• 0:20—Breasts, buns and brief lower frontal nudity
while making love with Miguel while two hookers
watch. Great!
• 0:23—Breasts, while lying on top of Miguel.
*Video Tapes:*
Sports Illustrated: The 1993 Swimsuit Video (1993)
. . . . . . . . . . . . . . . . . . . . . . . . . . . . . . . .Model
*Magazines:*
Sports Illustrated (Feb 14, 1994)
. . . . . . . . . . . . . . . . . . . . . . . Everybody Into the Pool

## Smith, Anna Nicole

a.k.a. Vickie Smith.
Model for *Guess?* jeans.
*Films:*
Naked Gun 33 1/3: The Final Insult (1993) . . . . . . Tanya
The Hudsucker Proxy (1994). . . . . . . . . . . . . . . . . .n.a.
*Music Videos:*
Will You Love Me Tomorrow/Bryan Ferry. . . . . . . . .n.a.
*Video Tapes:*
**Playboy Video Calendar 1993** (1992) . . . . . .January
•• 0:02—Breasts and buns during Country music number.
••• 0:03—Nude in outdoor Western setting by campfire.
**Playboy Video Centerfold: Tiffany Sloan** (1992)
. . . . . . . . . . . . . . . . . . . . . . . . Playmate Profile
••• 0:26—Nude in country bar.
••• 0:28—Nude at the beach.
••• 0:29—Nude in still photos.
••• 0:30—Nude in bed in Victorian fantasy.
••• 0:32—Nude, dancing in front of male body builders.
••• 0:34—Nude in campfire setting.

**Playboy Video Calendar 1994** (1993). . . . . . January
••• 0:04—Full frontal nudity, in country setting, washing herself and rolling around in the hay. B&W.
**Playboy's Playmate Review 1993** (1993)
. . . . . . . . . . . . . . . . . . . . . . . . . . . . . . .Miss May
••• 0:23—Breasts and buns, while at the beach.
••• 0:25—Nude, posing with male bodybuilders.
••• 0:26—Nude in Victorian style fantasy.
*Magazines:*
**Playboy** (May 1992). . . . . . . . . . . . . . . . . . . Playmate
••• 90-101—Nude.
**Playboy** (Dec 1992) . . . . . . . . . . . . . . . .Sex Stars 1992
••• 189—Breasts.
**Playboy's Playmate Review** (Jun 1993). . . . . . . .May
••• 40-49—Nude.
**Playboy** (Jun 1993). . . . . . . . . . . . Playmate of the Year
••• 130-139—Nude.
**Playboy's Blondes, Brunettes & Redheads**
(Sep 1993). . . . . . . . . . . . . . . . . . . . . . . . . . .Herself
•• 7—Breasts.
**Playboy's Nudes** (Dec 1993) . . . . . . . . . . . . . . Herself
••• 4—Full frontal nudity.
**Playboy** (Dec 1993) . . . . . . . . . . . . . . . .Sex Stars 1993
••• 174—Right breast and lower frontal nudity.
**Playboy** (Jan 1994). . . . . . . . . . . . 40 Memorable Years
••• 95—Full frontal nudity.
**Playboy** (Feb 1994)
. . . . . . . . . . . . . .My Sudsy Valentine/The Year in Sex
••• 66-75—Nude.
••• 117—Breasts.
**Playboy's Bathing Beauties** (Mar 1994) . . . . .Herself
• 5—Partial lower frontal nudity in wet swimsuit.

## Smith, Cheryl

a.k.a. Rainbeaux Smith.
*Films:*
Evel Knievel (1972). . . . . . . . . . . . . . . . . . . . . . . . n.a.
**Video Vixens** (1973) . . . . . . . . . . . . .Twinkle Twat Girl
••• 0:24—Full frontal nudity doing a commercial, sitting
next to pool.
**Caged Heat** (1974) . . . . . . . . . . . . . . . . . . . . . .Lavelle
*a.k.a. Renegade Girls*
• 0:04—Brief left breast, dreaming in her jail cell that
a guy is caressing her through the bars.
•• 0:25—Breasts in the shower scene.
•• 0:50—Brief nude in the solitary cell.
**The Swinging Cheerleaders** (1974) . . . . . . . .Andrea
•• 0:12—Breasts taking off her bra and putting sheer
blouse on.
• 0:17—Left breast, several times, sitting in bed with
Ross.
**Farewell, My Lovely** (1975; British). . . . . . . . . . Doris
• 0:56—Frontal nudity in bedroom in a bordello with
another guy before getting beaten by the madam.
**Drum** (1976). . . . . . . . . . . . . . . . . . . . . Sophie Maxwell
•• 0:54—Breasts in the stable trying to get Yaphet Kot-
to to make love with her.

**Massacre at Central High** (1976) . . . . . . . . . . . Mary
- • 0:27—Brief breasts in a classroom getting attacked by some guys.
- ••• 1:09—Nude walking around on a mountain side with Robert Carradine and Lani O'Grady.

**The Pom Pom Girls** (1976) . . . . . . . . . . . . . Roxanne
- • 1:02—Very brief breasts, taking off her dress in locker room while talking to Judy.
- • 1:03—Brief breasts, while putting her cheerleader top on.

**Revenge of the Cheerleaders** (1976) . . . . . . Heather
- • 0:00—Brief breasts changing tops in back of car. (Blonde on the far right.)
  0:28—Buns, in shower room scene.
  0:36—Full frontal nudity, but covered with bubbles.

Slumber Party '57 (1976) . . . . . . . . . . . . . . . . . . Sherry
The Choirboys (1977) . . . . . . . . . . . . . . . . . . . . . Tammy
**Cinderella** (1977) . . . . . . . . . . . . . . . . . . . . Cinderella
- •• 0:03—Breasts dancing and singing.
- ••• 0:30—Frontal nudity getting "washed" by her sisters for the Royal Ball.
- •• 0:34—Breasts in the forest during a dream.
- ••• 0:41—Breasts taking a bath. Frontal nudity drying herself off.
- • 1:16—Brief breasts with the Prince.
- • 1:30—Brief left breast after making love with the Prince to prove it was her.
- • 1:34—Brief side view of left breast making love in the Prince's carriage.

The Incredible Melting Man (1977) . . . . . . . . . . . Model
Laserblast (1978) . . . . . . . . . . . . . . . . . . . . . . . . Kathy
Up in Smoke (1978) . . . . . . . . . . . . . . Laughing Lady
**The Best of Sex and Violence** (1981) . . . . . Cinderella
- • 0:14—Breasts taking a bath in scene from *Cinderella*.

Cheech & Chong's Nice Dreams (1981)
. . . . . . . . . . . . . . . . . . . . . . . . . . . Blondie Group #1
**Parasite** (1982) . . . . . . . . . . . . . . . . . . . . Captive Girl
- •• 0:08—Breasts tied by wrists in kitchen.
- •• 0:12—Breasts knocking gun out of guy's hands standing behind fence.

Vice Squad (1982) . . . . . . . . . . . . . . . White Prostitute
*Magazines:*
**Penthouse** (May 1976)
. . . . . . . . . . . . . . . . . Easy Riders/Uncredited Woman
- ••• 62-71—Nude with a guy after horseback riding.

# Smith, Crystal
*Films:*
**Hot Dog... The Movie** (1984) . . . . . . . . . Motel Clerk
- •• 0:10—Nude getting out of spa and going to the front desk to sign people in.

*Magazines:*
**Playboy** (Sep 1971) . . . . . . . . . . . . . . . . . . Playmate

# Smith, Donna
*Video Tapes:*
Playmate Playoffs . . . . . . . . . . . . . . . . . . . . Playmate
**Playboy Video Calendar 1987** (1986) . . . . Playmate
**Playmates at Play** (1990) . . . . . . . . . . . . . . . Hoops

*Magazines:*
**Playboy** (Mar 1985) . . . . . . . . . . . . . . . . . . . Playmate
**Playboy's Girls of Summer '86** (Aug 1986) . . . Herself
- ••• 9—Full frontal nudity with hands over the upper half of her breasts.
- ••• 14-15—Breasts and buns.
- ••• 104-105—Full frontal nudity.

**Playboy's 1987 Book of Lingerie** (Mar 1987)
. . . . . . . . . . . . . . . . . . . . . . . . . . . . . . . . . . . . . Herself
- •• 25—Left breast and lower frontal nudity.
- ••• 80-81—Full frontal nudity.
- • 97—Buns.

**Playboy's Book of Lingerie** (Jan 1992) . . . . . . Herself
- •• 77—Buns and tip of left breast.

**Playboy's Calendar Playmates** (Nov 1992) . . . Herself
- •• 52—Buns and left breast.

# Smith, Julie Kristen
*Films:*
**Pretty Smart** (1986) . . . . . . . . Samantha Falconwright
- •• 0:20—Nude in her room when Daphne sees her.
- •• 0:26—Breasts in bed talking to Jennifer.
- •• 0:40—Breasts in bed.
- •• 0:52—Breasts sitting in lounge by the pool.
- • 0:57—Brief left breast, while brushing teeth.
- • 1:10—Brief right breast, while making love with boyfriend in bed.
- • 1:13—More brief right breast.
- ••• 1:14—Nude, sitting on pillow on top of her boyfriend in bed.

**Disorderlies** (1987) . . . . . . . . . . . . . Skinny Dipper #2
- • 0:56—Brief breasts and buns walking around near pool. Long shot.

Mankillers (1987) . . . . . . . . . . . . . . . . High School Girl
**Angel III: The Final Chapter** (1988) . . . . . . . Darlene
- ••• 0:40—Breasts during caveman shoot with a brunette girl.
- ••• 0:44—Breasts again dancing in caveman shoot.

*Video Tapes:*
**Penthouse Ready to Ride** (1992) . . . . . . . . . . Model
Score with Chicks (1992) . . . . . . . . . . . . . Cast Member
**Making of the "Carousel Girls' Calendar"** (1993) .
Miss February
- ••• 0:16—Breasts during photo shoot.
- ••• 0:19—Nude during interview segment.

**Penthouse's 25th Anniversary Swimsuit Video**
(1993) . . . . . . . . . . . . . . . . . . . . . . . . . . . . . . . . . Pet
**Playboy's Secret Confessions** (1993)
. . . . . . . . . . . . . . . . . . . High School Reunion/Deanna
- ••• 0:04—Breasts in house and in bed while making love with her old high school friend.

*CD-ROM:*
**Penthouse Interactive Virtual Photo Shoot, Disc 2**
(1993) . . . . . . . . . . . . . . . . . . . . . . . . . . . . . . . . . Pet
*Magazines:*
**Penthouse** (Feb 1993) . . . . . . . . . . . . . . . . . . . . Pet
- ••• 69-81—Nude.

## Smith, Laurie

Adult film actress.

*Films:*

**Paradise Motel** (1985) . . . . . . . . . . Honeymoon Wife
••• 0:02—Left breast, then breasts in Honeymoon Suite with her new husband, then making love in bed.

*Video Tapes:*

Nudes in Limbo (1983) . . . . . . . . . . . . . . . . . . . .Model

## Smith, Linda

*Films:*

Hardcore (1979) . . . . . . . . . . . Hope (Mistress Victoria)
**The Beastmaster** (1982) . . . . . . . . . . . . .Kiri's Friend
• 0:35—Breasts in a pond with Tanya Roberts.

## Smith, Madeline

*Films:*

The Killing of Sister George (1968) . . . . . . . . . . . . . Nun
Taste the Blood of Dracula (1970) . . . . . . . . . . . . . .Dolly
**Vampire Lovers** (1970; British) . . . . . . . . . . . . . .Emma
•• 0:32—Breasts trying on a dress in the bedroom after Carmilla has taken a bath.
• 0:49—Breasts in bed, getting her top pulled down by Carmilla.
Carry On Matron (1971) . . . . . . . . . . . . . . . Mrs. Pullitt
**Up Pompeii** (1971; British) . . . . . . . . . . . . . . . Erotica
Frankenstein and The Monster From Hell (1973) . . Sarah
Live and Let Die (1973; British) . . . . . . . . . Miss Caruso
Bawdy Adventures of Tom Jones (1976; British) . . Sophia

*TV:*

Doctor in the House (1970-73) . . . . . . . . . . . . . . Nurse

## Smith, Maggie

*Films:*

The Prime of Miss Jean Brodie (1969) . . . . . . Jean Brodie
(Academy Award for Best Actress.)
**California Suite** (1978) . . . . . . . . . . . . . Diana Barrie
(Academy Award for Best Supporting Actress.)
• 1:05—Very brief side of left breast, putting night-gown on over her head.
Clash of the Titans (1981) . . . . . . . . . . . . . . . . . Thetis
Quartet (1981; British/French) . . . . . . . . . . . . . . . .Lois
Lily in Love (1985) . . . . . . . . . . . . . . . . . . . Lily Wynn
A Private Function (1985) . . . . . . . . . . . . .Joyce Chilvers
A Room with a View (1986; British) . . . Charlotte Bartlett
The Lonely Passion of Judith Hearne (1988)
. . . . . . . . . . . . . . . . . . . . . . . . . Judith Hearne
Hook (1991) . . . . . . . . . . . . . . . . . . . . Granny Wendy
Sister Act (1992) . . . . . . . . . . . . . . . . . Mother Superior
The Secret Garden (1993) . . . . . . . . . . . . Mrs. Medlock
Sister Act 2: Back in the Habit (1993) . . Mother Superior

## Smith, Martha

*Films:*

Animal House (1978) . . . . . . . . . . . . . . . . Babs Jansen
**Blood Link** (1983) . . . . . . . . . . . . . . . . . . . . .Hedwig
•• 0:41—Breasts, wearing black panties while in bed with Keith.

•• 0:43—Brief breasts, while kneeling on bed, talking to Keith.
• 0:48—Right breast, while sitting in bed and talking. Shadow and scarf get in the way. Brief breasts.
• 0:49—Breasts, while getting slapped around by Keith.
••• 0:51—Breasts sitting up in bed when Craig and Keith meet each other for the first time.
• 1:13—Breasts, wearing red panties, with Keith before he kills her.
• 1:14—Brief buns, covered with blood when discovered by policemen.

*TV:*

Scarecrow and Mrs. King (1983-87)
. . . . . . . . . . . . . . . . . . . . . . . . .Francine Desmond

*Magazines:*

**Playboy** (Jul 1973) . . . . . . . . . . . . . . . . . . . . Playmate
••• 106-113—Full frontal nudity.

## Smith, Melanie

*Films:*

**The Baby Doll Murders** (1992) . . . . . . . .Peggy Davis
••• 0:09—Breasts, while taking off her blouse and getting into hot tub with Jeff Kober.
•• 0:10—Breasts in hot tub with Kober. Fence gets in the way.
•• 0:11—Breasts, getting out of the hot tub.
•• 0:46—Breasts in hot tub with Kober while making out.
Molly & Gina (1993) . . . . . . . . . . . . . . . . . . . . . n.a.
Trancers III (1993) . . . . . . . . . . . . . . . . . . . . . . .R.J.

*Made for TV Movies:*

Green Dolphin Beat (1994) . . . . . . . . . .Linda Rodriguez

## Smith, Rainbeaux

See: Smith, Cheryl.

## Smith, Vickie

See: Smith, Anna Nicole.

## Smith, Yeardley

*Films:*

Heaven Help Us (1985) . . . . . . . . . . . . . . . . . Cathleen
The Legend of Billie Jean (1985) . . . . . . . . . . . . . Putter
Maximum Overdrive (1986) . . . . . . . . . . . . . . . . Lonnie
**Ginger Ale Afternoon** (1989) . . . . . . .Bonnie Cleator
• 0:53—Brief upper half of left breast, taking off top in trailer with Hank.
Listen to Me (1989) . . . . . . . . . . . . . . . . . . . . . Cootz
City Slickers (1991) . . . . . . . . . . . . . . . . . . . . . Nancy
Toys (1992) . . . . . . . . . . . . . . . . . . . . . . .Researcher

*TV:*

The Simpsons (1989- ) . . . . . . . . . Voice of Lisa Simpson
Herman's Head (1991- ) . . . . . . . . . . . . . . .Louise Fitzer

# Snodgress, Carrie

*Films:*

**Diary of a Mad Housewife** (1970) . . . . . . Tina Balser
- ••• 0:01—Breasts taking off nightgown and getting dressed, putting on white bra while Richard Benjamin talks to her.
  0:36—Buns and brief side view of left breast, while kissing Frank Langella.
- • 0:41—Very brief breasts lying on floor when Langella pulls the blanket up.
- • 0:54—Breasts lying in bed with Langella.
  1:03—In white bra and panties getting dressed in Langella's apartment.
  1:10—In white bra and panties in Langella's apartment again.
- ••• 1:21—Breasts in the shower with Langella, then drying herself off.

The Fury (1978) . . . . . . . . . . . . . . . . . . . . . . . . . Hester
Homework (1982). . . . . . . . . . . . . . . . . . . . Dr. Delingua
Trick or Treats (1982) . . . . . . . . . . . . . . . . . . . . . Joan
A Night in Heaven (1983). . . . . . . . . . . . . Mrs. Johnson
Pale Rider (1985). . . . . . . . . . . . . . . . . . Sarah Wheeler
Murphy's Law (1986) . . . . . . . . . . . . . . . . Joan Freeman
Across the Tracks (1990) . . . . . . . . . . Rosemary Maloney
Mission of the Shark (1991) . . . . . . . . . . . . . . . . . . n.a.
The Ballad of Little Jo (1993). . . . . . . . . . . . Ruth Badger
*Made for TV Movies:*
Woman with a Past (1992) . . . . . . . . . . . . . . . . Florence

# Snyder, Susan Marie

*Films:*

**Sleepaway Camp II: Unhappy Campers** (1988)
. . . . . . . . . . . . . . . . . . . . . . . . . . . . . . . . . . . . . . . Mare
- • 0:08—Brief breasts lifting up her T-shirt.
- • 0:24—Brief breasts flashing in boy's cabin.
- • 0:33—Breasts in Polaroid photograph that Angela confiscates from the boys.

*TV:*

As the World Turns . . . . . . . . . . . . . . . . . . Julie Wendall
Santa Barbara . . . . . . . . . . . . . . . . . . . . . Laken Capwell

# Snyder, Suzanne

*Films:*

The Oasis (1984). . . . . . . . . . . . . . . . . . . . . . . . . Jennifer
Remo Williams: The Adventure Begins (1985)
. . . . . . . . . . . . . . . . . . . . . . . . . . . Nurse/Soap Opera
Weird Science (1985) . . . . . . . . . . . . . . . . . . . . . . . Deb
Night of the Creeps (1986). . . . . . . . . . . . . . . . . . . Lisa
Pretty Kill (1987). . . . . . . . . . . . . . . . Franci/Stella/Paul
Killer Klowns from Outer Space (1988) . . . . . . . . Debbie
The Night Before (1988) . . . . . . . . . . . . . . . . . . . . . Lisa
Retribution (1988) . . . . . . . . . . . . . . . . . . . . . . . . Angel
  0:50—Very, very brief blurry left breast getting up in bed with George after his nightmare.
The Return of the Living Dead II (1988) . . . . . . . Brenda

**Femme Fatale** (1990) . . . . . . . . . . . . . . . . . . . Andrea
- ••• 0:08—Breasts, nonchalantly taking off her top and posing for Billy Zane's painting. (She sometimes has a bag over her head.)
- •• 0:46—Breasts posing again with the bag on and off her head.

# Soares, Alana

*Films:*
Beverly Hills Cop II (1987) . . . . . . . . . Playboy Playmate
*Video Tapes:*
**Playboy Video Magazine, Volume 5** (1983)
. . . . . . . . . . . . . . . . . . . . . . . . . . . . . . . . . . . Playmate
- • 0:06—Brief breasts on chair.
*Magazines:*
**Playboy** (Mar 1983) . . . . . . . . . . . . . . . . . . . . Playmate
**Playboy's Girls of Summer '86** (Aug 1986). . . Herself
- ••• 49-51—Full frontal nudity.
**Playboy's 1987 Book of Lingerie** (Mar 1987)
. . . . . . . . . . . . . . . . . . . . . . . . . . . . . . . . . . . . Herself
- • 72—Upper half of left breast.
**Playboy's Nudes** (Oct 1990) . . . . . . . . . . . . . . Herself
- ••• 72—Breasts.
**Playboy's Book of Lingerie** (Jan 1991) . . . . . . Herself
- •• 18-19—Right breast and lower frontal nudity.
**Playboy's Book of Lingerie** (Mar 1992). . . . . . Herself
- ••• 64—Breasts.
**Playboy's Bathing Beauties** (Apr 1992). . . . . . Herself
- • 79—Half of buns and partial left breast.
**Playboy's Calendar Playmates** (Nov 1992). . . Herself
- ••• 25—Full frontal nudity.
**Playmates at Play** (Jul 1994) . . . . . . . . . . . . . Herself
- ••• 20-23—Full frontal nudity.

# Socas, Maria

*Films:*
**The Warrior and the Sorceress** (1984). . . . . . . Naja
(Breasts in every scene she's in.)
- ••• 0:15—Breasts wearing robe and bikini bottoms in room with Zeg. Sort of brief buns, leaving the room.
- •• 0:22—Breasts standing by a wagon at night.
- •• 0:27—Breasts in room with David Carradine. Dark. Most of buns when leaving the room.
- •• 0:31—Breasts and buns climbing down wall.
- • 0:34—Brief breasts, then left breast with rope around her neck at the well.
- • 0:44—Breasts when Carradine rescues her.
- • 0:47—Breasts walking around outside.
- • 0:57—More breasts outside.
- • 1:00—Breasts watching a guy pound a sword.
- • 1:05—Breasts under a tent after Carradine uses the sword. Long shot.
- • 1:09—Breasts during big fight scene.
- • 1:14—Breasts next to well. Long shot.
Soldier's Revenge (1986) . . . . . . . . . . . . . . . . . . Baetriz
Deathstalker II (1987). . . . . . . . . . . . . . Amazon Queen
  0:50—In see-through nightgown after telling Deathstalker she is going to marry him.
Hollywood Boulevard II (1989). . . . . . . . Amazon Queen

## Søeberg, Camilla

*Films:*
Twist & Shout (1986; Danish). . . . . . . . . . . . . . . .Anna
**Manifesto** (1988) . . . . . . . . . . . . . . . . . . . . . Svetlana
••• 0:15—Nude, in bathtub and bedroom with Emile. Long scene.
• 0:19—Brief left breast when Emile cuts off her hair.
•• 1:04—Left breast, several times when Emile is in her room. More left breast cleaning up after Emile accidentally dies.
• 1:15—Brief side of left breast, while making love with Eric Stoltz. Dark. Buns, getting out of bed.
•• 1:16—Breasts and buns unrolling Emile in the rug.
•• 1:23—Breasts sitting in bed with puppies.

## Solari, Suzanne

*Films:*
**Roller Blade** (1986) . . . . . . . . . . . Sister Sharon Cross
0:04—Buns, in G-string, lying in bed.
• 1:21—Brief upper half of right breast, taking off suit. Buns in G-string.
Hell Comes to Frogtown (1987) . . . . . . . . Runaway Girl
RollerBlade Warriors: Taken By Force (1988)
. . . . . . . . . . . . . . . . . . . . . . . . . . . . .Sharon Crosse
Class of Nuke 'Em High Part II: Subhumanoid Meltdown (1991). . . . . . . . . . . . . . . Toxie Squirrel Gang Member
*Magazines:*
**Playboy** (Apr 1993) . . . . . . . . . . . . . . . . . . . .Grapevine
• 178-179—Lower half of left breast. B&W.

## Soles, P.J.

P.J. stands for Pamela Jane.
Ex-wife of actor Dennis Quaid.
*Films:*
Carrie (1976) . . . . . . . . . . . . . . . . . . . . . . . . . Norma
**Halloween** (1978). . . . . . . . . . . . . . . . . . . . . . .Lynda
• 1:04—Brief right breast, sitting up in bed after making love in bed with Bob.
• 1:07—Brief breasts getting strangled by Michael in the bedroom.
Breaking Away (1979). . . . . . . . . . . . . . . . . . Suzy
Old Boyfriends (1979). . . . . . . . . . . . . . . . . . . Sandy
Rock 'n' Roll High School (1979). . . . . . . . . . Riff Randell
Private Benjamin (1980) . . . . . . . . Private Wanda Winter
Stripes (1981) . . . . . . . . . . . . . . . . . . . . . . . . . Stella
**Terror in the Aisles** (1984) . . . . . . . . . . . . . . .Lynda
• 0:24—Brief breasts in scene from *Halloween.*
Sweet Dreams (1985). . . . . . . . . . . . . . . . . . . Wanda
B.O.R.N. (1988) . . . . . . . . . . . . . . . . . . . . . . . . . Liz
Alienator (1989) . . . . . . . . . . . . . . . . . . . . . . . Tara
Soldier's Fortune (1991) . . . . . . . . . . . . . . . . .Debra
*Magazines:*
**Playboy** (Nov 1981) . . . . . . . . . . . Sex in Cinema 1981
•• 166—Breasts.

## • Somers, Gwen

*Films:*
Faith (1990). . . . . . . . . . . . . . . . . . . . . .Kate Davis
**Alien Intruder** (1992) . . . . . . . . . . . . . . . . . . .Annie
••• 0:19—Breasts, taking off her top in front of Lloyd while he sits in bathtub.
**Anthony's Desire** (1993). . . . . . . . . . . . . . . . . Jessica
••• 0:29—Nude, while lying on bed and talking. Long scene.
••• 1:09—Full frontal nudity, while on bed with Anthony and Desiree sitting next to her.
Good Girls Don't (1993) . . . . . . . . . . . . .Bimbo Betina
**Renegade: Fighting Cage** (1993) . . . . . . . . . . . Lena
(Nudity added for video release.)
• 1:07—Breasts, while making love with a guy a blonde woman in bed.
*Video Tapes:*
**Playboy's How to Reawaken Your Sexual Powers** (1992) . . . . . . . . . . . . . . . . . . . . . . . . .Cast Member
••• 0:21—Full frontal nudity in the forest with her lover.
••• 0:29—Nude on hammock on sailboat with her lover.
**Buck Naked Line Dancing** (1993) . . . . . . . . . Dancer
••• 0:00—Breasts throughout. She's usually in the back in the right, with a bandana in her pocket.
**Playboy's Secret Confessions** (1993)
. . . . . . . . . . . . . . . . . . . . . . . . .Teacher's Pet/Marilyn
•• 0:27—Breasts, while making love in bed with Warren. Full frontal nudity and brief buns, while standing on stairs with Jay.

## Somers, Kristi

*Films:*
Carnival of Love (1983) . . . . . . . . . . . . . . . . . . . . . Kristi
*a.k.a. Inside the Love House*
Rumble Fish (1983) . . . . . . . . . . . . . . . . . . . . . . . n.a.
**Hardbodies** (1984) . . . . . . . . . . . . . . . . . . . . .Michelle
•• 0:53—Nude, dancing on the beach while Ashley plays the guitar and sings.
Girls Just Want to Have Fun (1985). . . . . . . . . . . . .Rikki
**Mugsy's Girls** (1985) . . . . . . . . . . . . . . . . . . . . . Laurie
• 0:15—Brief breasts several times while mud wrestling.
•• 0:29—Breasts and buns in bathtub on bus.
• 0:34—Brief breasts holding up sign to get truck driver to stop.
Savage Streets (1985) . . . . . . . . . . . . . . . . . . .Valerie
0:24—In bra and panties in the locker room.
**Tomboy** (1985) . . . . . . . . . . . . . . . . . . . . . Seville Ritz
•• 0:14—Breasts taking a shower while talking to Betsy Russell.
• 0:53—Brief breasts stripping at a party.
Hell Comes to Frogtown (1987). . . . . . . . . . . . .Arabella
Return to Horror High (1987). . . . . . . . . . .Ginny McCall

# Somers, Suzanne

*Films:*
American Graffiti (1973) . . . . . . The Blonde in the T-bird
**Magnum Force** (1973) . . . . . . . . Uncredited Pool Girl
•• 0:26—In blue swimsuit getting into a swimming
pool, brief breasts a couple of times before getting
shot, brief breasts floating dead.
Yesterday's Hero (1979; British) . . . . . . . . Cloudy Martin
Nothing Personal (1980; Canadian) . . . . . . . . . Abigail
1:07—In wet T-shirt sitting with her feet in a pond
talking with Donald Sutherland.
Serial Mom (1993) . . . . . . . . . . . . . . . . . . . . . Herself
*Made for Cable Movies:*
Seduced by Evil (1994; USA) . . . . . . . . . . . .Lee Lindsay
*Miniseries:*
Hollywood Wives (1988) . . . . . . . . . . . . Gina Germaine
*Made for TV Movies:*
Keeping Secrets (1991) . . . . . . . . . . . . Suzanne Somers
*TV:*
Three's Company (1977-81) . . . . . . . . . . Chrissy Snow
She's the Sheriff (1987-89) . . . . . . Sheriff Hildy Granger
Step by Step (1991- ) . . . . . . . . . . . . . . . . . Carol Foster
*Magazines:*
**Playboy** (Feb 1980) . . . Suzanne Somers' Playmate Test
••• 136-145—Old photos taken before she was famous.
Nude.
**Playboy** (Dec 1984) . . . . . . . . . . . . Suzanne Take Two
••• 120-129—New photos. Breasts and buns.

# Sommer, Elke

*Films:*
**Sweet Ecstasy** (1962) . . . . . . . . . . . . . . . . . . . . . Elke
Nude.
A Shot in the Dark (1964) . . . . . . . . . . Maria Gambrelli
Boy, Did I Get a Wrong Number (1966) . . . . . . . . Didi
The Corrupt Ones (1966) . . . . . . . . . . . . . . . . . . . . Lily
The Oscar (1966) . . . . . . . . . . . . . . . . . . Kay Bergdahl
**The Invincible Six** (1969) . . . . . . . . . . . . . . . . . .Zari
• 0:44—Right breast under wet, skin-colored outfit af-
ter fight in pool.
•• 1:09—Right breast, while tending to her wound.
•• 1:10—Breasts, while making love in the dark.
**The House of Exorcism** (1975) . . . . . . . . . Lisa Reiner
*a.k.a. Lisa and the Devil*
••• 1:10—Breasts, lying on floor when Maximillian
opens her blouse.
Ten Little Indians (1975) . . . . . . . . . . . . . . . . . . . Vera
**Left for Dead** (1978) . . . . . . . . Magdalene Krushcen
•• 0:38—Left breast, while posing for photographer.
• 0:39—Very brief left breast in B&W photo.
0:58—Buns and breasts when police officers lift her
up to put plastic under her. Covered with blood,
can't see her face.
• 1:09—Very brief left breast in B&W photo.
The Prisoner of Zenda (1979) . . . . . . . . . The Countess
Lily in Love (1985) . . . . . . . . . . . . . . . . . Alicia Brown
Severed Ties (1992) . . . . . . . . . . . . . . Helena Harrison
*Magazines:*
Playboy (Sep 1970) . . . . . . . . . . . . . . . . . . . . . . . .n.a.

**Playboy** (Jan 1974) . . . . . . . . Twenty Years of Playboy
•• 209—Breasts getting into pool.
**Playboy** (Jan 1979) . . . . . . . . . . . . . 25 Beautiful Years
•• 159—Breasts getting into a pool.
**Playboy** (Jan 1989) . . . . . . . . Women of the Seventies
•• 217—Breasts getting into pool.

# Sommerfield, Diane

*Films:*
Love in a Taxi (1980) . . . . . . . . . . . . . . . . . . . . Carine
Back Roads (1981) . . . . . . . . . . . . . . . . . . . . . . . . Liz
**The Nightstalker** (1987) . . . . . . . . . . .Lonnie Roberts
• 0:35—Side view of right breast lying dead in
morgue.

# • Song, Cheryl

*Films:*
**Weekend Pass** (1984) . . . . . . . . . . . . . . . . Chop Suzi
• 0:26—Breasts while giving a guy a massage.
*TV:*
Soul Train . . . . . . . . . . . . . . . . . . . . . . . . . . . . Dancer

# Sorenson, Heidi

*Films:*
History of the World, Part I (1981) . . . . . . . .Vestal Virgin
Fright Night (1985) . . . . . . . . . . . . . . . . . . . . . Hooker
Spies Like Us (1985) . . . . . . . . . . .Fitz-Hume's Supervisor
Roxanne (1987) . . . . . . . . . . . . . . . . . . . . . . . .Trudy
For the Boys (1991) . . . . . . . . . . . . . . . . . . . Showgirl
*Made for Cable TV:*
**Dream On: Martin Tupper in "Magnum Farce"**
(1994; HBO) . . . . . . . . . . . . . . . . . . . . . . . . . . . . Jodi
••• 0:01—Buns in G-string panties, then breasts, while
making love on top of and under Martin.
••• 0:16—In white bra, then breasts and buns, while
making love on sofa with Mack to get even with
Martin. More breasts after getting caught and get-
ting dressed.
*Video Tapes:*
**Playboy Video Magazine, Volume 5** (1983)
. . . . . . . . . . . . . . . . . . . . . . . . . . . . . . . . . . . . Playmate
• 0:06—Brief breasts in library.
*Magazines:*
**Playboy** (Jul 1981) . . . . . . . . . . . . . . . . . . . . Playmate
**Playboy's Calendar Playmates** (Nov 1992) . . .Herself
••• 13—Full frontal nudity.
••• 25—Full frontal nudity.
**Playboy's Nudes** (Dec 1992) . . . . . . . . . . . . . .Herself
••• 6—Full frontal nudity.
**Playboy Presents Girl of the World** (May 1994)
. . . . . . . . . . . . . . . . . . . . . . . . . . . . . . . . . . . . .Herself
••• 3-7—Breasts.

# Soutendijk, Reneé

*Films:*
**Spetters** (1980; Dutch) . . . . . . . . . . . . . . . . . . Fientje
•• 1:12—Breasts making love in trailer with Jeff.
The Girl with the Red Hair (1983; Dutch) . . . . . . .Hannie
The Cold Room (1984) . . . . . . . . . . . . . . . . . . . . . Lili

**The Fourth Man** (1984; Dutch) . . . . . . . . . . .Christine
- ••• 0:27—Full frontal nudity removing robe, brief buns in bed, side view left breast, then breasts in bed with Gerard.
- • 0:32—Brief left breast in bed with Gerard after he hallucinates and she cuts his penis off.
- ••• 0:53—Left breast, then right breast in red dress when Gerard opens her dress.
- • 1:11—Breasts making love with Herman while Gerard watches through keyhole.

Grave Secrets (1990). . . . . . . . . . . . . . . . Iris Norwood

**Eve of Destruction** (1991). . Dr. Eve Simmons/Eve VIII
  0:17—Left breast, while on table as a robot, with half her skin removed. Possibly a special-effect body.
- • 0:22—Brief breasts in bathroom (as a robot), fixing her wound. Breasts sitting on bed, putting a large bandage over the wound.

*Made for Cable Movies:*
Murderers Among Us: The Simon Wiesenthal Story (1989; HBO) . . . . . . . . . . . . . . . . . . . . . . . . . . . Cyla
Keeper of the City (1991; Showtime) . . Vickie Benedetto

*Made for Cable TV:*
**The Hitchhiker: Murderous Feelings** . . Sara Kendal
- ••• 0:04—In bra, then breasts with stockings and a garter belt on couch with a guy.
- • 0:18—Right breast when mysterious attacker surprises her from behind.

## Spacek, Sissy

*Films:*
**Prime Cut** (1972) . . . . . . . . . . . . . . . . . . . . . . . .Poppy
- • 0:25—Brief side view of left breast lying in hay, then buns when Gene Hackman lifts her up to show to Lee Marvin.
- ••• 0:30—Breasts sitting in bed, then getting up to try on a dress while Marvin watches.
  0:32—Close up of breasts though sheer black dress in a restaurant.

Badlands (1973) . . . . . . . . . . . . . . . . . . . . . . . . . .Holly
Ginger in the Morning (1973). . . . . . . . . . . . . . Ginger

**Carrie** (1976). . . . . . . . . . . . . . . . . . . . . Carrie White
- •• 0:02—Nude, taking a shower, then having her first menstrual period in the girls' locker room.
- • 1:25—Brief breasts taking a bath to wash all the pig blood off her after the dance.

Three Women (1977) . . . . . . . . . . . . . . . . . Pinky Rose

**Welcome to L.A.** (1977). . . . . . . . . . . . Linda Murray
- •• 0:51—Brief breasts after bringing presents into Keith Carradine's bedroom.

Heart Beat (1979) . . . . . . . . . . . . . . . . .Carolyn Cassady
Coal Miner's Daughter (1980). . . . . . . . . . .Loretta Lynn
(Academy Award for Best Actress.)
Raggedy Man (1981) . . . . . . . . . . . . . . . . . . . . . . Nita
  0:43—Side view of left breast washing herself off while two guys peep from outside window. Long shot, don't really see anything.
Missing (1982) . . . . . . . . . . . . . . . . . . . . . Beth Horman
The River (1984) . . . . . . . . . . . . . . . . . . . . Mae Garvey
Marie (1986). . . . . . . . . . . . . . . . . . . . Marie Ragghianti

'night Mother (1986). . . . . . . . . . . . . . . . . Jessie Cates
Violets Are Blue (1986). . . . . . . . . . . . . . Gussie Sawyer
The Long Walk Home (1990) . . . . . . .Miriam Thompson
JFK (1991) . . . . . . . . . . . . . . . . . . . . . . . . . Liz Garrison
Hard Promises (1992). . . . . . . . . . . . . . . . Chris Coalter

*Made for Cable Movies:*
A Private Matter (1992; HBO) . . . . . . . . .Sherri Finkbine

*Made for TV Movies:*
A Place for Annie (1994) . . . . . . . . . . . . Susan Lansing

*Magazines:*
**Playboy** (Dec 1977) . . . . . . . . . . . . . .Sex Stars of 1977
- • 218—Left breast under sheer green dress.

## Spangler, Donna

*Films:*
Another Chance (1989) . . . . . . . . . . . . . . . . . . Cynthia
Guns (1990). . . . . . . . . . . . . . . . . . . . . . . Hugs Huggins
  0:27—Oil wrestling with Kym.
  0:28—Showering (in front) while talking to Kym (in back).
Carnal Crimes (1991). . . . . . . . . . . . . . . . . . . . . Esther

**Roots of Evil** (1991). . . . . . . . . . . . . . . . . . . . Scarlett
(Unrated version reviewed.)
- •• 0:04—Breasts, getting attacked by the crazy guy, then killed.
- • 0:07—Brief breasts, dead, covered with blood when Alex Cord discovers her.

*Video Tapes:*
**Sexy Lingerie II** (1990) . . . . . . . . . . . . . . . . . . Model
Wet and Wild II (1990). . . . . . . . . . . . . . . . . . . Model
**Sexy Lingerie III** (1991) . . . . . . . . . . . . . . . . . Model

*Magazines:*
**Playboy** (Dec 1989) . . . . . . . . . . . . . . . Lethal Women
- ••• 153—Full frontal nudity.
**Playboy's Book of Lingerie** (Mar 1991). . . . . . Herself
- • 22—Right breast.
- ••• 101—Breasts.
**Playboy's Book of Lingerie** (Jul 1991). . . . . . .Herself
- • 41—Lower frontal nudity.
**Playboy's Career Girls** (Aug 1992) . . . . Lethal Women
- ••• 104—Full frontal nudity.
**Playboy** (Aug 1993) . . . . . . . . . . . . . . . . . . Grapevine
- •• 159—Left breast. B&W.

## • Spaulding, Tracy

*Films:*
Armed for Action (1992) . . . . . . . . . . . . . . . . . . . Lori
**The Deadly Secret** (1993). . . . . . . . . . . Reyna Vaught
- •• 0:00—Breasts, several times during opening credits.
- ••• 0:25—Breasts, with Joe Estevez in study.
- • 0:35—Brief breasts.
- • 0:38—Brief breasts several times in B&W.
- •• 0:41—Buns in G-string and breasts while making love with Estevez in bed.
- • 0:44—Brief breasts, while getting out of bed and putting robe on.
- • 1:10—Brief breasts when Estevez comes up behind her and feels her breasts.

•• 1:11—Breasts, while making love with Estevez on bed.
•• 1:17—Breasts and brief buns in B&W day dream.
• 1:27—Brief right breast, while making love in flash-back.

## Speir, Dona

*Films:*
Doin' Time (1984) . . . . . . . . . . . . . . . . . . Card Holder
Dragnet (1987) . . . . . . . . . . . . . . . . . . . . . Baitmate
**Hard Ticket to Hawaii** (1987) . . . . . . . . . . . . Donna
  • 0:01—Breasts on boat kissing her boyfriend, Rowdy.
  ••• 0:23—Breasts in the spa with Hope Marie Carlton looking at diamonds they found.
  ••• 1:04—Breasts and buns with Rowdy after watching a video tape.
  •• 1:33—Breasts during the end credits.
Mortuary Academy (1988) . . . . . . . . . . . . . . . . Nurse
**Click: Calendar Girl Killer** (1989) . . . . . . . . . .Nancy
  0:00—Posing in yellow two piece swimsuit during photo session.
  0:06—In wet, white dress after being pushed into the spa.
  • 0:11—Brief glimpses of breasts during photo session. Buns and breasts under sheer fabric.
  •• 0:12—Brief buns, dropping the piece of fabric.
  0:28—Posing in yellow two piece swimsuit during photo session.
**Picasso Trigger** (1989) . . . . . . . . . . . . . . . . . . Donna
  0:17—In white lingerie on boat with Hope Marie Carlton.
  ••• 0:49—Breasts and buns standing, then making love in bed.
**Savage Beach** (1989) . . . . . . . . . . . . . . . . . . . . Dona
  0:06—Almost breasts in spa with the three other women.
  • 0:32—Breasts changing clothes in airplane with Hope Marie Carlton.
  •• 0:48—Nude, going for a swim on the beach with Carlton.
**Guns** (1990) . . . . . . . . . . . . . . . . . . . . . Donna Hamilton
  ••• 1:00—Breasts and buns in black G-string getting dressed in locker room. Then in black lingerie.
**Do or Die** (1991) . . . . . . . . . . . . . . . . . Donna Hamilton
  • 0:06—Brief breasts taking off towel and getting into spa.
  •• 0:32—Breasts, mostly right breast, changing clothes in back of airplane.
  ••• 1:21—Breasts and buns, in swimming pool with Erik Estrada.
**Fit To Kill** (1993) . . . . . . . . . . . . . . . . . Donna Hamilton
  •• 0:21—Breasts and buns in G-string, while undressing and putting dresses on with Vasquez.
  0:55—In two piece swimsuit.
  ••• 1:18—Buns in two piece swimsuit, then breasts during Kane's fantasy.
  1:29—In two piece swimsuit.

**Hard Hunted** (1993) . . . . . . . . . . . . . Donna Hamilton
  •• 1:22—Left breast, then breasts on beach with the bad guy, while making love and resting afterwards.
*Video Tapes:*
Playmate Playoffs . . . . . . . . . . . . . . . . . . . . . . . Playmate
**Playboy Video Calendar 1987** (1986) . . . . . Playmate
**Playboy Video Centerfold: Teri Weigel** (1986)
  . . . . . . . . . . . . . . . . . . . . . . . . . . . . . . . . . . . . . . Playmate
Glamour Through Your Lens—Outdoor Techniques
  (1989) . . . . . . . . . . . . . . . . . . . . . . . . . . . . . . . . . Herself
  0:22—Posing by Corvette in white shorts and red top.
  0:35—In white two piece swimsuit on lounge chair by the pool.
**Wet and Wild** (1989) . . . . . . . . . . . . . . . . . . . . Model
**Sexy Lingerie III** (1991) . . . . . . . . . . . . . . . . . Model
*Magazines:*
**Playboy** (Mar 1984) . . . . . . . . . . . . . . . . . . . . . Playmate
**Playboy's 1987 Book of Lingerie** (Mar 1987)
  . . . . . . . . . . . . . . . . . . . . . . . . . . . . . . . . . . . . . . . Herself
  ••• 87—Full frontal nudity.
  •• 88-89—Half of left breast and buns.
**Playboy's Nudes** (Oct 1990) . . . . . . . . . . . . . . Herself
  ••• 24—Full frontal nudity.
**Playboy's Book of Lingerie** (Mar 1991) . . . . . Herself
  • 54—Breasts under sheer black gown.
**Playboy's Bathing Beauties** (Apr 1992) . . . . . Herself
  • 79—Buns in T-back.
**Playboy's Girls of Summer '92** (Jun 1992) . . . Herself
  •• 4—Right breast.
**Playboy's Calendar Playmates** (Nov 1992) . . . Herself
  ••• 34—Full frontal nudity.
  ••• 54—Full frontal nudity.
**Playboy's Book of Lingerie** (Nov 1992) . . . . . Herself
  • 72—Lower frontal nudity.
  • 77—Lower frontal nudity.
**Playboy's Book of Lingerie** (Jan 1993) . . . . . . Herself
  • 40-41—Lower frontal nudity.
**Playboy's Book of Lingerie** (Mar 1993) . . . . . Herself
  •• 54-55—Buns.
**Playboy's Blondes, Brunettes & Redheads**
  (Sep 1993) . . . . . . . . . . . . . . . . . . . . . . . . . . . . . Herself
  • 16—Lower frontal nudity.
**Playboy's Video Playmates** (Sep 1993) . . . . . . Herself
  ••• 78-79—Breasts.
**Playboy's Book of Lingerie** (Jan 1994) . . . . . . Herself
  •• 56—Left breast.
**Playboy's Bathing Beauties** (Mar 1994) . . . . . Herself
  ••• 11—Breasts.
**Playboy Presents Playmates in Paradise**
  (Mar 1994) . . . . . . . . . . . . . . . . . . . . . . . . . . . Playmate
  ••• 54-57—Nude.

# • Speiss, Kimberly
*Films:*
Night of the Wilding (1990) . . . . . . . . . . . . . . . . .Doris
California Hot Wax (1992). . . . . . . . . . . . . . Bikini Girl
Last Dance (1992). . . . . . . . . . . . . . . . . . . . . . .Meryll
   1:03—Sort of buns, while dancing on stage.
**Psycho Cop 2** (1992) . . . . . . . . . . . . . . . . . . . . Chloe
   • 0:37—Buns, while falling off of desk with Tony, then
   standing up and talking to Sharon.

## Spelvin, Georgina
Adult flim actress.
*Films:*
**I Spit on Your Corpse** (1974) . . . . . . . . . . . . . Sandra
  *a.k.a. Girls for Rent*
   • 0:38—Flashing her left breast to get three guys to
   stop their car.
   ••• 0:39—Breasts, fighting with the three guys.
   • 0:47—Brief right breast in gaping blouse.
   ••• 0:53—Breasts outside, de-virginizing the backwoods
   kid.
   •• 1:08—Breasts, close-up view, showing her breasts to
   him.
   • 1:10—Buns, in lowered pants and left breast in open
   blouse.
**Honky Tonk Nights** (1978) . . . . . . . . . . . . . Georgia
   • 0:06—Breasts, lying with her head in a guy's lap.
Police Academy III: Back in Training (1986)
. . . . . . . . . . . . . . . . . . . . . . . . . . . . . . . .The Hooker
*Magazines:*
**Playboy** (Nov 1973) . . . . . . . . . . . Sex in Cinema 1973
   ••• 157—Breasts with a snake in photo from *The Devil in
   Miss Jones.*
**Playboy** (Dec 1973). . . . . . . . . . . . . Sex Stars of 1973
   • 210—Partial right breast and lower frontal nudity.

# • Spencer, Holly
*Films:*
Beach Beverly Hills (1992). . . . . . . .Bikini Audition Girl 1
**Secret Games 2—The Escort** (1993) . . . . . . . . . .Lisa
(Unrated version reviewed.)
   ••• 0:24—Nude, after taking off coat, covering Hewitt
   with birthday cake and in the shower with him and
   Stacey.
   •• 0:26—Breasts and buns while making love in bed
   with Stacey and Hewitt.
   •• 1:05—Breasts in flashbacks.

## Sportolaro, Tina
*Films:*
Sincerely Charlotte (1986; French) . . . . . . . . . . . . . .n.a.
Frantic (1988) . . . . . . . . . . . . . . . . . . . . . . . TWA Clerk
**The Passion of Beatrice** (1988; French)
. . . . . . . . . . . . . . . . . . . . . . Mère de François Enfant
   • 0:06—Brief breasts when the young François discov-
   ers her in bed with another man and kills him.
Paris By Night (1989; British) . . . . . . . . . . . . . . . Violet

## Spradling, Charlie
a.k.a. Charlie.
*Films:*
The Blob (1988). . . . . . . . . . . . . . . . . . . . . . . . . Co-ed
**Unexpected Encounters, Vol. 3** (1988)
. . . . . . . . . . . . . . . . . . . . . . . . . . . .Woman in House
   ••• 0:50—In lingerie, then breasts on sofa with the gardener.
**Meridian** (1989). . . . . . . . . . . . . . . . . . . . . . . . Gina
  *a.k.a. Kiss of the Beast*
  *a.k.a. Phantoms*
   •• 0:22—Breasts getting her blouse torn off by
   Lawrence while lying on the table.
   ••• 0:28—Breasts standing next to fireplace, then
   breasts on the couch. Hot!
**Twice Dead** (1989) . . . . . . . . . . . . . . . . . . . . . . .Tina
   •• 1:11—Breasts taking off jacket next to bed.
   ••• 1:14—Breasts making love with her boyfriend in
   bed.
   • 1:18—Brief breasts dead in bed.
**Mirror Mirror** (1990) . . . . . . . . . . . . . .Charleen Kane
   • 1:05—Very, very brief side of left breast, after taking
   of swimsuit in locker room.
   • 1:06—Buns, taking a shower. Brief breasts a couple
   of times when the hot water pipes break.
   1:09—Buns, lying on the floor, dead, covered with
   blisters.
**Puppet Master II** (1990). . . . . . . . . . . . . . . . .Wanda
   •• 1:04—Breasts getting out of bed and adjusting her
   panties.
Ski School (1990). . . . . . . . . . . . . . . . . . . . . . .Paulette
**Wild at Heart** (1990) . . . . . . . . . . . . . . . . . . . . Irma
   • 0:40—Brief breasts in bed during flashback.
The Doors (1991). . . . . . . . . . . . .CBS Girl Backstage
Bad Channels (1992) . . . . . . . . . . . . . . . . . . . . .Cookie
Caged Fear (1992). . . . . . . . . . . . . . . . . . . . . . . . .Joy
**To Sleep with a Vampire** (1992) . . . . . . . . . . . . Nina
   • 0:04—On stage in black lingerie, then buns in T-
   back.
   ••• 0:05—Breasts and buns in push up bra and T-back
   while dancing on stage.
   ••• 0:59—In red top and red T-back on stage, breasts
   and buns. Excellent close up of breasts.
   ••• 1:03—Breasts while making love on stage with Scott
   Valentine.
**Test Tube Teens From the Year 2000** (1993)
. . . . . . . . . . . . . . . . . . . . . . . . . . . . . . . . Girl on TV
  *a.k.a. Virgin Hunters*
   • 0:23—Breasts in scenes from *Meridian: Kiss of the
   Beast* being shown on TV.
Angel of Destruction (1994). . . . . . . . . . . . Brit Alwood
*TV:*
Twin Peaks (1990-91). . . . . . . . . . . . . . . . . . .Swabbie

## Springsteen, Pamela
Sister of singer Bruce Springsteen.
*Films:*
Fast Times at Ridgemont High (1982) . . . . .Dina Phillips
Reckless (1984) . . . . . . . . . . . . . . . . . . . . .Karen Sybern

My Science Project (1985) . . . Hall Monitor/Ellie's Friend
**Dixie Lanes** (1987) . . . . . . . . . . . . . . . . . . . . . . . Judy
•• 1:00—Breasts, turning around in pond, while talking
to Everett at night.
Modern Girls (1987) . . . . . . . . . . . . . . . . . . . . . Tanya
Scenes from the Goldmine (1987). . . . . . . . . . Stephanie
Sleepaway Camp II: Unhappy Campers (1988)
. . . . . . . . . . . . . . . . . . . . . . . . . . . . . . . . . . . Angela
Fast Food (1989). . . . . . . . . . . . . . . Mary Beth Bensen
Sleepaway Camp III: Teenage Wasteland (1989)
. . . . . . . . . . . . . . . . . . . . . . . . . . . . . Angela Baker
The Gumshoe Kid (1990) . . . . . . . . . . . . Mona Krause
*Made for TV Movies:*
My Mother's Secret Life (1984) . . . . . . . . . . . . . . Kelly

## Sprinkle, Annie
Adult film actress.
*Films:*
**Mondo New York** (1987) . . . . . . . . Model/Performer
• 0:17—Nude, painted body with other models dur-
ing "Rapping & Rocking" segment.
**Wimps** (1987) . . . . . . . . . . . . . . . . . . . Head Stripper
•• 1:12—Breasts on stage with two other strippers,
teasing Francis.
**Young Nurses in Love** (1987) . . . . . . . . . . Twin Falls
•• 0:23—Breasts getting measured by Dr. Spencer.
Shadows in the City (1991). . . . . . . . . . . . Ex-Girlfriend
*Made for Cable TV:*
Real Sex 2 (1991; HBO). . . . . . . . . . . . . . . . . Herself
**Real Sex 4** (1992; HBO)
. . . . . . . . . . . . . . Annie Sprinkle's One Woman Show
•• 0:00—Brief breasts during opening credits.
•• 0:01—Breasts several times during her show.
••• 0:09—Breasts with vibrator during a ceremonial sex
routine in her show.

## Squire, Janie
*Films:*
**Piranha** (1978) . . . . . . . . . . . . . . . . . . . . . . Barbara
•• 0:02—Breasts taking off her top to go swimming
with her boyfriend.
**Cheerleaders Wild Weekend** (1985)
. . . . . . . . . . . . . . . . . . . . . . . . . . . Donna/Darwell
••• 0:39—Breasts and brief buns, taking off her white
blouse during contest.
••• 0:41—Breasts with the other five girls during contest.
••• 0:43—Breasts while getting measured with the other two girls.

## • St. Claire, Jacqueline
*Films:*
**Hollywood Dreams** (1993) . . . . . . . . . . . . . Stripper
(Unrated version reviewed.)
•• 0:57—Breasts and buns in T-back, after stripping out
of outfit while dancing in bar set.
**Housewife From Hell** (1993) . . . . . . . . . . . Mary-Lou
••• 0:12—Breasts, while taking off blouse on bed with
John, then making love.

• 0:15—Brief frontal nudity while in bathroom with
John.
•• 0:16—Buns and breasts, while getting dressed in
bedroom while talking to John.
••• 0:40—In purple bra and panties, then buns and
breasts while in office with John.
• 1:01—Brief buns in bodysuit, while getting up out of
bed.

## St. Croix, Dominique
*Films:*
Recruits (1986; Canadian) . . . . . . . . . . . . . . . . . . . n.a.
*Video Tapes:*
**Penthouse Ready to Ride** (1992) . . . . . . . . . Model
**Penthouse Satin & Lace II: Hollywood Undercover**
(1992) . . . . . . . . . . . . . . . . . . . . . . . . . . . . . . . . Pet
**Penthouse The Great Pet Hunt—Part II** (1993)
. . . . . . . . . . . . . . . . . . . . . . . . . . . . . . . . . . . . . Pet
••• 0:10—Breasts and buns in T-back, then nude while
stripping out of dominatrix outfit on stage.
*CD-ROM:*
**Penthouse Interactive Virtual Photo Shoot, Disc 1**
(1993) . . . . . . . . . . . . . . . . . . . . . . . . . . . . . . . . Pet
*Magazines:*
**Penthouse** (Apr 1986) . . . . . . . . . . . . . . . . . . . . Pet

## St. George, Cathy
*Films:*
Star 80 (1983) . . . . . . . . . . . . . Playboy Mansion Guest
Beverly Hills Brats (1989) . . . . . . . . . . . . . . . . . . Sally
0:22—In sheer purple bra, while talking on the
phone.
*Video Tapes:*
**Playboy's Playmate Review 2** (1984) . . . . . Playmate
**Wet and Wild** (1989) . . . . . . . . . . . . . . . . . . Model
*Magazines:*
**Playboy** (Aug 1982) . . . . . . . . . . . . . . . . . . Playmate
**Playboy's Girls of Summer '86** (Aug 1986). . . Herself
•• 21—Right breast.
**Playboy's Book of Lingerie** (Jul 1991) . . . . . . . Herself
••• 46—Breasts.
**Playboy's Book of Lingerie** (Nov 1991) . . . . . Herself
• 82—Right breast.
**Playboy's Sisters** (Feb 1992) . . . . . . . . . . . . . . Herself
••• 20-29—Breasts.
**Playboy's Book of Lingerie** (Mar 1992). . . . . . Herself
•• 60—Right breast.
**Playboy's Bathing Beauties** (Apr 1992). . . . . . Herself
••• 72—Breasts.
••• 92—Breasts.
**Playboy's Book of Lingerie** (May 1992) . . . . . Herself
• 71—Partial lower frontal nudity.
**Playboy's Girls of Summer '92** (Jun 1992) . . . Herself
••• 40—Breasts.
••• 100—Full frontal nudity.
**Playboy's Book of Lingerie** (Sep 1992) . . . . . . Herself
•• 8—Left breast.
• 37—Lower frontal nudity.
••• 89—Breasts.

**Playboy's Calendar Playmates** (Nov 1992) . . Herself
••• 12—Full frontal nudity.
**Playboy's Book of Lingerie** (Nov 1992) . . . . . Herself
••• 60—Breasts.
**Playboy's Book of Lingerie** (Jan 1993) . . . . . . Herself
•• 71—Buns and side view of right breast.
**Playboy's Bathing Beauties** (Apr 1993) . . . . . Herself
•• 12—Left breast and partial buns.
••• 67—Breasts.
•• 83—Left breast and buns.
**Playboy's Book of Lingerie** (May 1993) . . . . . Herself
••• 43—Full frontal nudity.
**Playboy's Book of Lingerie** (Jul 1993) . . . . . . Herself
•• 67—Breasts under sheer top.
**Playboy's Blondes, Brunettes & Redheads**
(Sep 1993) . . . . . . . . . . . . . . . . . . . . . . . . . . Herself
•• 37—Partial breasts.
**Playboy's Book of Lingerie** (Nov 1993) . . . . . Herself
•• 22-23—Left breast.
**Playboy's Book of Lingerie** (Jan 1994) . . . . . . Herself
•• 52—Right breast and lower frontal nudity.
**Playboy's Bathing Beauties** (Mar 1994) . . . . . Herself
••• 20—Breasts.
**Playboy's Book of Lingerie** (May 1994) . . . . . Herself
•• 37—Left breast.
••• 63—Full frontal nudity.
••• 92-93—Full frontal nudity.
**Playboy's Book of Lingerie** (Jul 1994) . . . . . . Herself
••• 21—Full frontal nudity.
• 78—Lower frontal nudity.

## St. Jon, Ashley

*Adult Films:*
**Centerfold Celebrities 3** . . . . . . . . . . . . Herself/Nurse
Having sex with Paul Thomas.
*Films:*
**Takin' It Off** (1984) . . . . . . . . . . . . . . . . . . . . . . Sin
••• 0:20—Breasts and buns doing two dance routines
on stage.
•• 0:53—Nude, stripping and dancing in the library.
**Weekend Pass** (1984) . . . . . . . . . . . . . . Xylene B-12
•• 0:13—Breasts dancing on stage.
**The Wild Life** (1984) . . . . . . . . . . . . . . . . . Stripper #1
••• 0:47—Breasts and brief buns doing strip tease rou-
tine in front of Christopher Penn and his friends.
Sorority Girls and the Creature from Hell (1990)
. . . . . . . . . . . . . . . . . . . . . . . . . . . . . . . Bar Patron
*Video Tapes:*
**Centerfold Screen Test** (1985) . . . . . . . . . . . Herself
••• 0:32—Breasts and buns in G-string, taking off her fur
coat while auditioning in a car.
The Stripper of the Year (1986) . . . . . . . . . . . . . . Judge

## • Stafford, Jamie

a.k.a. Adult film actress Jamie Summers.
*Films:*
**Night Rhythms** (1992) . . . . . . . . . . . . . . . . . . . . Kit
(Unrated version reviewed.)
•• 0:40—Breasts in push-up bra in dressing room.

••• 0:51—Nude, in bed, making love with Lila and Martin Hewitt.
• 0:54—Buns, while watching TV while lying in bed.
••• 0:55—Nude, undressing to take a shower with Lila.
•• 1:23—In sheer black blouse, talking to Delia Sheppard in the radio station.
••• 1:25—Nude, in bed with Sheppard, then getting
dressed. Long scene.

## • Stagno, Lisa Marie

*Films:*
Liquid Dreams (1992) . . . . . . . . . . . . . Neuroid Reactor
(Unrated version reviewed.)
**Army of One** (1993) . . . . . . . . . . . .Rita's Body Double
•• 0:34—Breasts and buns, while undressing and get-
ting into shower. Body double for Kristian Alfonso.

## Stakis, Anastassia

*Films:*
**Nevada Heat** (1982) . . . . . . . . . . . . . . . . . . . . . Wooly
*a.k.a. Fake-Out*
• 0:13—Breasts in the shower room scene.
Siesta (1987) . . . . . . . . . . . . . . . . . . . . . . . . . . .Desdra

## Staley, Lora

*Films:*
**American Nightmare** (1981; Canadian)
. . . . . . . . . . . . . . . . . . . . . . . . . . . . . Louise Harmon
•• 0:44—Breasts and buns in G-string dancing on
stage.
••• 0:54—Breasts making love in bed with Eric.
• 0:59—Brief right breast, then breasts auditioning in
TV studio.
Thief (1981) . . . . . . . . . . . . . . . . . . . . . . . . . . . Paula
Risky Business (1983) . . . . . . . . . . . . . . . . . . . Call Girl
Deadly Weapon (1989) . . . . . . . . . . . . . . . . . . . Leslie
Samantha (1991) . . . . . . . . . . . . . . . . . . . . TV Reporter

## Staller, Ilona

a.k.a. Italian adult film actress Cicciolina.
Was a member of the Italian Parliament from 1987-92.
*Films:*
**Inhibition** (1984; Italian) . . . . . . . . . . . . . . . . . . Anna
••• 0:08—Nude taking a shower with Carol.
• 0:43—Brief full frontal nudity getting out of swimming pool.
••• 0:55—Breasts making love in the water with Robert.
••• 1:00—Full frontal nudity getting disciplined by Carol.
*Made for Cable TV:*
**Real Sex 3** (1992; HBO) . . . . . . . . . . . . . . . Cicciolina
•• 0:00—Breasts several times during the opening
credits.
• 0:16—Breasts several times.
• 0:17—Brief lower frontal nudity and buns. More
breasts in clips.
••• 0:20—More breasts clips.
• 0:24—More breasts shots.

*Magazines:*
**Playboy** (Feb 1988) . . . . . . . . . . . . . . . The Year in Sex
••• 134—Full frontal nudity.
**Playboy** (Feb 1991) . . . . . . . . . . . . . . . The Year in Sex
• Left breast, making the "victory" sign with her left hand.

## Stansfield, Claire

*Films:*
The Doors (1991) . . . . . . . . . . . . . . . Warhol Eurosnob
Nervous Ticks (1991) . . . . . . . . . . . . . . . . . . . . . . . Lu
Best of the Best 2 (1992). . . . . . . . . . . . . . . . . . Greta
The Swordsman (1992). . . . . . . . . . . . . . . . . . . . Julie
*Made for Cable TV:*
**Red Shoe Diaries: Bounty Hunter** (1993; Showtime)
. . . . . . . . . . . . . . . . . . . . . . . . . . The Bounty Hunter
• 0:16—Buns, in black G-string. Don't see her face.
• 0:19—Brief breasts several times, making love outside in the rain with Oliver. Hard to see because of the lightning effect.
••• 0:25—Breasts several times, making love with Oliver on the floor in the cafe.

## Starbuck, Cheryl

*Films:*
Angel III: The Final Chapter (1988) . . . . . . Video Girl #3
**Mortuary Academy** (1988) . . . . . . . . Linda Hollyhead
• 1:08—Breasts, dead, in morgue when Paul Bartel tries to make love with her.
Shy People (1988). . . . . . . . . . . . . . . . . . . . Stewardess

## Stark, Kimberleigh

*Films:*
Crime Lords (1990). . . . . . . . . . . . . Lieutenant Sylvestri
**Night of the Cyclone** (1990). . . . . . . . . . . . . . Venna
• 0:01—Brief left breast while posing for the painter.
• 0:40—Breasts on the boat, fighting with the businessman. Breasts on the floor, dead.
**Lethal Ninja** (1992) . . . . . . . . . . . . . . . . . . . . Farida
•• 1:01—Buns and breasts, while getting out of bath and putting on robe.
Cyborg Cop (1993). . . . . . . . . . . . . . . Woman Hostage
Woman of Desire (1993). . . . . . . . Nurse Vivian Donner

## Stark, Koo

Former girlfriend of Prince Andrew of England in 1982, before he met and married "Fergie."
Special Stills Photographer in the film *Aria.*
*Films:*
**Justine**. . . . . . . . . . . . . . . . . . . . . . . . . . . . Justine
•• 0:09—Breasts getting fondled by a nun.
• 0:16—Breasts getting attacked by a nun.
• 0:57—Breasts in open dress getting attacked by old guy.
••• 1:00—Breasts getting bathed, then lower frontal nudity.
• 1:28—Right breast and buns taking off clothes, then brief full frontal nudity getting dressed again.
• 1:32—Breasts getting thrown in to the water.

The Rocky Horror Picture Show (1975; British)
. . . . . . . . . . . . . . . . . . . . . . . . . . . . . Bridesmaid
**Emily** (1976; British) . . . . . . . . . . . . . . . . . . . . . Emily
•• 0:08—Breasts, lying in bed caressing herself while fantasizing about James.
••• 0:30—Breasts in studio posing for Augustine, then kissing her.
••• 0:42—Buns and breasts taking a shower after posing for Augustine.
•• 0:56—Left breast, under a tree with James.
• 1:16—Breasts in the woods seducing Rupert.
Cruel Passion (1978) . . . . . . . . . . . . . . . . . . . . . . n.a.
Electric Dreams (1984). . . . . . . . . . . Girl in Soap Opera

## • Stark, Melody

*Films:*
**Crackerjack** (1994) . . . . . . . . . . . . . . . . . . . Newlywed
• 0:33—Brief side view of left breast, while undressing in room with her husband.
••• 0:34—Breasts, when her husband plays with an ice cube on her breasts. Buns when the terrorists break into the room.
*Magazines:*
**Playboy's Girls of the World** (Oct 1992). . . . . Herself
••• 9—Full frontal nudity.

## Staunton, Imelda

*Films:*
Comrades (1986; British) . . . . . . . . . . . . Betsy Loveless
**Antonia & Jane** (1991; British) . . . . . . . Jane Hartman
• 0:08—Right breast, while lying in bed with Norman, reading a book to get him turned on.
Much Ado About Nothing (1993; British). . . . . Margaret
Peter's Friends (1993; British/U.S.) . . . . . . . . . . . . Mary

## Stavin, Mary

*Films:*
Octopussy (1983; British). . . . . . . . . . . . Octopussy Girl
A View to a Kill (1985) . . . . . . . . . . . . . Kimberley Jones
House (1986). . . . . . . . . . . . . . . . . . . . . . . . . . . Tanya
Open House (1987) . . . . . . . . . . . . . . . Katie Thatcher
**Howling V** (1989) . . . . . . . . . . . . . . . . . . . . . . . Anna
•• 1:09—Breasts three times drying herself off while Richard watches in the mirror. Possible body double.
*TV:*
Twin Peaks (1990-91). . . . . . . . . . . . . . . . . . . . . Heba

## • Steafel, Sheila

*Films:*
Baby Love (1969). . . . . . . . . . . . . . . . . . . . . . . Tessa
Goodbye Mr. Chips (1969; British). . . . . . . . . . . . Tilly
**Tropic of Cancer** (1970) . . . . . . . . . . . . . . . . . Tania
•• 0:25—Breasts, while ballet dancing in studio while wearing only a tutu.
Bloodbath at the House of Death (1985; British) . . . n.a.

## • Steel, Pippa

*Films:*
Lust for a Vampire (1970; British) ........ Susan Pelley
Take a Girl Like You (1970; British) .............. Ted
**Vampire Lovers** (1970; British).............. Laura
 • 0:24—Left breast in bed when the doctor pulls her top down to listen to her heart beat.
Young Winston (1972; British)...... Clementine Hozier

## • Steele, Vanessa

*Films:*
**Wet and Wild Summer!** (1992; Australian)
..................................Charlene
 •• 1:25—Breasts, opening her leather jacket to distract the other lifeguard boat.
Sniper (1993) ...................... Mrs. Alvarez

## Steenburgen, Mary

Ex-wife of actor Malcolm McDowell.
*Films:*
Goin' South (1978)..................... Julia Tate
Time After Time (1979; British) ........ Amy Robbins
**Melvin and Howard** (1980)........ Lynda Dummar
(Academy Award for Best Supporting Actress.)
 •• 0:31—Breasts and buns, ripping off barmaid outfit and walking out the door.
Ragtime (1981)......................... Mother
A Midsummer Night's Sex Comedy (1982)..... Adrian
Cross Creek (1983) ......... Marjorie Kinnan Rawlings
Romantic Comedy (1983)................. Phoebe
Dead of Winter (1987)
............... Julie Rose/Katie McGovern/Evelyn
End of the Line (1987) ........... Rose Pickett
Miss Firecracker (1989) ..................... Elain
Parenthood (1989) ............... Karen Buckman
Back to the Future, Part III (1990) ....... Clara Clayton
The Butcher's Wife (1991)................. Stella
Philadelphia (1993)................. Belinda Conine
What's Eating Gilbert Grape (1993)....... Betty Carver
*Made for TV Movies:*
One Magic Christmas (1985; U.S./Canadian)
.................................. Ginny Grainger
The Attic—The Hiding of Anne Frank (1988)
.................................. Miep Gies

## Stefanelli, Simonetta

*Films:*
**The Godfather** (1972) ................. Apollonia
 •• 1:50—Breasts in bedroom on honeymoon night.
Three Brothers (1982; Italian) .... Young Donato's Wife
*Magazines:*
**Playboy** (Nov 1972) ........... Sex in Cinema 1972
 • 161—Left breast, grainy photo from *The Godfather.*
**Playboy** (Mar 1974)...... The Don's Daughter-In-Law
 ••• 97-99—Breasts.

## Stein, Pamela J.

*Video Tapes:*
**Playboy Video Calendar 1989** (1988).... September
 ••• 0:33—Nude.
**Playboy Video Centerfold: Tawnni Cable** (1990)
.................................. Playmate
 ••• 0:14—Nude in Hawaii with Tawnni Cable and Jacqueline Sheen.
**Playboy Playmates in Paradise** (1992).... Playmate
*Magazines:*
**Playboy** (Nov 1987)................... Playmate
**Playboy's Nudes** (Oct 1990) .............. Herself
 ••• 73—Full frontal nudity.
**Playboy's Book of Lingerie** (Jan 1991) ...... Herself
 • 10—Partial right breast and lower frontal nudity.
**Playboy's Book of Lingerie** (Mar 1991)...... Herself
 •• 61—Left breast and lower frontal nudity.
**Playboy's Book of Lingerie** (Jul 1991)....... Herself
 ••• 56—Breasts.
**Playboy's Book of Lingerie** (Nov 1991) ..... Herself
 ••• 13—Full frontal nudity.
**Playboy's Book of Lingerie** (Mar 1992)...... Herself
 ••• 27—Breasts.
 ••• 49—Full frontal nudity.
**Playboy's Book of Lingerie** (May 1992) ..... Herself
 ••• 32—Breasts.
 •• 38—Buns.
 ••• 93—Breasts and buns.
**Playboy's Girls of Summer '92** (Jun 1992) ... Herself
 ••• 88—Full frontal nudity.
**Playboy's Calendar Playmates** (Nov 1992)... Herself
 •• 75—Left breast and most of right breast.
**Playboy's Book of Lingerie** (Nov 1992) ..... Herself
 •• 107—Left breast and lower frontal nudity.
**Playboy's Book of Lingerie** (Mar 1993)...... Herself
 • 37—Partial right breast.
 ••• 78—Full frontal nudity.
**Playboy's Book of Lingerie** (Jan 1994) ...... Herself
 ••• 95—Breasts.
**Playboy's Bathing Beauties** (Mar 1994) ..... Herself
 • 60—Half of left breast.
**Playboy's Girls of Summer '94** (Jul 1994).... Herself
 ••• 33—Breasts.
 ••• 36-37—Breasts.
**Playboy's Book of Lingerie** (Jul 1994)....... Herself
 ••• 50—Full frontal nudity.
 ••• 75—Breasts.

## Stenberg, Brigitta

*Films:*
Queens Logic (1991) .......... Girl in Club Bathroom
Homicidal Impulse (1992) .............. Receptionist
*a.k.a. Killer Instinct*
Raiders of the Sun (1992)..................... Vera
**Rapid Fire** (1992)...................... Rosalyn
 • 0:10—Brief side view of right breast, posing in art class. Don't see her face. Long shot breasts, getting up and putting on robe.
Stop! Or My Mom Will Shoot (1992) ...... Stewardess

## Stensgaard, Yutte

Real name is Jytte Stensgaard.
*Films:*
**Lust for a Vampire** (1970; British) . . . . . . . . Mircalla
••• 0:19—Breasts, three times, getting a massage from another school girl.
0:22—Very, very brief full frontal nudity while diving into the water. Long shot, don't see anything.
•• 0:53—Breasts outside with Lestrange. Left breast when lying down.
• 0:58—Breasts during Lestrange's dream.
Scream and Scream Again (1970; British) . . . . . . . Erika
The Buttercup Chain (1971; British) . . . . . . . . . . . n.a.

## Stephen, Karen

*Films:*
**Pick-Up Summer** (1979; Canadian) . . . . . . . . Donna
• 0:25—Very brief lower half of breast, pulling her T-shirt up to distract someone.
0:34—Very, very brief breasts when the boys spray her and she jumps up.
Happy Birthday to Me (1980; Canadian). . Miss Calhoun
Hog Wild (1980; Canadian). . . . . . . . . . . . . . . Brenda

## • Stephens, Yvette

*Films:*
**Carnal Crimes** (1991). . . . . . . . . . . . . . . . . . . .Mia
•• 0:25—Left breast, when Renny makes out with her.
••• 0:28—Brief left breast, then breasts posing with Linda.
••• 0:29—Full frontal nudity making love with Linda Carol and Renny.
• 0:48—Breasts and brief buns on TV.
• 0:50—Brief breasts in flashback.
*Magazines:*
Playboy (Sep 1994). . . . . . . . . . . . . . . . . . . .Grapevine

## Stephenson, Pamela

*Films:*
**Stand Up Virgin Soldiers** (1976) . . . . . . . . . . . Nurse
Breasts and brief buns after removing clothes and getting into bed.
History of the World, Part I (1981)
. . . . . . . . . . . . . . . . . . . . . . . . Mademoiselle Rimbaud
1:17—In lingerie, under blouse, when she flashes herself in front of Harvey Korman.
1:18—In lingerie again, flashing herself for Mel Brooks.
The Secret Policeman's Other Ball (1982; British) . . .n.a.
Finders Keepers (1983) . . . . . . . . . . . Georgiana Latimer
Scandalous (1983) . . . . . . . . . . . . . Fiona Maxwell Sayle
Superman III (1983) . . . . . . . . . . . . . .Lorelei Ambrosia
**Bloodbath at the House of Death** (1985; British)
. . . . . . . . . . . . . . . . . . . . . . . . . . . . . .Barbara Coyle
• 0:50—Very brief breasts getting clothes ripped off by an unseen being.
*TV:*
Saturday Night Live (1984-85) . . . . . . . . . . . . . .Regular

## • Sterling, Alicyn

See: Bittner, Carrie.

## Sterling, Gayle

Adult film actress.
*Films:*
**Simply Irresistible** (1983). . . . . . . . . . . . . . . . . Juliet
(R-rated version. *Irresistible* is the X-rated version.)
•• 0:40—Breasts and buns in bed with Walter.
0:46—In lingerie on bed.

## Stern, Ellen

*Films:*
The Duchess and the Dirtwater Fox (1976) . . . . . . Bride
**Jessi's Girls** (1976) . . . . . . . . . . . . . . . . . . . . . . . Kana
••• 1:10—Left breast, then breasts in bed with a guy.

## Stevens, Brinke

Ex-wife of *The Rocketeer* comic book creator David Stevens.
*Films:*
**The Slumber Party Massacre** (1982) . . . . . . . .Linda
•• 0:07—Buns, then breasts taking a shower during girls locker room scene.
**Sole Survivor** (1982) . . . . . . . . . . . . . . . . . . . Jennifer
•• 0:45—Breasts after taking off bra while playing strip poker.
**The Man Who Wasn't There** (1983) . . . . . .Nymphet
• 0:45—Buns and brief breasts in the girls' shower, when she gets shampoo from an invisible Steve Guttenberg.
**Private School** (1983) . . . . . . .Uncredited School Girl
•• 0:42—Brief breasts and buns in shower room scene. She's the brunette wearing a pony tail who passes in front of the chalkboard.
The Witching (1983) . . . . . . . . . Black Sabbath Member
*a.k.a. Necromancy*
(Originally filmed in 1971 as *Necromancy*, additional scenes were added and re-released in 1983.)
**Body Double** (1984) . . . . . . . . . . .Girl in Bathroom #3
• 1:12—Breasts sitting in chair in adult film preview that Craig Wasson watches on TV.
**Emmanuelle IV** (1984) . . . . . . .Uncredited Dream Girl
••• 0:19—Breasts, getting coached by Sylvia Kristel during dream-like sequence on how to get a guy aroused.
**Fatal Games** (1984) . . . . . . . . . Uncredited Shower Girl
• 0:14—Brief, out of focus side of left breast and upper half of buns, taking a shower in the background while two girls talk. (She's wearing a light blue towel around her hair.)
**Psycho III** (1986) . . . . . Body Double for Diana Scarwid
•• 0:30—Brief breasts and buns getting ready to take a shower, body doubling for Diana Scarwid.
**Nightmare Sisters** (1987). . . . . . . . . . . . . . . . .Marci
••• 0:39—Breasts wearing panties, while standing with Melody and Mickey after transforming from nerds to sexy women.

••• 0:40—Breasts while in the kitchen with Melody and Mickey.

••• 0:44—Nude in the bathtub with Melody and Mickey. Excellent, long scene.

••• 0:47—Breasts while in the bathtub. Nice close up.

••• 0:48—Still more buns and breasts in the bathtub.

**Slavegirls from Beyond Infinity** (1987)...... Shala

• 0:29—Chained up wearing black lingerie. Brief right breast.

• 0:31—Brief side view of left breast on table. Nice pan from her feet to her head while she's lying on her back.

Grandmother's House (1988) ............... Woman

**The Jigsaw Murders** (1988)............ Stripper #1

• 0:28—Very, very brief breasts posing for photographer in white bra and panties when camera passes between her and the other stripper.

**Phantom of the Mall: Eric's Revenge** (1988)
......................... Girl in Dressing Room

• 0:14—Breasts in dressing room and on B&W monitor several times (second room from the left).

**Sorority Babes in the Slimeball Bowl-O-Rama**
(1988)................................... Taffy

0:07—In panties getting spanked with Michelle Bauer.

• 0:12—Nude showering off whipped cream in bathtub while talking to a breasts Michelle Bauer. Excellent long scene!

Warlords (1988) ..................... Dow's Wife

**Murder Weapon** (1989)....... Girl in Shower on TV

• 1:00—Brief left breast on TV that the guys are watching. Scene from *Nightmare Sisters*.

**Bad Girls from Mars** (1990) ............... Myra

• 0:11—Brief side of left breast, then breasts getting massaged on diving board.

**Haunting Fear** (1990) ................... Victoria

••• 0:10—Full frontal nudity, taking a bath and getting out.

•• 0:22—Breasts, while changing into nightgown in bedroom.

••• 0:32—Breasts while lying on Coroner's table.

Mob Boss (1990)........................ Sara

Transylvania Twist (1990) ............... Betty Lou

**Roots of Evil** (1991) .................... Candy

(Unrated version reviewed.)

•• 1:33—Right breast, then breasts while sitting on bed talking to Deanna Lund.

Shadows in the City (1991)........... Fortune Teller

Spirits (1991) ..................... Amy Goldwyn

Munchie (1992) .................. Band Member

**Teenage Exorcist** (1992) ............... Dianne

• 1:03—Brief partial buns in sexy, skimpy outfit, while walking down stairs with Eddie Deezen.

• 1:06—More brief partial buns.

• 1:13—Partial buns, during struggle with Elena Sahagan.

• 1:13—More partial buns, while bending over Jay Richardson.

• 1:16—Partial buns under fishnet stockings with Deezen.

*Made for Cable Movies:*

Acting on Impulse (1993; Showtime)........ Waitress

*Video Tapes:*

**Dark Romances: Volume I and II** (1978) Various Parts

• 3:26—(1:39 into Volume II) Partial breasts in B&W segment while wearing a blonde wig.

**Playboy Video Magazine, Volume 1** (1982)
......................... Marie/Ribald Classic

• 0:01—Full frontal nudity.

•• 0:46—Breasts on the bed with Jean-Pierre.

••• 0:47—Breasts in bathtub. Full frontal nudity in front of fire.

•• 0:49—Breasts outside in the garden.

**More Candid Candid Camera** (1983)
......................... Horseriding Student

••• 0:00—Buns and lower frontal nudity, learning how to ride a horse "bareback" style.

**Playboy Video Magazine, Volume 4** (1983)
..................... Flashdancer/Dream Lover

• 0:15—Very brief lower frontal nudity and buns in orange lingerie.

••• 0:16—Nude, fighting over blue towel with Linnea Quigley in the shower.

••• 0:43—Nude in a sheet covered chair during fantasy sequence. Best for Brinke fans!

**Playboy Video Magazine, Volume 5** (1983)
......................... Candid Camera Girl

•• 0:18—Lots of buns shots, during prank learning how to ride a horse "bare back."

The Girls of Penthouse (1984) .... Ghost Town Woman

**Red Hot Rock** (1984)................... Miss Utah

*a.k.a. Sexy Shorts (on laser disc)*

• 0:41—Brief breasts several times in open-front swimsuit during beauty pageant during "Gimme Gimme Good Lovin'" by Helix.

**Scream Queen Hot Tub Party** (1991) ....... Herself

•• 0:07—Breasts, taking off white outfit and putting on black teddy.

• 0:12—Buns, while walking up the stairs.

•• 0:14—Buns and breasts in shower scene from *Slumber Party Massacre*.

••• 0:19—Breasts and buns, demonstrating the proper Scream Queen way to take a shower.

••• 0:44—Breasts taking off her swimsuit top and soaping up with the other girls.

••• 0:46—Breasts in still shot during the end credits.

**Brinke Stevens Private Collection Volume 1**
(1992) .................................. Herself

•• 0:16—Breasts in *Flashdancers* segment from *Playboy* video magazine.

•• 0:19—Nude in still photo sequence in shower with Linnea Quigley.

• 0:22—Brief breasts lying on slab from *Bad Girls from Beyond Infinity*.

• 0:30—Breasts scenes from *Nightmare Sisters*.

••• 0:41—Breasts, in scenes from that were cut from the U.S. version of *Bad Girls From Mars*.

- 0:43—Buns, in G-string outfit posing for photo session.

**Brinke Stevens Private Collection Volume 2**
(1994)................................ Herself
- 0:01—Buns in gynecology-at-home sketch from *Playboy.*
- •• 0:03—Breasts, while in garden as Marie, from *Ribald Classics.*
- 0:05—Breasts and partial buns in music video by Helix from *Red Hot Rock.*
- •• 0:09—Breasts, after taking off bra in strip-poker scene from *Sole Survivor.*
- ••• 0:10—Breasts with Sylvia Kristel from *Emmanuelle IV.*
- ••• 0:12—Breasts and buns, in screen tests for *The Girls of Penthouse.*
- ••• 0:16—Full frontal nudity, in screen tests for *The Girls of Penthouse.*

*Magazines:*
**Penthouse** (Jul 1982) ............ Marlene & Brinke
- •• 50-67—Left breast and buns.

## Stevens, Connie
*Films:*
**Scorchy** (1971) ..................... Jackie Parker
- •• 0:23—Open blouse, revealing left bra cup while talking on the telephone. Brief breasts swimming in the water after taking off bathing suit top.
- •• 0:52—Side view left breast, taking a shower.
- ••• 0:56—Brief right breast making love in bed with Greg Evigan. Breasts getting tied to the bed by the thieves. Kind of a long shot and a little dark and hard to see.
- 1:00—Brief breasts getting covered with a sheet by the good guy.
Grease 2 (1982) ..................... Miss Mason
Back to the Beach (1987) .................. Connie
Tapeheads (1988) ..................... June Tager
*Miniseries:*
Scruples (1980)................. Maggie McGregor
*Made for TV Movies:*
The Littlest Angel (1969)............ Flying Mistress
Playmates (1972) ................... Patti Holvey
Love's Savage Fury (1979)................... Dolby
*TV:*
Hawaiian Eye (1959-63) ...............Cricket Blake
Wendy and Me (1964-65)........... Wendy Conway

## Stevens, Stella
Mother of actor Andrew Stevens.
*Films:*
Li'l Abner (1959)............Appasionata von Climax
Girls! Girls! Girls! (1962) ............. Robin Gantner
The Nutty Professor (1963)............ Stella Purdy
**The Ballad of Cable Hogue** (1970)...........Hildy
- 1:12—Buns changing into nightgown in bedroom.
- 1:14—Brief top half of breasts in outdoor tub, then buns running into cabin when stagecoach arrives.
The Poseidon Adventure (1972) ..........Linda Rogo

**Slaughter** (1972) ...........................Ann
- •• 0:47—Left breast, several times in bed with Jim Brown.
- 0:55—Left breast, making love in bed with Brown again. Dark.
- 0:57—Brief right breast, in bed afterwards. Close up shot.
- ••• 1:14—Buns and breasts taking a shower and getting out. This is her best nude scene.
Arnold (1973) .............................Karen
The Manitou (1977)................. Amelia Crusoe
Chained Heat (1983; U.S./German) ........... Taylor
The Longshot (1986) ...................... Nicki
Down the Drain (1989) ...................Sophia
- 0:45—In black lingerie yelling at Dino in the bathroom.
Mom (1989) ........................ Beverly Hills
Last Call (1990) ......................... Betty
- 0:52—Very brief left nipple popping out of black lingerie top while making love with Jason on a pool table.
South Beach (1992) ....................... Nancy
The Terror Within II (1992)....................Kara
Body Chemistry 3: Point of Seduction (1993)
.......................... Frannie Sibley
Molly & Gina (1993) ........................ n.a.
Hard Drive (1994) .......................Susan
(Unrated version reviewed.)
*Made for Cable Movies:*
Attack of the 5' 2" Women (1994; Showtime) . Lawanda
*Made for Cable TV:*
Dream On: Over Your Dead Body (1990; HBO)
.......................... Lyla Murphy
*Made for TV Movies:*
Man Against the Mob (1988)............. Joey Day
*TV:*
Santa Barbara .......................Phyllis Blake
Ben Casey (1965)....................Jane Hancock
Flamingo Road (1981-82) ......... Lute-Mae Sanders
*Magazines:*
**Playboy** (Jan 1960)................. Playmate
**Playboy** (Dec 1973) .............Sex Stars of 1973
- •• 210—Breasts behind plants.
**Playboy** (Jan 1974)......... Twenty Years of Playboy
- 201-202—Buns, posing with a cross-eyed funny face.
Playboy (Jan 1989).............Women of the Sixties
161—Half of left breast behind pink material.
**Playboy** (Jan 1994)........... 40 Memorable Years
- 87—Buns and partial left breast.

## Stevenson, Cynthia
*Films:*
**The Player** (1992) ............... Bonnie Sherow
- •• 0:19—Breasts, sitting in spa with Tim Robbins.
Watch It (1993) ......................... Ellen
*Made for Cable TV:*
Dream On: Off-Off Broadway Bound (1994; HBO)
..............................Abby Kaplow

*TV:*
Cheers (1989) . . . . . . . . . . . . . . . . . . . . . . . . . . . . .n.a.
My Talk Show (1990) . . . . . . . . . . . . . . . . Jennifer Bass
Bob (1992-93) . . . . . . . . . . . . . . . . . . . . . . . . . .Tricia

## Stevenson, Judy

*Films:*
**Alvin Rides Again** (1974; Australian) . . . . . .Housewife
•• 0:01—Full frontal nudity, dropping her towel while Alvin washes her window.
Cathy's Child (1979; Australian) . . . . . . . . . . . . . . . . Lil

## Stevenson, Juliet

*Films:*
**Drowning by Numbers** (1988; British)
. . . . . . . . . . . . . . . . . . . . . . . . . . . .Cisse Colpitts 2
• 0:57—Lower frontal nudity and left breast, while trying to entice Hardy. Long shot.
The March (1990; British) . . . . . . . . . . . Uare Fitzgerald
Truly, Madly, Deeply (1991) . . . . . . . . . . . . . . . . .Nina
0:46—Very, very brief, blurry tip of left breast, when Alan Rickman pushes her out of the bedroom.
The Trial (1994; British) . . . . . . . . . . . .Fraulein Burstner
*Made for TV Movies:*
Masterpiece Theatre: A Doll's House (1992) . . . . . .Nora

## Stewart, Alexandra

*Films:*
**Kemek** . . . . . . . . . . . . . . . . . . . . . . . . . . . . . Marisa
• 0:26—Brief right breast while sitting up in bed.
0:42—In sheer white dress.
• 0:49—Right breast while kneeling in bed. Out of focus.
0:51—Very, very brief tip of right breast while crying in bed and talking to David Henison.
• 0:52—Brief breasts lying in bed with Henison.
The Bride Wore Black (1968; French/Italian)
. . . . . . . . . . . . . . . . . . . . . . . . . . . . .Miss Becker
**Because of the Cats** (1973) . . . . . . . . . . . . . Theodora
• 0:16—Breasts under sheer black blouse.
•• 0:43—Breasts, sitting up and covering herself while sunbathing outside.
Goodbye Emmanuelle (1977) . . . . : . . . . . . . Dorothee
The Uncanny (1977; British) . . . . . . . . . . . . .Mrs. Blake
**In Praise of Older Women** (1978; Canadian) . . Paula
•• 1:21—Breasts in bed with Tom Berenger.
•• 1:23—Nude, in and out of bed with Berenger.
The Last Chase (1980) . . . . . . . . . . . . . . . . . . . . Eudora
Agency (1981; Canadian) . . . . . . . . . . . . . . . . . . Mimi
Chanel Solitaire (1981) . . . . . . . . . . . . . . . . . . . .n.a.
Under the Cherry Moon (1986) . . . . . . . . Mrs. Sharon
Frantic (1988) . . . . . . . . . . . . . . . . . . . . . . . . . . . Edie
*Made for Cable TV:*
**The Hitchhiker: Shattered Vows** . . . . Jackie Winslow
• 0:04—In white bra and panties, then side view breasts making love in bed with Jeff.
*Magazines:*
**Playboy** (Oct 1978) . . . . . . Observing "Older Women"
•• 193-195—Nude.

## Stewart, Catherine Mary

*Films:*
Nighthawks (1981) . . . . . . . . . . . . . . . . . . . . . .Salesgirl
The Beach Girls (1982) . . . . . . . . . . . . . . . . Surfer Girl
The Last Starfighter (1984) . . . . . . . . . .Maggie Gordon
Night of the Comet (1984) . . . . . . . . . . . . . . .Regina
Mischief (1985) . . . . . . . . . . . . . . . . . . . . . . . Bunny
Dudes (1987) . . . . . . . . . . . . Jessie, Gas Station Owner
Nightflyers (1987) . . . . . . . . . . . . . . . . . . . . .Miranda
Scenes from the Goldmine (1987) . . . . . .Debi D'Angelo
World Gone Wild (1988) . . . . . . . . . . . . . . . . .Angie
Weekend at Bernie's (1989) . . . . . . . . . . Gwen Saunders
*a.k.a. Hot and Cold*
Cafe Romeo (1991) . . . . . . . . . . . . . . . . . . . . . . . . .Lia
Samurai Cowboy (1993) . . . . . . . . . . . . . . . . . . . . n.a.
*Made for Cable Movies:*
**Psychic** (1992; USA) . . . . . . . . . . . . . . . . . . . . Laurel
• 0:45—Very brief right breast, twice, at the end of love making scene with Zach Galligan.
The Sea Wolf (1993; TNT) . . . . . . . . . . . Flaxen Brewster
*Made for TV Movies:*
Ordeal in the Arctic (1993) . . . . . . . . . . . . . . . . Wilma
*TV:*
Hearts are Wild (1991) . . . . . . . . . . . . . . Kyle Hubbard

## Stewart, Liz

*Video Tapes:*
Playmate Playoffs . . . . . . . . . . . . . . . . . . . . . . .Playmate
**Playboy Video Magazine, Volume 10** (1986)
. . . . . . . . . . . . . . . . . . . . . . . . . . The Goldner Girls
•• 0:17—Breasts during modeling session for photographer David Goldner.
**Wet and Wild** (1989) . . . . . . . . . . . . . . . . . . . . Model
*Magazines:*
**Playboy** (Jul 1984) . . . . . . . . . . . . . . . . . . . . .Playmate
**Playboy's Girls of Summer '86** (Aug 1986). . . Herself
••• 68-69—Full frontal nudity.
**Playboy's 1987 Book of Lingerie** (Mar 1987)
. . . . . . . . . . . . . . . . . . . . . . . . . . . . . . . . . . .Herself
••• 26-27—Full frontal nudity.
•• 29—Side of left breast and buns.
• 76—Upper half of left breast and lower frontal nudity.
•• 99—Left breast and lower frontal nudity.
••• 105—Full frontal nudity.
**Playboy's Calendar Playmates** (Nov 1992). . . Herself
•• 46—Buns and side of right breast.
**Playboy's Nudes** (Dec 1993) . . . . . . . . . . . . . . Herself
••• 92—Full frontal nudity.

## Steyn, Jennifer

*Films:*
**Curse III: Blood Sacrifice** (1990) . . . . . . . . . . . Cindy
• 0:35—Side of left breast, kissing Roger while at the beach inside a tent. Upper half of left breast when blade tears through tent.
0:40—Breasts, covered with blood when Geoff looks in the tent.
Night of the Cyclone (1990) . . . . . . . . . . . . . . Celeste

**Demon Keeper** (1993) . . . . . . . . . . . . . .Ruth Stanley
- 0:31—Very brief right breast, while lying dead in bed next to Howard.
- • 0:37—Breasts after taking off robe in front of mirror.
- 0:39—Breasts, while caressed by devil creature. Close-up, don't see face.

Freefall (1993). . . . . . . . . . . . . . . . . . . . . . . Secretary

## Stiles, Shannon

*Films:*
**Bikini Island** (1991) . . . . . . . . . . . . . . . . . . . . .Nikki
- 0:35—Breasts in bed with Jack taking off her top while someone watches through keyhole.

*Video Tapes:*
Rock Video Girls 2 (1992) . . . . . . . . . . . . . . . . . Herself

## • Stillo, Janine

*Films:*
To Protect and Serve (1992) . . . . . . . . . . . . Counter Girl
*Made for Cable TV:*
**Red Shoe Diaries: The Game** (1994; Showtime)
. . . . . . . . . . . . . . . . . . . . . . . . . . . . . . . . . . . . Tara
- 0:14—Brief breasts, while arching her back while making love with Marty while Lily and John make love nearby.

## Stolze, Lena

*Films:*
Man Under Suspicion (1985) . . . . . . . . . . . . . . .Jessica
Maschenka (1987; British/German). . . . . . . . . . . .Klara
**The Nasty Girl** (1989; German) . . . . . . . . . . . . Sonja
 1:24—Most of her left breast in gaping nightgown while bending over to get earrings put on.
- 1:27—Brief breasts and lower frontal nudity, while swimming in water.

## Stone, Dee Wallace

See: Wallace Stone, Dee.

## Stone, Madison

a.k.a. Adult film actress Madison.
*Films:*
**Naked Obsession** (1990) . . . . . . . . . . . . . . . . Jezebel
- •• 0:35—In black leather outfit. Buns in G-string and breasts.
- •• 0:37—More breasts and buns.
- 0:38—More.
- •• 0:39—Brief full frontal nudity.

**Evil Toons** (1991) . . . . . . . . . . . . . . . . . . . . .Roxanne
- ••• 0:20—Buns in G-string, then breasts doing a strip routine in front of her girlfriends.
- ••• 0:33—Breasts, taking off blouse and putting on bra and panties. Buns in sheer panties.
- •• 0:36—Breasts on the floor, getting attacked by the monster.
- ••• 0:38—Breasts walking around, covered with blood, talking with Megan.
- •• 0:41—Breasts putting blouse on.
- 0:42—Breasts on couch with Biff.

- 0:55—Left breast in open blouse, seducing Burt.
- 0:59—Brief breasts several times, dead, when the other girls discover her.

## Stone, Sharon

*Films:*
Stardust Memories (1980) . . . . .Blonde on Passing Train
Deadly Blessing (1981). . . . . . . . . . . . . . . . . . . . Lana
**Irreconcilable Differences** (1984) . . . Blake Chandler
- •• 0:56—Breasts lowering her blouse in front of Ryan O'Neal during film test.

King Solomon's Mines (1985) . . . . . . . . . . . . . . Jessica
**Allan Quatermain and the Lost City of Gold**
 (1987) . . . . . . . . . . . . . . . . . . . . . . . . Jesse Huston
- 0:20—Very brief lower frontal nudity, seen under loose panties, when she stands up in back of car and pulls her dress off over her head. (Don't really see much, but for the sake of completeness...)

**Cold Steel** (1987). . . . . . . . . . . . . . . . .Kathy Conners
- 0:33—Brief left breast making love in bed with Brad Davis. Dark, hard to see. Brief breasts turning over after making love.

Police Academy 4: Citizens on Patrol (1987)
. . . . . . . . . . . . . . . . . . . . . . . . . . . . . Claire Matson
Above the Law (1988) . . . . . . . . . . . . . . . . .Sara Toscani
**Action Jackson** (1988) . . . . . . . . . . Patrice Dellaplane
- •• 0:34—Breasts in a steam room. Hard to see because of all the steam.
- 0:56—Brief right breast, dead, on the bed when police view her body.

**Blood and Sand** (1989; Spanish). . . . . . . . . .Doña Sol
 0:57—Very brief upper half of right breast, making love on table with Juan.
- •• 0:58—Left breast, making love in bed with Juan. Don't see her face well.
- ••• 1:04—Breasts quite a few times, making love with Juan in the woods.

**Scissors** (1990). . . . . . . . . . . . . . . . . Angela Anderson
 0:04—Upper half of left breast sitting up after attack in elevator.
- 0:12—Breasts changing clothes.
 0:36—In bra with Steve Railsback. Brief upper half of left breast. Dark.

**Total Recall** (1990) . . . . . . . . . . . . . . . . . . . . . . . Lori
- 0:04—Brief right breast in gaping lingerie when leaning over Arnold Schwarzenegger in bed.

he said, she said (1991) . . . . . . . . . . . . . . . . . . . .Linda
Where Sleeping Dogs Lie (1991) . . . . . . . . Serena Black
 0:43—In one piece black swimsuit.
**Year of the Gun** (1991). . . . . . . . . . . . . . Alison King
- 1:00—Brief left breast, while standing against the door, with Andrew McCarthy. Long shot.
- 1:01—Side of left breast, while making love on bed.

**Basic Instinct** (1992). . . . . . . . . . . Catherine Trammel
(Unrated Director's cut reviewed.)
- ••• 0:02—Buns and breasts while making love on top of Johnny in bed, then killing him.

- •• 0:21—Buns and left breast in mirror in her bedroom while Michael Douglas watches while waiting for her.
- • 0:26—Two brief crotch shots while crossing and uncrossing her legs during interrogation.
- •• 0:44—Nude, undressing in her house, while Douglas watches from outside. Medium long shot.
- ••• 1:10—Breasts while in bed with Douglas.
- ••• 1:13—Breasts and buns, tying Douglas up in bed and on top of him.
- •• 1:15—Buns, while sitting on top of Douglas.
- • 1:32—Very brief right breast, with Douglas in front of fireplace.
- ••• 1:43—Breasts, while taking off her blouse in Douglas' apartment.
- ••• 2:00—Breasts, while in bed on top of Douglas.

Diary of a Hitman (1992) . . . . . . . . . . . . . . . . . . . . .Kiki

**Intersection** (1993) . . . . . . . . . . . . . . . Sally Eastman
- • 0:18—Right breast behind glass blocks in shower, then very brief left breast in mirror when she adjusts her robe.

Last Action Hero (1993) . . . . . . . . . . . . . . . . . . Herself

**Sliver** (1993) . . . . . . . . . . . . . . . . . . . . . . Carly Norris
- • 0:14—Brief left breast, while in bathtub.
- • 0:43—Buns, in black bra, while making love on William Baldwin's lap.
- • 0:44—Half of right breast, while under Baldwin.
- •• 0:45—Brief left breast, while getting up out of bed. Side view breasts and buns, while getting dressed.
- •• 0:46—Buns and breasts, while taking off her top again.

*Miniseries:*
War and Remembrance (1988) . . . . . . . . . .Janice Henry
*Made for TV Movies:*
Calendar Girl Murders (1984) . . . . . . . . . . . . . . . .Cassie
Tears in the Rain (1988; British). . . . . . . . .Casey Cantrell
*TV:*
Bay City Blues (1983) . . . . . . . . . . . . . .Cathy St. Marie
*Magazines:*
**Playboy** (Jul 1990). . . . . . . . . . . . .Dishing with Sharon
- ••• 118-127—Breasts in B&W photos.

**Playboy** (Nov 1993) . . . . . . . . . . . Sex in Cinema 1993
- •• 133—Lower frontal nudity in interrogation chair scene from *Basic Instinct.*

**Playboy** (Dec 1993). . . . . . . . . . . . . . . Sex Stars 1993
- • 177—Right breast, slightly out of focus B&W photo.

Playboy (Jan 1994) . . . . . . . . . . . . . . Remember Sharon

## Stoner, Sherri

Story editor for Steven Spielberg.
She was Disney's animator's model for Ariel in *The Little Mermaid* and Belle in *Beauty and the Beast.*
*Films:*
Impulse (1984) . . . . . . . . . . . . . . . . . . . . . . Young Girl
Lovelines (1984) . . . . . . . . . . . . . . . . . . . . . . . . . Suzy
**Reform School Girls** (1986). . . . . . . . . . . . . . . .Lisa
- • 1:03—Very brief breasts and buns, lying on stomach in the restroom, getting branded by bad girls.

*Made for TV Movies:*
My Mother's Secret Life (1984) . . . . . . . . Laura Sievers

## • Stones, Tammy
*Films:*
Neurotic Cabaret (1991) . . . . . . . . . . . . . . . . . . .Terri
**Death Ring** (1992). . . . . . . . . . . . . . . . Cindy Maddin
- ••• 0:53—Breasts in open lingerie top in Skylord's apartment.

## Stowe, Madeleine
Wife of actor Brian Benben.
*Films:*
Stakeout (1987) . . . . . . . . . . . . . . . . . . . Maira McGuire
   0:43—Buns and brief side view of right breast getting a towel after taking a shower while Richard Dreyfuss watches her.
**Tropical Snow** (1989) . . . . . . . . . . . . . . . . . . . .Marina
- • 0:05—Very brief side view of left breast putting red dress on.
- • 0:11—Buns, lying in bed. Very brief right breast sitting up. (I wish they could have panned the camera to the right!)
- •• 0:24—Breasts in mirror putting red dress on.
   0:32—Buns, lying on top of Tavo in bed.
- • 0:54—Brief breasts making love in the water with Tavo. Then buns, lying on the beach (long shot.)
   1:22—Long shot side view of right breast in water with Tavo.

Worth Winning (1989). . . . . . . . . . . . Veronica Briskow
Closet Land (1990) . . . . . . . . . . . . . . . . . . The Author
**Revenge** (1990) . . . . . . . . . . . . . . . . . . . . . . . .Miryea
   0:44—Side view of buns when Kevin Costner pulls up her dress to make love with her.
   0:52—In white slip talking to Costner in bedroom.
- • 1:00—Buns, making love with Costner in jeep. Very brief breasts coming out of the water.
- • 1:07—Very brief breasts when Costner is getting beat up.

The Two Jakes (1990). . . . . . . . . . . . . . . .Lillian Bodine
   0:23—Very brief buns, when Jack Nicholson lifts her slip up in bed.
The Last of the Mohicans (1992) . . . . . . . . .Cora Munro
**Unlawful Entry** (1992) . . . . . . . . . . . . . . . .Karen Carr
- ••• 0:56—Breasts and partial buns, while making love on top of Kurt Russell in bed.

Another Stakeout (1993) . . . . . . . . . . . . . . . . . .Maria
**Blink** (1993) . . . . . . . . . . . . . . . . . . . . . Emma Brody
- • 1:04—Side of left breast while walking to look at roses.
- •• 1:06—Breasts, after taking off top and making love with Aidan Quinn.

China Moon (1993) . . . . . . . . . . . . . . . . . . . . . . . n.a.
**Short Cuts** (1993) . . . . . . . . . . . . . . . .Sherri Shepard
- •• 1:20—Left breast, while posing for painting by Julianne Moore.
- • 2:07—(0:24 into Part 2) Brief left breast, while turning over in bed.

Bad Girls (1994). . . . . . . . . . . . . . . . . . . Cody Zamora

*TV:*
The Gangster Chronicles (1981) . . . . . . . . .Ruth Lasker
*Magazines:*
**Playboy** (Aug 1994). . . . . . . . . . . . . . . . . . Potpourri
• 158—Left breast under sheer black dress. B&W.

# Strain, Julie

*Films:*
**Carnal Crimes** (1991). . . . . . . . . . . . . . . . . . . Ingrid
••• 0:55—Breasts and partial buns, wearing black garter
belt and stockings, making love with Renny in restroom. Long scene.
**Double Impact** (1991) . . . . . . . . . . . . . . . . . Student
• 0:09—Brief buns, while lying on floor in pink leotard
in exercise class.
**Mirror Images** (1991) . . . . . . . . . . . . . . . . . . . Gina
•• 0:48—Buns and right breast, making love in bed
with Kaitlin.
•• 0:49—Buns in black bra and panties.
• 0:57—Buns in black body suit.
••• 0:58—Breasts lying on bed, watching the slave girl
and guy with the mask make love.
**Out for Justice** (1991) . . . . . . . . . . . . . Roxanne Ford
• 0:53—Brief side view of right breast in Polaroid photograph that Steven Seagal looks at.
• 1:06—Brief side view of right breast in Polaroid
again.
• 1:11—Brief right breast, twice, dead in bed when
discovered by Seagal.
• 1:12—Briefly in Polaroid again.
**Sunset Heat** (1991)
. . . . . . . . . . . . . . . Carl's Breakfast Girl/Party Statuette
(Unrated version reviewed.)
•• 0:51—Breasts, covered with silver paint, made up to
look like a statue at the party.
Kuffs (1992) . . . . . . . . . . . . . . . . . . . . . . . . Kane's Girl
**Night Rhythms** (1992). . . . . . . . . . . . . . . . . . . Linda
(Unrated version reviewed.)
••• 0:03—In white bra, then left breast, while talking on
the phone and playing with herself.
**Psycho Cop 2** (1992) . . . . . . . . . . . . . . . . Stephanie
0:19—Brief buns, when elevator door opens.
••• 0:21—Buns in cowboy outfit, then breasts with red
star pasties while doing dance routine.
•• 0:25—Breasts and buns, while with the two other
dancers and the guys.
• 0:31—Breasts and buns, when Mike comes back.
• 0:33—Breasts, when the guys start worrying about
Mike.
• 0:38—Breasts, when putting them in Brian's face.
• 0:41—Breasts, when with Brian. Buns in cowboy
outfit for the rest of the film.
The Unnameable II (1992) . . . . . . . . . . . . . . Creature
**Witchcraft IV: Virgin Heart** (1992) . . . . . Belladonna
• 0:25—Buns, while dancing on stage in a red bra and
red G-string.
••• 0:27—Breasts, dancing on stage.
•• 0:46—Breasts on the floor with Santara.
• 0:49—Brief breasts in open dress on couch with Will.

• 1:15—Breasts, lying on couch in her dressing room
while Will tries to talk to her.
**Enemy Gold** (1993) . . . . . . . . . . . . . . . . .Jewel Panther
0:53—In two piece swimsuit.
••• 1:03—Breasts and buns in leather outfit while dancing with a sword in front of a fire.
**Fit To Kill** (1993) . . . . . . . . . . . . . . . . . . . .Blu Steele
•• 0:10—Buns in swimsuit while doing stretching exer-
cises.
•• 0:11—Breasts, undoing her swimsuit top.
•• 0:47—Breasts and buns in G-string, while making
love in the kitchen with Brett Clark.
0:49—In one piece swimsuit.
**Future Shock** (1993) . . . . . . . . . . . . . . .Female Dancer
• 0:03—Brief buns in sexy black G-string outfit with
black top, while dancing in front of guy sitting in
electric chair.
Naked Gun 33 1/3: The Final Insult (1993)
. . . . . . . . . . . . . . . . . . . . . . . . . . . . . . . . Dominatrix
**Money to Burn** (1994) . . . . . . . . . . . . . . . . . . . . . Jill
• 0:38—Brief buns in G-string under hiked up dress,
several times, while dancing in club.
•• 0:39—Stripping out of her dress down to red bra,
panties, garter belt and stockings, then breasts and
buns. More when making love with Ann on the
floor.
••• 0:42—Nude, waking up and getting dressed.
*Video Tapes:*
**Penthouse Centerfold—Julie Strain** (1991) . . . .Pet
**Sexy Lingerie III** (1991). . . . . . . . . . . . . . . . . Model
**Penthouse Fast Cars/Fantasy Women** (1992)
. . . . . . . . . . . . . . . . . . . . . . . . . . . . . . . . . . . Model
**Penthouse Pet of the Year Playoff 1992** (1992)
. . . . . . . . . . . . . . . . . . . . . . . . . . . . . . . . . . . . .Pet
••• 0:16—Nude at the beach, in the house, in the bath-
tub, outside, at a desk on a bed.
**Penthouse Ready to Ride** (1992) . . . . . . . . . Model
**Penthouse Satin & Lace II: Hollywood Undercover**
(1992) . . . . . . . . . . . . . . . . . . . . . . . . . . . . . . . .Pet
**Penthouse Satin & Lace: An Erotic History of
Lingerie** (1992) . . . . . . . . . . . . . . . . . . . . . . Model
••• 0:01—Nude with blonde woman.
••• 0:09—Nude with blonde woman in elevator.
••• 0:29—Nude outside.
••• 0:46—Full frontal nudity with three guys.
••• 0:49—Full frontal nudity with two blonde women.
**Sexy Lingerie IV** (1992) . . . . . . . . . . . . . . . . . Model
**Buck Naked Line Dancing** (1993) . . . . . . . . . Dancer
••• 0:00—Breasts and buns throughout. Sometimes
wearing pasties with tassels. If you are a faithful
reader of this book, you should be able to recognize
who she is!
**The Penthouse All-Pet Workout** (1993). . . . . . .Pet
• 0:00—Breasts during introduction.
•• 0:03—Brief nude shots while getting undressed and
suited up.
••• 0:06—Nude while posing outside.
••• 0:43—Nude with the other girls, exercising, working
with equipment, in the pool and spa.

**Penthouse Forum Letters: Volume 1** (1993)
. . . . . . . . . . . . . . Reach Out and Touch Someone/Wife
••• 1:09—Breasts on couch having phone sex with her
husband. Great if you also like to hear women talk
dirty.

**Hot Body Video Magazine: Hot Stuff** (1994) . . . n.a.

**Penthouse Pet of the Year Winners 1993: Mahalia
& Julie** (1994) . . . . . . . . . . . . . . . . . . . . . . . . . . . . Pet
• 0:00—Brief lower frontal nudity during introduc-
tion.
••• 0:01—Nude in bed.
••• 0:04—Nude in chair and making love with a guy.
••• 0:06—Nude, while touching herself while a trio of
women work on a film.
••• 0:10—Full frontal nudity, while making love with a
guy in a B&W movie.
••• 0:12—Nude in house in a bodysuit, then after ripping it off.
••• 0:16—Nude, while wearing a garter belt and stockings outside and in pool.
• 0:34—Nude during end credits.

*CD-ROM:*

**Penthouse Interactive Virtual Photo Shoot, Disc 1**
(1993) . . . . . . . . . . . . . . . . . . . . . . . . . . . . . . . . . . . . Pet

*Magazines:*

**Playboy** (May 1991) . . . . . . . . . . . . . . . . . . . Grapevine
•• 183—Left breast.
**Penthouse** (Jun 1991) . . . . . . . . . . . . . . . . . . . . . Pet
••• 71-85—Nude.
**Playboy** (Jul 1991) . . . . . . . . . . . . . The Height Report
••• 134-135—Full frontal nudity.
**Penthouse** (Feb 1992) . . . . . . . . . . . . . . . . . . . . Julie
••• 39-47—Nude in B&W photos.
**Penthouse** (Jun 1992) . . . . . . . . . Pet of the Year Playoff
••• 92-93—Nude.
**Penthouse** (Jan 1993) . . . . . . . . . . . . . Pet of the Year
••• 108-123—Nude.
**Penthouse** (Feb 1994) . . . . . . Julie and Jacqueline/Julie
••• 91-99—Nude.

# Strasberg, Susan

Daughter of acting teacher Lee Strasberg.
*Films:*
The Trip (1967) . . . . . . . . . . . . . . . . . . . . Sally Groves
The Brotherhood (1968) . . . . . . . . . . . . Emma Ginetta
Psych-Out (1968) . . . . . . . . . . . . . . . . . . . Jennie Davis
Psycho Sisters (1974) . . . . . . . . . . . . . . . . . . . Brenda
The Manitou (1977) . . . . . . . . . . . . . . . . Karen Tandy
1:33—Breasts, fighting the creature in bed. Really
bad special effects. Too dark to see anything.
Rollercoaster (1977) . . . . . . . . . . . . . . . . . . . . . Fran
**In Praise of Older Women** (1978; Canadian)
. . . . . . . . . . . . . . . . . . . . . . . . . . . . . . . . . . . . Bobbie
•• 1:03—Left breast, while making love in bed with
Tom Berenger.
••• 1:04—Breasts in bed after Berenger rolls off her.
Bloody Birthday (1980) . . . . . . . . . . . . . . . . . Miss Davis
Sweet Sixteen (1982) . . . . . . . . . . . . . . Joanne Morgan
The Delta Force (1986) . . . . . . . . . . . . . . Debra Levine

The Runnin' Kind (1988) . . . . . . . . . . . . . . Carol Curtis
The Light in the Jungle (1990) . . . . . . Helene Schweitzer
*TV:*
The Marriage (1954) . . . . . . . . . . . . . . . . Emily Marriott
Toma (1973-74) . . . . . . . . . . . . . . . . . . . . . Patty Toma

# Stratten, Dorothy

*Films:*
Americathon (1979) . . . . . . . . . . . . . . . . Playboy Bunny
**Autumn Born** (1979) . . . . . . . . . . . . . . . . . . . . . . Tara
0:03—In dressing room in beige bra, panties, garter
belt and stockings changing clothes. Long, close-up
lingering shots.
0:16—Unconscious in beige lingerie, then conscious, walking around the room.
0:21—In bra and panties getting her rear end
whipped while tied to the bed.
•• 0:26—Left breast taking bath, then right breast getting up, then breasts dressing.
• 0:30—Side view of left breast, then breasts climbing
back into bed.
0:35—In beige bra and panties in the shower with
her captor.
0:43—Quick cuts of various scenes.
••• 0:46—In white bra and panties, side view of left
breast and buns, then breasts in bathtub. Long
scene.
• 0:50—Side view of left breast and buns getting undressed. Nice buns shot. Right breast lying down in
chair.
• 1:03—Brief breasts shots during flashbacks.
Skatetown, U.S.A. (1979) . . . . . . . . Girl who orders Pizza
Galaxina (1980) . . . . . . . . . . . . . . . . . . . . . . Galaxina
They All Laughed (1981) . . . . . . . . . . . Dolores Martin
*Video Tapes:*
**Playboy Video Magazine, Volume 4** (1983)
. . . . . . . . . . . . . . . . . . . . . . . . . . . . . . . . . . . Playmate
• 1:09—Brief breasts in black lingerie during photo
shoot.
•• 1:13—Breasts and buns in bubble bath.
•• 1:19—Breasts posing in dance studio.
• 1:22—More brief breasts shots from photo shoot.
**Dorothy Stratten, The Untold Story** (1985)
. . . . . . . . . . . . . . . . . . . . . . . . . . . . . . . . . . . . Herself
•• 0:02—Breasts during photo session on sofa.
•• 0:03—Left breast in mirror before falling off sofa,
breasts after.
••• 0:06—Breasts outside in a field.
••• 0:14—Breasts and buns in still photos.
••• 0:17—Full frontal nudity while posing in front of
mirrored wall with a ballet rail.
••• 0:26—Breasts in still photos.
••• 0:39—Breasts in bathtub for Playmate of the Year
pictorial.
••• 1:02—Nude in classic pin-up girl poses.
••• 1:05—Breasts in bathtub and on sofa.

**Playboy's Playmates of the Year: The '80s** (1989)
. . . . . . . . . . . . . . . . . . . . Playmate of the Year 1980
••• 0:27—Breasts and buns in various settings during
photo session.
•• 0:32—Brief breasts holding flowers in a field.
•• 0:51—Breasts in field.
**Hugh Hefner: Once Upon a Time** (1992) . . . Herself
• 1:08—Right breast in bathtub.

*Magazines:*
**Playboy** (Aug 1979). . . . . . . . . . . . . . . . . Playmate
**Playboy** (Dec 1979). . . . . . . . . . . . . Sex Stars of 1979
••• 258—Breasts.
**Playboy** (Jun 1980) . . . . . . . . . . . Playmate of the Year
••• 168-179—Nude.
**Playboy** (Oct 1980). . . . . . . . . . . . . . .Girls of Canada
••• 151—Full frontal nudity.
**Playboy** (Dec 1980). . . . . . . . . . . . . Sex Stars of 1980
•• 247—Left breast.
**Playboy** (Jan 1989) . . . . . . . . . . Women of the Eighties
219—Full frontal nudity.
**Playboy's Nudes** (Oct 1990). . . . . . . . . . . . . . Herself
••• 102—Full frontal nudity.
**Playboy** (Jan 1994) . . . . . . . . . . .40 Memorable Years
••• 93—Full frontal nudity.

## Streep, Meryl

*Films:*
Julia (1977). . . . . . . . . . . . . . . . . . . . . . . .Anne Marie
The Deer Hunter (1978) . . . . . . . . . . . . . . . . . . . Linda
Kramer vs. Kramer (1979) . . . . . . . . . . . . Joanna Kramer
(Academy Award for Best Supporting Actress.)
Manhattan (1979). . . . . . . . . . . . . . . . . . . . . . . . .Jill
The Seduction of Joe Tynan (1979) . . . . . .Karen Traynor
The French Lieutenant's Woman (1981) . . . .Sarah/Anna
Sophie's Choice (1982) . . . . . . . . . . . . . . . . . Sophie
(Academy Award for Best Actress.)
**Still of the Night** (1982) . . . . . . . . . .Brooke Reynolds
0:22—Side view of right breast and buns taking off
robe for the massage guy. Long shot, don't see her
face.
Falling In Love (1984) . . . . . . . . . . . . . . .Molly Gilmore
**Silkwood** (1984) . . . . . . . . . . . . . . . . . .Karen Silkwood
• 0:24—Very brief glimpse of upper half of left breast
when she flashes it in nuclear reactor office.
Out of Africa (1985) . . . . . . . . . . . . . . . . . Karen Blixen
Plenty (1985) . . . . . . . . . . . . . . . . . . . . . . . . . Susan
Heartburn (1986) . . . . . . . . . . . . . . . . . . . . . Rachel
Ironweed (1987). . . . . . . . . . . . . . . . . . . . . . . . Helen
A Cry in the Dark (1988). . . . . . . . . . Lindy Chamberlain
1:44—Brief side view of right breast in jail being ex-
amined by two female guards. Don't see her face,
probably a body double.
She-Devil (1989). . . . . . . . . . . . . . . . . . . .Mary Fisher
Postcards from the Edge (1990) . . . . . . . . Suzanne Vale
Defending Your Life (1991). . . . . . . . . . . . . . . . . Julia
Death Becomes Her (1992). . . . . . . . . Madeline Ashton
The House of Spirits (1993). . . . . . . . . . . . . . . .Clara
*Miniseries:*
Holocaust (1978) . . . . . . . . . . . . . . . Inga Helms Weiss

## • Street, Rebecca

*Films:*
**Lonely Hearts** (1991) . . . . . . . . . . . . . . .Jane Ericson
• 1:12—Brief side of right breast, while making love
on top of Eric Roberts on couch.
Warlock: The Armageddon (1993) . . . . . . . . . . . .Kate

## Strickland, Connie

*Films:*
The Roommates (1973) . . . . . . . . . . . . . . . . . . . Alice
**Act of Vengeance** (1974) . . . . . . . . . . . . . . . Teresa
*a.k.a. The Rape Squad*
(Not to be confused with the film with the same name
starring Charles Bronson.)
• 0:37—Brief full frontal nudity under water, several
times, sitting in spa with other women. (She's the
blonde on the far right.)
**The Centerfold Girls** (1974). . . . . . . . . . . . . . Patsy
•• 1:07—Breasts in bathroom washing her halter top
just before getting killed.

## • Stringfield, Sherry

*TV:*
The Guiding Light . . . . . . . . . . . . . . . . . . . . . . Blake
NYPD Blue (1993-94). . . . . . . . . . . Laura Hughes Kelly
**NYPD Blue: True Confessions** (Oct 12, 1993) . . . . . .
Laura Hughes Kelly
•• 0:22—Brief buns and back side of right breast, twice,
getting out of bed and walking to get her robe.
ER (1994- ). . . . . . . . . . . . . . . . . . . . . . . . . . . . . n.a.

## Strohmeier, Tara

*Films:*
Candy Stripe Nurses (1974) . . . . . . . . . . . . . . . . Irene
Truck Turner (1974) . . . . . . . . . . . . . . . . . . . Turnpike
Cover Girl Models (1975). . . . . . . . . . . . . . . . .Mandy
**Hollywood Boulevard** (1976). . . . . . . . . . . .Jill McBain
•• 0:00—Breasts getting out of van and standing with
film crew.
• 0:31—Silhouette of breasts, while making love with
P.G.
••• 0:32—Breasts sunbathing with Bobbi and Candy.
••• 0:33—Breasts acting for film on hammock. Long
scene.
The Great Texas Dynamite Chase (1977) . . . . . . . . .Pam
**Kentucky Fried Movie** (1977) . . . . . . . . . . . . . . Girl
•• 1:16—In bra, then breasts making love on couch
with her boyfriend while people on the TV news
watch them.
**Malibu Beach** (1978). . . . . . . . . . . . . . . . Glorianna
• 0:08—Breasts kissing her boyfriend at the beach
when someone steals her towel.
**Van Nuys Blvd.** (1979). . . . . . . . . . . . . . . . .Wanda
•• 0:21—Breasts, while playing around with food with
Bobby in the back of his van.
• 0:51—Brief breasts, flashing while hitchhiking to get
a ride.
*Made for TV Movies:*
The Lakeside Killer (1979) . . . . . . . . . . . . . . . . Janie

## Strong, Brenda

*Films:*
**Weekend Warriors** (1986) . . . . . . . . Danny El Dubois
• 0:44—Breasts, lit from the side, standing in the dark.
Spaceballs (1987) . . . . . . . . . . . . . . . . . . . . . . . Nurse
Stepfather III: Father's Day (1992)
. . . . . . . . . . . . . . . . . . . . . . . Crime Search Reporter
Malice (1993) . . . . . . . . . . . . . . . . . . . . . . . . . Claudia
My Life (1993) . . . . . . . . . . . . . . . . . . . . . . . . . Laura
*Made for TV Movies:*
Island City (1994) . . . . . . . . . . . . . . . . . . . . . . . . n.a.
*TV:*
Twin Peaks (1990-91) . . . . . . . . . . . . . . . . . . . . Jones

## Struthers, Sally

*Films:*
**Five Easy Pieces** (1970) . . . . . . . . . . . . . . . . . . . Betty
0:15—In a bra sitting on a couch in the living room
with Jack Nicholson and another man and a woman.
•• 0:34—Brief breasts a couple of times making love
with Nicholson. Lots of great moaning, but hard to
see anything.
The Getaway (1972) . . . . . . . . . . . . . . . . . . Fran Clinton
1:15—In black bra getting out of bed and leaning
over injured bad guy to get something.
*Made for TV Movies:*
Hey, I'm Alive (1975). . . . . . . . . . . . . . . . Helen Klaben
Intimate Strangers (1977) . . . . . . . . . . . . . Janis Halston
In the Best Interest of the Children (1992)
. . . . . . . . . . . . . . . . . . . . . . . . . . . . . Patty Pepper
*TV:*
The Summer Smother's Show (1970) . . . . . . . . . Regular
The Tim Conway Comedy Hour (1970). . . . . . . . Regular
All In the Family (1971-78) . . . . . . . . Gloria Bunker Stivic
Gloria (1982-83) . . . . . . . . . . . . . . Gloria Bunker Stivic
9 to 5 (1986-88) . . . . . . . . . . . . . . Marsha Shrimpton

## Stuart, Cassie

*Films:*
**Ordeal by Innocence** (1984) . . . . . . . . Maureen Clegg
•• 1:14—Breasts in bed talking to Donald Sutherland.
**Secret Places** (1984; British) . . . . . . . . . . . . . . . Nina
• 0:07—Brief breasts, after pulling up her blouse to
show off her breasts to her girlfriends.
• 1:15—Brief left breast, getting into bathtub with the
help of her girlfriends. (She's drunk.)
Slayground (1984; British). . . . . . . . . . . . . . . . . Fran
Stealing Heaven (1988; British/Yugoslavian) . . Petronilla
Afraid of the Dark (1992; British/French)
. . . . . . . . . . . . . . . . . . . . . . . . Woman Neighbor

## Stuart, Wendy

*Films:*
**Incoming Freshman** (1979). . . . . . . . . Miss Seymour
••• 0:25—In purple bra and panties, then breasts and
buns stripping during Professor Bilbo's fantasy.
• 0:55—Buns and side of right breast in fantasy.
• 1:18—Breasts during end credits.
Model Behavior (1982) . . . . . . . . . . . . . . Lily White Girl

## Stubbs, Imogen

*Films:*
**Deadline** (1988) . . . . . . . . . . . . . . . Lady Romy-Burton
0:42—Doing handstands in a bikini top.
• 0:44—Brief left breast, while getting out of bed with
John Hurt. Full frontal nudity turning toward bed,
brief breasts getting back into bed.
**A Summer Story** (1988) . . . . . . . . . . . . . Megan David
•• 0:36—Left breast several times, then right breast
while making love with Frank in barn.
0:41—Very, very brief buns, frolicking in pond at
night with Frank.
1:03—Very brief silhouette of left breast during
Frank's flashback sequence.
Erik the Viking (1989; British) . . . . . . . . . . . . . . . . Aud
True Colors (1991) . . . . . . . . . . . . . . . . . . . . Diana Stiles
*Made for Cable Movies:*
**Fellow Traveller** (1989; HBO) . . . . . . . Sarah Aitchison
• 0:54—Breasts in bed with Asa. Very, very brief right
breast when he rolls off her.

## Styler, Trudie

Wife of singer/actor Sting.
*Films:*
**Fair Game** (1988; Italian) . . . . . . . . . . . . . . . . . . . Eva
0:14—Very, very brief blurry top of right breast in
gaping blouse, while standing up after changing
clothes.
• 0:37—Brief buns, kneeling in bathtub. Very brief
buns in the mirror several times putting on robe and
getting out of the bathtub.

## Sukowa, Barbara

*Films:*
Berlin Alexanderplatz (1983; West German) . . . . . . . n.a.
**The Sicilian** (1987) . . . . . . Camilia Duchess of Crotone
(Director's uncut version reviewed.)
•• 0:05—Buns and brief breasts taking a bath, three
times.
• 0:07—Brief right breast reading Time magazine. Full
frontal nudity in the mirror standing up in the tub.
• 0:08—Brief right breast standing at the window
watching Christopher Lambert steal a horse.
••• 1:01—In bra, then breasts in bedroom with Lam-
bert. More breasts, then nude. Long scene.
Voyager (1991; German/French) . . . . . . . . . . . Hannah
Zentropa (1991; Danish) . . . . . . . . Katharina Hartmann
(Subtitled.)
M. Butterfly (1993) . . . . . . . . . . . . . . Jeanne Gallimard
*Miniseries:*
Space (1987) . . . . . . . . . . . . . . . . . . . . . . . Liesl Kolff

## Sullivan, Sheila

*Films:*
Hickey and Boggs (1972) . . . . . . . . . . . . . . Edith Boggs
**A Name for Evil** (1973) . . . . . . . . . . . . Luanna Baxter
• 0:51—Full frontal nudity dancing in the bar with everybody.

- 0:54—Breasts while Robert Culp makes love with her.
- 0:56—Breasts getting dressed.
- 1:17—Nude, skinny dipping with Culp.

*Magazines:*

**Playboy** (Mar 1973). . . . . . . . . . . . . . . "Evil" Doings
- 147—Partial breasts.
- 149—Right breast while kissing Robert Culp.

## • Sumers, Stephanie

*Films:*

**Anthony's Desire** (1993) . . . . . . . . . . . . . . . . Dancer
- •• 0:22—Breasts, while on stage, lying in the lap of another woman. (She's wearing a choker.)

**Midnight Tease** (1994) . . . . . . . . . . . . . . . . Tiffany
- •• 0:00—Breasts and buns, while dancing during opening credits.
- ••• 0:07—Breasts and buns in T-back, while dancing on stage.
- ••• 0:09—Breasts, while dressing and talking to Samantha in dressing room.
- ••• 0:12—Nude, while making love on top of Samantha's stepfather, then getting killed in dream.
  0:14—Breasts while tied to pole in club with a slit throat and covered with blood.
- 0:50—Breasts with slit throat and blood in dream.

*Video Tapes:*

**Hot Body Video Magazine: Naughty But Nice** (1993). . . . . . . . . . . . . . . . . . . . . . . . . . . . . . . .n.a.
**Hot Body Video Magazine: Hot Stuff** (1994) . . .n.a.

## • Summer, Jamie

See: Stafford, Jamie.

## • Sunare

*Made for Cable TV:*

**Red Shoe Diaries: Jake's Story** (1993; Showtime)
. . . . . . . . . . . . . . . . . . . . . . . . . . . Woman in Trailer
(Available on video tape on *Red Shoe Diaries 4: Auto Erotica*.)
- ••• 0:10—Breasts and buns while posing with a tattooed guy while Sheryl takes photos.
- • 0:12—Brief breasts and buns in B&W flashback photos.

**Red Shoe Diaries: The Game** (1994; Showtime)
. . . . . . . . . . . . . . . . . . . Uncredited Woman with John
- • 0:21—Brief partial right breast while making love with John.
- • 0:23—Brief breasts, twice, while making love with John.

## Sutton, Lori

*Films:*

History of the World, Part I (1981). . . . . . . . Vestal Virgin
Looker (1981) . . . . . . . . . . . . . . . . . . . . . . . Reston Girl
Fast Times at Ridgemont High (1982) . . . . . . . Playmate
**Malibu Express** (1984) . . . . . . . . . . . . Beverly McAfee
- ••• 0:54—Breasts and buns, making love in bed with Cody.

**Up the Creek** (1984) . . . . . . . . . . . . . . . . . . . Cute Girl
- • 0:40—Brief breasts, twice, after ripping open her blouse to get a crowd excited while cheerleading.

**Night Patrol** (1985). . . . . . . . . . . . . . . . Edith Hutton
- ••• 0:47—In white bra, panties, garter belt and stockings, then breasts three times taking off bra in bedroom with the Police officer.

## Swafford, Jody

*Films:*

**Evils of the Night** (1985) . . . . . . . . . . . . . .Lotion Girl
- •• 0:12—Breasts while rubbing lotion on another girl.
- •• 0:13—More breasts with the other girl.
- • 0:14—Brief breasts when Eddie watches her.

*Video Tapes:*

**The Girls of Penthouse** (1984)
. . . . . . . . . . . . . . . . . . . . . . . . Ghost Town Woman
- ••• 0:29—In black lingerie, then full frontal nudity making love with cowboy.

## Swanson, Brenda

*Films:*

Dangerous Love (1988) . . . . . . . . . . . . . . . . . .Felicity
Skin Deep (1989) . . . . . . . . . . . . . . . . . . . . . . . .Emily
**Steel and Lace** (1990) . . . . . . . . . . . Miss Fairweather
- •• 0:58—Breasts in lunchroom, opening her blouse in front of one of the bad guys on the table.

Prototype X29A (1992) . . . . . . . . . . . Dr. Alexis Zalazny
Dead Connection (1993) . . . . . . . . . . . . . . . . . .Susan
**Indecent Behavior** (1993) . . . . . . . . . . . .Judith Miller
(Unrated version reviewed.)
- ••• 1:05—In white bra, then breasts, while making love with Carol in observation room.

*Video Tapes:*

**Inside Out 2** (1992)
. . . . Mrs. Jenkins/There's This Traveling Salesman, See
(Unrated version reviewed.)
  0:42—In braless, wet tank top, in barn.
- •• 0:43—Breasts, taking off her top in barn.

## Swanson, Jackie

*Films:*

**Lethal Weapon** (1987) . . . . . . . . . Amanda Hunsacker
- •• 0:01—Brief breasts standing on balcony rail getting ready to jump.

It's Alive III: Island of the Alive (1988) . . . . . . . . .Tenant
**Perfect Victims** (1988) . . . . . . . . . . . . . Carrie Marks
- •• 0:13—In bra, then left breast, while changing clothes by closet.
- • 0:23—Brief left breast, while lying on sofa when Brandon opens her robe. Brief right breast and lower frontal nudity when he rips off her panties.
  0:25—Right breast several more times, while lying on sofa while Brandon torments her.
- ••• 1:15—Left breast and buns, seen through clear shower door. Nice shot for bun lovers!
- • 1:16—Brief buns in the shower, seen from above.

*TV:*

Cheers (1989-93) . . . . . . . . . . . . . . . . . . . .Kelly Gaines

## Swift, Sally

a.k.a. Adult film actress Jennifer West.
Films:
**Auditions** (1978) . . . . . . . . . . . . . . . . . .Melinda Sale
••• 0:21—Full frontal nudity, undressing and masturbating during her audition.
•• 0:30—Breasts and buns, whipping Harry.
Hell Squad (1986). . . . . . . . . . . . . . . . . . . . . . . Ann

## • Swin, Monica

Films:
**Erotikill** (1973) . . . . . . . . . . . . . Princess de Rochefort
a.k.a. La Comtesse Noire
a.k.a. The Loves of Irina
•• 0:47—Breasts, getting her dress taken off and blood sucked.
•• 0:55—Breasts, lying on table in doctor's office.
Demoniac (1974; French/Spanish)
. . . . . . . . . . . . . . . . . . . . The Count's Sadistic Partner

## • Swinton, Tilda

Films:
The Last of England. . . . . . . . . . . . . . . . . . . . . . . .n.a.
Caravaggio (1986; British). . . . . . . . . . . . . . . . . . Lena
Aria (1987; U.S./British). . . . . . . . . . . . . . . Young Girl
War Requiem (1988; British) . . . . . . . . . . . . . . . Nurse
Edward II (1992; British) . . . . . . . . . . . . . . . . Isabella
**Orlando** (1993; British) . . . . . . . . . . . . . . . . Orlando
••• 0:56—Full frontal nudity while looking at herself in mirror.

## Sykes, Brenda

Films:
The Baby Maker (1970). . . . . . . . . . . . . . . . . . Francis
**Getting Straight** (1970) . . . . . . . . . . . . . . . . . .Luan
•• 0:53—Brief left breast, while scooting up in bed with Elliott Gould, then breasts, while getting back in bed.
The Liberation of L. B. Jones (1970). . . . . . . . . . . . Jelly
**Honky** (1971) . . . . . . . . . . . . . . . . . . . . Sheila Smith
••• 0:42—Breasts with her boyfriend, making love on the floor.
• 1:22—Brief breasts several times getting raped by two guys.
Pretty Maids All in a Row (1971) . . . . . . . Pamela Wilcox
Skin Game (1971). . . . . . . . . . . . . . . . . . . . . . Naomi
**Black Gunn** (1972) . . . . . . . . . . . . . . . . . . . . .Judith
• 0:45—Brief side view of right breast, while getting out of bed with Jim Brown.
Cleopatra Jones (1973) . . . . . . . . . . . . . . . . . Tiffany
**Mandingo** (1975) . . . . . . . . . . . . . . . . . . . . . . Ellen
• 0:58—Breasts in bed with Perry King.
**Drum** (1976) . . . . . . . . . . . . . . . . . . . . . . . .Calinda
• 0:19—Breasts standing next to bed with Ken Norton.
TV:
Ozzie's Girls (1973) . . . . . . .Brenda (Jennifer) MacKenzie
Executive Suite (1976-77) . . . . . . . . . Summer Johnson

Magazines:
**Playboy** (Oct 1972) . . . . . . . . .Brown, Black and White
• 88—Almost breasts.
**Playboy** (Nov 1972) . . . . . . . . . . Sex in Cinema 1972
• 162—Left breast, in a photo from Black Gunn.
**Playboy** (Dec 1975) . . . . . . . . . . . . . .Sex Stars of 1975
•• 185—Right breast.

## Tabrizi, Tera

Films:
Cool As Ice (1991) . . . . . . . . . . . . . . . . . . . Club Dancer
**White Sands** (1992)
. . . . . . .Body Double for Mary Elizabeth Mastrontonio
•• 1:10—Left breast and upper half of buns in the shower undressing in the shower with Willem Dafoe. Don't see face, so it's probably Tera.
Carlito's Way (1993). . . . . . . . . . . . . . . . . . . Club Date
Made for Cable Movies:
Red Shoe Diaries (1992; Showtime) . . . . . . Alex's Friend
(Unrated video tape version reviewed.)
Magazines:
**Playboy's Book of Lingerie** (Jan 1991) . . . . . .Herself
•• 14—Side of right breast and buns.
**Playboy's Book of Lingerie** (Mar 1991). . . . . .Herself
•• 62—Buns and side of right breast.
**Playboy's Book of Lingerie** (Sep 1991) . . . . . .Herself
••• 48—Breasts.
• 76-77—Right breast.
**Playboy's Book of Lingerie** (Nov 1991) . . . . .Herself
•• 104—Right breast.
•• 106-107—Buns and side of right breast.
**Playboy's Book of Lingerie** (Jan 1992) . . . . . .Herself
••• 3-7—Breasts and buns.
**Playboy's Book of Lingerie** (Mar 1992). . . . . .Herself
• 96-97—Breasts.
**Playboy's Bathing Beauties** (Apr 1992). . . . . .Herself
• 30-31—Right breast.
**Playboy's Career Girls** (Aug 1992) . . . .Double Visions
••• 38-39—Breasts and buns.
Playboy's Book of Lingerie (Sep 1992) . . . . . . . .Herself
**Playboy's Book of Lingerie** (Nov 1992) . . . . .Herself
•• 8—Left breast.
**Playboy's Nudes** (Dec 1992) . . . . . . . . . . . . .Herself
••• 62—Breasts.
**Playboy's Book of Lingerie** (Jan 1993) . . . . . .Herself
•• 36-37—Right breast.
**Playboy's Book of Lingerie** (Mar 1993) . . . . . .Herself
••• 48—Breasts.
**Playboy's Bathing Beauties** (Apr 1993). . . . . .Herself
•• 33—Left breast.
••• 50—Breasts.
**Playboy's Book of Lingerie** (May 1993) . . . . . .Herself
••• 79—Side of left breast and buns in thong.
**Playboy's Book of Lingerie** (Jul 1993) . . . . . . .Herself
•• 40—Right breast.
**Playboy's Blondes, Brunettes & Redheads**
(Sep 1993). . . . . . . . . . . . . . . . . . . . . . . . . . . . . .Herself
•• 53—Right breast and half of left breast.

**Playboy's Nudes** (Dec 1993) . . . . . . . . . . . . . Herself
•• 8—Breasts.
**Playboy's Book of Lingerie** (Jan 1994) . . . . . . Herself
•• 47—Right breast.

# Taggart, Sharon
*Films:*
**The Last Picture Show** (1971) . . . . . Charlene Duggs
•• 0:11—In bra, then breasts making out in truck with
Timothy Bottoms.
The Harrad Experiment (1973) . . . . . . . . . . . . .Barbara

# Tallman, Patricia
*Films:*
**Knightriders** (1981) . . . . . . . . . . . . . . . . . . . . . Julie
• 0:46—Brief breasts in the bushes in moonlight talk-
ing to her boyfriend while a truck driver watches.
Monkey Shines: An Experiment in Fear (1988)
. . . . . . . . . . . . . . . . . . . . . . Party Guest and Stunts
After Midnight (1989) . . . . . . . . . . . . . . . Stunt Player
Roadhouse (1989) . . . . . . . . . . . . . . . Bandstand Babe
Night of the Living Dead (1990) . . . . . . . . . . . .Barbara
Sweet Justice (1991) . . . . . . . . . . . . . . . . . . . . . .Josie
Army of Darkness (1992) . . . . . . . . . . . Possessed Witch
Benefit of the Doubt (1993; U.S./German)
. . . . . . . . . . . . . . . . . . . . . . . . . . . .Karen's Mother
Kalifornia (1993) . . . . . . . . . . . . . . . . . . . . . . . Stunts
(Unrated version reviewed.)
*Made for Cable Movies:*
Attack of the 50 ft. Woman (1993; HBO) . . . . . . .Stunts
*Made for Cable TV:*
Red Shoe Diaries: Double or Nothing (1993; Showtime)
. . . . . . . . . . . . . . . . . . . . . . . . . . . . . . . . . Stunts

# Tamerlis, Zoe
a.k.a. Zoë Tamerlaine and Zoe Lund.
*Films:*
Ms. 45 (1980) . . . . . . . . . . . . . . . . . . . . . . . . .Thana
**Special Effects** (1984) . . . . . . . . . . . . . Amelia/Elaine
0:01—Side view of right breast, wearing pasties during photo session.
• 0:16—Brief breasts sitting by pool with Eric Bogozian.
•• 0:19—Breasts getting into bed and in bed with
Bogozian.
• 0:22—Breasts, dead in spa while Bogozian washes
her off.
0:44—Brief breasts in moviola that Bogozian watches.
• 1:12—Breasts making love on bed with Keefe.
• 1:17—Breasts getting into bed during filming of
movie. Brief breasts during Bogozian's flashbacks.
1:20—More left breast shots on moviola getting
strangled.
••• 1:33—Breasts with Bogozian when he takes her
dress off.
• 1:35—Breasts sitting on bed kissing Bogozian. More
breasts and more flashbacks.
• 1:40—Brief breasts during struggle. Dark.

Heavy Petting (1989) . . . . . . . . . Herself/Writer, Actress
Bad Lieutenant (1992) . . . . . . . . . . . . . . . . . . . . . Zoe

# Tané
See: McClure, Tané.

# • Tanner, Joy
*Films:*
Liar's Edge (1991) . . . . . . . . . . . . . . . . . . . . . . . Ruth
**Prom Night IV: Deliver Us From Evil** (1991) . .Laura
(All nude scenes look like a body double.)
• 0:58—Buns, lying in bed with Jeff. Don't see her
face.
0:59—Very brief right breast, while making love with
Jeff, standing up. Don't see her face.
• 1:00—Buns and back half of right breast, getting out
of bed. Don't see her face.
•• 1:01—Breasts in shower. Don't see her face. It looks
like a body double because the double's breasts are
bigger than Joy's.

# Tate, Laura
*Films:*
**Dead Space** (1990) . . . . . . . . . . . . . .Marissa Salinger
•• 0:33—Breasts in bed with Marc Singer during her
dream.
Subspecies (1990) . . . . . . . . . . . . . . . . . . . . .Michelle

# Tate, Sharon
Late wife of director Roman Polanski.
Victim of the Manson Family murders on August 9, 1969.
*Films:*
**The Fearless Vampire Killers** (1967) . . . Sarah Shagal
• 0:24—Very, very brief breasts struggling in bathtub
with vampire. Hard to see.
**Valley of the Dolls** (1967) . . . . . . . . . . Jennifer North
• 1:21—In bra, acting in a movie. Very, very brief left
breast in bed with a guy (curtain gets in the way).
• 1:23—Very brief side view of right breast, while sit-
ting up in bed.
Ciao Frederico! (1971) . . . . . . . . . . . . . . . . . . . . . n.a.
*TV:*
The Beverly Hillbillies (1963-65) . . . . . . . . . . Janet Trego
Petticoat Junction (1963) . . . . . . . . . . . Billie Jo Bradley
*Magazines:*
**Playboy** (Mar 1967) . . . . . . . . . . . . . .The Tate Gallery
70-73—Breasts and buns, in photographs taken by
Roman Polanski on the set of *The Fearless Vampire
Killers.*
**Playboy** (Jan 1989) . . . . . . . . . . . .Women of the Sixties
• 160—Side view of right breast, taking a bubble
bath.

# Taye-Loren, Carolyn

*Films:*

Scanner Cop (1993) . . . . . . . Nurse in Emergency Room

**Witchcraft V: Dance with the Devil** (1993) . . . . Keli

••• 0:18—In pink bra and panties in her bedroom.

••• 1:01—Breasts while making love with Bill under leaky water pipes in the basement.

*Magazines:*

**Playboy** (May 1993) . . . . . . . . . . . . . . . . . . Grapevine

• 175—Buns in cowboy chaps and lower half of breasts. B&W.

# • Taylor, Courtney

*Films:*

Prom Night III (1989) . . . . . . . . . . . Mary Lou Maloney

**Sins of the Night** (1993) . . . . . . . . . . . . . . . Danielle

(Unrated version reviewed.)

• 1:20—In black bra and panties, then breasts in room with Deborah Shelton and Miles O'Keeffe. Medium long shot. Side of right breast in closer shot.

# Taylor, Elizabeth

Ex-wife (twice) of actor Richard Burton.

*Films:*

**Cleopatra** (1963) . . . . . . . . . . . . . . . . . . Cleopatra

• 0:28—Half of buns, lying face down, while getting a massage.

2:02—(0:08 into tape 2) Taking a bath—You can't see anything.

X, Y and Zee (1972) . . . . . . . . . . . . . . . . . . . . . Zee

1:11—Brief right breast, in bloody bathtub water, trying to commit suicide. Probably a body double— Don't see her face.

Ash Wednesday (1973) . . . . . . . . . . . . . . . . . . Barbara

• 0:10—Long shot breasts, closer shot of buns, getting prepared for plastic surgery in hospital. Don't see her face, probably a body double.

Psychotic (1975; Italian) . . . . . . . . . . . . . . . . . Lise

*a.k.a. Driver's Seat*

0:03—In sheer beige bra while in changing room.

0:34—In sheer white slip while walking around.

# Taylor, Kimberly

*Films:*

Bedroom Eyes II (1989) . . . . . . . . . . . . . . . . Michelle

**Cleo/Leo** (1989) . . . . . . . . . . . . . . . . . . . Store Clerk

••• 0:22—Breasts in white panties, changing in dressing room with Jane Hamilton. Very nice!

**Party Incorporated** (1989) . . . . . . . . . . . . . . . Felicia

*a.k.a. Party Girls*

•• 0:26—Breasts shaking her breasts trying an outfit on.

••• 0:39—Breasts and buns in G-string in the bar with the guys.

**Frankenhooker** (1990) . . . . . . . . . . . . . . . . . Amber

• 0:36—Brief left breast in green top during introduction to Jeffrey.

•• 0:37—Brief breasts during exam by Jeffrey. Then breasts getting breasts measured with calipers.

• 0:41—Brief right breast, twice, enjoying drugs.

•• 0:42—Breasts, getting off bed and onto another bed with Anise.

• 0:43—Breasts kneeling in bed screaming before exploding.

**Beauty School** (1993) . . . . . . . . . . . . . . . . . Kimberly

• 0:43—Buns in white lingerie on balcony. Long shot.

••• 0:44—Breasts doing breast exercises, then buns in G-string going for a swim. (She's on the far right.)

••• 0:45—Buns and breasts, getting out of the swimming pool.

••• 0:51—Breasts while making love with Quincy outside.

••• 1:22—Breasts, taking off her dress and making love with Quincy.

*Magazines:*

**Penthouse** (Dec 1988) . . . . . . . . . . . . . . . . . . . Pet

# Taylor, Lili

*Films:*

Mystic Pizza (1988) . . . . . . . . . . . . . . . . . Jojo Barboza

Born on the Fourth of July (1989) . . . . . . . . Jamie Wilson

Say Anything (1989) . . . . . . . . . . . . . . . . . . . Corey

**Bright Angel** (1990) . . . . . . . . . . . . . . . . . . . . . Lucy

• 0:26—Brief top of breasts under water, taking a bath in a pond.

•• 0:27—Breasts, walking out of the pond.

Dogfight (1991) . . . . . . . . . . . . . . . . . . . . . . . Rose

**Household Saints** (1992) . . . . . . . . . . . . . . . . Teresa

•• 1:35—Breasts while in her bedroom, after undressing in front of Leonard.

Rudy (1993) . . . . . . . . . . . . . . . . . . . . . . . . Sherry

Short Cuts (1993) . . . . . . . . . . . . . . . . . Honey Bush

Watch It (1993) . . . . . . . . . . . . . . . . . . . . . Brenda

# • Taylor, Lindsay

See: Mayo-Chandler, Karen.

# Taylor, Lisa

*Films:*

**Love Trap** (1977) . . . . . . . . . . . . . . . . . . . . Eleanor

*a.k.a. Let's Get Laid*

•• 0:37—Breasts, while answering and talking on the phone.

• 0:53—Partial lower frontal nudity while talking on the phone to Gordon. Brief breasts, while hanging up the phone.

• 1:33—Brief left breast while making love on bed with two guys.

**Eyes of Laura Mars** (1978) . . . . . . . . . . . . . . Michele

• 0:59—Very brief right breast, while on table just before getting killed.

Where the Buffalo Roam (1980) . . . . . . . . . . . . Ruthie

Windy City (1984) . . . . . . . . . . . . . . . . . . . . Sherry

## Taylor, Marianne

*Films:*
Vendetta (1986) . . . . . . . . . . . . . . . . . . . . . . . . . . .Star
**Bloodmatch** (1991) . . . . . . . . . . . . . . . Max Manduke
 • 0:13—Breasts and buns, making love in bed on top
 of Caldwell.

## Taylor, Vida

*Films:*
God Told Me To (1976) . . . . . . . .Mrs. Mulling as a Child
**Clash of the Titans** (1981) . . . . . . . . . . . . . . . .Danae
 • 0:11—Right breast while breast feeding her baby.
 Buns, walking on beach.

## Taylor-Young, Leigh

*Films:*
I Love You, Alice B. Toklas (1968) . . . . . . . . . . . . .Nancy
**The Big Bounce** (1969) . . . . . . . . . . . . . Nancy Barker
 (Not available on video tape.)
The Adventurers (1970) . . . . . . . . . . . . . . . . . Amparo
The Buttercup Chain (1971; British) . . . . . . . . . Manny
The Gang that Couldn't Shoot Straight (1971)
 . . . . . . . . . . . . . . . . . . . . . . . . . . .Angela Palumbo
The Horsemen (1971) . . . . . . . . . . . . . . . . . . . . . Zereh
Soylent Green (1973) . . . . . . . . . . . . . . . . . . . . . Shirl
Can't Stop the Music (1980) . . . . . . . . . .Claudia Walters
Looker (1981) . . . . . . . . . . . . . . . . . . . . . Jennifer Long
Jagged Edge (1985) . . . . . . . . . . . . . . . Virginia Howell
Secret Admirer (1985) . . . . . . . . . . . . . . Elizabeth Fimple
Accidents (1988) . . . . . . . . . . . . . . . . . . Beryl Chambers
Honeymoon Academy (1990) . . . . . . . . .Mrs. Doris Kent
*TV:*
Picket Fences . . . . . . . . . . . . . . . . . . . . . . . . . Rachel
The Devlin Connection (1982) . . . . . . . . .Lauren Dane
Dallas (1987-88) . . . . . . . . . . . . . . . . . . Kimberly Cryder

## Tedesco, Paola

*Films:*
The Gospel According to St. Matthew (1966; French/
 Italian) . . . . . . . . . . . . . . . . . . . . . . . . . . . . . Salome
Battle of the Amazons (1973; Italian/Spanish) . . . Valeria
Crime Boss (1976; Italian) . . . . . . . . . . . . . . . . . . . .n.a.
**I Hate Blondes** (1981; Italian) . . . . . . . . . . . . . .Teresa
 ••• 0:06—Breasts, sitting up in bed at night and turning
 on the light. Buns, while walking around the room.

## Tenison, Reneé

*Films:*
Shout (1991) . . . . . . . . . . . . . . . . . . . . . . . Girl in Bar
CB4 (1993) . . . . . . . . . . . . . . . . . . . . . . . . . . . . . Twin
*Video Tapes:*
**Playboy Video Calendar 1991** (1990) . . . . . . August
 ••• 0:31—Nude.
**Playboy Video Centerfold: Reneé Tenison** (1990)
 . . . . . . . . . . . . . . . . . . . . Playmate of the Year 1990
 ••• 0:00—Nude throughout.
**Wet and Wild III** (1991) . . . . . . . . . . . . . . . . . .Model

**The Best of Video Playmate Calendars** (1992)
 . . . . . . . . . . . . . . . . . . . . . . . . . . . . . . . . Playmate
 ••• 0:06—Nude in the desert.
 ••• 0:08—Nude working out in warehouse gym.
 ••• 0:10—Nude, taking a milk bath.
 ••• 0:11—Nude in bedroom.
*Magazines:*
**Playboy** (Nov 1989) . . . . . . . . . . . . . . . . . . . Playmate
**Playboy's Nudes** (Oct 1990) . . . . . . . . . . . . . . Herself
 •• 106-107—Left breast and lower frontal nudity.
**Playboy's Book of Lingerie** (Mar 1991) . . . . .Herself
 •• 23—Left breast and buns.
**Playboy's Book of Lingerie** (Sep 1991) . . . . . .Herself
 ••• 16-17—Full frontal nudity.
 ••• 60—Right breast and lower frontal nudity.
**Playboy's Book of Lingerie** (Nov 1991) . . . . .Herself
 •• 20—Left breast and lower frontal nudity.
**Playboy's Book of Lingerie** (Jan 1992) . . . . . .Herself
 • 70-71—Right breast.
**Playboy's Sisters** (Feb 1992) . . . . . . . . . . . . . .Herself
 ••• 12-19—Full frontal nudity.
**Playboy's Book of Lingerie** (Mar 1992) . . . . . .Herself
 ••• 56—Full frontal nudity.
**Playboy's Bathing Beauties** (Apr 1992) . . . . . .Herself
 ••• 36—Breasts.
 ••• 84-85—Breasts.
**Playboy's Book of Lingerie** (May 1992) . . . . .Herself
 •• 46-47—Buns and side of right breast.
**Playboy's Career Girls** (Aug 1992)
 . . . . . . . . . . . . . . . . . . . . . . . . Baywatch Playmates
 ••• 12—Full frontal nudity.
**Playboy's Book of Lingerie** (Sep 1992) . . . . . .Herself
 •• 108-109—Left breast and buns.
**Playboy's Calendar Playmates** (Nov 1992) . . .Herself
 •• 94—Right breast and lower frontal nudity.
 •• 102—Buns and right breast.
**Playboy's Book of Lingerie** (Nov 1992) . . . . .Herself
 •• 68—Buns and side of right breast.
**Playboy's Nudes** (Dec 1992) . . . . . . . . . . . . . .Herself
 ••• 68—Breasts.
**Playboy's Book of Lingerie** (Jan 1993) . . . . . .Herself
 ••• 86—Breasts.
**Playboy's Book of Lingerie** (Mar 1993) . . . . . .Herself
 ••• 76—Side view of left breast and buns.
**Playboy's Book of Lingerie** (May 1993) . . . . .Herself
 ••• 74—Breasts.
**Playboy's Girls of Summer '93** (Jun 1993) . . .Herself
 ••• 62—Full frontal nudity.
**Playboy's Wet & Wild Women** (Aug 1993) . . .Herself
 ••• 11—Full frontal nudity.
 ••• 26—Breasts.
 ••• 54—Breasts.
**Playboy's Blondes, Brunettes & Redheads**
 (Sep 1993) . . . . . . . . . . . . . . . . . . . . . . . . . .Herself
 •• 44-45—Buns.
**Playboy's Book of Lingerie** (Sep 1993) . . . . . .Herself
 ••• 44—Breasts.
**Playboy's Video Playmates** (Sep 1993) . . . . . .Herself
 ••• 80-83—Full frontal nudity.

**Playboy's Book of Lingerie** (Nov 1993) . . . . . Herself
••• 14—Breasts and buns.
**Playboy's Book of Lingerie** (Jan 1994). . . . . . Herself
••• 14—Breasts.
••• 76-77—Breasts.
**Playboy's Bathing Beauties** (Mar 1994). . . . . Herself
• 32—Left breast.
••• 68—Breasts.
**Playboy's Book of Lingerie** (May 1994). . . . . Herself
••• 11—Breasts.
**Playboy's Girls of Summer '94** (Jul 1994) . . . Herself
•• 23—Right breast.
••• 82—Breasts.
**Playboy's Book of Lingerie** (Jul 1994) . . . . . . Herself
••• 12-13—Breasts and buns.
••• 94-95—Breasts.
**Playboy's Book of Lingerie** (Sep 1994) . . . . . Herself
••• 68—Full frontal nudity.

## Tennant, Victoria

Ex-wife of comedian/actor Steve Martin.
*Films:*
The Ragman's Daughter (1974; British). . . Doris Randall
Horror Planet (1980; British) . . . . . . . . . . . . . . . Barbara
*a.k.a. Inseminoid*
All of Me (1984) . . . . . . . . . . . . . . . . . . . Terry Hoskins
The Holcroft Covenant (1985). . . . . . . Helden Tennyson
Flowers in the Attic (1987) . . . . . . . . . . . . . . . . Mother
Best Seller (1988) . . . . . . . . . . . . . . . . . Roberta Gillian
**Whispers** (1989) . . . . . . . . . . . . . . . . Hilary Thomas
• 0:43—Buns and side of right breast getting into
bathtub. Long shot, looks like a body double (the
ponytail in her hair changes position).
• 0:44—Buns and brief breasts running down the
stairs. Looks like the same body double.
A Handmaid's Tale (1990). . . . . . . . . . . . . . Aunt Lydia
L.A. Story (1991). . . . . . . . . . . . . . . . . . . . . . . . . Sara
The Plague (1992; French/British) . . . . . . . . . Alice Rieux

## Terashita, Jill

*Films:*
The Big Bet (1985) . . . . . . . . . . . . . . . . . . . . . . . Koko
Terminal Entry (1986) . . . . . . . . . . . . . . . . . . . . Gwen
Dirty Laundry (1987). . . . . . . . . . . . . . . . . . . . . . n.a.
**Night of the Demons** (1987) . . . . . . . . . . . . Frannie
(Unrated version reviewed.)
•• 0:57—Breasts while making love with her boyfriend
in a coffin.
**Sleepaway Camp III: Teenage Wasteland** (1989)
. . . . . . . . . . . . . . . . . . . . . . . . . . . . . . . . . . . . . Arab
• 0:16—Breasts putting sweatshirt on.
Why Me? (1990). . . . . . . . . . . . . . . . . . . . . . Hostess
Rapid Fire (1992) . . . . . . . . . . . . . . . . . . . . . . Stunts
*Magazines:*
**Playboy's Book of Lingerie** (Jan 1991) . . . . . . Herself
•• 23—Buns and partial left breast.
**Playboy's Book of Lingerie** (Jul 1991) . . . . . . Herself
• 44—Buns.

**Playboy's Book of Lingerie** (Nov 1991) . . . . . Herself
• 38—Right breast.
**Playboy's Book of Lingerie** (Mar 1992). . . . . . Herself
••• 72—Breasts.
**Playboy's Book of Lingerie** (May 1992) . . . . . Herself
•• 104-105—Left breast and side view of buns.
**Playboy's Book of Lingerie** (Jul 1992). . . . . . . Herself
••• 95—Breasts.
**Playboy's Book of Lingerie** (Sep 1992) . . . . . . Herself
••• 47—Full frontal nudity.
Playboy's Book of Lingerie (Jul 1993) . . . . . . . . . Herself
**Playboy's Blondes, Brunettes & Redheads**
(Sep 1993). . . . . . . . . . . . . . . . . . . . . . . . . . . . Herself
••• 57—Full frontal nudity.
**Playboy's Book of Lingerie** (Jan 1994) . . . . . . Herself
••• 67—Breasts.
**Playboy's Book of Lingerie** (Jul 1994). . . . . . . Herself
•• 27—Right breast and lower frontal nudity.

## Texter, Gilda

*Films:*
**Angels Hard as They Come** (1971) . . . . . . . . . Astrid
• 0:26—Brief breasts several times when bad guys try
to rape her. Dark.
**Vanishing Point** (1971). . . . . . . . . . . . . . Nude Rider
• 1:17—Breasts while riding motorcycle outside.
••• 1:19—Breasts riding motorcycle and walking
around without wearing any clothes. Long scene.

## Thackray, Gail

a.k.a. Robyn Harris and Gail Harris.
*Films:*
**Party Favors** (1987). . . . . . . . . . . . . . . . . . . . Nicole
• 0:04—Breasts in dressing room with the other three
girls changing into blue swimsuit.
• 0:11—Brief left breast in the swimsuit during dance
practice.
• 0:12—Breasts during dance practice.
• 0:17—More breasts during dance practice.
•• 0:42—Breasts doing strip routine at anniversary party. Great buns in G-string shots.
••• 1:01—Breasts and buns in G-string after stripping
from cheerleader outfit. Lots of bouncing breast
shots. Mingling with the men afterwards.
• 1:16—Nude by the swimming pool during the final
credits.
**Takin' It All Off** (1987) . . . . . . . . . . . Hannah McCall
••• 0:03—Breasts in red leotard and head band, in
dance studio.
••• 0:11—Full frontal nudity in the showers (she's in the
back on the right.)
••• 0:28—Nude, doing strip routine outside.
•• 1:24—Nude, dancing with the other girls on stage.
• 1:29—Breasts in crate backstage with Hadem.
Angel III: The Final Chapter (1988). . . . . . . . . . . . n.a.
**Death Feud** (1989) . . . . . . . . . . . . Harry's Girl Friend
•• 1:12—Breasts on bed with Harry.
1:16—In black lingerie on boat with Harry.

**The Haunting of Morella** (1989) . . . . . . . . . . . . Ilsa
•• 0:38—Breasts in bed with Niles. Buns also when getting out and getting dressed.
**Nudity Required** (1989). . . . . . . . . . . . . . . . . .Midge
•• 0:36—Breasts, asking Buddy a question. Brief breasts (tenth girl) standing in line.
••• 0:37—Breasts doing her song and tap dance audition.
• 0:44—Breasts while playing in pool.
**Hard to Die** (1990). . . . . . . . . . . . . . . . Dawn Grant
*a.k.a. Tower of Terror*
••• 0:31—Breasts, while taking a shower.
**Sorority House Massacre 2** (1990). . . . . . . . . . Linda
•• 0:25—In bra and panties, then breasts while changing clothes.
0:50—In wet lingerie.
**Sins of Desire** (1992) . . . . . . . . . . . Monica Waldman
(Unrated version reviewed.)
• 0:00—Breasts in quick clips, while making love with Scott during nightmare.
*Video Tapes:*
**The Girls of Malibu** (1986) . . . . . . . . . . . . . . . . .Gail
••• 0:28—In two piece swimsuit. Nude taking a shower and drying herself off.
**In Search of the Perfect 10** (1986) . . Perfect Girl #5
••• 0:31—Nude, while trying on all sorts of lingerie in dressing room.
**Starlet Screen Test** (1986). . . . . . . . . . . . . . . Susan
••• 0:31—In robe, on red sofa, then in bra and panties, then nude.
**The Stripper of the Year** (1986). . . . . . . . .Billy Jean
••• 0:32—Nude, stripping from red overalls and a hat.
•• 0:53—Breasts on stage with the other contestants.
**Trashy Ladies Wrestling** (1987) . . . . . . . . . . . . . Fifi
•• 0:02—Buns in G-string, black bra, garter belt and stockings. Breasts getting oil dribbled on her.
**Starlets Exposed! Volume II** (1991) . . . . . . . . . .Gail
(Same as *The Girls of Malibu*.)
••• 0:07—Nude, taking off robe, taking a shower, then drying herself off.

## Theel, Lynn
*Films:*
Fyre (1979). . . . . . . . . . . . . . . . . . . . . . . . . . . . . Fyre
**Humanoids from the Deep** (1980). . . . Peggy Larsen
• 0:22—Very, very brief half of right breast, when fight in parking lot startles her and her boyfriend in back of truck.
• 0:30—Brief breasts getting raped on the beach by a humanoid.
• 0:51—Brief breasts, dead, lying on the beach all covered with seaweed.
Without Warning (1980). . . . . . . . . . . . . . . . . . Beth
Hollywood Boulevard II (1989) . . . . . . . . .Ann Gregory

## Thelen, Jodi
*Films:*
**Four Friends** (1981). . . . . . . . . . . . . . . . . . . Georgia
•• 0:17—Left breast in open blouse three times with her three male friends.
0:58—In pink bra taking off her blouse.
The Black Stallion Returns (1983). . . . . . . . . . . . Tabari
Twilight Time (1983) . . . . . . . . . . . . . . . . . . . . . . Lena
*Made for TV Movies:*
Follow Your Heart (1990). . . . . . . . . . . . . . . . Cecile

## Theodore, Sondra
*Video Tapes:*
**Wet and Wild** (1989) . . . . . . . . . . . . . . . . . . Model
*Magazines:*
**Playboy** (Jul 1977) . . . . . . . . . . . . . . . . . . Playmate
••• 108-119—Nude.
**Playboy** (Oct 1977) . . . . . . . . . . . . . . . . Dear Playboy
••• 18—Full frontal nudity in small photo.
**Playboy** (Dec 1977)
. . . .Playboy's Playmate House Party/Sex Stars of 1977
••• 152-161—Nude.
••• 216—Full frontal nudity.
**Playboy** (Apr 1980) . . . . . .Playboy's Playmate Reunion
• 130—Buns.
**Playboy's Girls of Summer '86** (Aug 1986). . .Herself
•• 95—Left breast and lower frontal nudity.

## Thom, Cristy
*Films:*
Best of the Best 2 (1992) . . . . . . . . . . .Girl at Restaurant
**Meatballs 4** (1992) . . . . . . . . . . . . . . . . . . . . Hillary
••• 0:38—Breasts, taking off her blouse and washing herself off.
*Video Tapes:*
**Playboy Video Calendar 1992** (1991). . . .September
••• 0:35—Full frontal nudity walking and posing around the house.
••• 0:37—Nude in room of mirrors.
••• 0:38—Nude in bathtub.
**Playboy's Playmate Review 1992** (1992)
. . . . . . . . . . . . . . . . . . . . . . . . . . . Miss February
••• 0:22—Nude on motorcycle, then with a snake and then in a house.
**Wet and Wild IV** (1992) . . . . . . . . . . . . . . . . Model
*Magazines:*
**Playboy** (Feb 1991) . . . . . . . . . . . . . . . . . Playmate
••• Nude.
**Playboy's Book of Lingerie** (Jul 1992). . . . . .Herself
•• 26-27—Right breast and lower frontal nudity.
••• 41—Breasts.
••• 52-53—Breasts.
•• 64—Left breast and lower frontal nudity.
**Playboy's Book of Lingerie** (Sep 1992). . . . . .Herself
••• 44-45—Breasts.
•• 62—Right breast.
**Playboy's Calendar Playmates** (Nov 1992). . .Herself
••• 105—Full frontal nudity.

**Playboy's Book of Lingerie** (Nov 1992) . . . . . Herself
••• 22-23—Full frontal nudity.
**Playboy's Nudes** (Dec 1992) . . . . . . . . . . . . . Herself
••• 3—Full frontal nudity.
••• 43—Full frontal nudity.
**Playboy's Book of Lingerie** (Jan 1993) . . . . . . Herself
•• 19—Partial right breast and lower frontal nudity.
**Playboy** (Feb 1993) . . . . . . . . . . Being in Nothingness
• 130—Tip of left breast.
**Playboy's Book of Lingerie** (Mar 1993) . . . . . Herself
•• 67—Buns and tip of right breast.
**Playboy's Book of Lingerie** (May 1993) . . . . . Herself
••• 15—Breasts.
**Playboy's Girls of Summer '93** (Jun 1993) . . . Herself
••• 10—Full frontal nudity.
••• 32-33—Full frontal nudity.
••• 45—Breasts.
**Playboy's Book of Lingerie** (Jul 1993) . . . . . . Herself
••• 81—Breasts.
••• 97—Breasts.
**Playboy's Wet & Wild Women** (Aug 1993) . . Herself
•• 14—Side of right breast.
••• 20—Breasts.
• 44—Partial right breast.
••• 75—Full frontal nudity.
•• 97—Breasts under fishnet top and lower frontal nudity.
**Playboy's Book of Lingerie** (Nov 1993) . . . . . Herself
•• 59—Left breast.
••• 106-107—Full frontal nudity.
**Playboy's Nudes** (Dec 1993) . . . . . . . . . . . . . Herself
••• 18—Full frontal nudity.
**Playboy's Book of Lingerie** (May 1994) . . . . . Herself
•• 78—Left breast. Right breast and lower frontal nudity under sheer lingerie.
**Playboy's Girls of Summer '94** (Jul 1994) . . . Herself
••• 17—Full frontal nudity.

## Thomas, Betty

*Films:*
Chesty Anderson, U.S. Navy (1975) . . . . Party Guest #1
Jackson County Jail (1976) . . . . . . . . . . . . . . . Waitress
**Tunnelvision** (1976) . . . . . . . . . . . Brigit Bert Richards
**Loose Shoes** (1977) . . . . . . . . . . . . . . Biker Chick #1
• 0:02—Brief right breast dancing on the table during the *Skateboarders from Hell* sketch.
**Used Cars** (1980) . . . . . . . . . . . . . . . . . . . . . . .Bunny
0:37—Dancing on top of a car next to Kurt Russell wearing pasties to attract customers (wearing a brunette wig).
Homework (1982). . . . . . . . . . . . . . .Reddog's Secretary
Troop Beverly Hills (1989) . . . . . . . . . . . . Velda Plendor
*Made for TV Movies:*
Outside Chance (1978). . . . . . . . . . . . . . . . Katherine
*TV:*
Hill Street Blues (1981-87). . . . . . . . . . . . . . Lucy Bates
*Video Tapes:*
E. Nick: A Legend in His Own Mind (1984) . . . . . Herself

## Thomas, Heather

*Films:*
Zapped! (1982) . . . . . . . . . . . . . . . . . . . . . . Jane Mitchell
0:20—Brief open sweater, wearing a bra when Scott Baio uses telekinesis to open it.
1:28—Body double, very, very brief breasts in photo that Willie Aames gives to Robby.
1:29—Body double brief breasts when Baio drops her dress during the dance.
Cyclone (1986) . . . . . . . . . . . . . . . . . . . . Teri Marshall
Deathstone (1986; German) . . . . . . . . . . Merryl Davis
Red Blooded American Girl (1988) . . . . . Paula Bukowsky
1:19—Lower half of right breast when Andrew Stevens is on top of her. Very, very brief silhouette of right breast. Probably a body double.
Hidden Obsession (1992). . . . . . . . . . . . . . .Ellen Carlyle
1:00—In bra, while on kitchen counter with Jan-Michael Vincent when he rips open her blouse.
1:01—Squished breast, against Vincent while on the floor with him.
*TV:*
Co-ed Fever (1979) . . . . . . . . . . . . . . . . . . . . . . . .Sandi
The Fall Guy (1981-86) . . . . . . . . . . . . . . . . Jodi Banks
The Ultimate Challenge (1991) . . . . . . . . . . . . .Co-Host

## Thomas, Heidi

*Films:*
**Crack House** (1989). . . . . . . . . . . . . . . . . . . . . .Annie
• 1:09—Brief left breast and buns in a G string, on table getting raped by a gang.
• 1:14—Breasts in bathtub, dead.
Ricochet (1991) . . . . . . . . . . . . . . . . . . . . . . . Reporter
*Made for Cable TV:*
**Tales From the Crypt: Split Personality**
(1992; HBO). . . . . . . . . . . . . . . . . . . . . . . .Prostitute
•• 0:06—Breasts, lying in bed with Joe Pesci.

## • Thompson, Alina

*Films:*
**Trapped** (1993) . . . . . . . . . . . . . . . . . . . . . . . Monica
*a.k.a. The Killing Jar*
• 0:16—In sheer white lingerie outfit in bedroom with Alan.
• 0:26—Right breast while in bed with Alan in Laura's imagination.
••• 0:33—In two piece swimsuit, then nude, while making love with Alan outside by pool.
•• 0:37—Nude, undressing and going for a swim in the pool, then getting killed.
**Seduce Me: Pamela Principle 2** (1994). . . . . Pamela
••• 0:23—Buns in sexy swimsuit, then breasts during photo session.
• 0:33—Brief lower half of buns, while walking up stairs in short dress.
••• 0:35—Breasts and buns, opening towel, then getting dressed.
••• 0:37—Nude, changing clothes then posing for photos outside. Some in B&W. Long scene.

•• 0:44—Buns in G-string and left breast while making love with Charles in kitchen.
• 0:49—Brief right breast and buns in swimsuit bottom while getting out of spa.
••• 1:16—Breasts and buns, while making love in bed with Charles.

*Magazines:*
**Playboy** (Apr 1993) . . . . . . . . . . . . . . . . . . Tattoo You
••• 82-83—Breasts. Tattoo on side of her hip.

## Thompson, Brooke

*Video Tapes:*
**Hot Body International: #1 Miss Cancun** (1990)
. . . . . . . . . . . . . . . . . . . . . . . . . . . . . . . . Contestant
•• 0:40—Buns, in one piece swimsuit.
0:50—3rd runner up.
**Hot Body International: #2 Miss Puerto Vallarta** (1990). . . . . . . . . . . . . . . . . . . . . . . . . Contestant
••• 0:26—Buns in red one piece swimsuit. Brief left breast a couple of times when it accidentally falls out.
0:56—3rd runner up.
Hot Body International: #4 Spring Break (1992)
. . . . . . . . . . . . . . . . . . . . . . . . . . . . . . . . Contestant
0:10—Dancing in one piece swimsuit on stage.
0:38—Wet T-shirt contest. Buns in G-string.

## Thompson, Cynthia Ann

*Films:*
**Cave Girl** (1985) . . . . . . . . . . . . . . . . . . . . . . . . . Eba
• 0:41—Buns, standing in stream while bathing. Long shot.
•• 1:04—Breasts making love with Rex.
**Tomboy** (1985) . . . . . . . . . . . . . . . . . . . . . . . Amanda
• 0:23—Brief right breast getting out of car in auto repair shop.
•• 1:02—Breasts delivering drinks to two guys in the swimming pool.
Not of This Earth (1988) . . . . Third Hooker (black dress)

## Thompson, Emma

Wife of actor/director Kenneth Branagh.
*Films:*
Henry V (1989) . . . . . . . . . . . . . . . . . .Princess Katherine
**The Tall Guy** (1990; British) . . . . . . . . . . . . . . . . Kate
••• 0:33—Very brief right breast, brief buns, then breasts during funny love making scene with Jeff Goldblum.
Dead Again (1991) . . . . . . . . Margaret Strauss/Jane Doe
Impromptu (1991) . . . . . . . . . . . . . . . .Duchess d'Antan
Howards End (1992) . . . . . . . . . . . . . .Margaret Schlegel
(Academy Award for Best Actress.)
In the Name of the Father (1993; British/U.S.)
. . . . . . . . . . . . . . . . . . . . . . . . . . . . . Gareth Peirce
Much Ado About Nothing (1993; British) . . . . . Beatrice
Peter's Friends (1993; British/U.S.) . . . . . . . . . .Maggie
The Remains of the Day (1993; British/U.S.)
. . . . . . . . . . . . . . . . . . . . . . . . . . . . . . Miss Kenton

## Thompson, Lea

*Films:*
**All The Right Moves** (1983) . . . . . . . . . . . . . . . . Lisa
••• 1:00—Breasts and brief buns and lower frontal nudity, getting undressed and into bed with Tom Cruise in his bedroom.
Jaws 3 (1983) . . . . . . . . . . . . . . . . . . Kelly Ann Bukowski
Red Dawn (1984) . . . . . . . . . . . . . . . . . . . . . . . . . Erica
The Wild Life (1984) . . . . . . . . . . . . . . . . . . . . . . Anita
0:38—In bra and panties putting body stocking on.
Back to the Future (1985) . . . . . . Lorraine Baines-McFly
Howard the Duck (1986) . . . . . . . . . . . . Beverly Switzler
SpaceCamp (1986) . . . . . . . . . . . . . . . . . . . . . Kathryn
Some Kind of Wonderful (1987) . . . . . . . Amanda Jones
**Casual Sex?** (1988) . . . . . . . . . . . . . . . . . . . . . Stacy
0:27—Buns, lying down at nude beach with Victoria Jackson.
0:30—Buns at the beach. Pan shot from her feet to her head.
Going Undercover (1988; British) . .Marigold De La Hunt
The Wizard of Loneliness (1988) . . . . . . . . . . . . . Sybil
Back to the Future, Part II (1989)
. . . . . . . . . . . . . . . . . . . . . . . Lorraine Baines-McFly
Back to the Future, Part III (1990)
. . . . . . . . . . . . . . . . . Maggie McFly/Lorraine McFly
Article 99 (1992) . . . . . . . . . . . . . . Dr. Robin Van Dorn
The Beverly Hillbillies (1993) . . . . . . . . . . . . . .Laura
Dennis the Menace (1993) . . . . . . . . . . .Alice Mitchell
*Made for Cable Movies:*
Stolen Babies (1993; Lifetime) . . . . . . . . . . . . . . . n.a.
*Made for Cable TV:*
Tales From the Crypt: Only Sin Deep (1989; HBO)
. . . . . . . . . . . . . . . . . . . . . . . . . . . . . Sylvia Vane
*Made for TV Movies:*
The Substitute Wife (1994) . . . . . . . . . . . . . . . . . n.a.

## Thompson, Victoria

*Films:*
**The Harrad Experiment** (1973) . . . . . . . . Beth Hillyer
0:08—Buns, in the bathroom while talking to Harry.
• 0:10—Brief breasts getting into bed.
•• 0:21—Breasts in nude encounter group.
• 0:41—Breasts getting into the swimming pool with Don Johnson and Laurie Walters.
0:49—Buns, getting dressed after making love with Johnson.
**The Harrad Summer** (1974) . . . . . . . . . . Beth Hillyer
*a.k.a. Student Union*
•• 0:57—Buns and brief breasts running down hallway and jumping into bed, pretending to be asleep.
1:03—Buns, lying on inflatable lounge in the pool.
1:04—Buns, lying face down on lounge chair.
**Famous T & A** (1982) . . . . . . . . . . . . . . Beth Hillyer
(No longer available for purchase, check your video store for rental.)
• 1:07—Brief breasts and bun scene from *The Harrad Experiment*.
• 1:12—Brief nude, getting up from the floor with Don Johnson.

## Thomson, Anna

See: Levine Thomson, Anna.

## Thomson, Kim

*Films:*
The Lords of Discipline (1983)..................n.a.
Party Party (1983; British)................. Brenda
**Stealing Heaven** (1988; British/Yugoslavian) .. Heloise
• 0:42—Side of left breast kneeling on floor with steam. Long shot.
•• 0:43—Closer view of left breast.
••• 0:47—Breasts and very brief lower frontal nudity lying in bed with Abelard. More left breast afterwards.
• 1:07—Nude, left side view on top of Abelard in bed. Long shot.

## Thorn, Frankie

*Films:*
Lisa (1989)............................... Judy
**Bad Lieutenant** (1992)..................... Nun
• 0:18—Very brief lower frontal nudity, while getting raped by two guys in church.
•• 0:26—Full frontal nudity while lying on hospital bed during examination.
Liquid Dreams (1992)..................... Paula
(Unrated version reviewed.)

## Thorne, Dyanne

*Films:*
Point of Terror (1971)..................... Andrea
**Ilsa, She Wolf of the S.S.** (1974)............. Ilsa
•• 0:00—Buns, then breasts making love in bed.
••• 0:01—Breasts taking a shower.
•• 0:29—Buns and breasts in bed with Wolfe.
•• 0:32—Right breast several times in bed with Wolfe.
••• 0:48—In white bra, then breasts undressing for Wolfe.
•• 0:50—Right breast, while lying in bed.
1:18—In black bra, panties, garter belt and stockings, tied to the bed.
Chesty Anderson, U.S. Navy (1975) .......... Nurse
**Ilsa, Harem Keeper of the Oil Sheiks** (1978) ... Ilsa
**Ilsa, The Wicked Warden** (1980)............. Ilsa
*a.k.a. Ilsa—Absolute Power*
*a.k.a. Greta, The Mad Butcher.*
*Ilsa—Absolute Power* is about 4 minutes shorter.
Hellhole (1985)..........................Chrysta
Real Men (1987)........................... Dad

## Thornton, Ann

*Films:*
**Eureka** (1983; British)..............Jane (red dress)
• 1:17—Brief breasts during African voodoo ceremony.
Hope and Glory (1987; British)...... Honeymoon Wife

## Thornton, Sigrid

*Films:*
**The Day After Halloween** (1978; Australian) ..Angela
*a.k.a. Snapshot*
• 0:04—Very brief breasts in ad photos on wall.
•• 0:19—Breasts during modeling session at the beach.
••• 0:21—More breasts at the beach.
•• 0:37—Breasts in magazine ad several times.
• 0:43—Brief right breast in magazine ad.
• 0:46—Breasts in ad again.
• 1:18—Entering room covered with the ad.
1:20—In beige bra in room with weirdo guy.
The Man from Snowy River (1982; Australian) ... Jessica
Great Expectations (1987; Australian)......... Bridget
Slate, Wyn & Me (1987; Australian)...... Blanche/Max
The Lighthorsemen (1988; Australian) .......... Anne
Return to Snowy River (1988) .............. Jessica
Over the Hill (1991; Australian) ............ Elizabeth
*Made for Cable Movies:*
All the Rivers Run (1984; HBO)..........Philadelphia
*TV:*
Paradise (1989-90).................Amelia Lawson
Guns of Paradise (1991).............Amelia Lawson

## Thorson, Laura

See: Hays, Lauren.

## • Thorson, Linda

*Films:*
**Valentino** (1977; British)............. Billie Streeter
• 0:14—Brief left breast, under a guy in bed.
The Greek Tycoon (1978)...................Angela
Curtains (1983; Canadian)........... Brooke Parsons
Flanagan (1985)...........................Andrea
Sweet Liberty (1986).......................Grace
*TV:*
One Life to Live...................... Julia Medina
The Avengers (1968-69)................. Tara King

## Thulin, Ingrid

*Films:*
Brink of Life (1957; Swedish)................. Cecila
Wild Strawberries (1957; Swedish)......Marianne Borg
The Magician (1959)..................Manda Aman
The Four Horsemen of the Apocalypse (1962)
.......................Marguerite Laurier
The Winter Light (1963; Swedish) .... Marta Lundberg
Hour of the Wolf (1968; Swedish) ..... Veronica Vogler
**The Damned** (1969; German) .. Sophie Von Essenbeck
•• 1:23—Breasts in bed with Frederick. Long scene for a 1969 film.
• 2:03—Left breast in bed with Martin (her son in the film).
**Cries and Whispers** (1972; Swedish) ......... Karin
*a.k.a. Viskingar Och Rop*
•• 0:57—Breasts and buns, undressing and getting ready for bed. Something covers lower frontal nudity.
Moses (1976; British/Italian)................Miriam

**After the Rehearsal** (1984; Swedish) . . . . . . . . .Rakel
 • 0:33—Brief breasts, when pulling up her sweater to
 show Henrik how beautiful her breasts still look.

## Thurman, Uma

Ex-wife of actor Gary Oldman.
*Films:*
Kiss Daddy Goodnight (1987) . . . . . . . . . . . . . . . Laura
**Dangerous Liaisons** (1988) . . . . . . Cécile de Volanges
 ••• 0:59—Breasts taking off her nightgown in her bed-
 room with John Malkovich.
Johnny Be Good (1988) . . . . . . . . . . . . . Georgia Elkans
The Adventures of Baron Munchausen (1989; British/
German) . . . . . . . . . . . . . . . . . . . . . . . . . . . .Venus/Rose
 1:14—Brief upper half of right breast when the fly-
 ing ladies wrap her with the flowing cloth.
Henry & June (1990). . . . . . . . . . . . . . . . . . June Miller
**Where the Heart Is** (1990) . . . . . . . . Daphne McBain
 • 0:08—Breasts during art film, but her entire body is
 artfully painted to match the background paintings.
 The second segment.
 0:40—More breasts with body painted posing for
 her sister. Long shot.
 1:16—In slide of painting taken at 0:40.
 1:43—Same painting from 0:40 during the end
 credits.
Final Analysis (1992) . . . . . . . . . . . . . . . . . .Diana Baylor
Jennifer 8 (1992). . . . . . . . . . . . . . . . . . . . . . . . . Helena
 0:50—Body double did nude scene in bathroom.
**Mad Dog and Glory** (1993) . . . . . . . . . . . . . . . Glory
 •• 0:56—Left breast, while in bed with Robert De Niro.
 • 0:58—Very brief breasts when De Niro gets off her.
Even Cowgirls Get the Blues (1994) . . . .Sissy Hankshaw
*Made for TV Movies:*
Robin Hood (1991). . . . . . . . . . . . . . . . . . .Maid Marian
*Magazines:*
**Playboy** (Dec 1990). . . . . . . . . . . . . Sex Stars of 1990
 • 179—Left breast, while kneeling. B&W.

## Tia

*Video Tapes:*
Mermaid's Illustrated. . . . . . . . . . . . . . . . . . . . . . . .n.a.
**The Best of the Mermaids** (1992) . . . Sand and Lace
 ••• 1:12—Breasts and buns in G-string on boat, at the
 beach and while scuba diving.
**Mermaids of the Aztec Empire** (1992)
 . . . . . . . . . . . . . . . . . . . . . . . . . . . . . . Mona Brock
 •• 0:01—Breasts during opening credits.
 ••• 0:02—Breasts and buns in G-string at the beach during opening credits.
 •• 0:06—Breasts outside with Lori Pallett by pool and
 under water.
 •• 0:10—In bra and panties, then breasts in jewelry
 store fantasy.
 • 0:11—Buns, in swimsuit, by the pool.
 • 0:13—Brief buns, while turning over in the spa.
 •• 0:14—Breasts and buns in G-string bottom on boat.
 ••• 0:23—Breasts and buns at the beach. Long scene.

 ••• 0:31—Breasts and buns in G-string while snorkeling
 under water.
 ••• 0:37—Breasts and buns at the beach again.
 ••• 0:49—Breasts and buns in swimsuit bottoms undressing at the beach during the end credits.
Mermaids of Sand, Sea and Surf (1993) . . . . . . . . . n.a.

## Ticotin, Rachel

*Films:*
**Fort Apache, The Bronx** (1981). . . . . . . . . . . Isabelle
 • 1:25—Brief upper half of breasts in bathtub while
 Paul Newman pours bubble bath in.
Critical Condition (1987) . . . . . . . . . . . . . . . . . .Rachel
Total Recall (1990) . . . . . . . . . . . . . . . . . . . . . . .Melina
FX 2 (1991) . . . . . . . . . . . . . . . . . . . . . . . Kim Brandon
One Good Cop (1991). . . . . . . . . . . . . . . . . . . .Grace
Where The Day Takes You (1992). . . . . . Officer Landers
Falling Down (1993) . . . . . . . . . . . . . . . . . . . . .Sandra
*Made for Cable Movies:*
Prison Stories, Women on the Inside (1990; HBO) . . . Iris
 0:07—Brief buns, squatting while getting strip
 searched in jail. Don't see her face.
Keep the Change (1992; TNT) . . . . . . . . . . . . . .Astrid
Deconstructing Sarah (1994; USA). . . . . . . . . . . . n.a.
*Made for TV Movies:*
Spies, Lies & Naked Thighs (1988). . . . . . . . . . . .Sonia
From the Files of Joseph Wambaugh: A Jury of One
 (1992) . . . . . . . . . . . . . . . . . . . . . . . . Christine Avila
Thicker Than Blood: The Larry McLinden Story (1994)
 . . . . . . . . . . . . . . . . . . . . . . . . . . . . . . . . . . . . n.a.
*TV:*
For Love and Honor (1983) . . . . . . . . . Cpl. Grace Pavlik
Ohara (1987-88) . . . . . . . . . . . . . . . . . . . Teresa Storm
Crime & Punishment (1993) . . . . . . . . . . .Annette Rey

## • Tilly, Jennifer

Sister of actress Meg Tilly.
*Films:*
No Small Affair (1984) . . . . . . . . . . . . . . . . . . . . Mona
Moving Violations (1985). . . . . . . . . . . . . .Amy Hopkins
He's My Girl (1987) . . . . . . . . . . . . . . . . . . . . . . . Lisa
Remote Control (1987) . . . . . . . . . . . . . . . . . . .Allegra
High Spirits (1988). . . . . . . . . . . . . . . . . . . . .Miranda
Johnny Be Good (1988) . . . . . . . . . . . . . .Connie Hisler
Rented Lips (1988). . . . . . . . . . . . . . . . . . . Mona Lisa
The Fabulous Baker Boys (1989). . . . . . .Monica Moran
Far From Home (1989). . . . . . . . . . . . . . . . . . . .Amy
Let It Ride (1989) . . . . . . . . . . . . . . . . . . . . . . . Vicki
At Home with the Webbers (1992). . . . Miranda Webber
Scorchers (1992) . . . . . . . . . . . . . . . . . . . . . . . Talbot
**Shadow of the Wolf** (1992) . . . . . . . . . . . . . Iglyook
 • 0:21—Very brief right breast under Lou Diamond
 Phillips.
 • 0:22—Very, very brief left breast when Phillips is on
 top of her and holds her arms down.
 •• 1:27—Very brief breasts, after taking off her clothes,
 then making love with Phillips.

**The Getaway** (1993). . . . . . . . . . . . . . . . Fran Carvey
(Unrated version reviewed.)
  •• 1:12—Breasts and buns while making love on top of
    Michael Madsen in bed while her husband is tied to
    chair in bathroom.
    1:21—In white bra while lying in bed with Madsen.
    1:31—In lingerie while sitting in bed with Madsen.
Heads (1993) . . . . . . . . . . . . . . . . . . . . . Tina Abbot
**Made in America** (1993) . . . . . . . . . . . . . . . . . Stacy
  • 0:13—Very, very brief back side of left breast, while
    jumping up out of bed. Brief buns and very, very
    brief back side of left breast while doing cartwheels
    into the bathroom. Possible body double.
Double Cross (1994) . . . . . . . . . . . . . . . . . . . . Melissa
*Made for Cable TV:*
Dream On: What Women Want (1992; HBO) . . . . . Ryan
*TV:*
Shaping Up (1984) . . . . . . . . . . . . . . Shannon Winters
Key West (1993) . . . . . . . . . . . . . . . . . . . . . Savannah

## Tilly, Meg
Sister of actress Jennifer Tilly.
*Films:*
Fame (1980) . . . . . . . . . . . . . . . . . . . . Principal Dancer
Tex (1982) . . . . . . . . . . . . . . . . . . . . . . Jamie Collins
The Big Chill (1983) . . . . . . . . . . . . . . . . . . . . Chloé
One Dark Night (1983) . . . . . . . . . . . . . . . . . . . Julie
Psycho II (1983) . . . . . . . . . . . . . . . . . . . . . . Mary
    0:35—Buns and very brief breasts of body double,
    getting out of the shower while Anthony Perkins
    watches through a peep hole.
Impulse (1984) . . . . . . . . . . . . . . . . . . . . . . . Jenny
    0:58—In wet red swimsuit in photograph, then
    breasts in B&W photograph (don't see her face)
    when Tim Matheson looks at photos.
Agnes of God (1985). . . . . . . . . . . . . . . . . Sister Agnes
Off Beat (1986). . . . . . . . . . . . . . . . . . Rachel Wareham
Masquerade (1988). . . . . . . . . . . . . . . Olivia Lawrence
    0:55—In pink nightgown in bedroom.
**The Girl in a Swing** (1989; U.S./British). . Karin Foster
  •• 0:44—In white bra, then breasts and buns.
  •• 0:50—Nude, while swimming under water.
  ••• 1:14—Breasts while sitting on swing, then making
    love.
    1:18—In white bra, while sitting in front of a mirror.
  ••• 1:44—Breasts while at the beach.
Valmont (1989). . . . . . . . . . . . . . . . . . . . . . Tourvel
The Two Jakes (1990) . . . . . . . . . . . . . . . . Kitty Berman
Leaving Normal (1992). . . . . . . . . . . . . . . . Marianne
Body Snatchers (1994) . . . . . . . . . . . . . Carol Malone
*Made for Cable TV:*
Nightmare Classics: Carmilla (1989; HBO) . . . . Carmilla
Fallen Angels: Dead-End for Delia (1993; Showtime)
. . . . . . . . . . . . . . . . . . . . . . . . . . . Lois Weldon
(Available on video tape on *Fallen Angels Two.*)
*Made for TV Movies:*
In the Best Interest of the Child (1990) . . Jennifer Colton
*TV:*
Winnetaka Road (1994). . . . . . . . . . . . . . . . . George

## Ting, Chan
*Video Tapes:*
**Playboy International Playmates** (1993). . . . . . Ting
  ••• 0:00—Full frontal nudity, on sofa, caressing herself.
  ••• 0:02—Breasts in still photos.
  ••• 0:03—Full frontal nudity outside with statue.
  •• 0:22—Breasts in restaurant with another woman
    during food fight.
  ••• 0:53—Nude, stripping and dancing in basement
    during interrogation fantasy.
*Magazines:*
**Playboy Presents International Playmates**
(Feb 1992) . . . . . . . . . . . . . . . . . . . . . . . . Herself
  ••• 20-23—Nude.
**Playboy's Girls of the World** (Oct 1992). . . . . Herself
  ••• 60-61—Full frontal nudity.

## Tippo, Patti
*Films:*
**10 to Midnight** (1983) . . . . . . . . . . . . . . . . Party Girl
  •• 0:52—Breasts, making love with a guy in the laundry
    room at a party.
Omega Syndrome (1986) . . . . . . . . . . . . . . . . . Sally
Sid and Nancy (1986; British)
. . . . . . . . . . . . . . . . . Tanned and Sultry Blonde
Brain Dead (1989) . . . . . . . . . . . . . . . . . . . . Resident
Roadside Prophets (1992) . . . . . . . . . . . Casino Cashier
*Made for Cable Movies:*
Dangerous Heart (1994; USA) . . . . . . . . . Policewoman
*TV:*
Sledge Hammer! (1987-88) . . . . . . . . . . . Officer Daley

## Tolan, Kathleen
*Films:*
**Death Wish** (1974) . . . . . . . . . . . . . . . . . . Carol Toby
  • 0:09—Brief breasts and buns getting raped by three
    punks.
The Line (1982) . . . . . . . . . . . . . . . . . . . . . . . n.a.
The Rosary Murders (1987) . . . . . . . . . Sister Ann Vania

## Tolo, Marilu
*Films:*
The Oldest Profession (1967) . . . . . . . . . . "Anticipation"
    1:23—Brief side view of left breast walking to the
    bathroom. Shown as a negative image, so it's hard
    to see.
Confessions of a Police Captain (1971). . Serena Li Puma
**Bluebeard** (1972). . . . . . . . . . . . . . . . . . . . . Brigitt
  • 1:25—Breasts in sheer blue blouse arguing with Ri-
    chard Burton.
  •• 1:27—Breasts getting whipped by Burton.
Beyond Fear (1975) . . . . . . . . . . . . . . . . . . . . Nicole
The Greek Tycoon (1978). . . . . . . . . . . Sophia Matalas
*Magazines:*
**Playboy** (Nov 1978) . . . . . . . . . . . Sex in Cinema 1978
  • 184—Upper half of left breast.

# Tomasina, Jeana

*Films:*

Lovely But Deadly (1973) ... Woman with Stuck Zipper
History of the World, Part I (1981) . . . . . . . Vestal Virgin
Looker (1981) . . . . . . . . . . . . . . . . . . . . . . . . . . . . . Suzy
**The Beach Girls** (1982) . . . . . . . . . . . . . . . . . . .Ducky
   •• 0:12—Breasts and buns, lying on the beach with
      Ginger, while a guy looks through a telescope.
   ••• 0:54—Breasts on a sailboat with a guy.
   • 0:55—Brief breasts on the beach after being "saved"
      after falling off the boat.
   •• 1:12—Breasts in sauna with Ginger and an older
      guy.
Off the Wall (1982) . . . . . . . . . . . . . . . . . . . . . . . . .n.a.
10 to Midnight (1983) . . . . . . . . . . . . . . . . . . . . . Karen
   0:26—In white body suit, changing in bedroom
   while the killer watches from inside the closet.
**Double Exposure** (1983) . . . . . . . . . . . . . . . . . Renee
   • 0:20—Very brief glimpse of left breast under water
      in swimming pool.
Up the Creek (1984) . . . . . . . . . . . . . . . . . . . . . . Molly
*Music Videos:*
Gimme All Your Loving/Z.Z. Top . . . . . . . . . . . . . . Girl
Legs/Z.Z. Top . . . . . . . . . . . . . . . . . . . . . . . . Legs Girl
Sharp Dressed Man/Z.Z. Top. . . . . . . . . . . Girl in White
*Video Tapes:*
Playboy Video Magazine, Volume 2 (1983)
. . . . . . . . . . . . . . . . . . . . . Herself/Playboy Playoffs
**Playboy Video Magazine, Volume 5** (1983)
. . . . . . . . . . . . . . . . . . . . . . . . . . . . . . . . . Playmate
   • 0:06—Brief breasts on piano.
   • 0:12—Breasts, then full frontal nudity posing on pi-
      ano.
**Playboy Video Centerfold: Reneé Tenison** (1990)
   . . . . . . . . . Portrait of a Photographer: Richard Fegley
   •• 0:34—Full frontal nudity, posing on piano for cen-
      terfold photo.
*Magazines:*
**Playboy** (Nov 1980) . . . . . . . . . . . . . . . . . . Playmate
   ••• 144-155—Nude.
**Playboy's Calendar Playmates** (Nov 1992) . . Herself
   ••• 26—Full frontal nudity.

# Tomlin, Melanie

*Films:*

**Rich Girl** (1991) . . . . . . . . . . . . . . . . . . . . . . . Diana
   • 0:03—Half of left breast, while in bed with Jeffrey.
   • 0:04—Almost side of left breast again, while looking
      for her keys.
Traces of Red (1992) . . . . . . . . . . . . . . . . . . . . Amanda

# Tompkins, Angel

*Films:*

Hang Your Hat on the Wind (1969) . . . . . . . Fran Harper
**I Love My Wife** (1970) . . . . . . . . . . . . Helene Donnelly
**Prime Cut** (1972) . . . . . . . . . . . . . . . . . . . . Clarabelle
   • 1:03—Very brief left breast sitting up in bed to talk
      to Lee Marvin.

1:04—Very brief back side view of left breast jumping out of bed.
The Don is Dead (1973). . . . . . . . . . . . . . . . . . . . Ruby
How to Seduce a Woman (1973) . . . . . . . . . . . Pamela
   1:28—In bra and panties for a long time getting a
   massage in bedroom.
**The Teacher** (1974) . . . . . . . . . . . . . . . .Diane Marshall
   ••• 0:09—Breasts on a boat taking off her swimsuit.
   ••• 0:12—More breasts on the boat getting a suntan.
   ••• 0:36—Breasts taking off her top in bedroom, then
      buns and breasts taking a shower.
   • 0:41—Brief right breast lying back on bed.
   •• 0:43—Brief breasts opening her bathrobe for Jay
      North.
   •• 0:47—Side view of right breast lying on bed, then
      right breast from above.
   •• 0:52—Breasts in boat after making love.
Walking Tall, Part II (1975) . . . . . . . . . .Marganne Stilson
The Farmer (1977). . . . . . . . . . . . . . . . . . . . . . . Betty
The Bees (1978). . . . . . . . . . . . . . . . . . . Sandra Miller
One Man Jury (1978). . . . . . . . . . . . . . . . . . . . . Kitty
Alligator (1980) . . . . . . . . . . . . . . . . . . .News Reporter
**The Naked Cage** (1985) . . . . . . . . . . . . Diane Wallace
   •• 0:22—In lingerie, then breasts with Abbey.
   • 0:38—Brief right breast, in bed with Abbey.
Dangerously Close (1986) . . . . . . . . . . . . . Mrs. Waters
**Murphy's Law** (1986) . . . . . . . . . . . . . . . . . . . . . .Jan
   • 0:19—Breasts doing a strip routine on stage while
      Charles Bronson watches.
   • 0:27—Brief breasts doing another routine.
Amazon Women on the Moon (1987) . . . . . . .First Lady
   1:00—In white nightgown, then black bra, panties,
   garter belt and stockings.
A Tiger's Tale (1988). . . . . . . . . . . . . . . . . . . . La Vonne
Crack House (1989) . . . . . . . . . . . . . . . . . . . . Mother
Relentless (1989) . . . . . . . . . . . . . . . . . . . . . . Carmen
*Made for Cable TV:*
The Hitchhiker: Homebodies . . . . . . . . . . . Janet O'Mell
*TV:*
Search (1972-73) . . . . . . . . . . . . . . . . . .Gloria Harding
*Magazines:*
**Playboy** (Feb 1972) . . . . . . . . . . . . . . . . . . . . .Angel
   ••• 87-91—Lots of photos of her in a river.
**Playboy** (Jun 1972). . . . . . . . . . . . . . . . . . Prime Cut
   ••• 123—Breasts.
**Playboy** (Dec 1972) . . . . . . . . . . . . .Sex Stars of 1972
   ••• 210—Full frontal nudity.
**Playboy** (Dec 1973) . . . . . . . . . . . . .Sex Stars of 1973
   ••• 209—Full frontal nudity.
**Playboy** (Dec 1974) . . . . . . . . . . . . .Sex Stars of 1974
   ••• 211—Right breast and lower frontal nudity in water-
      fall.

# Toothman, Lisa

*Films:*

**Hard Rock Zombies** (1985) . . . . . . . . . . . . . . . . Elsa
- 0:01—Buns, undressing to go skinny dipping. Breasts long shot.
- ••• 0:32—Buns, while getting into the shower. Breasts and buns in the shower behind clear plastic curtain.

**RollerBlade Warriors: Taken By Force** (1988)
. . . . . . . . . . . . . . . . . . . . . . . . . . . . . . . . Slave Girl #1
- •• 0:21—Breasts after getting her top ripped off by two guys.
- ••• 0:23—Breasts, while walking through the desert.

The Girl I Want (1990) . . . . . . . . . . . . . . . . . . . . Girl 2

**Witchcraft III: The Kiss of Death** (1991). . Charlotte
- •• 1:02—Buns and breasts in shower with Louis while William has a bad dream.
- •• 1:12—Left breast, while on bed with Louis, against her will.

Eyes of the Serpent (1992) . . . . . . . . . . . . . . . . Neema

# • Torday, Terry

*Films:*

**Julia** (1974; German) . . . . . . . . . . . . . . . . . . . . . Yvonne
- 0:08—Brief right breast, while making love in train restroom.
- •• 0:18—Breasts, while in bed with Ralph. Dark, hard to see.
- 0:37—Breasts, while getting up to put swimsuit on.
- 0:41—Brief breasts, while getting dressed in bedroom with Ralph.
- •• 0:57—Full frontal nudity in bedroom seducing Patrick.
- •• 1:01—Breasts, while sitting up in bed eating breakfast with Patrick.

Hanna's War (1988) . . . . . . . . . . . . . Baroness Hatvany

# Torek, Denise

*Films:*

New York's Finest (1988). . . . . . . . . . . . . . . Hooker #2
**Sensations** (1988). . . . . . . . . . . . . . . . . Phone Girl #2
- 0:23—Breasts talking on the phone sex line.

# Torena, Lyllah

*Films:*

Fly Me (1973) . . . . . . . . . . . . . . . . . . . . . . . . . . . . . n.a.
**The Boob Tube** (1975) . . . . . . . . . . . . . . Natalie Nolan
- ••• 0:28—Breasts, putting on her blouse.
- 0:42—Breasts, getting raped by three Hell's Angel guys outside during flashback.
- •• 0:45—Breasts and buns, on bed, taking off her clothes with Dr. Carstairs.
- ••• 0:46—Breasts and buns, while making love with Dr. Carstairs in bed. Nice buns shot. More breasts after making love.
- 0:48—Breasts and buns, while making love in bed with Gretchen.
- •• 1:08—Left breast, while in front of Sid when her robe is pulled down by Gretchen.
- 1:10—Breasts on sofa with Gretchen.

- ••• 1:12—Breasts during orgy on couch.
- 1:16—Brief breasts in hallway.

# Toscano, Gabriela

*Films:*

South (1988; Argentinian/French) . . . . . . . . . . . Blondi
**Satanic Attraction** (1991; Italian). . . . . . . . Fernanda
- 0:43—Partial left breast, making love with Lionel. Brief side view of left breast, eating fruit afterwards.

# Tough, Kelly

*Video Tapes:*

**Playboy's Playmate Review** (1982) . . . . . . . Playmate
- ••• 0:27—Nude, camping, then in bedroom setting.

**Playmates at Play** (1990) . . . . . . . . . . . Making Waves

*Magazines:*

**Playboy** (Oct 1981) . . . . . . . . . . . . . . . . . . . Playmate
**Playboy's Girls of Summer '86** (Aug 1986). . . Herself
- ••• 55—Full frontal nudity.

# Townsend, K.C.

*Films:*

Husbands (1970) . . . . . . . . . . . . . . . . . . . . . . . Barmaid
**Is There Sex After Death?** (1975)
. . . . . . . . . . Round Table Discussion/Woman on Table
- •• 1:25—Full frontal nudity, while making love on table with a guy in front of a group of a discussion group of men.

**All That Jazz** (1979) . . . . . . . . . . . . . . . . . . . Stripper
- 0:20—Breasts backstage getting Joey excited before he goes on stage. Lit by red light.

Below the Belt (1980) . . . . . . . . . . . . . . . . . . . . Thalia
The Burning (1981) . . . . . . . . . . . . . . . . . . . . . Hooker

# Townsend, Patrice

*Films:*

**Sitting Ducks** (1978) . . . . . . . . . . . . . . . . . . . . . Jenny
- ••• 0:55—Breasts, taking off her blouse in room with Sid.
- •• 0:58—Buns and brief left breast, sitting up in bed with Simon after getting seen by Leona.

Always (1984) . . . . . . . . . . . . . . . . . . . . . . . . . . . Judy

# • Tracy

*Video Tapes:*

**Penthouse Pet of the Year Playoff 1993** (1993)
. . . . . . . . . . . . . . . . . . . . . . . . . . . . . . . . . . . . . . . Pet
- ••• 0:31—Nude on bed, in front of mirror while making herself up and getting dressed, in a house (sometimes wearing a black wig).

**Penthouse Pet of the Year Winners 1993: Mahalia & Julie** (1994)
. . . . . . . . . . . Sneak Preview of Pet of the Year Playoff
- ••• 0:25—In lingerie, then nude on bed and couch.

*Magazines:*

**Penthouse** (Jun 1992) . . . . . . . . . . . . . . . . . . . . . Pet
- ••• 67-81—Full frontal nudity.

# Trainor, Saxon

*Films:*
Scorchers (1992) . . . . . . . . . . . . . . . . . . . . . . . . Renee
The Legend of Wolf Mountain (1993) . . . . . . . . . Helen
*Made for Cable TV:*
Dream On: Home Sweet Homeboy (1993; HBO)
. . . . . . . . . . . . . . . . . . . . . . . . . . . . . . . . . . . . Carol
*Video Tapes:*
**Inside Out 2** (1992) . . . . . . . . . . . . . . . . . The Doctor
(Unrated version reviewed.)
• 0:52—Breasts in bed on top of Drake. B&W.

# Tranelli, Deborah

*Films:*
**Naked Vengeance** (1985) . . . . . . . . . . . . .Carla Harris
0:18—In black bra and panties in bedroom while a
guy peek in from the window.
• 0:25—In black bra, then breasts during gang rape.
••• 0:43—Nude, while walking into the water to seduce
a guy before killing him.
*Made for TV Movies:*
Mistress (1987) . . . . . . . . . . . . . . . . . . . . . . . . . .Clerk
*TV:*
Dallas (1989-90) . . . . . . . . . . . . . . . . . . . . . . . . Phyllis

# • Trapp, Robin

*Films:*
Look Who's Talking Too (1990) . . . . . . . . . . Cool Chick
**South Beach** (1992) . . . . . . . . . . . . . . . . . . . . . Casey
••• 0:59—Buns, while making love with Fred William-
son. Nice close-up of breasts.

# • Travis, Kylie

*Films:*
**Eyes of the Beholder** (1992) . . . . . . . .Holly Brandon
•• 1:08—Left breast, then breasts after taking her dress
top down in front of Janice.
*TV:*
Models Inc. (1994- ) . . . . . . . . . . . . . . . . . . Julie Dante

# Travis, Nancy

*Films:*
Three Men and a Baby (1987) . . . . . . . . . . . . . . . Sylvia
**Married to the Mob** (1988) . . . . . . . . . .Karen Lutnig
• 0:15—Buns and brief side view of right breast, with
Tony in hotel room. Brief breasts in the bathtub.
Air America (1990) . . . . . . . . . . . . . .Corinne Landreaux
**Internal Affairs** (1990) . . . . . . . . . . .Kathleen Avila
• 0:38—Side view of left breast when Raymond opens
the shower door to talk to her.
Loose Cannons (1990) . . . . . . . . . . . . . . . . . . . . . Riva
Three Men and a Little Lady (1990) . . . . . . . . . . Sylvia
Chaplin (1992; British/U.S.) . . . . . . . . . . . . .Joan Barry
Passed Away (1992) . . . . . . . . . . . . . .Cassie Slocombe
Greedy (1993) . . . . . . . . . . . . . . . . . . . . . . . . . . Robin
So, I Married an Axe Murderer (1993)
. . . . . . . . . . . . . . . . . . . . . . . . . . . . Harriet Michaels
The Vanishing (1993) . . . . . . . . . . . . . . . . . . Rita Baker

*Made for Cable TV:*
Fallen Angels: The Frightening Frammis (1993)
. . . . . . . . . . . . . . . . . . . . . . . . . . . . . . .Bette Allison
(Available on video tape on *Fallen Angels One.*)

# Travis, Stacey

*Films:*
Deadly Dreams (1988) . . . . . . . . . . . . . . . . . . Librarian
Phantasm II (1988) . . . . . . . . . . . . . . . . . . . . . . . . .Jeri
Dr. Hackenstein (1989) . . . . . . . . . . . . . . Melanie Victor
**Hardware** (1990) . . . . . . . . . . . . . . . . . . . . . . . . . .Jill
• 0:21—Almost breasts in shower. Brief left breast in
bed with Moses. Lit with blue light.
0:38—Brief breasts in bedroom seen by a guy
through telescope. Infrared-looking effect.
The Super (1991) . . . . . . . . . . . . . . . . . . . . . . . Heather
**Dracula Rising** (1992) . . . . . . . . . . . . . . . . . . Theresa
0:43—Very brief glimpses of body parts while swim-
ming under water. Hard to see.
•• 0:44—Breasts, while on rocks in front of waterfall
with Christopher Atkins. Long shot, then closer shot.
Nude under water, sometimes with another woman, sometimes with Atkins.
Caroline at Midnight (1993) . . . . . . . . Christine Jenkins
Only the Strong (1993) . . . . . . . . . . . . . . . . . . .Dianna
*Made for Cable Movies:*
Attack of the 5' 2" Women (1994; Showtime) . . .Christy

# Traylor, Susan

*Films:*
Bright Lights, Big City (1988) . . . . . . . . . . Leather Lady
Bail Jumper (1989) . . . . . . . . . . . . . . . . . . . . .Lawyer
The Bodyguard (1992) . . . . . . . . . . . . . .Dress Designer
**A River Runs Through It** (1992) . . . . . . . . Rawhide
• 1:17—Buns, sleeping in the woods with Neal. Don't
see her face.

# Treas, Terri

*Films:*
All That Jazz (1979) . . . . . . . . . . . . . . . . . . Fan Dancer
The Best Little Whorehouse in Texas (1982)
. . . . . . . . . . . . . . . . . . . . . . . . . . . Chicken Ranch Girl
1:12—Very brief, most of right breast, while wearing
cowboy hat and garter belt, straddling a football
player when Dom DeLuise bursts in with his video
crew.
The Nest (1987) . . . . . . . . . . . . . . . Dr. Morgan Hubbard
Deathstalker III: The Warriors From Hell (1988)
. . . . . . . . . . . . . . . . . . . . . . . . . . . . . . . . .Camlearde
The Terror Within (1988) . . . . . . . . . . . . . . . . . . Linda
**The Fabulous Baker Boys** (1989) . . . . . . . Girl in Bed
• 0:00—Brief upper half of right breast when sheet
falls down when she leans over in bed.
Frankenstein Unbound (1990) . . . . . . . .Computer Voice
House IV (1991) . . . . . . . . . . . . . . . . . . . . . . .Kelly Cobb
0:45—Very, very brief side view of right breast
(wearing pastie) getting into the shower.
1:08—In bra, in her bedroom after waking up in the
morning.

Rage and Honor (1992) . . . . . . . . . . . . . . Rita Carlson
*TV:*
Seven Brides for Seven Brothers (1982-83)
. . . . . . . . . . . . . . . . . . . . . . . . . . . . Hannah McFadden
Alien Nation (1989-91) . . . . . . . . . . . . . . Cathy Frankel

## Trentini, Peggy

*Films:*
**Young Doctors in Love** (1982) . . . . . . . . Christmas Elf
•• 0:55—Brief breasts greeting visitors to the party.
• 0:57—Breasts again sitting on couch.
Up the Creek (1984) . . . . . . . . . . . . . . . . . . . . . . . Co-Ed
Ghoulies IV (1993) . . . . . . . . . . . . . . . . . . . . . Monica
*Magazines:*
**Playboy** (Jan 1992) . . . . . . . . . The Swedish Bikini Team
Ulla Swensen.
••• 78-85—Breasts while stretching swimsuit top with
her hands. Breasts while standing on pool ladder.
Buns while holding surfboard (2nd from the right).
Breasts while holding her arms up. Right breast
while inside phone booth holding black phone.
Breasts standing and holding her left arm up.
Breasts, while feeding raccoon. Breasts, while lying
on sleeping bag with her left arm on her stomach.
**Playboy's Nudes** (Dec 1992) . . . . . . . . . . . . . Herself
••• 17—Breasts.

## Trickey, Paula

*Films:*
**Maniac Cop 2** (1990) . . . . . . . . . . . . . . . . . . Cheryl
•• 0:41—In orange two piece swimsuit on stage, then
breasts and buns in G-string.
Carnal Crimes (1991) . . . . . . . . . . . . . . . . . . . Jasmine
*Made for Cable TV:*
**Dream On: Futile Attraction** (1991; HBO). . . . Janice
•• 0:02—Breasts sitting in bed with Martin.
Sessions: Episode 3 (1991; HBO) . . . . . . Fantasy Woman
*TV:*
Trade Winds (1993- ) . . . . . . . . . . . . . . . . . . . . . . Lisa

## Trigger, Sarah

*Films:*
Kid (1990). . . . . . . . . . . . . . . . . . . . . . . . . . . . . Kate
0:36—Almost breasts in gaping T-shirt while wash-
ing a horse.
Bill and Ted's Bogus Journey (1991) . . . . . . . . . Joanna
Grand Canyon (1991) . . . . . . . . . . . . . . . . . . . Vanessa
**Paradise** (1991). . . . . . . . . . . . . . . . . . . . . . . Darlene
• 0:14—Brief breasts ironing her clothes in open win-
dow while Willard and Billie watch from their tree
house. Long shot after. Hard to see her face.
Pet Sematary II (1992) . . . . . . . . . . . Marjorie Hargrove
**Deadfall** (1993). . . . . . . . . . . . . . . . . . . . . . . . Diane
••• 0:42—In white bra and panties, after taking off dress
in motel room with Michael Biehn. Breasts, while
making love with him.
• 0:44—Right breast, while lying in bed with Biehn
when he changes positions and the covers move.

•• 0:45—Breasts, while wearing white panties, leaving
bed and getting dressed.
PCU (1994) . . . . . . . . . . . . . . . . . . . . . . . . . . . . . n.a.
*Made for Cable Movies:*
**Fellow Traveller** (1989; HBO) . . . . . . . . . . . . . Gloria
•• 0:02—Breasts, sitting up in bed, stretching, then
getting out.

## Trilling, Zoe

a.k.a. Geri Betzler.
*Films:*
The Borrower (1989) . . . . . . . . . . . . . . . . . . . . Astrid
**Nervous Ticks** (1991) . . . . . . . . . . . . . . . . . . . Marci
•• 0:24—Brief breasts in shower when Bill Pullman
opens the shower curtains.
Dr. Giggles (1992) . . . . . . . . . . . . . . . . . . . . . . Normi
**To Protect and Serve** (1992) . . . . . . . . . . . . Beverly
• 0:24—Breasts in bed with a guy. Lit with strobe
light.
Night of the Demons 2 (1994). . . . . . . . . . . . . Shirley
0:59—Very brief breasts before a special effect of her
breasts turning into a pair of hands that grab Rick.
More brief breasts, when hands change back into
breasts. Don't see her face.
*Made for TV Movies:*
Children of the Night (1985) . . . . . . . . . . . . . . Melody

## Tripoldi, Idy

*Films:*
**Auditions** (1978) . . . . . . . . . . . . . . . . . . Bonnie Tirol
••• 1:01—Full frontal nudity, taking off sweater.
•• 1:07—Breasts and buns during orgy scene.
**Fairytales** (1979) . . . . . . . . . . . . . . . . . . Naked Girl
••• 0:06—Nude, dancing in bedroom and getting in
and out of bed with The Prince.
**Famous T & A** (1982) . . . . . . . . . . . . . . . Bonnie Tirol
(No longer available for purchase, check your video
store for rental.)
••• 0:35—Full frontal nude scene from *Auditions*.

## Tripplehorn, Jeanne

*Films:*
**Basic Instinct** (1992). . . . . . . . . . . . . . Dr. Beth Garner
(Unrated Director's cut reviewed.)
••• 0:35—Briefly in bra, then breasts with Michael Dou-
glas in her apartment. Buns when he rips her panties
off.
••• 0:37—Breasts, sitting up, then getting up off the
floor.
The Firm (1993). . . . . . . . . . . . . . . . . . . Abby McDeere
The Night We Never Met (1993) . . . . . . . . . . . . Pastel
*Made for TV Movies:*
The Perfect Tribute (1991) . . . . . . . . . . . . . . . . . Julia

## Tristan, Dorothy

*Films:*
End of the Road (1969) . . . . . . . . . . . . . . . . . . . . n.a.
Klute (1971). . . . . . . . . . . . . . . . . . . . . . . Arlyn Page
Scarecrow (1973). . . . . . . . . . . . . . . . . . . . . . . Coley

Man on a Swing (1974) . . . . . . . . . . . . . . . . . . . . . .Janet
Swashbuckler (1976). . . . . . . . . . . . . . . . . . . . . . . .Alice
**California Dreaming** (1978) . . . . . . . . . . . . . . . . Fay
    0:05—In braless white top, jogging on the beach
    with Glynnis O'Connor.
    • 0:20—Brief breasts changing clothes while a group
    of boys peek through a hole in the wall.

## Truchon, Isabelle

*Films:*
**Backstab** (1990) . . . . . . . . . . . . . . . . . . . . . . . .Jennifer
  •• 0:08—In bra, then breasts in back seat of car with
    James Brolin. Don't see her face very well.
  • 0:16—Buns, black panties and stockings while on
    the floor with Brolin. Brief right breast.
  • 0:18—Brief buns in front of fireplace. Side view of
    right breast. Buns, while walking into the other
    room.
Jesus of Montreal (1990; French/Canadian)
  . . . . . . . . . . . . . . . . . . . . . . . . . . Richard's Girlfriend
If Looks Could Kill (1991) . . . . . . . . 1st Class Stewardess
  *a.k.a. Teen Agent*
Deadbolt (1992) . . . . . . . . . . . . . . . . . . . . . . . . . . . .n.a.

## • Trumbo, Karen

*Films:*
**Claire of the Moon** (1992) . . . . . . . Dr. Noel Benedict
  • 1:22—Very brief left breast, twice, in open jacket in
    restroom with her fantasy woman, then Claire.
  ••• 1:39—Breasts, while making love on bed with
    Claire. Long scene.
Hear No Evil (1993). . . . . . . . . . . . . . . . . Nadine Brock

## Tsopei, Corinna

*Films:*
Valley of the Dolls (1967) . . . . . . . . . . . . Telephone Girl
The Sweet Ride (1968) . . . . . . . . . . . . . . . . . Tennis Girl
  (Not available on video tape.)
**A Man Called Horse** (1970). . . . . . . . . . Running Deer
  • 1:03—Long shot of buns, before entering sweat
    house. Side view of left breast kneeling inside the
    sweat house.
    1:04—Partial left breast (shadows get in the way).
  • 1:15—Very brief breasts when startled by Richard
    Harris' screaming.
  • 1:22—Left nipple while in tepee with Harris.
  • 1:23—Side of left breast and right breast in tepee
    with Harris.

## • Tunney, Robin

*Films:*
Encino Man (1992) . . . . . . . . . . . . . . . . . . . . . . . . Ella
*Made for Cable TV:*
**Dream On: Silent Night, Holy Cow** (1993; HBO)
  . . . . . . . . . . . . . . . . . . . . . . . . . . . . . . . . Marybeth
  • 0:35—Very, very brief right breast, while lying down
    on the floor next to Jeremy.
*Made for TV Movies:*
JFK: Reckless Youth (1993). . . . . . . . . .Kathleen Kennedy

## Turner, Janine

*Films:*
Young Doctors in Love (1982) . . . . . . . . . . . . . Cameo
Tai-Pan (1986) . . . . . . . . . . . . . . . . . . . . . . . . Shevaun
**Monkey Shines: An Experiment in Fear** (1988)
  . . . . . . . . . . . . . . . . . . . . . . . . . . . . .Linda Aikman
    0:01—Side view of buns, lying in bed when Jason
    Beghe wakes up. Don't really see anything.
Steel Magnolias (1989) . . . . . . . Nancy Beth Marmillion
The Ambulance (1990) . . . . . . . . . . . . . . . . . . . .Cheryl
Cliffhanger (1993) . . . . . . . . . . . . . . . . .Jessie Deighan
*TV:*
Behind the Screen (1981). . . . . . . . . .Janie-Claire Willow
General Hospital (1982-83) . . . . . . . . . Laura Templeton
Northern Exposure (1990- ) . . . . . . . . Maggie O'Connell

## Turner, Kathleen

*Films:*
**Body Heat** (1981) . . . . . . . . . . . . . . . . . Maddy Walker
  • 0:22—Brief side view of left breast in bed with Will-
    iam Hurt.
  •• 0:24—Breasts in a shack with Hurt.
    0:32—Buns, getting dressed. Long shot, hard to see.
  • 0:54—Brief left breast in bathtub. Long shot, hard to
    see.
**The Man with Two Brains** (1983) . . Dolores Benedict
  • 0:08—Right breast when Steve Martin is operating
    on her in the operating room.
    0:22—In sheer lingerie in bedroom with Steve Mar-
    tin, teasing him and driving him crazy.
  • 0:36—Buns, in hotel room with a guy about to
    squeeze her buns when Steve Martin walks in.
**Crimes of Passion** (1984) . . .Joanna Crane/China Blue
  (Unrated version reviewed.)
  ••• 0:45—Breasts, wearing black panties and stockings,
    in bed with Bobby. Shadows of them making love
    on the wall.
  • 1:00—Right breast in back of a limousine with a rich
    couple.
    1:22—In blue bra and panties.
  • 1:27—Right breast in bed with Bobby.
Romancing the Stone (1984) . . . . . . . . . . . Joan Wilder
The Jewel of the Nile (1985). . . . . . . . . . . . Joan Wilder
**Prizzi's Honor** (1985) . . . . . . . . . . . . . . Irene Walker
  • 0:30—Very brief left breast making love with Jack
    Nicholson on bed.
Peggy Sue Got Married (1986). . . . . . . . . . . Peggy Sue
**Julia and Julia** (1987; Italian). . . . . . . . . . . . . . .Julia
  (This movie was shot using a high-definition video sys-
  tem and then transferred to film.)
  ••• 0:32—Breasts making love in bed with her husband.
  ••• 1:08—Breasts, then right breast making love in bed
    with Sting.
The Accidental Tourist (1988). . . . . . . . . . . . . .Sarah
Switching Channels (1988) . . . . . . . . . . . . . . .Christy
**The War of the Roses** (1989). . . . . . . . Barbara Rose
    0:04—In braless, wet white blouse.
    0:06—In braless, wet white blouse walking around
    on the sidewalk with Michael Douglas.

- 0:08—Very brief left breast, while lying in bed with Douglas and she moves the sheets.
- 0:33—Very, very brief lower frontal nudity, after squeezing Douglas' waist with her legs in bed.

V. I. Warshawski (1991). . . . . . . . . . . . . . . . . . . . . . Vic
0:21—Briefly in lingerie, changing clothes in back of cab.

House of Cards (1993) . . . . . . . . . . . . . Ruth Matthews
Naked in New York (1993) . . . . . . . . . . . . . . . . . .n.a.
Serial Mom (1993) . . . . . . . . . . . . . . . . . . . . . . Mom
Undercover Blues (1993). . . . . . . . . . . . . . . . Jane Blue
*Made for Cable Movies:*

**A Breed Apart** (1984; HBO). . . . . . . . . . Stella Clayton
- •• 1:12—Breasts in bed with Rutger Hauer, then left breast.

## • *Turpin, Bahni*

*Films:*
Daughters of the Dust (1991) . . . . . . . . . .Iona Peazant
Malcolm X (1992). . . . . . . . . . . . Follower at Temple #7
*Made for Cable Movies:*
**Rebel Highway: Girls in Prison** (1994; Showtime)
. . . . . . . . . . . . . . . . . . . . . . . . . . . . . . . . . .Melba
- 0:23—Back side of left breast, while in the showers with Ione Skye.

## Tuscany

a.k.a. Heather Tuscany.
*Films:*
**Angel of Passion** (1991) . . . . . . . . . . . . . . . . . . Ellen
- ••• 0:36—Buns and breasts making love with a guy on a boat.

**The Baby Doll Murders** (1992) . . . . . . Young Woman
- ••• 0:34—Breasts in bedroom with the suspected killer, then on bed.

*Video Tapes:*
Bikini Blitz (1990) . . . . . . . . . . . . . . . . . . . . . . .Model
0:09—Very brief partial back side view of left breast, pulling up bikini top.

*Magazines:*
**Playboy** (Sep 1992). . . . . . . . . . . . . . . . . . . .Grapevine
- 163—Lower half of left breast.

## Tweed, Shannon

Sister of model/actress Tracy Tweed.
*Films:*
**Of Unknown Origin** (1983; Canadian) . .Meg Hughes
- 0:00—Brief side view of right breast taking a shower.

**Hot Dog... The Movie** (1984) . . . . . . . . Sylvia Fonda
- ••• 0:42—Breasts getting undressed, then making love in bed and in hot tub with Harkin.

**The Surrogate** (1984; Canadian) . . . . . . . . . Lee Wake
- ••• 0:03—Breasts taking a Jacuzzi bath.
- 0:42—Brief breasts changing in bedroom, then in bra getting dressed. Long shot.
- ••• 1:02—Breasts in sauna talking with Frank. Long scene.

Meatballs III (1987). . . . . . . . . . . . . . The Love Goddess
Steele Justice (1987) . . . . . . . . . . . . . . . . . . . . Angela

Cannibal Women in the Avocado Jungle of Death (1988)
. . . . . . . . . . . . . . . . . . . . . . . . . . . Dr. Margot Hunt
**Lethal Woman** (1988). . . . . . . . . . . . . . . . . . . . .Tory
- ••• 1:01—Breasts at the beach with Derek. Brief buns in white bikini bottom.

**In the Cold of the Night** (1989) . . . . . . . . . . . Lena
- 0:02—Right breast while making love with Scott.

Night Visitor (1989) . . . . . . . . . . . . . . . . . . . Lisa Grace
**Last Call** (1990) . . . . . . . . . . . . . . . . . . Cindy/Audrey
- 0:12—In black body stocking, dancing on stage. Breasts and buns in G-string underneath.
- •• 0:29—Right breast, on the floor with William Katt.
- •• 0:39—Brief buns, rotating in chair with Katt. Breasts leaning against column.
- 0:40—Breasts on stair railing.
- 1:01—Left breast, while leaning against column and kissing Katt.
- 1:02—Left breast in bed with Katt.
- ••• 1:05—Breasts making love on roof with Katt.

**The Last Hour** (1990) . . . . . . . . . . . . . . . . . . . .Susan
*a.k.a. Concrete War*
- •• 0:05—Breasts in bed, making love with Eric.
- 0:07—Brief buns and side of left breast, in the shower.

Twisted Justice (1990) . . . . . . . . . . . . . . . . . . . Hinkle
Firing Line (1991). . . . . . . . . . . . . . . . . Sandra Spencer
Liar's Edge (1991) . . . . . . . . . . . . . . . . . . Heather Burnz
**Night Eyes 2** (1991). . . . . . . . . . . . . . . Marilyn Mejenes
- ••• 0:49—Buns and breasts making love with Andrew Stevens in bed.
- ••• 1:06—Breasts, making love with Stevens (nice use of raspberries).

The Naked Truth (1992). . . . . . . . .First Class Stewardess
**Sexual Response** (1992) . . . . . . . . . . . . . . . . . . . Eve
(Unrated version reviewed.)
- ••• 0:25—Breasts in studio with Edge, while he checks her out.
- ••• 0:29—Breasts, making love with him. Long scene.
- ••• 0:31—Full frontal nudity, lying in bed, then sitting up.
- ••• 0:43—Breasts, while making love in her house with Edge.
- •• 0:51—Breasts in pool at night with Edge.
- •• 0:52—Full frontal nudity, getting up out of bed and putting robe on.
- •• 0:55—Breasts in study with Edge.
- ••• 1:07—Breasts and buns, while taking a shower. Nude, getting out and drying herself off.

**Cold Sweat** (1993). . . . . . . . . . . . . . . . . . Beth Moore
- ••• 0:14—Breasts squished against the glass shower door while making out with Sean. More breasts and buns.
0:15—In bra, while sitting on bed.
- •• 0:17—Breasts and buns while playing with fluorescent paints with Adam Baldwin in bathtub. Kind of dark.
- ••• 0:43—Breasts and very brief lower frontal nudity while on bed with Sean.

•• 0:53—Buns and back side of left breast getting into bathtub. More breasts, twice, while in bathtub.

**Indecent Behavior** (1993) . . . . . . . . Rebecca Mathis
(Unrated version reviewed.)

• 0:12—Breasts seen through water in spa. Brief buns, getting out of spa.

•• 0:56—Breasts while making love with Gary Hudson.

••• 1:24—In bra and panties, then breasts and buns, while making love in observation room with Nick.

• 1:26—Breasts, while getting out of bed.

**Night Eyes 3** (1993) . . . . . . . . . . . . . . Zoe Clairmont

•• 0:16—Breasts, while getting her clothes ripped off by Dan, then sitting up in bed.

• 0:23—Brief full frontal nudity in shower behind the door.

••• 0:51—Breasts and buns, while making love in bed with Andrew Stevens.

• 0:53—Buns, while lying in bed afterwards.

••• 0:56—Nude, while getting into the shower and in the shower.

••• 1:01—Full frontal nudity, while taking off her robe in front of fireplace.

•• 1:02—Partial buns and breasts, while on top of Stevens.

• 1:15—Brief breasts in B&W photo from security video tape.

**Possessed by the Night** (1993) . . . . . . . . Carol McKay

0:40—Working out in wet, braless, white tank top.

•• 0:42—Breasts, while wiping off her sweat with the tank top.

••• 0:45—In bra on bed with Ted Prior, then breasts and brief lower frontal nudity, while making love with him.

**Scorned** (1993) . . . Patricia Langley/Amanda Chessfield

0:45—In bedroom in bra and panties when Robey peeks in through window.

•• 0:50—Breasts, after taking off bra with Robey, then in bed.

•• 0:59—Left breast and buns, while making love on top of Robey in bed.

•• 1:19—In bra, then breasts, while making love on bed with Robey.

**Hard Vice** (1994) . . . . . . . . . . . . . . . . . . . . . Andrea

•• 0:44—Breasts after taking off her top in front of Sam Jones.

**Model By Day** (1994) . . . . . . . . . . . . . . . . . . Shannon
(Shown on network TV without the nudity.)

• 0:42—Breasts, while letting the club owner feel her up before she beats him up.

*Made for Cable TV:*

**Hitchhiker: Videodate** . . . . . . . . . . . . . . . . . . . . n.a.
(Available on *The Hitchhiker, Volume 4.*)
The Hitchhiker: Doctor's Orders (1987; HBO)
. . . . . . . . . . . . . . . . . . . . . . . . . . . . . Dr. Rita de Roy

0:15—In black bra, panties, garter belt and stockings.

*TV:*

Falcon Crest (1982-83) . . . . . . . . . . . . . . . Diana Hunter
Fly By Night (1991) . . . . . . . . . . . . Sally "Slick" Monroe

*Video Tapes:*

**Playboy Video Magazine, Volume 1** (1982)
. . . . . . . . . . . . . . . . . . . . . . . . . Playmate of the Year

•• 0:02—Full frontal nudity, posing by bathtub for photo session.

••• 1:13—Nude, posing in bed.

••• 1:15—Full frontal nudity in photo session.

• 1:21—Full frontal nudity in front of piano, in bathtub and in bed.

**Playboy's Playmate Review** (1982) . . . . . . . Playmate

••• 0:47—Nude in bed, then in photo shoot by a table, then by a piano, then in bathtub.

**Playboy Video Magazine, Volume 5** (1983)
. . . . . . . . . . . . . . . . . . . . . . . . . . . . . . . . Playmate

• 0:05—Brief breasts in bathtub.

••• 0:13—Full frontal nudity in bedroom set.

**Playboy's Playmates of the Year: The '80s** (1989)
. . . . . . . . . . . . . . . . . . . . . Playmate of the Year 1982

••• 0:36—Full frontal nudity in photo session in a house.

••• 0:37—Nude in still photos. Nude posing by piano, in bathtub, in bed.

• 0:51—Full frontal nudity standing by bed.

**Playboy Video Centerfold: Reneé Tenison** (1990)
. . . . . . . . . . Portrait of a Photographer: Richard Fegley

••• 0:36—Full frontal nudity, posing by bed for centerfold photo.

*Magazines:*

**Playboy** (Nov 1981) . . . . . . . . . . . . . . . . . . . Playmate
**Playboy** (Nov 1983) . . . . . . . . . . Sex in Cinema 1983

•• 146—Breasts.

**Playboy's 1987 Book of Lingerie** (Mar 1987)
. . . . . . . . . . . . . . . . . . . . . . . . . . . . . . . . . Herself

••• 19—Breasts while sitting on bed.

••• 20-23—Full frontal nudity.

• 48—Lower frontal nudity.

• 93—Breasts.

**Playboy** (Jan 1989) . . . . . . . . . . Women of the Eighties

• 249—Full frontal nudity, lying in bed. B&W photo.

**Playboy's Nudes** (Oct 1990) . . . . . . . . . . . . . Herself

••• 108—Breasts.

**Playboy** (May 1991) . . . . . . . . . . . . . . . . Boss Tweeds

••• 144-153—Nude, with her sister, Tracy Tweed.

**Playboy** (Dec 1991) . . . . . . . . . . . . . . . Sex Stars 1991

••• 184—Breasts.

**Playboy's Sisters** (Feb 1992) . . . . . . . . . . . . . Herself

••• 4-11—Full frontal nudity.

**Playboy's Career Girls** (Aug 1992)
. . . . . . . . . . . . . . . . . . . . . . . . . Baywatch Playmates

••• 11—Breasts.

**Playboy's Calendar Playmates** (Nov 1992) . . . Herself

••• 17—Full frontal nudity.

••• 23—Full frontal nudity.

••• 31—Full frontal nudity.

**Playboy's Blondes, Brunettes & Redheads**
(Sep 1993) . . . . . . . . . . . . . . . . . . . . . . . . . . Herself

•• 31—Right breast.

**Playboy** (Jan 1994) . . . . . . . . . . . 40 Memorable Years

• 93—Side of right breast in B&W.

# Tweed, Tracy

Sister of *Playboy* Playmate/actress Shannon Tweed.
*Films:*
**Sunset Heat** (1991) . . . . . . . . . . . . . . . . . . . . . . Lena
(Unrated version reviewed.)
• • • 0:19—Breasts making love with Michael Paré. Nice,
long scene.
• • • 0:22—Breasts and buns, making love with Paré on
stairs, sofa and the floor.
• • • 0:24—Breasts, lying on the floor when the bad guys
come in. Brief partial right breast, standing up and
covering herself with a jacket.
Live Wire (1992) . . . . . . . . . . . . . . . . . . Rolls Royce Girl
(Unrated version on video tape reviewed, not the R-rated version shown on HBO. )
**Night Rhythms** (1992) . . . . . . . . . . . . . . . . . . . .Honey
(Unrated version reviewed.)
• • • 0:28—Breasts making love with Martin Hewitt in radio station. Nice, long scene.
• • • 0:31—Nude, getting up after changing positions.
• • 0:33—Breasts, lying dead on the floor.
**Night Eyes 3** (1993) . . . . . . . . . . . . . . . . . . Dana Gray
• • 0:25—Left breast, then breasts while in bed with
Edgar.
• • • 0:40—Breasts and side view of buns, while wearing
black G-string panties in dressing room while nonchalantly talking to Andrew Stevens.
*Magazines:*
**Playboy** (May 1991) . . . . . . . . . . . . . . . . . Boss Tweeds
• • • 144-153—Nude, with her sister, Shannon Tweed.
**Playboy** (Jul 1991) . . . . . . . . . . . . . . . The Height Report
• • 132-133—Buns, in chair.
**Playboy's Sisters** (Feb 1992) . . . . . . . . . . . . . Herself
• • • 4-11—Full frontal nudity.
**Playboy's Blondes, Brunettes & Redheads**
(Sep 1993) . . . . . . . . . . . . . . . . . . . . . . . . . . . Herself
• • 94-95—Buns.

# Twiggy

Famous '60s model.
Real name is Lesley Hornby.
Wife of British actor Leigh Lawson.
*Films:*
The Boy Friend (1971; British) . . . . . . . . . .Polly Browne
The Doctor and the Devils (1985) . . . . . . . . Jenny Bailey
Madame Sousatzka (1988) . . . . . . . . . . . . . . . . Jenny
Istanbul (1990) . . . . . . . . . . . . . . . . . . . . . . . . . . Maud
*Made for Cable TV:*
Tales From the Crypt: The New Arrival (1992; HBO)
. . . . . . . . . . . . . . . . . . . . . . . . . . . . . . . . . . . . Bonnie
**John Carpenter's Body Bags** (1993; Showtime)
. . . . . . . . . . . . . . . . . . . . . . . . . . . . . . . . . .Eye/Cathy
• 1:20—It looks like you get two very brief peeks at her
crotch between Mark Hamill's legs while he is on top
of her in bed. When she pushes him off her, she
quickly pulls her nightgown down.
*TV:*
Princesses (1991) . . . . . . . . . . . . . . . . . . . . . . . Georgy

# Twomey, Anne

*Films:*
Refuge (1981) . . . . . . . . . . . . . . . . . . . . . . . . . . . n.a.
The Imagemaker (1985). . . . . . . . . . . . Molly Grainger
0:11—Very, very brief breasts reading newspaper in
bedroom (wearing flesh colored tape over her nip-
ples). Then in white bra and panties talking to a guy
in bed.
1:04—In bra and skirt undressing in front of Michael
Nouri.
Deadly Friend (1986) . . . . . . . . . . . . . .Jeannie Conway
Last Rites (1988) . . . . . . . . . . . . . . . . . . . . . Zena Pace
Orpheus Descending (1990) . . . . . . . . . .Carol Cutrere
*Made for TV Movies:*
Bump in the Night (1991) . . . . . . . . . . . . . . . . . Sarah
The Secret (1992) . . . . . . . . . . . . . . . . . . . . Dr. Meyers

# Tylo, Hunter

a.k.a. Deborah Morehart.
Spokesmodel for Pantene shampoo.
Wife of actor Michael Tylo.
*Films:*
**The Initiation** (1984) . . . . . . . . . . . . . . . . . . . . Alison
• • • 0:33—Frontal nudity in shower, then getting out
and drying herself off.
• • • 0:57—Breasts, changing tops in sporting goods
store in mall.
Final Cut (1986). . . . . . . . . . . . . . . . . . . . . . . . .Annie
*TV:*
The Bold and the Beautiful . . . . . . . . . . . Taylor Hayes

# Tylyn

See: John, Tylyn.

# Tyrrell, Susan

Likes to show only one breast in nude scenes!
*Films:*
**The Steagle** (1971) . . . . . . . . . . . . . . . . . . . . . Louise
• 0:48—Brief left breast twice, lying on bed with Rich-
ard Benjamin.
Fat City (1972). . . . . . . . . . . . . . . . . . . . . . . . . . . Oma
**The Killer Inside Me** (1975) . . . . . . . . .Joyce Lakeland
• • 1:27—Very brief left breast, then very brief breasts
(both breasts!) in bed with Stacy Keach during flash-
back scene.
Andy Warhol's Bad (1977; Italian) . . . . . . . . Mary Aiken
I Never Promised You a Rose Garden (1977) . . . . . . Lee
Islands in the Stream (1977). . . . . . . . . . . . . . . . . Lil
Loose Shoes (1977) . . . . . . . . . . . . . . . . . . . . . Boobies
**Forbidden Zone** (1980). . . . . . . . . . . . . . Queen Doris
• • 0:19—Left breast sticking out of dress, sitting on big
dice with Herve Villechaize.
• • 1:02—Left breast sticking out of dress after fighting
with the Ex-Queen.
Fast Walking (1981) . . . . . . . . . . . . . . . . . . . . . . . Evie
**Night Warning** (1982) . . . . . . . . . . . . . .Cheryl Roberts
• 0:17—Left breast, sticking out of dress just before
she stabs the TV repairman.
Angel (1983) . . . . . . . . . . . . . . . . . . . . . . Solly Mosler

**Tales of Ordinary Madness** (1983; Italian) . . . . . Vera
- 0:19—Right nipple, seen in between strings in bra when she's lying on the floor.
- 0:20—Upper half of breasts, in between strings in bra. Lower frontal nudity.
- • 0:22—Lower frontal nudity and upper half of breasts in bra, while standing by the door. Brief buns, while getting carried to bed by Ben Gazzara.
- • 0:23—Upper half of breasts, buns and lower frontal nudity while lying in bed.

Avenging Angel (1985) . . . . . . . . . . . . . . . Solly Mosler
**Flesh + Blood** (1985) . . . . . . . . . . . . . . . . . . . . .Celine
- 1:35—Right breast sticking out of her dress when everybody throws their clothes into the fire.

The Offspring (1986) . . . . . . . . . . . . . . . Beth Chandler
The Underachievers (1987) . . . . . . . . . . . . . Mrs. Grant
Big Top Pee Wee (1988) . . . . . . . . . . . Midge Montana
**Far From Home** (1989) . . . . . . . . . . . . . .Agnes Reed
- 0:29—Very, very brief right breast in bathtub getting electrocuted.

Cry Baby (1990) . . . . . . . . . . . . . . . . . . . . . . Ramona
Rockula (1990) . . . . . . . . . . . . . . . .Chuck the Bartender
Motorama (1991) . . . . . . . . . . . . . . . . . . . . . Bartender

*Made for Cable TV:*
The Hitchhiker: In the Name of Love (1987; HBO)
. . . . . . . . . . . . . . . . . . . . . . . . . . . . . . . . . . . . .Doris

*Made for TV Movies:*
Sidney Sheldon's Windmill of the Gods (1988) . . .Neusa

*TV:*
Open All Night (1981-82) . . . . . . . . . Gretchen Feester

# Tyson, Cathy

*Films:*
Mona Lisa (1987) . . . . . . . . . . . . . . . . . . . . . . Simone
Business as Usual (1988; British) . . . . . . . Josie Patterson
**The Serpent and the Rainbow** (1988)
. . . . . . . . . . . . . . . . . . . . . .Dr. Marielle Duchamp
- 0:41—Brief breasts making love with Dennis. Probably a body double, don't see her face.

# Udenio, Fabiana

*Films:*
Boarding School (1976; German) . . . . . . . . . . . . . Gina
*a.k.a. Virgin Campus*
*a.k.a. The Passion Flower Hotel*
Hardbodies 2 (1986) . . . . . . . . . . . . . . . . Cleo/Princess
Summer School (1987) . . . . . . . . . . . . . . . .Anna-Maria
Bride of Re-Animator (1989) . . . . . . . Francesca Danelli
0:45—Most of her left breast in bed with Dan. His hand covers it most of the time.
Robocop 2 (1990) . . . . . . . . . . . . . . . Sunblock Woman
**Diplomatic Immunity** (1991) . . . . . . . . . . . . . Teresa
- • 1:06—Breasts in panties, on the floor with her hands tied behind her back when Klaus rips her blouse open to photograph her.

*Made for TV Movies:*
The Scarlet and the Black (1983) . . . . . .Guilia Lombardo
Journey to the Center of the Earth (1993)
. . . . . . . . . . . . . . . . . . . . . . . . . . . . . Sandy Miller

*TV:*
One Life to Live (1985-86) . . . . . . . . . . . . . . . .Gulietta

# Udy, Claudia
*Films:*
**American Nightmare** (1981; Canadian) . . . . .Andrea
- ••• 0:08—Buns, then breasts dancing on stage.
- • 0:22—Buns getting into bathtub. Breasts during struggle with killer.

**Joy** (1983; French/Canadian) . . . . . . . . . . . . . . . . .Joy
- •• 0:11—Nude, undressing, getting into bath then into and out of bed.
- ••• 0:14—Nude in bed with Marc.
- ••• 0:31—In swimsuits, posing for photos, then full frontal nudity.
- •• 0:54—Breasts sitting with Bruce at encounter group.
- • 1:04—Buns and breasts getting into bathtub.

Skullduggery (1983; Canadian) . . . . . . . . . . . . . . Dolly
**Out of Control** (1984) . . . . . . . . . . . . . . . . . . . . .Tina
0:19—In leopard skin pattern bra and panties.
- 0:28—In leopard bra and panties playing Strip Spin the Bottle, then very brief breasts taking off her top. Long shot.
- 0:47—Brief left breast getting raped by bad guy on the boat.
- 0:54—Brief left breast, then right breast making love with Cowboy.

Savage Dawn (1984) . . . . . . . . . . . . . . . . . .Katie Rand
**Nightforce** (1986) . . . . . . . . . . . . . . . Christy Hanson
- •• 0:07—Breasts making love in the stable with Steve during her engagement party.
- ••• 0:10—Nude, fantasizing in the shower.

The Pink Chiquitas (1986; Canadian) . . . . . . . . . .Helen
**Master of Dragonard Hill** (1987) . . . . . . . . .Arabella
- ••• 0:11—Nude, undressing to seduce Calabar. More breasts and buns while kissing him.
- •• 0:14—Silhouette of breasts while making love with Calabar, then breasts.
- • 0:58—Brief buns and side of right breast during flash back. Brief right breast when she gets out of bed.

Captive Rage (1988) . . . . . . . . . . . . . . . . . . . . . Chiga
**Dragonard** (1988) . . . . . . . . . . . . . . . . . . . . .Arabella
- •• 1:11—Breasts dressed as Cleopatra dancing a routine in front of a bunch of guys.

Edge of Sanity (1988) . . . . . . . . . . . . . . . . . . . . . Liza
Any Man's Death (1989) . . . . . . . . . . . . . . . . . . .Laura
Thieves of Fortune (1989) . . . . . . . . . . . . . . . Marissa

# Udy, Helene
*Films:*
Pick-Up Summer (1979; Canadian) . . . . . . . . . . . Suzy
0:34—Very, very brief breasts when the boys spray her and she jumps up.
Incubus (1981; Canadian) . . . . . . . . . . . . . Sally Harper
My Bloody Valentine (1981; Canadian) . . . . . . . .Sylvia
**One Night Only** (1984; Canadian) . . . . . . . . .Suzanne
- 0:50—Buns and right breast in bed talking with a guy.

- 1:12—Over the shoulder, brief left breast on top of a guy in bed.

Nightflyers (1987) . . . . . . . . . . . . . . . . . . . . . . . . .Lilly

**Pin** (1988) . . . . . . . . . . . . . . . . . . . . . Marcia Bateman

••• 1:03—Breasts in bedroom with Leon.

**Sweet Murder** (1990) . . . . . . . . . . . . . . . . .Lisa Smith

•• 0:44—Brief buns, twice, while standing in doorway in Dell's apartment.

•• 0:47—Breasts in bed while talking to Dell, then nude, getting out of bed while he's asleep.

- 0:48—Brief nude while stabbing Dell with a knife.

- 0:49—Buns and right breast while dragging Dell out of the bedroom.

*Made for TV Movies:*

Children of the Night (1985) . . . . . . . . . . . . . . . . Dallas

Toughlove (1985) . . . . . . . . . . . . . . . . . . . . . . . . .Randa

The Hollywood Detective (1989) . . . . . . Lois Wednesday

*TV:*

As the World Turns (1983) . . . . . . . . . . .Frannie Hughes

Dr. Quinn, Medicine Woman (1993- ) . . . . . . . . . .Myra

## • *Ullmann, Liv*

*Films:*

Hour of the Wolf (1968; Swedish) . . . . . . . . Alma Borg

Shame (1968) . . . . . . . . . . . . . . . . . . . . . . . . . . . . .n.a.

Cries and Whispers (1972; Swedish) . . . . . . . . . . Maria

*a.k.a. Viskingar Och Rop*

**Richard's Things** (1980; British) . . . . . . . . . . . . . Kate

- 0:12—Very, very brief left breast, while wrapping a towel around herself.

Dangerous Moves (1985; Swiss) . . . . . . . . . . . . Marina

Gaby, A True Story (1987) . . . . . . . . . . . . .Sari Brimmer

Mosca Addio (1987; Italian) . . . . . . . . . . . . . Ida Nudel

Mindwalk (1991) . . . . . . . . . . . . . . . . . . Sonia Hoffman

## • *Ulrich, Kim*

See: Johnston-Ulrich, Kim.

## *Unger, Deborah*

*Films:*

Prisoners of the Sun (1990; Australian) . . . . . Sister Littell

Till There Was You (1990; Australian) . . . . . . . . . . .Anna

**Whispers in the Dark** (1992) . . . . . . . . Eve Abergray

- 0:14—Breasts during dream visualizations. Don't see her face.

0:22—In black bra and panties, undressing in office in front of Annabella Sciorra.

- 0:24—Brief breasts during visualization by Sciorra. Don't see her face.

- 0:37—Brief breasts during Sciorra's dream.

- 0:38—Buns and side view of left breast, dead, while hanging by her neck.

*Made for Cable Movies:*

Hotel Room (1993; HBO) . . . . . . . Getting Rid of Robert

State of Emergency (1993; HBO) . . . . . . . . . Sue Payton

## *Vaccaro, Brenda*

*Films:*

**Midnight Cowboy** (1969) . . . . . . . . . . . . . . . . Shirley

- 1:30—Very, very brief out of focus left breast in open fur coat, lying down with Jon Voight.

- 1:31—Very brief left breast when falling back onto bed with Voight.

•• 1:32—Brief right breast, while rolling in bed with Voight.

I Love My Wife (1970) . . . . . . . . . . . . . . . Jody Burrows

Once is Not Enough (1975) . . . . . . . . . . . . . . . . .Linda

Airport '77 (1977) . . . . . . . . . . . . . . . . . . Eve Clayton

**House by the Lake** (1977; Canadian) . . . . . . . . .Diane

Breasts.

The First Deadly Sin (1980) . . . . . . . . . . Monica Gilbert

Chanel Solitaire (1981) . . . . . . . . . . . . . . . . . . . . . n.a.

Zorro, The Gay Blade (1981) . . . . . . . . . . . . . .Florinda

Supergirl (1984; British) . . . . . . . . . . . . . . . . . . Bianca

Water (1986; British) . . . . . . . . . . . . . . . . . . . . Bianca

Heart of Midnight (1988) . . . . . . . . . . . . . . . . . . Betty

Edgar Allan Poe's "The Masque of the Red Death" (1989) . . . . . . . . . . . . . . . . . . . . . . . . . . . . . . .Elaina

Ten Little Indians (1989) . . . . . . . . . . . Marion Marshall

*Made for Cable Movies:*

Red Shoe Diaries (1992; Showtime) . . . . . . . . . Martha

(Unrated video tape version reviewed.)

*Made for TV Movies:*

Paper Dolls (1982) . . . . . . . . . . . . . . . . . . . Julia Blake

*TV:*

Sara (1976) . . . . . . . . . . . . . . . . . . . . . Sara Yarnell

Dear Detective (1979)

. . . . . . . . . . . . . . . Detective Sergeant Kate Hudson

Paper Dolls (1984) . . . . . . . . . . . . . . . . . . . . Julia Blake

## *Vaccaro, Tracy*

*Films:*

The Man Who Loved Women (1983) . . . . . . . . . . .Legs

**Candy The Stripper** (1993) . . . . . . . . . . . . . . Candy

- 0:01—Very brief left breast, opening her blouse to flash a guy on the street.

••• 0:26—Breasts and buns in G-string, doing strip tease routine on stage.

••• 0:28—Breasts, while hiding behind bar with David after fight breaks out.

•• 0:38—Breasts in open blouse, showing her breasts to David.

••• 0:46—Breasts, while wearing panties, while in bedroom with Larry.

- 0:50—Wearing pasties, buns in G-string while posing for photographer.

- 0:56—Left breast in open robe in bedroom with Larry.

- 0:57—Breasts, while in bedroom, kissing Larry.

- 1:01—Breasts and buns in flashback on the bar.

••• 1:11—Breasts, while making out with David.

••• 1:13—Breasts, while making out with David on the floor.

•• 1:15—More breasts, while on the floor with David.

••• 1:28—Breasts and buns in G-string doing strip tease routine out of dress and lingerie.

*Magazines:*

**Playboy** (Oct 1983) . . . . . . . . . . . . . . . . . . . Playmate

**Playboy's Girls of Summer '86** (Aug 1986) . . Herself

•• 67—Left breast and lower frontal nudity.

**Playboy's 1987 Book of Lingerie** (Mar 1987)

. . . . . . . . . . . . . . . . . . . . . . . . . . . . . . . Herself

• 59—Lower frontal nudity.

••• 77—Breasts.

# • Vail, Lorin Jean

*Films:*

The Patriot (1986) . . . . . . . . . . . . . . . . . Howard's Girl

**Rest in Pieces** (1987) . . . . . . . . . . . . . . Helen Hewitt

•• 0:15—Breasts in the bubble bath.

• 0:17—Breasts hanging onto outside of tub after struggle.

• 0:25—Brief breasts making love in bed with Bob during concert. Dark.

• 0:26—Brief breasts lying under Bob in bed. Dark.

• 0:30—Brief left breast, getting out of bed and putting on robe.

• 0:58—Brief right breast, reaching around to put her right arm into sleeve of robe. Dark.

•• 1:00—Breasts, getting robe taking off and pushed into swimming pool. More breasts under the water.

• 1:01—More breasts in the swimming pool.

• 1:05—Brief side view of left breast getting out of bed and putting on robe.

# • Valandrey, Charlotte

*Films:*

**Red Kiss** (1985; French) . . . . . . . . . . . . . . . . . Nadia

• 0:52—Very brief right breast, in bed with the photographer. Very dark.

•• 1:21—Very brief right breast, then breasts with the photographer.

Orlando (1993; British) . . . . . . . . . . . . . . . . . . . Sasha

# Valen, Nancy

*Films:*

The Heavenly Kid (1985) . . . . . . . . . . . . . . . . Melissa

Porky's Revenge (1985; Canadian) . . . . . . . . . . Ginger

The Big Picture (1989) . . . . . . . . . . . . . . Young Sharon

**Listen to Me** (1989) . . . . . . . . . . . . . . . . . . . . . Mia

• 0:06—Very, very brief left breast in bed with Garson when Kirk Cameron first meets him.

Loverboy (1989) . . . . . . . . . . . . . . . . . . . Jenny Gordon

Final Embrace (1991) . . . . . . . Candy Vale/Laurel Parrish

*Made for TV Movies:*

Perry Mason: The Case of the Fatal Framing (1992)

. . . . . . . . . . . . . . . . . . . . . . . . . . . . . Mala Sikorski

*TV:*

Hull High (1990) . . . . . . . . . . . . . . . . . Donna Breedlove

# Valez, Karen

Ex-wife of actor Lee Majors.

*Video Tapes:*

**Playboy Video Magazine, Volume 7** (1985)

. . . . . . . . . . . . . . . . . . . . . . . . . . . . . . . Playmate

••• 1:01—Breasts and buns on lounge chair, rubbing oil on herself.

••• 1:04—Nude, undressing outside in gazebo and on porch.

••• 1:09—Full frontal nudity undressing in living room.

**Playboy's Playmates of the Year: The '80s** (1989)

. . . . . . . . . . . . . . . . . . . . . . Playmate of the Year 1985

••• 0:39—Breasts and buns, in lounge chair, rubbing oil on herself.

••• 0:42—Nude, in a gazebo.

•• 0:52—Right breast in open dress.

**Wet and Wild** (1989) . . . . . . . . . . . . . . . . . . . Model

*Magazines:*

Playboy (Dec 1984) . . . . . . . . . . . . . . . . . . . Playmate

**Playboy's Girls of Summer '86** (Aug 1986) . . . Herself

•• 6—Side of left breast and side of buns.

••• 23-27—Nude.

• 36—Partial left breast and partial lower frontal nudity.

**Playboy's 1987 Book of Lingerie** (Mar 1987)

. . . . . . . . . . . . . . . . . . . . . . . . . . . . . . . Herself

••• 33—Full frontal nudity.

•• 34—Side of right breast and buns.

• 49—Left breast.

••• 97—Breasts.

**Playboy's Nudes** (Oct 1990) . . . . . . . . . . . . . Herself

••• 97—Full frontal nudity.

**Playboy's Calendar Playmates** (Nov 1992) . . . Herself

••• 39—Full frontal nudity.

**Playboy Presents Playmates in Paradise**

(Mar 1994) . . . . . . . . . . . . . . . . . . . . . . . . Playmate

••• 76-79—Nude.

# van Breeschooten, Karin

Identical twin sister of Miryam van Breeschooten.

*Video Tapes:*

**Playboy Video Calendar 1990** (1989) . . . . . . October

••• 0:51—Nude.

**Playboy Video Centerfold: Dutch Twins** (1989)

. . . . . . . . . . . . . . . . . . . . . . . . . . . . . . . Playmate

••• 0:00—Nude throughout.

**The Best of Video Playmate Calendars** (1992)

. . . . . . . . . . . . . . . . . . . . . . . . . . . . . . . Playmate

•• 0:27—In lingerie and nude in modeling session, then running around house with her twin sister. Quick cuts.

••• 0:28—Nude, in a house with her twin sister, posing, bathing and dressing.

*Magazines:*

**Playboy** (Sep 1989) . . . . . . . . . . . . . . . . . . . Playmate

**Playboy's Nudes** (Oct 1990) . . . . . . . . . . . . . Herself

••• 75—Full frontal nudity.

**Playboy's Sisters** (Feb 1992) . . . . . . . . . . . . Herself

••• 98-105—Nude.

**Playboy's Calendar Playmates** (Nov 1992) . . Herself
••• 85—Full frontal nudity.
**Playboy's Blondes, Brunettes & Redheads**
(Sep 1993) . . . . . . . . . . . . . . . . . . . . . . . . . . Herself
••• 38—Breasts with her twin sister.
**Playboy** (Jan 1994) . . . . . . . . . . . . 40 Memorable Years
••• 94—Full frontal nudity.
**Playmates at Play** (Jul 1994) . . . . . . . . . . . . . Herself
••• 44—Full frontal nudity.
••• 78-81—Breasts and buns.
**Playboy's Girls of Summer '94** (Jul 1994) . . . Herself
••• 70—Full frontal nudity.

## van Breeschooten, Miryam

Identical twin sister of Karin van Breeschooten.
*Video Tapes:*
**Playboy Video Calendar 1990** (1989) . . . . . October
••• 0:51—Nude.
**Playboy Video Centerfold: Dutch Twins** (1989)
. . . . . . . . . . . . . . . . . . . . . . . . . . . . . . . . Playmate
••• 0:00—Nude throughout.
**The Best of Video Playmate Calendars** (1992)
. . . . . . . . . . . . . . . . . . . . . . . . . . . . . . . . Playmate
•• 0:27—In lingerie and nude in modeling session,
then running around house with her twin sister.
Quick cuts.
••• 0:28—Nude, in a house with her twin sister, posing,
bathing and dressing.
*Magazines:*
**Playboy** (Sep 1989) . . . . . . . . . . . . . . . . . . . Playmate
**Playboy's Nudes** (Oct 1990) . . . . . . . . . . . . . . Herself
••• 75—Full frontal nudity.
**Playboy's Sisters** (Feb 1992) . . . . . . . . . . . . . Herself
••• 98-105—Nude.
**Playboy's Calendar Playmates** (Nov 1992) . . Herself
••• 85—Full frontal nudity.
**Playboy's Blondes, Brunettes & Redheads**
(Sep 1993) . . . . . . . . . . . . . . . . . . . . . . . . . . Herself
••• 38—Breasts with her twin sister.
**Playboy** (Jan 1994) . . . . . . . . . . . . 40 Memorable Years
••• 94—Full frontal nudity.
**Playmates at Play** (Jul 1994) . . . . . . . . . . . . . Herself
••• 44—Full frontal nudity.
••• 78-81—Breasts and buns.
**Playboy's Girls of Summer '94** (Jul 1994) . . . Herself
••• 70—Full frontal nudity.

## Van De Ven, Monique

*Films:*
**Turkish Delight** (1974; Dutch) . . . . . . . . . . . . . . Olga
•• 0:24—Breasts when Rutger Hauer opens her blouse,
then nude on the bed.
•• 0:27—Breasts, waking up in bed.
••• 0:33—Breasts on bed with Hauer, then nude getting
up to fix flowers.
0:42—Buns, with Hauer at the beach.
•• 0:46—Breasts modeling for Hauer, then brief nude
running around outside.
•• 0:54—Breasts in bed with open blouse with flowers.

• 1:04—In wet T-shirt in the rain with Hauer, then
brief breasts coming down the stairs.
**Keetje Tippel** (1978; Dutch) . . . . . . . . . . . . . . . Katie
*a.k.a. Katie's Passion*
(Dutch with English subtitles.)
• 0:37—Brief buns when guy rips her panties off.
•• 0:43—Breasts in hospital when a group of doctors
examine her.
• 0:48—Left breast a couple of times talking to a doctor. Brief buns sitting down.
• 1:09—Brief buns, while getting into bed.
• 1:11—Very brief left breast in bed with Rutger Hauer
when he catches her eating her chocolate.
••• 1:15—Nude burning all her old clothes and getting
into bathtub.
The Assault (1986; Dutch)
. . . . . . . . . . . . . . . . . . . . Truus Coster/Saskia de Graaff
Amsterdamned (1988; Dutch) . . . . . . . . . . . . . . . Laura
Lily Was Here (1989; Dutch) . . . . . . . . . . . . . . Midwife
Paint It Black (1989) . . . . . . . . . . . . . . . . . . . . Kyla Leif

## Van Doren, Mamie

*Films:*
Running Wild (1955) . . . . . . . . . . . . . . . . . . Irma Bean
High School Confidential (1958) . . . . . . . Gwen Dulaine
Teacher's Pet (1958) . . . . . . . . . . . . . . . . Peggy De Fore
Sex Kittens Go to College (1960) . . . . Dr. Mathilda West
Three Nuts in Search of a Bolt (1964) . . . . . Saxie Symbol
Free Ride (1986) . . . . . . . . . . . . . . . . . Debbie Stockwell
*Magazines:*
**Playboy** (Jan 1989) . . . . . . . . . . . . Women of the Sixties
• 156—Breasts under sheer yellow dress in photo
from 1964.

## Van Kamp, Merete

*Films:*
**The Osterman Weekend** (1983) . . . . Zuna Brickman
•• 0:01—Breasts and brief buns in bed on a TV moni-
tor, then breasts getting injected by two intruders.
• 0:35—Brief breasts on video again while Rutger
Hauer watches in the kitchen on TV.
• 1:30—Breasts again on video during TV show.
You Can't Hurry Love (1984) . . . . . . . . . . . . . Monique
**Lethal Woman** (1988) . . . . . . . . . . . . Diana/Christine
• 1:23—Very brief side view of left breast, reaching for
towel after bath. Hard to see.
*Miniseries:*
Princess Daisy (1983) . . . . . . . . . . . . . . . . . . . . . Daisy
*TV:*
Dallas (1985-86) . . . . . . . . . . . . . . . . . . . . . . . . Grace

## Van Patten, Joyce

*Films:*
Making It (1971) . . . . . . . . . . . . . . . . . . . . Betty Fuller
**Housewife** (1972) . . . . . . . . . . . . . . . . . . Bernadette
• 0:46—Breasts and buns on pool table getting attacked by Yaphet Kotto. Probably a body double,
don't see her face.

1:04—Most of left breast getting on top of Kotto. In side view, you can see black tape over her nipple.
- 1:05—Brief side of right breast under Kotto's arm several times after she falls on the floor with him.

The Falcon and the Snowman (1985) . . . . . . Mrs. Boyce
St. Elmo's Fire (1985) . . . . . . . . . . . . . . . Mrs. Beamish
Billy Galvin (1986) . . . . . . . . . . . . . . . . . . . . . . . . Mae
Blind Date (1987) . . . . . . . . . . . . . . . . . Nadia's Mother
Monkey Shines: An Experiment in Fear (1988)
. . . . . . . . . . . . . . . . . . . . . . . . . . . . Dorothy Mann
Trust Me (1989) . . . . . . . . . . . . . . . . . . . Nettie Brown
*Made for TV Movies:*
Breathing Lessons (1994) . . . . . . . . . . . . . . . . Serena
*TV:*
The Good Guys (1968-70) . . . . . . . . . Claudia Gramus

## Van Tilborgh, Guusje

*Films:*
**A Zed and Two Noughts** (1985; British)
. . . . . . . . . . . . . . . . . . . . . . . . . . . . Caterina Bolnes
- 0:42—Brief lower frontal nudity when Oliver lifts her skirt up in restroom to check to see what kind of panties she's wearing.
- 0:51—Lower frontal nudity, then very brief breasts while posing for photo by Van Meegeren.

Zjoek (1987; Dutch) . . . . . . . . . . . . . . . . . . . . . . Olga

## Van Vooren, Monique

*Films:*
Tarzan and the She-Devil (1953) . . . . . . . . . . . . . Lyra
Gigi (1958) . . . . . . . . . . . . . . . . . . . . . . . . . Showgirl
Ash Wednesday (1973) . . . . . . . . . . . . German Woman
Sugar Cookies (1973) . . . . . . . . . . . . . . . . . . Helene
**Andy Warhol's Frankenstein** (1974; Italian/German/French) . . . . . . . . . . . . . . . . . . . . . . . . . . Katherine
- 0:47—Breasts in bed with Nicholas. Brief lower frontal nudity twice when he rolls on top of her.
- 1:21—Left breast letting Sascha, the creature, caress her breast
- 1:26—Breasts, dead, when her breasts pop out of her blouse.

Wall Street (1987) . . . . . . . . . . . . . . . . . . . . . . . . n.a.

## Vander Woude, Teresa

*Films:*
**Killer Workout** (1987) . . . . . . . . . . . . . . . . . . . Jaimy
*a.k.a. Aerobi-Cide*
- 0:43—Breasts in locker room with Tommy during his nightmare.

Night Visitor (1989) . . . . . . . . . . . . . . . . Kelly Fremont

## Vandernoot, Alexandra

*Films:*
Mascara (1987; French/Belgian) . . . . . . . . . . . . Euridice
*Made for Cable Movies:*
Doomsday Gun (1994; HBO) . . . . . . . . . . . . . . Marie

*Made for Cable TV:*
**Strangers: Windows** (1992; HBO) . . . . . . The Woman
(Available on video tape on *Strangers*.)
- 0:10—Breasts, making love with her lover while Timothy Hutton watches from across the street.
- 0:12—Right breast, while in bed struggling with her lover.
- 0:13—Right breast, while tied to bed when Hutton comes to rescue her.
- 0:14—Brief breasts while sitting on toilet.

*TV:*
Highlander: The Series (1992-93) . . . . . . . . . . . . Tessa

## Vanity

Singer.
a.k.a. D. D. Winters.
Real name is Denise Matthews.
Sister of model Patricia Matthews.
*Films:*
**Tanya's Island** (1980; Canadian) . . . . . . . . . . . . Tanya
0:04—Very brief breasts and buns covered with paint during B&W segment.
- 0:07—Nude caressing herself and dancing during the opening credits.
- 0:09—Nude making love on the beach.
0:11—Brief right breast, while talking to Lobo.
- 0:19—Brief breasts on the beach with Lobo, then more breasts while yelling at him.
- 0:28—Mostly breasts in flimsy halter top exploring a cave.
- 0:33—Full frontal nudity undressing in tent.
- 0:35—Left breast sleeping. Dark, hard to see.
0:37—Buns while sleeping.
- 0:40—Breasts superimposed over another scene.
0:48—Brief buns swimming in the ocean.
- 0:51—Full frontal nudity walking out of the ocean and getting dressed.
- 0:53—Brief breasts in open blouse.
- 1:08—Breasts in middle of compound when Lobo rapes her in front of Blue.
- 1:16—Full frontal nudity running through the jungle in slow motion. Brief buns.

Terror Train (1980; Canadian) . . . . . . . . . . . . . . Merry
**The Best of Sex and Violence** (1981) . . . . . . . Tanya
- 0:24—Buns and breasts in various scenes from *Tanya's Island*.

**Famous T & A** (1982) . . . . . . . . . . . . . . . . . . Tanya
(No longer available for purchase, check your video store for rental.)
- 1:02—Breasts scenes from *Tanya's Island*.

The Last Dragon (1985) . . . . . . . . . . . . . . . . . . Laura
**52 Pick-Up** (1986) . . . . . . . . . . . . . . . . . . . . Doreen
- 0:47—Breasts, stripping in room while Roy Scheider takes Polaroid pictures.
- 0:52—Breasts under sheer purple nightgown. Partial buns in G-string underneath also.

**Never Too Young to Die** (1986) . . . . . . Donja Deering
0:25—In white bra in the kitchen with John Stamos while he tends to her wounded arm.

- 1:04—Wearing a bikini swimsuit, putting on suntan lotion. Brief breasts in quick cuts making love with John in a cabin bedroom.

Deadly Illusion (1987) . . . . . . . . . . . . . . . . . . . . . Rina

**Action Jackson** (1988) . . . . . . . . . . . . . . . Sydney Ash

•• 0:29—Breasts in bed with Craig T. Nelson.

Neon City (1991) . . . . . . . . . . . . . . . . . . . . . . . . . Reno

Da Vinci's War (1992) . . . . . . . . . . . . . . . . . . . . . Lupe

South Beach (1992) . . . . . . . . . . . . . . Jennifer Derringer

*Made for Cable Movies:*

Memories of Murder (1990; Lifetime) . . . . . . . Carmen

*Made for Cable TV:*

**Tales From the Crypt: Dead Wait** (1991; HBO)

. . . . . . . . . . . . . . . . . . . . . . . . . . . . . . . . . . . Catarine

- 0:15—Brief breasts and buns several times in and out of bed with James Remar.

*Made for TV Movies:*

Jackie Collins' Lady Boss (1992) . . . . . . . . . . . . . . . n.a.

*Magazines:*

**Playboy** (Jan 1985) . . . . . . . . The Girls of Rock 'n' Roll

**Playboy** (May 1985) . . . . . . . . . . . . . . . . . . . . . . . . n.a.

**Playboy** (Sep 1986) . . . . . . . . . . . . . . Playboy Gallery

129—Photo taken Jan 1981

**Playboy** (Apr 1988) . . . . . . . . . . . . . . . . . . . . . Vanity

••• 68-79—Nude.

**Playboy** (Dec 1988) . . . . . . . . . . . . . Sex Stars of 1988

••• 185—Breasts.

**Playboy** (Jan 1989) . . . . . . . . . Women of the Eighties

•• 256—Right breast.

**Playboy** (Oct 1989) . . . . . . . . . . . . . . . . . . . Grapevine

• 175—Upper half breasts in B&W photo.

**Playboy's Nudes** (Oct 1990) . . . . . . . . . . . . . Herself

••• 25—Breasts.

## Vargas, Valentina

*Films:*

**The Name of the Rose** (1986) . . . . . . . . . . . The Girl

••• 0:46—Breasts and buns making love with Christian Slater in the monastery kitchen.

The Big Blue (1988) . . . . . . . . . . . . . . . . . . . . . Bonita

Street of No Return (1991; U.S./French) . . . . . . . . . Celia

**The Tigress** (1992) . . . . . . . . . . . . . . Tigress/Pauline

•• 0:06—Nude, undressing in room and lying in bed with James Remar.

•• 0:10—Nude, sitting up in bed, then getting out and leaving the room.

•• 0:18—Nude, getting out of bed and getting dressed.

•• 0:45—Right breast, while in room when Remar pulls her dress down.

•• 0:48—Buns, while in bed with Remar.

• 0:52—Brief breasts, while changing clothes in room.

••• 0:53—Breasts when Remar opens her blouse and massages her breasts.

• 1:03—Half of left breast while primping herself in front of mirror.

## Varsi, Diane

*Films:*

Peyton Place (1957) . . . . . . . . . . . . . Allison MacKenzie

Compulsion (1959) . . . . . . . . . . . . . . . . . . . Ruth Evans

Sweet Love, Bitter (1967) . . . . . . . . . . . . . . . . . . Della

Killers Three (1968) . . . . . . . . . . . . . . . . Carol Ward

Wild in the Streets (1968) . . . . . . . . . . . . . Sally Leroy

**Bloody Mama** (1970) . . . . . . . . . . . . . . Mona Gibson

••• 0:16—Breasts, sitting up in bed with Dan Stroud. Buns, when getting out of bed. Long scene.

Johnny Got His Gun (1971) . . . . . . . . . . . . 4th Nurse

I Never Promised You a Rose Garden (1977) . . . . . Sylvia

## • Vasilopoulos, Nicole

*Films:*

Class of Nuke 'Em High Part II: Subhumanoid Meltdown (1991) . . . . . . . . . . . . . . . . Bald Subhumanoid

**Warlords 3000** (1992) . . . . . . . . . . . . . . . . Ox's Wife

•• 0:23—Breasts, in open blouse in bedroom with Ox.

## Vasquez, Roberta

*Films:*

Easy Wheels (1989) . . . . . . . . . . . . . . . . . . . Tondalco

Picasso Trigger (1989) . . . . . . . . . . . . . . . . . Pantera

Street Asylum (1989) . . . . . . . . . . . . . . . . . . Kristen

**Guns** (1990) . . . . . . . . . . . . . . . . . . . . . Nicole Justin

•• 0:50—Right breast while making love on motorcycle with her boyfriend.

The Rookie (1990) . . . . . . . . . . . . . . . . Heather Torres

**Do or Die** (1991) . . . . . . . . . . . . . . . . . . Nicole Justin

0:06—Sort of breasts under water in spa.

•• 0:56—Breasts, making love with Bruce, outside.

Final Judgement (1992) . . . . . . . . . . . . . . . . . Whitney

Out for Blood (1992) . . . . . . . . . . . . . . . Detective Price

Sins of Desire (1992) . . . . . . . . . . . . . . . . Motel Girl

(Unrated version reviewed.)

**Fit To Kill** (1993) . . . . . . . . . . . . . . . . . Nicole Justin

•• 0:21—Breasts and buns in G-string, while undressing and putting dresses on with Speir.

••• 0:52—Breasts and buns, while making love with her boyfriend in bed.

0:55—In two piece swimsuit.

1:29—In two piece swimsuit.

**Hard Hunted** (1993) . . . . . . . . . . . . . . . Nicole Justin

•• 1:20—Breasts while making out with Bruce in the ocean.

*Video Tapes:*

Playmate Playoffs . . . . . . . . . . . . . . . . . . . . . Playmate

**Playboy Video Calendar 1987** (1986) . . . . . Playmate

**Wet and Wild** (1989) . . . . . . . . . . . . . . . . . Model

**Playmates at Play** (1990) . . . . . . . . . . . Hardbodies

*Magazines:*

**Playboy** (Nov 1984) . . . . . . . . . . . . . . . . . Playmate

**Playboy's Calendar Playmates** (Nov 1992) . . . Herself

••• 45—Full frontal nudity.

••• 52—Full frontal nudity.

**Playmates at Play** (Jul 1994) . . . . . . . . . . . . Herself

••• 74-77—Nude.

## Vaughn, Linda Rhys

*Video Tapes:*
**Playboy's Playmate Review** (1982) . . . . . . Playmate
••• 1:06—Nude on horseback, then next to stream.
**Playmates at Play** (1990) . . . . . . . . . . . . . .Bareback
*Magazines:*
**Playboy** (Apr 1982) . . . . . . . . . . . . . . . . . . Playmate
**Playboy's 1987 Book of Lingerie** (Mar 1987)
. . . . . . . . . . . . . . . . . . . . . . . . . . . . . . . . . Herself
••• 38—Full frontal nudity.
**Playboy's Calendar Playmates** (Nov 1992) . . Herself
••• 14—Full frontal nudity.

## Vega, Isela

*Films:*
**Bring Me the Head of Alfredo Garcia** (1974). . Elita
• 0:25—Brief right breast a couple of times, then brief
breasts in bed with Warren Oaks.
••• 0:44—Breasts when Kris Kristofferson rips her top
off. Long scene.
•• 0:52—Breasts sitting in shower with wet hair.
•• 1:49—Still from shower scene during credits.
**Drum** (1976) . . . . . . . . . . . . . . . . . . . . . . . Marianna
• 0:04—Breasts in bed with the maid, Rachel.
•• 0:22—Brief breasts standing next to the bed with
Maxwell.
The Streets of L.A. (1979) . . . . . . . . . . . . . . . . . .n.a.
Barbarosa (1982) . . . . . . . . . . . . . . . . . . . Josephina
Blood Screams (1986; U.S./Mexican) . . . . . . . . . . .n.a.
*Magazines:*
**Playboy** (Jul 1974) . . . . . . . . . . . . . . . .Viva Vegal
••• 80-83—Full frontal nudity.
**Playboy** (Nov 1974) . . . . . . . . . . Sex in Cinema 1974
••• 147—Breasts from *Bring Me the Head of Alfredo Gar-*
*cia.*
**Playboy** (Nov 1976) . . . . . . . . . . Sex in Cinema 1976
••• 155—Breasts in a photo from *Drum.*
**Playboy** (Feb 1977) . . . . . . . . . . . . . . . . Dear Playboy
••• 16—Full frontal nudity in small photo.

## • Vela, Rosie

*Films:*
The Two Jakes (1990) . . . . . . . . . . . . . . . . . . . . .n.a.
**Inside Edge** (1991) . . . . . . . . . . . . . . . . . Lisa Zamora
••• 1:06—Breasts, while making love with Michael Madsen in bed.

## Venora, Diane

*Films:*
Wolfen (1981). . . . . . . . . . . . . . . . . . . . Rebecca Neff
The Cotton Club (1984) . . . . . . . . . . . . .Gloria Swanson
**Terminal Choice** (1985; Canadian) . . . . . . . . . .Anna
0:44—In lingerie, talking to Frank.
• 0:48—Brief left breast, making love in bed with
Frank. Don't see her face.
F/X (1986) . . . . . . . . . . . . . . . . . . . . . . . . . . . Ellen
0:37—Walking around her apartment in a white slip.
Bird (1988) . . . . . . . . . . . . . . . Chan Richardson Parker

*TV:*
Thunder Alley (1994) . . . . . . . . . . . . . . . . Bobbi Turner

## • Venturelli, Silvana

*Films:*
**Macabre**. . . . . . . . . . . . . . . . . . . . . . . . . . . . .Annie
• 1:03—Very, very brief right breast, while wrapping a
robe around herself.
• 1:05—Brief right breast while lying on bed when
Gert checks her out.
**Camille 2000** (1969) . . . . . . . . . . . . . . . . . . . .Olympe
**The Lickerish Quartet** (1970; Italian) . . . .The Woman
*a.k.a. Erotic Illusion*
• 0:01—Brief right breast under a guy in B&W porno
film.
•• 0:03—Breasts, after taking off her top in film.
•• 0:05—Breasts while sitting on bed in film.
•• 0:06—Breasts, while in bed with another woman.
• 0:30—Breasts, while on couch with a guy in film.
• 0:32—Breasts on bed with guy in film.
• 0:47—Lower half of buns under mini-skirt while in library with the father.
••• 0:49—Nude, while in library on table and the floor
with the father.
••• 1:00—Nude, while undressing outside with the son
and making love.
•• 1:10—Breasts, while tied by wrists to bed in film.
A Long Ride From Hell (1970; Italian) . . . . . . . . . Ruth

## Venus, Brenda

*Films:*
Foxy Brown (1974) . . . . . . . . . . . . . . . . . . . . .Arabella
**The Eiger Sanction** (1975) . . . . . . . . . . . . . . George
• 0:50—Very brief breasts opening her blouse to get
Clint Eastwood to climb up a hill.
• 1:06—Breasts taking off her clothes in Eastwood's
room, just before she tries to kill him. Dark, hard to
see.
Swashbuckler (1976) . . . . . . . . . . . . . . . Bath Attendant
48 Hrs. (1982) . . . . . . . . . . . . . . . . . . . . . . . . Hooker
*Magazines:*
**Playboy** (Jul 1986) . . . . . . . . . . . . . . . . Henry's Venus
•• 72-79—B&W photos. Full frontal nudity with lots of
diffusion.

## Verkaik, Petra

*Films:*
Auntie Lee's Meat Pies (1991) . . . . . . . . . . . . . . Baby
Pyrates (1991) . . . . . . . . . . . . . . . . . . . . . . . . . Basia
*Video Tapes:*
**Playboy Video Calendar 1991** (1990). . . .November
••• 0:45—Nude.
**Sexy Lingerie II** (1990) . . . . . . . . . . . . . . . . . Model
**Wet and Wild II** (1990). . . . . . . . . . . . . . . . . Model
**Sexy Lingerie III** (1991). . . . . . . . . . . . . . . . . Model
**Wet and Wild III** (1991) . . . . . . . . . . . . . . . . . Model
**The Best of Wet and Wild** (1992). . . . . . . . . . Model
**Playboy Playmates in Paradise** (1992). . . . Playmate

*Magazines:*
**Playboy** (Dec 1989) . . . . . . . . . . . . . . . . . . . Playmate
**Playboy's Book of Lingerie** (Jan 1991) . . . . . . Herself
••• 29-31—Full frontal nudity.
**Playboy's Book of Lingerie** (Mar 1991) . . . . . Herself
• 22—Left breast.
• 100—Right breast.
**Playboy's Book of Lingerie** (Jul 1991) . . . . . . Herself
• 23—Lower frontal nudity.
**Playboy's Book of Lingerie** (Mar 1992) . . . . . Herself
••• 26—Full frontal nudity.
••• 57—Full frontal nudity.
**Playboy's Book of Lingerie** (May 1992) . . . . . Herself
•• 26-27—Right breast and partial lower frontal nudity.
•• 51—Right breast.
**Playboy's Girls of Summer '92** (Jun 1992) . . . Herself
•• 34—Buns and side of right breast.
**Playboy's Book of Lingerie** (Jul 1992) . . . . . . Herself
• 84—Lower frontal nudity.
**Playboy's Calendar Playmates** (Nov 1992) . . Herself
••• 96—Full frontal nudity.
**Playboy's Book of Lingerie** (Jan 1993) . . . . . . Herself
•• 108—Side view of right breast and buns.
**Playboy** (Feb 1993) . . . . . . . . . . . Being in Nothingness
••• 127—Full frontal nudity in yellow robe.
••• 135—Full frontal nudity.
**Playboy's Bathing Beauties** (Apr 1993) . . . . . Herself
••• 4—Breasts.
**Playboy's Book of Lingerie** (May 1993) . . . . . Herself
••• 86-87—Full frontal nudity.
**Playboy's Wet & Wild Women** (Aug 1993) . . Herself
•• 42—Buns.
**Playboy's Blondes, Brunettes & Redheads**
(Sep 1993) . . . . . . . . . . . . . . . . . . . . . . . . . . . Herself
••• 46—Full frontal nudity.
**Playboy's Video Playmates** (Sep 1993) . . . . . Herself
••• 84-85—Full frontal nudity.
**Playboy's Book of Lingerie** (Jan 1994) . . . . . . Herself
••• 28—Full frontal nudity.
**Playboy's Bathing Beauties** (Mar 1994) . . . . . Herself
••• 14-15—Nude.
**Playmates at Play** (Jul 1994) . . . . . . . . . . . . . Herself
••• 3-5—Breasts.
**Playboy's Girls of Summer '94** (Jul 1994) . . . Herself
••• 1-3—Breasts and buns.
••• 18-19—Breasts.
••• 88-89—Full frontal nudity.
**Playboy's Book of Lingerie** (Jul 1994) . . . . . . Herself
••• 57—Full frontal nudity.
**Playboy's Book of Lingerie** (Sep 1994) . . . . . Herself
•• 22—Left breast and lower frontal nudity.

# Vernon, Kate

Daughter of actor John Vernon.
*Films:*
Chained Heat (1983; U.S./German) . . . . . . . . Cellmate
Alphabet City (1984) . . . . . . . . . . . . . . . . . . . . .Angie
**Roadhouse 66** (1984) . . . . . . . . . . . .·. . . . Melissa Duran
• 1:03—Brief breasts in back of car with Judge Rein-
hold. Dark.
Pretty in Pink (1986) . . . . . . . . . . . . . . . . . . . . . Benny
The Last Days of Philip Banter (1987) . . . . . . . . . .Brent
**Hostile Takeover** (1988; Canadian). . . . . . . . . . .Sally
*a.k.a. Office Party*
• 0:35—Very brief, left breast undressing in office with ˎ
John Warner. Dark.
•• 0:39—Right breast, turning over in her sleep, then
playing with the chain.
Malcolm X (1992) . . . . . . . . . . . . . . . . . . . . . .Sophia
**Dangerous Touch** (1993) . . . . . . . . . . .Amanda Grace
0:19—Having sex with Lou Diamond Phillips in bed
during a party.
••• 0:29—Breasts, while making love with Phillips in
convertible car in the woods.
••• 0:36—In black leotard, garter belt and stockings,
then breasts while undressing in front of Phillips.
••• 0:38—More breasts when Phillips ties her hands to
the headboard.
••• 0:51—Breasts, while making love in bed with Nicole
while Phillips video tapes everything.
• 0:53—Breasts, on video monitor when she looks at
video tape of her with Nicole.
*Made for Cable TV:*
Tales From the Crypt: Till Death Do We Part
(1994; HBO). . . . . . . . . . . . . . . . . . . . . . . . . . Lucille
*Made for TV Movies:*
Daughters of Privilege (1990). . . . . . . . . . . . . . .Diana
House of Secrets (1993) . . . . . . . . . . . . . . .Laura Morrell
*TV:*
Falcon Crest (1984-85). . . . . . . . . . . . . Lorraine Prescott
Who's the Boss? (1990) . . . . . . . . . . . . Kathleen Sawyer

# Veronica, Christina

a.k.a. Christina Veronique.
*Films:*
**Sexpot** (1986) . . . . . . . . . . . . . . . . . . . . . . . . . . . Betty
••• 0:28—In bra, then breasts with her two sisters when
their bras pop off. (She's on the left.)
•• 0:46—Breasts taking off her top in boat with Gorilla.
• 0:54—Breasts lying on the grass with Gorilla.
• 1:28—Breasts during outtakes of 0:28 scene.
**Thrilled to Death** (1988) . . . . . . . . . . . . . . . . . Satin
•• 0:33—Breasts talking to Cliff during porno film
shoot.
**Girlfriend from Hell** (1989) . . . . . . . . . . . . . Dancer
••• 1:17—Breasts dancing on stage in club.
**Party Incorporated** (1989). . . . . . . . . . . . . Christina
*a.k.a. Party Girls*
••• 0:52—Buns and breasts dancing in front of everybody at party.
Roadhouse (1989) . . . . . . . . . . . . . . . . . Strip Joint Girl

A Woman Obsessed (1989) . . . . . . . . . Crystal the Maid
Corporate Affairs (1990) . . . . . . . . . . . Tanning Woman
   0:47—Side of right breast, getting tanned.
**They Bite** (1991) . . . . . . . . . . . . . . . . . . . . . . . Tammy
   ••• 0:20—Breasts in bed during porno movie shoot.
   ••• 0:55—Breasts, sunbathing on the beach while a guy
    rubs suntan lotion on her.
   • 1:03—Breasts on the beach during playback of film.
   •• 1:08—Breasts on boat, getting attacked by monster.
   • 1:09—Breasts in water, struggling with the monster.
   • 1:10—Brief breasts on beach during playback of
    film.
Dragon Fire (1993) . . . . . . . . . . . . . . . . . . . . . Dancer

## Verran, Michelle

a.k.a. Adult film actress Barbii.
*Films:*
**Sorority House Massacre 2** (1990) . . . . . . . Suzanne
   ••• 0:23—Buns in panties, then breasts changing
    clothes.

## Verrell, Cec

*Films:*
**Runaway** (1984) . . . . . . . . . . . . . . . . . . . . . . . Hooker
   •• 0:44—Breasts in hotel bathroom while Tom Selleck
    sneaks into her room.
Hollywood Vice Squad (1986) . . . . . . . . . . . . . . . . . Judy
Silk (1986) . . . . . . . . . . . . . . . . . . . . . Jenny Sleighton
**Hell Comes to Frogtown** (1987) . . . . . . . . Centinella
   •• 0:19—Breasts taking off her blouse and getting into
    sleeping bag with Roddy Piper. Brief breasts again
    after he throws her off him.
Transformations (1988) . . . . . . . . . . . . . . . . . . . Antonia
Three of Hearts (1993) . . . . . . . . . . . . . . . . . . . Allison
*TV:*
Supercarrier (1988)
   . . . . . . . . . . . . . . . Lt. Cmdr. Ruth "Beebee" Rutkowski
*Video Tapes:*
**Inside Out** (1992) . . . . . . . The Psychiatrist/Shrink Wrap
   ••• 0:18—In red bra, then breasts making love with the
    guy she picked up in the bar.
Inside Out 3 (1992). . . . . . . . . . . . . . . . . . Susan/Tango

## Veruschka

Model.
*Films:*
Blow-Up (1966; British/Italian) . . . . . . . . . . . Veruschka
The Bride (1985) . . . . . . . . . . . . . . . . . . . . . Countess
*Magazines:*
**Playboy** (Jan 1974) . . . . . . . . . . . . . . . . . Painted Lady
   ••• 122-129—Full frontal nudity in various artfully paint-
    ed body poses.
**Playboy** (Jan 1989) . . . . . . . . Women of the Seventies
   •• 214—Breasts wearing body paint.
**Playboy's Nudes** (Oct 1990). . . . . . . . . . . . . Herself
   •• 55—Full frontal nudity with a painted body.
**Playboy's Nudes** (Dec 1992) . . . . . . . . . . . . . Herself
   • 76-77—Nude with body painted to look like a gang-
    ster.

## Vetri, Victoria

a.k.a. *Playboy* Playmate Angela Dorian.
*Films:*
Rosemary's Baby (1968). . . . . . . . . . . . Terry Fionoffrio
**Group Marriage** (1972) . . . . . . . . . . . . . . . . . . . . . Jan
   ••• 0:28—Buns and breasts getting into bed with Den-
    nis, Sander and Chris. More breasts sitting in bed.
    Long scene.
   • 1:19—Brief side view of right breast in lifeguard
    booth.
**Invasion of the Bee Girls** (1973) . . . . . . . . Julie Zorn
   • 0:30—Brief breasts getting molested by jerks.
   ••• 1:19—Breasts in the bee transformer, then brief
    buns getting rescued.
*Made for TV Movies:*
Night Chase (1970) . . . . . . . . . . . . . . . . . Beverly Dorn
*Magazines:*
**Playboy** (Sep 1967) . . . . . . . . . . . . . . . . . . . . Playmate
   Used alternate name of Angela Dorian for the centerfold.
   Playmate of the Year 1968.
**Playboy** (Nov 1972) . . . . . . . . . . Sex in Cinema 1972
   • 166—Breasts in a photo from *Group Marriage.* Small
    photo, hard to see anything.
**Playboy** (Jan 1974) . . . . . . . . Twenty Years of Playmates
   •• 108—Left breast while wearing shawl.

## Vickers, Vicki

a.k.a. Adult film actress Raven.
a.k.a. Rachel Vickers.
*Films:*
**Angel Eyes** (1991) . . . . . . . . . . . . . . . . . . . . . Michelle
   ••• 0:02—Breasts and buns, while making love with
    Steven in bed. Long scene.
   ••• 0:18—Buns and breasts in shower. Partial lower
    frontal nudity.
   ••• 0:25—Right breast, then breasts while making love
    with Steven in bed while Angel watches. Long
    scene.
   •• 0:32—Breasts, while rolling over in bed.
   ••• 0:40—Breasts, getting into shower, washing herself
    and getting out.
   ••• 0:44—Buns and breasts while making love in bed
    with Steven.
   • 0:51—Brief left breast, while adjusting the covers in
    bed.
   ••• 0:53—Breasts in bed while making love in bed with
    Angel. Buns in G-string when getting out of bed.
   •• 0:55—Breasts, while bending over sink to wash her
    face. Right breast, while peeking around the door.
*Video Tapes:*
**The Girls of Penthouse** (1984) . . . . . . . . The Locket
   ••• 0:17—Breasts, then nude, making love.
**Penthouse Love Stories** (1986)
   . . . . . . . . . . . . . . . . . Snapshot and Loveboat Woman
   ••• 0:37—Nude, taking pictures of herself.
   •• 0:51—Breasts on hammock watching Julie Parton.
   •• 0:55—Left breast, twice while lying on hammock.

# • Vinni, Sasha

*Video Tapes:*

**Making of the "Carousel Girls' Calendar"** (1993)
. . . . . . . . . . . . . . . . . . . . . . . . . . . . . . Miss November
••• 1:13—Full frontal nudity during photo shoot.
••• 1:16—Nude during interview segment.

**Penthouse Pet of the Year Playoff 1993** (1993)
. . . . . . . . . . . . . . . . . . . . . . . . . . . . . . . . . . . Pet
••• 0:20—Nude, outside with a car, in a dance studio, in the back seat of a limousine, in a house, in the shower.

**Penthouse Pet of the Year Winners 1994: Sasha & Leslie** (1994) . . . . . . . . . . . . . . . . . . . Pet of the Year
••• 0:00—Breasts, outside of trailer.
••• 0:03—Nude on bed.
••• 0:08—Breasts, outside with tigers and nude while painted like a tiger.
••• 0:14—In lingerie and nude in room.
••• 0:19—Sunbathing nude outside.
••• 0:23—Nude in front of some seats.

*Magazines:*

**Penthouse** (Sep 1991) . . . . . . . . . . . . . . . . . . . . . Pet
••• 111-125—Nude.
**Penthouse** (Jun 1993) . . . . . . . . Pet of the Year Play-Off
••• 110-111—Nude.
**Penthouse** (Jan 1994) . . . . . . . . . . . . . . Pet of the Year
••• 117-127—Nude.
**Penthouse** (Sep 1994) . . . . . . . . . . . . . Sasha & Leslie
••• 208-219—Nude with Leslie Glass.

## Viva

*Films:*

Midnight Cowboy (1969) . . . . . . . . . Gretel McAlbertson
Cisco Pike (1971) . . . . . . . . . . . . . . . . . . . . . . . Merna
Play It Again, Sam (1972) . . . . . . . . . . . . . . . . . Jennifer
Forbidden Zone (1980) . . . . . . . . . . . . . . . . . . Ex-Queen
**Superstar: The Life and Times of Andy Warhol** (1990) . . . . . . . . . . . . . . . . . . . . . . . . . . . . . . Herself
• 0:26—Very brief right breast, while raising blouse to breast feed a baby.
• 0:49—Brief breasts, while lying in bed on right side of split screen in a clip from another film.
The Man Without a Face (1993) . . . . . . . . . Mrs. Cooper

# • Vives, Vivianne

*Films:*

**Hot Blood** (1989; Spanish) . . . . . . . . . . . . . . . Connie
• 1:19—Buns and very brief side view of left breast in bed with Julio.
•• 1:21—Breasts in bed several times, then lower frontal nudity with Julio.
All Tied Up (1992) . . . . . . . . . . . . . . . . . . . . . Carmen

## Vogel, Darlene

*Films:*

Back to the Future, Part II (1989) . . . . . . . . . . . . . Spike
**Ski School** (1990) . . . . . . . . . . . . . . . . . . . . . . . . Lori
• 1:03—Breasts in bed with Johnny.
Angel 4: Undercover (1993) . . . . . . . . . . . . . . . . Molly

## Vold, Ingrid

*Films:*

**Side Roads** (1988) . . . . . . . . . . . . . . . . Bonnie Velasco
• 0:29—Brief breasts in motel room, getting undressed and carried into bed by Joe.
0:30—In white lingerie, talking with Joe. Long scene.
0:56—In white bra and panties, changing clothes.
• 1:45—Brief breasts in mirror, getting out of bed.
Communion (1989) . . . . Uncredited Magician's Assistant
**Angel of Passion** (1991) . . . . . . . . . . . . . . . . Vanessa
• 1:01—Brief breasts posing on the couch for the photographer.
**To Sleep with a Vampire** (1992) . . . . . . . Stripper #1
••• 0:06—Breasts, while dancing on stage. (Wearing a wig.)
• 0:07—Brief breasts on stage (seen in B&W through the vampire's eyes.)
Good Girls Don't (1993) . . . . . . . . . . . . . Prison Guard

## Von Palleske, Heidi

*Films:*

**Dead Ringers** (1988) . . . . . . . . . . . . . . . . . . . . . Cary
• 0:45—Brief left breast sticking out of bathrobe, while talking to Jeremy Irons in the bathroom.
Blind Fear (1989; Canadian) . . . . . . . . . . . . . . . . Marla
Renegades (1989) . . . . . . . . . . . . . . . . . . . Hooker in Bar
White Light (1990) . . . . . . . . . . . . . . . . . Debra Halifax
Deceived (1991) . . . . . . . . . . . . . . . . . Mrs. Peabody
**Ramona** (1992) . . . . . . . . . . . . . . . . . . Ramona Soco
• 0:04—Brief breasts, while making love with Henry.
•• 0:06—Brief breasts, several times, while rolling over in bed.
• 1:13—Breasts, after taking off blouse in hotel room with Henry.

## Voorhees, Deborah

a.k.a. Debisue Voorhees.
*Films:*

Avenging Angel (1985) . . . . . . . . . . . . . . . . . . . . Roxie
**Friday the 13th, Part V—A New Beginning** (1985)
. . . . . . . . . . . . . . . . . . . . . . . . . . . . . . . . . . . Tina
••• 0:41—Breasts after making love with Eddie, then lying down and relaxing just before getting killed.
• 0:43—Buns and brief left breast when Eddie turns her over and discovers her dead.
**Appointment with Fear** (1988) . . . . . . . . . . . . . Ruth
• 0:21—Very, very brief side view of left breast taking off bra to go swimming, then very brief breasts getting out of the pool.

## Vorgan, Gigi

*Films:*

Jaws II (1978) . . . . . . . . . . . . . . . . . . . . . . . . . . Brook
**Hardcore** (1979) . . . . . . . . . . . . . . . . . . Teenage Girl
• 0:32—Breasts on sofa in Peter Boyle's apartment.
Caveman (1981) . . . . . . . . . . . . . . . . . Folg's Daughter
Children of a Lesser God (1986) . . . . . . . . . . Announcer
Rain Man (1988) . . . . . . . . . . . . . . Voice-Over Actress

Red Heat (1988) . . . . . . . . . . . . . . . . . . . . . . . . Audrey
Vital Signs (1989) . . . . . . . . . . . . . . . . . . . . . . . Nell
*TV:*
Knots Landing (1984) . . . . . . . . . . . . . . . . . . . . Carol

# Wagner, Lindsay

*Films:*
**Two People** (1973) . . . . . . . . . . . . .Deidre McCluskey
(Not available on video tape.)

# Wagner, Lori

*Films:*
**Caligula** (1980) . . . . . . . . . . . . . . . . . . . . . . Agrippina
(X-rated, 147 minute version.)
••• 1:16—Nude, making love with Anneka Di Lorenzo.
Long scene.
Trained to Kill (1988) . . . . . . . . . . . . . . Ace Duran's Girl
UHF (1989). . . . . . . . . . . . . . . . . . . . . . . Mud Wrestler
*Video Tapes:*
**Penthouse: On the Wild Side** (1988). . . . . . . . Lover
• 0:54—Nude with Anneka de Lorenzo during scenes
from *The Making of Caligula.*
*Magazines:*
**Penthouse** (May 1980) . . . . . . .The Making of Caligula
• 142—Lower frontal nudity and left breast.
**Penthouse** (Jun 1980) . . . . . . . . . . . . Anneka and Lori
••• 142-153—Nude (she has lighter hair) with Anneka
di Lorenzo.
**Penthouse** (Feb 1991) . . . . . . . Lori–Caligula Revisited
•• Nude in recent photos and Caligula photos.

# Wahl, Corinne

See: Alphen, Corrine.

# Walden, Lynette

*Films:*
Split Image (1982) . . . . . . . . . . . . . . . . . . . . .Sexy Girl
**Mobsters** (1991). . . . . . . . . . . . . . . . Cute Debutante
*a.k.a. Mobsters—The Evil Empire*
•• 0:32—Breasts when Richard Grieco undoes her
dress.
**Almost Blue** (1992) . . . . . . . . . . . . . . . . . . . .Jasmine
••• 0:34—Breasts in bed on top of Michael Madsen.
• 0:35—Brief breasts, while walking to the bed and lying down while wearing panties.
••• 1:08—In black bra, then breasts and brief partial
buns, while making love with Madsen on the sofa.
•• 1:10—Buns, while lying on sofa asleep with Madsen.
1:18—In black bra and panties in Madsen's apartment.
**The Silencer** (1992) . . . . . . . . . . . . . . . . . . . . Angel
••• 0:09—Breasts and buns, taking off clothes and getting into bathtub with her boyfriend.
•• 0:10—More breasts, while making love with him in
the bathtub.
0:28—Serious cleavage in open blouse in kitchen
with a new boyfriend.
0:40—Almost breasts, while making out with Tony.
Benny & Joon (1993) . . . . . . . . . . . . Female Customer

*Made for Cable TV:*
Fallen Angels: Murder, Obliquely (1993; Showtime)
. . . . . . . . . . . . . . . . . . . . . . Your Host "Fay Friendly"
(Available on video tape on *Fallen Angels One.*)
0:00—Briefly in black bra and lingerie, while getting
dressed during the introduction.
*Made for TV Movies:*
A Matter of Justice (1993) . . . . . . . . . . . . . . . . . . Patty
*TV:*
Fallen Angels (1993) . . . . . . . . Your Host "Fay Friendly"

# Walker, Arnetia

*Films:*
The Best Little Whorehouse in Texas (1982) . . . .Dogette
The Wizard of Speed & Time (1988)
. . . . . . . . . . . . . . . . . . . . . . .Tina Dreem/Running Girl
**Scenes from the Class Struggle in Beverly Hills**
(1989) . . . . . . . . . . . . . . . . . . . . . . . . . . . . . . To-Bel
• 0:37—Breasts making love with Frank on the sofa.
•• 1:10—Breasts in bed waking up with Howard.
••• 1:23—Breasts making love on top of Ed Begley, Jr. on
the floor.
Love Crimes (1991) . . . . . . . . . . . . . . . . Maria Johnson
(Unrated version reviewed.)
*Made for Cable Movies:*
Cast a Deadly Spell (1991; HBO) . . . . Hipolite Kropolkin
*TV:*
Nurses (1991- ) . . . . . . . . . . . . . . . . . . . . . . . . .Annie

# Walker, Christina

*Films:*
**The Banker** (1989) . . . . . . . . . . . . . . . . . . . . . . Girl
• 0:18—Breasts on bed with Jeff Conaway
The Malibu Beach Vampires (1991)
. . . . . . . . . . . . . . . . . . . Vice President Vampire Affairs

# Walker, Kathryn

*Films:*
Midnight Dancer (1987; Australian). . . . . . . . . . .Kathy
*a.k.a. Belinda*
**Dangerous Game** (1988; Australian). . . . . . . .Kathryn
• 1:19—Very, very brief breasts when her black top is
pulled up while struggling with Murphy.

# • Walker, Liza

*Films:*
**Twisted Obsession** (1990) . . . . . . . . . . .Jenny Greene
1:12—Lower frontal nudity while lying down. (Don't
see her face.)
• 1:35—Brief breasts in blue light when Jeff Goldblum
sees her.
Buddy's Song (1993; British) . . . . . . . . . . . . . . .Elaine

# Walker, Tracy

*Films:*
**Invisible Maniac** (1990) . . . . . . . . . . . . Telescope Gal
•• 0:01—Nude, taking off clothes during opening
credits. Nice dancing.
*Video Tapes:*
Bikini Blitz (1990) . . . . . . . . . . . . . . . . . . . . . . .Model

# Wallace Stone, Dee

a.k.a. Dee Wallace.
Wife of actor Christopher Stone.
*Films:*
The Hills Have Eyes (1977) . . . . . . . . . . . . Lynne Wood
**10** (1979) . . . . . . . . . . . . . . . . . . . . . . . . Mary Lewis
• 1:09—Brief side view of buns, while on the floor.
• 1:10—Brief upper half of buns, going into bathroom
and dropping her sheet.
The Howling (1981) . . . . . . . . . . . . . . . . . Karen White
E.T. The Extraterrestrial (1982) . . . . . . . . . . . . . .Mary
Cujo (1983) . . . . . . . . . . . . . . . . . . . . . . . . . . Donna
0:33—Brief left thigh and left bun, getting felt up by
Christopher Stone in the kitchen.
Secret Admirer (1985) . . . . . . . . . . . . . . . . .Connie Ryan
Critters (1986) . . . . . . . . . . . . . . . . . . . . . .Helen Brown
**Shadow Play** (1986) . . . . . . . . . . . . . . Morgan Hanna
• 1:06—Brief breasts making love with Ron Kuhlman.
Kind of dark and hard to see.
The Christmas Visitor (1987) . . . . . . . . . . . . .Elizabeth
Club Life (1987) . . . . . . . . . . . . . . . . . .Tilly Francesca
I'm Dangerous Tonight (1990) . . . . . . . . . . . . . Wanda
Alligator II: The Mutation (1991) . . . . . Christine Hodges
Popcorn (1991) . . . . . . . . . . . . . . . . . . . . . . Suzanne
Discretion Assured (1993) . . . . . . . . . . . . . . . Kitten
*Made for Cable TV:*
Rebel Highway: Runaway Daughters (1994; Showtime)
. . . . . . . . . . . . . . . . . . . . . . . . . . . .Mrs. Gordon
*Made for TV Movies:*
The Secret War of Jackie's Girls (1980) . . . . . . . . Maxine
Sins of Innocence (1986) . . . . . . . . . . . . . Vicki McGary
Addicted to his Love (1988) . . . . . . . Betty Ann Brennan
Stranger on My Land (1988) . . . . . . . . . . . . . . . Annie
Moment of Truth: Cradle of Conspiracy (1994)
. . . . . . . . . . . . . . . . . . . . . . . . . . .Suzanne Guthrie
Witness to the Execution (1994) . . . . . . . .Emily Dawson
*TV:*
Together We Stand (1986) . . . . . . . . . . . . .Lori Randall

# •Wallace, Julie T.

*Films:*
The Living Daylights (1987) . . . . . . . . . . . . . . . . .n.a.
Hawks (1988; British) . . . . . . . . . . . . . . . . Ward Sister
The Lunatic (1992) . . . . . . . . . . . . . . . . . . . . . . Inga
Anchoress (1993; British) . . . . . . . . . . . . . . . .Bertha
*Made for Cable Movies:*
**The Life and Loves of a She-Devil**
(1991; British; A&E) . . . . . . . . . . . . . . . . . . . . Ruth
• 0:54—(With commercials.) Brief buns, while walking
down hallway.

• 1:05—(Into part 2 with commercials.) brief side view
of buns while tied up in bed before getting spanked
by the judge.
• 1:06—(With commercials.) Brief buns again.

# Walter, Jessica

*Films:*
Lilith (1964) . . . . . . . . . . . . . . . . . . . . . . . . . . .Laura
Grand Prix (1966) . . . . . . . . . . . . . . . . . . . . . . . . .Pat
The Group (1966) . . . . . . . . . . Libby MacAusland
**Play Misty for Me** (1971) . . . . . . . . . . . . . . . Evelyn
• 0:13—Very brief right breast in bed with Clint East-
wood. Lit with blue light. Hard to see anything.
The Flamingo Kid (1984) . . . . . . . . . . . . . Phyllis Brody
Ghost in the Machine (1993) . . . . . . . . . . . . . .Elaine
PCU (1994) . . . . . . . . . . . . . . . . . . . . . . . . . . . n.a.
*Miniseries:*
Wheels (1978) . . . . . . . . . . . . . . . . . . . . . . Ursula
Bare Essence (1983) . . . . . . . . . . . . . . Ava Marshall
*Made for TV Movies:*
Leave of Absence (1994) . . . . . . . . . . . . . . . . .Bess
*TV:*
For the People (1965) . . . . . . . . . . . . . . Phyllis Koster
Amy Prentiss (1974-75) . . . . . . . . . . . . . Amy Prentiss
All That Glitters (1977) . . . . . . . . . . . . . . Joan Hamlyn
The Round Table (1992) . . . . . . . . . . . Anne McPherson

# Walter, Marianne

See: Nichols, Kelly.

# Walters, Julie

*Films:*
Educating Rita (1983; British) . . . . . . . . . . . . . . . Rita
**She'll be Wearing Pink Pyjamas** (1985; British)
. . . . . . . . . . . . . . . . . . . . . . . . . . . . . . . . .Fran
••• 0:07—Full frontal nudity taking a shower with the
other women. Long scene.
•• 0:58—Nude, undressing and going skinny dipping
in mountain lake, then getting out. Nice bun shot
walking into the lake.
**Personal Services** (1987) . . . . . . . . . . . Cynthia Payne
• 0:21—Very brief side view of left breast, while reaching to turn off radio in the bathtub. Her face is covered with cream.
Prick Up Your Ears (1987; British) . . . . . . . . .Elise Orton
Buster (1988) . . . . . . . . . . . . . . . . . . . . . . . . . .June
Stepping Out (1991) . . . . . . . . . . . . . . . . . . . . .Vera

# Walters, Laurie

*Films:*
**The Harrad Experiment** (1973) . . . . . . . Sheila Grove
• 0:29—Breasts, wearing white panties, while with
Don Johnson.
• 0:40—Nude taking off blue dress and getting into
the swimming pool with Johnson.
**The Harrad Summer** (1974) . . . . . . . . . Sheila Grove
*a.k.a. Student Union*
0:02—Breasts, while undressing in bathroom. Long
shot, out of focus.

•• 1:04—Breasts, while lying on lounge chair, then buns and more breasts getting up and pushing Harry into the pool.

**Famous T & A** (1982) . . . . . . . . . . . . . . . Sheila Grove
(No longer available for purchase, check your video store for rental.)
  • 1:08—Breasts scene from *The Harrad Experiment*.
  •• 1:11—Nude pool scene from *The Harrad Experiment*.
*Made for TV Movies:*
Eight is Enough: A Family Reunion (1987)
. . . . . . . . . . . . . . . . . . . . . . . . . .Joannie Bradford
*TV:*
Eight is Enough (1977-81) . . . . . . . . .Joannie Bradford

# •*Walthall, Romy*
See: Windsor, Romy.

# *Waltrip, Kim*
*Films:*
**Pretty Smart** (1986) . . . . . . . Sara Gentry (the teacher)
  •• 0:53—Breasts, while sunbathing with her students.
**Nights in White Satin** (1987) . . . . . . .Stevie Hughes
  0:37—In white wig, bra, panties, garter belt and stocking during photo session.
  0:39—Brief side view of left breast in black slip during photo session.
  • 0:53—Breasts in bathtub with Walker. Out of focus, hard to see.

# •*Waltz, Lisa*
*Films:*
Brighton Beach Memoirs (1986) . . . . . . . . . . . . . .Nora
The Opposite Sex ...and How to Live with Them (1992)
. . . . . . . . . . . . . . . . . . . . . . . . . . . . . . . Lizbeth
**Pet Sematary II** (1992) . . . . . . . . . . . Amanda Gilbert
  • 0:53—Very brief right breast, while in bed when Clancy Brown rips her nightgown off.
*Made for Cable Movies:*
Roswell (1994; Showtime). . . . . . . . . . . . . . . Janet Foss

# •*Ward, Mary B.*
*Films:*
**Playing For Keeps** (1986) . . . . . . . . . . . . . . . . . Chloe
  •• 0:49—Breasts, after taking off her sweatshirt outside at night in front of Danny.
Hangin' with the Homeboys (1991) . . . . . . . . . . . .Luna
*TV:*
TV 101 (1988-89) . . . . . . . . . . . . . . . . . . Penny Lipton

# *Ward, Pamela*
*Films:*
Hellhole (1985). . . . . . . . . . . . . . . . . . . . . . . . . Tina
**School Spirit** (1985). . . . . . . . . . Girl in Sorority Room
  ••• 0:15—Buns, then breasts in her room while Billy is invisible.
  ••• 0:16—More breasts and buns with other women in shower room.
The Women's Club (1987) . . . . . Fashion Show Woman
Knockouts (1992) . . . . . . . . . . . . . . . . . . . . . . . .n.a.

*Video Tapes:*
Battling Beauties (1983) . . . . . . . Foxy Boxer/Valley Girl

# *Ward, Rachel*
Wife of actor Bryan Brown.
*Films:*
**Night School** (1980) . . . . . . . . . . . . . . . . . . . . Elanor
  • 0:24—In sheer white bra and panties, taking off clothes to take a shower. Breasts taking off bra. Hard to see because she's behind a shower curtain.
  0:28—Buns, when her boyfriend rubs red paint all over her in the shower.
The Final Terror (1981). . . . . . . . . . . . . . . . . .Margaret
Sharky's Machine (1981) . . . . . . . . . . . . . . . .Dominoe
Dead Men Don't Wear Plaid (1982) . . . . . . Juliet Forrest
Against All Odds (1984) . . . . . . . . . . . . . . . Jessie Wyler
  0:49—Very brief buns lying down with Jeff Bridges.
  0:50—Wet white dress in water. Long shot, don't see anything.
  1:01—The sweaty temple scene. Erotic, but you don't really see anything.
The Good Wife (1987; Australian) . . . . . . . . Marge Hills
  *a.k.a. The Umbrella Woman*
Hotel Colonial (1988). . . . . . . . . . . . . . . . . Irene Costa
How to Get Ahead in Advertising (1988; British) . . .Julia
**After Dark, My Sweet** (1990) . . . . . . . .Fay Anderson
  • 1:22—Very, very brief half of right breast under Jason Patric in bed when he moves slightly.
Christopher Columbus: The Discovery (1992; U.S./ Spanish) . . . . . . . . . . . . . . . . . . . . . . . .Queen Isabella
Double Obsession (1992). . . . . . . . . . . . Grandmother
Wide Sargasso Sea (1993) . . . . . . . . . . Annette Cosway
  (Unrated version reviewed.)
*Made for Cable Movies:*
**Fortress** (1985; HBO) . . . . . . . . . . . . . . . . . Sally Jones
  • 0:38—Swimming in a sheer bra underwater.
Black Magic (1992; Showtime). . . . . . . . .Lillian Blatman
**Double Jeopardy** (1992; Showtime) . . . . . . Lisa Burns
  0:20—In shower with Bruce Boxleitner. You can see that she's wearing a towel around her midsection.
  0:21—Very brief left breast, in the shower with Boxleitner. Hard to see because of the shadows. Also steam on glass obscures her face.
  • 0:23—Very brief right breast, when Eddie opens her robe to rip her panties off. Hard to see because of the beveled glass in the door. Very, very brief right breast while getting attacked by Eddie when she reaches back to get a knife. Don't see her face clearly.
*Miniseries:*
The Thorn Birds (1983) . . . . . . . . . . . . . .Meggie Cleary
*Made for TV Movies:*
And the Sea Will Tell (1991) . . . . . . . . . . Jennifer Jenkins
*Magazines:*
**Playboy** (Mar 1984) . . . . . . . . . . . . . . . . . .Roving Eye
  ••• 203—Breasts in photos that weren't used in *Night School*.

# Warner, Julie

*Films:*
Flatliners (1990) . . . . . . . . . . . . . . One of Joe's Women
**Doc Hollywood** (1991) . . . . . . . . . . . . . . . . . . . . . .Lou
- 0:15—Silhouette of right breast while standing in lake during Michael J. Fox's dream. Possible lower frontal nudity since she is facing the camera, but since it is shot in silhouette, you can't see anything.
- ••• 0:16—Breasts several times, skinny dipping in lake, then getting out while Fox watches.
Mr. Saturday Night (1992) . . . . . . . . . . . . . . . . . Elaine
Indian Summer (1993) . . . . . . . . . . . . . . Kelly Berman

# Warner, Missy

Adult film actress.
*Video Tapes:*
**Big Bust Casting Call** (1992) . . . . . . . . . . . . . Herself
- ••• 0:31—In bra and G-string, undressing for audition, then nude in front of mirror.
**L.A. Strippers** (1992) . . . . . . . . . . . . . . Missy Warner
- ••• 0:01—Breasts dancing on stage during introduction.
- ••• 0:18—In raincoat, then lingerie, then nude dancing on stage. Long scene.

# Warner, T.C.

*Films:*
**The Art of Dying** (1991) . . . . . . . . . . . . . . . . . .Janet
    0:14—Buns, shackled up in S&M chamber with a customer.
- ••• 0:32—Breasts in the shower. Buns and side of right breast, before getting stabbed to death.
*Made for TV Movies:*
Overkill: The Aileen Wuornos Story (1992) . . . . . . . Amy
Lies of the Heart: The Story of Laurie Kellogg (1994)
  . . . . . . . . . . . . . . . . . . . . . . . . . . . . . .Nicole Pappas

# Warren, Jennifer

*Films:*
**Night Moves** (1975) . . . . . . . . . . . . . . . . . . . . . Paula
- •• 0:56—Breasts in bed with Gene Hackman.
- 0:57—Right breast after making love in bed with Hackman.
Another Man, Another Chance (1977; U.S./French)
  . . . . . . . . . . . . . . . . . . . . . . . . . . . . . . . . . . .Mary
Slap Shot (1977) . . . . . . . . . . . . . . . . . .Francine Dunlop
Ice Castles (1979) . . . . . . . . . . . . . . .Deborah Macland
*TV:*
Paper Dolls (1984) . . . . . . . . . . . . . . . . . .Dinah Caswell
*Magazines:*
**Playboy** (Nov 1975) . . . . . . . . . . . Sex in Cinema 1975
- ••• 132—Breasts in bed with Gene Hackman from *Night Moves.*

# Warren, Sandra

a.k.a. Sandee Currie.
*Films:*
Terror Train (1980; Canadian) . . . . . . . . . . . . . . Mitchy
Gas (1981; Canadian) . . . . . . . . . . . . . . Sarah Marshall

Curtains (1983; Canadian) . . . . . . . . . . . Tara Demillo
- 0:58—Side view of left breast practicing a scene in the play with Summers.
Terminal Choice (1985; Canadian) . . . . . . . Nurse Tipton

# Wasa, Maxine

*Films:*
**L.A. Bounty** (1989) . . . . . . . . . . . . . . . . . . . . . Model
- 0:07—Right breast while posing for Wings Hauser while he paints. Left breast, getting up. Long shot.
- 0:26—Left breast while posing on couch for Hauser.
- •• 0:38—Breasts lying on couch again.
**Savage Beach** (1989) . . . . . . . . . . . . . . . .Sexy Beauty
- ••• 0:08—Side view of left breast, in pool with Shane, then breasts getting out of pool.
- ••• 0:10—Breasts while Shane talks on the phone.
*Made for Cable TV:*
Dream On: The First Episode (1990; HBO)
  . . . . . . . . . . . . . . . . . . . . . . . . . . . . Andrea Kelly
*Video Tapes:*
**Wet and Wild** (1989) . . . . . . . . . . . . . . . . . . . Model
*Magazines:*
**Playboy** (Nov 1989) . . . . . . . . . . Sex in Cinema 1989
- •• 134—Side view of left breast from *Savage Beach.*

# Watkins, Michelle

*Films:*
Terms of Endearment (1983) . . . . . . . . . . . . . . Woman
**The Outing** (1987) . . . . . . . . . . . . . . . . . . . . . Faylene
- •• 0:12—Breasts taking off her top, standing by the edge of the swimming pool, then running breasts through the house with panties on.

# Watson, Alberta

*Films:*
**In Praise of Older Women** (1978; Canadian) . . Mitzi
- •• 0:51—Breasts sitting in chair talking with Tom Berenger, then more breasts lying in bed. Long scene.
Power Play (1978; Canadian) . . . . . . . . . . . . . . .Donna
  0:21—Brief breasts lying on table getting shocked through her nipples.
Stone Cold Dead (1979; Canadian) . . . . . . . Olivia Page
The Soldier (1982) . . . . . . . . . . . . . . . Susan Goodman
**The Keep** (1983) . . . . . . . . . . . . . . . . . . . . Eva Cuza
- 0:59—Very brief breasts making love with Scott Glenn, then brief lower frontal nudity.
Best Revenge (1984) . . . . . . . . . . . . . . . . . . . . . . n.a.
White of the Eye (1988) . . . . . . . . . . . . . . Ann Mason
The Hitman (1991) . . . . . . . . . . . . .Christine De Vera
Zebrahead (1992) . . . . . . . . . . . . . . . . . . . . . Phyliss
Spanking the Monkey (1994) . . . . . . . . . . . . . . . . n.a.
*Made for TV Movies:*
Women of Valor (1986) . . . . . . . . . . . . . . . . . .Helen
Relentless: Mind of a Killer (1993) . . . . . . Ellen Giancola
Jonathan Stone: Threat of Innocence (1994)
  . . . . . . . . . . . . . . . . . . . . Deborah Walsh Bradford

# • Watson, Virginia

*Films:*
**The Spring** (1989) . . . . . . . . . . . . . . . . . . . . Pafinya
  •• 0:45—Breasts taking off her top in front of Dack
    Rambo in his hotel room.
Dead On (1993) . . . . . . . . . . . . . . . . . . . . . . . Dorian
  (Unrated version reviewed.)
*Made for Cable Movies:*
Running Mates (1992; HBO) . . . . . . . .TV Anchorwoman

# Way, Renee

*Films:*
**The Newlydeads** (1988). . . . . . . . . . . . . . . . . Brenda
  • 0:19—Buns and side of right breast, while in spa
    with her boyfriend.
**Party Plane** (1988) . . . . . . . . . . . . . . . . . . . . .Andy
  ••• 0:01—Breasts, while taking off her blouse to fix the
    plane.
  ••• 0:06—Breasts, while sitting on edge of spa.
  ••• 0:11—Breasts again, when getting out of spa.
  • 0:12—Brief breasts after dropping her towel while
    talking to Tim.

# Wayne, April

Former model for Ujena Swimwear (*Swimwear Illustrated*
magazine).
*Films:*
**Moon in Scorpio** (1987). . . . . . . . . . . . . . . . . Isabel
  • 0:32—Brief right breast in bed with a guy.
  • 0:35—Brief breasts putting bathing suit on in a bath-
    room on a boat when a guy opens the door.
Party Camp (1987) . . . . . . . . . . . . . . . . Nurse Brenda
*Video Tapes:*
Swimwear Illustrated: On Location (1986)
  . . . . . . . . . . . . . . . . . . . . . . . . . . Swimsuit Model

# Wayne, Carol

*Films:*
The Party (1968). . . . . . . . . . . . . . . . . . . June Warren
Scavenger Hunt (1979). . . . . . . . . . . . . . . . . . . Nurse
Gypsy Angels (1980). . . . . . . . . . . . . . . . . . Waitress
Savannah Smiles (1983) . . . . . . . . . . . . . . . . Doreen
**Heartbreakers** (1984) . . . . . . . . . . . . . . . . . .Candy
    0:22—In black wig and bra posing for Peter Coyote
    in his studio.
  ••• 0:41—In white bra and panties, then brief breasts in
    the mirror stripping in front of Coyote and Nick
    Mancuso. Then brief breasts lying in bed with Coy-
    ote.
Surf II (1984). . . . . . . . . . . . . . . . . . . . . Mrs. O'Finlay
*TV:*
The Tonight Show . . . . . . . . . . . . . . . . . . . . .Regular
*Video Tapes:*
E. Nick: A Legend in His Own Mind (1984) . . . . . Regine
*Magazines:*
**Playboy** (Feb 1984) . . . . . . . . . 101 Nights with Johnny
  ••• 56-61—Full frontal nudity.

# Weatherly, Shawn

Miss South Carolina 1980.
Miss U.S.A. 1980.
Miss Universe 1980.
*Films:*
Cannonball Run II (1984) . . . . . . . . . . . . . . .Dean's Girl
Police Academy III: Back in Training (1986)
  . . . . . . . . . . . . . . . . . . . . . . . . . . . . .Cadet Adams
Party Line (1988) . . . . . . . . . . . . Asst. D.A. Stacy Sloane
Shadowzone (1989). . . . . . . . . . . . . . . . . .Dr. Kidwell
**Thieves of Fortune** (1989) . . . . . . . . . . . . . . . Peter
  • 1:09—Brief breasts several times, taking a shower
    (while wearing beard and moustache disguise).
  ••• 1:21—Breasts in white panties distracting tribe so
    she can get away.
**Amityville 1992: It's About Time** (1992) . . . . Andra
  ••• 0:07—Breasts, making love in bed on top of her hus-
    band. Nice and sweaty!
*TV:*
Shaping Up (1984) . . . . . . . . . . . . . Melissa McDonald
Baywatch (1988-90). . . . . . . . . . . . . . . . . . . . .Jil Riley

# Weaver, Jacki

*Films:*
**Alvin Purple** (1973; Australian) . . . . Second Sugar Girl
  •• 0:33—Brief full frontal nudity, lying in bean bag
    chair.
**Jock Petersen** (1974; Australian) . . . . . . Susie Petersen
  *a.k.a. Petersen*
  ••• 0:01—Full frontal nudity lying in bed with Jock.
Picnic at Hanging Rock (1975) . . . . . . . . . . . . . .Minnie
The Removalists (1975) . . . . . . . . . . . . . Marilyn Carter
Caddie (1976) . . . . . . . . . . . . . . . . . . . . . . . . . .Josie
Squizzy Taylor (1984). . . . . . . . . . . . . . . . . . . . Dolly

# Weaver, Sigourney

*Films:*
Annie Hall (1977). . . . . . . . . Alvy's Date Outside Theatre
Alien (1979). . . . . . . . . . . . . . . . . . . . . Lt. Ellen Ripley
Eyewitness (1981) . . . . . . . . . . . . . . . . . Tony Sokolow
Deal of the Century (1983) . . . . . . . . . . . . Mrs. De Voto
The Year of Living Dangerously (1983; Australian)
  . . . . . . . . . . . . . . . . . . . . . . . . . . . . . . . Jill Bryant
Ghostbusters (1984) . . . . . . . . . . . . . . . . Dana Barrett
Aliens (1986) . . . . . . . . . . . . . . . . . . . . Lt. Ellen Ripley
**Half Moon Street** (1986) . . . . . . . . . Lauren Slaughter
  *a.k.a. Escort Girl*
  • 0:05—Brief breasts in the bathtub.
  •• 0:11—Brief breasts in the bathtub again.
  • 0:18—Brief buns and side view of right breast while
    putting on makeup in front of the mirror. Wearing a
    black garter belt and stockings.
  ••• 0:39—Breasts, while riding exercise bike while being
    photographed, then brief breasts getting out of the
    shower.
    0:46—Very, very brief breasts wearing a sheer black
    blouse with no bra during daydream sequence.
  • 0:50—Brief breasts, while in bed with Michael
    Caine, then left breast.

1:16—In braless, wet, white blouse in bathroom after knocking a guy out.

**One Woman or Two** (1986; French) . . . . . . . . Jessica
*a.k.a. Une Femme Ou Deux*

1:30—In braless white blouse.

•• 1:31—Very brief side view of left breast in bed with Gerard Depardieu.

Gorillas in the Mist (1988). . . . . . . . . . . . . Dian Fossey

Ghostbusters II (1989). . . . . . . . . . . . . . . Dana Barrett

Working Girl (1989) . . . . . . . . . . . . . . Katherine Parker

1:22—In white lingerie, sitting in bed, then talking to Harrison Ford.

1492: Conquest of Paradise (1992; British/U.S./Spanish/French) . . . . . . . . . . . . . . . . . . . . . . Queen Isabella

Alien 3 (1992). . . . . . . . . . . . . . . . . . . Lt. Ellen Ripley

Dave (1993) . . . . . . . . . . . . . . . . . . . . . Ellen Mitchell

*Magazines:*

Playboy (Oct 1992). . . . . . . . . . . . . . . . . . . Grapevine

# Webb, Chloe

*Films:*

**Sid and Nancy** (1986; British). . . . . . . . . . . . . . Nancy

• 0:21—Left breast, under Sid's arm in bed with him. Covered up, hard to see.

•• 0:44—Breasts in bed after making love, then arguing with Sid.

**The Belly of an Architect** (1987; British/Italian)
. . . . . . . . . . . . . . . . . . . . . . . . . . Louisa Kracklite

•• 0:01—Very brief right breast, making love on train with Brian Dennehy. Brief side view of right breast sitting up and putting camisole top on.

• 0:56—Brief buns in room with Lambert Wilson.

• 1:07—Brief buns, lying in bed with Wilson.

1:27—Breasts B&W photos of a pregnant woman. Supposedly her, but probably not.

Twins (1988). . . . . . . . . . . . . . . . . . . . . . Linda Mason

Heart Condition (1990). . . . . . . . . . . . . Crystal Gerrity

0:00—In black lingerie, photographing the Senator with Peisha.

1:00—In black lingerie in bedroom with Bob Hoskins.

Queens Logic (1991). . . . . . . . . . . . . . . . . . . Patricia

A Dangerous Woman (1993). . . . . . . . . . . . . . . . Birdy

*Made for TV Movies:*

Lucky Day (1991) . . . . . . . . . . . . . . . Allison Campbell

Silent Cries (1993). . . . . . . . . . . . . . . . . . Dinki Denk

**Tales of the City** (1994). . . . . . . . . . . . . Mona Ramsey

•• 0:15—(Into Part 1) Breasts, while nonchalantly changing clothes in front of Mary Ann.

*TV:*

Thicke of the Night (1983) . . . . . . . . . . . . . . . Regular

China Beach (1988) . . . . . . . . . . . . . . . Laurette Barber

# Weber, Sharon Clark

See: Clark, Sharon.

# • Weeks, Kathe

*Made for Cable TV:*

**Tales From the Crypt: Death of Some Salesman** (1993; HBO). . . . . . . . . . . . . . . . . . . . . . . . . Stella

••• 0:02—Breasts, while making love in bed with Ed Begley Jr.

••• 0:03—Breasts, while sitting in bed and talking with Begley.

*Magazines:*

Playboy (Mar 1994) . . . . . . . . . . . . . . . . . . Grapevine

# • Weickgenant, Blair

*Films:*

**Smooth Talker** (1990). . . . . . . . . . . . . . . Lisa Charles

• 0:33—Breasts, lying in bed and sitting up during Carl's B&W fantasy.

Double Obsession (1992). . . . . . . . . . . Lillian Robinson

# Weigel, Teri

The first *Playboy* Playmate to star in adult films *after* she became a Playmate.

*Adult Films:*

**The Barlow Affairs** (1991) . . . . . . . . . . . . . . . . n.a.

**Lingerie Busters** (1991) . . . . . . . . . . . . . . . . . n.a.

**Starr** (1991) . . . . . . . . . . . . . . . . . . . . . . . . n.a.

**Wicked** (1991) . . . . . . . . . . . . . . . . . . . . . . . n.a.

*Films:*

**Cheerleader Camp** (1987) . . . . . . . . . . . . Pam Bently
*a.k.a. Bloody Pom Poms*

•• 0:12—Breasts taking off her swimsuit top while sunbathing.

**Glitch** (1988) . . . . . . . . . . . . . . . . . . . . . . . Lydia

0:41—In pink bathing suit talking to blonde guy.

• 0:54—Very brief side view of right breast in bathtub with dark haired guy.

Return of the Killer Tomatoes (1988) . . . Matt's Playmate

**The Banker** (1989) . . . . . . . . . . . . . . . . . . . . Jaynie

••• 0:02—Taking off dress, then in lingerie, then breasts making love with Osbourne in bed. More breasts after.

**Far From Home** (1989) . . . . . . . . . . . Woman in Trailer

•• 0:16—Breasts making love when Drew Barrymore peeks in window.

**Night Visitor** (1989) . . . . . . . . . . . . . Victim in Cellar

• 0:50—Brief out of focus breasts changing tops in the cellar.

• 0:55—Right breast, during ceremony. Very brief breasts just before being stabbed.

**Savage Beach** (1989). . . . . . . . . . . . . . . . . Anjelica

••• 0:33—Breasts taking off black teddy and getting into bed to make love.

•• 0:47—Breasts making love in the back seat of car.

**Marked for Death** (1990). . . . . . . . . . . . Sexy Girl #2

• 0:39—Brief breasts on bed with Jimmy when Steven Seagal bursts into the room. (She's the brunette.)

**Predator 2** (1990). . . . . . . . . . . . . . . Columbian Girl
• 0:22—Brief breasts making love on bed. More breasts several times being held on the floor, brief full frontal nudity getting up when the Predator starts his attack.
Auntie Lee's Meat Pies (1991) . . . . . . . . . . . . . . Coral
1:23—Breasts under sheer outfit.
1:29—Buns, while swimming in one piece swimsuit under water.
**Innocent Blood** (1992). . . . . . Melody Lounge Dancer
•• 1:32—Breasts (holding a red and white boa, in the middle of two other dancers), dancing in front of Robert Loggia.

*Video Tapes:*
**Playboy Video Centerfold: Teri Weigel** (1986)
. . . . . . . . . . . . . . . . . . . . . . . . . . . . . . . . Playmate
••• 0:00—Nude, in shower, taking a bath, in bedroom.
••• 0:15—Nude outside in spa, and modeling lingerie with Dona Speir and Hope Marie Carlton.
••• 0:18—Nude in bed taking of black lingerie outfit.
**Playboy Video Calendar 1988** (1987) . . . . Playmate
**Playboy's Fantasies** (1987) . . . . . . . . The Mannequin
••• 0:21—Nude, after coming to life from being a mannequin.
**Wet and Wild** (1989). . . . . . . . . . . . . . . . . . .Model
**Playboy's Fantasies II** (1990) . . . . . . . Grand Illusions
••• 0:31—Nude outside in the woods during a surveyor's fantasy.
**Sexy Lingerie II** (1990). . . . . . . . . . . . . . . . . .Model
**Wet and Wild II** (1990) . . . . . . . . . . . . . . . . .Model
**Secrets of Making Love... To the Same Person Forever** (1991). . . . . . . . . . . . . . . .Mirror, Spa & Bed
••• 0:33—Breasts and buns in front of mirror, in spa and tied up in bed.
• 0:48—Breasts and lower frontal nudity in spa and in bed.
**Sexy Lingerie III** (1991) . . . . . . . . . . . . . . . . .Model
**Inside Out 3** (1992) . . . . . . . . . . . Woman/The Portal
•• 0:27—Brief breasts, standing up in the water.
**Penthouse Fast Cars/Fantasy Women** (1992)
. . . . . . . . . . . . . . . . . . . . . . . . . . . . . . . . .Model

*Magazines:*
**Playboy** (Apr 1986). . . . . . . . . . . . . . . . . . Playmate
**Playboy's Book of Lingerie** (Mar 1991) . . . . . Herself
• 14—Lower frontal nudity in hot pink lingerie.
••• 30—Breasts.
**Penthouse** (May 1992). . . . . . . . . . . . . Shooting Star
••• 110-121—Nude.
**Playboy's Calendar Playmates** (Nov 1992) . . Herself
••• 61—Full frontal nudity.

# Weiss, Amy-Rochelle

*Films:*
**Round Trip to Heaven** (1992). . . . . . . . . . . . .Yvette
••• 0:19—In black bra and G-string in bedroom with Corey Feldman, then breasts and buns on top of him in bed.

**Secret Games 2—The Escort** (1993). . . . . . . Stacey
(Unrated version reviewed.)
••• 0:09—Full frontal nudity, while making love with Martin Hewitt in front of fireplace.
••• 0:16—Nude, while in bedroom then making love with Hewitt on dining room table.
•• 0:19—Breasts, while sitting in bed with Hewitt and talking.
••• 0:21—Breasts in video playback and in bed while talking with Hewitt on the phone.
••• 0:24—Nude, after taking off coat, covering Hewitt with birthday cake and in the shower with him and Lisa.
•• 0:26—Breasts and buns while making love in bed with Lisa and Hewitt.
• 0:37—Breasts, several times in flashback.
• 0:38—Breasts on video playback.
••• 0:41—Breasts, while making love with Hector in bed while Hewitt watches.
••• 0:54—Breasts, while modeling clothes for Hewitt in bedroom.
••• 0:57—Breasts, while making love with Hewitt in newlywed fantasy.
•• 1:04—Breasts and buns, while making love on top of Hewitt in flashbacks.
•• 1:11—Breasts, while in bed with Hector while talking on the phone.
•• 1:13—Breasts on video playback.
•• 1:16—Brief breasts on video playback.

*Made for Cable Movies:*
**The Hit List** (1993; Showtime)
. . . . . . . . . . . . . . . . . . . Body Double for Yancy Butler
• 0:31—Buns, taking off swimsuit in front of Jeff Fahey. Long shot, don't see her face.
1:00—Brief left breast in bed while making love with Fahey. Don't see her face very well.

*Music Videos:*
What Comes Naturally/Sheena Easton
. . . . . . . . . . . . . . . . . . . . . . Body Double for Sheena

*Video Tapes:*
**Sexy Lingerie III** (1991). . . . . . . . . . . . . . . . . Model
**Intimate Workout For Lovers** (1992)
. . . . . . . . . . . . . . . . . . . . . . . . . . . . Water Workout
••• 0:21—Nude, outside by swimming pool and in pool.
**Playboy's Erotic Fantasies** (1992) . . . . .Cast Member
**Playboy's Erotic Fantasies III** (1993)
. . . . . . . . . . . . . . . . . . . Morning Splendor/Horserider
••• 0:14—Breasts in push-up bra, buns in G-string panties, garter belt and lingerie. Then nude while making love in the stable with a guy.

*Magazines:*
**Playboy's Book of Lingerie** (Jul 1991). . . . . . .Herself
••• 87—Breasts.
••• 107—Breasts.
**Playboy's Book of Lingerie** (Nov 1991) . . . . .Herself
••• 52—Breasts.
**Playboy's Book of Lingerie** (Jan 1992) . . . . . .Herself
••• 66—Breasts.

**Playboy's Book of Lingerie** (Mar 1992) . . . . . Herself
••• 100-101—Buns and breasts.
**Playboy's Book of Lingerie** (May 1992) . . . . . Herself
••• 70—Full frontal nudity.
**Playboy** (Jul 1992) . . . . . . . . . . . . . . . . . . . . . Grapevine
••• 170—Breasts in swimming pool. B&W.

## Weiss, Roberta

*Films:*
Autumn Born (1979) . . . . . . . . . . . . . . . . . . . . Melissa
0:07—Buns, wearing panties and bending over desk
to get whipped.
**Cross Country** (1983; Canadian) . . . . . . . . . Alma Jean
•• 0:59—Breasts on bed with two other people.
**The Dead Zone** (1983) . . . . . . . . . . . . Alma Frechette
• 0:49—Briefly in beige bra, then brief breasts when
the killer rips her blouse open during Christopher
Walken's vision.
Abducted (1986; Canadian) . . . . . . . . . . . . . . . . Renee
*Made for Cable TV:*
**The Hitchhiker: And If We Dream** (1987; HBO)
. . . . . . . . . . . . . . . . . . . . . . . . . . . . . . Rosanne Lucas
(Available on *The Hitchhiker, Volume 3.*)
•• 0:11—Breasts and buns in barn making love with
Stephen Collins.
•• 0:17—Breasts in dream classroom with Collins.
• 0:23—Brief breasts in bed after second dream with
Collins.

## Welch, Lisa

*Films:*
Revenge of the Nerds (1984) . . . . . . . . . . . . . . . . Suzy
*Magazines:*
**Playboy** (Sep 1980) . . . . . . . . . . . . . . . . . . . Playmate
••• 118-129—Full frontal nudity.

## Welch, Tahnee

Daughter of actress Raquel Welch.
*Films:*
Cocoon (1985) . . . . . . . . . . . . . . . . . . . . . . . . . . Kitty
1:01—Buns walking into swimming pool.
**Lethal Obsession** (1987; German) . . . . Daniela Santini
*a.k.a. The Joker*
0:14—Buns, putting on robe after talking to John on
the phone.
• 0:15—Half of left breast, taking off coat to hug John
in the kitchen.
0:16—Sort of left breast, in bed with John. Too dark
to see anything.
1:16—Buns, getting an injection.
Cocoon, The Return (1988) . . . . . . . . . . . . . . . . Kitty
*TV:*
Falcon Crest (1987-89) . . . . . . . . . . . . . . . . . Shannon

## Weldon, Cirsten

*Films:*
**Hard to Die** (1990) . . . . . . . . . . . . . . Agent's Girlfriend
*a.k.a. Tower of Terror*
• 0:19—Breasts in bedroom with Tess's agent. Medium long shot.
The Doors (1991) . . . . . . . . . . . . . . . . . . . . . Girl in Car

## Weller, Mary Louise

*Films:*
The Evil (1977) . . . . . . . . . . . . . . . . . . . . Laurie Belden
**Animal House** (1978) . . . . . . . . . . Mandy Pepperidge
••• 0:38—In white bra, then breasts in bedroom while
John Belushi watches on a ladder through the window.
The Bell Jar (1979) . . . . . . . . . . . . . . . . . . . . . Doreen
Blood Tide (1982) . . . . . . . . . . . . . . . . . . . . . . Sherry
**Forced Vengeance** (1982) . . . . . . . . . . . Claire Bonner
• 1:04—Brief breasts, struggling with the bad guy.
• 1:08—Very brief right breast then left breast, while
lying dead on the floor.
Q (1982) . . . . . . . . . . . . . . . . . . . . . . . . Mrs. Pauley

## Welles, Gwen

*Films:*
A Safe Place (1971) . . . . . . . . . . . . . . . . . . . . . . Bari
**Hit!** (1973) . . . . . . . . . . . . . . . . . . . . . Sherry Nielson
••• 2:03—Breasts, taking off her clothes in front of a
woman before killing her.
California Split (1974) . . . . . . . . . . . . . . . . Susan Peters
**Nashville** (1975) . . . . . . . . . . . . . . . . . . . Sueleen Gay
•• 2:09—In bra singing to a room full of men, then
breasts doing a strip tease, buns walking up the
steps and out of the room.
**Between the Lines** (1977) . . . . . . . . . . . . . . . . Laura
•• 0:32—Buns and breasts drying off with a towel in
front of a mirror.
Desert Hearts (1986) . . . . . . . . . . . . . . . . . . . . Gwen
The Men's Club (1986) . . . . . . . . . . . . . . . . . Redhead
Sticky Fingers (1988) . . . . . . . . . . . . . . . . . . . Marcie
Eating (1990) . . . . . . . . . . . . . . . . . . . . . . . . . Sophie
*Magazines:*
**Playboy** (Nov 1972) . . . . . . Variation of a Vadim Theme
••• 111-115—Full frontal nudity.
**Playboy** (May 1975) . . . . . . . . . . The Splendor of Gwen
••• 96-99—Nude.
**Playboy** (Nov 1975) . . . . . . . . . . Sex in Cinema 1975
••• 131—Breasts in still photo from *Nashville.*
**Playboy** (Dec 1975) . . . . . . . . . . . . . Sex Stars of 1975
••• 188—Breasts and partial lower frontal nudity.

## Welles, Jennifer

*Films:*
**Sugar Cookies** (1973) . . . . . . . . . . . . Max's Secretary
• 0:28—Breasts in red panties in Max's office while he
talks on the phone, then lower frontal nudity.
•• 0:56—Full frontal nudity getting dressed.

**The Groove Tube** (1974) . . . . . . . . . The Geritan Girl
•• 0:21—Dancing nude around her husband, Chevy Chase.
**Is There Sex After Death?** (1975)
. . . . . . . . . . . . . . . . . Magic Act/Merkin's Assistant
•• 0:41—Brief left breast and buns, while helping Merkin, then full frontal nudity.
*Magazines:*
**Playboy** (Nov 1977) . . . . . . . . . . Sex in Cinema 1977
••• 164—Full frontal nudity from *Honeypie.*
**Playboy** (Dec 1977). . . . . . . . . . . . Sex Stars of 1977
••• 217—Full frontal nudity.

## Welles, Terri
*Films:*
**Looker** (1981) . . . . . . . . . . . . . . . . . . . . . . . . . . . Lisa
• 0:02—Brief breasts getting photographed for operation. In black bra and panties in her apartment a lot.
The Firm (1993) . . . . . . . . Woman Dancing With Avery
*Video Tapes:*
**Playboy's Playmates of the Year: The '80s** (1989)
. . . . . . . . . . . . . . . . . . . . Playmate of the Year 1981
••• 0:08—Nude in still photos.
••• 0:10—Nude at the beach.
••• 0:11—Nude in still photos.
•• 0:51—Breasts coming out of the water.
*Magazines:*
**Playboy** (Dec 1980). . . . . . . . . . . . . . . . . . Playmate
••• 184-197—Nude.
**Playboy** (Jun 1981) . . . . . . . . . . . Playmate of the Year
**Playboy's Girls of Summer '86** (Aug 1986) . . Herself
• 98—Right breast.
**Playboy's Nudes** (Oct 1990). . . . . . . . . . . . . Herself
• 103—Side view of left breast.
**Playboy** (Jan 1994) . . . . . . . . . . . 40 Memorable Years
••• 94—Full frontal nudity.

## Wells, Aarika
*Films:*
**Sharky's Machine** (1981). . . . . . . . . . . . . . . Tiffany
• 0:52—Brief side view breasts (mostly silhouette) in Rachel Ward's apartment.
Walking the Edge (1985). . . . . . . . . . . . . . . . . . Julia
*TV:*
Supertrain (1979) . . . . . . . . . . . . . . . . . . . . . . Gilda

## Wells, Victoria
*Films:*
**Cheech & Chong's Nice Dreams** (1981)
. . . . . . . . . . . . . . . . . . . . . . . . . . . Beach Girl #1
• 0:29—Brief breasts on the beach with two other girls. Long shot, unsteady, hard to see.
• 0:32—More brief breasts again.
• 0:33—More brief breasts again.
The Best Little Whorehouse in Texas (1982)
. . . . . . . . . . . . . . . . . . . . . . . . . . . Washing Girl
Losin' It (1982) . . . . . . . . . . . . . . . . . . . . . . . . . n.a.

## Wendel, Lara
*Films:*
Desire, The Interior Life (1980; Italian/German)
. . . . . . . . . . . . . . . . . . . . . . . . . . . . . . Desideria
Identification of a Woman (1983; Italian) . . . . . . . . . n.a.
Ghosthouse (1989; Italian). . . . . . . . . . . . . . . Martha
**Husbands and Lovers** (1991; Italian) . . . . . . . . Louisa
(Unrated version reviewed.)
••• 0:47—In bra and panties with Julian Sands, then breasts making love with him.
*Magazines:*
**Playboy** (Nov 1992) . . . . . . . . . . Sex in Cinema 1992
•• 144—Left breast with Julian Sands from *Husbands and Lovers.*

## Werchan, Bonnie
*Films:*
**Auditions** (1978) . . . . . . . . . . . . . . . . . Tracy Matthews
••• 0:02—Breasts, then full frontal nudity, undressing for her audition.
••• 0:31—Nude, undressing herself and Van.
•• 0:33—Buns and side of right breast, making love with Van.
•• 1:07—Breasts and buns during orgy scene.
Summer Camp (1979) . . . . . . . . . . . . . . . . . . . . . n.a.

## • West, Jennifer
See: Swift, Sally.

## • Westcott, Carrie
*Films:*
Ring of Fire II: Blood and Steel (1992)
. . . . . . . . . . . . . . . . . . . . . . Bad Girl Gang Member
*Video Tapes:*
**Playboy Night Dreams** (1993) . . . . . . . . . . . . . Detour
••• 0:04—Nude after stripping out of bra, panties, garter belt and stockings, after picking up a guy and making love in house.
**Wet and Wild: The Locker Room** (1994) . . Playmate
*Magazines:*
**Playboy** (Sep 1993) . . . . . . . . . . . . . . . . . . . Playmate
••• 102-113—Nude.
**Playboy** (Jan 1994) . . . . . . . . Playboy's Playmate Review
••• 202—Full frontal nudity.
**Playboy's Playmate Review** (May 1994)
. . . . . . . . . . . . . . . . . . . . . . . . . . Miss September
••• 74-81—Nude.
**Playboy's Girls of Summer '94** (Jul 1994) . . . . Herself
••• 10—Breasts.
•• 81—Left breast and lower frontal nudity.
**Playboy's Book of Lingerie** (Jul 1994) . . . . . . . Herself
••• 52-53—Breasts.
••• 93—Breasts.
**Playboy's Book of Lingerie** (Sep 1994) . . . . . . Herself
••• 12—Full frontal nudity.

# Wharton, Wally Anne

*Films:*

**Up in Smoke** (1978) . . . . . . . . . . . . . . . . . . : . . . . Debbie
   1:03—Brief back side of left breast, while in back of
   van with Cheech Marin.

**Cheerleaders Wild Weekend** (1985) . . . Lisa/Darwell
  •• 0:06—Breasts in back of school bus, flashing a guy
   in pickup truck, then pressing her breasts against the
   window.
  ••• 0:37—Breasts, opening her white blouse during
   contest.
  ••• 0:39—Breasts and brief buns, in white skirt during
   contest.

Last Resort (1985) . . . . . . . . . . . . . . . . . . . . . . Wanda

*Video Tapes:*

Thunder and Mud (1989) . . . . . . . . . . Wanda Wallinsky

*Magazines:*

**Playboy** (Nov 1985) . . . . . . . . . . . Sex in Cinema 1985
  •• 129—Breasts in back of bus from *Cheerleaders Wild
   Weekend.*

# Whirry, Shannon

*Films:*

Out for Justice (1991) . . . . . . . . . . . . . . . . Terry Malloy

**Animal Instincts** (1992). . . . . . . . . . . . . Joanne Cole
(Unrated version reviewed.)
   0:01—In bra and panties during opening credits.
  ••• 0:18—In white bra and panties in bed then full frontal nudity during her fantasies with several guys.
  •• 0:23—Breasts and buns, in various lingerie outfits, in
   front of mirror.
  •• 0:26—Full frontal nudity under sheer white body
   suit, trying to get Maxwell Caulfield interested in
   her.
  •• 0:28—Breasts while taking a bath.
  ••• 0:30—Nude in bed, making love with the Cable TV
   guy.
   0:36—In bra and panties, while talking on the telephone.
   0:38—In bra and panties, while in bed.
  ••• 0:43—In bra and panties, then nude while in bed
   with the Assistant DA while Caulfield watches on TV.
  ••• 0:46—Breasts, while sitting in bed with Caulfield.
  •• 0:50—Breasts with Delia Sheppard and a guy.
  ••• 0:51—In black bra and panties on TV after undressing as a businessman. Breasts in bed with a guy.
  ••• 0:54—Breasts in bedroom and on bed with Delia.
  ••• 0:59—In black bra and panties, then breasts and
   buns with Mitch Gaylord in bedroom while making
   love.
   1:03—In black bra, panties, garter belt and stockings in her bedroom.
  • 1:16—Buns in G-string and side of left breast, while
   in bed with Jan-Michael Vincent.

**Body of Influence** (1992). . . . . . . . . . . . . Laura/Lana
(Unrated version reviewed.)
  ••• 0:08—Breasts on bed with her lover during recollection for Jonathon.

  • 0:16—Left breast, while on bed, tied by wrists and
   getting raped during recollection.
  •• 0:26—In black bra, undressing in office. Right
   breast, while lying on desk. Buns in panties.
  ••• 0:44—In burgundy bra and panties with Jonathon in
   his house. Then nude, while making love in living
   room. Long scene.
  ••• 1:05—In black bra, then breasts and buns, while
   making love on top of Jonathon.
  ••• 1:08—Breasts, while sitting up in bed and talking to
   Jonathon.

**Animal Instincts 2** (1993) . . . . . . . . . . . . . . . Joanna
  ••• 0:11—Breasts, in bed with a fantasy lover while she
   imagines another guy watching them make love.
  ••• 0:30—Breasts, while rubbing lotion on herself in the
   backyard while Steve watches from his backyard.
  • 0:38—Brief breasts, while in her bedroom. Seen on
   video monitor.
  ••• 0:47—Full frontal nudity while making love with a
   guy she picks up in a bar while Steve watches on video monitor.
  ••• 0:49—Nude, while making love in bedroom with a
   woman she picks up in a bar.
  •• 0:53—Left breast, while opening her robe and talking on the phone.
  ••• 1:01—Nude, while posing for Eric in his studio.
  •• 1:04—Breasts, while taking a shower.
  • 1:05—Brief left breast in photos that Eric shows her.
  •• 1:07—In white bra and panties, then breasts and
   buns while making love with Eric.

**Mirror Images II** (1993) . . . . . . . . . . . . Carrie/Terrie
  ••• 0:03—Nude, while taking a shower during the
   opening credits. Then breasts, while making love on
   top of her twin sister's boyfriend in bed.
  • 0:19—Buns in panties and bra while trying on lingerie in front of mirror.
  ••• 0:25—Full frontal nudity while making love with her
   female psychologist, Dr. Rubin. Long scene.
  ••• 0:31—Nude, while making love outside in pool with
   Dan before getting caught by Phyllis
  ••• 0:39—In black bra, then full frontal nudity while
   making love on bed with Clete. She gives him a hot
   wax treatment. Long scene.
  • 0:49—Breasts, while making love in bed with a customer while Jake watches from outside the window.
   Long shot.
  ••• 0:56—In black bra and panties, the full frontal nudity while making love in bedroom with a customer.
  •• 1:01—In white bra, then breasts and buns in G-
   string with another woman in hotel room.
  ••• 1:10—Breasts, while making love in bed with Jake.
   Long scene.
  • 1:27—Breasts while making love with Jake (in B&W).

*Video Tapes:*

Eden 6 (1994) . . . . . . . . . . . . . . . . . . . . Lauren's Friend

# Whitaker, Christina

*Films:*

**The Naked Cage** (1985) . . . . . . . . . . . . . . . . . . . . .Rita
- ••• 0:08—Breasts in bed with Willy.
- • 0:55—Brief breasts in gaping sweatshirt during fight with Sheila.
- 1:28—Panties during fight with Shari Shattuck.
- 1:29—Sort of left breast in gaping dress.

Assault of the Killer Bimbos (1988) . . . . . . . . . Peaches
Midnight Cabaret (1988) . . . . . . . . . . . . . . . . . Dancer
Stormquest (1988) . . . . . . . . . . . . . . . . . . . . . . . . Asha
Vampire at Midnight (1988) . . . . . . . . . . . . . . . .Ingrid

*Made for Cable TV:*

**Love Street: Seven Fifteen** (1993; Showtime)
. . . . . . . . . . . . . . . . . . . . . . . . . . . . . . . . . . . Eve Sutter
- 0:08—In bra in motel room with Jack.
- ••• 0:09—Breasts and buns, while making love in bed with Jack.
- 0:14—In white bra, panties, garter belt and stockings while in motel room with Jack.
- • 0:15—Brief breasts while tied to the bed by her wrists.
- 0:18—In black bra, panties, garter belt and stocking in motel room with Jack.
- •• 0:19—Brief breasts, while dropping her towel.
- ••• 0:20—Breasts, while making love in bed with Jack.
- ••• 0:22—Breasts, while making love in bed.

# Whitcraft, Elizabeth

*Films:*

Birdy (1985) . . . . . . . . . . . . . . . . . . . . . . . . . Rosanne
**Angel Heart** (1987) . . . . . . . . . . . . . . . . . . . . . Connie
(Original Unedited Version reviewed.)
(Blonde hair.)
- •• 0:33—Breasts in bed talking with Mickey Rourke while taking off her clothes.

**Working Girl** (1989). . . . . . . . . . . . . Doreen DiMucci
(Brunette hair.)
- •• 0:29—Breasts on bed on Alec Baldwin when Melanie Griffith opens the door and discovers them.

GoodFellas (1990). . . . . . . . Tommy's Girlfriend at Copa
Where Sleeping Dogs Lie (1991) . . . . . Serena's Secretary

*Video Tapes:*

**Inside Out 2** (1992)
. . . . . . . . . . . . . . . Sarah/Some Guys Have All the Luck
(Unrated version reviewed.)
- ••• 1:10—Breasts taking off her top in bed. More breasts in bed. Brief partial buns.

**Eden 3** (1993) . . . . . . . . . . . . . . . . . . . . . . . . . . . Val
- •• 0:15—Left breast, while lying in bed under Lyle.
- ••• 0:29—Breasts while in room, then making love with Lyle.
- ••• 1:03—Breasts while taking off her swimsuit top outside in front of Lyle.

# • White, April Daisy

*Films:*

**Silent Madness** (1984) . . . . . . . . . . . . . . . . . . . .Susan
- • 0:06—Breasts, while changing tops at back of van.

**Violated** (1987) . . . . . . . . . . . . . . . . . . . . . . .Lisa Robb
- ••• 0:16—Breasts, while wearing panties while getting dressed in bedroom while talking to her little brother.
- •• 0:22—Breasts, after taking off her dress and diving into pool.
- •• 0:25—Full frontal nudity while getting raped in bedroom by Jack while Marilyn and Frank help.
- • 0:28—Breasts and lower frontal nudity while washing herself off in bathtub.
- •• 0:40—Breasts in flashback of rape scene.
- • 0:53—Full frontal nudity in flashback of rape scene.
- • 1:08—Breasts on video playback of taking her dress off by pool.

# • White, Carol

*Films:*

Never Let Go (1960; British). . . . . . . . . . . . . . . .Jackie
Daddy's Gone A-Hunting (1969) . . . . . . . .Cathy Palmer
The Man Who Had Power Over Women (1970; British)
. . . . . . . . . . . . . . . . . . . . . . . . . . . . . . . . . .Jody Pringle
Something Big (1971; British) . . . . . . . .Dover MacBride
Some Call It Loving (1972). . . . . . . . . . . . . . . Scarlett
Up the Sandbox (1972) . . . . . . . . . .Miss Spittlemeister
**The Squeeze** (1977; British) . . . . . . . . . . . . . . . . . . Jill
- ••• 0:58—Nude, after taking off her clothes in front of the three bad guys. Long scene.

*Magazines:*

**Playboy** (Nov 1973) . . . . . . . . . . . Sex in Cinema 1973
- •• 156—Breasts in photo from *Some Call It Loving.*

# White, Sheila

*Films:*

Here We Go Round the Mulberry Bush (1968; British)
. . . . . . . . . . . . . . . . . . . . . . . . . . . . . . . . . . . . . Paula
Oliver! (1968; British). . . . . . . . . . . . . . . . . . . . . . .Bet
Confessions of a Window Cleaner (1974; British) . . Rosie
Confessions of a Pop Performer (1975; British). . . . Rosie
Oh, Alfie! (1975; British). . . . . . . . . . . . . . . . . . .Norma
*a.k.a. Alfie Darling*

*Miniseries:*

**I, Claudius—Episode 12, A God in Colchester**
(1976; British) . . . . . . . . . . . . . . . . . . . Lady Messalina
(Available on video tape in *I, Claudius—Volume 6.*)
- •• 0:00—Left breast, in bed with Mnester.
- • 0:02—Buns, getting out of bed and putting on a sheer dress.
- • 0:18—Right breast, in bed with Silius.
- ••• 0:29—Breasts in bed with Silius.

# White, Vanna

*Films:*

**Gypsy Angels** (1980) . . . . . . . . . . . . . . . . . . . Mickey
    0:20—Dancing on stage in club in two piece swim-
    suit outfit.
    0:46—Silhouette of breasts from behind shower cur-
    tain.
   • 0:46—Partial right breast, while making out with Jeff
    outside by a fire.
    1:12—Back side of left breast while getting into bed
    during Jeff's flashback.
Graduation Day (1981) . . . . . . . . . . . . . . . . . . . . .Doris
Looker (1981) . . . . . . . . . . . . . . . . . . . . . . Reston Girl
Naked Gun 33 1/3: The Final Insult (1993) . . . . . Herself
*Made for TV Movies:*
The Goddess of Love (1988) . . . . . . . . . . . . . . . . Venus
*TV:*
Wheel of Fortune (1982- ) . . . . . . . . . . . . . . . .Hostess
*Video Tapes:*
Vanna White—Get Slim, Stay Slim . . . . . . . . . . Herself
*Magazines:*
**Penthouse** (Feb 1983) . . . . . Ad for Paradise Company
  •• 165—In lingerie in four small photos.
**Playboy** (May 1987) . . . . . . . . . . . . . . . . . . . . .Vanna
  ••• 134-143—In sheer lingerie from catalog she did be-
    fore *Wheel of Fortune.*
**Playboy** (Dec 1987) . . . . . . . . . . . . . Sex Stars of 1987
  ••• 150—In sheer black lingerie.
**Playboy** (Dec 1988) . . . . . . . . . . . . . Sex Stars of 1988
  •• 183—Right breast under lingerie.
**Playboy** (Jan 1994) . . . . . . . . . . . . . Remember Vanna
  •• 188-189—Breasts and buns in sheer lingerie.

# Whitfield, Lynn

*Films:*

Doctor Detroit (1983) . . . . . . . . . . . . . Thelma Cleland
Silverado (1985) . . . . . . . . . . . . . . . . . . . . . . . . . . .Ray
The Slugger's Wife (1985) . . . . . . . . . . . . . Tina Alvarado
Dead Aim (1987) . . . . . . . . . . . . . . . . . Sheila Freeman
Jaws: The Revenge (1987) . . . . . . . . . . . . . . . . . .Louisa
Taking the Heat (1993) . . . . . . . . . . . . . . . . . . .Carolyn
*Made for Cable Movies:*
**The Josephine Baker Story** (1991; HBO)
    . . . . . . . . . . . . . . . . . . . . . . . . . . . Josephine Baker
   • 0:00—Breasts while dancing during opening credits.
    Slow motion.
  •• 0:13—Breasts after taking off her dress top for the
    French painter.
 ••• 0:14—Breasts in the mirror and while dancing with
    the painter after making love. Nice. Dancer doing
    splits looks like a body double.
    0:16—Brief buns, in wet dress, getting out of swim-
    ming pool.
 ••• 0:31—Breasts while on stage doing the Banana
    Dance.
 ••• 0:33—Breasts, while doing the Banana Dance.
   • 2:02—Brief breasts while dancing in flashback.
State of Emergency (1993; HBO) . . . . . .Dehlia Johnson

*Miniseries:*
Women of Brewster Place (1989) . . . . . . . . . . . . . .Ciel
*Made for TV Movies:*
Triumph of the Heart: The Ricky Bell Story (1991)
  . . . . . . . . . . . . . . . . . . . . . . . . . . . . . . . . .Natala
The Cosby Mysteries (1994) . . . . . . . . . Barbara Lorenz
Thicker Than Blood: The Larry McLinden Story (1994)
  . . . . . . . . . . . . . . . . . . . . . . . . . . Bobbie Mallory
*TV:*
Heartbeat (1988-89) . . . . . . . . . . . . . .Dr. Cory Banks
Equal Justice (1991) . . . . . . . . . . . . . . Maggie Mayfield
The Cosby Mysteries (1994- ) . . . . . . . . Barbara Lorenz
*Magazines:*
**Playboy** (Apr 1991) . . . . . . . . . . . . . . . . . Grapevine
  ••• 170—Breasts in B&W photo from *The Josephine Bak-*
    *er Story.*
**Playboy** (Jan 1992) . . . . . . . . . . . . . . . The Year in Sex
  ••• 148—Breasts from *The Josephine Baker Story.*

# Whitlow, Jill

*Films:*

Porky's (1981; Canadian) . . . . . . . . . . . . . . . . . Mindy
Mask (1985) . . . . . . . . . . . . . . . . . . . . . .Annie Marie
Weird Science (1985) . . . . . . . . . . . . . Perfume Salesgirl
**Night of the Creeps** (1986) . . . . Cynthia Cronenberg
    0:31—In bra and panties taking off sweater.
   • 0:33—Brief breasts putting nightgown on over her
    head in her bedroom.
Thunder Run (1986) . . . . . . . . . . . . . . . . . . . . . . Kim
Twice Dead (1989) . . . . . . . . . . . . . . . . . .Robin/Myrna
    0:27—In white slip, getting ready for bed, then
    walking around the house.

# Whitman, Kari

a.k.a. Kari Kennel.
*Films:*
Masterblaster (1986) . . . . . . . . . . . . . . . . . . . Jennifer
Beverly Hills Cop II (1987) . . . . . . . . . . .Playboy Model
Phantom of the Mall: Eric's Revenge (1988)
  . . . . . . . . . . . . . . . . . . . . . . . . . . . Melody Austin
Men at Work (1990) . . . . . . . . . . . . . . . . . . . . . .Judy
Chained Heat 2 (1993) . . . . . . . . . . . Suzanne Morrison
Forced to Kill (1993) . . . . . . . . . . . . . . . . . . . Heather
*Video Tapes:*
**Rock Video Girls** (1991) . . . . . . . . . . . Small Town Girl
   • 0:31—Breasts under sheer white nightie.
**Playboy Playmates in Paradise** (1992) . . . . Playmate
*Magazines:*
**Playboy** (Feb 1988) . . . . . . . . . . . . . . . . . . . Playmate
**Playboy Presents Playmates in Paradise**
  (Mar 1994) . . . . . . . . . . . . . . . . . . . . . . . . . Playmate
  ••• 86-91—Full frontal nudity.

# Whitting, Robyn

*Films:*

Innocent Sally (1973) . . . . . . . . . . . . . . . . . . . . . . .n.a.
   *a.k.a. The Dirty Mind of Young Sally*
**Video Vixens** (1973). . . . . . . . . . . Patient and Virginia
  •• 0:40—Breasts, then nude on couch in psychiatrist's
    office. In B&W.
  •• 0:52—Full frontal nudity acting in bed with Rex for
    a film. In B&W.

# Whitton, Margaret

*Films:*

Love Child (1982) . . . . . . . . . . . . . . . . . Jacki Steinberg
National Lampoon Goes to the Movies (1982)
 . . . . . . . . . . . . . . . . . . . . . . . . . . . . . First Lady
   *a.k.a. Movie Madness*
9 1/2 Weeks (1986). . . . . . . . . . . . . . . . . . . . . Molly
The Best of Times (1986). . . . . . . . . . . . . . . . . . Darla
**Ironweed** (1987). . . . . . . . . . . . . . . . . . . . . . Katrina
  •• 1:19—Full frontal nudity leaving the house and
    walking down steps while young Francis brushes a
    horse.
**The Secret of My Success** (1987) . . . . . .Vera Prescott
  • 0:31—Very brief breasts taking off swimsuit top in
    swimming pool with Michael J. Fox.
Little Monsters (1989). . . . . . . . . . . . . . Holly Stevenson
Major League (1989). . . . . . . . . . . . . . . . Rachel Phelps
Big Girls Don't Cry... They Get Even (1991) . . . Melinda
The Man Without a Face (1993) . . . . . . . . . . Catherine
*Made for TV Movies:*
The Summer My Father Grew Up (1991) . . . . . . Naomi
Menendez: A Killing in Beverly Hills (1994)
 . . . . . . . . . . . . . . . . . . . . . . . . . . Leslie Abramson
*TV:*
Hometown (1985) . . . . . . . . . . . . . . Barbara Donnelly
Fine Romance (1989) . . . . . . . . . . . . . . . . . .Louisa
Good & Evil (1991). . . . . . . . . . . . . . . . . . . . Genny

# Widdoes, Kathleen

*Films:*

The Group (1966). . . . . . . . . . . . . . . . .Helena Davidson
Petulia (1968; U.S./British) . . . . . . . . . . . . . . . . .Wilma
The Sea Gull (1968) . . . . . . . . . . . . . . . . . . . . Masha
The Mephisto Waltz (1971). . . . . . . . . . . . Maggie West
Savages (1972) . . . . . . . . . . . . . . . . . . . . . . . Leslie
The End of August (1974). . . . . . . . . . . . . . . . . Adele
I'm Dancing as Fast as I Can (1981) . . . . . . Dr. Rawlings
Without a Trace (1983) . . . . . . . . . . . . . . . Ms. Hauser
*TV:*
As the World Turns . . . . . . . . . . . . . . . . Emma Snyder
*Magazines:*
**Playboy** (Mar 1972). . . . . . . . . . . . . . . . . . Savages
  • 142—Breasts.
  • 145—Breasts.

# Wiesmeier, Lynda

*Films:*

Joysticks (1983) . . . . . . . . . . . . . . . . . . . . . . Candy
**Private School** (1983) . . . . . . . . . . . . . . . .School Girl
  ••• 0:42—Nude in shower room scene. First blonde in
    shower on the left.
**Malibu Express** (1984) . . . . . . . . . . . . June Khnockers
  •• 0:04—Breasts in locker room taking jumpsuit off.
  • 1:16—Breasts leaning out of racing car window
    while a helicopter chases her and Cody.
**Preppies** (1984) . . . . . . . . . . . . . . . . . . . . . . .Trini
    0:54—In bra and panties, practicing sexual positions
    on beds with Margot.
  ••• 1:06—Breasts on bed with Mark.
**R.S.V.P.** (1984) . . . . . . . . . . . . . . . . . Jennifer Edwards
  •• 0:11—Breasts diving into the pool while Toby fanta-
    sizes about her being nude.
  • 0:19—Breasts in kitchen when Toby fantasizes about
    her again.
  ••• 1:21—Nude getting out of the pool and kissing To-
    by, when she really is nude.
Touch and Go (1984). . . . . . . . . . . . . . . . . Girl in Bar
**Wheels of Fire** (1984) . . . . . . . . . . . . . . . . . . .Arlie
   *a.k.a. Desert Warrior*
  ••• 0:18—Breasts on the ground, being held down by
    two bad guys, then getting tied to hood of car.
  •• 0:20—More breasts, long shot, tied to hood of car.
  • 0:22—More breasts while tied to the hood of the
    car.
  • 0:23—Breasts, being brought into tent.
  ••• 0:34—Breasts, chained up in tent and trying to es-
    cape. Long scene.
  •• 0:45—Left breast, while lying on cot.
  •• 0:47—Breasts outside, fighting off crowd of guys.
Avenging Angel (1985) . . . . . . . . . . . . . . . . . . Debbie
Real Genius (1985). . . . . . . . . . . . . . Chris' Girl at Party
Teen Wolf (1985) . . . . . . . . . . . . . . . . . . . . . . . n.a.
**Evil Town** (1987) . . . . . . . . . . . . . . . . . . . . Dianne
  ••• 0:09—Breasts, while on top of Tony outside while
    camping.
  •• 0:11—Right breast while making out with boyfriend
    outside. Breasts when getting up.
  • 0:13—Breasts in open blouse, while running from
    bad guy. Nice bouncing action.
  ••• 0:15—Breasts, while getting captured by bad guys.
  •• 0:17—Breasts, when getting out of car and brought
    into the house.
  •• 0:23—Breasts while tied up in chair.
Going Undercover (1988; British). . . . . . . . . Beach Girl
*Video Tapes:*
**Playboy's Playmate Review** (1982) . . . . . . . Playmate
  ••• 1:17—Nude undressing and taking a shower. Wow!
    Then in ballet studio.
**Playboy Video Magazine, Volume 2** (1983)
 . . . . . . . . . . . . . . . . . . . . . . . . . . . . . Playmate
  ••• 1:12—In bra, stockings and garter belt. Undressing
    then full frontal nudity taking a shower.
  ••• 1:18—Nude, working out in dance studio.

**Playboy Video Magazine, Volume 5** (1983)
. . . . . . . . . . . . . . . . . . . . . . . . . . . . . . . . . . . Playmate
- 0:06—Brief breasts in shower.

**Red Hot Rock** (1984) . . . . . . . . . . . . . .Girl in Shower
*a.k.a. Sexy Shorts (on laser disc)*
- 0:01—Brief upper half of buns, then breasts taking off bra while a guy peeks into the locker room during "Girls" by Dwight Tilley.
- 0:02—Brief full frontal nudity in the shower. (On the left.)

**Wet and Wild** (1989) . . . . . . . . . . . . . . . . . . . .Model
**Playmates at Play** (1990) . . . . . . . . . . . . .Hardbodies
*Magazines:*
**Playboy** (Jul 1982) . . . . . . . . . . . . . . . . . . . . Playmate
**Playboy's Calendar Playmates** (Nov 1992) . . Herself
- 26—Buns.

# • *Wilbur, Claire*

*Films:*
**Score** (1973) . . . . . . . . . . . . . . . . . . . . . . . . . Elvira
- 0:01—Brief breasts, while making love with Jack.
- 0:04—Brief buns, after taking off overcoat.
- 0:13—Left breast, while on bed in open blouse, lying on bed for Lynn Lowry to take a picture.
- ••• 0:20—Full frontal nudity after taking off her robe in front of Mike. Buns, while making love.
- 0:33—Brief breasts, while taking off bra.
- 0:53—Brief right breast while sitting back in bed.
- •• 0:59—Breasts, after taking off her dress to go to sleep with Betsy.
- 1:02—Brief left breast, while in bed with Betsy.
- ••• 1:09—Full frontal nudity while standing up in bed, making love with Betsy.
- ••• 1:12—Breasts, while making love with Lynn.
- 1:15—Breasts, while waking up in bed.
- 1:22—Right breast, while in bed with everybody.
- 1:24—Breasts, while in bed.

Teenage Hitchikers (1975). . . . . . . . . . . . . . . . . . .n.a.

# *Wilcox, Mary*

*Films:*
Lepke (1975; U.S./Israeli) . . . . . . . . . . . . . . . . Marion
*Magazines:*
**Playboy** (Oct 1974). . . . . . . . . . . . . . . . . .Lepke's Lady
- ••• 85-91—Nude.

**Playboy** (Nov 1975) . . . . . . . . . . . Sex in Cinema 1975
- 132—Side of left breast, while in bed with Tony Curtis in still photo from *Lepke*.

# *Wilcox, Toyah*

British singer.
*Films:*
Jubilee (1977) . . . . . . . . . . . . . . . . . . . . . . . . . . Mad
Quadrophenia (1979; British) . . . . . . . . . . . . . . Monkey
The Tempest (1979; British) . . . . . . . . . . . . . . . Miranda
**The Ebony Tower** (1985) . . . . . . . . . . . . . . . . . Freak
- 0:37—Full frontal nudity, undressing and going skinny dipping in lake. Long shot.

- 0:38—Buns and side of right breast, kneeling during picnic after swimming.
- 0:39—Buns, while lying down next to Lawrence Olivier.
- •• 0:40—Buns, while lying next to Greta Scacchi and talking to David.
- •• 0:44—More buns, while talking to David and watching him go swimming.

Anchoress (1993; British) . . . . . . . . . Pauline Carpenter

# *Wild, Kelley*

*Video Tapes:*
**The Best of the Mermaids** (1992) . . . . . .Heartstrings
- ••• 0:35—Nude, while playing harp.

**Hot Body International: #3 Lingerie Special**
(1992) . . . . . . . . . . . . . . . . . . . . . . . . . . .Contestant
- ••• 0:22—Buns in purple and black bra and G-string.
- ••• 0:55—1st place winner. Breasts, getting out of bed. Buns, in G-string. Breasts in bathtub.
- ••• 0:57—Buns and breasts, getting a massage.

**Hot Body International: #5 Miss Acapulco** (1992)
. . . . . . . . . . . . . . . . . . . . . . . . . . . . . . . .Contestant
- •• 0:01—Brief breasts while saying "Hi Mom!"
- ••• 0:39—Breasts, taking off her bikini top.
- •• 0:40—Buns, dancing in green two piece swimsuit.

Mermaids of Sand, Sea and Surf (1993) . . . . . . . . . . n.a.
Vixens of Bandelero (1993) . . . . . . . . . . . . . . . . . . n.a.
Mermaids at War (1994) . . . . . . . . . . . . . . . . . . . n.a.
*Magazines:*
**Penthouse** (May 1988) . . . . . . . . . . . . . . . . . . . .Pet

# *Wild, Sándra*

*Films:*
**Body Waves** (1991) . . . . . . . . . . . . . . . . . . . . . . Anita
- ••• 0:39—Breasts under sheer white robe, then breasts with Larry on chair.
- ••• 1:12—Breasts in bedroom with Larry.

California Hot Wax (1992) . . . . . . . . . . . . . . .Bikini Girl
**Sunset Grill** (1992) . . . . . . . . . . . . . . Mrs. Pietrowski
0:03—Out-of-focus breasts, while making love. Seen through telephoto camera lens.
- ••• 0:04—Breasts in bed with her lover, then nude while struggling in bedroom with her husband.

**Fit To Kill** (1993) . . . . . . . . . . . . . . . . . . . . . . . Sandy
- ••• 0:07—Breasts, while talking on phone while standing in spa. Buns in gold swimsuit bottom, while getting out. Breasts while pouring coffee.
- ••• 0:21—Breasts in spa in long shot. More breasts in closer shot while putting swimsuit on.
- 0:55—In two piece swimsuit.
- 1:11—Buns, while wearing a sexy black swimsuit/lingerie outfit.
- 1:30—In two piece swimsuit.

*Made for Cable TV:*
Sessions: Episode 2 (1991; HBO) . . . . . . . . . . . . Amber
*Video Tapes:*
**Wet and Wild** (1989) . . . . . . . . . . . . . . . . . . . . Model
**Sexy Lingerie II** (1990) . . . . . . . . . . . . . . . . . Model

**Inside Out 4** (1992) . . . . . . . Blonde Woman/The Thief
(Unrated version reviewed.)
••• 0:44—Breasts, sitting up in bed and getting out.
**Playboy's 101 Ways to Excite Your Lover** (1992)
. . . . . . . . . . . . . . . . . . . . . . . . . . . . . .Smell/Woman
••• 0:08—Nude in green robe in bedroom.
**Rock Video Girls 2** (1992) . . . . . . . . . . . . . . . Herself
0:00—Brief partial right breast, by water pump dur-
ing opening credits.
0:16—In sheer black blouse in B&W photo session.
0:19—In braless white tank top in music video.
••• 0:21—Breasts taking off her tank top by water pump
in music video.
*Magazines:*
**Playboy's Book of Lingerie** (Jul 1991) . . . . . . Herself
••• 58—Breasts.
**Playboy** (Aug 1991). . . . . . . . . . . . .California Dreamin'
•• 136—Side view of right breast, while bending over.
**Playboy's Book of Lingerie** (Sep 1991) . . . . . Herself
••• 11—Breasts.
**Playboy's Book of Lingerie** (Nov 1991) . . . . . Herself
••• 40—Breasts.
**Playboy's Book of Lingerie** (Jan 1992) . . . . . . Herself
••• 32—Breasts.
**Playboy's Girls of Summer '92** (Jun 1992). . . Herself
•• 26—Partial right breast and partial lower frontal nudity.
•• 38—Left breast.
**Playboy's Book of Lingerie** (Sep 1992) . . . . . Herself
•• 16—Right breast.
**Playboy's Nudes** (Dec 1992) . . . . . . . . . . . . . Herself
••• 91—Breasts.
**Playboy's Book of Lingerie** (Mar 1993) . . . . . Herself
••• 72—Breasts.
**Playboy's Wet & Wild Women** (Aug 1993) . . Herself
•• 51—Buns and side of right breast.
**Playboy's Blondes, Brunettes & Redheads**
(Sep 1993) . . . . . . . . . . . . . . . . . . . . . . . . . . Herself
••• 26—Breasts and buns.
**Playboy's Nudes** (Dec 1993) . . . . . . . . . . . . . Herself
•• 52—Buns.
• 74—Half of left breast.

# Wilde, Cecilia

*Films:*
**Psychos in Love** (1987) . . . . . . . . . . . . . . . . . . .Nikki
•• 0:08—Breasts, dancing on stage in a bar.
••• 0:14—Buns, in G-string while dancing on stage,
then breasts.
•• 0:45—Breasts, dancing on stage with a fluorescent
light.
Pledge Night (1988) . . . . . . . . . . . . . . . . . . . . Connie

# Wildman, Valerie

*Films:*
Splash (1984) . . . . . . . . . . . . . . . . . . . . .Wedding Guest
The Falcon and the Snowman (1985)
. . . . . . . . . . . . . . . . . . . . . . . . U.S. Embassy Official
A Fine Mess (1986) . . . . . . . . . . . . . . . . Anchorwoman

**Inner Sanctum** (1991). . . . . . . . . . . . . . Jennifer Reed
0:05—Wearing transparent light blue nightgown,
getting out of bed, into wheelchair.
•• 0:11—Right breast, while sitting on bed with Joseph
Bottoms.
Neon City (1991). . . . . . . . . . . . . . . . . . . . . . . . Sandy
Josh and S.A.M. (1993) . . . . . . . . Dallas Airline Officer
*Made for Cable TV:*
Tales From the Crypt: Came the Dawn (1993)
. . . . . . . . . . . . . . . . . . . . . . . Woman in Restaurant
*TV:*
Beverly Hills, 90210 (1993- ) . . . . . . . . . . . . . Christine

# Wildsmith, Dawn

Ex-wife of director Fred Olen Ray.
*Films:*
Armed Response (1986). . . . . . . . . . . . . . . . . . . . Thug
Cyclone (1986) . . . . . . . . . . . . . . . . . . . . . . . . . . Henna
Star Slammer—The Escape (1986). . . . . . . . . . . . Muffin
**Surf Nazis Must Die** (1986) . . . . . . . . . . . . . . . . Eva
• 0:25—Breasts being fondled at the beach wearing a
wet suit by Adolf. Mostly right breast.
Commando Squad (1987) . . . . . . . . . . . . . . . Consuela
Evil Spawn (1987) . . . . . . . . . . . . . . . . . . Evelyn Avery
a.k.a. Donna Shock in this film.
Phantom Empire (1987). . . . . . . . . . . . . Eddy Colchilde
**The Tomb** (1987) . . . . . . . . . . . . . . . . . . . Anna Conda
••• 0:54—Breasts taking off robe in room with Michelle
Bauer, then getting pushed onto a bed full of snakes.
B.O.R.N. (1988). . . . . . . . . . . . . . . . . . . . . . . . . Singer
Deep Space (1988) . . . . . . . . . . . . . . . . . . . . . . Janice
Hollywood Chainsaw Hookers (1988). . . . . . . . . . . Lori
It's Alive III: Island of the Alive (1988)
. . . . . . . . . . . . . . . . . . . . Uncredited Dancer in Club
Warlords (1988). . . . . . . . . . . . . . . . . . . . . . . . Danny
Alienator (1989). . . . . . . . . . . . . . . . . . . . . . .Caroline
Beverly Hills Vamp (1989) . . . . . . . Sherry Santa Monica
Nerds of a Feather (1989) . . . . . . Fortune Telling Client
The Alien Within (1990). . . . . . . . . . . . . . Evelyn Avery
Contains footage from *The Evil Spawn* woven together
with new material.
Demon Sword (1991) . . . . . . . . . . . . . . . . . . . Selena
a.k.a. Wizards of the Demon Sword

# • Wiley, Laurel

*Films:*
**Shock 'Em Dead** (1990) . . . . . . . . . . . . . . Monique
• 0:26—Brief breasts, pulling her top down to show
Martin her scar. Don't see her face.
**Test Tube Teens From the Year 2000** (1993)
. . . . . . . . . . . . . . . . . . . . . . . . . . . . . . . . . . .Annie
a.k.a. Virgin Hunters
••• 0:30—Breasts, taking off towel and in the showers
(she's on the right) with Victoria while Vin and Naldo
watch.
*Magazines:*
**Playboy's Book of Lingerie** (Nov 1992) . . . . .Herself
•• 64—Breasts.

**Playboy's Blondes, Brunettes & Redheads**
(Sep 1993) . . . . . . . . . . . . . . . . . . . . . . . . . . Herself
••• 97—Breasts.

# Wilkening, Catherine

*Films:*
Contrainte Par Corps (1988; French). . . . . . . . . . . Lola
Deux Minutes de Soleil en Plus (1988; French) . . . . Aina
**Jesus of Montreal** (1990; French/Canadian)
. . . . . . . . . . . . . . . . . . . . . . . . . . . . .Mireille Fontaine
• 1:08—Brief breasts starting to take off her sweatshirt
during an audition.

# Wilkes, Donna

*Films:*
Almost Summer (1978). . . . . . . . . . . . . . . . . Meredith
Jaws II (1978) . . . . . . . . . . . . . . . . . . . . . . . . . Jackie
Fyre (1979). . . . . . . . . . . . . . . . . . . . . . . . . . . Carol
Hard Knocks (1979) . . . . . . . . . . . . . . . . . . . . Chrissy
*a.k.a. Hollywood Knight*
**Schizoid** (1980). . . . . . . . . . . . . . . . . . . Allison Foles
0:12—Breasts taking off her bra in bathroom while
Klaus Kinski watches. Buns, getting into the shower.
Out of focus shots.
•• 0:13—Side view breasts getting into the shower.
Blood Song (1982) . . . . . . . . . . . . . . . . . . . . . Marion
*a.k.a. Dreamslayer*
Angel (1983). . . . . . . . . . . . . . . . . . . . . . Angel/Molly
Grotesque (1987) . . . . . . . . . . . . . . . . . . . . . . Kathy
*Made for TV Movies:*
The Courage and the Passion (1978). . . . . . . . . . Tracy
Born to Be Sold (1981) . . . . . . . . . . . . . . Cindy Carlson
*TV:*
Hello, Larry (1979) . . . . . . . . . . . . . . . . . . .Diane Adler
Days of Our Lives (1982-83) . . . . . . . . .Pamela Prentiss

# Wilkinson, June

*Films:*
The Immoral Mr. Teas (1959) . . . . . . . .Uncredited torso
**Talking Walls** (1982) . . . . . . . . . . . . . . . . . . . . Blonde
• 0:13—Brief left breast, in car room, getting green
towel yanked off.
0:14—Very, very brief left breast in car room again.
Dark.
•• 1:08—Brief breasts, getting green towel taken off.
Sno-Line (1984) . . . . . . . . . . . . . . . . . . . . . . . Audrey
Keaton's Cop (1990). . . . . . . . . .Archie "Big Mama" Gish
*Magazines:*
**Playboy** (Jan 1974) . . . . . . . . . Twenty Years of Playboy
• 200—Right breast, in bed, in small photo.
**Playboy** (May 1980) . . . . . . . . . . The World of Playboy
• 13—Partial right breast and half of buns.
**Playboy** (Jan 1989) . . . . . . . . . . . .Women of the Fifties
••• 116—Breasts, wearing a gold bikini bottom.

# Williams, Barbara

*Films:*
**Thief of Hearts** (1984) . . . . . . . . . . . . . .Mickey Davis
(Special Home Video Version reviewed.)
• 0:46—Right breast in bathtub when her husband
comes in and tries to read her diary.
••• 0:53—Breasts making love with Steven Bauer in his
condo.
Jo Jo Dancer, Your Life Is Calling (1986) . . . . . . . . Dawn
Tiger Warsaw (1988) . . . . . . . . . . . . . . . . . . . . .Karen
Watchers (1988) . . . . . . . . . . . . . . . . . . . . . . . Nora
City of Hope (1991) . . . . . . . . . . . . . . . . . . . . .Angela
Indecency (1992). . . . . . . . . . . . . . . . . . . . . . .Marie
**Oh, What a Night** (1992) . . . . . . . . . . . . . . . . . .Vera
•• 0:21—Very brief right breast, then very brief breasts,
while undressing to go for a swim while Corey Haim
watches without her knowledge. Brief breasts in the
water and getting out.
• 0:46—Breasts, while swimming the backstroke in
the water while Haim watches again.
••• 0:59—Breasts, while swimming the backstroke
again and getting out. (This time she knows that
Haim is watching.) Nice slow motion shot for a PG-
13 film! Very brief wet panties.
•• 1:15—Left breast, while lying down on her back
with Haim in a barn.
*Made for Cable Movies:*
Keeper of the City (1991; Showtime) . . . . . . . . . .Grace
Spencer: Ceremony (1993) . . . . . . . . . . . . . . . .Susan
*Made for TV Movies:*
Quiet Killer (1992) . . . . . . . . . . . . . . . . . . . . Charlene

# Williams, Carol Ann

*Films:*
1941 (1979). . . . . . . . . . . . . . . . . . . . . . . . USO Girl
Butch and Sundance: The Early Days (1979) . . . . . . Lilly
**The Hollywood Knights** (1980) . . . . . . . . . . . . . .Jane
• 0:51—Very brief breasts, opening her blouse to distract Dudley. Don't see her face.

# Williams, Cynda

*Films:*
**Mo' Better Blues** (1990) . . . . . . . . . Clarke Betancourt
•• 0:24—Breasts, then left breast after kissing Denzel
Washington.
••• 1:07—Breasts on bed when Denzel Washington ac-
cidentally calls her "Indigo."
•• 1:28—Left breast while making love in bed with
Wesley Snipes.
One False Move (1992) . . . . . . . . . . . . . . . . .Fantasia
*Made for TV Movies:*
Tales of the City (1994) . . . . . . . . . . . .D'orothea Wilson

# Williams, Edy

Ex-wife of director Russ Meyer.

*Films:*

The Secret Life of an American Wife (1968)
. . . . . . . . . . . . . . . . . . . . . . . . . . . . Susie Steinberg
    0:32—In blonde wig wearing black bra and panties getting into bed.
    1:15—In black bra and panties again coming out of bedroom into the hallway.

Beyond the Valley of the Dolls (1970) . . . . Ashley St. Ives

The Seven Minutes (1971) . . . . . . . . . . . . . Faye Osborn

**Dr. Minx** (1975) . . . . . . . . . . . . . . . . . . . . . . . . . . n.a.
Breasts.

**An Almost Perfect Affair** (1979) . . . . . . . . . Herself
  • 0:18—Breasts and buns, while showing off during Cannes Film Festival.
  • 0:38—Brief breasts in a photo of herself that she holds up.

**The Best of Sex and Violence** (1981). . . . . . . Herself
  •• 0:46—Breasts in various scenes from *Dr. Minx.*

**Famous T & A** (1982) . . . . . . . . . . . . . . . . . . . Herself
(No longer available for purchase, check your video store for rental.)
  •• 0:39—Breasts and bun scenes from *Dr. Minx.*

**Chained Heat** (1983; U.S./German) . . . . . . . . . Paula
  •• 0:30—Full frontal nudity in the shower, soaping up Twinks.
  •• 0:36—Breasts at night in bed with Twinks.

**Hollywood Hot Tubs** (1984) . . . . . . . . . . . . . Desiree
  ••• 0:26—Breasts, trying to seduce Shawn while he works on a hot tub.
    1:26—In black lingerie outfit in the hallway.
  • 1:30—Partial breasts with breasts sticking out of her bra while she sits by hot tub with Jeff.
  •• 1:32—Breasts in hot tub room with Shawn.
  • 1:36—Brief breasts while running around.
  • 1:38—Breasts again in the hot tub lobby.

**Hellhole** (1985). . . . . . . . . . . . . . . . . . . . . . . . . . Vera
  ••• 0:22—Breasts on bed posing for Silk.
  ••• 0:24—Breasts in white panties in shower, then fighting with another woman.
  ••• 1:03—Breasts in mud bath with another woman. Long scene.

Mankillers (1987) . . . . . . . . . . . . . . . Sergeant Roberts

**Rented Lips** (1988). . . . . . . . . . . . . . . Heather Darling
  • 0:15—Breasts in bed, under Robert Downey, Jr. during playback of porno movie.

Bad Manners (1989) . . . . . . . . . . . . . . . . . . . Mrs. Slatt

**Dr. Alien** (1989) . . . . . . . . . . . . . . . . . . . Buckmeister
*a.k.a. I Was a Teenage Sex Mutant*
  ••• 0:54—Breasts taking off her top in the women's locker room in front of Wesley.

**Nudity Required** (1989). . . . . . . . . . . . . . . . Isabella
  ••• 1:05—Breasts, with whip, while acting in movie.
  •• 1:07—More breasts in movie.
  •• 1:09—More right breast.
  •• 1:13—Breasts, during screening of the movie.

**Bad Girls from Mars** (1990). . . . . . . . . . . Emanuelle
  •• 0:17—Breasts, several times changing in back of convertible car.
  ••• 0:23—Breasts, changing out of wet dress in bathroom.
  ••• 0:30—Breasts taking off blouse to get into spa.
  • 0:32—Breasts in back of Porsche and getting out.
  ••• 0:35—Breasts in store, signing autograph for robber.
  • 0:46—Buns in G-string, then breasts taking off her top again.
  ••• 0:58—Breasts in T.J.'s office. More breasts when wrestling with Martine.
  • 1:05—Breasts while tied up.
  • 1:07—Breasts again.
  •• 1:17—Breasts while taking off her outfit during outtakes.

*Magazines:*

**Playboy** (Feb 1973) . . . . . . . . . . . . . . . . . Next Month
  • 210—Left breast in B&W photo.

**Playboy** (Mar 1973) . . . . . . . . . . . . . . . . . All About Edy
  ••• 135-141—Nude.

**Playboy** (Jan 1978). . . . . . . . . . . . . . . The Year in Sex
  • 201—Nude in swimming pool.

**Playboy** (Nov 1989) . . . . . . . . . . . Sex in Cinema 1989
  ••• 134—Breasts still from *Bad Girls From Mars.*

# Williams, JoBeth

*Films:*

**Kramer vs. Kramer** (1979) . . . . . . . . . Phyllis Bernard
  • 0:45—Buns and brief breasts in the hallway meeting Dustin Hoffman's son.

The Dogs of War (1980; British) . . . . . . . . . . . . . . Jessie

Stir Crazy (1980) . . . . . . . . . . . . . . . . . . . . . . . Meredith

Endangered Species (1982) . . . . . . . . . . . Harriet Purdue

Poltergeist (1982) . . . . . . . . . . . . . . . . . . Diane Freeling

The Big Chill (1983). . . . . . . . . . . . . . . . . . . . . . . Karen

American Dreamer (1984) . . . . . . . . . . . . Cathy Palmer

**Teachers** (1984). . . . . . . . . . . . . . . . . . . . . . . . . . Lisa
  • 1:39—Brief breasts taking off clothes and running down school hallway yelling at Nick Nolte.

Desert Bloom (1986) . . . . . . . . . . . . . . . . . . . . . . . Lily

Poltergeist II: The Other Side (1986) . . . . Diane Freeling

Memories of Me (1988) . . . . . . . . . . . . . Lisa McConnell

Welcome Home (1989) . . . . . . . . . . . . . . . . . . . . Sarah

Dutch (1991) . . . . . . . . . . . . . . . . . . . . . . . . . . Natalie
*a.k.a. Driving Me Crazy*

Switch (1991) . . . . . . . . . . . . . . . . . . . . Margo Brofman

Stop! Or My Mom Will Shoot (1992) . . . . . Gwen Harper

Wyatt Earp (1994) . . . . . . . . . . . . . . . . . . . . . . . . n.a.

*Made for Cable Movies:*

**Chantilly Lace** (1993; Showtime) . . . . . . . . . . Natalie
  • 0:59—Brief breasts, taking off her blouse in bedroom with the pizza boy.

Sex, Love and Cold Hard Cash (1993; USA) . . . . . . . n.a.

Parallel Lives (1994; Showtime) . . . . . . . . . Win Winslow

*Miniseries:*

The Day After (1983) . . . . . . . . . . . . . . . . . . . . . Nancy

*Made for TV Movies:*

Adam (1983) . . . . . . . . . . . . . . . . . . . . . . Reve Walsh

Baby M (1988) . . . . . . . . . . . . . .Mary Beth Whitehead
My Name is Bill W. (1989). . . . . . . . . . . . . .Lois Wilson
Child in the Night (1990) . . . . . . . . . .Dr. Jackie Hollis
Jonathan: The Boy Nobody Wanted (1992)
. . . . . . . . . . . . . . . . . . . . . . . . . . . Ginny Moore
Final Appeal (1993). . . . . . . . . . . . . . . . . . . . . .n.a.
*TV:*
Somerset (1975) . . . . . . . . . . . . . . . . . Carrie Wheeler
The Guiding Light (1977-81) . . . . . . . . Brandy Shelooe

## Williams, Vanessa

Dethroned Miss America 1984.
Singer.
Not to be confused with the actress Vanessa Williams.
*Films:*
The Pick-Up Artist (1987) . . . . . . . . . . . . . . . . . .Rae
Under the Gun (1989) . . . . . . . . . . Samantha Richards
Another You (1991) . . . . . . . . . . . . . . . . . . . . .Gloria
Harley Davidson and The Marlboro Man (1991)
. . . . . . . . . . . . . . . . . . . . . . . . . . . Lulu Daniels
*Miniseries:*
The Jacksons: An American Dream (1992)
. . . . . . . . . . . . . . . . . . . . . . . . Suzanne de Passe
*Made for TV Movies:*
Full Exposure: The Sex Tapes Scandal (1989). . Valentine
*TV:*
The Soul of VH-1 . . . . . . . . . . . . . . . . . . . . .Hostess
*Magazines:*
**Penthouse** (Sep 1984)
. . . . . . . . . . . . . . . . . .Here She Comes, Miss America
••• 66-75—B&W nude photos.
**Penthouse** (Nov 1984) . . . . . . . Tom Chaipel interview
••• 85-89—More B&W nude photos.

## Williams, Wendy O.

Lead singer of *The Plasmatics.*
*Adult Films:*
**800 Fantasy Lane** (1979). . . . . . . . . . . . . . . . . . .n.a.
Candy Goes to Hollywood (1979). . . . . . . . . . . . . .n.a.
*Films:*
**Reform School Girls** (1986). . . . . . . . . . . . . . Charlie
•• 0:26—Breasts talking to two girls in the shower.
Pucker Up and Bark Like a Dog (1989) . . . . . . . . Butch
*Magazines:*
**Playboy** (Aug 1980) . . . . . . . . . . . . . . . . . .Grapevine
• 263—Right breast with tape over the nipple.
**Playboy** (Oct 1986). . . . . . . . . . . . . . . Oh, Wendy O.!
•• 70-75—Breasts.

## • Willoughby, Marlene

Adult film actress.
*Films:*
Married to the Mob (1988). . . . . . . . . . . Mrs. Fat Man
*Magazines:*
**Penthouse** (Dec 1980) . . . . . . . . . . . Some Like It Hot
••• 176-185—Nude.

## Wilsey, Shannon

a.k.a. Adult film actress Savannah.
*Films:*
**Invisible Maniac** (1990) . . . . . . . . . . . . . . . . . . . Vicky
• 0:21—Buns and very, very brief side of left breast in
the shower with the other girls.
• 0:33—Right breast covered with bubbles.
••• 0:43—In bra, then breasts and lots of buns in locker
room with the other girls.
•• 0:44—Buns and left breast in the shower with the
other girls.
••• 1:04—Undressing in locker room in white bra and
panties, then breasts. More breasts taking a shower
and getting electrocuted.
**Sorority House Massacre 2** (1990) . . . . . . . . Satana
•• 0:43—Breasts and buns in G-string, dancing in club.
**Legal Tender** (1991) . . . . . . . . . . . . . . . . . . .Mal's Girl
•• 0:24—Breasts in bubble bath with brunette girl and
Morton Downey Jr.
•• 0:31—Breasts and buns in G-string bringing phone
to Downey.

## Wilson, Ajita

Transexual (she used to be a he).
*Films:*
**Love Lust and Ecstasy** (1978) . . . . . . . . . . . . . .Sara
•• 0:02—Nude taking a shower and getting into bed
with an old guy.
•• 0:04—Nude making love with a young guy.
•• 0:17—Breasts in bathtub, then making love on bed.
•• 0:22—Breasts making love in a swimming pool, in a
river, by a tree.
•• 0:26—Nude getting undressed and taking a shower.
•• 0:35—Full frontal nudity changing clothes.
••• 0:54—Full frontal nudity making love in bed.
**The Joy of Flying** (1979) . . . . . . . . . . Madame Gaballi
*a.k.a. Erotic Ways*
• 1:20—Full frontal nudity undressing for George.
• 1:23—Breasts, making love on top of George.
• 1:25—Left breast, while in bed with George.
**Catherine Cherie** (1982). . . . . . . . . .Dancer/Miss Ajita
• 0:23—Breasts and buns dancing in club. Covered
with paint. Long shot.
0:24—Brief buns, greeting Carlo after the show.
•• 0:43—Full frontal nudity in room with Carlo.
**A Man for Sale** (1982) . . . . . . . . . . . . .Dancer/Model
• 0:02—Breasts several times posing for photographer
with another model.
• 0:26—Breasts and buns, dancing in an erotic ballet
show.
Savage Island (1985) . . . . . . . . . . . . . . . . . . . . .Marie
**Twelfth Night** (1988; Italian). . . . . . . . . . . . . Antonia
•• 0:50—Buns, taking off her dress and walking into
stream with a guy.
• 0:51—Very brief breasts, making love with him in
the stream.
•• 1:11—Right breast, hanging out of black dress,
dancing in tavern.

# Wilson, Alisa

*Films:*

**The Terror on Alcatraz** (1986) . . . . . . . . . . . Clarissa
- 1:14—Brief breasts opening her blouse to distract Frank, so she can get away from him.

Loverboy (1989) . . . . . . . . . . . . . . . . . . .Nurse Darlene

Psycho Cop 2 (1992) . . . . . . . . . . . . . . Anchorwoman

# Wilson, Cheryl-Ann

*Films:*

Terminal Choice (1985; Canadian) . . . . . . . Nurse Fields

**Cellar Dweller** (1987) . . . . . . . . . . . . . . . . . . . . .Lisa
- •• 0:59—Brief right breast, then breasts taking a shower.

*TV:*

Days of Our Lives . . . . . . . . . . . . . . . . . . . . . . . . .n.a.

# • Wilson, Regan

*Films:*

**Blood Mania** (1970) . . . . . . . . . . . . . . . . . . . . Cheryl
- •• 0:07—Breasts and buns, while in bubble bath.
- 0:17—In bra, while undressing in bedroom. Very brief side of right breast, when putting on robe.
- 0:21—Very brief side of left breast, while leaning over to kiss Craig in bed.
- 0:34—Partial right breast, while on couch with the blackmailer.

*Magazines:*

**Playboy** (Oct 1967) . . . . . . . . . . . . . . . . . . Playmate

# Wilson, Seretta

*Films:*

**Tower of Evil** (1972; British) . . . . . . . . . . . . . . . . Mae
- 0:34—Very, very brief breasts, lying in bed in flashbacks. Then breasts, sleeping in bed.
- •• 0:35—Breasts, while sleeping in bed.
- 0:38—More breasts, while sleeping in bed.
- 0:39—Very, very brief breasts, getting the covers taken off before getting killed.
- 0:41—Very brief breasts, dead, covered with blood.

Beyond the Fog (1981; British) . . . . . . . . . . . . . . Mac

# Wilson, Sheree

*Films:*

**Fraternity Vacation** (1985) . . . . . . . . . . Ashley Taylor
- 0:43—In white leotard at aerobics class.
- 0:47—Breasts and buns of body double (Roberta Whitewood), while in the bedroom when the guys photograph her with a telephoto lens.
- 1:01—In white leotard exercising in living room with Leigh McCloskey.

Crimewave (1986) . . . . . . . . . . . . . . . . . . . . . .Nancy

*Made for Cable Movies:*

**Past Tense** (1994; Showtime) . . . . . . . . . .Emily Talbert
- •• 1:00—Left breast and most of right breast in open vest in front of Scott Glenn. Definitely not a body double!

*Miniseries:*

Kane & Abel (1985) . . . . . . . . . . . . . . . Melanie LeRoy

*TV:*

Our Family Honor (1985-86) . . . . . . . . . . . Rita Danzig

Dallas (1987-91) . . . . . . . . . . . . . . . . . . . . . . . April

Walker, Texas Ranger (1993- ) . . . . . . . . . . . Alex Cahill

# Winchester, Maude

*Films:*

**Birdy** (1985) . . . . . . . . . . . . . . . . . . . . Doris Robinson
- •• 1:32—Breasts in car letting Mathew Modine feel her.

Brain Dead (1989) . . . . . . . . . . . . . . . . . . . Crazy Anna

The Spirit of '76 (1991) . . . . . . . . . . . Cyndi the Waitress

Bram Stoker's Dracula (1992) . . . . . . . Downstairs Maid

A Few Good Men (1992) . . . . . . . . . . . . . . Aunt Ginny

Carnosaur (1993) . . . . . . . . . . . . . . . . . . . . .Downey

*Made for Cable Movies:*

Attack of the 50 ft. Woman (1993; HBO) . . . . . . .Donna

# Windsor, Romy

a.k.a. Romy Walthall.

*Films:*

**Thief of Hearts** (1984) . . . . . . . . . . . . . . . . . . Nicole

(Special Home Video Version reviewed.)
- ••• 0:12—Full frontal nudity with Steven Bauer getting dressed.

Up the Creek (1984) . . . . . . . . . . . . . . . . . . . . Corky

Howling IV: The Original Nightmare (1988) . . . . . .Marie

Big Bad John (1989) . . . . . . . . . . . . . . . Marie Mitchelle

Edgar Allan Poe's "The House of Usher" (1990) . . .Molly

*TV:*

Man of the People (1991) . . . . . . . . . . . . . . . . . Rita

Hotel Malibu (1994- ) . . . . . . . . . . . . . . . . . . . Nancy

# Winger, Debra

Ex-wife of actor Timothy Hutton.

*Films:*

**Slumber Party '57** (1976) . . . . . . . . . . . . . . . Debbie
- 0:10—Breasts with her five girl friends during swimming pool scene. Hard to tell who is who.
- ••• 0:53—Breasts three times, lying down, making out with Bud.

Thank God It's Friday (1978) . . . . . . . . . . . . . Jennifer

French Postcards (1979) . . . . . . . . . . . . . . . . Melanie

Urban Cowboy (1980) . . . . . . . . . . . . . . . . . . . Sissy

Cannery Row (1982) . . . . . . . . . . . . . . . . . . . . Suzy

**An Officer and a Gentleman** (1982) . . . Paula Pokrifki
- ••• 1:05—Brief side view of right breast, then breasts making love with Richard Gere in a motel.

Terms of Endearment (1983) . . Emma Greenway Horton

**Mike's Murder** (1984) . . . . . . . . . . . . . . . . . . . Betty
- 0:26—Brief left breast in bathtub.

Legal Eagles (1986) . . . . . . . . . . . . . . . . .Laura Kelly

Black Widow (1987) . . . . . . . . . . . . . . . . . Alexandra

Made in Heaven (1987) . . . . . . . . . . . . . . . . Emmett

Betrayed (1988) . . . . . . . . . . Katie Phillips/Cathy Weaver

Everybody Wins (1990) . . . . . . . . . . . . . Angela Crispini
- 0:50—Side view of left breast, lying on Nick Nolte in bed. Long shot.

**The Sheltering Sky** (1990) . . . . . . . . . . Kit Moresby
0:13—Upper half of lower frontal nudity in open
robe when John Malkovich caresses her stomach.
0:24—Buns, getting out of bed.
- 0:41—Very brief breasts grabbing sheets and getting out of bed with Tunner.
1:58—Lower frontal nudity and sort of buns, getting
undressed with Belqassim.
Leap of Faith (1992) . . . . . . . . . . . . . . . . . . . . . Jane
**A Dangerous Woman** (1993) . . . . . . .Martha Horgan
- 0:42—Very, very brief lower frontal nudity, then
buns, while masturbating in bed. Don't see her face.
Medium long shot.
Shadowlands (1993; British) . . . . . . . . . . .Joy Gresham
Wilder Napalm (1993) . . . . . . . . . . . . . . . . . . . Vida
*TV:*
Wonder Woman (1976-77) . . . . . . .Drusilla/Wonder Girl

# Winkler, Angela

*Films:*
**The Lost Honor of Katharina Blum** (1975; German)
. . . . . . . . . . . . . . . . . . . . . . . . . . . .Katharina Blum
•• 0:15—Full frontal nudity, while in bathroom, getting
strip searched by policewoman.
- 0:43—Brief right breast, after getting out of the
shower.
**The Tin Drum** (1979; German) . . . . . Agnes Matzerath
•• 0:38—Very brief right breast after taking off clothes
in room with Jan. Buns and side view of left breast in
bed with him.
Benny's Video (1992) . . . . . . . . . . . . . . . . . . . .Mother

# Winkler, K.C.

*Films:*
**H.O.T.S.** (1979) . . . . . . . . . . . . . . . . . . . . . .Cynthia
*a.k.a. T & A Academy*
- 0:27—Breasts in blue bikini bottom on balcony.
•• 0:31—Breasts in van making love, then arguing with
John.
**The Happy Hooker Goes Hollywood** (1980)
. . . . . . . . . . . . . . . . . . . . . . . . . . . . . . . . . . Amber
•• 0:41—Breasts in cowboy outfit on bed with a guy.
••• 0:43—Breasts, wearing a blue garter belt playing
pool with Susan Kiger.
Night Shift (1982) . . . . . . . . . . . . . . . . . . . . . Cheryl
They Call Me Bruce? (1982) . . . . . . . . . . . . . . . . .n.a.
Armed and Dangerous (1986) . . . . . . . . . . . . . . . Vicki
*TV:*
High Rollers . . . . . . . . . . . . . . . . . . . . . . . . . .Hostess
*Magazines:*
**Playboy** (Jan 1979) . . . . . . . . The Great Playmate Hunt
••• 190—Full frontal nudity.
**Playboy** (Oct 1985) . . . . . . . . . . . . . . . . . . . .Grapevine
- 241—In swimsuit, showing left breast. B&W.
**Playboy** (Mar 1986) . . . . . . . . . . . . . . . . . . . .Grapevine
- 176—In wet swimsuit. B&W.
**Playboy** (Sep 1989) . . . . . . . . . . . . . . Body by Winkler
••• 82-87—Nude.

**Playboy's Nudes** (Oct 1990) . . . . . . . . . . . . . .Herself
••• 42-43—Full frontal nudity.

# Winningham, Mare

*Films:*
**One Trick Pony** (1980) . . . . . . . . McDeena Dandridge
•• 0:14—Breasts in the bathtub with Paul Simon,
smoking a cigarette. Long scene.
**Threshold** (1983; Canadian) . . . . . . . .Carol Severance
- 0:56—Brief full frontal nudity, lying on operating table, then side view of left breast getting prepped for
surgery.
St. Elmo's Fire (1985) . . . . . . . . . . . . . . . . . . . .Wendy
Nobody's Fool (1986) . . . . . . . . . . . . . . . . . . . . . .Pat
Made in Heaven (1987) . . . . . . . . . . . . Brenda Carlucci
Shy People (1988) . . . . . . . . . . . . . . . . . . . . . Candy
Miracle Mile (1989) . . . . . . . . . . . . . . . . . .Julie Peters
Turner & Hooch (1989) . . . . . . . . . . . . . Emily Carson
Hard Promises (1992) . . . . . . . . . . . . . . . . . . . Dawn
Wyatt Earp (1994) . . . . . . . . . . . . . . . . . . . . . .n.a.
*Made for Cable Movies:*
Better Off Dead (1993; Lifetime) . . . . . . . . . . . . . . n.a.
Sexual Healing (1993; Showtime) . . . . . . . . . . . .Marla
*Miniseries:*
The Thorn Birds (1983) . . . . . . . . . . . . .Justine O'Neill
*Made for TV Movies:*
Helen Keller: The Miracle Continues (1984)
. . . . . . . . . . . . . . . . . . . . . . . . . . . . . .Helen Keller
Who is Julia? (1986) . . . . . . . . . . . . . .Mary Frances
A Winner Never Quits (1986) . . . . . . . . . . . . . . .Annie
Crossing to Freedom (1990) . . . . . . . . Nicole Rougeron
Love & Lies (1990) . . . . . . . . . . . . . . . . . . Kim Paris
She Stood Alone (1991) . . . . . . . . . . Prudence Crandall
Intruders (1992) . . . . . . . . . . . . . . . . . . .Mary Wilkes
Those Secrets (1992) . . . . . . . . . . . . . . . . . . . .Faye
Betrayed by Love (1994) . . . . . . . . . . . . . . . . . Dana
*Magazines:*
**Playboy** (Nov 1981) . . . . . . . . . . Sex in Cinema 1981
•• 170—Breasts in bathtub from *One Trick Pony.*

# Winters, D.D.

See: Vanity.

# Witherspoon, Reese

*Films:*
**The Man in the Moon** (1991) . . . . . . . . . . Dani Trant
- 0:09—Brief buns, running to go skinny dipping.
Don't see her face. Long shot of back side of left
breast while running on pier.
0:12—Brief buns, climbing up ladder. Tree branches
get in the way. Don't see her face again.
A Far Off Place (1993; U.S./British) . . . . . . Nonnie Parker
Jack the Bear (1993) . . . . . . . . . . . . . . . Karen Morris
*Made for Cable Movies:*
Wildflower (1991; Lifetime) . . . . . . . . . . . . Ellie Perkins
*Miniseries:*
Return to Lonesome Dove (1993) . . . . Ferris Dunnegan
*Made for TV Movies:*
Desperate Choices: To Save My Child (1992) . . . . Cassie

# Witt, Kathryn

*Films:*
**Lenny** (1974) . . . . . . . . . . . . . . . . . . . . . . . . . . Girl
- 0:43—Right breast with Valerie Perrine while Dustin Hoffman watches.

Looker (1981) . . . . . . . . . . . . . . . . . . . . Tina Cassidy
0:17—In beige lingerie undressing in her room.

Star 80 (1983) . . . . . . . . . . . . . . . . . . . . . . . . . Robin

**Cocaine Wars** (1986) . . . . . . . . . . . . . . . . . . . . . Janet
*a.k.a. Vice Wars*
- 0:36—Brief breasts and buns making love in bed with John Schneider.

Demon of Paradise (1987) . . . . . . . . . . . . . . . . . Annie

Philadelphia (1993) . . . . . . . . . . . . . . Melissa Benedict

*TV:*
Flying High (1978-79) . . . . . . . . . . . . . . . . Pam Bellagio

# Witter, Cherie

*Video Tapes:*
**Playboy Video Calendar 1987** (1986) . . . . Playmate

*Magazines:*
**Playboy** (Feb 1985) . . . . . . . . . . . . . . . . . . . Playmate

**Playboy's 1987 Book of Lingerie** (Mar 1987)
. . . . . . . . . . . . . . . . . . . . . . . . . . . . . . . . . . Herself
- • • 9—Full frontal nudity.
- • • 41—Full frontal nudity.

**Playboy's Calendar Playmates** (Nov 1992) . . Herself
- • • 49—Full frontal nudity.

# Witter, Karen

*Films:*
Dangerously Close (1986) . . . . . . . . . . . . . . . . . Betsy

The Perfect Match (1987) . . . . . . . . . . . . . . . . Tammy

Hero and the Terror (1988) . . . . . . . . . . . . . . Ginger

Mortuary Academy (1988) . . . . . . . . . . . . Christie Doll

Out of the Dark (1988) . . . . . . . . . . . . . . . . . Jo Ann

Paramedics (1988) . . . . . . . . . . . . . . . . . . . Danger Girl
0:03—In white bra and panties in bedroom with a heart attack victim while the paramedics try to save him.
0:07—In wet blouse after getting in a car crash with a guy in the fountain.

Silent Assassins (1988) . . . . . . . . . . . . . . Sushi Bar Girl

The Vineyard (1988) . . . . . . . . . . . . . . . . . . . . . . . n.a.

**Another Chance** (1989) . . . . . . . . . . . . Nancy Burton
- 0:44—Brief side view of right breast and buns getting out of bed.
0:45—In two piece swimsuit.

Edgar Allan Poe's "Buried Alive" (1989) . . . . . . . . . Janet

**Midnight** (1989) . . . . . . . . . . . . . . . . . . Missy Angel
- 0:32—In bed with Mickey. Nice squished breasts against him, but only a very brief side view of left breast.
0:48—In two piece swimsuit, going into the pool.
0:58—In nightgown, walking around with lots of makeup on her face.

Popcorn (1991) . . . . . . . . . . . . . . . . . . . . . . . . . . Joy

*TV:*
One Life to Live (1990-94) . . . . . . . . . Tina Lord Roberts

*Video Tapes:*
**Playboy's Playmate Review** (1982) . . . . . . . Playmate
- • • 0:00—Nude deep sea fishing, then sunbathing on sailboat.

**Playmates at Play** (1990) . . . . . . . . . . Making Waves

*Magazines:*
**Playboy** (Mar 1982) . . . . . . . . . . . . . . . . . . . Playmate

**Playboy's Girls of Summer '86** (Aug 1986) . . . Herself
- 76-77—Lower frontal nudity.

**Playboy** (Dec 1991) . . . . . . . . . . . . . . . Sex Stars 1991
- • • 182—Buns and side of left breast.

**Playboy's Calendar Playmates** (Nov 1992) . . . Herself
- • • 15—Full frontal nudity.

# Wolf, Rita

*Films:*
**My Beautiful Laundrette** (1985; British) . . . . . . Tania
- • • 0:15—Breasts holding blouse up, showing off her breasts outside window to Omar.

Slipstream (1990) . . . . . . . . . . . . . . . . . . . . . . . . Maya

# • Wolter, Sherilyn

*Films:*
**Eyewitness to Murder** (1989) . . . . . . . . . . . Suzanne
- 1:00—Very, very brief lower half of right breast while making love with Andrew Stevens. Don't see her face.

*TV:*
B.J. and the Bear (1981) . . . . . . . . . . . . . . Cindy Grant

# Wood, Cyndi

*Films:*
Apocalypse Now (1979) . . . . . . . . Playmate of the Year

**Van Nuys Blvd.** (1979) . . . . . . . . . . . . . . . . . . . Moon
- • • 0:57—Left breast outside on boat with Bobby, then breasts, while making love in bed with him.

*Video Tapes:*
**Playboy Video Centerfold: Teri Weigel** (1986)
. . . . . . . . . . . . . . . . . . . . . . . . . . . Playmate Update
- • • 0:25—Nude in still photos.

*Magazines:*
**Playboy** (Feb 1973) . . . . . . . . . . . . . . . . . . . Playmate
- • • 100-107—Full frontal nudity.

**Playboy** (Jun 1974) . . . . . . . . . . . Playmate of the Year
- • • 146-155—Nude.

Playboy (Jul 1976) . . . . . . . . . . . . . . . . . . . . . Cover
Breasts under sheer white outfit.

**Playboy** (Dec 1976) . . . . . . . . Portfolio: Pompeo Posar
- • • 111—Buns and back side of right breast.

**Playboy** (Apr 1980) . . . . . . Playboy's Playmate Reunion
- 126—Small breasts centerfold photo.

# Wood, Jane

Films:

The Ragman's Daughter (1974; British)
. . . . . . . . . . . . . . . . . . . . . . . . . Older Tony's Wife
Lassiter (1984) . . . . . . . . . . . . . . . . . . . . Mary Becker
**She'll be Wearing Pink Pyjamas** (1985; British)
. . . . . . . . . . . . . . . . . . . . . . . . . . . . . . . . . Jude
• 0:07—Nude, shaving her legs in the women's shower room.
Blood Red Roses (1986; Scottish) . . . . . . . . . . . . . . n.a.

# Wood, Janet

Films:

**Angels Hard as They Come** (1971) . . . . . . . . . . Vicki
•• 1:09—Breasts taking off her top, dancing with Clean Sheila at the biker's party.
•• 1:16—Breasts outside when the General rips her blouse open.
**The G.I. Executioner** (1971) . . . . . . . . Cynthia Jordan
a.k.a. Wit's End
a.k.a. Dragon Lady
•• 0:29—Breasts and buns in bed with Dave.
Terror House (1972) . . . . . . . . . . . . . . . . . . . . . . Pamela
**The Centerfold Girls** (1974) . . . . . . . . . . . . . . Linda
•• 0:14—Breasts putting on robe and getting out of bed.
**Slumber Party '57** (1976) . . . . . . . . . . . . . . . . Smitty
• 0:10—Breasts with her five girl friends during swimming pool scene. Hard to tell who is who.
•• 1:06—Left breast, then breasts in stable with David while his sister watches.

# Wood, Lana

Sister of the late actress Natalie Wood.

Films:

The Searchers (1956) . . . . . . . . . . . . . Debbie as a Child
Diamonds are Forever (1971; British) . . . Plenty O'Toole
**A Place Called Today** (1972) . . . . . . Carolyn Scheider
••• 0:40—Side view of left breast, then breasts lying down talking to Ron.
**Demon Rage** (1981) . . . . . . . . . . . . . . . . . . . . . . . Lisa
a.k.a. Dark Eyes
a.k.a. Demon Seed
• 0:00—Breasts when breasts pop out of nightgown while running from someone at the beach.
••• 0:09—Breasts and very brief partial lower frontal nudity in bed when sheets get pulled off her.
••• 0:19—Breasts, while taking a shower when she sees the spirit.
••• 0:26—Breasts and very brief lower frontal nudity while lying in bed when the spirit visits her and makes love.
••• 0:38—Breasts in bed, while making love with the spirit.
• 0:53—Brief breasts with the spirit, while making love in bed.
• 1:22—Brief full frontal nudity getting her nightgown torn off.

Made for TV Movies:

Nightmare in Badham County (1976) . . . . . . . . . Smitty
(Nudity added for video tape.)

TV:

The Long Hot Summer (1965-66) . . . . . . . . Eula Harker
Peyton Place (1966-67) . . . . . . . . . . . . . Sandy Webber
Capitol (1983) . . . . . . . . . . . . . . . . . . . . . . . Fran Bruke

Magazines:

**Playboy** (Apr 1971) . . . . . . The Well-Versed Lana Wood
••• 100-103—Breasts.
Playboy (Nov 1972) . . . . . . . . . . . . Sex in Cinema 1972
159—Hard to see anything.
**Playboy** (Sep 1987) . . . . . . . . . 25 Years of James Bond
••• 128—Breasts.

# Wood, Laurie

Video Tapes:

**Playboy Video Calendar 1990** (1989) . . . . . . . . April
••• 0:18—Nude.

Magazines:

**Playboy** (Mar 1989) . . . . . . . . . . . . . . . . . . . Playmate
**Playboy's Book of Lingerie** (Mar 1992) . . . . . . Herself
•• 88-89—Buns and right breast.
**Playboy's Book of Lingerie** (May 1992) . . . . . Herself
• 52—Left breast.
**Playboy's Book of Lingerie** (Sep 1992) . . . . . . Herself
•• 96—Buns and right breast.
**Playboy's Calendar Playmates** (Nov 1992) . . . Herself
••• 81—Full frontal nudity.

# Wood, Nicole

Video Tapes:

**Playboy Video Calendar 1994** (1993) . . . . . . October
••• 0:39—Nude while running around a house and posing.
••• 0:40—Nude while posing in water-theme backdrops in color and B&W.

Magazines:

**Playboy** (Apr 1993) . . . . . . . . . . . . . . . . . . . Playmate
••• 102-113—Nude.
**Playboy** (Jan 1994) . . . . . . . . Playboy's Playmate Review
••• 203—Full frontal nudity.
**Playboy's Playmate Review** (May 1994) . . . Miss April
••• 32-39—Nude.
**Playmates at Play** (Jul 1994) . . . . . . . . . . . . . Herself
••• 12-13—Breasts under sheer dress and lower frontal nudity.
**Playboy's Girls of Summer '94** (Jul 1994) . . . . Herself
••• 14-15—Full frontal nudity.
**Playboy's Book of Lingerie** (Sep 1994) . . . . . . Herself
• 9—Partial lower frontal nudity.
••• 81—Breasts.

# Wood-Sharkey, Rebecca

a.k.a. Rebecca Sharkey.

*Films:*

**Friday the 13th, Part V—A New Beginning** (1985)
................................ Lana
- 0:33—Brief breasts opening her dress while changing to go out with Billy.

Mask (1985) .............................. Angel

Barbarian Queen II: The Empress Strikes Back (1989)
.................................... Ziela

The Forgotten One (1989) ............... Barmaid

Switch (1991) .................... Gay Club Patron

# Woodell, Pat

*Films:*

**The Big Doll House** (1971) .............. Bodine
- 0:27—Brief breasts hung by wrists and whipped by a guard. Hair covers most of her breasts.

The Roommates (1973). .................. Heather

The Woman Hunt (1975; U.S./Philippines) ........n.a.

*TV:*

Petticoat Junction (1963-65) ........ Bobby Jo Bradley

# Woods, Barbara Alyn

*Films:*

Circuitry Man (1990) ...................... Yoyo

Delusion (1990) .......................... Julie

**Dance with Death** (1991) ................. Kelly
- ••• 0:16—In black bra, panties and stockings, doing strip tease on stage. Breasts and buns in G-string.
- •• 0:24—Breasts, dancing in red bra and panties.
- ••• 0:46—Breasts and buns in G-string, dancing on stage.
- • 0:47—Brief side view of left breast, while changing back stage. Buns seen in mirror.
- ••• 0:59—Breasts and buns, doing strip tease routine in Marilyn Monroe outfit.
- ••• 1:01—Breasts, making love in bed with Maxwell Caulfield.

**The Waterdance** (1991) ............Annabelle Lee
- • 1:24—Buns, in G-string, while on stage in a strip club.

We're Talkin' Serious Money (1991)
........................Baggage Claim Agent

**The Terror Within II** (1992) ............. Sharon
- •• 0:28—Buns and breasts while in bed with Jamie.

**Flesh and Bone** (1993)................... Cindy
- • 0:16—Partial buns, while lying on her stomach on bed.

Ghoulies IV (1993) ........................ Kate

*Made for Cable TV:*

**Dream On: It Came From Beneath the Sink**
(1992; HBO) ........................... Linda
- •• 0:01—Breasts, kneeling on bed in Martin's office in his dream. Brief buns, on top of him in bed.
- •• 0:02—Brief left breast with Martin in his dream.
- • 0:03—Brief breasts in flashback/daydream.
- •• 0:09—Breasts and buns in bed with Martin in more of his dreams.

- • 0:11—Breasts in flashback.
- • 0:13—Buns, several times in G-string at Martin's apartment.

*Video Tapes:*

**Eden** (1992) ........................ Eve Sinclair
- • 0:09—Buns and breasts, while kissing Grant outside during her fantasy.
- ••• 0:10—Breasts in pool and on beach, making love with Grant during more fantasy.
- • 0:24—Brief breasts, putting on lingerie.
- ••• 0:30—Breasts, while making love on table with Grant during another fantasy.
- • 0:54—Buns in maroon bra and T-back in her bedroom.
- ••• 0:55—Breasts and buns in the shower making love with Grant during her fantasy.
- • 1:18—Buns in lingerie in fantasy with Grant.
- ••• 1:19—Left breast, while on couch with Grant/Josh in her fantasy.

**Eden 2** (1992)........................ Eve Sinclair
- • 0:20—Brief breasts on boat in fantasy with Grant.
- • 0:43—In bra, then brief breasts in hay in a stable with Grant during a fantasy.
- • 1:01—Brief breasts in bubble bath. Don't see her face.
  1:02—Breasts under sheer nightgown.
- ••• 1:04—Breasts with Grant outside by pool, then in bathtub.
- •• 1:19—Breasts and buns in the shower with Steve then Grant during a fantasy.

**Inside Out** (1992) .............Terri/Brush Strokes
- ••• 0:07—Breasts and buns in G-string, undressing for Jack.
- ••• 0:08—Close-up of breasts as Jack paints on her with his paintbrush.
- ••• 0:09—Full frontal nudity, getting paint poured all over her body.
- • 0:11—Brief breasts, while holding onto chair while making love.

**Eden 3** (1993)........................ Eve Sinclair
  0:02—In wet white dress, while frolicking in the ocean with Josh.
- •• 0:10—Breasts, fantasizing about Grant during her massage.
- ••• 0:35—In white bra, then breasts during her fantasy while making love outside with Grant.
- • 0:47—In black bra and panties, then left breast while making love with Josh in bedroom.
- •• 0:49—Breasts, while crying in the shower.
- • 0:59—In wet nightgown, then buns and brief right breast while out in the rain with Grant.
- •• 1:26—Breasts while making love on the hood of a car with Grant.

Eden 4 (1993) ........................ Eve Sinclair
  0:41—In white lingerie after taking off her wedding dress on stairs with her husband.

**Eden 5** (1993) ....................... Eve Sinclair
- •• 0:37—Buns and breasts, while making love on beach with Grant in flashback.

•• 0:48—Breasts, while making love on beach at night with Paul.

•• 0:50—Brief buns in panties while frolicking in the surf with Paul. Breasts while making love.

• 1:01—Breasts, while making love with Grant.

• 1:28—In pink bra, then left breast with Grant in bed.

**Eden 6** (1994) . . . . . . . . . . . . . . . . . . . . . Eve Sinclair

• 0:54—Brief breasts, while fooling around in bed with Paul.

•• 1:34—Brief buns and breasts while making love with Paul in bed.

•• 2:01—Breasts, while making love with Paul. Half of right breast when Paul makes out with her.

• 2:04—Right breast, while making love with Paul.

• 2:17—Breasts, while making love on table with Paul.

*Magazines:*

**Playboy** (Jun 1993) . . . . . . . . . . . . . All About "Eden"

••• 80-81—Breasts.

**Playboy's Nudes** (Dec 1993) . . . . . . . . . . . . . Herself

••• 12—Full frontal nudity.

## Woods, Connie

*Films:*

The Forbidden Dance (1990) . . . . . . . . . . . . . . . . Trish

*Made for Cable TV:*

**Dream On: Futile Attraction** (1991; HBO). . .Darlene

•• 0:03—Breasts dressed as a cheerleader on top of Martin in bed.

*Video Tapes:*

**Night of the Living Babes** (1987). . . . . . . . . . . Lulu

• 0:46—Breasts and buns in lingerie, in a cell with Buck.

••• 0:48—More breasts in cell with Buck.

• 0:50—Breasts getting rescued with Michelle Bauer.

## Woods, Jerii

*Films:*

Switchblade Sisters (1975) . . . . . . . . . . . . . . . . . . .Toby

**Revenge of the Cheerleaders** (1976). . . . . . . . .Gail

• 0:00—Breasts, while changing clothes in front left seat of car.

0:05—Lower frontal nudity taking off cheerleader skirt in girl's restroom and putting on panties.

• 0:26—Brief right breast, while sitting in bleachers with the other cheerleaders.

••• 0:28—Nude in boy's shower room scene.

•• 0:37—Breasts, while sitting up in sleeping bag.

• 0:44—Brief breasts in front seat of car with David Hasselhoff.

••• 0:53—Nude with Leslie and hiker guy while frolicking in the woods.

•• 0:55—Nude some more making out with the hiker guy with Leslie.

••• 0:57—Nude, walking down road with Leslie when stopped by a policeman.

••• 1:23—Breasts during Hawaiian party.

## • Woodville, Kate

*Films:*

Black Gunn (1972) . . . . . . . . . . . . . . . . . . . . . . .Louella

**Sex Through a Window** (1977) . . . . . . .Sally Norman

•• 0:29—Left breast, after sitting up in bed after John sits up, then brief breasts while turning over in bed.

••• 1:15—Breasts, while making love in bed and after with John.

## Woronov, Mary

*Films:*

Bad Georgia Road . . . . . . . . . . . . . . . . . . . . . . Hackett

**Kemek** . . . . . . . . . . . . . . . . . . . . . . . . . . . . . . . . Mary

Seizure (1973) . . . . . . . . . . . . . . . . . . . . . . . . . . Mikki

**Sugar Cookies** (1973) . . . . . . . . . . . . . . . . . . . .Camila

••• 0:10—Breasts in bathtub, then wearing white panties exercising breasts on the floor. Long scene.

• 1:04—Breasts with Julie in the bathtub.

• 1:07—Brief breasts, then left breast, making love with Julie.

• 1:17—Brief right breast when Lynn Lowry yanks her dress up.

Silent Night, Bloody Night (1974) . . . . . . . . . . . . .Diane

**Death Race 2000** (1975). . . . . . . . . . . Calamity Jane

• 0:27—Brief breasts arguing with Matilda the Hun.

Hollywood Boulevard (1976) . . . . . . . . . Mary McQueen

Jackson County Jail (1976) . . . . . . . . . . . . . . . . . Pearl

Mr. Billion (1977). . . . . . . . . . . . . . . . . . . . . .Actress

The Lady in Red (1979) . . . . . . . . . Woman Bankrobber

Rock 'n' Roll High School (1979) . . . . . . . Evelyn Togar

**Angel of H.E.A.T.** (1981). . . . . . . . . .Samantha Vitesse

*a.k.a. The Protectors, Book I*

••• 0:11—Frontal nudity changing clothes on a boat dock after getting out of the lake.

•• 0:43—Breasts wrestling in the mud after wearing white bathing suit.

Heartbeeps (1981) . . . . . . . . . . . . . . Party House Owner

**Eating Raoul** (1982) . . . . . . . . . . . . . . . . . Mary Bland

••• 0:46—Breasts, while struggling with Ed Begley Jr. on the couch. More breasts while Raoul counts money on her stomach. Long scene.

• 0:53—Buns and side view of right breast, while in hospital room with Raoul. A little dark.

National Lampoon Goes to the Movies (1982)

. . . . . . . . . . . . . . . . . . . . . . . . . . . . . . . Secretary

*a.k.a. Movie Madness*

Get Crazy (1983) . . . . . . . . . . . . . . . . . . . . . Violetta

Night of the Comet (1984) . . . . . . . . . . . . . . . . Carol

Hellhole (1985) . . . . . . . . . . . . . . . . . . . . Dr. Fletcher

Chopping Mall (1986) . . . . . . . . . . . . . . . . Mary Bland

*a.k.a. Killbots*

Nomads (1986) . . . . . . . . . . . . . . . . . . Dancing Mary

Terrorvision (1986). . . . . . . . . . . . . . . . . . . . . Raquel

Mortuary Academy (1988). . . . . . . . . . . . Mary Purcell

Let It Ride (1989) . . . . . . . . . . . . . . . . . . . . . Quinella

**Scenes from the Class Struggle in Beverly Hills** (1989) . . . . . . . . . . . . . . . . . . . . . . . . . . . .Lizabeth

••• 1:06—In black lingerie, then breasts in bedroom, then in bed with Juan.

Club Fed (1990) . . . . . . . . . . . . . . . . . . . . . . . . . Jezebel
Dick Tracy (1990) . . . . . . . . . . . . . . . . . Welfare Person
Rock 'n' Roll High School Forever (1990). . Doctor Vadar
Warlock (1990) . . . . . . . . . . . . . . . . . . . . . . . Channeller
Watchers II (1990). . . . . . . . . . . . . . . . . . Dr. Glatman
Motorama (1991) . . . . . . . . . . . . . . . . .Kidnapping Wife
Where Sleeping Dogs Lie (1991). . . . . . . Woman Tourist
Good Girls Don't (1993) . . . . . . . . . . . . . . . . . . Wiltern
*Made for Cable Movies:*
Acting on Impulse (1993; Showtime) . . . . . Receptionist
*Made for TV Movies:*
A Bunny's Tale (1985) . . . . . . . . . . . . . . . . Miss Renfroe
*TV:*
Babylon 5 (1994- ) . . . . . . . . . . . . . . . . . . . . Ko D'arth

## • Wray, Fay
*Films:*
Doctor X (1932) . . . . . . . . . . . . . . . . . . . . . . . . . . . Joan
The Most Dangerous Game (1932) . . . . .Eve Trowbridge
**King Kong** (1933). . . . . . . . . . . . . . . . . . Ann Darrow
  • 1:12—Right breast, after surfacing from the water
    after jumping off cliff with Bruce Cabot.
Mystery of the Wax Museum (1933) . . Charlotte Duncan
The Vampire Bat (1933) . . . . . . . . . . . . . . . . Ruth Bertin
Viva Villa! (1934). . . . . . . . . . . . . . . . . . . . . . . .Teresa
The Evil Mind (1935; British). . . . . . . . . . . . . . . .Rene
  *a.k.a. The Clairvoyant*
Melody for Three (1941) . . . . . . . . . . . . . Mary Stanley
Small Town Girl (1953) . . . . . . . . . Mrs. Gordon Kimbell
Hell on Frisco Bay (1956) . . . . . . . . . . . .Kay Stanley
Rock, Pretty Baby (1956). . . . . . . . . . . . . . Beth Daley
Crime of Passion (1957) . . . . . . . . . . . . . . .Alice Pope
Tammy and the Bachelor (1957). . . . . . . . . Mrs. Brent

## Wren, Clare
*Films:*
No Man's Land (1988) . . . . . . . . . . . . . . . . . .Deborah
**Season of Fear** (1989) . . . . . . . . . . .Sarah Drummond
  0:23—Breasts in bed with Mick. Long shot, hard to
    see.
  0:25—Brief silhouette, behind shower door.
  • 0:42—Side view of left breast, on top of Mick. Very,
    very brief left breast, turning over when they hear a
    noise outside.
Steel and Lace (1990) . . . . . . . . . . . . . . . . . . . . .Gally
*TV:*
Young Riders (1990-92) . . . . . . . . . . . . . .Rachel Dunn

## Wright, Amy
*Films:*
The Deer Hunter (1978) . . . . . . . . . . . . . . Bridesmaid
**Girlfriends** (1978). . . . . . . . . . . . . . . . . . . . . . . . .Ceil
  • 0:42—Brief breasts getting out of bed to talk to Mel-
    anie Mayron.
The Amityville Horror (1979). . . . . . . . . . . . . . Jackie
Breaking Away (1979) . . . . . . . . . . . . . . . . . . . .Nancy
Wise Blood (1979; U.S./German). . . . . . . .Sabbath Lilly
Heartland (1980) . . . . . . . . . . . . . . . . . . . . . . . .Clara
Inside Moves (1980) . . . . . . . . . . . . . . . . . . . . . . Ann

Stardust Memories (1980) . . . . . . . . . . . . . . . .Shelley
The Accidental Tourist (1988). . . . . . . . . . . .Rose Leary
Crossing Delancey (1988) . . . . . . . . . . . . . . . . . .Ricki
Deceived (1991) . . . . . . . . . . . . . . . . . . . Evelyn Wade
Love Hurts (1991) . . . . . . . . . . . . . . . . Karen Weaver
Hard Promises (1992). . . . . . . . . . . . . . . . . . . . .Shelley
Josh and S.A.M. (1993) . . . . . . . . . . . . . . . . .Waitress
Robot in the Family (1993). . . . . . . . . . . . . . . . n.a.
*Made for TV Movies:*
Settle the Score (1989). . . . . . . . . . . . . . . . . . . .Becky
To Dance with the White Dog (1993). . . . . . . . . Carrie

## Wright, Jenny
*Films:*
The Executioner's Song (1982). . . . . . . . . . .April Baker
  (European Version reviewed.)
**Pink Floyd The Wall** (1982) . . . . . . American Groupie
  ••• 0:41—Breasts, while doing strip tease dance, in back
    of a truck while it's parked backstage.
**World According to Garp** (1982) . . . . . . . . .Curbie
  •• 0:33—Brief breasts behind the bushes with Robin
    Williams giving him "something to write about."
**The Wild Life** (1984). . . . . . . . . . . . . . . . . . . . .Eileen
  •• 0:22—In bra and panties, then breasts changing in
    her bedroom while Christopher Penn watches from
    the window.
St. Elmo's Fire (1985) . . . . . . . . . . . . . . . . . . . . Felicia
Near Dark (1987). . . . . . . . . . . . . . . . . . . . . . . . .Mae
Out of Bounds (1987) . . . . . . . . . . . . . . . . . . . .Dizz
The Chocolate War (1988). . . . . . . . . . . . . . . . Lisa
Valentino Returns (1988) . . . . . . . . . . . . Sylvia Fuller
I, Madman (1989) . . . . . . . . . . . . . . . . . . . . . Virginia
A Shock to the System (1990) . . . . . .Melanie O'Connor
**Young Guns II** (1990) . . . . . . . . . . Jane Greathouse
  • 1:07—Buns, taking off her clothes, getting on a
    horse and riding away. Hair covers breasts.
  • 1:38—Buns, while walking down stairs during epi-
    logue.
Queens Logic (1991) . . . . . . . . . . . . . . . . . . . . Asha
**The Lawnmower Man** (1992) . . . . . . . .Marnie Burke
  (Unrated Director's cut reviewed.)
  •• 1:04—Right breast, while in bed with Jeff Fahey.
  • 1:15—Brief right breast, while in bed under Fahey.
*TV:*
Capital News (1990) . . . . . . . . . . . . . . .Doreen Duncan

## Wright, Robin
Significant other of actor/director Sean Penn.
*Films:*
Hollywood Vice Squad (1986) . . . . . . . . . . . . . . Lori
The Princess Bride (1987). . . . . . . . . . . . . . . Buttercup
**State of Grace** (1990) . . . . . . . . . . . . . . . . Kathleen
  •• 0:38—Breasts making love standing up with Sean
    Penn in the hall. Dark.
  1:01—In bra on bed with Penn, than walking
    around while talking to him.
  • 1:58—Brief side of right breast taking off towel and
    putting on blouse.

**Denial** (1991) . . . . . . . . . . . . . . . . . . . . . . . . . Sarah
  • 0:37—Side view of buns, while lying on top of Jason
    Patric.
The Playboys (1992) . . . . . . . . . . . . . . . . Tara Maguire
Toys (1992). . . . . . . . . . . . . . . . . . . . . . . . Gwen Tyler
Forrest Gump (1994) . . . . . . . . . . . . . . . . . . . . . n.a.
*TV:*
Santa Barbara . . . . . . . . . . . . . . . . . . . . Kelly Capwell

## Wright, Sylvia

*Films:*
**Bloody Birthday** (1980) . . . . . . . . . . . . . . .Girl in Van
  ••• 0:45—Breasts undressing in a van and making out
    with a guy.
Terror on Tour (1980) . . . . . . . . . . . . . . . . . . . . Carol
**Malibu Hot Summer** (1981) . . . . . . . .Actress at Party
*a.k.a. Sizzle Beach*
(*Sizzle Beach* is the re-released version with Kevin Costner featured on the cover. It is missing all the nude
scenes during the opening credits before 0:06.)
  •• 0:01—Nude, standing up during opening credits.
  ••• 1:07—Breasts fixing her hair in front of mirror, then
    full frontal nudity talking to Howard.
  • 1:09—Breasts on top of Howard.

## Wyhl, Jennifer

*Made for Cable Movies:*
**Soft Touch** (1987; Playboy). . . . . . . . . . . . . . . .Nancy
(Shown on *The Playboy Channel* as *Birds in Paradise*.)
  • 0:00—Breasts during opening credits.
**Soft Touch II** (1987; Playboy) . . . . . . . . . . . . . .Nancy
(Shown on *The Playboy Channel* as *Birds in Paradise*.)
  • 0:01—Breasts during opening credits.
  • 0:05—Breasts in bed with Neill.
  • 0:18—Breasts undressing for robbers. Brief full fron-
    tal nudity.
  •• 0:57—Breasts in bed with Neill.
  •• 1:01—Full frontal nudity in bed with Neill.

## • Wylde, Kim

See: Gielser, Regina.

## Wyss, Amanda

*Films:*
Fast Times at Ridgemont High (1982) . . . . . . . . . . . .Lisa
Better Off Dead (1985) . . . . . . . . . . . . . . . . .Beth Truss
A Nightmare on Elm Street (1985) . . . . . . . . . Tina Gray
Silverado (1985) . . . . . . . . . . . . . . . . . . . . . . . .Phoebe
**Deadly Innocents** (1988) . . . . . . . . . . . .Andy/Angela
  •• 0:12—Breasts, taking off T-shirt and putting on lin-
    gerie.
  ••• 1:29—Right breast, twice, with Andrew Stevens.
Powwow Highway (1988; U.S./British) . . . Rabbit Layton
To Die For (1988) . . . . . . . . . . . . . . . . . . . . . Celia Kett
Black Magic Woman (1990) . . . . . . . . . . Diane Abbott
Shakma (1990) . . . . . . . . . . . . . . . . . . . . . . . . . Tracy
To Die For 2 (1991). . . . . . . . . . . . . . . . . . . . . . .Celia
*a.k.a. Son of Darkness: To Die For II*
Bloodfist IV: Die Trying (1992). . . . . . . . . . . . .Shannon

*Made for TV Movies:*
My Mother's Secret Life (1984) . . . . . . . . . . Tobi Jensen

## Xuxa

Real name is Maria da Garca Meneghel.
Brazilian children's television show host.
*Films:*
**Love Strange Love** (1982; Brazilian) . . . . . . . . Tamara
  •• 0:26—Breasts standing on table, getting measured
    for outfit.
  ••• 0:29—Breasts again when Hugo watches. Long
    scene.
  •• 0:58—Right breast when she lets Hugo caress it.
    (Film is reversed since mole above her right breast
    appears over the left.)
  • 1:00—More right breast.
  •• 1:09—Breasts, stripping out of bear costume during
    party.
  ••• 1:13—Breasts several times undressing in room.
    Long scene.
  •• 1:27—Side view of left breast in bed with Hugo.
*TV:*
Xuxa! (1994- ) . . . . . . . . . . . . . . . . . . . . . . . . Hostess

## Yarnall, Celeste

*Films:*
The Nutty Professor (1963) . . . . . . . . . .College Student
Bob & Carol & Ted & Alice (1969). . . . . . . . . . . .Susan
**The Velvet Vampire** (1971) . . . . . . . . . Diane Le Fanu
  • 0:32—Brief breasts, while zipping up her blouse af-
    ter trying to seduce Lee.
  • 0:42—Breasts in desert scene when Lee pulls her
    blouse down.
  ••• 0:45—Breasts, while on the floor, making love with
    Lee.
  •• 0:55—Breasts in desert scene with Lee.
  • 0:57—Side view of buns, lying on top of someone in
    a coffin.
  • 1:02—Breasts, while in bed with Lee.
The Mechanic (1972). . . . . . . . . . . . . . . The Mark's Girl
Scorpio (1973). . . . . . . . . . . . . . . . . . . . .Helen Thomas
Fatal Beauty (1987) . . . . . . . . . . . . . . . . . . . . . .Laura
Funny About Love (1990). . . . . . . . . . . . Delta Gamma
Ambition (1991) . . . . . . . . . . . . . Beverly Hills Shopper
Driving Me Crazy (1991) . . . . . . . . . . . . . . Volvo Boss
Born Yesterday (1993) . . . . . . . . . . . . . . . Mrs. Hedges

## Yates, Cassie

*Films:*
The Evil (1977). . . . . . . . . . . . . . . . . . . . . . . . . . Mary
**Rolling Thunder** (1977) . . . . . . . . . . . . . . . . . .Candy
  ••• 1:31—Breasts while undressing in bedroom with
    Tommy Lee Jones.
  • 1:32—Right breast, while sitting on bed with Jones.
  • 1:33—Right breast, when Jones sits up in bed.
**Convoy** (1978) . . . . . . . . . . . . . . . . . . . . . . . .Violet
  • 0:21—Very brief left breast, while in truck sleeper
    with Kris Kristofferson.
F.I.S.T. (1978). . . . . . . . . . . . . . . . . . . . . . . . . . .Molly

FM (1978). . . . . . . . . . . . . . . . . . . . . . . . . . .Laura Coe
**The Osterman Weekend** (1983). . . . . Betty Cardone
•• 0:48—Breasts getting into bed with Chris Sarandon
while Rutger Hauer watches on TV.
• 0:51—Right breast, making love with Sarandon.
Unfaithfully Yours (1984). . . . . . . . . . . . . Carla Robbins
*Made for TV Movies:*
Having Babies II (1977). . . . . . . . . . . . . . .Paula Plotkin
Who'll Save Our Children? (1978). . . . . . .Lurene Garver
Of Mice and Men (1981) . . . . . . . . . . . . . . . . . . Mae
Listen To Your Heart (1983). . . . . . . . . . . . . . . .Stacey
Moment of Truth: Stalking Back (1993). . . . Sandi Boyer
*TV:*
Rich Man, Poor Man—Book II (1976-77) . Annie Adams
Nobody's Perfect (1980) . . . Detective Jennifer Dempsey
Detective in the House (1985). . . . . . . . .Diane Wyman
Dynasty (1987) . . . . . . . . . . . . . . . . . . . . Sarah Curtis

# Yazel, Carrie Jean

*Films:*
**Death Becomes Her** (1992). . . . . . . . .Girl at Dakota's
• 0:27—Brief buns in mirror, hiding from Meryl Streep
at Dakota's.
**Mr. Baseball** (1992) . . . . . . . . . . . . . . . . Coed in Bed
• 0:03—Very, very brief upper half of right breast,
while sleeping when Tom Selleck gets out of bed.
*Video Tapes:*
**Playboy Video Calendar 1992** (1991) . . . . . . . . June
••• 0:22—Breasts and buns in kitchen shoot. More
when pouring honey on her body.
••• 0:25—Nude, dancing in bar fantasy.
**Sexy Lingerie III** (1991) . . . . . . . . . . . . . . . . . .Model
**The Best of Sexy Lingerie** (1992). . . . . . . . . .Model
**Playboy's Playmate Review 1992** (1992)
. . . . . . . . . . . . . . . . . . . . . . . . . . . . . . . . . Miss May
••• 0:14—Nude outside with piano, then outside in
doorway and then in a house.
*Magazines:*
**Playboy** (May 1991) . . . . . . . . . . . . . . . . . . Playmate
••• 110-121—Nude.
**Playboy's Book of Lingerie** (Jul 1992) . . . . . . Herself
••• 34—Full frontal nudity.
••• 42-43—Breasts.
**Playboy's Book of Lingerie** (Sep 1992) . . . . . Herself
•• 57—Buns and left breast.
**Playboy's Book of Lingerie** (Nov 1992) . . . . . Herself
•• 18—Left breast.
•• 33—Left breast and partial lower frontal nudity.
**Playboy** (Feb 1993). . . . . . . . . . . Being in Nothingness
• 126—Right breast and lower frontal nudity.
**Playboy** (Apr 1993). . . . . . . . . . . . . . . . . Tattoo You
••• 80—Full frontal nudity with temporary tattoos on
her stomach.
**Playboy's Book of Lingerie** (Jul 1993) . . . . . . Herself
••• 61—Full frontal nudity.
**Playboy's Wet & Wild Women** (Aug 1993) . . Herself
••• 24-25—Full frontal nudity.
• 28—Left breast and lower frontal nudity in lingerie.
••• 58—Breasts.

**Playboy's Video Playmates** (Sep 1993) . . . . . .Herself
••• 86-87—Full frontal nudity.
**Playboy's Book of Lingerie** (Jan 1994) . . . . . .Herself
••• 44—Breasts.
••• 94—Breasts.
**Playboy's Book of Lingerie** (Mar 1994). . . . . .Herself
•• 80-81—Right breast.
**Playboy's Book of Lingerie** (May 1994) . . . . . Herself
•• 88-89—Left breast.
**Playmates at Play** (Jul 1994) . . . . . . . . . . . . . .Herself
••• 3-5—Breasts.
**Playboy's Girls of Summer '94** (Jul 1994). . . .Herself
••• 71—Breasts.
••• 88—Full frontal nudity.
**Playboy's Book of Lingerie** (Jul 1994). . . . . . .Herself
•• 9—Breasts under sheer robe.

# York, Brittany

a.k.a. Alison Armitage.
*Films:*
**I Posed for Playboy** (1991). . . . . . . . . . . . . . .Herself
*a.k.a. Posing: Inspired by Three Real Stories*
(Shown on network TV without the nudity.)
(Nude scenes added for video tape.)
••• 0:20—Right breast, then breasts on motorcycle dur-
ing photo shoot.
••• 0:22—In T-shirt, then breasts during second photo
shoot.
**Miracle Beach** (1991) . . . . . . . . . . . . . . . . Girl in Bed
•• 0:14—Breasts, lying in bed next to Scotty, then sit-
ting up. She's on the right.
Secret Games (1991) . . . . . . . . . . . . . . . . . . . . . . .Nun
(Unrated version reviewed.)
*TV:*
Acapulco H.E.A.T. (1993- ) . . . . . . . . . . . . "Cat" Pascal
*Video Tapes:*
**Playboy Video Calendar 1992** (1991). . . .November
••• 0:43—Breasts in lingerie. Nude in studio shoot.
••• 0:45—In black body stocking and nude in oriental
style shoot.
**Wet and Wild III** (1991) . . . . . . . . . . . . . . . . . Model
**The Best of Video Playmate Calendars** (1992)
. . . . . . . . . . . . . . . . . . . . . . . . . . . . . . . . . Playmate
0:22—In lingerie.
••• 0:23—Nude in studio.
••• 0:25—In lingerie and nude in asian-style studio set-
ting.
**The Best of Wet and Wild** (1992). . . . . . . . . Model
**Sexy Lingerie IV** (1992) . . . . . . . . . . . . . . . . . Model
**Wet and Wild IV** (1992). . . . . . . . . . . . . . . . . Model
*Magazines:*
**Playboy** (Oct 1990) . . . . . . . . . . . . . . . . . . . .Playmate
••• 102—Nude.
**Playboy's Book of Lingerie** (Jul 1991). . . . . . .Herself
• 48—Upper half of left breast and upper half of buns.
**Playboy's Book of Lingerie** (Nov 1991) . . . . .Herself
• 9—Lower frontal nudity.
**Playboy's Book of Lingerie** (Mar 1992). . . . . .Herself
••• 55—Full frontal nudity.

**Playboy's Book of Lingerie** (Sep 1992) . . . . . Herself
•• 17—Left breast and lower frontal nudity.
•• 100—Left breast and buns.
**Playboy's Book of Lingerie** (Nov 1992) . . . . . Herself
• 55—Left breast.
**Playboy's Nudes** (Dec 1992) . . . . . . . . . . . . . Herself
•• 42—Right breast.
**Playboy's Book of Lingerie** (Jan 1993) . . . . . . Herself
••• 46-47—Breasts.
**Playboy** (Feb 1993) . . . . . . . . . . . Being in Nothingness
• 127—Half of left breast in sheer purple lingerie.
• 129—Most of right breast and lower frontal nudity.
••• 133—Full frontal nudity.
**Playboy's Book of Lingerie** (Mar 1993) . . . . . Herself
••• 64-65—Breasts.
**Playboy's Book of Lingerie** (May 1993) . . . . . Herself
••• 51-53—Full frontal nudity.
**Playboy's Book of Lingerie** (Jul 1993) . . . . . . Herself
••• 53—Breasts.
• 65—Breasts and buns under sheer white top.
**Playboy's Book of Lingerie** (Sep 1993) . . . . . Herself
• 21—Lower frontal nudity.
••• 52—Breasts.
••• 89—Breasts.
**Playboy's Video Playmates** (Sep 1993) . . . . . Herself
••• 88-91—Breasts.
**Playboy's Book of Lingerie** (Nov 1993) . . . . . Herself
• 40—Side view of buns.
**Playboy's Book of Lingerie** (Jan 1994) . . . . . . Herself
• 69—Lower frontal nudity.
**Playboy's Book of Lingerie** (Mar 1994) . . . . . Herself
• 47—Buns.
Sport (Mar 1994) . . . . . . . . . . . . . . . . Feel the H.E.A.T.
**Playboy's Book of Lingerie** (May 1994) . . . . . Herself
• 65—Lower frontal nudity.
••• 82-83—Full frontal nudity.

## York, Linda

*Films:*
Chain Gang Women (1972) . . . . . . . . . . . . . . . . . . .n.a.
**Video Vixens** (1973) . . . . . . . . . . . . . Dial-A-Snatch Girl
•• 0:34—Nude on a turntable during a commercial,
getting felt by four blindfolded guys.

## • York, Rachel

*Films:*
Billy Bathgate (1991) . . . . . . . . . . . Embassy Club Singer
Killer Instinct (1992) . . . . . . . . . . . . . . . . . . . .Lotti Coll
*a.k.a. Mad Dog Coll*
Dead Center (1993) . . . . . . . . . . . . . . . . . . . . . .Mary
**Taking the Heat** (1993) . . . . . . . . . . . . . . . . . . Susan
•• 0:19—Left breast, while enthusiastically making love
in bed on top of George Segal. Very, very brief
breasts when changing positions to under the
sheets.

## York, Susannah

*Films:*
Tunes of Glory (1960) . . . . . . . . . . . . . . Morag Sinclair
Tom Jones (1963) . . . . . . . . . . . . . . . . . . . . . . . .Sophie
A Man for All Seasons (1966) . . . . . . . . . Margaret More
**The Killing of Sister George** (1968)
. . . . . . . . . . . . . . . . . . . . . . . . . . . . . .Alice McNaught
0:19—Breasts under sheer blue nightgown.
0:59—In black bra and panties.
1:45—In black bra and panties getting undressed.
•• 2:07—(0:09 into tape 2) Breasts lying in bed with
another woman.
**Images** (1972; Irish) . . . . . . . . . . . . . . . . . . . . .Cathryn
• 0:59—Brief lower frontal nudity, then right breast ly-
ing on the bed.
1:38—Brief buns in the shower.
X, Y and Zee (1972) . . . . . . . . . . . . . . . . . . . . . . . Stella
That Lucky Touch (1975) . . . . . . . . . . . . Julia Richardson
**The Adventures of Eliza Fraser** (1976; Australian)
. . . . . . . . . . . . . . . . . . . . . . . . . . . . . . . .Elisa Fraser
• 1:10—Brief breasts twice during ceremony. Paint on
her face while running from hut.
• 1:30—Brief, upper half of left beast, while bathing in
river with Bracefell.
**The Silent Partner** (1978) . . . . . . . . . . . . . . . . .Julie
• 0:38—Very brief right breast pulling her dress back
up with Elliott Gould.
Superman (1978) . . . . . . . . . . . . . . . . . . . . . . . . .Lara
**The Shout** (1979) . . . . . . . . . . . . . . . . Rachel Fielding
•• 0:53—Brief breasts changing from a bathrobe to a
blouse in bedroom.
• 1:02—Brief nude in upstairs room getting ready to
make love with Alan Bates.
1:05—Brief buns, standing at end of hallway.
1:09—In white slip inside and outside house.
1:11—Breasts in bathtub with John Hurt.
• 1:18—Brief breasts getting up from bed with Bates.
Long shot, hard to see anything.
The Awakening (1980) . . . . . . . . . . . . . . . . Jane Turner
Falling in Love Again (1980) . . . . . . . . . . . . . .Sue Lewis
Pretty Kill (1987) . . . . . . . . . . . . . . . . . . . . . . . . .Toni
A Summer Story (1988) . . . . . . . . . . . Mrs. Narracrombe
Illusions (1992) . . . . . . . . . . . . . . . . . . . . . . .Dr. Sinclair

## Young, Dey

*Films:*
Rock 'n' Roll High School (1979) . . . . . . . Kate Rambeau
Dead Kids (1981; Australian/New Zealand) . . . .Caroline
*a.k.a. Strange Behavior*
Strange Invaders (1983) . . . . . . . . . . . . . . . Teen Girl
Doin' Time (1984) . . . . . . . . . . . . . . . . . . . Vicki Norris
The Running Man (1987) . . . . . . . . . . . . . . . . . . .Amy
Spaceballs (1987) . . . . . . . . . . . . . . . . . . . . . .Waitress
The Serpent and the Rainbow (1988) . . . . . Mrs. Cassedy
Spontaneous Combustion (1989) . . . . . . . . . . . . Rachel
Pretty Woman (1990) . . . . . . . . . . Snobby Saleswoman
Frankie & Johnny (1991) . . . . . . . . . . . Johnny's Ex-Wife
No Place to Hide (1991) . . . . . . . . . . . . . . . . . . .Karen
Back In the U.S.S.R. (1992) . . . . . . . . . . . . . . Claudia

**Conflict of Interest** (1992) . . . . . . . . . . . . . . . . . Vera
0:08—In bra, while sitting in Mick's lap.
- 0:31—Brief right breast, while turning over on her back in bed with Mick.
- • 0:32—Left breast, while in bed, getting kissed by Mick.

*Made for TV Movies:*
In the Shadows, Someone's Watching (1993)
. . . . . . . . . . . . . . . . . . . . . . . . . . . . . . Lydia Holroyd

## Young, Gabriela

*Video Tapes:*
**Intimate Workout For Lovers** (1992)
. . . . . . . . . . . . . . . . . . . . . . . . Romantic Relaxation
- •• 0:01—Nude, in bedroom, in bathtub and in bed.
**Playboy's 101 Ways to Excite Your Lover** (1992)
. . . . . . . . . . . . . . . . . . . . . . . . . . . . . Cast Member

*Magazines:*
**Playboy's Book of Lingerie** (Jan 1992) . . . . . . Herself
- •• 31—Buns and side of right breast.

## Young, Karen

*Films:*
**Deep in the Heart** (1983; British) . . . Kathleen Sullivan
*a.k.a. Handgun*
- 0:35—Buns and brief breasts undressing and getting forced into bed with Larry. (Her hair gets in the way.)
- •• 0:36—Brief breasts and buns, getting out of bed. Brief right breast when putting her dress on.
Almost You (1984) . . . . . . . . . . . . . . . Lisa Willoughby
1:00—Partial left breast while kissing Griffin Dunne in bed.
Birdy (1985) . . . . . . . . . . . . . . . . . . . . . Hannah Rourke
9 1/2 Weeks (1986). . . . . . . . . . . . . . . . . . . . . . . Sue
Heat (1987) . . . . . . . . . . . . . . . . . . . . . . . . . . . Holly
Jaws: The Revenge (1987). . . . . . . . . . . . . Carla Brody
Torch Song Trilogy (1988). . . . . . . . . . . . . . . . Laurel
**Criminal Law** (1989) . . . . . . . . . . . . . . . Ellen Falkner
- 1:21—Very brief buns, then brief breasts in bed with Ben.
**Night Game** (1989) . . . . . . . . . . . . . . . . . . . . . Roxy
0:02—In white slip with Roy Scheider.
- 0:06—Right breast, while in bed with Scheider after he answers the phone.

*Made for TV Movies:*
The Summer My Father Grew Up (1991) . . . . Chandelle

## Young, Robbin

*Films:*
For Your Eyes Only (1981). . . . . . . . . . Flower Shop Girl
Night Shift (1982). . . . . . . . . . . . . . . . . . . . . . . Nancy
*Magazines:*
**Playboy** (Jun 1981) . . . . . . . . . . . . . For Your Eyes Only
- ••• 126-127—Breasts (won a contest to appear in the film and in *Playboy* magazine).
**Playboy** (Dec 1981). . . . . . . . . . . . . . Sex Stars of 1981
- ••• 244—Frontal nudity.

## Young, Sean

*Films:*
Jane Austen in Manhattan (1980). . . . . . . . . . . Ariadne
Stripes (1981) . . . . . . . . . . . . . . . . . . . . Louise Cooper
Blade Runner (1982) . . . . . . . . . . . . . . . . . . . Rachael
Young Doctors in Love (1982) . . . . . Dr. Stephanie Brody
0:48—In white panties and camisole top in the surgery room with Michael McKean.
Dune (1984) . . . . . . . . . . . . . . . . . . . . . . . . . . Chani
On the back of the laser disc cover, there is a small photo of her in a sheer black blouse lying down with Kyle MacLachlan.
Baby... Secret of the Lost Legend (1985)
. . . . . . . . . . . . . . . . . . . . . . . Susan Matthew-Loomis
**No Way Out** (1987) . . . . . . . . . . . . . . . . Susan Atwell
0:11—In black stockings, garter belt & corset in love scene in back of limousine with Kevin Costner.
- ••• 0:13—Side view of left breast, then brief right breast, going into Nina's apartment with Costner.
0:21—In bed in pink lingerie and a robe talking on telephone when Costner is in Manila.
0:31—In corset and stockings with garter belt in bathroom talking to Costner.
Wall Street (1987) . . . . . . . . . . . . . . . . . . . Kate Gekko
**The Boost** (1989). . . . . . . . . . . . . . . . . . Linda Brown
- 0:16—Very, very brief breasts jumping into the swimming pool with James Woods. Very, very brief side view of right breast and buns, twice, getting out of the pool, sitting on edge, then getting pulled back in by James Woods.
- •• 0:17—Left breast, while in pool talking to Woods. Right breast visible under water.
0:48—Brief breasts under water in spa with Woods.
Cousins (1989). . . . . . . . . . . . . . . . . . . . Tish Kozinski
1:28—In black bra, in hotel room with William Petersen.
**Fire Birds** (1990) . . . . . . . . . . . . . . Billie Lee Guthrie
*a.k.a. Wings of the Apache*
- 0:52—Very, very brief right breast twice in bed with Nicolas Cage.
**A Kiss Before Dying** (1991) . . Ellen/Dorothy Carlsson
- •• 0:31—Brief breasts making love in bed with Matt Dillon. Kind of dark.
- 0:35—Brief side view or right breast in shower with Dillon. Don't see her face.
1:11—Very brief partial left breast in gaping pajama top when she leans over to turn off the light.
**Love Crimes** (1991) . . . . . . . . . . . . . . Dana Greenway
(Unrated version reviewed.)
- •• 0:20—Almost left breast, getting out of bathtub. Buns and partial lower frontal nudity, getting dressed.
- •• 0:55—Breasts in open blouse, yelling at Patrick Bergin.
- 0:57—Brief right breast, on bed in open blouse.
- ••• 0:59—Nude in bathtub.
- ••• 1:01—Breasts, making love with Bergin. Lit with red light.

••• 1:03—Full frontal nudity, getting covered with a towel.
• 1:08—Full frontal nudity, in Polaroid that Maria looks at.
• 1:11—More full frontal nudity in Polaroid.
1:21—Partial right breast, while taking a shower.
• 1:23—Brief breasts in the shower.
1:25—Very brief right breast in gaping robe.
1:27—Full frontal nudity in burning Polaroid.
Once Upon A Crime (1992) . . . . . . . . . . . . . . . . Phoebe
Ace Ventura: Pet Detective (1993). . . . . . . . . . . . . .Lois
1:17—In bra and panties after Ace manages to rip off all her clothes in order to prove she's a man.
Fatal Instinct (1993) . . . . . . . . . . . . . . . . . . Lola Cain
Hold Me, Thrill Me, Kiss Me (1993). . . . . . . . . . . Twinkle
(Unrated version reviewed.)
Model By Day (1994) . . . . . . . . . . . . . . . . . Mercedes
(Shown on network TV without the nudity.)
*Made for Cable Movies:*
**Blue Ice** (1992; Showtime) . . . . . . . . . .Stacy Mansdorf
• 0:17—Brief breasts and buns, while making love with Michael Caine.
• 0:18—Brief buns and partial back side of left breast, while sitting up in bed.
**Sketch Artist** (1992; Showtime). . . . . . . . . . . Rayanne
0:51—In black bra in bed with Jeff Fahey.
•• 0:52—Right breast, several times while making love in bed with Fahey.
*Made for TV Movies:*
Witness to the Execution (1994) . . . . . . . Jessica Traynor

# Zabou

*Films:*
**The Perils of Gwendoline in the Land of the Yik Yak** (1984; French). . . . . . . . . . . . . . . . . . . . . . . Beth
•• 0:36—Breasts, after taking off her blouse in the rain in the forest.
•• 0:57—Breasts while in torture chamber, getting rescued by Tawny Kitaen.
•• 1:04—Breasts after Kitaen escapes.
• 1:11—Buns, in costume during fight.
**One Woman or Two** (1986; French) . . . . . Constance
*a.k.a. Une Femme Ou Deux*
•• 0:28—Brief breasts pulling up her blouse for Gerard Depardieu.
C'est La Vie (1990; French) . . . . . . . . . . . . . . . . . Bella

# Zadora, Pia

Singer.
*Films:*
Santa Claus Conquers the Martians (1964) . . . . . Girmar
**Butterfly** (1982) . . . . . . . . . . . . . . . . . . . . . . . . .Kady
0:15—Silhouette changing while Stacy Keach watches.
•• 0:33—Breasts and buns getting into the bath.
••• 0:35—Breasts in bathtub when Keach is giving her a bath.

Nevada Heat (1982) . . . . . . . . . . . . . . . . . . . . .Bobbi
*a.k.a. Fake-Out*
• 0:14—Very brief partial right breast and brief buns, in the showers.
• 0:47—Side of left breast, while in bubble bath with Desi Arnaz, Jr.
**The Lonely Lady** (1983) . . . . . . . . . . JeniLee Randall
• 0:12—Brief breasts getting raped by Ray Liotta, after getting out of the pool.
•• 0:22—Brief breasts, then left breast, while making love with Walter.
•• 0:28—Side view breasts lying in bed with Walter.
•• 0:44—Buns and side view of left breast taking a shower.
• 0:46—Very brief right breast, in bed with George.
•• 1:05—Left breast, then brief breasts making love with Vinnie.
Voyage of the Rock Aliens (1985) . . . . . . . . . . . DeeDee
*a.k.a. When the Rains Begin to Fall*
Hairspray (1988) . . . . . . . . . . . . . . . . The Beatnik Chick
Naked Gun 33 1/3: The Final Insult (1993) . . . . . Herself
*Magazines:*
**Penthouse** (Oct 1983) . . . . . . . . . . . . . . . . . . . . .Pia
**Playboy** (Nov 1983) . . . . . . . . . . . Sex in Cinema 1983
•• 144—Frontal nudity.

# Zakovich, Danise

*Films:*
**Round Trip to Heaven** (1992) . . . . . . . .Miss Moscow
•• 1:06—Buns and upper half breasts, undressing in bedroom.
••• 1:07—Breasts, opening her towel for Zach Galligan.
• 1:12—Very brief right breast, while in bed with Galligan.
*Video Tapes:*
Inside Sports: Beauties on the Beach (1992). . . . . Model

# Zambelli, Zaira

*Films:*
**Bye Bye Brazil** (1980; Brazilian). . . . . . . . . . . . Dasdô
•• 1:11—Buns, then breasts outside by a boat with Cigano.
Fulaninha (1986; Brazilian). . . . . . . . . . . . . . . Sulamita

# Zane, Lisa

Sister of actor Billy Zane.
*Films:*
Gross Anatomy (1989) . . . . . . . . . . . . . . . . . . . . Luann
**Pucker Up and Bark Like a Dog** (1989)
. . . . . . . . . . . . . . . . . . . . . . . . . . . . . .Taylor Phillips
•• 0:52—Breasts in shower with Max. Left breast, while in bed.
**Bad Influence** (1990) . . . . . . . . . . . . . . . . . .Claire
• 0:39—Brief breasts on video tape seen on TV at party.
Femme Fatale (1990) . . . . . . . . . . . . . . . . . . . . Cynthia
Freddy's Dead: The Final Nightmare (1991)
. . . . . . . . . . . . . . . . . . . . . . . . . . .Maggie Burroughs

**Unveiled** (1993) . . . . . . . . . . Stephania Montgomery
• 1:06—Very, very brief left breast in gaping gown, while bending over to pick stuff up off the floor.
*Made for TV Movies:*
Dark Reflection (1994) . . . . . . . . . . . . . . . . . .Elizabeth

# Zann, Lenore
*Films:*
Black Mirror (1980; Canadian) . . . . . . . . . . . . . . . . .n.a.
Happy Birthday to Me (1980; Canadian) . . . . . .Maggie
The Hounds of Notre Dame (1980; Canadian)
. . . . . . . . . . . . . . . . . . . . . . . . . . . . . . . . . Lila Petrie
**American Nightmare** (1981; Canadian) . . . . . . . Tina
••• 0:25—Breasts and buns while dancing on stage.
•• 1:05—Breasts and buns while dancing on stage again.
Visiting Hours (1982; Canadian) . . . . . . . . . . . . . . .Lisa
0:39—In panties, while talking with Michael Ironside.
Murder By Phone (1983; Canadian) . . . .Connie Lawson
*a.k.a. Bells*
**One Night Only** (1984; Canadian) . . . . . . . . . . .Anne
•• 0:20—Breasts while getting dressed in bedroom with Jamie.
• 1:04—Right breast in bedroom with Jamie.
••• 1:19—Breasts and buns while making love with Jamie.
Def-Con 4 (1985) . . . . . . . . . . . . . . . . . . . . . . . . . J. J.
Return (1985) . . . . . . . . . . . . . . . . . . . . . . . . . Susan
Mania (1986; Canadian)
. . . . . . . . . . . . . . . .The Good Samaritan/Julie Somers
The Girl (1987; British) . . . . . . . . . . . . . . . . . . . .Viveca
Pretty Kill (1987) . . . . . . . . . . . . . . . . . . . . . . . Carrie
Geeks in Love (1992; Canadian) . . . . . . . . . . . . . . .n.a.
**Cold Sweat** (1993) . . . . . . . . . . . . . . Catherine Wicker
•• 0:04—Brief buns in panties, then partial lower frontal nudity in bra, panties, garter belt and stockings. Brief breasts while making love in office with David.
•• 0:46—Breasts in bubble bath while talking to Ben Cross.
••• 0:50—Breasts, while lying on bed and talking to Cross.
*Made for TV Movies:*
Love and Hate (1989) . . . . . . . . . . . . . . . . . . . . .Lynne
Tom Alone (1989) . . . . . . . . . . . . . . . . . . . . Lily Manse
*Magazines:*
**Playboy** (Jan 1992) . . . . . . . . . . . . . . .The Year in Sex
•• 145—Breasts in bed in photo from a stage play in Chicago.

# Zee, Ona
Adult film actress.
a.k.a. Ona Simms Wiegers.
*Films:*
**Enrapture** (1989) . . . . . . . . . . . . . . . . . . .Chase Webb
•• 0:13—In red bra, panties, garter belt and stockings. Buns in G-string, then breasts undressing when she doesn't know Keith is watching.

•• 0:17—Breasts when Keith fantasizes about her while he's making love with Martha.
•• 0:21—Breasts in back of limousine with a lucky guy.
••• 1:08—Full frontal nudity making love on top of Keith in bed.
The Art of Dying (1991) . . . . . . . . . . . . Frances Warner
*Made for Cable TV:*
**Real Sex 5** (1993; HBO) . . . . . . . . .Of Human Bondage
• 0:00—Brief left breast during opening credits.
••• 0:12—Breasts, leading Frank Zee up stairs and in bed. More breasts while spanking him.
••• 0:15—Breasts, getting clips put on her nipples. Buns in T-back while getting spanked.

# • Zenor, Suzanne
*Films:*
**Get to Know Your Rabbit** (1972) . . . . . . . . . . .Paula
• 0:06—Very brief buns, getting out of bed.
Play It Again, Sam (1972) . . . . . . . . . . Discotheque Girl
Lucky Lady (1973) . . . . . . . . . . . . . . . . . . . . . Brunette
The Way We Were (1973) . . . . . . . . . . . . Dumb Blonde
The Choirboys (1977) . . . . . . . . . . . . . Blonde at Party
Rabbit Test (1978) . . . . . . . . . . . . . . Mother of Triplets

# Zhivago, Stacia
*Films:*
**Sorority House Massacre 2** (1990) . . . . . . . Kimberly
••• 0:21—Nude, taking a shower.
0:50—In wet lingerie.
• 0:53—Buns, while going up the stairs.
0:55—Brief buns, while going up the stairs.
• 1:00—Brief breasts, sitting up in bathtub filled with bloody water to strangle Linda.
*Video Tapes:*
**Scream Queen Hot Tub Party** (1991) . . . . . Kimberly
••• 0:16—Nude, in shower scene from *Sorority House Massacre 2.*

# • Zimmie, Elizabeth
*Films:*
Sorority House Party (1992) . . . . Screaming Sorority Girl
**Killing Obsession** (1994) . . . . . . . . . . . . . . . . . Babs
• 0:43—Brief left breast, several times, while posing with Randy during photo shoot.

# Zinszer, Pamela
*Films:*
**The Happy Hooker Goes to Washington** (1977)
. . . . . . . . . . . . . . . . . . . . . . . . . . . . . . . . . .Linda
• 1:19—Brief breasts in raincoat flashing in front of congressional panel.
*Video Tapes:*
Playboy Video Magazine, Volume 2 (1983)
. . . . . . . . . . . . . . . . . . . . . .Herself/Playboy Playoffs
*Magazines:*
**Playboy** (Mar 1974) . . . . . . . . . . . . . . . . . . Playmate
••• 102-111—Nude.
**Playboy** (Jul 1980) . . . . . . . . . . . .The World of Playboy
••• 12—Breasts.

## Zucker, Miriam

*Films:*

**Prime Evil** (1987) . . . . . . . . . . . . . . . . . . Nancy Deans
•• 0:03—Breasts several times, during sacrificial cere-
mony.
**Senior Week** (1987) . . . . . . . . . . Princeton Dream Girl
•• 0:42—Breasts during dream.
Wildest Dreams (1987) . . . . . . . . . . . . . . . . . Customer
Alien Space Avenger (1988) . . . . . . . . Bordello Reporter
New York's Finest (1988). . . . . . . . . . . . . . . Mrs. Rush
**Sensations** (1988). . . . . . . . . . . . . . . . Cookie Woman
• 0:06—Breasts on couch making love with a guy
while Jenny and Brian watch.
A Woman Obsessed (1989). . . . . . . . . . . . . . . . Betsy

## Zuniga, Daphne

*Films:*

The Initiation (1984). . . . . . . . . . . . . . . . . . . Kelly Terry
0:34—Upper half of buns, putting on panties while
someone watches from inside the closet. Don't see
her face.
The Sure Thing (1985) . . . . . . . . . . . . Alison Bradbury
Visionquest (1985) . . . . . . . . . . . . . . . Margie Epstein
Modern Girls (1987) . . . . . . . . . . . . . . . . . . . . Margo
Spaceballs (1987) . . . . . . . . . . . . . . . . . . Princess Vespa
**Last Rites** (1988). . . . . . . . . . . . . . . . . . . . . . Angela
• 0:04—Very brief breasts running into the bathroom
to escape from being shot. Covered with blood,
don't see her face. Very brief right breast reaching
for a bathrobe. Don't really see anything.
0:40—Buns, behind a shower door.
0:50—Buns, getting out of bed and standing in front
of Tom Berenger.
The Fly II (1989) . . . . . . . . . . . . . . . . . . . . . . . . Beth
Gross Anatomy (1989) . . . . . . . . . . . . . Laurie Rorbach
**Staying Together** (1989). . . . . . . . . . . . Beverly Young
•• 0:56—Buns, lying in bed with Kit. Nice, long buns
scene.
Mad at the Moon (1993)
. . . . . . . . . . . . . . . . . Jenny's Mom as a Young Woman
*Made for Cable Movies:*
Prey of the Chameleon (1992; Showtime)
. . . . . . . . . . . . . . . . . . . . . . . . . . . Elizabeth Burrows
*Made for TV Movies:*
Quarterback Princess (1983) . . . . . . . . . . . . Kim Maida
*TV:*
Melrose Place (1992- ) . . . . . . . . . . . . . . . . Jo Reynolds
*Magazines:*
**Playboy** (Oct 1994). . . . . . . . . . . . . . . . . . . Grapevine
• 174—Side of left breast in gaping dress top. B&W.

# Actors

# Aames, Willie

*Films:*
Scavenger Hunt (1979) . . . . . . . . . . . . . Kenny Stevens
**Paradise** (1981). . . . . . . . . . . . . . . . . . . . . . . . David
  0:42—Buns, while walking into the ocean with a
  fishing net. Dark, hard to see anything.
  •• 1:12—Nude swimming with Phoebe Cates under
  water.
Zapped! (1982). . . . . . . . . . . . . . . . . . . . . . . Peyton
*Made for TV Movies:*
An Eight is Enough Wedding (1989) . . . . . . . . . Tommy
*TV:*
Swiss Family Robinson (1975-76) . . . . . . Fred Robinson
We'll Get By (1975). . . . . . . . . . . . . . . . . . Kenny Platt
Eight is Enough (1977-81) . . . . . . . . . Tommy Bradford
We're Movin' (1982). . . . . . . . . . . . . . . . . . . . . . Host
Charles in Charge (1984-85) . . . . . . . . Buddy Lembeck
Charles in Charge (1987-90) . . . . . . . . Buddy Lembeck

# • Abbananto, Sean

*Video Tapes:*
**Playboy Night Dreams** (1993) . . . Intimate Strangers
  ••• 0:15—Buns, while making love on top of his lover in
  bed.
Playboy's Erotic Fantasies III (1993) . . . . . . . . . . . . .n.a.
**Playboy's Sensual Fantasy for Lovers** (1993)
. . . . . . . . . . . . . . . . . . . . . . . . . . . . . . Film Fantasies
  •• 0:27—Buns while making love, in "sheik" fantasy
  with his lover.

# Abele, Jim

*Films:*
**Student Affairs** (1987) . . . . . . . . . Andrew Armstrong
  • 1:07—Buns, when his friends play a practical joke on
  him in the shower.
Wimps (1987) . . . . . . . . . . . . . . . . . . . .Charles Conrad

# Abraham, Ken

*Films:*
**Creepozoids** (1987) . . . . . . . . . . . . . . . . . . . . . Butch
  •• 0:16—Side view of buns, while standing in shower
  with Linnea Quigley.
Hobgoblins (1988) . . . . . . . . . . . . . . . . . . . . . . Thug
Vice Academy (1988) . . . . . . . . . . . . . . . . . . Dwayne
**Deadly Embrace** (1989) . . . . . . . . . . . Chris Thompson
  •• 0:17—Buns, while taking a shower.
  • 1:01—Brief buns, while making love on top of Lin-
  nea Quigley.
Girlfriend from Hell (1989) . . . . . . . . . . . . . . . Rocco
Ministry of Vengeance (1989) . . . . . . . . . . . . . Sparky
Marked for Murder (1990) . . . . . . . . . . . . . . . . .n.a.
Terror Night (1991). . . . . . . . . . . . . . . . . . . . . . .n.a.
Mind, Body & Soul (1992) . . . . . . . . . . . . . . . . Sean

# • Acovone, Jay

*Films:*
**Cruising** (1980). . . . . . . . . . . . . . . . . . . . . . Skip Lee
  • 0:56—Brief buns, when towel falls off after police
  burst into room.

Times Square (1980) . . . . . . . . . . . . . . . . . . . . . . n.a.
Cold Steel (1987). . . . . . . . . . . . . . . . . .Cooke Manero
Doctor Mordrid (1992) . . . . . . . . . . . . . . . . . . . Tony

# Addabbo, Anthony

*Made for Cable TV:*
**Red Shoe Diaries: Weekend Pass** (1993; Showtime)
. . . . . . . . . . . . . . . . . . . . . . . . . . . . . . . . . . .Eddie
  • 0:09—Lower half of buns, while walking in barracks
  in front of Jane.
  •• 0:11—Buns, while getting dressed. Out of focus.
*Made for TV Movies:*
Love on the Run (1994) . . . . . . . . . . . . . . . . . . . n.a.
*Video Tapes:*
**Inside Out 4** (1992). . . . . . . . . . . .Kenner/Put Asunder
(Unrated version reviewed.)
  ••• 0:22—Buns, while lying in bed with Dolores.
  •• 0:25—Buns, while lying in bed on top of Dolores.

# Adell, Steve

*Films:*
**Almost Pregnant** (1992) . . . . . . . . . . . .Muscle Man
(Unrated version reviewed.)
  • 0:04—Buns, while making love in bed with Tanya
  Roberts.
  •• 0:20—Buns, while on top of Roberts during Jeff Conaway's dream.

# • Adler, Bill

*Films:*
The Pom Pom Girls (1976) . . . . . . . . . . . . . . . . Duane
The Van (1977) . . . . . . . . . . . . . . . . . . . . . . . . Steve
Love and the Midnight Auto Supply (1978) . . . . .Ramon
Malibu Beach (1978) . . . . . . . . . . . . . . . . . . . . . n.a.
**Van Nuys Blvd.** (1979). . . . . . . . . . . . . . . . . . Bobby
  • 0:21—Brief buns, while making out with Wanda in
  the back of his van.
  • 0:58—Brief buns, while making love on top of
  Moon.

# Agterberg, Toon

*Films:*
**Spetters** (1980; Dutch) . . . . . . . . . . . . . . . . . . Hans
  ••• 0:35—Frontal nudity, measuring and comparing his
  manlihood with his friends in the auto shop.
  • 1:21—Buns, getting gang raped by gay guy he has
  been stealing money from.
Kafka (1992; U.S./French) . . . . . . . . . Youthful Anarchist

# Albert, Edward

Son of actor Eddie Albert.
*Films:*
Butterflies Are Free (1972) . . . . . . . . . . . . . . . . .Don
Forty Carats (1973) . . . . . . . . . . . . . . . . .Peter Latham
The Domino Principle (1977) . . . . . . . . . . . . Ross Pine
The Purple Taxi (1977; French/Italian/Irish) . . . . . . .Jerry
The Greek Tycoon (1978). . . . . . . . . . . . . . Nico Tomasis
Galaxy of Terror (1981) . . . . . . . . . . . . . . . . Cabren
House Where Evil Dwells (1982). . . . . . . . . . . . . . Ted

Ellie (1984) . . . . . . . . . . . . . . . . . . . . . . . . . . . . . . . Tom
Getting Even (1986) . . . . . . . . . . . . . . . . . . . . . Taggar
The Underachievers (1987) . . . . . . . . . . Danny Warren
The Rescue (1988) . . . . . . . . . . . . . Commander Merrill
Wild Zone (1989) . . . . . . . . . . . . . . . . . Colonel Lavera
Shootfighter: Fight to the Death (1992) . . . . . . . Mr. C.
Broken Trust (1993) . . . . . . . . . . . . . . . . . . Peter Wyatt
Demon Keeper (1993) . . . . . . . . . . . . . . . Remy Grilland
**The Ice Runner** (1993) . . . . . . . . . . . . . . . . . . Jeff West
  •• 0:51—Buns, taking off his pants in room with Lena
Red Sun Rising (1993) . . . . . . . . . . . . . . . . . . . . . Decklin
Sexual Malice (1993) . . . . . . . . . . . . . . . . . . . Richard
  (Unrated version reviewed.)
Hard Drive (1994) . . . . . . . . . . . . . . . . . . . . . Examiner
  (Unrated version reviewed.)
*Made for Cable Movies:*
Body Language (1992; USA) . . . . . . . . . . . . . . . Charles
*Made for Cable TV:*
The Hitchhiker: Man at the Window (1985; HBO)
. . . . . . . . . . . . . . . . . . . . . . . . . . . . . . . Arthur Brown
*Miniseries:*
The Last Convertible (1979) . . . . . . . . . . Ron Dalrymple
*TV:*
The Yellow Rose (1983-84) . . . . . . . . . Quisto Champion
Falcon Crest (1986-89) . . . . . . . . . . . . . Jeff Wainwright

## Alden, John

*Films:*
**The Young Warriors** (1983; U.S./Canadian) . . . Jorge
  • 0:16—Dropping his pants in a room during pledge
  at fraternity.
Making the Grade (1984) . . . . . . . . . Egbert Williamson

## Alexander, Jason

*Films:*
**The Burning** (1981) . . . . . . . . . . . . . . . . . . . . . . . Dave
  • 0:29—Buns, pulling swimsuit down and up to moon
  Glazer. (On the far left.)
Brighton Beach Memoirs (1986) . . . . . . . . . Pool Player
Jacob's Ladder (1990) . . . . . . . . . . . . . . . . . . . . . Geary
Pretty Woman (1990) . . . . . . . . . . . . . . . Philip Stuckey
White Palace (1990) . . . . . . . . . . . . . . . . Neil Horowitz
I Don't Buy Kisses Anymore (1992) . . . . . Bernie Fishbine
Coneheads (1993) . . . . . . . . . . . . . . . . . . . Larry Farber
*Made for Cable Movies:*
Sexual Healing (1993; Showtime) . . . . . . . . . . . . Frank
*Made for Cable TV:*
Dream On: oral sex, lies and videotape (1993; HBO)
. . . . . . . . . . . . . . . . . . . . . . . . . . . Randall Townsend
*TV:*
Seinfeld . . . . . . . . . . . . . . . . . . . . . . George Costanza
E/R (1984-85) . . . . . . . . . . . . . . . . . . . Harold Stickley

## Alexander, Sandy

*Films:*
**The People Next Door** (1970) . . . . . . . . . . . . . Elliot
  •• 0:38—Frontal nudity, sitting up in upper bunk bed,
  then nude getting out.
Vigilante (1983) . . . . . . . . . . . . . . . . . . . . . . Prisoner

## Alin, Jeff

*Films:*
**Coming Together** (1978) . . . . . . . . . . . Frank Hughes
  *a.k.a. A Matter of Love*
  • 1:05—Buns, while putting pants on with Richard.

## Altamura, John

*Films:*
Young Nurses in Love (1987) . . . . . . . . . . . . . . . . . n.a.
New York's Finest (1988) . . . . . . . . . . . . . Brian Morrison
The Toxic Avenger: Part II (1988) . . . . . . . Toxic Avenger
**Party Incorporated** (1989) . . . . . . . . . . . . . . . . . Burt
  *a.k.a. Party Girls*
  • 0:50—Buns, while undressing and showing off at
  the bar.
The Toxic Avenger III: The Last Temptation of Toxie
  (1989) . . . . . . . . . . . . . . . . . . . . . . . . Toxic Avenger
**The Marilyn Diaries** (1990) . . . . . . . . . . . . . Frankie
  • 0:13—Buns, while in hall after Marilyn Chambers
  takes his sheet away.
Affairs of the Heart (1992) . . . . . . . . . . . . . . . Jock #1

## Amer, Nicholas

*Miniseries:*
**I, Claudius—Episode 12, A God in Colchester**
  (1976; British) . . . . . . . . . . . . . . . . . . . . . . Mnester
  (Available on video tape in *I, Claudius—Volume 6.*)
  • 0:04—Brief buns, while in bed with Lady Messalina.

## • Amodeo, Luigi

*Films:*
Year of the Gun (1991) . . . . . . . . . . . . . Piero Gagliani
*Made for Cable TV:*
**Red Shoe Diaries: How I Met My Husband**
  (1993; Showtime) . . . . . . . . . . . . . . . . . . . . Giuseppe
  • 0:30—Brief buns, while on top of Neith Hunter on
  stage.

## • Anderson, Daniel

*Films:*
Seduce Me: Pamela Principle 2 (1994) . . . . . . . . . . Matt
*Video Tapes:*
Playboy's Erotic Fantasies III (1993) . . . . . . . . . . . . n.a.
**Playboy's Sensual Fantasy for Lovers** (1993)
. . . . . . . . . . . . . . . . . . . . . . . . . . . . . Secret Desires
  •• 0:39—Buns, while making love with his lover in bed.
**Penthouse Forum Letters: Volume 2** (1994)
. . . . . . . . . . . . . . . . . . . . . . The Good Samaritan/Driver
  ••• 0:11—Buns, while making love in back seat and on
  trunk of convertible.

## • Anderson, Kevin

*Films:*
Pink Nights (1985) . . . . . . . . . . . . . . . . . . . . . . . Danny
Orphans (1987) . . . . . . . . . . . . . . . . . . . . . . . . Phillip
Miles From Home (1988) . . . . . . . . . . . . Terry Roberts
In Country (1989) . . . . . . . . . . . . . . . . . . . . . . Lonnie
Orpheus Descending (1990) . . . . . . . . . . . Val Xavier

Liebestraum (1991). . . . . . . . . . . . . . . . Nick Kaminsky
(Unrated Director's cut reviewed.)
Sleeping with the Enemy (1991) . . . . . . . . . . . . . . .Ben
Hoffa (1992) . . . . . . . . . . . . . . . . . . . . Robert Kennedy
The Night We Never Met (1993). . . . . . . Brian McVeigh
Rising Sun (1993) . . . . . . . . . . . . . . . . Bob Richmond
*Made for Cable Movies:*
**The Wrong Man** (1993; Showtime) . . . . . . . . . . Alex
••• 1:24—Buns, while getting out of bed and washing
his face and getting back into bed.

## Anderson, Marc
*Films:*
**Coming Together** (1978). . . . . . . . . . Richard Duncan
*a.k.a. A Matter of Love*
•• 0:13—Buns, while kneeling and kissing Angie, then
more buns making love.
• 0:58—Buns, while making love with Vicky.
• 1:05—Buns, while putting pants on with Frank.

## • Andrew, Michael
*Films:*
**Hollywood Hot Tubs** (1984) . . . . . . . . . . . . . . . . Jeff
• 1:00—Buns, under water when Pam takes his swim
trunks off.

## Andrews, Anthony
*Films:*
Under the Volcano (1984). . . . . . . . . . . . . Hugh Firmin
The Second Victory (1986) . . . . . . . . . . . Major Hanlon
Hanna's War (1988) . . . . . Squadron Leader McCormick
The Lighthorsemen (1988; Australian)
. . . . . . . . . . . . . . . . . . . . . Major Meinertzhagen
*Miniseries:*
**Brideshead Revisited** (1981; British) . . Sebastian Flyte
•• 0:17—(Part 3 on TV or Book 2 on video tape.) Buns,
while standing on roof with Jeremy Irons after talk-
ing with Cordelia.
*Made for TV Movies:*
The Scarlet Pimpernel (1982) . . . . . . . Sir Percy Blakeney
Bluegrass (1988) . . . . . . . . . . . . . . . . . . . . . Fitzgerald
Danielle Steel's "Jewels" (1992) . . . . . . Duke of Whitfield

## Anglade, Jean-Hughes
*Films:*
**Betty Blue** (1986; French). . . . . . . . . . . . . . . . . .Zorg
••• 0:09—Frontal nudity.
•• 1:03—Nude trying to sleep in living room.
•• 1:39—Frontal nudity walking to the bathroom.
•• 1:45—Frontal nudity talking on the telephone.
La Femme Nikita (1991; French/Italian). . . . . . . .Marco
*a.k.a. Nikita*
Especially on Sunday (1993) . . . . . . . . . . . Motorcyclist

## Anthony, Corwyn
*Films:*
**Student Confidential** (1987). . . . . . . . . . . . . . .Greg
• 1:26—Buns, while getting into bed with Susan.

## Antin, Steve
*Films:*
The Last American Virgin (1982) . . . . . . . . . . . . . . Rick
Sweet Sixteen (1982). . . . . . . . . . . . . . . . . Hank Burke
The Goonies (1985) . . . . . . . . . . . . . . . . . . . . . . .Troy
Penitentiary III (1987). . . . . . . . . . . . . . . . . . . .Roscoe
**The Accused** (1988). . . . . . . . . . . . . . . . . . Bob Joiner
• 1:29—Buns, while raping Jodi Foster on the pinball
machine.
Survival Quest (1989). . . . . . . . . . . . . . . . . . . . Raider
Without You I'm Nothing (1990) . . . . . . . . . Steve Antin
Inside Monkey Zetterland (1993) . . . Monkey Zetterland
*TV:*
NYPD Blue: Serge the Coincierge (Mar 29, 1994). . . n.a.

## Ardi, Richard
*Films:*
Bikini Island (1991) . . . . . . . . . . . . . . Tasha's Girlfriend
*Video Tapes:*
**Intimate Workout For Lovers** (1992)
. . . . . . . . . . . . . . . . . . . . . . . . . . . . Morning Stretch
••• 0:29—Nude, in bed in the morning and on the pa-
tio.

## • Arenz, Michael D.
*Films:*
**Scorned** (1993) . . . . . . . . . . . . . . . . . . Robey Weston
•• 0:49—Buns, after taking off his clothes with Shannon Tweed.

## Arkin, Alan
*Films:*
The Russians are Coming, The Russians are Coming
(1966) . . . . . . . . . . . . . . . . . . . . . . . . . . . . Rozanov
Wait Until Dark (1967) . . . . . . . . . . . . . . . . . . . .Boat
Woman Times Seven (1967). . . . . . . . . . . . . . . . .Fred
The Heart is a Lonely Hunter (1968). . . . . . . John Singer
**Catch-22** (1970). . . . . . . . . . . . . . Captain Yossarian
• 0:52—Buns, while standing wearing only his hat,
talking to Dreedle. Don't see his face.
Last of the Red Hot Lovers (1972) . . . Barneau Cashman
Freebie and the Bean (1974) . . . . . . . . . . . . . . Bean
Hearts of the West (1975) . . . . . . . . . . . . . . . .Kessler
Rafferty and the Gold Dust Twins (1975) . . . . . . Rafferty
The Seven-Per-Cent Solution (1976) . . . Sigmund Freud
The In-Laws (1979) . . . . . . . . . . . . . Sheldon Kornpett
The Magician of Lublin (1979) . . . . . . . . . . . . . . .Yasha
Simon (1980). . . . . . . . . . . . . . Simon Mendelssohn
Chu Chu and the Philly Flash (1981) . . . . . . . . . . Flash
Improper Channels (1981; Canadian) . . . . . . . . Jeffrey
Bad Medicine (1985) . . . . . . . . . . . . . . . . Dr. Madera
Joshua Then and Now (1985; Canadian)
. . . . . . . . . . . . . . . . . . . . . . . . . . . Reuben Shapiro
Big Trouble (1986) . . . . . . . . . . . . . . .Leonard Hoffman
Coupe de Ville (1990) . . . . . . . . . . . . . . . Fred Libner
Edward Scissorhands (1990). . . . . . . . . . . . . . . . .Bill
Havana (1990). . . . . . . . . . . . . . . . . . . . . . Joe Volpi
The Rocketeer (1991). . . . . . . . . . . . . . . . . . . .Peevy
Glengarry Glen Ross (1992) . . . . . . . . . . . . . . George

Indian Summer (1993) . . . . . . . . . . . . . . . . . Unca Lou
Taking the Heat (1993) . . . . . . . . . . . . . Tommy Canard
*Made for Cable Movies:*
Cooperstown (1993; TNT) . . . . . . . . . . . . . . . . . . n.a.
Doomsday Gun (1994; HBO) . . . . . . . . . . . . . . . Yossi

## Armstrong, Jack
*Films:*
Bad Guys (1986) . . . . . . . . . . . . . . . . . . . . . Sod Buster
The Guyver (1991) . . . . . . . . . . . . . . . . . . . . . . . . Sean
*Video Tapes:*
**Eden** (1992) . . . . . . . . . . . . . . . . . . . . . . . . . . . . B.D.
••• 0:44—Buns, taking off clothes and frolicking on the
beach with Marnie.
••• 1:06—Buns, while making love in bed with Lacey.
• 1:10—Brief buns, while leaving room.
Eden 2 (1992) . . . . . . . . . . . . . . . . . . . . . . . . . . . B.D.
**Eden 4** (1993) . . . . . . . . . . . . . . . . . . . . . . . . . . B.D.
••• 1:25—Buns, while in bed with Melissa. Nice tan line.

## • Arngrim, Stefan
*Films:*
The Way West (1967) . . . . . . . . . . . . . . Billy Tadlock Jr.
**Fear No Evil** (1981) . . . . . . . . . . . . . . . . . . . . . Andrew
•• 0:37—Buns, in the back corner of the showers while
getting teased by the other boys.
• 0:45—Buns, while leaving bedroom during Julie's
dream encounter.
Class of 1984 (1982; Canadian) . . . . . . . . . . Drugstore
*TV:*
Land of the Giants (1968-70) . . . . . . . . Barry Lockridge

## Arnott, David
*Films:*
**Criss Cross** (1992) . . . . . . . . . . . . . . . . . . . . Chris Cross
•• 1:15—Brief buns, putting on his pants when his girl
friend's parents come home. Don't see his face.

## Ashby, Linden
*Films:*
**Night Angel** (1989) . . . . . . . . . . . . . . . . . . . . . . Craig
• 1:22—Buns, while kneeling down to pick up picture.
Don't see his face.
Into the Sun (1991) . . . . . . . . . . . . . . . . . . . . . Dragon
*Video Tapes:*
Inside Out 3 (1992) . . . . . . . . . . . . . . . . . . . Jed/Tango

## • Askwith, Robin
*Films:*
if... (1969; British) . . . . . . . . . . . . . . . . . . . . . Keating
**Tower of Evil** (1972; British) . . . . . . . . . . . . . . . . Des
• 0:35—Brief buns, getting up out of bed and putting
on his pants. Dark.
**Love Trap** (1977) . . . . . . . . . . . . . . . . . . . Gordon Laid
*a.k.a. Let's Get Laid*
• 0:39—Buns, while making love with girls in his
dream.

## • Asparagus, Fred
*Films:*
**Surf II** (1984) . . . . . . . . . . . . . . . . . . . . . . . . Fat Boy #1
• 0:19—Buns, when blue wet suit splits in the back
while at the beach.
This is Spinal Tap (1984) . . . . . . . . . Joe "Mama" Besser
Three Amigos (1986) . . . . . . . . . . . . . . . . . . Bartender

## Astin, Sean
Son of actress Patty Duke and actor John Astin.
*Films:*
The Goonies (1985) . . . . . . . . . . . . . . . . . . . . . Mikey
Like Father, Like Son (1987) . . . . . . . . . . . . . . . Trigger
White Water Summer (1987) . . . . . . Alan Block/Narrator
Staying Together (1989) . . . . . . . . Duncan McDermott
The War of the Roses (1989) . . . . . . . . . . . Josh, Age 17
Memphis Belle (1990) . . . . . . . . Richard "Rascal" Moore
**Toy Soldiers** (1991) . . . . . . . . . . . . . . . . . . Billy Tepper
• 1:08—Brief buns, while taking off his wet clothes af-
ter coming in through the window.
The Willies (1991) . . . . . . . . . . . . . . . . . . . . . Michael
Encino Man (1992) . . . . . . . . . . . . . . . . Dave Morgan
Where The Day Takes You (1992) . . . . . . . . . . . . Greg
Rudy (1993) . . . . . . . . . . . . . . . . . . . . . . . . . . . Rudy

## Atkins, Christopher
*Films:*
**Blue Lagoon** (1980) . . . . . . . . . . . . . . . . . . . . Richard
•• 0:27—Nude swimming underwater after growing
up from little children.
• 0:29—Buns, while underwater.
•• 1:03—Nude swimming under water.
• 1:05—Buns, while kissing Brooke Shields.
•• 1:09—Very brief frontal nudity in water slide with
Shields.
The Pirate Movie (1982; Australian) . . . . . . . . . Frederic
**A Night in Heaven** (1983) . . . . . . . . . . . . . . . . . . Rick
• 1:03—Very brief frontal nudity when he pulls down
his pants in hotel room with Leslie Ann Warren.
• 1:15—Brief buns while on boat with Leslie Ann Warren's angry husband.
Beaks The Movie (1987) . . . . . . . . . . . . . . . . . . Peter
Mortuary Academy (1988) . . . . . . . . . . . . . Sam Grimm
Listen to Me (1989) . . . . . . . . . . . . . . . Bruce Arlington
Shakma (1990) . . . . . . . . . . . . . . . . . . . . . . . . . Sam
Shoot (1991) . . . . . . . . . . . . . . . . . . . . . . . . . Spence
**Dracula Rising** (1992) . . . . . . . . . . . . . . . . . . . . Vlad
0:43—Very brief glimpses of body parts while swim-
ming under water. Hard to see.
• 0:44—Brief buns, under water.
**Wet and Wild Summer!** (1992; Australian)
. . . . . . . . . . . . . . . . . . . . . . . . . . . . Bobby McCain
••• 0:22—Buns, taking off swimsuit at the beach.
Die Watching (1993) . . . . . . . . . . . . . Michael Terrence
*Made for Cable Movies:*
Fatal Charm (1992; Showtime) . . . . . . . . Adam Brenner
*TV:*
Dallas (1983-84) . . . . . . . . . . . . . . . . . Peter Richards
Rock 'n' Roll Summer Action (1985) . . . . . . . . . . . Host

*Magazines:*
**Playboy** (Nov 1980) . . . . . . . . . . Sex in Cinema 1980
••• 183—Frontal nudity.
**Playgirl** (Sep 1982) . . . . . . . . . . . . . . . . . . . . Pictorial

## Atkins, Tom

*Films:*
The Detective (1968) . . . . . . . . . . . . . . . . . . . Harmon
The Owl and the Pussycat (1970)
. . . . . . . . . . . . . . . . . . . . . Gang Member in Car
Where's Poppa? (1970) . . . . . . Policeman in Apartment
Special Delivery (1976) . . . . . . . . . . . . . . . . . Zabelski
Escape from New York (1981) . . . . . . . . . . . . . . Rehme
**Halloween III: Season of the Witch** (1983)
. . . . . . . . . . . . . . . . . . . . . . . . . . . Daniel Challis
•• 0:42—Buns, getting out of bed and putting his
pants on.
The New Kids (1985) . . . . . . . . . . . "Mac" MacWilliams
Lethal Weapon (1987). . . . . . . . . . . . Michael Hunsaker
Maniac Cop (1988). . . . . . . . . . . . . . . . . . Lt. McCrae
Two Evil Eyes (1991) . . . . . . . . . . . . . . . . . . . Grogan
Bob Roberts (1992; U.S./British) . . . . . . Dr. Caleb Menck
Striking Distance (1993) . . . . . . . . . . . . . . Fred Hardy

## Babb, Roger

*Films:*
**Working Girls** (1987). . . . . . . . . . . . . . . . . . . . . Paul
• 1:18—Frontal nudity with Molly.

## Bacon, Kevin

Husband of actress Kyra Sedgwick.
*Films:*
Animal House (1978) . . . . . . . . . . . . . . . . . Chip Diller
**Friday the 13th** (1980) . . . . . . . . . . . . . . . . . . . Jack
• 0:39—Close up of buns when Marci squeezes them.
Only When I Laugh (1981) . . . . . . . . . . . . . . . . . Don
Diner (1982) . . . . . . . . . . . . . . . . . . . . . . . Fenwick
Forty Deuce (1982). . . . . . . . . . . . . . . . . . . . Rickey
Footloose (1984). . . . . . . . . . . . . . . Ren MacCormack
Enormous Changes at the Last Minute (1985). . . Dennis
Quicksilver (1986). . . . . . . . . . . . . . . . . . Jack Casey
End of the Line (1987) . . . . . . . . . . . . . . . . . Everett
Planes, Trains and Automobiles (1987) . . . . . . Taxi Racer
White Water Summer (1987) . . . . . . . . . . . . . . . . Vic
She's Having a Baby (1988). . . . . . Jefferson "Jake" Briggs
The Big Picture (1989) . . . . . . . . . . . . . Nick Chapman
Criminal Law (1989) . . . . . . . . . . . . . . . . Martin Thiel
Tremors (1989) . . . . . . . . . . . . . . . . . Valentine McKee
Flatliners (1990) . . . . . . . . . . . . . . . . David Labraccio
he said, she said (1991). . . . . . . . . . . . . . . Dan Hanson
JFK (1991). . . . . . . . . . . . . . . . . . . . Willie O'Keefe
**Pyrates** (1991) . . . . . . . . . . . . . . . . . . . . . . . . . Ari
• 0:06—Brief side view of buns several times while
making love with Kyra Sedgwick. Long shot.
•• 0:22—Buns in jock strap, while horsing around in
bed with Sedgwick.
Queens Logic (1991). . . . . . . . . . . . . . . . . . Dennis
A Few Good Men (1992). . . . . . . . . . . . Capt. Jack Ross
The Air Up There (1993) . . . . . . . . . . . . . . . . . . n.a.

*TV:*
The Guiding Light . . . . . . . . . . . . . . . . . . . Tim Werner

## Baggetta, Vincent

*Films:*
Two-Minute Warning (1976) . . . . . . . . . . . . Ted Shelley
**The Man Who Wasn't There** (1983) . . . . . . . . . Riley
• 0:23—Buns, while lying on the floor after fighting
with the other guys.
*TV:*
Chicago Story (1982). . . . . . . . . . . . . . . Lou Pellegrino

## Bahner, Blake

*Films:*
Black Belt II: Fatal Force (1988). . . . . . . . . . . Brad Snyder
**Sensations** (1988) . . . . . . . . . . . . . . . . . . Brian Ingles
•• 0:10—Very, very brief lower frontal nudity pushing
the covers off the bed, then buns, while getting out
of bed.
Caged Fury (1989). . . . . . . . . . . . . . . . . . . Buck Lewis
Lethal Pursuit (1989) . . . . . . . . . . . . . . . . . . Warren
Demon Sword (1991) . . . . . . . . . . . . . . . . . . . Thane
*a.k.a. Wizards of the Demon Sword*

## Baio, Scott

*Films:*
Bugsy Malone (1976). . . . . . . . . . . . . . . Bugsy Malone
Skatetown, U.S.A. (1979). . . . . . . . . . . . . . . . Richie
Foxes (1980) . . . . . . . . . . . . . . . . . . . . . . . . Brad
Zapped! (1982) . . . . . . . . . . . . . . . . . . . . . . Barney
**I Love N.Y.** (1987) . . . . . . . . . . . . . . . . Mario Colone
• 1:19—Brief, upper half of buns, while getting out of
bed. Dark, hard to see.
*Made for TV Movies:*
Happy Days Reunion (1992) . . Charles "Chachi" Arcola
*TV:*
Blansky's Beauties (1977) . . . . . . . . . Anthony DeLuca
Happy Days (1977-84) . . . . . . . . Charles "Chachi" Arcola
Who's Watching the Kids? (1978)
. . . . . . . . . . . . . . . . . . . Frankie "The Fox" Vitola
Joanie Loves Chachi (1982-83)
. . . . . . . . . . . . . . . . . . Charles "Chachi" Arcola
Charles in Charge (1984-85) . . . . . . . . . . . . Charles
Charles in Charge (1987-90) . . . . . . . . . . . . Charles
Baby Talk (1991-92) . . . . . . . . . . . . . . . . . . James
Diagnosis Murder (1994- ) . . . . . . . . . . . . Jack Stewart

## Baker, Henry Judd

*Films:*
Seizure (1973) . . . . . . . . . . . . . . . . . . . . . . . Jackal
**Cruising** (1980) . . . . . . . . . . . . . . . . . . . Tough Cop
•• 0:57—Buns in jock strap, while leaving interrogation
room.
• 0:58—Buns in jock strap, while getting up to slap
Skip Lee around.
Neighbors (1981) . . . . . . . . . . . . . . . . . . . Policeman
Vigilante (1983) . . . . . . . . . . . . . . . . . . . . . . Quinn
After Hours (1985) . . . . . . . . . . . . . . . . . . . . . . Jett
The Money Pit (1986) . . . . . . . . . . . . . . . . . . . Oscar

**Clean and Sober** (1988). . . . . . . . . . . . . . . . . .Xavier
  •• 0:15—Buns, when going crazy in drug rehabilitation
    room.
The Mighty Quinn (1989). . . . . . . . . . . . . . . Nicotine
The Super (1991) . . . . . . . . . . . . . .First Man on Stoop

# Baker, Scott
*Films:*
Delivery Boys (1984). . . . . . . . . . . . . . . . . Snooty Man
**Cleo/Leo** (1989) . . . . . . . . . . . . . . . . .Leo Blockman
  • 0:09—Very brief buns after getting his butt kicked.
The Butcher's Wife (1991). . . . . . . . . . . . . . Fire Eater

# • Baldwin, Adam
*Films:*
My Bodyguard (1980). . . . . . . . . . . . . . . . Linderman
Ordinary People (1980). . . . . . . . . . . . . . . .Still Man
D.C. Cab (1983) . . . . . . . . . . . . . . . . . . . . . . .Albert
Reckless (1984). . . . . . . . . . . . . . . . . .Randy Daniels
3:15—The Moment of Truth (1986) . . . . . .Jeff Hannah
Bad Guys (1986). . . . . . . . . . . . . . . . . . Skip Jackson
Full Metal Jacket (1987) . . . . . . . . . . . .Animal Mother
The Chocolate War (1988) . . . . . . . . . . . . . . . .Carter
Next of Kin (1989) . . . . . . . . . . . . . . . . Joey Rosselini
Predator 2 (1990) . . . . . . . . . . . . . . . . . . . . . Garber
Guilty by Suspicion (1991) . . . . . . . . . . . . . FBI Man
Deadbolt (1992). . . . . . . . . . . . . . . . . . . .Alec Danz
Radio Flyer (1992). . . . . . . . . . . . . . . . . .The King
Where The Day Takes You (1992) . . . . . . . . Officer Black
Bitter Harvest (1993). . . . . . . . . . . . . . .Bobby Brody Jr.
**Cold Sweat** (1993) . . . . . . . . . . . . . . Mitch Simmons
  • 0:17—Buns, while playing with fluorescent paint on
    Shannon Tweed in bathtub. Kind of dark.
*Made for Cable Movies:*
Blind Justice (1994; HBO) . . . . . . . . . . . . . Sgt. Hastings
*Made for TV Movies:*
Poison Ivy (1985) . . . . . . . . . . . . . . . . . . . . . . . Ike

# • Baldwin, Alec
Brother of actors William, Steven and Daniel Baldwin.
Husband of actress Kim Basinger.
*Films:*
Forever Lulu (1987). . . . . . . . . . . . . . . . . . . . Buck
Beetlejuice (1988). . . . . . . . . . . . .Adam Maitland
Married to the Mob (1988). . . . . . . . . . Frank De Marco
She's Having a Baby (1988). . . . . . . . . .Davis McDonald
Talk Radio (1988) . . . . . . . . . . . . . . . . . . . . Dan
Great Balls of Fire (1989). . . . . . . . .Jimmy Lee Swaggart
Working Girl (1989) . . . . . . . . . . . . . . . Mick Dugan
Alice (1990) . . . . . . . . . . . . . . . . . . . . . . . . .Ed
The Hunt for Red October (1990) . . . . . . . . . Jack Ryan
Miami Blues (1990). . . . . . . . . .Frederick J. Frenger, Jr.
The Marrying Man (1991). . . . . . . . . Charley Pearl
  *a.k.a. Too Hot to Handle*
Glengarry Glen Ross (1992) . . . . . . . . . . . . . Blake
Prelude to a Kiss (1992) . . . . . . . . . . . . Peter Hoskins
**The Getaway** (1993). . . . . . . . . . . . . . Doc McCoy
  (Unrated version reviewed.)
  •• 0:19—Buns, while pulling down his underwear.

**Malice** (1993) . . . . . . . . . . . . . . . . . . . . . . . . . .Jed
  • 0:24—Brief buns, while making love in bed with
    Tanya.
*Made for TV Movies:*
Code of Honor (1984) . . . . . . . . . . . . . . . . . . . .n.a.
  Original title: *Sweet Revenge.*
*TV:*
Knots Landing (1984-85) . . . . . . . . . . . . .Joshua Rush

# • Baldwin, Stephen
Brother of actors William, Alec and Daniel Baldwin.
*Films:*
The Beast (1988) . . . . . . . . . . . . . . . . . . . . . Golikov
Homeboy (1988) . . . . . . . . . . . . . . . Luna Park Drunk
Born on the Fourth of July (1989). . . . . . . Billy Vorsovich
Last Exit to Brooklyn (1990) . . . . . . . . . . . . . . . . Sal
Crossing the Bridge (1992) . . . . . . . . . Danny Morgan
**Bitter Harvest** (1993) . . . . . . . . . . . . . Travis Graham
  • 0:30—Buns, when Jennifer Rubin pulls his under-
    wear down. Don't see his face.
  •• 0:31—Buns, while lying in bed.
Posse (1993) . . . . . . . . . . . . . . . . . . . . . . . Little J
  0:50—Almost frontal nudity, when jumping into wa-
    ter. His hand covers his privates, then it's too blurry
    once her starts moving.
New Eden (1994). . . . . . . . . . . . . . . . . . . . . Adams
**Threesome** (1994) . . . . . . . . . . . . . . . . . . . Stuart
  0:33—Brief side view of buns while in shower.
  •• 0:53—Buns, while walking to rock at edge of lake
    and diving in.
  • 1:21—Buns, while lying in bed with Lara Flynn Boyle
    and Josh Charles.

# Baldwin, William
Brother of actors Alec, Steven and Daniel Baldwin.
*Films:*
Flatliners (1990). . . . . . . . . . . . . . . . . . Joe Hurley
**Backdraft** (1991). . . . . . . . . . . . . . . .Brian McCaffrey
  •• 0:33—Brief buns (on the left) in the shower room
    with Jason Gedrick.
**Sliver** (1993). . . . . . . . . . . . . . . . . . Zeke Hawkins
  ••• 1:03—Buns, while sneaking up behind Sharon Stone
    and making love while standing up.
**Three of Hearts** (1993). . . . . . . . . . . . . .Joe Casella
  •• 0:01—Brief buns in mirror, while walking out of
    bathroom.

# Ball, Rod
*Films:*
**Porky's** (1981; Canadian) . . . . . . . . . . . . . . . Steve
  • 0:18—Brief frontal nudity sitting on bench in the
    cabin.
  • 0:21—Very brief frontal nudity, following Meat out
    the front door of the cabin, then buns, while in front
    of the house.
Porky's II: The Next Day (1983; Canadian) . . . . . . .Steve
Rhinestone (1984) . . . . . . . . . . . . . . . . . . . .Heckler
Cape Fear (1991). . . . . . . . . . . . . . . . . . . .Prisoner

# Ball, Vincent

Films:
Where Eagles Dare (1969; British) . . . . . . . . . Carpenter
**Not Tonight Darling** (1971; British) . . . . . . . . . Alex
- 1:04—Buns, getting pushed out of the car with Ben the Click by the revengeful women. Long shot.
- 1:05—Full frontal nudity, while running after the car. Shaky camera.

Breaker Morant (1979; Australian). . . . . Lt. Ian Hamilton
Phar Lap (1984; Australian) . . . . . . . . Lachlan McKinnon
The Year My Voice Broke (1987; Australian)
. . . . . . . . . . . . . . . . . . . . . . . . . . . . . Headmaster
Frauds (1992; Australian) . . . . . . . . . . . . . . . . . Judge

# Banderas, Antonio

Films:
Labyrinth of Passion (1982; Spanish). . . . . . . . . . . . .n.a.
Matador (1986; Spanish) . . . . . . . . . . . . . . . . . Angel
Women on the Verge of a Nervous Breakdown
(1988; Spanish). . . . . . . . . . . . . . . . . . . . . . . .Carlos
**Tie Me Up! Tie Me Down!** (1990; Spanish) . . . . .Ricky
- 1:17—Buns in mirror on ceiling, while making love with Victoria Abril. Long shot.

Truth or Dare (1991) . . . . . . . . . . . . . . . . . . . . Himself
**The Mambo Kings** (1992) . . . . . . . . . . Nestor Castillo
- 0:48—Buns, while in bed on top of Maruschka Detmers.
- 1:10—Upper half of buns, sitting on side of bed, while putting his pants on.

The House of Spirits (1993). . . . . . . . . . . . . . . . Pedro
Philadelphia (1993). . . . . . . . . . . . . . . . Miguel Alvarez

# • Bangel, Harry

Films:
**Is There Sex After Death?** (1975)
. . . . . . . . . . . . . Round Table Discussion/Man on Table
•• 1:25—Buns, while making love on table with a guy in front of a group of a discussion group of men.

# Barbareschi, Luca

Films:
**Bye Bye Baby** (1989; Italian). . . . . . . . . . . . . . . Paulo
- 0:20—Brief buns, while on top of Brigitte Nielsen in bed.

# Barber, Paul

Films:
**The Long Good Friday** (1980; British) . . . . . . . .Erroll
- 0:42—Brief buns, getting cut on his rear end during interrogation.

# • Bardem, Javier

Films:
High Heels (1991; Spanish). . . . . . . . .TV Floor Manager
**Jamón, Jamón** (1992; Spanish). . . . . . . . . . . . . . Raul
••• 0:39—Nude, while practicing bullfighting outside at night with his friend, then running away when caught. Long scene. (He's wearing a necklace.)

# Barrett, Lance

Films:
**Not Tonight Darling** (1971; British) . . . . . . . . . Gary
- 0:43—Brief side view of buns, while standing up in bathtub.
- 0:44—Very, very brief frontal nudity, when it pokes out from under a towel while he stands up in bathtub.

# Barro, Cesare

Films:
**My Father's Wife** (1976; Italian) . . . . . . . . . . . Claudio
a.k.a. Confessions of a Frustrated Housewife
- 0:52—Buns, while bringing Patricia champagne.

Inhibition (1984; Italian) . . . . . . . . . . . . . . . . . . . n.a.

# Bates, Alan

Films:
Whistle Down the Wind (1961; British)
. . . . . . . . . . . . . . . . . . . . . Arthur Blakey, The Man
Zorba the Greek (1963) . . . . . . . . . . . . . . . . . . . .Basil
Georgy Girl (1966; British) . . . . . . . . . . . . . . . . . . Jos
**King of Hearts** (1966; French/Italian)
. . . . . . . . . . . . . . . . . . . . . Private Charles Plumpick
(Letterboxed French version with English subtitles.)
•• 1:39—Buns, while standing at the asylum gates while he holds a bird cage after taking his army uniform off.

**Women in Love** (1971) . . . . . . . . . . . . . . . . . . Rupert
- 0:25—Buns and brief frontal nudity walking around the woods rubbing himself with everything.
- 0:50—Buns, while making love with Ursula after a boy and girl drown in the river.
••• 0:54—Nude fighting with Oliver Reed in a room in front of a fireplace. Long scene.

Impossible Object (1973; French) . . . . . . . . . . . . .Harry
a.k.a. Story of a Love Story
An Unmarried Woman (1978) . . . . . . . . . . . . . . . .Saul
The Rose (1979). . . . . . . . . . . . . . . . . . . . . . . Rudge
The Shout (1979). . . . . . . . . . . . . . Charles Crossly
Nijinsky (1980; British). . . . . . . . . . . . .Sergei Diaghilev
Quartet (1981; British/French) . . . . . . . . . . H.J. Heidler
Return of the Soldier (1983; British) . . . . . . . . . . .Chris
The Wicked Lady (1983; British). . . . . . . . . Jerry Jackson
Duet for One (1987) . . . . . . . . . . . . . David Cornwallis
A Prayer for the Dying (1987) . . . . . . . . . . Jack Meehan
We Think the World of You (1988; British) . . . . . . .Frank
Club Extinction (1990). . . . . . . . . . . . . . . Dr. Marsfeldt
a.k.a. Doctor M
Hamlet (1990; British/French) . . . . . . . . . King Claudius
Mr. Frost (1990; French/British) . . . . Inspector Detweiler
Made for TV Movies:
Pack of Lies (1987). . . . . . . . . . . . . . . . . . . . . Stewart

# Battaglia, Matt

Made for Cable Movies:
**Chantilly Lace** (1993; Showtime)
. . . . . . . . . . . . . . . . . . . . . . . . . Chris the Pizza Boy
    0:00—Brief upper half of buns in bedroom with Jo-
    Beth Williams. Never see his face.

# Bauer, Steven

Films:
Scarface (1983). . . . . . . . . . . . . . . . . . . . . . . Manny Ray
**Thief of Hearts** (1984). . . . . . . . . . . . . . . Scott Muller
   (Special Home Video Version reviewed.)
  •• 0:53—Brief side view of buns, carrying Barbara Will-
    iams into bed.
Running Scared (1986). . . . . . . . . . . . . . . . . . . . Frank
The Beast (1988). . . . . . . . . . . . . . . . . . . . . . . . . . Taj
Wildfire (1988) . . . . . . . . . . . . . . . . . . . . . . . . . . Frank
Gleaming the Cube (1989) . . . . . . . . . . . . . Al Lucero
A Climate for Killing (1990). . . . . . . . . . . . Paul McGraw
False Arrest (1991) . . . . . . . . . . . . . . . . Det. Dan Ryan
   Video tape version is shorter than the miniseries that
   aired on TV. It also has nude scenes added.
**Sweet Poison** (1991) . . . . . . . . . . . . . . . . . . . .Bobby
  •• 1:06—Buns, while making love on top of Patricia
    Healy in bed. Don't see his face.
Raising Cain (1992). . . . . . . . . . . . . . . . . . . . . . . Jack
Snapdragon (1993). . . . . . . . . . . . . . . . . . . . . . David
Woman of Desire (1993). . . . . . . . . Jonathan/Ted Ashby
**Stranger By Night** (1994) . . . . . . . . Bobby Corcoran
  •• 0:57—Buns and brief frontal nudity, while making
    love in bed on top of Jennifer Rubin.
Made for Cable TV:
**Red Shoe Diaries: Safe Sex** (1992; Showtime)
. . . . . . . . . . . . . . . . . . . . . . . . . . The Man/Michael
   (Available on video tape on Red Shoe Diaries 2: Double
   Dare.)
  • 0:12—Buns, taking off his pants and making love
    with Joan Severance on the floor. Don't see his face
    very well, but it's him.
TV:
Wiseguy (1990). . . . . . . . . . . . . . . .Michael Santana
Magazines:
**Playgirl** (Nov 1987). . . . . . . . . . . . . . . . .Raw Footage
   35—Buns and blurred frontal nudity in stills from
   Thief of Hearts.

# Bean, Sean

Films:
How to Get Ahead in Advertising (1988; British)
. . . . . . . . . . . . . . . . . . . . . . . . . . . . . Carry Frisk
**Stormy Monday** (1988) . . . . . . . . . . . . . . . Brendan
  •• 0:37—Buns, putting on his underwear while Mela-
    nie Griffith watches.
War Requiem (1988; British) . . . . . . . . .German Soldier
The Field (1990) . . . . . . . . . . . . . . . . . .Tadgh McCabe
Lorna Doone (1990; British) . . . . . . . . . . . . . . . .n.a.
Patriot Games (1992) . . . . . . . . . . . . . . . Sean Miller
Black Beauty (1994) . . . . . . . . . . . . . . . . . . . . . .n.a.

# Beatty, Warren

Brother of actress/author Shirley MacLaine.
Husband of actress Annette Bening.
Films:
Splendor in the Grass (1961) . . . . . . . . . . Bud Stamper
Lilith (1964). . . . . . . . . . . . . . . . . . . . . . Vincent Bruce
Bonnie and Clyde (1967). . . . . . . . . . . . . . . . . .Clyde
McCabe and Mrs. Miller (1971) . . . . . . . .John McCabe
Dollars (1972) . . . . . . . . . . . . . . . . . . . . . . Joe Collins
The Parallax View (1974) . . . . . . . . . . . . . . . . . . .Joe
The Fortune (1975) . . . . . . . . . . . . . . . . . . . . . .Nicky
**Shampoo** (1975) . . . . . . . . . . . . . . . . . . . . . George
  • 0:42—Upper half of buns with pants a little bit down
    in the bathroom with Julie Christie.
  • 1:24—Buns, while making love with Christie when
    Goldie Hawn discovers them. Long shot, hard to
    see.
Heaven Can Wait (1978) . . . . . . . . . . . . Joe Pendleton
Reds (1981) . . . . . . . . . . . . . . . . . . . . . . . John Reed
Ishtar (1987) . . . . . . . . . . . . . . . . . . . . . Lyle Rogers
Dick Tracy (1990). . . . . . . . . . . . . . . . . . . Dick Tracy
Bugsy (1991) . . . . . . . . . . . . . Benjamin "Bugsy" Siegel
Truth or Dare (1991) . . . . . . . . . . . . . . . . . . Himself
TV:
The Many Loves of Dobie Gillis (1959-60)
. . . . . . . . . . . . . . . . . . . . . . . . Milton Armitage
Magazines:
**Playboy** (Nov 1975) . . . . . . . . . . Sex in Cinema 1975
  • 141—Upper half of buns on the bathroom floor with
    Julie Christie in still from Shampoo.

# Beckley, Tony

Films:
Get Carter (1971) . . . . . . . . . . . . . . . . . . . . . . Peter
Revenge of the Pink Panther (1978). . . . . . . . Guy Algo
**When a Stranger Calls** (1979). . . . . . . . Curt Duncan
  • 1:07—Side view of buns, while kneeling in restroom.

# Beghe, Jason

Films:
Compromising Positions (1985). . . . . . . . . . . Cupcake
**Monkey Shines: An Experiment in Fear** (1988)
. . . . . . . . . . . . . . . . . . . . . . . . . . . . . Allan Mann
  • 0:01—Side view of buns while on the floor, stretch-
    ing to go running.
The Chinatown Murders: Man Against the Mob (1989)
. . . . . . . . . . . . . . . . . . . . . . . . . . . . . . . . Sammy
Made for Cable Movies:
Bodily Harm (1989) . . . . . . . . . . . . . . . . . . . . . John
Full Eclipse (1993; HBO). . . . . . . . . . . . . .Doug Crane

## Begley, Ed, Jr.
*Films:*
Stay Hungry (1976)......................... Lester
Blue Collar (1978)........................Bobby Joe
Hardcore (1979)......................... Soldier
Private Lessons (1981)...................Jack Travis
Cat People (1982)..................... Joe Creigh
Eating Raoul (1982) ..................... Hippie
Young Doctors in Love (1982).... Young Simon's Father
Get Crazy (1983) ......................... Colin
Protocol (1984)......................... Hassler
Streets of Fire (1984)................... Ben Gunn
This is Spinal Tap (1984)........ John "Stumpy" Pepys
Transylvania 6-5000 (1985).............. Gil Turner
**Amazon Women on the Moon** (1987) ......Griffin
• 0:54—Buns, while walking around as the Son of the
   Invisible Man. This section is in B&W.
The Accidental Tourist (1988) ............... Charles
**Meet the Applegates** (1989)........Dick Applegate
• 0:46—Buns, while running around nuclear power
   plant after his pile of clothes are taken away by the
   janitor.
Scenes from the Class Struggle in Beverly Hills (1989)
.........................................Peter
**She-Devil** (1989)....................Bob Patchett
•• 0:32—Brief buns, when towel falls off outside after
   Rosanne Arnold takes off in a taxi.
Dark Horse (1992)...................... Jack Mills
Greedy (1993) ......................... Carl
Renaissance Man (1994)......................n.a.
*Made for Cable Movies:*
Mastergate (1992; Showtime)......... Steward Butler
Running Mates (1992; HBO).............. Chapman
Incident at Deception Ridge (1994; USA) .........n.a.
*Made for Cable TV:*
Tales From the Crypt: Death of Some Salesman
   (1993; HBO) ...................... Judd Campbell
*Made for TV Movies:*
A Shining Season (1979)....................n.a.
Spies, Lies & Naked Thighs (1988) ..............n.a.
In the Best Interest of the Child (1990) ..Howard Feldon
Chance of a Lifetime (1991) ................ Darrel
In the Line of Duty: Siege at Marion (1992)
.................................... Fred House
World War II: When Lions Roared (1994). .Harry Hopkins
*TV:*
Roll Out (1973-74) .......... Lt. Robert W. Chapman
St. Elsewhere (1982-88) .............Dr. Victor Erlich
Parenthood (1990) .................... Gil Buckman
Winnetaka Road (1994)................Glenn Barker

## Belle, Ekkhardt
*Films:*
**Julia** (1974; German)...................... Patrick
• 1:01—Very brief buns, while in bed with Terry.

## Beltran, Robert
*Films:*
Zoot Suit (1981) ..................... Lowrider
Eating Raoul (1982) .....................Raoul
Lone Wolf McQuade (1983).................. Kayo
Night of the Comet (1984) .................Hector
Gaby, A True Story (1987) ...................Luis
**Scenes from the Class Struggle in Beverly Hills**
   (1989) ...............................Juan
• 1:34—Brief buns, when his shorts are pulled down
   by Frank.
Crack Down (1990) ...................Juan Delgado
Bugsy (1991) .........................Alejandro
Kiss Me a Killer (1991) ..................... Tony
ShadowHunter (1992) ...............Frank Totsoni
*Made for Cable Movies:*
State of Emergency (1993; HBO) ..... Raoul Hernandez
*Made for TV Movies:*
The Chase (1991)..................... Mike Silva
Stormy Weathers (1992) ..................... Gio
Rio Shannon (1993).................. Tito Carson
*TV:*
Models Inc. (1994- ).......................Lt. Soto

## •Belushi, James
Brother of the late actor John Belushi.
*Films:*
Thief (1981).............................. Barry
Trading Places (1983).....................Harvey
The Man With One Red Shoe (1985) .......... Morris
About Last Night... (1986) ........... Bernie Litko
Jumpin' Jack Flash (1986).......... Sperry Repairman
Little Shop of Horrors (1986) .......... Patrick Martin
Salvador (1986) .......................Dr. Rock
The Principal (1987)..................Rick Latimer
Real Men (1987) ................... Nick Pirandelo
Red Heat (1988)............... Det. Dgt. Art Ridzik
Homer & Eddie (1989)............... Homer Lanza
K-9 (1989) ................... Thomas Dooley
The Palermo Connection (1989; Italian)
.......................... Carmine Bonavia
Masters of Menace (1990) ................. Gypsy
Mr. Destiny (1990)................... Larry Burrows
Taking Care of Business (1990)........ Jimmy Dworski
Curly Sue (1991) .....................Bill Dancer
Only the Lonely (1991) .......................Sal
Diary of a Hitman (1992) .................. Shandy
Once Upon A Crime (1992) ............ Neil Schwary
Traces of Red (1992) ................. Jack Dobson
Abraxas: Guardian of the Universe (1993) .... Principal
Last Action Hero (1993)................... Himself
*Made for Cable Movies:*
Best Legs in the 8th Grade (1984; HBO)..........n.a.
**Parallel Lives** (1994; Showtime) ........ Nick Dimas
• 0:34—Brief buns (he's on the right), while mooning
   the women in hallway during panty raid.
Royce (1994; Showtime) ............. Shane Royce
*Miniseries:*
Wild Palms (1993) .................. Harry Wyckoff

# Benben, Brian

Husband of actress Madeleine Stowe.
*Films:*
Clean and Sober (1988) . . . . . . . . . . . . . . Martin Laux
I Come in Peace (1990). . . . . . . . . . . . .Laurence Smith
*Made for Cable TV:*
**Dream On: Doing the Bossa Nova** (1990; HBO)
. . . . . . . . . . . . . . . . . . . . . . . . . . Martin Tupper
  • 0:07—Brief lower half of buns while making love on
  photocopier with Vicki Frederick.
**Dream On: Sex and the Single Parent** (1990; HBO)
. . . . . . . . . . . . . . . . . . . . . . . . . . Martin Tupper
  •• 0:11—Brief buns when Ms. Brodsky fantasizes about
  him when he walks out the classroom door.
**Dream On: And Bimbo Was His Name-O**
(1992; HBO) . . . . . . . . . . . . . . . . . . . . Martin Tupper
  • 0:07—Buns, four times, on top of Teri Garr in bed.
  Don't see his face, but it's him.
**Dream On: Come and Knock On Our Door...**
(1992; HBO) . . . . . . . . . . . . . . . . . . . . Martin Tupper
  •• 0:16—Buns, while getting out of bed in hotel room
  with Eddie.
**Dream On: Dance Ten, Sex Three** (1992; HBO)
. . . . . . . . . . . . . . . . . . . . . . . . . . Martin Tupper
  •• 0:24—Buns, while on top of Roxanne Hart in bed.
**Dream On: The Undergraduate** (1992; HBO)
. . . . . . . . . . . . . . . . . . . . . . . . . . Martin Tupper
  • 0:04—Brief lower half of buns, while standing up
  with Julie.
**Dream On: A Midsummer Night's Dream On**
(1993; HBO) . . . . . . . . . . . . . . . . . . . . Martin Tupper
  • 0:16—Brief upper half of buns, while leaving the
  room.
*TV:*
The Gangster Chronicles (1981) . . . . . . . Michael Lasker
Kay O'Brien (1986) . . . . . . . . . . . . . . . . Dr. Mark Doyle

# Beneyton, Yves

*Films:*
**The Lacemaker** (1977; French) . . . . . . . . . . François
  • 0:57—Buns, while walking to bed. Dark.

# Benjamin, Richard

Actor turned director.
Husband of actress Paula Prentiss.
*Films:*
**Goodbye, Columbus** (1969) . . . . . . . . . . . . . . . Neil
  • 1:11—Brief buns, while walking into the bathroom.
  Very, very brief frontal nudity. Blurry, hard to see
  anything.
Catch-22 (1970) . . . . . . . . . . . . . . . . . . . Major Danby
Diary of a Mad Housewife (1970) . . . . . .Jonathan Balser
The Marriage of a Young Stockbroker (1971)
. . . . . . . . . . . . . . . . . . . . . . . . . . . William Alren
The Steagle (1971) . . . . . . . . . . . . . . . . . .Harold Weiss
Portnoy's Complaint (1972) . . . . . . . Alexander Portnoy
The Last of Sheila (1973). . . . . . . . . . . . . . . . . . Tom
Westworld (1973) . . . . . . . . . . . . . . . . . . Peter Martin
Sunshine Boys (1975) . . . . . . . . . . . . . . . . . Ben Clark

House Calls (1978). . . . . . . . . . . Dr. Norman Solomon
Love at First Bite (1979) . . . . . . . . . . Dr. Jeff Rosenberg
Scavenger Hunt (1979) . . . . . . . . . . . . . . . . . . . Stuart
First Family (1980) . . . . . . . . Press Secretary Bunthorne
How to Beat the High Cost of Living (1980). . . . . Albert
The Last Married Couple in America (1980)
. . . . . . . . . . . . . . . . . . . . . . . . . . . .Marv Cooper
Saturday the 14th (1981). . . . . . . . . . . . . . . . . . John
*TV:*
He & She (1967-68). . . . . . . . . . . . . . . . Dick Hollister
Quark (1978) . . . . . . . . . . . . . . . . . . . Adam Quark

# Bennent, David

*Films:*
**The Tin Drum** (1979; German) . . . . . . . . . . . . . .Oskar
  • 1:41—Buns, changing clothes in bath house with
  Maria.
  • 2:06—Buns, getting out of bed and getting dressed.
Dog Day (1984; French) . . . . . . . . . . . . . . . . . .Chim
Legend (1986). . . . . . . . . . . . . . . . . . . . . . . . Gump

# Benson, Robby

*Films:*
Lucky Lady (1973) . . . . . . . . . . . . . . . . . . Billy Webber
Ode to Billy Joe (1976). . . . . . . . . . . . Billy Joe McAllister
One on One (1977) . . . . . . . . . . . . . . . . Henry Steele
The Chosen (1978; Italian/British) . . . . Danny Saunders
The End (1978) . . . . . . . . . . . . . . . . . . . . The Priest
Ice Castles (1979). . . . . . . . . . . . . . . . . Nick Peterson
Walk Proud (1979). . . . . . . . . . . . . . . . . . . . Emilio
Tribute (1980; Canadian) . . . . . . . . . . .Jud Templeton
National Lampoon Goes to the Movies (1982)
. . . . . . . . . . . . . . . . . . . . . . . . . . .Brent Falcone
  *a.k.a. Movie Madness*
Running Brave (1983; Canadian) . . . . . . . . . . . Billy Mills
Harry and Son (1984) . . . . . . . . . . . . . . . . .Howard
White Hot (1988). . . . . . . . . . . . . . . . . . . . . . Scott
**Modern Love** (1990) . . . . . . . . . . . . . . . . .Greg Frank
  •• 0:35—Brief buns while running out of room after
  finding out he's going to be a father.
  0:36—Long shot of buns, while standing on roof of
  house yelling the good news to the world.
At Home with the Webbers (1992). . . . . . . Roger Swade
**Invasion of Privacy** (1992) . . . . . . . . . . . . . Alex Pruitt
  (Unrated version reviewed.)
  •• 1:20—Buns, while making love on top of Lydie De-
  nier in bed.
*Made for Cable Movies:*
Homewrecker (1992; Sci-Fi) . . . . . . . . . . . . . . . . n.a.
*Made for TV Movies:*
All the Kind Strangers (1974) . . . . . . . . . . . . . . n.a.
Precious Victims (1993) . . . . . . . . . . . . . . . . . . n.a.
*TV:*
Tough Cookies (1986) . . . . . . . . . . . . . Det. Cliff Brady

# Berenger, Tom

*Films:*
Looking for Mr. Goodbar (1977) . . . . . . . . . . . . . . Gary
The Sentinel (1977). . . . . . . . . . . . . . . . . . . . .Man at End
**In Praise of Older Women** (1978; Canadian)
. . . . . . . . . . . . . . . . . . . . . . . . . . . . . . . . Andras Vayda
• 0:32—Buns, while in bed with Karen Black (seen in
  mirror). Long shot.
•• 1:04—Buns, while rolling off Susan Strasberg. Kind
  of dark.
•• 1:07—Very brief lower frontal nudity three times,
  standing up and picking up Strasberg.
• 1:20—Very brief frontal nudity turning over in bed
  waiting for Alexandra Stewart.
• 1:23—Very, very brief blurry frontal nudity turning
  over in bed after getting mad at Alexandra Stewart.
••• 1:42—Buns, while undressing with Helen Shaver.
  Very brief balls.
Butch and Sundance: The Early Days (1979)
. . . . . . . . . . . . . . . . . . . . . . . . . . . . . . . .Butch Cassidy
The Dogs of War (1980; British) . . . . . . . . . . . . . Drew
Beyond Obsession (1982) . . . . . . . . . . . . . . . .Matthew
The Big Chill (1983) . . . . . . . . . . . . . . . . . . . . . . Sam
Eddie and the Cruisers (1983) . . . . . . . . . . . . . . Frank
Fear City (1984) . . . . . . . . . . . . . . . . . . . . . .Matt Rossi
Rustler's Rhapsody (1985). . . . . . . . . . . . Rex O'Herlihan
Platoon (1986) . . . . . . . . . . . . . . . . . . . . . . . Barnes
Someone to Watch Over Me (1987) . . . : . .Mike Keagan
Betrayed (1988) . . . . . . . . . . . . . . . . . Gary Simmons
Last Rites (1988) . . . . . . . . . . . . . . . . . . . Michael
Shoot to Kill (1988). . . . . . . . . . . . . . . . Jonathan Knox
Born on the Fourth of July (1989) . . Recruiting Sergeant
Major League (1989). . . . . . . . . . . . . . . . . . Jake Taylor
The Field (1990) . . . . . . . . . . . . . . . . . . The American
Love at Large (1990). . . . . . . . . . . . . . . .Harry Dobbs
**At Play in the Fields of the Lord** (1991)
. . . . . . . . . . . . . . . . . . . . . . . . . . . . . . . . Lewis Moon
•• 0:45—Buns, while taking off his clothes after parachuting into the jungle.
••• 0:46—Nude, arriving at the Niaruna village.
• 0:47—Very brief buns and frontal nudity.
•• 0:50—Buns, while entering hut.
••• 0:52—Brief frontal nudity while standing up, then
  buns, while walking.
•• 0:54—Buns, while wearing G-string.
••• 0:55—More buns, wearing G-string, while walking
  in the forest.
•• 0:56—More buns, with Pindi.
• 1:31—(0:01 into tape 2) Buns, in G-string.
••• 2:14—(0:44 into tape 2) Buns, in G-string, with Pindi.
• 2:47—(1:17 into tape 2) Buns, outside in G-string.
•• 2:50—(1:20 into tape 2) Buns, in G-string when the
  white men in the helicopter fire bomb the village.
Shattered (1991). . . . . . . . . . . . . . . . . . . . Dan Merrick
Gettysburg (1993) . . . . . . Lieut. Gen. James Longstreet
Sliver (1993) . . . . . . . . . . . . . . . . . . . . . . Jack Landsford
Sniper (1993) . . . . . . . . . . . . . . . . . . . . Thomas Beckett
Chasers (1994) . . . . . . . . . . . . . . . . . . . . . Rock Reilly

*Made for Cable TV:*
Dream On: The Second Greatest Story Ever Told
(1991; HBO). . . . . . . . . . . . . . . . . . . . . .Nick Spencer
*TV:*
One Life to Live . . . . . . . . . . . . . . . . . . . . . . Tim Siegel
*Magazines:*
**Playboy** (Nov 1992) . . . . . . . . . . . Sex in Cinema 1992
•• 147—Frontal nudity from *At Play in the Fields of the
  Lord.*

# Berg, Peter

*Films:*
Never on Tuesday (1988) . . . . . . . . . . . . . . . . . . . .Eddie
Genuine Risk (1989). . . . . . . . . . . . . . . . . . . . . Henry
Heart of Dixie (1989) . . . . . . . . . . . . . . . . . . . . . Jenks
Race for Glory (1989). . . . . . . . . . . . . . Chris Washburn
Shocker (1989) . . . . . . . . . . . . . . . . . Jonathan Parker
Crooked Hearts (1991). . . . . . . . . . . . . . . . . . . . .Tom
Late for Dinner (1991) . . . . . . . . . . . . . Frank Lovegren
A Midnight Clear (1991) . . . . . . . . . . . . . . . . . .Miller
**Aspen Extreme** (1993) . . . . . . . . . . Dexter Rutecki
•• 1:14—Nude, running on road after getting beat up.
Fire in the Sky (1993). . . . . . . . . . . . . . David Whitlock
Unveiled (1993). . . . . . . . . . . . . . . . . . . . .Drug Dealer
**The Last Seduction** (1994). . . . . . . . . . . Mike Swale
•• 0:53—Buns, while getting up out of bed and walk-
  ing to bathroom.
*Made for Cable Movies:*
A Case for Murder (1993; USA) . . . . . . . . . . . . . . n.a.
*Made for TV Movies:*
Rise and Walk: The Dennis Byrd Story (1994)
. . . . . . . . . . . . . . . . . . . . . . . . . . . . . . .Dennis Byrd

# Berger, Helmut

*Films:*
**The Damned** (1969; German) . . Martin Von Essenbeck
• 2:03—Buns, while walking up to his mother and rip-
  ping her dress off. Dark, don't see his face.
Dorian Gray (1970; Italian/British/German)
. . . . . . . . . . . . . . . . . . . . . . . . . . . . . . . .Dorian Gray
The Garden of the Finzi-Continis (1971; Italian/German)
. . . . . . . . . . . . . . . . . . . . . . . . . . . . . . . . Alberto
Ash Wednesday (1973) . . . . . . . . . . . . . . . . . . Erich
Ludwig (1973; Italian) . . . . . . . . . . . . . . . . . . Ludwig
Conversation Piece (1974; Italian/French) . . . . . Konrad
**The Romantic Englishwoman** (1975; British/French)
. . . . . . . . . . . . . . . . . . . . . . . . . . . . . . . . . .Thomas
• 1:08—Upper half of buns, while sitting at edge of
  pool talking to Glenda Jackson.
Battle Force (1976). . . . . . . . . . . . . . . . . . . . . . . . n.a.
Code Name: Emerald (1985) . . . . . . . . . . . . .Ernst Ritter
The Godfather, Part III (1990). . . . . . . Frederick Keinszig
*TV:*
Dynasty (1983-84). . . . . . . . . . . . . . . . . Peter de Vilbis
*Magazines:*
**Playboy** (Nov 1976) . . . . . . . . . . . Sex in Cinema 1976
• 146—Partial buns, while sitting down in photo from
  *Romantic Englishwoman.*

# Bergin, Patrick

*Films:*

The Courier (1988; British) . . . . . . . . . . . . . . . . Christy

Mountains of the Moon (1989) . . . . . . . . Richard Burton

Highway to Hell (1991) . . . . . . . . . . . . . . . . . . . . Beezie

**Love Crimes** (1991) . . . . . . . . . . . . . . David Hanover

(Unrated version reviewed.)

• 1:02—Buns, during love scene with Sean Young. Lit with red light, don't see his face.

Sleeping with the Enemy (1991) . . . . . . . Martin Bruney

Map of the Human Heart (1992; Australian/Canadian)

. . . . . . . . . . . . . . . . . . . . . . . . . . . . . . Walter Russell

Patriot Games (1992) . . . . . . . . . . . . . Kevin O'Donnell

**Double Cross** (1994) . . . . . . . . . . . . . . . . Jack Conealy

• 0:24—Buns, while standing in shower with Kelly Preston. Don't see his face very well.

*Made for Cable Movies:*

Frankenstein (1993; TNT) . . . . . . Dr. Victor Frankenstein

They (1993; Showtime) . . . . . . . . . . . . . . Mark Samuels

# Berling, Peter

*Films:*

Aguirre, The Wrath of God (1972; West German)

. . . . . . . . . . . . . . . . . . . . . . . Don Fernando de Guzman

**Julia** (1974; German) . . . . . . . . . . . . . . . . . Alex Lovener

• 0:12—Brief buns, while playing the piano outside on the dock.

The Marriage of Maria Braun (1979; German) . . . Bronski

Fitzcarraldo (1982) . . . . . . . . . . . . . . . Opera Manager

Voyager (1991; German/French) . . . . . . . . . . . Baptist

# Bernard, Erick

*Films:*

**The Passion of Beatrice** (1988; French) . . . . L'amant

• 0:06—Brief buns, in bed with François' mother when discovered by François.

Cyrano De Bergerac (1990; French) . . . . . . . . . . Cadet

# Bernsen, Collin

Son of actress Jeanne Cooper.

Brother of actor Corbin Bernsen.

*Films:*

Dangerous Love (1988) . . . . . . . . . . . . . . . . . Brooks

Hangfire (1990) . . . . . . . . . . . . . . . . . . . . . . . . RTO

Mr. Destiny (1990) . . . . . . . . . . . . . . . Tom Robertson

**Puppet Master II** (1990) . . . . . . . . . . . . . . . Michael

•• 1:10—Buns, while putting out fire on the bed.

Double Trouble (1991) . . . . . . . . . . . . . Whitney Regan

Frozen Assets (1992) . . . . . . . . . . . . . . . . . . . Lomax

*Made for Cable Movies:*

Sketch Artist (1992; Showtime) . . . . . . . . . . . . Phillipe

*Video Tapes:*

Inside Out 3 (1992) . . . . . . . . . Dennis/The Wet Dream

# Bernsen, Corbin

Son of actress Jeanne Cooper.

Brother of actor Collin Bernsen.

Husband of actress Amanda Pays.

*Films:*

Three the Hard Way (1974) . . . . . . . . . . . . . . . . . Boy

S.O.B. (1981) . . . . . . . . . . . . . . . . . . . . . . . . . . n.a.

Dead Aim (1987) . . . . . . . . . . . . . . . . . . . . . Webster

Hello Again! (1987) . . . . . . . . . . . . . . . Jason Chadman

Bert Rigby, You're a Fool (1989) . . . . . . . . . Jim Shirley

Disorganized Crime (1989) . . . . . . . . . . . Frank Salazar

**Major League** (1989) . . . . . . . . . . . . . . . Roger Dorn

• 0:58—Brief buns, while running in locker room to cover himself with a towel when Rachel comes in to talk to the team.

Shattered (1991) . . . . . . . . . . . . . . . . . . . . Jeb Scott

Frozen Assets (1992) . . . . . . . . . . . . . . Zach Shepard

Final Mission (1993) . . . . . . . . . General Morgan Breslaw

A Brilliant Disguise (1994) . . . . . . . . . . . . Dr. Martin

Major League II (1994) . . . . . . . . . . . . . . . . . . . n.a.

*Made for Cable Movies:*

Dead on the Money (1991) . . . . . . . . . . . . . . . . n.a.

*Miniseries:*

Grass Roots (1992) . . . . . . . . . . . . . . . . . . . Will Lee

*Made for TV Movies:*

Line of Fire: The Morris Dees Story (1991) . . Morris Dees

Love Can Be Murder (1992) . . . . . . . . . . . . . . . n.a.

Beyond Suspicion (1993) . . . . . . . . . . . . . . . . . n.a.

I Know My Son Is Alive (1994) . . . . . . . . . . . . . Mark

*TV:*

L.A. Law (1986-94) . . . . . . . . . . . . . . . Arnie Becker

# Biehn, Michael

*Films:*

**Coach** (1978) . . . . . . . . . . . . . . . . . . . . . . . . . Jack

• 1:11—Upper half of buns, while in shower with Cathy Lee Crosby.

Hogwild (1980; Canadian) . . . . . . . . . . . . . . . . . Tim

The Fan (1981) . . . . . . . . . . . . . . . . . . Douglas Breen

The Lords of Discipline (1983) . . . . . . . . . . . Alexander

**The Terminator** (1984) . . . . . . . . . . . . . . Kyle Reese

• 0:06—Side view of buns after arriving from the future. Brief buns running down the alley. A little dark.

Aliens (1986) . . . . . . . . . . . . . . . . . . . Corporal Hicks

Rampage (1987) . . . . . . . . . . . . . . . . Anthony Fraser

In a Shallow Grave (1988) . . . . . . . . . . . Garnet Montrose

The Seventh Sign (1988) . . . . . . . . . . . . . Russell Quinn

The Abyss (1989) . . . . . . . . . . . . . . . Lieutenant Coffey

Navy SEALS (1990) . . . . . . . . . . . . . . . . . . . Curran

Timebomb (1990) . . . . . . . . . . . . . . . . . . . Eddy Kay

**K2** (1991) . . . . . . . . . . . . . . . . . . . . . Taylor Brooks

• 0:43—Brief buns, while standing up in pool outside.

**Deadfall** (1993) . . . . . . . . . . . . . . . . . . . . . . . . Joe

• 0:43—Buns, while making love on top of Sarah Trigger in bed.

Tombstone (1993) . . . . . . . . . . . . . . . . Johnny Ringo

*Made for Cable Movies:*

A Taste For Killing (1992; USA) . . . . . . . . . . . Bo Landry

Strapped (1993; HBO) . . . . . . . . . . . . . Mathew McRae

## Blackwood, Steve

*Made for Cable TV:*

**Dream On: Portrait by an Artist On the Young Man** (1993; HBO). . . . . . . . . . . . . . . Tatoo Customer
- •• 0:09—Buns, lying face down on table, getting a tatoo on his butt cheek.

## Blake, Robert

*Films:*

The Treasure of the Sierra Madre (1948) . . .Mexican Boy
PT 109 (1963). . . . . . . . . . . . . . . . . . . "Bucky" Harris
This Property is Condemned (1966) . . . . . . . . . Sidney
In Cold Blood (1967) . . . . . . . . . . . . . . . . .Perry Smith
Tell Them Willie Boy is Here (1969) . . . . . . . . . . . Willie
- 0:22—Sort of buns when Katherine Ross lies down with him. Very, very brief lower frontal nudity seen through spread legs (one frame). More buns. Long shot, hard to see.

Electra Glide in Blue (1973). . . . . . . . . John Wintergreen
Busting (1974) . . . . . . . . . . . . . . . . . . . . . . . . .Farrell
Coast to Coast (1980). . . . . . . . . . . . . Charlie Callahan
*Made for TV Movies:*
Of Mice and Men (1981) . . . . . . . . . . . . George Milton
Judgment Day: The John List Story (1993) . . . . John List
*TV:*
Baretta (1975-78) . . . . . . . . . . . . Detective Tony Baretta
Hell Town (1985) . . . . . . . . . . . . . . . Father Noah Rivers

## • Blasco, Daniel

*Films:*

Wild Orchid (1990). . . . . . . . . . . . . . . . . Man in Airport
*Made for Cable TV:*
**Red Shoe Diaries: Runway** (1994; Showtime) Miguel
- ••• 0:21—Buns, taking off his underwear and making love with Alia in front of two hookers.

## Blodgett, Michael

*Films:*

The Catalina Caper (1967) . . . . . . . . . . . . . .Bob Draper
The Trip (1967). . . . . . . . . . . . . . . . . . . . . . . . . . .n.a.
There Was a Crooked Man (1970). . . . . . Coy Cavendish
**The Velvet Vampire** (1971) . . . . . . . . . . . . . Lee Ritter
- •• 0:21—Buns, getting up out of bed during desert dream scene.
- ••• 0:42—Buns, in desert dream scene.
- •• 0:46—Buns, while on floor with Diane.

The Carey Treatment (1972) . . . . . . . . . .Roger Hudson
The Ultimate Thrill (1974). . . . . . . . . . . . . . . . . . Tom

## Blundell, Graeme

*Films:*

**Alvin Purple** (1973; Australian). . . . . . . . . Alvin Purple
- •• 0:21—Brief nude, while painting Samantha's body.
- •• 0:22—Buns and brief frontal nudity in bedroom with the Kinky Lady.
- • 0:25—Brief buns with Mrs. Warren—who turns out to be a man.
- • 0:26—Very brief frontal nudity running out of room, then buns going down the stairs.
- ••• 0:33—Nude, undressing and taking a shower. Shot at fast speed.
- •• 1:04—Nude, running away from the girl during showing of movie.
- • 1:21—Buns, while getting chased by a group of women down the street.

**Alvin Rides Again** (1974; Australian) . . . .Alvin Purple
- • 0:06—Buns, while running out of the office after he's awakened. Blurry.

Don's Party (1976; Australian) . . . . . . . . . . . . . . Simon
Pacific Banana (1980). . . . . . . . . . . . . . . . . . . . . .n.a.
The Year My Voice Broke (1987; Australian) . . Nils Olson

## Bluteau, Lothaire

*Films:*

**Jesus of Montreal** (1990; French/Canadian)
. . . . . . . . . . . . . . . . . . . . . . . . . . .Daniel Coulombe
- • 0:43—Buns, getting whipped while tied to a tree during a play. Long shot.
- • 0:44—Buns, during crucifixion during play.
- • 1:13—Upper half of frontal nudity when police arrest him during play.
- • 1:36—Very brief frontal nudity when the cross he's on falls over.

**Black Robe** (1991; Canadian/Australian)
. . . . . . . . . . . . . . . . . . . . . . . . . . . Father Laforgue
- • 0:18—Brief side view of buns, while hanging his rear end over the side of the canoe.
- • 1:04—Buns, while standing in Iroquois hut.

Orlando (1993; British) . . . . . . . . . . . . . . . .The Khan
*Made for TV Movies:*
Mrs. 'arris Goes to Paris (1992). . . . . . . . . . . . . Andre
*Magazines:*
**Playboy** (Nov 1990) . . . . . . . . . . Sex in Cinema 1990
- •• 141—Full frontal nudity from *Jesus of Montreal*.

## Bogosian, Eric

*Films:*

**Special Effects** (1984) . . . . . . . . . . . . . . . . . . .Neville
- • 0:21—Buns, while fighting with Zoe Tamerlis in bed. Medium long shot.

Talk Radio (1988). . . . . . . . . . . . . . . . Barry Champlain
Sex, Drugs, Rock & Roll (1991) . . . . . . . . . . . . Himself

## Bolano, Tony

*Films:*

**Cat Chaser** (1988) . . . . . . . . . . . . . . . . . . . . . Corky
- •• 1:16—Nude, undressing in bathroom with Andres, before getting shot by Charles Durning.

## Bolla, R.

Adult film actor.
*Adult Films:*
**Blonde Ambition** (1980; British). . . . . . . . . . . . . Erik
Frontal nudity in hard core sex scenes.
*Films:*
Deathmask (1983) . . . . . . . . . . . . . . . . . . . . . . .n.a.

# Bonanno, Louis

*Films:*
Sex Appeal (1986)........................Tony
Slammer Girls (1987).....................Cubby
Student Affairs (1987)............... Louie Balducci
**Wimps** (1987).........................Francis
- 1:13—Buns, while running into a restaurant kitchen.

Auntie Lee's Meat Pies (1991)................. Doc
Cool As Ice (1991) .............Sugar Shack Singer
*Video Tapes:*
Night of the Living Babes (1987).............Buck

# Bond, Steve

*Films:*
Tarzan and the Jungle Boy (1966)..............Erik
Massacre at Central High (1976).............. Craig
Gas Pump Girls (1978) ......................n.a.
**H.O.T.S.** (1979)..........................John
*a.k.a. T & A Academy*
- 0:32—Buns, while trapped in van with K. C. Winkler.

The Prey (1980) ..........................Joel
Magdelena (1988) .................Joseph Mohr
To Die For (1988) ........................ Tom
Picasso Trigger (1989)......................n.a.
To Die For 2 (1991)........................ Tom
*a.k.a. Son of Darkness: To Die For II*
*TV:*
Santa Barbara .......................Mack Blake
General Hospital (1983-86)..........Jimmy Lee Holt

# Bond, Tony

*Films:*
**Desert Passion** (1992) ..................... Nick
- 0:17—Buns, while making love on top of Heather in the desert. Long scene.
- 1:02—Buns, while making love with Heather during cowboy fantasy.

# Bondy, Christopher

*Made for Cable Movies:*
**Deadly Surveillance** (1991; Showtime) ...... Nickels
- 0:31—Buns, while dropping his towel to run after Michael.

# • Bonuglia, Maurizio

*Films:*
**The Seducers** (1970) ..................... Aldo
*a.k.a. Sensation*
*a.k.a. Top Sensation*
- 0:11—Very brief buns, when Mudy yanks his towel off and he jumps off boat into the water. Sort of buns, while swimming in the water.

Ludwig (1973; Italian).....................Mayor

# Boorman, Charley

Son of British director John Boorman.
*Films:*
Dream One (1984; British/French) ........ Cunegond

The Emerald Forest (1985)..............Tommy
- 0:23—Brief buns, while running through camp.
- 0:24—Brief buns, while running from waterfall and diving into pond.
- 0:30—Buns, during ceremony.
- 0:45—Buns, while running away from the Fierce People with his dad.
- 1:02—Buns while running on the rocks, then bun in hut.
- •• 1:31—Buns while climbing up the building.
- 1:35—Buns while running down the hall to save Kachiri.

Hope and Glory (1987; British)........ Luftwaffe Pilot

# Boretski, Paul

*Films:*
Spacehunter: Adventures in the Forbidden Zone (1983) ........................................ Jarrett
**Perfect Timing** (1984) ......................Joe
- •• 0:11—Brief frontal nudity and buns, while rolling over on the bed.
- 0:29—Frontal nudity on the roof in the snow with Bonnie.
- 0:35—Buns, while on bed getting slapped on the behind.
- 0:50—Buns, while in bed with Judy.
- •• 1:03—Brief frontal nudity on TV with Judy while he and Bonnie watch.

# Bottoms, Joseph

Brother of actors Sam and Timothy Bottoms.
*Films:*
The Dove (1974; British) ..........Robin Lee Graham
Crime and Passion (1976) .................... Larry
High Rolling (1977; Australian)................Texas
The Black Hole (1979) .......Lieutenant Charles Pizer
Cloud Dancer (1980) ..................Tom Loomis
**Surfacing** (1980) ..........................Joe
- 0:23—Buns, while in bed with Kathleen Beller.

King of the Mountain (1981) ................ Buddy
Blind Date (1984)................ Jonathon Ratcliffe
*a.k.a. Deadly Seduction*
(Not the same 1987 *Blind Date* with Bruce Willis.)
**Born to Race** (1988) .................. Al Pagura
- 0:55—Brief buns, while taking off bathrobe on deck and jumping into the lake.

**Inner Sanctum** (1991)...............Baxter Reed
- 0:10—Lower half of buns, while in office with Margaux Hemingway.
- ••• 0:43—Buns, while on sofa with Tanya Roberts.

Liar's Edge (1991) .................Dave Kirkpatrick
0:55—Almost buns, drying off after getting out of the shower.
*Made for Cable Movies:*
Treacherous Crossing (1992; USA) .............. n.a.
*Miniseries:*
Holocaust (1978)......................Rudi Weiss
*Made for TV Movies:*
Gunsmoke: To the Last Man (1992) ... Tommy Graham

## Bottoms, Sam

Brother of actors Joseph and Timothy Bottoms.
*Films:*
**The Last Picture Show** (1971) . . . . . . . . . . . . . Billy
- 0:41—Brief buns, after falling out of car with Jimmy Sue.

Class of '44 (1973) . . . . . . . . . . . . . . . . . . . . . Marty
The Outlaw Josey Wales (1976) . . . . . . . . . . . . . Jamie
Apocalypse Now (1979) . . . . . . . . . . . . . . . . . . Lance
Bronco Billy (1980) . . . . . . . . . . . . . . . . . . Leonard
Prime Risk (1985) . . . . . . . . . . . . . . . . . . . Bill Yeoman
Dolly Dearest (1992) . . . . . . . . . . . . . . . . . Eliot Reed
Sugar Hill (1993) . . . . . . . . . . . . . . . . Oliver Thompson
*Made for TV Movies:*
Cage Without a Key (1975) . . . . . . . . . . . . . . . . . n.a.

## Bottoms, Timothy

Brother of actors Joseph and Sam Bottoms.
*Films:*
Johnny Got His Gun (1971) . . . . . . . . . . . . Joe Bonham
The Last Picture Show (1971) . . . . . . . Sonny Crawford
The Paper Chase (1973) . . . . . . . . . . . . . . . . . . Hart
The White Dawn (1974) . . . . . . . . . . . . . . . . Daggett
Small Town in Texas (1976) . . . . . . . . . . . . . . . Poke
Rollercoaster (1977) . . . . . . . . . . . . . . . . .Young Man
The Other Side of the Mountain, Part II (1978)
. . . . . . . . . . . . . . . . . . . . . . . . . . . . . John Boothe
Hurricane (1979) . . . . . . . . . . . . . . . . . . . Jack Sanford
**The High Country** (1980; Canadian) . . . . . . . . . . Jim
- 1:19—Buns, while walking into the pond with Linda Purl.
- 1:24—Buns, while pulling underwear on after getting out of sleeping bag.

Hambone and Hillie (1984) . . . . . . . . . . . . . . Michael
**In the Shadow of Kilimanjaro** (1985)
. . . . . . . . . . . . . . . . . . . . . . . . . . . .Jack Ringtree
- • 0:18—Buns, three times, while in bedroom with Irene Miracle.
- 0:21—Brief buns, in mirror, while putting towel around himself.

Invaders from Mars (1986) . . . . . . . . . . George Gardner
What Waits Below (1986) . . . . . . . . . . . . . . Maj. Stevens
The Drifter (1988) . . . . . . . . . . . . . . . . . . . . .Arthur
Istanbul (1990) . . . . . . . . . . . . . . . . . . . . . . . Frank
Texasville (1990) . . . . . . . . . . . . . . . . . Sonny Crawford
*Made for Cable TV:*
The Hitchhiker: The Joker (1987; HBO) . . . . . . . . . .Peter
*Miniseries:*
East of Eden (1981) . . . . . . . . . . . . . . . . . . .Adam Trask

## • Bowen, Dennis

*Films:*
Gas Pump Girls (1978) . . . . . . . . . . . . . . . . . . . . . .n.a.
**Van Nuys Blvd.** (1979) . . . . . . . . . . . . . . . . . . . .Greg
- 0:53—Brief buns, while putting his underwear on after getting caught in the wrong bedroom.

Lisa (1989) . . . . . . . . . . . . . . . . . . . . Alison's Boyfriend
*TV:*
Welcome Back, Kotter (1975-77) . . . . . . . . Todd Ludlow

## Bowen, Michael

*Films:*
Forbidden World (1982) . . . . . . . . . . . . . . . Jimmy Swift
Valley Girl (1983) . . . . . . . . . . . . . . . . . . . . . Tommy
Night of the Comet (1984) . . . . . . . . . . . . . . . . Larry
The Wild Life (1984) . . . . . . . . . . . . . . . . . . . . . . . .Vince
The Check is in the Mail (1986) . . . . . . . . Gary Jackson
Echo Park (1986) . . . . . . . . . . . . . . . . . . . . .August
Iron Eagle (1986) . . . . . . . . . . . . . . . . . . . . Knotcher
Less than Zero (1987) . . . . . . . . . . . . . . . . . . . .Hop
**Mortal Passions** (1989) . . . . . . . . . . . . . . . . . . .Burke
- 0:42—Brief buns, while on top of Adele.

Kid (1990) . . . . . . . . . . . . . . . . . . . . . . . . . Harlan
Operation Lookout (1991) . . . . . . . . . . . . . . . .Slater
The Taking of Beverly Hills (1991)
. . . . . . . . . . . . . . . . . . . . . L.A. Cop at Roadblock
The Player (1992) . . . . . . . . . . . . . . . . . . . . Cameo
*Made for TV Movies:*
Bonnie and Clyde: The True Story (1992) . . Buck Barrow
Casualties of Love: The "Long Island Lolita" Story (1993)
. . . . . . . . . . . . . . . . . . . . . . . . . . . . .Paul Makely

## Bowie, David

Singer.
Husband of model/actress Iman.
*Films:*
The Man Who Fell to Earth (1976; British)
. . . . . . . . . . . . . . . . . . . . Thomas Jerome Newton
(Uncensored version reviewed.)
0:58—Brief buns, while turning over in bed with Candy Clark.
1:56—Frontal nudity and brief buns in bed with Clark. Don't see his face.

Just a Gigolo (1979; German) . . . . . . . . . . . . . . .Paul
The Hunger (1983) . . . . . . . . . . . . . . . . . . . . John
Merry Christmas, Mr. Lawrence (1983; Japanese/British)
. . . . . . . . . . . . . . . . . . . . . . . . . . . . . .Celliers
Yellowbeard (1983) . . . . . . . . . . . . . . . . . . . Henson
Into the Night (1985) . . . . . . . . . . . . . . . . . .Colin Morris
Absolute Beginners (1986; British) . . . . Vendice Partners
Labyrinth (1986) . . . . . . . . . . . . . . . . . . . . . .Jareth
The Last Temptation of Christ (1988) . . . . . Pontius Pilate
The Linguini Incident (1991) . . . . . . . . . . . . . . Monte
Twin Peaks: Fire Walk With Me (1992) . . . . Phillip Jeffries
*Made for Cable TV:*
Dream On: The Second Greatest Story Ever Told
(1991; HBO) . . . . . . . . . . . . . Sir Roland Moorecock

## Boxleitner, Bruce

*Films:*
Six Pack Annie (1975) . . . . . . . . . . . . . . . . . Bobby Joe
The Baltimore Bullet (1980) . . . . . . . . Billie Joe Robbins
Tron (1982) . . . . . . . . . . . . . . . . . . . . . Alan/Tron
Diplomatic Immunity (1991) . . . . . . . . . . Cole Hickel
Murderous Vision (1991) . . . . . . . . .Det. Kyle Robashaw
The Babe (1992) . . . . . . . . . . . . . . . Jumpin' Joe Dugan
Kuffs (1992) . . . . . . . . . . . . . . . . . . . . . . Brad Kuffs

**Made for Cable Movies:**
**Double Jeopardy** (1992; Showtime) . . . . . . .Jack Hart
••• 0:27—Buns, while standing and talking on the telephone.
Perfect Family (1992; USA) . . . . . . . . . . . . . . . . . . Alan
**Miniseries:**
The Last Convertible (1979) . . . . . . . . . . George Virdon
Till We Meet Again (1989). . . . . . . . . . . . . . . . . Jock
**Made for TV Movies:**
The Secret (1992) . . . . . . . . . . . . . . . . .Patrick Dunmore
House of Secrets (1993) . . . . . . . . . . . .Dr. Frank Ravinel
Gunsmoke: One Man's Justice (1994) . . . . . . . . . . .n.a.
Wyatt Earp: Return to Tombstone (1994) . . . . . . .Sheriff
**TV:**
How the West was Won (1978-79) . . . . . Luke Macahan
East of Eden (1981). . . . . . . . . . . . . . .Charles Trask
Bring 'Em Back Alive (1982-83). . . . . . . . . . . Frank Buck
Scarecrow and Mrs. King (1983-87)
. . . . . . . . . . . . . . . . . . . . . . Lee Stetson (Scarecrow)

## Boyle, Lance
**Films:**
**Maiden Quest** (1972). . . . . . . . . . . . . . . . . .Siegfried
*a.k.a. The Long Swift Sword of Siegfried*
•• 0:24—Buns, during orgy scene.

## Boyle, Peter
**Films:**
Medium Cool (1969) . . . . . . . . . . . Gun Clinic Manager
Diary of a Mad Housewife (1970)
. . . . . . . . . . . . . . . . .Man in Group Therapy Session
Joe (1970). . . . . . . . . . . . . . . . . . . . . . . . . . Joe Curran
T. R. Baskin (1971) . . . . . . . . . . . . . . . . .Jack Mitchell
The Candidate (1972). . . . . . . . . . . . . . . . . . . Lucas
Kid Blue (1973). . . . . . . . . . . . . . . . . . Preacher Bob
Steelyard Blues (1973) . . . . . . . . . . . Eagle Throneberry
Young Frankenstein (1974) . . . . . . . . . . . . . . Monster
Swashbuckler (1976). . . . . . . . . . . . . . . . Lord Durant
Taxi Driver (1976) . . . . . . . . . . . . . . . . . . . . . Wizard
F.I.S.T. (1978) . . . . . . . . . . . . . . . . . . . . Max Graham
Beyond the Poseidon Adventure (1979) . Frank Massetti
Hardcore (1979) . . . . . . . . . . . . . . . . . . . . Andy Mast
North Dallas Forty (1979) . . . . . . . . . . . . . . . Emmett
Where the Buffalo Roam (1980) . . . . . . . . . . . . .Lazlo
Outland (1981). . . . . . . . . . . . . . . . . . . . . . Sheppard
Hammett (1982). . . . . . . . . . . . . . . . . . . Jimmy Ryan
Yellowbeard (1983). . . . . . . . . . . . . . . . . . . . . Moon
Johnny Dangerously (1984) . . . . . . . . . . . . . Dundee
**The Dream Team** (1989) . . . . . . . . . . . . . . . Jack
•• 0:05—Buns, while getting up out of chair.
Kickboxer 2: The Road Back (1990). . . . . . Justin Maciah
Men of Respect (1990) . . . . . . . . . . . . . . . . . . Duffy
Nervous Ticks (1991) . . . . . . . . . . . . . . . .Ron Rudman
Honeymoon in Vegas (1992). . . . . . . . . . .Chief Orman
Solar Crisis (1992). . . . . . . . . . . . . . . . Arnold Teague
Taking the Heat (1993) . . . . . . . . . . . . . . . . . . Judge
**Made for Cable Movies:**
The Tragedy of Flight 103: The Inside Story (1990; HBO)
. . . . . . . . . . . . . . . . . . . . . . . . . . . . . . . Fred Ford

Royce (1994; Showtime) . . . . . . . . . . . . . . . .Huggins
**Miniseries:**
From Here to Eternity (1979) . . . . . . . . . . Fatso Judson
**Made for TV Movies:**
In the Line of Duty: Street War (1992)
. . . . . . . . . . . . . . . . . . . . . . . . . .Detective Dan Reilly
**TV:**
Joe Bash (1986) . . . . . . . . . . . . . . . . . . . Officer Joe Bash

## Bradshaw, Billy
**Films:**
Opportunity Knocks (1990) . . . . . . . . . . . . . . . .David
**The Other Woman** (1992) . . . . . . . . . . . . . . . . . Scott
(Unrated version reviewed.)
• 0:52—Half of buns, making love with Sally in the office screening room.

## Branagh, Kenneth
Director.
Husband of actress Emma Thompson.
**Films:**
**High Season** (1988; British) . . . . . . . . . . . . . Rich Lamb
• 0:56—Buns, while putting a wrap around Jacqueline Bisset after they fool around in the water.
A Month in the Country (1988; British) . . . . . . . Moon
Henry V (1989) . . . . . . . . . . . . . . . . . . . . . King Henry V
Dead Again (1991). . . . . . . Roman Strauss/Mike Church
Much Ado About Nothing (1993; British). . . . . Benedick
Peter's Friends (1993; British/U.S.) . . . . . . . . . . Andrew
Swing Kids (1993) . . . . . . . . . . . . . . . . . . . SS Official

## Brando, Marlon
**Films:**
A Streetcar Named Desire (1951). . . . . Stanley Kowalski
On the Waterfront (1954) . . . . . . . . . . . . . Terry Malloy
(Academy Award for Best Actor.)
The Nightcomers (1971; British) . . . . . . . . Peter Quint
0:30—Looks like you can see something between his legs, but most of his midsection is hidden by bed post.
The Godfather (1972) . . . . . . . . . . . .Don Vito Corleone
(Academy Award for Best Actor.)
**Last Tango In Paris** (1972). . . . . . . . . . . . . . . . .Paul
(X-rated, letterbox version.)
• 1:59—Brief buns, while pulling his pants down to moon a woman at a dance.
The Missouri Breaks (1976) . . . . . . . . . . . . Lee Clayton
A Dry White Season (1989) . . . . . . . . . . . .Ian McKenzie
The Freshman (1990). . . . . . . . . . . . .Carmine Sabatini
Christopher Columbus: The Discovery (1992; U.S./
Spanish). . . . . . . . . . . . . . . . . . . . . . . . Torquemada

## Brandon, Cory
**Films:**
**Auditions** (1978) . . . . . . . . . . . . . . . . . . . .Van Scott
•• 0:32—Frontal nudity when Tracy undresses him.

# Brandon, David

*Films:*

**The Naked Sun.** . . . . . . . . . . . . . . . . . . . . . . . Lucas
- • 0:58—Buns, while kneeling in bed, undressing Gina.
- ••• 1:00—Buns, while making love on top of Gina in bed.
- • 1:15—Buns, while making love with Gina.

The Boys From Brazil (1978) . . . . . . . . . . . . . . Schmidt
She (1983) . . . . . . . . . . . . . . . . . . . . . . . . Pretty Boy
Good Morning, Babylon (1987; Italian/French) . . . Grass
High-Frequency (1988; Italian) . . . . . . . . . . . . . . . Spy

# Brannan, Gavin

*Films:*

**Private Passions** (1983) . . . . . . . . . . . . . . . . . . . . Mark
- • 1:19—Buns, while lying in bed on top of Sybil Danning.

# Breeding, Larry

*Films:*

**Street Music** (1982) . . . . . . . . . . . . . . . . . . . . . . Eddie
- •• 1:09—Buns, while getting out of bed and putting his underwear on.

*TV:*

Who's Watching the Kids? (1978) . . . . . . . . Larry Parnell
The Last Resort (1979-80) . . . . . . . . . . . Michael Lerner

# Brenner, Christopher

*Films:*

**The Executioner** (1980) . . . . . . . . . . . . . Chicken Boy
- • 1:05—Buns, twice, while tied up on bed when Robert Ginty kills the bad guy.

# Bridges, Beau

*Films:*

Village of the Giants (1965) . . . . . . . . . . . . . . . . Fred
**Gaily, Gaily** (1969) . . . . . . . . . . . . . . . . . . . Ben Harvey
- •• 1:37—Brief buns, getting up from table and shaking.

The Landlord (1970) . . . . . . . . . . . . . . . . Elgar Enders
The Christian Licorice Store (1971) . . . . . . Franklin Kane
Adam's Women (1972; Australian) . . . . . . . . . . . Adam
Your Three Minutes Are Up (1973) . . . . . . . . . . Charlie
The Other Side of the Mountain (1975) . . . . . Dick Buek
Swashbuckler (1976) . . . . . . . . . . . . . . . . Major Folly
Greased Lightning (1977) . . . . . . . . . . . . . . . . . Hutch
Norma Rae (1979) . . . . . . . . . . . . . . . . . . . . . . Sonny
The Runner Stumbles (1979) . . . . . . . . . . . . . . . . Toby
Honky Tonk Freeway (1981) . . . . . . . . . Duane Hanson
Night Crossing (1981) . . . . . . . . . . . . . . Gunter Wetzel
Love Child (1982) . . . . . . . . . . . . . . . . . Jack Hansen
Heart Like a Wheel (1983) . . . . . . . . . . . Connie Kalitta
The Hotel New Hampshire (1984) . . . . . . . . . . . Father
The Killing Time (1987) . . . . . . . . Sheriff Sam Wayburn
The Iron Triangle (1988) . . . . . . . . . . . Captain Keene
The Wild Pair (1988) . . . . . . . . . . . . . . . . . . . . . n.a.
The Fabulous Baker Boys (1989) . . . . . . . . Frank Baker
The Wizard (1989) . . . . . . . . . . . . . . . . Sam Woods
Daddy's Dyin'... Who's Got the Will? (1990) . . . . Orville

Sidekicks (1992) . . . . . . . . . . . . . . . . . Jerry Gabrewski
Married to It (1993) . . . . . . . . . . . . . . . . John Morden
*Made for Cable Movies:*
Women & Men: Stories of Seduction (1990; HBO)
. . . . . . . . . . . . . . . . . . . . . . . . . . . Gerry Breen
Wildflower (1991; Lifetime) . . . . . . . . . . . Jack Perkins
Without Warning: The James Brady Story (1991)
. . . . . . . . . . . . . . . . . . . . . . . . . James Brady
*Made for Cable TV:*
Tales From the Crypt: Abra Cadaver (1991; HBO)
. . . . . . . . . . . . . . . . . . . . . . . . . . . . . Marty
*Miniseries:*
Space (1987) . . . . . . . . . . . . . . . Randy Claggett
*Made for TV Movies:*
Outrage! (1986) . . . . . . . . . . . . . . . . . Brad Gordon
Elvis and the Colonel: The Untold Story (1993)
. . . . . . . . . . . . . . . . . . . . . . . . . . Tom Parker
The Man with Three Wives (1993) . . . . . . . . . . . n.a.
Secret Sins of the Father (1994) . . . . . . . Tom Thielman
*TV:*
United States (1980) . . . . . . . . . . . . . Richard Chapin
Harts of the West (1993- ) . . . . . . . . . . . . . Dave Hart

# Bridges, Jeff

Son of actor Lloyd Bridges.
Brother of actor Beau Bridges.
*Films:*
The Last Picture Show (1971) . . . . . . . . . Duane Jackson
Fat City (1972) . . . . . . . . . . . . . . . . . . . . . . . . Ernie
The Last American Hero (1973) . . . . . . Elroy Jackson, Jr.
  *a.k.a. Hard Driver*
Thunderbolt and Lightfoot (1974) . . . . . . . . . Lightfoot
Hearts of the West (1975) . . . . . . . . . . . . . Lewis Tater
Rancho Deluxe (1975) . . . . . . . . . . . . . . . Jack McKee
King Kong (1976) . . . . . . . . . . . . . . . . Jack Prescott
Stay Hungry (1976) . . . . . . . . . . . . . . . . Craig Blake
The American Success Company (1979) . . . . . . . Harry
**Winter Kills** (1979) . . . . . . . . . . . . . . . . . Nick Kegan
- •• 0:50—Buns, while getting dressed after making love with Belinda Bauer.

Heaven's Gate (1980) . . . . . . . . . . . . . . . . . . . John
Cutter's Way (1981) . . . . . . . . . . . . . . . Richard Bone
  *a.k.a. Cutter and Bone*
Kiss Me Goodbye (1982) . . . . . . . . . . . . Rupert Baines
Tron (1982) . . . . . . . . . . . . . . . . . . . . . . . Flynn/Clu
Against All Odds (1984) . . . . . . . . . . . . . Terry Brogan
**Starman** (1984) . . . . . . . . . . . . . . . . . Scott/Starman
- • 0:11—Brief buns, while standing up after growing from DNA to a man.

Jagged Edge (1985) . . . . . . . . . . . . . . . Jack Forester
8 Million Ways to Die (1986) . . . . . . . Matthew Scudder
The Morning After (1986) . . . . . . . . . . . . . . . Turner
Nadine (1987) . . . . . . . . . . . . . . . Vernon Hightower
Tucker: The Man and His Dream (1988)
. . . . . . . . . . . . . . . . . . . . . . . . Preston Tucker
The Fabulous Baker Boys (1989) . . . . . . . . . Jack Baker
See You in the Morning (1989) . . . . . . . . . . . . Larry
Texasville (1990) . . . . . . . . . . . . . . . . Duane Jackson
The Fisher King (1991) . . . . . . . . . . . . . . . . . . . Jack

American Heart (1993) . . . . . . . . . . . . . . . . . . . . . . . Jack
Fearless (1993) . . . . . . . . . . . . . . . . . . . . . . . Max Klein
The Vanishing (1993) . . . . . . . . . . . . . Barney Cousins
Blown Away (1994). . . . . . . . . . . . . . . . . . . . . . . .n.a.

## Brockette, Gary

*Films:*

**The Last Picture Show** (1971) . . . . . . . Bobby Sheen
   • 0:36—Upper frontal nudity and buns, while getting
    out of pool and greeting Randy Quaid and Cybill
    Shepherd. More buns, getting back into the pool.
Ice Pirates (1984) . . . . . . . . . . . . . . . . . Percy the Robot
The Philadelphia Experiment (1984) . .Adjutant/Andrews
Mac and Me (1988) . . . . . . . . . . . . . . . . . . . . . Doctor

## Broderick, Matthew

Son of actor James Broderick.
*Films:*

Max Dugan Returns (1983). . . . . . . . . . . . . . . Michael
Wargames (1983) . . . . . . . . . . . . . . . . . . . . . . . David
Ladyhawke (1985) . . . . . . . . . . . . . . . . Phillipe Gaston
Ferris Bueller's Day Off (1986). . . . . . . . . . Ferris Bueller
Project X (1987) . . . . . . . . . . . . . . . . . . . .Jimmy Garrett
Biloxi Blues (1988) . . . . . . . . . . Eugene Morris Jerome
Torch Song Trilogy (1988). . . . . . . . . . . . . . . . . Alan
Family Business (1989) . . . . . . . . . . . .Adam McMullen
Glory (1989). . . . . . . . . . . . . . Col. Robert Gould Shaw
The Freshman (1990) . . . . . . . . . . . . . . Clark Kellogg
**Out on a Limb** (1992) . . . . . . . . . . . . . Bill Campbell
   ••• 0:16—Buns, while standing on road, holding a mail-
    box to hide his privates while a bus load of kids pass
    by. Brief buns when a car stops to pick him up.
The Night We Never Met (1993). . . . . . . . . Sam Lester
*TV:*
Master Harold...and the Boys (1985) . . . . . . . . . . .n.a.

## Brolin, James

*Films:*

The Boston Strangler (1968) . . . . . . . . . . . . . . .Sgt. Lisi
Westworld (1973) . . . . . . . . . . . . . . . . . . . . John Blane
Gable and Lombard (1976). . . . . . . . . . . . . .Clark Gable
The Car (1977) . . . . . . . . . . . . . . . . . . . . .Wade Parent
Capricorn One (1978). . . . . . . . . . . . Charles Brubaker
The Amityville Horror (1979). . . . . . . . . . George Lutz
Night of the Juggler (1980). . . . . . . . . . . . . Sean Boyd
High Risk (1981) . . . . . . . . . . . . . . . . . . . . . . . Stone
Pee Wee's Big Adventure (1985) . . . . . . . . . . . . ."P.W."
**Ted & Venus** (1991) . . . . . . . . . . . . . . . . . . . . . Max
   •• 0:22—Buns, while painting Carol Kane in his house
    when Bud Cort walks in. Don't see his face.
Gas Food Lodging (1992) . . . . . . . . . . . . . .John Evans
*Made for Cable Movies:*
Twin Sisters (1992) . . . . . . . . . . . . . . . . . . . Michael
Parallel Lives (1994; Showtime). Professor Spencer Jones
*Made for TV Movies:*
And the Sea Will Tell (1991) . . . . . . . . . . . . Mac Grant
Visions of Murder (1993). . . . . . . . . . . . . . . . . . Hal
*TV:*
Marcus Welby, M.D. (1969-76). . . . . . . Dr. Steven Kiley

Hotel (1983-88) . . . . . . . . . . . . . . . . . .Peter McDermott
Angel Falls (1993) . . . . . . . . . . . . . . . . . . . . Luke Larson

## Brosnan, Pierce

Husband of the late actress Cassandra Harris.
*Films:*

The Long Good Friday (1980; British). . . . .First Irishman
**Nomads** (1986) . . . . . . . . . . . . . . . . . . . . . . Pommier
   • 0:56—Buns, while taking his pants off by the win-
    dow. Kind of dark, hard to see.
The Fourth Protocol (1987; British) . . . . . . . . . Petrofsky
The Deceivers (1988). . . . . . . . . . . . . . . William Savage
Taffin (1988; U.S./British) . . . . . . . . . . . . . Mark Taffin
Mister Johnson (1991) . . . . . . . . . . . . . .Harry Rudbeck
Entangled (1992; Canadian/French). . . . . . . . .Caravan
The Lawnmower Man (1992). . . . . . . .Lawrence Angelo
   (Unrated Director's cut reviewed.)
**Live Wire** (1992) . . . . . . . . . . . . . . . . . Danny O'Neill
   (Unrated version on video tape reviewed, not the R-rat-
   ed version shown on HBO. )
   ••• 1:02—Buns, while making love in bed with Lisa Eil-
   bacher.
Mrs. Doubtfire (1993) . . . . . . . . . . . . . . . . . . . . . Stu
*Made for Cable Movies:*
The Heist (1989; HBO). . . . . . . . . . . . . Bobby Skinner
Death Train (1993; USA) . . . . . . . . . . . . . . . . . . n.a.
Don't Talk to Strangers (1994; USA). . . . . . . . . . n.a.
*Miniseries:*
James Clavell's Noble House (1988) . . . . . . . . . .Dunross
*TV:*
Remington Steele (1982-87) . . . . . . . Remington Steele

## Brown, Bryan

Husband of actress Rachel Ward.
*Films:*

Breaker Morant (1979; Australian) . . Lt. Peter Handcock
Cathy's Child (1979; Australian) . . . . . . . . . . . . . .Nicko
**Winter of Our Dreams** (1981) . . . . . . . . . . . . . . Reb
   • 0:48—Brief buns while falling into bed with Judy
    Davis.
The Empty Beach (1985) . . . . . . . . . . . . . . .Cliff Hardy
Parker (1985; British) . . . . . . . . . . . . . . . David Parker
Rebel (1985; Australian). . . . . . . . . . . . . . Tiger Kelly
F/X (1986) . . . . . . . . . . . . . . . . . . . . . . . . .Rollie Tyler
Tai-Pan (1986) . . . . . . . . . . . Dirk Struan/"Tai-Pan"
The Good Wife (1987; Australian) . . . . . . . . Sonny HIlls
   *a.k.a. The Umbrella Woman*
Cocktail (1988) . . . . . . . . . . . . . . . . . Doug Coughlin
Gorillas in the Mist (1988) . . . . . . . . . . . Bob Campbell
Prisoners of the Sun (1990; Australian)
   . . . . . . . . . . . . . . . . . . . . . . . . . . . . Captain Cooper
FX 2 (1991) . . . . . . . . . . . . . . . . . . . . . . . . .Rollie Tyler
Sweet Talker (1991; Australian) . . . . . . . Harry Reynolds
Blame It on the Bellboy (1992; British) . . .Charlton Black
*Made for Cable Movies:*
Dead In the Water (1991) . . . . . . . . . . . Charlie Deegan
Devlin (1991; Showtime) . . . . . . . . . . . Frank Devlin
The Last Hit (1993; USA) . . . . . . . . . . . . . . . . . . n.a.

*Miniseries:*
The Thorn Birds (1983) . . . . . . . . . . . . . . . Luke O'Neill

# Brown, Clancy
*Films:*
Bad Boys (1983) . . . . . . . . . . . . . . . . . . . Viking Lofgren
The Adventures of Buckaroo Banzai, Across the 8th
 Dimension (1984) . . . . . . . . . . . . . . . . . . . . . Rawhide
The Bride (1985). . . . . . . . . . . . . . . . . . . . . . . . . Viktor
Thunder Alley (1985) . . . . . . . . . . . . . . . . . . . . Weasel
Highlander (1986) . . . . . . . . . . . . . . . . . . . . Kuragan
Extreme Prejudice (1987) . . . . . . . . . Sgt. Larry McRose
Shoot to Kill (1988). . . . . . . . . . . . . . . . . . . . . . Steve
**Blue Steel** (1989) . . . . . . . . . . . . . . . . . . Nick Mann
 • 1:27—Upper half of buns, while lying on the bath-
    room floor. Don't see his face, so it could be any-
    body.
Season of Fear (1989) . . . . . . . . . . . . . . Ward St. Clair
Ambition (1991) . . . . . . . . . . . . . . . . . . . . . . . . . Albert
Pet Sematary II (1992) . . . . . . . . . . . . . . . Gus Gilbert
*Made for Cable Movies:*
Cast a Deadly Spell (1991; HBO). . . . . . . . Harry Borden
Past Midnight (1992; USA) . . . . . . . . . . . . . Steve Lundy
Last Light (1993; Showtime) . . . . . . . . Lionel McMannis
*Made for Cable TV:*
Tales From the Crypt: Halfway Horrible (1993; HBO)
 . . . . . . . . . . . . . . . . . . . . . . . . . . . . . . .Roger Lassen
*Made for TV Movies:*
Love, Lies and Murder (1991) . . . . . . . . . .David Brown
Desperate Rescue: The Cathy Mahone Story (1993)
 . . . . . . . . . . . . . . . . . . . . . . . . . . . . .Dave Chattelier
*TV:*
Earth 2 (1994- ) . . . . . . . . . . . . . . . . . . . . . . . .n.a.

# Brown, Dwier
*Films:*
House (1986) . . . . . . . . . . . . . . . . . . . . . . . Lieutenant
Field of Dreams (1989) . . . . . . . . . . . . . . .John Kinsella
The Guardian (1990). . . . . . . . . . . . . . . . . . . . . .Phil
 0:37—Soft of buns, while in bed with Carey Lowell.
    Don't see his face.
The Cutting Edge (1992) . . . . . . . . . . . . . . . . . . . Hale
Mom and Dad Save the World (1992). . . . . . . . . . . Sirk
Gettysburg (1993) . . . . . . . . . . . . . . . . .Captain Brewer

# Brown, Max M.
*Films:*
**Wolfen** (1981). . . . . . . . . . . . Christopher Van der Veer
 • 0:21—Brief frontal nudity, lying dead as a corpse on
    the coroner's table. Don't see his face.

# Brown, Murray
*Films:*
**Vampyres** (1974; British). . . . . . . . . . . . . . . . . .Ted
 •• 0:22—Buns, while making love in bed with Fran.
 • 0:56—Buns, while falling into bed.

# Brown, Timothy
*Films:*
Black Gunn (1972). . . . . . . . . . . . . . . . . . . . . . . Larry
Sweet Sugar (1972) . . . . . . . . . . . . . . . . . . . . . . Mojo
 *a.k.a. Hellfire on Ice*
Girls Are For Loving (1973) . . . . . . . . . . . . . . . . . n.a.
Nashville (1975). . . . . . . . . . . . . . . . . . .Tommy Brown
**Famous T & A** (1982) . . . . . . . . . . . . . . . . . . . . Mojo
 (No longer available for purchase, check your video
    store for rental.)
 • 1:05—Buns in outtake from *Sweet Sugar.*
Losin' It (1982). . . . . . . . . . . . . . . . . . . . . . . . . . . n.a.
*TV:*
M*A*S*H (1972) . . . . . . . . . . . . . . Spearchucker Jones

# Brown, Woody
*Films:*
Killer Party (1986) . . . . . . . . . . . . . . . . . . . . .Harrison
**The Accused** (1988). . . . . . . . . . . . . . . . . . . . .Danny
 • 1:28—Buns, while raping Jodi Foster on the pinball
    machine.
Off Limits (1988) . . . . . . . . . . . . . . . . . . . . . .Co-Pilot
**The Rain Killer** (1990). . . . . . . . . . . . Jordan Rosewall
 ••• 0:39—Buns, while getting into bed, kneeling next to
    bed, then getting into bed with Satin. Long scene.
Alligator II: The Mutation (1991) . . . . . . . . Rich Harmon
**Animal Instincts 2** (1993) . . . . . . . . . . . . . . . . Steve
 • 0:23—Brief buns while making love with Catherine
    in bed.
 • 1:20—Buns, twice, while making love on top of
    Catherine in bed.
Secret Games 3 (1994). . . . . . . . . . . . . . . . . . . . n.a.
*TV:*
Flamingo Road (1981-82) . . . . . . . . . . Skipper Weldon
The Facts of Life (1983-84). . . . . . . . . . . . . . . . . Cliff

# • Buckley, Keith
*Films:*
**Virgin Witch** (1971; British) . . . . . . . . . . . . . .Johnny
 • 1:20—Brief buns, with Betty during ceremony.
The Pied Piper (1972; British) . . . . .Mattio, Gypsy Leader
The Eagle Has Landed (1977; British) . . . . . . . . . . . n.a.
The Spy Who Loved Me (1977; British) . . . . . . . . . . n.a.
Excalibur (1981; British). . . . . . . . . . . . . . . . .Uryens
The Star Chamber (1983). . . . . . . . . . . . . . . . .Assassin
Half Moon Street (1986) . . . . . . . . . .Hugo Van arkady
 *a.k.a. Escort Girl*
Hawks (1988; British) . . . . . . . . . . . . . . Dutch Doctor

# Bullington, Perry
*Films:*
**Chatterbox** (1977) . . . . . . . . . . . . . . . . . . . . . . . Ted
 • 0:02—Buns, while stumbling around the room.

## Bumiller, William
*Films:*
Last Resort (1985) . . . . . . . . . . . . . . . . . . . . . . . Etienne
Guns (1990) . . . . . . . . . . . . . . . . . . . . . . . . . . . Lucas
**Overexposed** (1990) . . . . . . . . . . . . . . . . . . . . .Hank
• 0:54—Brief buns, while taking off his pants to get into bed with Catherine Oxenberg.
Do or Die (1991) . . . . . . . . . . . . . . . . . . . . . . . Lucas
Father Hood (1993) . . . . . . . . . . . . . . . . . . . . . Travis
*Made for TV Movies:*
Mistress (1987) . . . . . . . . . . . . . . . . . . . . . . . . . . .n.a.
*Video Tapes:*
Inside Out (1992) . . . . . . . . . . . . . . Jack/Brush Strokes

## • Burke, Robert
*Films:*
The Unbelievable Truth (1990) . . . . . . . . . . Josh Hutton
Rambling Rose (1991) . . . . . . . . Police Chief Dave Wilkie
**Dust Devil** (1992; British) . . . . . . . . . . . . . .Dust Devil
• 0:49—Buns, while making love on top of Chelsea Field.
Simple Men (1992; U.S./British) . . . . . . . . Bill McCabe
A Far Off Place (1993; U.S./British) . . . . . . . Paul Parker
Heaven and Earth (1993) . . . . . . . . . . . . . . . . GI Paul
Robocop 3 (1993) . . . . . . . . . .Robocop/Alex J. Murphy
Tombstone (1993) . . . . . . . . . . . . . . . . Frank McLaury

## Burns, Stephen W.
*Films:*
**Spiker** . . . . . . . . . . . . . . . . . . . . . . . . Sonny Flestow
• 0:03—Buns in room.
Herbie Goes Bananas (1980) . . . . . . . . . . . . . . . . Pete

## Burns, William
*Films:*
The Passover Plot (1976; Israeli) . . . . . . . . . . . . .Shimon
Mirrors (1978) . . . . . . . . . . . . . . . . . . . . . . . . . Gary
**Play Murder For Me** (1991) . . . . . . . . . . Fred Merritt
• 0:37—Buns, on couch, trying to attack Tracy Scoggins.
*Made for Cable TV:*
Red Shoe Diaries: Jake's Story (1993; Showtime)
. . . . . . . . . . . . . . . . . . . . . . . . . . . . . . . Howard
(Available on video tape on *Red Shoe Diaries 4: Auto Erotica*.)

## Burton, Jeff
*Films:*
**Planet of the Apes** (1968) . . . . . . . . . . . . . . Dodge
• 0:26—Very brief buns while taking off clothes to go skinny dipping. (Guy on the right.)
Sweet Charity (1969) . . . . . . . . . . . . . . . . . .Policeman

## • Burton, LeVar
*Films:*
Looking for Mr. Goodbar (1977) . . . . . . . .Cap Jackson
The Hunter (1980) . . . . . . . . . . . . . . . . . Tommy Price
The Supernaturals (1987) . . . . . .Private Michael Osgood
*Made for Cable Movies:*
**Parallel Lives** (1994; Showtime) . . . Dr. Franklin Carter
• 0:34—Brief buns (he's on the left), while mooning the women in hallway during panty raid.
*Miniseries:*
Roots (1977) . . . . . . . . . . . . . . . . . . . . Kunta Kinte
*Made for TV Movies:*
Firestorm: 72 Hours in Oakland (1993)
. . . . . . . . . . . . . . . . . . . . . Fire Chief J. Allan Mather
*TV:*
Reading Rainbow . . . . . . . . . . . . . . . . . . . . . . Host
Star Trek: The Next Generation (1987-94)
. . . . . . . . . . . . . . . . . . . . . . . . . .Gerodi La Forge

## Burton, Wendell
*Films:*
The Sterile Cuckoo (1969) . . . . . . . . . . . . . . . . .Jerry
**Fortune and Men's Eyes** (1971) . . . . . . . . . . . Smitty
• 1:40—Briefly nude, after getting stripped by guards in jail cell.
Heat (1987) . . . . . . . . . . . . . . . . . . . . . . . . . . . n.a.
*TV:*
The New Dick Van Dyke Show (1973) . . . .Lucas Preston
East of Eden (1981) . . . . . . . . . . . . . . . . Tom Hamilton

## • Buscemi, Steve
*Films:*
Kiss Daddy Goodnight (1987) . . . . . . . . . . . . . .Johnny
Call Me (1988) . . . . . . . . . . . . . . . . . . . Switch Blade
Heart of Midnight (1988) . . . . . . . . . . . . . . . . . Eddy
Vibes (1988) . . . . . . . . . . . . . . . . . . . . . . . . . .Fred
Bloodhounds of Broadway (1989) . . . . . .Whining Willie
Mystery Train (1989) . . . . . . . . . . . . . . . . . .Charlie
New York Stories (1989) . . . . . . . . . . . . Gregory Stark
Slaves of New York (1989) . . . . . . . . . . . . . .Wilfredo
Miller's Crossing (1990) . . . . . . . . . . . . . . . . . Mink
Tales From the Darkside, The Movie (1990)
. . . . . . . . . . . . . . . . . . . . . . . . Edward Bellingham
Barton Fink (1991) . . . . . . . . . . . . . . . . . . . . . Chet
Billy Bathgate (1991) . . . . . . . . . . . . . . . . . . . Chet
Zandalee (1991) . . . . . . . . . . . . . . . . . . . .Odd Man
Criss Cross (1992) . . . . . . . . . . . . . . . . . . . . . Louis
**In the Soup** (1992) . . . . . . . . . . . . . . . . . Aldolpho
•• 0:49—Buns in halfway up pants, while going to the door to see who's there.
Reservoir Dogs (1992) . . . . . . . . . . . . . . . . .Mr. Pink
Ed and His Dead Mother (1993) . . . . . . . . . . . . . n.a.
Rising Sun (1993) . . . . . . . . .Willy "The Weasel" Wilhelm
Twenty Bucks (1993) . . . . . . . . . . . . . . . . . . . . n.a.
Airheads (1994) . . . . . . . . . . . . . . . . . . . . . . . Rex
*Made for Cable TV:*
Tales From the Crypt: Forever Ambergris (1993; HBO)
. . . . . . . . . . . . . . . . . . . . . . . . . . . . . . . . . . Ike

# Butcher, Glenn

*Films:*
**Young Einstein** (1989; Australian) .. Ernest Rutherford
- 0:56—Buns, while standing in front of sink when Marie comes to rescue Einstein. (He's the one on the left.)

# Butler, Jerry

Adult film actor.
Real name is Paul Siederman.
Husband of actress Lisa Loring.
*Adult Films:*
**Bad Girls IV** . . . . . . . . . . . . . . . . . . . . . . . . . . . . .n.a.
*Films:*
Evils of the Night (1985) . . . . . . . . . . . . . . . . . . . Eddie
Deranged (1987) . . . . . . . . . . . . . . . . . . . . . . . Frank

# Byrd, George

*Films:*
**The Marriage of Maria Braun** (1979; German) . . Bill
- • 0:37—Very brief frontal nudity and buns in bedroom with Maria.
- • • 0:39—Nude, while fighting with Hermann. Long scene.

# Byrd, Tom

*Films:*
Twilight Zone—The Movie (1983) . . . . . . . . . . . . . G.I.
**Out Cold** (1989) . . . . . . . . . . . . . . . . . . Mr. Holstrom
- 0:10—Brief frontal nudity getting out of bed with Teri Garr when her husband comes home.
Young Guns II (1990) . . . . . . . . . . . . . . . . . .Pit Inmate
*Made for TV Movies:*
Wet Gold (1984) . . . . . . . . . . . . . . . . . . . . . . . . . . .Chris
*TV:*
Boone (1983-84) . . . . . . . . . . . . . . . . . .Boone Sawyer

# Byrne, Gabriel

Husband of actress Ellen Barkin.
*Films:*
Excalibur (1981; British) . . . . . . . . . . . . . . . . . . . . Uther
The Keep (1983) . . . . . . . . . . . . . . . . . . . . . . . .Kaempffer
Wagner (1983; British) . . . . . . . . . . . . . . . . . . Karl Ritter
Defense of the Realm (1986; British) . . . . . . Nick Mullen
Gothic (1986; British) . . . . . . . . . . . . . . . . . . . . . . Byron
Hello Again! (1987) . . . . . . . . . . . . . . . . . .Kevin Scanlon
Julia and Julia (1987; Italian) . . . . . . . . . . . . . . . . Paolo
(This movie was shot using a high-definition video system and then transferred to film.)
Lionheart (1987) . . . . . . . . . . . . . . . . . . The Black Prince
**Siesta** (1987) . . . . . . . . . . . . . . . . . . . . . . . . . . .Augustine
- 1:28—Brief buns and frontal nudity, while getting out of bed. Long shot, hard to see.
A Soldier's Tale (1988; New Zealand) . . . . . . . . . . . Saul
Dark Obsession (1989; British) . . . . . . . . . . . . . . . Hugo
*a.k.a. Diamond Skulls*
Miller's Crossing (1990) . . . . . . . . . . . . . . Tom Reagan
Shipwrecked (1990; Norwegian) . . . . . . Lt. John Merrick
Cool World (1992) . . . . . . . . . . . . . . . . . . . . Jack Deebs

**A Dangerous Woman** (1993) . . . . . . . . . . . . Mackey
- 0:57—Lower half of buns, while making love with Debra Winger on sofa.
Into the West (1993) . . . . . . . . . . . . . . . . . . Papa Riley
Point of No Return (1993) . . . . . . . . . . . . . . . . . . Bob
Trial By Jury (1994) . . . . . . . . . . . . . . . . . . . . . . . . n.a.
*Made for Cable Movies:*
Mussolini and I (1985; HBO) . . . . . . . .Vittorio Mussolini
*Miniseries:*
Christopher Columbus (1985) . . .Christopher Columbus

# Cable, Bill

*Films:*
Pee Wee's Big Adventure (1985) . . . . . . . . . . Policeman
**Basic Instinct** (1992) . . . . . . . . . . . . . . . . Johnny Boz
(Unrated Director's cut reviewed.)
- 0:05—Brief frontal nudity, when Michael Douglas looks at the stains on the bed with UV light.

# Cadman, Josh

*Films:*
**Goin' All the Way** (1981) . . . . . . . . . . . . . . . . .Bronk
- 1:05—Buns, while in the shower talking to Boom Boom.
Angel (1983) . . . . . . . . . . . . . . . . . . . . . . . . . . . Spike
**Surf II** (1984) . . . . . . . . . . . . . . . . . . . Johnny Big Head
- 0:05—Buns, mooning three girls who flash him.
Kuffs (1992) . . . . . . . . . . . . . . . . . . . . . . Bill Donnelly
*Made for TV Movies:*
Quarterback Princess (1983) . . . . . . . . . . . . . . . Brian

# Cage, Nicolas

Real name is Nicholas Coppola.
Nephew of director Francis Coppola.
Nephew of actress Talia Shire.
*Films:*
Fast Times at Ridgemont High (1982) . . . . . . Brad's Bud
Rumble Fish (1983) . . . . . . . . . . . . . . . . . . . . . Smokey
Valley Girl (1983) . . . . . . . . . . . . . . . . . . . . . . . Randy
The Cotton Club (1984) . . . . . . . . . . . . . .Vincent Dwyer
Racing with the Moon (1984) . . . . . . . . . . . . . .Nicky
Birdy (1985) . . . . . . . . . . . . . . . . . . . . . Al Columbato
The Boy in Blue (1986; Canadian) . . . . . . . . Ned Hanlan
Peggy Sue Got Married (1986) . . . . . . . . Charlie Bodell
Moonstruck (1987) . . . . . . . . . . . . . . Ronny Cammareri
Raising Arizona (1987) . . . . . . . . . . . . H.I. McDonnough
Vampire's Kiss (1989) . . . . . . . . . . . . . . . .Peter Loew
Fire Birds (1990) . . . . . . . . . . . . . . . . . . . .Jake Preston
*a.k.a. Wings of the Apache*
Wild at Heart (1990) . . . . . . . . . . . . . . . . . . . . . Sailor
**Zandalee** (1991) . . . . . . . . . . . . . . . . . Johnny Collins
- • 0:30—Buns, while making love in bed with Zandalee.
Honeymoon in Vegas (1992) . . . . . . . . . . . . . . . . Jack
Red Rock West (1992) . . . . . . . . . . . . . . . . . . Michael
Amos & Andrew (1993) . . . . . . . . . . . . . . Amos Odell
Deadfall (1993) . . . . . . . . . . . . . . . . . . . . . . . .Eddie
Guarding Tess (1993) . . . . . . . . . . . . . . Doug Chesnic
It Could Happen to You (1994) . . . . . . . . Charlie Lang

# • Cage, Patrick

*Films:*
Dying Young (1991) . . . . . . . . . . . . Shauna's Boyfriend
*Video Tapes:*
**Playboy's Erotic Weekend Getaways** (1992)
. . . . . . . . . . . . . . . . . . . . .Anticipation: The Mountains
• • • 0:04—Frontal nudity, while in front of fireplace with
his lover.
• • 0:05—Buns, while making love with her in front of
fireplace.
• • • 0:06—Buns, while getting into bathtub with his lover.
**Playboy's How to Reawaken Your Sexual Powers**
(1992). . . . . . . . . . . . . . . . . . . . . . . . . Cast Member
• • • 0:26—Nude at the beach while standing and touching his lover.
• • • 0:43—Nude outside by stream and on blanket with
his lover.

## Calderone, Paul

*Films:*
Band of the Hand (1986) . . . . . . . . . . . . . . . . . . . .Tito
The Chair (1988). . . . . . . . . . . . . . . . . . . . . . . . . .Pizza
Sticky Fingers (1988). . . . . . . . . . . . . . . . . . . . . .Speed
Sea of Love (1989) . . . . . . . . . . . . . . . . . . . . . Serafino
King of New York (1990). . . . . . . . . . . . . . Joey Dalesio
**Q & A** (1990) . . . . . . . . . . . . . . . . . . . Roger Montalvo
• 1:50—Brief buns, while on floor of boat, getting
strangled by Nick Nolte.
Bad Lieutenant (1992) . . . . . . . . . . . . . . . . . Cop One
Criss Cross (1992) . . . . . . . . . . . . . . . . . . . . . . .Blacky

## Calfa, Don

*Films:*
1941 (1979) . . . . . . . . . . . . . . . . . Telephone Operator
The Return of the Living Dead (1985) . . . . . . . . . .Ernie
**Chopper Chicks in Zombietown** (1989)
. . . . . . . . . . . . . . . . . . . . . . . . . . . . . Ralph Willum
• 0:41—Brief buns, while trapped in walk-in locker
with zombie Lucile. Don't see his face.
Weekend at Bernie's (1989). . . . . . . . . . . . . . . Paulie
*a.k.a. Hot and Cold*
Bugsy (1991) . . . . . . . . . . . . . . . . . . . . . Louie Dragna
Stay Tuned (1992). . . . . . . . . . . . . . . . . . . . . Wetzel
*TV:*
Park Place (1981) . . . . . . . . . . Howard "Howie" Beech
Legmen (1984). . . . . . . . . . . . . . . Oscar Armismendi
*Video Tapes:*
E. Nick: A Legend in His Own Mind (1984)
. . . . . . . . . . . . . . . . . . . . . . . . E. "Nick" Vanacuzzi

## Cali, Joseph

*Films:*
Saturday Night Fever (1977). . . . . . . . . . . . . . . . Joey
(R-rated version reviewed.)
Voices (1979) . . . . . . . . . . . . . . . . . . . . . . . . . . Pinky
The Competition (1980) . . . . . . . . . . . . . Jerry Di Salvo

**The Lonely Lady** (1983) . . . . . . . . . . .Vincent Dacosta
• 1:05—Buns, while near pool table and walking
around the house with Pia Zadora.
*TV:*
Flatbush (1979) . . . . . . . . . . . . . . Presto Prestopopolos
Today's F.B.I. (1981-82) . . . . . . . . . . . . . . . Nick Frazier

## Callow, Simon

Director.
*Films:*
Amadeus (1984) . . . . . . . . . . . . . .Emanuel Schikaneder
The Good Father (1986). . . . . . . : . . . . . . .Mark Varner
**A Room with a View** (1986; British)
. . . . . . . . . . . . . . . . . . . . . . . . The Reverend Mr. Beebe
• 1:04—Frontal nudity taking off clothes and jumping
into pond.
• • • 1:05—Nude running around with Freddy and
George in the woods. Lots of frontal nudity.
Maurice (1987; British). . . . . . . . . . . . . . . . . Mr. Ducie
Manifesto (1988) . . . . . . . . . . . . . . . . . Police Chief Hunt
Mr. & Mrs. Bridge (1990). . . . . . . . . . . . . . . . Dr. Sauer
Postcards from the Edge (1990) . . . . . . . Simon Asquith
Howards End (1992) . . . . . . . . . . . . . . . Music Lecturer
Soft Top, Hard Shoulder (1992; British)
. . . . . . . . . . . . . . . . . . . . . . . . . . Eddie Cherdowski
Four Weddings and a Funeral (1994; British) . . . .Gareth

## Calvin, John

*Films:*
California Dreaming (1978) . . . . . . . . . . . . . . . . . Rick
The Cheap Detective (1978) . . . . . . . . . . . . . . . . n.a.
Norma Rae (1979). . . . . . . . . . . . . . . . . . . Ellis Harper
Foolin' Around (1980) . . . . . . . . . . . . . . . . . . Whitley
Making Love (1982). . . . . . . . . . . . . . . . . . . . .David
Swordkill (1984). . . . . . . . . . . . . . Dr. Alan Richards
Back to the Beach (1987). . . . . . . . . . . . . . . . . . .Troy
Primary Target (1990) . . . . . . . . . . . . . . . . .Cromwell
Critters 3 (1991) . . . . . . . . . . . . . . . . . . . . . Clifford
**Almost Pregnant** (1992) . . . . . . . . . .Gordon Mallory
(Unrated version reviewed.)
• • 1:11—Buns, while on top of Tanya Roberts in bed.
*TV:*
The Paul Lynde Show (1972-73) . . . . . Howie Dickerson
From Here to Eternity (1980) . . . . . . Lt. Kenneth Barrett
Tales of the Gold Monkey (1982-83)
. . . . . . . . . . . . . . . . . . . . . . . . . Rev. Willie Tenboom

# • Cambridge, Godfrey

*Films:*
The President's Analyst (1967) . . . . . . . . . . Don Masters
Cotton Comes to Harlem (1970) . . . Grave Digger Jones
**Watermelon Man** (1970) . . . . . . . . . . . . . .Jeff Gerber
• 0:01—Brief buns, twice, while lying in tanning bed
during exercise session. He's made up to look like a
white guy. Don't see his face very well.
• 0:20—Brief buns, after pulling down his pajamas after "turning" into a black guy. Don't see his face.
Come Back Charleston Blue (1972)
. . . . . . . . . . . . . . . . . . . . . . . Grave Digger Jones

Son of Blob (1972) ..........................n.a.
*a.k.a. Beware! The Blob*
Friday Foster (1975) ................. Ford Malotte
Scott Joplin (1977) ................... Tom Turpin

## Campanaro, Philip

*Films:*
Sex Appeal (1986)........................ Ralph
**Slammer Girls** (1987)..................... Gary
- 0:48—Buns, while dancing in G-string in front of the girls in their prison cell.
- 0:49—More buns in G-string, while wrestling with Melody.

## Campbell, Nicholas

*Films:*
The Amateur (1982) .................... Schraeger
The Killer Instinct (1982; Canadian) ............. n.a.
*a.k.a. Trapped*
**Certain Fury** (1985) .................... Sniffer
- • 0:38—Buns, while getting undressed to rape Irene Cara.
Rampage (1987)....................Albert Morse
The Big Slice (1991) ............ Nick Papadopoulis
Naked Lunch (1991)........................Hank
Shadow of the Wolf (1992) .................. Scott
*Made for TV Movies:*
Children of the Night (1985) ................ Larry
Betrayal of Trust (1994)................Richard Noel

## • Campbell, William

*Films:*
The Rocketeer (1991) ...................... Cliff
Gettysburg (1993) .............. Lieutenant Pitzer
*Made for TV Movies:*
**Tales of the City** (1994).............. Jon Fielden
- • 0:38—(Into part 5) Brief buns, dropping his towel and entering room in bathhouse.
*TV:*
Dynasty (1984-85) .................... Luke Fuller
Crime Story (1986-88) ......... Detective Joey Indelli
Moon Over Miami (1993- )..................Walter

## • Carberry, Joseph

*Films:*
The Survivors (1983).......... Detective Matt Burke
Vigilante (1983) ......................... Ramon
Missing in Action (1984)................Carpenter
Verne Miller (1988)....................Hymie Ross
Presumed Innocent (1990) .......... Mr. McGaffney
*TV:*
**NYPD Blue: NYPD Lou** (Oct 2, 1993)........ Kevin
- 0:39—Brief buns, getting out of bed after getting caught by Andy's dad.

## • Carpenter, Peter

*Films:*
**Blood Mania** (1970) ..................... Craig
- 0:07—Buns, almost removing his pants and getting into bath tub with Cheryl.
- 0:20—Very brief side view of buns, while sitting in bed.
Point of Terror (1971)...................... Tony

## Carradine, David

Son of actor John Carradine.
Brother of actors Keith and Robert Carradine.
*Films:*
Macho Callahan (1970) ..... Colonel David Mountford
**Boxcar Bertha** (1972) .............. Big Bill Shelly
- 0:54—Buns, while putting pants on after hearing a gun shot.
Mean Streets (1973) ...................... Drunk
Death Race 2000 (1975) .............. Frankenstein
Bound For Glory (1976)............ Woody Guthrie
Cannonball (1976; U.S./Hong Kong)
......................"Cannonball" Buckman
Gray Lady Down (1977).............. Captain Gates
The Serpent's Egg (1977)........... Abel Rosenberg
Thunder and Lightning (1977).........Harley Thomas
Death Sport (1978) ................... Kaz Oshay
Circle of Iron (1979)................. Chang-Sha
Cloud Dancer (1980)...............Brad Randolph
The Long Riders (1980) ............. Cole Younger
Americana (1981) ....................... Soldier
Q (1982) ..................... Detective Shepard
Lone Wolf McQuade (1983)................Rawley
**On the Line** (1984; Spanish) .............. Bryant
- 0:11—Buns, while lying on a table, getting a massage by three women.
The Warrior and the Sorceress (1984)............Kain
Armed Response (1986)................... Jim Roth
P.O.W.: The Escape (1986) .......... Colonel Cooper
Warlords (1988)......................... Dow
Crime Zone (1989) ...................... Jason
Sonny Boy (1989) ....................... Pearl
Sundown: The Vampire in Retreat (1989).....Mardulak
Tropical Snow (1989)......................Oskar
Bird on a Wire (1990).................... Eugene
Dune Warriors (1990).................... Michael
Field of Fire (1990)............. General Corman
Double Trouble (1991)....................Mr. C
Evil Toons (1991) .................... Gideon Fisk
Martial Law (1991)..................Dalton Rhodes
Waxwork II: Lost in Time (1991).......... The Beggar
Animal Instincts (1992) .................. Lamberti
(Unrated version reviewed.)
Night Rhythms (1992) ................. Vincent
(Unrated version reviewed.)
Dead Center (1993)..................... Chavez
*Made for Cable Movies:*
Deadly Surveillance (1991; Showtime)...... Lieutenant
*Miniseries:*
North and South (1985) ............. Justin LaMotte

North and South, Book II (1986) . . . . . . . Justin LaMotte
*Made for TV Movies:*
A Winner Never Quits (1986) . . . . . . . . . . . . Pete Gray
*TV:*
Shane (1966) . . . . . . . . . . . . . . . . . . . . . . . . . . . Shane
Kung Fu (1972-75) . . . . . . . . . . . . . Kwai Chang Caine
Kung Fu: The Legend Continues (1993- )
. . . . . . . . . . . . . . . . . . . . . . . . . . . Kwai Chang Caine

## Carradine, Keith

Son of actor John Carradine.
Brother of actors David and Robert Carradine.
*Films:*
McCabe and Mrs. Miller (1971) . . . . . . . . . . . . Cowboy
Hex (1973) . . . . . . . . . . . . . . . . . . . . . . . . . . . Whizzer
Thieves Like Us (1974) . . . . . . . . . . . . . . . . . . Bowie
**Nashville** (1975) . . . . . . . . . . . . . . . . . . . . Tom Frank
• 0:47—Buns, while sitting on floor after getting out
of bed.
Lumiere (1976; French) . . . . . . . . . . . . . . David Foster
The Duellists (1977; British) . . . . . . . . . . . . . . D'Hubert
Welcome to L.A. (1977) . . . . . . . . . . . . . Carroll Barber
Pretty Baby (1978) . . . . . . . . . . . . . . . . . . . . . Bellocq
**An Almost Perfect Affair** (1979) . . . . . . . . . . . . . Hal
• 0:48—Brief buns, while getting into bathtub with
Monica Vitti.
Old Boyfriends (1979) . . . . . . . . . . . . . . . . . . . Wayne
The Long Riders (1980) . . . . . . . . . . . . . . . Jim Younger
Southern Comfort (1981) . . . . . . . . . . . . . . . . Spencer
Choose Me (1984) . . . . . . . . . . . . . . . . . . . . . Mickey
Maria's Lovers (1985) . . . . . . . . . . . . . . Clarence Butts
The Inquiry (1986) . . . . . . . . . . . . . . . . . . Titus Valerius
Trouble in Mind (1986) . . . . . . . . . . . . . . . . . . . Coop
Backfire (1987) . . . . . . . . . . . . . . . . . . . . Clinton James
**The Moderns** (1988) . . . . . . . . . . . . . . . . . Nick Hart
•• 1:17—Buns, while walking into bathroom with Lin-
da Fiorentino.
**The Capone** (1989) . . . . . . . . . . . . . . . . Mike Rourke
*a.k.a. Revenge of Al Capone*
(Originally a Made for TV Movie.)
• 1:01—Partial buns, while making love on top of De-
brah Farentino in bed.
Cold Feet (1989) . . . . . . . . . . . . . . . . . . . . . . . Monte
Daddy's Dyin'... Who's Got the Will? (1990) . . . Clarence
The Bachelor (1991) . . . . . . . . . . . . . . . Dr. Emil Grasler
The Ballad of the Sad Cafe (1991) . . . . . . . Marvin Macy
Street of No Return (1991; U.S./French) . . . . . . Michael
Criss Cross (1992) . . . . . . . . . . . . . . . . . . . . John Cross
*Made for Cable Movies:*
Judgement (1990; HBO) . . . . . . . . . . . . . . Perre Guitry
**Payoff** (1991; Showtime) . . . . . .Peter "Mac" MacAlister
• 0:01—Sort of buns, while in shower, seen from
above, looking down.
*Miniseries:*
Chiefs (1983) . . . . . . . . . . . . . . . . . Foxy Funderburke
*Made for TV Movies:*
A Rumor of War (1980) . . . . . . . . . . . . . . . . . . . . . n.a.
In the Best of Families, Marriage, Pride and Madness
(1994) . . . . . . . . . . . . . . . . . . . . . . . . . . . Tom Leary

## • Carradine, Robert

Son of actor John Carradine.
Brother of actors David and Keith Carradine.
*Films:*
Mean Streets (1973) . . . . . . . . . . . The Young Assassin
Cannonball (1976; U.S./Hong Kong) . . . . . .Jim Crandell
Jackson County Jail (1976) . . . . . . . . . . . . . . Bobby Ray
Massacre at Central High (1976) . . . . . . . . . . . Spoony
**The Pom Pom Girls** (1976) . . . . . . . . . . . . . Johnnie
• 0:28—Brief buns, while mooning the Hardin High
jocks out the back window of car.
•• 1:08—Buns, while in the showers with the other
boys.
Joyride (1977) . . . . . . . . . . . . . . . . . . . . . . . . . . John
Orca, The Killer Whale (1977) . . . . . . . . . . . . . . . Ken
Coming Home (1978) . . . . . . . . . . . . . . . . Bill Munson
The Big Red One (1980) . . . . . . . . . . . . . . . . . . . . Zab
The Long Riders (1980) . . . . . . . . . . . . . Bob Younger
Heartaches (1981; Canadian) . . . . . . . . Stanley Howard
T.A.G.: The Assassination Game (1982) . . . . . . . . . .Alex
Wavelength (1982) . . . . . . . . . . . . . . . . Bobby Sinclair
Revenge of the Nerds (1984) . . . . . . . . . Lewis Skolnick
Number One with a Bullet (1987)
. . . . . . . . . . . . . . . . . . . . . Nicholas "Nick" Berzack
Revenge of the Nerds II: Nerds in Paradise (1987)
. . . . . . . . . . . . . . . . . . . . . . . . . . . Lewis Skolnick
Buy and Cell (1988) . . . . . . . . . . . . . . . . Herbie Altman
Rude Awakening (1989) . . . . . . . . . . . . . . . . Sammy
Illusions (1992) . . . . . . . . . . . . . . . . .Greg Sanderson
The Player (1992) . . . . . . . . . . . . . . . . . . . . . Cameo
*Made for Cable Movies:*
Somebody Has to Shoot the Picture (1990; HBO) . . n.a.
Doublecrossed (1991; HBO) . . . . . . . . . . . Dave Booker
The Disappearance of Christina (1993) . . . . . . . . . . n.a.
*Made for Cable TV:*
John Carpenter's Body Bags (1993; Showtime)
. . . . . . . . . . . . . . . . . . . . . . The Gas Station/Bill
*Made for TV Movies:*
The Incident (1989) . . . . . . . . . . . . . . . . . . . . . . . n.a.
Clarence (1990) . . . . . . . . . . . . . . . . . . . . . . . . . n.a.
Revenge of the Nerds III: The Next Generation (1992)
. . . . . . . . . . . . . . . . . . . . . . . . . . . Lewis Skolnick
The Tommyknockers (1993) . . . . . . . . . . . . . . . Bryant
Revenge of the Nerds IV: Nerds in Love (1994) . . . Lewis

## • Carrey, Jim

*Films:*
Finders Keepers (1983) . . . . . . . . . . . . . Lane Biddlecoff
Once Bitten (1985) . . . . . . . . . . . . . . . . Mark Kendall
Peggy Sue Got Married (1986) . . . . . . . . . . . Walter Getz
The Dead Pool (1988) . . . . . . . . . . . . . . . . . . . . . n.a.
Earth Girls are Easy (1989) . . . . . . . . . . . . . . . . Wiploc
**Ace Ventura: Pet Detective** (1993) . . . . . Ace Ventura
•• 1:07—Buns, running to get into the shower after
burning his clothes.
The Mask (1994) . . . . . . . . . . . . . . . . . . Stanley Ipkiss
*TV:*
The Duck Factory (1984) . . . . . . . . . . . . . Skip Tarkenton
In Living Color (1990- ) . . . . . . . . . . . . . . Cast Member

## Carrier, Gene

*Video Tapes:*
**The Girls of Penthouse** (1984)
. . . . . . . . . . . . . . . . . . . . . . . . Ghost Town Cowboy
••• 0:31—Frontal nudity with Jody Swafford. Buns, while carrying her to couch and making love.

## • Carroll, Justin

*Films:*
**Mind Twister** (1992) . . . . . . . . . . . . . . . .Young Stud
(Unrated version reviewed.)
• 0:31—Brief buns in mirror, while getting out of bathtub after getting caught with Lisa by Daniel.
**Psycho Cop 2** (1992) . . . . . . . . . . . . . . . . . . . . Tony
•• 0:37—Buns, while making love on top of Chloe on desk, then standing up and talking to Sharon.
Stormswept (1994) . . . . . . . . . . . . . . . . . . . . . . Damon
*Video Tapes:*
Wet and Wild: The Locker Room (1994) . . Cast Member

## Carson, John David

*Films:*
**Pretty Maids All in a Row** (1971) . . . . . . . . . . Ponce
• 1:04—Very brief buns, sticking out from under sheet when he uses it to cover Angie Dickinson in bed.
The Day of the Dolphin (1973) . . . . . . . . . . . . . . Larry
Stay Hungry (1976) . . . . . . . . . . . . . . . . . . . . . .Halsey
Empire of the Ants (1977) . . . . . . . . . . . . . .Joe Morrison
The Fifth Floor (1978) . . . . . . . . . . . . . . Ronnie Denton
Charge of the Model T's (1979) . . . . . . . . . . . . . .n.a.
The Savage Is Loose (1979) . . . . . . . . . . . . . . . . David
The Light in the Jungle (1990) . . . . . . . Horton Herschel
Pretty Woman (1990) . . . . . . . . . . . . . . . . . . . . .Mark
*TV:*
Falcon Crest (1987-88) . . . . . . . . . . . . . . . . Jay Spence

## • Caruso, David

*Films:*
Without Warning (1980) . . . . . . . . . . . . . . . . . . . Tom
First Blood (1982) . . . . . . . . . . . . . . . . . . . . . . . Mitch
An Officer and a Gentleman (1982) . . . . Topper Daniels
Thief of Hearts (1984) . . . . . . . . . . . . . .Buddy Calamara
(Special Home Video Version reviewed.)
Blue City (1986) . . . . . . . . . . . . . . . . . . . . . Joey Rayford
China Girl (1987) . . . . . . . . . . . . . . . . . . . . . . . . . .n.a.
Twins (1988) . . . . . . . . . . . . . . . . . . . . . . . . .Al Greco
King of New York (1990) . . . . . . . . . . . . . . Dennis Gilley
Hudson Hawk (1991) . . . . . . . . . . . . . . . . . . . Kit Kat
Mad Dog and Glory (1993) . . . . . . . . . . . . . . . . . Mike
*Made for TV Movies:*
Judgment Day: The John List Story (1993)
. . . . . . . . . . . . . . . . . . . . . . . . . Chief Bob Richland
*TV:*
NYPD Blue (1993- ) . . . . . . . . . . . . . . . . . . . .John Kelly
**NYPD Blue: True Confessions** (Oct 12, 1993)
. . . . . . . . . . . . . . . . . . . . . . . . . . . . . . . . John Kelly
•• 0:22—Buns, while getting into shower with Lori.

**NYPD Blue: Personal Foul** (Oct 26, 1993)
. . . . . . . . . . . . . . . . . . . . . . . . . . . . . . . . John Kelly
••• 0:12—Buns, walking out of shower in police locker room.

## Case, Robert

*Films:*
**Hot Blood** (1989; Spanish) . . . . . . . . . . . . . . Ricardo
•• 1:20—Buns, with Alicia in stable.

## Casey, Bernie

Former football player.
*Films:*
Black Gunn (1972) . . . . . . . . . . . . . . . . . . . . . . .Seth
Boxcar Bertha (1972) . . . . . . . . . . . . . . . . .Von Morton
Cleopatra Jones (1973) . . . . . . . . . . . . . . . . . . Reuben
**The Man Who Fell to Earth** (1976; British) . . . Peters
(Uncensored version reviewed.)
• 1:42—Buns, while getting out of swimming pool during a black and white dream sequence.
Sharky's Machine (1981) . . . . . . . . . . . . . . . . . Arch
Never Say Never Again (1983) . . . . . . . . . . .Felix Leiter
Revenge of the Nerds (1984) . . . . . . . . . U. N. Jefferson
Spies Like Us (1985) . . . . . . . . . . . . . . Colonel Rhombus
Backfire (1987) . . . . . . . . . . . . . . . . . . . Clinton James
Steele Justice (1987) . . . . . . . . . . . . . . . . . . . . . .Reese
I'm Gonna Git You Sucka (1988) . . . . . . . . John Slade
Bill and Ted's Excellent Adventure (1989) . . . . . Mr. Ryan
Another 48 Hrs. (1990) . . . . . . . . . . . .Kirkland Smith
Street Knight (1992) . . . . . . . . . . . . . . . . .Raymond
Under Seige (1992) . . . . . . . . . . . . . Commander Harris
The Cemetery Club (1993) . . . . . . . . . . . . . . . John
*Made for Cable Movies:*
Chains of Gold (1991; Showtime) . . . . . . . . . Sgt. Palco
*Made for TV Movies:*
Brian's Song (1971) . . . . . . . . . . . . . . . . J.C. Caroline
Love is Not Enough (1978) . . . . . . . . . . . . Mike Harris
Ring of Passion (1978) . . . . . . . . . . . . . . . . Joe Louis
*TV:*
Harris and Company (1979) . . . . . . . . . . . . Mike Harris
Bay City Blues (1983) . . . . . . . . . . . . . . Ozzie Peoples

## Casey, Lawrence

*Films:*
**The Student Nurses** (1970) . . . . . . . . Dr. Jim Casper
*a.k.a. Young LA Nurses*
•• 0:52—Buns, while walking to Karen Carlson to talk.
The Great Waldo Pepper (1975) . . . . . . . . German Star
Borderline (1980) . . . . . . . . . . . . . . . . . . . Andy Davis
*TV:*
The Rat Patrol (1966-68) . . . . . . Private Mark Hitchcock

## Cassavetes, Nick

Son of actor John Cassavetes and actress Gena Rowlands.
*Films:*
Husbands (1970) . . . . . . . . . . . . . . . . . . . . . . . . Gus
Woman Under the Influence (1974) . . . . . . . . . . Adolph
Mask (1985) . . . . . . . . . . . . . . . . . . . . . . . . . . . . .T.J.
Black Moon Rising (1986) . . . . . . . . . . . . . . . . . . Luis

Quiet Cool (1986). . . . . . . . . . . . . . . . . . . . . .Valence
The Wraith (1986). . . . . . . . . . . . . . . . . . . . .Packard
Assault of the Killer Bimbos (1988) . . . . . . . . Wayne-O
Under the Gun (1989) . . . . . . . . . . . . . . Tony Braxton
Backstreet Dreams (1990). . . . . . . . . . . . Mikey Acosta
Delta Force 3: The Killing Game (1991)
. . . . . . . . . . . . . . . . . . . . . . . Major Charles Stewart
**Body of Influence** (1992). . . . . . . . . .Jonathon Brooks
(Unrated version reviewed.)
  • 1:06—Very, very brief frontal nudity, while in bed
    when Lana rolls on top of him and scoots up.
Sins of Desire (1992). . . . . . . . . . . . . . . Barry Mitchum
(Unrated version reviewed.)
Broken Trust (1993) . . . . . . . . . . . . . . . . . Alan Brogan
**Class of 1999 II: The Substitute** (1993)
. . . . . . . . . . . . . . . . . . . . . . . . . . . . . .Emmett Grazer
  • 1:01—Very briefly nude, while turning over in bed
    with Jenna.
**Sins of the Night** (1993) . . . . . . . . . . . . Jack Neitsche
(Unrated version reviewed.)
  •• 0:48—Buns, while making love in bed with Deborah
    Shelton.

## Cassidy, Rick
*Films:*
  **Auditions** (1978) . . . . . . . . . . . . . . . . . Charlie White
  ••• 0:04—Nude, undressing for his audition.
  •• 0:29—Buns, during sex scene with a woman.
  • 1:07—Buns in bed during orgy scene.
  •• 1:13—Nude on kneeling on bed.
*Video Tapes:*
  Love Skills: A Guide to the Pleasures of Sex (1984)
. . . . . . . . . . . . . . . . . . . . . . . . . . . . . . . . . .Model

## Castillo, Eduardo
*Films:*
  **Gnaw: Food of the Gods II** (1988; Canadian)
. . . . . . . . . . . . . . . . . . . . . . . . . . . . . . . . . .Carlos
  • 0:46—Buns, while walking through bushes to take a
    leak. More buns, while running away from the giant
    rats.

## • Castle, John
*Films:*
  Blow-Up (1966; British/Italian) . . . . . . . . . . . . . . Painter
  The Lion in the Winter (1968; British) . . .Prince Geoffrey
  The Promise (1969; British). . . . . . . . Marat Yestigneyev
  Man of La Mancha (1972). . . . . . . . Duke/Dr. Carrasco
  **The Adventures of Eliza Fraser** (1976; Australian)
. . . . . . . . . . . . . . . . . . . . . . . . . . . .Rory McBryde
    0:34—Upper half of buns, while in bed on top of Su-
    sannah York.
  •• 0:38—Buns, while jumping on York, then getting
    pushed out the door.
  The Incredible Sarah (1976; British). . . . . . . . . .Damala
  Eagle's Wing (1978; British). . . . . . . . . . . . . The Priest
  King David (1985). . . . . . . . . . . . . . . . . . . . . . .Abner
  Dealers (1989) . . . . . . . . . . . . . . . . . . . Frank Mallory
  Robocop 3 (1993). . . . . . . . . . . . . . . . . . .McDaggett

## Caulfield, Maxwell
*Films:*
  Grease 2 (1982). . . . . . . . . . . . . . . Michael Carrington
  Electric Dreams (1984). . . . . . . . . . . . . . . . . . . .Bill
  The Supernaturals (1987). . . . . . . . . . . . . . .Lt. Ray Ellis
  Sundown: The Vampire in Retreat (1989). . . . . . . Shane
  Project: Alien (1990) . . . . . . . . . . . . . . . George Abbott
  **Dance with Death** (1991). . . . . . . . . . . . Shaughnessy
    • 1:01—Brief side view of buns, while making love in
      bed with Kelly.
  Waxwork II: Lost in Time (1991). . . . . . . . . . . . .Mickey
  Alien Intruder (1992) . . . . . . . . . . . . . . . . . . . . .Nick
  Animal Instincts (1992) . . . . . . . . . . . . . . . .David Cole
  (Unrated version reviewed.)
  **In a Moment of Passion** (1992). . . . . . . Victor Brandt
    • 0:51—Partial buns, after killing Adriana in bed and
      rolling onto the floor.
  **Midnight Witness** (1992). . . . . . . . . . . . . . .Garland
    •• 1:11—Brief buns, getting out of bed and putting un-
      derwear on.
  Calendar Girl (1993) . . . . . . . . . . . . . . Man in Bathrobe
  Gettysburg (1993) . . . . . . . . . . . Colonel Strong Vincent
*Miniseries:*
  Dynasty: The Reunion (1991). . . . . . . . . . . . . . . Miles
*TV:*
  The Colbys (1985-87) . . . . . . . . . . . . . . . . Miles Colby

## Cazenove, Christopher
*Films:*
  There's a Girl in My Soup (1970) . . . . . . . . . . . . .Nigel
  East of Elephant Rock (1976; British) . .Robert Proudfoot
  Eye of the Needle (1981) . . . . . . . . . . . . . . . . .David
  **Heat and Dust** (1982). . . . . . . . . . . . . Douglas Rivers
    •• 1:25—Buns while lying in bed with Greta Scacchi
      under a mosquito net.
  Until September (1984) . . . . . . . . . . . . . . . . . . .Philip
  Mata Hari (1985) . . . . . . . . . . Captain Karl Von Byerling
  Souvenir (1988; British) . . . . . . . . . . . . . William Root
  Three Men and a Little Lady (1990) . . . . . . . . . Edward
  Aces: Iron Eagle III (1992). . . . . . . . . . . . . . . .Palmer
*Made for TV Movies:*
  Tears in the Rain (1988; British) . . . . . . . . . . . . Michael
  To Be The Best (1992) . . . . . . . . . . . . . Jonathan Ainsley
*TV:*
  Dynasty (1986-87). . . . . . . . . . . . . . . . Ben Carrington

## Ceinos, José Antonio
*Films:*
  **Black Venus** (1983) . . . . . . . . . . . . . . . . . . . .Armand
    • 0:14—Buns, while making love with Venus in bed.
  Patricia (1984) . . . . . . . . . . . . . . . . . . . . . . . .n.a.

## Chan, Jackie
*Films:*
  The Big Brawl (1980) . . . . . . . . . . . . . . . . . . . . .Jerry
  The Cannonball Run (1981) . . . . . . .Subaru Driver No. 1
  Cannonball Run II (1984). . . . . . . . . . . . . . . . .Jackie

**The Fearless Hyena, Part II** (1984; Chinese)
................................ Chan Lung
  • 0:06—Brief buns, jumping up in the water while trying to catch a fish. Don't see his face clearly.
The Protector (1985; Hong Kong/U.S.) ..... Billy Wong

## Chapman, Graham
*Films:*
Monty Python and the Holy Grail (1974; British)
................................King Arthur
**Monty Python's Life of Brian** (1979; British)
................................ Brian Called Brian
  ••• 1:03—Buns before opening window, frontal nudity after opening window and being surprised by his flock of followers, buns while putting clothes on. Funniest frontal nude scene.
The Secret Policeman's Other Ball (1982; British) ...n.a.
Monty Python's the Meaning of Life (1983; British)
................................n.a.
Yellowbeard (1983).................. Yellowbeard
The Secret Policeman's Private Parts (1984)........n.a.
*Made for TV Movies:*
How to Irritate People (1968; British) ...........n.a.
*TV:*
Monty Python's Flying Circus (British) ........Regular
The Big Show (1980) .....................Regular

## Charles, Emile
*Films:*
**Wonderland** (1989; British) ............... Eddie
  ••• 1:27—Nude, taking off his clothes and swimming under water with the dolphins. Long scene.

## • Charles, Josh
*Films:*
Dead Poets Society (1989) ......... Knox Overstreet
Don't Tell Mom the Babysitter's Dead (1991) .... Bryan
Crossing the Bridge (1992)............Mort Golden
**Threesome** (1994) .....................Eddy
  • 0:54—Brief buns, while running and jumping into the lake. Partial buns, while lying on lake shore in-between Lara Flynn Boyle and Stephen Baldwin.

## Charles, Timothy
*Films:*
**Uncaged** (1991) .......................Evan
*a.k.a. Angel in Red*
  • 0:42—Brief buns, while on the floor with Micki.

## Chase, Steve
*Video Tapes:*
Eden (1992) ............................ Josh
**Eden 2** (1992) ......................... Josh
  ••• 1:19—Buns in shower during Eve's fantasy.
**Eden 3** (1993) ......................... Josh
  •• 0:49—Buns, while coming into the shower to see what's wrong with Eve.
  •• 1:36—Buns, while getting into bed with Randi.

**Eden 5** (1993)..........................Josh
  ••• 0:19—Buns, when Randi takes his towel off.
  ••• 0:20—Buns, while making love with Randi.
**Eden 6** (1994).........................Josh
  •• 1:10—Buns, whilein bed with Randi.
  ••• 2:01—Buns, while making love with Randi.

## • Cheyne, Hank
*Films:*
**Killing Obsession** (1994) ................ Randy
  • 0:31—Upper half of buns, when making love with Annie in photo studio.

## Chicot, Etienne
*Films:*
Like a Turtle on Its Back (1981; French)
........................... Jean-Louis No. 2
**36 Fillette** (1988; French) ...............Maurice
  • 1:18—Very brief buns, getting up out of bed. Blurry.
Meeting Venus (1990; British) ............ Toushrau

## Chong, Tommy
*Films:*
Up in Smoke (1978)................... Man Stoner
**Cheech & Chong's Nice Dreams** (1981) .... Himself
  • 0:55—Out of focus buns, in mirror while lying in bed with Donna and Cheech. Very, very brief blurry out of focus frontal nudity in mirror when he gets out of bed.
Things Are Tough All Over (1982) ....... Prince Habib
Cheech & Chong's Still Smokin' (1983)........Chong
Yellowbeard (1983) ................... El Nebuloso
Far Out Man (1990)................... Far Out Man
The Spirit of '76 (1991) ................... Stoner

## Christopher, Gerard
*a.k.a. Jerry Dinome.*
Model turned actor.
*Films:*
**Tomboy** (1985) .....................Randy Star
  •• 0:59—Buns, while making love with Betsy Russell in the exercise room.
Dangerously Close (1986) ................... Lang
*TV:*
Superboy (1989-92)........... Clark Kent/Superboy

## Clark, Brett
*Films:*
Night Shift (1982) .................Nick "The Dick"
Bachelor Party (1984).......................Nick
Malibu Express (1984) ................... Shane
**Alien Warrior** (1985) ................... Buddy
  •• 0:03—Buns, while walking naked after getting transported to Earth.
Last Resort (1985) .....................Manuello
Off the Mark (1986).................... Superstud

**Young Lady Chatterley II** (1986)
. . . . . . . . . . . . . . . . . . . . . . . . . . Thomas "Gardener"
- •• 0:15—Brief buns, while pulling up his pants after getting caught with Monique Gabrielle in the woods by Adam West.
- • 0:16—Very brief buns, when Monique pulls his pants down again.

Eye of the Eagle (1987; Philippines). . . Sgt. Rick Stratton
Teen Witch (1989) . . . . . . . . . . . . . . . . . . . . . . Bruiser
Deathstalker IV: Match of Titans (1990). . . . . . . . .Vaniat
Inner Sanctum (1991). . . . . . . . . . . . . . . Neil Semple
Fit To Kill (1993) . . . . . . . . . . . . . . . . . . . . . . Burke
Hard Hunted (1993) . .. . . . . . . . . . . . . .Yacht Captain

## Clark, John

*Films:*
Jagged Edge (1985) . . . . . . . . . . . . . . . . . .Dr. Holloway
**Blood Frenzy** (1987). . . . . . . . . . . . . . . . . Crawford
- • 0:39—Buns, while falling out of motor home lavatory drunk.

## Clay, Nicholas

*Films:*
**Excalibur** (1981; British) . . . . . . . . . . . . . . . . Lancelot
- •• 1:13—Buns, while fighting with himself in a suit of armor.
- • 1:31—Brief buns, while running into the woods after waking up. Long shot, hard to see.

**Lady Chatterley's Lover** (1981; French/British)
. . . . . . . . . . . . . . . . . . . .Oliver Mellors (The Gardener)
- ••• 0:21—Nude, washing himself while Sylvia Kristel watches from the trees.

Evil Under the Sun (1982). . . . . . . . . . . Patrick Redfern
Lionheart (1987). . . . . . . . . . . . . . Charles de Montfort
*Made for TV Movies:*
Poor Little Rich Girl: The Barbara Hutton Story (1987)
. . . . . . . . . . . . . . . . . . . . . . . Prince Alexis Mdivani
*Video Tapes:*
**Playboy Video Magazine, Volume 2** (1983)
. . . . . . . . . . . . . . . . . . . . . . . . . . . . . . Gardener
- • 0:18—Buns, in scene from *Lady Chatterley's Lover.*

## Cleese, John

*Films:*
Interlude (1968; British) . . . . . . . . . . . . . . .TV Publicist
Monty Python and the Holy Grail (1974; British)
. . . . . . . . . . . . . . . . . . . . . . . . . . . . Black Knight
**Romance with a Double Bass** (1974; British)
. . . . . . . . . . . . . . . . . . . . . . . Musician Smychkov
- ••• 0:14—Brief buns while walking around with his bass and then the case.
- •• 0:16—Buns, while standing at the edge of the pond.
- •• 0:17—Buns, while running to jump in the water.
- ••• 0:18—Buns, while walking around.
- ••• 0:19—Buns, while walking around with his hands over his eyes.
- • 0:21—Brief long shot of buns, while walking around.
- • 0:22—More buns, while walking around outside.
- •• 0:24—Buns, while carrying bass into the house.

Monty Python's Life of Brian (1979; British)
. . . . . . . . . . . . . . . . . . . . . . . . . . Third Wise Man
Time Bandits (1981; British) . . . . . . . . . . . .Robin Hood
Monty Python's the Meaning of Life (1983; British)
. . . . . . . . . . . . . . . . . . . . . . . . . . . . . . . . . n.a.
Yellowbeard (1983) . . . . . . . . . . . . . . . . . . Blind Pew
Silverado (1985). . . . . . . . . . . . . . . . . .Sheriff Langston
Clockwise (1986; British) . . . . . . . . . . Brian Stimpson
**A Fish Called Wanda** (1988) . . . . . . . . . . . . . Archie
- • 1:13—Very brief upper half of buns, in house when he's surprised by the returning family. Looks like very, very brief frontal nudity when he stands up after pulling his underwear down.

The Big Picture (1989) . . . . . . . . . . . . . . . . Bartender
Erik the Viking (1989; British) . . . . . . . .Halfdan the Black
Bullseye! (1990) . . . . . .Man Who Looks Like John Cleese
Splitting Heirs (1993). . . . . . . . . . . . . . . . . Shadgrind
*Made for TV Movies:*
How to Irritate People (1968; British) . . . . . . . . . . . n.a.
*TV:*
Fawlty Towers (British) . . . . . . . . . . . . . . Basil Fawlty
Monty Python's Flying Circus (British) . . . . . . . . Regular

## Clementi, Pierre

*Films:*
The Conformist (1971; Italian/French) . . .Nino Seminara
**Steppenwolf** (1974) . . . . . . . . . . . . . . . . . . . . .Pablo
- • 1:40—Very brief frontal nudity, sleeping on floor with Dominique Sanda.

Sweet Movie (1975). . . . . . . . . . . . . . . . . . . . . n.a.
Quartet (1981; British/French) . . . . . . . . . . . . . . Theo
Exposed (1983) . . . . . . . . . . . . . . . . . . . . . . . . .Vic

## Coates, Kim

*Films:*
The Boy in Blue (1986; Canadian) . . .McCoy Man No. 2
**Red Blooded American Girl** (1988). . . . . . . . .Dennis
- • 0:01—Buns, while giving Rebecca a glass in bed.
- • 0:30—Very brief buns, while getting into bathtub.

Cold Front (1989; Canadian) . . . . . . . . . . . . . . Mantha
The Last Boy Scout (1991) . . . . . . . . . . . . . . . . Chet
Innocent Blood (1992). . . . . . . . . . . . . . . . . . . Ray
The Club (1993). . . . . . . . . . . . . . . . . . . Mr. Carver

## Cochran, Ian

*Films:*
**Bolero** (1984). . . . . . . . . . . . . . . . . . .Robert Stewart
- • 1:26—Buns, while making love with Catalina.

## Coe, George

*Films:*
The Stepford Wives (1975). . . . . . . . . . . Claude Axhelm
French Postcards (1979). . . . . . . . . . . . . . . Mr. Weber
Kramer vs. Kramer (1979) . . . . . . . . . . . Jim O'Connor
The First Deadly Sin (1980) . . . . . . . . . . . .Dr. Bernardi
Bustin' Loose (1981) . . . . . . . . . .Dr. Wilson T. Renfrew
The Amateur (1982). . . . . . . . . . . . . . . . . . Rutledge
The Entity (1983). . . . . . . . . . . . . . . . . . . Dr. Weber

Remo Williams: The Adventure Begins (1985)
.............................. Gen. Scott Watson
Head Office (1986) ................... Senator Issel
Blind Date (1987) ..................... Harry Gruen
Best Seller (1988) ....................... Graham
**Cousins** (1989) ....................... Uncle Phil
•• 0:08—Buns, while mooning everybody during wedding reception.
• 0:34—Buns again, during video playback.
The End of Innocence (1989) ................. Dad
The Mighty Ducks (1992) ........... Judge Weathers
*Made for TV Movies:*
My Wicked Ways... The Legend of Errol Flynn (1985)
.................................. Irving Jerome
*TV:*
Goodnight, Beantown (1983) ........... Dick Novak
Max Headroom (1987) ................ Ben Cheviot

## Coleman, Dabney

*Films:*
This Property is Condemned (1966) : ....... Salesman
I Love My Wife (1970)............... Frank Donnelly
Cinderella Liberty (1973)........... Executive Officer
The Dove (1974; British) ............ Charles Huntley
The Towering Inferno (1974) ...... Assistant Fire Chief
Bite the Bullet (1975) .................. Jack Parker
The Other Side of the Mountain (1975) ...Dave McCoy
Midway (1976)............... Captain Murray Arnold
Rolling Thunder (1977).................. Maxwell
Viva Knievel (1977) ............... Ralph Thompson
How to Beat the High Cost of Living (1980)
............................... Jack Heintzel
Melvin and Howard (1980)........ Judge Keith Hayes
Nothing Personal (1980; Canadian) .... Tom Dickerson
**Modern Problems** (1981) .................. Mark
••• 1:09—Buns, while taking off towel in front of Patti D'Arbanville.
On Golden Pond (1981) ................. Bill Ray
Tootsie (1982)........................... Ron
Young Doctors in Love (1982)....... Dr. Joseph Prang
Wargames (1983) ..................... McKittrick
Cloak and Dagger (1984) ...... Jack Flack/Hal Osborne
Meet the Applegates (1989) ............. Aunt Bea
Short Time (1990).................. Burt Simpson
Where the Heart Is (1990)........ Stewart McBain
Amos & Andrew (1993) ... Chief of Police Cecil Tolliver
The Beverly Hillbillies (1993) ........... Mr. Drysdale
*Made for Cable TV:*
Never Forget (1991; TNT).............. William Cox
*Made for TV Movies:*
Baby M (1988) ....................... Skoloff
*TV:*
That Girl (1966-67).............. Dr. Leon Bessemer
Mary Hartman, Mary Hartman (1975-78) .. Merle Jeeter
Apple Pie (1978)............... Fast Eddie Murtaugh
Buffalo Bill (1983-84) ............... Bill Bittinger
The Slap Maxwell Story (1987-88) ...... Slap Maxwell
Drexell's Class (1991-92)............... Otis Drexell
Madman of the People (1994- ) ............... n.a.

## Coleman, John

*Films:*
**Angel Eyes** (1991) ......................... Nick
••• 1:10—Buns, while making love on top of Angel on the floor.

## Coleman, Warren

*Films:*
**Young Einstein** (1989; Australian) ... Lunatic Professor
• 0:55—Buns while in Lunatic Asylum, taking a shower.
• 0:56—More buns while standing in front of sink when Marie comes to rescue Einstein. (He's the one on the right.)
• 0:58—Brief buns while crowding into the shower stall with the other Asylum people.

## Collver, Mark

*Films:*
**There's Nothing Out There** (1990) ........... Jim
•• 0:33—Buns, taking off his clothes to go skinny dipping in pond.

## • Colt, Aaron

*Video Tapes:*
**Penthouse Forum Letters: Volume 2** (1994)
.......................... The Big Switch/Steve
••• 0:32—Nude, getting into hot tub, then making love with Cindy on lounge chair.

## Conaway, Jeff

*Films:*
The Eagle Has Landed (1977; British)............ n.a.
I Never Promised You a Rose Garden (1977)
.................................. Lactamaeon
Grease (1978) ........................... Kenickie
**Covergirl** (1982; Canadian) ............ T. C. Sloane
•• 0:43—Very brief lower frontal nudity getting out of bed.
The Patriot (1986) ....................... Mitchell
The Sleeping Car (1990) .......... Bud Sorenson
Mirror Images (1991)...................... Jeffrey
A Time to Die (1991) ...................... Frank
Total Exposure (1991) .............. Peter Keynes
Alien Intruder (1992) .................... Borman
**Almost Pregnant** (1992) ......... Charlie Alderson
(Unrated version reviewed.)
••• 0:10—Buns, while making love on top of Tanya Roberts in bed.
•• 1:12—Buns in bed in alternate scenes with Roberts and Joan Severance.
Bikini Summer 2 (1992)..................... Stu
In a Moment of Passion (1992) ...... Werner Soehnen
L.A. Goddess (1992)....................... Sean
Sunset Strip (1992) ....................... Tony
*TV:*
Taxi (1978-83).................... Bobby Wheeler
Wizards and Warriors (1983) ..... Prince Erik Greystone
Berrengers (1985) ................... John Higgins

## Conlon, Tim

*Films:*
**Prom Night III** (1989) . . . . . . . . . . . . . . . . . . . . Alex
• 0:15—Brief buns and very brief balls when the flag
   he's wearing falls off.
*TV:*
Wild Oats (1994- ) . . . . . . . . . . . . . . . . . . . . . . . Jack

## Connery, Sean

*Films:*
Darby O'Gill and the Little People (1959)
. . . . . . . . . . . . . . . . . . . . . . . . . . . .Michael McBride
Dr. No (1962; British) . . . . . . . . . . . . . . . . James Bond
From Russia with Love (1963; British) . . . . . James Bond
Goldfinger (1964; British) . . . . . . . . . . . . . James Bond
Thunderball (1965; British) . . . . . . . . . . . . James Bond
A Fine Madness (1966) . . . . . . . . . . . . . Samson Shillitoe
You Only Live Twice (1967; British) . . . . . . . James Bond
Shalako (1968; British) . . . . . . . . . . . . . . . . .Shalako
The Molly Maguires (1970) . . . . . . . . . . . . . Jack Kehoe
The Anderson Tapes (1971). . . . . . . . . . . . . . Anderson
Diamonds are Forever (1971; British) . . . . . James Bond
Murder on the Orient Express (1974; British)
. . . . . . . . . . . . . . . . . . . . . . . Colonel Arbuthnot
Zardoz (1974; British) . . . . . . . . . . . . . . . . . . . .Zed
**The Man Who Would Be King** (1975)
. . . . . . . . . . . . . . . . . . . . . . . . . . . Daniel Dravot
••• 1:27—Buns, while standing with arms up, getting
   robe put on.
The Wind and the Lion (1975) . . . . . . . .Mulay el Raisuli
The Next Man (1976) . . . . . . . . . . Khalif Abdul-Muhsen
*a.k.a. Double Hit*
Robin and Marian (1976; British). . . . . . . . Robin Hood
A Bridge Too Far (1977; British). . . . Maj. Gen. Urquhart
Cuba (1979) . . . . . . . . . . . . . . . . . . . . .Major Depes
The Great Train Robbery (1979; British). . .Edward Pierce
Meteor (1979) . . . . . . . . . . . . . . . . . . Dr. Paul Bradley
Outland (1981). . . . . . . . . . . . . . . . . . . . . . O'Neill
Time Bandits (1981; British) . . . . . . . King Agamemnon
Wrong is Right (1982). . . . . . . . . . . . . . . . Patrick Hale
Sword of the Valiant (1984; British). . . . . Green Knight
Highlander (1986) . . . . . . . . . . . . . . . . . . . Ramirez
The Name of the Rose (1986) . . . . William of Baskerville
The Untouchables (1987) . . . . . . . . . . . . .James Malone
(Academy Award for Best Supporting Actor.)
Memories of Me (1988) . . . . . . . . . . . . . . . . .Himself
The Presidio (1988). . . . . . . . . . . Lt. Col. Alan Caldwell
Family Business (1989) . . . . . . . . . . . . .Jesse McMullen
Indiana Jones and the Last Crusade (1989)
. . . . . . . . . . . . . . . . . . . . . . . . . .Dr. Henry Jones
The Hunt for Red October (1990) . . Capt. Marko Ramius
The Russia House (1990). . . . . . . . . . . . . . Barley Blair
Highlander 2: The Quickening (1991) . . . . . . . Ramirez
Robin Hood: Prince of Thieves (1991) . . . .King Richard
Medicine Man (1992) . . . . . . . . . . .Dr. Robert Campbell
Rising Sun (1993) . . . . . . . . . . . . . . . . . .John Connor

## Conroy, Kevin

*Films:*
Battle in the Erogenous Zone . . . . . . . . . . . Mondo Ray
**Chain of Desire** (1992) . . . . . . . . . . . . . . . . . . . .Joe
•• 1:25—Buns, while pulling down his underwear to
   masturbate while watching a woman in her apart-
   ment do the same.
• 1:28—Brief side view of buns, after he's finished.
*Made for Cable Movies:*
The Secret Passion of Robert Clayton (1992; USA) . . n.a.
*Made for TV Movies:*
Island City (1994) . . . . . . . . . . . . . . . . . . . . . n.a.
*TV:*
Ohara (1987). . . . . . . . . . . . . . . .Capt. Lloyd Hamilton
Tour of Duty (1987-88) . . . . . . . . . Capt. Rusty Wallace

## • Constantine, Yorgo

*Films:*
**Return to Two Moon Junction** (1993) . . .Robert Lee
• 0:21—Upper half of buns, while sitting on chair and
   talking on telephone, then standing up.

## Cooper, Terence

*Films:*
Casino Royale (1967; British) . . . . . . . . . . . . . Cooper
**Heart of the Stag** (1983; New Zealand)
. . . . . . . . . . . . . . . . . . . . . . . . . .Robert Jackson
• 0:03—Buns, while making love in bed on top of his
   daughter. Don't see his face.
The Shrimp on the Barbie (1990). . . . . . . . .Ian Hobart

## Cooper, Trevor

*Films:*
Moonlighting (1982; British) . . . . . . . . . Hire Shop Man
The Whistle Blower (1987; British) . . . . Inspector Bourne
**Drowning by Numbers** (1988; British) . . . . . . . Hardy
•• 0:12—Full frontal nudity, lying in bed sleeping.

## Corbo, Robert

*Films:*
**Last Rites** (1988) . . . . . . . . . . . . . . . . . . . . . . Gino
• 0:03—Buns and frontal nudity in a room with
   Daphne Zuniga just before getting caught by another woman and shot.

## Corri, Nick

*Films:*
Gotcha! (1985) . . . . . . . . . . . . . . . . . . . . . . Manolo
A Nightmare on Elm Street (1985). . . . . . . . .Rod Lane
Lawless Land (1988). . . . . . . . . . . . . . . . . . . . n.a.
Slaves of New York (1989) . . . . . . . . . Marley Mantello
**Tropical Snow** (1989) . . . . . . . . . . . . . . . . . . Tavo
•• 0:11—Buns in bed with Madeleine Stowe.
•• 0:44—Buns, while standing naked in police station.
Predator 2 (1990) . . . . . . . . . . . . . . . . . . . .Detective
In the Heat of Passion (1991) . . . . . . . . . . . . .Charlie
(Unrated version reviewed.)

# Costello, Anthony

*Films:*

Blue (1968) . . . . . . . . . . . . . . . . . . . . . . . . . .Jess Parker
Will Penny (1968) . . . . . . . . . . . . . . . . . . . . . . Bigfoot
The Molly Maguires (1970) . . . . . . . . Frank McAndrew
**Doctor's Wives** (1971) . . . . . . . . . . #31 Mike Traynor
  • 0:52—Brief buns, while getting tape recorder and
    running back to bed.

# Costner, Kevin

*Films:*

Chasing Dreams (1981) . . . . . . . . . . . . . . . . . . . . . .n.a.
Malibu Hot Summer (1981) . . . . . . . . . . . . .John Logan
  *a.k.a. Sizzle Beach*
  (*Sizzle Beach* is the re-released version with Kevin Cost-
  ner featured on the cover. It is missing all the nude
  scenes during the opening credits before 0:06.)
Shadows Run Black (1981) . . . . . . . . . . . . Jimmy Scott
Night Shift (1982) . . . . . . . . . . . . . . . . . .Frat Boy #1
Stacy's Knights (1983). . . . . . . . . . . . . . . . . . . . .Will
Table for Five (1983) . . . . . . . . . . . . . . . . . Newlywed
Testament (1983) . . . . . . . . . . . . . . . . . . . . Phil Pitkin
**American Flyers** (1985) . . . . . . . . . . . . . . . . . Marcus
  • 0:53—Brief, upper half of buns, while riding bicycles
    when his pants get yanked down by David.
Fandango (1985) . . . . . . . . . . . . . . . . . . .Gardner Barnes
Silverado (1985) . . . . . . . . . . . . . . . . . . . . . . . . . Jake
No Way Out (1987) . . . . . . . . . . Lt. Cmdr. Tom Farrell
The Untouchables (1987) . . . . . . . . . . . . . . Eliot Ness
Bull Durham (1988) . . . . . . . . . . . . . . . . . .Crash Davis
Field of Dreams (1989) . . . . . . . . . . . . . . .Ray Kinsella
The Gunrunner (1989) . . . . . . . . . . . . . . Ted Beaubien
**Dances with Wolves** (1990) . . . . . . . Lt. John Dunbar
  •• 0:37—Brief buns, while washing his clothes in the
    pond.
  ••• 0:40—Buns, while standing by himself after scaring
    away Kicking Bird.
**Revenge** (1990). . . . . . . . . . . . . . . . . . . . . . . Cochran
  •• 1:14—Brief buns while getting out of bed and wrap-
    ping a sheet around himself.
JFK (1991) . . . . . . . . . . . . . . . . . . . . . . . Jim Garrison
Robin Hood: Prince of Thieves (1991)
  . . . . . . . . . . . . . . . . . . . . . . . . . . Robin of Locksley
    1:14—Body double's buns, while bathing under wa-
    terfall when Marian sees him. Hard to see because of
    the falling water. Body double was used because the
    water was so cold.
The Bodyguard (1992) . . . . . . . . . . . . . . . Frank Farmer
A Perfect World (1993) . . . . . . . . . . . . . . Butch Haynes
Wyatt Earp (1994). . . . . . . . . . . . . . . . . . . . . . . .n.a.

# Cramer, Grant

*Films:*

New Year's Evil (1981). . . . . . . . . . . . . . .Derek Sullivan
**Hardbodies** (1984) . . . . . . . . . . . . . . . . . . . . . . .Scotty
  • 0:03—Brief buns, while getting out of bed after
    making love with Kristi.
Killer Klowns from Outer Space (1988) . . . . . . . . . .Mike
Beverly Hills Brats (1989). . . . . . . . . . . . . . . .Officer #1

Hangfire (1990) . . . . . . . . . . . . . . . . . . . . . . . . Snake
Auntie Lee's Meat Pies (1991) . . . . . . . . . . . . . . . Phil
Driving Me Crazy (1991) . . . . . . . . . . . . . . . . . . Boris
Save Me (1993) . . . . . . . . . . . . . . . . . . Bond Trader #4
  (Unrated version reviewed.)
*Made for TV Movies:*
An Inconvenient Woman (1991) . . . . . . . . . . . . . Lonny

# Crawford, Johnny

Brother of actor Robert Crawford.
*Films:*

Space Children (1958) . . . . . . . . . . . . . . . . . . . . . Ken
The Restless Ones (1965) . . . . . . . . . . . . . David Winton
Village of the Giants (1965) . . . . . . . . . . . . . . .Horsey
El Dorado (1967) . . . . . . . . . . . . . . . . . Luke MacDonald
**The Naked Ape** (1972) . . . . . . . . . . . . . . . . . . . . . Lee
  (Not available on video tape.)
  Frontal nudity.
The Great Texas Dynamite Chase (1977) . . . . . . . . .Slim
Tilt (1978) . . . . . . . . . . . . . . . . . . . . . . . . . . .Mickey
*TV:*
The Rifleman (1958-63) . . . . . . . . . . . . . .Mark McCain
*Magazines:*
**Playboy** (Sep 1973) . . . . . . . . . . . . . The Naked Ape
  ••• 159-161—Nude.
**Playboy** (Dec 1973) . . . . . . . . . . . . .Sex Stars of 1973
  ••• 211—Frontal nudity.

# Crew, Carl

*Films:*

**Blood Diner** (1987) . . . . . . . . . . . . . . George Tutman
  • 1:02—Buns, while mooning Sheeba through the
    passenger window of a van.
The Underachievers (1987) . . . . . . . . . . . . . . . Thug 2

# • Cromwell, James

*Films:*

Murder by Death (1976) . . . . . . . . .Marcel the Chauffer
The Cheap Detective (1978) . . . . . . . . . . . . . Schnell
Nobody's Perfekt (1981) . . . . . . . . . . . . . . .Dr. Carson
The Man with Two Brains (1983) . . . . . . . . . . . .Realtor
The House of God (1984). . . . . . . . . . . . . Officer Quick
  (Not available on video tape.)
Oh God, You Devil! (1984). . . . . . . . . . . . . . . . .Priest
Revenge of the Nerds (1984) . . . . . . . . . . .Mr. Skolnick
**Tank** (1984) . . . . . . . . . . . . . . . . . . . . . Deputy Euclid
  •• 1:06—Buns, after James Garner makes him strip and
    handcuffed to telephone pole by Jenilee Harrison.
A Fine Mess (1986) . . . . . . . . . . . . . . . . Detective Blist
The Rescue (1988) . . . . . . . . . . . . . . Admiral Rothman
The Babe (1992) . . . . . . . . . . . . . . . . . .Brother Mathius
*TV:*
All In the Family (1974) . . . . . . . . . Stretch Cunningham
Hot I Baltimore (1975) . . . . . . . . . . . . . . . . . . Bill Lewis
The Nancy Walker Show (1976). . . . . . . . . . . . . . Glen
The Last Precinct (1986). . . . . . . . . . . . . Chief Bludhorn

# Crowe, Russell

*Films:*

Prisoners of the Sun (1990; Australian)
................... Lieutenant Jack Corbett
**Proof** (1991; Australian)....................Andy
•• 1:12—Buns, while making love on top of Celia on the couch.
Spotswood (1991; Australian) ............Kim Barrett
The Crossing (1992; Australian) .............Johnny
The Efficiency Expert (1992; Australian)......... Kim
Romper Stomper (1993; Australian) ......... Hando

# Cruise, Tom

Husband of actress Nicole Kidman.
Ex-husband of actress Mimi Rogers.
*Films:*

Endless Love (1981) ........................ Billy
**Taps** (1981) ....................... David Shawn
• 0:29—Very brief upper half of buns in shower.
Losin' It (1982) ........................... Woody
**All The Right Moves** (1983) ................Stef
•• 1:00—Very brief frontal nudity getting undressed in his bedroom with Lea Thompson.
The Outsiders (1983) .................Steve Randle
Risky Business (1983) ....................Joel
The Color of Money (1986)................Vincent
Legend (1986) ............................ Jack
Top Gun (1986) .........................Maverick
Cocktail (1988)................... Brian Hanagan
Rain Man (1988)...................Charlie Babbitt
**Born on the Fourth of July** (1989)....... Ron Kovic
• 0:47—Very brief buns, sort of, while in bed at hospital when his rear end is sticking through the bottom of a bed.
Days of Thunder (1990) ...............Cole Trickle
Far and Away (1992)................Joseph Donelly
1:02—Upper half of buns, bending over to fix his bedding while Nicole Kidman peeks through hole in room divider.
A Few Good Men (1992)......Lieutenant Daniel Kaffee
The Firm (1993) ..................Mitch McDeere

# Culp, Robert

*Films:*

PT 109 (1963)................... Ens. "Barney" Ross
Bob & Carol & Ted & Alice (1969) ............ Bob
Hickey and Boggs (1972) .............Frank Boggs
**A Name for Evil** (1973) ............John Blake
•• 0:52—Frontal nudity running through the woods with a woman.
• 1:07—Buns, while going skinny dipping. Lots of bun shots underwater.
The Great Scout and Cathouse Thursday (1976)
................................ Jack Colby
Goldengirl (1979) .....................Esselton
National Lampoon Goes to the Movies (1982)
............................. Fred Everest
*a.k.a. Movie Madness*
Turk 182 (1985) .................... Mayor Tyler

Big Bad Mama II (1987).............Daryl Pearson
Pucker Up and Bark Like a Dog (1989)........Gregor
Silent Night, Deadly Night III: Better Watch Out! (1989)
................................. Lt. Connely
Timebomb (1990) ..................Mr. Phillips
Murderous Vision (1991) ..............Dr. Bordinay
The Pelican Brief (1993) ..................President
*Made for TV Movies:*
Calendar Girl Murders (1984) ...............Trainor
Her Life as a Man (1984) ............Dave Fleming
Columbo Goes to College (1990)........Jordan Rowe
Voyage of Terror: The Achillie Largo Affair (1990)
................................General Davies
I Spy Returns (1994)...............Kelly Robinson
*TV:*
I Spy (1965-68) .................Kelly Robinson
Greatest American Hero (1981-83)........Bill Maxwell
*CD-ROM:*
Voyeur (1993) ....................... n.a.
*Magazines:*
**Playboy** (Mar 1973) ..............."Evil" Doings
• 148—Side view nude.

# • Culver, Calvin

*Films:*

**Ginger** (1970)........................ Rodney
••• 1:02—Frontal nudity, tied up spread eagle on the bed.
• 1:07—Brief frontal nudity when Ginger lies down on top of him.
**Score** (1973).......................... Jack
• 0:01—Buns, while making love in bed with Elvira.
• 0:33—Brief buns, after dressing up like a sailor.
•• 1:09—Buns, several times, while making love in bed with Eddie.
• 1:11—Buns, while getting into bed with Eddie.
• 1:21—Buns, while on bed.
• 1:22—Very brief buns, while on bed.
• 1:24—Very, very brief frontal nudity, while sitting down in bed next to Elvira.

# Curry, Steven

*Films:*

**Glen and Randa** (1971)................... Glen
••• 0:00—Nude in the woods with Randa. Long scene.
• 0:42—Frontal nudity while kneeling on the ground.

# Cvetkovic, Svetozar

*Films:*

**Montenegro** (1981; British/Swedish) .... Montenegro
••• 1:07—Frontal nudity taking a shower while Susan Anspach watches.
Manifesto (1988).........................Rudi

# • Czerny, Henry

*Films:*

**Cold Sweat** (1993)...............Sean Mathieson
•• 0:44—Buns, while on bed with Shannon Tweed.

# Dacus, Don

*Films:*

**Hair** (1979) .............................. Woof
 • 0:57—Buns, while taking off clothes and diving into pond with Treat Williams and Hud.

# Dafoe, Willem

*Films:*

**Roadhouse 66** (1984).............. Johnny Harte
 •• 1:02—Buns, standing up while kissing Jesse.
Streets of Fire (1984)..................... Raven
**To Live and Die in L.A.** (1985) ........ Eric Masters
 0:58—Side view of buns, while kneeling on floor, burning counterfeit money.
 0:59—Lower half of buns, while making love in bed with Debra Feuer in bed. Seen on TV.
 • 1:06—Buns, while sitting on bench in locker room, changing clothes.
**The Last Temptation of Christ** (1988) .. Jesus Christ
 • 1:56—Buns, getting beaten and whipped.
 • 1:57—Buns, while getting crown of thorns placed on his head.
 2:02—Side view of buns, while hanging on cross.
Mississippi Burning (1988) ..............Alan Ward
Off Limits (1988)..................... Bud McGriff
Born on the Fourth of July (1989) ........... Charlie
Triumph of the Spirit (1989) .......... Salamo Arouch
Cry Baby (1990) ...................Hateful Guard
Wild at Heart (1990) .................Bobby Peru
Flight of the Intruder (1991) ................. Cole
**Body of Evidence** (1992) ........... Frank Dulaney
 (Unrated version reviewed.)
 ••• 0:14—Buns, while making love in bed on top of Sharon.
 • 0:46—Several brief frontal nudity shots, when it pokes out from under Madonna while she's on top of him in bed behind the curtain.
**Light Sleeper** (1992) ................ John LeTour
 •• 0:44—Buns, while kneeling in bed, kissing Dana Delany.
White Sands (1992) ...................Ray Dolezal
Faraway, So Close (1993; German) ........Emit Flesti
Clear and Present Danger (1994) ..............n.a.

# Daltrey, Roger

Singer with *The Who* and on his own.
*Films:*

**Lisztomania** (1975; British)..............Franz Liszt
 • 0:01—Brief buns while standing on bed tying a sheet to make some pants. Dark, don't see his face.
Tommy (1975; British) ...................Tommy
The Kids are Alright (1979; British) ...........Himself
The Legacy (1979; British)..................Clive
 *a.k.a. The Legacy of Maggie Walsh*
McVicar (1980; British) ............... Tom McVicar
If Looks Could Kill (1991) ................... Blade
 *a.k.a. Teen Agent*
Cold Justice (1992; British) ............Keith Gibson

*Made for Cable TV:*
 Tales From the Crypt: Forever Ambergris (1993; HBO)
 ..............................Dalton

# Damian, Leo

*Films:*

The Last Temptation of Christ (1988) .. Person in Crowd
**Ghosts Can't Do It** (1989) ................ Fasto
 • 1:31—Brief, lower buns while sliding down stack of hay. Long shot.
**Hard Drive** (1994) ........................ Will
 (Unrated version reviewed.)
 • 0:04—Brief buns, while making love with the Candle Dream Girl.
 • 0:07—Buns, while making love in bed with Dream Girl.
 • 0:11—Partial buns, while making love in bed with Laura.
 •• 1:15—Buns, while making love with Christina Fulton on kitchen counter.

# • Damon, Matt

*Films:*

Mystic Pizza (1988) ....................Steamer
**School Ties** (1992)....................Charlie Dillon
 •• 1:09—Buns, in the showers with two other guys (He's on the left).
 • 1:12—Very brief buns, while on the floor after getting hit by David.
Geronimo: An American Legend (1993)
 ......................Lieutenant Britton Davis

# Danare, Malcolm

*Films:*

Christine (1983)....................... Moochie
Flashdance (1983) ......................... Cecil
The Lords of Discipline (1983) ..............Poteete
**Heaven Help Us** (1985)...................Caesar
 • 0:36—Buns, while walking to the pool after all the other guys jump in. Long shot.
National Lampoon's European Vacation (1985)
 ...................... The Froegers' Son
The Curse (1987).........................Cyrus
Popcorn (1991) ............................. Bud

# Daniels, Jeff

*Films:*

Ragtime (1981) ..................... O'Donnell
Terms of Endearment (1983) ...........Flap Horton
The Purple Rose of Cairo (1985)
 ...................Tom Baxter/Gil Shepherd
Heartburn (1986)....................... Richard
Marie (1986) ....................... Eddie Sisk
**Something Wild** (1986) ............Charles Driggs
 •• 0:16—Buns, while lying in bed after making love with Melanie Griffith.
The House on Carroll Street (1988) ......... Cochran
Sweet Hearts Dance (1988) ........... Sam Manners
Checking Out (1989)................. Ray Macklin

Arachnophobia (1990) . . . . . . . . . . . Dr. Ross Jennings
Welcome Home Roxy Carmichael (1990)
. . . . . . . . . . . . . . . . . . . . . . . . . . . .Denton Webb
The Butcher's Wife (1991). . . . . . . . . . . . . . . . . . Alex
**Love Hurts** (1991). . . . . . . . . . . . . . . . . Paul Weaver
••• 1:24—Buns, several times in motel room with Judith Ivey.
Teamster Boss (1992) . . . . . . . . . . . . . . . . . . . . Noonan
Gettysburg (1993) . . . . . . . . . Col. Joshua Chamberlain
Speed (1994) . . . . . . . . . . . . . . . . . . . . . . . . . .n.a.
*Made for Cable Movies:*
Disaster in Time (1992; Showtime) . . . . . . . Ben Wilson
a.k.a. Timescape

## Darling, Candy
Female impersonator.
The subject of Lou Reed's song "Walk on the Wild Side."
*Films:*
Lady Liberty (1972; Italian/French) . . . . . . .Transvestite
Silent Night, Bloody Night (1974). . . . . . . . . . . . . .n.a.
**Superstar: The Life and Times of Andy Warhol**
(1990). . . . . . . . . . . . . . . . . . . . . . . . . . . . .Himself
•• 0:39—Frontal nudity in B&W still photo.
• 1:13—Very brief frontal nudity in the same B&W still photo.

## Daughton, James
*Films:*
Animal House (1978) . . . . . . . . . . . . . .Greg Marmalard
**Malibu Beach** (1978) . . . . . . . . . . . . . . . . . . . . .Bobby
• 0:32—Buns, while running into the ocean with his friends.
**The Beach Girls** (1982) . . . . . . . . . . . . . . . . . . .Scott
• 0:33—Buns and very brief frontal nudity while taking off clothes and running into the ocean.
Blind Date (1984) . . . . . . . . . . . . . . . . . . . . . . David
a.k.a. Deadly Seduction
(Not the same 1987 *Blind Date* with Bruce Willis.)
Mortuary Academy (1988) . . . . . . . . Yuppie at Car Lot
Girlfriend from Hell (1989) . . . . . . . . . . . . . . . . David

## Daveau, Alan
*Films:*
**Screwballs** (1983). . . . . . . . . . . . . . . . . . Howie Bates
• 1:00—Buns, after losing at strip bowling.

## Davidson, Jaye
*Films:*
**The Crying Game** (1992). . . . . . . . . . . . . . . . . . Dil
••• 1:03—Brief full frontal nudity when Stephen Rea discovers Dil's a he.

## Davies, Stephen
*Films:*
**Inserts** (1976) . . . . . . . . . . . . . . . . . . . . . . . . . .Rex
•• 0:31—Buns and balls, while on bed with Veronica Cartwright, making a porno movie for Richard Dreyfuss.
Heart Beat (1979) . . . . . . . . . . . . . . . . . . . .Bob Bendix

The Long Good Friday (1980; British). . . . . . . . . . Tony
The Razor's Edge (1984). . . . . . . . . . . . . . . . . Malcolm
The Nest (1987). . . . . . . . . . . . . . . . . . . . . . . . . .Homer
Corporate Affairs (1990). . . . . . . . . . . . . . .Ukranian #2
The Berlin Conspiracy (1991) . . . . . . . . . Klaus Heinlein
Alien Intruder (1992) . . . . . . . . . . . . . . . . . . . . . . Peter
Rage and Honor (1992) . . . . . . . . . . . . . . . . . . . . Baby
*Made for TV Movies:*
Revenge of the Nerds IV: Nerds in Love (1994) . . . Chip
*Magazines:*
**Playboy** (Nov 1976) . . . . . . . . . . Sex in Cinema 1976
••• 155—Buns from *Inserts.*

## Davis, Brad
*Films:*
**Midnight Express** (1978; British) . . . . . . . .Billy Hayes
• 0:12—Buns, while standing naked in front of guards after getting caught trying to smuggle drugs.
**A Small Circle of Friends** (1980) . . . . . . .Leo DaVinci
•• 1:22—Brief buns, while dropping his pants with several other guys for Army draft inspection.
Chariots of Fire (1981) . . . . . . . . . . . . . .Jackson Scholz
Querelle (1982) . . . . . . . . . . . . . . . . . . . . . . . .Querella
Cold Steel (1987). . . . . . . . . . . . . . . . . Johnny Modine
Hangfire (1990) . . . . . . . . . . . . . . . Sheriff Ike Slayton
Rosalie Goes Shopping (1990) . . . . . . . . . .Liebling Ray
The Player (1992). . . . . . . . . . . . . . . . . . . . . . Cameo
*Made for Cable Movies:*
Blood Ties (1986; Italian; Showtime) . . . . . .Julian Salina
*Miniseries:*
Roots (1977) . . . . . . . . . . . . . . . . Ol' George Johnson
Chiefs (1983). . . . . . . . . . . . . . . . . . Chief Sonny Butts
*Made for TV Movies:*
Sybil (1976). . . . . . . . . . . . . . . . . . . . . . . . . . n.a.
A Rumor of War (1980) . . . . . . . . . . . . . . . . . . . n.a.

## • Davis, Buddy
*Video Tapes:*
**Penthouse Forum Letters: Volume 2** (1994)
. . . . . . . . . . . . . . . . . . . . . The Loving Nurse/Patient
••• 0:01—Buns and balls while making love in hospital bed with a nurse.

## Davis, Gene
*Films:*
Cruising (1980) . . . . . . . . . . . . . . . . . . . . . . . DaVinci
Night Games (1980) . . . . . . . . . . . . . . . . . . . .Timothy
**10 to Midnight** (1983) . . . . . . . . . . . . . .Warren Stacy
•• 0:08—Nude, running after girl in the woods.
•• 0:28—Buns, in Betty's bedroom, while attempting to get her diary.
•• 1:31—Buns, lots of times, while attacking the girls in their apartment.
•• 1:36—Buns and very brief frontal nudity leaving the apartment at the top of the stairs.
•• 1:37—Nude, running after Lisa Eilbacher in the street.
Messenger of Death (1988) . . . . . . . . . . .Junior Assassin
Universal Soldier (1992). . . . . . . . . . . . . . .Lieutenant

## Davis, Mac

Singer.

*Films:*

**North Dallas Forty** (1979) . . . . . . . . . . . . . . Maxwell
- 0:53—Brief buns while getting a can of Coke in the locker room.

Cheaper to Keep Her (1980) . . . . . . . . . . . Bill Dekkar
The Sting II (1983) . . . . . . . . . . . . . . . . . . . . Hooker
Blackmail (1991) . . . . . . . . . . . . . . . . . . . . . . Norm

*TV:*

The Mac Davis Show (1974-76) . . . . . . . . . . . . . Host

## Day, Clayton

*Films:*

**Deep In the Heart** (1983; British). . . . . . . Larry Keeler
*a.k.a. Handgun*
- 0:35—Buns, while in bedroom forcing Karen Young to have sex.

## Day-Lewis, Daniel

*Films:*

Gandhi (1982) . . . . . . . . . . . . . . . . . . . . . . . . Colin
The Bounty (1984) . . . . . . . . . . . . . . . . . . . . . Fryer
My Beautiful Laundrette (1985; British) . . . . . . . Johnny
A Room with a View (1986; British) . . . . . . . . Cecil Vyse
**Stars and Bars** (1988) . . . . . . . . . . . Henderson Bores
- • 1:21—Brief buns, while trying to open the window. Very, very brief frontal nudity when he throws the statue out the window. Blurry and dark. More buns, climbing out the window and into a trash dumpster.

The Unbearable Lightness of Being (1988) . . . . Thomas
My Left Foot (1989; British). . . . . . . . . . . .Christy Brown
(Academy Award for Best Actor.)
Eversmile New Jersey (1991) . . . . . . . . . . . . . . . .n.a.
The Last of the Mohicans (1992). . . . . . . . . . .Hawkeye
The Age of Innocence (1993) . . . . . . . . Newland Archer
In the Name of the Father (1993; British/U.S.)
. . . . . . . . . . . . . . . . . . . . . . . . . . . . . Gerry Conlon

## De La Brosse, Simon

*Films:*

Pauline at the Beach (1983; French) . . . . . . . . . Sylvain
**The Little Thief** (1989; French) . . . . . . . . . . . . Raoul
*a.k.a. La Petite Voleuse*
- 1:07—Very brief buns and frontal nudity while jumping into bed (seen in mirror).

Strike it Rich (1990). . . . . . . . . . . . . . . . . . . Philippe

## De Lint, Derek

*Films:*

Soldier of Orange (1977; Dutch). . . . . . . . . . . . . Alex
Mata Hari (1985) . . . . . . . . . . . . . . .Handsome Traveler
The Assault (1986; Dutch). . . . . . . . . . . Anton Steenwijk
Mascara (1987; French/Belgian) . . . . . . . . . Chris Brine
**Stealing Heaven** (1988; British/Yugoslavian) . .Abelard
- • • 0:47—Brief frontal nudity taking off his shirt. Then buns, while in bed making love with Kim Thomson.
- 1:07—Brief side view of buns under Kim. Long shot.

The Unbearable Lightness of Being (1988) . . . . . . Franz

*Made for Cable Movies:*
The Endless Game (1990; Showtime) . . . . . . . . Abramov
*Made for TV Movies:*
Burning Bridges (1990) . . . . . . . . . . . . . Gus Morgan
*TV:*
NYPD Blue: Serge the Coincierge (Mar 29, 1994)
. . . . . . . . . . . . . . . . . . . . . . . . . . . . . . . . .Serge

## de Meijo, Carlo

*Films:*

**Twelfth Night** (1988; Italian). . . . . . . . . . . . . Orsino
- 0:00—Buns, while standing up after bath. Out of focus.
- 0:49—Half of buns, while sitting on rock, talking to Viola.

## De Niro, Robert

*Films:*

Greetings (1968) . . . . . . . . . . . . . . . . . . . . .Jon Rubin
The Wedding Party (1969) . . . . . . . . . . . . . . . . Cecil
**Bloody Mama** (1970) . . . . . . . . . . . . . . .Lloyd Barker
0:03—Very briefly nude, having a towel fight with his brother. Blurry, hard to see.
Bang the Drum Slowly (1973) . . . . . . . . . Bruce Pearson
Mean Streets (1973) . . . . . . . . . . . . . . . . Johnny Boy
The Godfather, Part II (1974) . . . . . . . . . Vito Corleone
(Academy Award for Best Supporting Actor.)
**1900** (1976; Italian) . . . . . . . . . . . . Alfredo Berlinghieri
(NC-17 version reviewed.)
- • • 2:04—Frontal nudity in bed with a girl and Gérard Depardieu.
- • • 2:05—Buns, getting out of bed.
- • • 2:30—Buns, undressing and making love on top of Dominique Sanda in the hay. Long shot.
The Last Tycoon (1976) . . . . . . . . . . . . . . Monroe Stahr
Taxi Driver (1976) . . . . . . . . . . . . . . . . . .Travis Bickle
New York, New York (1977). . . . . . . . . . . . Jimmy Doyle
**The Deer Hunter** (1978). . . . . . . . . . . . . . . Michael
- • • 0:50—Nude, running in street, then more nude by basketball court. Brief frontal nudity getting covered by Christopher Walken's jacket. Long shot.
Raging Bull (1980) . . . . . . . . . . . . . . . . . .Jake La Motta
(Academy Award for Best Actor.)
True Confessions (1981). . . . . . . . . . . . . . Des Spellacy
King of Comedy (1983) . . . . . . . . . . . . . . Rupert Pupkin
Falling In Love (1984) . . . . . . . . . . . . . . . Frank Raftis
Once Upon a Time in America (1984) . . . . . . . .Noodles
(Long version reviewed.)
Brazil (1985; British). . . . . . . . . . . . . . . . . . . . .Tuttle
The Mission (1986; British). . . . . . . . . . . . . .Mendoza
Angel Heart (1987) . . . . . . . . . . . . . . . . Louis Cyphre
(Original Unedited Version reviewed.)
The Untouchables (1987). . . . . . . . . . . . . . . Al Capone
Midnight Run (1988). . . . . . . . . . . . . . . . .Jack Walsh
Jackknife (1989). . . . . . . . . . Joseph "Megs" Megessey
We're No Angels (1989). . . . . . . . . . . . . . . . . . .Ned
GoodFellas (1990) . . . . . . . . . . . . . . . .James Conway
Stanley and Iris (1990) . . . . . . . . Stanley Everett Cox
Awakenings (1991) . . . . . . . . . . . . . . Leonard Lowe

Backdraft (1991) . . . . . . . . . . . . . . . . . Donald Rimgale
Cape Fear (1991) . . . . . . . . . . . . . . . . . . . . . Max Cady
Guilty by Suspicion (1991) . . . . . . . . . . . David Merrill
Mistress (1991) . . . . . . . . . . . . . . . . . . . Evan M. Wright
Night and the City (1992). . . . . . . . . . . . Harry Fabian
A Bronx Tale (1993) . . . . . . . . . . . . . . . Lorenzo Anello
Mad Dog and Glory (1993). . .Wayne "Mad Dog" Dobie
This Boy's Life (1993) . . . . . . . . . . . . . . Dwight Hansen

## Deacon, Brian

*Films:*
The Triple Echo (1973; British) . . . . . . . . . . . . . Barton
Vampyres (1974; British) . . . . . . . . . . . . . . . . . . . . John
Jesus (1979) . . . . . . . . . . . . . . . . . . . . . . . . . . . . . Jesus
Nelly's Version (1983; British) . . . . . . . . . . . . . . David
**A Zed and Two Noughts** (1985; British)
. . . . . . . . . . . . . . . . . . . . . . . . . . . . . . . Oswald Deuce
- • 1:12—Buns (he's on the right), getting into bed with Alba and Oliver.
- •• 1:25—Nude (on the right), walking to chair and sitting down while Oliver does the same.
- ••• 1:27—Frontal nudity, standing up.
- ••• 1:50—Nude, injecting himself and lying down to time lapse photograph himself decay with Oliver.

## Deacon, Eric

*Films:*
**A Zed and Two Noughts** (1985; British)
. . . . . . . . . . . . . . . . . . . . . . . . . . . . . . . . Oliver Deuce
- •• 0:24—Buns in bed, then nude while throwing Venus out, then her clothes.
- ••• 0:30—Frontal nudity, sitting on bathroom floor.
- • 1:12—Buns (he's on the left), getting into bed with Alba and Oswald.
- •• 1:25—Nude (on the left), walking to chair and sitting down while Oswald does the same.
- ••• 1:27—Frontal nudity, standing up.
- ••• 1:50—Nude, injecting himself and lying down to time lapse photograph himself decay with Oswald.

## • DeLuise, Dom

Father of actor Peter DeLuise and actor Michael DeLuise.
*Films:*
Failsafe (1964). . . . . . . . . . . . . . . . . . . . . Sgt. Collins
Blazing Saddles (1974) . . . . . . . . . . . . . . Buddy Bizarre
The Adventure of Sherlock Holmes' Smarter Brother
(1975). . . . . . . . . . . . . . . . . . . . . . . . . . . . Gambetti
Silent Movie (1976). . . . . . . . . . . . . . . . . . . Dom Bell
The Cheap Detective (1978) . . . . . . . . . Pepe Damascus
**Fatso** (1980) . . . . . . . . . . . . . . . . . . Dominick DiNapoli
- • 0:26—Brief buns in open back hospital gown while walking in hallway past a woman.
The Last Married Couple in America (1980)
. . . . . . . . . . . . . . . . . . . . . . . . . . . . . Walter Holmes
Smokey and the Bandit II (1980). . . . . . . . . . . . . Doc
Wholly Moses (1980) . . . . . . . . . . . . . . . . . Shadrach
The Cannonball Run (1981) . . . . . . . . . . . . . . Victor
History of the World, Part I (1981). . . . . . Emperor Nero
The Best Little Whorehouse in Texas (1982) . . . . Melvin

Cannonball Run II (1984). . . . . . . . . . . . . Victor/Chaos
Johnny Dangerously (1984) . . . . . . . . . . . . . The Pope
Loose Cannons (1990) . . . . . . . . . Harry Gutterman
Driving Me Crazy (1991) . . . . . . . . . . . . . . . . . Mr. B
Robin Hood: Men in Tights (1993). . . . . . Don Giovanni
*TV:*
The Glen Campbell Goodtime Hour (1971-72) . Regular
Lotsa Luck (1973-74) . . . . . . . . . . . . Stanley Belmont
The Dom DeLuise Show (1987-88) . . . . . . . . . . . Host
Candid Camera (1991) . . . . . . . . . . . . . . . . . . Host

## • DeMarco, Douglass

*Films:*
**Anthony's Desire** (1993). . . . . . . . . . . . . . . Anthony
- ••• 0:17—Buns, while making love in bed with Desiree.
- •• 0:24—Buns, while making love in bed with Desiree, then getting up out of bed.
- • 0:45—Buns, while making love at the beach with Desiree.
- •• 0:46—Buns, while making love with Desiree in bed.
- ••• 1:14—Buns, walking to bed, kneeling, then making love in bed with Jessica.

## Dempsey, Patrick

*Films:*
Heaven Help Us (1985) . . . . . . . . . . . . . . . . . . Corbet
Can't Buy Me Love (1987) . . . . . . . . . . . . Ronald Miller
In the Mood (1987) . . . . . Ellsworth "Sonny" Wisecarver
**Meatballs III** (1987). . . . . . . . . . . . . . . . . . . . . Rudy
- •• 0:19—Buns, while in the shower when first being visited by Sally Kellerman.
Happy Together (1988) . . .Christopher "Chris" Wooden
**Some Girls** (1988) . . . . . . . . . . . . . . . . . . . . Michael
*a.k.a. Sisters*
- • 0:34—Brief frontal nudity, then buns while running all around the house chasing Jennifer Connelly.
Loverboy (1989) . . . . . . . . . . . . . . . . . . . Randy Bodek
Coupe de Ville (1990) . . . . . . . . . . . . . . Bobby Libner
Run (1990). . . . . . . . . . . . . . . . . . . . . Charlie Farrow
Mobsters (1991) . . . . . . . . . . . . . . . . . Meyer Lansky
*a.k.a. Mobsters—The Evil Empire*
**Bank Robber** (1993) . . . . . . . . . . . . . . . . . . . . Billy
- •• 1:21—Buns, while taking a shower.
Face the Music (1993) . . . . . . . . . . . . . . . . . . . n.a.
With Honors (1994) . . . . . . . . . . . . . . . . . . . . . n.a.
*Made for TV Movies:*
JFK: Reckless Youth (1993) . . . . . . . . . . John F. Kennedy
*TV:*
Fast Times (1986). . . . . . . . . . . . . . . . . Mike Damone

## Denison, Anthony John

*Films:*
**Little Vegas** (1990) . . . . . . . . . . . . . . . . . . . Carmine
- •• 0:53—Buns, getting into pond with Catherine O'Hara.
City of Hope (1991). . . . . . . . . . . . . . . . . . . . . Rizzo
The Harvest (1992) . . . . . . . . . . . . . . . Noel Guzman
A Brilliant Disguise (1994) . . . . . . . . . . . Andy Manola

*Made for Cable Movies:*
Sex, Love and Cold Hard Cash (1993; USA) . . . . . . . .n.a.
*Made for TV Movies:*
The Amy Fisher Story (1993) . . . . . . . . . Joey Buttafuoco
Getting Gotti (1994) . . . . . . . . . . . . . . . . . . . .John Gotti
*TV:*
Crime Story (1986) . . . . . . . . . . . . . . . . . . . . .Ray Luca

# Dennehy, Brian

*Films:*
Semi-Tough (1977) . . . . . . . . . . . . . . . . . . . T.J. Lambert
F.I.S.T. (1978) . . . . . . . . . . . . . . . . . . . . . . .Frank Vasko
Foul Play (1978) . . . . . . . . . . . . . . . . . . . . . . . . .Fergie
10 (1979) . . . . . . . . . . . . . . . . . . . . . . . . . . Bartender
Little Miss Marker (1980) . . . . . . . . . . . . . . . . . Herbie
First Blood (1982) . . . . . . . . . . . . . . . . . . . . . . Teasle
Split Image (1982) . . . . . . . . . . . . . . . . . . . . . . Kevin
Finders Keepers (1983) . . . . . . . . . . . . . . Mayor Fizzoli
Gorky Park (1983) . . . . . . . . . . . . . . . . .William Kirwill
Never Cry Wolf (1983) . . . . . . . . . . . . . . . . . . .Rosie
The River Rat (1984) . . . . . . . . . . . . . . . . . . . . . . Doc
Cocoon (1985) . . . . . . . . . . . . . . . . . . . . . . . .Walter
Silverado (1985) . . . . . . . . . . . . . . . . . . . . . . . .Cobb
Twice in a Lifetime (1985) . . . . . . . . . . . . . . . . . Nick
The Check is in the Mail (1986) . . . . . . .Richard Jackson
F/X (1986) . . . . . . . . . . . . . . . . . . . . .Leo McCarthy
Legal Eagles (1986) . . . . . . . . . . . . . . . . . Cavanaugh
**The Belly of an Architect** (1987; British/Italian)
. . . . . . . . . . . . . . . . . . . . . . . . . Stourley Kraclite
••• 0:12—Buns, while taking off underwear and getting
into bed with Chloe Webb. Kind of a long shot.
Best Seller (1988) . . . . . . . . . .Det. Lt. Dennis Meechum
Miles From Home (1988) . . . . . . . . . . Frank Roberts, Sr.
The Last of the Finest (1990) . . . . . . . . . . . . Frank Daly
Presumed Innocent (1990) . . . . . . . . Raymond Horgan
FX 2 (1991) . . . . . . . . . . . . . . . . . .Leo McCarthy
Gladiator (1992) . . . . . . . . . . . . . . . . . . . . . . .Horn
Teamster Boss (1992) . . . . . . . . . . . . . . Jackie Presser
*Made for Cable Movies:*
The Diamond Fleece (1992; USA)
. . . . . . . . . . . . . . . . . . . Lieutenant Merritt Outlaw
Foreign Affairs (1993; TNT) . . . . . . . . Chuck Mumpson
*Made for TV Movies:*
The Real American Hero (1978) . . . . . . . . . . . . . .n.a.
The Seduction of Miss Leona (1980) . . . . . .Bliss Dawson
A Killing in a Small Town (1990) . . . . . . . . . .Ed Reivers
Deadly Matrimony (1992) . . . . . . . . . . . . . . Jack Reed
To Catch a Killer (1992; Canadian) . . . John Wayne Gacy
Final Appeal (1993) . . . . . . . . . . . . . . . . . . . . .n.a.
Jack Reed: Badge of Honor (1993) . . . . . . . . . Jack Reed
Murder in the Heartland (1993) . . . . . . . . . . . . . .n.a.
Leave of Absence (1994) . . . . . . . . . . . . . . Sam Mercer
*TV:*
Big Shamus, Little Shamus (1979) . . . . . . . . Arnie Sutter
Star of the Family (1982) . . . . . . . . . . . . . .Buddy Krebs
Birdland (1994- ) . . . . . . . . . . . . . . . Dr. Brian McKenzie

# Denney, David

*Films:*
**Under Cover** (1987) . . . . . . . . . . . . . . . . Hassie Pearl
• 0:43—Brief buns while walking around boy's locker
room wearing his jock strap.
Rush Week (1989) . . . . . . . . . . . . . . . . . . . .Greg Ochs

# • Denton, Chris

*Films:*
**Bound and Gagged: A Love Story** (1993) . . . . . Cliff
•• 1:15—Buns, several times, while taking off his underwear in front of Elizabeth.

# Depardieu, Gérard

Father of actor Guillaume Depardieu.
*Films:*
**Going Places** (1974; French) . . . . . . . . . . .Jean-Claude
• 0:42—Upper half of buns and pubic hair, while talking to Pierrot.
•• 0:49—Buns while in bed, then more buns making
love to Miou-Miou. Nice up and down action.
• 0:50—Brief buns while switching places with Pierrot.
• 0:51—Brief frontal nudity getting out of bed. Dark,
hard to see. Subtitles get in the way.
**1900** (1976; Italian) . . . . . . . . . . . . . . . . . .Olmo Dalco
(NC-17 version reviewed.)
•• 2:03—Brief frontal nudity sitting at table with Robert
De Niro. Again when walking into the bedroom.
••• 2:04—Frontal nudity in bed with a girl and De Niro.
••• 2:07—Nude, getting up and walking around.
This Sweet Sickness (1977; French) . . . David Martineau
*a.k.a. dites-lui que je l'aime*
Get Out Your Handkerchiefs (1978) . . . . . . . . . . .Raoul
The Last Metro (1980) . . . . . . . . . . . . Bernard Granger
**Loulou** (1980; French) . . . . . . . . . . . . . . . . . .Loulou
• 0:07—Brief buns, while getting out of bed after it
breaks. Dark.
•• 0:36—Buns, while lying in bed with Isabelle Hup-
pert.
**The Moon in the Gutter** (1983; French/Italian)
. . . . . . . . . . . . . . . . . . . . . . . . . . . . . . .Gerard
*a.k.a. La Lune dans Le Caniveau*
• 1:26—Upper half of buns, while getting out of bed.
The Return of Martin Guerre (1983; French)
. . . . . . . . . . . . . . . . . . . . . . . . . Martin Guerre
Police (1985; French) . . . . . . . . . . . . . . . . . Mangin
Jean de Florette (1986; French) . . . . . . . . Jean Cadoret
Camille Claudel (1989; French) . . . . . . .Auguste Rodin
Cyrano De Bergerac (1990; French)
. . . . . . . . . . . . . . . . . . . . . . .Cyrano De Bergerac
Green Card (1990) . . . . . . . . . . . . . . . . . . . .Georges
Too Beautiful for You (1990; French) . . . . . . . . Bernard
Uranus (1991; French) . . . . . . . . . . . . . . . . .Leopold
1492: Conquest of Paradise (1992; British/U.S./Spanish/
French) . . . . . . . . . . . . . . . . . . .Christopher Columbus
All the Mornings of the World (1992; French)
. . . . . . . . . . . . . . . . . . . . . . . . . . . Marin Marais
*a.k.a. Tout Les Matins Du Monde*
My Father The Hero (1993) . . . . . . . . . . . . . . . André

# • Depardieu, Guillaume

Son of actor Gérard Depardieu.
*Films:*
**All the Mornings of the World** (1992; French)
. . . . . . . . . . . . . . . . . . . . . . . . . . Young Marin Marais
*a.k.a. Tout Les Matins Du Monde*
•• 1:08—Buns and balls from behind, while getting out of bed.

## Depp, Johnny

*Films:*
A Nightmare on Elm Street (1985) . . . . . . . . Glen Lantz
**Private Resort** (1985) . . . . . . . . . . . . . . . . . . . . Jack
•• 0:12—Buns, while in hotel room with Leslie Easterbrook.
Platoon (1986) . . . . . . . . . . . . . . . . . . . . . . . . .Lerner
Cry Baby (1990) . . . . . . . . . . . . . . . . . . . . . Cry-Baby
Edward Scissorhands (1990) . . . . . Edward Scissorhands
Freddy's Dead: The Final Nightmare (1991)
. . . . . . . . . . . . . . . . . . . . . . . . . . . . . . Glen Lantz
Benny & Joon (1993) . . . . . . . . . . . . . . . . . . . . Sam
What's Eating Gilbert Grape (1993) . . . . . . Gilbert Grape
*TV:*
21 Jump Street (1987-90) . . . . . . . . . . Tommy Hanson

## Dern, Bruce

Father of actress Laura Dern.
Ex-husband of actress Diane Ladd.
*Films:*
Marnie (1964) . . . . . . . . . . . . . . . . . . . . . . . . . Sailor
Hush...Hush, Sweet Charlotte (1965) . . . . John Mayhew
The Wild Angels (1966) . . . . . . . . . . . Loser (Joey Kerns)
Rebel Rousers (1967) . . . . . . . . . . . . . . . . . . . . . . J.J.
The St. Valentine's Day Massacre (1967) . . . . . John May
The Trip (1967) . . . . . . . . . . . . . . . . . . . . John, Guru
Waterhole 3 (1967) . . . . . . . . . . . . . . . . . . . . Deputy
Support Your Local Sheriff! (1969) . . . . . . . . .Joe Danby
Bloody Mama (1970) . . . . . . . . . . . . . . Kevin Kirkman
Silent Running (1971) . . . . . . . . . . . . . . . . . . . .Lowell
The Cowboys (1972) . . . . . . . . . . . . . . . . . Long Hair
King of Marvin Gardens (1972) . . . . . . . . .Jason Staebler
Thumb Tripping (1972) . . . . . . . . . . . . . . . . . .Smitty
The Great Gatsby (1974) . . . . . . . . . . . . Tom Buchanan
The Laughing Policeman (1974) . . . . . . . . . Leo Larsen
Smile (1974) . . . . . . . . . . . . . . . . . . . . . . . .Big Bob
**The Twist** (1976) . . . . . . . . . . . . . . . . . . . . . William
•• 0:45—Buns, while taking off his clothes and walking onto stage during a play. Long shot.
Black Sunday (1977) . . . . . . . . . . . . . . . . . . . Lander
**Coming Home** (1978) . . . . . . . . . . Captain Bob Hyde
•• 2:03—Buns, while taking off his clothes at the beach and running into the ocean.
The Driver (1978) . . . . . . . . . . . . . . . . . The Detective
Middle Age Crazy (1980; Canadian) . . . . . . . Bobby Lee
**Tattoo** (1981) . . . . . . . . . . . . . . . . . . . . . .Karl Kinski
•• 1:36—Buns, while making love with Maud Adams before she kills him.
Harry Tracy (1982; Canadian) . . . . . . . . . . .Harry Tracy
That Championship Season (1982) . . . George Sitkoswki

On the Edge (1985) . . . . . . . . . . . . . . . . . . . . . . .Wes
(Unrated version reviewed.)
• 0:52—Brief buns, seen from below while floating in a pond.
The Big Town (1987) . . . . . . . . . . . . . . . Mr. Edwards
1969 (1988) . . . . . . . . . . . . . . . . . . . . . . . . . . . Cliff
World Gone Wild (1988) . . . . . . . . . . . . . . . . .Ethan
The 'burbs (1989) . . . . . . . . . . . . . . . Mark Rumsfield
After Dark, My Sweet (1990) . . . . . . . . . . . Uncle Bud
Into the Badlands (1991) . . . . . . . . . . . . . . Barston
Diggstown (1992) . . . . . . . . . . . . . . . . . John Gillon
*a.k.a. Midnight Sting*
*Made for Cable Movies:*
The Court-Martial of Jackie Robinson (1990)
. . . . . . . . . . . . . . . . . . . . . . . . . . . . . .Ed Higgins
Amelia Earhart: The Final Flight (1994; TNT) G.P. Putnam
*Miniseries:*
Space (1987) . . . . . . . . . . . . . . . . . . . . Stanley Mott
*Made for TV Movies:*
Toughlove (1985) . . . . . . . . . . . . . . . . Rob Charters
It's Nothing Personal (1993) . . . . . . . . . . . Billy Archer
*TV:*
Stoney Burke (1962-63) . . . . . . . . . . . . . . E. J. Stocker

## Desarthe, Gerard

*Films:*
**A Love in Germany** (1984; French/German)
. . . . . . . . . . . . . . . . . . . . . . . . . . . . . Karl Wyler
• 0:28—Buns, while lying in bed with Maria.
Uranus (1991; French) . . . . . . . . . . . . . . . .Maxine Loin

# • Detroit, Peter

*Video Tapes:*
**Penthouse Forum Letters: Volume 2** (1994)
. . . . . . . . . . . . . . . . The Perfect Model/Photographer
••• 0:18—Nude, while making love with model in studio.

## Dewaere, Patrick

*Films:*
**Going Places** (1974; French) . . . . . . . . . . . . . .Pierrot
• 0:42—Upper half of buns while starting to leave the room. Surgical tape on his buns.
•• 0:48—Buns while in bed with Marie-Ange.
• 0:50—Brief buns, while switching places with Jean-Claude.
1:41—Sort of buns, while making love in back seat of car. Dark.
• 1:42—Buns, while getting out of car and pulling up his pants.
Catherine & Co. (1975; French) . . . . . . . . . . . .Francois
Beau Pere (1981; French) . . . . . . . . . . . . . . . . . Remi
**The Heat of Desire** (1982; French) . . . . . . Serge Laine
*a.k.a. Plein Sud*
• 0:17—Buns, while getting out of bed and going into Carol's "house" that she has made out of sheets.
0:20—Pubic hair, while lying on his back.
• 0:21—Side view of buns, while on the floor with Carol.

0:57—Brief side view of buns, while getting out of bed and putting on pants.
• 1:02—Buns, while getting into bed with Carol. Very, very brief frontal nudity hidden by subtitles.
• 1:14—Buns, while taking off pants and getting into bed.

## Dewee, Patrick
*Films:*
**Master of Dragonard Hill** (1987) . . . . . . . . . . Calabar
•• 0:14—Buns, while getting out of bed after being discovered in bed with Claudia Udy by her father.

## Diehl, John
*Films:*
Stripes (1981) . . . . . . . . . . . . . . . . . . . . . . . . . Cruiser
**Angel** (1983) . . . . . . . . . . . . . . . . . . . . . . . . Billy Boy
• 0:35—Buns, while washing blood off himself. Dark, hard to see. Long scene.
D.C. Cab (1983) . . . . . . . . . . . . . . . . . . . . . . Kidnapper
Joysticks (1983) . . . . . . . . . . . . . . . . . . . . . . . . . Arnie
National Lampoon's Vacation (1983)
. . . . . . . . . . . . . . . . . . . . . . . . Assistant Mechanic
City Limits (1984) . . . . . . . . . . . . . . . . . . . . . Whitey
A Climate for Killing (1990) . . . . . . . . . . . Wayne Paris
Kickboxer 2: The Road Back (1990) . . . . . . . . . Morrison
Motorama (1991) . . . . . . . . . . . . . . . . . . . . . . . . Phil
Whore (1991) . . . . . . . . . . . . . . . . . . . . . . . . Derelict
*a.k.a. If you're afraid to say it... Just see it*
Mikey (1992) . . . . . . . . . . . . . . . . . . . . . Neil Trenton
Mo' Money (1992) . . . . . . . . . . . . . . . . Keith Harding
The Paint Job (1992) . . . . . . . . . . . . . . . . . . . . . Father
Falling Down (1993) . . . . . . . . . . Dad (Back Yard Party)
Gettysburg (1993) . . . . . . . . . . . . . . . . Private Bucklin
Remote (1993) . . . . . . . . . . . . . . . . . . . . . . Delbert
*TV:*
Miami Vice (1984-89) . . . . . . . . . . Detective Larry Zito

## • DiFrancisco, Joey
*Video Tapes:*
Wet and Wild IV (1992) . . . . . . . . . . . . . . . . . . Extra
**Playboy's Secret Confessions** (1993)
. . . . . . . . . . . . . . . . . . . . . Jailhouse Rock/Rick
•• 0:34—Brief erect frontal nudity while in jail cell with Tina.
• 0:35—Very brief frontal nudity while grabbing his shirt and sitting up on bed.
**Playboy's Sensual Fantasy for Lovers** (1993)
. . . . . . . . . . . . . . . . . . . . . . . . . . . . . . Games
••• 0:06—Buns in G-string in bathroom with his lover, then nude, while making love in bed.
• 0:46—Buns during review.

## • Dingwall, Kelly
*Films:*
The Year My Voice Broke (1987; Australian) . . . . . . Barry
**The Custodian** (1993) . . . . . . . . . . . . . . . . . Reynolds
• 0:47—Buns, while in the shower.

## Dini, Memo
*Films:*
**Mediterraneo** (1991; Italian) . . . . . . . Libero Munaron
• 0:52—Buns, jumping into the water with his brother.
• 1:27—Buns, jumping into the water with his brother during end credits.

## Dinome, Jerry
See: Christopher, Gerard.

## DiStefano, Len
*Films:*
**Naked Instinct** (1993) . . . . . . . . . . . . . . . . . Poolman
••• 0:23—Nude, playing with himself while Joanne watches.

## Divine
Female impersonator.
Real name was Harris Glenn Milstead.
*Films:*
Mondo Trasho (1970) . . . . . . . . . . . . . Hit & Run Driver
Pink Flamingos (1972) . . . . . . . . . . . . . . . . . . . . . n.a.
**Female Trouble** (1974) . . . . . . . Dawn Davenport/Earl
• 0:15—Buns, wiggling and dancing in white bra and G-string on stage.
• 0:58—Close-up of penis, while showing it to Taffy. Don't see his face.
Polyester (1981) . . . . . . . . . . . . . . . . . Francine Fishpaw
Lust in the Dust (1985) . . . . . . . . . . . . . . . . . . . Rosie
0:03—Buns, while taking off clothes to go for a dip in a pond. Don't see his face.
0:07—Brief breasts, when a midget cowboy yanks "her" blouse down. Obviously a body double since Divine was really a man.
1:02—Buns, while walking into pond during flashback.
1:06—Buns, while lying face down on bed (on the left), showing her tattoo map with Laine Kazan. Don't see his face.
1:07—Close-up of right bun. Don't see his face.
Hairspray (1988) . . . . . . Edna Turnblad/Arvin Hodgepile
Out of the Dark (1988) . . . . . . . . . . . . . . . . . Langella

## • Dixon, Callum
*Films:*
**Waterland** (1992; British/U.S.) . . . . . . . . . . Freddie Parr
• 0:05—Brief buns, pulling down his pants with his friends to show Mary (He's the second from the right).

# Dolan, Michael

*Films:*
Hamburger Hill (1987) .................. Murphy
Light of Day (1987)................. Gene Bodine
Biloxi Blues (1988) ............. James J. Hennessey
**Necessary Roughness** (1991)
.................... Eric "Samurai" Hanson
  • 1:09—Buns, while taking a shower, kind of hard to
  see. (He's the guy in the middle.)

# • Donato, Len

*Films:*
**Killer Looks** (1994)..................... Mickey
(Unrated version reviewed.)
  • 0:43—Very, very brief buns, while rolling out of bed
  when Sara Suzanne Brown's husband comes home.
  • 0:51—Very, very brief buns in flashback.

# Dorison, Zag

*Films:*
**Deadly Innocents** (1988)............. Crazy Norm
  • 0:04—Buns, while standing on top of van and
  mooning the paramedics.

# Douglas, Kirk

Father of actor Michael Douglas.
*Films:*
Out of the Past (1947) ............... Whit Sterling
Champion (1949)................... Midge Kelly
A Letter to Three Wives (1949) ........ George Phipps
The Glass Menagerie (1950) ........... Jim O'Connor
Along the Great Divide (1951) .......... Len Merrick
The Big Carnival (1951) ............. Charles Tatum
Detective Story (1951) ................ Jim McLeod
The Big Sky (1952) ....................Deakins
20,000 Leagues Under the Sea (1954) ...... Ned Land
Man without a Star (1955) ........... Dempsey Rae
Ulysses (1955; Italian) ..................... Ulysses
Gunfight at the O.K. Corral (1957)
...................... John H. "Doc" Holliday
Paths of Glory (1957) ................. Colonel Dax
The Vikings (1958) ......................Einar
Last Train from Gun Hill (1959)........ Matt Morgan
Spartacus (1960)...................... Spartacus
Seven Days in May (1964)
.................. Colonel Martin "Jiggs" Casey
In Harm's Way (1965) .............. Paul Eddington
Cast a Giant Shadow (1966) ....Colonel Mickey Marcus
The Way West (1967) .......Senator William J. Tadlock
The Brotherhood (1968) ............. Frank Ginetta
**The Arrangement** (1969) ......Eddie and Evangelos
  • 0:25—Brief buns, while on the beach.
**There Was a Crooked Man** (1970)...Paris Pitman, Jr.
  • 0:11—Brief upper half of buns, while leaving bed-
  room wearing only his gun belt.
  •• 1:09—Brief buns and balls, while jumping into a bar-
  rel to take a bath in prison.
A Gunfight (1971)................... Will Tenneray
Once is Not Enough (1975) ........... Mike Wayne

The Chosen (1978; Italian/British) ............Caine
The Fury (1978)................... Peter Sandza
**Holocaust 2000** (1978).............. Robert Caine
  •• 0:52—Buns, during nightmare sequence. Long
  shots, hard to tell it's him.
The Villain (1979)..................... Cactus Jack
The Final Countdown (1980)
.................... Captain Matthew Yelland
**Saturn 3** (1980)...................... Adam
  • 0:57—Brief buns while fighting with Harvey Keitel,
  more brief buns sitting down in bed with Farrah
  Fawcett.
The Man from Snowy River (1982; Australian)
.......................... Spur/Harrison
Eddie Macon's Run (1983) ............... Marazack
**Tough Guys** (1986) ................. Archie Long
  • 1:36—Buns, while standing on moving train, moon-
  ing Charles Durning.
Oscar (1991) ...................... Snap's Father
Greedy (1993) ........................ Uncle Joe
*Made for Cable Movies:*
Drawl (1984; HBO) ............. Harry H. Holland
*Made for TV Movies:*
The Secret (1992) ................. Mike Dunmore

# Douglas, Michael

Son of actor Kirk Douglas.
*Films:*
Hail, Hero! (1969) ..................... Carl Dixon
Napolean and Samantha (1972) ............ Danny
Coma (1978) ................. Dr. Mark Bellows
The China Syndrome (1979) .........Richard Adams
Running (1979) ............... Michael Andropolis
It's My Turn (1980) ................... Ben Lewin
The Star Chamber (1983)............ Steven Hardin
Romancing the Stone (1984)........... Jack Colton
A Chorus Line (1985)................... Zack
The Jewel of the Nile (1985)............. Jack Colton
**Fatal Attraction** (1987) .......... Dan Gallagher
  •• 0:16—Brief buns, while pulling his pants down to
  make love with Glenn Close on the kitchen sink.
  • 0:17—Very brief buns while falling into bed with
  Close.
  • 0:22—Brief buns, while taking a shower.
Wall Street (1987) ................. Gordon Gekko
(Academy Award for Best Actor.)
Black Rain (1989)..................... Nick Conklin
The War of the Roses (1989) ........... Oliver Rose
  1:36—Almost buns, while cleaning himself in the bidet.
**Basic Instinct** (1992)............. Det. Nick Curran
(Unrated Director's cut reviewed.)
  •• 0:36—Brief buns, when pulling down his underwear
  to make love with Beth.
  •• 1:10—Buns and very, very brief frontal nudity, while
  on top of Sharon Stone in bed.
  •• 1:12—Brief buns, in overhead mirror over the bed.
  ••• 1:15—Buns, while walking to the bathroom.
  ••• 1:16—Buns, while walking back to the bedroom.

Shining Through (1992) . . . . . . . . . . . . . . . . Ed Leland
Falling Down (1993) . . . . . . . . . . . . . . . . . . . . . . D-FENS
TV:
The Streets of San Francisco (1972-76)
. . . . . . . . . . . . . . . . . . . . . . . . Inspector Steve Keller

# • Douglas, Nick
Video Tapes:
**The Lover's Guide to Sexual Ecstasy: A Sensual
Guide to Lovemaking** (1992)
. . . . . . . . . . . . . . . . . . . . The Intimate Appointment
••• 0:42—Buns, while making love on top of her lover.
• 1:01—Buns, while making love.
••• 1:04—Buns, while making love in G-spot position.

# Dourif, Brad
Films:
**One Flew Over the Cuckoo's Nest** (1975) . . . . . Billy
•• 1:50—Buns in hallway, putting on his pants after
getting caught with Candy.
Eyes of Laura Mars (1978) . . . . . . . . . . . . . . .Tommy Ludlow
Wise Blood (1979; U.S./German). . . . . . . . Hazel Motes
Ragtime (1981). . . . . . . . . . . . . . . . . . . .Younger Brother
Dune (1984) . . . . . . . . . . . . . . . . . . . . . . . Piter De Vries
Blue Velvet (1986). . . . . . . . . . . . . . . . . . . . . Raymond
Impure Thoughts (1986). . . . . . . . . . . Kevin Harrington
Fatal Beauty (1987) . . . . . . . . . . . . . . . . . . . . Leo Nova
Child's Play (1988) . . . . . . . . . . . . . . . .Charles Lee Ray
Mississippi Burning (1988) . . . . . . . . . . . . . Deputy Dell
Sonny Boy (1989) . . . . . . . . . . . . . . . . . . . . . . . Weasel
Spontaneous Combustion (1989) . . . . . . . . . . . . David
The Exorcist III (1990) . . . . . . . . . . . . . . James Venamon
Grim Prairie Tales (1990). . . . . . . . . . . . . . . . . . Farley
Hidden Agenda (1990; British) . . . . . . . . . . . . . . Paul
Stephen King's Graveyard Shift (1990)
. . . . . . . . . . . . . . . . . . . . . . . . . Tucker Cleveland
Body Parts (1991) . . . . . . . . . . . . . . . . . . . .Reno Lacey
Common Bonds (1991) . . . . . . . . . . . . . . . . . . Johnny
Horseplayer (1991) . . . . . . . . . . . . . . . . . .Bud Cowan
Jungle Fever (1991). . . . . . . . . . . . . . . . . . . . . Leslie
London Kills Me (1991; British) . . . . . . . . . Hemingway
Murder Blues (1991) . . . . . . . . . . . . . . . . . John Barnes
Critters 4: They're Invading Your Space (1992) . . Al Bert
Final Judgement (1992) . . . . . . . . . . . . Father Tyrone
Trauma (1992) . . . . . . . . . . . . . . . . . . . . . .Dr. Lloyd
Amos & Andrew (1993) . . . . Officer Donnie Donaldson
Color of Night (1994) . . . . . . . . . . . . . . . . . . . . . . n.a.
Made for Cable TV:
Tales From the Crypt: People Who Live in Brass Hearses
(1993; HBO) . . . . . . . . . . . . . . . . . . . . . . . . . . .Virgil
Miniseries:
Wild Palms (1993). . . . . . . . . . . . . . . . . Chickie Levitt
Made for TV Movies:
Desperado: The Outlaw Wars (1989). . . . . . Camillus Fly
TV:
Studs Lonigan (1979) . . . . . . . . . . . . . . . .Danny O'Neill

# Dow Smith, Shannon
Films:
**Invasion of Privacy** (1992) . . . . . . . . . . . Young Man
(Unrated version reviewed.)
••• 0:02—Buns, in bedroom with Alex's mother while
young Alex watches from the closet.
Video Tapes:
Playboy's Erotic Fantasies III (1993) . . . . . . . . . . . . n.a.

# • Drake, Paul
Films:
Sudden Impact (1983) . . . . . . . . . . . . . . . . . . . . Mick
Beverly Hills Cop (1984). . . . . . . . . . . . . . Holdup Man
**Midnight Cabaret** (1988) . . . . . . . . . . . . The Intruder
•• 0:03—Nude, while walking up steps and into apart-
ment after killing a guy in the street.
• 0:05—More buns, while walking around building.
Sometimes with a G-string, sometimes without.

# Dubac, Bob
Stand-up comedian.
Films:
**Stitches** (1985). . . . . . . . . . . . . . . . . . . .Al Rosenberg
• 0:03—Very brief buns, while walking around in
classroom. Made up to look like a bald corpse.
0:04—Brief buns, while chasing people down hallway. Don't see face. (He's in the middle, holding a
beer can.)

# Duchovny, David
Films:
New Year's Day (1989). . . . . . . . . . . . . . . . . . . . . Billy
**Julia Has Two Lovers** (1990). . . . . . . . . . . . . . Daniel
• 0:42—Frontal nudity, standing outside during Julia's
fantasy. Hard to see because vertical blinds get in the
way. Upper half of buns, while in bed with her (in
B&W).
• 0:54—Brief side view of buns, getting out of bed
and putting underwear on. Long shot.
Don't Tell Mom the Babysitter's Dead (1991). . . . .Bruce
**The Rapture** (1991). . . . . . . . . . . . . . . . . . . . . Randy
••• 0:24—Buns and brief frontal nudity getting out of
bed in Mimi Roger's bedroom.
Beethoven (1992) . . . . . . . . . . . . . . . . . . . . . . Brad
Chaplin (1992; British/U.S.) . . . . . . . . . . . . . . . . Rollie
Ruby (1992). . . . . . . . . . . . . . . . . . . . . Officer Tippit
Venice/Venice (1992) . . . . . . . . . . . . . . . . . . .Dylan
**Kalifornia** (1993). . . . . . . . . . . . . . . . Brian Kessler
(Unrated version reviewed.)
•• 0:34—Buns, while making love on bed in motel
room with Michelle Forbes.
Made for Cable Movies:
Red Shoe Diaries (1992; Showtime) . . . . . . . . . . . .Jake
(Unrated video tape version reviewed.)
Made for TV Movies:
Baby Snatcher (1992). . . . . . . . . . . . . . . . . . . . .David
TV:
The X-Files (1993- ) . . . . . . . . . . . . . . . . . Fox Mulder

## Dukes, David

*Films:*

The Strawberry Statement (1970) . . . . . . . . . . . . Guard
The Wild Party (1975) . . . . . . . . . . . . . James Morrison
A Little Romance (1979) . . . . . . . . . . George De Marco
The First Deadly Sin (1980) . . . . . . . . . . . Daniel Blank
Without a Trace (1983) . . . . . . . . . . . . . Graham Selky
The Men's Club (1986) . . . . . . . . . . . . . . . . . . Phillip
See You in the Morning (1989) . . . . . . . . . . . . . . Peter
A Handmaid's Tale (1990) . . . . . . . . . . . . . . . Doctor
The Rutanga Tapes (1991) . . . . . . . . . . . . .Bo Petersen
*Made for Cable Movies:*
Cat on a Hot Tin Roof (1984; HBO). . . . . . . . . . . .n.a.
The Josephine Baker Story (1991; HBO) . . . . Jo Bouillon
And the Band Played On (1992; HBO)
. . . . . . . . . . . . . . . . . . . . . . . . Dr. Mervyn Silverman
*Made for Cable TV:*
**The Hitchhiker: Remembering Melody**
(1984; HBO) . . . . . . . . . . . . . . . . . . . . . . . . . . . Ted
• 0:05—Buns, while taking a shower.
*Miniseries:*
Beacon Hill (1975) . . . . . . . . . . . . . . . . Robert Lassiter
79 Park Avenue (1977) . . . . . . . . . . . . . . Mike Koshko
The Winds of War (1983) . . . . . . . . . . . . . Leslie Slote
Space (1987) . . . . . . . . . . . . . . . . . Leopold Strabismus
*Made for TV Movies:*
She Woke Up (1992). . . . . . . . . . . . . . . . . . . . . Sloan
*TV:*
Sisters (1991-93). . . . . . . . . . . . . . . . . . . . . . . Wade
The Mommies (1993-94) . . . . . . . . . . . . . . . . . . .n.a.

## Dullea, Keir

*Films:*

David and Lisa (1962) . . . . . . . . . . . . . . . . . . . David
The Fox (1967) . . . . . . . . . . . . . . . . . . . . . . . . . Paul
2001: A Space Odyssey (1968; British/U.S.)
. . . . . . . . . . . . . . . . . . . . . . . . . . . . David Bowman
**Paperback Hero** (1973; Canadian). . . . . . . . . . . Rick
• 0:37—Partial buns, while rolling over in the shower
with Elizabeth Ashley.
• 0:40—Upper half of buns, while sitting up in the
shower.
Brainwaves (1983) . . . . . . . . . . . . . . . . . .Julian Bedford
The Next One (1983) . . . . . . . . . . . . . . . . . . . . Glenn
2010 (1984) . . . . . . . . . . . . . . . . . . . . . Dave Bowman
Blind Date (1984) . . . . . . . . . . . . . . . . . . Dr. Steiger
*a.k.a. Deadly Seduction*
(Not the same 1987 *Blind Date* with Bruce Willis.)
Oh, What a Night (1992) . . . . . . . . . . . . . . . .Thorvalo

## • Dumont, J. K.

*Films:*

**The Pamela Principle** (1992) . . . . . . . . Carl Breeding
(Unrated version reviewed.)
• 0:10—Buns, while making love with Anne in bed.

## Dunn, Matthew Cary

*Films:*

**The Bikini Carwash Company** (1992)
. . . . . . . . . . . . . . . . . . . . . . . . . . . Donovan Drake
(Unrated version reviewed.)
••• 0:44—Buns, while making love with Amy.

## • Dunn, Morrissey

*Films:*

**Cadillac Girls** (1993; Canadian). . . . . . . . . . . . . Miles
• 0:02—Buns, while getting out of bed with Page.

## Dunning, Judd

*Films:*

**Cabin Fever** (1992) . . . . . . . . . . . . . . . . .Jack Reynolds
••• 0:27—Nude in bed with Lenore.
••• 0:33—Buns, making love in bed with Lenore. Long
scene.
••• 0:35—More buns while making love.
••• 0:37—Still more buns while making love.

## Dye, Cameron

*Films:*

Valley Girl (1983) . . . . . . . . . . . . . . . . . . . . . . . .Fred
Body Rock (1984) . . . . . . . . . . . . . . . . . . . . . . E-Z
Heated Vengeance (1984) . . . . . . . . . . . . . . . . Bandit
The Joy of Sex (1984). . . . . . . . . . . . . . . . . Alan Holt
The Last Starfighter (1984). . . . . . . . . . . . . . . . Andy
Fraternity Vacation (1985) . . . . . . . . . . . . .Joe Gillespie
Scenes from the Goldmine (1987) . . . . . . Niles Dresden
Stranded (1987). . . . . . . . . . . . . . . . . . . . . .Lt. Scott
**Out of the Dark** (1988). . . . . . . . . . Kevin Silver/Bobo
• 0:32—Brief buns when Kristi yanks his underwear
down while he is throwing a basketball. Don't see
his face.
Men at Work (1990). . . . . . . . . . . . . . . . . . . Luzinski
*Made for Cable Movies:*
Last Light (1993; Showtime) . . . . . . . . . . . . .1st Inmate
*Made for TV Movies:*
Dark Reflection (1994) . . . . . . . . . . . . . . . . . . . Craig

## • Eagle, Jeff

*Films:*

**Hollywood Hot Tubs** (1984). . . . . . . . . . . . . Cameron
• 0:21—Brief buns, after pulling down his swimsuit to
get into hot tub with Dee-Dee.
Sex Appeal (1986) . . . . . . . . . . . . . . .Donald Cromronic
Slammer Girls (1987). . . . . . . . . . . . . . . . . Harry Wiener

## Earhar, Kirt

*Films:*

**Summer Job** (1989). . . . . . . . . . . . . . . . . . . . . . Tom
• 0:30—Buns in black G-string bikini when his swim
trunks get ripped off.
• 0:43—Buns in G-string underwear getting out of
bed and going to the bathroom.

# • East, Jeff

*Films:*

Tom Sawyer (1973). . . . . . . . . . . . . . Huckleberry Finn
Huckleberry Finn (1974) . . . . . . . . . . . Huckleberry Finn
**The Campus Corpse** (1977). . . . . . . . . . . . . . . Craig
    0:17—Side view of buns in jock strap after getting
    out of van for hazing.
  •• 0:19—Brief buns, while running and falling in the
    woods with Charlie Martin Smith.
  • 0:22—Buns, while running up rocks after Smith has
    broken his leg.
  • 0:23—Buns, while running down the road to get
    help.
  ••• 0:24—Buns, after arriving at cabin and standing out-
    side next to van.
Superman (1978) . . . . . . . . . . . . . . . Young Clark Kent
Klondike Fever (1980). . . . . . . . . . . . . . . . Jack London
Deadly Blessing (1981) . . . . . . . . . . . . . . John Schmidt
Up the Creek (1984) . . . . . . . . . . . . . . . . . . . . . Max
Pumpkinhead (1988) . . . . . . . . . . . . . . . . . . . . Chris

# • Eastwick, Robert

*Films:*

**Strike a Pose** (1993). . . . . . . . . . . . . . . . Nick Carter
  ••• 0:33—Buns, while standing up and making love
    with Miranda.
  •• 1:07—Brief partial frontal nudity while in bed with
    Miranda. Buns while getting out.

# Eastwood, Clint

Director.
Former Mayor of Carmel, California (1986-88).

*Films:*

For a Few Dollars More (1965; Italian/German)
. . . . . . . . . . . . . . . . . . . . The Man With No Name
A Fistful of Dollars (1967; Italian)
. . . . . . . . . . . . . . . . . . . . The Man With No Name
The Good, The Bad, and The Ugly (1967; Italian/
Spanish) . . . . . . . . . . . . . . . . . . . . . . . . . . Joe
Coogan's Bluff (1968) . . . . . . . . . . . . . . . . . Coogan
Hang 'em High (1968) . . . . . . . . . . . . . . . Jed Cooper
Where Eagles Dare (1969; British)
. . . . . . . . . . . . . . . . . Lieutenant Morris Schaffer
Kelly's Heroes (1970). . . . . . . . . . . . . . . . . . . . Kelly
Two Mules for Sister Sara (1970). . . . . . . . . . . . Hogan
The Beguiled (1971) . . . . . . . . . . . . . . . John McBurney
Dirty Harry (1971). . . . . . . . . . . . . . . . Harry Callahan
Play Misty for Me (1971). . . . . . . . . . . . . Dave Garland
Joe Kidd (1972). . . . . . . . . . . . . . . . . . . . . Joe Kidd
High Plains Drifter (1973) . . . . . . . . . . . . .The Stranger
Magnum Force (1973) . . . . . . . . . . . . . Harry Callahan
Thunderbolt and Lightfoot (1974)
. . . . . . . . . . . . . . . John "Thunderbolt" Doherty
The Eiger Sanction (1975). . . . . . . . . Jonathan Hemlock
The Enforcer (1976) . . . . . . . . . . . . . . Harry Callahan
The Outlaw Josey Wales (1976). . . . . . . . . .Josey Wales
The Gauntlet (1977) . . . . . . . . . . . . . . . Ben Shockley
Every Which Way But Loose (1978). . . . . . Philo Beddoe

Escape from Alcatraz (1979). . . . . . . . . . . Frank Morris
    0:07—Buns, while walking down jail hallway with
    two guards, don't see his face, so probably a body
    double.
Any Which Way You Can (1980) . . . . . . . . Philo Beddoe
Bronco Billy (1980) . . . . . . . . . . . . . . . . Bronco Billy
Firefox (1982) . . . . . . . . . . . . . . . . . . . .Mitchell Gant
Honkytonk Man (1982) . . . . . . . . . . . . . . . .Red Stovall
Sudden Impact (1983) . . . . . . . . . . . . . .Harry Callahan
City Heat (1984) . . . . . . . . . . . . . . . Lieutenant Speer
**Tightrope** (1984). . . . . . . . . . . . . . . . . . . Wes Block
  • 0:33—Buns, while on the bed on top of Becky. Slow
    pan, red light, covered with sweat. Possible body
    double because the camera gets out of focus for a
    bit as it pans up his back.
Pale Rider (1985) . . . . . . . . . . . . . . . . . . . Preacher
Heartbreak Ridge (1986) . . . . . . . . . . . . . . Highway
The Dead Pool (1988) . . . . . . . . . . . . .Harry Callahan
Pink Cadillac (1989). . . . . . . . . . . . . . . Tommy Nowak
The Rookie (1990) . . . . . . . . . . . . . . . . Nick Pulovski
White Hunter Black Heart (1990) . . . . . . . . John Wilson
Unforgiven (1992) . . . . . . . . . . . . . . . . William Munny
In the Line of Fire (1993) . . . . . . . . . . . .Frank Horrigan
A Perfect World (1993) . . . . . . . . . . . . . .Red Garnett

*TV:*

Rawhide (1959-66) . . . . . . . . . . . . . . . . Rowdy Yates

# • Eden, Daniel

*Films:*

**Fear No Evil** (1981) . . . . . . . . . . . . . . . . . . . . Tony
  • 0:21—Brief buns, while chasing after Marie in base-
    ment of school building. Long shot.
  •• 0:37—Buns and brief frontal nudity, after getting up
    off the shower floor.
St. Elmo's Fire (1985) . . . . . . . . . . . . . . . Street Tough

# Edwards, Anthony

*Films:*

Fast Times at Ridgemont High (1982) . . . . . Stoner Bud
Heart Like a Wheel (1983)
. . . . . . . . . . . . . . . . . John Muldowney, Age 15-23
Revenge of the Nerds (1984) . . . . . . . . . . . . . .Gilbert
Gotchal (1985) . . . . . . . . . . . . . . . . . .Jonathan Moore
The Sure Thing (1985) . . . . . . . . . . . . . . . . . . .Lance
Top Gun (1986) . . . . . . . . . . . . . . Lt. Nick Bradshaw
Summer Heat (1987) . . . . . . . . . . . . . . Aaron Walston
How I Got Into College (1989). . . . . . . . . Kip Hammet
**Downtown** (1990). . . . . . . . . . . . . . . . Alex Kearney
  • 0:19—Buns, while outside after getting his police
    uniform ripped off.
Delta Heat (1992) . . . . . . . . . . . . . . . . .Mike Bishop
Landslide (1992) . . . . . . . . . . . . . . . . . . .Bob Boyd
Pet Sematary II (1992) . . . . . . . . . . . . . Chase Matthews

*Made for Cable Movies:*

Hometown Boy Makes Good (1990; HBO). . Boyd Geary
Sexual Healing (1993; Showtime) . . . . . . . . . . . .David

*TV:*

It Takes Two (1982-83). . . . . . . . . . . . . . .Andy Quinn
ER (1994- ). . . . . . . . . . . . . . . . . . . . . . . . . . n.a.

## Edwards, Eric

Adult film actor.
*Adult Films:*
**Blonde Ambition** (1980; British) .. Stephen Carlisle III
Nude in hard core sex scenes.

## Eek-A-Mouse

Reggae singer.
*Films:*
**New Jack City** (1991) . . . . . . . . . . . . . . . . . Fat Smitty
• 0:15—Buns, when Wesley Snipes holds a gun to his
head and makes him walk nude outside.

## • Ehlers, Jerome

*Films:*
Quigley Down Under (1990). . . . . . . . . . . . . . . Coogan
**Fatal Bond** (1991; Australian) . . . . . . . . . . Joe Martinez
•• 0:08—Buns and lower frontal nudity while getting
up out of bed.

## • Elliott, Sam

*Films:*
Butch Cassidy and the Sundance Kid (1969)
. . . . . . . . . . . . . . . . . . . . . . . . . . . . . . .Card Player
The Games (1970) . . . . . . . . . . . . . . . . Richie Robinson
Frogs (1972). . . . . . . . . . . . . . . . . . . . . . . Pickett Smith
Molly and Lawless John (1972) . . . . . . . .Johnny Lawler
Lifeguard (1975) . . . . . . . . . . . . . . . . . . . . . . . . . Rick
**The Legacy** (1979; British) . . . . . . . . . . . Pete Danner
*a.k.a. The Legacy of Maggie Walsh*
••• 0:18—Buns, walking to shower. Don't see his face.
Mask (1985) . . . . . . . . . . . . . . . . . . . . . . . . . . . . .Gar
Fatal Beauty (1987). . . . . . . . . . . . . . . . . .Mike Marshak
Shakedown (1988) . . . . . . . . . . . . . . . . . .Richie Marks
Roadhouse (1989). . . . . . . . . . . . . . . . . Wade Garrett
Prancer (1990) . . . . . . . . . . . . . . . . . . . . . . John Riggs
Sibling Rivalry (1990) . . . . . . . . . . . . . . Charles Turner
Rush (1991) . . . . . . . . . . . . . . . . . . . . . . . Larry Dodd
Gettysburg (1993) . . . . . . . . . . . . . General John Buford
Tombstone (1993) . . . . . . . . . . . . . . . . . . . .Virgil Earp
*TV:*
Mission Impossible (1970-71) . . . . . . . . . . . . . . . Doug
Once an Eagle (1976-77) . . . . . . . . . . . . . Sam Damon
The Yellow Rose (1983-84) . . . . . . . . .Chance McKenzie

## Elwes, Cary

*Films:*
Another Country (1984; British) . . . . . . . . . . .Harcourt
Oxford Blues (1984) . . . . . . . . . . . . . . . . . . . . Lionel
The Bride (1985). . . . . . . . . . . . . . . . . . . . . . . . .Josef
**Lady Jane** (1987; British) . . . . . . . . . . Guilford Dudley
• 1:19—Brief buns, while getting out of bed.
The Princess Bride (1987) . . . . . . . Westley the Farmboy
Glory (1989). . . . . . . . . . . . . . . . . . . . . Cabot Forbes
Days of Thunder (1990) . . . . . . . . . . . . . Russ Wheeler
Hot Shots (1991) . . . . . . . . . . . . . . . . . Kent Gregory
Leather Jackets (1991). . . . . . . . . . . . . . . . . . Dobbs
Bram Stoker's Dracula (1992) . . .Lord Arthur Holmwood

**The Crush** (1993). . . . . . . . . . . . . . . . . . . . .Nick Eliot
•• 0:12—Brief buns in bathroom when Darian peeks in.
Don't see his face.
Robin Hood: Men in Tights (1993). . . . . . . .Robin Hood

## Emil, Michael

*Films:*
Tracks (1977). . . . . . . . . . . . . . . . . . . . . . . . . . Gene
**Sitting Ducks** (1978). . . . . . . . . . . . . . . . . . . Simon
•• 0:45—Buns, while getting out of the bathtub.
• 0:58—Buns, after getting out of bed and putting his
pants on to chase Leona.
Can She Bake a Cherry Pie? (1983) . . . . . . . . . . . . . Eli
Always (1984) . . . . . . . . . . . . . . . . . . . David's Brother
Insignificance (1985) . . . . . . . . . . . . . . . .The Professor
Someone To Love (1986) . . . . . . . . . . . . . Mickey Sapir
Deadly Illusion (1987) . . . . . . . . . . Medical Examiner
New Year's Day (1989). . . . . . . . . . . . . Dr. Stadthagen
Operation Lookout (1991) . . . . . . . . Professor Hardwick
Adventures in Spying (1992) . . . . . . Professor Hardwick

## • Enos, John

*Films:*
Death Becomes Her (1992) . . . . . . . . .Lisle's Bodyguard
Demolition Man (1993) . . . . . . . . . . . . . . . . .Prisoner
*Made for Cable TV:*
**Red Shoe Diaries: Naked in the Moonlight**
(1994; Showtime) . . . . . . . . . . . . . . . . . . . . .James
•• 0:14—Brief side view of buns, while making love
with Camille.
••• 0:22—Brief buns, several times while making love.

## • Esposito, Giancarlo

*Films:*
Running (1979) . . . . . . . . . . . . . Puerto Rican Teenager
**Taps** (1981). . . . . . . . . . . . . . . . . . . . . . J.C. Pierce
• 1:24—Brief upper half of buns in shower when the
water is turned off.
Trading Places (1983). . . . . . . . . . . . . . . . . .Cell Mate
The Cotton Club (1984). . . . . . . . . . . . . . Bumpy Hood
Desperately Seeking Susan (1985) . . . . . . .Street Vendor
Maximum Overdrive (1986). . . . . . . . . . . .Video Player
School Daze (1988) . . . . . . . . . . . . . . . . . Julian Eaves
Do the Right Thing (1989). . . . . . . . . . . . . Buggin Out
King of New York (1990) . . . . . . . . . . . . . . . . . .Lance
Mo' Better Blues (1990) . . . . . . . . . . . .Left Hand Lacey
Harley Davidson and The Marlboro Man (1991)
. . . . . . . . . . . . . . . . . . . . . . . . . . . . . . . .Jimmy Jiles
Amos & Andrew (1993) . . . . . . . . . . Rev. Fenton Brunch

## Esposito, J. Michael

*Films:*
**Fatal Skies** (1989) . . . . . . . . . . . . . . . . . . . . . .Duane
• 0:31—Buns, while standing in the water, then diving
in.

## Estevez, Emilio

Son of actor Martin Sheen.
Brother of actor Charlie Sheen.
Ex-husband of choreographer/singer Paula Abdul.
*Films:*
Tex (1982) . . . . . . . . . . . . . . . . . . . . . . Johnny Collins
Nightmares (1983) . . . . . . . . . . . . . . . . . . . . . . . . . J. J.
The Outsiders (1983) . . . . . . . . . . . . . Two-Bit Matthews
Repo Man (1984) . . . . . . . . . . . . . . . . . . . . . . . . . Otto
The Breakfast Club (1985). . . . . . . . . . . . Andrew Clark
St. Elmo's Fire (1985) . . . . . . . . . . . . . . . . . . . . Kirbo
That Was Then... This Is Now (1985). . . . . Mark Jennings
Maximum Overdrive (1986) . . . . . . . . . . . Bill Robinson
Wisdom (1986). . . . . . . . . . . . . . . . . . . . John Wisdom
Stakeout (1987) . . . . . . . . . . . . . . . . . . . . Bill Reimers
Never on Tuesday (1988) . . Uncredited Tow Truck Driver
**Young Guns** (1988). . . William H. Bonney (Billy the Kid)
 • 1:19—Brief buns while standing up in the bathtub.
Men at Work (1990) . . . . . . . . . . . . . . . James St. James
**Young Guns II** (1990)
 . . . . . . . . . . . . . . . William H. Bonney (Billy the Kid)
 •• 1:00—Buns, while getting up out of bed, putting his
 pants on.
Freejack (1992) . . . . . . . . . . . . . . . . . . . . Alex Furlong
The Mighty Ducks (1992) . . . . . . . . . . . Gordon Bombay
Another Stakeout (1993). . . . . . . . . . . . . Bill Reimers
Judgement Night (1993). . . . . . . . . . . . . . Frank Wyatt
**Loaded Weapon 1** (1993) . . . . . . . . . . . . . . Jack Colt
 •• 0:56—Buns, getting out of bed. It looks like he has
 his body all oiled up.
D2: The Mighty Ducks (1994). . . . . . . . Gordon Bombay

## Eubanks, Corey Michael

Son of producer/*The Newlywed Game* host Bob Eubanks.
*Films:*
**Payback** (1991). . . . . . . . . . . . . . . . . . . . . . . Clinton
 • 0:49—Brief buns, while putting his pants on after
 jerks tip his trailer over.
**Forced to Kill** (1993) . . . . . . . . . . . . . . . . . . Johnny
 •• 0:17—Buns, after Heather steals his towel. Don't see
 his face.

## Evans, Brian

*Films:*
**The Book of Love** (1991). . . . . . . . . . . . . . . Schank
 • 0:21—Buns, while tied up to cot with candle stuck
 in his rear end by the bad guys.

## Everett, Rupert

*Films:*
Dance with a Stranger (1985; British) . . . . David Blakely
Duet for One (1987) . . . . . . . . . . . Constantine Kassanis
Hearts of Fire (1987) . . . . . . . . . . . . . . . . . James Colt
The Right Hand Man (1987) . . . . . . . . Harry Ironminster
**The Comfort of Strangers** (1991) . . . . . . . . . . Colin
 •• 0:47—Buns, while walking around the room, look-
 ing for his clothes.
 • 1:05—Buns, while making love with Natasha Rich-
 ardson on bed. Lit with blue light.

## Fahey, Jeff

*Films:*
Silverado (1985). . . . . . . . . . . . . . . . . . . . . . . Tyree
Psycho III (1986) . . . . . . . . . . . . . . . . . . . . . . Duane
**Backfire** (1987) . . . . . . . . . . . . . . . . . . . . . Donnie
 • 0:22—Brief, partial buns while taking a shower, then
 very brief, out of focus frontal nudity in shower
 when blood starts to gush out of the shower head.
Split Decisions (1988) . . . . . . . . . . . . . . Ray McGuinn
Impulse (1989) . . . . . . . . . . . . . . . . . . . . . . . . Stan
The Serpent of Death (1989) . . . . . . . . . . . Jake Bonner
True Blood (1989) . . . . . . . . . . . Raymond Trueblood
Curiosity Kills (1990) . . . . . . . . . . . . . . . . . Matthew
The Last of the Finest (1990) . . . . . . . . . Rick Rodrigues
White Hunter Black Heart (1990) . . . . . . . . . Pete Verrill
Body Parts (1991) . . . . . . . . . . . . . . . . Bill Crushank
Iron Maze (1991). . . . . . . . . . . . . . . . . . . . . . Barry
The Lawnmower Man (1992). . . . . . . . . . . . Jobe Smith
 (Unrated Director's cut reviewed.)
Freefall (1993) . . . . . . . . . . . . . . . . . . . . Dea Dellum
Quick (1993) . . . . . . . . . . . . . . . . . . . . . . . Muncie
**Woman of Desire** (1993) . . . . . . . . . . . . . Jack Lynch
 • 0:01—Buns, while lying face down on sand at
 beach.
Wyatt Earp (1994) . . . . . . . . . . . . . . . . . . . . . n.a.
*Made for Cable Movies:*
**Sketch Artist** (1992; Showtime) . . . . . . . . . . . . Jack
 • 0:52—Brief upper half of buns in bed on top of Sean
 Young.
Blindsided (1993; USA) . . . . . . . . . . . . . Frank McKenna
**The Hit List** (1993; Showtime). . . . . . . . . Charlie Pike
 • 1:00—Buns, while making love with (supposedly)
 Yancy Butler. Don't see his face well.
*Made for Cable TV:*
Iran: Days of Crisis (1991; TNT) . . . . . . . . . . . . . . n.a.
*Made for TV Movies:*
Parker Kane (1990) . . . . . . . . . . . . . . . . . Parker Kane
In the Company of Darkness (1993). . . . . . Will McCaid

## Fairbanks Fogg, Kirk

*Films:*
**Alien Space Avenger** (1988) . . . . . . . . . . . . . . Matt
 • 0:22—Buns, while walking out of apartment after
 Ginny.

## Falconeti, Sonny

*Films:*
**Angel of Passion** (1991). . . . . . . . . . . . . . . . . Will
 • 0:22—Buns frolicking in the surf with Carol while
 wearing a G-string.

## Falk, Peter

*Films:*
Penelope (1966) . . . . . . . . . . . . . . . Lieutenant Bixbee
Anzio (1968; Italian). . . . . . . . . . . . . Corporal Rabinoff
Husbands (1970) . . . . . . . . . . . . . . . . . . . . . . Archie
Woman Under the Influence (1974). . . . . Nick Longhetti
Murder by Death (1976) . . . . . . . . . . . . . Sam Diamond
The Brink's Job (1978) . . . . . . . . . . . . . . . . Tony Pino

The Cheap Detective (1978) . . . . . . . . Lou Peckinpaugh
The In-Laws (1979) . . . . . . . . . . . . . . . . . . Vince Ricardo
...All the Marbles (1981) . . . . . . . . . . . . . . . . . . Harry
*a.k.a. The California Dolls*
Big Trouble (1986) . . . . . . . . . . . . . . . . . . Steve Rickey
Wings of Desire (1987) . . . . . . . . . . . . . . . . .Himself
*a.k.a. Der Himmel Uber Berlin*
Cookie (1989) . . . . . . . . . . . . .Dominick "Dino" Capisco
**In the Spirit** (1990) . . . . . . . . . . . . . . . . . Roger Flan
•• 0:17—Buns, three times while standing up, a little
embarrassed, talking to Crystal.
Tune in Tomorrow (1990) . . . . . . . . . Pedro Carmichael
*a.k.a. Aunt Julia and the Scriptwriter*
The Player (1992) . . . . . . . . . . . . . . . . . . . . . Cameo
Faraway, So Close (1993; German) . . . . . . . . . . Himself
*Made for TV Movies:*
Death Hits the Jackpot (1991) . . . . . . . . . . . . Columbo
Columbo: No Time To Die (1992) . . . . . . . . . Columbo
Columbo: It's All in the Game (1993) . . . . .Lt. Columbo
*TV:*
The Untouchables (1959-63). . . . . . . . . . . . Nate Selko
Columbo (1971-77) . . . . . . . . . . .Lieutenant Columbo

## Farmer, Gary
*Films:*
Police Academy (1984) . . . . . . . . .Sidewalk Store Owner
**Powwow Highway** (1988; U.S./British)
. . . . . . . . . . . . . . . . . . . . . . . . . . . . . . Philbert Bono
•• 1:00—Buns, while in bedroom getting out of bed to
wake up Buddy.
Renegades (1989) . . . . . . . . . . . . . . . . . . . . .George
Still Life (1990) . . . . . . . . . . . . . . . . . . . . . . . Billy
Blown Away (1992) . . . . . . . . . . . . . . . . . . Anderson
(Unrated version reviewed.)
The Dark Wind (1993)
. . . . . . . . . . . . . . . . .Sheriff Albert "Cowboy" Dashee
*Made for TV Movies:*
Plymouth (1991) . . . . . . . . . . . . . . . . . . . . . . .Todd

## •Faulkner, Graham
*Films:*
Brother Sun, Sister Moon (1973) . . . . . . . . . . . . . .n.a.
**Priest of Love** (1980) . . . . . . . . . . . . . .Cornish Farmer
• 0:52—Buns, after taking off clothes and getting into
water with D.H. Lawrence.
•• 0:55—Nude, getting off rock and getting dressed
when soldiers start harassing him.

## Fawcett, Greg
*Films:*
**Naked Instinct** (1993) . . . . . . . . . . . . . .Football Jock
••• 0:59—Buns, making love in bathtub with Joanne.

## Feldman, Corey
*Films:*
Time After Time (1979; British) . . . . . . . Boy at Museum
Friday the 13th, Part IV—The Final Chapter (1984)
. . . . . . . . . . . . . . . . . . . . . . . . . . . . . . . .Tommy
Gremlins (1984) . . . . . . . . . . . . . . . . . . . . . . Pete

Friday the 13th, Part V—A New Beginning (1985)
. . . . . . . . . . . . . . . . . . . . . . . . . . .Tommay at 12
The Goonies (1985) . . . . . . . . . . . . . . . . . . . .Mouth
Stephen King's "Silver Bullet" (1985) . . . . Marty Coslaw
The Lost Boys (1987) . . . . . . . . . . . . . . . . . .Edgar Frog
License to Drive (1988) . . . . . . . . . . . . . . . . . . Dean
The 'burbs (1989) . . . . . . . . . . . . . . . . . Ricky Butler
Dream A Little Dream (1989) . . . . . . . . . . . Bobby Keller
Edge of Honor (1990) . . . . . . . . . . . . . . . . . Butler
Rock 'n' Roll High School Forever (1990) . . . .Jesse Davis
**Blown Away** (1992). . . . . . . . . . . . . . . . . . . . . .Wes
(Unrated version reviewed.)
• 1:26—Buns, twice, getting out of bed. Dark, don't
see his face.
Meatballs 4 (1992) . . . . . . . . . . . . . . . . . Ricky Wade
Round Trip to Heaven (1992) . . . . . . . . . . . . . Larry
Lipstick Camera (1993) . . . . . . . . . . . . . . Joule Iverson
Loaded Weapon 1 (1993). . . . . . . . . . . . . Young Cop
Stepmonster (1993) . . . . . . . . . . . . . . . . . . . Phlegm
*TV:*
The Bad News Bears (1979-80) . . . . . . . . . . Regi Tower
Madame's Place (1982) . . . . . . . . . . . . . . . . .Buzzy

## Feldman, Marty
*Films:*
**Think Dirty** . . . . . . . . . . . . . . . . . . . . . . . . Teddy
*a.k.a. Every Home Should Have One*
•• 0:44—Buns, while running around in a "documentary" about Sweden with Julie Ege, then in a "Swedish" film.
**The Adventure of Sherlock Holmes' Smarter
Brother** (1975) . . . . . . . . . . . . . . . . . .Orville Sacker
•• 1:04—Buns, in ballroom with Gene Wilder, after a
buzz saw removes the back of their tuxedos.
*TV:*
The Marty Feldman Comedy Machine (1972) . . . . Host

## •Ferrer, Miguel
Husband of actress Leilani Sarelle.
Son of actor José Ferrer and actress Rosemary Clooney.
*Films:*
Lovelines (1984). . . . . . . . . . . . . . . . . . . . . Dragon
Star Trek III: The Search for Spock (1984)
. . . . . . . . . . . . . . . . . . . . . 1st Officer, USS Excelsior
Robocop (1987). . . . . . . . . . . . . . . . . .Robert Morton
Valentino Returns (1988) . . . . . . . . . . . . . . . . n.a.
Deepstar Six (1989) . . . . . . . . . . . . . . . . . . .Snyder
The Guardian (1990) . . . . . . . . . . . . . . . .Ralph Hess
Revenge (1990) . . . . . . . . . . . . . . . . . . . . .Amador
**The Harvest** (1992) . . . . . . . . . . . . . . . . Charlie Pope
• 1:21—Brief partial frontal nudity under sheets when
getting out of bed and putting on pants.
Twin Peaks: Fire Walk With Me (1992) . Albert Rosenfield
Another Stakeout (1993) . . . . . . . . . . . .Tony Castellano
Hot Shots! Part Deux (1993) . . . . . . . . . . . . Harbinger
Point of No Return (1993) . . . . . . . . . . . . . . Kaufman
*Made for Cable Movies:*
Incident at Deception Ridge (1994; USA) . . . . . . . . n.a.
Royce (1994; Showtime) . . . . . . . . . . . . . . .Gribbon

*TV:*
Shannon's Deal (1990-91) . . . . . . . . . DA Todd Spurrier
Broken Badges (1990-91) . . . . . . . . Deau Jack Bowman
Twin Peaks (1990-91) . . . . . . . . . . . . Albert Rosenfield

## Ferris, Larry
*Video Tapes:*
**Penthouse Love Stories** (1986) . . . . . . . Ecstacize Man
 •• 0:32—Frontal nudity and buns, with a woman in the shower.

## • Field, Norman
*Films:*
**Psycho From Texas** (1981) . . . . . . . . . . . . Salesman
 • 0:09—Buns, while making love with Wheeler's mother on bed.

## Field, Todd
a.k.a. William Field.
*Films:*
Radio Days (1987). . . . . . . . . . . . . . . . . . . . . Crooner
The End of Innocence (1989) . . . . . . . . . . . . . . . . n.a.
Eye of the Eagle II: Inside the Enemy (1989)
. . . . . . . . . . . . . . . . . . . . . . . . . . . . Anthony Glenn
Fat Man and Little Boy (1989). . . . . . . . . Robert Wilson
Gross Anatomy (1989) . . . . . . . . . . . . David Schreiner
**Back to Back** (1990). . . . . . . . . . . . . . . . . Todd Brand
 •• 0:33—Buns, while walking to and jumping into swimming pool.
Full Fathom Five (1990) . . . . . . . . . . . . . . . Johnson
Queens Logic (1991). . . . . . . . . . . . . . . . . . . . Cecil
jas Ruby in Paradise (1993) . . . . . . . . . . Mike McCaslin
*TV:*
Take Five (1987) . . . . . . . . . . . . . . . . . . . . Kevin Davis
Bakersfield P.D. (1993- ) . . . . . . . . . . . . . . . . . Lewis

## Fields, Robert
*Films:*
They Shoot Horses, Don't They? (1969) . . . . . . . . . . Joel
**The Sporting Club** (1971) . . . . . . . . . . Verner Stanton
 • 0:24—Buns, mooning the President out the window of a bus.
Rhinoceros (1973). . . . . . . . . . . . . . . . . . . Logician
Star 80 (1983). . . . . . . . . . . . . . . . . . . . . Director
Anna (1987) . . . . . . . . . . . . . . . . . . . . . . . . Daniel

## Finney, Albert
*Films:*
Wolfen (1981). . . . . . . . . . . . . . . . . . . . Dewey Wilson
Shoot the Moon (1982) . . . . . . . . . . . . George Dunlap
**Under the Volcano** (1984). . . . . . . . . Geoffrey Firmin
 ••• 0:49—Buns and brief frontal nudity in bathroom with Jacqueline Bisset and Anthony Andrews when they try to give him a shower.
 •• 0:52—Buns and very brief frontal nudity, putting on his underwear.
Orphans (1987) . . . . . . . . . . . . . . . . . . . . . Harold
Miller's Crossing (1990) . . . . . . . . . . . . . . . . . . Leo
The Playboys (1992) . . . . . . . . . . . . . . . . . . Hegarty

Rich in Love (1992) . . . . . . . . . . . . . . . . Warren Odom
*Made for Cable Movies:*
The Endless Game (1990; Showtime) . . . . . Alec Hillsden

## Firth, Colin
*Films:*
1919 (1984; British) . . . . . . . . . . . . . . Young Alexander
Another Country (1984; British) . . . . . . . . Tommy Judd
Apartment Zero (1988) . . . . . . . . . . . . . . Adrian LeDuc
A Month in the Country (1988; British) . . . . . . . . Birkin
Valmont (1989) . . . . . . . . . . . . . . . . . . . . . Valmont
Femme Fatale (1990) . . . . . . . . . . . . . . Joseph Prince
The Pleasure Principal (1991; British) . . . . . . . . . . . Dick
The Hour of the Pig (1993; British/French)
. . . . . . . . . . . . . . . . . . . . . . . . Richard Courtois
*Made for Cable Movies:*
**Hostages** (1993; HBO) . . . . . . . . . . . . John McCarthy
 • 0:09—Buns, while wearing blindfold, getting undressed and pushed into jail cell by captors.

## Firth, Peter
*Films:*
**Equus** (1977) . . . . . . . . . . . . . . . . . . . . . Alan Strang
 • 1:19—Frontal nudity standing in a field with a horse.
 ••• 2:00—Nude in loft above the horses in orange light with Jenny Agutter. Long scene.
**Joseph Andrews** (1977; British/French)
. . . . . . . . . . . . . . . . . . . . . . . . . Joseph Andrews
 •• 0:26—Buns, getting his clothes stolen by two guys in the woods.
 •• 0:27—More buns, while lying in the woods when discovered by a passing carriage. Very brief frontal nudity while walking to road. Buns when putting a coat on.
Tess (1979; French/British) . . . . . . . . . . . . Angel Clare
When Ya Comin' Back Red Ryder (1979)
. . . . . . . . . . . . . . . . . . . . . . . . . Stephen Ryder
 (Not available on video tape.)
Lifeforce (1985) . . . . . . . . . . . . . . . . . . . . . . Caine
Letter to Brezhnev (1986; British) . . . . . . . . . . . . Peter
Innocent Victim (1988) . . . . . . . . . . . . . . . . Terence
The Hunt for Red October (1990) . . . . . . . . . Ivan Putin
Shadowlands (1993; British). . . . . . . . . . . Doctor Craig
*Made for TV Movies:*
The Incident (1989) . . . . . . . . . . . . . . . . . . . . . n.a.
*Magazines:*
**Playboy** (Nov 1977) . . . . . . . . . . Sex in Cinema 1977
 • 157—Upper part of buns, while on horseback from *Equus*.

## • Fish, Troy
*Films:*
**Madman** (1982). . . . . . . . . . . . . . . . . . . . . . . . T.P.
 • 0:24—Brief buns, while getting into hot tub with Betsy.

# • Fisher, Don

*Video Tapes:*

**The Girls of Penthouse, Volume 2** (1993)

. . . . . . . . . . . . . . . . . . . . . . . . . . . . . . . Nightstalker

••• 0:41—Buns, while making love with his lover in alley.

# Fitzpatrick, Bob

*Films:*

Deranged (1987) . . . . . . . . . . . . . . . . . . . . . . . . Valet

**If Looks Could Kill** (1987) . . . . . . . . . . . . . . Doorman

••• 0:18—Buns, while undressing and getting into bed with the maid.

# Fletcher, Dexter

*Films:*

Bugsy Malone (1976) . . . . . . . . . . . . . . . . . . . Baby Face

The Elephant Man (1980) . . . . . . . . . . . . . . . . Bytes' Boy

The Long Good Friday (1980; British) . . . . . . . . . . . Kid

The Bounty (1984) . . . . . . . . . . . . . . . . . . . . . . . Ellison

Revolution (1986) . . . . . . . . . . . . . . . . . . . . Ned Dobb

Lionheart (1987) . . . . . . . . . . . . . . . . . . . . . . Michael

**The Rachel Papers** (1989; British) . . . Charles Highway

• 0:58—Very brief buns, while jumping into bed with Ione Skye.

Twisted Obsession (1990) . . . . . . . . . . Malcolm Greene

# Flower, George "Buck"

a.k.a. C. D. LaFleure.

*Films:*

Bad Georgia Road . . . . . . . . . . . . . . . . . . . . . . . Spiker

**Innocent Sally** (1973) . . . . . . . . . . . . . . . . . . . . . Toby

*a.k.a. The Dirty Mind of Young Sally*

• 0:50—Brief frontal nudity, changing places with Sally.

••• 0:53—Buns, while making love on top of Sally in back of van.

**Video Vixens** (1973) . . . . . . . . . . . . . . . . . . Rex Boorski

•• 0:52—Frontal nudity taking off his pants, then buns in bed with actress during filming of a movie. In B&W.

Delinquent School Girls (1974) . . . . . . . . . . . . . . . Earl

Alice Goodbody (1975) . . . . . . . . . . . . . . Roger Merkel

Johnny Firecloud (1975) . . . . . . . . . . . . . . . . . . Wade

Flicks (1981) . . . . . . . . . . . . . . . . . . . . . . . . . . . n.a.

Cheerleader Camp (1987) . . . . . . . . . . . . . . . . . . . Pop

*a.k.a. Bloody Pom Poms*

Code Name Zebra (1987) . . . . . . . . . . . . . . . . . Bundy

Party Favors (1987) . . . . . . . . . . . . . . . . . . . . . . . Pop

Takin' It All Off (1987) . . . . . . . . . . . . . . Allison's Father

Berserker (1988) . . . . . . . . . . . . . . . . . . . . . . . . . n.a.

Mac and Me (1988) . . . . . . . . . . . . . . . Security Guard

Sorority Babes in the Slimeball Bowl-O-Rama (1988)

. . . . . . . . . . . . . . . . . . . . . . . . . . . . . . . . . . Janitor

They Live (1988) . . . . . . . . . . . . . . . . . . . . . . . Drifter

Back to the Future, Part II (1989) . . . . . . . . . . . . . Bum

Blood Games (1989) . . . . . . . . . . . . . . . . . . . . . . n.a.

Nerds of a Feather (1989) . . . . . . . . . . . . . Bed Patient

Relentless (1989) . . . . . . . . . . . . . . . . . . . . . . . . n.a.

Sundown: The Vampire in Retreat (1989) . . . . . . . Bailey

The Turn-On (1989) . . . . . . . . . . Guy Giving Directions

*a.k.a. Le Clic*

Dragonfight (1990) . . . . . . . . . . . . . . . . . . . . . Jericho

Masters of Menace (1990) . . . . . Sheriff Hayward C. Julip

Puppet Master II (1990) . . . . . . . . . . . . . . . . Matthew

976-EVIL II: The Astral Factor (1991) . . . . . . . . . Turrell

Mirror Images (1991) . . . . . . . . . . . . . . . . . . Wolfman

Soldier's Fortune (1991) . . . . . . . . . . . . . . . . . . T. Max

Waxwork II: Lost in Time (1991) . . . . . . . . . Stepfather

Munchie (1992) . . . . . . . . . . . . . . . . . . . Rich Tramp

Warlock: The Armageddon (1993) . . . . . . Man in Crowd

*Made for Cable TV:*

John Carpenter's Body Bags (1993; Showtime)

. . . . . . . . . . . . . . . . . . . . . The Gas Station/Stranger

*Video Tapes:*

Inside Out 2 (1992)

. . . . . . . . Farmer/There's This Traveling Salesman, See

(Unrated version reviewed.)

# • Fonda, Peter

Son of actor Henry Fonda.

Father of actress Bridget Fonda.

*Films:*

Lilith (1964) . . . . . . . . . . . . . . . . . . . Stephen Evshevsky

The Wild Angels (1966) . . . . . . . . . . . . . . Heavenly Blues

**The Trip** (1967) . . . . . . . . . . . . . . . . . . . . Paul Groves

•• 0:27—Buns, while getting out of the swimming pool and being helped into the house.

Easy Rider (1969) . . . . . . . . . . . . . . . . . . . . . . . Wyatt

The Last Movie (1971) . . . . . . . . . . . . . . . . . . . Sheriff

Dirty Mary, Crazy Larry (1974) . . . . . . . . . . . . . . Larry

Killer Force (1975; Swiss/Irish) . . . . . . . . . Mike Bradley

Race with the Devil (1975) . . . . . . . . . . . . . . . . Roger

Fighting Mad (1976) . . . . . . . . . . . . . . . . . . . . . Tom

Futureworld (1976) . . . . . . . . . . . . . . Chuck Browning

High-Ballin' (1978) . . . . . . . . . . . . . . . . . . . . . . Rane

Wanda Nevada (1979) . . . . . . . . . . Beaudray Demerille

Split Image (1982) . . . . . . . . . . . . . . . . . . Kirklander

Spasms (1983; Canadian) . . . . . . . Dr. Thomas Brasilian

Certain Fury (1985) . . . . . . . . . . . . . . . . . . . Rodney

Fatal Mission (1990) . . . . . . . . . . . . . . . Ken Andrews

South Beach (1992) . . . . . . . . . . . . . . . . . . . . . . Jake

Bodies, Rest & Motion (1993) . . . . . . . Motorcycle Rider

Deadfall (1993) . . . . . . . . . . . . . . . . . . . . . . . . . n.a.

**Molly & Gina** (1993) . . . . . . . . . . . . . . . . . . . . Larry

••• 1:06—Buns, getting out of bed to look out the window.

*Magazines:*

**Playboy** (Nov 1976) . . . . . . . . . . Sex in Cinema 1976

• 146—Partial frontal nudity in photo from *Fighting Mad.*

# Forster, Robert

*Films:*

Justine (1969; Italian/Spanish) . . . . . . . . . . . . . Narouz

**Medium Cool** (1969) . . . . . . . . . . . . . . . . . . . . John

•• 0:36—Nude, running around the house frolicking with Ruth.

The Don is Dead (1973) . . . . . . . . . . . . . . . . . . Frank
Avalanche (1978) . . . . . . . . . . . . . . . . . . . . Nick Thorne
The Black Hole (1979). . . . . . . . . . . Capt. Dan Holland
**Vigilante** (1983) . . . . . . . . . . . . . . . . . . . . . . . . . Eddie
•• 0:55—Buns, in the prison showers with other prisoners (he's on the right.)
Hollywood Harry (1985) . . . . . . . . . . . . . . . Harry Petry
The Delta Force (1986) . . . . . . . . . . . . . . . . . . . . Abdul
The Banker (1989) . . . . . . . . . . . . . . . . . . . . . . . Dan
Satan's Princess (1989) . . . . . . . . . . . . . . . Lou Cherney
Committed (1990) . . . . . . . . . . . . . . . . . . . . Desmond
29th Street (1991) . . . . . . . . . . . . . Sergeant Tartaglia
Diplomatic Immunity (1991). . . . . . . . . . . . Stonebridge
In Between (1991) . . . . . . . . . . . . . . . . . . . . . . Paul
South Beach (1992) . . . . . . . . . . . . . . . . . . . . . . Ted
American Yakuza (1993) . . . . . . . . . . . . . . . . . Littman
Body Chemistry 3: Point of Seduction (1993)
. . . . . . . . . . . . . . . . . . . . . . . . . . . . . . . Bob Sibley
Maniac Cop 3: Badge of Silence (1993) . . . . . Dr. Powell
*TV:*
Banyon (1972-73). . . . . . . . . . . . . . . Miles C. Banyon
Nakia (1974). . . . . . . . . . . . . . . . . Deputy Nakia Parker
Once a Hero (1979) . . . . . . . . . . . . . . . . . . . Gumshoe

## Fox, Edward

Brother of actor James Fox.
*Films:*
The Long Duel (1967; British) . . . . . . . . . . . Hardwicke
**Day of the Jackal** (1973) . . . . . . . . . . . . . . The Jackal
• 1:40—Brief buns, twice, while in bedroom after killing Colette. Dark.
A Doll's House (1973; British) . . . . . . . . . . . . Krogstad
A Bridge Too Far (1977; British). . . . . . Lt. Gen. Horrocks
The Duellists (1977; British). . . . . . . . . . . . Col. Raynard
Soldier of Orange (1977; Dutch). . . . . . . . . Col. Rafelli
The Squeeze (1977; British). . . . . . . . . . . . . Foreman
The Big Sleep (1978; British) . . . . . . . . . . . . Joe Brody
The Cat and The Canary (1978; British). . . . . . Hendricks
Force Ten from Navarone (1978) . . . . . . . . . . . Miller
Nighthawks (1981) . . . . . . . . . . . . . . . . . . A.T.A.C. Man
Gandhi (1982) . . . . . . . . . . . . . . . . . . . . . Gen. Dyer
Never Say Never Again (1983) . . . . . . . . . . . . . . . . M
The Bounty (1984) . . . . . . . . . . . . . Captain Greetham
The Shooting Party (1985; British). . Lord Gilbert Hartup
Wild Geese II (1985; British) . . . . . . . . . . . Alex Faulkne

## Fox, James

a.k.a. William Fox.
Brother of actor Edward Fox.
*Films:*
The Miniver Story (1950) . . . . . . . . . . . . . . . . . Toby
The Lavender Hill Mob (1951; British) . . . . . . . . Gregory
The Chase (1966) . . . . . . . . . . . . . Jason "Jake" Rogers
Thoroughly Modern Millie (1967) . . . . . . . Jimmy Smith
Isadora (1968; British). . . . . . . . . . . . . . Gordon Craig
**Performance** (1970). . . . . . . . . . . . . . . . . . . . Chas
• 0:00—Very brief frontal nudity and buns while making love with a woman. Don't see his face.
• 0:02—Buns, while getting up next to his girlfriend.

• 0:24—Brief buns, while getting roughed up by bad guys.
Greystoke: The Legend of Tarzan, Lord of the Apes (1984) . . . . . . . . . . . . . . . . . . . . . . . . Lord Eskar
A Passage to India (1984; British) . . . . . . Richard Fielding
Absolute Beginners (1986; British) . . . Henley of Mayfair
The Whistle Blower (1987; British) . . . . . . . . . . . Lord
The Mighty Quinn (1989) . . . . . . . . . . . . . . . . Elgin
Afraid of the Dark (1992; British/French) . . . . . . . Frank
Hostage (1992) . . . . . . . . . . . . . . . . . . . . . Paynter
Patriot Games (1992). . . . . . . . . . . . . . . Lord Holmes
The Remains of the Day (1993; British/U.S.)
. . . . . . . . . . . . . . . . . . . . . . . . . Lord Darlington
*Made for Cable Movies:*
Doomsday Gun (1994; HBO) . . . . . . . . . . Whittington
*Made for TV Movies:*
Fall From Grace (1994). . . . . . . . . Colonel Henry Ridley

## •Fox, Michael J.

*Films:*
Midnight Madness (1980) . . . . . . . . . . . . . . . . Scott
Back to the Future (1985) . . . . . . . . . . . . Marty McFly
Teen Wolf (1985) . . . . . . . . . . . . . . . . . Scott Howard
Light of Day (1987) . . . . . . . . . . . . . . . . . Joe Rasnick
The Secret of My Success (1987) . . . . . . . Bentley Foster
Back to the Future, Part II (1989)
. . . . . . . . Marty McFly/Marty McFly Jr./Marlene McFly
Casualties of War (1989) . . . . . . . . . . . . . PFC Eriksson
Back to the Future, Part III (1990)
. . . . . . . . . . . . . . . . . . . . Marty McFly/Seamus McFly
Doc Hollywood (1991). . . . . . . . . . . . . . . Ben Stone
The Hard Way (1991). . . . . . . . . . . . . . . . Nick Lang
The Concierge (1993) . . . . . . . . . . . . . . Doug Ireland
For Love or Money (1993) . . . . . . . . . . . . . . . . n.a.
**Greedy** (1993) . . . . . . . . . . . . . . . . . . . . . . . Daniel
•• 0:28—Buns, after taking off his underwear, then leaving the hotel room and coming back in.
••• 0:30—Buns, while opening the door to greet Laura.
Life With Mikey (1993). . . . . . . . . . . . . . . . . . n.a.
*Made for Cable TV:*
Tales From the Crypt: The Trap (1991; HBO)
. . . . . . . . . . . . . . . . . . . . . . . . . . . . Prosecutor
*Made for TV Movies:*
Poison Ivy (1985). . . . . . . . . . . . . . . . . . . . . . n.a.
*TV:*
Palmertown, U.S.A. (1980-81) . . . . . . . . . Willy-Joe Hall
Family Ties (1982-89). . . . . . . . . . . . . . Alex P. Keaton

## Frank, Billy

*Films:*
Grotesque (1987). . . . . . . . . . . . . . . . . . . . . . n.a.
**Nudity Required** (1989) . . . . . . . . . . . . . . . . Buddy
••• 0:32—Buns, while walking around bathtub and talking to Scammer, then jumping into tub.
• 0:57—Side view of buns, behind textured shower door with Julie Newmar.
Lady Avenger (1991) . . . . . . . . . . . . . . . . . . . Arnie

# • Fraser, Brendan
*Films:*
Dogfight (1991) . . . . . . . . . . . . . . . . . . . . . . . .1st Sailor
Encino Man (1992) . . . . . . . . . . . . . . . . . . . . . . . . Link
**School Ties** (1992) . . . . . . . . . . . . . . . . . . David Greene
 •• 1:09—Buns, in the showers with two other guys
 (He's in the middle).
Twenty Bucks (1993). . . . . . . . . . . . . . . . . . . . . . .n.a.
Airheads (1994) . . . . . . . . . . . . . . . . . . . . . . . Chazz
**With Honors** (1994) . . . . . . . . . . . . . . Monty Kessler

# • Fraser, Shane
*Films:*
**Angel 4: Undercover** (1993) . . . . . . . . . . Piston Jones
 •• 0:28—Brief buns, while getting up off bed and putting on his pants.

# Frey, Sami
*Films:*
Sweet Movie (1975) . . . . . . . . . . . . . . . . . . . . . . . .n.a.
Nea (A Young Emmanuelle) (1976; French). . . . . . . Axel
The Little Drummer Girl (1984). . . . . . . . . . . . . . Khalil
**Black Widow** (1987) . . . . . . . . . . . . . . . . . . . . . Paul
 •• 1:18—Buns, while walking into swimming pool.
*Miniseries:*
War and Remembrance (1988) . . . . . . . . . . .Rabinovitz

# Friels, Colin
Husband of actress Judy Davis.
*Films:*
Monkey Grip (1983; Australian) . . . . . . . . . . . . . . Javo
**Kangaroo** (1986; Australian) . . . . . . . . .Richard Somers
 •• 1:08—Buns, while running into the ocean.
 • 1:09—Frontal nudity walking towards Judy Davis.
 Long shot, hard to see anything.
Malcolm (1986; Australian). . . . . . . . . . . . . . .Malcolm
High Tide (1987; Australian) . . . . . . . . . . . . . . . Mick
Warm Nights on a Slow Moving Train (1987) . .The Man
Ground Zero (1988; Australian) . . . . . . .Harvey Denton
Darkman (1990) . . . . . . . . . . . . . . . . Louis Strack, Jr.
Class Action (1991). . . . . . . . . . . . . . Michael Grazier

# Frye, Brittain
*Films:*
Less than Zero (1987) . . . . . . . . . . . . . . . . Teenager #2
**Hide and Go Shriek** (1988) . . . . . . . . . . . . Randy Flint
 • 0:51—Brief buns, while undressing and getting into
 bed. Long shot.
 • 0:52—Brief buns, while putting on his pants after
 getting out of bed.
 • 0:58—Very brief buns, while pulling up his pants.
 Dark.
Slumber Party Massacre 3 (1990) . . . . . . . . . . . . . .Ken

# Gains, Tyler
*Films:*
**Novel Desires** (1991) . . . . . . . . . . . . . . . . . Brian/Eric
 • 0:18—Buns, as Eric, making love with the Model on
 picnic table.

# • Galin, Alex
*Video Tapes:*
Playboy's 101 Ways to Excite Your Lover (1992)
 . . . . . . . . . . . . . . . . . . . . . . . . . . . . . . . . .Cast Member
Playboy's Erotic Fantasies (1992) . . . . . . . .Cast Member
**Playboy's How to Reawaken Your Sexual Powers**
 (1992) . . . . . . . . . . . . . . . . . . . . . . . . . . .Cast Member
 ••• 0:18—Nude while making love with his lover by lava
 flow.
 ••• 0:33—Nude, by waterfall with his lover.

# Gallagher, Peter
*Films:*
The Idolmaker (1980) . . . . . . . . . . . . . . . . . . . .Cesare
**Summer Lovers** (1982) . . . . . . . . . . . . Michael Pappas
 • 0:22—Buns, while running into the water after Vale-
 rie Quennessen.
 • 0:54—Frontal nudity getting ready to dive off a rock
 while Daryl Hannah and Quennessen watch. Long
 shot, hard to see anything.
Dreamchild (1986; British) . . . . . . . . . . . . . .Jack Dolan
sex, lies and videotape (1989) . . . . . . . . . . . . . . . John
Late for Dinner (1991) . . . . . . . . . . . . . .Bob Freeman
Bob Roberts (1992; U.S./British)
 . . . . . . . . . . . . . . . . . . . . . . News Anchor Dan Riley
The Player (1992). . . . . . . . . . . . . . . . . . . Larry Levy
Malice (1993) . . . . . . . . . . . . . . . . . . . . .Dennis Riley
Short Cuts (1993) . . . . . . . . . . . . . . . . Stormy Weathers
Watch It (1993) . . . . . . . . . . . . . . . . . . . . . . . John
*Made for Cable Movies:*
While Mile (1994; HBO). . . . . . . . . . . . . . Jack Robbins
*Made for Cable TV:*
Fallen Angels: The Frightening Frammis (1993)
 . . . . . . . . . . . . . . . . . . . . . . . . . . . . Mitch Allison
 (Available on video tape on *Fallen Angels One.*)
Fallen Angels: The Quiet Room (1993; Showtime)
 . . . . . . . . . . . . . . . . . . . . . . . . . . . . Dr. Yorgrau
 (Available on video tape on *Fallen Angels Two.*)
*Made for TV Movies:*
Skag (1980) . . . . . . . . . . . . . . . . . . . . . . John Skagska

# Galland, Philippe
*Films:*
**Overseas** (1991; French). . . . . . . . . . . . . . . . . . .Paul
 •• 0:13—Very, very brief, blurry tip of frontal nudity
 while jumping out of bathtub and standing on stool.
 Buns, while standing on stool.

# • Galligan, Zach
*Films:*
Gremlins (1984). . . . . . . . . . . . . . . . . . Billy Peltzer
Waxwork (1988) . . . . . . . . . . . . . . . . . . . . . . Mark
Rising Storm (1989) . . . . . . . . . . . . . . . .Artie Gage
Gremlins 2: The New Batch (1990) . . . . . . . Billy Peltzer
Waxwork II: Lost in Time (1991). . . . . . . .Mark Loftmore
Zandalee (1991) . . . . . . . . . . . . . . . . . . . . . . . Rog
**All Tied Up** (1992). . . . . . . . . . . . . . . . . . Brian Hartley
 •• 0:59—Buns after throwing off towel in his backyard.
 Don't see his face.

Round Trip to Heaven (1992) . . . . . . . . . . . . . . . Steve
Caroline at Midnight (1993) . . . . . . . . . . . . . Jerry Hutt
Ice (1993) . . . . . . . . . . . . . . . . . . . . . . . . . . . . . . Rick
Warlock: The Armageddon (1993) . . . . . . . . . Douglas
*Made for Cable Movies:*
Psychic (1992; USA) . . . . . . . . . . . . . . Patrick Costello
*Made for Cable TV:*
Tales From the Crypt: Strung Along (1992; HBO)
. . . . . . . . . . . . . . . . . . . . . . . . . . . . . . . . Rick/David
*Made for TV Movies:*
For Love and Glory (1993) . . . . . . . . . . . . . . . . . . n.a.

# Ganios, Tony
*Films:*
The Wanderers (1979) . . . . . . . . . . . . . . . . . . . . . Peppy
Back Roads (1981) . . . . . . . . . . . . . . . . . . . . . . Bartini
Continental Divide (1981) . . . . . . . . . . . . . . . . Possum
**Porky's** (1981; Canadian) . . . . . . . . . . . . . . . . . . Meat
•• 0:21—Brief buns, while running out of the cabin
during practical joke.
**Porky's Revenge** (1985; Canadian) . . . . . . . . . . Meat
•• 0:16—Buns, while getting out of swimming pool
(the fifth guy getting out). More buns running
around.
Die Hard 2 (1990) . . . . . . . . . . . . . . . . . . . . . . . Baker
The Taking of Beverly Hills (1991) . . . . . . . . . . EPA Man
Rising Sun (1993) . . . . . . . . . . . . . . . . Doorman Guard

# Garcia, Andres
*Films:*
**Tintorera** (1977) . . . . . . . . . . . . . . . . . . . . . . . Miguel
• 0:22—Brief buns, while walking down hallway to
look for Fiona Lewis. Dark.
• 0:27—Buns, after taking off his clothes to swim to
boat.
•• 0:28—Buns, while walking on boat deck.
• 0:41—Very brief frontal nudity in boat kitchen with
Susan George and Steven.
•• 0:42—Nude, picking up George and throwing her
overboard.

# Garfield, Allen
a.k.a. Allen Goorwitz.
*Films:*
Believe in Me (1971) . . . . . . . . . . . . . . . . . . . . Stutter
**Cry Uncle** (1971) . . . . . . . . . . . . . . . . . . . Jake Masters
• 0:03—Very brief partial frontal nudity, while spank-
ing Renee on the buns and hanging up the phone.
•• 0:24—Brief buns, then frontal nudity, while walking
away from the bathroom after talking to Cora.
• 0:39—Lower half of buns, getting washed by Debi
Morgan.
• 0:48—Buns, making love on top of Lena in bed.
•• 0:52—Buns, getting tied up by Larry and the two
girls.
• 0:59—Brief buns, while dropping his towel to get
into bed with Cora.
• 1:06—Buns, while making love on top of Connie,
not knowing she's dead.

The Candidate (1972) . . . . . . . . . . . . . . . . Howard Klein
Get to Know Your Rabbit (1972) . . . . . . . . . . . . . . . Vic
Slither (1973) . . . . . . . . . . . . . . . . . . Vincent J. Palmer
Busting (1974) . . . . . . . . . . . . . . . . . . . . . . . . . . Rizzo
The Conversation (1974) . . . . . . . . . . . . . Bernie Moran
The Front Page (1974) . . . . . . . . . . . . . . . . . . . Kruger
The Cotton Club (1984) . . . . . . . . . Abbadabba Berman
Teachers (1984) . . . . . . . . . . . . . . . . . . . . . Rosenberg
Desert Bloom (1986) . . . . . . . . . . . . . . . . . . Mr. Mosol
Beverly Hills Cop II (1987) . . . . . . . . . . . Harold Lutz
Night Visitor (1989) . . . . . . . . . . . . . . Zachary Willard
Club Fed (1990) . . . . . . . . . . . . . Harrison Farnsworth IV
Dick Tracy (1990) . . . . . . . . . . . . . . . . . . . . . Reporter
Miracle Beach (1991) . . . . . . . . . . . . . Magnus O'Leary
Until the End of the World (1991) . . . . . . . . . . . . Bernie
Cyborg 2: Glass Shadow (1993) . . . . . . . . Martin Dunn
Family Prayers (1993) . . . . . . . . . . . . . . . . . . . . Cantor

# Garfunkel, Art
*Films:*
Catch-22 (1970) . . . . . . . . . . . . . . . . . Captain Nately
Carnal Knowledge (1971) . . . . . . . . . . . . . . . . . Sandy
**Bad Timing: A Sensual Obsession** (1980)
. . . . . . . . . . . . . . . . . . . . . . . . . . . . . . . Alex Linden
• 0:55—Buns, while making love with Theresa Russell
on stairwell. Don't see his face.
• 0:57—Buns (Sort of see his balls through his legs),
while on top of Russell when visited by Harvey Keitel.
1:48—Side view of buns while in bed with an unconscious Russell.
Boxing Helena (1993) . . . . . . . . Dr. Lawrence Augustine

# Garrison, Bob
*Films:*
**Hollywood Hot Tubs 2—Educating Crystal** (1989)
. . . . . . . . . . . . . . . . . . . . . . . . . Billy "Derrick" Dare
• 0:53—Buns, while running up to hot dog stand.

# Gaylord, Mitch
Gymnast.
*Films:*
American Anthem (1987) . . . . . . . . . . . . . Steve Tevere
**American Tiger** (1989; Italian) . . . . . . . . . . . . . Scott
*a.k.a. American Rickshaw*
• 0:17—Buns, while on boat with Joanna. Long shot,
don't see his face.
Animal Instincts (1992) . . . . . . . . . . . . . . Rod Tennison
(Unrated version reviewed.)
Sexual Outlaws (1993) . . . . . . . . . . . . . Francis Badham

# Geary, Anthony
*Films:*
You Can't Hurry Love (1984) . . . . . . . . . . . . . . . . Tony
Disorderlies (1987) . . . . . . . . . . . . . . . . Winslow Lowry
Penitentiary III (1987) . . . . . . . . . . . . . . . . Serenghetti
Private Investigations (1987) . . . . . . . . . . . . . . . Larry
Dangerous Love (1988) . . . . . . . . . . . . . . . . . . Mickey
It Takes Two (1988) . . . . . . . . . . . . . . . . . . . . . Wheel

Pass the Ammo (1988) . . . . . . . . . . . . . . . . . . Stonewall
Crack House (1989) . . . . . . . . . . . . . . . . . . . . Dockett
UHF (1989). . . . . . . . . . . . . . . . . . . . . . . . . . . . .Philo
Night of the Warrior (1991) . . . . . . . . . . . . . . . . Lynch
**Scorchers** (1992). . . . . . . . . . . . . . . . . . . . . .Preacher
  ••• 0:01—Buns, while making love on top of Faye Dun-
    away on porch. More buns, afterwards.
*Made for Cable Movies:*
High Desert Kill (1989; USA) . . . . . . . . . . . . . . . . . Jim
*TV:*
General Hospital . . . . . . . . . . . . . . . . . . . . . . . . . Luke

## Gedrick, Jason
*Films:*
Massive Retaliation (1984) . . . . . . . . . . . . . . Eric Briscoe
**The Heavenly Kid** (1985). . . . . . . . . . . . . . . . . . Lenny
  •• 0:31—Brief buns, while in clothing store when Bob-
    by magically dresses him in better looking clothes.
Iron Eagle (1986) . . . . . . . . . . . . . . . . . . . . . . . . Doug
Born on the Fourth of July (1989) . . . . . . . . . .Martinez
Rooftops (1989) . . . . . . . . . . . . . . . . . . . . . . . . . . .T
Still Life (1990) . . . . . . . . . . . . . . . . . . . Peter Sherwood
**Backdraft** (1991) . . . . . . . . . . . . . . . Tim Krizminski
  •• 0:33—Brief buns (on the right) in the shower room
    with William Baldwin.
Queens Logic (1991). . . . . . . . . . . . . . . . . . . . . .n.a.
*TV:*
Class of '96 (1993) . . . . . . . . . . . . . . David Morrissey

## Gere, Richard
Husband of model Cindy Crawford.
*Films:*
Report to the Commissioner (1975) . . . . . . . . . . . Billy
**Looking for Mr. Goodbar** (1977) . . . . . . . . . . . Tony
  •• 1:00—Buns, while on Diane Keaton's floor doing
    push-ups, then running around in his jock strap.
Days of Heaven (1978) . . . . . . . . . . . . . . . . . . . . . Bill
Yanks (1979). . . . . . . . . . . . . . . . . . . . . . . . . . . Matt
**American Gigolo** (1980) . . . . . . . . . . . . . . . . . Julian
  •• 0:39—Buns and frontal nudity. Long shot, so it's
    hard to see anything.
An Officer and a Gentleman (1982) . . . . . . . Zack Mayo
**Beyond the Limit** (1983) . . . . . . . . . Dr. Eduardo Plarr
  • 0:21—Buns.
**Breathless** (1983) . . . . . . . . . . . . . . . . . . . . . . . Jesse
  •• 0:11—Frontal nudity dancing and singing in the
    shower. Hard to see because of the steam.
  •• 0:52—Buns, while taking his pants off to get into the
    shower with Valerie Kaprisky, then more buns in
    bed. Very brief frontal nudity. Dark, hard to see.
  • 0:53—Very, very brief top of frontal nudity popping
    up when Kaprisky gets out of bed.
The Cotton Club (1984) . . . . . . . . . . . . . . Dixie Dwyer
King David (1985). . . . . . . . . . . . . . . . . . . . . . David
No Mercy (1986) . . . . . . . . . . . . . . . . . . Eddie Jilletie
Power (1986) . . . . . . . . . . . . . . . . . . . . .Pete St. John
Miles From Home (1988) . . . . . . . . . . . . Frank Roberts
Internal Affairs (1990) . . . . . . . . . . . . . . . . Dennis Peck
Pretty Woman (1990) . . . . . . . . . . . . . . . . Edward Lewis

**Final Analysis** (1992). . . . . . . . . . . . . . . Dr. Isaac Barr
  ••• 0:21—Buns while, making love on top of Kim Bas-
    inger in bed.
Intersection (1993). . . . . . . . . . . . . . . Vincent Eastman
Mr. Jones (1993) . . . . . . . . . . . . . . . . . . . . . . .Mr. Jones
    0:52—Partial pubic hair, while sitting, getting a
    shower.
Sommersby (1993) . . . . . . . . . . . . . . . . Jack Sommersby
*Made for Cable Movies:*
And the Band Played On (1992; HBO) . . Choreographer

## Getty, Balthazar
Great-grandson of oil billionaire J. Paul Getty.
*Films:*
Lord of the Flies (1990) . . . . . . . . . . . . . . . . . . .Ralph
Young Guns II (1990). . . . . . . . . . . . . . .Tom O'Folliard
December (1991). . . . . . . . . . . . . . . . . . Allister Gibbs
My Heroes Have Always Been Cowboys (1991)
  . . . . . . . . . . . . . . . . . . . . . . . . . . . . . .Jud Meadows
**The Pope Must Die** (1991) . . . . . . . . . .Joe Don Dante
*a.k.a. The Pope Must Diet*
  • 0:46—Buns, making love with Luccia in his motor
    home.
Where The Day Takes You (1992). . . . . . . . . . . .Little J.

## Ghadban, Alle
*Films:*
Liar's Edge (1991) . . . . . . . . . . . . . . . . . .Tunnel Guard
**Prom Night IV: Deliver Us From Evil** (1991) . . . .Jeff
  • 0:37—Buns, mooning out the limousine window.
  • 0:59—Buns, standing up while carrying Laura. Don't
    see his face.

## •Giaimo, Anthony
*Films:*
My Girl (1991) . . . . . . . . . . . . . . . . . . . Carnival Barker
**Deadly Rivals** (1992) . . . . . . . . . . . . . .Bayne Murdoch
  •• 0:07—Buns, when bad guys rip his underwear off
    while he's hanging by his wrists so they can torture
    him into talking.

## Giamatti, Marcus
*Films:*
**Necessary Roughness** (1991) . . . . . . . . . . . . . Sargie
  • 1:09—Buns, while taking a shower. (He's the tall guy
    on the left.)

## •Gibb, Donald
*Films:*
Meatballs, Part II (1984). . . . . . . . . . . . . . . . .Mad Dog
**Revenge of the Nerds** (1984). . . . . . . . . . . . . . Ogre
  • 0:46—Brief buns, while mooning the nerds from
    back of flatbed truck. (He's the guy on the left.)
Lost in America (1985). . . . . . . . . . . . . . . . .Ex-Convict
Transylvania 6-5000 (1985) . . . . . . . . . . . . . . Wolfman
Bloodsport (1987) . . . . . . . . . . . . . . . . . Ray Jackson
Revenge of the Nerds II: Nerds in Paradise (1987) . Ogre

# Gibson, Mel

*Films:*

Mad Max (1979)........................... Max
Tim (1979) .......................... Tim Melville
**Gallipoli** (1981)..................... Frank Dunne
   •• 1:18—Buns, while running into the water. (He's the
   guy on the left.)
The Road Warrior (1981)..................... Max
The Year of Living Dangerously (1983; Australian)
   ....................................Guy Hamilton
The Bounty (1984) ............... Fletcher Christian
Mrs. Soffel (1984)..................... Ed Biddle
The River (1984) .................... Tom Garvey
Mad Max Beyond Thunderdome (1985)......... Max
**Lethal Weapon** (1987)...............Martin Riggs
   ••• 0:06—Buns, while getting out of bed and walking to
   the refrigerator.
Tequila Sunrise (1988)................... McKussie
Lethal Weapon 2 (1989)...............Martin Riggs
Air America (1990) .....................Gene Ryack
**Bird on a Wire** (1990) ............... Rick Jarmin
   •• 1:01—Brief close-up of buns when Rachel operates
   on his gunshot wound. Don't see his face, but it is
   him.
Hamlet (1990; British/French)...............Hamlet
**Forever Young** (1992) ....................Daniel
   •• 0:30—Buns, after getting out of suspended anima-
   tion chamber.
Lethal Weapon 3 (1992)...............Martin Riggs
The Man Without a Face (1993) .......Justin McCleod
Maverick (1994) .................... Bret Maverick

# • Gibson, Thomas

*Films:*

Far and Away (1992)..................... Stephen
The Age of Innocence (1993) ...........Stage Actor
*Made for TV Movies:*
**Tales of the City** (1994)...........Beauchamp Day
   • 0:38—(Into Part 3) Brief upper half of buns, while sit-
   ting on chair in front of bed.

# • Gift, Roland

Member of the rock group Fine Young Cannibals.
*Films:*
**Sammy and Rosie Get Laid** (1987; British)
   ................................... Danny/Victoria
   •• 1:08—Buns, while lying face down on bed with Ros-
   ie.
   • 1:10—Brief buns, while lying on top of Rosie. Seen
   in the middle of a three segment split screen.
Scandal (1989) ................Johnnie Edgecombe
(Unrated version reviewed.)

# Gillis, Jamie

Adult film actor.
*Adult Films:*
Centerfold Celebrities 3....................Himself
Blonde Ambition (1980; British) .........The Director

*Films:*
**Deranged** (1987)...................... Eugene
   • 1:06—Buns, while getting into bed with Jane Hamil-
   ton.
If Looks Could Kill (1987)............. Jack Devonoff
Young Nurses in Love (1987) ........... Dr. Spencer
Alien Space Avenger (1988) ........... Businessman
Enrapture (1989) .........................James

# Glenn, Scott

*Films:*

**The Baby Maker** (1970) .................... Tad
   • 1:30—Buns while in bed with Charlotte.
Angels Hard as They Come (1971)........ Long John
Hex (1973)............................Jimbang
Nashville (1975)................... Glenn Kelly
Fighting Mad (1976) .....................Charlie
Apocalypse Now (1979)................. Civilian
More American Graffiti (1979) ...............Newt
Cattle Annie and Little Britches (1980) ...... Bill Dalton
Urban Cowboy (1980)....................... Wes
The Challenge (1982) .........................Rich
Personal Best (1982) .............. Terry Tingloff
The Keep (1983) ............ Glaeken Trismegestus
The Right Stuff (1983) .............Alan Shepard
Silverado (1985).........................Emmett
Wild Geese II (1985; British)........... John Haddad
Off Limits (1988) .........Colonel Dexter Armstrong
Verne Miller (1988) ...................Verne Miller
Miss Firecracker (1989) .................Mac Sam
The Hunt for Red October (1990) ...... Bart Mancuso
Silence of the Lambs (1990)........... Jack Crawford
Backdraft (1991) .....................John Adcox
My Heroes Have Always Been Cowboys (1991)
   .......................................H.D. Dalton
The Player (1992)........................ Cameo
ShadowHunter (1992) ................. John Cain
*Made for Cable Movies:*
Women & Men 2: Three Short Stories (1991; HBO)
   ......................................... Henry
Extreme Justice (1993; HBO) ........... Dan Vaughn
Slaughter of the Innocents (1993; HBO)
   .............................. Stephen Broderick
**Past Tense** (1994; Showtime)......... Gene Ralston
   • 0:10—Very brief, partial buns, while making love
   with Lara Flynn Boyle on the floor.

# Goddard, Trevor

*Video Tapes:*
**Inside Out** (1992) ..... The Other Criminal/The Leda
   • 0:37—Buns, walking down the hallway and standing by Sherrie Rose's bed.

# Goldan, Wolf

*Films:*
**Melody in Love** (1978) ..................Octavio
   • 1:14—Buns, while making love in bed with Rachel
   and Angela.

# Goldblum, Jeff

Ex-husband of actress Geena Davis.

*Films:*

California Split (1974) . . . . . . . . . . . . . . . . Lloyd Harris

**Death Wish** (1974) . . . . . . . . . . . . . . . . . . . . Freak 1
- 0:10—Brief buns, while standing with pants down in living room raping Carol with his two punk friends.

Nashville (1975) . . . . . . . . . . . . . . . . . . . . Tricycle Man

Special Delivery (1976) . . . . . . . . . . . . . . . . . . . Snake

St. Ives (1976) . . . . . . . . . . . . . . . . . . . . . . . . . . Hood

Annie Hall (1977) . . . . . . . . . . . . . . . . . . . . Party Guest

Between the Lines (1977) . . . . . . . . . . . . . . . . . . Max

The Sentinel (1977) . . . . . . . . . . . . . . . . . . . . . . Jack

Invasion of the Body Snatchers (1978) . . . . Jack Bellicec

Remember My Name (1978) . . . . . . . . . . Mr. Nadd

Thank God It's Friday (1978) . . . . . . . . . . . . . . . Tony

The Big Chill (1983) . . . . . . . . . . . . . . . . . . . Michael

The Right Stuff (1983) . . . . . . . . . . . . . . . . . Recruiter

Threshold (1983; Canadian) . . . . . . . . . . Aldo Gehring

The Adventures of Buckaroo Banzai, Across the 8th Dimension (1984) . . . . . . . . . . . . . . . . . . New Jersey

Into the Night (1985) . . . . . . . . . . . . . . . . Ed Okin

Silverado (1985) . . . . . . . . . . . . . . . . . . . . . . . Slick

Transylvania 6-5000 (1985) . . . . . . . . . . . . Jack Harrison

The Fly (1986) . . . . . . . . . . . . . . . . . . . . Seth Brundle

Beyond Therapy (1987) . . . . . . . . . . . . . . . . . Bruce

Vibes (1988) . . . . . . . . . . . . . . . . . . . . . Nick Deezy

Earth Girls are Easy (1989) . . . . . . . . . . . . . . . . Mac

Mr. Frost (1990; French/British) . . . . . . . . . . . Mr. Frost

The Tall Guy (1990; British) . . . . . . . . . . . Dexter King
0:34—Brief right cheek of buns, while rolling around on the floor with Emma Thompson. Don't see his face.

Twisted Obsession (1990) . . . . . . . . . . . . . Daniel Gillis

The Favor, the Watch and the Very Big Fish (1991; French/British) . . . . . . . . . . . . . . . . . Pianist
*a.k.a. Rue Saint-Sulpice*

Deep Cover (1992) . . . . . . . . . . . . . . . . . . David Jason

Fathers and Sons (1992) . . . . . . . . . . . . . . . Max Fish

The Player (1992) . . . . . . . . . . . . . . . . . . . . Cameo

Shooting Elizabeth (1992; French) . . . . . . Harold Pigeon

Jurassic Park (1993) . . . . . . . . . . . . . . . . . . Ian Malcolm

*Made for Cable Movies:*

Lush Life (1993; Showtime) . . . . . . . . . . . . . . . . . Al

*TV:*

Tenspeed and Brown Shoe (1980)
. . . . . . . . . . . . . . . . . Lionel "Brown Shoe" Whitney

# Goldwyn, Tony

*Films:*

Friday the 13th, Part VI: Jason Lives (1986) . . . . . Darren

Gaby, A True Story (1987) . . . . . . . . . . . . . . . . . David

Ghost (1990) . . . . . . . . . . . . . . . . . . . . Carl Brunner

Kuffs (1992) . . . . . . . . . . . . . . . . . . . . Ted Bukovsky

**Traces of Red** (1992) . . . . . . . . . . . . . . . . Steve Frayn
•• 1:04—Buns, standing up from bed and putting on his underwear.

The Pelican Brief (1993) . . . . . . . . . . . . . Fletcher Coal

Taking the Heat (1993) . . . . . . . . . . . . . . . . Michael

*Made for Cable Movies:*

**Love Matters** (1993; Showtime) . . . . . . . . . . . . Geoff
(Unrated version reviewed.)
- 0:30—Brief buns, after getting out of bed to talk to Annette O'Toole.
- 0:33—Buns, while carrying Gina Gershon to the table.
- 0:34—Very, very brief blurry frontal nudity when Gershon pushes him back from kitchen island.
- ••• 0:53—Buns, in the bathroom, while putting cordless phone away.
- •• 0:56—Buns, while making love with Gershon in the shower.

Doomsday Gun (1994; HBO) . . . . . . . . . . . . . . Duvall

# Gomez, Panchito

*Films:*

Walk Proud (1979) . . . . . . . . . . . . . . . . . . . . Manuel

Borderline (1980) . . . . . . . . . . . . . . . . . Benito Morales

Max Dugan Returns (1983) . . . . . . . . . . . . . . . . Luis

Tuff Turf (1984) . . . . . . . . . . . . . . . . . . . . . . Mickey

3:15—The Moment of Truth (1986) . . . . . . . . Chooch

Return to Horror High (1987) . . . . . . . . . . . Choo Choo

**American Me** (1992) . . . . . . . . . . . . . . Young Santana
- 0:18—Brief buns, walking out of room in Juvenile Hall.
- 0:20—Brief buns, getting up out of bed to kill the guy who raped him.

# Gonzales, Joe

*Films:*

**Brain Damage** (1988) . . . . . . . . . . . . . . Guy in Shower
- 0:54—Buns, while taking a shower.

# Goodeve, Grant

*Films:*

License to Drive (1988) . . . . . . . . . . . . . . Mr. Nice Guy

**Take Two** (1988) . . . . . . . . Barry Griffith/Frank Bentley
- 0:31—Buns, while in bed with Robin Mattson.
- ••• 0:46—Buns, while getting into bed with Mattson again.

*Made for TV Movies:*

An Eight is Enough Wedding (1989) . . . . . . . . . . . David

*TV:*

Eight is Enough (1977-81) . . . . . . . . . . David Bradford

Dynasty (1983) . . . . . . . . . . . . . . . . . . . Chris Deegan

Northern Exposure (1990- ) . . . . . . . . . . . . . . . . Rick

# Gooding, Cuba, Jr.

*Films:*

Coming to America (1988) . . . . . . . Boy Getting Haircut

**Boyz N the Hood** (1991) . . . . . . . . . . . . . . . Tre Styles
- 0:42—Buns, in bed with Tisha. Don't see his face, but it is him.

A Few Good Men (1992) . . . . . Corporal Carl Hammaker

Gladiator (1992) . . . . . . . . . . . . . . . . . . . . Lincoln

Judgement Night (1993) . . . . . . . . . . . . Mike Peterson

Lightning Jack (1993; Australian) . . . . . . . . . Ben Doyle

*Made for Cable Movies:*
Daybreak (1993; HBO) . . . . . . . . . . . . . . . . . . . . . Torch

# Goodman, Caleb

*Films:*
**Up Yours** . . . . . . . . . . . . . . . . . . . . . . . . . . . . . . . . .Virgil
- 0:50—Buns, while dancing on roof of building with Mary Lou.

# Graham, Gary

*Films:*
The Hollywood Knights (1980) . . . . . . . . . Jimmy Shine
The Arrogant (1987) . . . . . . . . . . . . . . . . . . . . . .Giovanni
**The Last Warrior** (1989) . . . . . . . . . . . . . . . . . . . .Gibb
- 0:07—Brief buns, while taking off his towel when he sees a ship.
**Robot Jox** (1990) . . . . . . . . . . . . . . . . . . . . . . .Achilles
- 0:32—Very brief buns, getting dressed in his room while talking to Athena.
Man Trouble (1992) . . . . . . . . . . . . . . . . . . Butch Gable
*Made for TV Movies:*
Danger Island (1992) . . . . . . . . . . . . . . . . . . . . . . . Rick
In the Best Interest of the Children (1992). . .John Birney
Trouble Shooters: Trapped Beneath the Earth (1993)
. . . . . . . . . . . . . . . . . . . . . . . . . . . . . . . . . . . . . . . Jack
*TV:*
Alien Nation (1989-91) . . . . . . . . . . .Det. Matthew Sikes

# • Grannell, William

*Films:*
**Ginger** (1970) . . . . . . . . . . . . . . . . . . . . . .Jason Varone
- 0:55—Buns, while on top of Vicky in bed.

# Grant, David

*Films:*
The End of August (1974) . . . . . . . . . . . . . . . . . Robert
French Postcards (1979) . . . . . . . . . . . . . . . . . . . . Alex
Happy Birthday, Gemini (1980). . . . . . . .Randy Hastings
**American Flyers** (1985) . . . . . . . . . . . . . . . . . . David
- 0:05—Brief buns and very, very brief frontal nudity taking off shorts and walking to bathroom.
Bat 21 (1988) . . . . . . . . . . . . . . . . . . . . . .Ross Carver
Strictly Business (1991) . . . . . . . . . . . . . . . . . . . . David

# • Grant, Gerald

*Films:*
**Score** (1973) . . . . . . . . . . . . . . . . . . . . . . . . . . . Eddie
- 0:36—Buns, while changing clothes.
- 1:11—Buns, while lying in bed with Jack.
- 1:16—Buns, while sleeping in bed with Jack.

# Grant, Richard E.

*Films:*
Withnail and I (1987; British). . . . . . . . . . . . . . Withnail
**How to Get Ahead in Advertising** (1988; British)
. . . . . . . . . . . . . . . . . . . . . . . . . . . . . . . . . . . . Bagley
- 0:19—Brief buns, while wearing apron in kitchen all covered with food. Brief buns again talking with Rachel Ward at top of stairs.

Mountains of the Moon (1989) . . . . . . . . . . . Oliphant
Henry & June (1990) . . . . . . . . . . . . . . . . . . . . . .Hugo
Warlock (1990) . . . . . . . . . . . . . . . . . . . . . . . Redferne
Hudson Hawk (1991) . . . . . . . . . . . Darwin Mayflower
L.A. Story (1991) . . . . . . . . . . . . . . . . . . . . . . . .Roland
Bram Stoker's Dracula (1992) . . . . . . . . Dr. Jack Seward
The Player (1992). . . . . . . . . . . . . . . . . . . .Tom Oakley
The Age of Innocence (1993) . . . . . . . . . . Larry Lefferts

# Gravance, Louie

*Films:*
**Evilspeak** (1981) . . . . . . . . . . . . . . . . . . . . . . . . .Jo Jo
- • 0:07—Buns, in shower with three other guys. (He's the one in the foreground on the right.)

# Graves, Rupert

*Films:*
**A Room with a View** (1986; British)
. . . . . . . . . . . . . . . . . . . . . . . . . . Freddy Honeychurch
- • • 1:05—Nude running around with Mr. Beebe and George in the woods. Lots of frontal nudity.
Maurice (1987; British). . . . . . . . . . . . . . . Alec Scudder
A Handful of Dust (1988) . . . . . . . . . . . . . . John Beaver
The Children (1990; British/German) . . Gerald Ormerod
Damage (1992; French/British) . . . . . . . . . . . . Martyn
(Unrated Director's cut reviewed.)
Where Angels Fear to Tread (1992) . . . . Phillip Herriton
*Made for Cable Movies:*
Doomsday Gun (1994; HBO) . . . . . . . . . . . . . . .Jones

# Greene, Daniel

*Films:*
Pulsebeat (1984) . . . . . . . . . . . . . . . . . . . . . . . Roger
**Stitches** (1985). . . . . . . . . . . . . . . . . . . . .Ted Fletcher
- 0:45—Brief buns, twice, while pulling his pants down in front of visiting medical students.
Hands of Steel (1986) . . . . . . . . . . . . . . . Paco Querak
Weekend Warriors (1986). . . . . . . . . . . . Phil McCracken
Arthur 2 On the Rocks (1988) . . . . . . . . . . . . . . .Troy
Elvira, Mistress of the Dark (1988) . . . . . . . Bob Redding
American Tiger (1989; Italian) . . . . . . . . . . . . . .Francis
*a.k.a. American Rickshaw*
Skeleton Coast (1989) . . . . . . . . . . . . . . . .Rick Weston

# • Greenleaf, Jim

*Films:*
Joysticks (1983) . . . . . . . . . .Jonathan Andrew McDorfus
**Surf II** (1984) . . . . . . . . . . . . . . . . . . . . . . .Fat Boy #2
- 0:19—Buns, when yellow wet suit splits in the back while at the beach.

# Greenquist, Brad

*Films:*
**The Bedroom Window** (1987). . . . . . . . . .Henderson
- 0:35—Buns, turning off the light while Steve Guttenberg spies on him.
The Chair (1988) . . . . . . . . . . . . . . . . . . . .Mushmouth

# Greenwood, Bruce

*Films:*
Bear Island (1980; British/Canadian) . . . . . . . Technician
The Malibu Bikini Shop (1985) . . . . . . . . . . . . . .Todd
Summer Dreams: The Story of the Beach Boys (1990)
. . . . . . . . . . . . . . . . . . . . . . . . . . . . . .Dennis Wilson
(Originally a made for TV movie.)
**Wild Orchid** (1990) . . . . . . . . . . . Jermone McFarland
•• 1:02—Buns, while in room with Carré Otis.
Servants of Twilight (1991) . . . . . . . . . Charlie Harrison
Passenger 57 (1992) . . . . . . . . . . . . . . . .Stuart Ramsey
*Made for Cable Movies:*
Bitter Vengeance (1994; USA) . . . . . . . . . . . . . . .n.a.
*Made for Cable TV:*
The Hitchhiker: Shattered Vows. . . . . . . . . . . . . . Jeff
*Made for TV Movies:*
In the Line of Duty: The F.B.I. Murders (1988). . . . Dove
Adrift (1993) . . . . . . . . . . . . . . . . . . . . . . . . . .n.a.
Rio Diablo (1993) . . . . . . . . . . . . . . . . . . . . . .Jervis
Woman on the Run: The Lawrencia Bembenek Story
(1993). . . . . . . . . . . . . . . . . . . . . . . . Fred Schultz
Heart of a Child (1994) . . . . . . . . . . . . . Fred Schouten
*TV:*
Legmen (1984) . . . . . . . . . . . . . . . . . . . . Jack Gage
St. Elsewhere (1986-88) . . . . . . . . . . . . . Dr. Seth Griffin
Knots Landing (1991-93) . . . . . . . . . . . .Pierce Lawton
Hardball (1994- ) . . . . . . . . . . . . . . . . . . . Dave Logan

# Greer, Michael

*Films:*
The Curious Female (1969) . . . . . . . . . . . . . . . Bixby
The Gay Deceivers (1969) . . . . . . . . . . . . . . . Malcom
The Magic Garden of Stanley Sweetheart (1970)
. . . . . . . . . . . . . . . . . . . . . . . . . . . . . . . . Danny
**Fortune and Men's Eyes** (1971) . . . . . . . . . Queenie
•• 1:22—Brief frontal nudity after ripping off his under-
wear after singing number in drag.
Dead People (1974) . . . . . . . . . . . . . . . . . . . . Thom
Summer School Teachers (1975) . . . . . . John John Lacey
The Rose (1979) . . . . . . . . . . . . . . . . . . . . . Emcee
The Lonely Guy (1983) . . . . . . . . . . . . The Counterman
*TV:*
The Bobby Gentry Show (1974) . . . . . . . . . . . .Regular

# Gregory, André

*Films:*
My Dinner with Andre (1981) . . . . . . . . . . . . . .Andre
Author! Author! (1982) . . . . . . . . . . . . . . . . . . .J.J.
Always (1984) . . . . . . . . . . . . . . . . . Party Philosopher
Protocol (1984). . . . . . . . . . . . . . . .Nawaf Al Kabeer
The Mosquito Coast (1986) . . . . . . . . . . .Mr. Spellgood
Street Smart (1987) . . . . . . . . . . . . . . . . Ted Avery
The Last Temptation of Christ (1988) . . John the Baptist
**Some Girls** (1988). . . . . . . . . . . . . . . . . Mr. D'Arc
*a.k.a. Sisters*
• 1:24—Buns, while standing in the study looking at a
book. Very brief frontal nudity when he turns around
to sit at his desk.
The Bonfire of the Vanities (1990) . . . . . . Aubrey Buffing

The Linguini Incident (1991) . . . . . . . . . . . . . . Dante
Demolition Man (1993)
. . . . . . . . . . . . . . . .Warden William Smithers (Aged)

# Grieco, Richard

*Films:*
If Looks Could Kill (1991) . . . . . . . . . . . Michael Corbin
*a.k.a. Teen Agent*
Mobsters (1991) . . . . . . . . . . Benjamin "Bugsy" Siegel
*a.k.a. Mobsters—The Evil Empire*
**Tomcat: Dangerous Desires** (1993). . . . . . . . . . .Tom
• 1:04—Partial buns, while lying in bed with Imogen.
• 1:07—Brief buns, while answering the phone.
*Made for TV Movies:*
Born to Run (1993) . . . . . . . . . . . . . . .Nicky Donatello
Sin and Redemption (1994) . . . . . . . . . . . . . . .n.a.
*TV:*
21 Jump Street (1988-89) . . . . . . . . . . . Dennis Booker
Booker (1989-90). . . . . . . . . . . . . . . . Dennis Booker

# Griggs, Jeff

*Films:*
CIA—Code Name: Alexa (1992) . . . . . . . . . .Benedetti
Hit the Dutchman (1992). . . . . . . . . . . . . . .Peter Coll
(Unrated version reviewed.)
Killer Instinct (1992). . . . . . . . . . . . . . . . . .Peter Coll
*a.k.a. Mad Dog Coll*
*Video Tapes:*
**Eden** (1992) . . . . . . . . . . . . . . . . . . . . . . . . .Grant
••• 0:55—Buns, in the shower during Eve's fantasy.
**Eden 2** (1992). . . . . . . . . . . . . . . . . . . . . . . .Grant
•• 0:44—Buns on top of Eve in hay during her fantasy.
•• 1:04—Buns, while outside with Eve during her fantasy.
Eden 3 (1993) . . . . . . . . . . . . . . . . . . . . . . . .Grant
0:11—Partial buns, while climbing on top of mas-
sage table with Eve.
0:59—Side view of buns, while standing up outside
in the rain with Eve.
**Eden 5** (1993). . . . . . . . . . . . . . . . . . . . . . . .Grant
•• 0:16—Buns, in bedroom during Eve's flashback.
Playboy Celebrity Centerfold: Dian Parkinson (1993) . . .
Cast Member

# Groat, Rick

*Films:*
**L.A. Goddess** (1992) . . . . . . . . . . . . . . . . . . Sheriff
• 0:08—Upper half of buns, while making love with
Diane in motor home.

# Gross, Paul

*Films:*
Cold Comfort (1988) . . . . . . . . . . . . . . . . . .Stephen
Getting Married in Buffalo Jump (1992; Canadian)
. . . . . . . . . . . . . . . . . . . . . . . . . . . . . . . . .Alex
**Aspen Extreme** (1993) . . . . . . . . . . . . . . .T.J. Burke
• 1:21—Buns, behind shower door.
*TV:*
XXX's & OOO's (1994- ) . . . . . . . . . . . . . . Bucky Dean

# Gruner, Olivier

*Films:*
Angel Town (1990) . . . . . . . . . . . . . . . . . . . . . . .Jacques
**Nemesis** (1992) . . . . . . . . . . . . . . . . . . . . . . . . . . Alex
- 0:45—Brief buns, pointing gun at Deborah Shelton. (Don't see his face, but it is him.)

# Guest, Christopher

Husband of actress Jamie Lee Curtis.
*Films:*
The Hospital (1971) . . . . . . . . . . . . . . . . . . . . . Resident
The Hot Rock (1972) . . . . . . . . . . . . . . . . . . . .Policeman
Death Wish (1974) . . . . . . . . . . . . . . . Patrolman Reilly
The Fortune (1975) . . . . . . . . . . . . . . . . . . . . Boy Lover
**Girlfriends** (1978) . . . . . . . . . . . . . . . . . . . . . . . . . .Eric
- 1:04—Buns, while running after Melanie Mayron in her apartment, then hugging her.
The Last Word (1979) . . . . . . . . . . . . . . . . . . . . . . Roger
The Long Riders (1980) . . . . . . . . . . . . . . . Charlie Ford
Heartbeeps (1981) . . . . . . . . . . . . . . . . . . . . . . .Calvin
This is Spinal Tap (1984) . . . . . . . . . . . . . . Nigel Tufnel
Little Shop of Horrors (1986) . . . . . . . . . . . 1st Customer
Beyond Therapy (1987) . . . . . . . . . . . . . . . . . . Bob
Sticky Fingers (1988) . . . . . . . . . . . . . . . . . . . . . . Sam
A Few Good Men (1992) . . . . . . . . . . . . . . . Dr. Stone
*TV:*
Saturday Night Live (1984-85) . . . . . . . . . . . . .Regular

# Gulpilil, David

*Films:*
Mad Dog Morgan (1976; Australian) . . . . . . . . . . Billy
**The Last Wave** (1977) . . . . . . . . . . . . . . . . . Chris Lee
- 1:30—Buns, while standing naked in cave. Dark.
The Right Stuff (1983) . . . . . . . . . . . . . . . . . Aborigine
Crocodile Dundee (1986; Australian) . . . . . . Neville Bell
Until the End of the World (1991) . . . . . . . . . . . David

# Gunner, Robert

*Films:*
**Planet of the Apes** (1968) . . . . . . . . . . . . . . . .Landon
- 0:26—Very brief buns while taking off clothes to go skinny dipping. (Guy on the left.)

# Guttenberg, Steve

*Films:*
The Chicken Chronicles (1977) . . . . . . . . . David Kessler
The Boys From Brazil (1978) . . . . . . . . . . . Barry Kohler
Can't Stop the Music (1980) . . . . . . . . . . . . Jack Morell
Diner (1982) . . . . . . . . . . . . . . . . . . . . . . . . . . . Eddie
**The Man Who Wasn't There** (1983) . . . Sam Cooper
- 0:54—Buns, while dropping his pants in office with three other men.
- 1:46—Brief buns, while kissing Cindy during their wedding ceremony.
Police Academy (1984) . . . . . . . . . . . . Carey Mahoney
Bad Medicine (1985) . . . . . . . . . . . . . . . . . . .Jeff Marx
Cocoon (1985) . . . . . . . . . . . . . . . . . . . . . Jack Bonner
Police Academy II: Their First Assignment (1985)
. . . . . . . . . . . . . . . . . . . . . . . . . . . . Carey Mahoney

Police Academy III: Back in Training (1986)
. . . . . . . . . . . . . . . . . . . . . . . . . . . . Carey Mahoney
Short Circuit (1986) . . . . . . . . . . . . . . . Newton Crosby
Amazon Women on the Moon (1987) . . . . . .Jerry Stone
**The Bedroom Window** (1987) . . . . . . . Terry Lambert
- 0:05—Buns, while getting out of bed and walking to the bathroom.
Police Academy 4: Citizens on Patrol (1987)
. . . . . . . . . . . . . . . . . . . . . . . . . . . . Carey Mahoney
Three Men and a Baby (1987) . . . . . . . . . . . . Michael
Cocoon, The Return (1988) . . . . . . . . . . . . Jack Bonner
High Spirits (1988) . . . . . . . . . . . . . . . . . . . . . . . Jack
Surrender (1988) . . . . . . . . . . . . . . . . . . . . . . . Marty
Don't Tell Her It's Me (1990) . . . . . . . . . Gus Kubicek
Three Men and a Little Lady (1990) . . . . . . . . . Michael
*Miniseries:*
The Day After (1983) . . . . . . . . . . . . . . . . . . . .Stephen
*TV:*
Billy (1979) . . . . . . . . . . . . . . . . . . . . . . . Billy Fisher
No Soap, Radio (1982) . . . . . . . . . . . . . . . . . . Roger

# Haggerty, Dan

*Films:*
The Tender Warrior (1971) . . . . . . . . . . . . . . . . . .Cal
**Bury Me an Angel** (1972) . . . . . . . . . . . . . . . . . Ken
- 1:17—Brief buns, while making love with Dag in bed. Lit with red light. Kind of a long shot, don't see his face very well.
Hex (1973) . . . . . . . . . . . . . . . . . . . . . . . .Brother Billy
The Life and Times of Grizzly Adams (1974)
. . . . . . . . . . . . . . . . . . . . . . . . . James Capen Adams
King of the Mountain (1981) . . . . . . . . . . . . . . . Rick
Abducted (1986; Canadian) . . . . . . . . . . . . . . . . .Joe
Elves (1989) . . . . . . . . . . . . . . . . . . . . . Mike McGavin
Ice Pawn (1990) . . . . . . . . . . . . . . . . . . . . . . . . n.a.
Inheritor (1990) . . . . . . . . . . . . . . . . . . . . Dr. Berquist
Repo Jake (1990) . . . . . . . . . . . . . . . . . . . . . . . Jake
Soldier's Fortune (1991) . . . . . . . . . . . . . Hollis Bodine
Spirit of the Eagle (1991) . . . . . . . . Big Eli McDonaugh
*TV:*
The Life and Times of Grizzly Adams (1977-78)
. . . . . . . . . . . . . . . . . . . James "Grizzly" Adams
*Video Tapes:*
Best Chest in the U.S. (1987) . . . . . . . . . . . . . .Judge

# Haim, Corey

*Films:*
Firstborn (1984) . . . . . . . . . . . . . . . . . . . . . . . . Brian
Lucas (1986) . . . . . . . . . . . . . . . . . . . . . . Lucas Blye
The Lost Boys (1987) . . . . . . . . . . . . . . . . . . . . . .Sam
License to Drive (1988) . . . . . . . . . . . . . . . . . . . .Les
Watchers (1988) . . . . . . . . . . . . . . . . . . . . . . .Travis
Dream A Little Dream (1989) . . . . . . . . . . . . . . Dinger
Dream Machine (1990) . . . . . . . . . . . . . . Barry Davis
Fast Getaway (1990) . . . . . . . . . . . . . . . . . . . .Nelson
Prayer of the Rollerboys (1990) . . . . . . . . . . . . Griffin

**Blown Away** (1992) . . . . . . . . . . . . . . . . . . . . . . Rich
(Unrated version reviewed.)
- ••• 0:15—Buns, lying in bed with Nicole Eggert, then getting out and putting his pants on.
- •• 0:24—Buns, while making love in bed on top of Eggert.
- • 1:11—Buns, getting out of bed after Eggert.
The Double O Kid (1992) . . . . . . . . . . . . . . Lance Elliot
Just One of the Girls (1992). . . . . . . . . . . . Chris Calder
Oh, What a Night (1992) . . . . . . . . . . . . . . . . . . Eric
*CD-ROM:*
Double Switch (1994). . . . . . . . . . . . . . . . . . . . .n.a.

## Hall, Michael Keyes
*Films:*
**Blackout** (1989) . . . . . . . . . . . . . . . . . . . . Alan Boyle
- • 1:19—Buns and balls viewed from the rear while stabbing Richard in bed.

## • Hallett, Neil
*Films:*
Rotten to the Core (1965; British) . . Guard Commander
**Virgin Witch** (1971; British) . . . . . . . .Gerald Amberley
- • 1:23—Buns, after ceremony.

## Hamill, John
*Films:*
No Blade of Grass (1970; British). . . . . . Roger Burnham
Trog (1970; British). . . . . . . . . . . . . . . . . . . . . . . Cliff
The Beast in the Cellar (1971; British)
. . . . . . . . . . . . . . . . . . . . . . . . . . Cpl. Alan Marlow
**Tower of Evil** (1972; British) . . . . . . . . . . . . . . . . Gary
- • 0:40—Buns, walking with Penny, then more buns, rolling into the water, dead.
Travels with My Aunt (1972; British) . . . . Crowder's Man
Beyond the Fog (1981; British) . . . . . . . . . . . . . . Gary
*a.k.a. Tower of Evil*

## Hamill, Mark
*Films:*
Star Wars (1977). . . . . . . . . . . . . . . . . . Luke Skywalker
Corvette Summer (1978) . . . . . . . . . . . . .Kent Dantley
The Big Red One (1980) . . . . . . . . . . . . . . . . . . Griff
The Empire Strikes Back (1980). . . . . . . Luke Skywalker
The Night the Lights Went Out in Georgia (1981)
. . . . . . . . . . . . . . . . . . . . . . . . . . . . . . . Conrad
The Return of the Jedi (1983) . . . . . . . . Luke Skywalker
Black Magic Woman (1990) . . . . . . . . . . . . Brad Travis
Slipstream (1990) . . . . . . . . . . . . . . . . . . . . . . Tasker
The Guyver (1991) . . . . . . . . . . . . . . . . . . . . . . Max
Time Runner (1992) . . . . . . . . . . . . . . .Michael Raynor
Silk Degrees (1994). . . . . . . . . . . . . . . . . . . . Johnson
*Made for Cable TV:*
**John Carpenter's Body Bags** (1993; Showtime)
. . . . . . . . . . . . . . . . . . . . . . . . . . . . . . Eye/Brent
- •• 1:20—Buns, alternating on top of Twiggy and another woman in bed during visions.
*TV:*
The Texas Wheelers (1974-75) . . . . . . . Doobie Wheeler

## Hamilton, Gary
*Films:*
**Tower of Evil** (1972; British) . . . . . . . . . . . . . . . Brom
- •• 0:53—Buns in bed, while making love on top of Nora.

## Hamilton, Neil
*Films:*
**The Tall Guy** (1990; British) . . . . . . . . . .Naked George
- •• 0:04—Buns, while walking around apartment talking to Jeff Goldblum. Brief frontal nudity (out of focus).
- • 0:06—More buns, when getting introduced to Goldblum.
- • 1:22—Brief buns, during end credits.

## Hamlin, Harry
Ex-husband of actress Nicollette Sheridan.
*Films:*
Movie Movie (1978) . . . . . . . . . . . . . . . . . Joey Popchik
Clash of the Titans (1981) . . . . . . . . . . . . . . . Perseus
King of the Mountain (1981) . . . . . . . . . . . . . . . Steve
Making Love (1982). . . . . . . . . . . . . . . . . . . . . . Bart
Blue Skies Again (1983) . . . . . . . . . . . . . . . . . Sandy
Target: Favorite Son (1988) . . . . . . . . . . . . . . . . n.a.
Murder So Sweet (1993) . . . . . . . . . . . . . . . . . . n.a.
**Save Me** (1993) . . . . . . . . . . . . . . . . . . . . Jim Stevens
(Unrated version reviewed.)
- ••• 0:39—Buns, while making love on top of Lysette Anthony in bed.
- • 0:50—Brief buns, while getting out of spa with Anthony. Long shot.
*Made for Cable Movies:*
**Laguna Heat** (1987; HBO) . . . . . . . . . . .Tom Shephard
- • 0:50—Buns, while walking into the ocean with Catherine Hicks.
Dinner At Eight (1989). . . . . . . . . . . . . . Larry Renault
Deceptions (1990; Showtime) . . . . . . . . . .Nick Gentry
*Made for Cable TV:*
The Hitchhiker: The Curse . . . . . . . . . . . . . . . . .Jerry
(Available on *The Hitchhiker, Volume 1*.)
*Miniseries:*
Master of the Game (1984) . . . . . . . . . . .Tony Blackwell
Space (1987) . . . . . . . . . . . . . . . . . . . . . . . John Pope
*Made for TV Movies:*
Deadly Intentions...Again? (1991) . . . . . Charles Raynor
Deliver Them from Evil: The Taking of Alta View (1992)
. . . . . . . . . . . . . . . . . . . . . . . . Richard Worthington
Poisoned by Love: The Kern County Murders (1993)
. . . . . . . . . . . . . . . . . . . . . . . . . . . . . . . . . . n.a.
In the Best of Families, Marriage, Pride and Madness
(1994) . . . . . . . . . . . . . . . . . . . . . . . . . Fritz Klenner
*TV:*
Studs Lonigan (1979). . . . . . . . . . . . . . . Studs Lonigan
L.A. Law (1986-91) . . . . . . . . . . . . . . . Michael Kuzak

## Haney, Daryl
*Films:*
**Daddy's Boys** (1988). . . . . . . . . . . . . . . . . . . . . Jimmy
  • 0:17—Buns, while getting undressed in room with Christie.
The Unborn (1991). . . . . . . . . . . . . . . . . . . . Policeman
Uncaged (1991) . . . . . . . . . . . . . . . . . . . . John in Nova
  *a.k.a. Angel in Red*

## Hanks, Jim
Brother of actor Tom Hanks.
*Films:*
**Buford's Beach Bunnies** (1992) . . . . . . . Jeeter Buford
  • 0:17—Buns, getting his underwear yanked down by Dr. Van Horney. (Don't see his face.)

## • Hansman, Lance
*Video Tapes:*
Playboy's Erotic Fantasies II (1993) . . . . . . Cast Member
**Playboy's Secret Confessions** (1993)
  . . . . . . . . . . . . . . . . . . . . . . . . . . . . On the Air/Tony
  • 0:11—Buns, while making love with the D.J. in her radio station.

## • Harelik, Mark
*Films:*
**A Gnome Named Gnorm** (1993) . . . . . . . . Kaminsky
  • 1:05—Brief buns, twice, after waking up without any clothes on so that Gnorm can escape.

## • Harkness, Percy
*Films:*
**Caged Terror** (1971) . . . . . . . . . . . . . . . . . . . Richard
  • 0:29—Brief buns, while rolling over on Janet after rubbing blood on her.
  • 1:00—Buns, when getting into bed.
  •• 1:01—Frontal nudity, while getting out of bed to look out the window.
Golden Apples of the Sun (1971; Canadian) . . . . Richard

## Harmon, Mark
Husband of actress Pam Dawber.
*Films:*
Comes a Horseman (1978) . . . . . . . . . Billy Joe Meynert
Beyond the Poseidon Adventure (1979) . . Larry Simpson
Let's Get Harry (1986). . . . . . . . . . . . . . Harry Burke, Jr.
Summer School (1987) . . . . . . . . . . . . . . Freddy Shoop
Worth Winning (1989) . . . . . . . . . . . . . . Taylor Worth
Cold Heaven (1990) . . . . . . . . . . . . . . . Alex Davenport
Till There Was You (1990; Australian). . . . . . Frank Flynn
Wyatt Earp (1994). . . . . . . . . . . . . . . . . . . . . . . . n.a.
*Made for Cable Movies:*
**The Fourth Story** (1990; Showtime) . . David Shepard
  ••• 0:53—Buns, while getting out of bed with Mimi Rogers. More buns, while walking outside and around the house.
*Made for TV Movies:*
The Prince of Bel Air (1986). . . . . . . . . . . . . . . Robin

*TV:*
Centennial (1978-79). . . . . . . . . . . . . . John McIntosh
Sam (1978) . . . . . . . . . . . . . . . . . . . Officer Mike Breen
240 Robert (1979-80) . . . . . Deputy Dwayne Thibideaux
Flamingo Road (1981-82) . . . . . . . . . . Fielding Carlyle
St. Elsewhere (1983-86) . . . . . . . . . Dr. Robert Caldwell
Moonlighting (1987) . . . . . . . . . . . . . . Sam Crawford
Reasonable Doubts (1991-93) . . . . . . . . . . Dicky Cobb

## Harrelson, Woody
*Films:*
Wildcats (1986) . . . . . . . . . . . . . . . . . . . . Krushinski
Doc Hollywood (1991). . . . . . . . . . . . . . . . . . . . Hank
Ted & Venus (1991). . . . . . . Homeless Vietnam Veteran
**White Men Can't Jump** (1992) . . . . . . . . Billy Hoyle
  • 0:21—Very, very brief half of buns, while getting into shower.
  • 0:37—Very, very brief half of buns, while getting out of bed.
Indecent Proposal (1993). . . . . . . . . . . David Murphy
The Cowboy Way (1994) . . . . . . . . . . . . . Pepper Lewis
Natural Born Killers (1994). . . . . . . . . . . . . . Mickey
*TV:*
Cheers (1985-93). . . . . . . . . . . . . . . . . Woody Boyd

## Harris, Ed
Husband of actress Amy Madigan.
*Films:*
Borderline (1980). . . . . . . . . . . . . . . . . . . . Hotchkiss
**Knightriders** (1981) . . . . . . . . . . . . . . . . Billy Davis
  • 0:01—Buns, while kneeling in the woods. Long shot, hard to see.
  • 1:51—Upper half of buns, while standing in a pond doing something with a stick.
Creepshow (1982) . . . . . . . . . . . . . . . . . . . . . . Hank
The Right Stuff (1983) . . . . . . . . . . . . . . . John Glenn
Under Fire (1983). . . . . . . . . . . . . . . . . . . . . . Gates
A Flash of Green (1984) . . . . . . . . . . . . . . Jimmy Wing
Places in the Heart (1984) . . . . . . . . . . . Wayne Lomax
**Swing Shift** (1984) . . . . . . . . . . . . . . . . Jack Walsh
  • 0:03—Very brief frontal nudity when he sits down in chair wearing a towel around his waist.
Alamo Bay (1985) . . . . . . . . . . . . . . . . . . . . Shang
Code Name: Emerald (1985) . . . . . . . . . . . . Gus Lang
Sweet Dreams (1985). . . . . . . . . . . . . . . Charlie Dick
To Kill a Priest (1988) . . . . . . . . . . . . . . . . . . Stefan
Walker (1988) . . . . . . . . . . . . . . . . . William Walker
The Abyss (1989). . . . . . . . . . . Virgil "Bud" Brigman
Jackknife (1989). . . . . . . . . . . . . . . . . . . . . . Dave
State of Grace (1990). . . . . . . . . . . . . . . . . Frankie
Glengarry Glen Ross (1992) . . . . . . . . . . . . . . Dave
China Moon (1993) . . . . . . . . . . . . . . . . . . . . n.a.
The Firm (1993). . . . . . . . . . . . . . . . Wayne Tarrance
Needful Things (1993). . . . . . . . Sheriff Alan Pangborn
Milk Money (1994) . . . . . . . . . . . . . . . . . . . . . n.a.
*Made for Cable Movies:*
The Last Innocent Man (1987; HBO) . . . . . . . . . . n.a.
Paris Trout (1991; Showtime). . . . . . . . Harry Seagraves
Running Mates (1992; HBO) . . . . . . . . Hugh Hathaway

*Miniseries:*
Stephen King's "The Stand" (1994). . . . General Starkey

## Harris, Gregory Alan
*Films:*
**Conflict of Interest** (1992) . . . . . . . . . Jason Flannery
- 0:48—Brief buns, in the shower when Vera accidentally opens the door.

## Harris, Jim
*Films:*
**Squeeze Play** (1979). . . . . . . . . . . . . . . . . . . . . Wes
- •• 0:39—Buns, tied up in a room while people walking by look in through open door.
Waitress! (1982) . . . . . . . . . . . . . . . . . . . . . . . . Jerry
American Ninja 4: The Annihilation (1991) . . . . . . . .n.a.

## Harris, Richard
*Films:*
The Bible (1966) . . . . . . . . . . . . . . . . . . . . . . . . Cain
Hawaii (1966) . . . . . . . . . . . . . . . . . . . . Rafer Hoxworth
Camelot (1967) . . . . . . . . . . . . . . . . . . . .King Arthur
Cromwell (1970; British) . . . . . . . . . . . . . . Cromwell
**A Man Called Horse** (1970) . . . . . . . . . John Morgan
- 0:07—Brief buns, while taking a bath in the river.
- •• 0:10—Very, very brief partial frontal nudity, while falling into the water. Buns, getting dragged around by ropes on his neck.
- •• 0:14—Buns, while trying to run away from the Indians. Long shot.
- ••• 0:15—Buns and brief frontal nudity while running around. More buns while kneeling on the ground.
The Molly Maguires (1970). . James McParlan/McKenna
99 and 44/100% Dead (1974) . . . . . . . . .Harry Crown
Juggernaut (1974; British) . . . . . . . . . . . . . . . . . Fallon
Return of a Man Called Horse (1976) . . . . John Morgan
Robin and Marian (1976; British). . . . . . . .King Richard
The Cassandra Crossing (1977; British) . . . .Chamberlain
Orca, The Killer Whale (1977) . . . . . . . . . Captain Nolan
The Wild Geese (1978; British) . . . . . . . . .Rafer Janders
The Last Word (1979) . . . . . . . . . . . . . . . .Danny Travis
Tarzan, The Ape Man (1981) . . . . . . . . . . . . . . . Parker
**Your Ticket Is No Longer Valid** (1982) . . . . . . Jason
- 1:19—Buns, while taking off robe and sitting on the floor.
Triumphs of a Man Called Horse (1983; U.S./Mexican)
. . . . . . . . . . . . . . . . . . . . . . . . . . . Man Called Horse
Highpoint (1984; Canadian) . . . . . . . . . . . Louis Kinney
Martin's Day (1985; Canadian) . . . . . . . .Martin Steckert
Wetherby (1985; British) . . . . . . . . . . . . . . . Sir Thomas
The Field (1990) . . . . . . . . . . . . . . . . . . . .Bull McCabe
Patriot Games (1992) . . . . . . . . . . . . . . Paddy O'Neil
Unforgiven (1992) . . . . . . . . . . . . . . . . . . .English Bob
**Wrestling Ernest Hemingway** (1993) . . .Frank Joyce

## Harrison, Gregory
*Films:*
North Shore (1987) . . . . . . . . . . . . . . . . . . . . . Chandler
**Body Chemistry 2: Voice of a Stranger** (1991) . Dan
- ••• 0:45—Buns on stairs when Brenda finds him in the morning.
Cadillac Girls (1993; Canadian) . . . . . . . . . . . . . . .Sam
Caught in the Act (1993) . . . . . . . . . . . . Scott McNally
*Made for Cable Movies:*
Bare Essentials (1991). . . . . . . . . . . . . . . . . . . . . . .Bill
Duplicates (1992; USA) . . . . . . . . . . . . . .Bob Boxletter
*Made for TV Movies:*
A Family Torn Apart (1993) . . . . . . . . . . . . . .Tom Kelley
Lies of the Heart: The Story of Laurie Kellogg (1994)
. . . . . . . . . . . . . . . . . . . . . . . . . . . . . Bruce Kellogg
*TV:*
Logan's Run (1977-78). . . . . . . . . . . . . . . . . . . Logan
Centennial (1978-79). . . . . . . . . . . . . . . . . Levi Zandt
Trapper John, M.D. (1979-86)
. . . . . . . . . . . . . . .Dr. George "Gonzo" Alonzo Gates
Falcon Crest (1989-90). . . . . . . . . . . . . . Michael Sharpe
The Family Man (1990-91). . . . . . . . . . . . . .Jack Taylor
True Detectives (1990-91) . . . . . . . . . . . . . . . . . Host

## Hart, Geno
Identical twin brother of Dash Hart.
*Films:*
**Takin' It All Off** (1987) . . . . . . . . . . . . . . . . . . Adam
- •• 1:08—Buns, while in the shower with Allison.

## Hartman, Billy
*Films:*
**Slaughter High** (1986) . . . . . . . . . . . . . . . . . . . .Frank
- 1:00—Brief buns while in bed with Stella.

## Hasselhoff, David
Singer.
Husband of actress Pamela Bach.
Ex-husband of actress Catherine Hickland.
*Films:*
**Revenge of the Cheerleaders** (1976) . . . . . . . Boner
- 0:28—Buns in shower room scene.
- ••• 0:30—Frontal nudity in shower room scene while soaping Gail.
Starcrash (1979; Italian) . . . . . . . . . . . . . . . . . . . Simon
W. B., Blue and the Bean (1988). . . . . . . . . .White Bread
*a.k.a. Bail Out*
Witchery (1988). . . . . . . . . . . . . . . . . . . . . . . . . Gary
The Final Alliance (1990) . . . . . . . . . . . . . . Will Colton
*Made for TV Movies:*
The Cartier Affair (1985) . . . . . . . . . . . . . . Curt Taylor
Knight Rider 2000 (1991) . . . . . . . . . . . Michael Knight
*TV:*
The Young and the Restless (1975-82)
. . . . . . . . . . . . . . . . . .Dr. William "Snapper" Foster Jr.
Knight Rider (1982-86) . . . . . . . . . . . . . Michael Knight
Baywatch (1989-90). . . . . . . . . . . . . . . Mitch Bucannon
Baywatch (1991- ) . . . . . . . . . . . . . . . . Mitch Bucannon

# Hatch, Richard

*Films:*
Best Friends (1975) . . . . . . . . . . . . . . . . . . . . . . . Jesse
Charlie Chan & the Curse of the Dragon Queen (1981)
. . . . . . . . . . . . . . . . . . . . . . . . . . . . . . . . Lee Chan, Jr.
**Heated Vengeance** (1984). . . . . . . . . . . . . . Hoffman
••• 0:38—Buns, while making love in bed with Michelle
during his dream.
•• 0:40—Buns, while getting up out of bed and walk-
ing to bathroom.
Party Line (1988) . . . . . . . . . . . . . . . . Lt. Dan Bridges
Ghettoblaster (1989). . . . . . . . . . . . . . . . . . . . . Travis
Delta Force Commando 2: Priority Red One (1991)
. . . . . . . . . . . . . . . . . . . . . . . . . . . . . . Brett Haskell
*Made for TV Movies:*
Battlestar Gallactica (1978) . . . . . . . . . . Captain Apollo
*TV:*
All My Children . . . . . . . . . . . . . . . . . . . . . . . . . . Phil
The Streets of San Francisco (1976-77)
. . . . . . . . . . . . . . . . . . . . . . Inspector Dan Robbins
Mary Hartman, Mary Hartman (1977-78)
. . . . . . . . . . . . . . . . . . . . . . . . Harmon Farinella
Battlestar Galactica (1978-79) . . . . . . . . Captain Apollo

# Hauer, Rutger

*Films:*
Surrogate Romance. . . . . . . . . . . . . . . . . . . . . . . . n.a.
**Turkish Delight** (1974; Dutch). . . . . . . . . . . . . . Erik
••• 0:01—Brief nude walking around his apartment talking to a woman he has just picked up.
• 0:04—Buns, while in bed (covered with a sheet),
then very brief frontal nudity throwing another girl
out.
•• 0:36—Frontal nudity getting up to answer the door
with flowers.
•• 1:12—Frontal nudity lying in bed depressed.
•• 1:16—Buns, while making love with Olga in bed.
Soldier of Orange (1977; Dutch) . . . . . . . . Erik Lanshoff
**Keetje Tippel** (1978; Dutch). . . . . . . . . . . . . . Dandy
*a.k.a. Katie's Passion*
(Dutch with English subtitles.)
• 1:10—Buns seen through torn pants while he is
kneeling on the floor.
•• 1:12—Brief frontal nudity getting out of bed.
Spetters (1980; Dutch) . . . . . . . . . . . . . . . . . .Witkamp
Chanel Solitaire (1981) . . . . . . . . . . . Etienne De Balsan
Nighthawks (1981). . . . . . . . . . . . . . . . . . . . . Wulfgar
Blade Runner (1982) . . . . . . . . . . . . . . . . . Roy Batty
Eureka (1983; British) . . . . . . . .Claude Maillot Van Horn
The Osterman Weekend (1983) . . . . . . . . . John Tanner
**Flesh + Blood** (1985) . . . . . . . . . . . . . . . . . . . Martin
• 1:35—Buns, while in a jock strap running up stairs
after everybody throws their clothes into the fire.
Ladyhawke (1985) . . . . . . . . . . . . . Etienne of Navarre
The Hitcher (1986) . . . . . . . . . . . . . . . . . John Ryder
Wanted: Dead or Alive (1987). . . . . . . . . . Nick Randall
The Blood of Heroes (1989) . . . . . . . . . . . . . . .Sallow
*a.k.a. Salute of the Jugger*
Bloodhounds of Broadway (1989). . . . . . . . . The Brain

Blind Fury (1990) . . . . . . . . . . . . . . . . . . . . Nick Parker
Beyond Justice (1992) . . . . . . . . . . . . . . . Tom Burton
Buffy The Vampire Slayer (1992) . . . . . . . . . . . .Lothos
Split Second (1992) . . . . . . . . . . . . . . . . . . . . . .Stone
Surviving the Game (1993) . . . . . . . . . . . . . . . . n.a.
*Made for Cable Movies:*
A Breed Apart (1984; HBO) . . . . . . . . . . . . Jim Malden
Dead Lock (1991; HBO) . . . . . . . . . . .Frank Warren
Past Midnight (1992; USA). . . . . . . . . . . . .Ben Jordan
**Blind Side** (1993; HBO) . . . . . . . . . . . . . . . . . Shell
• 0:52—Buns, while making love on top of Mariska
Hargitay in bed.
Amelia Earhart: The Final Flight (1994; TNT)
. . . . . . . . . . . . . . . . . . . . . . . . . . . . . Fred Noonan
*Made for Cable TV:*
Voyage (1993; USA). . . . . . . . . . . . . . . . . . . . Morgan
*Magazines:*
**Playboy** (Nov 1974) . . . . . . . . . . . Sex in Cinema 1974
•• 151—Buns from *Turkish Delight.*

# Hauser, Wings

*Films:*
Homework (1982) . . . . . . . . . . . . . . . . . . . . . Reddog
Vice Squad (1982) . . . . . . . . . . . . . . . . . . . . . Ramrod
**Deadly Force** (1983) . . . . . . . . . . . . . Stoney Cooper
•• 0:44—Very brief buns, leaping out of bathtub when
gunman starts shooting. More buns, while lying on
the floor.
•• 0:49—Buns, while in hammock, lying on top of
Joyce Ingalls.
A Soldier's Story (1984) . . . . . . . . . . . . . . . . . Lt. Byrd
3:15—The Moment of Truth (1986) . . . . .Mr. Havilland
Jo Jo Dancer, Your Life Is Calling (1986) . . . . . . . . . Cliff
Nightmare At Noon (1987) . . . . . . . . . . . . Ken Griffith
*a.k.a. Deathstreet USA*
No Safe Haven (1987) . . . . . . . . . . . . . . . Clete Harris
Tough Guys Don't Dance (1987) . . . . . . . . . . Regency
The Wind (1987) . . . . . . . . . . . . . . . . . . . . . . . . Phil
The Carpenter (1988) . . . . . . . . . . . . . . . . . . . . . Ed
Dead Man Walking (1988). . . . . . . . . . . . .John Luger
Bedroom Eyes II (1989) . . . . . . . . . . . . . Harry Ross
L.A. Bounty (1989). . . . . . . . . . . . . . . . . . Cavanaugh
Street Asylum (1989) . . . . . . . . . . . . .Sgt. Arliss Ryder
Beastmaster 2: Through the Portal of Time (1990)
. . . . . . . . . . . . . . . . . . . . . . . . . . . . . . . . . Arklon
Coldfire (1990) . . . . . . . . . . . . . . . . . . . . . . . . Lars
Frame Up (1990) . . . . . . . . . . . . . . . . . . . Ralph Baker
Living to Die (1990). . . . . . . . . . . . . . Nick Carpenter
Pale Blood (1990) . . . . . . . . . . . . . . . . Van Vandameer
**The Art of Dying** (1991). . . . . . . . . . . . . . . . . . Jack
•• 0:28—Buns, while standing in kitchen making love
with Kathleen Kinmont.
Blood Money (1991) . . . . . . . . . . . . . . . . . . . . John
*a.k.a. The Killer's Edge*
Frame Up II (1991). . . . . . . . . . . . . . .Sheriff Ralph Baker
*a.k.a. Deadly Conspiracy*
In Between (1991) . . . . . . . . . . . . . . . . . . . . . . . Jack
Mind, Body & Soul (1992). . . . . . . . . . . John Stockton

*TV:*
The Young and the Restless (1977-81) . . . . .Greg Foster
Lightning Force (1991-92)
. . . . . . . . . . . . . Lieutenant Colonel "Trane" Coltrane
Roseanne (1992- ). . . . . . . . . . . . . . . . . . . .Ty Tilden

# Hayes, Alan

*Films:*
**Friday the 13th, Part IV—The Final Chapter**
(1984). . . . . . . . . . . . . . . . . . . . . . . . . . . . Paul
- 0:26—Brief buns, while swinging on a rope and jumping into the lake.

Neon Maniacs (1985) . . . . . . . . . . . . . . . . . . . . Steven

# Heard, John

*Films:*
**Between the Lines** (1977). . . . . . . . . . . . . . . . Harry
- • 1:17—Buns, while putting his pants on.

First Love (1977). . . . . . . . . . . . . . . . . . . . . . David
Chilly Scenes of Winter (1979) . . . . . . . . . . . . .Charles
Heart Beat (1979) . . . . . . . . . . . . . . . . . .Jack Kerouac
Cutter's Way (1981) . . . . . . . . . . . . . . . . . .Alex Cutter
*a.k.a. Cutter and Bone*
**Cat People** (1982). . . . . . . . . . . . . . . . .Oliver Yates
- 1:37—Very brief side view of buns, while taking off his pants and sitting on bed next to Kinski.
- • 1:50—Buns, while making love with Nastassja Kinski in bed in a cabin.

C.H.U.D. (1984) . . . . . . . . . . . . . . . . . .George Cooper
After Hours (1985) . . . . . . . . . . . . . . . . . . . Bartender
Heaven Help Us (1985). . . . . . . . . . . . Brother Timothy
Too Scared to Scream (1985) . . . . . . . . Lab Technician
The Trip to Bountiful (1986) . . . . . . . . . . . .Ludie Watts
Violated (1987). . . . . . . . . . . . . . . . . . . . . . .Skipper
Beaches (1988). . . . . . . . . . . . . . . . . . . John Pierce
Big (1988). . . . . . . . . . . . . . . . . . . . . . . . . . . Paul
The Milagro Beanfield War (1988). . . . . .Charlie Bloom
The End of Innocence (1989) . . . . . . . . . . . . . . Dean
Home Alone (1990) . . . . . . . . . . . . . . . . . . . .Peter
Deceived (1991) . . . . . . . . . . . . . . . . . Jack Saunders
Mindwalk (1991) . . . . . . . . . . . . . . .Thomas Harriman
Rambling Rose (1991). . . . . . . . . . . . .Willcox Hillyer
Gladiator (1992) . . . . . . . . . . . . . . . . . . . John Riley
Home Alone 2: Lost in New York (1992)
. . . . . . . . . . . . . . . . . . . . . . . . . .Peter McCallister
Radio Flyer (1992). . . . . . . . . . . . . . . . . Daugherty
Waterland (1992; British/U.S.). . . . . . . . . . .Lewis Scott
In the Line of Fire (1993). . . . . . . . . . . . Professor Riger
The Pelican Brief (1993) . . . . . . . . . . . . .Gavin Verheek
*Made for Cable Movies:*
Dead Ahead: The Exxon Valdez Disaster (1992; U.S./
British; HBO). . . . . . . . . . . . . . . . . . . . .Dan Lawn
*Made for TV Movies:*
Necessity (1988). . . . . . . . . . . . . . . . . . . . Charlie
Cross of Fire (1989). . . . . . . . . . . . . . Steve Stephenson
Spoils of War (1994) . . . . . . . . . . . . . . . . . . . .n.a.

# Hearne, Michael

*Films:*
**Young Lady Chatterley** (1977) . . . . . . . . . Hitchhiker
- ••• 0:52—Buns, several times in back of car with Harlee McBride.
- • 0:54—Brief buns when he's let out of the car.

# Hehn, Sascha

*Films:*
Naughty Nymphs (1972; German). . . . . . . . . . . . . n.a.
*a.k.a. Passion Pill Swingers*
*a.k.a. Don't Tell Daddy*
**Melody in Love** (1978) . . . . . . . . . . . . . . . . . Alain
- •• 1:08—Buns while outside with Melody. Very brief erect penis under covers.
- • 1:16—Buns, twice while making love with Melody near an erupting volcano.

**Patricia** (1984). . . . . . . . . . . . . . . . . . Harry Miller
- • 0:41—Lower half of buns, while scratching his butt in the hallway.

# • Hench, Richard

*Films:*
Bio-Hazard (1984) . . . . . . . . . . . . . . . . . . . . . n.a.
Star Slammer—The Escape (1986). . . . . . . . . . . .Garth
**Endangered** (1994) . . . . . . . . . . . . . . . . . . . Richard
- • 0:36—Long, long shot of buns, while walking on rocks.

# Hennessy, Michael

*Films:*
Extremities (1986) . . . . . . . . . . . . . . . . . Pizza Man
**Transformations** (1988) . . . . . . . . . . . . . . . Stephens
- • 1:07—Brief, partial buns, while pulling his pants down.

# • Henry, Gregg

*Films:*
Mean Dog Blues (1978) . . . . . . . . . . . . . . Paul Ramsey
Just Before Dawn (1980) . . . . . . . . . . . . . . . . . . n.a.
**The Patriot** (1986) . . . . . . . . . . . . . . . . . Matt Ryder
- • 0:49—Upper half of buns, while making love on top of Simone Griffeth (her leg gets in the way).

Fair Game (1988; Italian) . . . . . . . . . . . . . . . . . Gene
Raising Cain (1992) . . . . . . . . . . . . . . . . . . . Lt. Terri
*Made for TV Movies:*
Staying Afloat (1993). . . . . . . . . . . . . . . . . Ed Smith

# Herrier, Mark

*Films:*
Tank (1984) . . . . . . . . . . . . . . . . . . . . . . . . . Elliot
**Porky's Revenge** (1985; Canadian) . . . . . . . . . . . Billy
- •• 0:16—Buns, while getting out of swimming pool (the second guy getting out). More buns running around.

Real Men (1987) . . . . . . . . . . . . . . . . . . . .Bradshaw

## Hershberger, Gary

Films:

**Paradise Motel** (1985) . . . . . . . . . . . . . . . . . . . . Sam
•• 0:33—Buns, while running away from the Coach's house.
Free Ride (1986) . . . . . . . . . . . . . . . . . . . . . . . . Dan
Sneakers (1992) . . . . . . . . College Aged Martin Bishop
Twin Peaks: Fire Walk With Me (1992). . . . . Mike Nelson

## Heston, Charlton

Films:

The Ten Commandments (1956) . . . . . . . . . . . . .Moses
Ben-Hur (1959). . . . . . . . . . . . . . . . . . Judah Ben-Hur
  (Academy Award for Best Actor.)
El Cid (1961; U.S./Italian) . . Rodrigo Diaz de Bivar/El Cid
**Planet of the Apes** (1968). . . . . . . . . . . .George Taylor
• 0:26—Buns, seen through a waterfall and while walking on rocks. Long shots.
• 1:04—Buns while standing in middle of the room when the apes tear his loin cloth off.
The Omega Man (1971) . . . . . . . . . . . . . . . . . . Neville
Soylent Green (1973) . . . . . . . . . . . . . . Detective Thorn
The Three Musketeers (1973) . . . . . . .Cardinal Richelieu
Airport 1975 (1974) . . . . . . . . . . . . . . . .Alan Murdock
Earthquake (1974) . . . . . . . . . . . . . . . . . . . . . . .Graff
Midway (1976). . . . . . . . . . . . . . Captain Matt Garth
Gray Lady Down (1977) . . . . . . . . Capt. Paul Blanchard
Almost an Angel (1990) . . . . . . . . . . . . . . . . . .Moses
Solar Crisis (1992). . . . . . . . . . . .Admiral "Skeet" Kelso
Tombstone (1993) . . . . . . . . . . . . . . . .Henry Hooker
Wayne's World 2 (1993) . . . . . . . . . . . . . .Good Actor
TV:
The Colbys (1985-87) . . . . . . . . . . . . . . . . Jason Colby

## Hewitt, Martin

Films:

**Endless Love** (1981) . . . . . . . . . . . . . . . . . . . . . David
• 0:22—Buns when seen in front of fireplace in living room with Brooke Shields. Long shot.
• 0:27—Very brief buns in bedroom when Shields closes the door. Another long shot.
•• 0:28—Buns, while jumping into bed with Shields.
• 0:38—Buns, while lying on top of Shields in bed.
Yellowbeard (1983). . . . . . . . . . . . . . . . . . . . . . Dan
Out of Control (1984). . . . . . . . . . . . . . . . . . . .Keith
Alien Predators (1986). . . . . . . . . . . . . . . . . Michael
Killer Party (1986). . . . . . . . . . . . . . . . . . . . . . Blake
Operation: Paratrooper (1988) . . . . . . . . . . Phil Cooper
a.k.a. Private War
Two Moon Junction (1988). . . . . . . . . . . . . . . . Chad
**Crime Lords** (1990) . . . . . . . . . . . . . . . . . .Peter Russo
•• 0:50—Buns, while getting back into bed with two Chinese girls.
**Carnal Crimes** (1991). . . . . . . . . . . . . . . . . . . .Renny
•• 0:29—Buns, while making love with Linda Carol and Mia.

**Secret Games** (1991). . . . . . . . . . . . . . . . . . . . . Eric
(Unrated version reviewed.)
• 0:38—Brief side view of buns, while in bed with Julianne.
0:48—Almost buns, on top of Julianne in bed. (Her foot gets in the way.)
**Night Rhythms** (1992) . . . . . . . . . . . . . . . Nick West
(Unrated version reviewed.)
•• 0:29—Buns, while making love with Tracy Tweed.
••• 0:31—Buns, while making love with Tweed.
• 0:33—Partial buns, while getting up off the floor.
••• 1:18—Buns, while making love on top of Deborah Driggs in bed.
**Secret Games 2—The Escort** (1993) . . . . . .Kyle Lake
(Unrated version reviewed.)
••• 0:24—Buns, while making love with Stacey and Lisa in the shower.
•• 0:33—Buns, while making love in bed with Irene.
TV:
The Family Tree (1983) . . . . . . . . . . . . . Sam Benjamin

## Hewlett, David

Films:

The Dark Side (1987). . . . . . . . . . . . . . . . . .Chuckie
Pin (1988) . . . . . . . . . . . . . . . . . . . . . . . . . Leon
Desire and Hell at Sunset Motel (1990)
. . . . . . . . . . . . . . . . . . . . . . . Deadpan Winchester
**Where the Heart Is** (1990). . . . . . . . . . . . . . . Jimmy
• 0:56—Buns, while walking around the hall in an angel costume.
Scanners 2: The New Order (1991) . . . . . .David Kellum

## Hill, Bernard

Films:

The Bounty (1984). . . . . . . . . . . . . . . . . . . . . Cole
The Chain (1985; British) . . . . . . . . . . . . . . . . .Nick
No Surrender (1986; British) . . . . . . . . . . . . Bernard
**Drowning by Numbers** (1988; British) . . . . . Madgett
•• 0:35—Buns, getting out of bed to throw papers out the window.
Mountains of the Moon (1989) . . .Dr. David Livingstone
Shirley Valentine (1989; British) . . . . . . . . .Joe Bradshaw

## Hindley, Tommy

Films:

**Silent Night, Deadly Night 4: Initiation** (1990)
. . . . . . . . . . . . . . . . . . . . . . . . . . . . . . . . Hank
• 0:03—Brief buns, while carrying Kim onto bed.

## Hines, Gregory

Films:

History of the World, Part I (1981) . . . . . . . . . . Josephus
**Wolfen** (1981) . . . . . . . . . . . . . . . . . . . . .Whittington
• 1:24—Buns, twice when he moons Albert Finney, who is looking through a green-tinted night vision scope.
Deal of the Century (1983) . . . . . . . . . . Ray Kasternak
White Nights (1985) . . . . . . . . . . Raymond Greenwood
Running Scared (1986) . . . . . . . . . . . . . . . Ray Hughes

Tap (1989) . . . . . . . . . . . . . . . . . . . . . . Max Washington
Eve of Destruction (1991) . . . . . . . . . . . . Jim McQuade
A Rage in Harlem (1991). . . . . . . . . . . . . . . . . . Goldy
Renaissance Man (1994) . . . . . . . . . . . . . . . . . . . n.a.

## Hinton, Darby
*Films:*
Son of Flubber (1963). . . . . . . . . . . . Second Hobgoblin
Mr. Sycamore (1975) . . . . . . . . . . . . . . . . . . . . . Frank
The Treasure of Jamaica Reef (1976) . . . . . . . . . . . . n.a.
Black Oak Conspiracy (1977) . . . . . . . . . Miner in Cafe
Goodbye Franklin High (1978) . . . . . . . . . . . . . . . n.a.
Hi-Riders (1978) . . . . . . . . . . . . . . . . . . . . . . . . . n.a.
Without Warning (1980). . . . . . . . . . . . . . . . . . Randy
**Firecracker** (1981) . . . . . . . . . . . . . . . Chuck Donner
  • 1:01—Brief upper half of buns, then buns, while
    making love with Jillian Kesner in bed.
Wacko (1983) . . . . . . . . . . . . . . . . . . . . . . .Rookie Cop
**Malibu Express** (1984). . . . . . . . . . . . . Cody Abilene
  • 0:08—Brief buns, while taking a shower on his boat.
*TV:*
Daniel Boone (1964-70) . . . . . . . . . . . . . . Israel Boone
Days of Our Lives (1985). . . . . . . . . . . . . . . Ian Griffith

## Hodges, Tom
*Films:*
Lucas (1986). . . . . . . . . . . . . . . . . . . . . . . . . . Bruno
Revenge of the Nerds II: Nerds in Paradise (1987). . .n.a.
Steel Magnolias (1989). . . . . . . . . . . . . . .Louie Jones
Frame Up (1990). . . . . . . . . . . . . . . . . . . . Don Curran
**The Baby Doll Murders** (1992) . . . . . . . . . Les Parker
  • 0:35—Upper half of buns, while in bed with the
    young woman.
**Excessive Force** (1993). . . . . . . . . . . . . . . . . . Dylan
  • 0:16—Buns, while making love in the bathroom
    with Lisa.
  •• 0:17—Buns, while putting his pants on in bedroom.

## Hoffman, Dustin
*Films:*
The Graduate (1967) . . . . . . . . . . . . . . . Ben Braddock
John and Mary (1969). . . . . . . . . . . . . . . . . . . . . John
Midnight Cowboy (1969) . . . . . . . . . . . . . . . . . Ratso
**Little Big Man** (1970) . . . . . . . . . . . . . . . Jack Crabb
  • 1:28—Buns, twice, while leaving Digging Bear's bed
    for another sister's bed inside tepee.
Straw Dogs (1972) . . . . . . . . . . . . . . . . . . . . . David
Papillon (1973) . . . . . . . . . . . . . . . . . . . . Louis Dega
Lenny (1974) . . . . . . . . . . . . . . . . . . . . Lenny Bruce
All the President's Men (1976) . . . . . . . . .Carl Bernstein
**Marathon Man** (1976). . . . . . . . . . . . . . . . . . . .Babe
  •• 1:09—Buns, getting out of the bathtub and putting
    some pajamas on while someone lurks outside the
    bathroom.
Straight Time (1978). . . . . . . . . . . . . . . . Max Dembo
  0:38—Very, very brief tip of penis in jail shower
    scene after getting sprayed by guard. Don't really
    see anything.
Agatha (1979; British). . . . . . . . . . . . . . Wally Stanton

Kramer vs. Kramer (1979) . . . . . . . . . . . . . Ted Kramer
  (Academy Award for Best Actor.)
Tootsie (1982) . . . . . . . . . . . . . . . . . . . . . . Michael
Ishtar (1987) . . . . . . . . . . . . . . . . . . . . Chuck Clarke
Rain Man (1988) . . . . . . . . . . . . . . . .Raymond Babbitt
  (Academy Award for Best Actor.)
Family Business (1989). . . . . . . . . . . . . . . . . . . . Vito
Dick Tracy (1990). . . . . . . . . . . . . . . . . . . .Mumbles
Billy Bathgate (1991) . . . . . . . . . . . . . . Dutch Schultz
Hook (1991) . . . . . . . . . . . . . . . . . . . . Captain Hook
Hero (1992) . . . . . . . . . . . . . . . . . . Bernie LaPlante

## Hoffman, Thom
*Films:*
**The Fourth Man** (1984; Dutch). . . . . . . . . . .Herman
  • 1:00—Frontal nudity on cross when Gerard pulls his
    red trunks down. Long shot.
  •• 1:10—Nude in bathroom when Gerard comes in.
  ••• 1:11—Buns making love on bed with Christine while
    Gerard watches through keyhole.
Lily Was Here (1989; Dutch). . . . . . . . . . . . . . Arend
Orlando (1993; British) . . . . . . . . . . William of Orange

## Hofschneider, Marco
*Films:*
**Europa Europa** (1991; German)
  . . . . . . . . . . . . . . . . . . . . . .Young Salomon Perel
  ••• 0:03—Buns, while taking off underwear to take a
    bath.
  • 0:05—Very, very brief frontal nudity, getting into
    tub.
  ••• 0:06—Nude, getting out of the bathtub and run-
    ning to hide in a barrel.
  •• 0:45—Nude, running around in barn, trying to get
    away from his fellow German officer.
  • 1:19—Brief, discolored frontal nudity, after he tries
    to "create" a foreskin.
Foreign Student (1994) . . . . . . . . . . . . . . . . . . . n.a.

## Holbrook, Hal
Husband of actress Dixie Carter.
*Films:*
Wild in the Streets (1968) . . . . . . . .Senator John Fergus
The People Next Door (1970) . . . . . . . . David Hoffman
They Only Kill Their Masters (1972) . . . . . . . . . Watkins
Magnum Force (1973) . . . . . . . . . . .Lieutenant Briggs
**The Girl from Petrovka** (1974) . . . . . . . . . . . . .Joe
  • 0:40—Brief buns, while getting out of bed, putting
    on a robe and talking to Goldie Hawn.
Midway (1976) . . . . . . . .Commander Joseph Rochefort
The Fog (1980) . . . . . . . . . . . . . . . . . . . . . . Malone
The Kidnapping of the President (1980; Canadian)
  . . . . . . . . . . . . . . . . . . . . . . President Adam Scott
Creepshow (1982). . . . . . . . . . . . . . .Henry Northrup
Girls Nite Out (1982) . . . . . . . . . . . . . . . Jim MacVey
  *a.k.a. Scared to Death*
The Star Chamber (1983). . . . . . . . . .Benjamin Caulfield
Wall Street (1987) . . . . . . . . . . . . . . . Lou Mannheim
The Unholy (1988). . . . . . . . . . . . . Archbishop Mosley

The Firm (1993) . . . . . . . . . . . . . . . . . . Oliver Lambert
*Miniseries:*
Blue and the Gray (1982) . . . President Abraham Lincoln
North and South, Book II (1986) . . . . . Abraham Lincoln
*Made for TV Movies:*
A Killing in a Small Town (1990) . . . . . . . Dr. Beardsley
*TV:*
The Senator (1970-71) . . . . . . . . Senator Hayes Stowe
Evening Shade (1990- ) . . . . . . . . . . . . . . . Evan Evans

## Holmes, T. C.

*Video Tapes:*
**Intimate Workout For Lovers** (1992)
. . . . . . . . . . . . . . . . . . . . . . . . . . Intimate Harmony
••• 0:39—Nude, in dance studio and in the showers.

## Hooten, Peter

*Films:*
**Fantasies** (1974) . . . . . . . . . . . . . . . . . . . . . . . Damir
*a.k.a. Once Upon a Love*
• 1:06—Buns, while dropping his towel in front of Bo
Derek. Long shot, don't see his face.
• 1:18—Buns again. Same shot from 1:06.
The Student Body (1975) . . . . . . . . . . . . Carter Blalock
Orca, The Killer Whale (1977) . . . . . . . . . . . . . . . Paul
The Soldier (1982) . . . . . . . . . . . . . . . . . . . . . . . n.a.

## Hoover, Phil

*Films:*
The Thing with Two Heads (1972) . . . . . . . . .Policeman
**Policewomen** (1974) . . . . . . . . . . . . . . . . . . . . . Doc
•• 0:42—Buns, seen through shower door. More buns,
after Laura opens the door.
The Black Gestapo (1975) . . . . . . . . . . . . . . . . . . Vito
Race with the Devil (1975) . . . . . . . . . . . . . Mechanic
Baker's Hawk (1976) . . . . . . . . . . . . . . . . . . . . . Sled
Superchick (1978) . . . . . . . . . . . . . . . . . Tommy Hooks
Best Seller (1988) . . . . . . . . . . . . . . . . . . . . . . . Roud

## • Hopkins, Rod

*Video Tapes:*
**The Lover's Guide to Sexual Ecstasy: A Sensual
Guide to Lovemaking** (1992) . . . Advanced Foreplay
•• 0:25—Buns, while making love in bed with his lover.
•• 0:33—Buns, while making love some more.
••• 0:36—Buns, while making love in various positions.

## Hoppe, Nicholas

*Films:*
**Night Club** (1989) . . . . . . . . . . . . . . . . . . . . . . Nick
• 0:27—Brief buns, while making love on roof with
stripper. Long shot.
••• 0:37—Frontal nudity, getting up off the floor.
••• 0:47—Buns, while making love with Elizabeth
Kaitan.

## Hopper, Dennis

*Films:*
Rebel Without a Cause (1955) . . . . . . . . . . . . . . .Goon
Giant (1956) . . . . . . . . . . . . . . . . . . . Jordan Benedict III
Cool Hand Luke (1967) . . . . . . . . . . . . . . Bubalugats
The Trip (1967) . . . . . . . . . . . . . . . . . . . . . . . . . . .Max
Easy Rider (1969) . . . . . . . . . . . . . . . . . . . . . . . . Billy
**Bloodbath** (1976) . . . . . . . . . . . . . . . . . . . .Chicken
*a.k.a. The Sky is Falling*
Mad Dog Morgan (1976; Australian) . . . Daniel Morgan
The American Friend (1977) . . . . . . . . . . . . . . . Ripley
**Tracks** (1977) . . . . . . . . . . . . . . . . . . . . Sgt. Jack Falen
•• 0:58—Frontal nudity running through the train.
Long scene.
Reborn (1978) . . . . . . . . . . . . . . . . . . . .Rev. Tom Harley
King of the Mountain (1981) . . . . . . . . . . . . . . . . .Cal
Out of the Blue (1982) . . . . . . . . . . . . . . . . . . . . .Don
The Osterman Weekend (1983) . . . . . Richard Tremayne
Rumble Fish (1983) . . . . . . . . . . . . . . . . . . . . . Father
My Science Project (1985) . . . . . . . . . . . . . .Bob Roberts
Blue Velvet (1986) . . . . . . . . . . . . . . . . . .Frank Booth
Hoosiers (1986) . . . . . . . . . . . . . . . . . . . . . . Shooter
Running Out of Luck (1986) . . . . . . . . . . Video Director
The Texas Chainsaw Massacre 2 (1986)
. . . . . . . . . . . . . . . . . . . Lieutenant "Lefty" Enright
Black Widow (1987) . . . . . . . . . . . . . . . . . . . . . . Ben
River's Edge (1987) . . . . . . . . . . . . . . . . . . . . .Feck
Straight to Hell (1987; British) . . . . . . . . . . . I.G. Farben
Blood Red (1988) . . . . . . . . . . William Bradford Berrigan
Riders of the Storm (1988) . . . . . . . . . . . . . . Captain
Backtrack (1989) . . . . . . . . . . . . . . . . . . . . . . . .Milo
*a.k.a. Catch Fire*
**Chattahoochee** (1990) . . . . . . . . . . . Walker Benson
• 0:32—Brief buns, while leaving the shower room af-
ter talking to Gary Oldman.
Flashback (1990) . . . . . . . . . . . . . . . . . Huey Walker
Eye of the Storm (1991) . . . . . . . . . . . . . . . . .Marvin
The Indian Runner (1991) . . . . . . . . . . . . . . . Caesar
Sunset Heat (1991) . . . . . . . . . . . . . . . . Carl Madson
(Unrated version reviewed.)
Boiling Point (1992; U.S./French) . . . . . . . . . . . . . Red
Red Rock West (1992) . . . . . . . . . . . . . . . . . . . . Lyle
Super Mario Bros. (1993) . . . . . . . . . . . King Koopa
True Romance (1993) . . . . . . . . . . . . . Clifford Worley
(Unrated version reviewed.)
Chasers (1994) . . . . . . . . . . . . . . . . . . . . . . Doggie
Speed (1994) . . . . . . . . . . . . . . . . . . . . . . . . . . n.a.
*Made for Cable Movies:*
Doublecrossed (1991; HBO) . . . . . . . . . . . Barry Seal
Paris Trout (1991; Showtime) . . . . . . . . . . . . Paris Trout
**Nails** (1992; Showtime) . . . . . . . . . .Harry "Nails" Niles
••• 0:39—Buns, while getting out of the bathtub and
running outside after the guy who shot at him.
• 0:40—Very, very brief frontal nudity, dropping towel
to drape on his shoulder.
The Heart of Justice (1993; TNT) . . . . . . . . Austin Blair
*Magazines:*
**Playboy** (Feb 1977) . . . . . . . . . . . . . The Year in Sex
••• 141—Frontal nudity running through train.

# • *Hordern, Michael*

*Films:*
El Cid (1961; U.S./Italian) . . . . . . . . . . . . . . Don Diego
Cleopatra (1963). . . . . . . . . . . . . . . . . . . . . . . . .Cicero
Cast a Giant Shadow (1966) . . . . . . British Ambassador
A Funny Thing Happened on the Way to the Forum
    (1966). . . . . . . . . . . . . . . . . . . . . . . . . . . . . . . . . Senex
Taming of the Shrew (1966; U.S./Italian). . . . . Baptista
How I Won the War (1967) . . . . . . . . . . . . . . . Grapple
Where Eagles Dare (1969; British) . . Vice Admiral Rolland
Up Pompeii (1971; British) . . . . . . . . . . . . . . . Ludicrus
Lucky Lady (1973). . . . . . . . . . . . Captain Rockwell
Mackintosh Man (1973; British) . . . . . . . . . . . .Brown
**Joseph Andrews** (1977; British/French)
    . . . . . . . . . . . . . . . . . . . . . . . . . . . . . . .Parson Adams
    • 1:28—Brief buns, while running down the hall try-
        ing to get Mr. Didapper out of bed.
    •• 1:30—Buns, while getting back into bed.
The Medusa Touch (1978; British). . . . . . . . . . .Atropos
Gandhi (1982) . . . . . . . . . . . . . . . . .Sir Georg Hodge
The Missionary (1982; British). . . . . . . . . Slatterthwaite
Yellowbeard (1983). . . . . . . . . . . . . . . . . Dr. Gilpin
The Trouble with Spies (1984). . . . . . . . . . Jason Lock
Comrades (1986; British) . . . . . . . . . . . . .Mr. Pitt
Lady Jane (1987; British) . . . . . . . . . . . . Dr. Peckenham
Dark Obsession (1989; British) . . . . . . . . .Lord Crewne
*a.k.a. Diamond Skulls*

# *Horenstein, Jay*

*Films:*
**American Taboo** (1984). . . . . . . . . . . . . . . . . . Paul
    •• 0:33—Frontal nudity, getting out of shower and dry-
        ing himself off. Foggy.
    • 1:11—Buns, while on top of Lisa in bed.
    • 1:28—Buns, while making love with Lisa during
        flashback.

# *Houston, Robert*

*Films:*
The Hills Have Eyes (1977) . . . . . . . . . . . . Bobby Carter
**Cheerleaders Wild Weekend** (1985) . . . . . . . . Billy
    • 0:45—Brief buns, getting caught watching Frankie
        give Jeanne a bath.
The Hills Have Eyes, Part II (1989) . . . . . . . . . . .Bobby

# *Howard, Adam Coleman*

*Films:*
Quiet Cool (1986). . . . . . . . . . . . . . . . . .Joshua Greer
**Slaves of New York** (1989) . . . . . . . . . . . . . . Stash
    • 1:15—Buns, while putting on his pants and silhou-
        ette of penis. Dark, hard to see.
No Secrets (1991). . . . . . . . . . . . . . . . . . . . . Manny

# *Howard, Alan*

*Films:*
Americanization of Emily (1964) . . . . . . . . . Port Ensign
Oxford Blues (1984) . . . . . . . . . . . . . . . . . . . . .Simon

**The Cook, The Thief, His Wife & Her Lover**
    (1989; Dutch/French). . . . . . . . . . . . . . . . . . Michael
    •• 0:32—Buns, while then brief frontal nudity with
        Helen Mirren.
    • 0:42—Buns, while on top of Mirren.
    • 1:11—Buns, with Mirren in kitchen.
    ••• 1:14—Buns, while getting into meat truck. Frontal
        nudity getting hosed off and walking around with
        Mirren.

# *Howard, Clint*

Brother of actor/director Ron Howard.
*Films:*
Gentle Giant (1967). . . . . . . . . . . . . . . . .Mark Wedloe
Wild Country (1971) . . . . . . . . . . . . . . . Andrew Tanner
Salty (1975) . . . . . . . . . . . . . . . . . . . . . . . . . . . . Tim
Eat My Dust! (1976). . . . . . . . . . . . . . . . . . . .Georgie
Grand Theft Auto (1977) . . . . . . . . . . . . . . . . . . Ace
Harper Valley P.T.A. (1978) . . . . . . . . . . . . . . . Corley
Rock 'n' Roll High School (1979) . . . . . . . .Eaglebauer
**Evilspeak** (1981) . . . . . . . . . . . . . . . . . . . Coopersmith
    • 0:07—Buns, in shower with three other guys. (He's
        the second from the left.)
Night Shift (1982) . . . . . . . . . . . . . . . . . . . . . Jefferey
Splash (1984). . . . . . . . . . . . . . . . . . . . Wedding Guest
Cocoon (1985) . . . . . . . . . . . . . . . . . . . . John Dexter
Gung Ho (1985) . . . . . . . . . . . . . . . . . . . . . . .Paul
The Wraith (1986) . . . . . . . . . . . . . . . . . . Rughead
End of the Line (1987) . . . . . . . . . . . . . . . Les Sullivan
B.O.R.N. (1988). . . . . . . . . . . . . . . . . . . . . . . n.a.
Freeway (1988) . . . . . . . . . . . . . . . . . . . . .Ronnie
Parenthood (1989). . . . . . . . . . . . . . . . . . . . . Lou
Tango & Cash (1989). . . . . . . . . . . . . . . . . .Slinky
Disturbed (1990) . . . . . . . . . . . . . . . . . . . . . Brian
Backdraft (1991) . . . . . . . . . . . . . . . . . . . . . Ricco
The Rocketeer (1991). . . . . . . . . . . . . . . . . . .Monk
Far and Away (1992) . . . . . . . . . . . . . . . . . . .Flynn
Carnosaur (1993). . . . . . . . . . . . . . . . . . . . . .Friar
Forced to Kill (1993) . . . . . . . . . . . . . . . . . Drifter
Ticks (1993) . . . . . . . . . . . . . . . . . . . Jarvis Tanner
Leprechaun 2 (1994) . . . . . . . . . . . . . . . . . Tourist
*TV:*
Gentle Ben (1967-69) . . . . . . . . . . . . . . . Mark Wedloe
The Cowboys (1974) . . . . . . . . . . . . . . . . . . Steve

# *Howell, C. Thomas*

Ex-husband of actress Rae Dawn Chong.
*Films:*
E.T. The Extraterrestrial (1982) . . . . . . . . . . . . . . Tyler
The Outsiders (1983). . . . . . . . . . . . . . . Ponyboy Curtis
Grandview, U.S.A. (1984). . . . . . . . . . . . . .Tim Pearson
Red Dawn (1984). . . . . . . . . . . . . . . . . . . . . Robert
Tank (1984) . . . . . . . . . . . . . . . . . . . . . . . . . . . Billy
Secret Admirer (1985) . . . . . . . . . . . . . . .Michael Ryan
The Hitcher (1986). . . . . . . . . . . . . . . . . . . Jim Halsey
Soul Man (1986) . . . . . . . . . . . . . . . . . . Mark Watson
**A Tiger's Tale** (1988). . . . . . . . . . . . . . . Bubber Drumm
    • 0:38—Upper half of buns getting undressed in bed-
        room while Ann-Margret changes in the bathroom.

The Return of the Musketeers (1989) . . . . . . . . . Raoul
Curiosity Kills (1990) . . . . . . . . . . . . . . . . . . Cat Thomas
Far Out Man (1990) . . . . . . . . . . . . C. Thomas Howell
Kid (1990) . . . . . . . . . . . . . . . . . . . . . . . . . . . . . . . . Kid
Side Out (1990) . . . . . . . . . . . . . . . . . . . Monroe Clark
Breaking the Rules (1992) . . . . . . . . . . . Gene Michaels
Nickel & Dime (1992) . . . . . . . . . . . . . . . . . . Jack Stone
**To Protect and Serve** (1992) . . . . . . . . . . . . . . . Egan
••• 0:07—Buns, while getting out of bed to get dressed.
  Don't see his face.
Gettysburg (1993)

. . . . . . . . . . . . . . Lieutenant Thomas D. Chamberlain
Jailbait (1993) . . . . . . . . . . . . . . . . . . . . Sgt. Lee Teffler
That Night (1993) . . . . . . . . . . . . . . . . . . . . . . . . . Rick
*Made for Cable Movies:*
**Acting on Impulse** (1993; Showtime) . . . Paul Stevens
• 1:06—Buns in pulled down boxer shorts in hotel
  room with Linda Fiorentino.
*Made for TV Movies:*
Into the Homeland (1987) . . . . . . . . . . . . . . . . . . . n.a.
Dark Reflection (1994) . . . . . . . . . . . . . . . . . . . . . n.a.
*TV:*
Two Marriages (1983-84) . . . . . . . . . . . . Scott Morgan

## Howes, Dougie
*Films:*
**Salome's Last Dance** (1987) . . . . . . . . Phoney Salome
• 1:05—Very brief frontal nudity at the end of a dance
  routine when you think he's a female Salome.

## Howman, Karl
*Films:*
**The House on Straw Hill** (1976; British) . Small Youth
*a.k.a. Exposé*
•• 0:36—Buns, raping Linda Hayden in a field, while his
  friend holds a gun.

## Hudson, Gary
*Films:*
Skatetown, U.S.A. (1979) . . . . . . . . . . . . . . . . . . . n.a.
King of the Mountain (1981) . . . . . . . . . . . Gang Leader
Cameron's Closet (1989) . . . . . . . . . . . . . . Bob Froelich
Night Angel (1989) . . . . . . . . . . . . . . . . . . . . . . . Rod
Roadhouse (1989) . . . . . . . . . . . . . . . . . . . . . . . Steve
Mind Twister (1992) . . . . . . . . . . . . . . . Daniel Strahten
(Unrated version reviewed.)
**Wild Cactus** (1992) . . . . . . . . . . . . . . . . . . . . Randall
(Unrated version reviewed.)
• 0:11—Buns, getting up out of bed and putting on
  his pants.
••• 1:18—Buns, while making love in bed on top of Al-
  ex.
**Indecent Behavior** (1993) . . . . . . . . . . . Nick Sharkey
(Unrated version reviewed.)
•• 0:57—Buns, several times while on top of Shannon
  Tweed.
Martial Outlaw (1993) . . . . . . . . . . . . . . . . Jack White
Scanner Cop (1993) . . . . . . . . . . . . . . . . . Damon Pratt

**Sexual Intent** (1994) . . . . . . . . . . . . . . . . . . . . John
• 0:50—Brief upper half of buns, while making love
  with Barbara in her office.
• 0:58—Very brief upper half of buns in bathroom.
*TV:*
Sidekicks (1986-87) . . . . . . . . . . . . . . . . . . . . . Coach

## Huff, Brent
*Films:*
Coach (1978) . . . . . . . . . . . . . . . . . . . . . . . . . . . Keith
**The Perils of Gwendoline in the Land of the Yik
Yak** (1984; French) . . . . . . . . . . . . . . . . . . . Willard
• 0:51—Brief buns, in G-string while wearing cos-
  tume.
•• 0:52—Buns, in G-string, walking around with Tawny
  Kitaen in costumes.
•• 0:54—More buns, after the women realize he's a
  man.
••• 0:56—Buns, in jail while wearing only the G-string.
Deadly Passion (1985) . . . . . . . . . . . . . . . . Sam Black
Stormquest (1988) . . . . . . . . . . . . . . . . . . . . . . . Zar
Falling From Grace (1992) . . . . . . . . . . . Parker Parks
*Made for TV Movies:*
I Spy Returns (1994) . . . . . . . . . . . . . . . . . . . . Tilden

## Hughes, Brendan
*Films:*
Return to Horror High (1987) . . . . . . . . . . Steven Blake
Stranded (1987) . . . . . . . . . . . . . . . . . . . . . . . Prince
**To Die For** (1988) . . . . . . . . . . . . . . . . . Vlad Tepish
• 1:13—Buns, while making love with Kate.
Sundown: The Vampire in Retreat (1989) . . . . . . . James
Howling VI—The Freaks (1990) . . . . . . . . . . . . . . . Ian

## Hurt, John
*Films:*
10 Rillington Place (1971; British) . . . Timothy John Evans
The Ghoul (1975; British) . . . . . . . . . . . . . . . . . . . Tom
**East of Elephant Rock** (1976; British) . . . . . . . . Nash
••• 0:48—Frontal nudity, getting up out of bed and get-
  ting dressed.
The Disappearance (1977) . . . . . . . . . . . . . . . . . . n.a.
Midnight Express (1978; British) . . . . . . . . . . . . . Max
Alien (1979) . . . . . . . . . . . . . . . . . . . . . . . . . . . Kane
The Shout (1979) . . . . . . . . . . . . . . . . Anthony Fielding
The Elephant Man (1980) . . . . . . . . . . . . John Merrick
Heaven's Gate (1980) . . . . . . . . . . . . . . . . . . . Irvine
History of the World, Part I (1981) . . . . . . . . . . . Jesus
Night Crossing (1981) . . . . . . . . . . . . . . Peter Strelzyks
Partners (1982) . . . . . . . . . . . . . . . . . . . . . . . Kerwin
**The Osterman Weekend** (1983) . . . Lawrence Fassett
• 0:01—Buns, while getting out of bed and walking to
  the shower.
**1984** (1984) . . . . . . . . . . . . . . . . . . . . Winston Smith
• 1:11—Buns, while walking from the bed to the win-
  dow next to Suzanna Hamilton.
Champions (1984) . . . . . . . . . . . . . . . . . Bob Champion
The Hit (1984) . . . . . . . . . . . . . . . . . . . . . . . Braddock
Jake Speed (1986) . . . . . . . . . . . . . . . . . . . . . . . . Sid

Aria (1987; U.S./British). . . . . . . . . . . . . . . . . The Actor
From the Hip (1987) . . . . . . . . . . . . . . Douglas Benoit
Deadline (1988) . . . . . . . . . . . . . . . . . . . Granville Jones
White Mischief (1988). . . . . . . . . . . . . . . . . . . Colville
Scandal (1989) . . . . . . . . . . . . . . . . . . . .Stephen Ward
   (Unrated version reviewed.)
The Field (1990) . . . . . . . . . . . . . . . . . . Bird O'Donnell
Frankenstein Unbound (1990). . . . . . . . . . . . Buchanan
King Ralph (1991). . . . . . . . . . . . . . . . . . . . . . . Graves
Monolith (1993) . . . . . . . . . . . . . . . . . . . . . . . Villano
Even Cowgirls Get the Blues (1994) . . . . . . . . Countess

# Hurt, William

*Films:*

**Altered States** (1980) . . . . . . . . . . . . . . Eddie Jessup
   0:46—Brief pubic hair twice when Charles Haid and
   Bob Balaban help him out of isolation tank.
   • 0:54—Very brief buns, while standing in the shower
   when he starts transforming. More buns standing
   near door and walking to bed.
Body Heat (1981) . . . . . . . . . . . . . . . . . . . . .Ned Racine
Eyewitness (1981). . . . . . . . . . . . . . . . . . Daryll Deever
The Big Chill (1983) . . . . . . . . . . . . . . . . . . . . . . . Nick
Gorky Park (1983). . . . . . . . . . . . . . . . . . . Arkady Renko
Kiss of the Spider Woman (1985; U.S./Brazilian)
. . . . . . . . . . . . . . . . . . . . . . . . . . . . . . . . .Luis Molina
   (Academy Award for Best Actor.)
Children of a Lesser God (1986) . . . . . . . . . James Leeds
**Broadcast News** (1987) . . . . . . . . . . . . . . Tom Grunik
  •• 0:59—Brief buns when getting up from bed after
   making love with Jennifer. Shadow of semi-erect pe-
   nis on the wall when she notices it.
The Accidental Tourist (1988) . . . . . . . . . . . . . . Macon
A Time of Destiny (1988) . . . . . . . . . . . . . . . . . Martin
Alice (1990) . . . . . . . . . . . . . . . . . . . . . . . . . . . Doug
I Love You to Death (1990) . . . . . . . . . . . . . . . Harlan
The Doctor (1991) . . . . . . . . . . . . . . . . Dr. Jack McKee
Until the End of the World (1991)
. . . . . . . . . . . . . . . . . . . Sam Farber/Trevor McPhee
The Plague (1992; French/British) . . . . Dr. Bernard Rieux
Mr. Wonderful (1993) . . . . . . . . . . . . . . . . . . . . . Tom
Trial By Jury (1994) . . . . . . . . . . . . . . . . . . . . . . .n.a.

# Hurwitz, Stan

*Films:*
**Necromancer** (1988) . . . . . . . . . . . . . . .Paul DuShane
   • 0:46—Brief buns, when Julie pulls his underwear
   down. Don't see his face.

# Hutton, Timothy

Ex-husband of actress Debra Winger.
*Films:*
Ordinary People (1980). . . . . . . . . . . . . . . . . .Conrad
   (Academy Award for Best Supporting Actor.)
Taps (1981). . . . . . . . . . . . . . . . . . . . . .Brian Moreland
Daniel (1983) . . . . . . . . . . . . . . . . . . . .Daniel Isaacson
**Made in Heaven** (1987) . . . . . Mike Shea/Elmo Barnett
  •• 0:08—Buns, while standing in a room when he first
   gets to heaven.

Everybody's All-American (1988) . . . . . . . . . . . Donnie
A Time of Destiny (1988) . . . . . . . . . . . . Jack McKenna
Q & A (1990). . . . . . . . . . . . . . . . . . . . . . . . . Al Rielly
Torrents of Spring (1990). . . . . . . . . . . . Dimitri Sanin
The Dark Half (1993) . . . . . . . . . . . . . .Thad Beaumont
The Temp (1993) . . . . . . . . . . . . . . . . . . . Peter Derns
*Made for Cable Movies:*
Zelda (1993; TNT) . . . . . . . . . . . . . F. Scott Fitzgerald
*Made for Cable TV:*
Strangers: Windows (1992; HBO). . . . . . . . . . . . .Tom
   (Available on video tape on *Strangers*.)

# •Idle, Eric

*Films:*
Yellowbeard (1983) . . . . . . . . . . . Commander Clement
National Lampoon's European Vacation (1985)Bike Rider
The Adventures of Baron Munchausen (1989; British/
   German). . . . . . . . . . . . . . . . . . . . Desmond/Berthold
Nuns on the Run (1990; British). . . . . . . . . Brian Hope
Too Much Sun (1990) . . . . . . . . . . . . . . . Sonny Rivers
Mom and Dad Save the World (1992) . . . . . . . . . . Raff
**Splitting Heirs** (1993). . . . . . . . . . . . . . . . . . Tommy
 ••• 0:41—Buns, while hiding in Kitty's apartment after
   Rick Moranis shows up.
   0:43—Brief side view of buns, walking down the
   stairs while holding his clothes.
*TV:*
Monty Python's Flying Circus (British) . . . . . . . . Regular
*Magazines:*
**Playboy** (Nov 1976) . . . . . . . . .The Vatican Sex Manual
   • 134-135—Side view of buns, demonstrating differ-
   ent (non) sexual positions. B&W.

# Ipalé, Aharon

*Films:*
**Too Hot To Handle** (1975) . . . . .Dominco de la Torres
   • 0:39—Buns, while in bed with Cheri Caffaro. Dark,
   hard to see.
The Final Option (1982; British) . . . . . . . . . . . . Malek
One Man Out (1988). . . . . . . . . . . . . . . . .The General
Invisible: The Chronicles of Benjamin Knight (1993)
. . . . . . . . . . . . . . . . . . . . . . . . . . . . . . . . . . Petroff
Son of the Pink Panther (1993) . . . . . . . . General Jaffar
*Made for TV Movies:*
The Great Pretender (1991) . . . . . . . . . . . . . . . Bratso

# Irons, Jeremy

*Films:*
Nijinsky (1980; British). . . . . . . . . . . . . Mikhail Fokine
The French Lieutenant's Woman (1981) . . . Charles/Mike
Moonlighting (1982; British) . . . . . . . . . . . . . .Nowak
Betrayal (1983; British). . . . . . . . . . . . . . . . . . . Jerry
Swann in Love (1984; French/German) . .Charles Swann
   *a.k.a. Un Amour de Swann*
The Mission (1986; British). . . . . . . . . . . . . . . Gabriel
Reversal of Fortune (1990) . . . . . . . . . . Claus von Bülow
   (Academy Award for Best Actor.)

**Damage** (1992; French/British) . . .Dr. Stephen Fleming (Unrated Director's cut reviewed.)
- • 0:52—Brief buns, while sitting on floor and making love with Juliette Binoche.
- ••• 1:30—Buns, while making love on top of Binoche.
- ••• 1:31—Nude, getting out of bed and running down the stairs.

Kafka (1992; U.S./French) . . . . . . . . . . . . . . . . . Kafka
Waterland (1992; British/U.S.) . . . . . . . . . . . . Tom Crick
The House of Spirits (1993) . . . . . . . . . . Esteban Trueba
M. Butterfly (1993) . . . . . . . . . . . . . . . . René Gallimard
*Miniseries:*

**Brideshead Revisited** (1981; British) . . . Charles Ryder
- •• 0:17—(Part 3 on TV or Book 2 on video tape.) Buns, while standing on roof with Anthony Andrews after talking with Cordelia.

## •J.J.

*Video Tapes:*

**Playboy Night Dreams** (1993) . . . . . .Do Not Disturb
- ••• 0:40—Buns, while making love on bed with his lover.

## •Jackson, Samuel L.

*Films:*

Coming to America (1988) . . . . . . . . . . . . Holdup Man
School Daze (1988). . . . . . . . . . . . . . . . . . . . . . Leeds
Betsy's Wedding (1990) . . . . . . . . . . . . Taxi Dispatcher
The Exorcist III (1990) . . . . . . . . . . . . Dream Blind Man
GoodFellas (1990). . . . . . . . . . . . . . . . Stacks Edwards
Mo' Better Blues (1990) . . . . . . . . . . . . . . . . Madlock
A Shock to the System (1990). . . . . . . . . . . . . Ulysses
Jungle Fever (1991). . . . . . . . . . . . . . . . Gator Purify
Strictly Business (1991) . . . . . . . . . . . . . . . . Monroe
Fathers and Sons (1992) . . . . . . . . . . . . . . Marshall
Johnny Suede (1992) . . . . . . . . . . . . . . . . . . B-Bop
Juice (1992) . . . . . . . . . . . . . . . . . . . . . . . . . . Trip
Jumpin' at the Boneyard (1992) . . . . . . . . Mr. Simpson
Patriot Games (1992) . . . . . . . . . . . . . . Robby Jackson
White Sands (1992) . . . . . . . . . . . . . . . Greg Meeker
Amos & Andrew (1993) . . . . . . . . Andrew Sterling
Jurassic Park (1993). . . . . . . . . . . . . . . . . . . . . Arnold
Loaded Weapon 1 (1993) . . . . . . . . . . . . . . .Wes Luger
Menace II Society (1993) . . . . . . . . . . . . . Tat Lawson
The Meteor Man (1993) . . . . . . . . . . . . . . . . . . Dre
True Romance (1993) . . . . . . . . . . . . . . . . Big Don
(Unrated version reviewed.)
*Made for Cable Movies:*

**Against the Wall** (1994; HBO). . . . . . . . . . . . Jamael
- • 0:06—Buns, during strip-search while entering prison. (Seen through grate).

Assault at West Point: The Court Martial of Johnson Whittaker (1994; Showtime) . . . . . . . . . . . . . . . .n.a.

## Jagger, Mick

Singer with *The Rolling Stones.*
Significant Other of model/actress Jerry Hall.
*Films:*

Performance (1970) . . . . . . . . . . . . . . . . . . . . . Turner
0:48—Side view of buns, while getting out of bathtub.
Burden of Dreams (1982). . . . . . . . . . . . . . . . . n.a.
**Running Out of Luck** (1986) . . . . . . . . . . . . Himself
- • 0:42—Brief buns in mirror in room with Rae Dawn Chong lying in bed. Another buns long shot in bed on top of Chong.

Freejack (1992) . . . . . . . . . . . . . . . . . . . . . . .Vacendak

## Janes, Tom

*Films:*

**Nemesis** (1992) . . . . . . . . . . . . . . . . . . . . . . . .Billy
- •• 0:30—Buns, standing at the window, looking out.
- • 0:31—More buns.
- ••• 0:32—More buns, backing up and lying on bed.
- •• 0:37—Brief nude, getting punched by Deborah Shelton and sitting on bed.
- • 0:38—Brief buns, getting thrown against the wall.

## Janssen, David

*Films:*

To Hell and Back (1955) . . . . . . . . . . . . .Lieutenant Lee
The Green Berets (1968) . . . . . . . . . .George Beckworth
The Shoes of a Fisherman (1968) . . . . . . . .George Faber
Marooned (1969) . . . . . . . . . . . . . . . Ted Dougherty
Macho Callahan (1970) . . . . . . Diego "Macho" Callahan
**Once is Not Enough** (1975) . . . . . . . . . . . . .Tom Colt
- • 1:22—Buns, while taking off clothes and walking to the bathroom.

Two-Minute Warning (1976) . . . . . . . . . . . . . Steve
Golden Rendezvous (1977) . . . . . . . . . .Charles Conway
Inchon (1981) . . . . . . . . . . . . . . . . . . . . . .David Feld
*TV:*

Richard Diamond, Private Detective (1957-60)
. . . . . . . . . . . . . . . . . . . . . . . . . . . .Richard Diamond
The Fugitive (1963-67). . . . . . . . . . . .Dr. Richard Kimble
O'Hara, U.S. Treasury (1971-72). . . . . . . . . .Jim O'Hara
Harry-O (1974-76). . . . . . . . . . . . . . . . . Harry Orwell
Centennial (1978-79). . . . . . . . . . . . . . . . .Paul Garrett

## •Jarrett, Gabriel

*Films:*

Karate Kid, Part III (1989). . . . . . . . . . . . . . . . Rudy
**At Home with the Webbers** (1992) . . . . . . . Thomas
- •• 1:24—Buns, after pulling down his underwear in Jennifer Tilly's bedroom.

## •Jeffrey, Douglas

*Films:*

**Sexual Malice** (1993). . . . . . . . . . . . . . . . . . . Quinn
(Unrated version reviewed.)
- •• 0:26—Buns in G-string, while dancing on stage.
- • 0:36—Buns, while making love on top of Christine in bed.

••• 0:47—Buns, while standing at doorway, then making love with Christine while standing up.
••• 0:57—Buns, while making love with Christine in clothing store dressing room.

## Jenkins, John

*Films:*
**Patti Rocks** (1988) . . . . . . . . . . . . . . . . . . . . . . Eddie
• 1:07—Buns, while making love with Patti in bed.
The Cutting Edge (1992) . . . . . . . . . . .3rd Olympic Pair

## Jeremy, Ron

Adult film actor.
*Adult Films:*
Centerfold Celebrities 3. . . . . . . . . . . . . . . . . .Himself
*Films:*
52 Pick-Up (1986). . . . . . . . . . . . . . . . . . . . Party Goer
Valet Girls (1987) . . . . . . . . . . . Uncredited Party Goer
Spring Fever USA (1988). . . . . . . . . . . . . . . . . . . .n.a.
*a.k.a. Lauderdale*
Caged Fury (1989) . . . . . . . . . . . . . . . . . . . . . . . .n.a.
Dead Bang (1989). . . . . . . . . . . . . . . . . . . . . . . . .n.a.
They Bite (1991) . . . . . . . . . . . . . . . . . . . . . . . Darryl
The Sex Puppets (1992) . . . . . . . . . . . . . .Gino Carlotti
Housewife From Hell (1993) . . . . . . . . . . . . . . . Vince

## Jeter, Michael

*Films:*
**Hair** (1979) . . . . . . . . . . . . . . . . . . Woodrow Sheldon
• 1:06—Buns while in front of Army guys.
Ragtime (1981). . . . . . . . . . . . . . . . . . . . . . . . . . .n.a.
Soup for One (1982). . . . . . . . . . . . . . . . . . . . . . .n.a.
The Money Pit (1986). . . . . . . . . . . . . . . . . . . .Arnie
Dead Bang (1989). . . . . . . . . . . . . . . . . . . Dr. Krantz
Tango & Cash (1989) . . . . . . . . . . . . . . . . . . . Skinner
The Fisher King (1991) . . . . . . Homeless Cabaret Singer
Bank Robber (1993) . . . . . . . . . . . . . . . Night Clerk 1
Sister Act 2: Back in the Habit (1993) . . . Father Ignatius
*Made for TV Movies:*
My Old Man (1979) . . . . . . . . . . . . . . George Gardner
Gypsy (1993) . . . . . . . . . . . . . . . . . . . Mr. Goldstone
Tales of the City (1994). . . . . . . . . . . . . . Carson Callas
*TV:*
Evening Shade (1990- ). . . . . . . . . . . . . . Herman Stiles

## Jodorowsky, Axel

*Films:*
**Santa Sangre** (1989; Italian/Spanish) . . . . . . . . Fenix
•• 0:00—Buns, in room in an asylum.

## Johnson, Don

Husband of actress Melanie Griffith.
*Films:*
The Magic Garden of Stanley Sweetheart (1970)
. . . . . . . . . . . . . . . . . . . . . . . . . Stanley Sweetheart
Zachariah (1971) . . . . . . . . . . . . . . . . . . . . .Matthew
**The Harrad Experiment** (1973) . . . . . . . Stanley Cole
•• 0:18—Brief frontal nudity after getting out of the shower while Laurie Walters watches.

Return to Macon County (1975) . . . . . . . Harley McKay
A Boy and His Dog (1976) . . . . . . . . . . . . . . . . . .Vic
Melanie (1982) . . . . . . . . . . . . . . . . . . . . . . . . .Carl
Miami Vice (1984) . . . . . . . . . . . . . . . . Sonny Crockett
Cease Fire (1985). . . . . . . . . . . . . . . . . . Tim Murphy
Sweet Hearts Dance (1988) . . . . . . . . . . . . Wiley Boon
Dead Bang (1989) . . . . . . . . . . . . . .Detective Jerry Beck
**The Hot Spot** (1990) . . . . . . . . . . . . . .Harry Madox
•• 0:41—Brief buns, while pulling up his underwear, talking to Virginia Madsen.
• 1:17—Buns, while undressing to go swimming with Madsen.
• 1:18—Buns, while getting out of the water. Long shot.
Harley Davidson and The Marlboro Man (1991)
. . . . . . . . . . . . . . Robert Lee Anderson, Marlboro Man
Paradise (1991) . . . . . . . . . . . . . . . . . . . . . .Ben Reed
Born Yesterday (1993) . . . . . . . . . . . . . . . .Paul Verrall
Guilty as Sin (1993) . . . . . . . . . . . . . . David Greenhill
*Made for TV Movies:*
Beulah Land (1980) . . . . . . . . . . . . . . . .Bonard Davis
The Revenge of the Stepford Wives (1980). . Andy Brady
*TV:*
From Here to Eternity (1980) . . . . Jefferson Davis Prewitt
Miami Vice (1984-89) . . . . . . . . . . . . . Sonny Crockett

## Johnson, Joseph Alan

*Films:*
Grad Night (1980). . . . . . . . . . . . . . . . . . . . . . . . Bob
The Slumber Party Massacre (1982) . . . . . . . . . . . Neil
Hollywood Hot Tubs (1984) . . . . . . . . . Shawn's Friend
Berserker (1988). . . . . . . . . . . . . . . . . . . . . . . . .n.a.
**Iced** (1988) . . . . . . . . . . . . . . . . . . . . . . . . . . . Alex
• 0:46—Brief buns while in bathtub reminiscing about making love with a girl.

## •Johnson, Kenneth A.

*Films:*
Genuine Risk (1989). . . . . . . . . . . . . . . . . . . Bartender
**At Home with the Webbers** (1992) . . . . . . . . Chuck
• 0:55—Buns, while standing in chaps in living room with Jennifer Tilly and dancing with her.
• 0:58—Buns, while on the floor and in reflection in window while making love with Tilly.
*Made for Cable TV:*
Red Shoe Diaries: Accidents Happen (1993; Showtime)
. . . . . . . . . . . . . . . . . . . . . . . . . . . . . . . . . Tracer
(Available on video tape on *Red Shoe Diaries 4: Auto Erotica*.)

## Jones, Griff Rhys

*Films:*
**The Misadventures of Mr. Wilt** (1990). . . Henry Wilt
• 0:34—Sort of buns, while naked and tied to inflatable doll.
• 0:36—More buns, while up on balcony. Long shot.

# Jones, Sam

*Films:*

10 (1979) . . . . . . . . . . . . . . . . . . . . . . David Hanley
Flash Gordon (1980) . . . . . . . . . . . . . . . Flash Gordon
**My Chauffeur** (1986) . . . . . . . . . . . . . . . . . . . Battle
••• 0:42—Buns, while running around the park naked.
Jane and the Lost City (1987; British) . . . . "Jungle" Jack
Silent Assassins (1988) . . . . . . . . . . . . . . . . Sam Kettle
One Man Force (1989) . . . . . . . . . . . . . . . . . . . Pete
**Under the Gun** (1989) . . . . . . . . . . . . . . . . . Braxton
• 0:41—Brief buns, while taking a shower at Vanessa
Williams place. Don't see his face.
Driving Force (1990) . . . . . . . . . . . . . . . . . . . Steve
Da Vinci's War (1992) . . . . . . . . . . . . . . Jim Holbrook
Maximum Force (1992) . . . . . . . . . . . . Michael Crews
Night Rhythms (1992) . . . . . . . . . . . . . . . . Jackson
(Unrated version reviewed.)
The Other Woman (1992) . . . . . . . . . . . . Mike Florian
(Unrated version reviewed.)
South Beach (1992) . . . . . . . . . . . . . . . . . . . Billy
Fist of Honor (1993) . . . . . . . . . . . . . . . . . . . Fist
Hard Vice (1994) . . . . . . . . . . . . . . . . . . . . . Joe

*TV:*

Code Red (1981-82) . . . . . . . . . . . . . . Chris Rorchek
Highwayman (1987-88) . . . . . . . . . . . . . Highwayman

*Magazines:*

**Playgirl** (Jun 1975) . . . . . . . . . . . . Man of the Month
Frontal nudity.
**Playgirl** (Jun 1988) . . . . . . . . . Where Are They Now?
38—Frontal nudity.

# Jones, Tommy Lee

*Films:*

Jackson County Jail (1976) . . . . . . . . . . . . Coley Blake
Rolling Thunder (1977) . . . . . . . . . . . . . Johnny Vohden
The Betsy (1978) . . . . . . . . . . . . . . . . . Angelo Perino
Eyes of Laura Mars (1978) . . . . . . . . . . . . John Neville
Coal Miner's Daughter (1980)

. . . . . . . . . . . . . . . . . . Doolittle "Mooney" Lynn
Back Roads (1981) . . . . . . . . . . . . . . . . Elmore Pratt
**The Executioner's Song** (1982) . . . . . . . Gary Gillmore
(European Version reviewed.)
•• 0:48—Buns, while walking to kitchen after hitting
Rosanna Arquette.
Nate and Hayes (1983) . . . . . . . . . Captain Bully Hayes
The River Rat (1984) . . . . . . . . . . . . . . . . . . . Billy
Black Moon Rising (1986) . . . . . . . . . . . . . . . Quint
The Big Town (1987) . . . . . . . . . . . . . . . George Cole
Stormy Monday (1988) . . . . . . . . . . . . . . . . Cosmo
Fire Birds (1990) . . . . . . . . . . . . . . . . . . Brad Little
*a.k.a. Wings of the Apache*
Blue Skies (1991) . . . . . . . . . . . . . . . . Hank Marshall
JFK (1991) . . . . . . . . . . . . . . . . . . . . . Clay Shaw
Under Seige (1992) . . . . . . . . . . . . . . William Stronnix
The Fugitive (1993) . . . . . . . . . . . . . . Samuel Gerard
Heaven and Earth (1993) . . . . . . . . . . Sgt. Steve Butler
House of Cards (1993) . . . . . . . . . Dr. Jack Beerlander
Blown Away (1994) . . . . . . . . . . . . . . . . . . . . n.a.
The Client (1994) . . . . . . . . . . . . . . . . . . . . . n.a.

Natural Born Killers (1994) . . . Warden Dwight McClusky
*Made for Cable Movies:*
Cat on a Hot Tin Roof (1984; HBO) . . . . . . . Brick Pollitt
The Park is Mine (1985; HBO) . . . . . . . . . . . . . Mitch
**Gotham** (1988; Showtime) . . . . . . . . . . Eddie Mallard
*a.k.a. The Dead Can't Lie*
• 0:50—Buns, while walking over to Virginia Madsen.
Dark, hard to see anything.
*Miniseries:*
Lonesome Dove (1989) . . . . . . . . . . . Woodrow F. Call
*Made for TV Movies:*
The Amazing Howard Hughes (1977) . . Howard Hughes
Stranger on My Land (1988) . . . . . . . . . . . . . . . n.a.
*TV:*
One Life to Live (1971-75) . . . . . . . . . . Dr. Mark Toland

# Jones, Tyrone Granderson

*Films:*

**Angel III: The Final Chapter** (1988) . . . . . . L.A. Pimp
•• 0:32—Buns, while standing in alley after Angel
pushes him out of the car.
Twins (1988) . . . . . . . . . . . . . . . . . . . Mover #2
Harlem Nights (1989) . . . . . . . . . . . . . . Crapshooter

# Joshua, Larry

*Films:*

**The Burning** (1981) . . . . . . . . . . . . . . . . . . Glazer
•• 1:02—Buns, getting out of the sleeping bag after
making love with Sally.
Still of the Night (1982) . . . . . . . . . . . . . . . Mugger
Shakedown (1988) . . . . . . . . . . . . . . . . . . . . Rydel
Sea of Love (1989) . . . . . . . . . . . . . . . . . . . Dargan
Dances with Wolves (1990) . . . . . . . . . . . . Sgt. Bauer
Quick Change (1990) . . . . . . . . . . . . Steet Sign Worker
A Midnight Clear (1991) . . . . . . . . . . Lieutenant Ware
True Colors (1991) . . . . . . . . . . . . . . . . . . . David

# Julia, Raul

*Films:*

Panic in Needle Park (1971) . . . . . . . . . . . . . . Marco
The Gumball Rally (1976) . . . . . . . . . . . . . . . Franco
Eyes of Laura Mars (1978) . . . . . . . . . . . Michael Reisler
The Escape Artist (1982) . . . . . . . . . . . . . Stu Quinones
**One from the Heart** (1982) . . . . . . . . . . . . . . . Ray
• 1:20—Very brief buns while getting out of bed with
Teri Garr when Frederic Forrest crashes through the
ceiling.
The Tempest (1982) . . . . . . . . . . . . . . . . . Kalibanos
Compromising Positions (1985) . . . . . . . . David Suarez
Kiss of the Spider Woman (1985; U.S./Brazilian)

. . . . . . . . . . . . . . . . . . . . . . . . . . Valentin
The Morning After (1986) . . . . . . . . . . Joaquin Manero
Moon Over Parador (1988) . . . . . . Roberto Strausmann
The Pentinent (1988) . . . . . . . . . . . . . Ramon Guerola
Tequila Sunrise (1988) . . . . . . . . . . . . . . . Escalante
Trading Hearts (1988) . . . . . . . . . . . . . . . . Vinnie
Frankenstein Unbound (1990) . . . . . Victor Frankenstein
Presumed Innocent (1990) . . . . . . . . . . . . Sandy Stern
The Rookie (1990) . . . . . . . . . . . . . . . . . . . Strom

The Addams Family (1991) . . . . . . . . . Gomez Addams
The Plague (1992; French/British) . . . . . . . . . . .Cottard
Addams Family Values (1993) . . . . . . . Gomez Addams
*Made for Cable Movies:*
The Burning Season (1994; HBO) . . . . . . Chico Mendes

# Juliano, Al

*Films:*
**True Love** (1989). . . . . . . . . . . . . . . . . Male Stripper
• 0:43—Buns while in G-string dancing on stage in a club.

# Junior, Fábio

*Films:*
**Bye Bye Brazil** (1980; Brazilian) . . . . . . . . . . . . . . Ciço
•• 0:38—Buns, while backstage with Salomé.

# Kantor, Richard

*Films:*
Baby, It's You (1983) . . . . . . . . . . . . . . . . . . . . . . .Curtis
**Out of Control** (1984) . . . . . . . . . . . . . . . . . . . . .Gary
• 0:29—Buns, while pulling his underwear down during a game of strip spin the bottle.
*TV:*
Finder of Lost Loves (1984-85) . . . . . . . . Brian Fletcher

# • Karlen, John

*Films:*
**Daughters of Darkness** (1971; Belgian/French/
German/Italian) . . . . . . . . . . . . . . . . . . Stefan Chiltern
• 0:43—Brief buns, rolling over on Valerie in bed.
• 1:03—Buns, putting on his robe. Long shot.
Night of Dark Shadows (1971) . . . . . . . . . . Alex Jenkins
Small Town in Texas (1976). . . . . . . . . . . . . . . . Lenny
Gimme an "F" (1981) . . . . . . . . . . . . . . . . . .Dr. Spirit
*a.k.a. T & A Academy 2*
Pennies from Heaven (1981) . . . . . . . . . . Detective
Racing with the Moon (1984) . . . . . . . . . . . . Mr. Nash
Native Son (1986). . . . . . . . . . . . . . . . . . . . . . . . Max
The Dark Wind (1993). . . . . . . . . . . . . . . . . Jake West
Surf Ninjas (1993). . . . . . . . . . . . . . . . . . . . . . . . Mac
*Miniseries:*
The Winds of War (1983) . . . . . . . . . . Captain Connelly
*Made for TV Movies:*
In a Child's Name (1991) . . . . . . . . . . . . . Joe Silvano
*TV:*
Cagney & Lacey (1982-88) . . . . . . . . . . . Harvey Lacey
(Won an Emmy Award in 1986.)

# Katt, William

Son of actor Bill Williams and actress Barbara Hale.
*Films:*
Carrie (1976) . . . . . . . . . . . . . . . . . . . . . .Tommy Ross
First Love (1977). . . . . . . . . . . . . . . . . . . . .Elgin Smith
Big Wednesday (1978) . . . . . . . . . . . . . . . . . . . . Jack
Baby... Secret of the Lost Legend (1985)
. . . . . . . . . . . . . . . . . . . . . . . . . . . . . .George Loomis
House (1986) . . . . . . . . . . . . . . . . . . . . . . Roger Cobb
White Ghost (1988) . . . . . . . . . . . . . . . . .Steve Shepard

**Last Call** (1990) . . . . . . . . . . . . . . . . . . . . . Paul Avery
••• 0:29—Buns, while on floor with Shannon Tweed.
• 0:41—Brief buns, while getting up from bed and putting his pants on.
• 1:02—Brief buns, while in bed with Tweed.
**Naked Obsession** (1990). . . . . . . . . . . Franklyn Carlyle
• 0:46—Very, very brief buns, while turning over in bed with Maria Ford. Long shot.
House IV (1991) . . . . . . . . . . . . . . . . . . . . .Roger Cobb
Desperate Motive (1992) . . . . . . . . . . . Richard Sullivan
Stranger By Night (1994). . . . . . . . . . . . . . Troy Rooney
*TV:*
Greatest American Hero (1981-83). . . . . . . Ralph Hanley

# • Katz, Larry

*Video Tapes:*
**Playboy's Secret Confessions** (1993)
. . . . . . . . . . . . . . . . . . . . . . . . . . . . . Teacher's Pet/Jay
• 0:26—Buns, while getting his pants pulled down in bedroom by Ruth Ann.

# Katzur, Iftach

*Films:*
**Private Popsicle** (1982) . . . . . . . . . . . . . . . . . . Benji
•• 1:26—Buns, while walking around after Rena steals his clothes.
The Ambassador (1984). . . . . . . . . . . . . . . . . . . . n.a.
Up Your Anchor (1985) . . . . . . . . . . . . . . . . . . . . n.a.

# Kaye, Norman

*Films:*
**Lonely Hearts** (1983; Australian) . . . . . . . . . . . . Peter
• 1:03—Buns, while getting out of bed. Very brief frontal nudity.
**Man of Flowers** (1984; Australian) . . . Charles Bremer
••• 0:17—Nude, taking off robe in bathroom and talking on the phone. Long scene.
Turtle Beach (1992; Australian). . . . . . Sir Adrian Hobday
*a.k.a. The Killing Beach*

# • Keach, Stacy

Brother of actor James Keach.
*Films:*
The Heart is a Lonely Hunter (1968). . . . . . . . . . Blount
End of the Road (1969) . . . . . . . . . . . . . . . . . . . . n.a.
Fat City (1972). . . . . . . . . . . . . . . . . . . . . . . . . Tully
The Life and Times of Judge Roy Bean (1972). . .Bad Bob
The New Centurions (1972). . . . . . . . . . . . . Roy Fehler
Watched! (1973) . . . . . . . . . . . . . . Mike Mandell/Sonny
Luther (1974). . . . . . . . . . . . . . . . . . . Martin Luther
The Killer Inside Me (1975) . . . . . . . . . . . . . Lou Ford
Battle Force (1976). . . . . . . . . . . . . . . . . . . . . . . n.a.
Street People (1976) . . . . . . . . . . . . . . . . . . . . . Phil
Gray Lady Down (1977). . . . . . . . . . . . Captain Bennett
**The Squeeze** (1977; British) . . . . . . . . . . . Jim Naboth
••• 0:30—Buns and very brief frontal nudity after being forced to strip in basement.
•• 0:35—Buns, while walking down the street after being let go.

Up in Smoke (1978) . . . . . . . . . . . . . . . . . . . . Sergeant
The Ninth Configuration (1979) . . . . . . . . Colonel Kane
Slave of the Cannibal God (1979; Italian) . . . . . . . . .n.a.
The Long Riders (1980). . . . . . . . . . . . . . . Frank James
Cheech & Chong's Nice Dreams (1981) . . . . . The Sarge
Road Games (1981; Australian) . . . . . . . . . . . . Pat Quid
Butterfly (1982). . . . . . . . . . . . . . . . . . . . . . . Jeff Tyler
That Championship Season (1982) . . . . . . . James Daley
Armed and Dangerous (1986). . . . . . . . . . . . . . . Judge
Class of 1999 (1990). . . . . . . . . . . . . . Dr. Bob Forrest
False Identity (1990) . . . . . Ben Driscoll/Harlan Erickkson
Mission of the Shark (1991) . . . .Captain Charles McVay
Sunset Grill (1992) . . . . . . . . . . . . . . . . . . . . Shelgrove
Raw Justice (1994) . . . . . . . . . . . . . . . . . . . . . Jenkins
  a.k.a. Good Cop, Bad Cop
Made for Cable Movies:
The Forgotten (1989) . . . . . . . . . . . . . . . . . . . . .n.a.
Made for Cable TV:
John Carpenter's Body Bags (1993; Showtime)
. . . . . . . . . . . . . . . . . . . . . . . . . . . . . Hair/Richard
Miniseries:
Blue and the Gray (1982) . . . . . . . . . . . . . . . . . . .n.a.
Princess Daisy (1983) . . . . . . . . . . . . . . . . . . . . .n.a.
Mistral's Daughter (1984). . . . . . . . . . . . . . . . . . .n.a.
Made for TV Movies:
All the Kind Strangers (1974) . . . . . . . . . . . . . . .n.a.
A Rumor of War (1980). . . . . . . . . . . . . . . . . . . .n.a.
Rio Diablo (1993) . . . . . . . . . . . . . . . . . . . . . . Kansas
TV:
Get Smart (1966-67). . . . . . . . . . . . . . . . . . . . Carlson
Caribe (1975) . . . . . . . . . . . . . . . Lieutenant Ben Logan
Mike Hammer (1984-87) . . . . . . . . . . . .Mike Hammer
Missing Reward (1989-92) . . . . . . . . . . . . . . . . . Host

## Keaton, Buster

Director.
Films:
Our Hospitality (1923) . . . . . . . . . . . . . William McKay
Three Ages (1923) . . . . . . . . . . . . . . . . . . . . . . . .n.a.
College (1927) . . . . . . . . . . . . . . . . . . . . . . . . Ronald
The General (1927). . . . . . . . . . . . . . . . . . .Johnie Gray
**The Cameraman** (1928). . . . . . . . . . . . . . . . . . Buster
  • 0:38—Very brief buns, diving underwater after los-
    ing his swimsuit when his girlfriend tries to get him
    out of the pool.
Steamboat Bill, Jr. (1928). . . . . . . . . . . Steamboat Bill, Jr.
Parlor, Bedroom and Bath (1931) . . . . . . Reginald Irving
Old Spanish Custom (1936) . . . . . . . Leander Proudfoot
Li'l Abner (1940) . . . . . . . . . . . . . . .Lonesome Polecat
The Villain Still Pursued Her (1941) . . . . . . . . . . William
Forever and a Day (1943) . . . . . . . . . Dabb's Assistant
In the Good Old Summertime (1949) . . . . . . . . Hickey
Sunset Boulevard (1950). . . . . . . . . . . . . . . . . .Himself
Limelight (1952). . . . . . . . . . . . . . . Piano Accompanist
Around the World in 80 Days (1956). . . . . . . Conductor
The Adventures of Huckleberry Finn (1960)
. . . . . . . . . . . . . . . . . . . . . . . . . . . . . . . Lion Tamer
Days of Thrills and Laughter (1961). . . . . . . . . . . .n.a.
Great Chase (1963). . . . . . . . . . . . . . . . . . . . . . .n.a.

It's a Mad, Mad, Mad, Mad World (1963)
. . . . . . . . . . . . . . . . . . . . . . . . . . Jimmy the Crook
Beach Blanket Bingo (1965). . . . . . . . . . . . . . Himself
How to Stuff a Wild Bikini (1965) . . . . . . . . . . . Bwana
A Funny Thing Happened on the Way to the Forum
  (1966) . . . . . . . . . . . . . . . . . . . . . . . . . . . Erronius

## Keitel, Harvey

Films:
**Who's That Knocking at My Door?** (1968) . . . . .J.R.
  • 0:42—Buns, several times, while in bed and stand-
    ing up. Quick cuts.
Mean Streets (1973) . . . . . . . . . . . . . . . . . . . .Charlie
Alice Doesn't Live Here Anymore (1975) . . . . . . . . . Ben
Buffalo Bill and the Indians (1976) . . . . . . . . . . . . . Ed
Mother, Jugs & Speed (1976). . . . . . . . . . . . . . . Speed
Taxi Driver (1976) . . . . . . . . . . . . . . . . . . . . . . Sport
The Duellists (1977; British) . . . . . . . . . . . . . . .Feraud
Welcome to L.A. (1977). . . . . . . . . . . . . . . Ken Hood
Blue Collar (1978) . . . . . . . . . . . . . . . . . . . . . .Jerry
Eagle's Wing (1978; British) . . . . . . . . . . . . . . Henry
**Fingers** (1978) . . . . . . . . . . . . . . . . . Jimmy Angelelli
  • 0:39—Brief partial frontal nudity several times, visi-
    ble under his shirt, after getting his rectum exam-
    ined by a doctor.
Bad Timing: A Sensual Obsession (1980)
. . . . . . . . . . . . . . . . . . . . . . . . Inspector Netusil
Death Watch (1980; French/German) . . . . . . . . Roddy
  a.k.a. Death in Full View
Saturn 3 (1980) . . . . . . . . . . . . . . . . . . . . . . Benson
The Border (1982) . . . . . . . . . . . . . . . . . . . . . . .Cal
Exposed (1983) . . . . . . . . . . . . . . . . . . . . . . . Rivas
La Nuit de Varennes (1983; French/Italian)
. . . . . . . . . . . . . . . . . . . . . . . . . . . Thomas Paine
Dream One (1984; British/French) . . . . . . . Mr. Legend
Falling In Love (1984) . . . . . . . . . . . . . . . . . .Ed Lasky
Camorra (1986; Italian) . . . . . . . . . Frankie Acquasanta
The Inquiry (1986). . . . . . . . . . . . . . . . .Pontius Pilate
**The Men's Club** (1986) . . . . . . . . . . . . . Solly Berliner
  • 1:22—Buns, while getting up off the bed to talk to
    Allison.
Off Beat (1986) . . . . . . . . . . . . . . . . . . . Bank Robber
Star Knight (1986; Spanish) . . . . . . . . . . . . . Sir Clever
Wise Guys (1986). . . . . . . . . . . . . . . . . . Bobby Dilea
The Pick-Up Artist (1987). . . . . . . . . . . . . . . .Alonzo
Blindside (1988; Canadian) . . . . . . . . . . . . . .Gruber
The January Man (1988) . . . . . . . . . . . . .Frank Starkey
The Last Temptation of Christ (1988). . . . . . . . . .Judas
GoodFellas (1990). . . . . . . . . . . . . . . . . . . . . J. R.
The Two Jakes (1990). . . . . . . . . . . . . . . Jake Berman
Bugsy (1991) . . . . . . . . . . . . . . . . . . . . Mickey Cohen
Mortal Thoughts (1991). . . . . . . . Detective John Woods
Thelma and Louise (1991) . . . . . . . . . . . . . . . . . Hal
Two Evil Eyes (1991) . . . . . . . . . . . . . . . . . . . .Usher
**Bad Lieutenant** (1992). . . . . . . . . . . . . . . . . . . Lt.
  ••• 0:12—Full frontal nudity, while high on drugs in
    apartment with two other people.
Reservoir Dogs (1992) . . . . . . . . . . . . . Mr. White/Larry
Sister Act (1992) . . . . . . . . . . . . . . . . . Vince LaRocca

Dangerous Game (1993). . . . . . . . . . . . . . Eddie Israel
(Unrated version reviewed.)
Monkey Trouble (1993). . . . . . . . . . . The Organ Grinder
**The Piano** (1993) . . . . . . . . . . . . . . . . . . . . . . .Baines
  •• 0:43—Buns, after taking off his shirt to dust off piano.
  ••• 1:01—Frontal nudity while pulling back curtain to
  show himself to Holly Hunter.
  •• 1:02—Buns, while getting on bed with Hunter.
  •• 1:02—Brief frontal nudity while sitting down in bed.
  •• 1:18—Buns, while making love on top of Hunter.
Point of No Return (1993). . . . . . . . . Victor the Cleaner
Rising Sun (1993) . . . . . . . . . . . . . . . . . . Tom Graham

## Keith, David

*Films:*
The Rose (1979) . . . . . . . . . . . . . . . . . . . . . . . . . .Mal
Brubaker (1980) . . . . . . . . . . . . . . . . Larry Lee Bullen
The Great Santini (1980). . . . . . . . . . . . . . . Red Pettus
Back Roads (1981) . . . . . . . . . . . . . . . . . . . . . Mason
Take This Job and Shove It (1981) . . . . . . .Harry Meade
An Officer and a Gentleman (1982) . . . . . . . Sid Worley
Independence Day (1983) . . . . . . . . . . . . . Jack Parker
The Lords of Discipline (1983). . . . . . . . . . . . . . . .Will
Firestarter (1984) . . . . . . . . . . . . . . . .Andrew McGee
**Gulag** (1985) . . . . . . . . . . . . . . . . . . . . Mickey Almon
  •• 1:26—Buns, while standing outside with Malcolm
  McDowell in the snow being hassled by guards.
Heartbreak Hotel (1988) . . . . . . . . . . . . . .Elvis Presley
White of the Eye (1988) . . . . . . . . . . . . . . . Paul White
**Liar's Edge** (1991). . . . . . . . . . . . . . . Gary Kilpatrick
  • 0:31—Buns, with tattoo, when he kills the mystery
  woman under Niagara Falls. Don't see his face.
  • 0:55—Brief buns during flashback to 0:31 scene.
Caged Fear (1992) . . . . . . . . . . . . . . . . . Tommy Lang
Desperate Motive (1992) . . . . . . . . . . . . . . . . Harry
Raw Justice (1994) . . . . . . . . . . . . . . . . . . . . . Mace
  *a.k.a. Good Cop, Bad Cop*
*Made for TV Movies:*
Friendly Fire (1978). . . . . . . . . . . . . . . Young Hamilton
Whose Child Is This? The War for Baby Jessica (1993)
. . . . . . . . . . . . . . . . . . . . . . . . . . . . . Dan Schmidt
*TV:*
Co-ed Fever (1979). . . . . . . . . . . . . . . . . . . . . Tuck
Flesh and Blood (1991) . . . . . . . . . . . . . . . .Arlo Weed
XXX's & OOO's (1994- ) . . . . . . . . . . . . .Bullet Dobbs

## Keller, Todd

*Video Tapes:*
Nudes in Limbo (1983) . . . . . . . . . . . . . . . . . . .Model
**Penthouse Love Stories** (1986). . Service Station Man
  •• 0:11—Brief frontal nudity in bedroom with a woman.
**Penthouse: On the Wild Side** (1988)
. . . . . . . . . . . . . . . . . . . . . . . . . . . Bytes & Pieces
  ••• 0:09—Nude, making love with a female technician
  in the computer lab.

## Kennedy, Marklen

*Films:*
**Witchcraft V: Dance with the Devil** (1993)
. . . . . . . . . . . . . . . . . . . . . . . . . . . . . . . William
  • 1:03—Buns, while leaving the basement.

## Kerwin, Brian

*Films:*
Hometown, U.S.A. (1979) . . . . . . . . . T.J. Swackhammer
**Murphy's Romance** (1985). . . . .Bobbie Jack Moriarity
  •• 0:55—Brief buns while walking into the bathroom.
Nickel Mountain (1985). . . . . . . . . . . . . . . . George
King Kong Lives! (1986). . . . . . . . . . . . . Hank Mitchell
Torch Song Trilogy (1988) . . . . . . . . . . . . . . . . . Ed
Code Name: Chaos (1990) . . . . . . . . . . . . . . . . .Jim
Hard Promises (1992). . . . . . . . . . . . Walter Humphrey
Love Field (1993) . . . . . . . . . . . . . . . . . .Ray Hallett
*Made for Cable TV:*
Tales From the Crypt: Judy, You're Not Yourself Today
. . . . . . . . . . . . . . . . . . . . . . . . . . . . . . . Donald
*Miniseries:*
Blue and the Gray (1982). . . . . . . . . . . . . Malachi Hale
*Made for TV Movies:*
The Real American Hero (1978) . . . . . . . . . . . . . n.a.
Wet Gold (1984) . . . . . . . . . . . . . . . . . . . . . Kenny
Bluegrass (1988) . . . . . . . . . . . . . . . . . . . . . Dancy
Switched at Birth (1991) . . . . . . . . . . . . . Bob Mays
Against Her Will: An Incident in Baltimore (1992)
. . . . . . . . . . . . . . . . . . . . . . . . . . . . . Jack Adkins
*TV:*
The Chisholms (1979) . . . . . . . . . . . .Gideon Chisholm
Lobo (1979-81) . . . . . . . . . . . .Deputy Birdwell Hawkins
Angel Falls (1993) . . . . . . . . . . . . . . . . . . Eli Harrison

## Kime, Jeffrey

*Films:*
**Quartet** (1981; British/French) . . . . . . . . . . . . . .James
  •• 0:49—Nude, posing with two women for the por-
  nographer.
Joy (1983; French/Canadian) . . . . . . . . . . . . . Helmut
The State of Things (1983). . . . . . . . . . . . . . . . Mark

## King, Perry

*Films:*
Slaughterhouse Five (1972) . . . . . . . . . . . Robert Pilgrim
The Lords of Flatbush (1974) . . . . . . . . . . . . . . .Chico
**Mandingo** (1975). . . . . . . . . . . . . . . . . . .Hammond
  •• 0:17—Frontal nudity walking to bed to make love
  with Dite.
The Wild Party (1975) . . . . . . . . . . . . . . . Dale Sword
Lipstick (1976). . . . . . . . . . . . . . . . . . . . Steve Edison
Andy Warhol's Bad (1977; Italian) . . . . . . . . . . . . .L-T
The Choirboys (1977) . . . . . . . . . . . . . . . . . . . Slate
**A Different Story** (1979) . . . . . . . . . . . . . . . Albert
  (R-rated version reviewed.)
  • 1:33—Buns, through shower door, then brief buns
  while getting out of the shower to talk to Meg Fos-
  ter.
Search and Destroy (1981). . . . . . . . . . . . . . Kip Moore

Class of 1984 (1982; Canadian) . . . . . . . . . . . . . .Andy
Switch (1991) . . . . . . . . . . . . . . . . . . . . . Steve Brooks
*Made for Cable TV:*
Tales From the Crypt: Came the Dawn (1993) . . . Roger
*Miniseries:*
Captains and the Kings (1976) . . . . . . . Rory Armagh
Aspen (1977) . . . . . . . . . . . . . . . . . . . . . . . Lee Bishop
The Last Convertible (1979) . . . . . . . . . . Russ Currier
*Made for TV Movies:*
Love's Savage Fury (1979). . . . . . . Colonel Zachary Willis
Shakedown on Sunset Strip (1988) . . . . . . . . . . . . .n.a.
Roxanne: The Prize Pulitzer (1989)

. . . . . . . . . . . . . . . . . Herbert "Peter" Pulitzer
Danielle Steel's "Kaleidoscope" (1990) . . John Chapman
*TV:*
The Quest (1982) . . . . . . . . . . . . . . . .Dan Underwood
Riptide (1984-86) . . . . . . . . . . . . . . . . . . . Cody Allen
Almost Home (1993). . . . . . . . . . . . . . . Brian Morgan
Trouble with Larry (1993) . . . . . . . . . . . . . . . . .Boyd

# Kingsley, Ben
*Films:*
Gandhi (1982) . . . . . . . . . . . . . . . . Mahatma Gandhi
(Academy Award for Best Actor.)
Betrayal (1983; British) . . . . . . . . . . . . . . . . . . Robert
Harem (1985; French). . . . . . . . . . . . . . . . . . . Selim
Turtle Diary (1986; British) . . . . . . . . . William Snow
Maurice (1987; British) . . . . . . . . . . . . . . Lasker Jones
Pascali's Island (1988; British) . . . . . . . . . . .Basil Pascali
Without a Clue (1988) . . . . . . . . . . . . . . Dr. Watson
The Children (1990; British/German) . . . . Martin Boyne
**The Fifth Monkey** (1990) . . . . . . . . . . . . . . . . .Kunda
1:04—Brief buns, while standing under waterfall.
Don't see his face and water is in the way.
Slipstream (1990) . . . . . . . . . . . . . . . . . . . . . . .Avatar
Bugsy (1991) . . . . . . . . . . . . . . . . . . . . Meyer Lansky
Sneakers (1992) . . . . . . . . . . . . . . . . . . . . . Cosmo
Dave (1993) . . . . . . . . . . . . . . . Vice President Nance
Schindler's List (1993). . . . . . . . . . . . . . . Itzhak Stern
Searching for Bobby Fischer (1993). . . . Bruce Pandolfini
*Made for Cable Movies:*
**Murderers Among Us: The Simon Wiesenthal
Story** (1989; HBO) . . . . . . . . . . . . Simon Wiesenthal
•• 0:27—Buns and brief frontal nudity standing in and
leaving a line in a concentration camp.

# Kinski, Klaus
Father of actress Nastassja Kinski.
Real last name is Nakzsynski.
*Films:*
Doctor Zhivago (1965) . . . . . . . . . . . . . . . . Kostoyed
For a Few Dollars More (1965; Italian/German)

. . . . . . . . . . . . . . . . . . . . . . . . . . . .Hunchback
Venus in Furs (1970) . . . . . . . . . . . . . . . . . . . Ahmed
Original version.
Count Dracula (1971; Spanish/Italian). . . . . . . Renfield
Aguirre, The Wrath of God (1972; West German)
. . . . . . . . . . . . . . . . . . . . Don Lope de Aguirre

Web of the Spider (1972; Italian/French)

. . . . . . . . . . . . . . . . . . . . . . . Edgar Allan Poe
Lifespan (1975; U.S./British) . . . . . . . . . . Industrialist
Nosferatu, The Vampire (1979; French/German)

. . . . . . . . . . . . . . . . . . . . . . . . .Count Dracula
Love and Money (1980). . . . . . . . . Frederick Stockheinz
Schizoid (1980) . . . . . . . . . . . . . . . . . . Dr. Peter Fales
**The Story of "O" Continues** (1981; French)

. . . . . . . . . . . . . . . . . . . . . . . . . . . . Sir Stephen
*a.k.a. Les Fruits de la Passion*
• 0:40—Very, very brief part of buns while making
love on bed with Arielle Dombasle.
Android (1982) . . . . . . . . . . . . . . . . . . . . Dr. Daniel
Fitzcarraldo (1982)

. . . . . . . . . . . . . Brian Sweeney Fitzgerald/Fitzcarraldo
The Soldier (1982) . . . . . . . . . . . . . . . . . . . . Dracha
The Little Drummer Girl (1984) . . . . . . . . . . . . . Kurtz
Codename Wildgeese (1985; Italian/German) . . . . . n.a.
Creature (1985) . . . . . . . . . . . . . . . Hans Rudy Hofner
Crawlspace (1986). . . . . . . . . . . . . . Dr. Karl Gunther
Star Knight (1986; Spanish) . . . . . . . . . . . . . .Bolkius

# Kirby, Bruno
*a.k.a. B. Kirby, Jr.*
*Films:*
Cinderella Liberty (1973) . . . . . . . . . . . . . . . . Alcott
**The Harrad Experiment** (1973). . . . . . Harry Schacht
• 0:41—Brief frontal nudity, getting into the swim-
ming pool with Beth, Don Johnson and Laurie
Walters.
The Godfather, Part II (1974) . . . . . . . . Young Clemenza
Between the Lines (1977). . . . . . . . . . . . . . . . .David
Borderline (1980). . . . . . . . . . . . . . . . . . Jimmy Fante
Where the Buffalo Roam (1980) . . . . . . . . . .Marty Lewis
Modern Romance (1981). . . . . . . . . . . . . . . . . . .Jay
This is Spinal Tap (1984) . . . . . . . . . Tommy Pischedda
Birdy (1985). . . . . . . . . . . . . . . . . . . . . . . . Renaldi
Tin Men (1986) . . . . . . . . . . . . . . . . . . . . . . . n.a.
Good Morning, Vietnam (1987) . . . . . . Lt. Steven Hauk
Bert Rigby, You're a Fool (1989). . . . . . . . .Kyle DeForest
We're No Angels (1989). . . . . . . . . . . . . . . . Deputy
When Harry Met Sally... (1989) . . . . . . . . . . . . Jess
City Slickers (1991) . . . . . . . . . . . . . . . . . Ed Furillo
*Made for Cable Movies:*
Mastergate (1992; Showtime) . . . . . . . . . . .Abel Lamb
*Made for Cable TV:*
Tales From the Crypt: The Trap (1991; HBO)

. . . . . . . . . . . . . . . . . . . . . . . . . . . .Billy Paloma
Fallen Angels: I'll Be Waiting (1993; Showtime)

. . . . . . . . . . . . . . . . . . . . . . . . . . . .Tony Reseck
(Available on video tape on *Fallen Angels Two*.)
*TV:*
The Super (1972). . . . . . . . . . . . . . . . Anthony Girelli

# Kirby, Michael
*Films:*
**My Pleasure is My Business** (1974). . . . . . . . . . . Gus
• 0:41—Brief buns while making love with Xaviera
Hollander.

Bugsy Malone (1976) . . . . . . . . . . . . . . . . . . . . . Angelo
In Praise of Older Women (1978; Canadian) . . . . . . . n.a.
The Silent Partner (1978) . . . . . . . . . . . . . . . . Packard
Meatballs (1979; Canadian) . . . . . . . . . . . . . . . . Eddy
Crossover (1980; Canadian) . . . . . . . . . . . . . Dr. Turley
  a.k.a. Mr. Patman
Agency (1981; Canadian) . . . . . . . . . . . . . . . . . Peters
Shadows and Fog (1991) . . . . . . . . . . . . . . . . . . Killer
Six Degrees of Separation (1993) . . . . . Loft Party Guest

## Kirk, David
*Films:*
**Cry Uncle** (1971). . . . . . . . . . . . . . . . Jason Dominic
  • 0:16—Buns, in bed with three girls. Very hard to see
    because the negative image is projected.
Hurry Up, Or I'll Be 30 (1973) . . . . . . . . . . . Mr. Trapani

## Kleemann, Gunter
*Films:*
**I Spit on Your Grave** (1978) . . . . . . . . . . . . . . . Andy
(Uncut, unrated version reviewed.)
  • 0:33—Buns, while raping Jennifer.

## Kline, Kevin
Husband of actress Phoebe Cates.
*Films:*
Sophie's Choice (1982). . . . . . . . . . . . . .Nathan Landau
The Big Chill (1983) . . . . . . . . . . . . . . . . . . . . Harold
The Pirates of Penzance (1983) . . . . . . . . . . Pirate King
Silverado (1985) . . . . . . . . . . . . . . . . . . . . . . Paden
**Violets Are Blue** (1986) . . . . . . . . . . . . Henry Squires
  • 1:02—Brief buns, while standing up and putting on
    his shorts, on island with Sissy Spacek.
Cry Freedom (1987; British) . . . . . . . . . . Donald Woods
A Fish Called Wanda (1988) . . . . . . . . . . . . . . . . Otto
(Academy Award for Best Supporting Actor.)
The January Man (1988) . . . . . . . . . . . . . . Nick Starkey
**I Love You to Death** (1990). . . . . . . . . . . . . . . . Joey
  • 0:10—Buns, while wearing an apron walking from
    the bedroom in Victoria Jackson's apartment.
Grand Canyon (1991). . . . . . . . . . . . . . . . . . . Mack
Soapdish (1991) . . . . . . . . . . . . . . . . . Jeffrey Anderson
Chaplin (1992; British/U.S.). . . . . . . . .Douglas Fairbanks
**Consenting Adults** (1992). . . . . . . . . . .Richard Parker
  •• 0:39—Buns, while in bed with Melissa Moore, when
    he thinks it's Kay.
**Dave** (1993). . . . . . . . . . . . . . Bill Mitchell/Dave Kovic
  • 0:49—Buns, several times, seen through steamed up
    shower door. Don't see his face.
Princess Caraboo (1994) . . . . . . . . . . . . . . . . . . n.a.

## Klisser, Evan J.
*Films:*
American Ninja 3: Blood Hunt (1989) . . . . . . . . Dexter
**Prey for the Hunter** (1990). . . . . . . . . . . . . . Jason
  • 0:17—Buns, while wiping paint off his butt.

## Knight, Wyatt
*Films:*
Porky's (1981; Canadian) . . . . . . . . . . . .Tommy Turner
**Porky's Revenge** (1985; Canadian) . . . .Tommy Turner
  •• 0:16—Buns, while getting out of swimming pool
    (the first guy getting out). More buns running
    around.
  • 0:54—Buns, getting his underwear pulled down
    while trying to escape from a motel room from Bal-
    bricker.

## Knoph, Gregory
*Films:*
**Ilsa, She Wolf of the S.S.** (1974) . . . . . . . . . . .Wolfe
  • 0:31—Buns, while in bed with Ilsa.
  • 0:32—More buns, while in bed with Ilsa.
  ••• 0:46—Buns, while in bed with the two blonde fe-
    male guards.

## • Knox, Terence
*Films:*
Heart Like a Wheel (1983) . . . . . . . . . . . . .Jack's Friend
**Rebel Love** (1985) . . . . . . . . . . . Hightower/McHugh
  •• 0:49—Buns, while getting out of bath tub and chas-
    ing Jamie Rose around in cabin.
Children of the Corn II: The Final Sacrifice (1992)
  . . . . . . . . . . . . . . . . . . . . . . . . . . . . . . . .Garrett
*Made for TV Movies:*
A Mother's Right: The Elizabeth Morgan Story (1992)
  . . . . . . . . . . . . . . . . . . . . . . . . . . . .Eric Foretich
Overexposed (1992) . . . . . . . . . . . . . . . . Nick Kasten
Poisoned by Love: The Kern County Murders (1993)
  . . . . . . . . . . . . . . . . . . . . . . . . . . . .Bobby Ballew
*TV:*
The Road Home (1994- ) . . . . . . . . . . . . . . . . . . . n.a.

## Koenig, Tommy
*Films:*
**Stitches** (1985). . . . . . . . . . . . . . . . . . Barfer Bogan
  • 0:03—Brief buns, while getting off gurney. Made up
    to look like a bald corpse. Something is covering his
    frontal nudity. Brief buns, while walking in class-
    room.
  • 0:04—Brief buns, while chasing people down hall-
    way. Don't see face. (He's in front.)

## Kologie, Ron
*Films:*
**Iced** (1988) . . . . . . . . . . . . . . . . . . . . . . . . . . Carl
  • 0:39—Buns, while in bathroom snorting cocaine.

## Kotto, Yaphet
*Films:*
The Thomas Crown Affair (1968) . . . . . . . . . . . . . Carl
The Liberation of L. B. Jones (1970) . . Sonny Boy Mosby
Man and Boy (1971) . . . . . . . . . . . . . . . Nate Hodges
Across 110th Street (1972). . . . . . . . . . . .Det. Lt. Pople
Housewife (1972). . . . . . . . . . . . . . . . . . . . . . . Bone
Live and Let Die (1973; British) . . . . . . . . . . . Kananga

Truck Turner (1974) . . . . . . . . . . . . . . . . . . . . . Blue
Friday Foster (1975) . . . . . . . . . . . . . . . . Colt Hawkins
Report to the Commissioner (1975)
. . . . . . . . . . . . . . . . . . Richard "Crunch" Blackstone
Shark's Treasure (1975) . . . . . . . . . . . . . . . . . . . . .Ben
**Drum** (1976) . . . . . . . . . . . . . . . . . . . . . . . . . Blaise
• 1:02—Buns, while getting hung upside down in
barn and spanked along with Ken Norton.
Blue Collar (1978) . . . . . . . . . . . . . . . . . . . . . . Smokey
Alien (1979) . . . . . . . . . . . . . . . . . . . . . . . . . .Parker
Brubaker (1980) . . . . . . . . . . . . . . . . Dickie Coombes
Fighting Back (1982). . . . . . . . . . . .Ivanhoe Washington
The Star Chamber (1983) . . . . . . . . . Det. Harry Lowes
Warning Sign (1985). . . . . . . . . . . . . . .Major Connolly
Eye of the Tiger (1986) . . . . . . . . . . . . . .J. B. Deveraux
Pretty Kill (1987) . . . . . . . . . . . . . . . . . . . . . . Harris
The Running Man (1987) . . . . . . . . . . . . . . . Laughlin
The Jigsaw Murders (1988) . . . . . . . . . . . .Dr. Fillmore
Midnight Run (1988) . . . . . . . . . . . . . Alonzo Mosely
Ministry of Vengeance (1989) . . . . . . . . . Mr. Whiteside
Tripwire (1989) . . . . . . . . . . . . . . . . . . . . . Lee Pitt
Hangfire (1990) . . . . . . . . . . . . . . . Police Lieutenant
Freddy's Dead: The Final Nightmare (1991) . . . . . . Doc
Almost Blue (1992) . . . . . . . . . . . . . . . . . . . . . Terry
Intent to Kill (1992). . . . . . . . . . . . . . Captain Jackson
*Made for Cable Movies:*
The Park is Mine (1985; HBO). . . . . . . . . . . Eubanks
Extreme Justice (1993; HBO). . . . . . . . . . . . . . Larson
*Made for TV Movies:*
Raid on Entebbe (1977) . . . . . . President Idi Amin Dada
For Love and Honor (1983)
. . . . . . . . . . . . . . . . Platoon Sgt. James "China" Bell
It's Nothing Personal (1993) . . . . . . . . . . . . . . .Lt. Riley
*TV:*
Homicide: Life on the Street (1993) . . . . Lt. Al Giardello

## Kove, Martin

*Films:*
Savages (1972) . . . . . . . . . . . . . . . . . . . . . . . . .Archie
Capone (1975) . . . . . . . . . . . . . . . . . . . Pete Gusenberg
Death Race 2000 (1975) . . . . . . . . . . . . Nero the Hero
The Four Deuces (1975) . . . . . . . . . . . . . . . . . . .n.a.
White Line Fever (1975) . . . . . . . . . . . . . . . . . . Clem
The Wild Party (1975) . . . . . . . . . . . . . . . . . . . Editor
Mr. Billion (1977) . . . . . . . . . . . . . . . Texas Gambler
Seven (1979) . . . . . . . . . . . . . . . . . . . . . . . . . Skip
Blood Tide (1982) . . . . . . . . . . . . . . . . . . . . . . Neil
The Karate Kid (1984) . . . . . . . . . . . . . . . . . . .Kreese
Rambo: First Blood, Part II (1985) . . . . . . . . . Ericson
The Karate Kid, Part II (1986) . . . . . . . . . . . . .Kreese
Steele Justice (1987) . . . . . . . . . . . . . . . . . .John Steele
**White Light** (1990) . . . . . . . . . . . . . . . Sean Craig
1:23—Upper half of buns, while on the floor with
Rachel.
• 1:24—Very brief buns, while getting out of bed.
Firehawk (1992) . . . . . . . . . . . . . . . . . . . . . . .Stewart
Project: Shadowchaser (1992). . . . . . . . . . . . . . Dasilva
Shootfighter: Fight to the Death (1992) . . . . . . .Mr. Lee
Future Shock (1993) . . . . . . . . . . . . . Doctor Langdon

Renegade: Fighting Cage (1993) . . . . . . . Mitch Raines
(Nudity added for video release.)
To Be The Best (1993) . . . . . . . . . . . . . . . . . . . . . Rick
Endangered (1994) . . . . . . . . . . . . . . . . . . . . .DeVoe
*Made for Cable TV:*
Tales From the Crypt: Halfway Horrible (1993; HBO)
. . . . . . . . . . . . . . . . . . . . . . . . . . . . .Police Officer
*TV:*
Code R (1977) . . . . . . . . . . . . . . . . . . . . .George Baker
We've Got Each Other (1977-78) . . . . . . . .Ken Redford
Cagney & Lacey (1982-88) . . . . . . . . Det. Victor Isbecki
Hard Time on Planet Earth (1989) . . . . . . . . . . . . Jesse

## Krabbé, Jeroen

*Films:*
Soldier of Orange (1977; Dutch) . . . . . . . . . . . . . Gus
Spetters (1980; Dutch). . . . . . . . . . . . . . . . . Henkhof
**The Fourth Man** (1984; Dutch). . . . . . . . . . . .Gerard
••• 0:03—Frontal nudity getting out of bed and walking
down the stairs.
•• 0:26—Frontal nudity drying himself off and getting
into bed.
• 0:33—Buns, while getting out of bed.
A World Apart (1988; British) . . . . . . . . . . . . . . . . Gus
The Punisher (1989). . . . . . . . . . . . . . . Gianni Franco
Till There Was You (1990; Australian)
. . . . . . . . . . . . . . . . . . . . . . . . Robert "Viv" Vivaldi
The Prince of Tides (1991) . . . . . . . . Herbert Woodruff
Kafka (1992; U.S./French) . . . . . . . . . . . . . . Bizzlebek
The Fugitive (1993) . . . . . . . . . . . . . Dr. Charles Nichols
King of the Hill (1993) . . . . . . . . . . . . . . Mr. Kurlander
*Made for Cable Movies:*
Stalin (1992; HBO). . . . . . . . . . . . . . . . . . . . . . . n.a.
*Miniseries:*
Dynasty: The Reunion (1991). . . . . . . . Jeremy Van Dorn
*Made for TV Movies:*
Code Name: Dancer (1987) . . . . . . . . . . . . . . . Malarin

## • Krause, Brian

*Films:*
December (1991). . . . . . . . . . . . . . . . . . . Tim Mitchell
Return to the Blue Lagoon (1991) . . . . . . . . . . . Richard
Stephen King's Sleepwalkers (1992) . . . . . Charles Brady
**The Liars' Club** (1993) . . . . . . . . . . . . . . . . . .Pat
• 0:15—Buns, when raping Marla in the backyard.
*Made for Cable TV:*
Tales From the Crypt: House of Horror (1993; HBO)
. . . . . . . . . . . . . . . . . . . . . . . . . . . . . . . . . . n.a.

## Kristofferson, Kris

*Films:*
Cisco Pike (1971) . . . . . . . . . . . . . . . . . . . . Cisco Pike
Blume in Love (1973). . . . . . . . . . . . . . . . . . . . . Elmo
**Pat Garrett and Billy the Kid** (1973) . . . Billy the Kid
(Uncut Director's version reviewed.)
• 0:43—Buns, while getting into bed with a girl after
Harry Dean Stanton gets out. Long shot, hard to see.
Bring Me the Head of Alfredo Garcia (1974). . . . . . Paco
Alice Doesn't Live Here Anymore (1975) . . . . . . . .David

The Sailor Who Fell From Grace with the Sea (1976)
................................. Jim Cameron
A Star is Born (1976)..................... Johnny
Vigilante Force (1976)............... Aaron Arnold
Semi-Tough (1977)................... Shake Tiller
Convoy (1978) ......................Rubber Duck
Heaven's Gate (1980) ..................... Averill
Rollover (1981)........................ Hub Smith
Flashpoint (1984) .......................... Logan
Songwriter (1984).................... Blackie Buck
Trouble in Mind (1986)..................... Hawk
Big Top Pee Wee (1988) ............ Mace Montana
Welcome Home (1989)...................... Jake
Millenium (1990) ..................... Bill Smith
Night of the Cyclone (1990)................. Stan
No Place to Hide (1991)............... Joe Garvey
Original Intent (1992)............... Jack Saunders
*Made for Cable Movies:*
The Tracker (1988; HBO)............. Noble Adams
Another Pair of Aces (1991)........ Capt. Elvin Metcalf
(Video tape includes nude scenes not shown on cable
TV.)
Miracle in the Wilderness (1991; TNT) ...Jericho Adams
*Made for TV Movies:*
Trouble Shooters: Trapped Beneath the Earth (1993)
................................. Stan Mather
*Magazines:*
**Playboy** (Nov 1973) .......... Sex in Cinema 1973
• 151—Side view of buns in photo from *Pat Garrett
and Billy the Kid.*
**Playboy** (Jul 1976)..................Kris and Sarah
•• 126—Buns, while in bed with Sarah Miles.

## Krowchuk, Chad
*Films:*
**Bye Bye Blues** (1989; Canadian)
.................... Richard Cooper (5 Years)
• 0:41—Buns, getting out of bathtub and dried off.

## Kuhlman, Ron
*Films:*
To Be or Not To Be (1983).............. Polish Flyer
Splash (1984) .................... Man with Date
Omega Syndrome (1986) .................... n.a.
**Shadow Play** (1986)................. John Crown
• 1:06—Buns, while standing and holding Dee Wallace in his arms.
Flesh and Bone (1993) ............... Clem Willets
Kalifornia (1993) ................... Male Officer
(Unrated version reviewed.)
*Made for TV Movies:*
The Brady Brides (1981) ........ Phillip Covington III

## Lackey, Skip
*Films:*
**Once Bitten** (1985)...................... Russ
• 1:11—Brief buns while in the school showers trying to see if Mark got bitten by a vampire.

## Lafayette, John
*Films:*
**The Shaming** (1979) .....................Rafe
*a.k.a. Good Luck, Miss Wyckoff*
*a.k.a. The Sin*
•• 0:43—Very brief frontal nudity, taking off his jumpsuit in classroom with Anne Heywood.
• 0:52—Buns, while making love on top of Heywood in classroom.
Deadly Weapon (1989) ............... Sgt. Conroy
Switch (1991) ...................... Sgt. Phillips
Article 99 (1992) ................... Neurologist
Patriot Games (1992)..................... Winter
White Sands (1992) ..................... Demott
Greedy (1993) ........................ Wayne

## • Lagache, Frederic
*Films:*
**Emmanuelle, The Joys of a Woman** (1975)
................................. Christopher
• 0:17—Sort of frontal nudity standing up in bathtub getting introduced to Sylvia Kristel. He's covered with bubbles.

## Lambert, Christopher
Husband of actress Diane Lane.
*Films:*
Greystoke: The Legend of Tarzan, Lord of the Apes
(1984) ..................... John Clayton/Tarzan
Subway (1985; French) ....................Fred
**Highlander** (1986).............. Conner MacLeod
• 1:30—Buns while making love with Roxanne Hart.
**The Sicilian** (1987) ........... Salvatore Giullano
(Director's uncut version reviewed.)
•• 1:02—Buns, when the Duchess yanks his underwear down. Don't see his face, but probably him.
To Kill a Priest (1988) ................. Father Alek
Priceless Beauty (1989; Italian)............. Monroe
Why Me? (1990) ................... Gus Cardinale
Highlander 2: The Quickening (1991) ....... MacLeod
Knight Moves (1992) ............. Peter Sanderson
**Fortress** (1993; U.S./Australian) ....... John Brennick
• 0:18—Brief balls, twice, seen under Loryn Locklin while making love in bed.
Gunmen (1993) ................... Dani Servigo

## Lamden, Derek
*Films:*
**Baby Love** (1969)........................Nick
• 1:29—Brief buns while in shower when Luci opens the door.

## • Lancaster, Burt
*Films:*
**The Swimmer** ..................... Ned Merrill
• 0:43—Long shot of buns, while taking off his swim trunks to get into nudist colony.
•• 0:45—Buns, after turning away from table and walking to the pool.

Criss Cross (1948) . . . . . . . . . . . . . . . . .Steve Thompson
Sorry, Wrong Number (1948) . . . . . . .Henry Stevenson
The Flame and the Arrow (1950). . . . . . . . . . . . .Dardo
Jim Thorpe—All American (1951) . . . . . . . .Jim Thorpe
Vengeance Valley (1951) . . . . . . . . . . . .Owen Daybright
Come Back, Little Sheba (1952) . . . . . . . .Doc Delaney
The Crimson Pirate (1952) . . . . . . . . . . . . . . . . . Vallo
From Here to Eternity (1953) . .Sergeant Milton Warden
Apache (1954) . . . . . . . . . . . . . . . . . . . . . . . . . Massai
Vera Cruz (1954) . . . . . . . . . . . . . . . . . . . . . . .Joe Erin
Trapeze (1956) . . . . . . . . . . . . . . . . . . . . . Mike Ribble
Gunfight at the O.K. Corral (1957) . . . . . . . . Wyatt Earp
Run Silent, Run Deep (1958). . . . Lieutenant Jim Bledsoe
Elmer Gantry (1960) . . . . . . . . . . . . . . . Elmer Gantry
    (Academy Award for Best Actor.)
The Birdman of Alcatraz (1962). . . . . . . .Robert Stroud
Seven Days in May (1964) . . . . General James M. Scott
The Gypsy Moths (1969). . . . . . . . . . . . . .Mike Retting
Airport (1970). . . . . . . . . . . . . . . . . . Mel Bakersfeld
Lawman (1971). . . . . . . . . . . . . Marshal Jered Maddox
    (Not available on video tape.)
Valdez is Coming (1971) . . . . . . . . . . . . . . Bob Valdez
Ulzana's Raid (1972) . . . . . . . . . . . . . . . . . . Farrington
Scorpio (1973) . . . . . . . . . . . . . . . . . . . . . . . . . Cross
Conversation Piece (1974; Italian/French) . . . . .Professor
1900 (1976; Italian) . . . . . . . . . . . . Alfredo Berlingheri
    (NC-17 version reviewed.)
Moses (1976; British/Italian) . . . . . . . . . . . . . . .Moses
The Cassandra Crossing (1977; British) . . . . . MacKenzie
The Island of Dr. Moreau (1977) . . . . . . . . . Dr. Moreau
Go Tell the Spartans (1978). . . . . . . . .Major Asa Barker
**Cattle Annie and Little Britches** (1980) . . .Bill Doolin
    • 1:16—Very brief upper half of buns, while grabbing
      bad guy's arm and pulling him into hot spring.
Zulu Dawn (1980; British). . . . . . . . . . Colonel Durnford
Atlantic City (1981; French/Canadian) . . . . . . . . . . .Lou
The Osterman Weekend (1983) . . . . .Maxwell Danforth
Little Treasure (1985) . . . . . . . . . . . . . . .Teschemacher
Tough Guys (1986). . . . . . . . . . . . . . . . . Harry Doyle
Rocket Gibraltar (1988). . . . . . . . . . . . . Levi Rockwell
Field of Dreams (1989) . . . . . . . . . . . . . . .Dr. Graham
*Made for TV Movies:*
Scandal Sheet (1985) . . . . . . . . . . . . . Harold Fallen
Voyage of Terror: The Achillie Largo Affair (1990) . . .n.a.

# Landi, Sal
*Films:*
**Savage Streets** (1985) . . . . . . . . . . . . . . . . . . Fargo
    • 0:31—Brief buns, while standing up in bathroom af-
      ter raping Linnea Quigley.
Club Life (1987) . . . . . . . . . . . . . . . . . . . . . . . . Sonny
Sweet Revenge (1987) . . . . . . . . . . . . . . . . . . . .n.a.
Dangerous Love (1988). . . . . . . . . . . . . . . . . . . .n.a.
Back to Back (1990) . . . . . . . . . . . . . . . . . . . . . .n.a.
Think Big (1990). . . . . . . . . . . . . . . . . . . . Tough Guy
For the Boys (1991). . . . . . . . . . . . . . . . Marine Driver
South Central (1992) . . . . . . . . . . . . . . . . . Detective
Street Knight (1992) . . . . . . . . . . . . . . . . . . . .Parker

The Young and the Restless (1988-89) . . . Clint Radisson

# Landrum, Bill
*Films:*
**The Doors** (1991)
    . . . . . . . . Choreographer/Body Double for Val Kilmer
    •• 1:04—Buns, while making love in bed with Kathleen
      Quinlan.

# • Lane, Charles
*Films:*
True Identity (1991) . . . . . . . . . . . . . . . . . . . . .Duane
**Posse** (1993). . . . . . . . . . . . . . . . . . . . . . . . . .Weazie
    • 0:50—Very brief frontal nudity and buns, getting
      picked up and thrown in the water. Blurry.

# Lang, Perry
*Films:*
**Teen Lust** (1978) . . . . . . . . . . . . . . . . . . . . . . . Terry
    *a.k.a. Girls Next Door*
    • 0:01—Buns in jock strap getting his pants pulled
      down while he does pull-ups.
1941 (1979). . . . . . . . . . . . . . . . . . . . . . . . .Dennis
Alligator (1980) . . . . . . . . . . . . . . . . . . . . . . . . . Kelly
The Big Red One (1980). . . . . . . . . . . . . . . . . .Kaiser
Cattle Annie and Little Britches (1980) . . . . . . . . . Elrod
The Hearse (1980) . . . . . . . . . . . . . . . . . . . . . . .Paul
Body and Soul (1981) . . . . . . . . . . . . . .Charles Golphin
O'Hara's Wife (1982) . . . . . . . . . . . . . . . . . Rob O'Hara
T.A.G.: The Assassination Game (1982) . . . . . . . . Frank
**Spring Break** (1983; Canadian). . . . . . . . . . . . Adam
    • 0:27—Brief buns while opening his towel in the
      shower, mooning his three friends.
Sahara (1984) . . . . . . . . . . . . . . . . . . . . . . . . .Andy
Jocks (1986). . . . . . . . . . . . . . . . . . . . . . . . . . .Jeff
Mortuary Academy (1988). . . . . . . . . . . . .Max Grimm
Jacob's Ladder (1990) . . . . . . . . . . . . . .Jacob's Assailant
Little Vegas (1990) . . . . . . . . . . . . . . . . . . . . . Steve
Relentless 2: Dead On (1991). . . . . . . . . Ralph Bashi
Jennifer 8 (1992) . . . . . . . . . . . . . . . . . . . . . . .Travis
*Made for TV Movies:*
Betrayed by Love (1994) . . . . . . . . . . . . . Earl McNally
Bay City Blues (1983). . . . . . . . . . . . . . Frenchy Nuckles

# Langa, Steven
*Video Tapes:*
**Eden 3** (1993). . . . . . . . . . . . . . . . . . . . . . . . . . Lyle
    •• 0:14—Buns, while in bedroom with Val.

# Langlois, Eric
*Films:*
**Greystoke: The Legend of Tarzan, Lord of the
Apes** (1984) . . . . . . . . . . . . . . . .Tarzan Aged Twelve
    • 0:21—Nude, in old house in the jungle.
    • 0:25—Nude, swinging and running around in the
      jungle.
    • 0:27—More buns, in the jungle during attack.

# LaPaglia, Anthony

*Films:*
Betsy's Wedding (1990) . . . . . . . . . . . . . . . Stevie Dee
29th Street (1991) . . . . . . . . . . . . . . . . Frank Pesce, Jr.
he said, she said (1991) . . . . . . . . . . . . . . . . . . Mark
One Good Cop (1991) . . . . . . . . . . . . . Stevie Dirnma
**Innocent Blood** (1992) . . . . . . . . . . . . . . Joe Gennaro
•• 1:25—Brief buns, taking off his pants to get in to
bed with Anne Parillaud.
Whispers in the Dark (1992) . . . . . . . . . . .Morgenstern
The Custodian (1993) . . . . . . . . . . . . . . . . . . Quinlan
So, I Married an Axe Murderer (1993). . . . Tony Giardino
*Made for Cable Movies:*
Black Magic (1992; Showtime) . . . . . . . . . . . . . . Ross
Past Tense (1994; Showtime) . . . . . . . . . . Larry Talbert

# Larson, Eric

*Films:*
**Demon Wind** (1990) . . . . . . . . . . . . . . . . . . . . . Cory
•• 0:10—Buns, while standing outside at gas station.
Don't see his face.

# • LaSardo, Robert

*Films:*
Me & Him (1988; West German) . . . . . . . . . . . . . .Tony
Moving (1988) . . . . . . . . . . . . . . . . . . . . . . . . .Perry
*TV:*
**NYPD Blue: Tempest In a C-Cup** (Nov 16, 1993)
. . . . . . . . . . . . . . . . . . . . . . . . . . .Hector Hernandez
• 0:01—Brief buns, while running down hallway to try
escape from the police.

# Lattanzi, Matt

Husband of singer/actress Olivia Newton-John.
*Films:*
**Rich and Famous** (1981) . . . . . . . . . . . . . The Boy, Jim
••• 1:10—Buns, while making love with Jacqueline Bis-
set.
Grease 2 (1982) . . . . . . . . . . . . . . . . . . . . . . . .n.a.
My Tutor (1983) . . . . . . . . . . . . . . . . . . Bobby Chrystal
That's Life! (1986) . . . . . . . . . . . . . . . . . . Larry Bartlet
Roxanne (1987) . . . . . . . . . . . . . . . . . . . . . . . .Trent
Catch Me... If You Can (1989) . . . . . . . . . . . . . Dylan
Diving In (1990) . . . . . . . . . . . . . . . . . . . . Jerome Colter

# Lauer, Andrew

*Films:*
Blame It on the Night (1984) . . . . . . . . Boy in Audience
Never on Tuesday (1988) . . . . . . . . . . . . . . . . . Matt
Born on the Fourth of July (1989) . . . . . . . . . . . . . Vet
The Doors (1991) . . . . . . . . . . . . . . . . . .UCLA Student
**Necessary Roughness** (1991) . . . . . . . . Charlie Banks
• 1:09—Buns, while taking a shower. (He's the bru-
nette guy on the far right.)
*TV:*
Grand (1990) . . . . . . . . . . . . . Officer Wayne Kasmurski

# Laughlin, John

*Films:*
An Officer and a Gentleman (1982) . . . . . . . . . . . .Troy
**Crimes of Passion** (1984) . . . . . . . . . . . Bobby Grady
(Unrated version reviewed.)
• 0:50—Buns, while getting dressed after having sex
with Kathleen Turner. (Viewed through peep hole by
Anthony Perkins.)
**Footloose** (1984) . . . . . . . . . . . . . . . . . . . . . .Woody
•• 0:58—Buns and upper half of pubic hair, while tak-
ing a shower in the locker room and talking to Kevin
Bacon and Christopher Penn.
Space Rage (1987) . . . . . . . . . . . . . . . . . . . . . Walker
Midnight Crossing (1988) . . . . . . . . . . Jeffrey Schubb
The Hills Have Eyes, Part II (1989) . . . . . . . . . . . . .Hulk
Motorama (1991) . . . . . . . . . . . . Man at Wagon Wheel
The Lawnmower Man (1992) . . . . . . . . . . Jake Simpson
(Unrated Director's cut reviewed.)
Sexual Malice (1993) . . . . . . . . . . . . . . . . . . . . . Jack
(Unrated version reviewed.)
*Made for Cable Movies:*
Memphis (1991; TNT) . . . . . . . . . . . . . . . . . . . . n.a.
*Made for Cable TV:*
Tales From the Crypt: Food For Thought (1993; HBO)
. . . . . . . . . . . . . . . . . . . . . . . . . . . . . . . . Johnnie
*TV:*
The White Shadow (1980-81) . . . . . . . . Paddy Falahey

# Law, John Phillip

*Films:*
Barbarella (1968; French/Italian) . . . . . . . . . . . . .Pygar
The Last Movie (1971) . . . . . . . . . . . . . . . Little Brother
The Love Machine (1971) . . . . . . . . . . . .Robin Stone
The Golden Voyage of Sinbad (1974; British) . . . . Sinbad
Tarzan, The Ape Man (1981) . . . . . . . . . . . . . . .Holt
Night Train to Terror (1985) . . . . . . . . . . . Harry Billings
Rainy Day Friends (1985) . . . . . . . .Dr. Stephen Kendrick
American Commandos (1986) . . . . . . . . . . . . . . Kelly
No Time to Die (1986) . . . . . . . . . . . . . . . .Ted Barner
Moon in Scorpio (1987) . . . . . . . . . . . . . . . . . . Allen
Alienator (1989) . . . . . . . . . . . . . . . . . .Sheriff Ward
**Angel Eyes** (1991) . . . . . . . . . . . . . . . . . . . . Steven
• 0:04—Brief buns, while lying on top of Michelle in
bed.

# Lawrence, Bruno

*Films:*
Goodbye Pork Pie (1980; New Zealand) . . . . . Mulvaney
**Smash Palace** (1981; New Zealand) . . . . . . . .Al Shaw
••• 0:39—Buns while in bed after arguing, then making
up with Jacqui.
Treasure of the Yankee Zephyr (1981) . . . . . . . . . Barker
Warlords of the 21st Century (1982) . . . . . . . . . . Willie
*a.k.a. Battletruck*
Heart of the Stag (1983; New Zealand) . . . . Peter Daley
Utu (1984; New Zealand) . . . . . . . . . . . .Williamson
An Indecent Obsession (1985) . . . . . . . . . Matt Sawyer
**The Quiet Earth** (1985; New Zealand) . . .Zac Hobson
•• 0:02—Brief frontal nudity lying on the bed.

•• 0:04—Brief nude getting back into bed.

• 0:33—Very brief frontal nudity jumping out of the ocean. Blurry, hard to see anything.

•• 1:01—Frontal nudity during flashback lying in bed.

Rikky & Pete (1988; Australian) . . . . . . . . . . . . . . Sonny

Spotswood (1991; Australian) . . . . . . . . . . . . . . Robert

The Efficiency Expert (1992; Australian) . . . . . . . Robert

## Layne, Scott
*Films:*

**Vice Academy, Part 2** (1990) . . . . . . . . . . . .Petrolino

• 0:49—Buns, twice, while in men's locker room when Linnea Quigley and Ginger Lynn Allen come in.

## Le Fever, Chuck
*Films:*

**The Naked Gun 2 1/2: The Smell of Fear** (1991)
. . . . . . . . . . . . . . . . . . . . . . . . .Mr. Griffith's Stunt Butt

• 1:07—Side view of buns when Leslie Nielsen yanks Dr. Meinheimer's pants down.

## Le Gros, James
*Films:*

Solarbabies (1986) . . . . . . . . . . . . . . . . . . . . . . Metron

Fatal Beauty (1987) . . . . . . . . . . . . . . . . . . . .Zack Jaeger

Blood & Concrete: A Love Story (1991) . . . . . . . . Lance

Leather Jackets (1991) . . . . . . . . . . . . . . . . . . . . . Carl

Nervous Ticks (1991) . . . . . . . . . . . . . . . . . . . . . Rusty

**Point Break** (1991) . . . . . . . . . . . . . . . . . . . . . . Roach

• 0:07—Brief buns, twice, while mooning the bank security camera. Wearing Richard Nixon mask. Could be anybody.

• 0:11—Buns, on B&W monitor in the FBI office.

• 0:59—Buns, mooning his friends while riding surfboard. Can't see his face clearly.

The Rapture (1991) . . . . . . . . . . . . . . . . . . . . . .Tommy

My New Gun (1992) . . . . . . . . . . . . . . . . . . . . . Skippy

singles (1992) . . . . . . . . . . . . . . . . . . . . . . . . . . .Andy

Where The Day Takes You (1992) . . . . . . . . . . .Crasher

*Made for Cable Movies:*

Guncrazy (1992; Showtime) . . . . . . . . . . . . . . Howard

## • Ledingham, David
*Films:*

**Final Judgement** (1992) . . . . . . . . . . . . . Robert Sorel

• 0:12—Buns, while walking around in his studio.

## Lee, Jason Scott
*Films:*

Back to the Future, Part II (1989) . . . . . . . . . . . . Whitey

**Map of the Human Heart** (1992; Australian/Canadian) . . . . . . . . . . . . . . . . . . . . . . . . . . . . . . Avik

•• 1:14—Buns, while making love with Albertine on top of blimp.

Dragon: The Bruce Lee Story (1993) . . . . . . . Bruce Lee

## Lee, Mark
*Films:*

**Gallipoli** (1981) . . . . . . . . . . . . . . . . . Archy Hamilton

•• 1:18—Buns, while running into the water with Mel Gibson. (Mark is the guy on the right.)

Emma's War (1986) . . . . . . . . . . . . . . . . .John Davidson

## Legein, Marc
*Films:*

**The Secrets of Love—Three Rakish Tales** (1986)
. . . . . . . . . . . . . . . . . . . . . . . . . . . . . . . . . . . . . Luke

• 0:18—Buns, while in the hay with the Weaver's wife.

• 0:24—More buns.

## Leguizamo, John
Stand-up comedian.
*Films:*

**Casualties of War** (1989) . . . . . . . . . . . . . . . . . .Diaz

• 0:53—Buns, while pulling his pants down to rape Oahn.

Die Hard 2 (1990) . . . . . . . . . . . . . . . . . . . . . . .Burke

Revenge (1990) . . . . . . . . . . . . . . . . . . . . . . . Ignacio

Street Hunter (1990) . . . . . . . . . . . . . . . . . . . .Angel

Hangin' with the Homeboys (1991) . . . . . . . . . .Johnny

Out for Justice (1991) . . . . . . . . . . . . . . . Boy in Alley

Regarding Henry (1991). . . . . . . . . . . . . . . Gunman

Whispers in the Dark (1992). . . . . . . . . . . . Johnny C.

Carlito's Way (1993). . . . . . . . . . . . . . . .Benny Blanco

Super Mario Bros. (1993) . . . . . . . . . . . . . Luigi Mario

*Made for Cable TV:*

Spic-O-Rama (1993; HBO) . . . . . . . .Various Personalities

## • Leigh, Spencer
*Films:*

**The Last of England** . . . . . . . . . . . . . . . . . . . . . n.a.

••• 0:46—Buns, while undressing next to and in bed with a soldier (can't tell if it's a male or female soldier).

•• 0:48—Very brief frontal nudity in bed with the soldier.

Aria (1987; U.S./British) . . . . . . . . . . . . . . . Young Man

Prick Up Your Ears (1987; British) . . . . . . . . . Constable

War Requiem (1988; British). . . . . . . . . . . . . Soldier 1

## Leina, Jonathan
*Films:*

**Police** (1985; French) . . . . . . . . . . . . . . . . . . . Simon

•• 0:11—Upper half of buns and brief frontal nudity in police station. Typewriter gets in the way.

## Leinert, Mike
*Films:*

**Easy Wheels** (1989) . . . . . . . . . . . . . . . . . . . Meatball

• 0:52—Brief buns, while putting his pants on.

## Lemieux, Vincent

*Films:*
**Desert Passion** (1992) . . . . . . . . . . . . Man in Bondage
••• 0:45—Buns, while in cage during bondage fantasy
   with Heather.

## Lemmon, Jack

Father of actor Chris Lemmon.
*Films:*
It Should Happen to You (1954) . . . . . . . Pete Sheppard
Mister Roberts (1955) . . . . . . Ens. Frank Thurlowe Pulver
Fire Down Below (1957) . . . . . . . . . . . . . . . . . . . Tony
Bell, Book and Candle (1959) . . . . . . . . . Nicky Holroyd
Some Like it Hot (1959) . . . . . . . . . . . . . Jerry/Daphne
The Apartment (1960) . . . . . . . . . . . . . . . . C. C. Baxter
The Wackiest Ship in the Army (1961) . . Lt. Rip Crandall
Days of Wine and Roses (1962) . . . . . . . . . . . . . . . Joe
Irma La Douce (1963) . . . . . . . . . . . . . . . . . . . . Nestor
Good Neighbor Sam (1964) . . . . . . . . . . . . Sam Bissel
The Great Race (1965) . . . . . . . . . . . . . . Professor Fate
The Fortune Cookie (1966) . . . . . . . . . . . . Harry Hinkle
Luv (1967) . . . . . . . . . . . . . . . . . . . . . . . . Harry Berlin
The Odd Couple (1968) . . . . . . . . . . . . . . Felix Ungar
The April Fool's (1969) . . . . . . . . . . . . Howard Brubaker
The Out of Towners (1970) . . . . . . . . George Kellerman
**Avanti!** (1973) . . . . . . . . . . . . . . Wendell Armbruster
  (Not available on video tape. Shown on *The Arts and En-*
  *tertainment Channel* periodically. Scenes are listed as
  0:00 since I can't time correctly with the commercials.)
  • 0:00—Buns, while standing up in bathtub talking to
    Juliet Mills.
Save the Tiger (1973) . . . . . . . . . . . . . . . Harry Stoner
The Front Page (1974) . . . . . . . . . . . . . . Hildy Johnson
The Prisoner of Second Avenue (1975) . . . . . . . . . . Mel
Airport '77 (1977) . . . . . . . . . . . . . . . . Don Gallagher
The China Syndrome (1979) . . . . . . . . . . . . Jack Godell
Tribute (1980; Canadian) . . . . . . . . . . . Jack Templeton
Buddy Buddy (1981) . . . . . . . . . . . . . . . Victor Clooney
Missing (1982) . . . . . . . . . . . . . . . . . . . . . Ed Horman
Mass Appeal (1984) . . . . . . . . . . . . . . . . Father Farley
Macaroni (1985; Italian) . . . . . . . . . . . . . Robert Traven
That's Life! (1986) . . . . . . . . . . . . . . . . Harvey Fairchild
JFK (1991) . . . . . . . . . . . . . . . . . . . . . . . . Jack Martin
Glengarry Glen Ross (1992) . . . . . . . . . . Shelley Levine
Grumpy Old Men (1993) . . . . . . . . . . . John Gustafson
Short Cuts (1993) . . . . . . . . . . . . . . . . . . Paul Finnigan
*Made for Cable Movies:*
For Richer, For Poorer (1992; HBO) . . . . Aronn Katourian
*TV:*
That Wonderful Guy (1949-50) . . . . . . . . . . . . . Harold
Toni Twin Time (1950) . . . . . . . . . . . . . . . . . . . . Host
Ad Libbers (1951) . . . . . . . . . . . . . . . . . . . . . Regular
Heaven for Betsy (1952) . . . . . . . . . . . . . . . . Pete Bell

## Lennon, John

Late singer with *The Beatles* and on his own.
*Films:*
A Hard Day's Night (1964; British) . . . . . . . . . . . . John
Help! (1965; British) . . . . . . . . . . . . . . . . . . . . . John

How I Won the War (1967) . . . . . . . . . . . . . Gripweed
**Imagine: John Lennon** (1988) . . . . . . . . . . . Himself
  • 0:43—Nude in B&W photos from his White Album.
  0:57—Brief frontal nudity of album cover again during interview.

## • Leonardi, Marco

*Films:*
Cinema Paradiso (1988; Italian/French)
. . . . . . . . . . . . . . . . . . . . . . . . Salvatore as a Youth
The Palermo Connection (1989; Italian) . . . . . . . . n.a.
**Like Water for Chocolate** (1993; Mexican) . . . . Pedro
*a.k.a. Como Agua Para Chocolate*
  • 1:40—Frontal nudity, while lying on bed, dead.

## Lester, Jeff

*Films:*
**In the Cold of the Night** (1989) . . . . . . . Scott Bruin
  • 0:05—Very brief buns, while rolling over to strangle
    Shannon Tweed.
*TV:*
Once a Hero (1979) . . . . . . . Captain Justice/Brad Steele
Walking Tall (1981) . . . . . . . . . . Deputy Grady Spooner

## • Leto, Jared

*Made for Cable Movies:*
**Rebel Highway: Cool and the Crazy**
  (1994; Showtime) . . . . . . . . . . . . . . . . . . . . . Michael
  • 0:43—Brief buns, while making love in bed with Lor-
    raine.

## Levine, Mark

*Films:*
**Spring Fever USA** (1988) . . . . . . . . . . . . . Duke Dork
*a.k.a. Lauderdale*
  • 1:17—Buns, twice, while in boat hallway with his
    skinny brother after being tricked.

## Levisetti, Emile

*Films:*
**Sexual Response** (1992) . . . . . . . . . . . . . . . . . . Edge
  (Unrated version reviewed.)
  ••• 0:31—Buns, while standing and looking out the
    window, then sitting on the bed.
  ••• 0:43—Buns, while making love with Shannon
    Tweed.

## Levitt, Steve

*Films:*
Those Lips, Those Eyes (1980) . . . . . . . . . . . Westervelt
Private School (1983) . . . . . . . . . . . . . . . . . . . Bellboy
Last Resort (1985) . . . . . . . . . . . . . . . . . . . . . . Pierre
Hunk (1987) . . . . . . . . . . . . . . . . . Bradley Brinkman
**Blue Movies** (1988) . . . . . . . . . . . . . . . . . . . . . Buzz
  •• 0:46—Buns, while walking around naked when Ran-
    dy and Kathy make him and Cliff take their clothes
    off.
The Experts (1989) . . . . . . . . . . . . . . . . . . . . . . n.a.

## Levy, Eugene

*Films:*

Going Beserk (1983) . . . . . . . . . . . . . . . Sal di Pasquale
National Lampoon's Vacation (1983). . . . . Car Salesman
Splash (1984) . . . . . . . . . . . . . . . . . . Walter Kornbluth
**Armed and Dangerous** (1986) . . . . . . . Norman Kane
  • 1:02—Cheeks of his buns through the back of leath-
  er pants while dressed in drag with John Candy to
  escape from the bad cops.
Club Paradise (1986). . . . . . . . . . . . . . . Barry Steinberg
Father of the Bride (1991) . . . . . . . . Auditioning Singer
Stay Tuned (1992). . . . . . . . . . . . . . . . . . . . Crowley
*TV:*

Second City TV Comedy (1977-81) . . . . Earl Camembert
SCTV Network 90 (1981-83). . . . . . . . . . . . . . Regular

## •Lewis, Huey

Singer with the group *Huey Lewis and the News.*
*Films:*

Back to the Future (1985)
  . . . . . . . Uncredited Battle of the Bands Audition Judge
**Short Cuts** (1993). . . . . . . . . . . . . . . . . . . Vern Miller
  0:50—Brief frontal nudity, while pulling it out of his
  pants while standing on rock. The next shot of him
  urinating is a fake penis since it was difficult to urinate for so long on cue.

## •Leza, Daniel

*Made for Cable TV:*

**Red Shoe Diaries: Night of Abandon**
  (1993; Showtime) . . . . . . . . . . . . . . . . . . . . . . Man
  • 0:25—Brief buns, when rolling off the woman on
  the beach.

## Lhermitte, Thierry

*Films:*

Next Year if All Goes Well (1983; French) . . . . . Maxime
My Best Friend's Girl (1984; French) . . . . Pascal Saulnier
  *a.k.a. La Femme du Mon Ami*
My New Partner (1984; French) . . . . . . . . . . . Francois
  *a.k.a. Les Ripoux*
**Until September** (1984). . . . . . . . Xavier de la Pérouse
  •• 0:43—Buns, after making love with Karen Allen.
  0:53—Almost frontal nudity getting out of bathtub.

## •Liapis, Pete

*Films:*

Swordkill (1984) . . . . . . . . . . . . . . . . . . . Johnny Tooth
Ghoulies (1985) . . . . . . . . . . . . . . . . . Jonathan Graves
**Ghoulies IV** (1993) . . . . . . . . . . . . . . Jonathan Graves
  • 0:49—Brief buns, putting on his underwear. Don't
  see his face.

## Liebman, Ron

*Films:*

**Where's Poppa?** (1970) . . . . . . . . . Sidney Hocheiser
  • 0:45—Buns while running across the street, then in
  front of door in hall, then brief buns leaving George
  Segal's apartment.

The Hot Rock (1972) . . . . . . . . . . . . . . . . . . . . Murch
Slaughterhouse Five (1972) . . . . . . . . . . . Paul Lazzaro
Your Three Minutes Are Up (1973). . . . . . . . . . Mike
Won Ton Ton, The Dog Who Saved Hollywood (1976)
  . . . . . . . . . . . . . . . . . . . . . . . . . . . Rudy Montague
Norma Rae (1979) . . . . . . . . . . . . . . . . . . . . Reuben
Zorro, The Gay Blade (1981) . . . . . . . . . . . . Esteban
Romantic Comedy (1983) . . . . . . . . . . . . . . . . . Leo
Phar Lap (1984; Australian) . . . . . . . . . . . Dave Davis
*TV:*

Kaz (1978-79) . . . . . . . . . . . . . . Martin "Kaz" Kazinsky

## Lindon, Vincent

*Films:*

**Half Moon Street** (1986) . . . . . . . . . . . . . . . Sonny
  *a.k.a. Escort Girl*
  • 1:04—Buns, while getting out of bed with Sigourney Weaver.

## Liotta, Ray

*Films:*

The Lonely Lady (1983) . . . . . . . . . . . . . . . . . . . Joe
Something Wild (1986) . . . . . . . . . . . . . . Ray Sinclair
Dominick and Eugene (1988). . . . . . . . Eugene Luciano
Field of Dreams (1989). . . . . . . . . Shoeless Joe Jackson
GoodFellas (1990) . . . . . . . . . . . . . . . . . . Henry Hill
Article 99 (1992) . . . . . . . . . . . . . . . . . . . . Sturgess
**Unlawful Entry** (1992) . . . . . . Officer Pete Davis
  • 0:50—Brief, out of focus buns, while getting out of
  shower in locker room.
Corrina, Corrina (1994) . . . . . . . . . . . . . Manny Singer
No Escape (1994) . . . . . . . . . . . . . . . . . John Robbins
*Made for Cable Movies:*

Women & Men 2: Three Short Stories (1991; HBO)
  . . . . . . . . . . . . . . . . . . . . . . . . . . . . . . . Martin
*TV:*

Another World (1978-81). . . . . . . . . . . . . Joey Perrini
Casablanca (1983) . . . . . . . . . . . . . . . . . . . . Sacha
Our Family Honor (1985-86) . . . . . . Officer Ed Santini

## Lipton, Robert

*Films:*

Blue (1968) . . . . . . . . . . . . . . . . . . . . . . . . Antonio
Bullitt (1968) . . . . . . . . . . . . . . . . . . . . . . First Aide
Tell Them Willie Boy is Here (1969) . . . . . . Newcombe
God's Gun (1977) . . . . . . . . . . . . . . . . . . . . . . n.a.
  *a.k.a. A Bullet from God*
Death Spa (1987). . . . . . . . . . . . . . . . . . . . . . Tom
**Lethal Woman** (1988). . . . . . . . Major Derek Johnson
  • 1:02—Very brief frontal nudity in the ocean with Sh-
  annon Tweed, when the water goes down.
  • 1:05—Brief buns while in the water on the beach
  with Tweed.
A Woman, Her Men and Her Futon (1992). . . . . . . Max
*TV:*

The Survivors (1969-70). . . . . . . . . . . . . . . . . . Tom

# • Lister, Tom "Tiny", Jr.
*Films:*
Beverly Hills Cop II (1987) . . . . . . . . . . . . . . . . . . .Orvis
Extreme Prejudice (1987) . . . . . . . . . . . . . . . . Monday
Prison (1987) . . . . . . . . . . . . . . . . . . . . . . . . . . . . . . Tiny
No Holds Barred (1989) . . . . . . . . . . . . . . . . . . . . Zeus
Talkin' Dirty After Dark (1991) . . . . . . . . . . . . . . . Bigg
Universal Soldier (1992) . . . . . . . . . . . . . . . . . . . GR55
Immortal Combat (1993) . . . . . . . . . . . . . . . . Yanagi
The Meteor Man (1993) . . . . . . . . . . . . . . . . . . . . Digit
**Posse** (1993) . . . . . . . . . . . . . . . . . . . . . . . . . . Obobo
•• 0:50—Buns, while urinating in the water.

# Lithgow, John
*Films:*
Obsession (1976) . . . . . . . . . . . . . . . . . . Robert La Salle
The Big Fix (1978) . . . . . . . . . . . . . . . . . Sam Sebastian
All That Jazz (1979) . . . . . . . . . . . . . . . . Lucas Sergeant
Rich Kids (1979) . . . . . . . . . . . . . . . . . . . . Paul Philips
Blow Out (1981) . . . . . . . . . . . . . . . . . . . . . . . . . Burke
World According to Garp (1982) . . . . . . . . . . . .Roberta
Terms of Endearment (1983) . . . . . . . . . . . . . Sam Burns
Twilight Zone—The Movie (1983) . . Airplane Passenger
2010 (1984) . . . . . . . . . . . . . . . . . . . . . . . . Walter Curnow
The Adventures of Buckaroo Banzai, Across the 8th
  Dimension (1984) . . . . Dr. Emilio Lizardo/John Whorfin
Footloose (1984) . . . . . . . . . . . . . Reverend Shaw Moore
Santa Claus (1985) . . . . . . . . . . . . . . . . . . . . . . .Bozo
Harry and the Hendersons (1987) . . . George Henderson
The Manhattan Project (1987) . . . . . . John Mathewson
Distant Thunder (1988) . . . . . . . . . . . . . .Mark Lambert
Out Cold (1989) . . . . . . . . . . . . . . . . . . . . . .Dave Geary
Memphis Belle (1990) . . . . . . . . Colonel Bruce Derringer
At Play in the Fields of the Lord (1991) . . . .Leslie Huben
Ricochet (1991) . . . . . . . . . . . . . . . . . . Earl Talbot Blake
Raising Cain (1992) . . . . Carter/Cain/Dr. Nix/Josh/Margo
Cliffhanger (1993) . . . . . . . . . . . . . . . . . . . . . . . Qualen
The Pelican Brief (1993) . . . . . . . . . . . . . . .Smith Keen
Princess Caraboo (1994) . . . . . . . . . . . . . . . . . . . .n.a.
*Made for Cable Movies:*
The Glitter Dome (1984; HBO) . . . . . . . Marty Welborn
**Traveling Man** (1989; HBO) . . . . . . . . . . . Ben Cluett
  • 0:48—Brief buns, while trying to get the VCR away
    from Mona in her living room.
Love, Cheat & Steal (1993; Showtime)
  . . . . . . . . . . . . . . . . . . . . . . . . Paul Harrington
The Wrong Man (1993; Showtime) . . . . . . . .Phillip Mills
*Miniseries:*
The Day After (1983) . . . . . . . . . . . . . . . . . . Joe Huxley
*Made for TV Movies:*
The Boys (1991) . . . . . . . . . . . . . . . . . . . Artie Margulies
World War II: When Lions Roared (1994)
  . . . . . . . . . . . . . . . . . . . . . . . . Franklin D. Roosevelt

# Lloyd, Christopher
*Films:*
One Flew Over the Cuckoo's Nest (1975) . . . . . . . Taber
Goin' South (1978) . . . . . . . . . . . . . . . . . . . . . . Towfield
The Lady in Red (1979) . . . . . . . . . . . . . . . . . Frognose

Schizoid (1980) . . . . . . . . . . . . . . . . . . . . . . . . Gilbert
National Lampoon Goes to the Movies (1982)
  . . . . . . . . . . . . . . . . . . . . . . . . .Samuel Starkman
  *a.k.a. Movie Madness*
Mr. Mom (1983) . . . . . . . . . . . . . . . . . . . . . . . . Larry
To Be or Not To Be (1983) . . . . . . . . . . . .Capt. Schultz
The Adventures of Buckaroo Banzai, Across the 8th
  Dimension (1984) . . . . . . . . . . . . . John Bigboote
The Joy of Sex (1984) . . . . . . . . . . . Coach Hindenberg
Star Trek III: The Search for Spock (1984) . . . . . . . Kruge
Back to the Future (1985) . . . . . . . . .Dr. Emmett Brown
Clue (1985) . . . . . . . . . . . . . . . . . . . . .Professor Plum
Miracles (1986) . . . . . . . . . . . . . . . . . . . . . . . .Harry
Walk Like a Man (1987) . . . . . . . . . . . . . . . . . .Reggie
Eight Men Out (1988) . . . . . . . . . . . . . . . . . Bill Burns
**Track 29** (1988; British) . . . . . . . . . . . . Henry Henry
  • 0:34—Very brief side view of his buns, while lying in
    the hospital getting spanked by Sandra Bernhard.
Who Framed Roger Rabbit (1988) . . . . . . . Judge Doom
Back to the Future, Part II (1989) . . . .Dr. Emmett Brown
The Dream Team (1989) . . . . . . . . . . . . . . . . . Henry
Back to the Future, Part III (1990) . . . .Dr. Emmett Brown
Why Me? (1990) . . . . . . . . . . . . . . . . . . . .Bruno Daley
The Addams Family (1991) . . . . . . . . . . . .Uncle Fester
Suburban Commando (1991) . . . . . . . . Charlie Wilcox
Addams Family Values (1993) . . . . . . . . . . .Uncle Fester
Dennis the Menace (1993) . . . . . . . . . .Switchblade Sam
Twenty Bucks (1993) . . . . . . . . . . . . . . . . . . . . . . n.a.
Camp Nowhere (1994) . . . . . . . . . .Dennis Van Welker
*Made for Cable Movies:*
Dead Ahead: The Exxon Valdez Disaster (1992; U.S./
  British; HBO) . . . . . . . . . . . . . . . . . .Frank Iarossi
*TV:*
Taxi (1979-83) . . . . . . . . . . "Reverend Jim" Ignatowski

# • Lone, John
*Films:*
King Kong (1976) . . . . . . . . . . . . . . . . . . Chinese Cook
Iceman (1984) . . . . . . . . . . . . . . . . . . . . . . . . .Charlie
The Year of the Dragon (1985) . . . . . . . . . . . . .Joey Tai
The Last Emperor (1987) . . . . . . . . . Pu Yi as an Adult
The Moderns (1988) . . . . . . . . . . . . . . . . . . . .Stone
Echoes in Paradise (1989) . . . . . . . . . . . . . . . . . Raka
**M. Butterfly** (1993) . . . . . . . . . . . . . . . . Song Liling
  •• 1:24—Buns, after taking off his clothes in back of
    paddy wagon with Jeremy Irons.

# Lorello, John Paul
*Films:*
**Pleasure In Paradise** (1992) . . . . . . . . . . . . . Hansen
  • 0:17—Partial buns, while making love in bed on top
    of Sandra.
  ••• 0:57—Buns, while taking off clothes and getting
    into pool with Sandra.

# Louden, Jay
*Films:*
**Opposing Force** (1986) . . . . . . . . . . . . . . Stevenson
  *a.k.a. Hell Camp*

- 0:31—Buns, while getting yanked out of the line by Becker.
- 0:32—Buns, while getting sprayed with water and dusted with white powder. He's the first guy through.

## Louganis, Greg

Olympic diving champion.
*Films:*
Dirty Laundry (1987). . . . . . . . . . . . . . . . . . . . . . Larry
*Video Tapes:*
**Inside Out 3** (1992) . . . . . . . . . . Max/The Wet Dream
- •• 1:28—Buns, in G-string, while walking around after turning into a human being from a fish. Unfortunately, he's wearing some goofy looking fish make-up.
- •• 1:30—Buns, in G-string, while getting out of the bathtub.

## Lowe, Rob

*Films:*
Class (1983) . . . . . . . . . . . . . . . . . . . . . . . . . . . . . Skip
The Outsiders (1983) . . . . . . . . . . . . . . . . . . . .Sodapop
The Hotel New Hampshire (1984). . . . . . . . . . . . . John
Oxford Blues (1984) . . . . . . . . . . . . . . . Nick Di Angelo
St. Elmo's Fire (1985) . . . . . . . . . . . . . . . . . . . . . Billy
**About Last Night...** (1986) . . . . . . . . . . . . . . Danny
- •• 0:52—Buns and almost frontal nudity when he opens the refrigerator with Demi Moore.
**Youngblood** (1986) . . . . . . . . . . . . .Dean Youngblood
- ••• 0:16—Buns, standing in hallway in jockstrap and walking around while Cindy Gibb watches.
Square Dance (1987) . . . . . . . . . . . . . . . . . . . . . Rory
*a.k.a. Home is Where the Heart Is*
Illegally Yours (1988). . . . . . . . . . . . . . . . .Richard Dice
**Masquerade** (1988) . . . . . . . . . . . . . . . . . Tim Whalen
- ••• 0:04—Buns, while getting up from bed with Kim Cattrall.
- •• 0:30—Buns, while making love with Meg Tilly in bed.
**Bad Influence** (1990) . . . . . . . . . . . . . . . . . . . . Alex
- ••• 1:27—Buns, while going into the bathroom.
The Dark Backward (1991) . . . . . . . . . . . . . . Dirk Delta
The Finest Hour (1991) . . . . . . . . . . . . . . . . . . Hammer
Stroke of Midnight (1991; U.S./French). . . . . . . Salvitore
*a.k.a. If the Shoe Fits*
Wayne's World (1992). . . . . . . . . . . . . Benjamin Oliver
*Miniseries:*
Stephen King's "The Stand" (1994). . . . . . . Nick Andros
*TV:*
A New Kind of Family (1979-80) . . . . . . . Tony Flanagan
*Video Tapes:*
**Rob Lowe's Home Video** (1989) . . . . . . . . . . Himself
Nude. A little bit hard to tell it's him (it's a copy of a copy of a copy...) Rob's video tape of his sexual tryst with two teenage girls can be purchased from *Midnight Blue*. The address is located at the end of this book.

## • Löwitsch, Klaus

*Films:*
The Odessa File (1974; British/German)
. . . . . . . . . . . . . . . . . . . . . . . . .Gustav Mackensen
Rosebud (1975) . . . . . . . . . . . . . . . . . . . . . . . Schloss
Cross of Iron (1977) . . . . . . . . . . . . . . . . . . . . .Kruger
**Despair** (1978; German/French). . . . . . . . . . . . . .Felix
- •• 0:59—Buns, while reaching to get his pants and following Dirk Bogarde around the room.
The Marriage of Maria Braun (1979; German)
. . . . . . . . . . . . . . . . . . . . . . . . . . Hermann Braun
Desire, The Interior Life (1980; Italian/German)
. . . . . . . . . . . . . . . . . . . . . . . . . . . .Administrator
Night Crossing (1981) . . . . . . . . . . . . . . . . . Schmolk
Firefox (1982) . . . . . . . . . . . . . . . General Vladimirov

## Lundgren, Dolph

*Films:*
A View to a Kill (1985) . . . . . . . . . . . . . . . . . . . Venz
Masters of the Universe (1987). . . . . . . . . . . . .He-Man
**The Punisher** (1989) . . . . . . . . . . . . . . . .Frank Castle
- 0:06—Upper half of buns, while kneeling in his underground hideout. Don't see his face.
- 1:23—Same shot at 00:06 used again.
Red Scorpion (1989) . . . . . . . . . . . . . . . . Lt. Nikolai
Cover Up (1990) . . . . . . . . . . . . . . . . Mike Anderson
I Come in Peace (1990) . . . . . . . . . . . . . . . . Jack Caine
**Showdown in Little Tokyo** (1991)
. . . . . . . . . . . . . . . . . . . . . . . . . . Detective Kenner
- ••• 0:53—Buns, while getting out of bed to check on noise outside.
Universal Soldier (1992). . . . . . . . . . . . . .Andrew Scott
Army of One (1993). . . . . . . . . . . . . . . . . . . . . Santee

## Luther, Michael

*Films:*
**Malibu Beach** (1978). . . . . . . . . . . . . . . . . . . . .Paul
- 0:32—Buns, while running into the ocean with his friends.

## Lutze, Rick

*Films:*
**Auditions** (1978) . . . . . . . . . . . . . . . . . . . . Ron Wilson
- 1:00—Nude during audition.

## Lynch, John

*Films:*
**Cal** (1984; Irish). . . . . . . . . . . . . . . . . . . . . . . . . .Cal
- 1:20—Buns, while getting into bed with Helen Mirren.
Edward II (1992; British). . . . . . . . . . . . . . . . . Spencer
In the Name of the Father (1993; British/U.S.) . . Paul Hill
The Secret Garden (1993) . . . . . . . . . . . . . .Lord Craven
*Made for Cable Movies:*
**The Railway Station Man** (1992; TNT)
. . . . . . . . . . . . . . . . . . . . . . . . . .Damian Sweeney
- 0:37—Buns, taking off his clothes, running into the ocean and jumping around.

## Lyon, Steve

*Films:*

**Campus Man** (1987) . . . . . . . . . . . . . . . . Brett Wilson
  •• 0:25—Brief buns, while putting on swim trunks for photo session.
**Valet Girls** (1987) . . . . . . . . . . . . . . . . . . . . . Ike
  • 1:17—Brief side view of buns, twice, when the girls make him and his two friends climb the "HOLLY-WOOD" sign.

## Maccanti, Roberto

*Films:*

**1900** (1976; Italian) . . . . . . . . . . . . . . Olmo as a Child
  (NC-17 version reviewed.)
  •• 1:05—Frontal nudity undressing and showing the young Alfredo his penis.

## Macchia, John

*Films:*

**Pink Motel** (1982) . . . . . . . . . . . . . . . . . . . . . Skip
  •• 1:08—Buns, taking off underwear and getting into bed with Charlene. Very brief frontal nudity falling over the side of the bed.
Miracles (1986) . . . . . . . . . . . . . . . . . . . . . . Martin

## MacGowran, Jack

*Films:*

**Age of Consent** (1969; Australian) . . . . . . . . . Nat Kelly
  • 1:01—Brief buns, while running into the ocean when Miss Marley sees him.
  •• 1:02—Buns, running away from her to the cabin while holding a dog to cover up his private parts.

## Mackintosh, Steven

*Films:*

Prick Up Your Ears (1987; British) . . . . . . . . Simon Ward
Memphis Belle (1990) . . . . . . . . . . . . . . . . . . . . Stan
**London Kills Me** (1991; British) . . . . . . . . . Muffdiver
  •• 1:06—Brief buns and penis, while getting into bathtub with Clint and Sylvie.
The Muppet Christmas Carol (1992) . . . . . . . . . . . Fred

## • MacLachlan, Kent

*Films:*

**Endangered** (1994) . . . . . . . . . . . . . . . . . . . . Neil
  • 0:18—Very brief frontal nudity, while running and jumping into lake.
  •• 0:20—Very brief buns, while diving under water. More buns, while getting out and talking to bad guys.

## MacLachlan, Kyle

*Films:*

Dune (1984) . . . . . . . . . . . . . . . . Paul Atreides/Maudib
**Blue Velvet** (1986) . . . . . . . . . . . . . . . . . . . . Jeffrey
  ••• 0:40—Buns, when Isabella Rossellini takes his underwear off in her apartment.
  •• 0:41—Buns and very brief frontal nudity while running to closet.

The Hidden (1987) . . . . . . . . . . . . . . . . Lloyd Gallagher
Don't Tell Her It's Me (1990) . . . . . . . . . . . . . . . Trout
The Doors (1991) . . . . . . . . . . . . . . . Ray Manzarek
Rich in Love (1992) . . . . . . . . . . . . . . . Billy McQueen
Twin Peaks: Fire Walk With Me (1992) . . . . Dale Cooper
Where The Day Takes You (1992) . . . . . . . . . . . . . Ted
The Flintstones (1994) . . . . . . . . . . . . . Cliff Vandercave
The Trial (1994; British) . . . . . . . . . . . . . . . . Josef K.
*Made for Cable Movies:*
Against the Wall (1994; HBO) . . . . . . . . . . . Michael
Roswell (1994; Showtime) . . . . . . . . . . . . Jesse Marcel
*Made for Cable TV:*
Tales From the Crypt: Carrion Death (1991; HBO)
  . . . . . . . . . . . . . . . . . . . . . . . . . . . . . Earl Diggs
*TV:*
Twin Peaks (1990-91) . . . . . . . . . . . . . . . . Dale Cooper

## Madsen, Michael

Brother of actress Virginia Madsen.

*Films:*

Wargames (1983) . . . . . . . . . . . . . . . . . . . . . . Steve
The Natural (1984) . . . . . . . . . . . . . . . . Bump Bailey
Racing with the Moon (1984) . . . . . . . . . . . . . Frank
The End of Innocence (1989) . . . . . . . . . . . . . . n.a.
Kill Me Again (1989) . . . . . . . . . . . . . . . . . . . Vince
The Doors (1991) . . . . . . . . . . . . . . . . . . Tom Baker
**Fatal Instinct** (1991) . . . . . . . . . . . . . Cliff Burden
  *a.k.a. To Kill For*
  (Unrated version reviewed.)
  • 0:43—Half of buns, while lying in bed.
  •• 0:48—Upper half of buns, while making love in bed with Laura Johnson.
Inside Edge (1991) . . . . . . . . . . . . . . . Richard Montana
Thelma and Louise (1991) . . . . . . . . . . . . . . . . Jimmy
Almost Blue (1992) . . . . . . . . . . . . . . . Morris Poole
Reservoir Dogs (1992) . . . . . . . . . . . . . Mr. Blonde/Vic
Straight Talk (1992) . . . . . . . . . . . . . . . . . . . Steve
Trouble Bound (1992) . . . . . . . . . . . . . . . . . . Harry
Dead Connection (1993) . . . . . . . . . . . . . Matt Dickson
Free Willy (1993) . . . . . . . . . . . . . . . Glen Greenwood
The Getaway (1993) . . . . . . . . . . . . . . . Rudy Travis
  (Unrated version reviewed.)
**A House in the Hills** (1993) . . . . . . . . . . . . Mickey
  •• 0:36—Brief buns, after getting out of the shower.
Money for Nothing (1993) . . . . . . . . Detective Laurenzi
Wyatt Earp (1994) . . . . . . . . . . . . . . . . . . . . . n.a.
*Made for Cable Movies:*
Beyond the Law (1992; HBO) . . . . . . . . . . . . . Blood
*Made for Cable TV:*
**The Hitchhiker: Man at the Window** (1985; HBO)
  . . . . . . . . . . . . . . . . . . . . . . . . . John Hampton
  •• 0:09—Buns, while making love with his wife on the couch.
*Made for TV Movies:*
Baby Snatcher (1992) . . . . . . . . . . . . . . . Cal Hudson
*TV:*
Our Family Honor (1985-86) . . . . . . . . . . Augie Danzig

## Mahinda, Edwin
*Films:*
**The Kitchen Toto** (1987; British) . . . . . . . . . Mwangi
  • 0:24—Nude, getting a bath outside.

## Maiden, Tony
*Films:*
**Spaced Out** (1980; British) . . . . . . . . . . . . . . . . . Willy
*a.k.a. Outer Touch*
  • 0:38—Buns, while getting examined by Cosia.

## Malkovich, John
Ex-husband of actress Glenne Headly.
*Films:*
The Killing Fields (1984) . . . . . . . . . . . . . . . . . . . . . Al
Places in the Heart (1984) . . . . . . . . . . . . . . . . . Mr. Will
Eleni (1985) . . . . . . . . . . . . . . . . . . . . . . . . . . . . . Nick
The Glass Menagerie (1987) . . . . . . . . . . . . . . . . Tom
Making Mr. Right (1987) . . . . . . . . Dr. Jeff Peters/Ulysses
Miles From Home (1988) . . . . . . . . . . . . . Barry Maxwell
**The Sheltering Sky** (1990) . . . . . . . . . . . . . . . . . Port
  ••• 0:32—Frontal nudity and half of buns, while getting
    out of bed and opening door.
The Object of Beauty (1991) . . . . . . . . . . . . . . . . Jake
Queens Logic (1991). . . . . . . . . . . . . . . . . . . . . . Eliot
Shadows and Fog (1991) . . . . . . . . . . . . . . . . . .Clown
Alive (1992) . . . . . . . . . . . . . . . . .Nando, 20 Years Later
Jennifer 8 (1992). . . . . . . . . . . . . . . . . . . . . . St. Anne
Of Mice and Men (1992) . . . . . . . . . . . . . . . . Lennie
In the Line of Fire (1993). . . . . . . . . . . . . . Mitch Leary
*Made for Cable Movies:*
Old Times (1993) . . . . . . . . . . . . . . . . . . . . . . Deeley
Heart of Darkness (1994; TNT) . . . . . . . . . . . . . . Kurtz

## Malone, Joseph
*Films:*
Universal Soldier (1992) . . . . . . . . . . . . . . . . . . .Huey
*Video Tapes:*
**Inside Out** (1992) . . . . . . . . . . . . . Terry/My Better Half
  •• 1:25—Buns, while lying on the floor. Brief partial
    frontal nudity. Long shot.

## • Mann, Sam
*Films:*
Hard Rock Zombies (1985) . . . . . . . . . . . . . . . . .Bobby
Roller Blade (1986) . . . . . . . . . . . . . . . . . . . . . . Waco
**RollerBlade Warriors: Taken By Force** (1988)
. . . . . . . . . . . . . . . . . . . . . . . . . . . . . . Marachek
  •• 0:52—Buns, after pulling down his pants to rape
    Elizabeth Kaitan. Don't see his face.

## March, John
*Films:*
**Moon 44** (1990; West German) . . . . . .Moose Haggerty
  • 0:43—Brief buns while in shower room. (Sort of see
    frontal nudity through grating in the shower divid-
    er.)

## Marchand, Guy
*Films:*
Cousin, Cousine (1975; French) . . . . . . . . . . . . . Pascal
**Loulou** (1980; French) . . . . . . . . . . . . . . . . . . . André
  •• 0:59—Buns, while getting out of bed with Isabelle
    Huppert.
Clean Slate (1981; French) . . . . . . . . . . . . . .Chavasson
  *a.k.a. Coup de Torchon*
The Heat of Desire (1982; French) . . . . . . . . . . . .Max
  *a.k.a. Plein Sud*
Entre Nous (1983; French) . . . . . . . . . . . . . . .Michel
  *a.k.a. Coup de Foudre*
Petit Con (1986; French) . . . . . . . . . . . . . Bob Choupon
May Wine (1990; French). . . . . . . . . Dr. Paul Charmant

## Margold, William
*Films:*
Fantasm (1976; Australian). . . . . . . . . . . . . . . . . n.a.
**Auditions** (1978) . . . . . . . . . . . . . . . . . . . . Larry Krantz
  •• 0:23—Frontal nudity during his audition.
  •• 0:26—Frontal nudity during audition with Linnea
    Quigley and Harry.
  •• 0:30—Frontal nudity, tied up on table.

## Margotta, Michael
*Films:*
The Strawberry Statement (1970) . . . . . . . . . . . Swatch
**Drive, He Said** (1972) . . . . . . . . . . . . . . . . . . Gabriel
  •• 1:21—Running nude across the grass and up some
    stairs, then trashing a biology room at the university.
Times Square (1980) . . . . . . . . . . . . . . . . . . . . .Jo Jo
Can She Bake a Cherry Pie? (1983) . . . . . . . . . . . Larry
*Made for TV Movies:*
She Lives (1973). . . . . . . . . . . . . . . . . . . . . . . . . .Al

## Marin, Richard "Cheech"
*Films:*
Up in Smoke (1978). . . . . . . . . . . . . . . . Pedro De Pacas
Cheech & Chong's Next Movie (1980) . . . . . . . Himself
**Cheech & Chong's Nice Dreams** (1981) . . . . Himself
  • 0:57—Brief buns when climbing over railing to es-
    cape Donna's husband, Animal.
    1:00—Buns while hanging over the side of the out-
    door elevator is probably a stunt double.
**Things Are Tough All Over** (1982) . . . . . Mr. Slyman
  • 0:21—Buns while in the laundromat dryer.
Cheech & Chong's Still Smokin' (1983) . . . . . . . Cheech
Yellowbeard (1983) . . . . . . . . . . . . . . . . . . . El Segundo
Cheech & Chong's The Corsican Brothers (1984)
. . . . . . . . . . . . . . . . . . . . . . . . . . . Corsican Brother
After Hours (1985) . . . . . . . . . . . . . . . . . . . . . . . . Neil
Echo Park (1986) . . . . . . . . . . . . . . . . . . . . . . . . . .Sid
Born in East L.A. (1987) . . . . . . . . . . . . . .Rudy Robles
Rude Awakening (1989). . . . . . . . . . . . . . . . . . . Zeus
Far Out Man (1990). . . . . . . . . . . . . . . . . Cheech Marin
The Shrimp on the Barbie (1990) . . . . . . . Carlos Muñoz
*Made for Cable Movies:*
The Cisco Kid (1994; TNT) . . . . . . . . . . . . . . . . Pancho

*Made for Cable TV:*
Dream On: The Taking of Pablum 1-2-3, Part II
  (1994; HBO) . . . . . . . . . . . . . . . . . . . . . . . . . . . .Waiter
*TV:*
The Golden Palace (1992- ) . . . . . . . . . . . . . . . . . . . .n.a.

## Marinaro, Ed

Ex-Minnesota Viking football player.
*Films:*
Fingers (1978) . . . . . . . . . . . . . . . . . . . . . . . . . . . . . .Gino
**Dead Aim** (1987) . . . . . . . . .Malcolm "Mace" Douglas
  • 0:53—Buns, while in bed making love with Amber.
    Dark, hard to see.
Queens Logic (1991) . . . . . . . . . . . . . . . . . . . . . . . Jack
*Made for Cable TV:*
Dream On: The Taking of Pablum 1-2-3, Part I
  (1994; HBO) . . . . . . . . . . . . . . . . . . . . . . . . .Policeman
*Made for TV Movies:*
Policewoman Centerfold (1983) . . . . . . . . . . . . . . . Nick
Menu for Murder (1990) . . . . . . . . . . . . . . . Det. Russo
Amy Fisher: My Story (1992) . . . . . . . . Joey Buttafuoco
Passport to Murder (1993) . . . . . . . . . . . .Hank McKay
*TV:*
Laverne & Shirley (1980-81) . . . . . . . . Sonny St. Jacques
Hill Street Blues (1981-87) . . . . . . . . Sergeant Joe Coffey
Sisters (1991- ) . . . . . . . . . . . . . . . . . . . . Mitch Margolis

## Markle, Stephen

*Films:*
Ticket to Heaven (1981; Canadian) . . . . . . . . . . . . .Karl
**Perfect Timing** (1984) . . . . . . . . . . . . . . . . . . . Harry
  • 0:58—Buns, while making love with Lacy.

## Marotte, Carl

*Films:*
**Pick-Up Summer** (1979; Canadian) . . . . . . . . . . Steve
  • 0:18—Side view of buns, while hanging a B.A. out
    passenger window at Rod.
Gas (1981; Canadian) . . . . . . . . . . . . . . . . . . . . . .Bobby
My Bloody Valentine (1981; Canadian) . . . . . . . . . .Dave

## Marquette, Ron

*Films:*
Mobsters (1991) . . . . . . . . . . . . . . . . . . . . . . . .Maitre'D
  *a.k.a. Mobsters—The Evil Empire*
*Made for Cable TV:*
**Red Shoe Diaries: Bounty Hunter** (1993; Showtime)
  . . . . . . . . . . . . . . . . . . . . . . . . . . . . .Oliver Dunbar
  • 0:19—Brief buns, making love outside with the
    bounty hunter. Don't see his face.
  0:25—Partial buns, making love on the floor in the
    cafe.
**Red Shoe Diaries: Kidnap** (1994; Showtime) . . . Tom
  ••• 0:17—Buns, several times, while making love out-
    side at night with Sara.

## • Mars, Kenneth

*Films:*
The Producers (1968) . . . . . . . . . . . . . Franz Liebkind
The April Fool's (1969) . . . . . . . . . . . . . . . Don Hopkins
Butch Cassidy and the Sundance Kid (1969) . . Marshall
Viva Max! (1969) . . . . . . . . . . . . . . . . . . .Dr. Sam Gillison
**Desperate Characters** (1971) . . . . . . . Otto Bentwood
  •• 0:20—Buns, while changing clothes in the closet
    doorway.
What's Up Doc? (1972) . . . . . . . . . . . . . . Hugh Simon
The Parallax View (1974) . . . . . . . . . . . . . . . . . . Turner
Young Frankenstein (1974) . . . . . . . . . . Inspector Kemp
Night Moves (1975) . . . . . . . . . . . . . . . . . . . . . . .Nick
Yellowbeard (1983) . . . . . . . . . . . . . . . .Crisp/Verdugo
Protocol (1984) . . . . . . . . . . . . . . . . . . . . . . . . . . Lou
Fletch (1985) . . . . . . . . . . . . . . . . . . . . .Stanton Boyd
Beer (1986) . . . . . . . . . . . . . . . . . . . . . . A.J. Norbecker
Radio Days (1987) . . . . . . . . . . . . . . . . . Rabbi Braumel
For Keeps (1988) . . . . . . . . . . . . . . . . . .Mr. Bobrucz
Illegally Yours (1988) . . . . . . . . . . . . . . . Hal B. Keeler
Rented Lips (1988) . . . . . . . . . . . . . . . .Reverend Farrell
Police Academy 6: City Under Siege (1989) . . . . . Mayor
Shadows and Fog (1991) . . . . . . . . . . . . . . . Magician
*Made for Cable TV:*
Sex, Shock and Censorship in the 90's (1993; Showtime)
  . . . . . . . . . . . . . . . . . . . . . . . . . . . Reverend Pete
*TV:*
He & She (1967-68) . . . . . . . . . . . . . . Harry Zarakardos

## Marshall, Bryan

*Films:*
The Viking Queen (1967; British) . . . . . . . . . . Dominic
I Started Counting (1970; British) . . . . . . . . . . . George
**Because of the Cats** (1973) . . . . Inspector Vanderbelt
  ••• 0:16—Frontal nudity, getting up out of bed.
    • 0:27—Partial frontal nudity behind glass while tak-
      ing a shower.
The Tamarind Seed (1974; British) . . . .George MacLeod
The Spy Who Loved Me (1977; British)
  . . . . . . . . . . . . . .Commander Talbot, H.M.S. Ranger
The Long Good Friday (1980; British) . . . . . . . . . .Harris
**Bliss** (1985; Australian) . . . . . . . . . . . . . Adrian Clunes
  • 1:01—Very brief buns, while running to the bath-
    room.
The Punisher (1989) . . . . . . . . . . . . . . . . . Dino Moretti

## Marshall, David Anthony

*Films:*
Across the Tracks (1990) . . . . . . . . . . . . . . . . . . .Louie
**Another 48 Hrs.** (1990) . . . . . . . . . . . . . Willie Hickok
  • 0:57—Buns, while putting pants on after getting out
    of bed.
Criss Cross (1992) . . . . . . . . . . . . . . . . . . . . . Blondie
Jailbait (1993) . . . . . . . . . . . . . . . . . . . . . . . . . Tommy

## Marshall, James
Films:
**Cadence** (1991) . . . . . . . . . . . . . . . . . . . . . . . . . Lamar
A Few Good Men (1992)
. . . . . . . . . . . . . . . . . Pvt. First Class Louden Downey
**Gladiator** (1992). . . . . . . . . . . . . . . . . . .Tommy Riley
• 1:33—Brief buns, while wearing jock strap when
Brian Dennehy yanks his boxing shorts down in box-
ing ring.
Twin Peaks: Fire Walk With Me (1992). . . . .James Hurley

## Martin, Ray
Films:
**Young Lady Chatterley** (1977) . . .Ronnie (stable boy)
•• 1:35—Frontal nudity, covered with cake during cake
orgy.

## Martinez, Nacho
Films:
**Matador** (1986; Spanish) . . . . . . . . . . . .Diego Montes
••• 0:29—Buns, while making love with Eva in bed.
High Heels (1991; Spanish). . . . . . . . . . . . . . . . . Juan

## • Mason, Michael
Video Tapes:
**Playboy's Secret Confessions** (1993)
. . . . . . . . . . . . . . . . . . . . Here Comes the Judge/Spike
• 0:49—Very brief erect frontal nudity (seen under the
girl's legs).
• 0:51—Buns, while lying on top of the girl. Long
shot.

## Masterson, Sean
Made for Cable TV:
**Dream On: The Name of the Game is Five-Card
Stud** (1991; HBO) . . . . . . . . . . . . . . . . . . . . . .Carter
• 0:17—Brief buns, after losing his clothes during
poker game.
•• 0:18—Buns again getting up from the table.
Dream On: To the Moon, Alex (1992; HBO) . . . . .Carter
Dream On: Hack Like Me (1994; HBO) . . . . . . . . .Carter
Dream On: Judy and the Beast (1994; HBO) . . . . .Carter
Dream On: Where There's Smoke, You're Fired
(1994; HBO) . . . . . . . . . . . . . . . . . . . . . . . . . . .Carter

## Mateo, Steve
Films:
**Vice Academy, Part 3** (1991)
. . . . . . . . . . . . . . . . . . . . . . . Professor Dirk Kaufinger
•• 0:47—Buns, when Ginger Lynn Allen and Elizabeth
Kaitan come into his lab.
Video Tapes:
**B-Movie Queens Revealed: The Making of "Vice
Academy"** (1993) . . . . . . . . Professor Dirk Kaufinger
•• 0:17—Buns, in scene from Vice Academy 2.

## Mathers, James
Films:
**Aria** (1987; U.S./British) . . . . . . . . . . . . . . . Boy Lover
•• 1:00—Brief dark outline of frontal nudity in hotel
room, then buns while making love with Bridget
Fonda.
• 1:02—Frontal nudity under water in the bathtub
with her.

## Matheson, Tim
Films:
Yours, Mine and Ours (1968). . . . . . . . . .Mike Beardsley
Magnum Force (1973). . . . . . . . . . . . . . . . . . . . Sweet
Almost Summer (1978) . . . . . . . . . . . . . Kevin Hawkins
**Animal House** (1978) . . . . . . . . . Eric "Otter" Stratton
• 0:08—Buns, changing clothes in his bedroom while
talking to Boone.
1941 (1979). . . . . . . . . . . . . . . . . . . . . . . . . Birkhead
A Little Sex (1982) . . . . . . . . . . . . . . Michael Donovan
To Be or Not To Be (1983) . . . . . . . . Lieutenant Sobinski
The House of God (1984). . . . . . . . . . . . . . . Dr. Basch
(Not available on video tape.)
**Impulse** (1984). . . . . . . . . . . . . . . . . . . . . . . . Stuart
• 0:17—Buns, when getting out of bed with Meg Tilly.
Up the Creek (1984) . . . . . . . . . . . . . . . . Bob McGraw
Fletch (1985) . . . . . . . . . . . . . . . . . . . . .Alan Stanwyk
Speed Zone (1989) . . . . . . . . . . . . . . . . . . . . . . .Jack
Drop Dead Fred (1991) . . . . . . . . . . . . . . . . Charles
Quicksand: No Escape (1991) . . . . . . . Scott Reinhardt
Solar Crisis (1992) . . . . . . . . . . . . . . . . . Steve Kelso
Made for Cable Movies:
Buried Alive (1990; USA) . . . . . . . . . . . . . . . . . Clint
Made for Cable TV:
Fallen Angels: Since I Don't Have You (1993; Showtime)
. . . . . . . . . . . . . . . . . . . . . . . . . . .Howard Hughes
(Available on video tape on Fallen Angels One.)
Made for TV Movies:
The Quest (1976). . . . . . . . . . . . . . . Quentin Beaudine
Listen To Your Heart (1983) . . . . . . . . . . . . Josh Stearn
Joshua's Heart (1990). . . . . . . . . . . . . . . . . . . . .Tom
Stephen King's "Sometimes They Come Back" (1991)
. . . . . . . . . . . . . . . . . . . . . . . . . . . . . . .Jim Norman
The Woman Who Sinned (1991) . . . . . Michael Robeson
Dying to Love You (1993) . . . . . . . . . . . . . . . . n.a.
Relentless: Mind of a Killer (1993) . . . . . . . . . . . . n.a.
Shameful Secrets (1993) . . . . . . . . . . . . . . . . . n.a.
TV:
Window on Main Street (1961-62). . . . . . . Roddy Miller
The Virginian (1969-70). . . . . . . . . . . . . . . . . Jim Horn
Bonanza (1972-73) . . . . . . . . . . . . . . . . . . .Griff King
Tucker's Witch (1982-83) . . . . . . . . . . . . . . Rick Tucker
Just in Time (1988). . . . . . . . . . . . . . . . . Harry Stadlin
Charlie Hoover (1991-93) . . . . . . . . . . . .Charlie Hoover

## Mathews, Stephen Kean
Films:
**Young Lady Chatterley II** (1986). . . Robert Downing
• 0:59—Buns, while making love with Cynthia Chatterley outside on the grass.

## Matshikiza, John

*Films:*
**Dust** (1985; French/Belgian) . . . . . . . . . . . . . Hendrik
• 0:38—Buns, while on top of a girl, trying to rape her.
Cry Freedom (1987; British) . . . . . . . . . . . . . . Mapetla
Dust Devil (1992; British) . . . . . . . . . . . . Joe Niemand

## Mauro, Joseph E.

*Films:*
**Affairs of the Heart** (1992) . . . . . . . . . . Jealous Man
• 0:38—Buns in G-string, walking into room with the Jealous Woman.

## Maury, Derrel

*Films:*
**Massacre at Central High** (1976) . . . . . . . . . . . David
• 0:32—Buns, while romping around in the ocean with Kimberly Beck. Dark, long shot. Hard to see anything.
*TV:*
Apple Pie (1978) . . . . . . . . . . . . . . . . . Junior Hollyhock
Joanie Loves Chachi (1982-83) . . . . . . . . . . . . . Mario

## • Mavers, Gary

*Films:*
The Resurrected (1990; British) . . . . . . . Johnny Fodden
*Made for TV Movies:*
**Masterpiece Theatre: Body & Soul** (1994) . . . . . Hal
•• 3:42—Buns, twice, in bedroom with Kristin Scott-Thomas.

## Mazmanian, Marius

*Films:*
The Beauties and the Beast (1973) . . . . . . . . . . . . . n.a.
**Video Vixens** (1973) . . . . . . . . . . . . . . . . . Psychiatrist
•• 0:42—Buns and balls from behind, while frolicking on couch with his patient. In B&W.
The Vanishing (1993) . . . . . . . . . . . . . . . . . . . . Cook

## McCarthy, Andrew

*Films:*
Class (1983) . . . . . . . . . . . . . . . . . . . . . . . . . Jonathan
**Heaven Help Us** (1985) . . . . . . . . . . . . Michael Dunn
• 0:35—Upper half of buns, while standing by the pool next to Caesar when he blows his nose.
St. Elmo's Fire (1985) . . . . . . . . . . . . . . . . . . . Kevin
Pretty in Pink (1986) . . . . . . . . . . . . Blane McDonough
**Less than Zero** (1987) . . . . . . . . . . . . . . . . . . Clay
• 0:03—Very brief buns when getting out of bed to answer the phone.
Mannequin (1987) . . . . . . . . . . . . . . Jonathan Switcher
Fresh Horses (1988) . . . . . . . . . . . . . . . . Matt Larkin
Kansas (1988) . . . . . . . . . . . . . . . . . . . . . Wade Corey
Weekend at Bernie's (1989) . . . . . . . . . . . Larry Wilson
*a.k.a. Hot and Cold*
Club Extinction (1990) . . . . . . . . . . . . . . The Assassin
*a.k.a. Doctor M*
Year of the Gun (1991) . . . . . . . . . . . David Raybourne
Only You (1992) . . . . . . . . . . . . . . . . Clifford Godfrey

The Joy Luck Club (1993) . . . . . . . . . . . . . . . . . . . Ted
Weekend at Bernie's II (1993) . . . . . . . . . . Larry Wilson
*Made for Cable TV:*
Tales From the Crypt: Loved to Death (1991; HBO)
. . . . . . . . . . . . . . . . . . . . . . . . . . . . Edward Foster

## McCleery, Gary

*Films:*
**Hard Choices** (1986) . . . . . . . . . . . . . . . . . . . Bobby
•• 1:11—Buns, while making love on top of Laura.
The Chair (1988) . . . . . . . . . . . . . . . . . . . Rick Donner

## • McClure, Doug

*Films:*
Gidget (1959) . . . . . . . . . . . . . . . . . . . . . . . . Waikiki
Nobody's Perfect (1968) . . . . . . . . . . . . Doc Willougby
The Land That Time Forgot (1975; British) . . . . . . . Tyler
At the Earth's Core (1976; British) . . . . . . . . David Innes
The People That Time Forgot (1977; British)
. . . . . . . . . . . . . . . . . . . . . . . . . . . . Bowen Tyler
Humanoids from the Deep (1980) . . . . . . . . . . . . . . Jim
Firebird 2015 AD (1981) . . . . . . . . . . . . . . . . . . n.a.
**House Where Evil Dwells** (1982) . . . . . . . . . . . . Alex
• 1:00—Very brief, upper half of buns, while making love with Susan George on the floor.
Cannonball Run II (1984) . . . . . . . . . . . . . . The Slapper
52 Pick-Up (1986) . . . . . . . . . . . . . . . . . . . . Averson
Omega Syndrome (1986) . . . . . . . . . . Detective Milnor
Tapeheads (1988) . . . . . . . . . . . . . . . . . Sidney Tager
*Miniseries:*
Roots (1977) . . . . . . . . . . . . . . . . . . . . . Jemmy Brent
*Made for TV Movies:*
Battling for Baby (1992) . . . . . . . . . . . . . . . . . . David
*TV:*
The Virginian (1962-71) . . . . . . . . . . . . . . . . Trampas
Search (1972-73) . . . . . . . . . . . . . . . . . . C.R. Grover
The Barbary Coast (1975-76) . . . . . . . . . Cash Conover
Out of This World (1987-91) . . . . Mayor Kyle Applegate

## • McCollow, Mike

*Films:*
**Sexual Outlaws** (1993) . . . . . . . . . . . . . . . . . . John
••• 0:32—Buns, while making love on top of Annie in bed.

## McDonald, Joshua

*Films:*
**Eleven Days, Eleven Nights** (1988; Italian) . . Michael
• 0:33—Buns, when Sarah removes his underwear.

## • McDonough, Stephen

*Films:*
**Bank Robber** (1993) . . . . . . . . . . . . . . . . . . . Andy
• 1:11—Brief upper half of buns, while in bed with Olivia D'Abo.

# McDowell, Malcolm

Ex-husband of actress Mary Steenburgen.

*Films:*

**If...** (1969; British) . . . . . . . . . . . . . . . . . . Mick Travers
••• 0:42—Buns, while standing in cold shower as punishment. He's the third guy.
Long Ago Tomorrow (1970) . . . . . . . . . . Bruce Pritchard
**A Clockwork Orange** (1971) . . . . . . . . . . . . . . . Alex
• 0:27—Very brief nude having sex with two women in his bedroom. Shot at fast speed.
0:52—Upper half of frontal nudity getting admitted to jail.
O Lucky Man! (1973; British) . . . . . . . . . . . . Mick Travis
Voyage of the Damned (1976; British) . . . . . Max Gunter
Time After Time (1979; British) . . . . . . . Herbert G. Wells
**Caligula** (1980) . . . . . . . . . . . . . . . . . . . . . . Caligula
(X-rated, 147 minute version.)
• 0:05—Buns, while rolling around in bed with Drusilla.
• 0:36—Brief buns, while taking ring off of Peter O'Toole.
• 0:46—Very brief buns while running to bed.
0:51—Buns, while putting Drusilla down in bed.
• 1:14—Nude walking around outside in the rain. Dark, long shot.
2:23—Very brief buns while under his white robe.
**Cat People** (1982) . . . . . . . . . . . . . . . . . . Paul Gollier
• 1:06—Side view of buns, while lying on the bathroom floor. Partial lower frontal nudity when he gets up.
Blue Thunder (1983) . . . . . . . . . . . . . . . . . . Cochrane
Get Crazy (1983) . . . . . . . . . . . . . . . . . . . . . . Reggie
**Gulag** (1985) . . . . . . . . . . . . . . . . . . . . . . Englishman
•• 1:26—Buns, while standing outside with David Keith in the snow being hassled by guards.
Class of 1999 (1990) . . . . . . . . . . . . . Dr. Miles Langford
Disturbed (1990) . . . . . . . . . . . . . . . . Dr. Derek Russell
**Jezebel's Kiss** (1990) . . . . . . . . . . Benjamin J. Faberson
•• 1:12—Buns, while making love with Jezebel.
The Light in the Jungle (1990) . . . Dr. Albert Schweitzer
Moon 44 (1990; West German) . . . . . . . . . . Major Lee
Chain of Desire (1992) . . . . . . . . . . . . . . Hubert Bailey
The Player (1992) . . . . . . . . . . . . . . . . . . . . . Cameo
Bophal (1993) . . . . . . . . . . . . . . . . . . . . . De Villiers
*Made for Cable TV:*
Tales From the Crypt: The Reluctant Vampire
(1991; HBO) . . . . . . . . . . . . . . . . . . Longtooth
*Made for TV Movies:*
Seasons of the Heart (1994) . . . . . . . . Alfred McGinnis
*Video Tapes:*
**Penthouse: On the Wild Side** (1988) . . . . . . Caligula
••• 0:50—Nude, in rainstorm seen from above during *The Making of Caligula*. Kind of a long shot.

# McElroy, Scott

*Films:*

**Desert Passion** (1992) . . . . . . . . . . . . . Mr. Gunther
• 0:28—Buns, while making love with a girl during his desert fantasy.

# McGann, Paul

*Films:*

Withnail and I (1987; British) . . . . . . . . . . . . Marwood
Innocent Victim (1988) . . . . . . . . . . . . . . . . . . Barry
**The Rainbow** (1989) . . . . . . . . . . . Anton Skrebensky
•• 1:30—Buns, while opening a bottle of wine in room with Sammi Davis.
• 1:44—Very brief frontal nudity and buns when running up a hill with Amanda Donohoe.
The Monk (1990; British/Spanish) . . . . . Father Lorenzo
Paper Mask (1991; British) . . . . . . . . . . Matthew Harris
Afraid of the Dark (1992; British/French) . . . Tony Dalton
Alien 3 (1992) . . . . . . . . . . . . . . . . . . . . . . . Golic
The Three Musketeers (1993) . . . . . . . . . . Girard/Jussac

# McGill, Bruce

*Films:*

Animal House (1978) . . . . . . . . . . . . . . . . . . . D-Day
The Hand (1981) . . . . . . . . . . . . . . . . . Brian Ferguson
Tough Enough (1983) . . . . . . . . . . . . . . . . Tony Fallon
Silkwood (1984) . . . . . . . . . . . . . . . . . . Mace Hurley
Club Paradise (1986) . . . . . . . . . . . . Dave the Fireman
No Mercy (1986) . . . . . . . . . . . . . . . . . . . . . Lt. Hall
Wildcats (1986) . . . . . . . . . . . . . . . . . . . Dan Darwill
**Out Cold** (1989) . . . . . . . . . . . . . . . . Ernie Cannald
•• 0:12—Frontal nudity, while opening the shower door, talking to Teri Garr. Brief buns, when putting on underwear.
Little Vegas (1990) . . . . . . . . . . . . . . . . . . . Harvey
The Last Boy Scout (1991) . . . . . . . . . . Mike Matthews
My Cousin Vinny (1992) . . . . . . . . . . . . Sheriff Farley
Play Nice (1992) . . . . . . . . . . . . . . . . Captain Foxx
(Unrated version reviewed.)
Cliffhanger (1993) . . . . . . . . . . . . . . . Treasury Agent
A Perfect World (1993) . . . . . . . . . . . . . Paul Saunders
*Made for Cable TV:*
Tales From the Crypt: The Trap (1991; HBO)
. . . . . . . . . . . . . . . . . . . . . . . . . . . . Lou Paloma
*Made for TV Movies:*
Shoot First: A Cop's Vengeance (1991) . . . . . . . . Shifton
Desperate Choices: To Save My Child (1992) . . . . . Dan
Black Widow Murders: The Blanche Taylor Moore Story
(1993) . . . . . . . . . . . . . . . . . . . . . . . . Morgan
Shameful Secrets (1993) . . . . . . . Judge Ian Greenstein
*TV:*
Delta House (1979) . . . . . . . . . . . . . . . . . . . D-Day

# • McGinley, Ted

*Films:*

Young Doctors in Love (1982) . . . . . . . . Dr. Bucky DeVol
**Revenge of the Nerds** (1984) . . . . . . . . . . Stan Gable
• 0:46—Brief buns, while mooning the nerds from back of flatbed truck. (He's the guy in the middle.)
Physical Evidence (1989) . . . . . . . . . . . . . . . . . Kyle
Troop Beverly Hills (1989) . . . . . . . . . . . . . . Himself
Blue Tornado (1990) . . . . . . . . . . . . . . . . . . Philip
Wayne's World 2 (1993) . . . . . . . . . . . . . . Mr. Scream
*Made for Cable Movies:*
Linda (1993; USA) . . . . . . . . . . . . . . Brandon Jeffries

*Made for TV Movies:*
Revenge of the Nerds III: The Next Generation (1992)
. . . . . . . . . . . . . . . . . . . . . . . . . . . . . . . . Stan Gable
*TV:*
Dynasty (1986-87) . . . . . . . . . . . . . . . . . Clay Fallmont
Baby Talk (1991) . . . . . . . . . . . . . . . . . . . . . . . . . . Craig
Married ...with Children (1991- ) . . . . . . . . . . Jefferson

# • McHattie, Stephen

*Films:*
The People Next Door (1970) . . . . . . . . . . . . . . . . Artie
Moving Violation (1979) . . . . . . . . . . . . . . Eddie Moore
Death Valley (1982) . . . . . . . . . . . . . . . . . . . . . . . Hal
Belizaire the Cajun (1986) . . . . . . . . . James Willoughby
Caribe (1987) . . . . . . . . . . . . . . . . . . . . . . . . . . . . n.a.
Salvation! (1987) . . . . . . . . . . . Reverend Edward Randall
Call Me (1988) . . . . . . . . . . . . . . . . . . . . . . . . Jellybean
One Man Out (1988) . . . . . . . . . . . . . . . . . . . . . . . . n.a.
Sticky Fingers (1988) . . . . . . . . . . . . . . . . . . . . . . . n.a.
Bloodhounds of Broadway (1989) . . . . . . . . . Red Henry
**The Dark** (1993) . . . . . . . . . . . . . . . . . . . . . . . Hunter
  • 0:30—Partial upper half of buns, while making love
    on bed with Tracy.
Geronimo: An American Legend (1993) . . . Schoonover
*Made for TV Movies:*
Jonathan Stone: Threat of Innocence (1994) . . Lt. Durant
*TV:*
Centennial (1978-80) . . . . . . . . . . . . . . . Jake Pasquinel
Highcliff Manor (1979) . . . . . . . . Reverend Ian Glenville
Beauty and the Beast (1989-90) . . . . . . . . . . . . Gabriel

# McIntire, Tim

Son of actor John McIntire and actress Jeanette Nolan.
*Films:*
The Sterile Cuckoo (1969) . . . . . . . Charlie Schumacher
Aloha, Bobby and Rose (1975) . . . . . . . . . . . . Buford
The Gumball Rally (1976) . . . . . . . . . . . . . . . . . Smith
**The Choirboys** (1977) . . . . . . . . . . . . . . Roscoe Rules
  • 0:36—Long shot of buns, while handcuffed to tree
    by his friends.
  ••• 0:39—Buns, while handcuffed to tree and trying to
    get a gay passerby help him. Long scene.
Fast Walking (1981) . . . . . . . . . . . . . . . . . . . . . . Wasco
Sacred Ground (1984) . . . . . . . . . . . . . . . . . . . . . Matt
*Miniseries:*
Rich Man, Poor Man (1976) . . . . . . . . . . . Brad Knight
*TV:*
The Legend of Jesse James (1965-66) . . . . . Bob Younger

# McKechnie, J. R.

*Films:*
**The Burning** (1981) . . . . . . . . . . . . . . . . . . . . . . . Fish
  • 0:29—Buns, pulling swimsuit down and up to moon
    Glazer. (On the far right.)

# • McKellen, Ian

*Films:*
The Promise (1969; British) . . . . . . . . . . . . . . Leonidik
Thank You All Very Much (1969; British) . . . . . . . George

**Priest of Love** (1980) . . . . . . . . . . . . . . D.H. Lawrence
  • 0:17—Buns after dropping robe and walking around
    bed. Shadow of erection on wall.
  ••• 0:52—Frontal nudity, while swimming in water.
  • 0:54—Brief frontal nudity while drying himself off.
  • 1:20—Brief buns, after taking off robe and getting
    into bed with Dorothy.
The Keep (1983) . . . . . . . . . . . . . . . . . . . . . . Dr. Cuza
Plenty (1985) . . . . . . . . . . . . . . Sir Andrew Charleson
Scandal (1989) . . . . . . . . . . . . . . . . . . John Profumo
(Unrated version reviewed.)

# McKenna, Travis

*Films:*
**Cheerleader Camp** (1987) . . . . . . . . . . . Timmy Moser
*a.k.a. Bloody Pom Poms*
  0:05—Buns, while hanging a B.A. out the van win-
    dow. He's a very heavy guy.
Real Men (1987) . . . . . . . . . . . . . . . . . . . . . . . . . Oaf
Dead Women In Lingerie (1991) . . . . . . . . . . . . . Billy
Batman Returns (1992) . . . . . . . . . . . . . . . Fat Clown
*Made for TV Movies:*
Ride with the Wind (1994) . . . . . . . . . . . . . . . . Travis

# McKeon, Doug

*Films:*
Uncle Joe Shannon (1978) . . . . . . . . . . . . . . . Robbie
Night Crossing (1981) . . . . . . . . . . . . . Frank Strelzyks
On Golden Pond (1981) . . . . . . . . . . . . . . . Billy Ray
**Mischief** (1985) . . . . . . . . . . . . . . . . . . . . . Jonathan
  • 0:56—Brief buns, while putting on his underwear af-
    ter making love with Kelly Preston.
Turnaround (1987) . . . . . . . . . . . . . . . . . . . . . . . Ben
*TV:*
Centennial (1978-79) . . . . . . . . . . . . . Philip Wendell
Big Shamus, Little Shamus (1979) . . . . . . . . Max Sutter

# • McMahon, Julian

*Films:*
**Wet and Wild Summer!** (1992; Australian)
. . . . . . . . . . . . . . . . . . . . . . . . . . . . Mick Dooley
  •• 0:21—Buns, taking off his swimtrunks at the beach.

# McNamara, Brian

*Films:*
The Beat (1986) . . . . . . . . . . . . . . . . . . . . . Billy Kane
Short Circuit (1986) . . . . . . . . . . . . . . . . . . . . . Frank
In the Mood (1987) . . . . . . . . . . . . . . . . . . . George
Stealing Home (1988) . . . . . . . . . . Billy Wyatt as a Teen
Blackwater (1989) . . . . . . . . . . . . . . . . . . . . . Hewitt
Caddyshack II (1989) . . . . . . . . . . . . . . . . Todd Young
Arachnophobia (1990) . . . . . . . . . . . . . Chris Collins
Mystery Date (1991) . . . . . . . . . . . . . . Craig McHugh
**When the Party's Over** (1991) . . . . . . . . . . . . Taylor
  • 0:27—Brief buns, while pulling up his pants, after
    getting caught with Rae Dawn Chong by Will.
*Made for TV Movies:*
Triumph Over Disaster: The Hurricane Andrew Story
(1993) . . . . . . . . . . . . . . . . . . . . . . . . . . Cal Kessler

The Nutt House (1989) . . . . . . . . . . . . . Charles Nutt III
Under Suspicion (1994- ) . . . . . . . . . . . . . Farnsworth

## • *McNamara, William*

*Films:*
Dream A Little Dream (1989) . . . . . . . . . . . . . . . . . Joel
Terror at the Opera (1989; Italian). . . . . . . . . . . . Stefan
Stella (1990) . . . . . . . . . . . . . . . . . . . . . . . Pat Robbins
Texasville (1990) . . . . . . . . . . . . . . . . . . Dickie Jackson
Aspen Extreme (1993). . . . . . . . . . . . . . Todd Pounds
**Chasers** (1994) . . . . . . . . . . . . . . . . . . Eddie De Vane
  •• 1:08—Buns, while running around trying to catch
  Erika Eleniak. More buns, while getting back into the
  room.
*Made for TV Movies:*
Doing Time on Maple Drive (1992). . . . . . . . . . . . Matt
*TV:*
Island Son . . . . . . . . . . . . . . . . . . . . . . . Sam Kulani

## *McNichol, Peter*

*Films:*
**Dragonslayer** (1981) . . . . . . . . . . . . . . . . . . . . . Galen
  • 0:27—Very brief buns while diving into pond. Sort of
  frontal nudity swimming under water. Hard to see
  because the water is so murky.
American Blue Note (1991). . . . . . . . . . . . . Jack Solow

## *Meader, Vaughn*

*Films:*
Lepke (1975; U.S./Israeli) . . . . . . . . . . Walter Winchell
*Magazines:*
**Playboy** (Feb 1975) . . . . . . Linda Lovelace for President!
  •• 80—Buns in still photo with Linda Lovelace from the
  film.

## *Meadows, Stephen*

*Films:*
**Night Eyes** (1990) . . . . . . . . . . . . . . . Michael Vincent
(Unrated version reviewed.)
  • 0:27—Buns and balls in bed with Tanya Roberts
  while Andrew Stevens watches on monitor.
V. I. Warshawski (1991) . . . . . . . . . . . . . . . Boom-Boom
When the Party's Over (1991) . . . . . . . . . . . . . . . . n.a.
Ultraviolet (1992) . . . . . . . . . . . . . . . . . . . Sam Halsey

## *Mednick, Michael*

*Video Tapes:*
**Intimate Workout For Lovers** (1992)
  . . . . . . . . . . . . . . . . . . . . . . . . . . . . Water Workout
  ••• 0:21—Nude, outside by swimming pool and in
  pool.

## *Meek, Jeffrey*

*Films:*
Winter People (1989) . . . . . . . . . . . . . . . Cole Campbell
Heart Condition (1990) . . . . . . . . . . . . . . . . . . Graham
**Night of the Cyclone** (1990) . . . . . . . . . . . . . . Adam
  • 1:07—Brief buns, while putting on his pants, when
  he's interrupted in bed with Angelique. Long shot.
*TV:*
The Exile (1991) . . . . . . . . . . . . . . . . John Stone/Phillips
Raven (1992-93) . . . . . . . . . . . . . . . . . . . . . . Raven

## • *Melvin, Murray*

*Films:*
Damn the Defiant! (1962; British) . . . . . . . . . Wagstaffe
Start the Revolution Without Me (1970). . . . . Blind Man
Barry Lyndon (1975; British). . . . . . . . . . Reverend Runt
Bawdy Adventures of Tom Jones (1976; British) . . . . Blifil
Shout at the Devil (1976; British) . . . . Lieutenant Phipps
**Joseph Andrews** (1977; British/French)
  . . . . . . . . . . . . . . . . . . . . . . . . . . . Beau Didapper
  • 1:29—Buns, taking off his clothes to get into bed
  with Fanny when he accidentally gets into bed with
  another woman. More buns while on top of her in
  bed.
Crossed Swords (1978) . . . . . . . . . . . . . Prince's Dresser
Comrades (1986; British) . . . . . . . . . . . . . . . . . . Clerk
Little Dorrit (1988; British) . . . . . . . . . . Dancing Master

## *Melymick, Mark*

*Made for Cable Movies:*
**Devlin** (1991; Showtime) . . . . . . . . . . . . Jack Brennan
  • 0:08—Buns, lying on bed while tied up.

## *Metrano, Art*

*Films:*
They Only Kill Their Masters (1972) . . . . . . . . . Malcolm
The All-American Boy (1973) . . . . . . . Jay David Swooze
Seven (1979) . . . . . . . . . . . . . . . . . . . . . . . . Kinsella
Cheaper to Keep Her (1980) . . . . . . . . . . . Tony Turino
History of the World, Part I (1981) . . . Leonardo da Vinci
Malibu Express (1984) . . . . . . . . . . . . . . . . . . Matthew
**Police Academy II: Their First Assignment** (1985)
  . . . . . . . . . . . . . . . . . . . . . . . . . . . . . Lt. Mauser
  • 0:39—Buns, while in the locker room after the guys
  put epoxy resin in his shampoo.
Police Academy III: Back in Training (1986)
  . . . . . . . . . . . . . . . . . . . . . . Commandant Mauser
Toys (1992) . . . . . . . . . . . . . . . . . . . . . Guard at Desk

## *Meyer, Michael*

*Films:*
**Mirror Images** (1991) . . . . . . . . . . . . . . . . . . Georgio
  •• 0:15—Buns, while getting out of bed with Shauna.
*Video Tapes:*
Playboy's Erotic Fantasies III (1993) . . . . . . . . . . . n.a.
Playboy's Secret Confessions (1993)
  . . . . . . . . . . . . . . . . . . . . . . Teacher's Pet/Warren

# • Michael, Christopher

*Video Tapes:*

**Playboy Night Dreams** (1993)
. . . . . . . . . . . . . . . . . . . . . . . . .Arresting Development
•• 0:49—Buns, while making love with his lover after
she strips out of police officer uniform.

# • Michaels, David

*Video Tapes:*

**The Lover's Guide to Sexual Ecstasy: A Sensual
Guide to Lovemaking** (1992) . . . . . . . . . . Foreplay
•• 0:23—Buns, while making love with his lover.
••• 0:53—Buns, while making love in various positions.
•• 0:56—Buns, while making love in various positions.
•• 0:57—Buns, while making love standing up.

# • Milan, Thomas

*Films:*

**Secret Games 2—The Escort** (1993) . . . . . . . Hector
(Unrated version reviewed.)
• 0:43—Buns, while making love in bed with Stacey
while Martin Hewitt watches.

# Milian, Tomas

*Films:*

Salomé (1986; Italian) . . . . . . . . . . . . . . . . . . . . . .Herod
**Cat Chaser** (1988). . . . . . . . . . . . . . . Andres De Boya
•• 1:16—Full frontal nudity, undressing in bathroom
with Corky, before getting shot by Charles Durning.
Havana (1990) . . . . . . . . . . . . . . . . . . . . . . . . . .Menocal
Revenge (1990) . . . . . . . . . . . . . . . . . . . . . . . . . . Cesar
JFK (1991). . . . . . . . . . . . . . . . . . . . . . . . . . . Leopoldo

# • Milione, Lou

*Films:*

Taps (1981). . . . . . . . . . . . . . . . . . . . . . . . . . . . Cadet
**Six Degrees of Separation** (1993) . . . . . . . . Hustler
••• 0:39—Nude, in bed with Will Smith, then running
around house, terrorizing Donald Sutherland and
Stockard Channing.

# • Millbern, David

*Films:*

The Slumber Party Massacre (1982) . . . . . . . . . . . . Jeff
Sorceress (1982) . . . . . . . . . . . . . . . . . . . . . . . . . .n.a.
Bank Robber (1993) . . . . . . . . . . . . . . . . . .Wiretapper
*Video Tapes:*
**Playboy's Secret Confessions** (1993) . . . Twins/Stuart
•• 0:41—Buns, on floor with the twins and by himself.

# Mills, Thomas

*Films:*

**Luther the Geek** (1988). . . . . . . . . . . . . . . . . . Rob
• 0:27—Very brief buns when Stacey Haiduk gooses
him.

# Mirandola, Vasco

*Films:*

**Mediterraneo** (1991; Italian) . . . . . . . . Felice Munaron
• 0:52—Buns, jumping into the water with his brother.
• 1:27—Buns, jumping into the water with his brother
during end credits.

# Mitchell, Albert

*Films:*

**Naked Instinct** (1993). . . . . . . . . . . . . . . . . .Frat Bully
••• 0:42—Nude with Michelle Bauer.

# Mitchell, Mark

*Films:*

**The Outing** (1987). . . . . . . . . . . . . . . . . . . Mike Daley
• 1:08—Buns when his friend gets killed, then very
brief frontal nudity sitting up.

# Mitchell, Scott

*Films:*

Thou Shalt Not Kill…Except (1987) . . . . . . . Philo Crazy
Fatal Instinct (1991) . . . . . . . . . . . Beaumont Detective
*a.k.a. To Kill For*
(Unrated version reviewed.)
*Video Tapes:*
**Inside Out** (1992) . . . . . . . . Love the One You're With
•• 1:14—Very brief frontal nudity when the girl climbs
on top of him.

# Modine, Matthew

*Films:*

Baby, It's You (1983) . . . . . . . . . . . . . . . . . . . . . .Steve
Private School (1983). . . . . . . . . . . . . . . . . . . . . . .Jim
Streamers (1983) . . . . . . . . . . . . . . . . . . . . . . . . . Billy
The Hotel New Hampshire (1984) . . . . . . . . .Chip Dove
Mrs. Soffel (1984) . . . . . . . . . . . . . . . . . . . .Jack Biddle
**Birdy** (1985) . . . . . . . . . . . . . . . . . . . . . . . . . . . Birdy
• 1:25—Buns, while squatting on the end of his bed,
thinking he's a bird.
• 1:29—Buns, while sitting on the bed. Longer shot.
•• 1:33—Buns, while walking around naked in his bed-
room.
• 1:42—Buns, after waking up when Nicolas Cage
comes into his bedroom.
**Visionquest** (1985) . . . . . . . . . . . . . . . . Louden Swain
• 1:29—Very brief buns while taking off underwear to
get weighed for wrestling match.
Full Metal Jacket (1987) . . . . . . . . . . . . . . . .Private Joker
Orphans (1987) . . . . . . . . . . . . . . . . . . . . . . . . . Treat
Married to the Mob (1988) . . . . . . . . . . . Mike Downey
Gross Anatomy (1989) . . . . . . . . . . . . . . . . . Joe Slovac
Memphis Belle (1990) . . . . . . . . . . . . Dennis Dearborn
Pacific Heights (1990) . . . . . . . . . . . . . Drake Goodman
Equinox (1992) . . . . . . . . . . . .Henry Petosa/Freddy Ace
Wind (1992) . . . . . . . . . . . . . . . . . . . . . . . .Will Parker
Short Cuts (1993) . . . . . . . . . . . . Doctor Ralph Wyman
*Made for Cable Movies:*
And the Band Played On (1992; HBO) . . Dr. Don Francis

## Moir, Richard

*Films:*

In Search of Anna (1978; Australian) . . . . . . . . . . . Tony
Chain Reactions (1980; Australian)
. . . . . . . . . . . . . . . . . . . . . . . . Junior Constable Pillott
Heatwave (1983; Australian) . . . . . . . . . . . . . . . Steven
**An Indecent Obsession** (1985) . . . . . . . Luce Daggett
  • 0:31—Buns when at the beach with his pals. Don't
  see his face.

## • Molina, Alfred

*Films:*

Raiders of the Lost Ark (1981) . . . . . . . . . . . . . . . Satipo
Eleni (1985) . . . . . . . . . . . . . . . . . . . . . . Young Christos
Ladyhawke (1985) . . . . . . . . . . . . . . . . . . . . . . Cezar
Letter to Brezhnev (1986; British) . . . . . . . . . . . Sergei
**Prick Up Your Ears** (1987; British) . . Kenneth Halliwell
  • 0:40—Brief buns, getting into bed with Gary Old-
  man.
  • 1:42—Buns, while lying dead on the floor after kill-
  ing Gary Oldman.
Manifesto (1988) . . . . . . . . . . . . . . . . . . . . . . .Avanti
Enchanted April (1991; British) . . . . . . . Mellersh Wilkins
Not Without My Daughter (1991). . . . . . . . . . . Moody
The Trial (1994; British). . . . . . . . . . . . . . . . . . . Titorelli

## Monahan, Dan

*Films:*

Adventures of Huckleberry Finn (1978) . . . . Tom Sawyer
Only When I Laugh (1981) . . . . . . . . . . . . . . . . . Jason
**Porky's** (1981; Canadian) . . . . . . . . . . . . . . . Pee Wee
  • 0:22—Buns, while running down the road at night.
  Long shot.
**Porky's II: The Next Day** (1983; Canadian)
. . . . . . . . . . . . . . . . . . . . . . . . . . . . . . . Pee Wee
  • 0:39—Buns while at cemetery with Graveyard Glo-
  ria, then upper half of lower frontal nudity when he's
  holding her.
  • 0:40—Upper half of lower frontal nudity when he
  drops Gloria.
  • 0:42—Nude, trying to hide Steve.
  ••• 0:44—Nude when guys with shotguns shoot at him.
Up the Creek (1984) . . . . . . . . . . . . . . . . . . . . . . Max
**Porky's Revenge** (1985; Canadian) . . . . . . . . Pee Wee
  •• 0:02—Buns, when his graduation gown gets accidentally torn off during a dream.
  •• 0:16—Buns, while getting out of swimming pool
  (the fourth guy getting out). More buns while running around.
  •• 1:27—Buns, while getting his graduation gown
  town off.
From the Hip (1987) . . . . . . . . . . . . . . . . . . . . . Larry
The Prince of Pennsylvania (1988). . . Tommy Rutherford

## Montana, Michael

*Films:*

**Affairs of the Heart** (1992). . . . . . . . . . . . . . Richard
  •• 1:13—Buns, with Amy Lynn Baxter during smoky
  dream scene.

## Montgomery, Chad

*Films:*

**Nightmare at Shadow Woods** (1983). . . . . . . Gregg
a.k.a. Blood Rage
  • 0:52—Brief buns, while making love with Andrea on
  diving board just before getting killed.

## Moore, Dudley

*Films:*

The Wrong Box (1966; British) . . . . . . . . .John Finsbury
30 is a Dangerous Age, Cynthia (1968; British)
. . . . . . . . . . . . . . . . . . . . . . . . . . . . Rupert Street
Bedazzled (1968; British) . . . . . . . . . . . Stanley Moon
The Hound of the Baskervilles (1977). . . . . . . . . . n.a.
Foul Play (1978). . . . . . . . . . . . . . . . . . Stanley Tibbets
**10** (1979) . . . . . . . . . . . . . . . . . . . . . George Webber
  • 0:47—Buns, while at neighbor's party just before
  Julie Andrews sees him through a telescope.
Wholly Moses (1980) . . . . . . . . . . . . . Harvey/Herschel
Arthur (1981). . . . . . . . . . . . . . . . . . . . . .Arthur Bach
Six Weeks (1982) . . . . . . . . . . . . . . . . . . Patrick Dalton
Lovesick (1983) . . . . . . . . . . . . . . . . . . Saul Benjamin
Romantic Comedy (1983) . . . . . . . . . . . . . . . . . Jason
Best Defense (1984). . . . . . . . . . . . . . . . . .Wylie Cooper
Micki & Maude (1984). . . . . . . . . . . . . . . . Rob Salinger
Unfaithfully Yours (1984) . . . . . . . . . . .Claude Eastman
Santa Claus (1985). . . . . . . . . . . . . . . . . . . . . .Patch
Like Father, Like Son (1987) . . . . . . . Dr. Jack Hammond
Arthur 2 On the Rocks (1988) . . . . . . . . . . .Arthur Bach
Crazy People (1990). . . . . . . . . . . . . . . . . . . . Emory
Blame It on the Bellboy (1992; British) . . . Melvyn Orton
*Made for Cable Movies:*
Parallel Lives (1994; Showtime)
. . . . . . . . . . . . . Imaginary Friend/President Andrews
*TV:*
Dudley (1993) . . . . . . . . . . . . . . . . . . . . . Dudley Bristol
Daddy's Girls (1994- ) . . . . . . . . . . . . . . . . . . . . . . n.a.

## Moore, Kenny

*Films:*

**Personal Best** (1982). . . . . . . . . . . . . . . . .Denny Stiles
  •• 1:31—Nude, getting out of bed and walking to the
  bathroom.

## Moore, Michael J.

*Films:*

**Border Heat** (1988). . . . . . . . . . . . . . . . . . . .J. C. Ryan
  • 0:14—Buns, while taking off his clothes and getting
  into spa with Darlanne Fluegel.

## Moore, Stephen

*Films:*

The Last Shot You Hear (1969; British)
. . . . . . . . . . . . . . . . . . . . . . . . . . . Peter's Colleague
Rough Cut (1980; British) . . . . . . . . . . . . . . . . . . n.a.
Laughter House (1984; British). . . . . . . . . . . . Howard
Clockwise (1986; British) . . . . . . . . . . . . . . .Mr. Jolly
The Doctor (1991) . . . . . . . . . . . . . . . . . . . . Dominic

**Under Suspicion** (1992) . . . . . . . . . . . . . . . . . . Roscoe
- 1:01—Very, very brief frontal nudity when Frank pulls the sheet down after catching Roscoe in bed with a young boy.

## Moreno, Jaime

*Films:*
**Amor Ciego** (1980; Mexican) . . . . . . . . . . . . . .Daniel
- •• 0:51—Frontal nudity standing up from bed, then buns when Apollonia hugs him.
- 0:53—Buns, while making love in bed with Apollonia.

## Moriarity, Daniel

*Films:*
**The Other Woman** (1992) . . . . . . . . . . . . . . . . . Carl
(Unrated version reviewed.)
- 0:59—Buns, during photo shoot.
- ••• 1:15—Buns, while in the shower with Jessica.

## Moriarty, Michael

*Films:*
Hickey and Boggs (1972) . . . . . . . . . . . . . . . . . . Ballard
Bang the Drum Slowly (1973) . . . . . . . . Henry Wiggen
The Last Detail (1973) . . . . . . . . . . Marine Duty Officer
Report to the Commissioner (1975)
. . . . . . . . . . . . . . . . . . . . . . Beauregard "Bo" Lockley
**Reborn** (1978) . . . . . . . . . . . . . . . . . . . . . . . . . .Mark
- 0:38—Brief buns, while rolling off Maria in bed.
Who'll Stop the Rain? (1978) . . . . . . . . . . . . . . . .John
Q (1982) . . . . . . . . . . . . . . . . . . . . . . . . Jimmy Quinn
Odd Birds (1985) . . . . . . . . . . . . . Brother T.S. Murphy
Pale Rider (1985) . . . . . . . . . . . . . . . . . . . Hull Barret
The Stuff (1985) . . . . . . . . . . . .David "Moe" Rutherford
Troll (1986) . . . . . . . . . . . . . . . . . . . . . Harry Potter Sr.
Dark Tower (1987) . . . . . . . . . . . . . . Dennis Randall
The Hanoi Hilton (1987) . . . . . . . . Lt. Cmdr. Williamson
It's Alive III: Island of the Alive (1988) . . . . . . Steve Jarvis
A Return to Salem's Lot (1988) . . . . . . . . . . . . . . Joey
Full Fathom Five (1990) . . . . . . . . . . . . . . Mackenzie
*Made for TV Movies:*
Born Too Soon (1993) . . . . . . . . . . . . . . Fox Butterfield
*TV:*
Law & Order (1990- ) . . . . . . . .Assistant D.A. Ben Stone

## Morrissey, David

*Films:*
**Drowning by Numbers** (1988; British) . . . . . Bellamy
- 0:43—Buns, while on couch with Joely Richardson.
- •• 1:24—Nude, getting drowned in the swimming pool.
**Waterland** (1992; British/U.S.) . . . . . . . . . . .Dick Crick
- •• 1:04—Buns, after taking off his clothes on boat and diving into the water to commit suicide.
*Made for TV Movies:*
Mysteryl Cause Célèbre (1991) . . George Percy Bowman

## Morrow, Rob

*Films:*
**Private Resort** (1985) . . . . . . . . . . . . . . . . . . . . . Ben
- 0:36—Brief buns while standing with Hillary Shepard worshiping Baba Rama.
- •• 0:39—Buns while getting caught naked by Mrs. Rawlins, then more buns, while running through the halls.
*TV:*
Tattingers (1988-89) . . . . . . . . . . . . Marco Bellini
Northern Exposure (1990- ) . . . . . . . . . Joel Fleischman

## Mortensen, Viggo

*Films:*
Witness (1985) . . . . . . . . . . . . . . . . .Moses Hochleitner
Prison (1987) . . . . . . . . . . . . . . . . . . . . .Connie Burke
Salvation! (1987) . . . . . . . . . . . . . . . . . .Jerome Stample
Fresh Horses (1988) . . . . . . . . . . . . . . . . . . . . Green
Tripwire (1989) . . . . . . . . . . . . . . . . . . . . . . . . Hans
Leatherface: The Texas Chainsaw Massacre III (1990)
. . . . . . . . . . . . . . . . . . . . . . . . . . . . . . . . . . . Tex
**The Reflecting Skin** (1990; British) . . . Cameron Dove
- 1:09—Brief buns, lying on the floor with Dolphin.
Young Guns II (1990) . . . . . . . . . . . . . . . .John W. Poe
**The Indian Runner** (1991) . . . . . . . . . . . . . . . . Frank
- ••• 1:01—Brief frontal nudity in mirror, then in real life in room.
Boiling Point (1992; U.S./French) . . . . . . . . . . . .Ronnie
Deception (1992) . . . . . . . . . . . . . . . . . . . .Johnny Faro
*a.k.a. Ruby Cairo*
American Yakuza (1993) . . . . . . Nick Davis/David Brandt
Carlito's Way (1993) . . . . . . . . . . . . . . . . . . . . . Lalin

## Moses, Mark

*Films:*
Battle in the Erogenous Zone . . . . . . . . . . . . . . . . .Alan
Someone to Watch Over Me (1987) . . . . . Win Hockings
Born on the Fourth of July (1989) . . . .Optomistic Doctor
Dead Men Don't Die (1991) . . . . . . . . . . . . . . .Jordan
The Doors (1991) . . . . . . . . . . . . . . . . . Jac Holzman
*Made for Cable Movies:*
**The Tracker** (1988; HBO) . . . . . . . . . . . . . Tom Adams
- •• 0:35—Buns, while getting out of the river after washing himself, then getting hassled by some bandits.
*TV:*
Grand (1990) . . . . . . . . . . . . . . . . . . . . Richard Peyton

## Moss, Robert

*Films:*
**Spring Fever USA** (1988) . . . . . . . . . . . . . Dick Dork
*a.k.a. Lauderdale*
- 1:17—Buns, twice, while in boat hallway with his heavy brother after being tricked.

# • Mostel, Joshua

*Films:*

**Harry and Tonto** (1974) . . . . . . . . . . . . . . . Norman
- 1:16—Brief buns, when mooning a horse in a trailer out the back window of car. Don't see his face.

# Mulcahy, Jack

*Films:*

**Porky's** (1981; Canadian) . . . . . . . . . . . . . . Frank Bell
- 0:21—Very brief frontal nudity, getting up from bench. Then buns while in front of the cabin.

Porky's II: The Next Day (1983; Canadian) . . . Frank Bell

# Mulkey, Chris

*Films:*

Loose Ends (1975). . . . . . . . . . . . . . . . . . . . . Billy Regis
The Long Riders (1980). . . . . . . . . . . . . . . Vernon Biggs
48 Hrs. (1982). . . . . . . . . . . . . . . . . . . . . . . . . . . . . Cop
First Blood (1982) . . . . . . . . . . . . . . . . . . . . . . . . . Ward
Timerider (1983). . . . . . . . . . . . . . . . . . . . . . . . Daniels
Heartbreak Hotel (1988) . . . . . . . . . . . . . . Steve Ayres
**Patti Rocks** (1988) . . . . . . . . . . . . . . . . . . . . . . . Billy
- 0:24—Nude in restroom with Eddie, undressing and putting on underwear.

Denial (1991) . . . . . . . . . . . . . . . . . . . . . . . . . . . Chad
Deadbolt (1992) . . . . . . . . . . . . . . . . . . . . . . . . Jordan
Gas Food Lodging (1992) . . . . . . . . . . . . . . Raymond
The Silencer (1992). . . . . . . . . . . . . . . . . . . . . George
Bound and Gagged: A Love Story (1993) . . . . . . . Steve
Ghost in the Machine (1993) . . . . . . . . . . . . . . . Bram

# • Mullinar, Rod

*Films:*

Breaker Morant (1979; Australian)
. . . . . . . . . . . . . . . . . . . . . . . . Major Charles Bolton
Thirst (1979; Australian) . . . . . . . . . . . . . . . . . . Derek
**Breakfast in Paris** (1981) . . . . . . . . . . Michael Barnes
- 0:29—Buns, getting up and out of bed.

Dead Calm (1989) . . . . . . . . . . . . . . . . Russell Bellows
Echoes in Paradise (1989) . . . . . . . . . . . . . . . . . Terry

# • Munro, Lochlyn

*Films:*

Run (1990) . . . . . . . . . . . . . . . . . . . . . College Buddy
**I Posed for Playboy** (1991) . . . . . . . . . . . . . . . . Sam
*a.k.a. Posing: Inspired by Three Real Stories*
(Shown on network TV without the nudity.)
- 0:47—Buns, while wearing an apron in kitchen with Josie Bissett.

Trancers 4—Jack of Swords (1993) . . . . . . . . Sebastian
*Made for TV Movies:*
Moment of Truth: Broken Pledges (1994) . . . .Jeff Laneer

# Murdocco, Vince

*Films:*

**Flesh Gordon 2** (1990; Canadian) . . . . . Flesh Gordon
- 0:00—Buns, while trying to save Dale.

Kickboxer 2: The Road Back (1990). . . . . . Brian Wagner
Ring of Fire (1991) . . . . . . . . . . . . . . . . . . . . . .Chuck

Ring of Fire II: Blood and Steel (1992) . . . . . . . . Chuck
To Be The Best (1993) . . . . . . . . . . . . . . . . . . . . . n.a.

# • Murray, Johnathon

*Films:*

**Hollywood Dreams** (1993) . . . . . . . . . . . . . . . Steve
(Unrated version reviewed.)
- 0:47—Buns, after taking off his shorts with Natasha in dressing room.

# • Myers, Mike

*Films:*

Wayne's World (1992) . . . . . . . . . . . . Wayne Campbell
**So, I Married an Axe Murderer** (1993)
. . . . . . . . . . . . . .Charlie MacKenzie/Stuart MacKenzie
•• 1:00—Buns, when towel around his waist falls down when hugging Ralph. Don't see his face.
Wayne's World 2 (1993) . . . . . . . . . . . Wayne Campbell
*TV:*
Saturday Night Live (1989- ) . . . . . . . . . . . . . . Regular

# Nassi, Joe

*Films:*

**Sorority House Massacre** (1987) . . . . . . . . . . . .Craig
- 0:50—Buns, while running away from the killer that has just killed his girlfriend Tracy in a tepee.

# Naughton, David

*Films:*

Separate Ways (1979) . . . . . . . . . . . . . . . Jerry Lansing
Midnight Madness (1980) . . . . . . . . . . . . . . . . . Adam
**An American Werewolf in London** (1981)
. . . . . . . . . . . . . . . . . . . . . . . . . . . . David Kessler
- 0:24—Very brief buns while running naked through the woods.
- 0:58—Buns, during his transformation into a werewolf.
•• 1:09—Brief frontal nudity and buns after waking up in wolf cage at the zoo. Long shot, hard to see anything. More buns, while running around the zoo.
Hot Dog... The Movie (1984). . . . . . . . . . . . . . . .Dan
Not for Publication (1984) . . . . . . . . . . . . . . . . Barry
**Terror in the Aisles** (1984). . . . . . . . . . David Kessler
- 0:17—Brief buns during transformation into a werewolf from *An American Werewolf in London*.
Separate Vacations (1985) . . . . . . . . . . .Richard Moore
The Boy in Blue (1986; Canadian) . . . . . . . . . . . . . Bill
Kidnapped (1986) . . . . . . . . . . . . . . . Vince McCarthy
Overexposed (1990) . . . . . . . . . . . . . . . . . . . Phillip
The Sleeping Car (1990) . . . . . . . . . . . Jason McCree
Steel and Lace (1990) . . . . . . . . . . . . . . . . . .Dunn
Wild Cactus (1992) . . . . . . . . . . . . . . . . . . . .Philip
(Unrated version reviewed.)
Amityville: A New Generation (1993) . . . . . . Dick Cutler
*Made for Cable TV:*
John Carpenter's Body Bags (1993; Showtime)
. . . . . . . . . . . . . . . . . . . . . . . . The Gas Station/Pete
Sex, Shock and Censorship in the 90's (1993; Showtime)
. . . . . . . . . . . . . . . . . . . . . . . . . . . . . . . . . Brad

*Made for TV Movies:*
Getting Physical (1984). . . . . . . . . Officer Mickey Ritter
The Goddess of Love (1988) . . . . . . . . . . . . . . . . . . Ted
*TV:*
Makin' It (1979) . . . . . . . . . . . . . . . . . . Billy Manucci
At Ease (1983). . . . . . . . . . . . . . . . . .P.F.C. Tony Baker
My Sister Sam (1986-89). . . . . . . . . . . . . . . . . . Jack

## Nazario, Al
*Films:*
**Incoming Freshman** (1979). . . . . . . . . . . . . Mooner
  • 0:44—Buns, while mooning Professor Bilbo during
    his daydream.
  • 0:56—Buns again during Bilbo's daydream.
  • 1:19—Buns, during end credits.

## Neeson, Liam
Husband of actress Natasha Richardson.
*Films:*
Excalibur (1981; British) . . . . . . . . . . . . . . . . . . .Gawain
Krull (1983). . . . . . . . . . . . . . . . . . . . . . . . . . .Kegan
The Bounty (1984) . . . . . . . . . . . . . . . . . . . . .Churchill
The Innocent (1985; British) . . . . . . . . . . . . . . . . .n.a.
The Mission (1986; British) . . . . . . . . . . . . . Fielding
**Duet for One** (1987). . . . . . . . . . . . . . . . . . . Totter
  • 1:07—Buns, while behind shower door, getting out
    of shower. Very, very brief buns, falling into bed
    when robe flies up. Long shot.
Next of Kin (1989) . . . . . . . . . . . . . . . . . . . . . Briar
Darkman (1990) . . . . . . . . . Peyton Westlake/Darkman
The Big Man (1991; British) . . . . . . . . . Danny Scoular
  *a.k.a. Crossing the Line*
Deception (1992) . . . . . . . . . . . . . . . . . . .Fergus Lamb
  *a.k.a. Ruby Cairo*
Husbands and Wives (1992) . . . . . . . . . . . . . . Michael
Leap of Faith (1992) . . . . . . . . . . . . . . . . . . . . . .Will
Shining Through (1992) . . . . . . . . .Franz-Otto Dietrich
**Under Suspicion** (1992). . . . . . . . . . . . . . . . . .Tony
  • 0:02—Buns, making love in bathroom with Hazel in
    bathroom while standing up. (Don't see his face.)
  • 0:03—Brief nude, running outside at night to get
    away from the husband. Long shot.
  • 0:04—Very brief frontal nudity, helping Frank over
    the fence.
Ethan Frome (1993) . . . . . . . . . . . . . . . .Ethan Frome
Schindler's List (1993). . . . . . . . . . . . . Oskar Schindler

## Neidorf, David
*Films:*
Bull Durham (1988) . . . . . . . . . . . . . . . . . . . . .Bobby
Born on the Fourth of July (1989) . . . . . . . . . . . Patient
*Made for Cable Movies:*
**Rainbow Drive** (1990; Showtime) . . . .Bernie Maxwell
  • 1:16—Buns, while in shower room when Peter
    Weller is interrogating him.

## Neill, Sam
*Films:*
Sleeping Dogs (1977; New Zealand) . . . . . . . . . . Smith
Just Out of Reach (1979; Australian). . . . . . . . . . . Mike
My Brilliant Career (1979; Australian). . . Harry Beecham
The Final Conflict (1981) . . . . . . . . . . . . Damien Thorn
  *a.k.a. Omen III*
Possession (1981; French/German) . . . . . . . . . . . Marc
Enigma (1982). . . . . . . . . . . . . . . . . . . Dimitri Vasilkov
**Reilly: Ace of Spies** (1984) . . . . . . . . . . Sidney Reilly
  ••• 0:21—Buns, while getting out of bed and putting on
    his pants during an earthquake.
Plenty (1985). . . . . . . . . . . . . . . . . . . . . . . . . .Lazar
For Love Alone (1986; Australian). . . . . . . .James Quick
The Good Wife (1987; Australian) . . . . . .Neville Gifford
  *a.k.a. The Umbrella Woman*
A Cry in the Dark (1988) . . . . . . . .Michael Chamberlain
Dead Calm (1989) . . . . . . . . . . . . . . . . . . John Ingram
The Hunt for Red October (1990) . .Capt. Vasily Borodin
Until the End of the World (1991) . . . Eugene Fitzpatrick
Hostage (1992) . . . . . . . . . . . . . . . . . . . . . . . Rennie
Memoirs of an Invisible Man (1992). . . . . .David Jenkins
Jurassic Park (1993) . . . . . . . . . . . . . . . . . .Alan Grant
**The Piano** (1993). . . . . . . . . . . . . . . . . . . . Stewart
  • 1:30—Buns, while in bed with Holly Hunter. Don't
    see his face.
Sirens (1993; Australian) . . . . . . . . . . . Norman Lindsay
*Miniseries:*
Family Pictures (1993) . . . . . . . . . . . . . . .David Eberlin
*Made for TV Movies:*
One Against the Wind (1991). . . . . Capt. James Leggatt

## Nelson, Bob
*Films:*
**Sorceress** (1982) . . . . . . . . . . . . . . . . . . . . . Erlick
  • 0:43—Brief buns, just before being put to death.
  •• 0:45—Buns, while getting massaged.
The Falcon and the Snowman (1985). . . . . . .FBI Agent
Miracles (1986) . . . . . . . . . . . . . . . . Sargeant Levit
Brain Donors (1992). . . . . . . . . . . . . . . . . . . Jacques
This is My Life (1992). . . . . . . . . . . . . . . . . . . . . Ed

## Nelson, Haywood
*Films:*
Mixed Company (1974). . . . . . . . . . . . . . . . . .Freddie
**Evilspeak** (1981) . . . . . . . . . . . . . . . . . . . Kowalski
  0:07—Buns, twice, in shower with three other guys.
  (He's the only black guy.)
*TV:*
Grady (1975-76) . . . . . . . . . . . . . .Haywood Marshall
What's Happening!! (1976-79). . . . . . .Dwayne Clemens
What's Happening Now!! (1985-88) . .Dwayne Clemens

## Nero, Franco
*Films:*
Camelot (1967). . . . . . . . . . . . . . . . . . . . Sir Lancelot
**Submission** (1976; Italian) . . . . . . . . . . . . . . Armond
  • 0:32—Brief side view of buns when making love
    with Lisa on the bed.

The Day of the Cobra (1980) . . . . . . . . . . . . . . . . .n.a.
The Girl (1987; British) . . . . . . . . . . . . . . . . John Berg
Die Hard 2 (1990). . . . . . . . . . . . . . . . . . . Esperanza

## Newman, Paul

Husband of actress Joanne Woodward.
*Films:*
Silver Chalice (1954). . . . . . . . . . . . . . . . . . . . . . Basil
Somebody Up There Likes Me (1956) . . .Rocky Graziano
Cat on a Hot Tin Roof (1958) . . . . . . . . . . Brick Pollitt
The Left-Handed Gun (1958) . . . . . . . . . . Billy Bonney
The Long, Hot Summer (1958) . . . . . . . . . . .Ben Quick
The Young Philadelphians (1959) . . . . . . Tony Lawrence
Exodus (1960). . . . . . . . . . . . . . . . . . Are Ben Gannan
From the Terrace (1960) . . . . . . . . . . . . . Alfred Eaton
The Hustler (1961) . . . . . . . . . . . . . . "Fast" Eddie Felson
Paris Blues (1961) . . . . . . . . . . . . . . . . . . Ram Bowen
Sweet Bird of Youth (1962) . . . . . . . . . . Chance Wayne
Hud (1963). . . . . . . . . . . . . . . . . . . . . . .Hud Bannon
The Prize (1963) . . . . . . . . . . . . . . . . Andrew Craig
Harper (1966) . . . . . . . . . . . . . . . . . . . . . . . Harper
Torn Curtain (1966) . . . . . . . . .Prof. Michael Armstrong
**Cool Hand Luke** (1967) . . . . . . . . . . . . . . . . . . . . Luke
  • 1:38—Very brief buns, putting on white shirt before
    going into The Box. Very dark.
Hombre (1967). . . . . . . . . . . . . . . . . . . John Russell
Butch Cassidy and the Sundance Kid (1969)
. . . . . . . . . . . . . . . . . . . . . . . . Butch Cassidy
The Secret War of Harry Frigg (1969) . . . . . .Harry Frigg
Winning (1969). . . . . . . . . . . . . . . . . . . . . . . Frank
Sometimes a Great Notion (1971). . . . . .Hank Stamper
The Life and Times of Judge Roy Bean (1972)
. . . . . . . . . . . . . . . . . . . . . . . . Judge Roy Bean
Pocket Money (1972) . . . . . . . . . . . . . . . . .Jim Kane
Mackintosh Man (1973; British) . . . . . . . . . . . Rearden
The Sting (1973). . . . . . . . . Henry Gondorff/Mr. Shaw
The Towering Inferno (1974) . . . . . . . . .Doug Roberts
Buffalo Bill and the Indians (1976). . . . . . . Buffalo Bill
The Drowning Pool (1976) . . . . . . . . . . . . . . Harper
Silent Movie (1976). . . . . . . . . . . . . . . . . . . Himself
Slap Shot (1977). . . . . . . . . . . . . . . . Reggie Dunlop
Quintet (1979) . . . . . . . . . . . . . . . . . . . . . . Essex
When Time Ran Out! (1980). . . . . . . . . .Hank Anderson
Absence of Malice (1981) . . . . . . . . . . . . . . Gallagher
Fort Apache, The Bronx (1981) . . . . . . . . . . . Murphy
The Verdict (1982) . . . . . . . . . . . . . . . Frank Galvin
Harry and Son (1984) . . . . . . . . . . . . . . . . . Harry
The Color of Money (1986). . . . . . . . . . . . . . Eddie
  (Academy Award for Best Actor.)
Blaze (1989) . . . . . . . . . . . . . . . Gov. Earl K. Long
Fat Man and Little Boy (1989). . . . . Gen Leslie R. Groves
Mr. & Mrs. Bridge (1990) . . . . . . . . . . . . Walter Bridge

## Nicholson, Jack

*Films:*
The Little Shop of Horrors (1960) . . . . . . . Wilbur Force
Studs Lonigan (1960) . . . . . . . . . . . . . . Weary Reilly
The Raven (1963) . . . . . . . . . . . . . . . .Rexford Bedlo
The Terror (1963) . . . . . . . . . . . .Lt. Andre Duvalier

Ride in the Whirlwind (1965). . . . . . . . . . . . . . . .Wes
Rebel Rousers (1967) . . . . . . . . . . . . . . . . . . . Bunny
Easy Rider (1969) . . . . . . . . . . . . . . . .George Hanson
Five Easy Pieces (1970). . . . . . . . . . . . . Robert Dupea
On a Clear Day You Can See Forever (1970)
. . . . . . . . . . . . . . . . . . . . . . . . . . Tad Pringle
Carnal Knowledge (1971) . . . . . . . . . . . . . Jonathan
A Safe Place (1971) . . . . . . . . . . . . . . . . . . . Mitch
King of Marvin Gardens (1972) . . . . . .David Staebler
The Last Detail (1973) . . . . . . . . . . . . . . .Buddusky
**Chinatown** (1974) . . . . . . . . . . . . . . . . . . . . . . J.J.
  • 1:28—Very brief buns, while putting pants on and
    getting out of bed after making love with Faye Dun-
    away.
One Flew Over the Cuckoo's Nest (1975)
. . . . . . . . . . . . . . . . . . . . . . .R. P. McMurphy
  (Academy Award for Best Actor.)
The Passenger (1975; Italian) . . . . . . . . . . .David Locke
Tommy (1975; British) . . . . . . . . . . . . . . . Specialist
The Last Tycoon (1976) . . . . . . . . . . . . . . . Brimmer
The Missouri Breaks (1976) . . . . . . . . . . . Tom Logan
The Shooting (1976) . . . . . . . . . . . . . . . Billy Spear
Goin' South (1978) . . . . . . . . . . . . . . . Henry Moon
The Shining (1980) . . . . . . . . . . . . . . . .Jack Torrance
**The Postman Always Rings Twice** (1981)
. . . . . . . . . . . . . . . . . . . . . . . . Frank Chambers
  • 1:25—Buns, while lying across the bed.
**Reds** (1981) . . . . . . . . . . . . . . . . . Eugene O'Neill
  • 0:50—Buns, while standing in the water with Diane
    Keaton at night. Very long shot.
The Border (1982) . . . . . . . . . . . . . . . . . . .Charlie
Terms of Endearment (1983) . . . . . . . Garrett Breedlove
Prizzi's Honor (1985) . . . . . . . . . . . Charley Partanna
  (Academy Award for Best Supporting Actor.)
  2:05—Buns, sort of. Viewed from above while he
    takes a shower. Hard to see anything.
Heartburn (1986). . . . . . . . . . . . . . . . . . . . . Mark
Ironweed (1987) . . . . . . . . . . . . . . . . Francis Phelan
The Witches of Eastwick (1987) . . . . . . Daryl Van Horne
Batman (1989). . . . . . . . . . . . . . Jack Napier/The Joker
The Two Jakes (1990). . . . . . . . . . . . . . . . Jake Gittes
A Few Good Men (1992) . . . . .Colonel Nathan R. Jessep
Hoffa (1992) . . . . . . . . . . . . . . . . . . .Jimmy Hoffa
Man Trouble (1992). . . . . . . . . . . . . . . Harry Bliss
Wolf (1994) . . . . . . . . . . . . . . . . . . . . . . . . .n.a.

## Nock, Thomas

*Films:*
**Alpine Fire** (1985; Swiss) . . . . . . . . . . . . . . . . . . Bob
  • 0:08—Brief buns, while outside taking a bath.
Gemini: The Twin Stars (1988; U.S./Swiss) . . . . . Thomas

## Nolan, Tom

*Films:*
Fast Times at Ridgemont High (1982) . . . .Dennis Taylor
Up the Creek (1984) . . . . . . . . . . . . . . . . .Whitney
**School Spirit** (1985) . . . . . . . . . . . . . . . Billy Batson
  • 0:17—Buns in open hospital smock. More buns
    while running up stairs.

• 1:29—Brief buns, in hospital gown, while leaving
  Judy's room.
*TV:*
Jessie (1984) . . . . . . . . . . . . . . . . . . . . . . Officer Hubbell

## Nolte, Nick

*Films:*
Return to Macon County (1975) . . . . . . . . . Bo Hollinger
The Deep (1977) . . . . . . . . . . . . . . . . . . .David Sanders
Who'll Stop the Rain? (1978) . . . . . . . . . . . . . . . . . Ray
Heart Beat (1979) . . . . . . . . . . . . . . . . . Neal Cassady
**North Dallas Forty** (1979) . . . . . . . . . . . Phillip Elliott
  • 0:49—Brief buns, while pulling down underwear to
    get into whirlpool bath in locker room.
48 Hrs. (1982) . . . . . . . . . . . . . . . . . . . . . . . Jack Cates
Cannery Row (1982) . . . . . . . . . . . . . . . . . . . . . . Doc
Under Fire (1983) . . . . . . . . . . . . . . . . . . . . .Russel Price
Teachers (1984) . . . . . . . . . . . . . . . . . . . . . . . Alex
**Down and Out in Beverly Hills** (1986). . . Jerry Baskin
  • 0:28—Buns, while changing out of wet clothes on
    patio.
  • 1:37—Brief buns, while changing out of Santa Claus
    outfit.
**Weeds** (1987) . . . . . . . . . . . . . . . . . . . . .Lee Umstetter
  •• 0:51—Buns, while getting out of bed and putting
    his pants on.
New York Stories (1989) . . . . . . . . . . . . . .Lionel Dobie
Three Fugitives (1989) . . . . . . . . . . . . . . .Daniel Lucas
Another 48 Hrs. (1990) . . . . . . . . . . . . . . . . .Jack Cates
Everybody Wins (1990) . . . . . . . . . . . . . .Tom O'Toole
Q & A (1990) . . . . . . . . . . . . . . . . . . . . . .Mike Brennan
Cape Fear (1991) . . . . . . . . . . . . . . . . . Sam Bowden
The Prince of Tides (1991) . . . . . . . . . . . . .Tom Wingo
The Player (1992) . . . . . . . . . . . . . . . . . . . . . . Cameo
Gettysburg (1993) . . . . . . . . . . . . . . . . . . . . . . .n.a.
Lorenzo's Oil (1993) . . . . . . . . . . . . . . Augusto Odone
Blue Chips (1994) . . . . . . . . . . . . . . . . . . . . Pete Bell
I Love Trouble (1994) . . . . . . . . . . . . . . . . . . . . .n.a.
I'll Do Anything (1994) . . . . . . . . . . . . . . . Matt Hobbs
*Miniseries:*
Rich Man, Poor Man (1976) . . . . . . . . . . Tom Jordache

## Nordling, Jeffrey

*Films:*
Working Girl (1989) . . . . . . . . . . . . . . . . . .Tim Rourke
Ruby (1992) . . . . . . . . . . . . . . . . . . . . . . . . . . .Hank
*Made for Cable Movies:*
**And the Band Played On** (1992; HBO)
. . . . . . . . . . . . . . . . . . . . . . . . . . . . . .Gaetan Dugas
  • 0:14—Brief buns, while getting dressed in examina-
    tion room when Glenne Headly comes in.
Dangerous Heart (1994; USA) . . . . . . . . . . Lee McLean
*Made for TV Movies:*
Journey to the Center of the Earth (1993) . . Chris Turner
Baby Brokers (1994) . . . . . . . . . . . . . . . . . . . . . . John

## Norman, Zack

*Films:*
Tracks (1977) . . . . . . . . . . . . . . . . . . . . . . . . . . . Mojo
Fingers (1978) . . . . . . . . . . . . . . . . . . . . . . . . . . .Cop
**Sitting Ducks** (1978) . . . . . . . . . . . . . . . . . . . . . . . Sid
  • 0:42—Brief buns, getting into bathtub to talk with
    Simon.
Romancing the Stone (1984) . . . . . . . . . . . . . . . . . Ira
Cadillac Man (1990) . . . . . . . . . . . . . . Harry Munchack
At Home with the Webbers (1992) . . . . .Sledge Hammer
Venice/Venice (1992) . . . . . . . . . . . . . . . . . . . . Dennis
*Made for Cable Movies:*
Lush Life (1993; Showtime) . . . . . . . . . . . . . Beanstrom

## North, Jay

*Films:*
**Maya** (1965) . . . . . . . . . . . . . . . . . . . . . . . Terry Bowen
  ••• 0:33—Buns, drying himself off and putting on loin-
    cloth after getting wet from being in river.
Zebra in the Kitchen (1965) . . . . . . . . . . . . . . . . Chris
The Teacher (1974) . . . . . . . . . . . . . . . . . . . . . . n.a.
*TV:*
Dennis the Menace (1959-63) . . . . . . . . Dennis Mitchell
Maya (1967-68) . . . . . . . . . . . . . . . . . . Terry Bowen

## Norton, Ken

Former boxer.
*Films:*
**Mandingo** (1975) . . . . . . . . . . . . . . . . . . . . . . . .Mede
  •• 1:36—Buns, while standing in bed with Susan
    George. More buns when making love with her.
**Drum** (1976) . . . . . . . . . . . . . . . . . . . . . . . . . . .Drum
  • 1:02—Buns, while getting hung upside down in
    barn and spanked along with Yaphet Kotto.
Mugsy's Girls (1985) . . . . . . . . . . . . . . . . . Branscombe
*TV:*
The Gong Show (1976-80) . . . . . . . . . . . . . . . Panelist

## Norton, Richard

*Films:*
China O'Brien 2 (1984) . . . . . . . . . . . . . . Matt Conroy
Gymkata (1985) . . . . . . . . . . . . . . . . . . . . . . . . Zamir
Equalizer 2000 (1986) . . . . . . . . . . . . . . . . . . . . Slade
China O'Brien (1991) . . . . . . . . . . . . . . . . . . . . . Matt
Ironheart (1991) . . . . . . . . . . . . . . . . . . . . Milverstead
**Lady Dragon** (1992) . . . . . . . . . . . .Ludwig Hauptman
  •• 0:39—Buns, twice, in bedroom with Susan.
Rage and Honor (1992) . . . . . . . . . . . Preston Michaels
Raiders of the Sun (1992) . . . . . . . . . . . . . . . Brodie
  0:56—Brief buns, while making love on top of Sierra.
  Long shot, not much seen.
Deathfight (1993) . . . . . . . . . . . . . . . . . . . . . . . n.a.
Rage & Honor II: Hostile Takeover (1993)
. . . . . . . . . . . . . . . . . . . . . . . . . . . Preston Michaels

## Nouri, Michael

*Films:*

Flashdance (1983). . . . . . . . . . . . . . . . . . . .Nick Hurley
The Imagemaker (1985) . . . . . . . . . . . Roger Blackwell
**Thieves of Fortune** (1989). . . . . . . . . . . . . . .Juan Luis
 • 0:57—Buns, while taking a shower outside. Long
   shot.
Captain America (1990) . . . . . . . . . . . .Lt. Colonel Louis
Little Vegas (1990) . . . . . . . . . . . . . . . . . . . . Frank
Project: Alien (1990) . . . . . . . . . . . . . . . . . .Jeff Milker
Total Exposure (1991) . . . . . . . . . . . . . . . Dave Murphy
Black Ice (1992; U.S./Canadian) . . . . . . . . . . Ben Shorr
Da Vinci's War (1992) . . . . . . . . . . . . . . . China Smith
American Yakuza (1993) . . . . . . . . . . . . . . .Campaneia

*Made for Cable Movies:*

Psychic (1992; USA) . . . . . . . . . . . . .Professor Steering

*Miniseries:*

Beacon Hill (1975) . . . . . . . . . . . . . . . Giorgia Bellonci
The Last Convertible (1979) . . . . . Jean R.G.R. des Barres

*Made for TV Movies:*

Shattered Dreams (1990) . . . . . . . . . . . . . . . . .n.a.
Danielle Steel's "Changes" (1991). . . . . . . . . . . . .n.a.
In the Arms of a Killer (1992) . . . . . . . . . Brian Venible
Eyes of Terror (1994). . . . . . . . . . . . .Lt. David Zaccariah

*TV:*

The Gangster Chronicles (1981)
 . . . . . . . . . . . . . . . . . . . .Charles "Lucky" Luciano
Bay City Blues (1983) . . . . . . . . . . . . . . . . Joe Rohner
Downtown (1986-87). . . . . . . . . .Detective John Forney
Love & War (1992- ) . . . . . . . . . . . . . . . . . . . . . .n.a.

## • Novak, Alan

*Films:*

**Alice in Wonderland** (1977) . . . . . . . . . . .Mad Hatter
(R-rated version reviewed.)
 • 0:26—Frontal nudity, showing himself to Alice.

## Noy, Zachi

*Films:*

Popcorn and Ice Cream (1978; West German) . . Johnny
 *a.k.a. Sex and Ice Cream*
The Magician of Lublin (1979) . . . . . . . . . . . . . Bolek
Enter the Ninja (1981) . . . . . . . . . . . . . . . . The Hook
**Private Popsicle** (1982) . . . . . . . . . . . . . . . .Hughie
 • 0:09—Buns while in bed with Eva.
The Ambassador (1984) . . . . . . . . . . . . . . . . . . .n.a.
Up Your Anchor (1985). . . . . . . . . . . . . . . . . .Huey

## Nozick, Bruce

*Films:*

The Wanderers (1979). . . . . . . . . . . . . . . . . . . .n.a.
**Hit the Dutchman** (1992) . . . . Arthur "Dutch" Shultz
(Unrated version reviewed.)
 •• 0:36—Briefly nude, running after Frances in her
   room. More buns, while on the floor with her.

## Nureyev, Rudolf

Ballet dancer.

*Films:*

**Valentino** (1977; British) . . . . . . . . .Rudolph Valentino
 ••• 0:54—Nude, while on bed with Michelle Phillips.
 ••• 0:55—Frontal nudity while getting up and out of
   bed.
 • 0:58—Side view of buns while posing for photos.
**Exposed** (1983) . . . . . . . . . . . . . . . . . . Daniel Jelline
 ••• 0:54—Buns, while in bed with Nastassja Kinski.

*Magazines:*

**Playboy** (Nov 1977). . . . . . . . . . . Sex in Cinema 1977
 ••• 166—Partial frontal nudity from *Valentino*.

## O'Brien, Myles

*Films:*

**Evil Laugh** (1986) . . . . . . . . . . . . . . . . . . . . . . Mark
 0:30—Sort of buns and brief lower frontal nudity
 rolling over on top of Tina in bed. Very, very brief
 frontal nudity when she takes the sheet away from
 him.

## • O'Donnell, Chris

*Films:*

Men Don't Leave (1989) . . . . . . . . . . . . Chris Macauley
Blue Skies (1991) . . . . . . . . . . . . . . . . . . . . . . . .n.a.
Fried Green Tomatoes (1991). . . . . Buddy Threadgoode
 *a.k.a. Fried Green Tomatoes at the Whistle Stop Café*
Scent of a Woman (1992) . . . . . . . . . . . Charlie Simms
**School Ties** (1992). . . . . . . . . . . . . . . . . Chris Reece
 • 1:09—Brief upper half of buns, in the showers with
   two other guys (He's on the right).
The Three Musketeers (1993). . . . . . . . . . . D'Artagnan

## O'Hara, Adore

*Films:*

**Auditions** (1978) . . . . . . . . . . . . . . . . . Adore O'Hara
 •• 0:47—Nude, while singing opera.
The Hard Way (1991). . . . . . . . . . . . . . Dead Entertainer

## O'Keeffe, Miles

*Films:*

**Tarzan, The Ape Man** (1981). . . . . . . . . . . . . Tarzan
 • 0:45—Sort of buns, under loin cloth in the surf. Lots
   of other semi-bun shots in the loin cloth throughout
   the rest of the film.
 1:09—Buns, while in loin cloth at side of lake with Bo
   Derek.
 • 1:48—Buns, while in loin cloth, wrestling with orangutan during end credits.
Ator, The Fighting Eagle (1982) . . . . . . . . . . . . . . .Ator
S.A.S. San Salvador (1982). . . . . . . . . . . . . Prince Malko
The Blade Master (1984) . . . . . . . . . . . . . . . . . . .n.a.
 *a.k.a. Ator, The Invincible*
Sword of the Valiant (1984; British) . . . . . . . . . Gawain
Campus Man (1987) . . . . . . . . . . . . . . . . . Cactus Jack
Iron Warrior (1987) . . . . . . . . . . . . . . . . . . . . . . .Ator

**The Drifter** (1988) . . . . . . . . . . . . . . . . . . . . . . . Trey
- 0:11—Brief upper half of buns while on the motel floor with Kim Delaney.

Waxwork (1988) . . . . . . . . . . . . . . . . . . Count Dracula
Liberty & Bash (1989) . . . . . . . . . . . . . . . . . . . . Liberty
Zero Tolerance (1989) . . . . . . . . . . . . . . . . . . Kowalski
Cartel (1990) . . . . . . . . . . . . . . . . . . . . . Chuck Taylor
**Relentless 2: Dead On** (1991) . . . . . . . . . . . . Gregor
••• 0:17—Buns, while putting ice cubes into bathtub, then getting in.

Shoot (1991) . . . . . . . . . . . . . . . . . . . . . . . . . . King
Sins of the Night (1993) . . . . . . . . . . . . Tony Falcone
(Unrated version reviewed.)

*Made for Cable Movies:*
Acting on Impulse (1993; Showtime) . . . . . . . . . . John

# O'Malley, Michael

*Films:*
**Not Tonight Darling** (1971; British) . . . Ben the Click
- 1:04—Buns, getting pushed out of the car with Alex by the revengeful women. Long shot.
- 1:05—Full frontal nudity, while running after the car. Shaky camera.

# O'Neal, Ryan

Father of actress Tatum O'Neal.
Significant Other of actress Farrah Fawcett.
*Films:*
Love Story (1970) . . . . . . . . . . . . . . . . . Oliver Barret IV
What's Up Doc? (1972) . . . . Professor Howard Bannister
Paper Moon (1973) . . . . . . . . . . . . . . . . . . Moses Pray
The Thief Who Came to Dinner (1973) . . . . . . . Webster
Barry Lyndon (1975; British) . . . . . . . . . . Barry Lyndon
The Driver (1978) . . . . . . . . . . . . . . . . . . . The Driver
Oliver's Story (1978) . . . . . . . . . . . . . . . Oliver Barret IV
The Main Event (1979) . . . . Eddie "Kid Natural" Scanlon
Green Ice (1981; British) . . . . . . . . . . . . . . . . . Wiley
So Fine (1981) . . . . . . . . . . . . . . . . . . . . . . . Bobby
**Partners** (1982) . . . . . . . . . . . . . . . . . . . . . Benson
•• 0:48—Buns, while wearing Indian outfit for photo session with Robyn Douglass. Don't see his face.

Irreconcilable Differences (1984) . . . . . . . Albert Brodsky
Fever Pitch (1985) . . . . . . . . . . . . . . . . . . . . . Taggart
Tough Guys Don't Dance (1987) . . . . . . . . Tim Madden
Chances Are (1989) . . . . . . . . . . . . . . . . . Philip Train
*Made for TV Movies:*
Small Sacrifices (1989) . . . . . . . . . . . . . Lew Lewiston
*TV:*
Empire (1962-63) . . . . . . . . . . . . . . . . . . . Tal Garret
Peyton Place (1964-69) . . . . . . . . . . Rodney Harrington
Good Sports (1991) . . . . . . . . . . . . . . . Bobby Tannen

# O'Quinn, Terry

*Films:*
Heaven's Gate (1980) . . . . . . . . . . . Captain Minardi
Without a Trace (1983) . . . . . . . . . . . . . . . . . . Parent
Mrs. Soffel (1984) . . . . . . . . . . . . . . . Buck McGovern
Places in the Heart (1984) . . . . . . . . . . Buddy Kelsey
Mischief (1985) . . . . . . . . . . . . . . . Claude Harbrough

Stephen King's "Silver Bullet" (1985) . . Sheriff Joe Haller
SpaceCamp (1986) . . . . . . . . . . . . . . Launch Director
Black Widow (1987) . . . . . . . . . . . . . . . . . . . . . Bruce
**The Stepfather** (1987) . . . . . . . . . . . . . . Jerry Blake
••• 0:02—Buns, while getting undressed, frontal nudity in mirror as he gets into the shower.

Pin (1988) . . . . . . . . . . . . . . . . . . . . . . . . Dr. Linden
Young Guns (1988) . . . . . . . . . . . . . . . . Alex McSween
**The Forgotten One** (1989) . . . . . . . . . Bob Anderson
- 1:11—Brief buns while turning over in bed with Evelyn.

Stepfather 2 (1989) . . . . . . . . . . . . . . . The Stepfather
Blind Fury (1990) . . . . . . . . . . . . . . Frank Devereaux
Company Business (1990) . . . . . . . . . . Colonel Grissom
Prisoners of the Sun (1990; Australian) . . . Major Beckett
The Rocketeer (1991) . . . . . . . . . . . . . . Howard Hughes
The Cutting Edge (1992) . . . . . . . . . . . . . . . . . . Jack
Amityville: A New Generation (1993) . . . Detective Clark
Lipstick Camera (1993) . . . . . . . . . . . . Raymond Miller
Tombstone (1993) . . . . . . . . . . . . . . . . Mayor Clum
*Made for Cable Movies:*
The Good Fight (1992; Lifetime) . . . . . . . . . . . . Henry
Wild Card (1992; USA) . . . . . . . . . . . . . . . . . . Barlow
Don't Talk to Strangers (1994; USA) . . . . . . . . . . . n.a.
*Made for TV Movies:*
Danielle Steel's "Kaleidoscope" (1990) . . . . . . . . Henry
Perry Mason: The Case of the Desperate Deception (1990) . . . . . . . . . . . . . . . . . . . . . . Curt Mitchell
The Last to Go (1991) . . . . . . . . . . . . . . . . . . Daniel
Shoot First: A Cop's Vengeance (1991) . . . . Sgt. Nicholas
Deliver Them from Evil: The Taking of Alta View (1992) . . . . . . . . . . . . . . . . . . . . . . . . . Sgt. Don Bell
Born Too Soon (1993) . . . . . . . . . . . . . . . Dr. Friedman
Visions of Murder (1993) . . . . . . . . . . . . . Adm. Hager
Heart of a Child (1994) . . . . . . . . . . . . . Gordon Holc
MacShayne: Winner Takes All (1994) . . . . Danny Leggett

# O'Reilly, Cyril

*Films:*
**Bloody Birthday** (1980) . . . . . . . . . . . . . Guy in Van
- 0:46—Buns, while sitting up in van.

**Porky's** (1981; Canadian) . . . . . . . . . . . . . . . . . Tim
- 0:21—Very, very brief frontal nudity, getting up from bench. Then buns, while in front of the cabin.

Porky's II: The Next Day (1983; Canadian) . . . . . . . Tim
Purple Hearts (1984) . . . . . . . . . . . . . . . . . . . Zuma
Dance of the Damned (1988) . . . . . . . . . . . . Vampire
Across the Tracks (1990) . . . . . . . . . . . . Coach Ryder
Navy SEALS (1990) . . . . . . . . . . . . . . . . . . . . Rexer
The Cool Surface (1992) . . . . . . . . . . . . . Gary/Eric
The Philadelphia Experiment 2 (1993) . . . . . . . . Decker
*Made for TV Movies:*
A Place to Be Loved (1993) . . . . . . . . . . Ralph Kingsley

# O'Ross, Ed

*Films:*
The Cotton Club (1984) . . . . . . . . . . . . . . . . . . Monk
The Pope of Greenwich Village (1984)
. . . . . . . . . . . . . . . . . . . . . . Bartender at Sal's

Seven Minutes in Heaven (1986)..........Mall Security
Full Metal Jacket (1987)..........Walter J. Schinoski
The Hidden (1987)......................Cliff Willis
Lethal Weapon (1987)....................Mendez
Action Jackson (1988)....................Stringer
Red Heat (1988)..................Viktor Rostavili
Verne Miller (1988)..................Ralph Capone
Another 48 Hrs. (1990)..............Frank Cruise
Dick Tracy (1990)..........................Itchy
**Play Nice** (1992)...........Jack "Mouth" Penucci
(Unrated version reviewed.)
> • 0:35—Buns, while making love in bed with Jill.
> •• 0:46—Buns, while making love with Jill on the floor.
Universal Soldier (1992)..............Colonel Perry

# O, George
*Films:*
**Summer Job** (1989)..................... Herman
> • 0:17—Buns, while getting his underwear torn off by five angry women, then running back to his room.
Popcorn (1991).........................1st Hood
Folks! (1992).............................Doorman
*Made for Cable Movies:*
Chains of Gold (1991; Showtime).......Corner Man

# Occhipinti, Andrea
*Films:*
Priest of Love (1980)................Young Painter
**Bolero** (1984).................Angel the Bullfighter
> •• 0:57—Buns, while lying in bed with Bo Derek, then making love with her.
> • 1:39—Side view of buns, during fantasy love making session with Bo in fog.
Conquest (1984; Italian).....................Ilias
A Blade in the Dark (1986; Italian).............Bruno

# Ohrt, Christoph M.
*Video Tapes:*
**Eden** (1992)...............................Ian
> •• 1:14—Buns, while getting out of bed and getting his pants.

# Olandt, Ken
*Films:*
April Fool's Day (1986)..................... Rob
**Summer School** (1987)....................Larry
> •• 0:48—Brief buns while wearing a red G-string in a male stripper club.
Leprechaun (1992)......................Nathan
*Made for TV Movies:*
The Laker Girls (1990)...................... Rick
*TV:*
Supercarrier (1988).........Lt. Jack "Sierra" DiPalma
SuperForce (1990-92).................Zack Stone

# Olbrychski, Daniel
*Films:*
**The Tin Drum** (1979; German).........Jan Bronski
> • 0:07—Buns, standing while being examined by army draft inspectors.
> •• 0:38—Buns, in room with Agnes.
Bolero (1982; French).......................Karl
La Truit (The Trout) (1982; French).......Saint-Genis
A Love in Germany (1984; French/German)
.........................................Wiktorczyk
The Unbearable Lightness of Being (1988)
........................Interior Ministry Official

# Oldman, Gary
Ex-husband of actress Uma Thurman.
*Films:*
Sid and Nancy (1986; British).............Sid Vicious
**Prick Up Your Ears** (1987; British).........Joe Orton
> •• 1:38—Buns, after taking off underwear and getting into bed.
**Track 29** (1988; British)...................Martin
> • 1:24—Buns, while holding onto Christopher Lloyd and stabbing him.
We Think the World of You (1988; British)
.........................................Johnny Burney
**Criminal Law** (1989)...................Ben Chase
> • 1:21—Very, very brief blurry frontal nudity in bed with Ellen.
**Chattahoochee** (1990)..............Emmett Foley
> • 1:17—Brief buns, standing while guards search his clothes. Very, very brief frontal nudity turning around to get a high-pressure enema. Long shot, don't really see anything.
State of Grace (1990).......................Jackie
Heading Home (1991)...................Ian Tyson
JFK (1991)....................Lee Harvey Oswald
Rosencrantz and Guildenstern are Dead (1991)
.........................................Rosencrantz
Bram Stoker's Dracula (1992)......Dracula/Prince Vlad
True Romance (1993)................Drexl Spivey
(Unrated version reviewed.)
**Romeo Is Bleeding** (1994)..... Sgt. Jack Grimaldi
> •• 0:27—Buns, while mooning Annabella Sciorra for a Polaroid photograph.
*Made for Cable TV:*
Fallen Angels: Dead-End for Delia (1993; Showtime)
..............................Sgt. Pat Kelley
(Available on video tape on *Fallen Angels Two*.)

# • Olds, Gabriel
*Films:*
**Calendar Girl** (1993)................ Ned Bleuer
> •• 0:44—Buns, while walking behind and next to Jason Priestly at the nude beach.
> •• 0:46—Buns, while running after Priestly into the surf at the beach.

# Oliviero, Silvio

*Films:*
**Graveyard Shift** (1987) . . . . . . . . . . .Stephen Tsepes
- 0:09—Buns, while climbing into his coffin.

Nightstick (1987) . . . . . . . . . . . . . . . . . . . . . . . .Ismael
Psycho Girls (1987) . . . . . . . . . . . . . . . . . . . . . .n.a.
The Understudy: Graveyard Shift II (1988) . . . . . .Baisez

# • Olkewicz, Walter

*Films:*
**Brainwash** (1982) . . . . . . . . . . . . . . . . . Buddy Gordon
- 0:29—Buns, after being forced to strip in front of guys in meeting. Upper half of frontal nudity.
- 0:31—Brief frontal nudity, while getting put in cage and humiliated. Long shot.
- 0:33—Buns, while still in cage. Long shot.
- 0:36—Buns, while getting spanked.
- • 0:42—Frontal nudity, while standing in the center of the group.
- 0:43—Briefly nude, while getting his clothes.

Heartbreakers (1984) . . . . . . . . . . . . . . . . . . . Marvin
Making the Grade (1984) . . . . . . . . . . Coach Wordman
*TV:*
The Last Resort (1979-80) . . . . . . . . . . .Zach Comstock
Wizards and Warriors (1983) . . . . . . . . . . . . . . .Marko
Partners in Crime (1984) . . . . . . . . . . . . Harmon Shain

# Olmos, Edward James

Husband of actress Lorraine Bracco.
*Films:*
**Wolfen** (1981) . . . . . . . . . . . . . . . . . . . . . .Eddie Holt
- 1:04—Buns, while lapping water, then nude, running around the beach. Dark.
- • 1:05—Very brief frontal nudity, leaping off pier in front of Albert Finney.
- 1:12—Very brief frontal nudity, running under pier during Finney's vision.

Zoot Suit (1981) . . . . . . . . . . . . . . . . . . . . El Pachoco
Blade Runner (1982) . . . . . . . . . . . . . . . . . . . . . Gaff
Saving Grace (1986) . . . . . . . . . . . . . . . . . . . . Ciolino
Stand and Deliver (1988) . . . . . . . . . . . Jaime Escalante
Triumph of the Spirit (1989) . . . . . . . . . . . . . . .Gypsy
Talent for the Game (1991) . . . . . . . . . . . . Virgil Sweet
American Me (1992) . . . . . . . . . . . . . . . . . . . Santana
*Made for Cable Movies:*
The Burning Season (1994; HBO) . . . . . .Wilson Pinheiro
*Made for TV Movies:*
Menendez: A Killing in Beverly Hills (1994) . . . . . . . José
*TV:*
Miami Vice (1984-89) . . . . . . . . . . . .Lt. Martin Castillo

# Olsen, Arne

*Films:*
**Black Ice** (1992; U.S./Canadian) . . . . . . . . .Eric Weaver
- • 0:10—Buns, on top of Joanna Pacula's body double, while making love on bed.

# Ontkean, Michael

*Films:*
The Peace Killers (1971) . . . . . . . . . . . . . . . . . . . .Jeff
Hot Summer Week (1973; Canadian) . . . . . . . . . . .n.a.
**Slap Shot** (1977) . . . . . . . . . . . . . . . . . . . .Ned Braden
- • 1:56—Brief buns while wearing a jock strap, while skating off the hockey rink and carrying a trophy.

Voices (1979) . . . . . . . . . . . . . . . . . . . . Drew Rothman
**Willie and Phil** (1980) . . . . . . . . . . . . . . . . . . .Willie
- • 1:36—Buns, while taking off his swimsuit at the beach and jumping around.
- • 1:45—Buns, while getting into the hot tub. (He's on the left.)

Making Love (1982) . . . . . . . . . . . . . . . . . . . . . Zack
The Witching (1983) . . . . . . . . . . . . . . .Frank Brandon
*a.k.a. Necromancy*
(Originally filmed in 1971 as *Necromancy*, additional scenes were added and re-released in 1983.)
Just the Way You Are (1984) . . . . . . . . . . . . . . . . Peter
The Allnighter (1987) . . . . . . . . . . . . . . . Mickey Leroi
Maid to Order (1987) . . . . . . . . . . . . . . Nick McGuire
Clara's Heart (1988) . . . . . . . . . . . . . . . . . . . Bill Hart
Street Justice (1988) . . . . . . . . . . . . . . . . . . Curt Flynn
Bye Bye Blues (1989; Canadian) . . . . . . . . Teddy Cooper
Cold Front (1989; Canadian) . . . . . . . . .Derek McKenzie
Postcards from the Edge (1990) . . . . . . . Robert Murch
*Made for Cable Movies:*
The Blood of Others (1984; HBO) . . . . . . . . . . . . .n.a.
*Made for TV Movies:*
In a Child's Name (1991) . . . . . . . . . .Dr. Kenneth Taylor
Whose Child Is This? The War for Baby Jessica (1993)
. . . . . . . . . . . . . . . . . . . . . . . . . . . . . Jan DeBoer
*TV:*
The Rookies (1972-74) . . . . . . . . . . . Officer Willie Gillis
Twin Peaks (1990-91) . . . . . . . . . . . . .Harry S. Truman

# Osbon, Harry

*Films:*
**Auditions** (1978) . . . . . . . . . . . . . . . . . . .Harry Boran
- • • 0:26—Nude during audition with Linnea Quigley and Larry.
- • • 0:30—Frontal nudity, getting whipped while standing up, chained at the wrists.

# Osborn, Bill

*Films:*
A Midnight Clear (1991) . . . . . . . . . . . . . . . . Sargeant
*Made for Cable Movies:*
**Double Jeopardy** (1992; Showtime) . . . Eddie Brizzard
- • 0:23—Buns, several times, while in the kitchen attacking Rachel Ward more afterwards after she stabs him.

# Otto, Barry

*Films:*
**Bliss** (1985; Australian) . . . . . . . . . . . . . . . .Henry Joy
- • • 0:48—Buns, while peddling on exercise bike.
- • 0:58—Buns, while lying on the floor with Honey.

Takeover (1988; Australian) . . . . . George Oppenheimer

The Custodian (1993) . . . . . . . . . . . . . . . . . . Ferguson
Strictly Ballroom (1993; Australian) . . . . . Doug Hastings

# Owen, Clive

*Films:*

**Close My Eyes** (1991; British) . . . . . . . . . . . . . Richard
•• 0:09—Brief frontal nudity, then buns, while getting
up from the floor and talking on the telephone.
0:29—Side view of buns, while lying on floor with
Natalie.
••• 0:30—Buns, while getting up and walking around.
•• 0:32—Very brief frontal nudity, rolling over. Out of
focus buns, lying on his stomach.
•• 0:46—Buns, while lying in bed with Natalie.
•• 0:56—Buns, while getting out of bed and walking to
the window.

*Made for TV Movies:*
Class of '61 (1993) . . . . . . . . . . . . . . . . . . . Devin O'Neil

*Magazines:*
**Playboy** (Nov 1992) . . . . . . . . . . Sex in Cinema 1992
•• 146—Buns, while on the floor with Helen Fitzgerald
from *Close My Eyes.*

# Pace, Richard

*Films:*

**I Spit on Your Grave** (1978) . . . . . . . . . . . . . Matthew
(Uncut, unrated version reviewed.)
• 0:42—Buns, while undressing in the house to rape
Jennifer.
1:15—Silhouette of penis while getting hung (by
the neck) by Jennifer.

# Packer, David

*Films:*

**You Can't Hurry Love** (1984) . . . . . . . . . . . . . Eddie
• 0:59—Buns, in store taking his pants off while peo-
ple watch him from the sidewalk.
The Runnin' Kind (1988) . . . . . . . . . . . . . . . . Joey Curtis
Trust Me (1989) . . . . . . . . . . . . . . . . . . . . . . Sam Brown
Crazy People (1990) . . . . . . . . . . . . . . . . . Mark Olander

*Miniseries:*
V (1983) . . . . . . . . . . . . . . . . . . . . . . . Daniel Bernstein
V: The Final Battle (1984) . . . . . . . . . . Daniel Bernstein

*Made for TV Movies:*
Dayo (1992) . . . . . . . . . . . . . . . . . . . . . . . . . . . . . n.a.

*TV:*
The Best Times (1985) . . . . . . . . . Niel "Trout" Troutman
What's Alan Watching? (1989) . . . . . . . . . . . . . . . Jeff

# Palese, Joe

*Films:*
Fear City (1984) . . . . . . . . . . . . . . . . . . . . . . . . . Tony
Freeway (1988) . . . . . . . . . . . . . . . . . . . . . . . . Gomez
**Sinners!** (1990) . . . . . . . . . . . . . . . . . . . . . . . . . . Al
• 0:00—Brief buns, while on top of a woman. Don't
see his face.
Blood Money (1991) . . . . . . . . . . . . . . . . . . . . . Burt
*a.k.a. The Killer's Edge*

# • Palin, Michael

*Films:*
Monty Python and the Holy Grail (1974; British) . . . n.a.
Monty Python's Jabberwocky (1977) . . . Dennis Cooper
Monty Python's Life of Brian (1979; British) . . . . . . . n.a.
Time Bandits (1981; British) . . . . . . . . . . . . . . . . . n.a.
The Missionary (1982; British) . . . . . . . . . . . . . . . n.a.
The Secret Policeman's Other Ball (1982; British) . . . n.a.
The Secret Policeman's Private Parts (1984) . . . . . . . n.a.
Brazil (1985; British) . . . . . . . . . . . . . . . . . . . . Jack Lint
A Private Function (1985) . . . . . . . . . . . Gilbert Chilvers
A Fish Called Wanda (1988) . . . . . . . . . . . . . . . . . Ken

*Made for Cable TV:*
**Michael Palin's Pole to Pole** (1992; A&E) . . . . . Host
•• 0:41—(into volume 1 of the four volume set.) Buns,
taking off towel and jumping into lake with two
guys after sitting in sauna.

*Made for TV Movies:*
How to Irritate People (1968; British) . . . . . . . . . . . n.a.

*TV:*
Monty Python's Flying Circus (British) . . . . . . . . Regular
Ripping Yarns (British) . . . . . . . . . . . . . . . . . . . . n.a.

# Pankow, John

*Films:*
The Hunger (1983) . . . . . . . . . . 1st Phone Booth Youth
**To Live and Die in L.A.** (1985) . . . . . . . John Vukovich
•• 1:06—Buns, while changing in the locker room.
*batteries not included (1987) . . . . . . . . . . . . . . Kovacs
The Secret of My Success (1987) . . . . . . . . Fred Melrose
Monkey Shines: An Experiment in Fear (1988)
. . . . . . . . . . . . . . . . . . . . . . . . . . Geoffrey Fisher
Talk Radio (1988) . . . . . . . . . . . . . . . . . . . . . . . Dietz
Mortal Thoughts (1991) . . . . . . . . . . . . Arthur Kellogg
Year of the Gun (1991) . . . . . . . . . . . . . . Italo Bianchi
Stranger Among Us (1992) . . . . . . . . . . . . . . . Levine
*a.k.a. Close to Eden*

*TV:*
Mad About You . . . . . . . . . . . . . . . . . . . . . . . . . . Ira

# • Paramore, Kiri

*Films:*
The Last Days of Chez Nous (1991; Australian) . . . . . Tim
**Flirting** (1992; Australian) . . . . . . . . . . . . "Slag" Green
• 0:03—Brief buns, after showing his school mates his
whip marks (He's the guy in the middle).

# Paré, Michael

*Films:*
Eddie and the Cruisers (1983) . . . . . . . . . . . . . . . Eddie
The Philadelphia Experiment (1984) . . . . . David Herdeg
Streets of Fire (1984) . . . . . . . . . . . . . . . . . Tom Cody
Instant Justice (1987) . . . . . . . . . . . . Scott Youngblood
Space Rage (1987) . . . . . . . . . . . . . . . . . . . . . Grange
**The Women's Club** (1987) . . . . . . . . . . . . . . . Patrick
1:05—Brief buns, during nightmare. Hard to see be-
cause of fog.
• 1:06—Buns, while standing in hallway during night-
mare. Long shot.

Eddie and the Cruisers II: Eddie Lives (1989)
. . . . . . . . . . . . . . . . . . . . . . . Eddie Wilson/Joe West
Dragonfight (1990). . . . . . . . . . . . . . . . . . . Moorpark
The Last Hour (1990) . . . . . . . . . . . . . . . . . . . . . Jeff
*a.k.a. Concrete War*
Moon 44 (1990; West German) . . . . . . . . . Felix Stone
The Closer (1991). . . . . . . . . . . . . . . . . . . Larry Freed
Into the Sun (1991). . . . . . . . . . . Captain Paul Watkins
Killing Streets (1991). . . . . . . . . . . . . Chris/Craig Brandt
**Sunset Heat** (1991) . . . . . . . . . . . . . . . . . . Eric Wright
(Unrated version reviewed.)
• 0:00—Buns, while standing and looking out the
   window.
••• 0:22—Buns, while standing on stairs with Tracy
   Tweed, then making love with her on the floor.
• 0:24—Buns, while standing up and walking up the
   stairs.
Blink of an Eye (1992). . . . . . . . . . . . . . Sam Browning
Point of Impact (1993) . . . . . . . . . . . . . . . . . . . . Jack
*TV:*
Greatest American Hero (1981-83) . . . . . . Tony Villicana
Houston Knights (1987-88). . . . . . . Sgt. Joey La Fiamma

## • *Parker, Carl*

*Films:*
John and Mary (1969). . . . . . . . . . . . . . . Tennis Player
**Score** (1973) . . . . . . . . . . . . . . . . . . . . . . . . . . . Mike
••• 0:21—Buns, while talking with Elvira, then making
   love while Betsy watches.
• 1:22—Buns, while in bed.
In the Mood (1987) . . . . . . . . . . . . . . Bus Ticket Agent
The Runestone (1990). . . . . . . . . . . . Elevator Operator

## *Parker, Jameson*

*Films:*
**The Bell Jar** (1979) . . . . . . . . . . . . . . . . . . . . . Buddy
• 0:09—Frontal nudity silhouette standing in bed-
   room with Marilyn Hassett, then buns. Dark, hard to
   see.
A Small Circle of Friends (1980) . . . . . . . . . . Nick Baxter
White Dog (1982). . . . . . . . . . . . . . . . . . . Roland Gray
American Justice (1986) . . . . . . . . . . . . Dave Buchanon
Prince of Darkness (1987) . . . . . . . . . . . . . . . . Brian
Curse of the Crystal Eye (1993). . . . . . . . . . Luke Ward
*Made for TV Movies:*
Who is Julia? (1986) . . . . . . . . . . . . . . . . Don North
Dead Before Dawn (1993). . . . . . . . . . . . . . . . . n.a.
*TV:*
Simon & Simon (1981-89)
. . . . . . . . . . . . . . . . . . . . Andrew Jackson (A.J.) Simon

## • *Parker, Nathaniel*

*Films:*
War Requiem (1988; British) . . . . . . . . . . Wilfred Owen
Hamlet (1990; British/French). . . . . . . . . . . . . Laertes
The Bodyguard (1992) . . . . . . . . . . . . . . . Clive Healy

**Wide Sargasso Sea** (1993) . . . . . . . . . . . . . Rochester
(Unrated version reviewed.)
••• 0:44—Buns while standing at the window, then
   frontal nudity while walking back to bed.
•• 0:52—Buns, while making love making love in bed
   with Antoinette.
•• 1:16—Buns, while making love standing up outside
   with Amelie.
*Magazines:*
**Playboy** (Nov 1993) . . . . . . . . . . . Sex in Cinema 1993
•• 138—Full frontal nudity in video still from *Wide Sargasso Sea.*

## • *Parrish, Max*

*Films:*
**Hold Me, Thrill Me, Kiss Me** (1993) . . . . Eli/Bud/Fritz
(Unrated version reviewed.)
• 0:08—Buns, when Sabra pulls his shorts off to give
   him a massage.
•• 0:11—Buns, while standing up to put his jeans on.

## *Parvin, Steve*

*Films:*
**Wheels of Fire** (1984) . . . . . . . . . . . . . . . . . . . . . Bo
*a.k.a. Desert Warrior*
• 0:07—Buns, mooning out the window of the car.
• 0:20—Buns, trying to get away from the bad guys
   "initiation."

## *Pasdar, Adrian*

*Films:*
Solarbabies (1986). . . . . . . . . . . . . . . . . . . . . Darstar
Streets of Gold (1986) . . . . . . . . . . . . . . Timmy Boyle
Near Dark (1987). . . . . . . . . . . . . . . . . . . . . . Caleb
**Made in U.S.A.** (1988). . . . . . . . . . . . . . . . . . . . . Dar
• 0:12—Buns, while walking to sit down at the laun-
   dromat when he washes all his clothes with Christo-
   pher Penn.
Vital Signs (1989). . . . . . . . . . . . . . Michael Chatham
1:11—Upper half of buns, with his pants partially
   down in basement with Diane Lane.
Torn Apart (1990) . . . . . . . . . . . . . . . . . . Ben Arnon
Grand Isle (1991). . . . . . . . . . . . . . . . Robert Lebrun
Carlito's Way (1993). . . . . . . . . . . . . . . . . . . Frankie
*Made for Cable Movies:*
The Lost Capone (1990). . . . . . . . . . . . . . . . . Jimmy

## *Patinkin, Mandy*

*Films:*
French Postcards (1979). . . . . . . . . . . . . . . . . Sayyid
The Last Embrace (1979) . . . . . . . . . . . . . Commuter
Night of the Juggler (1980) . . . . . . . . . . . . . . Cabbie
Ragtime (1981) . . . . . . . . . . . . . . . . . . . . . . Tateh
Daniel (1983). . . . . . . . . . . . . . . . . . . Paul Isaacson
**Yentl** (1983) . . . . . . . . . . . . . . . . . . . . . . . Avigdor
•• 0:49—Buns, after taking off his clothes to go skinny
   dipping.
• 0:51—Brief buns while sitting down next to Barbra
   Streisand, the brief buns, while standing up.

- 0:52—Buns, while walking around and sitting down. Long shot.

Maxie (1985) . . . . . . . . . . . . . . . . . . . . . . . . . . . Nick
The Princess Bride (1987) . . . . . . . . . . . . Inigo Montoya
Alien Nation (1988) . . . . . . . . . . . . . . . . Sam Francisco
The House on Carroll Street (1988) . . . . . . . Ray Salwen
Dick Tracy (1990) . . . . . . . . . . . . . . . . . . . . . . . . 88 Keys
The Doctor (1991) . . . . . . . . . . . . . . . . . . . . . . Murray
Impromptu (1991) . . . . . . . . . . . . . . . Alfred DeMusset
True Colors (1991) . . . . . . . . . . . . . . . . . John Palmeri
Life With Mikey (1993) . . . . . . . . . . . . . . . . . Irate Man

## Patric, Jason

Son of actor/author Jason Miller.
Grandson of late actor/comedian Jackie Gleason.
*Films:*
Solarbabies (1986) . . . . . . . . . . . . . . . . . . . . . . . . Jason
The Lost Boys (1987) . . . . . . . . . . . . . . . . . . . Michael
**After Dark, My Sweet** (1990) . . Kevin "Collie" Collins
 •• 1:19—Buns, while taking off pants and getting into bed with Rachel Ward. More brief buns on top of her.
Frankenstein Unbound (1990) . . . . . . . . . . . . Lord Byron
Denial (1991) . . . . . . . . . . . . . . . . . . . . . . . . . Michael
Rush (1991) . . . . . . . . . . . . . . . . . . . . . . . Jim Raynor
Geronimo: An American Legend (1993)
. . . . . . . . . . . . . . . . . . Lieutenant Charles Gatewood
*Made for TV Movies:*
Toughlove (1985) . . . . . . . . . . . . . . . . . Gary Charters

## Patrick, Randal

*Films:*
Livin' Large (1991) . . . . . . . . . . . . . . . . . . . . . . . Jimmy
*Made for Cable Movies:*
**By Dawn's Early Light** (1990; HBO) . . . . . . . O'Toole
 • 0:14—Brief buns while in shower room getting dressed during red alert.

## • Patrick, Robert

*Films:*
Equalizer 2000 (1986) . . . . . . . . . . . . . . . . . . . . Deke
Eye of the Eagle (1987; Philippines) . . . . . Johnny Ransom
Zero Tolerance (1989) . . . . . . . . . . . . . . . . . . . . . Jeff
Die Hard 2 (1990) . . . . . . . . . . . . . . . . . . . . . O'Reilly
**Terminator 2: Judgement Day** (1991) . . . . . . T-1000
 • 0:00—Partial buns and very brief partial frontal nudity when kneeling down after arriving from the future.
The Cool Surface (1992) . . . . . . . . . . . . . . . Jarvis Scott
Wayne's World (1992) . . . . . . . . . . . . . . . . . . Bad Cop
Body Shot (1993) . . . . . . . . . . . . . . . . . . Mickey Dane
Fire in the Sky (1993) . . . . . . . . . . . . . . . Mike Rogers
Last Action Hero (1993) . . . . . . . . . . . . . . . Himself
*Made for Cable TV:*
Tales From the Crypt: The New Arrival (1992; HBO)
. . . . . . . . . . . . . . . . . . . . . . . . . . . . . . . . . . . . D.J.

## Patterson, Jimmy

*Films:*
**The Young Warriors** (1983; U.S./Canadian)
. . . . . . . . . . . . . . . . . . . . . . . . . . "Ice Test" Monty
 • 0:14—Buns, while dropping pants and sitting on a block of ice during pledge at fraternity.

## Pavesi, Paolo

*Films:*
**1900** (1976; Italian) . . . . . . . . . . . . . Alfredo as a Child
(NC-17 version reviewed.)
 • 1:05—Frontal nudity showing the young Olmo his penis.

## Paxton, Bill

*Films:*
Mortuary (1981) . . . . . . . . . . . . . . . . . . . . Paul Andrews
Stripes (1981) . . . . . . . . . . . . . . . . . . . . . . . . . . . n.a.
Impulse (1984) . . . . . . . . . . . . . . . . . . . . . . . . . Eddie
Streets of Fire (1984) . . . . . . . . . . . . . . . . . . . . Clyde
The Terminator (1984) . . . . . . . . . . . . . . . Punk Leader
Commando (1985) . . . . . . . . . . . . . . . Intercept Officer
**Weird Science** (1985) . . . . . . . . . . . . . . . . . . . . Chet
 •• 0:30—Buns, while taking off towel to give to his younger brother in the kitchen.
Aliens (1986) . . . . . . . . . . . . . . . . . . . . . Private Hudson
Near Dark (1987) . . . . . . . . . . . . . . . . . . . . . . Severen
Pass the Ammo (1988) . . . . . . . . . . . . . . . . . . . . Jesse
Brain Dead (1989) . . . . . . . . . . . . . . . . . . . Jim Reston
Next of Kin (1989) . . . . . . . . . . . . . . . . . Gerald Gates
Back to Back (1990) . . . . . . . . . . . . . . . . . . . Bo Brand
The Last of the Finest (1990) . . . . Howard "Hojo" Jones
Navy SEALS (1990) . . . . . . . . . . . . . . . . . . . . . Dane
Predator 2 (1990) . . . . . . . . . . . . . . . . . . . . . . Jerry
Slipstream (1990) . . . . . . . . . . . . . . . . . Matt Owens
**The Dark Backward** (1991) . . . . . . . . . . . . . . . . Gus
 •• 0:44—Buns, while taking off his jumpsuit and diving into bed with his three fat girlfriends.
One False Move (1992) . . . . . . . Dale "Hurricane" Dixon
Trespass (1992) . . . . . . . . . . . . . . . . . . . . . . . . Vince
The Vagrant (1992) . . . . . . . . . . . . . . Graham Krakowski
**Boxing Helena** (1993) . . . . . . . . . . . . . . Ray O'Malley
 • 0:17—Buns, while rolling over on top of Sherilyn Fenn in bed.
 •• 0:19—Very brief frontal nudity while sitting on bed. Seen behind side of liquor bottle.
Future Shock (1993) . . . . . . . . . . . . . . . . . . . . . Vince
Indian Summer (1993) . . . . . . . . . . . . . . . Jack Belston
**Monolith** (1993) . . . . . . . . . . . . . . . . . . . . . Tucker
 • 0:15—Brief buns, in shower when Lindsay Crouse comes in to visit and talk.
Tombstone (1993) . . . . . . . . . . . . . . . . . . Morgan Earp
True Lies (1994) . . . . . . . . . . . . . . . . . . . . . . . Simon
*Made for Cable TV:*
Tales From the Crypt: People Who Live in Brass Hearses
(1993; HBO) . . . . . . . . . . . . . . . . . . . . . . . . . Billy
*Made for TV Movies:*
Deadly Lessons (1983) . . . . . . . . . . . . . . . . . . . . n.a.

## Peck, Brian

*Films:*

**The Last American Virgin** (1982)........... Victor
  • 0:20—Buns, during penis measurement in boy's
    locker room. Don't see his face.

## • Penco, Tomás

*Films:*

**Jamón, Jamón** (1992; Spanish)........ Raul's Friend
  ••• 0:39—Nude, while practicing bullfighting outside at
    night with Raul, then running away when caught.
    Long scene.

## Penn, Christopher

Brother of actor Sean Penn.
Son of director Leo Penn.

*Films:*

All The Right Moves (1983)................... Brian
Rumble Fish (1983)........................... B.J.
Footloose (1984)........................... Willard
The Wild Life (1984) ................... Tom Drake
Pale Rider (1985)..................... Josh LaHood
At Close Range (1986) .......... Tommy Whitewood
**Made in U.S.A.** (1988) ...................... Tuck
  • 0:12—Buns, while walking to sit down at the laun-
    dromat when he washes all his clothes with Adrian
    Pasdar.
Best of the Best (1990) ..................... Travis
Future Kick (1991) ...........................Bang
Leather Jackets (1991).................. Big Steve
Mobsters (1991) ................... Tommy Reina
  *a.k.a. Mobsters—The Evil Empire*
Best of the Best 2 (1992)............. Travis Brickley
The Pickle (1992) ................... Gregory Stone
Reservoir Dogs (1992).............. Nice Guy/Eddie
Beethoven's 2nd (1993) .................... Floyd
Josh and S.A.M. (1993)..............Derek Baxter
Short Cuts (1993) ................... Jerry Kaiser
True Romance (1993) ................. Nicky Dimes
  (Unrated version reviewed.)

## Penn, Sean

Significant other of actress Robin Wright.
Ex-husband of singer/actress Madonna.
Brother of actor Christopher Penn.
Son of director Leo Penn.

*Films:*

Taps (1981)........................Alex Dwyer
Fast Times at Ridgemont High (1982)......Jeff Spicoli
**Bad Boys** (1983) ................... Mick O'Brien
  • 0:10—Brief buns while getting up off the floor with
    Ally Sheedy.
  •• 0:46—Buns while taking a shower.
Crackers (1984)........................... Dillard
Racing with the Moon (1984)... Henry "Hopper" Nash
The Falcon and the Snowman (1985) ..... Daulton Lee
At Close Range (1986) .......... Brad Whitewood, Jr.
Shanghai Surprise (1986) .......... Glendon Wasey
Colors (1988) ................... Danny McGavin

Judgment in Berlin (1988) .............. Gunther X
Casualties of War (1989) ......... Sergeant Meserve
We're No Angels (1989)......................Jim
State of Grace (1990)....................... Terry
Carlito's Way (1993)..................... Kleinfeld

## Pepe, Paul

*Films:*

**Saturday Night Fever** (1977) ........... Double J.
  (R-rated version reviewed.)
  • 0:22—Buns, while making love in back seat of car
    with a girl.

## Pereio, Paulo Cesar

*Films:*

**I Love You** (1982; Brazilian) ................Paulo
  *a.k.a. Eu Te Amo*
  • 0:35—Brief side view of buns and frontal nudity,
    while kneeling on the floor with Sonia Braga.
  • 0:38—Buns, in mirror, while walking in hallway.
  •• 0:59—Buns and part of frontal nudity covered with
    paint with Braga.
  • 1:36—Side view of buns, while making love on top
    of Braga.
  • 1:37—Brief buns while lying on floor with Braga. Lit
    with neon lights.

## Perez, Lazaro

*Films:*

**Fortune and Men's Eyes** (1971).............Catso
  •• 0:29—Brief buns, undressing and dressing during
    rape of another male inmate in jail cell.
The Gumball Rally (1976)......................Jose
The January Man (1988) ......................Ramon

## Perry, Jeff

*Films:*

Three Fugitives (1989) .................... Orderly
Body of Evidence (1992) ..................... Gabe
  (Unrated version reviewed.)
Hard Promises (1992)....................... Pinky
Life on the Edge (1992) ............... Ray Nelson
Storyville (1992)................... Peter Dandridge
**Naked Instinct** (1993)................... Frat Boy
  •• 0:40—Nude in fraternity house with Michelle Bauer.

## Peter, Jens

*Films:*

**Wild Orchid** (1990) ............. Voleyball Player
  ••• 1:29—Buns, while in room with Jacqueline Bisset
    and Carré Otis.

## Petersen, William L.

*Films:*

Thief (1981).............. Katz & Jammer Bartender
**To Live and Die in L.A.** (1985) ...... Richard Chance
  • 0:44—Brief frontal nudity, but hard to see anything
    because it's dark.
Manhunter (1986) ................... Will Graham

Cousins (1989) . . . . . . . . . . . . . . . . . . . . . . Tom Hardy
Young Guns II (1990) . . . . . . . . . . . . . . . . . Pat Garrett
Hard Promises (1992) . . . . . . . . . . . . . . . . Joey Coalter
Passed Away (1992) . . . . . . . . . . . . . . . Frank Scanlan
*Made for Cable Movies:*
Long Gone (1987; HBO) . . . . . . . . Cecil "Stud" Cantrell
Keep the Change (1992; TNT) . . . . . . . . . . Joe Starling
**Curaçao** (1993; Showtime) . . . . . . . . Stephen Guerin
*a.k.a. Deadly Currents*
•• 0:52—Buns, while getting up from bed and walking past Julie Carmen to the bathroom.
*Miniseries:*
The Kennedys of Massachusetts (1990)
. . . . . . . . . . . . . . . . . . . . . . . . . . . Joseph P. Kennedy
Return to Lonesome Dove (1993) . . . . . . Gideon Walker

## Phelps, Matthew
*Films:*
Dreamaniac (1987). . . . . . . . . . . . . . . . . . . . . . Foster
**Nightmare Sisters** (1987) . . . . . . . . . . . . . . . . . .J.J.
•• 0:53—Buns, while taking off his pants and getting into bed with Michelle Bauer.

## • Phillips, Lou Diamond
*Films:*
La Bamba (1987) . . . . . . . . . . . . . . . . . . . Ritchie Valens
Stand and Deliver (1988) . . . . . . . . . . . . . . . . . Angel
Young Guns (1988). . . . . . . . . . . . . . . Chavez Y Chavez
Disorganized Crime (1989) . . . . . . . . . . . . . . Ray Forgy
Renegades (1989) . . . . . . . . . . . . . . . . . . . . Hank Storm
The First Power (1990) . . . . . . . . . . . . . Russell Logan
A Show of Force (1990). . . . . . . . . . . . . . Jesus Fuentes
Young Guns II (1990) . . . . . . . . . . Jose Chavez Y Chavez
Ambition (1991) . . . . . . . . . . . . . . . . . . . . . . Mitchell
Shadow of the Wolf (1992) . . . . . . . . . . . . . . .Agaguk
**Dangerous Touch** (1993). . . . . . . . . Mick Burroughs
0:32—Sort of buns, while showering behind plastic curtain. Hard to see anything.
••• 0:38—Buns, after taking off his shorts in front of Kate Vernon.
0:41—Upper half of buns, while making love with Vernon on video playback.
• 1:06—Buns, while making love with Vernon. Long shot.
The Dark Wind (1993). . . . . . . . . . . . . Officer Jim Chee
*Made for Cable Movies:*
Extreme Justice (1993; HBO) . . . . . . . . . . . . Jeff Powers
*Made for Cable TV:*
Tales From the Crypt: Oil's Well That Ends Well (1993; HBO) . . . . . . . . . . . . . . . . . . . . . . . . . . Jerry

## • Picker, Josh
*Films:*
**Flirting** (1992; Australian) . . . . . . . . . . ."Backa" Bourke
• 0:03—Brief buns, after showing his school mates his whip marks (He's the guy on the left).

## • Pike, Gerry
*Films:*
**Killer Looks** (1994) . . . . . . . . . . . . . . . . . . . .Plumber
(Unrated version reviewed.)
•• 0:07—Buns, while making love with Sara Suzanne Brown, then getting dressed after getting caught by her husband.

## • Pilato, Josef
*Films:*
**Married People, Single Sex** (1993) . . . . . . . . . . Artie
• 1:18—Partial buns, while kneeling on bed while making love with Meg.

## • Pilgrim, George
*Made for Cable TV:*
**Red Shoe Diaries: Hotline** (1994; Showtime) . Adam
• 0:09—Brief lower half of buns, when Tess pulls down his underwear.

## Pitzalis, Fredrico
*Films:*
**Devil in the Flesh** (1986; French/Italian) . . . . .Andrea
• 0:57—Brief buns while in bed with Maruschka Detmers.
• 1:19—Frontal nudity when Detmers performs fellatio on him. Dark, hard to see.

## Placido, Donato
*Films:*
**Caligula** (1980) . . . . . . . . . . . . . . . . . . . . . .Proculus
(X-rated, 147 minute version.)
• 1:11—Frontal nudity taking his robe off for Malcolm McDowell. Buns, while getting raped by McDowell's fist.
*Magazines:*
**Playboy** (Nov 1980) . . . . . . . . . . . Sex in Cinema 1980
• 180—Buns in still from *Caligula*.

## Plank, Scott
*Films:*
A Chorus Line (1985) . . . . . . . . . . . . . . . . . . . . Dancer
Wired (1989) . . . . . . . . . . . . . . . . . . . . . .Herb Axelson
Mr. Baseball (1992) . . . . . . . . . . . . . . . . . . . .Ryan Ward
*Made for Cable TV:*
**Red Shoe Diaries: Accidents Happen** (1993; Showtime) . . . . . . . . . . . . . . . . . . . . . . . Zack
(Available on video tape on *Red Shoe Diaries 4: Auto Erotica*.)
• 0:15—Brief buns, getting out of bed after discovering he was making love with the maid rather than his wife.

## • Pollock, Daniel
*Films:*
Proof (1991; Australian) . . . . . . . . . . . . . . . . . . . Gary
**Romper Stomper** (1993; Australian) . . . . . . . . Davey
•• 1:11—Buns, while making love with Gabe in bed.

## Poole, David
*Films:*
**Naked Instinct** (1993) . . . . . . . . . . . . . . . Therapist
•• 1:09—Buns, while making love in bed with Michelle Bauer.
••• 1:10—Full frontal nudity, on the floor under Bauer.
••• 1:11—Nude, making love on top of Bauer.

## Popper, Alan
*Films:*
Kandyland (1987) . . . . . . . . . . . . . . . . . . . . Heckler
**Small Kill** (1991) . . . . . . . . . . . . . . . . Thomas Stanzak
• 0:21—Buns, while crazily running around outside in a jockstrap.

## • Porro, Mark Steven
*Made for Cable TV:*
**Love Street: Seven Fifteen** (1993; Showtime)
. . . . . . . . . . . . . . . . . . . . . . . . . . . . . . . Jack Lloyd
•• 0:09—Buns, while lying in bed with Eve.

## Potter, Michael
*Films:*
**Female Trouble** (1974) . . . . . . . . . . . . . . . . . . Gater
• 0:27—Nude, caught in bed with another woman by Divine.
••• 0:28—Buns, making love in bed on top of Divine.
••• 0:29—Frontal nudity, sitting in bed, talking to Taffy.
•• 0:31—More buns, while making love on top of Divine. Frontal nudity after sticking a carrot in her mouth.

## Potts, Daniel
*Films:*
**Greystoke: The Legend of Tarzan, Lord of the Apes** (1984) . . . . . . . . . . . . . . . . . . Tarzan Aged Five
• 0:17—Nude in the jungle.
• 0:19—More nude in the jungle.
Revolution (1986) . . . . . . . . . . . . . . . . . . . . . . Ahab

## • Powers, David
*Films:*
The Fiendish Plot of Dr. Fu Manchu (1980) . . . . . Bedser
*Video Tapes:*
**Penthouse Forum Letters: Volume 2** (1994)
. . . . . . . . . . . . . . . . . . . . . . . . The Big Switch/Dan
••• 0:32—Nude, getting into hot tub, then making love with Debbie on bench.

## • Praed, Michael
*Films:*
Nightflyers (1987) . . . . . . . . . . . . . . . . . . . . . . . Royd
**To Die For 2** (1991) . . . . . . . . . . . . . . . . . . . . . . Max
*a.k.a. Son of Darkness: To Die For II*
• 1:08—Side view of buns, after attacking a woman at her car.
*TV:*
Dynasty (1985-86) . . . . . . . . . . . . . . . . . Prince Michael

## Prescott, Robert
*Films:*
**Bachelor Party** (1984) . . . . . . . . . . . . . Richard Chance
• 1:18—Buns, after being hung out the window tied up with sheets by Tom Hanks and his friends.
The Joy of Sex (1984) . . . . . . . . . . Tom Pittman/Richard
Real Genius (1985) . . . . . . . . . . . . . . . . . . . . . . Kent

## Price, Alan
Singer/songwriter.
*Films:*
O Lucky Man! (1973; British) . . . . . . . . . . . . . . Himself
**Oh, Alfie!** (1975; British) . . . . . . . . . . . . . Alfie Elkins
*a.k.a. Alfie Darling*
•• 0:14—Buns washing himself off in the kitchen while talking to Louise's husband.

## Price, Marc
*Films:*
The Zoo Gang (1985) . . . . . . . . . . . . . . . . . . . . . Val
**Trick or Treat** (1986) . . . . . . . . . . . . Eddie Weinbauer
•• 0:04—Buns, while lying on the floor and also kneeling at boys' locker room door when the bullies leave him outside where the girls can see him.
• 0:12—Brief buns, in Polaroid photo of the previous incident.
The Rescue (1988) . . . . . . . . . . . . . . . . . . Max Rothman
Killer Tomatoes Eat France! (1992) . . . . . . . . . . Michael
*TV:*
Family Ties (1982-89) . . . . . . Irwin "Skippy" Handelman
Condo (1983) . . . . . . . . . . . . . . . . . . . . Billy Kirkridge

## • Priestley, Jason
*Films:*
The Boy Who Could Fly (1986) . . . . . . . . . . . . . . Gary
Nowhere to Run (1989) . . . . . . . . . . . . . . . . . . Howard
**Calendar Girl** (1993) . . . . . . . . . . . . . Roy Darpinian
••• 0:44—Buns, while walking to and at nude beach with his two buddies.
••• 0:46—Buns, while walking to the surf. Very, very brief frontal nudity when it pops up to his belly when he turns around to talk to his buddies.
Tombstone (1993) . . . . . . . . . . . . . . . Billy Breckenridge
*TV:*
Sister Kate (1989-90) . . . . . . . . . . . . . . . Tod Mahaffey
Beverly Hills, 90210 (1990- ) . . . . . . . . . Brandon Walsh

## Pringle, Bryan
*Films:*
Damn the Defiant! (1962; British) . . . . . . Sgt. Kneebone
Cromwell (1970; British) . . . . . . . . . . Trooper Hawkins
Monty Python's Jabberwocky (1977)
. . . . . . . . . . . . . . . . . . . . . . . . . Second Gate Guard
Brazil (1985; British) . . . . . . . . . . . . . . . . . . . . . Spiro
**Drowning by Numbers** (1988; British) . . . . . . . . Jake
• 0:04—Buns, while undressing with Nancy.
• 0:06—Nude, in the tub, drunk.
Getting It Right (1989) . . . . . . . . . . . . . . . . Mr. Lamb
Three Men and a Little Lady (1990) . . . . Old Englishman

# • Priola, Mark

*Video Tapes:*

**Playboy's How to Reawaken Your Sexual Powers**
(1992)......................... Cast Member
••• 0:04—Nude, while swimming under water, working
out on rock and on beach, and massaging his lover.

# • Prior, Ted

*Films:*

Killer Workout (1987) ............... Chuck Dawson
*a.k.a. Aerobi-Cide*
Hardcase and Fist (1988)................Bud McAll
Raw Nerve (1991).................. Jimmy Clayton
Double Threat (1992) ................... Mugger
(Unrated version reviewed.)
**Possessed by the Night** (1993)..... Howard Hansen
••• 0:07—Buns, while making love in bed with Sandahl
Bergman.
Raw Justice (1994) ..................... Bennett
*a.k.a. Good Cop, Bad Cop*

# Prochnow, Jürgen

*Films:*

The Lost Honor of Katharina Blum (1975; German)
........................... Ludwig Goetten
Das Boot (1982; German) ............. The Captain
The Keep (1983)........................Woorman
Dune (1984)................... Duke Leto Atreides
**Killing Cars** (1986) ................. Ralph Korda
• 0:48—Buns, while getting up from bed to look at
cigarette lighter. Slightly out of focus. Don't see his
face well.
Beverly Hills Cop II (1987).............Maxwell Dent
A Dry White Season (1989).............. Capt. Stolz
The Fourth War (1990) ......... Col. N.A. Valachev
Hurricane Smith (1990)............... Charlie Dowd
Kill Cruise (1990; German) ............. The Skipper
The Man Inside (1990) ............. Gunter Wallraff
Body of Evidence (1992)............. Dr. Alan Paley
(Unrated version reviewed.)
Interceptor (1992)....................... Phillips
Twin Peaks: Fire Walk With Me (1992)...... Woodsman
*Made for Cable Movies:*
Lie Down with Lions (1994; Lifetime) ........ Marteau
*Made for TV Movies:*
Danielle Steel's "Jewels" (1992)
.................... Joachim von Mannheim
The Fire Next Time (1993) ............. Larry Richter

# Pryor, Richard

Comedian.
*Films:*

Lady Sings the Blues (1972) ............. Piano Man
Some Call It Loving (1972) ................. Jeff
Hit! (1973) .................... Mike Willmer
Uptown Saturday Night (1974)
.................... Sharpe Eye Washington
Car Wash (1976)......................Daddy Rich
Silver Streak (1976)................Grover Muldoon

Greased Lightning (1977) ........... Wendell Scott
Which Way Is Up? (1977)
............. Leroy Jones/Rufus Jones/Rev. Thomas
Blue Collar (1978) .......................... Zeke
The Wiz (1978) .........................The Wiz
Richard Pryor—Live in Concert (1979)........ Himself
Stir Crazy (1980) ................... Harry Monroe
Wholly Moses (1980) ....................Pharaoh
Bustin' Loose (1981) ................. Joe Braxton
Richard Pryor Live on the Sunset Strip (1982)... Himself
Some Kind of Hero (1982) ............. Eddie Keller
The Toy (1982) .................... Jack Brown
Richard Pryor—Here and Now (1983) ........ Himself
Superman III (1983).................. Gus Gorman
Brewster's Millions (1985) ......Montgomery Brewster
Richard Pryor—Live and Smokin' (1985) ...... Himself
**Jo Jo Dancer, Your Life Is Calling** (1986)
.................... Jo Jo Dancer/Alter Ego
•• 0:06—Buns, while walking naked out of the hospital
waiting for the limousine.
Moving (1988)........................ Arlo Pear
Harlem Nights (1989) .................. Sugar Ray
See No Evil, Hear No Evil (1989) ............. Wally
Another You (1991) .................. Eddie Dash
*TV:*
The Richard Pryor Show (1977) ............. Host

# Pucci, Robert

*Films:*

**The Last Hour** (1990) ..................... Eric
*a.k.a. Concrete War*
• 0:05—Brief buns, while making love in bed with Shannon Tweed.
American Me (1992) ...................Bodyguard

# Purcell, James

*Films:*

S.O.B. (1981)............................. n.a.
Where Are the Children? (1986)......... Robin Legler
Bad Dreams (1988) ................. Paramedic
**Playroom** (1989) ........................Paul
*a.k.a. Schizo*
•• 0:25—Buns, while making love with Jamie Rose on a
chair.
White Light (1990)................... Bill Dockerty
The Hitman (1991) ........................Sal

# Quaid, Dennis

Brother of actor Randy Quaid.
Husband of actress Meg Ryan.
*Films:*

9/30/55 (1977) ...........................Frank
Our Winning Season (1978)............. Paul Morelli
Seniors (1978) ...........................Alan
Breaking Away (1979) ..................... Mike
Gorp (1980)..................... Mad Grossman
The Long Riders (1980) .................. Ed Miller
All Night Long (1981) ..............Freddie Dupler
Caveman (1981) ...........................Lar

The Night the Lights Went Out in Georgia (1981)
........................................Travis Child
Jaws 3 (1983) .........................Mike Brody
The Right Stuff (1983)..............Gordon Cooper
Tough Enough (1983)....................Art Long
Dreamscape (1984)..................Alex Gardner
Enemy Mine (1985) ...................Davidge
**The Big Easy** (1987)...............Remy McSwain
• 0:24—Brief buns when Ellen Barkin pulls his underwear down in bed.
••• 0:51—Buns, while putting underwear on after getting out of bed.
**Innerspace** (1987) ................Tuck Pendleton
•• 0:08—Buns, while standing naked in the street as taxi drives off with his towel. Kind of a long shot.
Suspect (1987) .....................Eddie Sanger
D.O.A. (1988) ....................Dexter Cornell
Everybody's All-American (1988).............Gavin
Great Balls of Fire (1989).............Jerry Lee Lewis
Come See the Paradise (1990) .........Jack McGurn
Postcards from the Edge (1990) .........Jack Falkner
1:03—Side view of buns, while leaning out of the shower, talking to Meryl Streep.
Flesh and Bone (1993) ............Arlis Sweeney
Undercover Blues (1993)................Jeff Blue
Wilder Napalm (1993) ..........Wallace Foudroyant
Wyatt Earp (1994)........................n.a.
*Made for TV Movies:*
Are You in the House Alone? (1978) ............Phil
Bill (1981) ......................Barry Morrow
Bill: On His Own (1983) .............Barry Morrow

## Quaid, Randy

Brother of actor Dennis Quaid.
*Films:*
**The Last Picture Show** (1971) .......Lester Marlow
• 0:38—Very brief frontal nudity jumping into pool after Cybill Shepherd jumps in.
The Last Detail (1973)..................Meadows
Lolly-Madonna XXX (1973)............Finch Feather
Paper Moon (1973)........................Leroy
Bound For Glory (1976) .............Luther Johnson
The Missouri Breaks (1976).............Little Tod
The Choirboys (1977)....................Proust
Midnight Express (1978; British) ........Jimmy Booth
Foxes (1980)..............................Jay
The Long Riders (1980)................Clell Miller
Heartbeeps (1981) ......................Charlie
National Lampoon's Vacation (1983).....Cousin Eddie
The Wild Life (1984) ...................Charlie
The Wraith (1986)...................Sheriff Loomis
No Man's Land (1988) .....Lieutenant Vincent Bracey
Bloodhounds of Broadway (1989).......Feet Samuels
National Lampoon's Christmas Vacation (1989)
.............................Cousin Eddie
Out Cold (1989) ...................Lester Atlas
Days of Thunder (1990) ...............Tim Daland
Quick Change (1990) .....................Loomis
Freaked (1993) ....................Eliah C. Skuggs

The Paper (1993) .....................McDougal
*Made for Cable Movies:*
Frankenstein (1993; TNT)................Creature
Next Door (1994; Showtime)........Lenny Benedetti
*Made for TV Movies:*
Murder in the Heartland (1993)................n.a.
Roommates (1994) ....................Jim Flynn
*TV:*
Saturday Night Live (1985-86)..............Regular
Davis Rules (1990-92) ...................Dwight

## Quarter, James

*Films:*
**Intimate Obsession** (1992)............Rick Simms
(Unrated version reviewed.)
• 0:16—Buns, while making love with Laura while Rachel watches from outside.
••• 0:18—Buns, while making love with Laura on chair and around the room.
•• 0:22—Buns, during Rachel's recollections.
••• 0:47—Buns, several times, while making love on top of Rachel.

## Quigley, Paxton

*Films:*
**The Boob Tube** (1975) ..........Dr. Henry Carstairs
• 0:13—Brief buns, in bed with Sharon Kelly.
•• 0:46—Buns, while making love in bed with Natalie.

## Quill, Tom

*Films:*
**Staying Together** (1989) ........Brian McDermott
• 0:03—Brief buns while getting out of bed with Stockard Channing. Hard to see because of the reflections in the window.

## Quinn, Aidan

Husband of actress Elizabeth Bracco.
*Films:*
**Reckless** (1984) ...................Johnny Rourke
• 1:03—Very brief frontal nudity and buns while running into Daryl Hannah's brother's room when her parents come home early.
• 1:12—Side view nude, taking a shower.
Desperately Seeking Susan (1985) ..............Dez
The Mission (1986; British)..................Felipe
Stakeout (1987).........Richard "Stick" Montgomery
Crusoe (1989) ........................Crusoe
Avalon (1990) ...................Jules Krichinsky
A Handmaid's Tale (1990) ...................Nick
The Lemon Sisters (1990)........Frankie McGuinness
At Play in the Fields of the Lord (1991)
.............................Martin Quarrier
The Playboys (1992) ......................Tom
Benny & Joon (1993).................Benny Pearl
**Blink** (1993) .............Detective John Hallstrom
•• 0:02—Buns, twice, after doing strip routine in bar and mooning Madeleine Stowe to get her attention.

*Made for Cable Movies:*
Lies of the Twins (1991; USA)
...................Jonathan & James McEwan
A Private Matter (1992; HBO) .......... Bob Finkbine

# Quinn, J. C.

*Films:*
Firepower (1979) ......................... Dunn
Brubaker (1980) ............................ n.a.
Times Square (1980)..................... Simon
Eddie Macon's Run (1983) ............. Shorter
C.H.U.D. (1984) ...................... Murphy
Silkwood (1984) ............... Curtis Schultz
Visionquest (1985) ......................Elmo
At Close Range (1986) .....................Boyd
Maximum Overdrive (1986) ........... Duncan
Barfly (1987)................................ Jim
Violated (1987)...................Kevin McBane
Big Business (1988)............... Garth Ratliff
The Abyss (1989) ............. "Sonny" Dawson
Gross Anatomy (1989) ............. Papa Slovak
Turner & Hooch (1989)............. Walter Boyett
Wired (1989)...................Comedy Coach
Days of Thunder (1990) ............... Waddell
Megaville (1990)..................... Newman
Prayer of the Rollerboys (1990)........... Jaworski
The Babe (1992)....................Jack Dunn
**Criss Cross** (1992)........................ Jetty
- 0:16—Brief buns, mooning umpire during baseball game.
The Program (1993) ...................Joe's Father

# Race, Hugo

*Films:*
Dogs In Space (1987; Australian) ............. Pierre
**In Too Deep** (1990; Australian) ..................Mark
- 0:39—Buns, while talking with Wendy when JoJo watches. Long shot.
- 0:41—Buns, while in bedroom talking with Wendy.
- 0:59—Brief buns, while walking past sliding glass door.
- •• 1:00—Nude, outside with Wendy, spraying her with a garden hose.
- •• 1:27—Buns, while getting up from the bed.

# •Rafter, Nick

*Films:*
**Seduce Me: Pamela Principle 2** (1994) .....Charles
- 0:59—Buns, while lying face down on bed, getting an oil massage by Pamela.

# Railsback, Steve

*Films:*
The Visitors (1972) .................Mike Nickerson
Angela (1977; Canadian) ................... Jean
The Deadly Games (1980).................... Billy
*a.k.a. The Eliminator*
The Stunt Man (1980)................... Cameron
Escape 2000 (1981) ....................... Paul

The Golden Seal (1983) ................... Jim Lee
Torchlight (1984)................... Jake Gregory
**Lifeforce** (1985)........................ Carlsen
- 1:26—Buns, while standing with Mathilda May after he stabs her with the sword. Surrounded by special effects.
Armed and Dangerous (1986) .......... The Cowboy
The Blue Monkey (1987) ....... Detective Jim Bishop
Scenes from the Goldmine (1987) .......Harry Spiros
The Wind (1987) ...................... Kesner
The Assassin (1989) ......... Hank Wright
Scissors (1990)........... Alex Morgan/Cole Morgan
Alligator II: The Mutation (1991) .......Vincent Brown
Quake (1992)........................Kyle Ryan
Sunstroke (1992) ............... Detective Biggs
Calendar Girl (1993) .............Roy's Father
Final Mission (1993)........... Colonel Olen Anderson
Private Wars (1993) .................. Jack Manning
Save Me (1993) ....................... Robbins
(Unrated version reviewed.)
*Made for Cable Movies:*
The Forgotten (1989)........................ n.a.
*Made for TV Movies:*
Helter Skelter (1976) .............Charles Manson
Good Cops, Bad Cops (1990) ........Jimmy Donnelly
Separated by Murder (1994) ........... Jesse Dixon

# Rajot, Pierre-Loup

*Films:*
**A Nos Amours** (1984; French) ............ Bernard
- 0:56—Brief buns, while walking around in the background. Long shot. Out of focus.
- 0:58—Partial frontal nudity, lying in bed talking to Sandrine Bonnaire.
Baton Rouge (1985; French) ...... Abadenour Colbert
Garcon! (1985; French) ..................Maurice

# Rally, Steve

*Films:*
Overkill (1987)......................Mickey Delano
*TV:*
Santa Barbara .............................. n.a.
The Young and the Restless ................... n.a.
*Video Tapes:*
Ultimate Sensual Massage (1991)............... n.a.
Playboy's 101 Ways to Excite Your Lover (1992)
...............................Cast Member
*Magazines:*
**Playgirl** (Sep 1984) .............Man of the Month
**Playgirl** (Jan 1985)................Man of the Year
**Playgirl** (Jun 1988).........The Return of Steve Rally
28-35—Nude.

# Rano, Corey

*Films:*
**Predator 2** (1990) ................. Ramon Vega
- 0:23—Buns, while hanging upside down several times.
- 0:26—Nude, hanging upside down, dead.

# Ratray, Peter

*Films:*
**Young Lady Chatterley** (1977)

. . . . . . . . . . . . . . . . . . . . . . . . . Paul (young gardener)
- • 0:37—Very brief buns, while pulling his pants up after getting caught with Janette.
- • 1:03—Buns, while making love with Harlee McBride
in the rain.
- •• 1:32—Buns, while in bed with McBride.

# Reed, Mathew

*Films:*
**Perfect** (1985). . . . . . . . . . . . . . . . . . . . . . . . . Roger
- • 1:01—Buns, while dancing in a jock strap at Chippendale's.

# Reed, Oliver

*Films:*
The Curse of the Werewolf (1961). . . . . . . . . . . . . . Leon
Oliver! (1968; British) . . . . . . . . . . . . . . . . . . . Bill Sikes
**Women in Love** (1971) . . . . . . . . . . . . . . Gerald Crich
- ••• 0:54—Nude, fighting with Alan Bates in a room in
front of a fireplace. Long scene.
The Three Musketeers (1973) . . . . . . . . . . . . . . . . .Althos
The Triple Echo (1973; British) . . . . . . . . . . . . .Sergeant
Blood in the Streets (1974; French/Italian) . Vito Cipriani
The Four Musketeers (1975) . . . . . . . . . . . . . . . . . Athos
Ten Little Indians (1975) . . . . . . . . . . . . . . . . . . Hugh
Tommy (1975; British) . . . . . . . . . . . . . . Frank Hobbs
Burnt Offerings (1976) . . . . . . . . . . . . . . . . . . . . .Ben
The Great Scout and Cathouse Thursday (1976)

. . . . . . . . . . . . . . . . . . . . . . . . . . . . . . .Joe Knox
The Big Sleep (1978; British) . . . . . . . . . . . . Eddie Mars
The Class of Miss MacMichael (1978) . . . Terence Sutton
The Prince and the Pauper (1978). . . . . . . .Miles Hendon
*a.k.a. Crossed Swords*
The Brood (1979; Canadian). . . . . . . . . . . . .Dr. Raglan
Dr. Heckyl and Mr. Hype (1980) . . . Dr. Heckyl/Mr. Hype
Condorman (1981). . . . . . . . . . . . . . . . . . . . . Krokov
Venom (1982; British) . . . . . . . . . . . . . . . . . . . .Dave
Spasms (1983; Canadian) . . . . . . . . . . . Suzanne Kincaid
The Sting II (1983) . . . . . . . . . . . . . . . Doyle Lonnegan
Black Arrow (1984) . . . . . . . . . . . . . Sir Daniel Brackley
**Castaway** (1986). . . . . . . . . . . . . . . Gerald Kingsland
- •• 1:46—Nude, doing things around the hut during
the storm.
Master of Dragonard Hill (1987) . . . . . . .Captain Shanks
Captive Rage (1988) . . . . . . . . . . . . General Belmondo
Dragonard (1988). . . . . . . . . . . . . . . . . .Captain Shanks
The Return of the Musketeers (1989) . . . . . . . . . . Athos
Skeleton Coast (1989) . . . . . . . . . . . . Captain Simpson
Edgar Allan Poe's "The House of Usher" (1990)

. . . . . . . . . . . . . . . . . . . . . . . . . . Roderick Usher
Hired to Kill (1990) . . . . . . . . . . . . . . . . . . . . . .Bartos
The Pit and the Pendulum (1991) . . . . . . . .The Cardinal
Severed Ties (1992). . . . . . . . . . . . . . .Dr. Hans Vaughan
*Miniseries:*
Christopher Columbus (1985). . . . . . . . . .Martin Pinzon
Return to Lonesome Dove (1993) . . . Gregor Dunnegan

*Made for TV Movies:*
The Lady and the Highwayman (1989) . . Sir Philip Gage

# Reems, Harry

Former adult film actor.
Is now married and selling real estate.
*Adult Films:*
**Deep Throat** (1972) . . . . . . . . . . . . . . . . . . . . . . n.a.
*Films:*
National Lampoon Goes to the Movies (1982)

. . . . . . . . . . . . . . . . . . . . . . . . . . .Vice Squad Cop
*a.k.a. Movie Madness*
R.S.V.P. (1984) . . . . . . . . . . . . . . . . . . .Grant Garrison
*Made for TV Movies:*
Dream House (1981) . . . . . . . . . . . . . . . . . . . . . Phil
*Magazines:*
**Playboy** (Aug 1973) . . . . . . . . . . . . . . . . . Porno Chic
- ••• 141—Full frontal nudity, standing outside.

# Rees, Roger

*Films:*
Star 80 (1983) . . . . . . . . . . . . . . . . . . . . .Aram Nicholas
**The Ebony Tower** (1985) . . . . . . . . . . .David Williams
- • 0:44—Buns, undressing to go skinny dipping. Long
shot.
Mountains of the Moon (1989) . . . . . . .Edgar Papworth
If Looks Could Kill (1991) . . . . . . . . . .Augustus Sternako
*a.k.a. Teen Agent*
Stop! Or My Mom Will Shoot (1992) . . . . . . . . .Parnell
Robin Hood: Men in Tights (1993)

. . . . . . . . . . . . . . . . . . . . . . . .Sheriff of Rottingham
*Made for TV Movies:*
Charles & Diana: Unhappily Ever After (1992)

. . . . . . . . . . . . . . . . . . . . . . . . . . . Prince Charles
The Tower (1993) . . . . . . . . . . . . . . . . . . . Mr. Littlehill
*TV:*
Cheers (1989-91) . . . . . . . . . . . . . . . . . Robin Colcord

# Reeves, Keanu

*Films:*
Flying (1986; Canadian). . . . . . . . . . . . . . . . . .Tommy
Youngblood (1986) . . . . . . . . . . . . . . . . . . . . . Hoover
River's Edge (1987) . . . . . . . . . . . . . . . . . . . . . . Matt
Dangerous Liaisons (1988). . . . . . . . .Chevalier Danceny
The Night Before (1988) . . . . . . . . . . Winston Connelly
Permanent Record (1988) . . . . . . . . . . .Chris Townsend
The Prince of Pennsylvania (1988) . . . .Rupert Marshetta
Bill and Ted's Excellent Adventure (1989)

. . . . . . . . . . . . . . . . . . . . Ted "Theodore" Logan
Parenthood (1989). . . . . . . . . . . . . . . . . . . . . . . Tod
I Love You to Death (1990) . . . . . . . . . . Marlon James
Tune in Tomorrow (1990) . . . . . . . . . . . Martin Loader
*a.k.a. Aunt Julia and the Scriptwriter*
Bill and Ted's Bogus Journey (1991)

. . . . . . . . . . . . . . . . . . . . Ted "Theodore" Logan
**My Own Private Idaho** (1991). . . . . . . . Scott Favor
- • 1:17—Very brief side view of buns, in quick cuts,
standing with Carmilla.

**Point Break** (1991). . . . . . . . . . . . . . . . . Johnny Utah
- 1:14—Very brief buns, while standing up to run after Tyler.

Bram Stoker's Dracula (1992) . . . . . . . Jonathan Harker
Freaked (1993) . . . . . . . . . . . . . . . . . Juan the Dog Boy
Little Buddha (1993). . . . . . . . . . . . . Prince Siddhârtha
Much Ado About Nothing (1993; British) . . . . Don John
Speed (1994) . . . . . . . . . . . . . . . . . . . . . . . Jack Traven

## Regehr, Duncan
*Films:*
The Monster Squad (1987) . . . . . . . . . . . Count Dracula
**The Banker** (1989) . . . . . . . . . . . . . . . . . . . . Osbourne
- 0:03—Buns, while getting out of bed with Teri Weigel. Don't see his face.

Gore Vidal's Billy the Kid (1989) . . . . . . . . Pat Garrett
*Made for TV Movies:*
My Wicked Ways... The Legend of Errol Flynn (1985)
. . . . . . . . . . . . . . . . . . . . . . . . . . . . . . Errol Flynn
Danielle Steel's "Once in a Lifetime" (1994)
. . . . . . . . . . . . . . . . . . . . . . . . . Justin Wakefield
*TV:*
Wizards and Warriors (1983). . . . . Prince Dirk Blackpool

## Reigrod, Jon
*Films:*
**The Boob Tube** (1975) . . . . . . . . . . . . . . . . . . Harvey
- 1:08—Buns, on sofa with Sharon and Dr. Carstairs.

## Reinhold, Judge
*Films:*
Stripes (1981) . . . . . . . . . . . . . . . . . . . . . . . . . . Elmo
Fast Times at Ridgemont High (1982) . . . Brad Hamilton
The Lords of Discipline (1983). . . . . . . . . . . Macabbee
Beverly Hills Cop (1984) . . . . . Detective Billy Rosewood
Gremlins (1984) . . . . . . . . . . . . . . . . . . . . . . Gerald
Roadhouse 66 (1984) . . . . . . . . Beckman Hallsgood, Jr.
Head Office (1986) . . . . . . . . . . . . . . . . . . . Jack Issel
Off Beat (1986) . . . . . . . . . . . . . . . . . . . . Joe Gower
Ruthless People (1986) . . . . . . . . . . . . . Ken Kessler
Beverly Hills Cop II (1987). . . . Detective Billy Rosewood
A Soldier's Tale (1988; New Zealand) . . . . . . . The Yank
Vice Versa (1988) . . . . . . . . . . . . . . . . . . Marshall
Near Mrs. (1990) . . . . . . . . . . . . . . . . . . . . . Claude
Rosalie Goes Shopping (1990) . . . . . . . . . . . . Priest
**Zandalee** (1991) . . . . . . . . . . . . . . . . Thierry Martin
••• 0:21—Buns while in bed with Zandalee.
- 0:23—Upper half of buns, while standing by the window.

Baby On Board (1992) . . . . . . . . . . . . . . . . . . Ernie
Over Her Dead Body (1992) . . . . . . . . . . . . . . Harry
*a.k.a. Enid Is Sleeping*
Bank Robber (1993) . . . . . . . . . . . . . . . Officer Gross
Beverly Hills Cop III (1994) . . . Detective Billy Rosewood
*Made for Cable Movies:*
Black Magic (1992; Showtime) . . . . . . . . . . Alex Gage
Four Eyes and Six Guns (1992; TNT) . . . . . . . . . . n.a.

## Reiser, Robert
*Films:*
**The Harrad Summer** (1974). . . . . . . . . . . . . Stanley
*a.k.a. Student Union*
- 0:57—Buns, while getting out of bed and hiding in closet.

## Rekert, Winston
*Films:*
Suzanne (1980; Canadian). . . . . . . . . . Nicky Callaghan
Heartaches (1981; Canadian). . . . . . . .Marcello Di Stassi
**Your Ticket Is No Longer Valid** (1982)
. . . . . . . . . . . . . . . . . . . . . . . Antonio Montoya
- 1:24—Buns, while in bed with Jennifer Dale.
Agnes of God (1985) . . . . . . . . . . . . . . . . . . . . . n.a.
Eternal Evil (1985; Canadian) . . . . . . . . . . . Paul Sharpe
*Made for Cable Movies:*
Glory! Glory! (1988; HBO) . . . . . . . . . . . . . . . . . n.a.

## Remar, James
*Films:*
Cruising (1980) . . . . . . . . . . . . . . . . . . . . . .Gregory
The Long Riders (1980) . . . . . . . . . . . . . . .Sam Starr
Clan of the Cave Bear (1985) . . . . . . . . . . . . . . Creb
Band of the Hand (1986) . . . . . . . . . . . . . . . .Nestor
Quiet Cool (1986) . . . . . . . . . . . . . . . . . . .Joe Dillon
Rent-a-Cop (1988) . . . . . . . . . . . . . . . . . . . Dancer
The Dream Team (1989) . . . . . . . . . . . . . . . Gianelli
Drugstore Cowboy (1989) . . . . . . . . . . . . . . Gentry
Silence Like Glass (1989) . . . . . . . . . . . . . . Charley
Tales From the Darkside, The Movie (1990) . . . . Preston
White Fang (1991). . . . . . . . . . . . . . . Beauty Smith
Confessions of a Hit Man (1992) . . . . . . . . . . . Bruno
Indecency (1992) . . . . . . . . . . . . . . . . . . . . Mick
**The Tigress** (1992). . . . . . . . . . . . . . . . . . . Andrei
•• 0:49—Buns, while getting into bathtub.
Blink (1993). . . . . . . . . . . . . . . . . .Thomas Ridgely
Fatal Instinct (1993) . . . . . . . . . . . . . . . Max Shady
*Made for Cable Movies:*
Dead Lock (1991; HBO). . . . . . . . . . . . . . . . . .Sam
Fatal Charm (1992; Showtime) . . . . . . . . . . . . Louise
*Made for Cable TV:*
The Hitchhiker: Homebodies . . . . . . . . . . . . . . Ron
Tales From the Crypt: Dead Wait (1991; HBO)
. . . . . . . . . . . . . . . . . . . . . . . . . Red Buckley
Strangers: The Last Game (1992; HBO) . . . . . . . Bernard
(Available on video tape on *Strangers*.)
*Made for TV Movies:*
Desperado: The Outlaw Wars (1989) . . . . . . . John Sikes

## Reves, Robbie
*Films:*
**Shadowzone** (1989) . . . . . . . . . . . . . . . . . . . . James
0:16—Frontal nudity long shot.
- 0:26—Frontal nudity lying under plastic bubble.

# Reynolds, Burt

Ex-husband of actress Loni Anderson.
*Films:*
Operation C.I.A. (1965) . . . . . . . . . . . . . Mark Andrews
Shark! (1969) . . . . . . . . . . . . . . . . . . . . . . . . . . . Caine
  *a.k.a. Maneaters!*
Deliverance (1972) . . . . . . . . . . . . . . . . . . . . . . Lewis
Everything You Wanted to Know About Sex, But Were
  Afraid to Ask (1972) . . . . . . . . . . . . . . . . Switchboard
Fuzz (1972). . . . . . . . . . . . . . . Detective Steve Carella
The Man Who Loved Cat Dancing (1973). . . Jay Grobart
White Lightning (1973). . . . . . . . . . . . . Gator McKlusky
The Longest Yard (1974). . . . . . . . . . . . . . . Paul Crewe
Hustle (1975) . . . . . . . . . . . . . Lieutenant Phil Gaines
Gator (1976). . . . . . . . . . . . . . . . . . . . . Gator McKlusky
Semi-Tough (1977). . . . . . . . . . . . . . Billy Clyde Puckett
Smokey and the Bandit (1977) . . . . . . . . . . . . .Bandit
The End (1978). . . . . . . . . . . . . . . . . . . Sonny Lawson
Hooper (1978) . . . . . . . . . . . . . . . . . . . Sonny Hooper
Starting Over (1979). . . . . . . . . . . . . . . . .Phil Potter
Rough Cut (1980; British) . . . . . . . . . . . . Jack Rhodes
Smokey and the Bandit II (1980). . . . . . . . . . . .Bandit
The Cannonball Run (1981) . . . . . . . . . . . . J. J. McClure
Paternity (1981) . . . . . . . . . . . . . . . . . . . . Buddy Evans
Sharky's Machine (1981). . . . . . . . . . . . . . . . . Sharky
Best Friends (1982). . . . . . . . . . . . . . . . Richard Babson
The Best Little Whorehouse in Texas (1982) . . . . Ed Earl
**The Man Who Loved Women** (1983). . David Fowler
  •• 1:25—Brief buns, while chiseling a statue after mak-
    ing love with Julie Andrews.
Smokey and the Bandit III (1983) . . . . . .The Real Bandit
Stroker Ace (1983) . . . . . . . . . . . . . . . . . . . Stroker Ace
Cannonball Run II (1984) . . . . . . . . . . . . . J. J. McClure
City Heat (1984) . . . . . . . . . . . . . . . . . . . Mike Murphy
Stick (1985) . . . . . . . . . . . . . . . . . . . . . . . . . . . Stick
Heat (1987) . . . . . . . . . . . . . . . . . . . . . . . . . . . Mex
Malone (1987) . . . . . . . . . . . . . . . . . . Richard Malone
Rent-a-Cop (1988) . . . . . . . . . . . . . . . . . . . . . Church
Breaking In (1989) . . . . . . . . . . . . . . . . Ernie Mullins
Physical Evidence (1989). . . . . . . . . . . . . . . . Joe Paris
Modern Love (1990). . . . . . . . . . . . . . . Colonel Parker
The Player (1992) . . . . . . . . . . . . . . . . . . . . . . Cameo
Cop and a Half (1993) . . . . . . . . . . . . . Nick McKenna
*Made for TV Movies:*
The Man From Left Field (1993) . . . . . . . . . . . . . . .n.a.
*TV:*
Riverboat (1959-60) . . . . . . . . . . . . . . . . . .Ben Frazer
Gunsmoke (1962-65) . . . . . . . . . . . . . . . . . Quint Asper
Hawk (1966). . . . . . . . . . . . . . . . . . . . .Lt. John Hawk
Dan August (1970-71) . . . . . . . . . . Det. Lt. Dan August
B. L. Stryker (1989-90) . . . . . . . . . . . . . . B. L. Stryker
Evening Shade (1990- ). . . . . . . . . . . . . Wood Newton
*Magazines:*
Cosmopolitan (Apr 1972) . . . . . . . . . . . . . . Centerfold

# Ribeiro, Marcelo

*Films:*
**Love Strange Love** (1982; Brazilian) . . . . Hugo (Child)
  • 0:20—Brief frontal nudity between his legs in bath-
    tub.

# Rice, Randy

*Films:*
**Pumping Iron II: The Women** (1985) . . . . . . Himself
  • 0:08—Buns in G-string, while dancing in women's
    club.

# • Richard, Pierre

*Films:*
**Tall Blond Man with One Black Shoe**
  (1973; French) . . . . . . . . . . . . . . . . . . . . . . . . .Francois
  •• 0:18—Buns, getting out of bathtub to answer the
    phone. Buns again, taking off towel and getting
    back in.
  • 0:19—Brief buns, getting out of bathtub to answer
    the phone again.

# • Richardson, John

*Films:*
**Marilyn Chambers' Bedtime Stories** (1993) . . Chris
  • 0:56—Brief buns, while making love in bed on top
    of Angelique.

# Rios, Javier

*Films:*
**Q & A** (1990) . . . . . . . . . . . . . . . . . . . . . . . . Boat Lover
  • 1:44—Brief buns, while on boat, getting pulled out
    of bed by Nick Nolte.

# Rivals, Jean Luc

*Films:*
**The Passion of Beatrice** (1988; French). . . . . . .Jehan
  • 0:57—Brief frontal nudity, getting dried off.

# Robbins, Tim

Significant Other of actress Susan Sarandon.
*Films:*
Toy Soldiers (1983) . . . . . . . . . . . . . . . . . . . . . . Bean
No Small Affair (1984) . . . . . . . . . . . . . . . . . . .Nelson
Fraternity Vacation (1985) . . . . . .Larry "Mother" Tucker
The Sure Thing (1985). . . . . . . . . . . . . . Gary Cooper
Howard the Duck (1986) . . . . . . . . . . . . . Phil Blumburtt
**Bull Durham** (1988) . . . Ebby Calvin "Nuke" La Loosh
  • 0:03—Buns, while in locker room making love with
    Millie when the coach sees them.
Five Corners (1988) . . . . . . . . . . . . . . . . . . . . .Harry
Tapeheads (1988) . . . . . . . . . . . . . . . . . . . Josh Tager
Erik the Viking (1989; British). . . . . . . . . . . . . . . Erik
Miss Firecracker (1989) . . . . . . . . . . Delmount Williams
Cadillac Man (1990) . . . . . . . . . . . . . . . . . . . . Larry
**Jacob's Ladder** (1990). . . . . . . . . . . . . . Jacob Singer
  •• 0:40—Buns, twice in bathroom, while getting ready
    for ice bath.
Jungle Fever (1991) . . . . . . . . . . . . . . . . . . . . . .Jerry

Bob Roberts (1992; U.S./British) . . . . . . . . Bob Roberts
**The Player** (1992) . . . . . . . . . . . . . . . . . . . . Griffin Mill
••• 1:46—Briefly nude, covered with mud, getting out
of mud bath.
Short Cuts (1993) . . . . . . . . . . . . . . . . .Gene Shepard
The Hudsucker Proxy (1994) . . . . . . . . . Norville Barnes
*Made for TV Movies:*
Quarterback Princess (1983) . . . . . . . . . . . . . . Marvin

## Roberts, Derrick
*Films:*
Wimps (1987) . . . . . . . . . . . . . . . . . . . . . . . . . . .n.a.
**Party Incorporated** (1989) . . . . . . . . . . . . . . . Louie
*a.k.a. Party Girls*
• 0:50—Brief buns, while undressing and showing off
at the bar.

## Roberts, Eric
Brother of actress Julia Roberts.
*Films:*
King of the Gypsies (1978) . . . . . . . . . . . . . . . . .Dave
Raggedy Man (1981) . . . . . . . . . . . . . . . . . . . . .Teddy
**Star 80** (1983) . . . . . . . . . . . . . . . . . . . Paul Snider
• 1:39—Buns, lying dead on floor, covered with blood
after shooting Dorothy, then himself.
The Pope of Greenwich Village (1984) . . . . . . . . Paulie
The Coca-Cola Kid (1985; Australian) . . . . . . . . Becker
Nobody's Fool (1986) . . . . . . . . . . . . . . . . . . . . Riley
Slow Burn (1986) . . . . . . . . . . . . . . . . . . Jacob Asch
Blood Red (1988) . . . . . . . . . . . . . . . . Marco Cologero
Rude Awakening (1989) . . . . . . . . . . . . . . . . . . Fred
The Ambulance (1990) . . . . . . . . . . . . . . . .Josh Baker
Best of the Best (1990) . . . . . . . . . . . . . . . . . . Alex
A Family Matter (1990) . . . . . . . . . . . . . Shaun McGinnis
Lonely Hearts (1991) . . . . . . . . . . . . . . . . . . . Frank
Best of the Best 2 (1992) . . . . . . . . . . . . . Alex Grady
Final Analysis (1992) . . . . . . . . . . . . . . . . Jimmy Evans
Freefall (1993) . . . . . . . . . . . . . . . . . . . . Grant Orion
The Hard Truth (1994) . . . . . . . . . Chandice Etheridge
*Made for Cable Movies:*
Descending Angel (1990; HBO) . . . . . . . . Michael Rossi
The Lost Capone (1990) . . . . . . . . . . . . . . . . . . . . Al
Love, Cheat & Steal (1993; Showtime) . . . . Reno Adams
*Made for Cable TV:*
Voyage (1993; USA) . . . . . . . . . . . . . . . . . . . . . . Gil
*Made for TV Movies:*
Fugitive Among Us (1992) . . . . . . . . . . . Cal Harper
Love, Honor & Obey: The Last Mafia Marriage (1993)
. . . . . . . . . . . . . . . . . . . . . . . . . . . . Bill Bonanno

## Robinson, David
*Films:*
**Revenge of the Cheerleaders** (1976) . . . . . . . Jordan
• 0:13—Buns when Tish plays with him while she's un-
der the counter.
Mephisto (1981; German) . . . . . . . . . . . . . . . . .n.a.
Buford's Beach Bunnies (1992)
. . . . . . . . . . . . . . . . . . .Forey, The Amazing Foreskin

## •Rohner, Clayton
*Films:*
April Fool's Day (1986) . . . . . . . . . . . . . . . . . . . Chaz
Just One of the Guys (1986) . . . . . . . . . . . . . . . . Rick
Modern Girls (1987) . . . . . . . . . . . . . Clifford/Bruno X
Bat 21 (1988) . . . . . . . . . . . Sergeant Harley Rumbaugh
Destroyer (1988) . . . . . . . . . . . . . . . . . . . .David Harris
I, Madman (1989) . . . . . . . . . . . . . . . . . . . . Richard
**Caroline at Midnight** (1993) . . . . . . . . . . . . . Jack
• 1:03—Very, very brief frontal nudity and sort of
buns, after pulling down his shorts and getting into
bathtub. Seen from above.
*TV:*
E.A.R.T.H. Force (1990) . . . . . . . . . . . . . .Dr. Carl Dana

## •Rooker, Michael
*Films:*
Henry: Portrait of a Serial Killer (1986) . . . . . . . . Henry
Above the Law (1988) . . . . . . . . . . . . . . . .Man in Bar
Eight Men Out (1988) . . . . . . . . . . . . . . Chick Gandil
Mississippi Burning (1988) . . . . . . . . . . . . Frank Bailey
Sea of Love (1989) . . . . . . . . . . . . . . . . . . . . . Terry
Days of Thunder (1990) . . . . . . . . . . . . . Rowdy Burns
JFK (1991) . . . . . . . . . . . . . . . . . . . . . . Bill Broussard
Cliffhanger (1993) . . . . . . . . . . . . . . . . . . Hal Tucker
The Dark Half (1993) . . . . . . . Sheriff Alan Pangborn
Tombstone (1993) . . . . . . . . . . . . Sherman McMasters
**The Hard Truth** (1994) . . . . . . . . . . . . . Jonah Mantz
•• 0:04—Buns, while standing in room with Lysette An-
thony.
••• 0:40—Buns, while making love with Anthony.

## Rose, Michael
*Films:*
**Breakfast in Bed** (1990) . . . . . . . . . Jonathan Maxwell
• 1:16—Half of buns, while lying in bed with Marilyn
Chambers.
*Video Tapes:*
Eden 4 (1993) . . . . . . . . . . . . . . . . . . . . . . . . . . n.a.

## Ross, Chelchie
*Films:*
On the Right Track (1981) . . . . . . . . . . . . . . Customer
**One More Saturday Night** (1986) . . . . . Dad Lundahl
• 0:39—Buns, squished against the car window in
back seat with Moira Harris.
The Untouchables (1987) . . . . . . . . . . . . . . . Reporter
Above the Law (1988) . . . . . . . . . . . . . . . . Nelson Fox
The Long Walk Home (1990) . . . . . . . . . . . . . . . . n.a.
Bill and Ted's Bogus Journey (1991) . . . . . . Colonel Oats
The Last Boy Scout (1991) . . . . . . . . . . Senator Baynard
Basic Instinct (1992) . . . . . . . . . . . . . . Captain Talcott
(Unrated Director's cut reviewed.)
Amos & Andrew (1993) . . . . . . . . . . . . . . . . . . . Earl
Rudy (1993) . . . . . . . . . . . . . . . . . . . . . . Dan Devine
*Made for Cable Movies:*
Rainbow Drive (1990; Showtime) . . . . . . . . Tom Cutter

*Made for Cable TV:*
Tales From the Crypt: Four Sided Triangle (1990; HBO)
.................................. George Yates
*Miniseries:*
The Burden of Proof (1992)......... Dr. Nate Cawley

## Ross, Willie

*Films:*
**The Cook, The Thief, His Wife & Her Lover**
(1989; Dutch/French)
.......................................Roy
0:03—Buns, while on ground covered with dog feces getting urinated on by Albert. (Talk about a bad
day!)
• 0:07—Buns, kneeling on ground while dogs walk
around.
• 0:09—Buns, while standing up.
Strike it Rich (1990).................Man at Theater

## Rossi, Leo

*Films:*
Grand Theft Auto (1977)..................... Sal
**Halloween II** (1981) ...................... Budd
• 0:48—Buns, while getting out of the whirlpool bath
to check the water temperature.
Brainwash (1982) ..................... Chris Morris
Heart Like a Wheel (1983)...........Jack Muldowney
River's Edge (1987)........................Jim
The Accused (1988) ........ Cliff "Scorpion" Albrect
Leonard, Part 6 (1988) ......................Chef
Relentless (1989)......................Sam Dietz
Fast Getaway (1990)....................... Sam
Maniac Cop 2 (1990) ......................Turkell
Too Much Sun (1990)............... George Bianco
Relentless 2: Dead On (1991) .............Sam Dietz
We're Talkin' Serious Money (1991) ......... Charlie
Relentless 3 (1992) ...................Sam Dietz
Where The Day Takes You (1992) .......... Mr. Burtis
Raw Justice (1994) ....................... Atkins
*a.k.a. Good Cop, Bad Cop*
*Made for Cable Movies:*
Rebel Highway: Reform School Girl (1994; Showtime)
............................... Disc Jockey
*Made for Cable TV:*
Rebel Highway: Runaway Daughters (1994; Showtime)
................................... Deputy 2
*TV:*
Partners in Crime (1984)..............Lt. Ed Vronsky
Tour of Duty (1988-90)................ Jake Bridger

## Rossovich, Rick

*Films:*
The Lords of Discipline (1983).................. Pig
Streets of Fire (1984)............... Officer Cooley
The Terminator (1984) .................... Matt
Warning Sign (1985)................... Bob
The Morning After (1986)................ Detective
Top Gun (1986) .....................Ron Kenner
Roxanne (1987) ..................Chris McDonell

Spellbinder (1988).................. Derek Clayton
**Paint It Black** (1989)............. Jonathan Dunbar
• 0:48—Upper half of buns while getting out of bed
with Julie Carmen.
Navy SEALS (1990) ........................Leary
Future Shock (1993)................ Frat Boy Leader
**Tropical Heat** (1993).................... Gravis
•• 0:11—Buns, several times, while in the swimming
pool with Carolyn.
•• 0:36—Buns, making love with Maryam D'Abo in waterfall.
•• 0:50—Very brief buns, while in bed on top of D'Abo.
•• 0:51—Buns, while lying on top of D'Abo in bed.
••• 0:52—Buns, getting out of bed and putting on his
pants.
*Made for Cable TV:*
**Tales From the Crypt: The Switch** (1990; HBO)
..................................... Hans
(Available on *Tales From the Crypt, Volume 3.*)
•• 0:23—Buns, while standing in front of mirror after
being transformed into a younger Carlton.
*Made for TV Movies:*
Deadly Lessons (1983) ....................Craig
The Gambler Returns: The Luck of the Draw (1991)
..................................Ethan Cassiday
*TV:*
MacGruder & Loud (1985) .................. Geller
Sons and Daughters (1990-91) ......... Spud Lincoln

## • Roundtree, Richard

*Films:*
**Shaft** (1971)......................... John Shaft
• 0:32—Brief lower half of buns, making love with a
woman. Hard to see because it is partly hidden by a
mobile. Don't see his face.
Shaft's Big Score (1972)................. John Shaft
Diamonds (1975)......................... Archie
Gypsy Angels (1980) ..................... n.a.
An Eye For an Eye (1981) ...........Captain Stevens
One Down, Two to Go (1982) ...............Ralph
Q (1982) ...................Sergeant Powell
The Big Score (1983) .................... Gordon
The Young Warriors (1983; U.S./Canadian)
................................ Sergeant John Austin
City Heat (1984) ...................... Dehl Swift
Jocks (1986)..................... Chip Williams
Opposing Force (1986) ...........Sergeant Stafford
*a.k.a. Hell Camp*
Angel III: The Final Chapter (1988). . Lieutenant Doniger
Maniac Cop (1988) ............ Commissioner Pike
Party Line (1988) .................. Captain Barnes
Crack House (1989) ............ Lieutenant Johnson
Night Visitor (1989) ............. Captain Crane
Bloodfist III: Forced to Fight (1991) ...... Samuel Stark
A Time to Die (1991) ...........Captain Ralph Phipps
Body of Influence (1992) .............. Harry Reams
(Unrated version reviewed.)
Deadly Rivals (1992) .............. Agent Peterson

Mind Twister (1992) . . . . . . . . . . . . . . . . . Frank Webb
(Unrated version reviewed.)
Amityville: A New Generation (1993) . . . . . . . . . . . .n.a.
Sins of the Night (1993) . . . . . . . . . . . . . . . . . . . . .n.a.
(Unrated version reviewed.)
*Made for TV Movies:*
Bonanza: The Return (1993) . . . . . . . . . . . . . . . .n.a.

## Rourke, Mickey

Husband of actress/model Carré Otis.
*Films:*
1941 (1979) . . . . . . . . . . . . . . . . . . . . . . . . . . . Reese
Fade to Black (1980) . . . . . . . . . . . . . . . . . . . . . . Richie
Heaven's Gate (1980) . . . . . . . . . . . . . . . . . . . . . .n.a.
Body Heat (1981) . . . . . . . . . . . . . . . . . . . . Teddy Lewis
Diner (1982) . . . . . . . . . . . . . . . . . . . . . . . . . . . Boogie
Eureka (1983; British) . . . . . . . . . . . . . . . . . . . Aurelio
Rumble Fish (1983) . . . . . . . . . . . . . . . . .Motorcycle Boy
The Year of the Dragon (1985) . . . . . . . . Stanley White
9 1/2 Weeks (1986) . . . . . . . . . . . . . . . . . . . . . . . John
**Angel Heart** (1987) . . . . . . . . . . . . . . . . Harry Angel
(Original Unedited Version reviewed.)
•• 1:28—Buns, while in bed with Lisa Bonet. Don't see
his face. It gets kind of bloody.
Barfly (1987) . . . . . . . . . . . . . . . . . . . . . . . . . . Henry
A Prayer for the Dying (1987) . . . . . . . . . Martin Fallon
Homeboy (1988) . . . . . . . . . . . . . . . . . . Johnny Walker
Johnny Handsome (1989) . . . . . . . . . . . . . . John Sedley
Desperate Hours (1990) . . . . . . . . . . .Michael Bosworth
Wild Orchid (1990) . . . . . . . . . . . . . . . . James Wheeler
Harley Davidson and The Marlboro Man (1991)
. . . . . . . . . . . . . . . . . . . . . . . . . . . Harley Davidson
White Sands (1992) . . . . . . . . . . . . . . German Lennox
*Made for Cable Movies:*
The Last Outlaw (1993; HBO) . . . . . . . . . . . . . . . .Graff
*Magazines:*
**Playgirl** (Nov 1987). . . . . . . . . . . . . . . .Raw Footage
35—Buns in stills from *Angel Heart.*

## Rowlatt, Michael

*Films:*
**Spaced Out** (1980; British) . . . . . . . . . . . . . . . Cliff
*a.k.a. Outer Touch*
• 0:42—Buns, while getting out of bed trying to get
away from Partha.

## Rubbo, Joe

*Films:*
**The Last American Virgin** (1982). . . . . . . . . . . David
• 0:45—Buns, in bed making love with Carmela while
his buddies watch through the key hole.
**Hot Chili** (1985) . . . . . . . . . . . . . . . . . . . . . . Arney
• 0:24—Brief buns while getting whipped by Brigitte.

## • Rusler, Robert

*Films:*
Weird Science (1985) . . . . . . . . . . . . . . . . . . . . . Max
Dangerously Close (1986). . . . . . . . . . . . . . . . . .n.a.

Nightmare on Elm Street 2: Freddy's Revenge (1986)
. . . . . . . . . . . . . . . . . . . . . . . . . . . . . . . . Grady
Thrashin' (1986) . . . . . . . . . . . . . . . . . . .Tommy Hook
Vamp (1986) . . . . . . . . . . . . . . . . . . . . . . . . . . . A.J.
Shag (1989) . . . . . . . . . . . . . . . . . . . . . Buzz Ravenel
**Final Embrace** (1991) . . . . . . . . . . . . . Kyle Lambdon
•• 0:05—Buns, while standing up next to bed and put-
ting his pants on.
• 1:00—Buns, while making love in bed with Laurel.
Crisis in the Kremlin (1992) . . . . . . . . . . . . . . . . n.a.
Amityville: A New Generation (1993). . . . . . . . . . Ray
*Made for TV Movies:*
Stephen King's "Sometimes They Come Back" (1991)
. . . . . . . . . . . . . . . . . . . . . . . . . . . . . . . . .n.a.
*TV:*
The Outsiders (1990) . . . . . . . . . . . . . . . . . Tim Shepard
The Outsiders (1990) . . . . . . . . . . . . . . . . . Tim Shepard
Angel Falls (1993) . . . . . . . . . . . . . . . . . . . . . . . n.a.

## Russ, Tim

*Films:*
Crossroads (1986) . . . . . . . . . . . . . . . . Robert Johnson
Spaceballs (1987). . . . . . . . . . . . . . . . . . . . . Trooper
Eve of Destruction (1991) . . . . . . . . . . . . . . . . Carter
**Night Eyes 2** (1991) . . . . . . . . . . . . . . Jesse Younger
•• 0:07—Buns, while getting out of bed and putting
his pants on.
Mr. Saturday Night (1992). . . . . . . . . .Assistant Director
*Made for Cable Movies:*
Fire With Fire (1986; Showtime). . . . . . . . . . . . . .Jerry
*TV:*
Highwayman (1987-88). . . . . . . . . . . . . . D.C. Montana

## Russell, Kurt

Significant Other of actress Goldie Hawn.
Ex-husband of actress Season Hubley.
Son of actor Bing Russell.
*Films:*
Follow Me Boys (1966) . . . . . . . . . . . . . . . . . . . .Whitey
The Horse in the Gray Flannel Suit (1968)
. . . . . . . . . . . . . . . . . . . . . . . . . . Ronnie Gardner
The Computer Wore Tennis Shoes (1969) . . . . . .Dexter
The Barefoot Executive (1971) . . . . . . . . . . Steven Post
Fool's Parade (1971). . . . . . . . . . . . . . . . Johnny Jesus
Now You See Him, Now You Don't (1972)
. . . . . . . . . . . . . . . . . . . . . . . . . . . .Dexter Riley
Charley & the Angel (1973) . . . . . . . . . . . . . .Ray Ferris
Superdad (1973) . . . . . . . . . . . . . . . . . . . . . . . . . Bart
The Strongest Man in the World (1975) . . . . . . . .Dexter
**Used Cars** (1980) . . . . . . . . . . . . . . . . . Rudy Russo
• 1:04—Very brief buns while putting on red under-
wear.
Escape from New York (1981) . . . . . . . . . . Snake Pliskin
The Thing (1982). . . . . . . . . . . . . . . . . . . . . MacReady
Silkwood (1984). . . . . . . . . . . . . . . . . . Drew Stephens
Swing Shift (1984) . . . . . . . . . . . . . . . . .Lucky Lockhart
The Mean Season (1985) . . . . . . . . . Malcolm Anderson
The Best of Times (1986) . . . . . . . . . . . Reno Hightower
Big Trouble in Little China (1986). . . . . . . . . Jack Burton

Overboard (1987) . . . . . . . . . . . . . . . . . . . Dean Proffitt
Tequila Sunrise (1988) . . . . . . . . . . . . . Lt. Nick Frescia
**Tango & Cash** (1989) . . . . . . . . . . . . . . . . . . . . . Cash
- •• 0:31—Brief buns while walking into the prison shower room with Sylvester Stallone.

Winter People (1989) . . . . . . . . . . . . . Wayland Jackson
Backdraft (1991) . . . . . . . . . . . . . . . . Stephen McCaffrey
Captain Ron (1992) . . . . . . . . . . . . . . . . . Captain Ron
Unlawful Entry (1992) . . . . . . . . . . . . . . . Michael Carr
Tombstone (1993) . . . . . . . . . . . . . . . . . . Wyatt Earp
*Made for TV Movies:*
The Quest (1976) . . . . . . . . . . . . . . . . . . . . Morgan
*TV:*
The Travels of Jamie McPheeters (1963-64) . . . . . . Jamie

## • Russell, Leigh
*Films:*
**Romper Stomper** (1993; Australian) . . . . . . Sonny Jim
- • 0:40—Brief buns, while mooning the Asian guys chasing him and his buddies.

## Russo, James
*Films:*
Fast Times at Ridgemont High (1982) . . . . . . . . Robber
A Stranger is Watching (1982) . . . . . Ronald Thompson
Vortex (1982) . . . . . . . . . . . . . . . . . . . Anthony Demmer
Exposed (1983) . . . . . . . . . . . . . . . . . . . . . . . . . . Nick
Beverly Hills Cop (1984) . . . . . . . . . . . . Mikey Tandino
The Cotton Club (1984) . . . . . . . . . . . . . . . Vince Hood
Once Upon a Time in America (1984) . . . . . . . . . Bugsy
(Long version reviewed.)
Extremities (1986) . . . . . . . . . . . . . . . . . . . . . . . . Joe
China Girl (1987) . . . . . . . . . . . . . . . . . . . . . . . Alby
The Blue Iguana (1988) . . . . . . . . . . . . . . . . . . . Reno
Freeway (1988) . . . . . . . . . . . . . . . . . . . Frank Quinn
We're No Angels (1989) . . . . . . . . . . . . . . . . . Bobby
**Cold Heaven** (1990) . . . . . . . . . . . . . . Daniel Corvin
- • 0:02—Buns, while standing at window, putting on underwear. Long shot.
- • 1:15—Brief buns while in bed with Theresa Russell.

Illicit Behavior (1991) . . . . . . . . . . . . . . . . . Bill Tanner
(Unrated version reviewed.)
A Kiss Before Dying (1991) . . . . . . . . . . . . . Dan Corelli
My Own Private Idaho (1991) . . . . . . . . . Richard Waters
Da Vinci's War (1992) . . . . . . . . . . . . . . . . . . . Mintz
Trauma (1992) . . . . . . . . . . . . . . . . . . . Captain Travis
Dangerous Game (1993) . . . . . . . . . . . . . . Frank Burns
(Unrated version reviewed.)
Bad Girls (1994) . . . . . . . . . . . . . . . . . . . Kid Jarrett
*Made for Cable Movies:*
Intimate Strangers (1991; Showtime) . . . . . Nick Ciccini
*Made for TV Movies:*
Desperate Rescue: The Cathy Mahone Story (1993)
. . . . . . . . . . . . . . . . . . . . . . . . . . . . Don Feeney

## Rust, Richard
*Films:*
**The Student Nurses** (1970) . . . . . . . . . . . . . . . . . Les
*a.k.a. Young LA Nurses*
- • 0:43—Buns, while lying in sand with Barbara Leigh.

The Last Movie (1971) . . . . . . . . . . . . . . . . . . . . Pisco
Kid Blue (1973) . . . . . . . . . . . . . . . . . Train Robber
The Great Gundown (1976) . . . . . . . . . . . . . . . Joe Riles

## Ryan, Eric
*Films:*
**The Bikini Carwash Company** (1992) . . . . . . Stanley
(Unrated version reviewed.)
- • 1:15—Buns, when Sunny yanks his short pants down.

## Rydell, Christopher
*Films:*
Gotcha! (1985) . . . . . . . . . . . . . . . . . . . Bob Jensen
Mask (1985) . . . . . . . . . . . . . . . . . High School Student
The Sure Thing (1985) . . . . . . . . . . . . . . . . . . . Charlie
The Check is in the Mail (1986) . . . . . . . . Drunken Sailor
**Blood and Sand** (1989; Spanish) . . . . . . . . . . . . Juan
- • 0:15—Buns, while running away after fighting bull. Dark, long shot.
- •• 0:18—Buns, seen between shower curtain when Sharon Stone watches.
- • 1:05—Buns, while on top of Stone. Long shot.

How I Got Into College (1989) . . . . . . . . . . . . . Oliver
Listen to Me (1989) . . . . . . . . . . . . . . . . . Tom Lloynd
Under the Boardwalk (1989) . . . . . . . . . . . . . . Tripper
Side Out (1990) . . . . . . . . . . . . . . . . . Wiley Hunter
For the Boys (1991) . . . . . . . . . . . . . . . . . . . Danny
Trauma (1992) . . . . . . . . . . . . . . . . . David Parsons
Flesh and Bone (1993) . . . . . . . . . . . . . . Resse Davies
*Made for TV Movies:*
In the Deep Woods (1992) . . . . . . . . . . . . . . . Tommy

## • Sabol, Dick
*Films:*
**Cotton Comes to Harlem** (1970) . . . . . . . . . . . Jarema
- ••• 0:31—Buns, in bedroom with Judy Pace, then running after her and getting caught in hallway outside of locked apartment.

Lady Liberty (1972; Italian/French) . . . . . . . . Colleague

## Sadler, William
*Films:*
**Die Hard 2** (1990) . . . . . . . . . . . . . . . Colonel Stuart
- •• 0:02—Buns, while exercising in hotel room before leaving for the airport.

Hard to Kill (1990) . . . . . . . . . . . . . . . . . Vernon Trent
The Hot Spot (1990) . . . . . . . . . . . . . . . Frank Sutton
Bill and Ted's Bogus Journey (1991)
. . . . . . . . . . . . . Grim Reaper/English Family Member
Rush (1991) . . . . . . . . . . . . . . . . . . . . . . . Monroe
Trespass (1992) . . . . . . . . . . . . . . . . . . . . . . . Don
Freaked (1993) . . . . . . . . . . . . . . . . . . . Dick Brian

*Made for TV Movies:*
Jack Reed: Badge of Honor (1993) . . . . . . . . . . . . .n.a.
Bermuda Grace (1994) . . . . . . . . . . . . . . . . . . . . . .n.a.

## Sador, Daniel

*Films:*
Sugar Cookies (1973) . . . . . . . . . . . . . . . . . . . . . . .Gus
    0:37—Buns while in bed with Dola, then running
    around.

## • Salinger, Matt

Son of writer J.D. Salinger.
*Films:*
**Revenge of the Nerds** (1984) . . . . . . . . . . . . . Burke
  • 0:46—Brief buns, while mooning the nerds from
    back of flatbed truck. (He's the guy on the right.)
Power (1986) . . . . . . . . . . . . . . . . . . . . Phillip Aarons
Captain America (1990)
 . . . . . . . . . . . . . . . . . Steve Rogers/Captain America
Firehawk (1992) . . . . . . . . . . . . . . . . . . . . . . . . . . .Tex
*TV:*
One Life to Live (1983) . . . . . . . . . . . . . . . . . . . .n.a.
Picket Fences (1993) . . . . . . . . . . . . . . . . . . . . . .n.a.
Second Chances (1993-94) . . . . . . . . . . . . . . . . .n.a.

## Sands, Julian

*Films:*
The Killing Fields (1984) . . . . . . . . . . . . . . . . . . Swain
Oxford Blues (1984) . . . . . . . . . . . . . . . . . . . . . . Colin
The Doctor and the Devils (1985) . . . . . . . . Dr. Murray
**Gothic** (1986; British) . . . . . . . . . . . . . . . . . . . Shelley
  •• 0:17—Buns, while standing on roof in the rain.
**A Room with a View** (1986; British)
 . . . . . . . . . . . . . . . . . . . . . . . . . . . . .George Emerson
  ••• 1:05—Nude running around with Freddy and Mr.
    Beebe in the woods. Lots of frontal nudity.
Siesta (1987) . . . . . . . . . . . . . . . . . . . . . . . . . . . . Kit
Vibes (1988) . . . . . . . . . . . . . . . . . . . Dr. Harrison Steele
**Blackwater** (1989) . . . . . . . . . . . . . . . . . . . . Wolfgang
  •• 1:00—Buns, while standing and talking to Stacey
    Dash.
Arachnophobia (1990) . . . . . . . . . . . Dr. James Atherton
Warlock (1990) . . . . . . . . . . . . . . . . . . . . . . . . Warlock
Grand Isle (1991) . . . . . . . . . . . . . . . . . . .Alcee Ambin
**Husbands and Lovers** (1991; Italian) . . . . . . . . .Stefan
  (Unrated version reviewed.)
  ••• 0:32—Frontal nudity, in the shower and getting out.
  ••• 0:35—Frontal nudity, getting into bed.
  ••• 1:13—Nude, taking a shower then getting out.
  •• 1:17—Very brief frontal nudity after making love
    with Joanna.
Impromptu (1991) . . . . . . . . . . . . . . . . . . . . . . . Liszt
Naked Lunch (1991) . . . . . . . . . . . . . . . . .Yves Cloquet
The Turn of the Screw (1992; British) . . . . . .Mr. Cooper
**Boxing Helena** (1993) . . . . . . . . . Dr. Nick Cavanaugh
  • 1:00—Brief buns, putting his pants on after Anne
    tries to get him excited.
  • 1:23—Buns, while making love with Fantasy Lover/
    Nurse.

Tale of a Vampire (1993) . . . . . . . . . . . . . . . . . .n.a.
Warlock: The Armageddon (1993) . . . . . . . . . .Warlock
*Made for Cable Movies:*
Crazy in Love (1992; TNT) . . . . . . . . . . . . . . . . .n.a.
*Made for TV Movies:*
Murder by Moonlight (1989) . . . . . . . . . . . . . . .n.a.
*Magazines:*
**Playboy** (Nov 1986) . . . . . . . . . . Sex in Cinema 1986
  • 128—Buns, in photo from *A Room with a View*. Kind
    of blurry.

## Sanville, Michael

*Films:*
**The First Turn-On!** (1983) . . . . . . . . . . . . . . . . Mitch
  • 1:18—Buns, while in cave orgy scene on top of An-
    nie.

## Sarafian, Deran

*Films:*
**10 to Midnight** (1983) . . . . . . . . . . . . . .Dale Anders
  • 0:08—Buns, while making love in van with Betty.

## Sarandon, Chris

Ex-husband of actress Susan Sarandon.
*Films:*
Dog Day Afternoon (1975) . . . . . . . . . . . . . . . . Leon
**Lipstick** (1976) . . . . . . . . . . . . . . . . . . .Gordon Stuart
  •• 0:50—Buns, while standing in his studio talking to
    Margaux Hemingway on the telephone.
The Sentinel (1977) . . . . . . . . . . . . . . . .Michael Lerman
Cuba (1979) . . . . . . . . . . . . . . . . . . . . . . Juan Polido
The Osterman Weekend (1983) . . . . . . .Joseph Cardone
Protocol (1984) . . . . . . . . . . . . . . . . Michael Ransome
Fright Night (1985) . . . . . . . . . . . . . . . . .Jerry Dandridge
The Princess Bride (1987) . . . . . . . . .Prince Humperdinck
Child's Play (1988) . . . . . . . . . . . . . . . . . Mike Norris
Collision Course (1989) . . . . . . . . . . . . . . . . Madras
Slaves of New York (1989) . . . . . . . . . . . .Victor Okrent
Whispers (1989) . . . . . . . . . . . . . . . . . .Detective Tony
The Resurrected (1990; British)
 . . . . . . . . . . . . . .Charles Dexter Ward/Joseph Curwen
Dark Tide (1993) . . . . . . . . . . . . . . . . . . . . . . . . Tim
*Made for TV Movies:*
Mayflower Madam (1987) . . . . . . . . . . . . . . . . Matt
A Murderous Affair: The Carolyn Warmus Story (1992)
 . . . . . . . . . . . . . . . . . . . . . . . . . . . . . . . . . . . . .n.a.
David's Mother (1994) . . . . . . . . . . . . . . . . . . .Philip

## Savage, John

*Films:*
**The Killing Kind** (1973) . . . . . . . . . . . Terry Lambert
  • 0:00—Upper half of buns when other guys pull his
    shorts down during rape of girl.
  •• 0:58—Buns while in shower when Mrs. Lambert
    opens the curtains to take a picture.
The Deer Hunter (1978) . . . . . . . . . . . . . . . .Steven
Hair (1979) . . . . . . . . . . . . . . . . . . . . . . . . . .Claude

**Cattle Annie and Little Britches** (1980)
. . . . . . . . . . . . . . . . . . . . . . . . . Bittercreek Newcomb
- 0:38—Brief buns, running and jumping into lake.
- 0:40—Buns, climbing on rocks. Long, long shot.

The Amateur (1982) . . . . . . . . . . . . . . . . . Charles Heller
The Beat (1986) . . . . . . . . . . . . . . . . . . . Frank Ellsworth
Hotel Colonial (1988) . . . . . . . . . . . . . . . . Marco Venieri
Do the Right Thing (1989) . . . . . . . . . . . . . . . . Clifton
The Godfather, Part III (1990) . . . . . . . . Andrew Hagen
Hunting (1990; Australian) . . . . . . . . . Michael Bergman
Primary Motive (1992) . . . . . . . . . . . . Wallace Roberts
CIA II: Target Alexa (1993) . . . . . . . . . . . . . . Kluge
Killing Obsession (1994) . . . . . . . . . . . . . . . . . . Albert
*Made for TV Movies:*
All the Kind Strangers (1974) . . . . . . . . . . . . . . . n.a.

# • Scandlin, Rick
*Films:*
**Hollywood Dreams** (1993) . . . . . . . . . . . . . . . . Lou
(Unrated version reviewed.)
•• 0:21—Buns, while taking off his shorts outside with Sara, then making love.

# • Schafer, John Clayton
*Films:*
Lights Out. . . . . . . . . . . . . . . . . . . . . . . . . . . . . . n.a.
**Return to Two Moon Junction** (1993). . . Jake Gilbert
••• 0:59—Buns, while making love with Savannah.
*TV:*
Seaquest DSV . . . . . . . . . . . . . . . . . . . . . . . . . . n.a.

# • Scheider, Roy
*Films:*
The Seven-Ups . . . . . . . . . . . . . . . . . . Buddy Manucci
Sorceror . . . . . . . . . . . . . . . . . . . . . . . . Jackie Scanlon
The French Connection (1971) . . . . . . . . . Buddy Russo
Klute (1971) . . . . . . . . . . . . . . . . . . . . . Frank Ligourin
Jaws (1975). . . . . . . . . . . . . . . Police Chief Martin Brody
Marathon Man (1976) . . . . . . . . . . . . . . . Doc Levy
Jaws II (1978) . . . . . . . . . . . . . Police Chief Martin Brody
**All That Jazz** (1979) . . . . . . . . . . . . . . . . Joe Gideon
- 1:42—Very brief partial buns while wearing open back hospital gown and dancing around in basement.
- 1:47—Very brief buns in hospital gown while getting escorted out of the cafeteria.

The Last Embrace (1979). . . . . . . . . . . . . Harry Hannan
Still of the Night (1982) . . . . . . . . . . . . . . . . Sam Rice
Blue Thunder (1983). . . . . . . . . . . . . . . . . . . Murphy
2010 (1984) . . . . . . . . . . . . . . . . . . . . Heywood Floyd
52 Pick-Up (1986). . . . . . . . . . . . . . . . . Harry Mitchell
The Men's Club (1986) . . . . . . . . . . . . . . . Cavanaugh
Cohen and Tate (1989). . . . . . . . . . . . . . . . . . Cohen
Listen to Me (1989) . . . . . . . . . . . . . . Charlie Nichols
Night Game (1989) . . . . . . . . . . . . . . . . . . . . . . n.a.
The Fourth War (1990) . . . . . . . . . Colonel Jack Knowles
The Russia House (1990). . . . . . . . . . . . . . . . Russell
Naked Lunch (1991). . . . . . . . . . . . . . . . Dr. Benway
Romeo Is Bleeding (1994). . . . . . . . . . . . . Don Falcone

*Made for Cable Movies:*
Tiger Town (1984; Disney). . . . . . . . . . . . . . . . . . n.a.
Somebody Has to Shoot the Picture (1990; HBO) . . n.a.
*TV:*
Seaquest DSV (1993- ) . . . . . . . . Capt. Nathan Bridger

# Schneider, John
*Films:*
**Eddie Macon's Run** (1983) . . . . . . . . . . Eddie Macon
- 0:15—Brief left side view of buns when beginning to cross the stream. Dark, hard to see.

Cocaine Wars (1986) . . . . . . . . . . . . . . . . . . . . Cliff
*a.k.a. Vice Wars*
The Curse (1987). . . . . . . . . . . . . . . . . . . . Carl Willis
Ministry of Vengeance (1989) . . . . . . . . . David Miller
Speed Zone (1989) . . . . . . . . . . . . . . . Cannonballer
*Made for TV Movies:*
Dream House (1981) . . . . . . . . . . . . . . Charlie Cross
Highway Heartbreaker (1992) . . . . . . . . . . . . . . n.a.
Desperate Journey: The Allison Wilcox Story (1993)
. . . . . . . . . . . . . . . . . . . . . . . . . . . . . . . . . . . Eddie
*TV:*
The Dukes of Hazzard (1979-85) . . . . . . . . . . Bo Duke
Heaven Help Us (1994- ) . . . . . . . . . . . . Doug Monroe

# • Schoffield, Dean
*Films:*
**Double Exposure** (1993). . . . . . . . . . . . Maria's Lover
•• 0:05—Buns, while making love with Jennifer Gatti in B&W.
•• 0:40—Buns, while making love in bed on top of Gatti in B&W.

# Schott, Bob
*Films:*
**The Working Girls** (1973) . . . . . . . . . . . . . . Roger
- 0:07—Buns, while getting out of bed to meet Honey.

Force Five (1981). . . . . . . . . . . . . . . . . . . . . . . Carl
Bloodfist III: Forced to Fight (1991) . . . . . . . Weird Willy
Out for Blood (1992) . . . . . . . . . . . . . . . . Mad Biker
In the Line of Fire (1993) . . . . . . . . . Jimmy Hendrickson

# Schwarzenegger, Arnold
Husband of Kennedy clan member/news reporter Maria Shriver.
*Films:*
Hercules in New York (1969) . . . . . . . . . . . Hercules
*a.k.a. Hercules Goes Bananas*
The Long Goodbye (1973). . . . . . . . . . . . . . Hoods
Stay Hungry (1976) . . . . . . . . . . . . . . . . . Joe Santo
Pumping Iron (1977) . . . . . . . . . . . . . . . . . Himself
The Villain (1979). . . . . . . . . . . . . Handsome Stranger
Conan the Barbarian (1982). . . . . . . . . . . . . . Conan
Conan the Destroyer (1984). . . . . . . . . . . . . . Conan
**The Terminator** (1984). . . . . . . . . . . The Terminator
••• 0:03—Buns, while kneeling by garbage truck, walking to look at the city and walking toward the three punks at night.

Commando (1985) . . . . . . . . . . . . . . . . . . . . . . . Matrix
Red Sonja (1985) . . . . . . . . . . . . . . . . . . . . . . Kalidor
Raw Deal (1986) . . . . . . . . . . . . . . . . . Mark Kaminsky
Predator (1987) . . . . . . . . . . . . . Major Dutch Schaefer
The Running Man (1987) . . . . . . . . . . . . . Ben Richards
**Red Heat** (1988) . . . . . . . . . . . . . . . . . . . Ivan Danko
 •• 0:02—Buns while in the sauna and outside fighting
 in the snow.
Twins (1988). . . . . . . . . . . . . . . . . . . Julius Benedict
Kindergarten Cop (1990) . . . . . . . . . . . . . . . Kimble
Total Recall (1990) . . . . . . . . . . . . . . . . . Doug Quaid
Terminator 2: Judgement Day (1991) . . . The Terminator
Beretta's Island (1993). . . . . . . . . . . . . . . . . Himself
Dave (1993) . . . . . . . . . . . . . . . . . . . . . . . . . Himself
Last Action Hero (1993) . . . . . . . . . . . . . . . Jack Slater
True Lies (1994) . . . . . . . . . . . . . . . . . Harry Tasker
*Made for TV Movies:*
The Jayne Mansfield Story (1980) . . . . . Mickey Hargitay
*Music Videos:*
You Could Be Mine/Guns N' Roses (1991). . . Terminator
*Magazines:*
Playboy (Sep 1976). . . . . . . . . . . . . . . . . . . . Grapevine
**Playboy** (Jan 1993) . . . . . . . . . . . . . . . The Year in Sex
 ••• 151—Full frontal nudity in old B&W bodybuilding
 photo that was published in the March 1992 issue of
 *Spy* magazine.

## Scofield, Dean
*Films:*
Animal Instincts 2 (1993) . . . . . . . . . . . . . . . . . . David
*Video Tapes:*
**Eden 2** (1992) . . . . . . . . . . . . . . . . . . . . . Paul Murdoch
 • 0:57—Buns, while making love on top of Juliet in
 bed.
Eden 3 (1993). . . . . . . . . . . . . . . . . . . . Paul Murdoch
**Eden 6** (1994) . . . . . . . . . . . . . . . . . . . . Paul Murdoch
 •• 2:17—Brief buns, while making love with Eve on ta-
 ble.

## Scorpio, Bernie
Identical twin brother of Lennie Scorpio.
*Films:*
**Video Vixens** (1973). . . . . . . . . . . . . . . . Turnip Twin
 ••• 1:05—Frontal nudity standing next to his identical
 twin brother after their trial.

## Scorpio, Lennie
Identical twin brother of Bernie Scorpio.
*Films:*
**Video Vixens** (1973). . . . . . . . . . . . . . . . Turnip Twin
 •• 1:03—Frontal nudity, then buns while on top of victim in bed.
 ••• 1:05—Frontal nudity standing next to his identical
 twin brother after their trial.

## Scott, Campbell
Son of actress Colleen Dewhurst and actor George C.
 Scott.
*Films:*
Five Corners (1988) . . . . . . . . . . . . . . . . . . . . . . . Cop
Longtime Companion (1990). . . . . . . . . . . . . . . . Willy
The Sheltering Sky (1990) . . . . . . . . . . . . . . . Turner
Dead Again (1991). . . . . . . . . . . . . . . . . . . . . . Doug
**Dying Young** (1991) . . . . . . . . . . . . . . Victor Geddes
 • 1:04—Brief buns, after running out of the house
 wrapped in a blanket and tossing it off. Long shot.
singles (1992) . . . . . . . . . . . . . . . . . . . . . . . . . Steve
*Made for TV Movies:*
The Perfect Tribute (1991) . . . . . . . . . . . . . . . . n.a.

## Scuddamore, Simon
*Films:*
**Slaughter High** (1986) . . . . . . . . . . . . . . . . . . Marty
 • 0:05—Nude in girl's shower room when his classmates pull a prank on him.

## Segado, Alberto
*Films:*
**Two to Tango** (1988) . . . . . . . . . . . . . . . . Lucky Lara
 • 0:29—Buns while on top of Adrienne Sachs, making
 love with her in bed.

## Selby, David
*Films:*
Night of Dark Shadows (1971)
 . . . . . . . . . . . . . . . . . . . . . . Quentin/Charles Collins
Up the Sandbox (1972) . . . . . . . . . . . . . Paul Reynolds
**The Girl in Blue** (1973; Canadian). . . . . . . . . . . Scott
 *a.k.a. U-turn*
 • 0:10—Brief buns while getting out of bed and put-
 ting on pants. Dark.
 0:44—Left half of buns while in shower.
 •• 1:14—Buns, while walking into the bathroom.
Super Cops (1974) . . . . . . . . . . . . . . . . . . . Bob Hantz
Rich Kids (1979). . . . . . . . . . . . . . . . . . . . Steve Sloan
Raise the Titanic (1980; British) . . . . . Dr. Gene Seagram
Rich and Famous (1981) . . . . . . . . . . . . . . Doug Blake
Dying Young (1991). . . . . . . . . . . . . . . Richard Geddes
Intersection (1993). . . . . . . . . . . . . . . Richard Quarry
*Made for TV Movies:*
Grave Secrets: The Legacy of Hilltop Drive (1992)
 . . . . . . . . . . . . . . . . . . . . . . . . . . . . Shag Williams
*TV:*
Dark Shadows . . . . . . . . . . . . . . . . . . . . . . . Quentin
Flamingo Road (1981-82) . . . . . . . . . . Michael Tyrone
Falcon Crest (1982-86). . . . . . . . . . . Richard Channing

## Selleck, Tom
*Films:*
The Seven Minutes (1971) . . . . . . . . . . . . . Phil Sanford
Terminal Island (1973) . . . . . . . . . . . Dr. Norman Milford
Coma (1978) . . . . . . . . . . . . . . . . . . . . . . . . . . Sean
High Road to China (1983) . . . . . . . . . . . . . O'Malley

**Lassiter** (1984) . . . . . . . . . . . . . . . . . . . . . . . . Lassiter
- 1:00—Buns, while getting out of bed after making love with Lauren Hutton.

Runaway (1984) . . . . . . . . . . . . . . . . . . . . . . . . Ramsay
Three Men and a Baby (1987) . . . . . . . . . . . . . . . . Peter
Her Alibi (1989) . . . . . . . . . . . . . . . . . Phil Blackwood
An Innocent Man (1989) . . . . . . . . . . Jimmy Rainwood
Quigley Down Under (1990) . . . . . . . Matthew Quigley
Three Men and a Little Lady (1990) . . . . . . . . . . . Peter
Christopher Columbus: The Discovery (1992; U.S./
  Spanish) . . . . . . . . . . . . . . . . . . . . . King Ferdinand
Folks! (1992) . . . . . . . . . . . . . . . . . . . . . . . . Jon Aldrich
**Mr. Baseball** (1992) . . . . . . . . . . . . . . . . . . . Jack Elliot
- ••• 0:03—Buns and partial pubic hair, while holding his clothes against his crotch while sneaking out of co-ed's bed.
- •• 0:23—Upper half of buns, after taking off towel. Buns and partial pubic hair (medium long shot), while sitting in tub.
- 1:19—Brief buns, taking off towel and sitting down in washing off area.

*Miniseries:*
The Sacketts (1979) . . . . . . . . . . . . . . . . . Orrin Sackett
*Made for TV Movies:*
The Shadow Riders (1982) . . . . . . . . . . . . . Mac Traven
*TV:*
The Young and the Restless (1974-75) . . . . Jed Andrews
The Rockford Files (1979-80) . . . . . . . . . . . Lance White
Magnum P.I. (1980-88) . . . . . . . . . . . Thomas Magnum

## Serbedzija, Rade
*Films:*
Hanna's War (1988) . . . . . . . . . . . . . . . . . Captain Ivan
**Manifesto** (1988) . . . . . . . . . . . . . . . . . . . . . . Emile
- 0:18—Buns, while under sheet and getting out of bed.

## Serna, Pepe
*Films:*
The Student Nurses (1970) . . . . . . . . . . . . . . . . . . . Luis
  *a.k.a. Young LA Nurses*
Group Marriage (1972) . . . . . . . . . . . . . . . . . . Ramon
The New Centurions (1972) . . . . . . . . . . Young Mexican
Hangup (1974) . . . . . . . . . . . . . . . . . . . . . . . Enrique
**The Day of the Locust** (1975) . . . . . . . . . . . . Miguel
- 2:01—Buns while on top of Karen Black, then buns while jumping out of bed.
**The Killer Inside Me** (1975) . . . . . . . . . Johnny Lopez
- 0:15—Brief upper half of buns, twice, getting strip searched at police station.
- •• 0:16—Very, very brief frontal nudity getting restrained by policemen.
Car Wash (1976) . . . . . . . . . . . . . . . . . . . . . . Chuco
Swashbuckler (1976) . . . . . . . . . . . . . Street Entertainer
The Jerk (1979) . . . . . . . . . . . . . . . . . . . . . . Punk #1
Walk Proud (1979) . . . . . . . . . . . . . . . . . . . . . Cesar
Honeysuckle Rose (1980) . . . . . . . . . . . . . . . . Rooster
Inside Moves (1980) . . . . . . . . . . . . . . . . . . . Herrada
Vice Squad (1982) . . . . . . . . . . . . . . . . . Pete Mendez

Deal of the Century (1983) . . . . . . . . . . . . . . . Vardis
Heartbreaker (1983) . . . . . . . . . . . . . . . . . . . . . . Loco
Scarface (1983) . . . . . . . . . . . . . . . . . . . . . . . . . Angel
The Adventures of Buckaroo Banzai, Across the 8th
  Dimension (1984) . . . . . . . . . . . . . . . . Reno Nevada
Red Dawn (1984) . . . . . . . . . . . . . . . Aardvark's Father
Fandango (1985) . . . . . . . . . Gas Station Mechanic
Silverado (1985) . . . . . . . . . . . . . . . . . . . . . . . Scruffy
Out of Bounds (1987) . . . . . . . . . . . . . . . . . . . Murano
Postcards from the Edge (1990) . . . . . . . . . . . . . Raoul
The Rookie (1990) . . . . . . . . . . . . . . . Lt. Ray Garcia
American Me (1992) . . . . . . . . . . . . . . . . . . . . Mundo
Only You (1992) . . . . . . . . . . . . . . . . . . Dock Official
*TV:*
Second Chances (1993- ) . . . . . . . . . . . . . . . . . . . . Sal
Hotel Malibu (1994- ) . . . . . . . . . . . . . . . . . . . . . . Sal
*Magazines:*
**Playboy** (Nov 1975) . . . . . . . . . . Sex in Cinema 1975
- 140—Buns, in grainy photo from *The Day of the Locust*.

## Shane, Michael Jay
*Films:*
Click: Calendar Girl Killer (1989) . . . . . . . . . . . . . Jessie
**Savage Beach** (1989) . . . . . . . . . . . . . Shane Abeline
- •• 0:08—Buns, while getting out of pool.
Guns (1990) . . . . . . . . . . . . . . . . . . . . . Shane Abilene
**Do or Die** (1991) . . . . . . . . . . . . . . . . Shane Abeline
- ••• 1:10—Buns, while making love with Atlanta, outside at night.
Fit To Kill (1993) . . . . . . . . . . . . . . . . . Shane Abilene
Hard Hunted (1993) . . . . . . . . . . . . . . . Shane Abilene
*Video Tapes:*
Playboy's 101 Ways to Excite Your Lover (1992)
  . . . . . . . . . . . . . . . . . . . . . . . . . . . . Cast Member
*Magazines:*
**Playgirl** (Sep 1988) . . . . . . . . . . . Man for September
- 44-51—Frontal nudity, side view of buns.

## Shannon, George
*Films:*
**Sugar Cookies** (1973) . . . . . . . . . . . . . . . . . . . . Max
- •• 0:14—Buns, while on top of Mary Woronov in bed.
**Indecent Behavior** (1993) . . . . . . . . . . Fredric Lang
  (Unrated version reviewed.)
- 0:07—Side view of buns, while making love with Carol.

## Sharkey, Ray
*Films:*
The Lords of Flatbush (1974) . . . . . . . . . . . . . Student
Trackdown (1976) . . . . . . . . . . . . . . . . . . . . . . Flash
Stunts (1977) . . . . . . . . . . . . . . . . . . . . . . . . Pauley
Paradise Alley (1978) . . . . . . . . . . . . . . . . . . . . Legs
Who'll Stop the Rain? (1978) . . . . . . . . . . . . . Smitty
Heart Beat (1979) . . . . . . . . . . . . . . . . . . . . . . . . Ira
The Idolmaker (1980) . . . . . . . . . . . . Vince Vacarddi
Love and Money (1980) . . . . . . . . . . . . . . Byron Levin

**Willie and Phil** (1980) . . . . . . . . . . . . . . . . . . . . .Phil
  •• 1:45—Buns, while getting into the hot tub. (He's on
    the right.)
Some Kind of Hero (1982) . . . . . . . . . . . . . . . . .Vinnie
Body Rock (1984) . . . . . . . . . . . . . . . . . . . . . . Terrence
Hellhole (1985). . . . . . . . . . . . . . . . . . . . . . . . . . Silk
Wise Guys (1986) . . . . . . . . . . . . . . . . . . . . . . .Marco
Private Investigations (1987) . . . . . . . . . . . . . . . .n.a.
The Capone (1989). . . . . . . . . . . . . . . . . . . .Al Capone
*a.k.a. Revenge of Al Capone*
(Originally a Made for TV Movie.)
**Scenes from the Class Struggle in Beverly Hills**
(1989). . . . . . . . . . . . . . . . . . . . . . . . . . . . . . . Frank
  • 1:10—Brief buns while sleeping in bed with Zandra.
**Act of Piracy** (1990). . . . . . . . . . . . . . . . . .Jack Wilcox
  • 0:33—Brief side view of buns while on top of Laura
    in bed.
  •• 0:35—Brief buns, while getting out of bed and put-
    ting on robe.
The Rain Killer (1990) . . . . . . . . . . . . . . . . Vince Capra
Relentless 2: Dead On (1991) . . . . . . . . . . . Kyle Volsone
**Caged Fear** (1992) . . . . . . . . . . . . . . . . . .Warden Hayes
  • 0:44—Buns, while lying dead on ground when po-
    lice are checking the crime scene. Don't see his face.
Round Trip to Heaven (1992) . . . . . . . . . . . . Stoneface
Zebrahead (1992). . . . . . . . . . . . . . . . . . Richard Glass
Cop and a Half (1993) . . . . . . . . . . . . . . . .Fountain
*Made for TV Movies:*
In the Line of Duty: Street War (1992)
. . . . . . . . . . . . . . . . . . . . . . Detective Victor Tomasino
*TV:*
Wiseguy (1987). . . . . . . . . . . . . . . . . Sonny Steelgrave
Man in the Family (1991) . . . . . . . . . . . . . . . . . . Sal

## Shea, John
*Films:*
**Hussy** (1980; British) . . . . . . . . . . . . . . . . . . . . . .Emory
  •• 0:29—Buns while making love with Helen Mirren in
    bed. Half of lower frontal nudity when she rolls off
    him.
Missing (1982) . . . . . . . . . . . . . . . . . . Charles Horman
Windy City (1984). . . . . . . . . . . . . . . . . . Danny Morgan
Unsettled Land (1987) . . . . . . . . . . . . . . . . . . . . .n.a.
A New Life (1988) . . . . . . . . . . . . . . . . . . . . . . Doc
Harlequin Romance: Magic Moments (1989)
. . . . . . . . . . . . . . . . . . . . . . . . . . . . . Troy Gardner
Freejack (1992) . . . . . . . . . . . . . . . . . . . . . . Morgan
Honey, I Blew Up the Kid (1992) . . . . . . . . . Hendrickson
**Backstreet Justice** (1993) . . . . . . . . . . . . . . . . . Nick
  •• 0:33—Buns, while making love on top of Linda Ko-
    zlowski.
*Made for Cable Movies:*
Ladykiller (1992; USA). . . . . . . . . . . . . . . Jack Packard
Notorious (1992; Lifetime) . . . . . . . . . . . . . . . .n.a.
*Made for Cable TV:*
The Hitchhiker: Minuteman. . . . . . . . . . . . . . . Jeremy
Tales From the Crypt: As Ye Sow (1993; HBO)
. . . . . . . . . . . . . . . . . . . . . . . . . . . . . . .Father John

Small Sacrifices (1989) . . . . . . . . . . . . . . Frank Joziak
*TV:*
Lois & Clark: The New Adventures of Superman (1993- )
. . . . . . . . . . . . . . . . . . . . . . . . . . . . .Lex Luthor

## Sheen, Martin
Father of actors Emilio Estevez and Charlie Sheen.
*Films:*
Rage (1972). . . . . . . . . . . . . . . . . . . . Major Holliford
Badlands (1973). . . . . . . . . . . . . . . . . . . . . . . . Kit
The Little Girl Who Lives Down the Lane
(1976; Canadian). . . . . . . . . . . . . . . . . . Frank Hallet
The Cassandra Crossing (1977; British) . . . . . . .Navarro
Eagle's Wing (1978; British) . . . . . . . . . . . . . . . . Pike
**Apocalypse Now** (1979) . . . . . . . . . . . Captain Willard
  • 0:07—Brief buns, while in bedroom after opening
    door for military guys.
The Final Countdown (1980) . . . . . . . . . . . Warren Lasky
Enigma (1982). . . . . . . . . . . . . . . . . . . Alex Holbeck
Gandhi (1982). . . . . . . . . . . . . . . . . . . . . . Walker
That Championship Season (1982) . . . . . . . . . Tom Daley
The Dead Zone (1983). . . . . . . . . . . . . . Greg Stillson
Man, Woman and Child (1983) . . . . . . . .Bob Beckwith
Firestarter (1984) . . . . . . . . . . . . . . . . Capt. Hollister
The Believers (1987). . . . . . . . . . . . . . Dr. Cal Jamison
Siesta (1987) . . . . . . . . . . . . . . . . . . . . . . . . Del
Wall Street (1987) . . . . . . . . . . . . . . . . . .Carl Fox
Beverly Hills Brats (1989) . . . . . . . . . . .Dr. Jeffrey Miller
Cold Front (1989; Canadian) . . . . . . . . . . . . John Hyde
The Maid (1990) . . . . . . . . . . . . . . . . .Anthony Wayne
Cadence (1991) . . . . . . . . . .Sergeant Otis V. McKinney
Original Intent (1992) . . . . . . . . . . . . . . . . . . .Joe
Gettysburg (1993) . . . . . . . . . . . . . . Gen. Robert E. Lee
Hear No Evil (1993) . . . . . . . . . . . . . . . .Lt. Philip Brock
*Made for Cable Movies:*
The Guardian (1984; HBO) . . . . . . . . . . .Charles Hyatt
Conspiracy: The Trial of the Chicago 8 (1987) . . . . . n.a.
Roswell (1994; Showtime) . . . . . . . . . . . . . Townsend
*Made for Cable TV:*
Tales From the Crypt: Well Cooked Hams (1993; HBO)
. . . . . . . . . . . . . . . . . . . . . . . Zorbin/Franz/Thomas
*Miniseries:*
Queen (1993) . . . . . . . . . . . . . . . . . James Jackson, Sr.
*Made for TV Movies:*
Samaritan: The Mitch Snyder Story (1986)
. . . . . . . . . . . . . . . . . . . . . . . . . . . . .Mitch Snyder
Shattered Spirits (1986) . . . . . . . . . . . Lyle Mollencamp
A Matter of Justice (1993) . . . . . . . . . . . . . Jack Brown
One of Her Own (1994). . . . . Assistant DA Pete Maresca

## Sheffer, Craig
*Films:*
Voyage of the Rock Aliens (1985) . . . . . . . . . . . .Frankie
*a.k.a. When the Rains Begin to Fall*
Split Decisions (1988) . . . . . . . . . . . . . Eddie McGuinn
Blue Desert (1990). . . . . . . . . . . . . . . . Randall Atkins

**Instant Karma** (1990) . . . . . . . . . . . . . . .Zane Smith
  • 1:15—Brief buns while on top of Penelope. Don't
    see his face.
    1:18—Very brief buns again in flashback.
Night Breed (1990). . . . . . . . . . . . . . . . . . . . . . .Boone
Eye of the Storm (1991) . . . . . . . . . . . . . . . . . . .Ray
A River Runs Through It (1992) . . . . . . Norman Maclean
Fire in the Sky (1993) . . . . . . . . . . . . . . . Allan Dallis
The Program (1993) . . . . . . . . . . . . . . . . . . . .Joe Kane
*Made for Cable Movies:*
Fire With Fire (1986; Showtime) . . . . . . . . . . . . .Joe Flsk
*TV:*
The Hamptons (1983). . . . . . . . . . . . . . Brian Chadway

## Shellen, Steve

*Films:*
**Gimme an "F"** (1981). . . . . . . . . . . . Tommy Hamilton
  *a.k.a. T & A Academy 2*
      0:56—Dancing in his underwear in the boy's shower
      room while the girls peek in at him.
  • 0:57—Brief upper half of buns.
**Talking Walls** (1982) . . . . . . . . . . . . . . . . .Paul Barton
  •• 0:58—Buns, while taking off his clothes and running
      down railroad tracks.
**Burglar** (1987) . . . . . . . . . . . . . . Christopher Marshall
  • 0:26—Buns, while in front of closet that Whoopi
      Goldberg is hiding in. Don't see his face, but proba-
      bly him.
Modern Girls (1987) . . . . . . . . . . . . . . . . . . . . . Brad
The Stepfather (1987). . . . . . . . . . . . . . . . . Jim Ogilvie
American Gothic (1988) . . . . . . . . . . . . . . . . . . Paul
Casual Sex? (1988) . . . . . . . . . . . . . . . . . . . . . . Nick
Murder One (1988; Canadian) . . . . . . . Wayne Coleman
Damned River (1990) . . . . . . . . . . . . . . . . . . . . . Ray
Still Life (1990) . . . . . . . . . . . . . . . . . . . . .Teddy Bulloch
The Bodyguard (1992) . . . . . . . . . . . . . . Tom Winston
**A River Runs Through It** (1992) . . . . . . . . Neal Burns
  • 1:17—Buns, sleeping in the woods with Rawhide.
      Don't see his face.
  •• 1:19—Buns, while walking to his house with help
      from his friends after getting badly sunburned.
Model By Day (1994) . . . . . . . . . . . . . Lt. Eddie Walker
(Shown on network TV without the nudity.)
*Made for Cable TV:*
**The Hitchhiker: Love Sounds**. . . . . . . . . . . . . Kerry
  •• 0:15—Brief buns, while making love in the house
      with Belinda Bauer.
  •• 0:22—Buns, while making love in the boat with Bau-
      er.
**Tales From the Crypt: Lover Come Hack To Me**
(1989; HBO) . . . . . . . . . . . . . . . . . . . . . . .Charles
  • 0:10—Buns, while getting undressed with his new-
      lywed wife in a strange house.
*Made for TV Movies:*
A Touch of Scandal (1984) . . . . . . . . . . .Billy Podovsky
Greyhounds (1994). . . . . . . . . . . . . . . . . . Evan Long

## • Sherwood, David

*Films:*
American Ninja 4: The Annihilation (1991). . . . . . . . n.a.
Curse of the Crystal Eye (1993) . . . . . . . . . Emilio Ferrari
**Demon Keeper** (1993) . . . . . . . . . . . . Howard Stanley
  • 0:40—Brief buns, while making love on top of Ruth
      in bed. Don't see his face.

## • Shipp, John Wesley

*Films:*
The Neverending Story II: The Next Chapter (1991)
. . . . . . . . . . . . . . . . . . . . . . . . . . . . . Barney Bux
*Made for TV Movies:*
Green Dolphin Beat (1994) . . . . . . . . . . . .Terry Latner
*TV:*
The Guiding Light . . . . . . . . . . . . . . . . . . . .Kelly Nelson
The Flash (1990-91) . . . . . . . . . . . . Barry Allen/The Flash
**NYPD Blue: Steroid Roy** (Feb 8, 1994). . . .Roy Larson
  ••• 0:25—Brief buns, while in police locker room, when
      talking to Kelly and Sipowicz.

## Shirin, Moti

*Films:*
**The Little Drummer Girl** (1984) . . . . . . . . . . .Michel
  •• 1:07—Nude, in a prison cell when Diane Keaton
      looks at his scars.
Unsettled Land (1987) . . . . . . . . . . . . . . . . . . . . .Salim

## Shore, Pauly

Son of comic Sammy Shore and Comedy Store owner
  Mitzi Shore.
*Films:*
For Keeps (1988) . . . . . . . . . . . . . . . . . . . . . . . . Retro
**Phantom of the Mall: Eric's Revenge** (1988). . Buzz
  •• 1:06—Buns, while mooning security guard on B&W
      surveillance monitor.
Wedding Band (1989) . . . . . . . . . . . . . . . . . . .Nicky
Class Act (1992). . . . . . . . . . . . . . . . . . . . . . . . . n.a.
Encino Man (1992) . . . . . . . . . . . . . . . . Stoney Brown
**Son-In-Law** (1993) . . . . . . . . . . . . . . . . . . . . . .Crawl
  •• 0:37—Buns while wearing cowboy chaps with no
      pants underneath while trying clothes on in store.
In the Army Now (1994) . . . . . . . . . . . . . . . . . . . n.a.
*TV:*
Totally Pauly . . . . . . . . . . . . . . . . . . . . . . . . . . Host

## Sibbit, John

*Films:*
**Love Circles Around the World** (1984) . . . . . . .Jack
  • 0:06—Very brief frontal nudity pulling his under-
      wear down and getting into bed.
  •• 0:19—Buns, while trying to run away from Brigid af-
      ter she yanks his underwear off.

## Siegel, David

*Films:*
**Private Passions** (1983) . . . . . . . . . . . . . . . . . .Toni
  • 0:29—Buns, with Laura. Don't see his face.

## Sills, David

*Films:*

**Breakfast in Bed** (1990) . . . . . . . . . . Henry Huntley
- •• 0:25—Buns, while in bed with Wendy.
- •• 0:35—Brief buns, while standing up in boat with Wendy.

## • Silver, Michael

*Films:*

**Jason Goes to Hell—The Final Friday** (1993)
. . . . . . . . . . . . . . . . . . . . . . Luke, the boy camper
(Unrated Director's Original Cut reviewed.)
- •• 0:26—Side view of buns, after taking off wet shorts after skinny dipping with his friends. Very, very brief frontal nudity. Hard to see because it's dark.
- • 0:29—Brief buns, several times, while in tent.

## Simione, Dan

*TV:*

General Hospital . . . . . . . . . . . . . . . . . . . . . . . . n.a.

*Magazines:*

**Playgirl** (Sep 1989) . . . . . . . . . . . . . . . . . The Natural
36-43—Upper half of buns, partial pubic hair.

## • Simmonds, John

*Video Tapes:*

**Playboy's How to Reawaken Your Sexual Powers** (1992). . . . . . . . . . . . . . . . . . . . . . . . . Cast Member
- ••• 0:12—Nude with his lover in the woods, a stream, a pond and under a waterfall.
- ••• 0:45—Nude, outside by beach with his lover. Also on air mattresses and snorkeling under water.

Penthouse Forum Letters: Volume 1 (1993). . . . . . . . n.a.

## Simon, Mark

*Video Tapes:*

**Inside Out 4** (1992) . . . . . William/What Anna Wants...
(Unrated version reviewed.)
- • 1:09—Buns and very brief frontal nudity, making out with Claudia while Anna takes photos.

## Simons, Alan

*Films:*

**Auditions** (1978) . . . . . . . . . . . . . . . . . . . . . Alan Cole
- • 0:18—Nude, undressing and caressing himself during his audition.
- •• 0:37—Buns, when his underwear is pulled down.

## Singer, Marc

Brother of actress Lori Singer.

*Films:*

Go Tell the Spartans (1978). . . . . . . . Captain Al Olivetti
The Beastmaster (1982) . . . . . . . . . . . . . . . . . . . . . Dar
If You Could See What I Hear (1982). . . . . . Tom Sullivan
Born to Race (1988) . . . . . . . . . . . . . . Kenny Landruff
In the Cold of the Night (1989) . . . . . . . . . Ken Strom
Beastmaster 2: Through the Portal of Time (1990) . . Dar

Body Chemistry (1990). . . . . . . . . . . Dr. Tom Redding
- • 0:18—Buns, standing up in hallway holding Claire while making love. Long shot.

Dead Space (1990) . . . . . . . . . . . . . . . . . . Steve Krieger
A Man Called Serge (1990) . . . . . . . . . . . . . Von Kraut
Watchers II (1990) . . . . . . . . . . . . . . . . . . Paul Ferguson
The Berlin Conspiracy (1991) . . . . . . . . . .Harry Spangler
Sweet Justice (1991). . . . . . . . . . . . . . . . . . Steve Colton
Ultimate Desires (1991) . . . . . . . . . . . .Jonathan Sullivan
　*a.k.a. Silhouette*
Silk Degrees (1994) . . . . . . . . . . . . . . . . . . . . . . .Baker

*Made for Cable Movies:*

High Desert Kill (1989; USA) . . . . . . . . . . . . . . . . Brad
The Sea Wolf (1993; TNT) . . . . . . . . . . . . . . . . . . n.a.

*Miniseries:*

V (1983) . . . . . . . . . . . . . . . . . . . . . . . .Mike Donovan
V: The Final Battle (1984). . . . . . . . . . . .Mike Donovan

*Made for TV Movies:*

Her Life as a Man (1984) . . . . . . . . . . . . . Mark Rogers

*TV:*

V: The Series (1984-85) . . . . . . . . . . . . .Mike Donovan
Dallas (1986-87) . . . . . . . . . . . . . . . . . . . .Matt Cantrell

## Singleton, Andrew

*Films:*

**Death Merchant** (1990) . . . . . . . . . . . . . . .McKinley
- • 0:47—Brief buns, while pulling up his pants, getting up out of bed with Natasha.

## Sinise, Gary

Husband of actress Moira Harris.

*Films:*

**A Midnight Clear** (1991) . . . . . . . . . . . . . . . Mother
- • 0:03—Long shot of buns, when he runs into stream.

Of Mice and Men (1992) . . . . . . . . . . . . . . . . George
Jack the Bear (1993). . . . . . . . . . . . . . . . . . . .Norman
Forrest Gump (1994) . . . . . . . . . . . . . . . . . . . . n.a.

*Miniseries:*

Stephen King's "The Stand" (1994) . . . . . . .Stu Redman

## Skarsgard, Stellan

*Films:*

**The Unbearable Lightness of Being** (1988)
. . . . . . . . . . . . . . . . . . . . . . . . . . . . The Engineer
- • 2:18—Buns, while making love with Tereza in his apartment.

Wind (1992) . . . . . . . . . . . . . . . . . . . . . . . Joe Heiser

## Skerritt, Tom

*Films:*

Fuzz (1972) . . . . . . . . . . . . . . . . . . .Detective Bert Kling
**Big Bad Mama** (1974). . . . . . . . . . . . . . . . Fred Diller
- • 1:18—Brief buns, while lying down with Angie Dickinson in barn.

Thieves Like Us (1974) . . . . . . . . . . . . . . . . .Dee Mobley
The Devil's Rain (1975; U.S./Mexican) . . . . Tom Preston
The Turning Point (1977). . . . . . . . . . . . Wayne Rogers
Up in Smoke (1978). . . . . . . . . . . . . . . . . . .Strawberry
Alien (1979). . . . . . . . . . . . . . . . . . . . . . . . . . . . Dallas

Ice Castles (1979) . . . . . . . . . . . . . . . . Marcus Winston
Fighting Back (1982). . . . . . . . . . . . . . John D'Angelo
The Dead Zone (1983) . . . . . . . . Sheriff Bannerman
**Opposing Force** (1986) . . . . . . . . . . . . . . . . . . Logan
  *a.k.a. Hell Camp*
> • 0:33—Very brief buns, while getting sprayed with
> water and dusted with white powder.
> •• 1:11—Brief buns, while jumping out of tree to knock
> out Tuan.

Top Gun (1986) . . . . . . . . . . . . . . Cmdr. Mike Metcalf
The Big Town (1987) . . . . . . . . . . . . . . . .Phil Carpenter
Maid to Order (1987) . . . . . . . . . Charles Montgomery
Poltergeist III (1988) . . . . . . . . . . . . . . . Bruce Gardner
Steel Magnolias (1989) . . . . . . . . . . . .Drum Eatenton
The Rookie (1990). . . . . . . . . . . . . .Eugene Ackerman
Big Man on Campus (1991) . . . . . . . . . . . Dr. Webster
Knight Moves (1992) . . . . . . . . . . . . . .Frank Sedman
**Poison Ivy** (1992) . . . . . . . . . . . . . . . . .Darryl Cooper
  (Unrated version reviewed.)
> •• 1:22—Buns, several times, while making love with
> Ivy by the piano when Sara Gilbert walks in.

A River Runs Through It (1992) . . . . . Reverend Maclean
singles (1992) . . . . . . . . . . . . . . . . . . . . . Mayor Weber
Wild Orchid II: Two Shades of Blue (1992) . . . . . . .Ham
*Made for TV Movies:*
Calendar Girl Murders (1984) . . . . . . . . . . . . . . Stoner
A Touch of Scandal (1984) . . . . . . . . . . . Father Dwelle
*TV:*
Ryan's Four (1983) . . . . . . . . . . . . . . Dr. Thomas Ryan
Picket Fences (1992- ) . . . . . . . . . . Sheriff Jimmy Brock

## Slater, Christian

*Films:*
The Legend of Billie Jean (1985) . . . . . . . . . . . . . . Binx
**The Name of the Rose** (1986). . . . . . . . Adso of Melk
> • 0:48—Buns, while making love with The Girl in the
> monastery kitchen.

Tucker: The Man and His Dream (1988) . . . . . . . . Junior
Gleaming the Cube (1989) . . . . . . . . . . . . . Brian Kelly
Heathers (1989) . . . . . . . . . . . . . . . . . . . . . . . . . .J.D.
The Wizard (1989) . . . . . . . . . . . . . . . . . . Nick Woods
Pump Up the Volume (1990) . . . . . . . . . . .Mark Hunter
Tales From the Darkside, The Movie (1990). . . . . .Andy
Young Guns II (1990) . . . . . . . Arkansas Dave Rudbaugh
**Mobsters** (1991). . . . . . . . . . . Charlie "Lucky" Luciano
  *a.k.a. Mobsters—The Evil Empire*
> 0:45—Very, very brief buns during love scene. Don't
> see his face.

Robin Hood: Prince of Thieves (1991) . . . . . Will Scarlett
Star Trek VI: The Undiscovered Country (1991)
. . . . . . . . . . . . . . . .Excelsior Communications Officer
Kuffs (1992) . . . . . . . . . . . . . . . . . . . .George Kuffs
Where The Day Takes You (1992) . . . . . . . . . . . . Rocky
Jimmy Hollywood (1993) . . . . . . . . . . . . . . . .William
**True Romance** (1993) . . . . . . . . . . . Clarence Worley
  (Unrated version reviewed.)
> • 0:11—Wide screen laser disc version only: Partial
> buns, while lying in bed with Patricia Arquette.

Untamed Heart (1993) . . . . . . . . . . . . . . . . . . . Adam

*Made for TV Movies:*
Living Proof: The Hank Williams, Jr. Story (1983)
. . . . . . . . . . . . . . . . . . . . . . . . . . . . Walt Willey

## • Slattery, Tony

*Films:*
How to Get Ahead in Advertising (1988; British) . . .Basil
The Crying Game (1992) . . . . . . . . . . . . . . . . . . . n.a.
**Peter's Friends** (1993; British/U.S.) . . . . . . . . . . Brian
> • 0:25—Buns, while lying on his stomach in bed with
> Sarah.

## Sloane, Lance

*Films:*
**The Big Bet** (1985) . . . . . . . . . . . . . . . . . . . . . Chris
> •• 0:38—Buns, while taking off robe and getting into
> bed with Angela Roberts after visiting Mrs. Roberts.
> •• 0:52—Buns, while on elevator floor with Monique
> Gabrielle during his daydream.
> • 1:07—Buns, while getting into tub with Kimberly
> Evenson during video tape fantasy. Long shot.

## Smith, Charlie Martin

*Films:*
The Culpepper Cattle Co. (1972) . . . . . . . . . . Tim Slater
Fuzz (1972) . . . . . . . . . . . . . . . . . . . . . . . . . . . . Baby
American Graffiti (1973). . . . . . . . . . . . Terry the Toad
Pat Garrett and Billy the Kid (1973) . . . . . . . . . Bowdre
  (Uncut Director's version reviewed.)
Rafferty and the Gold Dust Twins (1975) . . . . . . . .Alan
No Deposit, No Return (1976) . . . . . . . . . . Longnecker
**The Campus Corpse** (1977) . . . . . . . . . . . . . .Barney
> • 0:19—Brief buns, while running down mountain
> side during hazing.

The Buddy Holly Story (1978) . . . . . . . . . . . . .Ray Bob
More American Graffiti (1979) . . . . . . . . Terry the Toad
Herbie Goes Bananas (1980) . . . . . . . . . . . . . . .D. J.
**Never Cry Wolf** (1983) . . . . . . . . . . . . . . . . . Tyler
> • 0:32—Buns while warming himself and drying his
> clothes after falling through the ice.
> • 1:18—Very brief frontal nudity running and jumping
> off a rock into the pond.
> • 1:20—Buns while running in meadow with the cari-
> bou.
> • 1:23—Brief silhouette of lower frontal nudity while
> scampering up a hill. More buns when chasing the
> caribou.

Starman (1984) . . . . . . . . . . . . . . . . . . . . . .Shermin
The Untouchables (1987). . . . . . . . . . . . Oscar Wallace
The Hot Spot (1990) . . . . . . . . . . . . . . . . .Lon Gulick
Deep Cover (1992) . . . . . . . . . . . . . . . . . . . . .Carver
Fifty-Fifty (1993) . . . . . . . . . . . . . . . . . . Martin Sprue
*Made for Cable Movies:*
And the Band Played On (1992; HBO) . . Dr. Harold Jaffe
Boris and Natasha (1992; Showtime) . . . . . . Hotel Clerk
Roswell (1994; Showtime) . . . . . . . . . . . Sheriff Wilcox
*Made for Cable TV:*
Tales From the Crypt: Halfway Horrible (1993; HBO)
. . . . . . . . . . . . . . . . . . . . . . . . . . . . . . . . . . . Colin

# • Smith, Danny
*Films:*
Iced (1988) ................................. Jeff
The Pamela Principle (1992) ................. n.a.
(Unrated version reviewed.)
**Hollywood Dreams** (1993) ............... Robby
(Unrated version reviewed.)
• 0:28—Partial buns, while making love with Natasha and Tiffany on the floor.

# • Smith, Reid "Chip"
*Films:*
**Blood Mania** (1970) ................... Poolboy
• 0:11—Upper half of buns, getting out of pool with Victoria.
Into the Night (1985) ............... Sheriff Peterson
Trapped (1993).................... Alan Armstrong
*a.k.a. The Killing Jar*
*TV:*
Chase (1973-74)............. Officer Norm Hamilton
The Chisholms (1980)............... Lester Hackett

# Smits, Jimmy
*Films:*
Running Scared (1986) .............. Julio Gonzales
Terror on the Blacktop (1987) ................ Bo
**Old Gringo** (1989) ................... Arroyo
• 1:26—Half of his buns while on bed with Jane Fonda. Long shot, don't see his face.
Vital Signs (1989) ............... Dr. David Redding
Fires Within (1991) ...................... Nestor
**Switch** (1991) .................... Walter Stone
••• 1:21—Buns, while stretching after waking up in the morning. A bit on the dark side.
*Made for Cable Movies:*
The Cisco Kid (1994; TNT) .............. Cisco Kid
*Made for TV Movies:*
The Broken Cord (1992) .............. David Moore
The Tommyknockers (1993) ... James "Gard" Gardener
*TV:*
L.A. Law (1986-91) ................. Victor Sifuentes

# • Snyder, Todd
*Video Tapes:*
**Playboy Night Dreams** (1993) ........ Night Watch
••• 0:22—Buns, while making love with his lover on car in parking structure.
**Playboy's Sensual Fantasy for Lovers** (1993)
.............................. Pretending
••• 0:14—Buns, after taking off his clothes outside to clean himself off, then frontal nudity while making love in stable.
• 0:47—Brief frontal nudity during review.

# • Sommer, Robert
*Films:*
**Auditions** (1978) ................. Frank Murphy
••• 0:33—Nude, during dungeon scene.
• 1:07—Buns during orgy scene.
Hanna K. (1984) ................. Court President
Saving Grace (1986) ................... Mr. Carver

# • Sorvino, Paul
*Films:*
A Touch of Class (1972) .............. Walter Menkes
The Day of the Dolphin (1973) ........... Mahoney
The Gambler (1974) ...................... Hips
I Will, I Will... For Now (1976) ........ Lous Springer
Bloodbrothers (1978). ............. Chubby DeCoco
The Brink's Job (1978) .............. Jazz Maffie
Cruising (1980) ................. Captain Edelson
Melanie (1982) ................. Walter Greer
Off the Wall (1982) ...................... Warden
The Stuff (1985)................... Colonel Spears
Turk 182 (1985)........................ Himself
A Fine Mess (1986) ................. Tony Pazzo
Dick Tracy (1990)................... Lips Manlis
GoodFellas (1990) ................. Paul Cicero
Age Isn't Everything (1991) ...................Max
The Rocketeer (1991). ............. Eddie Valentine
Backstreet Justice (1993) ....... Captain Phil Giarrusso
The Firm (1993) ................. Joey Morolto
*Made for Cable Movies:*
**Parallel Lives** (1994; Showtime) ........ Ed Starling
• 0:16—Brief upper half of buns, while getting pantsed in room by the guys.
*Miniseries:*
Chiefs (1983) ............................. n.a.
*Made for TV Movies:*
My Mother's Secret Life (1984) ............... n.a.

# Spader, James
*Films:*
Tuff Turf (1984) ................... Morgan Hiller
Pretty in Pink (1986) ............... Steff McKee
Baby Boom (1987)................. Ken Arrenberg
Jack's Back (1987) ............... John/Rick Wesford
Less than Zero (1987) ......................Rip
Mannequin (1987)....................... Richards
The Rachel Papers (1989; British) ........... De Forest
sex, lies and videotape (1989) ........ Graham Dalton
Bad Influence (1990) ................. Michael Boll
**White Palace** (1990) ............... Max Baron
•• 0:38—Buns, while taking off clothes and getting into bed with Susan Sarandon. Don't see his face.
True Colors (1991)................... Tim Garrity
Bob Roberts (1992; U.S./British)
................. News Anchor Chuck Marin
Storyville (1992).................. Cray Fowler
Dreamlover (1994)........................ Ray
Wolf (1994) ............................. n.a.
*TV:*
The Family Tree (1983) ............... Jake Nichols

# Spanjer, Maarten

*Films:*

**Spetters** (1980; Dutch) . . . . . . . . . . . . . . . . . . . . . Jeff
••• 0:35—Frontal nudity, measuring and comparing his
manlihood with his friends in the auto shop.
 • 1:12—Buns while climbing into bed in trailer with
Reneé Soutendijk.

# Spano, Joe

*Films:*

American Graffiti (1973) . . . . . . . . . . . . . . . . . . . . . Vic
Roadie (1980) . . . . . . . . . . . . . . . . . . . . . . . . . . . . . .Ace
**Terminal Choice** (1985; Canadian) . . . . . . .Frank Holt
••• 0:34—Buns, taking off towel and getting dressed in
locker room while talking to Anna.
 • 0:49—Buns, while making love in bed with Anna.
Long shot, don't see his face.

*Made for Cable Movies:*

Fever (1991; HBO) . . . . . . . . . . . . . . . . . . . . . .Junkman

*Made for TV Movies:*

The Girl Who Came Between Them (1990). . . . . . . . Jim
The Flood: Who Will Save Out Children? (1993)
. . . . . . . . . . . . . . . . . . . . . . . . . . . . . . . .Richard Koons

*TV:*

Hill Street Blues (1981-87). . . . . . . . . .Henry Goldblume

# Spano, Vincent

*Films:*

Over the Edge (1979) . . . . . . . . . . . . . . . . . . . . . .Mark
Baby, It's You (1983) . . . . . . . . . . . . . . . . . . . . . . Sheik
The Black Stallion Returns (1983) . . . . . . . . . . . . . Raj
Rumble Fish (1983). . . . . . . . . . . . . . . . . . . . . . Steve
Alphabet City (1984). . . . . . . . . . . . . . . . . . . . Johnny
**Creator** (1985) . . . . . . . . . . . . . . . . . . . . . . . . . .Boris
 • 0:28—Brief buns, while in shower room with David
Ogden Stiers after working out in a gym.
 • 0:57—Brief buns, before taking a shower.
Maria's Lovers (1985) . . . . . . . . . . . . . . . . . Al Griselli
Good Morning, Babylon (1987; Italian/French)
. . . . . . . . . . . . . . . . . . . . . . . . . . . . Nicola Bonnano
And God Created Woman (1988) . . . . . . . . .Billy Moran
(Unrated version.)
City of Hope (1991) . . . . . . . . . . . . . . . . . . . . . . Nick
Oscar (1991). . . . . . . . . . . . . .Anthony Rossano, C.P.A.
Alive (1992) . . . . . . . . . . . . . . . . . . . . . Antonio Balbi
Indian Summer (1993) . . . . . . . . . . . . Matthew Berman

*Made for Cable Movies:*

Blood Ties (1986; Italian; Showtime). . . . . . . Mark Ciuni
Afterburn (1992; HBO) . . . . . . . . . . . . . . Ted Harduvel

*Made for Cable TV:*

Tales From the Crypt: Two for the Show (1993; HBO)
. . . . . . . . . . . . . . . . . . . . . . . . . . . . . . . . .Officer Fine

# Speakman, Jeff

*Films:*

Side Roads (1988) . . . . . . . . . . . . . . . . . .Joseph Velasco
Lionheart (1990) . . . . . . . . . . . .Mansion Security Man
The Perfect Weapon (1991) . . . . . . . . . . . . Jeff Sanders
**Street Knight** (1992). . . . . . . . . . . . . . . . . . . . . .Jake
••• 0:05—Buns, while getting out of bed at night.

# Spechtenhauser, Robert Egon

*Films:*

**Bizarre** (1986; Italian). . . . . . . . . . . . . . . . . . Edward
 • 0:29—Partial buns, while taking a shower when Lau-
rie peeks in at him.
 • 0:31—Brief buns, while on top of Laurie in the water.
••• 0:36—Buns, while on bed with Laurie. (He's made
up to look like a woman.)

# • Spengler, Volker

*Films:*

**Despair** (1978; German/French). . . . . . . . . . . .Ardalion
 • 1:06—Buns, in his studio with Lydia when Dirk Bogarde looks for a painting.
The Marriage of Maria Braun (1979; German)
. . . . . . . . . . . . . . . . . . . . . . . . . . . . . . . .Conductor

# Spicer, Jerry

*Films:*

Liquid Dreams (1992) . . . . . . . . . . . Hot Box Escort #2
(Unrated version reviewed.)
**Sunset Grill** (1992) . . . . . . . . . . . . . . . . . . . . .Lover
 • 0:04—Very brief frontal nudity and very brief buns,
getting caught in bed with Mrs. Pietrowski.
Witchcraft 6: The Devil's Mistress (1993) . . . . . . . . Will
(Unrated version reviewed.)
Money to Burn (1994) . . . . . . . . . . . . . . . . . . . Kevin

# Springfield, Rick

Singer.

*Films:*

**Hard to Hold** (1984) . . . . . . . . . . . . . . James Roberts
 • 0:06—Buns, while running down the hall getting
chased by a bunch of young girls.
•• 0:15—Buns, while lying in bed sleeping.

*Made for TV Movies:*

Battlestar Gallactica (1978) . . . . . . . . . . .Lieutenant Zac
Nick Knight (1989) . . . . . . . . . . . . . . . . . . . . . . .Nick
In the Shadows, Someone's Watching (1993)
. . . . . . . . . . . . . . . . . . . . . . . . . . . . . . Paul Merritt

*TV:*

General Hospital . . . . . . . . . . . . . . . . Dr. Noah Drake
The Human Target (1992) . . . . . . .Christopher Chance
High Tide (1994- ) . . . . . . . . . . . . . . . . . . . . . . . n.a.

# • Stadele, Owen

*Films:*

**Airborne** (1993). . . . . . . . . . . . . . . . . . . . . . . Blane
 • 1:05—Brief buns, while wearing a jockstrap after his
sweat pants are yanked down by Mitchell during
street hockey game.

# Stallone, Sylvester

Ex-husband of actress Brigitte Nielsen.

*Adult Films:*

**The Italian Stallion** (1970) . . . . . . . . . . . . . . . . Stud
X-rated film that Stallone did before he got famous.
Originally called *A Party at Kitty and Stud's*. Re-titled and
re-released in 1985. He has lots of nude scenes in this
film.

*Films:*

The Lords of Flatbush (1974). . . . . . . . . Stanley Rosiello
Capone (1975) . . . . . . . . . . . . . . . . . . . . . . Frank Nitti
Death Race 2000 (1975) . . . . . Machine Gun Joe Viterbo
Farewell, My Lovely (1975; British) . . . . . . . Kelly/Jonnie
Cannonball (1976; U.S./Hong Kong). . . . . . . . . . . . .n.a.
Rocky (1976). . . . . . . . . . . . . . . . . . . . . Rocky Balboa
F.I.S.T. (1978) . . . . . . . . . . . . . . . . . . . . Johnny Kouak
Paradise Alley (1978). . . . . . . . . . . . . . . Cosmo Carboni
Rocky II (1979) . . . . . . . . . . . . . . . . . . . Rocky Balboa
Nighthawks (1981) . . . . . . . . . . . . . . . . . Deke De Silva
Victory (1981). . . . . . . . . . . . . . . . . . . . Robert Hatch
First Blood (1982) . . . . . . . . . . . . . . . . . . . . . Rambo
Rocky III (1982) . . . . . . . . . . . . . . . . . . . Rocky Balboa
Rhinestone (1984). . . . . . . . . . . . . . . . . . . . . . Nick
Rambo: First Blood, Part II (1985) . . . . . . . . . . . Rambo
   0:49—Brief, sort of buns, while wearing a small loin-
   cloth and getting lifted out of muddy water by his
   wrists.
Rocky IV (1985). . . . . . . . . . . . . . . . . . . Rocky Balboa
Cobra (1986) . . . . . . . . . . . . . . . . . . . Marion Cobretti
Over the Top (1987) . . . . . . . . . . . . . . . . Lincoln Hawk
Lock Up (1989) . . . . . . . . . . . . . . . . . . . . . . . Frank
**Tango & Cash** (1989) . . . . . . . . . . . . . . . .Ray Tango
   •• 0:31—Brief buns while walking into the prison
   shower room with Kurt Russell.
**Rocky V** (1990) . . . . . . . . . . . . . . . . . . Rocky Balboa
   • 0:03—Side view of buns, while standing in the
   shower. Long shot.
Oscar (1991). . . . . . . . . . . . . Angelo "Snaps" Provolone
**Stop! Or My Mom Will Shoot** (1992). . Joe Bomowski
   • 0:22—Upper half of buns behind shower door when
   his mom talks to him in the bathroom.
Cliffhanger (1993). . . . . . . . . . . . . . . . . Gabe Walker
Demolition Man (1993) . . . . . . . . . . . . . .John Spartan

*Made for Cable TV:*

Dream On: The Second Greatest Story Ever Told
   (1991; HBO) . . . . . . . . . . . . . . . . . . . . . . . .Himself

*Magazines:*

**Playboy** (Feb 1980). . . . . . . . . . . . . . The Year in Sex
   • 159—Partial buns in still from *The Italian Stallion*.

# Stanton, Harry Dean

*Films:*

Two-Lane Blacktop . . . . . . . . . . . . Oklahoma Hitchhiker
The Adventures of Huckleberry Finn (1960)
   . . . . . . . . . . . . . . . . . . . . . . . . . . . Slave Catcher
How the West was Won (1963). . . . . . . . . . . . . Outlaw
Ride in the Whirlwind (1965) . . . . . . . . . . . Blind Dick
Cool Hand Luke (1967). . . . . . . . . . . . . . . . . . .Tramp
Rebel Rousers (1967). . . . . . . . . . . . . . . . . . . Rebel

Kelly's Heroes (1970) . . . . . . . . . . . . . . . . . . .Willard
**Cisco Pike** (1971) . . . . . . . . . . . . . . . . . Jesse Dupre
   • 1:00—Brief upper half of buns, while standing up in
   bathtub to greet Kris Kristofferson.
Pat Garrett and Billy the Kid (1973) . . . . . . . . . . . Luke
   (Uncut Director's version reviewed.)
The Godfather, Part II (1974) . . . . . . . . . . . . .FBI No. 1
Farewell, My Lovely (1975; British). . . . . . . . .Billy Rolfe
Rafferty and the Gold Dust Twins (1975) . . Billy Winston
Rancho Deluxe (1975) . . . . . . . . . . . . . . . . . . . .Curt
The Missouri Breaks (1976) . . . . . . . . . . . . . . . Calvin
Straight Time (1978) . . . . . . . . . . . . . . . . Jerry Schue
Alien (1979). . . . . . . . . . . . . . . . . . . . . . . . . Brett
The Rose (1979). . . . . . . . . . . . . . . . . . . . Billie Ray
Wise Blood (1979; U.S./German) . . . . . . . . .Ash Hawks
The Black Marble (1980) . . . . . . . . . . . . . .Philo Sinner
Death Watch (1980; French/German)
   . . . . . . . . . . . . . . . . . . . . . . . . Vincent Ferriman
   *a.k.a. Death in Full View*
Private Benjamin (1980). . . . . . . . . . . Sgt. Jim Ballard
Escape from New York (1981) . . . . . . . . . . . . . Brian
One from the Heart (1982) . . . . . . . . . . . . . . . Moe
Young Doctors in Love (1982) . . . . . . Dr. Oliver Ludwig
Christine (1983). . . . . . . . . . . . . . . . . .Rudolph Junkins
The Bear (1984). . . . . . . . . . . . . . . . . Coach Thomas
Paris, Texas (1984; French/German). . . . . . . . . .Travis
Red Dawn (1984). . . . . . . . . . . . . . . . . . Mr. Eckert
Repo Man (1984). . . . . . . . . . . . . . . . . . . . . .Bud
Fool For Love (1985) . . . . . . . . . . . . . . . . Old Man
Pretty in Pink (1986) . . . . . . . . . . . . . . . Jack Walsh
Slam Dance (1987) . . . . . . . . . . . . . . . . . . Smiley
The Last Temptation of Christ (1988) . . . . . . . Saul/Paul
Mr. North (1988) . . . . . . . . . . . . . . . .Henry Simmons
Stars and Bars (1988). . . . . . . . . . . . . . .Loomis Gage
Dream A Little Dream (1989) . . . . . . . . . . . Ike Baker
The Fourth War (1990). . . . . . . . . . . . Gen. Hackworth
Wild at Heart (1990) . . . . . . . . . . . . .Johnnie Farragut
Man Trouble (1992) . . . . . . . . . . . . . . Redmond Layls
Twin Peaks: Fire Walk With Me (1992) . . . . . . Carl Rodd

*Made for Cable Movies:*

Hostages (1993; HBO) . . . . . . . . . . . . . . . Frand Reed
Hotel Room (1993; HBO). . . . . . . . . . . . . . . . .Tricks
Against the Wall (1994; HBO) . . . . . . . . . . . . . . Hal

*Made for TV Movies:*

One Magic Christmas (1985; U.S./Canadian). . . Gideon

# Staskel, James

*Films:*

An Innocent Man (1989) . . . . . . . . . . . . . . . . . . n.a.

*Video Tapes:*

**Inside Out 3** (1992). . . . . . . . . . .Tom/The Houseguest
   •• 1:04—Buns, while getting into bathtub to get
   cleaned up by Marilyn Hassett.

# • Steadman, Ken

*Films:*

**Beach Babes From Beyond** (1993) . . . . . . . . . .Jerry
   • 0:42—Brief buns, when swimsuit falls down while
   playing in the surf.

627

Lovers' Lovers (1993) . . . . . . . . . . . . . . Make Out Guy
**Mirror Images II** (1993) . . . . . . . . . . . . . . . . . . . Dan
- •• 0:33—Buns, while running from the spa to the
house after getting caught with Shannon Whirry.

## Steiner, John
*Films:*
**Beyond the Door II** (1977; Italian) . . . . . . . . . . Bruno
- • 0:12—Brief buns, while making love with Dora on
the sofa. Dark.
Yor: The Hunter from the Future (1983) . . . . . . Overlord
Cut and Run (1985; Italian) . . . . . . . . . . . . . . . . Vlado

## • Stepp, Craig
*Films:*
Legal Tender (1991) . . . . . . . . . . . . . . . . . . . . . . n.a.
*Video Tapes:*
**Playboy Night Dreams** (1993) . . . . . . . . . . Fall Guy
- • 0:33—Brief side view of buns, while making love
with his lover on pool chair.
Eden 6 (1994) . . . . . . . . . . . . . . . . . . . . . . . . . . . n.a.

## Stern, Daniel
*Films:*
Breaking Away (1979) . . . . . . . . . . . . . . . . . . . . Cyril
Starting Over (1979) . . . . . . . . . . . . . . . . . . Student 2
It's My Turn (1980) . . . . . . . . . . . . . . . . . . Cooperman
**A Small Circle of Friends** (1980) . . . . . . . . Crazy Kid
- • 1:22—Brief buns, while dropping his pants with sev-
eral other guys for Army draft inspection.
Stardust Memories (1980) . . . . . . . . . . . . . . . . . Actor
Honky Tonk Freeway (1981) . . . . . . . . . . . . . . . . n.a.
I'm Dancing as Fast as I Can (1981) . . . . . . . . . . . Jim
Diner (1982) . . . . . . . . . . . . . . . . . . . . . . . . Shrevie
Blue Thunder (1983) . . . . . . . . . . . . . . . . Lymangood
Get Crazy (1983) . . . . . . . . . . . . . . . . . . . . . . . Neil
C.H.U.D. (1984) . . . . . . . . . . . . . . . . . . The Reverend
Frankenweenie (1984) . . . . . . . . . . . . . Ben Frankenstein
Key Exchange (1985) . . . . . . . . . . . . . . . . . . Michael
The Boss' Wife (1986) . . . . . . . . . . . . . . . . Joel Keefer
Born in East L.A. (1987) . . . . . . . . . . . . . . . . . . Jimmy
D.O.A. (1988) . . . . . . . . . . . . . . . . . . Hal Petersham
The Milagro Beanfield War (1988) . . . . . . . . Herbie Platt
Friends, Lovers & Lunatics (1989) . . . . . . . . . . . . Mat
Little Monsters (1989) . . . . . . . . . . . . . . Glen Stevenson
Coupe de Ville (1990) . . . . . . . . . . . . . . . Marvin Libner
Home Alone (1990) . . . . . . . . . . . . . . . . . . . . . Marv
My Blue Heaven (1990) . . . . . . . . . . . . . . . Will Stubbs
City Slickers (1991) . . . . . . . . . . . . . . . . . Phil Berquist
Home Alone 2: Lost in New York (1992)
. . . . . . . . . . . . . . . . . . . . . . . . . Marvin Murchins
Rookie of the Year (1993) . . . . . . . . . . . . . . . Brickma
City Slickers II: The Legend of Curly's Gold (1994) . . Phil
*Made for Cable Movies:*
The Court-Martial of Jackie Robinson (1990)
. . . . . . . . . . . . . . . . . . . . . . . . . . . William Cline
*TV:*
Hometown (1985) . . . . . . . . . . . . . . . . . Joey Nathan

## Stevens, Andrew
Son of actress Stella Stevens.
Ex-husband of actress Kate Jackson.
*Films:*
Massacre at Central High (1976) . . . . . . . . . . . . . Mark
Vigilante Force (1976) . . . . . . . . . . . . . . . . Paul Sinton
The Boys in Company C (1978) . . . . . . . . Billy Ray Pike
The Fury (1978) . . . . . . . . . . . . . . . . . . . . Robin Sandza
Death Hunt (1981) . . . . . . . . . . . . . . . . . . . . . Alvin
The Seduction (1982) . . . . . . . . . . . . . . . . . . . Derek
10 to Midnight (1983) . . . . . . . . . . . . . . . Paul McAnn
Deadly Innocents (1988) . . . . . . . . . . . . Bob Appling
Red Blooded American Girl (1988)
. . . . . . . . . . . . . . . . . . . Owen Augustus Urban III
The Terror Within (1988) . . . . . . . . . . . . . . . . . David
Down the Drain (1989) . . . . . . . . . . . . . . Victor Scalia
Eyewitness to Murder (1989) . . . . . . . . . . . . . . Page
**Night Eyes** (1990) . . . . . . . . . . . . . . . . . . . . . . Will
(Unrated version reviewed.)
- ••• 1:11—Buns while in the shower.
- ••• 1:26—Side view of buns with Tanya Roberts seen
through a window.
**Night Eyes 2** (1991) . . . . . . . . . . . . . . . Will Griffith
- • 1:07—Partial buns, in mirror, while lying on the floor
with Shannon Tweed.
Deadly Rivals (1992) . . . . . . . . . . . . Kevin Fitzgerald
Double Threat (1992) . . . . . . . . . . . . . . . . Eric Cline
(Unrated version reviewed.)
Maximum Force (1992) . . . . . . . . . . . . . . . . Tommy
Munchie (1992) . . . . . . . . . . . . . . . . . . . . . . Elliott
The Terror Within II (1992) . . . . . . . . David Pennington
Body Chemistry 3: Point of Seduction (1993) . . Alan Clay
**Night Eyes 3** (1993) . . . . . . . . . . . . . . Will Griffith
- •• 0:53—Buns, while making love on top of Shannon
Tweed in bed.
- •• 1:01—Buns, while making love with Shannon
Tweed. First seen on B&W security monitor, then in
real life.
Scorned (1993) . . . . . . . . . . . . . . . . . Alex Weston
Munchie Strikes Back (1994) . . . . . . . . . Shelby Carlisle
*Miniseries:*
The Bastard (1978) . . . . . . . . . . . . . . . . . Philip Kent
*TV:*
Code Red (1981-82) . . . . . . . . . . . . . . . . Ted Rorchek
Emerald Point N.A.S. (1983-84)
. . . . . . . . . . . . . . . . Lieutenant Glenn Matthews
Dallas (1987-89) . . . . . . . . . . . . . . . . . Casey Denault

## Stevens, Fisher
*Films:*
**The Burning** (1981) . . . . . . . . . . . . . . . . Woodstock
- • 0:29—Buns, pulling swimsuit down and up to moon
Glazer. (2nd from the right.)
Baby, It's You (1983) . . . . . . . . . . . . . . Stage Manager
The Brother From Another Planet (1984)
. . . . . . . . . . . . . . . . . . . . . . . . . . Card Trickster
The Flamingo Kid (1984) . . . . . . . . . . . . . Hawk Ganz
My Science Project (1985) . . . . . . . . . . . Vince Latello
The Boss' Wife (1986) . . . . . . . . . . . . . Carlos Delgado

Short Circuit (1986) . . . . . . . . . . . . . . . . Ben Jabituya
Short Circuit 2 (1988) . . . . . . . . . . . . . . . Ben Jabituya
Bloodhounds of Broadway (1989) . . . . . . . Hotfoot Harry
Reversal of Fortune (1990) . . . . . . . . . . David Marriott
The Marrying Man (1991). . . . . . . . . . . . . . . . . Sammy
  a.k.a. Too Hot to Handle
Mystery Date (1991) . . . . . . . . . . . . . . . . . . . . . Dwight
When the Party's Over (1991) . . . . . Alexander Midnight
Bob Roberts (1992; U.S./British) . . . . Reporter Rock Bork
Super Mario Bros. (1993) . . . . . . . . . . . . . . . . . . . Iggy
TV:
The Guiding Light (1977) . . . . . . . . . . . . . . . . . . . n.a.
Key West (1993) . . . . . . . . . . . . . . . . . . Seamus O'Neill

# • Stevenson, Eugene
Films:
**The Pamela Principle** (1992) . . . . . . . Steve Breeding
(Unrated version reviewed.)
  ••• 0:46—Buns, while making love on top of his girl-
    friend on the living room floor. Nice close-ups.

# Stevenson, Parker
Husband of actress Kirstie Alley.
Films:
Lifeguard (1975) . . . . . . . . . . . . . . . . . . . . . . . . . . Chris
Stroker Ace (1983) . . . . . . . . . . . . . . . . . Aubrey James
**Stitches** (1985) . . . . . . . . . . . . . . . . . Bobby Stevens
  • 0:04—Brief buns, while chasing people down hall-
    way. Don't see face. (He's in the last one.)
Made for Cable TV:
The Hitchhiker: Best Shot (1987; HBO) . . . . . . . . . Brett
Miniseries:
North and South, Book II (1986) . . . . . . . . Billy Hazard
Made for TV Movies:
Shadow of a Stranger (1992) . . . . . . . . . . . Ted Clinton
TV:
The Hardy Boys Mysteries (1977-79) . . . . . . Frank Hardy
Falcon Crest (1984-85) . . . . . . . . . . . . . . Joel McCarthy
Probe (1988). . . . . . . . . . . . . . . . . . . . . . Austin James
Baywatch (1989-90) . . . . . . . . . . . . . . . Craig Pomeroy

# Stewart, Robin
Films:
Damn the Defiant! (1962; British) . . . . . . . . . . . Pardoe
Cromwell (1970; British) . . . . . . . . . . . . Prince of Wales
Horror House (1970; British) . . . . . . . . . . . . . . . Henry
**The Adventures of a Private Eye** (1974; British)
. . . . . . . . . . . . . . . . . . . . . . . . . . . . . Scott West
  • 0:23—Buns, dancing around after getting caught in
    a mousetrap.
  • 0:35—Buns, while in boat on top of Clarissa
  •• 0:36—Brief full frontal nudity, getting up and diving
    off boat.
  • 0:58—Buns, while on couch with the Inspector's
    Wife.
  • 1:17—Buns, while standing in bathroom at Lisa's
    place.
Pacific Banana (1980) . . . . . . . . . . . . . . . . . . . . . n.a.

# • Stiglitz, Hugo
Films:
Survive (1977; Mexican) . . . . . . . . . . . . . . . . Francisco
**Tintorera** (1977) . . . . . . . . . . . . . . . . . . . . . . Steven
  0:11—Brief partial buns, while lying in bed with Fio-
    na Lewis.
  • 0:41—Side view of buns, while searing apron in boat
    galley.
Under the Volcano (1984) . . . . . . . . . . . . . . Sinarquista
The Treasure of the Amazon (1985; Mexican)
. . . . . . . . . . . . . . . . . . . . . . . . . . . . . Boat Captain
Killing Machine (1986; Spanish/Mexican) . . . . . . . Picot

# Sting
Singer with The Police and on his own.
Husband of actress Trudi Styler.
Real name is Gordon Matthew Sumner.
Films:
Quadrophenia (1979; British) . . . . . . . . . . The Ace Face
**Brimstone and Treacle** (1982; British)
. . . . . . . . . . . . . . . . . . . . . . . . . . . . Martin Taylor
  • 1:19—Buns, while making love with Suzanna Hamil-
    ton on her bed. Dark, hard to see.
Dune (1984) . . . . . . . . . . . . . . . . . . . . . . . Feyd Rautha
The Bride (1985) . . . . . . . . . . . . . . . . . . . Frankenstein
Plenty (1985) . . . . . . . . . . . . . . . . . . . . . . . . . . . Mick
**Julia and Julia** (1987; Italian). . . . . . . . . . . . . Daniel
(This movie was shot using a high-definition video sys-
tem and then transferred to film.)
  •• 1:11—Buns, while sleeping in bed when Kathleen
    Turner leaves. Don't see his face very well.
Stormy Monday (1988) . . . . . . . . . . . . . . . . . . . Finney

# Stockwell, Guy
Brother of actor Dean Stockwell.
Films:
Tobruk (1966) . . . . . . . . . . . . . . . . . . Lt. Max Mohnfeld
Airport 1975 (1974). . . . . . . . . . . . . . . . . . Col. Moss
It's Alive (1974) . . . . . . . . . . . . . . . . . . . . . . . Clayton
**Santa Sangre** (1989; Italian/Spanish). . . . . . . . Orgo
  •• 0:38—Buns, several times, when Concha catches
    him with the tattooed lady. (He's a heavy guy.)
  • 0:39—Buns, lying dead on the ground after he cuts
    his own throat.
TV:
Adventures in Paradise (1959-62). . . . . . . . Chris Parker

# Stockwell, John
Films:
So Fine (1981) . . . . . . . . . . . . . . . . . . . . . . . . . . . Jim
Losin' It (1982). . . . . . . . . . . . . . . . . . . . . . . . . Spider
Christine (1983). . . . . . . . . . . . . . . . . . . . . . . Dennis
Eddie and the Cruisers (1983) . . . . . . . . . . . . . Keith
City Limits (1984) . . . . . . . . . . . . . . . . . . . . . . . . Lee
My Science Project (1985) . . . . . . . . Michael Harlan
**Dangerously Close** (1986) . . . . . . . . Randy McDevill
  • 0:33—Brief buns while in steamy locker room.
Top Gun (1986). . . . . . . . . . . . . . . . . . . . . . . Cougar
Millions (1990). . . . . . . . . . . . . . . . . . . David Phipps

*Miniseries:*
North and South (1985) . . . . . . . . . . . . . . Billy Hazard

## Stoddard, Peter

*Films:*
**Naked Instinct** (1993) . . . . . . . . . .Hot Tub Repairman
- 0:28—Buns, getting into tub with Joanne.
- ••• 0:30—Full frontal nudity, while lying on side of tub with Joanne.
- ••• 0:36—Full frontal nudity, standing up in tub.

## Stokes, Barry

*Films:*
**Happy Housewives** . . . . . . . . . . . . . . . . . . . . . . Bob
- 0:31—Brief buns, while running away from Mrs. Elgin and her daughter in the barn.

**Spaced Out** (1980; British) . . . . . . . . . . . . . . . . Oliver
*a.k.a. Outer Touch*
- 0:54—Buns, while undressing to get in bed with Prudence.

**Alien Prey** (1984; British) . . . . . . . . . . . . . . . . Anders
- •• 1:19—Buns, while getting on top of Glory Annen in bed.

## Stoltz, Eric

*Films:*
Fast Times at Ridgemont High (1982) . . . . . . Stoner Bud
Lucky 13 (1984) . . . . . . . . . . . . . . . . . . . . Danny Hicks
*a.k.a. Running Hot*
*a.k.a. Highway to Hell*
Surf II (1984). . . . . . . . . . . . . . . . . . . . . . . . . .Chuck
The Wild Life (1984) . . . . . . . . . . . . . . . . . Bill Conrad
Code Name: Emerald (1985). . . . . . . . . .Andy Wheeler
Mask (1985) . . . . . . . . . . . . . . . . . . . . . Rocky Dennis
The New Kids (1985) . . . . . . . . . . . . . . . . . . . .Mark
Lionheart (1987). . . . . . . . . . . . . . . . . . .Robert Nerra
Sister Sister (1987) . . . . . . . . . . . . . . . . Matt Rutledge
Some Kind of Wonderful (1987) . . . . . . . .Keith Nelson
**Haunted Summer** (1988). . . . . . . . . . . .Percy Shelley
- ••• 0:09—Nude, under the waterfall and walking around in the river. Long scene.

**Manifesto** (1988) . . . . . . . . . . . . . . . . . . . Christopher
- 1:16—Buns, while helping Camilla unroll Emile in the rug.

The Fly II (1989) . . . . . . . . . . . . . . . . . . . . . . Martin
Say Anything (1989). . . . . . . . . . . . . . . . . . . . Vahlere
Memphis Belle (1990). . . . . . . . . . . . . . . Danny Daily
The Waterdance (1991) . . . . . . . . . . . . . . Joel Garcia
singles (1992). . . . . . . . . . . . . . . . . . . . . . . . Mime
Bodies, Rest & Motion (1993). . . . . . . . . . . . . . Sid
Naked in New York (1993) . . . . . . . . . . . . Jake Briggs
*Made for Cable Movies:*
Foreign Affairs (1993; TNT). . . . . . . . . . . .Fred Turner
The Heart of Justice (1993; TNT). . . . . . . David Leader
*Made for TV Movies:*
Paper Dolls (1982) . . . . . . . . . . . . . . . . . . . . . Steve
Roommates (1994). . . . . . . . . . . . . . . . . .Bill Thomas

## Stone, Christopher

Husband of actress Dee Wallace Stone.
*Films:*
**The Grasshopper** (1970). . . . . . . . . . . . . . Jay Rigney
*a.k.a. The Passing of Evil*
*a.k.a. Passions*
- 0:26—Buns, seen through shower door when Jacqueline Bisset comes in to join him.
- 1:17—Brief buns while lying in bed talking to Bisset.

**The Howling** (1981) . . . . . . . . . . R. William "Bill" Neill
- 0:48—Brief buns, rolling over while making love with Elizabeth Brooks in front of a campfire.

Cujo (1983) . . . . . . . . . . . . . . . . . . . . . . . . . . Steve
The Annihilators (1985) . . . . . . . . . . . . . . Bill Esker
Blue Movies (1988) . . . . . . . . . . . . . . . . . . . . Brad
*Made for Cable Movies:*
Dying to Remember (1993; USA). . . . . . . . . . . . . n.a.
*Made for Cable TV:*
Rebel Highway: Runaway Daughters (1994; Showtime)
. . . . . . . . . . . . . . . . . . . . . . . . . . . . Mr. Gordon
*Miniseries:*
Blue and the Gray (1982). . . . . . . . . . . Major Fairbairn
*TV:*
The Interns (1970-71) . . . . . . . . . . . . .Dr. Pooch Hardin
Spencer's Pilots (1976) . . . . . . . . . . . . .Cass Garrett
Harper Valley P.T.A. (1981-82) . . . . . . . . Tom Meechum
Dallas (1984) . . . . . . . . . . . . . . . . . . . Dave Stratton
The New Lassie (1989-91) . . . . . . . . . Chris McCullough

## • Strathairn, David

*Films:*
Return of the Secaucus Seven (1980) . . . . . . . . . . . Ron
Lovesick (1983) . . . . . . . . . . . . . . . . . . . . . Zuckerman
The Brother From Another Planet (1984) . . Man in Black
Iceman (1984). . . . . . . . . . . . . . . . . . . . . Dr. Singe
At Close Range (1986) . . . . . . . . . . . . . . . .Tony Pine
Matewan (1987) . . . . . . . . . . . .Police Chief Sid Hatfield
Call Me (1988). . . . . . . . . . . . . . . . . . . . . . . . .Sam
Dominick and Eugene (1988). . . . . . . . Martin Chernak
Eight Men Out (1988) . . . . . . . . . . . . . Eddie Cicotte
Stars and Bars (1988) . . . . . . . . . . . . . . . . . .Charlie
The Feud (1990) . . . . . . . . . . . . . . . . The Stranger
Memphis Belle (1990) . . . . . . . . . .Commanding Officer
Big Girls Don't Cry... They Get Even (1991)
. . . . . . . . . . . . . . . . . . . . . . . . . . . Keith Powers
City of Hope (1991) . . . . . . . . . . . . . . . . . .Asteroid
Bob Roberts (1992; U.S./British). . . . . . . . . Mack Laflin
A League of Their Own (1992). . . . . . . . Ira Lowenstein
Sneakers (1992). . . . . . . . . . . . . . . . . . . . .Whistler
**A Dangerous Woman** (1993). . . . . . . . . . . . . Getzo
- 1:20—Brief upper half of buns, when Debra Winger interrupts him while he's pulling up his underwear.

The Firm (1993). . . . . . . . . . . . . . . . . . .Ray McDeere
Passion Fish (1993) . . . . . . . . . . . . . . . . . . .Rennie

## Street, Elliot

*Films:*
Honky (1971). . . . . . . . . . . . . . . . . . . . . . . . . . n.a.
Welcome Home, Soldier Boys (1972) . . . . . . . .Fat Back

**The Harrad Experiment** (1973) . . . . . . . . . . . Wilson
•• 0:44—Frontal nudity taking off clothes and getting
into the swimming pool.

## Strohmyer, Scott
Films:
**The Bikini Carwash Company** (1992) . . . . Big Bruce
(Unrated version reviewed.)
•• 0:18—Buns, while walking on beach with Rita.

## Sullivan, William Bell
Films:
**Diamond Run** (1988; Indonesian). . . . . . . . . . . Nicky
a.k.a. Java Burn
•• 0:08—Buns, while lying in bed, then getting up.
The Hunt for Red October (1990)
. . . . . . . . . . . . . . . . . . . . . . Lt. Cmdr. Mike Hewitt

## Sutherland, Donald
Father of actor Kiefer Sutherland.
Films:
Die, Die, My Darling (1965) . . . . . . . . . . . . . . Joseph
Dr. Terror's House of Horrors (1965) . . . . . . . Bob Carroll
The Dirty Dozen (1967) . . . . . . . . . . . . . Vernon Pinkley
Kelly's Heroes (1970). . . . . . . . . . . . . . . . . . . Oddball
M*A*S*H (1970) . . . . . . . . . . . . . . . . . .Hawkeye Pierce
Start the Revolution Without Me (1970)
. . . . . . . . . . . . . . . .Charles Coupe/Pierre De Sisi
Johnny Got His Gun (1971). . . . . . . . . . . . .Jesus Christ
Klute (1971) . . . . . . . . . . . . . . . . . . . . . . .John Klute
**Don't Look Now** (1973). . . . . . . . . . . . . John Baxter
• 0:27—Buns, while in the bathroom with Julie
Christie.
Steelyard Blues (1973) . . . . . . . . . . . . . . . Jesse Veldini
The Day of the Locust (1975) . . . . . . . . . . . . . Homer
1900 (1976; Italian) . . . . . . . . . . . . . . . . . . .Attila
(NC-17 version reviewed.)
The Disappearance (1977) . . . . . . . . . . . . . . . . Jay
The Eagle Has Landed (1977; British) . . . . . Liam Devlin
Kentucky Fried Movie (1977) . . . . . . . . . . . . .Clumsy
**Animal House** (1978). . . . . . . . . . . . . .Dave Jennings
• 1:22—Buns, while reaching up in kitchen to get
something when his sweater goes up. Out of focus.
Invasion of the Body Snatchers (1978)
. . . . . . . . . . . . . . . . . . . . . . . Matthew Bennell
The Great Train Robbery (1979; British). . . . . . . . Agan
Murder by Decree (1979) . . . . . . . . . . . . .Robert Lees
Bear Island (1980; British/Canadian) . . . . . Frank Lansing
Nothing Personal (1980; Canadian)
. . . . . . . . . . . . . . . . . . . . . Professor Roger Keller
Ordinary People (1980). . . . . . . . . . . . . . . . . .Calvin
Eye of the Needle (1981) . . . . . . . . . . . . . . . . Faber
Gas (1981; Canadian) . . . . . . . . . . . . . . . Nick the Noz
Max Dugan Returns (1983). . . . . . . . . . . . . . .Brian
Threshold (1983; Canadian) . . . . . . . . . . . . . Dr. Vrain
Crackers (1984). . . . . . . . . . . . . . . . . . . . . Weslake
Ordeal by Innocence (1984) . . . . . . . . . . Arthur Calgary
Heaven Help Us (1985) . . . . . . . . . . . . .Brother Thadeus
Revolution (1986) . . . . . . . . . . . . . Sergeant Major Peasy

The Rosary Murders (1987) . . . . . . . . . . Father Koesler
Lock Up (1989) . . . . . . . . . . . . . . . .Warden Drumgoole
Lost Angels (1989) . . . . . . . . . . . . . . . Dr. Charles Loftis
Backdraft (1991) . . . . . . . . . . . . . . . . . .Ronald Bartel
Eminent Domain (1991). . . . . . . . . . . . . . . . . .Joseph
JFK (1991) . . . . . . . . . . . . . . . . . . . . . . .Colonel "X"
Quicksand: No Escape (1991) . . . . . . . . . . . . . . Doc
Buffy The Vampire Slayer (1992) . . . . . . . . . . . . Merrick
Shadow of the Wolf (1992) . . . . . . . . . . . . .Henderson
Benefit of the Doubt (1993; U.S./German)
. . . . . . . . . . . . . . . . . . . . . . . . . . Frank Braswell
Dr. Bethune (1993; Canadian/French)
. . . . . . . . . . . . . . . . . . . . . . . . .Norman Bethune
Six Degrees of Separation (1993) . . . . . . . Flan Kittredge
Made for Cable Movies:
The Railway Station Man (1992; TNT)
. . . . . . . . . . . . . . . . . . . . . . . . . Roger Hawthorne
Made for TV Movies:
Oldest Living Confederate Widow Tells All (1994)
. . . . . . . . . . . . . . . . . . . . . . . . . .William (older)

## Sutherland, Kiefer
Son of actor Donald Sutherland.
Films:
Max Dugan Returns (1983) . . . . . . . . . . . . . . . . .Bill
Bay Boy (1985; Canadian) . . . . . . . . . Donald Campbell
At Close Range (1986) . . . . . . . . . . . . . . . . . . . Tim
Stand By Me (1986). . . . . . . . . . . . . . . . .Ace Merrill
The Killing Time (1987) . . . . . . . . . . . . . Brian Costello
The Lost Boys (1987) . . . . . . . . . . . . . . . . . .David
1969 (1988). . . . . . . . . . . . . . . . . . . . . . . . Scott
Bright Lights, Big City (1988). . . . . . . . . . . Tad Allagash
Promised Land (1988) . . . . . . . . . . . . . . . Danny Rivers
Young Guns (1988) . . . . . . . . . . Josiah "Doc" Scurlock
Chicago Joe and the Showgirl (1989; British)
. . . . . . . . . . . . . . . . . . . . . . . . . . . Karl Hulten
Renegades (1989) . . . . . . . . . . . . . . . .Buster McHenry
Flashback (1990) . . . . . . . . . . . . . . . . . .John Buckner
Flatliners (1990). . . . . . . . . . . . . . . . . . .Nelson Wright
Young Guns II (1990) . . . . . . . . . . . . . . . Doc Scurlock
Article 99 (1992) . . . . . . . . . . . . . . . . . Peter Morgan
A Few Good Men (1992)
. . . . . . . . . . . . . . . . . Lieutenant Jonathan Kendrick
Twin Peaks: Fire Walk With Me (1992) . . . . .Sam Stanley
The Three Musketeers (1993). . . . . . . . . . . . . .Athos
The Vanishing (1993). . . . . . . . . . . . . . . Jeff Harriman
The Cowboy Way (1994) . . . . . . . . . . . . . Sonny Gilstrap
Made for Cable Movies:
**Last Light** (1993; Showtime) . . . . . . . . Denver Bayliss
• 0:03—Side view of buns, in solitary confinement
cell. Dark. Covered with feces.
• 0:05—Brief buns, while walking in jail hallway. Still
covered with feces.
• 0:06—Buns, while standing in front of security cage,
getting clothes. Long scene, but still covered with
feces.

## • Sutton, Dudley

*Films:*
The Leather Boys (1965; British) . . . . . . . . . . . . . . Pete
Cry of the Penguins (1972; British) . . . . . . . . . Starshot
The Pink Panther Strikes Again (1976) . . . . . . . McLaren
Valentino (1977; British) . . . . . . . . . . . . . . . . . . . Willie
The Big Sleep (1978; British) . . . . . . . . . . . . . . . Lanny
The Island (1980) . . . . . . . . . . . . . . . . . . . . . . Dr. Brazil
Brimstone and Treacle (1982; British) . . . . . . . . Stroller
The Trail of the Pink Panther (1982) . . . . . . . . . . . . .n.a.
The Rainbow (1989) . . . . . . . . . . . . . . . . . . MacAllister
**Edward II** (1992; British) . . . . . . . Bishop of Winchester
   • 0:08—Brief side view nude, after getting beaten.
Orlando (1993; British) . . . . . . . . . . . . . . . King James I

## Swayze, Patrick

Brother of actor Don Swayze.
*Films:*
Skatetown, U.S.A. (1979) . . . . . . . . . . . . . . . . . . . .Ace
The Outsiders (1983) . . . . . . . . . . . . . . . . . . . . . . Darrel
Uncommon Valor (1983) . . . . . . . . . . . . . . . . . . . .Scott
Grandview, U.S.A. (1984) . . . . . . . Ernie "Slam" Webster
Red Dawn (1984) . . . . . . . . . . . . . . . . . . . . . . . . . . Jed
Youngblood (1986) . . . . . . . . . . . . . . . . . . Derek Sutton
Dirty Dancing (1987) . . . . . . . . . . . . . . Johnny Castle
Steel Dawn (1988) . . . . . . . . . . . . . . . . . . . . . . . Nomad
Tiger Warsaw (1988) . . . . . . . . . . Chuck "Tiger" Warsaw
Next of Kin (1989) . . . . . . . . . . . . . . . . . . Truman Gates
**Roadhouse** (1989) . . . . . . . . . . . . . . . . . . . . . Dalton
   ••• 0:30—Brief buns getting out of bed while Kathleen
      Wilhoite watches.
Ghost (1990) . . . . . . . . . . . . . . . . . . . . . . .Sam Wheat
Point Break (1991) . . . . . . . . . . . . . . . . . . . . . . . Bodhi
City of Joy (1992) . . . . . . . . . . . . . . . . . . . . . . . . . Max
Father Hood (1993) . . . . . . . . . . . . . . . . . . Jack Charles
*Miniseries:*
North and South (1985) . . . . . . . . . . . . . . . .Orry Main
North and South, Book II (1986) . . . . . . . . . .Orry Main
*TV:*
Renegades (1983) . . . . . . . . . . . . . . . . . . . . . . .Bandit

## Tabor, Erin

*Films:*
**I Spit on Your Grave** (1978) . . . . . . . . . . . . . Johnny
(Uncut, unrated version reviewed.)
   • 0:25—Buns, while undressing to rape Jennifer.
   • 1:20—Buns, while undressing at gun point.

## • Taylor, Noah

*Films:*
Dogs In Space (1987; Australian) . . . . . . . . . . . . . .n.a.
The Year My Voice Broke (1987; Australian)
. . . . . . . . . . . . . . . . . . . . . . . . . . .Danny Embling
**Flirting** (1992; Australian) . . . . . . . . . .Danny Embling
   • 0:03—Close up of buns, when his school mates
      check out his whip marks with flashlight. Don't see
      his face.

## Taylor, Zach

*Films:*
**Group Marriage** (1972) . . . . . . . . . . . . . . . . . . . . Phil
   •• 0:43—Buns, while walking on beach with Jan.
Dazed and Confused (1993) . . . . . . . . . . . . . 1st Geek

## Tepper, William

*Films:*
Drive, He Said (1972) . . . . . . . . . . . . . . . . . . . . .Hector
Breathless (1983) . . . . . . . . . . . . . . . . . . . . . . . . .Paul
Bachelor Party (1984) . . . . . . . . . . . . . . . Dr. Stan Gassko
**Miss Right** (1987; Italian) . . . . . . . . . . . . . .Terry Bartell
   • 0:47—Buns, while jumping out of bed with Karen
      Black when the bed catches fire.

## Terrell, John Canada

*Films:*
Recruits (1986; Canadian) . . . . . . . . . . . . . . . . .Winston
**She's Gotta Have It** (1987) . . . . . . . . . . . Greer Childs
   •• 0:27—Buns and very brief frontal nudity, while get-
      ting into bed with Nola. More quick shots of buns in
      bed.
Rooftops (1989) . . . . . . . . . . . . . . . . . . . . . . .Junkie Cop
**Def by Temptation** (1990) . . . . . . . . . . Bartender #1
   •• 0:09—Nude, running through house trying to get
      away from The Temptress.
The Return of Superfly (1990) . . . . . . Detective Loomey
The Five Heartbeats (1991) . . . . Michael "Flash" Turner
Boomerang (1992) . . . . . . . . . . . . . . . . . . . . . . . .Todd

## Terry, Nigel

*Films:*
The Lion in the Winter (1968; British) . . . . . . Prince John
Excalibur (1981; British) . . . . . . . . . . . . . . . King Arthur
**Deja Vu** (1984) . . . . . . . . . . . . . . . . . . . . Michel/Greg
   • 1:17—Very brief buns, while jumping out of bed
      when Jaclyn Smith tries to kill him with a knife.
Sylvia (1985; New Zealand) . . . . . . . . . . . . .Aden Morris
War Requiem (1988; British) . . . . . . . . . . . . . Abraham
Christopher Columbus: The Discovery (1992; U.S./
   Spanish) . . . . . . . . . . . . . . . . . . . . . . . . . . .Roldan
Edward II (1992; British) . . . . . . . . . . . . . . . .Mortimer
*TV:*
Covington Cross (1992-93) . . . . . . . . . . . . . . . . . Gray

## • Thewlis, David

Husband of actress Sara Sugarman.
*Films:*
Little Dorrit (1988; British) . . . . . . . . . . George Braddle
The Resurrected (1990; British) . . . . . . . . Kevin Deakin
Life is Sweet (1991; British) . . . . . . . . . . Nicola's Lover
Afraid of the Dark (1992; British/French)
. . . . . . . . . . . . . . . . . . . . . . Tom Miller/Locksmith
Damage (1992; French/British) . . . . . . . . . . . .Detective
(Unrated Director's cut reviewed.)
**Naked** (1993; British) . . . . . . . . . . . . . . . . . . . .Johnny
   •• 0:17—Frontal nudity, while getting up out of bed.
      Dark.
Black Beauty (1994) . . . . . . . . . . . . . . . . . . . . . . . n.a.

*Made for TV Movies:*
Mystery! Prime Suspect 3 (1994) . . . . . . . .James Jackson

# • Thomas, Hugh
*Films:*
**if...** (1969; British) . . . . . . . . . . . . . . . . . . . . . . .Denson
• 0:43—Brief buns, while getting out of bathtub in boy's shower room.
O Lucky Man! (1973; British). . . . . . . . . . . . . . . . .n.a.
Rough Cut (1980; British) . . . . . . . . . . . . . . . . . . . .n.a.
The Tall Guy (1990; British) . . . . . . . . . . Dr. Karabekian

# Thompson, Jack
*Films:*
Libido (1973; Australian) . . . . . . . . . . . . . . . . . . . . . .Ken
**Jock Petersen** (1974; Australian). . . . . . . Tony Petersen
*a.k.a. Petersen*
••• 0:13—Buns, while making love with Wendy Hughes on the floor.
••• 0:20—Frontal nudity under tarp with Moira during protest.
• 0:22—Buns while in bed with Suzy.
•• 0:44—Nude running around the beach with Hughes.
•• 0:50—Frontal nudity undressing, then buns while lying in bed.
Mad Dog Morgan (1976; Australian)
. . . . . . . . . . . . . . . . . . . . . . . Detective Manwaring
Breaker Morant (1979; Australian). . . Major J. F. Thomas
The Earthling (1980) . . . . . . . . . . . . . . . . . . . Ross Daley
The Man from Snowy River (1982; Australian). . . Clancy
Merry Christmas, Mr. Lawrence (1983; Japanese/British)
. . . . . . . . . . . . . . . . . . . . . . . . . . . . . . Hicksley-Ellis
Sunday Too Far Away (1983; Australian) . . . . . . . Foley
Burke and Wills (1985; Australian)
. . . . . . . . . . . . . . . . . . . . . .Robert O'Hara Burke
Flesh + Blood (1985). . . . . . . . . . . . . . . . . .Hawkwood
Ground Zero (1988; Australian) . . . . . . . . . .Trebilcock
Deception (1992) . . . . . . . . . . . . . . . . . . . . . . . . . .Ed
*a.k.a. Ruby Cairo*
Trouble in Paradise (1992). . . . . . . . . . Jake La Fontaine
Turtle Beach (1992; Australian) . . . . . . . . . . . . Ralph
*a.k.a. The Killing Beach*
Wind (1992) . . . . . . . . . . . . . . . . . . . . . . .Jack Neville
A Far Off Place (1993; U.S./British) . . . . . . .John Ricketts

# Thomsen, Kevin
*Films:*
**Cleo/Leo** (1989) . . . . . . . . . . . . . . . . . . . . . .Bob Miller
• 1:07—Brief frontal nudity, then buns while making love with Jane Hamilton on bed.
Enrapture (1989). . . . . . . . . . . . . . . . . . . . . . . .Keith

# • Thomson, Gordon
*Films:*
**Candy The Stripper** (1993) . . . . . . . . . . . . . . David
•• 1:15—Buns, while on the floor, making out on top of Candy.

# • Tiernan, Andrew
*Films:*
**Edward II** (1992; British) . . . . . . . . . . . . . . Gaveston
• 0:16—Sort of side view of buns, while squatting on throne.
The Trial (1994; British) . . . . . . . . . . . . . . . Berthold

# Tierney, Aidan
*Films:*
**Family Viewing** (1987; Canadian) . . . . . . . . . . . . Van
•• 0:26—Brief buns, while getting up out of bed and putting on his underwear.

# Tobias, Oliver
*Films:*
Romance of a Horse Thief (1971) . . . . . .Zanvill Kradnick
'Tis a Pity She's a Whore (1972; Italian) . . . . . . Giovanni
**The Stud** (1978; British) . . . . . . . . . . . . . . .Tony Blake
• 1:06—Buns, running away from the pool.
**The Wicked Lady** (1983; British) . . . . . . . Kit Locksby
• 0:58—Buns, with Caroline in living room.
Mata Hari (1985) . . . . . . . . . . . . . . . . . . . . . . . Ladoux

# Torgl, Mark
*Films:*
**The First Turn-On!** (1983) . . . . . . . . . . . . . .Dwayne
• 1:02—Buns, while dropping his pants for Michelle.

# Torn, Rip
*Films:*
Tropic of Cancer (1970) . . . . . . . . . . . . . . .Henry Miller
**Payday** (1972) . . . . . . . . . . . . . . . . . . . . Maury Dann
• 1:21—Brief buns while getting up out of bed.
Slaughter (1972) . . . . . . . . . . . . . . . . . . . . . . . .Hoffo
The Man Who Fell to Earth (1976; British)
. . . . . . . . . . . . . . . . . . . . . . . . . . . . .Nathan Bryce
(Uncensored version reviewed.)
Coma (1978) . . . . . . . . . . . . . . . . . . . . . . . .Dr. George
The Seduction of Joe Tynan (1979) . . . . Senator Kittner
Heartland (1980) . . . . . . . . . . . . . . . . . . . . . . . .Clyde
One Trick Pony (1980) . . . . . . . . . . . . . . . . .Walter Fox
Airplane II: The Sequel (1982) . . . . . . . . . . . .Hruger
The Beastmaster (1982) . . . . . . . . . . . . . . . . . . .Maax
A Stranger is Watching (1982) . . . . . . . . . . Artie Taggart
Cross Creek (1983) . . . . . . . . . . . . . . . . . Marsh Turner
Flashpoint (1984). . . . . . . . . . . . . . . . . . . . Sheriff Wells
Songwriter (1984) . . . . . . . . . . . . . . . . . Dino McLeish
Summer Rental (1985) . . . . . . . . . . . . . . . . . . .Scully
Beer (1986) . . . . . . . . . . . . . . . . . . . Buzz Beckerman
Extreme Prejudice (1987). . . . . . . . Sheriff Hank Pearson
Silence Like Glass (1989) . . . . . . . . . . . Dr. Markowitz
Defending Your Life (1991) . . . . . . . . . . Bob Diamond
Beautiful Dreamers (1992; Canadian). . . . Walt Whitman
Dolly Dearest (1992) . . . . . . . . . . . . . . . .Karl Resnick
Robocop 3 (1993) . . . . . . . . . . . . . . . . . . .The CEO
*Made for Cable Movies:*
Laguna Heat (1987; HBO) . . . . . . . . . . . . . . . . . .n.a.

Another Pair of Aces (1991) . . . . . . . Capt. Jack Parsons
(Video tape includes nude scenes not shown on cable
TV.)
Beyond the Law (1992; HBO) . . . . . . . . . . . . . Prescott
Dead Ahead: The Exxon Valdez Disaster (1992; U.S./
British; HBO) . . . . . . . . . . . . . . . . . . . . . . . . . . Yost
*Miniseries:*
North and South, Book III: Heaven and Hell (1994)
. . . . . . . . . . . . . . . . . . . . . . . . . . . . . . . . . Adolphus
*Made for TV Movies:*
Death Hits the Jackpot (1991) . . . . . . . . . . Leon Lamarr
My Son Johnny (1991) . . . . . . . . . . . . . Brian Stansbury
A Mother's Right: The Elizabeth Morgan Story (1992)
. . . . . . . . . . . . . . . . . . . . . . . . . . . . . . .Bill Morgan
Heart of a Child (1994) . . . . . . . . . . .Dr. Leonard Bailey
*TV:*
The Larry Sanders Show (1992- ) . . . . . . . . . . . . . Artie

# • Tortorich, Vincent
*Video Tapes:*
Playboy's Erotic Fantasies (1992) . . . . . . . Cast Member
**Playboy's How to Reawaken Your Sexual Powers**
(1992). . . . . . . . . . . . . . . . . . . . . . . . . Cast Member
••• 0:21—Nude in the forest with his lover.
••• 0:29—Nude on hammock on sailboat with his lover.

# Tovatt, Patrick
*Films:*
On the Nickel (1980) . . . . . . . . . . . . . . . . . . . . . .n.a.
**Ellie** (1984) . . . . . . . . . . . . . . . . . . . . . . . . . . . . Art
• 1:19—Brief blurry buns while falling down the stairs.

# Trujillo, Raoul
*Films:*
White Light (1990) . . . . . . . . . . . . . . . . . . . . . Hatchet
**The Adjuster** (1991; Canadian)
. . . . . . . . . . . . . . . . . . . . . . Matthew, Larry's Lover
• 0:59—Buns, in B&W photo that Elias Koteas looks at.
• 1:32—Buns in the same B&W photo.
• 1:33—Buns, while sleeping in motel room while
Koteas walks around.
Black Robe (1991; Canadian/Australian) . . . . Kiotseaton
Scanners 2: The New Order (1991). . . . . . . . . . . . Drak

# Tubb, Barry
*Films:*
The Legend of Billie Jean (1985) . . . . . . . . . . . . . Hubie
Mask (1985) . . . . . . . . . . . . . . . . . . . . . . . . . . Dewey
Top Gun (1986) . . . . . . . . . . . . . . . . . . . . .Henry Ruth
**Valentino Returns** (1988) . . . . . . . . . . . Wayne Gibbs
•• 1:15—Buns, while fighting two other guys after skinny dipping with Jenny Wright at night. Very, very
brief, blurry frontal nudity after getting hit and rolling into the water.
**Warm Summer Rain** (1989) . . . . . . . . . . . . . . . Guy
•• 0:23—Lower frontal nudity getting off Kelly Lynch in
bed.
0:25—Side view of buns while dreaming in bed.

•• 0:58—Frontal nudity kneeling on floor and behind
the table while washing Lynch.
• 1:00—Buns while getting washed by Lynch.
• 1:07—Brief buns while making love with Lynch.
Quick cuts.
••• 1:09—Nude picking up belongings and running out
of burning house with Lynch.
Guilty by Suspicion (1991) . . . . . . . . . . . . . Jerry Cooper
*Miniseries:*
Return to Lonesome Dove (1993) . . . . . . . . . . . Jasper
*TV:*
Bay City Blues (1983) . . . . . . . . . . . . . . Mickey Wagner

# • Turco, Paolo
*Films:*
**The Lickerish Quartet** (1970; Italian). . . . . . . . . Son
*a.k.a. Erotic Illusion*
••• 1:00—Nude, while undressing outside with the girl.
That Splendid November (1971; Italian/French). . . Nino
Bread and Chocolate (1978; Italian). . . . . . . . . .Commis

# Turturro, John
Husband of actress Katherine Borowitz.
*Films:*
Exterminator 2 (1984) . . . . . . . . . . . . . . . . . Guy No. 1
The Flamingo Kid (1984) . . . . . . . . . . Ted From Pinky's
Desperately Seeking Susan (1985) . . . . . . . . . . . . Ray
Gung Ho (1985) . . . . . . . . . . . . . . . . . . . . . . .Willie
To Live and Die in L.A. (1985) . . . . . . . . . . . Carl Cody
The Color of Money (1986) . . . . . . . . . . . . . . . .Julian
Hannah and Her Sisters (1986). . . . . . . . . . . . . Writer
Off Beat (1986) . . . . . . . . . . . . . . . . . . . Neil Pepper
The Sicilian (1987) . . . . . . . . . . . . . . . . Aspanu Pisciotta
(Director's uncut version reviewed.)
Five Corners (1988) . . . . . . . . . . . . . . . Heinz Sabantino
Backtrack (1989) . . . . . . . . . . . . . . . . . . . . . . Pinella
*a.k.a. Catch Fire*
Do the Right Thing (1989). . . . . . . . . . . . . . . . . Dino
**Men of Respect** (1990) . . . . . . . . . . . . Mike Battaglia
0:21—Side view of buns, lying in bed with Ruthie.
• 0:25—Brief upper half of buns, putting on robe and
leaving room.
•• 0:45—Buns, while washing blood off himself in
bathroom with Ruthie's help.
Miller's Crossing (1990) . . . . . . . . . . . .Bernie Bernbaum
Mo' Better Blues (1990) . . . . . . . . . . . . .Moe Flatbush
State of Grace (1990). . . . . . . . . . . . . . . . . . . . .Nick
Barton Fink (1991) . . . . . . . . . . . . . . . . . Barton Fink
Brain Donors (1992). . . . . . . . . . . . . Roland T. Flakfizer
**Mac** (1992) . . . . . . . . . . . . . . . .Niccolo "Mac" Vitelli
• 1:08—Brief buns, while getting out of bed. Don't
see his face.
Fearless (1993). . . . . . . . . . . . . . . . . . . Bill Pearlman

# Tyson, Richard
*Films:*
Three O'Clock High (1987) . . . . . . . . . . . .Buddy Revell
**Two Moon Junction** (1988) . . . . . . . . . . . . . . . .Perry
• 0:58—Very, very brief buns while wrestling with April in a motel room. Dark, hard to see.
Kindergarten Cop (1990) . . . . . . . . . . . . . . . . .Crisp
The Babe (1992) . . . . . . . . . . . . . . . . . . . . . . Guy Bush
**Dark Tide** (1993) . . . . . . . . . . . . . . . . . . . . . .Dak
•• 0:41—Brief buns, after taking off shorts and diving into underground pool.
• 0:42—Buns, seen under water while he's swimming.
• 0:44—Brief buns, while making love with Brigitte Bako in underground pool.
*Made for Cable TV:*
Red Shoe Diaries: Talk To Me Baby (1992; Showtime)
. . . . . . . . . . . . . . . . . . . . . . . . . . . . . . . . . . Bud
(Available on video tape on *Red Shoe Diaries 3: Another Woman's Lipstick.*)
*TV:*
Hardball (1989-90) . . . . . . . . . . Joe "Kaz" Kaczierowski

# Underwood, Jay
*Films:*
The Boy Who Could Fly (1986) . . . . . . . . . . . . . . . .Eric
**The Invisible Kid** (1988) . . . . . . . . . . . Grover Dunn
• 0:27—Brief buns while running around the school halls after becoming visible with his friend, Milton.
Uncle Buck (1989). . . . . . . . . . . . . . . . . . . . . . . Bug
The Gumshoe Kid (1990) . . . . . . . . . . . . .Jeff Sherman
To Die For 2 (1991). . . . . . . . . . . . . . . . . . . . . Danny
*a.k.a. Son of Darkness: To Die For II*
*Made for Cable Movies:*
Not Quite Human (1987; Disney) . . . . . . . . . . . . . Chip
Not Quite Human II (1989; Disney). . . . . . . . . . . . Chip
Still Not Quite Human (1992; Disney). . . . . . . . . . Chip

# Urena, Fabio
*Films:*
**The Bronx War** (1989) . . . . . . . . . . . . . . . . . . . .Tony
• 0:54—Buns, getting up out of bed with Alicia and getting dressed.
Falling Down (1993) . . . . . . . . . . . . . . .Gang Member 4

# Valentine, Scott
*Films:*
**Deadtime Stories** (1985) . . . . . . . . . . . . . . . .Peter
• 0:19—Buns, while getting out of bath.
My Demon Lover (1987). . . . . . . . . . . . . . . . . . .Kaz
**Write to Kill** (1990) . . . . . . . . . . . . . . . Clark Sanford
• 1:03—Very brief partial frontal nudity, leaping out of bed.
**Double Obsession** (1992) . . . . . . . . . . . .Steve Burke
• 0:48—Brief buns, when leaving Maryam D'Abo in bathroom.
Homicidal Impulse (1992). . . . . . . . . . . . . . .Tim Casey
*a.k.a. Killer Instinct*
(Unrated version reviewed.)
To Sleep with a Vampire (1992) . . . . . . . . . . . Vampire

The Unborn II (1993) . . . . . . . . . . . . . . . . . John Edson
*Made for Cable Movies:*
After the Shock (1990) . . . . . . . . . . . . . . . . Shannon
The Secret Passion of Robert Clayton (1992; USA)
. . . . . . . . . . . . . . . . . . . . . . . . . . Robert Clayton, Jr.
*Made for TV Movies:*
Perry Mason: The Case of the Fatal Framing (1992)
. . . . . . . . . . . . . . . . . . . . . . . . . . . . Damian Blakely
*TV:*
Family Ties (1985-89). . . . . . . . . . . . . . . . Nick Moore

# Van Damme, Jean-Claude
Husband of actress Darcy LaPier.
*Films:*
No Retreat, No Surrender (1986) . . . . . .Ivan the Russian
**Bloodsport** (1987) . . . . . . . . . . . . . . . . . . . . . . .Frank
•• 0:50—Brief buns while putting underwear on after spending the night with Janice.
Black Eagle (1988) . . . . . . . . . . . . . . . . . . . . . .Andrei
Cyborg (1989). . . . . . . . . . . . . . . Gibson Rickenbacker
Kick Boxer (1989). . . . . . . . . . . . . . . . . Kurt Sloane
Death Warrant (1990) . . . . . . . . . . . . . . . .Louis Burke
**Lionheart** (1990) . . . . . . . . . . . . . . . . . . . . . . . Lyon
••• 0:47—Buns, while putting on robe after getting out of bed.
**Double Impact** (1991). . . . . . . . . . . . . . . . Chad/Alec
• 1:11—Very brief buns, while making love with Danielle. Dark.
**Universal Soldier** (1992). . . . . . . . . . . . . Luc Devreux
••• 0:34—Buns, while standing in front of air conditioner.
••• 0:35—Buns, while walking in motel parking lot after Ally Walker. Partial buns, while lying on ground.
Hard Target (1993) . . . . . . . . . . . . . Chance Boudreaux
Last Action Hero (1993) . . . . . . . . . . . . . . . . Himself
**Nowhere to Run** (1993) . . . . . . . . . . . . . . . . . .Sam
•• 0:24—Buns, while walking out of and backing into lake. Kind of a long shot.
**Timecop** (1994). . . . . . . . . . . . . . . . . . . . . . . . .n.a.
*Music Videos:*
Time Won't Let Me/The Smithereens (1986)
. . . . . . . . . . . . . . . . . . . . . . . .Time Machine Operator

# Van Hetenryck, Kevin
*Films:*
**Basket Case** (1982) . . . . . . . . . . . . . . . .Duane Bradley
•• 1:21—Frontal nudity, twice, running around at night.
**Basket Case 2** (1989) . . . . . . . . . . . . . .Duane Bradley
• 0:34—Buns while standing in front of mirror looking at the large scar on the side of his body.
Basket Case 3: The Progeny (1991) . . . . .Duane Bradley

## Van Hoffman, Brant

*Films:*
Police Academy (1984) . . . . . . . . . . . . . . Kyle Blankes
**The Further Adventures of Tennessee Buck** (1987)
. . . . . . . . . . . . . . . . . . . . . . . . . . . . Ken Manchester
 • 0:38—Brief buns, behind a mosquito net while making love with his disinterested wife.
Guilty by Suspicion (1991) . . . . . . . . . . . . . . . . Stanley

## Van Patten, Nels

Son of actor Dick Van Patten.
*Films:*
Lunch Wagon (1981) . . . . . . . . . . . . . . . . . . . . .Scotty
 *a.k.a. Lunch Wagon Girls*
 *a.k.a. Come 'N' Get It*
The Young Warriors (1983; U.S./Canadian) . . . . . . Roger
One Last Run (1990). . . . . . . . . . . . . . . . . . . . Charlie
**Mirror Images** (1991) . . . . . . . . . . . . . . . . Joey Zoom
 •• 0:08—Buns, while in bed and getting out of bed with Shauna.
 •• 0:29—Buns, while on top of Kaitlin.
Live Wire (1992) . . . . . . . . . . . . . . . Racquetball Player (Unrated version on video tape reviewed, not the R-rated version shown on HBO. )
**Mind Twister** (1992) . . . . . . . . . . . . . . . . .Roy Gerard (Unrated version reviewed.)
 •• 0:17—Buns, while making love with Heather on sofa.

## Van Tongeren, Hans

*Films:*
**Spetters** (1980; Dutch) . . . . . . . . . . . . . . Ron Hartman
 ••• 0:35—Frontal nudity, measuring and comparing his manlihood with his friends in the auto shop.
Summer Lovers (1982) . . . . . . . . . . . . . . . . . Jan Tolin

## Vavrin, Michael

*Films:*
**Naked Instinct** (1993) . . . . . . . . . . . . Virgin Rich Kid
 ••• 0:07—Nude, taking off his underwear in bed and masturbating while Michelle Bauer watches, then making love with her. Long scene.
 ••• 0:13—Buns, while making love on top of Bauer.

## Vazquez, Yul

*Films:*
The Mambo Kings (1992) . . . . . . . . . . . . . . . . . .Flaco
*Made for Cable TV:*
**Tales From the Crypt: On a Dead Man's Chest** (1992; HBO) . . . . . . . . . . . . . . . . . . . . . . . . . Danny
 ••• 0:06—Buns, while making love on top of Sherrie Rose, then getting out of bed.

## • Venentini, Venentine

*Films:*
**Emmanuelle, The Joys of a Woman** (1975)
. . . . . . . . . . . . . . . . . . . . . . . . . . . . . . . Polo Player
 • 0:52—Nude in locker room when Sylvia Kristel secretly watches him.

 • 0:53—Left side of buns, while making love with Kristel.
*Magazines:*
**Playboy** (Mar 1976) . . . . . . . . . . Encore Emmanuellel
 •• 78—Buns as tattooed polo player.

## Ventura, Clyde

*Films:*
Bury Me an Angel (1972) . . . . . . . . . . . . . . . . . Bernie
Gator Bait (1973) . . . . . . . . . . . . . . . . . . . . . . n.a.
**Terminal Island** (1973) . . . . . . . . . . . . . . . . . Dillon
 •• 0:42—Buns, while taking off pants in front of Phyllis Davis, then covered with honey and bees, then running to jump into a pond.
Serial (1980) . . . . . . . . . . . . . . . . . . . . . . . Donald

## Villard, Tom

*Films:*
Parasite (1982). . . . . . . . . . . . . . . . . . . . . . . . Zeke
Surf II (1984) . . . . . . . . . . . . . . . . . Jacko O'Finlay
Heartbreak Ridge (1986) . . . . . . . . . . . . . . . . Profile
**The Trouble with Dick** (1986) . . . . . . . .Dick Kendred
 0:30—Side view of buns, while leaving Haley's room.
 • 0:58—Buns from under his shirt, getting out of bed to open the door.
Weekend Warriors (1986). . . . . . . . . . . . .Mort Seblinsky
My Girl (1991) . . . . . . . . . . . . . . . . . . . . . . . Justin
Popcorn (1991) . . . . . . . . . . . . . . . . . . . . . . . Toby
Whore (1991) . . . . . . . . . . . . . . . . . . . . . . . Hippy
 *a.k.a. If you're afraid to say it... Just see it*
Shakes the Clown (1992) . . . . . . . . . . . Dirthead in Car
*TV:*
We Got It Made (1983-84). . . . . . . . . . . . .Jay Bostwick

## Vincent, Jan-Michael

*Films:*
Going Home (1971). . . . . . . . . . . . . . . Jimmy Graham
The Mechanic (1972). . . . . . . . . . . . . . Steve McKenna
The World's Greatest Athlete (1973). . . . . . . . . . .Nanu
**Buster and Billie** (1974) . . . . . . . . . . . . . Buster Lane
 ••• 1:06—Frontal nudity taking off his underwear and walking to Billie. Buns, in slow motion, while swinging into the water.
Bite the Bullet (1975) . . . . . . . . . . . . . . . . . . . Carbo
White Line Fever (1975) . . . . . . . . . . . Carrol Jo Hummer
Baby Blue Marine (1976) . . . . . . . . Marion Hedgepeth
Vigilante Force (1976) . . . . . . . . . . . . . . Ben Arnold
Damnation Alley (1977) . . . . . . . . . . . . . . . .Tanner
Big Wednesday (1978) . . . . . . . . . . . . . . . . . . Matt
Hooper (1978) . . . . . . . . . . . . . . . . . . . . . . . . . Ski
Defiance (1980) . . . . . . . . . . . . . . . . . . . . . Tommy
The Return (1980) . . . . . . . . . . . . . . . . . . . . Deputy
Hard Country (1981) . . . . . . . . . . . Kyle Richardson
Born in East L.A. (1987) . . . . . . . . . . . . . .McCalister
Enemy Territory (1987) . . . . . . . . . . . . . . . Parker
Alienator (1989). . . . . . . . . . . . . . . . . . . Commander
Deadly Embrace (1989) . . . . . . . . . . . Stewart Morland
Demonstone (1990). . . . . . . . . . . . . . . .Andrew Buck

Hangfire (1990) . . . . . . . . . . . . . . . . . . . . . . .Hawks
Haunting Fear (1990) . . . . . . . . . . . . . . . . .James Trent
Beyond the Call of Duty (1991). . . . . . . . . . Len Jordan
The Divine Enforcer (1991) . . . . . . . . . . Father Thomas
Raw Nerve (1991). . . . . . . . . . . . . . . . . . . . Bruce Ellis
Xtro 2, The Second Encounter (1991)
. . . . . . . . . . . . . . . . . . . . . . . . . Dr. Ron Shepherd
Animal Instincts (1992) . . . . . . . . . . . . . . . .Fletcher Ross
(Unrated version reviewed.)
Hidden Obsession (1992) . . . . . . . . . . . . . Ben Scanlon
Midnight Witness (1992). . . . . . . . . . . . . . . . . . Lance
Sins of Desire (1992). . . . . . . . . . . . . . .Warren Robillard
(Unrated version reviewed.)
Indecent Behavior (1993) . . . . . . . . . . . . . Tom Mathis
(Unrated version reviewed.)
*Miniseries:*
The Winds of War (1983) . . . . . . . . . . . . .Byron Henry
*TV:*
The Survivors (1969-70) . . . . . . . . . . . .Jeffrey Hastings
Airwolf (1984-86) . . . . . . . . . . . . . .Stringfellow Hawke
*Magazines:*
**Playboy** (Nov 1974) . . . . . . . . . . Sex in Cinema 1974
• 154—Frontal nudity in very blurry still from *Buster
and Billie.*
**Playboy** (Dec 1974). . . . . . . . . . . . . Sex Stars of 1974
••• 210—Full frontal nudity.

## Vogel, Jack
*Films:*
Demon Wind (1990). . . . . . . . . . . . . . . . . . . . .Stacey
**Presumed Guilty** (1990) . . . . . . . . . . . . Jessie Weston
•• 0:19—Buns, while getting out of the shower.
Lock n' Load (1991) . . . . . . . . . . . . . . . .Paul McMillan

## Voight, Jon
*Films:*
**Midnight Cowboy** (1969) . . . . . . . . . . . . . .Joe Buck
• 0:00—Very brief side view of buns, picking up bar of
soap from the shower floor.
• 0:20—Brief buns, while running into bedroom and
jumping onto bed with Sylvia Miles.
• 0:50—Very brief buns, during struggle with a group
of men. More buns when they hold his legs.
• 1:32—Buns, while in bed with Brenda Vaccaro.
Catch-22 (1970) . . . . . . . . . . . . . . . Milo Minderbinder
Deliverance (1972) . . . . . . . . . . . . . . . . . . . . . . . . .Ed
**The All-American Boy** (1973) . . . . . . . . . . Vic Bealer
• 0:06—Very brief partial buns, while getting up off
the floor with Janelle.
•• 0:37—Buns, while getting into shower.
Conrack (1974). . . . . . . . . . . . . . . . . . . Pat Conroy
The Odessa File (1974; British/German) . . . .Peter Miller
**End of the Game** (1976; Italian/German)
. . . . . . . . . . . . . . . . . . . . . . . . . . Walter Tschanz
•• 0:29—Brief frontal nudity, getting up from bed to
talk to Jacqueline Bisset in the bathroom. Brief buns
and more partial frontal nudity. (Amazing for a PG
movie in 1975!)

Coming Home (1978) . . . . . . . . . . . . . . .Luke Martin
(Academy Award for Best Actor.)
The Champ (1979) . . . . . . . . . . . . . . . . . . . . . . .Bill
Table for Five (1983) . . . . . . . . . . . . . . . . . J. P. Tannen
Runaway Train (1985) . . . . . . . . . . . . . . . . . .Manny
Desert Bloom (1986) . . . . . . . . . . . . . . . . . . . . .Jack
*Made for Cable Movies:*
Chernobyl: The Final Warning (1991). . . . . . . . . . . n.a.
The Last of His Tribe (1992; HBO) . . . . . . . . Dr. Kroeber
*Miniseries:*
Return to Lonesome Dove (1993)
. . . . . . . . . . . . . . . . . . . . .Captain Woodrow Call

## Vu-An, Eric
*Films:*
**The Sheltering Sky** (1990) . . . . . . . . . . . . . Belqassim
• 1:59—Buns, while rolling over in bed with Debra
Winger. Long shot, don't see his face.

## • Walker, Robert, Jr.
*Films:*
Gone with the West (1962) . . . . . . . . . . . . . . . . . n.a.
Ensign Pulver (1964) . . . . . . . . . . . . . . . . . . . . . . n.a.
**Road to Salina** (1969; French/Italian) . . . . . . . .Jonas
••• 0:23—Nude, running on beach and swimming un-
der water with Billie.
•• 0:24—Buns, while lying on beach with Billie.
• 0:44—Brief frontal nudity while in tent on beach.
Brief frontal nudity while standing up in the water.
Little Moon & Jud McGraw (1976). . . . . . . . . . . . n.a.
*a.k.a. Gone with the West*
Heated Vengeance (1984) . . . . . . . . . . . . . . . . . n.a.
Angkor: Cambodia Express (1985; Thai/Italian) . . . . . . .
Andy Cameron
Evil Town (1987) . . . . . . . . . . . . . . . . . . . . . . Mike

## Wallace, Eric
*Video Tapes:*
**Intimate Workout For Lovers** (1992)
. . . . . . . . . . . . . . . . . . . . . . . . Romantic Relaxation
••• 0:01—Nude, in bedroom, in bathtub and in bed.
Playboy's 101 Ways to Excite Your Lover (1992)
. . . . . . . . . . . . . . . . . . . . . . . . . . . .Cast Member

## Walsh, M. Emmet
*Films:*
Alice's Restaurant (1969) . . . . . . . . . .Group W Sergeant
Get to Know Your Rabbit (1972) . . . . . . . . . Mr. Wendel
Serpico (1973). . . . . . . . . . . . . . . . . . . . . .Gallagher
Slap Shot (1977) . . . . . . . . . . . . . . . . . . . .Dickie Dunn
**Straight Time** (1978) . . . . . . . . . . . . . . . .Earl Frank
• 0:47—Buns, while handcuffed to fence in the mid-
dle of the road with his pants down.
The Fish That Saved Pittsburgh (1979). . . Wally Cantrell
The Jerk (1979) . . . . . . . . . . . . . . . . . . . . . . Madman
**Fast Walking** (1981) . . . . . . . . . . . . Sgt. George Sager
• 0:59—Frontal nudity standing in the doorway of
Evie's mobile home yelling at James Woods after he
interrupts Walsh making love with Evie.

Blade Runner (1982) . . . . . . . . . . . . . . . . . . . . .Bryant
Scandalous (1983) . . . . . . . . . . . . . . . Simon Reynolds
Blood Simple (1984) . . . . . . . . . . . .Private Detective
Missing in Action (1984) . . . . . . . . . . . . . . . . . Tuck
Fletch (1985) . . . . . . . . . . . . . . . . . . . . . . Dr. Dolan
Back to School (1986) . . . . . . . . . . . . .Coach Turnbull
The Best of Times (1986) . . . . . . . . . . . . . . . Charlie
Critters (1986) . . . . . . . . . . . . . . . . . . . . . . . . Harv
Wildcats (1986) . . . . . . . . . . . . . . . . . . . . . . . .Coes
Harry and the Hendersons (1987) . . . . . . . . George, Sr.
Clean and Sober (1988) . . . . . . . . . . . . Richard Dirks
The Milagro Beanfield War (1988) . . . . . . . . . Governor
No Man's Land (1988) . . . . . . . . . . . . . .Captain Haun
Sunset (1988) . . . . . . . . . . . . . . . . . . . . .Chief Dibner
Catch Me... If You Can (1989) . . . . . . .Johnny Phatmun
The Mighty Quinn (1989) . . . . . . . . . . . . . . . . . Miller
Red Scorpion (1989) . . . . . . . . . . . . . .Dewey Ferguson
Sundown: The Vampire in Retreat (1989) . . . . . . .Mort
Thunderground (1989) . . . . . . . . . . . . . . . . . . Wedge
Chattahoochee (1990) . . . . . . . . . . . . . . . . . . .Morris
Narrow Margin (1990) . . . . . . Sergeant Dominick Benti
Killer Image (1991) . . . . . . . . . . . . . . . . . .John Kane
Equinox (1992) . . . . . . . . . . . . . . . . . . . . .Pete Petosa
The Naked Truth (1992) . . . . . . . . . Garcia/Gesundheim
White Sands (1992) . . . . . . . . . . . . . . . . Bert Gibson
Bitter Harvest (1993) . . . . . . . . . . . . . Sheriff Bob Brody
Wilder Napalm (1993) . . . . . . . . . . . . . . . . Fire Chief
*Made for Cable Movies:*
The Fourth Story (1990; Showtime) . . . . . . . . . . Harry
Four Eyes and Six Guns (1992; TNT) . . . . . . . . . . . .n.a.
*Miniseries:*
The Right of the People (1986) . . . . . . . . . . . . . .Mayor
Brotherhood of the Rose (1989) . . . . . . . . . . . . . Hardy
*Made for TV Movies:*
Love & Lies (1990) . . . . . . . . . . . . . . . . . .Clyde Wilson
*TV:*
The Sandy Duncan Show (1972) . . . . . . . .Alex Lembeck
Dear Detective (1979) . . . . . . . . . . . . . . . Capt. Gorcey
East of Eden (1981) . . . . . . . . . . . . . . . . . Sheriff Quinn
UNSUB (1989) . . . . . . . . . . . . . . . . . . . . . . . . . Ned

## Walter, Tracey

*Films:*
Ginger (1970) . . . . . . . . . . . . . . . . . . . . Ginger's Brother
Goin' South (1978) . . . . . . . . . . . . . . . . . . . . . Coogan
Hardcore (1979) . . . . . . . . . . . . . . . . . . . Main Teller
The Hunter (1980) . . . . . . . . . . . . . . . . . Rocco Mason
The Hand (1981) . . . . . . . . . . . . . . . . . . . . . . . Cop
Honkytonk Man (1982) . . . . . . . . . . . . . . . . . . .Pooch
Timerider (1983) . . . . . . . . . . . . . . . . . . Carl Dorsett
Conan the Destroyer (1984) . . . . . . . . . . . . . Malak
Repo Man (1984) . . . . . . . . . . . . . . . . . . . . . . . Miller
At Close Range (1986) . . . . . . . . . . . . . . . . . Patch
Something Wild (1986) . . . . . . . . . . The Country Squire
Malone (1987) . . . . . . . . . . . . . . . . . . . Calvin Bollard
Married to the Mob (1988) . . . . . . . . Mr. Chicken Lickin'
Mortuary Academy (1988) . . . . . . . . . . . . . Dickson
Batman (1989) . . . . . . . . . . . . . . . . . . . .Bob the Goon
Homer & Eddie (1989) . . . . . . . . . . . . . Tommy Dearly

Under the Boardwalk (1989) . . . . . . . . . . . . . . . Bum
Delusion (1990) . . . . . . . . . . . . . . . . . Bus Ticket Cashier
Pacific Heights (1990) . . . . . . . . . . . . . . . Exterminator
Silence of the Lambs (1990) . . . . . . . . . . . . . . . Lamar
The Two Jakes (1990) . . . . . . . . . . . . . . . Tyrone Otley
Young Guns II (1990) . . . . . . . . . . . . . . . Beever Smith
**City Slickers** (1991) . . . . . . . . . . . . . . . . . . .Cookie
  • 1:16—Very brief buns, mooning everybody while
      riding stagecoach. Happy face painted on his rear.
      Hard to tell if it's him.
Liquid Dreams (1992) . . . . . . . . . . . . . . . . . . . . Cecil
  (Unrated version reviewed.)
Amos & Andrew (1993) . . . . . . . . . . . Bloodhound Bob
Cyborg 2: Glass Shadow (1993) . . . . . . . . . . . Wild Card
Philadelphia (1993) . . . . . . . . . . . . . . . . . . Librarian
*Made for Cable Movies:*
Guncrazy (1992; Showtime) . . . . . . . . . . . . . . . Elton
*Made for Cable TV:*
Sex, Shock and Censorship in the 90's (1993; Showtime)
. . . . . . . . . . . . . . . . . . . . . . . . . . . . . Leonard Eels
*Made for TV Movies:*
Ride with the Wind (1994) . . . . . . . . . . . . . . . .Francis

## *Warburton, Patrick*

*Films:*
Battle in the Erogenous Zone . . . . . . . . . . . . . Pool Boy
**Master of Dragonard Hill** (1987) . . . .Richard Abdee
  0:07—Very brief buns in mirror. Hard to see.

## *Ward, Fred*

*Films:*
Escape from Alcatraz (1979) . . . . . . . . . . . John Anglin
Southern Comfort (1981) . . . . . . . . . . . . . . . . .Reece
The Right Stuff (1983) . . . . . . . . . . . . . . . . Gus Grissom
Timerider (1983) . . . . . . . . . . . . . . . . . Lyle Swann
Uncommon Valor (1983) . . . . . . . . . . . . . . . . Wilkes
Silkwood (1984) . . . . . . . . . . . . . . . . . . . . . .Morgan
Swing Shift (1984) . . . . . . . . . . . . . . . Biscuits Toohey
Remo Williams: The Adventure Begins (1985)
. . . . . . . . . . . . . . . . . . . . . . . . . . .Remo Williams
Secret Admirer (1985) . . . . . . . . . . . . . . . . .Lou Fimple
Big Business (1988) . . . . . . . . . . . . . . .Roone Dimmick
Off Limits (1988) . . . . . . . . . . . . . . . . . . . . . . . Dix
The Prince of Pennsylvania (1988) . . . . . . . . . . . . Gary
Backtrack (1989) . . . . . . . . . . . . . . . . . . . . . Pauling
  *a.k.a. Catch Fire*
Tremors (1989) . . . . . . . . . . . . . . . . . . . . . . Eal Bass
**Henry & June** (1990) . . . . . . . . . . . . . . . .Henry Miller
  ••• 1:39—Buns, twice, while making love with Maria de
      Madeiros.
Miami Blues (1990) . . . . . . . . . . Sergeant Hoke Moseley
Bob Roberts (1992; U.S./British)
. . . . . . . . . . . . . . . . . . . . News Anchor Chip Dailey
Equinox (1992) . . . . . . . . . . . . . . . . . . . . . Mr. Paris
The Player (1992) . . . . . . . . . . . . . . . . . . . . . Walter
Thunderheart (1992) . . . . . . . . . . . . . . . . . Jack Milton
The Dark Wind (1993) . . . . . . . Lieutenant Joe Leaphorn
Naked Gun 33 1/3: The Final Insult (1993) . . . . . Rocco

Short Cuts (1993) . . . . . . . . . . . . . . . . . . . . Stuart Kane
1:45—(0:2 into Part 2) Partial buns, while sliding into bed with Anne Archer.
*Made for Cable Movies:*
Cast a Deadly Spell (1991; HBO). . . . H. Phillip Lovecraft
Four Eyes and Six Guns (1992; TNT) . . . . . . . Wyatt Earp
*Made for Cable TV:*
The Hitchhiker: Dead Heat (1987; HBO) . . . . . . .Luther

## Ward, Wally
*Films:*
Weird Science (1985) . . . . . . . . . . . . . . . . . A Weenie
Thunder Run (1986) . . . . . . . . . . . . . . . . . . . . . . Paul
The Chocolate War (1988) . . . . . . . . . . . . . . . .Archie
**The Invisible Kid** (1988) . . . . . . . . . Milton McClane
• 0:27—Brief buns while running around the school halls after becoming visible with his friend, Grover.
*Made for TV Movies:*
Children of the Night (1985) . . . . . . . . . . . . . . Kevin
*TV:*
Fast Times (1986) . . . . . . . . . . . . . . . . . . . Mark Ratner

## Warden, Jack
*Films:*
You're in the Army Now (1951) . . . . . . . . . . . . .Morse
The Sporting Club (1971) . . . . . . . . . . . . . . . . . .Olive
The Man Who Loved Cat Dancing (1973) . . . . . . Dawes
Shampoo (1975). . . . . . . . . . . . . . . . . . . . . Lester Carr
All the President's Men (1976) . . . . . . . Harry Rosenfeld
Death on the Nile (1978; British). . . . . . . . . Dr. Bessner
Heaven Can Wait (1978). . . . . . . . . . . . . . .Max Corkle
...and Justice for All (1979) . . . . . . . . . . . Judge Rayford
Being There (1979). . . . . . . . . . . . . . . President Bobby
Beyond the Poseidon Adventure (1979)
. . . . . . . . . . . . . . . . . . . . . . . . . . .Harold Meredith
The Champ (1979) . . . . . . . . . . . . . . . . . . . . . .Jackie
Used Cars (1980) . . . . . . . . . . . Roy L. Fuchs/Luke Fuchs
Chu Chu and the Philly Flash (1981) . . . . . .Commander
So Fine (1981) . . . . . . . . . . . . . . . . . . . . . . . . . . Jack
The Verdict (1982) . . . . . . . . . . . Mickey Morrissey
Crackers (1984). . . . . . . . . . . . . . . . . . . . . . . Garvey
**Problem Child** (1990) . . . . . . . . . . . "Big" Ben Healy
• 1:07—Buns, on TV in bar, mooning into the camera when he doesn't know it is on. (Yes, it is him.)
Problem Child II (1991). . . . . . . . . . . . "Big" Ben Healy
Night and the City (1992). . . . . . . . . . . . Al Grossman
Passed Away (1992) . . . . . . . . . . . . . . . . Jack Scanlan
Toys (1992). . . . . . . . . . . . . . . . . . . Old General Zevo
Guilty as Sin (1993). . . . . . . . . . . . . . . . . . . . . . Moe
*TV:*
The Bad News Bears (1979-80) . . . . .Morris Buttermaker
Crazy Like a Fox (1984-86) . . . . . . . . . . . . . Harry Fox

## Warden, Jonathan
*Films:*
**Greetings** (1968) . . . . . . . . . . . . . . . . . . . .Paul Shaw
•• 1:15—Buns, while making love in bed with the Nymphomaniac. Shot at high speed. More buns, while getting out from under her.

## • Warnock, Grant
*Films:*
**Waterland** (1992; British/U.S.). . . . . . . . . Young Tom
• 0:05—Brief buns, pulling down his pants with his friends to show Mary (He's on the far right).

## Warren, Michael
*Films:*
Butterflies Are Free (1972) . . . . . . . . . . . . . . . . Roy
**Drive, He Said** (1972) . . . . . . . . . . . . . Easly Jefferson
• 0:09—Buns and very brief frontal nudity in the shower room with the other basketball players.
Cleopatra Jones (1973) . . . . . . . . . . . . . . . . . . Andy
Fast Break (1979) . . . . . . . . . . . . . . . . . . . . Preacher
Heaven is a Playground (1991). . . . . . . . .Byron Harper
Storyville (1992). . . . . . . . . . . . . . . . . . .Nathan Lefleur
*Made for Cable TV:*
Dream On: The Taking of Pablum 1-2-3, Part I (1994; HBO). . . . . . . . . . . . . . . . . . . . . . . Policeman
*TV:*
Sierra (1974) . . . . . . . . . . . . . . . . . . . Ranger P.J. Lewis
Paris (1979-80) . . . . . . . . . . . . . . . . . . . . Willie Miller
Hill Street Blues (1981-87) . . . . . . . . Officer Bobby Hill

## • Warwick, Richard
*Films:*
Romeo and Juliet (1968; British/Italian) . . . . . . .Gregory
**if...** (1969; British) . . . . . . . . . . . . . . . . . . . . Wallace
•• 0:42—Buns, while standing in cold shower as punishment. He's the second guy.
First Love (1970; German/Swiss) . Lieutenant Belovzorov
Nicholas and Alexandra (1971; British)
. . . . . . . . . . . . . . . . . . . . . . . .Grand Duke Dmitru
Confessions of a Pop Performer (1975; British). . . . . n.a.
International Velvet (1978; British) . . . . . . . . . . . . Tim
Hamlet (1990; British/French) . . . . . . . . . . . . Bernardo
White Hunter Black Heart (1990) . . . . . . . . . Basil Fields

## Washington, Denzel
*Films:*
Carbon Copy (1981) . . . . . . . . . . . . . . . . . . . Roger
A Soldier's Story (1984) . . . . . . . . . . . . . Pfc. Peterson
Power (1986). . . . . . . . . . . . . . . . . . . . Arnold Billings
**Cry Freedom** (1987; British). . . . . . . . . . . . Steve Biko
• 1:05—Side view of buns, while lying on the floor after getting beat up. Dark, hard to see anything.
• 1:07—Buns again. Dark.
1:26—Buns in B&W photo. Supposed to be him, but probably not. Don't see face.
Glory (1989) . . . . . . . . . . . . . . . . . . . . . . . . . . Trip
(Academy Award for Best Supporting Actor.)
The Mighty Quinn (1989) . . . . . . . . . . . . . . . . Xavier
Heart Condition (1990) . . . . . . . . . . . . Napoleon Stone
Mo' Better Blues (1990) . . . . . . . . . . . . . . Bleek Gilliam
**Ricochet** (1991) . . . . . . . . . . . . . . . . . . . .Nick Styles
• 0:13—Almost very brief frontal nudity in locker room when Lindsay Wagner comes to talk. (It looks like he's wearing something over his penis.)
Malcolm X (1992) . . . . . . . . . . . . . . . . . . .Malcolm X

**Mississippi Masala** (1992) . . . . . . . . . . . . .Demetrius
•• 1:17—Buns, getting up out of bed and putting on his pants.
Much Ado About Nothing (1993; British) . . . Don Pedro
The Pelican Brief (1993) . . . . . . . . . . . . .Gary Grantham
Philadelphia (1993) . . . . . . . . . . . . . . . . . . . . . Joe Miller
*TV:*
St. Elsewhere (1982-88) . . . . . . . . . .Dr. Phillip Chandler

# Wass, Ted
*Films:*
Curse of the Pink Panther (1983) . . . . . . . . Clifton Sleigh
Oh God, You Devil! (1984) . . . . . . . . . . . Bobby Shelton
**Sheena** (1984) . . . . . . . . . . . . . . . . . . . . . . . Vic Casey
• 1:48—Buns, after getting pulled out of the ground after tribal healing ceremony.
Long Shot (1986) . . . . . . . . . . . . . . . . . . . . . . Stump
*Made for TV Movies:*
Pancho Barnes (1988) . . . . . . . . . . . . . . . . Frank Clarke
Danielle Steel's "Star" (1993) . . . . . . . . . . . . . . .Ernie
Triumph Over Disaster: The Hurricane Andrew Story (1993) . . . . . . . . . . . . . . . . . . . . . . . . Bryan Norcross
*TV:*
Soap (1977-81) . . . . . . . . . . . . . . . . . . Danny Dallas
Men (1989) . . . . . . . . . . . . . . . . Dr. Steven Ratajkowski
Blossom (1991- ) . . . . . . . . . . . . . . . . . . . . Nick Russo

# • Wasser, Ed
*Films:*
**Stormswept** (1994) . . . . . . . . . . . . . . . . . . . . .Eugene
••• 1:30—Buns, while making love with Brianna in pantry.

# Wasson, Craig
*Films:*
Rollercoaster (1977) . . . . . . . . . . . . . . . . . . . . Hippie
The Boys in Company C (1978) . . . . . . . . Dave Bisbee
Go Tell the Spartans (1978). . Corporal Stephen Courcey
Carny (1980) . . . . . . . . . . . . . . . . . . . . . . . Mickey
Schizoid (1980) . . . . . . . . . . . . . . . . . . . . . . . Doug
Four Friends (1981) . . . . . . . . . . . . . . . . . Danilo Prozor
**Ghost Story** (1981) . . . . . . . . . . . . . . . . . . Don/David
•• 0:08—Brief frontal nudity falling out the window, then buns, while landing next to the pool.
• 0:41—Buns, while making love with Alice Krige in bedroom.
Second Thoughts (1983) . . . . . . . . . . . . . . . . . . . .Will
Body Double (1984) . . . . . . . . . . . . . . . . . . . . . . Jake
The Men's Club (1986) . . . . . . . . . . . . . . . . . . . Paul
A Nightmare on Elm Street 3: The Dream Warriors (1987) . . . . . . . . . . . . . . . . . Dr. Neil Goldman
Malcolm X (1992) . . . . . . . . . . . . . . . . . . . .T.V. Host
*Made for Cable Movies:*
Strapped (1993; HBO) . . . . . . . . . . . . . . . . . . . .Ben
*Made for TV Movies:*
Skag (1980) . . . . . . . . . . . . . . . . . . .David Skagska
Why Me? (1984) . . . . . . . . . . . . . . . . . . Brian Harmon
*TV:*
Phyllis (1977) . . . . . . . . . . . . . . . . . . Mark Valenti

# Waters, John
(Not to be confused with John Waters the director.)
*Films:*
**The Adventures of Eliza Fraser** (1976; Australian)
. . . . . . . . . . . . . . . . . . . . . . . . . . . Dave Bracefell
• 0:27—Side view of buns, while undressing and getting into bed.
•• 0:29—Nude, walking around outside. Buns, while standing in doorway.
•• 0:32—Brief pubic hair, then buns while getting off bed to hide under it.
•• 0:38—Buns, after getting out from under bed and standing up after McBride leaves.
•• 1:23—Buns in loincloth after joining the tribe.
*Made for Cable Movies:*
All the Rivers Run (1984; HBO) . . . . . . . . . . . . .Brenton

# Waterston, Sam
*Films:*
Savages (1972) . . . . . . . . . . . . . . . . . . . . . . . .James
The Great Gatsby (1974) . . . . . . . . . . . . .Nick Carraway
Rancho Deluxe (1975) . . . . . . . . . . . . . . . Cecil Colson
Capricorn One (1978) . . . . . . . . . . . . . . . .Peter Willis
Eagle's Wing (1978; British) . . . . . . . . . . . White Bull
Interiors (1978) . . . . . . . . . . . . . . . . . . . . . . . Mike
Heaven's Gate (1980) . . . . . . . . . . . . . . . . . . Canton
Hopscotch (1980) . . . . . . . . . . . . . . . . . . . . Cutter
**Sweet William** (1980; British) . . . . . . . . . . . . William
• 0:27—Buns, seen through a window in the door, standing on balcony with Jenny Agutter.
The Killing Fields (1984) . . . . . . . . . . .Sydney Schanberg
Warning Sign (1985) . . . . . . . . . . . . . . . . . Cal Morse
Just Between Friends (1986) . . . . . . . . . . Harry Crandall
September (1987) . . . . . . . . . . . . . . . . . . . . . Peter
Trade Secrets (1989; French) . . . . . . . . . . . . . . .Gerry
Welcome Home (1989) . . . . . . . . . . . . . . . . . .Woody
The Man in the Moon (1991) . . . . . . . . .Matthew Trant
Mindwalk (1991) . . . . . . . . . . . . . . . . . . Jack Edwards
Serial Mom (1993) . . . . . . . . . . . . . . . . . . . . . .Dad
*Made for Cable Movies:*
Finnegan Begin Again (1985) . . . . . . . . Paul Broadbent
The Nightmare Years (1989) . . . . . . . . . . . . . William
Assault at West Point: The Court Martial of Johnson Whittaker (1994; Showtime) . . . . . . . . . . . . . . . n.a.
*Made for Cable TV:*
Tales From the Crypt: As Ye Sow (1993; HBO)
. . . . . . . . . . . . . . . . . . . . . . . . . . . G.G. Devoe
*Miniseries:*
Q.E.D. (1982) . . . . . . . . . . . . . . .Quentin E. Deverill
*Made for TV Movies:*
David's Mother (1994) . . . . . . . . . . . . . . . . . . . John
*TV:*
I'll Fly Away (1991-93) . . . . . . . . . . . . . Forrest Bedford

# Waybill, John "Fee"

Lead singer of *The Tubes.*
*Films:*
Ladies and Gentlemen, The Fabulous Stains (1982)
........................................Lou Corpse
(Not available on video tape.)
*Video Tapes:*
**Red Hot Rock** (1984) ....................Himself
*a.k.a. Sexy Shorts (on laser disc)*
- ••• 0:13—Nude, getting dressed in locker room during "Sports Fans" by The Tubes.
- • 0:29—Buns, in G-string S&M outfit during "Mondo Bondage" by The Tubes.

# Weaving, Hugo

*Films:*
The Right Hand Man (1987) ............ Ned Devine
**...Almost** (1990; Australian) .................. Jake
0:52—Very brief out of focus buns when he drops his pants in front of Rosanna Arquette. Don't see his face. Note in the very next scene, he's wearing underwear!
Proof (1991; Australian) .................. Martin
Frauds (1992; Australian) ................Jonathan
The Custodian (1993) .....................Church
The Adventures of Priscilla, Queen of the Desert (1994)
........................................Mitzi

# Weber, Dewey

*Films:*
**Chain of Desire** (1992).............David Bango
- ••• 0:48—Buns, while getting out of bathtub and drying himself off while talking to Ken.

# Weber, Steven

*Films:*
The Flamingo Kid (1984)................Paul Hirsch
Flanagan (1985) ...........................Sean
Hamburger Hill (1987) .............. Sgt. Worcester
**Single White Female** (1992) ..........Sam Rawson
- •• 1:12—Very brief frontal nudity, getting out of bed with Jennifer Jason Leigh. Upper half of buns, while putting on his pants.
The Temp (1993) ...................Brad Montroe
*Made for TV Movies:*
In the Company of Darkness (1993) ....... Kyle Timer
Betrayed by Love (1994)..................Jeff Avery

# Wehe, Oliver

*Films:*
**Erendira** (1983; Brazilian) ................. Ulysses
- • 1:24—Buns, while getting into bed with Erendira.

# Welker, Michael

*Films:*
**Drop Dead Fred** (1991) ........ Waiter at Wine Gala
- • 1:12—Buns, when toga falls off while he's carrying trays.

# Weller, Peter

*Films:*
Just Tell Me What You Want (1980) ...Steven Routledge
Shoot the Moon (1982)............. Frank Henderson
Of Unknown Origin (1983; Canadian) .....Bart Hughes
The Adventures of Buckaroo Banzai, Across the 8th Dimension (1984) ............... Buckaroo Banzai
Firstborn (1984)............................Sam
**A Killing Affair** (1985) ............ Baston Morris
- • 1:20—Brief buns, getting out of bed, standing up and putting his pants on.
Robocop (1987).............Alex Murphy/Robocop
The Tunnel (1987; Spanish) ..............Juan Pablo
**Cat Chaser** (1988) .................George Moran
- •• 0:24—Very, very brief frontal nudity, twice when he is kneeling and takes his pants off. Buns, while making love on top of Kelly McGillis.
Shakedown (1988)................. Roland Dalton
Leviathan (1989) .................... William Beck
Robocop 2 (1990) ...........Alex Murphy/Robocop
Naked Lunch (1991) .....................Bill Lee
Road to Ruin (1992)....................Jack Sloan
Sunset Grill (1992) ...................Ryder Hart
Fifty-Fifty (1993) ....................Jake Wyer
*Made for Cable Movies:*
**Apology** (1986; HBO)............... Rad Hungare
- • 1:04—Brief buns, while putting pants on, getting out of bed to chase after intruder at night.
Rainbow Drive (1990; Showtime)...... Mike Gallagher
Women & Men: Stories of Seduction (1990; HBO)
........................................Hobie
*Made for TV Movies:*
The Substitute Wife (1994).................... n.a.

# • Wells, Win

*Films:*
**Bloodbath** (1976) ........................ Alice
*a.k.a. The Sky is Falling*
- • 1:23—Very brief buns, while crawling away from a bull.
1:24—Very, very brief buns, while getting horned by one of the bull's horns.

# Welsh, Kenneth

*Films:*
**Covergirl** (1982; Canadian) ....... Harrison Chandler
- • 1:23—Brief buns, while seen on video tape used to get him in trouble. Long shot.
Of Unknown Origin (1983; Canadian) .........James
Falling In Love (1984) .....................Doctor
Heartburn (1986)..................... Dr. Appel
The House on Carroll Street (1988) .........Hackett
Physical Evidence (1989) ............Harry Norton
The Freshman (1990).............Dwight Armstrong
The Big Slice (1991)..................Lt. Bernard
*Made for TV Movies:*
Adrift (1993) .............................. n.a.
Woman on the Run: The Lawrencia Bembenek Story (1993) ........................Don Eisenberg

# • West, Timothy
Films:
The Looking Glass War (1970; British) . . . . . . . . . Taylor
Day of the Jackal (1973) . . . . . . . . . . . . . . . Berthier
Hedda (1975; British) . . . . . . . . . . . . . . . . . . . Tesman
**Joseph Andrews** (1977; British/French)
. . . . . . . . . . . . . . . . . . . . . . . . . . . Mr. Tow-Wouse
• 0:31—Buns, when getting caught in the hay with
Betty by Mrs. Tow-Wouse.
Agatha (1979; British) . . . . . . . . . . . . . . . . . . Ken Ward
Rough Cut (1980; British) . . . . . . . . . . . . Nigel Lawton
Cry Freedom (1987; British) . . . . . . . . . Captain de Wet
Consuming Passions (1988; U.S./British) . . . . . . Dr. Rees

# Weston, Jack
Films:
Fuzz (1972) . . . . . . . . . . . . . . . . Detective Meyer Meyer
Gator (1976) . . . . . . . . . . . . . . . . . . . . Irving Greenfield
The Ritz (1976) . . . . . . . . . . . . . . . . . . Gaetano Proclo
Cuba (1979) . . . . . . . . . . . . . . . . . . . . . . . . Gutman
Can't Stop the Music (1980) . . . . . . . . . . Benny Murray
**Four Seasons** (1981) . . . . . . . . . . . . . . Danny Zimmer
• 0:48—Brief buns in water while skinny dipping with
Rita Moreno.
High Road to China (1983) . . . . . . . . . . . . . . . Struts
Dirty Dancing (1987) . . . . . . . . . . . . . Max Kellerman
Ishtar (1987) . . . . . . . . . . . . . . . . . . . . . Marty Freed
Short Circuit 2 (1988) . . . . . . . . . . . . . . Oscar Baldwin

# Whiting, Leonard
Films:
Legend of Young Dick Turpin (1965; British) . . . . . Jimmy
**Romeo and Juliet** (1968; British/Italian) . . . . . . Romeo
•• 1:34—Buns, while in bed with Juliet, then getting
out to stretch. Long scene.
Say Hello to Yesterday (1970; British) . . . . . . . . . . Boy

# Wilborn, Carlton
Films:
Without You I'm Nothing (1990) . . . . . . . Ballet Dancer
**Truth or Dare** (1991) . . . . . . . . . . . . . . . . . . Dancer
1:39—Frontal nudity showing himself to Madonna.
Dark, hard to see. B&W.
1:43—Very brief frontal nudity getting into bed with
Madonna. Too dark to see anything. B&W.
• 1:45—Brief buns, while in bed with Madonna. B&W.

# Wilby, James
Films:
Maurice (1987; British) . . . . . . . . . . . . . . Maurice Hall
A Handful of Dust (1988) . . . . . . . . . . . . . . Tony Last
**A Summer Story** (1988) . . . . . . . . . . . . Frank Ashton
• 0:08—Buns, in creek with Mr. Garten while skinny
dipping.
Howards End (1992) . . . . . . . . . . . . . . Charles Wilcox
Made for TV Movies:
Masterpiece Theatre: Adam Bede (1992)
. . . . . . . . . . . . . . . . . . . . . Capt. Arthur Donnithorne

# Wilder, Gene
Films:
The Producers (1968) . . . . . . . . . . . . . . . . . Leo Bloom
Quackser Fortune has a Cousin in the Bronx (1970; Irish)
. . . . . . . . . . . . . . . . . . . . . . . . Quackser Fortune
Start the Revolution Without Me (1970)
. . . . . . . . . . . . . . . . . . . Claude Coupe/Philippe De Sisi
Willy Wonka and the Chocolate Factory (1971)
. . . . . . . . . . . . . . . . . . . . . . . . . . . . Willy Wonka
Everything You Wanted to Know About Sex, But Were
Afraid to Ask (1972) . . . . . . . . . . . . . . . . Dr. Ross
Blazing Saddles (1974) . . . . . . . . . . . . . . . . . . . . Jim
The Little Prince (1974; British) . . . . . . . . . . . . The Fox
Young Frankenstein (1974) . . . . . . . . . . Dr. Frankenstein
**The Adventure of Sherlock Holmes' Smarter
Brother** (1975) . . . . . . . . . . . . . . . Sigerson Holmes
•• 1:04—Buns, in ballroom with Marty Feldman, after
a buzz saw removes the back of their tuxedos.
Silver Streak (1976) . . . . . . . . . . . . . . George Caldwell
The World's Greatest Lover (1977) . . . . . . Rudy Valentine
The Frisco Kid (1979) . . . . . . . . . . . . . . Avram Belinsky
Stir Crazy (1980) . . . . . . . . . . . . . . . . . Skip Donahue
Hanky Panky (1982) . . . . . . . . . . . . . . Michael Jordon
**The Woman in Red** (1984) . . . . . . . . . Theodore Pierce
• 1:15—Side view of buns while getting back into bed
with Kelly Le Brock after getting out to take his un-
derwear off the lamp.
Haunted Honeymoon (1986) . . . . . . . . . . . Larry Abbot
See No Evil, Hear No Evil (1989) . . . . . . . . . . . . Dave
Funny About Love (1990) . . . . . . . . . . . Duffy Bergman
Another You (1991) . . George Washington/Abe Fielding
TV:
Something Wilder (1994- ) . . . . . . . . . . . . . . . . . n.a.

# Wilder, James
Films:
Zombie High (1987) . . . . . . . . . . . . . . . . . . . . Barry
a.k.a. The School That Ate My Brain
Murder One (1988; Canadian) . . . . . . . . . . . Carl Isaacs
Scorchers (1992) . . . . . . . . . . . . . . . . . . . . . Dolan
Made for Cable Movies:
**Prey of the Chameleon** (1992; Showtime) . . . . . . J.D.
• 0:32—Upper half of buns, while getting out of bed.
Made for TV Movies:
Confessions: Two Faces of Evil (1994) . . . . . . . . . . n.a.
Tonya & Nancy: The Inside Story (1994) . . . Jeff Gillooly
TV:
Equal Justice (1990-91) . . . . . . . . . . . Christopher Searls
Route 66 (1993) . . . . . . . . . . . . . . . . . . . . . . . Nick
Models Inc. (1994- ) . . . . . . . . . . . . . . . Adam Louder

# • Williams, Clarence, III
Films:
Purple Rain (1984) . . . . . . . . . . . . . . . . . . . . Father
Made for Cable Movies:
**Against the Wall** (1994; HBO) . . . . . . . . . . . . Choko
• 0:14—Brief upper half of buns, before putting on
towel in shower room.

TV:
  The Mod Squad (1968-73) . . . . . . . . . . . . . Linc Hayes

# Williams, Hutch

Films:
  **Naked Instinct** (1993) . . . . . . . . . . . . Military Recruit
  ••• 0:51—Nude, dancing after stripping in front of
     Joanne.

# Williams, Jason

Films:
  Alice in Wonderland (1977) . . . . . . . . . . . . . . . . . .n.a.
  (R-rated version reviewed.)
  Time Walker (1982). . . . . . . . . . . . . . . . . . . . . . . Jeff
  Down and Out in Beverly Hills (1986) . . . . . . . . . Lance
  **Danger Zone II: Reaper's Revenge** (1988) . . . Wade
  •• 0:06—Buns, while getting out of bed and putting
     pants on.
  Vampire at Midnight (1988) . . . . Detective Roger Sutter
  Society (1989). . . . . . . . . . . . . . . . . . . . . Jason's Friend
  Danger Zone III: Steel Horse War (1991) . . . Wade Olsen

# Williams, Robin

Films:
  Can I Do It 'Til I Need Glasses? (1976) . . . . . . . . . . .n.a.
  Popeye (1980) . . . . . . . . . . . . . . . . . . . . . . . . . Popeye
  World According to Garp (1982). . . . . . . . . . T.S. Garp
  The Survivors (1983). . . . . . . . . . . . . . Donald Quinelle
  Moscow on the Hudson (1984). . . . . . . Vladimir Ivanoff
  The Best of Times (1986). . . . . . . . . . . . . . Jack Dundee
  Club Paradise (1986). . . . . . . . . . . . . . . . .Jack Moniker
  Good Morning, Vietnam (1987) . . . . . .Adrian Cronauer
  The Adventures of Baron Munchausen (1989; British/
  German) . . . . . . . . . . . . . . . . . . . . . King of the Moon
  Dead Poets Society (1989) . . . . . . . . . . . .John Keating
  Cadillac Man (1990) . . . . . . . . . . . . . . . . .Joey O'Brien
  Awakenings (1991) . . . . . . . . . . . . Dr. Malcolm Sayer
  Dead Again (1991) . . . . . . . . . . . . . . Dr. Cozy Carlisle
  **The Fisher King** (1991) . . . . . . . . . . . . . . . . . . . .Parry
  ••• 0:58—Nude, dancing around in the park at night
     with Jeff Bridges.
  Hook (1991) . . . . . . . . . . . . . . . Peter Pan/Peter Banning
  Shakes the Clown (1992) . . Uncredited Gerry the Mime
  Toys (1992). . . . . . . . . . . . . . . . . . . . . . . . Leslie Zevo
  Mrs. Doubtfire (1993) . . . . Daniel Hillard/Mrs. Doubtfire
  Being Human (1994) . . . . . . . . . . . . . . . . . . . . Hector
TV:
  Mork & Mindy (1978-82) . . . . . . . . . . . . . . . . . . Mork

# Williams, Treat

Films:
  The Ritz (1976) . . . . . . . . . . . . . . . . . . . . Michael Brick
  The Eagle Has Landed (1977; British)
  . . . . . . . . . . . . . . . . . . . . . . . .Captain Happy Clark
  1941 (1979) . . . . . . . . . . . . . . . . . . . . . . . . . . Sitarski
  **Hair** (1979) . . . . . . . . . . . . . . . . . . . . . . . . . . . Berger
  • 0:57—Buns, while taking off clothes and diving into
     pond with Hud and Woof.
  Why Would I Lie? (1980). . . . . . . . . . . . . . . . . .Cletus

Prince of the City (1981) . . . . . . . . . . . . . Daniel Ciello
Pursuit of D.B. Cooper (1981) . . . . . . . . . . . . . .Meade
**Flashpoint** (1984) . . . . . . . . . . . . . . . . . . . . . . . Ernie
  •• 0:03—Buns, putting on pants in locker room while
     talking to Kris Kristofferson.
Once Upon a Time in America (1984)
. . . . . . . . . . . . . . . . . . . . . . . . . . . .Jimmy O'Donnell
  (Long version reviewed.)
Smooth Talk (1985) . . . . . . . . . . . . . . . . . .Arnold Friend
The Men's Club (1986) . . . . . . . . . . . . . . . . . . . Terry
Dead Heat (1988) . . . . . . . . . . . . . . . . . Roger Mortis
Heart of Dixie (1989) . . . . . . . . . . . . . . . . . . . . Hoyt
Sweet Lies (1989). . . . . . . . . . . . . . . . . . . . . . . .Peter
  0:52—Side view of buns while in bed with Joanna
     Pacula. Very, very brief, blurry frontal nudity getting
     out of bed. Don't really see anything.
Till Death Do Us Part (1991). . . . . . . . . . . . Alan Palliko
Made for Cable Movies:
  **Third Degree Burn** (1989; HBO). . . . . . . Scott Weston
  • 0:43—Brief buns while taking off his robe with Vir-
     ginia Madsen in his bedroom.
  The Water Engine (1992; TNT). . . . . . . . . Dave Murray
  **Parallel Lives** (1994; Showtime) . . . . . . .Peter Barnum
  • 0:34—Brief buns (he's in the middle), while moon-
     ing the women in hallway during panty raid.
Made for Cable TV:
  Tales From the Crypt: None but the Lonely Heart
     (1992; HBO). . . . . . . . . . . . . . . . . . . . . . .Howard
Made for TV Movies:
  Deadly Matrimony (1992) . . . . . . . . . . . . Alan Masters
TV:
  Eddie Dodd (1991) . . . . . . . . . . . . . . . . . .Eddie Dodd
  Good Advice (1993- ) . . . . . . . . . . . . . . . .Jack Harold

# Williamson, Fred

Films:
  Just Tell Me That You Love Me, Junie Moon . . . . . . . n.a.
  Black Caesar (1973) . . . . . . . . . . . . . . . . . Tommy Gibbs
  **Hell Up in Harlem** (1973) . . . . . . . . . . . Tommy Gibbs
  ••• 0:42—Buns, while in bed making love with Marga-
     ret Avery.
  That Man Bolt (1973). . . . . . . . . . . . . . . . .Jefferson Bolt
  Boss (1974) . . . . . . . . . . . . . . . . . . . . . . . Boss Nigger
     a.k.a. Boss Nigger
  Three the Hard Way (1974) . . . . . . . . . . .Jagger Daniels
  Adios Amigo (1975) . . . . . . . . . . . . . . . . . . . . . . Ben
  Bucktown (1975) . . . . . . . . . . . . . . . . . . . . . . . . Duke
  Take a Hard Ride (1975; U.S./Italian) . . . . . . . . . . Tyree
  Mean Johnny Barrows (1976). . . . . . . . Johnny Barrows
  One Down, Two to Go (1982) . . . . . . . . . . . . . . . .Cal
  The Big Score (1983) . . . . . . . . . . . . . . . . . .Frank Hooks
  The Bronx Warriors (1983; Italian) . . . . . . . . . .The Ogre
  Vigilante (1983) . . . . . . . . . . . . . . . . . . . . . . . . .Nick
  White Fire (1985). . . . . . . . . . . . . . . . . . . . . . . .Noah
  Foxtrap (1986; U.S./Italian) . . . . . . . . . . . . .Thomas Fox
  The Messenger (1987; Italian) . . . .Jake Sebastian Turner
  Delta Force Commando 2: Priority Red One (1991)
  . . . . . . . . . . . . . . . . . . . . . . . . . . . Capt. Sam Beck
  South Beach (1992) . . . . . . . . . . . . . . . Mack Derringer

*Miniseries:*
Wheels (1978). . . . . . . . . . . . . . . . Leonard Wingate
*TV:*
Julia (1970-71) . . . . . . . . . . . . . . . . . . . .Steve Bruce
Half Nelson (1985) . . . . . . . . . . . . . . . . Chester Long

## Wilson, Dorien

*Made for Cable TV:*
**Dream On: Come and Knock On Our Door...**
(1992; HBO) . . . . . . . . . . . . . . . . . . . . . Eddie Charles
•• 0:16—Buns, while getting out of bed in hotel room
with Martin.
**Dream On: A Midsummer Night's Dream On**
(1993; HBO) . . . . . . . . . . . . . . . . . . . . . Eddie Charles
• 0:14—Brief partial buns, while making love with
Cara while standing up.
**Dream On: Depth Be Not Proud** (1993; HBO)
. . . . . . . . . . . . . . . . . . . . . . . . . . . . Eddie Charles
•• 0:10—Brief buns, pulling up his underwear.

## Wilson, Lambert

*Films:*
Chanel Solitaire (1981) . . . . . . . . . . . . . . . . . . . . .n.a.
Sahara (1984) . . . . . . . . . . . . . . . . . . . . . . . . . . . .Jaffar
Red Kiss (1985; French). . . . . . . . . . . . . . . . Stephane
**Rendez-Vous** (1986; French). . . . . . . . . . . . . Quentin
• 0:22—Very brief buns, while falling with Juliet onto
net during play.
**The Belly of an Architect** (1987; British/Italian)
. . . . . . . . . . . . . . . . . . . . . . . . . . Caspasian Speckler
•• 0:56—Buns, several time in room with Chloe Webb
while Brian Dennehy watches through keyhole.
• 1:04—Upper half of buns, while lying in bed with
Webb. Long shot.
*Made for Cable Movies:*
Frankenstein (1993; TNT) . . . . . . . . . . . . . . . . Clerval
*Made for Cable TV:*
**Strangers: Small Sounds and Tilting Shadows**
(1992). . . . . . . . . . . . . . . . . . . . . . . . . . . . The Guy
(Available on video tape on *Strangers*.)
• 0:04—Brief buns, while making love on top of Joan
Chen in bed.

## Wilson, Robert Brian

*Films:*
**Silent Night, Deadly Night** (1984). . . . . . . Billy at 18
• 0:30—Sort of buns while in bed with Pamela.

## Wilson, Roger

*Films:*
Blow Out (1981) . . . . . . . . . . . . . . . . . . . .Coed Lover
Porky's (1981; Canadian) . . . . . . . . . . . . . . . . Mickey
**Thunder Alley** (1985). . . . . . . . . . . . . . . . . . . Richie
• 0:55—Buns, while diving into the water. Long, long,
long shot.
• 1:15—Brief buns, while wrestling on bed with Star.
**Second Time Lucky** (1986) . . . . . . . . . . Adam Smith
•• 0:13—Buns, while in the Garden of Eden.
•• 0:30—Buns, while standing out in the rain.

Aspen Extreme (1993) . . . . . . . . . . . . . . . . . . Jake Neil
*TV:*
Seven Brides for Seven Brothers (1982-83)
. . . . . . . . . . . . . . . . . . . . . . . . . . Daniel McFadden

## Winchester, Jeff

*Films:*
**Olivia** (1983) . . . . . . . . . . . . . . . . . . . . . . . . Richard
*a.k.a. A Taste of Sin*
• 1:17—Buns, while getting stuffed into trunk by Olivia. Dark.

## Winn, David

*Films:*
**My Therapist** (1983) . . . . . . . . . . . . . . . . Mike Jenner
•• 0:19—Buns, while making love with Marilyn Cham-
bers in bed.

## •Wise, Darren

*Video Tapes:*
**Playboy Night Dreams** (1993) . . . . . . . . . . . .Detour
••• 0:06—Buns, when his lover pulls down his underwear.
**Playboy's Secret Confessions** (1993)
. . . . . . . . . . . . . . . . . . . . . . . . . .Wash and Wax/Dennis
•• 0:19—Buns, while making love outside with a girl by
a car.

## Wolf, Axel

*Video Tapes:*
Sexy Lingerie III (1991) . . . . . . . . . . . . . Additional Cast
**Intimate Workout For Lovers** (1992)
. . . . . . . . . . . . . . . . . . . . . . . . . . . .Sensual Exercise
••• 0:11—Nude, exercising in living room and exercise
room.

## •Wolf, Scott

*Films:*
**Teenage Bonnie and Klepto Clyde** (1993) . . . .Clyde
• 0:53—Brief buns, while standing on hood of car,
while mooning an old guy who is staring at him.

## •Wolff, Frank

*Films:*
Atlas (1961) . . . . . . . . . . . . . . . . . . . . . . . . . . . . n.a.
The Last Gun (1964; Italian). . . . . . . . . . . . . . . . n.a.
**The Lickerish Quartet** (1970; Italian). . . . . . Husbnad
*a.k.a. Erotic Illusion*
•• 0:51—Brief nude, several times, while rolling around
on library floor with the girl.
When Women Had Tails (1970; Italian) . . . . . . . . n.a.
When Women Lost Their Tails (1971; Italian) . . . . . n.a.

## Woltz, Randy

*Films:*
**The Young Warriors** (1983; U.S./Canadian)
. . . . . . . . . . . . . . . . . . . . . . . . . . . "Brick Test" Frank
• 0:16—Dropping his pants in a room during pledge
at fraternity.

## • Wood, David

*Films:*

**if...** (1969; British) . . . . . . . . . . . . . . . . . . . . . . Johnny
- • 0:41—Buns, while standing in cold shower as punishment. He's the first guy.

ffolkes (1980; British) . . . . . . . . . . . . . . . . . . . . Herring
Sweet William (1980; British) . . . . . . . . . . . . . . . Vicar

## Wood, Timothy

*Films:*

**Love Circles Around the World** (1984) . . . . Michael
- •• 1:29—Frontal nudity, lying in bed with Jill after making love while video taping it.

## Woods, James

*Films:*

Hickey and Boggs (1972) . . . . . . . . . . . . . . . . .Lt. Wyatt
The Visitors (1972) . . . . . . . . . . . . . . . . . . . Bill Schmidt
The Way We Were (1973) . . . . . . . . . . Frankie McVeigh
The Gambler (1974) . . . . . . . . . . . . . . . . . Bank Officer
Distance (1975) . . . . . . . . . . . . . . . . . . . . . . . . .Larry
Night Moves (1975) . . . . . . . . . . . . . . . . . . . . Quentin
The Choirboys (1977) . . . . . . . . . . . . . . . . Bloomguard
**The Onion Field** (1979) . . . . . . . . . . .Gregory Powell
- •• 1:33—Buns, while taking a shower in the prison.

The Black Marble (1980) . . . . . . . . . . . . . . . . . Fiddler
Eyewitness (1981) . . . . . . . . . . . . . . . . . . . . . . . . Aldo
Fast Walking (1981) . . . . . . . . . . . Fast-Walking Miniver
Split Image (1982) . . . . . . . . . . . . . . . . . . . . . . Prattt
Videodrome (1983; Canadian) . . . . . . . . . . . .Max Renn
Against All Odds (1984) . . . . . . . . . . . . . . . . . Jake Wise
Once Upon a Time in America (1984) . . . . . . . . . . Max
(Long version reviewed.)
Cat's Eye (1985) . . . . . . . . . . . . . . . . . . . . . . .Morrison
Joshua Then and Now (1985; Canadian)
. . . . . . . . . . . . . . . . . . . . . . . . . . . . Joshua Shapiro
Salvador (1986) . . . . . . . . . . . . . . . . . . . Richard Boyle
Best Seller (1988) . . . . . . . . . . . . . . . . . . . . . . . . Cleve
Cop (1988) . . . . . . . . . . . . . . . . . . . . . . .Lloyd Hopkins
The Boost (1989) . . . . . . . . . . . . . . . . . . Lenny Brown
Immediate Family (1989) . . . . . . . . . . . Michael Spector
True Believer (1989) . . . . . . . . . . . . . . . . . . Eddie Dodd
The Hard Way (1991) . . . . . . . . . . . . . . . . . .John Moss
Chaplin (1992; British/U.S.) . . . . . . . . . . .Lawyer Scott
Diggstown (1992) . . . . . . . . . . . . . . . . . . . Gabriel Caine
*a.k.a. Midnight Sting*
Straight Talk (1992) . . . . . . . . . . . . . . . . . . . . . . Jack
The Getaway (1993) . . . . . . . . . . . . . . . . . Jack Benyon
(Unrated version reviewed.)
*Made for Cable Movies:*
Women & Men: Stories of Seduction (1990; HBO)
. . . . . . . . . . . . . . . . . . . . . . . . . . . . . . . . . . Robert
Citizen Cohn (1992; HBO) . . . . . . . . . Roy Marcus Cohn
**Next Door** (1994; Showtime) . . . . . . . . . . Matt Coler
- • 0:30—Brief buns, while mooning out the window while Randy Quaid sprays the outside of the window with water.

*Made for Cable TV:*
Dream On: oral sex, lies and videotape (1993; HBO)
. . . . . . . . . . . . . . . . . . . . . . . . . .Dennis Youngblood
Fallen Angels: Since I Don't Have You (1993; Showtime)
. . . . . . . . . . . . . . . . . . . . . . . . . . . . . Hickey Cohen
(Available on video tape on *Fallen Angels One.*)
*Miniseries:*
Holocaust (1978) . . . . . . . . . . . . . . . . . . . . Karl Weiss
*Made for TV Movies:*
My Name is Bill W. (1989) . . . . . . . . . . . . . . Bill Wilson
The Boys (1991) . . . . . . . . . . . . . . . . . . . Walter Farmer
Jane's House (1994) . . . . . . . . . . . . . . . . . . . . . . . n.a.

## Woods, Michael

*Films:*

**Lady Beware** (1987) . . . . . . . . . . . . . . . . . . . .Jack Price
- •• 0:43—Buns, while lying down in Diane Lane's bed.

FX 2 (1991) . . . . . . . . . . . . . . . . . . . . . Second Mobster
Straight Talk (1992) . . . . . . . . . . . . . . . . . Photographer
**Blindfold: Acts of Obsession** (1993) . . . .Mike Dalton
- ••• 0:07—Buns, while making love with Shannen Doherty on lit table. Long shot.
- • 0:08—Brief buns in the shower with Doherty.

*Made for Cable TV:*
Red Shoe Diaries: Double Dare (1992; Showtime) . . n.a.
(Available on video tape on *Red Shoe Diaries 2: Double Dare.*)
*Made for TV Movies:*
Omen IV: The Awakening (1991) . . . . . . . . . Gene York
Double Edge (1992) . . . . . . . . . . . . . . . . . . . . . . .Paul
*TV:*
Bare Essence (1983) . . . . . . . . . . . . . . . . . Sean Benedict
Our Family Honor (1985-86) . . . . . . Jerry Cole (Danzig)
Capital News (1990) . . . . . . . . . . . . . . . .Clay Gibson

## • Woon

*Films:*

**Immortal Combat** (1993) . . . . . . . . . . . . . . . . Osato
- • 0:01—Buns, getting up out of bed with Meg Foster.

## Wright, Dorsey

*Films:*

**Hair** (1979) . . . . . . . . . . . . . . . . . . . . . . . . . . . . .Hud
- • 0:57—Buns, while taking off clothes and diving into pond with Treat Williams and Woof.

Ragtime (1981) . . . . . . . . . . . . . . . . . . . . . . . . . . n.a.
The Hotel New Hampshire (1984) . . . . . . . . Junior Jones

## Wright, Edward

*Films:*

**Necromancer** (1988) . . . . . . . . . . . . . . . Carl Caulder
- • 0:41—Buns, while taking off his towel and walking into shower.

# Wright, Ken
*Films:*
Skatetown, U.S.A. (1979) . . . . . . . . . . . . . . . . . . . . .n.a.
**Opposing Force** (1986) . . . . . . . . . . . . . . . . Conway
*a.k.a. Hell Camp*
- 0:33—Brief buns, while getting his poncho after being sprayed with water and dusted with white powder.

The Hanoi Hilton (1987) . . . . . . . . . . . . . . . . .Kennedy

# Wright, Patrick
*Films:*
The Abductors (1971). . . . . . . . . . . . . . . . . . . . .Jablon
**Young Lady Chatterley** (1977) . . Flash Back Gardener
••• 0:02—Nude, washing himself, outside while Lady Frances Chatterley watches.
- 0:05—Buns, while in house with Lady Chatterley.
- 0:06—More buns, while on the floor.
- 0:33—Buns, with Lady Chatterley by the pond.

**If You Don't Stop It You'll Go Blind** (1979) . . . .n.a.

# Yaari, Yossi
*Films:*
**Auditions** (1978) . . . . . . . . . . . . . . . .Moshe Mitzvah
- 1:10—Buns, while taking off his clothes during orgy scene.

# York, Michael
*Films:*
Taming of the Shrew (1966; U.S./Italian). . . . . Lucentio
Accident (1967; British). . . . . . . . . . . . . . . . . .William
Romeo and Juliet (1968; British/Italian) . . . . . . . .Tybalt
**Justine** (1969; Italian/Spanish). . . . . . . . . . . . . .Darley
••• 0:13—Buns, seen in mirror while fooling around in bedroom with Melissa.

Zeppelin (1971; British). . . . . . Geoffrey Richter-Douglas
Cabaret (1972) . . . . . . . . . . . . . . . . . . . . Brian Roberts
The Three Musketeers (1973) . . . . . . . . . . . .D'Artagnan
Murder on the Orient Express (1974; British)
. . . . . . . . . . . . . . . . . . . . . . . . . . Count Andrenyi
The Four Musketeers (1975) . . . . . . . . . . . . .D'Artagnan
Logan's Run (1976). . . . . . . . . . . . . . . . . . . . .Logan
The Island of Dr. Moreau (1977) . . . .Andrew Braddock
The Last Remake of Beau Geste (1977) . . . . .Beau Geste
Riddle of the Sands (1984; British). . . Charles Carruthers
Success is the Best Revenge (1984; British) . . Alex Rodak
Lethal Obsession (1987; German) . . . . . . . . .Dr. Proper
*a.k.a. The Joker*
Phantom of Death (1987; Italian) . . . . . . . . . . . Robert
Midnight Cop (1988; Italian) . . . . . . . . . . . .Karstens
The Return of the Musketeers (1989) . . . . . .D'Artagnan
Barbara Cartland's "Duel of Hearts" (1990; British)
. . . . . . . . . . . . . . . . . . . . . Gevase Warlingham
Discretion Assured (1993). . . . . . . . . . . . . . . .Trevor
Wide Sargasso Sea (1993). . . . . . . . . . . . . .Paul Mason
(Unrated version reviewed.)
*Miniseries:*
Space (1987) . . . . . . . . . . . . . . . . . . . . .Dieter Kolff

*Made for TV Movies:*
Fall From Grace (1994). . . . . . . . . . . . . . .Stromelburg
*TV:*
Knots Landing (1987-88) . . . . . . . . . . . . .Charles Scott

# Young Evans, Mitchell
*Video Tapes:*
**Inside Out 4** (1992). . . . . . . . . . . . . .Dave/Video Mate
(Unrated version reviewed.)
- 1:17—Buns, with Sharon Kane in his living room in fast speed.

# Young, Aden
*Films:*
**Black Robe** (1991; Canadian/Australian)
. . . . . . . . . . . . . . . . . . . . . . . . . . . . . . Daniel
- 0:29—Brief buns, while making love with Annuka in the woods at night.
•• 1:04—Buns, while standing in Iroquois hut.

Over the Hill (1991; Australian) . . . . . . . . . . . . . .Nick
Sniper (1993). . . . . . . . . . . . . . . . . . . . Doug Papich

# Youngs, Jim
*Films:*
The Wanderers (1979) . . . . . . . . . . . . . . . . . . Buddy
The Executioner's Song (1982). . . . . . . . . Sterling Baker
(European Version reviewed.)
Footloose (1984) . . . . . . . . . . . . . . . . . . . . . Chuck
**Out of Control** (1984). . . . . . . . . . . . . . . . .Cowboy
- 0:54—Buns, while making love with Claudia Udy.

Hot Shot (1986). . . . . . . . . . . . . . . . . . . . . . . n.a.
Nobody's Fool (1986) . . . . . . . . . . . . . . . . . . . Billy
Youngblood (1986) . . . . . . . . . . . Kelly Youngblood
You Talkin' To Me (1987) . . . . . . . . . . . Bronson Green
Cyborg 2: Glass Shadow (1993). . . . .Pinwheel Exec #1

# Yurasek, John
*Films:*
**Less than Zero** (1987). . . . . . . . . . . . . . . Naked Man
- 1:22—Brief buns while standing up when Andrew McCarthy discovers him with Robert Downey, Jr.

# Zane, Billy
Husband of actress Lisa Collins.
Brother of actress Lisa Zane.
*Films:*
Back to the Future (1985) . . . . . . . . . . . . . . . . Match
Critters (1986). . . . . . . . . . . . . . . . . . . .Steve Elliot
Back to the Future, Part II (1989) . . . . . . . . . . . Match
**Dead Calm** (1989) . . . . . . . . . . . . . . Hughie Warriner
- 1:01—Buns, while walking around on the boat.

Femme Fatale (1990). . . . . . . . . . . . . . .Elijah Hooper
Megaville (1990) . . . . . . . . . . . . . . . .Palinov/Jensen
Memphis Belle (1990) . . . . . . . . . . . "Val" Valentine
Millions (1990). . . . . . . . . . . . . . . . .Maurizo Ferreti
Blood & Concrete: A Love Story (1991) . . . . .Joey Turks
Betrayal of the Dove (1992) . . . . . . . . . . Dr. Jesse Peter

**Lake Consequence** (1992) . . . . . . . . . . . . . . . . . Billy
(Unrated version reviewed.)
  • 0:52—Brief upper half of buns in spa.
  ••• 1:08—Buns, while making love on top of Joan Severance in field. Don't see his face.
Flashfire (1993) . . . . . . . . . . . . . . . . . . . . . Jack Flinder
Orlando (1993; British) . . . . . . . . . . . . . . . Shelmerdine
Poetic Justice (1993) . . . . . . . . . . . . . . . . . . . . Brad
Posse (1993) . . . . . . . . . . . . . . . . . . . Colonel Graham
Sniper (1993) . . . . . . . . . . . . . . . . . . . . Richard Miller
Tombstone (1993) . . . . . . . . . . . . . . . . . . . Mr. Fabian
*Made for Cable TV:*
Tales From the Crypt: Well Cooked Hams (1993; HBO)
  . . . . . . . . . . . . . . . . . . . . . . . . . . . Miles Federman
*Made for TV Movies:*
The Case of the Hillside Strangler (1989)
  . . . . . . . . . . . . . . . . . . . . . . . . . Kenneth Bianchi
Running Delilah (1992) . . . . . . . . . . . . . . . . . . Paul
*TV:*
Twin Peaks (1990-91) . . . . . . . . . . John Justice Wheeler

# Zee, Frank
Husband of adult film actress Ona Zee.
*Made for Cable TV:*
**Real Sex 5** (1993; HBO) . . . . . . . . Of Human Bondage
  ••• 0:12—Buns in T-back, undressing in front of Ona Zee, then lying across her lap while getting spanked.

# Zelnicker, Michael
*Films:*
**Pick-Up Summer** (1979; Canadian) . . . . . . . . . . . Greg
  • 0:04—Brief buns, while hanging a B.A. out the back window of the van.
Hog Wild (1980; Canadian) . . . . . . . . . . . . . . . . . Pete
Touch and Go (1984) . . . . . . . . . . . . . . . . . McDonald
Bird (1988) . . . . . . . . . . . . . . . . . . . . . . . Red Rodney
Naked Lunch (1991) . . . . . . . . . . . . . . . . . . . Martin
Queens Logic (1991) . . . . . . . . . . . . . . . . . . . Marty

# Titles

## 10 (1979)

Julie Andrews . . . . . . . . . . . . . . . . . . . . . . . . . . . Sam
Brian Dennehy . . . . . . . . . . . . . . . . . . . . . . Bartender
Bo Derek . . . . . . . . . . . . . . . . . . . . . . . Jennifer Hanley
  - 1:19—In yellow swimsuit running in slow motion towards Dudley Moore in his daydream.
  - • 1:29—Brief buns and breasts taking off towel and putting on robe when Moore visits her. Long shot, hard to see.
  - • 1:36—Brief breasts taking off dress trying to seduce Moore. Dark, hard to see.
  - • 1:37—Breasts, lying in bed. Dark, hard to see.
  - •• 1:41—Breasts, going to fix the skipping record. Long shot, hard to see. Buns, while jumping back into bed.
  - • 1:43—Breasts and buns, while sitting up in bed.
  - • 1:44—Breasts and buns in bed when Moore gets out.
Sam Jones . . . . . . . . . . . . . . . . . . . . . . . . David Hanley
Dudley Moore . . . . . . . . . . . . . . . . . . . George Webber
  - • 0:47—Buns, while at neighbor's party just before Julie Andrews sees him through a telescope.
Dee Wallace Stone . . . . . . . . . . . . . . . . . . . Mary Lewis
  - • 1:09—Brief side view of buns, while on the floor.
  - • 1:10—Brief upper half of buns, going into bathroom and dropping her sheet.

## 10 to Midnight (1983)

Gene Davis . . . . . . . . . . . . . . . . . . . . . . . Warren Stacy
  - •• 0:08—Nude, running after girl in the woods.
  - •• 0:28—Buns, in Betty's bedroom, while attempting to get her diary.
  - •• 1:31—Buns, lots of times, while attacking the girls in their apartment.
  - •• 1:36—Buns and very brief frontal nudity leaving the apartment at the top of the stairs.
  - •• 1:37—Nude, running after Lisa Eilbacher in the street.
Lisa Eilbacher . . . . . . . . . . . . . . . . . . . . . Laurie Kessler
Jean Manson . . . . . . . . . . . . . . . . . . . . . . . . . . Margo
  - ••• 1:25—Breasts in hotel room with killer when he tries to elude Charles Bronson.
  - • 1:26—Brief right breast, lying in bed, covered with sheet.
Kelly Preston . . . . . . . . . . . . . . . . . . . . . . . . . Doreen
Ola Ray . . . . . . . . . . . . . . . . . . . . . . . . . . . . . . . . . Ola
  - • 1:30—Very brief buns and very brief left breast, taking off robe and getting into the shower.
  - •• 1:31—Breasts in the shower.
  - •• 1:32—More breasts in the shower.
  - • 1:39—Very brief breasts, dead, covered with blood in the shower.
Deran Sarafian . . . . . . . . . . . . . . . . . . . . . Dale Anders
  - • 0:08—Buns, while making love in van with Betty.
Andrew Stevens . . . . . . . . . . . . . . . . . . . . Paul McAnn
Patti Tippo . . . . . . . . . . . . . . . . . . . . . . . . . Party Girl
  - •• 0:52—Breasts, making love with a guy in the laundry room at a party.

Jeana Tomasina . . . . . . . . . . . . . . . . . . . . . . . . . Karen
  - 0:26—In white body suit, changing in bedroom while the killer watches from inside the closet.

## 18 Again! (1988)

Connie Gauthier . . . . . . . . . . . . . . . . . . . Artist's Model
  - •• 0:29—Very brief breasts, then buns taking her robe off during art class.
Anita Morris . . . . . . . . . . . . . . . . . . . . . . . . Madeline
Jennifer Runyon . . . . . . . . . . . . . . . . . . . . . . . . Robin

## 1900 (1976; Italian)

(NC-17 version reviewed.)
Stefania Casini . . . . . . . . . . . . . . . . . . . . . Epileptic Girl
  - •• 2:02—Breasts taking off her top, more breasts in bed with Robert De Niro and Gerard Depardieu.
  - ••• 2:04—Breasts sitting up in bed, then nude while having a seizure.
Robert De Niro . . . . . . . . . . . . . . . . Alfredo Berlinghieri
  - ••• 2:04—Frontal nudity in bed with a girl and Gérard Depardieu.
  - ••• 2:05—Buns, getting out of bed.
  - ••• 2:30—Buns, undressing and making love on top of Dominique Sanda in the hay. Long shot.
Gérard Depardieu . . . . . . . . . . . . . . . . . . . Olmo Dalco
  - •• 2:03—Brief frontal nudity sitting at table with Robert De Niro. Again when walking into the bedroom.
  - ••• 2:04—Frontal nudity in bed with a girl and De Niro.
  - ••• 2:07—Nude, getting up and walking around.
Burt Lancaster . . . . . . . . . . . . . . . . . Alfredo Berlingheri
Roberto Maccanti . . . . . . . . . . . . . . . . . Olmo as a Child
  - •• 1:05—Frontal nudity undressing and showing the young Alfredo his penis.
Paolo Pavesi . . . . . . . . . . . . . . . . . . . Alfredo as a Child
  - • 1:05—Frontal nudity showing the young Olmo his penis.
Ty Randolph . . . . . . . . . . . . . . . . . . . . . . . . . . . . n.a.
Dominique Sanda . . . . . . . . . . . . . . . . . . . . . . . . . Ada
  - ••• 2:30—Left breast, then breasts in hay with Robert De Niro. Long shot of full frontal nudity while lying in the hay.
  - ••• 2:48—(0:08 into tape 2.) Nude under thin fabric dancing with De Niro for photographer.
Stefania Sandrelli . . . . . . . . . . . . . . . . . . Anita Foschi
Donald Sutherland . . . . . . . . . . . . . . . . . . . . . . . Attila

## 1941 (1979)

Nancy Allen . . . . . . . . . . . . . . . . . . . . . . . . . . Donna
  - 0:17—Wearing red bra in cockpit of airplane with Tim Matheson.
  - 1:12—In red bra again with Matheson in the airplane.
Susan Backlinie . . . . . . . . . . . . . . . . . . . Polar Bear Girl
  - • 0:02—Brief breasts and buns, while taking off robe and running into the ocean. Dark, hard to see. This is a parody of her part in Jaws.
  - 0:05—Buns, while hanging on submarine periscope.
  - 0:06—Very, very brief left breast when getting back into the water.
Don Calfa . . . . . . . . . . . . . . . . . . . . Telephone Operator
Perry Lang . . . . . . . . . . . . . . . . . . . . . . . . . . . . Dennis

Tim Matheson. . . . . . . . . . . . . . . . . . . . . . . . Birkhead
Mickey Rourke. . . . . . . . . . . . . . . . . . . . . . . Reese
Carol Ann Williams . . . . . . . . . . . . . . . . . . . . USO Girl
Treat Williams . . . . . . . . . . . . . . . . . . . . . . . Sitarski

### 1984 (1984)
Suzanna Hamilton. . . . . . . . . . . . . . . . . . . . . Julia
- •• 0:38—Full frontal nudity taking off her clothes in the woods with John Hurt.
- ••• 0:52—Nude in secret room standing and drinking and talking to Hurt. Long scene.
- • 1:11—Side view of left breast kneeling down.
- •• 1:12—Breasts after picture falls off the view screen on the wall.

John Hurt . . . . . . . . . . . . . . . . . . . . . Winston Smith
- • 1:11—Buns, while walking from the bed to the window next to Suzanna Hamilton.

### 2020 Texas Gladiators (1983; Italian)
Sabrina Siani . . . . . . . . . . . . . . . . . . . . . . . . Maida
- •• 0:07—Left breast, in open white dress after gang rape.
- • 0:34—Breasts during rape.

### 36 Fillette (1988; French)
Etienne Chicot . . . . . . . . . . . . . . . . . . . . . . . Maurice
- • 1:18—Very brief buns, getting up out of bed. Blurry.

### 3:15—The Moment of Truth (1986)
Adam Baldwin. . . . . . . . . . . . . . . . . . . . . . . . Jeff Hannah
Wendy Barry . . . . . . . . . . . . . . . . . . . . . . . . . Lora
Deborah Foreman . . . . . . . . . . . . . . . . Sherry Havilland
- 0:26—Very brief blurry buns and side view of left breast jumping out of bed when her parents come home. Long shot, hard to see anything.

Gina Gershon . . . . . . . . . . . . . . . One of the Cobrettes
Panchito Gomez . . . . . . . . . . . . . . . . . . . . . Chooch
Wings Hauser . . . . . . . . . . . . . . . . . . . . Mr. Havilland

### 48 Hrs. (1982)
Greta Blackburn . . . . . . . . . . . . . . . . . . . . . . . Lisa
- •• 0:13—Breasts and buns in bathroom in hotel room with James Remar.

Denise Crosby. . . . . . . . . . . . . . . . . . . . . . . . Sally
- 0:47—Very, very brief side view of half of left breast, while swinging baseball bat at Eddie Murphy.
- • 1:24—Very brief side view of right breast when James Remar pushes her onto bed.
- • 1:25—Very brief breasts then very brief side view of right breast attacking Nick Nolte.

Sandy Martin . . . . . . . . . . . . . . . . . . . . Policewoman
Chris Mulkey. . . . . . . . . . . . . . . . . . . . . . . . . . Cop
Nick Nolte. . . . . . . . . . . . . . . . . . . . . . . . Jack Cates
Annette O'Toole . . . . . . . . . . . . . . . . . . . . . Elaine
Ola Ray . . . . . . . . . . . . . . . . . . . . . Vroman's Dancers
Suzanne M. Regard . . . . . . . . . . . . . . . Cowgirl Dancer
- 0:39—Dancer in red-neck bar wearing silver star pasties.

Brenda Venus . . . . . . . . . . . . . . . . . . . . . . . Hooker

### 52 Pick-Up (1986)
Ann-Margret . . . . . . . . . . . . . . . . . . . Barbara Mitchell
Vanity . . . . . . . . . . . . . . . . . . . . . . . . . . . . Doreen
- ••• 0:47—Breasts, stripping in room while Roy Scheider takes Polaroid pictures.
- • 0:52—Breasts under sheer purple nightgown. Partial buns in G-string underneath also.

Ron Jeremy . . . . . . . . . . . . . . . . . . . . . . Party Goer
Amber Lynn . . . . . . . . . . . . . . . . . . . . . . Party Goer
- • 0:23—Breasts opening her blouse while being video taped at party.
- • 0:24—Breasts and buns on TV. B&W.
- • 0:26—Left breast, then breasts being video taped with another woman.

Doug McClure . . . . . . . . . . . . . . . . . . . . . . Averson
Kelly Preston . . . . . . . . . . . . . . . . . . . . . . . . . Cini
- • 0:09—Brief buns in video tape made by blackmailers.
- • 0:36—Breasts, tied to chair on video tape made by blackmailers.
- 0:39—Very brief breasts covered with blood after being shot.

Roy Scheider . . . . . . . . . . . . . . . . . . . . . Harry Mitchell

### 8 Million Ways to Die (1986)
Rosanna Arquette . . . . . . . . . . . . . . . . . . . . . Sarah
- 1:00—In a bra in Jeff Bridges' apartment.

Jeff Bridges. . . . . . . . . . . . . . . . . . Matthew Scudder
Alexandra Paul . . . . . . . . . . . . . . . . . . . . . . . Sunny
- •• 0:24—Full frontal nudity, standing in bathroom while Jeff Bridges watches.

### 9 1/2 Ninjas (1990)
Andee Gray . . . . . . . . . . . . . . . . . . . . . . Lisa Thorne
- •• 1:02—Breasts making love with Joe in the rain.
- • 1:19—Brief breasts during flashback.

Sharon Lee Jones . . . . . . . . . . . . . . . . . . . . . Zelda
- • 0:52—Breasts eating Chinese food in the shower with Joe.

### 9 1/2 Weeks (1986)
Kim Basinger . . . . . . . . . . . . . . . . . . . . . . Elizabeth
- • 0:27—Blindfolded while Mickey Rourke plays with an ice cube on her. Brief right breast.
- 0:36—Masturbating while watching slides of art.
- 0:41—Playing with food at the refrigerator with Rourke. Messy, but erotic.
- • 0:54—Very brief left breast, while rolling over in bed.
- 0:58—Making love with Rourke in clock tower.
- ••• 1:11—In wet lingerie, then breasts making love in a wet stairwell with Rourke.
- • 1:19—Doing a sexy dance for Rourke in a white slip.
- • 1:22—Buns, showing off to Rourke on building.
- • 1:44—Brief buns, putting on pants and getting out of bed.

Mickey Rourke . . . . . . . . . . . . . . . . . . . . . . . John
Margaret Whitton . . . . . . . . . . . . . . . . . . . . . Molly
Karen Young . . . . . . . . . . . . . . . . . . . . . . . . . Sue

### 976-EVIL (1988)

Lezlie Deane . . . . . . . . . . . . . . . . . . . . . . . . . . . .Suzie
- 0:34—Brief right breast in open leather jacket, making love on top of Spike. Brief breasts several times getting off him.
- • 0:37—Brief breasts opening jacket after putting on underwear.

### 976-EVIL II: The Astral Factor (1991)

Deborah Dutch . . . . . . . . . . . . . . . . . Commerical Wife
George "Buck" Flower. . . . . . . . . . . . . . . . . . . .Turrell
Monique Gabrielle . . . . . . . . . . . . . . . . . . . .Miss Lawlor
Karen Mayo-Chandler . . . . . . . . . . . . . . . . . . . .Laurie
- •• 0:00—Breasts in shower room, then putting on wet T-shirt.
- 0:01—Running around the school hallways wearing white panties and wet, white T-shirt.

Brigitte Nielsen . . . . . . . . . . . . . . . . . . . . . . . . Agnes

### A Nos Amours (1984; French)

Sandrine Bonnaire. . . . . . . . . . . . . . . . . . . . . Suzanne
- 0:17—Brief breasts, pulling dress top down to put on nightgown.
- •• 0:34—Breasts sitting up in bed talking to Bernard. Brief side view of buns.
- 0:42—Very brief side view of left breast while waking up in bed.
- 0:57—Very brief lower frontal nudity, while getting out of bed with Martine and her boyfriend. Long shot of buns, while hugging Bernard in the background (out of focus).

Maïté Maillé . . . . . . . . . . . . . . . . . . . . . . . . . Martine
Pierre-Loup Rajot. . . . . . . . . . . . . . . . . . . . . . Bernard
- 0:56—Brief buns, while walking around in the background. Long shot. Out of focus.
- 0:58—Partial frontal nudity, lying in bed talking to Sandrine Bonnaire.

### About Last Night... (1986)

James Belushi . . . . . . . . . . . . . . . . . . . . . . .Bernie Litko
Rob Lowe . . . . . . . . . . . . . . . . . . . . . . . . . . . Danny
- •• 0:52—Buns and almost frontal nudity when he opens the refrigerator with Demi Moore.

Demi Moore . . . . . . . . . . . . . . . . . . . . . . . . . .Debbie
0:32—In white bra getting dressed.
- 0:34—Brief upper half of right breast in the bathtub with Rob Lowe.
0:35—In white bra getting dressed.
- 0:50—Side view of right breast, then very brief breasts.
- ••• 0:51—Buns and breasts in bed with Lowe, arching her back, then lying in bed when he rolls off her.
- •• 0:52—Breasts and buns in kitchen with Lowe.

Elizabeth Perkins . . . . . . . . . . . . . . . . . . . . . . . . Joan

### The Abyss (1989)

Michael Biehn . . . . . . . . . . . . . . . . . Lieutenant Coffey
Ed Harris . . . . . . . . . . . . . . . . . . . Virgil "Bud" Brigman
Mary Elizabeth Mastrantonio. . . . . . . . Lindsey Brigman
- 1:41—Breasts during C.P.R. scene.

J. C. Quinn . . . . . . . . . . . . . . . . . . . . "Sonny" Dawson

### The Accused (1988)

Steve Antin. . . . . . . . . . . . . . . . . . . . . . . . . Bob Joiner
- 1:29—Buns, while raping Jodi Foster on the pinball machine.

Woody Brown . . . . . . . . . . . . . . . . . . . . . . . . .Danny
- 1:28—Buns, while raping Jodi Foster on the pinball machine.

Jodie Foster . . . . . . . . . . . . . . . . . . . . . . . Sarah Tobias
- 1:27—Brief breasts a few times during rape scene on pinball machine by Dan and Bob.

Kelly McGillis . . . . . . . . . . . . . . . . . . Kathryn Murphy
Leo Rossi . . . . . . . . . . . . . . . . . Cliff "Scorpion" Albrect

### Ace Ventura: Pet Detective (1993)

Jim Carrey . . . . . . . . . . . . . . . . . . . . . . . . .Ace Ventura
- •• 1:07—Buns, running to get into the shower after burning his clothes.

Courteney Cox. . . . . . . . . . . . . . . . . . . . . . . . Melissa
Rebecca Ferratti . . . . . . . . . . . . . . . . . . . . Sexy Woman
Sean Young . . . . . . . . . . . . . . . . . . . . . . . . . . . . Lois
1:17—In bra and panties after Ace manages to rip off all her clothes in order to prove she's a man.

### Act of Piracy (1990)

Belinda Bauer. . . . . . . . . . . . . . . . . . . . Sandy Andrews
Nancy Mulford. . . . . . . . . . . . . . . . . . . .Laura Warner
- 0:11—Very brief left breast under Gary Busey in bed. Dark, hard to see.
0:12—In white lingerie, walking around on the boat shooting everybody.
- 0:34—Brief, upper half of left breast, in bed with Ray Sharkey.
0:35—In white nightgown.

Ray Sharkey . . . . . . . . . . . . . . . . . . . . . . . . Jack Wilcox
- 0:33—Brief side view of buns while on top of Laura in bed.
- •• 0:35—Brief buns, while getting out of bed and putting on robe.

### Act of Vengeance (1974)

*a.k.a. The Rape Squad*
(Not to be confused with the film with the same name starring Charles Bronson.)

Anneka di Lorenzo . . . . . . . . . . . . . . . . . . . . . . . Chris
- ••• 1:07—Buns and breasts, getting dressed in house. Seen from outside through simulated camera viewfinder.

Patricia Estrin . . . . . . . . . . . . . . . . . . . . . . . . . .Angie
- 0:37—Brief full frontal nudity, several times, under water in spa. (She's third from the right.)

Jo Ann Harris . . . . . . . . . . . . . . . . . . . . . . . . . . Linda
- ••• 0:06—Breasts, taking off blouse for rapist, getting fondled by him, running away, then getting hit.
- 0:09—Brief left breast, while getting her blouse afterwards. Dark.
- 0:37—Breasts under water with other women in spa. (She's the third from the left.)

Jennifer Lee . . . . . . . . . . . . . . . . . . . . . . . . . . . Nancy
- 0:38—Breasts looking up in spa while talking to another woman.

Lisa Moore . . . . . . . . . . . . . . . . . . . . . . . . . . . Karen
- ••• 0:24—Breasts after rapist cuts her dress open and fondles her breasts while she has a cloth stuffed in her mouth.
- • 0:37—Buns and breasts, walking into the spa to join the other women.
- • 1:27—Brief breasts during fight while tied up in cage. Dark.

Connie Strickland . . . . . . . . . . . . . . . . . . . . . . .Teresa
- • 0:37—Brief full frontal nudity under water, several times, sitting in spa with other women. (She's the blonde on the far right.)

### Acting on Impulse *(1993; Made for Cable Movie)*
Elvira. . . . . . . . . . . . . . . . . . . . . . . . . . . . . . . . . .Roxy
Nancy Allen . . . . . . . . . . . . . . . . . . . . . . Cathy Tomas
Linda Fiorentino . . . . . . . . . . . . . . . . . . . Susan Gittes
C. Thomas Howell. . . . . . . . . . . . . . . . . . Paul Stevens
- • 1:06—Buns in pulled down boxer shorts in hotel room with Linda Fiorentino.

Miles O'Keeffe. . . . . . . . . . . . . . . . . . . . . . . . . . John
Brinke Stevens. . . . . . . . . . . . . . . . . . . . . . Waitress
Mary Woronov . . . . . . . . . . . . . . . . . . . . Receptionist

### Action Jackson *(1988)*
Vanity. . . . . . . . . . . . . . . . . . . . . . . . . . . .Sydney Ash
- •• 0:29—Breasts in bed with Craig T. Nelson.

Deborah Dutch. . . . . . . . . . . . . . . . . . . . . . . . . .n.a.
Susan Lentini. . . . . . . . . . . . . . . . . . . . . . VW Driver
Ed O'Ross . . . . . . . . . . . . . . . . . . . . . . . . . . . Stringer
Melissa Prophet. . . . . . . . . . . . . . . . . . . .Newscaster
Sharon Stone . . . . . . . . . . . . . . . . Patrice Dellaplane
- •• 0:34—Breasts in a steam room. Hard to see because of all the steam.
- • 0:56—Brief right breast, dead, on the bed when police view her body.

### The Adjuster *(1991; Canadian)*
Jennifer Dale . . . . . . . . . . . . . . . . . . . . . . . . . .Arianne
- ••• 0:46—Breasts, while making love on top of Elias Koteas and discussing her insurance adjustments. Dark but nice.

Gabrielle Rose . . . . . . . . . . . . . . . . . . . . . . . . . Mimi
Raoul Trujillo . . . . . . . . . . . . . . . Matthew, Larry's Lover
- • 0:59—Buns, in B&W photo that Elias Koteas looks at.
- • 1:32—Buns in the same B&W photo.
- • 1:33—Buns, while sleeping in motel room while Koteas walks around.

### The Adultress *(1973)*
Tyne Daly . . . . . . . . . . . . . . . . . . . . . . . . . . . . . Inez
- • 0:21—Brief side view of right breast in room with Carl. Brief out of focus breasts in bed.
- •• 0:51—Breasts outside with Hank.
- ••• 0:53—Breasts on a horse with Hank.

### The Adventure of Sherlock Holmes' Smarter Brother *(1975)*
Dom DeLuise . . . . . . . . . . . . . . . . . . . . . . . .Gambetti
Marty Feldman. . . . . . . . . . . . . . . . . . . . .Orville Sacker
- •• 1:04—Buns, in ballroom with Gene Wilder, after a buzz saw removes the back of their tuxedos.

Gene Wilder. . . . . . . . . . . . . . . . Sigerson Holmes
- •• 1:04—Buns, in ballroom with Marty Feldman, after a buzz saw removes the back of their tuxedos.

### The Adventures of a Private Eye *(1974; British)*
Nicola Austine . . . . . . . . . . . . . . . . . . . . . . Wife in Bed
- •• 0:00—Breasts and buns, getting out of bed to take a shower.

Linda Regan. . . . . . . . . . . . . . . . . . . . . . . . . Clarissa
- • 0:34—Full frontal nudity in boat with Scott.
- • 0:36—Very brief side view of left breast, getting up and diving off boat.

Robin Stewart . . . . . . . . . . . . . . . . . . . . .Scott West
- • 0:23—Buns, dancing around after getting caught in a mousetrap.
- • 0:35—Buns, while in boat on top of Clarissa.
- •• 0:36—Brief full frontal nudity, getting up and diving off boat.
- • 0:58—Buns, while on couch with the Inspector's Wife.
- • 1:17—Buns, while standing in bathroom at Lisa's place.

### The Adventures of Eliza Fraser *(1976; Australian)*
Abigail . . . . . . . . . . . . . . . . . . . . . . . . . . .Buxom Girl
- • 0:01—Breasts when Martin pulls the sheets off her.

John Castle. . . . . . . . . . . . . . . . . . . . . . . Rory McBryde
0:34—Upper half of buns, while in bed on top of Susannah York.
- •• 0:38—Buns, while jumping on York, then getting pushed out the door.

John Waters . . . . . . . . . . . . . . . . . . . Dave Bracefell
- • 0:27—Side view of buns, while undressing and getting into bed.
- •• 0:29—Nude, walking around outside. Buns, while standing in doorway.
- • 0:32—Brief pubic hair, then buns while getting off bed to hide under it.
- •• 0:38—Buns, after getting out from under bed and standing up after McBride leaves.
- •• 1:23—Buns in loincloth after joining the tribe.

Susannah York . . . . . . . . . . . . . . . . . . . . . . .Elisa Fraser
- • 1:10—Brief breasts twice during ceremony. Paint on her face while running from hut.
- • 1:30—Brief, upper half of left beast, while bathing in river with Bracefell.

### Affairs of the Heart *(1992)*
John Altamura . . . . . . . . . . . . . . . . . . . . . . . . Jock #1
Amy Lynn Baxter . . . . . . . . . . . . . . . . . . . . . . .Josie Hart
- •• 0:00—Breasts during opening credits.
- •• 0:02—Breasts and buns in G-string, while posing for photos.

••• 1:09—Breasts posing in santa cap during photo session.

•• 1:13—Breasts with Richard during smoky dream scene.

Cody Carmack . . . . . . . . . . . . . . . . . . . . . . . . . . . .Itchy

••• 0:45—Breasts taking off her bikini top with her husband.

Lorna Courtney. . . . . . . . . . . . . . . . . . . . . . . . . . . Jane

••• 1:04—Breasts, making love in front of a fire in sleeping bag with Dick.

Isabelle Fortea . . . . . . . . . . . . . . . . . . . . . . . . . Karen

••• 1:06—Breasts making love in cabin with Tom.

Joan Gerardi . . . . . . . . . . . . . . . . . . Miss Valentine's Day

••• 0:15—Breasts, posing for photos in red bottoms.

Melissa Leigh. . . . . . . . . . . . . . . . . . . . .Jealous Woman

••• 0:38—Buns, then breasts with the Jealous Man.

Joseph E. Mauro . . . . . . . . . . . . . . . . . . . . Jealous Man

• 0:38—Buns in G-string, walking into room with the Jealous Woman.

Michael Montana . . . . . . . . . . . . . . . . . . . . . .Richard

•• 1:13—Buns, with Amy Lynn Baxter during smoky dream scene.

Beckie Mullen . . . . . . . . . . . . . . . . . . . . . . . Pool Girl

••• 0:52—Breasts, after taking off her bikini top, then diving into pool.

•• 0:53—Breasts, lying on towel on diving board, then turning over.

Angela Nicholas . . . . . . . . . . . . . . . . . . . . . .Dreamgirl

•• 0:14—In bra, then left breast while in bed with the Geek.

### Afraid of the Dark (1992; British/French)

James Fox . . . . . . . . . . . . . . . . . . . . . . . . . . . . . Frank

Clare Holman . . . . . . . . . . . . . . . . . . . . . . . . . . . Rose

••• 0:38—Breasts, while wearing white panties, garter belt and stockings while posing for photographer in studio on a wooden horse. Long scene.

Paul McGann . . . . . . . . . . . . . . . . . . . . Tony Dalton

Cassie Stuart . . . . . . . . . . . . . . . . . . .Woman Neighbor

David Thewlis . . . . . . . . . . . . . . . .Tom Miller/Locksmith

### After Dark, My Sweet (1990)

Bruce Dern . . . . . . . . . . . . . . . . . . . . . . . . . .Uncle Bud

Jeanie Moore. . . . . . . . . . . . . . . . . . . . . . . . . Nanny

Jason Patric . . . . . . . . . . . . . . . Kevin "Collie" Collins

•• 1:19—Buns, while taking off pants and getting into bed with Rachel Ward. More brief buns on top of her.

Rachel Ward . . . . . . . . . . . . . . . . . . . . . . . Fay Anderson

• 1:22—Very, very brief half of right breast under Jason Patric in bed when he moves slightly.

### After Hours (1985)

Rosanna Arquette . . . . . . . . . . . . . . . . . . . . . . . .Marcy

0:48—In bed, dead, in panties. Arm covers breasts.

Henry Judd Baker . . . . . . . . . . . . . . . . . . . . . . . . Jett

Linda Fiorentino . . . . . . . . . . . . . . . . . . . . . . . . Kiki

0:11—In black bra and skirt doing paper maché.

•• 0:19—Breasts taking off bra in doorway while Griffin Dunne watches.

Teri Garr . . . . . . . . . . . . . . . . . . . . . . . . . . . . . Julie

John Heard. . . . . . . . . . . . . . . . . . . . . . . . Bartender

Richard "Cheech" Marin . . . . . . . . . . . . . . . . . . . .Neil

### After School (1987)

Renee Coleman . . . . . . . . . . . . . . . . . September Lane

•• 0:35—Breasts and buns getting into bathtub. Almost lower frontal nudity.

Sherrie Rose . . . . . . . . . . . . . . . . . . First Tribe Member

### After the Rehearsal (1984; Swedish)

Lena Olin . . . . . . . . . . . . . . . . . . . . . . . .Anna Egerman

Ingrid Thulin . . . . . . . . . . . . . . . . . . . . . . . . . Rakel

• 0:33—Brief breasts, when pulling up her sweater to show Henrik how beautiful her breasts still look.

### Against the Wall (1994; Made for Cable Movie)

Samuel L. Jackson . . . . . . . . . . . . . . . . . . . . . . .Jamael

• 0:06—Buns, during strip-search while entering prison. (Seen through grate).

Kyle MacLachlan . . . . . . . . . . . . . . . . . . . . . Michael

Harry Dean Stanton . . . . . . . . . . . . . . . . . . . . . . Hal

Clarence Williams, III . . . . . . . . . . . . . . . . . . . . Choko

• 0:14—Brief upper half of buns, before putting on towel in shower room.

### Agatha (1979; British)

Dustin Hoffman . . . . . . . . . . . . . . . . . . . . Wally Stanton

Vanessa Redgrave. . . . . . . . . . . . . . . . . . Agatha Christie

• 0:38—Buns, while lying face down and getting a massage. Then wearing a wet gown in bathtub.

Timothy West. . . . . . . . . . . . . . . . . . . . . . . Ken Ward

### Age of Consent (1969; Australian)

Clarissa Kaye-Mason. . . . . . . . . . . . . . . . . . . . . . Meg

• 0:05—Brief breasts, crawling on the bed to watch TV.

Jack MacGowran . . . . . . . . . . . . . . . . . . . . . Nat Kelly

• 1:01—Brief buns, while running into the ocean when Miss Marley sees him.

•• 1:02—Buns, running away from her to the cabin while holding a dog to cover up his private parts.

Helen Mirren . . . . . . . . . . . . . . . . . . . . . . . . . . . . Cora

• 0:48—Breasts several times in the mirror. Brief lower frontal nudity, kneeling on the floor.

•• 0:55—Brief breasts and buns quite a few time, snorkeling under water.

••• 1:20—Breasts and half of buns, posing in the water for James Mason. Then getting out.

### Agony of Love (1966)

Pat Barringer . . . . . . . . . . . . . . . . . . . . .Barbara Thomas

0:09—Undressing for a customer down to a white bra.

•• 0:10—Breasts, after taking off bra, then on bed with the customer. Upper half of buns in pulled down panties.

••• 0:16—Breasts and buns, standing in front of bathroom mirror, then taking a bath and drying herself off.

•• 0:19—Breasts, while making love with the Beatnik and his girlfriend.

- 0:29—Brief breasts several times during nightmare with money.
  0:36—In black bra, undressing in room with two Conventioneers.
- 0:38—Brief breasts while wearing panties, in bed with a Conventioneer.
- ••• 0:42—Breasts, while lying on bed and getting out of bed after making love with the Conventioneer.
- 0:43—Breasts, while sitting up after making love with the other Conventioneer.
- 0:54—In white bra and panties on bed, then breasts several times with a customer.
- •• 1:02—In white bra, taking off her clothes in front of a customer. Then breasts while wearing panties while she poses and he messily eats a lot of food.
- 1:16—Brief breasts, while turning over in bed before seeing her husband.

## Airborne *(1993)*
Brittney Powell . . . . . . . . . . . . . . . . . . . . . . . . . . .Nikki
Owen Stadele . . . . . . . . . . . . . . . . . . . . . . . . . . . Blane
- 1:05—Brief buns, while wearing a jockstrap after his sweat pants are yanked down by Mitchell during street hockey game.

## Alamo Bay *(1985)*
Ed Harris . . . . . . . . . . . . . . . . . . . . . . . . . . . . . .Shang
Amy Madigan . . . . . . . . . . . . . . . . . . . . . . . . . . Glory
- •• 0:28—Breasts while lying in motel bed with Ed Harris.
- •• 0:30—Breasts while sitting up in the bed.
  0:40—Walking in parking lot in a wet T-shirt.

## Albino *(1976)*
a.k.a. *Night of the Askari*
Sybil Danning . . . . . . . . . . . . . . . . . . . . . . . . . . . Sally
- 0:19—Breasts, then full frontal nudity getting raped by the Albino and his buddies.

## Alexa *(1988)*
Ruth Corrine Collins . . . . . . . . . . . . . . . . . . . . . Marshall
- 0:01—Breasts a couple of times taking blue dress off and putting it on again. Long shot.
Christine Moore . . . . . . . . . . . . . . . . . . . . . . . . . Alexa
  0:04—In red slip in bedroom.
  0:06—In black bra, on bed with Tommy.
  0:11—In black lingerie talking on phone in bed.
- •• 0:24—Breasts lying in bed with Anthony while reminiscing.
- •• 1:08—Breasts in bed with Anthony again.

## Alice Goodbody *(1975)*
Angela Carnon . . . . . . . . . . . . . . . . . . . . Harmonica Girl
- ••• 1:07—Buns and lower frontal nudity playing a harmonica without her mouth. (Never see her face.)
- 1:20—Buns, during end credits.
George "Buck" Flower. . . . . . . . . . . . . . . Roger Merkel
Sharon Kelly . . . . . . . . . . . . . . . . . . . . Alice Goodbody
- 0:01—Brief breasts in mirror, getting dressed.
- ••• 0:16—In bra, then full frontal nudity, undressing in Arnold's place. More breasts in the shower with him.

- ••• 0:17—Frontal nudity, while lying in bed and making out with Arnold.
- 0:27—Breasts with Roger while he eats all sorts of food off her body.
- 0:28—Breasts, lying in bed with Roger afterwards.
- ••• 0:37—Right breast, then frontal nudity while talking to Rex.
- ••• 0:38—Breasts when Rex carries her to bed and makes love with her, while admiring himself.
- ••• 0:47—Breasts with bandages on her face.
- ••• 0:51—Breasts, taking off her robe and getting into bed. (Bandages are still on her face.)
- •• 1:09—Buns, undressing and getting into bed.
- 1:21—Brief breasts in mirror in bed with Rex during the end credits.

## Alice in Wonderland *(1977)*
(R-rated version reviewed.)
Kristine DeBell . . . . . . . . . . . . . . . . . . . . . . . . . . Alice
- 0:10—Brief left breast, several times after shrinking.
- 0:12—In braless wet sheet, after getting out of the water.
- 0:14—Brief lower frontal nudity in open sheet during song and dance number.
- •• 0:16—Lower frontal nudity and breasts while getting licked by her new friends.
- •• 0:18—Full frontal nudity while putting new dress on.
- 0:19—Left breast in gaping dress when sitting down on rock.
- ••• 0:22—Breasts, after taking off dress and playing with herself.
- 0:40—Brief right breast, while lying on the ground with Tweedledum and Tweedledee.
- 0:42—Brief breasts under dress while singing and dancing.
- •• 0:51—Full frontal nudity on bed with the king.
- ••• 0:59—Full frontal nudity getting bathed and primped by two women, then making love with them, then with the Queen. Brief buns, when getting up.
- 1:05—Right breast in dress, while running from the Queen.
- •• 1:07—Nude while making love with her boyfriend after returning from Wonderland.
- ••• 1:10—Breasts, while running around in field in white dress, then riding a horse. Full frontal nudity in waterfall.
- ••• 1:15—Nude during end credits.
Juliet Graham . . . . . . . . . . . . . . . . . . . . . . . The Queen
- ••• 0:51—Full frontal nudity in garter belt and stockings while walking, then talking with Alice.
- ••• 0:54—Full frontal nudity during trial.
  0:58—Breasts in quick cuts.
- 1:05—Full frontal nudity, while running after Alice.
- •• 1:13—Breasts during the end credits.
Alan Novak . . . . . . . . . . . . . . . . . . . . . . . Mad Hatter
- 0:26—Frontal nudity, showing himself to Alice.
Jason Williams . . . . . . . . . . . . . . . . . . . . . . . . . . . n.a.

### Alice's Restaurant (1969)
Shelley Plimpton . . . . . . . . . . . . . . . . . . . . . . . Reenie
•• 0:21—Breasts, taking off her blouse while sitting on bed and talking to Arlo Guthrie.
M. Emmet Walsh. . . . . . . . . . . . . . . Group W Sergeant

### Alien Intruder (1992)
Melinda Armstrong . . . . . . . . . . . . . . . . . . . .Tammy
•• 0:29—In two piece swimsuit, then nude in shower during Maxwell Caulfield's virtual reality experience.
• 0:30—Very, very brief right breast, while putting on robe while walking on balcony.
• 0:54—Breasts, while lying dead on beach.
Maxwell Caulfield . . . . . . . . . . . . . . . . . . . . . . . Nick
Jeff Conaway . . . . . . . . . . . . . . . . . . . . . . . . . Borman
Stephen Davies . . . . . . . . . . . . . . . . . . . . . . . .Peter
Jane Hamilton . . . . . . . . . . . . . . . . . . . . . .Turk's Mama
Lauren Hays . . . . . . . . . . . . . . . . . . . . . . . . . . Roni
Adrianne Sachs . . . . . . . . . . . . . . . . . . . . . . . .Yvonne
Tracy Scoggins . . . . . . . . . . . . . . . . . . . . . . Ariel
  0:31—In one piece swimsuit, while walking out of surf at beach in front of Maxwell Caulfield.
• 0:54—Breasts and buns (mostly silhouette) while straddling Caulfield on bed.
Gwen Somers . . . . . . . . . . . . . . . . . . . . . . . . . Annie
••• 0:19—Breasts, taking off her top in front of Lloyd while he sits in bathtub.

### Alien Prey (1984; British)
Glory Annen . . . . . . . . . . . . . . . . . . . . . . . . . . .Jessica
• 0:22—Breasts unbuttoning blouse to sunbathe.
•• 0:34—Breasts taking off top, getting into bed with Josephine, then making love with her.
  0:36—Buns, rolling on top of Josephine.
••• 0:38—More breasts when Josephine is playing with her.
  0:39—More buns in bed. Long shot.
• 0:46—Left breast and buns standing up in bathtub.
•• 1:05—Breasts getting out of bed and putting a dress on.
•• 1:19—Breasts in bed with Anders. Brief buns when he rips her panties off.
Sally Faulkner . . . . . . . . . . . . . . . . . . . . . . . Josephine
• 0:32—Very, very brief left breast taking off top.
  0:36—Buns, in bed with Glory Annen.
• 0:37—Breasts on her back in bed with Annen.
Barry Stokes . . . . . . . . . . . . . . . . . . . . . . . . . Anders
•• 1:19—Buns, while getting on top of Glory Annen in bed.

### Alien Space Avenger (1988)
Vicki Darnell . . . . . . . . . . . . . . . . . . . . . . Bordello Lady
Kirk Fairbanks Fogg . . . . . . . . . . . . . . . . . . . . . . .Matt
• 0:22—Buns, while walking out of apartment after Ginny.
Jamie Gillis . . . . . . . . . . . . . . . . . . . . . . .Businessman
Gina Mastrogiacomo. . . . . . . . . . . . . . . . . . . . . Ginny
••• 0:19—Breasts in bed, making love with Matt. Breasts and buns, getting out and getting dressed.

Angela Nicholas . . . . . . . . . . . . . . . . . . . . . . . . . Doris
• 0:56—Brief breasts making whoopee with Jaimie Gillis.
••• 0:57—More breasts making love on top of Gillis while killing him.
Elisa Pensler Gabrielli . . . . . . . . . . . . . Red Riding Hood
Miriam Zucker . . . . . . . . . . . . . . . . . . . .Bordello Reporter

### Alien Warrior (1985)
Tally Chanel . . . . . . . . . . . . . . . . . . . . . . . . . . . Barbara
•• 0:46—In white lingerie, then breasts and buns while undressing in room with the Police Captain.
• 1:03—Brief breasts and buns in flashback of 0:46 scene.
Brett Clark . . . . . . . . . . . . . . . . . . . . . . . . . . . Buddy
•• 0:03—Buns, while walking naked after getting transported to Earth.
Lydia Finzi . . . . . . . . . . . . . . . . . . . . . . . . . Beverly

### The Alien Within (1990)
Contains footage from *The Evil Spawn* woven together with new material.
Suzanne Ager. . . . . . . . . . . . . . . . . . . . . . . . .Erin West
Bobbie Bresee . . . . . . . . . . . . . . . . . . . . . Lynn Roman
• 0:12—Very brief half of right breast in bed with a guy.
••• 0:37—Breasts and side view of buns in bathroom looking at herself in the mirror, then taking a shower.
Pamela Gilbert . . . . . . . . . . . . . . . . . . . . . Elaine Talbot
••• 0:48—Nude taking off black lingerie and going swimming in pool.
••• 0:55—Breasts in the pool, then full frontal nudity getting out.
Melissa Anne Moore. . . . . . . . . . . . . . . .Monica Roarke
•• 0:52—Left breast, taking off her purple dress.
••• 1:18—Breasts, lying on bed when the monster strangles her and pulls her top down.
• 1:19—Left breast, while lying in bed, then getting up.
Dawn Wildsmith . . . . . . . . . . . . . . . . . . . . Evelyn Avery

### All That Jazz (1979)
Leah Ayres-Hamilton . . . . . . . . . . . . .Nurse Capobianco
Sandahl Bergman. . . . . . . . . . . . . . . . . . . . . .Sandra
•• 0:51—Breasts and buns in T-back while dancing on scaffolding during a dance routine.
Vicki Frederick . . . . . . . . . . . . . . . . . . . .Menage Partner
Deborah Geffner . . . . . . . . . . . . . . . . . . . . . . Victoria
• 0:16—Brief breasts taking off her blouse and walking up the stairs while Roy Scheider watches. A little out of focus.
Jessica Lange . . . . . . . . . . . . . . . . . . . . . . Angelique
John Lithgow . . . . . . . . . . . . . . . . . . . Lucas Sergeant
Sue Paul. . . . . . . . . . . . . . . . . . . . . . . . . . . . Stacy
• 1:18—Brief right breast in bed with Roy Scheider at the hospital.
Roy Scheider . . . . . . . . . . . . . . . . . . . . . . . Joe Gideon
• 1:42—Very brief partial buns while wearing open back hospital gown and dancing around in basement.

• 1:47—Very brief buns in hospital gown while getting escorted out of the cafeteria.
K.C. Townsend . . . . . . . . . . . . . . . . . . . . . . . Stripper
• 0:20—Breasts backstage getting Joey excited before he goes on stage. Lit by red light.
Terri Treas . . . . . . . . . . . . . . . . . . . . . . . . Fan Dancer

## ...All the Marbles (1981)
a.k.a. The California Dolls
Angela Aames . . . . . . . . . . . . . . . . . . . . . . . . . . Louise
•• 0:20—Breasts in Peter Falk's motel room talking with Iris, then sitting on the bed.
Peter Falk . . . . . . . . . . . . . . . . . . . . . . . . . . . . Harry
Vicki Frederick . . . . . . . . . . . . . . . . . . . . . . . . . . Iris
• 1:03—Brief side view of left breast, while crying in the shower after fighting with Peter Falk.
Laurene Landon . . . . . . . . . . . . . . . . . . . . . . Molly
Tracy Reed . . . . . . . . . . . . . . . . . . . . . . . . . . Diane

## All the Mornings of the World (1992; French)
a.k.a. Tout Les Matins Du Monde
Anne Brochet . . . . . . . . . . . . . . . . . . . . . . Madeleine
• 0:46—Nude by river bank while running to hide behind tree when seen by Marin. Long shot.
•• 0:56—Left breast, while opening her dress and letting Marin feel and kiss her breast.
• 1:06—Brief breasts, after opening her blouse for Marin in the hallway.
• 1:08—Brief upper half of right breast while holding Marin's hand.
•• 1:20—Lower frontal nudity under nightgown, while getting out of bed.
Gérard Depardieu . . . . . . . . . . . . . . . . . . . Marin Marais
Guillaume Depardieu . . . . . . . . . . . Young Marin Marais
•• 1:08—Buns and balls from behind, while getting out of bed.

## All The Right Moves (1983)
Tom Cruise . . . . . . . . . . . . . . . . . . . . . . . . . . . . Stef
•• 1:00—Very brief frontal nudity getting undressed in his bedroom with Lea Thompson.
Christopher Penn . . . . . . . . . . . . . . . . . . . . . . Brian
Lea Thompson . . . . . . . . . . . . . . . . . . . . . . . . . Lisa
••• 1:00—Breasts and brief buns and lower frontal nudity, getting undressed and into bed with Tom Cruise in his bedroom.

## All Tied Up (1992)
Zach Galligan . . . . . . . . . . . . . . . . . . . . . . Brian Hartley
•• 0:59—Buns after throwing off towel in his backyard. Don't see his face.
Tracy Griffith . . . . . . . . . . . . . . . . . . . . Sharon Stevens
Teri Hatcher . . . . . . . . . . . . . . . . . . . . . Linda Alissio
Vivianne Vives . . . . . . . . . . . . . . . . . . . . . . . Carmen

## The All-American Boy (1973)
Anne Archer . . . . . . . . . . . . . . . . . . . Drenna Valentine
Rosalind Cash . . . . . . . . . . . . . . . . . . . . . . . . Poppy
Jeanne Cooper . . . . . . . . . . . . . . . . . . . . Nola Bealer
Art Metrano . . . . . . . . . . . . . . . . . Jay David Swooze

E.J. Peaker . . . . . . . . . . . . . . . . . . . . . . . . Janelle Sharkey
••• 0:37—Breasts and buns, while in bathroom with Jon Voight.
Jon Voight . . . . . . . . . . . . . . . . . . . . . . . . . . . Vic Bealer
• 0:06—Very brief partial buns, while getting up off the floor with Janelle.
•• 0:37—Buns, while getting into shower.

## All-American Murder (1991)
Josie Bissett . . . . . . . . . . . . . . . . . . . . . . . . Tally Fuller
1:01—Brief breasts in Polaroid photographs that Charlie Schlatter looks at. Hard to see.
• 1:07—Very brief breasts several times during B&W flashbacks.
• 1:12—Breasts on top of the Dean during Joanna Cassidy's B&W flashbacks. Quick cuts.
Joanna Cassidy . . . . . . . . . . . . . . . . . . . . Erica Darby
J. C. Quinn . . . . . . . . . . . . . . . . . . . . . . . . . . . . n.a.

## Allan Quatermain and the Lost City of Gold (1987)
Elvira . . . . . . . . . . . . . . . . . . . . . . . . . . . . . . Sorais
Sharon Stone . . . . . . . . . . . . . . . . . . . Jesse Huston
• 0:20—Very brief lower frontal nudity, seen under loose panties, when she stands up in back of car and pulls her dress off over her head. (Don't really see much, but for the sake of completeness...)

## Alley Cat (1982)
Karen Mani . . . . . . . . . . . . . . . . . . . . . . . . . . Billie
• 0:01—Brief breasts in panties taking night gown off during opening credits.
0:17—In two piece swimsuit sitting by the pool.
••• 0:38—Brief side view of right breast and buns getting into the shower. Full frontal nudity in the shower.
••• 0:48—Breasts during women's prison shower room scene. Long scene.
Moriah Shannon . . . . . . . . . . . . . . . . . . . . . . . Sam

## Alligator Eyes (1990)
Annabelle Larsen . . . . . . . . . . . . . . . . . . . . . Pauline
•• 0:42—Nude, getting up from bed and walking around.

## Allonsanfan (1974; Italian)
Italian with English subtitles.
Mimsy Farmer . . . . . . . . . . . . . . . . . . . . . . . Mirella
•• 1:14—Buns, while lying in bed with Marcello Mastroianni. Breasts, sitting up in bed. (Subtitles get in the way.)
1:15—Buns, while standing up with Mastroianni.
1:34—Very brief part of right breast, under her arm while kneeling on bed.
Lea Massari . . . . . . . . . . . . . . . . . . . . . . . . Charlotte
• 0:32—Buns, while undressing in bedroom in front of Marcello Mastroianni.

## ...Almost (1990; Australian)
Rosanna Arquette . . . . . . . . . . . . . . . . . . . . . . Wendy
Susan Lyons . . . . . . . . . . . . . . . . . . . . . . . . . Caroline

Hugo Weaving . . . . . . . . . . . . . . . . . . . . . . . . . . . Jake
0:52—Very brief out of focus buns when he drops
his pants in front of Rosanna Arquette. Don't see his
face. Note in the very next scene, he's wearing underwear!

### Almost Blue *(1992)*
Yaphet Kotto. . . . . . . . . . . . . . . . . . . . . . . . . . . . .Terry
Michael Madsen . . . . . . . . . . . . . . . . . . . .Morris Poole
Lynette Walden. . . . . . . . . . . . . . . . . . . . . . . .Jasmine
••• 0:34—Breasts in bed on top of Michael Madsen.
• 0:35—Brief breasts, while walking to the bed and lying down while wearing panties.
••• 1:08—In black bra, then breasts and brief partial
buns, while making love with Madsen on the sofa.
•• 1:10—Buns, while lying on sofa asleep with Madsen.
1:18—In black bra and panties in Madsen's apartment.

### An Almost Perfect Affair *(1979)*
Keith Carradine. . . . . . . . . . . . . . . . . . . . . . . . . . . Hal
• 0:48—Brief buns, while getting into bathtub with
Monica Vitti.
Edy Williams . . . . . . . . . . . . . . . . . . . . . . . . . Herself
• 0:18—Breasts and buns, while showing off during
Cannes Film Festival.
• 0:38—Brief breasts in a photo of herself that she
holds up.

### Almost Pregnant *(1992)*
(Unrated version reviewed.)
Steve Adell . . . . . . . . . . . . . . . . . . . . . . . Muscle Man
• 0:04—Buns, while making love in bed with Tanya
Roberts.
•• 0:20—Buns, while on top of Roberts during Jeff Conaway's dream.
John Calvin . . . . . . . . . . . . . . . . . . . . . Gordon Mallory
•• 1:11—Buns, while on top of Tanya Roberts in bed.
Lisa Comshaw. . . . . . . . . . . . . . . . . . . . . Body Double
Jeff Conaway. . . . . . . . . . . . . . . . . . . . Charlie Alderson
••• 0:10—Buns, while making love on top of Tanya Roberts in bed.
•• 1:12—Buns in bed in alternate scenes with Roberts
and Joan Severance.
Lezlie Deane . . . . . . . . . . . . . . . . . . . . . . . Party Girl
Tanya Roberts . . . . . . . . . . . . . . . . . . . . Linda Alderson
••• 0:04—Breasts and buns, in bed with a guy. Long
scene.
• 0:10—Brief right breast, while under Conaway in
bed.
• 0:18—Brief left breast, while in bed with another
guy during Conaway's dream.
0:40—Very brief side view of buns, in lingerie, walking down stairs.
• 1:08—Buns, lying in bed while Gordon writes.
••• 1:11—Breasts and buns in bed.
••• 1:12—Nude with Conaway.
Joan Severance . . . . . . . . . . . . . . . . . Maureen Mallory
••• 0:58—In belly dancer outfit in bedroom with Jeff
Conaway, then breasts.

•• 1:06—In black leather outfit, then breasts and buns
in G-string. Her hair gets in the way a lot.
•• 1:09—Brief breasts and buns in various sexual positions in bed with Conaway.

### Alpine Fire *(1985; Swiss)*
Thomas Nock. . . . . . . . . . . . . . . . . . . . . . . . . . . Bob
• 0:08—Brief buns, while outside taking a bath.

### Altered States *(1980)*
Drew Barrymore. . . . . . . . . . . . . . . . . . .Margaret Jessup
Blair Brown . . . . . . . . . . . . . . . . . . . . . . . . .Emily Jessup
• 0:10—Brief left breast making love with William Hurt
in red light from an electric heater.
•• 0:34—Breasts lying on her stomach during Hurt's
mushroom induced hallucination.
1:39—Buns, sitting in hallway with Hurt after the
transformations go away.
William Hurt. . . . . . . . . . . . . . . . . . . . . . . . .Eddie Jessup
0:46—Brief pubic hair twice when Charles Haid and
Bob Balaban help him out of isolation tank.
• 0:54—Very brief buns, while standing in the shower
when he starts transforming. More buns standing
near door and walking to bed.

### Alvin Purple *(1973; Australian)*
Abigail . . . . . . . . . . . . . . . . . . . . . . . Girl in See-Through
0:01—On bus in see-through top. Hard to see any-
thing.
Graeme Blundell . . . . . . . . . . . . . . . . . . . . .Alvin Purple
•• 0:21—Brief nude, while painting Samantha's body.
•• 0:22—Buns and brief frontal nudity in bedroom with
the Kinky Lady.
• 0:25—Brief buns with Mrs. Warren—who turns out
to be a man.
• 0:26—Very brief frontal nudity running out of room,
then buns going down the stairs.
••• 0:33—Nude, undressing and taking a shower. Shot
at fast speed.
•• 1:04—Nude, running away from the girl during
showing of movie.
• 1:21—Buns, while getting chased by a group of
women down the street.
Lynette Curran. . . . . . . . . . . . . . . . . . . .First Sugar Girl
•• 0:02—Brief full frontal nudity when Alvin opens the
door.
Kris McQuade . . . . . . . . . . . . . . . . . . . . . . . Samantha
••• 0:21—Breasts and buns, while painting Alvin's body.
Debbie Nankervis. . . . . . . . . . . . . . . Girl in Blue Movie
•• 1:04—Nude, running after Alvin in bedroom during
showing of movie.
Elke Neidhardt . . . . . . . . . . . . . . . Woman in Blue Movie
•• 1:07—In red bra, then full frontal nudity in bedroom
with Alvin during showing of film.
Anne Pendlebury . . . . . . . . . . . . . . . . . . Woman with Pin
•• 0:48—Right breast and lower frontal nudity, while
lying in bed, talking with Alvin.
Jacki Weaver. . . . . . . . . . . . . . . . . . . . Second Sugar Girl
•• 0:33—Brief full frontal nudity, lying in bean bag
chair.

## Alvin Rides Again (1974; Australian)
Abigail . . . . . . . . . . . . . . . . . . . . . . . . . . . . . . Mae
••• 0:12—Breasts in store with Alvin.
Graeme Blundell . . . . . . . . . . . . . . . . . . . . Alvin Purple
• 0:06—Buns, while running out of the office after he's awakened. Blurry.
Chantal Contouri . . . . . . . . . . . . . . . Boobs La Touche
• 1:15—Very brief lower frontal nudity, putting panties on in the car. Brief breasts, putting red dress on.
Kris McQuade. . . . . . . . . . . . . . . . . . . . . . . . . Mandy
••• 0:48—Full frontal nudity, taking off red dress and getting into bed with Alvin. More breasts lying in bed. Long scene.
Debbie Nankervis . . . . . . . . . . . . . . . Woman Cricketer
Candy Raymond . . . . . . . . . . . . . . . . . . . . . Girl in Office
• 0:05—Lower frontal nudity and buns, in office with Alvin.
Judy Stevenson . . . . . . . . . . . . . . . . . . . . . . .Housewife
•• 0:01—Full frontal nudity, dropping her towel while Alvin washes her window.

## Always (1984)
Michael Emil . . . . . . . . . . . . . . . . . . . . . .David's Brother
André Gregory . . . . . . . . . . . . . . . Party Philosopher
Melissa Leo . . . . . . . . . . . . . . . . . . . . . . . . . . .Peggy
• 1:33—Very, brief breasts and buns, jumping over inflatable lounge in pool. Long shot.
Patrice Townsend . . . . . . . . . . . . . . . . . . . . . . Judy

## The Amateur (1982)
Nicholas Campbell . . . . . . . . . . . . . . . . . . . .Schraeger
George Coe . . . . . . . . . . . . . . . . . . . . . . . .Rutledge
Chapelle Jaffe . . . . . . . . . . . . . . . . . . . . . . .Gretchen
• 1:19—Breasts (mostly right breast), while lying on operating table when doctors try to reviver her after John Savage gives her a poison pill.
• 1:20—More right breast again.
Marthe Keller . . . . . . . . . . . . . . . . . . . . . . .Elisabeth
John Savage . . . . . . . . . . . . . . . . . . . . . Charles Heller

## Amazon Women on the Moon (1987)
Corinne Alphen. . . . . . . . . . . . . . . . . . . . . . . . .Shari
••• 1:13—In black bra, then breasts on TV while Ray watches.
Rosanna Arquette . . . . . . . . . . . . . . . . . . . . . . Karen
Belinda Balaski. . . . . . . . . . . . . . . . . . . . . Bernice Pitnik
Ed Begley, Jr. . . . . . . . . . . . . . . . . . . . . . . . . .Griffin
• 0:54—Buns, while walking around as the Son of the Invisible Man. This section is in B&W.
Lana Clarkson . . . . . . . . . . . . . . . . . . . . . . . Alpha Beta
Sybil Danning . . . . . . . . . . . . . . . . . . . .Queen Lara
Monique Gabrielle . . . . . . . . . . . . . . . . . . Taryn Steele
••• 0:05—Nude during Penthouse Video sketch. Long sequence of her nude in unlikely places.
Steve Guttenberg . . . . . . . . . . . . . . . . . . . . Jerry Stone
Tracey E. Hutchinson. . . . . . . . . . . . . . . . . . . . Floozie
1:18—Brief right breast, while hitting balloon while Carrie Fisher talks to a guy. This sketch is in B&W and appears after the first batch of credits.
Michelle Pfeiffer . . . . . . . . . . . . . . . . . .Brenda Landers

Kelly Preston . . . . . . . . . . . . . . . . . . . . . . . . . . .Violet
Angel Tompkins . . . . . . . . . . . . . . . . . . . . . . .First Lady
1:00—In white nightgown, then black bra, panties, garter belt and stockings.

## Amazons (1986)
Danitza Kingsley. . . . . . . . . . . . . . . . . . . . . . . Tshingi
••• 0:30—Breasts and buns quite a few times with Colungo out of and in bed.
Ty Randolph. . . . . . . . . . . . . . . . . . . . . . . . . . .Dyala
•• 0:22—Breasts skinny dipping then getting dressed with Tashi.
•• 0:24—Brief breasts getting her top opened by bad guys then fighting them.
Penelope Reed . . . . . . . . . . . . . . . . . . . . . . . . Tashi
•• 0:22—Breasts and buns undressing to go skinny dipping. More breasts getting dressed.
• 0:24—Brief breasts getting top opened by bad guys.

## The Ambassador (1984)
Ellen Burstyn . . . . . . . . . . . . . . . . . . . . . . . Alex Hacker
••• 0:06—Breasts opening her robe to greet her lover.
••• 0:07—Brief breasts making love in bed.
••• 0:29—Breasts in a movie while her husband, Robert Mitchum, watches.
Iftach Katzur. . . . . . . . . . . . . . . . . . . . . . . . . . n.a.
Zachi Noy . . . . . . . . . . . . . . . . . . . . . . . . . . . n.a.

## Ambition (1991)
Katherine Armstrong . . . . . . . . . . . . . . . . . . .Roseanne
••• 1:13—Buns in G-string, then breasts in Clancy Brown's apartment.
Clancy Brown. . . . . . . . . . . . . . . . . . . . . . . . Albert
Karen Landry . . . . . . . . . . . . . . . . Woman in Bookstore
Lou Diamond Phillips . . . . . . . . . . . . . . . . . . .Mitchell
Celeste Yarnall . . . . . . . . . . . . . . . Beverly Hills Shopper

## The American Angels, Baptism of Blood (1989)
Mimi Lesseos . . . . . . . . . . . . . . . . . . . Magnificent Mimi
Jan MacKenzie . . . . . . . . . . . . . . . . . . . . . Luscious Lisa
0:07—Buns in G-string on stage in club. More buns getting lathered up for wrestling match.
• 0:11—Breasts and buns when a customer takes her top off. She's covered with shaving cream.
•• 0:12—Breasts taking a shower when Diamond Dave looks in to talk to her.
• 0:56—Right breast, while in wrestling ring with Dave.

## American Flyers (1985)
Rae Dawn Chong. . . . . . . . . . . . . . . . . . . . . . .Sarah
Kevin Costner. . . . . . . . . . . . . . . . . . . . . . . . Marcus
• 0:53—Brief, upper half of buns, while riding bicycles when his pants get yanked down by David.
David Grant . . . . . . . . . . . . . . . . . . . . . . . . . .David
• 0:05—Brief buns and very, very brief frontal nudity taking off shorts and walking to bathroom.
Katherine Kriss . . . . . . . . . . . . . . . . . . . . . . . . . .Vera

Alexandra Paul .......................... Becky
- 0:50—Very brief right breast, then very brief half of left breast changing tops with David Grant. Brief side view of right breast. Dark.
- 1:13—Brief breasts in white panties getting into bed with David Grant.

### American Gigolo (1980)
Michele Drake................. 1st Girl on Balcony
- 0:03—Breasts on the balcony while Richard Gere and Lauren Hutton talk.
Richard Gere........................... Julian
- 0:39—Buns and frontal nudity. Long shot, so it's hard to see anything.
Lauren Hutton........................ Michelle
- 0:37—Left breast, making love with Richard Gere in bed in his apartment.

### American Heart (1993)
Jeff Bridges ............................. Jack
Shareen Mitchell........................ Diane
- 1:09—Breasts and buns in sheer black panties while dancing in peep show with three other women.
- 1:10—Breasts, while in dressing room. Seen on B&W monitor.
- 1:11—Breasts under sheer top while in dressing room, putting makeup on and getting a drink.

### American Me (1992)
Panchito Gomez ................. Young Santana
- 0:18—Brief buns, walking out of room in Juvenile Hall.
- 0:20—Brief buns, getting up out of bed to kill the guy who raped him.
Grace Morley ...................... JD's Friend
Edward James Olmos ................. Santana
Robert Pucci ...................... Bodyguard
Pepe Serna .......................... Mundo

### American Nightmare (1981; Canadian)
Alexandra Paul ........... Isabelle Blake/Tanya Kelly
- 0:02—Left breast while smoking in bed. Breasts before getting killed. Long scene.
Lora Staley ..................... Louise Harmon
- 0:44—Breasts and buns in G-string dancing on stage.
- 0:54—Breasts making love in bed with Eric.
- 0:59—Brief right breast, then breasts auditioning in TV studio.
Claudia Udy .......................... Andrea
- 0:08—Buns, then breasts dancing on stage.
- 0:22—Buns getting into bathtub. Breasts during struggle with killer.
Lenore Zann ............................ Tina
- 0:25—Breasts and buns while dancing on stage.
- 1:05—Breasts and buns while dancing on stage again.

### The American Success Company (1979)
Belinda Bauer .......................... Sarah
Jeff Bridges ............................ Harry

Bianca Jagger........................... Corinne
- 0:35—Breasts under see-through black top while sitting on bed.

### American Taboo (1984)
Jay Horenstein ............................ Paul
- 0:33—Frontal nudity, getting out of shower and drying himself off. Foggy.
- 1:11—Buns, while on top of Lisa in bed.
- 1:28—Buns, while making love with Lisa during flashback.

### American Tiger (1989; Italian)
*a.k.a. American Rickshaw*
Mitch Gaylord ........................... Scott
- 0:17—Buns, while on boat with Joanna. Long shot, don't see his face.
Daniel Greene ......................... Francis
Sherrie Rose ........................... Mary Jo

### An American Werewolf in London (1981)
Jenny Agutter........................ Alex Price
- 0:41—Brief right breast in bed with David Naughton. Dark, hard to see.
Linzi Drew ....................... Brenda Bristols
- 1:26—Side view of left breast in porno movie while David Naughton talks to his friend, Jack.
- 1:27—Brief breasts in movie talking on the phone.
David Naughton ................. David Kessler
- 0:24—Very brief buns while running naked through the woods.
- 0:58—Buns, during his transformation into a werewolf.
- 1:09—Brief frontal nudity and buns after waking up in wolf cage at the zoo. Long shot, hard to see anything. More buns, while running around the zoo.

### Amityville 1992: It's About Time (1992)
Shawn Weatherly........................ Andra
- 0:07—Breasts, making love in bed on top of her husband. Nice and sweaty!

### The Amityville Horror (1979)
James Brolin........................ George Lutz
Margot Kidder ..................... Kathleen Lutz
- 0:21—Brief right breast in reflection in mirror while doing dance stretching exercises in the bedroom. Hard to see because of the pattern on the mirror tiles.
- 0:22—Cleavage in open blouse while talking to James Brolin.
- 0:23—Very brief partial right breast, on the floor, kissing Brolin.
Helen Shaver ......................... Carolyn
Amy Wright ............................ Jackie

### Amityville II: The Possession (1982)
Rutanya Alda ................... Deloris Montelli
Diane Franklin ................. Patricia Montelli
- 0:41—Half of right breast, while sitting on bed talking to her brother.

### Amityville: A New Generation (1993)

Barbara Howard . . . . . . . . . . . . . . . . . . . . . Jane Cutler
David Naughton . . . . . . . . . . . . . . . . . . . . . Dick Cutler
Julia Nickson . . . . . . . . . . . . . . . . . . . . . . . . . . . Suki
- •• 0:28—Left breast, with David Naughton while taking off her coveralls.
- • 0:29—Very brief back side of left breast, putting on her coverall strap.

Terry O'Quinn. . . . . . . . . . . . . . . . . . . Detective Clark
Richard Roundtree. . . . . . . . . . . . . . . . . . . . . . . .n.a.
Robert Rusler. . . . . . . . . . . . . . . . . . . . . . . . . . . . Ray
Lala Sloatman . . . . . . . . . . . . . . . . . . . . . . . . Lianie
- •• 0:14—Breasts, undressing and making love with Keyes.

### Amor Ciego (1980; Mexican)

Apollonia. . . . . . . . . . . . . . . . . . . . . . . . . . . . . .Patty
- • 0:32—Breasts getting out of hammock.
- ••• 0:52—Right breast, standing up, then breasts kissing Daniel. More breasts in bed.
- ••• 0:59—Buns, making love in bed, then breasts afterwards.
- •• 1:11—Breasts, taking off her towel and putting Daniel's hand on her left breast.
- •• 1:15—Breasts, turning over, then lying in bed.

Jaime Moreno . . . . . . . . . . . . . . . . . . . . . . . . .Daniel
- ••• 0:51—Frontal nudity standing up from bed, then buns when Apollonia hugs him.
- • 0:53—Buns, while making love in bed with Apollonia.

### And God Created Woman (1988)

(Unrated version.)
Rebecca De Mornay . . . . . . . . . . . . . . . . . . . . . Robin
- •• 0:06—Brief Left breast and buns in gymnasium with Vincent Spano. Brief right breast making love.
- • 0:53—Brief buns and breasts in the shower when Spano sees her.
- •• 1:02—Brief left breast with Langella on the floor.
- ••• 1:12—Breasts making love with Spano in a museum.

Pat Lee . . . . . . . . . . . . . . . . . . . . . . . . . . . . . Inmate
Vincent Spano. . . . . . . . . . . . . . . . . . . . Billy Moran

### ...and God created woman (1957; French)

Brigitte Bardot. . . . . . . . . . . . . . . . . . . . . . . . Juliette
- • 0:40—Very brief side view of right breast getting out of bed.

### And the Band Played On

(1992; Made for Cable Movie)
Nathalie Baye . . . . . . . . . . . . . . . . . . Dr. Francoise Barre
David Dukes . . . . . . . . . . . . . . . . Dr. Mervyn Silverman
Richard Gere . . . . . . . . . . . . . . . . . . . . . Choreographer
Anjelica Huston . . . . . . . . . . . . . . . . . Dr. Betsy Reisz
Matthew Modine . . . . . . . . . . . . . . . . . .Dr. Don Francis
Jeffrey Nordling. . . . . . . . . . . . . . . . . .Gaetan Dugas
- • 0:14—Brief buns, while getting dressed in examination room when Glenne Headly comes in.

Charlie Martin Smith. . . . . . . . . . . . . . .Dr. Harold Jaffe

### Android (1982)

Brie Howard . . . . . . . . . . . . . . . . . . . . . . . . . Maggie
- • 0:25—Buns, then breasts in bedroom when Klaus Kinski watches her on video monitor.
- • 0:54—Brief side of right breast, while sitting on Max's lap and kissing him.
- 0:59—Partial left breast, while lying dead in bed.
- 1:09—Brief side view of left breast while lying dead in bed.

Klaus Kinski . . . . . . . . . . . . . . . . . . . . . . . . Dr. Daniel

### Andy Warhol's Frankenstein (1974; Italian/German/French)

Dalila Di'Lazzaro. . . . . . . . . . . . . . . . . . . . . .The Girl
- •• 0:09—Breasts lying on platform in the lab.
- • 0:37—Close up of left breast while the Count cuts her stitches. (Pretty bloody.)
- 0:43—Breasts, covered with blood, strapped to table
- • 0:49—Breasts on table, all wired up.
- • 1:03—Right breast lying on table. Long shot.
- • 1:05—More right breast, long shot.
- •• 1:06—More breasts on table, then standing in the lab.
- •• 1:20—Brief right breast when Otto pulls her top down.
- • 1:23—Breasts on table again, then walking around. (Scar on chest.) Lower frontal nudity when Otto pulls her bandage down, then more gross breasts when he removes her guts.

Monique Van Vooren . . . . . . . . . . . . . . . . . . .Katherine
- •• 0:47—Breasts in bed with Nicholas. Brief lower frontal nudity twice when he rolls on top of her.
- • 1:21—Left breast letting Sascha, the creature, caress her breast
- • 1:26—Breasts, dead, when her breasts pop out of her blouse.

### Angel (1983)

Josh Cadman . . . . . . . . . . . . . . . . . . . . . . . . . . Spike
John Diehl . . . . . . . . . . . . . . . . . . . . . . . . .Billy Boy
- • 0:35—Buns, while washing blood off himself. Dark, hard to see. Long scene.

Elaine Giftos. . . . . . . . . . . . . . . . . . . . . Patricia Allen
Donna McDaniel . . . . . . . . . . . . . . . . . . . . . . .Crystal
- • 0:19—Brief breasts, dead in bed when the killer pulls the covers down.

Graem McGavin . . . . . . . . . . . . . . . . . . . . . Lana
- •• 0:31—Breasts standing in hotel bathroom talking to her John.

Susan Tyrrell. . . . . . . . . . . . . . . . . . . . . .Solly Mosler
Donna Wilkes. . . . . . . . . . . . . . . . . . . . .Angel/Molly

### Angel 4: Undercover (1993)

Rebekka Armstrong . . . . . . . . . . . . . . . Catfight Groupie
- • 0:41—Brief breasts, while with a band member and another woman in dressing room.

Kerrie Clark . . . . . . . . . . . . . . . . . . . . . . . . . . Paula
- ••• 0:26—Breasts, while making love with Piston in bedroom.

•• 0:28—Very briefly nude, getting up out of bed. Breasts, while taking a shower.

Shane Fraser . . . . . . . . . . . . . . . . . . . . . . . Piston Jones
•• 0:28—Brief buns, while getting up off bed and putting on his pants.

Nicolette Janssen. . . . . . . . . . . . . Music Video Groupie
• 1:00—Breasts, while backstage with the drummer and the other groupie.

Sam Phillips. . . . . . . . . . . . . . . . . . . . . . . . . . . Jade
• 0:18—Breasts in open robe, while sitting on dressing room counter in front of Piston.

Darlene Vogel . . . . . . . . . . . . . . . . . . . . . . . . Molly

### An Angel at My Table (1990; Australian/New Zealand)

Kerry Fox. . . . . . . . . . . . . . . . . . . . . . . . . . . .Janet
• 1:45—Brief breasts and partial lower frontal nudity while in bathtub.
•• 2:06—Left breast while sitting on bed with her boyfriend.
• 2:07—Nude, while swimming in the water.
•• 2:09—Long shot of right breast, while lying on rock outside, then breasts in a closer shot.

### Angel Eyes (1991)

Suzanne Ager . . . . . . . . . . . . . . . . . . . .Nurse Stewart
John Coleman. . . . . . . . . . . . . . . . . . . . . . . . . . Nick
••• 1:10—Buns, while making love on top of Angel on the floor.

Monique Gabrielle . . . . . . . . . . . . . . . . . . . . Angel
••• 0:18—Nude, in shower with Michelle.
• 0:32—Brief breasts in robe in her bedroom.
••• 0:45—Left breast and lower frontal nudity, while caressing herself while watching Steven and Michelle make love in bed.
••• 0:47—Right breast, then breasts in bed while fantasizing Steven is making love with her. Then breasts in open robe.
••• 0:54—Breasts and buns, while making love in bed with Michelle. Very nice!
••• 1:10—Nude, while making love with Nick on the floor. (This scene was really worn down on the video tape that I rented—I think I know why!)

John Phillip Law. . . . . . . . . . . . . . . . . . . . . . Steven
• 0:04—Brief buns, while lying on top of Michelle in bed.

Sazzy Lee . . . . . . . . . . . . . . . . . . . . . . . . . . . Amy
Paula Reve'e . . . . . . . . . . . . . . . . . . . . . . . . . Julie
•• 0:13—Breasts, while standing in yellow bikini bottoms and rubbing lotion on herself.
• 0:23—Breasts, while lying on pool float in the pool.
• 0:25—More breasts while on pool float.

Vicki Vickers . . . . . . . . . . . . . . . . . . . . . Michelle
••• 0:02—Breasts and buns, while making love with Steven in bed. Long scene.
••• 0:18—Buns and breasts in shower. Partial lower frontal nudity.
••• 0:25—Right breast, then breasts while making love with Steven in bed while Angel watches. Long scene.

•• 0:32—Breasts, while rolling over in bed.
••• 0:40—Breasts, getting into shower, washing herself and getting out.
••• 0:44—Buns and breasts while making love in bed with Steven.
• 0:51—Brief left breast, while adjusting the covers in bed.
••• 0:53—Breasts in bed while making love in bed with Angel. Buns in G-string when getting out of bed.
•• 0:55—Breasts, while bending over sink to wash her face. Right breast, while peeking around the door.

### Angel Fist (1992)

Melissa Anne Moore. . . . . . . . . . . . . . . . . . . . . .Lorda
•• 0:03—Breasts and buns, in the showers.
•• 0:35—Nude, behind Katara in the showers.
••• 1:03—Breasts when she gets a bad guy to open her blouse and untie her. Very brief breasts during fight scenes.

Catya Sassoon . . . . . . . . . . . . . . . . . . . .Katara/Kat Lang
• 0:19—Brief breasts, dropping towel and putting on shirt in front of Alcatraz.
•• 0:31—Right breast, while in the shower.
••• 0:32—Breasts in red panties, doing martial arts on a couple of bad guys in her apartment.
••• 0:35—Full frontal nudity in the showers.
••• 0:49—Breasts, while making love on bed with Alcatraz. Long scene.

### Angel Heart (1987)

(Original Unedited Version reviewed.)

Lisa Bonet . . . . . . . . . . . . . . . . . . . .Epiphany Proudfoot
0:53—In wet top, talking with Mickey Rourke outside.
• 1:01—Brief left breast, twice, in open dress during voodoo ceremony.
••• 1:27—Breasts in bed with Rourke. It gets kind of bloody.
• 1:32—Breasts in bathtub.
• 1:48—Breasts in bed, dead. Covered with a bloody sheet.

Robert De Niro. . . . . . . . . . . . . . . . . . . . . Louis Cyphre
Judith Drake. . . . . . . . . . . . . . . . . . . . . . . . Izzy's Wife
Charlotte Rampling . . . . . . . . . . . Margaret Krusemark
• 1:10—Brief left breast, lying dead on the floor, covered with blood.
• 1:46—Very brief left breast during flashback of the dead-on-the-floor-covered-with-blood scene.

Mickey Rourke . . . . . . . . . . . . . . . . . . . . . . Harry Angel
•• 1:28—Buns, while in bed with Lisa Bonet. Don't see his face. It gets kind of bloody.

Elizabeth Whitcraft. . . . . . . . . . . . . . . . . . . . . . Connie
•• 0:33—Breasts in bed talking with Mickey Rourke while taking off her clothes.

### Angel III: The Final Chapter (1988)

Maud Adams . . . . . . . . . . . . . . . . . . . . . . . . . Nadine
Laura Albert . . . . . . . . . . . . . . . . . . . . . . .Nude Dancer
• 0:00—Brief breasts dancing in a casino. Wearing red G-string.
• 0:01—Brief breasts dancing in background.

- 0:06—Side view of left breast and buns, while yelling at Molly for taking her picture.

Toni Basil ............................... Hillary

Barbara Hammond ................. Video Girl #2
- 0:34—Breasts (on the right) on video monitor during audition tape talking with her roommate.

Tyrone Granderson Jones ............. L.A. Pimp
- • 0:32—Buns, while standing in alley after Angel pushes him out of the car.

Mitzi Kapture ..................... Molly Stewart

Roxanne Kernohan ................. White Hooker

Kim McKamy .................... Video Girl #1

Richard Roundtree............. Lieutenant Doniger

Julie Kristen Smith...................... Darlene
- • • 0:40—Breasts during caveman shoot with a brunette girl.
- • • 0:44—Breasts again dancing in caveman shoot.

Cheryl Starbuck.................... Video Girl #3

Gail Thackray ............................ n.a.

## Angel in Red
See: Uncaged.

## Angel of Destruction (1994)
Maria Ford .......................... Jo Alwood
- • • 0:41—Breast and buns in panties while using martial arts on the bad guys!
- • • 0:45—Breasts, while making love with Aaron in bed.
- • • 0:59—Breasts and buns in G-string after stripping and dancing on stage.

Charlie Spradling.................... Brit Alwood

## Angel of H.E.A.T. (1981)
*a.k.a. The Protectors, Book I*

Marilyn Chambers................ Angel Harmony
- • 0:15—Full frontal nudity making love with an intruder on the bed.
- • 0:17—Breasts in a bathtub.
- • • 0:40—Breasts in a hotel room with a short guy.
- • 0:52—Breasts getting out of a wet suit.
- • • 1:01—Breasts sitting on floor with some robots.
- • 1:29—Breasts in bed with Mark.

Remy O'Neill..................... Andrea Shockley
- • • 0:43—Breasts, wearing a blue swimsuit, wrestling in the mud with Mary Woronov.

Mary Woronov ............... Samantha Vitesse
- • • 0:11—Frontal nudity changing clothes on a boat dock after getting out of the lake.
- • • 0:43—Breasts wrestling in the mud after wearing white bathing suit.

## Angel of Passion (1991)
Tuscany................................ Ellen
- • • 0:36—Buns and breasts making love with a guy on a boat.

Venus De Light ........................ Carol
- • 0:15—Breasts taking a shower.
- • • 0:19—Breasts and buns in G-string dancing outside next to pool at a birthday party.
- • • 0:23—Breasts and buns in red lingerie in camper, then breasts while making love on top of Will.

Sonny Falconeti ......................... Will
- • 0:22—Buns frolicking in the surf with Carol while wearing a G-string.

Pamela Jackson........................ Eileen
- • • • 1:13—Breasts and upper half of buns while on bed with Eric making love.

Kathleen Kane ....................... Suzette
- • • 1:08—Breasts while posing for Marty in the house.

Lisa Petruno .................... Sheryl Diamond
- • • 0:00—Making love with the husband on the stairs.

Ingrid Vold........................... Vanessa
- • 1:01—Brief breasts posing on the couch for the photographer.

## Angels Hard as They Come (1971)
Scott Glenn ......................... Long John

Gilda Texter ........................... Astrid
- • 0:26—Brief breasts several times when bad guys try to rape her. Dark.

Janet Wood ............................ Vicki
- • • 1:09—Breasts taking off her top, dancing with Clean Sheila at the biker's party.
- • • 1:16—Breasts outside when the General rips her blouse open.

## Animal House (1978)
Karen Allen................ Katherine "Katy" Fuller
- 1:21—Brief buns putting on shirt when Boone visits her at her house.

Kevin Bacon ........................ Chip Diller

James Daughton ................. Greg Marmalard

Sarah Holcomb .................. Clorette DePasto
- • • 0:56—Brief breasts lying on bed after passing out in Tom Hulce's bed during toga party.

Sunny Johnson...................... Otter's Co-Ed

Tim Matheson ................ Eric "Otter" Stratton
- • 0:08—Buns, changing clothes in his bedroom while talking to Boone.

Bruce McGill .......................... D-Day

Martha Smith ...................... Babs Jansen

Donald Sutherland.................. Dave Jennings
- • 1:22—Buns, while reaching up in kitchen to get something when his sweater goes up. Out of focus.

Mary Louise Weller.............. Mandy Pepperidge
- • • • 0:38—In white bra, then breasts in bedroom while John Belushi watches on a ladder through the window.

## Animal Instincts (1992)
(Unrated version reviewed.)

David Carradine........................ Lamberti

Maxwell Caulfield.................... David Cole

Mitch Gaylord ..................... Rod Tennison

Erika Nann .......................... Dianne

Delia Sheppard ....................... Ingrid
- • • 0:50—Breasts, while in bed with her lover and Joanne.
- • • 0:54—Breasts, while in bed with only Joanne.

Jan-Michael Vincent ................. Fletcher Ross

Shannon Whirry.................... Joanne Cole
- 0:01—In bra and panties during opening credits.

••• 0:18—In white bra and panties in bed then full frontal nudity during her fantasies with several guys.

•• 0:23—Breasts and buns, in various lingerie outfits, in front of mirror.

•• 0:26—Full frontal nudity under sheer white body suit, trying to get Maxwell Caulfield interested in her.

•• 0:28—Breasts while taking a bath.

••• 0:30—Nude in bed, making love with the Cable TV guy.

0:36—In bra and panties, while talking on the telephone.

0:38—In bra and panties, while in bed.

••• 0:43—In bra and panties, then nude while in bed with the Assistant DA while Caulfield watches on TV.

••• 0:46—Breasts, while sitting in bed with Caulfield.

•• 0:50—Breasts with Delia Sheppard and a guy.

••• 0:51—In black bra and panties on TV after undressing as a businessman. Breasts in bed with a guy.

••• 0:54—Breasts in bedroom and on bed with Delia.

••• 0:59—In black bra and panties, then breasts and buns with Mitch Gaylord in bedroom while making love.

1:03—In black bra, panties, garter belt and stockings in her bedroom.

• 1:16—Buns in G-string and side of left breast, while in bed with Jan-Michael Vincent.

### Animal Instincts 2 (1993)

Debra Beatty . . . . . . . . . . . . . . . . . . . . . . . . . Cindy

•• 0:24—Full frontal nudity, while posing for Eric in his studio and putting a robe on.

Woody Brown . . . . . . . . . . . . . . . . . . . . . . . . . Steve

• 0:23—Brief buns while making love with Catherine in bed.

• 1:20—Buns, twice, while making love on top of Catherine in bed.

Shannon McLeod . . . . . . . . . . . . . . . . . . . Miss Geary

•• 0:14—In black bra, then breasts and buns in panties after taking off her top while trying to tease Steve.

••• 0:20—Breasts, after taking off bra and making love with a guy in bed.

Elizabeth Sandifer . . . . . . . . . . . . . . . . . . . Catherine

••• 0:23—In white bra and panties, then breasts and brief buns, while making love with Steve in bed.

• 1:16—Brief breasts, while undressing in her room when Steve sees her from outside. Long shot.

• 1:18—Breasts, while in bedroom with Steve, then making love on bed.

Dean Scofield . . . . . . . . . . . . . . . . . . . . . . . . David

Shannon Whirry . . . . . . . . . . . . . . . . . . . . . . Joanna

••• 0:11—Breasts, in bed with a fantasy lover while she imagines another guy watching them make love.

••• 0:30—Breasts, while rubbing lotion on herself in the backyard while Steve watches from his backyard.

• 0:38—Brief breasts, while in her bedroom. Seen on video monitor.

••• 0:47—Full frontal nudity while making love with a guy she picks up in a bar while Steve watches on video monitor.

••• 0:49—Nude, while making love in bedroom with a woman she picks up in a bar.

•• 0:53—Left breast, while opening her robe and talking on the phone.

••• 1:01—Nude, while posing for Eric in his studio.

•• 1:04—Breasts, while taking a shower.

• 1:05—Brief left breast in photos that Eric shows her.

•• 1:07—In white bra and panties, then breasts and buns while making love with Eric.

### Anna (1987)

Robert Fields . . . . . . . . . . . . . . . . . . . . . . . . . Daniel

Sally Kirkland . . . . . . . . . . . . . . . . . . . . . . . . . . Anna

•• 0:28—Breasts in the bathtub talking to Daniel.

### Another 48 Hrs. (1990)

Bernie Casey . . . . . . . . . . . . . . . . . . . . Kirkland Smith

Nancy Everhard . . . . . . . . . . . . . . . . . . . Female Doctor

Page Leong . . . . . . . . . . . . . . . . . . . . . . . . Angel Lee

• 1:00—Brief breasts getting out of bed with Willie.

David Anthony Marshall . . . . . . . . . . . . . . Willie Hickok

• 0:57—Buns, while putting pants on after getting out of bed.

Francesca "Kitten" Natividad . . . . . . . . . . Girl in Movie

• 1:04—Brief breasts on movie screen when two motorcycles crash through it.

Yana Nirvana . . . . . . . . . . . . . . . . . . . . . . CHP Officer

Nick Nolte . . . . . . . . . . . . . . . . . . . . . . . . Jack Cates

Ed O'Ross . . . . . . . . . . . . . . . . . . . . . . . . Frank Cruise

### Another Chance (1989)

Vanessa Angel . . . . . . . . . . . . . . . . . . . Jacky Johansson

• 0:26—Sort of breasts under water in spa. Hard to see because of the bubbles.

Leslee Bremmer . . . . . . . . . Girl in Womanizer's Meeting

Barbara Edwards . . . . . . . . . . . . . . Diana the Temptress

••• 0:38—Breasts in trailer with Johnny.

Bruce Greenwood . . . . . . . . . . . . . . . . . . . . . . . . n.a.

Donna Spangler . . . . . . . . . . . . . . . . . . . . . . Cynthia

Karen Witter . . . . . . . . . . . . . . . . . . . . . Nancy Burton

• 0:44—Brief side view of right breast and buns getting out of bed.

0:45—In two piece swimsuit.

### Another Pair of Aces (1991; Made for Cable Movie)

(Video tape includes nude scenes not shown on cable TV.)

Kris Kristofferson . . . . . . . . . . . . . . Capt. Elvin Metcalf

Joan Severance . . . . . . . . . . . . . . . . . . . Susan Davis

•• 1:00—Brief breasts several times, making love with Kris Kristofferson in bed.

Rip Torn . . . . . . . . . . . . . . . . . . . . . . Capt. Jack Parsons

### Another Time, Another Place (1983; British)

Phyllis Logan . . . . . . . . . . . . . . . . . . . . . . . . . . Janie

••• 0:31—Breasts, washing herself off after working in the fields. Nice close-up shot.

•• 0:53—Full frontal nudity, after undressing then getting into bed.

••• 1:08—Breasts in front of a group of men.

## Anthony's Desire (1993)

Annastasia Alexander . . . . . . . . . . . . . . . . . . . Dancer
- ••• 0:04—Nude, on stage stripping out of black dress. Wearing gloves.
- •• 0:22—Full frontal nudity, while stretching in the background on the left.
- •• 0:54—Breasts while lying on her back in the middle of the group of women.
- • 1:02—Breasts, while sitting in the background on the left.

Debra Beatty. . . . . . . . . . . . . . . . . . . . . . . . . Dancer
- ••• 0:04—Full frontal nudity, while stripping out of green dress on stage with other women.
- •• 0:22—Breasts, while sitting on stage on the right.
- • 1:02—Left breast, while sitting behind Annastasia Alexander on the left side of the stage.

Nicole Broderson. . . . . . . . . . . . . . . . . . . . . . Dancer
- • 0:54—Buns, while sitting on her stomach in the middle of the group of women. Tattoo on her right butt cheek.

Douglass DeMarco . . . . . . . . . . . . . . . . . . . . Anthony
- ••• 0:17—Buns, while making love in bed with Desiree.
- •• 0:24—Buns, while making love in bed with Desiree, then getting up out of bed.
- • 0:45—Buns, while making love at the beach with Desiree.
- •• 0:46—Buns, while making love with Desiree in bed.
- ••• 1:14—Buns, walking to bed, kneeling, then making love in bed with Jessica.

Kelly Jackson . . . . . . . . . . . . . . . . . . . . . . . . . Dancer
- •• 0:54—Left breast, while lying on her side in a group of women. She's near the top of the screen.
- •• 1:02—Breasts, while playing the violin on stage.

Ashlie Rhey . . . . . . . . . . . . . . . . . . . . . . . . . . Dancer
- • 0:22—Breasts, while lying on her back under another woman on stage.
- • 0:54—Left breast and brief lower frontal nudity, while lying down with other women. She's at the bottom of the screen.

Gwen Somers . . . . . . . . . . . . . . . . . . . . . . . . .Jessica
- ••• 0:29—Nude, while lying on bed and talking. Long scene.
- ••• 1:09—Full frontal nudity, while on bed with Anthony and Desiree sitting next to her.

Stephanie Sumers . . . . . . . . . . . . . . . . . . . . . Dancer
- •• 0:22—Breasts, while on stage, lying in the lap of another woman. (She's wearing a choker.)

## Antonia & Jane (1991; British)

Saskia Reeves. . . . . . . . . . . . . . . . . . . . Antonia McGill
- •• 0:42—Brief partial left breast, while lying in bed on top of her lover. Breasts, turning over on her back.
- • 0:44—Breasts, leaning over her lover while is tied and blindfolded in bed.

Imelda Staunton . . . .`. . . . . . . . . . . . . Jane Hartman
- • 0:08—Right breast, while lying in bed with Norman, reading a book to get him turned on.

## Any Man's Death (1989)

Nancy Mulford . . . . . . . . . . . . . . . . . . . . . . . . . Tara

Mia Sara. . . . . . . . . . . . . . . . . . . . . . . . . . . Gerlind
- • 0:50—Brief right nipple when John Savage undoes her top. Don't see her face.

Claudia Udy . . . . . . . . . . . . . . . . . . . . . . . . . . .Laura

## Aphrodite (1982; German/French)

Catherine Jourdan . . . . . . . . . . . . . . . . . . . . . Valerie
- • 0:34—Brief upper half of breasts in bathtub.

Valerie Kaprisky . . . . . . . . . . . . . . . . . . . . . . Pauline
- ••• 0:12—Nude, washing herself off in front of a two-way mirror while a man on the other side watches.

## Apocalypse Now (1979)

Sam Bottoms . . . . . . . . . . . . . . . . . . . . . . . .Lance
Colleen Camp . . . . . . . . . . . . . . . . . . . . . . . . . Playmate
Linda Carpenter . . . . . . . . . . . . . . . . . . . . . . . Playmate
- • 1:01—Breasts in centerfold photo, hung up for display. Long shot.

Scott Glenn . . . . . . . . . . . . . . . . . . . . . . . . . Civilian
Martin Sheen . . . . . . . . . . . . . . . . . . . . Captain Willard
- • 0:07—Brief buns, while in bedroom after opening door for military guys.

Cyndi Wood. . . . . . . . . . . . . . . . . Playmate of the Year

## Apology (1986; Made for Cable Movie)

Peter Weller . . . . . . . . . . . . . . . . . . . . . . . . Rad Hungare
- • 1:04—Brief buns, while putting pants on, getting out of bed to chase after intruder at night.

## Appassionata (1979; Italian)

Eleonora Giorgi . . . . . . . . . . . . . . . . . . . . . . . Nicola
- • 0:14—Very brief left breast in open blouse with Emilio in his dentist office. Breasts several times.
- •• 0:41—Full frontal nudity in bedroom when Emilio comes in. Dark.
- ••• 0:54—Nude in office with Emilio in stockings and garter belt.
- • 1:35—Brief right breast in bed with Emilio. Dark.

Ornella Muti. . . . . . . . . . . . . . . . . . . . . . . . . Virginia
- • 0:32—Brief breasts in bathroom when her father rips open her T-shirt while looking for hickeys.

  0:57—Partial left breast, leaning over to tempt her father.

  1:07—In white bra, changing clothes during party.

  1:21—In white bra, in bathroom, giving herself hickeys.

  1:25—In white bra in bed, showing her father her pubic hair.
- • 1:35—Buns, getting out of bed with her father. Brief side of left breast when leaving the room.

## Appointment with Fear (1988)

Pamela Bach . . . . . . . . . . . . . . . . . . . . . . . . Samantha
- • 0:56—Breasts getting into the spa. Long shot, hard to see.

Michele Little . . . . . . . . . . . . . . . . . . . . . . . . . Carol
Deborah Voorhees . . . . . . . . . . . . . . . . . . . . . . . Ruth
- • 0:21—Very, very brief side view of left breast taking off bra to go swimming, then very brief breasts getting out of the pool.

## Apprentice to Murder (1987)

Rutanya Alda . . . . . . . . . . . . . . . . . . . . . . . . Elma Kelly
Mia Sara . . . . . . . . . . . . . . . . . . . . . . . . . . . . . . Alice
  • 0:29—Left side view breasts making love with Chad Lowe.

## Aria (1987; U.S./British)

Beverly D'Angelo . . . . . . . . . . . . . . . . . . . . . . . Gilda
Linzi Drew . . . . . . . . . . . . . . . . . . . . . . . . . . . . . Girl
  • 1:09—Breasts on operating table after car accident. Hair is all covered with bandages.
  •• 1:10—Breasts getting shocked to start her heart.
Sandrine Dumas . . . . . . . . . . . . . . . . . . . . . . . . . . . n.a.
Bridget Fonda . . . . . . . . . . . . . . . . . . . . . . Girl Lover
  ••• 0:59—Brief right breast, then buns and breasts lying down on bed in hotel room in Las Vegas.
  •• 1:02—Breasts in the bathtub with her boyfriend.
Elizabeth Hurley . . . . . . . . . . . . . . . . . . . . . Marietta
  • 0:46—Brief breasts, turning around while singing to a guy.
  • 0:47—Buns while standing and hugging him.
John Hurt . . . . . . . . . . . . . . . . . . . . . . . . . The Actor
Spencer Leigh . . . . . . . . . . . . . . . . . . . . Young Man
James Mathers . . . . . . . . . . . . . . . . . . . . . Boy Lover
  •• 1:00—Brief dark outline of frontal nudity in hotel room, then buns while making love with Bridget Fonda.
  • 1:02—Frontal nudity under water in the bathtub with her.
Anita Morris . . . . . . . . . . . . . . . . . . . . . . . . . Phoebe
Theresa Russell . . . . . . . . . . . . . . . . . . . . . King Zog
Tilda Swinton . . . . . . . . . . . . . . . . . . . . . Young Girl

## Arizona Heat (1988)

Denise Crosby . . . . . . . . . . . . . . . . . . . . . . . Jill Andrews
  • 1:13—Brief upper half of left breast in shower with Larry.

## Armed and Dangerous (1986)

Teagan Clive . . . . . . . . . . . . . . . . . . . . . . Staff Member
Christine Dupree . . . . . . . . . . . . . . . . . . . Peep Show Girl
  • 0:58—Very, very brief breasts shots behind glass dancing in front of John Candy and Eugene Levy.
Stacy Keach . . . . . . . . . . . . . . . . . . . . . . . . . . . Judge
Eugene Levy . . . . . . . . . . . . . . . . . . . . . Norman Kane
  • 1:02—Cheeks of his buns through the back of leather pants while dressed in drag with John Candy to escape from the bad cops.
Steve Railsback . . . . . . . . . . . . . . . . . . . The Cowboy
Meg Ryan . . . . . . . . . . . . . . . . . . . . Maggie Cavanaugh
K.C. Winkler . . . . . . . . . . . . . . . . . . . . . . . . . . Vicki

## Armed Response (1986)

Kai Baker . . . . . . . . . . . . . . . . . . . . . . . . . . . . . Pam
Michelle Bauer . . . . . . . . . . . . . . . . . . . . . . Stripper
  • 0:41—Breasts, dancing on stage.
Bobbie Bresee . . . . . . . . . . . . . . . . . . . . . . . . . Anna
David Carradine . . . . . . . . . . . . . . . . . . . . Jim Roth
Laurene Landon . . . . . . . . . . . . . . . . . . . . Deborah
Dawn Wildsmith . . . . . . . . . . . . . . . . . . . . . . Thug

## Army Brats (1984; Dutch)

Akkemay . . . . . . . . . . . . . . . . . . . . . Madeline Gisberts
  •• 0:22—Breasts in the shower with her boyfriend.
  • 0:26—Brief breasts, taking off towel and putting on robe while arguing with her mother.
  • 0:32—Brief breasts while changing tops.
  • 0:47—Brief breasts while sunbathing outside (seen through binoculars).
  • 1:24—Breasts in bed with her boyfriend.

## Army of One (1993)

Khandi Alexander . . . . . . . . . . . . . . . . . . . . . Maralena
Dolph Lundgren . . . . . . . . . . . . . . . . . . . . . . . Santee
Michelle Phillips . . . . . . . . . . . . . . . . . . . . . . . Esther
Lisa Marie Stagno . . . . . . . . . . . Rita's Body Double
  •• 0:34—Breasts and buns, while undressing and getting into shower. Body double for Kristian Alfonso.

## The Arrangement (1969)

Kirk Douglas . . . . . . . . . . . . . . . . . Eddie and Evangelos
  • 0:25—Brief buns, while on the beach.
Faye Dunaway . . . . . . . . . . . . . . . . . . . . . . . . . Gwen
  • 0:25—Brief buns in various scenes while at the beach with Kirk Douglas.
Dianne Hull . . . . . . . . . . . . . . . . . . . . . . . . . . . Ellen
Deborah Kerr . . . . . . . . . . . . . . . . . . . . . . . . Florence
  • 0:36—Buns, behind curtain, while taking off her night gown. Brief long shot of left breast, behind curtain, getting into bed.

## The Arrogant (1987)

Teresa Gilmore-Capps . . . . . . . . . . . . . . . . . . Charlotte
  • 0:23—Brief breasts, making love in a barn.
Gary Graham . . . . . . . . . . . . . . . . . . . . . . . Giovanni
Sylvia Kristel . . . . . . . . . . . . . . . . . . . . . . . . . . Julie
  • 0:14—In wet blouse, in lake.
  • 0:22—In wet blouse again, walking out of the lake.
  • 0:44—Brief breasts several times, in gaping dress.

## The Art of Dying (1991)

Wings Hauser . . . . . . . . . . . . . . . . . . . . . . . . . . Jack
  •• 0:28—Buns, while standing in kitchen making love with Kathleen Kinmont.
Kathleen Kinmont . . . . . . . . . . . . . . . . . . . . Holly
  • 0:28—Brief left breast, making love with Wings Hauser in the kitchen. Brief breasts when he pours milk on her.
  •• 0:33—Breasts in bathtub with Hauser. Intercut with Janet getting stabbed.
T.C. Warner . . . . . . . . . . . . . . . . . . . . . . . . . . Janet
  0:14—Buns, shackled up in S&M chamber with a customer.
  ••• 0:32—Breasts in the shower. Buns and side of right breast, before getting stabbed to death.
Ona Zee . . . . . . . . . . . . . . . . . . . . . . Frances Warner

## Ashanti, Land of No Mercy (1979)

Beverly Johnson . . . . . . . . . . . . . . . Dr. Anansa Linderby
  •• 0:07—Buns and brief side view of breasts, taking off clothes to go skinny dipping.

- •• 0:08—Briefly nude, running to put her clothes back on.
- • 1:15—Right breast in gaping dress while bending over to bury dead bad guy.

### Aspen Extreme (1993)

Peter Berg . . . . . . . . . . . . . . . . . . . . . . . Dexter Rutecki
- •• 1:14—Nude, running on road after getting beat up.

Paul Gross . . . . . . . . . . . . . . . . . . . . . . . . . . T.J. Burke
- • 1:21—Buns, behind shower door.

William McNamara . . . . . . . . . . . . . . . . . Todd Pounds
Teri Polo . . . . . . . . . . . . . . . . . . . . . . . . . Robin Hand
Nicolette Scorsese . . . . . . . . . . . . . . . . . . . . . . . . Tina
Roger Wilson . . . . . . . . . . . . . . . . . . . . . . . . . Jake Neil

### The Assassin (1989)

Elpidia Carrillo . . . . . . . . . . . . . . . . . . . . . . . . Elena
Steve Railsback . . . . . . . . . . . . . . . . . . . . Hank Wright
Andaluz Russell . . . . . . . . . . . . . . . . .Amanda Portales
- • 0:21—Brief breasts while changing clothes in room with the other assassins.

### Assault of the Killer Bimbos (1988)

Nick Cassavetes. . . . . . . . . . . . . . . . . . . . . Wayne-O
Elizabeth Kaitan. . . . . . . . . . . . . . . . . . . . . . . . Lulu
- •• 0:41—Brief breasts during desert musical sequence, opening her blouse, then taking off her shorts, then putting on a light blue dress. Don't see her face.

Christina Whitaker. . . . . . . . . . . . . . . . . . . . Peaches

### Assault of the Party Nerds (1989)

Michelle Bauer . . . . . . . . . . . . . . . . . . . . . . Muffin
- • 0:16—Side view of left breast kissing Bud.
- ••• 0:20—Breasts lying in bed seen from Bud's point of view, then sitting up by herself.
- • 1:15—Brief right breast, then breasts in bed with Scott.

Linnea Quigley . . . . . . . . . . . . . . . . . . . . . . . .Bambi
- ••• 0:25—Breasts straddling Cliff in bed.

### At Home with the Webbers (1992)

Robby Benson. . . . . . . . . . . . . . . . . . . . Roger Swade
Gabriel Jarrett . . . . . . . . . . . . . . . . . . . . . . . Thomas
- •• 1:24—Buns, after pulling down his underwear in Jennifer Tilly's bedroom.

Kenneth A. Johnson. . . . . . . . . . . . . . . . . . .Chuck
- • 0:55—Buns, while standing in chaps in living room with Jennifer Tilly and dancing with her.
- • 0:58—Buns, while on the floor and in reflection in window while making love with Tilly.

Zack Norman . . . . . . . . . . . . . . . . . . . . Sledge Hammer
Jennifer Tilly . . . . . . . . . . . . . . . . . . Miranda Webber

### At Play in the Fields of the Lord (1991)

Kathy Bates. . . . . . . . . . . . . . . . . . . . . Hazel Quarrier
- • 2:22—(0:52 into tape 2) Nude, covered with mud and leaves, going crazy outside after her son dies.

Tom Berenger. . . . . . . . . . . . . . . . . . . . . . Lewis Moon
- •• 0:45—Buns, while taking off his clothes after parachuting into the jungle.
- ••• 0:46—Nude, arriving at the Niaruna village.
- • 0:47—Very brief buns and frontal nudity.

- •• 0:50—Buns, while entering hut.
- ••• 0:52—Brief frontal nudity while standing up, then buns, while walking.
- •• 0:54—Buns, while wearing G-string.
- ••• 0:55—More buns, wearing G-string, while walking in the forest.
- •• 0:56—More buns, with Pindi.
- • 1:31—(0:01 into tape 2) Buns, in G-string.
- ••• 2:14—(0:44 into tape 2) Buns, in G-string, with Pindi.
- • 2:47—(1:17 into tape 2) Buns, outside in G-string.
- •• 2:50—(1:20 into tape 2) Buns, in G-string when the white men in the helicopter fire bomb the village.

Daryl Hannah. . . . . . . . . . . . . . . . . . . . Andy Huben
2:09—(0:39 into tape 2) Brief buns, swimming in water.
- ••• 2:10—(0:40 into tape 2) Buns, getting out and resting by tree. Long shot, then breasts in (excellent!) closer shot. Very brief top of lower frontal nudity. (Skip tape 1 and fast forward to this!)
- •• 2:11—(0:41 into tape 2) Brief buns, running away after kissing Tom Berenger.

John Lithgow . . . . . . . . . . . . . . . . . . . . . Leslie Huben
Aidan Quinn. . . . . . . . . . . . . . . . . . . Martin Quarrier

### Atlantic City (1981; French/Canadian)

Burt Lancaster . . . . . . . . . . . . . . . . . . . . . . . . . Lou
Susan Sarandon . . . . . . . . . . . . . . . . . . . . . . .Sally
- •• 0:50—Left breast cleaning herself with lemon juice while Burt Lancaster watches through window.

### Attack of the 50 ft. Woman
*(1993; Made for Cable Movie)*

Cristi Conaway. . . . . . . . . . . . . . . . . . . . . . .Honey
0:12—In black bra and panties while getting dressed in motel room with Daniel Baldwin.
- • 0:16—Very brief buns and back side of left breast, after getting out of bed and walking to the bathroom. 1:07—In black bra, while dancing in front of Baldwin in beauty shop.

Frances Fisher. . . . . . . . . . . . . . . . . . . . .Dr. Cushing
Daryl Hannah. . . . . . . . . . . . . . . . . . .Nancy Archer
Hilary Shepard . . . . . . . . . . . . . . . . . . . . . . . Nurse
Patricia Tallman . . . . . . . . . . . . . . . . . . . . . Stunts
Maude Winchester. . . . . . . . . . . . . . . . . . .Donna

### Auditions (1978)

Cory Brandon. . . . . . . . . . . . . . . . . . . . . .Van Scott
- •• 0:32—Frontal nudity when Tracy undresses him.

Rick Cassidy . . . . . . . . . . . . . . . . . . . . .Charlie White
- ••• 0:04—Nude, undressing for his audition.
- •• 0:29—Buns, during sex scene with a woman.
- • 1:07—Buns in bed during orgy scene.
- •• 1:13—Nude on kneeling on bed.

Marita Ditmar . . . . . . . . . . . . . . . . . . . . . Frieda Volker
- •• 1:05—Breasts and partial buns with another woman and a guy.

Mara Lutra . . . . . . . . . . . . . . . . . . . .Jenny Marino
- •• 0:58—Nude during her audition.
- •• 1:07—Breasts and buns during orgy scene.

Rick Lutze . . . . . . . . . . . . . . . . . . . . . . . . . . Ron Wilson
- 1:00—Nude during audition.

William Margold . . . . . . . . . . . . . . . . . . . . . Larry Krantz
- •• 0:23—Frontal nudity during his audition.
- •• 0:26—Frontal nudity during audition with Linnea Quigley and Harry.
- • 0:30—Frontal nudity, tied up on table.

Adore O'Hara . . . . . . . . . . . . . . . . . . . . . Adore O'Hara
- •• 0:47—Nude, while singing opera.

Harry Osbon . . . . . . . . . . . . . . . . . . . . . . . Harry Boran
- ••• 0:26—Nude during audition with Linnea Quigley and Larry.
- •• 0:30—Frontal nudity, getting whipped while standing up, chained at the wrists.

Rhonda Petty . . . . . . . . . . . . . . . . . . . . . .Patty Rhodes
- •• 0:26—Breasts during audition.
- •• 0:30—Breasts, standing next to Larry and full frontal nudity straddling him on the table.

Linnea Quigley . . . . . . . . . . . . . . . . . . . . Sally Webster
- ••• 0:06—Breasts and buns, undressing and dancing during her audition.
- ••• 0:26—Full frontal nudity, acting with two guys.

Alan Simons . . . . . . . . . . . . . . . . . . . . . . . . . Alan Cole
- • 0:18—Nude, undressing and caressing himself during his audition.
- •• 0:37—Buns, when his underwear is pulled down.

Robert Sommer. . . . . . . . . . . . . . . . . . . .Frank Murphy
- ••• 0:33—Nude, during dungeon scene.
- • 1:07—Buns during orgy scene.

Sally Swift . . . . . . . . . . . . . . . . . . . . . . . . .Melinda Sale
- ••• 0:21—Full frontal nudity, undressing and masturbating during her audition.
- •• 0:30—Breasts and buns, whipping Harry.

Idy Tripoldi . . . . . . . . . . . . . . . . . . . . . . . . Bonnie Tirol
- ••• 1:01—Full frontal nudity, taking off sweater.
- • 1:07—Breasts and buns during orgy scene.

Bonnie Werchan . . . . . . . . . . . . . . . . . Tracy Matthews
- ••• 0:02—Breasts, then full frontal nudity, undressing for her audition.
- ••• 0:31—Nude, undressing herself and Van.
- •• 0:33—Buns and side of right breast, making love with Van.
- • 1:07—Breasts and buns during orgy scene.

Yossi Yaari . . . . . . . . . . . . . . . . . . . . . . .Moshe Mitzvah
- • 1:10—Buns, while taking off his clothes during orgy scene.

## Auntie Lee's Meat Pies (1991)

Karen Black. . . . . . . . . . . . . . . . . . . . . . . . Auntie Lee
Louis Bonanno . . . . . . . . . . . . . . . . . . . . . . . . . Doc
Grant Cramer . . . . . . . . . . . . . . . . . . . . . . . . . . .Phil
Ava Fabian . . . . . . . . . . . . . . . . . . . . . . . . Magnolia
- 1:29—Buns, while swimming in one piece swimsuit under water.

Pia Reyes . . . . . . . . . . . . . . . . . . . . . . . . . . . . . Sky
- •• 1:10—Breasts in basement with her rock star boyfriend.
- •• 1:15—Breasts in basement with her pot smoking boyfriend.

Kristine Rose. . . . . . . . . . . . . . . . . . . . . . . . . . . Fawn
- •• 1:12—Breasts in Stonehedge bedroom with her rock star boyfriend. More breasts in silhouette.
- • 1:28—Buns, in G-string in swimming pool.

Petra Verkaik . . . . . . . . . . . . . . . . . . . . . . . . . . Baby
Teri Weigel. . . . . . . . . . . . . . . . . . . . . . . . . . . . Coral
- 1:23—Breasts under sheer outfit.
- 1:29—Buns, while swimming in one piece swimsuit under water.

## Autumn Born (1979)

Dorothy Stratten . . . . . . . . . . . . . . . . . . . . . . . . .Tara
- 0:03—In dressing room in beige bra, panties, garter belt and stockings changing clothes. Long, close-up lingering shots.
- 0:16—Unconscious in beige lingerie, then conscious, walking around the room.
- 0:21—In bra and panties getting her rear end whipped while tied to the bed.
- •• 0:26—Left breast taking bath, then right breast getting up, then breasts dressing.
- • 0:30—Side view of left breast, then breasts climbing back into bed.
- 0:35—In beige bra and panties in the shower with her captor.
- 0:43—Quick cuts of various scenes.
- ••• 0:46—In white bra and panties, side view of left breast and buns, then breasts in bathtub. Long scene.
- • 0:50—Side view of left breast and buns getting undressed. Nice buns shot. Right breast lying down in chair.
- • 1:03—Brief breasts shots during flashbacks.

Roberta Weiss. . . . . . . . . . . . . . . . . . . . . . . . Melissa
- 0:07—Buns, wearing panties and bending over desk to get whipped.

## Avanti! (1973)

(Not available on video tape. Shown on *The Arts and Entertainment Channel* periodically. Scenes are listed as 0:00 since I can't time correctly with the commercials.)

Jack Lemmon . . . . . . . . . . . . . . . . . .Wendell Armbruster
- • 0:00—Buns, while standing up in bathtub talking to Juliet Mills.

Juliet Mills . . . . . . . . . . . . . . . . . . . . . Pamela Piggott
- 0:00—Buns, climbing out of the water onto a rock.
- • 0:00—Side view of right breast while lying on rock and talking to Jack Lemmon.
- ••• 0:00—Brief breasts while waving to fishermen on a passing boat.
- 0:00—Brief buns putting something up in the closet in Jack Lemmon's hotel room.

## Avenging Angel (1985)

Laura Burkett . . . . . . . . . . . . . . . . . . . . . .Blonde Hooker
Charlene Jones. . . . . . . . . . . . . . . . . . . . . . . . . Hooker
Karen Mani . . . . . . . . . . . . . . . . . . . . . . .Janie Soon Lee
- ••• 0:06—Nude taking a shower, right breast in mirror drying herself off, then in bra getting dressed.

Betsy Russell. . . . . . . . . . . . . . . . . Angel/Molly Stewart
Susan Tyrrell. . . . . . . . . . . . . . . . . . . . . . . .Solly Mosler

Deborah Voorhees . . . . . . . . . . . . . . . . . . . . . . . Roxie
Lynda Wiesmeier . . . . . . . . . . . . . . . . . . . . . . . Debbie

## *Ay, Carmela!* (1991; Spanish)

Carmen Maura . . . . . . . . . . . . . . . . . . . . . . . . Carmela
- •• 0:42—Showing her left breast to the Lieutenant to explain why she had a Republican flag. Subtitles get in the way.
- •• 1:38—Breasts taking off flag on stage during play. Subtitles get in the way again.

## *The Baby Doll Murders* (1992)

Tuscany. . . . . . . . . . . . . . . . . . . . . . . . Young Woman
- ••• 0:34—Breasts in bedroom with the suspected killer, then on bed.

Alretha Baker. . . . . . . . . . . . . . . . . . . . . . . . . . . . n.a.
Shana Golden . . . . . . . . . . . . . . . . . . . . . . Prostitute
Tom Hodges . . . . . . . . . . . . . . . . . . . . . . . Les Parker
- • 0:35—Upper half of buns, while in bed with the young woman.

Joanne Lara . . . . . . . . . . . . . . . . . . . . . . . . Mrs. Jayson
- ••• 0:44—Breasts, while taking a shower, getting out, drying herself off, walking to bed and talking on the phone. Long scene.
- •• 0:46—Breasts, on bed while getting killed and afterwards.

Julie McCullough. . . . . . . . . . . . . . . . . . . . . . . . Betty
  0:58—In black bra and panties.
Melanie Smith. . . . . . . . . . . . . . . . . . . . Peggy Davis
- ••• 0:09—Breasts, while taking off her blouse and getting into hot tub with Jeff Kober.
- •• 0:10—Breasts in hot tub with Kober. Fence gets in the way.
- •• 0:11—Breasts, getting out of the hot tub.
- •• 0:46—Breasts in hot tub with Kober while making out.

## *Baby Love* (1969)

Linda Hayden . . . . . . . . . . . . . . . . . . . . . . . . . . Luci
  0:32—Buns, standing in room when Nick sneaks in.
  0:34—Very brief right breast, while throwing doll at Robert.
- • 0:39—Breasts in mirror taking a bath. Long shot. Brief left breast hidden by steam.
- • 0:52—Brief breasts taking off her top to show Nick while sunbathing.
  1:25—Brief breasts calling Robert from window. Long shot.
  1:27—Very brief breasts sitting up while talking to Robert.
- • 1:28—Breasts in open robe struggling with Robert.

Derek Lamden. . . . . . . . . . . . . . . . . . . . . . . . . . Nick
- • 1:29—Brief buns while in shower when Luci opens the door.

Sheila Steafel. . . . . . . . . . . . . . . . . . . . . . . . . . Tessa

## *The Baby Maker* (1970)

Scott Glenn. . . . . . . . . . . . . . . . . . . . . . . . . . . Tad
- • 1:30—Buns while in bed with Charlotte.

Barbara Hershey. . . . . . . . . . . . . . . . . . . . . . . . Tish
- • 0:14—Side view of left breast taking off dress and diving into the pool. Long shot and dark. Buns in water.
  0:23—Left breast (out of focus) under sheet in bed.

Helena Kallianiotes . . . . . . . . . . . . . . . . . . . . . .Wanda
- • 1:30—Brief breasts when Barbara Hershey sees her in bed with Tad.

Brenda Sykes . . . . . . . . . . . . . . . . . . . . . . . . . Francis

## *Baby, It's You* (1983)

Rosanna Arquette. . . . . . . . . . . . . . . . . . . . . . . . Jill
- •• 1:17—Left breast, making love in bed with Vincent Spano.

Richard Kantor . . . . . . . . . . . . . . . . . . . . . . . .Curtis
Marta Kober. . . . . . . . . . . . . . . . . . . . . . . . . Debra
Matthew Modine. . . . . . . . . . . . . . . . . . . . . . . Steve
Vincent Spano . . . . . . . . . . . . . . . . . . . . . . . . Sheik
Fisher Stevens . . . . . . . . . . . . . . . Stage Manager

## *Bachelor Party* (1984)

Angela Aames . . . . . . . . . . . . . . . . . . Mrs. Klupner
Toni Alessandrini  Desiree, Woman Dancing with Donkey
  1:24—Buns, in G-string, while dancing with donkey during party.
Brett Clark . . . . . . . . . . . . . . . . . . . . . . . . . .Nick
Monique Gabrielle . . . . . . . . . . . . . . . . . . . Tracey
- •• 1:11—Full frontal nudity in the hotel bedroom with Tom Hanks as his bachelor party gift.
Annie Gaybis . . . . . . . . . . . . . . . . . . . . . Hooker
Rosanne Katon. . . . . . . . . . . . . Bridal Shower Hooker
Tawny Kitaen . . . . . . . . . . . . . . . .Debbie Thompson
Rebecca Perle . . . . . . . . . . . . . Screaming Woman
Robert Prescott. . . . . . . . . . . . . . . . Richard Chance
- • 1:18—Buns, after being hung out the window tied up with sheets by Tom Hanks and his friends.
William Tepper. . . . . . . . . . . . . . . . . Dr. Stan Gassko

## *Back In the U.S.S.R.* (1992)

Natalya Negoda . . . . . . . . . . . . . . . . . . . . . . . Lena
- •• 0:46—Side view of left breast, making love with Sloan in the bathtub. Brief right breast when Dimitri comes into the bathroom.
Dey Young. . . . . . . . . . . . . . . . . . . . . . . . Claudia

## *Back to Back* (1990)

Apollonia . . . . . . . . . . . . . . . . . . . . . . . Jesse Duro
Susan Anspach. . . . . . . . . . . . . . . .Madeline Hix
Todd Field . . . . . . . . . . . . . . . . . . . . .Todd Brand
- •• 0:33—Buns, while walking to and jumping into swimming pool.
Bill Paxton . . . . . . . . . . . . . . . . . . . . . . . Bo Brand

## *Back to School* (1986)

Adrienne Barbeau . . . . . . . . . . . . . . . . . . . . . Vanessa
Leslie Huntly. . . . . . . . . . . . . . . . . . . . . . Coed #1
- •• 0:14—Brief breasts in the shower room when Rodney Dangerfield first arrives on campus.
Sally Kellerman. . . . . . . . . . . . . . . . . . . . . . .Diane
Becky LeBeau . . . . . . . . . . . . Bubbles, the Hot Tub Girl
M. Emmet Walsh . . . . . . . . . . . . . . . . Coach Turnbull

## Backdraft (1991)

William Baldwin . . . . . . . . . . . . . . . . . Brian McCaffrey
- •• 0:33—Brief buns (on the left) in the shower room with Jason Gedrick.

Rebecca De Mornay . . . . . . . . . . . . . .Helen McCaffrey
Robert De Niro . . . . . . . . . . . . . . . . . . Donald Rimgale
Jason Gedrick . . . . . . . . . . . . . . . . . . . . Tim Krizminski
- •• 0:33—Brief buns (on the right) in the shower room with William Baldwin.

Scott Glenn . . . . . . . . . . . . . . . . . . . . . . . .John Adcox
Clint Howard. . . . . . . . . . . . . . . . . . . . . . . . . Ricco
Jennifer Jason Leigh. . . . . . . . . . . . . . .Jennifer Vaitkus
- • 1:16—Very, very brief left breast on back of fire truck with William Baldwin. (Right after someone knocks open a door with an axe.)

Kurt Russell . . . . . . . . . . . . . . . . . . . . .Stephen McCaffrey
Donald Sutherland . . . . . . . . . . . . . . . . . Ronald Bartel

## Backfire (1987)

Karen Allen . . . . . . . . . . . . . . . . . . . . . . . . . . . .Mara
- • 0:48—Lots of buns, then brief breasts with Keith Carradine in the bedroom.
- • 1:00—Brief breasts in the shower.

Keith Carradine . . . . . . . . . . . . . . . . . . . . Clinton James
Bernie Casey . . . . . . . . . . . . . . . . . . . . . . Clinton James
Jeff Fahey . . . . . . . . . . . . . . . . . . . . . . . . . . Donnie
- • 0:22—Brief, partial buns while taking a shower, then very brief, out of focus frontal nudity in shower when blood starts to gush out of the shower head.

## Backstab (1990)

June Chadwick . . . . . . . . . . . . .Mrs. Caroline Chambers
Meg Foster . . . . . . . . . . . . . . . . . . . . . . .Sara Rudnick
Isabelle Truchon . . . . . . . . . . . . . . . . . . . . .Jennifer
- •• 0:08—In bra, then breasts in back seat of car with James Brolin. Don't see her face very well.
- • 0:16—Buns, black panties and stockings while on the floor with Brolin. Brief right breast.
- • 0:18—Brief buns in front of fireplace. Side view of right breast. Buns, while walking into the other room.

## Backstreet Dreams (1990)

Nick Cassavetes. . . . . . . . . . . . . . . . . . . Mikey Acosta
Maria Celedonio . . . . . . . . . . . . . . . . . . . . . Maria M.
Sherilyn Fenn . . . . . . . . . . . . . . . . . . . . . . . . . . Lucy
- • 0:00—Right breast while sleeping in bed with Dean. Medium long shot.

Meg Register. . . . . . . . . . . . . . . . . . . . . . . . . .Candy
Brooke Shields. . . . . . . . . . . . . .Stephanie "Stevie" Bloom

## Backstreet Justice (1993)

Linda Kozlowski. . . . . . . . . . . . . . . . . . . Kerri Finnegan
- ••• 0:31—Breasts in open dress and while making love in bedroom with John Shea.

John Shea . . . . . . . . . . . . . . . . . . . . . . . . . . . Nick
- •• 0:33—Buns, while making love on top of Linda Kozlowski.

Paul Sorvino . . . . . . . . . . . . . . . .Captain Phil Giarrusso

## Backtrack (1989)

*a.k.a. Catch Fire*

Jodie Foster . . . . . . . . . . . . . . . . . . . . . . Anne Benton
- • 0:50—Breasts behind textured shower door.
- ••• 0:51—Breasts, leaning out of the shower to get her towel. Very, very brief side of left breast and buns, while drying herself off in bedroom. Side of left breast and buns, while putting on slip.

Dennis Hopper. . . . . . . . . . . . . . . . . . . . . . . . . .Milo
Helena Kallianiotes . . . . . . . . . . . . . . . . . . . Grace Carelli
John Turturro . . . . . . . . . . . . . . . . . . . . . . . . Pinella
Fred Ward . . . . . . . . . . . . . . . . . . . . . . . . . Pauling

## Bad Boys (1983)

Clancy Brown. . . . . . . . . . . . . . . . . . . . . Viking Lofgren
Sean Penn . . . . . . . . . . . . . . . . . . . . . . . Mick O'Brien
- • 0:10—Brief buns while getting up off the floor with Ally Sheedy.
- •• 0:46—Buns while taking a shower.

Ally Sheedy . . . . . . . . . . . . . . . . . . . . . .J. C. Walenski
- • 0:12—Very, very brief left breast, while kneeling on floor next to bed when Sean Penn leaves. A little blurry and a long shot.

## Bad Georgia Road

George "Buck" Flower . . . . . . . . . . . . . . . . . . . . Spiker
Carol Lynley . . . . . . . . . . . . . . . . . . . . . . . .Molly Golden
- • 1:02—Very brief upper half of right breast, after hitting the water in anger after her clothes are stolen.

Mary Woronov. . . . . . . . . . . . . . . . . . . . . . . . Hackett

## Bad Girls from Mars (1990)

Jasaé . . . . . . . . . . . . . . . . . . . . . . . . . . . . . . . Terry
- ••• 0:03—Breasts taking off her top.
- •• 0:05—More breasts going into dressing room.

Dana Bentley Konkel . . . . . . . . . . . . . . . . . . . . Martine
- •• 0:28—Breasts taking off her blouse in office.
- •• 0:59—Breasts several times wrestling with Edy Williams.

Sherri Graham . . . . . . . . . . . . . . . . . . . . . . . . Swimmer
- •• 0:22—Very brief breasts diving into, then climbing out of pool.

Brinke Stevens . . . . . . . . . . . . . . . . . . . . . . . . . Myra
- • 0:11—Brief side of left breast, then breasts getting massaged on diving board.

Edy Williams . . . . . . . . . . . . . . . . . . . . . . Emanuelle
- •• 0:17—Breasts, several times changing in back of convertible car.
- ••• 0:23—Breasts, changing out of wet dress in bathroom.
- ••• 0:30—Breasts taking off blouse to get into spa.
- • 0:32—Breasts in back of Porsche and getting out.
- • 0:35—Breasts in store, signing autograph for robber.
- • 0:46—Buns in G-string, then breasts taking off her top again.
- ••• 0:58—Breasts in T.J.'s office. More breasts when wrestling with Martine.
- • 1:05—Breasts while tied up.
- • 1:07—Breasts again.

•• 1:17—Breasts while taking off her outfit during out-takes.

## Bad Influence *(1990)*
Charisse Glenn . . . . . . . . . . . . . Stylish Eurasian Woman
••• 1:26—Breasts and partial lower frontal nudity making love on Rob Lowe.
• 1:28—Very brief left breast in bed with the blonde woman.
Rob Lowe . . . . . . . . . . . . . . . . . . . . . . . . . . . . . . Alex
••• 1:27—Buns, while going into the bathroom.
James Spader . . . . . . . . . . . . . . . . . . . . . . Michael Boll
Lisa Zane. . . . . . . . . . . . . . . . . . . . . . . . . . . . . . . Claire
• 0:39—Brief breasts on video tape seen on TV at party.

## Bad Lieutenant *(1992)*
Paul Calderone . . . . . . . . . . . . . . . . . . . . . . Cop One
Harvey Keitel . . . . . . . . . . . . . . . . . . . . . . . . . . .Lt.
••• 0:12—Full frontal nudity, while high on drugs in apartment with two other people.
Zoe Tamerlis . . . . . . . . . . . . . . . . . . . . . . . . . . .Zoe
Frankie Thorn . . . . . . . . . . . . . . . . . . . . . . . . . Nun
• 0:18—Very brief lower frontal nudity, while getting raped by two guys in church.
•• 0:26—Full frontal nudity while lying on hospital bed during examination.

## Bad Manners *(1989)*
Karen Black . . . . . . . . . . . . . . . . . . .Mrs. Fitzpatrick
Kimmy Robertson . . . . . . . . . . . . . . . . Sarah Fitzpatrick
•• 0:38—Breasts and buns taking off robe and getting into the shower when Mouse takes a picture of her.
1:16—In white bra when Piper rips her blouse open while she's tied up on the piano.
1:18—Briefly on piano again.
Edy Williams . . . . . . . . . . . . . . . . . . . . . . . Mrs. Slatt

## Bad Timing: A Sensual Obsession *(1980)*
Art Garfunkel. . . . . . . . . . . . . . . . . . . . . .Alex Linden
• 0:55—Buns, while making love with Theresa Russell on stairwell. Don't see his face.
• 0:57—Buns (Sort of see his balls through his legs), while on top of Russell when visited by Harvey Keitel.
1:48—Side view of buns while in bed with an unconscious Russell.
Harvey Keitel. . . . . . . . . . . . . . . . . . . . . .Inspector Netusil
Theresa Russell . . . . . . . . . . . . . . . . . . . .Milena Flaherty
0:14—Buns and breasts under short, sheer blouse.
0:17—Almost brief right breast in bed during Art Garfunkel's flashback. Very brief left breast kneeling on bed with him.
• 0:31—Full frontal nudity in bed with Garfunkel. Intercut with tracheotomy footage. Kind of gross.
•• 0:32—Right breast, while sitting in bed talking to Garfunkel.
• 0:41—Brief breasts several times on operating table.
• 0:55—Full frontal nudity making love on stairwell with Garfunkel. Quick cuts.

• 0:56—Brief breasts twice after stairwell episode while throwing a fit.
•• 1:45—In bra, then breasts passed out on bed while Garfunkel cuts her clothes off. Brief full frontal nudity.
•• 1:48—More breasts cuts while Garfunkel makes love to her while she's unconscious from an overdose of drugs.

## The Bagdad Café *(1988)*
Marianne Sägebrecht. . . . . . . . . . . . . . . . . . . . . .Jasmin
•• 1:09—Right breast slowly lowering her top, posing while Jack Palance paints.
•• 1:12—More breasts posing for Palance.

## Baja Oklahoma *(1988; Made for Cable Movie)*
Alice Krige . . . . . . . . . . . . . . . . . . . . . . . . . . .Patsy Cline
Karen Laine . . . . . . . . . . . . . . . . . . . . . .Girl at Drive-In
• 0:04—Left breast, in truck with a jerk guy. Dark, hard to see anything.
Julia Roberts. . . . . . . . . . . . . . . . . . . . . . . . . . . Candy

## The Ballad of Cable Hogue *(1970)*
Stella Stevens . . . . . . . . . . . . . . . . . . . . . . . . . . . . Hildy
1:12—Buns changing into nightgown in bedroom.
• 1:14—Brief top half of breasts in outdoor tub, then buns running into cabin when stagecoach arrives.

## The Ballad of Little Jo *(1993)*
Suzy Amis . . . . . . . . . . . . . . . . . . . . . . . .Jo Monaghan
• 0:12—Buns and left breast in reflection in mirror. Hard to see her face clearly.
••• 1:16—Breasts, while on bed with Tinman.
Melissa Leo . . . . . . . . . . . . . . . . . . . . . . Mrs. Grey
Carrie Snodgress . . . . . . . . . . . . . . . . . . . . Ruth Badger

## The Baltimore Bullet *(1980)*
Bruce Boxleitner. . . . . . . . . . . . . . . . . . .Billie Joe Robbins
Cissie Colpitts-Cameron . . . . . . . . . . . . . . . . . . . . .Sugar
• 0:09—Breasts behind shower door after James Coburn gets out.
Joyce Mandel . . . . . . . . . . . . . . . . . . . . . . . .Waitress

## Bank Robber *(1993)*
Lisa Bonet . . . . . . . . . . . . . . . . . . . . . . . . . . . Priscilla
•• 0:36—Buns, while lying on bed, waiting for Patrick Dempsey.
•• 0:37—Breasts, while making love in bed with Dempsey.
•• 1:05—Brief breasts while making love in bed with Dempsey.
Olivia D'Abo. . . . . . . . . . . . . . . . . . . . . . . . . . Selina
• 0:03—Very, very brief right breast, while pulling the sheets over herself in bed. Brief breasts, while getting out of bed.
• 0:04—Brief, upper half of left breast at doorway, then brief partial left breast in mirror.
• 0:21—Brief side of right breast, while making love in bed with Chris.
• 1:10—Brief breasts, while turning over in bed after making love with Andy.

Patrick Dempsey . . . . . . . . . . . . . . . . . . . . . . . . . . Billy
•• 1:21—Buns, while taking a shower.
Mariska Hargitay . . . . . . . . . . . . . . . . . . Marissa Benoit
Michael Jeter . . . . . . . . . . . . . . . . . . . . . . . Night Clerk 1
Paula Kelly . . . . . . . . . . . . . . . . . . . . . . . . . . . . . Mother
Stephen McDonough . . . . . . . . . . . . . . . . . . . . . Andy
• 1:11—Brief upper half of buns, while in bed with
Olivia D'Abo.
David Millbern . . . . . . . . . . . . . . . . . . . . . . Wiretapper
Judge Reinhold . . . . . . . . . . . . . . . . . . . . . Officer Gross

## The Banker (1989)
Robert Forster . . . . . . . . . . . . . . . . . . . . . . . . . . . . Dan
E.J. Peaker . . . . . . . . . . . . . . . . . . . . . . . . . . . . . Renee
Duncan Regehr . . . . . . . . . . . . . . . . . . . . . . . Osbourne
• 0:03—Buns, while getting out of bed with Teri Wei-
gel. Don't see his face.
Debi Richter . . . . . . . . . . . . . . . . . . . . . . . . . . Melanie
Christina Walker . . . . . . . . . . . . . . . . . . . . . . . . . Girl
• 0:18—Breasts on bed with Jeff Conaway
Teri Weigel . . . . . . . . . . . . . . . . . . . . . . . . . . . . Jaynie
••• 0:02—Taking off dress, then in lingerie, then breasts
making love with Osbourne in bed. More breasts after.

## Barbarella (1968; French/Italian)
Jane Fonda . . . . . . . . . . . . . . . . . . . . . . . . . Barbarella
•• 0:04—Breasts getting out of space suit during open-
ing credits in zero gravity. Hard to see because the
frame is squeezed so the lettering will fit.
John Phillip Law. . . . . . . . . . . . . . . . . . . . . . . . . Pygar
Anita Pallenberg . . . . . . . . . . . . . . . . The Black Queen

## Barbarian Queen (1985)
Lana Clarkson . . . . . . . . . . . . . . . . . . . . . . . . Amethea
•• 0:38—Brief breasts during attempted rape.
••• 0:48—Breasts being tortured with metal hand then
raped by torturer.
Dawn Dunlap . . . . . . . . . . . . . . . . . . . . . . . . Taramis
• 0:00—Breasts, in the woods getting raped.
Katt Shea . . . . . . . . . . . . . . . . . . . . . . . . . . . . Estrild
• 0:31—Brief breasts, when her top gets torn off by
guards.

## Barbarian Queen II: The Empress Strikes Back
(1989)
Orietta Aguilar . . . . . . . . . . . . . . . . . . . . . . . Erigina
•• 0:14—Breasts during fight in mud with Lana Clark-
son.
Lana Clarkson . . . . . . . . . . . . . . . . . . . . . . . . . Athelia
••• 0:14—Breasts during fight with Erigina in mud.
More breasts afterwards.
••• 0:31—Left breast, while making love with Aurion
outside.
••• 0:43—Breasts, tied up to torture rack.
••• 0:49—More breasts, tied up to torture rack.
•• 0:51—Brief right breast then breasts several times,
while lying down, tied to the rack.
• 0:54—Very brief breasts when Aurion covers her up.
Rebecca Wood-Sharkey . . . . . . . . . . . . . . . . . . . . Ziela

## Barbarians at the Gate
(1993; Made for Cable Movie)
Joanna Cassidy . . . . . . . . . . . . . . . . . . Linda Robinson
Leilani Sarelle . . . . . . . . . . . . . . . . . . . . . Laurie Johnson
0:57—In black bra and panties after taking off dress.
• 0:59—Side view of right breast, twice, while taking
off bra and putting on T-shirt.

## Barfly (1987)
Faye Dunaway . . . . . . . . . . . . . . . . . . . . . Wanda Wilcox
• 0:58—Brief upper half of breasts in bathtub talking
to Mickey Rourke.
Alice Krige . . . . . . . . . . . . . . . . . . . . . . . . . . . . . Tully
Sandy Martin . . . . . . . . . . . . . . . . . . . . . . . . . . Janice
J. C. Quinn . . . . . . . . . . . . . . . . . . . . . . . . . . . . . Jim
Mickey Rourke . . . . . . . . . . . . . . . . . . . . . . . . . Henry

## Basic Instinct (1992)
(Unrated Director's cut reviewed.)
Bill Cable . . . . . . . . . . . . . . . . . . . . . . . . . . Johnny Boz
• 0:05—Brief frontal nudity, when Michael Douglas
looks at the stains on the bed with UV light.
Michael Douglas . . . . . . . . . . . . . . . . . Det. Nick Curran
•• 0:36—Brief buns, when pulling down his underwear
to make love with Beth.
•• 1:10—Buns and very, very brief frontal nudity, while
on top of Sharon Stone in bed.
•• 1:12—Brief buns, in overhead mirror over the bed.
••• 1:15—Buns, while walking to the bathroom.
••• 1:16—Buns, while walking back to the bedroom.
Chelchie Ross . . . . . . . . . . . . . . . . . . . . Captain Talcott
Leilani Sarelle . . . . . . . . . . . . . . . . . . . . . . . . . . Roxy
Sharon Stone . . . . . . . . . . . . . . . . Catherine Trammel
••• 0:02—Buns and breasts while making love on top of
Johnny in bed, then killing him.
•• 0:21—Buns and left breast in mirror in her bedroom
while Michael Douglas watches while waiting for
her.
• 0:26—Two brief crotch shots while crossing and uncrossing her legs during interrogation.
•• 0:44—Nude, undressing in her house, while Douglas watches from outside. Medium long shot.
••• 1:10—Breasts while in bed with Douglas.
••• 1:13—Breasts and buns, tying Douglas up in bed
and on top of him.
••• 1:15—Buns, while sitting on top of Douglas.
• 1:32—Very brief right breast, with Douglas in front
of fireplace.
••• 1:43—Breasts, while taking off her blouse in Douglas' apartment.
••• 2:00—Breasts, while in bed on top of Douglas.
Jeanne Tripplehorn . . . . . . . . . . . . . . . . Dr. Beth Garner
••• 0:35—Briefly in bra, then breasts with Michael Douglas in her apartment. Buns when he rips her panties
off.
••• 0:37—Breasts, sitting up, then getting up off the
floor.

### Basic Training (1984)
Angela Aames . . . . . . . . . . . . . . . . . . . . . . . . . . .Cheryl
 • 0:19—Brief breasts in bathtub.
Erika Dockery . . . . . . . . . . . . . . . . . . . . . . . . Salesgirl 2
 • 0:00—Brief breasts standing behind the desk.
Ann Dusenberry . . . . . . . . . . . . . . . . . . Melinda Griffin
 ••• 1:13—Breasts in Russian guy's bedroom.
Barbara Peckinpaugh. . . . . . . . . . . . . . . . . . Salesgirl 1
 • 0:00—Breasts, while on desk.
Rhonda Shear . . . . . . . . . . . . . . . . . . . . . . . . . Debbie
 •• 0:07—Breasts making love with Mark.
 0:15—In bra, making love on Mark's desk.

### Basket Case (1982)
Kevin Van Hetenryck . . . . . . . . . . . . . . . Duane Bradley
 •• 1:21—Frontal nudity, twice, running around at
 night.

### Basket Case 2 (1989)
Heather Rattray. . . . . . . . . . . . . . . . . . . . . . . . . Susan
 • 1:20—Brief right breast twice, when white blouse
 gapes open in bedroom with Duane. Special effect
 scar on her stomach makes it a little unappealing
 looking.
Annie Ross. . . . . . . . . . . . . . . . . . . . . . . .Granny Ruth
Kevin Van Hetenryck . . . . . . . . . . . . . . . Duane Bradley
 • 0:34—Buns while standing in front of mirror looking
 at the large scar on the side of his body.

### Basket Case 3: The Progeny (1991)
Carla Morrell. . . . . . . . . . . . . . . . . . . . . . . . . Twin #1
 •• 0:41—Breasts in bed with her twin sister and Du-
 ane's brother.
 • 1:29—Brief breast, lying in bed with her twin sister
 and Duane's brother after the end credits.
Carmen Morrell. . . . . . . . . . . . . . . . . . . . . . . Twin #2
 •• 0:41—Breasts in bed with her twin sister and Duane's brother.
 • 1:29—Brief breast, lying in bed with her twin sister
 and Duane's brother after the end credits.
Heather Rattray. . . . . . . . . . . . . . . . . . . . . . . . Susan
Annie Ross. . . . . . . . . . . . . . . . . . . . . . . .Granny Ruth
Kevin Van Hetenryck . . . . . . . . . . . . . . . Duane Bradley

### Bay Boy (1985; Canadian)
Isabelle Mejias. . . . . . . . . . . . . . . . . . . . . .Mary McNeil
 •• 1:28—Brief breasts in her bedroom with Kiefer Sutherland, then brief breasts in bed with him.
Kiefer Sutherland. . . . . . . . . . . . . . . . Donald Campbell

### Beach Babes From Beyond (1993)
Sara Bellomo. . . . . . . . . . . . . . . . . . . . . . . . . . .Xena
 ••• 0:01—Breasts and very brief lower frontal nudity
 while in shower and getting dressed with Luna and
 Sola during opening credits.
 ••• 0:32—Buns, in swimsuit at the beach.
 • 0:58—Buns, while dancing in swimsuits and boots
 on stage at beach during bikini contest.

Angela Cornell . . . . . . . . . . . . . . . . . . . . . Sally's Model
 ••• 0:20—Breasts, while posing in spa outside (she's on
 the left) during catalog photo session with two other models.
 • 1:02—Brief breasts, when swimsuit top flies off while
 dancing on stage during bikini contest (she's the
 second one).
Nikki Fritz. . . . . . . . . . . . . . . . . . . . . . . . . Sally's Model
 ••• 0:20—Breasts, while posing in spa outside (she's on
 the right) during catalog photo session with two
 other models.
 ••• 0:22—Nude, in bedroom during Hassler's fantasy.
 • 1:02—Brief breasts, twice, when swimsuit top flies
 off while dancing on stage during bikini contest
 (she's the last one).
Tamara Landry. . . . . . . . . . . . . . . . . . . . . . . . . Luna
 •• 0:02—Breasts, while taking off pink top, getting
 dressed and talking with Xena and Sola.
 ••• 0:34—Breast, while making love in back of van with
 Jerry.
 •• 0:39—Buns, in swimsuit at the beach.
 • 0:58—Buns, while dancing in swimsuits and boots
 on stage at beach during bikini contest.
Linnea Quigley. . . . . . . . . . . . . . . . . . . . . . . . .Sally
Ken Steadman . . . . . . . . . . . . . . . . . . . . . . . . . .Jerry
 • 0:42—Brief buns, when swimsuit falls down while
 playing in the surf.

### Beach Balls (1988)
Leslie Danon . . . . . . . . . . . . . . . . . . . . . . . . Kathleen
 • 1:06—In bra, then brief breasts in car with Doug.

### The Beach Girls (1982)
Debra Blee. . . . . . . . . . . . . . . . . . . . . . . . . . . .Sarah
 ••• 1:22—Brief breasts opening her swimsuit top on the
 beach.
Corinne Bohrer. . . . . . . . . . . . . . . . . . Champagne Girl
James Daughton . . . . . . . . . . . . . . . . . . . . . . . . Scott
 • 0:33—Buns and very brief frontal nudity while taking off clothes and running into the ocean.
Tessa Richarde . . . . . . . . . . . . . . . . . . . . . . . Doreen
Catherine Mary Stewart . . . . . . . . . . . . . . . . Surfer Girl
Jeana Tomasina . . . . . . . . . . . . . . . . . . . . . . . Ducky
 •• 0:12—Breasts and buns, lying on the beach with
 Ginger, while a guy looks through a telescope.
 ••• 0:54—Breasts on a sailboat with a guy.
 • 0:55—Brief breasts on the beach after being "saved"
 after falling off the boat.
 •• 1:12—Breasts in sauna with Ginger and an older
 guy.

### Beaks The Movie (1987)
Christopher Atkins . . . . . . . . . . . . . . . . . . . . . . Peter
Michelle Johnson . . . . . . . . . . . . . . . . . . . . . . Vanessa
 • 0:26—Brief breasts covered with bubbles after taking a bath. Don't see her face.
 • 0:31—Brief breasts covered with bubbles after getting out of bathtub with Christopher Atkins. Don't
 see her face.

## The Beast Within *(1982)*

Bibi Besch . . . . . . . . . . . . . . . . . . . . Caroline MacCleary
- •• 0:06—Breasts, getting her blouse torn off by the beast while she is unconscious. Dark, hard to see her face.

Kitty Moffat. . . . . . . . . . . . . . . . . . . . Amanda Platt
- •• 1:32—Breasts, getting her dress torn off by the beast while she is unconscious. Don't see her face, could be a body double.

## The Beastmaster *(1982)*

Tanya Roberts . . . . . . . . . . . . . . . . . . . . . . . . . Kiri
- ••• 0:35—Breasts in a pond while Marc Singer watches, then breasts getting out of the water when his pet ferrets steal her towel.

Marc Singer . . . . . . . . . . . . . . . . . . . . . . . . . . Dar
Linda Smith. . . . . . . . . . . . . . . . . . . . . . Kiri's Friend
- • 0:35—Breasts in a pond with Tanya Roberts.

Rip Torn . . . . . . . . . . . . . . . . . . . . . . . . . . . Maax

## Beauty School *(1993)*

Jane Hamilton . . . . . . . . . . Countess Sophia Von Spatula
- • 0:18—Left breast while leaning up while lying on massage table.
- • 1:11—Partial left breast while lying in bed. Breasts, when sitting up.
- ••• 1:15—Breasts while lying in bed.

Dana Hardin . . . . . . . . . . . . . . . . . . . . . . . . Ashley
- • 0:58—Breasts, dancing in cage in club.

Sylvia Kristel . . . . . . . . . . . . . . . . . . . . . . . . Sylvia
- • 1:27—Brief breasts in bed with the private investigator.

Theresa Lynn. . . . . . . . . . . . . . . . . . . . Countess's Girl
Lisa Madison. . . . . . . . . . . . . . . . . . . . . . . . Kristina
- •• 0:02—Breasts making out with a guy in bedroom.
- ••• 1:23—Breasts making out with a guy.

Susan Napoli. . . . . . . . . . . . . . . . . . . . . . . Otis' Girl
- •• 0:21—Breasts undoing her swimsuit top for Mr. Otis.

J. J. North . . . . . . . . . . . . . . . . . . . . . . . . . . Renee
- ••• 0:44—Breasts while doing breast exercises, then buns in G-string going for a swim. (She's on the far left.)
- • 0:46—Brief breasts, while standing in pool.
- •• 0:57—Breasts and buns in G-string while undressing in locker room.

Carina Ragnarsson. . . . . . . . . . . . . . . . . . . . Heather
- •• 0:40—Breasts, dancing with her top down on stage in club.

Kimberly Taylor. . . . . . . . . . . . . . . . . . . . . Kimberly
- • 0:43—Buns in white lingerie on balcony. Long shot.
- ••• 0:44—Breasts doing breast exercises, then buns in G-string going for a swim. (She's on the far right.)
- ••• 0:45—Buns and breasts, getting out of the swimming pool.
- ••• 0:51—Breasts while making love with Quincy outside.
- ••• 1:22—Breasts, taking off her dress and making love with Quincy.

## Because of the Cats *(1973)*

Sylvia Kristel . . . . . . . . . . . . . . . . . . . . . . . . . . n.a.
- • 1:09—Breasts and buns, under water with Case.

Bryan Marshall . . . . . . . . . . . . . . . Inspector Vanderbelt
- ••• 0:16—Frontal nudity, getting up out of bed.
- • 0:27—Partial frontal nudity behind glass while taking a shower.

Alexandra Stewart . . . . . . . . . . . . . . . . . . . . Theodora
- • 0:16—Breasts under sheer black blouse.
- •• 0:43—Breasts, sitting up and covering herself while sunbathing outside.

## Becoming Colette *(1992; French/German/U.S.)*

Virginia Madsen . . . . . . . . . . . . . . . . . . . . . . . Polaire
- •• 0:48—Breasts in bed, with Mathilda May.
- •• 0:49—Side view of left breast in bed with May and Klaus Maria Brandauer.

Mathilda May. . . . . . . . . . . . . . . . . . . Gabrielle Colette
- •• 0:01—Left breast, in open dress top, on stage during play.
- •• 0:16—Breasts, sitting up in bed.
- •• 0:48—Left breast, then breasts in bed with Virginia Madsen.
- •• 0:49—Side view of right breast in bed with Madsen and Klaus Maria Brandauer.
- •• 1:13—Upper half of buns and right breast, while making love in bed on top of Brandauer.

## Bedroom Eyes
*(1985; Made for Cable Movie; Canadian)*

Dayle Haddon . . . . . . . . . . . . . . . . . . . . . . . . . Alixe
- 1:06—Getting undressed in tap pants and white camisole top while Harry watches in the mirror.

Barbara Law. . . . . . . . . . . . . . . . . . . . . . . . . Jobeth
- • 0:02—Breasts taking off clothes while Harry watches through the window.
- •• 0:07—Breasts and buns, kissing a woman.
- • 0:14—Breasts during Harry's flashback when he talks to the psychiatrist.
- •• 0:23—Breasts and buns dancing in bedroom.
- •• 0:57—Breasts with Mary, kissing on floor.
- 1:17—In beige bra, panties, garter belt and stockings in bed with Harry.
- • 1:23—Brief breasts on top of Harry.

## Bedroom Eyes II *(1989)*

Linda Blair . . . . . . . . . . . . . . . . . . . . . Sophie Stevens
- 0:31—Buns, in bed with Wings Hauser.
- • 0:33—Brief left breast under bubbles in the bathtub. Don't see her face.

Jennifer Delora . . . . . . . . . . . . . . . . . . . . . Gwendolyn
- •• 0:04—Undressing in hotel room with Vinnie. Breasts, then making love.

Jane Hamilton . . . . . . . . . . . . . . . . . . JoBeth McKenna
- • 0:50—Breasts knifing Linda Blair, then fighting with Wings Hauser.

Wings Hauser. . . . . . . . . . . . . . . . . . . . . . Harry Ross

Kathy Shower . . . . . . . . . . . . . . . . . . . . . . .Carolyn Ross
- •• 0:22—Breasts in the artist's studio fighting with her lover while Wings Hauser watches through the window.

Kimberly Taylor. . . . . . . . . . . . . . . . . . . . . . . Michelle

### The Bedroom Window (1987)

Brad Greenquist . . . . . . . . . . . . . . . . . . . . . Henderson
- • 0:35—Buns, turning off the light while Steve Guttenberg spies on him.

Steve Guttenberg . . . . . . . . . . . . . . . . . . .Terry Lambert
- •• 0:05—Buns, while getting out of bed and walking to the bathroom.

Isabelle Huppert . . . . . . . . . . . . . . . . . Sylvia Wentworth
- •• 0:06—Briefly nude while looking out the window at attempted rape.

Elizabeth McGovern . . . . . . . . . . . . . . . . . . . . . Denise
- 1:25—Silhouette of breasts on shower curtain when Steve Guttenberg peeks in the bathroom.

### The Beguiled (1971)

Clint Eastwood . . . . . . . . . . . . . . . . . . . .John McBurney
Jo Ann Harris. . . . . . . . . . . . . . . . . . . . . . . . . . . . Carol
- • 1:09—Right breast, while in bed under Clint Eastwood at night.
- • 1:10—Brief left breast and side view of buns on top of Eastwood in bed. Brief buns, when discovered by Edwina.
- • 1:11—Very brief right breast, covering herself up in bed. Very brief breasts shadow on the wall, then very, very brief right breast covering herself with a sheet and walking out the door.

Mae Mercer . . . . . . . . . . . . . . . . . . . . . . . . . . Hallie
- • 1:28—Very brief breasts in ripped open dress during flashback.

### Behind Locked Doors (1969)

Madeleine Le Roux . . . . . . . . . . . . . . . . Woman at Party
- • 0:07—Breasts after taking off bra while making out with guy in barn.

### The Believers (1987)

Jennifer Lee. . . . . . . . . . . . . . . . . . . . Calder's Assistant
Helen Shaver. . . . . . . . . . . . . . . . . . . . . Jessica Halliday
- • 0:38—Brief glimpse of right breast while lying in bed with Martin Sheen.
- 1:17—Buns, getting out of bed.

Martin Sheen . . . . . . . . . . . . . . . . . . . . .Dr. Cal Jamison

### The Bell Jar (1979)

Roxanne Hart . . . . . . . . . . . . . . . . . . . . . . . . . . . . .n.a.
Marilyn Hassett . . . . . . . . . . . . . . . . Esther Greenwood
- • 0:10—In bra, then brief breasts in bed with Buddy. Dark, hard to see.
- •• 1:09—Breasts taking off her clothes and throwing them out the window while yelling.

Jameson Parker . . . . . . . . . . . . . . . . . . . . . . . .Buddy
- • 0:09—Frontal nudity silhouette standing in bedroom with Marilyn Hassett, then buns. Dark, hard to see.

Mary Louise Weller . . . . . . . . . . . . . . . . . . . . . .Doreen

### The Belly of an Architect (1987; British/Italian)

Stefania Casini . . . . . . . . . . . . . . . . . . . . .Flavia Speckler
- ••• 1:15—Lower frontal nudity, in open robe with Brian Dennehy. Then buns and breasts on couch. Kind of a long shot.

Brian Dennehy . . . . . . . . . . . . . . . . . . .Stourley Kraclite
- ••• 0:12—Buns, while taking off underwear and getting into bed with Chloe Webb. Kind of a long shot.

Chloe Webb. . . . . . . . . . . . . . . . . . . . . . Louisa Kracklite
- •• 0:01—Very brief right breast, making love on train with Brian Dennehy. Brief side view of right breast sitting up and putting camisole top on.
- • 0:56—Brief buns in room with Lambert Wilson.
- • 1:07—Brief buns, lying in bed with Wilson.
- 1:27—Breasts B&W photos of a pregnant woman. Supposedly her, but probably not.

Lambert Wilson . . . . . . . . . . . . . . . . Caspasian Speckler
- •• 0:56—Buns, several time in room with Chloe Webb while Brian Dennehy watches through keyhole.
- • 1:04—Upper half of buns, while lying in bed with Webb. Long shot.

### Beretta's Island (1993)

Jo Champa. . . . . . . . . . . . . . . . . . . . . . . . . . . Celeste
Elizabeth Kaitan . . . . . . . . . . . . . . . . . . . . . . . .Linda
- •• 1:33—Breasts, while playing with Franco Columbu in the ocean at the end of the film, during the end credits and after.

Arnold Schwarzenegger . . . . . . . . . . . . . . . . . . Himself

### The Berlin Affair (1985; Italian/German)

Gudrun Landgrebe. . . . . . . . . . . Louise Von Hollendorf
- • 0:23—Very brief inner half of left breast, twice, while making out with Mio.

### Best Friends (1982)

Goldie Hawn . . . . . . . . . . . . . . . . . . . Paula McCullen
- • 0:18—Very, very brief side view of right breast getting into the shower with Burt Reynolds.
- • 1:14—Upper half of left breast in the shower, twice.

Burt Reynolds. . . . . . . . . . . . . . . . . . . . . Richard Babson

### The Best Little Whorehouse in Texas (1982)

Dom DeLuise . . . . . . . . . . . . . . . . . . . . . . . . . .Melvin
Annie Gaybis . . . . . . . . . Uncredited Chicken Ranch Girl
- • 1:12—Brief breasts, twice, smoking a joint in bed with a football player when Dom DeLuise busts in with his news crew.

Sandy Johnson . . . . . . . . . . . . . . . . . Chicken Ranch Girl
Burt Reynolds. . . . . . . . . . . . . . . . . . . . . . . . . .Ed Earl
Terri Treas . . . . . . . . . . . . . . . . . . . . Chicken Ranch Girl
- 1:12—Very brief, most of right breast, while wearing cowboy hat and garter belt, straddling a football player when Dom DeLuise bursts in with his video crew.

Arnetia Walker . . . . . . . . . . . . . . . . . . . . . . . .Dogette
Victoria Wells . . . . . . . . . . . . . . . . . . . . . . . Washing Girl

## The Best of Sex and Violence (1981)

Elvira . . . . . . . . . . . . . . . . . . . . . . . . . . . . . Katya
- •• 0:40—Brief breasts dancing on stage in scene from *Working Girls.*

Vanity . . . . . . . . . . . . . . . . . . . . . . . . . . . . . Tanya
- • 0:24—Buns and breasts in various scenes from *Tanya's Island.*

Angela Aames . . . . . . . . . . . . . . . . . . . . Little Bo Peep
- • 0:18—Brief breasts in scene from *Fairytales.*
- • 0:20—Brief right breast in scene from *Fairytales.*

Phyllis Davis . . . . . . . . . . . . . . . . . . . . . . . . Sugar/Joy
- •• 0:56—Breasts after bath and in bed in scenes from *Sweet Sugar.*
- ••• 0:59—Breasts and buns walking out of lake in scene from *Terminal Island.*

Uschi Digard . . . . . . . . . . . . . . . . . Truck Stop Woman
- • 0:47—Breasts getting chased by policeman in parking lot in scene from *Truck Stop Women.*

Laura Gemser . . . . . . . . . . . . . . . . . . . . . . .Emanuelle
- • 0:23—Side of left breast while getting clothes taken off by a guy. Long shot. Scene from *Emanuelle Around the World.*

Claudia Jennings . . . . . . . . . . . . . . . . . . . . . . . Rose
- •• 0:46—Breasts taking off her blouse in scene from *Truck Stop Women.*

Laura Jane Leary . . . . . . . . . . . . . . . . . . . . Girl Victim
- • 0:00—Getting clothes ripped off, then in bra and panties, then breasts.

Joan Prather . . . . . . . . . . . . . . . . . . . . . . . . Herself
- •• 0:38—Breasts getting her breasts squeezed by an attacker. Dark.

Cheryl Smith . . . . . . . . . . . . . . . . . . . . . . .Cinderella
- • 0:14—Breasts taking a bath in scene from *Cinderella.*

Edy Williams . . . . . . . . . . . . . . . . . . . . . . . . Herself
- •• 0:46—Breasts in various scenes from *Dr. Minx.*

## Betrayal of the Dove (1992)

Bobbi Brown . . . . . . . . . . . . . . . . . . . . . . . . Dancer
- •• 1:03—Buns in outfit, then breasts while dancing on stage in club.

Kelly Le Brock . . . . . . . . . . . . . . . . . . . . . . . . Una

Helen Slater . . . . . . . . . . . . . . . . . . . . . . . . .Ellie
- • 0:29—Brief tip of right breast while in bed with Billy Zane.
- •• 0:30—Brief right breast, while in pool with Zane. Brief breasts in bed, then left breast.
- ••• 0:31—Very, very brief breasts, then more breasts while in bed with Zane.

Billy Zane . . . . . . . . . . . . . . . . . . . . . . .Dr. Jesse Peter

## The Betsy (1978)

Jane Alexander . . . . . . . . . . . . . . . . . . . Alicia Hardeman

Kathleen Beller . . . . . . . . . . . . . . . . . . . Betsy Hardeman
- ••• 0:12—Nude getting into swimming pool.
- •• 1:14—Breasts lying under Tommy Lee Jones.

Lesley-Anne Down . . . . . . . . . . . . . . Lady Bobby Ayres
- • 0:38—Brief left breast and upper half of buns, while with Tommy Lee Jones.
- • 0:57—Very brief left breast in bed with Jones.

Tommy Lee Jones . . . . . . . . . . . . . . . . . .Angelo Perino

Katharine Ross . . . . . . . . . . . . . . . . . . . . Sally Hardeman
- • 1:02—Very brief upper half of left breast, while breast feeding baby in front of Laurence Olivier.

## Betty Blue (1986; French)

Jean-Hughes Anglade . . . . . . . . . . . . . . . . . . . . . . Zorg
- ••• 0:09—Frontal nudity.
- •• 1:03—Nude trying to sleep in living room.
- •• 1:39—Frontal nudity walking to the bathroom.
- •• 1:45—Frontal nudity talking on the telephone.

Béatrice Dalle . . . . . . . . . . . . . . . . . . . . . . . . . . Betty
- ••• 0:01—Breasts making love in bed with Zorg. Long sequence.
- ••• 0:30—Nude on bed having sex with boyfriend.
- ••• 1:03—Nude trying to sleep in living room.
- ••• 1:21—Breasts in white tap pants in hallway.
- ••• 1:29—Breasts lying down with Zorg.
- ••• 1:39—Breasts sitting on bathtub crying & talking.

## Between the Lines (1977)

Allison Argo . . . . . . . . . . . . . . . . . . . . . . . . . . Dancer
- • 0:28—Breasts dancing on stage.

Lindsay Crouse . . . . . . . . . . . . . . . . . . . . . . .Abbie
- • 0:52—Brief side view of right breast, lying in bed with John Heard.

Jeff Goldblum . . . . . . . . . . . . . . . . . . . . . . . . . .Max

John Heard . . . . . . . . . . . . . . . . . . . . . . . . . . .Harry
- •• 1:17—Buns, while putting his pants on.

Marilu Henner . . . . . . . . . . . . . . . . . . . . . . .Danielle
- 0:27—Dancing on stage wearing pasties.

Bruno Kirby . . . . . . . . . . . . . . . . . . . . . . . . . .David

Gwen Welles . . . . . . . . . . . . . . . . . . . . . . . . .Laura
- •• 0:32—Buns and breasts drying off with a towel in front of a mirror.

## Beverly Hills Cop II (1987)

Rebecca Ferratti . . . . . . . . . . . . . . . . . .Playboy Playmate

Allen Garfield . . . . . . . . . . . . . . . . . . . . Harold Lutz

Kymberly Herrin . . . . . . . . . . . . . . . . . .Playboy Playmate

Venice Kong . . . . . . . . . . . . . . . . . . . . .Playboy Playmate

Luann Lee . . . . . . . . . . . . . . . . . . . . . .Playboy Playmate

Carrie Leigh . . . . . . . . . . . . . . . . . . . . . . . . . .Herself

Tom "Tiny" Lister, Jr. . . . . . . . . . . . . . . . . . . . . . Orvis

Brigitte Nielsen . . . . . . . . . . . . . . . . . . . . . Karla Fry

Kym Paige . . . . . . . . . . . . . . . . . . . . . .Playboy Playmate

Jürgen Prochnow . . . . . . . . . . . . . . . . Maxwell Dent

Ola Ray . . . . . . . . . . . . . . . . . . . . . . .Playboy Playmate

Judge Reinhold . . . . . . . . . . . .Detective Billy Rosewood

Teal Roberts . . . . . . . . . . . . . . . . . . . . . . . . Stripper
- •• 0:45—Breasts and buns, wearing G-string at the 385 North Club.

Peggy Sands . . . . . . . . . . . . . . . . . . . . . . Stripper
- • 0:48—Very brief breasts, dancing at the 385 North Club.

Alana Soares . . . . . . . . . . . . . . . . . . . .Playboy Playmate

Kari Whitman . . . . . . . . . . . . . . . . . . . . .Playboy Model

## Beverly Hills Vamp (1989)

Michelle Bauer . . . . . . . . . . . . . . . . . . . . . . . . Kristina
- • 0:12—Buns and brief side view of right breast in bed biting a guy.

0:33—In red slip, with Kyle.
- •• 0:38—Breasts trying to get into Kyle's pants.
  1:09—In black lingerie attacking Russell in bed with Debra Lamb and Jillian Kesner.
  1:19—In black lingerie enticing Mr. Pendleton into bedroom.
  1:22—In black lingerie, getting killed as a vampire by Kyle.

Britt Ekland . . . . . . . . . . . . . . . . . . . Madam Cassandra
Greta Gibson. . . . . . . . . . . . . . . . . Screen Test Starlet
- •• 0:53—Breasts and brief buns in G-string lying on Mr. Pendleton's desk.

Jillian Kesner . . . . . . . . . . . . . . . . . . . . . . . . .Claudia
0:06—In white lingerie riding a guy like a horse.
0:33—In white slip with Brock.
0:42—Almost breasts in bed with Brock. Too dark to see anything.
1:09—In white nightgown attacking Russell in bed with Debra Lamb and Michelle Bauer.
1:17—In white nightgown, getting killed as a vampire by Kyle.

Debra Lamb . . . . . . . . . . . . . . . . . . . . . . . . . .Jessica
0:33—In black slip, with Russell.
- ••• 0:36—Breasts and buns in red G-string posing for Russell while he photographs her.
- ••• 0:41—More breasts posing on bed.
  1:09—In white nightgown attacking Russell in bed with Michelle Bauer and Jillian Kesner.
  1:19—In white nightgown, getting killed as a vampire by Kyle.

Dawn Wildsmith . . . . . . . . . . . . . .Sherry Santa Monica

## Beyond Erotica (1979)

Andrea Rau . . . . . . . . . . . . . . . . . . . . . . . . . . . . Lola
- • 0:26—Breasts, undressing in her bedroom.
- •• 0:30—Nude, undressing, then lying in bed, then trying on bunny costume.
- • 0:47—Left breast, while lying on the floor.
- • 0:56—Brief buns, running around in her cell.
- • 0:57—Brief nude, behind wall with holes in it.
- • 0:59—Left breast, seen though hole in the wall.
- •• 1:10—Breasts in her bedroom.
- • 1:23—Left breast, in flashback to 0:47 scene.

## Beyond Obsession (1982)

Tom Berenger. . . . . . . . . . . . . . . . . . . . . .Matthew
Eleonora Giorgi . . . . . . . . . . . . . . . . . . . . . . . . .Nina
- •• 0:01—Breasts, taking off her top and getting into the shower with Tom Berenger.
- •• 0:59—Right breast in bed with Marcello Mastroianni, brief right breast after.

## Beyond the Door II (1977; Italian)

Daria Nicolodi. . . . . . . . . . . . . . . . . . . . . . . . . .Dora
- • 0:30—Buns, in the shower.
- • 0:47—Brief left breast in gaping nightgown, sitting up in bed.

John Steiner . . . . . . . . . . . . . . . . . . . . . . . . . Bruno
- • 0:12—Brief buns, while making love with Dora on the sofa. Dark.

## Beyond the Door III (1989; Yugoslavian)

Mary Kohnert. . . . . . . . . . . . . . . . . . . . . . . . . . Beverly
- •• 0:03—Breasts taking a shower.

## Beyond the Law (1992; Made for Cable Movie)

Linda Fiorentino . . . . . . . . . . . . . . . . . . . . . . . . Renee
- ••• 0:52—Breasts while making love with Charlie Sheen. Brief buns in T-back panties.

Michael Madsen. . . . . . . . . . . . . . . . . . . . . . .Blood
Rip Torn . . . . . . . . . . . . . . . . . . . . . . . . . . . .Prescott

## Beyond the Limit (1983)

Elpidia Carrillo . . . . . . . . . . . . . . . . . . . . . . . . Clara
- •• 0:31—Breasts making love with Richard Gere. Long scene.
- •• 1:08—Breasts talking to Gere. Another long scene.

Richard Gere . . . . . . . . . . . . . . . . . . . . .Dr. Eduardo Plarr
- • 0:21—Buns.

## Big Bad Mama (1974)

Angie Dickinson . . . . . . . . . . . . . . . . . Wilma McClatchie
- • 0:38—Buns, getting into bed with Tom Skerritt. Brief right breast, while on top of him.
- ••• 0:48—Breasts in bed with William Shatner.
- • 1:00—Very brief breasts, pulling the sheets up while lying in bed with Shatner.
- ••• 1:18—Breasts and brief full frontal nudity putting a shawl and then a dress on.

Sally Kirkland . . . . . . . . . . . . . . . . . . . . Barney's Woman
- •• 0:13—Breasts and buns waiting for Barney then throwing shoe at Billy Jean.
- • 1:23—Brief breasts, covering herself up scene from 0:13 during end credits.

Robin Lee. . . . . . . . . . . . . . . . . . . . . . . Polly McClatchie
- • 0:08—Brief left breast in gaping dress when cops try to pull her car over.
- • 0:22—In see-through dress on stage with her sister and a stripper.
- • 0:32—Brief breasts running around the bedroom chasing her sister.
- • 0:52—Buns, taking off her nightgown and getting into bed with Tom Skerritt.

Joan Prather . . . . . . . . . . . . . . . . . . . . . . . . Jane Kingston
- •• 1:15—Breasts and buns in the bathroom with Tom Skerritt.

Susan Sennet . . . . . . . . . . . . . . . . . . . . . . . Billy Jean
- • 0:50—Breasts and buns getting onto bed with Tom Skerritt.
- •• 0:51—Breasts and buns, getting out of bed with Skerritt.
- • 0:52—Brief buns, getting back into bed with Skerritt along with Polly.

Tom Skerritt. . . . . . . . . . . . . . . . . . . . . . . . . Fred Diller
- • 1:18—Brief buns, while lying down with Angie Dickinson in barn.

## Big Bad Mama II (1987)

Danielle Brisebois . . . . . . . . . . . . . Billy Jean McClatchie
- ••• 0:12—Breasts with Julie McCullough playing in a pond underneath a waterfall.

0:36—In a white slip standing at the door talking to McCullough, then talking to Angie Dickinson.

Robert Culp........................Daryl Pearson

Angie Dickinson ...............Wilma McClatchie
- 0:48—Very brief full frontal nudity putting on her shawl scene from *Big Bad Mama* superimposed over a car chase scene.
- 0:52—Breasts and brief buns (probably a body double) in bed with Robert Culp. You don't see her face with the body.

Kelli Maroney...................Willie McClatchie

Julie McCullough................Polly McClatchie
- 0:12—Breasts with Danielle Brisebois playing in a pond underneath a waterfall.
- 0:36—In lingerie, then breasts sitting on Jordan who is tied up in bed.

Linda Shayne........................Bank Teller

## The Big Bet (1985)

Stephanie Blake.....................Mrs. Roberts
- 0:04—Breasts sitting on bed, then making love with Chris.
- 0:37—Nude on bed with Chris. Shot at fast speed, he runs between bedrooms.
- 0:59—Full frontal nudity in bed again. Shot at fast speed.

Elizabeth Cochrell ...............Sister in Stag Film
- 1:05—Breasts and buns, undressing and getting into bathtub in a video tape that Chris is watching.
- 1:08—Breasts again on video tape, when Chris watches it on TV at home.

Kim Evenson...........................Beth
- 0:36—Right breast, sitting on couch with Chris.
- 0:45—Brief breasts, twice, taking off swimsuit top.
- 0:54—Brief breasts three times in elevator when Chris pulls her sweater up.
- 1:06—Nude when Chris fantasizes about her being in the video tape that he's watching. Long shot.
- 1:19—In white bra and panties, then nude while undressing for Chris.

Monique Gabrielle ..........Fantasy Girl in Elevator
- 0:51—In purple bra, then eventually nude in elevator with Chris.

Sylvia Kristel .........................Michelle
- 0:07—Left breast in open nightgown while Chris tries to fix her sink.
- 0:20—Breasts dressing while Chris watches through binoculars.
- 0:28—Breasts undressing while Chris watches through binoculars.
- 0:40—Breasts getting out of the shower and drying herself off.
- 1:00—Breasts getting into bed while Chris watches through binoculars.
- 1:13—Breasts in bedroom with Chris, then making love.

Sheila Lussier...............................n.a.

Lance Sloane.............................Chris
- 0:38—Buns, while taking off robe and getting into bed with Angela Roberts after visiting Mrs. Roberts.

- 0:52—Buns, while on elevator floor with Monique Gabrielle during his daydream.
- 1:07—Buns, while getting into tub with Kimberly Evenson during video tape fantasy. Long shot.

Jill Terashita ...............................Koko

## The Big Bird Cage (1972)

Teda Bracci ...........................Bull Jones
- 0:15—Breasts in front of the guard, Rocco.
- 0:51—Very brief right breast, then left breast during fight with Pam Grier. Brief left breast standing up in rice paddy.

Anitra Ford............................Terry
- 0:15—Left breast and buns taking shower. Brief lower frontal nudity after putting shirt on when leaving.
- 0:19—Brief lower frontal nudity turing around.
- 0:44—Brief left breast during gang rape.
- 1:14—Brief left breast in gaping dress. Dark.

Pam Grier.............................Blossom

Candice Roman .........................Carla
- 0:16—Buns, while in the shower.

## The Big Chill (1983)

Tom Berenger ...........................Sam

Glenn Close ............................Sara
- 0:27—Breasts sitting down in the shower crying.

Jeff Goldblum.........................Michael

William Hurt............................Nick

Kevin Kline ............................Harold

Mary Kay Place..........................Meg

Meg Tilly .............................Chloé

JoBeth Williams .........................Karen

## The Big Doll House (1971)

Roberta Collins.........................Alcott
- 0:33—Breasts in shower. Seen through blurry window by prison worker, Fred. Blurry, but nice.
- 0:34—Brief left breast, while opening her blouse for Fred.

Pam Grier.............................Grear
- 0:28—Very brief most of right breast rolling over in bed.
- 0:32—Breasts getting her back washed by Collier. Arms in the way a little bit.
- 0:44—Left breast covered with mud sticking out of her top after wrestling with Alcott.

Brooke Mills............................Harrad
- 0:28—Side of right breast, while lying in bed before rolling over.

Christiane Schmidtmer................Miss Dietrich

Pat Woodell............................Bodine
- 0:27—Brief breasts hung by wrists and whipped by a guard. Hair covers most of her breasts.

## The Big Easy (1987)

Ellen Barkin .........................Anne Osborne

0:21—White panties in lifted up dress in bed with Dennis Quaid.

0:32—Brief buns jumping up in kitchen after pinching a guy who she thinks is Quaid.

Dennis Quaid . . . . . . . . . . . . . . . . . . . . . . Remy McSwain
- • 0:24—Brief buns when Ellen Barkin pulls his under-wear down in bed.
- ••• 0:51—Buns, while putting underwear on after get-ting out of bed.

### The Big Hurt (1987; Australian)
Nikki Lane . . . . . . . . . . . . . . . . . . . . . . . . Tank Girl #1
- • 1:26—Possible full frontal nudity standing in water filled tube. Can't recognize her because wearing a swim mask and breathing apparatus.

### The Big Man (1991; British)
*a.k.a. Crossing the Line*
Julie Graham . . . . . . . . . . . . . . . . . . . . . . . . Melanie
- •• 1:09—Breasts when Liam Neeson undresses her and starts to make love with her.
Liam Neeson . . . . . . . . . . . . . . . . . . . . . Danny Scoular

### The Big Sleep (1978; British)
Candy Clark . . . . . . . . . . . . . . . . . . Camilla Sternwood
- ••• 0:18—Breasts, sitting in a chair when Robert Mitchum comes in after a guy is murdered.
- • 0:30—Brief breasts in a photograph that Mitchum is looking at.
  0:38—Breasts in the photos again. Out of focus.
- •• 0:39—Breasts sitting in chair during recollection of the murder.
- •• 1:03—Very brief full frontal nudity in bed, throwing open the sheets for Mitchum.
  1:05—Very, very brief buns, getting up out of bed.
Joan Collins . . . . . . . . . . . . . . . . . . . . . . . Agnes Lozelle
Edward Fox . . . . . . . . . . . . . . . . . . . . . . . . . Joe Brody
Sarah Miles . . . . . . . . . . . . . . . . Charlotte Sternwood
Diana Quick . . . . . . . . . . . . . . . . . . . . . . Mona Grant
Oliver Reed . . . . . . . . . . . . . . . . . . . . . . Eddie Mars
Dudley Sutton . . . . . . . . . . . . . . . . . . . . . . . Lanny

### The Big Town (1987)
Suzy Amis . . . . . . . . . . . . . . . . . . . . . Aggie Donaldson
Lolita Davidovich . . . . . . . . . . . . . . Black Lace Stripper
Bruce Dern . . . . . . . . . . . . . . . . . . . . . . Mr. Edwards
Lee Grant . . . . . . . . . . . . . . . . . . Ferguson Edwards
Tommy Lee Jones . . . . . . . . . . . . . . . . . . . George Cole
Diane Lane . . . . . . . . . . . . . . . . . . . . . . . Lorry Dane
  0:51—Doing a strip routine in the club wearing a G-string and pasties while Matt Dillon watches.
- ••• 1:17—Breasts making love on bed with Dillon in ho-tel room.
  1:27—Brief left breast wearing pasties walking into dressing room while Dillon plays craps.
Tom Skerritt . . . . . . . . . . . . . . . . . . . . . Phil Carpenter

### The Bikini Carwash Company (1992)
(Unrated version reviewed.)
Suzanne Ager . . . . . . . . . . . . . . . . . . . . . . . . . Foxy
- • 0:59—Buns in G-string, doing strip routine.
Rikki Brando . . . . . . . . . . . . . . . . . . . . . . . . . . Amy
- • 0:15—Brief breasts when Stanley steals her bikini top.
- • 0:30—Brief breasts during water fight.

- • 0:31—Brief breasts at car wash.
- • 0:43—Brief right breast, while making love with Donovan.
- •• 0:44—Buns and breasts, making love with Donovan.
- •• 0:59—Breasts, making out in car with Donovan.
- ••• 1:00—More breasts in car with Donovan.
- • 1:02—Brief breasts in car wash.
- •• 1:12—Breasts posing for photos.
Sara Suzanne Brown . . . . . . . . . . . . . . . . . . . . . Sunny
- • 0:15—Brief breasts when Stanley steals her bikini top.
- • 0:25—Breasts, washing windshield and side win-dow.
- ••• 0:26—More breasts while window washing.
- •• 0:30—Breasts during water fight.
- •• 0:31—Breasts at car wash.
- • 0:35—Breasts running after a guy who stole her bi-kini top.
- ••• 0:46—Breasts and buns in G-string, hand washing a customer with Rita.
- ••• 0:47—Breasts and buns, dancing inside car wash.
- •• 0:53—Breasts outside at car wash.
- ••• 1:02—Nude, soaped up in car wash with Melissa and Rita.
- ••• 1:12—Breasts, posing for photos.
- ••• 1:15—Breasts when Stanley takes her top off.
Neriah Davis . . . . . . . . . . . . . . . . . . . . . . . . . . . Rita
- ••• 0:15—Breasts taking off her bikini top so Stanley can "catch some fish" with it.
- ••• 0:18—Breasts and buns, making love with Big Bruce.
- • 0:43—Breasts and buns, making love with Big Bruce. (same as 0:18)
- ••• 0:45—Brief left breast, getting dressed. Then buns, after forgetting to put on her bikini bottoms.
- ••• 0:46—Breasts and buns in G-string, hand washing a customer with Sunny.
- ••• 0:47—Buns, bending over while wearing a cowboy outfit.
- ••• 0:48—Breasts and buns, dancing inside car wash with Sunny and Melissa.
- ••• 1:02—Nude, soaped up in car wash with Sunny and Melissa.
- •• 1:11—Buns, posing while wearing cowboy outfit.
- ••• 1:13—Breasts and buns.
Kristie Ducati . . . . . . . . . . . . . . . . . . . . . . . . Melissa
- • 0:13—Buns in G-string, while at the beach.
- ••• 0:20—Breasts, taking off her bikini top in shack with Jack.
- •• 0:26—Nude, changing clothes in car wash.
- •• 0:30—Breasts during water fight.
- • 0:32—Brief breasts in Jack's fantasy.
- • 0:45—Brief left breast and buns, dressing.
- ••• 0:47—Breasts and buns, dancing inside car wash.
- ••• 1:02—Nude, soaped up in car wash with Rita and Sunny.
- ••• 1:07—Breasts and buns, making love in shack with Jack. Wow!
- ••• 1:12—Breasts, posing for photos.

Matthew Cary Dunn . . . . . . . . . . . . . . Donovan Drake
••• 0:44—Buns, while making love with Amy.
Jennifer Irwin. . . . . . . . . . . . . . . .Awesome Beach Girl
•• 0:00—Buns, on beach in a very small swimsuit.
••• 0:02—Brief right breast, turning over, then breasts
while yelling at Jack.
Eric Ryan . . . . . . . . . . . . . . . . . . . . . . . . . . . . Stanley
• 1:15—Buns, when Sunny yanks his short pants
down.
Scott Strohmyer . . . . . . . . . . . . . . . . . . . . Big Bruce
•• 0:18—Buns, while walking on beach with Rita.

### The Bikini Carwash Company II (1993)
(Unrated version reviewed.)
Melissa Barrick. . . . . . . . . . . . . . . . . . . . . . . . . Cyndi
••• 0:38—In black lingerie, then breasts during kitchen
commercial.
••• 0:42—Breasts and buns under black body stocking
in "Rock Me" music video number.
••• 0:46—In lingerie, then breasts during repairman
commercial.
• 0:52—Brief breasts, while making out on kitchen table.
• 1:28—Breasts during music video number at the
carwash.
Rikki Brando . . . . . . . . . . . . . . . . . . . . . . . . . . . Amy
••• 0:09—Breasts with the other three girls, celebrating
in office during music video number.
•• 1:09—Buns in lingerie, then breasts in dressing
room with Marshall.
Sara Suzanne Brown . . . . . . . . . . . . . . . . . . . .Sunny
••• 0:09—Breasts with the other three girls, celebrating
in office during music video number.
•• 0:16—Breasts at carwash during music video number. (Wearing yellow bikini bottoms.)
• 0:24—Buns in lingerie in offices of The Miracle Network with Rita.
• 0:27—Brief breasts, twice, while flashing her breasts
in office.
••• 1:16—In black lingerie, then breasts in office fantasy.
• 1:29—Breasts and buns in bikini bottoms during
music video number at the carwash.
Carrie Chambers . . . . . . . . . . . . . . . . . . . .Chairwoman
• 0:26—Brief back side of left breast in her office with
Derek.
Neriah Davis . . . . . . . . . . . . . . . . . . . . . . . . . . . .Rita
••• 0:09—Breasts with the other three girls, celebrating
in office during music video number.
••• 0:16—Breasts at carwash during music video number. (Wearing pink bikini bottoms.)
• 0:24—Buns in lingerie in offices of The Miracle Network with Sunny.
• 0:27—Brief breasts while flashing her breasts in office.
••• 0:35—Breasts and buns in studio when she's caught
without her clothes on.
• 1:15—Brief breasts and buns during clean up at the
studio.
•• 1:29—Breasts and buns in swimsuit during music
video number at the carwash.

Kristie Ducati . . . . . . . . . . . . . . . . . . . . . . . . . Melissa
•• 0:00—Breasts in back of limousine with a guy.
••• 0:09—Breasts with the other three girls, celebrating
in office during music video number.
•• 0:16—Breasts at carwash during music video number. (Wearing orange bikini bottoms.)
••• 1:20—Breasts and buns while making love with
Derek in the TV studio.
•• 1:29—Breasts and buns in bikini bottoms during
music video number at the carwash.
Beckie Mullen. . . . . . . . . . . . . . . . . . . . School Teacher

### Bikini Island (1991)
Richard Ardi . . . . . . . . . . . . . . . . . . . . .Tasha's Girlfriend
Holly Floria. . . . . . . . . . . . . . . . . . . . . . . . Annie Kelly
• 0:03—Buns in panties, then breasts in shower (seen
through plastic shower curtain). Don't see her face.
0:28—Buns in one piece white swimsuit at the
beach.
• 0:35—Buns in the shower. Don't see her face.
Cyndi Pass . . . . . . . . . . . . . . . . . . . . . . . . . . . . . Kari
• 0:47—Brief upper half of right breast, while chang-
ing swimsuit tops at the beach.
• 0:55—Side of left breast, while taking off her top on
bed with Jack.
0:59—Buns, in black bra and panties after Max disappears.
Shannon Stiles . . . . . . . . . . . . . . . . . . . . . . . . . Nikki
• 0:35—Breasts in bed with Jack taking off her top
while someone watches through keyhole.

### Bikini Summer (1991)
Rebekah Alfred. . . . . . . . . . . . . . . . . D.A. Rachel Green
•• 1:20—In bra, then breasts and buns in dressing
room, trying on swimsuit after everyone has left.
Melinda Armstrong . . . . . . . . . . . . . . . . . . . . . Cheryl
• 0:07—Very brief breasts and partial buns, in bathroom when Chet interrupts her.
0:25—Close-up of buns, bending over while wearing a swimsuit.
••• 0:35—Nude in swimming pool and talking to Burt.
Nice, long scene.
•• 0:49—Breasts and buns, trying on swimsuits, then
having a water fight with Shelley Michelle.
0:51—Buns, in swimsuit at the beach.
••• 1:17—Full frontal nudity in swimming pool flashback.
Michelle Grassnick . . . . . . . . . . . . . . . . . . . . . Debbie
Lori Jo Hendrix . . . . . . . . . . . . . . . . .Smart Girl on Beach
Jennifer Irwin . . . . . . . . . . . . . . . . . . . . . . . . . Mindy
Kelli Konop. . . . . . . . . . . . . . . . . . . . . . . . . . . . Rene
Shelley Michelle . . . . . . . . . . . . . . . . . . . . . . . . . Jazz
•• 0:33—Breasts and buns in the shower while Max
peeks through hole.
•• 0:49—Breasts and buns, trying on swimsuits, then
having a water fight with Cheryl.
Nicole Sassaman . . . . . . . . . . . . . . . . . . Band Member

## Bikini Summer 2 (1992)
Avalon Anders . . . . . . . . . . . . . . . . . . . . . . . . Clarice
- ••• 0:11—Breasts in sexy outfit, acting as a dominatrix with Harry in his office.
- •• 0:13—More breasts in Harry's office.
- • 0:33—Buns and brief left breast, teasing Harry.
- ••• 0:37—In black body stocking then breasts with Harry in his office.
- ••• 0:41—More breasts in white corset with Harry.

Melinda Armstrong . . . . . . . . . . . . . . . . . . . . . Venessa
- ••• 0:05—Breasts and buns, taking a shower.
- ••• 0:52—Breasts, taking off swimsuit top in bedroom. Breasts and buns, taking a shower.
- ••• 0:54—Breasts and buns in T-back panties, taking off robe and getting into bed, then sitting up to eat breakfast.

Carrie Bittner . . . . . . . . . . . . . . . . . . . . . . . . Sandra
- • 0:15—Buns in two piece swimsuit, while walking with Sandy.
- •• 0:38—Breasts (she's the blonde), taking off her T-shirt and jumping into the pool with Sandra.
- • 0:40—Very brief breasts, running past some guys.
- ••• 0:42—More breasts, while running around the backyard.
- ••• 0:44—More breasts and buns in swimsuits, while running around some more.

Jeff Conaway . . . . . . . . . . . . . . . . . . . . . . . . . . . Stu
Tracy Dali . . . . . . . . . . . . . . . . . . . . . . . . . . . . Anita
- • 0:49—Buns, in black lingerie after taking off her maid outfit in front of Harry.
- ••• 0:51—Breasts in back seat of limousine, while making love with Harry.
- • 0:55—Brief buns, while bending over in maid outfit.

Maureen Flaherty . . . . . . . . . . . . . . . . . . . . . Bridget
- •• 0:04—Breasts, waking up in bed in the morning with William.
- ••• 0:29—Breasts in bed with William.

Jessica Hahn . . . . . . . . . . . . . . . . . . . . . . . . . Marilyn
- • 0:03—In black bra in bed with Harry, then buns in black G-string, climbing on his back.

Tammy Marcel . . . . . . . . . . . . . . . . . . . . . . . . Sandy
- • 0:15—Buns in two piece swimsuit, while walking with Sandra.
- •• 0:38—Breasts (she's the brunette), taking off her T-shirt and jumping into the pool with Sandra.
- • 0:40—Very brief breasts, running past some guys.
- ••• 0:42—More breasts, while running around the backyard.
- ••• 0:44—More breasts and buns in swimsuits, while running around some more.

## Bilitis (1977; French)
Patti D'Arbanville . . . . . . . . . . . . . . . . . . . . . . . Bilitis
- ••• 0:25—Breasts copying Melissa undressing.
- •• 0:27—Breasts on tree.
- ••• 0:31—Full frontal nudity taking off swimsuit with Melissa.
- 0:36—Buns, cleaning herself in the bathroom.
- •• 0:59—Breasts and buns making love with Melissa.

Catherine Leprince . . . . . . . . . . . . . . . . . . . . . . Helene
- •• 0:13—Breasts taking off dress and getting into bed with Bilitis.

## Billy Bathgate (1991)
Steve Buscemi . . . . . . . . . . . . . . . . . . . . . . . . . Chet
Dustin Hoffman . . . . . . . . . . . . . . . . . Dutch Schultz
Moira Kelly . . . . . . . . . . . . . . . . . . . . . . . . . Rebecca
Nicole Kidman . . . . . . . . . . . . . . . . . . . . Drew Preston
- •• 0:42—Briefly nude, throwing off towel in front of a vanity with three mirrors.
- •• 0:52—Very brief full frontal nudity underwater. Brief full frontal nudity getting out of water and putting on dress.

Rachel York . . . . . . . . . . . . . . . . . Embassy Club Singer

## Bio-Hazard (1984)
Richard Hench . . . . . . . . . . . . . . . . . . . . . . . . . . n.a.
Angelique Pettyjohn . . . . . . . . . . . . . . . . . . . Lisa Martyn
- •• 0:30—Partial left breast on couch with Mitchell. In beige bra and panties talking on telephone, breast almost falling out of bra.
- ••• 1:15—Left breast, on couch with Mitchell, in out-take scene during the end credits.
- • 1:16—Upper half of left breast on couch again during a different take.

## Bird on a Wire (1990)
David Carradine . . . . . . . . . . . . . . . . . . . . . . Eugene
Mel Gibson . . . . . . . . . . . . . . . . . . . . . . . Rick Jarmin
- •• 1:01—Brief close-up of buns when Rachel operates on his gunshot wound. Don't see his face, but it is him.

Goldie Hawn . . . . . . . . . . . . . . . . . . . Marianne Graves
- • 0:31—Buns, in open dress climbing up ladder with Mel Gibson.
- • 1:18—Very brief top of right breast rolling over on top of Gibson in bed. Don't see her face.

Joan Severance . . . . . . . . . . . . . . . . . . . . Rachel Varnay

## Birdy (1985)
Sandra Beall . . . . . . . . . . . . . . . . . . . . . . . . . Shirley
Nicolas Cage . . . . . . . . . . . . . . . . . . Al Columbato
Bruno Kirby . . . . . . . . . . . . . . . . . . . . . . . . . . Renaldi
Matthew Modine . . . . . . . . . . . . . . . . . . . . . . . Birdy
- • 1:25—Buns, while squatting on the end of his bed, thinking he's a bird.
- • 1:29—Buns, while sitting on the bed. Longer shot.
- •• 1:33—Buns, while walking around naked in his bedroom.
- • 1:42—Buns, after waking up when Nicolas Cage comes into his bedroom.

Elizabeth Whitcraft . . . . . . . . . . . . . . . . . . . . . Rosanne
Maude Winchester . . . . . . . . . . . . . . . Doris Robinson
- •• 1:32—Breasts in car letting Mathew Modine feel her.

Karen Young . . . . . . . . . . . . . . . . . . . . Hannah Rourke

## The Bitch (1979; British)
Joan Collins . . . . . . . . . . . . . . . . . . . . Fontaine Khaled
- 0:01—In long slip getting out of bed and putting a bathrobe on.

• 0:03—Brief breasts in the shower with a guy.
•• 0:24—Brief breasts taking black corset off for the chauffeur in the bedroom, then buns getting out of bed and walking to the bathroom.
0:39—Making love in bed wearing a blue slip.
• 1:01—Left breast after making love in bed.
Sue Lloyd . . . . . . . . . . . . . . . . . . . . . . . Vanessa Grant
• 1:12—Side view of left breast and breasts in the swimming pool.
Pamela Salem . . . . . . . . . . . . . . . . . . . . . . . . . . Lynn
•• 0:46—Breasts in bed making love with a guy after playing at a casino.

## Bits and Pieces (1985)
Sandy Brooke . . . . . . . . . . . . . . . . . . . . . Mrs. Talbot
••• 1:03—Breasts in bathtub washing herself before the killer drowns her. Very brief right breast when struggling.
• 1:09—Brief breasts under water in bathtub, dead.
Tally Chanel . . . . . . . . . . . . . . . . . . . . . . . . . . Jennifer
0:58—In the woods with the killer, seen briefly in bra and panties before and after being killed.
Sheila Lussier . . . . . . . . . . . . . . . . . . . . . . . . . . Tanya
•• 0:07—In bra, tied down by Arthur, then brief breasts as he cuts her bra off before he kills her. Brief right breast several times with blood on her.

## Bitter Harvest (1993)
Adam Baldwin . . . . . . . . . . . . . . . . . . . Bobby Brody Jr.
Stephen Baldwin . . . . . . . . . . . . . . . . . . Travis Graham
• 0:30—Buns, when Jennifer Rubin pulls his underwear down. Don't see his face.
•• 0:31—Buns, while lying in bed.
Patsy Kensit . . . . . . . . . . . . . . . . . . . . . . . Jolene Leder
••• 0:40—In black bodysuit, then left breast while making love with Stephen Baldwin in bed. Breasts in bathtub.
• 0:41—Left breast, while lying in bathtub with Baldwin.
•• 0:49—Brief breasts in bed with Baldwin and Jennifer Rubin.
Jennifer Rubin . . . . . . . . . . . . . . . . . . . Kelly Ann Walsh
• 0:21—Brief breasts while wearing panties, trying on clothes in front of closet mirror.
•• 0:28—Brief breasts, then left breast while adjusting her robe so Stephen Baldwin can give her a massage.
••• 0:30—Breasts, after taking off robe, walking to bedroom with Baldwin and making love.
0:33—Very brief upper half of right breast when she adjusts her position while lying in bed.
M. Emmet Walsh . . . . . . . . . . . . . . . . Sheriff Bob Brody

## Bizarre (1986; Italian)
Florence Guerin . . . . . . . . . . . . . . . . . . . . . . . . Laurie
•• 0:03—Breasts on bed with Guido. Lower frontal nudity while he molests her with a pistol.
••• 0:18—Nude after taking off her clothes in hotel room with a guy. Nice.
••• 0:30—Full frontal nudity making love with Edward in the water.

• 0:34—Brief side of right breast, taking off robe in bathroom with Edward. (He's made himself up to look like a woman.)
••• 0:36—Breasts in white panties making love with Edward.
•• 0:40—Breasts and brief lower frontal nudity in Guido's office with him.
••• 0:45—Nude, playing outside with Edward, then making love with his toe.
•• 0:47—Breasts getting out of bed and putting a blouse on.
•• 0:49—Breasts with Edward when Guido comes in.
• 1:11—Breasts sitting in chair talking to Edward.
• 1:20—Lower frontal nudity, putting the phone down there.
• 1:28—Buns and lower frontal nudity on bed when Guido rips her clothes off and rapes her.
Robert Egon Spechtenhauser . . . . . . . . . . . . . . Edward
• 0:29—Partial buns, while taking a shower when Laurie peeks in at him.
• 0:31—Brief buns, while on top of Laurie in the water.
••• 0:36—Buns, while on bed with Laurie. (He's made up to look like a woman.)

## Black Belt (1992)
Sean'a Arthur . . . . . . . . . . . . . . . . . . . . . . . . Reporter
Deirdre Imershein . . . . . . . . . . . . . . . . . . . . . Shanna
••• 1:08—Breasts in bed, making love with Don "The Dragon" Wilson.
Mia M. Ruiz . . . . . . . . . . . . . . . . . . . . . . . . . . Hooker
••• 0:04—Breasts, while sitting on bed.
0:16—Breasts, while dead on bed, covered with blood.

## Black Emanuelle (1976)
Laura Gemser . . . . . . . . . . . . . . . . . . . . . . . Emanuelle
• 0:00—Brief breasts daydreaming on airplane.
• 0:19—Left breast in car kissing a guy at night.
•• 0:27—Breasts in shower with a guy.
••• 0:30—Full frontal nudity making love with a guy in bed.
••• 0:37—Breasts taking pictures with Karin Schubert.
•• 0:41—Full frontal nudity lying on bed dreaming about the day's events while masturbating, then full frontal nudity walking around.
•• 0:49—Breasts in studio with Johnny.
••• 0:52—Brief right breast making love on the side of the road. Full frontal nudity by the pool kissing Gloria.
•• 1:00—Nude, taking a shower, then answering the phone.
•• 1:04—Breasts on boat after almost drowning.
•• 1:08—Full frontal nudity dancing with African tribe, then making love with the leader.
•• 1:14—Full frontal nudity taking off clothes by waterfall with Johnny.
•• 1:23—Breasts making love with the field hockey team on a train.
Karin Schubert . . . . . . . . . . . . . . . . . . . . Anne Danielli
• 0:06—Brief breasts adjusting a guy's tie.

- ••• 0:14—Breasts making love in gas station with the gas station attendant.
- ••• 0:37—Nude, running in the jungle while Laura Gemser takes pictures of her.
- • 0:40—Breasts, kissing Gemser.
- • 0:44—Right breast, making love with Johnny in bed.

### Black Gunn (1972)

Jeannie Bell . . . . . . . . . . . . . . . . . . . . . . . . . . . . . Lisa
Timothy Brown . . . . . . . . . . . . . . . . . . . . . . . . . Larry
Bernie Casey . . . . . . . . . . . . . . . . . . . . . . . . . . . . Seth
Luciana Paluzzi . . . . . . . . . . . . . . . . . . . . . . . . . . Toni
Brenda Sykes . . . . . . . . . . . . . . . . . . . . . . . . . . Judith
- • 0:45—Brief side view of right breast, while getting out of bed with Jim Brown.

Kate Woodville . . . . . . . . . . . . . . . . . . . . . . . . Louella

### Black Ice (1992; U.S./Canadian)

Michael Nouri . . . . . . . . . . . . . . . . . . . . . . . . Ben Shorr
Arne Olsen . . . . . . . . . . . . . . . . . . . . . . . . . Eric Weaver
- •• 0:10—Buns, on top of Joanna Pacula's body double, while making love on bed.

Joanna Pacula . . . . . . . . . . . . . . . . . . . . . . . . . Vanessa

### Black Moon Rising (1986)

Nick Cassavetes . . . . . . . . . . . . . . . . . . . . . . . . . . Luis
Linda Hamilton . . . . . . . . . . . . . . . . . . . . . . . . . . Nina
- • 0:50—Brief left breast, while making love in bed with Tommy Lee Jones.

Tommy Lee Jones . . . . . . . . . . . . . . . . . . . . . . . Quint
Lisa London . . . . . . . . . . . . . . . . . . . . . . . . . Redhead

### Black Rainbow (1989; British)

Rosanna Arquette . . . . . . . . . . . . . . . . . . Martha Travis
0:48—In black bra, panties, garter belt and stockings in while talking to Tom Hulce.
- ••• 0:50—Breasts in bed with Hulce, then walking to bathroom.

### Black Robe (1991; Canadian/Australian)

Lothaire Bluteau . . . . . . . . . . . . . . . . . Father Laforgue
- • 0:18—Brief side view of buns, while hanging his rear end over the side of the canoe.
- • 1:04—Buns, while standing in Iroquois hut.

Raoul Trujillo . . . . . . . . . . . . . . . . . . . . . . . . Kiotseaton
Aden Young . . . . . . . . . . . . . . . . . . . . . . . . . . . Daniel
- • 0:29—Brief buns, while making love with Annuka in the woods at night.
- •• 1:04—Buns, while standing in Iroquois hut.

### Black Venus (1983)

José Antonio Ceinos . . . . . . . . . . . . . . . . . . . Armand
- • 0:14—Buns, while making love with Venus in bed.

Monique Gabrielle . . . . . . . . . . . . . . . . . . . . . . Ingrid
- ••• 0:03—Nude in Sailor Room at the bordello.
- ••• 1:01—Breasts and buns, taking off clothes for Madame Lilli's customers.

Florence Guerin . . . . . . . . . . . . . . . . . . . . . . . . Louise
- •• 0:45—Nude talking, then making love with Venus in bed.
- ••• 1:16—Nude frolicking on the beach with Venus.

- ••• 1:18—Nude in bedroom getting out of wet clothes with Venus.
- • 1:21—Buns in bed with Jacques and Venus.

Josephine Jaqueline Jones . . . . . . . . . . . . . . . . . . Venus
- •• 0:05—Breasts in Jungle Room.
- ••• 0:11—Nude, in bedroom, posing for Armand while he sketches.
- • 0:14—Breasts and buns making love with Armand in bed.
- •• 0:17—Nude, posing for Armand while he models in clay, then on the bed, kissing him.
- • 0:21—Brief nude getting dressed.
- ••• 0:38—Nude, making love in bed with Karin Schubert.
  0:45—Nude, talking and then making love in bed with Louise.
- •• 0:50—Breasts when Pierre brings everybody in to see her.
- •• 0:57—Breasts in silhouette while Armand fantasizes about his statue coming to life.
- ••• 1:04—Nude.
- ••• 1:07—Nude with the two diplomats on the bed.
- ••• 1:16—Nude frolicking on the beach with Louise.
- ••• 1:18—Breasts in bedroom getting out of wet clothes with Louise.
- •• 1:21—Breasts in bed with Jacques.
- •• 1:24—Full frontal nudity getting out of bed.

Karin Schubert . . . . . . . . . . . . . . . . . . . . . . . . . . Marie
- •• 0:38—Nude in bed with Venus, making love.

### Black Widow (1987)

Rutanya Alda . . . . . . . . . . . . . . . . . . . . . . . . . . . Irene
Sami Frey . . . . . . . . . . . . . . . . . . . . . . . . . . . . . . Paul
- •• 1:18—Buns, while walking into swimming pool.

Dennis Hopper . . . . . . . . . . . . . . . . . . . . . . . . . . . Ben
Terry O'Quinn . . . . . . . . . . . . . . . . . . . . . . . . . . Bruce
Theresa Russell . . . . . . . . . . . . . . . . . . . . . . Catherine
- • 0:28—Briefly nude, making love in cabin.
- •• 1:18—Nude in pool with Paul.

Debra Winger . . . . . . . . . . . . . . . . . . . . . . . Alexandra

### The Black Windmill (1974; British)

Delphine Seyrig . . . . . . . . . . . . . . . . . . . . Ceil Burrows
- •• 0:34—Right breast and buns, undressing and getting into bed to pose for a photo taken by John Vernon.

### Blackout (1989)

Michael Keyes Hall . . . . . . . . . . . . . . . . . . . Alan Boyle
- • 1:19—Buns and balls viewed from the rear while stabbing Richard in bed.

Carol Lynley . . . . . . . . . . . . . . . . . . . . . . . . Esther Boyle
- •• 1:01—Brief breasts leaning against the wall while someone touches her left breast.

Gail O'Grady . . . . . . . . . . . . . . . . . . . . . . Caroline Boyle

### Blackwater (1989)

Denise Crosby . . . . . . . . . . . . . . . . . . . . . . . . . . Sally
Stacey Dash . . . . . . . . . . . . . . . . . . . . . . . . . . Minnie
- • 0:37—Upper half of buns and back side of right breast, while walking to and sitting on edge of bed.

- 0:44—Very brief side view of left breast, while propping herself up while lying on couch.
- 0:59—Brief right breast, while in bed on top of Julian Sands.

Brian McNamara........................ Hewitt
Julian Sands......................... Wolfgang
- •• 1:00—Buns, while standing and talking to Stacey Dash.

### Blade Runner (1982)

Joanna Cassidy.......................... Zhora
- •• 0:54—Breasts getting dressed after taking a shower while talking with Harrison Ford.

Daryl Hannah............................. Pris
Rutger Hauer......................... Roy Batty
Edward James Olmos ..................... Gaff
M. Emmet Walsh.........................Bryant
Sean Young............................Rachael

### Blame It on Rio (1984)

Michelle Johnson..................Jennifer Lyons
- •• 0:19—Breasts on the beach greeting Michael Caine and Joseph Bologna with Demi Moore, then brief breasts in the ocean.
- 0:26—Breasts taking her clothes off for Caine on the beach. Dark, hard to see.
- •• 0:27—Breasts seducing Caine. Dark, hard to see.
- ••• 0:56—Full frontal nudity taking off robe and sitting on bed to take a Polaroid picture of herself.
- 0:57—Very brief breasts in the Polaroid photo showing it to Caine.
- 1:02—Brief breasts taking off her top in front of Caine while her dad rests on the sofa.

Demi Moore ........................ Nicole Hollis
- 0:19—Very brief right breast turning around to greet Michael Caine and Joseph Bologna.

### Blaze (1989)

Lolita Davidovich..................... Blaze Starr
- 0:09—In bra doing her first strip routine. Very brief side views of left breast under hat.
- 0:15—Strip tease routine in front of Paul Newman. At the end, she takes off bra to reveal pasties.
- 0:42—In black bra and panties with Newman.
- •• 0:48—Breasts on top of Newman, then side view of left breast.

Paul Newman .................. Gov. Earl K. Long

### Blind Date (1984)

a.k.a. Deadly Seduction
(Not the same 1987 Blind Date with Bruce Willis.)
Kirstie Alley ........................ Claire Parker
- 0:12—Brief breasts making love in bed with Joseph Bottoms. Dark, hard to see anything.

Joseph Bottoms.................. Jonathon Ratcliffe
Lana Clarkson ......................... Rachel
- 0:52—Brief breasts rolling over in bed when Joseph Bottoms sneaks in. Dark, hard to see.
- 1:11—In two piece swimsuit during a modeling assignment.
- 1:18—In two piece swimsuit by pool.

James Daughton ........................David
Keir Dullea ......................... Dr. Steiger
Valeria Golino.................... Girl in Bikini
Marina Sirtis........................ Hooker
- ••• 0:21—Breasts walking to and lying in bed just before taxi driver kills her.

### Blind Justice (1994; Made for Cable Movie)

Adam Baldwin ..................... Sgt. Hastings
Elisabeth Shue ........................Caroline
- 0:36—Very, very brief right breast in gaping dress after getting up slightly after Armand Assante falls over.
- 0:39—Brief upper half of right breast with part of nipple sticking out of camisole top while sitting on bed.

### Blind Side (1993; Made for Cable Movie)

Tamara Clatterbuck ..................Barbara Hall
- •• 1:13—In bra and panties, outside with Rutger Hauer by the spa. Then breasts several times.

Rebecca De Mornay................... Lynn Kaines
Mariska Hargitay ...................... Melanie
Rutger Hauer ........................... Shell
- 0:52—Buns, while making love on top of Mariska Hargitay in bed.

Diana Lee-Hsu ..................... Mrs. Dance

### Blind Vision (1990)

Deborah Shelton ................ Leanne Dunaway
- ••• 0:25—Breasts, making love with her boyfriend on the floor. Some shots are a body double.

### Blindfold: Acts of Obsession (1993)

Shannen Doherty................. Madeleine Dalton
- ••• 0:07—Breasts, while making love.
- •• 0:08—Breasts while making love in the shower with Mike.
- ••• 0:21—Breasts, in bed, while making love with Mike.
- •• 0:39—Breasts, during photo session with pillows while posing for Mike. More breast flashes while in bed.
  1:06—In black bra on desk in Judd Nelson's office. Brief, partial right breast, when he caresses it.

Aleksandra Kaniak ......................Natalie
Michael Woods ..................... Mike Dalton
- ••• 0:07—Buns, while making love with Shannen Doherty on lit table. Long shot.
- 0:08—Brief buns in the shower with Doherty.

### Blindside (1988; Canadian)

Lolita Davidovich .......................Adele
- •• 0:32—Breasts dancing on stage.
  0:39—Sort of buns bending over and pointing a gun through her legs in front of mirror.

Lori Hallier ............................Julie
Harvey Keitel ..........................Gruber

### Blindsided (1993; Made for Cable Movie)

Jeff Fahey........................ Frank McKenna
Stephanie Menuez .................. Racehorse Girl

Mia Sara . . . . . . . . . . . . . . . . . . . . . . Chandler Strange
- • 0:16—Very brief right breast while making love under Jeff Fahey.

## Blink (1993)

Aidan Quinn . . . . . . . . . . . . . Detective John Hallstrom
- •• 0:02—Buns, twice, after doing strip routine in bar and mooning Madeleine Stowe to get her attention.

James Remar . . . . . . . . . . . . . . . . . . . . Thomas Ridgely
Madeleine Stowe . . . . . . . . . . . . . . . . . . . .Emma Brody
- • 1:04—Side of left breast while walking to look at roses.
- •• 1:06—Breasts, after taking off top and making love with Aidan Quinn.

## Bliss (1985; Australian)

Gia Carides . . . . . . . . . . . . . . . . . . . . . . . . . . Lucy Joy
- • 1:25—Brief breasts during nightmare. Cockroaches crawl out of cut between her breasts. Pretty gross. (The cockroaches—not her.)

Lynette Curran . . . . . . . . . . . . . . . . . . . . . . Bettina Joy
Helen Jones . . . . . . . . . . . . . . . . . . . . . . Honey Barbara
- ••• 0:58—Breasts, lying on the floor with Harry. Brief part of lower frontal nudity. Long scene.
- • 1:01—Brief breasts on bed when Adrian runs to the bathroom.
  1:24—Left breast while standing outside with arms outstretched.
- • 1:39—Buns, while swimming. Long shot of buns while walking up rocks.

Bryan Marshall . . . . . . . . . . . . . . . . . . . . .Adrian Clunes
- • 1:01—Very brief buns, while running to the bathroom.

Barry Otto . . . . . . . . . . . . . . . . . . . . . . . . . . Henry Joy
- ••• 0:48—Buns, while peddling on exercise bike.
- •• 0:58—Buns, while lying on the floor with Honey.

## Blood & Concrete: A Love Story (1991)

Jennifer Beals . . . . . . . . . . . . . . . . . . . . . . . . . . . Mona
- • 0:10—Buns, in pulled up slip on bed with Billy Zane. Brief, out-of-focus shot of her left breast. Don't see her face.

James Le Gros . . . . . . . . . . . . . . . . . . . . . . . . . . Lance
Billy Zane . . . . . . . . . . . . . . . . . . . . . . . . . .Joey Turks

## Blood and Sand (1989; Spanish)

Christopher Rydell . . . . . . . . . . . . . . . . . . . . . . . . Juan
- • 0:15—Buns, while running away after fighting bull. Dark, long shot.
- •• 0:18—Buns, seen between shower curtain when Sharon Stone watches.
- • 1:05—Buns, while on top of Stone. Long shot.

Sharon Stone . . . . . . . . . . . . . . . . . . . . . . . .Doña Sol
  0:57—Very brief upper half of right breast, making love on table with Juan.
- •• 0:58—Left breast, making love in bed with Juan. Don't see her face well.
- ••• 1:04—Breasts quite a few times, making love with Juan in the woods.

## Blood Diner (1987)

Cynthia Baker . . . . . . . . . . . . . . . . . . . . . . . . . . Cindy
- ••• 0:44—Nude outside by fire with her boyfriend, then fighting a guy with an axe.

Carl Crew . . . . . . . . . . . . . . . . . . . . . . . .George Tutman
- • 1:02—Buns, while mooning Sheeba through the passenger window of a van.

Tanya Papanicolas . . . . . . . . . . . . . . . . . Sheetar & Bitsy
- • 0:15—Brief breasts as photographer during topless aerobics photo shoot.
- • 0:24—Breasts, dead on operating table, then dead, standing up.

## Blood Frenzy (1987)

John Clark . . . . . . . . . . . . . . . . . . . . . . . . . . .Crawford
- • 0:39—Buns, while falling out of motor home lavatory drunk.

Lisa Loring . . . . . . . . . . . . . . . . . . . . . . . . . . . . Dory
  0:27—In sheer bra, taking off her blouse and dribbling water on herself.

Wendy MacDonald . . . . . . . . . . . . . . . . . . . .Dr. Shelley

## Blood Link (1983)

Sarah Langenfeld . . . . . . . . . . . . . . . . . . . . . . Christine
- •• 1:01—Breasts while taking her top off in bed with Craig.
- • 1:04—Breasts in bed with Keith.

Penelope Milford . . . . . . . . . . . . . . . . . . . . .Julie Warren
- •• 0:22—Breasts while in bed with Craig. Very brief left breast, when she grabs the pillow.
- •• 1:24—In black bra in greenhouse with Keith, then breasts.
- • 1:27—Brief buns, while on top of Keith. Long shot.
- •• 1:28—Right breast, when Keith tries to strangle her.
- ••• 1:35—Breasts, while in bedroom with Keith.

Martha Smith . . . . . . . . . . . . . . . . . . . . . . . . . Hedwig
- •• 0:41—Breasts, wearing black panties while in bed with Keith.
- •• 0:43—Brief breasts, while kneeling on bed, talking to Keith.
- • 0:48—Right breast, while sitting in bed and talking. Shadow and scarf get in the way. Brief breasts.
- • 0:49—Breasts, while getting slapped around by Keith.
- ••• 0:51—Breasts sitting up in bed when Craig and Keith meet each other for the first time.
- • 1:13—Breasts, wearing red panties, with Keith before he kills her.
- • 1:14—Brief buns, covered with blood when discovered by policemen.

## Blood Mania (1970)

Peter Carpenter . . . . . . . . . . . . . . . . . . . . . . . . . Craig
- • 0:07—Buns, almost removing his pants and getting into bath tub with Cheryl.
- • 0:20—Very brief side view of buns, while sitting in bed.

Vicki Peters . . . . . . . . . . . . . . . . . . . . . . . . . . . . . .Gail
- •• 1:04—Breasts, while making love with Dr. Cooper in front of the fire. Seen through flames. Intercut with a rape scene.
- • 1:10—Brief breasts in bathroom. More brief breasts, while getting beaten to death by Victoria and drug around on rug.
- • 1:15—Very brief breasts, while dead, covered with blood when discovered by Craig.
- • 1:17—Brief breasts while being placed in car. Covered with blood.

Reid "Chip" Smith. . . . . . . . . . . . . . . . . . . . . . Poolboy
- • 0:11—Upper half of buns, getting out of pool with Victoria.

Regan Wilson . . . . . . . . . . . . . . . . . . . . . . . . . .Cheryl
- •• 0:07—Breasts and buns, while in bubble bath.
- • 0:17—In bra, while undressing in bedroom. Very brief side of right breast, when putting on robe.
- • 0:21—Very brief side of left breast, while leaning over to kiss Craig in bed.
- • 0:34—Partial right breast, while on couch with the blackmailer.

### Blood on Satan's Claw (1971; British)
*a.k.a. Satan's Skin*
Linda Hayden . . . . . . . . . . . . . . . . . . . . . . .Angel Blake
- •• 0:40—Breasts, while undressing in front of priest to tempt him.

### Blood Relations (1989)
Lydie Denier . . . . . . . . . . . . . . . . . . . . . . . . . . . Marie
- •• 0:07—Left breast making love with Thomas on stairway.
- • 0:44—Brief left breast in bed with Thomas' father. Very brief cuts of her breasts in B&W.
  0:47—Getting out of swimming pool in a one piece swimsuit.
- ••• 0:54—Full frontal nudity undressing for the Grandfather.
Carrie Leigh . . . . . . . . . . . . . . . . . . Thomas' Girlfriend

### Blood Sisters (1986)
Amy Brentano. . . . . . . . . . . . . . . . . . . . . . . . . . Linda
- ••• 0:12—Breasts, getting out of bed.
- •• 0:14—Breasts, walking around. Right breast, in bed with Russ. Brief upper half of buns.
Ruth Corrine Collins . . . . . . . . . . . . . . . . . . . Prostitute
Gretchen Kingsley. . . . . . . . . . . . . . . . . . . . . . . . Ellen
- •• 0:32—Breasts, changing clothes to go to sleep in bedroom.
- ••• 0:50—Breasts in bed with Jim.
Maria Machart . . . . . . . . . . . . . . . . . . . . . . . . Marnie
- •• 0:45—In bra, then brief breasts putting on nightgown and caressing herself.

### Blood Ties (1986; Made for Cable Movie; Italian)
Maria Conchita Alonso . . . . . . . . . . . . . . . . . . Caterina
- •• 0:35—Brief breasts when Vincent Spano rips her dress off.
Brad Davis. . . . . . . . . . . . . . . . . . . . . . . . Julian Salina

Barbara De Rossi . . . . . . . . . . . . . . . . . . . . . . . Luisa
- • 0:58—Brief breasts on couch when bad guy rips her clothes off.
Vincent Spano . . . . . . . . . . . . . . . . . . . . . . .Mark Ciuni

### Blood Ties (1991)
Michelle Johnson . . . . . . . . . . . . . . . . . . . . . . . Celia
Kim Johnston-Ulrich . . . . . . . . . . . . . . . . . . . . .Loren
- • 1:21—Very brief breasts, while rolling over in bed with Harry.

### Bloodbath (1976)
*a.k.a. The Sky is Falling*
Carroll Baker . . . . . . . . . . . . . . . . . . . . . . . . Treasure
- • 0:16—Outline of left breast in see-through blouse when kneeling in the ocean to urinate.
- • 0:50—Very brief buns, while mooning her mute lover.
Dennis Hopper. . . . . . . . . . . . . . . . . . . . . . . .Chicken
Win Wells. . . . . . . . . . . . . . . . . . . . . . . . . . . . Alice
- • 1:23—Very brief buns, while crawling away from a bull.
  1:24—Very, very brief buns, while getting horned by one of the bull's horns.

### Bloodbath at the House of Death (1985; British)
Sheila Steafel . . . . . . . . . . . . . . . . . . . . . . . . . . n.a.
Pamela Stephenson . . . . . . . . . . . . . . . . . Barbara Coyle
- • 0:50—Very brief breasts getting clothes ripped off by an unseen being.

### Bloodfist III: Forced to Fight (1991)
Pat Anderson . . . . . . . . . . . . . . . . . . . . . . . . . .Elaine
- • 0:55—Buns and breasts in clip from movie *TNT Jackson* that the inmates watch while Diddler gets stabbed to death.
Jeannie Bell . . . . . . . . . . . . . . . . . . . . . . . TNT Jackson
- •• 0:55—Breasts several times in movie *TNT Jackson* that the inmates watch while Diddler gets stabbed to death.
Richard Roundtree . . . . . . . . . . . . . . . . . . Samuel Stark
Bob Schott. . . . . . . . . . . . . . . . . . . . . . . . . Weird Willy

### Bloodlust: Subspecies III (1993)
Denice Duff . . . . . . . . . . . . . . . . . . . . Michelle Morgan
Melanie Shatner . . . . . . . . . . . . . . . . . . Rebecca Morgan
- • 0:04—Very brief left breast and buns, while taking off blood-stained dress and putting on a coat. Long shot.

### Bloodmatch (1991)
Hope Marie Carlton . . . . . . . . . . . . . . . . . .Connie Angel
Marianne Taylor. . . . . . . . . . . . . . . . . . . . Max Manduke
- • 0:13—Breasts and buns, making love in bed on top of Caldwell.

### Bloodsport (1987)
Leah Ayres-Hamilton . . . . . . . . . . . . . . . . . . . . . Janice
Donald Gibb . . . . . . . . . . . . . . . . . . . . . . . Ray Jackson
Jean-Claude Van Damme . . . . . . . . . . . . . . . . . . . .Frank
- •• 0:50—Brief buns while putting underwear on after spending the night with Janice.

## Bloodstone (1988)

Laura Albert . . . . . . . . . . . . . . . . . . . . . . . . . . Kim Chi
- 0:05—Very brief side view of left breast turning around in pool to look at a guy.

## Bloodstone: Subspecies II (1992)

Denice Duff. . . . . . . . . . . . . . . . . . . . . Michelle Morgan
- 0:10—Very, very brief left breast under sheer part of dress while taking it off. Back side of right breast while putting on sweater.
- •• 0:16—Breasts, while crying in the shower.

Melanie Shatner . . . . . . . . . . . . . . . . . .Rebecca Morgan
- 0:34—Upper half of buns and breasts behind translucent plastic shower door. Hard to see.

## Bloodsuckers (1970; British)

Imogen Hassall . . . . . . . . . . . . . . . . . . . . . . . . .Chriseis
- 0:05—Right breast, while standing up at the beach and kissing Richard.

## Bloody Birthday (1980)

Julie Brown . . . . . . . . . . . . . . . . . . . . . . . . . . . Beverly
- ••• 0:13—Dancing in red bra, then breasts while two boys peek through hole in the wall, then buns. Nice, long scene.
  0:48—In bedroom wearing red bra.
  1:03—In bedroom again in the red bra.

Erica Hope. . . . . . . . . . . . . . . . . . . . . . . . . . . . Annie
- 0:04—Brief breasts in cemetery, making out with Duke.

Cyril O'Reilly . . . . . . . . . . . . . . . . . . . . . Guy in Van
- 0:46—Buns, while sitting up in van.

Susan Strasberg. . . . . . . . . . . . . . . . . . . . .Miss Davis
Sylvia Wright. . . . . . . . . . . . . . . . . . . . . . Girl in Van
- ••• 0:45—Breasts undressing in a van and making out with a guy.

## Bloody Friday (1973)

*a.k.a. Single Girls*

Robyn Hilton. . . . . . . . . . . . . . . . . . . . . . . . . Denise
Chéri Howell . . . . . . . . . . . . . . . . . . . . . . . .Shannon
- 1:01—Breasts and buns after "accidentally" dropping her towel in front of Bud.

Claudia Jennings . . . . . . . . . . . . . . . . . . . . Allison
- 0:40—Breasts, taking off her dress to sunbathe on rock at the beach. Long shot. Side view of right breast, putting dress back on when George talks to her.
- •• 0:57—Breasts, drying herself off after shower.

Joan Prather . . . . . . . . . . . . . . . . . . . . . . . . . . Lola
- •• 1:06—Breasts, acting out her fantasy with Blue just before getting killed. Dark.

## Bloody Mama (1970)

Robert De Niro . . . . . . . . . . . . . . . . . . . . . Lloyd Barker
  0:03—Very briefly nude, having a towel fight with his brother. Blurry, hard to see.
Bruce Dern . . . . . . . . . . . . . . . . . . . . Kevin Kirkman
Diane Varsi . . . . . . . . . . . . . . . . . . . . . . . Mona Gibson
- ••• 0:16—Breasts, sitting up in bed with Dan Stroud. Buns, when getting out of bed. Long scene.

## Bloody Trail (1972)

Rickey Richardson. . . . . . . . . . . . . . . . . . . . . .Miriam
- 1:01—Peek at left breast in torn blouse.
- 1:05—Right breast while sleeping, dark, hard to see.

## Blow Out (1981)

Nancy Allen . . . . . . . . . . . . . . . . . . . . . . . . . . . .Sally
- 0:58—Brief upper half of right breast with the sheet pulled up in B&W photograph that John Travolta examines.

Amanda Cleveland. . . . . . . . . . . . . . . . . . . . Coed Lover
- 0:01—Left breast in room while someone watches from the outside.

Missy Cleveland . . . . . . . . . . . . . . . . . . . . Shower Victim
- •• 0:02—Breasts in shower and on TV monitor while killer stalks outside.

John Lithgow . . . . . . . . . . . . . . . . . . . . . . . . . . .Burke
Cindy Manion . . . . . . . . . . . . . . . . . . . . . . Dancing Coed
Missy O'Shea . . . . . . . . . . . . . . . . . . . . . . Dancing Coed
  0:00—Dancing in sheer nightgown while a campus guard watches from outside the window.
Robin Sherwood. . . . . . . . . . . . . . . . . . . . . Screamer
Roger Wilson . . . . . . . . . . . . . . . . . . . . . . Coed Lover

## Blow-Up (1966; British/Italian)

Veruschka. . . . . . . . . . . . . . . . . . . . . . . . . . Veruschka
Jane Birkin . . . . . . . . . . . . . . . . . . . . . . . . .Teenager
- 1:06—Breasts, while changing clothes in David Hemming's studio.
- 1:08—Brief breasts while frolicking with Hemmings and the other teenage girl in the studio. Very, very brief lower frontal nudity under Hemmings.

John Castle. . . . . . . . . . . . . . . . . . . . . . . . . .Painter
Sarah Miles . . . . . . . . . . . . . . . . . . . . . . . . Patricia
Vanessa Redgrave. . . . . . . . . . . . . . . . . . . . . . .Jane

## Blown Away (1992)

(Unrated version reviewed.)
Nicole Eggert . . . . . . . . . . . . . . . . . . . . . . . .Megan
- •• 0:15—Breasts and buns, getting out of bed with Haim.
- ••• 0:21—Right breast then breasts and buns, while standing in bedroom, making out with Corey Haim.
- •• 0:24—Breasts, while making love in bed with Haim.
- • 0:26—Left breast, while in shower with Haim.
- ••• 0:46—Breasts, while making love, sitting on Haim's lap in front of fire.
- • 1:00—Upper half of buns, in bed with Haim.
- • 1:10—Brief breasts and buns, while getting out of bed.
- • 1:26—Very brief half of right breast and buns in T-back under sheer nightgown, while making love in bed on top of Corey Feldman.
- • 1:28—Very brief right breast, while getting shot by policeman.

Gary Farmer. . . . . . . . . . . . . . . . . . . . . . . .Anderson
Corey Feldman. . . . . . . . . . . . . . . . . . . . . . . . . .Wes
- • 1:26—Buns, twice, getting out of bed. Dark, don't see his face.

Corey Haim . . . . . . . . . . . . . . . . . . . . . . . . . . . Rich
- ••• 0:15—Buns, lying in bed with Nicole Eggert, then getting out and putting his pants on.
- •• 0:24—Buns, while making love in bed on top of Eggert.
- • 1:11—Buns, getting out of bed after Eggert.

### Blue Desert (1990)

Vali Ashton . . . . . . . . . . . . . . . . . . . . . . . . . . . . . .n.a.
Courteney Cox . . . . . . . . . . . . . . . . . . . . . Lisa Roberts
0:52—Silhouette of right breast, standing up with Steve. Probably a body double. Very, very brief right nipple between Steve's arms lying in bed. Dark, hard to see.
- •• 0:53—Left breast, lying in bed under Steve. A little hard to see her face, but it sure looks like her to me! 1:14—Buns and part of left breast getting towel. Looks like a body double.
Craig Sheffer . . . . . . . . . . . . . . . . . . . . . . Randall Atkins

### Blue Ice (1992; Made for Cable Movie)

Sean Young . . . . . . . . . . . . . . . . . . . . . . .Stacy Mansdorf
- • 0:17—Brief breasts and buns, while making love with Michael Caine.
- • 0:18—Brief buns and partial back side of left breast, while sitting up in bed.

### Blue Lagoon (1980)

Christopher Atkins . . . . . . . . . . . . . . . . . . . . . .Richard
- •• 0:27—Nude swimming underwater after growing up from little children.
- • 0:29—Buns, while underwater.
- •• 1:03—Nude swimming under water.
- • 1:05—Buns, while kissing Brooke Shields.
- •• 1:09—Very brief frontal nudity in water slide with Shields.
Brooke Shields . . . . . . . . . . . . . . . . . . . . . . . Emmeline
0:27—Nude swimming underwater after growing up from little children.
0:43—More underwater swimming.
1:00—Breasts body double lying on a rock.
1:09—Right breast of body double in hammock.
1:24—Body double breast feeding the baby.

### The Blue Max (1966)

Ursula Andress . . . . . . . . . . . . . . . . . . . Countess Kasti
- • 1:26—Very, very brief half of left breast, lying on her back in bed.
- • 1:47—(0:04 into tape 2) Very brief half of right breast, while kneeling down in front of Peppard in hotel room. Very, very brief breasts under towel around her neck when she stands up.
- • 1:48—(0:05 into tape 2) Very, very brief silhouette of right breast, while lying back down in bed with George Peppard in bedroom.

### Blue Movies (1988)

Vickie Benson . . . . . . . . . . . . . . . . . . . . . . . . . Andrea
Lucinda Crosby . . . . . . . . . . . . . . . . . . . . .Randy Moon
- • 0:10—Breasts in a spa, in a movie.
- •• 0:11—Breasts, kneeling on a table, shooting a porno movie.
- ••• 0:32—Breasts auditioning for Buzz.
- • 1:02—Breasts on desk in a movie.
Steve Levitt . . . . . . . . . . . . . . . . . . . . . . . . . . . . Buzz
- •• 0:46—Buns, while walking around naked when Randy and Kathy make him and Cliff take their clothes off.
Darian Mathias . . . . . . . . . . . . . . . . . . . . . . . . . .Kathy
- • 0:37—Very brief breasts twice acting for the first time in a porno film.
0:39—Breasts from above during screening of movie. Hard to see.
Christopher Stone . . . . . . . . . . . . . . . . . . . . . . . Brad

### Blue Steel (1989)

Clancy Brown . . . . . . . . . . . . . . . . . . . . . . . . .Nick Mann
- • 1:27—Upper half of buns, while lying on the bathroom floor. Don't see his face, so it could be anybody.
Jamie Lee Curtis . . . . . . . . . . . . . . . . . . . Megan Turner
1:27—Very, very brief buns twice when rolling out of bed, trying to get her gun. Dark.
Elizabeth Peña . . . . . . . . . . . . . . . . . . . . . . . Tracy Perez

### Blue Velvet (1986)

Laura Dern . . . . . . . . . . . . . . . . . . . . . . . Sandy Williams
Brad Dourif . . . . . . . . . . . . . . . . . . . . . . . . . .Raymond
Dennis Hopper . . . . . . . . . . . . . . . . . . . . . . .Frank Booth
Kyle MacLachlan . . . . . . . . . . . . . . . . . . . . . . . . Jeffrey
- ••• 0:40—Buns, when Isabella Rossellini takes his underwear off in her apartment.
- •• 0:41—Buns and very brief frontal nudity while running to closet.
Isabella Rossellini . . . . . . . . . . . . . . . . . . . . . .Dorothy
0:34—In black bra and panties, in her apartment while Kyle MacLachlan watches from inside closet.
- • 0:36—Buns, after taking off panties in her bathroom. Long shot.
0:45—Partial lower frontal nudity, under robe while lying on the floor after Dennis Hopper pushes her down.
- • 1:08—Brief full frontal nudity, while frolicking with MacLachlan in bed.
- • 1:27—Very, very brief lower frontal nudity, while rolling over in bed in MacLachlan's flashback.
- • 1:40—Nude, standing on porch, bruised.
- • 1:41—Briefly, nude, sitting in car. Long shot. Brief right breast, while getting covered up.
- •• 1:42—Brief breasts at Laura Dern's house.

### Bluebeard (1972)

Agostina Belli . . . . . . . . . . . . . . . . . . . . . . . . . .Caroline
- • 1:31—Brief left breast lying on grass getting a tan.
- •• 1:32—Breasts taking off clothes and lying on the couch.
Sybil Danning . . . . . . . . . . . . . . . . . . . . . The Prostitute
- • 1:08—Brief breasts kissing Nathalie Delon showing her how to make love to her husband.
- • 1:09—Brief left breast, lying on the floor with Delon just before Richard Burton kills both of them.

Nathalie Delon . . . . . . . . . . . . . . . . . . . . . . . . . . . Erika
- • 1:03—Breasts in bed, showing Richard Burton her breasts.
- • 1:09—Brief right breast lying on the floor with Sybil Danning just before Richard Burton kills both of them.

Joey Heatherton . . . . . . . . . . . . . . . . . . . . . . . . .Anne
- • 0:25—Breasts under black see-through nightie while Richard Burton photographs her. Very brief right breast.
- ••• 1:46—Brief breasts opening her dress top to taunt Richard Burton.

Karin Schubert . . . . . . . . . . . . . . . . . . . . . . . . . Greta
- • 1:43—Brief breasts, spinning around, unwrapping herself from a red towel for Richard Burton.

Marilu Tolo . . . . . . . . . . . . . . . . . . . . . . . . . . . . Brigitt
- • 1:25—Breasts in sheer blue blouse arguing with Richard Burton.
- •• 1:27—Breasts getting whipped by Burton.

## Blume in Love (1973)

Susan Anspach . . . . . . . . . . . . . . . . . . . . . Nina Blume
Kris Kristofferson . . . . . . . . . . . . . . . . . . . . . . . . .Elmo
Marsha Mason . . . . . . . . . . . . . . . . . . . . . . . . . .Arlene
- • 0:22—Side view of right breast, then brief breasts lying in bed with George Segal.
- • 0:35—Very brief right breast while reaching over the bed.
- •• 0:54—Brief breasts twice, reaching over to get a pillow while talking to Segal.

Erin O'Reilly. . . . . . . . . . . . . . . . . . . . . . . . . . . Cindy
- • 0:40—Breasts and buns, getting out of bed with George Segal.

## Boarding School (1976; German)

*a.k.a. Virgin Campus*
*a.k.a. The Passion Flower Hotel*

Nastassja Kinski . . . . . . . . . . . . . . . . . . Deborah Collins
- • 0:15—Brief breasts in the shower with her roommates. Hard to tell who is who.
- • 1:11—Left breast, then breasts in the shower (She's the second from the right) consoling Marie-Louise.
- • 1:16—Breasts under sheer nightie.
- ••• 1:32—Breasts making love with Sinclair.

Fabiana Udenio. . . . . . . . . . . . . . . . . . . . . . . . . Gina

## Bobbie Jo and the Outlaw (1976)

Belinda Balaski. . . . . . . . . . . . . . . . . .Essie Beaumont
- ••• 0:29—Breasts in pond with Marjoe Gortner and Lynda Carter.
- • 0:43—Very brief breasts, when Gortner pushes her into a pond.

Lynda Carter . . . . . . . . . . . . . . . . . . . . Bobbie Jo Baker
0:10—Partial side of left breast, changing blouses in her bedroom.
- ••• 0:17—Left breast, several times, while making love with Marjoe Gortner.
- •• 0:27—Brief left breast, making love with Gortner again at night.
- • 0:31—Very brief left breast, then very brief breasts in pond with Gortner experimenting with mushrooms.

## Body and Soul (1981)

Azizi Johari . . . . . . . . . . . . . . . . . . . . . . . . Pussy Willow
- ••• 0:31—Breasts sitting on bed with Leon Isaac Kennedy, then left breast, while lying in bed.

Rosanne Katon . . . . . . . . . . . . . . . . . . . . . . . . Melody
- • 0:04—Left breast several times making love in restroom with Leon Isaac Kennedy.

Perry Lang . . . . . . . . . . . . . . . . . . . . . . .Charles Golphin
Ola Ray . . . . . . . . . . . . . . . . . . . . . . . . . . . Hooker #1
- • 0:54—Brief breasts sitting on top of Leon Isaac Kennedy in bed with two other hookers.

Laurie Senit . . . . . . . . . . . . . . . . . . . . . . . Hooker #3
- • 0:54—Brief breasts lying next to Leon Isaac Kennedy in bed with two other hookers.

## Body Chemistry (1990)

Mary Crosby . . . . . . . . . . . . . . . . . . . . . . . . . . .Marlee
Lisa Pescia . . . . . . . . . . . . . . . . . . . . . . . . . . . . .Claire
- ••• 0:18—Breasts making love with Marc Singer standing up, then at foot of bed.
- 0:35—In purple bra in van with Singer.
- 0:55—Buns, standing in hallway. Long shot.

Marc Singer . . . . . . . . . . . . . . . . . . . . . .Dr. Tom Redding
- • 0:18—Buns, standing up in hallway holding Claire while making love. Long shot.

## Body Chemistry 2: Voice of a Stranger (1991)

Maria Ford . . . . . . . . . . . . . . . . . . . . . Uncredited Victim
- •• 0:37—Breasts in bed during flashback. (This scene is from *Naked Obsession*.)

Monique Gabrielle . . . . . . . . . . . . .Brunette in Flashback
- • 0:19—Very brief buns and left breast in bed.

Gregory Harrison . . . . . . . . . . . . . . . . . . . . . . . . .Dan
- ••• 0:45—Buns on stairs when Brenda finds him in the morning.

Lisa Pescia . . . . . . . . . . . . . . . . . . . . . Claire Archer
- • 0:42—Brief buns and side of left breast, making love on stairs with Dan.
- ••• 0:52—Breasts and buns, in bathtub, standing up, sitting back down while talking with Dan.
- • 1:07—Buns, in leather outfit in radio control booth with Morton Downey Jr.
- • 1:18—Very brief buns and left breast on the stairs in flashback.

## Body Chemistry 3: Point of Seduction (1993)

Antonia Dorian. . . . . . . . . . . . . . . . . . . . . . . . . .Krissy
Morgan Fairchild . . . . . . . . . . . . . . . . . . . . .Beth Clancey
Robert Forster . . . . . . . . . . . . . . . . . . . . . . . Bob Sibley
Becky LeBeau . . . . . . . . . . . . . . . . . . . . . . . . Margaret
- •• 0:04—Full frontal nudity, seen on TV monitor, while taking her clothes off on bed during call-in show.

Shari Shattuck . . . . . . . . . . . . . . . . . . . Dr. Claire Archer
- •• 0:15—Breasts, while making love on bed with Andrew Stevens at night during storm.
- ••• 0:28—Side view of buns and breasts, while making love with Stevens on bed.
- ••• 0:57—Breasts, taking off robe in front of Stevens. More breasts and buns while making love with him.

Delia Sheppard . . . . . . . . . . . . . . . . . . . . . . .Wilhemina

Andrew Stevens . . . . . . . . . . . . . . . . . . . . . Alan Clay
Stella Stevens . . . . . . . . . . . . . . . . . . . . .Frannie Sibley

### Body Double (1984)

Barbara Crampton . . . . . . . . . . . . . . . . . . . .Carol Sculley
- •• 0:04—Brief right breast, while making love in bed with another man when her husband walks in.

Alexandra Day. . . . . . . . . . . . . . . . . Girl in Bathroom #1
Melanie Griffith . . . . . . . . . . . . . . . . . . . . . . Holly Body
- •• 0:20—Breasts in brunette wig dancing around in bedroom while Craig Wasson watches through a telescope.
- • 0:28—Breasts in bedroom again while Wasson and the Indian welding on the satellite dish watch.
- •• 1:12—Breasts and buns on TV that Wasson is watching.
- •• 1:13—Breasts and buns on TV after Wasson buys the video tape.
- • 1:19—Brief buns in black leather outfit in bathroom during filming of movie.
- • 1:20—Brief buns again in the black leather outfit.

Barbara Peckinpaugh. . . Girl #2 (Holly Does Hollywood)
- • 1:12—Brief breasts in orgy scene in adult film preview that Craig Wasson watches on TV. (Lettering gets in the way.)

Ty Randolph . . . . . . . . . . . . . . . . . . . . . . . . . . . Mindi
- ••• 1:50—Breasts in the shower during filming of movie with Craig Wasson made up as a vampire.

Linda Shaw . . . . . . . . . . . . . . . . . . . . . . . .Linda Shaw
- • 1:11—Left breast on monitor while Craig Wasson watches TV.

Deborah Shelton. . . . . . . . . . . . . . . . . . . . . . . Gloria
Brinke Stevens. . . . . . . . . . . . . . . Girl in Bathroom #3
- • 1:12—Breasts sitting in chair in adult film preview that Craig Wasson watches on TV.

Craig Wasson . . . . . . . . . . . . . . . . . . . . . . . . . . . Jake

### Body Heat (1981)

Jane Hallaren. . . . . . . . . . . . . . . . . . . . . . . . . . Stella
William Hurt . . . . . . . . . . . . . . . . . . . . . . . . Ned Racine
Mickey Rourke. . . . . . . . . . . . . . . . . . . . . Teddy Lewis
Kathleen Turner . . . . . . . . . . . . . . . . . . Maddy Walker
- • 0:22—Brief side view of left breast in bed with William Hurt.
- •• 0:24—Breasts in a shack with Hurt.
- 0:32—Buns, getting dressed. Long shot, hard to see.
- • 0:54—Brief left breast in bathtub. Long shot, hard to see.

### Body of Evidence (1992)

(Unrated version reviewed.)
Madonna . . . . . . . . . . . . . . . . . . . . . Rebecca Carlson
- • 0:01—Breasts, while making love on TV during video playback.
- • 0:03—Breasts and buns some more on TV.
- • 0:20—Upper half of buns, getting acupuncture.
- ••• 0:41—Breasts on stairs and in bed with Willem Dafoe.
- •• 0:42—Breasts on bed behind curtains with Dafoe.
- • 0:43—Brief right breast, while licking champagne off Dafoe's chest.

- ••• 0:45—Full frontal nudity, while climbing on top of Dafoe and making love. Seen through curtains.
- • 0:55—Lower frontal nudity, while making love with Dafoe in parking garage.
- ••• 1:07—Very, very brief left breast when Dafoe grabs her arm. Breasts opening her robe and lying on the floor and playing with herself while Dafoe watches.
- •• 1:10—Buns, while lying on the floor when Dafoe rips her panties off.
- ••• 1:11—Full frontal nudity on TV during video playback.

Anne Archer. . . . . . . . . . . . . . . . . . . . . . Joanne Braslow
- 1:12—Nude scene on video playback is body double Shawn Lusader.

Willem Dafoe. . . . . . . . . . . . . . . . . . . . . . Frank Dulaney
- ••• 0:14—Buns, while making love in bed on top of Sharon.
- • 0:46—Several brief frontal nudity shots, when it pokes out from under Madonna while she's on top of him in bed behind the curtain.

Julianne Moore. . . . . . . . . . . . . . . . . . Sharon Dulaney
- ••• 0:14—Breasts in bed, while making love with Willem Dafoe, then breasts and buns getting out of bed to take a shower.

Jeff Perry . . . . . . . . . . . . . . . . . . . . . . . . . . . . . Gabe
Jürgen Prochnow . . . . . . . . . . . . . . . . Dr. Alan Paley

### Body of Influence (1992)

(Unrated version reviewed.)
Diana Barton . . . . . . . . . . . . . . . . . . . . . . . . Jennifer
Sandahl Bergman. . . . . . . . . . . . . . . . . . . . . Clarissa
- 0:32—In white bra, white panties and black stockings in psychiatrist's office.
- 0:41—In bra and panties on TV during video playback.

Nick Cassavetes . . . . . . . . . . . . . . . Jonathon Brooks
- • 1:06—Very, very brief frontal nudity, while in bed when Lana rolls on top of him and scoots up.

Anna Karin. . . . . . . . . . . . . . . . . . . . . . . . . . . . Beth
Sandra Margot. . . . . . . . . . . . . . . . . . . . . . Margaret
- ••• 0:03—Breasts and buns in black G-string panties, while undressing for Jonathon.

Monique Parent. . . . . . . . . . . . . . . . . . . Chic Woman
- •• 0:57—Buns in lingerie and breasts undressing in front of Jonathan and Lana at gunpoint.

Heather Parkhurst. . . . . . . . . . . . Woman in Apartment
Ashlie Rhey. . . . . . . . . . . . . . . . . . . . . . . . Dominatrix
Richard Roundtree . . . . . . . . . . . . . . . . Harry Reams
Shannon Whirry. . . . . . . . . . . . . . . . . . . . .Laura/Lana
- ••• 0:08—Breasts on bed with her lover during recollection for Jonathon.
- • 0:16—Left breast, while on bed, tied by wrists and getting raped during recollection.
- •• 0:26—In black bra, undressing in office. Right breast, while lying on desk. Buns in panties.
- ••• 0:44—In burgundy bra and panties with Jonathon in his house. Then nude, while making love in living room. Long scene.
- ••• 1:05—In black bra, then breasts and buns, while making love on top of Jonathon.

••• 1:08—Breasts, while sitting up in bed and talking to Jonathon.

## Body Shot (1993)

Michelle Johnson. . . . . . . . . . . . . . . . . Danielle Wilde
　0:23—Brief buns in T-back under fishnet outfit.
•　0:28—Brief buns, when dropping robe.
Barbara Patrick . . . . . . . . . . . . . . . . . . . . . . . .Candy
••　0:06—Breasts, while sitting on couch in Robert Patrick's studio.
Robert Patrick . . . . . . . . . . . . . . . . . . . . Mickey Dane

## Body Snatchers (1994)

Gabrielle Anwar. . . . . . . . . . . . . . . . . . . Marti Malone
•　0:49—Very, very brief breast while in bathtub when pod creature falls on top of her.
••• 1:13—Several brief breast shots, while sitting up, looking at Tim and writhing around on bed in infirmary.
Meg Tilly. . . . . . . . . . . . . . . . . . . . . . . Carol Malone

## Body Waves (1991)

Sean'a Arthur . . . . . . . . . . . . . . . . . . . . . . Dream Girl
••　0:02—Brief buns in swimsuit, walking into office.
•••　0:03—Breasts, taking off her bathing suit top during Rick's dream.
••　0:07—Breasts and side view of buns in swimsuit bottom, during Dooner's fantasy.
Sherrie Rose . . . . . . . . . . . . . . . . . . . . . . . Suzanne
Sándra Wild . . . . . . . . . . . . . . . . . . . . . . . . .Anita
•••　0:39—Breasts under sheer white robe, then breasts with Larry on chair.
•••　1:12—Breasts in bedroom with Larry.

## Bolero (1984)

Ian Cochran . . . . . . . . . . . . . . . . . . . . . . Robert Stewart
•　1:26—Buns, while making love with Catalina.
Olivia D'Abo . . . . . . . . . . . . . . . . . . . . . . . . Paloma
•　0:38—Nude covered with bubbles taking a bath.
•　1:05—Brief breasts in the steam room with Bo.
•　1:32—Breasts in the steam room talking with Bo. Hard to see because it's so steamy.
Bo Derek. . . . . . . . . . . . . . . . . . . . . Ayre McGillvary
•　0:04—Brief breasts, stripping to panties, outside after graduating from school.
•••　0:19—Breasts making love with Arabian guy covered with honey, messy.
•••　0:58—Breasts making love in bed with Angel.
•••　1:38—Breasts during fantasy love making session with Angel in fog.
Ana Obregon . . . . . . . . . . . . . . . . . . . . Catalina Terry
•　1:32—Brief breasts making love with Robert.
Andrea Occhipinti . . . . . . . . . . . . .Angel the Bullfighter
••　0:57—Buns, while lying in bed with Bo Derek, then making love with her.
•　1:39—Side view of buns, during fantasy love making session with Bo in fog.

## Bonnie's Kids (1973)

Tiffany Bolling . . . . . . . . . . . . . . . . . . . . . . . . .Ellie
••　0:21—Breasts, modeling in office.

•　1:16—Brief right breast making love in bed.
Robin Mattson . . . . . . . . . . . . . . . . . . . . . . . . . Myra
•　0:05—Brief side view of right breast, changing in bedroom while two men watch from outside.
•••　0:07—Breasts washing herself in the bathroom.

## The Boob Tube (1975)

Elana Casey . . . . . . . . . . . . . . . . . . . . Greta Van Allen
•　0:27—Buns, while lying in bed with Dr. Carstens.
•••　0:48—Breasts, taking off her blouse in bed, then making love with Natalie.
•　1:01—Buns and side of left breast on sofa.
•••　1:11—Nude, opening the door.
•••　1:12—Breasts during orgy on the couch.
•　1:16—Brief breasts in hallway.
Sharon Kelly. . . . . . . . . . . . . . . . . . . . Selma Carpenter
•••　0:06—Breasts and buns, trying to seduce Dr. Carstairs.
•••　0:10—Breasts and buns, having fun by herself on the bed while Dr. Carstairs watches. Nice close-ups.
•••　0:11—More breasts and buns in bed with Dr. Carstairs.
•　1:03—Breasts under sheer nightie while Harvey checks her sink.
•　1:09—Breasts and buns, on sofa, then leaving the room.
••　1:11—Breasts and buns, entering the room.
•••　1:12—Breasts during orgy on couch.
•　1:16—Brief breasts in hallway.
Paxton Quigley . . . . . . . . . . . . . . . Dr. Henry Carstairs
•　0:13—Brief buns, in bed with Sharon Kelly.
••　0:46—Buns, while making love in bed with Natalie.
Jon Reigrod . . . . . . . . . . . . . . . . . . . . . . . . . .Harvey
•　1:08—Buns, on sofa with Sharon and Dr. Carstairs.
Becky Sharpe . . . . . . . . . . . . . . . . . . . . Massage Girl
••　0:20—Right breast, then breasts, while getting massaged by Sid on the table.
Lyllah Torena . . . . . . . . . . . . . . . . . . . . Natalie Nolan
•••　0:28—Breasts, putting on her blouse.
•　0:42—Breasts, getting raped by three Hell's Angel guys outside during flashback.
•••　0:45—Breasts and buns, on bed, taking off her clothes with Dr. Carstairs.
•••　0:46—Breasts and buns, while making love with Dr. Carstairs in bed. Nice buns shot. More breasts after making love.
••　0:48—Breasts and buns, while making love in bed with Gretchen.
••　1:08—Left breast, while in front of Sid when her robe is pulled down by Gretchen.
•　1:10—Breasts on sofa with Gretchen.
•••　1:12—Breasts during orgy on couch.
•　1:16—Brief breasts in hallway.

## The Book of Love (1991)

Josie Bissett . . . . . . . . . . . . . . . . . . . . . . . . . . . . Lily
Brian Evans. . . . . . . . . . . . . . . . . . . . . . . . . .Schank
•　0:21—Buns, while tied up to cot with candle stuck in his rear end by the bad guys.

Leesa Rowland . . . . . . . . . . . . . . . . . . . . Honeymoon
0:56—Stripping in tent at carnival, wearing pasties.

### Boomerang (1992)

Robin Givens. . . . . . . . . . . . . . . . . . . . . . . .Jacqueline
0:50—Very brief half of left breast, lying with her back on bed with Eddie Murphy when she first puts her arm under his arm.
•• 1:02—Very brief side view of right breast, while making love on top of Murphy in bed.
1:42—In black bra and panties, in bed with Murphy.

Grace Jones. . . . . . . . . . . . . . . . . . . . . . . . .Strangé
• 0:35—Brief buns, under stockings during conference room meeting.
1:19—Brief buns and back side of left breast, several times on TV monitor during editing of a commercial.
• 1:29—Very brief breasts ripping off dress during a commercial.

John Canada Terrell. . . . . . . . . . . . . . . . . . . . . Todd

### The Boost (1989)

James Woods . . . . . . . . . . . . . . . . . . . . . Lenny Brown
Sean Young. . . . . . . . . . . . . . . . . . . . . . . . Linda Brown
• 0:16—Very, very brief breasts jumping into the swimming pool with James Woods. Very, very brief side view of right breast and buns, twice, getting out of the pool, sitting on edge, then getting pulled back in by James Woods.
•• 0:17—Left breast, while in pool talking to Woods. Right breast visible under water.
0:48—Brief breasts under water in spa with Woods.

### The Border (1982)

Elpidia Carrillo. . . . . . . . . . . . . . . . . . . . . . . . Maria
• 1:19—Half of right breast and half of left breast, after opening her blouse in shack with Jack Nicholson.
Harvey Keitel. . . . . . . . . . . . . . . . . . . . . . . . . . . Cal
Jack Nicholson . . . . . . . . . . . . . . . . . . . . . . . Charlie
Valerie Perrine. . . . . . . . . . . . . . . . . . . . . . . . .Marcy

### Border Heat (1988)

Darlanne Fluegel. . . . . . . . . . . . . . . . . . . Peggy Martin
0:23—In black bra straddling Ryan in the bedroom.
Michael J. Moore. . . . . . . . . . . . . . . . . . . . . J. C. Ryan
• 0:14—Buns, while taking off his clothes and getting into spa with Darlanne Fluegel.

### Born on the Fourth of July (1989)

Stephen Baldwin. . . . . . . . . . . . . . . . . . Billy Vorsovich
Tom Berenger. . . . . . . . . . . . . . . . . . Recruiting Sergeant
Tom Cruise. . . . . . . . . . . . . . . . . . . . . . . . . Ron Kovic
• 0:47—Very brief buns, sort of, while in bed at hospital when his rear end is sticking through the bottom of a bed.
Willem Dafoe . . . . . . . . . . . . . . . . . . . . . . . . Charlie
Vivica Fox . . . . . . . . . . . . . . . . . . . . . . . . . . . Hooker
• 0:50—Brief right breast, while taking off bra on top of patient in hospital. Dark.
Jason Gedrick . . . . . . . . . . . . . . . . . . . . . . .Martinez

Cordelia Gonzalez . . . . . . . . . . . . . . . . . . . Maria Elena
••• 1:43—Breasts in black panties, then full frontal nudity in bed with Tom Cruise.
Andrew Lauer. . . . . . . . . . . . . . . . . . . . . . . . . . . Vet
Mark Moses . . . . . . . . . . . . . . . . .Optomistic Doctor
Billie Neal. . . . . . . . . . . . . . . . . . . .Nurse Washington
David Neidorf . . . . . . . . . . . . . . . . . . . . . . . .Patient
Kyra Sedgwick . . . . . . . . . . . . . . . . . . . . . . . .Donna
Lili Taylor . . . . . . . . . . . . . . . . . . . . . . . Jamie Wilson

### Born to Race (1988)

Joseph Bottoms . . . . . . . . . . . . . . . . . . . . .Al Pagura
• 0:55—Brief buns, while taking off bathrobe on deck and jumping into the lake.
La Gena Hart . . . . . . . . . . . . . . . . . . . . . . . . . .Jenny
Marla Heasley. . . . . . . . . . . . . Andrea Lombardo
• 0:52—Buns, outside at night while kissing Joseph Bottoms.
Marc Singer . . . . . . . . . . . . . . . . . . . Kenny Landruff

### The Borrower (1989)

Mädchen Amick. . . . . . . . . . . . . . . . . . . . . . .Megan
Geri Betzler . . . . . . . . . . . . . . . . . . . . . . . . . .Astrid
Rae Dawn Chong. . . . . . . . . . . . . . . . . Diana Pierce
Tamara Clatterbuck . . . . . . . . . . . . . . Michele Chodiss
Lorrie Marlow. . . . . . . . . . . . . . . . . . . . Nurse Wilson
• 0:57—Brief left breast and upper half of right breast, while making love with a doctor in operating room.
Zoe Trilling. . . . . . . . . . . . . . . . . . . . . . . . . .Astrid

### The Boss' Wife (1986)

Arielle Dombasle . . . . . . . . . . . . . .Mrs. Louise Roalvang
• 1:01—Brief breasts getting a massage by the swimming pool.
••• 1:07—Breasts trying to seduce Daniel Stern at her place.
•• 1:14—Brief breasts in Stern's shower.
Melanie Mayron. . . . . . . . . . . . . . . . . . . .Janet Keefer
Daniel Stern. . . . . . . . . . . . . . . . . . . . . . . . Joel Keefer
Fisher Stevens . . . . . . . . . . . . . . . . . . Carlos Delgado

### Bound and Gagged: A Love Story (1993)

Ginger Lynn Allen . . . . . . . . . . . . . . . . . . . . . . .Leslie
••• 0:13—Breasts, while making love on kitchen counter with Chris Mulkey, then on the floor.
0:43—Very, very brief inner half of right breast, when her blouse is opened by Elizabeth.
• 0:48—Breasts, in back seat of car when a guy tries to "help" her.
Karen Black . . . . . . . . . . . . . . . . . . . . . . . . . . Carla
Chris Denton . . . . . . . . . . . . . . . . . . . . . . . . . . Cliff
•• 1:15—Buns, several times, while taking off his underwear in front of Elizabeth.
Chris Mulkey . . . . . . . . . . . . . . . . . . . . . . . . . Steve
Mary Ella Ross . . . . . . . . . . . . . . . . . . . . . . . . .Lida
• 0:05—Partial right breast, when getting caught making love in bed. Breasts, while in bed afterwards.
• 0:54—Right breast, while in bed with Chris Mulkey and Cliff during Cliff's dream.
• 0:58—Brief breasts, while making love with her lover when Cliff looks through skylight.

## Boxcar Bertha (1972)

David Carradine . . . . . . . . . . . . . . . . . . . . . Big Bill Shelly
- 0:54—Buns, while putting pants on after hearing a gun shot.

Bernie Casey . . . . . . . . . . . . . . . . . . . . . . . . Von Morton

Barbara Hershey . . . . . . . . . . . . . . . . . Bertha Thompson
- •• 0:10—Breasts making love with David Carradine in a railroad boxcar, then brief buns walking around when the train starts moving.
- 0:52—Nude, side view in house with David Carradine.
  0:54—Buns, putting on dress after hearing a gun shot.

## Boxing Helena (1993)

Sherilyn Fenn . . . . . . . . . . . . . . . . . . . . . . . . Helena
  0:11—In bra, undressing in bedroom while Julian Sands watches from outside in tree.
- ••• 0:13—Right breast, then breasts, while making love.
- 0:17—Very, very brief left breast when rolling over in bed.
- 0:18—Breasts, while getting out of bed after getting interrupted by a phone call.
  1:39—Briefly in bra in flashback.

Art Garfunkel . . . . . . . . . . . . . . . Dr. Lawrence Augustine

Bill Paxton . . . . . . . . . . . . . . . . . . . . . . . Ray O'Malley
- 0:17—Buns, while rolling over on top of Sherilyn Fenn in bed.
- •• 0:19—Very brief frontal nudity while sitting on bed. Seen behind side of liquor bottle.

Meg Register . . . . . . . . . . . . . . . . . . Marion Cavanaugh
- •• 0:06—Right breast in open dress in Julian Sand's flashback.

Julian Sands . . . . . . . . . . . . . . . . . . Dr. Nick Cavanaugh
- 1:00—Brief buns, putting his pants on after Anne tries to get him excited.
- 1:23—Buns, while making love with Fantasy Lover/ Nurse.

Nicolette Scorsese . . . . . . . . . . . . . Fantasy Lover/Nurse
- ••• 1:22—In black bra, panties and stockings then buns and breasts while making love with Julian Sands while Sherilyn Fenn watches.

## A Boy and His Dog (1976)

Suzanne Benton . . . . . . . . . . . . . . . . . . . . . Quilla June
- •• 0:29—Nude, getting dressed while Don Johnson watches.
- 0:45—Right breast lying down with Johnson after making love with him.

Don Johnson . . . . . . . . . . . . . . . . . . . . . . . . . . . Vic

## The Boy in Blue (1986; Canadian)

Melody Anderson . . . . . . . . . . . . . . . . . . . . . . Dulcie
- 0:07—Brief cleavage while making love with Nicolas Cage, then very brief top half of right breast when a policeman scares her.

Nicolas Cage . . . . . . . . . . . . . . . . . . . . Ned Hanlan

Kim Coates . . . . . . . . . . . . . . . . . . . . McCoy Man No. 2

Cynthia Dale . . . . . . . . . . . . . . . . . . . . . . . . Margaret
- ••• 1:15—Breasts standing in a loft kissing Nicolas Cage.

David Naughton . . . . . . . . . . . . . . . . . . . . . . . . Bill

## The Boys From Brazil (1978)

David Brandon . . . . . . . . . . . . . . . . . . . . . . . Schmidt

Steve Guttenberg . . . . . . . . . . . . . . . . . . Barry Kohler

Linda Hayden . . . . . . . . . . . . . . . . . . . . . . . . . Nancy
- 0:44—Very brief right breast, in mirror. Very, very brief left breast, twice, while in bed.
- 0:50—Very brief breasts, gagged, lying dead on bed.

## Boys Night Out (1987)

Teri Lynn Peake . . . . . . . . . . . . . . . . . . . . . . . . Maid
- ••• 0:25—Buns in G-string, then breasts doing a strip routine. Long scene.

## Boyz N the Hood (1991)

Angela Bassett . . . . . . . . . . . . . . . . . . . . . Reva Styles

Cuba Gooding, Jr. . . . . . . . . . . . . . . . . . . . . Tre Styles
- 0:42—Buns, in bed with Tisha. Don't see his face, but it is him.

Tammy Hansen . . . . . . . . . . . . . . . . . . . . . . . . Rosa

Nia Long . . . . . . . . . . . . . . . . . . . . . . . . . . Brandi
  1:16—In bra, lying in bed with Tre.
- 1:17—Left breast, while in bed with Tre. Don't see her face, but it is her.

Leonette Scott . . . . . . . . . . . . . . . . . . . . . . . Tisha
- 0:42—Side view of left breast in bed with Tre. Don't see her face.

## The Brain (1988)

Christine Kossack . . . . . . . . . . . . . . . . . . . . . . Vivian
- •• 0:24—Breasts on monitor, then breasts in person during Jim's fantasy.
- •• 1:11—Breasts again in the basement during Jim's hallucination.

## Brain Damage (1988)

Vicki Darnell . . . . . . . . . . . . . . . . . . Blonde in Hell Club

Joe Gonzales . . . . . . . . . . . . . . . . . . . . . Guy in Shower
- 0:54—Buns, while taking a shower.

## Brainwash (1982)

Yvette Mimieux . . . . . . . . . . . . . . . . . . . . . Bianca Ray

Walter Olkewicz . . . . . . . . . . . . . . . . . . . Buddy Gordon
- 0:29—Buns, after being forced to strip in front of guys in meeting. Upper half of frontal nudity.
- 0:31—Brief frontal nudity, while getting put in cage and humiliated. Long shot.
- 0:33—Buns, while still in cage. Long shot.
- 0:36—Buns, while getting spanked.
- •• 0:42—Frontal nudity, while standing in the center of the group.
- 0:43—Briefly nude, while getting his clothes.

Cindy Pickett . . . . . . . . . . . . . . . . . . . . . Lyn Nilsson
  1:24—In sheer beige bra and panties, while getting her clothes taken off in front of group.

Leo Rossi . . . . . . . . . . . . . . . . . . . . . . . Chris Morris

## *Brainwaves* (1983)

Corinne Alphen . . . . . . . . . . . . . . . . . . . . . Lelia Adams
- 0:03—Brief side of right breast, reaching out to turn off the water faucets in the bathtub.
- 0:05—Full frontal nudity, getting electrocuted in the bubble bath.
- 0:50—Brief right breast, during Kaylie's vision.

Keir Dullea . . . . . . . . . . . . . . . . . . . . . Julian Bedford
Suzanna Love . . . . . . . . . . . . . . . . . . . . Kaylie Bedford

## *Bram Stoker's Dracula* (1992)

Cary Elwes . . . . . . . . . . . . . . . . . .Lord Arthur Holmwood
Sadie Frost . . . . . . . . . . . . . . . . . . . . . . . . . . . . . Lucy
- 0:41—Left breast, while making love with Dracula on bench outside at night during the rain.
- • 0:58—Breasts in bed, quite a few times, after getting bit by Dracula and getting a blood transfusion.
- 1:12—Brief right breast in gaping nightgown.
- 1:19—Left breast, while lying in bed when Dracula pays a return visit.
- 1:20—Brief left breast, when the wolf Dracula jumps on the bed.

Richard E. Grant . . . . . . . . . . . . . . . . . Dr. Jack Seward
Honey Lauren . . . . . . . . . . . . . . . . . . . Peep Show Girl
Gary Oldman . . . . . . . . . . . . . . . . . Dracula/Prince Vlad
Keanu Reeves . . . . . . . . . . . . . . . . . . . Jonathan Harker
Maude Winchester . . . . . . . . . . . . . . .Downstairs Maid

## *Breakfast in Bed* (1990)

Marilyn Chambers . . . . . . . . . . . . . . Marilyn Valentine
- • 0:04—Full frontal nudity, getting out of bubble bath and drying herself off while talking to her manager.
- • • 0:21—Breasts, taking off swimsuit top and sunbathing. Nude, swimming underwater.
- • 0:53—In bra, then breasts making love.
- 1:01—In black bra and panties, undressing in her room.
- • 1:16—Full frontal nudity, getting out of bed, putting on robe, then getting back in with Jonathan.

Courtney James . . . . . . . . . . . . . . . . . . . . . . . . .Mitzi
- • • 0:36—Breasts, walking into the pool. Also seen from under water.
- • • 0:37—Breasts and bun in G-string, getting out of pool.
- 0:39—Breasts on the beach with Mr. Stewart.

Michael Rose . . . . . . . . . . . . . . . . . .Jonathan Maxwell
- 1:16—Half of buns, while lying in bed with Marilyn Chambers.

David Sills . . . . . . . . . . . . . . . . . . . . . . . Henry Huntley
- • 0:25—Buns, while in bed with Wendy.
- • 0:35—Brief buns, while standing up in boat with Wendy.

## *Breakfast in Paris* (1981)

Rod Mullinar . . . . . . . . . . . . . . . . . . . . Michael Barnes
- • 0:29—Buns, getting up and out of bed.

Barbara Parkins . . . . . . . . . . . . . . . . . . . Jackie Wyatt
- • • 0:41—Right breast, while rolling over in bed. Breasts when sitting up in bed.

## *Breaking All the Rules* (1985; Canadian)

Papusha Demitro . . . . . . . . . . . . . . . . . . . . . . . . Patty
Rachel Hayward . . . . . . . . . . . . . . . . . . . . . . . . .Angie
- • • • 0:16—Breasts changing in the bathroom.
- • 0:43—Brief breasts after being felt up on roller coaster.

## *Breathless* (1983)

Richard Gere . . . . . . . . . . . . . . . . . . . . . . . . . . . Jesse
- • • 0:11—Frontal nudity dancing and singing in the shower. Hard to see because of the steam.
- • • 0:52—Buns, while taking his pants off to get into the shower with Valerie Kaprisky, then more buns in bed. Very brief frontal nudity. Dark, hard to see.
- • 0:53—Very, very brief top of frontal nudity popping up when Kaprisky gets out of bed.

Valerie Kaprisky . . . . . . . . . . . . . . . . . Monica Poiccard
0:23—Brief side view of left breast in her apartment. Long shot, hard to see anything.
- • • • 0:47—Breasts in her apartment with Richard Gere kissing.
- • • 0:52—Brief full frontal nudity standing in the shower when Gere opens the door, afterwards, buns in bed.
- • • 0:53—Breasts, holding up two dresses for Gere to pick from, then breasts putting the black dress on.
- 1:23—Breasts behind a movie screen with Gere. Lit with red light.

William Tepper . . . . . . . . . . . . . . . . . . . . . . . . . . . .Paul

## *A Breed Apart* (1984; Made for Cable Movie)

Jane Bentzen . . . . . . . . . . . . . . . . . . . . . . . . Reporter
- • • • 0:55—Left breast in bed with Powers Booth, then full frontal nudity getting out of bed and putting her clothes on.

Rutger Hauer . . . . . . . . . . . . . . . . . . . . . . . Jim Malden
Kathleen Turner . . . . . . . . . . . . . . . . . . Stella Clayton
- • • 1:12—Breasts in bed with Rutger Hauer, then left breast.

## *Breeders* (1986)

LeeAnne Baker . . . . . . . . . . . . . . . . . . . . . . . Kathleen
- • • • 0:28—Nude, undressing from her nurse outfit in the kitchen, then taking a shower.
- 0:59—Brief breasts in alien nest. (She's the blonde in front.)
- • • 1:08—Breasts in alien nest.
- 1:09—Breasts in alien nest again. (Behind Alec.)
- 1:11—Breasts behind Alec again. Then long shot when nest is electrocuted. (On the left.)

Amy Brentano . . . . . . . . . . . . . . . . . . . . . . . . . . Gail
- 0:59—Long shot of buns, getting into the nest.
- 1:07—Breasts in nest, throwing her head back.
- • • 1:08—Brief breasts, writhing around in the nest, then breasts, arching her back.
- 1:11—Breasts, long shot, just before the nest is destroyed.

Adriane Lee . . . . . . . . . . . . . . . . . . . . . . . . . . . . .Alec
- • • 0:49—Breasts, undressing while talking on the phone.

- 1:07—Brief breasts, covered with goop, in the alien nest.
- 1:08—Brief breasts in nest behind Frances Raines.
- 1:09—Brief breasts behind Raines again.
- 1:11—Breasts, lying back in the goop, then long shot breasts.

Natalie O'Connell . . . . . . . . . . . . . . . . . . . . . . . Donna
- 0:02—Very brief left breast, getting her blouse ripped by creature.
- •• 0:44—Breasts, sitting up in hospital bed, then buns, walking down the hall.
- ••• 0:47—More breasts and buns, walking around outside.
- 1:10—Brief breasts, standing up in the alien nest.

Frances Raines . . . . . . . . . . . . . . . . . . Karinsa Marshall
- ••• 0:12—Nude stretching and exercising in photo studio.
- 0:16—Brief full frontal nudity, getting attacked by the creature.
- ••• 0:53—Breasts and buns, taking off her blouse and walking down the hall and into the basement. Long scene.
- 1:07—Very brief right breast in the alien nest with the other women.
- 1:10—Brief breasts standing up.

### *Brewster McCloud* (1970)
Shelley Duvall . . . . . . . . . . . . . . . . . . . . . . . . Suzanne
Sally Kellerman . . . . . . . . . . . . . . . . . . . . . . . . Louise
     0:43—Brief back side of right breast giving a boy a bath.
- •• 1:07—Breasts, playing in a fountain.

Jennifer Salt . . . . . . . . . . . . . . . . . . . . . . . . . . . Hope

### *Bride of Re-Animator* (1989)
Kathleen Kinmont . . . . . . . . . . . . . . . . Gloria/The Bride
- 0:58—Brief breasts several times with her top pulled down to defibrillate her heart.
     1:17—Breasts under gauze. Her body has gruesome looking special effects appliances all over it.
     1:22—More breasts under gauze.
     1:24—More breasts. Pretty unappealing.
     1:27—Brief buns, when turning around after ripping out her own heart.

Fabiana Udenio . . . . . . . . . . . . . . . . . Francesca Danelli
     0:45—Most of her left breast in bed with Dan. His hand covers it most of the time.

### *The Bride Wore Black* (1968; French/Italian)
Jeanne Moreau . . . . . . . . . . . . . . . . . . . . . . . Julie Kohler
     0:00—Left breast in B&W photo of a painting, that is coming off a printing press.
     0:29—Left breast, in painting on the wall.
- 1:24—Brief breasts, taking her dress in front of a patterned mirror.
     1:37—Breasts in painting when the police photograph it.

Alexandra Stewart . . . . . . . . . . . . . . . . . . . .Miss Becker

### *Bright Angel* (1990)
Valerie Perrine . . . . . . . . . . . . . . . . . . . . . . . . .Alleen

Mary Kay Place . . . . . . . . . . . . . . . . . . . . . . . . . . .Judy
Lili Taylor . . . . . . . . . . . . . . . . . . . . . . . . . . . . . Lucy
- 0:26—Brief top of breasts under water, taking a bath in a pond.
- •• 0:27—Breasts, walking out of the pond.

### *A Brilliant Disguise* (1994)
Lysette Anthony . . . . . . . . . . . . . . . . . . .Michele Ramsey
- •• 0:44—Breasts and buns, while making love with Andy.

Corbin Bernsen . . . . . . . . . . . . . . . . . . . . . . . Dr. Martin
Dawn Ann Billings . . . . . . Brunette in French Restaurant
Devin De Vasquez . . . . . . . . . . . . . . . . . . . . . . .Gianna
Anthony John Denison . . . . . . . . . . . . . . . .Andy Manola
Christina Fulton . . . . . . . . . . . . . . . . . . . . . . . .Marlene
Beverly Johnson . . . . . . . . . . . . . . . . . . . . . . . Barbara
Cherie Michan . . . . . . . . . . . . . . . . . . . . . . . . . Selma
Elizabeth Nottoli . . . . . . . . . . . . . Janet/Fashion Model
Kathy Shower . . . . . . . . . . . . . . . . . . . . . . . Lila Foster

### *Brimstone and Treacle* (1982; British)
Sting . . . . . . . . . . . . . . . . . . . . . . . . . . . .Martin Taylor
- 1:19—Buns, while making love with Suzanna Hamilton on her bed. Dark, hard to see.

Suzanna Hamilton . . . . . . . . . . . . . . . . . . Patricia Bates
- •• 0:47—Breasts in bed when Sting opens her blouse and fondles her.
- •• 1:18—Breasts in bed when Sting fondles her again.
- 1:20—Brief lower frontal nudity writhing around on the bed after Denholm Elliott comes downstairs.

Dudley Sutton . . . . . . . . . . . . . . . . . . . . . . . . .Stroller

### *Bring Me the Head of Alfredo Garcia* (1974)
Kris Kristofferson . . . . . . . . . . . . . . . . . . . . . . . Paco
Isela Vega . . . . . . . . . . . . . . . . . . . . . . . . . . . . . Elita
- 0:25—Brief right breast a couple of times, then brief breasts in bed with Warren Oaks.
- ••• 0:44—Breasts when Kris Kristofferson rips her top off. Long scene.
- •• 0:52—Breasts sitting in shower with wet hair.
- •• 1:49—Still from shower scene during credits.

### *Broadcast News* (1987)
Lois Chiles . . . . . . . . . . . . . . . . . . . . . . .Jennifer Mack
Holly Hunter . . . . . . . . . . . . . . . . . . . . . . . Jane Craig
William Hurt . . . . . . . . . . . . . . . . . . . . . . . .Tom Grunik
- •• 0:59—Brief buns when getting up from bed after making love with Jennifer. Shadow of semi-erect penis on the wall when she notices it.

### *Broken Trust* (1993)
Edward Albert . . . . . . . . . . . . . . . . . . . . . . . Peter Wyatt
Nick Cassavetes . . . . . . . . . . . . . . . . . . . . . .Alan Brogan
Wendy MacDonald . . . . . . . . . . . . . . .Dr. Joyce Radley

### *The Bronx War* (1989)
Fabio Urena . . . . . . . . . . . . . . . . . . . . . . . . . . . . Tony
- 0:54—Buns, getting up out of bed with Alicia and getting dressed.

### *Brubaker* (1980)
Jane Alexander . . . . . . . . . . . . . . . . . . . . . . . . .Lillian

Linda Haynes. . . . . . . . . . . . . . . . . . . . . . . . . Carol
• 1:03—Breasts getting dressed with Huey in bed-
room when Robert Redford comes in.
David Keith. . . . . . . . . . . . . . . . . . . . . Larry Lee Bullen
Yaphet Kotto. . . . . . . . . . . . . . . . . . . . Dickie Coombes
J. C. Quinn . . . . . . . . . . . . . . . . . . . . . . . . . . . .n.a.

## Bucktown (1975)
Pam Grier . . . . . . . . . . . . . . . . . . . . . . . . . . Aretha
••• 0:29—Left breast, while in bed with Fred Williamson.
Fred Williamson . . . . . . . . . . . . . . . . . . . . . . . .Duke

## Buford's Beach Bunnies (1992)
Suzanne Ager . . . . . . . . . . . . . . . . . . .`. . .Boopsie Underall
•• 0:19—Breasts in the shower.
• 0:20—Brief breasts when her towel falls off in front
of telegram guy.
• 0:36—Buns, in red two piece swimsuit at the beach.
• 0:37—Buns, while walking up the stairs.
0:38—In white lingerie in her bedroom with Jeeter.
Avalon Anders. . . . . . . . . . . . . . . . . . . . .Santa's Helper
Stephanie Anderson . . . . . . . . . . . . . . . . . . . . .Marilyn
Rikki Brando . . . . . . . . . . . . . . . . . . . . Lauren Beatty
•• 0:54—Breasts in bed with Jeeter.
Jim Hanks . . . . . . . . . . . . . . . . . . . . . . . . .Jeeter Buford
• 0:17—Buns, getting his underwear yanked down by
Dr. Van Horney. (Don't see his face.)
Francesca "Kitten" Natividad. . . . . . . . . . . . Madam #1
Monique Parent . . . . . . . . . . . . . . . . . Amber Dexterous
•• 0:09—Breasts, fooling around with a customer in
the restroom.
• 0:11—More breasts, with the customer.
• 0:42—Left breast in gaping vest, trying to get into
Jeeter's pants.
••• 1:14—Breasts in bedroom with a customer.
David Robinson. . . . . . . . . Forey, The Amazing Foreskin

## Bull Durham (1988)
Kevin Costner . . . . . . . . . . . . . . . . . . . . . . .Crash Davis
David Neidorf . . . . . . . . . . . . . . . . . . . . . . . . . .Bobby
Tim Robbins . . . . . . . . . . . . . Ebby Calvin "Nuke" La Loosh
• 0:03—Buns, while in locker room making love with
Millie when the coach sees them.
Jenny Robertson . . . . . . . . . . . . . . . . . . . . Millie
Susan Sarandon . . . . . . . . . . . . . . . . . . . . Annie Savoy
1:39—Brief right breast peeking out from under her
dress after crawling on the kitchen floor to get a
match.

## Bulletproof (1988)
Lydie Denier . . . . . . . . . . . . . . . . . . . . . . . . . Tracy
•• 0:14—Breasts in Gary Busey's bathtub.
0:20—Brief buns, putting on shirt after getting out
of bed. Very, very brief side view of left breast.
Darlanne Fluegel. . . . . . . . . . . . . . . .Devon Shepard

## Bullies (1985)
Olivia D'Abo . . . . . . . . . . . . . . . . . . . . . .Becky Cullen
•• 0:39—In wet white T-shirt swimming in river while
Matt watches.

## Burglar (1987)
Steve Shellen . . . . . . . . . . . . . . . . . Christopher Marshall
• 0:26—Buns, while in front of closet that Whoopi
Goldberg is hiding in. Don't see his face, but probably him.

## The Burning (1981)
Jason Alexander . . . . . . . . . . . . . . . . . . . . . . . Dave
• 0:29—Buns, pulling swimsuit down and up to moon
Glazer. (On the far left.)
Leah Ayres-Hamilton . . . . . . . . . . . . . . . . . . . .Michelle
Carrick Glenn. . . . . . . . . . . . . . . . . . . . . . . . . .Sally
••• 0:19—Breasts, taking a shower in the outdoor showers.
• 0:20—Very brief breasts, putting her T-shirt back on.
Carolyn Houlihan. . . . . . . . . . . . . . . . . . . . . .Karen
•• 0:45—Nude, going skinny dipping with Eddy in lake
at night.
••• 0:46—Brief breasts several times in the lake with Eddy, then breasts and buns getting out. Nice buns
shot.
•• 0:47—Nude, walking around in the woods, looking
for her clothes.
Holly Hunter. . . . . . . . . . . . . . . . . . . . . . . .Sophie
Larry Joshua . . . . . . . . . . . . . . . . . . . . . . . Glazer
•• 1:02—Buns, getting out of the sleeping bag after
making love with Sally.
J. R. McKechnie . . . . . . . . . . . . . . . . . . . . . . . Fish
• 0:29—Buns, pulling swimsuit down and up to moon
Glazer. (On the far right.)
Fisher Stevens . . . . . . . . . . . . . . . . . . . . . Woodstock
• 0:29—Buns, pulling swimsuit down and up to moon
Glazer. (2nd from the right.)
K.C. Townsend. . . . . . . . . . . . . . . . . . . . . . . Hooker

## Bury Me an Angel (1972)
Dan Haggerty . . . . . . . . . . . . . . . . . . . . . . . . Ken
• 1:17—Brief buns, while making love with Dag in
bed. Lit with red light. Kind of a long shot, don't see
his face very well.
Dixie Lee Peabody . . . . . . . . . . . . . . . . . . . . .Dag
0:11—Very brief silhouette of left breast, while getting into bed.
• 0:13—Very brief right breast, while getting back into
bed.
••• 0:41—Nude, skinny dipping in river and getting
out.
• 1:16—Breasts making love in bed with Dan Haggerty. Lit with red light.
Clyde Ventura . . . . . . . . . . . . . . . . . . . . . . . Bernie

## Bushido Blade (1979; British/U.S.)
Laura Gemser. . . . . . . . . . . . . . . . . . . . . . . . .Tomoe
• 1:08—Brief right breast taking off her top in bedroom with Captain Hawk.

## Buster and Billie (1974)
Joan Goodfellow . . . . . . . . . . . . . . . . . . . . . . Billie
0:33—Brief breasts in truck with Jan-Michael Vin-
cent. Dark, hard to see.

- 1:06—Buns, then brief breasts in the woods with Vincent.
- 1:25—Brief left breast getting raped by jerks.

Pamela Sue Martin . . . . . . . . . . . . . . . . . . Margie Hooks
Jan-Michael Vincent . . . . . . . . . . . . . . . . . .Buster Lane
- ••• 1:06—Frontal nudity taking off his underwear and walking to Billie. Buns, in slow motion, while swinging into the water.

### Butterfly (1982)
Stacy Keach. . . . . . . . . . . . . . . . . . . . . . . . . .Jeff Tyler
Pia Zadora. . . . . . . . . . . . . . . . . . . . . . . . . . . . .Kady
　　0:15—Silhouette changing while Stacy Keach watches.
- •• 0:33—Breasts and buns getting into the bath.
- ••• 0:35—Breasts in bathtub when Keach is giving her a bath.

### Buying Time (1987)
Laura Cruikshank. . . . . . . . . . . . . . . . . . . . . . .Jessica
- •• 0:52—Breasts several times making love with Ron on pool table.

### By Dawn's Early Light (1990; Made for Cable Movie)
Rebecca De Mornay . . . . . . . . . . . . . . . Cindy Moreau
Randal Patrick . . . . . . . . . . . . . . . . . . . . . . . . O'Toole
- • 0:14—Brief buns while in shower room getting dressed during red alert.

### By Design (1982; Canadian)
Sara Botsford. . . . . . . . . . . . . . . . . . . . . . . . . . Angie
- • 0:23—Full frontal nudity in the ocean. Long shot, hard to see anything.
- • 1:08—Brief side view of left breast making love in bed while talking on the phone.

Patty Duke . . . . . . . . . . . . . . . . . . . . . . . . . . . Helen
- •• 0:49—Left breast, lying in bed.
- •• 1:05—Brief left breast sitting on bed.
- • 1:06—Brief left breast, then brief right breast lying in bed with the photographer.

### Bye Bye Baby (1989; Italian)
Carol Alt . . . . . . . . . . . . . . . . . . . . . . . . . . . . Sandra
　　0:09—Part of right breast, while in the shower.
　　0:22—Wearing a white bra, while taking off her blouse in the doctor's office.
Luca Barbareschi . . . . . . . . . . . . . . . . . . . . . . . . Paulo
- • 0:20—Brief buns, while on top of Brigitte Nielsen in bed.
Brigitte Nielsen . . . . . . . . . . . . . . . . . . . . . . . . . .Lisa
- • 0:20—Brief side view of right breast, while lying on a guy in bed. Nice buns shot also.

### Bye Bye Blues (1989; Canadian)
Rebecca Jenkins. . . . . . . . . . . . . . . . . . . . Daisy Cooper
- • 0:01—Brief breasts, getting out of bathtub. Very brief buns, while running outside and putting on robe to get away from snake.
- • 0:42—Upper half of breasts, while in bathtub.
- • 0:45—Very brief left breast under water in bathtub.
Chad Krowchuk . . . . . . . . . . Richard Cooper (5 Years)
- • 0:41—Buns, getting out of bathtub and dried off.

Michael Ontkean . . . . . . . . . . . . . . . . . . . Teddy Cooper

### Bye Bye Brazil (1980; Brazilian)
Betty Faria . . . . . . . . . . . . . . . . . . . . . . . . . . . Salomé
- •• 0:28—Breasts, wearing red panties, backstage with Cigano.
- • 0:29—Left breast while sitting in a chair.
- •• 0:38—Breasts backstage with Ciço.
- • 1:24—Buns, under a mosquito net with a customer.
Fábio Junior . . . . . . . . . . . . . . . . . . . . . . . . . . . .Ciço
- •• 0:38—Buns, while backstage with Salomé.
Zaira Zambelli . . . . . . . . . . . . . . . . . . . . . . . . Dasdô
- •• 1:11—Buns, then breasts outside by a boat with Cigano.

### C.O.D. (1983)
Corinne Alphen . . . . . . . . . . . . . . . . Cheryl Westwood
- • 0:21—Brief breasts changing clothes in dressing room while talking to Zacks.
- • 1:25—Brief breasts taking off her blouse in dressing room scene.
　　1:26—In green bra, talking to Albert.
　　1:28—In green bra during fashion show.
Carole Davis . . . . . . . . . . . . . . . . . . . . Contessa Bazzini
- • 1:25—Brief breasts in dressing room scene in black panties, garter belt and stockings when she takes off her robe.
　　1:29—In black top during fashion show.
Samantha Fox . . . . . . . . . . . . . . . . . . . . Female Reporter
Teresa Ganzel. . . . . . . . . . . . . . . . . . . . . . . Lisa Foster
- • 0:46—Right breast hanging out of dress while dancing at disco with Zack.
- • 1:25—Brief side view of left breast taking off purple robe in dressing room scene. Then in white bra talking to Albert.
　　1:29—In white bra during fashion show.
Marilyn Joi . . . . . . . . . . . . . . . . . . . . . . . Debbie Winter
- •• 1:16—Breasts during photo session.
- • 1:25—Brief breasts taking off robe wearing red garter belt during dressing room scene.
　　1:26—In red bra, while talking to Albert.
　　1:30—In red bra during fashion show.
Olivia Pascal . . . . . . . . . . . . . . . . . . . . . . . . Holly Fox
　　1:30—In white top during fashion show.

### Cabin Fever (1992)
Judd Dunning . . . . . . . . . . . . . . . . . . . . . .Jack Reynolds
- ••• 0:27—Nude in bed with Lenore.
- ••• 0:33—Buns, making love in bed with Lenore. Long scene.
- ••• 0:35—More buns while making love.
- ••• 0:37—Still more buns while making love.
Belinda Farrell . . . . . . . . . . . . . . . . . . . .Lenore Hoffman
- • 0:00—Brief right breast in gaping nightie when bending over.
- ••• 0:07—Breasts on the floor with Jack during her fantasy. Long scene.
- ••• 0:16—Breasts, sitting on floor, while playing with herself and fantasizing about Jack.
- ••• 0:20—Breasts and buns, undressing and getting into bathtub.

- 0:23—Brief lower frontal nudity and right breast in open robe.
- •• 0:27—Nude in bed with Jack and rolling over and getting out of bed.
- 0:30—Brief breasts opening her blouse in front of Jack.
- ••• 0:32—Nude, making love in bed with Jack. Nice, long scene.
- 0:41—Right breast, while sitting in bed and putting on a blouse.
- 0:43—In white lingerie in the house.

## Cabo Blanco (1982)
Ana de Sade . . . . . . . . . . . . . . . . . . . . . . . . . . . . Rosa
- 0:34—Brief breasts, lying in bed and talking to a guy.
- 0:36—Brief right breast, twice, when he gets out of bed to look out the window.
Dominique Sanda . . . . . . . . . . . Marie Claire Allesandri
- 1:27—Buns, swimming in pool. Long shot.

## Caddyshack (1980)
Sarah Holcomb . . . . . . . . . . . . . . . Maggie O'Hooligan
Cindy Morgan. . . . . . . . . . . . . . . . . . Lacey Underall
0:50—Very, very brief side view of left breast sliding into the swimming pool. Very blurry.
- •• 0:58—Breasts in bed with Danny three times.

## Cadillac Girls (1993; Canadian)
Jennifer Dale . . . . . . . . . . . . . . . . . . . . . . . . . . . Sally
- ••• 0:41—In bra, then breasts while making love in bedroom with Gregory Harrison.
Morrissey Dunn. . . . . . . . . . . . . . . . . . . . . . . . Miles
- 0:02—Buns, while getting out of bed with Page.
Gregory Harrison. . . . . . . . . . . . . . . . . . . . . . . . Sam
Mia Kirshner . . . . . . . . . . . . . . . . . . . . . . . . . . Page
- 0:02—Back half of breast in mirror when Miles gets out of bed. Long shot.

## Cadillac Man (1990)
Fran Drescher . . . . . . . . . . . . . . . . . . . . . Joy Munchack
- 0:07—Very brief right breast several times while in bed with Robin Williams.
Zack Norman . . . . . . . . . . . . . . . . . Harry Munchack
Lori Petty. . . . . . . . . . . . . . . . . . . . . . . . . . . . . . Lila
Pamela Reed . . . . . . . . . . . . . . . . . . . . . . . . . . Tina
Tim Robbins . . . . . . . . . . . . . . . . . . . . . . . . . Larry
Annabella Sciorra . . . . . . . . . . . . . . . . . . . . . Donna
Robin Williams . . . . . . . . . . . . . . . . . . . . Joey O'Brien

## Caged Fear (1992)
Karen Black . . . . . . . . . . . . . . . . . . . . . . . . . . Blanche
Loretta Devine. . . . . . . . . . . . . . . . . . . . . . . . . Judy
Jo Ann Harris . . . . . . . . . . . . . . . . . . . Big As A House #1
David Keith . . . . . . . . . . . . . . . . . . . . . . Tommy Lang
Ray Sharkey. . . . . . . . . . . . . . . . . . . . Warden Hayes
- 0:44—Buns, while lying dead on ground when police are checking the crime scene. Don't see his face.
Charlie Spradling. . . . . . . . . . . . . . . . . . . . . . . . . Joy

## Caged Fury (1984)
Taaffe O'Connell . . . . . . . . . . . . . . . . . . . . . . . Honey
- •• 0:17—Breasts on bed with a guard. Mostly left breast.
0:40—Very, very brief tip of left breast peeking out between arms in shower.
- 1:06—Very brief breasts getting blouse ripped open by a guard in the train.

## Caged Fury (1989)
Blake Bahner . . . . . . . . . . . . . . . . . . . . . . . . Buck Lewis
April Dawn Dollarhide . . . . . . . . . . . . . Rhonda Wallace
- 0:54—Briefly nude, after dropping towel and joining Kat in the showers.
Ron Jeremy. . . . . . . . . . . . . . . . . . . . . . . . . . . n.a.
Alison Le Priol. . . . . . . . . . . . . . . . . . . Blonde Escapee
- 0:00—In bra and panties, then buns in G-string. Then brief breasts while crawling on the floor.
Janine Lindemulder . . . . . . . . . . . . . . . . . . . . . . Lulu
0:14—Dancing in bar in black bra and G-string.
- 0:15—Brief breasts dancing in front of Erik Estrada.
Sandra Margot. . . . . . . . . . . . . . . . . . . . Crazy Daisy
1:10—Buns in G-string and bra dancing for some men.
- •• 1:11—Breasts after taking off bra.
Roxanna Michaels . . . . . . . . . . . Katherine "Kat" Collins
0:32—In white bra in open blouse on couch with Jack Carter.
- 0:39—Breasts while getting searched upon entering prison with other topless women.
Melissa Anne Moore. . . . . . . . . . . . . . . . . . . . Gloria
Ty Randolph. . . . . . . . . . . . . . . . . Warden Sybil Thorn
- •• 0:53—Breasts and buns undressing for bath, then in the bathtub.
Elena Sahagun . . . . . . . . . . . . . . . . . Tracy Collins
0:51—In bra when Buck holds her hostage.
- •• 0:58—Left breast while taking a shower.

## Caged Heat (1974)
*a.k.a. Renegade Girls*
Juanita Brown . . . . . . . . . . . . . . . . . . . . . . . Maggie
- 0:25—Breasts in shower scene.
Deborah Clearbranch. . . . . . . . . . . . . . . . . . Debbie
Roberta Collins. . . . . . . . . . . . . . . . . . . . . . . Belle
- 0:11—Very brief breasts getting blouse ripped open by Juanita.
- ••• 1:01—Breasts while the prison doctor has her drugged so he can take pictures of her.
Erica Gavin. . . . . . . . . . . . . . . . . . . . Jacqueline Wilson
- 0:08—Buns, getting strip searched before entering prison.
- •• 0:25—Breasts in shower scene.
- 0:30—Brief side view of left breast in another shower scene.
Cheryl Smith . . . . . . . . . . . . . . . . . . . . . . . . . Lavelle
- 0:04—Brief left breast, dreaming in her jail cell that a guy is caressing her through the bars.
- •• 0:25—Breasts in the shower scene.
- •• 0:50—Brief nude in the solitary cell.

## *Caged Heat 2: Stripped of Freedom* (1993)

Pamella D'Pella . . . . . . . . . . . . . . . . . . . . . . . . . Paula
••• 0:13—Breasts, while making love with the warden on sofa in his office.
••• 0:42—Brief buns in T-back and breasts, while dancing for the warden in his office.
Susan Harvey . . . . . . . . . . . . . . . . . . . . . . . . . . Lucy
• 1:00—Brief breasts, while in her cell, flashing to distract a guard.
Jewel Shepard . . . . . . . . . . . . . . . . . . . . . . . . Amanda
•• 0:15—In bra and panties, then breasts, while undressing for strip search in the warden's office.
•• 0:49—Breasts, after getting her prison shirt ripped open, then whipped in front of the other prisoners.

## *Caged Terror* (1971)

Percy Harkness . . . . . . . . . . . . . . . . . . . . . . . . Richard
• 0:29—Brief buns, while rolling over on Janet after rubbing blood on her.
• 1:00—Buns, when getting into bed.
•• 1:01—Frontal nudity, while getting out of bed to look out the window.

## *Cal* (1984; Irish)

John Lynch . . . . . . . . . . . . . . . . . . . . . . . . . . . . . Cal
• 1:20—Buns, while getting into bed with Helen Mirren.
Helen Mirren . . . . . . . . . . . . . . . . . . . . . . . Marcella
1:18—In a white bra and slip.
•• 1:20—Brief frontal nudity taking off clothes and getting into bed with Cal in his cottage, then right breast making love.

## *Calendar Girl* (1993)

Stephanie Anderson . . . . . . . . . . . . . . Marilyn Monroe
• 0:44—Buns and long shot of left breast at the nude beach while wearing a wig.
• 0:46—Buns, standing up at the beach, taking off her wig while the bad guys talk to the boys in the water.
Maxwell Caulfield . . . . . . . . . . . . . . . . Man in Bathrobe
Gabriel Olds . . . . . . . . . . . . . . . . . . . . . . . . Ned Bleuer
•• 0:44—Buns, while walking behind and next to Jason Priestly at the nude beach.
•• 0:46—Buns, while running after Priestly into the surf at the beach.
Jason Priestley . . . . . . . . . . . . . . . . . . . Roy Darpinian
••• 0:44—Buns, while walking to and at nude beach with his two buddies.
••• 0:46—Buns, while walking to the surf. Very, very brief frontal nudity when it pops up to his belly when he turns around to talk to his buddies.
Steve Railsback . . . . . . . . . . . . . . . . . . . . Roy's Father

## *California Casanova* (1991)

Michelle Johnston . . . . . . . . . . . . . . . . . . . . . . Laura
0:12—Buns, in black G-string, while dancing on stage.
• 0:18—Brief breasts under sheer black top, while dancing in front of a guy in pool house.

## *California Dreaming* (1978)

Kirsten Baker . . . . . . . . . . . . . . . . . . . . . . . . . .Karen
John Calvin . . . . . . . . . . . . . . . . . . . . . . . . . . . Rick
Stacey Nelkin . . . . . . . . . . . . . . . . . . . . . . . . . Marsha
Glynnis O'Connor . . . . . . . . . . . . . . . . . . . . . . Corky
•• 0:11—Breasts pulling her top over her head when T.T. is using the bathroom.
1:12—In white bra, in bed with T.T.
••• 1:14—Breasts in bed with T.T.
Tanya Roberts . . . . . . . . . . . . . . . . . . . . Stephanie
Dorothy Tristan . . . . . . . . . . . . . . . . . . . . . . . . . Fay
0:05—In braless white top, jogging on the beach with Glynnis O'Connor.
• 0:20—Brief breasts changing clothes while a group of boys peek through a hole in the wall.

## *California Hot Wax* (1992)

Sharon Cain . . . . . . . . . . . . . . . . . . . . . . . . . . .Loretta
•• 0:55—Breasts, changing in car wash maintenance room in front of Scott.
•• 0:59—Breasts in and out of swimming pool with Scott.
Jacqueline Jade . . . . . . . . . . . . . . . . . . . . . .Bikini Girl
Carla Morrell . . . . . . . . . . . . . . . . . . . . . . . .Bikini Girl
Carmen Morrell . . . . . . . . . . . . . . . . . . . . . .Bikini Girl
Kimberly Speiss . . . . . . . . . . . . . . . . . . . . . .Bikini Girl
Sándra Wild . . . . . . . . . . . . . . . . . . . . . . . . .Bikini Girl

## *California Suite* (1978)

Jane Fonda . . . . . . . . . . . . . . . . . . . . . . Hannah Warren
Sheila Frazier . . . . . . . . . . . . . . . . . . . Bettina Panama
Denise Galik . . . . . . . . . . . . . . . . . . . . . . . . . . Bunny
Maggie Smith . . . . . . . . . . . . . . . . . . . .Diana Barrie
• 1:05—Very brief side of left breast, putting nightgown on over her head.

## *Caligula* (1980)

(X-rated, 147 minute version.)
Adrianna Asti . . . . . . . . . . . . . . . . . . . . . . . . . . . .Ennia
• 0:27—Breasts at side of bed with Malcolm McDowell when he feels her breasts.
•• 0:54—Breasts lying down surrounded by slaves. Mostly her right breast.
Mirella D'Angelo . . . . . . . . . . . . . . . . . . . . . . . . .Livia
•• 1:08—Buns and breasts in kitchen with Malcolm McDowell. Full frontal nudity on table when he rapes her in front of her husband-to-be.
Anneka di Lorenzo . . . . . . . . . . . . . . . . . . . . . .Messalina
••• 1:16—Nude, making love with Lori Wagner. Long scene.
Malcolm McDowell . . . . . . . . . . . . . . . . . . . . .Caligula
• 0:05—Buns, while rolling around in bed with Drusilla.
• 0:36—Brief buns, while taking ring off of Peter O'Toole.
• 0:46—Very brief buns while running to bed.
0:51—Buns, while putting Drusilla down in bed.
• 1:14—Nude walking around outside in the rain. Dark, long shot.
2:23—Very brief buns while under his white robe.

Helen Mirren.........................Caesonia
    1:02—Side view of buns with Malcolm McDowell
- 1:13—Brief breasts several times getting out of bed to run after McDowell. Dark.
    1:15—Very brief left breast taking off her dress to dry McDowell off.

Donato Placido.......................Proculus
- 1:11—Frontal nudity taking his robe off for Malcolm McDowell. Buns, while getting raped by McDowell's fist.

Teresa Ann Savoy.....................Druscilla
- •• 0:01—Nude, running around in the forest with Malcolm McDowell.
- • 0:05—Buns, rolling in bed with McDowell. Very brief breasts getting out of bed.
- • 0:26—Left breast several times in bed.
- • 0:46—Brief right breast in bed with McDowell again.
- • 1:15—Left breast with McDowell and Helen Mirren.
- • 1:22—Very brief left breast getting up in open dress.
- •• 1:45—Full frontal nudity, then buns when dead and McDowell tries to revive her.

Lori Wagner..........................Agrippina
- ••• 1:16—Nude, making love with Anneka Di Lorenzo. Long scene.

## Call Me (1988)

Steve Buscemi.....................Switch Blade
Patricia Charbonneau.....................Anna
- •• 1:18—Brief left breast making love in bed with a guy, then breasts putting blouse on and getting out of bed.

Patti D'Arbanville.......................Coni
Stephen McHattie......................Jellybean
David Strathairn..........................Sam

## The Cameraman (1928)

Buster Keaton.........................Buster
- • 0:38—Very brief buns, diving underwater after losing his swimsuit when his girlfriend tries to get him out of the pool.

## The Campus Corpse (1977)

Jeff East...............................Craig
    0:17—Side view of buns in jock strap after getting out of van for hazing.
- •• 0:19—Brief buns, while running and falling in the woods with Charlie Martin Smith.
- • 0:22—Buns, while running up rocks after Smith has broken his leg.
- • 0:23—Buns, while running down the road to get help.
- ••• 0:24—Buns, after arriving at cabin and standing outside next to van.

Lani O'Grady.......................Campus Girl
Charlie Martin Smith......................Barney
- • 0:19—Brief buns, while running down mountain side during hazing.

## Campus Man (1987)

Kim Delaney.....................Dayna Thomas

Morgan Fairchild.............Katherine Van Buren
Steve Lyon..........................Brett Wilson
- •• 0:25—Brief buns, while putting on swim trunks for photo session.

Miles O'Keeffe.......................Cactus Jack

## Can It Be Love (1992)

*a.k.a. Spring Break Sorority Babes*
Lorissa McComas.......................Montana
- ••• 0:55—Breasts and buns, changing into lingerie behind two way mirror while David watches.

Blake Pickett...........................Dyanne

## Can She Bake a Cherry Pie? (1983)

Karen Black...............................Zee
    0:40—Sort of left breast squished against a guy, while kissing him in bed.
- • 1:02—Very brief upper half of left breast in bed when she reaches up to touch her hair.

Michael Emil..............................Eli
Frances Fisher..........................Louise
Michael Margotta........................Larry

## Candy Stripe Nurses (1974)

Elana Casey...........................Zouzou
Kimberly Hyde..........................April
Sally Kirkland.................Woman in Clinic
Robin Mattson........................Dianne
- •• 0:22—Nude in gym with the basketball player.
- ••• 0:40—Nude in bed with the basketball player.

Candice Rialson........................Sandy
- •• 0:05—Breasts in hospital linen closet with a guy.
- •• 0:08—Breasts smoking and writing in bathtub.
- • 0:14—Breasts in hospital bed.

Maria Rojo...........................Marisa
- •• 0:29—Breasts making love with convict.
- • 0:52—Brief breasts during attempted rape in kitchen pantry.

Tara Strohmeier..........................Irene

## Candy The Stripper (1993)

Gordon Thomson.......................David
- •• 1:15—Buns, while on the floor, making out on top of Candy.

Tracy Vaccaro..........................Candy
- • 0:01—Very brief left breast, opening her blouse to flash a guy on the street.
- ••• 0:26—Breasts and buns in G-string, doing strip tease routine on stage.
- ••• 0:28—Breasts, while hiding behind bar with David after fight breaks out.
- •• 0:38—Breasts in open blouse, showing her breasts to David.
- ••• 0:46—Breasts, while wearing panties, while in bedroom with Larry.
- • 0:50—Wearing pasties, buns in G-string while posing for photographer.
- • 0:56—Left breast in open robe in bedroom with Larry.
- • 0:57—Breasts, while in bedroom, kissing Larry.
- • 1:01—Breasts and buns in flashback on the bar.

••• 1:11—Breasts, while making out with David.

••• 1:13—Breasts, while making out with David on the floor.

•• 1:15—More breasts, while on the floor with David.

••• 1:28—Breasts and buns in G-string doing strip tease routine out of dress and lingerie.

## Candyman (1992)

Kasi Lemmons . . . . . . . . . . . . . . . . . . Bernadette Walsh

Carolyn Lowery . . . . . . . . . . . . . . . . . . . . . . . . . Stacey

Virginia Madsen . . . . . . . . . . . . . . . . . . . . . . Helen Lyle

• 0:47—In bloody bra, while undressing after she was arrested. Side of right breast, after taking off bra. Bloody.

• 0:54—Brief left breast, while in bathtub. Lower half of right breast, after sitting up.

## Capone (1975)

Susan Blakely . . . . . . . . . . . . . . . . . . . . . . Iris Crawford

•• 1:13—Breasts, taking off her clothes outside in front of Ben Gazzara.

• 1:22—Left breast, while lying in bed with Gazzara.

••• 1:23—Nude, getting out of bed and getting dressed, then more breasts while fooling around with Gazzara.

Martin Kove . . . . . . . . . . . . . . . . . Pete Gusenberg

Sylvester Stallone . . . . . . . . . . . . . . . . . . . Frank Nitti

## The Capone (1989)

*a.k.a. Revenge of Al Capone*

(Originally a Made for TV Movie.)

Keith Carradine . . . . . . . . . . . . . . . . . . . . Mike Rourke

• 1:01—Partial buns, while making love on top of Debrah Farentino in bed.

Debrah Farentino . . . . . . . . . . . . . . . . . . . . . . . Jennie

• 1:01—Breasts, while making love in bed with Keith Carradine.

Ray Sharkey . . . . . . . . . . . . . . . . . . . . . . . . Al Capone

## Captain Ron (1992)

Mary Kay Place . . . . . . . . . . . . . . . . . Katherine Harvey

• 0:32—Brief right breast, then brief breasts in shower in boat with Martin Short. Overhead view. Hard to see her face, but it is her.

0:34—Buns, seen through shower door is a stunt double.

Kurt Russell . . . . . . . . . . . . . . . . . . . . . . Captain Ron

## Captive Rage (1988)

Maureen Kedes . . . . . . . . . . . . . . . . . . . . . . . . . . . Jan

•• 0:31—Breasts, getting chained to bed and raped by guards.

Oliver Reed . . . . . . . . . . . . . . . . . General Belmondo

Claudia Udy . . . . . . . . . . . . . . . . . . . . . . . . . . . Chiga

## Carlito's Way (1993)

John Leguizamo . . . . . . . . . . . . . . . . . . Benny Blanco

Penelope Ann Miller . . . . . . . . . . . . . . . . . . . . . . Gail

••• 0:59—Breasts, while dancing on stage in club in auburn wig.

••• 1:18—Breasts, after opening her robe and enticing Al Pacino in her apartment.

Viggo Mortensen . . . . . . . . . . . . . . . . . . . . . . . . Lalin

Adrian Pasdar . . . . . . . . . . . . . . . . . . . . . . . . Frankie

Sean Penn . . . . . . . . . . . . . . . . . . . . . . . . . Kleinfeld

Tera Tabrizi . . . . . . . . . . . . . . . . . . . . . . . . Club Date

## Carmen (1983; Spanish)

Laura Del Sol . . . . . . . . . . . . . . . . . . . . . . . . Carmen

• 1:14—Left breast, while lying in bed with Antonio.

• 1:27—Brief partial left breast, standing up when Antonio catches her in wardrobe room with another dancer.

## Carnal Crimes (1991)

Jasaé . . . . . . . . . . . . . . . . . . . . . . . . . . . . . . Christa

••• 0:19—Full frontal nudity in lingerie, making love with a guy while Linda Carol secretly watches.

Linda Carol . . . . . . . . . . . . . . . . . . . . . . . . . . . Elise

• 0:01—Very brief left breast, while rolling over in bed.

• 0:05—In wet lingerie and very brief side view of right breast in shower fantasy.

• 0:07—Breasts in B&W photo collage.

• 0:09—Full frontal nudity under sheer nightie, trying to get Stanley into bed.

• 0:11—Breasts in B&W photo again.

• 0:24—Brief right breast outside window opening her top while watching Renny & Mia make out.

• 0:26—Brief upper half of right breast when bum molests her.

••• 0:28—Breasts posing for Renny with Mia.

••• 0:29—Full frontal nudity making love with Renny and Mia.

• 0:30—Brief buns, sleeping in bed.

••• 0:38—Breasts making love with the baker. Long scene.

• 0:49—Breasts in B&W photo again.

• 1:02—Brief side view of right breast in gaping blouse.

• 1:33—Side view of buns in dominatrix outfit.

Sherri Graham . . . . . . . . . . . . . . . . . . . . Party Girl #1

Martin Hewitt . . . . . . . . . . . . . . . . . . . . . . . . . Renny

•• 0:29—Buns, while making love with Linda Carol and Mia.

Deirdre Morrow . . . . . . . . . . . . . . . . . . . . . Leggy Girl

• 1:22—Buns, in G-string, leaning over to talk to Renny and Stanley.

Donna Spangler . . . . . . . . . . . . . . . . . . . . . . . Esther

Yvette Stephens . . . . . . . . . . . . . . . . . . . . . . . . . Mia

•• 0:25—Left breast, when Renny makes out with her.

••• 0:28—Brief left breast, then breasts posing with Linda.

••• 0:29—Full frontal nudity making love with Linda Carol and Renny.

• 0:48—Breasts and brief buns on TV.

• 0:50—Brief breasts in flashback.

Julie Strain . . . . . . . . . . . . . . . . . . . . . . . . . . Ingrid

••• 0:55—Breasts and partial buns, wearing black garter belt and stockings, making love with Renny in restroom. Long scene.

Paula Trickey . . . . . . . . . . . . . . . . . . . . . . . Jasmine

### Carnal Knowledge (1971)

Ann-Margret . . . . . . . . . . . . . . . . . . . . . . . . . . . . Bobbie
- •• 0:48—Breasts and buns making love in bed with Jack Nicholson, then getting out of bed and into shower with Jack.
- • 1:07—Brief side view of left breast putting a bra on in the bedroom.

Candice Bergen. . . . . . . . . . . . . . . . . . . . . . . . . . . Susan
Art Garfunkel. . . . . . . . . . . . . . . . . . . . . . . . . . . . . Sandy
Carol Kane . . . . . . . . . . . . . . . . . . . . . . . . . . . . .Jennifer
Jack Nicholson . . . . . . . . . . . . . . . . . . . . . . . .Jonathan

### Carnival of Love (1983)

*a.k.a. Inside the Love House*
Becky LeBeau . . . . . . . . . . . . . . . . . . . . . . . . . . . .Nancy
Kristi Somers . . . . . . . . . . . . . . . . . . . . . . . . . . . . . Kristi

### Caroline at Midnight (1993)

Julie Baltay . . . . . . . . . . . . . . . . . . . . . . . . . . .Dream Lover
- • 0:31—Right breast, while in bed during Jack's dream. Don't see her face.

Zach Galligan . . . . . . . . . . . . . . . . . . . . . . . . . Jerry Hutt
Susan Harvey . . . . . . . . . . . . . . . . . . . . . . . . . . . . . Lilli
- •• 0:03—Breasts, while being held by Stan, while Judd Nelson tries to get information from Miguel.

Virginia Madsen . . . . . . . . . . . . . . . . . . . . . Susan Prince
Clayton Rohner . . . . . . . . . . . . . . . . . . . . . . . . . . . Jack
- • 1:03—Very, very brief frontal nudity and sort of buns, after pulling down his shorts and getting into bathtub. Seen from above.

Mia Sara . . . . . . . . . . . . . . . . . . . . . . . . . . . . .Victoria
- ••• 0:24—Breasts, while making love with Jack.
- •• 0:30—Left breast, in open robe in bedroom with Tim Daly.
- ••• 0:51—Breasts, while making love on top and under Jack in bed. Nice!

Stacey Travis . . . . . . . . . . . . . . . . . . . . . Christine Jenkins

### Carrie (1976)

Nancy Allen. . . . . . . . . . . . . . . . . . . . . . .Chris Hargenson
- •• 0:01—Nude, in slow motion in girls' locker room behind Amy Irving.

William Katt . . . . . . . . . . . . . . . . . . . . . . . .Tommy Ross
P.J. Soles . . . . . . . . . . . . . . . . . . . . . . . . . . . . . . . Norma
Sissy Spacek . . . . . . . . . . . . . . . . . . . . . . . Carrie White
- •• 0:02—Nude, taking a shower, then having her first menstrual period in the girls' locker room.
- • 1:25—Brief breasts taking a bath to wash all the pig blood off her after the dance.

### Cartel (1990)

Miles O'Keeffe. . . . . . . . . . . . . . . . . . . . . . Chuck Taylor
Suzanne Slater . . . . . . . . . . . . . . . . . . . . . . . . . .Nancy
0:28—In red two piece swimsuit modeling on motorcycle.
0:35—Brief bra and panties on bed during struggle.
- • 0:36—Breasts during brutal rape/murder scene.

### Casanova (1987)

Marina Baker. . . . . . . . . . . . . . . . . . . . . . . . . . Lucretia
Faye Dunaway. . . . . . . . . . . . . . . . . . . . . . . . Countess

Sylvia Kristel . . . . . . . . . . . . . . . . . . . . . . . . . . . . n.a.
Traci Lin . . . . . . . . . . . . . . . . . . . . . . . . . . . . . . Heidi
- • 1:56—Very, very brief right breast while bending over to help Richard Chamberlain. Long, long shot.

Rose McVeigh . . . . . . . . . . . . . . . . . . . . . Captain's Wife
Ornella Muti. . . . . . . . . . . . . . . . . . . . . . . . . .Henriette
Hanna Schygulla . . . . . . . . . . . . . . Casanova's Mother

### Castaway (1986)

Frances Barber . . . . . . . . . . . . . . . . .Sister Saint Winifred
Amanda Donohoe . . . . . . . . . . . . . . . . . . . .Lucy Irvine
- ••• 0:22—Breasts talking to Reed.
- •• 0:32—Nude on beach after helicopter leaves.
- •• 0:48—Full frontal nudity lying on her back on the rocks at the beach.
- ••• 0:51—Breasts on rock when Reed takes a blue sheet off her, then catching a shark.
- ••• 0:54—Nude yelling at Reed at the campsite, then walking around looking for him.
- ••• 1:01—Breasts getting seafood out of a tide pool.
- •• 1:03—Breasts lying down at night talking with Reed in the moonlight.
- ••• 1:18—Breasts taking off bathing suit top after the visitors leave, then arguing with Reed.

Georgina Hale . . . . . . . . . . . . . . . Sister Saint Margaret
Virginia Hey . . . . . . . . . . . . . . . . . . . . . . . . . . . Janice
Oliver Reed . . . . . . . . . . . . . . . . . . . . Gerald Kingsland
- •• 1:46—Nude, doing things around the hut during the storm.

### Casual Sex? (1988)

Victoria Jackson . . . . . . . . . . . . . . . . . . . . . . . Melissa
0:30—Brief buns lying down with Lea Thompson at a nude beach.
0:33—Brief buns wrapping a towel around herself just before getting a massage. Long shot, hard to see.
1:06—Brief buns getting out of bed.
Steve Shellen . . . . . . . . . . . . . . . . . . . . . . . . . . .Nick
Lea Thompson . . . . . . . . . . . . . . . . . . . . . . . . . Stacy
0:27—Buns, lying down at nude beach with Victoria Jackson.
0:30—Buns at the beach. Pan shot from her feet to her head.

### Casualties of War (1989)

Michael J. Fox . . . . . . . . . . . . . . . . . . . . . . PFC Eriksson
John Leguizamo . . . . . . . . . . . . . . . . . . . . . . . . .Diaz
- • 0:53—Buns, while pulling his pants down to rape Oahn.

Sean Penn . . . . . . . . . . . . . . . . . . . . . Sergeant Meserve

### Cat Chaser (1988)

Brooke Becker . . . . . . . . . . . . . . . . . . . . . . . . . . Philly
Tony Bolano. . . . . . . . . . . . . . . . . . . . . . . . . . . . Corky
- •• 1:16—Nude, undressing in bathroom with Andres, before getting shot by Charles Durning.

Kelly McGillis . . . . . . . . . . . . . . . . . . . . . Mary De Boya
- ••• 0:23—Breasts on the floor with Peter Weller. Long scene.

••• 1:04—Full frontal nudity taking off her slip and getting raped by her husband's pistol. Kind of dark.

•• 1:06—Brief buns, getting pushed around the house. Right breast while signing a paper.

Tomas Milian . . . . . . . . . . . . . . . . . . . . . Andres De Boya

•• 1:16—Full frontal nudity, undressing in bathroom with Corky, before getting shot by Charles Durning.

Sherrie Rose . . . . . . . . . . . . . . . Uncredited Waitress

Adrianne Sachs . . . . . . . . . . . . . . . . . . . .Anita De Boya

Peter Weller. . . . . . . . . . . . . . . . . . . . . . George Moran

•• 0:24—Very, very brief frontal nudity, twice when he is kneeling and takes his pants off. Buns, while making love on top of Kelly McGillis.

## Cat in the Cage *(1978)*

Colleen Camp. . . . . . . . . . . . . . . . . . . . . Gilda Riener

• 0:36—Very brief left breast twice, while making love in bed with Bruce.

Sybil Danning . . . . . . . . . . . . . . . . . . . . . . .Susan Khan

• 0:24—Brief breasts getting slapped around by Ralph.

• 0:25—Brief left breast several times smoking and talking to Ralph, brief left breast getting up.

•• 0:30—Full frontal nudity getting out of the pool.

• 0:52—Black bra and panties undressing and getting into bed with Ralph. Brief left breast and buns.
1:02—In white lingerie in bedroom.
1:10—In white slip looking out window.
1:15—In black slip.

• 1:18—Very brief right breast several times, struggling with an attacker on the floor.

## Cat People *(1982)*

Ed Begley, Jr. . . . . . . . . . . . . . . . . . . . . . . Joe Creigh

John Heard . . . . . . . . . . . . . . . . . . . . . . . Oliver Yates

• 1:37—Very brief side view of buns, while taking off his pants and sitting on bed next to Kinski.

•• 1:50—Buns, while making love with Nastassja Kinski in bed in a cabin.

Nastassja Kinski . . . . . . . . . . . . . . . . . . . . . Irena Gallier

••• 1:03—Nude at night, walking around outside chasing a rabbit.

•• 1:35—Breasts taking off blouse, walking up the stairs and getting into bed.

• 1:37—Brief right breast, lying in bed with John Heard.

•• 1:38—Breasts getting out of bed and walking to the bathroom.

•• 1:40—Brief buns, getting back into bed. Breasts in bed.

•• 1:47—Full frontal nudity, walking around in the cabin at night.

• 1:49—Breasts, tied to the bed by Heard.

Lynn Lowry. . . . . . . . . . . . . . . . . . . . . . . . . .Ruthie

• 0:16—In black bra in Malcolm McDowell's hotel room, then brief breasts when bra pops open after crawling down the stairs.

Malcolm McDowell . . . . . . . . . . . . . . . . . . Paul Gollier

• 1:06—Side view of buns, while lying on the bathroom floor. Partial lower frontal nudity when he gets up.

Annette O'Toole. . . . . . . . . . . . . . . . . . . . Alice Perrin

••• 1:30—In a bra, then breasts undressing in locker room.

• 1:31—Some breasts shots of her in the pool. Distorted because of the water.

• 1:33—Brief right breast, after getting out of the pool.

Tessa Richarde . . . . . . . . . . . . . . . . . . . . . . . . . Billie

•• 1:00—Breasts in bed with Malcolm McDowell trying to get him excited.

## Catch-22 *(1970)*

Alan Arkin . . . . . . . . . . . . . . . . . . . . Captain Yossarian

• 0:52—Buns, while standing wearing only his hat, talking to Dreedle. Don't see his face.

Richard Benjamin. . . . . . . . . . . . . . . . . . . Major Danby

Suzanne Benton. . . . . . . . . . . . . . . . . Dreedle's WAC

Olimpia Carlisi . . . . . . . . . . . . . . . . . . . . . . . . Luciana

• 1:04—Breasts lying in bed talking with Alan Arkin.

Art Garfunkel . . . . . . . . . . . . . . . . . . . . Captain Nately

Paula Prentiss. . . . . . . . . . . . . . . . . . . . Nurse Duckett

• 0:22—Full frontal nudity on platform in the water, throwing her dress to Alan Arkin during his dream. Long shot, over exposed, hard to see.

Jon Voight . . . . . . . . . . . . . . . . . . . Milo Minderbinder

## Catherine & Co. *(1975; French)*

Jane Birkin . . . . . . . . . . . . . . . . . . . . . . . . . Catherine

• 0:07—Breasts, standing up in the bathtub to open the door for another woman.

•• 0:09—Side view of left breast, while taking off her blouse in bed.

••• 0:10—Breasts, sitting up and turning the light on, smoking a cigarette.

••• 0:17—Right breast, while making love in bed.

•• 0:24—Breasts taking off her dress, then buns jumping into bed.

•• 0:36—Buns and left breast posing for a painter.

• 0:45—Breasts taking off dress, walking around the house. Left breast, inviting the neighbor in.

Patrick Dewaere . . . . . . . . . . . . . . . . . . . . . . .Francois

## Catherine Cherie *(1982)*

Ajita Wilson . . . . . . . . . . . . . . . . . . . .Dancer/Miss Ajita

• 0:23—Breasts and buns dancing in club. Covered with paint. Long shot.
0:24—Brief buns, greeting Carlo after the show.

•• 0:43—Full frontal nudity in room with Carlo.

## Cathy's Curse *(1976; Canadian)*

Beverley Murray. . . . . . . . . . . . . . . . . . . . . . . . Vivian

• 1:13—Very, very brief left breast, while jumping around in bathtub, brushing leaches off her body.

### Cattle Annie and Little Britches (1980)

Scott Glenn . . . . . . . . . . . . . . . . . . . . . . . . .Bill Dalton
Burt Lancaster . . . . . . . . . . . . . . . . . . . . . . .Bill Doolin
- 1:16—Very brief upper half of buns, while grabbing bad guy's arm and pulling him into hot spring.

Diane Lane . . . . . . . . . . . . . . . . . . . . . . . . . . . Jenny
0:40—Briefly in braless, wet long johns while standing in lake.

Perry Lang. . . . . . . . . . . . . . . . . . . . . . . . . . . .Elrod
Amanda Plummer . . . . . . . . . . . . . . . . . . . . . : Annie
- 0:39—Breasts visible under braless, wet long johns while standing in lake.

John Savage . . . . . . . . . . . . . . . Bittercreek Newcomb
- 0:38—Brief buns, running and jumping into lake.
- 0:40—Buns, climbing on rocks. Long, long shot.

### Cave Girl (1985)

Jasaé . . . . . . . . . . . . . . . . . . . . . . . Locker Room Student
- • 0:05—Breasts with four other girls in the girls' locker room undressing, then running after Rex. She's sitting on a bench, wearing red and white panties.

Michelle Bauer . . . . . . . . . . . . . . . Locker Room Student
- • 0:05—Breasts with four other girls in the girls' locker room undressing, then running after Rex. She's the first to take her top off, wearing white panties, running and carrying a tennis racket.

Susan Mierisch . . . . . . . . . . . . . . Locker Room Student
- • 0:05—Breasts with four other girls in the girls' locker room undressing, then running after Rex. She's blonde, wearing red panties and a necklace.

Cynthia Ann Thompson . . . . . . . . . . . . . . . . . . .Eba
- 0:41—Buns, standing in stream while bathing. Long shot.
- • 1:04—Breasts making love with Rex.

### CB4 (1993)

Khandi Alexander . . . . . . . . . . . . . . . . . . . . . . . Sissy
- 0:51—In bra and brief partial buns in panties on bed on top of Chris Rock. Side view of right breast, twice, while letting Allen Payne and Chris Rock poke it (Don't see her face, probably a body double).

Reneé Tenison . . . . . . . . . . . . . . . . . . . . . . . . . Twin

### Cellar Dweller (1987)

Pamela Bellwood. . . . . . . . . . . . . . . . . . . . . Amanda
Cheryl-Ann Wilson . . . . . . . . . . . . . . . . . . . . . .Lisa
- • 0:59—Brief right breast, then breasts taking a shower.

### The Centerfold Girls (1974)

Jennifer Ashley. . . . . . . . . . . . . . . . . . . . . . . .Charly
- 0:34—Breasts taking off blouse while changing clothes.
- • 0:49—Breasts and buns posing for photographer outside with Glory.

Jaime Lyn Bauer . . . . . . . . . . . . . . . . . . . . . . Jackie
- • 0:04—Breasts getting out of bed and walking around the house.
- • • 0:14—Breasts getting undressed in the bathroom.
- • 0:15—Brief breasts and buns putting on robe and getting out of bed, three times.

Tiffany Bolling . . . . . . . . . . . . . . . . . . . . . . . . .Vera
- 1:02—Brief breasts in photograph.
- • • 1:12—Breasts in the shower.
- 1:21—Brief breasts in motel bed getting raped by two guys after they drug her beer.

Teda Bracci . . . . . . . . . . . . . . . . . . . . . . . . . . . Rita
- 0:18—Breasts taking off her clothes in the living room in front of everybody.

Kitty Carl . . . . . . . . . . . . . . . . . . . . . . . . . . . Sandi
- • 0:45—Breasts taking off her top while sitting on the bed with Perry.
0:51—Breasts on the beach, dead. Long shot, hard to see.

Talie Cochrane. . . . . . . . . . . . . . . . . . . . . . . .Donna
Anneka di Lorenzo . . . . . . . . . . . . . . . . . . . . . .Pam
Ruthy Ross . . . . . . . . . . . . . . . . . . . . . . . . . . Glory
- • • 0:49—Breasts and buns posing for photographer outside with Charly.

Connie Strickland. . . . . . . . . . . . . . . . . . . . . . Patsy
- • 1:07—Breasts in bathroom washing her halter top just before getting killed.

Janet Wood . . . . . . . . . . . . . . . . . . . . . . . . . . Linda
- • 0:14—Breasts putting on robe and getting out of bed.

### Certain Fury (1985)

Nicholas Campbell. . . . . . . . . . . . . . . . . . . . Sniffer
- • 0:38—Buns, while getting undressed to rape Irene Cara.

Irene Cara . . . . . . . . . . . . . . . . . . . . . . . . . . . Tracy
0:32—Getting undressed to take a shower. Very brief side views of left breast.
0:35—Very brief breasts in shower after Tatum O'Neal turns on the kitchen faucet. Hard to see because of the shower door.
- • 0:36—Frontal nudity and side view of buns, behind shower door while Sniffer comes into the bathroom.
- • 0:39—Breasts several times when Sniffer tries to rape her and she fights back.
- 0:41—Buns, kneeling on floor. Overhead view.

Peter Fonda . . . . . . . . . . . . . . . . . . . . . . . . . Rodney
Tatum O'Neal . . . . . . . . . . . . . . . . . . . . . . . .Scarlet

### A Certain Sacrifice (1981)

Madonna. . . . . . . . . . . . . . . . . . . . . . . . . . . Bruna
- • • 0:22—Breasts during weird rape/love scene with one guy and two girls.
- 0:40—Brief right breast in open top lying on floor after getting attacked by guy in back of restaurant.
- 0:57—Brief breasts during love making scene, then getting smeared with blood.

### Chain of Desire (1992)

Angel Aviles . . . . . . . . . . . . . . . . . . . . . . . . . . . . Isa
- 0:14—In bra in bed with Jesus, then breasts. Dark.

Kevin Conroy. . . . . . . . . . . . . . . . . . . . . . . . . . .Joe
- • 1:25—Buns, while pulling down his underwear to masturbate while watching a woman in her apartment do the same.
- 1:28—Brief side view of buns, after he's finished.

Linda Fiorentino . . . . . . . . . . . . . . . . . . Alma D'Angeli
  • 0:09—Very brief left breast, while rolling over in bed.
Malcolm McDowell. . . . . . . . . . . . . . . . . Hubert Bailey
Assumpta Serna . . . . . . . . . . . . . . . . . . . . . . . Cleo
Dewey Weber . . . . . . . . . . . . . . . . . . . . . .David Bango
  ••• 0:48—Buns, while getting out of bathtub and dry-
    ing himself off while talking to Ken.

## Chained Heat (1983; U.S./German)

Jennifer Ashley. . . . . . . . . . . . . . . . . . . . . . . .Grinder
Greta Blackburn . . . . . . . . . . . . . . . . . . . . . . . Lulu
Linda Blair. . . . . . . . . . . . . . . . . . . . . . . . . . . Carol
  ••• 0:30—Breasts in the shower.
  •• 0:56—In bra, then breasts in the Warden's office
    when he rapes her.
Christina Cardan. . . . . . . . . . . . . . . . . . . . Miss King
Sybil Danning . . . . . . . . . . . . . . . . . . . . . . . . Erika
  ••• 0:30—Breasts in the shower with Linda Blair.
Monique Gabrielle . . . . . . . . . . . . . . . . . . . . Debbie
  ••• 0:08—Nude, stripping for the Warden in his office.
  ••• 0:09—Nude, getting into the spa with the Warden.
Sharon Hughes . . . . . . . . . . . . . . . . . . . . . . . . Val
  •• 0:30—Brief breasts in the shower with Linda Blair.
  •• 0:51—Buns, in lingerie, stripping for a guy.
  •• 1:04—Breasts in the spa with the Warden.
Marcia Karr . . . . . . . . . . . . . . . . . . . . . . . . . Twinks
  ••• 0:30—Breasts, getting soaped up by Edy Williams in
    the shower.
  • 0:37—Brief breasts, taking off her top in bed with
    Edy Williams at night.
  •• 0:40—Breasts in cell getting raped by the guard.
Louisa Moritz . . . . . . . . . . . . . . . . . . . . . . . Bubbles
Stella Stevens . . . . . . . . . . . . . . . . . . . . . . . .Taylor
Kate Vernon . . . . . . . . . . . . . . . . . . . . . . . .Cellmate
Edy Williams . . . . . . . . . . . . . . . . . . . . . . . . . Paula
  •• 0:30—Full frontal nudity in the shower, soaping up
    Twinks.
  •• 0:36—Breasts at night in bed with Twinks.

## Chained Heat 2 (1993)

Kimberly Kates . . . . . . . . . . . . . . . Alexandra Morrison
  ••• 0:30—Full frontal nudity, while in the shower with
    Tina.
  • 0:56—Buns, in G-string under sheer blue dress dur-
    ing casino party.
  •• 1:04—Breasts, while sitting up in bed and getting
    out. Wearing panties and stockings.
Brigitte Nielsen . . . . . . . . . . . . . . . . . . . .Magda Kassar
  0:36—In black body suit in bedroom with Rosa.
  1:00—In lingerie, in bedroom with Alex.
Kari Whitman . . . . . . . . . . . . . . . . .Suzanne Morrison

## The Challenge (1982)

Donna Kei Benz. . . . . . . . . . . . . . . . . . . . . . . Akiko
  • 1:23—Breasts making love with Scott Glenn in mo-
    tel room. Could be a body double. Dark, hard to see
    anything.
Scott Glenn. . . . . . . . . . . . . . . . . . . . . . . . . . Rich

## A Change of Seasons (1980)

Bo Derek . . . . . . . . . . . . . . . . . . . . . Lindsey Routledge
  •• 0:00—Breasts in hot tub during the opening credits.
  • 0:25—Side view of left breast in the shower talking
    to Anthony Hopkins.
Shirley MacLaine . . . . . . . . . . . . . . . . . . . . .Karen Evans

## Chantilly Lace (1993; Made for Cable Movie)

Matt Battaglia . . . . . . . . . . . . . . . . . Chris the Pizza Boy
  0:00—Brief upper half of buns in bedroom with Jo-
  Beth Williams. Never see his face.
Lindsay Crouse. . . . . . . . . . . . . . . . . . . . . . . . Rheza
Ally Sheedy . . . . . . . . . . . . . . . . . . . . . . . . Elizabeth
Helen Slater . . . . . . . . . . . . . . . . . . . . . . . . Hannah
JoBeth Williams . . . . . . . . . . . . . . . . . . . . .Natalie
  • 0:59—Brief breasts, taking off her blouse in bed-
    room with the pizza boy.

## Chaplin (1992; British/U.S.)

Geraldine Chaplin . . . . . . . . . . . . . . . Hannah Chaplin
David Duchovny . . . . . . . . . . . . . . . . . . . . . . . Rollie
Vicki Frederick . . . . . . . . . . . . . . . . . . . . Party Guest
Milla Jovovich. . . . . . . . . . . . . . . . . . . . Mildred Harris
  • 0:55—Top of left breast peeking over top of lingerie
    while sitting on bed talking to Chaplin.
  • 0:56—Buns, after taking off lingerie and standing in
    front of Chaplin.
Moira Kelly. . . . . . . . . . . . . . Hetty Kelly/Oona O'Neill
  •• 0:20—Brief breasts, while changing in dressing
    room when surprised by Chaplin.
Kevin Kline. . . . . . . . . . . . . . . . . . . Douglas Fairbanks
Diane Lane. . . . . . . . . . . . . . . . . . . Paulette Goddard
  • 1:33—Upper half of breasts, while lying in bed.
Penelope Ann Miller. . . . . . . . . . . . . . . . Edna Purviance
Nancy Travis . . . . . . . . . . . . . . . . . . . . . Joan Barry
James Woods . . . . . . . . . . . . . . . . . . . . Lawyer Scott

## Chasers (1994)

Tom Berenger . . . . . . . . . . . . . . . . . . . . . . Rock Reilly
Erika Eleniak. . . . . . . . . . . . . . . . . . . . . .Toni Johnson
  0:47—Buns in white bra and panties, while climbing
    out of hole in ground.
  ••• 1:03—In bra, then breasts and buns, while making
    love in bed with William McNamara.
Marilu Henner . . . . . . . . . . . . . . . . . . . . . . . . Katie
Dennis Hopper. . . . . . . . . . . . . . . . . . . . . . . Doggie
William McNamara . . . . . . . . . . . . . . . .Eddie De Vane
  •• 1:08—Buns, while running around trying to catch
    Erika Eleniak. More buns, while getting back into the
    room.

## Chattahoochee (1990)

Dennis Hopper. . . . . . . . . . . . . . . . . . . . .Walker Benson
  • 0:32—Brief buns, while leaving the shower room af-
    ter talking to Gary Oldman.
Frances McDormand . . . . . . . . . . . . . . . . . . Mae Foley
Gary Oldman . . . . . . . . . . . . . . . . . . . . Emmett Foley
  • 1:17—Brief buns, standing while guards search his
    clothes. Very, very brief frontal nudity turning
    around to get a high-pressure enema. Long shot,
    don't really see anything.

Pamela Reed . . . . . . . . . . . . . . . . . . . . . . . . . . Earlene
M. Emmet Walsh . . . . . . . . . . . . . . . . . . . . . . . . Morris

## Chatterbox (1977)
Perry Bullington . . . . . . . . . . . . . . . . . . . . . . . . . Ted
- 0:02—Buns, while stumbling around the room.

Candice Rialson . . . . . . . . . . . . . . . . . . . . . . . . . Penny
- •• 0:01—Left breast, in bed with Ted, then breasts getting out of bed.
- 0:10—In white bra wrestling on couch with another woman.
- ••• 0:15—Side view of right breast then breasts during demonstration on stage.
- ••• 0:26—Breasts in bed talking on phone.
- 0:32—In open dress letting her "chatterbox" sing during talk show. Something covers pubic area.
- •• 0:35—Breasts during photo shoot.
- •• 0:38—Breasts again for more photos while opening a red coat.
- •• 0:43—Breasts in bed with Ted.
- ••• 0:55—Breasts taking off white dress, walking up the stairs and opening the door.
- •• 1:09—Breasts opening her raincoat for Ted.

## Cheech & Chong's Nice Dreams (1981)
Sandra Bernhard . . . . . . . . . . . . . . . . . . . . . . . Girl Nut
Shelby Chong . . . . . . . . . . . . . . . . . . . . . . . Body Builder
Tommy Chong . . . . . . . . . . . . . . . . . . . . . . . . Himself
- 0:55—Out of focus buns, in mirror while lying in bed with Donna and Cheech. Very, very brief blurry out of focus frontal nudity in mirror when he gets out of bed.

Evelyn Guerrero . . . . . . . . . . . . . . . . . . . . . . . Donna
- 0:43—Brief left breast sticking out of her spandex outfit, sitting down at table in restaurant.
- 0:56—In burgundy lingerie in her apartment with Cheech Marin.

Stacy Keach . . . . . . . . . . . . . . . . . . . . . . . The Sarge
Richard "Cheech" Marin . . . . . . . . . . . . . . . . . . Himself
- 0:57—Brief buns when climbing over railing to escape Donna's husband, Animal.
- 1:00—Buns while hanging over the side of the outdoor elevator is probably a stunt double.

Linnea Quigley . . . . . . . . . . . . . . . . . Blondie Group #2
Roselyn Royce . . . . . . . . . . . . . . . . . . . . Beach Girl #3
- 0:29—Brief breasts on the beach with two other girls. Long shot, unsteady, hard to see.
- 0:32—More brief breasts again.
- 0:33—More brief breasts again.

Cheryl Smith . . . . . . . . . . . . . . . . . . . . Blondie Group #1
Victoria Wells . . . . . . . . . . . . . . . . . . . . Beach Girl #1
- 0:29—Brief breasts on the beach with two other girls. Long shot, unsteady, hard to see.
- 0:32—More brief breasts again.
- 0:33—More brief breasts again.

## Cheech & Chong's Still Smokin' (1983)
Tommy Chong . . . . . . . . . . . . . . . . . . . . . . . Chong
Richard "Cheech" Marin . . . . . . . . . . . . . . . . . Cheech

Linnea Quigley . . . . . . . . . . . . . . . . . Uncredited Spa Girl
- •• 0:42—Breasts, looking into two-way mirror. (She's the last girl.)
- 0:53—Breasts, walking in front of Cheech in the shower room.
- •• 1:00—Breasts, sitting on the floor with five other naked girls with Cheech.

## Cheerleader Camp (1987)
a.k.a. Bloody Pom Poms
Vickie Benson . . . . . . . . . . . . . . . . . . . . . . . Miss Tipton
- 0:27—Brief breasts undressing in her bedroom.

Rebecca Ferratti . . . . . . . . . . . . . . . . . . . . Theresa Salazar
George "Buck" Flower . . . . . . . . . . . . . . . . . . . . . Pop
Travis McKenna . . . . . . . . . . . . . . . . . . . . Timmy Moser
0:05—Buns, while hanging a B.A. out the van window. He's a very heavy guy.

Krista Pflanzer . . . . . . . . . . . . . . . . . . . . . . . . Suzy
- 0:11—Breasts several times sunbathing on the rocks.
- 0:14—Brief breasts in flashback.
- 0:17—Breasts on TV in Timmy's video tape of sunbathing on the rocks.

Betsy Russell . . . . . . . . . . . . . . . . . . . . Alison Wentworth
Teri Weigel . . . . . . . . . . . . . . . . . . . . . . . Pam Bently
- •• 0:12—Breasts taking off her swimsuit top while sunbathing.

## Cheerleaders Wild Weekend (1985)
Kristine DeBell . . . . . . . . . . . . . . . . . . . . . Debbie/Pierce
Elizabeth Halsey . . . . . . . . . . . . . . . . . . . . Susan/Pierce
- ••• 0:40—Breasts in red panties, in contest.
- ••• 0:41—Breasts with the other five girls during contest.
- ••• 0:43—Breasts during getting measured with the other two girls.

Robert Houston . . . . . . . . . . . . . . . . . . . . . . . . Billy
- 0:45—Brief buns, getting caught watching Frankie give Jeanne a bath.

Tracey Ann King . . . . . . . . . . . . . . . . . . . . LaSalle/Polk
- 0:00—Brief breasts while tying her shoelace in locker room.
- 0:33—Brief breasts in catfight with another girl in cabin.
- ••• 0:39—Breasts, taking off her yellow blouse during contest.
- ••• 0:41—Breasts with the other five girls during contest.
- 0:42—Breasts, losing contest.

Janie Squire . . . . . . . . . . . . . . . . . . . . . Donna/Darwell
- ••• 0:39—Breasts and brief buns, taking off her white blouse during contest.
- ••• 0:41—Breasts with the other five girls during contest.
- ••• 0:43—Breasts while getting measured with the other two girls.

Wally Anne Wharton . . . . . . . . . . . . . . . . . Lisa/Darwell
- •• 0:06—Breasts in back of school bus, flashing a guy in pickup truck, then pressing her breasts against the window.

••• 0:37—Breasts, opening her white blouse during contest.

••• 0:39—Breasts and brief buns, in white skirt during contest.

## Chesty Anderson, U.S. Navy (1975)
Uschi Digard . . . . . . . . . . . . . . . .Baron's Girlfriend #1
Shari Eubank . . . . . . . . . . . . . . . . . . . . . . . . . Chesty
    0:03—In bra sitting on bed, talking to Baby.
    0:41—In bra and panties during fight in barracks.
    • 0:58—Brief right breast, while making love with Fred Willard.
Lynne Guthrie . . . . . . . . . . . . . . . . . . . . . Lt. Ambrose
Rosanne Katon . . . . . . . . . . . . . . . . . . . . . . . .Cocoa
    0:02—In bra with the other girls in barracks.
    •• 0:40—Breasts when bra pops open during fight in barracks.
Joyce Mandel . . . . . . . . . . . . . . . . . . . . . . . . . Suzi
    0:02—In bra with the other girls in barracks.
    •• 0:15—Buns and very brief back side of left breast, taking off towel and putting on robe.
Betty Thomas . . . . . . . . . . . . . . . . . . . . Party Guest #1
Dyanne Thorne . . . . . . . . . . . . . . . . . . . . . . . . Nurse

## Chickboxer (1992)
Michelle Bauer . . . . . . . . . . . . .Greta "Chickboxer" Holtz
    0:39—In sexy pink outfit.
    ••• 0:57—Full frontal nudity, making love with a guy in bed.

## The Children (1980)
Gale Garnett . . . . . . . . . . . . . . . . . . . . .Cathy Freeman
Rita Montone . . . . . . . . . . . . . . . . . . . . . Dee Dee Shore
    •• 0:20—Breasts, lying on chair by pool before talking to the Sheriff.

## Children of a Lesser God (1986)
William Hurt . . . . . . . . . . . . . . . . . . . . . . James Leeds
E. Katherine Kerr . . . . . . . . . . . . . . . . . . Mary Lee Ochs
Marlee Matlin . . . . . . . . . . . . . . . . . . . . . . . . . Sarah
    • 0:44—Brief buns under water in swimming pool. Don't see her face.
    0:47—Part of left breast while hugging William Hurt (seen from under water).
Gigi Vorgan . . . . . . . . . . . . . . . . . . . . . . . Announcer

## Chinatown (1974)
Faye Dunaway . . . . . . . . . . . . . . . . . . . . . . . .Evelyn
    • 1:26—Very brief right breast, in bed talking to Jack Nicholson.
    • 1:28—Very brief right breast in bed talking to Nicholson. Very brief flash of right breast under robe when she gets up to leave the bedroom.
Jack Nicholson . . . . . . . . . . . . . . . . . . . . . . . . .J.J.
    • 1:28—Very brief buns, while putting pants on and getting out of bed after making love with Faye Dunaway.

## The Choirboys (1977)
Jeannie Bell . . . . . . . . . . . . . . . . . . . . Fanny Forbes
Blair Brown . . . . . . . . . . . . . . . . . . . . . .Kimberly Lyles

Phyllis Davis . . . . . . . . . . . . . . . . . . . . . . . . Foxy/Gina
    •• 0:29—Breasts wearing pasties, under sheer pink robe.
    1:24—In black bra, panties, garter belt and stockings.
Perry King . . . . . . . . . . . . . . . . . . . . . . . . . . . Slate
Tim McIntire . . . . . . . . . . . . . . . . . . . . . Roscoe Rules
    • 0:36—Long shot of buns, while handcuffed to tree by his friends.
    ••• 0:39—Buns, while handcuffed to tree and trying to get a gay passerby help him. Long scene.
Randy Quaid . . . . . . . . . . . . . . . . . . . . . . . . . Proust
Cheryl Smith . . . . . . . . . . . . . . . . . . . . . . . Tammy
James Woods . . . . . . . . . . . . . . . . . . . . . . Bloomguard
Suzanne Zenor . . . . . . . . . . . . . . . . . . . Blonde at Party

## Chopper Chicks in Zombietown (1989)
Don Calfa . . . . . . . . . . . . . . . . . . . . . . . .Ralph Willum
    • 0:41—Brief buns, while trapped in walk-in locker with zombie Lucile. Don't see his face.
Vicki Frederick . . . . . . . . . . . . . . . . . . . . . . . . Jewel
Gretchen Palmer . . . . . . . . . . . . . . . . . . . . . . Rusty
Jamie Rose . . . . . . . . . . . . . . . . . . . . . . . . . . Dede

## Chopping Mall (1986)
*a.k.a. Killbots*
Angela Aames . . . . . . . . . . . . . . . . . . . . . Miss Vanders
Barbara Crampton . . . . . . . . . . . . . . . . . . . . . Suzie
    •• 0:22—Brief breasts taking off top in furniture store in front of her boyfriend on the couch.
Kelli Maroney . . . . . . . . . . . . . . . . . . . . . . . . Alison
Toni Naples . . . . . . . . . . . . . . . . . . . Bathing Beauty
Suzanne Slater . . . . . . . . . . . . . . . . . . . . . . .Leslie
    •• 0:28—Brief breasts in bed showing breasts to Mike.
    0:31—Walking around the mall in panties and a blouse.
Mary Woronov . . . . . . . . . . . . . . . . . . . . Mary Bland

## The Church (1991; Italian)
*a.k.a. La Chiesa*
Asia Argento . . . . . . . . . . . . . . . . . . . . . . . . . Lotte
Barbara Cupisti . . . . . . . . . . . . . . . . . . . . . . . . . Lisa
    • 0:28—Very brief back side of right breast, while sitting up in bed. Side of right breast, while scooting over on bed while talking to Evald.
    • 0:48—Very brief left breast in gaping nightgown, while scrambling for the phone. Very brief right breast in gaping nightgown when getting up off ground after jumping through window.
    • 1:25—Breasts, while lying on slab and getting painted.
    • 1:31—Breasts, while getting raped by beast.

## CIA—Code Name: Alexa (1992)
Jeff Griggs . . . . . . . . . . . . . . . . . . . . . . . .Benedetti
Kathleen Kinmont . . . . . . . . . . . . . . . . . . . . . . Alexa
    • 1:04—Very brief buns and very, very brief right breast and brief left breast while making love with Lorenzo Lamas in bed.

### Cinderella (1977)

Linda Gildersleeve . . . . . . . . . . . . . . Farm Girl (redhead)
- ••• 0:21—Breasts and buns with her brunette sister in their house making love with the guy who is looking for Cinderella.
- •• 1:24—Full frontal nudity with her sister again when the Prince goes around to try and find Cinderella.

Elizabeth Halsey . . . . . . . . . . . . . . . Farm Girl (brunette)
- ••• 0:21—Nude with her redhead sister in their house making love with the guy who is looking for Cinderella.
- •• 1:24—Breasts with her sister again when the Prince goes around to try and find Cinderella.

Yana Nirvana . . . . . . . . . . . . . . . . . . . . . . . . . Drucella
- • 0:02—Breasts taking off clothes with her sister Maribella to let Cinderella wash.
- • 0:06—Brief breasts sitting up in bed with Maribella.

Mariwin Roberts . . . . . . . . . . . . . . . . Trapper's Daughter
- ••• 0:11—Frontal nudity getting a bath outside by her blonde sister. Long scene.

Cheryl Smith . . . . . . . . . . . . . . . . . . . . . . . . Cinderella
- ••• 0:03—Breasts dancing and singing.
- ••• 0:30—Frontal nudity getting "washed" by her sisters for the Royal Ball.
- •• 0:34—Breasts in the forest during a dream.
- ••• 0:41—Breasts taking a bath. Frontal nudity drying herself off.
- • 1:16—Brief breasts with the Prince.
- • 1:30—Brief left breast after making love with the Prince to prove it was her.
- • 1:34—Brief side view of left breast making love in the Prince's carriage.

### Cinderella Liberty (1973)

Dabney Coleman . . . . . . . . . . . . . . . . . Executive Officer
Bruno Kirby . . . . . . . . . . . . . . . . . . . . . . . . . . . . Alcott
Sally Kirkland . . . . . . . . . . . . . . . . . . . . . . . Fleet Chick
Marsha Mason . . . . . . . . . . . . . . . . . . . . Maggie Paul
- 0:09—Brief panties shot leaning over pool table when James Caan watches.
- •• 0:17—Side view of left breast in room with Caan. Brief right breast sitting down on bed.
- ••• 0:38—Breasts sitting up in bed, yelling at Caan.
- • 0:54—Very brief left breast turning over in bed and sitting up.

### Circle of Two (1980)

Tatum O'Neal . . . . . . . . . . . . . . . . . . . . Sarah Norton
- •• 0:56—Breasts standing behind a chair in Richard Burton's studio talking to him.

### Cisco Pike (1971)

Viva . . . . . . . . . . . . . . . . . . . . . . . . . . . . . . . Merna
Joy Bang . . . . . . . . . . . . . . . . . . . . . . . . . . . . . . Lynn
- 0:45—Very, very brief right breast, seen under Kris Kristofferson's arm at the beginning of the scene in bed with Merna.

Karen Black . . . . . . . . . . . . . . . . . . . . . . . . . . . . Sue
- •• 0:47—Breasts, getting dressed in bedroom.

Kris Kristofferson . . . . . . . . . . . . . . . . . . . . Cisco Pike

Harry Dean Stanton . . . . . . . . . . . . . . . . . . Jesse Dupre
- • 1:00—Brief upper half of buns, while standing up in bathtub to greet Kris Kristofferson.

### City Limits (1984)

Kim Cattrall . . . . . . . . . . . . . . . . . . . . . . . . . Wickings
- •• 1:02—Right breast, while sitting up in bed with a piece of paper stuck to her.

Rae Dawn Chong . . . . . . . . . . . . . . . . . . . . . . . . Yogi
John Diehl . . . . . . . . . . . . . . . . . . . . . . . . . . . Whitey
John Stockwell . . . . . . . . . . . . . . . . . . . . . . . . . . Lee

### City of Hope (1991)

Angela Bassett . . . . . . . . . . . . . . . . . . . . . . . . Reesha
- •• 1:20—Breasts in bed with Joe Morton.

Anthony John Denison . . . . . . . . . . . . . . . . . . . . Rizzo
Gina Gershon . . . . . . . . . . . . . . . . . . . . . . . . . Laurie
Vincent Spano . . . . . . . . . . . . . . . . . . . . . . . . . . Nick
David Strathairn . . . . . . . . . . . . . . . . . . . . . . Asteroid
Barbara Williams . . . . . . . . . . . . . . . . . . . . . . Angela

### City Slickers (1991)

Bruno Kirby . . . . . . . . . . . . . . . . . . . . . . . Ed Furillo
Helen Slater . . . . . . . . . . . . . . . . . . . Bonnie Rayburn
Yeardley Smith . . . . . . . . . . . . . . . . . . . . . . . Nancy
Daniel Stern . . . . . . . . . . . . . . . . . . . . . Phil Berquist
Tracey Walter . . . . . . . . . . . . . . . . . . . . . . . . Cookie
- • 1:16—Very brief buns, mooning everybody while riding stagecoach. Happy face painted on his rear. Hard to tell if it's him.

### Claire of the Moon (1992)

Karen Trumbo . . . . . . . . . . . . . . . . . Dr. Noel Benedict
- • 1:22—Very brief left breast, twice, in open jacket in restroom with her fantasy woman, then Claire.
- ••• 1:39—Breasts, while making love on bed with Claire. Long scene.

### Clash of the Titans (1981)

Ursula Andress . . . . . . . . . . . . . . . . . . . . . Aphrodite
Claire Bloom . . . . . . . . . . . . . . . . . . . . . . . . . Hera
Judi Bowker . . . . . . . . . . . . . . . . . . . . . Andromeda
- • 1:41—Buns and partial side view of right breast getting out of bath. Don't see her face.

Harry Hamlin . . . . . . . . . . . . . . . . . . . . . . . Perseus
Maggie Smith . . . . . . . . . . . . . . . . . . . . . . . . Thetis
Vida Taylor . . . . . . . . . . . . . . . . . . . . . . . . . Danae
- • 0:11—Right breast while breast feeding her baby. Buns, walking on beach.

### Class (1983)

Jacqueline Bisset . . . . . . . . . . . . . . . . . . . . . . . Ellen
Candace Collins . . . . . . . . . . . . . . . . . . . . Buxom Girl
Lolita Davidovich . . . . . . . . . . . . . . . . 1st Girl (motel)
Rob Lowe . . . . . . . . . . . . . . . . . . . . . . . . . . . Skip
Virginia Madsen . . . . . . . . . . . . . . . . . . . . . . . . Lisa
- •• 0:20—Brief left breast when Andrew McCarthy accidentally rips her blouse open at the girl's school.

Andrew McCarthy . . . . . . . . . . . . . . . . . . . . Jonathan

### Class of 1999 II: The Substitute (1993)

Nick Cassavetes . . . . . . . . . . . . . . . . . . . Emmett Grazer
- 1:01—Very briefly nude, while turning over in bed with Jenna.

Caitlin Dulany . . . . . . . . . . . . . . . . . . . Jenna McKensie
- •• 1:01—Breasts, while making love in bed with Emmett.
- ••• 1:02—More breasts while making love. Intercut with John shooting a machine gun.

### Class of Nuke 'Em High (1986)

Janelle Brady . . . . . . . . . . . . . . . . . . . . . . . . . . . Chrissy
- •• 0:26—Breasts sitting on bed in the attic with Warren.
- 0:31—Brief breasts scene from 0:26 superimposed over Warren's nightmare.

### Class of Nuke 'Em High Part II: Subhumanoid Meltdown (1991)

Jackie Moen . . . . . . . . . . . . . . Diane/Bald Subhumanoid
Leesa Rowland . . . . . . . . . . . . . . . . . . . . . . . . . Victoria
- •• 0:24—Breasts in room with Roger. Special effect mouth in her stomach.
- 0:25—Most of side of left breast, while making love on top of Roger.

Darla Slavens. . . . . . . . . . . . . . . . . . Plain White Rapper
Suzanne Solari. . . . . . . . . Toxie Squirrel Gang Member
Nicole Vasilopoulos . . . . . . . . . . . . . Bald Subhumanoid

### Clean and Sober (1988)

Henry Judd Baker . . . . . . . . . . . . . . . . . . . . . . . Xavier
- •• 0:15—Buns, when going crazy in drug rehabilitation room.

Brian Benben . . . . . . . . . . . . . . . . . . . . . Martin Laux
Claudia Christian. . . . . . . . . . . . . . . . . . . . . . . . . Iris
Harley Jane Kozak . . . . . . . . . . . . . Ralston Receptionist
Stephanie Menuez . . . . . . . . . . . . . . . . . . . Ticket Agent
Rachel Ryan. . . . . . . . . . . . . Uncredited Dead Girlfriend
- 0:02—Buns, lying dead in Michael Keaton's bed. Don't see her face, but it's her.

M. Emmet Walsh . . . . . . . . . . . . . . . . . . . Richard Dirks

### Clean Slate (1981; French)

a.k.a. Coup de Torchon

Isabelle Huppert . . . . . . . . . . . . . . . . . . . . . . Rosalie
- •• 0:50—Breasts and buns, after taking off her slip in bedroom in front of Lucien.
- ••• 1:13—Breasts, after sitting up in bed, then full frontal nudity, after getting out of bed.

Guy Marchand . . . . . . . . . . . . . . . . . . Chavasson
Irene Skobline . . . . . . . . . . . . . . . . . . . . . . . . . . Anne
- •• 1:07—Breasts, while taking a shower and getting spied on by Nono.

### Cleo/Leo (1989)

Ginger Lynn Allen . . . . . . . . . . . . . . . . . . . . . . . Karen
- ••• 0:39—Full frontal nudity getting out of the shower, getting dried with a towel by Jane Hamilton, then in nightgown.
- ••• 0:57—Full frontal nudity getting out of the shower and dried off again.

Scott Baker. . . . . . . . . . . . . . . . . . . . . . Leo Blockman
- 0:09—Very brief buns after getting his butt kicked.

Ruth Corrine Collins . . . . . . . . . . . . . . . . . . . . . . . Sally
- ••• 0:08—Breasts getting dress pulled off by Leo.

Jennifer Delora . . . . . . . . . . . . . . . . . . . . . . . Bernice
Jane Hamilton . . . . . . . . . . . . . . . . . . . . . Cleo Clock
- •• 0:13—Nude undressing in front of three guys.
- 0:21—Breasts changing in dressing room.
- ••• 0:22—Breasts changing in dressing room with the Store Clerk.
- 0:40—In bra and panties.
- •• 1:07—Left breast and lower frontal nudity making love with Bob on bed.

Kimberly Taylor . . . . . . . . . . . . . . . . . . . . . Store Clerk
- ••• 0:22—Breasts in white panties, changing in dressing room with Jane Hamilton. Very nice!

Kevin Thomsen . . . . . . . . . . . . . . . . . . . . . Bob Miller
- 1:07—Brief frontal nudity, then buns while making love with Jane Hamilton on bed.

### Cleopatra (1963)

Michael Hordern . . . . . . . . . . . . . . . . . . . . . . Cicero
Elizabeth Taylor . . . . . . . . . . . . . . . . . . . . . Cleopatra
- 0:28—Half of buns, lying face down, while getting a massage.
- 2:02—(0:08 into tape 2) Taking a bath—You can't see anything.

### Click: Calendar Girl Killer (1989)

Lisa Axelrod . . . . . . . . . . . . . . . . . . . . . . . . . Jennifer
Tracy Dali . . . . . . . . . . . . . . . . . . . . . . . . . . . . . June
Michael Jay Shane . . . . . . . . . . . . . . . . . . . . . . Jessie
Dona Speir . . . . . . . . . . . . . . . . . . . . . . . . . . . Nancy
- 0:00—Posing in yellow two piece swimsuit during photo session.
- 0:06—In wet, white dress after being pushed into the spa.
- 0:11—Brief glimpses of breasts during photo session. Buns and breasts under sheer fabric.
- •• 0:12—Brief buns, dropping the piece of fabric.
- 0:28—Posing in yellow two piece swimsuit during photo session.

### A Climate for Killing (1990)

Steven Bauer . . . . . . . . . . . . . . . . . . . . . Paul McGraw
John Diehl . . . . . . . . . . . . . . . . . . . . . . . . Wayne Paris
Dedee Pfeiffer. . . . . . . . . . . . . . . . . . . . . . . . . Donna
Sherrie Rose . . . . . . . . . . . . . . . . . . . . . . . Rita Paris
- •• 1:30—Breasts in bed while Wayne recollects his crime to John Beck.

Katharine Ross . . . . . . . . . . . . . . . . . . . . Grace Hines
Mia Sara. . . . . . . . . . . . . . . . . . . . . . . . . . Elise Shipp

### A Clockwork Orange (1971)

Adrienne Corri . . . . . . . . . . . . . . . . . . Mrs. Alexander
- •• 0:11—Breasts through cut-outs in her top, then full frontal nudity getting raped by Malcolm McDowell and his friends.

Malcolm McDowell . . . . . . . . . . . . . . . . . . . . . . . Alex
- 0:27—Very brief nude having sex with two women in his bedroom. Shot at fast speed.

0:52—Upper half of frontal nudity getting admitted to jail.

### Close My Eyes (1991; British)

Helen FitzGerald . . . . . . . . . . . . . . . . . . . . . Scottish Girl
•• 0:08—Nude, lying down, then getting up in room with Richard.
Clive Owen . . . . . . . . . . . . . . . . . . . . . . . . . . . . Richard
•• 0:09—Brief frontal nudity, then buns, while getting up from the floor and talking on the telephone.
 0:29—Side view of buns, while lying on floor with Natalie.
••• 0:30—Buns, while getting up and walking around.
•• 0:32—Very brief frontal nudity, rolling over. Out of focus buns, lying on his stomach.
•• 0:46—Buns, while lying in bed with Natalie.
•• 0:56—Buns, while getting out of bed and walking to the window.
Saskia Reeves. . . . . . . . . . . . . . . . . . . . Natalie Gillespie
•• 0:29—Very brief right breast, twice, then breasts twice in room with Richard.
••• 0:31—Full frontal nudity, getting up and getting dressed.
••• 0:45—In white bra, then breasts standing, then lying on the floor with Richard.
•• 0:46—Buns, while lying in bed with Richard. Nude, getting out of bed and putting on robe.
• 0:56—Right breast, while lying in bed.

### Club Extinction (1990)

*a.k.a. Doctor M*
Alan Bates . . . . . . . . . . . . . . . . . . . . . . . Dr. Marsfeldt
Jennifer Beals . . . . . . . . . . . . . . . . . . . . . . Sonja Vogler
• 1:16—Brief side of left breast rolling over in bed with Hartmann. Don't see her face, but probably her.
•• 1:17—Brief breasts in bed with Hartmann when he kisses her right breast, then brief right breast.
Andrew McCarthy . . . . . . . . . . . . . . . . . . . The Assassin

### Coach (1978)

Michael Biehn . . . . . . . . . . . . . . . . . . . . . . . . . . . Jack
• 1:11—Upper half of buns, while in shower with Cathy Lee Crosby.
Cathy Lee Crosby . . . . . . . . . . . . . . . . . . . . . . Randy
• 0:31—Very brief side view of left breast when Michael Biehn opens the door while she's putting on her top.
 0:52—In wet white T-shirt at the beach and in her house with Biehn.
 1:11—Very, very brief breasts in shower room with Biehn. Blurry, hard to see anything.
Brent Huff . . . . . . . . . . . . . . . . . . . . . . . . . . . . . Keith
Rosanne Katon . . . . . . . . . . . . . . . . . . . . . . . . . . Sue
• 0:10—Very brief breasts flashing her breasts along with three of her girlfriends for their four boyfriends.
Lenka Novak . . . . . . . . . . . . . . . . . . . . . . . . . Marilyn
• 0:10—Very brief breasts flashing her breasts along with her girlfriends for their boyfriends.

### The Coca-Cola Kid (1985; Australian)

Kris McQuade . . . . . . . . . . . . . . . . . . . . . . . . Juliana

Eric Roberts . . . . . . . . . . . . . . . . . . . . . . . . . . Becker
Greta Scacchi . . . . . . . . . . . . . . . . . . . . . . . . . . Terri
••• 0:49—Nude taking a shower with her daughter.
•• 1:20—Brief breasts wearing a Santa Claus outfit while in bed with Eric Roberts.

### Cocaine Wars (1986)

*a.k.a. Vice Wars*
John Schneider. . . . . . . . . . . . . . . . . . . . . . . . . . Cliff
Kathryn Witt. . . . . . . . . . . . . . . . . . . . . . . . . . . Janet
• 0:36—Brief breasts and buns making love in bed with John Schneider.

### Cocktail (1988)

Bryan Brown . . . . . . . . . . . . . . . . . . . . . Doug Coughlin
Tom Cruise . . . . . . . . . . . . . . . . . . . . . . . Brian Hanagan
Gina Gershon . . . . . . . . . . . . . . . . . . . . . . . . . . Coral
• 0:31—Very, very brief right breast romping around in bed with Tom Cruise.
Kelly Lynch . . . . . . . . . . . . . . . . . . . . . . . Kerry Coughlin
 0:45—Buns, wearing a two piece swimsuit at the beach.
 1:01—Buns, in string bikini swimsuit on boat with Tom Cruise and Bryan Brown.
Elisabeth Shue . . . . . . . . . . . . . . . . . . . . Jordan Mooney
 0:52—Side view of left breast while standing up in waterfall with Tom Cruise when she takes off her swimsuit top.

### Coffy (1973)

Pam Grier. . . . . . . . . . . . . . . . . . . . . . . . . . . . . Coffy
• 0:05—Upper half of right breast in bed with a guy.
 0:19—Buns, walking past the fireplace, seen through a fish tank.
•• 0:25—Breasts in open dress getting attacked by two masked burglars.
••• 0:38—Buns and breasts undressing in bedroom. Wow!
• 0:42—Brief right breast when breast pops out of dress while she's leaning over. Dark, hard to see.
 0:49—In black bra and panties in open dress with a guy in the bedroom.

### Cold Comfort (1988)

Jayne Eastwood . . . . . . . . . . . . . . . . . . . . Mrs. Brocket
Paul Gross . . . . . . . . . . . . . . . . . . . . . . . . . . . Stephen
Margaret Langrick . . . . . . . . . . . . . . . . . . . . . . Dolores
•• 0:16—In tank top and panties, then breasts undressing in front of Stephen.
• 0:19—Very brief side of left breast and buns getting robe.
•• 0:41—Doing strip tease in front of her dad and Stephen. In black bra and panties, then breasts.
• 0:42—Very brief breasts jumping into bed.

### Cold Feet (1989)

Keith Carradine . . . . . . . . . . . . . . . . . . . . . . . . Monte
Sally Kirkland . . . . . . . . . . . . . . . . Maureen Linoleum
• 0:56—In black bra and panties taking off her dress in bedroom with Keith Carradine. Brief right breast pulling bra down.

- 0:58—Brief side view of right breast sitting up in bed talking to Carradine.

## Cold Heaven (1990)
Mark Harmon . . . . . . . . . . . . . . . . . . . .Alex Davenport
Theresa Russell . . . . . . . . . . . . . . . . . Marie Davenport
- 0:09—Very brief upper half of right breast, when it pops out of her swimsuit top when struggling to get Mark Harmon onto boat.
- 0:18—Side of left breast while washing herself at the sink.
- 1:14—Brief breasts several times, making love in bed with James Russo.

James Russo . . . . . . . . . . . . . . . . . . . . . Daniel Corvin
- 0:02—Buns, while standing at window, putting on underwear. Long shot.
- 1:15—Brief buns while in bed with Theresa Russell.

## Cold Steel (1987)
Jay Acovone . . . . . . . . . . . . . . . . . . . . . Cooke Manero
Brad Davis. . . . . . . . . . . . . . . . . . . . .Johnny Modine
Sharon Stone . . . . . . . . . . . . . . . . . . . Kathy Conners
- 0:33—Brief left breast making love in bed with Brad Davis. Dark, hard to see. Brief breasts turning over after making love.

## Cold Sweat (1993)
Adam Baldwin. . . . . . . . . . . . . . . . . . . Mitch Simmons
- 0:17—Buns, while playing with fluorescent paint on Shannon Tweed in bathtub. Kind of dark.

Henry Czerny . . . . . . . . . . . . . . . . . . . Sean Mathieson
•• 0:44—Buns, while on bed with Shannon Tweed.

Shannon Tweed . . . . . . . . . . . . . . . . . . . Beth Moore
••• 0:14—Breasts squished against the glass shower door while making out with Sean. More breasts and buns.
0:15—In bra, while sitting on bed.
•• 0:17—Breasts and buns while playing with fluorescent paints with Adam Baldwin in bathtub. Kind of dark.
••• 0:43—Breasts and very brief lower frontal nudity while on bed with Sean.
•• 0:53—Buns and back side of left breast getting into bathtub. More breasts, twice, while in bathtub.

Lenore Zann . . . . . . . . . . . . . . . . . . . Catherine Wicker
•• 0:04—Brief buns in panties, then partial lower frontal nudity in bra, panties, garter belt and stockings. Brief breasts while making love in office with David.
•• 0:46—Breasts in bubble bath while talking to Ben Cross.
••• 0:50—Breasts, while lying on bed and talking to Cross.

## Coldfire (1990)
Lisa Axelrod. . . . . . . . . . . . . . . . . . . . . . . . . Dancer
- 0:11—Breasts, twice, dancing on stage.
- 0:13—Brief breasts, getting pushed off the stage.

Darcy De Moss . . . . . . . . . . . . . . . . . . . . . . . Maria
••• 0:27—Partial right breast and buns, lying in bed with Nick. Left breast, then breasts making love with him.

•• 0:30—Breasts in bathtub with Nick.
Wings Hauser. . . . . . . . . . . . . . . . . . . . . . . . . . Lars

## Collector's Item (1988)
a.k.a. The Trap
Laura Antonelli. . . . . . . . . . . . . . . . . . . . Marie Colbert
0:18—In white lingerie with Tony Musante.
- 0:20—Lower frontal nudity, then right breast making love with Musante. Dark.
0:37—In black bra, garter belt and stockings in open robe undressing for Musante.
0:41—In the same lingerie again dropping robe and getting dressed.

Blanca Marsillach . . . . . . . . . . . . . . . . . . . Jacqueline
•• 0:52—In white bra cleaning up Tony Musante in bed, then breasts.
1:04—Lower frontal nudity while watching Musante and Laura Antonelli making love in bed.
- 1:18—Breasts getting dressed. A little dark.
•• 1:22—Breasts changing clothes in bedroom while Antonelli talks to her.

Cristina Marsillach . . . . . . . . . . . . . . . . . Young Marie
•• 0:12—Right breast in elevator with Tony Musante.
•• 0:36—Breasts in open blouse, then full frontal nudity in hut with Musante.

## The Color of Money (1986)
Tom Cruise . . . . . . . . . . . . . . . . . . . . . . . Vincent
Mary Elizabeth Mastrantonio . . . . . . . . . . . . . . Carmen
- 0:41—Brief breasts in bathroom mirror drying herself off while Paul Newman talks to Tom Cruise. Long shot, hard to see.

Paul Newman . . . . . . . . . . . . . . . . . . . . . . .Eddie
Helen Shaver . . . . . . . . . . . . . . . . . . . . . . . Janelle
John Turturro. . . . . . . . . . . . . . . . . . . . . . . .Julian

## Colors (1988)
Maria Conchita Alonso. . . . . . . . . . . . . . Louisa Gomez
••• 0:48—Breasts making love in bed with Sean Penn.
Sean Penn . . . . . . . . . . . . . . . . . . . . .Danny McGavin

## The Comfort of Strangers (1991)
Rupert Everett . . . . . . . . . . . . . . . . . . . . . . . Colin
•• 0:47—Buns, while walking around the room, looking for his clothes.
- 1:05—Buns, while making love with Natasha Richardson on bed. Lit with blue light.

Helen Mirren . . . . . . . . . . . . . . . . . . . . . . .Caroline
Natasha Richardson . . . . . . . . . . . . . . . . . . . Mary
••• 0:45—Breasts sleeping in bed. Long shot. Then closer breasts after waking up. Long scene.
•• 1:05—Breasts making love with Colin. Lit with blue light.
•• 1:06—Right breast, lying in bed with Colin. Lit with blue light.

## Coming Home (1978)
Robert Carradine . . . . . . . . . . . . . . . . . . . .Bill Munson
Bruce Dern. . . . . . . . . . . . . . . . . . . . . Captain Bob Hyde
•• 2:03—Buns, while taking off his clothes at the beach and running into the ocean.

Jane Fonda . . . . . . . . . . . . . . . . . . . . . . . . .Sally Hyde
•• 1:26—Making love in bed with Jon Voight. Breasts only when her face is visible. Buns and brief left breast when you don't see a face is a body double.
Penelope Milford. . . . . . . . . . . . . . . . . . . . Viola Munson
• 1:19—Doing strip tease in room with Jane Fonda and two guys. Sort of right breast peeking out between her arms when she changes her mind.
Jon Voight. . . . . . . . . . . . . . . . . . . . . . . Luke Martin

## Coming to America (1988)
Victoria Dillard . . . . . . . . . . . . . . . . . . . . . . .Bather
•• 0:04—Breasts, standing up in royal bathtub to announce "The royal penis is clean, Your Highness."
Cuba Gooding, Jr. . . . . . . . . . . . . . . Boy Getting Haircut
Samuel L. Jackson . . . . . . . . . . . . . . . . . . . .Holdup Man
Bianca McEachin. . . . . Uncredited Miss Black Awareness
• 0:37—Buns, wearing pink sequined, two piece swimsuit on stage during Black Awareness meeting.

## Coming Together (1978)
*a.k.a. A Matter of Love*
Jeff Alin . . . . . . . . . . . . . . . . . . . . . . . . . Frank Hughes
• 1:05—Buns, while putting pants on with Richard.
Marc Anderson . . . . . . . . . . . . . . . . . . Richard Duncan
•• 0:13—Buns, while kneeling and kissing Angie, then more buns making love.
• 0:58—Buns, while making love with Vicky.
• 1:05—Buns, while putting pants on with Frank.
Christy Neal . . . . . . . . . . . . . . . . . . . . . . Vicky Hughes
0:12—In bra and panties, in bedroom with Frank.
• 0:30—Brief right breast in shower with Angie.
• 0:37—Breasts and buns making love standing up in front of sliding glass door with Frank. Quick cuts.
• 0:49—Brief breasts again during flashbacks.
•• 0:57—Breasts with Angie and Richard.
• 1:05—Breasts on beach with Angie. Long shot.

## Commando (1985)
Ava Cadell. . . . . . . . . . . . . . . . . . . . . . . . . Girl in Bed
• 0:46—Very brief breasts three times in bed when Arnold Schwarzenegger knocks a guy through the motel door into her room.
Rae Dawn Chong . . . . . . . . . . . . . . . . . . . . . . Cindy
Chelsea Field. . . . . . . . . . . . . . . . . . . . . . Stewardess
Bill Paxton. . . . . . . . . . . . . . . . . . . . . Intercept Officer
Arnold Schwarzenegger . . . . . . . . . . . . . . . . . Matrix

## Common Bonds (1991)
Rae Dawn Chong . . . . . . . . . . . . . . . . . . . Ilene Curtis
Brad Dourif. . . . . . . . . . . . . . . . . . . . . . . . . . Johnny
Tasmin Kelsey . . . . . . . . . . . . . . . . . . . . . . . . Ginger
• 0:04—Breasts in hotel room with the cop when Michael Ironside bursts into the room. Long shot. More out of focus breasts shots in the mirror.

## The Company of Wolves (1985)
Danielle Dax . . . . . . . . . . . . . . . . . . . . . . . Wolfgirl
• 1:26—Brief buns and breasts running around outside. Her hair is in the way a lot.

## Con el Corazón en la Mano (1988; Mexican)
Maria Conchita Alonso. . . . . . . . . . . . . . . . . . . .n.a.
• 0:38—Very, very brief right breast, while turning over in bed with her husband.
• 0:39—Breasts several times, taking a bath.
•• 1:15—Breasts while ripping off her dress. Long shot, side view, standing while kissing a guy.

## Conan the Barbarian (1982)
Sandahl Bergman. . . . . . . . . . . . . . . . . . . . . . . .Valeria
•• 0:49—Brief left breast making love with Arnold Schwarzenegger.
Valerie Quennessen. . . . . . . . . . . . . . . . . .The Princess
Arnold Schwarzenegger . . . . . . . . . . . . . . . . . . . Conan

## The Concrete Jungle (1982)
Greta Blackburn . . . . . . . . . . . . . . . . . . . . . Lady in Bar
Sondra Currie. . . . . . . . . . . . . . . . . . . . . . . .Katherine
Aimée Eccles . . . . . . . . . . . . . . . . . . . . . . . . Spider
Marcia Karr . . . . . . . . . . . . . . . . . . . . . . . . Marcy
Camille Keaton. . . . . . . . . . . . . . . . . . . . . . . . Rita
• 0:41—In black bra, then breasts getting raped by Stone. Brief lower frontal nudity sitting up afterwards.

## Confessions of a Serial Killer (1987)
Eleese Lester. . . . . . . . . . . . . . . . . . . . . . .Karen Grimes
• 0:34—Buns, tied and gaged to bed before being raped and killed.

## Conflict of Interest (1992)
Gregory Alan Harris . . . . . . . . . . . . . . . . . Jason Flannery
• 0:48—Brief buns, in the shower when Vera accidentally opens the door.
Heather Parkhurst. . . . . . . . . . . . . . . . . . . .Francesca
Dey Young. . . . . . . . . . . . . . . . . . . . . . . . . . .Vera
0:08—In bra, while sitting in Mick's lap.
• 0:31—Brief right breast, while turning over on her back in bed with Mick.
•• 0:32—Left breast, while in bed, getting kissed by Mick.

## The Conformist (1971; Italian/French)
Pierre Clementi . . . . . . . . . . . . . . . . . . . .Nino Seminara
Dominique Sanda . . . . . . . . . . . . . . . . . . Anna Quadri
•• 1:01—Breasts, taking off leotard for Marcello.
Stefania Sandrelli . . . . . . . . . . . . . . . . . . . . .Giulia
• 0:41—Right breast, while in train with her husband.
• 1:07—Very brief, upper half of buns, while turning around.

## Consenting Adults (1992)
Kevin Kline. . . . . . . . . . . . . . . . . . . . . . Richard Parker
•• 0:39—Buns, while in bed with Melissa Moore, when he thinks it's Kay.
Mary Elizabeth Mastrantonio . . . . . . . . . Priscilla Parker
Rebecca Miller . . . . . . . . . . . . . . . . . . . . . . .Kay Otis
• 0:28—Buns and brief side view of left breast, while getting out of tub. Seen through shutters while Kevin Kline watches through the window.

Melissa Anne Moore . . . . . . . . . . . . . . . . Trudy Seaton
- 0:37—Buns, while lying in bed when Kevin Kline takes the place of the husband.

Billie Neal . . . . . . . . . . . . . . . . . . . . . Annie Duttonville

### Contempt (1963; French/Italian)
Brigitte Bardot. . . . . . . . . . . . . . . . . . . . . . Camille Javal
- 0:04—Buns.
  0:52—Almost buns walking through door after bath.
- 0:54—Buns, while lying on rug.
- 1:30—Buns, while lying on beach. Long shot.

### The Conversation (1974)
Allen Garfield . . . . . . . . . . . . . . . . . . . . . Bernie Moran
Teri Garr . . . . . . . . . . . . . . . . . . . . . . . . . . . . . . Amy
Elizabeth MacRae . . . . . . . . . . . . . . . . . . . . Meredith
- 1:14—Breasts and buns, getting undressed in work area with Gene Hackman. Long shot, dark.

### Convoy (1978)
Kris Kristofferson . . . . . . . . . . . . . . . . . . . . Rubber Duck
Ali MacGraw. . . . . . . . . . . . . . . . . . . . . . . . . Melissa
Cassie Yates. . . . . . . . . . . . . . . . . . . . . . . . . . Violet
- 0:21—Very brief left breast, while in truck sleeper with Kris Kristofferson.

### The Cook, The Thief, His Wife & Her Lover
(1989; Dutch/French)
Alan Howard . . . . . . . . . . . . . . . . . . . . . . . . . Michael
- •• 0:32—Buns, while then brief frontal nudity with Helen Mirren.
- 0:42—Buns, while on top of Mirren.
- 1:11—Buns, with Mirren in kitchen.
- ••• 1:14—Buns, while getting into meat truck. Frontal nudity getting hosed off and walking around with Mirren.

Helen Mirren. . . . . . . . . . . . . . . . . . . . Georgina Spica
  0:22—In black bra in restroom performing fellatio on Michael.
- •• 0:32—In lingerie undressing, then lower frontal nudity, buns and left breast in kitchen with Michael.
- 0:42—Buns and right breast, while making love with Michael again.
- •• 0:57—Breasts sitting and talking with Michael.
  1:01—Buns, kneeling on table.
- 1:05—Brief breasts, while leaning back on table with Michael.
  1:07—Lower frontal nudity opening her coat for Michael.
- 1:11—Buns and breasts in kitchen.
- ••• 1:14—Buns, getting into meat truck. Full frontal nudity in truck and walking around with Michael.

Willie Ross . . . . . . . . . . . . . . . . . . . . . . . . . . . . Roy
  0:03—Buns, while on ground covered with dog feces getting urinated on by Albert. (Talk about a bad day!)
- 0:07—Buns, kneeling on ground while dogs walk around.
- 0:09—Buns, while standing up.

### Cool Blue (1990)
Judie Aronson. . . . . . . . . . . . . . . . . . . . . . . . . Cathy
- •• 1:03—Breasts in bed on top of Woody Harrelson.
Ely Pouget . . . . . . . . . . . . . . . . . . . . . . . . . Christiane
- •• 0:18—Side view of right breast, then breasts with Woody Harrelson.

### Cool Hand Luke (1967)
Dennis Hopper. . . . . . . . . . . . . . . . . . . . . . Bubalugats
Paul Newman . . . . . . . . . . . . . . . . . . . . . . . . . Luke
- 1:38—Very brief buns, putting on white shirt before going into The Box. Very dark.
Harry Dean Stanton . . . . . . . . . . . . . . . . . . . . Tramp

### The Cool Surface (1992)
Teri Hatcher. . . . . . . . . . . . . . . . . . . . . . . Dani Payson
- ••• 0:20—Close-up of left breast, while lying in bed with Robert Patrick during daydream.
- ••• 0:27—Breasts, while standing in front of Patrick when he takes off her lingerie.
- 0:29—Brief right breast, when Patrick gets out of bed.
Cyril O'Reilly . . . . . . . . . . . . . . . . . . . . . . Gary/Eric
Robert Patrick. . . . . . . . . . . . . . . . . . . . . Jarvis Scott

### Corporate Affairs (1990)
Ria Coyne. . . . . . . . . . . . . . . . . . . . . . . . . . Mistress
- •• 0:10—Left breast several times in back of car with Arthur.
Mary Crosby . . . . . . . . . . . . . . . . . . . . Jessica Pierce
  0:27—In bra while sitting in Arthur's lap in chair.
  1:04—In pink bra with Peter Scolari.
Stephen Davies . . . . . . . . . . . . . . . . . . . . . Ukranian #2
Kim Gillingham . . . . . . . . . . . . . . . . . . Ginny Malmquist
- 1:09—Breasts, climbing out of cubicle.
Lisa Moncure . . . . . . . . . . . . . . . . . . . . . Carolyn Bean
- 1:07—Very, very brief left breast, while kicking Douglas out of cubicle.
Elena Sahagun . . . . . . . . . . . . . . . . . . . . . . . . Stacy
Jeanne Sal . . . . . . . . . . . . . . . . . . . . . . . . . . Sandy
- 0:38—Left breast in open dress while sneaking around the office with Buster.
Christina Veronica . . . . . . . . . . . . . . Tanning Woman
  0:47—Side of right breast, getting tanned.

### Corvette Summer (1978)
Mark Hamill . . . . . . . . . . . . . . . . . . . . . . . Kent Dantley
Annie Potts. . . . . . . . . . . . . . . . . . . . . . . . . Vanessa
- 0:51—Silhouette of right breast in van with Mark Hamill. Out of focus breasts washing herself in the van while talking to him. Don't really see anything.

### Cotton Comes to Harlem (1970)
Godfrey Cambridge . . . . . . . . . . . . . Grave Digger Jones
Judy Pace. . . . . . . . . . . . . . . . . . . . . . . . . . . . Iris
- •• 0:28—Buns and breasts, taking off dress and getting into shower.
- ••• 0:29—Breasts and buns while getting out of the shower.
- 0:30—Upper half of breasts in mirror while sitting at vanity.

••• 0:31—Brief breasts, unwrapping from towel and lying on bed. Breasts, while lying in bed. Breasts and buns while getting out of bed.
Dick Sabol............................... Jarema
••• 0:31—Buns, in bedroom with Judy Pace, then running after her and getting caught in hallway outside of locked apartment.

### Cousin, Cousine (1975; French)
Marie-Christine Barrault ................... Marthe
•• 1:05—Breasts in bed with her lover, cutting his nails.
• 1:07—Brief side view of right breast, while giving him a bath.
••• 1:16—Breasts with penciled tattoos all over her body.
1:33—Braless in see-through white blouse saying "good bye" to everybody.
Guy Marchand ........................... Pascal
Marie-France Pisier ....................... Karine

### Cousins (1989)
George Coe ........................... Uncle Phil
•• 0:08—Buns, while mooning everybody during wedding reception.
• 0:34—Buns again, during video playback.
William L. Petersen ..................... Tom Hardy
Isabella Rossellini..................... Maria Hardy
Sean Young......................... Tish Kozinski
1:28—In black bra, in hotel room with William Petersen.

### Covergirl (1982; Canadian)
Jeff Conaway....................... T. C. Sloane
•• 0:43—Very brief lower frontal nudity getting out of bed.
Irena Ferris ........................... Kit Paget
•• 0:19—Brief breasts taking off robe and getting into bathtub with Dee.
• 0:43—Very brief right breast sticking out of nightgown.
• 0:46—Upper half of left breast during modeling session.
• 0:47—Breasts in mirror in dressing room.
0:49—Brief breasts getting attacked by Joel.
• 0:53—Brief left breast, putting another blouse on.
• 0:53—Brief left breast, putting on blouse.
Roberta Leighton ................... Dee Anderson
0:16—Almost breasts, while making love dressed like a nun.
Michele Scarabelli ................... Snow Queen
Kenneth Welsh ..................... Harrison Chandler
• 1:23—Brief buns, while seen on video tape used to get him in trouble. Long shot.

### Crack House (1989)
Anthony Geary ......................... Dockett
Richard Roundtree............... Lieutenant Johnson
Heidi Thomas ........................... Annie
• 1:09—Brief left breast and buns in a G string, on table getting raped by a gang.
• 1:14—Breasts in bathtub, dead.

Angel Tompkins......................... Mother

### Crackerjack (1994)
Nastassja Kinski ........................... K.C.
Melody Stark ......................... Newlywed
• 0:33—Brief side view of left breast, while undressing in room with her husband.
••• 0:34—Breasts, when her husband plays with an ice cube on her breasts. Buns when the terrorists break into the room.

### Crash and Burn (1990)
Katherine Armstrong ..................... Christine
••• 1:00—Breasts taking a shower before being killed.

### Crawlspace (1986)
Klaus Kinski ..................... Dr. Karl Gunther
Tané McClure ....................... Sophie Fisher
• 0:00—Nipples, sticking out of holes that she cuts in her red bra. Brief breasts in bed making love with Hank. Dark.

### Crazy Mama (1975)
Sally Kirkland ........................... Ella Mae
Cloris Leachman........................... Melba
• 0:53—Brief left breast under clear plastic blouse while washing her boyfriend's hair in the sink.
Linda Purl............................... Cheryl
0:05—In pink, two piece swimsuit at the beach.
• 0:52—Very brief buns, then brief breasts when Snake and Donny Most keep opening the door after she has taken a shower. Long shot, hard to see.

### Creator (1985)
Mariel Hemingway........................... Meli
0:38—Brief breasts cooling herself off by pulling up T-shirt in front of a fan.
• 1:10—Brief breasts flashing David Ogden Stiers during football game to distract him.
Virginia Madsen......................... Barbara
0:53—Walking on beach in a blue one piece swimsuit with Vincent Spano.
••• 0:58—Nude in shower with Spano.
Vincent Spano ........................... Boris
• 0:28—Brief buns, while in shower room with David Ogden Stiers after working out in a gym.
• 0:57—Brief buns, before taking a shower.

### Creature (1985)
Klaus Kinski ..................... Hans Rudy Hofner
Marie Laurin....................... Susan Delambre
•• 0:41—Breasts and brief buns with blood on her shoulders, getting Jon to take his helmet off.
Diane Salinger ....................... Melanie Bryce

### Creatures the World Forgot (1971; British)
Julie Ege............................. Nala, The Girl
0:56—Very brief breasts several times (it looks like a stunt double) fighting in cave with The Dumb Girl. Hard to see.
• 1:32—Very, very brief half of right breast when fighting a snake that is wrapped around her face.

Marcia Fox . . . . . . . . . . . . . . . . . . . . . The Dumb Girl
- • 0:51—Right breast, then brief breasts turning around by the pool.
- • 0:58—Brief breasts fighting with Julie Ege.
- • 1:20—Very brief right breast when The Dark Boy gets his leg cut.

### Creepozoids (1987)
Ken Abraham . . . . . . . . . . . . . . . . . . . . . . . . . . Butch
- •• 0:16—Side view of buns, while standing in shower with Linnea Quigley.
Kim McKamy . . . . . . . . . . . . . . . . . . . . . . . . . . Kate
Linnea Quigley . . . . . . . . . . . . . . . . . . . . . . . Blanca
- •• 0:15—Breasts taking off her top to take a shower.
- •• 0:16—Right breast, while standing in shower with Butch.
- • 0:24—Right breast several times while sleeping in bed with Butch.

### Creepshow 2 (1987)
Lois Chiles . . . . . . . . . . . . . . . . . . . . . . . . Annie Lansing
- •• 0:59—Brief breasts getting out of boyfriend's bed, then getting dressed.

### Cries and Whispers (1972; Swedish)
*a.k.a. Viskingar Och Rop*
Harriet Andersson . . . . . . . . . . . . . . . . . . . . . . . Agnes
Ingrid Thulin . . . . . . . . . . . . . . . . . . . . . . . . . Karin
- •• 0:57—Breasts and buns, undressing and getting ready for bed. Something covers lower frontal nudity.
Liv Ullmann . . . . . . . . . . . . . . . . . . . . . . . . . . Maria

### Crime Lords (1990)
Susan Byun . . . . . . . . . . . . . . . . . . . . . . . . Monahan
- •• 1:06—Left breast, then right breast, while making out with Wayne Crawford on the couch.
Martin Hewitt . . . . . . . . . . . . . . . . . . . . . Peter Russo
- •• 0:50—Buns, while getting back into bed with two Chinese girls.
Kimberleigh Stark . . . . . . . . . . . . . . Lieutenant Sylvestri

### Crime Zone (1989)
David Carradine . . . . . . . . . . . . . . . . . . . . . . . . Jason
Sherilyn Fenn . . . . . . . . . . . . . . . . . . . . . . . . . Helen
- 0:16—In black lingerie and stockings in bedroom.
- •• 0:23—Breasts wearing black panties making love with Bone. Dark, long shot.

### Crimes of Passion (1984)
(Unrated version reviewed.)
John Laughlin . . . . . . . . . . . . . . . . . . . . Bobby Grady
- • 0:50—Buns, while getting dressed after having sex with Kathleen Turner. (Viewed through peep hole by Anthony Perkins.)
Annie Potts . . . . . . . . . . . . . . . . . . . . . . . Amy Grady
Janice Renney . . . . . . . . . . . . . . . . . . . . . . . Stripper
- ••• 0:06—Breasts and buns dancing while Anthony Perkins watches.
- 1:00—Buns again.

Kathleen Turner . . . . . . . . . . . Joanna Crane/China Blue
- ••• 0:45—Breasts, wearing black panties and stockings, in bed with Bobby. Shadows of them making love on the wall.
- • 1:00—Right breast in back of a limousine with a rich couple.
- 1:22—In blue bra and panties.
- • 1:27—Right breast in bed with Bobby.

### Criminal Law (1989)
Kevin Bacon . . . . . . . . . . . . . . . . . . . . . . . Martin Thiel
Gary Oldman . . . . . . . . . . . . . . . . . . . . . . . Ben Chase
- • 1:21—Very, very brief blurry frontal nudity in bed with Ellen.
Karen Young . . . . . . . . . . . . . . . . . . . . Ellen Falkner
- • 1:21—Very brief buns, then brief breasts in bed with Ben.

### Criss Cross (1992)
David Arnott . . . . . . . . . . . . . . . . . . . . . . . Chris Cross
- •• 1:15—Brief buns, putting on his pants when his girl friend's parents come home. Don't see his face.
Steve Buscemi . . . . . . . . . . . . . . . . . . . . . . . . . Louis
Paul Calderone . . . . . . . . . . . . . . . . . . . . . . . Blacky
Keith Carradine . . . . . . . . . . . . . . . . . . . . John Cross
Cathryn De Prume . . . . . . . . . . . . . . . . . . . . Oakley
Goldie Hawn . . . . . . . . . . . . . . . . . . . . . Tracy Cross
- •• 0:23—Buns and breasts in pasties, dancing on stage in club while her son watches.
Anna Levine Thomson . . . . . . . . . . . . . . . . . . Monica
David Anthony Marshall . . . . . . . . . . . . . . . . . Blondie
Annie McEnroe . . . . . . . . . . . . . . . . . . . . . Mrs. Sivil
J. C. Quinn . . . . . . . . . . . . . . . . . . . . . . . . . . . Jetty
- • 0:16—Brief buns, mooning umpire during baseball game.

### Critters 2: The Main Course (1988)
Roxanne Kernohan . . . . . . . . . . . . . . . . . . . . . . . . Lee
- •• 0:37—Brief breasts after transforming from an alien into a Playboy Playmate.

### Critters 4: They're Invading Your Space (1992)
Angela Bassett . . . . . . . . . . . . . . . . . . . . . . . . . . Fran
- 0:24—Side view of body in silhouette while taking a shower.
- •• 0:25—Buns in nice, tilt-up shot with partial back side view of right breast, but you don't see her face.
Brad Dourif . . . . . . . . . . . . . . . . . . . . . . . . . . Al Bert

### Crocodile Dundee (1986; Australian)
David Gulpilil . . . . . . . . . . . . . . . . . . . . . . Neville Bell
Linda Kozlowski . . . . . . . . . . . . . . . . . . . Sue Charlton
- •• 0:31—Buns in black one piece swimsuit with thong back after she takes off her skirt to fill her canteen with water.

### Crooked Hearts (1991)
Peter Berg . . . . . . . . . . . . . . . . . . . . . . . . . . . . Tom
Wendy Gazelle . . . . . . . . . . . . . . . . . . . . . . . . Eileen
Marg Helgenberger . . . . . . . . . . . . . . . . . . . . Jennetta

Jennifer Jason Leigh . . . . . . . . . . . . . . . . . . . . . . Harriet
•• 1:10—In black bra, then breasts in bathtub with
Tom.
Juliette Lewis . . . . . . . . . . . . . . . . . . . . . . . . . . . . . Cassie
Cindy Pickett . . . . . . . . . . . . . . . . . . . . . . . . . . . . . . . . Jill

### Cross Country (1983; Canadian)
Nina Axelrod . . . . . . . . . . . . . . . . . . . . . . . . . . Lois Hayes
0:28—Brief buns and sort of breasts, getting fondled
by Richard.
1:05—Very, very brief breasts fighting outside the
motel in the rain with Johnny.
Roberta Weiss . . . . . . . . . . . . . . . . . . . . . . . Alma Jean
•• 0:59—Breasts on bed with two other people.

### Cross My Heart (1987)
Joanna Kerns . . . . . . . . . . . . . . . . . . . . . . . . . . . . . Nancy
Annette O'Toole . . . . . . . . . . . . . . . . . . . . . . . . . . Kathy
0:44—In pink bra standing in bedroom with Martin
Short.
•• 0:46—Left breast, in bed with Short.
•• 0:48—Breasts in bed when Short heads under the
covers.
•• 0:49—Brief breasts again getting her purse.
• 1:05—Brief breasts and buns, dressing after Short
finds out about her daughter.

### Cross of Iron (1977)
Senta Berger . . . . . . . . . . . . . . . . . . . . . . . . . . . . . . . Eva
• 0:55—Brief buns, while taking off her nightgown in
bedroom.
Klaus Löwitsch . . . . . . . . . . . . . . . . . . . . . . . . . . Kruger

### Crossover (1980; Canadian)
a.k.a. Mr. Patman
Fionnula Flanagan . . . . . . . . . . . . . . . . . . . . . . Abadaba
• 0:27—Brief breasts opening her robe and flashing
James Coburn.
Tabitha Harrington . . . . . . . . . . . . . . . . . Montgomery
• 0:11—Brief right breast, then brief full frontal nudity
lying in bed, then struggling with James Coburn in
her room. Wearing white makeup on her face.
•• 0:29—Nude walking in to room to talk with Coburn,
then breasts and brief buns leaving.
Michael Kirby . . . . . . . . . . . . . . . . . . . . . . . . Dr. Turley
Kate Nelligan . . . . . . . . . . . . . . . . . . . . . . . . . Peabody

### Cruising (1980)
Jay Acovone . . . . . . . . . . . . . . . . . . . . . . . . . . . Skip Lee
• 0:56—Brief buns, when towel falls off after police
burst into room.
Karen Allen . . . . . . . . . . . . . . . . . . . . . . . . . . . . . Nancy
Henry Judd Baker . . . . . . . . . . . . . . . . . . . . Tough Cop
•• 0:57—Buns in jock strap, while leaving interrogation
room.
• 0:58—Buns in jock strap, while getting up to slap
Skip Lee around.
Gene Davis . . . . . . . . . . . . . . . . . . . . . . . . . . . . DaVinci
James Remar . . . . . . . . . . . . . . . . . . . . . . . . . Gregory
Paul Sorvino . . . . . . . . . . . . . . . . . . . . Captain Edelson

### The Crush (1993)
Cary Elwes . . . . . . . . . . . . . . . . . . . . . . . . . Nick Eliot
•• 0:12—Brief buns in bathroom when Darian peeks in.
Don't see his face.
Jennifer Rubin. . . . . . . . . . . . . . . . . . . . . . . . . . . . Amy
Alicia Silverstone . . . . . . . . . . . . . . . . . Darian Forrester
• 0:31—Buns, after dropping her shirt while Nick is
hiding in her closet. Don't see her face. Brief buns,
when walking into bathroom. Don't see her face.

### Cry Freedom (1987; British)
Kevin Kline . . . . . . . . . . . . . . . . . . . . . . . . Donald Woods
John Matshikiza . . . . . . . . . . . . . . . . . . . . . . . Mapetla
Denzel Washington . . . . . . . . . . . . . . . . . . . . Steve Biko
• 1:05—Side view of buns, while lying on the floor after getting beat up. Dark, hard to see anything.
• 1:07—Buns again. Dark.
1:26—Buns in B&W photo. Supposed to be him, but
probably not. Don't see face.
Timothy West. . . . . . . . . . . . . . . . . . . . Captain de Wet

### Cry of a Prostitute: Love Kills (1975; Italian)
Barbara Bouchet. . . . . . . . . . . . . . . . . . . . . . . . . Margie
• 0:30—Brief left breast, lying in bed with Rico.
• 0:31—Brief breasts in bed, with Rico when he starts
making love with her.
•• 0:50—Breasts in panties and robe, walking angrily
around her room.
0:56—In braless blouse in Bedroom with Tony.

### Cry Uncle (1971)
Maureen Byrnes . . . . . . . . . . . . . . . . . . . . . . Lena Right
• 0:16—Breasts and buns in bed with two other girls
while spanking Dominic. Hard to see because the
negative image is projected.
••• 0:46—Brief breasts with Connie when Jake peeks in
the window. Full frontal nudity, talking with Jake at
the doorway.
• 0:48—Breasts, making love with Jake in bed.
•• 0:49—Nude, getting out of bed after knocking out
Jake.
••• 0:50—Full frontal nudity, while interrogating Jake.
•• 0:53—Breasts, in room with gun while covering
Jake.
•• 0:54—Full frontal nudity, while shooting gun and
leaving.
Allen Garfield . . . . . . . . . . . . . . . . . . . . . . Jake Masters
• 0:03—Very brief partial frontal nudity, while spank-
ing Renee on the buns and hanging up the phone.
•• 0:24—Brief buns, then frontal nudity, while walking
away from the bathroom after talking to Cora.
• 0:39—Lower half of buns, getting washed by Debi
Morgan.
• 0:48—Buns, making love on top of Lena in bed.
•• 0:52—Buns, getting tied up by Larry and the two
girls.
• 0:59—Brief buns, while dropping his towel to get
into bed with Cora.
• 1:06—Buns, while making love on top of Connie,
not knowing she's dead.

David Kirk . . . . . . . . . . . . . . . . . . . . . . Jason Dominic
- 0:16—Buns, in bed with three girls. Very hard to see because the negative image is projected.

Madeleine Le Roux . . . . . . . . . . . . . . . . . Cora Merrill
- ••• 0:22—Breasts and buns, undressing in bathroom while talking to Jake.
- ••• 0:27—Nude, taking off her dress in front of Keith and making love with him on the sofa. Long scene.
- 0:42—Brief breasts, sitting up in bed when door is slammed in Jake's face.
- 0:59—Full frontal nudity, while standing in bedroom doorway.
- 1:11—Breasts under sheer red and black nightie, then making love with Jake. Long scene.
- 1:18—Brief buns, while taking off her panties.

Debbi Morgan . . . . . . . . . . . . . . . . . . . . . Olga Winter
- ••• 0:40—Breasts and buns, taking off her blouse and skirt in room with Jake. Long scene.

Nancy Salmon. . . . . . . . . . . . . . . . . . . . . . . . Connie
- 0:16—Breasts and buns in bed with two other girls while spanking Dominic. Hard to see because the negative image is projected.
- 0:26—Full frontal nudity in B&W photo that Keith shows Cora.
- 0:45—Brief breasts in the same B&W photo.
- 0:46—Brief right breast with Lena when Jake peeks in the window.
- 0:48—Breasts, fixing drugs while sitting on bed.
- ••• 0:51—Breasts, while sitting on bed, then full frontal nudity getting out of bed.
- 1:04—Buns, while lying on bed.
- •• 1:06—Full frontal nudity, rolling off bed and onto the floor, when Jake discovers she's dead.

## The Crying Game (1992)

Jaye Davidson . . . . . . . . . . . . . . . . . . . . . . . . . . Dil
- ••• 1:03—Brief full frontal nudity when Stephen Rea discovers Dil's a he.

Miranda Richardson . . . . . . . . . . . . . . . . . . . . . Jude
Tony Slattery. . . . . . . . . . . . . . . . . . . . . . . . . . . n.a.

## Crystal Heart (1987)

Tawny Kitaen . . . . . . . . . . . . . . . . . . . . Alley Daniels
- •• 0:46—Breasts and buns, while "making love" with Lee Curreri through the glass.
- •• 0:50—Nude, crashing through glass shower door, covered with blood during her nightmare.
- 1:14—Brief breasts making love with Curreri in and falling out of bed.

Marina Saura. . . . . . . . . . . . . . . . . . . . . . . . Justine

## Curaçao (1993; Made for Cable Movie)
### a.k.a. Deadly Currents

William L. Petersen . . . . . . . . . . . . . . . Stephen Guerin
- •• 0:52—Buns, while getting up from bed and walking past Julie Carmen to the bathroom.

## The Curious Female (1969)

Elaine Edwards . . . . . . . . . . . . . . . . . . . . . Mrs. Wilde
- 0:56—Breasts in bed with a young man before Joan walks in the room.

Michael Greer . . . . . . . . . . . . . . . . . . . . . . . . . Bixby
Charlene Jones . . . . . . . . . . . . . . . Pearl Lucomb/Girl #2
- 0:14—Brief breasts, twice, while taking a shower.
- 0:29—Buns, while running in slow motion to the pool.
- 0:30—Buns, while lying down.
  1:08—Breasts while making love with a guy. Hard to see because of psychedelic light.
- •• 1:09—Breasts while turning over on her back with Andre.

Angelique Pettyjohn . . . . . . . . . . . . Susan Rome/Girl #1
- ••• 0:29—Buns, while running in slow motion to the pool, then putting on towel. Breasts on diving board.
- ••• 0:30—Breasts and buns, while on inflatable mattress in pool.
- 0:52—Breasts while talking on the phone.
- 0:55—Breasts while making love in bed with a guy.
- 1:01—Brief breasts, while jumping into pool. Long shot.

## Curse III: Blood Sacrifice (1990)

Jenilee Harrison . . . . . . . . . . . . . . Elizabeth Armstrong
- ••• 0:43—Breasts sitting in bathtub. Almost side of right breast when wrapping a towel around herself.

Jennifer Steyn. . . . . . . . . . . . . . . . . . . . . . . . . Cindy
- 0:35—Side of left breast, kissing Roger while at the beach inside a tent. Upper half of left breast when blade tears through tent.
  0:40—Breasts, covered with blood when Geoff looks in the tent.

## Curtains (1983; Canadian)

Samantha Eggar. . . . . . . . . . . . . . Samantha Sherwood
Linda Thorson . . . . . . . . . . . . . . . . . . . Brooke Parsons
Sandra Warren . . . . . . . . . . . . . . . . . . . . . Tara Demillo
- 0:58—Side view of left breast practicing a scene in the play with Summers.

## The Custodian (1993)

Kelly Dingwall . . . . . . . . . . . . . . . . . . . . . . . Reynolds
- 0:47—Buns, while in the shower.

Anthony LaPaglia . . . . . . . . . . . . . . . . . . . . . Quinlan
Kerry Mack. . . . . . . . . . . . . . . . . . . . . . . Policewoman
Barry Otto . . . . . . . . . . . . . . . . . . . . . . . . . Ferguson
Hugo Weaving . . . . . . . . . . . . . . . . . . . . . . . Church

## Cut and Run (1985; Italian)

Karen Black . . . . . . . . . . . . . . . . . . . . . . . . . . Karin
Lisa Blount . . . . . . . . . . . . . . . . . . . . . . . Fran Hudson
Valentina Forte. . . . . . . . . . . . . . . . . . . . . . . . . Ana
- ••• 0:29—Brief left breast being made love to in bed. Then breasts sitting up in bed and left side view and buns taking a shower.

John Steiner. . . . . . . . . . . . . . . . . . . . . . . . . . Vlado

## Cutter's Way (1981)
### a.k.a. Cutter and Bone

Jeff Bridges. . . . . . . . . . . . . . . . . . . . . . Richard Bone
Julia Duffy . . . . . . . . . . . . . . . . . . . . . . . Young Girl
Ann Dusenberry . . . . . . . . . . . . . . . . . . . Valerie Duran

Lisa Eichhorn. . . . . . . . . . . . . . . Maureen "Mo" Cutter
 • 1:07—Brief right breast, wearing bathrobe, lying on
    lounge chair while Jeff Bridges looks at her.
John Heard . . . . . . . . . . . . . . . . . . . . . . . Alex Cutter

### Cutting Class (1988)
Brenda Lynn Klemme . . . . . . . . . . . . . . . . . Colleen
    0:32—In bra in locker room. Very, very brief buns
       cheerleading without any panties on.
 • 0:37—More very brief buns, ducking under bleach-
       ers.
Jill Schoelen. . . . . . . . . . . . . . . . . . . . . Paula Carson
    0:58—Side view of left breast, while taking off robe.
       Long shot. Almost breasts turing around.
 • 1:00—Very, very brief breasts in mirror when Gary
    helps put her robe on. (Out of focus.)

### Cyborg (1989)
Dayle Haddon. . . . . . . . . . . . . . . . . . . . Pearl Prophet
Debi Richter . . . . . . . . . . . . . . . . . . . . . Nady Simmons
    0:28—Buns, after taking off clothes and running into
       the ocean.
 • 0:30—Brief left breast by the fire showing herself to
       Jean-Claude Van Damme.
Jean-Claude Van Damme . . . . . . . . Gibson Rickenbacker

### Cyborg 2: Glass Shadow (1993)
Allen Garfield . . . . . . . . . . . . . . . . . . . . . Martin Dunn
Renee Griffin . . . . . . . . . . . . . . . . . . . . . . . . . . Dreena
 • 0:04—Brief breasts, several times, while making love
    with a guy before she blows up.
Tracey Walter . . . . . . . . . . . . . . . . . . . . . . . Wild Card
Jim Youngs . . . . . . . . . . . . . . . . . . . . Pinwheel Exec #1

### Cyborg Cop (1993)
Alonna Shaw. . . . . . . . . . . . . . . . . . . . . . . . . . Cathy
 ••• 0:58—Breasts, while making love with Jack.
Kimberleigh Stark . . . . . . . . . . . . . . . Woman Hostage

### Cyclone (1986)
Michelle Bauer . . . . . . . . . . . . Uncredited Shower Girl
 • 0:06—Very brief buns and side of left breast walking
    around in locker room. (Passes several times in front
    of camera.)
Martine Beswicke . . . . . . . . . . . . . . . . . . . . . Waters
Ashley Ferrare . . . . . . . . . . . . . . . . . . . . Carla Hastings
    0:04—Working out at health club with Heather Th-
       omas.
Pamela Gilbert . . . . . . . . . . . . Uncredited Shower Girl
    0:06—Buns and breasts (she's the brunette) in the
       showers. Long shot.
Heather Thomas . . . . . . . . . . . . . . . . . . . . Teri Marshall
Dawn Wildsmith . . . . . . . . . . . . . . . . . . . . . . Henna

### D.C. Cab (1983)
Adam Baldwin. . . . . . . . . . . . . . . . . . . . . . . . . Albert
Irene Cara . . . . . . . . . . . . . . . . . . . . . . . . . . Herself
John Diehl. . . . . . . . . . . . . . . . . . . . . . . . . . Kidnapper
Deborah Dutch . . . . . . . . . . . . . . . . . . . . . . . . . n.a.
Jill Schoelen . . . . . . . . . . . . . . . . . . . . . . . . Claudette

Moriah Shannon . . . . . . . . . . . . . Venus Club Passenger
 •• 0:16—In bra, then breasts, undressing in back seat
    of cab.
 •• 0:17—Breasts when Albert tries to get his fare.
 • 0:18—Breasts, then buns when Gary Busey takes her
    money. Buns and very brief lower frontal nudity run-
    ning out of the club after him.

### Da Vinci's War (1992)
Vanity . . . . . . . . . . . . . . . . . . . . . . . . . . . . . . . . Lupe
Kim Burnette . . . . . . . . . . . . . . . . . . . . . . . . Monique
 ••• 0:49—Breasts, kneeling by herself, while putting on
    a show for the bad guy.
Sam Jones . . . . . . . . . . . . . . . . . . . . . . . Jim Holbrook
Melissa Anne Moore. . . . . . . . . . . . . . . . . . . . . . Fred
 ••• 0:14—Breasts and buns, with Michael Nouri in his
    workout room.
Michael Nouri . . . . . . . . . . . . . . . . . . . . China Smith
James Russo . . . . . . . . . . . . . . . . . . . . . . . . . . . Mintz
Kimberly Ryusaki . . . . . . . . . . . . . Cocktail Waitress #3

### Daddy's Boys (1988)
Laura Burkett . . . . . . . . . . . . . . . . . . . . . . . . . Christie
 ••• 0:17—Breasts in room with Jimmy.
 •• 0:20—Left breast, while making love with Jimmy in
    bed again.
 • 0:21—Brief breasts during Jimmy's nightmare.
 • 0:43—Brief breasts in bed again, then getting
    dressed.
 • 0:53—Brief breasts in bed consoling Jimmy.
 • 1:11—Left breast, while in bed with Jimmy.
Daryl Haney . . . . . . . . . . . . . . . . . . . . . . . . . . Jimmy
 • 0:17—Buns, while getting undressed in room with
    Christie.
Linda Shayne . . . . . . . . . . . . . . . . . . . . . . . Nanette

### Damage (1992; French/British)
(Unrated Director's cut reviewed.)
Juliette Binoche . . . . . . . . . . . . . . . . . . . . . . . . Anna
 • 0:52—Brief breasts while sitting on floor and making
    love with Jeremy Irons.
 •• 1:31—Breasts on bed after getting caught with by
    Iron's son.
Leslie Caron . . . . . . . . . . . . . . . . . . Elizabeth Prideaux
Rupert Graves . . . . . . . . . . . . . . . . . . . . . . . . Martyn
Jeremy Irons. . . . . . . . . . . . . . . . Dr. Stephen Fleming
 • 0:52—Brief buns, while sitting on floor and making
    love with Juliette Binoche.
 ••• 1:30—Buns, while making love on top of Binoche.
 ••• 1:31—Nude, getting out of bed and running down
    the stairs.
Miranda Richardson . . . . . . . . . . . . . . . . . . . . Ingrid
 ••• 1:40—Breasts, while standing in front of Jeremy
    Irons in the bedroom.
David Thewlis. . . . . . . . . . . . . . . . . . . . . . . Detective

### The Damned (1969; German)
Helmut Berger . . . . . . . . . . . . . . Martin Von Essenbeck
 • 2:03—Buns, while walking up to his mother and rip-
    ping her dress off. Dark, don't see his face.
Charlotte Rampling . . . . . . . . . . . . Elizabeth Thallman

Ingrid Thulin . . . . . . . . . . . . . . . . Sophie Von Essenbeck
- •• 1:23—Breasts in bed with Frederick. Long scene for a 1969 film.
- • 2:03—Left breast in bed with Martin (her son in the film).

### Damned River (1990)
Lisa Aliff. . . . . . . . . . . . . . . . . . . . . . . . . . . . . . . . .Anne
  0:28—Silhouette of breasts while undressing in tent.
- • 0:32—Very, very brief top of right breast in open blouse, then half of right breast in wet blouse washing her hair.
- • 0:50—Very brief breasts struggling with Ray when he rips her top open. Don't see her face.
Steve Shellen. . . . . . . . . . . . . . . . . . . . . . . . . . . . .Ray

### Dance of the Damned (1988)
Starr Andreeff . . . . . . . . . . . . . . . . . . . . . . . . . . . . .Jodi
- •• 0:03—Breasts dancing in black bikini bottoms on stage in a club.
  1:06—In black bra, panties, garter belt and stockings dancing in bar just for the vampire.
- •• 1:08—Breasts in the bar with the vampire.
Maria Ford . . . . . . . . . . . . . . . . . . . . . . . . . . Teacher
- • 0:11—Brief breasts during dance routine in club wearing black panties, garter belt and stockings.
Deborah Ann Nassar . . . . . . . . . . . . . . . . . . . La Donna
- • 0:07—Brief breasts during dance routine in club.
Cyril O'Reilly . . . . . . . . . . . . . . . . . . . . . . . . . Vampire

### Dance with a Stranger (1985; British)
Rupert Everett . . . . . . . . . . . . . . . . . . . . . David Blakely
Miranda Richardson . . . . . . . . . . . . . . . . . . . .Ruth Ellis
  0:08—Very brief upper half of left breast, twice, while in bed making love with David.
  0:18—Very brief tip of left breast getting into bed with David. Dark.
- • 0:20—Very, very brief side view of left breast, putting robe on in bed.

### Dance with Death (1991)
Sean'a Arthur . . . . . . . . . . . . . . . . . . . . . . . . . Sherilyn
- • 0:42—Buns, while dancing on stage with Lola.
Alretha Baker. . . . . . . . . . . . . . . . . . . . . . . . . . . .Sunny
- ••• 0:23—Breasts and buns in G-string, dancing on stage and falling off because she's on drugs.
Tracey Burch. . . . . . . . . . . . . . . . . . . . . . . . . . Whitney
- ••• 0:03—Breasts and buns in G-string, dancing on stage.
- ••• 0:05—More breasts and buns while dancing.
Maxwell Caulfield . . . . . . . . . . . . . . . . . . .Shaughnessy
- • 1:01—Brief side view of buns, while making love in bed with Kelly.
Jill Pierce . . . . . . . . . . . . . . . . . . . . . . . . . . . . . Lola
- •• 0:07—Breasts and buns, dancing in wedding outfit on stage.
- • 0:11—Breasts and buns in G-string, dancing on stage. Long shot, seen in mirror. Buns while getting tips.
  0:28—Buns, dancing on stage in the background.

- • 0:42—Buns in G-string dancing with Sherilyn on stage.
- • 0:56—Brief breasts on stage when Kelly talks to her. 1:11—Buns, while dancing on stage.
Catya Sassoon . . . . . . . . . . . . . . . . . . . . . . . . . . . Jodie
- ••• 0:29—Breasts and buns in G-string, while dancing on stage.
- ••• 0:37—Breasts and buns, dancing on stage. Her body is painted gold.
- ••• 0:38—More breasts and buns.
Barbara Alyn Woods. . . . . . . . . . . . . . . . . . . . . . Kelly
- ••• 0:16—In black bra, panties and stockings, doing strip tease on stage. Breasts and buns in G-string.
- •• 0:24—Breasts, dancing in red bra and panties.
- ••• 0:46—Breasts and buns in G-string, dancing on stage.
- • 0:47—Brief side view of left breast, while changing back stage. Buns seen in mirror.
- ••• 0:59—Breasts and buns, doing strip tease routine in Marilyn Monroe outfit.
- ••• 1:01—Breasts, making love in bed with Maxwell Caulfield.

### Dances with Wolves (1990)
Kevin Costner. . . . . . . . . . . . . . . . . . . . .Lt. John Dunbar
- •• 0:37—Brief buns, while washing his clothes in the pond.
- ••• 0:40—Buns, while standing by himself after scaring away Kicking Bird.
Larry Joshua . . . . . . . . . . . . . . . . . . . . . . . . Sgt. Bauer

### Danger Zone II: Reaper's Revenge (1988)
Stephanie Blake . . . . . . . . . . . . Tattooed Topless Dancer
- ••• 0:47—Breasts, dancing on stage in bikini bottoms.
Alisha Das . . . . . . . . . . . . . . . . . . . . . . . . . . Francine
Jane Higginson. . . . . . . . . . . . . . . . . . . . . . . . .Donna
- •• 0:17—Breasts unconscious on sofa while the bad guys take Polaroid photos of her.
- • 0:18—Brief breasts in the photo that Wade looks at.
- • 0:22—Brief left breast adjusting her blouse outside. Long shot.
- • 0:34—Left breast in another Polaroid photograph. 0:45—In black bra, panties and stockings posing on motorcycle for photograph.
Jason Williams . . . . . . . . . . . . . . . . . . . . . . . . . .Wade
- •• 0:06—Buns, while getting out of bed and putting pants on.

### Dangerous Game (1988; Australian)
Kathryn Walker. . . . . . . . . . . . . . . . . . . . . . . .Kathryn
- • 1:19—Very, very brief breasts when her black top is pulled up while struggling with Murphy.

### Dangerous Game (1993)
(Unrated version reviewed.)
Madonna. . . . . . . . . . . . . . . . . . . . . .Sarah Jennings
  0:13—In braless tank top in room with James Russo.
- • 0:45—Brief buns in G-string, falling over back of sofa on video playback.
- •• 0:53—Nude, while getting out of bed and getting dressed.

- 1:00—Brief buns, when getting her panties ripped off by Russo.

Christina Fulton . . . . . . . . . . . . . . . . . . . . . . . Blonde
Harvey Keitel . . . . . . . . . . . . . . . . . . . . . . Eddie Israel
Annie McEnroe . . . . . . . . . . . . . . . . . . . . . . . . . Cameo
James Russo . . . . . . . . . . . . . . . . . . . . . . .Frank Burns

### Dangerous Liaisons (1988)
Glenn Close . . . . . . . . . . . . . . . . . Marquise de Merteuil
Michelle Pfeiffer . . . . . . . . . . . . . . . Madame de Tourvel
Keanu Reeves . . . . . . . . . . . . . . . . . Chevalier Danceny
Uma Thurman . . . . . . . . . . . . . . . . . Cécile de Volanges
- ••• 0:59—Breasts taking off her nightgown in her bed-room with John Malkovich.

### Dangerous Love (1988)
Teri Austin . . . . . . . . . . . . . . . . . . . . . . . . .Dominique
Brenda Bakke . . . . . . . . . . . . . . . . . . . . . . . . . . .Chris
Collin Bernsen . . . . . . . . . . . . . . . . . . . . . . . . . Brooks
Eloise Broady . . . . . . . . . . . . . . . . . . . . . . . . . . . Bree
- ••• 0:06—Breasts changing into lingerie in the mirror.
Anthony Geary . . . . . . . . . . . . . . . . . . . . . . . . Mickey
Kimberly Kates . . . . . . . . . . . . . . . . . . . . . . . . . Susan
Sal Landi . . . . . . . . . . . . . . . . . . . . . . . . . . . . . .n.a.
Nicole Picard . . . . . . . . . . . . . . . . . . . . . . . . . . . Jane
Brenda Swanson . . . . . . . . . . . . . . . . . . . . . . Felicity

### Dangerous Obsession (1990; Italian)
Corrine Clery . . . . . . . . . . . . . . . . . . . . Carol Simpson
- 0:14—Right breast sticking out of lingerie while ly-ing in bed.
- •• 0:36—Full frontal nudity lying in bed waiting for her husband, then with him, then getting out of bed.
Blanca Marsillach . . . . . . . . . . . . . . . . . . . . . .Jessica
- 0:02—Left breast, getting fondled by Johnny in re-cording studio. Lower frontal nudity when he pulls down her panties.
- •• 0:05—Breasts while opening her blouse when Johnny plays his saxophone.
- 0:17—Lower frontal nudity on the stairs with Johnny, then brief breasts.
- 0:29—Brief breasts in video tape on T.V.
- 0:40—Breasts while changing blouses.
- ••• 0:56—Full frontal nudity masturbating while looking at pictures of Johnny. Buns, then more full frontal nudity getting video taped.
- ••• 0:58—Breasts in bed with a gun. Nude walking around the house. Long scene.
- 1:05—Brief breasts on beach taking off sweater and burying a dog.
- 1:06—Brief full frontal nudity during video taping session.
- •• 1:07—Breasts while cleaning up Dr. Simpson.
- ••• 1:13—Breasts, taking chains off Dr. Simpson, then lying in bed. Full frontal nudity making love with him.

### Dangerous Touch (1993)
Monique Parent . . . . . . . . . . . . . . . . . . . . . . . .Nicole
- •• 0:47—Full frontal nudity, while in the shower when surprised by Kate Vernon.

- ••• 0:49—Full frontal nudity, after dropping towel to join Lou Diamond Phillips and Vernon in bed.
- ••• 0:51—Breasts, while handcuffed in bed with Vernon.
Lou Diamond Phillips . . . . . . . . . . . . . . Mick Burroughs
  0:32—Sort of buns, while showering behind plastic curtain. Hard to see anything.
- ••• 0:38—Buns, after taking off his shorts in front of Kate Vernon.
  0:41—Upper half of buns, while making love with Vernon on video playback.
- 1:06—Buns, while making love with Vernon. Long shot.
Kate Vernon . . . . . . . . . . . . . . . . . . . . . . .Amanda Grace
  0:19—Having sex with Lou Diamond Phillips in bed during a party.
- ••• 0:29—Breasts, while making love with Phillips in convertible car in the woods.
- ••• 0:36—In black leotard, garter belt and stockings, then breasts while undressing in front of Phillips.
- ••• 0:38—More breasts when Phillips ties her hands to the headboard.
- ••• 0:51—Breasts, while making love in bed with Nicole while Phillips video tapes everything.
- 0:53—Breasts, on video monitor when she looks at video tape of her with Nicole.

### A Dangerous Woman (1993)
Gabriel Byrne . . . . . . . . . . . . . . . . . . . . . . . . .Mackey
- 0:57—Lower half of buns, while making love with Debra Winger on sofa.
Barbara Hershey . . . . . . . . . . . . . . . . . . . . . Frances
David Strathairn . . . . . . . . . . . . . . . . . . . . . . . Getzo
- 1:20—Brief upper half of buns, when Debra Winger interrupts him while he's pulling up his underwear.
Chloe Webb . . . . . . . . . . . . . . . . . . . . . . . . . . . Birdy
Debra Winger . . . . . . . . . . . . . . . . . . . . . Martha Horgan
- 0:42—Very, very brief lower frontal nudity, then buns, while masturbating in bed. Don't see her face. Medium long shot.

### Dangerously Close (1986)
Gerard Christopher . . . . . . . . . . . . . . . . . . . . . . Lang
Carey Lowell . . . . . . . . . . . . . . . . . . . . . . . . . . .Julie
Dedee Pfeiffer . . . . . . . . . . . . . . . . . . . . . . . . . Nicki
Robert Rusler . . . . . . . . . . . . . . . . . . . . . . . . . .n.a.
John Stockwell . . . . . . . . . . . . . . . . . . Randy McDevill
- 0:33—Brief buns while in steamy locker room.
Angel Tompkins . . . . . . . . . . . . . . . . . . . . .Mrs. Waters
Karen Witter . . . . . . . . . . . . . . . . . . . . . . . . . . Betsy

### The Dark (1993)
Cynthia Belliveau . . . . . . . . . . . . . . . . . . . . . . .Tracy
- •• 0:29—In slip, then bra, then breasts while making love on bed in motel with Hunter.
Stephen McHattie . . . . . . . . . . . . . . . . . . . . . .Hunter
- 0:30—Partial upper half of buns, while making love on bed with Tracy.

### The Dark Backward (1991)
Lara Flynn Boyle . . . . . . . . . . . . . . . . . . . . . .Rosarita
Claudia Christian . . . . . . . . . . . . . . . . . . . . . . . . Kitty

Rob Lowe . . . . . . . . . . . . . . . . . . . . . . . . . . Dirk Delta
Bill Paxton. . . . . . . . . . . . . . . . . . . . . . . . . . . . . . .Gus
   •• 0:44—Buns, while taking off his jumpsuit and diving
      into bed with his three fat girlfriends.

### Dark Obsession *(1989; British)*
*a.k.a. Diamond Skulls*
Gabriel Byrne . . . . . . . . . . . . . . . . . . . . . . . . . Hugo
Amanda Donohoe. . . . . . . . . . . . . . . . . . . . . . . Ginny
   •• 0:01—Breasts getting felt by a pair of hands.
   ••• 0:41—Left breast, breasts, brief lower frontal nudity
      while making love with Gabriel Byrne.
   • 0:47—In black bra and panties, then full frontal nu-
      dity getting into tub. Right breast while sitting in the
      tub.
Sadie Frost . . . . . . . . . . . . . . . . . . . . . . . . . Rebecca
   • 0:22—Very brief right breast in bed after she rolls off
      Jamie.
   ••• 0:33—Breasts several times while making love with
      Jamie when Gabriel Byrne interrupts them.
Michael Hordern . . . . . . . . . . . . . . . . . . . . .Lord Crewne

### Dark Side of the Moon *(1989)*
Wendy MacDonald . . . . . . . . . . . . . . . . . . . . . . . Alex
   • 0:54—In bra, then brief breasts having it torn off.
      Don't see her face.
Camilla More . . . . . . . . . . . . . . . . . . . . . . . . . . . Lesli

### Dark Tide *(1993)*
Brigitte Bako . . . . . . . . . . . . . . . . . . . . . . . . . . . Andi
      0:16—In wet white blouse, coming out of the water.
   • 0:26—Very brief tip of left breasts in bathtub. Brief
      breasts, while covering up when Richard Tyson looks
      at her.
   • 0:27—Right breast, under water after Tyson leaves.
   ••• 0:43—Breasts, while making love with Tyson in un-
      derground pool. Great!
   ••• 1:05—Breasts, while sitting in bathtub, with a snake
      crawling up her chest.
Chris Sarandon . . . . . . . . . . . . . . . . . . . . . . . . . .Tim
Richard Tyson . . . . . . . . . . . . . . . . . . . . . . . . . . .Dak
   •• 0:41—Brief buns, after taking off shorts and diving
      into underground pool.
   • 0:42—Buns, seen under water while he's swimming.
   • 0:44—Brief buns, while making love with Brigitte
      Bako in underground pool.

### Dark Universe *(1993)*
Blake Pickett . . . . . . . . . . . . . . . . . . . . . . . Kim Masters
   ••• 0:45—Breasts, in open blouse, while outside in the
      woods with Jack.

### Darling Lili *(1970)*
Julie Andrews . . . . . . . . . . . . . . . . . . . . . . . Lili Smith
   • 1:12—Very, very brief left breast, when doing strip
      tease and tossing aside yellow outfit to duck behind
      curtain.

### Daughter of Death *(1982)*
*a.k.a. Julie Darling*
Sybil Danning . . . . . . . . . . . . . . . . . . . . . . . . . Susan
   •• 0:36—Breasts in bed with Anthony Franciosa.

   • 0:38—Brief right breast under Franciosa.
Cindy Girling . . . . . . . . . . . . . . . . . . . . . . . . . . . Irene
   •• 0:12—Breasts in bathtub and getting out.
Isabelle Mejias . . . . . . . . . . . . . . . . . . . . . . . . . . Julie

### Daughters of Darkness *(1971; Belgian/French/German/Italian)*
John Karlen . . . . . . . . . . . . . . . . . . . . . . .Stefan Chiltern
   • 0:43—Brief buns, rolling over on Valerie in bed.
   • 1:03—Buns, putting on his robe. Long shot.
Andrea Rau . . . . . . . . . . . . . . . . . . . . . . . . . . . Ilona
   • 0:39—Buns and side of right breast, kneeling on
      floor while bending over the toilet.
   • 0:56—Brief breasts on top of Stefan in bed.
   ••• 1:00—Left breast, while standing in bathroom
      watching Stefan take a shower.
   ••• 1:01—Breasts when Stefan tries to drag her into the
      shower.
   • 1:02—Breasts, lying dead on the floor.
   • 1:03—Breasts, lying dead on the floor. Long shot.
Delphine Seyrig . . . . . . . . . Countess Elisabeth Bathory

### Dave *(1993)*
Ben Kingsley. . . . . . . . . . . . . . . . .Vice President Nance
Kevin Kline . . . . . . . . . . . . . . . Bill Mitchell/Dave Kovic
   • 0:49—Buns, several times, seen through steamed up
      shower door. Don't see his face.
Arnold Schwarzenegger . . . . . . . . . . . . . . . . . Himself
Sigourney Weaver . . . . . . . . . . . . . . . . . .Ellen Mitchell

### The Day After Halloween *(1978; Australian)*
*a.k.a. Snapshot*
Chantal Contouri . . . . . . . . . . . . . . . . . . . . . Madeline
Sigrid Thornton . . . . . . . . . . . . . . . . . . . . . . . .Angela
   • 0:04—Very brief breasts in ad photos on wall.
   •• 0:19—Breasts during modeling session at the beach.
   ••• 0:21—More breasts at the beach.
   •• 0:37—Breasts in magazine ad several times.
   • 0:43—Brief right breast in magazine ad.
   • 0:46—Breasts in ad again.
   • 1:18—Entering room covered with the ad.
      1:20—In beige bra in room with weirdo guy.

### The Day of the Cobra *(1980)*
Sybil Danning . . . . . . . . . . . . . . . . . . . . . . . . .Brenda
   • 0:41—Buns and side view of right breast getting out
      of bed and putting robe on with Lou. Long shot.
Franco Nero. . . . . . . . . . . . . . . . . . . . . . . . . . . . n.a.

### Day of the Jackal *(1973)*
Edward Fox . . . . . . . . . . . . . . . . . . . . . . . . . The Jackal
   • 1:40—Brief buns, twice, while in bedroom after kill-
      ing Colette. Dark.
Olga Georges-Picot . . . . . . . . . . . . . . . . . . . . .Denise
   • 0:55—Brief breasts and buns, getting out of bed to
      use the phone.
Delphine Seyrig . . . . . . . . . . . . . . . . . . . . . . . Colette
   • 1:25—Side view of right breast while lying in bed
      with the Jackal. Dark.

- 1:40—Very brief side view of left breast, when she rolls on her back. Brief side view of left breast after the Jackal kills her.

Timothy West . . . . . . . . . . . . . . . . . . . . . . . Berthier

### The Day of the Locust (1975)

Karen Black . . . . . . . . . . . . . . . . . . . . . . . . . . . Faye
Pepe Serna . . . . . . . . . . . . . . . . . . . . . . . . . . Miguel
- 2:01—Buns while on top of Karen Black, then buns while jumping out of bed.

Donald Sutherland . . . . . . . . . . . . . . . . . . . . Homer

### Daybreak (1993; Made for Cable Movie)

Cuba Gooding, Jr. . . . . . . . . . . . . . . . . . . . . . . . Torch
Moira Kelly . . . . . . . . . . . . . . . . . . . . . . . . . . . . Blue
- ••• 0:43—Right breast, then breasts while making out with Cuba Gooding Jr.
- ••• 1:14—Breasts when Gooding has to take her top off in front of a guard.

### Dead Aim (1987)

Corbin Bernsen . . . . . . . . . . . . . . . . . . . . . . Webster
Sandi Brannon . . . . . . . . . . . . . . . . . . . . . . . . Misty
- 0:05—Buns in G-string, while dancing on stage during opening credits.
- 0:09—Breasts, while dancing on stage with the other girls (wearing a white bottom).
- ••• 1:02—Breasts and buns in G-string doing dance routine.
- 1:14—Very brief right breast, several times, while covered with blood, lying dead on bed.

Carol Chambers . . . . . . . . . . . . . . . . . . . . . . . Nicole
- 0:15—Buns in G-string.

Shirlene Foss . . . . . . . . . . . . . . . . . . . . . . . . . . B.J.
- 0:14—Buns in G-string and white top.
- 0:55—Brief buns in G-string while dancing on stage in bridal outfit.

Cassandra Gava . . . . . . . . . . . . . . . . . . . . . . . Amber
- 0:14—Buns, while sitting on chair on stage.
- 0:52—Very brief breasts, while making love with Ed Marinaro in bed. Very dark, hard to see.

Ed Marinaro . . . . . . . . . . . . . . Malcolm "Mace" Douglas
- 0:53—Buns, while in bed making love with Amber. Dark, hard to see.

Lynn Whitfield . . . . . . . . . . . . . . . . . . . . Sheila Freeman

### Dead and Buried (1981)

Melody Anderson . . . . . . . . . . . . . . . . . . . . . . . Janet
Lisa Blount . . . . . . . . . . . . . . . . . . . Girl on the Beach
- 0:06—Brief breasts on the beach getting her picture taken by a photographer.

### Dead Boyz Can't Fly (1992)

Ruth Corrine Collins . . . . . . . . . . . . . . . Myra Kandinsky
- 0:14—Brief breasts while getting raped by Buzz in elevator.

Jennifer Delora . . . . . . . . . . . . . . . . . . . . . . . . Helen
Sheila Kennedy . . . . . . . . . . . . . . . . . . . . . . Lorraine
- 0:00—Breasts and buns in G-string, while dancing in smoke filled club.

- •• 0:16—Buns in G-string and breasts, while dancing in club.

Delia Sheppard . . . . . . . . . . . . . . . . . . . . . . . . Angie
- •• 1:01—In white bra and panties, then breasts in doctor's office when bad guy pretends to be a doctor and examines her.

### Dead Calm (1989)

Nicole Kidman . . . . . . . . . . . . . . . . . . . . Rae Ingram
- 1:00—Brief buns and breasts on the floor with the Billy Zane.

Rod Mullinar . . . . . . . . . . . . . . . . . . . Russell Bellows
Sam Neill . . . . . . . . . . . . . . . . . . . . . . . John Ingram
Billy Zane . . . . . . . . . . . . . . . . . . . . . Hughie Warriner
- 1:01—Buns, while walking around on the boat.

### Dead Connection (1993)

Lisa Bonet . . . . . . . . . . . . . . . . . . . . Catherine Briggs
- 0:58—Breasts, while making love in bed with Michael Madsen.

Susan Byun . . . . . . . . . . . . . . . . . . . . . . . . . . Sarah
- 0:50—Very, very brief left breast while catching shirt that Michael Madsen throws to her.

Michael Madsen . . . . . . . . . . . . . . . . . . Matt Dickson
Brenda Swanson . . . . . . . . . . . . . . . . . . . . . . Susan

### Dead On (1993)

(Unrated version reviewed.)
Lynn Oddo . . . . . . . . . . . . . . . . . . . . . . . . . . . Lisa
- •• 1:00—Breasts, while getting dressed after spending the night in Matt McCoy's bed.

Tracy Scoggins . . . . . . . . . . . . . . . . Marla Beaumont
- 0:00—Partial breasts in shower during opening credits. Brief breasts when getting out of shower.
- 0:19—Brief left breast while in bathtub when she reaches up to turn off the speaker phone.

Shari Shattuck . . . . . . . . . . . . . . . . . Erin Davenport
- ••• 0:15—Breasts and buns in panties, while making out with Matt McCoy in doorway, then making love on the floor. Wow!
- ••• 0:29—Breasts, while making love with McCoy in her studio. Shot almost in silhouette.
- 0:49—Brief breasts, while rolling over in bed to answer the phone.

Virginia Watson . . . . . . . . . . . . . . . . . . . . . . Dorian

### Dead Ringers (1988)

Genevieve Bujold . . . . . . . . . . . . . . . . . Claire Niveau
- •• 0:49—Very brief right breast in bed with Jeremy Irons, then brief breasts reaching for pills and water. Dark, hard to see.

Heidi Von Palleske . . . . . . . . . . . . . . . . . . . . . Cary
- 0:45—Brief left breast sticking out of bathrobe, while talking to Jeremy Irons in the bathroom.

### Dead Solid Perfect (1988; Made for Cable Movie)

Corinne Bohrer . . . . . . . . . . . . . . . . . . . Janie Rimmer
- ••• 0:31—Nude, getting out of bed to get some ice for Randy Quaid. Nice scene!

Kathryn Harrold . . . . . . . . . . . . . . . . . . Beverly T. Lee

### Dead Space (1990)
Marc Singer . . . . . . . . . . . . . . . . . . . . . . . Steve Krieger
Laura Tate. . . . . . . . . . . . . . . . . . . . . . Marissa Salinger
  •• 0:33—Breasts in bed with Marc Singer during her
     dream.

### The Dead Zone (1983)
Brooke Adams. . . . . . . . . . . . . . . . . . . . Sarah Bracknell
Chapelle Jaffe . . . . . . . . . . . . . . . . . . . . . . . . . . . . . n.a.
Martin Sheen . . . . . . . . . . . . . . . . . . . . . .Greg Stillson
Tom Skerritt . . . . . . . . . . . . . . . . . Sheriff Bannerman
Roberta Weiss . . . . . . . . . . . . . . . . . . . . Alma Frechette
  • 0:49—Briefly in beige bra, then brief breasts when
    the killer rips her blouse open during Christopher
    Walken's vision.

### Dead-End Drive-In (1986; Australian)
Natalie McCurry . . . . . . . . . . . . . . . . . . . . . . . Carmen
  •• 0:19—Breasts in red car with Ned Manning.

### Deadfall (1993)
Michael Biehn . . . . . . . . . . . . . . . . . . . . . . . . . . . . . Joe
  • 0:43—Buns, while making love on top of Sarah Trig-
    ger in bed.
Nicolas Cage. . . . . . . . . . . . . . . . . . . . . . . . . . Eddie
Peter Fonda . . . . . . . . . . . . . . . . . . . . . . . . . . . . . n.a.
Sarah Trigger . . . . . . . . . . . . . . . . . . . . . . . . Diane
  ••• 0:42—In white bra and panties, after taking off dress
    in motel room with Michael Biehn. Breasts, while
    making love with him.
  • 0:44—Right breast, while lying in bed with Biehn
    when he changes positions and the covers move.
  •• 0:45—Breasts, while wearing white panties, leaving
    bed and getting dressed.

### Deadline (1988)
John Hurt . . . . . . . . . . . . . . . . . . . . . . Granville Jones
Imogen Stubbs . . . . . . . . . . . . . . . . Lady Romy-Burton
    0:42—Doing handstands in a bikini top.
  • 0:44—Brief left breast, while getting out of bed with
    John Hurt. Full frontal nudity turning toward bed,
    brief breasts getting back into bed.

### Deadly Blessing (1981)
Jeff East. . . . . . . . . . . . . . . . . . . . . . . . John Schmidt
Lisa Hartman Black . . . . . . . . . . . . . . . . . . . . . . . .Faith
    1:31—It looks like brief left breast after getting hit
    with a rock by Maren Jensen, but it's a special-effect
    appliance over her breasts because she's supposed
    to be a male in the film.
Maren Jensen . . . . . . . . . . . . . . . . . . . . . . . Martha
  •• 0:27—Breasts and buns changing into a nightgown
    while a creepy guy watches through the window.
    0:52—Buns, getting into the bathtub. Kind of
    steamy and hard to see.
  • 0:56—Brief breasts in bathtub with snake. (Notice
    that she gets into the tub naked, but is wearing
    black panties in the water).
Colleen Riley . . . . . . . . . . . . . . . . . . . . . . . Melissa
Sharon Stone . . . . . . . . . . . . . . . . . . . . . . . .Lana

### Deadly Companion (1979)
Susan Clark . . . . . . . . . . . . . . . . . . . . . . . .Paula West
  • 0:19—Brief left breast, while consoling Michael Sar-
    razin in bed, then brief side view of left breast.
  • 0:20—Brief breasts sitting up in bed.
Pita Oliver . . . . . . . . . . . . . . . . . . . . . . . . . . .Lorraine
  • 0:14—Very brief left breast, then very brief breasts
    sitting up in bed during Michael Sarrazin's day-
    dream. Dark.
    1:32—Brief full frontal nudity, dead on bed when
    Susan Clark comes into the bedroom.

### Deadly Dreams (1988)
Juliette Cummins . . . . . . . . . . . . . . . . . . . . Maggie Kallir
  • 0:25—Breasts on bed, taking off her blouse and kiss-
    ing Alex.
  ••• 0:55—Breasts and brief buns, making love with Jack
    in bed.
Stacey Travis . . . . . . . . . . . . . . . . . . . . . . . Librarian

### Deadly Embrace (1989)
Ken Abraham . . . . . . . . . . . . . . . . . . . . Chris Thompson
  •• 0:17—Buns, while taking a shower.
  • 1:01—Brief buns, while making love on top of Lin-
    nea Quigley.
Michelle Bauer . . . . . . . . . . . . . . . .Female Spirit of Sex
  •• 0:22—Breasts caressing herself during fantasy se-
    quence.
  ••• 0:28—Breasts taking off tube top and caressing her-
    self.
  ••• 0:40—Breasts and buns kissing blonde guy. Nice
    close up of him kissing her breasts.
  • 0:42—Side of left breast lying down with the guy.
  • 1:03—Buns and side of right breast with the guy.
Ruth Corrine Collins . . . . . . . . . . . . . . . Dede Magnolia
Linnea Quigley. . . . . . . . . . . . . . . . . . . . . Michelle Arno
  •• 0:15—In white lingerie, then breasts and buns dur-
    ing Chris' fantasy.
  •• 0:34—Breasts and buns caressing herself.
  •• 0:43—Breasts again.
    0:46—Brief breasts.
  •• 0:50—Breasts and buns undressing.
  ••• 0:58—Breasts in bed on top of Chris, then making
    love.
  • 1:02—Breasts and buns on top of Chris while Char-
    lotte watches on T.V.
    1:11—Breasts in Chris' fantasy.
  • 1:12—Breasts and buns in playback of video tape.
Ty Randolph. . . . . . . . . . . . . . . . . .Charlotte Morland
    0:19—In yellow one piece swimsuit by the pool with
    Chris.
    0:27—In wet, white T-shirt in the kitchen with Chris.
  •• 0:28—Breasts taking off her top. Mostly side view of
    left breast.
  • 0:29—More left breast, while in bed with Chris.
  ••• 0:30—Breasts, making love in bed with Chris.
  • 1:10—Brief right breast, on T.V. when she replays
    video tape for Linnea Quigley.
Jan-Michael Vincent . . . . . . . . . . . . . . Stewart Morland

### Deadly Eyes *(1982; Canadian)*
Sara Botsford . . . . . . . . . . . . . . . . . . . . . Kelly Leonard
- 0:42—Breasts several times, making love with Paul.
Lisa Langlois . . . . . . . . . . . . . . . . . . . . . . . . . Trudy

### Deadly Force *(1983)*
Marilyn Chambers. . . . . . . . . . . . Actress in Video Tape
- 0:25—Breasts in adult video tape on projection TV.
Gina Gallego. . . . . . . . . . . . . . . . . . . . . . . . . . Maria
Wings Hauser . . . . . . . . . . . . . . . . . . . Stoney Cooper
- •• 0:44—Very brief buns, leaping out of bathtub when gunman starts shooting. More buns, while lying on the floor.
- •• 0:49—Buns, while in hammock, lying on top of Joyce Ingalls.
Joyce Ingalls . . . . . . . . . . . . . . . . . . . . . Eddie Cooper
- •• 0:48—Breasts, making out with Wings Hauser on hammock.

### The Deadly Games *(1980)*
*a.k.a. The Eliminator*
Colleen Camp. . . . . . . . . . . . . . . . . . . . . . . . .Randy
Denise Galik . . . . . . . . . . . . . . . . . . . . . . . . . . .Mary
- 1:13—Left breast, twice, making love on top of Roger in bed.
Jo Ann Harris. . . . . . . . . . . . . . . . . . . . . . . . .Keegan
- 0:48—Breasts in the shower. Hard to see because of the pattern on the glass.
Alexandra Morgan . . . . . . . . . . . . . . . . . . . . . Linda
- •• 0:03—In bra, standing in doorway at night, then breasts. Dark.
- 0:04—Very brief left breast and lots of cleavage in open blouse talking on the phone.
  0:05—Most of right breast, standing up.
Steve Railsback . . . . . . . . . . . . . . . . . . . . . . . . Billy

### Deadly Innocents *(1988)*
Mary Crosby . . . . . . . . . . . . . . . . . . . . . .Beth/Cathy
- 0:00—Very, very brief right breast in gaping nightgown when her husband grabs her wrist.
- 0:38—Brief upper back half of left breast in bathroom mirror after taking off her nightgown.
Zag Dorison . . . . . . . . . . . . . . . . . . . . . Crazy Norm
- 0:04—Buns, while standing on top of van and mooning the paramedics.
Andrew Stevens . . . . . . . . . . . . . . . . . . Bob Appling
Amanda Wyss . . . . . . . . . . . . . . . . . . . . .Andy/Angela
- •• 0:12—Breasts, taking off T-shirt and putting on lingerie.
- ••• 1:29—Right breast, twice, with Andrew Stevens.

### Deadly Passion *(1985)*
Ingrid Boulting . . . . . . . . . . . . . . . Martha Greenwood
- 0:46—Brief buns taking off clothes and jumping into pool. Long shot.
- •• 0:47—Breasts getting out of pool and kissing Brent Huff. Right breast in bed.
- 0:54—Breasts in whirlpool bath with Huff.
- ••• 1:02—Breasts, wearing white panties and massaging herself in front of a mirror.

- •• 1:31—Breasts taking off clothes and jumping into bed with Huff.
Brent Huff . . . . . . . . . . . . . . . . . . . . . . . . . Sam Black
Susan Isaacs . . . . . . . . . . . . . . . . . . . . . . . . . . .Trixie
- •• 0:02—Breasts sitting up in bed talking to Brent Huff.

### Deadly Rivals *(1992)*
Brooke Becker . . . . . . . . . . . . . . . . . . . . .Shallie Kittle
- 0:14—Breasts visible under sheer white blouse while talking to Andrew Stevens in auditorium.
Anthony Giaimo. . . . . . . . . . . . . . . . . .Bayne Murdoch
- •• 0:07—Buns, when bad guys rip his underwear off while he's hanging by his wrists so they can torture him into talking.
Margaux Hemingway. . . . . . . . . .Agent Linda Howerton
Randi Ingerman . . . . . . . . . . . . . . . . .Rachel Richmond
- ••• 0:18—Breasts, while in bed in open robe with Rudy.
- 0:20—Right breast in open robe before killing Rudy.
- 0:46—Brief buns in panties, while trying to kill strong bad guy.
Richard Roundtree . . . . . . . . . . . . . . . . Agent Peterson
Andrew Stevens . . . . . . . . . . . . . . . . .Kevin Fitzgerald

### The Deadly Secret *(1993)*
Tracy Hagemann . . . . . . . . . . . . . . . . . . . . . . .Sarah
- 0:37—Brief buns in panties.
- 1:22—Very brief right breast, several times, during rape on beach.
Tracy Spaulding. . . . . . . . . . . . . . . . . . . Reyna Vaught
- •• 0:00—Breasts, several times during opening credits.
- ••• 0:25—Breasts, with Joe Estevez in study.
- 0:35—Brief breasts.
- 0:38—Brief breasts several times in B&W.
- •• 0:41—Buns in G-string and breasts while making love with Estevez in bed.
- 0:44—Brief breasts, while getting out of bed and putting robe on.
- 1:10—Brief breasts when Estevez comes up behind her and feels her breasts.
- •• 1:11—Breasts, while making love with Estevez on bed.
- •• 1:17—Breasts and brief buns in B&W day dream.
- 1:27—Brief right breast, while making love in flashback.

### Deadly Strangers *(1974; British)*
Hayley Mills . . . . . . . . . . . . . . . . . . . . . . . . . . . Belle
  1:02—Buns in bathtub when her uncle watches her.
  1:05—In black bra, garter belt and panties while Steven fantasizes as he sees her through a keyhole.
- ••• 1:13—In white bra and panties while Steven watches through keyhole, then breasts after taking off bra and reading a newspaper.
  1:15—In white bra, getting dressed.

### Deadly Surveillance *(1991; Made for Cable Movie)*
Susan Almgren. . . . . . . . . . . . . . . . . . . . . . . .Rachel
  0:00—Very, very brief right breast, while getting dressed. Don't see her face. B&W.
- 0:12—Breasts in the shower. Long shot.
- •• 0:34—Breasts in the shower with Nickels.

••• 0:54—Buns, in black panties and bra, then breasts in room with Michael Ironside.
Christopher Bondy . . . . . . . . . . . . . . . . . . . . . . . Nickels
• 0:31—Buns, while dropping his towel to run after Michael.
David Carradine . . . . . . . . . . . . . . . . . . . . . Lieutenant

## Deadly Vengeance (1985)
(Althought the copyright on the movie states 1985, it looks more like the 1970's.)
Grace Jones. . . . . . . . . . . . . . . . . . . . . Slick's Girlfriend
••• 0:06—Right breast, then breasts in bed with Slick.
•• 0:13—Left breast, when Slick sits up in bed, then full frontal nudity after he gets up.

## Deadtime Stories (1985)
Cathryn De Prume . . . . . . . . . . . . . . . . . . . Goldi-lox
•• 1:08—Breasts taking a shower, quick cuts.
Nicole Picard. . . . . . . . . . . . . .Rachel (Red Riding Hood)
• 0:48—Very brief right breast in shack with boy-friend.
Scott Valentine . . . . . . . . . . . . . . . . . . . . . . . . .Peter
• 0:19—Buns, while getting out of bath.

## Death Becomes Her (1992)
Stephanie Anderson . . . . . . . . . . . . . . . Marilyn Monroe
Donna Baltron. . . . . . . . . . . . . . Madeline Body Double
Catherine Bell . . . . . . . . . . . . . . . . . . . Lisle Body Double
•• 1:19—Buns, while getting out of swimming pool and drying herself off. (2 long shots and 1 close-up.)
John Enos . . . . . . . . . . . . . . . . . . . Lisle's Bodyguard
Goldie Hawn . . . . . . . . . . . . . . . . . . . . . . . Helen Sharp
Michelle Johnson. . . . . . . . . . . . . . . . . . . . . . . . .Anna
Barbara Ann Klein . . . . . . . . .Goldie Hawn's Stunt Double
Isabella Rossellini. . . . . . . . . . . . . . . . .Lisle Von Rhuman
Meryl Streep . . . . . . . . . . . . . . . . . . . . Madeline Ashton
Carrie Jean Yazel . . . . . . . . . . . . . . . . . . Girl at Dakota's
• 0:27—Brief buns in mirror, hiding from Meryl Streep at Dakota's.

## Death Feud (1989)
Greta Blackburn . . . . . . . . . . . . . . . . . . . . . . . . . Jenny
0:29—In sexy black dress talking to Frank Stallone.
1:04—In black lingerie on couch.
Lisa Loring . . . . . . . . . . . . . . . . . . . . . . . . . . Roxey
0:06—Dancing in club with feathery pasties. Later, wearing the same thing under a sheer negligee.
0:41—Dancing again with the same pasties.
1:20—Dancing with red tassel pasties.
Karen Mayo-Chandler . . . . . . . . . . . . . . . . . . . . .Anne
0:26—In lingerie with a customer.
•• 0:36—In white lingerie, then breasts several times outside taking off robe.
Erika Nann . . . . . . . . . . . . . . . . . . . . . . . . . Hooker
Gail Thackray . . . . . . . . . . . . . . . . .Harry's Girl Friend
•• 1:12—Breasts on bed with Harry.
1:16—In black lingerie on boat with Harry.

## Death Game, The Seducers (1977)
*a.k.a. Mrs. Manning's Weekend*
Colleen Camp . . . . . . . . . . . . . . . . . . . . . . . . .Donna
0:16—Buns, in spa with Sondra Locke trying to get George in with them.
• 0:47—Brief breasts jumping up and down on the bed while George is tied up.
•• 1:16—Breasts behind stained glass door taunting George. Hard to see.
Sondra Locke . . . . . . . . . . . . . . . . . . . . . . . Jackson
0:16—Buns and brief right breast in spa with Colleen Camp trying to get George in with them.
• 0:48—Brief breasts running around the room trying to keep George away from the telephone.

## Death Merchant (1990)
Dana Bentley Konkel . . . . . . . . . . . . . Jason's Girlfriend
• 0:35—Brief breasts undressing for shower during dream.
Martina Castel . . . . . . . . . . . . . . . . . . . . . . . Martina
Andrew Singleton . . . . . . . . . . . . . . . . . . . . .McKinley
• 0:47—Brief buns, while pulling up his pants, getting up out of bed with Natasha.

## Death of a Soldier (1985; Australian)
Nikki Lane . . . . . . . . . . . . . . . . . . . . . . . Stripper in Bar
•• 0:49—Nude, dancing on stage.

## Death Race 2000 (1975)
David Carradine. . . . . . . . . . . . . . . . . . . . . Frankenstein
Roberta Collins . . . . . . . . . . . . . . . . Matilda the Hun
•• 0:27—Breasts being interviewed and arguing with Calamity Jane.
Simone Griffeth . . . . . . . . . . . . . . . . . . . . . .Annie Smith
• 0:32—Side view of left breast, while holding David Carradine. Dark, hard to see.
••• 0:56—Breasts and buns getting undressed and lying on bed with Carradine.
Martin Kove . . . . . . . . . . . . . . . . . . . . . . . Nero the Hero
Louisa Moritz . . . . . . . . . . . . . . . . . . . . . . . . . . . Myra
• 0:28—Breasts and buns getting a massage and talking to David Carradine.
Sylvester Stallone . . . . . . . . . . .Machine Gun Joe Viterbo
Mary Woronov. . . . . . . . . . . . . . . . . . . . Calamity Jane
• 0:27—Brief breasts arguing with Matilda the Hun.

## Death Ring (1992)
Isabel Glasser . . . . . . . . . . . . . . . . . . . . . . .Lauren Sadler
•• 0:11—Breasts, after taking off swimsuit top on chair outside with Mike Norris.
Tammy Stones . . . . . . . . . . . . . . . . . . Cindy Maddin
••• 0:53—Breasts in open lingerie top in Skylord's apartment.

## Death Spa (1987)
Brenda Bakke. . . . . . . . . . . . . . . . . . . . . . . . . .Laura
••• 0:05—Very brief lower frontal nudity, while taking off pants in locker room. Don't see her face. Then nude, in steam room.
Rosalind Cash. . . . . . . . . . . . . . . . . . . . . Sgt. Stone
Cindi Dietrich. . . . . . . . . . . . . . . . . . . . . . . . . .Linda

Chelsea Field . . . . . . . . . . . . . . . . . . . . . . . . . . . Darla
Robert Lipton . . . . . . . . . . . . . . . . . . . . . . . . . . . Tom
Tané McClure . . . . . . . . . . . . . . . . . . . . . . . . . . .Vicky
- •• 1:10—Breasts in sauna with Tom.
- • 1:19—Brief breasts during the fire.

Shari Shattuck . . . . . . . . . . . . . . . . . . . . . . . Catherine

## Death Wish (1974)

Jeff Goldblum . . . . . . . . . . . . . . . . . . . . . . . . . Freak 1
- • 0:10—Brief buns, while standing with pants down in living room raping Carol with his two punk friends.

Christopher Guest . . . . . . . . . . . . . . . . . Patrolman Reilly
Kathleen Tolan . . . . . . . . . . . . . . . . . . . . . . . Carol Toby
- • 0:09—Brief breasts and buns getting raped by three punks.

## Death Wish II (1982)

Roberta Collins . . . . . . . . . . . . . . . . . . . Woman at Party
Silvana Gallardo . . . . . . . . . . . . . . . . . . . . . . . Rosario
- • 0:11—Buns, on bed getting raped by gang. Brief breasts on bed and floor.
- • 0:13—Nude, trying to get to the phone. Very brief full frontal nudity, lying on her back on the floor after getting hit.

Ava Lazar . . . . . . . . . . . . . . . . . . Girl in TV Soap Opera
Melody Santangelo . . . . . . . . . . . . . . . . . Tourist's Wife
- • 0:37—Breasts, being held as a shield by a gang member in parking garage.

Robin Sherwood . . . . . . . . . . . . . . . . . . . . Carol Kersey
- • 0:15—Breasts after getting raped by gang member in their hideout.

## Death Wish III (1985)

Marina Sirtis . . . . . . . . . . . . . . . . . . . . . . . . . . . Maria
- • 0:42—Breasts getting blouse ripped open next to a car by the bad guys.
- • 0:43—More breasts on mattress at the bad guy's hangout.

## Deathrow Game Show (1988)

Esther Alise . . . . . . . . . . . . . . . . . . . . . . . . . Groupie
- •• 0:08—Breasts in bed with Chuck.

Debra Lamb . . . . . . . . . . . . . . . . . . . . Shanna Shallow
- ••• 0:23—Breasts dancing in white G-string and garter belt during the show.

## Deathstalker (1983)

Barbi Benton . . . . . . . . . . . . . . . . . . . . . . . . . . Codille
- •• 0:39—Breasts struggling while chained up and everybody is fighting.
- • 0:47—Right breast, struggling on the bed with Deathstalker.

Lana Clarkson . . . . . . . . . . . . . . . . . . . . . . . . .Kaira
- •• 0:26—Breasts when her cape opens, while talking to Deathstalker and Oghris.
- ••• 0:29—Breasts lying down by the fire when Deathstalker comes to make love with her.
- • 0:49—Brief breasts with gaping cape, sword fighting with a guard.

## Deathstalker II (1987)

Christine Dupree
- . . . . . . . . . .Uncredited Body Double for Toni Naples
- • 0:55—Brief breasts in strobe lights making love with the bad guy. Hard to see because of blinking lights.

Monique Gabrielle . . . . . . . Reena the Seer/Princess Evie
- • 0:57—Brief breasts getting dress torn off by guards.
- ••• 1:01—Breasts making love with Deathstalker.
- • 1:24—Breasts, laughing during the blooper scenes during the end credits.

Toni Naples . . . . . . . . . . . . . . . . . . . . . . . . . Sultana
Maria Socas . . . . . . . . . . . . . . . . . . . . . Amazon Queen
- 0:50—In see-through nightgown after telling Deathstalker she is going to marry him.

## Deathstalker III: The Warriors From Hell (1988)

Carla Herd . . . . . . . . . . . . . . . . . . . . . . . Carlisa/Elizena
- • 0:20—Side view of right breast, while making love in tent when guard looks in.
- •• 0:46—Breasts taking a bath.

Terri Treas . . . . . . . . . . . . . . . . . . . . . . . . . .Camlearde

## Deathstalker IV: Match of Titans (1990)

Brett Clark . . . . . . . . . . . . . . . . . . . . . . . . . . . . . Vaniat
Maria Ford . . . . . . . . . . . . . . . . . . . . . . . . . . . .Dionara
- •• 0:13—Brief buns, then breasts, getting dressed in cave.
- • 0:19—Left breast, while kissing Deathstalker in bed.

Michelle Moffett . . . . . . . . . . . . . . . . . . . . . . . . Kana
- ••• 0:52—Very brief left breast, then breasts sitting on bed while trying to seduce Vaniat.
- ••• 0:59—Breasts on bed, trying to seduce Vaniat. More breasts, getting out of bed and getting dressed.

Anya Pencheva . . . . . . . . . . . . . . . . . . . . . . . .Janeris
- • 0:16—Brief left breast in open top, while wrestling with Maria Ford in the water.
- • 0:36—Brief left breast, while kissing her lover slave girl during brief orgy scene.

## Deceit (1989)

Sam Phillips . . . . . . . . . . . . . . . . . . . . . . . .Eve Bendibuckle
- • 0:25—In bra and panties after Bailey forces her to strip. Buns in panties. Dressed like this until 1:22.

## Deceptions (1990; Made for Cable Movie)

Harry Hamlin . . . . . . . . . . . . . . . . . . . . . . . .Nick Gentry
Nicollette Sheridan . . . . . . . . . . . . . . Adrienne Erickson
- • 0:35—Very, very brief silhouette of breasts, while hugging Harry Hamlin when the camera tilts down from her head to her buns.

## The Deep (1977)

Jacqueline Bisset . . . . . . . . . . . . . . . . . . . . . . . Gail Berke
- ••• 0:01—Scuba diving underwater in a wet T-shirt.
- • 0:08—More wet T-shirt, getting out of water, onto boat.

Nick Nolte . . . . . . . . . . . . . . . . . . . . . . . David Sanders

## Deep Cover (1992)

Victoria Dillard . . . . . . . . . . . . . . . . . . . . . . . . . . Betty
- • 0:52—Brief breasts, taking off her blouse to make love with Larry Fishburne.

Jeff Goldblum . . . . . . . . . . . . . . . . . . . . . . David Jason
Charlie Martin Smith. . . . . . . . . . . . . . . . . . . . . Carver

## Deep in the Heart *(1983; British)*
*a.k.a. Handgun*
Clayton Day . . . . . . . . . . . . . . . . . . . . . . . .Larry Keeler
- 0:35—Buns, while in bedroom forcing Karen Young to have sex.

Karen Young . . . . . . . . . . . . . . . . . . Kathleen Sullivan
- 0:35—Buns and brief breasts undressing and getting forced into bed with Larry. (Her hair gets in the way.)
- • 0:36—Brief breasts and buns, getting out of bed. Brief right breast when putting her dress on.

## The Deer Hunter *(1978)*
Rutanya Alda. . . . . . . . . . . . . . . . . . . . . . . . . . Angela
Robert De Niro . . . . . . . . . . . . . . . . . . . . . . . Michael
- • 0:50—Nude, running in street, then more nude by basketball court. Brief frontal nudity getting covered by Christopher Walken's jacket. Long shot.

John Savage . . . . . . . . . . . . . . . . . . . . . . . . . Steven
Meryl Streep . . . . . . . . . . . . . . . . . . . . . . . . . Linda
Amy Wright . . . . . . . . . . . . . . . . . . . . . . Bridesmaid

## Def by Temptation *(1990)*
John Canada Terrell. . . . . . . . . . . . . . . . Bartender #1
- • 0:09—Nude, running through house trying to get away from The Temptress.

## Defenseless *(1991)*
Barbara Hershey . . . . . . . . . . . . . . . . . . T. K. Katwuller
Sandy Martin . . . . . . . . . . . . . . . . . . . . . . . . . . Judge
Sheree North . . . . . . . . . . . . . . . . . . . . . Mrs. Bodeck
Kellie Overbey. . . . . . . . . . . . . . . . . . . . . Janna Seldes
- ••• 0:58—Brief breasts, nonchalantly changing into swimsuit at the beach.
- •• 1:22—Breasts, posing on bed with her father in video playback.

## Deja Vu *(1984)*
Claire Bloom . . . . . . . . . . . . . . . . . . . . Eleanor Harvey
Nigel Terry . . . . . . . . . . . . . . . . . . . . . . .Michel/Greg
- • 1:17—Very brief buns, while jumping out of bed when Jaclyn Smith tries to kill him with a knife.

## Delinquent School Girls *(1974)*
George "Buck" Flower. . . . . . . . . . . . . . . . . . . . .Earl
Sharon Kelly . . . . . . . . . . . . . . . . . . . . . . . . . . Greta
- • 0:05—Left breast in mirror while practicing martial arts.

## Delivery Boys *(1984)*
Scott Baker . . . . . . . . . . . . . . . . . . . . . Snooty Man
Samantha Fox. . . . . . . . . . . . . . . Woman in Tuxedo
Annabelle Gurwitch. . . . . . . . . . . Woman with Big Hat
Jane Hamilton. . . . . . . . . . . . . . . . . . . . . . . Art Snob
Suzanne Remey Lawrence. . . . . . . . . . . . . . . . Nurse
0:34—In bra and panties after doing a strip tease with another nurse while dancing in front of a boy who is lying on an operating table.

Kelly Nichols . . . . . . . . . . . . . . . . . . . . . . . Elizabeth
- • 0:44—Top half of right breast, while eating rolls with a young boy.

Taija Rae . . . . . . . . . . . . . . . . . . . . . . . . . . . . Nurse
0:34—In bra and panties after doing a strip tease with another nurse while dancing in front of a boy who is lying on an operating table.

## Delta Fox *(1977)*
Priscilla Barnes . . . . . . . . . . . . . . . . . . . . . . . .Karen
0:36—Left breast undressing in room for David. Very dark, hard to see.
- • 0:38—Very brief breasts struggling with a bad guy and getting slammed against the wall.
0:39—Very brief blurry left breast running in front of the fireplace.
- • 0:40—Breasts sneaking out of house. Brief breasts getting into Porsche.
- • 0:49—Brief right breast reclining onto bed with David. Side view of left breast several times while making love.
1:29—Very brief side view of left breast in David's flashback.

## Delta Heat *(1992)*
Linda Doná . . . . . . . . . . . . . . . . . . . . . . . Tine Tulane
Anthony Edwards. . . . . . . . . . . . . . . . . .Mike Bishop
Betsy Russell. . . . . . . . . . . . . . . . . . . . . . . . . . Vicki
0:52—Dancing in front of Anthony Edwards in sexy two piece outfit.
- • 0:54—Brief buns and partial side of right breast, walking from bed, past two guys. (More buns seen in mirror.)

## Delusion *(1990)*
Barbra Horan . . . . . . . . . . . . . . . . . . . . . . . . . Carly
Tamara Landry. . . . . . . . . . . . . . . . . . . . . . .Arabella
Jennifer Rubin. . . . . . . . . . . . . . . . . . . . . . . . .Patti
- • 0:34—Brief buns, pulling her panties down to moon the guys before entering the lake.
0:37—Walking out of the lake in red bra and panties. More in red bra while playing with her lizard.
0:46—Very briefly in wet bra, coming up for air from the water. Slow motion.
- ••• 1:07—Breasts in motel bathroom, drying her hair. More breasts in the motel room with George.
- • 1:12—Right breast, in open blouse, while sitting on the bed, talking with George.

Tracey Walter. . . . . . . . . . . . . . . . Bus Ticket Cashier
Barbara Alyn Woods. . . . . . . . . . . . . . . . . . . . .Julie

## Demolition Man *(1993)*
John Enos. . . . . . . . . . . . . . . . . . . . . . . . . .Prisoner
André Gregory. . . . . . .Warden William Smithers (Aged)
Susan Lentini . . . . . . . . . . . . . . . . . . . . TV Reporter
Brandy Sanders . . . . . . . . . . . . . . . . . Fiber Op Girl
- • 1:13—Very brief breasts, after accidentally calling the wrong number on her video phone.

Sylvester Stallone . . . . . . . . . . . . . . . . . . John Spartan

**The Demon** *(1981; South African)*
Jennifer Holmes . . . . . . . . . . . . . . . . . . . . . . . . . . . .Mary
•• 0:22—Breasts in dressing room.
• 1:18—Brief side of left breast, taking off robe to take a bath.
• 1:26—Breasts, crawling around in the rafters. Dark.
••• 1:29—Breasts climbing through a hole in the roof, then landing on the bed. More breasts in the bathroom.

**Demon Keeper** *(1993)*
Edward Albert . . . . . . . . . . . . . . . . . . . . . .Remy Grilland
Katrina Maltby . . . . . . . . . . . . . . . . . . . . . . Hilary Jackson
••• 0:27—Breasts, several times, while in black panties, after taking off robe and getting massaged by Dorothy.
Adrienne Pearce . . . . . . . . . . . . . . . . . . . . . Dia Gregory
0:51—Very brief right breast under wet nightgown, while being carried back into the house.
David Sherwood . . . . . . . . . . . . . . . . . . Howard Stanley
• 0:40—Brief buns, while making love on top of Ruth in bed. Don't see his face.
Jennifer Steyn . . . . . . . . . . . . . . . . . . . . . . .Ruth Stanley
• 0:31—Very brief right breast, while lying dead in bed next to Howard.
•• 0:37—Breasts after taking off robe in front of mirror.
• 0:39—Breasts, while caressed by devil creature. Close-up, don't see face.

**Demon of Paradise** *(1987)*
Laura Banks . . . . . . . . . . . . . . . . . . . . . . . . . . . . . . Cahill
Leslie Huntly . . . . . . . . . . . . . . . . . . . . . . . . . . . Gobby
•• 0:51—Breasts taking off her top on a boat, then swimming in the ocean.
Kathryn Witt . . . . . . . . . . . . . . . . . . . . . . . . . . . Annie

**Demon Rage** *(1981)*
*a.k.a. Dark Eyes*
*a.k.a. Demon Seed*
Britt Ekland . . . . . . . . . . . . . . . . . . . . . . . . Ann-Marie
Lana Wood . . . . . . . . . . . . . . . . . . . . . . . . . . . . . .Lisa
• 0:00—Breasts when breasts pop out of nightgown while running from someone at the beach.
••• 0:09—Breasts and very brief partial lower frontal nudity in bed when sheets get pulled off her.
••• 0:19—Breasts, while taking a shower when she sees the spirit.
••• 0:26—Breasts and very brief lower frontal nudity while lying in bed when the spirit visits her and makes love.
••• 0:38—Breasts in bed, while making love with the spirit.
• 0:53—Brief breasts with the spirit, while making love in bed.
• 1:22—Brief full frontal nudity getting her nightgown torn off.

**Demon Seed** *(1977)*
Julie Christie . . . . . . . . . . . . . . . . . . . . . .Susan Harris
• 0:25—Side view of left breast, getting out of bed.
•• 0:30—Breasts and buns getting out of the shower while the computer watches with its camera.

**Demon Wind** *(1990)*
Eric Larson . . . . . . . . . . . . . . . . . . . . . . . . . . . . Cory
•• 0:10—Buns, while standing outside at gas station. Don't see his face.
Sandra Margot . . . . . . . . . . . . . . . . . . . Beautiful Demon
•• 0:50—Breasts trying to tempt Stacy and Chuck out of the cabin.
Mia M. Ruiz . . . . . . . . . . . . . . . . . . . . . . . . . . . . Reana
Jack Vogel . . . . . . . . . . . . . . . . . . . . . . . . . . . Stacey

**Demonic Toys** *(1991)*
Kristine Rose . . . . . . . . . . . . . . . . . . . . . . . . . Miss July
• 0:25—Breasts in centerfold photo in magazine.
•• 0:59—Breasts in warehouse as a ghost in front of Mark.
Tracy Scoggins . . . . . . . . . . . . . . . . . . . . . . . Judith Gray

**Demonstone** *(1990)*
Nancy Everhard . . . . . . . . . . . . . . . . . . . . . . .Sharon Gale
• 0:47—Very, very brief backside view of tip of left breast after bending over to pick up robe off the floor.
Jan-Michael Vincent . . . . . . . . . . . . . . . . . .Andrew Buck

**Demonwarp** *(1988)*
Michelle Bauer . . . . . . . . . . . . . . . . . . . . . . . . . . . Betsy
•• 0:41—Breasts, taking off her T-shirt to get a tan in the woods.
•• 0:43—Left breast, lying down, then brief breasts getting up when the creature attacks.
•• 0:47—Breasts putting blood-stained T-shirt back on.
•• 1:19—Breasts, strapped to table, getting ready to be sacrificed.
• 1:22—Breasts on stretcher, dead.
Pamela Gilbert . . . . . . . . . . . . . . . . . . . . . Carrie Austin
••• 0:20—In bra, then breasts in bed with Jack.
••• 0:22—Right breast, then breasts lying in bed, making love with Jack.
•• 1:23—Breasts, strapped to table.
• 1:24—Breasts several more times on the table.
•• 1:25—Breasts getting up and getting dressed.
Colleen McDermott . . . . . . . . . . . . . . . . . . . . . . Cindy
•• 0:23—Breasts and buns drying herself off after taking a shower.
• 0:24—Very brief lower frontal nudity, under her towel, trying to run up the stairs.

**Denial** *(1991)*
Rae Dawn Chong . . . . . . . . . . . . . . . . . . . . . . . .Julie
Christine Harnos . . . . . . . . . . . . . . . . . . . . . . . . . .Sid
Chris Mulkey . . . . . . . . . . . . . . . . . . . . . . . . . . .Chad
Jason Patric . . . . . . . . . . . . . . . . . . . . . . . . . . Michael
Robin Wright . . . . . . . . . . . . . . . . . . . . . . . . . . .Sarah
• 0:37—Side view of buns, while lying on top of Jason Patric.

## Deranged *(1987)*

Jerry Butler . . . . . . . . . . . . . . . . . . . . . . . . . Frank
Jennifer Delora . . . . . . . . . . . . . . . . . . . . . . .Maryann
 • 1:09—Breasts in bed with Frank. Long shot.
Bob Fitzpatrick . . . . . . . . . . . . . . . . . . . . . . . . .Valet
Jamie Gillis . . . . . . . . . . . . . . . . . . . . . . . . . Eugene
 • 1:06—Buns, while getting into bed with Jane Hamilton.
Nancy Groff . . . . . . . . . . . . . . . . . . . . . . . . . Teacher
Jane Hamilton . . . . . . . . . . . . . . . . . . . . . . . . . Joyce
 • 0:29—Buns, getting undressed to take a shower. Side of left breast.
 • 0:37—Side view of left breast, taking off towel and putting blouse on. Long shot.
 • 1:01—Breasts, changing blouses in her bedroom.
 • 1:05—Breasts in bedroom, taking off her blouse with Jamie Gillis.
 • 1:07—Breasts in bed when Jennifer wakes her up.

## Descending Angel *(1990; Made for Cable Movie)*

Diane Lane . . . . . . . . . . . . . . . . . . . . . . Irina Stroia
 • 0:01—Brief right breast, while making love with Eric Roberts on train during opening credits.
 •• 0:44—In white camisole top with Roberts, then breasts lying in bed with him.
Eric Roberts. . . . . . . . . . . . . . . . . . . . . . Michael Rossi

## Desert Hearts *(1986)*

Patricia Charbonneau . . . . . . . . . . . . . . . . .Cay Rivvers
 ••• 1:09—Brief breasts making love in bed with Helen Shaver.
Denise Crosby. . . . . . . . . . . . . . . . . . . . . . . . . . Pat
Helen Shaver. . . . . . . . . . . . . . . . . . . . . . .Vivian Bell
 • 1:05—Brief breasts in bed in hotel room.
 ••• 1:09—Breasts making love in bed with Patricia Charbonneau.
Gwen Welles. . . . . . . . . . . . . . . . . . . . . . . . . Gwen

## Desert Passion *(1992)*

Tony Bond . . . . . . . . . . . . . . . . . . . . . . . . . . Nick
 ••• 0:17—Buns, while making love on top of Heather in the desert. Long scene.
 • 1:02—Buns, while making love with Heather during cowboy fantasy.
Carrie Janisse. . . . . . . . . . . . . . . . . . . . . . Heather
 •• 0:04—In gold bra and panties, then breasts making love with an actor on bed.
 ••• 0:17—In white bra, then full frontal nudity, making love in the desert with Nick. Long scene.
 •• 0:43—Breasts in S&M outfit during bondage fantasy.
 •• 0:54—Nude (near window), while talking to Maggie in the shower room.
 ••• 1:01—Breasts during cowboy fantasy outside. Long scene.
Vincent Lemieux . . . . . . . . . . . . . . . . . . .Man in Bondage
 ••• 0:45—Buns, while in cage during bondage fantasy with Heather.

Scott McElroy. . . . . . . . . . . . . . . . . . . . . . Mr. Gunther
 • 0:28—Buns, while making love with a girl during his desert fantasy.
Nicole Sassaman . . . . . . . . . . . . . . . . . . . . . .Linda
 •• 0:34—Breasts in spa with Maggie. In the background while Maggie makes love with Mr. Sasso.
 • 0:37—Brief left breast and buns in the spa. Breasts in spa in the background.
 ••• 0:55—Nude, getting out of the pool.

## Desire *(1989; Italian)*

Josie Bissett . . . . . . . . . . . . . . . . . . . . . . . Jessica Harrison
 ••• 0:28—Breasts and buns, while making love in bed with her boyfriend. Long scene.
 •• 0:32—Brief breasts, getting out of bed and getting dressed.
 ••• 0:45—Breasts, while making love with the taxi boy.
 ••• 0:51—Breasts, playing the piano while getting caressed and kissed.
 ••• 0:55—Breasts, while lying in bed.
 •• 1:16—Breasts in bed with an older man.
 • 1:17—Brief breasts in bed while wearing a brunette wig (she's supposed to be her mother).
 • 1:20—Side view of left breast on top of a guy in bed in slow motion. (Wearing a wig).
 • 1:21—More left breast (still wearing wig).
 • 1:27—Left breast, while in bed in flashbacks.

## Despair *(1978; German/French)*

Andrea Ferréol . . . . . . . . . . . . . . . . . . . . . . . . . . Lydia
 • 0:07—Long shot of right breast and very brief lower frontal nudity and buns, while crawling into bed. Left breast in closer shot, while lying in bed with Dirk Bogarde.
 •• 0:24—Long shot of right breast and buns, while crawling into bed again. Breasts and buns in closer shot in bed.
 •• 1:21—Nude, when Bogarde takes off her clothes in the hallway.
 • 1:24—Brief breasts when Bogarde walks by her.
 ••• 1:25—Nude in hall and bedroom while talking to Bogarde. Long shot of buns. Full frontal nudity while sitting on bed, then following Bogarde around until he leaves.
Klaus Löwitsch . . . . . . . . . . . . . . . . . . . . . . . . . .Felix
 •• 0:59—Buns, while reaching to get his pants and following Dirk Bogarde around the room.
Volker Spengler . . . . . . . . . . . . . . . . . . . . . . .Ardalion
 • 1:06—Buns, in his studio with Lydia when Dirk Bogarde looks for a painting.

## Desperate Characters *(1971)*

Carol Kane. . . . . . . . . . . . . . . . . . . . . . . . . .Young Girl
Shirley MacLaine . . . . . . . . . . . . . . . Sophie Bentwood
 •• 1:21—Left breast, while standing with Kenneth Mars, when he takes off her blouse.
 ••• 1:22—Breasts, while on bed, reluctantly kissing Kenneth Mars.
Kenneth Mars. . . . . . . . . . . . . . . . . . . . . . Otto Bentwood
 •• 0:20—Buns, while changing clothes in the closet doorway.

### Desperate Crimes (1991; Italian)
Denise Crosby . . . . . . . . . . . . . . . . . . . . . . Bella Blu
Randi Ingerman . . . . . . . . . . . . . . . . . . . . . . . . Nina
Elizabeth Kaitan. . . . . . . . . . . . . . . . . . . . . Jamie Lee
- 0:04—Brief right breast, when getting her jacket opened by a bad guy, then more right breast after getting shot.

Traci Lords . . . . . . . . . . . . . . . . . . . . . . . . . . . Laura

### Desperate Hours (1990)
Lindsay Crouse . . . . . . . . . . . . . . . . . . . . . Chandler
Kelly Lynch . . . . . . . . . . . . . . . . . . . . . .Nancy Breyers
- 0:10—Brief breasts, walking on sidewalk with Mickey Rourke when her breasts pop out of her suit.
- 1:19—Brief breasts, getting wired with a hidden microphone in bathroom.

Mimi Rogers . . . . . . . . . . . . . . . . . . . . . .Nora Cornell
Mickey Rourke. . . . . . . . . . . . . . . . .Michael Bosworth

### Desperately Seeking Susan (1985)
Madonna . . . . . . . . . . . . . . . . . . . . . . . . . . . . Susan
    0:09—Briefly in black bra taking off her blouse in bus station restroom.
    1:16—In black bra getting out of pool and lying down on lounge chair.

Rosanna Arquette . . . . . . . . . . . . . . . . . Roberta Glass
- 0:46—Breasts getting dressed when Aidan Quinn sees her through the fish tank. Long shot, hard to see.

Anne Carlisle. . . . . . . . . . . . . . . . . . . . . . . . .Victoria
Giancarlo Esposito. . . . . . . . . . . . . . . . . Street Vendor
Anna Levine Thomson. . . . . . . . . . . . . . . . . . Crystal
Ann Magnuson . . . . . . . . . . . . . . . . . . Cigarette Girl
Aidan Quinn . . . . . . . . . . . . . . . . . . . . . . . . . . .Dez
John Turturro . . . . . . . . . . . . . . . . . . . . . . . . . .Ray

### Devil in the Flesh (1986; French/Italian)
Maruschka Detmers . . . . . . . . . . . . . . . . . Giulia Dozza
- 0:20—Very brief side view of left breast and buns going past open door way to get a robe.
- •• 0:27—Nude, talking to Andrea's dad in his office.
- 0:55—Breasts putting a robe on. Dark.
- •• 0:57—Breasts and buns in bedroom with Andrea.
- •• 1:09—Breasts in hallway with Andrea.
    1:19—Performing fellatio on Andrea. Dark, hard to see.
- ••• 1:22—Full frontal nudity holding keys for Andrea to see, brief buns.
    1:42—Lower frontal nudity dancing in living room in red robe.

Fredrico Pitzalis . . . . . . . . . . . . . . . . . . . . . Andrea
- 0:57—Brief buns while in bed with Maruschka Detmers.
- 1:19—Frontal nudity when Detmers performs fellatio on him. Dark, hard to see.

### Devlin (1991; Made for Cable Movie)
Bryan Brown . . . . . . . . . . . . . . . . . . . . . Frank Devlin
Lisa Eichhorn. . . . . . . . . . . . . . . . . . . . .Anita Brennan
Frances Fisher . . . . . . . . . . . . . . . . . . . . . Maryellen

Mark Melymick . . . . . . . . . . . . . . . . . . . . Jack Brennan
- 0:08—Buns, lying on bed while tied up.

Gabrielle Rose . . . . . . . . . . . . . . . Sister Anne Elizabeth

### Devonsville Terror (1983)
Suzanna Love. . . . . . . . . . . . . . . . . . . . .Jessica Scanlon
- •• 0:30—Breasts as an apparition, getting Mr. Gibbs attention.
- 0:36—Brief breasts during flashback to 0:30 scene.
- 0:43—Brief right breast during Ralph's past-life recollection.

### Dial Help (1988)
Charlotte Lewis . . . . . . . . . . . . . . . . . . . .Jenny Cooper
    1:06—Black panties and bare back dressing in black corset top and stockings. Yowza!
- •• 1:09—Brief right breast while rolling around in the bathtub.

### Diamond Run (1988; Indonesian)
*a.k.a. Java Burn*
Ava Lazar . . . . . . . . . . . . . . . . . . . . . . . . . Samantha
- •• 0:07—Brief breasts, several times, making love in bed with Nicky. Hard to see her face.

William Bell Sullivan . . . . . . . . . . . . . . . . . . . . . .Nicky
- •• 0:08—Buns, while lying in bed, then getting up.

### Diary of a Mad Housewife (1970)
Richard Benjamin. . . . . . . . . . . . . . . . . Jonathan Balser
Peter Boyle. . . . . . . . . . . Man in Group Therapy Session
Carrie Snodgress . . . . . . . . . . . . . . . . . . . .Tina Balser
- ••• 0:01—Breasts taking off nightgown and getting dressed, putting on white bra while Richard Benjamin talks to her.
    0:36—Buns and brief side view of left breast, while kissing Frank Langella.
- 0:41—Very brief breasts lying on floor when Langella pulls the blanket up.
- 0:54—Breasts lying in bed with Langella.
    1:03—In white bra and panties getting dressed in Langella's apartment.
    1:10—In white bra and panties in Langella's apartment again.
- ••• 1:21—Breasts in the shower with Langella, then drying herself off.

### Diary of Forbidden Dreams (1973; Italian)
Sydne Rome. . . . . . . . . . . . . . . . . . . . . . . . .The Girl
- ••• 0:06—Brief breasts taking off torn T-shirt in a room, then breasts sitting on edge of bed.
- ••• 0:09—Nude getting out of shower, drying herself off and getting dressed.
- 0:20—Brief side view of right breast, while talking to Marcello Mastroianni in her room.
- •• 0:22—Brief breasts putting shirt on.
- •• 1:28—Breasts outside on stairs fighting for her shirt.
- 1:30—Brief buns and breasts climbing onto truck.

### Die Hard (1988)
Cheryl Baker. . . . . . . . . . . . . . . . . . . Woman with Man
- 0:22—Brief breasts in office with a guy when the terrorists first break into the building.

731

Bonnie Bedelia . . . . . . . . . . . . . . . . . . . . . Holly McClane
Terri Lynn Doss . . . . . . . . . . . . . . . . . . . . . Girl at Airport
Kym Malin . . . . . . . . . . . . . . . . . . . . . . . . . . . Hostage

### *Die Hard 2* (1990)
Bonnie Bedelia . . . . . . . . . . . . . . . . . . . . . Holly McClane
Tony Ganios . . . . . . . . . . . . . . . . . . . . . . . . . . . Baker
John Leguizamo . . . . . . . . . . . . . . . . . . . . . . . . Burke
Franco Nero . . . . . . . . . . . . . . . . . . . . . . . Esperanza
Robert Patrick . . . . . . . . . . . . . . . . . . . . . . . . O'Reilly
William Sadler . . . . . . . . . . . . . . . . . . . Colonel Stuart
- •• 0:02—Buns, while exercising in hotel room before leaving for the airport.

### *Die Watching* (1993)
Avalon Anders . . . . . . . . . . . . . . . . . . . . . . . . . . Marie
- ••• 0:40—In pink outfit doing strip tease while getting videotaped by Christopher Atkins, then breasts. Long scene.
- • 0:52—Brief breasts, seen on TV monitor.

Vali Ashton . . . . . . . . . . . . . . . . . . . . . . . Nola Carlisle
0:41—Very, very briefly in pink bra in Christopher Atkins' hallucinations.
- • 1:00—Buns in white panties and right breast while making love with Atkins.

Christopher Atkins . . . . . . . . . . . . . . . Michael Terrence
Melanie Good . . . . . . . . . . . . . . . . . . . . . Sheila Walsh
- ••• 0:05—In white bodysuit dancing while Christopher Atkins video tapes her. Then breasts through bodysuit, then breasts after she rips the bodysuit open.
- ••• 0:07—Breasts in ripped bodysuit while taped down in chair before Atkins kills her.

Erika Nann . . . . . . . . . . . . . . . . . . . . . . . . . . Gabrielle
- •• 0:51—Right breast, while caressing with herself while Christopher Atkins videotapes her before killing her. Her right hand is handcuffed to shelves.

### *A Different Story* (1979)
(R-rated version reviewed.)
Linda Carpenter . . . . . . . . . . . . . . . . . . . . . . Chastity
- • 1:33—Very brief breasts in shower, shutting the door when Meg Foster discovers her with Perry King.

Meg Foster . . . . . . . . . . . . . . . . . . . . . . . . . . . Stella
0:12—In white bra and panties exercising and changing clothes in her bedroom.
- •• 0:53—Breasts sitting on Perry King, rubbing cake all over each other on bed.
- • 0:59—Brief buns and side view of right breast, while getting into bed with King.

Perry King . . . . . . . . . . . . . . . . . . . . . . . . . . . Albert
- • 1:33—Buns, through shower door, then brief buns while getting out of the shower to talk to Meg Foster.

### *Dinosaur Island* (1993)
Julie Baltay . . . . . . . . . . . . . . . . . . . . . . . . Cave Girl
Michelle Bauer . . . . . . . . . . . . . . . . . . . . . . . . . June
- ••• 0:20—Breasts (she has white necklaces on), while bathing in a stream with April and May, then bathing the guys.

- ••• 0:22—More breasts, while bathing the guys.
- • 0:38—Brief upper half of left breast, popping out of bikini top after winning fight with the Queen.
- ••• 1:07—Breasts, while making love outside at night with Turbo.

Antonia Dorian . . . . . . . . . . . . . . . . . . . . . . . . April
- ••• 0:20—Breasts (she has white head band on), while bathing in a stream with May and June, then bathing the guys.
- ••• 0:22—More breasts, while bathing the guys.
- ••• 0:53—Breasts, while making love outside with Skeemer.

Griffin Drew . . . . . . . . . . . . . . . . . . . . . . . . . . . May
- ••• 0:20—Breasts (she has dark necklaces on), while bathing in a stream with April and June, then bathing the guys.
- ••• 0:22—More breasts, while bathing the guys.
- ••• 0:30—Breasts, while helping Wayne's arm feel better in prehistoric spa.
- ••• 0:31—Breasts and buns, while making love with Wayne in spa.
- • 1:15—Side of left breast during end credits.

Deborah Dutch . . . . . . . . . . . . . . . . . . . . . . Cave Girl
Nikki Fritz . . . . . . . . . . . . . . . . . . . . . . . High Priestess
- •• 0:00—Breasts (painted blue) and buns in G-string, while dancing during sacrifice ceremony.

Becky LeBeau . . . . . . . . . . . . . . . . . . . . Virgin Sacrifice
- ••• 0:00—Breasts, after getting her bikini top ripped off while tied by her wrists during sacrifice ceremony.

Toni Naples . . . . . . . . . . . . . . . . . . . Queen Morganna
- • 0:37—Brief left breast, popping out of bikini top when June starts dragging her around by her hair.

### *Diplomatic Immunity* (1991)
Bruce Boxleitner . . . . . . . . . . . . . . . . . . . . Cole Hickel
Robert Forster . . . . . . . . . . . . . . . . . . . . . Stonebridge
Meg Foster . . . . . . . . . . . . . . . . . . . . . Gerta Hermann
Fabiana Udenio . . . . . . . . . . . . . . . . . . . . . . . Teresa
- •• 1:06—Breasts in panties, on the floor with her hands tied behind her back when Klaus rips her blouse open to photograph her.

### *Dirty Hands* (1975; French)
Romy Schneider . . . . . . . . . . . . . . . . . . . . . . . . Julie
- • 0:01—Buns and right breast getting a tan, lying on the grass after a man's kite lands on her.
- • 0:09—Side view of right breast, while lying in bed with a man, then breasts.
- • 1:04—Breasts lying on floor, then brief breasts sitting up and looking at something on the table.

### *Disaster in Time* (1992; Made for Cable Movie)
a.k.a. *Timescape*
Mimi Craven . . . . . . . . . . . . . . . . . . . . . . . . Carolyn
Emilia Crow . . . . . . . . . . . . . . . . . . . . . . . . . Reeve
- • 0:18—Side view of left breast, sitting in front of vanity while Jeff Daniels watches. Long shot.

Jeff Daniels . . . . . . . . . . . . . . . . . . . . . . . Ben Wilson
Marilyn Lightstone . . . . . . . . . . . . . . . . Madame Iovine

## Discretion Assured (1993)

Elizabeth Gracen . . . . . . . . . . . . . . . . . . . . . . Miranda
- 0:28—Brief buns when Michael York removes her panties.
- 0:39—Breasts and buns, while making love with York.
- 1:09—Back side of right and buns, while rubbing lotion on herself. Brief left breast, while putting on robe. Medium long shots.
- 1:22—Brief breasts, when York rips her dress open during argument.

Dee Wallace Stone . . . . . . . . . . . . . . . . . . . . . Kitten
Michael York . . . . . . . . . . . . . . . . . . . . . . . . . .Trevor

## Disorderlies (1987)

Anthony Geary . . . . . . . . . . . . . . . . . . . . Winslow Lowry
Julie Kristen Smith . . . . . . . . . . . . . . . Skinny Dipper #2
- 0:56—Brief breasts and buns walking around near pool. Long shot.

## Diva (1982; French)

Thuy Ann Luu . . . . . . . . . . . . . . . . . . . . . . . . . . . Alba
- 0:13—Breasts in B&W photos when record store clerk asks to see her portfolio.
- 0:15—More of the B&W photos on the wall.
1:27—Very brief upper half of left breast taking off top, seen through window. Long shot.

## The Divine Enforcer (1991)

Carrie Chambers . . . . . . . . . . . . . . . . . . . . . . . . . Kim
- 1:21—Upper half of right breast in bra, while strapped into a chair by Dan Stroud.

Jan-Michael Vincent . . . . . . . . . . . . . . . Father Thomas

## The Divine Nymph (1977; Italian)

Laura Antonelli . . . . . . . . . . . . . . . . Manoela Roderighi
- 0:10—Full frontal nudity reclining in chair.
- 0:18—Right breast in open blouse sitting in bed. Lower frontal nudity while getting up.

## Diving In (1990)

Yolanda Jilot . . . . . . . . . . . . . . . . . . . . Amanda Lansky
0:32—In red, one piece swimsuit, getting out of the pool to talk to Wayne.
0:54—In blue, one piece swimsuit, getting out of the pool.
- 0:55—Brief breasts, in open blouse, getting dressed while talking to Burt Young.

Matt Lattanzi . . . . . . . . . . . . . . . . . . . . . Jerome Colter

## Dixie Lanes (1987)

Karen Black . . . . . . . . . . . . . . . . . . . . . . . . . . .Zelma
Tina Louise . . . . . . . . . . . . . . . . . . . . . . . . . . Violet
Pamela Springsteen . . . . . . . . . . . . . . . . . . . . . . Judy
- 1:00—Breasts, turning around in pond, while talking to Everett at night.

## Do or Die (1991)

Cynthia Brimhall . . . . . . . . . . . . . . . . . . . . . Edy Stark
- 0:31—Most of buns, wearing white lingerie outfit, singing and dancing at night.

- 0:36—Breasts and buns, making love with Lucas on floor in front of fire.

William Bumiller . . . . . . . . . . . . . . . . . . . . . . .Lucas
Ava Cadell . . . . . . . . . . . . . . . . . . . . . . . . . . . . Ava
- 0:20—Buns and brief breasts, getting dressed in motor home. Lots of buns shots, wearing swimsuit.

Carolyn Liu . . . . . . . . . . . . . . . . . . . . . . . . . . . Silk
- 0:14—Breasts, getting up off massage table and putting robe on.
- 1:04—Breasts in bed with Pat Morita.

Stephanie Schick . . . . . . . . . . . . . . . . . . . . Atlanta Lee
- 1:09—Breasts making love with Shane outside at night.
- 1:15—Brief breasts in background, getting dressed. Out of focus.

Michael Jay Shane . . . . . . . . . . . . . . . . . . Shane Abeline
- 1:10—Buns, while making love with Atlanta, outside at night.

Dona Speir . . . . . . . . . . . . . . . . . . . . . Donna Hamilton
- 0:06—Brief breasts taking off towel and getting into spa.
- 0:32—Breasts, mostly right breast, changing clothes in back of airplane.
- 1:21—Breasts and buns, in swimming pool with Erik Estrada.

Roberta Vasquez . . . . . . . . . . . . . . . . . . . . Nicole Justin
0:06—Sort of breasts under water in spa.
- 0:56—Breasts, making love with Bruce, outside.

## Do the Right Thing (1989)

Giancarlo Esposito . . . . . . . . . . . . . . . . . . . . Buggin Out
Joie Lee . . . . . . . . . . . . . . . . . . . . . . . . . . . . . .Jade
Rosie Perez . . . . . . . . . . . . . . . . . . . . . . . . . . . . .Tina
- 1:22—Breasts when Spike Lee rubs ice all over her. Don't see her face, but it's her.

John Savage . . . . . . . . . . . . . . . . . . . . . . . . . . Clifton
John Turturro . . . . . . . . . . . . . . . . . . . . . . . . . . Dino

## Doc Hollywood (1991)

Cristi Conaway . . . . . . . . . . . . . . . . . . . . .Receptionist
Bridget Fonda . . . . . . . . . . . . . . . . . . . . . Nancy Lee
Michael J. Fox . . . . . . . . . . . . . . . . . . . . . . Ben Stone
Woody Harrelson . . . . . . . . . . . . . . . . . . . . . . . Hank
Julie Warner . . . . . . . . . . . . . . . . . . . . . . . . . . . Lou
- 0:15—Silhouette of right breast while standing in lake during Michael J. Fox's dream. Possible lower frontal nudity since she is facing the camera, but since it is shot in silhouette, you can't see anything.
- 0:16—Breasts several times, skinny dipping in lake, then getting out while Fox watches.

## Doctor Mordrid (1992)

Jay Acovone . . . . . . . . . . . . . . . . . . . . . . . . . . . Tony
Julie Michaels . . . . . . . . . . . . . . . . . . . . . . . . . . Irene
- 0:00—Breasts and buns, while talking with Brian Thompson, then getting picked up and placed on table.

## Doctor's Wives *(1971)*

Anthony Costello . . . . . . . . . . . . . . . . #31 Mike Traynor
- 0:52—Brief buns, while getting tape recorder and running back to bed.

## The Dolls

*a.k.a. The Story of the Dolls*

Tetchie Agbayani . . . . . . . . . . . . . . . . . . . . . . . . . . Lee
- 0:12—Brief right breast, several times, while fighting with Pedro on the beach.
- ••• 0:24—Breasts and buns, while undressing and taking a bubble bath with the other models.
- •• 0:39—Buns and right breast, then full fronal nudity while posing on beach for Tom.
- ••• 0:41—Full frontal nudity, while making love on the beach with Tom.
- •• 0:57—Buns, while making love with Tom.
- 0:58—Breasts in magazine photos.
- 1:01—Brief breasts in magazine photos.
- 1:03—Nude in magazine photos.
- •• 1:04—Nude, while running on beach in flashback.
- 1:10—Very brief right breast, during tribal ceremony.
- ••• 1:12—Breasts, getting paint taken off her in bed, then sitting up.
- 1:24—Brief buns, while on the ground with Tom.

## Domino *(1989)*

Brigitte Nielsen . . . . . . . . . . . . . . . . . . . . . . . . Domino
- 0:05—Right breast, lying down next to swimming pool, breasts getting out.
- ••• 1:04—Right breast, caressing herself in a white lingerie body suit, wearing a black wig.

## Don't Answer the Phone *(1979)*

Pamela Bryant . . . . . . . . . . . . . . . . . . . . . . . . . Sue Ellen
- •• 0:28—Breasts in the killer's photo studio when he rips her jacket off and kills her.

Denise Galik . . . . . . . . . . . . . . . . . . . . . . . . . . . . . Lisa
Flo Gerrish . . . . . . . . . . . . . . . . . . . . . . Dr. Lindsay Gale
- 1:05—Very brief breasts rolling over in bed with McCabe. Brief breasts when he pulls the covers down.
- 1:19—Side view of right breast, several times, while taking off blouse and putting nightgown on.

Suzanne Severeid . . . . . . . . . . . . . . . . . . . . . . . Hooker
- 0:43—Very brief right breast in open blouse after the killer strangles her.

## Don't Go Near the Park *(1979)*

Linnea Quigley . . . . . . . . . . . . . . . . . . . . Bondi's Mother
  0:08—Full frontal nudity, behind shower door.
- 0:09—Brief left breast, while wrapping a towel around herself.
- ••• 0:19—Left breast, while lying in bed with Mark.

## Don't Look Now *(1973)*

Julie Christie . . . . . . . . . . . . . . . . . . . . . . . Laura Baxter
- 0:27—Brief breasts in bathroom with Donald Sutherland.
- •• 0:30—Breasts making love with Sutherland in bed.

Donald Sutherland . . . . . . . . . . . . . . . . . . . John Baxter
- 0:27—Buns, while in the bathroom with Julie Christie.

## Don't Open Till Christmas *(1984; British)*

Pat Astley . . . . . . . . . . . . . . . . . . . . . . . . . . . . . . Sharon
- ••• 0:19—Breasts in sexy gold outfit while posing for photo session. Nice, long scene.
- •• 0:22—Breasts flashing while wearing a Santa outfit for Cliff.
- •• 0:24—Breasts in Santa outfit when the killer checks her out while holding a razor.
- •• 0:26—Breasts, sitting on bed opening her robe for policemen.

Belinda Mayne . . . . . . . . . . . . . . . . . . . . . . . . . . . Kate
Caroline Munro . . . . . . . . . . . . . . . . . . . . . . . Herself

## Dona Flor and Her Two Husbands *(1978; Brazilian)*

Sonia Braga . . . . . . . . . . . . . . . . . . . . . . . . . . . . . Flor
- 0:13—Buns and brief breasts with her husband.
- •• 0:15—Breasts lying on the bed.
  0:17—Buns, getting out of bed.
- ••• 0:54—Breasts making love on the bed with her husband.
- 0:57—Breasts lying on the bed.
- ••• 1:41—Breasts kissing her first husband.

## Doom Asylum *(1987)*

Ruth Corrine Collins . . . . . . . . . . . . . . . . . . . . . . Tina
- •• 0:19—Breasts pulling up her top while yelling at kids below.

Patty Mullen . . . . . . . . . . . . . . . Judy LaRue/Kiki LaRue

## The Doors *(1991)*

Josie Bissett . . . . . . . . . . . . . Robby Krieger's Girlfriend
Christina Fulton . . . . . . . . . . . . . . . . . . . . . . . . . Nico
- •• 0:56—Breasts, after taking off her top in elevator with Val Kilmer.

Bill Landrum. Choreographer/Body Double for Val Kilmer
- •• 1:04—Buns, while making love in bed with Kathleen Quinlan.

Andrew Lauer . . . . . . . . . . . . . . . . . . . . . UCLA Student
Karina Lombard . . . . . . . . . . . . . . . . . . Warhol Actress
Kyle MacLachlan . . . . . . . . . . . . . . . . Ray Manzarek
Michael Madsen . . . . . . . . . . . . . . . . . . . . . Tom Baker
Debi Mazar . . . . . . . . . . . . . . . . . . . . . . Whiskey Girl
Annie McEnroe . . . . . . . . . . . . . . . . . . . . . . Secretary
Mark Moses . . . . . . . . . . . . . . . . . . . . . . . Jac Holzman
Kathleen Quinlan . . . . . . . . . . . . . . . Patricia Kennealy
- ••• 1:00—Brief left breast, while in bed with Val Kilmer, breasts (while wearing glasses) out of bed.
- 1:02—Left breast, while crawling on the floor.
- ••• 1:03—Nude, dancing around her apartment with Kilmer.

Mimi Rogers . . . . . . . . . . . . . Magazine Photographer
Jennifer Rubin . . . . . . . . . . . . . . . . . . . . . . . . . . Edie
Meg Ryan . . . . . . . . . . . . . . . . . . . . Pamela Courson
- •• 1:06—Right breast, while lying in bed with Val Kilmer.

Charlie Spradling . . . . . . . . . . . . . . . CBS Girl Backstage
Claire Stansfield . . . . . . . . . . . . . . . . . Warhol Eurosnob

Cirsten Weldon . . . . . . . . . . . . . . . . . . . . . . Girl in Car

### *Doppelganger: The Evil Within* (1992)
Drew Barrymore . . . . . . . . . . . . . . . . . . . Holly Gooding
- •• 0:23—Breasts in shower when water turns blood red. Great shot, but ruined by the red water.
- • 0:26—Brief side of left breast in kitchen with Patrick.

Leslie Hope . . . . . . . . . . . . . . . . . . . . . . . . . Elizabeth
Sally Kellerman . . . . . . . . . . . . . . . . . . . . . . . Sister Jan

### *Double Cross* (1994)
Patrick Bergin . . . . . . . . . . . . . . . . . . . . . . Jack Conealy
- • 0:24—Buns, while standing in shower with Kelly Preston. Don't see his face very well.

Kelly Preston . . . . . . . . . . . . . . . . . . . . . Vera Blanchard
- • 0:08—In bra, panties, garter belt and stockings in hotel room with Patrick Bergin. Buns and partial left breast, when he rips off her panties. Don't see her face.
- • 0:24—Buns, while getting into the shower. Don't see her face.

Jennifer Tilly . . . . . . . . . . . . . . . . . . . . . . . . . . Melissa

### *Double Exposure* (1983)
Pamela Hensley . . . . . . . . . . . . . . . . . Sergeant Fontain
Victoria Jackson . . . . . . . . . . . . . . . Racetrack Model #1
Sally Kirkland . . . . . . . . . . . . . . . . . . . . . . . . . . Hooker
- •• 0:26—Breasts in alley getting killed.

Terry Moore . . . . . . . . . . . . . . . . . . . . Married Woman
Joanna Pettet . . . . . . . . . . . . . . . . . . . . Mindy Jordache
- •• 0:55—Breasts, making love in bed with Adrian.

Misty Rowe . . . . . . . . . . . . . . . . . . . . . . . . . . . . Bambi
Kathy Shower . . . . . . . . . . . . . . . . . . . Mudwrestler #1
Jeana Tomasina . . . . . . . . . . . . . . . . . . . . . . . . Renee
- • 0:20—Very brief glimpse of left breast under water in swimming pool.

### *Double Exposure* (1993)
Jennifer Gatti . . . . . . . . . . . . . . . . . . . . . . Maria Putnam
- •• 0:06—Breasts in B&W, while making love with a guy.
- • 0:25—In bra, then brief lower frontal nudity and brief buns in B&W.
- •• 0:39—Breasts, while making love on top of a guy in B&W.
- •• 0:40—Breasts again while on top of and below the guy in B&W.
- • 1:22—Brief left breast in bed with Dedee Pfeiffer (in color).
- • 1:23—Brief right breast while in bed with Pfeiffer.

Dedee Pfeiffer . . . . . . . . . . . . . . . . . . . . . . Linda Mack
- • 1:22—Brief left breast while in bed with Jennifer Gatti.
- •• 1:23—Left breast, quite a few times, while lying on her back.

Dean Schoffield . . . . . . . . . . . . . . . . . . . . Maria's Lover
- •• 0:05—Buns, while making love with Jennifer Gatti in B&W.
- •• 0:40—Buns, while making love in bed on top of Gatti in B&W.

### *Double Impact* (1991)
Shelley Michelle . . . . . . . . . . . . . . . Uncredited Student
Alonna Shaw . . . . . . . . . . . . . . . . . . . . . Danielle Shaw
- •• 1:09—Breasts, in white panties, changing out of her wet clothes on boat.
- •• 1:10—Breasts and buns several times, making love with Chad during Alex's jealous fantasy.
- • 1:11—More breasts and buns in fantasy.
- • 1:12—More breasts.

Julie Strain . . . . . . . . . . . . . . . . . . . . . . . . . . . Student
- • 0:09—Brief buns, while lying on floor in pink leotard in exercise class.

Jean-Claude Van Damme . . . . . . . . . . . . . . . . Chad/Alec
- • 1:11—Very brief buns, while making love with Danielle. Dark.

### *Double Jeopardy* (1992; Made for Cable Movie)
Bruce Boxleitner . . . . . . . . . . . . . . . . . . . . . . . Jack Hart
- ••• 0:27—Buns, while standing and talking on the telephone.

Bill Osborn . . . . . . . . . . . . . . . . . . . . . . . Eddie Brizzard
- •• 0:23—Buns, several times, while in the kitchen attacking Rachel Ward more afterwards after she stabs him.

Rachel Ward . . . . . . . . . . . . . . . . . . . . . . . . . Lisa Burns
- 0:20—In shower with Bruce Boxleitner. You can see that she's wearing a towel around her midsection.
- 0:21—Very brief left breast, in the shower with Boxleitner. Hard to see because of the shadows. Also steam on glass obscures her face.
- • 0:23—Very brief right breast, when Eddie opens her robe to rip her panties off. Hard to see because of the beveled glass in the door. Very, very brief right breast while getting attacked by Eddie when she reaches back to get a knife. Don't see her face clearly.

### *The Double Life of Veronique* (1991; French)
Sandrine Dumas . . . . . . . . . . . . . . . . . . . . . Catherine
Irène Jacob . . . . . . . . . . . . . . . . . . . . Veronika/Véronique
- •• 0:04—Left breast, then breasts lying in bed with her boyfriend.
- 0:22—In bra and panties in her bedroom.
- ••• 0:28—Brief lower frontal nudity, then breasts while making love with her boyfriend.
- • 0:41—Brief left breast, while sitting up in bed to answer the phone.

### *Double Obsession* (1992)
Maryam D'Abo . . . . . . . . . . . . . . . . . . . . . Claire Burke
- • 0:34—Breasts, while taking a shower. Seen behind plastic shower curtain.

Margaux Hemingway . . . . . . . . . . . . . . Heather Dwyer
- •• 0:31—Right breast, while wearing Indian headress and making love on top of Fredric Forrest in bed.

Scott Valentine . . . . . . . . . . . . . . . . . . . . . . Steve Burke
- • 0:48—Brief buns, when leaving Maryam D'Abo in bathroom.

Rachel Ward . . . . . . . . . . . . . . . . . . . . . . Grandmother
Blair Weickgenant . . . . . . . . . . . . . . . . Lillian Robinson

## Double Threat *(1992)*

(Unrated version reviewed.)

Sally Kirkland . . . . . . . . . . . . . . . . . . . . Monica Martel
- 0:13—In lingerie outfit while playing with herself. Partial left breast.
- • 0:51—Brief left breast, then breasts while dressing in bathroom.

Ted Prior . . . . . . . . . . . . . . . . . . . . . . . . . Mugger

Sherrie Rose . . . . . . . . . . . . . . . . . . . . . . . Lisa Shane
- 0:09—Buns in lingerie, while sleeping in bed.
- 0:23—Buns in white lingerie while acting in movie with Andrew Stevens.
- ••• 0:47—Right breast, then breasts while making love with Stevens in bed.

Andrew Stevens . . . . . . . . . . . . . . . . . . . . Eric Cline

## Down and Out in Beverly Hills *(1986)*

Nick Nolte. . . . . . . . . . . . . . . . . . . . . . . .Jerry Baskin
- 0:28—Buns, while changing out of wet clothes on patio.
- 1:37—Brief buns, while changing out of Santa Claus outfit.

Elizabeth Peña. . . . . . . . . . . . . . . . . . . . . . Carmen

Jason Williams. . . . . . . . . . . . . . . . . . . . . . . Lance

## Down by Law *(1986)*

Ellen Barkin . . . . . . . . . . . . . . . . . . . . . . . Laurette

Billie Neal . . . . . . . . . . . . . . . . . . . . . . . . . Bobbie
- •• 0:11—Breasts lying in bed, talking to Jack. Medium long shot. Long scene.
- ••• 0:12—Side view of right breast, partial lower frontal nudity, lying in bed.
- •• 0:13—More breasts, medium long shot again, lying in bed.
- •• 0:14—Right breast when Jack covers her up with sheet.

## Down the Drain *(1989)*

Teri Copley . . . . . . . . . . . . . . . . . . . . . . Kathy Miller
- 0:04—Full frontal nudity making love on couch with Andrew Stevens. Looks like a body double.
- 0:31—In two piece swimsuit, then body double nude doing strip tease for Stevens. Notice body double isn't wearing earrings.
- 0:33—Buns, (probably the body double) on top of Stevens.
- 1:21—In black bra in motel room when bad guy opens her blouse.

Trisha Lane . . . . . . . . . . . . . . . . . . . . . . . . Robin

Andrew Stevens . . . . . . . . . . . . . . . . . . Victor Scalia

Stella Stevens . . . . . . . . . . . . . . . . . . . . . . Sophia
- 0:45—In black lingerie yelling at Dino in the bathroom.

## Downtown *(1990)*

Anthony Edwards . . . . . . . . . . . . . . . . . .Alex Kearney
- 0:19—Buns, while outside after getting his police uniform ripped off.

Penelope Ann Miller . . . . . . . . . . . . . . . . Lori Mitchell

## Dr. Alien *(1989)*

*a.k.a. I Was a Teenage Sex Mutant*

Laura Albert . . . . . . . . . . . . . . . . . . . . . .Rocker Chick #3
- ••• 0:21—Breasts in black outfit during dream sequence with two other rocker chicks.

Ginger Lynn Allen . . . . . . . . . . . . . . . . .Rocker Chick #1
- ••• 0:21—Breasts in red panties during dream sequence with two other rocker chicks.

Michelle Bauer . . . . . . . . . . . . . . . . . . . Coed #1
- ••• 0:53—Breasts taking off her top (she's on the left) in the women's locker room after another coed takes hers off in front of Wesley.

Julie Gray . . . . . . . . . . . . . . . . . . . . . . . . Karla
- ••• 0:44—In white bra, then breasts in Janitor's room with Wesley.

Elizabeth Kaitan . . . . . . . . . . . . . . . . . . . . .Waitress

Linnea Quigley. . . . . . . . . . . . . . . . . . .Rocker Chick #2
- ••• 0:21—Breasts in white outfit during dream sequence with two other rocker chicks.

Karen Russell . . . . . . . . . . . . . . . . . . . . . . Coed #2
- ••• 0:53—Breasts taking off her top (she's on the right) in the women's locker room before another coed takes her's off in front of Wesley.

Edy Williams. . . . . . . . . . . . . . . . . . . . .Buckmeister
- ••• 0:54—Breasts taking off her top in the women's locker room in front of Wesley.

## Dr. Caligari *(1989)*

Laura Albert . . . . . . . . . . . . . . . . . . . . . Mrs. Van Houten
- ••• 0:05—Breasts taking off yellow towel, then sitting in bathtub.
- •• 0:07—Lying down, making love with guy wearing a mask.
- ••• 0:10—Breasts taking orange bra off, then lying back and playing with herself.
- •• 0:11—More breasts, lying on the floor.
- •• 0:12—More breasts, lying on the floor again.
- 0:30—Brief left breast with big tongue.

Catherine Case. . . . . . . . . Patient with Extra Hormones

Debra De Liso . . . . . . . . . . . . . . . . . . . . . Grace Butter

## Dr. Jekyll and Sister Hyde *(1971)*

Martine Beswicke . . . . . . . . . . . . . . . . . . . Sister Hyde
- 0:25—Breasts, opening her blouse and examining her breasts after transforming from a man.
- 0:27—Left breast, feeling herself.
- 0:44—Brief buns, taking off coat to put on a dress.

## Dracula Rising *(1992)*

Christopher Atkins . . . . . . . . . . . . . . . . . . . . . .Vlad
- 0:43—Very brief glimpses of body parts while swimming under water. Hard to see.
- 0:44—Brief buns, under water.

Stacey Travis . . . . . . . . . . . . . . . . . . . Theresa
- 0:43—Very brief glimpses of body parts while swimming under water. Hard to see.
- •• 0:44—Breasts, while on rocks in front of waterfall with Christopher Atkins. Long shot, then closer shot. Nude under water, sometimes with another woman, sometimes with Atkins.

## Dracula's Widow *(1988)*

Rachel Jones . . . . . . . . . . . . . . . . . . . . . . . . . Jenny
- 0:54—Brief left breast, then brief breasts, twice, lying in the bathtub, getting stabbed by Sylvia Kristel.

Sylvia Kristel . . . . . . . . . . . . . . . . . . . . . . . . Vanessa

## Dragon Fire *(1993)*

Monique Parent . . . . . . . . . . . . . . . . . . . . . . . Dancer
- • 0:57—Breasts and buns in T-back, while dancing on stage painted with fluorescent paint. Lit with black-light.

Pamela Runo . . . . . . . . . . . . . . . . . . . . . . . . . . Marta
- • • 0:25—Breasts and buns in T-back, while doing strip routine on stage. Lit with strobe lights.
- • 0:29—Breasts and buns in T-back, while dancing on stage.
- • • 0:49—Breasts, while making love in bed with Powers.

Christina Veronica . . . . . . . . . . . . . . . . . . . . . Dancer

## Dragon: The Bruce Lee Story *(1993)*

Lauren Holly . . . . . . . . . . . . . . . . . . . . . . . Linda Lee
- 0:39—Very, very brief tip of left breast when making love with Jason Scott Lee (when she moves her hand from the front of his shoulder to the back).

Jason Scott Lee . . . . . . . . . . . . . . . . . . . . . Bruce Lee
Lala Sloatman . . . . . . . . . . . . . . . . . . . . Sherry Schnell

## Dragonard *(1988)*

Oliver Reed . . . . . . . . . . . . . . . . . . . . . Captain Shanks
Annabel Schofield . . . . . . . . . . . . . . . . . . . . . Honore
- 0:26—Brief side view of left breast, brief breasts lying down, then left breast again in stable with Abdee.

Claudia Udy . . . . . . . . . . . . . . . . . . . . . . . . Arabella
- • • 1:11—Breasts dressed as Cleopatra dancing a routine in front of a bunch of guys.

## Dragonslayer *(1981)*

Caitlin Clarke. . . . . . . . . . . . . . . . . . . . . . . . Valerian
0:27—Body double's very brief side of left breast from under water.

Peter McNichol. . . . . . . . . . . . . . . . . . . . . . . . Galen
- 0:27—Very brief buns while diving into pond. Sort of frontal nudity swimming under water. Hard to see because the water is so murky.

## Dream Lover *(1986)*

Kristy McNichol. . . . . . . . . . . . . . . . . Kathy Gardner
- 0:17—Very, very brief right breast getting out of bed, then walking around in a white top and underwear.
0:21—Walking around in the white top again. Same scene used in flashbacks at 0:34, 0:46 and 0:54.

## The Dream Team *(1989)*

Peter Boyle . . . . . . . . . . . . . . . . . . . . . . . . . . . Jack
- • • 0:05—Buns, while getting up out of chair.
Laura Harrington. . . . . . . . . . . . . . . . . . . . . . . Nurse
Christopher Lloyd . . . . . . . . . . . . . . . . . . . . . Henry
James Remar . . . . . . . . . . . . . . . . . . . . . . . . Gianelli

## Dressed to Kill *(1980)*

Nancy Allen . . . . . . . . . . . . . . . . . . . . . . . Liz Blake
- 1:21—In black bra, panties and stockings in Michael Caine's office.
- • 1:36—Breasts (from above), buns and brief right breast in shower.

Angie Dickinson . . . . . . . . . . . . . . . . . . . Kate Miller
- 0:01—Brief side view behind shower door. Long shot, hard to see.
0:02—Frontal nude scene in shower is a body double, Victoria Lynn Johnson.
0:24—Brief buns getting out of bed after coming home from museum with a stranger.

Victoria Lynn Johnson
. . . . . . . . . . . . . . . Body Double for Angie Dickinson
- • • 0:02—Frontal nudity in the shower body doubling for Angie Dickinson.

## The Drifter *(1988)*

Timothy Bottoms . . . . . . . . . . . . . . . . . . . . . Arthur
Kim Delaney. . . . . . . . . . . . . . . . . . . . . Julia Robbins
- 0:11—Brief breasts making love with Miles O'Keeffe on motel floor.
- • • 0:21—Breasts in bed talking with Timothy Bottoms.

Miles O'Keeffe . . . . . . . . . . . . . . . . . . . . . . . . . Trey
- 0:11—Brief upper half of buns while on the motel floor with Kim Delaney.

## Drive, He Said *(1972)*

Karen Black . . . . . . . . . . . . . . . . . . . . . . . . . . Olive
- 1:05—Brief breasts screaming in the bathtub when she gets scared when a bird flies in.
1:19—Brief lower frontal nudity running out of the house in her bathrobe.

June Fairchild . . . . . . . . . . . . . . . . . . . . . . . Sylvie
- 0:16—Buns and brief breasts walking around in the dark while Gabriel shines a flashlight on her.
- 1:01—Breasts, then brief nude getting dressed while Gabriel goes crazy and starts trashing a house.

Michael Margotta . . . . . . . . . . . . . . . . . . . . Gabriel
- • • 1:21—Running nude across the grass and up some stairs, then trashing a biology room at the university.

William Tepper. . . . . . . . . . . . . . . . . . . . . . . . Hector
Michael Warren . . . . . . . . . . . . . . . . . Easly Jefferson
- 0:09—Buns and very brief frontal nudity in the shower room with the other basketball players.

## Drop Dead Fred *(1991)*

Phoebe Cates. . . . . . . . . . . . . . . . . . . . . Elizabeth
Bridget Fonda . . . . . . . . . . . . . . . . . . . . Annabella
Marsha Mason . . . . . . . . . . . . . . . . . . . . . . . Polly
Tim Matheson . . . . . . . . . . . . . . . . . . . . . . Charles
Michael Welker . . . . . . . . . . . . . . Waiter at Wine Gala
- 1:12—Buns, when toga falls off while he's carrying trays.

## Drowning by Numbers *(1988; British)*

Trevor Cooper . . . . . . . . . . . . . . . . . . . . . . . . Hardy
- • • 0:12—Full frontal nudity, lying in bed sleeping.

Jane Gurnett . . . . . . . . . . . . . . . . . . . . . . . . . . .Nancy
- ••• 0:04—Nude, undressing inside and running outside, taking a bath with Jake. Long scene.
- ••• 0:06—More breasts and buns, in the bathtub next to Jake.
- • 0:10—Left breast, passed out in bathtub.
- • 0:11—More left breast in bathtub.
- • 0:15—Left breast, while in wheelbarrow.
- • 0:16—Full frontal nudity when the women pull her onto the bed.

Bernard Hill . . . . . . . . . . . . . . . . . . . . . . . . . . Madgett
- •• 0:35—Buns, getting out of bed to throw papers out the window.

David Morrissey . . . . . . . . . . . . . . . . . . . . . . Bellamy
- • 0:43—Buns, while on couch with Joely Richardson.
- •• 1:24—Nude, getting drowned in the swimming pool.

Bryan Pringle . . . . . . . . . . . . . . . . . . . . . . . . . . Jake
- • 0:04—Buns, while undressing with Nancy.
- • 0:06—Nude, in the tub, drunk.

Joely Richardson . . . . . . . . . . . . . . . . . .Cisse Colpitts 3
- • 0:28—Breasts, taking off swimsuit and drying herself off. Long shot.
- ••• 0:43—Breasts and buns, making love on couch with Bellamy.
- • 1:23—Breasts under water in pool with Bellamy.
- • 1:24—Breasts getting out of pool.
- ••• 1:25—Breasts standing up and putting swimsuit back on.
- •• 1:37—Left breast, while in car with Madgett.

Juliet Stevenson . . . . . . . . . . . . . . . . . . .Cisse Colpitts 2
- • 0:57—Lower frontal nudity and left breast, while trying to entice Hardy. Long shot.

### Drum (1976)

Pam Grier . . . . . . . . . . . . . . . . . . . . . . . . . . . Regine
- • 0:58—Very brief breasts getting undressed and into bed with Maxwell.

Paula Kelly . . . . . . . . . . . . . . . . . . . . . . . . . . . Rachel

Yaphet Kotto . . . . . . . . . . . . . . . . . . . . . . . . . . Blaise
- • 1:02—Buns, while getting hung upside down in barn and spanked along with Ken Norton.

Fiona Lewis . . . . . . . . . . . . . . . . . . . . Augusta Chauvet
- ••• 0:57—Breasts taking a bath, getting out, then having Pam Grier dry her off.

Ken Norton . . . . . . . . . . . . . . . . . . . . . . . . . . . Drum
- • 1:02—Buns, while getting hung upside down in barn and spanked along with Yaphet Kotto.

Cheryl Smith . . . . . . . . . . . . . . . . . . . . Sophie Maxwell
- •• 0:54—Breasts in the stable trying to get Yaphet Kotto to make love with her.

Brenda Sykes . . . . . . . . . . . . . . . . . . . . . . . . . .Calinda
- • 0:19—Breasts standing next to bed with Ken Norton.

Isela Vega . . . . . . . . . . . . . . . . . . . . . . . . Marianna
- • 0:04—Breasts in bed with the maid, Rachel.
- •• 0:22—Brief breasts standing next to the bed with Maxwell.

### Duet for One (1987)

Julie Andrews . . . . . . . . . . . . . . . . . .Stephanie Anderson
- • 0:28—Very brief left breast in gaping blouse in bathroom splashing water on her face because she feels sick, then wet T-shirt.
- ••• 1:06—Breasts stretching, lying in bed.
- • 1:07—Very brief buns and very brief right breast, when she rolls off the bed onto the floor.
  1:30—In wet white blouse from perspiring after taking an overdose of pills.

Alan Bates . . . . . . . . . . . . . . . . . . . . . . David Cornwallis

Rupert Everett . . . . . . . . . . . . . . . Constantine Kassanis

Cathryn Harrison . . . . . . . . . . . . . . . Penny Smallwood

Macha Meril . . . . . . . . . . . . . . . . . . . . . . . . . . . . Anya

Liam Neeson . . . . . . . . . . . . . . . . . . . . . . . . . . Totter
- • 1:07—Buns, while behind shower door, getting out of shower. Very, very brief buns, falling into bed when robe flies up. Long shot.

### Dune Warriors (1990)

David Carradine . . . . . . . . . . . . . . . . . . . . . . . . Michael

Maria Isabel Lopez . . . . . . . . . . . . . . . . . . . . . .Miranda
- •• 0:25—Breasts in underground lake with Val.
- ••• 0:43—Breasts making love with a guy in bed.

Jillian McWhirter . . . . . . . . . . . . . . . . . . . . . . . . . .Val
- • 0:25—Brief right breast with Miranda in underground lake. (Her hair is in the way of her left breast.)

### Dust (1985; French/Belgian)

Jane Birkin . . . . . . . . . . . . . . . . . . . . . . . . . . .Magda
  1:17—Brief breasts and buns, taking off robe and pounding the wall. Very dark.

John Matshikiza . . . . . . . . . . . . . . . . . . . . . . . Hendrik
- • 0:38—Buns, while on top of a girl, trying to rape her.

### Dust Devil (1992; British)

Robert Burke . . . . . . . . . . . . . . . . . . . . . . . Dust Devil
- • 0:49—Buns, while making love on top of Chelsea Field.

Chelsea Field . . . . . . . . . . . . . . . . . . . . Wendy Robinson
- • 0:22—Very, very brief partial left breast, when standing up in bathtub.
  0:50—Putting on bra, while sitting on bed.

John Matshikiza . . . . . . . . . . . . . . . . . . . . Joe Niemand

Terri Norton . . . . . . . . . . . . . . . . . . . . Saartjie Haarhoff
- • 0:06—Breasts and brief side view of buns, while making love in bed with Dust Devil before he breaks her neck.

Marianne Sägebrecht . . . . . . . . . . . . . . . . Dr. Leidzinger

### Dying Young (1991)

Ellen Burstyn . . . . . . . . . . . . . . . . . . . . . . Mrs. O'Neil

Patrick Cage . . . . . . . . . . . . . . . . . . . . Shauna's Boyfriend

Julia Roberts . . . . . . . . . . . . . . . . . . . . . . . Hilary O'Neil

Campbell Scott . . . . . . . . . . . . . . . . . . . . Victor Geddes
- • 1:04—Brief buns, after running out of the house wrapped in a blanket and tossing it off. Long shot.

David Selby . . . . . . . . . . . . . . . . . . . . . . Richard Geddes

### East of Elephant Rock (1976; British)
Judi Bowker.........................Eve Proudfoot
Christopher Cazenove.............Robert Proudfoot
John Hurt.................................Nash
••• 0:48—Frontal nudity, getting up out of bed and getting dressed.

### Easy Kill (1989)
Jane Badler..............................Jade
• 0:35—Brief breasts, while sitting in spa with slit wrists. Brief crotch shot when Frank Stallone carries her out of the spa.
• 0:43—Brief right breast, while making love in bed with Stallone.
• 1:07—Left breast, while making love in bed with Stallone. Don't see her face.

### Easy Money (1983)
Sandra Beall.....................Maid of Honor
Jennifer Jason Leigh................Allison Capuletti
Kimberly McArthur...................Ginger Jones
•• 0:47—Breasts sunbathing in the backyard when seen by Rodney Dangerfield.

### Easy Rider (1969)
Toni Basil...............................Mary
• 1:24—Brief right breast (her hair gets in the way) and very, very brief buns, taking off clothes in graveyard during hallucination sequence.
1:26—Very brief buns, climbing on something (seen through fish-eye lens).
• 1:27—Buns, while lying down (seen through fish-eye lens).
Karen Black..............................Karen
Peter Fonda.............................Wyatt
Dennis Hopper...........................Billy
Jack Nicholson..................George Hanson

### Easy Wheels (1989)
Eileen Davidson........................She Wolf
Mike Leinert..........................Meatball
• 0:52—Brief buns, while putting his pants on.
Karen Russell...........................Candy
Roberta Vasquez......................Tondalco

### Eating (1990)
Nelly Alard...............................n.a.
••• 0:06—Breasts, several times while sunbathing, then getting up and walking by pool, sitting down and tying a blouse around her waist.
Toni Basil..............................Jackie
Rachelle Carson..........................Cathy
Mary Crosby..............................Kate
Daphna Kastner.........................Jennifer
Elizabeth Kemp..........................Nancy
Taryn Power.............................Anita
Lisa Richards............................Helene
0:12—Brief right breast, while putting a sweater over her head.
Savannah Smith Bouchér..................Eloise
Gwen Welles............................Sophie

### Eating Raoul (1982)
Ed Begley, Jr.............................Hippie
Robert Beltran...........................Raoul
Mary Woronov.......................Mary Bland
••• 0:46—Breasts, while struggling with Ed Begley Jr. on the couch. More breasts while Raoul counts money on her stomach. Long scene.
• 0:53—Buns and side view of right breast, while in hospital room with Raoul. A little dark.

### The Ebony Tower (1985)
Roger Rees.........................David Williams
• 0:44—Buns, undressing to go skinny dipping. Long shot.
Greta Scacchi...........................Mouse
• 0:37—Full frontal nudity, undressing and going skinny dipping in lake. Long shot.
• 0:41—Brief lower half of left breast, while lying down next to Toyah Wilcox.
• 0:43—Brief nude walking into the lake.
Toyah Wilcox.............................Freak
• 0:37—Full frontal nudity, undressing and going skinny dipping in lake. Long shot.
• 0:38—Buns and side of right breast, kneeling during picnic after swimming.
• 0:39—Buns, while lying down next to Lawrence Olivier.
•• 0:40—Buns, while lying next to Greta Scacchi and talking to David.
•• 0:44—More buns, while talking to David and watching him go swimming.

### Echo Park (1986)
Elvira...................................Sheri
Michael Bowen..........................August
Susan Dey......................Meg "May" Greer
• 1:17—Brief glimpse of right breast, while doing a strip tease at a party.
Richard "Cheech" Marin......................Sid

### Ecstasy (1932)
Hedy Lamarr..........................The Wife
• 0:25—Brief breasts starting to run after a horse in a field.
• 0:26—Long shot running through the woods, side view naked, then brief breasts hiding behind a tree.

### Eddie Macon's Run (1983)
Leah Ayres-Hamilton.......................Chris
Kirk Douglas...........................Marazack
Lisa Dunsheath...........................Kay
J. C. Quinn............................Shorter
John Schneider......................Eddie Macon
• 0:15—Brief left side view of buns when beginning to cross the stream. Dark, hard to see.

### Edgar Allan Poe's "Buried Alive" (1989)
Ginger Lynn Allen.......................Debbie
• 0:12—Very, very brief left breast, while struggling with the other girls in the kitchen.
Nia Long...............................Fingers

Karen Witter . . . . . . . . . . . . . . . . . . . . . . . . . . . . Janet

### Edge of Sanity (1988)
Glynnis Barber. . . . . . . . . . . . . . . . . . . . Elisabeth Jekyll
Sarah Maur-Thorp. . . . . . . . . . . . . . . . . . . . Susannah
- 0:00—Left breast, while pulling down top to show the little boy in the barn.
- •• 0:09—Breasts, while talking to the two doctors after they examine her back.
- •• 0:50—Breasts in red room with Anthony Perkins and Johnny.
- 0:56—Very brief breasts in nun outfit.
- 1:10—Brief breasts in Perkins' hallucination at Flora's whorehouse.

Claudia Udy . . . . . . . . . . . . . . . . . . . . . . . . . . . . Liza

### Edward II (1992; British)
John Lynch . . . . . . . . . . . . . . . . . . . . . . . . . . Spencer
Dudley Sutton. . . . . . . . . . . . . . . Bishop of Winchester
- 0:08—Brief side view nude, after getting beaten.

Tilda Swinton . . . . . . . . . . . . . . . . . . . . . . . . . Isabella
Nigel Terry . . . . . . . . . . . . . . . . . . . . . . . . . Mortimer
Andrew Tiernan . . . . . . . . . . . . . . . . . . . . . Gaveston
- 0:16—Sort of side view of buns, while squatting on throne.

### The Eiger Sanction (1975)
Clint Eastwood . . . . . . . . . . . . . . . . Jonathan Hemlock
Candice Rialson. . . . . . . . . . . . . . . . . . . . . Art Student
Brenda Venus. . . . . . . . . . . . . . . . . . . . . . . . George
- 0:50—Very brief breasts opening her blouse to get Clint Eastwood to climb up a hill.
- 1:06—Breasts taking off her clothes in Eastwood's room, just before she tries to kill him. Dark, hard to see.

### Eleven Days, Eleven Nights (1988; Italian)
Joshua McDonald . . . . . . . . . . . . . . . . . . . . . Michael
- 0:33—Buns, when Sarah removes his underwear.

Jessica Moore . . . . . . . . . . . . . . . . . . . . Sarah Asproon
- 0:03—Breasts opening her raincoat on boat for Michael, then making love.
- 0:11—Buns, taking off robe in front of Michael.
- •• 0:16—Right breast, on T.V., then side of breast.
- •• 0:29—Breasts with Michael, changing clothes with him in restroom.
- ••• 0:33—Breasts in motel room with Michael, then making love.
- 0:44—Brief breasts and buns when leaving Michael all tied up.
- •• 0:51—Breasts and buns in recording studio with Michael.
- 1:17—Breasts during flashbacks.
- ••• 1:19—Nude, making love with Michael on bed.

### Eleven Days, Eleven Nights 2 (1990)
Ruth Corrine Collins . . . . . . . . . . . . . . Dana Durrington
- ••• 0:14—Breasts while wearing stockings and making out with George on bed.

Laura Gemser . . . . . . . . . . . . . . . . . . . . . Jackie Forrest

Kristine Rose. . . . . . . . . . . . . . . . . . . . . Sarah Asproon
- •• 0:18—Breasts, while getting undressed and into bathtub.
- ••• 0:20—Breasts and buns while washing herself in bathtub while being secretly videotaped.
  0:32—In lingerie with panties, garter belt and stockings after hopping on stage in club and dancing and stripping, showing off to Sonny.
- •• 0:38—Left breast, while making love in kitchen with Bob, while being watched on video monitor.
  0:57—In black bra, panties, garter belt and stockings after taking off dress with George.
- 1:09—Breasts, while pretending Francis with Sonny. Left breast afterwards.

### Ellie (1984)
Edward Albert . . . . . . . . . . . . . . . . . . . . . . . . . . Tom
Sheila Kennedy. . . . . . . . . . . . . . . . . . . . . . Ellie May
- •• 0:29—Full frontal nudity posing for Billy while he takes pictures of her just before he falls over a cliff.
  0:38—In white bra and panties, in barn loft with Frank.
  0:58—In white bra and panties struggling to get away from Edward Albert.
- 1:16—In bra and panties taking off dress with Art. Breasts taking off bra and throwing them on antlers. Brief breasts many times while frolicking around.

Patrick Tovatt . . . . . . . . . . . . . . . . . . . . . . . . . . Art
- 1:19—Brief blurry buns while falling down the stairs.

### Emanuelle in Bangkok (1977)
Laura Gemser . . . . . . . . . . . . . . . . . . . . . Emanuelle
- •• 0:07—Breasts making love with a guy.
- •• 0:12—Full frontal nudity changing in hotel room.
- ••• 0:17—Full frontal nudity getting a bath, then massaged by another woman.
- •• 0:35—Breasts during orgy scene.
- •• 0:53—Breasts in room with a woman, then taking a shower.
- •• 1:01—Breasts in tent with a guy and woman.
- •• 1:08—Full frontal nudity dancing in a group of guys.
- •• 1:16—Full frontal nudity taking a bath with a woman.
- •• 1:18—Breasts on bed making love with a guy.

### Emanuelle the Seductress (1979; Greek)
Laura Gemser. . . . . . . . . . . . . . . . . . . . . . . Emanuelle
- 0:01—Full frontal nudity lying in bed with Mario.
- 0:02—Brief breasts riding horse on the beach.
- •• 0:42—Breasts making love then full frontal nudity getting dressed with Tommy.
- ••• 0:48—Breasts undressing in bedroom, then in white panties, then nude talking to Alona.
- •• 0:54—Breasts walking around in a skirt.
- •• 1:02—Breasts outside taking a shower, then on lounge chair making love with Tommy.

### Emanuelle's Amazon Adventure (1977)
Laura Gemser. . . . . . . . . . . . . . . . . . . . . . . Emanuelle
- 0:17—Brief left breast in flashback sequence in bed with a man.

- 0:21—Brief breasts making love in bed.
- 0:25—Brief breasts in the water with a blonde woman.
- •• 1:10—Full frontal nudity painting her body.
- 1:11—Brief breasts in boat.
- 1:13—Nude walking out of the water trying to save Isabelle.
- 1:14—Brief breasts getting into the boat with Isabelle.

## Embryo (1976)

Barbara Carrera . . . . . . . . . . . . . . . . . . . . . . . Victoria
  0:36—Almost breasts meeting Rock Hudson for the first time. Hair covers breasts.
  1:09—In see through top in bedroom with Hudson.
- •• 1:10—Brief buns and breasts in the mirror after making love with Hudson.
- 1:11—Left breast sticking out of bathrobe.

## The Emerald Forest (1985)

Tetchie Agbayani . . . . . . . . . . . . . . . . . . . . . . Caya
- 1:48—Breasts in the river when Kachiri is match making all the couples together.

Charley Boorman . . . . . . . . . . . . . . . . . . . . . . Tommy
- 0:23—Brief buns, while running through camp.
- 0:24—Brief buns, while running from waterfall and diving into pond.
- 0:30—Buns, during ceremony.
- 0:45—Buns, while running away from the Fierce People with his dad.
- 1:02—Buns while running on the rocks, then bun in hut.
- •• 1:31—Buns while climbing up the building.
- 1:35—Buns while running down the hall to save Kachiri.

Meg Foster . . . . . . . . . . . . . . . . . . . . . Jean Markham
Dira Paes. . . . . . . . . . . . . . . . . . . . . . . . . . . . Kachiri
- •• 0:24—Brief buns while running from waterfall and diving into the pond.
- 0:33—Breasts while in water talking to Tomme.
- 0:56—Left breast in courtyard when Tomme proposes marriage to her.
- 0:57—Left breast in forest with Tomme. Long shot.
- •• 1:01—Breasts, by the river.
- •• 1:04—Breasts and buns during wedding ceremony.
- •• 1:16—Breasts with the other tribe women after being captured by the fierce people.
- 1:18—Breasts with the other girls being herded into the building.
- •• 1:38—Breasts, in forest taking off clothes.
- 1:40—Buns, returning to the forest.
- 1:48—Breasts while in the river.

## Emily (1976; British)

Sarah Brackett. . . . . . . . . . . . . . . . . . . . . . Margaret
- 0:09—Buns, while looking out the window at Koo Stark.

Jeannie Collings. . . . . . . . . . . . . . . . . . . . . . Rosalind
- 1:05—Brief breasts on the couch with Gerald while Richard watches.

Jane Hayden. . . . . . . . . . . . . . . . . . . . . . . . . . Rachel
- •• 1:09—Breasts in bed with Billy.

Ina Skriver . . . . . . . . . . . . . . . . . . . . . . . . Augustine
- ••• 0:43—Breasts getting into the shower with Koo Stark to give her a massage.

Koo Stark . . . . . . . . . . . . . . . . . . . . . . . . . . . Emily
- •• 0:08—Breasts, lying in bed caressing herself while fantasizing about James.
- ••• 0:30—Breasts in studio posing for Augustine, then kissing her.
- ••• 0:42—Buns and breasts taking a shower after posing for Augustine.
- •• 0:56—Left breast, under a tree with James.
- 1:16—Breasts in the woods seducing Rupert.

## Emmanuelle (1974)

(R-rated version reviewed.)
Christine Boisson . . . . . . . . . . . . . . . . . . . Marie-Ange
- •• 0:16—Full frontal nudity diving into swimming pool. Also buns, under water.
- ••• 0:19—Breasts outside in hanging chair with Sylvia Kristel.

Marika Green. . . . . . . . . . . . . . . . . . . . . . . . . . Bee
- 0:46—Nude, undressing outside with Sylvia Kristel. Brief full frontal nudity, when leaving blanket.
- •• 0:47—Breasts, getting dressed.
- 0:50—Upper half of buns, while lying down, talking to Kristel.

Sylvia Kristel. . . . . . . . . . . . . . . . . . . . . . Emmanuelle
- 0:00—Very brief left breast in robe, while sitting on bed.
- 0:02—Breasts in B&W photos.
- 0:10—Breasts and buns, making love in bed with her husband under a net.
- 0:13—Brief breasts taking off bikini top by swimming pool.
- ••• 0:14—Breasts getting up from chair, then full frontal nudity while talking to Ariane.
- ••• 0:15—Nude, swimming under water. Nice.
- 0:18—Partial left breast, while sleeping in bed.
- •• 0:24—Breasts, making love with a stranger on an airplane.
- •• 0:31—Breasts with Ariane in the squash court.

## Emmanuelle 5 (1986)

Michele Burger. . . . . . . . . . . . . . . . . . . . . . Girl No. 3
- ••• 0:42—Breasts, while talking with the two other girls. Wearing a blue head band.
- •• 0:44—Breasts, while drinking champagne with the other harem girls.

Monique Gabrielle . . . . . . . . . . . . . . . . . . . Emmanuelle
- ••• 0:01—Breasts and buns with a guy on rocks near the ocean in a film.
- ••• 0:05—Nude on boat after escaping from the crowd at Cannes who rip her clothes off.
- •• 0:09—Brief breasts taking off her jacket in restaurant. Breasts on boat with Charles.
- ••• 0:10—Full frontal nudity, making love on boat with Charles.

••• 0:17—In black lingerie, then full frontal nudity while posing for Phillip.

•• 0:26—Full frontal nudity while changing clothes in her room.

••• 0:38—Full frontal nudity while undressing in room with other harem girls.

••• 0:40—Breasts, getting fixed up by three harem girls.

••• 0:52—Buns and breasts while making love with Phillip outside.

••• 1:07—Breasts in bed with Charles.

• 1:09—Very brief right breast, in airplane cockpit with Charles.

Roxanna Michaels . . . . . . . . . . . . . . . . . . . . . Girl No. 2

••• 0:42—Breasts, while talking with the two other girls.

••• 0:43—Breasts, talking to Eddie and Monique Gabrielle.

•• 0:48—Breasts, during rescue/escape.

Heidi Paine . . . . . . . . . . . . . . . . . . . . . . . . . . Girl No. 1

••• 0:42—Breasts, while talking with the two other girls. Wearing a red turban.

•• 0:44—Breasts, while drinking champagne with the other harem girls.

## Emmanuelle IV (1984)

Sophie Berger . . . . . . . . . . . . . . . . . . . . . . . . . . Maria

•• 0:46—Full frontal nudity putting on robe.

0:49—Buns, taking off robe in front of Mia Nygren.

Sylvia Kristel . . . . . . . . . . . . . . . . . . . . . . . . . Sylvia

•• 0:00—Breasts in photos during opening credits.

Mia Nygren. . . . . . . . . . . . . . . . . . . . . . Emmanuelle IV

0:13—Buns, lying on table after plastic surgery.

••• 0:15—Full frontal nudity walking around looking at her new self in the mirror.

• 0:20—Brief breasts a couple of times making love on top of a guy getting coached by Sylvia Kristel in dream-like sequence.

•• 0:22—Full frontal nudity taking off blouse in front of Dona.

0:25—Almost making love with a guy in bar.

••• 0:30—Nude undressing in front of Maria.

•• 0:39—Full frontal nudity taking her dress off and getting covered with a white sheet.

••• 0:40—Full frontal nudity lying down and then putting dress back on.

•• 0:45—Full frontal nudity during levitation trick.

0:49—Right bra cup reclining on bed.

• 0:52—Brief breasts in stable.

••• 0:54—Breasts taking off black dress in chair. Brief lower frontal nudity.

0:57—Brief lower frontal nudity putting on white panties.

• 1:00—Brief breasts when Susanna takes her dress off.

• 1:03—Brief right breast making love on ground with a boy.

••• 1:07—Breasts while walking on beach.

• 1:09—Breasts with Dona. Dark.

Deborah Power . . . . . . . . . . . . . . . . . . . . . . . . Dona

• 1:09—Buns, while lying down and getting a massage from Mia Nygren.

Brinke Stevens . . . . . . . . . . . . . . Uncredited Dream Girl

••• 0:19—Breasts, getting coached by Sylvia Kristel during dream-like sequence on how to get a guy aroused.

## Emmanuelle, The Joys of a Woman (1975)

Laura Gemser. . . . . . . . . . . . . . . . . . . Massage Woman

Sylvia Kristel . . . . . . . . . . . . . . . . . . . . . . . .Emmanuelle

• 0:18—Breasts making love with her husband in bedroom.

•• 0:22—Breasts, then full frontal nudity, undressing in bedroom, then making love with her husband.

••• 0:32—Breasts with acupuncture needles stuck in her. More breasts masturbating while fantasizing about Christopher.

• 0:53—Right breast, while making love with polo player in locker room.

••• 0:58—Nude, getting massaged by another woman.

••• 1:14—Right breast in bedroom in open dress, then breasts with Jean in bed. Flashback of her with three guys in a bordello.

Frederic Lagache . . . . . . . . . . . . . . . . . . . . Christopher

• 0:17—Sort of frontal nudity standing up in bathtub getting introduced to Sylvia Kristel. He's covered with bubbles.

Catherine Rivet. . . . . . . . . . . . . . . . . . . . . Anna-Maria

••• 0:58—Nude, while getting massaged by Laura Gemser.

••• 1:25—Nude making love with Sylvia Kristel and Jean.

Venentine Venentini . . . . . . . . . . . . . . . . . . . .Polo Player

• 0:52—Nude in locker room when Sylvia Kristel secretly watches him.

• 0:53—Left side of buns, while making love with Kristel.

## End of the Game (1976; Italian/German)

Jacqueline Bisset. . . . . . . . . . . . . . . . . . . . Anna Crawley

Jon Voight . . . . . . . . . . . . . . . . . . . . . . . . Walter Tschanz

•• 0:29—Brief frontal nudity, getting up from bed to talk to Jacqueline Bisset in the bathroom. Brief buns and more partial frontal nudity. (Amazing for a PG movie in 1975!)

## Endangered (1994)

Richard Hench . . . . . . . . . . . . . . . . . . . . . . . . Richard

• 0:36—Long, long shot of buns, while walking on rocks.

Sandra Hess . . . . . . . . . . . . . . . . . . . . . . . . . . . .Kate

•• 0:18—Very brief breasts, while jumping up and splashing water in the lake. Brief breasts while standing up in lake (closer shot).

•• 0:19—Buns, while getting out of the lake and getting blanket.

• 0:20—Brief breasts, while turning around and putting on blouse.

•• 0:38—Buns and back side of left breast while taking a bath outside. Breasts in long shot, then closer shot.

Martin Kove . . . . . . . . . . . . . . . . . . . . . . . . . . . DeVoe

Kent MacLachlan. . . . . . . . . . . . . . . . . . . . . . . Neil
- 0:18—Very brief frontal nudity, while running and jumping into lake.
- 0:20—Very brief buns, while diving under water. More buns, while getting out and talking to bad guys.

## Endgame (1983)
Laura Gemser . . . . . . . . . . . . . . . . . . . . . . . . .Lilith
- 1:10—Brief breasts a couple of times getting blouse ripped open by a gross looking guy.

## Endless Love (1981)
Tom Cruise. . . . . . . . . . . . . . . . . . . . . . . . . . . Billy
Jami Gertz. . . . . . . . . . . . . . . . . . . . . . . . . . . .Patty
Martin Hewitt . . . . . . . . . . . . . . . . . . . . . . . . David
- 0:22—Buns when seen in front of fireplace in living room with Brooke Shields. Long shot.
- 0:27—Very brief buns in bedroom when Shields closes the door. Another long shot.
- 0:28—Buns, while jumping into bed with Shields.
- 0:38—Buns, while lying on top of Shields in bed.
Shirley Knight . . . . . . . . . . . . . . . . . . . . . . . .Anne
Penelope Milford. . . . . . . . . . . . . . . . . . . . . . Ingrid
Brooke Shields. . . . . . . . . . . . . . . . . . . . . . . Jade
0:37—Body double, side view of right breast in bed with David.
1:08—Body double very brief left breast, in bed with another guy during David's dream.

## Endless Night (1977)
Britt Ekland . . . . . . . . . . . . . . . . . . . . . . . . . . Greta
- 1:21—Brief breasts several times with Michael.
Hayley Mills. . . . . . . . . . . . . . . . . . . . . . . . . .Ellie

## Enemies, A Love Story (1989)
Anjelica Huston. . . . . . . . . . . . . . . . . . . . . . .Tamara
Lena Olin . . . . . . . . . . . . . . . . . . . . . . . . . . . Masha
- 0:16—In white bra, then brief breasts several times in bed with Ron Silver. Breasts again after making love and starting to make love again.

## Enemy Gold (1993)
Tai Collins. . . . . . . . . . . . . . . . . . . . . . . . . . .Ava Noble
- 0:20—Breasts and very brief lower frontal nudity in sauna. Breasts and buns, getting out of the sauna and into the shower.
- 1:26—Breasts, while making love with Mark.
Kym Malin . . . . . . . . . . . . . . . . . . . . . .Cowboy's Hostess
Suzi Simpson. . . . . . . . . . . . . . . . . . . . . . . .Becky Midnite
- 0:09—Breasts, while undressing and changing clothes in bathroom.
- 0:33—Breasts and buns, while making love with Chris.
- 1:05—Breasts and buns while taking a shower outside.
- 1:11—Buns in panties, while standing outside when the boys return.
Julie Strain. . . . . . . . . . . . . . . . . . . . . . Jewel Panther
0:53—In two piece swimsuit.

- 1:03—Breasts and buns in leather outfit while dancing with a sword in front of a fire.

## Enigma (1982)
Brigitte Fossey . . . . . . . . . . . . . . . . . . . . . . . .Karen
- 0:39—Brief breasts after undressing in jail cell. Very brief lower frontal nudity and buns, shielding herself from the light.
- 0:40—Breasts getting interrogated.
Sam Neill . . . . . . . . . . . . . . . . . . . . . . . Dimitri Vasilkov
Martin Sheen . . . . . . . . . . . . . . . . . . . . . . . Alex Holbeck

## Enrapture (1989)
Deborah Blaisdell . . . . . . . . . . . . . . . . . . . . . . Martha
- 0:10—Breasts undressing in her apartment with Keith.
- 0:17—Left breast, in bed with Keith, then brief breasts.
Jamie Gillis . . . . . . . . . . . . . . . . . . . . . . . . . .James
Jane Hamilton . . . . . . . . . . . . . . . . . . . . . . . .Annie
Felicia Peluso . . . . . . . . . . . . . . . . . . . . . . . .Ingenue
Kevin Thomsen . . . . . . . . . . . . . . . . . . . . . . . Keith
Ona Zee. . . . . . . . . . . . . . . . . . . . . . . Chase Webb
- 0:13—In red bra, panties, garter belt and stockings. Buns in G-string, then breasts undressing when she doesn't know Keith is watching.
- 0:17—Breasts when Keith fantasizes about her while he's making love with Martha.
- 0:21—Breasts in back of limousine with a lucky guy.
- 1:08—Full frontal nudity making love on top of Keith in bed.

## Enter the Dragon (1973)
Ahna Capri. . . . . . . . . . . . . . . . . . . . . . . . . . .Tania
- 0:47—Very brief left breast three times in open blouse in bed with John Saxon.

## The Entity (1983)
Margaret Blye. . . . . . . . . . . . . . . . . . . . . . . Cindy Nash
George Coe . . . . . . . . . . . . . . . . . . . . . . . . . Dr. Weber
Barbara Hershey. . . . . . . . . . . . . . . . . . . Carla Moran
- 0:33—Breasts and buns getting undressed before taking a bath. Don't see her face.
0:59—"Breasts" during special effect when The Entity fondles her breasts with invisible fingers while she sleeps.
- 1:32—"Breasts" again getting raped by The Entity while Alex Rocco watches helplessly.

## Entre Nous (1983; French)
a.k.a. Coup de Foudre
Miou-Miou. . . . . . . . . . . . . . . . . . . . . . . . Madeleine
Isabelle Huppert. . . . . . . . . . . . . . . . . Helen Webber
- 1:01—Brief breasts in shower room talking about her breasts with Miou-Miou.
Guy Marchand. . . . . . . . . . . . . . . . . . . . . . . .Michel

## Equus (1977)
Jenny Agutter. . . . . . . . . . . . . . . . . . . . . . . .Jill Mason
- 2:00—Nude in loft above the horses in orange light, then making love with Alan.

Peter Firth . . . . . . . . . . . . . . . . . . . . . . . .Alan Strang
- 1:19—Frontal nudity standing in a field with a horse.
- 2:00—Nude in loft above the horses in orange light with Jenny Agutter. Long scene.

### *Erendira* (1983; Brazilian)
Blanca Guerra . . . . . . . . . . . . . . . . . . . . Ulysses' Mother
Claudia Ohana . . . . . . . . . . . . . . . . . . . . . . . . Erendira
- 0:14—Breasts while getting fondled by a guy against her will.
- 0:26—Breasts while lying in bed sweating and crying after having to have sex with an army of men.
- 1:04—Breasts while lying in bed sleeping.
  1:08—Brief breasts while getting out of bed. Long shot, hard to see.
- 1:24—Breasts and buns while on bed with Ulysses.
Irene Papas . . . . . . . . . . . . . . . . . . . . .The Grandmother
Oliver Wehe . . . . . . . . . . . . . . . . . . . . . . . . . . Ulysses
- 1:24—Buns, while getting into bed with Erendira.

### *Erotic Images* (1983)
Alexandra Day . . . . . . . . . . . . . . . . . . .Logan's Girlfriend
- 0:37—Breasts getting out of bed while Logan talks on the phone to Britt Ekland.
Britt Ekland . . . . . . . . . . . . . . . . . . . . . . . . . .Julie Todd
- 0:16—Brief side view of left breast in bed with Glenn.
- 0:29—In bra, then breasts in bed with Glenn.
  0:33—In bra, in open robe looking at herself in the mirror.
  1:27—In black bra, talking to Sonny.
Meredith Kennedy . . . . . . . . . . . . . . . . . . . . . Ginger
- 1:04—Breasts on the couch with two guys.
Alexandra Morgan . . . . . . . . . . . . . . . . . Emily Stewart
- 0:57—In black lingerie, then breasts on the living room floor with Glenn.
- 1:05—Breasts in bed, making love with Glenn.
- 1:12—Breasts in the kitchen with Glenn.
- 1:21—Right breast, on couch with Glenn.
Remy O'Neill . . . . . . . . . . . . . . . . . . . . . .Vickie Coleman
- 0:04—Breasts while sitting in chaise lounge talking to Britt Ekland about sex survey. Long scene.
- 0:06—Breasts while in bed with Marvin. Brief lower frontal nudity.
- 0:07—Brief left breast while in spa with TV repairman, then brief breasts.
Julia Parton . . . . . . . . . . . . . . . . . . . . . . Marvin's Nurse
- 0:08—Brief breasts in office with Marvin. Dark, hard to see.
Barbara Peckinpaugh . . . . . . . . . . . . . . . . Cheerleader
- 0:07—Breasts dancing in an office with another cheerleader.

### *Erotikill* (1973)
*a.k.a. La Comtesse Noire*
*a.k.a. The Loves of Irina*
Lina Romay . . . . . . . . . . . . . . . . . . . . . . . . . . . . Irina
- 0:00—Full frontal nudity, wearing a belt and cape walking towards the camera during the opening credits.

- 0:08—Full frontal nudity on bed, then walking around while wearing a cape. Out of focus.
- 0:17—Full frontal nudity, lying in bed and drinking.
- 0:31—Very brief right breast during struggle with another woman on bed.
- 0:32—Full frontal nudity, while walking through the woods with a cape and belt.
- 0:33—Breasts, flapping her cape.
- 0:43—Breasts under sheer black nightgown.
- 0:45—Full frontal nudity when the other woman takes her nightgown off.
- 0:47—Full frontal nudity biting another woman and sucking her blood.
- 1:05—Full frontal nudity sitting down in bath filled with red water.
- 1:07—More breasts and brief buns doing pelvic thrusts in bathtub. Out of focus sometimes.
- 1:08—Nude in bathtub.
Monica Swin . . . . . . . . . . . . . . . . .Princess de Rochefort
- 0:47—Breasts, getting her dress taken off and blood sucked.
- 0:55—Breasts, lying on table in doctor's office.

### *Eternity* (1989)
Eileen Davidson . . . . . . . . . . . . . . . . . . . . Dahlia/Valerie
  0:33—In black bra and panties in dressing room. Brief buns standing in bathtub during Jon Voight's flashback.
- 0:52—Brief left breast, then breasts, in bed with Voight. Don't see face.

### *Eureka* (1983; British)
Rutger Hauer . . . . . . . . . . . . . . Claude Maillot Van Horn
Emma Relph . . . . . . . . . . . . . . . . . . . . .Mary (blue dress)
- 1:17—Brief breasts during African voodoo ceremony.
Mickey Rourke . . . . . . . . . . . . . . . . . . . . . . . . .Aurelio
Theresa Russell . . . . . . . . . . . . . . . . . . . . . . . . .Tracy
  0:38—In lingerie talking to Rutger Hauer.
- 0:40—Right breast, lying in bed with Hauer.
- 1:04—Very brief left breast in bed with Hauer, then brief lower frontal nudity and brief buns when Gene Hackman bursts into the room.
- 1:09—Breasts on a boat with Hauer.
- 1:41—Left breast peeking out from under black top while lying in bed.
- 1:59—Full frontal nudity kicking off sheets in the bed.
Ann Thornton . . . . . . . . . . . . . . . . . . . . Jane (red dress)
- 1:17—Brief breasts during African voodoo ceremony.

### *Europa Europa* (1991; German)
Julie Delpy . . . . . . . . . . . . . . . . . . . . . . . . . . . . . . .Leni
Marco Hofschneider . . . . . . . . . . . .Young Salomon Perel
- 0:03—Buns, while taking off underwear to take a bath.
- 0:05—Very, very brief frontal nudity, getting into tub.
- 0:06—Nude, getting out of the bathtub and running to hide in a barrel.

•• 0:45—Nude, running around in barn, trying to get away from his fellow German officer.

• 1:19—Brief, discolored frontal nudity, after he tries to "create" a foreskin.

## Eve of Destruction (1991)

Gregory Hines . . . . . . . . . . . . . . . . . . . . . . Jim McQuade
Tim Russ . . . . . . . . . . . . . . . . . . . . . . . . . . . Carter
Reneé Soutendijk . . . . . . . . . . Dr. Eve Simmons/Eve VIII
    0:17—Left breast, while on table as a robot, with half her skin removed. Possibly a special-effect body.

• 0:22—Brief breasts in bathroom (as a robot), fixing her wound. Breasts sitting on bed, putting a large bandage over the wound.

## An Evening with Kitten (1983)

Francesca "Kitten" Natividad . . . . . . . . . . . . . . . Herself
   •• 0:02—Breasts busting out of her blouse.
   •• 0:09—Breasts while in miniature city scene.
   • 0:11—Brief breasts while on stage.
   • 0:20—Left breast, in bed with a vampire.
   ••• 0:21—Breasts and buns in G-string during dance in large champagne glass prop. Long scene.
   ••• 0:24—Breasts on beach in mermaid costume with little shell pasties.
   ••• 0:25—Breasts while in the glass again.
   •• 0:28—Breasts while in and out of glass.
   •• 0:29—Brief breasts during end credits.

## Every Breath (1992)

Cynthia Brimhall . . . . . . . . . . . . . . . . . . . . . . . . Kris
Joanna Pacula . . . . . . . . . . . . . . . . . . . . . . . . Lauren
   • 0:21—Very, very brief right breast in jacket while kissing Judd Nelson in bedroom.
   ••• 0:36—Brief back side of right breast, then breasts while kissing Nelson outside by pool.
   0:43—In black bra and panties in bedroom with Bob.
   ••• 1:10—Breasts and buns while in the shower.

## Every Time We Say Goodbye (1986)

Cristina Marsillach . . . . . . . . . . . . . . . . . . . . . . Sarah
   1:00—In white slip in her bedroom.
   1:03—In white slip again.
   •• 1:09—Right breast, then brief breasts lying in bed with Tom Hanks.

## Everybody's All-American (1988)

Timothy Hutton . . . . . . . . . . . . . . . . . . . . . . Donnie
Jessica Lange . . . . . . . . . . . . . . . . . . . . . . . . . . Babs
   0:32—Brief breasts under sheer nightgown in bedroom with Dennis Quaid.
   • 0:54—Buns and very, very brief side view of left breast by the campfire by the lake with Timothy Hutton at night. Might be a body double.
Dennis Quaid . . . . . . . . . . . . . . . . . . . . . . . . . Gavin

## Everybody's Fine (1991; Italian)

a.k.a. Stanno Tutti Bene
Valeria Cavalli . . . . . . . . . . . . . . . . . . . . . . . . Tosca
   0:49—In white bra and panties during lingerie modeling assignment.

• 0:54—Brief glimpses of left breast, after taking off her dress backstage at fashion show. Left breast, while breast feeding her baby.

## The Evil Below (1991)

Sheri Able . . . . . . . . . . . . . . . . . . . . . . . . . . . Tracy
   • 0:10—Buns, in two piece swimsuit on boat.
   0:16—In wet T-shirt getting on boat after diving.
   • 0:21—Right breast, with Max behind curtain. Hard to see.
June Chadwick . . . . . . . . . . . . . . . . . . Sarah Livingston
   • 0:08—Very, very brief left breast, while on the floor with Max after he takes off her bra.
   0:39—In red, one piece swimsuit on boat.
   • 0:45—Very brief left breast, while on the floor with Max. Different angle from 0:08.

## Evil Laugh (1986)

Kim McKamy . . . . . . . . . . . . . . . . . . . . . . . . Connie
Myles O'Brien . . . . . . . . . . . . . . . . . . . . . . . . . Mark
   0:30—Sort of buns and brief lower frontal nudity rolling over on top of Tina in bed. Very, very brief frontal nudity when she takes the sheet away from him.

## Evil Spawn (1987)

Bobbie Bresee . . . . . . . . . . . . . . . . . . . . . Lynn Roman
   • 0:14—Very brief half of right breast in bed with a guy.
   0:26—In red one piece swimsuit.
   ••• 0:36—Breasts and side view of buns in bathroom looking at herself in the mirror, then taking a shower.
Pamela Gilbert . . . . . . . . . . . . . . . . . . . . Elaine Talbot
   ••• 0:46—Nude taking off black lingerie and going swimming in pool. Hubba, hubba!
   ••• 0:49—Breasts in the pool, then full frontal nudity getting out.
Dawn Wildsmith . . . . . . . . . . . . . . . . . . Evelyn Avery

## Evil Spirits (1990)

Martine Beswicke . . . . . . . . . . . . . . . . . . . . . Vanya
Karen Black . . . . . . . . . . . . . . . . . . . . . Ella Purdy
Dori Courtney . . . . . . . . . . . . . . . . . . . . Bank Teller
Debra Lamb . . . . . . . . . . . . . . . . . . . . . . . . . . Tina
   ••• 0:22—Breasts, while dancing in her bedroom while Michael Berryman watches through peep hole. Most of her buns in underwear. Long scene.

## Evil Toons (1991)

Suzanne Ager . . . . . . . . . . . . . . . . . . . . . . . . Terry
   ••• 0:31—Breasts and buns in G-string, taking off clothes to put on her pajamas.
   •• 1:09—Right breast, while on the floor getting her pajamas ripped open by Roxanne.
   •• 1:10—Brief breasts when Roxanne rips the pajamas all the way down.
Michelle Bauer . . . . . . . . . . . . . . . . . . . . Mrs. Burt
   •• 0:48—Breasts opening her lingerie for Burt. Buns, while walking away in G-string.
David Carradine . . . . . . . . . . . . . . . . . . Gideon Fisk

Barbara Dare. . . . . . . . . . . . . . . . . . . . . . . . . . . . . Jan
••• 0:30—Breasts, taking off robe and putting on red
    nightgown.
•• 1:06—Breasts when her top is pulled down by Rox-
    anne.
Monique Gabrielle . . . . . . . . . . . . . . . . . . . . . Megan
    0:21—In bra in open blouse when Roxanne tries to
    get her to do a strip tease.
••• 0:25—In bra, then breasts undressing in front of mir-
    ror.
Madison Stone . . . . . . . . . . . . . . . . . . . . . . . Roxanne
••• 0:20—Buns in G-string, then breasts doing a strip
    routine in front of her girlfriends.
••• 0:33—Breasts, taking off blouse and putting on bra
    and panties. Buns in sheer panties.
•• 0:36—Breasts on the floor, getting attacked by the
    monster.
••• 0:38—Breasts walking around, covered with blood,
    talking with Megan.
•• 0:41—Breasts putting blouse on.
• 0:42—Breasts on couch with Biff.
• 0:55—Left breast in open blouse, seducing Burt.
• 0:59—Brief breasts several times, dead, when the
    other girls discover her.

**Evil Town** (1987)
Robert Walker, Jr. . . . . . . . . . . . . . . . . . . . . . . . . Mike
Lynda Wiesmeier. . . . . . . . . . . . . . . . . . . . . . . Dianne
••• 0:09—Breasts, while on top of Tony outside while
    camping.
•• 0:11—Right breast while making out with boyfriend
    outside. Breasts when getting up.
• 0:13—Breasts in open blouse, while running from
    bad guy. Nice bouncing action.
•• 0:15—Breasts, while getting captured by bad guys.
•• 0:17—Breasts, when getting out of car and brought
    into the house.
•• 0:23—Breasts while tied up in chair.

**Evils of the Night** (1985)
Jerry Butler . . . . . . . . . . . . . . . . . . . . . . . . . . . . Eddie
Bridget Holloman . . . . . . . . . . . . . . . . . . . . . Heather
Tina Louise . . . . . . . . . . . . . . . . . . . . . . . . . . . . . Cora
Amber Lynn . . . . . . . . . . . . . . . . . . . . . . . . . . . . Joyce
• 0:14—Brief breasts, taking her pink swimsuit top off
    for Eddie.
•• 0:17—Breasts with Eddie in deserted house. Dark.
•• 0:19—Full frontal nudity when Eddie takes her
    shorts off. Dark.
• 0:21—Right breast, while in bed with Eddie. Still
    dark.
• 0:22—More right breast.
•• 0:23—Full frontal nudity in bed when Eddie gets
    out.
•• 0:24—Nude, while getting out of bed and getting
    dressed. Dark.
Julie Newmar . . . . . . . . . . . . . . . . . . . . .Doctor Zarma
Jody Swafford . . . . . . . . . . . . . . . . . . . . . . . Lotion Girl
•• 0:12—Breasts while rubbing lotion on another girl.
•• 0:13—More breasts with the other girl.

• 0:14—Brief breasts when Eddie watches her and her
    friend.

**Evilspeak** (1981)
Louie Gravance . . . . . . . . . . . . . . . . . . . . . . . . .Jo Jo
•• 0:07—Buns, in shower with three other guys. (He's
    the one in the foreground on the right.)
Lynn Hancock . . . . . . . . . . . . . . . . . . . .Miss Friedemyer
•• 0:56—In bra, then breasts taking off bra in front of
    fireplace. Buns in panties, walking up the stairs.
••• 0:57—Breasts and buns in the shower, then getting
    killed by pigs.
Clint Howard . . . . . . . . . . . . . . . . . . . . . Coopersmith
• 0:07—Buns, in shower with three other guys. (He's
    the second from the left.)
Haywood Nelson . . . . . . . . . . . . . . . . . . . . . Kowalski
    0:07—Buns, twice, in shower with three other guys.
    (He's the only black guy.)

**Excalibur** (1981; British)
Katrine Boorman . . . . . . . . . . . . . . . . . . . . . . Igrayne
• 0:14—Right breast, then breasts in front of the fire
    when Uther tricks her into thinking that he is her
    husband and makes love to her.
Keith Buckley . . . . . . . . . . . . . . . . . . . . . . . . . .Uryens
Gabriel Byrne. . . . . . . . . . . . . . . . . . . . . . . . . .Uther
Nicholas Clay. . . . . . . . . . . . . . . . . . . . . . . .Lancelot
•• 1:13—Buns, while fighting with himself in a suit of
    armor.
• 1:31—Brief buns, while running into the woods after
    waking up. Long shot, hard to see.
Cherie Lunghi . . . . . . . . . . . . . . . . . . . . . . .Guenevere
• 1:25—Brief breasts in the forest kissing Lancelot.
Helen Mirren . . . . . . . . . . . . . . . . . . . . . . . Morgana
• 1:31—Side view of left breast under a fishnet outfit
    climbing into bed.
Liam Neeson . . . . . . . . . . . . . . . . . . . . . . . . . Gawain
Nigel Terry. . . . . . . . . . . . . . . . . . . . . . . King Arthur

**Excessive Force** (1993)
Liza Cruzat . . . . . . . . . . . . . . . . . . . . . . . . . . Hooker
Tom Hodges . . . . . . . . . . . . . . . . . . . . . . . . .Dylan
• 0:16—Buns, while making love in the bathroom
    with Lisa.
•• 0:17—Buns, while putting his pants on in bedroom.
Charlotte Lewis . . . . . . . . . . . . . . . . . . . . Anna Gilmour
••• 0:54—Brief right breast, then breasts while in bed
    with Thomas Ian Griffith.

**The Executioner** (1980)
Christopher Brenner. . . . . . . . . . . . . . . . . Chicken Boy
• 1:05—Buns, twice, while tied up on bed when Rob-
    ert Ginty kills the bad guy.
Samantha Eggar. . . . . . . . . . . . . . . Dr. Megan Stewart
    1:23—In body suit, briefly sitting up in hospital bed
    with Christopher George.

### The Executioner's Song (1982)

(European Version reviewed.)

Rosanna Arquette . . . . . . . . . . . . . . . . . . . Nicole Baker
- ••• 0:30—Brief breasts in bed, then getting out of bed. Buns, walking to kitchen.
- ••• 0:41—Breasts in bed with Tommy Lee Jones.
- ••• 0:48—Breasts on top of Jones making love.
- •• 1:36—Right breast and buns, standing up getting strip searched before visiting Jones in prison.

Tommy Lee Jones . . . . . . . . . . . . . . . . . . Gary Gillmore
- •• 0:48—Buns, while walking to kitchen after hitting Rosanna Arquette.

Jenny Wright. . . . . . . . . . . . . . . . . . . . . . April Baker
Jim Youngs . . . . . . . . . . . . . . . . . . . . . Sterling Baker

### Exposed (1983)

Iman. . . . . . . . . . . . . . . . . . . . . . . . . . . . . . .Model
Bibi Andersson . . . . . . . . . . . . . . . . . . . . Margaret
Pierre Clementi . . . . . . . . . . . . . . . . . . . . . . . . Vic
Janice Dickinson . . . . . . . . . . . . . . . . . . . . . .Model
Harvey Keitel . . . . . . . . . . . . . . . . . . . . . . . .Rivas
Nastassja Kinski. . . . . . . . . . . . Elizabeth Carlson
- •• 0:54—Breasts in bed with Rudolf Nureyev.

Rudolf Nureyev . . . . . . . . . . . . . . . . . .Daniel Jelline
- ••• 0:54—Buns, while in bed with Nastassja Kinski.

James Russo . . . . . . . . . . . . . . . . . . . . . . . . . Nick

### Extreme Justice (1993; Made for Cable Movie)

Julie Austin . . . . . . . . . . . . . . . . . . . . . . . . Cindy
Chelsea Field. . . . . . . . . . . . . . . . . . .Kelly Daniels
- • 0:18—In white bra, then brief left breast on sofa with Lou Diamond Phillips.

Scott Glenn. . . . . . . . . . . . . . . . . . . . .Dan Vaughn
Yaphet Kotto . . . . . . . . . . . . . . . . . . . . . . Larson
Lou Diamond Phillips . . . . . . . . . . . . . . Jeff Powers

### Extreme Prejudice (1987)

Maria Conchita Alonso . . . . . . . . . . . . . Sarita Cisneros
- •• 0:27—Brief breasts in the shower while Nick Nolte is in the bathroom talking to her.

Clancy Brown . . . . . . . . . . . . . . . .Sgt. Larry McRose
Tom "Tiny" Lister, Jr.. . . . . . . . . . . . . . . . . . Monday
Rip Torn . . . . . . . . . . . . . . . . . . .Sheriff Hank Pearson

### Extremities (1986)

Farrah Fawcett . . . . . . . . . . . . . . . . . . . . . Marjorie
- • 0:37—Brief side view of right breast when Joe pulls down her top in the kitchen. Can't see her face, but reportedly her.

Michael Hennessy . . . . . . . . . . . . . . . . . . . .Pizza Man
Sandy Martin . . . . . . . . . . . . . . . . . . . .Officer Sudow
James Russo . . . . . . . . . . . . . . . . . . . . . . . . . . . Joe

### Eye of the Needle (1981)

Christopher Cazenove. . . . . . . . . . . . . . . . . . . David
Kate Nelligan . . . . . . . . . . . . . . . . . . . . . . . . . . Lucy
- •• 0:52—Brief left breast, while drying herself off in the bathroom when Donald Sutherland accidentally sees her.
  1:15—Top half of buns, making love in bed with Sutherland.

- 1:26—Breasts making love in bed with Sutherland after he killed her husband. Dark, hard to see.

Donald Sutherland . . . . . . . . . . . . . . . . . . . . . .Faber

### Eyes of a Stranger (1981)

Jennifer Jason Leigh . . . . . . . . . . . . . . . . . . . . .Tracy
- • 1:15—Very brief breasts lying in bed getting attacked by rapist.
- •• 1:19—Left breast, while cleaning herself in bathroom.

### Eyes of Fire (1983)

Karlene Crockett . . . . . . . . . . . . . . . . . . . . . . . Leah
- • 0:44—Brief breasts sitting up in the water and scaring Mr. Dalton.
- 1:16—Breasts talking to Dalton who is trapped in a tree. Brief breasts again when he pulls the creature out of the tree.

### Eyes of Laura Mars (1978)

Brad Dourif . . . . . . . . . . . . . . . . . . . . Tommy Ludlow
Faye Dunaway . . . . . . . . . . . . . . . . . . .Laura Mars
Darlanne Fluegel . . . . . . . . . . . . . . . . . . . . .Lulu
Tommy Lee Jones. . . . . . . . . . . . . . . .John Neville
Raul Julia . . . . . . . . . . . . . . . . . . . .Michael Reisler
Lisa Taylor . . . . . . . . . . . . . . . . . . . . . . Michele
- • 0:59—Very brief right breast, while on table just before getting killed.

### Eyes of the Beholder (1992)

Toni Kalem. . . . . . . . . . . . . . . . . . . . .Doctor Gruber
Joanna Pacula. . . . . . . . . . . . . . . . . . .Diana Carlyle
Kylie Travis . . . . . . . . . . . . . . . . . . . . Holly Brandon
- •• 1:08—Left breast, then breasts after taking her dress top down in front of Janice.

### Eyes of the Serpent (1992)

Diana Frank . . . . . . . . . . . . . . . . . . . . . . . . .Fiona
- •• 1:05—Buns and breasts, several times while making love in bed with Galen.

Lisa Toothman . . . . . . . . . . . . . . . . . . . . . . . Neema

### Eyewitness to Murder (1989)

Andrew Stevens . . . . . . . . . . . . . . . . . . . . . . Page
Sherilyn Wolter. . . . . . . . . . . . . . . . . . . . .Suzanne
- • 1:00—Very, very brief lower half of right breast while making love with Andrew Stevens. Don't see her face.

### The Fabulous Baker Boys (1989)

Beau Bridges . . . . . . . . . . . . . . . . . . . . . Frank Baker
Jeff Bridges. . . . . . . . . . . . . . . . . . . . . . . Jack Baker
Michelle Pfeiffer . . . . . . . . . . . . . . . . . Susie Diamond
Jennifer Tilly . . . . . . . . . . . . . . . . . . . .Monica Moran
Terri Treas . . . . . . . . . . . . . . . . . . . . . . Girl in Bed
- • 0:00—Brief upper half of right breast when sheet falls down when she leans over in bed.

### Fade to Black (1980)

Linda Kerridge . . . . . . . . . . . . . . . . . . . . . . Marilyn
- • 0:44—Breasts in the shower.

Mickey Rourke . . . . . . . . . . . . . . . . . . . . . . . Richie

Marya Small . . . . . . . . . . . . . . . . . . . . . . . . .Doreen

### Fair Game (1985; Australian)
Cassandra Delaney . . . . . . . . . . . . . . . . . . . . . .Jessica
- • 0:15—Buns and brief side of left breast, taking off her outfit and lying on bed.
- • 0:16—Breasts rolling over in bed.
  0:19—Brief, out of focus buns, in Polaroid photograph taped to inside of the refrigerator.
- • 0:32—Brief left breast, taking off outfit to take a shower.
- •• 0:48—Brief breasts when the bad guys cut her blouse open. Breasts several times, while tied to front of truck.
- • 0:49—Brief left breast while getting up off the ground.
  0:50—Half of right breast, while sitting in the shower. Dark.

### Fair Game (1988; Italian)
Gregg Henry. . . . . . . . . . . . . . . . . . . . . . . . . . . Gene
Trudie Styler . . . . . . . . . . . . . . . . . . . . . . . . . . . Eva
  0:14—Very, very brief blurry top of right breast in gaping blouse, while standing up after changing clothes.
- • 0:37—Brief buns, kneeling in bathtub. Very brief buns in the mirror several times putting on robe and getting out of the bathtub.

### Fairytales (1979)
Angela Aames . . . . . . . . . . . . . . . . . . . . . . Little Bo Peep
- ••• 0:14—Nude with The Prince in the woods.
Nai Bonet . . . . . . . . . . . . . . . . . . . . . . . . .Sheherazade
- • 0:29—Buns and very brief left breast doing a belly dance and rubbing oil on herself.
Marita Ditmar . . . . . . . . . . . . . . . . . . . . . . .S & M Dancer
- • 0:38—Breasts wearing masks with two other S&M Dancers.
Lindsay Freeman . . . . . . . . . . . . . . . . . . . . . . . . . .Jill
- •• 0:24—Nude on hill with Jack.
Annie Gaybis. . . . . . . . . . . . . . . . . . . . . . Snow White
- ••• 0:21—Nude in room with the seven little dwarfs singing and dancing.
Evelyn Guerrero . . . . . . . . . . . . . . . . . . . .S & M Dancer
- •• 0:38—Breasts wearing masks with two other blonde S&M Dancers.
- •• 0:56—Full frontal nudity dancing with the other S&M Dancers again.
Linnea Quigley . . . . . . . . . . . . . . . . . . . . . . Dream Girl
- • 1:07—Breasts waking up after being kissed by The Prince.
Mariwin Roberts . . . . . . . . . . . . . . . . Elevator Operator
- • 0:20—Brief full frontal nudity in the elevator.
- •• 0:23—Breasts again, closer shot.
Idy Tripoldi . . . . . . . . . . . . . . . . . . . . . . . . Naked Girl
- ••• 0:06—Nude, dancing in bedroom and getting in and out of bed with The Prince.

### Fall From Innocence (1988)
Isabelle Mejias . . . . . . . . . . . . . . . . . . . Marsa Cummins
Amanda Smith . . . . . . . . . . . . . . . . . . . . . .Janis Cummins
- • 0:05—Brief right breast while lying in bed when Bob gets out.
- • 0:48—Left breast, in open nightie top, while walking down hallway.
  0:52—Very brief side view of right breast standing up from the bed.

### Fame (1980)
Irene Cara . . . . . . . . . . . . . . . . . . . . . . . . . . . . . . Coco
  1:16—In leotard, dancing and talking to Hillary.
- • 1:57—Brief breasts during "audition" on a B&W TV monitor.
Meg Tilly . . . . . . . . . . . . . . . . . . . . . . . Principal Dancer

### A Family Matter (1990)
Carol Alt. . . . . . . . . . . . . . . . . . . . . . . . . . . . . Nancy
- •• 1:08—Buns, in panties. Brief side view of left breast with Eric Roberts.
Josie Bell. . . . . . . . . . . . . . . . . . . . . . . . . . . . . Cissy
Eric Roberts . . . . . . . . . . . . . . . . . . . . . Shaun McGinnis

### Family Viewing (1987; Canadian)
Gabrielle Rose . . . . . . . . . . . . . . . . . . . . . . . . . .Sandra
- • 0:27—Brief left breast, lying down with Stan. Seen on TV that Van watches.
- • 0:29—Same 0:27 scene again.
Aidan Tierney. . . . . . . . . . . . . . . . . . . . . . . . . . . . Van
- •• 0:26—Brief buns, while getting up out of bed and putting on his underwear.

### Famous T & A (1982)
(No longer available for purchase, check your video store for rental.)
Elvira . . . . . . . . . . . . . . . . . . . . . . . . . . . . . . .Katya
- ••• 0:28—Breasts scene from *Working Girls*.
Vanity . . . . . . . . . . . . . . . . . . . . . . . . . . . . . Tanya
- • 1:02—Breasts scenes from *Tanya's Island*.
Angela Aames . . . . . . . . . . . . . . . . . . . Little Bo Peep
- • 0:50—Breasts scene from *Fairytales*.
Ursula Andress . . . . . . . . . . . . . . . . . . . . . . .Herself
- ••• 0:15—Full frontal nudity scenes from *Slave of the Cannibal God*.
Brigitte Bardot . . . . . . . . . . . . . . . . . . . . . . . . . .Joan
- • 0:25—Buns, then brief breasts in scene from *Ms. Don Juan*.
Jacqueline Bisset. . . . . . . . . . . . . . . . . . . . . . . .Jenny
- ••• 0:31—Breasts scene from *Secrets*.
Timothy Brown . . . . . . . . . . . . . . . . . . . . . . . . . Mojo
- • 1:05—Buns in outtake from *Sweet Sugar*.
Pamela Collins . . . . . . . . . . . . . . . . . . . . . . Dolores
- ••• 1:05—Breasts in scenes and outtakes from *Sweet Sugar*.
Sybil Danning . . . . . . . . . . . . . . . . . . . . . . . . Hostess
- • 0:00—Brief side view of buns and partial left breast, getting dressed.
Phyllis Davis . . . . . . . . . . . . . . . . . . . . . . . . .Sugar/Joy
- ••• 0:02—Nude in lots of great out-takes from *Terminal Island*. Check this out if you are a Phyllis Davis fan!

••• 0:51—Breasts in scenes from *Sweet Sugar.* Includes more out-takes.

••• 1:04—More out-takes from *Sweet Sugar.*

Uschi Digard . . . . . . . . . . . . . . . . . . . .Truck Stop Woman
•• 0:44—Breasts scenes from *Harry, Cherry & Raquel* and *Truck Stop Women.*

Ella Edwards . . . . . . . . . . . . . . . . . . . . . . . . . . . .Simone
•• 1:07—Buns and breasts in outtakes from *Sweet Sugar.*

Laura Gemser . . . . . . . . . . . . . . . . . . . . . . .Emanuelle
••• 0:55—Breasts scenes from *Emanuelle Around the World.*

Claudia Jennings . . . . . . . . . . . . . . . . . . . . . . . . Rose
•• 0:26—Breasts scenes from *Single Girls* and *Truck Stop Women.*

Laura Jane Leary . . . . . . . . . . . . . . . . Motorcycle Rider
• 0:29—Lower nudity, riding a motorcycle with only a jacket on.

Barbara Leigh . . . . . . . . . . . . . . . . . . . .Bunny Campbell
••• 0:45—Breasts scene from *Terminal Island.* Includes additional takes that weren't used.

Ornella Muti . . . . . . . . . . . . . . . . . . . . . . . . . . . .Lisa
• 0:07—Breasts in scenes from *Summer Affair.* Nude underwater and running around the beach.

Joan Prather . . . . . . . . . . . . . . . . . . . . . . . . . . . Herself
•• 0:49—Brief breasts in scene from *Bloody Friday.*

Victoria Thompson . . . . . . . . . . . . . . . . . . . .Beth Hillyer
• 1:07—Brief breasts and bun scene from *The Harrad Experiment.*
• 1:12—Brief nude, getting up from the floor with Don Johnson.

Idy Tripoldi . . . . . . . . . . . . . . . . . . . . . . . Bonnie Tirol
••• 0:35—Full frontal nude scene from *Auditions.*

Laurie Walters . . . . . . . . . . . . . . . . . . . . . Sheila Grove
• 1:08—Breasts scene from *The Harrad Experiment.*
•• 1:11—Nude pool scene from *The Harrad Experiment.*

Edy Williams . . . . . . . . . . . . . . . . . . . . . . . . . . Herself
•• 0:39—Breasts and bun scenes from *Dr. Minx.*

## The Fanatasist *(1986; Irish)*

Moira Harris . . . . . . . . . . . . . . . . . . . . .Patricia Teeling
• 1:24—Brief breasts and buns climbing onto couch for the weird photographer.
• 1:28—Brief right breast leaning over to kiss the photographer.
• 1:31—Very brief side view of left breast in bathtub.

Gabrielle Reidy . . . . . . . . . . . . . . . . . . . .Kathy O'Malley
• 0:03—Breasts getting attacked in a room.

## Fanny Hill *(1981; British)*

Lisa Raines Foster. . . . . . . . . . . . . . . . . . . . .Fanny Hill
•• 0:09—Nude, getting into bathtub, then drying herself off.
• 0:10—Full frontal nudity getting into bed.
••• 0:12—Full frontal nudity making love with Phoebe in bed.
••• 0:30—Nude, making love in bed with Charles.
•• 0:49—Breasts, whipping her lover, Mr. H., in bed.
•• 0:53—Nude getting into bed with William while Hannah watches through the keyhole.

••• 1:26—Nude, getting out of bed, then running down the stairs to open the door for Charles.

## Fantasies *(1974)*
*a.k.a. Once Upon a Love*

Bo Derek . . . . . . . . . . . . . . . . . . . . . . . . . Anastasia
• 0:03—Left breast, in bathtub.
•• 0:15—Breasts taking off top, then right breast, in bathtub.
• 0:43—Breasts getting her dress top pulled down.
• 0:59—Brief breasts in the water. Very brief full frontal nudity walking back into the house.
• 1:00—Buns and left breast several times outside the window.
• 1:17—Upper left breast, in bathtub again.

Peter Hooten . . . . . . . . . . . . . . . . . . . . . . . . . Damir
• 1:06—Buns, while dropping his towel in front of Bo Derek. Long shot, don't see his face.
• 1:18—Buns again. Same shot from 1:06.

## Far and Away *(1992)*

Tom Cruise . . . . . . . . . . . . . . . . . . . . . .Joseph Donelly
1:02—Upper half of buns, bending over to fix his bedding while Nicole Kidman peeks through hole in room divider.

Thomas Gibson . . . . . . . . . . . . . . . . . . . . . .Stephen

Clint Howard . . . . . . . . . . . . . . . . . . . . . . . . . Flynn

Michelle Johnson . . . . . . . . . . . . . . . . . . . . . .Grace

Nicole Kidman . . . . . . . . . . . . . . . . . . Shannon Christie
1:03—Back half of right breast, seen through sheer room divider when she changes clothes.

## Far From Home *(1989)*

Drew Barrymore. . . . . . . . . . . . . . . . . . . .Joleen Cox
0:40—In wet T-shirt in water with Jimmy.

Jennifer Tilly . . . . . . . . . . . . . . . . . . . . . . . . . . . .Amy

Susan Tyrrell . . . . . . . . . . . . . . . . . . . . . Agnes Reed
• 0:29—Very, very brief right breast in bathtub getting electrocuted.

Teri Weigel. . . . . . . . . . . . . . . . . . . .Woman in Trailer
•• 0:16—Breasts making love when Drew Barrymore peeks in window.

## Far Out Man *(1990)*

Rae Dawn Chong . . . . . . . . . . . . . . . . Rae Dawn Chong

Shelby Chong . . . . . . . . . . . . . . . . . . . . . . . . . .Tree
• 0:11—Very brief side view of left breast, in gaping blouse when she leans over to light a joint.

Tommy Chong. . . . . . . . . . . . . . . . . . . . Far Out Man

C. Thomas Howell . . . . . . . . . . . . . . .C. Thomas Howell

Richard "Cheech" Marin . . . . . . . . . . . . . Cheech Marin

Penelope Reed . . . . . . . . . . . . . . . . . . . . Stewardess

Peggy Sands . . . . . . . . . . . . . . . . . . . . . . . . . Misty
••• 0:50—Breasts and buns in black G-string, undressing and getting into bathtub with Tommy Chong.

## Farewell, My Lovely *(1975; British)*

Charlotte Rampling . . . . . . . . . . . . . . . . . . . . . Velma

Cheryl Smith . . . . . . . . . . . . . . . . . . . . . . . . . Doris
• 0:56—Frontal nudity in bedroom in a bordello with another guy before getting beaten by the madam.

Sylvester Stallone . . . . . . . . . . . . . . . . . . . . Kelly/Jonnie
Harry Dean Stanton. . . . . . . . . . . . . . . . . . . . Billy Rolfe

### Fast Times at Ridgemont High (1982)

Nicolas Cage. . . . . . . . . . . . . . . . . . . . . . . . Brad's Bud
Phoebe Cates . . . . . . . . . . . . . . . . . . . . . Linda Barrett
  ••• 0:50—Breasts getting out of swimming pool during Judge Reinhold's fantasy.
Lana Clarkson . . . . . . . . . . . . . . . . . . . . . . Mrs. Vargas
Anthony Edwards . . . . . . . . . . . . . . . . . . . . Stoner Bud
Ava Lazar . . . . . . . . . . . . . . . . . . . . . . . . . . Playmate
Jennifer Jason Leigh . . . . . . . . . . . . . . . . Stacy Hamilton
  • 0:18—Left breast, while making out with Ron in a dugout.
  ••• 1:00—Breasts in poolside dressing room.
Kelli Maroney . . . . . . . . . . . . . . . . . . . . . . . . . Cindy
Tom Nolan . . . . . . . . . . . . . . . . . . . . . . Dennis Taylor
Sean Penn. . . . . . . . . . . . . . . . . . . . . . . . .Jeff Spicoli
Judge Reinhold . . . . . . . . . . . . . . . . . . Brad Hamilton
James Russo . . . . . . . . . . . . . . . . . . . . . . . . . Robber
Pamela Springsteen . . . . . . . . . . . . . . . . . Dina Phillips
Eric Stoltz . . . . . . . . . . . . . . . . . . . . . . . . Stoner Bud
Lori Sutton . . . . . . . . . . . . . . . . . . . . . . . . . Playmate
Amanda Wyss . . . . . . . . . . . . . . . . . . . . . . . . . . .Lisa

### Fast Walking (1981)

Kay Lenz . . . . . . . . . . . . . . . . . . . . . . . . . . . . Moke
  • 0:26—Brief breasts closing the door after pulling James Woods into the room.
  0:42—Caressing herself under her dress while in prison visiting room, talking to George.
  ••• 1:27—Right breast in store. Breasts getting hosed down and dried off outside by James Woods.
  • 1:32—Brief left breast, making love with Woods.
Tim McIntire. . . . . . . . . . . . . . . . . . . . . . . . . Wasco
Susan Tyrrell . . . . . . . . . . . . . . . . . . . . . . . . . . Evie
M. Emmet Walsh. . . . . . . . . . . . . . Sgt. George Sager
  • 0:59—Frontal nudity standing in the doorway of Evie's mobile home yelling at James Woods after he interrupts Walsh making love with Evie.
James Woods . . . . . . . . . . . . . . . . Fast-Walking Miniver

### Fatal Attraction (1987)

Anne Archer . . . . . . . . . . . . . . . . . . . . Ellen Gallagher
  0:51—In white bra, sitting in front of mirror, getting ready for a party.
Glenn Close . . . . . . . . . . . . . . . . . . . . . . .Alex Forrest
  •• 0:17—Left breast when she opens her top to let Michael Douglas kiss her. Then very brief buns, falling into bed with him.
  • 0:20—Brief right breast in freight elevator with Douglas.
  ••• 0:32—Breasts in bed talking to Douglas. Long scene, sheet keeps changing positions between cuts.
Michael Douglas . . . . . . . . . . . . . . . . . . Dan Gallagher
  •• 0:16—Brief buns, while pulling his pants down to make love with Glenn Close on the kitchen sink.
  • 0:17—Very brief buns while falling into bed with Close.
  • 0:22—Brief buns, while taking a shower.

### Fatal Attraction (1981; Canadian)

*a.k.a. Head On*
Sally Kellerman. . . . . . . . . . . . . . . . . . . . .Michelle Keys
  • 0:46—Brief breasts in building making out with a guy. Dark, hard to see.
  1:19—Brief half of left breast, after struggling with a guy.

### Fatal Bond (1991; Australian)

Linda Blair . . . . . . . . . . . . . . . . . . . . . . . . . . . Leonie
  •• 0:25—Brief right breast out of her slip, while making love on top of Joe in bed.
  1:00—Breasts and buns, while washing herself off in shower. Seen behind textured glass door.
Jerome Ehlers . . . . . . . . . . . . . . . . . . . . Joe Martinez
  •• 0:08—Buns and lower frontal nudity while getting up out of bed.

### Fatal Charm (1992; Made for Cable Movie)

Christopher Atkins . . . . . . . . . . . . . . . . . Adam Brenner
Tracy Dali. . . . . . . . . . . . . . . . . . . . . . . .Dream Girl
  •• 0:11—Breasts in van with Christopher Atkins. Lots of diffusion.
  • 0:20—Brief breasts in van during Amanda Peterson's fantasy.
James Remar . . . . . . . . . . . . . . . . . . . . . . . . Louise

### Fatal Games (1984)

Angela Bennett . . . . . . . . . . . . . . . . . . .Sue Allen Baines
  •• 0:21—Full frontal nudity in the sauna with Teal Roberts.
  • 0:23—Nude, running around the school, trying to get away from the killer. Dark.
Sally Kirkland . . . . . . . . . . . . . . . . . . . . . Diane Paine
Melissa Prophet . . . . . . . . . . . . . . . . . . . Nancy Wilson
  • 0:14—Buns and side view of left breast in shower with other girls. Long shot. (She's wearing a white towel on her head.)
Linnea Quigley . . . . . . . . . . . . . . . . . . . . . . . .Athelete
Teal Roberts . . . . . . . . . . . . . . . . . . . . . . . Lynn Fox
  ••• 0:08—Breasts on bed and floor when Frank takes her clothes off, more breasts in shower.
  •• 0:21—Breasts in sauna with Sue.
Brinke Stevens . . . . . . . . . . . . . Uncredited Shower Girl
  • 0:14—Brief, out of focus side of left breast and upper half of buns, taking a shower in the background while two girls talk. (She's wearing a light blue towel around her hair.)

### Fatal Instinct (1991)

*a.k.a. To Kill For*
(Unrated version reviewed.)
Laura Johnson . . . . . . . . . . . . . . . . . .Catherine Merrims
  • 0:45—Brief left breast in open robe, getting out of bed.
  ••• 0:47—Breasts in bed talking with Michael Madsen, then making love.
  ••• 0:51—Breasts in the bathtub when Bill comes in. Partial lower frontal nudity when standing up.
  •• 0:52—Brief buns and breasts getting dressed in bedroom.

- 0:59—In wet T-shirt in pool. Brief buns, underwater, more when getting out.

Michael Madsen . . . . . . . . . . . . . . . . . . . . Cliff Burden
- 0:43—Half of buns, while lying in bed.
- • 0:48—Upper half of buns, while making love in bed with Laura Johnson.

Kim McKamy . . . . . . . . . . . . . Frank Stegner's Girlfriend
- • 0:01—Breasts, opening her towel in front of Frank at night before he gets shot.

Scott Mitchell . . . . . . . . . . . . . . . . . Beaumont Detective

## Fatal Justice (1992)
Suzanne Ager . . . . . . . . . . . . . . . . . . . . . . . Diana
- • • 0:12—In black body suit, then breasts and buns in G-string while making love with her boyfriend.
- 0:36—Breasts while changing clothes behind room divider. Hard to see.

## Fatal Mission (1990)
Tia Carrere . . . . . . . . . . . . . . . . . . . . . . Mai Chang
- 0:22—Side view of right breast while changing tops. Dark.

Peter Fonda. . . . . . . . . . . . . . . . . . . . . . Ken Andrews

## Fatal Pulse (1987)
Roxanne Kernohan . . . . . . . . . . . . . . . . . . . . . Ann
- 0:58—Brief breasts in yellow outfit before getting thrown out of the window.

Christie Mucciante . . . . . . . . . . . . . . . . . . . . Karen
- • 0:52—Breasts, getting dressed for bed.

Sky Nicholas . . . . . . . . . . . . . . . . . . . . . . . Sheila
- • • 0:36—Breasts in bathtub, taking a bath, then getting killed. Long scene.

## Fatal Skies (1989)
Kim Anderson . . . . . . . . . . . . . . . . . . . . . . . Cindy
- 0:48—Buns in lingerie, while posing for Lance in his office.

Veronica Carothers . . . . . . . . . . . . . . . . . . . . Toni
- • 0:31—Buns, while putting on swimsuit bottom.
- • 0:32—Breasts, while putting on swimsuit top.

J. Michael Esposito . . . . . . . . . . . . . . . . . . . Duane
- 0:31—Buns, while standing in the water, then diving in.

Melissa Anne Moore . . . . . . . . . . . . . . . . . . . Suzy

## Fatso (1980)
Dom DeLuise . . . . . . . . . . . . . . . Dominick DiNapoli
- 0:26—Brief buns in open back hospital gown while walking in hallway past a woman.

## Fear (1991; Made for Cable Movie)
Michelle Foreman . . . . . . . . . . . . . . . Gale the Stripper
- 0:50—Breasts and buns dancing in bar. Hard to see because seen through the killer's eyes.

Lauren Hutton. . . . . . . . . . . . . . . . . . . Jessica Moreau
Ally Sheedy . . . . . . . . . . . . . . . . . . . . . Cayce Bridges

## Fear City (1984)
Maria Conchita Alonso . . . . . . . . . . . . . Silver Chavez
Tom Berenger . . . . . . . . . . . . . . . . . . . . . . Matt Rossi

Rae Dawn Chong. . . . . . . . . . . . . . . . . . . . . Leila
- • • 0:26—Breasts and buns, dancing on stage.
- 0:50—Brief breasts in the hospital getting a shock to get her heart started.

Emilia Crow . . . . . . . . . . . . . . . . . . . . . . . . Bibi
- • 0:16—Breasts, dancing at the Metropole club.
- 1:00—Breasts, dancing on the stage.

Melanie Griffith . . . . . . . . . . . . . . . . . . . . Loretta
  0:04—Buns, in blue G-string, dancing on stage.
- • 0:07—Breasts, dancing on stage.
- • • 0:23—Breasts dancing on stage wearing a red G-string.

Tracy Griffith . . . . . . . . . . . . . . . . . Sandra Cook
Janet Julian. . . . . . . . . . . . . . . . . . . . . . . . . Ruby
Joy Michael . . . . . . . . . . . . . . . . . . . Metropole Dancer
Joe Palese. . . . . . . . . . . . . . . . . . . . . . . . . . Tony
Ola Ray . . . . . . . . . . . . . . . . . . . . . Honey Powers

## The Fear Inside (1992; Made for Cable Movie)
Jennifer Rubin. . . . . . . . . . . . . . . . . . . Jane Caswell
- 0:26—Breasts with Peter. Hard to see because of the strobe light effect.
- 0:53—Buns and partial left breast visible under water while skinny dipping in pool.
  0:55—Full frontal nudity under water. Hard to see because of the distortion.

## Fear No Evil (1981)
Stefan Arngrim. . . . . . . . . . . . . . . . . . . . . . Andrew
- • 0:37—Buns, in the back corner of the showers while getting teased by the other boys.
- 0:45—Buns, while leaving bedroom during Julie's dream encounter.

Daniel Eden . . . . . . . . . . . . . . . . . . . . . . . . Tony
- 0:21—Brief buns, while chasing after Marie in basement of school building. Long shot.
- • 0:37—Buns and brief frontal nudity, after getting up off the shower floor.

## Fear of Scandal (1992; Italian)
Linda Carol . . . . . . . . . . . . . . . . . . . . . . . . . Anna
- 0:21—Brief left breast, while making love with a guy in bed.
- 0:42—Left breast, while making love in bed.
- • 0:43—Breasts, while covering herself with the bed covers.

## Fearless (1978)
Joan Collins . . . . . . . . . . . . . . . . . . . . . . Bridgitte
- 0:01—In bra and panties, then brief right breast during opening credits.
- • 0:41—Breasts after doing a strip tease routine on stage.
- 1:17—Undressing in front of Wally in white bra and panties, then right breast.
- 1:20—Brief right breast lying dead on couch.

## The Fearless Hyena, Part II (1984; Chinese)
Jackie Chan . . . . . . . . . . . . . . . . . . . . . . Chan Lung
- 0:06—Brief buns, jumping up in the water while trying to catch a fish. Don't see his face clearly.

### The Fearless Vampire Killers (1967)

Fiona Lewis . . . . . . . . . . . . . . . . . . . . . . . . . . . Maid
Sharon Tate. . . . . . . . . . . . . . . . . . . . . Sarah Shagal
- 0:24—Very, very brief breasts struggling in bathtub with vampire. Hard to see.

### Felicity (1978; Australian)

Glory Annen . . . . . . . . . . . . . . . . . . . . . . . . . . Felicity
- • 0:02—Breasts taking off leotard in girl's shower room, then nude taking a shower.
- 0:05—Buns, then left breast, then right breast undressing to go skinny dipping.
- • 0:10—Breasts and buns at night at the girl's dormitory with Jenny.
- • 0:15—Breasts undressing in room in front of Christine.
- 0:16—Left breast, while touching herself in bed.
- • • 0:20—Lots of lower frontal nudity trying on clothes, bras and panties in dressing room. Brief breasts and buns.
- • • 0:25—Buns and breasts taking a bath. Full frontal nudity when Steve peeks in at her.
- 0:31—Brief full frontal nudity losing her virginity on car with Andrew.
- • • 0:38—Full frontal nudity in bath with Mei Ling and two other girls, then getting massaged. Long scene.
- • • 0:58—Full frontal nudity in bed with Miles.
- • • 1:13—Full frontal nudity with Mei Ling making love on bed. Long scene.
- 1:20—Left breast, while making love standing up.
- • 1:21—Breasts and buns making love with Miles.
- • 1:27—Nude making love again with Miles.
- 1:29—Buns, in the water with Miles.

Joni Flynn . . . . . . . . . . . . . . . . . . . . . . . . . Mei Ling
- • • 0:38—Nude in bath with Glory Annen and two other girls, then getting massaged. Long scene.
- • • 0:43—Breasts and buns, making love on boat with a guy.
- • • 1:13—Nude, making love in bed with Glory. Long scene.

### Fellow Traveller (1989; Made for Cable Movie)

Imogen Stubbs . . . . . . . . . . . . . . . . . . . Sarah Aitchison
- 0:54—Breasts in bed with Asa. Very, very brief right breast when he rolls off her.

Sarah Trigger . . . . . . . . . . . . . . . . . . . . . . . . Gloria
- • 0:02—Breasts, sitting up in bed, stretching, then getting out.

### Female Trouble (1974)

Divine . . . . . . . . . . . . . . . . . . . . . Dawn Davenport/Earl
- 0:15—Buns, wiggling and dancing in white bra and G-string on stage.
- 0:58—Close-up of penis, while showing it to Taffy. Don't see his face.

Elizabeth Coffey . . . . . . . . . . . . . . . . . . . . . . Ernestine
- 1:24—Right breast, while lying on cot in jail cell with Divine.
- 1:25—More right breast.
- 1:26—Brief lower frontal nudity when kissing Divine.

Edith Massey . . . . . . . . . . . . . . . . . . . . . . . . . . . . Ida
- • 0:20—Breasts, massaging her breasts in front of the mirror.

Michael Potter . . . . . . . . . . . . . . . . . . . . . . . . . . . Gater
- 0:27—Nude, caught in bed with another woman by Divine.
- • • • 0:28—Buns, making love in bed on top of Divine.
- • • • 0:29—Frontal nudity, sitting in bed, talking to Taffy.
- • • 0:31—More buns, while making love on top of Divine. Frontal nudity after sticking a carrot in her mouth.

### Femme Fatale (1990)

Lisa Blount . . . . . . . . . . . . . . . . . . . . . . . . . . . Jenny
Colin Firth . . . . . . . . . . . . . . . . . . . . . . . . Joseph Prince
Suzanne Snyder . . . . . . . . . . . . . . . . . . . . . . . . Andrea
- • • • 0:08—Breasts, nonchalantly taking off her top and posing for Billy Zane's painting. (She sometimes has a bag over her head.)
- • • 0:46—Breasts posing again with the bag on and off her head.

Billy Zane . . . . . . . . . . . . . . . . . . . . . . Elijah Hooper
Lisa Zane . . . . . . . . . . . . . . . . . . . . . . . . Cynthia

### Fever (1991; Made for Cable Movie)

Teresa Gilmore-Capps . . . . . . . . . . . . . . . . . . . Jeanine
Marcia Gay Harden . . . . . . . . . . . . . . . . . . . . . . Lacy
- 0:18—Brief breasts making love in bed with Sam Neill.
- • • 1:31—In bra in bed with bad guy, then breasts when he opens her bra. Kind of dark.

Joe Spano. . . . . . . . . . . . . . . . . . . . . . . . . . Junkman

### Fever Pitch (1985)

Catherine Hicks . . . . . . . . . . . . . . . . . . . . . . . . . Flo
- 0:11—Brief left breast, while sitting on bed in hotel room talking with Ryan O'Neal.

Cherie Michan . . . . . . . . . . . . . . . . . . . Rose O'Sharon
Ryan O'Neal . . . . . . . . . . . . . . . . . . . . . . . . Taggart

### The Fifth Floor (1978)

John David Carson . . . . . . . . . . . . . . . . Ronnie Denton
Patti D'Arbanville . . . . . . . . . . . . . . . . . . . . Cathy Burke
Sharon Farrell . . . . . . . . . . . . . . . . . . . . . . . . Melanie
Dianne Hull . . . . . . . . . . . . . . . . . . . . . Kelly McIntyre
- • • 0:29—Breasts and buns in shower while Carl watches, then brief full frontal nudity running out of the shower.
- • • 1:09—Breasts in whirlpool bath getting visited by Carl again, then raped.

### The Fifth Monkey (1990)

Vera Fischer . . . . . . . . . . . . . . . . . . . . . . . Mrs. Watts
Ben Kingsley. . . . . . . . . . . . . . . . . . . . . . . . . Kunda
- 1:04—Brief buns, while standing under waterfall. Don't see his face and water is in the way.

### The Final Alliance (1990)
David Hasselhoff . . . . . . . . . . . . . . . . . . . . . Will Colton
Jeanie Moore. . . . . . . . . . . . . . . . . . . . . . . . . . . . Carrie
- • 1:03—Brief breasts getting into bed with David Hasselhoff, then brief right breast twice in bed with him. A little dark.

### Final Analysis (1992)
Kim Basinger. . . . . . . . . . . . . . . . . . . . . . .Heather Evans
- •• 0:21—Right breast, while making love in bed under Richard Gere.

Richard Gere. . . . . . . . . . . . . . . . . . . . . . . Dr. Isaac Barr
- ••• 0:21—Buns while, making love on top of Kim Basinger in bed.

Shelley Michelle . . . . . . . Body Double for Kim Basinger
Eric Roberts. . . . . . . . . . . . . . . . . . . . . . . . . Jimmy Evans
Uma Thurman. . . . . . . . . . . . . . . . . . . . . . Diana Baylor

### Final Embrace (1991)
Linda Doná . . . . . . . . . . . . . . . . . . . . . . . . . . . . . . Jeri
Robert Rusler. . . . . . . . . . . . . . . . . . . . . Kyle Lambdon
- •• 0:05—Buns, while standing up next to bed and putting his pants on.
- • 1:00—Buns, while making love in bed with Laurel.

Nancy Valen . . . . . . . . . . . . . . Candy Vale/Laurel Parrish

### Final Exam (1981)
Deanna Robbins . . . . . . . . . . . . . . . . . . . . . . . . . .Lisa
- •• 1:13—Buns and breasts, after taking off dress and covering herself with a sheet in studio.

### Final Judgement (1992)
Karen Black. . . . . . . . . . . . . . . . . . . . . . . . Mrs. Sorrel
Brad Dourif . . . . . . . . . . . . . . . . . . . . . .Father Tyrone
Maria Ford . . . . . . . . . . . . . . . . . . . . . . . . . . . .Nicole
- ••• 0:20—Breasts and buns in G-string while stripping and dancing on stage. Nice bending over action.
- ••• 0:39—In red bra and panties, then breasts and buns while dancing on stage.
- ••• 0:52—Breasts and buns in G-string while dancing on stage.
- • 0:56—Very, very brief breast, while putting a towel around herself after getting out of the shower.
- •• 0:58—Breasts while making love with Brad Dourif in bed during daydream.

Lisa Inouye . . . . . . . . . . . . . . . . . . . . . . . . . . . . Lily
- •• 0:32—Breasts, walking up behind Rob in room, then making love. Brief buns in G-string, getting out of bed. Side view of breasts in mirror.
- • 1:01—Buns in lingerie in mirror.

David Ledingham . . . . . . . . . . . . . . . . . Robert Sorel
- • 0:12—Buns, while walking around in his studio.

Toni Naples. . . . . . . . . . . . . . . . . . . . . . . . Dancer #2
- • 0:51—Breasts, while dancing on stage, wearing sunglasses.

Sherrie Rose . . . . . . . . . . . . . . . . . . . Amanda Peterson
Roberta Vasquez . . . . . . . . . . . . . . . . . . . . . . Whitney

### Final Mission (1993)
Corbin Bernsen . . . . . . . . . . . . General Morgan Breslaw
Elizabeth Gracen . . . . . . . . . . . . . . . . . . . . . Caitlin Cole
- ••• 0:28—Breasts, while making out with Billy Wirth.
- • 0:53—Breasts, while making love on bed with Wirth at night.

Steve Railsback. . . . . . . . . . . . . Colonel Olen Anderson

### Final Round (1993)
Kathleen Kinmont . . . . . . . . . . . . . . . . . . . . . . Jordan
- 0:17—In black bra, panties, garter belt and stockings in room with Lorenzo Lamas.
- ••• 0:18—Breasts, while making love on the floor with Lamas.

### The Finest Hour (1991)
Tracy Griffith . . . . . . . . . . . . . . . . . . . . . . . . . Barbara
- • 0:21—In wet, braless, white dress, getting out of the water after canoe tips over.
- • 1:02—Swimming with Mazzoli under water in ocean in a wet, braless, white dress.
- • 1:03—Brief side view of right breast, while taking the wet dress off.

Rob Lowe. . . . . . . . . . . . . . . . . . . . . . . . . . . . Hammer

### Fingers (1978)
Tisa Farrow. . . . . . . . . . . . . . . . . . . . . . . . . . . . Carol
Harvey Keitel . . . . . . . . . . . . . . . . . . Jimmy Angelelli
- • 0:39—Brief partial frontal nudity several times, visible under his shirt, after getting his rectum examined by a doctor.

Ed Marinaro. . . . . . . . . . . . . . . . . . . . . . . . . . . Gino
Zack Norman. . . . . . . . . . . . . . . . . . . . . . . . . . .Cop
Tanya Roberts . . . . . . . . . . . . . . . . . . . . . . . . . Julie

### The Finishing Touch (1991)
Delia Goldson . . . . . . . . . . . . . . . . . . .Sorvino's Model
- •• 1:06—In lingerie outfit, then breasts while handcuffed to bed while getting video taped by Sorvino.

### Fiona (1978; British)
Linda Regan. . . . . . . . . . . . . . . . . . . . . . . . Secretary
Fiona Richmond . . . . . . . . . . . . . . Fiona Richmond
- •• 0:23—Breasts on boat with a blonde woman rubbing oil on her.
- •• 0:27—In a bra, then frontal nudity stripping in a guy's office for an audition.
- •• 0:35—Breasts, then frontal nudity lying down during photo session.
- • 0:51—Breasts walking around her apartment in boots.
- •• 1:00—Breasts with old guy ripping each other's clothes off.
- •• 1:08—Frontal nudity taking off clothes for a shower.

### Fire Birds (1990)
a.k.a. Wings of the Apache
Nicolas Cage . . . . . . . . . . . . . . . . . . . . . .Jake Preston
Tommy Lee Jones. . . . . . . . . . . . . . . . . . . . Brad Little
Sean Young . . . . . . . . . . . . . . . . . . . Billie Lee Guthrie
- • 0:52—Very, very brief right breast twice in bed with Nicolas Cage.

### Firecracker (1981)

Darby Hinton . . . . . . . . . . . . . . . . . . . . Chuck Donner
- • 1:01—Brief upper half of buns, then buns, while making love with Jillian Kesner in bed.

Jillian Kesner . . . . . . . . . . . . . . . . . . . . . Susanne Carter
0:42—In bra and panties, while running around, trying to get away from bad guys.
- ••• 0:44—Breasts, while fighting bad guys after her bra comes off. Nice!
- ••• 0:58—In panties on bed, then buns as Darby Hinton cuts her clothes off with a knife. Breasts while making love with him in bed.

### Firehouse (1987)

Ruth Corrine Collins . . . . . . . . . . . . . . . . . . . Bubbles
Gianna Rains . . . . . . . . . . . . . . . . . . . . . Barrett Hopkins
- ••• 0:33—Breasts taking a shower, then drying herself just before the fire alarm goes off.
- •• 0:56—Breasts making love with the reporter on the roof of a building.

### Fires Within (1991)

Greta Scacchi . . . . . . . . . . . . . . . . . . . . . . . . Isabel
- • 0:18—Upper half of buns, very brief breasts in bed. 0:19—In bra, changing clothes.
- • 0:38—Very brief breasts in bed.

Jimmy Smits . . . . . . . . . . . . . . . . . . . . . . . . Nestor

### First Love (1977)

Beverly D'Angelo. . . . . . . . . . . . . . . . . . . . . Shelley
0:05—Very, very brief half of left breast when her jacket opens up while talking to William Katt.
0:11—In white bra and black panties in Katt's bedroom.
- • 1:10—Brief breasts taking off her top in bedroom with Katt.

Susan Dey. . . . . . . . . . . . . . . . . . . . . . Caroline Hedges
- ••• 0:31—Breasts making love in bed with William Katt. Long scene.
- • 0:51—Breasts taking off her top in her bedroom with Katt.

John Heard . . . . . . . . . . . . . . . . . . . . . . . David
William Katt . . . . . . . . . . . . . . . . . . . . . . . Elgin Smith

### First Name: Carmen (1983; French)

Maruschka Detmers . . . . . . . . . . . . . . . . . . . . Carmen
- ••• 0:36—Breasts while standing by window with a guy.
- •• 0:40—Breasts several times while in bedroom with Joseph.
- • 0:42—Lower frontal nudity (out of focus) while talking to Joseph. Long scene.
- • 0:44—Brief lower frontal nudity with Joseph.
- • 0:46—More lower frontal nudity.
- •• 0:58—Nude, after Joseph takes off her robe.
- •• 1:07—Breasts while undressing in bedroom.
- ••• 1:08—Breasts in red panties, getting out of bed and walking through the house, sitting on couch and lying on bed. Long scene.
- ••• 1:13—Brief full frontal nudity in bathroom and in shower.

Myriem Roussel. . . . . . . . . . . . . . . . . . . . . . . n.a.

### The First Nudie Musical (1979)

Leslie Ackerman . . . . . . . . . . . . . . . . . . . . . . . Susie
Alexandra Morgan . . . . . . . . . . . . . . . . . . . Mary La Rue
- • 0:54—Breasts, singing and dancing during dancing dildo routine.
- ••• 1:04—Full frontal nudity in bed trying to do a take. 1:07—Breasts in bed with a guy with a continuous erection.
- •• 1:17—Breasts in bed in another scene.

### The First Power (1990)

Susan Giosa . . . . . . . . . . . . . . . . . . . . . . . . Carmen
0:12—In bra when the killer opens her blouse.
- • 0:22—Brief right breast, lying dead with a bloody pentagram cut into her stomach.

Tracy Griffith . . . . . . . . . . . . . . . . . . . . Tess Seaton
Lou Diamond Phillips . . . . . . . . . . . . . . . . Russell Logan
Melanie Shatner. . . . . . . . . . . . . . . . . . . . . . Shopgirl

### The First Turn-On! (1983)

Georgia Harrell. . . . . . . . . . . . . . . . . . . Michelle Farmer
- ••• 1:17—Breasts and brief buns in cave with everybody during orgy scene.

Sheila Kennedy. . . . . . . . . . . . . . . . . . . . . Dreamgirl
- • 0:52—In red two piece swimsuit, then breasts when the top falls down during Danny's daydream.
- • 0:59—Right breast, while in bed with Danny.

Michael Sanville . . . . . . . . . . . . . . . . . . . . . . . Mitch
- • 1:18—Buns, while in cave orgy scene on top of Annie.

Mark Torgl . . . . . . . . . . . . . . . . . . . . . . . Dwayne
- • 1:02—Buns, while dropping his pants for Michelle.

### A Fish Called Wanda (1988)

John Cleese . . . . . . . . . . . . . . . . . . . . . . . Archie
- • 1:13—Very brief upper half of buns, in house when he's surprised by the returning family. Looks like very, very brief frontal nudity when he stands up after pulling his underwear down.

Jamie Lee Curtis . . . . . . . . . . . . . . . . . . . . . Wanda
0:21—In black bra and panties changing in the bedroom talking to Kevin Kline.
0:35—In black bra sitting on bed getting undressed.

Kevin Kline. . . . . . . . . . . . . . . . . . . . . . . . Otto
Michael Palin . . . . . . . . . . . . . . . . . . . . . . . . Ken

### The Fisher King (1991)

Jeff Bridges. . . . . . . . . . . . . . . . . . . . . . . . . Jack
Michael Jeter . . . . . . . . . . . . . Homeless Cabaret Singer
Amanda Plummer . . . . . . . . . . . . . . . . . . . . . Lydia
Robin Williams . . . . . . . . . . . . . . . . . . . . . . Parry
- ••• 0:58—Nude, dancing around in the park at night with Jeff Bridges.

### Fist of Honor (1993)

Joey House. . . . . . . . . . . . . . . . . . . . . . . . . Gina
- • 0:19—Side of right breast and buns, after undressing in front of Sam Jones.

Sam Jones . . . . . . . . . . . . . . . . . . . . . . . . . Fist

## Fit To Kill (1993)

Cynthia Brimhall . . . . . . . . . . . . . . . . . . . . . Edy Stark
•• 1:00—Breasts under sheer white body suit while posing for her boyfriend while he photographs her.

Ava Cadell . . . . . . . . . . . . . . . . . . . . . . . . . . . . . . Ava
1:10—In black bra and panties, while talking on the phone.
•• 1:13—Half of right breast, sticking out of bra. Buns in G-string.
•• 1:14—Left breast, while making love with Petrov in radio station while still talking on the air.
••• 1:17—Breasts in spa with Petrov.

Brett Clark . . . . . . . . . . . . . . . . . . . . . . . . . . . Burke

Carolyn Liu . . . . . . . . . . . . . . . . . . . . . . . . . . . Silk
• 0:09—Buns in body suit, while in room with Kane.
•• 0:11—Breasts while making love in bed with Kane.
••• 0:46—Breasts, while taking off lingerie on boat with Kane.
0:49—In two piece swimsuit.

Michael Jay Shane . . . . . . . . . . . . . . . . . . Shane Abilene

Dona Speir . . . . . . . . . . . . . . . . . . . . . Donna Hamilton
•• 0:21—Breasts and buns in G-string, while undressing and putting dresses on with Vasquez.
0:55—In two piece swimsuit.
••• 1:18—Buns in two piece swimsuit, then breasts during Kane's fantasy.
1:29—In two piece swimsuit.

Julie Strain . . . . . . . . . . . . . . . . . . . . . . . . . . Blu Steele
•• 0:10—Buns in swimsuit while doing stretching exercises.
•• 0:11—Breasts, undoing her swimsuit top.
•• 0:47—Breasts and buns in G-string, while making love in the kitchen with Brett Clark.
0:49—In one piece swimsuit.

Roberta Vasquez . . . . . . . . . . . . . . . . . . . . . Nicole Justin
•• 0:21—Breasts and buns in G-string, while undressing and putting dresses on with Speir.
••• 0:52—Breasts and buns, while making love with her boyfriend in bed.
0:55—In two piece swimsuit.
1:29—In two piece swimsuit.

Sándra Wild . . . . . . . . . . . . . . . . . . . . . . . . . . . . Sandy
••• 0:07—Breasts, while talking on phone while standing in spa. Buns in gold swimsuit bottom, while getting out. Breasts while pouring coffee.
••• 0:21—Breasts in spa in long shot. More breasts in closer shot while putting swimsuit on.
0:55—In two piece swimsuit.
• 1:11—Buns, while wearing a sexy black swimsuit/lingerie outfit.
1:30—In two piece swimsuit.

## Five Easy Pieces (1970)

Susan Anspach . . . . . . . . . . . . . . . . Catherine Van Oost
Toni Basil . . . . . . . . . . . . . . . . . . . . . . . . Terry Grouse
Karen Black . . . . . . . . . . . . . . . . . . . . Rayette Dipesto
0:48—In sheer black nightie in bathroom, then walking to bedroom with Jack Nicholson.
Helena Kallianiotes . . . . . . . . . . . . . . . . . Palm Apodaca
Jack Nicholson . . . . . . . . . . . . . . . . . . . . Robert Dupea

Sally Struthers . . . . . . . . . . . . . . . . . . . . . . . . . . Betty
0:15—In a bra sitting on a couch in the living room with Jack Nicholson and another man and a woman.
•• 0:34—Brief breasts a couple of times making love with Nicholson. Lots of great moaning, but hard to see anything.

## A Flash of Green (1984)

Blair Brown . . . . . . . . . . . . . . . Catherine "Kat" Hubble
• 1:30—Very brief right breast moving around in bed with Ed Harris.
Joan Goodfellow . . . . . . . . . . . . . . . . . . . . . Mitchie
Ed Harris . . . . . . . . . . . . . . . . . . . . . . . . . Jimmy Wing

## Flashdance (1983)

Belinda Bauer . . . . . . . . . . . . . . . . . . . . . . Katie Hurley
Jennifer Beals . . . . . . . . . . . . . . . . . . . . . . . . . . . Alex
Malcolm Danare . . . . . . . . . . . . . . . . . . . . . . . . . Cecil
Monique Gabrielle . . . . . . . . . . . . . Uncredited Stripper
•• 1:27—Buns, in G-string, walking down walkway of stage in club. Brief breasts, accepting a bill in her red G-string.
Marine Jahan
. . . . . . . . . Uncredited Dance Double for Jennifer Beals
Sunny Johnson . . . . . . . . . . . . . . . . . . . . . Jennie Szabo
• 1:28—Breasts, while sitting on stage and moving her legs around.
• 1:29—Very brief left breast in open rain coat, when Jennifer Beals grabs money outside.
Dirga McBroom . . . . . . . . . . . . . . . . . . . . . . . Heels
Michael Nouri . . . . . . . . . . . . . . . . . . . . . Nick Hurley

## Flashfire (1993)

Kristin Minter . . . . . . . . . . . . . . . . . . . . . . . . Lisa Cates
•• 0:18—In black bra, panties, garter belt and stockings, then breasts while in hotel room with Artie.
•• 0:20—Breasts while making love in bed with Artie.
•• 0:21—Breasts when hit men burst into the room and kill Artie.
• 0:49—Buns in panties and side of right breast while undressing when Billy Zane sees her.
••• 1:11—Breasts, while making love on bed in a boat with Zane.
Billy Zane . . . . . . . . . . . . . . . . . . . . . . . . Jack Flinder

## Flashpoint (1984)

Kris Kristofferson . . . . . . . . . . . . . . . . . . . . . . Logan
Rip Torn . . . . . . . . . . . . . . . . . . . . . . . . . Sheriff Wells
Treat Williams . . . . . . . . . . . . . . . . . . . . . . . . Ernie
•• 0:03—Buns, putting on pants in locker room while talking to Kris Kristofferson.

## Flesh + Blood (1985)

Nancy Cartwright . . . . . . . . . . . . . . . . . . . . Kathleen
• 0:28—Brief breasts showing Jennifer Jason Leigh how to make love. Long shot.
Rutger Hauer . . . . . . . . . . . . . . . . . . . . . . . . . Martin
• 1:35—Buns, while in a jock strap running up stairs after everybody throws their clothes into the fire.
Jennifer Jason Leigh . . . . . . . . . . . . . . . . . . . . Agnes
• 0:45—Brief right breast, while being held down.

•• 1:05—Full frontal nudity getting into the bath with Rutger Hauer and making love.

••• 1:16—Full frontal nudity getting out of bed with Hauer and walking to the window.

•• 1:35—Full frontal nudity, while throwing clothes into the fire.

•• 1:36—Breasts, when Hauer removes sheet that covers her.

•• 1:37—Buns and long shot brief side view of right breast, while walking to the castle behind Hauer. Brief breasts when stopped on stairs while watching Tom Burlinson throw food into well.

Blanca Marsillach . . . . . . . . . . . . . . . . . . . . . . . . . . Clara

•• 0:11—Full frontal nudity on bed having convulsions after getting hit on the head with a sword.

Marina Saura . . . . . . . . . . . . . . . . . . . . . . . . . . . . . . Polly

• 0:59—Brief left breast during feast in the castle.

• 1:09—Breasts on balcony of the castle with everybody during the day.

Jack Thompson . . . . . . . . . . . . . . . . . . . . . . Hawkwood

Susan Tyrrell . . . . . . . . . . . . . . . . . . . . . . . . . . . . Celine

• 1:35—Right breast sticking out of her dress when everybody throws their clothes into the fire.

## Flesh and Bone (1993)

Ron Kuhlman . . . . . . . . . . . . . . . . . . . . . . Clem Willets

Gwyneth Paltrow . . . . . . . . . . . . . . . . . . . . . . . Ginnie

•• 1:09—Left breast, while in motel room, talking with Meg Ryan.

Dennis Quaid . . . . . . . . . . . . . . . . . . . . . Arlis Sweeney

Meg Ryan . . . . . . . . . . . . . . . . . . . . . . . . . Kay Davies

•• 0:59—Right breast, several times, while making love with Dennis Quaid in bed.

Christopher Rydell. . . . . . . . . . . . . . . . . . . Resse Davies

Barbara Alyn Woods . . . . . . . . . . . . . . . . . . . . . . Cindy

• 0:16—Partial buns, while lying on her stomach on bed.

## Flesh Gordon 2 (1990; Canadian)

Morgan Fox . . . . . . . . . . . . . . . . . . . Robunda Hooters

•• 0:12—Breasts, while opening her top to get Flesh Gordon excited.

• 1:07—Brief breasts when her top is opened by the Evil Presence to get Flesh aroused.

Kathleen Kane. . . . . . . . . . . . . . . . . . . . . . . Girl in Car

Robyn Kelly. . . . . . . . . . . . . . . . . . . . . . . . Dale Ardor

•• 0:24—Brief breasts in push-up bra when Dr. Jerkoff rips her jacket open.

• 0:49—Brief buns, while acting like a dog on all fours on the floor.

Melissa Mounds . . . . . . . . . . . . . . . . Bazonga Bomber

••• 0:46—Breasts standing by table with Flesh Gordon and Dr. Jerkoff.

••• 0:48—More breasts with Dr. Jerkoff.

Vince Murdocco . . . . . . . . . . . . . . . . . . . Flesh Gordon

•• 0:00—Buns, while trying to save Dale.

## Flirting (1992; Australian)

Nicole Kidman . . . . . . . . . . . . . . . . . . . Nicola Radcliffe

Thandie Newton . . . . . . . . . . . . . . . . Thandiwe Adjewa

•• 1:30—Brief breasts, getting out of bed and putting a coat on over herself after getting caught with Danny.

Kiri Paramore . . . . . . . . . . . . . . . . . . . . . . "Slag" Green

• 0:03—Brief buns, after showing his school mates his whip marks (He's the guy in the middle).

Josh Picker . . . . . . . . . . . . . . . . . . . . . "Backa" Bourke

• 0:03—Brief buns, after showing his school mates his whip marks (He's the guy on the left).

Noah Taylor. . . . . . . . . . . . . . . . . . . . Danny Embling

• 0:03—Close up of buns, when his school mates check out his whip marks with flashlight. Don't see his face.

## The Fly (1986)

Joy Boushel . . . . . . . . . . . . . . . . . . . . . . . . . . . . Tawny

• 0:54—Very brief breasts viewed from below when Jeff Goldblum pulls her by the arm to get her out of bed.

Geena Davis. . . . . . . . . . . . . . . . . . . . Veronica Quaife

0:40—Brief almost side view of left breast getting out of bed.

Jeff Goldblum. . . . . . . . . . . . . . . . . . . . . Seth Brundle

## Footloose (1984)

Kevin Bacon. . . . . . . . . . . . . . . . . Ren MacCormack

Elizabeth Gorcey . . . . . . . . . . . . . . . . . . . . . Wendy Jo

John Laughlin. . . . . . . . . . . . . . . . . . . . . . . . . Woody

•• 0:58—Buns and upper half of pubic hair, while taking a shower in the locker room and talking to Kevin Bacon and Christopher Penn.

John Lithgow . . . . . . . . . . . . . . . Reverend Shaw Moore

Christopher Penn . . . . . . . . . . . . . . . . . . . . . . Willard

Lori Singer . . . . . . . . . . . . . . . . . . . . . . Ariel Moore

Jim Youngs. . . . . . . . . . . . . . . . . . . . . . . . . . Chuck

## For Your Love Only (1979; German)

Nastassja Kinski . . . . . . . . . . . . . . . . . . . . . . . . Zena

•• 0:04—Breasts, twice, in the woods with her teacher, Victor, while Michael watches through the bushes.

• 0:15—Brief right breast, in the woods with Michael.

•• 0:58—Partial left breast, sitting up in bed with Victor. Breasts walking around and putting on robe.

## Forbidden World (1982)

Michael Bowen . . . . . . . . . . . . . . . . . . . . Jimmy Swift

June Chadwick. . . . . . . . . . . . . . . . . Dr. Barbara Glaser

•• 0:29—Breasts in bed making love with Jesse Vint.

•• 0:54—Breasts taking a shower with Dawn Dunlap.

Dawn Dunlap. . . . . . . . . . . . . . . . . . . . Tracy Baxter

• 0:27—Brief breasts getting ready for bed.

••• 0:37—Nude in steam bath.

•• 0:54—Breasts in shower with June Chadwick.

## Forbidden Zone (1980)

Viva . . . . . . . . . . . . . . . . . . . . . . . . . . . . . Ex-Queen

Gisele Lindley. . . . . . . . . . . . . . . . . . . . . The Princess

••• 0:21—Breasts in jail cell.

••• 0:39—Breasts turning a table around.
•• 0:45—Breasts bending over, making love with a frog.
•• 0:51—Breasts in a cave.
•• 0:53—More breasts scenes.
•• 1:06—Even more breasts scenes.
Susan Tyrrell . . . . . . . . . . . . . . . . . . . . . . Queen Doris
• 0:19—Left breast sticking out of dress, sitting on big dice with Herve Villechaize.
•• 1:02—Left breast sticking out of dress after fighting with the Ex-Queen.

### Force Ten from Navarone (1978)
Barbara Bach . . . . . . . . . . . . . . . . . . . . . . . . . . Maritza
• 0:32—Brief breasts taking a bath in the German officer's room.
Edward Fox . . . . . . . . . . . . . . . . . . . . . . . . . . . . Miller

### Forced to Kill (1993)
Corey Michael Eubanks . . . . . . . . . . . . . . . . . . . Johnny
•• 0:17—Buns, after Heather steals his towel. Don't see his face.
Clint Howard . . . . . . . . . . . . . . . . . . . . . . . . . .Drifter
Kari Whitman . . . . . . . . . . . . . . . . . . . . . . . Heather

### Forced Vengeance (1982)
Susie Hall . . . . . . . . . . . . . . . . . . . . . . . . . . . Dancer
• 0:57—Breasts, dancing in club with an Asian dancer.
Mary Louise Weller . . . . . . . . . . . . . . . . . Claire Bonner
• 1:04—Brief breasts, struggling with the bad guy.
• 1:08—Very brief right breast then left breast, while lying dead on the floor.

### Foreign Body (1986; British)
Amanda Donohoe . . . . . . . . . . . . . . . . . . . . . . Susan
0:37—Undressing in her bedroom down to lingerie. Very brief side view of right breast, then brief left breast putting blouse on.
•• 0:40—Breasts opening her blouse for Ram.
Anna Massey . . . . . . . . . . . . . . . . . . . . . . Miss Furze
Sinitta Renet . . . . . . . . . . . . . . . . . . Lovely Indian Girl
• 0:06—Buns, then breasts in bedroom.

### Forever Lulu (1987)
Alec Baldwin . . . . . . . . . . . . . . . . . . . . . . . . . . . Buck
Deborah Harry . . . . . . . . . . . . . . . . . . . . . . . . Lulu
Hanna Schygulla . . . . . . . . . . . . . . . . . . . . . . . Elaine
• 1:03—Brief breasts in and getting out of bubble bath.

### Forever Young (1992)
Jamie Lee Curtis . . . . . . . . . . . . . . . . . . . . . . . Claire
1:00—In bra, while getting dressed.
Mel Gibson . . . . . . . . . . . . . . . . . . . . . . . . . .Daniel
•• 0:30—Buns, after getting out of suspended animation chamber.
Isabel Glasser . . . . . . . . . . . . . . . . . . . . . . . . Helen
Ava Lazar . . . . . . . . . . . . . . . . . Waitress at Diner ('92)

### The Forgotten One (1989)
Elisabeth Brooks . . . . . . . . . . . . . . . . . . . . . . . . Carla
Kristy McNichol . . . . . . . . . . . . . . . . . .Barbara Stupple
0:06—Jogging in braless pink top, then talking to Terry O'Quinn.
1:33—In pink top, lying in bed.
Terry O'Quinn . . . . . . . . . . . . . . . . . . . . . Bob Anderson
• 1:11—Brief buns while turning over in bed with Evelyn.
Rebecca Wood-Sharkey . . . . . . . . . . . . . . . . . .Barmaid

### Fort Apache, The Bronx (1981)
Kathleen Beller . . . . . . . . . . . . . . . . . . . . . . . . Theresa
Pam Grier . . . . . . . . . . . . . . . . . . . . . . . . .Charlotte
Paul Newman . . . . . . . . . . . . . . . . . . . . . . . . . Murphy
Rachel Ticotin . . . . . . . . . . . . . . . . . . . . . . . . Isabelle
• 1:25—Brief upper half of breasts in bathtub while Paul Newman pours bubble bath in.

### Fortress (1985; Made for Cable Movie)
Rachel Ward . . . . . . . . . . . . . . . . . . . . . . . Sally Jones
• 0:38—Swimming in a sheer bra underwater.

### Fortress (1993; U.S./Australian)
Christopher Lambert . . . . . . . . . . . . . . . . John Brennick
• 0:18—Brief balls, twice, seen under Loryn Locklin while making love in bed.
Loryn Locklin . . . . . . . . . . . . . . . . . . Karen Brennick
• 0:18—Lower half of buns, under lingerie while making love on top of Christopher Lambert in bed.

### Fortune and Men's Eyes (1971)
Wendell Burton . . . . . . . . . . . . . . . . . . . . . . . . Smitty
• 1:40—Briefly nude, after getting stripped by guards in jail cell.
Michael Greer . . . . . . . . . . . . . . . . . . . . . . . .Queenie
•• 1:22—Brief frontal nudity after ripping off his underwear after singing number in drag.
Lazaro Perez . . . . . . . . . . . . . . . . . . . . . . . . . .Catso
•• 0:29—Brief buns, undressing and dressing during rape of another male inmate in jail cell.

### Four Friends (1981)
Jodi Thelen . . . . . . . . . . . . . . . . . . . . . . . . . . Georgia
•• 0:17—Left breast in open blouse three times with her three male friends.
0:58—In pink bra taking off her blouse.
Craig Wasson . . . . . . . . . . . . . . . . . . . . . .Danilo Prozor

### Four Seasons (1981)
Bess Armstrong . . . . . . . . . . . . . . . . . . . . Ginny Newley
0:26—In two piece swimsuit on boat putting lotion on herself.
• 0:38—Brief buns twice skinny dipping in the water with Nick.
0:40—In one piece swimsuit.
Jack Weston . . . . . . . . . . . . . . . . . . . . . Danny Zimmer
• 0:48—Brief buns in water while skinny dipping with Rita Moreno.

## The Fourth Man (1984; Dutch)

Thom Hoffman . . . . . . . . . . . . . . . . . . . . . . Herman
- 1:00—Frontal nudity on cross when Gerard pulls his red trunks down. Long shot.
- •• 1:10—Nude in bathroom when Gerard comes in.
- ••• 1:11—Buns making love on bed with Christine while Gerard watches through keyhole.

Jeroen Krabbé . . . . . . . . . . . . . . . . . . . . . . . Gerard
- ••• 0:03—Frontal nudity getting out of bed and walking down the stairs.
- •• 0:26—Frontal nudity drying himself off and getting into bed.
- 0:33—Buns, while getting out of bed.

Reneé Soutendijk. . . . . . . . . . . . . . . . . . . . .Christine
- ••• 0:27—Full frontal nudity removing robe, brief buns in bed, side view left breast, then breasts in bed with Gerard.
- 0:32—Brief left breast in bed with Gerard after he hallucinates and she cuts his penis off.
- ••• 0:53—Left breast, then right breast in red dress when Gerard opens her dress.
- 1:11—Breasts making love with Herman while Gerard watches through keyhole.

## The Fourth Protocol (1987; British)

Pierce Brosnan . . . . . . . . . . . . . . . . . . . . .Petrofsky
Joanna Cassidy . . . . . . . . . . . . . . . . . . . . . Vassilieva
- 1:39—Brief left breast. She's lying dead in Pierce Brosnan's bathtub.
- 1:49—Same thing, different angle.

## The Fourth Story (1990; Made for Cable Movie)

Mark Harmon . . . . . . . . . . . . . . . . . . . David Shepard
- ••• 0:53—Buns, while getting out of bed with Mimi Rogers. More buns, while walking outside and around the house.

Mimi Rogers . . . . . . . . . . . . . . . . . Valerie McCoughlin
M. Emmet Walsh. . . . . . . . . . . . . . . . . . . . . . . Harry

## Fox Style (1974)

Jovita Bush . . . . . . . . . . . . . . . . . . . . . . . . . . Bonnie
- 1:02—Brief right breast while in dressing room, changing clothes.

Denise Denise. . . . . . . . . . . . . . . . . . . . . . . . . . Cindy
- 0:42—Brief breasts rolling over on her stomach on river bank with A. J.
- 1:21—Most of right breast, in bed with A. J.

## Foxtrap (1986; U.S./Italian)

Beatrice Palme . . . . . . . . . . . . . . . . . . . . . Marianna
- •• 0:41—Brief breasts and buns in bed with Fred Williamson, then more breasts making love.

Fred Williamson . . . . . . . . . . . . . . . . . . . . Thomas Fox

## Foxy Brown (1974)

Juanita Brown . . . . . . . . . . . . . . . . . . . . . . . .Claudia
Pam Grier . . . . . . . . . . . . . . . . . . . . . . . . Foxy Brown
- 0:05—Breasts, getting out of bed and taking off nightgown.
- 0:40—Brief left breast, while getting dressed.
- 1:04—Upper half of breasts, while tied to bed.

---

- ••• 1:05—Right breast, then breasts rolling over in bed.

Kimberly Hyde . . . . . . . . . . . . . . . . . . . . . . . Jennifer
Brenda Venus. . . . . . . . . . . . . . . . . . . . . . . .Arabella

## Frame Up (1990)

Frances Fisher. . . . . . . . . . . . . . . . . . . . . Jo Westlake
- •• 0:52—Breasts, lying back in bed with Wings Hauser.
- •• 0:54—Left breast, while lying in bed with Hauser.

Wings Hauser. . . . . . . . . . . . . . . . . . . . . Ralph Baker
Tom Hodges . . . . . . . . . . . . . . . . . . . . . Don Curran

## Frances (1982)

Anjelica Huston . . . . .Hospital Sequence: Mental Patient
Jessica Lange . . . . . . . . . . . . . . . . . . . . . Frances Farmer
- 0:41—Very brief upper half of left breast, while lying on bed and throwing a newspaper.
- 0:50—Brief full frontal nudity covered with bubbles standing up in bathtub and wrapping a towel around herself. Long shot, hard to see.
- 1:01—Brief buns and right breast running into the bathroom when the police bust in. Very, very brief full frontal nudity, then buns closing the bathroom door. Reportedly her, even though you don't see her face clearly.

## Frank and I (1983)

Sophie Favier . . . . . . . . . . . . . . . . . . . . . . . . . Maud
- 0:16—Nude, undressing then breasts lying in bed with Charles.
- 0:40—Brief breasts in bed with Charles.

Jennifer Inch. . . . . . . . . . . . . . . . . . . . Frank/Frances
- 0:10—Brief buns, getting pants pulled down for a spanking.
- ••• 0:22—Nude getting undressed and walking to the bed.
- 0:24—Brief nude when Charles pulls the sheets off her.
- 0:32—Brief buns, getting spanked by two older women.
- ••• 0:38—Full frontal nudity getting out of bed and walking to Charles at the piano.
- •• 0:45—Full frontal nudity lying on her side by the fireplace. Dark, hard to see.
- •• 1:09—Brief breasts making love with Charles on the floor.
- ••• 1:11—Nude taking off her clothes and walking toward Charles at the piano.

## Frankenhooker (1990)

Lia Chang . . . . . . . . . . . . . . . . . . . . . . . . . .Crystal
- 0:38—Buns, when Jeffrey draws a check mark on her.
- 0:40—Brief buns, fighting with the other girls over the drugs.

Vicki Darnell. . . . . . . . . . . . . . . . . . . . . . . . . .Sugar
- 0:36—Brief middle part of each breast through slit bra during introduction to Jeffrey.
- •• 0:37—Breasts, sticking out of black lingerie while getting legs measured.
- 0:38—Right breast, while sitting in chair.

- 0:39—Breasts through slit lingerie three times while folding clothes.
  0:40—Buns, fighting over drugs.
- ••• 0:41—Very brief right breast, sitting on bed (on the right) enjoying drugs. Breasts dancing with the other girls.

Jennifer Delora . . . . . . . . . . . . . . . . . . . . . . . . Angel
- 0:40—Brief breasts during introduction to Jeffrey.
- ••• 0:41—Breasts dancing in room with the other hookers. (Nice tattoos!)

Charlotte J. Helmcamp . . . . . . . . . . . . . . . . . Honey
- •• 0:26—Breasts yanking down her top outside of Jeffrey's car window.

Heather Hunter . . . . . . . . . . . . . . . . . . . . Chartreuse
- 0:36—Brief breasts during introduction to Jeffrey.
- 0:37—Brief breasts bending over behind Sugar.
- ••• 0:41—Brief breasts and buns, running in front of bed. A little blurry. Then breasts and buns dancing with the other girls.
- 0:43—Breasts dodging flying leg with Sugar.
- •• 0:44—Breasts, crawling on the floor.

Patty Mullen . . . . . . . . . . . . . . . . . . . . . . .Elizabeth
- •• 1:01—Breasts and buns in garter belt and stockings, in room with a customer.

Susan Napoli . . . . . . . . . . . . . . . . . . . . . . . . . Anise
- 0:42—Brief left breast on bed with Amber, taking off her top. Brief breasts after Angel explodes.
- 0:43—Breasts, kneeling on bed screaming before exploding.

Kimberly Taylor . . . . . . . . . . . . . . . . . . . . . . Amber
- 0:36—Brief left breast in green top during introduction to Jeffrey.
- •• 0:37—Brief breasts during exam by Jeffrey. Then breasts getting breasts measured with calipers.
- 0:41—Brief right breast, twice, enjoying drugs.
- •• 0:42—Breasts, getting off bed and onto another bed with Anise.
- 0:43—Breasts kneeling in bed screaming before exploding.

## Frankenstein General Hospital *(1988)*
Rebunkah Jones . . . . . . . . . . . . . . . . . . . Elizabeth Rice
- •• 1:05—Breasts in the office letting Mark Blankfield examine her back.

Kathy Shower . . . . . . . . . . . . . . . . . Dr. Alice Singleton
  0:35—In white lingerie outfit pacing around in her office.
- 1:15—Brief breasts running out of her office after the monster, putting her lab coat on.

## Frankenstein Unbound *(1990)*
Myriam Cyr . . . . . . . . . . . . . . . . . . . . Information Officer
Bridget Fonda . . . . . . . . . . . . . . . . . . . . . . . . . .Mary
John Hurt . . . . . . . . . . . . . . . . . . . . . . . . . Buchanan
Raul Julia . . . . . . . . . . . . . . . . . . . Victor Frankenstein
Jason Patric . . . . . . . . . . . . . . . . . . . . . . Lord Byron
Catherine Rabett . . . . . . . . . . . . . . . . . . . . . .Elizabeth
  1:10—Very brief left breast, while lying dead after getting shot by Frankenstein. Unappealing looking because of all the gruesome makeup.

Terri Treas . . . . . . . . . . . . . . . . . . . . . . Computer Voice

## Frantic *(1988)*
Emmanuelle Seigner . . . . . . . . . . . . . . . . . . . .Michelle
- 1:02—Brief side view of right breast, while changing blouses in bedroom.

Tina Sportolaro . . . . . . . . . . . . . . . . . . . . TWA Clerk
Alexandra Stewart . . . . . . . . . . . . . . . . . . . . . .Edie

## Fraternity Vacation *(1985)*
Barbara Crampton . . . . . . . . . . . . . . . . . . . . .Chrissie
- ••• 0:16—Breasts and buns in bedroom with two guys taking off her swimsuit.

Cameron Dye . . . . . . . . . . . . . . . . . . . .Joe Gillespie
Kathleen Kinmont . . . . . . . . . . . . . . . . . . . .Marianne
- ••• 0:16—Breasts and buns taking off her swimsuit in bedroom with two guys.

Julie Payne . . . . . . . . . . . . . . . . . . . . . . Naomi Tvedt
Tim Robbins . . . . . . . . . . . . . . .Larry "Mother" Tucker
Sheree Wilson . . . . . . . . . . . . . . . . . . . .Ashley Taylor
  0:43—In white leotard at aerobics class.
- 0:47—Breasts and buns of body double (Roberta Whitewood), while in the bedroom when the guys photograph her with a telephoto lens.
  1:01—In white leotard exercising in living room with Leigh McCloskey.

## Freddy's Dead: The Final Nightmare *(1991)*
Lezlie Deane . . . . . . . . . . . . . . . . . . . . . . . . .Tracy
Johnny Depp . . . . . . . . . . . . . . . . . . . .Glen Lantz
Yaphet Kotto . . . . . . . . . . . . . . . . . . . . . . . . . . Doc
Linnea Quigley . . . . . . . . .Soul from Freddy's Chest
- 1:25—Brief breasts, struggling in Freddy's stomach during the end credits special-effects review.

Lisa Zane . . . . . . . . . . . . . . . . . . . .Maggie Burroughs

## Free Ride *(1986)*
Tally Chanel . . . . . . . . . . . . . . . . . . . . . . . . . . Candy
- 0:53—Brief buns, wearing G-string, taking off her clothes on porch. Long shot.
- 0:57—Brief breasts in bedroom with Dan.

Elizabeth Cochrell . . . . . . . . . . . . . . . . . . Nude Girl #1
- 0:25—Brief buns taking a shower with another girl.

Gary Hershberger . . . . . . . . . . . . . . . . . . . . . . . .Dan
Rebecca Lynn . . . . . . . . . . . . . . . . . . . . Nude Girl #2
- 0:25—Brief buns taking a shower with another girl.

Renée Props . . . . . . . . . . . . . . . . . . . . . . . . . .Kathy
- 0:13—Brief breasts in the shower while Dan watches.

Mamie Van Doren . . . . . . . . . . . . . . . .Debbie Stockwell

## Freefall *(1993)*
Jeff Fahey . . . . . . . . . . . . . . . . . . . . . . . .Dea Dellum
Pamela Gidley . . . . . . . . . . . . . . . . . . . . . Katy Mazur
- 0:29—Brief back side of left breast and upper half of buns, while making love with Eric Roberts in bed. Almost breasts when Roberts lies back down. Breasts later on don't show her face.
- 0:40—Right breast with Roberts in flashback. Don't see her face again.

Terri Norton . . . . . . . . . . . . . . . . . . . . . . . . . .Susan

Eric Roberts . . . . . . . . . . . . . . . . . . . . . . . Grant Orion
Jennifer Steyn . . . . . . . . . . . . . . . . . . . . . . . Secretary

### *Freelance* (British)
*a.k.a. Con Man*
Luan Peters . . . . . . . . . . . . . . . . . . . . . . . . . Rosemary
- 0:25—Right breast and buns, while making love with Gary and Mitch.
- 0:26—Left breast, twice, while making love with Gary and Mitch.

### *Freeway* (1988)
Darlanne Fluegel . . . . . . . . . . . . Sarah "Sunny" Harper
- 0:27—In bra in bathroom taking a pill, then very, very brief right breast, getting into bed.
- 0:28—Brief left breast putting on robe and getting out of bed.

Clint Howard . . . . . . . . . . . . . . . . . . . . . . . . . . Ronnie
Joe Palese . . . . . . . . . . . . . . . . . . . . . . . . . . . Gomez
James Russo . . . . . . . . . . . . . . . . . . . . . Frank Quinn

### *French Postcards* (1979)
George Coe . . . . . . . . . . . . . . . . . . . . . . Mr. Weber
David Grant . . . . . . . . . . . . . . . . . . . . . . . . . . Alex
Mandy Patinkin . . . . . . . . . . . . . . . . . . . . . . . . Sayyid
Marie-France Pisier . . . . . . . . . . . . . . . Madame Tessier
- • 0:16—In white bra, then breasts in dressing room while a guy watches without her knowing.

Valerie Quennessen . . . . . . . . . . . . . . . . . . . . . . . Toni
Debra Winger . . . . . . . . . . . . . . . . . . . . . . . Melanie

### *French Quarter* (1978)
Lindsay Bloom . . . . "Big Butt" Annie/Policewoman in Bar
Susan Clark . . . . . . . . . . . . . . . . . . . . . Bag Stealer/Sue
Alisha Fontaine
. . . . . . . . . Gertrude "Trudy" Dix/Christine Delaplane
- 0:12—Dancing on stage for the first time. Buns in G-string. Breasts in large black pasties.
- 0:47—Brief left breast several times, posing for Mr. Beloq.
- 0:49—Left breast again.
- • 1:13—Breasts during auction.
- • 1:18—Brief breasts, then buns making love with Tom, then breasts again.
- 1:26—Brief breasts getting her top pulled down during party.
- 1:31—Brief breasts getting tied down during voodoo ceremony.
- • 1:32—More breasts tied down during ceremony.

Ann Michelle
. . . . . . "Coke Eye" Laura/Policewoman in French Hotel
- 0:42—Right breast, when Josie wakes her up.
- ••• 0:43—Breasts in bed, caressing Josie's breasts.
- •• 0:58—Breasts during voodoo ceremony. Close ups of breasts with snake.
- 1:19—Brief breasts, sitting in bed.
- ••• 1:20—More breasts sitting in bed, talking to a customer. Long scene.

Laura Misch Owens . . . . . . . . "Ice Box" Josie/Girl on Bus
- 0:41—Breasts under sheer white nightgown.

- ••• 0:43—Full frontal nudity taking off nightgown, wearing garter belt. Getting into bed with Laura.

### *The French Woman* (1979)
*a.k.a. Madame Claude*
Dayle Haddon . . . . . . . . . . . . . . . . . . . . . . Elizabeth
- 0:15—Very, very brief breasts in dressing room.
- 0:49—Breasts on bed with Madame Claude.
- 0:55—Breasts kissing Pierre, then buns while lying on the floor.
  1:10—In two piece swimsuit on sailboat.
- 1:11—Left breast, then buns at the beach with Frederick.

Vibeke Knudsen . . . . . . . . . . . . . . . . . . . . . Anne-Marie
- 0:04—Breasts in chair in office with Robert Webber.
- 0:09—Breasts walking on beach with Japanese Businessman.
- ••• 0:11—Breasts on bed with David while she talks on the telephone. Then hot scene making love with him in the shower.
- 1:19—Breasts in bed with a customer when David comes over.

### *Frenzy* (1972; British)
Barbara Leigh-Hunt . . . . . . . . . . . . . . . . Brenda Blaney
- 0:31—Left breast, while sitting in chair with the necktie killer. Don't see her face.

Anna Massey . . . . . . . . . . . . . . . . . . . . Babs Milligan
- •• 0:45—Breasts getting out of bed and then buns, walking to the bathroom. Probably a body double.

### *Friday Foster* (1975)
Godfrey Cambridge . . . . . . . . . . . . . . . . . Ford Malotte
Pam Grier . . . . . . . . . . . . . . . . . . . . . . . . Friday Foster
- ••• 0:29—Breasts, several times, while taking a shower while Carl Weathers stalks around in her apartment.
- ••• 1:12—Upper half of breast, while in bubble bath with Blake. Breasts in bed with him.

Yaphet Kotto . . . . . . . . . . . . . . . . . . . . . . . Colt Hawkins

### *Friday the 13th* (1980)
Kevin Bacon . . . . . . . . . . . . . . . . . . . . . . . . . . . . . . Jack
- 0:39—Close up of buns when Marci squeezes them.

### *Friday the 13th, Part II* (1981)
Kirsten Baker . . . . . . . . . . . . . . . . . . . . . . . . . . . . Terry
- •• 0:45—Breasts and buns taking off clothes to go skinny dipping.
- 0:47—Very brief breasts jumping up in the water.
- 0:48—Full frontal nudity and buns getting out of the water. Long shot.

Marta Kober . . . . . . . . . . . . . . . . . . . . . . . . . . . Sandra

### *Friday the 13th, Part III* (1982)
Annie Gaybis . . . . . . . . . . . . . . . . . . . . . . . . . Cashier
Tracie Savage . . . . . . . . . . . . . . . . . . . . . . . . Debbie
  0:32—In blue, two piece swimsuit.
- 0:59—Brief breasts, while getting back into the shower after shutting the door.
- 1:00—Very brief right breast, while getting towel.

## Friday the 13th, Part IV—The Final Chapter (1984)

Judie Aronson . . . . . . . . . . . . . . . . . . . . . . . .Samantha
- 0:26—Brief breasts and very brief buns taking clothes off to go skinny dipping.
- 0:29—Brief breasts under water pretending to be dead.
- •• 0:39—Breasts and brief buns taking off her T-shirt to go skinny dipping at night.

Kimberly Beck . . . . . . . . . . . . . . . . . . . . . . . . . . Trish
Corey Feldman . . . . . . . . . . . . . . . . . . . . . . . .Tommy
Alan Hayes . . . . . . . . . . . . . . . . . . . . . . . . . . . Paul
- 0:26—Brief buns, while swinging on a rope and jumping into the lake.

Barbara Howard . . . . . . . . . . . . . . . . . . . . . . . . Sara
0:52—In white bra and panties putting on a robe in the bedroom getting ready for her boyfriend.
- 1:01—Buns, through shower door.

Camilla More . . . . . . . . . . . . . . . . . . . . . . . . . . Tina
- 0:26—Very brief breasts in the lake jumping up with her twin sister to show they are skinny dipping.
- 0:48—Left breast, in bed with Crispin Glover.

Carey More . . . . . . . . . . . . . . . . . . . . . . . . . . . . Terri
- 0:26—Very brief breasts in the lake jumping up with her twin sister to show they are skinny dipping.

## Friday the 13th, Part VII: The New Blood (1988)

Elizabeth Kaitan. . . . . . . . . . . . . . . . . . . . . . . . Robin
- 0:53—Brief left breast in bed making love with a guy.
- 0:55—Brief breasts sitting up in bed after making love and the sheet falls down.
- •• 1:00—Brief breasts again sitting up in bed and putting a shirt on over her head.

Heidi Kozak. . . . . . . . . . . . . . . . . . . . . . . . . . . Sandra
- 0:36—Buns, while taking off clothes to go skinny dipping. Brief breasts under water just before getting killed by Jason.

## Friday the 13th, Part V—A New Beginning (1985)

Juliette Cummins. . . . . . . . . . . . . . . . . . . . . . . Robin
- ••• 1:01—Breasts, wearing panties getting undressed and climbing into bed just before getting killed.
1:05—Very brief breasts, covered with blood when Reggie discovers her dead.

Corey Feldman . . . . . . . . . . . . . . . . . . . . Tommay at 12
Melanie Kinnaman . . . . . . . . . . . . . . . . . . Pam Roberts
1:08—In wet white blouse coming back into the house from the rain.

Deborah Voorhees . . . . . . . . . . . . . . . . . . . . . . Tina
- ••• 0:41—Breasts after making love with Eddie, then lying down and relaxing just before getting killed.
- 0:43—Buns and brief left breast when Eddie turns her over and discovers her dead.

Rebecca Wood-Sharkey . . . . . . . . . . . . . . . . . . . . . Lana
- 0:33—Brief breasts opening her dress while changing to go out with Billy.

## Friendly Favors (1983)
*a.k.a. Six Swedes on a Pump*

Brigitte Lahaie . . . . . . . . . . . . . . . . . . . . . . . . .Greta
- •• 0:02—Full frontal nudity riding a guy in bed. (She's wearing a necklace.)
- ••• 0:39—Full frontal nudity having fun on "exercise bike."
- ••• 0:46—Full frontal nudity taking off clothes and running outside with the other girls. Nice slow motion shots.
- •• 0:53—Breasts, making love with Kerstin.
- ••• 1:01—Full frontal nudity in room with the Italian.
- ••• 1:15—Full frontal nudity in room with guy from the band.

## From Beyond (1986)

Barbara Crampton . . . . . . . . . Dr. Katherine McMichaels
- •• 0:44—Brief breasts after getting blouse torn off by the creature in the laboratory.
0:51—Buns getting on top of Jeffrey Combs in black leather outfit.

## Full Contact (1992)

Denise Buick. . . . . . . . . . . . . . . . . . . . . . . . . . . Tori
- ••• 0:31—Buns in T-back, then in bra, then breasts, while doing strip routine on stage.
- •• 0:39—Buns in T-back and breasts while dancing on stage.
- •• 1:02—Breasts and buns, while making love with Luke.

## The Funhouse (1981)

Elizabeth Berridge . . . . . . . . . . . . . . . . . . . . . . .Amy
- •• 0:03—Brief breasts taking off robe to get into the shower, then very brief breasts getting out to chase Joey.

Sylvia Miles . . . . . . . . . . . . . . . . . . . . . . Madame Zena

## The Further Adventures of Tennessee Buck (1987)

Kathy Shower. . . . . . . . . . . . . . . . . .Barbara Manchester
0:22—In white lingerie in her hut getting dressed.
- ••• 0:57—Breasts getting rubbed with oil by the cannibal women. Nice close up shots.
- •• 1:02—Breasts in a hut with the Chief of the tribe.

Brant Van Hoffman. . . . . . . . . . . . . . . .Ken Manchester
- 0:38—Brief buns, behind a mosquito net while making love with his disinterested wife.

## Future Kick (1991)

Linda Doná . . . . . . . . . . . . . . . . . . . . . . . . . . . Tye
Maria Ford . . . . . . . . . . . . . . . . . . . . . . . . . . Dancer
Meg Foster. . . . . . . . . . . . . . . . . . . . . . Nancy Morgan
Lisa Glaser . . . . . . . . . . . . . . . . . . Uncredited Dancer
- 0:36—Breasts, dancing on stage in white outfit. (Taken from *Stripped to Kill II*.)

Christopher Penn . . . . . . . . . . . . . . . . . . . . . . . Bang

## Future Shock (1993)

Martin Kove . . . . . . . . . . . . . . . . . . . . Doctor Langdon
Bill Paxton . . . . . . . . . . . . . . . . . . . . . . . . . . .Vince
Rick Rossovich . . . . . . . . . . . . . . . . . . Frat Boy Leader
Pamela Runo . . . . . . . . . . . . . . . . . . . . . . . . . . Model

Julie Strain. . . . . . . . . . . . . . . . . . . . . Female Dancer
- 0:03—Brief buns in sexy black G-string outfit with black top, while dancing in front of guy sitting in electric chair.

### The G.I. Executioner (1971)
*a.k.a. Wit's End*
*a.k.a. Dragon Lady*
Angelique Pettyjohn . . . . . . . . . . . . . . . . . . . . Bonnie
- •• 0:16—Doing a strip routine on stage. Buns in G-string, very brief side view of right breast, then breasts at end.
- •• 0:40—Breasts, lying asleep in bed.
- ••• 0:58—Breasts and buns, undressing in front of Dave, getting into bed, fighting an attacker and getting shot. Long scene.
- • 1:14—Breasts, lying shot in rope net.

Victoria Racimo. . . . . . . . . . . . . . . . . . . . .Foon Mae Lee
- • 0:12—Nude in bathroom mirror getting dressed.
- • 0:54—Brief breasts undressing and getting into bed. (See reflection in glass on headboard.)
- • 1:15—Sort of buns, lying in Dave's lap. Then left breast.
- 1:18—Buns, tied up by wrists. Sort of breasts being turned around (hair is in the way).

Janet Wood. . . . . . . . . . . . . . . . . . . . . Cynthia Jordan
- •• 0:29—Breasts and buns in bed with Dave.

### Gabriela (1984; Brazilian)
Sonia Braga. . . . . . . . . . . . . . . . . . . . . . Gabriela
- •• 0:26—Breasts leaning back out the window making love on a table with Marcello Mastroianni.
- ••• 0:27—Nude, taking a shower outside and cleaning herself up.
- • 0:32—Right breast in bed.
- •• 0:38—Nude, making love with Mastroianni on the kitchen table.
- •• 0:45—Nude, getting in bed with Mastroianni.
- 1:13—Full frontal nudity, on bed with another man, then getting beat up by Mastroianni.
- ••• 1:17—Nude, changing clothes in the bedroom.
- •• 1:32—Breasts and buns making love outside with Mastroianni. Lots of passion!

### Gaby, A True Story (1987)
Robert Beltran. . . . . . . . . . . . . . . . . . . . . . .Luis
Tony Goldwyn . . . . . . . . . . . . . . . . . . . . . David
Rachel Levin . . . . . . . . . . . . . . . . . . . . . Gaby
- • 0:56—Right breast, then breasts on the floor making love with another handicapped boy, Fernando.
Liv Ullmann. . . . . . . . . . . . . . . . . . . . .Sari Brimmer

### Gaily, Gaily (1969)
Beau Bridges. . . . . . . . . . . . . . . . . . . . .Ben Harvey
- •• 1:37—Brief buns, getting up from table and shaking.
Margot Kidder. . . . . . . . . . . . . . . . . . . . .Adeline

### Galactic Gigolo (1988)
*a.k.a. Club Earth*
LeeAnne Baker . . . . . . . . . . . . . . . . . . . . . . Lucy
- • 0:08—Breasts in hot tub behind Eoj.
Ruth Corrine Collins . . . . . . . . . . . . . . .Dr. Ruth Pepper
- •• 0:47—Breasts, while stripping in front of Eoj.
- • 0:49—Breasts, while getting tied up by Sammy.
- • 0:53—Breasts in open cape while in family room.
- • 0:55—Breasts, while getting rescued.
Courtney James . . . . . . . . . . . . . . . . . . . . . . Lisa
Angela Nicholas . . . . . . . . . . . . . . .Peggy Sue Peggy
- • 0:21—Brief right breast in open blouse leaving room with Eoj.
Karen Nielsen. . . . . . . . . . . . . . . . . .Kathy/Cheerleader
- •• 0:27—Breasts (she's on the left) while in hot tub with Eoj and Sandy.
Lisa Petruno . . . . . . . . . . . . . . . . . . . . . Sandy
- •• 0:27—Breasts (she's on the right) while in hot tub with Eoj and Kathy.

### Galaxy of Terror (1981)
Edward Albert . . . . . . . . . . . . . . . . . . . . . Cabren
Taaffe O'Connell . . . . . . . . . . . . . . . . . . . . .Damelia
- •• 0:42—Breasts getting raped by a giant alien slug. Nice and slimy.
- 0:46—Buns, covered with slime being discovered by her crew mates.

### Gallipoli (1981)
Mel Gibson . . . . . . . . . . . . . . . . . . . . . Frank Dunne
- •• 1:18—Buns, while running into the water. (He's the guy on the left.)
Mark Lee . . . . . . . . . . . . . . . . . . . . . Archy Hamilton
- •• 1:18—Buns, while running into the water with Mel Gibson. (Mark is the guy on the right.)

### The Game is Over (1966)
Jane Fonda . . . . . . . . . . . . . . . . . . . . . Renee Saccard
- • 0:15—Very brief left breast, getting out of bed. Breasts in mirror when running to the door.
- • 0:16—Brief breasts, several times, while behind sheer white curtain.
- • 0:17—Very brief breasts, while falling onto bed.
- •• 0:18—Breasts, while lying in bed with the guy.

### Games Girls Play (1974; British)
*a.k.a. The Bunny Caper*
*a.k.a. Sex Play*
Erin Geraghty. . . . . . . . . . . . . . . . . . . . . Ducky
- • 1:11—In bra and panties, then breasts running around outside.
Christina Hart. . . . . . . . . . . . . . . . . . . . Bunny O'Hara
- • 0:00—Brief lower frontal nudity and buns when her dress blows up from the wind.
- •• 0:01—Full frontal nudity in slow motion, jumping into bed. Then nude, twirling around in another room.
- ••• 0:18—Nude, undressing with the other girls, then walking around the house to the pool, then swimming nude.
- • 1:01—Brief breasts getting dressed.

## Games That Lovers Play (1970)
Penny Brahms . . . . . . . . . . . . . . . . . . . . . . . Constance
  •• 0:08—Breasts outside with a customer.
  •• 0:10—Breasts again putting dress back on.
Joanna Lumley . . . . . . . . . . . . . . . . . . . . . . . . . Fanny
  •• 0:17—Nude, getting out of bed and putting on robe.
  • 0:50—Right breast, while in bed with Jonathan.
  •• 1:18—Breasts sitting in bed, talking on the phone.
  •• 1:29—Brief breasts several times in bed with Constance and a guy. Breasts after and during the end credits.

## The Garden of the Finzi-Continis (1971; Italian/German)
Helmut Berger. . . . . . . . . . . . . . . . . . . . . . . . Alberto
Dominique Sanda . . . . . . . . . . . . . . . . . . . . . . Micol
  0:24—In braless wet white T-shirt after getting caught in a rainstorm.
  • 1:12—Breasts sitting on a bed after turning a light on so the guy standing outside can see her.

## Gas Food Lodging (1992)
Brooke Adams. . . . . . . . . . . . . . . . . . . . . . . . . Nora
James Brolin . . . . . . . . . . . . . . . . . . . . . . . John Evans
Chris Mulkey. . . . . . . . . . . . . . . . . . . . . . . Raymond
Ione Skye . . . . . . . . . . . . . . . . . . . . . . . . . . . Trudi
  ••• 0:38—Breasts, taking off her blouse in a cave with her boyfriend, then making love.
  • 0:40—Brief right breast, while sitting up.

## Gator Bait (1973)
Janit Baldwin. . . . . . . . . . . . . . . . . . . . . . . . . . Julie
  •• 0:27—Breasts and buns walking into a pond, then getting out and getting dressed.
  • 0:35—Very brief right breast, twice, popping out of her dress when the bad guys hold her.
  • 0:40—Brief left breast struggling against two guys on the bed.
Claudia Jennings . . . . . . . . . . . . . . . . . . Desiree Tibidoe
  • 0:06—Brief left and right breasts during boat chase sequence.
Clyde Ventura. . . . . . . . . . . . . . . . . . . . . . . . . . n.a.

## Gator Bait II—Cajun Justice (1988)
Jan MacKenzie. . . . . . . . . . . . . . . . . . . . . Angelique
  0:13—Most of right breast while kissing her husband.
  0:29—Most of right breast while in bed.
  •• 0:34—Buns and side view of left breast, taking a bath outside. Brief breasts a couple of times while the bad guys watch.
  • 0:41—Brief side view of left breast taking off towel in front of the bad guys.
  1:05—Brief buns occasionally when her blouse flaps up during boat chase.

## The Gauntlet (1977)
Clint Eastwood . . . . . . . . . . . . . . . . . . . . Ben Shockley
Sondra Locke . . . . . . . . . . . . . . . . . . . . . . . Gus Mally
  •• 1:10—Brief right breast, then breasts getting raped by two biker guys in a box car while Clint Eastwood is tied up.

## Gemini Affair (1974)
Kathy Kersh . . . . . . . . . . . . . . . . . . . . . . . . . Jessica
  0:10—In white bra and black panties changing in front of Marta Kristen.
  •• 0:11—Nude getting into bed with Kristen.
  • 0:12—Brief breasts turning over onto her stomach in bed.
  •• 0:17—Nude, standing up in bed and jumping off.
  ••• 0:57—Nude in bed with Kristen.
  •• 1:04—Left breast sitting up in bed after Kristen leaves.
Marta Kristen . . . . . . . . . . . . . . . . . . . . . . . . . . Julie
  ••• 0:32—Breasts wearing beige panties talking with Jessica in the bathroom.
  • 0:56—Very, very brief left breast and lower frontal nudity standing next to bed with a guy. Very brief left breast in bed with him.
  ••• 0:59—Breasts and buns making love in bed with Jessica. Wowzers!

## Genuine Risk (1989)
Peter Berg . . . . . . . . . . . . . . . . . . . . . . . . . . . Henry
Kenneth A. Johnson . . . . . . . . . . . . . . . . . . . Bartender
Michelle Johnson . . . . . . . . . . . . . . . . . . . . . . . . Girl
  0:27—In black bra in room with Henry.
  0:29—In bra in open top coming out of the bathroom.
  • 0:43—On bed in black bra and panties with Henry. Left breast peeking out of the top of her bra.

## Get Out Your Handkerchiefs (1978)
Gérard Depardieu . . . . . . . . . . . . . . . . . . . . . . Raoul
Carole Laure. . . . . . . . . . . . . . . . . . . . . . . . Solange
  •• 0:21—Breasts sitting in bed listening to her boyfriend talk.
  •• 0:31—Breasts sitting in bed knitting.
  • 0:41—Upper half of left breast in bed.
  •• 0:47—Left breast, while sitting in bed and the three guys talk.
  • 1:08—Brief right breast when the little boy peeks at her while she sleeps.
  1:10—Lower frontal nudity while he looks at her some more.
  ••• 1:17—Full frontal nudity taking off nightgown while sitting on bed for the little boy.

## Get to Know Your Rabbit (1972)
Allen Garfield . . . . . . . . . . . . . . . . . . . . . . . . . . Vic
Samantha Jones . . . . . . . . . . . . . . . . . . . . . . . Susan
  •• 0:27—Right breast, after taking the bra off.
  0:27—In red bra, in front of Allen Garfield and Tommy Smothers.
  • 0:28—Right breast, while dancing with Smothers in the store.

Anne Randall . . . . . . . . . . . . . . . . . . . . . . Stewardess
Katharine Ross . . . . . . . . . . . . . . . Terrific-Looking Girl
M. Emmet Walsh . . . . . . . . . . . . . . . . . . Mr. Wendel
Suzanne Zenor . . . . . . . . . . . . . . . . . . . . . . . . Paula
• 0:06—Very brief buns, getting out of bed.

### The Getaway (1972)
Ali MacGraw . . . . . . . . . . . . . . . . . . . . . . Carol McCoy
0:16—In wet white blouse after jumping in pond
with Steve McQueen.
• 0:19—Very brief left breast lying back in bed kissing
McQueen.
Sally Struthers . . . . . . . . . . . . . . . . . . . . . Fran Clinton
1:15—In black bra getting out of bed and leaning
over injured bad guy to get something.

### The Getaway (1993)
(Unrated version reviewed.)
Alec Baldwin . . . . . . . . . . . . . . . . . . . . . . . Doc McCoy
•• 0:19—Buns, while pulling down his underwear.
Kim Basinger . . . . . . . . . . . . . . . . . . . . . . Carol McCoy
•• 0:18—In bra and panties in bedroom with Alec Baldwin, then nude (kind of silhouette).
• 0:25—Very brief left breast and lower frontal nudity
while pulling down towel behind steamy shower
door. Hard to see.
• 1:29—Side view of buns in the shower.
••• 1:30—Breasts and buns, while making love with
Baldwin. Nice. Very, very brief lower frontal nudity.
1:32—In white bra and panties in hotel room.
Michael Madsen . . . . . . . . . . . . . . . . . . . . .Rudy Travis
Jennifer Tilly . . . . . . . . . . . . . . . . . . . . . . . Fran Carvey
•• 1:12—Breasts and buns while making love on top of
Michael Madsen in bed while her husband is tied to
chair in bathroom.
1:21—In white bra while lying in bed with Madsen.
1:31—In lingerie while sitting in bed with Madsen.
James Woods . . . . . . . . . . . . . . . . . . . . . . Jack Benyon

### Getting It Right (1989)
Helena Bonham Carter . . . . . . . . . . . Minerva Munday
•• 0:18—Breasts a couple of times in bed talking to
Gavin. It's hard to recognize her because she has lots
of makeup on her face.
Jane Horrocks . . . . . . . . . . . . . . . . . . . . . . . . . Jenny
Bryan Pringle . . . . . . . . . . . . . . . . . . . . . . . Mr. Lamb
Lynn Redgrave . . . . . . . . . . . . . . . . . . . . . . . . . Joan
•• 0:46—Brief right breast, then brief breasts on couch
seducing Gavin. More right breast shot when wrestling with him.

### Getting Straight (1970)
Candice Bergen . . . . . . . . . . . . . . . . . . . . . . . . . . Jan
Brenda Sykes . . . . . . . . . . . . . . . . . . . . . . . . . . .Luan
•• 0:53—Brief left breast, while scooting up in bed with
Elliott Gould, then breasts, while getting back in
bed.

### Ghost Story (1981)
Alice Krige . . . . . . . . . . . . . . . . . . . . . . . . . . Alma/Eva
• 0:41—Brief breasts making love in bedroom with
Craig Wasson.
•• 0:44—Breasts in bathtub with Wasson.
•• 0:46—Breasts sitting up in bed.
••• 0:49—Buns, then breasts standing on balcony turning and walking to bedroom talking to Wasson.
Craig Wasson . . . . . . . . . . . . . . . . . . . . . . .Don/David
•• 0:08—Brief frontal nudity falling out the window,
then buns, while landing next to the pool.
• 0:41—Buns, while making love with Alice Krige in
bedroom.

### Ghosts Can't Do It (1989)
Leo Damian . . . . . . . . . . . . . . . . . . . . . . . . . . . . Fasto
• 1:31—Brief, lower buns while sliding down stack of
hay. Long shot.
Bo Derek . . . . . . . . . . . . . . . . . . . . . . . . . . . . . .Kate
••• 0:26—In one piece swimsuit on beach, then full
frontal nudity taking it off. Brief buns covered with
sand on her back. Long scene.
••• 0:32—Breasts, sitting and washing herself. Very brief
buns, jumping into tub.
•• 0:48—Full frontal nudity taking a shower.
• 0:49—Very, very brief breasts and buns jumping into
pool. Long shot. Full frontal nudity under water.
0:52—Very, very brief partial breasts pulling a guy
into the pool
1:00—In wet dress, dancing sexily in the rain.
•• 1:12—Breasts behind mosquito net with her boyfriend.
Julie Newmar . . . . . . . . . . . . . . . . . . . . . . . . . .Angel

### Ghoulies IV (1993)
Lynn Danielson . . . . . . . . . . . . . . . . . . . Female Victim
Antonia Dorian . . . . . . . . . . . . . . . . . . . . . Lady in Red
Pete Liapis . . . . . . . . . . . . . . . . . . . . . Jonathan Graves
• 0:49—Brief buns, putting on his underwear. Don't
see his face.
Peggy Trentini . . . . . . . . . . . . . . . . . . . . . . . . Monica
Barbara Alyn Woods . . . . . . . . . . . . . . . . . . . . .Kate

### The Gift (1982; French)
Clio Goldsmith . . . . . . . . . . . . . . . . . . . . . . . Barbara
•• 0:39—Brief breasts several times in the bathroom,
then right breast in bathtub.
• 0:49—Breasts lying in bed sleeping.
0:51—Very brief left breast turning over in bed.
• 0:52—Brief right breast then buns, reaching for
phone while lying in bed.
1:16—Very brief left breast getting out of bed. Dark,
hard to see.

### Gimme an "F" (1981)
*a.k.a. T & A Academy 2*
Daphne Ashbrook . . . . . . . . . . . . . . . . . .Phoebe Willis
Jennifer Cooke . . . . . . . . . . . . . . . . . . . .Pam Bethlehem
1:10—Wearing United States flag pasties frolicking
with Dr. Spirit. Nice bouncing action.
1:38—Still of pasties scene during end credits.

Darcy De Moss . . . . . . . . . . . . . . . One of the "Ducks"
Julie Gray . . . . . . . . . . . . . . . . . . . . . . Falcon Marsha
John Karlen . . . . . . . . . . . . . . . . . . . . . . . . .Dr. Spirit
Valerie McIntosh . . . . . . . . . . . . . .One of the "Vikings"
Steve Shellen. . . . . . . . . . . . . . . . . . Tommy Hamilton
    0:56—Dancing in his underwear in the boy's shower
    room while the girls peek in at him.
    • 0:57—Brief upper half of buns.
Cindy Silver. . . . . . . . . . . . . . . . . . One of the "Ducks"

### Ginger (1970)

Cheri Caffaro. . . . . . . . . . . . . . . . . . . . . . . . . Ginger
  ••• 1:06—Breasts, taking off her top in front of Rodney
    and lying on top of him in bed.
  •• 1:10—Full frontal nudity, getting up off the bed.
  • 1:22—Sort of breasts during recollection of her rape.
    Hard to see.
  • 1:23—Breasts, taking off her towel in front of Jimmy.
  ••• 1:32—Nude, on bed handcuffed behind her back by
    Rex, then getting molested by him. Long scene.
Calvin Culver. . . . . . . . . . . . . . . . . . . . . . . . .Rodney
  ••• 1:02—Frontal nudity, tied up spread eagle on the
    bed.
  • 1:07—Brief frontal nudity when Ginger lies down on
    top of him.
William Grannell . . . . . . . . . . . . . . . . . . . .Jason Varone
  •• 0:55—Buns, while on top of Vicky in bed.
Tracey Walter . . . . . . . . . . . . . . . . . . . . Ginger's Brother

### Ginger Ale Afternoon (1989)

Yeardley Smith . . . . . . . . . . . . . . . . . . Bonnie Cleator
  • 0:53—Brief upper half of left breast, taking off top in
    trailer with Hank.

### The Girl from Petrovka (1974)

Goldie Hawn. . . . . . . . . . . . . . . . . . . . . . . Oktyabrina
    1:30—Very, very brief breasts in bed with Hal Hol-
    brook. Don't really see anything—it lasts for about
    one frame.
Hal Holbrook. . . . . . . . . . . . . . . . . . . . . . . . . . . Joe
  • 0:40—Brief buns, while getting out of bed, putting
    on a robe and talking to Goldie Hawn.

### The Girl in a Swing (1989; U.S./British)

Meg Tilly. . . . . . . . . . . . . . . . . . . . . . . . Karin Foster
  •• 0:44—In white bra, then breasts and buns.
  •• 0:50—Nude, while swimming under water.
  ••• 1:14—Breasts while sitting on swing, then making
    love.
    1:18—In white bra, while sitting in front of a mirror.
  ••• 1:44—Breasts while at the beach.

### The Girl in Blue (1973; Canadian)

*a.k.a. U-turn*
Maud Adams. . . . . . . . . . . . . . . . . . . . .Paula/Tracy
  • 1:16—Side view of right breast, while sitting on bed
    with Scott.
    1:19—In two piece swimsuit getting out of lake.
Gay Rowan . . . . . . . . . . . . . . . . . . . . . . . . . Bonnie
  • 0:06—Left breast, in bed with Scott.
  • 0:31—Brief breasts in bathtub.

  • 0:48—Right breast, while in shower talking to Scott.
    Brief breasts (long shot) on balcony throwing water
    down at him.
  • 1:21—Brief right breast and buns getting out of bed
    and running out of the room.
David Selby . . . . . . . . . . . . . . . . . . . . . . . . . . . Scott
  • 0:10—Brief buns while getting out of bed and put-
    ting on pants. Dark.
    0:44—Left half of buns while in shower.
  •• 1:14—Buns, while walking into the bathroom.

### Girl on a Motorcycle (1968; French/British)

*a.k.a. Naked Under Leather*
Marianne Faithfull . . . . . . . . . . . . . . . . . . . .Rebecca
  •• 0:05—Nude, getting out of bed and walking to the
    door.
  • 0:38—Brief side view of left breast putting night-
    gown on.
  • 1:23—Brief breasts while lying down and talking
    with Alain Delon.
  • 1:30—Very brief right breast a couple of times mak-
    ing love with Delon.
Catherine Jourdan . . . . . . . . . . . . . . . . . . . . . Catherine

### A Girl to Kill For (1989)

Karen Medak . . . . . . . . . . . . . . . . . . . . . . . . . . . Sue
  ••• 0:17—Breasts showering at the beach after surfing
    with Chuck.
    0:38—In bra lying on desk in office with Chuck.
  •• 1:08—Breasts in spa when Chuck takes her shirt off.
    Then miscellaneous shots making love.

### Girlfriend from Hell (1989)

Ken Abraham. . . . . . . . . . . . . . . . . . . . . . . . . Rocco
James Daughton . . . . . . . . . . . . . . . . . . . . . .David
Lezlie Deane. . . . . . . . . . . . . . . . . . . . . . . . . .Diane
Christina Veronica . . . . . . . . . . . . . . . . . . . . . Dancer
  ••• 1:17—Breasts dancing on stage in club.

### Girlfriends (1978)

Christopher Guest . . . . . . . . . . . . . . . . . . . . . . . Eric
  • 1:04—Buns, while running after Melanie Mayron in
    her apartment, then hugging her.
Melanie Mayron. . . . . . . . . . . . . . . . .Susan Weinblatt
  • 0:14—Buns, very brief lower frontal nudity and brief
    left breast getting dressed in bathroom.
Anita Skinner . . . . . . . . . . . . . . . . . . . . . Anne Munroe
Amy Wright . . . . . . . . . . . . . . . . . . . . . . . . . . . Ceil
  • 0:42—Brief breasts getting out of bed to talk to Mel-
    anie Mayron.

### Gladiator (1992)

Cara Buono . . . . . . . . . . . . . . . . . . . . . . . . . . Dawn
Brian Dennehy . . . . . . . . . . . . . . . . . . . . . . . . . Horn
Cuba Gooding, Jr. . . . . . . . . . . . . . . . . . . . . . Lincoln
John Heard. . . . . . . . . . . . . . . . . . . . . . . John Riley
James Marshall . . . . . . . . . . . . . . . . . . . . Tommy Riley
  • 1:33—Brief buns, while wearing jock strap when
    Brian Dennehy yanks his boxing shorts down in box-
    ing ring.
Debra Sandlund . . . . . . . . . . . . . . . . . . . . . . Charlene

## Glen and Randa (1971)

Steven Curry . . . . . . . . . . . . . . . . . . . . . . . . . . . . Glen
- ••• 0:00—Nude in the woods with Randa. Long scene.
- • 0:42—Frontal nudity while kneeling on the ground.

Shelley Plimpton . . . . . . . . . . . . . . . . . . . . . . . . Randa
- ••• 0:01—Nude in the woods with Glen. Long scene.
- • 0:40—Lower nudity, while lying on the ground when Glen tickles her.

## Glitch (1988)

Laura Albert . . . . . . . . . . . . . . . . . . . . . . . . . . . Topless
- • 0:35—Brief breasts auditioning for two guys by taking off her top.

Christina Cardan . . . . . . . . . . . . . . . . . . . . . . Non SAG
- • 0:47—Brief breasts in spa taking off her swimsuit top.

Teri Weigel . . . . . . . . . . . . . . . . . . . . . . . . . . . . Lydia
- 0:41—In pink bathing suit talking to blonde guy.
- • 0:54—Very brief side view of right breast in bathtub with dark haired guy.

## Gnaw: Food of the Gods II (1988; Canadian)

Eduardo Castillo . . . . . . . . . . . . . . . . . . . . . . . . . Carlos
- • 0:46—Buns, while walking through bushes to take a leak. More buns, while running away from the giant rats.

## A Gnome Named Gnorm (1993)

Claudia Christian. . . . . . . . . . . . . . . . . . . . . . Samantha
Mark Harelik . . . . . . . . . . . . . . . . . . . . . . . . . . Kaminsky
- • 1:05—Brief buns, twice, after waking up without any clothes on so that Gnorm can escape.

## God's Gun (1977)

*a.k.a. A Bullet from God*
Sybil Danning . . . . . . . . . . . . . . . . . . . . . . . . . . . Jenny
- • 1:09—Right breast popping out of dress with a guy in the barn during flashback.

Robert Lipton . . . . . . . . . . . . . . . . . . . . . . . . . . . . .n.a.

## The Godfather (1972)

Marlon Brando . . . . . . . . . . . . . . . . . Don Vito Corleone
Diane Keaton . . . . . . . . . . . . . . . . . . . . . . Kay Adams
Simonetta Stefanelli . . . . . . . . . . . . . . . . . . . Apollonia
- •• 1:50—Breasts in bedroom on honeymoon night.

## Goin' All the Way (1981)

Josh Cadman . . . . . . . . . . . . . . . . . . . . . . . . . . . Bronk
- • 1:05—Buns, while in the shower talking to Boom Boom.

Gina Calabrese . . . . . . . . . . . . . . . . . . . . . . . . . . .n.a.
- •• 0:12—Left breast, in the girls' locker room shower. Standing on the left.

Eileen Davidson. . . . . . . . . . . . . . . . . . . . . . . . . . . BJ
- ••• 0:12—Breasts in the girls' locker room shower. Standing next to Monica.
- ••• 0:22—Exercising in her bedroom in braless pink T-shirt, then breasts talking on the phone to Monica.

Sherrie Miller . . . . . . . . . . . . . . . . . . . . . . . . . . Candy
- 0:47—Brief right breast getting out of bubble bath.
- •• 0:49—Breasts with Artie during his fantasy.

## Going Places (1974; French)

Miou-Miou . . . . . . . . . . . . . . . . . . . . . . . Marie-Ange
- ••• 0:14—Breasts sitting in bed, filing her nails. Full frontal nudity standing up and getting dressed.
- •• 0:48—Breasts in bed with Pierrot and Jean-Claude.
- • 0:51—Left breast under Pierrot.
- ••• 0:52—Buns in bed when Jean-Claude rolls off her. Full frontal nudity sitting up with the two guys in bed.
- •• 1:21—Brief breasts opening the door. Breasts and panties walking in after the two guys.
- • 1:27—Partial left breast taking off dress and walking into house.
- 1:28—Very brief breasts while closing the shutters.
- •• 1:31—Full frontal nudity in open dress running after the two guys. Long shot. Full frontal nudity putting her wet dress on.
- • 1:41—Breasts while in back of car. Dark.

Gérard Depardieu . . . . . . . . . . . . . . . . . . . . Jean-Claude
- • 0:42—Upper half of buns and pubic hair, while talking to Pierrot.
- •• 0:49—Buns while in bed, then more buns making love to Miou-Miou. Nice up and down action.
- • 0:50—Brief buns while switching places with Pierrot.
- • 0:51—Brief frontal nudity getting out of bed. Dark, hard to see. Subtitles get in the way.

Patrick Dewaere . . . . . . . . . . . . . . . . . . . . . . . . . Pierrot
- • 0:42—Upper half of buns while starting to leave the room. Surgical tape on his buns.
- •• 0:48—Buns while in bed with Marie-Ange.
- • 0:50—Brief buns, while switching places with Jean-Claude.
- 1:41—Sort of buns, while making love in back seat of car. Dark.
- • 1:42—Buns, while getting out of car and pulling up his pants.

Brigitte Fossey . . . . . . . . . . . . . . . . . . . . . Young Mother
- ••• 0:32—In bra, then breasts in open blouse on the train when she lets Pierrot suck the milk out of her breasts.

Isabelle Huppert . . . . . . . . . . . . . . . . . . . . . . . Jacqueline
- • 1:53—Brief upper half of left breast making love with Jean-Claude.

Jeanne Moreau. . . . . . . . . . . . . . . . . . . . . .Jeanne Pirolle

## The Golden Voyage of Sinbad (1974; British)

John Phillip Law . . . . . . . . . . . . . . . . . . . . . . . . .Sinbad
Caroline Munro . . . . . . . . . . . . . . . . . . . . . . .Margiana
- 0:51—Very brief right nipple, sticking out of top when Sinbad carries her from the boat to the shore. Long shot.

## Good Morning, Babylon (1987; Italian/French)

Desiree Becker . . . . . . . . . . . . . . . . . . . . . . . . . . Mabel
- • 1:06—Brief breasts in the woods making love.

David Brandon . . . . . . . . . . . . . . . . . . . . . . . . . . Grass
Greta Scacchi. . . . . . . . . . . . . . . . . . . . . . . . . . . Edna
- •• 1:05—Breasts in the woods making love with Vincent Spano.

Vincent Spano . . . . . . . . . . . . . . . . . . . . Nicola Bonnano

**The Good Mother** (1988)
Tracy Griffith . . . . . . . . . . . . . . . . . . . . . . . . . . . .Babe
  • 0:06—Brief breasts opening her blouse to show a
    young Anna what it's like being pregnant.
Diane Keaton . . . . . . . . . . . . . . . . . . . . . . . . . .Anna

**The Good Wife** (1987; Australian)
a.k.a. The Umbrella Woman
Bryan Brown . . . . . . . . . . . . . . . . . . . . . . . . Sonny Hills
Helen Jones. . . . . . . . . . . . . . . . . . . . . . . .Rosie Gibbs
Clarissa Kaye-Mason . . . . . . . . . . . . . . . . Mrs. Jackson
Susan Lyons . . . . . . . . . . . . . . . . . . . . . . .Mrs. Fielding
  • 1:22—Very brief breasts coming in from the balco-
    ny.
Sam Neill . . . . . . . . . . . . . . . . . . . . . . . Neville Gifford
Rachel Ward . . . . . . . . . . . . . . . . . . . . . . . Marge Hills

**Goodbye Emmanuelle** (1977)
Olga Georges-Picot. . . . . . . . . . . . . . . . . . . . . . . .n.a.
Sylvia Kristel . . . . . . . . . . . . . . . . . . . . . . Emmanuelle
  •• 0:03—Full frontal nudity in bath and getting out.
  •• 0:04—Full frontal nudity taking off dress.
  ••• 0:06—Full frontal nudity in bed with Angelique.
  ••• 0:26—Breasts with photographer in old house.
    0:42—Brief side view of right breast, in bed with
    Jean.
  ••• 1:03—Full frontal nudity on beach with movie direc-
    tor.
  •• 1:06—Full frontal nudity lying on beach sleeping.
  •• 1:28—Side view of left breast lying on beach with
    Gregory while dreaming.
Alexandra Stewart. . . . . . . . . . . . . . . . . . . . . Dorothee

**Goodbye Pork Pie** (1980; New Zealand)
Bruno Lawrence . . . . . . . . . . . . . . . . . . . . . . Mulvaney
Claire Oberman. . . . . . . . . . . . . . . . . . . . . . . . . . Shirl
  •• 0:44—Breasts while in freight car with Gerry.

**Goodbye, Columbus** (1969)
Richard Benjamin . . . . . . . . . . . . . . . . . . . . . . . Neil
  • 1:11—Brief buns, while walking into the bathroom.
    Very, very brief frontal nudity. Blurry, hard to see
    anything.
Ali MacGraw. . . . . . . . . . . . . . . . . . . . . . . . . Brenda
  • 0:50—Very brief side view of left breast, taking off
    dress before running and jumping into a swimming
    pool. Brief right breast jumping into pool.
  • 1:11—Very brief side view of right breast in bed with
    Richard Benjamin. Brief buns, getting out of bed and
    walking to the bathroom.

**Goodbye, Norma Jean** (1975)
Patch Mackenzie. . . . . . . . . . . . . . . . . . . .Ruth Latimer
Misty Rowe. . . . . . . . . . . . . . . . . . . . .Norma Jean Baker
    0:02—In white bra putting makeup on.
  •• 0:08—In white bra and panties, then breasts.
  • 0:14—Brief breasts in bed getting raped.
    0:31—Very, very brief silhouette of right breast, in
    bed with Rob.
  ••• 0:59—Breasts during shooting of stag film, then in
    B&W when some people watch the film.

**Gorky Park** (1983)
Brian Dennehy . . . . . . . . . . . . . . . . . . . . . William Kirwill
William Hurt. . . . . . . . . . . . . . . . . . . . . . .Arkady Renko
Joanna Pacula. . . . . . . . . . . . . . . . . . . . . . . . . . .Irina
  •• 1:20—Brief breasts in bed making love with William
    Hurt.

**Gotcha!** (1985)
Nick Corri . . . . . . . . . . . . . . . . . . . . . . . . . . . . Manolo
Anthony Edwards. . . . . . . . . . . . . . . . . .Jonathan Moore
Linda Fiorentino. . . . . . . . . . . . . . . . . . . . . . . . .Sasha
  •• 0:53—Brief breasts getting searched at customs.
Kari Lizer . . . . . . . . . . . . . . . . . . . . . . . . . . . . Muffy
Christopher Rydell . . . . . . . . . . . . . . . . . . . Bob Jensen

**Gotham** (1988; Made for Cable Movie)
a.k.a. The Dead Can't Lie
Tommy Lee Jones. . . . . . . . . . . . . . . . . . Eddie Mallard
  • 0:50—Buns, while walking over to Virginia Madsen.
    Dark, hard to see anything.
Virginia Madsen . . . . . . . . . . . . . . . . . . Rachel Carlyle
  • 0:50—Brief breasts in the shower when Tommy Lee
    Jones comes over to her apartment, then breasts
    while lying on the floor.
  •• 1:12—Breasts, while dead, in the freezer when Jones
    comes back to her apartment, then brief breasts.
  • 1:18—Breasts while in the bathtub under water.

**Gothic** (1986; British)
Gabriel Byrne . . . . . . . . . . . . . . . . . . . . . . . . . . .Byron
Myriam Cyr . . . . . . . . . . . . . . . . . . . . . . . . . . . . .Claire
  •• 0:53—Left breast, then breasts while lying in bed
    with Gabriel Byrne.
  • 0:55—Brief left breast lying in bed. Long shot.
  • 1:02—Breasts, while sitting on pool table opening
    her top for Julian Sands. Special effect with eyes in
    her nipples.
  • 1:12—Buns and brief breasts covered with mud.
Natasha Richardson . . . . . . . . . . . . . . . . . . . . . Mary
Julian Sands . . . . . . . . . . . . . . . . . . . . . . . . . . .Shelley
  •• 0:17—Buns, while standing on roof in the rain.

**Graduation Day** (1981)
Erica Hope . . . . . . . . . . . . . . . . . . . . . . . . . . . .Diane
  • 1:02—Brief breasts in open blouse running away
    from the killer.
Patch Mackenzie . . . . . . . . . . . . . . . . . . Anne Ramstead
E.J. Peaker . . . . . . . . . . . . . . . . . . . . . . . . . . . Blondie
Linnea Quigley. . . . . . . . . . . . . . . . . . . . . . . . Dolores
  •• 0:36—Breasts by the piano in classroom with Mr.
    Roberts unbuttoning her blouse.
Linda Shayne . . . . . . . . . . . . . . . . . . .Uncredited Paula
Vanna White . . . . . . . . . . . . . . . . . . . . . . . . . . . Doris

**Grand Canyon** (1991)
Sharon Lee Jones . . . . . . . . . . . . . . . . . . . . Studio Girl
Kevin Kline. . . . . . . . . . . . . . . . . . . . . . . . . . . . . Mack
Mary-Louise Parker. . . . . . . . . . . . . . . . . . . . . . .Dee
  • 1:00—Breasts, pulling sheet down, while lying in
    bed during dream sequence.
Sarah Trigger . . . . . . . . . . . . . . . . . . . . . . . . . Vanessa

## Grand Isle *(1991)*

Ellen Burstyn . . . . . . . . . . . . . . . . . .Mademoiselle Reisa
Kelly McGillis. . . . . . . . . . . . . . . . . . . . . Edna Pontellier
- ••• 1:08—Breasts while on the floor making love with Julian Sands.
- ••• 1:19—Breasts, twice, in open robe while sketching while lying on the floor.
- ••• 1:30—Buns and breasts after taking off clothes at the beach.
- ••• 1:31—Nude, quite a few times, while swimming under water. Seen from under water.
- •• 1:32—Breasts, while doing the backstroke above water.

Adrian Pasdar . . . . . . . . . . . . . . . . . . . .Robert Lebrun
Julian Sands. . . . . . . . . . . . . . . . . . . . . . Alcee Ambin

## Grandview, U.S.A. *(1984)*

Jamie Lee Curtis . . . . . . . . . . . . . Michelle "Mike" Cody
- ••• 1:00—Left breast, lying in bed with C. Thomas Howell.

C. Thomas Howell. . . . . . . . . . . . . . . . . . . Tim Pearson
Jennifer Jason Leigh. . . . . . . . . . . . . . . .Candy Webster
Patrick Swayze . . . . . . . . . . . . . . .Ernie "Slam" Webster

## The Grasshopper *(1970)*

*a.k.a. The Passing of Evil*
*a.k.a. Passions*
Jacqueline Bisset . . . . . . . . . . . . . . . . . .Christine Adams
- 0:21—In flesh-colored Las Vegas-style showgirl costume. Partial buns.
- 0:27—More showgirl shots.
- 1:14—In black two piece swimsuit.
- 1:16—Brief, almost left breast while squished against Jay in the shower.

Christopher Stone. . . . . . . . . . . . . . . . . . . . .Jay Rigney
- 0:26—Buns, seen through shower door when Jacqueline Bisset comes in to join him.
- • 1:17—Brief buns while lying in bed talking to Bisset.

## Graveyard Shift *(1987)*

Sugar Bouche . . . . . . . . . . . . . . . . . . . .Fabulous Frannie
- ••• 0:12—Breasts doing a stripper routine on stage.
- • 0:24—Brief breasts in the shower.

Kim Cayer. . . . . . . . . . . . . . . . . . . . . . . . . . . . . Suzy
- •• 0:06—In black bra, then brief left breast when vampire rips the bra off.
- • 0:53—Brief breasts in junk yard with garter belt, black panties and stockings.

Silvio Oliviero . . . . . . . . . . . . . . . . . . . .Stephen Tsepes
- • 0:09—Buns, while climbing into his coffin.

## The Great Bikini Off-Road Adventure *(1994)*

Avalon Anders. . . . . . . . . . . . . . . . . . . . .Paulina Smalls
- •• 0:01—Breasts, while sunbathing and lying on ground and spraying herself with water.
- •• 0:16—Breasts, while sunbathing outside on the rocks with Tisha.
- ••• 0:21—Breasts, while undoing her swimsuit top in front of two guys out in the desert.
- • 0:31—Brief buns, while in swimsuit.

- ••• 0:44—Breasts, while posing on a jeep for a customer with a camera.
- ••• 0:50—Breasts and buns, while posing outside for a customer.
- ••• 1:02—Breasts and buns during water fight.

Lauren Hays. . . . . . . . . . . . . . . . . . . . . . . . . Lori Baker
- • 1:06—Buns in swimsuit while giving a tour.
- ••• 1:11—In bra in house with her boyfriend, then breasts while making love with him.

## Greedy *(1993)*

Khandi Alexander. . . . . . . . . . . . . . . . . . . . . . . . .Laura
Ed Begley, Jr. . . . . . . . . . . . . . . . . . . . . . . . . . . . . Carl
Colleen Camp . . . . . . . . . . . . . . . . . . . . . . . . . .Patti
Olivia D'Abo. . . . . . . . . . . . . . . . . . . . . . . . . . .Molly
Kirk Douglas. . . . . . . . . . . . . . . . . . . . . . . .Uncle Joe
Michael J. Fox . . . . . . . . . . . . . . . . . . . . . . . . Daniel
- •• 0:28—Buns, after taking off his underwear, then leaving the hotel room and coming back in.
- ••• 0:30—Buns, while opening the door to greet Laura.

Joyce Hyser . . . . . . . . . . . . . . . . . . . . . . . . . . Muriel
John Lafayette . . . . . . . . . . . . . . . . . . . . . . . .Wayne
Nancy Travis . . . . . . . . . . . . . . . . . . . . . . . . . .Robin

## Greetings *(1968)*

Robert De Niro. . . . . . . . . . . . . . . . . . . . . .Jon Rubin
Jonathan Warden . . . . . . . . . . . . . . . . . . . . Paul Shaw
- •• 1:15—Buns, while making love in bed with the Nymphomaniac. Shot at high speed. More buns, while getting out from under her.

## Greystoke: The Legend of Tarzan, Lord of the Apes *(1984)*

James Fox. . . . . . . . . . . . . . . . . . . . . . . . . Lord Eskar
Christopher Lambert . . . . . . . . . . . John Clayton/Tarzan
Eric Langlois. . . . . . . . . . . . . . . . . . . Tarzan Aged Twelve
- • 0:21—Nude, in old house in the jungle.
- • 0:25—Nude, swinging and running around in the jungle.
- • 0:27—More buns, in the jungle during attack.

Daniel Potts . . . . . . . . . . . . . . . . . . . . Tarzan Aged Five
- • 0:17—Nude in the jungle.
- • 0:19—More nude in the jungle.

## The Grifters *(1990)*

Annette Bening . . . . . . . . . . . . . . . . . . . .Myra Langtry
- •• 0:36—In bra and panties in her apartment, then breasts lying in bed "paying" her rent. Kind of dark.
- ••• 1:06—Nude, walking down the hall to the bedroom and into bed.
- 1:30—Very brief right breast, dead in morgue. Long shot.

Anjelica Huston . . . . . . . . . . . . . . . . . . . . . Lilly Dillon

## Grim Prairie Tales *(1990)*

Brad Dourif . . . . . . . . . . . . . . . . . . . . . . . . . .Farley
Lisa Eichhorn . . . . . . . . . . . . . . . . . . . . . . Maureen
Michelle Joyner . . . . . . . . . . . . . . . . . . . . . . . . .Jenny
- • 0:35—Very brief right breast, then left breast while making love with Marc McClure. Kind of dark.

## The Groove Tube (1974)

Jennifer Welles . . . . . . . . . . . . . . . . . . . The Geritan Girl
- •• 0:21—Dancing nude around her husband, Chevy Chase.

## Group Marriage (1972)

Aimée Eccles . . . . . . . . . . . . . . . . . . . . . . . . . . Chris
   0:15—Buns, getting into bed.
- • 1:15—Brief side view of left breast and buns getting into the shower.

Claudia Jennings . . . . . . . . . . . . . . . . . . . . . . . . Elaine
- ••• 1:02—Breasts under mosquito net in bed with Phil. Long scene.

Pepe Serna . . . . . . . . . . . . . . . . . . . . . . . . . . Ramon

Zach Taylor . . . . . . . . . . . . . . . . . . . . . . . . . . . Phil
- •• 0:43—Buns, while walking on beach with Jan.

Victoria Vetri . . . . . . . . . . . . . . . . . . . . . . . . . . Jan
- ••• 0:28—Buns and breasts getting into bed with Dennis, Sander and Chris. More breasts sitting in bed. Long scene.
- • 1:19—Brief side view of right breast in lifeguard booth.

## The Guardian (1990)

Dwier Brown . . . . . . . . . . . . . . . . . . . . . . . . . . . Phil
   0:37—Soft of buns, while in bed with Carey Lowell. Don't see his face.

Miguel Ferrer . . . . . . . . . . . . . . . . . . . . . Ralph Hess

Carey Lowell . . . . . . . . . . . . . . . . . . . . . . . . . . Kate
- •• 0:37—Right breast twice, in bed with Phil.

Jenny Seagrove . . . . . . . . . . . . . . . . . . . . . . . Camilla
- ••• 0:21—Side view of left breast, while in bathtub with the baby. Right breast, then breasts.
   0:23—Buns, drying herself off. Long shot.
- •• 0:38—Breasts, mostly left breast on top of Phil. Don't see her face, probably a body double.
   0:46—Buns, skinny dipping. Long shot.
- •• 0:47—Breasts healing her wound by a tree. Side view of right breast.
- • 1:18—Very brief breasts under sheer gown in forest just before getting hit by a Jeep.
   1:24—Very briefly breasts scaring Carey Lowell. Body is painted all over.

## Gulag (1985)

David Keith . . . . . . . . . . . . . . . . . . . . . Mickey Almon
- •• 1:26—Buns, while standing outside with Malcolm McDowell in the snow being hassled by guards.

Malcolm McDowell . . . . . . . . . . . . . . . . . Englishman
- •• 1:26—Buns, while standing outside with David Keith in the snow being hassled by guards.

Nancy Paul . . . . . . . . . . . . . . . . . . . . . . . . . . Susan
- •• 0:42—Buns, then breasts taking a shower while David Keith daydreams while he's on a train.

## The Gumshoe Kid (1990)

Tracy Scoggins . . . . . . . . . . . . . . . . . . . . Rita Benson
   0:33—In two piece white swimsuit. Nice bun shot while Jay Underwood hides in the closet.

- ••• 1:10—Side view of left breast in the shower with Underwood. Excellent slow motion breasts shot while turning around. Brief side view of right breast in bed afterwards.

Pamela Springsteen . . . . . . . . . . . . . . . . . Mona Krause

Jay Underwood . . . . . . . . . . . . . . . . . . . . . Jeff Sherman

## Guncrazy (1992; Made for Cable Movie)

Drew Barrymore . . . . . . . . . . . . . . . . . . . . . . . . . Anita
   1:00—Briefly in wet blouse in shower with her boyfriend. Seen from above.
- • 1:24—Brief buns, while in bed on top of her boyfriend. Don't see her face.

James Le Gros . . . . . . . . . . . . . . . . . . . . . . . . . Howard

Ione Skye . . . . . . . . . . . . . . . . . . . . . . . . . . . . . . Joy

Tracey Walter . . . . . . . . . . . . . . . . . . . . . . . . . . Elton

## Guns (1990)

Cynthia Brimhall . . . . . . . . . . . . . . . . . . . . Edy Stark
   0:26—Buns, in G-string singing and dancing at club.
- •• 0:27—Breasts in dressing room.
   0:53—Buns, in black one piece outfit and stockings, singing in club. Nice legs!

William Bumiller . . . . . . . . . . . . . . . . . . . . . . . . Lucas

Allegra Curtis . . . . . . . . . . . . . . . . . . . . . . . . . Robyn

Phyllis Davis . . . . . . . . . . . . . . . . . Kathryn Hamilton

Devin De Vasquez . . . . . . . . . . . . . . . . . . . . . . Cash
- • 1:12—Brief side of right breast and buns undressing for bath.

Liv Lindeland . . . . . . . . . . . . . . . . . . . . . . . . . . . Ace

Lisa London . . . . . . . . . . . . . . . . . . . . . . . . . . Rocky

Kym Malin . . . . . . . . . . . . . . . . . . . . . . . . . . . . Kym
   0:27—Oil wrestling with Hugs.
- ••• 0:28—Showering (in back) while talking to Hugs (in front).

Michael Jay Shane . . . . . . . . . . . . . . . . . . Shane Abilene

Donna Spangler . . . . . . . . . . . . . . . . . . . Hugs Huggins
   0:27—Oil wrestling with Kym.
   0:28—Showering (in front) while talking to Kym (in back).

Dona Speir . . . . . . . . . . . . . . . . . . . . . Donna Hamilton
- ••• 1:00—Breasts and buns in black G-string getting dressed in locker room. Then in black lingerie.

Roberta Vasquez . . . . . . . . . . . . . . . . . . . Nicole Justin
- •• 0:50—Right breast while making love on motorcycle with her boyfriend.

## Gypsy Angels (1980)

Marilyn Hassett . . . . . . . . . . . . . . . . . . . . . . . . . Jan

Richard Roundtree . . . . . . . . . . . . . . . . . . . . . . . n.a.

Carol Wayne . . . . . . . . . . . . . . . . . . . . . . . . Waitress

Vanna White . . . . . . . . . . . . . . . . . . . . . . . . . Mickey
   0:20—Dancing on stage in club in two piece swimsuit outfit.
   0:46—Silhouette of breasts from behind shower curtain.
- • 0:46—Partial right breast, while making out with Jeff outside by a fire.
   1:12—Back side of left breast while getting into bed during Jeff's flashback.

## The Gypsy Moths (1969)

Bonnie Bedelia . . . . . . . . . . . . . . . . . . . . . . Annie Burke
- • 0:28—Very, very brief right breast, while opening and folding her robe together while walking up the stairs. Partially hidden by shadow.

Deborah Kerr . . . . . . . . . . . . . . . . . . .Elizabeth Brandon
- ••• 0:52—Buns and left breast, while making love with Burt Lancaster on sofa.

Burt Lancaster . . . . . . . . . . . . . . . . . . . . . .Mike Retting

Sheree North . . . . . . . . . . . . . . . . . . . . . . . . Waitress
- •• 0:37—Breasts while dancing on stage in pink pasties and pink bikini bottoms.
- • 0:53—Most of left breast, while lying in bed next to Gene Hackman.

## H.O.T.S. (1979)

*a.k.a. T & A Academy*

Angela Aames . . . . . . . . . . . . . . . .Boom-Boom Bangs
- • 0:21—Breasts parachuting into pool.
- • 0:39—Breasts in bathtub playing with a seal.
- • 1:33—Breasts while playing football.

Lindsay Bloom. . . . . . . . . . . . . . . . . Melody Ragmore
- • 0:28—Very brief right breast on balcony.
- • 1:34—Brief breasts during football game throwing football as quarterback.

Steve Bond . . . . . . . . . . . . . . . . . . . . . . . . . . . . John
- • 0:32—Buns, while trapped in van with K. C. Winkler.

Pamela Bryant. . . . . . . . . . . . . . . . . . . . . . Teri Lynn
- • 1:33—Breasts during football game.

Sandy Johnson . . . . . . . . . . . . . . . . . . . . . Stephanie
- •• 0:27—Breasts on balcony in red bikini bottoms.
- •• 1:34—Breasts during football game during huddle with all the other girls.

Susan Lynn Kiger. . . . . . . . . . . . . . . . . Honey Shayne
- • 0:00—Breasts in shower room with the other girls.
- •• 0:33—Breasts in pool making love with Doug.
- • 1:33—Breasts in football game.

Lisa London. . . . . . . . . . . . . . . . . . . . . Jennie O'Hara
- • 1:22—Breasts changing clothes by the closet while a crook watches her.
- • 1:33—Breasts playing football.

K.C. Winkler . . . . . . . . . . . . . . . . . . . . . . . . .Cynthia
- • 0:27—Breasts in blue bikini bottom on balcony.
- •• 0:31—Breasts in van making love, then arguing with John.

## Hail, Mary (1985; French)

*a.k.a. Je Vous Salve, Marie*

Juliette Binoche. . . . . . . . . . . . . . . . . . . . . . . Juliette

Myriem Roussel . . . . . . . . . . . . . . . . . . . . . . . .Mary
- • 0:56—Brief full frontal nudity in bathroom.
- ••• 0:57—Full frontal nudity in bathtub, washing herself while kneeling.
- ••• 1:13—Nude, undressing and putting on nightgown in bedroom.
- • 1:17—Brief breasts, while moving around under sheets in bed.
- ••• 1:18—Breasts, while sitting on bed.
- • 1:19—Lower frontal nudity and tops of breasts while undressing and bending over in gaping top.

- •• 1:22—Close-up of lower frontal nudity, while in bedroom with Joseph.
- •• 1:23—Lower frontal nudity and buns, after lifting up her blouse.
- • 1:30—Very, very brief right breast, while rolling around in bed under the sheets.
- ••• 1:31—Lower frontal nudity, then breasts, while in bed. Nice close-ups.
- ••• 1:33—Lower frontal nudity and breasts, while lying in bed on her back.

## Hair (1979)

Beverly D'Angelo . . . . . . . . . . . . . . . . . . . . . . Sheila
- • 0:59—In white bra and panties, then breasts on rock near pond. Medium long shot.
- ••• 1:01—Breasts in panties getting out of the pond.
- • 1:38—Side view of right breast changing clothes in car with George.

Don Dacus . . . . . . . . . . . . . . . . . . . . . . . . . . . Woof
- • 0:57—Buns, while taking off clothes and diving into pond with Treat Williams and Hud.

Michael Jeter . . . . . . . . . . . . . . . . . .Woodrow Sheldon
- • 1:06—Buns while in front of Army guys.

John Savage. . . . . . . . . . . . . . . . . . . . . . . . . .Claude

Treat Williams . . . . . . . . . . . . . . . . . . . . . . . . Berger
- • 0:57—Buns, while taking off clothes and diving into pond with Hud and Woof.

Dorsey Wright . . . . . . . . . . . . . . . . . . . . . . . . . .Hud
- • 0:57—Buns, while taking off clothes and diving into pond with Treat Williams and Woof.

## Half Moon Street (1986)

*a.k.a. Escort Girl*

Keith Buckley . . . . . . . . . . . . . . . . . . . .Hugo Van arkady

Vincent Lindon. . . . . . . . . . . . . . . . . . . . . . . . Sonny
- • 1:04—Buns, while getting out of bed with Sigourney Weaver.

Janet McTeer . . . . . . . . . . . . . Van Arkady's Ambassador

Sigourney Weaver . . . . . . . . . . . . . . . Lauren Slaughter
- • 0:05—Brief breasts in the bathtub.
- •• 0:11—Brief breasts in the bathtub again.
- • 0:18—Brief buns and side view of right breast while putting on makeup in front of the mirror. Wearing a black garter belt and stockings.
- ••• 0:39—Breasts, while riding exercise bike while being photographed, then brief breasts getting out of the shower.
- 0:46—Very, very brief breasts wearing a sheer black blouse with no bra during daydream sequence.
- • 0:50—Brief breasts, while in bed with Michael Caine, then left breast.
- 1:16—In braless, wet, white blouse in bathroom after knocking a guy out.

## Halloween (1978)

Jamie Lee Curtis . . . . . . . . . . . . . . . . . . . . . . . Laurie

Sandy Johnson . . . . . . . . . . . . . . . . . Judith Meyers
- 0:06—Very brief breasts covered with blood on floor after Michael stabs her to death.

P.J. Soles . . . . . . . . . . . . . . . . . . . . . . . . . Lynda
- 1:04—Brief right breast, sitting up in bed after making love in bed with Bob.
- 1:07—Brief breasts getting strangled by Michael in the bedroom.

### Halloween II (1981)
Jamie Lee Curtis . . . . . . . . . . . . . . . . . . . . . Laurie
Leo Rossi . . . . . . . . . . . . . . . . . . . . . . . . . . . Budd
- 0:48—Buns, while getting out of the whirlpool bath to check the water temperature.
Pamela Susan Shoop . . . . . . . . . . . . . . . . . . . . Karen
••• 0:48—Breasts getting into the whirlpool bath with Budd in the hospital.

### Halloween III: Season of the Witch (1983)
Tom Atkins . . . . . . . . . . . . . . . . . . . . . Daniel Challis
•• 0:42—Buns, getting out of bed and putting his pants on.
Stacey Nelkin . . . . . . . . . . . . . . . . . Ellie Grimbridge
- 0:37—Brief right breast, behind shower door, when getting out of the shower.

### Hamburger—The Motion Picture (1986)
Debra Blee . . . . . . . . . . . . . . . . . . . . . . Mia Vunk
0:25—Briefly in wet dress in the swimming pool.
Randi Brooks . . . . . . . . . . . . . . . . . . . . . . . .Mrs. Vunk
•• 0:52—Brief breasts in helicopter with a guy.
Karen Mayo-Chandler . . . . . . . . .Dr. Victoria Gotbottom
- 0:03—Brief breasts in her office trying to help, then seduce Russell.
Maria Richwine . . . . . . . . . . . . . . . . . . . . . . .Conchita
•• 0:49—Breasts trying to seduce Russell in a room.

### The Hand (1981)
Annie McEnroe . . . . . . . . . . . . . . . . . . . . Stella Roche
•• 0:51—Breasts undressing for Michael Caine.
Bruce McGill . . . . . . . . . . . . . . . . . . . . Brian Ferguson
Tracey Walter . . . . . . . . . . . . . . . . . . . . . . . . Cop

### The Hand That Rocks the Cradle (1992)
Rebecca De Mornay . . . . . . . . . . . . . . . . . . . . Peyton
- 0:29—Upper half of right breast, breast feeding Claire's baby.
0:36—Partial right breast, breast feeding the baby again.
1:25—Briefly in wet nightgown in the kitchen with Michael.
Julianne Moore . . . . . . . . . . . . . . . . . . . . . . Marlene
Annabella Sciorra . . . . . . . . . . . . . . . . . . . Claire Bartel
- 0:08—Brief side of right breast in open gown, while lying on Dr. Mott's examination table.
0:38—Partial right breast, trying to breast feed her baby.

### A Handmaid's Tale (1990)
David Dukes . . . . . . . . . . . . . . . . . . . . . . . . . Doctor
Faye Dunaway . . . . . . . . . . . . . . . . . . . . . Serena Joy
Elizabeth McGovern . . . . . . . . . . . . . . . . . . . Moira
Aidan Quinn . . . . . . . . . . . . . . . . . . . . . . . . . Nick

Natasha Richardson . . . . . . . . . . . . . . . . . . . . . . .Kate
•• 0:30—Breasts twice at the window getting some fresh air.
- 0:59—Breasts making love with Aidan Quinn.
••• 1:00—Breasts after Quinn rolls off her.
Victoria Tennant. . . . . . . . . . . . . . . . . . . . Aunt Lydia

### Hanover Street (1979)
Lesley-Anne Down . . . . . . . . . . . . . . Margaret Sallinger
- 0:22—In bra and slip, then brief breasts in bedroom with Harrison Ford.
Patsy Kensit . . . . . . . . . . . . . . . . . . . . .Sarah Sallinger

### The Happy Hooker (1975)
Denise Galik . . . . . . . . . . . . . . . . . . . . . . . . . . Cynthia
Anita Morris . . . . . . . . . . . . . . Linda Jo/Mary Smith
- 0:59—Breasts lying on table while a customer puts ice cream all over her.
- 1:24—Breasts covered with whipped cream getting it sprayed off with champagne by another customer.
Lynn Redgrave . . . . . . . . . . . . . . . . . Xaviera Hollander
0:43—In black bra and panties doing a strip tease routine in a board room while Tom Poston watches.

### The Happy Hooker Goes Hollywood (1980)
Martine Beswicke . . . . . . . . . . . . . . . . Xaviera Hollander
•• 0:05—Brief breasts in bedroom with Policeman.
••• 0:22—Brief buns, jumping into the swimming pool, then breasts next to the pool with Adam West.
- 0:27—Breasts in bed with West, then breasts waking up.
Lindsay Bloom . . . . . . . . . . . . . . . . . . . . . . . . . Chris
Tanya Boyd . . . . . . . . . . . . . . . . . . . . . . . . . . .Sylvie
- 0:39—Brief breasts in jungle room when an older customer accidentally comes in.
Liz Glazowski . . . . . . . . . . . . . . . . . . . . . . . . . . . Liz
Kim Hopkins. . . . . . . . . . . . . . . . . . . . Young Xaviera
Susan Lynn Kiger . . . . . . . . . . . . . . . . . . . . . . Susie
- 0:42—Breasts, singing "Happy Birthday" to a guy tied up on the bed.
••• 0:43—Breasts, wearing a red garter belt playing pool with K.C. Winkler.
Lisa London . . . . . . . . . . . . . . . . . . . . . . . . . Laurie
Alexandra Morgan . . . . . . . . . . . . . . . . . . . . . . .Max
K.C. Winkler. . . . . . . . . . . . . . . . . . . . . . . . . .Amber
•• 0:41—Breasts in cowboy outfit on bed with a guy.
••• 0:43—Breasts, wearing a blue garter belt playing pool with Susan Kiger.

### The Happy Hooker Goes to Washington (1977)
Dawn Clark . . . . . . . . . . . . . . . . . . . . . . . . . Candy
- 1:18—Breasts, covered with spaghetti in a restaurant.
Cissie Colpitts-Cameron . . . . . . . . . . . . Miss Goodbody
- 0:29—Very brief breasts when her top pops open during the senate hearing.
Raven De La Croix . . . . . . . . Uncredited Ice Cream Girl
- 0:31—Brief breasts, while lying on table, getting her rear end covered with ice cream.

Linda Gildersleeve . . . . . . . . . . . . . . . . Honeymoon Wife
• 0:35—Brief breasts in a diner during the filming of a commercial.
Joey Heatherton . . . . . . . . . . . . . . . . . Xaviera Hollander
Joyce Jillson . . . . . . . . . . . . . . . . . . . . . . . . . . . . . Herself
Marilyn Joi . . . . . . . . . . . . . . . . . . . . . . . . . . . . . Sheila
• 0:09—Left breast while on a couch.
• 0:47—Brief breasts during car demonstration.
•• 1:14—Breasts in military guy's office.
Bonnie Large . . . . . . . . . . . . . . . . . . . . Carolyn (Model)
• 0:06—Breasts during photo shoot.
Louisa Moritz . . . . . . . . . . . . . . . . . . .Natalie Naussbaum
• 0:39—Brief breasts and buns, lying down on top of Larry Storch in tennis court.
Pamela Zinszer . . . . . . . . . . . . . . . . . . . . . . . . . Linda
• 1:19—Brief breasts in raincoat flashing in front of congressional panel.

## Happy Housewives (British)

Ava Cadell . . . . . . . . . . . . . . . . . . . . . . . . . Schoolgirl
0:39—Buns, getting caught by the Squire and getting spanked.
Jeannie Collings . . . . . . . . . . . . . . . . . . . . . .Mrs. Wain
• 0:16—Very, very brief right breast with the Newsagent's Daughter and Bob in the bathtub.
Sue Lloyd . . . . . . . . . . . . . . . . . . . . . . . . . The Blonde
Nita Lorraine . . . . . . . . . . . . . . . . . . . . . . Jenny Elgin
• 0:31—Brief side view of left breast and buns in barn chasing after Bob.
• 0:32—Brief breasts in open dress talking to policeman.
Helli Louise . . . . . . . . . . . . . . . . Newsagent's Daughter
•• 0:16—Breasts with Mrs. Wain and Bob in the bathtub.
Penny Meredith . . . . . . . . . . . . . . . . . . . . Margaretta
• 0:02—Brief right breast, while talking on the telephone while Bob makes love with her.
•• 0:19—Breasts while standing up in bathtub and talking to Bob.
• 0:34—In sheer black lingerie.
• 1:05—Brief breasts pulling her top down when interrupted by the policeman at the window.
Barry Stokes . . . . . . . . . . . . . . . . . . . . . . . . . . . Bob
• 0:31—Brief buns, while running away from Mrs. Elgin and her daughter in the barn.

## Happy Together (1988)

Patrick Dempsey . . . . . . . Christopher "Chris" Wooden
Helen Slater . . . . . . . . . . . . . . . Alexandra "Alex" Page
•• 0:17—Brief right breast changing clothes while talking to Patrick Dempsey. Unfortunately, she has a goofy expression on her face.
0:57—In red lingerie tempting Dempsey. Later, panties under panty hose when Dempsey pulls her dress up while she's on roller skates.
1:07—Very brief panties under panty hose again straddling Dempsey in the hallway.
1:14—Panties under white stockings while changing in the closet.

## Hard Choices (1986)

Margaret Klenck . . . . . . . . . . . . . . . . . . . . . . . . .Laura
•• 1:10—Left breast, then breasts making love with Bobby. Nice close up shot.
• 1:11—Very brief half of left breast and lower frontal nudity getting back into bed. Long shot.
Gary McCleery . . . . . . . . . . . . . . . . . . . . . . . . . Bobby
•• 1:11—Buns, while making love on top of Laura.

## Hard Drive (1994)

(Unrated version reviewed.)
Edward Albert . . . . . . . . . . . . . . . . . . . . . . Examiner
Robin Joi Brown . . . . . . . . . . . . . . . .Assistant Examiner
Leo Damian . . . . . . . . . . . . . . . . . . . . . . . . . . . . Will
• 0:04—Brief buns, while making love with the Candle Dream Girl.
• 0:07—Buns, while making love in bed with Dream Girl.
• 0:11—Partial buns, while making love in bed with Laura.
•• 1:15—Buns, while making love with Christina Fulton on kitchen counter.
Christina Fulton . . . . . . . . . . . . . . . . . . . . Dana/Delilah
• 0:23—Brief lower frontal nudity, brief left breast and brief buns while getting attacked on bed by Will.
• 0:25—Buns, while lying on bed after getting shot.
• 0:26—Brief buns and left breast in Will's flashback.
•• 1:15—Left breast, while making love with Will on kitchen counter.
Deanne Power . . . . . . . . . . . . . . . .Candle Dream Girl
•• 0:03—Left breast, then breasts, while making love with Will on the floor surrounded by lit candles.
• 0:05—Brief breasts on the floor again.
Stella Stevens . . . . . . . . . . . . . . . . . . . . . . . . .Susan

## Hard Hunted (1993)

Cynthia Brimhall . . . . . . . . . . . . . . . . . . . . . Edy Stark
••• 0:50—Breasts in bedroom while making love with Lucas.
•• 1:18—Left breast, then breasts in bed with Lucas.
Ava Cadell . . . . . . . . . . . . . . . . . . . . . . . . . . . . Ava
0:08—In two piece swimsuit in radio station.
••• 0:38—Breasts in spa with Becky while doing radio show.
1:19—In white fishnet top while talking on the radio.
Brett Clark . . . . . . . . . . . . . . . . . . . . . . Yacht Captain
Carolyn Liu . . . . . . . . . . . . . . . . . . . . . . . . . . . . Silk
• 0:02—Buns, while in lingerie on boat with Mr. Kane.
••• 0:08—Breasts, while taking off her dress top on boat in front of Mr. Kane, then in bed with him.
• 0:10—Brief breasts, while lying in bed with the plastic explosive on the safe blows up.
Beckie Mullen . . . . . . . . . . . . . . . . . . . . . . . .Becky
0:07—In red, two piece swimsuit in radio station with Shane.
•• 0:38—Breasts and buns in G-string in spa with Ava doing radio show.
••• 0:56—Breasts while getting out of spa and getting coffee.

Michael Jay Shane . . . . . . . . . . . . . . . . . . Shane Abilene
Dona Speir . . . . . . . . . . . . . . . . . . . . . . Donna Hamilton
- •• 1:22—Left breast, then breasts on beach with the bad guy, while making love and resting afterwards.
Roberta Vasquez . . . . . . . . . . . . . . . . . . . . Nicole Justin
- •• 1:20—Breasts while making out with Bruce in the ocean.

### Hard Rock Zombies (1985)
Annabelle Larsen . . . . . . . . . . . . . . . . . . . . . . Groupie
Sam Mann . . . . . . . . . . . . . . . . . . . . . . . . . . . Bobby
Lisa Toothman . . . . . . . . . . . . . . . . . . . . . . . . . Elsa
- • 0:01—Buns, undressing to go skinny dipping. Breasts long shot.
- ••• 0:32—Buns, while getting into the shower. Breasts and buns in the shower behind clear plastic curtain.

### Hard Ticket to Hawaii (1987)
Cynthia Brimhall . . . . . . . . . . . . . . . . . . . . . . . . . Edy
- •• 0:47—Breasts changing out of a dress into a blouse and pants.
- •• 1:33—Breasts during the end credits.
Hope Marie Carlton . . . . . . . . . . . . . . . . . . . . . . Taryn
- •• 0:07—Breasts taking a shower outside while talking to Dona Speir.
- ••• 0:23—Breasts in the spa with Speir looking at diamonds they found.
- ••• 0:40—Breasts and buns on the beach making love with her boyfriend, Jimmy John.
- •• 1:33—Breasts during the end credits.
Patty Duffek . . . . . . . . . . . . . . . . . . . . . . . . Patticakes
- •• 0:48—Breasts talking to Michelle after swimming.
Dona Speir . . . . . . . . . . . . . . . . . . . . . . . . . . Donna
- • 0:01—Breasts on boat kissing her boyfriend, Rowdy.
- ••• 0:23—Breasts in the spa with Hope Marie Carlton looking at diamonds they found.
- ••• 1:04—Breasts and buns with Rowdy after watching a video tape.
- •• 1:33—Breasts during the end credits.

### Hard to Die (1990)
*a.k.a. Tower of Terror*
Bridget Carney . . . . . . . . . . . . . . . . . . . Shayne Hobbie
- ••• 0:24—Breasts and buns while taking a shower. Long scene.
Deborah Dutch . . . . . . . . . . . . . . . . . . . . Jackie Webster
- •• 0:25—Breasts and buns, while taking a shower.
Monique Gabrielle . . . . . . . . . . . . . . . . . . . . Fifi Latour
Karen Mayo-Chandler . . . . . . . . . . . . . . . . Diana Farrow
- •• 0:10—Breasts, putting on her dress in office with Mr. Plimpton.
Melissa Anne Moore . . . . . . . . . . . . . . . . Tess Cochran
- ••• 0:21—Breasts taking off her top, then more lengthy breasts while taking a shower. Long scene.
Toni Naples . . . . . . . . . . . . . . . . . . . . . . . Sgt. Shawlee
Gail Thackray . . . . . . . . . . . . . . . . . . . . . Dawn Grant
- ••• 0:31—Breasts, while taking a shower.
Cirsten Weldon . . . . . . . . . . . . . . . . . . Agent's Girlfriend
- • 0:19—Breasts in bedroom with Tess's agent. Medium long shot.

### Hard to Hold (1984)
Janet Eilber . . . . . . . . . . . . . . . . . . . . . . . Diana Lawson
Monique Gabrielle . . . . . . . . . . . . . . . . . . . . Wife #1
Sharon Hughes . . . . . . . . . . . . . . . . . . . . . . . . . Wife
Charlene Jones . . . . . . . . . . . . . . . . . . . . . . . . . . Wife
Rick Springfield . . . . . . . . . . . . . . . . . . . James Roberts
- • 0:06—Buns, while running down the hall getting chased by a bunch of young girls.
- •• 0:15—Buns, while lying in bed sleeping.

### The Hard Truth (1994)
Lysette Anthony . . . . . . . . . . . . . . . . . . . . Lisa Kantrell
-     0:04—In black bra and panties.
-     0:22—In black bra in office with Jonah.
- ••• 0:39—In black bra, then breasts, while making love with Jonah.
Loretta Devine . . . . . . . . . . . . . . . . . . Nichols' Secretary
Eric Roberts . . . . . . . . . . . . . . . . . . . . Chandice Etheridge
Michael Rooker . . . . . . . . . . . . . . . . . . . . Jonah Mantz
- •• 0:04—Buns, while standing in room with Lysette Anthony.
- ••• 0:40—Buns, while making love with Anthony.

### Hard Vice (1994)
Rebecca Ferratti . . . . . . . . . . . . . . . . . . . . . Christine
- ••• 0:02—Buns and breasts, getting out of bubble bath and making love on top of a customer in bed. Breasts while taking a shower.
- ••• 0:21—Breasts, while making love in bed with another customer.
- •• 0:22—Breasts and buns, while taking a shower.
-     1:04—Buns in panties, while standing in bedroom. Long shot.
-     1:06—Upper half of buns in the shower.
Sam Jones . . . . . . . . . . . . . . . . . . . . . . . . . . . . . . Joe
Shannon Tweed . . . . . . . . . . . . . . . . . . . . . . . . Andrea
- •• 0:44—Breasts after taking off her top in front of Sam Jones.

### Hardbodies (1984)
Julie Always . . . . . . . . . . . . . . . Photo Session Hardbody
- •• 0:40—Breasts with other girls posing breasts getting pictures taken by Rounder. She's wearing blue dress with a white belt.
Leslee Bremmer . . . . . . . . . . . Photo Session Hardbody
- • 0:02—Breasts in the surf when her friends take off her swimsuit top during the opening credits.
- •• 0:40—Breasts with other topless girls posing for photographs taken by Rounder. She takes off her dress and is wearing a black G-string.
Roberta Collins . . . . . . . . . . . . . . . . . . . . . . . . Lana
Grant Cramer . . . . . . . . . . . . . . . . . . . . . . . . . Scotty
- • 0:03—Brief buns, while getting out of bed after making love with Kristi.
Darcy De Moss . . . . . . . . . . . . . . . . . . . . . . . . . Dede
- ••• 0:55—Breasts in the back seat of the limousine with Rounder.
Erika Dockery . . . . . . . . . . . . . . . . . . Hardbody in Car
Jackie Easton . . . . . . . . . . . . . . . Girl in Dressing Room
- •• 0:27—Breasts taking off dress to try on swimsuit.

•• 0:40—Breasts with other topless girls posing for photographs taken by Rounder. She's wearing a white skirt.

Marcia Karr . . . . . . . . . . . . . . . . . . Hardbody On Stairs
Kathleen Kinmont . . . . . . . . . . . . . . . . . . . Pretty Skater
Teal Roberts . . . . . . . . . . . . . . . . . . . . . . . . Kristi Kelly

•• 0:03—Breasts in bed after making love with Scotty, then putting her sweater on.

••• 0:47—Breasts standing in front of closet mirrors talking about breasts with Kimberly.

••• 0:56—Breasts making love with Scotty on the beach.

• 1:22—Breasts on fancy car bed with Scotty.

Cindy Silver . . . . . . . . . . . . . . . . . . . . . . . . . . Kimberly

•• 0:07—Brief breasts on beach when a dog steals her bikini top.

••• 0:47—Breasts standing in front of closet mirrors talking about breasts with Kristi.

Kristi Somers . . . . . . . . . . . . . . . . . . . . . . . . . . Michelle

•• 0:53—Nude, dancing on the beach while Ashley plays the guitar and sings.

## *Hardbodies 2* (1986)

Brenda Bakke . . . . . . . . . . . . . . . . . . . . . . . . Morgan

•• 0:34—Buns, getting into bathtub, then breasts, taking a bath.

Roberta Collins . . . . . . . . . . . . . . . . . . . . . Lana Logan
Fabiana Udenio . . . . . . . . . . . . . . . . . . . . Cleo/Princess

## *Hardcase and Fist* (1988)

Maureen La Vette . . . . . . . . . . . . . . . . . . . . Nora Wilde

•• 0:24—Breasts, getting out of spa when Tony starts shooting gun in the house.

Debra Lamb . . . . . . . . . . . . . . . . . . . . . . . . . Chieko

• 1:08—Buns in G-string while dancing on stage in a club.

••• 1:09—Breasts while dancing on stage and doing some fire eating. Nice, long scene.

•• 1:13—Breasts, three times, while peeking from behind curtain.

Ted Prior . . . . . . . . . . . . . . . . . . . . . . . . . Bud McAll

## *Hardcore* (1979)

Leslie Ackerman . . . . . . . . . . . . . . . . . . . . . . . Felice

• 0:44—Breasts in porno house with George C. Scott.

Ed Begley, Jr. . . . . . . . . . . . . . . . . . . . . . . . . . Soldier
Bibi Besch . . . . . . . . . . . . . . . . . . . . . . . . . . . Mary
Peter Boyle . . . . . . . . . . . . . . . . . . . . . . . Andy Mast
Season Hubley . . . . . . . . . . . . . . . . . . . . . . . . . Niki

• 0:27—Breasts acting in a porno movie.

••• 1:05—Full frontal nudity talking to George C. Scott in a booth. Panties mysteriously appear later on.

Linda Smith . . . . . . . . . . . . . . . . Hope (Mistress Victoria)
Gigi Vorgan . . . . . . . . . . . . . . . . . . . . . . . Teenage Girl

• 0:32—Breasts on sofa in Peter Boyle's apartment.

Tracey Walter . . . . . . . . . . . . . . . . . . . . . Main Teller

## *Hardware* (1990)

Stacey Travis . . . . . . . . . . . . . . . . . . . . . . . . . . . Jill

• 0:21—Almost breasts in shower. Brief left breast in bed with Moses. Lit with blue light.

0:38—Brief breasts in bedroom seen by a guy through telescope. Infrared-looking effect.

## *Harem* (1985; French)

Rosanne Katon . . . . . . . . . . . . . . . . . . . . . . . . . . Judy
Ben Kingsley . . . . . . . . . . . . . . . . . . . . . . . . . . Selim
Nastassja Kinski . . . . . . . . . . . . . . . . . . . . . . . . Diane

• 0:14—Breasts getting into swimming pool.

•• 1:04—Breasts in motel room with Ben Kingsley.

## *Harley Davidson and The Marlboro Man* (1991)

Tia Carrere . . . . . . . . . . . . . . . . . . . . . . . . . . Kimiko
Giancarlo Esposito . . . . . . . . . . . . . . . . . . . Jimmy Jiles
Chelsea Field . . . . . . . . . . . . . . . . . . . . Virginia Slim

• 0:40—Side of left breast, sitting up in bed. Very brief buns standing up. Don't see her face very well.

Don Johnson . . . . . Robert Lee Anderson, Marlboro Man
Mickey Rourke . . . . . . . . . . . . . . . . . . . Harley Davidson
Vanessa Williams . . . . . . . . . . . . . . . . . . . Lulu Daniels

## *The Harrad Experiment* (1973)

Don Johnson . . . . . . . . . . . . . . . . . . . . . Stanley Cole

•• 0:18—Brief frontal nudity after getting out of the shower while Laurie Walters watches.

Bruno Kirby . . . . . . . . . . . . . . . . . . . . . Harry Schacht

• 0:41—Brief frontal nudity, getting into the swimming pool with Beth, Don Johnson and Laurie Walters.

Elliot Street . . . . . . . . . . . . . . . . . . . . . . . . . . Wilson

•• 0:44—Frontal nudity taking off clothes and getting into the swimming pool.

Sharon Taggart . . . . . . . . . . . . . . . . . . . . . Barbara
Victoria Thompson . . . . . . . . . . . . . . . . . . Beth Hillyer

0:08—Buns, in the bathroom while talking to Harry.

• 0:10—Brief breasts getting into bed.

•• 0:21—Breasts in nude encounter group.

• 0:41—Breasts getting into the swimming pool with Don Johnson and Laurie Walters.

0:49—Buns, getting dressed after making love with Johnson.

Laurie Walters . . . . . . . . . . . . . . . . . . . . Sheila Grove

• 0:29—Breasts, wearing white panties, while with Don Johnson.

• 0:40—Nude taking off blue dress and getting into the swimming pool with Johnson.

## *The Harrad Summer* (1974)

*a.k.a. Student Union*

Sherry Miles . . . . . . . . . . . . . . . . . . . . . . . . . . . Dee
Lisa Moore . . . . . . . . . . . . . . . . . . . . . . . . . . Arnae
Robert Reiser . . . . . . . . . . . . . . . . . . . . . . . Stanley

• 0:57—Buns, while getting out of bed and hiding in closet.

Patrice Rohmer . . . . . . . . . . . . . . . . . . . . . . . Marcia

• 0:33—Brief breasts, starting to take off her blouse in motel room with Harry.

Victoria Thompson . . . . . . . . . . . . . . . . . . Beth Hillyer

•• 0:57—Buns and brief breasts running down hallway and jumping into bed, pretending to be asleep.

1:03—Buns, lying on inflatable lounge in the pool.

1:04—Buns, lying face down on lounge chair.

Laurie Walters . . . . . . . . . . . . . . . . . . . . . . Sheila Grove
- 0:02—Breasts, while undressing in bathroom. Long shot, out of focus.
- •• 1:04—Breasts, while lying on lounge chair, then buns and more breasts getting up and pushing Harry into the pool.

## Harry and Tonto (1974)
Ellen Burstyn . . . . . . . . . . . . . . . . . . . . . . . . . Shirley
Melanie Mayron . . . . . . . . . . . . . . . . . . . . . . . Ginger
- • 0:57—Very brief breasts in motel room with Art Carney taking off her towel and putting on blouse. Long shot, hard to see.
Joshua Mostel . . . . . . . . . . . . . . . . . . . . . . . Norman
- • 1:16—Brief buns, when mooning a horse in a trailer out the back window of car. Don't see his face.

## The Harvest (1992)
Anthony John Denison . . . . . . . . . . . . . . Noel Guzman
Miguel Ferrer . . . . . . . . . . . . . . . . . . . . . . Charlie Pope
- • 1:21—Brief partial frontal nudity under sheets when getting out of bed and putting on pants.
Leilani Sarelle . . . . . . . . . . . . . . . . . . . . Natalie Caldwell
- •• 1:13—Side view of buns, then breasts, while in car with Miguel Ferrer. Don't see her face very well.
- ••• 1:19—Full frontal nudity, while making love with Ferrer in bed.

## The Haunted (1976)
Ann Michelle . . . . . . . . . . . . . . . Abanaki/Jennifer Baines
- ••• 0:03—Breasts while on horseback as Abanaki.
- •• 0:06—Breasts, while riding on horseback in the desert.
- • 0:48—Breasts while lying on towel outside with Patrick at night.
- •• 1:19—Breasts while riding the horse again.

## Haunted Summer (1988)
Alice Krige . . . . . . . . . . . . . . . . . . . . . . . . Mary Godwin
Eric Stoltz . . . . . . . . . . . . . . . . . . . . . . . Percy Shelley
- ••• 0:09—Nude, under the waterfall and walking around in the river. Long scene.

## Haunting Fear (1990)
Karen Black . . . . . . . . . . . . . . . . . . . . Dr. Julia Harcourt
Sherri Graham . . . . . . . . . . . . . . . . . . . . Visconti's Girl
- • 0:45—Buns in swimming pool. (Breasts seen under water.)
- • 0:47—Breasts, giving Visconti a massage while he talks on the phone.
Delia Sheppard . . . . . . . . . . . . . . . . . . . . . . . . . Lisa
- ••• 0:13—Breasts on desk, making love with Terry.
- ••• 1:10—Full frontal nudity, making love in bed with Terry. Long scene.
Brinke Stevens . . . . . . . . . . . . . . . . . . . . . . . . Victoria
- ••• 0:10—Full frontal nudity, taking a bath and getting out.
- •• 0:22—Breasts, while changing into nightgown in bedroom.
- ••• 0:32—Breasts while lying on Coroner's table.
Jan-Michael Vincent . . . . . . . . . . . . . . . . . James Trent

## The Haunting of Morella (1989)
Lana Clarkson . . . . . . . . . . . . . . . . . . . . . . . Coel Deveroux
- ••• 0:17—Breasts, taking a bath, then getting out and wrapping a towel around herself.
- ••• 1:00—Breasts in white panties, standing under a waterfall.
Deborah Dutch . . . . . . . . . . . . . . . . . . . . . Serving Girl
- ••• 0:14—Breasts and buns, taking off pink tap pants and getting into bath.
- • 0:15—Buns, lying dead on the floor, covered with blood.
Nicole Eggert . . . . . . . . . . . . . . . . . . . . Morella/Lenora
Maria Ford . . . . . . . . . . . . . . . . . . . . . . . . . . . . Diane
- ••• 1:00—Breasts taking off nightgown and swimming in pond, then walking to waterfall.
Gail Thackray . . . . . . . . . . . . . . . . . . . . . . . . . . . Ilsa
- •• 0:38—Breasts in bed with Niles. Buns also when getting out and getting dressed.

## Havana (1990)
Alan Arkin . . . . . . . . . . . . . . . . . . . . . . . . . Joe Volpi
Lise Cutter . . . . . . . . . . . . . . . . . . . . . . . . . . . Patty
- • 0:44—Most of side of left breast with Robert Redford. Very, very brief part of right breast while he turns her around. Very brief left breast when Redford puts a cold glass on her chest. Dark, hard to see.
Tomas Milian . . . . . . . . . . . . . . . . . . . . . . Menocal
Lena Olin . . . . . . . . . . . . . . . . . . . . . Bobby Duran
Karen Russell . . . . . . . . . . . . . . . . . . . . Dancer #2

## He Knows You're Alone (1980)
Elizabeth Kemp . . . . . . . . . . . . . . . . . . . . . . Nancy
- ••• 1:12—Breasts, taking off robe and taking a shower.
Patsy Pease . . . . . . . . . . . . . . . . . . . . . . . . . . Joyce
- • 0:42—Very, very brief left breast in open blouse when she turns around to turn off the lights.

## he said, she said (1991)
Kevin Bacon . . . . . . . . . . . . . . . . . . . . . . . Dan Hanson
Ashley Gardner . . . . . . . . . . . . . . . . . . . . . . . . Susan
- • 1:05—Brief upper half of right breast, when her breast pops out of her dress while talking to Kevin Bacon and Elizabeth Perkins at restaurant.
Anthony LaPaglia . . . . . . . . . . . . . . . . . . . . . . . Mark
Elizabeth Perkins . . . . . . . . . . . . . . . . . . . . Lorie Bryer
- • 1:15—Brief breasts getting into the shower with Kevin Bacon.
Sharon Stone . . . . . . . . . . . . . . . . . . . . . . . . . . Linda

## The Head of the Family (1967; Italian/French)
Claudine Auger . . . . . . . . . . . . . . . . . . . . . . . Adriana
- • 1:18—Very brief side of right breast, while putting Marco's shirt on.
Leslie Caron . . . . . . . . . . . . . . . . . . . . . . . . . . Paola
- • 0:22—Very brief upper half of left breast while sitting at drafting table and breast feeding her baby.

## Hear My Song (1991; British)
Tara Fitzgerald . . . . . . . . . . . . . . . . . . . . . Nancy Doyle
- •• 0:07—Brief breasts in bed, then nude, getting out of bed and getting dressed while angry at Micky.

### Hear No Evil (1993)
Marlee Matlin . . . . . . . . . . . . . . . . . . . . Jillian Shananhan
•• 0:30—Brief breasts, getting out of the bathtub.
Martin Sheen . . . . . . . . . . . . . . . . . . . Lt. Philip Brock
Karen Trumbo. . . . . . . . . . . . . . . . . . . . . Nadine Brock

### Heart Beat (1979)
Stephen Davies . . . . . . . . . . . . . . . . . . . . . . . Bob Bendix
Ann Dusenberry . . . . . . . . . . . . . . . . . . . . . . . . Stevie
•• 0:41—Full frontal nudity frolicking in bathtub with
Nick Nolte.
John Heard . . . . . . . . . . . . . . . . . . . . . . . Jack Kerouac
Nick Nolte. . . . . . . . . . . . . . . . . . . . . Neal Cassady
Ray Sharkey. . . . . . . . . . . . . . . . . . . . . . . . . . . . Ira
Sissy Spacek . . . . . . . . . . . . . . . . . . . . Carolyn Cassady

### Heart of Midnight (1988)
Steve Buscemi. . . . . . . . . . . . . . . . . . . . . . . . . . Eddy
Jennifer Jason Leigh. . . . . . . . . . . . . . . . . . . . . . Carol
• 0:27—Very brief side view of right breast, while
reaching for soap in the shower.
Brenda Vaccaro . . . . . . . . . . . . . . . . . . . . . . . . . Betty

### Heart of the Stag (1983; New Zealand)
Terence Cooper . . . . . . . . . . . . . . . . . . Robert Jackson
• 0:03—Buns, while making love in bed on top of his
daughter. Don't see his face.
Bruno Lawrence . . . . . . . . . . . . . . . . . . . . . Peter Daley
Mary Regan. . . . . . . . . . . . . . . . . . . . . . . Cathy Jackson
• 0:03—Brief right breast twice, very brief lower frontal nudity in bed with her father.
•• 1:06—Breasts in bed, ripping her blouse open while
yelling at her father.

### Heartbreak Ridge (1986)
Clint Eastwood . . . . . . . . . . . . . . . . . . . . . . . Highway
Marsha Mason . . . . . . . . . . . . . . . . . . . . . . . . Aggie
Rebecca Perle . . . . . . . . . . . . . . . . . Student in Shower
• 1:48—Very brief breasts getting out of shower when
the Marines rescue the students.
Tom Villard . . . . . . . . . . . . . . . . . . . . . . . . . . Profile

### Heartbreaker (1983)
Apollonia. . . . . . . . . . . . . . . . . . . . . . . . . . . . . Rose
Dawn Dunlap . . . . . . . . . . . . . . . . . . . . . . . . . . . Kim
• 0:49—Breasts putting on dress in bedroom.
0:51—Very, very brief right breast in open dress during rape attempt. Dark.
•• 1:02—Left breast, lying on bed with her boyfriend.
Long scene.
Pepe Serna . . . . . . . . . . . . . . . . . . . . . . . . . . Loco

### Heartbreakers (1984)
Kathryn Harrold . . . . . . . . . . . . . . . . . . . . . . . . Cyd
0:02—In black bra and panties changing clothes in
Peter Coyote's studio.
Carole Laure . . . . . . . . . . . . . . . . . . . . . . . Liliane
• 0:56—Brief breasts making love in car with Nick
Mancuso. Dark, hard to see.
• 1:25—In sheer black dress, then brief right breast
making love in art gallery with Peter Coyote.
Walter Olkewicz . . . . . . . . . . . . . . . . . . . . . . Marvin

Jamie Rose . . . . . . . . . . . . . . . . . . . . . . . . . . . Libby
••• 0:09—Breasts in bed talking with Nick Mancuso and
Peter Coyote.
Carol Wayne . . . . . . . . . . . . . . . . . . . . . . . . . . Candy
0:22—In black wig and bra posing for Peter Coyote
in his studio.
••• 0:41—In white bra and panties, then brief breasts in
the mirror stripping in front of Coyote and Nick
Mancuso. Then brief breasts lying in bed with Coyote.

### Hearts and Armour (1983)
Barbara De Rossi . . . . . . . . . . . . . . . . . . . . Bradamante
•• 1:05—Breasts while sleeping with Ruggero.
Tanya Roberts . . . . . . . . . . . . . . . . . . . . . . . . Angelica

### Heat and Dust (1982)
Christopher Cazenove . . . . . . . . . . . . . . . Douglas Rivers
•• 1:25—Buns while lying in bed with Greta Scacchi
under a mosquito net.
Julie Christie. . . . . . . . . . . . . . . . . . . . . . . . . . . . Anne
Greta Scacchi. . . . . . . . . . . . . . . . . . . . . . Olivia Rivers
•• 1:25—Buns, lying in bed under a mosquito net with
Douglas, then breasts rolling over.

### The Heat of Desire (1982; French)
a.k.a. Plein Sud
Patrick Dewaere . . . . . . . . . . . . . . . . . . . Serge Laine
• 0:17—Buns, while getting out of bed and going into
Carol's "house" that she has made out of sheets.
0:20—Pubic hair, while lying on his back.
• 0:21—Side view of buns, while on the floor with
Carol.
0:57—Brief side view of buns, while getting out of
bed and putting on pants.
• 1:02—Buns, while getting into bed with Carol. Very,
very brief frontal nudity hidden by subtitles.
• 1:14—Buns, while taking off pants and getting into
bed.
Clio Goldsmith. . . . . . . . . . . . . . . . . . . . . . . . . Carol
• 0:09—Breasts and buns, getting out of bed in train
to look out the window. Dark.
• 0:12—Brief breasts in bathroom mirror when Serge
peeks in.
•• 0:19—Full frontal nudity in the bathtub.
•• 0:20—Nude, sitting on the floor with Serge's head in
her lap.
•• 0:21—Buns, lying face down on floor. Very brief
breasts. A little dark. Then breasts sitting up and
drinking out of bottle.
• 0:22—Right breast, in gaping robe sitting on floor
with Serge.
• 0:24—Partial left breast consoling Serge in bed.
• 0:25—Breasts sitting on chair on balcony, then walking inside. Dark.
• 0:56—Breasts walking from bathroom and getting
into bed. Dark.
• 0:57—Brief right breast, while on couch with Guy
Marchand.
•• 0:58—Breasts getting dressed while Serge is yelling.
Guy Marchand. . . . . . . . . . . . . . . . . . . . . . . . . . Max

### Heated Vengeance (1984)

Cameron Dye . . . . . . . . . . . . . . . . . . . . . . . . . Bandit
Richard Hatch . . . . . . . . . . . . . . . . . . . . . . . Hoffman
- ••• 0:38—Buns, while making love in bed with Michelle during his dream.
- •• 0:40—Buns, while getting up out of bed and walking to bathroom.

Robert Walker, Jr. . . . . . . . . . . . . . . . . . . . . . . . . n.a.

### Heaven Help Us (1985)

Malcolm Danare . . . . . . . . . . . . . . . . . . . . . . Caesar
- • 0:36—Buns, while walking to the pool after all the other guys jump in. Long shot.

Patrick Dempsey . . . . . . . . . . . . . . . . . . . . . . Corbet
John Heard . . . . . . . . . . . . . . . . . . . Brother Timothy
Andrew McCarthy. . . . . . . . . . . . . . . . . .Michael Dunn
- • 0:35—Upper half of buns, while standing by the pool next to Caesar when he blows his nose.

Yeardley Smith . . . . . . . . . . . . . . . . . . . . . .Cathleen
Donald Sutherland . . . . . . . . . . . . . . . Brother Thadeus

### Heaven's Gate (1980)

Jeff Bridges . . . . . . . . . . . . . . . . . . . . . . . . . . . . John
Isabelle Huppert . . . . . . . . . . . . . . . . . . . . . . . . Ella
- •• 1:10—Nude running around the house and in bed with Kris Kristofferson.
- ••• 1:18—Nude, taking a bath in the river.
- • 2:24—Very brief left breast getting raped by three guys.

John Hurt . . . . . . . . . . . . . . . . . . . . . . . . . . Irvine
Kris Kristofferson . . . . . . . . . . . . . . . . . . . . . . Averill
Terry O'Quinn. . . . . . . . . . . . . . . . Captain Minardi
Mickey Rourke. . . . . . . . . . . . . . . . . . . . . . . . .n.a.
Sam Waterston . . . . . . . . . . . . . . . . . . . . . . Canton

### Heavenly Bodies (1985)

Jo Anne Bates . . . . . . . . . . . . . . . Girl in Locker Room
Sugar Bouche . . . . . . . . . . . . . . . . . . . . . . Stripper
- • 0:16—Breasts doing stripper-gram for Steve.

Cynthia Dale. . . . . . . . . . . . . . . . . . . Samantha Blair
- • 0:30—Brief breasts fantasizing about making love with Steve while doing aerobic exercises.

Laura Henry . . . . . . . . . . . . . . . . . . . . . . . . Debbie
- • 0:46—Brief breasts making love while her boyfriend, Jack, watches TV.

### The Heavenly Kid (1985)

Jason Gedrick . . . . . . . . . . . . . . . . . . . . . . . Lenny
- •• 0:31—Brief buns, while in clothing store when Bobby magically dresses him in better looking clothes.

Nancy Valen . . . . . . . . . . . . . . . . . . . . . . . Melissa

### The Heist (1989; Made for Cable Movie)

Pierce Brosnan . . . . . . . . . . . . . . . . . . . Bobby Skinner
Wendy Hughes . . . . . . . . . . . . . . . . . . . . . . . Susan
- • 0:52—Very brief side view of right breast making love in bed with Pierce Brosnan.

### Hell Comes to Frogtown (1987)

Sandahl Bergman . . . . . . . . . . . . . . . . . . . . Spangle
Suzanne Solari. . . . . . . . . . . . . . . . . . . Runaway Girl
Kristi Somers . . . . . . . . . . . . . . . . . . . . . . Arabella

Cec Verrell . . . . . . . . . . . . . . . . . . . . . . . . . Centinella
- •• 0:19—Breasts taking off her blouse and getting into sleeping bag with Roddy Piper. Brief breasts again after he throws her off him.

### Hell High (1989)

Karen Russell . . . . . . . . . . . . . . . . . . . . . . . Teen Girl
- •• 0:04—Breasts in shack with Teen Boy while little girl watches through a hole in the wall.

### Hell Up in Harlem (1973)

Margaret Avery . . . . . . . . . . . . . . . . . . .Sister Jennifer
- ••• 0:42—Breasts in bed, while making love with Fred Williamson.

Gloria Hendry. . . . . . . . . . . . . . . . . . Helen Bradley
Fred Williamson . . . . . . . . . . . . . . . . . Tommy Gibbs
- ••• 0:42—Buns, while in bed making love with Margaret Avery.

### Hellhole (1985)

Lamya Derval . . . . . . . . . . . . . . . . . . . . . . . .Jacuzzi Girl
- ••• 1:08—Breasts (she's on the right) sniffing glue in closet with another woman.
- ••• 1:12—Full frontal nudity in Jacuzzi room with Mary Woronov.

Terry Moore. . . . . . . . . . . . . . . . . . Sidnee Hammond
Ray Sharkey . . . . . . . . . . . . . . . . . . . . . . . . . Silk
Dyanne Thorne . . . . . . . . . . . . . . . . . . . Chrysta
Pamela Ward . . . . . . . . . . . . . . . . . . . . . . . .Tina
Edy Williams. . . . . . . . . . . . . . . . . . . . . . . . .Vera
- ••• 0:22—Breasts on bed posing for Silk.
- ••• 0:24—Breasts in white panties in shower, then fighting with another woman.
- ••• 1:03—Breasts in mud bath with another woman. Long scene.

Mary Woronov. . . . . . . . . . . . . . . . . . . . .Dr. Fletcher

### Hello Again! (1987)

Corbin Bernsen . . . . . . . . . . . . . . . . . . .Jason Chadman
Gabriel Byrne . . . . . . . . . . . . . . . . . . . . Kevin Scanlon
Shelley Long . . . . . . . . . . . . . . . . . . . . Lucy Chadman
- • 0:58—Brief buns, in hospital gown, walking down hallway.

### Hello Mary Lou: Prom Night II (1987)

Beverly Hendry. . . . . . . . . . . . . . . . . . Monica Walters
- • 1:03—Brief side view of buns and breasts, while getting undressed in locker room.
- • 1:04—Nude in shower room with Vicki.

Wendy Lyon . . . . . . . . . . . . . . . . . . Vicki Carpenter
0:58—Very, very brief left breast, while turning around after getting sucked into the blackboard.
- ••• 1:04—Nude in shower with Monica. Nude a lot walking around shower room.
- ••• 1:06—Full frontal nudity, walking in locker room, stalking Monica.

### Hellraiser (1987)

Clare Higgins . . . . . . . . . . . . . . . . . . . . . . . . . .Julia
- • 0:17—Very, very brief left breast and buns making love with Frank.
1:10—In white bra in bedroom putting necklace on.

### Hellraiser III: Hell on Earth (1992)

(Unrated version reviewed.)

Paula Marshall. . . . . . . . . . . . . . . . . . . . . . . . . . . . Terri
- • 0:47—Very, very brief left breast under gaping blouse, while spinning around to get up off the floor to run to the door.

### Hellraiser II—Hellbound (1988)

Catherine Chevalier. . . . . . . . . . . . . . . Tiffany's Mother
Clare Higgins . . . . . . . . . . . . . . . . . . . . . . . . . . Julia
- • 0:20—Very, very brief right breast, lying in bed with Frank. Scene from *Hellraiser*.

### Hellroller (1992)

Michelle Bauer . . . . . . . . . . . . . . . . . . . .Michelle Novak
  0:26—Undressing in motel room down to white body suit, then exercising.
- ••• 0:30—Breasts taking a bath.
  0:35—Dead in bathroom, covered with blood and with her guts hanging out.
Ruth Corrine Collins . . . . . . . . . . . . . Eugene's Mother
Elizabeth Kaitan. . . . . . . . . . . . . . . . . . . . . . . . . .Lizzy
Hyapatia Lee. . . . . . . . . . . . . . . . . . . . . . . . . . Dancer
- ••• 0:43—Breasts, dancing in room by herself.
- ••• 0:45—Breasts and buns, while taking a shower.

### Henry & June (1990)

Maria De Medeiros . . . . . . . . . . . . . . . . . . . . . Anais Nin
- • 0:50—Brief right breast, popping out of dress top.
- •• 0:52—Breasts lying in bed with Richard E. Grant.
- •• 1:13—Breasts in bed with Fred Ward, buns getting out. Right breast standing by the window.
- ••• 1:31—Breasts in bed with Brigitte Lahaie.
  1:37—Nude under sheer black patterned dress.
- •• 1:43—Close up of right breast as Ward plays with her.
- •• 2:01—Left breast, then breasts after taking off her top in bed with Uma Thurman.
Richard E. Grant . . . . . . . . . . . . . . . . . . . . . . . . Hugo
Brigitte Lahaie. . . . . . . . . . . . . . . . . . . . . .Harry's Whore
- •• 0:23—Brief buns and breasts under sheer white dress going up stairs with Fred Ward.
- •• 1:22—Breasts in sheer white dress again. Nude under dress walking up stairs.
- ••• 1:23—Breasts and buns making love with another woman while Anais and Hugo watch.
- • 1:31—Breasts in bed with Anais. Intercut with Uma Thurman, so hard to tell who is who.
Maïté Maillé . . . . . . . . . . . . . . . . . . . . . .Frail Prostitute
- • 1:22—In black see-through dress.
- ••• 1:23—Breasts making love with Brigitte Lahaie in front of Anais and Hugo.
Uma Thurman. . . . . . . . . . . . . . . . . . . . . . June Miller
Fred Ward. . . . . . . . . . . . . . . . . . . . . . . . Henry Miller
- ••• 1:39—Buns, twice, while making love with Maria de Medeiros.

### Hexed (1993)

*a.k.a. All Shook Up*

Laura Banks . . . . . . . . . . . . . . . . . . . . . . . .1st Reporter
Claudia Christian . . . . . . . . . . . . . . . . . . . . . . . .Hexina
- • 0:30—Tip of right breast, several times, while lying on her back in bed. (You can tell when the body double is used because of the bad wig.)
- •• 0:31—Brief right breast, several times, while making love in bed.
- • 0:34—Very brief inside of right breast in gaping coat, while raising knife. Brief buns, while getting pushed off bed.
Teresa Ganzel. . . . . . . . . . . . . . . . . . . . . . 3rd Reporter
Shelley Michelle . . . . . .Body Double for Claudia Christian
- •• 0:31—Breasts, while making love on top of Matthew in bed.
- • 0:32—Buns and right breast, getting out of bed.
- • 0:57—Buns and brief left breast, while standing up in bed.

### Hide and Go Shriek (1988)

Donna Baltron . . . . . . . . . . . . . . . . . . . . . Judy Ramerize
- •• 0:56—In white bra and panties, then breasts after undressing seductively in front of her boyfriend.
Brittain Frye . . . . . . . . . . . . . . . . . . . . . . . . Randy Flint
- • 0:51—Brief buns, while undressing and getting into bed. Long shot.
- • 0:52—Brief buns, while putting on his pants after getting out of bed.
- • 0:58—Very brief buns, while pulling up his pants. Dark.
Rebunkah Jones . . . . . . . . . . . . . . . . . . . .Bonnie Williams
- •• 0:27—Breasts taking off her blouse. More breasts sitting in bed.
Annette Sinclair . . . . . . . . . . . . . . . . . . . . . Kim Downs
- • 0:51—Brief breasts and buns, undressing and getting into bed. Long shot.
- •• 0:57—Breasts, getting up and out of bed, then getting dressed.
- • 1:02—Breasts and buns, tied up on top of freight elevator.
- • 1:05—Breasts on top of elevator.
- • 1:17—Breasts on top of elevator fighting with the killer. Lit with red light.

### Hider in the House (1989)

Rebekka Armstrong . . . . . . . . . . . . . Attractive Woman
- • 0:47—Brief breasts in bed with Mimi Roger's husband when she surprises them.
Mimi Rogers. . . . . . . . . . . . . . . . . . . . . . Julie Dreyer

### The High Country (1980; Canadian)

Timothy Bottoms. . . . . . . . . . . . . . . . . . . . . . . . . . .Jim
- • 1:19—Buns, while walking into the pond with Linda Purl.
- • 1:24—Buns, while pulling underwear on after getting out of sleeping bag.
Linda Purl. . . . . . . . . . . . . . . . . . . . . . . . . . . .Kathy
- • 1:03—Brief buns, while taking a shower in the waterfall.

## High Heels (1991; Spanish)

Victoria Abril . . . . . . . . . . . . . . . . . . . . . . Rebecca Giner
- 0:31—Breasts, when her dress falls down slightly while hanging on a pole and making love with Lethal.

Javier Bardem . . . . . . . . . . . . . . . . . . . TV Floor Manager
Nacho Martinez . . . . . . . . . . . . . . . . . . . . . . . . . . Juan
Carmen Maura . . . . . . . . . . . . . . . . . . . . . . . . . . Tina

## High Heels (1972; French)

*a.k.a. Docteur Popaul*

Laura Antonelli . . . . . . . . . . . . . . . . . . . . . . Martine
  0:35—Breasts undressing while Jean-Paul Belmondo watches. Long, long shot.
- 0:36—Briefly nude when Belmondo watches through opera glasses.
- ••• 0:53—Breasts and buns, getting out of bed and walking around.
- 0:55—Buns, getting a shot while lying on examination table.
- •• 0:56—Breasts, twice, sitting naked on examination table.
- 1:30—Brief side of right breast during flashback of 0:56 scene.
  1:31—Brief full frontal nudity, running around her house while Mia Farrow watches. Long shot.

Mia Farrow . . . . . . . . . . . . . . . . . . . . . Christine Du Pont

## High Season (1988; British)

Jacqueline Bisset . . . . . . . . . . . . . . . . . . . Katherine Shaw
- 0:56—Brief breasts doing the backstroke in the water with Kenneth Branagh, then left breast while lying down. Hard to see, everything is lit with blue light.

Kenneth Branagh . . . . . . . . . . . . . . . . . . . . . Rich Lamb
- 0:56—Buns, while putting a wrap around Jacqueline Bisset after they fool around in the water.

Irene Papas . . . . . . . . . . . . . . . . . . . . . . . . . Penelope

## High Stakes (1989)

Kathy Bates . . . . . . . . . . . . . . . . . . . . . . . . . . . . Jill
Maia Danziger . . . . . . . . . . . . . . . . . . . . . . . . Veronica
Sally Kirkland . . . . . . . . . . . . . Melanie "Bambi" Rose
- 0:01—In two piece costume, doing a strip tease routine on stage. Buns in G-string, then very, very brief breasts while flashing.
  1:11—In black bra cutting her hair in front of a mirror.

## Higher Education (1987; Canadian)

Lori Hallier . . . . . . . . . . . . . . . . . . . . . . . Nicole Hubert
- 0:44—Right breast, twice, while making love with Andy in bed.

Jennifer Inch . . . . . . . . . . . . . . . . . . . . . Gladys/Glitter
Isabelle Mejias . . . . . . . . . . . . . . . . . . . . . Carrie Hanson

## Highlander (1986)

Clancy Brown . . . . . . . . . . . . . . . . . . . . . . . . . Kuragan
Sean Connery . . . . . . . . . . . . . . . . . . . . . . . . Ramirez
Roxanne Hart . . . . . . . . . . . . . . . . . . . . . Brenda Wyatt
- 1:30—Brief breasts making love with Christopher Lambert. Dark, hard to see.

Christopher Lambert . . . . . . . . . . . . . Conner MacLeod
- 1:30—Buns while making love with Roxanne Hart.

## The Hills Have Eyes, Part II (1989)

Robert Houston . . . . . . . . . . . . . . . . . . . . . . . . Bobby
Penny Johnson . . . . . . . . . . . . . . . . . . . . . . . . . . Sue
- 0:49—Brief breasts in bus, trying to get Foster's attention.

John Laughlin . . . . . . . . . . . . . . . . . . . . . . . . . . . Hulk
Colleen Riley . . . . . . . . . . . . . . . . . . . . . . . . . . . Jane
- 0:55—Very brief left breast, twice, while taking a shower outside when Foster talks to her.

## Hired to Kill (1990)

Barbara Lee Alexander . . . . . . . . . . . . . . . . . . . Sheila
  0:19—In white bra, spraying on perfume.
Jordana Capra . . . . . . . . . . . . . . . . . . . . . . Joanna
  0:18—Very briefly in black bra, putting on lipstick.
  0:19—In black bra, talking to Sivi, in front of the mirror.
Cynthia Lee . . . . . . . . . . . . . . . . . . . . . . Armwrestler
Michelle Moffett . . . . . . . . . . . . . . . . . . . . . . . . Ana
- 0:46—Left breast in dress, then breasts when Oliver Reed lowers her top.
- 0:47—More breasts in open dress top.
- •• 1:04—Very, very brief tip of right breast, lying on table when Brian Thompson rips her blouse open. More breasts, lying on the table. Dark.

Oliver Reed . . . . . . . . . . . . . . . . . . . . . . . . . Bartos
Penelope Reed . . . . . . . . . . . . . . . . . . . . . . . Katrina

## The Hit List (1993; Made for Cable Movie)

Jeff Fahey . . . . . . . . . . . . . . . . . . . . . . . Charlie Pike
- 1:00—Buns, while making love with (supposedly) Yancy Butler. Don't see his face well.

La Joy Farr . . . . . . . . . . . . . . . . . . . . . . . . . . . Linda
Shelley Michelle . . . . . . . . . . . . . . . . . . . . . . Dancer
Amy-Rochelle Weiss . . . . . Body Double for Yancy Butler
- 0:31—Buns, taking off swimsuit in front of Jeff Fahey. Long shot, don't see her face.
  1:00—Brief left breast in bed while making love with Fahey. Don't see her face very well.

## Hit the Dutchman (1992)

(Unrated version reviewed.)

Jeff Griggs . . . . . . . . . . . . . . . . . . . . . . . . . Peter Coll
Sally Kirkland . . . . . . . . . . . . . . Emma Flegenheimer
Bruce Nozick . . . . . . . . . . . . . Arthur "Dutch" Shultz
- •• 0:36—Briefly nude, running after Frances in her room. More buns, while on the floor with her.

Elena Skorohodove . . . . . . . . . . . . . . . . . . . . Anastasia
- •• 1:17—Breasts, making love with Arthur in bedroom.
- ••• 1:19—Nude, making love in bed with Arthur and afterwards.
- •• 1:23—Breasts in bed with Arthur.

## Hit! (1973)

Richard Pryor . . . . . . . . . . . . . . . . . . . . . . Mike Willmer
Gwen Welles . . . . . . . . . . . . . . . . . . . . . Sherry Nielson
••• 2:03—Breasts, taking off her clothes in front of a woman before killing her.

## The Hitchhikers (1971)

Misty Rowe . . . . . . . . . . . . . . . . . . . . . . . . . . . .Maggie
• 0:00—Brief side view of left breast getting dressed.
• 0:17—Very brief breasts getting dress ripped open, then raped in van.
• 0:48—Brief right breast while getting dressed.
• 1:09—Left breast, making love with Benson.
• 1:10—Brief breasts taking a bath in tub.
• 1:13—Very brief right breast in car with another victim.

## Hitz (1992)

a.k.a. Judgment
Karen Black . . . . . . . . . . . . . . . . . . . . . . Tiffany Powers
Emilia Crow . . . . . . . . . . . . . . . . . . . . . Chelsea Walker
••• 0:27—Breasts and very brief upper half of lower frontal nudity, making love in bed with Jimmy. Lit with red light.

## Hold Me, Thrill Me, Kiss Me (1993)

(Unrated version reviewed.)
Andrea Naschak . . . . . . . . . . . . . . . . . . . . . . . Sabra
• 0:04—Buns in yellow and orange two piece swimsuit while dancing on stage.
• 0:08—Buns in G-string and out of it in trailer with Max.
• 0:09—Very brief left breast under sheer black blouse.
0:25—Buns, while on stage in black outfit.
• 0:46—Buns and most of breast, while dancing on stage in sexy outfit.
Max Parrish . . . . . . . . . . . . . . . . . . . . . . . Eli/Bud/Fritz
• 0:08—Buns, when Sabra pulls his shorts off to give him a massage.
•• 0:11—Buns, while standing up to put his jeans on.
Nicole Sassaman . . . . . . . . . . . . . . . . . . . Girl on a Leash
Sean Young. . . . . . . . . . . . . . . . . . . . . . . .Twinkle

## Hollywood Boulevard (1976)

Candice Rialson. . . . . . . . . . . . . . . . Candy Wednesday
•• 0:29—Breasts getting her blouse ripped off by actors during a film.
••• 0:32—Breasts sunbathing with Bobbi and Jill.
•• 0:45—Brief breasts in the films she's watching at the drive-in. Same as 0:29.
Tara Strohmeier . . . . . . . . . . . . . . . . . . . . .Jill McBain
•• 0:00—Breasts getting out of van and standing with film crew.
• 0:31—Silhouette of breasts, while making love with P.G.
••• 0:32—Breasts sunbathing with Bobbi and Candy.
••• 0:33—Breasts acting for film on hammock. Long scene.
Mary Woronov . . . . . . . . . . . . . . . . . Mary McQueen

## Hollywood Boulevard II (1989)

Ginger Lynn Allen . . . . . . . . . . . . . . . . Candy Chandler
•• 0:33—Breasts in screening room with Woody, the writer.
Michelle Moffett. . . . . . . . . . . . . . . . . . . .Mary Randolf
Ty Randolph. . . . . . . . . . Amazon Warrior from Brooklyn
Penelope Reed . . . . . . . . . Amazon Warrior with Crystal
Maria Socas . . . . . . . . . . . . . . . . . . . . Amazon Queen
Lynn Theel . . . . . . . . . . . . . . . . . . . . . . Ann Gregory

## Hollywood Chainsaw Hookers (1988)

Esther Alise. . . . . . . . . . . . . . . . . . . . . . . . . . . . . Lisa
••• 0:25—Breasts playing with a baseball bat while a John photographs her.
Michelle Bauer . . . . . . . . . . . . . . . . . . . . . . .Mercedes
••• 0:09—Nude in motel room with a John just before chainsawing him to pieces.
Tricia Brown. . . . . . . . . . . . . . . . . . . . . . . . . .Ilsa
•• 0:37—Breasts while Jack is tied up in bed.
Linnea Quigley. . . . . . . . . . . . . . . . . . . . . Samantha
• 0:32—Breasts, dancing on stage.
• 1:02—Breasts, (but her body is painted) dancing in a ceremony.
Dawn Wildsmith . . . . . . . . . . . . . . . . . . . . . . . Lori

## Hollywood Dreams (1993)

(Unrated version reviewed.)
Debra Beatty . . . . . . . . . . . . . . . . . . . . . . . . . . .Sara
••• 0:11—Breasts after taking off her top in office for audition in front of Lou.
••• 0:19—Nude, diving into pool and getting out, then making love at Lou's.
•• 0:24—Left breast and partial lower frontal nudity while lying on bed on a set.
•• 0:39—Breasts while making love with Robby on bed in bedroom set.
• 1:06—Side of right breast while getting made up.
Kelly Jackson . . . . . . . . . . . . . . . . . . . . . . . . Veronica
•• 0:08—Nude, while making love with Steve on the floor.
• 0:14—In black lingerie, then left breast after undressing in office for audition in front of Lou.
• 0:25—Buns and breasts while in shower set during filming.
• 0:52—Breasts, while making love on couch with Steve.
••• 1:15—Nude, after taking off her dress in bedroom and making love with Robby.
• 1:19—Brief left breast while hugging Robby.
Johnathon Murray . . . . . . . . . . . . . . . . . . . . . . Steve
• 0:47—Buns, after taking off his shorts with Natasha in dressing room.
Kathy Pasmore. . . . . . . . . . . . . . . . . . . . . . . .Tiffany
••• 0:15—Breasts and buns, while sitting on desk in Lou's office.
••• 0:27—Getting a massage while wearing a sexy suit, then breasts and buns in T-back while making out with Natasha.
•• 0:28—Breasts and buns, while making love with Natasha and Robby.

• 1:06—Breasts in background while getting dressed.

Rick Scandlin. . . . . . . . . . . . . . . . . . . . . . . . . . . .Lou
 •• 0:21—Buns, while taking off his shorts outside with Sara, then making love.

Danny Smith. . . . . . . . . . . . . . . . . . . . . . . . . . . .Robby
 • 0:28—Partial buns, while making love with Natasha and Tiffany on the floor.

Jacqueline St. Claire. . . . . . . . . . . . . . . . . . . . . . Stripper
 •• 0:57—Breasts and buns in T-back, after stripping out of outfit while dancing in bar set.

### Hollywood Hot Tubs (1984)

Michael Andrew . . . . . . . . . . . . . . . . . . . . . . . . . Jeff
 • 1:00—Buns, under water when Pam takes his swim trunks off.

Jeff Eagle. . . . . . . . . . . . . . . . . . . . . . . . . . . Cameron
 • 0:21—Brief buns, after pulling down his swimsuit to get into hot tub with Dee-Dee.

Joseph Alan Johnson . . . . . . . . . . . . . . . Shawn's Friend

Becky LeBeau . . . . . . . . . . . . . . . . . . . . . . . . . Veronica
 •• 0:49—Breasts changing in the locker room with other girl soccer players while Jeff watches.
 • 0:54—Breasts in hot tub with the other girls and Shawn.

Donna McDaniel. . . . . . . . . . . . . . . . . . . Leslie Maynard

Remy O'Neill. . . . . . . . . . . . . . . . . . . . . . . . .Pam Landers
 • 1:00—Brief right breast in hot tub with Jeff.

Alexis Schreiner. . . . . . . . . . . . . . . . . . . . . . . Soccer Girl

Katt Shea . . . . . . . . . . . . . . . . . . . . . . . . . . . .Dee-Dee
 • 0:21—Breasts with her boyfriend while Shawn is working on the hot tub.

Jewel Shepard . . . . . . . . . . . . . . . . . . . . . .Crystal Landers

Edy Williams . . . . . . . . . . . . . . . . . . . . . . . . . . . Desiree
 ••• 0:26—Breasts, trying to seduce Shawn while he works on a hot tub.
  1:26—In black lingerie outfit in the hallway.
 • 1:30—Partial breasts with breasts sticking out of her bra while she sits by hot tub with Jeff.
 •• 1:32—Breasts in hot tub room with Shawn.
 • 1:36—Brief breasts while running around.
 • 1:38—Breasts again in the hot tub lobby.

### Hollywood Hot Tubs 2—Educating Crystal (1989)

Martina Castel. . . . . . . . . . . . . . . . . . . . . . . . . Hardie

Tally Chanel . . . . . . . . . . . . . . . . . . . . . . . .Mindy Wright

Dori Courtney. . . . . . . . . . . . . . . . . . . . . . . Hot Tub Girl
 •• 1:00—Breasts stuck in the spa and getting her hair freed.

Bob Garrison. . . . . . . . . . . . . . . . . .Billy "Derrick" Dare
 • 0:53—Buns, while running up to hot dog stand.

Remy O'Neill. . . . . . . . . . . . . . . . . . . . . . . . .Pam Landers
  0:57—Swinging tassels on the tips of her belly dancing top.

Jewel Shepard. . . . . . . . . . . . . . . . . . . . Crystal Landers
  0:38—In white slip during Gary's fantasy.
 • 1:12—Brief left breast, while lying down, kissing Gary.

### The Hollywood Knights (1980)

Dawn Clark . . . . . . . . . . . . . . . . . . . . . . Pom Pom Girl
 •• 0:01—Breasts sunbathing outside with Fran Drescher and another Pom Pom Girl.
 • 0:11—In bra, then brief breasts, changing clothes at night.
 • 0:20—Breasts in B&W Polaroid photograph. Long shot.

Michele Drake . . . . . . . . . . . . . . . . . . . . . . .Cheerleader
 • 0:28—Brief lower nudity in raised cheerleader outfit doing cheers in front of school assembly.

Fran Drescher. . . . . . . . . . . . . . . . . . . . . . . . . . .Sally

Debra Feuer . . . . . . . . . . . . . . . . . . . . . . . . . . .Cheetah

Gary Graham . . . . . . . . . . . . . . . . . . . . . . .Jimmy Shine

Kim Hopkins. . . . . . . . . . . . . . . . . . . . . . Pom Pom Girl
 • 0:01—Breasts, sunbathing outside with her two girl-friends.

Joyce Hyser . . . . . . . . . . . . . . . . . . . Brenda Weintraub

Michelle Pfeiffer . . . . . . . . . . . . . . . . . . . . . .Suzi Q.

Carol Ann Williams. . . . . . . . . . . . . . . . . . . . . . .Jane
 • 0:51—Very brief breasts, opening her blouse to distract Dudley. Don't see her face.

### Holocaust 2000 (1978)

Agostina Belli . . . . . . . . . . . . . . . . . . . . . . . . .Sara Golen
 •• 0:50—Breasts in bed making love with Kirk Douglas.

Kirk Douglas. . . . . . . . . . . . . . . . . . . . . . Robert Caine
 •• 0:52—Buns, during nightmare sequence. Long shots, hard to tell it's him.

### Home Movies (1980)

Nancy Allen . . . . . . . . . . . . . . . . . . . . . . . Kristina
 • 1:14—Very brief left breast when bending over while sitting on bed and again when reaching up to touch Keith Gordon's face.

### Homework (1982)

Michelle Bauer . . . . . . . . . . . Uncredited Dream Groupie
 ••• 1:01—Breasts with two other groupies, groping Tommy while he sings. (She has a flower in her hair and is the only brunette.)

Joan Collins . . . . . . . . . . . . . . . . . . . . . . . . . . . .Diane

Wings Hauser. . . . . . . . . . . . . . . . . . . . . . . . . . .Reddog

Joy Michael
 . . . . . . . . Diane, Age 16/Body Double for Joan Collins
 •• 0:39—In bra, then breasts in car making out with her boyfriend.
 •• 1:18—Breasts, taking off her bra and making love with Tommy. (Supposed to be Joan Collins.)

Barbara Peckinpaugh . . . . . Uncredited Magazine Model
 ••• 0:01—Brief breasts in magazine layout. In lingerie, then breasts in Tommy's photo session fantasy.

Carrie Snodgress . . . . . . . . . . . . . . . . . . . . Dr. Delingua

Betty Thomas. . . . . . . . . . . . . . . . . . . Reddog's Secretary

## Homicidal Impulse (1992)

*a.k.a. Killer Instinct*

(Unrated version reviewed.)

Vanessa Angel . . . . . . . . . . . . . . . . . . . . . . . . .Deborah
- •• 0:13—In bra, then breasts making love with Scott Valentine in his office on top of the photocopier (Don't see her face).
- •• 0:24—Breasts and buns, while making love in bed (you can see her face a little bit).
- ••• 0:30—In black bra, then breasts while making love (don't see her face).
- • 0:39—Very brief breasts in flashes during Valentine's drug induced visions.

Brigitta Stenberg . . . . . . . . . . . . . . . . . . . . Receptionist

Scott Valentine . . . . . . . . . . . . . . . . . . . . . . .Tim Casey

## Honey (1980; Italian)

Donatella Damiani . . . . . . . . . . . . . . . . .. The Landlady
- • 0:24—Very, very brief right breast dodging Clio Goldsmith's hand while playfully drying her off with a towel.

  0:34—Showing lots of cleavage while massaging a guy.

Clio Goldsmith . . . . . . . . . . . . . . . . . . . . . . . . . Annie
- •• 0:05—Nude kneeling in a room.
- •• 0:20—Nude getting into the bathtub.
- •• 0:42—Nude getting changed.
- ••• 0:44—Nude while hiding under the bed.
- •• 0:58—Nude getting disciplined, taking off clothes, then kneeling.

## Honky (1971)

Elliot Street . . . . . . . . . . . . . . . . . . . . . . . . . . . . .n.a.

Brenda Sykes . . . . . . . . . . . . . . . . . . . . . . . Sheila Smith
- ••• 0:42—Breasts with her boyfriend, making love on the floor.
- • 1:22—Brief breasts several times getting raped by two guys.

## Honky Tonk Nights (1978)

Serena . . . . . . . . . . . . . . . . . . . . . . . . . . . . Dolly Pop
- • 0:04—Breasts in open blouse, getting restrained after getting in a fight with a guy who tries to molest her.
- ••• 0:10—Breasts in bed with Bobby, then putting on a robe.
- ••• 0:38—Breasts standing in doorway, then in kitchen with Bill.

Carol Doda . . . . . . . . . . . . . . . . . . . . . . . Belle Barnette
- ••• 0:17—Breasts changing blouses in bedroom with Doris Ann.
- • 0:28—Left breast several times while making out with a guy.
- ••• 1:11—Breasts in bedroom with Doris Ann during flashback. (Different camera angle than 0:17.)

Amanda Jones . . . . . . . . . . . . . . . . . . . . . . . . . . .Honey
- •• 0:41—Breasts outside by car with Dan.
- ••• 0:42—Breasts and buns, in the woods with Dan.

Georgina Spelvin . . . . . . . . . . . . . . . . . . . . . . Georgia
- • 0:06—Breasts, lying with her head in a guy's lap.

## Horror Planet (1980; British)

*a.k.a. Inseminoid*

Jennifer Ashley . . . . . . . . . . . . . . . . . . . . . . . . . . . Holly

Stephanie Beacham . . . . . . . . . . . . . . . . . . . . . .Kate

Judy Geeson . . . . . . . . . . . . . . . . . . . . . . . . . . Sandy
- •• 0:31—Brief breasts on the operating table.
- • 0:32—Brief full frontal nudity on table.
- • 0:37—Brief full frontal nudity during flashbacks.

Victoria Tennant . . . . . . . . . . . . . . . . . . . . . . . Barbara

## Hospital Massacre (1982)

*a.k.a. X-Ray*

Barbi Benton . . . . . . . . . . . . . . . . . . . . . . .Susan Jeremy

  0:29—Undressing behind a curtain while the Doctor watches her silhouette.
- ••• 0:31—Breasts getting examined by the Doctor. First sitting up, then lying down.
- ••• 0:34—Great close up shot of breasts while the Doctor uses stethoscope on her.

## Hostages (1993; Made for Cable Movie)

Kathy Bates . . . . . . . . . . . . . . . . . . . . . . . . . . Peggy Say

Colin Firth . . . . . . . . . . . . . . . . . . . . . . . . John McCarthy
- • 0:09—Buns, while wearing blindfold, getting undressed and pushed into jail cell by captors.

Natasha Richardson . . . . . . . . . . . . . . . . . . . . Jill Morrell

Harry Dean Stanton . . . . . . . . . . . . . . . . . . Frand Reed

## Hostile Takeover (1988; Canadian)

*a.k.a. Office Party*

Jayne Eastwood . . . . . . . . . . . . . . . . . . . . . Mrs. Talmage

Cindy Girling . . . . . . . . . . . . . . . . . . . . . . Mrs. Gayford

Kate Vernon . . . . . . . . . . . . . . . . . . . . . . . . . . . . .Sally
- • 0:35—Very brief, left breast undressing in office with John Warner. Dark.
- •• 0:39—Right breast, turning over in her sleep, then playing with the chain.

## Hot Blood (1989; Spanish)

Robert Case . . . . . . . . . . . . . . . . . . . . . . . . . . . Ricardo
- •• 1:20—Buns, with Alicia in stable.

Sylvia Kristel . . . . . . . . . . . . . . . . . . . . . . . . . . .Sylvia
- • 0:44—Buns, getting molested by Dom Luis.

Alicia Moro . . . . . . . . . . . . . . . . . . . . . . . . . . . . . Alicia
- • 0:00—Buns and lower frontal nudity in stable with Ricardo. Long shot.
- • 0:06—In bra and panties with Julio, then buns and breasts. Looks like a body double because hair doesn't match.

Vivianne Vives . . . . . . . . . . . . . . . . . . . . . . . . . Connie
- • 1:19—Buns and very brief side view of left breast in bed with Julio.
- •• 1:21—Breasts in bed several times, then lower frontal nudity with Julio.

## The Hot Box (1972)

Andrea Cagan . . . . . . . . . . . . . . . . . . . . . . . . . . Bunny
- •• 0:16—Breasts cleaning herself off in stream behind Ellie and getting out.
- • 0:21—Breasts sleeping in hammock. (She's the third girl from the front, stretching.)

••• 0:45—Breasts in stream while bathing with the other three girls.

Margaret Markov . . . . . . . . . . . . . . . . . . . . Lynn Forrest
- • 0:12—Breasts when bad guy cuts her swimsuit top open.
- •• 0:16—Breasts in stream consoling Bunny.
- • 0:21—Breasts in the furthest hammock from camera. Long shot.
- ••• 0:45—Breasts bathing in stream with the other girls.

Rickey Richardson . . . . . . . . . . . . . . . . . Ellie St. George
- •• 0:16—Breasts cleaning herself off in stream and getting out.
- • 0:21—Breasts sleeping in hammocks. (She's the second one from the front.)
- • 0:26—Breasts getting accosted by the People's Army guys.
- ••• 0:43—Full frontal nudity making love with Flavio.
- ••• 0:45—Breasts in stream bathing with the other three girls.
- • 1:01—Breasts taking off top in front of soldiers.

Laurie Rose . . . . . . . . . . . . . . . . . . . . . . . . . . . . . . Sue
- •• 0:16—Breasts cleaning herself off in stream and getting out.
- •• 0:21—Breasts sleeping in hammocks. (She's the first one from the front.)
- • 0:26—Breasts getting accosted by the People's Army guys.
- ••• 0:45—Breasts in stream bathing with the other three girls.
- • 0:58—Full frontal nudity getting raped by Major Dubay.

## Hot Child in the City (1987)
Leah Ayres-Hamilton . . . . . . . . . . . . . . . . . . . . . Rachel
0:38—In braless white T-shirt walking out by the pool and inside her sister's house.
- • 1:12—Very brief breasts in the shower with a guy. Long shot, hard to see anything.

Shari Shattuck. . . . . . . . . . . . . . . . . . . . . . . . . Abby

## Hot Chili (1985)
Victoria Barrett . . . . . . . . . . . . . . . Victoria Stevenson
- • 0:55—Very brief close up shot of right breast when it pops out of her dress. Don't see her face.

Bea Fiedler . . . . . . . . . . . . . . . . . . . . The Music Teacher
- •• 0:08—Breasts, while playing the cello and being fondled by Ricky.
0:29—Buns, while playing the violin.
- •• 0:34—Nude during fight in restaurant with Chi Chi. Hard to see because of the flashing light.
- ••• 0:36—Breasts lying on inflatable lounge in pool, playing a flute.
- ••• 0:43—Left breast, while playing a tuba.
- ••• 1:01—Breasts and buns, while dancing in front of Mr. Lieberman.
- • 1:07—Buns, then right breast while dancing with Stanley.

Flo Gerrish. . . . . . . . . . . . . . . . . . . . . . . . Mrs. Baxter

Katherine Kriss . . . . . . . . . . . . . . . . . . . . . Allison Baxter
- ••• 0:56—Breasts getting out of the pool and talking to Ricky.
- • 1:09—Buns and side view of left breast, while lying down and kissing Ricky.

Louisa Moritz . . . . . . . . . . . . . . . . . . . . . . . . . Chi Chi
0:06—Brief buns turning around in white apron after talking with the boys.
- •• 0:34—Nude during fight in restaurant with the Music Teacher. Hard to see because of the flashing light.

Taaffe O'Connell . . . . . . . . . . . . . . . . . . . . . . Brigitte
- ••• 0:21—Breasts while lying on the bed. Shot with lots of diffusion.
- • 0:30—Brief breasts while playing the drums.
- • 1:11—Brief breasts in bed while making love with Ernie, next to her drunk husband.

Joe Rubbo . . . . . . . . . . . . . . . . . . . . . . . . . . . . .Arney
- • 0:24—Brief buns while getting whipped by Brigitte.

## Hot Chocolate (1992)
Bo Derek . . . . . . . . . . . . . . . . . . . . . . . . . B.J. Cassidy
- • 0:30—Brief side view of right breast, while pulling sheets up on herself in bed.

## Hot Dog... The Movie (1984)
David Naughton . . . . . . . . . . . . . . . . . . . . . . . . .Dan
Crystal Smith . . . . . . . . . . . . . . . . . . . . . . . Motel Clerk
- •• 0:10—Nude getting out of spa and going to the front desk to sign people in.

Shannon Tweed . . . . . . . . . . . . . . . . . . Sylvia Fonda
- ••• 0:42—Breasts getting undressed, then making love in bed and in hot tub with Harkin.

## Hot Moves (1984)
Monique Gabrielle . . . . . . . . . . . . . . . . . . . . . . Babs
- • 0:29—Nude on the nude beach.
- •• 1:07—Breasts on and behind the sofa with Barry trying to get her top off.

Gayle Gannes. . . . . . . . . . . . . . . . . . . . . . . . . . .Jamie
- • 1:09—Breasts, taking off her white blouse and getting in bed with Joey.

Suzi Horne . . . . . . . . . . . . . . . . . . . . . . . . . . Hooker #1
Debi Richter . . . . . . . . . . . . . . . . . . . . . . . . . . . Heidi
0:06—Brief left bun, pulling pink swimsuit bottom aside for the boys at the beach.
- • 0:29—Breasts on nude beach.
- ••• 1:09—Breasts, taking off her red dress in bed with Michael.

Jill Schoelen . . . . . . . . . . . . . . . . . . . . . . . . Julie Ann

## Hot Resort (1984)
Victoria Barrett. . . . . . . . . . . . . . . . . . . . . . . . . .Jane
Dana Kaminsky . . . . . . . . . . . . . . . . . . . . . . . Melanie
- •• 1:02—Breasts taking off her white dress in a boat.

Linda Kenton . . . . . . . . . . . . . . Mrs. Geraldine Miller
- • 0:11—Very brief right breast, while in back of car with a guy.
- • 0:16—Right breast, while passed out in closet with a bunch of guys.
- • 0:24—Brief upper half of right breast, while on boat with a guy.

- 0:46—Brief breasts in Volkswagen.
- 0:51—Brief breasts in bathtub with Bronson Pinchot.
- 1:24—Brief breasts making love on a table while covered with food.

Cynthia Lee................................Alice
- 1:08—Breasts in the bathtub.

## The Hot Spot (1990)

Debra Cole........................ Irene Davey
- 1:26—Breasts sunbathing next to Jennifer Connelly at side of lake. Long shot.
- 1:27—Breasts talking with Connelly some more.

Jennifer Connelly.................... Gloria Harper
1:01—In black bra and panties walking out of lake with Don Johnson.
1:26—Buns, lying next to Irene next to lake. Long shot.
- 1:27—Breasts, talking to Irene next to lake. Wow!

Don Johnson..................... Harry Madox
- 0:41—Brief buns, while pulling up his underwear, talking to Virginia Madsen.
- 1:17—Buns, while undressing to go swimming with Madsen.
- 1:18—Buns, while getting out of the water. Long shot.

Virginia Madsen ................... Dolly Harshaw
- 0:41—Side view of left breast while sitting on bed talking to Don Johnson.
- 0:47—Tip of right breast when Johnson kisses it.
- 1:16—Buns, undressing for a swim outside at night. Breasts hanging on rope.
- 1:18—Buns, getting out of water with Johnson. Long shot.
- 1:21—Left breast when robe gapes open while sitting up.
1:23—Brief lower frontal nudity and buns in open robe after jumping off tower at night.
1:24—Breasts at bottom of hill with Johnson. Long shot.
1:45—Nude, very, very briefly running out of house. Very blurry, could be anybody.

William Sadler.....................Frank Sutton
Charlie Martin Smith.................. Lon Gulick

## Hot T-Shirts (1980)

Corinne Alphen........................... Judy
0:55—In braless T-shirt as a car hop.
- 1:10—In yellow outfit dancing in wet T-shirt contest. Brief breasts while flashing the crowd.

## Hot Target (1985)

Simone Griffeth.................. Christine Webber
- 0:09—Breasts taking off top for shower, then breasts and brief frontal nudity taking shower.
- 0:19—Breasts in bed after making love with Steve Marachuck.
- 0:21—Buns, getting out of bed and walking to bathroom.
- 0:23—Breasts in bed with Marachuck again.

- 0:34—Breasts in the woods with Marachuck while cricket match goes on.

## Hot Under the Collar (1991)

Melinda Clarke.......................... Monica
Karman Kruschke ......................... Sherry
Tané McClure .......................... Rowena
0:28—In red bra and panties in her room, trying to seduce Max. Almost right breast when she pulls her bra strap down.
- 0:32—Breasts in bed with Max.

## A House in the Hills (1993)

Michael Madsen.......................Mickey
- 0:36—Brief buns, after getting out of the shower.

Helen Slater .......................Alex Weaver
- 0:15—Breasts, while in bedroom in front of mirror, trying on various lingerie. Very nice!
0:36—Sort of breasts, in shower when Michael Madsen brings her a dress. Shower door is too fogged up to see anything.

## The House of Exorcism (1975)

*a.k.a. Lisa and the Devil*

Sylva Koscina ...........................Sophia
- 0:24—Breasts, while making love in bed with George the chauffeur.

Elke Sommer .......................Lisa Reiner
- 1:10—Breasts, lying on floor when Maximillian opens her blouse.

## House of the Rising Sun (1987)

Jamie Barrett ........................... Janet
- 1:04—Very brief breasts making love with Louis.

James Daughton ........................ n.a.

## The House on Carroll Street (1988)

Jeff Daniels........................ Cochran
Kelly McGillis ........................... Emily
- 0:39—Brief breasts reclining into the water in the bathtub.

Mandy Patinkin ..................... Ray Salwen
Kenneth Welsh...................... Hackett

## House on Sorority Row (1983)

Eileen Davidson ........................ Vicki
- 0:16—Breasts and buns in room making love with her boyfriend.
0:19—In white bikini top by the pool.

Harley Jane Kozak.........................Diane
Kate McNeil.......................Katherine

## The House on Straw Hill (1976; British)

*a.k.a. Exposé*

Linda Hayden..................... Linda Hindstatt
- 0:28—Breasts getting undressed in her room.
- 0:47—Breasts, masturbating in bed.
- 1:06—Right breast, in bed with Fiona Richmond.

Karl Howman........................Small Youth
- 0:36—Buns, raping Linda Hayden in a field, while his friend holds a gun.

Fiona Richmond . . . . . . . . . . . . . . . . . . . . . . . Suzanne
••• 0:05—Buns and breasts undressing and getting into bed and making love with Udo Kier.
•• 0:56—In black bra, then breasts undressing in front of Kier.
••• 1:00—Breasts in bedroom, then making love with Kier.
1:03—Brief buns, lying on Linda's bed.
1:05—Buns, lying on Linda's bed.
1:06—Right breast, in bed with Linda.
•• 1:07—Breasts in bed with Linda.
• 1:09—Buns and side of left breast getting up from bed.
• 1:11—Full frontal nudity, getting stabbed in the bathroom. Covered with blood.

### House Where Evil Dwells (1982)
Edward Albert . . . . . . . . . . . . . . . . . . . . . . . . . . .Ted
Susan George . . . . . . . . . . . . . . . . . . . . . . . . . Laura
••• 0:21—Breasts in bed making love with Edward Albert.
•• 0:59—Breasts making love again.
Doug McClure . . . . . . . . . . . . . . . . . . . . . . . . . . Alex
• 1:00—Very brief, upper half of buns, while making love with Susan George on the floor.

### Household Saints (1992)
Lili Taylor . . . . . . . . . . . . . . . . . . . . . . . . . . . .Teresa
•• 1:35—Breasts while in her bedroom, after undressing in front of Leonard.

### Housewife (1972)
Yaphet Kotto. . . . . . . . . . . . . . . . . . . . . . . . . . . .Bone
Joyce Van Patten . . . . . . . . . . . . . . . . . . . . Bernadette
• 0:46—Breasts and buns on pool table getting attacked by Yaphet Kotto. Probably a body double, don't see her face.
1:04—Most of left breast getting on top of Kotto. In side view, you can see black tape over her nipple.
• 1:05—Brief side of right breast under Kotto's arm several times after she falls on the floor with him.

### Housewife From Hell (1993)
Lisa Comshaw. . . . . . . . . . . . . . . . . . . . . . . . . Melissa
•• 0:03—Nude, after taking off robe in front of bathroom mirror (while wearing glasses), then getting into shower.
•• 0:04—Breasts, while sitting in bathtub and talking to John.
••• 0:36—Breasts, while sitting in bubble bath and talking to John.
• 0:48—In bra, buns in T-back while dancing in garage in between two other dancers.
• 1:00—Breasts under white bodysuit.
Jerica Fox . . . . . . . . . . . . . . . . . . . . . . . . . . . Party Girl
••• 0:53—In red bra and panties, then breasts while dancing beside spa, then getting into spa and sitting in spa.
Ron Jeremy . . . . . . . . . . . . . . . . . . . . . . . . . . . . Vince

Jennifer Peace. . . . . . . . . . . . . . . . . . . . . . . . . . . Sue
•• 0:27—Breasts, while undoing her dress in John's office.
Jacqueline St. Claire . . . . . . . . . . . . . . . . . . . .Mary-Lou
••• 0:12—Breasts, while taking off blouse on bed with John, then making love.
• 0:15—Brief frontal nudity while in bathroom with John.
•• 0:16—Buns and breasts, while getting dressed in bedroom while talking to John.
••• 0:40—In purple bra and panties, then buns and breasts while in office with John.
• 1:01—Brief buns in bodysuit, while getting up out of bed.

### How Funny Can Sex Be? (1973)
Laura Antonelli. . . . . . . . . . . Miscellaneous Personalities
• 0:01—Brief breasts taking off swimsuit.
• 0:04—Brief breasts in bathtub covered with bubbles.
0:13—Lying in bed in sheer nightgown.
0:18—Lying in bed again.
• 0:26—Breasts getting into bed.
• 0:36—Breasts making love in elevator behind frosted glass. Shot at fast speed.
• 1:08—In sheer white nun's outfit during fantasy sequence. Brief breasts and buns. Nice slow motion.
1:16—In black nightie.
• 1:24—In black bra and panties, then breasts while changing clothes.

### How to Beat the High Cost of Living (1980)
Richard Benjamin . . . . . . . . . . . . . . . . . . . . . . . Albert
Dabney Coleman . . . . . . . . . . . . . . . . . . . . Jack Heintzel
Jane Curtin. . . . . . . . . . . . . . . . . . . . . . . . . . . .Elaine
1:28—In pink bra, distracting everybody in the mall so her friends can steal money.
• 1:29—Close up breasts, taking off her bra. Probably a body double.
Sybil Danning . . . . . . . . . . . . . . . . . . . . . . . .Charlotte
Jessica Lange . . . . . . . . . . . . . . . . . . . . . . . . . Louise

### How to Get Ahead in Advertising (1988; British)
Sean Bean . . . . . . . . . . . . . . . . . . . . . . . . . Carry Frisk
Richard E. Grant. . . . . . . . . . . . . . . . . . . . . . . . Bagley
• 0:19—Brief buns, while wearing apron in kitchen all covered with food. Brief buns again talking with Rachel Ward at top of stairs.
Jacqueline Pearce . . . . . . . . . . . . . . . . . . . . . . . Maud
Tony Slattery . . . . . . . . . . . . . . . . . . . . . . . . . . .Basil
Rachel Ward. . . . . . . . . . . . . . . . . . . . . . . . . . .Julia

### How to Seduce a Woman (1973)
Alexandra Hay . . . . . . . . . . . . . . . . . . . . . . Nell Brinkman
• 1:05—Brief right breast in mirror taking off black dress.
••• 1:06—Breasts posing for pictures. Long scene.
• 1:47—Breasts during flashback. Lots of diffusion.
Angel Tompkins . . . . . . . . . . . . . . . . . . . . . . . Pamela
1:28—In bra and panties for a long time getting a massage in bedroom.

## The Howling (1981)

Belinda Balaski . . . . . . . . . . . . . . . . . . . . . . Terry Fisher
Elisabeth Brooks . . . . . . . . . . . . . . . . . . . . . . . . Marsha
- •• 0:46—Full frontal nudity taking off her robe in front of a campfire.
- • 0:48—Breasts sitting on Bill by the fire.

Christopher Stone. . . . . . . . . . . . . R. William "Bill" Neill
- • 0:48—Brief buns, rolling over while making love with Elizabeth Brooks in front of a campfire.

Dee Wallace Stone . . . . . . . . . . . . . . . . . . Karen White

## Howling II: Your Sister is a Werewolf (1984)

Sybil Danning . . . . . . . . . . . . . . . . . . . . . . . . . . Stirba
- • 0:35—Left breast, then breasts with Mariana in bedroom about to have sex with a guy.
- • 1:20—Very brief breasts during short clips during the end credits. Same shot repeated about 10 times.

Marsha A. Hunt. . . . . . . . . . . . . . . . . . . . . . . Mariana
- •• 0:33—Breasts in bedroom with Sybil Danning and a guy.

Annie McEnroe . . . . . . . . . . . . . . . . . . . . . . . . . Jenny

## Howling III: The Marsupials (1987)

Imogen Annesley . . . . . . . . . . . . . . . . . . . . . . .Jerboa
- • 0:42—Very brief breasts taking off dress in barn to give birth. Breasts are covered with makeup.

## Howling IV: The Original Nightmare (1988)

Lamya Derval . . . . . . . . . . . . . . . . . . . . . . . . . .Elanor
- •• 0:32—Brief left breast, then breasts making love with Richard. Nice silhouette on the wall.

Suzanne Severeid . . . . . . . . . . . . . . . . . . . . . . Janice
Romy Windsor . . . . . . . . . . . . . . . . . . . . . . . . Marie

## Howling V (1989)

Elizabeth Shé. . . . . . . . . . . . . . . .Mary Lou Summers
- • 0:33—Buns and side view of right breast getting into pool with Donovan.
- • 0:36—Very brief full frontal nudity climbing out of pool with Donovan.

Mary Stavin. . . . . . . . . . . . . . . . . . . . . . . . . . . .Anna
- •• 1:09—Breasts three times drying herself off while Richard watches in the mirror. Possible body double.

## Humanoids from the Deep (1980)

Denise Galik . . . . . . . . . . . . . . . . . . . . . . . .Linda Beale
Lisa Glaser. . . . . . . . . . . . . . . . . . . . . . . . . . . . Becky
- ••• 0:34—Full frontal nudity, undressing in tent with Billy and his ventriloquist dummy.
- • 0:35—Nude, running on the beach at night, trying to escape the humanoids.

Doug McClure . . . . . . . . . . . . . . . . . . . . . . . . . . Jim
Linda Shayne. . . . . . . . . . . . . . . . . . . . . Miss Salmon
- • 1:06—Breasts after getting bathing suit ripped off by a humanoid.

Lynn Theel . . . . . . . . . . . . . . . . . . . . . Peggy Larsen
- • 0:22—Very, very brief half of right breast, when fight in parking lot startles her and her boyfriend in back of truck.
- • 0:30—Brief breasts getting raped on the beach by a humanoid.

- • 0:51—Brief breasts, dead, lying on the beach all covered with seaweed.

## Humongous (1982; Canadian)

Janit Baldwin . . . . . . . . . . . . . . . . . . . . Carla Simmons
Joy Boushel . . . . . . . . . . . . . . . . . . . . . . . Donna Blake
- •• 0:09—Breasts looking out the window. More breasts in the room in the mirror.
- • 0:48—Breasts undoing her top to warm up Bert.

Shay Garner . . . . . . . . . . . . . . . . . . . . . . . Ida Parsons
- • 0:05—Brief left breast and brief lower frontal nudity getting her clothes ripped off by a guy. Don't see her face.

Janet Julian. . . . . . . . . . . . . . . . . . . . . . Sandy Ralston

## Hundra (1983)

Laurene Landon . . . . . . . . . . . . . . . . . . . . . . . Hundra
- • 0:29—Very brief breasts, several times, riding her horse in the surf. Partial buns. Blurry.

## The Hunger (1983)

David Bowie. . . . . . . . . . . . . . . . . . . . . . . . . . . John
Catherine Deneuve . . . . . . . . . . . . . . . . . . . . .Miriam
- • 0:08—Brief breasts taking a shower with David Bowie. Probably a body double, you don't see her face.

Ann Magnuson . . . . . . . . . . .Young Woman from Disco
- • 0:05—Brief breasts in kitchen with David Bowie just before he kills her.

John Pankow . . . . . . . . . . . . . . 1st Phone Booth Youth
Susan Sarandon . . . . . . . . . . . . . . . Sarah Roberts
- ••• 0:59—In a wine stained white T-shirt, then breasts during love scene with Catherine Deneuve.

## Hunting (1990; Australian)

Kerry Armstrong. . . . . . . . . . . . . . . . . . .Michelle Harris
- • 0:29—Side view of left breast in steamy shower.
- •• 0:35—Breasts, making love with John Savage in bed. Seen on video monitors.
- • 1:00—Breasts and upper half of buns, making love with Savage.
- • 1:02—Brief buns, turning over in bed.
- • 1:26—Very, very brief breasts, getting her dress top yanked down. Breasts, long shot, getting raped on dining table. Left breast, lying on the floor afterwards.

John Savage. . . . . . . . . . . . . . . . . . . Michael Bergman

## Hurricane (1979)

Timothy Bottoms . . . . . . . . . . . . . . . . . . . .Jack Sanford
Mia Farrow. . . . . . . . . . . . . . . . . . .Charlotte Bruckner
- • 0:39—Brief left breast in open dress top while crawling under bushes at the beach.

## Hurricane Smith (1990)

Cassandra Delaney. . . . . . . . . . . . . . . . . . . . . . .Julie
- •• 0:45—Breasts, while making love with Carl Weathers in bed.

Jürgen Prochnow . . . . . . . . . . . . . . . . . . Charlie Dowd

## Husbands and Lovers (1991; Italian)
(Unrated version reviewed.)

Joanna Pacula . . . . . . . . . . . . . . . . . . . . . . . . Helena
- ••• 0:03—Breasts, making love on top of Julian Sands in bed. Left breast, while lying in bed after.
- ••• 0:10—Nude, walking around and getting into bed with Sands.
- ••• 0:18—Breasts in bathroom, brushing her teeth, then getting dressed.
- ••• 0:32—Buns and breasts, getting into the shower with Sands.
- • 0:35—Brief breasts getting into bed.
- •• 0:37—Breasts in white panties, putting on stockings.
- •• 0:59—Buns, getting spanked by Paolo.
- ••• 1:17—Buns, then breasts making love in bed with Sands. Nude getting out of bed.
- • 1:19—Brief breasts, putting on stockings, then white bra and panties.
- • 1:21—Buns, in greenhouse with Paolo when he beats her.

Julian Sands. . . . . . . . . . . . . . . . . . . . . . . . . . Stefan
- ••• 0:32—Frontal nudity, in the shower and getting out.
- ••• 0:35—Frontal nudity, getting into bed.
- ••• 1:13—Nude, taking a shower then getting out.
- •• 1:17—Very brief frontal nudity after making love with Joanna.

Lara Wendel . . . . . . . . . . . . . . . . . . . . . . . . . Louisa
- ••• 0:47—In bra and panties with Julian Sands, then breasts making love with him.

## Hussy (1980; British)
Helen Mirren. . . . . . . . . . . . . . . . . . . . . . . . . . Beaty
- •• 0:22—Left breast, then side of right breast, while lying in bed with John Shea.
- ••• 0:29—Nude, making love in bed with Shea.
- •• 0:31—Full frontal nudity in bathtub.

John Shea . . . . . . . . . . . . . . . . . . . . . . . . . . . Emory
- •• 0:29—Buns while making love with Helen Mirren in bed. Half of lower frontal nudity when she rolls off him.

## Hustle (1975)
Catherine Bach . . . . . . . . . . . . . . . . . . . Peggy Summers
Eileen Brennan . . . . . . . . . . . . . . . . . . . Paula Hollinger
Catherine Deneuve . . . . . . . . . . . . . . . . . Nicole Britton
Sharon Kelly . . . . . . . . . . . . . . . . . . . . . Gloria Hollinger
- • 0:12—Brief breasts several times getting rolled out of freezer, dead.
- • 1:03—In pasties, dancing behind curtain when Gloria's father imagines the dancer is Gloria.
- • 1:42—In black lingerie, brief buns and side views of breast in bed in film.

Burt Reynolds . . . . . . . . . . . . . . Lieutenant Phil Gaines
Patrice Rohmer . . . . . . . . . . . . . . . . . . . Linda (Dancer)
- • 1:03—In pasties, dancing on stage behind beaded curtain. Buns in G-string.

## I Don't Give a Damn (1985; Israeli)
a.k.a. Lo Sam Zayin

Liora Grossman . . . . . . . . . . . . . . . . . . . . . . . Maya
- • 1:11—Brief right breast, while posing for Rafi in the kitchen.

## I Hate Blondes (1981; Italian)
Corrine Clery . . . . . . . . . . . . . . . . . . . . . . . . Angelica
- • 1:17—Left breast and upper half of buns, in bedroom with a guy when he tries to seduce her.

Paola Tedesco . . . . . . . . . . . . . . . . . . . . . . . . Teresa
- ••• 0:06—Breasts, sitting up in bed at night and turning on the light. Buns, while walking around the room.

## I Love N.Y. (1987)
Scott Baio. . . . . . . . . . . . . . . . . . . . . . . Mario Colone
- • 1:19—Brief, upper half of buns, while getting out of bed. Dark, hard to see.

## I Love You (1982; Brazilian)
a.k.a. Eu Te Amo

Sonia Braga . . . . . . . . . . . . . . . . . . . . . . . . . Maria
- ••• 0:34—Full frontal nudity making love with Paulo.
- •• 0:36—Breasts sitting on the edge of the bed.
- • 0:49—Breasts running around the house teasing Paulo.
- •• 0:50—Brief nude in blinking light. Don't see her face.
- • 0:53—Breasts eating fruit with Paulo.
- ••• 0:54—Breasts wearing white panties in front of windows with Paulo. Long scene.
- • 1:03—Left breast standing talking to Paulo.
- • 1:10—Left breast talking to Paulo.
- • 1:15—Very brief full frontal nudity, several times, in Paulo's flashback in blinking light scene.
- ••• 1:23—Breasts with Paulo during an argument. Dark, but long scene.
- •• 1:28—Breasts walking around Paulo's place with a gun. Dark.
- • 1:33—Various breasts scenes.

Vera Fischer . . . . . . . . . . . . . . . . . . . Barbara Bergman
- ••• 0:31—Left breast while in front of TV and in chair with Paulo.
- •• 0:46—Left breast sticking out of nightgown. Silhouette of breasts while getting up. Full frontal nudity after taking off nightgown.
- ••• 0:47—Nude in bed with Paulo.
- ••• 1:05—Breasts on couch with Paulo.
- • 1:09—Breasts on TV while opening her dress.

Paulo Cesar Pereio . . . . . . . . . . . . . . . . . . . . . Paulo
- • 0:35—Brief side view of buns and frontal nudity, while kneeling on the floor with Sonia Braga.
- • 0:38—Buns, in mirror, while walking in hallway.
- •• 0:59—Buns and part of frontal nudity covered with paint with Braga.
- • 1:36—Side view of buns, while making love on top of Braga.
- • 1:37—Brief buns while lying on floor with Braga. Lit with neon lights.

### *I Love You to Death* (1990)

Phoebe Cates . . . . . . . . . . . . . . . Uncredited Girl in Bar
William Hurt . . . . . . . . . . . . . . . . . . . . . . . Harlan
Victoria Jackson . . . . . . . . . . . . . . . . . . . . . . Lacey
Michelle Joyner . . . . . . . . . . . . . . . . . . . . Donna Joy
Kevin Kline . . . . . . . . . . . . . . . . . . . . . . . . . Joey
- 0:10—Buns, while wearing an apron walking from the bedroom in Victoria Jackson's apartment.

Keanu Reeves . . . . . . . . . . . . . . . . . . . Marlon James

### *I Never Promised You a Rose Garden* (1977)

Bibi Andersson . . . . . . . . . . . . . . . . . . . . . Dr. Fried
Jeff Conaway . . . . . . . . . . . . . . . . . . . . . Lactamaeon
Kathleen Quinlan . . . . . . . . . . . . . . . . . . . . Deborah
- 0:27—Breasts changing in a mental hospital room with the orderly.
- 0:52—Brief breasts riding a horse in a hallucination sequence. Blurry, hard to see. Then close up of left breast (could be anyone's).

Susan Tyrrell . . . . . . . . . . . . . . . . . . . . . . . . . Lee
Diane Varsi . . . . . . . . . . . . . . . . . . . . . . . . . Sylvia

### *I Posed for Playboy* (1991)

*a.k.a. Posing: Inspired by Three Real Stories*
(Shown on network TV without the nudity.)
Josie Bissett . . . . . . . . . . . . . . . . . . . Claire Baywood
- 0:09—Close-up of left breast, while on couch with Nick. Don't see her face.

Lynda Carter . . . . . . . . . . . . . . . Meredith Lanahan
Lochlyn Munro . . . . . . . . . . . . . . . . . . . . . . . Sam
- • 0:47—Buns, while wearing an apron in kitchen with Josie Bissett.

Brittany York . . . . . . . . . . . . . . . . . . . . . . Herself
- • • 0:20—Right breast, then breasts on motorcycle during photo shoot.
- • • 0:22—In T-shirt, then breasts during second photo shoot.

### *I Spit on Your Corpse* (1974)

*a.k.a. Girls for Rent*
Talie Cochrane . . . . . . . . . . . . . . . . . . . . . Hitchhiker
- 0:47—Brief right breast, then breasts getting shot. More breasts, dead, covered with blood.

Mikel James . . . . . . . . . . . . . . . . . . . . . . . . Laura
Susan McIver . . . . . . . . . . . . . . . . . . . . . . . Donna
- • • 0:24—Breasts undressing for a guy. More breasts and buns making love in bed with him, then getting out of bed.

Georgina Spelvin . . . . . . . . . . . . . . . . . . . . Sandra
- 0:38—Flashing her left breast to get three guys to stop their car.
- • • 0:39—Breasts, fighting with the three guys.
- • • 0:47—Brief right breast in gaping blouse.
- • • 0:53—Breasts outside, de-virginizing the backwoods kid.
- • • 1:08—Breasts, close-up view, showing her breasts to him.
- • 1:10—Buns, in lowered pants and left breast in open blouse.

### *I Spit on Your Grave* (1978)

(Uncut, unrated version reviewed.)
Camille Keaton . . . . . . . . . . . . . . . . . . . . . . . Jennifer
- 0:05—Breasts undressing to go skinny dipping in lake.
- • • 0:23—Left breast sticking out of bathing suit top, then breasts after top is ripped off. Right breast several times.
- 0:25—Breasts, getting raped by the jerks.
- 0:27—Buns and brief full frontal nudity, crawling away from the jerks.
- 0:29—Nude, walking through the woods.
- 0:32—Breasts, getting raped again.
- 0:36—Breasts and buns after rape.
- 0:38—Buns, walking to house.
- 0:40—Buns and lower frontal nudity in the house.
- 0:41—More breasts and buns on the floor.
- 0:45—Nude, very dirty after all she's gone through.
- 0:51—Full frontal nudity while lying on the floor.
- 0:52—Side of left breast while in bathtub.
- • • 1:13—Full frontal nudity seducing Matthew before killing him.
- • • • 1:23—Full frontal nudity in front of mirror, then getting into bathtub. Long scene.

Gunter Kleemann . . . . . . . . . . . . . . . . . . . . . . . Andy
- 0:33—Buns, while raping Jennifer.

Richard Pace . . . . . . . . . . . . . . . . . . . . . . . Matthew
- 0:42—Buns, while undressing in the house to rape Jennifer.
- 1:15—Silhouette of penis while getting hung (by the neck) by Jennifer.

Erin Tabor . . . . . . . . . . . . . . . . . . . . . . . . . Johnny
- 0:25—Buns, while undressing to rape Jennifer.
- 1:20—Buns, while undressing at gun point.

### *I, the Jury* (1982)

Corinne Bohrer . . . . . . . . . . . . . . . . Soap Opera Actress
Bobbi Burns . . . . . . . . . . . . . . . . . . . . . . . Sheila Kyle
- 0:01—Brief side view of right breast, while in bed with Armand Assante.

Barbara Carrera . . . . . . . . . . . . . . Dr. Charolette Bennett
- • • • 1:02—Nude on bed making love with Armand Assante. Very sexy.
- 1:45—Brief breasts, while in hallway kissing Assante.
- 1:46—Brief left breast, while falling to the floor. Breasts while lying on the floor wounded.

Samantha Fox . . . . . . . . . . . . . Uncredited Orgy Woman
Lee Anne Harris . . . . . . . . . . . . . . . . . . . . . . 1st twin
- • • • 0:48—Breasts on bed talking to Armand Assante.
- 0:52—Full frontal nudity on bed wearing red wig, talking to the maniac.
- 0:54—Brief breasts, dead on bed when discovered by Assante.

Lynette Harris . . . . . . . . . . . . . . . . . . . . . . 2nd twin
- • • • 0:48—Breasts on bed talking to Armand Assante.
- 0:52—Full frontal nudity on bed wearing red wig, talking to the maniac.
- 0:54—Brief breasts, dead on bed when discovered by Assante.

Laurene Landon . . . . . . . . . . . . . . . . . . . . . . . Velda

## The Ice Runner (1993)
Edward Albert . . . . . . . . . . . . . . . . . . . . . . . Jeff West
- •• 0:51—Buns, taking off his pants in room with Lena

## Iced (1988)
Debra De Liso . . . . . . . . . . . . . . . . . . . . . . . . . . Trina
- • 0:11—In a bra, then brief nude making love with Cory in hotel room.

Elizabeth Gorcey . . . . . . . . . . . . . . . . . . . . . . . Diane
Joseph Alan Johnson . . . . . . . . . . . . . . . . . . . . . Alex
- • 0:46—Brief buns while in bathtub reminiscing about making love with a girl.

Ron Kologie . . . . . . . . . . . . . . . . . . . . . . . . . . . Carl
- • 0:39—Buns, while in bathroom snorting cocaine.

Lisa Loring . . . . . . . . . . . . . . . . . . . . . . . Jeanette
- • 0:46—Brief left breast in bathtub.
- • 0:53—Buns and brief right breast in bathtub with Alex.
- •• 1:05—Brief lower frontal nudity and buns, while getting into hot tub. Breasts in hot tub just before getting electrocuted.
- •• 1:13—Full frontal nudity lying dead in the hot tub.
- • 1:18—Brief full frontal nudity lying dead in the hot tub again.

Danny Smith . . . . . . . . . . . . . . . . . . . . . . . . . . . Jeff

## If Looks Could Kill (1987)
Bob Fitzpatrick . . . . . . . . . . . . . . . . . . . . . Doorman
- ••• 0:18—Buns, while undressing and getting into bed with the maid.

Jamie Gillis . . . . . . . . . . . . . . . . . . . . . Jack Devonoff
Jane Hamilton . . . . . . . . . . . . . . . . . . . . . . Mary Beth
Gretchen Kingsley . . . . . . . . . . . . . . . . . . . . . Elizabeth
Jeanne Marie . . . . . . . . . . . . . . . . . . . Jeannie Burns
- •• 0:06—Breasts taking off her robe and kissing George.

Sharon Moran . . . . . . . . . . . . . . . . . . . . . Madonna Maid
- •• 0:17—Full frontal nudity after Laura leaves the apartment.

## If You Don't Stop It You'll Go Blind (1979)
Talie Cochrane . . . . . . . . . . . . . . . . . . . . . . . . . . n.a.
Sandra Dempsey . . . . . . . . . . . . . . . . . . . . . . . . . n.a.
Uschi Digard . . . . . . . . . . . . . . . . . . Various Characters
- •• 0:02—Breasts in bed and closets during opening credits.
- • 0:03—Breasts, pulling up her T-shirt during beginning credits.
- • 0:23—Brief breasts raising her hand in classroom.
- 0:25—In braless, wet tank top, washing her car.
- ••• 0:26—Breasts, while showing them to a guy and letting him feel them.
- • 0:36—Brief upper half of left breast, when it sticks out of her dress.
- ••• 0:52—Full frontal nudity (Contestant #1) on bed, waiting for Omar.
- •• 1:17—Breasts in class during end credits.

Becky Sharpe . . . . . . . . . . . . . . . . . . . . . . . . . . . n.a.
Patrick Wright . . . . . . . . . . . . . . . . . . . . . . . . . . . n.a.

## if... (1969; British)
Robin Askwith . . . . . . . . . . . . . . . . . . . . . . . . Keating
Mary MacLeod . . . . . . . . . . . . . . . . . . . . . . Mrs. Kemp
- •• 1:27—Buns and side of left breast while walking around deserted boy's dormitory (B&W).

Malcolm McDowell . . . . . . . . . . . . . . . . . Mick Travers
- ••• 0:42—Buns, while standing in cold shower as punishment. He's the third guy.

Hugh Thomas . . . . . . . . . . . . . . . . . . . . . . . . Denson
- • 0:43—Brief buns, while getting out of bathtub in boy's shower room.

Richard Warwick . . . . . . . . . . . . . . . . . . . . . Wallace
- •• 0:42—Buns, while standing in cold shower as punishment. He's the second guy.

David Wood . . . . . . . . . . . . . . . . . . . . . . . . . . Johnny
- • 0:41—Buns, while standing in cold shower as punishment. He's the first guy.

## Illegal Entry (1992)
Barbara Lee Alexander . . . . . . . . . . . . . . . Pamela Raby
- ••• 1:02—Breasts, while making out with her boyfriend.
- •• 1:15—Breasts, while making love on piano with her boyfriend.

## Illicit Behavior (1991)
(Unrated version reviewed.)
Sondra Currie . . . . . . . . . . . . . . . . . . . . . . . . Yolanda
Pamella D'Pella . . . . . . . . . . . . . . . . . . . . . . Marilyn
Jenilee Harrison . . . . . . . . . . . . . . . . Charlene Lernoux
James Russo . . . . . . . . . . . . . . . . . . . . . . . Bill Tanner
Joan Severance . . . . . . . . . . . . . . . . . . . . Melissa Yarnell
- • 0:12—Buns, while making love standing up in the kitchen with Jack Scalia. Don't see face.
- ••• 0:13—Breasts on table making love with Scalia. Don't see her face.
- •• 0:54—Right breast and buns, while taking off stockings, panties and bra in bathtub. Don't see face.
- •• 1:10—Breasts and buns in car with Davi. (Sometimes you see her face with her breasts, sometimes not.)
- •• 1:16—Right breast, while lying in bed and talking to Davi.

## Ilsa, She Wolf of the S.S. (1974)
Gregory Knoph . . . . . . . . . . . . . . . . . . . . . . . . Wolfe
- • 0:31—Buns, while in bed with Ilsa.
- • 0:32—More buns, while in bed with Ilsa.
- ••• 0:46—Buns, while in bed with the two blonde female guards.

Dyanne Thorne . . . . . . . . . . . . . . . . . . . . . . . . . Ilsa
- •• 0:00—Buns, then breasts making love in bed.
- ••• 0:01—Breasts taking a shower.
- ••• 0:29—Buns and breasts in bed with Wolfe.
- •• 0:32—Right breast several times in bed with Wolfe.
- ••• 0:48—In white bra, then breasts undressing for Wolfe.
- •• 0:50—Right breast, while lying in bed.
- 1:18—In black bra, panties, garter belt and stockings, tied to the bed.

**The Image** *(1990; Made for Cable Movie)*
Marsha Mason . . . . . . . . . . . . . . . . . . Jean Cromwell
• 0:08—Two brief side views of left breast standing in bathroom after Albert Finney gets out of the shower.

**Images** *(1972; Irish)*
Cathryn Harrison. . . . . . . . . . . . . . . . . . Susannah
Susannah York . . . . . . . . . . . . . . . . . . . . Cathryn
• 0:59—Brief lower frontal nudity, then right breast lying on the bed.
1:38—Brief buns in the shower.

**Imagine: John Lennon** *(1988)*
John Lennon . . . . . . . . . . . . . . . . . . . . . . Himself
• 0:43—Nude in B&W photos from his White Album.
0:57—Brief frontal nudity of album cover again during interview.
Yoko Ono . . . . . . . . . . . . . . . . . . . . . . . Herself
• 0:43—Nude in B&W photos from John Lennon's White Album.
0:57—Brief full frontal nudity from album cover again during an interview.
1:27—Almost breasts in bed with Lennon.

**Immoral Tales** *(1975)*
Paloma Picasso . . . . . . . . . . Countess Erzsebet Bathory
••• 0:59—Nude, getting her clothes ripped off by a bunch of women in a room.
• 1:00—Brief nude, walking away from the women.
•• 1:02—Nude, bathing in blood.
••• 1:05—Nude, walking down stairs. Then in bed with another woman.
••• 1:08—Nude in bed and sitting up.

**Immortal Combat** *(1993)*
Woon . . . . . . . . . . . . . . . . . . . . . . . . . . . Osato
• 0:01—Buns, getting up out of bed with Meg Foster.
Meg Foster . . . . . . . . . . . . . . . . . . . . . . . . Quinn
Tom "Tiny" Lister, Jr.. . . . . . . . . . . . . . . . . Yanagi
Kim Morgan Greene . . . . . . . . . . . . . . . . . . Karen

**Immortal Sins** *(1992; Spanish)*
Maryam D'Abo . . . . . . . . . . . . . . . . . . . . . Susan
Shari Shattuck . . . . . . . . . . . . . . . . . . . . . Diana
• 0:13—Very brief breasts during Mike's dream.
• 0:32—Breasts several times, while making love with Mike.
•• 0:44—Left breast while making love with Mike.
••• 1:09—Breasts making love with Mike.
••• 1:18—Still more breasts making love with Mike.
1:20—Almost full frontal nudity, while standing in doorway. (Hard to see because of shadows.)

**Immortalizer** *(1990)*
Rebekka Armstrong. . . . . . . . . . . . . . . . . . . . June
• 0:16—Breasts getting blouse taken off by nurse.
••• 0:29—Breasts when a worker fondles her while she's asleep.
Raye Hollitt . . . . . . . . . . . . . . . . . . . . . . Queenie

**Impulse** *(1989)*
Jeff Fahey . . . . . . . . . . . . . . . . . . . . . . . . . Stan

Theresa Russell . . . . . . . . . . . . . . . . . . . . . . Lottie
•• 0:37—Left breast, while making love with Stan in bed.

**Impulse** *(1984)*
Tim Matheson . . . . . . . . . . . . . . . . . . . . . . Stuart
• 0:17—Buns, when getting out of bed with Meg Tilly.
Bill Paxton . . . . . . . . . . . . . . . . . . . . . . . . Eddie
Sherri Stoner . . . . . . . . . . . . . . . . . . . . Young Girl
Meg Tilly . . . . . . . . . . . . . . . . . . . . . . . . . Jenny
0:58—In wet red swimsuit in photograph, then breasts in B&W photograph (don't see her face) when Tim Matheson looks at photos.

**In a Moment of Passion** *(1992)*
Maxwell Caulfield. . . . . . . . . . . . . . . . . Victor Brandt
• 0:51—Partial buns, after killing Adriana in bed and rolling onto the floor.
Jeff Conaway . . . . . . . . . . . . . . . . . . Werner Soehnen
Chase Masterson . . . . . . . . . . . . . . . Tammy Brandon
• 0:36—Very brief side of left breast, when dancing in a restaurant with Maxwell Caulfield in front of a lot of people.
• 1:01—Brief left breast, while making love with Caulfield.

**In Harm's Way** *(1965)*
Barbara Bouchet. . . . . . . . . . . . . . . . . Liz Eddington
• 0:05—Very, very brief right breast, while waving to Hugh O'Brian from the water (B&W).
Kirk Douglas. . . . . . . . . . . . . . . . . . Paul Eddington
Paula Prentiss . . . . . . . . . . . . . . . . . . . . . . . Bev

**In Praise of Older Women** *(1978; Canadian)*
Tom Berenger . . . . . . . . . . . . . . . . . . Andras Vayda
• 0:32—Buns, while in bed with Karen Black (seen in mirror). Long shot.
•• 1:04—Buns, while rolling off Susan Strasberg. Kind of dark.
•• 1:07—Very brief lower frontal nudity three times, standing up and picking up Strasberg.
• 1:20—Very brief frontal nudity turning over in bed waiting for Alexandra Stewart.
• 1:23—Very, very brief blurry frontal nudity turning over in bed after getting mad at Alexandra Stewart.
••• 1:42—Buns, while undressing with Helen Shaver. Very brief balls.
Karen Black . . . . . . . . . . . . . . . . . . . . . . . Maya
•• 0:35—Breasts in bed with Tom Berenger.
Michael Kirby. . . . . . . . . . . . . . . . . . . . . . . n.a.
Marilyn Lightstone . . . . . . . . . . . . . . . . . . . Klari
• 0:45—Left breast, twice, while on floor with Tom Berenger before being discovered by Karen Black.
Marianne McIssac . . . . . . . . . . . . . . . . . . . Julika
•• 0:23—Breasts and buns, getting into bed with Tom Berenger.
Helen Shaver . . . . . . . . . . . . . . . . Ann MacDonald
••• 1:40—Blue bra and panties, then breasts with Tom Berenger.
••• 1:42—Nude lying in bed with Berenger, then getting out and getting dressed.

Alexandra Stewart . . . . . . . . . . . . . . . . . . . . . . . Paula
  •• 1:21—Breasts in bed with Tom Berenger.
  •• 1:23—Nude, in and out of bed with Berenger.
Susan Strasberg . . . . . . . . . . . . . . . . . . . . . . . . Bobbie
  •• 1:03—Left breast, while making love in bed with
    Tom Berenger.
  ••• 1:04—Breasts in bed after Berenger rolls off her.
Alberta Watson . . . . . . . . . . . . . . . . . . . . . . . . . . Mitzi
  •• 0:51—Breasts sitting in chair talking with Tom Be-
    renger, then more breasts lying in bed. Long scene.

### In the Cold of the Night *(1989)*
Melinda Armstrong . . . . . . . . . . . . . . . . . . Laser Model 2
Tammy Hansen . . . . . . . . . . . . . . . . . . . . . . . . Model 2
Jeff Lester . . . . . . . . . . . . . . . . . . . . . . . . Scott Bruin
  • 0:05—Very brief buns, while rolling over to strangle
    Shannon Tweed.
Shelley Michelle . . . . . . . . . . . . . . . . . . . . . . Model 3
Adrianne Sachs . . . . . . . . . . . . . . . . . . Kimberly Shawn
  ••• 0:52—Buns and breasts in shower, then making love
    with Scott. Long, erotic scene.
  • 0:59—Brief breasts in outdoor spa.
  •• 1:06—Breasts making love on Scott's lap in bed.
Marc Singer . . . . . . . . . . . . . . . . . . . . . . . . Ken Strom
Shannon Tweed . . . . . . . . . . . . . . . . . . . . . . . . . Lena
  • 0:02—Right breast while making love with Scott.

### In the Heat of Passion *(1991)*
(Unrated version reviewed.)
Nick Corri . . . . . . . . . . . . . . . . . . . . . . . . . . Charlie
Sally Kirkland . . . . . . . . . . . . . . . . . . . . Dr. Lee Adams
  ••• 0:21—In black bra, then breasts making love with
    Charlie while her husband is downstairs.
  • 0:23—Brief breasts in the shower when her husband
    opens the shower curtain.
  •• 0:29—Breasts with Charlie in stall in women's re-
    stroom.
  •• 0:42—Breasts teasing Charlie from the bathroom.
  • 0:45—Right breast, then breasts in bed with Charlie.
  • 1:11—Very brief buns, while on the couch with
    Charlie.

### In the Shadow of Kilimanjaro *(1985)*
Timothy Bottoms . . . . . . . . . . . . . . . . . . Jack Ringtree
  •• 0:18—Buns, three times, while in bedroom with
    Irene Miracle.
  • 0:21—Brief buns, in mirror, while putting towel
    around himself.
Irene Miracle . . . . . . . . . . . . . . . . . . . . . Lee Ringtree
  • 0:18—Brief breasts in bed with Timothy Bottoms.
    Kind of hard to see anything because it's dark.

### In the Soup *(1992)*
Jennifer Beals . . . . . . . . . . . . . . . . . . . . . . . Angelica
Steve Buscemi . . . . . . . . . . . . . . . . . . . . . . . Aldolpho
  •• 0:49—Buns in halfway up pants, while going to the
    door to see who's there.
Carol Kane . . . . . . . . . . . . . . . . . . . . . . . . . Barbara
Debi Mazar . . . . . . . . . . . . . . . . . . . . . . . . . . . Suzi

### In the Spirit *(1990)*
Olympia Dukakis . . . . . . . . . . . . . . . . . . . . . . . . . Sue
Peter Falk . . . . . . . . . . . . . . . . . . . . . . . . . Roger Flan
  •• 0:17—Buns, three times while standing up, a little
    embarrassed, talking to Crystal.
Melanie Griffith . . . . . . . . . . . . . . . . . . . . . . . Lureen

### In Too Deep *(1990; Australian)*
Hugo Race . . . . . . . . . . . . . . . . . . . . . . . . . . . . Mark
  • 0:39—Buns, while talking with Wendy when JoJo
    watches. Long shot.
  • 0:41—Buns, while in bedroom talking with Wendy.
  • 0:59—Brief buns, while walking past sliding glass
    door.
  •• 1:00—Nude, outside with Wendy, spraying her with
    a garden hose.
  • 1:27—Buns, while getting up from the bed.

### Incoming Freshman *(1979)*
Alice Barrett . . . . . . . . . . . . . . . . . . . . Boxing Student
  •• 0:43—Breasts answering a question during Professor
    Bilbo's fantasy.
  • 0:55—Breasts in another of Bilbo's fantasy.
  • 1:18—Breasts during end credits.
Georgia Harrell . . . . . . . . . . . . . . . . . . . . . . . Student
Marilyn Faith Hickey . . . . . . . Sargeant Laverne Finterplay
  • 0:06—Breasts and buns when Professor Bilbo fanta-
    sizes about her.
  • 0:56—Breasts and buns during Bilbo's fantasy.
  • 1:18—Breasts during end credits.
Al Nazario . . . . . . . . . . . . . . . . . . . . . . . . . . Mooner
  • 0:44—Buns, while mooning Professor Bilbo during
    his daydream.
  • 0:56—Buns again during Bilbo's daydream.
  • 1:19—Buns, during end credits.
Wendy Stuart . . . . . . . . . . . . . . . . . . . . . Miss Seymour
  ••• 0:25—In purple bra and panties, then breasts and
    buns stripping during Professor Bilbo's fantasy.
  • 0:55—Buns and side of right breast in Bilbo's fanta-
    sy.
  • 1:18—Breasts during end credits.

### Indecent Behavior *(1993)*
(Unrated version reviewed.)
Gary Hudson . . . . . . . . . . . . . . . . . . . . . Nick Sharkey
  •• 0:57—Buns, several times while on top of Shannon
    Tweed.
Michelle Moffett . . . . . . . . . . . . . . . . . . . . Carol Leiter
  •• 0:07—Breasts, while making love under Frederic be-
    hind 2-way glass.
  •• 0:10—Breasts and buns, while making love on top of
    Frederic. The camera move around a lot, so it's kind
    of hard to see.
  •• 0:24—In black bra and panties, then breasts and
    buns, while making love with Robert while being
    observed behind 2-way glass.
  •• 1:06—Breasts while making love with Brenda and
    getting video taped.

Brandy Sanders . . . . . . . . . . . . . . . . . . . . . . . Elaine Croft
   0:31—Half of left breast, while playing with herself
   while listening in on intercom.
••• 0:59—Breasts and side view of buns, while taking off
   her clothes in front of Jan-Michael Vincent.
••• 1:10—Breasts, taking off her top in front of Vincent.
George Shannon . . . . . . . . . . . . . . . . . . . . . Fredric Lang
  • 0:07—Side view of buns, while making love with
   Carol.
Brenda Swanson . . . . . . . . . . . . . . . . . . . . Judith Miller
••• 1:05—In white bra, then breasts, while making love
   with Carol in observation room.
Shannon Tweed . . . . . . . . . . . . . . . . . Rebecca Mathis
  • 0:12—Breasts seen through water in spa. Brief buns,
   getting out of spa.
  •• 0:56—Breasts while making love with Gary Hudson.
••• 1:24—In bra and panties, then breasts and buns,
   while making love in observation room with Nick.
  • 1:26—Breasts, while getting out of bed.
Jan-Michael Vincent . . . . . . . . . . . . . . . . . Tom Mathis

## An Indecent Obsession (1985)
Wendy Hughes . . . . . . . . . . . . . . . . . . Honour Langtry
   0:32—Possibly Wendy breasts, could be Sue because Luce is fantasizing about Wendy while making
   love with Sue. Dark, long shot, hard to see.
  •• 1:10—Left breast, making love in bed with Wilson.
Bruno Lawrence . . . . . . . . . . . . . . . . . . . . . Matt Sawyer
Richard Moir . . . . . . . . . . . . . . . . . . . . . . . Luce Daggett
  • 0:31—Buns when at the beach with his pals. Don't
   see his face.

## Indecent Proposal (1993)
Catlyn Day . . . . . . . . . . . . . . . . . . . . . . . Wine Goddess
Woody Harrelson . . . . . . . . . . . . . . . . . . David Murphy
Demi Moore . . . . . . . . . . . . . . . . . . . . . . Diana Murphy
  •• 0:05—In black bra, brief buns and breasts while
   making out with Woody Harrelson on the kitchen
   floor.
  • 0:37—Upper half of right breast, while lying in bed
   with Harrelson.
  • 0:40—Upper half of right breast, while lying in bed
   and talking with Harrelson. Very brief right breast,
   when lifting sheet over her head.

## The Indian Runner (1991)
Patricia Arquette . . . . . . . . . . . . . . . . . . . . . . Dorothy
Valeria Golino . . . . . . . . . . . . . . . . . . . . . . . . . . Maria
Dennis Hopper . . . . . . . . . . . . . . . . . . . . . . . . . Caesar
Viggo Mortensen . . . . . . . . . . . . . . . . . . . . . . . Frank
  ••• 1:01—Brief frontal nudity in mirror, then in real life
   in room.

## The Inheritance (1978; Italian)
Adrianna Asti . . . . . . . . . . . . . . . . . . . . Teta Ferramonti
Dominique Sanda . . . . . . . . . . . . . . . . . . . . . . . . Irene
  •• 0:18—Full frontal nudity getting undressed and lying on the bed with her new husband.
  ••• 0:37—Full frontal nudity lying in bed with her lover.
  • 1:19—Very brief right breast, while undoing top for
   Anthony Quinn.

••• 1:22—Left breast, lying in bed. Full frontal nudity
   jumping out of bed after realizing that Quinn is
   dead.

## Inhibition (1984; Italian)
Cesare Barro . . . . . . . . . . . . . . . . . . . . . . . . . . . . . n.a.
Ilona Staller . . . . . . . . . . . . . . . . . . . . . . . . . . . . Anna
  ••• 0:08—Nude taking a shower with Carol.
  • 0:43—Brief full frontal nudity getting out of swimming pool.
  ••• 0:55—Breasts making love in the water with Robert.
  ••• 1:00—Full frontal nudity getting disciplined by Carol.

## The Initiation (1984)
Hunter Tylo . . . . . . . . . . . . . . . . . . . . . . . . . . . Alison
  ••• 0:33—Frontal nudity in shower, then getting out
   and drying herself off.
  ••• 0:57—Breasts, changing tops in sporting goods
   store in mall.
Daphne Zuniga . . . . . . . . . . . . . . . . . . . . . . Kelly Terry
   0:34—Upper half of buns, putting on panties while
   someone watches from inside the closet. Don't see
   her face.

## Inner Sanctum (1991)
Suzanne Ager . . . . . . . . . . . . . . . . . . . . . . . . . Maureen
Michelle Bauer . . Body Double for Margaux Hemingway
  • 0:09—Left breast, body double in office for Margaux
   Hemingway.
  •• 0:23—Breasts body double for Hemingway, while in
   bed with Joseph Bottoms.
Joseph Bottoms . . . . . . . . . . . . . . . . . . . . . Baxter Reed
  • 0:10—Lower half of buns, while in office with Margaux Hemingway.
  ••• 0:43—Buns, while on sofa with Tanya Roberts.
Brett Clark . . . . . . . . . . . . . . . . . . . . . . . . Neil Semple
Margaux Hemingway . . . . . . . . . . . . . . . Anna Rawlins
  • 0:09—Brief buns and tip of left breast in office with
   Joseph Bottoms.
  ••• 0:23—In bra with Bottoms, then breasts, while in
   bed. (When you don't see her face, it's Michelle Bauer doing the body double work.)
Tanya Roberts . . . . . . . . . . . . . . . . . . . . . . Lynn Foster
  • 0:35—Right breast, several times, while looking out
   the window.
  • 0:40—Buns in lingerie on sofa with Joseph Bottoms,
   then breasts while making love.
  ••• 0:57—In black lingerie under trench coat, stripping
   for Bret Clark. Buns, then breasts making love.
Valerie Wildman . . . . . . . . . . . . . . . . . . . . Jennifer Reed
   0:05—Wearing transparent light blue nightgown,
   getting out of bed, into wheelchair.
  •• 0:11—Right breast, while sitting on bed with Joseph
   Bottoms.

## Innerspace (1987)
Fiona Lewis . . . . . . . . . . . . . . . . . . Dr. Margaret Canker
Dennis Quaid . . . . . . . . . . . . . . . . . . . . Tuck Pendleton
  •• 0:08—Buns, while standing naked in the street as
   taxi drives off with his towel. Kind of a long shot.

Meg Ryan . . . . . . . . . . . . . . . . . . . . . . . . . . . . Lydia

### The Innocent (1976; Italian)
Laura Antonelli . . . . . . . . . . . . . . . . . . . . . . . Julianna
- ••• 0:41—Breasts in bed with her husband.
- ••• 0:53—Full frontal nudity in bed when her husband lifts her dress up.

### Innocent Blood (1992)
Angela Bassett. . . . . . . . . . . . . . . . U.S. Attorney Sinclair
Kim Coates . . . . . . . . . . . . . . . . . . . . . . . . . . . . . Ray
Anthony LaPaglia . . . . . . . . . . . . . . . . . . . Joe Gennaro
- •• 1:25—Brief buns, taking off his pants to get in to bed with Anne Parillaud.
Anne Parillaud. . . . . . . . . . . . . . . . . . . . . . . . . Marie
- ••• 0:03—Nude in her apartment.
- • 1:17—Brief buns, taking off coat and getting into bed.
- 1:21—Very brief partial buns, while sitting up in bed.
- •• 1:24—Breasts, taking off sheet and kneeling over in bed to get handcuffs put on.
- ••• 1:25—Breasts and buns, while making love in bed with Anthony LaPaglia.
Linnea Quigley . . . . . . . . . . . . . . . . . . . . . . . . . Nurse
Teri Weigel . . . . . . . . . . . . . . . Melody Lounge Dancer
- • 1:32—Breasts (holding a red and white boa, in the middle of two other dancers), dancing in front of Robert Loggia.

### Innocent Sally (1973)
*a.k.a. The Dirty Mind of Young Sally*
Angela Carnon . . . . . . . . . . . . . . . . . . . . . . . . . . .n.a.
George "Buck" Flower. . . . . . . . . . . . . . . . . . . . .Toby
- • 0:50—Brief frontal nudity, changing places with Sally.
- ••• 0:53—Buns, while making love on top of Sally in back of van.
Sharon Kelly . . . . . . . . . . . . . . . . . . . . . . . . . . . Sally
- ••• 0:35—Breasts, undressing in back of van. Long scene.
- ••• 0:37—Full frontal nudity, on pillow in back of van while caressing herself. Another long scene.
- ••• 0:39—More full frontal nudity in van.
- ••• 0:47—Right breast, then full frontal nudity, making love with Toby in van. Long scene.
- ••• 1:05—Breasts, making love in bed with another guy. Long scene.
- ••• 1:10—Full frontal nudity, making more love. Long scene.
- •• 1:19—Breasts, after making love.
- ••• 1:23—Full frontal nudity, while making love with a guy.
Robyn Whitting. . . . . . . . . . . . . . . . . . . . . . . . . . .n.a.

### Innocent Victim (1988)
Peter Firth . . . . . . . . . . . . . . . . . . . . . . . . . . Terence
Paul McGann . . . . . . . . . . . . . . . . . . . . . . . . .Barry
Helen Shaver. . . . . . . . . . . . . . . . . . . . Benet Archdale
- • 1:05—Very brief side of left breast on top of a guy in bed.

### Inserts (1976)
Veronica Cartwright. . . . . . . . . . . . . . . . . . . . Harlene
- •• 0:16—Breasts sitting on bed with Richard Dreyfuss.
- ••• 0:31—Nude on bed with Stephen Davies making a porno movie for Dreyfuss. Long scene.
Stephen Davies . . . . . . . . . . . . . . . . . . . . . . . . . Rex
- •• 0:31—Buns and balls, while on bed with Veronica Cartwright, making a porno movie for Richard Dreyfuss.
Jessica Harper. . . . . . . . . . . . . . . . . . . . . Cathy Cake
- ••• 1:15—Breasts in garter belt and stockings, lying in bed for Richard Dreyfuss. Long scene.

### Inside Edge (1991)
Michael Madsen. . . . . . . . . . . . . . . Richard Montana
Rosie Vela. . . . . . . . . . . . . . . . . . . . . . . . .Lisa Zamora
- ••• 1:06—Breasts, while making love with Michael Madsen in bed.

### Instant Karma (1990)
Rebekka Armstrong . . . . . . . . . . . . . . . . . . . . .Jamie
Hedy Lamarr . . . . . . . . . . . . . . . . . . . . Movie Goddess
Craig Sheffer . . . . . . . . . . . . . . . . . . . . . Zane Smith
- • 1:15—Brief buns while on top of Penelope. Don't see his face.
- 1:18—Very brief buns again in flashback.
Annette Sinclair . . . . . . . . . . . . . . . . . . . . . . . . .Amy

### Internal Affairs (1990)
Pamella D'Pella. . . . . . . . . . . . . . . . . . . . . . . . Cheryl
Victoria Dillard . . . . . . . . . . . . . . . . . . . . . . . . . Kee
Richard Gere . . . . . . . . . . . . . . . . . . . . Dennis Peck
Faye Grant . . . . . . . . . . . . . . . . . . . . . . . . . . . Penny
- • 0:50—Right breast, while straddling Richard Gere while she talks on the telephone.
Billie Neal. . . . . . . . . . . . . . . . . . . . . . . .Dorian's Wife
Nancy Travis . . . . . . . . . . . . . . . . . . Kathleen Avila
- • 0:38—Side view of left breast when Raymond opens the shower door to talk to her.

### Intersection (1993)
Lolita Davidovich . . . . . . . . . . . . . . . . . .Olivia Marshak
- • 0:01—Breasts during Richard Gere's flashback. Don't see her face.
- • 0:04—Very brief right breast while rolling over in bed.
- •• 1:15—Brief breasts while pulling up her pajama tops during game of charades.
Richard Gere . . . . . . . . . . . . . . . . . . . . Vincent Eastman
Christine Lippa . . . . . . . . . . . . . . . . . . . . .Step Magazine
David Selby . . . . . . . . . . . . . . . . . . . . . Richard Quarry
Sharon Stone . . . . . . . . . . . . . . . . . . . . . .Sally Eastman
- • 0:18—Right breast behind glass blocks in shower, then very brief left breast in mirror when she adjusts her robe.

### Intimate Obsession (1992)
(Unrated version reviewed.)
Kristie Ducati . . . . . . . . . . . . . . . . . . . . . . . . . . Laura
- ••• 0:15—Breasts while making love with Rick while Rachel watches from outside. Long scene.

••• 0:17—More breasts, while making love on top of Rick.

••• 0:18—Buns and more breasts while making love.

••• 0:19—Brief partial lower frontal nudity and more breasts while making love with Rick.

•• 0:21—Breasts during Rachel's recollections.

Valerie Hartman . . . . . . . . . . . . . . . . . . . . . . . . . Karen

Heather McTague . . . . . . . . . . . . . . . . Beth Thompson

••• 0:38—Nude, while making love with Tom in bedroom. (She's wearing a dark wig and sunglasses.) Long scene.

• 1:04—Breasts on TV in video playback that Rachel watches.

• 1:10—Left breast, while sitting on couch and kissing Tom.

James Quarter . . . . . . . . . . . . . . . . . . . . . . . Rick Simms

• 0:16—Buns, while making love with Laura while Rachel watches from outside.

••• 0:18—Buns, while making love with Laura on chair and around the room.

••• 0:22—Buns, during Rachel's recollections.

••• 0:47—Buns, several times, while making love on top of Rachel.

### Intimate Strangers *(1991; Made for Cable Movie)*

Tia Carrere . . . . . . . . . . . . . . . . . . . . . . . . . . . . . Mino

• 0:34—In black lingerie in Nick's apartment. Very brief side of right breast in bed with him.

Paige French . . . . . . . . . . . . . . . . . . . . . . Meg Wheeler

Deborah Harry . . . . . . . . . . . . . . . . . . . . Cory Wheeler

James Russo . . . . . . . . . . . . . . . . . . . . . . Nick Ciccini

### Into the Fire *(1988)*

*a.k.a. Legend of Lone Wolf*

Susan Anspach . . . . . . . . . . . . . . . . . Rosalind Winfield

•• 0:22—Left breast, under trench coat when she first comes into the house, briefly again in the kitchen.

•• 0:31—Breasts in bedroom standing up with Wade.

Olivia D'Abo . . . . . . . . . . . . . . . . . . . . . . . . . . . Liette

0:07—Very, very brief silhouette of left breast in bed with Wade.

•• 0:32—Breasts on bed with Wade. A little bit dark and hard to see.

•• 1:10—Breasts in the bathtub. (Note her panties when she gets up.)

### Into the Night *(1985)*

David Bowie . . . . . . . . . . . . . . . . . . . . . . . Colin Morris

Sue Bowser . . . . . . . . . . . . . . . . . . . . . . Girl on Boat

•• 0:24—Breasts taking off blouse with Jake on his boat after Michelle Pfeiffer leaves.

Jeff Goldblum . . . . . . . . . . . . . . . . . . . . . . . Ed Okin

Kathryn Harrold . . . . . . . . . . . . . . . . . . . . . . .Christie

Tracey E. Hutchinson. . . . . . . . . . . . . . . Federal Agent

Irene Papas . . . . . . . . . . . . . . . . . . . . .Shaheen Parvizi

Dedee Pfeiffer . . . . . . . . . . . . . . . . . . . . . . . . Hooker

Michelle Pfeiffer . . . . . . . . . . . . . . . . . . . . . . . Diana

•• 0:27—Brief buns while in bathroom.

• 0:28—Brief side nudity, twice, walking past doorway. Medium long shot.

Peggy Sands . . . . . . . . . . . . . . . . . . .Shameless Woman

• 0:43—Breasts putting dress on after coming out of men's restroom stall after a man leaves the stall first.

Reid "Chip" Smith . . . . . . . . . . . . . . . . Sheriff Peterson

### Invasion of Privacy *(1992)*

(Unrated version reviewed.)

Robby Benson . . . . . . . . . . . . . . . . . . . . . Alex Pruitt

•• 1:20—Buns, while making love on top of Lydie Denier in bed.

Diana Cuevas. . . . . . . . . . . . . . . . . . . . Alex's Mother

•• 0:01—Left breast, while in bedroom with her lover, while young Alex watches from closet.

Lydie Denier. . . . . . . . . . . . . . . . . . . . . . . . . . Vicky

• 0:54—Brief breasts in her apartment dancing in front of Robby Benson while he video tapes her.

••• 1:19—Breasts on top of Benson in bed.

Shannon Dow Smith . . . . . . . . . . . . . . . . . Young Man

••• 0:02—Buns, in bedroom with Alex's mother while young Alex watches from the closet.

### Invasion of the Bee Girls *(1973)*

Anna Aries . . . . . . . . . . . . . . . . . . . . . . . . . Cora Kline

•• 0:55—Buns and breasts getting transformed into a Bee Girl.

••• 1:00—Breasts getting out of the bee transformer.

Anitra Ford. . . . . . . . . . . . . . . . . . . . .Dr. Susan Harris

••• 0:47—Breasts and buns undressing in front of a guy in front of a fire.

Susan Player Jarreau . . . . . . . . . . . . . . . . . . . . . Girl

Beverly Powers. . . . . . . . . . . . . . . . . .Harriet Williams

• 1:14—In white bra and panties, then right breast and buns, taking off her clothes for her husband.

Victoria Vetri . . . . . . . . . . . . . . . . . . . . . . . Julie Zorn

• 0:30—Brief breasts getting molested by jerks.

••• 1:19—Breasts in the bee transformer, then brief buns getting rescued.

### Invasion of the Body Snatchers *(1978)*

Brooke Adams . . . . . . . . . . . . . . . . . . Elizabeth Driscoll

0:49—All covered in pod gunk in her bedroom when Donald Sutherland discovers her. Don't really see anything.

•• 1:43—Brief breasts behind plants when Sutherland sees her change into a pod person. Hard to see because plants are in the way.

• 1:48—Breasts walking through the pod factory pointing out Sutherland to everybody. Long shot, hard to see.

Veronica Cartwright. . . . . . . . . . . . . . . . .Nancy Bellicec

Jeff Goldblum. . . . . . . . . . . . . . . . . . . . . .Jack Bellicec

Donald Sutherland . . . . . . . . . . . . . . . . Matthew Bennell

### The Invincible Six *(1969)*

Elke Sommer . . . . . . . . . . . . . . . . . . . . . . . . . . . . Zari

• 0:44—Right breast under wet, skin-colored outfit after fight in pool.

•• 1:09—Right breast, while tending to her wound.

•• 1:10—Breasts, while making love in the dark.

## The Invisible Kid (1988)
Karen Black . . . . . . . . . . . . . . . . . . . . . . . . . . . . Mom
Jay Underwood . . . . . . . . . . . . . . . . . . . . Grover Dunn
- 0:27—Brief buns while running around the school halls after becoming visible with his friend, Milton.
Wally Ward . . . . . . . . . . . . . . . . . . . . . Milton McClane
- 0:27—Brief buns while running around the school halls after becoming visible with his friend, Grover.

## Invisible Maniac (1990)
Dana Bentley Konkel . . . . . . . . . . . . . . . . . Newscaster
- 1:22—Brief breasts on monitor doing the news.
Stephanie Blake. . . . . . . . . . . . . . . . . . . . . . .Mrs. Cello
- •• 0:42—Breasts opening her blouse for Chet.
- •• 0:52—Breasts in her office trying to seduce Dr. Smith. Nice close up of right breast.
Debra Lamb . . . . . . . . . . . . . . . . . . . . . . . . . . . .Betty
- 0:21—Buns and very brief side view of right breast in the shower with the other girls.
- ••• 0:43—In bra, then breasts and buns standing on the left in the locker room with the other girls.
- 0:44—Buns and brief breasts in the shower with the other girls.
- •• 0:56—In bra, then breasts getting killed by Dr. Smith.
- 0:58—Brief breasts, dead, discovered by April and Joan.
Melissa Anne Moore . . . . . . . . . . . . . . . . . . . . .Bunny
- 0:21—Buns in shower with the other girls.
- ••• 0:43—In bra, then breasts sitting with yellow towel in locker room with the other girls.
- 0:44—Breasts in shower with the other girls.
- ••• 1:09—In bra, then breasts making out in Principal's Office with Chet. Long scene.
Tracy Walker . . . . . . . . . . . . . . . . . . . . . . Telescope Gal
- •• 0:01—Nude, taking off clothes during opening credits. Nice dancing.
Shannon Wilsey. . . . . . . . . . . . . . . . . . . . . . . . . . .Vicky
- 0:21—Buns and very, very brief side of left breast in the shower with the other girls.
- 0:33—Right breast covered with bubbles.
- ••• 0:43—In bra, then breasts and lots of buns in locker room with the other girls.
- •• 0:44—Buns and left breast in the shower with the other girls.
- ••• 1:04—Undressing in locker room in white bra and panties, then breasts. More breasts taking a shower and getting electrocuted.

## Invisible: The Chronicles of Benjamin Knight (1993)
Aharon Ipalé . . . . . . . . . . . . . . . . . . . . . . . . . . . Petroff
Jennifer Nash. . . . . . . . . . . . . . . . . . . . . . . . . . . .Zanna
- 0:15—Buns, while making love in bed with Wade. Don't see her face well.

## Ironheart (1991)
Karman Kruschke . . . . . . . . . . . . . . . . . . . . . . . . .Kristi
- •• 0:55—Buns and brief side of left breast, getting out of bed with John. Brief breasts in bathroom.

Melanie Mosely . . . . . . . . . . . . . . . . . . . . . Pretty Girl
- •• 0:18—Breasts, while getting her T-shirt ripped off by four jerks. Long shot and closer shots.
Richard Norton . . . . . . . . . . . . . . . . . . . . Milverstead

## Ironweed (1987)
Carroll Baker . . . . . . . . . . . . . . . . . . . . . Annie Phelan
Jack Nicholson . . . . . . . . . . . . . . . . . . . . Francis Phelan
Meryl Streep . . . . . . . . . . . . . . . . . . . . . . . . . .Helen
Margaret Whitton . . . . . . . . . . . . . . . . . . . . . .Katrina
- •• 1:19—Full frontal nudity leaving the house and walking down steps while young Francis brushes a horse.

## Irreconcilable Differences (1984)
Drew Barrymore. . . . . . . . . . . . . . . . . . . . Casey Brodsky
Dana Kaminsky . . . . . . . . . . . . . . Woman in Dress Shop
Shelley Long . . . . . . . . . . . . . . Lucy Van Patten Brodsky
Ryan O'Neal. . . . . . . . . . . . . . . . . . . . . .Albert Brodsky
Sharon Stone . . . . . . . . . . . . . . . . . . . . Blake Chandler
- •• 0:56—Breasts lowering her blouse in front of Ryan O'Neal during film test.

## Is There Sex After Death? (1975)
Harry Bangel . . . Round Table Discussion/Man on Table
- •• 1:25—Buns, while making love on table with a guy in front of a group of a discussion group of men.
Mary Elaine Monti . . . . . . . . . . . . Stag Film Scene/Sue
- •• 0:53—Buns and right breast, while in bed with a guy during filming of stag film.
- •• 1:00—Breasts and buns, while in bed with Fred.
K.C. Townsend. .Round Table Discussion/Woman on Table
- •• 1:25—Full frontal nudity, while making love on table with a guy in front of a group of a discussion group of men.
Jennifer Welles . . . . . . . . Magic Act/Merkin's Assistant
- •• 0:41—Brief left breast and buns, while helping Merkin, then full frontal nudity.

## Isadora (1968; British)
James Fox. . . . . . . . . . . . . . . . . . . . . . Gordon Craig
Vanessa Redgrave. . . . . . . . . . . . . . . . . Isadora Duncan
0:47—Brief glimpses of breasts and buns dancing around in her boyfriend's house at night. Hard to see anything.
- 2:19—Very brief breasts dancing on stage after coming back from Russia.

## Ishtar (1987)
Isabelle Adjani . . . . . . . . . . . . . . . . . . . . . . Shirra Assel
- 0:27—Very brief left breast flashing herself to Dustin Hoffman at the airport while wearing sunglasses.
Warren Beatty . . . . . . . . . . . . . . . . . . . . . Lyle Rogers
Dustin Hoffman . . . . . . . . . . . . . . . . . . . .Chuck Clarke
Carol Kane. . . . . . . . . . . . . . . . . . . . . . . . . . . . Carol
Jack Weston . . . . . . . . . . . . . . . . . . . . . .Marty Freed

## The Island (1980)
Angela Punch McGregor . . . . . . . . . . . . . . . . . . . Beth
- •• 0:45—Breasts taking off poncho to make love with Michael Caine in hut after rubbing stuff on him.

0:50—Braless under poncho walking towards Caine.
Dudley Sutton . . . . . . . . . . . . . . . . . . . . . . . .Dr. Brazil

## Island of 1000 Delights *(German)*
Bea Fiedler . . . . . . . . . . . . . . . . . . . . . . . . . . . . Julia
- •• 0:25—Full frontal nudity washing herself in bathtub, then nude taking off her towel for Michael.
- •• 0:27—Breasts lying on floor after making love, then buns walking to chair.
- •• 0:46—Full frontal nudity taking off her dress and kissing Howard.
- •• 0:50—Breasts in white bikini bottoms coming out of the water to greet Howard.
- ••• 1:06—Breasts sitting in the sand near the beach, then nude talking with Sylvia.
- ••• 1:17—Right breast (great close up) making love with Sylvia.
- ••• 1:18—Breasts above Sylvia.

Scarlett Gunden . . . . . . . . . . . . . . . . . . . . . . . Francine
- ••• 0:02—Breasts on beach dancing with Ching. Upper half of buns sitting down.
- 0:20—Dancing braless in sheer brown dress.
- •• 0:44—Full frontal nudity getting tortured by Ming.
- • 1:16—Breasts on beach after Ching rescues her.

Olivia Pascal . . . . . . . . . . . . . . . . . . . . . . . . . . Peggy
- •• 0:16—Breasts, tied up while being tortured by two guys. Upper half lower frontal nudity.
- •• 0:23—Full frontal nudity lying in bed, then buns running out the door. Full frontal nudity running up stairs, nude hiding in bedroom.
- 0:33—In braless black dress.
- ••• 0:57—Nude, taking off her clothes in shower with Michael.
- • 1:26—Brief breasts running on the beach with Michael.

## It's Called Murder Baby *(1982)*
(R-rated version of the adult film *Dixie Ray, Hollywood Star*.)
Judy Carr. . . . . . . . . . . . . . . . . . . . . . . . . .Adrian Ross
- • 1:21—Brief breasts, sitting up on bed in background.

Lisa De Leeuw . . . . . . . . . . . . . . . . . . . . . . . Dixie Ray
- • 0:26—Lower frontal nudity, raising her dress at the beach to prove to Nick that she never wears panties.
- ••• 0:42—Nude on table, getting massaged by Adrian.
- •• 0:49—Full frontal nudity when Nick leaves the room.
- •• 1:21—Breasts, getting up to get dressed.
- • 1:22—Brief lower frontal nudity in open robe, while walking around the house.
- ••• 1:24—Breasts, opening her nightgown in front of Nick.

Samantha Fox . . . . . . . . . . . . . . . . . . . . . .Lisa Benson
- ••• 1:10—In bra, then breasts in bedroom in front of Nick and Sherry.
- •• 1:11—Breasts, sleeping on bed, then waking up and getting out.
- • 1:18—Brief breasts in B&W flashback.

Jane Hamilton . . . . . . . . . . . . . . . . . . . . . . . . . Sherry
- • 0:59—Buns, raising her skirt for Nick.
- • 1:11—Left breast, sleeping in bed, then waking up and getting out.

Kelly Nichols . . . . . . . . . . . . . . . . . . . . . . . . . . Leslie

## It's My Turn *(1980)*
Jill Clayburgh . . . . . . . . . . . . . . . . . . . Kate Gunzinger
- • 1:10—Brief upper half of left breast in bed with Michael Douglas after making love.

Michael Douglas . . . . . . . . . . . . . . . . . . . . Ben Lewin
Jennifer Salt . . . . . . . . . . . . . . . . . . . . . . . . . . Maisie
Daniel Stern . . . . . . . . . . . . . . . . . . . . . . Cooperman

## Jackson County Jail *(1976)*
Robert Carradine . . . . . . . . . . . . . . . . . . . .Bobby Ray
Marciee Drake . . . . . . . . . . . . Candy (David's Girlfriend)
- • 0:04—Brief breasts wrapping towel around herself, in front of Howard Hesseman. Long shot.

Tommy Lee Jones. . . . . . . . . . . . . . . . . . . Coley Blake
Yvette Mimieux . . . . . . . . . . . . . . . . . . . .Dinah Hunter
- • 0:39—Breasts in jail cell getting raped by policeman.

Patrice Rohmer. . . . . . . . . . . . . . . . . . . . .Cassie Anne
Betty Thomas. . . . . . . . . . . . . . . . . . . . . . .Waitress
Mary Woronov . . . . . . . . . . . . . . . . . . . . . . . Pearl

## Jacob's Ladder *(1990)*
Jason Alexander . . . . . . . . . . . . . . . . . . . . . . . Geary
Perry Lang . . . . . . . . . . . . . . . . . . . Jacob's Assailant
Billie Neal. . . . . . . . . . . . . . . . . . . . . . . . . . . Della
Elizabeth Peña . . . . . . . . . . . . . . . . . . . . . . .Jezzie
- • 0:14—Side view of right breast taking off robe and getting into shower with Tim Robbins.
- ••• 0:16—Breasts several times opening dress and putting pants on. Then in black bra.
- •• 0:31—Very, very brief breasts in bed with Robbins, then left breast a lot. Dark.

Tim Robbins. . . . . . . . . . . . . . . . . . . . Jacob Singer
- •• 0:40—Buns, twice in bathroom, while getting ready for ice bath.

## Jagged Edge *(1985)*
Jeff Bridges. . . . . . . . . . . . . . . . . . . . . . . Jack Forester
John Clark . . . . . . . . . . . . . . . . . . . . . . . . Dr. Holloway
Glenn Close . . . . . . . . . . . . . . . . . . . . . .Teddy Barnes
- 0:46—Side view of left breast, making love in bed with Jeff Bridges.
- 1:38—Very brief side view of right breast running down the hall taking off her blouse. Back is toward camera. Blurry shot.

Maria Mayenzet . . . . . . . . . . . . . . . . . . . Page Forrester
- • 0:02—Very brief breast, on bed when the killer rips her pajamas open. Long shot.

Leigh Taylor-Young . . . . . . . . . . . . . . . Virginia Howell

## Jailbait *(1993)*
Melinda Armstrong . . . . . . . . . . . . . . . . . . . . . . Dawn
- • 0:43—Brief buns in G-string, then breasts, while talking to C. Thomas Howell in room in sex club.

Angel Aviles . . . . . . . . . . . . . . . . . . . . . . . . Pizza Girl

Krista Errickson . . . . . . . . . . . . . . . . . . . . . Merci Cooper
   0:11—In black bra, panties, garter belt and stock-
    ings in room with Tommy.
•• 0:12—Breasts, while in bed handcuffing Tommy to
    the bed.
   0:19—In black bra in motel room.
   1:11—Back half of left breast, while making love
    with a guy.
C. Thomas Howell . . . . . . . . . . . . . . . . . Sgt. Lee Teffler
David Anthony Marshall . . . . . . . . . . . . . . . . . . .Tommy

### Jailbait Babysitter (1978)
Mariwin Roberts . . . . . . . . . . . . . . . . . . . . . . . . . Trisha
•• 0:08—Breasts and buns, taking off her dress and
    getting into van with Cal.
•• 0:18—Breasts and buns in shower with Marion while
    Mike and Cal help them.

### Jakarta (1988)
Sue Francis Pai . . . . . . . . . . . . . . . . . . . . . . . . . . . Esha
• 1:01—Brief right breast, while making love in the
    courtyard with Falco.
   1:13—Brief side of right breast while kissing Falco.
•• 1:13—Side view of right breast, then brief breasts
    twice, making love under a mosquito net with Falco.
    Hard to see her face clearly.

### James Joyce's Women (1983)
Fionnula Flanagan . . . . . . . . . . . . . . . . . . . Molly Bloom
• 0:48—Brief breasts getting out of bed.
••• 0:56—Breasts getting back into bed.
••• 1:02—Full frontal nudity masturbating in bed talk-
    ing to herself. Very long scene—9 minutes!

### Jamón, Jamón (1992; Spanish)
Javier Bardem . . . . . . . . . . . . . . . . . . . . . . . . . . . Raul
••• 0:39—Nude, while practicing bullfighting outside at
    night with his friend, then running away when
    caught. Long scene. (He's wearing a necklace.)
Penelope Cruz . . . . . . . . . . . . . . . . . . . . . . . . . . .Silvia
••• 0:11—Right breast, then breasts, while making out
    with José Luis.
• 0:46—Breasts, while kneeling on ground in dream
    sequence.
• 1:02—Left breast sticking out of dress while José Luis
    has a temper tantrum.
   1:03—In braless, wet white dress.
   1:05—Partial buns, while kissing Raul.
••• 1:09—Breasts, while making love with Raul.
Anna Galiena . . . . . . . . . . . . . . . . . . . . . . . . . Carmen
•• 0:35—Breasts out of the top of her dress, while in
    the back of the restaurant with José Luis.
Tomás Penco . . . . . . . . . . . . . . . . . . . . . . . Raul's Friend
••• 0:39—Nude, while practicing bullfighting outside at
    night with Raul, then running away when caught.
    Long scene.
Stefania Sandrelli . . . . . . . . . . . . . . . . . . . . . .Conchita

### The January Man (1988)
Harvey Keitel . . . . . . . . . . . . . . . . . . . . . Frank Starkey
Kevin Kline . . . . . . . . . . . . . . . . . . . . . . . Nick Starkey

Mary Elizabeth Mastrantonio . . . . . . . Bernadette Flynn
• 0:40—Breasts in bed with Kevin Kline. Side view of
    left breast squished against Kline.
••• 0:42—Breasts after Kline gets out of bed. Brief shot,
    but very nice!
Billie Neal . . . . . . . . . . . . . . . . . . . . . . . . . . . . . Gwen
Lazaro Perez . . . . . . . . . . . . . . . . . . . . . . . . . . .Ramon
Susan Sarandon . . . . . . . . . . . . . . . . . Christine Starkey

### Jason Goes to Hell—The Final Friday (1993)
(Unrated Director's Original Cut reviewed.)
Kathryn Atwood . . . . . . . . . . Alexis, the blonde camper
•• 0:26—Breasts, after taking off wet blouse after skin-
    ny dipping with her friends.
Michelle Clunie . . . . . Deborah, the dark-haired camper
• 0:29—Brief right breast, while on top of Luke in tent.
••• 0:31—Breasts, while making love with Luke in tent
    before getting killed.
Barbara Ann Klein . . . . . . . . . . . . . . . . . . . . . . . Stunts
Julie Michaels . . . . . . . . . . . . . . .Elizabeth Marcus F.B.I.
•• 0:03—In white bra and panties, then buns and
    breasts while starting to take a shower. More breasts
    after grabbing towel.
Michael Silver . . . . . . . . . . . . . . . Luke, the boy camper
•• 0:26—Side view of buns, after taking off wet shorts
    after skinny dipping with his friends. Very, very brief
    frontal nudity. Hard to see because it's dark.
• 0:29—Brief buns, several times, while in tent.

### Jaws (1975)
Susan Backlinie . . . . . . . . . . . . . . . . . . . .Chrissie Watkins
• 0:02—Brief back side of right breast, while taking off
    her clothes and running on the beach. Seen mostly
    in sihouette.
• 0:03—Brief left breast (seen from the shark's point-
    of-view from underneath), while swimming in the
    water. Dark.
Roy Scheider . . . . . . . . . . . . . Police Chief Martin Brody

### Jekyll & Hyde... Together Again (1982)
Elvira . . . . . . . . . . . . . . . . . . . . . . . . . . . . . Busty Nurse
• 0:56—Brief right breast, peeking out from smock in
    operating room. (She's wearing a surgical mask.)
Bess Armstrong . . . . . . . . . . . . . . . . . . . . . . . . . . Mary
Krista Errickson . . . . . . . . . . . . . . . . . . . . . . . . . . . .Ivy
   0:31—In red bra and panties in bedroom with Mark
    Blankfield.
Noelle North . . . . . . . . . . . . . . . . . . . . . . . . . . Student

### Jennifer (1978)
Lisa Pelikan . . . . . . . . . . . . . . . . . . . . . . . . . . . Jennifer
• 0:45—Back side of right breast, in the showers by
    herself.
• 0:49—Full frontal nudity, falling into the pool from
    ladder. (Possibly a stunt double.)

### Jennifer 8 (1992)
Perry Lang . . . . . . . . . . . . . . . . . . . . . . . . . . . . .Travis
John Malkovich . . . . . . . . . . . . . . . . . . . . . . . St. Anne
Uma Thurman . . . . . . . . . . . . . . . . . . . . . . . .Helena
   0:50—Body double did nude scene in bathroom.

## Jessi's Girls (1976)

Regina Carroll . . . . . . . . . . . . . . . . . . . . . . . . . . . Claire
- •• 0:58—Breasts and buns in hay with Indian guy. Don't see her face.

Sondra Currie . . . . . . . . . . . . . . . . . . . . . . . . . . .Jessica
- • 0:02—Nude in water cleaning up, then brief left breast getting dressed.
- • 0:07—Breasts getting raped by four guys. Fairly long scene.
- • 0:37—Breasts kissing Clay under a tree. Hard to see because of the shadows.

Ellen Stern. . . . . . . . . . . . . . . . . . . . . . . . . . . . .Kana
- ••• 1:10—Left breast, then breasts in bed with a guy.

## Jesus of Montreal (1990; French/Canadian)

Lothaire Bluteau . . . . . . . . . . . . . . . . . Daniel Coulombe
- • 0:43—Buns, getting whipped while tied to a tree during a play. Long shot.
- • 0:44—Buns, during crucifixion during play.
- • 1:13—Upper half of frontal nudity when police arrest him during play.
- • 1:36—Very brief frontal nudity when the cross he's on falls over.

Isabelle Truchon . . . . . . . . . . . . . . . Richard's Girlfriend
Catherine Wilkening . . . . . . . . . . . . . .Mireille Fontaine
- • 1:08—Brief breasts starting to take off her sweatshirt during an audition.

## Jezebel's Kiss (1990)

Katherine Barrese . . . . . . . . . . . . . . . . . . . . . . Jezebel
- •• 0:36—Full frontal nudity washing herself off in kitchen after having sex with the sheriff.
- • 0:42—Brief buns, going for a swim in the ocean. Dark.
- ••• 0:48—Breasts taking off her robe in front of Hunt, then making love with him.
- • 0:58—Brief right breast and buns while Malcolm McDowell watches through slit in curtain. Long shot.
- • 1:09—Right breast and buns getting undressed. Long shot. Closer shot of buns, putting robe on.
- ••• 1:12—Breasts making love with McDowell. More breasts after.

Meg Foster . . . . . . . . . . . . . . . . . . . . .Amanda Faberson
Malcolm McDowell. . . . . . . . . . . Benjamin J. Faberson
- •• 1:12—Buns, while making love with Jezebel.

## The Jigsaw Murders (1988)

Laura Albert . . . . . . . . . . . . . . . . . . . . . .Blonde Stripper
- ••• 0:19—Breasts and buns in black G-string, stripping during bachelor party in front of a group of policemen.

Michelle Bauer . . . . . . . . . . . . . . . . . . . . Cindy Jakulski
- 0:20—Brief buns on cover of puzzle box during bachelor party.
- • 0:21—Brief breasts in puzzle on underside of glass table after the policemen put the puzzle together.
- • 0:29—Very brief breasts when the police officers show the photographer the puzzle picture.

- • 0:43—Very brief breasts long shots in some pictures that the photographer is watching on a screen.

Catherine Case. . . . . . . . . . . . . . . . . . . . . Stripper #2
- • 0:27—Brief breasts in black peek-a-boo bra posing for photographer.

Michelle Johnson . . . . . . . . . . . . . . . . . Kathy DaVonzo
- 0:51—Posing in leotards in dance studio.
- 1:07—Posing in lingerie on bed.
- 1:20—In light blue dance outfit.
- 1:27—Posing in blue swimsuit.

Yaphet Kotto . . . . . . . . . . . . . . . . . . . . . . . Dr. Fillmore
Brinke Stevens . . . . . . . . . . . . . . . . . . . . . Stripper #1
- • 0:28—Very, very brief breasts posing for photographer in white bra and panties when camera passes between her and the other stripper.

## Jo Jo Dancer, Your Life Is Calling (1986)

Tanya Boyd . . . . . . . . . . . . . . . . . . . . . . . . . . . .Alicia
Wings Hauser. . . . . . . . . . . . . . . . . . . . . . . . . . . .Cliff
Paula Kelly . . . . . . . . . . . . . . . . . . . . . . . . . .Satin Doll
- 0:26—Doing a strip tease in the night club wearing gold pasties and a gold G-string.

Richard Pryor . . . . . . . . . . . . . . . Jo Jo Dancer/Alter Ego
- •• 0:06—Buns, while walking naked out of the hospital waiting for the limousine.

Barbara Williams. . . . . . . . . . . . . . . . . . . . . . Dawn

## Jock Petersen (1974; Australian)
*a.k.a. Petersen*

Belinda Giblin. . . . . . . . . . . . . . . . . . . . . Moira Winton
- •• 0:21—Left breast several times, under a cover with Jock, then buns when cover is removed.

Wendy Hughes . . . . . . . . . . . . . . . . . . . . Patricia Kent
- ••• 0:12—Breasts in her office with Tony.
- • 0:13—Breasts making love with Tony on the floor.
- •• 0:44—Nude running around the beach with Tony.
- •• 0:50—Nude in bed making love with Tony.
- • 1:24—Full frontal nudity when Tony rapes her in her office.

Anne Pendlebury . . . . . . . . . . . . . . . . . . . . . . . Peggy
Jack Thompson . . . . . . . . . . . . . . . . . . . Tony Petersen
- ••• 0:13—Buns, while making love with Wendy Hughes on the floor.
- ••• 0:20—Frontal nudity under tarp with Moira during protest.
- • 0:22—Buns while in bed with Suzy.
- •• 0:44—Nude running around the beach with Hughes.
- •• 0:50—Frontal nudity undressing, then buns while lying in bed.

Jacki Weaver. . . . . . . . . . . . . . . . . . . . . Susie Petersen
- ••• 0:01—Full frontal nudity lying in bed with Jock.

## Joe (1970)

Peter Boyle. . . . . . . . . . . . . . . . . . . . . . . . . .Joe Curran
Susan Sarandon . . . . . . . . . . . . . . . . . .Melissa Compton
- • 0:02—Breasts and very brief lower frontal nudity taking off clothes and getting into bathtub with Frank.

## Johnny Firecloud *(1975)*

George "Buck" Flower . . . . . . . . . . . . . . . . . . . . . . Wade
Christina Hart . . . . . . . . . . . . . . . . . . . . . . . . . . . . . June
•• 0:22—Breasts, lying in bed with Johnny.
••• 0:26—Breasts, opening her blouse in barn in front of Johnny.
Sacheen Littlefeather . . . . . . . . . . . . . . . . . . . . . Nenya
••• 0:55—Breasts, getting raped by jerks on desk in classroom.

## Johnny Handsome *(1989)*

Ellen Barkin . . . . . . . . . . . . . . . . . . . . . . . . Sunny Boyd
Elizabeth McGovern . . . . . . . . . . . . . . Donna McCarty
•• 0:47—Right breast, while in bed with Mickey Rourke.
Mickey Rourke . . . . . . . . . . . . . . . . . . . . . . John Sedley

## Jokes My Folks Never Told Me *(1976)*

Raven De La Croix . . . . . . . . . . . . . . . . . . . . . . . . . n.a.
Marciee Drake . . . . . . . . . . . . . . . . . . . . . . . . . . . . n.a.
Deborah Dutch . . . . . . . . . Girl on Bed/Confessional Girl
•• 0:33—Left breast, while sitting on bed (on the right) talking to the sweater girl.
Jackie Giroux . . . . . . . . . . . . . . . . . . . . . . . . . . . . . n.a.
Sandy Johnson . . . . . . . . . . . . . . . . . . . . . . . . . . . n.a.
Mariwin Roberts . . . . . . . . . . . . . . . . . . . . . . . . . . n.a.

## Joseph Andrews *(1977; British/French)*

Ann-Margret . . . . . . . . . . . . . . . . . . . . . . . . Lady Boaby
0:19—Standing in pool in wet dress.
0:23—Upper half of breasts in black outfit in bed. Hard to see because of the shadows.
Peter Firth . . . . . . . . . . . . . . . . . . . . . . Joseph Andrews
•• 0:26—Buns, getting his clothes stolen by two guys in the woods.
•• 0:27—More buns, while lying in the woods when discovered by a passing carriage. Very brief frontal nudity while walking to road. Buns when putting a coat on.
Michael Hordern . . . . . . . . . . . . . . . . . . . Parson Adams
• 1:28—Brief buns, while running down the hall trying to get Mr. Didapper out of bed.
•• 1:30—Buns, while getting back into bed.
Murray Melvin . . . . . . . . . . . . . . . . . . . Beau Didapper
• 1:29—Buns, taking off his clothes to get into bed with Fanny when he accidentally gets into bed with another woman. More buns while on top of her in bed.
Natalie Ogle . . . . . . . . . . . . . . . . . . . . . . . . . . . Fanny
• 1:15—Very brief side of left breast, getting her blouse ripped off to get flogged.
•• 1:20—Breasts while hugging Joseph Andrews after he beats up the guy who was attacking her.
•• 1:21—Right breast while walking, then breasts after taking off her blouse in front of Joseph.
•• 1:35—Breasts, after undressing and getting into bed.
Timothy West . . . . . . . . . . . . . . . . . . . Mr. Tow-Wouse
• 0:31—Buns, when getting caught in the hay with Betty by Mrs. Tow-Wouse.

## The Josephine Baker Story *(1991; Made for Cable Movie)*

David Dukes . . . . . . . . . . . . . . . . . . . . . . . . Jo Bouillon
Lynn Whitfield . . . . . . . . . . . . . . . . . . . Josephine Baker
• 0:00—Breasts while dancing during opening credits. Slow motion.
•• 0:13—Breasts after taking off her dress top for the French painter.
••• 0:14—Breasts in the mirror and while dancing with the painter after making love. Nice. Dancer doing splits looks like a body double.
0:16—Brief buns, in wet dress, getting out of swimming pool.
••• 0:31—Breasts while on stage doing the Banana Dance.
••• 0:33—Breasts, while doing the Banana Dance.
• 2:02—Brief breasts while dancing in flashback.

## Joy *(1983; French/Canadian)*

Nancy Cser . . . . . . . . . . . . . . . . . . . . . . . Unidentified
Jeffrey Kime . . . . . . . . . . . . . . . . . . . . . . . . . . . Helmut
Claudia Udy . . . . . . . . . . . . . . . . . . . . . . . . . . . . . . Joy
•• 0:11—Nude, undressing, getting into bath then into and out of bed.
••• 0:14—Nude in bed with Marc.
••• 0:31—In swimsuits, posing for photos, then full frontal nudity.
•• 0:54—Breasts sitting with Bruce at encounter group.
• 1:04—Buns and breasts getting into bathtub.

## The Joy of Flying *(1979)*

*a.k.a. Erotic Ways*
Olivia Pascal . . . . . . . . . . . . . . . . . . . . . . . . . . . Maria
•• 0:39—Breasts wearing panties, in bedroom with George, then nude.
•• 0:46—Nude with George in bathroom.
Ajita Wilson . . . . . . . . . . . . . . . . . . . Madame Gaballi
•• 1:20—Full frontal nudity undressing for George.
•• 1:23—Breasts, making love on top of George.
•• 1:25—Left breast, while in bed with George.

## Joy: Chapter II *(1985; French)*

*a.k.a. Joy and Joan*
Brigitte Lahaie . . . . . . . . . . . . . . . . . . . . . . . . . . . . Joy
• 0:01—Left breast in coat during photo session.
••• 0:11—Nude, getting into bubble bath and out with Bruce.
• 0:20—Breasts, lying in bed after party.
•• 0:22—Breasts, talking on the phone.
••• 0:27—Nude, getting a massage from Milaka. Nice.
• 0:32—Breasts changing clothes.
••• 0:45—In bra, then breasts changing clothes with Joanne.
•• 0:47—Full frontal nudity, masturbating in bed. Medium long shot.
••• 0:54—Nude, making love with Joanne on train. Nice, long scene!
• 1:03—Breasts in the water with Joanne.
•• 1:08—Breasts, getting molested by a bunch of guys in the shower.

- 1:10—Right breast, lying next to a pool.
- •• 1:17—Nude in bubble bath with Joanne and getting out.
- • 1:23—Buns, dancing with Joanne.
- ••• 1:27—Nude, making love with Joanne and Mark.

Maria Isabel Lopez . . . . . . . . . . . . . . . . . . . . . . Milaka
- •• 0:10—Breasts, showing Joy her breasts at Bruce's request.
- ••• 0:27—Breasts, taking off her robe and massaging Joy.

## Joyride (1977)
Robert Carradine. . . . . . . . . . . . . . . . . . . . . . . . John
Melanie Griffith . . . . . . . . . . . . . . . . . . . . . . . .Susie
- • 0:05—Breasts in back of station wagon with Robert Carradine, hard to see anything.
- •• 0:59—Brief breasts in spa with everybody.
- • 1:11—Brief breasts in shower with Desi Arnaz, Jr.

Anne Lockhart. . . . . . . . . . . . . . . . . . . . . . . . . Cindy
- •• 0:59—Brief breasts in the spa with everybody.
- ••• 1:00—Breasts, standing in the kitchen kissing Desi Arnaz Jr.

## Joysticks (1983)
Corinne Bohrer . . . . . . . . . . . . . . . . . . . . . Patsy Rutter
John Diehl. . . . . . . . . . . . . . . . . . . . . . . . . . ./Arnie
Jim Greenleaf . . . . . . . . . . . Jonathan Andrew McDorfus
Erin Halligan . . . . . . . . . . . . . . . . . . . . . . . . . Sandy
- •• 1:08—Right breast, then breasts and lower frontal nudity in bed with Jefferson surrounded by candles.

Becky LeBeau . . . . . . . . . . . . . . . . . . . . . . . . .Liza
Kym Malin . . . . . . . . . . . . . . . . . . . . . . . . . . Lola
- • 0:03—Breasts with Alva showing a nerd their breasts by pulling their blouses open.
- ••• 0:18—Breasts during strip-video game with Jefferson, then in bed with him.
- • 0:57—Breasts during fantasy sequence, lit with red lights, hard to see anything.
- • 1:02—Brief breasts in slide show in courtroom.

Lynda Wiesmeier. . . . . . . . . . . . . . . . . . . . . . . .Candy

## Julia (1974; German)
Ekkhardt Belle . . . . . . . . . . . . . . . . . . . . . . . . Patrick
- • 1:01—Very brief buns, while in bed with Terry.

Peter Berling . . . . . . . . . . . . . . . . . . . . . . .Alex Lovener
- • 0:12—Brief buns, while playing the piano outside on the dock.

Gisela Hahn. . . . . . . . . . . . . . . . . . . . . . . . Miriam
- •• 0:12—Breasts tanning herself outside.
- • 1:14—Brief breasts sitting in the rain.

Sylvia Kristel . . . . . . . . . . . . . . . . . . . . . . . . Julia
- 0:23—Brief breasts in the lake.
- •• 0:25—Breasts on deck in the lake.
- • 0:28—Brief breasts changing clothes at night. Long shot.
- •• 0:34—Breasts on boat with two boys.
- •• 0:42—Breasts taking off her towel.
- • 1:12—Breasts on tennis court with Patrick.

Terry Torday . . . . . . . . . . . . . . . . . . . . . . . . .Yvonne
- • 0:08—Brief right breast, while making love in train restroom.

- •• 0:18—Breasts, while in bed with Ralph. Dark, hard to see.
- • 0:37—Breasts, while getting up to put swimsuit on.
- • 0:41—Brief breasts, while getting dressed in bedroom with Ralph.
- •• 0:57—Full frontal nudity in bedroom seducing Patrick.
- •• 1:01—Breasts, while sitting up in bed eating breakfast with Patrick.

## Julia and Julia (1987; Italian)
(This movie was shot using a high-definition video system and then transferred to film.)
Sting . . . . . . . . . . . . . . . . . . . . . . . . . . . . . Daniel
- •• 1:11—Buns, while sleeping in bed when Kathleen Turner leaves. Don't see his face very well.

Gabriel Byrne. . . . . . . . . . . . . . . . . . . . . . . . .Paolo
Kathleen Turner . . . . . . . . . . . . . . . . . . . . . . . .Julia
- ••• 0:32—Breasts making love in bed with her husband.
- ••• 1:08—Breasts, then right breast making love in bed with Sting.

## Julia Has Two Lovers (1990)
David Duchovny . . . . . . . . . . . . . . . . . . . . . . . Daniel
- • 0:42—Frontal nudity, standing outside during Julia's fantasy. Hard to see because vertical blinds get in the way. Upper half of buns, while in bed with her (in B&W).
- • 0:54—Brief side view of buns, getting out of bed and putting underwear on. Long shot.

Daphna Kastner . . . . . . . . . . . . . . . . . . . . . . . .Julia
- • 0:11—Brief breasts, changing blouses while talking on the telephone.
- • 0:25—Partial left breast, while in bubble bath.
- • 0:29—Right breast, while in bubble bath.
- • 0:30—Breasts in mirror, getting out of bathtub.
- • 0:53—Left breast, while lying in bed with David Duchovny. Long shot.

## Jungle Fever (1991)
Brad Dourif . . . . . . . . . . . . . . . . . . . . . . . . . .Leslie
Samuel L. Jackson. . . . . . . . . . . . . . . . . . .Gator Purify
Gina Mastrogiacomo . . . . . . . . . . . . . . . . . . . Louise
Debi Mazar . . . . . . . . . . . . . . . . . . . . . . . . .Denise
Lonette McKee. . . . . . . . . . . . . . . . . . . . . . . . Drew
- •• 0:04—Left breast while making love with Wesley Snipes in bed.
- • 2:03—Brief left breast in bed with Snipes again.

Tim Robbins. . . . . . . . . . . . . . . . . . . . . . . . . .Jerry
Annabella Sciorra . . . . . . . . . . . . . . . . . . . . Angie Tucci
0:32—In black bra

## Jungle Warriors (1985)
Ava Cadell . . . . . . . . . . . . . . . . . . . . . . . . . . Didi Belair
- • 0:50—Brief breasts getting yellow top ripped open by Sybil Danning.

Sybil Danning . . . . . . . . . . . . . . . . . . . . . . . . .Angel
0:53—Buns, getting a massage while lying face down.

Suzi Horne ........................ Pam Ross
- 0:51—Brief breasts twice during jail scene. Wearing a white blouse, with a yellow shirt underneath. Brief buns. Don't see her face.

Louisa Moritz ................... Laura McCashin

### Just Before Dawn (1980)
Gregg Henry......................................n.a.
Jamie Rose............................... Megan
  0:33—Breasts in pond. Long shot.
- 0:34—Brief breasts in pond, closer shot.
-- 0:36—Brief upper half of left breast, then brief breasts several times splashing in the water.
- 0:37—Breasts getting out of the water.

### Just One of the Guys (1986)
Sherilyn Fenn .......................... Sandy
Joyce Hyser.......................Terry Griffith
  0:10—In two piece swimsuit by the pool with her boyfriend.
-- 1:27—Brief breasts opening her blouse to prove that she is really a girl.
Clayton Rohner............................. Rick

### Just Tell Me What You Want (1980)
Leslie Easterbrook ................. Hospital Nurse
Ali MacGraw..................... Bones Burton
-- 0:16—Breasts getting dressed in her bedroom.
-- 1:26—Brief breasts in bathroom getting ready to take a shower.
Peter Weller.................... Steven Routledge

### Just the Way You Are (1984)
Kaki Hunter................................Lisa
Kristy McNichol.......................... Susan
- 0:50—Very brief left breast showing her friend that she's not too hot because there is nothing under her white coat. Medium long shot.
Michael Ontkean..........................Peter
Alexandra Paul ........................ Bobbie

### Just You and Me, Kid (1979)
Brooke Shields........................... Kate
- 0:07—Brief buns, running down stairs after her towel gets caught in fence.

### Justine
Koo Stark ........................... Justine
-- 0:09—Breasts getting fondled by a nun.
- 0:16—Breasts getting attacked by a nun.
- 0:57—Breasts in open dress getting attacked by old guy.
--- 1:00—Breasts getting bathed, then lower frontal nudity.
- 1:28—Right breast and buns taking off clothes, then brief full frontal nudity getting dressed again.
- 1:32—Breasts getting thrown in to the water.

### Justine (1969; Italian/Spanish)
Anouk Aimee........................... Justine
-- 0:36—Nude, while frolicking in the ocean.
Robert Forster.........................Narouz

Anna Karina ........................... Melissa
-- 0:13—Half of right breast, while fooling around in bed with Michael York.
Michael York ...........................Darley
--- 0:13—Buns, seen in mirror while fooling around in bedroom with Melissa.

### K2 (1991)
Michael Biehn .......................Taylor Brooks
- 0:43—Brief buns, while standing up in pool outside.
Patricia Charbonneau................. Jacki Metcalfe
Annie Grindlay............................ Lisa
Julia Nickson ........................... Cindy
- 0:26—Briefly nude, getting up out of bed and putting robe on.
Kehli O'Byrne..............................Pam

### Kalifornia (1993)
(Unrated version reviewed.)
David Duchovny ..................... Brian Kessler
-- 0:34—Buns, while making love on bed in motel room with Michelle Forbes.
Michelle Forbes ................... Carrie Loughlin
- 0:34—Very, very brief upper half of lower frontal nudity while in bed with David Duchovny.
Ron Kuhlman......................Male Officer
Juliette Lewis ..................... Adele Corners
-- 0:09—Left breast, after opening robe to say "goodbye" to Brad Pitt.
Patricia Tallman ......................... Stunts

### Kandyland (1987)
Sandahl Bergman................... Harlow Divine
Catlyn Day...............................Diva
--- 0:50—Breasts wearing pasties doing strip routine.
- 1:06—Brief breasts talking on the telephone in dressing room.
- 1:12—Brief breasts during dance routine with the other girls.
Kim Evenson ............................ Joni
  0:26—In purple bra and white panties practicing dancing on stage.
--- 0:31—Breasts doing first dance routine.
-- 0:45—Brief breasts during another routine with bubbles floating around.
Alan Popper........................... Heckler

### Kangaroo (1986; Australian)
Judy Davis .......................Harriet Somers
Colin Friels ..................... Richard Somers
-- 1:08—Buns, while running into the ocean.
- 1:09—Frontal nudity walking towards Judy Davis. Long shot, hard to see anything.

### The Keep (1983)
Gabriel Byrne......................... Kaempffer
Scott Glenn ................. Glaeken Trismegestus
Ian McKellen ........................ Dr. Cuza
Jürgen Prochnow ..................... Woorman

Alberta Watson . . . . . . . . . . . . . . . . . . . . . . . .Eva Cuza
- 0:59—Very brief breasts making love with Scott Glenn, then brief lower frontal nudity.

### Keeper of the City (1991; Made for Cable Movie)
Gina Gallego. . . . . . . . . . . . . . . . . . . . . . . . . . . Elena
- 0:19—Brief half of left breast, getting out of bed and putting on black bra. Wearing black panties.

Reneé Soutendijk. . . . . . . . . . . . . . . .Vickie Benedetto
Barbara Williams . . . . . . . . . . . . . . . . . . . . . . . Grace

### Keetje Tippel (1978; Dutch)
a.k.a. Katie's Passion
(Dutch with English subtitles.)
Rutger Hauer. . . . . . . . . . . . . . . . . . . . . . . . . Dandy
- 1:10—Buns seen through torn pants while he is kneeling on the floor.
- 1:12—Brief frontal nudity getting out of bed.

Monique Van De Ven . . . . . . . . . . . . . . . . . . . . . .Katie
- 0:37—Brief buns when guy rips her panties off.
- 0:43—Breasts in hospital when a group of doctors examine her.
- 0:48—Left breast a couple of times talking to a doctor. Brief buns sitting down.
- 1:09—Brief buns, while getting into bed.
- 1:11—Very brief left breast in bed with Rutger Hauer when he catches her eating his chocolate.
- 1:15—Nude burning all her old clothes and getting into bathtub.

### Kemek
Alexandra Stewart. . . . . . . . . . . . . . . . . . . . . . . Marisa
- 0:26—Brief right breast while sitting up in bed.
  0:42—In sheer white dress.
- 0:49—Right breast while kneeling in bed. Out of focus.
  0:51—Very, very brief tip of right breast while crying in bed and talking to David Henison.
- 0:52—Brief breasts lying in bed with Henison.

Mary Woronov . . . . . . . . . . . . . . . . . . . . . . . . . .Mary

### Kentucky Fried Movie (1977)
Uschi Digard . . . . . . . . . . . . . . . . . . Woman in Shower
- 0:09—Breasts getting them massaged in the shower, then squished breasts against the shower door.

Marilyn Joi. . . . . . . . . . . . . . . . . . . . . . . . Cleopatra
- 1:11—Breasts in bed with Schwartz.

Lenka Novak. . . . . . . . . . . . . . . . . . . Linda Chambers
- 0:09—Breasts sitting on a couch with two other girls.

Tara Strohmeier . . . . . . . . . . . . . . . . . . . . . . . . Girl
- 1:16—In bra, then breasts making love on couch with her boyfriend while people on the TV news watch them.

Donald Sutherland . . . . . . . . . . . . . . . . . . . . .Clumsy

### The Key (1985; Italian)
a.k.a. La Chiave
Barbara Cupisti. . . . . . . . . . . . . . . . . . . . . . . . . n.a.
Stefania Sandrelli . . . . . . . . . . . . . . . . . . . . . . Teresa
- ••• 0:31—Nude when Nino examines her while she's passed out. Long scene.
- •• 0:42—Full frontal nudity in bathtub while Nino peeks in over the door.
- •• 1:04—In lingerie, then breasts and buns, undressing sexily in front of Nino.
- •• 1:16—Left breast, sticking out of nightgown so Nino can suck on it.
- ••• 1:19—Breasts and buns making love in bed with Laszlo.
- •• 1:21—Breasts and buns getting up and cleaning herself.
- •• 1:28—Breasts sitting in bed talking to Nino.
- ••• 1:30—Nude, getting on top of Nino in bed.

### Key Exchange (1985)
Brooke Adams . . . . . . . . . . . . . . . . . . . . . . . . . Lisa
  0:10—Nude on bicycle with her boyfriend, but you can't see anything because of his strategically placed arms.
- 0:45—Very brief right breast getting into the shower with her boyfriend, then hard to see behind the shower curtain.

Kerry Armstrong. . . . . . . . . . . . . . . . . . . . The Beauty
Sandra Beall . . . . . . . . . . . . . . . . . . . . . . . . . . Marcy
- ••• 1:14—Breasts on bed taking off her clothes and talking to Daniel Stern.

Terri Garber . . . . . . . . . . . . . . . . . . . . . . . . . . .Amy
Daniel Stern . . . . . . . . . . . . . . . . . . . . . . . . .Michael

### Kickboxer 4—The Aggressor (1993)
Jill Pierce . . . . . . . . . . . . . . . . . . . . . . . . . Darcy Cove
- •• 0:44—Breasts, while in room with Lando after taking off her dress.
- 1:04—Left breast, after sitting up in bed.
- 1:05—Brief breasts while lying back down on bed.

### Kidnapped (1986)
Barbara Crampton . . . . . . . . . . . . . . . . . . . . . . .Bonnie
  0:35—In white bra and panties in hotel room.
- ••• 0:37—Breasts getting tormented by a bad guy in bed.
- •• 1:12—Breasts opening her pajamas for David Naughton.
- •• 1:14—Breasts in white panties getting dressed.

Kim Evenson . . . . . . . . . . . . . . . . . . . . . . . . . Debbie
- 0:25—Right breast in bed talking on the phone. Long shot, hard to see.
  0:30—In blue nightgown in room.
- ••• 1:28—Breasts getting her arm prepared for a drug injection. Long scene.
- ••• 1:30—Breasts acting in a movie. Long shot, then close up. Wearing a G-string.

David Naughton . . . . . . . . . . . . . . . . .Vince McCarthy

## Kill (1971; French/Spanish/German)

a.k.a. Kill! Kill! Kill!

Jean Seberg . . . . . . . . . . . . . . . . . . . . . . . . Emily
- 0:42—Side view of right breast and buns. Don't see her face.
- 0:45—More right breast a couple of times. Still don't see her face.

## Kill Crazy (1989)

Danielle Brisebois . . . . . . . . . . . . . . . . . . . . . . Libby
- •• 0:39—Breasts taking off top to go skinny dipping with Rachel.
- • 0:46—Very brief right breast, while lying on ground with a bad guy while getting raped. Buns, getting turned over before being shot.

Rachelle Carson . . . . . . . . . . . . . . . . . . . . . . . Rachel
- •• 0:39—Breasts taking off top to go skinny dipping with Libby.

## Kill Cruise (1990; German)

Elizabeth Hurley . . . . . . . . . . . . . . . . . . . . . . . . Lou
- • 0:15—Very brief breasts during strip tease routine on stage.
- • 1:09—Side of right breast, while making love with Jürgen Prochnow.
- • 1:15—Very brief right breast in open blouse, several times when Prochnow throws Patsy Kensit overboard.
- 1:25—Most of side of right breast, while consoling Kensit.

Patsy Kensit. . . . . . . . . . . . . . . . . . . . . . . . . . . . Su
Jürgen Prochnow . . . . . . . . . . . . . . . . . . . The Skipper

## The Killer Elite (1975)

Uschi Digard . . . . . . . . . . . . . . . . Uncredited Party Girl
- • 0:00—Brief right breast, while sitting in front of Robert Duvall at a party. Long shot. Continuity error: Note the next time you see her, the blouse is closed!

## Killer Image (1991)

Krista Errickson . . . . . . . . . . . . . . . . . . . . . . . Shelley
Barbara Gajewskia. . . . . . . . . . . . . . . . . . . . . . . Stacey
- • 0:22—Very, very brief left breast, taking off bra at window with M. Emmet Walsh.

M. Emmet Walsh. . . . . . . . . . . . . . . . . . . . . . John Kane

## The Killer Inside Me (1975)

Stacy Keach. . . . . . . . . . . . . . . . . . . . . . . . . . Lou Ford
Pepe Serna . . . . . . . . . . . . . . . . . . . . . . Johnny Lopez
- • 0:15—Brief upper half of buns, twice, getting strip searched at police station.
- •• 0:16—Very, very brief frontal nudity getting restrained by policemen.

Susan Tyrrell . . . . . . . . . . . . . . . . . . Joyce Lakeland
- •• 1:27—Very brief left breast, then very brief breasts (both breasts!) in bed with Stacy Keach during flashback scene.

## Killer Looks (1994)

(Unrated version reviewed.)

Sara Suzanne Brown. . . . . . . . . . . . . . . . . . . . . .Diane
- • 0:01—Buns, while in two piece swimsuit in pool.
- • 0:02—Buns and breasts after getting out of pool and taking off swimsuit top.
- ••• 0:04—Full frontal nudity while making love with the plumber.
- ••• 0:26—Breasts, while making love in spa with her husband.
- • 0:30—Breasts, while putting bra on in bedroom.
- ••• 0:41—Nude while making love with Mickey in bed.
- • 0:47—Briefly nude, while getting into bed.
- • 0:50—Full frontal nudity in flashbacks while on bed with Mickey.
- • 0:59—Breasts in open dress top, while trying to get back away from Cynthia's advances.
- •• 1:23—In bra and panties, then breasts, while blindfolded and making out with Janine Lindemulder and Lené Hefner on stairway.
- ••• 1:25—Nude, while in the shower.

Len Donato . . . . . . . . . . . . . . . . . . . . . . . . . . . .Mickey
- • 0:43—Very, very brief buns, while rolling out of bed when Sara Suzanne Brown's husband comes home.
- • 0:51—Very, very brief buns in flashback.

Lené Hefner . . . . . . . . . . . . . . . . . . . . . . .Angela's Lover
- •• 0:22—In white dress, then breasts, while Janine Lindemulder makes out with her in parking lot.
- •• 1:11—In black dress, then breasts and buns, while making out with Lindemulder.
- •• 1:18—Breasts, while sunbathing outside by pool with Lindemulder.

Diane Hurley . . . . . . . . . . . . . . . . . . . . . . . . Cynthia
- •• 0:57—Nude, while trying to make out with Sara Suzanne Brown.
- ••• 0:59—Full frontal nudity while making love with Vince on sofa.

Janine Lindemulder . . . . . . . . . . . . . . . . . . . . .Angela
- ••• 1:12—In white lingerie, then breasts while making out with Lené Hefner and Mickey's lover.
- •• 1:18—Breasts, while sunbathing outside by pool with Hefner.
- • 1:23—Breasts while making out on stairway with Hefner and Sara Suzanne Brown.

Gerry Pike . . . . . . . . . . . . . . . . . . . . . . . . . . . .Plumber
- •• 0:07—Buns, while making love with Sara Suzanne Brown, then getting dressed after getting caught by her husband.

## Killer Workout (1987)

a.k.a. Aerobi-Cide

Marcia Karr . . . . . . . . . . . . . . . . . . . . . . . . . . . Rhonda
- 1:03—Breasts, opening her jacket to show the policeman her scars. Unappealing.
- 1:12—Breasts in locker room, killing a guy. Covered with the special effects scars.

Ted Prior . . . . . . . . . . . . . . . . . . . . . . . Chuck Dawson
Teresa Vander Woude . . . . . . . . . . . . . . . . . . . . . .Jaimy
- •• 0:43—Breasts in locker room with Tommy during his nightmare.

## A Killing Affair (1985)

Sandi Brannon . . . . . . . . . . . . . . . . . . . . . . . . . . . Sara
•• 0:08—Breasts, sitting up in bed, then kissing Pink.
Susie Hall . . . . . . . . . . . . . . . . . . . . . . . . . . . Blanche
Peter Weller. . . . . . . . . . . . . . . . . . . . . . . Baston Morris
• 1:20—Brief buns, getting out of bed, standing up and putting his pants on.

## Killing Cars (1986)

Senta Berger . . . . . . . . . . . . . . . . . . . . . . . . . . Marie
Jürgen Prochnow . . . . . . . . . . . . . . . . . Ralph Korda
• 0:48—Buns, while getting up from bed to look at cigarette lighter. Slightly out of focus. Don't see his face well.

## Killing Heat (1981)

Karen Black. . . . . . . . . . . . . . . . . . . . . . . Mary Turner
•• 0:41—Full frontal nudity giving herself a shower in the bedroom.

## The Killing Kind (1973)

Sue Bernard . . . . . . . . . . . . . . . . . . . . . . . . . . . . Tina
• 0:00—Breasts during gang rape.
• 0:19—Breasts again during flashback.
• 1:12—Brief breasts again several times during flashbacks.
John Savage . . . . . . . . . . . . . . . . . . . . .Terry Lambert
• 0:00—Upper half of buns when other guys pull his shorts down during rape of girl.
•• 0:58—Buns while in shower when Mrs. Lambert opens the curtains to take a picture.

## Killing Obsession (1994)

Hank Cheyne . . . . . . . . . . . . . . . . . . . . . . . . .Randy
• 0:31—Upper half of buns, when making love with Annie in photo studio.
Victoria Dillard . . . . . . . . . . . . . . . . . . . . . .Jean Wilson
Hyapatia Lee. . . . . . . . . . . . . . . . . . . . . . Annie Smith
••• 0:12—Breasts and buns in G-string, while dancing on bar.
•• 0:15—Breasts, while changing clothes in bathroom, then walking to John Savage.
• 0:18—Brief right breast, while lying dead on floor.
John Savage . . . . . . . . . . . . . . . . . . . . . . . . .Albert
Elizabeth Zimmie . . . . . . . . . . . . . . . . . . . . . . . Babs
• 0:43—Brief left breast, several times, while posing with Randy during photo shoot.

## The Killing of a Chinese Bookie (1976)

Azizi Johari . . . . . . . . . . . . . . . . . . . . . . . . . . Rachel
• 1:14—Brief breasts, while dancing on stage.
• 1:15—Breasts dancing in red light, then coming over to talk to Ben Gazzara.
• 1:26—Brief side view of right breast, while taking a shower.

## The Killing of Sister George (1968)

Madeline Smith. . . . . . . . . . . . . . . . . . . . . . . . Nun
Susannah York . . . . . . . . . . . . . . . . . . Alice McNaught
0:19—Breasts under sheer blue nightgown.
0:59—In black bra and panties.
1:45—In black bra and panties getting undressed.

•• 2:07—(0:09 into tape 2) Breasts lying in bed with another woman.

## Killing Streets (1991)

Michael Paré . . . . . . . . . . . . . . . . . .Chris/Craig Brandt
Jennifer Runyon . . . . . . . . . . . . . . . . . . . Sandra Ross
• 1:00—In white lingerie then brief breasts taking off lingerie in bed with Michael Paré. Hard to see.

## The Killing Time (1987)

Beau Bridges . . . . . . . . . . . . . . . Sheriff Sam Wayburn
Camelia Kath . . . . . . . . . . . . . . . . . . . . . .Laura Winslow
• 0:32—Very brief right breast, while making love with Beau Bridges. Hard to see anything. Dark, lit with red light.
• 0:43—Brief breasts lying in bed getting photographed with Beau Bridges to frame Kiefer Sutherland for a murder.
Kiefer Sutherland . . . . . . . . . . . . . . . . . . Brian Costello

## King David (1985)

John Castle. . . . . . . . . . . . . . . . . . . . . . . . . . . Abner
Richard Gere . . . . . . . . . . . . . . . . . . . . . . . . . .David
Alice Krige . . . . . . . . . . . . . . . . . . . . . . . . Bathsheba
•• 1:16—Full frontal nudity getting a bath outside at dusk while Richard Gere watches.
Cherie Lunghi . . . . . . . . . . . . . . . . . . . . . . . .Michal
•• 0:28—Breasts lying in bed with Richard Gere. (Her hair is in the way a little bit.)

## King Kong (1933)

Fay Wray . . . . . . . . . . . . . . . . . . . . . . . . . .Ann Darrow
• 1:12—Right breast, after surfacing from the water after jumping off cliff with Bruce Cabot.

## King Kong Lives! (1986)

Linda Hamilton . . . . . . . . . . . . . . . . . . Amy Franklin
• 0:47—Very, very brief right breast getting out of sleeping bag after camping out near King Kong.
Brian Kerwin. . . . . . . . . . . . . . . . . . . . . Hank Mitchell

## King of Hearts (1966; French/Italian)

(Letterboxed French version with English subtitles.)
Alan Bates . . . . . . . . . . . . . . . Private Charles Plumpick
•• 1:39—Buns, while standing at the asylum gates while he holds a bird cage after taking his army uniform off.
Genevieve Bujold . . . . . . . . . . . . . . . . . . . . Colombine

## King of Marvin Gardens (1972)

Ellen Burstyn . . . . . . . . . . . . . . . . . . . . . . . . . . .Sally
• 0:50—Brief breasts, while kneeling on the floor and turning around to shoot squirt guns.
Bruce Dern. . . . . . . . . . . . . . . . . . . . . . Jason Staebler
Jack Nicholson . . . . . . . . . . . . . . . . . . . .David Staebler

## King of New York (1990)

Ariane . . . . . . . . . . . . . . . . . . . . . . . .Dinner Guest
Vanessa Angel . . . . . . . . . . . . . . . . . . . British Female
Paul Calderone. . . . . . . . . . . . . . . . . . . . .Joey Dalesio
David Caruso . . . . . . . . . . . . . . . . . . . . Dennis Gilley
Giancarlo Esposito . . . . . . . . . . . . . . . . . . . . . . .Lance

Janet Julian . . . . . . . . . . . . . . . . . . . . . . . .Jennifer
  • 0:26—Very brief left breast, standing in subway car kissing Christopher Walken. Don't see her face.
Phoebe Légerè . . . . . . . . . . . . . . . . .Bordello Woman

### King of the Gypsies (1978)
Danielle Brisebois . . . . . . . . . . . . . . . . . . . . Young Tita
Annette O'Toole . . . . . . . . . . . . . . . . . . . . . . . Sharon
Annie Potts . . . . . . . . . . . . . . . . . . . . . . . . . . .Persa
Eric Roberts. . . . . . . . . . . . . . . . . . . . . . . . . . .Dave
Susan Sarandon . . . . . . . . . . . . . . . . . . . . . . . . Rose
  • 0:49—Brief right breast during fight with Judd Hirsch.
Brooke Shields. . . . . . . . . . . . . . . . . . . . . . . . . .Tita

### King of the Kickboxers (1990)
Sherrie Rose . . . . . . . . . . . . . . . . . . . . . . . . . . Molly
  • 1:05—Very brief buns in G-string and partial side of left breast, while getting into tub with Jake.

### The King's Whore (1990; French/British)
Valeria Golino . . . . . . . . . . . . . . . . . . . . Jeanne de Luyes
  •• 0:08—Right breast, while making out with Alexander.
  • 1:01—Brief upper half of breasts, while lying in bed with Timothy Dalton.
  ••• 1:02—Breasts and buns when Dalton beats her up and throws her out of the room.
  •• 1:16—Right breast when Dalton helps her with her skin disease.
  • 1:19—Brief right breast when Dalton takes off her bandages.
  • 1:20—Upper half of breasts while in bathtub. (She still has the skin disease.)

### The Kiss (1988)
Céline Lomez . . . . . . . . . . . . . . . . . . . . . . . Aunt Irene
Joanna Pacula . . . . . . . . . . . . . . . . . . . . . . . . . Felice
  •• 0:49—Side view breasts making love with a guy. Intercut with Meredith Salenger seeing a model of a body spurt blood.
  • 0:57—Breasts covered with body paint doing a ceremony in a hotel room.
  •• 1:24—Brief right breast, while making love with a guy on bed while Salenger is asleep in the other room.

### A Kiss Before Dying (1991)
Lia Chang . . . . . . . . . . . . . . . . . . . . . . . Shoe Saleslady
Joie Lee. . . . . . . . . . . . . . . . . . . . . . . . . . . . . . Cathy
Billie Neal . . . . . . . . . . . . . . . . . . . . . . . . . . . Nurse
James Russo . . . . . . . . . . . . . . . . . . . . . . . Dan Corelli
Sean Young. . . . . . . . . . . . . . . Ellen/Dorothy Carlsson
  •• 0:31—Brief breasts making love in bed with Matt Dillon. Kind of dark.
  • 0:35—Brief side view or right breast in shower with Dillon. Don't see her face.
  1:11—Very brief partial left breast in gaping pajama top when she leans over to turn off the light.

### Kiss of the Beast
See: Meridian.

### The Kitchen Toto (1987; British)
Phyllis Logan . . . . . . . . . . . . . . . . . . . . . Janet Graham
Edwin Mahinda . . . . . . . . . . . . . . . . . . . . . . . .Mwangi
  • 0:24—Nude, getting a bath outside.

### Klute (1971)
Rosalind Cash. . . . . . . . . . . . . . . . . . . . . . . . . . . .Pat
Jane Fonda. . . . . . . . . . . . . . . . . . . . . . . . Bree Daniel
  • 0:27—Side view of left and right breasts stripping in the old man's office.
Roy Scheider . . . . . . . . . . . . . . . . . . . . . Frank Ligourin
Donald Sutherland . . . . . . . . . . . . . . . . . . . . John Klute
Dorothy Tristan . . . . . . . . . . . . . . . . . . . . . .Arlyn Page

### Knight Moves (1992)
Holly Chester . . . . . . . . . . . . . . . . . . . . . . . Officer No. 2
Rachel Hayward . . . . . . . . . . . . . . . . . . . . . .Last Victim
  • 1:05—Very, very brief breasts screaming when the killer pulls the covers on the bed and flashes with a camera.
Christopher Lambert . . . . . . . . . . . . . . .Peter Sanderson
Diane Lane. . . . . . . . . . . . . . . . . . . . . . .Kathy Sheppard
  •• 0:45—Breasts while making love with Christopher Lambert in bed.
Kehli O'Byrne . . . . . . . . . . . . . . . . . . . Debi Rutledge
  •• 0:08—Breasts and partial lower frontal nudity, while making love in bed with Christopher Lambert.
Tom Skerritt. . . . . . . . . . . . . . . . . . . . . . . Frank Sedman

### Knightriders (1981)
Ed Harris . . . . . . . . . . . . . . . . . . . . . . . . . . Billy Davis
  • 0:01—Buns, while kneeling in the woods. Long shot, hard to see.
  • 1:51—Upper half of buns, while standing in a pond doing something with a stick.
Amy Ingersoll . . . . . . . . . . . . . . . . . . . . . . . . . Linet
  • 0:00—Very brief left breast, while lying down, then sitting up in woods next to Ed Harris.
Patricia Tallman . . . . . . . . . . . . . . . . . . . . . . . .Julie
  • 0:46—Brief breasts in the bushes in moonlight talking to her boyfriend while a truck driver watches.

### Knockouts (1992)
Leigh Betchley . . . . . . . . . . . . . . . . . . . . . . . .Brooke
  • 0:04—Brief breasts while putting on white bra in dressing room.
  • 0:26—Very brief left breast after winning strip poker game.
  ••• 0:41—Breasts while taking off lingerie, while wearing blue panties.
  ••• 0:44—Breasts while posing in space costume for photographs.
  • 0:46—Brief right breast while posing in front of blinds.
Tally Chanel. . . . . . . . . . . . . . . . . . . . Samantha Peters
  •• 0:15—Breasts taking off swimsuit top and getting ready for a bath.

- ••• 0:16—Breasts and buns, while undressing and getting into bathtub while Garth peeks in.
- ••• 0:25—Breasts during strip poker game.
- •• 0:26—Breasts and buns in G-string while walking to her bedroom.
- • 0:29—Breasts while sitting on the bed.
- ••• 0:39—In white lingerie, then breasts while posing for photographs.
- •• 0:42—Breasts while Wesley helps put her top on.
- •• 0:43—Breasts while taking a shower (seen on TV monitor).
- ••• 0:47—Breasts while making love with Wesley.
- • 0:59—Brief breasts while punching a bag (seen in mostly silhouette).
- • 1:16—Breasts in shower in video playback.

Michelle Grassnick . . . . . . . . . . . . . . . . . . . . . Margo
- ••• 0:04—Breasts while lifting weights.
- ••• 0:35—Breasts, several times in locker room with her girlfriends.
- •• 0:59—Breasts, while putting swimsuit on (she's on the left).
- 1:10—Buns, in outfit during wrestling match.
- • 1:12—Brief right breast, when it falls out of her top.

Chona Jason . . . . . . . . . . . . . . . . . . . . . . . . . Ninja
- ••• 0:03—Breasts while doing sit-ups.
- • 1:05—Wearing a sheer black body stocking during kick fighting match.

Deanne Power. . . . . . . . . . . . . . . . . . .Julie the Secretary
Paula Reve'e . . . . . . . . . . . . . . . . . . . . . . . . .Candy
- •• 0:04—Breasts, going to look in the guy's locker room.
- •• 0:23—Breasts during strip poker game.
- •• 0:27—Breasts while sitting on chest of drawers.
- ••• 0:43—In lingerie, then breasts while posing for photographs.
- •• 0:59—Breasts while working out (seen mostly in silhouette).

Cindy Rome . . . . . . . . . . . . . . . . . . . . . . . . . Vicki
- • 0:04—Breasts while putting on makeup in front of mirror. Long shot. Breasts walking in front of Brooke in pink G-string and white tights when Garth peeks in the locker room.
- • 0:14—Buns in G-string swimsuit. Brief breasts while lying down in lounge chair.
- • 0:25—Brief breasts, after losing her tennis shoe during strip poker game.
- • 0:28—Breasts while in bedroom.
- ••• 0:37—In red, white and blue swimsuit, then breasts and buns while posing for photographs.
- ••• 0:45—Breasts and buns in G-string, while posing for October photograph.
- •• 0:59—Breasts while talking on the phone, combing her hair and doing her nails. Seen mostly in silhouette.

Nicole Sassaman . . . . . . . . . . . . . . . . . . . . . Hallie
Pamela Ward. . . . . . . . . . . . . . . . . . . . . . . . . .n.a.

## *Kramer vs. Kramer* (1979)

Jane Alexander . . . . . . . . . . . . . . . . . .Margaret Phelps
Iris Alhanti. . . . . . . . . . . . . . . . . . . . . . . . . . . .n.a.

George Coe . . . . . . . . . . . . . . . . . . . . . . . Jim O'Connor
Dustin Hoffman . . . . . . . . . . . . . . . . . . . . . Ted Kramer
Meryl Streep . . . . . . . . . . . . . . . . . . . . . .Joanna Kramer
JoBeth Williams . . . . . . . . . . . . . . . . . . . .Phyllis Bernard
- • 0:45—Buns and brief breasts in the hallway meeting Dustin Hoffman's son.

## *L'Annee Des Meduses* (1987; French)

Caroline Cellier. . . . . . . . . . . . . . . Claude, Chris' Mother
- •• 0:02—Breasts taking off top at the beach.
- •• 0:56—Breasts on boat at night with Romain.
- •• 1:06—Breasts on the beach with Valerie Kaprisky.
- • 1:14—Left breast, lying on beach with Romain at night.

Valerie Kaprisky . . . . . . . . . . . . . . . . . . . . . . . . Chris
- •• 0:06—Breasts pulling down swimsuit at the beach.
- ••• 0:24—Full frontal nudity while taking off dress with older man.
- ••• 0:42—Breasts walking around the beach talking to everybody.
- •• 0:46—Breasts on the beach taking a shower.
- ••• 1:02—Breasts on the beach with her mom.
- ••• 1:37—Nude dancing on the boat for Romain.
- ••• 1:42—Breasts walking from the beach to the bar.
- • 1:43—Breasts in swimming pool.

Barbara Nielsen . . . . . . . . . . . . . . . . . . . . . . Barbara
- • 0:37—Brief breasts taking off T-shirt at the beach.
- •• 0:40—Breasts at the beach with Valerie Kaprisky.
- •• 1:04—Breasts while sitting on Kaprisky at the beach.
- •• 1:08—Right breast, lying on the beach with Kaprisky.
- •• 1:41—Breasts on the beach taking off her top.
- ••• 1:43—Nude, in the swimming pool.

## *L.A. Bounty* (1989)

Sybil Danning . . . . . . . . . . . . . . . . . . . . . . . . . Ruger
Wings Hauser. . . . . . . . . . . . . . . . . . . . . . . Cavanaugh
Lenore Kasdorf. . . . . . . . . . . . . . . . . . . . Kelly Rhodes
Maxine Wasa . . . . . . . . . . . . . . . . . . . . . . . . Model
- • 0:07—Right breast while posing for Wings Hauser while he paints. Left breast, getting up. Long shot.
- • 0:26—Left breast while posing on couch for Hauser.
- •• 0:38—Breasts lying on couch again.

## *L.A. Goddess* (1992)

Tally Chanel . . . . . . . . . . . . . . . . . . . . . . . . . Beverly
- •• 0:08—Breasts, while getting dressed in bathroom with Kathy.
- •• 0:17—Breasts and buns, while getting out of the shower.
- 0:37—In two piece swimsuit.
- ••• 1:07—Buns (nice crotch shot) and breasts in bed while making love with Jeff Conaway and talking on the phone.

Jeff Conaway . . . . . . . . . . . . . . . . . . . . . . . . . Sean
Rick Groat . . . . . . . . . . . . . . . . . . . . . . . . . Sheriff
- • 0:08—Upper half of buns, while making love with Diane in motor home.

Wendy MacDonald . . . . . . . . . . . . . . . . . . . . . .Diane
- 0:06—In red and black bra and panties in motor home.

•• 0:08—Side of left breast, then breasts while making love with the Sheriff actor in motor home.
• 1:06—Brief buns, while flashing while dancing on table during party.

Kathy Shower . . . . . . . . . . . . . . . . . . . . . . Lisa Moore
•• 0:00—Full frontal nudity, getting out of the shower. 0:17—In white body suit.
•• 0:45—Side view of buns and breasts, getting into and in bathtub.
••• 0:53—Nude in spa with Damian.
• 0:56—Left breast, while lying in park with Damian. 0:58—Breasts while making love in bed with Damian.
• 1:20—Brief breasts in spa with Damian in flashback.

### L.A. Story (1991)
Iman . . . . . . . . . . . . . . . . . . . . . . . . . . . . . . . .Cynthia
Cheryl Baker . . . . . . . . . . . . . Changing Room Woman
• 0:18—Brief breasts in dressing room, when Steve Martin sees her.
Frances Fisher . . . . . . . . . . . . . . . . . . . . . . . . June
Richard E. Grant . . . . . . . . . . . . . . . . . . . . . Roland
Marilu Henner. . . . . . . . . . . . . . . . . . . . . . . . Trudi
Victoria Tennant . . . . . . . . . . . . . . . . . . . . . . Sara

### La Bamba (1987)
Elizabeth Peña. . . . . . . . . . . . . . . . . . . . Rosie Morales
• 0:06—Brief side view of right breast taking a shower outside when two young boys watch her from a water tower. Long shot, hard to see.
Lou Diamond Phillips . . . . . . . . . . . . . . Ritchie Valens

### La Belle Noiseuse (1992; French)
Emmanuelle Béart. . . . . . . . . . . . . . . . . . . . Marianne
•• 1:11—Full frontal nudity, after taking off robe and posing in studio.
•• 1:24—Left breast and lower frontal nudity while posing.
•• 1:27—Full frontal nudity after finishing posing and putting on robe.
•• 1:34—Nude, after taking off robe and getting ready to pose.
••• 1:38—Nude, after taking off robe and getting ready to pose while leaning on stool.
••• 1:43—Nude, after taking off robe and posing while sitting on chair.
•• 1:49—Nude, lying on chair after taking off robe.
•• 1:51—Nude, after taking off robe and posing on floor.
••• 1:53—Nude, while kneeling on bench while posing.
••• 1:57—Full frontal nudity while posing on stool, then sitting on chairs and sitting on floor. Long scene.
• 2:03—(0:00 into tape 2) Full frontal nudity while posing on bench.
•• 2:06—(0:03 into tape 2) Nude, while getting off bench and putting on robe.
•• 2:10—(0:07 into tape 2) Breasts and buns, after taking off robe and sitting on bench.
••• 2:16—(0:13 into tape 2) Breasts, while posing on stool, then full frontal nudity, getting up off stool and putting on robe.

••• 2:33—(0:30 into tape 2) Nude, after taking off robe, and posing on mattress on the floor.
••• 2:42—(0:39 into tape 2) Nude, while walking around the studio, looking at the paintings, then sitting on mattress on the floor. Long scene.
•• 2:57—(0:54 into tape 2) Buns and breasts, while sitting on mattress on the floor. Full frontal nudity while lying down, then getting up, putting on robe and walking away.
•• 3:17—(1:14 into tape 2) Breasts and buns, while standing and posing.
•• 3:20—(1:17 into tape 2) Right beast, while standing and posing. Long shot at first, then closer shot.
Jane Birkin . . . . . . . . . . . . . . . . . . . . . . . . . . . . . Liz

### La Cicala (The Cricket) (1983)
Barbara De Rossi . . . . . . . . . . . . . . . . . . . . .Saveria
•• 0:39—Nude swimming under waterfall with Clio Goldsmith.
•• 0:43—Breasts undressing in room with Goldsmith.
• 0:57—Brief right breast changing into dress in room.
• 1:05—In wet white lingerie in waterfall with a guy, then in a wet dress.
1:26—Very brief buns in bed with Anthony Franciosa.
•• 1:28—Breasts in bathroom with Franciosa.
• 1:36—Brief right breast making love with trucker.
Clio Goldsmith . . . . . . . . . . . . . . . . . . . . . . . . Cicala
•• 0:26—Nude when Wilma brings her in to get Anthony Franciosa excited again.
•• 0:39—Nude swimming under waterfall with Barbara de Rossi.
••• 0:43—Full frontal nudity undressing in room with de Rossi.

### La Femme Nikita (1991; French/Italian)
a.k.a. Nikita
Jean-Hughes Anglade. . . . . . . . . . . . . . . . . . . . Marco
Jeanne Moreau. . . . . . . . . . . . . . . . . . . . . . .Amande
Anne Parillaud . . . . . . . . . . . . . . . . . . . . . . . Nikita
• 0:59—Very brief right nipple, peeking out of her top when she sits up in bed.

### La Lectrice (1989; French)
a.k.a. The Reader
Miou-Miou. . . . . . . . . . . . . . . . . . . . Constance/Marie
1:06—Making love with a guy while reading to him in bed.
• 1:18—Full frontal nudity lying in bed. Close-up pan shot from lower frontal nudity, then left breast, then right breast.
• 1:20—Very brief right breast, then lower frontal nudity getting dressed.
Maria De Medeiros. . . . . . . . . . . . . . . . . . Silent Nurse

### The Lacemaker (1977; French)
Yves Beneyton . . . . . . . . . . . . . . . . . . . . . . . François
• 0:57—Buns, while walking to bed. Dark.
Isabelle Huppert. . . . . . . . . . . . . . . . . . . . . Beatrice
• 0:50—Briefly nude while getting into bed.

- 0:57—Breasts under shawl, then nude while getting into bed.
- •• 0:58—Breasts, lying in bed.
- • 1:04—Nude, in her apartment.
- ••• 1:22—Nude, in her apartment with François.

### Lady Avenger (1991)
Michelle Bauer . . . . . . . . . . . . . . . . . . . . . . . Annalee
- ••• 0:30—Breasts, making love in bed on top of J.C.
- ••• 0:52—Breasts, making love in bed on top of Ray.
Billy Frank . . . . . . . . . . . . . . . . . . . . . . . . . . . .Arnie
Peggy Sands . . . . . . . . . . . . . . . . . . . . . . . . . .Maggie
- ••• 0:18—Breasts in bed with Kevin.

### Lady Beware (1987)
Diane Lane . . . . . . . . . . . . . . . . . . . . . . . Katya Yarno
0:10—Walking around in her apartment in a red silk teddy getting ready for bed.
0:14—Lying down in white semi-transparent pajamas after fantasizing.
0:24—In black bra in apartment.
- ••• 0:46—Breasts in her apartment and in bed making love with Mack.
- •• 0:52—Brief breasts during Jack's flashback when he is in the store.
- •• 0:59—Brief side view breasts in bed with Mack again during another of Jack's flashbacks.
- • 1:02—Very brief breasts in bed with Mack.
1:06—Brief breasts lying in bed behind thin curtain in another of Jack's flashbacks.
Michael Woods . . . . . . . . . . . . . . . . . . . . . . Jack Price
- •• 0:43—Buns, while lying down in Diane Lane's bed.

### Lady Chatterley's Lover (1981; French/British)
Nicholas Clay . . . . . . . . . .Oliver Mellors (The Gardener)
- ••• 0:21—Nude, washing himself while Sylvia Kristel watches from the trees.
Sylvia Kristel . . . . . . . . . . . . . . . . Constance Chatterley
- •• 0:25—Nude in front of mirror.
- • 0:59—Brief breasts with the Gardener.
- • 1:04—Brief breasts.
- ••• 1:16—Nude in bedroom with the Gardener.

### Lady Cocoa (1974)
Lola Falana . . . . . . . . . . . . . . . . . . . . . . . . . . . Coco
- • 0:45—Left breast lying on bed, pulling up yellow towel. Long shot, hard to see.
- ••• 1:23—Breasts on boat with a guy.

### Lady Dragon (1992)
Richard Norton . . . . . . . . . . . . . . . . Ludwig Hauptman
- •• 0:39—Buns, twice, in bedroom with Susan.

### The Lady in Red (1979)
Christopher Lloyd . . . . . . . . . . . . . . . . . . . . Frognose
Pamela Sue Martin . . . . . . . . . . . . . . . . Polly Franklin
- • 0:07—Right breast, while in bedroom with a guy clutching her clothes.
- ••• 0:20—Breasts in jail with a group of women prisoners waiting to be examined by a nurse.

Francesca "Kitten" Natividad . . . . .Uncredited Partygoer
- • 0:39—Brief breasts outside during party.
Mary Woronov . . . . . . . . . . . . . . . .Woman Bankrobber

### Lady Jane (1987; British)
Helena Bonham Carter. . . . . . . . . . . . . Lady Jane Grey
- • 1:19—Breasts kneeling on the bed with Guilford.
- • 2:09—Side view of right breast and very, very brief breasts sitting by fire with Guilford.
Cary Elwes . . . . . . . . . . . . . . . . . . . . .Guilford Dudley
- • 1:19—Brief buns, while getting out of bed.
Michael Hordern . . . . . . . . . . . . . . . . . Dr. Peckenham
Sara Kestelman. . . . . . . . . . . . . . . . . . . Frances Grey

### Lady on the Bus (1978; Brazilian)
Sonia Braga . . . . . . . . . . . . . . . . . . . . . . . . . . . n.a.
- • 0:11—Brief left breast.
- ••• 0:12—Breasts, then buns, then full frontal nudity in bed getting her slip torn off by her newlywed husband. Long struggle scene.
- •• 0:39—Right breast standing with half open dress, then breasts lying in bed, then getting into the pool.
- ••• 0:48—Breasts and buns on the beach after picking up a guy on the bus.
- • 0:54—Brief breasts in bed dreaming.
- • 1:02—Brief breasts in waterfall with bus driver.
- • 1:05—Breasts in cemetery after picking up another guy on the bus.
- • 1:13—Breasts on the ground with another guy from a bus.
- • 1:16—Left breast sitting on sofa while her husband talks.

### Laguna Heat (1987; Made for Cable Movie)
Rutanya Alda . . . . . . . . . . . . . . . . . . . . . . . . . . . n.a.
Harry Hamlin . . . . . . . . . . . . . . . . . . . .Tom Shephard
- • 0:50—Buns, while walking into the ocean with Catherine Hicks.
Catherine Hicks . . . . . . . . . . . . . . . . . . Jane Algernon
- •• 0:50—Breasts and buns, running around the beach with Harry Hamlin.
- •• 1:05—Brief breasts in bed making love with Harry Hamlin, having her head hit the headboard.
Rip Torn. . . . . . . . . . . . . . . . . . . . . . . . . . . . . . . n.a.

### The Lair of the White Worm (1988; British)
Sammi Davis-Voss . . . . . . . . . . . . . . . . . . . Mary Trent
Amanda Donohoe . . . . . . . . . . . . . . Lady Sylvia Marsh
- • 0:52—Nude, opening a tanning table and turning over.
- • 0:57—Brief left breast licking the blood off a phallic-looking thing.
- • 1:19—Brief breasts jumping out to attack Angus, then walking around her underground lair (her body is painted for the rest of the film).
- • 1:22—Breasts walking up steps with a large phallic thing strapped to her body.
Linzi Drew . . . . . . . . . . . . . . . . . . . . . . . . . Maid/Nun
Tina Shaw . . . . . . . . . . . . . . . . . . . . . . . . . Maid/Nun

## Lake Consequence (1992)

(Unrated version reviewed.)

May Karasun . . . . . . . . . . . . . . . . . . . . . . . . . . . Grace
- • 0:24—Brief breasts, coming up for air from under water in lake.
- •• 0:25—Breasts, getting out of the water to get Joan Severance.
- ••• 0:26—Breasts, lying on float in the middle of the lake with Severance.
- ••• 0:28—Full frontal nudity and brief buns, diving into the lake.
- •• 0:29—Buns and breasts, greeting Billy Zane after getting out of the lake.
- • 0:30—Full frontal nudity, drying herself off and getting dressed. Long shot.
- • 0:47—Left breast, while making out with Xiao in bar.
- ••• 0:50—Breasts close-up getting acupuncture.
- ••• 0:53—Breasts, walking to spa.
- •• 0:55—Breasts in spa with Severance and Zane.
- •• 0:57—Right breast while making love with Zane in spa.

Joan Severance . . . . . . . . . . . . . . . . . . . . . . . . . .Irene
- • 0:02—Left breast, while lying in bed.
- • 0:41—Brief breasts several times while making love with Billy Zane.
- ••• 0:50—Full frontal nudity in spa in bathhouse, while making love with Zane.
- ••• 0:54—Breasts in spa making out with Zane and Grace.
- • 1:06—Brief glimpses of right breast in open coat, while struggling in a field with Zane.
- ••• 1:07—Breasts in field with Zane. Oh yeah!
- •• 1:19—Brief side view breasts and buns in bedroom with Zane.

Billy Zane . . . . . . . . . . . . . . . . . . . . . . . . . . . . Billy
- • 0:52—Brief upper half of buns in spa.
- ••• 1:08—Buns, while making love on top of Joan Severance in field. Don't see his face.

## Las Vegas Weekend (1986)

Vickie Benson . . . . . . . . . . . . . . . . . . . . . . . . Amanda
- • 1:12—Breasts and buns, while making love in bed with Percy.

Tamara Landry . . . . . . . . . . . . . . . . . . . . . . . . . . Lea

## Lassiter (1984)

Lauren Hutton . . . . . . . . . . . . . . . . . . . Kari Von Fursten
- • 0:18—Brief breasts over-the-shoulder shot making love with a guy on the bed just before killing him.

Belinda Mayne . . . . . . . . . . . . . . . . . .Helen Boardman
- ••• 0:06—In bra then breasts letting Tom Selleck undress her while her husband is in the other room.

Tom Selleck. . . . . . . . . . . . . . . . . . . . . . . . . . Lassiter
- • 1:00—Buns, while getting out of bed after making love with Lauren Hutton.

Jane Seymour . . . . . . . . . . . . . . . . . . . . . . . . . . Sara
- • 0:10—Buns and brief side view of right breast lying on stomach on bed with Tom Selleck.

Jane Wood . . . . . . . . . . . . . . . . . . . . . . . Mary Becker

## The Last American Virgin (1982)

Steve Antin. . . . . . . . . . . . . . . . . . . . . . . . . . . . Rick
Diane Franklin . . . . . . . . . . . . . . . . . . . . . . . . .Karen
- ••• 1:06—Breasts in room above the bleachers with Jason.
- •• 1:17—Breasts and almost lower frontal nudity taking off her panties in the clinic.

Louisa Moritz . . . . . . . . . . . . . . . . . . . . . . . .Carmela
- ••• 0:42—Breasts and buns in her bedroom with Rick.

Brian Peck . . . . . . . . . . . . . . . . . . . . . . . . . . . Victor
- • 0:20—Buns, during penis measurement in boy's locker room. Don't see his face.

Tessa Richarde . . . . . . . . . . . . . . . . . . . . . . . .Brenda
- •• 0:15—Brief breasts walking into the living room when Gary's parents come home.

Kimmy Robertson. . . . . . . . . . . . . . . . . . . . . . . Rose
Joe Rubbo . . . . . . . . . . . . . . . . . . . . . . . . . . .David
- • 0:45—Buns, in bed making love with Carmela while his buddies watch through the key hole.

## The Last Boy Scout (1991)

Denise Ames . . . . . . . . . . . . . . . . . . . . Jacuzzi Party Girl
- • 0:11—Brief breasts getting out of the Jacuzzi.

Sara Suzanne Brown. . . . . . . . . . . . . . . . . . . . . Dancer
- • 0:19—Brief breasts and buns while dancing in club.

Kim Coates. . . . . . . . . . . . . . . . . . . . . . . . . . . . Chet
Chelsea Field . . . . . . . . . . . . . . . . . .Sarah Hollenbeck
Bruce McGill . . . . . . . . . . . . . . . . . . . . Mike Matthews
Teal Roberts. . . . . . . . . . . . . . . . . . . . . . . . . . Dancer
Chelchie Ross. . . . . . . . . . . . . . . . . . Senator Baynard

## Last Call (1990)

Crisstyn Dante . . . . . . . . . . . . . . . . . . . . . . . . Hooker
William Katt . . . . . . . . . . . . . . . . . . . . . . . . Paul Avery
- ••• 0:29—Buns, while on floor with Shannon Tweed.
- • 0:41—Brief buns, while getting up from bed and putting his pants on.
- • 1:02—Brief buns, while in bed with Tweed.

Stella Stevens . . . . . . . . . . . . . . . . . . . . . . . . . . Betty
0:52—Very brief left nipple popping out of black lingerie top while making love with Jason on a pool table.

Shannon Tweed . . . . . . . . . . . . . . . . . . . . Cindy/Audrey
- • 0:12—In black body stocking, dancing on stage. Breasts and buns in G-string underneath.
- •• 0:29—Right breast, on the floor with William Katt.
- •• 0:39—Brief buns, rotating in chair with Katt. Breasts leaning against column.
- • 0:40—Breasts on stair railing.
- • 1:01—Left breast, while leaning against column and kissing Katt.
- • 1:02—Left breast in bed with Katt.
- ••• 1:05—Breasts making love on roof with Katt.

## Last Dance (1992)

Monica Akesson . . . . . . . . . . . . . . . . . . . . . Body Double
Elaine Hendrix . . . . . . . . . . . . . . . . . . . . . . . . . Kelly
- ••• 0:20—Breasts and buns in bed with Jim. Don't see her face, probably a body double.
- •• 0:52—Buns in white lingerie outfit.

Erica Ringstrom . . . . . . . . . . . . . . . . . . . . . . . . Heather
- •• 0:48—Buns in G-string, dancing on stage during DTV contest.

Kimberly Speiss . . . . . . . . . . . . . . . . . . . . . . . . Meryll
- 1:03—Sort of buns, while dancing on stage.

### The Last Days of Chez Nous (1991; Australian)

Kerry Fox . . . . . . . . . . . . . . . . . . . . . . . . . . . . . Vicki
- 1:03—Upper half of buns, while standing on balcony with a sheet wrapped around herself.

Lisa Harrow . . . . . . . . . . . . . . . . . . . . . . . . . . . Beth
- • 1:10—Brief breasts, while moving around in bed with Bruno Ganz.

Kiri Paramore . . . . . . . . . . . . . . . . . . . . . . . . . . Tim

### The Last Detail (1973)

Nancy Allen . . . . . . . . . . . . . . . . . . . . . . . . . . . Nancy
Carol Kane . . . . . . . . . . . . . . . . . . . . . Young Whore
- • 1:02—Brief breasts sitting on bed talking with Randy Quaid. Her hair is in the way, hard to see.

Michael Moriarty . . . . . . . . . . . . . . Marine Duty Officer
Jack Nicholson . . . . . . . . . . . . . . . . . . . . . . Buddusky
Randy Quaid . . . . . . . . . . . . . . . . . . . . . . . Meadows

### The Last Embrace (1979)

Janet Margolin . . . . . . . . . . . . Ellie "Eva" Fabian
- • 1:10—Brief breasts in bathtub with Bernie, before strangling him.
- •• 1:14—Right breast, while reaching for the phone in bed with Roy Scheider.
- • 1:20—Left breast in photo that Scheider is looking at with a magnifying glass (it's supposed to be her grandmother).
- 1:22—Almost breasts in the shower talking to Scheider.

Mandy Patinkin . . . . . . . . . . . . . . . . . . . . . Commuter
Roy Scheider . . . . . . . . . . . . . . . . . . . . . Harry Hannan

### The Last Emperor (1987)

Joan Chen . . . . . . . . . . . . . . . . . . . . . . . . . Wan Jung
Jade Go . . . . . . . . . . . . . . . . . . . . . . . . . . . . . . Ar Mo
- • 0:10—Right breast in open top after breast feeding the young Pu Yi.
- • 0:20—Right breast in open top telling Pu Yi a story.
- • 0:29—Right breast in open top breast feeding an older Pu Yi. Long shot.

John Lone . . . . . . . . . . . . . . . . . . . . Pu Yi as an Adult

### Last Exit to Brooklyn (1990)

Stephen Baldwin . . . . . . . . . . . . . . . . . . . . . . . . Sal
Maia Danziger . . . . . . . . . . . . . . . . . . . Mary Black
- 0:10—Out of focus buns and right breast taking off her slip.
- • 0:12—Very brief breasts making love with Harry. Breasts after.

Jennifer Jason Leigh . . . . . . . . . . . . . . . . . . . . . Tralata
- •• 1:28—Breasts, opening her blouse in bar after getting drunk.
- • 1:33—Breasts getting drug out of car, placed on mattress, then basically raped by a long line of guys. Long, painful-to-watch scene.

- 1:35—Breasts lying on mattress when Spook comes to save her.

### The Last Hour (1990)

*a.k.a. Concrete War*

Raye Hollitt . . . . . . . . . . . . . . . . . . . . . . . . . . . Adler
Michael Paré . . . . . . . . . . . . . . . . . . . . . . . . . . . Jeff
Robert Pucci . . . . . . . . . . . . . . . . . . . . . . . . . . . Eric
- • 0:05—Brief buns, while making love in bed with Shannon Tweed.

Shannon Tweed . . . . . . . . . . . . . . . . . . . . . . Susan
- •• 0:05—Breasts in bed, making love with Eric.
- • 0:07—Brief buns and side of left breast, in the shower.

### The Last Innocent Man
### (1987; Made for Cable Movie)

Ed Harris . . . . . . . . . . . . . . . . . . . . . . . . . . . . . n.a.
Roxanne Hart . . . . . . . . . . . . . . . . . . . . . . . . . . n.a.
- ••• 1:06—Breasts in bed making love, then sitting up and arguing with Ed Harris in his apartment.

### Last Light (1993; Made for Cable Movie)

Clancy Brown . . . . . . . . . . . . . . . . . . Lionel McMannis
Cameron Dye . . . . . . . . . . . . . . . . . . . . . 1st Inmate
Lynne Moody . . . . . . . . . . . . . . . . . Hope Whitmore
Amanda Plummer . . . . . . . . . . . . . . . Lillian Burke
Kathleen Quinlan . . . . . . . . . . . . . . . . . . Kathy Rubicek
Kiefer Sutherland . . . . . . . . . . . . . . . . Denver Bayliss
- • 0:03—Side view of buns, in solitary confinement cell. Dark. Covered with feces.
- • 0:05—Brief buns, while walking in jail hallway. Still covered with feces.
- • 0:06—Buns, while standing in front of security cage, getting clothes. Long scene, but still covered with feces.

### The Last Married Couple in America (1980)

Priscilla Barnes . . . . . . . . . . . . . . . . . . . Helena Dryden
Richard Benjamin . . . . . . . . . . . . . . . . . . Marv Cooper
Sondra Currie . . . . . . . . . . . . . . . . . . . . . . . . . . Lainy
- •• 1:32—Breasts taking off her clothes in bedroom in front of Natalie Wood, George Segal and her husband.

Dom DeLuise . . . . . . . . . . . . . . . . . . . Walter Holmes
Catherine Hickland . . . . . . . . . . . . . . . . . . . Rebecca
Jenny Neumann . . . . . . . . . . . . . . . . . . . . . . . Nurse

### The Last of England (British)

Spencer Leigh . . . . . . . . . . . . . . . . . . . . . . . . . . n.a.
- ••• 0:46—Buns, while undressing next to and in bed with a soldier (can't tell if it's a male or female soldier).
- •• 0:48—Very brief frontal nudity in bed with the soldier.

Tilda Swinton . . . . . . . . . . . . . . . . . . . . . . . . . . n.a.

### The Last Picture Show (1971)

Sam Bottoms . . . . . . . . . . . . . . . . . . . . . . . . . . Billy
- • 0:41—Brief buns, after falling out of car with Jimmy Sue.

Timothy Bottoms . . . . . . . . . . . . . . . Sonny Crawford

Eileen Brennan . . . . . . . . . . . . . . . . . . . . . . .Genevieve
Jeff Bridges . . . . . . . . . . . . . . . . . . . . . Duane Jackson
Gary Brockette . . . . . . . . . . . . . . . . . . . . Bobby Sheen
- 0:36—Upper frontal nudity and buns, while getting out of pool and greeting Randy Quaid and Cybill Shepherd. More buns, getting back into the pool.
Ellen Burstyn . . . . . . . . . . . . . . . . . . . . . . . .Lois Farrow
Kimberly Hyde . . . . . . . . . . . . . . . Annie-Annie Martin
- •• 0:36—Full frontal nudity, getting out of pool to meet Randy Quaid and Cybill Shepherd.
- • 0:37—Breasts several times, sitting at edge of pool with Bobby.
- • 0:38—More breasts, sitting on edge of pool in background.
Cloris Leachman . . . . . . . . . . . . . . . . . . . Ruth Popper
Randy Quaid . . . . . . . . . . . . . . . . . . . . . .Lester Marlow
- • 0:38—Very brief frontal nudity jumping into pool after Cybill Shepherd jumps in.
Cybill Shepherd. . . . . . . . . . . . . . . . . . . . . .Jacy Farrow
- •• 0:37—Undressing on diving board. Very brief left breast falling onto diving board. Brief breasts tossing bra aside.
- • 0:38—Brief left breast jumping into the water.
- ••• 1:05—Breasts and buns in motel room with Jeff Bridges.
Sharon Taggart . . . . . . . . . . . . . . . . . . Charlene Duggs
- •• 0:11—In bra, then breasts making out in truck with Timothy Bottoms.

## Last Resort (1985)
Brenda Bakke . . . . . . . . . . . . . . . . . . . . . . Veroneeka
- •• 0:36—Breasts in the woods with Charles Grodin.
William Bumiller . . . . . . . . . . . . . . . . . . . . . . Etienne
Brett Clark. . . . . . . . . . . . . . . . . . . . . . . . . . Manuello
Steve Levitt . . . . . . . . . . . . . . . . . . . . . . . . . . Pierre
Wally Anne Wharton . . . . . . . . . . . . . . . . . . . . Wanda

## Last Rites (1988)
Tom Berenger. . . . . . . . . . . . . . . . . . . . . . . Michael
Robert Corbo . . . . . . . . . . . . . . . . . . . . . . . . . Gino
- • 0:03—Buns and frontal nudity in a room with Daphne Zuniga just before getting caught by another woman and shot.
Anne Twomey. . . . . . . . . . . . . . . . . . . . . . .Zena Pace
Daphne Zuniga . . . . . . . . . . . . . . . . . . . . . . . Angela
- • 0:04—Very brief breasts running into the bathroom to escape from being shot. Covered with blood, don't see her face. Very brief right breast reaching for a bathrobe. Don't really see anything.
0:40—Buns, behind a shower door.
0:50—Buns, getting out of bed and standing in front of Tom Berenger.

## The Last Seduction (1994)
Peter Berg . . . . . . . . . . . . . . . . . . . . . . . . Mike Swale
- •• 0:53—Buns, while getting up out of bed and walking to bathroom.
Linda Fiorentino . . . . . . . . . . . . . . . . Bridget Gregory
- •• 0:31—Breasts, while walking around the house, gathering her clothes and getting dressed.

- 0:37—Brief side view of buns during pan shot from her feet to her head, while she's lying in bed.
- •• 0:50—Very brief breasts, buns, then left breast while making love in bed with Peter Berg.
1:41—Breasts under sheer white blouse.

## Last Summer (1969)
Catherine Burns . . . . . . . . . . . . . . . . . . . . . . . . Rhoda
- • 1:31—Very brief breasts struggling with Stacy, Peter and Dan. Long shot.
Barbara Hershey . . . . . . . . . . . . . . . . . . . . . . . Sandy
- • 0:19—Breasts after taking off her swimsuit top on sailboat with Richard Thomas. Hair is in the way.
- • 1:30—Very brief right breast, after taking off her top in the woods.

## Last Tango In Paris (1972)
(X-rated, letterbox version.)
Marlon Brando. . . . . . . . . . . . . . . . . . . . . . . . . .Paul
- • 1:59—Brief buns, while pulling his pants down to moon a woman at a dance.
Maria Schneider . . . . . . . . . . . . . . . . . . . . . . .Jeanne
- • 0:15—Lower frontal nudity and very brief buns, rolling on the floor.
- • 0:44—Breasts in jeans, walking around the apartment.
- •• 0:53—Left breast, while lying down, then walking to Marlon Brando, then breasts.
- ••• 0:55—Breasts, kneeling while talking to Brando.
- • 0:56—Side of left breast.
- • 0:57—Breasts, rolling off the bed, onto the floor.
- •• 1:01—Right breast, in bathroom. Breasts in mirror.
- • 1:03—Brief breasts in bathroom with Brando while she puts on makeup.
- ••• 1:04—Nude, in bathroom with Brando, then sitting on counter.
- • 1:27—Brief lower frontal nudity, pulling up her dress in elevator.
- • 1:30—Breasts in bathtub with Brando.
- ••• 1:32—Nude, standing up in bathtub while Brando washes her. More breasts, getting out. Long scene.

## The Last Temptation of Christ (1988)
David Bowie. . . . . . . . . . . . . . . . . . . . . . .Pontius Pilate
Willem Dafoe . . . . . . . . . . . . . . . . . . . . . . . Jesus Christ
- • 1:56—Buns, getting beaten and whipped.
- • 1:57—Buns, while getting crown of thorns placed on his head.
2:02—Side view of buns, while hanging on cross.
Leo Damian . . . . . . . . . . . . . . . . . . . . Person in Crowd
André Gregory . . . . . . . . . . . . . . . . . . . .John the Baptist
Barbara Hershey . . . . . . . . . . . . . . . . . Mary Magdelene
- • 0:16—Brief buns behind curtain. Brief right breast making love, then brief breasts.
0:17—Buns, while sleeping.
- •• 0:20—Breasts, tempting Jesus.
- • 2:12—Brief tip of left breast, lying on ground under Jesus.
- • 2:13—Left breast while caressing her pregnant belly.
Harvey Keitel . . . . . . . . . . . . . . . . . . . . . . . . . . . Judas
Harry Dean Stanton . . . . . . . . . . . . . . . . . . . . Saul/Paul

## The Last Tycoon (1976)

Ingrid Boulting . . . . . . . . . . . . . . . . . . Kathleen Moore
- 0:56—Buns and side of right breast taking off her dress in unfinished beach house in front of Robert De Niro.
- •• 0:58—More buns, lying down afterwards.
- 1:00—Buns, getting up and putting dress on. Very brief side of left breast.
- 1:02—Brief right breast when De Niro takes her dress off.

Robert De Niro . . . . . . . . . . . . . . . . . . . Monroe Stahr
Anjelica Huston . . . . . . . . . . . . . . . . . . . . . . . Edna
Jeanne Moreau . . . . . . . . . . . . . . . . . . . . . . . . Didi
Jack Nicholson . . . . . . . . . . . . . . . . . . . . . Brimmer
Theresa Russell . . . . . . . . . . . . . . . . . . Cecilia Brady

## The Last Warrior (1989)

Gary Graham . . . . . . . . . . . . . . . . . . . . . . . . . . Gibb
- 0:07—Brief buns, while taking off his towel when he sees a ship.

Maria Holvöe . . . . . . . . . . . . . . . . . . . . . . Katherine
- •• 1:24—Right breast, after the Japanese warrior removes her dress.

## The Last Wave (1977)

David Gulpilil . . . . . . . . . . . . . . . . . . . . . . Chris Lee
- 1:30—Buns, while standing naked in cave. Dark.

## The Last Winter (1983; Israeli)

Yona Elian . . . . . . . . . . . . . . . . . . . . . . . . . . . Maya
- •• 0:48—Breasts taking off her robe to get into pool.
  0:49—Buns, lying on marble slab with Kathleen Quinlan.

Kathleen Quinlan . . . . . . . . . . . . . . . . . . . . . Joyce
- •• 0:48—Brief side view of left breast taking off her robe and diving into pool Very brief buns.
  0:49—Buns, lying on marble slab, talking with Maya.
  0:50—Very brief right breast sitting up. Long shot, hard to see.

## Laura (1979)

a.k.a. Shattered Innocence
Maud Adams . . . . . . . . . . . . . . . . . . . . . . . . . Sarah
Dawn Dunlap . . . . . . . . . . . . . . . . . . . . . . . . Laura
- 0:20—Brief side view of left breast and buns talking to Maud Adams, then brief side view of right breast putting on robe.
- ••• 0:23—Nude, dancing while being photographed.
- ••• 1:15—Nude, letting Paul feel her so he can sculpt her, then making love with him.
  1:22—Buns, putting on panties talking to Maud Adams.

Maureen Kerwin . . . . . . . . . . . . . . . . . . . . Martine
- 0:03—Brief full frontal nudity getting out of bed and putting white bathrobe on.

## The Lawnmower Man (1992)

(Unrated Director's cut reviewed.)
Pierce Brosnan . . . . . . . . . . . . . . . . Lawrence Angelo

Jeff Fahey . . . . . . . . . . . . . . . . . . . . . . . . . Jobe Smith
John Laughlin . . . . . . . . . . . . . . . . . . . . Jake Simpson
Jenny Wright . . . . . . . . . . . . . . . . . . . . Marnie Burke
- •• 1:04—Right breast, while in bed with Jeff Fahey.
- 1:15—Brief right breast, while in bed under Fahey.

## Leather Jackets (1991)

Ginger Lynn Allen . . . . . . . . . . . . . . . . . . . . . . Bree
- •• 0:39—Breasts on stage for Mickey's bachelor party. Buns, in G-string. Made up to look like Geisha Girls.

Cary Elwes . . . . . . . . . . . . . . . . . . . . . . . . . . Dobbs
Bridget Fonda . . . . . . . . . . . . . . . . . . . . . . . Claudi
- 0:15—Brief breasts on bed with Mickey.

James Le Gros . . . . . . . . . . . . . . . . . . . . . . . . . Carl
Christopher Penn . . . . . . . . . . . . . . . . . . Big Steve
Mary Ella Ross . . . . . . . . . . . . . . . . Student Girl #2

## Left for Dead (1978)

Cindy Girling . . . . . . . . . . . . . . . . . . . . Pauline Corte
- •• 0:19—Nude, taking off shirt in bedroom.

Elke Sommer . . . . . . . . . . . . . . . Magdalene Krushcen
- •• 0:38—Left breast, while posing for photographer.
- 0:39—Very brief left breast in B&W photo.
  0:58—Buns and breasts when police officers lift her up to put plastic under her. Covered with blood, can't see her face.
- 1:09—Very brief left breast in B&W photo.

## The Legacy (1979; British)

a.k.a. The Legacy of Maggie Walsh
Roger Daltrey . . . . . . . . . . . . . . . . . . . . . . . . Clive
Sam Elliott . . . . . . . . . . . . . . . . . . . . . . Pete Danner
- ••• 0:18—Buns, walking to shower. Don't see his face.

Katharine Ross . . . . . . . . . . . . . . . . . Maggie Walsh

## Legal Tender (1991)

Wendy MacDonald . . . . . . . . . . . . . . . Verna Wheeler
  0:22—Brief buns in lingerie in Morton Downey Jr.'s office. Don't see her face.
- •• 1:20—Long shot of buns and side of left breast taking off robe in front of Downey. Breasts on bed with him.

Jacqueline Palmer . . . . . . . . . . . . . . . . . . Mal's Girl
- 0:24—Breasts in bubble bath with blonde girl and Morton Downey Jr.
- •• 0:31—Breasts outside by the swimming pool.

Tanya Roberts . . . . . . . . . . . . . . . . . . Rikki Rennick
- 0:41—Buns and breasts making love with Robert Davi. Don't see her face.

Craig Stepp . . . . . . . . . . . . . . . . . . . . . . . . . . . n.a.
Shannon Wilsey . . . . . . . . . . . . . . . . . . . . Mal's Girl
- •• 0:24—Breasts in bubble bath with brunette girl and Morton Downey Jr.
- •• 0:31—Breasts and buns in G-string bringing phone to Downey.

## The Legend of Hell House (1973; British)

Pamela Franklin . . . . . . . . . . . . . . . . . . Florence Tanner
- 1:03—Silhouette of breasts while taking off nightgown and getting into bed.

## Lenny (1974)

Dustin Hoffman . . . . . . . . . . . . . . . . . . . . . Lenny Bruce
Valerie Perrine . . . . . . . . . . . . . . . . . . . . . . Honey Bruce
    0:04—Doing a strip tease on stage down to pasties
    and buns in a G-string. No nudity, but still nice.
••• 0:14—Breasts in bed when Dustin Hoffman pulls the
    sheet off her then makes love.
•• 0:17—Breasts sitting on the floor in a room full of
    flowers when Hoffman comes in.
    0:24—Left breast wearing pastie doing dance in
    flashback.
• 0:43—Right breast with Kathryn Witt.
Kathryn Witt . . . . . . . . . . . . . . . . . . . . . . . . . . . . Girl
• 0:43—Right breast with Valerie Perrine while Dustin
    Hoffman watches.

## Less than Zero (1987)

Michael Bowen . . . . . . . . . . . . . . . . . . . . . . . . . Hop
Brittain Frye . . . . . . . . . . . . . . . . . . . . . . Teenager #2
Jami Gertz . . . . . . . . . . . . . . . . . . . . . . . . . . . Blair
Neith Hunter . . . . . . . . . . . . . . . . . . . . . . . . . . Alana
Andrew McCarthy . . . . . . . . . . . . . . . . . . . . . . Clay
• 0:03—Very brief buns when getting out of bed to
    answer the phone.
James Spader . . . . . . . . . . . . . . . . . . . . . . . . . Rip
John Yurasek . . . . . . . . . . . . . . . . . . . . . . Naked Man
• 1:22—Brief buns while standing up when Andrew
    McCarthy discovers him with Robert Downey, Jr.

## Lethal Ninja (1992)

Kimberleigh Stark . . . . . . . . . . . . . . . . . . . . . Farida
•• 1:01—Buns and breasts, while getting out of bath
    and putting on robe.

## Lethal Obsession (1987; German)

a.k.a. The Joker

Tahnee Welch . . . . . . . . . . . . . . . . . . . Daniela Santini
    0:14—Buns, putting on robe after talking to John on
    the phone.
• 0:15—Half of left breast, taking off coat to hug John
    in the kitchen.
    0:16—Sort of left breast, in bed with John. Too dark
    to see anything.
    1:16—Buns, getting an injection.
Michael York . . . . . . . . . . . . . . . . . . . . . . . Dr. Proper

## Lethal Pursuit (1989)

Blake Bahnit . . . . . . . . . . . . . . . . . . . . . . . . Warren
Mitzi Kapture . . . . . . . . . . . . . . . . . . . . . . Debra J.
•• 0:32—Breasts in motel shower, then getting out.
    (You can see the top of her swimsuit bottom.)
    0:47—In wet tank top talking with Warren.

## Lethal Weapon (1987)

Tom Atkins . . . . . . . . . . . . . . . . . . . . Michael Hunsaker
Cheryl Baker . . . . . . . . . . . . . . . . . Girl in Shower #1
Terri Lynn Doss . . . . . . . . . . . . . . . . . Girl in Shower #2
Mel Gibson . . . . . . . . . . . . . . . . . . . . . . . Martin Riggs
••• 0:06—Buns, while getting out of bed and walking to
    the refrigerator.

Ed O'Ross . . . . . . . . . . . . . . . . . . . . . . . . . Mendez
Jackie Swanson . . . . . . . . . . . . . . . . Amanda Hunsacker
•• 0:01—Brief breasts standing on balcony rail getting
    ready to jump.

## Lethal Weapon 2 (1989)

Mel Gibson . . . . . . . . . . . . . . . . . . . . . . Martin Riggs
Patsy Kensit . . . . . . . . . . . . . . . . . . . Rika Van Den Haas
•• 1:15—Right breast lying in bed with Mel Gibson.
•• 1:19—Breasts in bed with Gibson.

## Lethal Woman (1988)

Robert Lipton . . . . . . . . . . . . . . . . . Major Derek Johnson
• 1:02—Very brief frontal nudity in the ocean with Sh-
    annon Tweed, when the water goes down.
• 1:05—Brief buns while in the water on the beach
    with Tweed.
Adrienne Pearce . . . . . . . . . . . . . . . . . . . . . . . Trudy
Shannon Tweed . . . . . . . . . . . . . . . . . . . . . . . . Tory
••• 1:01—Breasts at the beach with Derek. Brief buns in
    white bikini bottom.
Merete Van Kamp . . . . . . . . . . . . . Diana/Christine
• 1:23—Very brief side view of left breast, reaching for
    towel after bath. Hard to see.

## Letter to Brezhnev (1986; British)

Peter Firth . . . . . . . . . . . . . . . . . . . . . . . . . . . Peter
Alfred Molina . . . . . . . . . . . . . . . . . . . . . . . . Sergei
Alexandra Pigg . . . . . . . . . . . . . . . . . . . . . . . Elaine
•• 0:57—Brief breasts in bed with a guy.

## Letters to an Unknown Lover (1985)

Andrea Ferréol . . . . . . . . . . . . . . . . . . . . . . . . Julia
Cherie Lunghi . . . . . . . . . . . . . . . . . . . . . . . Helene
    0:40—In white slip in her bedroom.
Mathilda May . . . . . . . . . . . . . . . . . . . . . . . . Agnes
• 0:43—Upper half of breasts in bathtub when Gervais
    opens the door.
••• 0:58—Buns and breasts taking off her robe in Ger-
    vais' room.

## Lianna (1982)

Linda Griffiths . . . . . . . . . . . . . . . . . . . . . . . Lianna
    0:22—In sheer white bra while changing blouses.
•• 0:29—Breasts and buns, making love in bed with
    Ruth. Dark.
•• 1:26—Right breast, then breasts while lying in bed
    with Cindy. Long, dark scene.
•• 1:42—Left breast while lying in bed with Ruth.
Jane Hallaren . . . . . . . . . . . . . . . . . . . . . . . . . Ruth
• 0:29—Brief left breast lying under Lianna during
    love making scene in bed. Dark.
Betsy Julia Robinson . . . . . . . . . . . . . . . . . . . . Cindy
•• 1:26—Breasts, getting into bed and in bed with Li-
    anna.

## Liar's Edge (1991)

Joseph Bottoms . . . . . . . . . . . . . . . . . Dave Kirkpatrick
    0:55—Almost buns, drying off after getting out of
    the shower.
Alle Ghadban . . . . . . . . . . . . . . . . . . . . . Tunnel Guard

David Keith . . . . . . . . . . . . . . . . . . . . . . Gary Kilpatrick
- 0:31—Buns, with tattoo, when he kills the mystery woman under Niagara Falls. Don't see his face.
- 0:55—Brief buns during flashback to 0:31 scene.

Joy Tanner. . . . . . . . . . . . . . . . . . . . . . . . . . . . . Ruth
Shannon Tweed . . . . . . . . . . . . . . . . . . Heather Burnz

### The Liars' Club (1993)
Shevonne Durkin. . . . . . . . . . . . . . . . . . . . . . Marla
- 0:13—Very, very brief tip of right breast when standing up when Pat sees her. Left breast when he opens her dress top. Brief lower frontal nudity (dark) when he undoes her panties. Very, very brief left breast when she starts to fall backward.
- •• 0:15—Right breast, then both breasts, when getting raped. (Don't see her face in close-ups.)

Brian Krause . . . . . . . . . . . . . . . . . . . . . . . . . . . . . Pat
- 0:15—Buns, when raping Marla in the backyard.

### The Lickerish Quartet (1970; Italian)
a.k.a. Erotic Illusion
Erika Remberg. . . . . . . . . . . . . . . . . . . . . . . . . . Wife
- •• 1:14—Nude, getting up off sofa and sitting back down, then in B&W film.
- •• 1:15—Breasts, while the girl feels her up. Close-up shot.
- 1:26—Right breast, while in bed in film.

Paolo Turco. . . . . . . . . . . . . . . . . . . . . . . . . . . . . Son
- ••• 1:00—Nude, while undressing outside with the girl.

Silvana Venturelli. . . . . . . . . . . . . . . . . . . . The Woman
- 0:01—Brief right breast under a guy in B&W porno film.
- •• 0:03—Breasts, after taking off her top in film.
- •• 0:05—Breasts while sitting on bed in film.
- •• 0:06—Breasts, while in bed with another woman.
- 0:30—Breasts, while on couch with a guy in film.
- 0:32—Breasts, while on bed with guy in film.
- 0:47—Lower half of buns under mini-skirt while in library with the father.
- ••• 0:49—Nude, while in library on table and the floor with the father.
- ••• 1:00—Nude, while undressing outside with the son and making love.
- •• 1:10—Breasts, while tied by wrists to bed in film.

Frank Wolff . . . . . . . . . . . . . . . . . . . . . . . . . . . Husbnad
- •• 0:51—Brief nude, several times, while rolling around on library floor with the girl.

### Liebestraum (1991)
(Unrated Director's cut reviewed.)
Kevin Anderson. . . . . . . . . . . . . . . . . . . Nick Kaminsky
Pamela Gidley. . . . . . . . . . . . . . . . . . . . . . .Jane Kessler
     0:37—Caressing her right breast during dream. Don't see anything.
- 1:07—Buns, while taking a shower. Almost breasts, but her arm gets in the way.

Catherine Hicks. . . . . . . . . . . . . . . . . . . . . Mary Parker
Ele Keats . . . . . . . . . . . . . . . . . . Actress on Soap Opera

### Lies (1984; British)
Miriam Byrd-Nethery . . . . . . . . . . . . . . . . . . . . . . . n.a.
Ann Dusenberry. . . . . . . . . . . . . . . . . . . .Robyn Wallace
- •• 0:10—Breasts opening the shower curtain in front of her boyfriend.
- 0:11—Right breast while kissing her boyfriend.

### The Life and Loves of a She-Devil
(1991; Made for Cable Movie; British)
Julie T. Wallace. . . . . . . . . . . . . . . . . . . . . . . . . . Ruth
- 0:54—(With commercials.) Brief buns, while walking down hallway.
- 1:05—(Into part 2 with commercials.) brief side view of buns while tied up in bed before getting spanked by the judge.
- 1:06—(With commercials.) Brief buns again.

### Life is Sweet (1991; British)
Jane Horrocks. . . . . . . . . . . . . . . . . . . . . . . . . . . Nicola
- 0:50—Breasts in bed with her boyfriend. Hard to see because she has chocolate all over her chest.

David Thewlis. . . . . . . . . . . . . . . . . . . . . . Nicola's Lover

### Lifeforce (1985)
Peter Firth . . . . . . . . . . . . . . . . . . . . . . . . . . . . . .Caine
Emma Jacobs . . . . . . . . . . . . . . . . . . . . . Crew Member
Mathilda May. . . . . . . . . . . . . . . . . . . . . . Space Girl
- 0:08—Full frontal nudity in glass case upside down.
- 0:13—Breasts, lying down in space shuttle. Lit with blue light.
- ••• 0:16—Breasts while sitting up in lab to suck the life out of military guard. Brief full frontal nudity.
- •• 0:17—Breasts again in the lab.
- •• 0:19—Breasts while walking around, then buns.
- ••• 0:20—Breasts, while walking down the stairs. Brief nude fighting with the guards.
- •• 0:44—Breasts with Steve Railsback during his nightmare. Lit with red light.
- 1:10—Brief breasts in space shuttle with Railsback.

Steve Railsback. . . . . . . . . . . . . . . . . . . . . . . . Carlsen
- 1:26—Buns, while standing with Mathilda May after he stabs her with the sword. Surrounded by special effects.

### Lifeguard (1975)
Anne Archer. . . . . . . . . . . . . . . . . . . . . . . . . . . Cathy
- 1:04—Very brief nipple while kissing Sam Elliott. Need to crank the brightness on your TV to the maximum. It appears in the lower right corner of the screen as the camera pans from right to left.

Sharon Clark . . . . . . . . . . . . . . . . . . . . . . . . . . . . .Tina
- 0:07—Brief side view of right breast undressing and getting into the shower.
- 0:08—Buns and brief breasts wrestling with Sam Elliott on the bed.

Sam Elliott . . . . . . . . . . . . . . . . . . . . . . . . . . . . . Rick
Kathleen Quinlan . . . . . . . . . . . . . . . . . . . . . .Wendy
Parker Stevenson . . . . . . . . . . . . . . . . . . . . . . . . Chris

## *Light Sleeper* (1992)
Willem Dafoe . . . . . . . . . . . . . . . . . . . . . John LeTour
•• 0:44—Buns, while kneeling in bed, kissing Dana Delany.
Dana Delany . . . . . . . . . . . . . . . . . . . . . . . Marianne
••• 0:46—Right breast, while lying on the floor with Willem Dafoe. Brief left breast when getting up. Lit with green light. (If this was anyone else, it would only get one •.)
Susan Sarandon . . . . . . . . . . . . . . . . . . . . . . . Ann

## *Like Water for Chocolate* (1993; Mexican)
*a.k.a. Como Agua Para Chocolate*
Marco Leonardi . . . . . . . . . . . . . . . . . . . . . . . . Pedro
• 1:40—Frontal nudity, while lying on bed, dead.
Claudette Maille . . . . . . . . . . . . . . . . . . . . . Gertrudis
•• 0:30—Breasts and buns while taking a shower. Nude, running out of shower house after it catches fire, running and jumping on horse with a guy.
• 1:36—Brief side view of left breast in shower flashback.

## *Link* (1986)
Elisabeth Shue . . . . . . . . . . . . . . . . . . . . . . Jane Chase
• 0:50—Brief right breast and buns, side view of a body double, standing in bathroom getting ready to take a bath while Link watches.

## *Lionheart* (1990)
Lisa Pelikan . . . . . . . . . . . . . . . . . . . . . . . . . . Helena
Jeff Speakman . . . . . . . . . . Mansion Security Man
Jean-Claude Van Damme . . . . . . . . . . . . . . . . . . Lyon
••• 0:47—Buns, while putting on robe after getting out of bed.

## *Lipstick* (1976)
Margaux Hemingway . . . . . . . . . . . . . Chris McCormick
•• 0:10—Brief breasts opening the shower door to answer the telephone.
•• 0:19—Brief breasts during rape attempt, including close-up of side view of left breast.
0:24—Buns, lying on bed while rapist runs a knife up her leg and back while she's tied to the bed.
•• 0:25—Brief breasts getting out of bed.
Mariel Hemingway . . . . . . . . . . . . . .Kathy McCormick
Perry King . . . . . . . . . . . . . . . . . . . . . . Steve Edison
Chris Sarandon . . . . . . . . . . . . . . . . . . . Gordon Stuart
•• 0:50—Buns, while standing in his studio talking to Margaux Hemingway on the telephone.

## *Lipstick Camera* (1993)
Sandahl Bergman . . . . . . . . . . . . . . . . . . . .Lilly Miller
• 0:19—Buns, while in T-back panties, while making love with Flynn in bed.
• 1:18—Buns on monitor during video playback.
Corey Feldman . . . . . . . . . . . . . . . . . . . .Joule Iverson
Ele Keats . . . . . . . . . . . . . . . . . . . . . . . . . Omy Clark
• 0:57—In bra, while making out with Flynn, then left breast while lying back with him.
Charlotte Lewis . . . . . . . . . . . . . . . . . . . Roberta Dailey
Terry O'Quinn . . . . . . . . . . . . . . . . . . . Raymond Miller

## *Listen to Me* (1989)
Christopher Atkins . . . . . . . . . . . . . . . . . Bruce Arlington
Jami Gertz . . . . . . . . . . . . . . . . . . . . . Monica Tomanski
Christopher Rydell . . . . . . . . . . . . . . . . . . .Tom Lloyd
Roy Scheider . . . . . . . . . . . . . . . . . . . . . Charlie Nichols
Annette Sinclair . . . . . . . . . . . . . . . . . . . . . Fountain Girl
Yeardley Smith . . . . . . . . . . . . . . . . . . . . . . . . . . Cootz
Nancy Valen . . . . . . . . . . . . . . . . . . . . . . . . . . . . . Mia
• 0:06—Very, very brief left breast in bed with Garson when Kirk Cameron first meets him.

## *Lisztomania* (1975; British)
Nell Campbell . . . . . . . . . . . . . . . . . . . . . . . . . . Olga
••• 1:04—Breasts in bed several times with Roger Daltrey when Ringo Starr comes in.
•• 1:06—Breasts in bed, sitting up and drinking.
••• 1:07—More breasts in bed with a gun after Starr leaves.
Roger Daltrey . . . . . . . . . . . . . . . . . . . . . . . Franz Liszt
• 0:01—Brief buns while standing on bed tying a sheet to make some pants. Dark, don't see his face.
Anulka Dziubinska . . . . . . . . . . . . . . . . . Lola Montez
•• 0:08—Breasts sitting on Roger Daltrey's lap, kissing him. Nice close up.
• 0:21—Breasts, backstage with Daltrey after the concert.
• 0:39—Breasts, wearing pasties, during Daltrey's nightmare/song and dance number.
Sara Kestelman . . . . . . . . . . . . . . . . . Princess Carolyn
Fiona Lewis . . . . . . . . . . . . . . . . . . . . . Countess Marie
•• 0:00—Breasts in bed getting breasts kissed by Roger Daltrey to the beat of a metronome.
• 0:01—Brief breasts swinging a chandelier to Daltrey.
•• 0:03—Brief breasts and buns while running from chair (long shot). Brief breasts when catching a candle on the bed.
•• 0:04—Brief left breast when her dress top is cut down. Left breast, sitting inside a piano with Daltrey.

## *Little Big Man* (1970)
Faye Dunaway . . . . . . . . . . . . . . . . . . . . . Mrs. Pendrake
Aimée Eccles . . . . . . . . . . . . . . . . . . . . . . . . Sunshine
Dustin Hoffman . . . . . . . . . . . . . . . . . . . . .Jack Crabb
• 1:28—Buns, twice, while leaving Digging Bear's bed for another sister's bed inside tepee.

## *Little Darlings* (1980)
Krista Errickson . . . . . . . . . . . . . . . . . . . . . . . . .Cinder
Kristy McNichol . . . . . . . . . . . . . . . . . . . . . . . . .Angel
Tatum O'Neal . . . . . . . . . . . . . . . . . . . . . . . . . . Ferris
• 0:35—Very, very brief half of left nipple, sticking out of swimsuit top when she comes up for air after falling into the pool to get Armand Assante's attention.

## *The Little Drummer Girl* (1984)
Sami Frey . . . . . . . . . . . . . . . . . . . . . . . . . . . Khalil
Diane Keaton . . . . . . . . . . . . . . . . . . . . . . . . . . Charlie
Klaus Kinski . . . . . . . . . . . . . . . . . . . . . . . . . . . Kurtz
Moti Shirin . . . . . . . . . . . . . . . . . . . . . . . . . . .Michel
•• 1:07—Nude, in a prison cell when Diane Keaton looks at his scars.

### Little Moon & Jud McGraw (1976)

*a.k.a. Gone with the West*

Stefanie Powers. . . . . . . . . . . . . . . . . . . . . . . .Little Moon
  • 0:29—Buns, taking a bath outside. At first, hidden behind a bush, then not. Long shot, Don't see her face. Partial right breast, but her hair gets in the way.
Robert Walker, Jr. . . . . . . . . . . . . . . . . . . . . . . . . .n.a.

### Little Nikita (1988)

Loretta Devine. . . . . . . . . . . . . . . . . .Verna McLaughlin
  • 1:03—Very brief left breast in bed after Sidney Poitier jumps out of bed when River Phoenix bursts into their bedroom.

### A Little Sex (1982)

Kate Capshaw. . . . . . . . . . . . . . . . . . . . . . . . Katherine
  • 0:10—Brief buns under T-shirt, when running away from table after stuffing a pancake down Tim Matheson's underwear.
  • 0:29—Breasts, while sitting on bed next to Matheson. Seen through out-of-focus candles.
Lisa Dunsheath . . . . . . . . . . . . . . Lucy (Down-On Girl)
Carolyn Houlihan . . . . . . . . . . . . . .Bathing Suit Model
Wendie Malick . . . . . . . . . . . . . . . . . . . . . Philomena
  • 0:39—Very, very brief side of left breast in gaping robe when she bends over to put her cigarette down.
Tim Matheson. . . . . . . . . . . . . . . . . . Michael Donovan

### The Little Thief (1989; French)

*a.k.a. La Petite Voleuse*

Nathalie Cardone . . . . . . . . . . . . . . . . . . . Mauricette
  •• 1:19—Breasts in convent arguing with a nun, then getting a shot.
Simon De La Brosse. . . . . . . . . . . . . . . . . . . . Raoul
  • 1:07—Very brief buns and frontal nudity while jumping into bed (seen in mirror).
Charlotte Gainsbourg . . . . . . . . . . . . . .Janine Castang
  •• 0:41—Breasts twice, taking off blouse in bedroom with Michel.

### Little Vegas (1990)

Anthony John Denison . . . . . . . . . . . . . . . . . Carmine
  •• 0:53—Buns, getting into pond with Catherine O'Hara.
Perry Lang. . . . . . . . . . . . . . . . . . . . . . . . . . . . Steve
Bruce McGill . . . . . . . . . . . . . . . . . . . . . . . . Harvey
Michael Nouri . . . . . . . . . . . . . . . . . . . . . . . . Frank

### Little Vera (1988; U.S.S.R.)

Natalya Negoda . . . . . . . . . . . . . . . . . . . . . . . Vera
  0:15—Very brief breasts and buns getting dressed. Dark, hard to see.
  ••• 0:50—Breasts making love with Sergei.
  •• 1:05—Breasts taking off her dress in the kitchen.

### Live Wire (1992)

(Unrated version on video tape reviewed, not the R-rated version shown on HBO. )
Pierce Brosnan . . . . . . . . . . . . . . . . . . . .Danny O'Neill
  ••• 1:02—Buns, while making love in bed with Lisa Eilbacher.

Lisa Eilbacher . . . . . . . . . . . . . . . . . . . . . . . Terry O'Neill
  ••• 1:01—Brief breasts several times and partial buns, in bath tub and in bed with Pierce Brosnan. Some of the love making scenes in bed were cut for the R-rated version.
Tracy Tweed . . . . . . . . . . . . . . . . . . . . . Rolls Royce Girl
Nels Van Patten . . . . . . . . . . . . . . . . . Racquetball Player

### The Living Daylights (1987)

Maryam D'Abo. . . . . . . . . . . . . . . . . . . . Kara Milovy
Virginia Hey . . . .Rubavitch (Colonel Pushkin's girlfriend)
  • 1:10—Brief side view of left breast when James Bond uses her to distract bodyguard.
Catherine Rabett . . . . . . . . . . . . . . . . . . . . . . . . n.a.
Julie T. Wallace. . . . . . . . . . . . . . . . . . . . . . . . . n.a.

### Living to Die (1990)

Rebecca Barrington . . . . . . . . . . . . . . Married Woman
  • 0:23—In red bra, blindfolded and tied to a lounge chair, then breasts while getting photographed.
  • 0:27—Breasts in chair when Wings Hauser talks to her.
Darcy De Moss. . . . . . . . . . . . . . . . . . . .Maggie Sams
  0:11—Taking off clothes to white bra, panties, garter belt and stockings in hotel room with a customer.
  • 0:32—Buns, getting out of spa while Wings Hauser watches without her knowing.
  0:33—Buns, in long shot when Hauser fantasizes about dancing with her.
  ••• 0:56—In black bra, then breasts and buns making love with Hauser.
  • 1:20—Breasts in mirror taking off black top for the bad guy.
Wings Hauser. . . . . . . . . . . . . . . . . . . . Nick Carpenter
Wendy MacDonald . . . . . . . . . . . Rookie Policewoman

### Loaded Guns (1975)

Ursula Andress. . . . . . . . . . . . . . . . . . . . . . . .Laura
  0:32—Buns, lying in bed with a guy.
  ••• 0:33—Breasts and buns getting out of bed. Full frontal nudity in elevator.
  •• 0:40—Nude getting out of bed and putting dress on.
  ••• 0:48—Nude getting into bathtub, breasts in tub, nude getting out and drying herself off.
  1:00—Buns while getting undressed and hopping into bed.
  • 1:02—Brief side view of right breast while getting dressed.

### Loaded Weapon 1 (1993)

Emilio Estevez. . . . . . . . . . . . . . . . . . . . . . . . Jack Colt
  •• 0:56—Buns, getting out of bed. It looks like he has his body all oiled up.
Corey Feldman. . . . . . . . . . . . . . . . . . . . . Young Cop
Samuel L. Jackson. . . . . . . . . . . . . . . . . . . Wes Luger
Beverly Johnson . . . . . . . . . . . . . . . . . . . . Doris Luger
  0:50—In gold, braless, semi-sheer blouse.
Karman Kruschke . . . . . . . . . . . . . . One of the Cindys

### Logan's Run (1976)
Jenny Agutter . . . . . . . . . . . . . . . . . . . . . . . . . . .Jessica
• 1:05—Very brief breasts and buns changing into fur
coat in ice cave with Michael York.
Farrah Fawcett . . . . . . . . . . . . . . . . . . . . . . . . . . .Holly
Laura Hippe . . . . . . . . . . . . . New You Shop Customer
Candice Rialson. . . . Uncredited Girl with Richard Jordan
Michael York . . . . . . . . . . . . . . . . . . . . . . . . . . . .Logan

### London Kills Me (1991; British)
Brad Dourif . . . . . . . . . . . . . . . . . . . . . . . . Hemingway
Rowena King . . . . . . . . . . . . . . . . . . . . . . . . . Melanie
Steven Mackintosh . . . . . . . . . . . . . . . . . . . . Muffdiver
•• 1:06—Brief buns and penis, while getting into bath-
tub with Clint and Sylvie.
Emer McCourt . . . . . . . . . . . . . . . . . . . . . . . . . Sylvie
• 1:02—Left breast in open blouse, while sleeping.
••• 1:05—Breasts, while sitting in bathtub with Clint.
Long scene.
Fiona Shaw . . . . . . . . . . . . . . . . . . . . . . . . . Headley

### The Lonely Guy (1983)
Lamya Derval . . . . . . . .One of "The Seven Deadly Sins"
Robyn Douglass . . . . . . . . . . . . . . . . . . . . . . Danielle
• 0:05—Upper half of right breast in sheer nightgown
in bed with Raoul while talking to Steve Martin.
Great nightgown!
0:33—In sheer beige negligee lying on couch talk-
ing to Martin on the phone.
• 1:03—Very, very brief peek at left nipple when she
flashes it for Martin so he'll let her into his party.
Michael Greer . . . . . . . . . . . . . . . . . . . The Counterman
Elizabeth Kaitan. . . . . . . . . . . . . . . . . . . . . . . . . .n.a.
Marie Laurin . . . . . . . . .One of "The Seven Deadly Sins"
Julie Payne . . . . . . . . . . . . . . . . . . . . . .Rental Agent

### Lonely Hearts (1983; Australian)
Wendy Hughes . . . . . . . . . . . . . . . . . . . . . . .Patricia
• 1:05—Brief breasts getting out of bed and putting a
dress on. Dark, hard to see.
Norman Kaye . . . . . . . . . . . . . . . . . . . . . . . . . .Peter
• 1:03—Buns, while getting out of bed. Very brief
frontal nudity.
Kris McQuade . . . . . . . . . . . . . . . . . . . . . .Rosemarie

### Lonely Hearts (1991)
Bibi Besch . . . . . . . . . . . . . . . . . . . . . . . Maria Wilson
0:05—Almost breasts in bed with Eric Roberts.
Joanna Cassidy . . . . . . . . . . . . . . . . . . . . Erin Randall
Beverly D'Angelo. . . . . . . . . . . . . . . . . . . . . . .Alma
0:33—Most of left breast, while making love in bed
with Eric Roberts.
• 0:57—Brief side view of right breast, while getting
into shower with Roberts.
• 0:58—Very brief left breast in shower after Roberts
gets pushed by Louise.
• 0:59—Very brief buns, when Roberts punches Louise
through the shower door.
Sharon Farrell . . . . . . . . . . . . . . . . . . . . . . . .Louise
•• 0:52—Breasts, while lying back on bed in room with
Eric Roberts.

Eric Roberts . . . . . . . . . . . . . . . . . . . . . . . . . . . Frank
Rebecca Street . . . . . . . . . . . . . . . . . . . . .Jane Ericson
• 1:12—Brief side of right breast, while making love
on top of Eric Roberts on couch.

### The Lonely Lady (1983)
Glory Annen. . . . . . . . . . . . . . . . . . . . . . . . . Marion
• 0:07—Brief left breast in back seat of car with Ray Liotta. Dark, hard to see.
Bibi Besch . . . . . . . . . . . . . . . . . . . . . . . . . Veronica
Joseph Cali. . . . . . . . . . . . . . . . . . . . . .Vincent Dacosta
• 1:05—Buns, while near pool table and walking
around the house with Pia Zadora.
Ray Liotta. . . . . . . . . . . . . . . . . . . . . . . . . . . . .Joe
Carla Romanelli . . . . . . . . . . . . . . . . Carla Maria Peroni
•• 1:10—Brief breasts taking off her top to make love
with Pia Zadora while a guy watches.
Pia Zadora . . . . . . . . . . . . . . . . . . . . . JeniLee Randall
• 0:12—Brief breasts getting raped by Ray Liotta, after
getting out of the pool.
•• 0:22—Brief breasts, then left breast, while making
love with Walter.
•• 0:28—Side view breasts lying in bed with Walter.
•• 0:44—Buns and side view of left breast taking a
shower.
• 0:46—Very brief right breast, in bed with George.
•• 1:05—Left breast, then brief breasts making love
with Vinnie.

### The Long Good Friday (1980; British)
Paul Barber. . . . . . . . . . . . . . . . . . . . . . . . . . . Erroll
• 0:42—Brief buns, getting cut on his rear end during
interrogation.
Pierce Brosnan . . . . . . . . . . . . . . . . . . . .First Irishman
Stephen Davies . . . . . . . . . . . . . . . . . . . . . . . . Tony
Dexter Fletcher. . . . . . . . . . . . . . . . . . . . . . . . .Kid
Patti Love. . . . . . . . . . . . . . . . . . . . . . . . . . . Carol
Bryan Marshall . . . . . . . . . . . . . . . . . . . . . . . .Harris
Helen Mirren . . . . . . . . . . . . . . . . . . . . . . . Victoria

### The Long Riders (1980)
David Carradine . . . . . . . . . . . . . . . . . . . . .Cole Younger
Keith Carradine . . . . . . . . . . . . . . . . . . . . . .Jim Younger
Robert Carradine . . . . . . . . . . . . . . . . . . . Bob Younger
Christopher Guest . . . . . . . . . . . . . . . . . . .Charlie Ford
Stacy Keach . . . . . . . . . . . . . . . . . . . . . . Frank James
Chris Mulkey . . . . . . . . . . . . . . . . . . . . .Vernon Biggs
Dennis Quaid. . . . . . . . . . . . . . . . . . . . . . Ed Miller
Randy Quaid . . . . . . . . . . . . . . . . . . . . . Clell Miller
Pamela Reed . . . . . . . . . . . . . . . . . . . . . Belle Starr
• 0:18—Buns, while standing up in bathtub to hug
David Carradine. (Don't see her face.)
James Remar . . . . . . . . . . . . . . . . . . . . . . .Sam Starr
Savannah Smith Bouchér . . . . . . . . . . . . . . . . . . . . . Zee

### Looker (1981)
Donna Kei Benz . . . . . . . . . . . . . . . . . . . . . . . Ellen
Randi Brooks . . . . . . . . . . . . . . . . . . . . .Girl in Bikini
Pamela Bryant . . . . . . . . . . . . . . . . . . . . .Reston Girl
Ashley Cox. . . . . . . . . . . . . . . . . . . . . . . . . Candy

Susan Dey.............................Cindy
  0:28—In white one piece swimsuit shooting a commercial at the beach.
  • 0:36—Buns, then brief breasts in computer imaging
  device. Breasts in computer monitor.
Melissa Prophet..............Commercial Script Girl
Lori Sutton.........................Reston Girl
Leigh Taylor-Young.................Jennifer Long
Jeana Tomasina.........................Suzy
Terri Welles..............................Lisa
  • 0:02—Brief breasts getting photographed for operation. In black bra and panties in her apartment a
  lot.
Vanna White........................Reston Girl
Kathryn Witt.......................Tina Cassidy
  0:17—In beige lingerie undressing in her room.

## Looking for Mr. Goodbar (1977)
Tom Berenger.............................Gary
LeVar Burton.......................Cap Jackson
Richard Gere.............................Tony
  •• 1:00—Buns, while on Diane Keaton's floor doing
  push-ups, then running around in his jock strap.
Caren Kaye..............................Rhoda
Diane Keaton...........................Theresa
  •• 0:11—Right breast in bed making love with her
  teacher, Martin, then putting blouse on.
  • 0:31—Brief left breast over the shoulder when the
  Doctor playfully kisses her breast.
  •• 1:04—Brief breasts smoking in bed in the morning,
  then more breasts after Richard Gere leaves.
  ••• 1:17—Breasts making love with Gere after doing a
  lot of cocaine.
  • 1:31—Brief breasts in the bathtub when James
  brings her a glass of wine.
  2:00—Getting out of bed in a bra.
  •• 2:02—Breasts during rape by Tom Berenger, before
  he kills her. Hard to see because of strobe lights.

## Loose Shoes (1977)
Louisa Moritz.........................Margie
Misty Rowe.............................Louise
Robin Sherwood....................Biker Chic #2
Betty Thomas.....................Biker Chick #1
  • 0:02—Brief right breast dancing on the table during
  the *Skateboarders from Hell* sketch.
Susan Tyrrell........................Boobies

## Lost Angels (1989)
Frances Fisher.....................Judith Loftis
Jane Hallaren......................Grace Willig
Nina Siemaszko........................Merilee
  • 0:38—Brief breasts and buns, running through
  courtyard. Long shot, don't really see anything.
  • 0:45—Buns, sitting at table outside, undressing and
  rubbing feces (yuck!) on herself.
Donald Sutherland...............Dr. Charles Loftis

## The Lost Empire (1983)
Angela Aames...................Heather McClure
  ••• 0:31—Breasts and buns taking a shower while Angel
  and White Star talk to her.
Deborah Blaisdell.....................Girl Recruit
  • 0:42—Brief buns and breasts, turning over on exam
  table.
Raven De La Croix.....................White Star
  ••• 1:05—Breasts with a snake after being drugged by
  the bad guy.
  •• 1:07—Breasts lying on a table.
  •• 1:08—Breasts, getting up off table and punching a
  guy.
Annie Gaybis.......................Prison Referee
  • 0:30—Breasts when her top gets ripped off by Angelique Pettyjohn during cat fight.
Tina Merkle.........................Girl Recruit
Angelique Pettyjohn.....................Whiplash
  0:29—In a sexy, black leather outfit fighting in prison with Heather.
Linda Shayne......................Cindy Blake

## The Lost Honor of Katharina Blum (1975; German)
Jürgen Prochnow.................Ludwig Goetten
Angela Winkler.................Katharina Blum
  •• 0:15—Full frontal nudity, while in bathroom, getting
  strip searched by policewoman.
  • 0:43—Brief right breast, after getting out of the
  shower.

## Loulou (1980; French)
Gérard Depardieu.......................Loulou
  • 0:07—Brief buns, while getting out of bed after it
  breaks. Dark.
  •• 0:36—Buns, while lying in bed with Isabelle Huppert.
Isabelle Huppert...........................Nelly
  • 0:06—Very, very brief breasts leaning over in bed.
  • 0:18—Brief breasts getting out of bed.
  • 0:27—Brief breasts turning over in bed.
  •• 0:36—Breasts lying in bed talking on phone. Mostly
  right breast.
  • 0:40—Lower frontal nudity and buns taking off
  panties and getting into bed.
  •• 0:59—Left breast in bed with André, then breasts
  taking him to the bathroom.
Guy Marchand.........................André
  •• 0:59—Buns, while getting out of bed with Isabelle
  Huppert.

## The Love Butcher (1982)
Marilyn Jones..........................Lena
Robin Sherwood........................Sheila
  • 0:39—Very brief buns, while putting on swimsuit
  bottom.
  • 0:40—Brief breasts several times, while struggling in
  pool with killer when he kills her with garden hose.
  • 0:41—Buns, while getting carried out of pool by killer. Breasts under water in bathtub, dead.

• 0:43—Brief breasts, while throwing bikini top while in pool.

## Love Child (1982)

Beau Bridges . . . . . . . . . . . . . . . . . . . . . . . Jack Hansen
Cheryl King . . . . . . . . . . . . . . . . . . . . . . . Van Inmate
Amy Madigan . . . . . . . . . . . . . . . . . . Terry Jean Moore
  • 0:08—Brief side view of right breast and buns taking a shower in jail while the guards watch.
  •• 0:53—Brief breasts and buns, making love with Beau Bridges in a room at the women's prison.
Margaret Whitton . . . . . . . . . . . . . . . . . Jacki Steinberg

## Love Circles Around the World (1984)

Sophie Berger . . . . . . . . . . . . . . . . . . . . . . . . Dagmar
  ••• 0:38—Breasts in women's restroom in casino making love with a guy in a tuxedo.
  ••• 0:43—Breasts in steam room wearing a towel around her waist, then making love.
Josephine Jaqueline Jones . . . . . . . . . . . . . . . Brigid
  •• 0:18—Breasts, then nude running around her apartment chasing Jack.
  • 0:30—Breasts, making love with Count Crispa in his hotel room.
John Sibbit . . . . . . . . . . . . . . . . . . . . . . . . . . . . . Jack
  • 0:06—Very brief frontal nudity pulling his underwear down and getting into bed.
  •• 0:19—Buns, while trying to run away from Brigid after she yanks his underwear off.
Timothy Wood . . . . . . . . . . . . . . . . . . . . . . . Michael
  •• 1:29—Frontal nudity, lying in bed with Jill after making love while video taping it.

## Love Crimes (1991)

(Unrated version reviewed.)
Patrick Bergin . . . . . . . . . . . . . . . . . . . . David Hanover
  • 1:02—Buns, during love scene with Sean Young. Lit with red light, don't see his face.
Fern Dorsey . . . . . . . . . . . . . . . . . . . . . . . . .Colleen Dells
  ••• 0:03—Breasts, getting photographed by Patrick Bergin.
Arnetia Walker. . . . . . . . . . . . . . . . . . . . Maria Johnson
Sean Young. . . . . . . . . . . . . . . . . . . . Dana Greenway
  •• 0:20—Almost left breast, getting out of bathtub. Buns and partial lower frontal nudity, getting dressed.
  •• 0:55—Breasts in open blouse, yelling at Patrick Bergin.
  • 0:57—Brief right breast, on bed in open blouse.
  ••• 0:59—Nude in bathtub.
  ••• 1:01—Breasts, making love with Bergin. Lit with red light.
  • 1:03—Full frontal nudity, getting covered with a towel.
  • 1:08—Full frontal nudity, in Polaroid that Maria looks at.
  • 1:11—More full frontal nudity in Polaroid.
  1:21—Partial right breast, while taking a shower.
  • 1:23—Brief breasts in the shower.
  1:25—Very brief right breast in gaping robe.
  1:27—Full frontal nudity in burning Polaroid.

## Love Hurts (1991)

Jeff Daniels . . . . . . . . . . . . . . . . . . . . . . . . .Paul Weaver
  ••• 1:24—Buns, several times in motel room with Judith Ivey.
Cloris Leachman. . . . . . . . . . . . . . . . . . . . Ruth Weaver
Amy Wright . . . . . . . . . . . . . . . . . . . . . . Karen Weaver

## A Love in Germany (1984; French/German)

Marie-Christine Barrault . . . . . . . . . . . . . . . .Maria Wyler
  • 0:23—Right breast, in bed with her lover when Pauline peeks from across the way.
  •• 0:28—Right breast in bedroom with Karl. Very brief lower frontal nudity getting back into bed. Long scene.
  ••• 0:43—Breasts in bedroom with Karl. Subtitles get in the way! Long scene.
Gerard Desarthe. . . . . . . . . . . . . . . . . . . . . . Karl Wyler
  • 0:28—Buns, while lying in bed with Maria.
Daniel Olbrychski . . . . . . . . . . . . . . . . . . . .Wiktorczyk
Hanna Schygulla . . . . . . . . . . . . . . . . . . . Pauline Kropp

## Love Letters (1984)

*a.k.a. Passion Play*
Jamie Lee Curtis . . . . . . . . . . . . . . . . . . . . . Anna Winter
  ••• 0:31—Breasts in bathtub reading a letter, then breasts in bed making love with James Keach.
  • 0:36—Brief breasts in lifeguard station with Keach.
  ••• 0:44—Brief breasts admiring a picture taken of her by Keach.
  ••• 0:46—Breasts and buns in bedroom undressing with Keach.
  • 0:49—Breasts in black and white Polaroid photographs that Keach is taking.
  1:02—In white slip in her house with Keach.
  • 1:07—Right breast, sticking out of slip, then right breast, while sleeping in bed with Keach.
Sally Kirkland . . . . . . . . . . . . . . . . . . . . . . . . . Hippie
Amy Madigan . . . . . . . . . . . . . . . . . . . . . . .Wendy

## Love Lust and Ecstasy (1978)

Ajita Wilson . . . . . . . . . . . . . . . . . . . . . . . . . . . . .Sara
  •• 0:02—Nude taking a shower and getting into bed with an old guy.
  •• 0:04—Nude making love with a young guy.
  •• 0:17—Breasts in bathtub, then making love on bed.
  •• 0:22—Breasts making love in a swimming pool, in a river, by a tree.
  •• 0:26—Nude getting undressed and taking a shower.
  •• 0:35—Full frontal nudity changing clothes.
  ••• 0:54—Full frontal nudity making love in bed.

## The Love Machine (1971)

Madeleine Collinson. . . . . . . . . . . . . . . . . . . . . Sandy
  •• 1:22—Breasts in shower with Robin and her sister when Dyan Cannon discovers them all together. Can't tell who is who.
Mary Collinson. . . . . . . . . . . . . . . . . . . . . . . Debbie
  •• 1:22—Breasts in shower with Robin and her sister when Dyan Cannon discovers them all together. Can't tell who is who.

Alexandra Hay. . . . . . . . . . . . . . . . . . . .Tina St. Claire
- • 0:34—Brief breasts in bed with Robin.
- • 0:38—Brief breasts coming around the corner putting blue bathrobe on.

Claudia Jennings. . . . . . . . . . . . . . . . . . . . . . .Darlene

John Phillip Law. . . . . . . . . . . . . . . . . . . Robin Stone

## Love Matters (1993; Made for Cable Movie)
(Unrated version reviewed.)

Kate Burton. . . . . . . . . . . . . . . . . . . . . . .Deborah
- • 0:05—Brief breasts, getting turned over on bed during video playback.
- • 0:09—Very brief side view of right breast, while making love in bed with Tony Goldwyn during video playback.

Gina Gershon . . . . . . . . . . . . . . . . . . . . . . . . . . Heat
- • 0:33—Brief left breast when Tony Goldwyn lays her down.
- ••• 0:34—Breasts, while on table with Goldwyn. More breasts while making love on kitchen island. Buns when running away.
- •• 0:44—Breasts, after turning over and lying under Goldwyn.
- • 0:53—Partial left breast, while in shower, talking to Goldwyn.

Tony Goldwyn . . . . . . . . . . . . . . . . . . . . . Geoff
- • 0:30—Brief buns, after getting out of bed to talk to Annette O'Toole.
- • 0:33—Buns, while carrying Gina Gershon to the table.
- • 0:34—Very, very brief blurry frontal nudity when Gershon pushes him back from kitchen island.
- ••• 0:53—Buns, in the bathroom, while putting cordless phone away.
- •• 0:56—Buns, while making love with Gershon in the shower.

Annette O'Toole . . . . . . . . . . . . . . . . . . . . . . Julie

## Love Scenes (1984)
*a.k.a. Ecstacy*

Tiffany Bolling . . . . . . . . . . . . . . . . . . . . . . . . . Val
- •• 0:01—Side view of left breast in bed with Peter.
- ••• 0:06—Breasts getting photographed by Britt Ekland in the house.
- • 0:09—Brief breasts opening her bathrobe to show Peter.
- • 0:12—Breasts in bathtub with Peter.
- ••• 0:19—Breasts lying in bed talking with Peter, then making love.
- • 0:43—Breasts acting in a movie when Rick opens her blouse.
- • 0:57—Nude behind shower door, then breasts getting out and talking to Peter.
- •• 0:59—Breasts making love tied up on bed with Rick during filming of movie.
- •• 1:07—Breasts, then full frontal nudity acting with Elizabeth during filming of movie.
- •• 1:17—Full frontal nudity getting out of pool.
- •• 1:26—Breasts with Peter on the bed.

Britt Ekland . . . . . . . . . . . . . . . . . . . . . . . . . Annie

Monique Gabrielle . . . . . . . . . . . . . . . . . . . Uncredited
- ••• 1:11—Full frontal nudity making love with Rick on bed.

Julie Newmar . . . . . . . . . . . . . . . . . . . . . . . . Belinda

## Love Strange Love (1982; Brazilian)

Xuxa . . . . . . . . . . . . . . . . . . . . . . . . . . . . . Tamara
- •• 0:26—Breasts standing on table, getting measured for outfit.
- ••• 0:29—Breasts again when Hugo watches. Long scene.
- •• 0:58—Right breast when she lets Hugo caress it. (Film is reversed since mole above her right breast appears over the left.)
- • 1:00—More right breast.
- • 1:09—Breasts, stripping out of bear costume during party.
- ••• 1:13—Breasts several times undressing in room. Long scene.
- •• 1:27—Side view of left breast in bed with Hugo.

Vera Fischer . . . . . . . . . . . . . . . . . . . . . . . . . . . . Anna
- • 0:23—Brief breasts and lower frontal nudity in bathtub. Breasts and buns, getting out.
- • 0:38—Breasts making love with Dr. Osmar.
- • 0:39—Brief buns, while lying in bed.
- •• 1:19—Breasts in bed with Dr. Osmar when Hugo watches.

Marcelo Ribeiro . . . . . . . . . . . . . . . . . . . . . Hugo (Child)
- • 0:20—Brief frontal nudity between his legs in bathtub.

## Love Trap (1977)
*a.k.a. Let's Get Laid*

Robin Askwith . . . . . . . . . . . . . . . . . . . . . . Gordon Laid
- • 0:39—Buns, while making love with girls in his dream.

Linda Hayden. . . . . . . . . . . . . . . . . . . . . . . . . . Gloria

Fiona Richmond. . . . . . . . . . . . . . . . . Maxine Lupercal
- •• 0:10—Nude, while in the shower/tub.
- • 0:21—Brief left breast when her lingerie is torn off in Gordon's hand.
- ••• 0:24—Nude, while doing strip routine on stage (wearing a big blonde wig).
-    0:26—Breasts, with a guy in bedroom.
- • 0:27—Breasts and buns in bed with him.
- •• 0:56—Nude, after stripping out of Nazi uniform, then bra and panties, then making love with two girls.
- •• 1:09—Breasts, while in bubble bath, talking to Gordon, then standing up.
- • 1:34—Brief breasts when Gordon pulls her dress top down during filming.

Lisa Taylor . . . . . . . . . . . . . . . . . . . . . . . . . . Eleanor
- •• 0:37—Breasts, while answering and talking on the phone.
- • 0:53—Partial lower frontal nudity while talking on the phone to Gordon. Brief breasts, while hanging up the phone.
- • 1:33—Brief left breast while making love on bed with two guys.

### Love, Cheat & Steal (1993; Made for Cable Movie)
Mädchen Amick . . . . . . . . . . . . . . . Lauren Harrington
- 0:01—Silhouette of side view of a breast, while kneeling above Eric Roberts. Don't see her face.
- 0:14—Almost buns, while in bedroom with John Lithgow.
- • 0:26—Buns, when Roberts rips her pants off. Don't see her face.
- • 0:47—Brief back side of right breast, twice, getting out of bed and putting on robe.

Susan Lentini . . . . . . . . . . . . . . . . . . . . . . . . . Nun
John Lithgow . . . . . . . . . . . . . . . . . . . . Paul Harrington
Eric Roberts . . . . . . . . . . . . . . . . . . . . . . . . Reno Adams

### The Lover (1992)
(Unrated version reviewed.)
Jane March . . . . . . . . . . . . . . . . . . . . . . . . . . The Girl
- •• 0:32—Full frontal nudity in bed with her lover.
- ••• 0:40—Left breast, while making love under her lover.
- ••• 0:42—Full frontal nudity, while lying in bed. Long shot.
- •• 0:43—Buns, while standing in tub, getting washed by her lover.
- ••• 0:44—Breasts, while lying in bed, talking with her lover. Long scene.
- •• 0:47—Left breast, while making love in bed.
- • 0:48—Full frontal nudity, while lying in bed.
- •• 0:54—Breasts while making love on the floor with her lover.
- ••• 0:56—More full frontal nudity on the floor.
- ••• 0:59—Nude, walking around and watering the plants, getting into bed, then making love.
- • 1:02—Brief breasts while making love.
- • 1:17—Breasts washing herself with her lover. Hard to see because bars get in the way.

### Lovers Like Us (1975)
a.k.a. The Savage
Catherine Deneuve . . . . . . . . . . . . . . . . . . . . . . .Nelly
- • 1:06—Brief left upper half of left breast in bed with Yves Montand. Dark.
- ••• 1:09—Breasts sitting up in bed.

### Lovers' Lovers (1993)
Jennifer Ciesar . . . . . . . . . . . . . . . . . . . . . . . . Blaire
- •• 0:29—Breasts and buns while in the shower.
- • 1:07—In white bra and brief breasts while making love with Michael on bed.
- 1:13—In white bra and panties in bedroom.

Ken Steadman. . . . . . . . . . . . . . . . . . . Make Out Guy

### The Loves of a French Pussycat (1976)
Sybil Danning . . . . . . . . . . . . . . . . . . . . . . . . . Andrea
- ••• 0:18—Breasts dancing with her boss, then in bed.
- •• 0:24—Breasts and buns in swimming pool.
- 0:40—In sheer white bra and panties doing things around the house. Long sequence.
- • 0:46—Breasts in bathtub with a guy.
- • 1:03—Left breast sticking out of bra, then breasts.

### The Loves of a Wall Street Woman (1989)
Tara Buckman . . . . . . . . . . . . . . . . . . . . . Brenda Baxter
- • 0:00—Breasts taking a shower, opening the door and getting a towel.
- •• 0:06—Breasts changing clothes in locker room in black panties. Nice legs!
- ••• 0:18—Breasts in bed making love with Alex.
- •• 0:31—Breasts in bed with Alex making love.
- •• 0:40—Breasts in black panties dressing in locker room.
- • 0:46—Brief breasts lying in bed, talking to her lover, side view of buns. Long shot.
- ••• 1:16—Breasts making love in bed with Alex.

### Loving Lulu (1992)
Sandahl Bergman. . . . . . . . . . . . . . . . . . . . . . . . .Lulu
- 0:34—In red bra and blue panties with Sam.
- ••• 0:35—Breasts, making love with Sam.
- • 0:42—Brief buns and brief breasts in shower with Sam.
- • 0:57—Brief right breast in bathroom, twice, with Sam.

Tanya Boyd . . . . . . . . . . . . . . . . . . . . . . .Background

### Lower Level (1990)
Elizabeth Gracen . . . . . . . . . . . . . . . . . . . . . . . . Hillary
- • 0:11—Breasts in back seat of BMW making love with Craig. Long shot.
- 0:12—Very, very brief partial left breast afterwards.
- • 0:13—Brief right breast and lower frontal nudity getting dressed. Then in black lingerie.
- 0:14—In wet black lingerie under fire sprinkler in parking garage.
- •• 0:23—In black lingerie, then brief breasts changing in her office while Sam secretly watches.

Shari Shattuck . . . . . . . . . . . . . . . . . . . . . .Dawn Simms

### Lucky 13 (1984)
a.k.a. Running Hot
a.k.a. Highway to Hell
Monica Carrico . . . . . . . . . . . . . . . . Charlene Andrews
- 0:09—Lying on bed in white bra and open dress top.
- 0:18—Walking around in panties and a blouse.
- •• 0:49—Breasts sitting on a rock after skinny dipping with Eric Stoltz.
- •• 0:51—Breasts and buns after getting out of water and picking up clothes.
- •• 1:03—Breasts in bed making love with Stoltz.
- ••• 1:15—Breasts lying in bed with Stoltz.

Juliette Cummins . . . . . . . . . . . . . . . . . . . . . . . . .Jenny
Eric Stoltz. . . . . . . . . . . . . . . . . . . . . . . . Danny Hicks

### Lunch Wagon (1981)
a.k.a. Lunch Wagon Girls
a.k.a. Come 'N' Get It
Pamela Bryant . . . . . . . . . . . . . . . . . . . . . . . . . Marcy
- •• 0:04—Breasts while changing tops in room in gas station with Rosanne Katon while a guy watches through key hole.
- • 0:55—Left breast, several times, in van with Bif.

Rosanne Katon . . . . . . . . . . . . . . . . . . . . . . .Shannon
- 0:01—Brief breasts getting dressed.
- 0:04—Brief side view of left breast changing tops in room in gas station with Pamela Bryant while a guy watches through key hole.
- 0:10—Breasts changing again in gas station.

Candy Moore . . . . . . . . . . . . . . . . . . . . . . . . . Diedra
- 0:53—Breasts under sheer robe, then breasts on couch with Arnie.

Louisa Moritz . . . . . . . . . . . . . . . . . . . . . . . .Sunshine
- 0:37—Breasts in spa taking off her swimsuit top.

Nels Van Patten. . . . . . . . . . . . . . . . . . . . . . . . .Scotty

## Lurkers (1987)

Ruth Corrine Collins . . . . . . . . . . . . . . . . .Jane (Model)
0:12—Undressing in white bra (on the right) with another model.
- 0:13—Breasts, changing clothes with the other model.

Annie Grindlay . . . . . . . . . . . . . . . . . . . . . .Lulu (Model)
- 0:12—Undressing in sheer bra (on the left) with another model.
- 0:13—Breasts, changing clothes with the other model.

Nancy Groff . . . . . . . . . . . . . . . . . . . . . . . . . . . .Rita
- 1:07—Partial right breast in bathroom with another woman while Cathy talks.

Christine Moore . . . . . . . . . . . . . . . . . . . . . . . . Cathy
- 0:19—Breasts in bed, making love with her boyfriend.
- 0:42—Brief breasts in bubble bath during hallucination scene with her mother.

## Lust for a Vampire (1970; British)

Luan Peters . . . . . . . . . . . . . . . . . . . . . . . . . . . Trudi
Pippa Steel . . . . . . . . . . . . . . . . . . . . . . . Susan Pelley
Yutte Stensgaard. . . . . . . . . . . . . . . . . . . . . . Mircalla
- 0:19—Breasts, three times, getting a massage from another school girl.
0:22—Very, very brief full frontal nudity while diving into the water. Long shot, don't see anything.
- 0:53—Breasts outside with Lestrange. Left breast when lying down.
- 0:58—Breasts during Lestrange's dream.

## Luther the Geek (1988)

Stacy Haiduk. . . . . . . . . . . . . . . . . . . . . . . . . . Beth
0:24—In bra and panties after undressing to take a shower.
- 0:26—Breasts with Rob in the shower. Wow!
- 0:28—Breasts taking off her robe in bed, then making love with Rob.

Thomas Mills. . . . . . . . . . . . . . . . . . . . . . . . . . . Rob
- 0:27—Very brief buns when Stacey Haiduk gooses him.

## M•A•S•H (1970)

Sally Kellerman . . . . . . . . Margaret "Hot Lips" Houlihan
- 0:42—Very, very brief left breast opening her blouse for Frank in her tent.

- 1:11—Very, very brief buns and side view of right breast during shower prank. Long shot, hard to see.
- 1:54—Very brief breasts in a slightly different angle of the shower prank during the credits.

Donald Sutherland. . . . . . . . . . . . . . . . . Hawkeye Pierce

## M. Butterfly (1993)

Jeremy Irons. . . . . . . . . . . . . . . . . . . . . René Gallimard
Annabel Leventon . . . . . . . . . . . . . . . . . . . . Frau Baden
- 0:50—Breasts, while sitting on bed and talking to Jeremy Irons.

John Lone. . . . . . . . . . . . . . . . . . . . . . . Song Liling
- 1:24—Buns, after taking off his clothes in back of paddy wagon with Jeremy Irons.

Barbara Sukowa . . . . . . . . . . . . . . . . . .Jeanne Gallimard

## Mac (1992)

Ellen Barkin . . . . . . . . . . . . . . . . . . . . . . . . . . .Oona
John Turturro . . . . . . . . . . . . . . . . Niccolo "Mac" Vitelli
- 1:08—Brief buns, while getting out of bed. Don't see his face.

## Macabre (Italian/Spanish)

Silvana Venturelli . . . . . . . . . . . . . . . . . . . . . . .Annie
- 1:03—Very, very brief right breast, while wrapping a robe around herself.
- 1:05—Brief right breast while lying on bed when Gert checks her out.

## Macbeth (1972)

Francesca Annis . . . . . . . . . . . . . . . . . . . . Lady Macbeth
- 1:41—Buns, while walking around after the bad guys have attacked and looted the castle. Side view of left breast, hard to see because it's covered by her hair.

## Macho Callahan (1970)

David Carradine . . . . . . . . . . . Colonel David Mountford
David Janssen. . . . . . . . . . . . . .Diego "Macho" Callahan
Jean Seberg . . . . . . . . . . . . . . . . . . . . . . . . Alexandra
- 0:36—Brief buns and partial breast in mirror. (Don't see her face clearly.)
- 1:01—Very brief left breast when David Janssen rips her blouse open. Brief breasts during struggle with him before he rapes her. Brief left breast during rape. (Never see face with body.)

## Mad Dog and Glory (1993)

David Caruso . . . . . . . . . . . . . . . . . . . . . . . . Mike
Robert De Niro. . . . . . . . . . . Wayne "Mad Dog" Dobie
Uma Thurman . . . . . . . . . . . . . . . . . . . . . . . . . Glory
- 0:56—Left breast, while in bed with Robert De Niro.
- 0:58—Very brief breasts when De Niro gets off her.

## Made in America (1993)

Nia Long . . . . . . . . . . . . . . . . . . . . . . . . Zora Mathews
Jennifer Tilly. . . . . . . . . . . . . . . . . . . . . . . . . . .Stacy
- 0:13—Very, very brief back side of left breast, while jumping up out of bed. Brief buns and very, very brief back side of left breast while doing cartwheels into the bathroom. Possible body double.

### Made in Heaven (1987)
Ellen Barkin . . . . . . . . . . . . . . . . . . . . . . . . . . . .Lucille
Timothy Hutton . . . . . . . . . . . . Mike Shea/Elmo Barnett
•• 0:08—Buns, while standing in a room when he first
gets to heaven.
Kelly McGillis. . . . . . . . . . . Annie Packert/Ally Chandler
Amanda Plummer . . . . . . . . . . . . . . . . . . . . Wiley Foxx
Debra Winger . . . . . . . . . . . . . . . . . . . . . . Emmett
Mare Winningham . . . . . . . . . . . . . . . Brenda Carlucci

### Made in U.S.A. (1988)
Judy Baldwin. . . . . . . . . . . . . . . . . . . . . . . . . Dorie
Cindi Dietrich . . . . . . . . . . . . . . . . . . . . . . . . . . .n.a.
Adrian Pasdar . . . . . . . . . . . . . . . . . . . . . . . . . . . .Dar
• 0:12—Buns, while walking to sit down at the laun-
dromat when he washes all his clothes with Christopher Penn.
Christopher Penn . . . . . . . . . . . . . . . . . . . . . . . .Tuck
• 0:12—Buns, while walking to sit down at the laundromat when he washes all his clothes with Adrian
Pasdar.
Lori Singer. . . . . . . . . . . . . . . . . . . . . . . . . . . . Annie
• 0:26—Brief left breast and very brief lower frontal
nudity in the back of a convertible with Dar at night.
0:44—In white, braless tank top talking to a used car
salesman.

### Mademoiselle (1966; French/British)
Jeanne Moreau . . . . . . . . . . . . . . . . . . . . Mademoiselle
1:00—Almost breasts, while putting tape over her
nipples.
•• 1:17—Right breast, while opening her blouse in field
in front of her lover. Don't see her face.

### Madman (1982)
Troy Fish . . . . . . . . . . . . . . . . . . . . . . . . . . . . . . .T.P.
• 0:24—Brief buns, while getting into hot tub with
Betsy.
Gaylen Ross. . . . . . . . . . . . . . . . . . . . . . . . . . . Betsy
• 0:24—Very brief full frontal nudity, getting into hot
tub with T.P.

### Magic (1978)
Ann-Margret . . . . . . . . . . . . . . . . . . . . Peggy Ann Snow
••• 0:44—Right breast, lying on her side in bed talking
to Anthony Hopkins.

### The Magic Bubble (1992)
Colleen Camp. . . . . . . . . . . . . . . . . . . . . . . .Deborah
Dayle Haddon. . . . . . . . . . . . . . . . . . . . . . . . . Susan
Shelley Michelle . . . . . . . . . . . . . . . . . . . Body Double
Diane Salinger. . . . . . . . . . . . . . . . . . . . . . . . . Julia
• 0:11—Very, very brief breasts after whipping off
towel in front of her husband. Very, very brief buns,
walking away. Back side of right breast, while pulling
back curtain in front of her husband while he sits on
the toilet.
• 1:21—Very brief side of left breast while putting on
nightgown.

### Magnum Force (1973)
Margaret Avery . . . . . . . . . . . . . . . . . . . . . . .Prostitute
Clint Eastwood. . . . . . . . . . . . . . . . . . . . .Harry Callahan
Hal Holbrook . . . . . . . . . . . . . . . . . . . . .Lieutenant Briggs
Tim Matheson . . . . . . . . . . . . . . . . . . . . . . . . . . Sweet
Suzanne Somers. . . . . . . . . . . . . . Uncredited Pool Girl
•• 0:26—In blue swimsuit getting into a swimming
pool, brief breasts a couple of times before getting
shot, brief breasts floating dead.

### Mahler (1974; British)
Georgina Hale . . . . . . . . . . . . . . . . . . . . . . Alma Mahler
•• 1:00—Breasts during musical number.

### Maiden Quest (1972)
*a.k.a. The Long Swift Sword of Siegfried*
Lance Boyle . . . . . . . . . . . . . . . . . . . . . . . . . Siegfried
•• 0:24—Buns, during orgy scene.
Sybil Danning . . . . . . . . . . . . . . . . . . . . . . .Kriemhild
• 0:02—Breasts in bath, surrounded by topless blonde
servants.
• 0:04—Breasts in the bath again.
••• 0:10—Nude in tub surrounded by breasts servant
girls.
••• 0:12—Breasts on bed, getting rubbed with oint-
ment by the servant girls.
•• 0:35—Breasts while in bed with Siegfried.
• 1:00—Breasts in bed with Siegfried.
••• 1:19—Breasts in bed with Siegfried.

### Major League (1989)
Tom Berenger . . . . . . . . . . . . . . . . . . . . . .Jake Taylor
Corbin Bernsen . . . . . . . . . . . . . . . . . . . . Roger Dorn
• 0:58—Brief buns, while running in locker room to
cover himself with a towel when Rachel comes in to
talk to the team.
Margaret Whitton . . . . . . . . . . . . . . . . . .Rachel Phelps

### Malibu Beach (1978)
Bill Adler. . . . . . . . . . . . . . . . . . . . . . . . . . . . . . n.a.
James Daughton . . . . . . . . . . . . . . . . . . . . . . . Bobby
• 0:32—Buns, while running into the ocean with his
friends.
Kim Lankford . . . . . . . . . . . . . . . . . . . . . . . . . Dina
0:32—Buns, running into the ocean.
• 0:34—Brief right breast getting out of the ocean.
• 1:16—Right breast on beach at night with boyfriend.
• 1:19—Brief breasts at top of the stairs.
•• 1:20—Brief breasts when her parent's come home.
• 1:21—Breasts in bed with her boyfriend.
Michael Luther. . . . . . . . . . . . . . . . . . . . . . . . .Paul
• 0:32—Buns, while running into the ocean with his
friends.
Susan Player Jarreau . . . . . . . . . . . . . . . . . . . . . . .Sally
• 0:28—Side view of left breast with boyfriend at
night on the beach. Long shot.
0:32—Buns, running into the ocean with her two
male friends.
0:33—Brief side view of left breast in water. Long
shot.

- 0:34—Brief breasts while in the ocean, then breasts while getting dressed by the fire.

Tara Strohmeier . . . . . . . . . . . . . . . . . . . . . . Glorianna
- 0:08—Breasts kissing her boyfriend at the beach when someone steals her towel.

### *The Malibu Bikini Shop* (1985)
Debra Blee . . . . . . . . . . . . . . . . . . . . . . . . . . . Jane
Bruce Greenwood . . . . . . . . . . . . . . . . . . . . . . Todd
Barbra Horan. . . . . . . . . . . . . . . . . . . . . . . . Ronnie
- 0:33—In wet tank top during Alan's fantasy.
- 1:13—Most of side of left breast, while kissing Alan in the spa.

Rita Jenrette . . . . . . . . . . . . . . . . . . . . . . . Aunt Ida
Jeana Loring . . . . . . . . . . . . . . . . . . . . Margie Hill
- 0:43—Breasts, dancing on stage during bikini contest (Contestant #4).

Gretchen Palmer . . . . . . . . . . . . . . . . . . . . . Woman
Bobbi Pavis . . . . . . . . . . . . . . . . . . . . . Stunning Girl
- 0:19—Breasts trying on bikini behind two-way glass.

Allene Simmons . . . . . . . . . . . . . . . . . . . Milinda Riley

### *Malibu Express* (1984)
Brett Clark. . . . . . . . . . . . . . . . . . . . . . . . . . . Shane
Sybil Danning . . . . . . . . . . . . . . . . . . . Countess Luciana
- 0:13—Brief breasts making love in bed with Cody.

Barbara Edwards . . . . . . . . . . . . . . . . . . . . . . . . May
- 0:10—Breasts taking a shower with Kimberly McArthur on the boat.
- 1:05—Breasts serving Cody coffee while he talks on the telephone.

Robyn Hilton. . . . . . . . . . . . . . . . . . . . Maid Marian
Darby Hinton . . . . . . . . . . . . . . . . . . . Cody Abilene
- 0:08—Brief buns, while taking a shower on his boat.

Kimberly McArthur . . . . . . . . . . . . . . . . . . . . Faye
- 0:10—Breasts taking a shower on the boat with Barbara Edwards.

Shanna McCullough . . . . . . . . . Uncredited Massage Girl
- 0:33—Breasts, several times while giving a guy a rub down.

Art Metrano . . . . . . . . . . . . . . . . . . . . . . . Matthew
Lorraine Michaels . . . . . . . . . . . . . . . . Liza Chamberlin
- 0:23—Breasts in the shower making love with Shane, while getting photographed by a camera.

Shelly Taylor Morgan . . . . . . . . . . . Anita Chamberlain
- 0:22—Breasts doing exercises on the floor.
- 0:26—Breasts making love with Shane in bed while being video taped. Then right breast while standing by door.

Suzanne M. Regard. . . . . . . . . . . . . . . . . . Sexy Sally
- 0:50—Brief breasts, while talking on the telephone.
- 1:06—Breasts, while talking on the telephone.

Lori Sutton . . . . . . . . . . . . . . . . . . . . Beverly McAfee
- 0:54—Breasts and buns, making love in bed with Cody.

Lynda Wiesmeier. . . . . . . . . . . . . . . . . June Khnockers
- 0:04—Breasts in locker room taking jumpsuit off.
- 1:16—Breasts leaning out of racing car window while a helicopter chases her and Cody.

### *Malibu Hot Summer* (1981)
*a.k.a. Sizzle Beach*
(*Sizzle Beach* is the re-released version with Kevin Costner featured on the cover. It is missing all the nude scenes during the opening credits before 0:06.)
Terry Congie . . . . . . . . . . . . . . . . . . . . Janice Johnson
- 0:09—Buns in the shower. Hard to see through the door.
- 0:29—Breasts taking off her top and getting into bed with Steve, then making love.
  0:54—In blue bikini top talking on the phone.
- 1:09—Side view of left breast kissing Gary during the party.
- 1:11—Breasts making love with Gary the next morning after the party.

Kevin Costner. . . . . . . . . . . . . . . . . . . . . . John Logan
Roselyn Royce . . . . . . . . . . . . . . . . . . . . Cheryl Rielly
- 0:15—On exercise bike, then breasts getting into bed.
- 0:16—Breasts sitting up in bed, buns going to closet to get dressed to go jogging.
  0:26—In pink two piece swimsuit running to answer the phone.
- 0:52—Breasts on boat with Brent.

Sylvia Wright . . . . . . . . . . . . . . . . . . . Actress at Party
- 0:01—Nude, standing up during opening credits.
- 1:07—Breasts fixing her hair in front of mirror, then full frontal nudity talking to Howard.
- 1:09—Breasts on top of Howard.

### *Malice* (1993)
Alec Baldwin . . . . . . . . . . . . . . . . . . . . . . . . . . Jed
- 0:24—Brief buns, while making love in bed with Tanya.

Debrah Farentino. . . . . . . . . . . . . . . . . . . . . Tanya
- 0:25—Very brief upper half of right breast, while in bed with Alec Baldwin.
- 0:26—Brief buns and breasts, while running into the bathroom. Medium long shot.

Peter Gallagher . . . . . . . . . . . . . . . . . . . Dennis Riley
Nicole Kidman . . . . . . . . . . . . . . . . . . . . . . . . Tracy
- 0:13—Very brief left breast then buns, when leaning over Bill Pullman in bed.

Gwyneth Paltrow . . . . . . . . . . . . . . . . . . . Paula Bell
Brenda Strong . . . . . . . . . . . . . . . . . . . . . . Claudia

### *Malicious* (1974; Italian)
Laura Antonelli. . . . . . . . . . . . . . . . . . . . . . Angela
- 1:14—Breasts after undressing while two boys watch from above.
- 1:27—Breasts, undressing under flashlight. Hard to see because the light is moving around a lot.
- 1:29—Breasts and buns running around the house.

### *The Mambo Kings* (1992)
Antonio Banderas. . . . . . . . . . . . . . . . . Nestor Castillo
- 0:48—Buns, while in bed on top of Maruschka Detmers.
- 1:10—Upper half of buns, sitting on side of bed, while putting his pants on.

Stephanie Blake. . . . . . . . . . . . . . . . . . . . . . Stripper
Maruschka Detmers . . . . . . . . . . . . . . Dolores Fuentes
•• 0:47—Breasts several times, making love in bed with Antonio Banderas.
Valerie McIntosh . . . . . . . . . . . . . . . . . . . . . .Tracy Blair
•• 1:10—Breasts, getting her bathing suit after Armand Assante discovers her with Antonio Banderas.
Yul Vazquez. . . . . . . . . . . . . . . . . . . . . . . . . . .Flaco

### A Man Called Horse (1970)

Richard Harris . . . . . . . . . . . . . . . . . . . . John Morgan
• 0:07—Brief buns, while taking a bath in the river.
•• 0:10—Very, very brief partial frontal nudity, while falling into the water. Buns, getting dragged around by ropes on his neck.
•• 0:14—Buns, while trying to run away from the Indians. Long shot.
••• 0:15—Buns and brief frontal nudity while running around. More buns while kneeling on the ground.
Corinna Tsopei . . . . . . . . . . . . . . . . . . . . Running Deer
• 1:03—Long shot of buns, before entering sweat house. Side view of left breast kneeling inside the sweat house.
1:04—Partial left breast (shadows get in the way).
1:15—Very brief breasts when startled by Richard Harris' screaming.
• 1:22—Left nipple while in tepee with Harris.
• 1:23—Side of left breast and right breast in tepee with Harris.

### A Man for Sale (1982)

Ajita Wilson. . . . . . . . . . . . . . . . . . . . . . Dancer/Model
• 0:02—Breasts several times posing for photographer with another model.
• 0:26—Breasts and buns, dancing in an erotic ballet show.

### A Man in Love (1987)

Jamie Lee Curtis . . . . . . . . . . . . . . . . . . . . Susan Elliot
Greta Scacchi . . . . . . . . . . . . . . . . . . . . . . Jane Steiner
••• 0:31—Breasts with Peter Coyote.
•• 1:04—Buns and left breast in bed with Coyote.
1:10—Brief side view breasts, putting black dress on.
• 1:24—Brief breasts in bed.

### The Man in the Moon (1991)

Sam Waterston . . . . . . . . . . . . . . . . . . . Matthew Trant
Reese Witherspoon . . . . . . . . . . . . . . . . . . . Dani Trant
• 0:09—Brief buns, running to go skinny dipping. Don't see her face. Long shot of back side of left breast while running on pier.
0:12—Brief buns, climbing up ladder. Tree branches get in the way. Don't see her face again.

### Man of Flowers (1984; Australian)

Alyson Best . . . . . . . . . . . . . . . . . . . . . . . . . . . . .Lisa
•• 0:04—Undressing out of clothes, in bra, panties and stockings in front of Charles, then full frontal nudity, then getting dressed.
•• 0:13—Full frontal nudity after taking off robe and sitting on chair for art class.

• 0:36—Brief breasts while in bed with a guy.
Norman Kaye. . . . . . . . . . . . . . . . . . . Charles Bremer
••• 0:17—Nude, taking off robe in bathroom and talking on the phone. Long scene.

### The Man Who Fell to Earth (1976; British)
(Uncensored version reviewed.)

David Bowie. . . . . . . . . . . . . . Thomas Jerome Newton
0:58—Brief buns, while turning over in bed with Candy Clark.
1:56—Frontal nudity and brief buns in bed with Clark. Don't see his face.
Bernie Casey . . . . . . . . . . . . . . . . . . . . . . . . Peters
• 1:42—Buns, while getting out of swimming pool during a black and white dream sequence.
Candy Clark. . . . . . . . . . . . . . . . . . . . . . . . .Mary-Lou
•• 0:42—Breasts in the bathtub, washing her hair and talking to David Bowie.
•• 0:55—Breasts sitting on bed and blowing out a candle.
••• 0:56—Breasts in bed with Bowie.
••• 1:26—Full frontal nudity climbing into bed with Bowie after he reveals his true alien self.
1:56—Nude with Bowie making love and shooting a gun.
Claudia Jennings . . . . . . . . . Uncredited Girl by the Pool
• 1:42—Breasts, standing by the pool and kissing Bernie Casey.
Rip Torn. . . . . . . . . . . . . . . . . . . . . . . . .Nathan Bryce

### The Man Who Loved Cat Dancing (1973)

Sarah Miles . . . . . . . . . . . . . . . . . . Catherine Crocker
•• 1:04—Back of left breast, then breasts, after taking off her blouse, then washing herself in water.
• 1:20—Brief left breast, while in bed with Burt Reynolds.
Burt Reynolds. . . . . . . . . . . . . . . . . . . . . Jay Grobart
Jack Warden. . . . . . . . . . . . . . . . . . . . . . . . . . Dawes

### The Man Who Loved Women (1983)

Julie Andrews . . . . . . . . . . . . . . . . . . . . . . .Marianna
Jennifer Ashley . . . . . . . . . . . . . . . . . . David's Mother
Kim Basinger . . . . . . . . . . . . . . . . . . . . .Louise "Lulu"
Jill Carroll . . . . . . . . . . . . . . . . . . . . Sue the Baby Sitter
Denise Crosby . . . . . . . . . . . . . . . . . . . . . . . . .Enid
Cindi Dietrich. . . . . . . . . . . . . . . . . . . . . . . . . Darla
Marilu Henner . . . . . . . . . . . . . . . . . Agnes Chapman
•• 0:18—Brief breasts in bed with Burt Reynolds.
Sharon Hughes . . . . . . . . . . . . . . . . . . . . . . . Nurse
Burt Reynolds. . . . . . . . . . . . . . . . . . . . .David Fowler
•• 1:25—Brief buns, while chiseling a statue after making love with Julie Andrews.
Tracy Vaccaro. . . . . . . . . . . . . . . . . . . . . . . . .Legs

### The Man Who Wasn't There (1983)

Vincent Baggetta . . . . . . . . . . . . . . . . . . . . . . . Riley
• 0:23—Buns, while lying on the floor after fighting with the other guys.
Deborah Dutch . . . . . . . . . . . . . . . . . . . Miss Dawson

Steve Guttenberg . . . . . . . . . . . . . . . . . . . . Sam Cooper
- ••• 0:54—Buns, while dropping his pants in office with three other men.
- • 1:46—Brief buns, while kissing Cindy during their wedding ceremony.

Lisa Langlois . . . . . . . . . . . . . . . . . . . . . . . .Cindy Worth
- •• 0:58—Nude running away from two policemen after turning visible.
- ••• 1:08—Breasts in white panties dancing in her apartment with an invisible Steve Guttenberg.
   1:47—Very, very brief upper half of left breast, while throwing bouquet at wedding.

Brinke Stevens. . . . . . . . . . . . . . . . . . . . . . . Nymphet
- • 0:45—Buns and brief breasts in the girls' shower, when she gets shampoo from an invisible Steve Guttenberg.

### The Man Who Would Be King (1975)
Sean Connery . . . . . . . . . . . . . . . . . . . . . Daniel Dravot
- ••• 1:27—Buns, while standing with arms up, getting robe put on.

### The Man with Two Brains (1983)
Randi Brooks . . . . . . . . . . . . . . . . . . . . . . . . . . . . . Fran
- •• 1:11—Brief breasts showing Steve Martin her breasts in front of the hotel. Buns, changing in the hotel room, then wearing black see-through negligee.

James Cromwell . . . . . . . . . . . . . . . . . . . . . . . Realtor
Kathleen Turner . . . . . . . . . . . . . . . . Dolores Benedict
- • 0:08—Right breast when Steve Martin is operating on her in the operating room.
   0:22—In sheer lingerie in bedroom with Steve Martin, teasing him and driving him crazy.
- • 0:36—Buns, in hotel room with a guy about to squeeze her buns when Steve Martin walks in.

### Mandingo (1975)
Susan George . . . . . . . . . . . . . . . . . . . . . . . . Blanche
- • 1:36—Brief breasts in bed with Ken Norton.

Perry King . . . . . . . . . . . . . . . . . . . . . . . . . Hammond
- •• 0:17—Frontal nudity walking to bed to make love with Dite.

Debbi Morgan . . . . . . . . . . . . . . . . . . . . . . . . . Dite
- • 0:17—Breasts in bed talking to Perry King.

Ken Norton. . . . . . . . . . . . . . . . . . . . . . . . . . Mede
- •• 1:36—Buns, while standing in bed with Susan George. More buns when making love with her.

Brenda Sykes. . . . . . . . . . . . . . . . . . . . . . . . . Ellen
- • 0:58—Breasts in bed with Perry King.

### The Manhunters (1980; French/Spanish/German)
Ursula Buchfellner . . . . . . . . . . . . . . . . .Laura Crawford
- • 0:06—Buns and side view breasts, walking around the house. Long shot.
- • 0:08—Breasts taking a bath.
- •• 0:10—Breasts in the bathtub.
- • 0:15—Full frontal nudity getting pulled out of the tub unconscious.
- • 0:19—Brief right breast when a kidnapper opens her blouse while she's tied up.

0:43—Very brief breasts running through the jungle.
- • 0:58—Brief lower frontal nudity, then breasts captured by the natives.
- •• 1:04—Breasts, unconscious, while tribe women undress her.
- •• 1:05—Full frontal nudity tied to a pole.
- •• 1:06—Nude, getting dragged into a hut.
- •• 1:10—Full frontal nudity taking a shower under waterfall with three tribe women.
- •• 1:12—Full frontal nudity, lying down while three tribe women put flowers on her.
- •• 1:23—Breasts and buns, getting carried away by the cannibal creature.
- • 1:26—Buns, being carried by the creature.
- •• 1:27—Breasts on the ground.
- •• 1:29—Buns and right breast, getting carried down the mountain side.
- ••• 1:30—Breasts on the boat with Peter.

Gisela Hahn . . . . . . . . . . . . . . . . . . . . . . . . . . . . . n.a.

### Maniac Cop 2 (1990)
Claudia Christian . . . . . . . . . . . . . . . . . . Susan Riley
Laurene Landon . . . . . . . . . . . . . . . . Teresa Mallory
Leo Rossi . . . . . . . . . . . . . . . . . . . . . . . . . . . Turkell
Paula Trickey . . . . . . . . . . . . . . . . . . . . . . . . . Cheryl
- •• 0:41—In orange two piece swimsuit on stage, then breasts and buns in G-string.

### Manifesto (1988)
Gabrielle Anwar . . . . . . . . . . . . . . . . . . . . . . . . . . .Tina
Simon Callow. . . . . . . . . . . . . . . . . . .Police Chief Hunt
Svetozar Cvetkovic. . . . . . . . . . . . . . . . . . . . . . .Rudi
Alfred Molina . . . . . . . . . . . . . . . . . . . . . . . . . Avanti
Rade Serbedzija . . . . . . . . . . . . . . . . . . . . . . . .Emile
- • 0:18—Buns, while under sheet and getting out of bed.

Camilla Søeberg. . . . . . . . . . . . . . . . . . . . . .Svetlana
- ••• 0:15—Nude, in bathtub and bedroom with Emile. Long scene.
- • 0:19—Brief left breast when Emile cuts off her hair.
- •• 1:04—Left breast, several times when Emile is in her room. More left breast cleaning up after Emile accidentally dies.
- • 1:15—Brief side of left breast, while making love with Eric Stoltz. Dark. Buns, getting out of bed.
- •• 1:16—Breasts and buns unrolling Emile in the rug.
- • 1:23—Breasts sitting in bed with puppies.

Eric Stoltz . . . . . . . . . . . . . . . . . . . . . . . .Christopher
- • 1:16—Buns, while helping Camilla unroll Emile in the rug.

### Manon of the Spring (1987; French)
Emmanuelle Béart . . . . . . . . . . . . . . . . . . . . . Manon
- • 0:11—Brief nude dancing around a spring playing a harmonica.

### Map of the Human Heart (1992; Australian/Canadian)
Patrick Bergin. . . . . . . . . . . . . . . . . . . . Walter Russell
Clotilde Courau . . . . . . . . . . . . . . . . . . . . . . . . Rainee

Jason Scott Lee . . . . . . . . . . . . . . . . . . . . . . . . . . Avik
 •• 1:14—Buns, while making love with Albertine on
   top of blimp.
Jeanne Moreau . . . . . . . . . . . . . . . . . . . . . Sister Banville
Anne Parillaud. . . . . . . . . . . . . . . . . . . . . . . .Albertine
 • 1:14—Partial left breast (close-up), then right breast,
   while making love with Avik on top of blimp.

### Marathon Man (1976)
Dustin Hoffman. . . . . . . . . . . . . . . . . . . . . . . . .Babe
 •• 1:09—Buns, getting out of the bathtub and putting
   some pajamas on while someone lurks outside the
   bathroom.
Marthe Keller . . . . . . . . . . . . . . . . . . . . . . . . . . .Elsa
 •• 0:42—Breasts lying on the floor after Dustin Hoff-
   man rolls off her.
Roy Scheider . . . . . . . . . . . . . . . . . . . . . . . . Doc Levy

### Mardi Gras for the Devil (1993)
Margaret Avery . . . . . . . . . . . . . . . . . . . . . . Miss Sadie
Lydie Denier . . . . . . . . . . . . . . . . . . . . . . . . . . Valerie
 ••• 0:50—Breasts, while making love in bed with Robert
   Davi.
Lesley-Anne Down . . . . . . . . . . . . . . . . . . . . .Christine
Trisha Lane . . . . . . . . . . . . . . . . . . . . . . . . . . . Jackie
 •• 0:03—Breasts, while in panties, while simulating sex
   in front of Michael Ironside.

### Maria's Lovers (1985)
Keith Carradine . . . . . . . . . . . . . . . . . . . Clarence Butts
Nastassja Kinski . . . . . . . . . . . . . . . . . . . . .Maria Bosic
   0:59—In a black bra.
 • 1:12—Brief right breast, while looking at herself in
   the mirror.
Anna Levine Thomson. . . . . . . . . . . . . . . . . . . . Kathy
Anita Morris . . . . . . . . . . . . . . . . . . . . . . . Mrs. Wynic
Vincent Spano. . . . . . . . . . . . . . . . . . . . . . . Al Griselli

### Marilyn Chambers' Bedtime Stories (1993)
Marilyn Chambers . . . . . . . . . . . . . . . . Marilyn Chambers
 •• 0:02—Breasts, after taking off towel, then opening
   and adjusting robe.
 • 0:04—Brief breasts in bedroom, taking off robe.
 • 1:02—Brief right breast on TV.
 •• 1:14—Breasts while making love with Bob on bed.
 •• 1:15—Breasts while making love with Bob on bed.
Camille Donatacci . . . . . . . . . . . . . . . . . . . . .Angelique
 ••• 0:34—Breasts and buns while changing lingerie in
   bedroom.
 ••• 0:42—Breasts, while making love with Chris on sofa.
 ••• 0:55—In pink bra and panties then right breast and
   buns in Chris' bedroom.
Isabelle Fortea . . . . . . . . . . . . . . . . . . . . . . . . Tatiana
 ••• 0:18—Breasts and buns in red G-string, after taking
   off dress with Bart's help.
 ••• 0:25—Breasts and buns with Bart, then in shower.
   Squished breasts against the glass.
 • 0:33—Breasts in open solid color robe in bathroom.
 • 1:17—Breasts in out take with Bart.
Joan Gerardi . . . . . . . . . . . . . . . . . . . . . . . . . . Jane

Theresa Lynn . . . . . . . . . . . . . . . . . . . . . . . . . Melissa
 •• 0:07—Breasts and buns in G-string, while changing
   lingerie in bedroom in front of mirror.
 •• 0:22—Breasts, while on sofa, practicing her acting
   with Bart.
 •• 0:29—Breasts, while making love with Bart on sofa.
 •• 0:33—Breasts, while in bathroom with blue towel.
 •• 1:17—Breasts, while on couch with Bart in out take.
John Richardson . . . . . . . . . . . . . . . . . . . . . . . . Chris
 • 0:56—Brief buns, while making love in bed on top
   of Angelique.
Donna Salvatore. . . . . . . . . . . . . . . . . . . . . . . Letitia
 • 0:01—Brief breasts in shower through hole in wall
   during opening credits.
 •• 0:11—Breasts, getting out of shower when Bart
   peeks through hole in wall.
 •• 0:32—Buns in T-back and breasts, while dancing
   with Bart.
 • 0:33—Breasts in open polka dot robe.
 • 1:17—Brief breasts in shower out take.

### The Marilyn Diaries (1990)
John Altamura . . . . . . . . . . . . . . . . . . . . . . . . .Frankie
 • 0:13—Buns, while in hall after Marilyn Chambers
   takes his sheet away.
Tara Buckman . . . . . . . . . . . . . . . . . . . . . . . . . .Jane
 •• 0:53—Breasts and buns, taking off robe and getting
   into bathtub. Left breast, in tub reading diary.
 •• 0:54—Breasts in and getting out of tub. Very brief
   lower frontal nudity.
 •• 1:27—Breasts in bathtub talking with John.
Marilyn Chambers . . . . . . . . . . . . . . . . . . . . . Marilyn
 •• 0:02—Breasts in bathroom with a guy during party.
 •• 0:26—In bra and panties in Istvan's studio, then
   breasts.
 ••• 0:27—Breasts in panties when Istvan opens her
   blouse.
 •• 0:45—Breasts in trench coat, opening it up to give
   the Iranian secret documents.
 • 0:47—Breasts when the Rebel Leader opens her
   trench coat.
 •• 0:48—Breasts with Colonel South.
 •• 0:57—Breasts opening her top for Hollywood producer.
 • 1:10—In swimsuit, then breasts with Roger.
 ••• 1:13—In black lingerie, then breasts making love
   with Chet.
 • 1:19—Left breast, in flashback with Roger.
 •• 1:25—In slip, then right breast, then breasts with
   Chet.

### Marked for Death (1990)
Tracey Burch . . . . . . . . . . . . . . . . . . . . . . .Sexy Girl #1
 • 0:39—Brief breasts on bed with Jimmy when Steven
   Seagal bursts into the room. (She's the blonde.)
Leslie Danon . . . . . . . . . . . . . . . . . . . . . . . . .Girl #1
Elizabeth Gracen . . . . . . . . . . . . . . . . . . . . . . Melissa
   0:45—Very brief part of right breast in gaping
   blouse, while crawling on the floor.
Joanna Pacula. . . . . . . . . . . . . . . . . . . . . . . . . Leslie

Elena Sahagun . . . . . . . . . . . . . . . . . . . . . . Carmen
  • 0:06—Breasts in room, shooting Steven Seagal's
    partner.
Teri Weigel . . . . . . . . . . . . . . . . . . . . . . Sexy Girl #2
  • 0:39—Brief breasts on bed with Jimmy when Steven
    Seagal bursts into the room. (She's the brunette.)

### The Marriage of Maria Braun (1979; German)
Peter Berling . . . . . . . . . . . . . . . . . . . . . . . . Bronski
George Byrd . . . . . . . . . . . . . . . . . . . . . . . . . . . . Bill
  •• 0:37—Very brief frontal nudity and buns in bedroom
    with Maria.
  ••• 0:39—Nude, while fighting with Hermann. Long
    scene.
Klaus Löwitsch. . . . . . . . . . . . . . . . . . Hermann Braun
Hanna Schygulla . . . . . . . . . . . . . . . . . . . Maria Braun
  • 0:22—Brief upper half of right breast, when peeking
    from behind divider in doctor's office.
  • 0:33—Buns, while lying in bed with her lover.
  • 0:34—Brief buns and left breast, while standing up
    in doctor's office. Subtitles get in the way.
  •• 1:15—Buns, while dropping sheet in room with her
    boss.
    1:48—In lingerie and stockings with her husband.
Volker Spengler. . . . . . . . . . . . . . . . . . . . . Conductor

### Married People, Single Sex (1993)
Chase Masterson. . . . . . . . . . . . . . . . . . . . . . . . Beth
  • 0:30—Buns in lingerie, while trying on clothes with
    her girlfriends.
Shelley Michelle . . . . . . . . . . . . . . . . . . . . . . . Carol
  ••• 0:54—Breasts and buns in G-string, garter belt and
    stockings while dancing on stage.
  ••• 1:05—Breasts and buns in black G-string, after
    opening her bathrobe and giving Will a private
    dance in the kitchen.
Josef Pilato . . . . . . . . . . . . . . . . . . . . . . . . . . Artie
  • 1:18—Partial buns, while kneeling on bed while
    making love with Meg.
Darla Slavens. . . . . . . . . . . . . . . . . . . . . . . . . . Fran
  •• 0:03—In white bra and buns in panties while un-
    dressing in bedroom. Full frontal nudity, walking to
    closet.
  •• 0:10—In white bra, then breasts while undressing in
    bedroom.
  ••• 0:53—Left breast in mirror, while trying out vibrator.

### Married to the Mob (1988)
Alec Baldwin . . . . . . . . . . . . . . . . . . . . Frank De Marco
Matthew Modine . . . . . . . . . . . . . . . . . . Mike Downey
Michelle Pfeiffer . . . . . . . . . . . . . . . . Angela de Marco
Nancy Travis . . . . . . . . . . . . . . . . . . . . . Karen Lutnig
  • 0:15—Buns and brief side view of right breast, with
    Tony in hotel room. Brief breasts in the bathtub.
Tracey Walter . . . . . . . . . . . . . . . . . Mr. Chicken Lickin'
Marlene Willoughby . . . . . . . . . . . . . . . Mrs. Fat Man

### The Married Woman (1964; French)
Macha Meril . . . . . . . . . . . . . . . . . . . . . . . . . . . . n.a.
  • 0:07—Brief glimpses of breasts while walking
    around inside house.

  • 0:08—Brief side of left breast, when climbing
    through window from outside.

### Martial Law II: Undercover (1992)
Bridget Carney. . . . . . . . . . . . . . . . . . . . . Flash Dancer
Deborah Driggs . . . . . . . . . . . . . . . . . . . . . . . . Tiffany
  • 0:59—Side of left breast, while taking off lingerie
    and getting into bed with Billy Drago.
  • 1:00—Breasts, rolling off Drago after he passes out.
Denice Duff . . . . . . . . . . . . . . . . . . . . . . Nancy Borelli
Sherrie Rose . . . . . . . . . . . . . . . . . . . . . . . . . . . . Bree
Kimber Sissons . . . . . . . . . . . . . . . . . . . . . . . Celeste

### Mary, Mary, Bloody Mary (1975)
Cristina Ferrare. . . . . . . . . . . . . . . . . . . . . . . . . Mary
  •• 0:07—Brief breasts making love with some guy on
    the couch just before she kills him.
  ••• 0:41—Breasts when Greta helps pull down Ferrare's
    top to take a bath.
    1:12—Bun and brief silhouette of left breast getting
    out of bed and getting dressed.
Helena Rojo . . . . . . . . . . . . . . . . . . . . . . . . . . Greta
  • 0:42—Buns and brief breasts getting into bathtub
    with Cristina Ferrare.

### Mascara (1987; French/Belgian)
Derek De Lint. . . . . . . . . . . . . . . . . . . . . Chris Brine
Charlotte Rampling . . . . . . . . . . . . . . . . . Gaby Hart
  • 1:03—Brief breasts putting on sweater when Micha-
    el Sarrazin watches through binoculars.
  • 1:18—Right breast, while making love with Chris.
Alexandra Vandernoot . . . . . . . . . . . . . . . . . . Euridice

### Masquerade (1988)
Kim Cattrall . . . . . . . . . . . . . Mrs. Brooke Morrison
  ••• 0:04—Breasts in bed with Rob Lowe.
    0:47—In white teddy after having sex with Lowe.
Dana Delany . . . . . . . . . . . . . . . . . . . . Anne Briscoe
Rob Lowe. . . . . . . . . . . . . . . . . . . . . . . . Tim Whalen
  ••• 0:04—Buns, while getting up from bed with Kim
    Cattrall.
  ••• 0:30—Buns, while making love with Meg Tilly in
    bed.
Meg Tilly . . . . . . . . . . . . . . . . . . . . . Olivia Lawrence
    0:55—In pink nightgown in bedroom.

### Massacre at Central High (1976)
Kimberly Beck . . . . . . . . . . . . . . . . . . . . . . . Theresa
  • 0:32—Nude romping in the ocean with David. Long
    shot, dark, hard to see anything.
  •• 0:42—Breasts on the beach making love with An-
    drew Stevens after a hang glider crash.
Steve Bond. . . . . . . . . . . . . . . . . . . . . . . . . . Craig
Robert Carradine . . . . . . . . . . . . . . . . . . . . . . Spoony
Derrel Maury . . . . . . . . . . . . . . . . . . . . . . . . . . David
  • 0:32—Buns, while romping around in the ocean
    with Kimberly Beck. Dark, long shot. Hard to see
    anything.
Lani O'Grady . . . . . . . . . . . . . . . . . . . . . . . . . . Jane
  ••• 1:09—Breasts walking out of a tent and getting back
    into it with Rainbeaux Smith and Robert Carradine.

Cheryl Smith. . . . . . . . . . . . . . . . . . . . . . . . . . . .Mary
- • 0:27—Brief breasts in a classroom getting attacked by some guys.
- ••• 1:09—Nude walking around on a mountain side with Robert Carradine and Lani O'Grady.

Andrew Stevens . . . . . . . . . . . . . . . . . . . . . . . . .Mark

## Master of Dragonard Hill (1987)

Patrick Dewee. . . . . . . . . . . . . . . . . . . . . . . . . .Calabar
- •• 0:14—Buns, while getting out of bed after being discovered in bed with Claudia Udy by her father.

Oliver Reed . . . . . . . . . . . . . . . . . . . . . . .Captain Shanks
Kimber Sissons . . . . . . . . . . . . . . . . . . . . . . . .Jane Abdee
- •• 0:08—Breasts making love in bed with Richard.

Claudia Udy . . . . . . . . . . . . . . . . . . . . . . . . . . Arabella
- ••• 0:11—Nude, undressing to seduce Calabar. More breasts and buns while kissing him.
- •• 0:14—Silhouette of breasts while making love with Calabar, then breasts.
- • 0:58—Brief buns and side of right breast during flash back. Brief right breast when she gets out of bed.

Patrick Warburton . . . . . . . . . . . . . . . . Richard Abdee
0:07—Very brief buns in mirror. Hard to see.

## Masterblaster (1986)

Tracey E. Hutchinson. . . . . . . . . . . . . . . . . . . . . .Lisa
- ••• 0:57—Breasts taking a shower (wearing panties).

Kari Whitman . . . . . . . . . . . . . . . . . . . . . . . . . .Jennifer

## Mata Hari (1985)

Christopher Cazenove. . . . . . .Captain Karl Von Byerling
Derek De Lint . . . . . . . . . . . . . . . .Handsome Traveler
Sylvia Kristel . . . . . . . . . . . . . . . . . . . . . . . . Mata Hari
- ••• 0:11—Breasts making love with a guy on a train.
- •• 0:31—Breasts standing by window after making love with the soldier.
- • 0:35—Breasts making love in empty house by the fireplace.
- •• 0:52—Breasts masturbating in bed wearing black stockings.
- • 1:02—Breasts during sword fight with another topless woman.
- • 1:03—Breasts in bed smoking opium and making love with two women.

Oliver Tobias . . . . . . . . . . . . . . . . . . . . . . . . .Ladoux

## Matador (1986; Spanish)

Antonio Banderas . . . . . . . . . . . . . . . . . . . . . . Angel
Nacho Martinez . . . . . . . . . . . . . . . . . . . .Diego Montes
- ••• 0:29—Buns, while making love with Eva in bed.

Carmen Maura . . . . . . . . . . . . . . . . . . . . . . . . . . Julie
Assumpta Serna . . . . . . . . . . . . . . . . . . Maria Cardinal
- • 0:03—Breasts taking off wrap and making love with a guy just before she kills him.
- ••• 1:38—Breasts on floor with Diego. Long shot, hard to see. Breasts in front of the fire.
- • 1:41—Brief breasts making love with Diego.
- • 1:43—Breasts lying on floor dead.

## Mausoleum (1983)

Bobbie Bresee . . . . . . . . . . . . . . . . . . . . . Susan Farrell
- ••• 0:25—Breasts and buns wrapping a towel around herself in her bedroom.
- •• 0:26—Breasts on the balcony showing herself to the gardener.
- • 0:29—Breasts in the garage with the gardener. Brief, dark, hard to see.
- • 0:32—Brief left breast, while kissing Marjoe Gortner.
- • 1:10—Breasts in the bathtub talking to Gortner. Long shot.

Laura Hippe . . . . . . . . . . . . . . . . . . . . . . . . . Aunt Cora

## Maximum Force (1992)

Sam Jones . . . . . . . . . . . . . . . . . . . . . . .Michael Crews
Sherrie Rose . . . . . . . . . . . . . . . . . . . . . . Cody Randal
- • 0:59—Breasts, while in bed with Sam Jones.

Andrew Stevens . . . . . . . . . . . . . . . . . . . . . . . . . Tommy

## Maya (1965)

Jay North . . . . . . . . . . . . . . . . . . . . . . . . Terry Bowen
- ••• 0:33—Buns, drying himself off and putting on loincloth after getting wet from being in river.

## Me & Him (1988; West German)

Robert LaSardo. . . . . . . . . . . . . . . . . . . . . . . . . Tony
Carey Lowell . . . . . . . . . . . . . . . . . . . . . Janet Anderson
- • 0:37—Very brief upper half of right breast sticking out of nightgown after turning over in bed with Griffin Dunne.

## Mean Dog Blues (1978)

Christina Hart. . . . . . . . . . . . . . . . . . . . Gloria Kinsman
- • 1:24—Brief breasts, in house with Gregg Henry.

Gregg Henry . . . . . . . . . . . . . . . . . . . . . . Paul Ramsey
Kay Lenz . . . . . . . . . . . . . . . . . . . . . . . Linda Ramsey
Tina Louise. . . . . . . . . . . . . . . . . . . . . . .Donna Lacey
- • 1:16—Very brief side view of right breast, while getting up off massage table. Don't see her face very well.

## The Mean Season (1985)

Mariel Hemingway. . . . . . . . . . . . . . .Christine Connelly
- •• 0:15—Breasts taking a shower.

Kurt Russell . . . . . . . . . . . . . . . . . . Malcolm Anderson

## Mean Streets (1973)

Jeannie Bell . . . . . . . . . . . . . . . . . . . . . . . . . . . .Diane
- • 0:07—Breasts dancing on stage with pasties on.
- • 1:00—Breasts backstage wearing pasties.

David Carradine. . . . . . . . . . . . . . . . . . . . . . . . Drunk
Robert Carradine . . . . . . . . . . . . . . . The Young Assassin
Robert De Niro. . . . . . . . . . . . . . . . . . . . . . Johnny Boy
Harvey Keitel . . . . . . . . . . . . . . . . . . . . . . . . .Charlie

## Meatballs 4 (1992)

Neriah Davis. . . . . . . . . . . . . . . . . . . . . . . . . . .Neriah
- • 0:05—Very brief buns, while getting her red towel pulled up by another girl while walking to the showers.

Kristie Ducati. . . . . . . . . . . . . . . . . . . . . . . . . . . .Kristi
- 0:05—Very, very brief buns, getting her light blue robe pulled up by Neriah while walking to the showers. Long shot.
- 0:06—Brief side of left breast, while taking a shower with three other girls. (She's on the far right in the first shot.)
- •• 0:37—Breasts, four times, while playing strip charades.
- 0:54—Left breast, while riding behind a guy on a four wheel motorcycle. (She's the one closest to the camera.)

Corey Feldman . . . . . . . . . . . . . . . . . . . . . .Ricky Wade
Paige French . . . . . . . . . . . . . . . . . . . . . . Jennifer Lipton
- •• 0:27—Breasts outside with Wes.
- 0:29—Brief breasts getting up when splashed with water.

Lauren Hays . . . . . . . . . . . . . . . . . . . . . . . . . . . Lauren
- 0:05—Brief breasts (she's on the far right), while taking off her black top in cabin with Miche and Hillary.

Monique Noel. . . . . . . . . . . . . . . . . . . . . . . . .Lovelie #1
Cristy Thom . . . . . . . . . . . . . . . . . . . . . . . . . . . .Hillary
- ••• 0:38—Breasts, taking off her blouse and washing herself off.

## Meatballs III (1987)

Caroline Arnold. . . . . . . . . . . . . . . Ida (Girl in VW Bug)
Patrick Dempsey . . . . . . . . . . . . . . . . . . . . . . . . . .Rudy
- •• 0:19—Buns, while in the shower when first being visited by Sally Kellerman.

Sally Kellerman . . . . . . . . . . . . . . . . . . . . Roxy Du Jour
Isabelle Mejias. . . . . . . . . . . . . . . . . . . . . . . . . Wendy
Shannon Tweed . . . . . . . . . . . . . . . The Love Goddess

## Mediterraneo (1991; Italian)

Vana Barba . . . . . . . . . . . . . . . . . . . . . . . . . .Vassilissa
- •• 1:03—Side of left breast, while in bed with Antonio.

Memo Dini . . . . . . . . . . . . . . . . . . . . . . Libero Munaron
- 0:52—Buns, jumping into the water with his brother.
- 1:27—Buns, jumping into the water with his brother during end credits.

Irene Grazioli. . . . . . . . . . . . . . . . . . . . . . . . Pastorella
- ••• 0:36—Breasts with the Munaron brothers.
- 0:52—Brief breasts, swimming in water.

Vasco Mirandola . . . . . . . . . . . . . . . . . . .Felice Munaron
- 0:52—Buns, jumping into the water with his brother.
- 1:27—Buns, jumping into the water with his brother during end credits.

## Medium Cool (1969)

Peter Boyle . . . . . . . . . . . . . . . . . . . Gun Clinic Manager
Robert Forster . . . . . . . . . . . . . . . . . . . . . . . . . . . .John
- •• 0:36—Nude, running around the house frolicking with Ruth.

Mariana Hill. . . . . . . . . . . . . . . . . . . . . . . . . . . . .Ruth
- 0:18—Close-up of breast in bed with John.
- •• 0:36—Nude, running around the house frolicking with John.

## Meet the Applegates (1989)

Ed Begley, Jr. . . . . . . . . . . . . . . . . . . . . . Dick Applegate
- 0:46—Buns, while running around nuclear power plant after his pile of clothes are taken away by the janitor.

Dabney Coleman . . . . . . . . . . . . . . . . . . . . . . Aunt Bea
Savannah Smith Bouchér . . . . . . . . . . . . . . . . . . Dottie

## Melanie (1982)

Don Johnson . . . . . . . . . . . . . . . . . . . . . . . . . . .Carl
Glynnis O'Connor . . . . . . . . . . . . . . . . . . . . . .Melanie
- 0:08—Very brief right breast, while turning over in bed next to Don Johnson.
- •• 0:09—Breasts, while sitting up and putting on a T-shirt, then getting out of bed.

Paul Sorvino. . . . . . . . . . . . . . . . . . . . . . . Walter Greer

## Melody in Love (1978)

Wolf Goldan. . . . . . . . . . . . . . . . . . . . . . . . . . .Octavio
- 1:14—Buns, while making love in bed with Rachel and Angela.

Scarlett Gunden. . . . . . . . . . . . . . . . . . . . . . . .Angela
- ••• 0:17—Full frontal nudity taking off dress and dancing in front of statue.
- ••• 0:50—Nude with a guy on a boat.
- •• 0:53—Breasts on another boat with Octavio.
- •• 0:59—Buns and breasts in bed talking to Rachel.
- •• 1:12—Full frontal nudity getting a tan on boat with Rachel.
- 1:14—Breasts making love in bed with Rachel and Octavio.

Sascha Hehn . . . . . . . . . . . . . . . . . . . . . . . . . Alain
- •• 1:08—Buns while outside with Melody. Very brief erect penis under covers.
- 1:16—Buns, twice while making love with Melody near an erupting volcano.

## Melvin and Howard (1980)

Martine Beswicke . . . . . . . . . . . . . . . Real Estate Woman
Dabney Coleman . . . . . . . . . . . . . . . . Judge Keith Hayes
Denise Galik . . . . . . . . . . . . . . . . . . . . . . . . . . . Lucy
Pamela Reed . . . . . . . . . . . . . . . . . . . . Bonnie Dummar
Mary Steenburgen . . . . . . . . . . . . . . . . . . Lynda Dummar
- •• 0:31—Breasts and buns, ripping off barmaid outfit and walking out the door.

## Men of Respect (1990)

Peter Boyle. . . . . . . . . . . . . . . . . . . . . . . . . . . . .Duffy
John Turturro . . . . . . . . . . . . . . . . . . . Mike Battaglia
- 0:21—Side view of buns, lying in bed with Ruthie.
- 0:25—Brief upper half of buns, putting on robe and leaving room.
- •• 0:45—Buns, while washing blood off himself in bathroom with Ruthie's help.

## The Men's Club (1986)

Penny Baker. . . . . . . . . . . . . . . . . . . . . . . . . . . . .Lake
- •• 1:13—Breasts while lying in bed with Treat Williams.

David Dukes. . . . . . . . . . . . . . . . . . . . . . . . . . . Phillip

Ann Dusenberry . . . . . . . . . . . . . . . . . . . . . . . . . . Page
- •• 1:04—Breasts while lying in bed after making love with Roy Scheider.

Gina Gallego . . . . . . . . . . . . . . . . . . . . . . . . . . Felicia

Marilyn Jones . . . . . . . . . . . . . . . . . . . . . . . . Allison
- •• 1:21—Breasts, while in bedroom talking to Harvey Keitel, then putting on dress.

Harvey Keitel . . . . . . . . . . . . . . . . . . . . . . Solly Berliner
- • 1:22—Buns, while getting up off the bed to talk to Allison.

Jennifer Jason Leigh . . . . . . . . . . . . . . . . . . . . . Teensy

Cindy Pickett . . . . . . . . . . . . . . . . . . . . . . . . . . Hannah

Roy Scheider . . . . . . . . . . . . . . . . . . . . . . . Cavanaugh

Helen Shaver . . . . . . . . . . . . . . . . . Sarah (uncredited)
- •• 0:13—Breasts under Roy Scheider in bed, then breasts again, getting back into bed.

Craig Wasson . . . . . . . . . . . . . . . . . . . . . . . . . . Paul

Gwen Welles . . . . . . . . . . . . . . . . . . . . . . . Redhead

Treat Williams . . . . . . . . . . . . . . . . . . . . . . . . Terry

### The Mephisto Waltz *(1971)*

Jacqueline Bisset . . . . . . . . . . . . . . . . . . . Paula Clarkson
- • 0:48—Very brief right and side view of left breast in bed with Alan Alda.
  1:36—Sort of left breast getting undressed for witchcraft ceremony. Long shot side views of right breast, but you can't see her face.
- •• 1:45—Very brief breasts twice under bloody water in blood covered bathtub, dead. Discovered by Kathleen Widdoes.

Barbara Parkins . . . . . . . . . . . . . . . . . . . . . . Roxanne
- • 1:26—Left breast, while kissing Alan Alda during witchcraft sequence.

Kathleen Widdoes . . . . . . . . . . . . . . . . . . Maggie West

### Meridian *(1989)*
*a.k.a. Kiss of the Beast*
*a.k.a. Phantoms*

Sherilyn Fenn . . . . . . . . . . . . . . . . . . . . . . . Catherine
- •• 0:23—White bra and panties, getting clothes taken off by Lawrence, then breasts.
- ••• 0:28—Breasts in bed with Oliver.
- •• 0:51—Breasts getting her blouse ripped open lying in bed.
  1:11—Briefly in white panties and bra putting red dress on.

Charlie Spradling . . . . . . . . . . . . . . . . . . . . . . . . Gina
- •• 0:22—Breasts getting her blouse torn off by Lawrence while lying on the table.
- ••• 0:28—Breasts standing next to fireplace, then breasts on the couch. Hot!

### Metamorphosis *(1989)*

Laura Gemser . . . . . . . . . . . . . . . . . . . . . . Prostitute
- • 0:37—Very brief breasts several times in Peter's flashback.
- • 0:43—Very brief breasts in flashback again.

### Miami Blues *(1990)*

Alec Baldwin . . . . . . . . . . . . . . . Frederick J. Frenger, Jr.

Martine Beswicke . . . . . . . . . . . . . . . . . . . . . . Noira

Kerrie Clark . . . . . . . . . . . . . . . . . . . . . . . . . . Hooker

Jennifer Jason Leigh . . . . . . . . . . . . . . Susie Waggoner
- 0:07—Very brief upper half of right breast, while changing clothes behind Alec Baldwin.
- ••• 0:10—Breasts in panties, taking off red dress and getting into bed.
  0:24—Very, very brief half of right breast while taking a bath. Long shot.
- 0:33—Breasts making love with Baldwin in the kitchen.

Fred Ward . . . . . . . . . . . . . . . . Sergeant Hoke Moseley

### Midnight *(1989)*

Kathleen Kinmont . . . . . . . . . . . . . . . . . . . . . . . Party

Lynn Redgrave . . . . . . . . . . . . . . . . . . . . . . . Midnight

Karen Witter . . . . . . . . . . . . . . . . . . . . . . . Missy Angel
- 0:32—In bed with Mickey. Nice squished breasts against him, but only a very brief side view of left breast.
  0:48—In two piece swimsuit, going into the pool.
  0:58—In nightgown, walking around with lots of makeup on her face.

### Midnight Cabaret *(1988)*

Esther Alise . . . . . . . . . . . . . . . . . . . . . . . . . . . Dancer

Lydie Denier . . . . . . . . . . . . . . . . . . . . Woman in White

Paul Drake . . . . . . . . . . . . . . . . . . . . . . . The Intruder
- •• 0:03—Nude, while walking up steps and into apartment after killing a guy in the street.
- • 0:05—More buns, while walking around building. Sometimes with a G-string, sometimes without.

Laura Harrington . . . . . . . . . . . . . . . . . Tanya Richards
- • 0:33—Very, very brief upper half of right breast while leaning back.
- • 0:34—Very, very brief left breast when a guy sticks his tongue out.
- • 0:43—Brief breasts when short guys rip her dress off.
- • 0:49—Very brief right breast in gaping nightgown, while bending over to put pants on.
- • 1:08—Brief breasts while making love with a guy.

Debra Lamb . . . . . . . . . . . . . . . . . . . . . . . . . . Dancer

Christina Whitaker . . . . . . . . . . . . . . . . . . . . . . Dancer

### A Midnight Clear *(1991)*

Peter Berg . . . . . . . . . . . . . . . . . . . . . . . . . . . . Miller

Larry Joshua . . . . . . . . . . . . . . . . . . . Lieutenant Ware

Bill Osborn . . . . . . . . . . . . . . . . . . . . . . . . . Sergeant

Gary Sinise . . . . . . . . . . . . . . . . . . . . . . . . . . Mother
- • 0:03—Long shot of buns, when he runs into stream.

### Midnight Cowboy *(1969)*

Viva . . . . . . . . . . . . . . . . . . . . . . . Gretel McAlbertson

Dustin Hoffman . . . . . . . . . . . . . . . . . . . . . . . Ratso

Sylvia Miles . . . . . . . . . . . . . . . . . . . . . . . . . . . Cass
- • 0:20—Brief buns, running into bedroom and jumping onto bed with Jon Voight. More when changing the TV channel with the remote control. Most of her right breast in bed under Voight.

Jennifer Salt . . . . . . . . . . . . . . . . . . . . . . . . . . Annie
- • 0:31—Very brief buns, while running away from some bad guys in flashback.

- 0:42—Brief left breast on bed with Voight in flash-back.
- 0:49—Very brief breasts in car in B&W flashback. More brief breasts and buns in car and running on porch.

Brenda Vaccaro . . . . . . . . . . . . . . . . . . . . . . Shirley
- 1:30—Very, very brief out of focus left breast in open fur coat, lying down with Jon Voight.
- 1:31—Very brief left breast when falling back onto bed with Voight.
- 1:32—Brief right breast, while rolling in bed with Voight.

Jon Voight . . . . . . . . . . . . . . . . . . . . . . . . . Joe Buck
- 0:00—Very brief side view of buns, picking up bar of soap from the shower floor.
- 0:20—Brief buns, while running into bedroom and jumping onto bed with Sylvia Miles.
- 0:50—Very brief buns, during struggle with a group of men. More buns when they hold his legs.
- 1:32—Buns, while in bed with Brenda Vaccaro.

## Midnight Crossing (1988)
Kim Cattrall . . . . . . . . . . . . . . . . . . . . Alexa Schubb
0:39—In wet white blouse, arguing in the water with her husband.
Crisstyn Dante . . . . . . . . . Body Double for Kim Cattrall
- 0:29—Brief left breast making love on small boat, body double for Kim Cattrall.
Faye Dunaway . . . . . . . . . . . . . . . . . . Helen Barton
John Laughlin . . . . . . . . . . . . . . . . . . . Jeffrey Schubb

## Midnight Dancer (1987; Australian)
a.k.a. Belinda
Robyn Moase . . . . . . . . . . . . . . . . . . . . . . . . Brenda
- 0:43—Brief breasts while putting on black top.
Mary Regan . . . . . . . . . . . . . . . . . . . . . . . . Crystal
- 0:29—Breasts in dressing room, undressing and rubbing makeup on herself.
- 0:56—In bra, then breasts in panties, changing clothes and getting into bed.
Kathryn Walker . . . . . . . . . . . . . . . . . . . . . . Kathy

## Midnight Express (1978; British)
Brad Davis . . . . . . . . . . . . . . . . . . . . . . . Billy Hayes
- 0:12—Buns, while standing naked in front of guards after getting caught trying to smuggle drugs.
John Hurt . . . . . . . . . . . . . . . . . . . . . . . . . . . Max
Irene Miracle . . . . . . . . . . . . . . . . . . . . . . . Susan
- 1:39—Breasts in prison visiting booth showing her breasts to Brad Davis so he can masturbate.
Randy Quaid . . . . . . . . . . . . . . . . . . . . Jimmy Booth

## Midnight Tease (1994)
Lisa Boyle . . . . . . . . . . . . . . . . . . . . . . . Samantha
- 0:02—Breasts in lingerie outfit, walking up to her stepfather and slicing his throat.
- 0:11—Buns in T-back and in bra, while undressing, then lying on bed.
- 0:12—Breasts in lingerie outfit, while killing her stepfather in dream.

- 0:24—Breasts, after opening her leather jacket on table in front of Dr. Saul.
- 0:37—Breasts, while making love with Dr. Saul in his office.
- 0:44—Breasts and buns in T-back while dancing on stage with Mantra.
- 0:47—Breasts while talking with Mantra in dressing room.
- 0:50—Breasts in lingerie outfit in dream, while slitting Mantra's throat.
- 0:53—Full frontal nudity while taking a shower behind clear plastic curtain.
- 0:58—In white bra and panties, then breasts and buns after stripping out of schoolgirl outfit. Intercut with flashbacks of her stepfather's suicide.
Nicole Grey . . . . . . . . . . . . . . . . . . . . . . . . Dusty
- 0:17—Breasts after stripping out of policewoman's uniform on stage.
Ashlie Rhey . . . . . . . . . . . . . . . . . . . . . . . . Mantra
- 0:00—Breasts and buns during opening credits.
- 0:42—Buns and breasts in black dominatrix outfit while dancing on stage with Samantha.
- 0:47—Breasts while talking with Samantha in dressing room.
- 0:50—Breasts, while whipping Samantha's stepfather in dream while Samantha kills her.
Stephanie Sumers . . . . . . . . . . . . . . . . . . . Tiffany
- 0:00—Breasts and buns, while dancing during opening credits.
- 0:07—Breasts and buns in T-back, while dancing on stage.
- 0:09—Breasts, while dressing and talking to Samantha in dressing room.
- 0:12—Nude, while making love on top of Samantha's stepfather, then getting killed in dream.
0:14—Breasts while tied to pole in club with a slit throat and covered with blood.
- 0:50—Breasts with slit throat and blood in dream.

## Midnight Witness (1992)
Lisa Boyle . . . . . . . . . . . . . . . . . . . . . . . . . Heidi
- 1:11—Breasts, while getting out of bed. Buns and breasts some more, seen in mirror.
Maxwell Caulfield . . . . . . . . . . . . . . . . . . . Garland
- 1:11—Brief buns, getting out of bed and putting underwear on.
Kelli Maroney . . . . . . . . . . . . . . . . . . . . . . Devon
Karen Moncrieff . . . . . . . . . . . . . . . . . . . . . Katy
- 1:08—Very brief buns, while making love with Paul in bed in motel (don't see her face). Very brief part of right nipple. Very brief right breast, when falling back onto bed (medium long shot).
Jan-Michael Vincent . . . . . . . . . . . . . . . . . . Lance

## Mike's Murder (1984)
Kym Malin . . . . . . . . . . . . . . . . . . . Beautiful Girl #1
Debra Winger . . . . . . . . . . . . . . . . . . . . . . . Betty
- 0:26—Brief left breast in bathtub.

## Mikey (1992)

Josie Bissett . . . . . . . . . . . . . . . . . . . . . . . . . . . . . Jessie
    0:44—In black bra and panties, in bedroom with David.
    0:58—In red one piece body leotard while in a spa with David.

Mimi Craven . . . . . . . . . . . . . . . . . . . . . . Rachel Trenton
  •• 0:52—Breasts, sitting in bathtub when Mikey comes into the bathroom to talk.

John Diehl . . . . . . . . . . . . . . . . . . . . . . . . . Neil Trenton

## Millions (1990)

Carol Alt . . . . . . . . . . . . . . . . . . . . . . . . . . . . . . . . . Beta
Catherine Hickland . . . . . . . . . . . . . . . . . . . . . . . Connie
  • 0:36—Buns, getting out of bed to open safe. Don't see her face, probably a body double because the hair is too dark.
  • 1:20—Buns, walking away from John Stockwell. Very brief back side of right breast, when she bends over to pick up blouse. Don't see her face.

Lauren Hutton . . . . . . . . . . . . . . . . . . . . . . . . Christina
Alexandra Paul . . . . . . . . . . . . . . . . . . . . . . . . . . . Julia
    0:19—In black stockings and body suit, changing clothes.
  ••• 0:44—Breasts while making love in bed with Billy Zane.
  • 0:59—Breasts in bed with Zane.

John Stockwell . . . . . . . . . . . . . . . . . . . . David Phipps
Billy Zane . . . . . . . . . . . . . . . . . . . . . . . Maurizo Ferreti

## Mind Twister (1992)

(Unrated version reviewed.)
Justin Carroll . . . . . . . . . . . . . . . . . . . . . . . Young Stud
  • 0:31—Brief buns in mirror, while getting out of bathtub after getting caught with Lisa by Daniel.

Deborah Dutch . . . . . . . . . . . . . . . . . . . Sheila Harrison
  •• 0:01—Brief breasts, after smashing her head through window to scream for help. Left breast, while dead on the floor.
  •• 0:04—Breasts, while dead on the floor when photographed by police.
  •• 0:05—More brief left breast shots while on the floor. Breasts, while getting put in body bag.
  •• 1:22—In bra, then breasts on TV monitor during video playback that Heather watches.

Maria Ford . . . . . . . . . . . . . . . . . . . . . Melanie Duncan
Gary Hudson . . . . . . . . . . . . . . . . . . . . . Daniel Strahten
Erika Nann . . . . . . . . . . . . . . . . . . . . . . . Lisa Strahten
  ••• 0:28—Breasts, while making love in candlelit bathtub with a young stud.
    0:33—In black lingerie in bedroom with Daniel.
  • 0:37—Breasts, while in bed with Daniel.
    0:42—In sheer black body suit in bathroom while talking to Daniel.
    0:49—In black bra, panties, garter belt and stockings.
    0:54—In black lingerie outfit.
  ••• 0:56—Breasts and buns, while making love with Heather while getting videotaped by Daniel.

  • 1:22—In lingerie on TV monitor during video playback. Buns, while wrestling with Sheila.

Richard Roundtree . . . . . . . . . . . . . . . . . . . . Frank Webb
Suzanne Slater . . . . . . . . . . . . . . . . . . . . . Heather Black
  ••• 0:17—Breasts and partial buns, while making love on sofa with Roy. Long scene.
  • 0:39—Inside half of left breast in open robe when pizza delivery guy sees her.
    0:54—In pink bra and panties in S&M room with Lisa.
  ••• 0:56—Breasts and buns, while in bed with Lisa while getting videotaped by Daniel. A little bit of fluorescent paint added to her breasts for color. Great!

Nels Van Patten . . . . . . . . . . . . . . . . . . . . . . Roy Gerard
  •• 0:17—Buns, while making love with Heather on sofa.

## Mind, Body & Soul (1992)

Ken Abraham . . . . . . . . . . . . . . . . . . . . . . . . . . . . . Sean
Toni Alessandrini . . . . . . . . . . . . . . . . . . . Priestess Tura
  •• 1:05—Breasts under fishnet body stocking during occult dance in a house.

Ginger Lynn Allen . . . . . . . . . . . . . . . . . . . . . . . Brenda
  •• 0:13—Breasts in open blouse while getting raped in jail by a guard.
  ••• 0:17—Breasts while talking with her boyfriend in open blouse and dripping candle wax on him.
  ••• 1:10—Breasts while lying in bed with her boyfriend, Sean.

Veronica Carothers . . . . . . . . . . . . . . . . . . . Sacrifice Girl
  ••• 0:02—Breasts when her dress is ripped open during occult ceremony while tied by her wrists.
  •• 0:26—Left breast several times and very, very brief right breast in black outfit (her face is covered with a hood) during occult ceremony.

Wings Hauser . . . . . . . . . . . . . . . . . . . . . . John Stockton

## Miracle Beach (1991)

Monique Gabrielle . . . . . . . . . . . . . . . . . . . Cindy Beatty
  •• 0:03—Breasts in bed with a guy when Scotty comes home. Breasts getting out of bed and getting dressed. (Note in first shot when she's lying in bed, she doesn't have a dress around her waist, then in the next shot when she stands up, she does.)

Allen Garfield . . . . . . . . . . . . . . . . . . . Magnus O'Leary
Michelle Grassnick . . . . . . . . . . . . . . . Miss Great Britain
  • 0:35—Brief buns in swimsuit bottom, then right breast, while lying in bed, talking with Lars.
  ••• 1:03—Breasts, while trying on swimsuits backstage.

Wendy Kaye . . . . . . . . . . . . . . . . . . . . . . . . . . Girl in Bed
  • 0:14—Breasts, lying in bed next to Scotty, then sitting up. She's on the left.

Brittany York . . . . . . . . . . . . . . . . . . . . . . . . . Girl in Bed
  •• 0:14—Breasts, lying in bed next to Scotty, then sitting up. She's on the right.

## Mirror Images (1991)

Lee Anne Beaman . . . . . . . . . . . . . . . . . . . . . . Rebecca
  ••• 1:11—Buns in G-string, then breasts in conference room, undressing in front of Jeff Conaway and Carter.

Jeff Conaway............................Jeffrey
George "Buck" Flower...................Wolfman
Michael Meyer ........................ Georgio
•• 0:15—Buns, while getting out of bed with Shauna.
Deirdre Morrow ...................... Slave Girl
••• 0:58—Buns in G-string, then breasts with masked guy.
••• 1:00—Breasts on bed with masked guy and Julie Strain.
Delia Sheppard ................... Kaitlin/Shauna
•• 0:07—Right breast, while undressing in front of vanity mirror.
•• 0:08—More breasts as Shauna in bed.
0:12—Buns, while dancing on stage with a band, wearing a sexy outfit.
••• 0:14—Breasts in bed with Georgio.
••• 0:27—Breasts and buns in G-string, making love with Joey. Long scene.
••• 0:33—Buns in black bra and panties, walking around her sister's apartment. Long scene.
••• 0:39—Right breast, while with a guy with a mask.
••• 0:41—Nude, taking a shower. Great!
••• 0:43—Breasts in bedroom after her shower.
•• 0:48—Left breast, while making love in bed with Julie Strain.
••• 1:29—Breasts in bed in lingerie with the policeman.
Julie Strain................................Gina
•• 0:48—Buns and right breast, making love in bed with Kaitlin.
•• 0:49—Buns in black bra and panties.
• 0:57—Buns in black body suit.
••• 0:58—Breasts lying on bed, watching the slave girl and guy with the mask make love.
Nels Van Patten......................Joey Zoom
•• 0:08—Buns, while in bed and getting out of bed with Shauna.
•• 0:29—Buns, while on top of Kaitlin.

### Mirror Images II (1993)
Sara Suzanne Brown ................... Prostitute
••• 0:13—In red bra and panties, then breasts and buns while making love with Clete in motel room. Long scene.
Ken Steadman............................ Dan
•• 0:33—Buns, while running from the spa to the house after getting caught with Shannon Whirry.
Shannon Whirry .................... Carrie/Terrie
••• 0:03—Nude, while taking a shower during the opening credits. Then breasts, while making love on top of her twin sister's boyfriend in bed.
• 0:19—Buns in panties and bra while trying on lingerie in front of mirror.
••• 0:25—Full frontal nudity while making love with her female psychologist, Dr. Rubin. Long scene.
••• 0:31—Nude, while making love outside in pool with Dan before getting caught by Phyllis.
••• 0:39—In black bra, then full frontal nudity while making love on bed with Clete. She gives him a hot wax treatment. Long scene.

• 0:49—Breasts, while making love in bed with a customer while Jake watches from outside the window. Long shot.
••• 0:56—In black bra and panties, the full frontal nudity while making love in bedroom with a customer.
•• 1:01—In white bra, then breasts and buns in G-string with another woman in hotel room.
••• 1:10—Breasts, while making love in bed with Jake. Long scene.
• 1:27—Breasts while making love with Jake (in B&W).

### Mirror Mirror (1990)
Karen Black ....................... Mrs. Gordon
Charlie Spradling .................. Charleen Kane
• 1:05—Very, very brief side of left breast, after taking of swimsuit in locker room.
• 1:06—Buns, taking a shower. Brief breasts a couple of times when the hot water pipes break.
1:09—Buns, lying on the floor, dead, covered with blisters.

### The Misadventures of Mr. Wilt (1990)
Griff Rhys Jones ....................... Henry Wilt
• 0:34—Sort of buns, while naked and tied to inflatable doll.
• 0:36—More buns, while up on balcony. Long shot.
Diana Quick................................Sally

### Mischief (1985)
Jami Gertz ............................Rosalie
Doug McKeon ........................Jonathan
• 0:56—Brief buns, while putting on his underwear after making love with Kelly Preston.
Terry O'Quinn .................. Claude Harbrough
Kelly Preston ................... Marilyn McCauley
••• 0:56—In a bra, then breasts, brief buns and brief partial lower frontal nudity, while seducing and making love with Doug McKeon in her bedroom.
Catherine Mary Stewart ................... Bunny

### Miss Right (1987; Italian)
Karen Black ............................Amy
• 0:47—Brief breasts jumping out of bed and running to get a bucket of water to put out a fire.
Dalila Di'Lazzaro ..................... Art Student
Clio Goldsmith.............................n.a.
Margot Kidder ............................Juliet
Marie-France Pisier........................Bebe
•• 0:07—Breasts in open top dress when the reporter discovers her in a dressing room behind a curtain.
William Tepper......................Terry Bartell
• 0:47—Buns, while jumping out of bed with Karen Black when the bed catches fire.

### Missing in Action (1984)
Joseph Carberry .................... Carpenter
Lenore Kasdorf............................Ann
• 0:41—Very brief breasts when Chuck Norris sneaks back in room and jumps into bed with her.
M. Emmet Walsh ......................... Tuck

### Mission Manila (1989)
Tetchie Agbayani . . . . . . . . . . . . . . . . . . . . . . . . Maria
Maria Isabel Lopez . . . . . . . . . . . . . . . . . . . . . . Jessie
- 0:22—Brief right breast several times in bed while Harry threatens her with knife.

### Mississippi Masala (1992)
Sarita Choudhury . . . . . . . . . . . . . . . . . . . . . .Mina
- 1:11—Right breast when Denzel Washington sucks on it.
Denzel Washington. . . . . . . . . . . . . . . . . . . .Demetrius
- 1:17—Buns, getting up out of bed and putting on his pants.

### Mississippi Mermaid (1969; French)
Catherine Deneuve . . . . . . Julie Roussel/Marion Vergano
- 1:04—Breasts, changing from a blouse to a sweater while standing up in parked car.
- 1:26—Brief breasts, taking off her blouse in bedroom.

### Mistress of the Apes (1979; British)
Barbara Leigh . . . . . . . . . . . . . . . . . . . . . . . . . . Laura
- 0:44—Breasts, washing her blouse in river and putting it on. (Seen through binoculars.)
- 0:46—Breasts, getting her blouse ripped off by jerks.
Suzy Mandel. . . . . . . . . . . . . . . . . . . . . . . . . Secretary
Jenny Neumann . . . . . . . . . . . . . . . . . . . .Susan Jamison
- 0:23—Brief side of right breast, getting ready for bed in her tent.
- 0:25—Brief half of right breast in open blouse. Very brief right breast, when pushing a guy away.
- 1:08—Back side of left breast and brief breasts while washing her blouse in river and putting it on.

### Mo' Better Blues (1990)
Giancarlo Esposito. . . . . . . . . . . . . . . . . Left Hand Lacey
Samuel L. Jackson . . . . . . . . . . . . . . . . . . . . . . Madlock
Tracy Camilla Johns. . . . . . . . . . . . . . . . . Club Patron
Joie Lee. . . . . . . . . . . . . . . . . . . . . . . . . Indigo Downes
- 1:06—Right breast while in bed with Denzel Washington.
- 1:08—Very, very brief right breast while pounding the bed and yelling at Denzel Washington.
John Turturro . . . . . . . . . . . . . . . . . . . . . Moe Flatbush
Denzel Washington. . . . . . . . . . . . . . . . . .Bleek Gilliam
Cynda Williams . . . . . . . . . . . . . . . . . Clarke Betancourt
- 0:24—Breasts, then left breast after kissing Denzel Washington.
- 1:07—Breasts on bed when Denzel Washington accidentally calls her "Indigo."
- 1:28—Left breast while making love in bed with Wesley Snipes.

### Mob Boss (1990)
Jasaé. . . . . . . . . . . . . . . . . . . . . . . . . . . . . . . . . Bar Girl
- 0:46—Breasts serving drinks to the guys at the table.
Suzanne Ager . . . . . . . . . . . . . . . . . . . . . . . Pool Girl
Teagan Clive. . . . . . . . . . . . . . . . . . . . . . . . . . .Noelle

Dori Courtney . . . . . . . . . . . . . . . . . . . . . . . . . Kathryn
- 0:31—In black bra, talking with Eddie Deezen, then breasts. Nice close-up. Long scene.
Morgan Fairchild . . . . . . . . . . . . . . . . . . . . . . . Gina
Sherri Graham . . . . . . . . . . . . . . . . . . . . . . . . Bar Girl
- 0:46—Breasts and buns, dancing on stage. Medium long shot.
Debra Lamb. . . . . . . . . . . . . . . . . . . . . . . . .Janise
Karen Russell . . . . . . . . . . . . . . . . . . . . . . . . . Mary
Brinke Stevens . . . . . . . . . . . . . . . . . . . . . . . . . Sara

### Mobsters (1991)
a.k.a. Mobsters—The Evil Empire
Leslie Bega . . . . . . . . . . . . . . . . . . . . . . Anna Lansky
Lara Flynn Boyle . . . . . . . . . . . . . . . . . .Mara Motes
Patrick Dempsey . . . . . . . . . . . . . . . . . .Meyer Lansky
Ava Fabian . . . . . . . . . . . . . . . . . . . . . . . . Cute Girl
Jennifer Gatti . . . . . . . . . . . . . . . . . . . . . . Secretary
Richard Grieco . . . . . . . . . . . Benjamin "Bugsy" Siegel
Ron Marquette. . . . . . . . . . . . . . . . . . . . Maitre'D
Monique Noel . . . . . . . . . . . . . . . . . . . . . . Showgirl
Christopher Penn . . . . . . . . . . . . . . . Tommy Reina
Bianca Rossini. . . . . . . . . . . . . . . . Rosalie Luciano
Karen Russell . . . . . . . . . . . . . . . . . . . . . . Showgirl
Christian Slater. . . . . . . . . . . . .Charlie "Lucky" Luciano
- 0:45—Very, very brief buns during love scene. Don't see his face.
Lynette Walden . . . . . . . . . . . . . . . . . .Cute Debutante
- 0:32—Breasts when Richard Grieco undoes her dress.

### Model Behavior (1982)
Jade Go . . . . . . . . . . . . . . . . . . . . . . . . . . Golden Girl
Jane Hamilton . . . . . . . . . Uncredited Adult Film Actress
- 0:50—Breasts on TV monitors during playback of adult video.
Kelly Nichols . . . . . . . . . . . . . . . . . . . . . . . Anne #2
- 0:40—Breasts, taking off her top first, with the other Anne in front of Dino.
Missy O'Shea . . . . . . . . . . . . . . . . . . . . . Anne #1
- 0:40—Breasts, taking off her top second, with the other Anne in front of Dino.
Frances Raines . . . . . . . . . . . . . . . . . . . . . Lily White Girl
Wendy Stuart. . . . . . . . . . . . . . . . . . . . . . Lily White Girl

### Model By Day (1994)
(Shown on network TV without the nudity.)
Kim Cayer . . . . . . . . . . . . . . . . . . . . . . . Young Woman
Steve Shellen . . . . . . . . . . . . . . . . . . . . . .Lt. Eddie Walker
Shannon Tweed . . . . . . . . . . . . . . . . . . . . . . . Shannon
- 0:42—Breasts, while letting the club owner feel her up before she beats him up.
Sean Young . . . . . . . . . . . . . . . . . . . . . . . . .Mercedes

### Modern Love (1990)
Robby Benson . . . . . . . . . . . . . . . . . . . . . . .Greg Frank
- 0:35—Brief buns while running out of room after finding out he's going to be a father.
0:36—Long shot of buns, while standing on roof of house yelling the good news to the world.
Burt Reynolds. . . . . . . . . . . . . . . . . . . . Colonel Parker

## Modern Problems (1981)

Dabney Coleman . . . . . . . . . . . . . . . . . . . . . . . . Mark
••• 1:09—Buns, while taking off towel in front of Patti
D'Arbanville.
Patti D'Arbanville . . . . . . . . . . . . . . . . . . . . . . Darcy
• 0:48—Very brief right breast in bed after Chevy
Chase has telekinetic sex with her.

## Modern Romance (1981)

Jane Hallaren. . . . . . . . . . . . . . . . . . . . . . . . . . Ellen
Kathryn Harrold . . . . . . . . . . . . . . . . . . . Mary Harvard
• 0:46—Very brief breasts and buns taking off robe
and getting into bed with Albert Brooks.
1:05—In pink lingerie opening her blouse to undo
her skirt while talking to Brooks.
Bruno Kirby. . . . . . . . . . . . . . . . . . . . . . . . . . . . Jay

## The Moderns (1988)

Genevieve Bujold . . . . . . . . . . . . . . . . . .Libby Valentin
Keith Carradine. . . . . . . . . . . . . . . . . . . . . . Nick Hart
•• 1:17—Buns, while walking into bathroom with Lin-
da Fiorentino.
Geraldine Chaplin. . . . . . . . . . . . . . . . . Nathalie de Ville
Linda Fiorentino . . . . . . . . . . . . . . . . . . . .Rachel Stone
• 0:40—Breasts sitting in bathtub while John Lone
shaves her armpits.
• 0:41—Right breast while turning over onto stomach
in bathtub.
•• 1:18—Breasts getting out of tub while covered with
bubbles to kiss Keith Carradine.
John Lone . . . . . . . . . . . . . . . . . . . . . . . . . . . Stone

## Molly & Gina (1993)

Frances Fisher . . . . . . . . . . . . . . . . . . . . . . . . . . .n.a.
Peter Fonda. . . . . . . . . . . . . . . . . . . . . . . . . . . .Larry
••• 1:06—Buns, getting out of bed to look out the win-
dow.
Shana Golden . . . . . . . . . . . . . . . . . . . . . . . . . Sherry
•• 1:05—Breasts, while making love on top of Peter
Fonda in bed.
• 1:06—Brief right breast, after rolling over after Fonda leaves the room.
• 1:08—Brief buns in G-string after tossing off her
robe.
Penny Johnson . . . . . . . . . . . . . . . . . . . . . . . . . . n.a.
Joanne Lara. . . . . . . . . . . . . . . . . . . . . . . . . . . . .n.a.
••• 0:00—Breasts and buns in G-string while dancing on
stage during opening credits.
Melanie Smith. . . . . . . . . . . . . . . . . . . . . . . . . . .n.a.
Stella Stevens . . . . . . . . . . . . . . . . . . . . . . . . . . .n.a.

## Mondo New York (1987)

Phoebe Légerè . . . . . . . . . . . . . . . . . . . . . . . .Singer
0:01—On stage, singing "Marilyn Monroe." Buns
and most of lower frontal nudity while writhing on
stage in a mini-skirt.
Ann Magnuson . . . . . . . . . . . . . . . . . . Poetry Reader
Annie Sprinkle. . . . . . . . . . . . . . . . . . Model/Performer
• 0:17—Nude, painted body with other models dur-
ing "Rapping & Rocking" segment.

## Money for Nothing (1993)

Fionnula Flanagan . . . . . . . . . . . . . . . . . . . . .Mrs. Coyle
Michael Madsen. . . . . . . . . . . . . . . . .Detective Laurenzi
Debi Mazar . . . . . . . . . . . . . . . . . . . . . . . Monica Russo
•• 0:39—Breasts, while making love in bed with John
Cusack while covered with money.
0:42—Brief buns in black panties and bra while getting dressed.
1:22—In black bra in bathroom while coloring Cusack's hair.

## Money to Burn (1994)

Diana Cuevas. . . . . . . . . . . . . . . . . . . . . . . Beach Girl
Melanie Good . . . . . . . . . . . . . . . . . . . . . . . . . . .Ann
• 0:40—Buns in fishnet body suit, breasts under the
suit, while making love with Julie Strain on the floor.
Kymberly Herrin. . . . . . . . . . . . . . . . . . . . . . . .Linda
Ashlie Rhey. . . . . . . . . . . . . . . . . . . . . . . . . . . Gina
• 1:02—Nude in bathtub with Don Swayze.
Nicole Sassaman . . . . . . . . . . . . . . . . . . Rich Girl #1
Jerry Spicer. . . . . . . . . . . . . . . . . . . . . . . . . . . .Kevin
Julie Strain . . . . . . . . . . . . . . . . . . . . . . . . . . . . . Jill
• 0:38—Brief buns in G-string under hiked up dress,
several times, while dancing in club.
•• 0:39—Stripping out of her dress down to red bra,
panties, garter belt and stockings, then breasts and
buns. More when making love with Ann on the
floor.
••• 0:42—Nude, waking up and getting dressed.

## Monika (1952; Swedish)

a.k.a. Sommaren Med Monika
Harriet Andersson. . . . . . . . . . . . . . . . . . . . . Monika
• 0:42—Brief back side of left breast, while sitting
down next to water. Buns while getting up to run to
water.
• 1:33—Buns and long shot of right breast in Harry's
flashback. This scene lasts longer than the 0:42 one.

## Monkey Shines: An Experiment in Fear (1988)

Jason Beghe. . . . . . . . . . . . . . . . . . . . . . . . Allan Mann
• 0:01—Side view of buns while on the floor, stretch-
ing to go running.
Kate McNeil. . . . . . . . . . . . . . . . . . . . . .Melanie Parker
• 1:07—Brief upper half of right breast, while making
love with Allan. Dark, hard to see anything.
John Pankow . . . . . . . . . . . . . . . . . . . . Geoffrey Fisher
Patricia Tallman . . . . . . . . . . . . Party Guest and Stunts
Janine Turner . . . . . . . . . . . . . . . . . . . . .Linda Aikman
0:01—Side view of buns, lying in bed when Jason
Beghe wakes up. Don't really see anything.
Joyce Van Patten . . . . . . . . . . . . . . . . . .Dorothy Mann

## Monolith (1993)

John Hurt. . . . . . . . . . . . . . . . . . . . . . . . . . . .Villano
Bill Paxton . . . . . . . . . . . . . . . . . . . . . . . . . . . .Tucker
• 0:15—Brief buns, in shower when Lindsay Crouse
comes in to visit and talk.

## Monsignor (1982)

Genevieve Bujold . . . . . . . . . . . . . . . . . . . . . . . . Clara
- ••• 1:05—Breasts getting undressed and climbing into bed while talking to Christopher Reeve.

Pamela Prati . . . . . . . . . . . . . . . . . . . . . 1st Roman Girl
- • 1:22—Brief breasts (on the left, wearing necklaces) next to a guy sitting in a chair, with another Roman girl on the right.

## Montenegro (1981; British/Swedish)

Susan Anspach . . . . . . . . . . . . . . . . . . . Marilyn Jordan
- •• 1:08—Full frontal nudity taking a shower.
- • 1:28—Right breast making love with Montenegro.

Svetozar Cvetkovic . . . . . . . . . . . . . . . . . . . Montenegro
- ••• 1:07—Frontal nudity taking a shower while Susan Anspach watches.

## Monty Python's Jabberwocky (1977)

Deborah Fallender. . . . . . . . . . . . . . . . . . . . The Princess
- • 0:56—Buns and brief full frontal nudity in bath when Michael Palin accidentally enters the room.
  0:57—Breasts under sheer white robe.

Michael Palin. . . . . . . . . . . . . . . . . . . . Dennis Cooper
Bryan Pringle. . . . . . . . . . . . . . . . . Second Gate Guard

## Monty Python's Life of Brian (1979; British)

Graham Chapman . . . . . . . . . . . . . . Brian Called Brian
- ••• 1:03—Buns before opening window, frontal nudity after opening window and being surprised by his flock of followers, buns while putting clothes on. Funniest frontal nude scene.

John Cleese. . . . . . . . . . . . . . . . . . . . . Third Wise Man
Michael Palin. . . . . . . . . . . . . . . . . . . . . . . . . . . n.a.

## Moon 44 (1990; West German)

Lisa Eichhorn. . . . . . . . . . . . . . . . . . . . . Terry Morgan
John March. . . . . . . . . . . . . . . . . . . . . Moose Haggerty
- • 0:43—Brief buns while in shower room. (Sort of see frontal nudity through grating in the shower divider.)

Malcolm McDowell. . . . . . . . . . . . . . . . . . Major Lee
Michael Paré . . . . . . . . . . . . . . . . . . . . . . . Felix Stone

## Moon in Scorpio (1987)

Donna Kei Benz. . . . . . . . . . . . . . . . . . Nurse Mitchell
Britt Ekland . . . . . . . . . . . . . . . . . . . . . . . . . . . . Linda
Jillian Kesner . . . . . . . . . . . . . . . . . . . . . . . . . . Claire
- •• 0:39—Breasts sitting on deck of boat with bathing suit top down.

John Phillip Law. . . . . . . . . . . . . . . . . . . . . . . Allen
April Wayne . . . . . . . . . . . . . . . . . . . . . . . . . Isabel
- • 0:32—Brief right breast in bed with a guy.
- • 0:35—Brief breasts putting bathing suit on in a bathroom on a boat when a guy opens the door.

## The Moon in the Gutter (1983; French/Italian)

*a.k.a. La Lune dans Le Caniveau*

Victoria Abril . . . . . . . . . . . . . . . . . . . . . . . . . . Bella
- • 0:28—Left breast, while riding on swing and getting felt by Gérard Depardieu.
- •• 1:26—Breasts, while lying in bed. Dark.

- ••• 1:27—Nude, getting out of bed and arguing with Depardieu. Long scene. Subtitles get in the way sometimes.
- •• 1:50—Upper half of right breast, popping out of the top of her dress when Depardieu leans her back on the counter.

Katia Berger . . . . . . . . . . . . . . . . . . . . . . . . . . . n.a.
Gérard Depardieu . . . . . . . . . . . . . . . . . . . . . . Gerard
- • 1:26—Upper half of buns, while getting out of bed.

Nastassja Kinski . . . . . . . . . . . . . . . . . . . . . . Loretta

## Moontrap (1989)

Leigh Lombardi . . . . . . . . . . . . . . . . . . . . . . . . Mera
- •• 1:08—Breasts with Walter Koenig in moon tent.

## The Morning After (1986)

Kathy Bates . . . . . . . . . . . . . . Woman on Mateo Street
Jeff Bridges. . . . . . . . . . . . . . . . . . . . . . . . . . Turner
Jane Fonda. . . . . . . . . . . . . . . . . . . . Alex Sternbergen
- • 1:08—Brief breasts making love with Jeff Bridges.

Raul Julia . . . . . . . . . . . . . . . . . . . . . Joaquin Manero
Rick Rossovich . . . . . . . . . . . . . . . . . . . . . Detective
Diane Salinger . . . . . . . . . . . . . . . . . . . Isabel Harding

## Mortal Passions (1989)

Michael Bowen . . . . . . . . . . . . . . . . . . . . . . . . Burke
- • 0:42—Brief buns, while on top of Adele.

Krista Errickson. . . . . . . . . . . . . . . . . . . . . . . . Emily
- •• 0:08—Brief breasts in bed with Darcy, while tied to the bed. Breasts getting untied and rolling over.
- • 0:11—Very brief right breast, rolling back on top of Darcy.
- ••• 0:40—Breasts after dropping her sheet for Burke, then making love with him.
- •• 0:46—Breasts getting into bed with her husband.

Cassandra Gava . . . . . . . . . . . . . . . . . . . . . . . Cinda
Sheila Kelley. . . . . . . . . . . . . . . . . . . . . . . . . . Adele

## Mortuary Academy (1988)

Rebekka Armstrong . . . . . . . . . . . . . . . . . . . . . Nurse
Christopher Atkins . . . . . . . . . . . . . . . . . . Sam Grimm
Vickie Benson . . . . . . . . . . . . . . . . . . . . . . Salesgirl
Laurie Ann Carr . . . . . . . . . . . . . . . . . . . . . . . Nurse
Lynn Danielson . . . . . . . . . . . . . . . . . Valerie Levitt
James Daughton . . . . . . . . . . . . . . Yuppie at Car Lot
Perry Lang . . . . . . . . . . . . . . . . . . . . . . Max Grimm
Kym Paige . . . . . . . . . . . . . . . . . . . . . . . . . . Nurse
Bobbi Pavis. . . . . . . . . . . . . . . . . . . . . Sexy Dancer
Dona Speir . . . . . . . . . . . . . . . . . . . . . . . . . Nurse
Cheryl Starbuck . . . . . . . . . . . . . . . . Linda Hollyhead
- • 1:08—Breasts, dead, in morgue when Paul Bartel tries to make love with her.

Tracey Walter. . . . . . . . . . . . . . . . . . . . . . . Dickson
Karen Witter. . . . . . . . . . . . . . . . . . . . . Christie Doll
Mary Woronov. . . . . . . . . . . . . . . . . . Mary Purcell

## Moscow on the Hudson (1984)

Maria Conchita Alonso. . . . . . . . . . . . . Lucia Lombardo
- •• 1:17—Breasts in bathtub with Robin Williams.

Robin Williams . . . . . . . . . . . . . . . . . Vladimir Ivanoff

### Motel Hell (1980)

Nina Axelrod............................Terry
   0:58—In wet white T-shirt, tubin' with Ida.
•• 1:01—Breasts sitting up in bed to kiss Vincent.
• 1:04—Very brief breasts in tub when Bruce breaks
    the door down, then getting out of tub.
Rosanne Katon ........................... Suzi

### Mountains of the Moon (1989)

Patrick Bergin ..................... Richard Burton
Richard E. Grant ......................Oliphant
Bernard Hill.................Dr. David Livingstone
Anna Massey...................... Mrs. Arundell
Roger Rees ...................... Edgar Papworth
Fiona Shaw ........................... Isabel
•• 0:33—Breasts and very brief lower frontal nudity let-
    ting Patrick Bergin wax the hair off her legs.
•• 1:43—Breasts in bed after Bergin returns from Afri-
    ca.

### Mr. Baseball (1992)

Mary Kohnert ...................... Player's Wife
Scott Plank ......................... Ryan Ward
Tom Selleck......................... Jack Elliot
••• 0:03—Buns and partial pubic hair, while holding his
    clothes against his crotch while sneaking out of co-
    ed's bed.
•• 0:23—Upper half of buns, after taking off towel.
    Buns and partial pubic hair (medium long shot),
    while sitting in tub.
• 1:19—Brief buns, taking off towel and sitting down
    in washing off area.
Carrie Jean Yazel ..................... Coed in Bed
• 0:03—Very, very brief upper half of right breast,
    while sleeping when Tom Selleck gets out of bed.

### Ms. Don Juan (1973)

Brigitte Bardot........................... Joan
• 0:19—Left breast in bathtub.
•• 1:19—Breasts through fish tank. Buns and left
    breast, then brief breasts in mirror with Paul.
Jane Birkin.............................Clara
   0:58—Lower frontal nudity lying in bed with Brigitte
    Bardot.
   1:00—Brief breasts in bed with Bardot. Long shot.
•• 1:01—Full frontal nudity getting dressed. Brief
    breasts in open blouse.

### Mugsy's Girls (1985)

Ken Norton...................... Branscombe
Darcy Nychols................. Madame Antoinette
Kristi Somers ...........................Laurie
• 0:15—Brief breasts several times while mud wres-
    tling.
•• 0:29—Breasts and buns in bathtub on bus.
• 0:34—Brief breasts holding up sign to get truck driv-
    er to stop.

### Murder Weapon (1989)

Michelle Bauer .............. Girl in Shower on TV
• 1:00—Brief left breast on TV that the guys are
    watching. Scene from Nightmare Sisters.
Victoria Nesbitt ........................... Vicki
••• 0:05—Breasts in bed with a guy after taking off her
    swimsuit top, then making love on top of him. Long
    scene.
Linnea Quigley......................... Dawn
• 0:08—Buns and very brief side of left breast walking
    into shower. Long shot.
•• 0:40—Breasts taking off her top in car.
•• 0:48—Breasts and buns taking off her top in bed-
    room.
••• 0:50—Breasts in bed on top of a guy. Excellent long
    scene. Brief buns, getting out of bed.
Karen Russell ...........................Amy
• 0:34—Brief breasts in shower.
   0:58—In black bra and panties in bedroom.
Brinke Stevens ................. Girl in Shower on TV
• 1:00—Brief left breast on TV that the guys are
    watching. Scene from Nightmare Sisters.

### Murderers Among Us: The Simon Wiesenthal Story
(1989; Made for Cable Movie)

Ben Kingsley.................... Simon Wiesenthal
•• 0:27—Buns and brief frontal nudity standing in and
    leaving a line in a concentration camp.
Reneé Soutendijk ...........................Cyla

### Murphy's Law (1986)

Leigh Lombardi ..................... Stewardess
Karen Price............................. Stunts
Carrie Snodgress ................... Joan Freeman
Angel Tompkins ...........................Jan
• 0:19—Breasts doing a strip routine on stage while
    Charles Bronson watches.
• 0:27—Brief breasts doing another routine.

### Murphy's Romance (1985)

Sally Field........................Emma Moriarity
Brian Kerwin.................Bobbie Jack Moriarity
•• 0:55—Brief buns while walking into the bathroom.
Anna Levine Thomson .....................Wanda

### The Mutilator (1983)

Frances Raines ...........................Linda
•• 0:35—Breasts, while in swimming pool, just before
    getting killed.

### My Beautiful Laundrette (1985; British)

Daniel Day-Lewis .........................Johnny
Rita Wolf ............................Tania
•• 0:15—Breasts holding blouse up, showing off her
    breasts outside window to Omar.

### My Best Friend's Girl (1984; French)
a.k.a. La Femme du Mon Ami

Isabelle Huppert..................Vivian Arthund
• 0:40—Brief left breast peeking out of bathrobe walk-
    ing around in living room.

1:00—Buns, making love with Thierry Lhermitte while his friend watches.

Thierry Lhermitte . . . . . . . . . . . . . . . . . Pascal Saulnier

## My Chauffeur *(1986)*

Cindy Beal. . . . . . . . . . . . . . . . . . . . . . . . . . . . .Beebop
Vickie Benson . . . . . . . . . . . . . . . . . . . . . . . Party Girl
Jeannine Bisignano . . . . . . . . . . . . . . . . . . . . . Party Girl
  • 1:23—Breasts, several times, taking off her white blouse in the back of the limousine. (She's the only brunette.)
Leslee Bremmer. . . . . . . . . . . . . . . . . . . . . . Party Girl
  1:19—Dancing in yellow outfit at a club. Most of buns.
  • 1:24—Buns and brief breasts in back of the limousine, taking off her yellow outfit.
  • 1:25—Breasts sleeping when Penn and Teller leave the limousine.
Sam Jones . . . . . . . . . . . . . . . . . . . . . . . . . . Battle
  ••• 0:42—Buns, while running around the park naked.
Sheila Lussier. . . . . . . . . . . . . . . . . . . . . . . . Party Girl
  • 1:23—Brief breasts taking off her blue blouse in the back of the limousine.
Darian Mathias . . . . . . . . . . . . . . . . . . . . . . . . .Dolly

## My Father The Hero *(1993)*

Gérard Depardieu . . . . . . . . . . . . . . . . . . . . . . André
Katherine Heigl . . . . . . . . . . . . . . . . . . . . . . . . .Nicole
  • 0:14—Buns in white, T-back swimsuit, getting up of lounge chair and walking while Gérard Depardieu tries to cover her up.
Lauren Hutton. . . . . . . . . . . . . . . . . . . . . . . . Megan

## My Father's Wife *(1976; Italian)*

*a.k.a. Confessions of a Frustrated Housewife*

Carroll Baker . . . . . . . . . . . . . . . . . . . . . . . . . . . Lara
  • 0:03—Right breast making love in bed with her husband, Antonio.
  •• 0:06—Breasts standing in front of bed talking to Antonio.
  ••• 0:18—Breasts kneeling in bed, then getting out and putting a robe on while wearing beige panties.
Cesare Barro . . . . . . . . . . . . . . . . . . . . . . . . . . .Claudio
  • 0:52—Buns, while bringing Patricia champagne.
Femi Benussi . . . . . . . . . . . . . . . . . . . . . . . . . . Patricia
  • 0:33—Close up view of left breast.
  •• 0:51—Right breast, while making love in bed with Claudio. Breasts after.

## My First Wife *(1985; Australian)*

Neela Dey . . . . . . . . . . . . . . . . . . . . . .Migrant Teacher
Wendy Hughes . . . . . . . . . . . . . . . . . . . . . . . Helen
  1:00—Brief breasts and lower frontal nudity under water during husband's dream. Don't see her face.
  •• 1:08—In bra, then breasts on the floor with her husband.
  •• 1:10—Breasts in bed lying down, then fighting with her husband. A little dark.
Anna-Maria Monticelli. . . . . . . . . . . . . . . . . . . . .Hillary

## My Man Adam *(1986)*

Veronica Cartwright . . . . . . . . . . . . . . . . . . .Elaine Swit
  • 1:09—Side view of right breast lying on tanning table when Adam steals her car keys. Long shot, hard to see.
Lydia Finzi . . . . . . . . . . . . . . . . . . . . . . . . Sunbather
  • 0:32—Brief breasts sunbathing by the swimming pool when Adam jumps into the pool and angers her.

## My Own Private Idaho *(1991)*

Chiara Caselli . . . . . . . . . . . . . . . . . . . . . . . . Carmella
  • 1:17—Breasts and buns in very brief, quick cuts with Keanu Reeves.
Melanie Mosely . . . . . . . . . . . . . . . . . . . Lounge Hostess
Keanu Reeves. . . . . . . . . . . . . . . . . . . . . . . Scott Favor
  • 1:17—Very brief side view of buns, in quick cuts, standing with Carmilla.
James Russo . . . . . . . . . . . . . . . . . . . . . . . Richard Waters

## My Pleasure is My Business *(1974)*

Jayne Eastwood . . . . . . . . . . . . . . . . . . . . . . . . Isabella
  • 1:16—Breasts in bed trying to get His Excellency's attention.
  •• 1:28—Breasts sitting up in bed with blonde guy.
Xaviera Hollander. . . . . . . . . . . . . . . . . . . . . . .Gabriele
  •• 0:14—Full frontal nudity in everybody's daydream.
  •• 0:39—Breasts sitting up in bed and putting on a blouse.
  •• 0:40—Breasts getting back into bed.
  ••• 0:59—Breasts and buns taking off clothes to go swimming in the pool, swimming, then getting out.
  •• 1:09—Breasts, buns and very brief lower frontal nudity, underwater in indoor pool with Gus.
  • 1:31—Buns and very brief side view of right breast, undressing at party.
Michael Kirby. . . . . . . . . . . . . . . . . . . . . . . . . . . . Gus
  • 0:41—Brief buns while making love with Xaviera Hollander.

## My Therapist *(1983)*

Marilyn Chambers . . . . . . . . . . . . . . . . . . . .Kelly Carson
  •• 0:01—Breasts in sex therapy class.
  •• 0:07—Breasts, then full frontal nudity undressing for Rip. Long scene.
  ••• 0:10—Breasts undressing at home, then full frontal nudity making love on couch. Long scene. Nice. Then brief side view of right breast in shower.
  • 0:18—Breasts on sofa with Mike.
  •• 0:21—Breasts taking off and putting red blouse on at home.
  ••• 0:26—Nude in bedroom by herself masturbating on bed.
  ••• 0:32—Breasts exercising on the floor, buns in bed with Mike, breasts in bed getting covered with whipped cream.
  •• 0:41—Left breast and lower frontal nudity fighting with Don while he rips off her clothes.
  •• 1:08—Breasts and brief buns in bed.
  1:12—In braless pink T-shirt at the beach.

Danielle Martin . . . . . . . . . . . . . . . . . . . . . . . Francine
•• 0:29—In bra, garter belt, stockings and panties, then breasts in room with Rip.
David Winn . . . . . . . . . . . . . . . . . . . . . . . Mike Jenner
•• 0:19—Buns, while making love with Marilyn Chambers in bed.

## *My Tutor* (1983)
Caren Kaye . . . . . . . . . . . . . . . . . . . . . . . Terry Green
•• 0:25—Breasts walking into swimming pool.
•• 0:52—Breasts in the pool with Matt Lattanzi.
••• 0:55—Right breast, lying in bed making love with Lattanzi.
Matt Lattanzi . . . . . . . . . . . . . . . . . . . . Bobby Chrystal
Graem McGavin . . . . . . . . . . . . . . . . . . . . . . . . Sylvia
••• 0:21—In white bra, then breasts in back seat of a car in a parking lot with Matt Lattanzi.
Shelly Taylor Morgan . . . . . . . . . . . . . . . . . . . . Louisa
Francesca "Kitten" Natividad . . . . . . . . . . . . Anna Maria
••• 0:10—Breasts in room with Matt Lattanzi, then lying in bed.
Katt Shea . . . . . . . . . . . . . . . . . . . . . . . Mud Wrestler
• 0:48—Brief breasts when a guy rips her dress off.
Jewel Shepard . . . . . . . . . . . . . . . . . Girl in Phone Booth
• 0:40—Brief left breast in car when Matt Lattanzi fantasizes about making love with her.

## *Mystery Train* (1989)
Steve Buscemi . . . . . . . . . . . . . . . . . . . . . . . . Charlie
Youki Kudoh . . . . . . . . . . . . . . . . . . . . . . . . Mitzuko
•• 0:30—In black bra, in bed. Breasts making love with Jun in bed.
0:37—In black bra, while packing suitcase.

## *Nails* (1992; Made for Cable Movie)
Anne Archer . . . . . . . . . . . . . . . . . . . . . . . Mary Niles
0:16—Breasts and buns belong to body double Shelley Michelle.
Teresa Crespo . . . . . . . . . . . . . . . . . . . Elena Hernandez
•• 0:44—Breasts, taking off her top in room with Dennis Hopper.
Dennis Hopper . . . . . . . . . . . . . . . . Harry "Nails" Niles
••• 0:39—Buns, while getting out of the bathtub and running outside after the guy who shot at him.
• 0:40—Very, very brief frontal nudity, dropping towel to drape on his shoulder.
Shelley Michelle . . . . . . . . . . . . . . . . . . . Body Double
•• 0:16—Breasts and buns, several times body double for Anne Archer during love scene with Dennis Hopper.

## *Naked* (1993; British)
Katrin Cartlidge . . . . . . . . . . . . . . . . . . . . . . . Sophie
•• 0:16—Breasts, while making love around the house with Johnny.
•• 1:17—In black bra and panties in bed with a guy. Breasts, while putting on her dress while sitting on bed.
• 1:23—Brief right breast in gaping dress, when getting up off the floor.

David Thewlis . . . . . . . . . . . . . . . . . . . . . . . . . Johnny
•• 0:17—Frontal nudity, while getting up out of bed. Dark.

## *The Naked Cage* (1985)
Lucinda Crosby . . . . . . . . . . . . . . . . . . . . . . . Rhonda
Flo Gerrish . . . . . . . . . . . . . . . . . . . . . . . . . Mother
Leslie Huntly . . . . . . . . . . . . . . . . . . . . . . . Peaches
Lisa London . . . . . . . . . . . . . . . . . . . . . . . . . Abbey
•• 0:22—Breasts in S&M costume with Angel Tompkins.
•• 0:38—Left breast making out in bed with Angel Tompkins.
Valerie McIntosh . . . . . . . . . . . . . . . . . . . . . . . Ruby
••• 0:24—Breasts and buns in infirmary, then getting attacked by Smiley. Brief lower frontal nudity.
• 0:28—Breasts, while hanging by rope, dead.
Stacey Shaffer . . . . . . . . . . . . . . . . . . . . . . . . . Amy
••• 1:03—Nude in shower room getting hassled by the other girls.
Shari Shattuck . . . . . . . . . . . . . . . . . . . . . . Michelle
•• 0:42—Buns and breasts in shower, then getting slashed by Rita during a dream.
•• 1:00—Left breast getting attacked by Smiley in jail cell, then fighting back.
1:28—In panties, during fight with Rita.
Angel Tompkins . . . . . . . . . . . . . . . . . . . Diane Wallace
•• 0:22—In lingerie, then breasts with Abbey.
• 0:38—Brief right breast, in bed with Abbey.
Christina Whitaker . . . . . . . . . . . . . . . . . . . . . . Rita
••• 0:08—Breasts in bed with Willy.
• 0:55—Brief breasts in gaping sweatshirt during fight with Sheila.
1:28—Panties during fight with Shari Shattuck.
1:29—Sort of left breast in gaping dress.

## *Naked Country* (1985; Australian)
Neela Dey . . . . . . . . . . . . . . . . . . . . . . . . . . Menyan
• 0:27—Breasts when meeting Mary and Lance.
•• 0:28—Breasts during wedding ceremony.
• 1:03—Brief left breast, while on top of cliff.
1:11—Very, very brief breasts during struggle in cave.

## *The Naked Gun 2 1/2: The Smell of Fear* (1991)
Chuck Le Fever . . . . . . . . . . . . . . Mr. Griffith's Stunt Butt
• 1:07—Side view of buns when Leslie Nielsen yanks Dr. Meinheimer's pants down.
Gina Mastrogiacomo . . . . . . "Is this some kind of bust?"

## *Naked Instinct* (1993)
Michelle Bauer . . . . . . . . . . . . . . . . . . . . . . Michelle
••• 0:10—Full frontal nudity with Virgin Rich Kid after taking off her maid outfit and making love with him on bed. Long scene.
••• 0:13—More full frontal nudity with him on top of her.
••• 0:43—Full frontal nudity with Frat Bully and making love with him. Long scene.
••• 1:07—Breasts and buns in red panties, making love with the Therapist. Long scene.

••• 1:10—Full frontal nudity making love on the floor, with her on top.

••• 1:11—More full frontal nudity with him on top.

••• 1:13—More full frontal nudity making love on her hands and knees.

Len DiStefano . . . . . . . . . . . . . . . . . . . . . . . . . Poolman

••• 0:23—Nude, playing with himself while Joanne watches.

Greg Fawcett . . . . . . . . . . . . . . . . . . . . . . . Football Jock

••• 0:59—Buns, making love in bathtub with Joanne.

Albert Mitchell . . . . . . . . . . . . . . . . . . . . . . . Frat Bully

••• 0:42—Nude with Michelle Bauer.

Jeff Perry . . . . . . . . . . . . . . . . . . . . . . . . . . . . . Frat Boy

•• 0:40—Nude in fraternity house with Michelle Bauer.

David Poole . . . . . . . . . . . . . . . . . . . . . . . . . . Therapist

•• 1:09—Buns, while making love in bed with Michelle Bauer.

••• 1:10—Full frontal nudity, on the floor under Bauer.

••• 1:11—Nude, making love on top of Bauer.

Deanne Power . . . . . . . . . . . . . . . . . . . . . . . . . . Joanne

••• 0:19—Breasts, in open robe and red panties, watching the pool man masturbate while she plays with herself.

••• 0:28—Nude, taking off robe and getting into tub, then making love with the Hot Tub Repairman.

••• 0:32—More nude, while making love with him. Long scene.

••• 0:36—Full frontal nudity, standing in tub with him.

••• 0:54—Nude, making love with the Military Recruit. Long scene.

••• 0:59—Nude, making love with the Football Jock.

Peter Stoddard . . . . . . . . . . . . . . . . Hot Tub Repairman

• 0:28—Buns, getting into tub with Joanne.

••• 0:30—Full frontal nudity, while lying on side of tub with Joanne.

••• 0:36—Full frontal nudity, standing up in tub.

Michael Vavrin . . . . . . . . . . . . . . . . . . . Virgin Rich Kid

••• 0:07—Nude, taking off his underwear in bed and masturbating while Michelle Bauer watches, then making love with her. Long scene.

••• 0:13—Buns, while making love on top of Bauer.

Hutch Williams . . . . . . . . . . . . . . . . . . . Military Recruit

••• 0:51—Nude, dancing after stripping in front of Joanne.

## Naked Obsession (1990)

Ria Coyne . . . . . . . . . . . . . . . . . . . . . . . . . . . . Cynthia

•• 0:11—Breasts on stage, dancing in black lingerie.

• 0:13—Buns in G-string while dancing.

•• 0:14—More breasts and buns while dancing.

Maria Ford . . . . . . . . . . . . . . . . . . . . . . . Lynne Hauser

0:16—Dancing on stage doing strip tease. Wearing bra, panties, garter belt and stockings.

••• 0:18—Buns in G-string.

••• 0:20—Breasts and buns in G-string, dancing on stage in front of William Katt. Long scene.

••• 0:23—Nude, dancing with Katt's necktie.

•• 0:34—Nude, on stage at end of another dance routine.

•• 0:44—Breasts in her apartment with Katt.

••• 0:45—Breasts and buns on top of Katt in bed while he gently strangles her with his necktie for oxygen deprivation.

•• 0:47—Breasts in bed after making love with Katt.

Sherri Graham . . . . . . . . . . . . . . . . . . . . . . . . Waitress

William Katt . . . . . . . . . . . . . . . . . . . . . Franklyn Carlyle

• 0:46—Very, very brief buns, while turning over in bed with Maria Ford. Long shot.

Wendy MacDonald . . . . . . . . . . . . . . . Saundra Carlyle

••• 0:28—In black bra, panties and stockings on the dining table during William Katt's fantasy, then breasts.

Elena Sahagun . . . . . . . . . . . . . . . . . . . . . . . . . . Becky

1:07—Dancing on stage in white outfit (She's got a mask over her face).

••• 1:10—In white bra, panties, garter belt and stockings while wearing the mask. Breasts and buns in G-string.

Madison Stone . . . . . . . . . . . . . . . . . . . . . . . . Jezebel

•• 0:35—In black leather outfit. Buns in G-string and breasts.

•• 0:37—More breasts and buns.

• 0:38—More.

•• 0:39—Brief full frontal nudity.

## The Naked Sun (Brazilian)

David Brandon . . . . . . . . . . . . . . . . . . . . . . . . . . Lucas

• 0:58—Buns, while kneeling in bed, undressing Gina.

••• 1:00—Buns, while making love on top of Gina in bed.

• 1:15—Buns, while making love with Gina.

## The Naked Truth (1992)

Donna Baltron . . . . . . . . . . . . . . . . . . . . . . . Miss Cuba

Maureen Flaherty . . . . . . . . . . . . . . . . . . . Miss Romania

0:24—In sexy red swimsuit in the boy's hotel room with the other contestants.

Julie Gray . . . . . . . . . . . . . . . . . . . . . . . Miss Hungary

Shelley Michelle . . . . . . . . . . . . . . . . . . . Miss Honduras

•• 0:18—Nude, changing into "something more comfortable" in front of the two Franks.

• 0:22—Buns, in pink sequined G-string two piece swimsuit.

Natasha Pavlova . . . . . . . . . . . . . . . . . . . . . Miss Bolivia

Shannon Tweed . . . . . . . . . . . . . . First Class Stewardess

M. Emmet Walsh . . . . . . . . . . . . . . Garcia/Gesundheim

## Naked Vengeance (1985)

Deborah Tranelli . . . . . . . . . . . . . . . . . . . . Carla Harris

0:18—In black bra and panties in bedroom while a guy peek in from the window.

• 0:25—In black bra, then breasts during gang rape.

••• 0:43—Nude, while walking into the water to seduce a guy before killing him.

## Naked Warriors (1973)

a.k.a. The Arena

Pam Grier . . . . . . . . . . . . . . . . . . . . . . . . . . . Mamawi

•• 0:08—Brief left breast, then lower frontal nudity and side view of right breast getting washed down in court yard.

••• 0:52—Breasts getting oiled up for a battle. Wow!

Lucretia Love. . . . . . . . . . . . . . . . . . . . . . . . . Deidre
- • 0:07—Brief breasts getting clothes torn off by guards.
- •• 0:08—Brief nude getting washed down in court yard.
  1:08—Brief buns, while bent over riding a horse.

Margaret Markov . . . . . . . . . . . . . . . . . . . . . . Bodicia
- • 0:07—Brief breasts getting clothes torn off by guards.
- • 0:13—Breasts getting her dress ripped off, then raped during party.
- • 0:19—Brief left breast, on floor making love, then right breast and buns.
  0:45—In sheer white dress consoling Septimus, then walking around.
- • 0:52—Brief breasts sitting down, listening to Cornelia.

## *A Name for Evil* (1973)
Robert Culp. . . . . . . . . . . . . . . . . . . . . . . John Blake
- •• 0:52—Frontal nudity running through the woods with a woman.
- • 1:07—Buns, while going skinny dipping. Lots of bun shots underwater.

Samantha Eggar . . . . . . . . . . . . . . . . . . . . .Joanna Blake
- • 0:42—Very brief breasts turning over in bed with Robert Culp. Dark, hard to see.

Sheila Sullivan . . . . . . . . . . . . . . . . . . . . .Luanna Baxter
- • 0:51—Full frontal nudity dancing in the bar with everybody.
- • 0:54—Breasts while Robert Culp makes love with her.
- • 0:56—Breasts getting dressed.
- • 1:17—Nude, skinny dipping with Culp.

## *The Name of the Rose* (1986)
Sean Connery . . . . . . . . . . . . . . . William of Baskerville
Christian Slater . . . . . . . . . . . . . . . . . Adso of Melk
- • 0:48—Buns, while making love with The Girl in the monastery kitchen.

Valentina Vargas . . . . . . . . . . . . . . . . . . . . . The Girl
- ••• 0:46—Breasts and buns making love with Christian Slater in the monastery kitchen.

## *Nashville* (1975)
Karen Black. . . . . . . . . . . . . . . . . . . . . . . Connie White
Timothy Brown . . . . . . . . . . . . . . . . . . . Tommy Brown
Keith Carradine. . . . . . . . . . . . . . . . . . . . . Tom Frank
- • 0:47—Buns, while sitting on floor after getting out of bed.

Geraldine Chaplin. . . . . . . . . . . . . . . . . . . . . . .Opal
Shelley Duvall . . . . . . . . . . . . . . . . . . . . . . .L.A. Jane
Scott Glenn. . . . . . . . . . . . . . . . . . . . . . . Glenn Kelly
Jeff Goldblum . . . . . . . . . . . . . . . . . . . . . .Tricycle Man
Cristina Raines. . . . . . . . . . . . . . . . . . . . . . . .Mary
Gwen Welles . . . . . . . . . . . . . . . . . . . . . Sueleen Gay
- •• 2:09—In bra singing to a room full of men, then breasts doing a strip tease, buns walking up the steps and out of the room.

## *The Nasty Girl* (1989; German)
Lena Stolze. . . . . . . . . . . . . . . . . . . . . . . . . . .Sonja
  1:24—Most of her left breast in gaping nightgown while bending over to get earrings put on.
- • 1:27—Brief breasts and lower frontal nudity, while swimming in water.

## *National Lampoon Goes to the Movies* (1982)
*a.k.a. Movie Madness*
Robby Benson . . . . . . . . . . . . . . . . . . . . . . .Brent Falcone
Candy Clark . . . . . . . . . . . . . . . . . . . . . . . Susan Cooper
Robert Culp . . . . . . . . . . . . . . . . . . . . . . .Fred Everest
Olympia Dukakis . . . . . . . . . . . . . . . . . . . . . .Helena
Ann Dusenberry. . . . . . . . . . . . . . . . . . . . . Dominique
Teresa Ganzel. . . . . . . . . . . . . . . . . . . . . . . .Diana
- ••• 0:19—Breasts, while lying in bed with Peter Riegert. Nice, long scene.

Diane Lane. . . . . . . . . . . . . . . . . . . . . . . . . . Lisa
Christopher Lloyd. . . . . . . . . . . . . . .Samuel Starkman
Harry Reems. . . . . . . . . . . . . . . . . . . . Vice Squad Cop
Margaret Whitton . . . . . . . . . . . . . . . . . . .First Lady
Mary Woronov. . . . . . . . . . . . . . . . . . . . . Secretary

## *National Lampoon's Class Reunion* (1982)
Misty Rowe . . . . . . . . . . . . . . . . . . . . . Cindy Shears
- • 0:37—Very brief breasts running around school stage in Hawaiian hula dance outfit.

Marya Small . . . . . . . . . . . . . . . . . . . . . . Iris Augen

## *National Lampoon's Vacation* (1983)
Beverly D'Angelo . . . . . . . . . . . . . . . . . . Ellen Griswold
- •• 0:18—Brief breasts taking a shower in the motel.
- • 1:19—Brief breasts taking off shirt and jumping into the swimming pool.

John Diehl . . . . . . . . . . . . . . . . . . . Assistant Mechanic
Eugene Levy. . . . . . . . . . . . . . . . . . . . . .Car Salesman
Randy Quaid . . . . . . . . . . . . . . . . . . . . . Cousin Eddie
Tessa Richarde . . . . . . . . . . . . . . . . . . . . . .Motel Guest

## *Naughty Nymphs* (1972; German)
*a.k.a. Passion Pill Swingers*
*a.k.a. Don't Tell Daddy*
Sybil Danning . . . . . . . . . . . . . . . . . . . . . Elizabeth
- ••• 0:21—Nude taking a bath while yelling at her two sisters.
- • 0:30—Breasts and buns throwing Nicholas out of her bedroom.
- •• 0:38—Full frontal nudity running away from Burt.

Sascha Hehn . . . . . . . . . . . . . . . . . . . . . . . . . . n.a.

## *The Naughty Stewardesses* (1978)
*a.k.a. Fresh Air*
Donna Desmond . . . . . . . . . . . . . . . . . . . . . .Margie
- •• 0:12—Breasts leaning out of the shower.

Mikel James . . . . . . . . . . . . . . . . . . . . . . .Diane
- •• 0:34—Breasts in bed waiting for Ben then in bed with him.

Tracey Ann King. . . . . . . . . . . . . . . . . . . . . Barbara
- •• 0:56—Breasts dancing by the pool in front of everybody.

## Necessary Roughness (1991)

Michael Dolan . . . . . . . . . . . . . . Eric "Samurai" Hanson
- 1:09—Buns, while taking a shower, kind of hard to see. (He's the guy in the middle.)

Marcus Giamatti . . . . . . . . . . . . . . . . . . . . . . . Sargie
- 1:09—Buns, while taking a shower. (He's the tall guy on the left.)

Harley Jane Kozak . . . . . . . . . . . . . . . . . Suzanne Carter
Andrew Lauer . . . . . . . . . . . . . . . . . . . . . Charlie Banks
- 1:09—Buns, while taking a shower. (He's the brunette guy on the far right.)

## Necromancer (1988)

Carla Baron . . . . . . . . . . . . . . . . . . . . . . . . . . . . . Gail
- 0:42—Brief breasts getting out of bed with Paul. Dark.

Stan Hurwitz . . . . . . . . . . . . . . . . . . . . . Paul DuShane
- 0:46—Brief buns, when Julie pulls his underwear down. Don't see his face.

Elizabeth Kaitan . . . . . . . . . . . . . . . . . . . . Julie Johnson
- 0:41—Breasts in the shower with Carl.
- 0:45—Very brief side view of right breast, taking off dress in front of Paul.
  1:01—In red and black lingerie.

Shannon McLeod . . . . . . . . . . . . . . . . . . . . . . . . Edna
Edward Wright . . . . . . . . . . . . . . . . . . . . Carl Caulder
- 0:41—Buns, while taking off his towel and walking into shower.

## Necropolis (1987)

LeeAnne Baker . . . . . . . . . . . . . . . . . . . . . . . . . . . Eva
- 0:04—Right breast, while dancing in skimpy black outfit during vampire ceremony.
- 0:38—Brief breasts in front of three evil things. (Before she has special make up to make it look like she has six breasts).

Adriane Lee . . . . . . . . . . . . . . . . . . . . . Cult Member

## Negatives (1968; British)

Glenda Jackson . . . . . . . . . . . . . . . . . . . . . . . . Vivan
- 0:27—Brief breasts, putting on fur coat in front of mirror.
- 0:30—Very brief left breast, while covering herself with fur coat before sitting up.

## Nemesis (1992)

Jennifer Gatti . . . . . . . . . . . . . Rosaria/German National
Olivier Gruner . . . . . . . . . . . . . . . . . . . . . . . . . . Alex
- 0:45—Brief buns, pointing gun at Deborah Shelton. (Don't see his face, but it is him.)

Marjean Holden . . . . . . . . . . . . . . . . . . . . . . . . . San
Tom Janes . . . . . . . . . . . . . . . . . . . . . . . . . . . . Billy
- • 0:30—Buns, standing at the window, looking out.
- 0:31—More buns.
- • • 0:32—More buns, backing up and lying on bed.
- • • 0:37—Brief nude, getting punched by Deborah Shelton and sitting on bed.
- 0:38—Brief buns, getting thrown against the wall.

Deborah Shelton . . . . . . . . . . . . . . . . . . . . . . Julian
- 0:30—Buns, while lying on bed.
- • 0:31—Buns, while standing up and hugging Billy.

- 0:36—Buns, while standing at window. Side view of left breast.
- • • • 0:37—Full frontal nudity, punching Billy and getting dressed. Looking good! Very buff—she worked out for three and a half hours a day.
  0:53—Special effect left breast, sticking through hole in her bullet-ridden blouse.

## Neon Maniacs (1985)

Alan Hayes . . . . . . . . . . . . . . . . . . . . . . . . . . . Steven
Marta Kober . . . . . . . . . . . . . . . . . . . . . . . . . Lorraine
Susan Mierisch . . . . . . . . . . . . . . . . . . Young Lover
- 0:07—Very brief upper half of right breast while kissing her boyfriend at night.

Leilani Sarelle . . . . . . . . . . . . . . . . . . . . . . . . . Natalie

## Nervous Ticks (1991)

Peter Boyle . . . . . . . . . . . . . . . . . . . . . . Ron Rudman
Julie Brown . . . . . . . . . . . . . . . . . . . . . Nancy Rudman
Lenore Kasdorf . . . . . . . . . . . . . . . . . . . . . . . . . Katie
James Le Gros . . . . . . . . . . . . . . . . . . . . . . . . . . Rusty
Claire Stansfield . . . . . . . . . . . . . . . . . . . . . . . . . . Lu
Zoe Trilling . . . . . . . . . . . . . . . . . . . . . . . . . . . Marci
- • 0:24—Brief breasts in shower when Bill Pullman opens the shower curtains.

## Network (1976)

Faye Dunaway . . . . . . . . . . . . . . . . Diana Christensen
- 1:10—Brief left breast twice, taking off clothes in room with William Holden.

## Nevada Heat (1982)

a.k.a. Fake-Out
Connie Hair . . . . . . . . . . . . . . . . . . . . . . . . . . Roberta
- 0:13—Breasts in the shower scene.
- 0:14—Brief breasts in the shower again. Brief buns in shower (Long shot).

Camelia Kath . . . . . . . . . . . . . . . . . . . . . . . Voice #4
Anastassia Stakis . . . . . . . . . . . . . . . . . . . . . . . Wooly
- 0:13—Breasts in the shower room scene.

Pia Zadora . . . . . . . . . . . . . . . . . . . . . . . . . . . Bobbi
- 0:14—Very brief partial right breast and brief buns, in the showers.
- 0:47—Side of left breast, while in bubble bath with Desi Arnaz, Jr.

## Never Cry Wolf (1983)

Brian Dennehy . . . . . . . . . . . . . . . . . . . . . . . . . Rosie
Charlie Martin Smith . . . . . . . . . . . . . . . . . . . . . Tyler
- 0:32—Buns while warming himself and drying his clothes after falling through the ice.
- 1:18—Very brief frontal nudity running and jumping off a rock into the pond.
- 1:20—Buns while running in meadow with the caribou.
- 1:23—Brief silhouette of lower frontal nudity while scampering up a hill. More buns when chasing the caribou.

### Never on Tuesday (1988)
Peter Berg............................ Eddie
Claudia Christian...................... Tuesday
- 0:43—Brief side view of right breast in the shower with Eddie during his fantasy.

Emilio Estevez.......... Uncredited Tow Truck Driver
Andrew Lauer...........................Matt

### Never Too Young to Die (1986)
Vanity......................... Donja Deering
0:25—In white bra in the kitchen with John Stamos while he tends to her wounded arm.
- 1:04—Wearing a bikini swimsuit, putting on suntan lotion. Brief breasts in quick cuts making love with John in a cabin bedroom.

Tara Buckman................. Sacrificed Punkette

### New Eden (1994)
Stephen Baldwin....................... Adams
Lisa Bonet.............................. Lily
- 1:02—Brief back side of left breast while in bed with Stephen Baldwin.

### New Jack City (1991)
Eek-A-Mouse........................Fat Smitty
- 0:15—Buns, when Wesley Snipes holds a gun to his head and makes him walk nude outside.

Tracy Camilla Johns......................Unigua
- 0:40—Buns, while dancing in red bra, panties, garter belt and stockings.
- 0:53—Buns and right breast in bed with Wesley Snipes.

### New Year's Evil (1981)
Teri Copley.......................Teenage Girl
- 0:49—Brief right breast in the back of the car with her boyfriend at a drive-in movie. Breast is half sticking out of her white bra. Dark, hard to see anything.

Grant Cramer .....................Derek Sullivan
Louisa Moritz ......................... Sally
Taaffe O'Connell........................ Jane

### New York Nights (1981)
Corinne Alphen.................... The Debutante
- 0:10—Breasts, making love in the back seat of a limousine with the rock star.
- 1:38—Breasts dancing in the bedroom while the Financier watches from the bed.

Bobbi Burns ......................The Authoress
- 0:16—Breasts on the couch outside with the rock star, then breasts in bed.

Cynthia Lee....................... The Porn Star
- 1:15—Breasts in the steam room talking to the prostitute.
- 1:26—Breasts in office with the financier and making love on his desk.

Missy O'Shea ...................... The Model
0:30—In white bra in restroom making love with the photographer.

### New York's Finest (1988)
John Altamura .....................Brian Morrison
Ruth Corrine Collins................. Joy Sugarman
- 0:04—Brief breasts with a bunch of hookers.
- 0:36—Breasts with her two friends doing push-ups on the floor.
- 1:02—Breasts making love on top of a guy talking about diamonds.

Jennifer Delora ................... Loretta Michaels
- 0:02—Brief breasts pretending to be a black hooker.
- 0:04—Brief breasts with a bunch of hookers.
- 0:36—Breasts with her two friends doing push-ups on the floor.

Jane Hamilton .......................... Bunny
Karen Nielsen........................Hooker #1
Heidi Paine........................ Carley Pointer
- 0:04—Brief breasts with a bunch of hookers.
- 0:36—Breasts with her two friends doing push-ups on the floor.

Denise Torek ....................... Hooker #2
Miriam Zucker ...................... Mrs. Rush

### The Newlydeads (1988)
Rebecca Barrington ..................... Blanche
- 0:08—Right breast, while making out with her fiancee, Bull, in the car.
  1:00—In white body suit, while lying on the floor.
- 1:01—Right breast, peeking out of the top of her body suit.
- 1:02—Brief buns, while on the floor with Bull.

Michele Burger........................Bikini Girl
Roxanna Michaels ...................... Lynda
0:23—In lacy black bra and panties, while in bed.
- 0:44—Breasts, while in the shower.
- 0:47—Brief breast, while dead on the shower floor after being stabbed.

Renee Way ...........................Brenda
- 0:19—Buns and side of right breast, while in spa with her boyfriend.

### Next Door (1994; Made for Cable Movie)
Kate Capshaw ...................... Karen Coler
Randy Quaid .....................Lenny Benedetti
James Woods ......................Matt Coler
- 0:30—Brief buns, while mooning out the window while Randy Quaid sprays the outside of the window with water.

### Next Year if All Goes Well (1983; French)

Isabelle Adjani . . . . . . . . . . . . . . . . . . . . . . . . . .Isabelle
- 0:27—Brief right breast, lying in bed with Maxime.

Thierry Lhermitte . . . . . . . . . . . . . . . . . . . . . . Maxime

### Nickel Mountain (1985)

Brian Kerwin . . . . . . . . . . . . . . . . . . . . . . . . . . .George
Heather Langencamp . . . . . . . . . . . . . . . . . . . . . Callie
- ••• 0:24—Breasts in bed lying with Willard.
- • 0:29—Side view of left breast and brief breasts falling on bed with Willard.
- 0:29—In white panties, peeking out the window.

### Nicole (1972)

a.k.a. The Widow's Revenge
Catherine Bach . . . . . . . . . . . . . . . . . . . . . . . . . . . . .Sue
- •• 1:01—Brief breasts, twice, undressing to put on nightgown on boat. Nice shots, but too brief.
- •• 1:10—Very brief side view of breasts, three times, getting felt by Leslie Caron. Don't see either Bach's or Caron's face.

Leslie Caron . . . . . . . . . . . . . . . . . . . . . . . . . . . .Nicole

### Night Angel (1989)

Linden Ashby . . . . . . . . . . . . . . . . . . . . . . . . . . . Craig
- • 1:22—Buns, while kneeling down to pick up picture. Don't see his face.

Lisa Axelrod . . . . . . . . . . . . . . . . . . . . . . . . . . . . Double
Karen Black . . . . . . . . . . . . . . . . . . . . . . . . . . . . . .Rita
Debra Feuer . . . . . . . . . . . . . . . . . . . . . . . . . . . .Kirstie
- • 0:46—Brief side of left breast. Dark.

Gary Hudson . . . . . . . . . . . . . . . . . . . . . . . . . . . . . Rod

### Night Breed (1990)

Catherine Chevalier . . . . . . . . . . . . . . . . . . . . . . Rachel
- • 1:12—Breasts in police jail, going through a door and killing a cop.

Craig Sheffer . . . . . . . . . . . . . . . . . . . . . . . . . . . .Boone

### Night Call Nurses (1972)

a.k.a. Young LA Nurses 2
Patti T. Byrne . . . . . . . . . . . . . . . . . . . . . . . . . .Barbara
- •• 0:59—Breasts several times in bed with the Doctor.

Alana Collins . . . . . . . . . . . . . . . . . . . . . . . . . . . . Janis
- •• 0:12—Breasts in bed with Zach.
- 0:24—In white two piece swimsuit on boat.
- •• 0:28—Breasts and buns on bed with Kyle.
- • 0:52—Brief right breast twice in shower with Kyle.

Lynne Guthrie . . . . . . . . . . . . . . . . . . . . . . . . .Cynthia
- • 0:00—Breasts on hospital roof taking off robe and standing on edge just before jumping off.

Mitte Lawrence . . . . . . . . . . . . . . . . . . . . . . . . Sandra
- •• 0:49—Breasts in bed with a guy.

Dixie Lee Peabody . . . . . . . . . . . . . . . . . . . . . . . Robin
- •• 0:35—Breasts taking off clothes in encounter group.
- • 0:39—Brief breasts in Barbara's flashback.

### Night Club (1989)

Nicholas Hoppe . . . . . . . . . . . . . . . . . . . . . . . . . Nick
- • 0:27—Brief buns, while making love on roof with stripper. Long shot.
- ••• 0:37—Frontal nudity, getting up off the floor.

---

- ••• 0:47—Buns, while making love with Elizabeth Kaitan.

Elizabeth Kaitan . . . . . . . . . . . . . . . . . . . . . . Beth/Liza
- •• 0:31—Left breast, while pulling down blouse and caressing herself.
- •• 0:33—Left breast in pulled down blouse on stairwell with Nick.
- ••• 0:36—Breasts on warehouse floor with Nick.
- ••• 0:46—Full frontal nudity, taking off her dress in front of Nick.
- ••• 1:03—Breasts, making love with another guy in front of Nick.

### Night Eyes (1990)

(Unrated version reviewed.)
Yvette Buchanan . . . . . . . . . . . . . . . . . . . . . . . .Baby Doll
- • 0:07—Brief left breast, then breasts making love in bathroom with Ronee.

Barbara Ann Klein . . . . . . . . . . . . . . . . Sleeping Woman
- • 0:02—Brief breasts struggling with burglar/rapist.

Stephen Meadows . . . . . . . . . . . . . . . .Michael Vincent
- • 0:27—Buns and balls in bed with Tanya Roberts while Andrew Stevens watches on monitor.

Tanya Roberts . . . . . . . . . . . . . . . . . . . . . . . . . . . Nikki
- 0:18—In white one piece swimsuit by the pool.
- • 0:20—Side view of left breast, while getting dressed while sitting on bed.
- 0:25—In white lingerie, making love in bed with Michael.
- 0:30—Repeat of last scene on TV when Andrew Stevens brings the video tape home to watch.
- 0:55—Making love with Stevens. Don't see anything, but still steamy. Bubble covered left breast in tub with Stevens.
- ••• 1:09—Breasts giving Stevens a massage, then making love. Nice! Buns and left breast, while in the shower making love.
- • 1:27—Buns, making love with Stevens in a chair.

Andrew Stevens . . . . . . . . . . . . . . . . . . . . . . . . . . . Will
- ••• 1:11—Buns while in the shower.
- ••• 1:26—Side view of buns with Tanya Roberts seen through a window.

### Night Eyes 2 (1991)

Tim Russ . . . . . . . . . . . . . . . . . . . . . . . . . . Jesse Younger
- •• 0:07—Buns, while getting out of bed and putting his pants on.

Lisa Saxton . . . . . . . . . . . . . . . . . . . . . . . . . .Car Rental Girl
- ••• 0:05—Breasts and buns, making love in bed with Jesse.
- • 0:09—Buns, on TV when video tape is played back.

Andrew Stevens . . . . . . . . . . . . : . . . . . . . . . . Will Griffith
- • 1:07—Partial buns, in mirror, while lying on the floor with Shannon Tweed.

Shannon Tweed . . . . . . . . . . . . . . . . . Marilyn Mejenes
- ••• 0:49—Buns and breasts making love with Andrew Stevens in bed.
- ••• 1:06—Breasts, making love with Stevens (nice use of raspberries).

## *Night Eyes 3* (1993)

Monique Parent . . . . . . . . . . . . . . . . . . . . . . . . Brandy
- ••• 0:09—Breasts and buns in G-string, stripping out of her clothes in Zoe's house in front of Dan.

Andrew Stevens . . . . . . . . . . . . . . . . . . . . . . Will Griffith
- •• 0:53—Buns, while making love on top of Shannon Tweed in bed.
- •• 1:01—Buns, while making love with Shannon Tweed. First seen on B&W security monitor, then in real life.

Shannon Tweed . . . . . . . . . . . . . . . . . . Zoe Clairmont
- •• 0:16—Breasts, while getting her clothes ripped off by Dan, then sitting up in bed.
- • 0:23—Brief full frontal nudity in shower behind the door.
- ••• 0:51—Breasts and buns, while making love in bed with Andrew Stevens.
- • 0:53—Buns, while lying in bed afterwards.
- ••• 0:56—Nude, while getting into the shower and in the shower.
- ••• 1:01—Full frontal nudity, while taking off her robe in front of fireplace.
- • 1:02—Partial buns and breasts, while on top of Stevens.
- • 1:15—Brief breasts in B&W photo from security video tape.

Tracy Tweed . . . . . . . . . . . . . . . . . . . . . . . Dana Gray
- •• 0:25—Left breast, then breasts while in bed with Edgar.
- ••• 0:40—Breasts and side view of buns, while wearing black G-string panties in dressing room while nonchalantly talking to Andrew Stevens.

## *A Night Full of Rain* (1978; Italian)

Candice Bergen. . . . . . . . . . . . . . . . . . . . . . . . . . Lizzy
- •• 1:04—Right breast, while in car with Giancarlo Giannini.

## *Night Game* (1989)

Roy Scheider. . . . . . . . . . . . . . . . . . . . . . . . . . . . .n.a.
Karen Young . . . . . . . . . . . . . . . . . . . . . . . . . . . .Roxy
    0:02—In white slip with Roy Scheider.
- • 0:06—Right breast, while in bed with Scheider after he answers the phone.

## *Night Games* (1980)

Joanna Cassidy . . . . . . . . . . . . . . . . . . . . . . Julie Miller
    0:44—Buns, skinny dipping in the pool with Cindy Pickett.
- •• 0:45—Brief full frontal nudity sitting up.

Gene Davis . . . . . . . . . . . . . . . . . . . . . . . . . . Timothy
Cindy Pickett. . . . . . . . . . . . . . . . . . . . Valerie St. John
- •• 0:05—Brief breasts, while getting scared by her husband in the shower.
- • 0:45—Buns and breasts by and in the swimming pool with Joanna Cassidy.
    0:46—Breasts under sheer blue dress during fantasy sequence with Cassidy.
- • 0:48—Brief full frontal nudity getting out of the pool, then breasts lying down with Cassidy.

    1:03—Dancing at night in a see through nightgown.
- ••• 1:14—Full frontal nudity standing up in bathtub, then breasts during fantasy with a guy in gold.
- •• 1:18—Breasts, while getting out of pool at night.
- ••• 1:24—Breasts, while sitting up in bed and stretching.

## *A Night in Heaven* (1983)

Christopher Atkins . . . . . . . . . . . . . . . . . . . . . . . . Rick
- • 1:03—Very brief frontal nudity when he pulls down his pants in hotel room with Leslie Ann Warren.
- • 1:15—Brief buns while on boat with Leslie Ann Warren's angry husband.

Sandra Beall . . . . . . . . . . . . . . . . . . . . . . . . . . . .Slick
- • 1:09—Brief close up of left breast in shower with Christopher Atkins.

Veronica Gamba . . . . . . . . . . . . . . . . . . . . . . Tammy
Rose McVeigh . . . . . . . . . . . . . . . . . . . . . . . . Alison
Carrie Snodgress . . . . . . . . . . . . . . . . . . Mrs. Johnson

## *Night Moves* (1975)

Susan Clark . . . . . . . . . . . . . . . . . . . . . . . . . . . Ellen
- • 1:09—Brief breasts in bed with Gene Hackman.

Melanie Griffith . . . . . . . . . . . . . . . . . . . Delly Grastner
- • 0:42—Brief breasts changing tops outside while talking with Gene Hackman.
- • 0:46—Nude, saying "hi" from under water beneath a glass bottom boat.
- • 0:47—Brief side view of right breast getting out of the water.

Kenneth Mars. . . . . . . . . . . . . . . . . . . . . . . . . . .Nick
Jennifer Warren . . . . . . . . . . . . . . . . . . . . . . . Paula
- •• 0:56—Breasts in bed with Gene Hackman.
- • 0:57—Right breast after making love in bed with Hackman.

James Woods . . . . . . . . . . . . . . . . . . . . . . . . .Quentin

## *Night of the Creeps* (1986)

Suzanne Snyder . . . . . . . . . . . . . . . . . . . . . . . . . Lisa
Jill Whitlow. . . . . . . . . . . . . . . . . . Cynthia Cronenberg
    0:31—In bra and panties taking off sweater.
- • 0:33—Brief breasts putting nightgown on over her head in her bedroom.

## *Night of the Cyclone* (1990)

Marisa Berenson. . . . . . . . . . . . . . . . . . . . . .Francoise
Alla Korot. . . . . . . . . . . . . . . . . . . . . . . . . Angelique
- • 0:21—Right breast, then brief breasts getting out of the shower.

Kris Kristofferson . . . . . . . . . . . . . . . . . . . . . . . .Stan
Jeffrey Meek. . . . . . . . . . . . . . . . . . . . . . . . . . Adam
- • 1:07—Brief buns, while putting on his pants, when he's interrupted in bed with Angelique. Long shot.

Kimberleigh Stark. . . . . . . . . . . . . . . . . . . . . . Venna
- • 0:01—Brief left breast while posing for the painter.
- • 0:40—Breasts on the boat, fighting with the businessman. Breasts on the floor, dead.

Jennifer Steyn. . . . . . . . . . . . . . . . . . . . . . . . Celeste

### Night of the Demons (1987)
(Unrated version reviewed.)

Amelia Kinkade . . . . . . . . . . . . . . . . . . . . . . . Angela
- 0:47—Brief buns in panties, garter belt and stockings under dress while doing sexy dance in living room.

Cathy Podewell . . . . . . . . . . . . . . . . . . . . . . . . . Judy
- 0:06—Brief buns, while changing clothes and talking on the phone.
- 0:07—In white bra after taking off her sweater.

Linnea Quigley . . . . . . . . . . . . . . . . . . . . . . . Suzanne
- 0:10—Buns in panties under short skirt, while bending over to distract the convenience store clerks.
- •• 0:52—Breasts twice, opening her dress top while acting weird. Pushes a tube of lipstick into her left breast. (Don't try this at home kids!)
- 0:56—Lower frontal nudity, lifting her skirt up for Jay.

Jill Terashita . . . . . . . . . . . . . . . . . . . . . . . . . Frannie
- •• 0:57—Breasts while making love with her boyfriend in a coffin.

### Night of the Living Babes (1987)

Blondi . . . . . . . . . . . . . . . . Mondo Zombie Girl Darlene
- ••• 0:12—Breasts wearing dark purple wig and long gloves, with the other Mondo Zombie Girls.
- ••• 0:16—More breasts and buns in bed with Buck.
- 0:50—Breasts on the couch with the other Zombie Girls.
- 0:52—Breasts on the couch again.

Michelle Bauer . . . . . . . . . . . . . . . . . . . . . . . . . Sue
- •• 0:44—Breasts chained up with Chuck and Buck.
- ••• 0:46—More breasts chained up.
- 0:50—Breasts getting rescued with Lulu.

Louis Bonanno . . . . . . . . . . . . . . . . . . . . . . . . Buck

Teri Lynn Peake . . . . . . . . . . . . . . . . . . . . Vesuvia
- ••• 0:25—Breasts and buns in G-string, dancing in front of Chuck and Buck. Long scene.

Connie Woods . . . . . . . . . . . . . . . . . . . . . . . Lulu
- 0:46—Breasts and buns in lingerie, in a cell with Buck.
- ••• 0:48—More breasts in cell with Buck.
- 0:50—Breasts getting rescued with Michelle Bauer.

### Night of the Warrior (1991)

Bridget Carney . . . . . . . . . . . . . . . . . . . . . . . Sarah
Anthony Geary . . . . . . . . . . . . . . . . . . . . . . . . Lynch
Kathleen Kinmont . . . . . . . . . . . . . . Katherine Pierce
- 0:29—Very brief upper half of right breast, leaning out of the shower to get a towel.
- 0:46—Very, very brief part of buns, lifting her leg up while kissing Lorenzo Lamas at the art gallery.
- 1:10—Brief right breast, while making love with Lamas on motorcycle.

Teal Roberts . . . . . . . . . . . . . . . . . . . . . . . Still Model

### Night of the Wilding (1990)

Julie Austin . . . . . . . . . . . . . . . . . . . . . . . . . . Betty
- 0:13—In bra and panties, undressing in bedroom.

- •• 0:14—Side of left breast, taking off bra in bathroom. Breasts in shower.
- 0:16—More breasts in the shower.
- 0:17—Breasts behind shower door.

Kimberly Speiss . . . . . . . . . . . . . . . . . . . . . . . . Doris

### Night Patrol (1985)

Linda Blair . . . . . . . . . . . . . . . . . . . . . . . . . . . . Sue
- 1:19—Brief left breast, in bed with The Unknown Comic.

Francesca "Kitten" Natividad . . . . . . . . Hippie Woman
- •• 1:01—Breasts in kitchen with Pat Paulsen, the other police officer and her hippie boyfriend.

Lori Sutton . . . . . . . . . . . . . . . . . . . . . . . Edith Hutton
- ••• 0:47—In white bra, panties, garter belt and stockings, then breasts three times taking off bra in bedroom with the Police officer.

### The Night Porter (1974; Italian/U.S.)

Charlotte Rampling . . . . . . . . . . . . . . . . . . . . . Lucia
- •• 0:11—Side nudity being filmed with a movie camera in the concentration camp line.
- 0:13—Nude running around a room while a Nazi taunts her by shooting his gun near her.
- ••• 1:12—Breasts doing a song and dance number wearing pants, suspenders and a Nazi hat. Long scene.

### Night Rhythms (1992)
(Unrated version reviewed.)

Carrie Bittner . . . . . . . . . . . . . . . . . . . . . . . . . Elaine
- ••• 0:06—Right breast, then breasts and lower frontal nudity while talking on the phone and playing with herself. Long scene.

David Carradine . . . . . . . . . . . . . . . . . . . . . Vincent
Deborah Driggs . . . . . . . . . . . . . . . . . . . . Cinnamon
- ••• 1:15—Left breast, then lower frontal nudity, making love with Martin Hewitt in bed.
- ••• 1:19—Breasts, sitting on bed and talking to Hewitt.

Martin Hewitt . . . . . . . . . . . . . . . . . . . . . . Nick West
- •• 0:29—Buns, while making love with Tracy Tweed.
- ••• 0:31—Buns, while making love with Tweed.
- 0:33—Partial buns, while getting up off the floor.
- ••• 1:18—Buns, while making love on top of Deborah Driggs in bed.

Sam Jones . . . . . . . . . . . . . . . . . . . . . . . . . Jackson
Erika Nann . . . . . . . . . . . . . . . . . . . . . . . . . . . Alex
- ••• 1:00—Buns in G-string and bra, then breasts, undressing in front of Martin Hewitt and making love with him.

Kristine Rose . . . . . . . . . . . . . . . . . . . . . . . . Marilyn
- ••• 0:17—Taking off her blouse at bar with Martin Hewitt, then nude, making love on the bar with him.

Delia Sheppard . . . . . . . . . . . . . . . . . . . . . . Bridget
- ••• 1:25—Full frontal nudity, making love with Kit in bed. Long scene.

Jamie Stafford . . . . . . . . . . . . . . . . . . . . . . . . . . Kit
- •• 0:40—Breasts in push-up bra in dressing room.
- ••• 0:51—Nude, in bed, making love with Lila and Martin Hewitt.
- 0:54—Buns, while watching TV while lying in bed.

••• 0:55—Nude, undressing to take a shower with Lila.

•• 1:23—In sheer black blouse, talking to Delia Sheppard in the radio station.

••• 1:25—Nude, in bed with Sheppard, then getting dressed. Long scene.

Julie Strain.............................. Linda

••• 0:03—In white bra, then left breast, while talking on the phone and playing with herself.

Tracy Tweed ............................Honey

••• 0:28—Breasts making love with Martin Hewitt in radio station. Nice, long scene.

••• 0:31—Nude, getting up after changing positions.

•• 0:33—Breasts, lying dead on the floor.

### Night School (1980)

Rachel Ward ...........................Elanor

• 0:24—In sheer white bra and panties, taking off clothes to take a shower. Breasts taking off bra. Hard to see because she's behind a shower curtain.

0:28—Buns, when her boyfriend rubs red paint all over her in the shower.

### Night Shift (1982)

Brett Clark...................... Nick "The Dick"

Kevin Costner .....................Frat Boy #1

Ashley Cox ...................... Jenny Lynn

Shannen Doherty ..................... Bluebird

Dawn Dunlap .......................Maxine

Monique Gabrielle ...................... Tessie

• 0:55—Brief breasts on college guy's shoulders during party in the morgue.

Cassandra Gava......................... J. J.

Clint Howard.........................Jefferey

Ava Lazar ...........................Sharon

Shelley Long ................... Belinda Keaton

0:20—In black teddy and robe talking to Henry Winkler in the hallway.

0:37—In panties, socks and tank top cooking breakfast in Winkler's kitchen.

Ola Ray .............................. Dawn

K.C. Winkler ........................Cheryl

Robbin Young.........................Nancy

### The Night They Raided Minsky's (1968)

Britt Ekland ................. Rachel Schpitendavel

• 1:34—Brief breasts, when her dress accidentally falls down during strip tease routine on stage. Probably a body double because you don't see her face. (A reader has a letter from the director who says it's a body double.)

### Night Train to Terror (1985)

Meredith Kennedy ................. Dead Redhead

• 0:16—Right breast, while strapped to gurney, before getting killed with a saw.

John Phillip Law. .................. Harry Billings

### Night Visitor (1989)

Allen Garfield ..................... Zachary Willard

Richard Roundtree.................. Captain Crane

Shannon Tweed .......................Lisa Grace

Teresa Vander Woude ............... Kelly Fremont

Teri Weigel......................... Victim in Cellar

• 0:50—Brief out of focus breasts changing tops in the cellar.

• 0:55—Right breast, during ceremony. Very brief breasts just before being stabbed.

### Night Warning (1982)

Julia Duffy ...........................Julie Linden

0:44—Upper half of left breast.

• 0:46—Brief breasts when her boyfriend pulls the sheets down.

•• 0:47—Brief breasts when Susan Tyrrell opens the bedroom door.

Susan Tyrrell.......................Cheryl Roberts

• 0:17—Left breast, sticking out of dress just before she stabs the TV repairman.

### The Nightcomers (1971; British)

Stephanie Beacham ............ Miss Margaret Jessel

• 0:13—Brief left breast lying in bed having her breasts fondled.

••• 0:30—Breasts in bed with Marlon Brando while a little boy watches through the window.

•• 0:55—Breasts in bed pulling the sheets down.

Marlon Brando........................ Peter Quint

0:30—Looks like you can see something between his legs, but most of his midsection is hidden by bed post.

### Nightfall (1988)

Andra Millian ............................Anna

• 0:12—Very brief breasts making love with David Birney.

• 0:41—Very brief breasts making love in front of a fire.

0:58—Same scene in a flashback while the guy is talking to another woman.

### Nightforce (1986)

Linda Blair .............................. Carla

Kathleen Kinmont ........................ Cindy

Claudia Udy.....................Christy Hanson

•• 0:07—Breasts making love in the stable with Steve during her engagement party.

••• 0:10—Nude, fantasizing in the shower.

### The Nightman (1992)

Joanna Kerns ...................... Eve Rhodes

0:44—Side view of buns in panties, garter belt and stockings making love with Tom. Don't see her face.

•• 0:47—Buns, while rolling over in bed and sitting up.

••• 0:57—Breasts and buns, while making love with Tom in bed. Don't see her face. Probably a body double.

Jenny Robertson............... Dr. Margaret Rhodes

• 1:25—Brief right breast in gaping dress when she looks at old things hidden under floor boards.

### Nightmare at Shadow Woods (1983)

a.k.a. Blood Rage

Jane Bentzen................................. Julie
   0:38—In red lingerie, black stockings and garter belt in her apartment with Phil.

Chad Montgomery.........................Gregg
   • 0:52—Brief buns, while making love with Andrea on diving board just before getting killed.

### A Nightmare on Elm Street 3: The Dream Warriors (1987)

Stacey Alden............................. Marcie
   ••• 0:49—Breasts and buns in white G-string, taking off nurse's uniform and seducing Joey in hospital room. Then giving him the tongue before turning into Freddy Kruger.

Patricia Arquette.................... Kristen Parker

Heather Langencamp .............Nancy Thompson

Jennifer Rubin ............................. Taryn

Craig Wasson .................. Dr. Neil Goldman

### A Nightmare on Elm Street 4: The Dream Master (1988)

Hope Marie Carlton.................... Pin-Up Girl
   • 0:21—Brief breasts swimming in a waterbed.

Linnea Quigley ............ Soul from Freddy's Chest
   • 1:23—Brief breasts twice, trying to get out of Freddy's body. Don't see her face clearly.

### Nightmare Sisters (1987)

Michelle Bauer .......................... Mickey
   ••• 0:39—Breasts standing in panties with Melody and Marci after transforming from nerds to sexy women.
   ••• 0:40—Breasts in the kitchen with Melody and Marci.
   ••• 0:44—Full frontal nudity in the bathtub with Melody and Marci. Excellent, long scene.
   ••• 0:47—Breasts in the bathtub. Nice close up.
   ••• 0:48—Still more breasts in the bathtub.
   •• 0:53—Breasts in bed with J.J.

Sandy Brooke .................. Amanda Detweiler

Matthew Phelps ............................J.J.
   •• 0:53—Buns, while taking off his pants and getting into bed with Michelle Bauer.

Linnea Quigley .........................Melody
   ••• 0:39—Breasts, wearing panties, while standing with Mickey and Marci after transforming from nerds to sexy women.
   ••• 0:40—Breasts in the kitchen with Mickey and Marci.
   ••• 0:44—Breasts in the bathtub with Mickey and Marci. Excellent, long scene.
   ••• 0:46—Breasts, while in the bathtub. Nice close up.
   ••• 0:48—Still more breasts, while in the bathtub.
   ••• 0:55—Breasts, while dancing and singing in front of Kevin. Long scene.
   •• 0:57—Breasts while on the couch with Bud.

Brinke Stevens.......................... Marci
   ••• 0:39—Breasts wearing panties, while standing with Melody and Mickey after transforming from nerds to sexy women.

   ••• 0:40—Breasts while in the kitchen with Melody and Mickey.

   ••• 0:44—Nude in the bathtub with Melody and Mickey. Excellent, long scene.

   ••• 0:47—Breasts while in the bathtub. Nice close up.

   ••• 0:48—Still more buns and breasts in the bathtub.

### Nights in White Satin (1987)

Kim Waltrip ...................... Stevie Hughes
   0:37—In white wig, bra, panties, garter belt and stocking during photo session.
   0:39—Brief side view of left breast in black slip during photo session.
   • 0:53—Breasts in bathtub with Walker. Out of focus, hard to see.

### The Nightstalker (1987)

Tally Chanel ............................Brenda
   • 0:54—Brief frontal nudity lying dead in bed covered with paint. Long shot, hard to see anything.

Joan Chen ........................... Mai Wong

Lydie Denier...................... First Victim
   ••• 0:03—Breasts making love with big guy.

Marcia Karr ....................... H.J. Salters

Sheila Lussier ............................ n.a.

Ola Ray ............................Sable Fox

Diane Sommerfield...............Lonnie Roberts
   • 0:35—Side view of right breast lying dead in morgue.

### Nightwish (1988)

(Unedited version reviewed.)

Alisha Das ................................ Kim
   •• 1:09—Brief breasts, then left breast in open dress caressing herself while lying on the ground.

Elizabeth Kaitan .........................Donna
   • 0:04—In wet T-shirt, then brief breasts taking it off during experiment. Long shot.
   • 1:10—Briefly in braless, see-through purple dress.

### Nijinsky (1980; British)

Alan Bates .......................Sergei Diaghilev

Leslie Browne........................... Romula
   • 1:34—Very brief breasts, twice, on the floor when Nijinsky rips her dress off. Dark.

Jeremy Irons....................... Mikhail Fokine

### Ninja Academy (1990)

Michele Burger.......................... Nudist

Becky LeBeau ........................... Nudist
   •• 0:26—Nude, carrying plate, then going to swing at nudist colony. Then playing volleyball (she's the first one to hit the ball).

Bonnie Paine ........................... Nudist
   • 0:26—Brief buns and breasts playing volleyball. (She's the second blonde on the far side of the net who misses the ball.)

### No Place to Hide (1991)
Drew Barrymore . . . . . . . . . . . . . . . . . . . . Tinsel Hanley
Lydie Denier . . . . . . . . . . . . . . . . . . . . . Pamela Hanley
- 0:03—Breasts, after opening her ballet costume in the wings backstage before getting sliced up with a knife.
Kris Kristofferson . . . . . . . . . . . . . . . . . . . . Joe Garvey
Dey Young . . . . . . . . . . . . . . . . . . . . . . . . . . . Karen

### No Small Affair (1984)
Judy Baldwin . . . . . . . . . . . . . . . . . . . . . . . . Stephanie
- ••• 0:36—In white bra, panties and garter belt, then breasts in Jon Cryer's bedroom trying to seduce him.
Elizabeth Daily . . . . . . . . . . . . . . . . . . . . . . . . . Susan
Demi Moore . . . . . . . . . . . . . . . . . . . . . . . . . . Laura
- 1:34—Very, very brief side view of left breast in bed with Jon Cryer.
Tim Robbins . . . . . . . . . . . . . . . . . . . . . . . . . Nelson
Jennifer Tilly . . . . . . . . . . . . . . . . . . . . . . . . . . Mona

### No Way Out (1987)
Iman . . . . . . . . . . . . . . . . . . . . . . . . . . . . Nina Beka
Kevin Costner . . . . . . . . . . . . . . . Lt. Cmdr. Tom Farrell
Sean Young . . . . . . . . . . . . . . . . . . . . . . . Susan Atwell
0:11—In black stockings, garter belt & corset in love scene in back of limousine with Kevin Costner.
- ••• 0:13—Side view of left breast, then brief right breast, going into Nina's apartment with Costner.
0:21—In bed in pink lingerie and a robe talking on telephone when Costner is in Manila.
0:31—In corset and stockings with garter belt in bathroom talking to Costner.

### Nomads (1986)
Pierce Brosnan . . . . . . . . . . . . . . . . . . . . . . Pommier
- 0:56—Buns, while taking his pants off by the window. Kind of dark, hard to see.
Lesley-Anne Down . . . . . . . . . . . . . . . . . . . . . . Flax
Anna-Maria Monticelli . . . . . . . . . . . . . . . . . . . . Niki
- 0:57—Left breast, making love in bed with Pierce Brosnan. Dark, hard to see anything.
Mary Woronov . . . . . . . . . . . . . . . . . . . Dancing Mary

### North Dallas Forty (1979)
Peter Boyle . . . . . . . . . . . . . . . . . . . . . . . . . Emmett
Mac Davis . . . . . . . . . . . . . . . . . . . . . . . . . . Maxwell
- 0:53—Brief buns while getting a can of Coke in the locker room.
Dayle Haddon . . . . . . . . . . . . . . . . . . . . . . Charlotte
Nick Nolte . . . . . . . . . . . . . . . . . . . . . . Phillip Elliott
- 0:49—Brief buns, while pulling down underwear to get into whirlpool bath in locker room.
Savannah Smith Bouchér . . . . . . . . . . . . . . . . Joanne
- 0:27—Very brief breasts in bed tossing around with Nick Nolte.

### Not of This Earth (1988)
Ava Cadell . . . . . . . . . . . . . . . . . . . . . . Second Hooker
- •• 0:41—Breasts in cellar with Paul just before getting killed with two other hookers. Wearing a gold dress.
Kim Dawson . . . . . . . . . . . . . . . . . . . . . Girl in House

Monique Gabrielle . . . . . . . . . . . . . . . . . . . . . . Agnes
Roxanne Kernohan . . . . . . . . . . . . . . . . . . . Lead Hooker
- ••• 0:41—Breasts in cellar with Paul just before getting killed with two other hookers. Wearing a blue top.
Becky LeBeau . . . . . . . . . . . . . . . . . Happy Birthday Girl
- ••• 0:47—Breasts doing a Happy Birthday stripper-gram for the old guy.
Traci Lords . . . . . . . . . . . . . . . . . . . . . . . . . . Nadine
- •• 0:25—Buns and side view of left breast drying herself off with a towel while talking to Jeremy.
0:27—In blue swimsuit by swimming pool.
- •• 0:42—Breasts in bed making love with Harry.
0:46—Walking around the house in white lingerie.
Kelli Maroney . . . . . . . . . . . . . . . . . Nurse Mary Oxford
Taaffe O'Connell . . . . . . . . . . . . . . . . . . . . . Damelia
- 0:04—Brief breasts and buns from *Galaxy of Terror* during the opening credits.
Rebecca Perle . . . . . . . . . . . . . . . . . . . . . . Alien Girl
0:53—In black swimsuit wearing sunglasses.
Cynthia Ann Thompson . . . . . Third Hooker (black dress)

### Not Quite Paradise (1986; British)
*a.k.a. Not Quite Jerusalem*
Joanna Pacula . . . . . . . . . . . . . . . . . . . . . . . . . . Gila
- 1:04—Left breast, lying in bed with Sam Robards.

### Not Tonight Darling (1971; British)
Nicola Austine . . . . . . . . . . At the West Side Health Club
Vincent Ball . . . . . . . . . . . . . . . . . . . . . . . . . . . . Alex
- 1:04—Buns, getting pushed out of the car with Ben the Click by the revengeful women. Long shot.
- 1:05—Full frontal nudity, while running after the car. Shaky camera.
Lance Barrett . . . . . . . . . . . . . . . . . . . . . . . . . . . Gary
- 0:43—Brief side view of buns, while standing up in bathtub.
- 0:44—Very, very brief frontal nudity, when it pokes out from under a towel while he stands up in bathtub.
Michael O'Malley . . . . . . . . . . . . . . . . . . . Ben the Click
- 1:04—Buns, getting pushed out of the car with Alex by the revengeful women. Long shot.
- 1:05—Full frontal nudity, while running after the car. Shaky camera.
Luan Peters . . . . . . . . . . . . . . . . . . . . . . . . . . Karen
- •• 0:04—Breasts and buns, taking off nightie and getting into bathtub.
- 0:05—Most of right breast, while sitting in tub, wishing her husband would look at her.
- •• 0:20—Breasts, while in bathroom, taking off her nightie while Eddie watches through binoculars.
0:21—In black bra and panties in Eddie's fantasy in store.
- •• 0:26—Right breast, while sitting in bathtub. Brief full frontal nudity when getting out.
- ••• 0:38—In white bra, then breasts, while undressing in room with Alex.
- ••• 0:39—Right breast, while making love in bed with Alex. Brief breasts in close-up.
0:42—Breasts under sheer top.

- 0:58—Buns, while getting massaged by Joan at the health club.

## Nothing Underneath (1985; Italian)
*a.k.a. Sotto Il Vestito Niente*

Anna Galiena . . . . . . . . . . . . . . . . . . . . . . . . . . . . . .n.a.
Renee Simonsen . . . . . . . . . . . . . . . . . . . . . . . .Barbara
- 0:51—Brief side view of left breast, changing backstage during fashion show.

## Novel Desires (1991)
Monica Akesson . . . . . . . . . . . . . . . . . . . . . . . . .Model
- ••• 0:17—Buns, then breasts while making love outside during story.
- ••• 0:18—Breasts making love on picnic table with Eric.
Leigh Betchley. . . . . . . . . . . . . . . . . . . . . . . . . . Susan
- ••• 0:13—Breasts in warehouse making love with Sandman. Long scene.
- ••• 0:15—More breasts while talking to Sandman.
Tyler Gains . . . . . . . . . . . . . . . . . . . . . . . . . Brian/Eric
- • 0:18—Buns, as Eric, making love with the Model on picnic table.
Lysa Hayland. . . . . . . . . . . . . . . . . . . . . . . . . . Linda
Gina Jourard . . . . . . . . . . . . . . . . . . . . . . . . . . .Shari
- •• 0:00—Right breast, then breasts in bed with Brian.
- •• 0:03—Breasts while taking a shower.
- •• 0:04—Brief tip of left breast while putting on a stocking. Breasts while getting dressed.

## Nowhere to Hide (1987)
Amy Madigan. . . . . . . . . . . . . . . . . . . Barbara Cutter
- • 1:04—Brief side view of right breast taking off towel to get dressed in cabin. Long shot, hard to see.

## Nowhere to Run (1993)
Rosanna Arquette . . . . . . . . . . . . . . . . . . . . . . .Clydie
- ••• 0:11—In white bra and panties, undressing in bathroom, then nude, getting into the shower while Jean-Claude Van Damme peeks in through the window.
- ••• 1:01—In bra, then breasts while making love in bed with Van Damme.
Jean-Claude Van Damme . . . . . . . . . . . . . . . . . . Sam
- •• 0:24—Buns, while walking out of and backing into lake. Kind of a long shot.

## Nudity Required (1989)
Pamela Bach . . . . . . . . . . . . . . . . . . . . . . . . . Dee Dee
Billy Frank . . . . . . . . . . . . . . . . . . . . . . . . . . . .Buddy
- ••• 0:32—Buns, while walking around bathtub and talking to Scammer, then jumping into tub.
- • 0:57—Side view of buns, behind textured shower door with Julie Newmar.
Becky LeBeau . . . . . . . . . . . . . . . . . . . . . . . . Melanie
- •• 0:35—Breasts, taking off pink swimsuit.
- •• 0:36—Brief breasts (third girl) standing in line.
- • 0:37—Breasts, standing behind Scammer.
- • 0:39—Very brief breasts.
- •• 0:41—Breasts while sitting next to Scammer by the pool.

Caroline Lomas . . . . . . . . . . . . . . . . . . . . . . . . .Caroline
- •• 0:36—Brief breasts (fifth girl) standing in line.
- •• 0:37—Breasts doing puppet routine for audition.
- •• 0:38—Breasts while yelling for not having a script.
- • 0:39—Breasts.
- • 0:44—Breasts while sitting on the edge of the pool.
Brooke Moore . . . . . . . . . . . . . . . . . . . . . . . .Bikini Girl
Julie Newmar. . . . . . . . . . . . . . . . . . . . . . . . . . .Irina
- • 0:57—Side of left breast and side view of buns behind textured shower door with Buddy.
Heidi Paine. . . . . . . . . . . . . . . . . . . . . . . . . . . . . .Jane
Ty Randolph. . . . . . . . . . . . . . . . . . . . . . . . . .Brenda
Misty Regan . . . . . . . . . . . . . . . . . . . . . Featured Dancer
- • 0:02—Breasts dancing on stage in club.
- • 0:04—Breasts and buns, on stage in G-string.
Gail Thackray. . . . . . . . . . . . . . . . . . . . . . . . . . . Midge
- •• 0:36—Breasts, asking Buddy a question. Brief breasts (tenth girl) standing in line.
- ••• 0:37—Breasts doing her song and tap dance audition.
- • 0:44—Breasts while playing in pool.
Edy Williams. . . . . . . . . . . . . . . . . . . . . . . . . . Isabella
- ••• 1:05—Breasts, with whip, while acting in movie.
- •• 1:07—More breasts in movie.
- •• 1:09—More right breast.
- •• 1:13—Breasts, during screening of the movie.

## Nudo di Donna (1984; Italian)
*a.k.a. Portrait of a Woman, Nude*

Eleonora Giorgi . . . . . . . . . . . . . . . . . . . . . . . . .Laura
- • 0:11—Very brief left breast, while taking off robe. Subtitles get in the way.
- • 0:12—Right breast, while in the shower, getting consoled.
- • 0:13—Brief upper half breasts, getting into bed.
- •• 0:14—Breasts in bed.
- •• 0:36—Nude, mostly buns, sleeping in bed when Sandro pulls back the covers.
- • 1:12—Brief right breast, while in bed with Sandro. 1:13—Right breast under sheer dress.

## Object of Desire (1991)
Tara Buckman . . . . . . . . . . . . . . . . . . . . . . . . . .Angie
- • 0:12—Breasts, leaning up on massage table.
- ••• 0:14—Breasts, getting dressed so Derrick can see.
- •• 0:23—Breasts, making love with Derrick in her dressing room.
- ••• 0:28—Breasts in bathtub with Derrick.
- • 0:43—Right breast, while making love in bed with Derrick.
- • 0:50—Side view of buns, while lying in bed.
- •• 0:51—Right breast, while sitting up in bed, then full frontal nudity.
- ••• 0:55—Breasts, opening her blouse in Steve's office in front of him.
- ••• 1:09—Full frontal nudity, posing for photographer in studio. Also side view of his buns.
- • 1:12—Brief breasts in magazine photos.
- ••• 1:18—Breasts changing clothes in dressing room.
Laura Gemser. . . . . . . . . . . . . Uncredited Photographer

## Obsession: A Taste For Fear (1987)
Teagan Clive . . . . . . . . . . . . . . . . . . Teagan Morrison
- 0:15—Brief upper half of right breast, when she lies back down in bed.
- 0:29—Buns, while lying dead, covered with plastic wrap.
- 0:37—Very brief buns in flashback to 0:29 scene.

Virginia Hey . . . . . . . . . . . . . . . . . . . . . . . . Diane
- 0:02—Breasts, lying in sauna.
- 0:04—Buns and very brief side view of right breast dropping towel to take a shower.
- • 0:14—Brief right breast in bed when sheet falls down.
- 0:37—Most of left breast, while crying.
- 0:39—Breasts, lying in bed talking to Kim.
- ••• 1:03—Breasts waking up in bed.
- 1:05—Breasts, getting ready to get dressed. Long shot.
- ••• 1:17—Breasts in hallway with Valerie.
- 1:19—Brief lower frontal nudity and right breast in bed with Valerie, then buns in bed.
- ••• 1:20—Breasts getting dressed, walking and running around the house when Valerie gets killed.
- 1:26—Breasts tied up in chair while Paul torments her. Lit with red light.

## The Octagon (1980)
Carol Bagdasarian . . . . . . . . . . . . . . . . . . . . . Aura
- 1:18—Brief side view of right breast, while sitting on bed next to Chuck Norris and taking her blouse off.

Karen Carlson . . . . . . . . . . . . . . . . . . . . . . Justine
Kim Lankford . . . . . . . . . . . . . . . . . . . . . . . Nancy

## Of Unknown Origin (1983; Canadian)
Jennifer Dale . . . . . . . . . . . . . . . . . . . . Lorrie Wells
Shannon Tweed . . . . . . . . . . . . . . . . . Meg Hughes
- 0:00—Brief side view of right breast taking a shower.

Peter Weller . . . . . . . . . . . . . . . . . . . . . Bart Hughes
Kenneth Welsh . . . . . . . . . . . . . . . . . . . . . . James

## Off Limits (1988)
Woody Brown . . . . . . . . . . . . . . . . . . . . . . . Co-Pilot
Willem Dafoe . . . . . . . . . . . . . . . . . . . . Bud McGriff
Scott Glenn . . . . . . . . . . . . . Colonel Dexter Armstrong
Thuy Ann Luu . . . . . . . . . . . . . . . . . . . . . . . . . Lanh
- •• 0:48—Breasts dancing on stage in a nightclub.

Fred Ward . . . . . . . . . . . . . . . . . . . . . . . . . . . . Dix

## Off the Mark (1986)
Brett Clark . . . . . . . . . . . . . . . . . . . . . . . Superstud
Becky LeBeau . . . . . . . . . . . . . . Uncredited Shower Girl
- 0:52—Brief breasts, after taking off her pink T-shirt in locker room. Brief buns, while walking into showers (2nd to the last girl).

## Off the Wall (1982)
Rosanna Arquette . . . . . . . . . . . . . . . . . . . . . . Pam
Jenny Neumann . . . . . . . . . . . . . . . . . . . . . . Linda
Roselyn Royce . . . . . . . . . . . . . . . . . Buxom Blonde
- 0:35—Left breast, while kissing an inmate in visiting room while the guards watch.

- •• 0:51—Left breast again, while kissing inmate through bars while the guards watch.

Paul Sorvino . . . . . . . . . . . . . . . . . . . . . . . . Warden
Jeana Tomasina . . . . . . . . . . . . . . . . . . . . . . . n.a.

## An Officer and a Gentleman (1982)
Lisa Blount . . . . . . . . . . . . . . . . . . . Lynette Pomeroy
1:25—In a red bra and tap pants in a motel room with David Keith.

David Caruso . . . . . . . . . . . . . . . . . . Topper Daniels
Lisa Eilbacher . . . . . . . . . . . . . . . . . . . Casey Seeger
Richard Gere . . . . . . . . . . . . . . . . . . . . Zack Mayo
David Keith . . . . . . . . . . . . . . . . . . . . . Sid Worley
John Laughlin . . . . . . . . . . . . . . . . . . . . . . . . Troy
Debra Winger . . . . . . . . . . . . . . . . . Paula Pokrifki
- ••• 1:05—Brief side view of right breast, then breasts making love with Richard Gere in a motel.

## The Offspring (1986)
Martine Beswicke . . . . . . . . . . . . . . . Katherine White
Miriam Byrd-Nethery . . . . . . . . . . . . . Eileen Burnside
- 0:26—Breasts in bathtub filled with ice while her husband tries to kill her with an ice pick.
- 0:29—Very brief right breast, dead in bathtub while her husband is downstairs.

Susan Tyrrell . . . . . . . . . . . . . . . . . . . Beth Chandler

## Oh, Alfie! (1975; British)
*a.k.a. Alfie Darling*
Minah Bird . . . . . . . . . . . . . . . . . . . . . . . . Gloria
Joan Collins . . . . . . . . . . . . . . . . . . . . . . . . . . Fay
0:28—In white bra and panties, running to answer the phone, then talking to Alfie.
- ••• 1:00—Breasts lying in bed after Alfie rolls off her.

Patsy Kensit . . . . . . . . . . . . . . . . . . . . . . . Penny
Rula Lenska . . . . . . . . . . . . . . . . . . . . . . . Louise
- 0:12—Breasts, then left breast in bed after making love with Alfie.

Vicki Michelle . . . . . . . . . . . . . . . . . . . . . . . Bird
Alan Price . . . . . . . . . . . . . . . . . . . . . Alfie Elkins
- •• 0:14—Buns washing himself off in the kitchen while talking to Louise's husband.

Annie Ross . . . . . . . . . . . . . . . . . . . . . . . . Claire
- •• 1:34—Breasts on top of Alfie in open black dress while he's lying injured in bed.

Sheila White . . . . . . . . . . . . . . . . . . . . . . . Norma

## Oh, What a Night (1992)
Genevieve Bujold . . . . . . . . . . . . . . . . . . . . . . Eva
Keir Dullea . . . . . . . . . . . . . . . . . . . . . . Thorvalo
Corey Haim . . . . . . . . . . . . . . . . . . . . . . . . . Eric
Barbara Williams . . . . . . . . . . . . . . . . . . . . . Vera
- •• 0:21—Very brief right breast, then very brief breasts, while undressing to go for a swim while Corey Haim watches without her knowledge. Brief breasts in the water and getting out.
- 0:46—Breasts, while swimming the backstroke in the water while Haim watches again.

••• 0:59—Breasts, while swimming the backstroke again and getting out. (This time she knows that Haim is watching.) Nice slow motion shot for a PG-13 film! Very brief wet panties.
•• 1:15—Left breast, while lying down on her back with Haim in a barn.

### Old Gringo (1989)
Jane Fonda . . . . . . . . . . . . . . . . . . . . . . Harriet Winslow
• 1:24—Side of left breast, while undressing in front of Jimmy Smits. Sort of brief right breast, while lying in bed and hugging him.
Jimmy Smits . . . . . . . . . . . . . . . . . . . . . . . . Arroyo
• 1:26—Half of his buns while on bed with Jane Fonda. Long shot, don't see his face.

### Olivia (1983)
a.k.a. A Taste of Sin
Suzanna Love . . . . . . . . . . . . . . . . . . . . . . . Olivia
•• 0:34—Buns and breasts making love in bed with Mike.
•• 0:58—Breasts and buns making love with Mike in the shower.
• 1:08—Very brief full frontal nudity getting into bed with Richard. Dark, long shot.
•• 1:09—Buns, lying in bed. Dark. Full frontal nudity getting out of bed and going to the bathroom.
Jeff Winchester . . . . . . . . . . . . . . . . . . . . . . Richard
• 1:17—Buns, while getting stuffed into trunk by Olivia. Dark.

### The Omega Man (1971)
Anna Aries. . . . . . . . . . . . . . Woman in Cemetary Crypt
Rosalind Cash . . . . . . . . . . . . . . . . . . . . . . . . Lisa
•• 1:09—Side view of left breast and upper half of buns getting out of bed. Buns and breasts sitting in bed.
• 1:21—Side view breasts in beige underwear while trying on clothes.
Charlton Heston . . . . . . . . . . . . . . . . . . . . . Neville

### On the Edge (1985)
(Unrated version reviewed.)
Bruce Dern . . . . . . . . . . . . . . . . . . . . . . . . . Wes
• 0:52—Brief buns, seen from below while floating in a pond.
Pam Grier . . . . . . . . . . . . . . . . . . . . . . . . . . Cora
0:18—In leotards, leading an aerobics dance class.
•• 0:42—Breasts in the mirror, then full frontal nudity making love with Bruce Dern standing up. Then brief left breast. A little dark.

### On the Line (1984; Spanish)
Victoria Abril . . . . . . . . . . . . . . . . . . . . . . Engracia
••• 0:16—Breasts getting undressed to make love with Mitch.
• 0:29—Very brief breasts, making love in bed with Mitch.
0:54—In white lingerie getting dressed.
David Carradine . . . . . . . . . . . . . . . . . . . . . Bryant
• 0:11—Buns, while lying on a table, getting a massage by three women.

### Once Bitten (1985)
Jim Carrey . . . . . . . . . . . . . . . . . . . . . . Mark Kendall
Lauren Hutton . . . . . . . . . . . . . . . . . . . . . Countess
Skip Lackey . . . . . . . . . . . . . . . . . . . . . . . . . Russ
• 1:11—Brief buns while in the school showers trying to see if Mark got bitten by a vampire.
Carey More . . . . . . . . . . . . . . . Moll Flanders Vampire

### Once is Not Enough (1975)
Kirk Douglas. . . . . . . . . . . . . . . . . . . . . Mike Wayne
David Janssen. . . . . . . . . . . . . . . . . . . . . . Tom Colt
• 1:22—Buns, while taking off clothes and walking to the bathroom.
Brenda Vaccaro . . . . . . . . . . . . . . . . . . . . . . Linda

### Once Upon a Time in America (1984)
(Long version reviewed.)
Jennifer Connelly . . . . . . . . . . . . . . . . Young Deborah
Robert De Niro. . . . . . . . . . . . . . . . . . . . . Noodles
Darlanne Fluegel . . . . . . . . . . . . . . . . . . . . . Eve
Olga Karlatos . . . . . . . . . Woman in the Puppet Theatre
•• 0:11—Right breast twice when bad guy pokes at her nipple with a gun.
Elizabeth McGovern . . . . . . . . . . . . . . . . . . Deborah
• 2:33—(0:32 into tape 2) Brief glimpses of left breast when Robert De Niro tries to rape her in the back seat of a car.
James Russo . . . . . . . . . . . . . . . . . . . . . . . Bugsy
Treat Williams . . . . . . . . . . . . . . . . Jimmy O'Donnell
James Woods . . . . . . . . . . . . . . . . . . . . . . . . Max

### One Deadly Summer (1984; French)
Isabelle Adjani . . . . . . . . . . . . . . . . . . . . . . Eliane
•• 0:21—Brief breasts changing in the window for Florimond.
••• 0:32—Nude, walking in and out of the barn.
• 0:36—Brief left breast lying in bed when Florimond gets up.
• 0:40—Buns and breasts taking a bath.
• 1:41—Part of right breast, getting felt up by an old guy, then right breast then brief breasts.
•• 1:47—Breasts in bedroom with Florimond.
1:49—In white bra and panties talking with Florimond.

### One Flew Over the Cuckoo's Nest (1975)
Brad Dourif . . . . . . . . . . . . . . . . . . . . . . . . . Billy
•• 1:50—Buns in hallway, putting on his pants after getting caught with Candy.
Christopher Lloyd. . . . . . . . . . . . . . . . . . . . Taber
Louisa Moritz . . . . . . . . . . . . . . . . . . . . . . . Rose
Jack Nicholson . . . . . . . . . . . . . . . . . R. P. McMurphy
Marya Small . . . . . . . . . . . . . . . . . . . . . . . Candy
• 1:00—Very brief side view of left breast, bending over to pick up her clothes on boat.

### One from the Heart (1982)
Teri Garr. . . . . . . . . . . . . . . . . . . . . . . . . Frannie
•• 0:09—Brief breasts getting out of the shower.
0:10—In a bra, getting dressed in bedroom.

- •• 0:40—Side view of right breast changing in. bedroom while Frederic Forrest watches.
- ••• 1:20—Brief breasts in bed when standing up after Forrest drops in though the roof while she's in bed with Raul Julia.

Raul Julia . . . . . . . . . . . . . . . . . . . . . . . . . . . . . . Ray
- • 1:20—Very brief buns while getting out of bed with Teri Garr when Frederic Forrest crashes through the ceiling.

Nastassja Kinski . . . . . . . . . . . . . . . . . . . . . . . . . Leila
- • 1:13—Brief breasts in open blouse when she leans forward after walking on a ball.

Harry Dean Stanton. . . . . . . . . . . . . . . . . . . . . . Moe

## One Man Army (1993)
Melissa Anne Moore . . . . . . . . . . . . . . . . Natalie Pierce
- ••• 0:26—Breasts, while taking a shower and drying herself off.
- ••• 0:29—Breasts, while making love with Jerry Trimble in bed.
- •• 0:33—Left breasts, while taking off her blouse to go for a swim. Breasts while in water after getting shot in the arm.

## One Man Force (1989)
Blueberry . . . . . . . . . . . . . . . . . . Santiago's Girlfriend
Maria Celedonio . . . . . . . . . . . . . . . . . . . . . . . . . Maria
- • 0:30—Brief breasts, twice, hiding John Matuzak in her apartment. Long shot.

Sharon Farrell . . . . . . . . . . . . . . . . . . . . . . . Shirley
Sam Jones . . . . . . . . . . . . . . . . . . . . . . . . . . . . . Pete
Stacey Q . . . . . . . . . . . . . . . . . . . . . . . . . . . . . . Lea

## One Million Heels B.C. (1993)
Michelle Bauer . . . . . . . . . . . . . . . . . . . . . . Cavegirl
- ••• 0:10—Half of right breast, while in skimpy top, under Rose in bed. Nude in the shower with Rose.
- •• 0:12—Breasts, while sitting on bed.
- ••• 0:13—Full frontal nudity while trying on lingerie.
- ••• 0:21—Nude, while soaping Savannah and Rose in the spa.
- • 0:25—Brief full frontal nudity taking off her towel in bedroom.
- ••• 0:26—Breasts and buns, while getting dressed on bed.

Jerica Fox . . . . . . . . . . . . . . . . . . . . . . . . . . . Savannah
- ••• 0:16—In lingerie, then nude while dancing in living room with Rose.
- ••• 0:21—Full frontal nudity, while soaping Rose and Bauer in the spa.
- • 0:25—Brief full frontal nudity taking off her towel in bedroom.
- ••• 0:26—Full frontal nudity, while getting dressed.

## One More Saturday Night (1986)
Moira Harris . . . . . . . . . . . . . . . . . . . . . . . . . . . Peggy
Bess Meyer . . . . . . . . . . . . . . . . . . . . . . . . . . . . Tobi
- • 1:02—Brief breasts in bed with Tom Davis.

Chelchie Ross . . . . . . . . . . . . . . . . . . . . . Dad Lundahl
- • 0:39—Buns, squished against the car window in back seat with Moira Harris.

Nina Siemaszko . . . . . . . . . . . . . . . . . . . . Karen Lundahl

## One Night Only (1984; Canadian)
Wendy Lands . . . . . . . . . . . . . . . . . . . . . . . . . . . . Jane
- •• 0:36—Breasts taking a bath while Jamie watches through keyhole.
- •• 0:38—Brief left breast in open robe.
- • 1:15—Brief breasts in bed with policeman.

Helene Udy . . . . . . . . . . . . . . . . . . . . . . . . . Suzanne
- • 0:50—Buns and right breast in bed talking with a guy.
- • 1:12—Over the shoulder, brief left breast on top of a guy in bed.

Lenore Zann. . . . . . . . . . . . . . . . . . . . . . . . . . . Anne
- •• 0:20—Breasts while getting dressed in bedroom with Jamie.
- • 1:04—Right breast in bedroom with Jamie.
- ••• 1:19—Breasts and buns while making love with Jamie.

## One Trick Pony (1980)
Blair Brown . . . . . . . . . . . . . . . . . . . . . . . . . . Marion
Joan Hackett. . . . . . . . . . . . . . . . . . . . . . . . Lonnie Fox
- ••• 1:21—Nude getting out of bed and getting dressed while talking to Paul Simon.

Rip Torn . . . . . . . . . . . . . . . . . . . . . . . . . Walter Fox
Mare Winningham . . . . . . . . . . . McDeena Dandridge
- •• 0:14—Breasts in the bathtub with Paul Simon, smoking a cigarette. Long scene.

## One Woman or Two (1986; French)
*a.k.a. Une Femme Ou Deux*
Zabou . . . . . . . . . . . . . . . . . . . . . . . . . . . . . Constance
- •• 0:28—Brief breasts pulling up her blouse for Gerard Depardieu.

Sigourney Weaver . . . . . . . . . . . . . . . . . . . . . Jessica
1:30—In braless white blouse.
- •• 1:31—Very brief side view of left breast in bed with Gerard Depardieu.

## The Onion Field (1979)
James Woods . . . . . . . . . . . . . . . . . . . . Gregory Powell
- •• 1:33—Buns, while taking a shower in the prison.

## Open House (1987)
Roxanne Baird . . . . . . . . . . . . . . . . . . . . . . . Allison
- •• 1:12—Buns and brief side view of left breast walking to swimming pool, then breasts getting out of the pool before the killer gets her.

Adrienne Barbeau. . . . . . . . . . . . . . . . . . Lisa Grant
- • 0:27—In black lace lingerie, then very brief half of left breast making love with Joseph Bottoms on the floor.
- •• 1:15—Brief side view of right breast getting out of bed at night to look at something in her briefcase.
- ••• 1:16—Brief breasts taking off bathrobe and getting back into bed. Kind of dark.

Tiffany Bolling . . . . . . . . . . . . . . . . . . . . . Judy Roberts
Cathryn Hartt. . . . . . . . . . . . . . . . . . . . . . . . . . Melody
Mary Stavin . . . . . . . . . . . . . . . . . . . . . Katie Thatcher

## Opposing Force (1986)
*a.k.a. Hell Camp*
Lisa Eichhorn . . . . . . . . . . . . . . . . . . . . . Lieutenant Casey
- 0:17—Wet T-shirt after going through river.
- ••• 0:33—Breasts getting sprayed with water and dusted with white powder.
- •• 1:03—Breasts after getting raped by Anthony Zerbe in his office, while another officer watches.
- ••• 1:05—Breasts and buns, getting dressed.
Jay Louden . . . . . . . . . . . . . . . . . . . . . . . . . . . . . . Stevenson
- 0:31—Buns, while getting yanked out of the line by Becker.
- 0:32—Buns, while getting sprayed with water and dusted with white powder. He's the first guy through.
Richard Roundtree. . . . . . . . . . . . . . . Sergeant Stafford
Tom Skerritt . . . . . . . . . . . . . . . . . . . . . . . . . . . . . . . Logan
- 0:33—Very brief buns, while getting sprayed with water and dusted with white powder.
- •• 1:11—Brief buns, while jumping out of tree to knock out Tuan.
Ken Wright . . . . . . . . . . . . . . . . . . . . . . . . . . . . Conway
- 0:33—Brief buns, while getting his poncho after being sprayed with water and dusted with white powder.

## Ordeal by Innocence (1984)
Faye Dunaway. . . . . . . . . . . . . . . . . . . . . Rachel Argyle
Sarah Miles . . . . . . . . . . . . . . . . . . . . . . Mary Durrant
Diana Quick . . . . . . . . . . . . . . . . . . . . . .Gwenda Vaughn
Cassie Stuart . . . . . . . . . . . . . . . . . . . . . .Maureen Clegg
- •• 1:14—Breasts in bed talking to Donald Sutherland.
Donald Sutherland . . . . . . . . . . . . . . . . . Arthur Calgary

## Orlando (1993; British)
Lothaire Bluteau . . . . . . . . . . . . . . . . . . . . . . The Khan
Thom Hoffman . . . . . . . . . . . . . . . . . William of Orange
Mary MacLeod . . . . . . . . . . . . . . . . . . . . . .First Woman
Dudley Sutton. . . . . . . . . . . . . . . . . . . . . . . King James I
Tilda Swinton . . . . . . . . . . . . . . . . . . . . . . . . Orlando
- ••• 0:56—Full frontal nudity while looking at herself in mirror.
Charlotte Valandrey . . . . . . . . . . . . . . . . . . . . . Sasha
Billy Zane . . . . . . . . . . . . . . . . . . . . . . . . . Shelmerdine

## Orpheus Descending (1990)
Kevin Anderson. . . . . . . . . . . . . . . . . . . . . Val Xavier
Vanessa Redgrave . . . . . . . . . . . . . . . . . .Lady Torrance
- •• 1:18—Buns, after taking off her robe and opening curtains to see Kevin Anderson. Shadow of left breast on curtain.
Anne Twomey. . . . . . . . . . . . . . . . . . . . . Carol Cutrere

## The Osterman Weekend (1983)
Meg Foster . . . . . . . . . . . . . . . . . . . . . . . . .Ali Tanner
- 0:14—Very, very brief tip of right breast after getting nightgown out of closet.
Rutger Hauer. . . . . . . . . . . . . . . . . . . . . . . John Tanner
Dennis Hopper . . . . . . . . . . . . . . . . . . .Richard Tremayne

John Hurt. . . . . . . . . . . . . . . . . . . . . . . Lawrence Fassett
- 0:01—Buns, while getting out of bed and walking to the shower.
Burt Lancaster . . . . . . . . . . . . . . . . . . Maxwell Danforth
Chris Sarandon. . . . . . . . . . . . . . . . . . . .Joseph Cardone
Helen Shaver . . . . . . . . . . . . . . . . . . . Virginia Tremayne
- •• 0:24—Breasts in an open blouse yelling at her husband in the bedroom.
- 0:41—Breasts in the swimming pool when everyone watches on the TV.
Merete Van Kamp . . . . . . . . . . . . . . . . . Zuna Brickman
- •• 0:01—Breasts and brief buns in bed on a TV monitor, then breasts getting injected by two intruders.
- 0:35—Brief breasts on video again while Rutger Hauer watches in the kitchen on TV.
- 1:30—Breasts again on video during TV show.
Cassie Yates . . . . . . . . . . . . . . . . . . . . . . . Betty Cardone
- •• 0:48—Breasts getting into bed with Chris Sarandon while Rutger Hauer watches on TV.
- 0:51—Right breast, making love with Sarandon.

## Other Side of Midnight (1977)
Marie-France Pisier. . . . . . . . . . . . . . . . . . . .Noëlle Page
- 0:10—Very brief breasts in bed with Lanchon.
  0:28—Buns, in bed with John Beck. Medium long shot.
  0:45—In white bra, in dressing room talking to Henri.
  0:50—Breasts in bathtub, giving herself an abortion with a coat hanger. Painful to watch!
- •• 1:11—Breasts wearing white slip in room getting dressed in front of Henri.
- ••• 1:17—Full frontal nudity in front of fireplace with Armand, rubbing herself with oil, then making love with ice cubes. Very nice!
- 1:35—Full frontal nudity taking off dress for Constantin in his room.
Susan Sarandon . . . . . . . . . . . . . . . .Catherine Douglas
- 1:10—Breasts in bedroom with John Beck. Long shot, then right breast while lying in bed.
  2:18—In wet white nightgown running around outside during a storm.

## The Other Woman (1992)
(Unrated version reviewed.)
Lee Anne Beaman . . . . . . . . . . . . . . . . .Jessica Mathews
- ••• 0:17—Nude, undressing and getting into the shower.
- •• 0:40—Breasts in the bathtub.
- •• 0:51—Buns, while lying in bed in the fetal position.
- ••• 1:09—Nude, on the floor making love with Traci. Interesting camera angles.
- ••• 1:13—Nude, getting up and out of bed, taking a shower, then making love with Carl. Long scene.
- •• 1:23—Breasts on floor with Traci during video playback on TV.
- ••• 1:34—Buns, in long shot, taking off robe to greet Zmed. Breasts and buns in bed with him.

Billy Bradshaw. . . . . . . . . . . . . . . . . . . . . . . . . . .Scott
- 0:52—Half of buns, making love with Sally in the office screening room.

Regina Gielser . . . . . . . . . . . . . . . . . . . . . . . Neighbor
- •• 0:49—Breasts and buns, while in bed with Jessica's mother during young Jessica's flashback.

Sam Jones . . . . . . . . . . . . . . . . . . . . . . . . . Mike Florian

Melissa Anne Moore . . . . . . . . . . . . . . . . . . . . . Elysse
- •• 0:58—Breasts, taking off her blouse while taking pictures during photo shoot.

Daniel Moriarity . . . . . . . . . . . . . . . . . . . . . . . . . Carl
- 0:59—Buns, during photo shoot.
- ••• 1:15—Buns, while in the shower with Jessica.

Jenna Persaud . . . . . . . . . . . . . . . . . . . . . . . Traci Collins
- •• 0:21—Breasts under sheer black top in her apartment with her boyfriend.
- ••• 0:22—Breasts taking off her top and getting milk poured on her.
- ••• 0:23—Breasts and buns, making love in kitchen while Jessica secretly watches.
- •• 0:31—Breasts posing with Sheila at the beach for Elysse.
- ••• 0:32—Full frontal nudity at the beach some more.
- 0:33—Breasts and buns, running in the surf. Long shot.
- •• 0:40—Breasts, during Jessica's flashbacks.
- ••• 0:53—Nude, taking a shower, drying herself off and putting on robe.
- ••• 0:57—Breasts posing with Carl during photo shoot.
- •• 0:59—More breasts during photo shoot.
- ••• 1:09—Breasts and buns, on the floor making love with Jessica. Interesting camera angles.
- 1:23—Breasts, while on the floor with Jessica during video playback on TV.

## Out Cold (1989)

Lisa Blount . . . . . . . . . . . . . . . . . . . . . . . . . . .Phyllis

Tom Byrd . . . . . . . . . . . . . . . . . . . . . . . Mr. Holstrom
- 0:10—Brief frontal nudity getting out of bed with Teri Garr when her husband comes home.

Teri Garr . . . . . . . . . . . . . . . . . . . . . . . Sunny Cannald

Debra Lamb . . . . . . . . . . . . . . . . . . . Panetti's Dancer
- 1:04—Brief breasts dancing in G-string on stage. Don't see her face.

John Lithgow . . . . . . . . . . . . . . . . . . . . . . .Dave Geary

Bruce McGill . . . . . . . . . . . . . . . . . . . . . . Ernie Cannald
- •• 0:12—Frontal nudity, while opening the shower door, talking to Teri Garr. Brief buns, when putting on underwear.

Randy Quaid . . . . . . . . . . . . . . . . . . . . . . . Lester Atlas

## Out for Justice (1991)

Jo Champa . . . . . . . . . . . . . . . . . . . . . . . Vicky Felino

Gina Gershon . . . . . . . . . . . . . . . . . . . . . Patti Modono

John Leguizamo . . . . . . . . . . . . . . . . . . . . .Boy in Alley

Shareen Mitchell . . . . . . . . . . . . . . . . . . . . .Laurie Lupo

Julie Strain. . . . . . . . . . . . . . . . . . . . . . . . Roxanne Ford
- 0:53—Brief side view of right breast in Polaroid photograph that Steven Seagal looks at.

- 1:06—Brief side view of right breast in Polaroid again.
- 1:11—Brief right breast, twice, dead in bed when discovered by Seagal.
- 1:12—Briefly in Polaroid again.

Shannon Whirry . . . . . . . . . . . . . . . . . . . . . Terry Malloy

## Out of Control (1984)

Cindi Dietrich. . . . . . . . . . . . . . . . . . . . . . . . . .Robin
- 0:29—Breasts taking off her red top. Long shot.

Sherilyn Fenn . . . . . . . . . . . . . . . . . . . . . . . . . . Katie
  0:19—In wet white T-shirt in pond with the other girls.

Martin Hewitt. . . . . . . . . . . . . . . . . . . . . . . . . . Keith

Richard Kantor . . . . . . . . . . . . . . . . . . . . . . . . . Gary
- 0:29—Buns, while pulling his underwear down during a game of strip spin the bottle.

Betsy Russell . . . . . . . . . . . . . . . . . . . . . . . . Chrissie
  0:19—In white corset and panties in the pond.
- •• 0:29—Breasts taking off her top while playing Strip Spin the Bottle.
  0:30—Buns, taking off her panties.

Claudia Udy . . . . . . . . . . . . . . . . . . . . . . . . . . . .Tina
  0:19—In leopard skin pattern bra and panties.
- 0:28—In leopard bra and panties playing Strip Spin the Bottle, then very brief breasts taking off her top. Long shot.
- 0:47—Brief left breast getting raped by bad guy on the boat.
- 0:54—Brief left breast, then right breast making love with Cowboy.

Jim Youngs. . . . . . . . . . . . . . . . . . . . . . . . . .Cowboy
- 0:54—Buns, while making love with Claudia Udy.

## Out of Season (1975; British)

Susan George. . . . . . . . . . . . . . . . . . . . . . . .Joanna
- 1:24—Nude, while walking in front of Cliff Robertson. Long shot.

Vanessa Redgrave. . . . . . . . . . . . . . . . . . . . . . . .Ann
- 0:35—Breasts, while putting on slip in bedroom.
- 0:53—Full frontal nudity, after throwing open bed covers for Cliff Robertson. Don't see her face.

## Out of the Blue (1982)

Sharon Farrell . . . . . . . . . . . . . . . . . . . . . . . . .Kathy
- 1:18—Left breast, when Don Gordon pulls it out of her nightgown and fondles it.

Dennis Hopper. . . . . . . . . . . . . . . . . . . . . . . . .Don

Michele Little . . . . . . . . . . . . . . . . . . . . . . Girl in Car

## Out of the Dark (1988)

Divine . . . . . . . . . . . . . . . . . . . . . . . . . . . .Langella

Starr Andreeff . . . . . . . . . . . . . . . . . . . . . . Camille

Karen Black . . . . . . . . . . . . . . . . . . . . . . . . . . Ruth

Teresa Crespo . . . . . . . . . . . . . . . . . . . . . . Debbie

Lynn Danielson . . . . . . . . . . . . . . . . . . . . . . . Kristi
- 0:09—Brief breasts getting out of bed. More breasts outside getting photographed.
- •• 1:01—Breasts in motel room making love with Kevin.
- 1:06—Left breast, while getting out of bed.

Cameron Dye . . . . . . . . . . . . . . . . . . Kevin Silver/Bobo
- 0:32—Brief buns when Kristi yanks his underwear down while he is throwing a basketball. Don't see his face.

Silvana Gallardo . . . . . . . . . . . . . . . . . . . . . McDonald
Karen Mayo-Chandler . . . . . . . . . . . . . . . . . . . Barbara
- 0:16—Brief breasts pulling red dress down wearing black stocking in Kevin's studio.
- ••• 0:17—Breasts and buns posing during photo shoot.

Karen Witter . . . . . . . . . . . . . . . . . . . . . . . . . . . Jo Ann

### Out on a Limb (1992)
Matthew Broderick . . . . . . . . . . . . . . . . . . Bill Campbell
- ••• 0:16—Buns, while standing on road, holding a mailbox to hide his privates while a bus load of kids pass by. Brief buns when a car stops to pick him up.

### Out on Bail (1988)
Adrienne Pearce . . . . . . . . . . . . . . . . . . . . . . . Maggie
Kathy Shower . . . . . . . . . . . . . . . . . . . . . . . Sally Anne
- 1:01—Brief breasts in shower with Robert Ginty.

### The Outing (1987)
Mark Mitchell . . . . . . . . . . . . . . . . . . . . . . Mike Daley
- 1:08—Buns when his friend gets killed, then very brief frontal nudity sitting up.

Michelle Watkins . . . . . . . . . . . . . . . . . . . . . . . Faylene
- •• 0:12—Breasts taking off her top, standing by the edge of the swimming pool, then running breasts through the house with panties on.

### Outland (1981)
Peter Boyle . . . . . . . . . . . . . . . . . . . . . . . . . Sheppard
Sean Connery . . . . . . . . . . . . . . . . . . . . . . . . . O'Neill
Sharon Duce . . . . . . . . . . . . . . . . . . . . . . . Prostitute
- 0:30—Right breast, lying down in room with drug crazed guy.
- 0:32—Breasts going into medical scanning device.

### The Outlaw Josey Wales (1976)
Sam Bottoms . . . . . . . . . . . . . . . . . . . . . . . . . Jamie
Clint Eastwood . . . . . . . . . . . . . . . . . . . . . Josey Wales
Sondra Locke . . . . . . . . . . . . . . . . . . . . . . Laura Lee
- •• 1:20—Briefly nude in rape scene.

### Over the Hill (1991; Australian)
Olympia Dukakis . . . . . . . . . . . . . . . . . . . . . . . Alma
- •• 0:56—Breasts, while getting them breasts painted for tribal ceremony.

Sigrid Thornton . . . . . . . . . . . . . . . . . . . . . . Elizabeth
Aden Young . . . . . . . . . . . . . . . . . . . . . . . . . . . Nick

### Overexposed (1990)
Karen Black . . . . . . . . . . . . . . . . . . . . . Mrs. Trowbridge
William Bumiller . . . . . . . . . . . . . . . . . . . . . . . . Hank
- 0:54—Brief buns, while taking off his pants to get into bed with Catherine Oxenberg.

Shelley Michelle . . Body Double for Catherine Oxenberg
- •• 0:54—Left breast several times, buns when taking off panties, lower frontal nudity while in bed with Hank. Wearing a wig with wavy hair.

David Naughton . . . . . . . . . . . . . . . . . . . . . . . Phillip

### Overseas (1991; French)
Marianne Basler . . . . . . . . . . . . . . . . . . . . . . . Gritte
Philippe Galland . . . . . . . . . . . . . . . . . . . . . . . . Paul
- •• 0:13—Very, very brief, blurry tip of frontal nudity while jumping out of bathtub and standing on stool. Buns, while standing on stool.

Nicole Garcia . . . . . . . . . . . . . . . . . . . . . . . . . . Zon
- 0:11—In sparkly bra, while admiring herself in the mirror.
- 0:12—Brief breasts behind mosquito net while in bed.
- 0:13—Brief breasts while playing with Paul in the bathroom. Very brief left breast, while reaching for towel.

### Pacific Banana (1980)
Alyson Best. . . . . . . . . . . . . . . . . . . . . . . . . . . . n.a.
Graeme Blundell . . . . . . . . . . . . . . . . . . . . . . . n.a.
Luan Peters . . . . . . . . . . . . . . . . . . . . . Candy Bubbles
- •• 1:00—Breasts several times flashing her breasts for Martin.

Robin Stewart . . . . . . . . . . . . . . . . . . . . . . . . . . n.a.

### Pacific Heights (1990)
Beverly D'Angelo . . . . . . . . . . . . . . . . . . . . . . . Ann
- 0:01—Sort of breasts in reflection on TV screen, then right breast, in bed with Michael Keaton.
  0:03—Very brief buns, turning over on bed when two guys burst in to the house.

Melanie Griffith . . . . . . . . . . . . . . . . . . . . Patty Parker
Matthew Modine . . . . . . . . . . . . . . . . Drake Goodman
Tracey Walter . . . . . . . . . . . . . . . . . . . . . Exterminator

### Paint It Black (1989)
Sally Kirkland . . . . . . . . . . . . . . . . . . . . . Marion Easton
  0:05—Most of left breast, while sitting in bed talking to Rick Rossovich.

Rick Rossovich . . . . . . . . . . . . . . . . . . Jonathan Dunbar
- 0:48—Upper half of buns while getting out of bed with Julie Carmen.

Monique Van De Ven . . . . . . . . . . . . . . . . . . . Kyla Leif

### Pale Blood (1990)
Darcy De Moss . . . . . . . . . . . . . . . . . . . . . . . . Cherry
- 0:33—Very, very brief left breast, while opening her robe while posing on couch.

Diana Frank . . . . . . . . . . . . . . . . . . . . . . . . . . Jenny
- •• 0:21—Breasts lying on the bed with Michael when he bites her.
- 0:36—Close up of left breast on TV monitor that Wings Hauser is editing with. Don't see face.
- 0:42—Brief left breast on TV monitor several times while Hauser examines the bite marks.
- 1:03—Very brief breasts when Hauser pulls her dress top down to look at her bite mark.

Wings Hauser . . . . . . . . . . . . . . . . . . . . Van Vandameer

## The Pamela Principle (1992)

(Unrated version reviewed.)

Melissa Barrick. . . . . . . . . Uncredited Steve's Girlfriend
- ••• 0:45—Breasts and buns in red G-string, then lower frontal nudity, while playing strip-card game in living room with Steve.

J. K. Dumont. . . . . . . . . . . . . . . . . . . . . Carl Breeding
- • 0:10—Buns, while making love with Anne in bed.

Regina Gielser. . . . . . . . . . . . . . . . . . . . . . . Felicia
- ••• 1:27—Buns in bed with Carl and Pamela, then breasts.

Tamara Landry . . . . . . . . . . . . . . . . . . . Anne Breeding
- ••• 0:08—Buns, while lying in bed with Carl, then breasts and lower frontal nudity.
- •• 0:28—Breasts, while sitting up in bed.
- ••• 0:48—Breasts, waking up in bed, then buns and lower frontal nudity getting out.
- ••• 0:57—Breasts, while making love with Carl in the kitchen, then buns in bed.
- ••• 1:03—Buns and breasts while in the shower.

Danny Smith. . . . . . . . . . . . . . . . . . . . . . . . . . . .n.a.

Eugene Stevenson. . . . . . . . . . . . . . . . Steve Breeding
- ••• 0:46—Buns, while making love on top of his girlfriend on the living room floor. Nice close-ups.

## Paper Mask (1991; British)

Amanda Donohoe. . . . . . . . . . . . . . . Christine Taylor
- 0:53—Breasts in bed under Matthew then on top of him.

Barbara Leigh-Hunt. . . . . . . . . . . . . . . Celia Mumford
Paul McGann . . . . . . . . . . . . . . . . . . . .Matthew Harris

## Paperback Hero (1973; Canadian)

Elizabeth Ashley . . . . . . . . . . . . . . . . . . . . . . Loretta
- ••• 0:37—Nude in shower with Keir Dullea. Long scene.
- ••• 0:39—Breasts, straddling Dullea in the shower.

Keir Dullea . . . . . . . . . . . . . . . . . . . . . . . . . . Rick
- • 0:37—Partial buns, while rolling over in the shower with Elizabeth Ashley.
- • 0:40—Upper half of buns, while sitting up in the shower.

Dayle Haddon. . . . . . . . . . . . . . . . . . . . . . Joanna
- 0:31—Lower half of buns, under T-shirt while standing behind a bar with Keir Dullea.

## Papillon (1973)

Ratna Assan. . . . . . . . . . . . . . . . . . . . . . . . . Zoraima
- • 1:54—Breasts, first seeing Steve McQueen.
- •• 1:55—Breasts, helping clean up McQueen on the beach and in the ocean.
- •• 1:56—Breasts, walking on the beach with McQueen.
- •• 1:57—Breasts, getting off boat and watching a guy open oysters.
- •• 2:00—Breasts, on beach, walking with McQueen while holding a torch.

Dustin Hoffman. . . . . . . . . . . . . . . . . . . . Louis Dega

## Paradise (1981)

Willie Aames. . . . . . . . . . . . . . . . . . . . . . . . .David
- 0:42—Buns, while walking into the ocean with a fishing net. Dark, hard to see anything.
- •• 1:12—Nude swimming with Phoebe Cates under water.

Phoebe Cates. . . . . . . . . . . . . . . . . . . . . . . .Sarah
- •• 0:23—Buns and breasts taking a shower in a cave while Willie Aames watches.
- 0:36—In wet white dress in a pond with Aames.
- • 0:40—Very brief left breast caressing herself while looking at her reflection in the water.
- • 0:43—Buns, getting out of bed to check out Aames' body while he sleeps.
- • 0:46—Buns, washing herself in a pond at night.
- •• 0:55—Side view of her silhouette at the beach at night. Nude swimming in the water, viewed from below.
- •• 1:10—Breasts making love with Aames. It looks like a body double. Don't see her face.
- ••• 1:12—Nude swimming under water with Aames.
- •• 1:16—Breasts making love with Aames again. It looks like the body double again.

## Paradise (1991)

Melanie Griffith . . . . . . . . . . . . . . . . . . . . . Lily Reed
Don Johnson . . . . . . . . . . . . . . . . . . . . . .Ben Reed
Sarah Trigger . . . . . . . . . . . . . . . . . . . . . . .Darlene
- • 0:14—Brief breasts ironing her clothes in open window while Willard and Billie watch from their tree house. Long shot after. Hard to see her face.

## Paradise Motel (1985)

Leslee Bremmer . . . . . . . . Uncredited Girl Leaving Room
- • 0:38—Breasts buttoning her pink sweater, leaving motel room.

Gary Hershberger. . . . . . . . . . . . . . . . . . . . . .Sam
- •• 0:33—Buns, while running away from the Coach's house.

Colleen McDermott . . . . . . . . . . . . . . . . . . . Debbie
- •• 0:24—Breasts in motel room with Mic, when Sam lets them use a room.

Laurie Smith. . . . . . . . . . . . . . . . . . Honeymoon Wife
- ••• 0:02—Left breast, then breasts in Honeymoon Suite with her new husband, then making love in bed.

## Parallel Lives (1994; Made for Cable Movie)

James Belushi . . . . . . . . . . . . . . . . . . . . . Nick Dimas
- • 0:34—Brief buns (he's on the right), while mooning the women in hallway during panty raid.

James Brolin . . . . . . . . . . . . . . .Professor Spencer Jones
LeVar Burton . . . . . . . . . . . . . . . . . .Dr. Franklin Carter
- • 0:34—Brief buns (he's on the left), while mooning the women in hallway during panty raid.

Lindsay Crouse. . . . . . . . . . . . . . . . . . . . . .Una Pace
- • 0:12—Very brief right breast in gaping dress, while bending over to make her bed on the sofa.

Dudley Moore . . . . Imaginary Friend/President Andrews
Ally Sheedy . . . . . . . . . . . . . . . . . . . . . . . . . Louise

Helen Slater. . . . . . . . . . . . . . . . . . . . . . Elsa Freedman
Paul Sorvino . . . . . . . . . . . . . . . . . . . . . . . Ed Starling
- • 0:16—Brief upper half of buns, while getting pantsed in room by the guys.

JoBeth Williams . . . . . . . . . . . . . . . . . . . . Win Winslow
Treat Williams . . . . . . . . . . . . . . . . . . . . Peter Barnum
- • 0:34—Brief buns (he's in the middle), while mooning the women in hallway during panty raid.

### *Paranoia* (1969; Italian/French)
Carroll Baker . . . . . . . . . . . . . . . . . . . . . . Kathryn West
- • 0:13—Buns and partial glimpses of breasts, in shower with Peter.
- • 0:16—Very, very brief upper half of right breast when Peter rips her dress.
- •• 0:17—Buns, while lying in bed with Peter.
  0:25—Brief buns, under mesh black robe.

### *Parasite* (1982)
Cherie Currie. . . . . . . . . . . . . . . . . . . . . . . . . Dana
Demi Moore . . . . . . . . . . . . . . . . . . . . . .Patricia Welles
Cheryl Smith . . . . . . . . . . . . . . . . . . . . . . Captive Girl
- •• 0:08—Breasts tied by wrists in kitchen.
- •• 0:12—Breasts knocking gun out of guy's hands standing behind fence.

Tom Villard . . . . . . . . . . . . . . . . . . . . . . . . . . . . .Zeke

### *The Park is Mine* (1985; Made for Cable Movie)
Tommy Lee Jones . . . . . . . . . . . . . . . . . . . . . . . Mitch
Yaphet Kotto. . . . . . . . . . . . . . . . . . . . . . . . Eubanks
Helen Shaver. . . . . . . . . . . . . . . . . . . . . .Valery Weaver
- • 0:46—Very brief breasts undressing then very, very brief left breast, while catching clothes from Tommy Lee Jones.

### *Partners* (1982)
Iris Alhanti. . . . . . . . . . . . . . . . . . . . . . . . . . Jogger
- •• 0:21—Breasts in the shower when Ryan O'Neal opens the shower curtain.

Jennifer Ashley. . . . . . . . . . . . . . . . . . . . . Secretary
Robyn Douglass . . . . . . . . . . . . . . . . . . . . . . . .Jill
- •• 1:00—Brief breasts taking off her top and getting into bed with Ryan O'Neal.

Denise Galik . . . . . . . . . . . . . . . . . . . . . . . . .Clara
John Hurt . . . . . . . . . . . . . . . . . . . . . . . . . . Kerwin
Ryan O'Neal . . . . . . . . . . . . . . . . . . . . . . . . Benson
- •• 0:48—Buns, while wearing Indian outfit for photo session with Robyn Douglass. Don't see his face.

### *Party Camp* (1987)
Jewel Shepard . . . . . . . . . . . . . . . . . . . . . Dyanne Stein
- ••• 0:57—In white bra and panties, then breasts playing strip poker with the boys.

April Wayne . . . . . . . . . . . . . . . . . . . . . . Nurse Brenda

### *Party Favors* (1987)
Blondi. . . . . . . . . . . . . . . . . . . . . . . . . . . . . . .Bobbi
- •• 0:04—Breasts in dressing room, taking off red top and putting on black one.
- • 0:23—Brief breasts when blouse pops off while delivering pizza.

- ••• 0:27—Breasts and buns in G-string doing a strip routine outside.
- • 0:31—Brief breasts flapping her blouse to cool off.
- ••• 1:04—Breasts doing a strip routine in a little girl outfit. Buns, in G-string. More breasts after.
- • 1:16—Nude taking off swimsuit next to pool during final credits.

April Dawn Dollarhide . . . . . . . . . . . . . . . . . . . . n.a.
George "Buck" Flower . . . . . . . . . . . . . . . . . . . . Pop
Jill Johnson . . . . . . . . . . . . . . . . . . . . . . . . . . . .Trixie
- •• 0:04—Breasts in dressing room, taking off blue dress and putting on red swimsuit.
- ••• 0:35—Breasts in doctors office taking off her clothes.
- ••• 1:03—Breasts doing strip routine in cowgirl costume. More breasts after.
- • 1:16—Breasts taking off swimsuit next to pool during final credits.

Gail Thackray . . . . . . . . . . . . . . . . . . . . . . . . . Nicole
- • 0:04—Breasts in dressing room with the other three girls changing into blue swimsuit.
- • 0:11—Brief left breast in the swimsuit during dance practice.
- • 0:12—Breasts during dance practice.
- • 0:17—More breasts during dance practice.
- •• 0:42—Breasts doing strip routine at anniversary party. Great buns in G-string shots.
- ••• 1:01—Breasts and buns in G-string after stripping from cheerleader outfit. Lots of bouncing breast shots. Mingling with the men afterwards.
- • 1:16—Nude by the swimming pool during the final credits.

### *Party Incorporated* (1989)
a.k.a. *Party Girls*
John Altamura . . . . . . . . . . . . . . . . . . . . . . . . . .Burt
- • 0:50—Buns, while undressing and showing off at the bar.

Marilyn Chambers . . . . . . . . . . . . . . . .Marilyn Sanders
- ••• 0:56—In lingerie, then breasts in bedroom with Weston. Nice!
- • 1:11—Brief breasts on the beach when Peter takes her swimsuit top off.

Ruth Corrine Collins . . . . . . . . . . . . . . . . . . . . Betty
- • 0:07—Breasts on desk with Dickie. Long shot.
- •• 1:08—Breasts in bed with Weston when Marilyn Chambers comes in.

Jane Hamilton
. . . . . . . . . Uncredited Whipped Cream Wrestling Girl
Susan Napoli . . . . . . . . . . . . . . . . .Uncredited Party Girl
- • 0:05—Brief breasts, while wearing a mask and dancing during party with two other girls.
- • 0:08—Brief breasts again.

Karen Nielsen. . . . . . . . . . . . . . . . . . . . . . . . .Diane
Derrick Roberts. . . . . . . . . . . . . . . . . . . . . . . . Louie
- • 0:50—Brief buns, while undressing and showing off at the bar.

Kimberly Taylor . . . . . . . . . . . . . . . . . . . . . . . Felicia
- •• 0:26—Breasts shaking her breasts trying an outfit on.

••• 0:39—Breasts and buns in G-string in the bar with the guys.

Christina Veronica . . . . . . . . . . . . . . . . . . . . . . Christina
••• 0:52—Buns and breasts dancing in front of everybody at party.

### Party Line *(1988)*
Greta Blackburn . . . . . . . . . . . . . . . . . . . . . . Angelina
• 0:01—Partial side of left breast in open dress, while standing and kissing Curtis.
•• 0:02—Breasts in bed with Curtis. Brief breasts after rolling off him when Leif Garrett comes in.
0:13—In bra and panties in bed.

Richard Hatch . . . . . . . . . . . . . . . . . . . Lt. Dan Bridges
Karen Mayo-Chandler . . . . . . . . . . . . . . . . . Sugar Lips
0:52—In black bra and panties.
0:57—Black panties, while hiking up her skirt and sitting of Leif Garrett's lap.
•• 0:58—Breasts, opening her blouse while sitting on Garrett's lap.
1:01—Brief breasts, while lying dead in field, covered with blood.

Richard Roundtree. . . . . . . . . . . . . . . . Captain Barnes
Shawn Weatherly . . . . . . . . . . . Asst. D.A. Stacy Sloane

### Party Plane *(1988)*
Laura Albert . . . . . . . . Uncredited Auditioning Woman
•• 0:30—Breasts, taking off blue dress during audition. She's wearing a white ribbon in her ponytail.

Michele Burger . . . . . . . . . . . . . . . . . . . . . . . . Carol
• 0:31—Breasts, squirting whipped cream on herself for her audition.
•• 0:38—Breasts doing a strip tease routine on the plane.
••• 1:02—Breasts mud wrestling with Renee on the plane.
• 1:09—Breasts in the cockpit, covered with mud.
• 1:17—Breasts in serving cart.

Iris Condon . . . . . . . . . . . . . . . . . . . . . . . . . . . Renee
• 0:29—Buns, in white lingerie during audition.
••• 0:48—Breasts plane doing a strip tease routine.
••• 1:02—Breasts on plane mud wrestling with Carol.
• 1:12—Left breast, covered with mud, holding the Mad Bomber.
• 1:17—Left breast, then breasts in trunk with the Doctor.

Jill Johnson . . . . . . . . . . . . . . . . . . . . . . . . . . Laurie
••• 0:06—Breasts and buns changing clothes and getting into spa with her two girlfriends. (She's wearing a black swimsuit bottom.)
••• 0:11—Breasts getting out of spa.
•• 0:16—Breasts in pool after being pushed in and her swimsuit top comes off.
•• 0:20—In bra and panties, then breasts on plane doing a strip tease.

Jacqueline Palmer . . . . . . . . . . . . . . . . . . . . . Suzie
••• 0:06—Breasts and buns changing clothes and getting into spa with her two girlfriends. (She's the dark haired one.)
••• 0:11—Breasts again, getting out of spa.

••• 0:23—In bra, then breasts doing strip tease routine on plane.
•• 0:35—Breasts doing another routine on the plane.

Renee Way . . . . . . . . . . . . . . . . . . . . . . . . . . . . Andy
••• 0:01—Breasts, while taking off her blouse to fix the plane.
••• 0:06—Breasts, while sitting on edge of spa.
••• 0:11—Breasts again, when getting out of spa.
• 0:12—Brief breasts after dropping her towel while talking to Tim.

### Pascali's Island *(1988; British)*
Ben Kingsley. . . . . . . . . . . . . . . . . . . . . . . Basil Pascali
Helen Mirren . . . . . . . . . . . . . . . . . . . . . Lydia Neuman
• 1:00—Left breast, lying in bed with Charles Dance. Long shot.

### The Passion of Beatrice *(1988; French)*
Erick Bernard . . . . . . . . . . . . . . . . . . . . . . . . . . L'amant
• 0:06—Brief buns, in bed with François' mother when discovered by François.

Julie Delpy . . . . . . . . . . . . . . . . . . . . . . . . . . Béatrice
• 0:58—Left breast, then breasts getting out of bed.
••• 1:11—Side view of right breast, holding dress after getting raped by her father. Nude, running to the door and barricading it with furniture.
•• 1:12—More nude, arranging furniture.
••• 1:13—Full frontal nudity, wiping her crotch and burning her clothes.
• 1:36—More of right breast, when her father puts soot on her face.
•• 1:37—Brief left breast, then breasts and brief buns standing with soot on her face. Long shot.
••• 1:44—Breasts taking a bath. Subtitles get in the way a bit.

Maïté Maillé. . . . . . . . . . . . . . . . . . . . . . . . La Noiraude
• 1:24—Brief left breast, showing Béatrice how she was abused.

Isabelle Nanty . . . . . . . . . . . . . . . . . . . . . . La Nourrice
•• 1:53—Right breast, offering her breast milk to Arnaud.

Jean Luc Rivals . . . . . . . . . . . . . . . . . . . . . . . . . . Jehan
• 0:57—Brief frontal nudity, getting dried off.

Tina Sportolaro . . . . . . . . . . . . Mère de François Enfant
• 0:06—Brief breasts when the young François discovers her in bed with another man and kills him.

### Past Midnight *(1992; Made for Cable Movie)*
Clancy Brown. . . . . . . . . . . . . . . . . . . . . . . Steve Lundy
Rutger Hauer . . . . . . . . . . . . . . . . . . . . . . . Ben Jordan
Natasha Richardson . . . . . . . . . . . . . . . Laura Matthews
••• 0:48—Breasts while making love in bed with Rutger Hauer.
• 1:10—Very brief side of left breast, while getting into the shower.

### Past Tense *(1994; Made for Cable Movie)*
Lara Flynn Boyle . . . . . . . . . . . Tory Bass/Sabrina James
• 0:10—In black bra with Scott Glenn. Brief breasts two times. You don't see her face very well and one is a medium long shot.

- 0:13—Supposedly her breasts, while making love with another guy during video playback on TV.
- 0:15—Very brief buns in flashback while on top of Glenn on the floor. Medium long shot.
- 0:28—Breasts, several times, during video playback on TV. Don't see her face very well.

Scott Glenn. . . . . . . . . . . . . . . . . . . . Gene Ralston
- 0:10—Very brief, partial buns, while making love with Lara Flynn Boyle on the floor.

Anthony LaPaglia . . . . . . . . . . . . . . . . . Larry Talbert
Sheree Wilson . . . . . . . . . . . . . . . . . . . Emily Talbert
- •• 1:00—Left breast and most of right breast in open vest in front of Scott Glenn. Definitely not a body double!

### Pat Garrett and Billy the Kid (1973)
(Uncut Director's version reviewed.)
Rutanya Alda. . . . . . . . . . . . . . . . . . . . . .Ruthie Lee
- •• 1:35—Breasts, while sitting on bed with James Coburn. (She's the only girl wearing a necklace.)

Rita Coolidge . . . . . . . . . . . . . . . . . . . . Maria
- •• 1:48—Brief right breast, while sitting on bed and getting undressed with Kris Kristofferson.

Kris Kristofferson . . . . . . . . . . . . . . . . . . Billy the Kid
- 0:43—Buns, while getting into bed with a girl after Harry Dean Stanton gets out. Long shot, hard to see.

Charlie Martin Smith. . . . . . . . . . . . . . . . .Bowdre
Harry Dean Stanton. . . . . . . . . . . . . . . . . . Luke

### Patricia (1984)
José Antonio Ceinos . . . . . . . . . . . . . . . . . . . .n.a.
Sascha Hehn . . . . . . . . . . . . . . . . . . . . . . Harry Miller
- 0:41—Lower half of buns, while scratching his butt in the hallway.

Anne Parillaud. . . . . . . . . . . . . . . . . . . . . Patricia Cook
- •• 0:25—Breasts, opening her jumpsuit top to get attention while trying to hitchhike.
- •• 0:30—Breasts in white panties, running around at a seminary, trying to get away from a group of guys.
- •• 0:31—Breasts in confessional booth.
- 0:32—Running around some more.
- •• 0:37—Nude making love with Priscilla on bed.
- 0:46—Sort of briefly breasts running around in skimpy costume.
- ••• 0:49—Dancing in two piece swimsuit, then breasts.
- 0:50—Breasts while lying on her stomach.
- 0:52—Brief breasts running into the ocean.
- 0:53—Brief breasts under water.
- 0:55—More brief breasts shots under the water.
- ••• 0:56—Nude, getting out of the ocean and lying down on the beach.
- 1:09—Breasts taking off her dress and playing bullfight with Harry.
- 1:10—Nude, dancing in her room. Hard to see because the curtains get in the way.
- 1:24—Brief buns while making love with Harry.
- 1:26—Brief breasts while making love with Harry.
- ••• 1:27—Full frontal nudity making love on top of Harry in bed.

### The Patriot (1986)
Jeff Conaway . . . . . . . . . . . . . . . . . . . . . . . . .Mitchell
Simone Griffeth . . . . . . . . . . . . . . . . . . . . . . . Sean
- •• 0:49—Brief breasts lying in bed, making love with Ryder.

Gregg Henry . . . . . . . . . . . . . . . . . . . . . . Matt Ryder
- 0:49—Upper half of buns, while making love on top of Simone Griffeth (her leg gets in the way).

Lorin Jean Vail . . . . . . . . . . . . . . . . . . . . .Howard's Girl

### Patti Rocks (1988)
John Jenkins . . . . . . . . . . . . . . . . . . . . . . . . .Eddie
- 1:07—Buns, while making love with Patti in bed.

Karen Landry . . . . . . . . . . . . . . . . . . . . . . . .Patti
0:48—Buns, walking from bathroom to bedroom and shutting the door. Long shot.
- 0:48—Very brief right breast in shower with Billy.
- •• 1:04—Breasts in bed with Eddie while Billy is out in the living room.

Chris Mulkey . . . . . . . . . . . . . . . . . . . . . . . Billy
- •• 0:24—Nude in restroom with Eddie, undressing and putting on underwear.

### Patty Hearst (1989)
Dana Delany . . . . . . . . . . . . . . . . . . . . . . . . . Gelina
Frances Fisher. . . . . . . . . . . . . . . . . . . . . . .Yolanda
Natasha Richardson . . . . . . . . . . . . . . . . . Patricia Hearst
- •• 0:13—Breasts, blindfolded in the bathtub while talking to a woman member of the S.L.A.

### Pauline at the Beach (1983; French)
Simon De La Brosse . . . . . . . . . . . . . . . . . . . .Sylvain
Arielle Dombasle . . . . . . . . . . . . . . . . . . . . . . Marion
- 0:24—Brief breasts lying in bed with a guy when her cousin looks in the window.
- •• 0:43—Brief breasts in house kissing Henri, while he takes her white dress off.
- •• 0:59—Breasts walking down the stairs in a white bikini bottom while putting a white blouse on.

### Payback (1988)
Michele Burger. . . . . . . . . . . . . . . . . . . . . . . .Laura
- 0:08—Brief breasts sitting up in bed just before getting shot, then brief breasts twice, dead in bed.

Jean Carol . . . . . . . . . . . . . . . . . . . . . .Donna Nathan
- ••• 0:24—Breasts opening her pink robe for Jason while reclining on couch.

### Payback (1991)
Corey Michael Eubanks . . . . . . . . . . . . . . . . . . Clinton
- 0:49—Brief buns, while putting his pants on after jerks tip his trailer over.

### Payday (1972)
Ahna Capri. . . . . . . . . . . . . . . . . . . . . . . . . Mayleen
- 0:20—Left breast in bed sleeping, then right breast with Rip Torn.
- ••• 0:21—Breasts sitting up in bed smoking a cigarette and talking to Torn. Long scene.

Rip Torn. . . . . . . . . . . . . . . . . . . . . . . . . Maury Dann
- 1:21—Brief buns while getting up out of bed.

## Payoff (1991; Made for Cable Movie)

Keith Carradine . . . . . . . . . . . . . .Peter "Mac" MacAlister
- 0:01—Sort of buns, while in shower, seen from above, looking down.

## Peace Maker (1990)

Hilary Shepard . . . . . . . . . . . . . . . . . . . . . .Dori Caisson
- 1:08—Brief upper half of buns, taking off shirt and getting into shower. Brief side view of upper half of left breast, twice while making love with Townsend.

## Pennies from Heaven (1981)

Josh Cadman. . . . . . . . . . . . . . . . . . . . . . . . . . . .n.a.
Jessica Harper . . . . . . . . . . . . . . . . . . . . . . . . . Joan
- 0:43—Brief breasts opening her nightgown for Steve Martin.
John Karlen . . . . . . . . . . . . . . . . . . . . . . . Detective

## The People Next Door (1970)

Sandy Alexander . . . . . . . . . . . . . . . . . . . . . . . .Elliot
- • 0:38—Frontal nudity, sitting up in upper bunk bed, then nude getting out.
Hal Holbrook. . . . . . . . . . . . . . . . . . . . David Hoffman
Cloris Leachman . . . . . . . . . . . . . . . . . . . . . . . . Tina
- 0:59—Buns and very brief side view of right breast, while getting up out of bed and putting on a robe.
Stephen McHattie. . . . . . . . . . . . . . . . . . . . . . . Artie

## Perfect (1985)

Jamie Lee Curtis . . . . . . . . . . . . . . . . . . . .Jessie Wilson
0:14—No nudity, but doing aerobics in leotards.
0:26—More aerobics in leotards.
0:40—More aerobics, mentally making love with John Travolta while leading the class.
1:19—More aerobics when photographer is shooting pictures.
1:32—In red leotard after the article comes out in Rolling Stone.
Chelsea Field . . . . . . . . . . . . . . . . . . . . . . . . .Randy
Marilu Henner. . . . . . . . . . . . . . . . . . . . . . . . . Sally
0:13—Working out on exercise machine.
Charlene Jones . . . . . . . . . . . . . . . . . . . . . Shotsy
- 0:17—Breasts stripping on stage in a club. Buns in G-string.
Mathew Reed . . . . . . . . . . . . . . . . . . . . . . . . . Roger
- 1:01—Buns, while dancing in a jock strap at Chippendale's.

## Perfect Strangers (1984)

Anne Carlisle. . . . . . . . . . . . . . . . . . . . . . . . . Sally
- 0:34—Left breast, while making love in bed with Johnny.
Ann Magnuson . . . . . . . . . . . . . . . . . . . . . . . .Maida

## Perfect Timing (1984)

Jo Anne Bates . . . . . . . . . . . . . . . . . . . . . . . . Karen
- ••• 0:21—Nude, getting ready to get her picture taken.
Paul Boretski . . . . . . . . . . . . . . . . . . . . . . . . . . Joe
- •• 0:11—Brief frontal nudity and buns, while rolling over on the bed.
- • 0:29—Frontal nudity on the roof in the snow with Bonnie.

- 0:35—Buns, while on bed getting slapped on the behind.
- 0:50—Buns, while in bed with Judy.
- •• 1:03—Brief frontal nudity on TV with Judy while he and Bonnie watch.
Nancy Cser . . . . . . . . . . . . . . . . . . . . . . . . . . . .Lacy
0:54—In white lingerie, taking off clothes for Harry and posing.
- ••• 0:56—Breasts getting photographed by Harry.
- 0:58—Breasts, making love with Harry.
- 1:01—Breasts.
Papusha Demitro . . . . . . . . . . . . . . . .Bonnie O. Bendix
- •• 0:26—Nude, taking off dress in photo studio and kissing Joe.
- 0:29—Breasts walking with Joe through the living room, then brief nude on the roof.
- •• 0:32—Nude, walking into the kitchen and getting chocolate out of the refrigerator.
- •• 0:34—Nude in bed with Joe.
- ••• 0:45—Nude in bedroom with Joe.
- •• 1:03—Nude on bed with Joe.
Alexandra Innes . . . . . . . . . . . . . . . . . . . . . . . Salina
- •• 1:06—Right breast and buns, posing for Harry.
Stephen Markle . . . . . . . . . . . . . . . . . . . . . . . . .Harry
- 0:58—Buns, while making love with Lacy.
Mary Beth Rubens . . . . . . . . . . . . . . . . . . . . . . .Judy
- 0:04—In a bra, then breasts in bedroom with Joe.
- •• 0:05—Nude, walking to kitchen, then talking with Harry.
- 0:08—Left breast seen through the camera's view finder.
- 0:10—Nude, getting dressed in bedroom.
0:49—In red bra and panties.
- •• 0:50—Nude, in bed with Joe.
- ••• 1:00—Nude, discovering Joe's hidden video camera, then going downstairs.
Michele Scarabelli . . . . . . . . . . . . . . . . . . . .Charlotte
- •• 1:11—Brief buns, then breasts in bed with Harry.
- 1:18—Breasts in bed with Harry during the music video.

## Perfect Victims (1988)

Nicolette Scorsese . . . . . . . . . . . . . . . . . .Melissa Cody
0:13—In white bra and panties, changing clothes by closet while talking to Carrie.
0:21—In white bra again when Brandon rips her blouse open while she's drugged out.
Deborah Shelton . . . . . . . . . . . . . . . . . . . . .Liz Winters
0:55—Very brief, upper half of breasts, lying back in bubble bath.
Jackie Swanson. . . . . . . . . . . . . . . . . . . . . Carrie Marks
- •• 0:13—In bra, then left breast, while changing clothes by closet.
- 0:23—Brief left breast, while lying on sofa when Brandon opens her robe while she's drugged out. Brief right breast and lower frontal nudity when he rips off her panties.
0:25—Right breast several more times, while lying on sofa while Brandon torments her.

••• 1:15—Left breast and buns, seen through clear shower door. Nice shot for bun lovers!

• 1:16—Brief buns in the shower, seen from above.

## Performance (1970)

James Fox . . . . . . . . . . . . . . . . . . . . . . . . . . . . . Chas
- • 0:00—Very brief frontal nudity and buns while making love with a woman. Don't see his face.
- • 0:02—Buns, while getting up next to his girlfriend.
- • 0:24—Brief buns, while getting roughed up by bad guys.

Mick Jagger . . . . . . . . . . . . . . . . . . . . . . . . . . . Turner
0:48—Side view of buns, while getting out of bathtub.

Anita Pallenberg . . . . . . . . . . . . . . . . . . . . . . . .Pherber
- • 0:44—Side view of left breast, while in bed with Mick Jagger.
- ••• 0:47—Breasts and buns, while in bathtub with Lucy and Jagger.
- • 0:50—Buns, injecting herself with drugs.
- •• 1:20—Right breast, while lying on the floor. Then breasts and buns, in bed with Chas.

Ann Sidney . . . . . . . . . . . . . . . . . . . . . . . . . . . Dana
- • 0:01—Very brief breasts and buns.
- • 0:24—Brief breasts with Chas in flashbacks.

## The Perils of Gwendoline in the Land of the Yik Yak (1984; French)

Zabou . . . . . . . . . . . . . . . . . . . . . . . . . . . . . . . Beth
- •• 0:36—Breasts, after taking off her blouse in the rain in the forest.
- •• 0:57—Breasts while in torture chamber, getting rescued by Tawny Kitaen.
- •• 1:04—Breasts after Kitaen escapes.
- • 1:11—Buns, in costume during fight.

Brent Huff . . . . . . . . . . . . . . . . . . . . . . . . . . . . Willard
- • 0:51—Brief buns, in G-string while wearing costume.
- •• 0:52—Buns, in G-string, walking around with Tawny Kitaen in costumes.
- •• 0:54—More buns, after the women realize he's a man.
- ••• 0:56—Buns, in jail while wearing only the G-string.

Tawny Kitaen . . . . . . . . . . . . . . . . . . . . . . . Gwendoline
- ••• 0:36—Breasts in the rain in the forest, taking off her top. More breasts with Willard.
- •• 0:52—Buns, while walking around with Willard in costumes.
- • 0:55—Buns, falling into jail cell, then in jail cell in costume.
- • 0:57—Buns, while rescuing Beth in torture chamber.
- •• 1:01—Breasts in S&M costume in front of mirrors.
- • 1:04—Brief breasts escaping from chains.
- • 1:07—Buns, in costume while riding chariot and next to wall.
- • 1:09—Buns, while standing up.
- •• 1:11—Buns, in costume during fight. Wearing green ribbon.
- •• 1:18—Breasts making love with Willard.

## Personal Best (1982)

Patrice Donnelly . . . . . . . . . . . . . . . . . . . . . Tory Skinner
- •• 0:16—Full frontal nudity after making love with Mariel Hemingway.
- •• 0:30—Full frontal nudity in steam room.
  1:06—Breasts in shower.

Scott Glenn . . . . . . . . . . . . . . . . . . . . . . . . .Terry Tingloff

Mariel Hemingway . . . . . . . . . . . . . . . . . . . . . Chris Cahill
- •• 0:16—Brief lower frontal nudity getting examined by Patrice Donnelly, then breasts after making love with her.
- •• 0:30—Breasts in the steam room talking with the other women.

Kenny Moore . . . . . . . . . . . . . . . . . . . . . . . .Denny Stiles
- •• 1:31—Nude, getting out of bed and walking to the bathroom.

## Personal Services (1987)

Julie Walters . . . . . . . . . . . . . . . . . . . . . . . Cynthia Payne
- • 0:21—Very brief side view of left breast, while reaching to turn off radio in the bathtub. Her face is covered with cream.

## Pet Sematary II (1992)

Clancy Brown . . . . . . . . . . . . . . . . . . . . . . . Gus Gilbert

Anthony Edwards . . . . . . . . . . . . . . . . . Chase Matthews

Darlanne Fluegel . . . . . . . . . . . . . . . . . . .Renee Hallow
- • 1:04—Probably a body double wearing a dog mask, breasts on top of Anthony Edwards during nightmare, lit with blue light.

Sarah Trigger . . . . . . . . . . . . . . . . . . . . Marjorie Hargrove

Lisa Waltz . . . . . . . . . . . . . . . . . . . . . . . .Amanda Gilbert
- • 0:53—Very brief right breast, while in bed when Clancy Brown rips her nightgown off.

## Peter's Friends (1993; British/U.S.)

Kenneth Branagh . . . . . . . . . . . . . . . . . . . . . . . Andrew

Tony Slattery . . . . . . . . . . . . . . . . . . . . . . . . . . Brian
- • 0:25—Buns, while lying on his stomach in bed with Sarah.

Imelda Staunton. . . . . . . . . . . . . . . . . . . . . . . . Mary

Emma Thompson . . . . . . . . . . . . . . . . . . . . . . . Maggie

## Petit Con (1986; French)

Souad Amidou . . . . . . . . . . . . . . . . . . . . . . . . Salima
- •• 0:42—Breasts, after taking off her top and getting into bed, while Michel watches her.
- • 0:50—Breasts, while lying in bed, then making love with Michel. Dark.
- • 0:53—Breasts, getting out of bed and getting back in.

Caroline Cellier. . . . . . . . . . . . . . . . . . . .Annie Choupon

Claudine Delvaux . . . . . . . . . . . . . . . . . . . . . . Maryse
- •• 0:28—Right breast, while getting felt up by her husband in front of Michel.

Guy Marchand . . . . . . . . . . . . . . . . . . . . . Bob Choupon

## Pets (1974)

Joan Blackman . . . . . . . . . . . . . . . . . . . . .Geraldine Mills
- • 0:46—Brief side view of left breast, while getting out of bed after making love with Bonnie.

Candice Rialson . . . . . . . . . . . . . . . . . . . . . . . . Bonnie
- •• 0:26—Breasts dancing in field while Dan is watching her while he's tied up.
- ••• 0:33—Breasts making love on top of Dan while he's still tied up.
  0:35—Running through woods in braless orange top.
- •• 0:40—Breasts getting into bath at Geraldine's house.
- • 0:45—Breasts posing for Geraldine.
  0:54—In black and red lingerie outfit getting ready for bed.
- ••• 1:02—Breasts taking off lingerie in bed with Ron, then making love with him.
  1:34—Almost breasts, getting whipped by Vincent.

## Phantasm II (1988)
Sam Phillips . . . . . . . . . . . . . . . . . . . . . . . . . . Alchemy
- •• 1:00—Breasts making love in bed with Lance.
Stacey Travis . . . . . . . . . . . . . . . . . . . . . . . . . . . . . Jeri

## Phantom Empire (1987)
Michelle Bauer . . . . . . . . . . . . . . . . . . . . . Cave Bunny
  0:32—Running around in the cave a lot in two piece loincloth swimsuit.
- •• 1:13—Breasts after losing her top during a fight, more breasts until Andrew puts his jacket on her.
Tricia Brown . . . . . . . . . . . . . . . . . . . . . . . . . Cavegirl
Sybil Danning . . . . . . . . . . . . . . . . . . . .The Alien Queen
Dawn Wildsmith . . . . . . . . . . . . . . . . . . Eddy Colchilde

## Phantom of the Mall: Eric's Revenge (1988)
Crisstyn Dante . . . . . . . . Body Double for Ms. Whitman
- •• 0:25—Breasts in bed about five times with Peter.
Morgan Fairchild . . . . . . . . . . . . . . . . . . .Karen Wilton
Pauly Shore . . . . . . . . . . . . . . . . . . . . . . . . . . . Buzz
- •• 1:06—Buns, while mooning security guard on B&W surveillance monitor.
Kimber Sissons . . . . . . . . . . . . . . . . . . . . . . . .Suzie
  0:14—Briefly in bra, in dressing room on B&W security monitor.
Brinke Stevens . . . . . . . . . . . . . . .Girl in Dressing Room
- • 0:14—Breasts in dressing room and on B&W monitor several times (second room from the left).
Kari Whitman . . . . . . . . . . . . . . . . . . . . Melody Austin

## Phoenix the Warrior (1988)
Veronica Carothers . . . . . . . . . . . . . . . . . . . . . .Suga
Roxanne Kernohan . . . . . . . . . . . . . . . . . . . . . Meda
- ••• 0:15—Breasts in waterfall (she's the white girl).
Kathleen Kinmont . . . . . . . . . . . . . . . . . . . . . Phoenix
Peggy Sands . . . . . . . . . . . . . . . . . . . . . . . . . . . Keela

## The Piano (1993)
Holly Hunter . . . . . . . . . . . . . . . . . . . . . . . . . . .Ada
- ••• 1:02—Nude, while sitting on bed.
- ••• 1:18—Buns then breasts while lying next to Harvey Keitel in bed.
- • 1:19—Very brief left nipple when kissing. Close-up shot.

Harvey Keitel . . . . . . . . . . . . . . . . . . . . . . . . . . Baines
- •• 0:43—Buns, after taking off his shirt to dust off piano.
- ••• 1:01—Frontal nudity while pulling back curtain to show himself to Holly Hunter.
- •• 1:02—Buns, while getting on bed with Hunter.
- •• 1:02—Brief frontal nudity while sitting down in bed.
- •• 1:18—Buns, while making love on top of Hunter.
Genevieve Lemon . . . . . . . . . . . . . . . . . . . . . . Nessie
Sam Neill . . . . . . . . . . . . . . . . . . . . . . . . . . . . Stewart
- • 1:30—Buns, while in bed with Holly Hunter. Don't see his face.

## Picasso Trigger (1989)
Steve Bond . . . . . . . . . . . . . . . . . . . . . . . . . . . n.a.
Cynthia Brimhall . . . . . . . . . . . . . . . . . . . . . . . . Edy
- •• 0:59—Breasts in weight room with a guy.
Hope Marie Carlton . . . . . . . . . . . . . . . . . . . . .Taryn
  0:17—In white lingerie on boat with Dona Speir.
- ••• 0:56—Breasts and buns in spa with a guy.
Patty Duffek . . . . . . . . . . . . . . . . . . . . . . . . Patticakes
- •• 1:04—Breasts taking a Jacuzzi bath.
Liv Lindeland . . . . . . . . . . . . . . . . . . . . . . . . . .Inga
Kym Malin . . . . . . . . . . . . . . . . . . . . . . . . . . . .Kym
- •• 1:04—Breasts taking a shower.
Dona Speir . . . . . . . . . . . . . . . . . . . . . . . . . .Donna
  0:17—In white lingerie on boat with Hope Marie Carlton.
- ••• 0:49—Breasts and buns standing, then making love in bed.
Roberta Vasquez . . . . . . . . . . . . . . . . . . . . . Pantera

## Pick-Up Summer (1979; Canadian)
Joy Boushel . . . . . . . . . . . . . . . . . . . . . . . . . . .Sally
- ••• 0:56—Breasts playing pinball, then running around.
Carl Marotte . . . . . . . . . . . . . . . . . . . . . . . . . . Steve
- • 0:18—Side view of buns, while hanging a B.A. out passenger window at Rod.
Karen Stephen . . . . . . . . . . . . . . . . . . . . . . . .Donna
- • 0:25—Very brief lower half of breast, pulling her T-shirt up to distract someone.
  0:34—Very, very brief breasts when the boys spray her and she jumps up.
Helene Udy . . . . . . . . . . . . . . . . . . . . . . . . . . . Suzy
  0:34—Very, very brief breasts when the boys spray her and she jumps up.
Michael Zelnicker . . . . . . . . . . . . . . . . . . . . . . . Greg
- • 0:04—Brief buns, while hanging a B.A. out the back window of the van.

## The Pickle (1992)
Linda Carlson . . . . . . . . . . . . . . . . . . . . . .Bernadette
- •• 0:12—In white bra and panties under stockings, after taking off her clothes in hotel room in front of Danny Aiello, then breasts.
Clotilde Courau . . . . . . . . . . . . . . . . . . . . .Francoise
  0:54—In white bra in hotel room with Danny Aiello.
- • 0:58—Brief half of right breast in gaping bra when she helps Aiello back onto bed.
Rebecca Miller . . . . . . . . . . . . . . . . . . . . . . . . Carrie
Christopher Penn . . . . . . . . . . . . . . . . . .Gregory Stone

Isabella Rossellini . . . . . . . . . . . . . . . . . . Actress in Film
Ally Sheedy . . . . . . . . . . . . . . . . . . . . . . . . Molly-Girl

### *Pin* (1988)
David Hewlett . . . . . . . . . . . . . . . . . . . . . . . . . . Leon
Terry O'Quinn . . . . . . . . . . . . . . . . . . . . . Dr. Linden
Helene Udy . . . . . . . . . . . . . . . . . . . . Marcia Bateman
••• 1:03—Breasts in bedroom with Leon.

### *Pink Floyd The Wall* (1982)
Nell Campbell . . . . . . . . . . . . . . . . . . . . . . . Groupie
Jenny Wright . . . . . . . . . . . . . . . . . .American Groupie
••• 0:41—Breasts, while doing strip tease dance, in back
    of a truck while it's parked backstage.

### *Pink Motel* (1982)
Terri Berland . . . . . . . . . . . . . . . . . . . . . . . . Marlene
   0:47—In red bra, while in bed with Max.
   0:56—In red bra and panties, while standing up
   with Max.
••• 1:18—Breasts, dropping her sheet in room in front
    of Max and Skip.
Cathryn Hartt . . . . . . . . . . . . . . . . . . . . . . .Charlene
••• 1:18—Breasts, dropping her sheet in room in front
    of Max and Skip.
John Macchia . . . . . . . . . . . . . . . . . . . . . . . . Skip
•• 1:08—Buns, taking off underwear and getting into
    bed with Charlene. Very brief frontal nudity falling
    over the side of the bed.
Kathi Sawyer-Young . . . . . . . . . . . . . . . . . . . . . Lola
   0:14—In bra, panties, garter belt and stockings in
   motel room.
   0:31—In bra and panties while listening to Mark's
   football stories.
• 0:36—Brief breasts, after opening her bra and falling
    onto bed with Mark.
••• 0:41—Breasts and buns in panties, trying to coax
    Mark out of the bathroom. Long scene.
•• 1:13—Breasts, while lying in bed with Mark.

### *Piranha* (1978)
Belinda Balaski . . . . . . . . . . . . . . . . . . . . . . . . Betsy
Heather Menzies . . . . . . . . . . . . . . . Maggie McKeown
. . . . . . . . . . . . . . . . . . . . . . . . . . . . . . . . .Barbara
•• 0:02—Breasts taking off her top to go swimming
    with her boyfriend.

### *A Place Called Today* (1972)
Cheri Caffaro . . . . . . . . . . . . . . . . . . Cindy Cartwright
•• 0:14—Full frontal nudity covered with oil or some-
    thing writhing around on the bed.
• 1:21—Brief side view of right breast undressing in
    the bathroom.
• 1:23—Brief full frontal nudity getting kidnapped by
    two guys.
• 1:30—Nude when they take off the blanket.
• 1:35—Brief breasts just before getting killed.
Lana Wood . . . . . . . . . . . . . . . . . . . . Carolyn Scheider
••• 0:40—Side view of left breast, then breasts lying
    down talking to Ron.

### *The Plague* (1992; French/British)
Sandrine Bonnaire . . . . . . . . . . . . . . . Martine Rambert
••• 0:53—Breasts, while in bathroom, examining herself
    for the plague.
William Hurt . . . . . . . . . . . . . . . . . . . . Dr. Bernard Rieux
Raul Julia . . . . . . . . . . . . . . . . . . . . . . . . . . . . Cottard
Victoria Tennant . . . . . . . . . . . . . . . . . . . . .Alice Rieux

### *Planet of the Apes* (1968)
Jeff Burton . . . . . . . . . . . . . . . . . . . . . . . . . . .Dodge
• 0:26—Very brief buns while taking off clothes to go
    skinny dipping. (Guy on the right.)
Robert Gunner . . . . . . . . . . . . . . . . . . . . . . . . Landon
• 0:26—Very brief buns while taking off clothes to go
    skinny dipping. (Guy on the left.)
Charlton Heston . . . . . . . . . . . . . . . . . . . George Taylor
• 0:26—Buns, seen through a waterfall and while
    walking on rocks. Long shots.
• 1:04—Buns while standing in middle of the room
    when the apes tear his loin cloth off.

### *Play Misty for Me* (1971)
Clint Eastwood . . . . . . . . . . . . . . . . . . . . . Dave Garland
Donna Mills . . . . . . . . . . . . . . . . . . . . . . . . . . . .Tobie
• 1:10—Brief side view of right breast hugging Clint
    Eastwood in a pond near a waterfall. Long shot, hard
    to see.
Jessica Walter . . . . . . . . . . . . . . . . . . . . . . . . . Evelyn
• 0:13—Very brief right breast in bed with Clint East-
    wood. Lit with blue light. Hard to see anything.

### *Play Murder For Me* (1991)
William Burns . . . . . . . . . . . . . . . . . . . . . . . .Fred Merritt
• 0:37—Buns, on couch, trying to attack Tracy Scog-
    gins.
Tracy Scoggins . . . . . . . . . . . . . . . . . . . . Tricia Merritt
•• 0:37—Right breast, then breasts when her husband
    sexually attacks her.

### *Play Nice* (1992)
(Unrated version reviewed.)
Robey . . . . . . . . . . . . . . . . . . . . . . . . . . .Jill/Rapunzel
• 0:28—Side view of right breast, while sitting on top
    of a victim in bed. Don't see her face.
••• 0:35—Breasts, making love in bed with Jack. Nice,
    long scene.
•• 0:46—Breasts, making love on the floor with Jack.
••• 1:09—Breasts in bed on top of Jack, then getting out
    of bed and getting dressed.
Ann Dusenberry . . . . . . . . . . . . . . . . . . Pam Crichmore
Bruce McGill . . . . . . . . . . . . . . . . . . . . . Captain Foxx
Ed O'Ross . . . . . . . . . . . . . . . . . . . Jack "Mouth" Penucci
• 0:35—Buns, while making love in bed with Jill.
•• 0:46—Buns, while making love with Jill on the floor.

### *Playbirds* (1978; British)
Pat Astley . . . . . . . . . . . . . . . . . . . . . . .Doreen Hamilton
•• 0:00—Breasts posing for photo session.
Suzy Mandel . . . . . . . . . . . . . . . . . . . . . . . . . . . Lena
•• 0:12—Nude stripping in Playbird office.

Mary Millington . . . . . . . . . . . . . . . . . . Lucy Sheridan
- ••• 0:55—White bra, black garter belt, panties and stockings then nude taking off her clothes during the policewoman audition.
- • 1:00—Breasts giving an old man a massage in a massage parlor.
- ••• 1:05—Breasts making love with another woman from the massage parlor.
- ••• 1:14—Nude doing a photo session for *Playbird* magazine.

### The Player (1992)
Leah Ayres-Hamilton . . . . . . . . . . . . . . . . . . . . . Sandy
Karen Black . . . . . . . . . . . . . . . . . . . . . . . . . . . Cameo
Michael Bowen . . . . . . . . . . . . . . . . . . . . . . . . . Cameo
Robert Carradine . . . . . . . . . . . . . . . . . . . . . . . Cameo
Cathy Lee Crosby . . . . . . . . . . . . . . . . . . . . . . Cameo
Brad Davis . . . . . . . . . . . . . . . . . . . . . . . . . . . . Cameo
Peter Falk . . . . . . . . . . . . . . . . . . . . . . . . . . . . Cameo
Peter Gallagher . . . . . . . . . . . . . . . . . . . . . Larry Levy
Teri Garr . . . . . . . . . . . . . . . . . . . . . . . . . . . . . Cameo
Gina Gershon . . . . . . . . . . . . . . . . . . . Whitney Gersh
Scott Glenn . . . . . . . . . . . . . . . . . . . . . . . . . . . Cameo
Jeff Goldblum . . . . . . . . . . . . . . . . . . . . . . . . . Cameo
Richard E. Grant . . . . . . . . . . . . . . . . . . . Tom Oakley
Anjelica Huston . . . . . . . . . . . . . . . . . . . . . . . Cameo
Sally Kellerman . . . . . . . . . . . . . . . . . . . . . . . Cameo
Sally Kirkland . . . . . . . . . . . . . . . . . . . . . . . . . Cameo
Marlee Matlin . . . . . . . . . . . . . . . . . . . . . . . . Cameo
Malcolm McDowell . . . . . . . . . . . . . . . . . . . . Cameo
Jennifer Nash . . . . . . . . . . . . . . . . . . . . . . . . . Cameo
Nick Nolte . . . . . . . . . . . . . . . . . . . . . . . . . . . Cameo
Burt Reynolds . . . . . . . . . . . . . . . . . . . . . . . . Cameo
Tim Robbins . . . . . . . . . . . . . . . . . . . . . . Griffin Mill
- ••• 1:46—Briefly nude, covered with mud, getting out of mud bath.
Julia Roberts . . . . . . . . . . . . . . . . . . . . . . . . . Cameo
Mimi Rogers . . . . . . . . . . . . . . . . . . . . . . . . . Cameo
Annie Ross . . . . . . . . . . . . . . . . . . . . . . . . . . . Cameo
Susan Sarandon . . . . . . . . . . . . . . . . . . . . . . Cameo
Greta Scacchi . . . . . . . . . . . . . . . June Gudmundsdottir
Cynthia Stevenson . . . . . . . . . . . . . . Bonnie Sherow
- •• 0:19—Breasts, sitting in spa with Tim Robbins.
Fred Ward . . . . . . . . . . . . . . . . . . . . . . . . . . . Walter

### Playing For Keeps (1986)
Mary B. Ward . . . . . . . . . . . . . . . . . . . . . . . . Chloe
- •• 0:49—Breasts, after taking off her sweatshirt outside at night in front of Danny.

### Playroom (1989)
a.k.a. *Schizo*
Lisa Aliff . . . . . . . . . . . . . . . . . . . . . . . . . . . . . Jenny
- •• 0:23—Breasts making love on top of Christopher.
James Purcell . . . . . . . . . . . . . . . . . . . . . . . . . . Paul
- •• 0:25—Buns, while making love with Jamie Rose on a chair.
Jamie Rose . . . . . . . . . . . . . . . . . . . . . . . . . . Marcy

### Pleasure in Paradise (1992)
Toni Alessandrini . . . . . . . . . . . . . . . . . Lingerie Girl/First
- •• 0:51—In black lingerie, then breasts and buns in G-string, while dancing in bar.
Linda Brown . . . . . . . . . . . . . . . . . . . . . . . . Heather
- • 0:02—Full frontal nudity, while getting out of the shower and wrapping a towel around herself.
- ••• 0:41—Breasts while in bed, making love with Rob. Long scene.
Diane Colton . . . . . . . . . . . . . . . . . . . . . . . . Tiffany
- ••• 0:27—In black bra, then breasts while making love with Hansen. Long scene.
Jacqueline Jade . . . . . . . . . . . . . . . . . . . . . . . . Carol
- •• 0:01—Left breast, then breasts while making love in field with a guy at night.
Gina Jourard . . . . . . . . . . . . . . . . . . . . . . . . Woman
- ••• 0:06—Breasts, while making in love in bed with Hansen.
- • 0:39—Breasts on bed with Hansen.
John Paul Lorello . . . . . . . . . . . . . . . . . . . . . Hansen
- • 0:17—Partial buns, while making love in bed on top of Sandra.
- ••• 0:57—Buns, while taking off clothes and getting into pool with Sandra.
Honey Smax . . . . . . . . . . . . . . . . . . . . . . . . Sandra
- ••• 0:14—Breasts in lingerie, while making love in bed with Hansen. Long scene.
- ••• 0:57—Nude in pool, while making love with Hansen, then getting out. Long scene.

### Point Blank (1967)
Angie Dickinson . . . . . . . . . . . . . . . . . . . . . . . . Chris
- 0:46—In white slip when John Vernon opens her dress.
- • 0:51—Breasts in background putting dress on. Kind of a long shot.

### Point Break (1991)
Debra Lamb . . . . . . . . Uncredited Flame Blower at Party
James Le Gros . . . . . . . . . . . . . . . . . . . . . . . . Roach
- • 0:07—Brief buns, twice, while mooning the bank security camera. Wearing Richard Nixon mask. Could be anybody.
- • 0:11—Buns, on B&W monitor in the FBI office.
- • 0:59—Buns, mooning his friends while riding surfboard. Can't see his face clearly.
Julie Michaels . . . . . . . . . . . . . . . . . . . . Freight Train
- • 0:53—Brief breasts in the shower.
- • 0:54—Nude, beating up Keanu Reeves in the bathroom during shoot-out. Full frontal nudity while stabbing an FBI agent.
Lori Petty . . . . . . . . . . . . . . . . . . . . . . . . . . . Tyler
- • 1:14—Very brief buns, running out of Keanu Reeves' bedroom.
Keanu Reeves . . . . . . . . . . . . . . . . . . . . . Johnny Utah
- • 1:14—Very brief buns, while standing up to run after Tyler.
Patrick Swayze . . . . . . . . . . . . . . . . . . . . . . . Bodhi

## Point of Impact (1993)
Barbara Carrera . . . . . . . . . . . . . . . . . . . . . . . . . . . Eva
- • 0:39—In wet white swimsuit, after getting out of swimming pool.
- • 0:40—Very brief breasts, while swimming under water past underwater window.
  0:49—In black lingerie, taking off clothes on bed with Michael Paré.
- •• 0:51—Close up of left breast, while making love with Paré.
- • 0:53—Brief left breast, after getting out of bed.
- ••• 0:59—Breasts and buns in T-back, while swimming under water in pool.
- •• 1:00—Breasts, while making love outside with Paré.
- •• 1:02—Breasts in shower with Paré and on bed in wet sheet.
Michael Paré . . . . . . . . . . . . . . . . . . . . . . . . . . . . Jack

## Point of No Return (1993)
Gabriel Byrne . . . . . . . . . . . . . . . . . . . . . . . . . . . Bob
Olivia D'Abo . . . . . . . . . . . . . . . . . . . . . . . . . . Angela
Miguel Ferrer . . . . . . . . . . . . . . . . . . . . . . . . Kaufman
Bridget Fonda . . . . . . . . . . . . . . . . . . . . . . . . . .Maggie
- • 0:49—Brief right breast, while making love with J.P.
Harvey Keitel . . . . . . . . . . . . . . . . . . . . Victor the Cleaner

## Poison Ivy (1992)
(Unrated version reviewed.)
Drew Barrymore . . . . . . . . . . . . . . . . . . . . . . . . . . . . Ivy
  1:00—In wet bra on hood of car in rain with Tom Skerritt.
Julie Jay . . . . . . . . . . . . . . . . . . . . . . . Nurse at Desk
Tom Skerritt . . . . . . . . . . . . . . . . . . . .Darryl Cooper
- •• 1:22—Buns, several times, while making love with Ivy by the piano when Sara Gilbert walks in.

## Police (1985; French)
Sandrine Bonnaire . . . . . . . . . . . . . . . . . . . . . . . Lydie
- ••• 0:49—Full frontal nudity, undressing in front of Gérard Depardieu, then getting out of the shower.
Gérard Depardieu . . . . . . . . . . . . . . . . . . . . . .Mangin
Jonathan Leina . . . . . . . . . . . . . . . . . . . . . . . .Simon
- •• 0:11—Upper half of buns and brief frontal nudity in police station. Typewriter gets in the way.
Sophie Marceau . . . . . . . . . . . . . . . . . . . . . . . . Noria
- • 0:10—Brief left breast in window during police strip search.
- • 1:36—Right and left breasts several times, while in bed with Gérard Depardieu

## Police Academy II: Their First Assignment (1985)
Julie Brown . . . . . . . . . . . . . . . . . . . . . . . . . . . Chloe
Colleen Camp . . . . . . . . . . . . . . . . . . . . . . . Kirkland
Steve Guttenberg . . . . . . . . . . . . . . . . Carey Mahoney
Art Metrano . . . . . . . . . . . . . . . . . . . . . . . Lt. Mauser
- • 0:39—Buns, while in the locker room after the guys put epoxy resin in his shampoo.

## Policewomen (1974)
Jeannie Bell . . . . . . . . . . . . . . . . . . . . . . . . . .Pam Harris
- •• 0:02—Buns and breasts changing clothes during prison break.
- ••• 1:28—Brief breasts changing into military clothes outside next to truck.
Sondra Currie . . . . . . . . . . . . . . . . . . . . . . . . . Lacy Bond
- ••• 0:50—Breasts and buns taking off sheer robe and getting into bed, then making love with Frank.
Phil Hoover . . . . . . . . . . . . . . . . . . . . . . . . . . . . Doc
- •• 0:42—Buns, seen through shower door. More buns, after Laura opens the door.
Susan McIver . . . . . . . . . . . . . . . . . . . . . . . . . .Laura
- •• 0:42—Breasts and buns, taking off two piece swimsuit and getting into the shower with Doc.
- • 0:44—Breasts in the shower after Doc leaves.
Laurie Rose . . . . . . . . . . . . . . . . . . . . . . . . . .Janette
- • 0:02—Brief side of left breast, changing clothes during prison break.

## The Pom Pom Girls (1976)
Bill Adler . . . . . . . . . . . . . . . . . . . . . . . . . . . . Duane
Jennifer Ashley . . . . . . . . . . . . . . . . . . . . . . . . Laurie
- • 1:02—Brief breasts (on the left), taking off her white blouse in locker room. Brief buns, taking off panties and pulling down her cheerleader body suit.
Robert Carradine . . . . . . . . . . . . . . . . . . . . . . . Johnnie
- • 0:28—Brief buns, while mooning the Hardin High jocks out the back window of car.
- •• 1:08—Buns, while in the showers with the other boys.
Susan Player Jarreau . . . . . . . . . . . . . . . . . . . . . .Sue Ann
- • 0:14—Breasts, while making out with Jesse in the back of his van while parked at burger joint.
- • 0:47—Breasts, while making out with Jesse in the back of his van while parked at school.
- • 1:02—Brief buns, taking off her panties in locker room with the other girls.
Cheryl Smith . . . . . . . . . . . . . . . . . . . . . . . . Roxanne
- • 1:02—Very brief breasts, taking off her dress in locker room while talking to Judy.
- • 1:03—Brief breasts, while putting her cheerleader top on.

## Popcorn and Ice Cream (1978; West German)
a.k.a. Sex and Ice Cream
Ursula Buchfellner . . . . . . . . . . . . . . . . . . . . . . Yvonne
- ••• 0:30—Nude with the hotel manager, Vivi and Bea.
- • 0:40—Breasts in open dress at the disco.
Bea Fiedler . . . . . . . . . . . . . . . . . . . . . . . .Policewoman
- ••• 0:47—Full frontal nudity getting dressed.
- ••• 1:13—Right breast, then breasts in bed with a lover.
- ••• 1:14—Full frontal nudity in bed some more.
Zachi Noy . . . . . . . . . . . . . . . . . . . . . . . . . . . .Johnny
Olivia Pascal . . . . . . . . . . . . . . . . . . . . . . . . . . Vivi
- • 0:26—Full frontal nudity (she's on the right), covered with soap, taking a shower with Bea.

### *The Pope Must Die* (1991)
*a.k.a. The Pope Must Diet*
Beverly D'Angelo . . . . . . . . . . . . . . . . .Veronica Dante
Balthazar Getty . . . . . . . . . . . . . . . . . . . Joe Don Dante
- 0:46—Buns, making love with Luccia in his motor home.

### *Porky's* (1981; Canadian)
Rod Ball. . . . . . . . . . . . . . . . . . . . . . . . . . . . . . Steve
- 0:18—Brief frontal nudity sitting on bench in the cabin.
- 0:21—Very brief frontal nudity, following Meat out the front door of the cabin, then buns, while in front of the house.

Kim Cattrall. . . . . . . . . . . . . . . . . . . . . . . Honeywell
- 0:58—Brief buns, then very brief lower frontal nudity after removing skirt to make love in the boy's locker room.

Susan Clark . . . . . . . . . . . . . . . . . . . . . Cherry Forever
Tony Ganios . . . . . . . . . . . . . . . . . . . . . . . . . . .Meat
- • 0:21—Brief buns, while running out of the cabin during practical joke.

Kaki Hunter. . . . . . . . . . . . . . . . . . . . . . . . . . Wendy
- 1:02—Brief full frontal nudity, then brief breasts in the shower scene.

Wyatt Knight. . . . . . . . . . . . . . . . . . . . Tommy Turner
Pat Lee . . . . . . . . . . . . . . . . . . . . . . . . . . Stripper
- 0:33—Brief breasts dancing on stage at Porky's showing her breasts to Pee Wee.

Dan Monahan. . . . . . . . . . . . . . . . . . . . . . Pee Wee
- 0:22—Buns, while running down the road at night. Long shot.

Jack Mulcahy. . . . . . . . . . . . . . . . . . . . . Frank Bell
- 0:21—Very brief frontal nudity, getting up from bench. Then buns while in front of the cabin.

Cyril O'Reilly . . . . . . . . . . . . . . . . . . . . . . . . . .Tim
- 0:21—Very, very brief frontal nudity, getting up from bench. Then buns, while in front of the cabin.

Allene Simmons . . . . . . . . . . . . . . . . . . . . . . Jackie
- 1:02—Breasts in the shower scene.

Jill Whitlow . . . . . . . . . . . . . . . . . . . . . . . . .Mindy
Roger Wilson. . . . . . . . . . . . . . . . . . . . . . . . Mickey

### *Porky's II: The Next Day* (1983; Canadian)
Rod Ball. . . . . . . . . . . . . . . . . . . . . . . . . . . . . Steve
Cissie Colpitts-Cameron . Graveyard Gloria/Sandy Le Toi
0:26—Buns in G-string at carnival.
- •• 0:39—Breasts and buns in G-string, stripping for Pee Wee at cemetery.
- •• 0:40—More breasts, pretending to die.
- • 0:42—Breasts, being carried by Meat.

Kaki Hunter. . . . . . . . . . . . . . . . . . . . . . . . . Wendy
Dan Monahan. . . . . . . . . . . . . . . . . . . . . . Pee Wee
- • 0:39—Buns while at cemetery with Graveyard Gloria, then upper half of lower frontal nudity when he's holding her.
- • 0:40—Upper half of lower frontal nudity when he drops Gloria.
- • 0:42—Nude, trying to hide Steve.
- ••• 0:44—Nude when guys with shotguns shoot at him.

Jack Mulcahy . . . . . . . . . . . . . . . . . . . . . . .Frank Bell
Cyril O'Reilly . . . . . . . . . . . . . . . . . . . . . . . . . . . Tim

### *Porky's Revenge* (1985; Canadian)
Kim Evenson . . . . . . . . . . . . . . . . . . . . . . . . . . .Inga
- •• 0:02—Right breast, while opening her graduation gown during Pee Wee's dream.
- •• 1:27—Breasts showing Pee Wee that she doesn't have any clothes under her graduation gown.

Tony Ganios. . . . . . . . . . . . . . . . . . . . . . . . . . Meat
- •• 0:16—Buns, while getting out of swimming pool (the fifth guy getting out). More buns running around.

Mark Herrier. . . . . . . . . . . . . . . . . . . . . . . . . Billy
- •• 0:16—Buns, while getting out of swimming pool (the second guy getting out). More buns running around.

Kaki Hunter . . . . . . . . . . . . . . . . . . . . . . . .Wendy
1:22—In white bra and panties taking off her clothes to jump off a bridge.

Wyatt Knight . . . . . . . . . . . . . . . . . . . . Tommy Turner
- •• 0:16—Buns, while getting out of swimming pool (the first guy getting out). More buns running around.
- • 0:54—Buns, getting his underwear pulled down while trying to escape from a motel room from Balbricker.

Rose McVeigh . . . . . . . . . . . . . . . . . . . . .Miss Webster
- ••• 0:39—In black bra, panties, garter belt and stockings then breasts in her apartment with Mr. Dobish while Pee Wee and his friends secretly watch.

Dan Monahan . . . . . . . . . . . . . . . . . . . . . . . Pee Wee
- •• 0:02—Buns, when his graduation gown gets accidentally torn off during a dream.
- •• 0:16—Buns, while getting out of swimming pool (the fourth guy getting out). More buns while running around.
- •• 1:27—Buns, while getting his graduation gown town off.

Nancy Valen. . . . . . . . . . . . . . . . . . . . . . . . .Ginger

### *Portfolio* (1983)
Carol Alt. . . . . . . . . . . . . . . . . . . . . . . . . . . .Herself
- 0:28—Brief right breast, while adjusting black, see-through blouse.
0:31—Brief side view of a little bit of right breast while changing clothes backstage at a fashion show.

Kelly Lynch. . . . . . . . . . . . . . . . . . . . . . Elite Model
Shari Shattuck . . . . . . . . . . . . . . . . . . . . . Elite Model

### *Posed for Murder* (1988)
Charlotte J. Helmcamp. . . . . . . . . . . . . . .Laura Shea
- • 0:00—Breasts in photos during opening credits.
- ••• 0:22—Posing for photos in sheer green teddy, then breasts in sailor's cap, then great breasts shots wearing just a G-string.
0:31—Very brief right breast in photo on desk.
0:44—In black one piece swimsuit.
- ••• 0:52—Breasts in bed making love with her boyfriend.

**Posse** (1993)
Stephen Baldwin . . . . . . . . . . . . . . . . . . . . . . . . . Little J
  0:50—Almost frontal nudity, when jumping into wa-
  ter. His hand covers his privates, then it's too blurry
  once her starts moving.
Pam Grier . . . . . . . . . . . . . . . . . . . . . . . . . . . . Phoebe
Charles Lane . . . . . . . . . . . . . . . . . . . . . . . . . Weazie
  • 0:50—Very brief frontal nudity and buns, getting
  picked up and thrown in the water. Blurry.
Tom "Tiny" Lister, Jr. . . . . . . . . . . . . . . . . . . . . . Obobo
  •• 0:50—Buns, while urinating in the water.
Salli Richardson . . . . . . . . . . . . . . . . . . . . . . . . . . Lana
  • 1:10—Brief buns, while taking off her dress in front
  of Mario Van Peebles, then brief breasts (don't see
  her face).
  •• 1:11—Breasts, while making love with Van Peebles
  in bed.
Billy Zane . . . . . . . . . . . . . . . . . . . . Colonel Graham

**Possessed by the Night** (1993)
Sandahl Bergman . . . . . . . . . . . . . . . . . . Peggy Hansen
  ••• 0:06—Breasts and buns, while making love with Ted
  Prior in bed.
  • 0:08—More right breast and buns, while lying in
  bed after making love.
  0:26—In white bra and panties in bedroom with Pri-
  or.
  0:58—Briefly in bra in bathroom.
  • 0:59—Breasts, while in bathtub.
  1:02—In white bra and panties, after undressing
  while Shannon Tweed hold Prior at gunpoint.
  ••• 1:03—Breasts, while lying in bed after Prior rips her
  bra and panties off.
  •• 1:14—Breasts, while changing tops in bedroom.
Sandy Korn
  . . . . . . . . Uncredited Body Double for Shannon Tweed
  ••• 1:05—Breasts and buns in panties, while caressing
  herself. Did this because the film makers didn't need
  to have Tweed come back to shoot only this one in-
  sert scene.
Ted Prior . . . . . . . . . . . . . . . . . . . . . Howard Hansen
  ••• 0:07—Buns, while making love in bed with Sandahl
  Bergman.
Amy Rochelle . . . . . . . . . . . . . . . . . Bikini Woman/Tina
  ••• 0:16—Breasts, while giving Scott a back rub, then
  leaving the room.
Shannon Tweed . . . . . . . . . . . . . . . . . . . Carol McKay
  0:40—Working out in wet, braless, white tank top.
  •• 0:42—Breasts, while wiping off her sweat with the
  tank top.
  ••• 0:45—In bra on bed with Ted Prior, then breasts and
  brief lower frontal nudity, while making love with
  him.

**Possession** (1981; French/German)
Isabelle Adjani . . . . . . . . . . . . . . . . . . . . Anna/Helen
  • 0:04—Breasts in bed.
  • 0:16—Breasts lying in bed when Sam Neill pulls the
  covers over her.

  ••• 0:47—Right breast, then breasts lying in bed with
  Neill.
  • 1:08—Right breast, while lying on the floor with
  Neill, then sitting up.
Sam Neill . . . . . . . . . . . . . . . . . . . . . . . . . . . . Marc

**The Postman Always Rings Twice** (1981)
Anjelica Huston . . . . . . . . . . . . . . . . . . . . . . . Madge
  • 1:30—Brief side view left breast sitting in trailer with
  Jack Nicholson.
Jessica Lange . . . . . . . . . . . . . . . . . . . Cora Papadakis
  0:17—Making love with Jack Nicholson on the kitch-
  en table. No nudity, but still exciting.
  0:18—Pubic hair peeking out of right side of her
  panties when Nicholson grabs her crotch.
  • 1:03—Very, very brief breasts, then very, very brief
  right breast twice, when Nicholson rips her dress
  down to simulate a car accident.
  1:26—Brief lower frontal nudity when Nicholson
  starts crawling up over her in bed.
Jack Nicholson . . . . . . . . . . . . . . . . . . . Frank Chambers
  • 1:25—Buns, while lying across the bed.

**Powwow Highway** (1988; U.S./British)
Gary Farmer . . . . . . . . . . . . . . . . . . . . . . . Philbert Bono
  •• 1:00—Buns, while in bedroom getting out of bed to
  wake up Buddy.
Amanda Wyss . . . . . . . . . . . . . . . . . . . . . Rabbit Layton

**Predator 2** (1990)
Maria Conchita Alonso . . . . . . . . . . . . . . . . . . . . Leona
Adam Baldwin . . . . . . . . . . . . . . . . . . . . . . . . . Garber
Elpidia Carrillo . . . . . . . . . . . . . . . . . . . . . . . . . . Anna
Nick Corri . . . . . . . . . . . . . . . . . . . . . . . . . . Detective
Bill Paxton . . . . . . . . . . . . . . . . . . . . . . . . . . . . Jerry
Corey Rano . . . . . . . . . . . . . . . . . . . . . Ramon Vega
  • 0:23—Buns, while hanging upside down several
  times.
  • 0:26—Nude, hanging upside down, dead.
Teri Weigel . . . . . . . . . . . . . . . . . . . . . . Columbian Girl
  • 0:22—Brief breasts making love on bed. More
  breasts several times being held on the floor, brief
  full frontal nudity getting up when the Predator
  starts his attack.

**Preppies** (1984)
Nitchie Barrett . . . . . . . . . . . . . . . . . . . . . . . . Roxanne
  • 0:11—Brief breasts changing into waitress costumes
  with her two friends.
Sharon Cain . . . . . . . . . . . . . . . . . . . . Exotic Dancer
Cindy Manion . . . . . . . . . . . . . . . . . . . . . . . . . . . . . . Jo
  • 0:11—Brief breasts changing into waitress costumes
  with her two friends.
  • 0:44—Breasts during party with the three preppie
  guys.
Katt Shea . . . . . . . . . . . . . . . . . . . . . . . . . Margot
  ••• 0:20—Breasts teasing Richard through the glass
  door of her house.
  0:54—In bra and panties with Trini, practicing sexual positions on the bed.
  • 1:07—Brief breasts after taking off bra in bed.

Lynda Wiesmeier . . . . . . . . . . . . . . . . . . . . . . . . . . Trini
   0:54—In bra and panties, practicing sexual positions on beds with Margot.
••• 1:06—Breasts on bed with Mark.

### Presumed Guilty (1990)
Holly Floria . . . . . . . . . . . . . . . . . . . . . . . . Mary Austin
  • 1:02—Side view of left breast, very brief lower frontal nudity and buns, while making love with Jessie.
Jack Vogel . . . . . . . . . . . . . . . . . . . . . . . Jessie Weston
  •• 0:19—Buns, while getting out of the shower.

### Presumed Innocent (1990)
Bonnie Bedelia . . . . . . . . . . . . . . . . . . . . Barbara Sabich
Joseph Carberry . . . . . . . . . . . . . . . . . . . Mr. McGaffney
Brian Dennehy . . . . . . . . . . . . . . . . . Raymond Horgan
Raul Julia . . . . . . . . . . . . . . . . . . . . . . . . . Sandy Stern
Greta Scacchi . . . . . . . . . . . . . . . . . . .Carolyn Polhemus
  • 0:46—Left breast, while making love on desk with Harrison Ford.
  • 0:53—Buns, lying in bed on top of Ford.

### Pretty Baby (1978)
Keith Carradine . . . . . . . . . . . . . . . . . . . . . . . . Bellocq
Mae Mercer . . . . . . . . . . . . . . . . . . .Mama Mosebery
Susan Sarandon . . . . . . . . . . . . . . . . . . . . . . . Hattie
   0:12—Feeding a baby with her left breast, while sitting by the window in the kitchen.
   0:24—Brief side view, taking a bath.
••• 0:39—Breasts on the couch when Keith Carradine photographs her.
Brooke Shields . . . . . . . . . . . . . . . . . . . . . . . . . Violet
  • 0:57—Breasts and buns taking a bath.
  • 1:26—Breasts posing on couch for Keith Carradine.
  • 1:28—Buns, getting thrown out of the room, then trying to get back in.

### Pretty Maids All in a Row (1971)
Joy Bang . . . . . . . . . . . . . . . . . . . . . . . . . . . . . .Rita
  • 0:57—Brief breasts in car with Rock Hudson.
  • 1:01—Right breast, in car with Hudson. Dark. More right breast, while getting dressed.
Gretchen Burrell . . . . . . . . . . . . . . . . . . . . Marjorie
  • 0:05—Partial side of right breast, in office with Rock Hudson.
  • 0:07—Breasts on the couch in Hudson's office.
Joanna Cameron . . . . . . . . . . . . . . . . . . . . . . .Yvonne
John David Carson . . . . . . . . . . . . . . . . . . . . . Ponce
  • 1:04—Very brief buns, sticking out from under sheet when he uses it to cover Angie Dickinson in bed.
Angie Dickinson . . . . . . . . . . . . . . . . . . . . Miss Smith
  • 1:04—Buns, in long shot, while lying on bed with Ponce.
Aimée Eccles . . . . . . . . . . . . . . . . . . . . . . . . . . .Hilda
  • 1:06—Partial buns while sitting on desk in Rock Hudson's office. Her hair covers most of her right breast.
June Fairchild . . . . . . . . . . . . . Sonya "Sonny" Swingle
  • 1:10—Brief breasts and lower frontal nudity, taking Polaroid photos of herself in Rock Hudson's office.

Barbara Leigh . . . . . . . . . . . . . . . . . . . . . . .Jean McDrew
  • 0:30—Brief partial side view of right breast when she leans over chess board on bed to touch Rock Hudson.
Margaret Markov . . . . . . . . . . . . . . . . . . . . . . . . Polly
Brenda Sykes . . . . . . . . . . . . . . . . . . . .Pamela Wilcox

### Pretty Smart (1986)
Patricia Arquette . . . . . . . . . . . . . . . . . . . . . . . . Zero
Julie Kristen Smith . . . . . . . . . . . Samantha Falconwright
  •• 0:20—Nude in her room when Daphne sees her.
  •• 0:26—Breasts in bed talking to Jennifer.
  •• 0:40—Breasts in bed.
  • 0:52—Breasts sitting in lounge by the pool.
  • 0:57—Brief left breast, while brushing teeth.
  • 1:10—Brief right breast, while making love with boyfriend in bed.
  • 1:13—More brief right breast.
  ••• 1:14—Nude, sitting on pillow on top of her boyfriend in bed.
Kim Waltrip . . . . . . . . . . . . . . . .Sara Gentry (the teacher)
  •• 0:53—Breasts, while sunbathing with her students.

### Pretty Woman (1990)
Jason Alexander . . . . . . . . . . . . . . . . . . . . Philip Stuckey
Judy Baldwin . . . . . . . . . . . . . . . . . . . . . . . . . . .Susan
John David Carson . . . . . . . . . . . . . . . . . . . . . . . . Mark
Lucinda Crosby . . . . . . . . . . . . . . . . . . . . Olsen Sister
Richard Gere . . . . . . . . . . . . . . . . . . . . . . .Edward Lewis
Shelley Michelle . . . . . . . . Body Double for Julia Roberts
   0:04—In black panties and bra, waking up and getting dressed.
Julia Roberts . . . . . . . . . . . . . . . . . . . . . . .Vivian Ward
  • 1:30—Very, very brief tip of left breast, then right breast, then left breast seen through head board, in bed with Gere. It's her—look especially at the vertical vein that pops out in the middle of her forehead whenever her blood pressure goes up.
Dey Young . . . . . . . . . . . . . . . . . . Snobby Saleswoman

### The Prey (1980)
Steve Bond . . . . . . . . . . . . . . . . . . . . . . . . . . . . . Joel
Gayle Gannes . . . . . . . . . . . . . . . . . . . . . . . . . . . Gail
  • 0:36—Brief breasts putting T-shirt on before the creature attacks her.

### Prey for the Hunter (1990)
Evan J. Klisser . . . . . . . . . . . . . . . . . . . . . . . . . . .Jason
  • 0:17—Buns, while wiping paint off his butt.

### Prey of the Chameleon
*(1992; Made for Cable Movie)*
Linda Carol . . . . . . . . . . . . . . . . . . . . . . . . . . . Nurse
  • 0:00—Breasts several times, making love with a guy in restroom. Dark.
   0:08—Buns, of dead body, lying on ground. Don't see face.
Lisa London . . . . . . . . . . . . . . . . . . . . . . . . . . . Alice
Michelle McBride . . . . . . . . . . . . . . . . . . . . . . .Leslie
Alexandra Paul . . . . . . . . . . . . . . . . . . . . . . . . Carrie

James Wilder . . . . . . . . . . . . . . . . . . . . . . . . . . . . . J.D.
- 0:32—Upper half of buns, while getting out of bed.

Daphne Zuniga . . . . . . . . . . . . . . . . . Elizabeth Burrows

### *Priceless Beauty* (1989; Italian)

Christopher Lambert . . . . . . . . . . . . . . . . . . . . Monroe

Diane Lane . . . . . . . . . . . . . . . . . . . . . . China/Anna
- • 0:34—Breasts in bed with Christopher Lambert.
- • 0:35—Brief left breast, then side of right breast on top of Lambert.

Claudia Ohana . . . . . . . . . . . . . . . . . . . . . . . . . Lisa

### *Prick Up Your Ears* (1987; British)

Frances Barber . . . . . . . . . . . . . . . . . . . . Leonie Orton

Spencer Leigh . . . . . . . . . . . . . . . . . . . . . . Constable

Steven Mackintosh . . . . . . . . . . . . . . . . Simon Ward

Alfred Molina . . . . . . . . . . . . . . . . . . Kenneth Halliwell
- 0:40—Brief buns, getting into bed with Gary Oldman.
- 1:42—Buns, while lying dead on the floor after killing Gary Oldman.

Gary Oldman . . . . . . . . . . . . . . . . . . . . . . . Joe Orton
- •• 1:38—Buns, after taking off underwear and getting into bed.

Vanessa Redgrave . . . . . . . . . . . . . . . . . Peggy Ramsay

Julie Walters . . . . . . . . . . . . . . . . . . . . . . . Elise Orton

### *Priest of Love* (1980)

Sarah Brackett . . . . . . . . . . . . . . . . . . . . Athsah Brester

Graham Faulkner . . . . . . . . . . . . . . . . . . Cornish Farmer
- 0:52—Buns, after taking off clothes and getting into water with D.H. Lawrence.
- •• 0:55—Nude, getting off rock and getting dressed when soldiers start harassing him.

Ian McKellen . . . . . . . . . . . . . . . . . . . . . D.H. Lawrence
- 0:17—Buns after dropping robe and walking around bed. Shadow of erection on wall.
- ••• 0:52—Frontal nudity, while swimming in water.
- 0:54—Brief frontal nudity while drying himself off.
- 1:20—Brief buns, after taking off robe and getting into bed with Dorothy.

Sarah Miles . . . . . . . . . . . . . . . . . . . . . . . . . Film Star

Andrea Occhipinti . . . . . . . . . . . . . . . . . Young Painter

### *Prime Cut* (1972)

Janit Baldwin . . . . . . . . . . . . . . . . . . . . . . . . . Violet
- 0:25—Very brief nude, being swung around when Gene Hackman lifts her up to show to Lee Marvin.
- 0:41—Brief breasts putting on a red dress.

Sissy Spacek . . . . . . . . . . . . . . . . . . . . . . . . . Poppy
- 0:25—Brief side view of left breast lying in hay, then buns when Gene Hackman lifts her up to show to Lee Marvin.
- ••• 0:30—Breasts sitting in bed, then getting up to try on a dress while Marvin watches.
- 0:32—Close up of breasts though sheer black dress in a restaurant.

Angel Tompkins . . . . . . . . . . . . . . . . . . . . Clarabelle
- 1:03—Very brief left breast sitting up in bed to talk to Lee Marvin.

1:04—Very brief back side view of left breast jumping out of bed.

### *Prime Evil* (1987)

Amy Brentano . . . . . . . . . . . . . . . . . . . . . . . . . Brett
- ••• 1:13—Breasts removing her gown (she's in the middle) with Cathy and Judy.

Ruth Corrine Collins . . . . . . . . . . . . . . . . . . . . . Cathy
- ••• 0:15—Breasts making love with her boyfriend in bed.
- • 0:16—More breasts sitting up and getting out of bed.
- ••• 0:27—Breasts, sitting up while the priest talks to her.
- •• 1:13—Left breast, while removing her gown (she's on the left) with Brett and Judy.

Jeanne Marie . . . . . . . . . . . . . . . . . . . . . . . . . Judy
- 1:13—Breasts after removing her gown (she's on the right) with Cathy and Brett.

Christine Moore . . . . . . . . . . . . . . Alexandra Parkman
- 0:09—In white bra in locker room.

Miriam Zucker . . . . . . . . . . . . . . . . . . . . . Nancy Deans
- •• 0:03—Breasts several times, during sacrificial ceremony.

### *The Prime of Miss Jean Brodie* (1969)

Pamela Franklin . . . . . . . . . . . . . . . . . . . . . . . Sandy
- •• 1:21—Breasts posing as a model for Teddy's painting. Brief right breast, while kissing him. Long shot of buns, while getting dressed.

Maggie Smith . . . . . . . . . . . . . . . . . . . . . Jean Brodie

### *Prime Target* (1991)

Jenilee Harrison . . . . . . . . . . . . . . . . . Kathy Bloodstone
- ••• 0:12—Breasts, lying back in bed with David Heavener. Short, but sweet!
- • 0:13—Partial right breast, under Heavener's arm.

Sandra Margot . . . . . . . . . . . . . . . . . . . . Girl in Shower
- ••• 0:52—Side view of left breast and buns, taking a shower.
- • 0:53—Buns, in hotel room after getting out of the shower.

### *The Prince of Pennsylvania* (1988)

Bonnie Bedelia . . . . . . . . . . . . . . . . . . . . Pam Marshetta
- 0:12—In black bra in open blouse in kitchen. Long scene.

Amy Madigan . . . . . . . . . . . . . . . . . . . Carla Headlee
- • 0:37—Left breast and buns, while getting out of bed with Keanu Reeves and putting on a robe.

Dan Monahan . . . . . . . . . . . . . . . . Tommy Rutherford

Keanu Reeves . . . . . . . . . . . . . . . . . . . . Rupert Marshetta

Fred Ward . . . . . . . . . . . . . . . . . . . . . . . . . . . . Gary

### *Prison Stories, Women on the Inside*
(1990; Made for Cable Movie)

Rae Dawn Chong . . . . . . . . . . . . . . . . . . . . . . Rhonda
- • 0:26—Very brief right breast several times in prison shower with Annabella Sciorra.

Lolita Davidovich . . . . . . . . . . . . . . . . . . . . . . Lorretta

Silvana Gallardo . . . . . . . . . . . . . . . . . . . . . . Mercedes

Annabella Sciorra . . . . . . . . . . . . . . . . . . . . . . Nicole

Rachel Ticotin . . . . . . . . . . . . . . . . . . . . . . . . . . . Iris
  0:07—Brief buns, squatting while getting strip
  searched in jail. Don't see her face.

## Private Lessons (1981)
Ed Begley, Jr. . . . . . . . . . . . . . . . . . . . . . . . .Jack Travis
Pamela Bryant. . . . . . . . . . . . . . . . . . . . . . . . . . Joyce
  • 0:03—Very brief right breast, changing in the house
  while Billy and his friend peep from outside.
Sylvia Kristel . . . . . . . . . . . . . . . . . . . . . . . . . .Mallow
  • 0:20—Very brief breasts sitting up next to the pool
  when the sprinklers go on.
  •• 0:24—Breasts and buns, stripping for Billy. Some
  shots might be a body double.
  • 0:51—Breasts in bed when she "dies" with Howard
  Hesseman.
  • 1:28—Breasts making love with Billy. Some shots
  might be a body double.

## Private Passions (1983)
Gavin Brannan . . . . . . . . . . . . . . . . . . . . . . . . .Mark
  • 1:19—Buns, while lying in bed on top of Sybil Danning.
Sybil Danning . . . . . . . . . . . . . . . . . . . . . . Katherine
David Siegel . . . . . . . . . . . . . . . . . . . . . . . . . . Toni
  • 0:29—Buns, with Laura. Don't see his face.

## Private Popsicle (1982)
Bea Fiedler . . . . . . . . . . . . . . . . . . . . . . . . . . . Eva
  •• 0:04—In black bra with Bobby. Upper half of left
  breast, very brief side of right breast, then breasts.
  ••• 0:06—Full frontal nudity with Bobby in bed.
  •• 0:07—More breasts with Bobby.
  ••• 0:08—Breasts on bed with Hughie.
  •• 0:09—More breasts when her husband gets into
  bed.
Iftach Katzur . . . . . . . . . . . . . . . . . . . . . . . . . .Benji
  •• 1:26—Buns, while walking around after Rena steals
  his clothes.
Zachi Noy. . . . . . . . . . . . . . . . . . . . . . . . . . .Hughie
  • 0:09—Buns while in bed with Eva.

## Private Resort (1985)
Vickie Benson . . . . . . . . . . . . . . . . . . . . . Bikini Girl
  • 0:28—In blue two piece swimsuit, showing her
  buns, then brief breasts with Reeves.
  1:11—Buns, in locker room, trying to slap Reeves.
Johnny Depp. . . . . . . . . . . . . . . . . . . . . . . . . Jack
  •• 0:12—Buns, while in hotel room with Leslie Easterbrook.
Leslie Easterbrook . . . . . . . . . . . . . . . . . . . Bobbie Sue
  •• 0:14—Very brief buns taking off swimsuit, then
  breasts under sheer white nightgown.
Lisa London. . . . . . . . . . . . . . . . . . . . . . . . . . .Alice
  0:51—In beige bra and panties several times with
  Rob Morrow and Johnny Depp while she's drunk.
Rob Morrow . . . . . . . . . . . . . . . . . . . . . . . . . .Ben
  • 0:36—Brief buns while standing with Hillary Shepard worshiping Baba Rama.

  •• 0:39—Buns while getting caught naked by Mrs.
  Rawlins, then more buns, while running through the
  halls.
Hilary Shepard . . . . . . . . . . . . . . . . . . . . . . . . Shirley
  ••• 0:36—Breasts, then buns, taking off her dress in
  front of Rob Morrow.

## Private Road (1987)
Mitzi Kapture . . . . . . . . . . . . . . . . . . . . .Helen Milshaw
  0:50—Wearing a white bra during a strip-spin-the-
  bottle game.
  •• 1:29—Nude, while making love in bed with Greg
  Evigan.

## Private School (1983)
Phoebe Cates. . . . . . . . . . . . . . . . . . . . . . . Christine
  1:21—Brief buns lying in sand with Mathew Mod-
  ine.
  1:24—Upper half of buns flashing with the rest of
  the girls during graduation ceremony.
Sylvia Kristel. . . . . . . . . . . . . . . . . . . . Ms. Copuletta
  0:57—In wet white dress after falling in the pool.
Steve Levitt . . . . . . . . . . . . . . . . . . . . . . . Bellboy
Kari Lizer . . . . . . . . . . . . . . . . . . . . . . . . . . . Rita
  • 0:30—Very brief left breast popping out of cheerleader's outfit along with the Coach.
Matthew Modine . . . . . . . . . . . . . . . . . . . . . . .Jim
Julie Payne . . . . . . . . . . . . . . . . . . . . . . Coach Whelan
  • 0:30—Very, very brief left breast popping out of
  cheerleader's outfit along with Rita.
Betsy Russell. . . . . . . . . . . . . . . . .Jordan Leigh-Jensen
  0:02—Taking a shower behind a frosted door.
  • 0:04—Very, very brief right breast and buns when
  Bubba takes her towel off through window.
  ••• 0:19—Breasts riding a horse after Kathleen Wilhoite
  steals her blouse.
  0:35—In jogging outfit stripping down to black bra
  and panties, brief upper half of buns.
  1:15—In white bra and panties, in room with Bubba.
  1:24—Upper half of buns flashing with the rest of
  the girls during graduation ceremony.
Brinke Stevens . . . . . . . . . . . . . . .Uncredited School Girl
  •• 0:42—Brief breasts and buns in shower room scene.
  She's the brunette wearing a pony tail who passes in
  front of the chalkboard.
Lynda Wiesmeier . . . . . . . . . . . . . . . . . . . .School Girl
  ••• 0:42—Nude in shower room scene. First blonde in
  shower on the left.

## Prizzi's Honor (1985)
Anjelica Huston . . . . . . . . . . . . . . . . . . Maerose Prizzi
Jack Nicholson . . . . . . . . . . . . . . . . . . Charley Partanna
  2:05—Buns, sort of. Viewed from above while he
  takes a shower. Hard to see anything.
Kathleen Turner . . . . . . . . . . . . . . . . . . . Irene Walker
  • 0:30—Very brief left breast making love with Jack
  Nicholson on bed.

### Problem Child (1990)
Jack Warden . . . . . . . . . . . . . . . . . . . . "Big" Ben Healy
- 1:07—Buns, on TV in bar, mooning into the camera when he doesn't know it is on. (Yes, it is him.)

### Programmed to Kill (1987)
*a.k.a. The Retaliator*
Sandahl Bergman . . . . . . . . . . . . . . . . . . . . Samira
- 0:11—Brief side view of right breast taking off T-shirt and leaning over to kiss a guy. Don't see her face.

### Project: Alien (1990)
Maxwell Caulfield . . . . . . . . . . . . . . George Abbott
Darlanne Fluegel . . . . . . . . . . . . . . . ."Bird" McNamara
- 0:18—Buns, getting out of bed and putting on a kimono.
Michael Nouri . . . . . . . . . . . . . . . . . . . . . . Jeff Milker

### Prom Night (1980)
Jamie Lee Curtis . . . . . . . . . . . . . . . . . . . . . . Kim
Pita Oliver . . . . . . . . . . . . . . . . . . . . . . . . . . . Vicki
- 0:35—Brief buns, mooning Mr. Sykes outside of tennis court.
Mary Beth Rubens . . . . . . . . . . . . . . . . . . . . . . Kelly
- 0:59—Very brief right breast making out with Drew in the locker room.
- 1:02—Brief upper half of breasts, standing up to put dress on. Dark.

### Prom Night III (1989)
Tim Conlon . . . . . . . . . . . . . . . . . . . . . . . . . . Alex
- 0:15—Brief buns and very brief balls when the flag he's wearing falls off.
Courtney Taylor . . . . . . . . . . . . . . Mary Lou Maloney

### Prom Night IV: Deliver Us From Evil (1991)
Alle Ghadban . . . . . . . . . . . . . . . . . . . . . . . . . Jeff
- 0:37—Buns, mooning out the limousine window.
- 0:59—Buns, standing up while carrying Laura. Don't see his face.
Joy Tanner. . . . . . . . . . . . . . . . . . . . . . . . . . . Laura
- 0:58—Buns, lying in bed with Jeff. Don't see her face.
  0:59—Very brief right breast, while making love with Jeff, standing up. Don't see her face.
- 1:00—Buns and back half of right breast, getting out of bed. Don't see her face.
- 1:01—Breasts in shower. Don't see her face. It looks like a body double because the double's breasts are bigger than Joy's.

### Promised Land (1988)
Debi Richter . . . . . . . . . . . . . . . . . . . . . . . Pammie
Meg Ryan . . . . . . . . . . . . . . . . . . . . . . . . . Beverly
- 0:22—Very brief side view of left breast in bed with Kiefer Sutherland.
Kiefer Sutherland . . . . . . . . . . . . . . . . . . . .Danny Rivers

### Promises, Promises (1963)
Jayne Mansfield . . . . . . . . . . . . . . . . . . . Sandy Brooks
  0:02—Bubble bath scene.

- ••• 0:04—Breasts drying herself off with a towel. Same shot also at 0:48.
- ••• 0:06—Breasts in bed. Same shot also at 0:08, 0:39 and 0:40.
- ••• 0:59—Buns, kneeling next to bathtub, right breast in bathtub, then breasts drying herself off.

### Proof (1991; Australian)
Russell Crowe. . . . . . . . . . . . . . . . . . . . . . . . . Andy
- •• 1:12—Buns, while making love on top of Celia on the couch.
Daniel Pollock . . . . . . . . . . . . . . . . . . . . . . . . Gary
Hugo Weaving . . . . . . . . . . . . . . . . . . . . . . . .Martin

### Prospero's Books (1991; Dutch/French/Italian)
Isabelle Pasco. . . . . . . . . . . . . . . . . . . . . . .Miranda
- 0:13—Tip of left breast, when it peeks out between an opening in her blouse, while lying in bed as John Gielgud sits beside her on the bed.

### The Prowler (1981)
Lisa Dunsheath . . . . . . . . . . . . . . . . . . . . . . . Sherry
- 0:20—Very brief breasts in the shower (overhead view).
- •• 0:21—More breasts and buns in shower, then breasts when Carl opens the door.
- 0:22—More breasts from overhead.
- •• 0:23—Breasts, getting killed by the prowler with a pitchfork.
- 1:23—Breasts, dead in the bathtub when Pam discovers her.

### Psychic (1992; Made for Cable Movie)
Zach Galligan. . . . . . . . . . . . . . . . . . . Patrick Costello
Michael Nouri . . . . . . . . . . . . . . . . . Professor Steering
Andrea Roth. . . . . . . . . . . . . . . . . . . . . . April Morris
- 1:01—Brief buns, partially covered with leaves, lying dead in park.
Catherine Mary Stewart . . . . . . . . . . . . . . . . . Laurel
- 0:45—Very brief right breast, twice, at the end of love making scene with Zach Galligan.

### Psycho Cop 2 (1992)
Barbara Lee Alexander . . . . . . . . . . . . . . . . . .Sharon
Brittany Ashland. . . . . . . . . . . . . . . . Go Go Dancer #1
- 0:21—Breasts on film that the guys are watching at bachelor party. (She's the blonde one.)
- 1:17—Breasts and buns in panties in film during end credits.
Justin Carroll . . . . . . . . . . . . . . . . . . . . . . . . . Tony
- •• 0:37—Buns, while making love on top of Chloe on desk, then standing up and talking to Sharon.
Kimberly Speiss . . . . . . . . . . . . . . . . . . . . . . . Chloe
- 0:37—Buns, while falling off of desk with Tony, then standing up and talking to Sharon.
Julie Strain . . . . . . . . . . . . . . . . . . . . . . . Stephanie
  0:19—Brief buns, when elevator door opens.
- ••• 0:21—Buns in cowboy outfit, then breasts with red star pasties while doing dance routine.
- •• 0:25—Breasts and buns, while with the two other dancers and the guys.

- 0:31—Breasts and buns, when Mike comes back.
- 0:33—Breasts, when the guys start worrying about Mike.
- 0:38—Breasts, when putting them in Brian's face.
- 0:41—Breasts, when with Brian. Buns in cowboy outfit for the rest of the film.

Alisa Wilson . . . . . . . . . . . . . . . . . . . . Anchorwoman

## Psycho From Texas (1981)
Angela Field . . . . . . . . . . . . . . . . . . .Wheeler's Mother
- •• 0:09—Breasts and buns, while making love in bed with the salesman.

Norman Field . . . . . . . . . . . . . . . . . . . Salesman
- • 0:09—Buns, while making love with Wheeler's mother on bed.

Linnea Quigley . . . . . . . . . . . . . . . . . . . . . . Barmaid
- ••• 1:16—Nude, after taking off her dress and dancing in front of Wheeler. (He pours beer on her.) Long scene.

## Psycho III (1986)
Juliette Cummins. . . . . . . . . . . . . . . . . . . . . . .Red
- ••• 0:39—Breasts making love with Duke in his motel room, then getting thrown out.

Jeff Fahey . . . . . . . . . . . . . . . . . . . . . . . . . Duane
Katt Shea . . . . . . . . . . . . . . . . . . . . . . . . . .Patsy
Brinke Stevens. . . . . . . . Body Double for Diana Scarwid
- •• 0:30—Brief breasts and buns getting ready to take a shower, body doubling for Diana Scarwid.

## Psycho IV: The Beginning
(1990; Made for Cable Movie)
Olivia Hussey. . . . . . . . . . . . . . . . . . . . . .Norma Bates
- •• 0:49—Breasts in motel room mirror while young Norman, watches through peephole.

## Psychopathia Sexualis (1966)
a.k.a. On Her Bed of Roses
Pat Barringer. . . . . . . . . . . . . . . . . . . . . . . . . Dancer
- ••• 0:34—Breasts, while belly dancing during party (she's the second dancer). Long scene.

## Psychos in Love (1987)
LeeAnne Baker . . . . . . . . . . . . . . . . . . .Heavy Metal Girl
- ••• 0:25—Breasts, undressing in room in front of Joe.

Patti Chambers . . . . . . . . . . . . . . . . . . . . . Girl in Bed
- •• 0:02—Breasts, sitting in bed and stretching, just before getting killed.

Ruth Corrine Collins . . . . . . . . . . . . . . . . . . . . Susan
- ••• 0:42—Breasts, dancing and undressing in living room in front of Joe when caught by Kate.

Angela Nicholas . . . . . . . . . . . . . . . . . . . . . Diane
- •• 0:04—Breasts while taking a shower, before being killed.

Cecilia Wilde. . . . . . . . . . . . . . . . . . . . . . . . .Nikki
- • 0:08—Breasts, dancing on stage in a bar.
- ••• 0:14—Buns, in G-string while dancing on stage, then breasts.
- •• 0:45—Breasts, dancing on stage with a fluorescent light.

## Pucker Up and Bark Like a Dog (1989)
Iris Condon . . . . . . . . . . . . . . . . . . . . . Stretch Woman
Robert Culp . . . . . . . . . . . . . . . . . . . . . . . . .Gregor
Wendy O. Williams. . . . . . . . . . . . . . . . . . . . .Butch
Lisa Zane . . . . . . . . . . . . . . . . . . . . . . Taylor Phillips
- •• 0:52—Breasts in shower with Max. Left breast, while in bed.

## Pump Up the Volume (1990)
Samantha Mathis. . . . . . . . . . . . . . . . . . . . .Nora Diniro
- •• 1:13—Breasts taking off sweater on patio with Christian Slater.

Christian Slater. . . . . . . . . . . . . . . . . . . . . Mark Hunter

## Pumping Iron II: The Women (1985)
Randy Rice. . . . . . . . . . . . . . . . . . . . . . . . . . Himself
- • 0:08—Buns in G-string, while dancing in women's club.

## The Punisher (1989)
Nancy Everhard . . . . . . . . . . . . . . . . . . . . . Sam Leary
Jeroen Krabbé . . . . . . . . . . . . . . . . . . Gianni Franco
Dolph Lundgren. . . . . . . . . . . . . . . . . . . .Frank Castle
- • 0:06—Upper half of buns, while kneeling in his underground hideout. Don't see his face.
- • 1:23—Same shot at 00:06 used again.

Bryan Marshall . . . . . . . . . . . . . . . . . . . . . Dino Moretti

## Puppet Master (1989)
Barbara Crampton . . . . . . . . . . . . . . Woman at Carnival
Irene Miracle . . . . . . . . . . . . . . . . . . . . . Dana Hadley
Kathryn O'Reilly . . . . . . . . . . . . . . . . . Carissa Stamford
- • 0:41—Left breast in bathtub, covered with bubbles.
- • 0:43—Brief left breast getting out of tub. Nipple covered with bubbles.
  0:50—Riding on Frank in bed. Don't see anything, but still exciting. Very brief buns under sheer nightgown when she gets off Frank.
  1:11—Right breast under sheer black nightgown, dead sitting at the table. Blood on her face.

## Puppet Master II (1990)
Collin Bernsen . . . . . . . . . . . . . . . . . . . . . . . Michael
- •• 1:10—Buns, while putting out fire on the bed.

George "Buck" Flower . . . . . . . . . . . . . . . . . Matthew
Charlie Spradling . . . . . . . . . . . . . . . . . . . . .Wanda
- •• 1:04—Breasts getting out of bed and adjusting her panties.

## Puppet Master III: Toulon's Revenge (1990)
Michelle Bauer. . . . . . . . . . . . . . . . . . . . . . . . .Lili
- • 0:15—Brief breasts bringing the phone to the General while he takes a bath.
- •• 0:43—Breasts, twice, making love on top of the General.

## Purgatory (1988)
Adrienne Pearce. . . . . . . . . . . . . . . . . . . . . . . Janine
- •• 0:51—Brief breasts in shower scene with Kirsten.

Tanya Roberts . . . . . . . . . . . . . . . . . . . . Carly Arnold
- • 0:29—Nude, getting into the shower.
- • 0:42—Very brief breasts in bed with the Warden.

0:43—In white lingerie in whorehouse.

•• 0:57—Left breast, then brief breasts in bed talking to Tommy.

## Purple Hearts (1984)

Annie McEnroe . . . . . . . . . . . . . . . . . . . . . . . .Hallaway

•• 1:23—Brief breasts coming out of the bathroom surprising Ken Wahl and Cheryl Ladd.

Cyril O'Reilly . . . . . . . . . . . . . . . . . . . . . . . . . . . Zuma

## Purple Rain (1984)

Apollonia. . . . . . . . . . . . . . . . . . . . . . . . . Apollonia

•• 0:20—Brief breasts taking off jacket before jumping into lake.

0:41—In lingerie making love with Prince.

1:06—In black lingerie and stockings singing on stage.

Clarence Williams, III . . . . . . . . . . . . . . . . . . . . .Father

## Pyrates (1991)

Kevin Bacon . . . . . . . . . . . . . . . . . . . . . . . . . . . Ari

• 0:06—Brief side view of buns several times while making love with Kyra Sedgwick. Long shot.

•• 0:22—Buns in jock strap, while horsing around in bed with Sedgwick.

Kyra Sedgwick. . . . . . . . . . . . . . . . . . . . . . . . . Sam

••• 0:19—In sheer lingerie on top of Kevin Bacon in bed, then breasts.

0:21—Partial buns, bouncing in bed with Bacon.

• 0:22—Brief buns, lying on top of Bacon.

• 0:26—Breasts under water in hot tub with Bacon.

Petra Verkaik. . . . . . . . . . . . . . . . . . . . . . . . .Basia

## Q (1982)

Bobbi Burns . . . . . . . . . . . . . . . . . . . . . . . . .Sunbather

•• 0:06—Breasts taking off swimsuit top and rubbing lotion on herself.

David Carradine . . . . . . . . . . . . . . . Detective Shepard

Candy Clark . . . . . . . . . . . . . . . . . . . . . . . . . . Joan

Michael Moriarty. . . . . . . . . . . . . . . . . . . Jimmy Quinn

Richard Roundtree. . . . . . . . . . . . . . . . Sergeant Powell

Mary Louise Weller . . . . . . . . . . . . . . . . . .Mrs. Pauley

## Q & A (1990)

Paul Calderone . . . . . . . . . . . . . . . . . . Roger Montalvo

• 1:50—Brief buns, while on floor of boat, getting strangled by Nick Nolte.

Timothy Hutton . . . . . . . . . . . . . . . . . . . . . . .Al Rielly

Nick Nolte. . . . . . . . . . . . . . . . . . . . . . . . Mike Brennan

Javier Rios . . . . . . . . . . . . . . . . . . . . . . . Boat Lover

• 1:44—Brief buns, while on boat, getting pulled out of bed by Nick Nolte.

## Quackser Fortune has a Cousin in the Bronx (1970; Irish)

Margot Kidder. . . . . . . . . . . . . . . . . . . . . . . . . Zazel

•• 1:03—Breasts undressing on a chair, then brief right, then breasts when Gene Wilder kisses her.

• 1:05—Side view of left breast, then buns, getting out of bed.

Gene Wilder . . . . . . . . . . . . . . . . . . . . Quackser Fortune

## Quake (1992)

Erika Anderson . . . . . . . . . . . . . . . . . . . . . . Jenny Sutton

• 0:05—Breasts, getting out of the shower and drying herself off. More breasts, putting on bra.

• 0:40—Breasts in photos from 0:05 in darkroom.

•• 0:50—Breasts on table when Steve Railsback rips her bra off.

•• 0:51—Breasts, in drugged sleep while Railsback takes pictures of her.

• 0:52—More breasts asleep, then awake.

Steve Railsback. . . . . . . . . . . . . . . . . . . . . . .Kyle Ryan

## Quartet (1981; British/French)

Isabelle Adjani . . . . . . . . . . . . . . . . . . . . . Marya Zelli

•• 1:06—Breasts in bed with Alan Bates.

Alan Bates . . . . . . . . . . . . . . . . . . . . . . . . H.J. Heidler

Pierre Clementi . . . . . . . . . . . . . . . . . . . . . . . Theo

Jeffrey Kime . . . . . . . . . . . . . . . . . . . . . . . . . . .James

•• 0:49—Nude, posing with two women for the pornographer.

Maggie Smith . . . . . . . . . . . . . . . . . . . . . . . . . . Lois

## Quest For Fire (1981)

Joy Boushel . . . . . . . . . . . . . . . . . . . . . . Tribe Member

Rae Dawn Chong. . . . . . . . . . . . . . . . . . . . . . . . Ika

0:37—Breasts and buns, running away from the bad tribe.

0:40—Breasts and buns, following the three guys.

0:41—Brief breasts behind rocks.

• 0:43—Brief side view of left breast, healing Noah's wound.

• 0:50—Right breast, while sleeping by the fire.

0:53—Long shot, side view of left breast after making love.

• 0:54—Breasts shouting to the three guys.

• 1:07—Breasts standing with her tribe.

• 1:10—Breasts and buns, walking through camp at night.

• 1:18—Breasts in a field.

• 1:20—Left breast, turning over to demonstrate the missionary position. Long shot.

• 1:25—Buns and brief left breast running out of bear cave.

## Quick (1993)

Tia Carrere. . . . . . . . . . . . . . . . . . . . . Janet Sakamoto

Jeff Fahey. . . . . . . . . . . . . . . . . . . . . . . . . . Muncie

Teri Polo. . . . . . . . . . . . . . . . . . . . . . . . . . . .Quick

•• 0:42—Breasts, taking off her blouse in front of mirror, then putting on black bra.

•• 1:06—In black bra, then breasts (mostly right breast) while making love in car with Herschel.

## The Quiet Earth (1985; New Zealand)

Bruno Lawrence . . . . . . . . . . . . . . . . . . . . . . .Zac Hobson

•• 0:02—Brief frontal nudity lying on the bed.

•• 0:04—Brief nude getting back into bed.

• 0:33—Very brief frontal nudity jumping out of the ocean. Blurry, hard to see anything.

•• 1:01—Frontal nudity during flashback lying in bed.

Alison Routledge . . . . . . . . . . . . . . . . . . . . . . Joanne
    0:49—Brief buns, after making breakfast for Zac.
  •• 1:24—Breasts in guard tower making love with Api.

### *R.P.M.* (1970)

Ann-Margret . . . . . . . . . . . . . . . . . . . . . . . . . .Rhoda
  •• 0:07—Brief left breast and buns getting out of bed
    talking with Anthony Quinn.
    0:30—In fishnet top.
Teda Bracci . . . . . . . . . . . . . . . . . . . . . . . . . Student

### *R.S.V.P.* (1984)

Jane Hamilton . . . . . . . . . . . . . . . . Mrs. Ellen Edwards
Tamara Landry . . . . . . . . . . . . . . . . . . . . . . . . .Vicky
  •• 0:43—Breasts sitting in van taking her top off.
  •• 0:48—Breasts making love in the van with two guys.
Suzanne Remey Lawrence . . . . . . . . . . . . . . . . Stripper
  •• 0:56—Breasts dancing in a radio station in front of a
    D.J.
Harry Reems . . . . . . . . . . . . . . . . . . . . . Grant Garrison
Laurie Senit . . . . . . . . . . . . . . . . . . . . . . Sherry Worth
  •• 1:00—Breasts in the shower with Harry Reems.
  •• 1:06—Breasts again.
Katt Shea . . . . . . . . . . . . . . . . . . . . . . .Rhonda Rivers
  • 0:31—Side view of left breast, making love in bed
    with Jonathan.
Allene Simmons . . . . . . . . . . . . . . . .Patty De Fois Gras
  •• 0:13—Breasts taking off red top behind the bar with
    the bartender.
  •• 0:38—Breasts in bed with Mr. Edwards, then buns
    running to hide in the closet.
  •• 0:41—Frontal nudity in room with Mr. Anderson.
  ••• 0:51—Breasts talking to Toby in the hallway trying
    to get help for the Governor.
Lynda Wiesmeier . . . . . . . . . . . . . . . . .Jennifer Edwards
  •• 0:11—Breasts diving into the pool while Toby fanta-
    sizes about her being nude.
  • 0:19—Breasts in kitchen when Toby fantasizes about
    her again.
  ••• 1:21—Nude getting out of the pool and kissing To-
    by, when she really is nude.

### *Rabid* (1977; Canadian)

Marilyn Chambers . . . . . . . . . . . . . . . . . . . . . . Rose
  •• 0:14—Breasts in bed.
  •• 1:04—Breasts in closet selecting clothes.
  •• 1:16—Breasts in white panties getting out of bed.

### *The Rachel Papers* (1989; British)

Dexter Fletcher . . . . . . . . . . . . . . . . . . .Charles Highway
  • 0:58—Very brief buns, while jumping into bed with
    Ione Skye.
Siri Neal . . . . . . . . . . . . . . . . . . . . . . . . . . . . . Suki
Ione Skye . . . . . . . . . . . . . . . . . . . . . . . . . . Rachel
  •• 0:58—Breasts getting undressed and into bed with
    Charles. Long shot, then breasts in bed.
  ••• 1:03—Brief breasts in three scenes. From above in
    bathtub, in bed and in bathtub again.
  •• 1:04—Left breast, making love sitting up with
    Charles.
  • 1:06—Brief breasts sitting up in bathtub.

  • 1:08—Brief breasts long shot getting dressed in
    Charles' room.
  • 1:28—Brief breasts kissing Charles in bed during his
    flashback.
James Spader . . . . . . . . . . . . . . . . . . . . . . . . .De Forest

### *Racing with the Moon* (1984)

Rutanya Alda . . . . . . . . . . . . . . . . . . . . . . . . Mrs. Nash
Nicolas Cage . . . . . . . . . . . . . . . . . . . . . . . . . .Nicky
Barbara Howard . . . . . . . . . . . . . . . . . . . . Gatsby Girl
Carol Kane . . . . . . . . . . . . . . . . . . . . . . . . . .Annie
John Karlen . . . . . . . . . . . . . . . . . . . . . . . . Mr. Nash
Michael Madsen . . . . . . . . . . . . . . . . . . . . . . . Frank
Elizabeth McGovern . . . . . . . . . . . . . . . . Caddie Winger
  • 0:45—Upper half of breast in pond with Sean Penn.
Sean Penn . . . . . . . . . . . . . . . Henry "Hopper" Nash

### *A Rage in Harlem* (1991)

Robin Givens . . . . . . . . . . . . . . . . . . . . . . . Imabelle
  ••• 0:32—Buns, while lying in bed with Forest Whitaker.
Gregory Hines . . . . . . . . . . . . . . . . . . . . . . . . . Goldy

### *Ragtime* (1981)

Jeff Daniels . . . . . . . . . . . . . . . . . . . . . . . . . O'Donnell
Brad Dourif . . . . . . . . . . . . . . . . . . . . Younger Brother
Michael Jeter . . . . . . . . . . . . . . . . . . . . . . . . . n.a.
Elizabeth McGovern . . . . . . . . . . . . . . . . .Evelyn Nesbit
  ••• 0:52—Breasts in living room sitting on couch and ar-
    guing with a lawyer. Very long scene.
Mandy Patinkin . . . . . . . . . . . . . . . . . . . . . . . .Tateh
Mary Steenburgen . . . . . . . . . . . . . . . . . . . . Mother
Dorsey Wright . . . . . . . . . . . . . . . . . . . . . . . . . n.a.

### *The Railway Station Man*
### (1992; Made for Cable Movie)

Julie Christie . . . . . . . . . . . . . . . . . . . . . . . . Helen Cuffe
  • 0:35—Buns, undressing to go skinny dipping. Brief
    side of left breast, running into the ocean. Long
    shot.
  • 0:37—Buns, while walking out of the surf. Long
    shot.
John Lynch . . . . . . . . . . . . . . . . . . . . .Damian Sweeney
  • 0:37—Buns, taking off his clothes, running into the
    ocean and jumping around.
Donald Sutherland . . . . . . . . . . . . . . Roger Hawthorne

### *The Rain Killer* (1990)

Kirsten Ashley . . . . . . . . . . . . . . . . . . . . . . . . Dancer #2
  • 0:32—Nude, dancing on stage in club. Backlit too
    much.
  • 0:49—Buns, then brief nude on stage in club. Slight-
    ly out of focus.
Woody Brown . . . . . . . . . . . . . . . . . . .Jordan Rosewall
  ••• 0:39—Buns, while getting into bed, kneeling next to
    bed, then getting into bed with Satin. Long scene.
Maria Ford . . . . . . . . . . . . . . . . . . . . . . . . . . . Satin
  •• 0:29—Nude, dancing on stage in club. Backlit too
    much.
  ••• 0:37—Breasts in bedroom with Jordan, taking off
    her clothes, getting tied to bed. Long scene.
  • 0:41—Breasts lying on her back on bed, dead.

- 0:48—Same scene from 0:41 when Rosewall looks at B&W police photo.

Ray Sharkey . . . . . . . . . . . . . . . . . . . . . . . Vince Capra

### Rain Man (1988)

Tom Cruise . . . . . . . . . . . . . . . . . . . . . . . Charlie Babbitt
Valeria Golino . . . . . . . . . . . . . . . . . . . . . . . . . Suzanna
- 0:35—Very brief left breast four times and very, very brief right breast once with open blouse fighting with Tom Cruise after getting out of the bathtub.
Dustin Hoffman. . . . . . . . . . . . . . . . Raymond Babbitt
Gigi Vorgan. . . . . . . . . . . . . . . . . . . Voice-Over Actress

### The Rain People (1969)

Shirley Knight . . . . . . . . . . . . . . . . . . . . . . . . Natalie
- 0:15—Breasts walking around in motel room and getting into bed. Long shot.
- 1:36—Very brief buns, with sheet wrapped around her, trying to get out of trailer.

### The Rainbow (1989)

Sammi Davis-Voss . . . . . . . . . . . . . . . Ursula Brangwen
- ••• 0:21—Breasts and buns with Amanda Donohoe undressing, running outside in the rain, jumping into the water, then talking by the fireplace.
- ••• 0:30—Breasts and buns posing for a painter.
- 1:33—Brief right breast and buns getting out of bed.
- ••• 1:44—Nude running outside with Donohoe.
Amanda Donohoe. . . . . . . . . . . . . . . . . Winifred Inger
- ••• 0:21—Nude with Sammi Davis undressing, running outside in the rain, jumping into the water, then talking by the fireplace.
- ••• 0:43—Full frontal nudity taking off nightgown and getting into bed with Davis, then right breast.
- ••• 1:44—Nude running outside with Davis.
Glenda Jackson . . . . . . . . . . . . . . . . . . Anna Brangwen
Paul McGann . . . . . . . . . . . . . . . . . . . Anton Skrebensky
- •• 1:30—Buns, while opening a bottle of wine in room with Sammi Davis.
- 1:44—Very brief frontal nudity and buns when running up a hill with Amanda Donohoe.
Dudley Sutton. . . . . . . . . . . . . . . . . . . . . . . MacAllister

### Rainbow Drive (1990; Made for Cable Movie)

Kathryn Harrold . . . . . . . . . . . . . . . . . . . . . Christine
David Neidorf . . . . . . . . . . . . . . . . . . . . Bernie Maxwell
- 1:16—Buns, while in shower room when Peter Weller is interrogating him.
Chelchie Ross . . . . . . . . . . . . . . . . . . . . . . Tom Cutter
Peter Weller. . . . . . . . . . . . . . . . . . . . . Mike Gallagher

### Rambling Rose (1991)

Robert Burke . . . . . . . . . . . . . . Police Chief Dave Wilkie
Laura Dern . . . . . . . . . . . . . . . . . . . . . . . . . . . . . Rose
- •• 0:23—Right breast several times, while lying on bench with Robert Duvall while Lucas Haas peeks in.
John Heard . . . . . . . . . . . . . . . . . . . . . . Willcox Hillyer

### Ramona (1992)

Heidi Von Palleske. . . . . . . . . . . . . . . . . Ramona Soco
- 0:04—Brief breasts, while making love with Henry.

- •• 0:06—Brief breasts, several times, while rolling over in bed.
- 1:13—Breasts, after taking off blouse in hotel room with Henry.

### Rapid Fire (1992)

Kate Hodge . . . . . . . . . . . . . . . . . . . . . . . Karla Withers
- 1:06—Brief breasts, taking off her blouse in bed on top of Brandon Lee. Don't see her face well.
Barbara Ann Klein. . . . . . . . . . . . . . . . . . . . . . Stunts
Brigitta Stenberg . . . . . . . . . . . . . . . . . . . . . . Rosalyn
- 0:10—Brief side view of right breast, posing in art class. Don't see her face. Long shot breasts, getting up and putting on robe.
Jill Terashita . . . . . . . . . . . . . . . . . . . . . . . . . . Stunts

### The Rapture (1991)

Carole Davis. . . . . . . . . . . . . . . . . . . . . . . . . . . Angie
- 0:20—Buns, on top of Vic in bed. Most of side of her right breast.
- 0:21—Very brief right breast, then very brief breasts while turning around to talk.
David Duchovny . . . . . . . . . . . . . . . . . . . . . . . Randy
- ••• 0:24—Buns and brief frontal nudity getting out of bed in Mimi Roger's bedroom.
James Le Gros. . . . . . . . . . . . . . . . . . . . . . . . . Tommy
Stephanie Menuez . . . . . . . . . . . . . . . . . . . . . . Diane
- ••• 0:06—Breasts in furniture store with Mimi Rogers, Vic and Randy.
Mimi Rogers. . . . . . . . . . . . . . . . . . . . . . . . . . Sharon
- 0:08—Most of her left breast, while lying in bed with Randy
- •• 0:36—Very brief side view of right breast, dropping nightgown and walking into closet.

### Raw Force (1981)

Britt Helfer . . . . . . . . . . . . . . . . . . . . . . . . Girl in Cabin
Jennifer Holmes . . . . . . . . . . . . . . . . . . . . . Ann Davis
Camille Keaton. . . . . . . . . . . . . . . . . . . . Girl in Toilet
- •• 0:28—Breasts in bathroom with a guy.
- •• 0:29—Breasts in bathroom again with the guy.
- 0:31—Breasts in bathroom again when he rips her pants off.
Jillian Kesner. . . . . . . . . . . . . . . . . . . . Cookie Winchell
Jewel Shepard . . . . . . . . . . . . . . . . . . . . Drunk Sexpot
- 0:31—Breasts in black swimsuit, when a guy adjusts her straps and it falls open.

### Raw Justice (1994)

a.k.a. Good Cop, Bad Cop
Pamela Anderson . . . . . . . . . . . . . . . . . . . . . . Sarah
- ••• 0:40—Breasts, while making out with David Keith in building while standing up.
- •• 0:58—Breasts, while making love with Robert Hayes in hotel room.
Stacy Keach . . . . . . . . . . . . . . . . . . . . . . . . . Jenkins
David Keith . . . . . . . . . . . . . . . . . . . . . . . . . . . Mace
Ted Prior . . . . . . . . . . . . . . . . . . . . . . . . . . . Bennett
Leo Rossi . . . . . . . . . . . . . . . . . . . . . . . . . . . Atkins

### The Razor's Edge (1984)

Stephen Davies . . . . . . . . . . . . . . . . . . . . . . . . Malcolm
Catherine Hicks . . . . . . . . . . . . . . . . . . . . . . . . Isabel
- 0:43—Brief upper half of left breast, in bed after seeing a cockroach.
Theresa Russell . . . . . . . . . . . . . . . . . . . . . . . Sophie

### Re-Animator (1985)

(Unrated version reviewed.)
Barbara Crampton . . . . . . . . . . . . . . . . . .Megan Halsey
- • 0:10—Brief buns putting panties on, then breasts, putting bra on after making love with Dan.
- • 1:09—Full frontal nudity, lying unconscious on table getting strapped down.
- 1:10—Breasts getting her breasts fondled by a headless body.
- 1:19—Breasts on the table.

### Real Men (1987)

James Belushi . . . . . . . . . . . . . . . . . . . . . Nick Pirandelo
Mark Herrier . . . . . . . . . . . . . . . . . . . . . . . . Bradshaw
Travis McKenna . . . . . . . . . . . . . . . . . . . . . . . . . . Oaf
Suzanne Slater . . . . . . . . . . . . . . . . . . . . Woman in Bed
- 0:07—Brief left breast, in bed with James Belushi.
Dyanne Thorne . . . . . . . . . . . . . . . . . . . . . . . . . . . Dad

### Rebel (1985; Australian)

Bryan Brown . . . . . . . . . . . . . . . . . . . . . . . . Tiger Kelly
Cassandra Delaney . . . . . . . . . . . All-Girl Band Member
Rainee Skinner . . . . . . . . . . . . . . . . . . . . Prostitute in bed
- 0:37—Brief breasts sitting up in bed.

### Rebel Highway: Cool and the Crazy
(1994; Made for Cable Movie)

Christine Harnos . . . . . . . . . . . . . . . . . . . . . . . Lorraine
- •• 0:43—Breasts, several times, while making love in bed with Michael.
Jared Leto . . . . . . . . . . . . . . . . . . . . . . . . . . Michael
- 0:43—Brief buns, while making love in bed with Lorraine.
Alicia Silverstone . . . . . . . . . . . . . . . . . . . . . . . .Roslyn
- 0:27—Very brief tip of right breast, twice, when Joey kicks off his shoe and drops his pants. Medium long shot, don't see her face clearly.
- 0:28—Very brief tip of right breast, twice, when Joey kneels down and lies back. Once more when she lies down on him. Medium long shot, don't see her face well.

### Rebel Highway: Girls in Prison
(1994; Made for Cable Movie)

Tamara Clatterbuck . . . . . . . . . . . . Actress on Newsreel
Anne Heche . . . . . . . . . . . . . . . . . . . . . . . . . . .Jennifer
- •• 1:02—Breasts, while walking in showers past the other girls, taking a shower and dropping a bar of soap.
Nicolette Scorsese . . . . . . . . . . . . . . . . . . . . . . . Suzy
Ione Skye . . . . . . . . . . . . . . . . . . . . . . . . . . . . . Carol
- 0:23—Right breast, while in the showers with Melba.

- 1:02—Very, very brief breasts, while washing Melba's back in the showers.
Bahni Turpin . . . . . . . . . . . . . . . . . . . . . . . . . . . Melba
- 0:23—Back side of left breast, while in the showers with Ione Skye.

### Rebel Highway: Reform School Girl
(1994; Made for Cable Movie)

Aimee Graham . . . . . . . . . . . . . . . . . . . Donna Patterson
0:48—In white bra in shack with Carmen.
- 0:49—Breasts, while making out in shack with Carmen.
- 0:51—Brief breasts while in shower.
Elisa Pensler Gabrielli . . . . . . . . . . . . . . . . . Velmont Girl
Leo Rossi . . . . . . . . . . . . . . . . . . . . . . . . . . Disc Jockey

### Rebel Love (1985)

Terence Knox . . . . . . . . . . . . . . . . . Hightower/McHugh
- •• 0:49—Buns, while getting out of bath tub and chasing Jamie Rose around in cabin.
Jamie Rose . . . . . . . . . . . . . . . . . . . .Columbine Cromwell
- 0:43—Very, very brief tip of right breast, while making love in bed under Terence Knox.

### Reborn (1978)

Dennis Hopper . . . . . . . . . . . . . . . . . . . Rev. Tom Harley
Michael Moriarty . . . . . . . . . . . . . . . . . . . . . . . . Mark
- 0:38—Brief buns, while rolling off Maria in bed.
Antonella Murgia . . . . . . . . . . . . . . . . . . . . . . . .Maria
- 0:35—Breasts in bed with Michael Moriarty.
- •• 0:37—More breasts in bed with Moriarty.
- ••• 0:38—Nude, getting out of bed.
- ••• 0:39—Nude, walking around in bedroom.

### Reckless (1984)

Adam Baldwin . . . . . . . . . . . . . . . . . . . . . Randy Daniels
Daryl Hannah . . . . . . . . . . . . . . . . . . . . . Tracey Prescott
0:48—In a white bra fighting in gymnasium with Johnny then in pool area in bra and panties.
- ••• 0:52—Breasts in furnace room of school making love with Johnny. Lit with red light.
Toni Kalem . . . . . . . . . . . . . . . . . . . . . . . . . . . .Donna
Aidan Quinn . . . . . . . . . . . . . . . . . . . . . .Johnny Rourke
- 1:03—Very brief frontal nudity and buns while running into Daryl Hannah's brother's room when her parents come home early.
- 1:12—Side view nude, taking a shower.
Pamela Springsteen . . . . . . . . . . . . . . . . . .Karen Sybern

### Recruits (1986; Canadian)

Lolita Davidovich . . . . . . . . . . . . . . . . . . . . . . . . .Susan
- 0:19—Very brief breasts when Steve bumps into her in the shower room.
- •• 0:54—Right breast, then breasts while making out with Steve in car.
- •• 0:56—Breasts, twice, while driving around in car with Steve, the Governor and his wife.
- •• 0:58—Breasts, while getting out of the car.
Dominique St. Croix . . . . . . . . . . . . . . . . . . . . . . n.a.
John Canada Terrell . . . . . . . . . . . . . . . . . . . . .Winston

### Red Blooded American Girl (1988)
Kim Coates . . . . . . . . . . . . . . . . . . . . . . . . . . . . Dennis
- 0:01—Buns, while giving Rebecca a glass in bed.
- 0:30—Very brief buns, while getting into bathtub.

Lydie Denier . . . . . . . . . . . . . . . . . . . . Rebecca Murrin
••• 0:00—Breasts in bed wearing panties, garter belt and stockings. Buns, rolling over. Long scene.

Andrew Stevens . . . . . . . . . . Owen Augustus Urban III
Heather Thomas . . . . . . . . . . . . . . . . . Paula Bukowsky
1:19—Lower half of right breast when Andrew Stevens is on top of her. Very, very brief silhouette of right breast. Probably a body double.

### Red Heat (1987; U.S./German)
Linda Blair. . . . . . . . . . . . . . . . . . . . . . . Chris Carlson
0:09—In blue nightgown in the bedroom with her boyfriend, almost breasts.
••• 0:56—Breasts in shower room scene.
••• 1:01—Brief breasts getting raped by Sylvia Kristel while the male guard watches.

Sue Kiel. . . . . . . . . . . . . . . . . . . . . . . . . . . . . . Hedda
- 0:56—Brief breasts in shower room scene (third girl behind Linda Blair). Long shot, hard to see.

Sylvia Kristel . . . . . . . . . . . . . . . . . . . . . . . . . Sofia
0:23—In red lingerie.
•• 0:56—Breasts in shower room scene.
- 1:01—Brief breasts raping Linda Blair.

### Red Heat (1988)
James Belushi . . . . . . . . . . . . . . . . .Det. Dgt. Art Ridzik
Gina Gershon . . . . . . . . . . . . . . . . . . . . . .Cat Manzetti
Ed O'Ross . . . . . . . . . . . . . . . . . . . . . . Viktor Rostavili
Gretchen Palmer. . . . . . . . . . . . . . . . . . . . . . . Hooker
- 1:20—Breasts and buns in hotel during shoot out.

Arnold Schwarzenegger . . . . . . . . . . . . . . . . Ivan Danko
•• 0:02—Buns while in the sauna and outside fighting in the snow.

Gigi Vorgan. . . . . . . . . . . . . . . . . . . . . . . . . . Audrey

### Red Kiss (1985; French)
Marthe Keller . . . . . . . . . . . . . . . . . . . . . . . . Bronka
Isabelle Nanty . . . . . . . . . . . . . . . . . . . . . . . . Jeanine
Charlotte Valandrey . . . . . . . . . . . . . . . . . . . . Nadia
- 0:52—Very brief right breast, in bed with the photographer. Very dark.
•• 1:21—Very brief right breast, then breasts with the photographer.

Lambert Wilson. . . . . . . . . . . . . . . . . . . . . . Stephane

### Red Shoe Diaries (1992; Made for Cable Movie)
(Unrated video tape version reviewed.)
Brigitte Bako . . . . . . . . . . . . . . . . . . . . . . . . . . Alex
- 0:26—Buns and breasts, getting out of bathtub with Jake.
- 0:35—Very brief buns when Tom rips off her panties.
•• 0:36—Several brief breasts shots while making love with Tom in bed.
- 0:40—Brief breasts, leaning back on bed with Tom.

David Duchovny. . . . . . . . . . . . . . . . . . . . . . . . Jake

Leana Hall . . . . . . . . . . . . . . . . . . . . . . . . . . . Ingrid
Anna Karin . . . . . . . . . . . . . . . . . . . . . . . . .Heidi #1
••• 1:29—Breasts, three times, making love with Tom.
Tera Tabrizi . . . . . . . . . . . . . . . . . . . . . . Alex's Friend
Brenda Vaccaro . . . . . . . . . . . . . . . . . . . . . . . Martha

### Red Sonja (1985)
Sandahl Bergman. . . . . . . . . . . . . . . . . .Queen Gedren
Brigitte Nielsen. . . . . . . . . . . . . . . . . . . . . Red Sonja
- 0:01—Half of right nipple through torn outfit, while sitting up.
Arnold Schwarzenegger . . . . . . . . . . . . . . . . . .Kalidor

### Red-Headed Stranger (1986)
Morgan Fairchild . . . . . . . . . . . . . . . . . . . . . .Kaysha
- 0:03—Bathing in stream in wet white dress. Long shot, then closer shot.
Katharine Ross . . . . . . . . . . . . . . . . . . . . . . . . Laurie

### Red-Headed Woman (1932)
Jean Harlow . . . . . . . . . . . . . . . . . . . . . . . Lil Andrews
- 0:17—Very, very brief right breast when Una Merkel passes over a pajama top and Harlow raises it over her head to put it on.

### Reds (1981)
Warren Beatty . . . . . . . . . . . . . . . . . . . . . . . John Reed
Diane Keaton . . . . . . . . . . . . . . . . . . . . . .Louise Bryant
- 0:50—Buns, while standing in the water with Jack Nicholson at night. Very long shot.
Jack Nicholson . . . . . . . . . . . . . . . . . . . Eugene O'Neill
- 0:50—Buns, while standing in the water with Diane Keaton at night. Very long shot.

### The Reflecting Skin (1990; British)
Viggo Mortensen . . . . . . . . . . . . . . . . . Cameron Dove
- 1:09—Brief buns, lying on the floor with Dolphin.

### Reform School Girls (1986)
Michelle Bauer . . . . . . . . . . . . . Uncredited Shower Girl
•• 0:25—Breasts, then nude in the shower.
Leslee Bremmer . . . . . . . . . . . . . Uncredited Shower Girl
•• 0:25—Brief breasts in the shower three times. Walking from left to right in the background, full frontal nudity by herself with wet hair, breasts walking from left to right.
Linda Carol . . . . . . . . . . . . . . . . . . . . Jennifer Williams
•• 0:05—Nude in the shower.
- 0:56—Breasts in the back of a truck with Norton.
•• 1:13—Breasts getting hosed down by Edna.
Sybil Danning . . . . . . . . . . . . . . . . . . . . .Warden Sutter
Darcy De Moss. . . . . . . . . . . . . . . . . . . . . . . . Knox
Sheila Lussier . . . . . . . . . . . . . . . . . . . . . . . . . . . n.a.
Lorrie Marlow. . . . . . . . . . . . . . . . . . . . . . . . . Shelly
Sherri Stoner . . . . . . . . . . . . . . . . . . . . . . . . . . Lisa
- 1:03—Very brief breasts and buns, lying on stomach in the restroom, getting branded by bad girls.
Wendy O. Williams. . . . . . . . . . . . . . . . . . . . .Charlie
•• 0:26—Breasts talking to two girls in the shower.

## Reilly: Ace of Spies (1984)

Jeananne Crowley . . . . . . . . . . . . . . . . . . . . . . Margaret
- •• 0:52—Brief breasts, opening her blouse for her invalid husband.

Sam Neill . . . . . . . . . . . . . . . . . . . . . . . . . Sidney Reilly
- ••• 0:21—Buns, while getting out of bed and putting on his pants during an earthquake.

## The Reincarnation of Peter Proud (1975)

Margot Kidder. . . . . . . . . . . . . . . . . . . . . . Marcia Curtis
- • 1:29—Brief breasts sitting in bathtub masturbating while remembering getting raped by husband.

Cornelia Sharpe. . . . . . . . . . . . . . . . . . . . . Nora Hayes
- •• 0:03—Breasts in bed with Michael Sarrazin, then buns when getting out of bed.

## The Rejuvenator (1988)

Vivian Lanko . . . . . . . . . . . . . . . . . . . . Elizabeth Warren
- • 0:31—Brief breasts in bed with Dr. Ashton while making love. Don't see her face well.

## Relentless 2: Dead On (1991)

Shelby Chong . . . . . . . . . . . . . . . . . . . . . . . . Waitress
Meg Foster . . . . . . . . . . . . . . . . . . . . . . . Carol Dietz
Barbara Ann Klein . . . . . . . . . . . . . . . . . . . . . Realtor
Perry Lang. . . . . . . . . . . . . . . . . . . . . . . . Ralph Bashi
Miles O'Keeffe . . . . . . . . . . . . . . . . . . . . . . . Gregor
- ••• 0:17—Buns, while putting ice cubes into bathtub, then getting in.

Leo Rossi. . . . . . . . . . . . . . . . . . . . . . . . . Sam Dietz
Ray Sharkey. . . . . . . . . . . . . . . . . . . . . Kyle Volsone

## Relentless 3 (1992)

Leo Rossi . . . . . . . . . . . . . . . . . . . . . . . . . Sam Dietz
Savannah Smith Bouchér . . . . . . . . . . . . . . Marianne
- • 0:10—Very brief breast when Walter starts to kiss it. 0:36—In black bra, then in white bra, while sitting in chair, getting photographed by Walter.

## Remember My Name (1978)

Geraldine Chaplin . . . . . . . . . . . . . . . . . . . . . . Emily
- • 1:23—Very brief left breast, lying in bed, then right breast, with Anthony Perkins.

Jeff Goldblum . . . . . . . . . . . . . . . . . . . . . . Mr. Nadd

## Rendez-Vous (1986; French)

Juliette Binoche . . . . . . . . . . . . . . . Anne "Nina" Larrieu
- • 0:07—Brief breasts in dressing room when Paulot surprises her and Fred.
- ••• 0:25—Side of left breast, then breasts and buns in empty apartment with Paulot.
- •• 0:32—Full frontal nudity in bed with Quentin.
- •• 0:35—Buns, then brief breasts in bed with Paulot and Quentin. Full frontal nudity getting out.
- •• 1:08—Breasts taking off her top in front of Paulot in the dark, then breasts lying on the floor.
- • 1:11—Right breast, making love on the stairs. Dark.

Olimpia Carlisi. . . . . . . . . . . . . . . . . . . . . . . . . n.a.
Caroline Faro. . . . . . . . . . . . . . . . . . . . . . . Juliette
- • 0:22—Buns, walking up stairs, then full frontal nudity on second floor during play. Buns, while hugging Romeo and falling back into a net.

Lambert Wilson . . . . . . . . . . . . . . . . . . . . . Quentin
- • 0:22—Very brief buns, while falling with Juliet onto net during play.

## Renegade: Fighting Cage (1993)

(Nudity added for video release.)

Cie Allman . . . . . . . . . . . . . . . . . . . . . . . . . Cheetah
- •• 0:46—Breasts in bed, while making love with a guy.

Cheryl Bachman. . . . . . . . . . . . . . . . . . Ring Card Girl
Marjean Holden . . . . . . . . . . . . . Tigress/Sharon Miller
Kathleen Kinmont . . . . . . . . . . . . . . . . . . . Cheyenne
Martin Kove . . . . . . . . . . . . . . . . . . . . . Mitch Raines
Tamara Landry . . . . . . . . . . . . . . . . . . . . . . . Ellen
- •• 1:06—Breasts and buns in panties, making love with a guy and another woman.

Ashlie Rhey. . . . . . . . . . . . . . . . . . . . . . . . Redhead
- ••• 1:14—Breasts and buns, while in a room with a guy, then making love with him on a small table.

Gwen Somers. . . . . . . . . . . . . . . . . . . . . . . . . Lena
- • 1:07—Breasts, while making love with a guy a blonde woman in bed.

## Rented Lips (1988)

Eileen Brennan . . . . . . . . . . . . . . . . . . Hotel Desk Clerk
Catlyn Day. . . . . . . . . . . . . . . . . . . . . . . . . Dancer
Page Leong . . . . . . . . . . . . . . . . . . . . . . . . Dancer
Kenneth Mars. . . . . . . . . . . . . . . . . Reverend Farrell
Jennifer Tilly . . . . . . . . . . . . . . . . . . . . . . Mona Lisa
Edy Williams . . . . . . . . . . . . . . . . . . Heather Darling
- • 0:15—Breasts in bed, under Robert Downey, Jr. during playback of porno movie.

## Repo Jake (1990)

Dana Bentley Konkel . . . . . . . . . . . . . . . . . . . Jenny
Dan Haggerty . . . . . . . . . . . . . . . . . . . . . . . . Jake
Bonnie Paine . . . . . . . . . . . . . . . . . . . . . . . R.V. Girl
- •• 0:28—Breasts (mostly left breast) while in R.V. with her boyfriend.
- •• 0:29—More breasts, while making love with him.

Jacqueline Palmer. . . . . . . . . . . . . . . . . . . Porn Gal
- ••• 0:47—Breasts and buns, while on bed, acting in a movie.

## Repossessed (1990)

Belle Avery . . . . . . . . . . . . . . . . . . . Gym Receptionist
Linda Blair . . . . . . . . . . . . . . . . . . . . . . Nancy Aglet
Charlotte J. Helmcamp. . . . . . . . . . . . . Incredible Girl
Melissa Anne Moore. . . . . . . . . . . . . . Bimbo Student
- •• 0:05—Breasts pulling her top down in classroom in front of Leslie Nielsen.

## Rest in Pieces (1987)

Lorin Jean Vail . . . . . . . . . . . . . . . . . . . . Helen Hewitt
- •• 0:15—Breasts in the bubble bath.
- • 0:17—Breasts hanging onto outside of tub after struggle.
- • 0:25—Brief breasts making love in bed with Bob during concert. Dark.
- • 0:26—Brief breasts lying under Bob in bed. Dark.
- • 0:30—Brief left breast, getting out of bed and putting on robe.

- 0:58—Brief right breast, reaching around to put her right arm into sleeve of robe. Dark.
- • 1:00—Breasts, getting robe taking off and pushed into swimming pool. More breasts under the water.
- 1:01—More breasts in the swimming pool.
- 1:05—Brief side view of left breast getting out of bed and putting on robe.

### Return (1985)
Karlene Crockett . . . . . . . . . . . . . . . . . . . . . . . . Diana
- 0:46—Breasts sitting up and getting out of bed. Long shot.

Lisa Richards . . . . . . . . . . . . . . . . . . . . . . Ann Stoving
Lenore Zann . . . . . . . . . . . . . . . . . . . . . . . . . . Susan

### The Return of Martin Guerre (1983; French)
Nathalie Baye . . . . . . . . . . . . . . . . . Bertrande de Rols
- 0:59—Brief side view of left breast, making love in bed on top of Martin. Don't see her face.

Gérard Depardieu . . . . . . . . . . . . . . . . . Martin Guerre

### The Return of the Living Dead (1985)
Don Calfa . . . . . . . . . . . . . . . . . . . . . . . . . . . . Ernie
Linnea Quigley . . . . . . . . . . . . . . . . . . . . . . . . . Trash
- ••• 0:19—Breasts and buns, strip tease and dancing in cemetery. (Lower frontal nudity is covered with some kind of make-up appliance).
- •• 0:25—Breasts and buns, while in cemetery with her boyfriend.
- 0:37—Breasts and buns, while running around in cemetery when it starts to rain.
- 0:38—Breasts, while running to the car in the rain (very long shot). Brief breasts while in back seat of car.
- 0:42—Breasts, while in back seat of car.
- 0:44—Breasts, while in back seat of car, trying to hold the convertible top closed.
- 0:46—Brief buns, while running up stairs.
- 0:49—Buns, while running into the cemetery. 1:04—Brief right breast, while in cemetery after seeing a zombie.
- 1:05—Brief breasts, while walking from the cemetery on the street to catch a streetperson.
- 1:21—Brief breasts, while running to munch on a policeman in blockade.
- 1:25—Brief breasts in still photo.
- 1:27—Breasts, during end credits in cemetery with her boyfriend.

Jewel Shepard . . . . . . . . . . . . . . . . . . . . . . . . . Casey

### Return of the Living Dead 3 (1993)
Melinda Clarke . . . . . . . . . . . . . . . . . . . . . Julie Walker
- •• 0:16—Breasts, while in bed talking with her boyfriend, Curt.
- 0:17—More breasts, while getting out of bed when Curt's dad comes home.
- 1:07—Breasts under skimpy outfit after doing some severe body piercing.
- •• 1:25—Brief breasts when getting rescued by Curt.

Pia Reyes . . . . . . . . . . . . . . . . . . . . . . . . . . . . Alicia

### Return to Frogtown (1992)
*a.k.a. Frogtown II*
Denice Duff . . . . . . . . . . . . . . . . . . . . . . . . Dr. Spangle
Rhonda Shear . . . . . . . . . . . . . . . . . . . . . . . . . . Fuzzy
Linda Singer . . . . . . . . . . . . . . . . . . . . . . . Nurse Cloris
0:48—Buns, in sexy outfit in room with Robert D'Zar.
- 0:50—Brief top of breasts, sticking out of her top while she's on top of D'Zar.

### Return to Horror High (1987)
Darcy De Moss . . . . . . . . . . . . . . . . . . . . . . Sheri Haines
- 0:21—Very brief left breast when her sweater gets lifted up while she's on some guy's back.

Panchito Gomez . . . . . . . . . . . . . . . . . . . . . Choo Choo
Brendan Hughes . . . . . . . . . . . . . . . . . . . Steven Blake
Maureen McCormick . . . . . . . . . . . . . . . . Officer Tyler
Remy O'Neill . . . . . . . . . . . . . . . . . . . . Esther Molvania
Kristi Somers . . . . . . . . . . . . . . . . . . . . . Ginny McCall

### A Return to Salem's Lot (1988)
Katja Crosby . . . . . . . . . . . . . . . . . . . . . . . . . . Cathy
- •• 0:36—Breasts making love in bed with Joey.
- 0:48—Side view of right breast kissing Joey outside next to a stream.

Michael Moriarty . . . . . . . . . . . . . . . . . . . . . . . . Joey

### Return to the Blue Lagoon (1991)
Milla Jovovich . . . . . . . . . . . . . . . . . . . . . . . . . . Lilli
- 0:49—Brief upper half breasts in front of mirror.
- 1:07—Very brief breasts under water with Richard. Brief breasts under waterfall with Richard. 1:09—Brief partial left breast on hilltop with Richard. Necklace gets in the way.
- 1:20—Briefly in wet beige blouse, standing up.
- 1:26—Side view of right breast three times, washing make up off her face in the pond.
- •• 1:28—Side view of right breast again. Very brief left breast, while picking up her top off rock. 1:30—Side of left breast, lying on bed while held down.

Brian Krause . . . . . . . . . . . . . . . . . . . . . . . Richard
Lisa Pelikan . . . . . . . . . . . . . . . . . . . . . . . . . . Sarah

### Return to Two Moon Junction (1993)
Melinda Clarke . . . . . . . . . . . . . . Savannah Delongpre
- •• 0:37—Lying in bed in wet white lingerie, then left breast (close-up shot) while fantasizing about Jake.
- 0:44—Upper half of buns, while in bed with Jake.
- •• 0:45—Buns and back half of right breast, while standing up and putting on dress.
- ••• 0:59—Breasts and very brief lower frontal nudity while making love with Jake.
- •• 1:01—Buns, while getting out of bed and putting a shirt on.
- 1:09—Breasts, with Jake in bed.

Yorgo Constantine . . . . . . . . . . . . . . . . . . . Robert Lee
- 0:21—Upper half of buns, while sitting on chair and talking on telephone, then standing up.

John Clayton Schafer . . . . . . . . . . . . . . . . . Jake Gilbert
- ••• 0:59—Buns, while making love with Savannah.

### Reuben, Reuben *(1983)*

E. Katherine Kerr . . . . . . . . . . . . . . . . . . . . Lucille Haxby
- 0:51—Brief left breast in bedroom, undressing in front of Tom Conti.

Kelly McGillis. . . . . . . . . . . . . . . . . . . . .Geneva Spofford

### Reunion *(1989; French/German)*

Maureen Kerwin . . . . . . . . . . . . Lisa, Henry's Daughter
Amelie Pick . . . . . . . . . . . . . . . . . . . . . . . .Young Lover
- 0:47—Brief breasts, twice, while making out in the woods with her boyfriend while two boys watch.

### Revenge *(1990)*

Kevin Costner . . . . . . . . . . . . . . . . . . . . . . . . Cochran
- •• 1:14—Brief buns while getting out of bed and wrapping a sheet around himself.

Miguel Ferrer . . . . . . . . . . . . . . . . . . . . . . . Amador
Sally Kirkland. . . . . . . . . . . . . . . . . . . . . . . Rock Star
John Leguizamo . . . . . . . . . . . . . . . . . . . . .Ignacio
Tomas Milian . . . . . . . . . . . . . . . . . . . . . . . Cesar
Madeleine Stowe . . . . . . . . . . . . . . . . . . . . Miryea
   0:44—Side view of buns when Kevin Costner pulls up her dress to make love with her.
   0:52—In white slip talking to Costner in bedroom.
   - 1:00—Buns, making love with Costner in jeep. Very brief breasts coming out of the water.
   - 1:07—Very brief breasts when Costner is getting beat up.

### Revenge of the Cheerleaders *(1976)*

David Hasselhoff . . . . . . . . . . . . . . . . . . . . . . . . Boner
- 0:28—Buns in shower room scene.
- ••• 0:30—Frontal nudity in shower room scene while soaping Gail.

Helen Lang . . . . . . . . . . . . . . . . . . . . . . . . . . Leslie
- 0:00—Left breast, changing in back seat of car.
- •• 0:07—Breasts in girl's restroom powdering herself.
- ••• 0:53—Nude with Gail and hiker guy frolicking in the woods.
- •• 0:55—Nude some more making out with the hiker guy with Gail.
- ••• 0:57—Nude walking down road with Gail when stopped by a policeman.
- ••• 1:24—Breasts during Hawaiian party. Nice dancing during the end credits.

David Robinson. . . . . . . . . . . . . . . . . . . . . . . . Jordan
- 0:13—Buns when Tish plays with him while she's under the counter.

Patrice Rohmer . . . . . . . . . . . . . . . . . . . . . . .Sesame
- 0:28—Brief breasts and buns in the boys shower room.

Cheryl Smith. . . . . . . . . . . . . . . . . . . . . . . . Heather
- 0:00—Brief breasts changing tops in back of car. (Blonde on the far right.)
   0:28—Buns, in shower room scene.
   0:36—Full frontal nudity, but covered with bubbles.

Jerii Woods . . . . . . . . . . . . . . . . . . . . . . . . . . . .Gail
- 0:00—Breasts, while changing clothes in front left seat of car.

0:05—Lower frontal nudity taking off cheerleader skirt in girl's restroom and putting on panties.
- 0:26—Brief right breast, while sitting in bleachers with the other cheerleaders.
- ••• 0:28—Nude in boy's shower room scene.
- •• 0:37—Breasts, while sitting up in sleeping bag.
- 0:44—Brief breasts in front seat of car with David Hasselhoff.
- ••• 0:53—Nude with Leslie and hiker guy while frolicking in the woods.
- •• 0:55—Nude some more making out with the hiker guy with Leslie.
- ••• 0:57—Nude, walking down road with Leslie when stopped by a policeman.
- ••• 1:23—Breasts during Hawaiian party.

### Revenge of the Nerds *(1984)*

Robert Carradine . . . . . . . . . . . . . . . . . . . Lewis Skolnick
Bernie Casey . . . . . . . . . . . . . . . . . . . . . . U. N. Jefferson
James Cromwell . . . . . . . . . . . . . . . . . . . . . .Mr. Skolnick
Anthony Edwards. . . . . . . . . . . . . . . . . . . . . . . .Gilbert
Donald Gibb . . . . . . . . . . . . . . . . . . . . . . . . . . Ogre
- 0:46—Brief buns, while mooning the nerds from back of flatbed truck. (He's the guy on the left.)

Ted McGinley. . . . . . . . . . . . . . . . . . . . . . .Stan Gable
- 0:46—Brief buns, while mooning the nerds from back of flatbed truck. (He's the guy in the middle.)

Julie Montgomery . . . . . . . . . . . . . . . . . . . . . . Betty
- •• 0:49—Breasts, after taking off robe to take a shower.
- 1:10—Breasts in photo in pie pan.

Matt Salinger . . . . . . . . . . . . . . . . . . . . . . . .Burke
- 0:46—Brief buns, while mooning the nerds from back of flatbed truck. (He's the guy on the right.)

Lisa Welch . . . . . . . . . . . . . . . . . . . . . . . . Suzy

### Revenge of the Ninja *(1983)*

Ashley Ferrare. . . . . . . . . . . . . . . . . . . . . . . . . Cathy
   0:33—In white lingerie sitting on couch with Dave.
   - 0:48—Brief breasts getting attacked by the Sumo Servant in the bedroom.
   1:13—In wet white tank top talking on the phone.

### Rich and Famous *(1981)*

Candice Bergen . . . . . . . . . . . . . . . . . Merry Noel Blake
Jacqueline Bisset. . . . . . . . . . . . . . . . . . . . Liz Hamilton
Matt Lattanzi . . . . . . . . . . . . . . . . . . . . . . The Boy, Jim
- ••• 1:10—Buns, while making love with Jacqueline Bisset.

Meg Ryan . . . . . . . . . . . . . . . . . . . .Debbie at 18 years
David Selby . . . . . . . . . . . . . . . . . . . . . . . . Doug Blake

### Rich Girl *(1991)*

Daphne Cheung . . . . . . . . . . . . . . . Oriental Temptress
- 1:14—Breasts, taking off her jacket in back room trying to get Rick to do drugs.

Cherie Currie . . . . . . . . . . . . . . . . . . . . . . . . .Michelle
Maureen Flaherty . . . . . . . . . . . . . . Girl in Restroom #1
Jill Schoelen . . . . . . . . . . . . . . . . . . . . . . . . .Courtney
Melanie Tomlin . . . . . . . . . . . . . . . . . . . . . . . .Diana
- 0:03—Half of left breast, while in bed with Jeffrey.

- 0:04—Almost side of left breast again, while looking for her keys.

### Richard's Things (1980; British)
Amanda Redman . . . . . . . . . . . . . . . . . . . . . . . . . Josie
- •• 0:51—Breasts, while lying in bed talking to Liv Ullman.
Liv Ullmann. . . . . . . . . . . . . . . . . . . . . . . . . . . . Kate
- 0:12—Very, very brief left breast, while wrapping a towel around herself.

### Ricochet (1991)
Victoria Dillard . . . . . . . . . . . . . . . . . . . . . . . . Alice
Linda Doná . . . . . . . . . . . . . . . . . . . . . . . . . . . Wanda
- •• 1:03—Breasts, undoing her dress, then buns, getting on bed to make love with Denzel Washington while he's drugged.
- 1:16—Buns, on top of Washington during video playback.
Susan Lentini. . . . . . . . . . . . . . . . . . . . . . . . . Reporter
John Lithgow . . . . . . . . . . . . . . . . . . . . Earl Talbot Blake
Heidi Thomas . . . . . . . . . . . . . . . . . . . . . . . . Reporter
Denzel Washington. . . . . . . . . . . . . . . . . . Nick Styles
- 0:13—Almost very brief frontal nudity in locker room when Lindsay Wagner comes to talk. (It looks like he's wearing something over his penis.)

### Rikky & Pete (1988; Australian)
Tetchie Agbayani . . . . . . . . . . . . . . . . . . . . . . . .Flossie
- 0:58—Brief upper half of left breast in bed with Pete when Rikky accidentally sees them in bed.
- ••• 1:30—Breasts in black panties dancing outside the jail while Pete watches from inside.
Bruno Lawrence . . . . . . . . . . . . . . . . . . . . . . . .Sonny

### Ring of Fire (1991)
Maria Ford . . . . . . . . . . . . . . . . . . . . . . . . . . . . . Julie
- •• 1:12—In black lingerie, then breasts, making love with Don Wilson.
- 1:14—Brief left breast, lying in bed, while he undresses her.
- ••• 1:15—Breasts, several, lying on her back in bed while making love.
- 1:17—Brief breasts, sitting up in bed afterward.
Vince Murdocco . . . . . . . . . . . . . . . . . . . . . . . . .Chuck
Lisa Saxton . . . . . . . . . . . . . . . . . . . . . . . . . . . Linda
- •• 0:10—Breasts and buns in several times, making love with Brad. Intercut with martial arts fight.
- 0:18—Brief buns, in G-string swimsuit, getting into spa with Brad. Breasts in spa.
- ••• 0:22—Breasts and buns in bathroom, while talking to Maria Ford.

### Rising Sun (1993)
Kevin Anderson. . . . . . . . . . . . . . . . . . . . Bob Richmond
Steve Buscemi. . . . . . . . . . . Willy "The Weasel" Wilhelm
Tia Carrere . . . . . . . . . . . . . . . . . . . . . . . . Jingo Asakuma
Sean Connery . . . . . . . . . . . . . . . . . . . . . . .John Connor
Tony Ganios . . . . . . . . . . . . . . . . . . . . . Doorman Guard
Tylyn John. . . . . . . . . . . . . . . . . . . . . . . . . . .Redhead

- ••• 0:56—Breasts, while sitting next to Eddie and when he licks sake off her left breast.
- •• 0:58—Breasts and buns, while jumping onto and riding on Wesley Snipes' back.
Harvey Keitel . . . . . . . . . . . . . . . . . . . . . . .Tom Graham
Shelley Michelle . . . . . . . . . . . . . . . . . . . . . . . . .Blonde
- 0:44—Very, very brief buns in black G-string, when her dress flies up while spinning around during party.
- •• 0:56—Breasts, while lying down on her back with sushi on her front. More breasts when police bust in.
Tatjana Patitz . . . . . . . . . . . . . . . . . . Cheryl Lynn Austin
- 0:06—Upper half of buns and side of right breast, while sitting in front of vanity in her apartment.
- •• 0:10—Very brief lower frontal nudity and breasts, getting her dress ripped open while on board room table.
- 0:52—Very brief right breast, on video monitor during playback of murder surveillance video.
- 1:44—Brief half of right breast in open dress during Wesley Snipes' daydream after being shot. Out of focus.

### Risky Business (1983)
Cynthia Baker. . . . . . . . . . . . . . . . . . . . . . . Test Teacher
Candace Collins . . . . . . . . . . . . . . . . . . . . . . . . Call Girl
Tom Cruise . . . . . . . . . . . . . . . . . . . . . . . . . . . . . Joel
Rebecca De Mornay . . . . . . . . . . . . . . . . . . . . . . . Lana
- 0:28—Brief nude standing by the window with Tom Cruise.
Lora Staley . . . . . . . . . . . . . . . . . . . . . . . . . . . Call Girl

### River of Death (1990)
Sarah Maur-Thorp . . . . . . . . . . . . . . . . .Anna Blakesley
- 0:14—Very brief left breast while in tent with Michael Dudikoff.

### A River Runs Through It (1992)
Emily Lloyd . . . . . . . . . . . . . . . . . . . . . . . Jessie Burns
Craig Sheffer . . . . . . . . . . . . . . . . . . . .Norman Maclean
Steve Shellen . . . . . . . . . . . . . . . . . . . . . . . .Neal Burns
- 1:17—Buns, sleeping in the woods with Rawhide. Don't see his face.
- •• 1:19—Buns, while walking to his house with help from his friends after getting badly sunburned.
Tom Skerritt. . . . . . . . . . . . . . . . . . . . .Reverend Maclean
Susan Traylor . . . . . . . . . . . . . . . . . . . . . . . . . Rawhide
- 1:17—Buns, sleeping in the woods with Neal. Don't see her face.

### River's Edge (1987)
Danyi Deats . . . . . . . . . . . . . . . . . . . . . . . . . . . . .Jamie
- 0:03—Breasts, dead lying next to river with her killer. (All the shots of her breasts in this film aren't exciting unless you like looking at dead bodies).
- 0:15—Close up breasts, then full frontal nudity when Crispin Glover pokes her with a stick.
  0:16—Full frontal nudity when the three boys leave.
  0:22—Full frontal nudity when all the kids come to see her body. (She's starting to look very discolored).
  0:24—Right breast when everybody leaves.

0:30—Right breast when they come to dump her body in the river.
Dennis Hopper . . . . . . . . . . . . . . . . . . . . . . . . . . Feck
Keanu Reeves . . . . . . . . . . . . . . . . . . . . . . . . . . Matt
Leo Rossi. . . . . . . . . . . . . . . . . . . . . . . . . . . . . . . Jim
Ione Skye . . . . . . . . . . . . . . . . . . . . . . . . . . Clarissa

### Road to Ruin (1992)
Eleonore Klarwein . . . . . . . . . . . . . . . . . . . . Girl Friend
•• 0:03—Breasts and buns, getting out of bed and walking into bathroom.
Carey Lowell . . . . . . . . . . . . . . . . . . . . . . Jessie Taylor
• 0:25—Lower half of buns, while sitting in bed with Peter Weller.
0:26—Very, very brief buns, when Weller pulls her onto the bed.
Peter Weller. . . . . . . . . . . . . . . . . . . . . . . . . Jack Sloan

### Road to Salina (1969; French/Italian)
Mimsy Farmer. . . . . . . . . . . . . . . . . . . . . . . . . . . Billie
••• 0:23—Breasts and buns, undressing and running to beach with Jonas. Nude, while swimming under water.
•• 0:24—Buns and breasts, while lying on the beach with Jonas.
• 0:40—Buns and brief right breast while taking a shower. Seen through lattice work.
•• 0:41—Nude in bed with Jonas.
• 0:42—Breasts, while making love with Jonas in tent.
• 0:44—Breasts and buns, while running out of the tent into the water. Nude in the water.
0:56—Brief right breast in bed with Jonas.
• 1:28—Buns and brief breasts after taking a shower outside and wrapping a towel around herself.
• 1:29—Brief nude, while rolling over in bed.
Robert Walker, Jr. . . . . . . . . . . . . . . . . . . . . . . . Jonas
••• 0:23—Nude, running on beach and swimming under water with Billie.
•• 0:24—Buns, while lying on beach with Billie.
• 0:44—Brief frontal nudity while in tent on beach. Brief frontal nudity while standing up in the water.

### Roadhouse (1989)
Jasaé. . . . . . . . . . . . . . . . . . . . . . . . . . . Strip Joint Girl
Laura Albert . . . . . . . . . . . . . . . . . . . . . . Strip Joint Girl
•• 0:45—Breasts and buns dancing on stage, wearing a hat.
Lisa Axelrod. . . . . . . . . . . . . . . . . . . . . . . . . Party Girl
Cheryl Baker . . . . . . . . . . . . . . . . Well-Endowed Wife
Sylvia Baker. . . . . . . . . . . . . . . . . . . . . . Table Dancer
Michele Burger . . . . . . . . . . . . . . . . . . Strip Joint Girl
Terri Lynn Doss . . . . . . . . . . . . . . . . . . Cody's Girlfriend
Sam Elliott. . . . . . . . . . . . . . . . . . . . . . . Wade Garrett
Kymberly Herrin . . . . . . . . . . . . . . . . . . . . Party Girl
Gary Hudson. . . . . . . . . . . . . . . . . . . . . . . . . . Steve
Pamela Jackson . . . . . . . . . . . . . . . . . Strip Joint Girl
Susan Lentini. . . . . . . . . . . . . . . . . Bandstand Babe
Kelly Lynch . . . . . . . . . . . . . . . . . . . . . . . . . . . . Doc
•• 1:04—Breasts and buns getting out of bed with a sheet wrapped around her.
Kym Malin . . . . . . . . . . . . . . . . . . . . . . . . Party Girl

Julie Michaels . . . . . . . . . . . . . . . . . . . . . . . . . Denise
••• 1:18—Breasts dancing on stage in club in front of Patrick Swayze.
Monique Noel . . . . . . . . . . . . . . Uncredited Barfly
Heidi Paine. . . . . . . . . . . . . . . . . . . . . . . . . Party Girl
Jacqueline Palmer. . . . . . . . . . . . . . . . . . . Party Girl
Patrick Swayze . . . . . . . . . . . . . . . . . . . . . . . Dalton
••• 0:30—Brief buns getting out of bed while Kathleen Wilhoite watches.
Patricia Tallman . . . . . . . . . . . . . . . . . Bandstand Babe
Christina Veronica . . . . . . . . . . . . . . Strip Joint Girl

### Roadhouse 66 (1984)
Willem Dafoe . . . . . . . . . . . . . . . . . . . . Johnny Harte
•• 1:02—Buns, standing up while kissing Jesse.
Kaaren Lee. . . . . . . . . . . . . . . . . . . . . . . Jesse Duran
•• 1:00—Breasts, taking off her top to go skinny dipping with Willem Dafoe. Dark.
Judge Reinhold. . . . . . . . . . . . . Beckman Hallsgood, Jr.
Kate Vernon . . . . . . . . . . . . . . . . . . . . Melissa Duran
• 1:03—Brief breasts in back of car with Judge Reinhold. Dark.

### Robin Hood: Prince of Thieves (1991)
Sean Connery . . . . . . . . . . . . . . . . . . . . King Richard
Kevin Costner. . . . . . . . . . . . . . . Robin of Locksley
1:14—Body double's buns, while bathing under waterfall when Marian sees him. Hard to see because of the falling water. Body double was used because the water was so cold.
Mary Elizabeth Mastrantonio . . . . . . . . . . . . . . Marian
Christian Slater. . . . . . . . . . . . . . . . . . . Will Scarlett

### Robot Jox (1990)
Gary Graham . . . . . . . . . . . . . . . . . . . . . . . Achilles
• 0:32—Very brief buns, getting dressed in his room while talking to Athena.
Anne-Marie Johnson. . . . . . . . . . . . . . . . . . . Athena
•• 0:35—Buns, walking to the showers after talking to Achilles and Tex.

### The Rocky Horror Picture Show (1975; British)
Nell Campbell . . . . . . . . . . . . . . . . . . . . . . Columbia
• 1:17—Top of breasts popping out of her blouse during song and dance on stage.
Patricia Quinn . . . . . . . . . . . . . . . . . . . . . Magenta
Susan Sarandon . . . . . . . . . . . . . . . . . Janet Weiss
Koo Stark . . . . . . . . . . . . . . . . . . . . . . Bridesmaid

### Rocky V (1990)
Delia Sheppard . . . . . . . . . . . . . . . . . . . . . . Karen
Sylvester Stallone . . . . . . . . . . . . . . . . . Rocky Balboa
• 0:03—Side view of buns, while standing in the shower. Long shot.

### Roller Blade (1986)
Michelle Bauer . . . . . . . . . . . . . . . . . . . . . Bod Sister
• 0:11—Breasts, being held by Satacoy's Devils.
••• 0:13—More breasts and buns in G-string during fight. Long scene.
• 0:16—Brief breasts twice, getting saved by the Sisters.

•• 0:33—Breasts during ceremony with the other two Bod Sisters. Buns also.

••• 0:35—Full frontal nudity after dip in hot tub. (Second to leave the tub.)

•• 0:40—Nude, on skates with the other two Bod Sisters. (She's on the left.)

Sam Mann . . . . . . . . . . . . . . . . . . . . . . . . . Waco

Barbara Peckinpaugh. . . . . . . . . . . . . . . . . . Bod Sister

•• 0:33—Breasts during ceremony. Cut on her throat is unappealing.

••• 0:35—Full frontal nudity after dip in hot tub with the other two Bod Sisters. (She's the first to leave.)

•• 0:40—Nude, on skates with the other two Bod Sisters. (She's in the middle.)

Suzanne Solari. . . . . . . . . . . . . . . . . Sister Sharon Cross

0:04—Buns, in G-string, lying in bed.

• 1:21—Brief upper half of right breast, taking off suit. Buns in G-string.

### RollerBlade Warriors: Taken By Force (1988)

Susan Jones. . . . . . . . . . . . . . . . . . . . . . . Slave Girl #2

•• 0:20—Breasts, while getting hassled by two guys.

••• 0:23—Breasts, while walking through the desert.

Elizabeth Kaitan. . . . . . . . . . . . . . . . . . . Gretchen Hope

• 0:51—Breasts, while tied to large spool and getting raped by Marachek.

• 1:03—Very brief breasts, several times, while getting raped in B&W vision.

Kathleen Kinmont . . . . . . . . . . . . . . . . . . . Karin Crosse

Sam Mann . . . . . . . . . . . . . . . . . . . . . . . . . Marachek

•• 0:52—Buns, after pulling down his pants to rape Elizabeth Kaitan. Don't see his face.

Suzanne Solari. . . . . . . . . . . . . . . . . . . . . Sharon Crosse

Lisa Toothman . . . . . . . . . . . . . . . . . . . . . Slave Girl #1

•• 0:21—Breasts after getting her top ripped off by two guys.

••• 0:23—Breasts, while walking through the desert.

### Rolling Thunder (1977)

Dabney Coleman . . . . . . . . . . . . . . . . . . . . . Maxwell

Linda Haynes. . . . . . . . . . . . . . . . . . . . . Linda Forchet

Tommy Lee Jones . . . . . . . . . . . . . . . . . Johnny Vohden

Lisa Richards . . . . . . . . . . . . . . . . . . . . . . . . . . Janet

Cassie Yates. . . . . . . . . . . . . . . . . . . . . . . . . . Candy

••• 1:31—Breasts while undressing in bedroom with Tommy Lee Jones.

• 1:32—Right breast, while sitting on bed with Jones.

• 1:33—Right breast, when Jones sits up in bed.

### Romance with a Double Bass (1974; British)

Connie Booth . . . . . . . . . . . . . . . . . . Princess Costanza

•• 0:10—Very brief buns, going into the water to retrieve her fishing float, then full frontal nudity while yelling at a guy who steals her clothes.

•• 0:11—Full frontal nudity, while walking around, looking for her clothes.

••• 0:18—Breasts, while holding her hand over her eyes.

•• 0:20—Brief left breast, while reaching up to close the bass case.

John Cleese . . . . . . . . . . . . . . . . . . Musician Smychkov

••• 0:14—Brief buns while walking around with his bass and then the case.

•• 0:16—Buns, while standing at the edge of the pond.

•• 0:17—Buns, while running to jump in the water.

••• 0:18—Buns, while walking around.

••• 0:19—Buns, while walking around with his hands over his eyes.

• 0:21—Brief long shot of buns, while walking around.

•• 0:22—More buns, while walking around outside.

•• 0:24—Buns, while carrying bass into the house.

### The Romantic Englishwoman (1975; British/French)

Helmut Berger . . . . . . . . . . . . . . . . . . . . . . . Thomas

• 1:08—Upper half of buns, while sitting at edge of pool talking to Glenda Jackson.

Nathalie Delon. . . . . . . . . . . . . . . . . . . . . . . Miranda

Glenda Jackson. . . . . . . . . . . . . . . . . . . . . . Elizabeth

• 0:30—Brief full frontal nudity outside, taking robe off in front of Michael Caine.

• 0:31—Buns, walking back into the house.

• 1:08—Side view of right breast sitting at edge of pool talking to Thomas.

• 1:45—Very, very brief breasts while in bed talking with Thomas.

Kate Nelligan . . . . . . . . . . . . . . . . . . . . . . . . . Isabel

### Romeo and Juliet (1968; British/Italian)

Olivia Hussey . . . . . . . . . . . . . . . . . . . . . . . . . Juliet

• 1:37—Very brief breasts rolling over and getting out of bed with Romeo.

Richard Warwick . . . . . . . . . . . . . . . . . . . . . Gregory

Leonard Whiting . . . . . . . . . . . . . . . . . . . . . . . Romeo

•• 1:34—Buns, while in bed with Juliet, then getting out to stretch. Long scene.

Michael York . . . . . . . . . . . . . . . . . . . . . . . . . Tybalt

### Romeo Is Bleeding (1994)

Juliette Lewis . . . . . . . . . . . . . . . . . . . . . . . . . Sheri

Gary Oldman . . . . . . . . . . . . . . . . . . Sgt. Jack Grimaldi

•• 0:27—Buns, while mooning Annabella Sciorra for a Polaroid photograph.

Lena Olin . . . . . . . . . . . . . . . . . . . . . . Mona Demakov

•• 1:20—Breasts under leather outfit with fake arm.

•• 1:22—More breasts in the leather outfit.

• 1:29—Buns in sexy black bodysuit.

Roy Scheider . . . . . . . . . . . . . . . . . . . . . Don Falcone

Annabella Sciorra . . . . . . . . . . . . . . . . . . . . . . Natalie

### Romper Stomper (1993; Australian)

Russell Crowe. . . . . . . . . . . . . . . . . . . . . . . . . Hando

Daniel Pollock . . . . . . . . . . . . . . . . . . . . . . . . Davey

•• 1:11—Buns, while making love with Gabe in bed.

Leigh Russell. . . . . . . . . . . . . . . . . . . . . . Sonny Jim

• 0:40—Brief buns, while mooning the Asian guys chasing him and his buddies.

### A Room with a View (1986; British)
Helena Bonham Carter . . . . . . . . . . . Lucy Honeychurch
Simon Callow . . . . . . . . . . . . . . The Reverend Mr. Beebe
- • 1:04—Frontal nudity taking off clothes and jumping into pond.
- ••• 1:05—Nude running around with Freddy and George in the woods. Lots of frontal nudity.
Daniel Day-Lewis. . . . . . . . . . . . . . . . . . . . . Cecil Vyse
Rupert Graves . . . . . . . . . . . . . . . Freddy Honeychurch
- ••• 1:05—Nude running around with Mr. Beebe and George in the woods. Lots of frontal nudity.
Julian Sands. . . . . . . . . . . . . . . . . . . . George Emerson
- ••• 1:05—Nude running around with Freddy and Mr. Beebe in the woods. Lots of frontal nudity.
Maggie Smith . . . . . . . . . . . . . . . . . . Charlotte Bartlett

### Roots of Evil (1991)
(Unrated version reviewed.)
Jasaé . . . . . . . . . . . . . . . . . . . . . . . . Subway Hooker
- ••• 1:05—Breasts taking off her top in subway stairwell, then getting killed by the bad guy.
Yvette Buchanan . . . . . . . . . . . . . . . . . . . . . . . Hooker
Daphne Cheung . . . . . . . . . . . . . . . . . . . . . . . . Tina
- ••• 0:09—Breasts in alley with a customer.
Jillian Kesner . . . . . . . . . . . . . . . . . . . . . . . . Brenda
- ••• 0:27—Breasts, giving Alex Cord a back massage in bed.
- • 0:30—Brief breasts, getting up out of bed.
Deanna Lund . . . . . . . . . . . . . . . . . . . . . . . . Marissa
- • 0:19—Most of left breast, then brief right breast, while making love in bed with Johnny.
- • 0:20—More right breast, while making love.
- •• 0:21—Still more right breast.
- ••• 1:33—Right breast, then breasts while lying in bed with Brinke Stevens.
Jewel Shepard . . . . . . . . . . . . . . . . . . . . . . . . Wanda
- • 1:31—Brief right breast, a couple of times, when it pops out of her blouse while she's in police station.
Delia Sheppard . . . . . . . . . . . . . . . . . . . . . . Monica
- ••• 0:04—Breasts and buns in G-string, dancing on stage.
- • 0:07—Breasts and buns, while on stage when wounded guy disturbs her act.
- ••• 0:38—Buns in outfit, then breasts dancing on stage.
- ••• 0:41—More buns and breasts in bed, making love with Johnny. Long scene.
Donna Spangler . . . . . . . . . . . . . . . . . . . . . . Scarlett
- •• 0:04—Breasts, getting attacked by the crazy guy, then killed.
- • 0:07—Brief breasts, dead, covered with blood when Alex Cord discovers her.
Brinke Stevens. . . . . . . . . . . . . . . . . . . . . . . .Candy
- •• 1:33—Right breast, then breasts while sitting on bed talking to Deanna Lund.

### The Rosebud Beach Hotel (1985)
Julie Always. . . . . . . . . . . . . . . . . . . . . . . . .Bellhop
- •• 0:22—Breasts, in open blouse, undressing with two other bellhops. She's the blonde on the left.

- •• 0:44—Breasts, playing spin the grenade, with two guys and the two other bellhops. She's on the left.
Colleen Camp . . . . . . . . . . . . . . . . . . . . . . . . . Tracy
- 0:07—In white lingerie in hotel room with Peter Scolari.
- 0:28—In black one piece swimsuit on lounge chair, then walking on the beach.
Cherie Currie . . . . . . . . . . . . . . . . . . . . . . . . Cherie
- 1:13—Singing with her twin sister in braless pink T-shirt on the beach.
Fran Drescher. . . . . . . . . . . . . . . . . . . . . . . . .Linda
Monique Gabrielle . . . . . . . . . . . . . . . . . . . . . . Lisa
- •• 0:22—Breasts and buns undressing in hotel room with two other girls. She's on the right.
- •• 0:44—Breasts taking off her red top in basement with two other girls and two guys.
- • 0:56—In black see-through nightie in hotel room with Peter Scolari.
Dirga McBroom . . . . . . . . . . . . . . . . . . . . . . . Bellhop
- • 0:49—Buns, then breasts, standing with the other bell hops, outfitted with military attire. (She's the one at the far end, furthest from the camera.)
Tina Merkle . . . . . . . . . . . . . . . . . . . . . . . . . . . Bellhop
- • 0:49—Breasts, standing in line. Closest to the camera.
Julia Parton. . . . . . . . . . . . . . . . . . . . . . . . . . Bellhop
- •• 0:49—Buns, then breasts, standing in line. Second from the camera.

### Rosemary's Baby (1968)
Mia Farrow. . . . . . . . . . . . . . . . . . Rosemary Woodhouse
- • 0:10—Brief left breast in room in new apartment on floor with John Cassavetes. Hard to see anything.
- • 0:43—Brief close up of her breasts while she's sitting on a boat during a nightmare.
- •• 0:44—Buns walking on boat, then breasts during impregnation scene with the devil.
Victoria Vetri . . . . . . . . . . . . . . . . . . . . Terry Fionoffrio

### Round Numbers (1990)
India Allen . . . . . . . . . . . . . . . . . . . . . . Swimsuit Model
Hope Marie Carlton . . . . . . . . . . . . . . . . . . . . . Mitzi
- • 0:39—Left breast, twice, while turning around in steam room in Kate Mulgrew's imagination.
Samantha Eggar. . . . . . . . . . . . . . . . . . . . . . . . Anne

### Round Trip to Heaven (1992)
Tara Buckman . . . . . . . . . . . . . . . . . . . . . . . Phyllis
Corey Feldman. . . . . . . . . . . . . . . . . . . . . . . . Larry
Zach Galligan. . . . . . . . . . . . . . . . . . . . . . . . . Steve
Lauren Hays. . . . . . . . . . . . . . . . . . . . . . .Contestant
Julie McCullough . . . . . . . . . . . . . . . . . . . . . Lucille
Cyndi Pass . . . . . . . . . . . . . . . . . . . . . . . . . . Cindy
Brittney Powell. . . . . . . . . . . . . . . . . . . . .Contestant
- • 0:36—Brief breasts, while putting on dark gray, one piece swimsuit in dressing room.
Kristine Rose. . . . . . . . . . . . . . . . . . . . . . . . . . Tina
Ray Sharkey . . . . . . . . . . . . . . . . . . . . . . Stoneface

Amy-Rochelle Weiss ........................Yvette
••• 0:19—In black bra and G-string in bedroom with Corey Feldman, then breasts and buns on top of him in bed.

Danise Zakovich ................... Miss Moscow
•• 1:06—Buns and upper half breasts, undressing in bedroom.
••• 1:07—Breasts, opening her towel for Zach Galligan.
• 1:12—Very brief right breast, while in bed with Galligan.

### Runaway (1984)
Kirstie Alley .............................. Jackie
1:04—Briefly in white bra getting scanned at the police station for bugging devices.
Tom Selleck............................Ramsay
Cec Verrell ............................. Hooker
•• 0:44—Breasts in hotel bathroom while Tom Selleck sneaks into her room.

### Running Out of Luck (1986)
Rae Dawn Chong ...................... Slave Girl
•• 0:42—Left breast, while hugging Mick Jagger, then again while lying in bed with him.
•• 1:12—Left breast painting some kind of drug laced solution on herself.
•• 1:14—Right breast, while in prison office offering her breast to the warden.
• 1:21—Buns and left breast, in bed with Jagger during a flashback.
Jerry Hall ............................... Herself
Dennis Hopper .................... Video Director
Mick Jagger............................Himself
• 0:42—Brief buns in mirror in room with Rae Dawn Chong lying in bed. Another buns long shot in bed on top of Chong.

### Running Scared (1986)
Steven Bauer............................ Frank
Darlanne Fluegel ................... Anna Costanzo
Gregory Hines...................... Ray Hughes
Tracy Reed ..........................Maryann
• 0:18—Brief buns.
• 1:30—Very brief breasts in bed with Gregory Hines.
Jimmy Smits ...................... Julio Gonzales

### Rush (1991)
Sam Elliott..........................Larry Dodd
Jennifer Jason Leigh...................Kristen Cates
• 1:09—Brief buns, when Jason Patric takes off her pajama bottoms and forces himself on her.
Jason Patric........................... Jim Raynor
William Sadler........................ Monroe

### Rush Week (1989)
Laura Burkett................... Rebecca Winters
•• 0:43—Breasts in the shower, talking to Jonelle.
• 0:55—Brief breasts getting dressed after modeling session.
David Denney...................... Greg Ochs

Kathleen Kinmont ............. Julie Ann McGuffin
• 0:07—Brief breasts several times during modeling session. Buns in G-string getting dressed. Long shot.

### Ruthless People (1986)
Jeannine Bisignano................. Hooker in Car
0:17—Breasts, hanging out of the car. Long, long shot, don't see anything.
• 0:40—Breasts in the same scene three times on TV while Danny De Vito watches.
• 0:49—Left breast hanging out of the car when the Chief of Police watches on TV. Closest shot.
1:15—Same scene again in department store TV's. Long shot, hard to see.
Laura Cruikshank ....................... n.a.
Anita Morris............................ Carol
Judge Reinhold...................... Ken Kessler
Helen Slater ......................Sandy Kessler

### S.A.S. San Salvador (1982)
Sybil Danning ................. Countess Alexandra
• 0:07—Brief left breast, while lying on the couch and kissing Malko.
Monika Kaelin ......................... n.a.
Miles O'Keeffe ..................... Prince Malko

### S.O.B. (1981)
Julie Andrews ........................ Sally Miles
•• 1:19—Breasts pulling the top off her red dress during the filming of a movie.
Rosanna Arquette........................ Babs
• 0:21—Brief breasts taking off white T-shirt on the deck of the house. Long shot, hard to see.
Marisa Berenson........................Mavis
•• 1:20—Breasts in bed with Robert Vaughn.
Corbin Bernsen ........................ n.a.
Gisele Lindley......................... n.a.
James Purcell .......................... n.a.
Gay Rowan............................ n.a.

### Sacrilege (1986)
Myriem Roussel ......... Sister Virginia Maria di Leva
••• 0:50—Full frontal nudity, while making love with a guy, while two other sisters watch.

### The Sailor Who Fell From Grace with the Sea (1976)
Kris Kristofferson ................... Jim Cameron
Sarah Miles ...................... Anne Osborne
• 0:18—Breasts sitting at the vanity getting dressed while her son watches through peephole.
•• 0:23—Breasts, fantasizing about her husband.
•• 0:42—Breasts, then nude, while making love with Kris Kristofferson.
• 1:15—Brief right breast, while in bed with Kristofferson.

### Salmonberries (1991; German)
k.d. lang.............................Kotzebue
••• 0:13—Brief full frontal nudity while standing in the library.

### *Salomé* (1986; Italian)

Jo Champa . . . . . . . . . . . . . . . . . . . . . . . . . . . . . Salomé
- •• 1:12—Nude under blue dress while dancing around.
- • 1:20—Full frontal nudity under sheer blue dress while in jail cell.
- • 1:27—Full frontal nudity in sheer dress while walking around.

Tomas Milian . . . . . . . . . . . . . . . . . . . . . . . . . . . Herod

Pamela Salem . . . . . . . . . . . . . . . . . . . . . . . . . Herodias
- • 0:05—Brief left breast, when her top gets ripped off.
- • 0:26—Left breast when servant girl helps take her dress off.
- • 0:27—Left breast and lower frontal nudity while standing in front of pool. Medium long shot.

### *Salome's Last Dance* (1987)

Linzi Drew . . . . . . . . . . . . . . . . . . . . . . . . . . . . 1st Slave
- •• 0:08—Breasts in black costume around a cage.
- •• 0:52—Breasts during dance number.

Dougie Howes . . . . . . . . . . . . . . . . . . . . .Phoney Salome
- • 1:05—Very brief frontal nudity at the end of a dance routine when you think he's a female Salome.

Glenda Jackson . . . . . . . . . . . . . . . Herodias/Lady Alice

Tina Shaw . . . . . . . . . . . . . . . . . . . . . . . . . . . . 2nd Slave
- •• 0:08—Breasts in black costume around a cage.
- •• 0:52—Breasts during dance number.

### *Salvador* (1986)

James Belushi . . . . . . . . . . . . . . . . . . . . . . . . Dr. Rock

Elpidia Carrillo . . . . . . . . . . . . . . . . . . . . . . . . . . Maria
- • 0:21—Very brief right breast, lying in a hammock with James Woods.

Cynthia Gibb . . . . . . . . . . . . . . . . . . . . . Cathy Moore

James Woods . . . . . . . . . . . . . . . . . . . . . Richard Boyle

### *Sammy and Rosie Get Laid* (1987; British)

Frances Barber . . . . . . . . . . . . . . . . . . . . . . Rosie Hobbs
- • 1:09—Very brief breasts, while bending over to kiss Danny. More brief breasts while making love (short cuts).
  1:21—Partial right breast while sitting in bubble bath with Sammy.

Claire Bloom . . . . . . . . . . . . . . . . . . . . . . . . . . . Alice

Wendy Gazelle . . . . . . . . . . . . . . . . . . . . . . . . . .Anna
- •• 0:03—Buns, while lying in bed with Sammy.
- • 1:10—Breasts, while lying under Sammy. Seen on the top of a three segment split screen. Don't see her face.

Roland Gift . . . . . . . . . . . . . . . . . . . . . Danny/Victoria
- •• 1:08—Buns, while lying face down on bed with Rosie.
- • 1:10—Brief buns, while lying on top of Rosie. Seen in the middle of a three segment split screen.

### *Santa Sangre* (1989; Italian/Spanish)

Blanca Guerra . . . . . . . . . . . . . . . . . . . . . . . . .Concha
  0:34—Half of buns, in sexy circus outfit.

Axel Jodorowsky . . . . . . . . . . . . . . . . . . . . . . . Fenix
- •• 0:00—Buns, in room in an asylum.

Guy Stockwell . . . . . . . . . . . . . . . . . . . . . . . . . . . Orgo
- •• 0:38—Buns, several times, when Concha catches him with the tattooed lady. (He's a heavy guy.)
- • 0:39—Buns, lying dead on the ground after he cuts his own throat.

### *Satan's Princess* (1989)

Lydie Denier. . . . . . . . . . . . . . . . . . . . .Nicole St. James
- • 0:27—Full frontal nudity, getting out of pool.
- ••• 0:28—Full frontal nudity, next to bed and in bed with Karen.
- ••• 0:45—Breasts and buns, making love in bed with Robert Forster.

Robert Forster . . . . . . . . . . . . . . . . . . . . . Lou Cherney

Leslie Huntly. . . . . . . . . . . . . . . . . . . . Karen Rhodes
- ••• 0:27—Breasts sitting on bed and in bed with Nicole.

Marilyn Joi . . . . . . . . . . . . . . . . . . . . . . . . . . Hooker

Caren Kaye. . . . . . . . . . . . . . . . . . . . . . . . . . . . Leah

Debra Lamb . . . . . . . . . . . . . . . . . . . . . Fire Eater/Dancer
- •• 0:23—Breasts in G-string doing a fire dance in club.
- • 0:25—Breasts, doing more dancing. Long shot.

Rena Riffel . . . . . . . . . . . . . . . . . . . . . . . . . .Erica Dunn
- •• 0:16—Breasts getting white dress torn open, then killed with a knife.

### *Satanic Attraction* (1991; Italian)

Gabriela Toscano . . . . . . . . . . . . . . . . . . . . . Fernanda
- • 0:43—Partial left breast, making love with Lionel. Brief side view of left breast, eating fruit afterwards.

### *Saturday Night Fever* (1977)

(R-rated version reviewed.)

Joseph Cali. . . . . . . . . . . . . . . . . . . . . . . . . . . . .Joey

Paul Pepe. . . . . . . . . . . . . . . . . . . . . . . . . . . Double J.
- • 0:22—Buns, while making love in back seat of car with a girl.

### *Saturday Night Special* (1994)

(Unrated version reviewed.)

Maria Ford . . . . . . . . . . . . . . . . . . . . . . . . . . Darlene
- ••• 0:37—Breasts, while making love with Travis in the woods.
- ••• 0:50—Breasts, while making love with Travis on bed. Buns, when lying down afterwards. Great!

### *Saturn 3* (1980)

Kirk Douglas . . . . . . . . . . . . . . . . . . . . . . . . . Adam
- • 0:57—Brief buns while fighting with Harvey Keitel, more brief buns sitting down in bed with Farrah Fawcett.

Farrah Fawcett . . . . . . . . . . . . . . . . . . . . . . . . .Alex
- •• 0:17—Brief right breast taking off towel and running to Kirk Douglas after taking a shower.

Harvey Keitel . . . . . . . . . . . . . . . . . . . . . . . . . Benson

### *Savage Attraction* (1983; Australian)

Kerry Mack. . . . . . . . . . . . . . . . . . . Christine Maresch
- ••• 0:10—Breasts, getting out of shower and putting on robe.
- • 0:11—Breasts behind shower door, making love with Walter.
- •• 0:17—Breasts sitting at the end of the bed.

•• 0:59—Breasts undressing in bedroom, then in bathtub with Walter.
••• 1:04—Breasts getting her blouse unbuttoned, then breasts in bed with Walter.
1:19—On boat, in semi-sheer white blouse.

## Savage Beach (1989)

Hope Marie Carlton. . . . . . . . . . . . . . . . . . . . . . . Taryn
0:06—Almost breasts in spa with the three other women.
• 0:32—Breasts changing clothes in airplane with Dona Speir.
• 0:48—Nude, going for a swim on the beach with Speir.
Patty Duffek . . . . . . . . . . . . . . . . . . . . . . . Patticakes
• 0:06—Breasts in spa with Lisa London, Dona Speir and Hope Marie Carlton.
•• 0:50—Breasts changing clothes.
Lisa London. . . . . . . . . . . . . . . . . . . . . . . . . . . . Rocky
• 0:06—Breasts in spa with Patty Duffek, Dona Speir and Hope Marie Carlton.
•• 0:50—Breasts changing clothes.
Michael Jay Shane. . . . . . . . . . . . . . . . . .Shane Abeline
•• 0:08—Buns, while getting out of pool.
Dona Speir . . . . . . . . . . . . . . . . . . . . . . . . . . . Dona
0:06—Almost breasts in spa with the three other women.
• 0:32—Breasts changing clothes in airplane with Hope Marie Carlton.
•• 0:48—Nude, going for a swim on the beach with Carlton.
Maxine Wasa. . . . . . . . . . . . . . . . . . . . . . Sexy Beauty
••• 0:08—Side view of left breast, in pool with Shane, then breasts getting out of pool.
••• 0:10—Breasts while Shane talks on the phone.
Teri Weigel . . . . . . . . . . . . . . . . . . . . . . . . . .Anjelica
••• 0:33—Breasts taking off black teddy and getting into bed to make love.
•• 0:47—Breasts making love in the back seat of car.

## Savage Dawn (1984)

Wendy Barry. . . . . . . . . . . . . . . . . . . . . . . Lipservice
• 1:01—Breasts, after taking off top in room in front of Richard Lynch.
•• 1:03—Breasts and buns after getting up with Lynch, then getting dressed.
Karen Black. . . . . . . . . . . . . . . . . . . . . . . . . . Rachel
Elizabeth Kaitan. . . . . . . . . . . . . . . . . . . . . Becky Sue
• 0:17—Right breast, while getting mauled by the bad guys.
Janice Renney . . . . . . . . . . . . . . . . . . . . . . . . Susan
Claudia Udy . . . . . . . . . . . . . . . . . . . . . Katie Rand

## Savage Messiah (1972; British)

Helen Mirren. . . . . . . . . . . . . . . . .Gosh Smith-Boyle
••• 0:39—Full frontal nudity, posing for sketches while walking up and down stairs and around. Nice long scene.
•• 1:15—Brief buns, while covering herself up.

## Savage Streets (1985)

Linda Blair . . . . . . . . . . . . . . . . . . . . . . . . .Brenda
••• 1:05—Breasts sitting in the bathtub thinking.
Debra Blee . . . . . . . . . . . . . . . . . . . . . . . . . . . Rachel
0:20—In a bra in the girls locker room.
Marcia Karr . . . . . . . . . . . . . . . . . . . . . . . . . Stevie
Sal Landi . . . . . . . . . . . . . . . . . . . . . . . . . . .Fargo
• 0:31—Brief buns, while standing up in bathroom after raping Linnea Quigley.
Rebecca Perle. . . . . . . . . . . . . . . . . . . . Cindy Clark
0:24—In bra and panties, fighting with Brenda in the locker room.
•• 0:53—Brief breasts in biology class getting her top torn off by Linda Blair.
Linnea Quigley. . . . . . . . . . . . . . . . . . . . . . .Heather
• 0:28—Breasts getting raped by the jerks.
Suzanne Slater . . . . . . . . . . . . . . . . . . . . . . Uncredited
•• 0:09—Breasts being held by jerks when they yank her tube top down.
Kristi Somers . . . . . . . . . . . . . . . . . . . . . . . .Valerie
0:24—In bra and panties in the locker room.

## Save Me (1993)

(Unrated version reviewed.)
Lysette Anthony. . . . . . . . . . . . . . . . . . . . . . . . Ellie
0:22—Brief buns in body suit, when Harry Hamlin picks her up in back room of lingerie store.
0:31—Upper half of right breast in bra, while making love in convertible Mustang with Hamlin.
••• 0:39—Nude, while sleeping then making love in bed with Hamlin.
•• 0:49—Breasts in spa with Hamlin. Long shot of buns, when getting out. Breasts again while putting on swimsuit.
••• 0:52—In bra, then breasts while making love with Hamlin in front of fireplace.
• 1:05—Breasts, when Hamlin forces himself on her in stairway of parking garage.
Grant Cramer. . . . . . . . . . . . . . . . . . . . Bond Trader #4
Harry Hamlin . . . . . . . . . . . . . . . . . . . . . . . Jim Stevens
••• 0:39—Buns, while making love on top of Lysette Anthony in bed.
• 0:50—Brief buns, while getting out of spa with Anthony. Long shot.
Olivia Hussey . . . . . . . . . . . . . . . . . . . . . . . . . . Gail
Steve Railsback. . . . . . . . . . . . . . . . . . . . . . . . Robbins
Ashlie Rhey. . . . . . . . . . . . . . . . . . . . . . . . . Customer
••• 0:21—Nude, while trying on lingerie after Lysette Anthony shows Harry Hamlin secret one-way mirror in dressing room in lingerie store.
Kristine Rose. . . . . . . . . . . . . . . . . . . . . . . . . Cheryl

## Say Yes (1986)

Lissa Layng. . . . . . . . . . . . . . . . . . . . . . . . . .Annie
•• 1:06—Breasts, getting her dress ripped off.
• 1:07—More breasts, putting on jacket in restroom.

## Scandal *(1989)*

(Unrated version reviewed.)

Britt Ekland . . . . . . . . . . . . . . . . . . . Mariella Novotny
- •• 0:31—Breasts lying on table with John Hurt.
- • 0:51—Right breast talking with Hurt and Christine.

Bridget Fonda . . . . . . . . . . . . . . . . . . Mandy Rice-Davis
- • 0:20—Brief breasts dressed as an Indian dancing while Christine tries to upstage her.
  - 0:54—In white lingerie, then lower frontal nudity in sheer nightgown in room with a guy.
  - 1:05—Brief buns walking back into bedroom. Long shot.

Roland Gift . . . . . . . . . . . . . . . . . . Johnnie Edgecombe
John Hurt . . . . . . . . . . . . . . . . . . . . . Stephen Ward
Ian McKellen . . . . . . . . . . . . . . . . . . . . John Profumo

## Scanners III: The Takeover *(1992)*

Liliana Komorowska . . . . . . . . . . . . . . . . Helena Monet
- •• 0:32—Breasts in and out of spa, talking with her dad.
- • 0:35—Brief right breast, while sitting up.

## Scarecrow *(1973)*

Rutanya Alda. . . . . . . . . . . . . . . . . . Woman in Camper
Eileen Brennan . . . . . . . . . . . . . . . . . . . . . Darlene
- • 0:27—Brief breasts in bed when Gene Hackman takes off her bra and grabs her breasts.

Dorothy Tristan . . . . . . . . . . . . . . . . . . . . . . Coley

## Scarface *(1983)*

Angela Aames . . . . . . . . . . . Woman at the Babylon Club
Steven Bauer . . . . . . . . . . . . . . . . . . . . Manny Ray
Lana Clarkson . . . . . . . . . . . Woman at the Babylon Club
Emilia Crow . . . . . . . . . . . . . . . . . . . . . Echevera
Mary Elizabeth Mastrantonio. . . . . . . . . . . . . . . . Gina
- • 2:36—(0:39 into tape 2) Very, very brief left breast when she gets shot and her nightgown opens up when she gets hit.

Shelly Taylor Morgan . . . . . Woman at the Babylon Club
Michelle Pfeiffer . . . . . . . . . . . . . . . . . . . . Elvira
Pepe Serna . . . . . . . . . . . . . . . . . . . . . . Angel
Katt Shea . . . . . . . . . . . . . Woman at the Babylon Club

## Scarred *(1983)*

Annie Gaybis. . . . . . . . . . . . . . . . . . . . . Movie Girl
- •• 0:32—Breasts, straddling a guy in bed during filming of a movie.

Jennifer Mayo . . . . . . . . . . . . . . . . . . . . . . Ruby
- ••• 0:18—Breasts, undressing in bedroom in front of a customer, lying in bed, then making love. Long scene.
- • 0:21—Breasts, while lying in bed afterward.
- • 0:27—Breasts in bathtub, getting red paint washed off by a friend.
- • 0:29—Left breast, while sitting in bathtub.

Alexis Schreiner. . . . . . . . . . . . . . . . . . . Movie Girl
- • 0:32—Breasts, while dancing during filming of a movie. (She's the auburn hair colored girl wearing a gold necklace.)

## Scenes from the Class Struggle in Beverly Hills *(1989)*

Ed Begley, Jr. . . . . . . . . . . . . . . . . . . . . . . Peter
Robert Beltran . . . . . . . . . . . . . . . . . . . . . . . Juan
- • 1:34—Brief buns, when his shorts are pulled down by Frank.

Jacqueline Bisset. . . . . . . . . . . . . . . . . . . . . Clare
Ray Sharkey . . . . . . . . . . . . . . . . . . . . . . . Frank
- • 1:10—Brief buns while sleeping in bed with Zandra.

Arnetia Walker . . . . . . . . . . . . . . . . . . . . . To-Bel
- • 0:37—Breasts making love with Frank on the sofa.
- •• 1:10—Breasts in bed waking up with Howard.
- ••• 1:23—Breasts making love on top of Ed Begley, Jr. on the floor.

Mary Woronov. . . . . . . . . . . . . . . . . . . . Lizabeth
- ••• 1:06—In black lingerie, then breasts in bedroom, then in bed with Juan.

## Schizo *(1977; British)*

*a.k.a. Amok*

*a.k.a. Blood of the Undead*

Stephanie Beacham . . . . . . . . . . . . . . . . . . . Beth
Lynne Frederick . . . . . . . . . . . . . . . . . . . Samantha
  - 0:26—In white bra and panties, while changing clothes in bedroom.
- •• 0:29—Breasts and buns, while walking to and taking a shower.
- • 0:56—Brief frontal nudity, while getting into bed.

## Schizoid *(1980)*

Flo Gerrish . . . . . . . . . . . . . . . . . . . . . . . . Pat
Mariana Hill . . . . . . . . . . . . . . . . . . . . . . . Julie
  - 0:58—Left breast, while making love in bed with Klaus Kinski. Dark, hard to see.

Klaus Kinski . . . . . . . . . . . . . . . . Dr. Peter Fales
Christopher Lloyd. . . . . . . . . . . . . . . . . . . Gilbert
Craig Wasson. . . . . . . . . . . . . . . . . . . . . . Doug
Donna Wilkes. . . . . . . . . . . . . . . . . . Allison Foles
  - 0:12—Breasts taking off her bra in bathroom while Klaus Kinski watches. Buns, getting into the shower. Out of focus shots.
- •• 0:13—Side view breasts getting into the shower.

## School Spirit *(1985)*

Leslee Bremmer . . . . . . . . . . . . . . . . . . . . Sandy
- • 1:18—Breasts on a guy's shoulder in pool. (She's on the right, wearing red swimsuit bottoms.)

Linda Carol . . . . . . . . . . . . . . . . . . . . . . Hogette
Roberta Collins. . . . . . . . . . . . . . . Helen Grimshaw
Jackie Easton . . . . . . . . . . . . . . . . . . . . Hogette
Julie Gray . . . . . . . . . . . . . . . . . . . . . . Kendall
Marlene Janssen . . . . . . . . . . . . . . Sleeping Princess
- •• 0:16—Breasts in shower room, shaving her legs.
- •• 0:42—Breasts and buns, sleeping when old guy goes invisible to peek at her.

Marta Kober. . . . . . . . . . . . . . . . . . . . . Ursula
Becky LeBeau . . . . . . . . . . . . . . . . . . . . Hogette
- • 1:07—Breasts sliding down water slide at dance, wearing black and white swimsuit bottoms.

Tom Nolan . . . . . . . . . . . . . . . . . . . . . . . . Billy Batson
- 0:17—Buns in open hospital smock. More buns while running up stairs.
- 1:29—Brief buns, in hospital gown, while leaving Judy's room.

Pamela Ward . . . . . . . . . . . . . . . . Girl in Sorority Room
- ••• 0:15—Buns, then breasts in her room while Billy is invisible.
- ••• 0:16—More breasts and buns with other women in shower room.

## School Ties (1992)

Matt Damon . . . . . . . . . . . . . . . . . Charlie Dillon
- •• 1:09—Buns, in the showers with two other guys (He's on the left).
- 1:12—Very brief buns, while on the floor after getting hit by David.

Brendan Fraser . . . . . . . . . . . . . . . . . . . . David Greene
- •• 1:09—Buns, in the showers with two other guys (He's in the middle).

Chris O'Donnell . . . . . . . . . . . . . . . . . . . . Chris Reece
- 1:09—Brief upper half of buns, in the showers with two other guys (He's on the right).

## Scissors (1990)

Vicki Frederick . . . . . . . . . . . . . . . . . . . . . Nancy Leahy
Michelle Phillips . . . . . . . . . . . . . . . . . . . . Ann Carter
Steve Railsback . . . . . . . . . . Alex Morgan/Cole Morgan
Sharon Stone . . . . . . . . . . . . . . . . . . Angela Anderson
- 0:04—Upper half of left breast sitting up after attack in elevator.
- •• 0:12—Breasts changing clothes.
- 0:36—In bra with Steve Railsback. Brief upper half of left breast. Dark.

## Scorchers (1992)

Faye Dunaway . . . . . . . . . . . . . . . . . . . . . . . . . . Thais
Anthony Geary . . . . . . . . . . . . . . . . . . . . . . . . Preacher
- ••• 0:01—Buns, while making love on top of Faye Dunaway on porch. More buns, afterwards.

Emily Lloyd . . . . . . . . . . . . . . . . . . . . . . . . . Splendid
Jennifer Tilly . . . . . . . . . . . . . . . . . . . . . . . . . Talbot
Saxon Trainor . . . . . . . . . . . . . . . . . . . . . . . . . Renee
James Wilder . . . . . . . . . . . . . . . . . . . . . . . . . Dolan

## Scorchy (1971)

Connie Stevens . . . . . . . . . . . . . . . . . . . . . Jackie Parker
- •• 0:23—Open blouse, revealing left bra cup while talking on the telephone. Brief breasts swimming in the water after taking off bathing suit top.
- •• 0:52—Side view left breast, taking a shower.
- ••• 0:56—Brief right breast making love in bed with Greg Evigan. Breasts getting tied to the bed by the thieves. Kind of a long shot and a little dark and hard to see.
- 1:00—Brief breasts getting covered with a sheet by the good guy.

## Score (1973)

Calvin Culver . . . . . . . . . . . . . . . . . . . . . . . . . . . . Jack
- 0:01—Buns, while making love in bed with Elvira.
- 0:33—Brief buns, after dressing up like a sailor.
- •• 1:09—Buns, several times, while making love in bed with Eddie.
- •• 1:11—Buns, while getting into bed with Eddie.
- 1:21—Buns, while on bed.
- 1:22—Very brief buns, while on bed.
- 1:24—Very, very brief frontal nudity, while sitting down in bed next to Elvira.

Gerald Grant . . . . . . . . . . . . . . . . . . . . . . . . . . . Eddie
- •• 0:36—Buns, while changing clothes.
- •• 1:11—Buns, while lying in bed with Jack.
- •• 1:16—Buns, while sleeping in bed with Jack.

Lynn Lowry . . . . . . . . . . . . . . . . . . . . . . . . . . . Betsy
- 0:35—Left breast, sticking out of lingerie outfit.
- 0:38—Brief full frontal nudity, in lingerie outfit while dancing.
- 0:40—Breasts, in lingerie, while sitting on the floor with Eddie.
- 1:01—Brief lower frontal nudity while in bed with Elvira.
- 1:06—Brief left breast in reflection in mirror.
- 1:07—Breasts in lingerie in bed with Elvira.
- •• 1:15—Brief right breast and lower frontal nudity in bed with Elvira.
- •• 1:22—Full frontal nudity, while in bed, then talking to Eddie.

Carl Parker . . . . . . . . . . . . . . . . . . . . . . . . . . . . Mike
- ••• 0:21—Buns, while talking with Elvira, then making love while Betsy watches.
- 1:22—Buns, while in bed.

Claire Wilbur . . . . . . . . . . . . . . . . . . . . . . . . . . Elvira
- 0:01—Brief breasts, while making love with Jack.
- 0:04—Brief buns, after taking off overcoat.
- 0:13—Left breast, in open blouse, lying on bed for Lynn Lowry to take a picture.
- ••• 0:20—Full frontal nudity after taking off her robe in front of Mike. Buns, while making love.
- 0:33—Brief breasts, while taking off bra.
- 0:53—Brief right breast while sitting back in bed.
- •• 0:59—Breasts, after taking off her dress to go to sleep with Betsy.
- 1:02—Brief left breast, while in bed with Betsy.
- ••• 1:09—Full frontal nudity while standing up in bed, making love with Betsy.
- ••• 1:12—Breasts, while making love with Lynn.
- 1:15—Breasts, while waking up in bed.
- 1:22—Right breast, while in bed with everybody.
- 1:24—Breasts, while in bed.

## Scorned (1993)

Michael D. Arenz . . . . . . . . . . . . . . . . . . Robey Weston
- •• 0:49—Buns, after taking off his clothes with Shannon Tweed.

Kim Morgan Greene . . . . . . . . . . . . . . . Marina Weston
- •• 0:42—Brief breasts, while sitting in bubble bath and getting out. Buns, when Shannon Tweed helps dry her off.

••• 1:09—Left breast, then breasts while in bed when Tweed makes love with her.
• 1:28—Breasts, while crying in shower after discovering her birds are dead.
Andrew Stevens . . . . . . . . . . . . . . . . . . . . Alex Weston
Shannon Tweed . . . Patricia Langley/Amanda Chessfield
0:45—In bedroom in bra and panties when Robey peeks in through window.
•• 0:50—Breasts, after taking off bra with Robey, then in bed.
•• 0:59—Left breast and buns, while making love on top of Robey in bed.
• 1:19—In bra, then breasts, while making love on bed with Robey.

## Scream Dream (1989)
Melissa Anne Moore . . . . . . . . . . . . . . .Jamie Summers
••• 0:39—Breasts in black panties in room with Derrick. Then straddling him.
•• 0:58—Breasts in dressing room pulling her top down during transformation into monster.

## Screen Test (1986)
Michelle Bauer . . . . . . . . . . . . . . . . . Dancer/Ninja Girl
•• 0:04—Breasts dancing on stage.
••• 0:42—Nude, with Monique Gabrielle, making love in a boy's dream.
Deborah Blaisdell . . . . . . . . . . . . . . . . . . . . . . Dancer
• 1:20—Brief breasts, twice, dancing on stage. Long shot.
Monique Gabrielle . . . . . . . . . . . . . . . . . . . . . Roxanne
•• 0:06—Breasts taking off clothes in back room in front of a young boy.
••• 0:42—Nude, with Michelle Bauer, seducing a boy in his day dream.
•• 1:20—Breasts taking off her top for a guy.

## Screwball Hotel (1988)
Corinne Alphen. . . . . . . . . . . . . . . . . . . . .Cherry Amour
• 0:46—Buns, in black outfit on bed with Norman.
Gianna Amore. . . . . . . . . . . . . . . . . . . . . . .Mary Beth
Lisa Bradford-Aiton . . . . . . . . . . . . . . . . . . Punk Singer
Andi Bruce . . . . . . . . . . . . . . . . . . . . . . . . . Bobbi Jo
Lori Deann Pallett . . . . . . . . . . . . . . . . . . . . . .Candy
••• 0:26—Breasts in the shower while Herbie is accidentally in there with her.
Reneé Shugart. . . . . . . . . . . . . . . . . . . . . . Blue Bell

## Screwballs (1983)
Kim Cayer . . . . . . . . . . . . . . Brunette Cheerleader
Alan Daveau . . . . . . . . . . . . . . . . . . . . . Howie Bates
• 1:00—Buns, after losing at strip bowling.
Raven De La Croix. . . . . . . . . . . . . . Miss Anna Tomical
••• 1:08—Breasts during strip routine in nightclub.
Linda Shayne. . . . . . . . . . . . . . . . . . Bootsie Goodhead
••• 0:43—Right breast, while in back of van at drive-in theater, then breasts.

## Season of Fear (1989)
Clancy Brown. . . . . . . . . . . . . . . . . . . . . Ward St. Clair
Clare Wren. . . . . . . . . . . . . . . . . . . . . Sarah Drummond
0:23—Breasts in bed with Mick. Long shot, hard to see.
0:25—Brief silhouette, behind shower door.
• 0:42—Side view of left breast, on top of Mick. Very, very brief left breast, turning over when they hear a noise outside.

## Second Time Lucky (1986)
Diane Franklin . . . . . . . . . . . . . . . . . . . . . . . . . . . Eve
0:07—In white bra and panties in frat house bedroom taking off her wet dress.
•• 0:13—Breasts a lot during first sequence in the Garden of Eden with Adam.
••• 0:28—Brief full frontal nudity running to Adam after trying an apple.
• 0:41—Left breast, while taking top of dress down.
••• 1:01—Breasts, opening her blouse in defiance, while standing in front of a firing squad.
Roger Wilson . . . . . . . . . . . . . . . . . . . . . Adam Smith
• 0:13—Buns, while in the Garden of Eden.
•• 0:30—Buns, while standing out in the rain.

## Secret Admirer (1985)
C. Thomas Howell . . . . . . . . . . . . . . . . . . .Michael Ryan
Kelly Preston . . . . . . . . . . . . . . Deborah Anne Fimple
•• 0:53—Brief breasts in car with C. Thomas Howell.
• 1:17—Very brief breasts in and out of bed.
Leigh Taylor-Young . . . . . . . . . . . . . . . Elizabeth Fimple
Dee Wallace Stone . . . . . . . . . . . . . . . . . . Connie Ryan
Fred Ward . . . . . . . . . . . . . . . . . . . . . . . .Lou Fimple

## Secret Fantasy (1981)
Laura Antonelli. . . . . . . . . . . . . . . . . . . Costanza Vivaldi
••• 0:16—In black bra in Doctor's office, then left breast, then breasts getting examined.
•• 0:18—In black bra and panties in another Doctor's office. Breasts and buns.
•• 0:19—Breasts getting X-rayed. Brief breasts lying down.
•• 0:32—Breasts and buns when Nicolo drugs her and takes Polaroid photos of her.
•• 0:49—Breasts and buns posing around the house for Nicolo while he takes Polaroid photos.
•• 0:53—Breasts and buns during Nicolo's dream.
••• 1:12—Breasts in Doctor's office.
•• 1:14—Breasts and buns in room with another guy.
•• 1:16—Breasts on train while workers "accidentally" see her.
•• 1:20—Breasts on bed after being carried from bathtub.
•• 1:25—Breasts dropping dress during opera.
•• 1:27—More breasts scenes from 0:49.

## Secret Games (1991)
(Unrated version reviewed.)
Michele Brin. . . . . . . . . . . . . . . . . . . . . . . . . Julianne
•• 0:03—Left breast, while lying in bed with Billy Drago.

••• 0:08—Breasts and buns, while taking a shower.

•• 0:09—Breasts under sheer white robe, trying to entice Drago.

••• 0:34—Breasts, sunbathing with the other girls. (She's wearing brown framed sunglasses.)

••• 0:38—Breasts in bed, making love with Martin Hewitt.

••• 0:43—Buns and breasts making love in bed with Drago.

••• 0:48—Breasts, while tied to the bed.

••• 0:54—In white bra and panties, then nude taking them off and putting new ones on.

••• 1:10—Breasts, while lying in bed with Hewitt.

••• 1:13—Breasts and buns, making love with Hewitt in bathtub.

•• 1:15—Breasts under sheer robe.

•• 1:32—Buns in G-string, then breasts, getting into bed and making love with Drago.

Martin Hewitt . . . . . . . . . . . . . . . . . . . . . . . . . . . Eric

• 0:38—Brief side view of buns, while in bed with Julianne.

0:48—Almost buns, on top of Julianne in bed. (Her foot gets in the way.)

Monique Parent . . . . . . . . . . . . . . . . . . . . . . . . Robin

• 0:33—Right breast, buns and crotch, while in bed with Julianne.

Catya Sassoon . . . . . . . . . . . . . . . . . . . . . . . . Sandra

••• 0:21—Breasts during modeling session with the other girls. (She's the only brunette.)

••• 0:26—Breasts, making love in bed with Emil.

•• 0:34—Breasts in yellow bikini bottoms, sunbathing with the other girls.

••• 0:40—Breasts, getting out of the swimming pool and lying on lounge chair.

Delia Sheppard . . . . . . . . . . . . . . . . . . . . . . . Celeste

• 0:38—Breasts under sheer black body suit.

0:45—Buns, under sheer robe.

•• 0:48—Breasts with her lover, while watching Julianne and Eric on TV.

Brittany York . . . . . . . . . . . . . . . . . . . . . . . . . . . Nun

### Secret Games 2—The Escort (1993)

(Unrated version reviewed.)

Sara Suzanne Brown . . . . . . . . . . . . . . . . . . . . . . . Irene

••• 0:32—Undressing in bedroom, then nude while making love with Martin Hewitt in bed.

• 0:53—Breasts, while making love next to dining room table with Hewitt.

•• 1:00—Breasts, while lying in bed with Hewitt.

•• 1:20—Nude, while in bed with Hewitt in bed.

Martin Hewitt . . . . . . . . . . . . . . . . . . . . . . . Kyle Lake

••• 0:24—Buns, while making love with Stacey and Lisa in the shower.

•• 0:33—Buns, while making love in bed with Irene.

Thomas Milan . . . . . . . . . . . . . . . . . . . . . . . . Hector

• 0:43—Buns, while making love in bed with Stacey while Martin Hewitt watches.

Jennifer Peace . . . . . . . . . . . . . . . . . . . . . . . . . Darci

••• 0:47—Full frontal nudity, while making love with Martin Hewitt in bed.

• 1:05—Breasts, in flashbacks.

Holly Spencer . . . . . . . . . . . . . . . . . . . . . . . . . . . Lisa

••• 0:24—Nude, after taking off coat, covering Hewitt with birthday cake and in the shower with him and Stacey.

•• 0:26—Breasts and buns while making love in bed with Stacey and Hewitt.

•• 1:05—Breasts in flashbacks.

Amy-Rochelle Weiss . . . . . . . . . . . . . . . . . . . . . Stacey

••• 0:09—Full frontal nudity, while making love with Martin Hewitt in front of fireplace.

••• 0:16—Nude, while in bedroom then making love with Hewitt on dining room table.

•• 0:19—Breasts, while sitting in bed with Hewitt and talking.

••• 0:21—Breasts in video playback and in bed while talking with Hewitt on the phone.

••• 0:24—Nude, after taking off coat, covering Hewitt with birthday cake and in the shower with him and Lisa.

•• 0:26—Breasts and buns while making love in bed with Lisa and Hewitt.

• 0:37—Breasts, several times in flashback.

• 0:38—Breasts on video playback.

••• 0:41—Breasts, while making love with Hector in bed while Hewitt watches.

••• 0:54—Breasts, while modeling clothes for Hewitt in bedroom.

••• 0:57—Breasts, while making love with Hewitt in newlywed fantasy.

•• 1:04—Breasts and buns, while making love on top of Hewitt in flashbacks.

•• 1:11—Breasts, while in bed with Hector while talking on the phone.

•• 1:13—Breasts on video playback.

• 1:16—Brief breasts on video playback.

### The Secret of My Success (1987)

Michael J. Fox . . . . . . . . . . . . . . . . . . . . . Bentley Foster

John Pankow . . . . . . . . . . . . . . . . . . . . . . . Fred Melrose

Helen Slater . . . . . . . . . . . . . . . . . . . . . . . . . . . Christy

Margaret Whitton . . . . . . . . . . . . . . . . . . . Vera Prescott

• 0:31—Very brief breasts taking off swimsuit top in swimming pool with Michael J. Fox.

### Secret Places (1984; British)

Jenny Agutter . . . . . . . . . . . . . . . . . . . . . . . Miss Lowrie

Claudine Auger . . . . . . . . . . . . . . . . . . . . Sophy Meister

Cassie Stuart . . . . . . . . . . . . . . . . . . . . . . . . . . . Nina

• 0:07—Brief breasts, after pulling up her blouse to show off her breasts to her girlfriends.

• 1:15—Brief left breast, getting into bathtub with the help of her girlfriends. (She's drunk.)

### Secret Sins (1992)

Michelle McIntosh . . . . . . . . . . . . . . . . . . . . Sara Jenson

• 0:29—Tip of right breast, sticking out of bubbles in bubble bath, then putting on bra in bedroom while wearing panties.

•• 0:43—Breasts, while making love with Johnny on sofa and in living room.

## Secrets (1971)

Jacqueline Bisset . . . . . . . . . . . . . . . . . . . . . . . Jenny
- 0:49—Very brief lower frontal nudity, putting panties on while wearing a black dress.
- ••• 1:02—Brief buns and a lot of breasts on bed making love with Raoul.

## The Secrets of Love—Three Rakish Tales (1986)

Lucienne Bruinooge . . . . . . . . . . . . . . . . . . . . Marietta
- • 0:02—Buns, while getting spanking.
- •• 0:27—Breasts, while lying in bed.

Olivia Brunaux. . . . . . . . . . . . . . . . . . . . . . . .Célestine
- • 1:03—Brief breasts and buns fantasizing.
- ••• 1:14—Breasts and buns in the greenhouse making love.
- ••• 1:18—Breasts while kneeling in the greenhouse and making love.

Marc Legein . . . . . . . . . . . . . . . . . . . . . . . . . . . Luke
- • 0:18—Buns, while in the hay with the Weaver's wife.
- • 0:24—More buns.

Tina Shaw. . . . . . . . . . . . . . . . . . . . . The Weaver's Wife
- • 0:10—Breasts in bed with Luke.
- ••• 0:17—Breasts in the barn.

## Seduce Me: Pamela Principle 2 (1994)

India Allen. . . . . . . . . . . . . . . . . . . . . . . . . . . . Elaine
- •• 0:19—Breasts when Charles opens her pajamas in bed to try to make love with her.
- ••• 0:27—Breasts and buns, while taking a shower.
- •• 1:13—Nude, walking outside and getting into spa, then in spa. Medium long shots.
- ••• 1:25—Nude, while making love with her lover in shower while Charles watches from outside.

Daniel Anderson . . . . . . . . . . . . . . . . . . . . . . . .Matt

Sara Bellomo. . . . . . . . . . . . . . . . . . . . . . . . . . . Inger
- •• 0:33—Breasts, twice, while walking past Charles in house.
- • 0:50—Breasts, while sitting in spa. (She's on the left.)
- •• 1:01—Breasts, while making love (loudly) on bed when Charles passes by open door. Dark.

Shannon McLeod . . . . . . . . . . . . . . . . . . . . . Melinda
- • 0:50—Very brief breasts, while in spa.

Shauna O'Brien. . . . . . . . . . . . . . . . . . . . . . . Michelle
- ••• 0:15—Breasts and buns in G-string, after taking off lingerie for photo session.

Tonya Poole . . . . . . . . . . . . . . . . . . . . . . . . . . . . Eve
- ••• 0:58—Breasts, while posing during photo shoot in studio.

Nick Rafter . . . . . . . . . . . . . . . . . . . . . . . . . . Charles
- • 0:59—Buns, while lying face down on bed, getting an oil massage by Pamela.

Cathleen Raymond . . . . . . . . . . . . . . . . . . . . . Cindy
- • 0:03—Breast, while in background, changing clothes. Out of focus.
- ••• 0:04—Breasts and buns in G-string, after taking off lingerie during photo session. Long scene.

Elizabeth Sandifer . . . . . . . . . . . . . . . . . . . . . . . .Jill
- • 1:13—Buns and breasts, while walking to spa, then in spa. Medium long shot.

Alina Thompson. . . . . . . . . . . . . . . . . . . . . . . Pamela
- ••• 0:23—Buns in sexy swimsuit, then breasts during photo session.
- • 0:33—Brief lower half of buns, while walking up stairs in short dress.
- ••• 0:35—Breasts and buns, opening towel, then getting dressed.
- ••• 0:37—Nude, changing clothes then posing for photos outside. Some in B&W. Long scene.
- •• 0:44—Buns in G-string and left breast while making love with Charles in kitchen.
- • 0:49—Brief right breast and buns in swimsuit bottom while getting out of spa.
- ••• 1:16—Breasts and buns, while making love in bed with Charles.

## The Seducers (1970)

*a.k.a. Sensation*
*a.k.a. Top Sensation*

Maurizio Bonuglia . . . . . . . . . . . . . . . . . . . . . . Aldo
- • 0:11—Very brief buns, when Mudy yanks his towel off and he jumps off boat into the water. Sort of buns, while swimming in the water.

Edwige Fenech. . . . . . . . . . . . . . . . . . . . . . . . . . Ulla
- • 0:10—Very brief side of right breast, after Tony pulls her top down.
- • 0:11—Brief buns, under towel while walking in hallway.
- ••• 0:13—Breasts, after taking off her top and rubbing suntan lotion on Paula.
- • 0:22—Brief left breast, after opening her robe to let a goat lick her while Aldo takes pictures.
- •• 1:10—Breasts, while on boat deck with Andrew.
- •• 1:12—Breasts, a couple of more times with Andrew.

Rosalba Neri. . . . . . . . . . . . . . . . . . . . . . . . . . Paula
- •• 0:06—Breasts, under lots of necklaces, in cabin with Mudy. Partial buns in panties.
- ••• 0:12—Buns, while sunbathing on boat, then brief left breast.
- •• 0:13—Right breast with Ulla on boat deck.
- • 0:35—Brief buns, pulling down her swimsuit bottom to show off her tan.
- • 0:54—Brief breasts, while on boat deck with Andrew.
- • 1:05—Upper half of buns, when Andrew pulls her swimsuit down.

## The Seduction (1982)

Colleen Camp . . . . . . . . . . . . . . . . . . . . . . . . . .Robin

Morgan Fairchild . . . . . . . . . . . . . . . . . . . . . . . .Jamie
- • 0:02—Brief breasts under water, swimming in pool.
- • 0:05—Very brief left breast, getting out of the pool to answer the telephone.
- 0:13—In white bra changing clothes while listening to telephone answering machine.
- 0:50—In white lingerie in her bathroom while Andrew Stevens watches from inside the closet.
- •• 0:51—Breasts pinning her hair up for her bath, then brief left breast in bathtub covered with bubbles.

- 1:21—Breasts getting into bed. Kind of dark, hard to see anything.

Cathryn Hartt . . . . . . . . . . . . . . . . . Teleprompter Girl
Andrew Stevens . . . . . . . . . . . . . . . . . . . . . . . . Derek

### See No Evil, Hear No Evil (1989)
Richard Pryor . . . . . . . . . . . . . . . . . . . . . . . . . . Wally
Joan Severance . . . . . . . . . . . . . . . . . . . . . . . . . . Eve
- •• 1:08—Breasts in and leaning out of the shower while Gene Wilder tries to get her bag.

Gene Wilder . . . . . . . . . . . . . . . . . . . . . . . . . . . .Dave

### Senior Week (1987)
Vicki Darnell . . . . . . . . . . . . . .Everett's Dream Teacher
- •• 0:03—Breasts during classroom fantasy.

Miriam Zucker. . . . . . . . . . . . . . Princeton Dream Girl
- •• 0:42—Breasts during dream.

### Seniors (1978)
Priscilla Barnes. . . . . . . . . . . . . . . . . . . . . . . . Sylvia
- •• 0:18—Breasts at the top of the stairs while Arnold climbs up the stairs while the rest of the guys watch.

Dennis Quaid . . . . . . . . . . . . . . . . . . . . . . . . . Alan

### Sensations (1988)
Blake Bahner . . . . . . . . . . . . . . . . . . . . . . .Brian Ingles
- •• 0:10—Very, very brief lower frontal nudity pushing the covers off the bed, then buns, while getting out of bed.

Jennifer Delora . . . . . . . . . . . . . . . . . . . . .Della Randall
- • 0:11—Brief breasts talking to Jenny to wake her up.
- • 0:13—Brief breasts a couple of times in open robe.
- •• 0:38—Breasts making love with a guy on bed.

Jane Hamilton . . . . . . . . . . . . . . . . . . . . . . . . . Tippy
Rebecca Lynn . . . . . . . . . . . . . . . . . . . . Jenny Hunter
- • 0:11—Breasts, sleeping on couch.
- • 0:23—Breasts talking on the telephone.
- •• 1:09—Breasts making love in bed with Brian.

Karen Nielsen . . . . . . . . . . . . . . . . . . . Scared Woman
Jacqueline Palmer . . . . . . . . . . . . . . . . . . . . . . Tess
Denise Torek . . . . . . . . . . . . . . . . . . . . Phone Girl #2
- • 0:23—Breasts talking on the phone sex line.

Miriam Zucker. . . . . . . . . . . . . . . . . . . .Cookie Woman
- • 0:06—Breasts on couch making love with a guy while Jenny and Brian watch.

### The Sensuous Nurse (1975; Italian)
Ursula Andress. . . . . . . . . . . . . . . . . . . . . . . . . .Anna
- •• 0:16—Breasts and buns in bed after making love with Benito.
- •• 0:22—Nude swimming in pool while Adonais watches.
- ••• 0:50—Nude slowly stripping and getting in bed with Adonais.
- ••• 1:10—Nude getting into bed.

Luciana Paluzzi . . . . . . . . . . . . . . . . . . . . . . . . .n.a.
- •• 0:20—Breasts in room, ripping off her clothes and reluctantly making love with Benito.

Carla Romanelli. . . . . . . . . . . . . . . . . . . . . . . . Tosca
- •• 0:06—Breasts, then nude standing in the winery, then running around.

- •• 0:41—Nude, in basement, playing army, then making love with bearded guy.

### A Sensuous Summer (1991)
Lori Jo Hendrix . . . . . . . . . . . . . . . . . Dream Girl/Beach
- ••• 0:16—Nude on beach with dark haired girl in Jinx's dream.
- •• 0:24—Breasts while kneeling on one knee in Jinx's dream.
- •• 0:39—Breasts again while kneeling on one knee in Jinx's dream.

Gina Jourard. . . . . . . . . . . . . . . . . . . . . . . . . . . Tracy
- ••• 0:09—Breasts while making love in bed with Alex.
- 0:21—In two different bras in bedroom with Alex.

Brittany McCrena. . . . . . . . . . . . . . . . . . . . . . . . Jill
- •• 0:00—Breasts while making love in bed with Bobby in flashback.
- •• 0:11—Breasts while making love with Bobby in flashback. Buns in swimsuit.
- ••• 0:59—In black bra then breasts while making love with Bobby.

### The Sentinel (1977)
Tom Berenger . . . . . . . . . . . . . . . . . . . . . . Man at End
Beverly D'Angelo . . . . . . . . . . . . . . . . . . . . . . .Sandra
- 0:25—Masturbating in red leotard and tights on couch in front of Cristina Raines.
- • 0:33—Brief breasts playing cymbals during Raines' nightmare (in B&W).
- 1:24—Brief breasts long shot with zombie make up, munching on a dead Chris Sarandon.

Jeff Goldblum. . . . . . . . . . . . . . . . . . . . . . . . . . Jack
Sylvia Miles . . . . . . . . . . . . . . . . . . . . . . . . . . Gerde
- • 0:33—Brief left breast, three times, standing behind Beverly D'Angelo. Right breast, ripping dress of Christina Raines. B&W dream.
- 1:23—Brief breasts, three times, with D'Angelo made up to look like zombies, munching on a dead Chris Sarandon.
- 1:27—Very brief right breast during big zombie scene.
- • 1:28—Brief breasts when the zombies start dying.

Cristina Raines . . . . . . . . . . . . . . . . . . . . Alison Parker
- • 0:18—Briefly in sheer beige bra, putting her blouse on.
- • 0:33—Very, very brief left breast immediately after Sylvia Miles rips her dress off. B&W dream sequence.

Chris Sarandon. . . . . . . . . . . . . . . . . .Michael Lerman

### Separate Vacations (1985)
Susan Almgren. . . . . . . . . . . . . . . . . . . Helene Gilbert
- •• 1:05—Breasts and buns in G-string before getting into bed and then in bed with David Naughton.
- • 1:07—Breasts and buns in bed, then in bathroom with Naughton.

Nancy Cser . . . . . . . . . . . . . . . . . . . . . . . Stewardess
Jennifer Dale . . . . . . . . . . . . . . . . . . . . . Sarah Moore
- • 0:17—Brief right breast in bed with her husband after son accidentally comes into their bedroom.
- 0:20—In a bra and slip showing the baby sitter the house before leaving.

•• 1:14—Breasts on bed with Jeff after having a fight with her husband.

• 1:19—Brief right breast, in bed with her husband.

Blanca Guerra . . . . . . . . . . . . . . . . . . . . . . . . . . . Alicia

• 0:56—Breasts on the bed with David Naughton when she turns out to be a hooker.

Laura Henry . . . . . . . . . . . . . . . . . . . . . . . . . . . . .Nancy

Sherrie Miller. . . . . . . . . . . . . . . . . . . . . . . . . . . Sandy

David Naughton . . . . . . . . . . . . . . . . . . . Richard Moore

## Separate Ways (1979)

Karen Black . . . . . . . . . . . . . . . . . . . . . Valentine Colby

• 0:04—Breasts and in panties changing while her husband talks on the phone, then in bra. Long shot.

•• 0:18—Breasts in bed, while making love with Tony Lo Bianco.

•• 0:36—Breasts taking a shower, then getting out.

Pamela Bryant. . . . . . . . . . . . . . . . . Cocktail Waitress

Sybil Danning . . . . . . . . . . . . . . . . . . . . . . . . . .Mary

David Naughton . . . . . . . . . . . . . . . . . . . .Jerry Lansing

## Serial (1980)

Pamela Bellwood. . . . . . . . . . . . . . . . . . . . . . . Carol

Sally Kellerman . . . . . . . . . . . . . . . . . . . . . . . Martha

• 0:03—Breasts sitting on the floor with a guy.

Patch Mackenzie . . . . . . . . . . . . . . . . . . . . . . . Stella

• 0:59—Brief breasts in mirror in swinger's club with Martin Mull.

Stacey Nelkin . . . . . . . . . . . . . . . . . . . . . . . Marlene

Robin Sherwood . . . . . . . . . . . . . . . . . . . . . Woman

Clyde Ventura . . . . . . . . . . . . . . . . . . . . . . . . .Donald

## The Serpent and the Rainbow (1988)

Cathy Tyson . . . . . . . . . . . . . . . Dr. Marielle Duchamp

• 0:41—Brief breasts making love with Dennis. Probably a body double, don't see her face.

Dey Young . . . . . . . . . . . . . . . . . . . . . . Mrs. Cassedy

## The Serpent of Death (1989)

Jeff Fahey . . . . . . . . . . . . . . . . . . . . . . . . Jake Bonner

Camilla More . . . . . . . . . . . . . . . . . . . . . . . . . .Rene

•• 0:15—Brief breasts in bed with Jeff Fahey.

•• 1:22—Brief left breast while in bed, then breasts and buns, getting out of bed (in mirror).

## Serpico (1973)

Cornelia Sharpe. . . . . . . . . . . . . . . . . . . . . . . Leslie

•• 0:41—Breasts in bathtub with Al Pacino.

M. Emmet Walsh. . . . . . . . . . . . . . . . . . . . . Gallagher

## Seven (1979)

Susan Lynn Kiger. . . . . . . . . . . . . . . . . . . . . .Jennie

••• 0:58—Breasts, while sitting on bed, then getting up and walking around in the kitchen, making coffee, then putting her swimsuit top on.

• 1:15—Brief breasts, while taking off swimsuit top to change outside by car.

Martin Kove . . . . . . . . . . . . . . . . . . . . . . . . . . Skip

Barbara Leigh . . . . . . . . . . . . . . . . . . . . . . . . . Alexa

0:17—Briefly in braless, semi-sheer yellow blouse.

Art Metrano . . . . . . . . . . . . . . . . . . . . . . . . .Kinsella

## The Seventh Sign (1988)

Michael Biehn . . . . . . . . . . . . . . . . . . . . . . .Russell Quinn

Demi Moore. . . . . . . . . . . . . . . . . . . . . . . . .Abby Quinn

• 1:03—Brief breasts, taking off bathrobe to take a bath. Her pregnant belly is not real—it's a full body prosthetic. Brief breasts when sitting in bathtub.

• 1:04—Brief tip of left breast, while sitting in bathtub and rubbing her belly.

## A Severed Head (1971; British)

Claire Bloom . . . . . . . . . . . . . . . . . . . . . . .Honor Klein

• 1:10—Breasts leaning up then right beast while sitting up in bed with Richard Attenborough.

Jennie Linden . . . . . . . . . . . . . . . . . . . . . .Georgie Hands

0:02—Buns, rolling over on the floor with Ian Holm.

## Sex Appeal (1986)

Louis Bonanno . . . . . . . . . . . . . . . . . . . . . . . . . . . Tony

Philip Campanaro . . . . . . . . . . . . . . . . . . . . . . .Ralph

Tally Chanel. . . . . . . . . . . . . . . . . . . . . . . . . . Corinne

• 1:22—Brief breasts at the door of Tony's apartment when he opens the door while fantasizing about her.

Jeff Eagle . . . . . . . . . . . . . . . . . . . . . .Donald Cromronic

Samantha Fox . . . . . . . . . . . . . . . . . . . . . . . . Sheila

••• 1:14—In black lingerie, then breasts and buns in black G-string with Rhonda. Long scene.

Jane Hamilton . . . . . . . . . . . . . . . . . . . . . . . Monica

••• 0:58—Breasts dancing on the bed with Tony in his apartment. Long scene.

Kim Kafkaloff . . . . . . . . . . . . . . . . . . . . . . Stephanie

•• 0:29—Buns, in G-string in Tony's bachelor pad. Breasts dancing and on bed.

Marcia Karr . . . . . . . . . . . . . . . . . . . . . . . Christina

• 1:12—Brief left breast, then in bra and panties on bed with her boyfriend.

Taija Rae . . . . . . . . . . . . . . . . . . . . . . . . . Rhonda

•• 1:14—In black lingerie, then breasts in black push-up teddy with Sheila.

## Sex Crimes (1991)

Kirsten Ashley. . . . . . . . . . . . . . . . . . . . . . . Dancer

Grace Morley. . . . . . . . . . . . . . . . . . . . . . . . . . Cynthia

• 0:13—Buns in swimsuit in club. Very, very brief left breast, while taking off her swimsuit top in dressing room.

• 0:36—Buns in G-string and red pasties while dancing in club. More in dressing room.

Maria Richwine . . . . . . . . . . . . . . . . . . . . . . .Rosanna

• 0:09—Very brief tip of right breast, while sitting in bathtub, covered with bruises and cuts after getting raped.

• 1:19—Brief breast in mirror, while taking a shower.

## Sex on the Run (1979; German/French/Italian)
*a.k.a. Some Like It Cool*
*a.k.a. Casanova and Co.*

Jeannie Bell . . . . . . . . . . . . . . . . . . . . . . . .Slave Girl

••• 0:01—Breasts, reading book in large bath with Marisa Berenson.

••• 0:24—Breasts, giving Berenson a back massage.

Marisa Berenson . . . . . . . . . . . . . . . . . . . . . . . . . . .n.a.
    1:23—Almost right breast, while in bed with Tony
    Curtis when she rolls over him.
Britt Ekland . . . . . . . . . . . . . . . . . . . . . .Countess Trivulsi
   • 0:44—Left breast while making love in bed with
    Tony Curtis (don't see her face).
Andrea Ferréol. . . . . . . . . . . . . . . . . . . . . . . . Beatrice
Sylva Koscina . . . . . . . . . . . . . . . . . . . . . . . Jelsamina
  ••• 0:28—Breasts and brief buns dropping her top for
    Tony Curtis, then walking around with the "other"
    Tony Curtis.
  •• 1:20—Breasts talking to her husband.
Marisa Mell . . . . . . . . . . . . . . . . . . . . . . . . Francesca
   • 0:52—Very, very brief left breast, while getting out
    of bed with Tony Curtis.
    1:12—Braless in white nightgown.
Lillian Müller . . . . . . . . . . . . . . . . . . . . . . . . . Angela
  ••• 0:15—Second woman (blonde) to take off her
    clothes with the other two women, nude. Long
    scene.
Olivia Pascal . . . . . . . . . . . . . . . . . . . . . .Convent Girl
  ••• 0:15—First woman (brunette) to take off her clothes
    with the other two women, full frontal nudity. Long
    scene.
Carla Romanelli. . . . . . . . . . . . . . . . . . . . . . . Dice Girl
  •• 0:58—Breasts and buns with two other women, los-
    ing their clothes during dice game.

### Sex Through a Window *(1977)*
Jackie Giroux. . . . . . . . . . . . . . . . . . . . . . . . . .Barbie
Cheryl King. . . . . . . . . . . . . . . . . . . . . . . . . . . Nurse
   • 0:19—In bra and panties, under sheer white panty-
    hose, then breasts after taking off bra, while John
    watches her through a telephoto lens.
Kate Woodville . . . . . . . . . . . . . . . . . . . . Sally Norman
  •• 0:29—Left breast, after sitting up in bed after John
    sits up, then brief breasts while turning over in bed.
  ••• 1:15—Breasts, while making love in bed and after
    with John.

### Sex with a Smile *(1976; Italian)*
Barbara Bouchet . . . . . . . ."One for the Money" segment
  ••• 0:50—Breasts sitting up in bed with a guy in bed,
    then lying down, wearing glasses.
Edwige Fenech . . . . . . . . . . . . . . . . . . . . . Dream Girl
  •• 0:03—Breasts tied to bed with two holes cut in her
    red dress top.
    0:09—Buns, in jail cell in court when the guy pulls
    her panties down with his sword.
  •• 0:13—Brief breasts in bed with Dracula taking off
    her top and hugging him.
   • 0:16—Breasts in bathtub. Long shot.
Dayle Haddon. . . . . . . . . . . . . . . . . . . . . . . The Girl
  •• 0:23—Breasts, covered with bubbles in the bathtub.
   • 0:43—Buns, taking off robe to take a shower, then
    brief breasts with Marty Feldman.
Sydne Rome . . . . . . . . . . . . . "A Dog's Day" segment

### Sexpot *(1986)*
Ruth Corrine Collins . . . . . . . . . . . . . . . . Ivy Barrington
  •• 0:09—Breasts on table, taking her dress off for Phil-
    lip.
   • 0:41—Buns, in Damon's arms.
  •• 0:51—Left breast, while in shower talking to Boop-
    sie.
Jennifer Delora . . . . . . . . . . . . . . . . . . . . . . . Barbara
  ••• 0:28—In bra, then breasts with her two sisters when
    their bras pop off. (She's in the middle.)
  •• 0:36—Breasts on bed with Gorilla.
   • 1:32—Breasts during outtakes of 0:28 scene.
Jane Hamilton . . . . . . . . . . . . . . . . . . . . . . . . . Beth
  ••• 0:28—In bra, then breasts with her two sisters when
    their bras pop off. (She's on the right.)
   • 1:32—Breasts during outtakes of 0:28 scene.
Christina Veronica . . . . . . . . . . . . . . . . . . . . . . Betty
  ••• 0:28—In bra, then breasts with her two sisters when
    their bras pop off. (She's on the left.)
  •• 0:46—Breasts taking off her top in boat with Gorilla.
  •• 0:54—Breasts lying on the grass with Gorilla.
   • 1:28—Breasts during outtakes of 0:28 scene.

### Sexual Intent *(1994)*
Michele Brin. . . . . . . . . . . . . . . . . . . . .Barbara Hayden
   • 0:28—Breasts, on balcony after John talks to her on
    cellular phone. Long shot.
   • 0:47—Breasts during fantasy with John while she's
    watching video tape of an interview.
  ••• 0:49—In bra and panties, then breasts and buns
    while making love with John in her office.
  •• 0:54—Breasts, while sitting in bathtub.
Gary Hudson . . . . . . . . . . . . . . . . . . . . . . . . . John
   • 0:50—Brief upper half of buns, while making love
    with Barbara in her office.
   • 0:58—Very brief upper half of buns in bathroom.

### Sexual Malice *(1993)*
(Unrated version reviewed.)
Edward Albert . . . . . . . . . . . . . . . . . . . . . . . Richard
Diana Barton . . . . . . . . . . . . . . . . . . . . . . . Christine
   • 0:13—Brief buns in panties, taking off robe and get-
    ting into bed.
  ••• 0:32—Breasts in shower, then nude getting out and
    putting on a robe.
  •• 0:33—Left breast in open robe, looking at herself in
    the mirror.
  ••• 0:36—Breasts and buns in hotel room when takes
    her robe off and makes love with her in bed.
  •• 0:42—Breasts while making love in surf under pier at
    the beach.
  ••• 0:48—In white bra, panties and stockings, then
    buns and breasts while making love.
  •• 0:55—Breasts and buns while making love in dress-
    ing room of clothing store.
  ••• 1:04—Breasts, while in bed with a black girl while
    Quinn takes photos.
   • 1:13—Breasts, while in spa with Edward Albert.
Douglas Jeffrey. . . . . . . . . . . . . . . . . . . . . . . . Quinn
  •• 0:26—Buns in G-string, while dancing on stage.

- 0:36—Buns, while making love on top of Christine in bed.
- ••• 0:47—Buns, while standing at doorway, then making love with Christine while standing up.
- ••• 0:57—Buns, while making love with Christine in clothing store dressing room.

John Laughlin . . . . . . . . . . . . . . . . . . . . . . . . . . . Jack
Sam Phillips. . . . . . . . . . . . . . . . . . . . . . . . . . .Nicole
- ••• 1:30—Brief buns in raised skirt, then breasts, while making love with Edward Albert on sofa.

Kathy Shower . . . . . . . . . . . . . . . . . . . . . Laura Altman
- ••• 0:10—Breasts, while making love on pool table with a guy when Christine peeks in room.

## Sexual Outlaws (1993)
Kim Dawson . . . . . . . . . . . . . . . . . . . . . . . . . Jeannie
- ••• 0:05—Breasts and buns in panties, then nude while changing lingerie, then posing on bed.
- ••• 0:07—Breasts and buns, while posing on bed.
- ••• 0:09—Breasts, while in bed with Rita.

Mitch Gaylord. . . . . . . . . . . . . . . . . . . Francis Badham
Nicole Grey. . . . . . . . . . . . . . . . . . . . . . . . . . . .Rita
- ••• 0:09—Breasts, after taking off her top with Jeannie, then making love in hotel room.

Mike McCollow. . . . . . . . . . . . . . . . . . . . . . . . . John
- ••• 0:32—Buns, while making love on top of Annie in bed.

Monique Parent . . . . . . . . . . . . . . . . Uncredited Annie
- ••• 0:31—In green bra, while sitting on bed and posing for John, then breasts while making love with him.

Jennifer Peace . . . . . . . . . . . . . . . . . . . . . . . . .Betty
- ••• 0:10—Breasts, in lingerie and after taking it off with Frank while acting for a video.
- ••• 0:13—Breasts with Frank and Harriet for video.

## Sexual Response (1992)
(Unrated version reviewed.)
Emile Levisetti . . . . . . . . . . . . . . . . . . . . . . . . .Edge
- ••• 0:31—Buns, while standing and looking out the window, then sitting on the bed.
- ••• 0:43—Buns, while making love with Shannon Tweed.

Shannon Tweed . . . . . . . . . . . . . . . . . . . . . . . . Eve
- ••• 0:25—Breasts in studio with Edge, while he checks her out.
- ••• 0:29—Breasts, making love with him. Long scene.
- ••• 0:31—Full frontal nudity, lying in bed, then sitting up.
- ••• 0:43—Breasts, while making love in her house with Edge.
- •• 0:51—Breasts in pool at night with Edge.
- •• 0:52—Full frontal nudity, getting up out of bed and putting robe on.
- •• 0:55—Breasts in study with Edge.
- ••• 1:07—Breasts and buns, while taking a shower. Nude, getting out and drying herself off.

## Shadow of the Wolf (1992)
Nicholas Campbell . . . . . . . . . . . . . . . . . . . . .Scott
Lou Diamond Phillips . . . . . . . . . . . . . . . . . . .Agaguk
Donald Sutherland . . . . . . . . . . . . . . . . . . Henderson

Jennifer Tilly . . . . . . . . . . . . . . . . . . . . . . . . . Iglyook
- • 0:21—Very brief right breast under Lou Diamond Phillips.
- • 0:22—Very, very brief left breast when Phillips is on top of her and holds her arms down.
- •• 1:27—Very brief breasts, after taking off her clothes, then making love with Phillips.

## Shadow Play (1986)
Ron Kuhlman . . . . . . . . . . . . . . . . . . . . . . . .John Crown
- • 1:06—Buns, while standing and holding Dee Wallace in his arms.

Cloris Leachman. . . . . . . . . . . . . . . . . . Millie Crown
Dee Wallace Stone . . . . . . . . . . . . . . . . Morgan Hanna
- • 1:06—Brief breasts making love with Ron Kuhlman. Kind of dark and hard to see.

## ShadowHunter (1992)
Robert Beltran . . . . . . . . . . . . . . . . . . . . . .Frank Totsoni
Scott Glenn . . . . . . . . . . . . . . . . . . . . . . . . John Cain
Gloria Reuben . . . . . . . . . . . . . . . . . . . . . . . . .Cayla
- • 0:07—Buns, lifting up her skirt to tempt Scott Glenn. Don't see her face and slightly out of focus.

## Shadows Run Black (1981)
Terry Congie . . . . . . . . . . . . . . . . . . . . . . . Lee Faulkner
- •• 0:22—Breasts, going for a swim in pool at night.
- • 0:23—Breasts under water.

Kevin Costner. . . . . . . . . . . . . . . . . . . . . .Jimmy Scott
Barbara Peckinpaugh . . . . . . . . . . . . . . . . . . . . Sandy
- ••• 0:57—Full frontal nudity, undressing in bedroom.
- •• 0:58—Buns and very, very brief breasts getting into the shower.
- ••• 0:59—Full frontal nudity, drying herself off. Nude, walking around the house. Long scene.
- •• 1:01—Nude, in the bathroom, trying to avoid the killer.

## Shadowzone (1989)
Maureen Flaherty . . . . . . . . . . . . . . . . . . . . . . . .Jenna
- •• 0:13—Breasts lying under plastic cover.
- • 0:18—Breasts on table getting operated on.
- •• 1:11—Breasts again under plastic cover several times.
- •• 1:17—Brief breasts again, then full frontal nudity.
- • 1:24—Breasts alive under the plastic cover.

Robbie Reves . . . . . . . . . . . . . . . . . . . . . . . . . .James
  0:16—Frontal nudity long shot.
- • 0:26—Frontal nudity lying under plastic bubble.

Shawn Weatherly . . . . . . . . . . . . . . . . . . . . .Dr. Kidwell

## Shaft (1971)
Richard Roundtree . . . . . . . . . . . . . . . . . . . . John Shaft
- • 0:32—Brief lower half of buns, making love with a woman. Hard to see because it is partly hidden by a mobile. Don't see his face.

## The Shaming (1979)
a.k.a. *Good Luck, Miss Wyckoff*
a.k.a. *The Sin*
Anne Heywood . . . . . . . . . . . . . . . . . . . Evelyn Wyckoff
• • • 0:49—Right breast, then breasts in open blouse after
    being raped by Rafe in her classroom.
    0:52—Breasts on classroom floor, making love with
    Rafe.
John Lafayette . . . . . . . . . . . . . . . . . . . . . . . . . . Rafe
• • 0:43—Very brief frontal nudity, taking off his jump-
    suit in classroom with Anne Heywood.
• 0:52—Buns, while making love on top of Heywood
    in classroom.

## Shampoo (1975)
Warren Beatty . . . . . . . . . . . . . . . . . . . . . . . . George
• 0:42—Upper half of buns with pants a little bit down
    in the bathroom with Julie Christie.
• 1:24—Buns, while making love with Christie when
    Goldie Hawn discovers them. Long shot, hard to
    see.
Julie Christie . . . . . . . . . . . . . . . . . . . . . . . . . Jackie
Lee Grant . . . . . . . . . . . . . . . . . . . . . . . . . . . Felicia
• 0:03—Brief breasts in bed sitting up and putting bra
    on talking to Warren Beatty. Long shot, hard to see.
Goldie Hawn . . . . . . . . . . . . . . . . . . . . . . . . . . . . Jill
Sharon Kelly . . . . . . . . . . . . . . . . . . . . . Painted Lady
• 1:17—Brief breasts covered with tattoos all over her
    body during party. Lit with strobe light.
Susan McIver . . . . . . . . . . . . . . . . . . . . . . . Customer
Jack Warden . . . . . . . . . . . . . . . . . . . . . . Lester Carr

## Sharky's Machine (1981)
Bernie Casey . . . . . . . . . . . . . . . . . . . . . . . . . . Arch
Sue Francis Pai . . . . . . . . . . . . . . . . . . . . . . Siakwan
Burt Reynolds . . . . . . . . . . . . . . . . . . . . . . . Sharky
Rachel Ward . . . . . . . . . . . . . . . . . . . . . . . Dominoe
Aarika Wells . . . . . . . . . . . . . . . . . . . . . . . . . Tiffany
• 0:52—Brief side view breasts (mostly silhouette) in
    Rachel Ward's apartment.

## Shattered (1991)
Tom Berenger . . . . . . . . . . . . . . . . . . . Dan Merrick
Corbin Bernsen . . . . . . . . . . . . . . . . . . . . . Jeb Scott
Greta Scacchi . . . . . . . . . . . . . . . . . . . Judith Merrick
• • 0:14—Breasts, turning over in bed.
• 0:16—Breasts in a strip of B&W photos that Tom Be-
    renger looks at.
• 0:36—Breasts in B&W photos in Bob Hoskins' office.
    Brief breasts in flashback.
• • 1:24—Breasts during love-making flashback.

## She (1983)
Sandahl Bergman . . . . . . . . . . . . . . . . . . . . . . . . She
• • 0:22—Breasts getting into a pool of water to clean
    her wounds after sword fight.
David Brandon . . . . . . . . . . . . . . . . . . . . . Pretty Boy

## She'll be Wearing Pink Pyjamas (1985; British)
Maureen O'Brien . . . . . . . . . . . . . . . . . . . . . . . . Joan
• 0:46—Brief breasts making love in bed with Tom.
    Dark.
Julie Walters . . . . . . . . . . . . . . . . . . . . . . . . . . . Fran
• • • 0:07—Full frontal nudity taking a shower with the
    other women. Long scene.
• • 0:58—Nude, undressing and going skinny dipping
    in mountain lake, then getting out. Nice bun shot
    walking into the lake.
Jane Wood . . . . . . . . . . . . . . . . . . . . . . . . . . . . Jude
• 0:07—Nude, shaving her legs in the women's show-
    er room.

## She's Gotta Have It (1987)
Tracy Camilla Johns . . . . . . . . . . . . . . . . . Nola Darling
• • • 0:05—Breasts, making love in bed with Jamie.
• • 0:25—Brief left breast taking off leotard with Greer.
    More breasts waiting for him to undress.
• 0:27—Breasts and buns in bed with Greer.
• 0:38—Breasts, close up of breast, while making love
    with Spike Lee.
• • 0:41—Left breast, while lying in bed with Lee.
• • 1:05—Breasts, twice, in bed masturbating.
Joie Lee . . . . . . . . . . . . . . . . . . . . Clorinda Bradford
John Canada Terrell . . . . . . . . . . . . . . . . . Greer Childs
• • 0:27—Buns and very brief frontal nudity, while get-
    ting into bed with Nola. More quick shots of buns in
    bed.

## She-Devil (1989)
Nitchie Barrett . . . . . . . . . . . . . . . . . . . . Bob's Secretary
Ed Begley, Jr. . . . . . . . . . . . . . . . . . . . . Bob Patchett
• • 0:32—Brief buns, when towel falls off outside after
    Rosanne Arnold takes off in a taxi.
Sylvia Miles . . . . . . . . . . . . . . . . . . . . . . . Mrs. Fisher
Meryl Streep . . . . . . . . . . . . . . . . . . . . . Mary Fisher

## Sheba, Baby (1975)
Pam Grier . . . . . . . . . . . . . . . . . . . . . . . Sheba Shayne
• 0:26—Side view of left breast, while lying in bed
    with Brick.

## Sheena (1984)
Nancy Paul . . . . . . . . . . . . . . . . . . . . . . . Betsy Ames
Tanya Roberts . . . . . . . . . . . . . . . . . . . . . . . . Sheena
• • 0:18—Breasts and buns taking a shower under a wa-
    terfall. Full frontal nudity (long shot), diving into the
    water.
• • • 0:54—Nude taking a bath in a pond while Ted Wass
    watches.
Ted Wass . . . . . . . . . . . . . . . . . . . . . . . . . . Vic Casey
• 1:48—Buns, after getting pulled out of the ground
    after tribal healing ceremony.

## The Sheltering Sky (1990)
Amina Annabi . . . . . . . . . . . . . . . . . . . . . . . . Mahrnia
• • 0:20—Left breast, then breasts in tent with John
    Malkovich.
• • 0:22—Right breast while lying down with Malkov-
    ich, breasts when he gets up.

John Malkovich . . . . . . . . . . . . . . . . . . . . . . . . . . . Port
••• 0:32—Frontal nudity and half of buns, while getting
     out of bed and opening door.
Campbell Scott . . . . . . . . . . . . . . . . . . . . . . . . . Turner
Eric Vu-An . . . . . . . . . . . . . . . . . . . . . . . . . . . Belqassim
  • 1:59—Buns, while rolling over in bed with Debra
     Winger. Long shot, don't see his face.
Debra Winger . . . . . . . . . . . . . . . . . . . . Kit Moresby
     0:13—Upper half of lower frontal nudity in open
     robe when John Malkovich caresses her stomach.
     0:24—Buns, getting out of bed.
  • 0:41—Very brief breasts grabbing sheets and get-
     ting out of bed with Tunner.
     1:58—Lower frontal nudity and sort of buns, getting
     undressed with Belqassim.

### *The Shining* (1980)
Lia Beldam . . . . . . . . . . . . . . . . Young Woman in Bath
••• 1:12—Full frontal nudity getting out of bathtub
     while Jack Nicholson watches.
Shelley Duvall . . . . . . . . . . . . . . . . . Wendy Torrance
Jack Nicholson . . . . . . . . . . . . . . . . . . . . . Jack Torrance

### *Shining Through* (1992)
Michael Douglas . . . . . . . . . . . . . . . . . . . . . . Ed Leland
Melanie Griffith . . . . . . . . . . . . . . . . . . . . . . . Linda Voss
•• 0:22—Breasts, making love in bed on top of Michael
     Douglas.
Liam Neeson . . . . . . . . . . . . . . . . . . Franz-Otto Dietrich
Joely Richardson . . . . . . . . . . . . .Margrete von Eberstien

### *Shirley Valentine* (1989; British)
Pauline Collins. . . . . . . . . . . . . . . . . . . Shirley Valentine
  • 0:13—Brief left breast giving Joe a shampoo in the
     bathtub.
•• 1:17—Breasts jumping from the boat into the water
     in slow motion. Very brief breasts in the water.
•• 1:19—Buns, hugging Tom Conti, left breast several
     times kissing him.
Bernard Hill . . . . . . . . . . . . . . . . . . . . . Joe Bradshaw
Joanna Lumley . . . . . . . . . . . . . . . . . . . . . . . Marjorie

### *Shock 'Em Dead* (1990)
Suzanne Ager . . . . . . . . . . . . . . . . . . . . . Groupie 3
Kathleen Kane. . . . . . . . . . . . . . . . . . . . . . Pizza Girl 2
Traci Lords . . . . . . . . . . . . . . . . . . . . . . Lindsay Roberts
Jackie Moen . . . . . . . . . . . . . . . . . . . . . . . .Groupie 4
•• 1:05—Breasts, taking off her top to tempt Martin.
Karen Russell . . . . . . . . . . . . . . . . . . . . . . . . Michelle
•• 0:16—In lingerie, then breasts twice with Martin.
Laurel Wiley . . . . . . . . . . . . . . . . . . . . . . . .Monique
  • 0:26—Brief breasts, pulling her top down to show
     Martin her scar. Don't see her face.

### *Short Cuts* (1993)
Anne Archer . . . . . . . . . . . . . . . . . . . . . . .Claire Kane
     1:49—(0:6 into Part 2) Very brief side view of buns,
     while hiking up nightgown and sitting on edge of
     tub.
Peter Gallagher . . . . . . . . . . . . . . . . . Stormy Weathers

Jennifer Jason Leigh . . . . . . . . . . . . . . . . . . . . Lois Kaiser
Jack Lemmon . . . . . . . . . . . . . . . . . . . . . .Paul Finnigan
Huey Lewis. . . . . . . . . . . . . . . . . . . . . . . . . . .Vern Miller
     0:50—Brief frontal nudity, while pulling it out of his
     pants while standing on rock. The next shot of him
     urinating is a fake penis since it was difficult to uri-
     nate for so long on cue.
Frances McDormand . . . . . . . . . . . . . . Betty Weathers
  • 0:46—Very brief left breast and partial lower frontal
     nudity, while walking past doorway. Brief left breast
     and lower frontal nudity, while peeking around
     doorway and wrapping a towel around herself.
Matthew Modine . . . . . . . . . . . . . Doctor Ralph Wyman
Julianne Moore. . . . . . . . . . . . . . . . . . . . Marian Wyman
••• 2:22—(0:39 into Part 2) Buns and lower frontal nu-
     dity in top part of outfit, after having to take off the
     skirt to clean it. Long scene.
Christopher Penn . . . . . . . . . . . . . . . . . . . . .Jerry Kaiser
Tim Robbins. . . . . . . . . . . . . . . . . . . . . . . Gene Shepard
Annie Ross . . . . . . . . . . . . . . . . . . . . . . . . Tess Trainer
Lori Singer . . . . . . . . . . . . . . . . . . . . . . . . Zoe Trainer
•• 0:48—Nude, stripping out of her clothes, then
     jumping in pool and floating. Seen through a fence.
Madeleine Stowe . . . . . . . . . . . . . . . . . . .Sherri Shepard
•• 1:20—Left breast, while posing for painting by
     Julianne Moore.
  • 2:07—(0:24 into Part 2) Brief left breast, while turn-
     ing over in bed.
Lili Taylor . . . . . . . . . . . . . . . . . . . . . . . . . . .Honey Bush
Fred Ward . . . . . . . . . . . . . . . . . . . . . . . . . Stuart Kane
     1:45—(0:2 into Part 2) Partial buns, while sliding
     into bed with Anne Archer.

### *The Shout* (1979)
Alan Bates . . . . . . . . . . . . . . . . . . . . . . . Charles Crossly
John Hurt. . . . . . . . . . . . . . . . . . . . . .Anthony Fielding
Susannah York . . . . . . . . . . . . . . . . . . . Rachel Fielding
•• 0:53—Brief breasts changing from a bathrobe to a
     blouse in bedroom.
  • 1:02—Brief nude in upstairs room getting ready to
     make love with Alan Bates.
     1:05—Brief buns, standing at end of hallway.
     1:09—In white slip inside and outside house.
     1:11—Breasts in bathtub with John Hurt.
  • 1:18—Brief breasts getting up from bed with Bates.
     Long shot, hard to see anything.

### *Showdown in Little Tokyo* (1991)
Tia Carrere . . . . . . . . . . . . . . . . . . . . . . . . . . . Minako
  • 0:50—Buns and side view of left breast, taking off
     robe and getting into outdoor tub with Dolph
     Lundgren. Don't see her face.
  • 0:52—Left breast, while making love in bed with
     Lundgren. Don't see her face again.
Renee Griffin . . . . . . . . . . . . . . . . . . . . . . . . . .Angel
•• 0:15—In black bra. Breasts in lingerie and stockings
     (mostly right breast) just before getting killed.
  • 0:34—Right breast, on TV during playback of her ex-
     ecution.

Dolph Lundgren . . . . . . . . . . . . . . . . . Detective Kenner
••• 0:53—Buns, while getting out of bed to check on noise outside.

### The Sicilian (1987)
(Director's uncut version reviewed.)
Christopher Lambert . . . . . . . . . . . . . Salvatore Giullano
•• 1:02—Buns, when the Duchess yanks his underwear down. Don't see his face, but probably him.
Barbara Sukowa . . . . . . . . . Camilia Duchess of Crotone
•• 0:05—Buns and brief breasts taking a bath, three times.
• 0:07—Brief right breast reading Time magazine. Full frontal nudity in the mirror standing up in the tub.
• 0:08—Brief right breast standing at the window watching Christopher Lambert steal a horse.
••• 1:01—In bra, then breasts in bedroom with Lambert. More breasts, then nude. Long scene.
John Turturro . . . . . . . . . . . . . . . . . . Aspanu Pisciotta

### Sid and Nancy (1986; British)
Gary Oldman . . . . . . . . . . . . . . . . . . . . Sid Vicious
Patti Tippo . . . . . . . . . . . . . .Tanned and Sultry Blonde
Chloe Webb . . . . . . . . . . . . . . . . . . . . . . . . Nancy
• 0:21—Left breast, under Sid's arm in bed with him. Covered up, hard to see.
•• 0:44—Breasts in bed after making love, then arguing with Sid.

### Side Out (1990)
Hope Marie Carlton. . . . . . . . . . . . . . . . . . .Vanna
C. Thomas Howell. . . . . . . . . . . . . . . . Monroe Clark
Harley Jane Kozak . . . . . . . . . . . . . . . . . . .Kate Jacobs
• 0:53—Brief left breast, then out of focus left breast, while in bed with Peter Horton.
Christopher Rydell. . . . . . . . . . . . . . . . . Wiley Hunter

### Side Roads (1988)
Jeff Speakman. . . . . . . . . . . . . . . . . . . Joseph Velasco
Ingrid Vold . . . . . . . . . . . . . . . . . . . . . Bonnie Velasco
• 0:29—Brief breasts in motel room, getting undressed and carried into bed by Joe.
0:30—In white lingerie, talking with Joe. Long scene.
0:56—In white bra and panties, changing clothes.
• 1:45—Brief breasts in mirror, getting out of bed.

### Siesta (1987)
Ellen Barkin . . . . . . . . . . . . . . . . . . . . . . . . Diane
••• 0:03—Brief full frontal nudity long shot taking off red dress, breasts, brief buns standing up, then full frontal nudity lying down.
1:22—Right nipple sticking out of dress while imagining she's with Gabriel Byrne instead of the reality of getting raped by taxi driver.
• 1:23—Brief lower frontal nudity, very brief silhouette of a breast, then brief buns some more while with Byrne. Dark, hard to see.
• 1:24—Lower frontal nudity, with torn dress while lying in bed after the taxi driver gets up.

1:26—Very brief lower frontal nudity, while running down road and her dress flies up as police cars pass by.
1:28—Very brief side view of right breast putting on dress in bed just before Isabella Rossellini comes into the bedroom to attack her. Long distance shot.
Gabriel Byrne. . . . . . . . . . . . . . . . . . . . . Augustine
• 1:28—Brief buns and frontal nudity, while getting out of bed. Long shot, hard to see.
Jodie Foster . . . . . . . . . . . . . . . . . . . . . . . . Nancy
0:47—In a black slip combing Ellen Barkin's hair.
0:50—In a slip again in bedroom with Barkin.
Grace Jones . . . . . . . . . . . . . . . . . . . . . . Conchita
Isabella Rossellini . . . . . . . . . . . . . . . . . . . . .Marie
Julian Sands . . . . . . . . . . . . . . . . . . . . . . . . . Kit
Martin Sheen. . . . . . . . . . . . . . . . . . . . . . . . . Del
Anastassia Stakis. . . . . . . . . . . . . . . . . . . .Desdra

### Silence Like Glass (1989)
Jami Gertz . . . . . . . . . . . . . . . . . . . . . . . Eva March
1:31—Very brief left breast on operating table, getting defibrillated. Possible body double. The Doctor's arm covers her face.
Dayle Haddon . . . . . . . . . . . . . . . . . . . Darlene Meyers
James Remar . . . . . . . . . . . . . . . . . . . . . . . Charley
Rip Torn. . . . . . . . . . . . . . . . . . . . . . . Dr. Markowitz

### The Silencer (1992)
Chris Mulkey . . . . . . . . . . . . . . . . . . . . . . . George
Lynette Walden . . . . . . . . . . . . . . . . . . . . . . .Angel
••• 0:09—Breasts and buns, taking off clothes and getting into bathtub with her boyfriend.
•• 0:10—More breasts, while making love with him in the bathtub.
0:28—Serious cleavage in open blouse in kitchen with a new boyfriend.
0:40—Almost breasts, while making out with Tony.

### Silent Madness (1984)
Elizabeth Kaitan . . . . . . . . . . . . . . . . . . . . Barbara
April Daisy White . . . . . . . . . . . . . . . . . . . . . .Susan
• 0:06—Breasts, while changing tops at back of van.

### Silent Night, Deadly Night (1984)
Tara Buckman . . . . . . . . . . . . . . . . . . . . .Mother (Ellie)
• 0:12—Brief right breast twice when the killer dressed as Santa Claus, rips her blouse open. Breasts lying dead with slit throat.
• 0:18—Very, very brief breasts during Billy's flashback.
• 0:43—Brief breasts a couple of times again in another of Billy's flashbacks.
Toni Nero. . . . . . . . . . . . . . . . . . . . . . . . . Pamela
• 0:30—Brief right breast twice just before Billy gets stabbed during fantasy scene.
• 0:42—Breasts in stock room when Andy attacks her.
• 0:44—Breasts while in stock room struggling with Billy, then getting killed by him.

Linnea Quigley . . . . . . . . . . . . . . . . . . . . . . . . . Denise
- ••• 0:52—Breasts while on pool table with Tommy, then putting on shorts and walking around the house. More breasts, while impaled on antlers.

Robert Brian Wilson. . . . . . . . . . . . . . . . . . . . Billy at 18
- • 0:30—Sort of buns while in bed with Pamela.

### Silent Night, Deadly Night 4: Initiation (1990)

Maud Adams. . . . . . . . . . . . . . . . . . . . . . . . . . . . .Fima
Tommy Hindley . . . . . . . . . . . . . . . . . . . . . . . . .Hank
- • 0:03—Brief buns, while carrying Kim onto bed.

Marjean Holden . . . . . . . . . . . . . . . . . . . . . . . . . . Jane
Neith Hunter. . . . . . . . . . . . . . . . . . . . . . . . . . . . . Kim
- • 0:03—Brief breasts several times in bed with Hank.
- • 0:47—Brief breasts during occult ceremony when a worm comes out of her mouth.
- • 1:05—Right breast, while lying on floor. Long shot. 1:06—Breasts, covered with gunk, transforming into a worm.
- • 1:07—Very brief side of right breast, while sitting up.

### Silent Night, Deadly Night III: Better Watch Out! (1989)

Robert Culp. . . . . . . . . . . . . . . . . . . . . . . . .Lt. Connely
Laura Herring . . . . . . . . . . . . . . . . . . . . . . . . . . .Jerri
- ••• 0:48—Breasts in bathtub with her boyfriend Chris.

### Silent Night, Deadly Night, Part 2 (1986)

Tara Buckman . . . . . . . . . . . . . . . . . . . . . . . .Mother
- • 0:09—Very brief right breast, with Santa Claus during flashback.
- • 0:14—Very brief breasts on ground during flashback.
- • 0:22—Very, very brief blurry breasts during flashback.
- • 0:47—Very, very brief breasts during flashback.

Elizabeth Kaitan. . . . . . . . . . . . . . . . . . . . . . . .Jennifer
0:58—Most of right breast, then buns, while kissing Ricky.

Toni Nero . . . . . . . . . . . . . . . . . . . . . . . . . . . Pamela
- •• 0:22—Breasts in back of toy store in flashback from *Silent Night, Deadly Night.*

Linnea Quigley . . . . . . . . . . . . . . . . . . . . . . . . . Denise
- ••• 0:26—Breasts on pool table and getting dressed flashback from *Silent Night, Deadly Night.*

### The Silent Partner (1978)

Gail Dahms . . . . . . . . . . . . . . . . . . . . . . . . . .Louise
- • 0:31—Right breast in bathroom with another guy when Elliott Gould surprises them.

Michael Kirby . . . . . . . . . . . . . . . . . . . . . . . .Packard
Céline Lomez . . . . . . . . . . . . . . . . . . . . . . . . Elaine
- • 1:05—Side view of left breast, then breasts, then buns with Elliott Gould.

Susannah York . . . . . . . . . . . . . . . . . . . . . . . . . Julie
- • 0:38—Very brief right breast pulling her dress back up with Elliott Gould.

### Silent Rage (1982)

Toni Kalem. . . . . . . . . . . . . . . . . . . . . . . . Alison Halman
- •• 0:22—Side view of left breast, then breasts, while in bed with Chuck Norris.
- •• 0:46—Right breast, while lying in bed with Norris. 1:01—Briefly in bra, undressing in bedroom to take a shower.

### Silent Scream (1980)

Rebecca Balding. . . . . . . . . . . . . . . . . . . . Scotty Parker
- • 0:50—Brief right breast while making love in bed with Jack.

### Silk 2 (1989)

Monique Gabrielle . . . . . . . . . . . Jenny "Silk" Sleighton
- ••• 0:27—Breasts, then full frontal nudity taking a shower while killer stalks around outside. 0:28—Very, very brief blurry right breast in open robe when she's on the sofa during fight.
- • 0:29—Brief breasts doing a round house kick on the bad guy. Right breast several times during the fight.
- ••• 0:55—Breasts taking off her blouse and making love on bed. Too much diffusion!

### Silk Degrees (1994)

India Allen . . . . . . . . . . . . . . . . . . . . . . . . . . . . Sheila
- •• 0:02—Breasts, while making love in bed with Degril-lo.

Katherine Armstrong . . . . . . . . . . . . . . . . . . . Nicole
- • 1:05—Very, very brief breast, while in water, while killing Mark Hamill.

Adrienne Barbeau. . . . . . . . . . . . . . . . . . . . . .Violet
Mark Hamill . . . . . . . . . . . . . . . . . . . . . . . . .Johnson
Angela Melini. . . . . . . . . . . . . . . . . . . . . . . . .Bonnie
Deborah Shelton . . . . . . . . . . . . . . . . . . . Alex Ramsey
- • 0:49—Full frontal nudity behind plastic shower curtain.
- •• 0:56—Breasts, while making love with Marc Singer in cabin.

Marc Singer . . . . . . . . . . . . . . . . . . . . . . . . . . .Baker

### Silkwood (1984)

E. Katherine Kerr . . . . . . . . . . . . . . . . . . . Gilda Schultz
Bruce McGill . . . . . . . . . . . . . . . . . . . . . Mace Hurley
J. C. Quinn. . . . . . . . . . . . . . . . . . . . . . . . Curtis Schultz
Kurt Russell . . . . . . . . . . . . . . . . . . . . . Drew Stephens
Meryl Streep . . . . . . . . . . . . . . . . . . . Karen Silkwood
- • 0:24—Very brief glimpse of upper half of left breast when she flashes it in nuclear reactor office.

Fred Ward . . . . . . . . . . . . . . . . . . . . . . . . . . . .Morgan

### Simply Irresistible (1983)

(R-rated version. *Irresistible* is the X-rated version.)
Nicole Black. . . . . . . . . . . . . . . . . . . . . . . . . Mata Hari
1:07—Pulling up her dress, then stripping in front of two guys in prison.
- •• 1:14—Full frontal nudity tied to a chair.

Samantha Fox . . . . . . . . . . . . . . . . . . . . . .Arlene Brooks
- • 1:20—In see-through white nightgown, then brief peeks at right breast when nightgown gapes open.

Gina Gianetti . . . . . . . . . . . . . . . . . . . . . . . .Sunshine
•• 0:49—Breasts in motel room with Walter and Juliet.
Dorothy LeMay . . . . . . . . . . . . . . . . . . . . . . .Hitchhiker
••• 0:09—Nude in office with Walter.
Gayle Sterling . . . . . . . . . . . . . . . . . . . . . . . . . . .Juliet
•• 0:40—Breasts and buns in bed with Walter.
0:46—In lingerie on bed.

### *Sinbad and the Eye of the Tiger* (1977; U.S./British)
Taryn Power . . . . . . . . . . . . . . . . . . . . . . . . . . . Dione
1:16—Very brief buns, skinny dipping in pond with
Jane Seymour. Long shot, but still pretty amazing for
a G-rated film.
1:18—Very brief partial side view of right breast,
running away from the troglodyte.
Jane Seymour . . . . . . . . . . . . . . . . . . . . . . . . . . Farah
1:16—Very brief buns, skinny dipping in pond with
Taryn Power. Long shot, but still pretty amazing for
a G-rated film.
1:17—Very brief partial right breast (arm covers
most of it) screaming when scared by the troglodyte.

### *Sincerely Charlotte* (1986; French)
Caroline Faro. . . . . . . . . . . . . . . .Irene the Baby Sitter
Isabelle Huppert . . . . . . . . . . . . . . . . . . . . . . Charlotte
0:20—Brief breasts while in bathtub. Long shot, out
of focus.
1:07—Very brief left breast changing into red dress
in the back seat of the car.
•• 1:15—Breasts in bed with Mathieu. Kind of dark.
Tina Sportolaro . . . . . . . . . . . . . . . . . . . . . . . . . . .n.a.

### *Single White Female* (1992)
Bridget Fonda . . . . . . . . . . . . . . . . . . . . . . . . . . Allie
• 0:04—Very, very brief right breast, while getting out
of bed with Sam. Very brief side view of right breast,
then buns, while walking to turn off answering machine.
• 0:05—Brief breasts, grabbing her clothes.
• 0:34—Buns and brief breasts, getting out of bed.
Dark.
• 1:18—Brief right breast, in gaping nightgown while
kneeling on bathroom floor after throwing up in the
toilet.
1:20—Brief silhouette of left breast, while changing
clothes.
Jennifer Jason Leigh . . . . . . . . . . . . . . . . . Hedy Carlson
••• 0:18—Breasts, changing clothes in her room in front
of Bridget Fonda.
• 0:29—Upper half of breasts, while in bathtub.
•• 0:37—Breasts, masturbating in bed while Fonda
peeks in bedroom.
••• 1:04—Breasts in the shower, then full frontal nudity,
getting out.
•• 1:09—Breasts, getting into bed with Sam.
1:10—Breasts in bed with Sam.
Steven Weber . . . . . . . . . . . . . . . . . . . . . .Sam Rawson
•• 1:12—Very brief frontal nudity, getting out of bed
with Jennifer Jason Leigh. Upper half of buns, while
putting on his pants.

### *Sinners!* (1990)
Wendy MacDonald . . . . . . . . . . . . . . . . . . . . . . . . .Fran
Joe Palese. . . . . . . . . . . . . . . . . . . . . . . . . . . . . . . . . .Al
• 0:00—Brief buns, while on top of a woman. Don't
see his face.

### *Sins of Desire* (1992)
(Unrated version reviewed.)
Nick Cassavetes . . . . . . . . . . . . . . . . . . Barry Mitchum
Becky LeBeau . . . . . . . . . . . . . . . . . . . . . . . . . . Sandy
••• 0:23—Nude, stripping and dancing (she's the
blonde on the left) with Clarise in front of Mr.
O'Connor. Long scene.
Monique Parent . . . . . . . . . . . . . . . . . . . . . . . . . Clarise
••• 0:23—Nude, stripping and dancing (she's the red-
head on the right) with Sandy in front of Mr. O'Connor. Long scene.
Tanya Roberts . . . . . . . . . . . . . . . . . . . . . . . Kay Egan
• 0:50—Buns, while in panties in bed with Barry.
••• 0:51—Nude, while making love in bed with Barry.
Long scene.
• 1:06—Breasts under patterned black body suit with
Jessica.
• 1:10—Brief left breast, under body suit.
Pamela Runo . . . . . . . . . . . . . . . . . . . . . . . . . . Rachel
••• 0:12—Right breast while in bubble bath, covered
with bubbles, then rinsed off. Breasts and buns, getting out and walking down hall.
Delia Sheppard . . . . . . . . . . . . . . . . . . . .Jessica Callister
••• 0:10—Full frontal nudity, while tied by her wrists in
bed with Scott.
••• 0:45—Breasts and buns, while making love on the
floor with Scott. Nice close-ups.
Gail Thackray . . . . . . . . . . . . . . . . . . . . Monica Waldman
• 0:00—Breasts in quick clips, while making love with
Scott during nightmare.
Roberta Vasquez. . . . . . . . . . . . . . . . . . . . . . Motel Girl
Jan-Michael Vincent . . . . . . . . . . . . . . . Warren Robillard

### *Sins of the Night* (1993)
(Unrated version reviewed.)
Lee Anne Beaman . . . . . . . . . . . . . . . . . . . . . Sue Ellen
•• 0:46—In black bra and G-string panties under sheer
robe while drunk in her house, then breasts.
Michele Brin. . . . . . . . . . . . . . . . . . . . . . . Laura Winters
• 0:05—In black bra and panties in her house with her
lover. Brief buns in G-string while Jack takes photos.
••• 0:06—Breasts, while making love with her lover.
Long scene.
•• 0:14—Breasts and buns, getting out of bed.
Nick Cassavetes . . . . . . . . . . . . . . . . . . . . .Jack Neitsche
•• 0:48—Buns, while making love in bed with Deborah
Shelton.
Michelle Moffett. . . . . . . . . . . . . . . . . . . . . . . . . . . Kay
••• 0:20—In black bra, then breasts and lower frontal
nudity while making love in bed with Jack. Long
scene.
•• 0:22—Breasts and very brief buns, getting out of
bed.
Miles O'Keeffe . . . . . . . . . . . . . . . . . . . .Tony Falcone

Richard Roundtree. . . . . . . . . . . . . . . . . . . . . . . . . .n.a.
Deborah Shelton. . . . . . . . . . . . . . . .Roxanne Flowers
> 0:00—Doing strip tease dance in black bra and panties during the opening credits.
> 0:39—In white bra and panties when Miles O'Keeffe forces her to dance and strip in front of him.
> ••• 0:48—Breasts, while making love with Jack. Some nice close-ups! Great, long scene.
> 0:55—In blonde wig in red bra and red panties in room with Ted.
> •• 0:58—Breasts during Jack's recollections.
> ••• 1:03—Breasts and buns, while making love with Jack. Long scene.
> 1:13—In blonde wig in red bra and panties on video tape.

Courtney Taylor . . . . . . . . . . . . . . . . . . . . . . . Danielle
> • 1:20—In black bra and panties, then breasts in room with Deborah Shelton and Miles O'Keeffe. Medium long shot. Side of right breast in closer shot.

## Sister Sister (1987)

Jennifer Jason Leigh. . . . . . . . . . . . . . . . . Lucy Bonnard
> •• 0:01—Breasts making love during a dream.
> 0:52—In lingerie talking with Eric Stoltz.
> •• 0:53—Left breast, while making love with Stoltz in her bedroom.
> • 0:58—Breasts in bathtub surrounded by candles.

Eric Stoltz . . . . . . . . . . . . . . . . . . . . . . . Matt Rutledge

## Sisters (1973)

Margot Kidder. . . . . . . . . . . . . . . . . . . .Danielle Breton
> • 0:11—Very brief left breast, undressing while walking down hallway. Long shot.
> • 0:14—Breasts opening her robe on couch for her new boyfriend. Shadows make it hard to see.

Jennifer Salt. . . . . . . . . . . . . . . . . . . . . . . .Grace Collier

## Sitting Ducks (1978)

Michael Emil . . . . . . . . . . . . . . . . . . . . . . . . . . .Simon
> •• 0:45—Buns, while getting out of the bathtub.
> • 0:58—Buns, after getting out of bed and putting his pants on to chase Leona.

Zack Norman . . . . . . . . . . . . . . . . . . . . . . . . . . . Sid
> • 0:42—Brief buns, getting into bathtub to talk with Simon.

Patrice Townsend . . . . . . . . . . . . . . . . . . . . . . Jenny
> ••• 0:55—Breasts, taking off her blouse in room with Sid.
> •• 0:58—Buns and brief left breast, sitting up in bed with Simon after getting seen by Leona.

## Six Degrees of Separation (1993)

Michael Kirby . . . . . . . . . . . . . . . . . . . . Loft Party Guest
Lou Milione. . . . . . . . . . . . . . . . . . . . . . . . . . . Hustler
> ••• 0:39—Nude, in bed with Will Smith, then running around house, terrorizing Donald Sutherland and Stockard Channing.

Donald Sutherland . . . . . . . . . . . . . . . . .Flan Kittredge

## Sketch Artist (1992; Made for Cable Movie)

Belle Avery . . . . . . . . . . . . . . . . . . . . . . . . . . . . .Krista
> • 1:11—Right breast, while making love with Paul by swimming pool. Long shot, don't see her face very well.

Drew Barrymore. . . . . . . . . . . . . . . . . . . . . . . . . Daisy
Collin Bernsen . . . . . . . . . . . . . . . . . . . . . . . Phillipe
Jeff Fahey . . . . . . . . . . . . . . . . . . . . . . . . . . . . . . Jack
> • 0:52—Brief upper half of buns in bed on top of Sean Young.

Stacy Haiduk . . . . . . . . . . . . . . . . . . . . . . . . . .Claire
Charlotte Lewis . . . . . . . . . . . . . . . . . . . . . . . . Leese
> ••• 0:02—Breasts making love on sofa. Buns in G-string, side of right breast, while changing CD. (Does this woman have the most awesome waist-to-chest ratio or what?)

Sean Young . . . . . . . . . . . . . . . . . . . . . . . Rayanne
> 0:51—In black bra in bed with Jeff Fahey.
> •• 0:52—Right breast, several times while making love in bed with Fahey.

## Ski School (1990)

Ava Fabian. . . . . . . . . . . . . . . . . . . . . . . . . . . Victoria
> ••• 0:53—In white bra and panties, then breasts making love with Johnny.

Charlie Spradling . . . . . . . . . . . . . . . . . . . . .Paulette
Darlene Vogel . . . . . . . . . . . . . . . . . . . . . . . . . . . Lori
> • 1:03—Breasts in bed with Johnny.

## Skin Art (1993)

Ariane . . . . . . . . . . . . . . . . . . . . . . . . . . . . . . . . . .Lin
> • 1:00—Left breast when Will pulls her lingerie top down and kisses her.

## Skin Deep (1989)

Diana Barton . . . . . . . . . . . . . . . . . . . . . . . . . .Helena
Denise Crosby . . . . . . . . . . . . . . . . . . . . . .Angie Smith
Chelsea Field . . . . . . . . . . . . . . . . . . . . . . . . . . .Amy
Raye Hollitt . . . . . . . . . . . . . . . . . . . . . . . . . . .Lonnie
> • 0:26—Brief side view breasts and buns getting undressed and into bed with John Ritter.

Heidi Paine. . . . . . . . . . . . . . . . . . . . . . . . . . . . . .Tina
> • 0:01—Brief side view breasts sitting on John Ritter's lap while Denise Crosby watches.

Brenda Swanson . . . . . . . . . . . . . . . . . . . . . . . . Emily

## Slam Dance (1987)

Virginia Madsen. . . . . . . . . . . . . . . . . Yolanda Caldwell
Mary Elizabeth Mastrantonio . . . . . . . . . . . Helen Drood
Lisa Niemi . . . . . . . . . . . . . . . . . . . . . . . . . Ms. Schell
> ••• 0:54—Nude in Tom Hulce's apartment.
> • 1:00—Breasts, dead, lying on the floor in Hulce's apartment.

Harry Dean Stanton . . . . . . . . . . . . . . . . . . . . Smiley

## Slammer Girls (1987)

Louis Bonanno. . . . . . . . . . . . . . . . . . . . . . . . .Cubby
Sharon Cain. . . . . . . . . . . . . . . . . . . . . . . . . . . . Rita
> • 0:23—Brief breasts changing clothes under table in the prison cafeteria.

•• 1:01—Breasts walking around an electric chair trying to distract a prison guard.

Philip Campanaro . . . . . . . . . . . . . . . . . . . . . . . . Gary
• 0:48—Buns, while dancing in G-string in front of the girls in their prison cell.
• 0:49—More buns in G-string, while wrestling with Melody.

Tally Chanel . . . . . . . . . . . . . . . . . . . . . . . Candy Treat
• 0:56—Buns, in G-string, doing a dance routine wearing feathery pasties for the Governor in the hospital.

Jeff Eagle . . . . . . . . . . . . . . . . . . . . . . . Harry Wiener

Samantha Fox . . . . . . . . . . . . . . . . . . . . . . . Mosquito
•• 0:17—Breasts in the shower hassling Melody with Tank.

Jane Hamilton . . . . . . . . . . . . . . . . . . . Miss Crabapples

Devon Jenkin . . . . . . . . . . . . . . . . . . Melody Campbell
0:08—In lingerie in her bedroom, then in jail.
• 0:12—Brief breasts getting lingerie ripped off by the prison matron.
• 0:16—Brief breasts getting blouse ripped off by Tank in the shower.

Kim Kafkaloff . . . . . . . . . . . . . . . . . . . . . . . . . Ginny
• 0:23—Brief breasts changing clothes under table in the prison cafeteria.

Sharon Kelly . . . . . . . . . . . . . . . . . . . . . . . Professor
• 0:23—Brief breasts changing clothes under table in the prison cafeteria.
•• 0:34—Breasts squishing breasts against the window during prison visiting hours.
•• 0:36—Breasts with an inflatable male doll.

Adriane Lee . . . . . . . . . . . . . . . . . . . . . Dead Convict

Maria Machart . . . . . . . . . . . . . . . . . . . . . . . Hooker
•• 0:06—Breasts, getting fondled by a cop.

Darcy Nychols . . . . . . . . . . . . . . . . . . . . . . . . . Tank
• 0:17—Breasts ripping blouse open while hassling Melody.

## Slap Shot (1977)

Lindsay Crouse . . . . . . . . . . . . . . . . . . . Lily Braden

Melinda Dillon . . . . . . . . . . . . . . . . . . . . . Suzanne
••• 0:30—Right breast, lying in bed with Paul Newman, then breasts sitting up and talking. Nice, long scene.

Paul Newman . . . . . . . . . . . . . . . . . . . Reggie Dunlop

Michael Ontkean . . . . . . . . . . . . . . . . . . Ned Braden
•• 1:56—Brief buns while wearing a jock strap, while skating off the hockey rink and carrying a trophy.

M. Emmet Walsh . . . . . . . . . . . . . . . . . . . Dickie Dunn

Jennifer Warren . . . . . . . . . . . . . . . . . Francine Dunlop

## The Slasher (1975)

Sylva Koscina . . . . . . . . . . . . . . . . . . . . . . . Barbara
•• 0:17—Left breast lying down getting a massage.
•• 1:18—Breasts undressing and putting a robe on at her lover's house. Left breast after getting stabbed.

## Slaughter (1972)

Marlene Clark . . . . . . . . . . . . . . . . . . . . Kim Walker
• 0:11—Very brief buns and right breast, getting thrown out of room by Jim Brown.

Stella Stevens . . . . . . . . . . . . . . . . . . . . . . . . . . Ann
•• 0:47—Left breast, several times in bed with Jim Brown.
• 0:55—Left breast, making love in bed with Brown again. Dark.
• 0:57—Brief right breast, in bed afterwards. Close up shot.
••• 1:14—Buns and breasts taking a shower and getting out. This is her best nude scene.

Rip Torn . . . . . . . . . . . . . . . . . . . . . . . . . . . . Hoffo

## Slaughter High (1986)

Billy Hartman . . . . . . . . . . . . . . . . . . . . . . . . . Frank
• 1:00—Brief buns while in bed with Stella.

Caroline Munro . . . . . . . . . . . . . . . . . . . . . . . Carol
0:19—Walking around her house in lingerie and a robe.

Simon Scuddamore . . . . . . . . . . . . . . . . . . . . Marty
• 0:05—Nude in girl's shower room when his classmates pull a prank on him.

## Slaughterhouse Five (1972)

Perry King . . . . . . . . . . . . . . . . . . . . . Robert Pilgrim

Ron Liebman . . . . . . . . . . . . . . . . . . . . Paul Lazzaro

Valerie Perrine . . . . . . . . . . . . . . . . Montana Wildhack
• 0:39—Breasts in *Playboy* magazine as a Playmate.
• 0:43—Breasts getting into the bathtub.
••• 1:27—Breasts in a dome with Michael Sacks.

## Slaughterhouse Rock (1988)

Toni Basil . . . . . . . . . . . . . . . . . . . . . Sammy Mitchell

Hope Marie Carlton . . . . . . . . . . . . . . . Krista Halpern
• 0:09—Brief right breast, taking off her top in bedroom with her boyfriend.
•• 0:49—Breasts, getting raped by Richard as he turns into a monster.

## Slave of the Cannibal God (1979; Italian)

Ursula Andress . . . . . . . . . . . . . . . . . . . . . . . . n.a.
•• 0:33—Breasts taking off shirt and putting on a T-shirt.
••• 1:07—Nude getting tied to a pole by the Cannibal People and covered with red paint.
1:20—Brief peek at buns under her skirt when running away from the Cannibal People.

Stacy Keach . . . . . . . . . . . . . . . . . . . . . . . . . . n.a.

## Slavegirls from Beyond Infinity (1987)

Cindy Beal . . . . . . . . . . . . . . . . . . . . . . . . . . . Tisa
0:25—Walking around in white bra and panties.
••• 0:36—Breasts on beach wearing white panties.
• 1:05—Left breast leaning back on table while getting attacked by Zed.

Elizabeth Kaitan . . . . . . . . . . . . . . . . . . . . . . Daria
••• 0:38—Breasts undressing and jumping into bed with Rik.

Brinke Stevens . . . . . . . . . . . . . . . . . . . . . . . Shala
• 0:29—Chained up wearing black lingerie. Brief right breast.

- 0:31—Brief side view of left breast on table. Nice pan from her feet to her head while she's lying on her back.

## Slavers (1977)
Britt Ekland ............................Anna
- 0:40—Breasts undressing in front of Ron Ely.

## Slaves of New York (1989)
Steve Buscemi........................ Wilfredo
Nick Corri ...................... Marley Mantello
Adam Coleman Howard ................... Stash
- 1:15—Buns, while putting on his pants and silhouette of penis. Dark, hard to see.
Jennifer Lee .........................n.a.
Madeleine Potter........................ Daria
- 1:14—Breasts making love with Stash on chair. Mostly see left breast. Dark.
Chris Sarandon ..................... Victor Okrent

## Sleepaway Camp II: Unhappy Campers (1988)
Carol Chambers ...................... Brooke
Valerie Hartman .........................Ally
- 0:06—Breasts waking up and stretching in bed, then standing next to bathroom.
- 0:33—Breasts in Polaroid photographs that Angela confiscates from the boys.
- 0:39—In beige bra, then breasts in restroom stall with Rob.
- 0:43—Breasts making love in the woods with Rob, then getting dressed. Nice!
Susan Marie Snyder........................Mare
- 0:08—Brief breasts lifting up her T-shirt.
- 0:24—Brief breasts flashing in boy's cabin.
- 0:33—Breasts in Polaroid photograph that Angela confiscates from the boys.
Pamela Springsteen...................... Angela

## Sleepaway Camp III: Teenage Wasteland (1989)
Tracy Griffith......................Marcia Holland
Pamela Springsteen.................Angela Baker
Jill Terashita............................ Arab
- 0:16—Breasts putting sweatshirt on.

## The Sleeping Car (1990)
Judie Aronson ............................ Kim
- 0:42—Brief breasts on top of David Naughton making love. Brief breasts three times after he hallucinates.
Jeff Conaway........................ Bud Sorenson
Sandra Margot ................. 19-Year Old Girl
- 0:00—Brief breasts shots taking off clothes then making love with a guy. Left breast while making love.
Dani Minnick........................ Joanne
David Naughton ................... Jason McCree

## Sliver (1993)
William Baldwin .................... Zeke Hawkins
- 1:03—Buns, while sneaking up behind Sharon Stone and making love while standing up.
Tom Berenger.................... Jack Landsford

Colleen Camp ...................... Judy Marks
Sharon Stone ......................... Carly Norris
- 0:14—Brief left breast, while in bathtub.
- 0:43—Buns, in black bra, while making love on William Baldwin's lap.
- 0:44—Half of right breast, while under Baldwin.
- 0:45—Brief left breast, while getting up out of bed. Side view breasts and buns, while getting dressed.
- 0:46—Buns and breasts, while taking off her top again.

## Sloane (1984)
Debra Blee ...................... Cynthia Thursby
- 0:15—Very brief breasts during attempted rape.
Ann Milhench ..................... Janice Thursby
- 0:02—Breasts and buns getting out of shower and being held by kidnappers.

## Slow Burn (1986)
Beverly D'Angelo ................... Laine Fleischer
- 1:01—Breasts making love with Eric Roberts. Don't see her face. Part of lower frontal nudity showing tattoo.
Eric Roberts ........................ Jacob Asch

## Slumber Party '57 (1976)
Bridget Holloman..................... Bonnie May
- 0:10—Breasts with her five girl friends during swimming pool scene. Hard to tell who is who.
- 0:26—Left breast in truck with her cousin Cal.
Joyce Jillson ......................... Gladys
Janice Karman ......................... Hank
- 1:06—Breasts, sitting watching Smitty and David make love in the stable.
Noelle North ...........................Angie
- 0:37—Buns, then breasts in bed with a party guest of her parents.
Cheryl Smith ...................... Sherry
Debra Winger ...................... Debbie
- 0:10—Breasts with her five girl friends during swimming pool scene. Hard to tell who is who.
- 0:53—Breasts three times, lying down, making out with Bud.
Janet Wood ...................... Smitty
- 0:10—Breasts with her five girl friends during swimming pool scene. Hard to tell who is who.
- 1:06—Left breast, then breasts in stable with David while his sister watches.

## The Slumber Party Massacre (1982)
Debra De Liso ........................... Kim
- 0:08—Very brief breasts getting soap from Trish in the shower.
- 0:29—In beige bra and panties, then breasts putting on a U.S.A. shirt while changing with the other girls.
Joseph Alan Johnson......................... Neil
Michele Michaels ...................... Trish
- 0:01—Breasts, in white panties, while getting dressed.
- 0:08—Buns, then brief breasts while passing the soap to Kim.

•• 0:29—Breasts, in white panties, while putting shirt on while two boys watch from outside.

David Millbern . . . . . . . . . . . . . . . . . . . . . . . . . . . Jeff

Brinke Stevens. . . . . . . . . . . . . . . . . . . . . . . . . Linda

•• 0:07—Buns, then breasts taking a shower during girls locker room scene.

### Slumber Party Massacre II (1987)

Juliette Cummins. . . . . . . . . . . . . . . . . . . . . . . Sheila

•• 0:24—In black bra, then breasts in living room during a party with her girlfriends.

Heidi Kozak . . . . . . . . . . . . . . . . . . . . . . . . . . . . Sally

Kimberly McArthur . . . . . . . . . . . . . . . . . . . . . . . Amy

### A Small Circle of Friends (1980)

Karen Allen . . . . . . . . . . . . . . . . . . . . . . . . . . . Jessica

• 0:47—Brief breasts in bathroom with Brad Davis. Don't see her face.

• 0:48—Very brief breasts, pushing Davis off her. Then very, very brief half of left breast turning around to walk to the mirror.

Brad Davis. . . . . . . . . . . . . . . . . . . . . . . Leo DaVinci

•• 1:22—Brief buns, while dropping his pants with several other guys for Army draft inspection.

Shelley Long . . . . . . . . . . . . . . . . . . . . . . . . . . . Alice

Jameson Parker . . . . . . . . . . . . . . . . . . . . . . Nick Baxter

Daniel Stern . . . . . . . . . . . . . . . . . . . . . . . Crazy Kid

• 1:22—Brief buns, while dropping his pants with several other guys for Army draft inspection.

### Small Kill (1991)

Rebecca Ferratti. . . . . . . . . . . . . . . . . . . Diana Conti

Alan Popper . . . . . . . . . . . . . . . . . . . . . Thomas Stanzak

• 0:21—Buns, while crazily running around outside in a jockstrap.

### Smash Palace (1981; New Zealand)

Bruno Lawrence . . . . . . . . . . . . . . . . . . . . . . . Al Shaw

••• 0:39—Buns while in bed after arguing, then making up with Jacqui.

Anna-Maria Monticelli. . . . . . . . . . . . . . . Jacqui Shaw

0:21—Silhouette of right breast changing while sitting on the edge of the bed.

••• 0:39—Breasts in bed after arguing, then making up with Bruno Lawrence.

### Smile (1974)

Colleen Camp. . . . . . . . . . . . . . . . . Connie Thompson

0:47—Side profile of right breast and buns in dressing room while Little Bob is outside taking pictures.

Bruce Dern . . . . . . . . . . . . . . . . . . . . . . . . . . .Big Bob

Melanie Griffith . . . . . . . . . . . . . . . . . . . . . . Karen Love

0:07—Brief glimpse at panties, bending over to pick up dropped box.

• 0:34—Very, very brief side view of right breast in dressing room, just before passing behind a rack of clothes.

• 0:47—Very brief side view of right breast, then side view of left breast when Little Bob is outside taking pictures.

• 0:48—Very brief breasts as Polaroid photograph that Little Bob took develops.

• 1:51—Breasts in the same Polaroid in the policeman's sun visor.

Annette O'Toole. . . . . . . . . . . . . . . . . . . . Doria Houston

0:34—In white bra and panties in dressing room.

1:06—In white bra and slip talking to Joan Prather in bedroom.

Joan Prather . . . . . . . . . . . . . . . . . . . . . . . . . . .Robin

• 0:47—Brief buns in dressing room, while taking off pants while Little Bob is outside taking pictures. (She's wearing a pink ribbon in her hair.)

### Smoke Screen (1988)

Kim Cattrall . . . . . . . . . . . . . . . . . . . . . Odessa Muldoon

0:31—Brief half of right breast sitting in bed with sheet pulled up on her.

•• 1:16—Breasts in bed on top of Gerald.

••• 1:17—Breasts lying in bed under Gerald while he kisses her breasts.

### Smooth Talker (1990)

Suzanne Ager. . . . . . . . . . . . . . . . . Candy (The 976-GIRL)

• 0:23—Left breast and partial buns, while lying on the floor dead.

• 0:24—More left breast, while lying dead on the floor. Lit with red light.

• 0:35—Left breast, while lying dead on the floor. Very brief buns in G-string.

Julie Austin . . . . . . . . . . . . . . . . . . . . . . . . Ms. Weston

Blair Weickgenant . . . . . . . . . . . . . . . . . . Lisa Charles

• 0:33—Breasts, lying in bed and sitting up during Carl's B&W fantasy.

### SnakeEater (1988)

Josie Bell. . . . . . . . . . . . . . . . . . . . . . . . . . . The Kid

• 0:39—Very brief side view of right breast and buns, while walking past open doorway while Lorenzo Lamas watches. Medium long shot.

### SnakeEater III ...His Law (1992)

Holly Chester . . . . . . . . . . . . . . . . . . . . . . . . . . .Fran

••• 0:30—Breasts and buns in G-string while dancing on stage in club.

Tracy Cook. . . . . . . . . . . . . . . . . . . . . . Hildy Gardener

••• 0:27—Breasts, while making love with Lorenzo Lamas in bedroom.

### Snapdragon (1993)

Pamela Anderson . . . . . . . . . . . . . . . . . . . . . . . .Felicity

• 0:06—Brief side view of right breast, while making love on top of a guy in bed before killing him.

• 0:26—Right breast, while making love on top of another guy in bed before killing him.

••• 0:55—Breasts and buns, while making love in bed on top of Steven Bauer in his dream.

• 1:06—In white bra and panties, then left breast and buns while making love on top of Bauer on the floor.

••• 1:22—Breasts and buns, while making love with Bauer.

Steven Bauer . . . . . . . . . . . . . . . . . . . . . . . . .David

Chelsea Field . . . . . . . . . . . . . . . . . . . . . . . .Peckham
  0:11—In black bra, while making love on top of
  Steven Bauer in bed.
Diana Lee-Hsu . . . . . . . . . . . . . . . . . . . Professor Huan

### *So, I Married an Axe Murderer* (1993)
Anthony LaPaglia . . . . . . . . . . . . . . . . . Tony Giardino
Debi Mazar . . . . . . . . . . . . . . . .Tony's Girlfriend Susan
Mike Myers . . . . . . Charlie MacKenzie/Stuart MacKenzie
 •• 1:00—Buns, when towel around his waist falls down
  when hugging Ralph. Don't see his face.
Amanda Plummer . . . . . . . . . . . . . . . . . .Rose Michaels
Nancy Travis . . . . . . . . . . . . . . . . . . . Harriet Michaels

### *Society* (1989)
Devin De Vasquez . . . . . . . . . . . . . . . . . . . . . Clarisa
 ••• 0:37—Breasts, making love in bed with Billy.
 • 0:40—Left breast, while on sofa with Billy when her
  mother comes home.
Heidi Kozak . . . . . . . . . . . . . . . . . . . . . . . . . . .Shauna
Caroline Lomas . . . . . . . . . . . . . . . . . . . . . . . . . .n.a.
Jason Williams . . . . . . . . . . . . . . . . . . . . Jason's Friend

### *Soft Touch* (1987; Made for Cable Movie)
(Shown on *The Playboy Channel* as *Birds in Paradise*.)
Jennifer Inch . . . . . . . . . . . . . . . . . . . . .Tracy Anderson
 • 0:01—Full frontal nudity during the opening credits.
 • 0:02—Breasts with her two girlfriends during the
  opening credits.
 ••• 0:17—Breasts exercising on the floor, walking
  around the room, the lying on bed. Long scene.
 • 0:20—Full frontal nudity getting out of bed.
 •• 0:23—Breasts in bed.
 ••• 0:50—Breasts sunbathing on boat with Carrie.
 •• 1:01—Full frontal nudity, sitting on towel, watching
  Carrie.
 • 1:02—Full frontal nudity, waving to a dolphin.
 •• 1:04—Breasts at night by campfire with Carrie.
 ••• 1:05—Brief left breast, then breasts putting on skirt
  and walking around the island.
 •• 1:13—Breasts in hut with island guy.
 • 1:19—Breasts in stills during the end credits.
Jeanine Louise . . . . . . . . . . . . . . . . . . . Carrie Crawford
 • 0:00—Breasts during opening credits.
 • 0:02—Breasts with her two girlfriends during the
  opening credits.
 • 0:03—Brief breasts getting out of the shower.
 • 0:17—Breasts seen in mirror, while taking a shower.
 ••• 0:19—Full frontal nudity during pillow fight on bed.
 •• 0:23—Breasts in bed with the other two girls.
 • 0:27—Breasts in T-shirt, leaning over to wash car.
 • 0:32—Breasts with Neill in open dress.
 ••• 0:35—Dancing on stage in red lingerie, then breasts
  and buns in G-string.
 •• 0:41—Full frontal nudity walking in water with a
  guy.
 ••• 0:50—Breasts sunbathing on the boat with Tracy.
 • 1:01—Nude, swinging into water. Long shot.
 • 1:02—Buns, waving to a dolphin.
 • 1:04—Breasts at night by campfire with Tracy.
 • 1:05—Brief left breast, while sleeping.

 • 1:06—Breasts when Tracy wakes her up.
 • 1:19—Breasts in stills during the end credits.
Sue Morrow . . . . . . . . . . . . . . . . . . . . . . . Ashley Keyes
 • 0:01—Breasts during opening credits.
 • 0:02—Breasts with her two girlfriends during the
  opening credits.
 •• 0:19—Breasts taking off her T-shirt in bed. More
  breasts sleeping, then waking up.
 • 0:20—Breasts getting out of bed.
 •• 0:22—Breasts making love with a guy.
 • 0:23—Breasts in bed.
 •• 0:53—Breasts on bed with Ensign Landers.
 ••• 0:59—Breasts and buns in play pool with Landers.
 • 1:19—Breasts in stills during end credits.
Jennifer Wyhl . . . . . . . . . . . . . . . . . . . . . . . . . . Nancy
 • 0:00—Breasts during opening credits.

### *Soft Touch II* (1987; Made for Cable Movie)
(Shown on *The Playboy Channel* as *Birds in Paradise*.)
Jennifer Inch . . . . . . . . . . . . . . . . . . . . .Tracy Anderson
 • 0:01—Breasts during opening credits.
 • 0:02—Breasts with her two girlfriends during opening credits.
 •• 0:14—Breasts dancing in Harry's bar by herself.
 • 0:27—Full frontal nudity on stage at Harry's after
  robbers tell her to strip.
 • 0:29—Side of left breast tied to Neill on bed.
 • 0:31—Breasts tied up when Ashley and Carrie discover her.
 •• 0:52—Full frontal nudity during strip poker game,
  then covered with whipped cream.
 • 0:57—Full frontal nudity getting out of bed.
Jeanine Louise . . . . . . . . . . . . . . . . . . . .Carrie Crawford
 • 0:00—Breasts during opening credits.
 • 0:02—Breasts with her two girlfriends during opening credits.
 •• 0:24—Breasts in bed feeling herself.
 •• 0:41—Full frontal nudity undressing and putting
  swimsuit on.
 • 0:51—Breasts with her diving instructor.
Sue Morrow . . . . . . . . . . . . . . . . . . . . . . . Ashley Keyes
 • 0:01—Breasts during opening credits.
 • 0:02—Breasts with her two girlfriends during the
  opening credits.
 •• 0:26—Breasts while sunbathing on boat.
 • 0:50—Brief breasts in the water.
 • 0:52—Breasts during strip poker game, then covered with whipped cream.
 • 0:56—Full frontal nudity getting out of bed.
Jennifer Wyhl . . . . . . . . . . . . . . . . . . . . . . . . . . Nancy
 • 0:01—Breasts during opening credits.
 • 0:05—Breasts in bed with Neill.
 • 0:18—Breasts undressing for robbers. Brief full frontal nudity.
 •• 0:57—Breasts in bed with Neill.
 •• 1:01—Full frontal nudity in bed with Neill.

### *Solar Crisis* (1992)
Brenda Bakke . . . . . . . . . . . . . . . . . . . . .Claire Beeson
Peter Boyle . . . . . . . . . . . . . . . . . . . . . .Arnold Teague

Silvana Gallardo . . . . . . . . . . . . . . . . . . . . . . . . . T.C.
Charlton Heston . . . . . . . . . . . . . .Admiral "Skeet" Kelso
Tim Matheson. . . . . . . . . . . . . . . . . . . . . . . Steve Kelso
Annabel Schofield . . . . . . . . . . . . . . . . . . . Alex Noffe
- •• 0:34—Breasts in the shower.
- •• 0:35—Breasts, sitting in chair, getting her mind probed.
- •• 0:54—Brief breasts during recollection of shower scene. Slightly distorted and out of focus.

### Soldier Blue *(1970)*
Candice Bergen. . . . . . . . . . . . . . Cresta Marybelle Lee
- • 0:57—Close-up of buns, in open skirt while in back of wagon when Peter Strauss tries to cover her up. Don't see her face.

### Soldier of Orange *(1977; Dutch)*
Derek De Lint . . . . . . . . . . . . . . . . . . . . . . . . . . . Alex
Edward Fox . . . . . . . . . . . . . . . . . . . . . . . . . Col. Rafelli
Rutger Hauer. . . . . . . . . . . . . . . . . . . . . Erik Lanshoff
Jeroen Krabbé . . . . . . . . . . . . . . . . . . . . . . . . . . .Gus
Susan Penhaligon . . . . . . . . . . . . . . . . . . . . . Susan
- • 1:34—Brief breasts kissing her boyfriend when Rutger Hauer sees them through the window. Medium long shot.
- ••• 1:36—Breasts in bed with her boyfriend and Hauer.

### A Soldier's Tale *(1988; New Zealand)*
Marianne Basler . . . . . . . . . . . . . . . . . . . . . . . Belle
- • 0:19—Brief breasts, while undressing in bedroom for Gabriel Byrne.
- •• 0:21—Breasts in bed with Byrne.
- •• 1:02—Buns and brief breasts while washing herself when Byrne sees her.
Gabriel Byrne . . . . . . . . . . . . . . . . . . . . . . . . . . Saul
Judge Reinhold . . . . . . . . . . . . . . . . . . . . . The Yank

### Sole Survivor *(1982)*
Anita Skinner. . . . . . . . . . . . . . . . . . . . Denise Watson
- . 0:29—Very, very brief right breast in bed with Dr. Richardson. Brief side view of right breast when he jumps out of bed.
  1:13—In bra, zipping up pants.
Brinke Stevens. . . . . . . . . . . . . . . . . . . . . . . .Jennifer
- •• 0:45—Breasts after taking off bra while playing strip poker.

### Some Call It Loving *(1972)*
Tisa Farrow . . . . . . . . . . . . . . . . . . . . . . . . . .Jennifer
- ••• 1:17—Breasts in bed with Troy.
Brandy Herred. . . . . . . . . . . . . . . . . . . . . Cheerleader
- ••• 1:12—Nude dancing in a club doing a strip tease dance in a cheerleader outfit.
Richard Pryor . . . . . . . . . . . . . . . . . . . . . . . . . . Jeff
Carol White. . . . . . . . . . . . . . . . . . . . . . . . . . Scarlett

### Some Girls *(1988)*
*a.k.a. Sisters*
Jennifer Connelly. . . . . . . . . . . . . . . . . . . . .Gabriella
Patrick Dempsey . . . . . . . . . . . . . . . . . . . . . Michael
- • 0:34—Brief frontal nudity, then buns while running all around the house chasing Jennifer Connelly.

André Gregory. . . . . . . . . . . . . . . . . . . . . . Mr. D'Arc
- • 1:24—Buns, while standing in the study looking at a book. Very brief frontal nudity when he turns around to sit at his desk.
Sheila Kelley. . . . . . . . . . . . . . . . . . . . . . . . . Irenka
- • 0:13—Breasts and buns getting something at the end of the hall while Michael watches. Long shot, hard to see.
- • 1:01—Breasts in window while Michael watches from outside. Long shot, hard to see.
  1:17—In black slip seducing Michael after funeral.

### Something Wild *(1986)*
Jeff Daniels. . . . . . . . . . . . . . . . . . . . . .Charles Driggs
- •• 0:16—Buns, while lying in bed after making love with Melanie Griffith.
Melanie Griffith . . . . . . . . . . . . . "Lulu"/Audrey Hankel
- ••• 0:16—Strips to breasts in bed with Jeff Daniels.
- • 0:24—Buns and brief breasts, while looking out the window.
Anna Levine Thomson . . . . . . . . . . . . .The Girl in 3F
Ray Liotta. . . . . . . . . . . . . . . . . . . . . . . . Ray Sinclair
Tracey Walter. . . . . . . . . . . . . . . . . The Country Squire

### Son-In-Law *(1993)*
Cindy Pickett . . . . . . . . . . . . . . . . . . . . . . . Connie
Pauly Shore . . . . . . . . . . . . . . . . . . . . . . . . . .Crawl
- •• 0:37—Buns while wearing cowboy chaps with no pants underneath while trying clothes on in store.

### Sorceress *(1982)*
Ana de Sade. . . . . . . . . . . . . . . . . . . . . . . . . Delisia
Lee Anne Harris . . . . . . . . . . . . . . . . . . . . . . . Mira
- ••• 0:11—Breasts (on the left) greeting the creature with her sister. Upper half of buns, getting dressed.
- ••• 0:29—Breasts (she's the second one) undressing with her sister in front of Erlick and Baldar.
Lynette Harris. . . . . . . . . . . . . . . . . . . . . . . . . Mara
- ••• 0:11—Breasts (on the right) greeting the creature with her sister.
- ••• 0:29—Breasts (she's the first one) undressing with her sister in front of Erlick and Baldar.
David Millbern . . . . . . . . . . . . . . . . . . . . . . . . . n.a.
Bob Nelson . . . . . . . . . . . . . . . . . . . . . . . . . Erlick
- • 0:43—Brief buns, just before being put to death.
- •• 0:45—Buns, while getting massaged.

### Sorority Babes in the Slimeball Bowl-O-Rama *(1988)*
Carla Baron . . . . . . . . . . . . . . . . . . . . . . . . .Frankie
Michelle Bauer . . . . . . . . . . . . . . . . . . . . . . . . . Lisa
  0:07—In panties getting spanked with Brinke Stevens.
- ••• 0:12—Breasts brushing herself in the front of mirror while Stevens takes a shower.
- • 0:14—Brief full frontal nudity when the three nerds fall into the bathroom.
  0:33—In black bra, panties, garter belt and stockings asking for Keith.
  0:35—Wearing the same lingerie, on top of Keith in the locker room.

- ••• 0:40—Breasts taking off her bra.
- ••• 0:43—More breasts undoing garter belt.
- •• 0:46—More breasts in locker room.
- •• 0:47—More breasts taking off stockings.
- • 1:04—Full frontal nudity sitting on the floor by herself.
- •• 1:05—Full frontal nudity getting up after the lights go out. Kind of dark.

George "Buck" Flower.....................Janitor
Linnea Quigley...........................Spider
Brinke Stevens............................Taffy
  0:07—In panties getting spanked with Michelle Bauer.
- ••• 0:12—Nude showering off whipped cream in bathtub while talking to a breasts Michelle Bauer. Excellent long scene!

## Sorority Girls and the Creature from Hell (1990)

Dori Courtney.........................Belinda
- •• 0:06—Breasts, drying herself off after shower. (Wearing panties.)
- ••• 0:08—More breasts, still drying herself off.
- • 0:12—Brief right breast, while in car with J.J.
- ••• 0:35—Breasts in spa with J.J.
- • 0:37—Buns, then left breast, while in spa during Gerald's fantasy.
- ••• 0:41—Breasts taking off her top by stream while J.J. gets killed.
- •• 0:43—Breasts, running around at night getting chased by the creature.

Vicki Darnell............................Dancer
  0:17—Breasts in bar in open blouse, dancing on stage. Lit with red light.
  • 0:24—More breasts dancing on stage.

Deborah Dutch.......................Mary Anne
  0:08—Very brief, side of left breast changing clothes in background.
- • 0:32—Lower half of left breast, dancing in cabin.

Kelli Lee............. Nude Double for Dori Courtney
- • 0:23—Breasts in bedroom with J.J.
- • 0:36—Breasts getting playfully strangled by Skip in the spa. Buns, getting out.

Ashley St. Jon........................ Bar Patron

## Sorority House Massacre (1987)

Joe Nassi.................................. Craig
- • 0:50—Buns, while running away from the killer that has just killed his girlfriend Tracy in a tepee.

Nicole Rio.................................. Tracy
- •• 0:20—In a sheer bra changing clothes with two other girls in a bedroom.
- •• 0:49—Breasts in a tepee with her boyfriend, Craig, just before getting killed.

## Sorority House Massacre 2 (1990)

Dana Bentley Konkel....................... Janey
- ••• 0:23—Breasts in bedroom talking to Suzanne and looking in the mirror. Buns, while getting dressed in black bodysuit.
  0:48—Left breast, sticking out of bodysuit, covered with blood, when the girls discover her dead.

Bridget Carney........................... Candy
- ••• 0:40—Breasts and buns in G-string, dancing in club.

Melissa Anne Moore....................... Jessica
- ••• 0:22—Breasts, talking to Kimberly, then taking a shower.
  0:50—In wet lingerie.
- • 0:53—Buns, while going up the stairs.

Toni Naples........................ Sgt. Shawlee
Gail Thackray............................Linda
- •• 0:25—In bra and panties, then breasts while changing clothes.
  0:50—In wet lingerie.

Michelle Verran .......................Suzanne
- ••• 0:23—Buns in panties, then breasts changing clothes.

Shannon Wilsey ........................ Satana
- •• 0:43—Breasts and buns in G-string, dancing in club.

Stacia Zhivago ........................ Kimberly
- ••• 0:21—Nude, taking a shower.
  0:50—In wet lingerie.
- • 0:53—Buns, while going up the stairs.
  0:55—Brief buns, while going up the stairs.
- • 1:00—Brief breasts, sitting up in bathtub filled with bloody water to strangle Linda.

## Sorority House Party (1992)

Avalon Anders ..........................Miranda
- • 1:05—Breasts and buns under sheer purple body suit.
  1:18—Briefly hanging out of car to flash her bra to distract bad guys.

Debra Beatty ............. Mennonite Fury Woman
April Lerman ............................Alex
  0:49—In bra while starting to make love with Jamie Z.
- ••• 0:50—Breasts, while making love on bed with Jamie Z.
  1:00—Right breast, while in bubble bath with Jamie.

Nicole Sassaman ...............Topless Sorority Girl
- •• 0:39—Breasts, opening Alex's bedroom door to ask for a bra.

Elizabeth Zimmie ...........Screaming Sorority Girl

## South Beach (1992)

Vanity ........................ Jennifer Derringer
Peter Fonda ............................. Jake
Robert Forster ........................... Ted
Sam Jones ............................. Billy
Stella Stevens........................... Nancy
Robin Trapp.............................Casey
- ••• 0:59—Buns, while making love with Fred Williamson. Nice close-up of breasts.

Fred Williamson ................... Mack Derringer

## South of Reno (1987)

Lisa Blount .........................Anette Clark
  1:02—In black bra getting blouse torn open while lying down.

Danitza Kingsley.........................Louise
Julie Montgomery .......................Susan
- • 1:22—Brief breasts kissing Martin. Dark, hard to see.

1:25—In motel room wearing black top and panties, then pink spandex top with the panties.

### The Southern Star *(1969; French/British)*
Ursula Andress . . . . . . . . . . . . . . . . . . . . . . Erica Kramer
- 1:07—Buns, walking into lake to wash herself. Long shot.
- 1:08—Breasts seen through water while she talks to George Segal.

### Spaced Out *(1980; British)*
*a.k.a. Outer Touch*
Glory Annen . . . . . . . . . . . . . . . . . . . . . . . . . Cosia
- ••• 0:23—Breasts talking to the other two space women. Long scene.
- 0:31—Very brief breasts changing clothes while dancing.
- 0:43—Breasts in bed with Willy.
- ••• 1:08—Breasts lying down.

Ava Cadell . . . . . . . . . . . . . . . . . . . . . . . . . . . . Partha
- •• 0:41—Left breast making love on bed with Cliff.
- •• 0:42—Nude wrestling on bed with Cliff.
- 0:43—Brief left breast lying in bed alone.
- •• 1:08—Breasts sitting on bed.

Kate Ferguson . . . . . . . . . . . . . . . . . . . . . . . Skipper
- 1:07—Brief breasts making love with Willy in bed. Lit with red light.

Tony Maiden . . . . . . . . . . . . . . . . . . . . . . . . . . . Willy
- 0:38—Buns, while getting examined by Cosia.

Michael Rowlatt . . . . . . . . . . . . . . . . . . . . . . . Cliff
- 0:42—Buns, while getting out of bed trying to get away from Partha.

Barry Stokes . . . . . . . . . . . . . . . . . . . . . . . . Oliver
- 0:54—Buns, while undressing to get in bed with Prudence.

### Speaking Parts *(1989; Canadian)*
Gabrielle Rose . . . . . . . . . . . . . . . . . . . . . . . . Clara
- •• 0:41—Right breast, on TV monitor, masturbating with Lance. Then breasts getting dressed.

### Special Effects *(1984)*
Eric Bogosian . . . . . . . . . . . . . . . . . . . . . . Neville
- 0:21—Buns, while fighting with Zoe Tamerlis in bed. Medium long shot.

Zoe Tamerlis . . . . . . . . . . . . . . . . . . . . . Amelia/Elaine
- 0:01—Side view of right breast, wearing pasties during photo session.
- 0:16—Brief breasts sitting by pool with Eric Bogozian.
- •• 0:19—Breasts getting into bed and in bed with Bogozian.
- 0:22—Breasts, dead in spa while Bogozian washes her off.
- 0:44—Brief breasts in moviola that Bogozian watches.
- •• 1:12—Breasts making love on bed with Keefe.
- 1:17—Breasts getting into bed during filming of movie. Brief breasts during Bogozian's flashbacks.
- 1:20—More left breast shots on moviola getting strangled.

- ••• 1:33—Breasts with Bogozian when he takes her dress off.
- 1:35—Breasts sitting on bed kissing Bogozian. More breasts and more flashbacks.
- 1:40—Brief breasts during struggle. Dark.

### The Specialist *(1975)*
Ahna Capri . . . . . . . . . . . . . . . . . . . . . . . . Londa Wyeth
- ••• 0:10—Breasts, while in bed, talking on the phone.
- ••• 0:28—Breasts on couch, posing for Bert.
- •• 1:09—Breasts, sitting up in bed and putting robe on.

Christiane Schmidtmer . . . . . . . . . . . . . . . Nude Model
- ••• 0:12—Breasts, posing for artist, then buns when she gets up to leave.

### Spellbinder *(1988)*
Alexandra Morgan . . . . . . . . . . . . . . . . . . . . . Pamela
Kelly Preston . . . . . . . . . . . . . . . . . . . . . . Miranda Reed
- ••• 0:19—Breasts in bed making love with Timothy Daly.
- 1:26—Dancing around in a sheer white gown with nothing underneath during cult ceremony at the beach.

Rick Rossovich . . . . . . . . . . . . . . . . . . . . . Derek Clayton

### Spetters *(1980; Dutch)*
Toon Agterberg . . . . . . . . . . . . . . . . . . . . . . . . Hans
- ••• 0:35—Frontal nudity, measuring and comparing his manlihood with his friends in the auto shop.
- 1:21—Buns, getting gang raped by gay guy he has been stealing money from.

Rutger Hauer . . . . . . . . . . . . . . . . . . . . . . . . Witkamp
Jeroen Krabbé . . . . . . . . . . . . . . . . . . . . . . . . Henkhof
Reneé Soutendijk . . . . . . . . . . . . . . . . . . . . . . . Fientje
- •• 1:12—Breasts making love in trailer with Jeff.

Maarten Spanjer . . . . . . . . . . . . . . . . . . . . . . . . . Jeff
- ••• 0:35—Frontal nudity, measuring and comparing his manlihood with his friends in the auto shop.
- 1:12—Buns while climbing into bed in trailer with Reneé Soutendijk.

Hans Van Tongeren . . . . . . . . . . . . . . . . . Ron Hartman
- ••• 0:35—Frontal nudity, measuring and comparing his manlihood with his friends in the auto shop.

### Spiker
Stephen W. Burns . . . . . . . . . . . . . . . . . Sonny Flestow
- 0:03—Buns in room.

### Spirits *(1991)*
Michelle Bauer . . . . . . . . . . . . . . . . . . . . . . Sister Mary
- ••• 0:21—Breasts, taking off nun's habit, trying to seduce Erik Estrada. Brief lower frontal nudity and buns also. Long scene.

Kaitlin Hopkins . . . . . . . . . . . . Succubus/Mrs. Heron
- •• 0:36—Breasts, several times, in bed on top of Harry. Then in gross make-up.

Carol Lynley . . . . . . . . . . . . . . . . . . . . . . . . Sister Jillian
Sandra Margot . . . . . . . . . . . . . . . . . . . . . . Nun Demon
Brinke Stevens . . . . . . . . . . . . . . . . . . . . Amy Goldwyn

## Splash (1984)

Daryl Hannah . . . . . . . . . . . . . . . . . . . . . . . . . Madison
  0:24—Partial buns, while running into the water at the beach. Looks like hair is taped to her buns.
  • 0:27—Brief right breast, swimming under water, entering the sunken ship.
  • 0:28—Buns, while walking around the Statue of Liberty.
  • 1:26—Brief right, then left breast while in tank when Eugene Levy looks at her.
  • 1:44—Brief right breast, under water when frogman grabs her from behind.
Clint Howard . . . . . : . . . . . . . . . . . .Wedding Guest
Amy Ingersoll . . . . . . . . . . . . . . . . . . . . . Reporter
Ron Kuhlman . . . . . . . . . . . . . . . . . . . Man with Date
Eugene Levy . . . . . . . . . . . . . . . . . . . Walter Kornbluth
Valerie Wildman . . . . . . . . . . . . . . . . . . .Wedding Guest

## Split Second (1992)

Kim Cattrall . . . . . . . . . . . . . . . . . . . . . . . . Michelle
  •• 0:43—Breasts in the shower.
  •• 0:45—Breasts in the shower, when Rutger Hauer opens the curtains.
Rutger Hauer . . . . . . . . . . . . . . . . . . . . . . . . Stone
Tina Shaw . . . . . . . . . . . . . . . . . . . Nightclub Stripper
  •• 0:07—Breasts, dancing in club in black S&M outfit, wearing a mask over her head.

## Splitting Heirs (1993)

John Cleese . . . . . . . . . . . . . . . . . . . . . . . . .Shadgrind
Sadie Frost . . . . . . . . . . . . . . . . . . . . . . . . . Angela
Barbara Hershey . . . . . . . . . . . . . . . . .Duchess Lucinda
Eric Idle . . . . . . . . . . . . . . . . . . . . . . . . . . . . .Tommy
  ••• 0:41—Buns, while hiding in Kitty's apartment after Rick Moranis shows up.
  0:43—Brief side view of buns, walking down the stairs while holding his clothes.
Catherine Zeta Jones . . . . . . . . . . . . . . . . . . . . . Kitty
  • 0:39—Swimming in lap pool (hard to see anything because of the water distortion.) Brief buns and back half of left breast, while getting out of the pool. Long shot.
  0:41—Very, very brief inside half of left breast, while throwing Eric Idle's second shoe to him.

## The Sporting Club (1971)

Margaret Blye . . . . . . . . . . . . . . . . . . . . . . . . Janey
  • 0:31—Breasts, sunbathing on rock when seen by James. Medium long shot.
Robert Fields . . . . . . . . . . . . . . . . . . . . . Verner Stanton
  • 0:24—Buns, mooning the President out the window of a bus.
Jo Ann Harris . . . . . . . . . . . . . . . . . . . . . . . . .Lu
  ••• 0:55—Breasts (mostly right breast) while in the woods, talking to James.
Jack Warden . . . . . . . . . . . . . . . . . . . . . . . . . .Olive

## The Spring (1989)

Shari Shattuck . . . . . . . . . . . . . . . . . . . . . . . .Dyanne
  • 0:00—Nude, several times, swimming under the water. Shot from under water.

  • 0:50—Breasts and buns, swimming under water.
  •• 0:51—Breasts, getting out of the water.
  •• 0:59—Brief breasts, turning over in bed with Dack Rambo.
  • 1:05—Standing up in wet lingerie, then swimming under water.
Virginia Watson . . . . . . . . . . . . . . . . . . . . . . Pafinya
  •• 0:45—Breasts taking off her top in front of Dack Rambo in his hotel room.

## Spring Break (1983; Canadian)

Corinne Alphen . . . . . . . . . . . . . . . . . . . . . . . . .Joan
  0:32—Taking a shower in a two piece bathing suit in an outdoor shower at the beach.
Sheila Kennedy . . . . . . . . . . . . . . . . . . . . . . . . Carla
  •• 0:49—Breasts during wet T-shirt contest.
Perry Lang . . . . . . . . . . . . . . . . . . . . . . . . . . Adam
  • 0:27—Brief buns while opening his towel in the shower, mooning his three friends.

## Spring Fever USA (1988)

*a.k.a. Lauderdale*
Amy Lynn Baxter . . . . . . . . . . . . . . Amy (Car Wash Girl)
Ron Jeremy . . . . . . . . . . . . . . . . . . . . . . . . . . . n.a.
Mark Levine . . . . . . . . . . . . . . . . . . . . . . .Duke Dork
  • 1:17—Buns, twice, while in boat hallway with his skinny brother after being tricked.
Janine Lindemulder . . . . . . . . . . . . . . . . Heather Lipton
  •• 0:14—Taking off her stockings, then brief breasts undressing for bath, then taking a bath.
Cari Mayor . . . . . . . . . . . . . . . . . . . . Girl on Campus
Robert Moss . . . . . . . . . . . . . . . . . . . . . . Dick Dork
  • 1:17—Buns, twice, while in boat hallway with his heavy brother after being tricked.
Anne Marie Oliver . . . . . . . . . . . . . . . . .Rita Durango
  •• 1:02—Breasts, during wet T-shirt contest.
Sherrie Rose . . . . . . . . . . . . . . . . . . . . . . Vinyl Vixen #1
Reneé Shugart . . . . . . . . . . . . . . . . . . .Beach Beauty

## Spring Symphony (1983)

Nastassja Kinski . . . . . . . . . . . . . . . . . . . . . . . Clara
  0:29—Brief left breast, when it pops out of her corset when she tries on a dress.

## The Squeeze (1977; British)

Edward Fox . . . . . . . . . . . . . . . . . . . . . . . . . Foreman
Stacy Keach . . . . . . . . . . . . . . . . . . . . . . . . Jim Naboth
  ••• 0:30—Buns and very brief frontal nudity after being forced to strip in basement.
  •• 0:35—Buns, while walking down the street after being let go.
Carol White . . . . . . . . . . . . . . . . . . . . . . . . . . . Jill
  ••• 0:58—Nude, after taking off her clothes in front of the three bad guys. Long scene.

## Squeeze Play (1979)

Jim Harris . . . . . . . . . . . . . . . . . . . . . . . . . . . .Wes
  •• 0:39—Buns, tied up in a room while people walking by look in through open door.
Jennifer Hetrick . . . . . . . . . . . . . . . . . . . . . . Samantha
  •• 0:00—Breasts in bed after making love.

- 0:26—Right breast, brief breasts with Wes on the floor.
- 0:37—In bra, in bedroom with Wes.

## Stacey! (1973)
*a.k.a. Stacey and Her Gangbusters*
Anitra Ford . . . . . . . . . . . . . . . . . . . . . . Tish Chambers
- •• 0:13—Breasts in bed making love with Frank.
Cristina Raines . . . . . . . . . . . . . . . . . . .Pamela Chambers
Anne Randall. . . . . . . . . . . . . . . . . . . . . . Stacey Hansen
- ••• 0:01—Breasts taking off her driving jump suit.
- ••• 0:12—Breasts changing clothes.
- ••• 0:39—Breasts in bed with Bob.

## Star 80 (1983)
Carroll Baker . . . . . . . . . . . . . . . . . .Dorothy's Mother
Lonnie Chin . . . . . . . . . . . . . . Playboy Mansion Guest
Robert Fields . . . . . . . . . . . . . . . . . . . . . . . . . Director
Deborah Geffner. . . . . . . . . . . . . . . . . . . . . . . . Billie
Tabitha Harrington . . . . . . . . . . . . . . . . . . . . . Blonde
Mariel Hemingway . . . . . . . . . . . . . . . .Dorothy Stratten
- • 0:00—Breasts in still photos during opening credits.
- • 0:02—Breasts lying on bed in Paul's flashbacks.
- ••• 0:22—Breasts during Polaroid photo session with Paul
- • 0:25—Breasts during professional photography session. Long shot.
- • 0:36—Brief breasts during photo session.
- • 0:57—Right breast, in centerfold photo on wall.
- • 1:04—Upper half of breasts, in bathtub.
- • 1:05—Brief breasts in photo shoot flashback.
- • 1:17—Brief breasts during layout flashbacks.
- • 1:20—Very brief breasts in photos on the wall.
- •• 1:33—Breasts undressing before getting killed by Paul. More brief breasts layout flashbacks.
Lorraine Michaels . . . . . . . . . . . . . . . .Paul's Party Guest
Roger Rees . . . . . . . . . . . . . . . . . . . . . Aram Nicholas
Eric Roberts. . . . . . . . . . . . . . . . . . . . . . . Paul Snider
- • 1:39—Buns, lying dead on floor, covered with blood after shooting Dorothy, then himself.
Cathy St. George. . . . . . . . . . . Playboy Mansion Guest
Kathryn Witt . . . . . . . . . . . . . . . . . . . . . . . . . . . Robin

## Star Slammer—The Escape (1986)
Bobbie Bresee . . . . . . . . . . . . . . . . . . . . . . . . Marai
Sandy Brooke . . . . . . . . . . . . . . . . . . . . . . . . Taura
- ••• 0:21—Breasts in jail putting a new top on. In braless white T-shirt for most of the rest of the film.
- •• 1:09—Breasts changing into a clean top.
Richard Hench. . . . . . . . . . . . . . . . . . . . . . . . Garth
Dawn Wildsmith . . . . . . . . . . . . . . . . . . . . . Muffin

## Starman (1984)
Karen Allen . . . . . . . . . . . . . . . . . . . . . . .Jenny Hayden
Jeff Bridges . . . . . . . . . . . . . . . . . . . . . Scott/Starman
- • 0:11—Brief buns, while standing up after growing from DNA to a man.
Pat Lee . . . . . . . . . . . . . . . . . . . . . . . . . .Bracero Wife
Charlie Martin Smith. . . . . . . . . . . . . . . . . . . Shermin

## Stars and Bars (1988)
Ingrid Buxbaum . . . . . . . . . . . . . . . . . . . . Photographer
Daniel Day-Lewis . . . . . . . . . . . . . . . . .Henderson Bores
- •• 1:21—Brief buns, while trying to open the window. Very, very brief frontal nudity when he throws the statue out the window. Blurry and dark. More buns, climbing out the window and into a trash dumpster.
Harry Dean Stanton . . . . . . . . . . . . . . . . .Loomis Gage
David Strathairn . . . . . . . . . . . . . . . . . . . . . . . .Charlie

## Starting Over (1979)
Candice Bergen . . . . . . . . . . . . . . . . . . . . .Jessica Potter
1:01—In a sheer blouse sitting on couch talking to Burt Reynolds.
- • 1:29—Very, very brief left breast in bed with Reynolds when he undoes her top. You see her breast just before the scene dissolves into the next one. Long shot, hard to see.
Jill Clayburgh . . . . . . . . . . . . . . . . . . Marilyn Holmberg
- • 0:45—Very brief upper half of breasts taking a shower while Burt Reynolds waits outside.
Mary Kay Place. . . . . . . . . . . . . . . . . . . . . . . . . .Marie
Burt Reynolds. . . . . . . . . . . . . . . . . . . . . . Phil Potter
Daniel Stern . . . . . . . . . . . . . . . . . . . . . . . . Student 2

## State of Grace (1990)
Sandra Beall . . . . . . . . . . . . . . . . . . . . . . . .Steve's Date
Ed Harris . . . . . . . . . . . . . . . . . . . . . . . . . . .Frankie
Gary Oldman . . . . . . . . . . . . . . . . . . . . . . . . . .Jackie
Sean Penn . . . . . . . . . . . . . . . . . . . . . . . . . . . Terry
John Turturro . . . . . . . . . . . . . . . . . . . . . . . . . .Nick
Robin Wright . . . . . . . . . . . . . . . . . . . . . . . Kathleen
- •• 0:38—Breasts making love standing up with Sean Penn in the hall. Dark.
1:01—In bra on bed with Penn, than walking around while talking to him.
- • 1:58—Brief side of right breast taking off towel and putting on blouse.

## State Park (1988; Canadian)
Crisstyn Dante . . . . . . . . . . . . . . . . . . . . . Blond in Net
- • 0:45—Very, very brief left breast putting swimsuit top back on after being rescued from net by the guy in the bear costume.
Shana Golden . . . . . . . . . . . . . . . . . . . Blond in Shower
- • 0:46—Breasts taking a shower outside while park ranger watches. Long shot.
Jennifer Inch. . . . . . . . . . . . . . . . . . . . . . . . . . Linnie
- • 0:34—Brief right breast, undoing swimsuit top while sunbathing.
- • 0:39—Brief breasts, taking off swimsuit top while cutting Raymond's hair.
Isabelle Mejias . . . . . . . . . . . . . . . . . . . . . . . Marsha

## Stateline Motel (1975; Italian)
*a.k.a. Last Chance for a Born Loser*
Ursula Andress . . . . . . . . . . . . . . . . . . . .Michelle Nolton
- ••• 0:34—Left breast, then breasts on bed with Oleg.
Barbara Bach . . . . . . . . . . . . . . . . . . . . . . . . . . .Emily

### Stay As You Are (1978; Italian)
English language version.
Barbara De Rossi . . . . . . . . . . . . . . . . . . . . . . . . . . . .n.a.
Nastassja Kinski . . . . . . . . . . . . . . . . . . . . . . Francesca
- 0:07—Left breast, while sleeping in bed.
- 1:00—Breasts, undressing and sitting in bed. Brief side of left breast, while lying in bed.
- ••• 1:02—Buns, while lying in bed, then full frontal nudity sitting up and covering herself with a sheet.
- ••• 1:27—Left breast, then breasts and brief buns in bed with Marcello Mastroianni. Long scene.
- ••• 1:28—Breasts, sitting up in bed, talking with Mastroianni.
- ••• 1:30—Nude, fooling around at the table with Mastroianni. Long scene. Nice bun shots.
- •• 1:33—Breasts in bedroom at night. Mostly silhouette.

### Stay Hungry (1976)
Ed Begley, Jr. . . . . . . . . . . . . . . . . . . . . . . . . . . . . Lester
Jeff Bridges . . . . . . . . . . . . . . . . . . . . . . . . Craig Blake
John David Carson . . . . . . . . . . . . . . . . . . . . .Halsey
Joanna Cassidy . . . . . . . . . . . . . . . . . . . . . Joe Mason
Sally Field . . . . . . . . . . . . . . . . . . Mary Kay Farnsworth
- 0:27—Buns, then very, very brief side view of left breast jumping back into bed. Very fast, everything is a blur, hard to see anything.
Laura Hippe . . . . . . . . . . . . . . . . . . . . . . . . May Ruth
- 1:19—Brief buns, hanging upside down in gym.
Helena Kallianiotes . . . . . . . . . . . . . . . . . . . . . . .Anita
Arnold Schwarzenegger . . . . . . . . . . . . . . . . Joe Santo

### Staying Together (1989)
Sean Astin . . . . . . . . . . . . . . . . . . . Duncan McDermott
Melinda Dillon . . . . . . . . . . . . . . . .Eileen McDermott
Sheila Kelley . . . . . . . . . . . . . . . . . . . . . . . Beth Harper
Tom Quill . . . . . . . . . . . . . . . . . . . . . Brian McDermott
- 0:03—Brief buns while getting out of bed with Stockard Channing. Hard to see because of the reflections in the window.
Daphne Zuniga . . . . . . . . . . . . . . . . . . . .Beverly Young
- •• 0:56—Buns, lying in bed with Kit. Nice, long buns scene.

### The Steagle (1971)
Richard Benjamin . . . . . . . . . . . . . . . . . . . .Harold Weiss
Cloris Leachman . . . . . . . . . . . . . . . . . . . . . . Rita Weiss
Susan Tyrrell . . . . . . . . . . . . . . . . . . . . . . . . . .Louise
- 0:48—Brief left breast twice, lying on bed with Richard Benjamin.

### Stealing Heaven (1988; British/Yugoslavian)
Victoria Burgoyne . . . . . . . . . . . . . . . . . . . . . Prostitute
- 0:28—Left breast, taking off her top. Side view of right breast and buns.
- •• 0:29—Breasts lying in bed.
Derek De Lint . . . . . . . . . . . . . . . . . . . . . . . . .Abelard
- ••• 0:47—Brief frontal nudity taking off his shirt. Then buns, while in bed making love with Kim Thomson. 1:07—Brief side view of buns under Kim. Long shot.
Cassie Stuart . . . . . . . . . . . . . . . . . . . . . . . Petronilla

Kim Thomson. . . . . . . . . . . . . . . . . . . . . . . . Heloise
- 0:42—Side of left breast kneeling on floor with steam. Long shot.
- •• 0:43—Closer view of left breast.
- ••• 0:47—Breasts and very brief lower frontal nudity lying in bed with Abelard. More left breast afterwards.
- 1:07—Nude, left side view on top of Abelard in bed. Long shot.

### Steaming (1985; British)
Felicity Dean . . . . . . . . . . . . . . . . . . . . . . . . . . Dawn
- •• 1:12—Breasts painting on herself.
Patti Love. . . . . . . . . . . . . . . . . . . . . . . . . . . . . .Josie
- 0:08—Frontal nudity, getting undressed.
- 0:45—Brief breasts.
- 1:30—Breasts, jumping around in the pool.
Sarah Miles . . . . . . . . . . . . . . . . . . . . . . . . . . .Sarah
- •• 0:23—Breasts while getting into pool with Vanessa Redgrave.
- •• 0:49—Breasts while getting undressed.
- •• 1:31—Nude while lying down next to pool.
Vanessa Redgrave. . . . . . . . . . . . . . . . . . . . . . Nancy
- 1:32—Buns and brief side view of right breast getting into pool.

### Steel and Lace (1990)
Stacy Haiduk . . . . . . . . . . . . . . . . . . . . . . . . . Alison
David Naughton . . . . . . . . . . . . . . . . . . . . . . . .Dunn
Brenda Swanson . . . . . . . . . . . . . . . Miss Fairweather
- •• 0:58—Breasts in lunchroom, opening her blouse in front of one of the bad guys on the table.
Clare Wren. . . . . . . . . . . . . . . . . . . . . . . . . . . . Gally

### The Stepfather (1987)
Terry O'Quinn . . . . . . . . . . . . . . . . . . . . . . . Jerry Blake
- ••• 0:02—Buns, while getting undressed, frontal nudity in mirror as he gets into the shower.
Gabrielle Rose . . . . . . . . . . . . . . . . . . . . . . .Dorothy
Jill Schoelen . . . . . . . . . . . . . . . . . . . Stephanie Maine
- •• 1:16—Buns and brief side of right breast, while getting into the shower. Breasts in the shower.
Steve Shellen . . . . . . . . . . . . . . . . . . . . . .Jim Ogilvie

### Stepfather III: Father's Day (1992)
Priscilla Barnes . . . . . . . . . . . . . . . . . . . .Christine Davis
- 1:27—Very brief buns, sitting down in bubble bath.
Season Hubley . . . . . . . . . . . . . . . . .Jennifer Ashley
Brenda Strong . . . . . . . . . . . . . .Crime Search Reporter

### Steppenwolf (1974)
Pierre Clementi . . . . . . . . . . . . . . . . . . . . . . . . .Pablo
- 1:40—Very brief frontal nudity, sleeping on floor with Dominique Sanda.
Carla Romanelli . . . . . . . . . . . . . . . . . . . . . . . .Maria
- ••• 0:59—Breasts sitting on bed with John Huston. Long scene.
Dominique Sanda . . . . . . . . . . . . . . . . . . . . Hermine
1:40—Brief lower frontal nudity, sleeping with a guy.
- 1:41—Very brief left breast, waking up and rolling over to hug John Huston.

### Stewardess School (1987)
Sandahl Bergman . . . . . . . . . . . . . . . . . Wanda Polanski
Corinne Bohrer . . . . . . . . . . . . . . . . . . . . Cindy Adams
Vicki Frederick . . . . . . . . . . . . . . . . . . . . Miss Grummet
Leslie Huntly . . . . . . . . . . . . . . . . . . . . . Alison Hanover
•• 0:46—Breasts, doing a strip tease on a table at a party at her house.
Julie Montgomery . . . . . . . . . . . . . . . . . . Pimmie Polk

### Still of the Night (1982)
Sara Botsford . . . . . . . . . . . . . . . . . . . . . . . Gail Phillips
Larry Joshua . . . . . . . . . . . . . . . . . . . . . . . . Mugger
Roy Scheider . . . . . . . . . . . . . . . . . . . . . . . . Sam Rice
Meryl Streep . . . . . . . . . . . . . . . . . . . . Brooke Reynolds
0:22—Side view of right breast and buns taking off robe for the massage guy. Long shot, don't see her face.

### Stitches (1985)
Lucinda Crosby . . . . . . . . . . . . . . . . . . . . . Nurse #5
Bob Dubac . . . . . . . . . . . . . . . . . . . . . . . . Al Rosenberg
• 0:03—Very brief buns, while walking around in classroom. Made up to look like a bald corpse.
0:04—Brief buns, while chasing people down hallway. Don't see face. (He's in the middle, holding a beer can.)
Deborah Fallender . . . . . . . . . . . . . . . . . . . . Nurse #1
Daniel Greene . . . . . . . . . . . . . . . . . . . . . . Ted Fletcher
• 0:45—Brief buns, twice, while pulling his pants down in front of visiting medical students.
Tommy Koenig . . . . . . . . . . . . . . . . . . . . . Barfer Bogan
• 0:03—Brief buns, while getting off gurney. Made up to look like a bald corpse. Something is covering his frontal nudity. Brief buns, while walking in classroom.
• 0:04—Brief buns, while chasing people down hallway. Don't see face. (He's in front.)
Jenny Neumann . . . . . . . . . . . . . . . . . . . . . . . Joan
Rebecca Perle . . . . . . . . . . . . . . . . . . . . . Bambi Belinka
••• 0:33—Breasts during female medical student's class where they examine each other.
• 1:00—Brief breasts on bed with Parker Stevenson when discovered by Nancy.
Parker Stevenson . . . . . . . . . . . . . . . . . . . Bobby Stevens
• 0:04—Brief buns, while chasing people down hallway. Don't see face. (He's in the last one.)

### Stone Cold (1991)
Laura Albert . . . . . . . . . . . . . . . . . . . . . Joe's Girlfriend
• 0:11—Buns, in bed when waking up. Very brief right breast.
Tracey E. Hutchinson . . . . . . . . . . . . . Pool Playing Chick
• 0:25—Brief breasts, playing pool with the guys.
Brenda Lynn Klemme . . . . . . . . . . . . . . . . . . . . . Marie

### Stone Cold Dead (1979; Canadian)
Jennifer Dale . . . . . . . . . . . . . . . . . Claudia Grissom
••• 0:05—Breasts, dancing on stage.
Linnea Quigley . . . . . . . . . . . . . . . . . . . . . . First Victim
• 0:03—Very brief right breast after getting shot through shower door. Buns after falling to the floor.

Alberta Watson . . . . . . . . . . . . . . . . . . . . . . Olivia Page

### Stop! Or My Mom Will Shoot (1992)
Vanessa Angel . . . . . . . . . . . . . . . . . . . . . . Stewardess
Marjean Holden . . . . . . . . . . . . . . . . . . . . . Stewardess
Julie Montgomery . . . . . . . . . . . . . . . . . . . . Secretary
Roger Rees . . . . . . . . . . . . . . . . . . . . . . . . . Parnell
Sylvester Stallone . . . . . . . . . . . . . . . . . . Joe Bomowski
• 0:22—Upper half of buns behind shower door when his mom talks to him in the bathroom.
Brigitta Stenberg . . . . . . . . . . . . . . . . . . Stewardess
JoBeth Williams . . . . . . . . . . . . . . . . . . . Gwen Harper

### Stormquest (1988)
Kai Baker . . . . . . . . . . . . . . . . . . . . . . . . . . . . . Arr
• 0:37—Very, very brief left breast, while struggling with Zar in the water.
Brent Huff . . . . . . . . . . . . . . . . . . . . . . . . . . . Zar
Christina Whitaker . . . . . . . . . . . . . . . . . . . . . . Asha

### Stormswept (1994)
Justin Carroll . . . . . . . . . . . . . . . . . . . . . . . Damon
Kathleen Kinmont . . . . . . . . . . . . . . . . . . . . Missy
Lorissa McComas . . . . . . . . . . . . . . . . . . . . . . Kelly
••• 0:53—Breasts, while making love in bed with Brianna.
••• 1:33—Nude, after taking off her robe in room in front of Eugene.
Melissa Anne Moore . . . . . . . . . . . . . . . . . . . . Dottie
•• 0:33—Breasts, when her towel falls off while talking to Brianna.
• 0:40—Breasts in open robe, while sitting on bed.
••• 1:10—Breasts, while making love on table with Damon.
Ed Wasser . . . . . . . . . . . . . . . . . . . . . . . . . . Eugene
••• 1:30—Buns, while making love with Brianna in pantry.

### Stormy Monday (1988)
Sting . . . . . . . . . . . . . . . . . . . . . . . . . . . . . Finney
Sean Bean . . . . . . . . . . . . . . . . . . . . . . . . . Brendan
•• 0:37—Buns, putting on his underwear while Melanie Griffith watches.
Catherine Chevalier . . . . . . . . . . . . . . Cosmo's Secretary
Melanie Griffith . . . . . . . . . . . . . . . . . . . . . . . Kate
0:03—Buns and side of right breast, behind shower door. Don't see anything because of the glass.
• 1:11—Very brief left breast, while making love in bed with Brendan.
Tommy Lee Jones . . . . . . . . . . . . . . . . . . . . . . Cosmo

### The Story of "O" (1975; French)
Corrine Clery . . . . . . . . . . . . . . . . . . . . . . . . . . . . O
•• 0:04—Breasts in the back of car when her boyfriend pulls her blouse down and rips her bra off.
••• 0:08—Breasts, getting made up by two women.
•• 0:10—Left breast, while getting checked out.
•• 0:13—Frontal nudity, chained to chandelier and whipped.
•• 0:14—Breasts on couch.
•• 0:16—Breasts getting out of tub and sitting on bed.

••• 0:18—Breasts and brief buns, getting out of bed and whipped. Frontal nudity, getting up.
••• 0:20—Frontal nudity with two guys.
••• 0:22—Breasts, sitting in front of a mirror.
•• 0:24—Breasts, watching another woman have sex in library.
••• 0:27—Breasts sitting at table and eating.
••• 0:29—Breasts getting a bath.
•• 0:30—Breasts being led around blindfolded.
•• 0:33—Brief breasts, getting whipped and eating.
••• 0:42—Buns, while bent over sofa.
••• 0:43—Breasts with older man on sofa.
••• 0:44—Nude, taking off her skirt.
••• 0:59—Frontal nudity, reclining on bed, then sitting up.
•• 1:02—Breasts in room with older man when he opens her blouse.
••• 1:05—Breasts and buns in bedroom.
••• 1:06—Nude with other women, getting dressed in a corset.
••• 1:08—Breasts, getting chained to posts and whipped.
•• 1:13—Breasts in bed with another woman.
•• 1:14—Breasts before getting branded.
••• 1:17—Frontal nudity, getting out of tub and putting on robe.
•• 1:19—Breasts getting her blouse opened and breast sucked.
••• 1:21—Nude, making love in bed. Slightly overexposed.
••• 1:26—Tied up to posts by wrists.
•• 1:32—Breasts in open cape, while wearing a mask. Frontal nudity getting cape removed.
Vibeke Knudsen . . . . . . . . . . . . . . . . . . . . . . . . . . . n.a.

## The Story of "O" Continues (1981; French)
### a.k.a. Les Fruits de la Passion
Arielle Dombasle . . . . . . . . . . . . . . . . . . . . . . Nathalie
• 0:17—Brief left breast, lying on her stomach in bed with Klaus Kinski.
••• 0:40—Full frontal nudity on bed, making love in front of O.
• 1:00—Very, very brief left breast, while grabbing her blouse out of Kinski's hands.
Isabelle Illiers . . . . . . . . . . . . . . . . . . . . . . . . . . . . O
••• 0:06—Breasts in chair, getting made up.
•• 0:08—Breasts and buns, walking up stairs.
• 0:10—Breasts sitting in bed.
•• 0:11—Breasts sitting in bed putting up Klaus Kinski's picture on the wall.
•• 0:12—Breasts and buns getting out of bed and walking around the room.
• 0:13—Tip of right breast, while looking out the window.
•• 0:18—Breasts looking out the window.
• 0:24—Brief left breast, under her dress.
• 0:26—Tips of breasts, sticking out of dress top.
•• 0:27—Breasts and buns in chair, more in room with a customer.
• 0:35—Breasts, sitting while looking at Kinski.

•• 0:36—Brief left breast, then full frontal nudity lying on bed during fantasy.
0:40—Full frontal nudity, getting chained up by Kinski.
•• 0:58—Full frontal nudity running in slow-motion during boy's fantasy.
• 1:02—Breasts in room with the boy.
• 1:04—Breasts making love with the boy.
Klaus Kinski . . . . . . . . . . . . . . . . . . . . . . . Sir Stephen
• 0:40—Very, very brief part of buns while making love on bed with Arielle Dombasle.

## The Story of Fausta (1988; Brazilian)
Betty Faria . . . . . . . . . . . . . . . . . . . . . . . . . . . . Fausta
• 1:10—Left breast, while leaning out of the shower to talk to Lourdes.

## Storyville (1992)
Charlotte Lewis . . . . . . . . . . . . . . . . . . . . . . . . . . Lee
•• 0:17—Buns, taking off martial arts outfit and getting into hot tub. Brief breasts, sitting down (medium long shot).
• 0:18—Brief upper half of breasts, in hot tub with James Spader.
Jeff Perry . . . . . . . . . . . . . . . . . . . . . . . Peter Dandridge
James Spader . . . . . . . . . . . . . . . . . . . . . . Cray Fowler
Michael Warren . . . . . . . . . . . . . . . . . . . . Nathan Lefleur

## Straight Time (1978)
Kathy Bates . . . . . . . . . . . . . . . . . . . . . . . . Selma Darin
Dustin Hoffman . . . . . . . . . . . . . . . . . . . . . Max Dembo
0:38—Very, very brief tip of penis in jail shower scene after getting sprayed by guard. Don't really see anything.
Theresa Russell . . . . . . . . . . . . . . . . . . . . . Jenny Mercer
••• 1:00—Left breast, while in bed with Dustin Hoffman. Don't see her face.
Harry Dean Stanton . . . . . . . . . . . . . . . . . . Jerry Schue
M. Emmet Walsh . . . . . . . . . . . . . . . . . . . . Earl Frank
• 0:47—Buns, while handcuffed to fence in the middle of the road with his pants down.

## Strange Shadows in an Empty Room (1976)
Tisa Farrow . . . . . . . . . . . . . . . . . . . . . . . . . . . . . n.a.
Carole Laure . . . . . . . . . . . . . . . . . . . . . . . . . . Louise
••• 1:29—Brief breasts, while running around the house and frolicking with Mrs. Wilkinson and Fred. Breasts while in slow motion, when beating Mrs. Wilkinson to death.

## The Stranger (1986)
Bonnie Bedelia . . . . . . . . . . . . . . . . . . . . . Alice Kildee
• 0:15—Brief right breast sticking up from behind her lover's arm making love in bed during flashback sequence (B&W).
• 0:19—Brief left breast turning over in hospital bed when a guy walks in. Long shot, hard to see.
•• 0:38—Right breast again making love (B&W).

### Stranger By Night (1994)
Steven Bauer . . . . . . . . . . . . . . . . . . . . . Bobby Corcoran
•• 0:57—Buns and brief frontal nudity, while making
love in bed on top of Jennifer Rubin.
William Katt . . . . . . . . . . . . . . . . . . . . . . . Troy Rooney
Jennifer Rubin . . . . . . . . . . . . . . . . . . . . Anne Richmond
••• 0:57—Breasts, while making love in bed with Steven
Bauer.

### Straw Dogs (1972)
Susan George . . . . . . . . . . . . . . . . . . . . . . . . . . . Amy
•• 0:32—Breasts taking off sweater, tossing it down to
Dustin Hoffman, then looking out the door at the
workers.
••• 1:00—Breasts on couch getting raped by one of the
construction workers.
Dustin Hoffman. . . . . . . . . . . . . . . . . . . . . . . . David

### Street Hunter (1990)
John Leguizamo . . . . . . . . . . . . . . . . . . . . . . . . Angel
Susan Napoli. . . . . . . . . . . . . . . . . . . . . . . Eddie's Girl
•• 0:40—Breasts in bed with Eddie (she's on the left,
wearing white panties).

### Street Knight (1992)
Bernie Casey . . . . . . . . . . . . . . . . . . . . . . . Raymond
Jennifer Gatti. . . . . . . . . . . . . . . . . . . . . . . . Rebecca
Sal Landi . . . . . . . . . . . . . . . . . . . . . . . . . . . Parker
Jeff Speakman . . . . . . . . . . . . . . . . . . . . . . . . . Jake
••• 0:05—Buns, while getting out of bed at night.

### Street Music (1982)
Larry Breeding. . . . . . . . . . . . . . . . . . . . . . . . Eddie
•• 1:09—Buns, while getting out of bed and putting
his underwear on.
Elizabeth Daily. . . . . . . . . . . . . . . . . . . . . . . Sadie
• 0:00—Nude behind shower door (can't see any-
thing), then brief right breast while reaching for
towel.
•• 0:24—Partial lower frontal nudity and left breast
with Eddie.
• 1:07—Brief breasts while on top of Eddie on the
floor.
• 1:08—Brief breasts while getting dressed.

### Streets (1989)
Starr Andreeff . . . . . . . . . . . . . . . Policewoman on Horse
Christina Applegate. . . . . . . . . . . . . . . . . . . . . Dawn
1:09—Very, very brief almost side view of left breast,
while kissing her boyfriend. His hand is over her
breast. Not really a nude scene, but I'm including it
because people might send this in as an addition.
Julie Jay . . . . . . . . . . . . . . Dawn's Tattooed Roommate
• 0:20—Brief breasts, twice, pulling her blouse closed
when Christina Applegate talks to her.
Kay Lenz . . . . . . . . . . . . . . . . . . . . . . . . . . Sergeant

### Streets of Fire (1984)
Ed Begley, Jr.. . . . . . . . . . . . . . . . . . . . . . Ben Gunn
Willem Dafoe . . . . . . . . . . . . . . . . . . . . . . . . Raven
Elizabeth Daily. . . . . . . . . . . . . . . . . . . . . Baby Doll

Marine Jahan . . . . . . . . . . . . . . . . . . "Torchie's" Dancer
0:28—Buns in G-string dancing in club.
0:34—More dancing.
• 0:35—Very brief right breast under body stocking,
then almost breasts under stocking when taking off
T-shirt.
Diane Lane. . . . . . . . . . . . . . . . . . . . . . . . . Ellen Aim
Amy Madigan . . . . . . . . . . . . . . . . . . . . . . . McCoy
Michael Paré . . . . . . . . . . . . . . . . . . . . . . Tom Cody
Bill Paxton . . . . . . . . . . . . . . . . . . . . . . . . . . .Clyde
Rick Rossovich . . . . . . . . . . . . . . . . . . . Officer Cooley

### Streets of Rage (1993)
Mimi Lesseos . . . . . . . . . . . . . . . . . . . . . Melody Sails
• 0:33—Buns and brief side view of breasts after taking off robe and getting into shower. Breasts, sort of
visible behind shower door.

### Streetwalkin' (1985)
Khandi Alexander . . . . . . . . . . . . . . . . . . . . . . . . Star
Samantha Fox . . . . . . . . . . . . . . . . . . . . Topless Dancer
• 0:22—Breasts, dancing on stage in nightclub (She's
the one wearing a head band).
• 0:27—More breasts, dancing on stage.
• 0:29—More breasts, dancing on stage.
• 0:56—Breasts, giving Antonio Fargas a massage at
the bar.
Melissa Leo . . . . . . . . . . . . . . . . . . . . . . . .Cookie
• 0:05—Brief breasts taking off red blouse in front of
mirror.
•• 0:15—Breasts, stripping and taking off her top for a
customer.
• 0:18—Brief right breast, having sex with her pimp
on the floor.
• 0:44—Breasts, taking off her top and sitting on bed
with a customer (long shot seen in mirror).
0:53—Buns, in body suit, in hotel room with customer.
Julie Newmar . . . . . . . . . . . . . . . . . . . . . .Queen Bee

### Strike a Pose (1993)
Debra Beatty . . . . . . . . . . . . . . . . . . . . . . . . Model
Michele Brin. . . . . . . . . . . . . . . . . . . . Miranda Cross
••• 0:06—Breasts, while making love with Nick at night
outside by a fire. Long scene.
••• 0:32—In black bra and panties, then breasts while
making love with Nick. Long scene.
• 0:40—Buns in panties that are squished against a
glass door.
••• 1:06—Brief left breast in bed, then breasts and buns
while making love with Nick.
Diana Cuevas. . . . . . . . . . . . . . . . . . . . . . . . Model
Robert Eastwick . . . . . . . . . . . . . . . . . . . . Nick Carter
••• 0:33—Buns, while standing up and making love
with Miranda.
•• 1:07—Brief partial frontal nudity while in bed with
Miranda. Buns while getting out.
Tamara Landry. . . . . . . . . . . . . . . . . . . . . . . . Candy
••• 0:23—In black bra, panties and stockings, then nude
with Carl. Long scene.
••• 1:01—Breasts, while making love on bed.

### Stripes (1981)

Sue Bowser . . . . . . . . . . . . . . . . . . . . . . Mud Wrestler
Dawn Clark . . . . . . . . . . . . . . . . . . . . . . Mud Wrestler
John Diehl . . . . . . . . . . . . . . . . . . . . . . . . . . . . Cruiser
Roberta Leighton . . . . . . . . . . . . . . . . . . . . . . .Anita
- 0:07—Breasts, wearing blue panties, while putting her shirt on and talking to Bill Murray.
Bill Paxton . . . . . . . . . . . . . . . . . . . . . . . . . . . . . .n.a.
Judge Reinhold . . . . . . . . . . . . . . . . . . . . . . . . .Elmo
P.J. Soles . . . . . . . . . . . . . . . . . . . . . . . . . . . . Stella
Sean Young . . . . . . . . . . . . . . . . . . . . Louise Cooper

### Stripped to Kill (1987)

Michelle Foreman . . . . . . . . . . . . . . . . . . . . . . Angel
- ••• 0:02—Breasts dancing on stage for Norman Fell.
Debra Lamb . . . . . . . . . . . . . . . . . . . . Amateur Dancer
Kay Lenz . . . . . . . . . . . . . . . . . . . . Cody Sheehan
- •• 0:23—Breasts dancing on stage.
- ••• 0:47—Breasts dancing in white lingerie.
Deborah Ann Nassar . . . . . . . . . . . . . . . . . . . . . Dazzle
- ••• 0:07—Breasts wearing a G-string dancing on stage with a motorcycle prop.

### Stripped to Kill II (1988)

Jeannine Bisignano . . . . . . . . . . . . . . . . . . . . . .Sonny
0:06—Buns, while wearing a black bra in dressing room.
- ••• 0:38—Breasts and buns during strip dance routine in white lingerie.
Maria Ford . . . . . . . . . . . . . . . . . . . . . . . . . . . Shady
- •• 0:21—Breasts, dancing on table in front of the detective. Buns, walking away.
- • 0:40—Brief upper half of left breast in the alley with the detective.
- •• 0:52—Breasts and buns during dance routine.
Lisa Glaser . . . . . . . . . . . . . . . . . . . . . . . . . . .Victoria
- •• 0:01—Breasts and buns in G-string doing a strip dance routine during Shadey's nightmare.
Marjean Holden . . . . . . . . . . . . . . . . . .Something Else
- •• 0:17—Breasts during strip dance routine.
Debra Lamb . . . . . . . . . . . . . . . . . . . . . . . . Mantra
- •• 0:04—Breasts during strip dance routine.
- ••• 0:42—Breasts in black lingerie during strip dance routine.
Karen Mayo-Chandler . . . . . . . . . . . . . . . . . .Cassandra
0:06—Black bra and panties in dressing room.
- •• 0:18—Breasts taking off her top for a customer.

### Stripper (1985)

Sara Costa . . . . . . . . . . . . . . . . . . . . . . . . . . . Herself
- ••• 0:16—Breasts doing strip dance routine.
- ••• 0:46—Breasts and buns dancing on stage in a G-string.
- ••• 1:12—Breasts doing another strip routine.
Venus De Light . . . . . . . . . . . . . . . . . . . . . . . Herself
- • 0:59—Brief breasts, on stage, blowing fire.
- ••• 1:07—Breasts and buns in black G-string, doing routine on stage, using fire.

Suzanne Primeaux . . . . . . . . . . . . . . . . . . . . . . .Herself
- •• 0:03—Breasts dancing on stage, kneeling on her left knee. Very brief buns in G-string.

### The Stud (1978; British)

Minah Bird . . . . . . . . . . . . . . . . . . . . . . . . . . .Molly
- •• 0:26—Breasts in bed when Tony is talking on the telephone.
Joan Collins . . . . . . . . . . . . . . . . . . . . . . . . Fontaine
- • 0:10—Brief left breast making love with Tony in the elevator.
0:27—Brief buns in panties, stockings and garter belt in Tony's apartment.
0:58—Brief black bra and panties under fur coat in back of limousine with Tony.
- • 1:03—Brief breasts taking off dress to get in pool.
- • 1:04—Nude in the pool with Tony.
Emma Jacobs . . . . . . . . . . . . . . . . . . . . . . . Alexandra
- •• 0:44—In bra, then breasts taking bra off in bedroom.
- • 0:48—Close up of breasts making love with Tony in his dark apartment.
- • 1:14—Breasts in bed with Tony, yelling at him.
Sue Lloyd . . . . . . . . . . . . . . . . . . . . . . . . . . Vanessa
- • 1:04—Breasts in the swimming pool with Joan Collins and Tony.
Natalie Ogle . . . . . . . . . . . . . . . . . . . . . . . . .Maddy
Oliver Tobias . . . . . . . . . . . . . . . . . . . . . . .Tony Blake
- • 1:06—Buns, running away from the pool.

### Student Affairs (1987)

Jim Abele . . . . . . . . . . . . . . . . . . . . . Andrew Armstrong
- • 1:07—Buns, when his friends play a practical joke on him in the shower.
Deborah Blaisdell . . . . . . . . . . . . . . . . . . . . . . . Kelly
- ••• 0:26—Breasts sitting up in bed talking to a guy.
Louis Bonanno . . . . . . . . . . . . . . . . . . . . Louie Balducci
Jane Hamilton . . . . . . . . . . . . . . . . . . . . . . . . Veronica
- •• 0:48—Breasts changing in dressing room, showing herself off to a guy.
- • 0:51—Brief breasts in a school room during a movie.
- •• 0:56—In black lingerie outfit, then breasts in bedroom while she tape records everything.
Jeanne Marie . . . . . . . . . . . . . . . . . . . . . . . Robin Ready
- • 0:35—Brief breasts wearing black panties in bed trying to seduce a guy.
- ••• 0:41—Breasts making love with another guy, while banging her back against the wall.
- • 0:44—Very brief breasts in VW with a nerd.
- • 1:09—Very brief breasts falling out of a trailer home filled with water.

### The Student Body (1975)

June Fairchild . . . . . . . . . . . . . . . . . . . . . . .Mitzi Mashall
- • 0:15—Brief breasts and buns, running and jumping into the pool during party. Brief long shot breasts, while in the pool.
- •• 0:21—Breasts getting into bed.
Peter Hooten . . . . . . . . . . . . . . . . . . . . . . Carter Blalock
Jillian Kesner . . . . . . . . . . . . . . . . . . . . . . Carrie Rafferty
- •• 0:29—Left breast, making out with Carter in the car.

### Student Confidential (1987)
Corwyn Anthony. . . . . . . . . . . . . . . . . . . . . . . . . Greg
- 1:26—Buns, while getting into bed with Susan.

Katherine Kriss. . . . . . . . . . . . . . . . . . . . . Elaine's Friend
Susie Scott . . . . . . . . . . . . . . . . . . . . . . Susan Bishop
- 0:02—Lying in bed covered with a gold sheet. Sort of right breast through her hair.
- • 1:26—Full frontal nudity standing in front of Greg.

### The Student Nurses (1970)
*a.k.a. Young LA Nurses*

Karen Carlson . . . . . . . . . . . . . . . . . . . . . . . . . Phred
- 0:08—Breasts in bed with the wrong guy.
  0:19—In bra, on sofa with Dr. Jim Casper.
- • • 0:50—In bed with Jim, breasts and buns getting out, then breasts sitting in chair. Long scene.
- 1:02—Brief breasts in bed.

Lawrence Casey . . . . . . . . . . . . . . . . . Dr. Jim Casper
- • 0:52—Buns, while walking to Karen Carlson to talk.

Elaine Giftos . . . . . . . . . . . . . . . . . . . . . . . . . Sharon
- 1:14—Brief breasts undressing and getting into bed with terminally ill boy. Dark, hard to see.

Barbara Leigh . . . . . . . . . . . . . . . . . . . . . . . Priscilla
- • • 0:43—Breasts on the beach with Les. Long scene.

Richard Rust . . . . . . . . . . . . . . . . . . . . . . . . . . Les
- 0:43—Buns, while lying in sand with Barbara Leigh.

Pepe Serna . . . . . . . . . . . . . . . . . . . . . . . . . . . Luis

### The Stunt Man (1980)
Barbara Hershey . . . . . . . . . . . . . . . . . . . . . . . Nina
- 1:29—Buns and side view of left breast in bed in a movie within a movie while everybody is watching in a screening room.

Steve Railsback . . . . . . . . . . . . . . . . . . . . . Cameron

### Submission (1976; Italian)
Andrea Ferréol. . . . . . . . . . . . . . . . . . . . . . . . Juliet
- • 0:43—Breasts in room with Franco Nero and Elaine.

Lisa Gastoni. . . . . . . . . . . . . . . . . . . . . . . . . Elaine
  0:28—Lower frontal nudity on the floor behind the counter with Franco Nero.
- 0:30—Left breast, while talking on the phone with her husband while Nero fondles her.
- • 0:32—Breasts and buns, making love on bed with Nero. Slightly out of focus.
- • 0:33—Breasts getting out of bed to talk to her daughter.
- • • 0:43—Breasts in room with Juliet and Nero. Long scene.
- • • 0:45—More breasts on the floor yelling at Nero.
  0:54—Brief lower frontal nudity in slip, sitting on floor with Nero.
- • • 0:57—Left breast, while wearing slip, walking in front of pharmacy. Then full frontal nudity while wearing only stockings. Long scene.
- • 1:00—Breasts in pharmacy with Nero, singing and dancing.
- • 1:28—Breasts when Nero cuts her slip open. Nice close up.
- • 1:29—Breasts getting up out of bed.

Franco Nero. . . . . . . . . . . . . . . . . . . . . . . . . Armond
- 0:32—Brief side view of buns when making love with Lisa on the bed.

### Subspecies (1990)
Michelle McBride . . . . . . . . . . . . . . . . . . . . . . Lillian
- 0:34—Left breast, while sleeping in bed when the vampire comes to get her.

Laura Tate . . . . . . . . . . . . . . . . . . . . . . . . . Michelle

### Sudden Impact (1983)
Paul Drake . . . . . . . . . . . . . . . . . . . . . . . . . . . Mick
Clint Eastwood. . . . . . . . . . . . . . . . . . Harry Callahan
Sondra Locke . . . . . . . . . . . . . . . . . . Jennifer Spencer
Lisa London . . . . . . . . . . . . . . . . . . . . Young Hooker
- • 1:04—Breasts in bathroom, walking to Nick in the bed.

### Sudden Thunder (1990)
Andrea Lamatsch . . . . . . . . . . . . . . . . . . Patricia Merrill
- 0:18—Right breast, while getting raped by jerks in the woods and brief breasts after escaping from them.
- • • 0:27—Nude, while skinny dipping in pond (some body parts are visible under the water).

### Sugar Cookies (1973)
Maureen Byrnes. . . . . . . . . . . . . . . . . . . . . . . . Dola
- • 0:37—Right breast while Gus is on top of her, then breasts and buns.

Lynn Lowry . . . . . . . . . . . . . . . . . . . . . . Alta/Julie
- • • 0:03—Brief breasts falling out of hammock, then breasts on couch with Max, then nude. Long scene. (Brunette wig as Alta.)
  0:13—Brief right breast in B & W photo.
- 0:14—Left breast while lying on autopsy table.
- • 0:20—Breasts in movie.
- • 0:52—Breasts taking off clothes for Mary Woronov. Breasts on bed. (Blonde as Julie.)
- • • 1:00—Breasts and buns with Woronov in bedroom, nude while wrestling with her.
- 1:04—Breasts with Woronov in bathtub.
- • • 1:06—Nude in bed with Woronov. Long scene.
- • 1:11—Right breast outside displaying herself to Max.
- 1:16—Right breast, then breasts making love with Woronov.
- • • 1:20—Nude with Woronov and Max. Long scene.

Daniel Sador . . . . . . . . . . . . . . . . . . . . . . . . . . Gus
  0:37—Buns while in bed with Dola, then running around.

George Shannon . . . . . . . . . . . . . . . . . . . . . . . . Max
- • 0:14—Buns, while on top of Mary Woronov in bed.

Monique Van Vooren. . . . . . . . . . . . . . . . . . . Helene
Jennifer Welles . . . . . . . . . . . . . . . . . . . Max's Secretary
- 0:28—Breasts in red panties in Max's office while he talks on the phone, then lower frontal nudity.
- • 0:56—Full frontal nudity getting dressed.

Mary Woronov. . . . . . . . . . . . . . . . . . . . . . . . Camila
- • • 0:10—Breasts in bathtub, then wearing white panties exercising breasts on the floor. Long scene.

- 1:04—Breasts with Julie in the bathtub.
- 1:07—Brief breasts, then left breast, making love with Julie.
- 1:17—Brief right breast when Lynn Lowry yanks her dress up.

## Summer Affair (1979)
Ornella Muti . . . . . . . . . . . . . . . . . . . . . . . . . . . . Lisa
- 0:44—Silhouette of breasts in cave by the water.
- 1:00—Brief breasts getting chased around in the grass and by the beach.

## Summer Dreams: The Story of the Beach Boys (1990)
(Originally a made for TV movie.)
Linda Doná . . . . . . . . . . . . . . . . . . . . . . . . . . . . . . n.a.
- 1:06—Silhouette of breasts while making love with Dennis Wilson.
Bruce Greenwood . . . . . . . . . . . . . . . . . . Dennis Wilson

## Summer Heat (1987)
Kathy Bates . . . . . . . . . . . . . . . . . . . . . . . Ruth Stanton
Miriam Byrd-Nethery . . . . . . . . . . . . . . . . Aunt Patty
Anthony Edwards . . . . . . . . . . . . . . . . . . Aaron Walston
Lori Singer . . . . . . . . . . . . . . . . . . . . . . . . . . . . . . . . Roxy
- •• 0:36—Breasts in bed with Jack. Kind of dark and hard to see.

## Summer Job (1989)
Amy Lynn Baxter . . . . . . . . . . . . . . . . . . . . . . . . Susan
- •• 0:10—Breasts changing in room with the other three girls. More breasts sitting on bed.
  0:15—In white bra, looking at herself in mirror.
- 0:34—Brief breasts when her swimsuit top pops off after saving a guy in swimming pool.
- 0:45—In white lingerie, brief breasts on stairs, flashing her breasts (wearing curlers).
  1:00—Brief buns in two piece swimsuit turning around.
- 1:23—Breasts pulling her top down talking to Mr. Burns.
Kirt Earhar . . . . . . . . . . . . . . . . . . . . . . . . . . . . . . . Tom
- 0:30—Buns in black G-string bikini when his swim trunks get ripped off.
- 0:43—Buns in G-string underwear getting out of bed and going to the bathroom.
Chona Jason . . . . . . . . . . . . . . . . . . . . . . . Beautiful Lady
Cari Mayor . . . . . . . . . . . . . . . . . . . . . . . . . . . . Donna
- 0:10—Brief breasts twice, taking off her top before and after Herman comes into the room.
George O . . . . . . . . . . . . . . . . . . . . . . . . . . . . Herman
- 0:17—Buns, while getting his underwear torn off by five angry women, then running back to his room.
Anne Marie Oliver . . . . . . . . . . . . . . . Kathy's Friend #2
Sherrie Rose . . . . . . . . . . . . . . . . . . . . . . Kathy Shields
  0:25—In bed wearing white bra and panties talking to Bruce. Long scene.
  0:52—Buns, walking around in swimsuit and jacket.
- •• 0:53—Breasts taking off swimsuit top kneeling by the phone, then brief buns standing up.

- 1:15—In yellow two piece swimsuit walking on the beach.
- •• 1:24—Brief breasts taking off her yellow top on the beach talking to Bruce.
Reneé Shugart . . . . . . . . . . . . . . . . . . . . . . . . . . Karen
- 0:15—In lingerie reading a magazine.
- 0:42—Breasts taking off her top. Long shot, dark.
- 0:45—In white lingerie, standing on stairs, then very brief left breast flashing.

## Summer Lovers (1982)
Peter Gallagher . . . . . . . . . . . . . . . . . . . Michael Pappas
- 0:22—Buns, while running into the water after Valerie Quennessen.
- 0:54—Frontal nudity getting ready to dive off a rock while Daryl Hannah and Quennessen watch. Long shot, hard to see anything.
Daryl Hannah . . . . . . . . . . . . . . . . . . Cathy Featherstone
- 0:07—Very brief breasts getting out of bed.
  0:17—In a two piece swimsuit.
  0:54—Buns, lying on rock with Valerie Quennessen watching Michael dive off a rock.
  0:56—In a swimsuit again.
- 1:03—Brief right breast sweeping the balcony.
Valerie Quennessen . . . . . . . . . . . . . . . . . . . . . . . . Lina
- 0:12—Breasts, while on balcony.
- ••• 0:19—Nude on the beach with Michael.
- 0:23—Brief breasts in a cave with Michael.
- •• 0:30—Breasts, while lying on the floor with Michael.
  0:54—Buns, lying on a rock with Daryl Hannah watching Michael dive off a rock.
- 1:03—Left breast, while in bed.
- •• 1:05—Breasts while dancing on the balcony.
  1:09—Breasts while on the beach.
Hans Van Tongeren . . . . . . . . . . . . . . . . . . . . . Jan Tolin

## Summer Night (1987; Italian)
Mariangela Melato . . . . . . . . . . . . . . . . . . Signora Bolk
- •• 0:26—Breasts behind gauze net over bed making love with a German guy.
- •• 1:02—Breasts while on the bed making love with the prisoner.
- •• 1:09—Breasts again.
- ••• 1:13—Buns, while walking out of the ocean, then breasts.

## Summer School (1987)
Kirstie Alley . . . . . . . . . . . . . . . . . . . . . . Robin Bishop
Mark Harmon . . . . . . . . . . . . . . . . . . . . . Freddy Shoop
Ken Olandt . . . . . . . . . . . . . . . . . . . . . . . . . . . . . Larry
- •• 0:48—Brief buns while wearing a red G-string in a male stripper club.
Fabiana Udenio . . . . . . . . . . . . . . . . . . . . . Anna-Maria

## Summer School Teachers (1975)
Pat Anderson . . . . . . . . . . . . . . . . . . . . . . . . . . . . Sally
- •• 0:52—Breasts and buns, posing for photos, then in bed with Bob.
- 1:05—Side view of right breast in photo in magazine.
Michael Greer . . . . . . . . . . . . . . . . . . . John John Lacey

Rhonda Leigh Hopkins . . . . . . . . . . . . . . . . . . . Denise
• 0:45—Breasts making love with a guy. Close up of a breast.

Candice Rialson . . . . . . . . . . . . . . . . . . . . . . . Conklin T.
• 0:14—Breasts and buns when Mr. Lacy fantasizes about what she looks like. Don't see her face, but it looks like her.
••• 0:38—Breasts outside with other teacher, kissing on the ground.

### *A Summer Story* (1988)

Imogen Stubbs . . . . . . . . . . . . . . . . Megan David
•• 0:36—Left breast several times, then right breast while making love with Frank in barn.
0:41—Very, very brief buns, frolicking in pond at night with Frank.
1:03—Very brief silhouette of left breast during Frank's flashback sequence.

James Wilby . . . . . . . . . . . . . . . . . . . . . . Frank Ashton
• 0:08—Buns, in creek with Mr. Garten while skinny dipping.

Susannah York . . . . . . . . . . . . . . . . . Mrs. Narracrombe

### *Summer's Games* (1987)

Amy Lynn Baxter . . . . . . . . . . Boxer/Girl from Penthouse
•• 0:04—Breasts opening her swimsuit top after contest. (1st place winner.)
•• 0:18—Breasts during boxing match.

Andi Bruce . . . . . . . . . . . . . . . . . . . . . . . News Anchor
0:12—Brief right breast, while turning around to look at monitor.
• 0:42—Breasts turning around to look at the monitor.

Lori Deann Pallett . . . . . . . . . . . . . . . . . . Torch Carrier
• 0:00—Half breasts running in short T-shirt carrying torch.
•• 0:04—Breasts opening her swimsuit top after contest. (2nd place winner.)

Teri Lynn Peake . . . . . . . . . . . . . . . . . . . Penthouse Girl
Cindy Rome . . . . . . . . . . . . . . . . . . . . . . . . . . . . Boxer

### *Sunset Grill* (1992)

Stacy Keach . . . . . . . . . . . . . . . . . . . . . . . . . . Shelgrove
Alexandra Paul . . . . . . . . . . . . . . . . . . . . . . . . . . Anita
••• 1:14—Breasts and upper talk of buns, while on top of Peter Weller in bed. Nice.
•• 1:15—Very brief buns, while rolling over on her back, then right breast.

Lori Singer . . . . . . . . . . . . . . . . . . . . . . . . . . . . Loren
•• 0:57—Breasts, taking off bra and putting on robe.
• 0:58—Brief full frontal nudity sitting down in open robe. Left breast, while sitting down in tub.
••• 0:59—Breasts and buns, with Peter Weller in bathtub.
••• 1:15—Breasts, sitting up in bed after making love with Weller. Covered with sweat.

Jerry Spicer . . . . . . . . . . . . . . . . . . . . . . . . . . . . Lover
• 0:04—Very brief frontal nudity and very brief buns, getting caught in bed with Mrs. Pietrowski.

Peter Weller . . . . . . . . . . . . . . . . . . . . . . . . Ryder Hart

Sándra Wild . . . . . . . . . . . . . . . . . . . . . . Mrs. Pietrowski
0:03—Out-of-focus breasts, while making love. Seen through telephoto camera lens.
••• 0:04—Breasts in bed with her lover, then nude while struggling in bedroom with her husband.

### *Sunset Heat* (1991)
(Unrated version reviewed.)

Daphne Ashbrook . . . . . . . . . . . . . . . . . . . . . . . . Julie
• 1:06—Brief breasts in silhouette, while making love with Michael Paré. Dark.
•• 1:07—More breasts, on top of Paré, then lying down.

Bridget Butler . . . . . . . . . . . . . . . . . . Lady in New York
• 0:00—Buns, lying in bed.
• 0:01—Buns, when Michael Paré takes off her shirt. Buns and partial left breast lying on him in bed.

Kerrie Clark . . . . . . . . . . . . . . . . . . . . . Brandon's Model
Tracy Dali . . . . . . . . . . . . . . . . . . . . . . . Carl's Pool Girl
•• 1:08—Breasts in pool with Dennis Hopper. Breasts and buns, getting out of pool while wearing a G-string.

Dennis Hopper . . . . . . . . . . . . . . . . . . . . . . Carl Madson
Michael Paré . . . . . . . . . . . . . . . . . . . . . . . Eric Wright
• 0:00—Buns, while standing and looking out the window.
••• 0:22—Buns, while standing on stairs with Tracy Tweed, then making love with her on the floor.
• 0:24—Buns, while standing up and walking up the stairs.

Elena Sahagun . . . . . . . . . . . . . . . . . . . . Brandon's Model
Julie Strain . . . . . . . . Carl's Breakfast Girl/Party Statuette
•• 0:51—Breasts, covered with silver paint, made up to look like a statue at the party.

Tracy Tweed . . . . . . . . . . . . . . . . . . . . . . . . . . . . Lena
••• 0:19—Breasts making love with Michael Paré. Nice, long scene.
••• 0:22—Breasts and buns, making love with Paré on stairs, sofa and the floor.
••• 0:24—Breasts, lying on the floor when the bad guys come in. Brief partial right breast, standing up and covering herself with a jacket.

### *Sunset Strip* (1992)

Bridget Butler . . . . . . . . . . . . . . . . . . . . . . . . . Candice
Michelle Clunie . . . . . . . . . . . . . . . . . . . . . . . . Jonesy
••• 0:23—In black skirt and bra, then breasts and buns in G-string, doing routine on stage.
• 1:16—Breasts in music video.

Jeff Conaway . . . . . . . . . . . . . . . . . . . . . . . . . . . Tony
Michelle Foreman . . . . . . . . . . . . . . . . . . . . . . Heather
•• 0:29—In black bra and G-string, practicing her dance routine in her living room.
0:42—Brief back side of left breast, while in the shower.
0:46—In black bra and G-string, practicing some more.
•• 1:24—Buns in G-string, while dancing during contest.

•• 1:28—Breasts in the shower with Jeff Conaway. Don't see her face well, but it looks like her.

••• 1:30—Buns in G-string dancing on stage and breasts (finally!) at the end.

Lori Jo Hendrix . . . . . . . . . . . . . . . . . . . . . . . . Tammy

•• 0:54—Breasts, taking off her swimsuit top for Crystal's video camera.

••• 1:12—Breasts and buns in G-string, doing strip routine on stage.

• 1:16—Breasts in music video.

Rebecca Lynn . . . . . . . . . . . . . . . . . . . . . . . . Crystal

•• 0:17—Breasts and buns in G-string, dancing on stage.

• 0:38—In red dress, then breasts doing strip routine.

• 1:03—In dress, then breasts while stripping. Buns in body stocking.

• 1:16—Breasts in music video.

Shelley Michelle . . . . . . . . . . . . . . . . . . . . . . . Veronica

## Superchick (1978)

Uschi Digard . . . . . . . . . . . . . . . . . . . . . . . . . Mayday

••• 0:42—Buns and breasts getting whipped acting during the making of a film, then talking to three people.

Flo Gerrish. . . . . . . . . . . . . . . . . . . . . . Funky Jane

Phil Hoover . . . . . . . . . . . . . . . . . . . . Tommy Hooks

Joyce Jillson . . . . . . . . . . . . . . . Tara B. True/Superchick

• 0:03—Brief upper half of right breast leaning back in bathtub.

•• 0:06—Breasts in bed throwing cards up.

• 0:16—Brief breasts under net on boat with Johnny.

• 0:29—Brief right breast several times in airplane restroom with a Marine.

1:12—Buns, frolicking in the ocean with Johnny. Don't see her face.

• 1:27—Close up of breasts (probably body double) when sweater pops open.

Candy Samples . . . . . . . . . . . . . . . . . . . . Lady on Boat

••• 0:08—Breasts in bed with Johnny on boat.

## Superfly (1972)

Sheila Frazier. . . . . . . . . . . . . . . . . . . . . . . . Georgia

•• 0:40—Breasts and buns, making love in the bathtub with Superfly.

## Superstar: The Life and Times of Andy Warhol (1990)

Viva. . . . . . . . . . . . . . . . . . . . . . . . . . . . . Herself

• 0:26—Very brief right breast, while raising blouse to breast feed a baby.

• 0:49—Brief breasts, while lying in bed on right side of split screen in a clip from another film.

Candy Darling. . . . . . . . . . . . . . . . . . . . . . . . Himself

•• 0:39—Frontal nudity in B&W still photo.

• 1:13—Very brief frontal nudity in the same B&W still photo.

## Surf II (1984)

Fred Asparagus. . . . . . . . . . . . . . . . . . . . . . Fat Boy #1

• 0:19—Buns, when blue wet suit splits in the back while at the beach.

Corinne Bohrer. . . . . . . . . . . . . . . . . . . . . Cindy Lou

Josh Cadman . . . . . . . . . . . . . . . . . . . Johnny Big Head

• 0:05—Buns, mooning three girls who flash him.

Jim Greenleaf . . . . . . . . . . . . . . . . . . . . . . Fat Boy #2

• 0:19—Buns, when yellow wet suit splits in the back while at the beach.

Britt Helfer . . . . . . . . . . . . . . . . . . . . . Hot Potato #2

•• 0:25—Breasts taking off bikini top with her friend in lifeguard station at beach with Eric Stoltz and his friend.

•• 0:27—Brief breasts with her friend, after dropping towel when she raises her hands for the police.

Linda Kerridge . . . . . . . . . . . . . . . . . . . . . . . Sparkle

Joy Michael . . . . . . . . . . . . . . . . . . . . . Hot Potato #1

•• 0:25—Breasts taking off bikini top with her friend in lifeguard station at beach with Eric Stoltz and his friend.

•• 0:27—Brief breasts with her friend, after dropping towel when she raises her hands for the police.

Eric Stoltz. . . . . . . . . . . . . . . . . . . . . . . . . . Chuck

Tom Villard . . . . . . . . . . . . . . . . . . . Jacko O'Finlay

Carol Wayne . . . . . . . . . . . . . . . . . . . Mrs. O'Finlay

## Surf Nazis Must Die (1986)

Bobbie Bresee . . . . . . . . . . . . . . . . . . Smeg's Mom

Cristina Garcia . . . . . . . . . . . . . . . . . . . . . . .Waitress

• 0:21—Breasts pulling her top up for Wheels while sitting on his lap.

Dawn Wildsmith . . . . . . . . . . . . . . . . . . . . . . Eva

• 0:25—Breasts being fondled at the beach wearing a wet suit by Adolf. Mostly right breast.

## Surfacing (1980)

Kathleen Beller. . . . . . . . . . . . . . . . . . . . . . . . .Kate

0:22—Very brief buns, pulling down pants to change. Dark, hard to see.

0:23—Very brief right breast undressing. Dark, hard to see.

• 0:24—Very, very brief breasts turning over in bed.

0:25—Buns, standing next to bed.

••• 1:23—Breasts washing herself in the water. One long shot, one side view of right breast.

Joseph Bottoms . . . . . . . . . . . . . . . . . . . . . . . . .Joe

• 0:23—Buns, while in bed with Kathleen Beller.

## The Surrogate (1984; Canadian)

Carole Laure. . . . . . . . . . . . . . . . . Anouk Vanderlin

• 0:48—Very brief breasts when Frank rips her blouse open in his apartment.

Barbara Law. . . . . . . . . . . . . . . . . Maggie Simpson

Marilyn Lightstone. . . . . . . . . . . . . Dr. Harriet Forman

Shannon Tweed . . . . . . . . . . . . . . . . . . . . .Lee Wake

••• 0:03—Breasts taking a Jacuzzi bath.

• 0:42—Brief breasts changing in bedroom, then in bra getting dressed. Long shot.

••• 1:02—Breasts in sauna talking with Frank. Long scene.

## Survival Quest (1989)
Steve Antin . . . . . . . . . . . . . . . . . . . . . . . . . . . . Raider
Traci Lin . . . . . . . . . . . . . . . . . . . . . . . . . . . . . . Olivia
• 0:50—Breasts, while bathing in a stream while seen by Gray. Long shot.

## Survivor (1987)
Sue Kiel . . . . . . . . . . . . . . . . . . . . . . . . . . The Woman
••• 0:33—Right breast, then breasts and buns making love with Survivor in hammock. Long scene.

## Suzanne (1980; Canadian)
Jennifer Dale . . . . . . . . . . . . . . . . . . . . . . . . Suzanne
•• 0:29—Breasts when boyfriend lifts her sweatshirt up when she's sitting on couch doing homework.
•• 0:53—Breasts with Nicky on the floor.
Winston Rekert . . . . . . . . . . . . . . . . . . Nicky Callaghan

## Suzanne (1973)
a.k.a. The Second Coming of Suzanne
(Suzanne has nudity in it, The Second Coming of Suzanne has the nudity cut out.)
Sondra Locke . . . . . . . . . . . . . . . . . . . . . . . Suzanne
•• 0:27—Breasts sitting, looking at a guy. Brief left breast several times lying down.
••• 0:29—Breasts lying down.

## Swamp Thing (1981)
Adrienne Barbeau . . . . . . . . . . . . . . . . . . . . Alice Cable
• 1:03—Side view of left breast washing herself off in the swamp. Long shot.
Karen Price . . . . . . . . . . . . . . . . . . . . . . . . Messenger

## Swann in Love (1984; French/German)
a.k.a. Un Amour de Swann
Marie-Christine Barrault . . . . . . . . . . .Madame Verdunn
Jeremy Irons . . . . . . . . . . . . . . . . . . . . . Charles Swann
Ornella Muti . . . . . . . . . . . . . . . . . . . . .Odette de Crêcy
•• 1:15—Brief left breast, making love with Jeremy Irons.
••• 1:28—Breasts sitting on bed talking to Irons.

## Swashbuckler (1976)
Rutanya Alda . . . . . . . . . . . . . . . . . . . . . Bath Attendant
Peter Boyle . . . . . . . . . . . . . . . . . . . . . . . . Lord Durant
Beau Bridges . . . . . . . . . . . . . . . . . . . . . Major Folly
Genevieve Bujold . . . . . . . . . . . . . . . . . . Jane Barnet
• 1:00—Very brief side view nude, diving from the ship into the water. Long shot, don't really see anything.
• 1:01—Buns and brief side of left breast seen from under water.
Anjelica Huston . . . . . . . . . . . . . . Woman of Dark Visage
Lisa Moore . . . . . . . . . . . . . . . . . . . . . . . Pirates' Lady
Pepe Serna . . . . . . . . . . . . . . . . . . . . Street Entertainer
Dorothy Tristan . . . . . . . . . . . . . . . . . . . . . . . . . Alice
Brenda Venus . . . . . . . . . . . . . . . . . . . . Bath Attendant

## Sweet Country (1985)
Jane Alexander . . . . . . . . . . . . . . . . . . . . . . . . . Anna
• 1:39—Brief side view of left breast after getting out of bed.
Carole Laure . . . . . . . . . . . . . . . . . . . . . . . . . . . Eva
•• 0:31—Breasts changing in apartment while Randy Quaid watches.
• 0:43—Nude in auditorium with other women prisoners.
••• 1:13—Nude in bed with Quaid.
Irene Papas . . . . . . . . . . . . . . . . . . . . . . .Mrs. Araya
Joanna Pettet . . . . . . . . . . . . . . . . . . . . . . . . Monica

## Sweet Justice (1991)
Catherine Hickland . . . . . . . . . . . . . . . . . . . .Chris Barnes
• 0:52—Brief buns and left breast, getting into spa. (You don't see her face clearly, it looks like a body double because her hair is different.)
•• 0:53—Brief upper half of left breast, while sitting in spa. This is definitely her!
Marjean Holden . . . . . . . . . . . . . . . . . . . . . . . . . . MJ
Kathleen Kinmont . . . . . . . . . . . . . . . . . . . . . Heather
Cheryl Paris . . . . . . . . . . . . . . . . . . . . . . . . .Suzanne
0:10—In black bra, outside with Marc Singer.
•• 0:12—Brief breasts while making love with Singer standing up by tree.
Marc Singer . . . . . . . . . . . . . . . . . . . . . . . Steve Colton
Patricia Tallman . . . . . . . . . . . . . . . . . . . . . . . .Josie

## Sweet Killing (1992; Canadian/French)
Andrea Ferréol . . . . . . . . . . . . . . . . . . . . . .Louise Cross
Leslie Hope . . . . . . . . . . . . . . . . . . . . . . . . . .Eva Bishop
•• 0:36—Right breast and partial left breast, while making love with Alan.

## Sweet Murder (1990)
Embeth Davidtz . . . . . . . . . . . . . . . . . . . Laurie Shannon
0:22—In white bra and panties in bedroom with Lisa.
• 0:40—Brief breasts behind wet shower door. Can't really see anything.
Helene Udy . . . . . . . . . . . . . . . . . . . . . . . Lisa Smith
•• 0:44—Brief buns, twice, while standing in doorway in Dell's apartment.
• 0:47—Breasts in bed while talking to Dell, then nude, getting out of bed while he's asleep.
• 0:48—Brief nude while stabbing Dell with a knife.
• 0:49—Buns and right breast while dragging Dell out of the bedroom.

## Sweet Perfection (1988)
a.k.a. The Perfect Model
Liza Cruzat . . . . . . . . . . . . . . . . . . . . . . . Linda Johnson
• 0:31—Left breast, in bed with Mario. Don't see her face. Probably a body double.

## Sweet Poison (1991)
Steven Bauer . . . . . . . . . . . . . . . . . . . . . . . . . . Bobby
•• 1:06—Buns, while making love on top of Patricia Healy in bed. Don't see his face.

Patricia Healy . . . . . . . . . . . . . . . . . . . . . . . .Charlene
- 0:01—Breasts and buns, while straddling her husband in bed.
  0:45—In white bra and panties, taking off her clothes and going for a dip in the river.
- ••• 1:05—Breasts, dropping her towel in front of Bauer in the bathroom.
- •• 1:08—Side view breasts, straddling Bauer in bed.

### Sweet Revenge (1987)
Nancy Allen . . . . . . . . . . . . . . . . . . . . . . . . Jillian Grey
Gina Gershon . . . . . . . . . . . . . . . . . . . . . . . . . . . K.C.
- 0:41—Brief breasts in water under a waterfall with Lee.
Sal Landi. . . . . . . . . . . . . . . . . . . . . . . . . . . . . . . .n.a.
Michele Little . . . . . . . . . . . . . . . . . . . . . . . . . . .Lee
- 0:41—Brief breasts in water under a waterfall with K.C.

### Sweet Sixteen (1982)
Steve Antin . . . . . . . . . . . . . . . . . . . . . . .Hank Burke
Sharon Farrell . . . . . . . . . . . . . . . . . . . . . . . . Kathy
Aleisa Shirley. . . . . . . . . . . . . . . . . . . . Melissa Morgan
- 0:16—Side view of body, nude, taking a shower.
- 1:11—Breasts undressing to go skinny dipping with Hank. Dark, hard to see.
- 1:13—Breasts, getting out of the water.
Susan Strasberg. . . . . . . . . . . . . . . . . . . .Joanne Morgan

### Sweet Sugar (1972)
*a.k.a. Hellfire on Ice*
Timothy Brown . . . . . . . . . . . . . . . . . . . . . . . . Mojo
Pamela Collins. . . . . . . . . . . . . . . . . . . . . . . .Dolores
- 0:26—Brief breasts when doctor tears her bra off.
- ••• 0:50—Breasts in the shower with Phyllis Davis.
Phyllis Davis . . . . . . . . . . . . . . . . . . . . . . . . . Sugar
- ••• 0:34—Breasts in bed with a guard.
- ••• 0:50—Breasts in the shower with Dolores.
- •• 0:57—Brief breasts in the bathroom.
Ella Edwards . . . . . . . . . . . . . . . . . . . . . . . .Simone
- 0:58—Breasts in bed with Mojo.
Jackie Giroux. . . . . . . . . . . . . . . . . . . . . . . . . Fara
- •• 0:33—Breasts, skinny dipping in stream with Dolores.

### Sweet William (1980; British)
Jenny Agutter . . . . . . . . . . . . . . . . . . . . . . . . . Ann
  0:27—Buns, while standing on balcony with Sam Waterston.
- •• 0:28—Breasts sitting on edge of the bed while talking with Waterston.
- 0:44—Brief left breast when Waterston takes her blouse off in the living room.
Anna Massey. . . . . . . . . . . . . . . . . . . . . . . . . . .Edna
Sam Waterston . . . . . . . . . . . . . . . . . . . . . . . William
- 0:27—Buns, seen through a window in the door, standing on balcony with Jenny Agutter.
David Wood . . . . . . . . . . . . . . . . . . . . . . . . .Vicar

### Sweetie (1989; Australian)
Genevieve Lemon . . . . . . . . . . . . . . . . . . . . . . Sweetie
- •• 1:23—Breasts in tree house (she's covered with paint).
- 1:25—Brief buns, mooning her dad.

### Swept Away (1975; Italian)
*a.k.a. Swept Away...by an unusual destiny in the blue sea of august*
Mariangela Melato. . . . . . . . . . . . . . . .Raffaela Lenzetti
- •• 1:10—Breasts on the sand when Giancarlo Giannini catches her and makes love with her.

### The Swimmer
Burt Lancaster . . . . . . . . . . . . . . . . . . . . . . Ned Merrill
- 0:43—Long shot of buns, while taking off his swim trunks to get into nudist colony.
- •• 0:45—Buns, after turning away from table and walking to the pool.

### The Swindle (1991)
Jasaé . . . . . . . . . . . . . . . . . . . . . . . . . . . . . . . . Nina
- ••• 0:28—Nude, posing for Tom while he video tapes her. Long scene.
- ••• 0:31—Nude, making love with Tom.
- ••• 0:36—Breasts in back of limousine with Dude.
Monica Akesson. . . . . . . . . . . . . . . . . Tom's Last Hurrah
- ••• 1:17—Breasts, then full frontal nudity, posing on couch for Tom.
Gloria Pryor . . . . . . . . . . . . . . . . . . . . . . . . . Claudia
- 1:15—Breasts with Tom.

### Swing Shift (1984)
Alana Collins . . . . . . . . . . . . . . . . . . . . . . Frankie Parker
  0:11—Buns in B&W photo that Christine Lahti shows to Fred Ward. Possible photo composite.
Ed Harris . . . . . . . . . . . . . . . . . . . . . . . . . . .Jack Walsh
- 0:03—Very brief frontal nudity when he sits down in chair wearing a towel around his waist.
Goldie Hawn . . . . . . . . . . . . . . . . . . . . . . . Kay Walsh
Holly Hunter. . . . . . . . . . . . . . . . . . . Jeannie Sherman
Penny Johnson. . . . . . . . . . . . . . . . . . . . . . Genevieve
Lisa Pelikan. . . . . . . . . . . . . . . . . . . . . Violet Mulligan
Kurt Russell . . . . . . . . . . . . . . . . . . . . .Lucky Lockhart
Fred Ward . . . . . . . . . . . . . . . . . . . . . Biscuits Toohey

### The Swinging Cheerleaders (1974)
Colleen Camp . . . . . . . . . . . . . . . . . . . . . . . Mary Ann
Sandra Dempsey . . . . . . . . . . . . . . . . .1st Girl at Tryout
Rosanne Katon. . . . . . . . . . . . . . . . . . . . . . . . . Lisa
- •• 0:25—Breasts taking off her blouse in her teacher's office. Half of right breast while he talks on the phone.
Cheryl Smith . . . . . . . . . . . . . . . . . . . . . . . . .Andrea
- •• 0:12—Breasts taking off her bra and putting sheer blouse on.
- 0:17—Left breast, several times, sitting in bed with Ross.

## Switch (1991)

Lysette Anthony . . . . . . . . . . . . . . . . . . . . . . . . . . Liz
- 0:05—Brief breasts in spa with JoBeth Williams and Felicia, trying to kill Steve.

Ellen Barkin . . . . . . . . . . . . . . . . . Amanda Brooks/Steve
Linda Doná . . . . . . . . . . . . . . . . . . . . . . . Gay Club Patron
Perry King . . . . . . . . . . . . . . . . . . . . . . . . . Steve Brooks
John Lafayette . . . . . . . . . . . . . . . . . . . . . . . Sgt. Phillips
Karen Medak. . . . . . . . . . . . . . . . . . . . . . Saleswoman
Jackie Moen . . . . . . . . . . . . . . . . . . . Girl at City Grille
Jimmy Smits . . . . . . . . . . . . . . . . . . . . . .Walter Stone
- ••• 1:21—Buns, while stretching after waking up in the morning. A bit on the dark side.

JoBeth Williams . . . . . . . . . . . . . . . . . . . Margo Brofman
Rebecca Wood-Sharkey. . . . . . . . . . . . . Gay Club Patron

## Switchblade Sisters (1975)

Marlene Clark . . . . . . . . . . . . . . . . . . . . . . . . . . Muff
Janice Karman. . . . . . . . . . . . . . . . . . . . . . . . . Bunnie
Robin Lee . . . . . . . . . . . . . . . . . . . . . . . . . . . . . Lace
- 0:48—Breasts sitting up in bed to talk to Dominic. Dark.

Joanne Nail . . . . . . . . . . . . . . . . . . . . . . . . . .Maggie
- 0:21—Very, very brief right breast in ripped blouse when she tries to rip Dominic's shirt off.

Jerii Woods . . . . . . . . . . . . . . . . . . . . . . . . . . . . .Toby

## The Sword and the Sorcerer (1982)

Kathleen Beller . . . . . . . . . . . . . . . . . . . . . . . . . Alana
- 0:54—Side view of buns, lying face down getting oil rubbed all over her.

Shelly Taylor Morgan . . . . . . . . . . . . . . . . . . . . Bar-Bra
- 0:54—Brief breasts when Lee Horsley crashes through the window and almost lands on her.

## Sylvester (1985)

Melissa Gilbert . . . . . . . . . . . . . . . . . . . . . . . . . Charlie
- 0:23—Very, very brief breasts struggling with a guy in truck cab. Seen through a dirty windshield.
- •• 0:24—Very brief left breast after Richard Farnsworth runs down the stairs to help her. Seen from the open door of the truck.

## Taffin (1988; U.S./British)

Pierce Brosnan . . . . . . . . . . . . . . . . . . . . . . .Mark Taffin
Alison Doody . . . . . . . . . . . . . . . . . . . . . . . Charlotte
- 0:14—Very, very brief side view of right breast when Pierce Brosnan rips her blouse open. Long shot, hard to see.

Tina Shaw. . . . . . . . . . . . . . . . . . . . . . .Lola the Stripper
- •• 1:04—Breasts doing routine in a club.

## Tai-Pan (1986)

Bryan Brown . . . . . . . . . . . . . . . . . Dirk Struan/"Tai-Pan"
Joan Chen. . . . . . . . . . . . . . . . . . . . . . . . . . May May
  0:55—In sheer top sitting on bed talking to Bryan Brown.
- 0:56—Brief left breast washing herself, hard to see anything.
  1:14—Sheer top again.
  1:30—Sheer top again.

---

Kyra Sedgwick . . . . . . . . . . . . . . . . . . . . . . . . . .Tess
Janine Turner . . . . . . . . . . . . . . . . . . . . . . . . Shevaun

## Tainted

Shari Shattuck . . . . . . . . . . . . . . . . . . . . . . . . . Cathy
- •• 0:09—Buns, while lying on top of Frank.
- ••• 0:27—Breasts in bubble bath, getting up, drying herself off, then putting on white bra while wearing panties.
  0:28—In white bra and panties, masturbating on chair.
  0:30—Briefly in white bra and panties, getting attacked by rapist.
- ••• 0:49—Breasts taking a shower.
- 0:51—Brief side view of left breast in the shower again.

## Take Two (1988)

Grant Goodeve . . . . . . . . . . Barry Griffith/Frank Bentley
- 0:31—Buns, while in bed with Robin Mattson.
- ••• 0:46—Buns, while getting into bed with Mattson again.

Robin Mattson . . . . . . . . . . . . . . . . . . . . . Susan Bentley
  0:21—Exercising in yellow outfit while Frank Stallone plays music.
- •• 0:25—Brief breasts taking a shower.
  0:26—Showing Grant Goodeve her new two piece swimsuit.
- ••• 0:29—Breasts in bed with Goodeve.
- ••• 0:45—Right breast in shower, then breasts getting into bed.
- 0:47—Brief breasts getting out of bed and putting an overcoat on.
  0:51—One piece swimsuit by the swimming pool.
  1:12—In two piece swimsuit at the beach.
- ••• 1:28—Breasts taking a shower after shooting Goodeve in bed.

Karen Mayo-Chandler . . . . . . . . . . . . . . . . . .Dorothy
- •• 1:17—Brief breasts on bed when her gold dress is pulled down a bit.

Suzanne Slater . . . . . . . . . . . . . . . . . . . . . . . . .Sherrie
- •• 0:11—Breasts in office talking with Grant Goodeve, wearing panties, garter belt and stockings.
- 1:00—Breasts undressing to get into hot tub wearing black underwear bottom.

## Takin' It All Off (1987)

George "Buck" Flower . . . . . . . . . . . . . Allison's Father
Geno Hart . . . . . . . . . . . . . . . . . . . . . . . . . . . . Adam
- •• 1:08—Buns, while in the shower with Allison.

Becky LeBeau . . . . . . . . . . . . . . . . . . . . . . . . .Becky
- •• 0:03—Breasts in pink leotard in dance studio.
- ••• 0:11—Nude in the showers (she's in the back on the left).
- •• 0:16—Breasts and brief full frontal nudity getting introduced to Allison.
- ••• 0:23—In black bra and panties, then nude doing a strip routine outside.
- 0:35—Brief full frontal nudity pushing Elliot into the pool.
- 0:36—Brief breasts in studio with Allison again.

- 0:36—Brief left breast in dance studio with Allison.
- •• 1:23—Nude, dancing with the other girls on stage.

Francesca "Kitten" Natividad. . . . . . . . . . Betty Bigones
- ••• 0:12—Nude, washing herself in the shower.
- •• 0:39—Nude, on stage in a giant glass, then breasts backstage in her dressing room.
- • 0:42—Breasts in flashbacks from *Takin' It Off*.
  0:46—Breasts in group in the studio.
- ••• 0:53—Nude, dancing on the deck outside. Some nice slow motion shots.
- •• 1:16—Breasts on stage in club.
- ••• 1:23—Nude, dancing with the other girls on stage.

Jean Poremba . . . . . . . . . . . . . . . . . . . . . . Allison
- • 0:36—Buns in G-string andl in pink bra.
- ••• 0:49—In white lingerie, then breasts, then nude dancing.
- ••• 0:58—Breasts and buns in G-string, dancing outside when she hears the music.
- ••• 0:59—Nude dancing in a park.
- •• 1:01—Nude dancing in a laundromat.
- ••• 1:03—Nude dancing in a restaurant.
- ••• 1:07—Nude in shower with Adam.
- •• 1:13—Breasts dancing for the music in a studio.
- ••• 1:23—Nude, dancing with the other girls on stage.

Gail Thackray . . . . . . . . . . . . . . . . . . . .Hannah McCall
- ••• 0:03—Breasts in red leotard and head band, in dance studio.
- ••• 0:11—Full frontal nudity in the showers (she's in the back on the right.)
- ••• 0:28—Nude, doing strip routine outside.
- •• 1:24—Nude, dancing with the other girls on stage.
- • 1:29—Breasts in crate backstage with Hadem.

## Takin' It Off (1984)

Francesca "Kitten" Natividad. . . . . . . . . . Betty Bigones
- •• 0:01—Breasts dancing on stage.
- ••• 0:04—Breasts and buns dancing on stage.
- ••• 0:29—Breasts in the Doctor's office.
- ••• 0:32—Nude dancing in the Psychiatrists' office.
- ••• 0:39—Nude in bed with a guy during fantasy sequence playing with vegetables and fruits.
- •• 0:49—Breasts in bed covered with popcorn.
- • 0:51—Nude doing a dance routine in the library.
- ••• 1:09—Nude splashing around in a clear plastic bathtub on stage.
- •• 1:20—Nude at a fat farm dancing.
- •• 1:24—Nude running in the woods in slow motion.

Angelique Pettyjohn . . . . . . . . . . . . . . . . . . Anita Little
Ashley St. Jon . . . . . . . . . . . . . . . . . . . . . . . . . . Sin
- ••• 0:20—Breasts and buns doing two dance routines on stage.
- •• 0:53—Nude, stripping and dancing in the library.

## Taking Care of Business (1990)

James Belushi . . . . . . . . . . . . . . . . . . . . Jimmy Dworski
Jill Johnson . . . . . . . . . . . . . . . . . . . . Tennis Court Girl
Loryn Locklin. . . . . . . . . . . . . . . . . . . . . . . . . . Jewel
- • 0:42—Buns and very brief side view, twice, seen through door, changing by the pool. Then in black two piece swimsuit.

## Taking the Heat (1993)

Alan Arkin . . . . . . . . . . . . . . . . . . . . . . Tommy Canard
Peter Boyle. . . . . . . . . . . . . . . . . . . . . . . . . . .Judge
Tony Goldwyn . . . . . . . . . . . . . . . . . . . . . . . Michael
Lynn Whitfield . . . . . . . . . . . . . . . . . . . . . . . . Carolyn
Rachel York . . . . . . . . . . . . . . . . . . . . . . . . . . .Susan
- •• 0:19—Left breast, while enthusiastically making love in bed on top of George Segal. Very, very brief breasts when changing positions to under the sheets.

## Tales From the Darkside, The Movie (1990)

Steve Buscemi . . . . . . . . . . . . . . . . . Edward Bellingham
Rae Dawn Chong . . . . . . . . . . . . . . . . . . . . . . Carola
- • 1:09—Left breast in blue light, twice, with James Remar. Don't see her face.

Deborah Harry . . . . . . . . . . . . . . . . . . . . . . . . Betty
Julianne Moore. . . . . . . . . . . . . . . . . . . . . . . .Susan
James Remar . . . . . . . . . . . . . . . . . . . . . . . Preston
Christian Slater. . . . . . . . . . . . . . . . . . . . . . . . Andy

## Tales of Ordinary Madness (1983; Italian)

Katia Berger . . . . . . . . . . . . . . . . . . . . . . .Girl on Beach
- ••• 1:30—Full frontal nudity, taking off her clothes in front of Ben Gazzara at the beach.

Judith Drake. . . . . . . . . . . . . . . . . . . . . . . Fat Woman
- • 0:49—Buns, in bra and panties in her bedroom with Ben Gazzara, then left breast when he fondles her.

Ornella Muti. . . . . . . . . . . . . . . . . . . . . . . . . . .Cass
- •• 0:37—Buns, four times, while standing at window in room with Ben Gazzara. Medium long shot.
- • 1:06—Buns, while standing at the beach and feeding the seagulls. One medium long shot and one long shot.

Susan Tyrrell. . . . . . . . . . . . . . . . . . . . . . . . . .Vera
- • 0:19—Right nipple, seen in between strings in bra when she's lying on the floor.
- • 0:20—Upper half of breasts, in between strings in bra. Lower frontal nudity.
- •• 0:22—Lower frontal nudity and upper half of breasts in bra, while standing by the door. Brief buns, while getting carried to bed by Ben Gazzara.
- •• 0:23—Upper half of breasts, buns and lower frontal nudity while lying in bed.

## Talking Walls (1982)

Judy Baldwin . . . . . . . . . . . . . . . . . . . . . . . . . . n.a.
Sybil Danning . . . . . . . . . . . . . . . . . . . . Bathing Beauty
Sally Kirkland . . . . . . . . . . . . . . . . . . . . . . . . Hooker
Marie Laurin. . . . . . . . . . . . . . . . . . . . . . . . . .Jeanne
Kathi Sawyer-Young. . . . . . . . . . . . . . . . . . . . . . n.a.
Steve Shellen . . . . . . . . . . . . . . . . . . . . . . Paul Barton
- •• 0:58—Buns, while taking off his clothes and running down railroad tracks.

June Wilkinson . . . . . . . . . . . . . . . . . . . . . . .Blonde
- • 0:13—Brief left breast, in car room, getting green towel yanked off.
  0:14—Very, very brief left breast in car room again. Dark.
- •• 1:08—Brief breasts, getting green towel taken off.

### Tall Blond Man with One Black Shoe (1973; French)

Mireille Darc . . . . . . . . . . . . . . . . . . . . . . . . . . . Christine
   0:55—Upper half of buns in low, low cut back of
   dress.
   1:03—Almost left breast, in bed with a guy.
Pierre Richard . . . . . . . . . . . . . . . . . . . . . . . . . Francois
  •• 0:18—Buns, getting out of bathtub to answer the
    phone. Buns again, taking off towel and getting
    back in.
  • 0:19—Brief buns, getting out of bathtub to answer
    the phone again.

### The Tall Guy (1990; British)

Jeff Goldblum . . . . . . . . . . . . . . . . . . . . . . Dexter King
   0:34—Brief right cheek of buns, while rolling around
   on the floor with Emma Thompson. Don't see his
   face.
Neil Hamilton . . . . . . . . . . . . . . . . . . . . . Naked George
  •• 0:04—Buns, while walking around apartment talk-
    ing to Jeff Goldblum. Brief frontal nudity (out of fo-
    cus).
  • 0:06—More buns, when getting introduced to
    Goldblum.
  • 1:22—Brief buns, during end credits.
Anna Massey . . . . . . . . . . . . . . . . . . . . . . . . . . . . . Mary
Hugh Thomas . . . . . . . . . . . . . . . . . . . . Dr. Karabekian
Emma Thompson . . . . . . . . . . . . . . . . . . . . . . . . Kate
  ••• 0:33—Very brief right breast, brief buns, then
    breasts during funny love making scene with Jeff
    Goldblum.

### Tango & Cash (1989)

Dori Courtney . . . . . . . . . . . . . . . . . . Dressing Room Girl
  • 1:06—Breasts, sitting in chair looking in the mirror
    in the background. Long shot.
Teri Hatcher . . . . . . . . . . . . . . . . . . . . . . . . . . . . . Kiki
Clint Howard . . . . . . . . . . . . . . . . . . . . . . . . . . . Slinky
Michael Jeter . . . . . . . . . . . . . . . . . . . . . . . . . . Skinner
Roxanne Kernohan . . . . . . . . . . . . . Dressing Room Girl
  • 1:06—Brief breasts in dressing room with three oth-
    er girls. She's the second one in the middle.
Tamara Landry . . . . . . . . . . . . . . . . . . . . . Girl in Bar
Christie Mucciante . . . . . . . . . . . . . Dressing Room Girl
  • 1:06—Brief breasts in dressing room. (She's the first
    topless blonde.)
Kurt Russell . . . . . . . . . . . . . . . . . . . . . . . . . . . . . Cash
  •• 0:31—Brief buns while walking into the prison
    shower room with Sylvester Stallone.
Sylvester Stallone . . . . . . . . . . . . . . . . . . . Ray Tango
  •• 0:31—Brief buns while walking into the prison
    shower room with Kurt Russell.

### Tank (1984)

James Cromwell . . . . . . . . . . . . . . . . . . . . Deputy Euclid
  •• 1:06—Buns, after James Garner makes him strip and
    handcuffed to telephone pole by Jenilee Harrison.
Jenilee Harrison . . . . . . . . . . . . . . . . . . . . . . . . . Sarah
Mark Herrier . . . . . . . . . . . . . . . . . . . . . . . . . . . . Elliot
C. Thomas Howell . . . . . . . . . . . . . . . . . . . . . . . . Billy

### Tanya's Island (1980; Canadian)

Vanity . . . . . . . . . . . . . . . . . . . . . . . . . . . . . Tanya
   0:04—Very brief breasts and buns covered with
   paint during B&W segment.
  ••• 0:07—Nude caressing herself and dancing during
    the opening credits.
  •• 0:09—Nude making love on the beach.
    0:11—Brief right breast, while talking to Lobo.
  •• 0:19—Brief breasts on the beach with Lobo, then
    more breasts while yelling at him.
  • 0:28—Mostly breasts in flimsy halter top exploring a
    cave.
  • 0:33—Full frontal nudity undressing in tent.
  • 0:35—Left breast sleeping. Dark, hard to see.
    0:37—Buns while sleeping.
    0:40—Breasts superimposed over another scene.
    0:48—Brief buns swimming in the ocean.
  •• 0:51—Full frontal nudity walking out of the ocean
    and getting dressed.
  • 0:53—Brief breasts in open blouse.
  •• 1:08—Breasts in middle of compound when Lobo
    rapes her in front of Blue.
  • 1:16—Full frontal nudity running through the jungle
    in slow motion. Brief buns.

### Taps (1981)

Tom Cruise . . . . . . . . . . . . . . . . . . . . . . . David Shawn
  • 0:29—Very brief upper half of buns in shower.
Giancarlo Esposito . . . . . . . . . . . . . . . . . . . . J.C. Pierce
  • 1:24—Brief upper half of buns in shower when the
    water is turned off.
Timothy Hutton . . . . . . . . . . . . . . . . . . . Brian Moreland
Lou Milione . . . . . . . . . . . . . . . . . . . . . . . . . . . Cadet
Sean Penn . . . . . . . . . . . . . . . . . . . . . . . . . Alex Dwyer

### Target (1985)

Ilona Grubel . . . . . . . . . . . . . . . . . . . . . . . . . . . . Carla
  • 1:12—Brief breasts in bed with Matt Dillon.

### Tarzan, The Ape Man (1981)

Bo Derek . . . . . . . . . . . . . . . . . . . . . . . . . . . . . . Jane
  ••• 0:43—Nude taking a bath in the ocean, then in a
    wet white dress.
  • 1:35—Brief breasts painted all white.
  • 1:45—Breasts washing all the white paint off in the
    river with Tarzan.
  •• 1:47—Breasts during the ending credits playing
    with Tarzan and the orangutan. (When I saw this
    film in a movie theater, the entire audience actually
    stayed to watch the credits!)
Richard Harris. . . . . . . . . . . . . . . . . . . . . . . . . Parker
John Phillip Law . . . . . . . . . . . . . . . . . . . . . . . . . Holt
Miles O'Keeffe . . . . . . . . . . . . . . . . . . . . . . . . . Tarzan
  • 0:45—Sort of buns, under loin cloth in the surf. Lots
    of other semi-bun shots in the loin cloth throughout
    the rest of the film.
    1:09—Buns, while in loin cloth at side of lake with Bo
    Derek.
  • 1:48—Buns, while in loin cloth, wrestling with oran-
    gutan during end credits.

### *Tattoo* (1981)

Maud Adams. . . . . . . . . . . . . . . . . . . . . . . . . Maddy
- • 0:22—Very brief breasts taking off clothes and putting a bathrobe on.
- •• 0:23—Breasts opening bathrobe so Bruce Dern can start painting.
- •• 0:25—Brief breasts getting into the shower to take off body paint.
- •• 0:58—Brief breasts and buns getting out of bed.
- •• 1:04—Breasts, knocked out on table before Dern starts tattooing her.
- ••• 1:07—Breasts looking at herself in the mirror with a few tattoos on.
- •• 1:24—Breasts lying on table masturbating while Dern watches through peep hole in the door.
- ••• 1:36—Full frontal nudity taking off robe then making love with Dern (her body is covered with tattoos).

Bruce Dern . . . . . . . . . . . . . . . . . . . . . . . .Karl Kinski
- •• 1:36—Buns, while making love with Maud Adams before she kills him.

E. Katherine Kerr . . . . . . . . . . . . . . . . . . . . . . Wife

### *Taxi Dancers* (1993)

Brittany McCrena . . . . . . . . . . . . . . . . . . . . . . Billie
- •• 0:16—Breasts, while changing clothes in room with Star.
- ••• 0:27—Breasts, while making love on billiard table with Bobby.
- ••• 0:44—Breasts (mostly left breast) while making love with Bobby in van.
- 0:45—Partial right breast, when waking up in the morning with Bobby.

### *The Teacher* (1974)

Jay North . . . . . . . . . . . . . . . . . . . . . . . . . . . .n.a.
Angel Tompkins . . . . . . . . . . . . . . . . . . Diane Marshall
- ••• 0:09—Breasts on a boat taking off her swimsuit.
- ••• 0:12—More breasts on the boat getting a suntan.
- ••• 0:36—Breasts taking off her top in bedroom, then buns and breasts taking a shower.
- • 0:41—Brief right breast lying back on bed.
- •• 0:43—Brief breasts opening her bathrobe for Jay North.
- •• 0:47—Side view of right breast lying on bed, then right breast from above.
- •• 0:52—Breasts in boat after making love.

### *Teachers* (1984)

Laura Dern . . . . . . . . . . . . . . . . . . . . . . . . . . Diane
Allen Garfield . . . . . . . . . . . . . . . . . . . . . . Rosenberg
Lee Grant . . . . . . . . . . . . . . . . . . . . . . . . . Dr. Burke
Julia Jennings. . . . . . . . . . . . . . . . . . . . . . The Blonde
- •• 0:05—Brief left breast, while sitting up in bed with Nick Nolte.

Nick Nolte. . . . . . . . . . . . . . . . . . . . . . . . . . . Alex
JoBeth Williams . . . . . . . . . . . . . . . . . . . . . . . .Lisa
- • 1:39—Brief breasts taking off clothes and running down school hallway yelling at Nick Nolte.

### *Ted & Venus* (1991)

Elvira . . . . . . . . . . . . . . . . . . . . . . . . . . . . . . Lisa
James Brolin. . . . . . . . . . . . . . . . . . . . . . . . . .Max
- •• 0:22—Buns, while painting Carol Kane in his house when Bud Cort walks in. Don't see his face.

Pamella D'Pella. . . . . . . . . . . . . . . . . . . . . . Gloria
- ••• 0:17—Breasts while undressing in locker room while talking to Linda.

Woody Harrelson . . . . . . . . . Homeless Vietnam Veteran
Carol Kane . . . . . . . . . . . . Colette/Colette's Twin Sister

### *Teen Lust* (1978)

*a.k.a. Girls Next Door*
Kirsten Baker . . . . . . . . . . . . . . . . . . . . . . Carol Hill
- • 0:45—Brief side view of left breast, while changing clothes in her bedroom.

Perry Lang . . . . . . . . . . . . . . . . . . . . . . . . . . Terry
- • 0:01—Buns in jock strap getting his pants pulled down while he does pull-ups.

### *Teenage Bonnie and Klepto Clyde* (1993)

Maureen Flannigan . . . . . . . . . . . . . . . . . . . . .Bonnie
- • 0:26—Very brief breasts, while climbing into back seat of car.
- ••• 0:34—In black bra and panties, lying on bed when Clyde pours money all over her. Right breast after taking off bra. Breasts while making love.

Connie Hair . . . . . . . . . . . . . . . . . . . . . . . . .Waitress
Scott Wolf . . . . . . . . . . . . . . . . . . . . . . . . . .Clyde
- • 0:53—Brief buns, while standing on hood of car, while mooning an old guy who is staring at him.

### *Teenage Exorcist* (1992)

Jasaé . . . . . . . . . . . . . . . . . . . . . . . . . . Dead Woman
- • 0:01—Brief breasts, dead with a slashed throat, on stairway when discovered by the maid.
- • 0:16—Brief breasts, several times, during nightmare while Brinke Stevens is sleeping.

Elena Sahagun . . . . . . . . . . . . . . . . . . . . . . .Sally
- • 0:09—Brief side view of right breast and buns in panties, while putting robe on.
- • 0:31—Buns and brief side of right breast, while getting into the shower.
- •• 0:32—Buns and right breast, while getting soaped up by creature's hand. Sort of frontal nudity behind fabric shower curtain.

Brinke Stevens . . . . . . . . . . . . . . . . . . . . Dianne
- • 1:03—Brief partial buns in sexy, skimpy outfit, while walking down stairs with Eddie Deezen.
- • 1:06—More brief partial buns.
- • 1:13—Partial buns, during struggle with Elena Sahagan.
- • 1:13—More partial buns, while bending over Jay Richardson.
- • 1:16—Partial buns under fishnet stockings with Deezen.

### *Teenage Seductress*

Sondra Currie. . . . . . . . . . . . . . . . . . . . . . . . . Terry
- ••• 0:14—Buns, while taking off robe in bedroom. Breasts, while looking at herself in bathroom mirror.

• 0:16—Breasts, while in front of mirror again. More breasts while taking a shower.
• 0:24—Breasts, while in bed, trying to get Preston to join her.
• 1:14—Brief partial right breast, while lying on bed with Preston.

### The Tempest (1982)
Raul Julia . . . . . . . . . . . . . . . . . . . . . . . . . . . . . . Kalibanos
Susan Sarandon . . . . . . . . . . . . . . . . . . . . . . . Aretha
0:58—In braless white tank top washing clothes with Molly Ringwald in the ocean.
1:53—In wet white T-shirt on balcony during rainstorm with Jason Robards and Raul Julia.
1:55—In wet white T-shirt on the beach.
• 1:57—Brief right, then left breasts in open T-shirt saving someone in the water.

### Tender Loving Care (1974)
Donna Desmond . . . . . . . . . . . . . . . . . . . .Karen Jordan
••• 0:26—Breasts on waterbed with Reno, brief lower frontal nudity, making love. Long scene.
• 0:39—Breasts and very brief buns getting out of bed.
•• 0:55—Brief buns and breasts on bed with Dr. Traynor.

### Terminal Choice (1985; Canadian)
Teri Austin. . . . . . . . . . . . . . . . . . . . . . . . Lylah Crane
0:14—Full frontal nudity, covered with blood on operating table. Long shot.
0:21—Right breast, on table being examined by Ellen Barkin. Dead, covered with dried blood.
0:26—Very brief left breast under plastic on table, hard to see.
Ellen Barkin . . . . . . . . . . . . . . . . . . . . . Mary O'Connor
Chapelle Jaffe . . . . . . . . . . . . . . . . . . . . . .Mrs. Dodson
Joe Spano . . . . . . . . . . . . . . . . . . . . . . . . . . . .Frank Holt
••• 0:34—Buns, taking off towel and getting dressed in locker room while talking to Anna.
• 0:49—Buns, while making love in bed with Anna. Long shot, don't see his face.
Diane Venora . . . . . . . . . . . . . . . . . . . . . . . . . . . .Anna
0:44—In lingerie, talking to Frank.
• 0:48—Brief left breast, making love in bed with Frank. Don't see her face.
Sandra Warren . . . . . . . . . . . . . . . . . . Nurse Tipton
Cheryl-Ann Wilson . . . . . . . . . . . . . . . . . Nurse Fields

### Terminal Entry (1986)
Barbara Edwards . . . . . . . . . . . . . . . . . . . Lady Electric
••• 0:05—Breasts taking a shower and getting a towel during video game scene.
Jill Terashita. . . . . . . . . . . . . . . . . . . . . . . . . . . . Gwen

### Terminal Exposure (1988)
Tara Buckman. . . . . . . . . . . . . . . . . . . . . . . . . . .n.a.
Hope Marie Carlton. . . . . . . . . . . . . . . . . . . .Christie
••• 1:11—Breasts in bathtub licking ice cream off a guy.
Ava Fabian . . . . . . . . . . . . . . . . . . . . . . . . Bruce's Girl

Luann Lee . . . . . . . . . . . . . . . . . . . . . . . . . Bruce's Girl
Nicole Rio . . . . . . . . . . . . . . . . . . . . . . . Hostage Girl

### Terminal Island (1973)
Phyllis Davis . . . . . . . . . . . . . . . . . . . . . . . . .Joy Lange
••• 0:39—Breasts and buns in a pond, full frontal nudity getting out, then more breasts putting blouse on while a guy watches.
Marta Kristen . . . . . . . . . . . . . . . . . . . . . . . .Lee Phillips
Barbara Leigh. . . . . . . . . . . . . . . . . . . . Bunny Campbell
••• 0:22—Breasts and buns undressing in room while Bobbie watches from the bed.
Tom Selleck . . . . . . . . . . . . . . . . . . . .Dr. Norman Milford
Clyde Ventura . . . . . . . . . . . . . . . . . . . . . . . . . Dillon
•• 0:42—Buns, while taking off pants in front of Phyllis Davis, then covered with honey and bees, then running to jump into a pond.

### The Terminator (1984)
Michael Biehn . . . . . . . . . . . . . . . . . . . . . . Kyle Reese
• 0:06—Side view of buns after arriving from the future. Brief buns running down the alley. A little dark.
Linda Hamilton . . . . . . . . . . . . . . . . . . Sarah Connor
•• 1:18—Brief breasts about four times making love on top of Michael Biehn in motel room.
Bill Paxton . . . . . . . . . . . . . . . . . . . . . . . . .Punk Leader
Rick Rossovich . . . . . . . . . . . . . . . . . . . . . . . . Matt
Arnold Schwarzenegger . . . . . . . . . . . . . The Terminator
••• 0:03—Buns, while kneeling by garbage truck, walking to look at the city and walking toward the three punks at night.

### Terminator 2: Judgement Day (1991)
Linda Hamilton . . . . . . . . . . . . . . . . . . . . Sarah Connor
Robert Patrick. . . . . . . . . . . . . . . . . . . . . . . . . T-1000
• 0:00—Partial buns and very brief partial frontal nudity when kneeling down after arriving from the future.
Arnold Schwarzenegger . . . . . . . . . . . . The Terminator

### Terms of Endearment (1983)
Jeff Daniels. . . . . . . . . . . . . . . . . . . . . . . . . .Flap Horton
John Lithgow . . . . . . . . . . . . . . . . . . . . . . Sam Burns
Shirley MacLaine . . . . . . . . . . . . . . . . .Aurora Greenway
1:00—Very, very brief right breast wrestling with Jack Nicholson in the ocean when she finally frees his hand from her breast. One frame. Hard to see, but for the sake of thoroughness....
Jack Nicholson . . . . . . . . . . . . . . . . . . Garrett Breedlove
Michelle Watkins . . . . . . . . . . . . . . . . . . . . . . Woman
Debra Winger. . . . . . . . . . . . . Emma Greenway Horton

### Terror at the Opera (1989; Italian)
Barbara Cupisti . . . . . . . . . . . . . . . . . . . . . . . n.a.
Cristina Marsillach . . . . . . . . . . . . . . . . . . . . . . Betty
• 0:23—Brief left breast during nightmare. Brief breasts, sitting up in bed and screaming.
William McNamara . . . . . . . . . . . . . . . . . . . Stefan
Daria Nicolodi . . . . . . . . . . . . . . . . . . . . . . . . Mira

### Terror in the Aisles (1984)
Nancy Allen . . . . . . . . . . . . . . . . . . . . . . . . . . Hostess

Kirsten Baker . . . . . . . . . . . . . . . . . . . . . . . . . .Terry
•• 1:03—Breasts and buns, undressing to go skinny dipping from *Friday the 13th, Part II.*
Morgan Fairchild. . . . . . . . . . . . . . . . . . . . . . . . Jamie
•• 1:06—Breasts in mirror in scene from *The Seduction.*
• 1:08—Brief left breast, getting out of pool from *The Seduction.*
Sandy Johnson . . . . . . . . . . . . . . . . . . . Judith Meyers
• 0:15—Brief breasts in scene from *Halloween.*
Victoria Lynn Johnson . Body Double for Angie Dickinson
• 1:07—Breasts in shower from Angie Dickinson's shower scene in *Dressed to Kill.*
David Naughton . . . . . . . . . . . . . . . . . . . David Kessler
• 0:17—Brief buns during transformation into a werewolf from *An American Werewolf in London.*
P.J. Soles . . . . . . . . . . . . . . . . . . . . . . . . . . . . .Lynda
• 0:24—Brief breasts in scene from *Halloween.*

### The Terror on Alcatraz (1986)
Sandy Brooke . . . . . . . . . . . . . . . . . . . . . . . . . Mona
• 0:05—Right breast on bed getting burned with a cigarette by Frank.
Alisa Wilson. . . . . . . . . . . . . . . . . . . . . . . . Clarissa
• 1:14—Brief breasts opening her blouse to distract Frank, so she can get away from him.

### Terror Train (1980; Canadian)
Vanity . . . . . . . . . . . . . . . . . . . . . . . . . . . . . Merry
Joy Boushel . . . . . . . . . . . . . . . . . . . . . . . . . . . Pet
•• 0:49—Breasts wearing panties in sleeper room on train with Mo.
Jamie Lee Curtis . . . . . . . . . . . . . . . . . . . . . . Alena
Sandra Warren . . . . . . . . . . . . . . . . . . . . . . Mitchy

### The Terror Within II (1992)
Clare Hoak . . . . . . . . . . . . . . . . . . . . . . . . . . Ariel
• 0:25—Brief side view of right breast, while in front of fire with Andrew Stevens.
Andrew Stevens . . . . . . . . . . . . . . . .David Pennington
Stella Stevens . . . . . . . . . . . . . . . . . . . . . . . . Kara
Barbara Alyn Woods . . . . . . . . . . . . . . . . . . Sharon
•• 0:28—Buns and breasts while in bed with Jamie.

### Tess (1979; French/British)
Arielle Dombasle. . . . . . . . . . . . . . . . . Mercy Chant
Peter Firth . . . . . . . . . . . . . . . . . . . . . . .Angel Clare
Suzanna Hamilton. . . . . . . . . . . . . . . . . . . . . . Izz
Nastassja Kinski . . . . . . . . . . . . . . . . . Tess Durbeyfield
• 0:47—Brief left breast, opening blouse in field to feed her baby.

### Test Tube Teens From the Year 2000 (1993)
*a.k.a. Virgin Hunters*
Robin Joi Brown . . . . . . . . . . . . . . . . . . . . .Victoria
••• 0:31—Breasts, in the showers (she's on the left) with Annie while Vin and Naldo watch.
Sara Suzanne Brown . . . . . . . . . . . . . . . . . . . Reena
•• 0:03—In black bra and panties, then buns in panties and breasts stripping out of her jumpsuit during Vin's day dream.
Morgan Fairchild. . . . . . . . . . . . . . . .Camella Swales

Charlie Spradling . . . . . . . . . . . . . . . . . . . . . Girl on TV
• 0:23—Breasts in scenes from *Meridian: Kiss of the Beast* being shown on TV.
Laurel Wiley . . . . . . . . . . . . . . . . . . . . . . . .Annie
••• 0:30—Breasts, taking off towel and in the showers (she's on the right) with Victoria while Vin and Naldo watch.

### Texas Detour (1977)
Priscilla Barnes . . . . . . . . . . . . . . . . . . Claudia Hunter
••• 1:03—Breasts, changing clothes and walking around in bedroom. Wearing white panties. This is her best breasts scene.
• 1:11—Breasts sitting up in bed with Patrick Wayne.
Lindsay Bloom . . . . . . . . . . . . . . . . . . . Sugar McCarthy

### Texas Lightning (1980)
Maureen McCormick . . . . . . . . . . . . . . . . . . . . . . Fay
1:04—Very brief upper half of right breast popping out of slip while struggling on bed with two jerks. Long shot, hard to see.

### That Cold Day in the Park (1969)
Suzanne Benton. . . . . . . . . . . . . . . . . . . . . . . Nina
• 0:38—Side view of left breast putting top on. Long shot.
• 1:05—Breasts taking off her clothes and getting into the bathtub. Another long shot.

### That Obscure Object of Desire (1977; French/Spanish)
Carole Bouquet . . . . . . . . . . . . . . . . . . . . Conchita
••• 0:53—Breasts in bedroom.
••• 1:01—Breasts in bed with Fernando Rey.
Angela Molina . . . . . . . . . . . . . . . . . . . . . . Conchita
• 0:53—Brief breasts in bathroom.
•• 1:20—Nude dancing in front of a group of tourists.
• 1:29—Brief breasts behind a gate taunting Fernando Rey.

### There Was a Crooked Man (1970)
Michael Blodgett . . . . . . . . . . . . . . . . . . Coy Cavendish
Jeanne Cooper . . . . . . . . . . . . . . . . . . . . . .Prostitute
• 0:18—Brief left breast trying to seduce the sheriff, Henry Fonda, in a room.
Kirk Douglas. . . . . . . . . . . . . . . . . . . . Paris Pitman, Jr.
• 0:11—Brief upper half of buns, while leaving bedroom wearing only his gun belt.
•• 1:09—Brief buns and balls, while jumping into a barrel to take a bath in prison.
Lee Grant. . . . . . . . . . . . . . . . . . . . . . . .Mrs. Bullard
Pamela Hensley . . . . . . . . . . . . . . . . . . . . . . Edwina
• 0:12—Very brief left breast lying on pool table with a guy.

### There's a Girl in My Soup (1970)
Christopher Cazenove . . . . . . . . . . . . . . . . . . . . Nigel
Gabrielle Drake . . . . . . . . . . . . . Julia Halford-Smythe
• 0:09—In beige bra with Peter Sellers, brief left breast in bed with him. Don't see her face well, but it is her.

Goldie Hawn . . . . . . . . . . . . . . . . . . . . . . . . . . Marion
- 0:37—Buns and very brief right side view of her body getting out of bed and walking to a closet to get a robe. Long shot.

Geraldine Sherman . . . . . . . . . . . . . . . . . . . . . Caroline
- •• 0:43—Breasts in bed, then getting out after Goldie Hawn splashes water on her.

### There's Nothing Out There (1990)
Mark Collver . . . . . . . . . . . . . . . . . . . . . . . . . . . . . . Jim
- •• 0:33—Buns, taking off his clothes to go skinny dipping in pond.

### They Bite (1991)
Ron Jeremy . . . . . . . . . . . . . . . . . . . . . . . . . . . . . Darryl
Susie Owens . . . . . . . . . . . . . . . . . . . . . . . . . . . . Kate
- 1:01—Right breast, while lying on the beach after getting attacked.
- ••• 1:02—Breasts and buns, while in bed on top of a guy before killing him.

Blake Pickett . . . . . . . . . . . . . . . . . . . . . . . . . . . Model
0:00—Posing for photographer in two piece swimsuit.
- ••• 0:03—Left breast, then breasts and buns, taking off swimsuit for the photographer. More breasts in the water, struggling with the monster.

Christina Veronica . . . . . . . . . . . . . . . . . . . . . . Tammy
- ••• 0:20—Breasts in bed during porno movie shoot.
- ••• 0:55—Breasts, sunbathing on the beach while a guy rubs suntan lotion on her.
- 1:03—Breasts on the beach during playback of film.
- •• 1:08—Breasts on boat, getting attacked by monster.
- 1:09—Breasts in water, struggling with the monster.
- 1:10—Brief breasts on beach during playback of film.

### They Only Kill Their Masters (1972)
Hal Holbrook . . . . . . . . . . . . . . . . . . . . . . . . . . Watkins
Art Metrano . . . . . . . . . . . . . . . . . . . . . . . . . . . Malcolm
Katharine Ross . . . . . . . . . . . . . . . . . . . . . . . . . . Kate
- 1:00—Very brief upper half of buns and very, very brief back side of right breast, when getting out of bed.

### They're Playing with Fire (1984)
Sybil Danning . . . . . . . . . . . . . . . . . . . . . Diane Stevens
0:04—In two piece swimsuit on boat. Long scene.
- ••• 0:08—Breasts and buns making love on top of Jay in bed on boat. Nice!
- •• 0:10—Breasts and buns getting out of shower, then brief side view of right breast.
0:43—In black bra and slip, in boat with Jay.
- •• 0:47—In black bra and slip, at home with Michael, then panties, then breasts and buns getting into shower.
- ••• 1:12—In white bra and panties in room with Jay then breasts.

### Thief of Hearts (1984)
(Special Home Video Version reviewed.)
Steven Bauer . . . . . . . . . . . . . . . . . . . . . . . . Scott Muller
- •• 0:53—Brief side view of buns, carrying Barbara Williams into bed.

David Caruso . . . . . . . . . . . . . . . . . . . . . Buddy Calamara
Annette Sinclair . . . . . . . . . . . . . . . . . . . . College Girl #1
Barbara Williams . . . . . . . . . . . . . . . . . . . . Mickey Davis
- 0:46—Right breast in bathtub when her husband comes in and tries to read her diary.
- ••• 0:53—Breasts making love with Steven Bauer in his condo.

Romy Windsor . . . . . . . . . . . . . . . . . . . . . . . . . . Nicole
- ••• 0:12—Full frontal nudity with Steven Bauer getting dressed.

### Thieves Like Us (1974)
Keith Carradine . . . . . . . . . . . . . . . . . . . . . . . . Bowie
Shelley Duvall . . . . . . . . . . . . . . . . . . . . . . . . . Keechie
- 1:16—Brief upper half of left breast, several times, while in bathtub.
- •• 1:17—Brief breasts and partial lower frontal nudity, then buns, standing up, getting out of tub and drying herself off.
- •• 1:18—Brief back side of right breast, while putting on nightgown.

Tom Skerritt . . . . . . . . . . . . . . . . . . . . . . . . Dee Mobley

### Thieves of Fortune (1989)
Michael Nouri . . . . . . . . . . . . . . . . . . . . . . . . Juan Luis
- 0:57—Buns, while taking a shower outside. Long shot.

Claudia Udy . . . . . . . . . . . . . . . . . . . . . . . . . Marissa
Shawn Weatherly . . . . . . . . . . . . . . . . . . . . . . . Peter
- 1:09—Brief breasts several times, taking a shower (while wearing beard and moustache disguise).
- ••• 1:21—Breasts in white panties distracting tribe so she can get away.

### Things Are Tough All Over (1982)
Tommy Chong . . . . . . . . . . . . . . . . . . . . . Prince Habib
Evelyn Guerrero . . . . . . . . . . . . . . . . . . . . . . . Donna
Richard "Cheech" Marin . . . . . . . . . . . . . . . Mr. Slyman
- 0:21—Buns while in the laundromat dryer.

### Think Dirty (British)
*a.k.a. Every Home Should Have One*
Julie Ege . . . . . . . . . . . . . . . . . . . . . . . . . . . . . . . Inga
- 0:43—Brief full frontal nudity, twice, in photo that Marty Feldman looks at.
- •• 0:44—Brief breasts in another photo. Breasts and buns, while running around in a "documentary" about Sweden with Marty Feldman, then in a "Swedish" film.

Marty Feldman . . . . . . . . . . . . . . . . . . . . . . . . . Teddy
- •• 0:44—Buns, while running around in a "documentary" about Sweden with Julie Ege, then in a "Swedish" film.

Annabel Leventon . . . . . . . . . . . . Chandler's Secretary

### Third Degree Burn (1989; Made for Cable Movie)
Virginia Madsen . . . . . . . . . . . . . . . . . . . . Anne Scholes
Treat Williams . . . . . . . . . . . . . . . . . . . . . Scott Weston
- 0:43—Brief buns while taking off his robe with Virginia Madsen in his bedroom.

### The Thomas Crown Affair (1968)
Faye Dunaway. . . . . . . . . . . . . . . . . . . Vicki Anderson
Yaphet Kotto. . . . . . . . . . . . . . . . . . . . . . . . . . . Carl
Judy Pace . . . . . . . . . . . . . . . . . . . . . . . . . Pretty Girl

### Those Lips, Those Eyes (1980)
Steve Levitt . . . . . . . . . . . . . . . . . . . . . . . . Westervelt
Glynnis O'Connor . . . . . . . . . . . . . . . . . . . . Ramona
- 0:37—Left breast in car with Tom Hulce. Dark, hard to see.
- • 1:12—Breasts and buns on bed with Tom Hulce. Dark.

### Three of Hearts (1993)
William Baldwin . . . . . . . . . . . . . . . . . . . . Joe Casella
- • 0:01—Brief buns in mirror, while walking out of bathroom.
Sherilyn Fenn . . . . . . . . . . . . . . . . . . . . . . . . . . Ellen
Aleksandra Kaniak . . . . . . . . . . . . . . . . . . . . . .Bride
Tawny Kitaen . . . . . . . . . . . . . . . . . . . .Woman in Bar
Kelly Lynch . . . . . . . . . . . . . . . . . . . . . . . . . Connie
Cec Verrell . . . . . . . . . . . . . . . . . . . . . . . . . Allison

### Threesome (1994)
Stephen Baldwin. . . . . . . . . . . . . . . . . . . . . . . Stuart
0:33—Brief side view of buns while in shower.
- • 0:53—Buns, while walking to rock at edge of lake and diving in.
- 1:21—Buns, while lying in bed with Lara Flynn Boyle and Josh Charles.
Lara Flynn Boyle . . . . . . . . . . . . . . . . . . . . . . . . Alex
0:34—Briefly in braless, white blouse while in bed with Stephen Baldwin and Josh Charles.
- 0:52—Buns, while walking and diving into lake to go skinny dipping.
- 0:54—Partial buns, while lying on lake shore with Baldwin and Charles.
- 1:21—Partial buns, while lying in bed between Baldwin and Charles.
Josh Charles . . . . . . . . . . . . . . . . . . . . . . . . .Eddy
- 0:54—Brief buns, while running and jumping into the lake. Partial buns, while lying on lake shore in between Lara Flynn Boyle and Stephen Baldwin.

### Threshold (1983; Canadian)
Jeff Goldblum . . . . . . . . . . . . . . . . . . . . Aldo Gehring
Donald Sutherland . . . . . . . . . . . . . . . . . . . .Dr. Vrain
Mare Winningham . . . . . . . . . . . . . . . Carol Severance
- 0:56—Brief full frontal nudity, lying on operating table, then side view of left breast getting prepped for surgery.

### Thrilled to Death (1988)
Rebecca Lynn . . . . . . . . . . . . . . . . . . . .Elaine Jackson
- 0:01—Breasts twice when Baxter opens her blouse.
- • 0:31—Breasts in locker room talking to Nan.

Christine Moore . . . . . . . . . . . . . . . . . . . . . Nan Christie
0:31—In bra in women's locker room.
- ••• 0:38—Breasts in office with Mr. Dance just before killing him.
Karen Nielsen. . . . . . . . . . . . . . . . . . . . . . . . . . . . n.a.
Christina Veronica . . . . . . . . . . . . . . . . . . . . . . Satin
- •• 0:33—Breasts talking to Cliff during porno film shoot.

### Thumb Tripping (1972)
Bruce Dern. . . . . . . . . . . . . . . . . . . . . . . . . . . Smitty
Meg Foster. . . . . . . . . . . . . . . . . . . . . . . . . . . . Shay
- 1:19—Very, very brief breasts leaning back in field with Jack. Long shot.
- 1:20—Breasts at night. Face is turned away from the camera.
Mariana Hill . . . . . . . . . . . . . . . . . . . . . . . . . . . . Lynn
- 1:14—In black bra, then very, very brief left breast when Jack comes to cover her up.
- 1:19—Breasts frolicking in the water with Gary.
1:20—In white swimsuit, dancing in bar.

### Thunder Alley (1985)
Clancy Brown. . . . . . . . . . . . . . . . . . . . . . . . .Weasel
Melanie Kinnaman. . . . . . . . . . . . . . . . . . . . . . . Star
- 0:52—Brief breasts under water in pool talking to Richie. Side view of right breast, talking to Donnie.
- •• 1:14—Breasts and buns, making love on bed with Richie, then getting out.
Susan McIver . . . . . . . . . . . . . . . . . . . . . . . Redhead
Jill Schoelen . . . . . . . . . . . . . . . . . . . . . . . . . . Beth
- 0:55—Very, very brief left breast and side view of buns, when Richie sits up while she's lying on her stomach on rocks.
Roger Wilson . . . . . . . . . . . . . . . . . . . . . . . . Richie
- 0:55—Buns, while diving into the water. Long, long, long shot.
- 1:15—Brief buns, while wrestling on bed with Star.

### Thunderbolt and Lightfoot (1974)
Catherine Bach. . . . . . . . . . . . . . . . . . . . . . Melody
Jeff Bridges. . . . . . . . . . . . . . . . . . . . . . . . . Lightfoot
Clint Eastwood. . . . . . . . . . John "Thunderbolt" Doherty
June Fairchild . . . . . . . . . . . . . . . . . . . . . . . . . Gloria
- 0:20—Very brief right breast and buns, while getting dressed in the bathroom after making love with Clint Eastwood.
Claudia Lennear. . . . . . . . . . . . . . . . . . . . . Secretary
Leslie Oliver . . . . . . . . . . . . . . . . . . . . . Teenage Girl
- •• 1:16—Brief breasts in bed when robbers break in and George Kennedy watches her.
- 1:31—Brief buns, tied up with her boyfriend in bed.
Luanne Roberts . . . . . . . . . . . . . . Suburban Housewife
- 0:57—Brief full frontal nudity standing behind a sliding glass door tempting Jeff Bridges.

### Tie Me Up! Tie Me Down! (1990; Spanish)
Victoria Abril . . . . . . . . . . . . . . . . . . . . . Marina Osorio
- ••• 0:24—Full frontal nudity playing with a frogman toy in the bathtub.

- 0:34—Buns and brief side of right breast, getting dressed.
- 0:44—Breasts while changing clothes, then on TV while Maximo watches.
- 1:09—Breasts while changing clothes.
- 1:16—Right breast, then breasts while making love in bed with Ricky.

Antonio Banderas . . . . . . . . . . . . . . . . . . . . . . . .Ricky
- 1:17—Buns in mirror on ceiling, while making love with Victoria Abril. Long shot.

### *Tiffany Jones* (British)
Anouska Hempel . . . . . . . . . . . . . . . . . . . .Tiffany Jones
- 0:02—Brief breasts walking in from the surf in wet white dress.
- 0:13—Breasts in bath. Buns also, getting out.
- 0:18—Brief left breast, taking off her top in front of bright light.
- 0:23—Breasts, several times, changing clothes in her bedroom.
- 0:24—Breasts walking around her apartment in white panties.
- 0:31—Breasts in bubble bath.
- 0:32—Brief left breast, wrapping an orange towel around herself.
- 0:39—Lying on table in black and red bra, then breasts. More right breast.
- 0:41—Side view breasts, covered with sweat.
- 0:55—Breasts, partial lower frontal nudity, taking a shower.
- 1:26—Breasts, running outside in a field when guys rip off her dress.

### *A Tiger's Tale* (1988)
Ann-Margret . . . . . . . . . . . . . . . . . . . . . . . . . . . Rose
- 0:45—Side view of left breast in bra, then breasts jumping up after fire ants start biting her. Brief buns running along a hill. Long shot, probably a body double.

C. Thomas Howell . . . . . . . . . . . . . . . . . Bubber Drumm
- 0:38—Upper half of buns getting undressed in bedroom while Ann-Margret changes in the bathroom.

Traci Lin . . . . . . . . . . . . . . . . . . . . . . . . . . . . . Penny
Leigh Lombardi . . . . . . . . . . . . . . . . . . . . . . . . Marcia
Kelly Preston . . . . . . . . . . . . . . . . . . . . . . . . . Shirley
- 0:03—Breasts in the car, letting C. Thomas Howell open her blouse and look at her breasts.

Angel Tompkins . . . . . . . . . . . . . . . . . . . . . . La Vonne

### *Tigers in Lipstick* (1979)
Ursula Andress . . . . . . . . . . The Stroller and The Widow
- 0:02—In black bra, panties and garter belt and stockings opening her fur coat to cause an accident.
- 0:48—In slip posing for photographer.
- 0:50—Very brief breasts when top of slip accidentally falls down.
- 0:51—More breasts with the photographer.

Laura Antonelli . . . . . . . . . . . . . . . . . . . . . The Pick Up
- 0:24—In brown lingerie lying in bed, then getting dressed.

- 0:34—In same lingerie, getting undressed, then in bed.

Sylvia Kristel . . . . . . . . . . . . . . . . . . . . . . . . . .The Girl
- 0:04—Breasts in photograph on the sand.
- 0:06—Braless in sheer nightgown lying in bed.
- 0:09—Breasts lying in bed with The Arab.
- 0:16—Lying in bed in red lingerie, then left breast for awhile.

### *Tightrope* (1984)
Randi Brooks . . . . . . . . . . . . . . . . . . . . . . . .Jamie Cory
- 0:20—Nude, taking off her robe and getting into the spa.
- 0:24—Buns and side of left breast, dead in the spa while Clint Eastwood looks at her.

Genevieve Bujold . . . . . . . . . . . . . . . . .Beryl Thibodeaux
Clint Eastwood . . . . . . . . . . . . . . . . . . . . . . . Wes Block
- 0:33—Buns, while on the bed on top of Becky. Slow pan, red light, covered with sweat. Possible body double because the camera gets out of focus for a bit as it pans up his back.

Margaret Howell . . . . . . . . . . . . . . . . . . . . .Judy Harper
- 0:44—Brief left breast viewed from above in a room with Clint Eastwood.

Rebecca Perle . . . . . . . . . . . . . . . . . . . . . Becky Jacklin
Jamie Rose . . . . . . . . . . . . . . . . . . . . . . . Melanie Silber
- 0:07—Buns, lying face down on bed, dead.

### *The Tigress* (1992)
Belinda Mayne . . . . . . . . . . . . . . . . . . . . . . . . . . . Elsy
James Remar . . . . . . . . . . . . . . . . . . . . . . . . . . Andrei
- 0:49—Buns, while getting into bathtub.

Valentina Vargas . . . . . . . . . . . . . . . . . . . .Tigress/Pauline
- 0:06—Nude, undressing in room and lying in bed with James Remar.
- 0:10—Nude, sitting up in bed, then getting out and leaving the room.
- 0:18—Nude, getting out of bed and getting dressed.
- 0:45—Right breast, while in room when Remar pulls her dress down.
- 0:48—Buns, while in bed with Remar.
- 0:52—Brief breasts, while changing clothes in room.
- 0:53—Breasts when Remar opens her blouse and massages her breasts.
- 1:03—Half of left breast while primping herself in front of mirror.

### *Till Death Do Us Part* (1991)
Embeth Davidtz . . . . . . . . . . . . . . . . . . . . . . . . . . Cat
0:10—In white bra in front of mirror with Treat Williams.

Rebecca Jenkins . . . . . . . . . . . . . . . . . Sandra Stockton
Jennifer Runyon . . . . . . . . . . . . . . . . . . . . . . . . . .Judy
- 1:02—Breasts and buns in T-back, undressing in bathroom. Don't see her face.

Leilani Sarelle . . . . . . . . . . . . . . . . . . . . . . . . . . Gloria
Treat Williams . . . . . . . . . . . . . . . . . . . . . Alan Palliko

### Till Marriage Do Us Part (1974; Italian)
Laura Antonelli . . . . . . . . . . . . . . . . . . . . . . . Eugenia
- •• 0:58—Breasts in the barn lying on hay after guy takes off her clothes.
- •• 1:02—Full frontal nudity standing up in bathtub while maid washes her.
- •• 1:07—Right breast with chauffeur in barn.
- •• 1:36—Breasts surrounded by feathers on the bed while priest is talking.

Karin Schubert . . . . . . . . . . . . . . . . . . . . . . . . . .Evelyn

### A Time to Die (1991)
Nitchie Barrett. . . . . . . . . . . . . . . . . . . . . . . . . Sheila
- • 0:12—Buns, getting out of bed.
- •• 0:16—Breasts making love in bed with Sam.

Daphne Cheung . . . . . . . . . . . . . . . . . . . . .Sunshine
Jeff Conaway. . . . . . . . . . . . . . . . . . . . . . . . . Frank
Traci Lords . . . . . . . . . . . . . . . . . . . . . . . . . . . Jackie
Nicole Picard. . . . . . . . . . . . . . . . . . . . . . . . . . Patti
Richard Roundtree. . . . . . . . . . . . Captain Ralph Phipps

### Time Walker (1982)
Nina Axelrod. . . . . . . . . . . . . . . . . . . . . . . . . .Susie
Greta Blackburn . . . . . . . . . . . . . . . . . . . . . . . Sherri
Melissa Prophet. . . . . . . . . . . . . . . . . . . . . . . .Jennie
- • 0:27—Brief breasts putting bra on while a guy watches from outside the window.
  1:17—Very, very brief right breast in shower when the mummy comes to get the crystal.

Allene Simmons . . . . . . . . . . . . . . . . . . . . . . Nurse
Jason Williams. . . . . . . . . . . . . . . . . . . . . . . . . . Jeff

### Timebomb (1990)
Michael Biehn . . . . . . . . . . . . . . . . . . . . . . . Eddy Kay
Julie Brown . . . . . . . . . Uncredited Waitress at Al's Diner
Robert Culp. . . . . . . . . . . . . . . . . . . . . . . Mr. Phillips
Patsy Kensit. . . . . . . . . . . . . . . . . . . Dr. Anna Nolmar
- •• 1:15—Breasts, mostly left breast, making love with Michael Biehn in bed. Partial buns also.

Tracy Scoggins . . . . . . . . . . . . . . . . . . . . . . Ms. Blue

### The Tin Drum (1979; German)
David Bennent . . . . . . . . . . . . . . . . . . . . . . . . Oskar
- • 1:41—Buns, changing clothes in bath house with Maria.
- • 2:06—Buns, getting out of bed and getting dressed.

Andrea Ferréol. . . . . . . . . . . . . . . . . . . . . . Lina Greff
Daniel Olbrychski . . . . . . . . . . . . . . . . . . . Jan Bronski
- • 0:07—Buns, standing while being examined by army draft inspectors.
- •• 0:38—Buns, in room with Agnes.

Angela Winkler . . . . . . . . . . . . . . . . . Agnes Matzerath
- •• 0:38—Very brief right breast after taking off clothes in room with Jan. Buns and side view of left breast in bed with him.

### Tintorera (1977)
Jennifer Ashley. . . . . . . . . . . . . . . . . . . . . . . . Kelly
- • 0:27—Buns and brief side of left breast, taking off her dress to swim to boat. She's the first one to take off her dress.

- •• 0:28—Breasts and buns, while on boat deck and getting into hammock with Steven.
- •• 0:29—Breasts, while sleeping in hammock and getting out. Brief nude in water, while swimming from the boat.
- • 1:11—Breasts, while taking off her yellow top. Dark.
- • 1:12—Brief breasts, while doing backstroke in water near Cynthia.
- • 1:14—Brief breasts, while getting pulled out of the water by Steven, then lying on her back on beach.

Priscilla Barnes . . . . . . . . . . . . . . . . . . . . Girl from Bar
- • 1:12—Brief breasts, while pouring beer over her head. Breasts seen from under water, while she turns around while wearing white panties. Breasts, while dropping her beer in the water.
- • 1:14—Breasts, while on the beach after the shark attack (on the left).

Andres Garcia. . . . . . . . . . . . . . . . . . . . . . . .Miguel
- • 0:22—Brief buns, while walking down hallway to look for Fiona Lewis. Dark.
- • 0:27—Buns, after taking off his clothes to swim to boat.
- •• 0:28—Buns, while walking on boat deck.
- • 0:41—Very brief frontal nudity in boat kitchen with Susan George and Steven.
- •• 0:42—Nude, picking up George and throwing her overboard.

Susan George. . . . . . . . . . . . . . . . . . . . . . Gabriella
- • 0:42—Brief breasts waking up Steven in hammock.

Fiona Lewis . . . . . . . . . . . . . . . . . . . . . . . . Patricia
- • 0:20—Brief side view (silhouette) of left breast in hallway. Breasts and buns, while walking to the ocean (long shot).
- •• 0:22—Nude, while swimming under water just before getting eaten by a shark. Don't see her face.

Laura Lyons . . . . . . . . . . . . . . . . . . . . . . . . Cynthia
- • 0:27—Buns and brief side of left breast, taking off her dress to swim to boat. She's the second one to take off her dress.
- • 0:28—Full frontal nudity, while dancing on boat deck.
- • 0:29—Left breast and brief buns, while getting into hammock with Steven.
- • 0:30—Brief buns, while swimming in water.

Hugo Stiglitz . . . . . . . . . . . . . . . . . . . . . . . Steven
  0:11—Brief partial buns, while lying in bed with Fiona Lewis.
- • 0:41—Side view of buns, while searing apron in boat galley.

### TNT Jackson (1975)
Pat Anderson . . . . . . . . . . . . . . . . . . . . . . . . .Elaine
- •• 0:58—Buns and breasts, getting out of the shower and putting robe on.

Jeannie Bell . . . . . . . . . . . . . . . . . Diana "TNT" Jackson
- ••• 0:43—Breasts, getting her blouse ripped off by the bad guys. More breasts during fight (notice her panties change from black to white to black).
- • 0:45—Brief breasts, almost hitting Joe.
- ••• 0:50—Breasts, while making love with Charlie.

### To Die For (1988)
Steve Bond . . . . . . . . . . . . . . . . . . . . . . . . . . . Tom
Eloise Broady. . . . . . . . . . . . . . . . . . . . . . . Girl at Party
Ava Fabian . . . . . . . . . . . . . . . . . . . . . . . . . . Franny
Brendan Hughes . . . . . . . . . . . . . . . . . . . .Vlad Tepish
  • 1:13—Buns, while making love with Kate.
Remy O'Neill. . . . . . . . . . . . . . . . . . . . . . . . Jane
Amanda Wyss . . . . . . . . . . . . . . . . . . . . . . Celia Kett

### To Die For 2 (1991)
*a.k.a. Son of Darkness: To Die For II*
Rosalind Allen . . . . . . . . . . . . . . . . . . . . . . . . . . Nina
  • 0:37—Breasts a few times in bed, while making love
    with Max.
Kathryn Atwood . . . . . . . . . . . . . . . . . . . . . . . .n.a.
Steve Bond . . . . . . . . . . . . . . . . . . . . . . . . . . . Tom
Remy O'Neill. . . . . . . . . . . . . . . . . . . . . . . . . . Jane
Michael Praed . . . . . . . . . . . . . . . . . . . . . . . . . Max
  • 1:08—Side view of buns, after attacking a woman at
    her car.
Jay Underwood . . . . . . . . . . . . . . . . . . . . . . . . Danny
Amanda Wyss . . . . . . . . . . . . . . . . . . . . . . .Celia

### To Kill a Clown (1971)
Blythe Danner. . . . . . . . . . . . . . . . . . . . . . . .Lily Frischer
  • 1:10—Side view of left breast sitting on bed talking
    to Alan Alda. Hair covers breast, hard to see. Buns,
    getting up and running out of the house.

### To Live and Die in L.A. (1985)
Willem Dafoe . . . . . . . . . . . . . . . . . . . . . Eric Masters
  0:58—Side view of buns, while kneeling on floor,
    burning counterfeit money.
  0:59—Lower half of buns, while making love in bed
    with Debra Feuer in bed. Seen on TV.
  • 1:06—Buns, while sitting on bench in locker room,
    changing clothes.
Debra Feuer . . . . . . . . . . . . . . . . . . . . . Bianca Torres
  0:58—Side view of buns, lying on bed while watch-
    ing Willem Dafoe burn the counterfeit money. Long
    shot.
  • 1:47—Brief breasts on video tape being played back
    on TV in empty house, hard to see anything.
Darlanne Fluegel. . . . . . . . . . . . . . . . . . . .Ruth Lanier
  •• 0:44—Brief breasts and buns, in bed when William
    Petersen comes home.
  1:29—In stockings on couch with Petersen.
  • 1:50—Very brief breasts on bed with Petersen in a
    flashback.
Jackie Giroux. . . . . . . . . . . . . . . . . . . . . . . Claudia Leith
John Pankow. . . . . . . . . . . . . . . . . . . . . . . John Vukovich
  •• 1:06—Buns, while changing in the locker room.
William L. Petersen . . . . . . . . . . . . . . . Richard Chance
  • 0:44—Brief frontal nudity, but hard to see anything
    because it's dark.
John Turturro . . . . . . . . . . . . . . . . . . . . . . .Carl Cody

### To Protect and Serve (1992)
Lezlie Deane. . . . . . . . . . . . . . . . . . . . . . . . . . . .Harriet
  • 0:47—Brief breasts in front of fireplace with C. Tho-
    mas Howell. Hard to see because candles get in the
    way.
  • 0:51—Brief breasts, getting up off the floor.
  • 1:18—Brief side view of left breast in mirror in bath-
    room. Long shot.
C. Thomas Howell . . . . . . . . . . . . . . . . . . . . . . Egan
  ••• 0:07—Buns, while getting out of bed to get dressed.
    Don't see his face.
Janine Stillo . . . . . . . . . . . . . . . . . . . . . . Counter Girl
Zoe Trilling. . . . . . . . . . . . . . . . . . . . . . . . . Beverly
  • 0:24—Breasts in bed with a guy. Lit with strobe
    light.

### To Sleep with a Vampire (1992)
Kristine Rose. . . . . . . . . . . . . . . . . . . . . . . . Prom Queen
Charlie Spradling . . . . . . . . . . . . . . . . . . . . . . . . Nina
  • 0:04—On stage in black lingerie, then buns in T-
    back.
  ••• 0:05—Breasts and buns in push up bra and T-back
    while dancing on stage.
  ••• 0:59—In red top and red T-back on stage, breasts
    and buns. Excellent close up of breasts.
  ••• 1:03—Breasts while making love on stage with Scott
    Valentine.
Scott Valentine. . . . . . . . . . . . . . . . . . . . . . .Vampire
Ingrid Vold . . . . . . . . . . . . . . . . . . . . . . . Stripper #1
  ••• 0:06—Breasts, while dancing on stage. (Wearing a
    wig.)
  • 0:07—Brief breasts on stage (seen in B&W through
    the vampire's eyes.)

### To the Devil, a Daughter (1976)
Nastassja Kinski . . . . . . . . . . . . . . . . Catherine Beddows
  ••• 1:24—Full frontal nudity, taking off her robe outside
    and walking towards Richard Widmark in slow mo-
    tion.

### The Tomb (1987)
Michelle Bauer . . . . . . . . . . . . . . . . . . . . . . . . Nefartis
Sybil Danning . . . . . . . . . . . . . . . . . . . . . . . . . .Jade
Francesca "Kitten" Natividad . . . . . . . . . . . . . . Stripper
  ••• 0:19—Breasts and buns in G-string dancing on
    stage.
  • 0:21—Brief breasts again.
Dawn Wildsmith . . . . . . . . . . . . . . . . . . . . . Anna Conda
  ••• 0:54—Breasts taking off robe in room with Michelle
    Bauer, then getting pushed onto a bed full of snakes.

### Tomboy (1985)
Michelle Bauer . . . . . . . . . . . Uncredited Girl in Corvette
  • 1:16—Brief breasts, while opening her dress in Cor-
    vette.
Gerard Christopher . . . . . . . . . . . . . . . . . . . .Randy Star
  •• 0:59—Buns, while making love with Betsy Russell in
    the exercise room.
Betsy Russell . . . . . . . . . . . . . Tomasina "Tommy" Boyd
  •• 0:44—In wet T-shirt, then brief breasts after landing
    in the water with her motorcycle.

•• 0:59—Breasts making love with the race car driver in an exercise room.

Kristi Somers . . . . . . . . . . . . . . . . . . . . . . . Seville Ritz
•• 0:14—Breasts taking a shower while talking to Betsy Russell.
• 0:53—Brief breasts stripping at a party.

Cynthia Ann Thompson . . . . . . . . . . . . . . . . Amanda
• 0:23—Brief right breast getting out of car in auto repair shop.
•• 1:02—Breasts delivering drinks to two guys in the swimming pool.

## Tomcat: Dangerous Desires (1993)

Maryam D'Abo . . . . . . . . . . . . . . . . . . . . . . . . . . Jacki
••• 0:07—Breasts in bathroom mirror with Richard Grieco.

Richard Grieco . . . . . . . . . . . . . . . . . . . . . . . . . . Tom
• 1:04—Partial buns, while lying in bed with Imogen.
• 1:07—Brief buns, while answering the phone.

Christine Lippa . . . . . . . . . . . . . . . . . . . . . . . . . Randi
• 0:56—Buns, while lying on bed and talking to Richard Grieco.

Natalie Radford . . . . . . . . . . . . . . . . . . . . . . . Imogen
••• 1:04—Brief left breast, then breasts and lower frontal nudity in bed with Richard Grieco.
•• 1:08—Brief buns and breasts in bed some more.
•• 1:09—More breasts while sitting in bed and watching video tape on TV.

## Too Hot To Handle (1975)

Cheri Caffaro . . . . . . . . . . . . . . . . . . . . . Samantha Fox
•• 0:06—Breasts wearing a black push-up bra and buns in black G-string.
• 0:13—Full frontal nudity lying on boat.
••• 0:39—Breasts making love in bed with Dominco.
••• 0:55—Full frontal nudity taking off clothes and lying in bed.
• 1:06—Brief left breast in bed with Dominco.

Aharon Ipalé . . . . . . . . . . . . . . . . Dominco de la Torres
• 0:39—Buns, while in bed with Cheri Caffaro. Dark, hard to see.

## Too Scared to Scream (1985)

Anne Archer . . . . . . . . . . . . . . . . . . . . . . . . . . Kate
Victoria Bass . . . . . . . . . . . . . . . . . . Cynthia Oberman
••• 0:08—Breasts and buns, undressing and hanging up her dress in closet. More walking to shower.
•• 0:10—Brief breasts, getting out of the shower.

John Heard . . . . . . . . . . . . . . . . . . . . . Lab Technician

## The Toolbox Murders (1978)

Marciee Drake . . . . . . . . . . . . . . . . . . . . . . . . Debbie
•• 0:09—In wet blouse, then breasts taking it off and putting a dry one on.

Evelyn Guerrero . . . . . . . . . . . . . . . . . . . . . . . Maria
Kelly Nichols . . . . . . . . . . . . . . . . . . . . . . . Dee Ann
••• 0:22—Right breast, then breasts taking a bath and enjoying herself. Long scene. Nude, running around trying to get away from the killer.
0:32—Breasts, while dead in her apartment and later on the coroner's table.

## Top Model (1989; Italian)

Laura Gemser . . . . . . . . . . . . . . . . . . . . Dorothy/Eve
• 0:44—Brief right breast and buns, frolicking with the cowboy.

Jessica Moore . . . . . . . . . . . . . . . . . Sarah Asproon/Gloria
••• 0:03—Nude, posing for photographer customer in his loft with mannequins, then talking on the phone.
• 0:08—Breasts in dressing room, when seen by Cliff.
•• 0:23—Buns and brief side of right breast, undressing in front of a customer.
•• 0:24—Breasts, rubbing oil on him.
•• 0:30—Full frontal nudity, in her bedroom when Peter blackmails her.
••• 0:35—Nude in photographer customer's loft again.
• 0:40—Brief buns, turning over in bed.
• 0:43—Breasts on couch, making love (disinterestedly) with cowboy.
• 0:56—Buns and partial right breast, while getting dressed.
••• 1:00—Breasts making love with Cliff on sofa, then sleeping afterward.
•• 1:04—Nude, undressing and walking down hallway.
•• 1:08—Nude, in hotel room, making love with Cliff.
••• 1:19—Buns, with Cliff in stairwell. Breasts and buns in bathroom with him.

## Total Exposure (1991)

Martina Castel . . . . . . . . . . . . . . . . . . . . . . . . Cissy
• 1:06—Breasts in spa being questioned by a guy with a gun.

Jeff Conaway . . . . . . . . . . . . . . . . . . . . Peter Keynes
Deborah Driggs . . . . . . . . . . . . . . . . . . . . . . . . Kathy
••• 0:08—Breasts dancing in front of Jeff Conaway, then making love in bed with him. Long scene.
• 0:22—Brief side view breasts in B&W photos that Conaway looks at.
• 0:24—Brief buns in black G-string and side of right breast changing clothes in locker room.
•• 0:25—Breasts and buns, trying to beat up Season Hubley.

Season Hubley . . . . . . . . . . . . . . . . . . Andi Robinson
0:07—Buns, getting into hot tub. Probably a body double.

Michael Nouri . . . . . . . . . . . . . . . . . . . Dave Murphy
Kristine Rose . . . . . . . . . . . . . . . . . . . . . . . . . . . Rita

## Total Recall (1990)

Arnold Schwarzenegger . . . . . . . . . . . . . . Doug Quaid
Sharon Stone . . . . . . . . . . . . . . . . . . . . . . . . . . . Lori
• 0:04—Brief right breast in gaping lingerie when leaning over Arnold Schwarzenegger in bed.

Rachel Ticotin . . . . . . . . . . . . . . . . . . . . . . . Melina

## Totally Exposed (1991)

Tina Bockrath . . . . . . . . . . . . . . . . . . . Lillian Tucker
•• 0:00—Buns and breasts, turning over on tanning table during opening credits.
• 0:01—Brief full frontal nudity, lying on tanning table.

•• 0:03—Brief nude, getting out of bed and putting on towel while talking to Bill.

••• 1:01—Full frontal nudity, turning over in tanning table. Full frontal nudity, dropping her towel in reception area.

••• 1:02—Buns, walking back to the room. Nude, taking off towel and lying on massage table.

••• 1:04—Nude, sitting up on table and standing up with Bill.

Jacqueline Jade . . . . . . . . . . . . . . . . . . . . . . Eleanor

••• 0:05—Full frontal nudity, taking off towel and lying on tanning table.

•• 0:08—Nude, on massage table, talking with Bill.

•• 0:09—Brief breasts, turning over on table, trying to make the moves on Bill.

•• 0:10—Brief breasts, sitting up.

•• 0:57—Nude, taking off towel and getting on massage table.

••• 0:58—Full frontal nudity, turning over to talk to Bill.

Kelli Konop . . . . . . . . . . . . . . . . . . . . . . . . . . . . Sue

• 0:18—Undressing to take a shower. Brief right breast, bending over to take off panties. Brief side view of left breast, while getting into the shower.

• 0:19—Sort of breasts, while washing herself in the shower. Her arms get in the way.

1:12—In white bra, while making out with Bill on bed.

Honey Smax . . . . . . . . . . . . . . . . . . . . . . . Linda

•• 0:41—Full frontal nudity, taking off towel in massage room.

## The Touch (1971; U.S./Swedish)

Bibi Andersson . . . . . . . . . . . . . . . . . . . Karen Vergerus

• 0:31—Breasts in bed with Elliott Gould.

••• 0:56—Breasts kissing Gould.

1:13—Very, very brief right breast washing Gould's hair in the sink.

## Tough Guys (1986)

Kirk Douglas . . . . . . . . . . . . . . . . . . . . . . Archie Long

• 1:36—Buns, while standing on moving train, mooning Charles Durning.

Darlanne Fluegel . . . . . . . . . . . . . . . . . . . . . Skye Foster

• 0:47—Very brief side view of right breast, leaning over to kiss Kirk Douglas.

Burt Lancaster . . . . . . . . . . . . . . . . . . . . . . Harry Doyle

Lisa Pescia . . . . . . . . . . . . . . . . . . . . . . . . Customer #1

Hilary Shepard . . . . . . . . . . . . . . . . . . . . . . . . . Sandy

## Tough Guys Don't Dance (1987)

Frances Fisher . . . . . . . . . . . . . . . . . . . . . Jessica Pond

Wings Hauser . . . . . . . . . . . . . . . . . . . . . . . Regency

Ryan O'Neal . . . . . . . . . . . . . . . . . . . . . . Tim Madden

Isabella Rossellini . . . . . . . . . . . . . . . . . . . Madeleine

Debra Sandlund . . . . . . . . . . . . . . . . . . . . Patty Lareine

•• 1:24—Breasts ripping her blouse off to kiss the policeman after they have killed and buried another woman.

• 1:24—Very brief left breast, twice, in bed with Ryan O'Neal. Long shot.

## Tower of Evil (1972; British)

Robin Askwith . . . . . . . . . . . . . . . . . . . . . . . . . Des

• 0:35—Brief buns, getting up out of bed and putting on his pants. Dark.

John Hamill . . . . . . . . . . . . . . . . . . . . . . . . . . Gary

• 0:40—Buns, walking with Penny, then more buns, rolling into the water, dead.

Gary Hamilton . . . . . . . . . . . . . . . . . . . . . . . . . Brom

•• 0:53—Buns in bed, while making love on top of Nora.

Seretta Wilson . . . . . . . . . . . . . . . . . . . . . . . . . . Mae

• 0:34—Very, very brief breasts, lying in bed in flashbacks. Then breasts, sleeping in bed.

•• 0:35—Breasts, while sleeping in bed.

• 0:38—More breasts, while sleeping in bed.

• 0:39—Very, very brief breasts, getting the covers taken off before getting killed.

• 0:41—Very brief breasts, dead, covered with blood.

## The Toxic Avenger (1985)

Cindy Manion . . . . . . . . . . . . . . . . . . . . . . . . Julie

0:14—In two piece swimsuit in locker room with Melvin.

••• 0:15—Breasts, after untying her swimsuit top in front of Melvin.

## The Toxic Avenger: Part II (1988)

John Altamura . . . . . . . . . . . . . . . . . . . . Toxic Avenger

Phoebe Légerè . . . . . . . . . . . . . . . . . . . . . . . . Claire

• 0:31—Brief right breast, while caressing herself while making out with the Toxic Avenger.

## Toy Soldiers (1983)

Terri Garber . . . . . . . . . . . . . . . . . . . . . . . . . . Amy

• 0:18—Brief right breast taking off her tank top when the army guys force her. Her head is down.

Tim Robbins . . . . . . . . . . . . . . . . . . . . . . . . . . Bean

Tracy Scoggins . . . . . . . . . . . . . . . . . . . . . . Monique

## Toy Soldiers (1991)

Sean Astin . . . . . . . . . . . . . . . . . . . . . . . Billy Tepper

• 1:08—Brief buns, while taking off his wet clothes after coming in through the window.

## Traces of Red (1992)

Victoria Bass . . . . . . . . . . . . . . . . . . . . . . Susan Dobson

James Belushi . . . . . . . . . . . . . . . . . . . . . . . Jack Dobson

Katheryn Culliver Pierce . . . . . . . . . . . . . Kimberly Davis

•• 0:11—Breasts in bed, dead with blood on her during James Belushi's recollection.

Tony Goldwyn . . . . . . . . . . . . . . . . . . . . . . Steve Frayn

•• 1:04—Buns, standing up from bed and putting on his underwear.

Faye Grant . . . . . . . . . . . . . . . . . . . . . . . . . Beth Frayn

0:52—Buns in T-back under sheer dress.

Michelle Joyner . . . . . . . . . . . . . . . . . . . Morgan Cassidy

• 0:08—In black bra, in bedroom with James Belushi. Brief breasts making love.

•• 0:24—Left breast, while lying dead in bed when Belushi sees her.

Melanie Tomlin . . . . . . . . . . . . . . . . . . . . . . Amanda

## *Track 29* (1988; British)

Sandra Bernhard . . . . . . . . . . . . . . . . . . . . . .Nurse Stein
Colleen Camp . . . . . . . . . . . . . . . . . . . . . . . . .Arlanda
Christopher Lloyd . . . . . . . . . . . . . . . . . . . .Henry Henry
- 0:34—Very brief side view of his buns, while lying in the hospital getting spanked by Sandra Bernhard.

Gary Oldman . . . . . . . . . . . . . . . . . . . . . . . . . Martin
- 1:24—Buns, while holding onto Christopher Lloyd and stabbing him.

Theresa Russell . . . . . . . . . . . . . . . . . . . . . Linda Henry

## *The Tracker* (1988; Made for Cable Movie)

Kris Kristofferson . . . . . . . . . . . . . . . . . . . Noble Adams
Mark Moses . . . . . . . . . . . . . . . . . . . . . . . . Tom Adams
- •• 0:35—Buns, while getting out of the river after washing himself, then getting hassled by some bandits.

## *Tracks* (1977)

Michael Emil . . . . . . . . . . . . . . . . . . . . . . . . . Gene
Dennis Hopper . . . . . . . . . . . . . . . . . . . Sgt. Jack Falen
- •• 0:58—Frontal nudity running through the train. Long scene.

Sally Kirkland . . . . . . . . . . . . . . . . . . . . . . Uncredited
Zack Norman . . . . . . . . . . . . . . . . . . . . . . . . . Mojo
Taryn Power . . . . . . . . . . . . . . . . . . . . . . . Stephanie
- 0:32—Brief side view of right breast changing in her room on the train. Don't see her face.
- 1:15—Brief left breast making love with Dennis Hopper in a field.

## *Trading Places* (1983)

James Belushi . . . . . . . . . . . . . . . . . . . . . . . . Harvey
Jamie Lee Curtis . . . . . . . . . . . . . . . . . . . . . . Ophelia
- ••• 1:00—Breasts in black panties after taking red dress off in bathroom while Dan Aykroyd watches.
- ••• 1:09—Breasts and black panties taking off halter top and pants getting into bed with a sick Aykroyd.

Giancarlo Esposito . . . . . . . . . . . . . . . . . . . Cell Mate

## *The Tragedy of a Ridiculous Man* (1981; Italian)

Anouk Aimee . . . . . . . . . . . . . . . . . . .Barbara Spaggiari
Olimpia Carlisi . . . . . . . . . . . . . . . . . . . . . . .Chiromat
Laura Morante . . . . . . . . . . . . . . . . . . . . . . . . Laura
- ••• 1:30—Breasts taking off her sweater in front of Primo because she's "uneasy."

## *Transformations* (1988)

Michael Hennessy . . . . . . . . . . . . . . . . . . . . Stephens
- 1:07—Brief, partial buns, while pulling his pants down.

Ann Margaret Hughes . . . . . . . . . . . . . . . . . . . . .Myra
- 0:42—Right breast, then breasts under Rex Smith in bed.
- 0:43—More breasts, dead in bed.

Lisa Langlois . . . . . . . . . . . . . . . . . . . . . . . . Miranda
Pamela Prati . . . . . . . . . . . . . . . . . . . .Woman Succubus
- ••• 0:05—Breasts and buns making love on top of Rex Smith in bed. She starts transforming into a creature.

- 0:21—Brief breasts again during Smith's flashback.
- 0:24—Brief breasts again, while transforming.
- 0:26—Brief breasts again, while transforming.

Cec Verrell . . . . . . . . . . . . . . . . . . . . . . . . . Antonia

## *Trapped* (1993)

*a.k.a. The Killing Jar*

Cie Allman . . . . . . . . . . . . . . . . . . . . .Buxom Blonde
Pamela Bryant . . . . . . . . . . . . . . . . . . . Laura Armstrong
- 0:03—In white lingerie in house, showing it off to her husband.
- 0:04—Brief breasts on TV monitor.
- 0:05—Brief buns and right breast in mirror while changing clothes in the bathroom.
- •• 0:11—Breasts, while starting to make love in backyard with Curtis.
- 0:15—Brief breasts in bathroom with her husband while he fantasizes about Monica.
- 0:24—Breasts, while on TV.
- •• 0:27—Breasts, while in shower, getting out and getting dressed.
- 0:29—Brief right breast when it slips out of nightgown while she lies in bed.
- 0:32—Brief left breast when masked guy cuts her nightgown strap open.
- 0:48—Brief side of left breast on TV.
- ••• 0:50—Nude, getting into bathtub, in bathtub, then getting dragged around house by guy.

Reid "Chip" Smith . . . . . . . . . . . . . . . . Alan Armstrong
Alina Thompson . . . . . . . . . . . . . . . . . . . . . . Monica
- 0:16—In sheer white lingerie outfit in bedroom with Alan.
- 0:26—Right breast while in bed with Alan in Laura's imagination.
- ••• 0:33—In two piece swimsuit, then nude, while making love with Alan outside by pool.
- •• 0:37—Nude, undressing and going for a swim in the pool, then getting killed.

## *Trauma* (1992)

Asia Argento . . . . . . . . . . . . . . . . . . . . . .Aura Petrescu
- •• 0:27—Breasts, after taking off bra in bathroom.

Brad Dourif . . . . . . . . . . . . . . . . . . . . . . . . Dr. Lloyd
Laura Johnson . . . . . . . . . . . . . . . . .Grace Harrington
- 0:38—Breast, while making love in bed with David and after he leaves.

James Russo . . . . . . . . . . . . . . . . . . . . . Captain Travis
Christopher Rydell . . . . . . . . . . . . . . . . . . David Parsons

## *Traveling Man* (1989; Made for Cable Movie)

Ingrid Buxbaum . . . . . . . . . . . . . . . .Uncredited Salesgirl
- ••• 0:05—Breasts and buns while wearing G-string, dancing during sales meeting.

John Lithgow . . . . . . . . . . . . . . . . . . . . . . Ben Cluett
- 0:48—Brief buns, while trying to get the VCR away from Mona in her living room.

## *Traxx* (1988)

Priscilla Barnes . . . . . . . . . . . . . Mayor Alexandria Cray
Gwendolyn Hajek . . . . . . . . . . . . . . . . . . . . . Playmate

Suzanne Primeaux. . . . . . . . . . . . . . . . . . . . Hooker #1
•• 0:37—Breasts, dancing on stage while wearing a mask.

### Treacherous (1993)

### Tribute (1980; Canadian)
Robby Benson. . . . . . . . . . . . . . . . . . . . Jud Templeton
Kim Cattrall. . . . . . . . . . . . . . . . . . . . . Sally Haines
Gale Garnett. . . . . . . . . . . . . . . . . . . . . . . . . Hilary
••• 1:39—Breasts, while taking off her nurse outfit in front of Jack Lemmon. (Pretty amazing for a PG movie!)
• 1:42—Brief half of right breast, while standing up.
Jack Lemmon . . . . . . . . . . . . . . . . . . . . Jack Templeton

### Trick or Treat (1986)
Marc Price. . . . . . . . . . . . . . . . . . . . Eddie Weinbauer
•• 0:04—Buns, while lying on the floor and also kneeling at boys' locker room door when the bullies leave him outside where the girls can see him.
• 0:12—Brief buns, in Polaroid photo of the previous incident.

### The Trip (1967)
Michael Blodgett. . . . . . . . . . . . . . . . . . . . . . . .n.a.
Bruce Dern . . . . . . . . . . . . . . . . . . . . . John, Guru
Peter Fonda . . . . . . . . . . . . . . . . . . . . . Paul Groves
•• 0:27—Buns, while getting out of the swimming pool and being helped into the house.
Dennis Hopper . . . . . . . . . . . . . . . . . . . . . . . Max
Susan Strasberg. . . . . . . . . . . . . . . . . . Sally Groves

### The Trojan Women (1972; British)
Genevieve Bujold . . . . . . . . . . . . . . . . . . . Cassandra
Irene Papas . . . . . . . . . . . . . . . . . . . . . . . . . . Helen
• 1:11—Very brief breasts, kneeling down to bathe in a pan of water. Seen between slats in wall. Long shot.
• 1:12—Brief breasts and very brief side view of buns, standing up and moving away from the slat wall when the women start throwing stones.
Vanessa Redgrave . . . . . . . . . . . . . . . . . .Andromache

### Tropic of Cancer (1970)
Ellen Burstyn . . . . . . . . . . . . . . . . . . . . . . . Mona
••• 0:02—Full frontal nudity, while lying on bed.
•• 0:03—Right breast while lying on her back in bed.
•• 0:04—Nude, getting out of bed to get bugs off her.
Magali Noel . . . . . . . . . . . . . . . . . . . . The Princess
••• 0:17—In sheer bra, then breasts after taking off her bra while sitting in bed in front of a guy.
Sheila Steafel . . . . . . . . . . . . . . . . . . . . . . . Tania
•• 0:25—Breasts, while ballet dancing in studio while wearing only a tutu.
Rip Torn . . . . . . . . . . . . . . . . . . . . . Henry Miller

### Tropical Heat (1993)
Lee Anne Beaman . . . . . . . . . . . . . . . . . . . . .Carolyn
••• 0:10—Nude, taking her clothes off outside by swimming pool, then getting in and making love with Rick Rossovich. Long scene.

•• 0:14—Breasts, while sitting at bar in swimming pool with Rossovich.
Maryam D'Abo. . . . . . . . . . . . . . . . . . . . . . Beverly
•• 0:36—Breasts, several times, while in waterfall with Rick Rossovich.
••• 0:47—Breasts in bathtub, giving Rossovich a shave.
• 0:49—Partial left breast, while lying in bed and making love with Rossovich.
• 0:50—Brief breasts in bed, while under Rossovich.
••• 0:51—Breasts while in bed with Rossovich.
Rick Rossovich . . . . . . . . . . . . . . . . . . . . . Gravis
•• 0:11—Buns, several times, while in the swimming pool with Carolyn.
•• 0:36—Buns, making love with Maryam D'Abo in waterfall.
• 0:50—Very brief buns, while in bed on top of D'Abo.
•• 0:51—Buns, while lying on top of D'Abo in bed.
••• 0:52—Buns, getting out of bed and putting on his pants.

### Tropical Snow (1989)
David Carradine. . . . . . . . . . . . . . . . . . . . . .Oskar
Nick Corri . . . . . . . . . . . . . . . . . . . . . . . . . Tavo
•• 0:11—Buns while in bed with Madeleine Stowe.
•• 0:44—Buns, while standing naked in police station.
Madeleine Stowe . . . . . . . . . . . . . . . . . . . . .Marina
• 0:05—Very brief side view of left breast putting red dress on.
• 0:11—Buns, lying in bed. Very brief right breast sitting up. (I wish they could have panned the camera to the right!)
•• 0:24—Breasts in mirror putting red dress on.
0:32—Buns, lying on top of Tavo in bed.
• 0:54—Brief breasts making love in the water with Tavo. Then buns, lying on the beach (long shot.)
1:22—Long shot side view of right breast in water with Tavo.

### Trouble Bound (1992)
Ginger Lynn Allen . . . . . . Uncredited Adult Film Actress
•• 0:22—Breasts on TV in motel room that Kit and Harry are watching.
Patricia Arquette. . . . . . . . . . . . . . . . . . . . . . Kit
Michael Madsen. . . . . . . . . . . . . . . . . . . . . .Harry

### Trouble in Mind (1986)
Genevieve Bujold . . . . . . . . . . . . . . . . . . . . .Wanda
Keith Carradine . . . . . . . . . . . . . . . . . . . . . .Coop
Kris Kristofferson . . . . . . . . . . . . . . . . . . . . .Hawk
Lori Singer . . . . . . . . . . . . . . . . . . . . . . . Georgia
• 1:01—Very brief left breast, in bed with Kris Kristofferson.

### The Trouble with Dick (1986)
Susan Dey . . . . . . . . . . . . . . . . . . . . . . . . .Diane
Elaine Giftos . . . . . . . . . . . . . . . . . . . . . . Sheila
Elizabeth Gorcey . . . . . . . . . . . . . . . . . . . . .Haley
• 0:13—Very brief left breast in gaping T-shirt while she lies on bed, plays with a toy and laughs.
0:26—Lower half of buns under robe on sofa with Dick.

0:27—Half of right breast on top of Dick in bed.

Tom Villard . . . . . . . . . . . . . . . . . . . . . . Dick Kendred

0:30—Side view of buns, while leaving Haley's room.

- 0:58—Buns from under his shirt, getting out of bed to open the door.

### Truck Stop Women (1974)

Uschi Digard . . . . . . . . . . . . . . . . . .Truck Stop Woman

- •• 0:18—Breasts getting arrested in the parking lot by the police officer, then buns and breasts getting frisked in a room.

Claudia Jennings . . . . . . . . . . . . . . . . . . . . . . . . Rose

- • 0:27—Brief breasts taking off blouse and getting into bed.

0:48—Brief side view of right breast in mirror, getting dressed.

- • 1:10—Brief breasts wrapping and unwrapping a towel around herself.

### True Blood (1989)

Jeff Fahey . . . . . . . . . . . . . . . . . . . .Raymond Trueblood

Sherilyn Fenn . . . . . . . . . . . . . . . . . . . . . Jennifer Scott

- • 1:22—Very brief right breast in closet trying to stab Spider with a piece of mirror.

### True Love (1989)

Al Juliano. . . . . . . . . . . . . . . . . . . . . . . . Male Stripper

- • 0:43—Buns while in G-string dancing on stage in a club.

Annabella Sciorra . . . . . . . . . . . . . . . . . . . . . . Donna

### True Romance (1993)

(Unrated version reviewed.)

Patricia Arquette . . . . . . . . . . . . . . . Alabama Whitman

- • 0:11—Brief breasts, while lying in bed with Christian Slater. Wide screen laser disc version only: Right breast two more times and partial left breast (••).

Dennis Hopper . . . . . . . . . . . . . . . . . . . . Clifford Worley

Samuel L. Jackson . . . . . . . . . . . . . . . . . . . . . Big Don

Anna Levine Thomson. . . . . . . . . . . . . . . . . . . . Lucy

Gary Oldman . . . . . . . . . . . . . . . . . . . . . Drexl Spivey

Christopher Penn . . . . . . . . . . . . . . . . . . . Nicky Dimes

Christian Slater . . . . . . . . . . . . . . . . . . Clarence Worley

- • 0:11—Wide screen laser disc version only: Partial buns, while lying in bed with Patricia Arquette.

### Truth or Dare (1991)

Madonna . . . . . . . . . . . . . . . . . . . . . . . . . . Herself

- ••• 0:44—Brief breasts changing clothes backstage. B&W.

1:16—Wearing a bra, in a store, trying on earrings. B&W.

1:35—Very brief half of left breast, while wearing robe and jumping up. B&W.

1:43—Sort of breasts in bed with her dancers. Her hands cover her breasts. B&W.

Antonio Banderas . . . . . . . . . . . . . . . . . . . .Himself

Warren Beatty. . . . . . . . . . . . . . . . . . . . . . .Himself

Sandra Bernhard . . . . . . . . . . . . . . . . . . . . . Herself

Carlton Wilborn . . . . . . . . . . . . . . . . . . . . . . Dancer

1:39—Frontal nudity showing himself to Madonna. Dark, hard to see. B&W.

1:43—Very brief frontal nudity getting into bed with Madonna. Too dark to see anything. B&W.

- • 1:45—Brief buns, while in bed with Madonna. B&W.

### Tuff Turf (1984)

Panchito Gomez. . . . . . . . . . . . . . . . . . . . .Mickey

Kim Richards . . . . . . . . . . . . . . . . . Frankie Croyden

1:07—In black lingerie getting dressed.

- • 1:29—Brief breasts supposedly of a body double (Fiona Morris) in bedroom with James Spader but I have heard from a very reliable source that it really was her.

Catya Sassoon . . . . . . . . . . . . . . . . . . . . . . . Feather

James Spader . . . . . . . . . . . . . . . . . . . . . Morgan Hiller

### The Tunnel (1987; Spanish)

Jane Seymour. . . . . . . . . . . . . . . . . . . . . . . . .Maria

- • 0:29—Very brief left breast, while in bed with Peter Weller when the sheet is pulled down.

- •• 0:44—Brief right beast, while getting dressed, throwing off her robe.

Peter Weller . . . . . . . . . . . . . . . . . . . . . . . .Juan Pablo

### Tunnelvision (1976)

Betty Thomas. . . . . . . . . . . . . . . . Brigit Bert Richards

### Turkish Delight (1974; Dutch)

Rutger Hauer . . . . . . . . . . . . . . . . . . . . . . . . . . Erik

- ••• 0:01—Brief nude walking around his apartment talking to a woman he has just picked up.

- • 0:04—Buns, while in bed (covered with a sheet), then very brief frontal nudity throwing another girl out.

- •• 0:36—Frontal nudity getting up to answer the door with flowers.

- •• 1:12—Frontal nudity lying in bed depressed.

- •• 1:16—Buns, while making love with Olga in bed.

Monique Van De Ven. . . . . . . . . . . . . . . . . . . . . Olga

- •• 0:24—Breasts when Rutger Hauer opens her blouse, then nude on the bed.

- •• 0:27—Breasts, waking up in bed.

- ••• 0:33—Breasts on bed with Hauer, then nude getting up to fix flowers.

0:42—Buns, with Hauer at the beach.

- •• 0:46—Breasts modeling for Hauer, then brief nude running around outside.

- •• 0:54—Breasts in bed with open blouse with flowers.

- • 1:04—In wet T-shirt in the rain with Hauer, then brief breasts coming down the stairs.

### The Turn-On (1989)

*a.k.a. Le Clic*

George "Buck" Flower . . . . . . . . . Guy Giving Directions

Maria Ford . . . . . . . . . . . . . . . . . . . . . . . . . . . . .Maria

- ••• 0:21—Breasts, then nude while dancing on stage after getting turned on by the black box.

Florence Guerin . . . . . . . . . . . . . . . Claudia Christiani

- •• 0:02—Buns and breasts in mirror.

••• 0:34—Breasts, while looking at herself in dressing room mirror and caressing herself.

•• 0:54—Breasts, while walking through the woods and taking off her clothes.

••• 0:56—Nude, while playing with herself in the woods, then getting tied up and carried away on a guy's shoulders. Long scene.

••• 1:07—Breasts and buns, while on the beach with Dr. Fez. Nude, fighting with her husband and running away into the house.

Debra Lamb . . . . . . . . . . . . . . Assistant in White Dress

Toni Naples. . . . . . . . . . . . . . . . . . . . . . . Harold's Wife

••• 0:31—Nude, during ceremony and after getting turned on by the black box.

## The Turning Point (1977)

Leslie Browne . . . . . . . . . . . . . . . . . . . . Emilia Rogers

• 0:51—Brief side view of right breast, while lying in bed with Mikhail Baryshnikov at the end of the love scene. Don't see her face.

Shirley MacLaine. . . . . . . . . . . . . . . . . . . . . . DeeDee

Tom Skerritt . . . . . . . . . . . . . . . . . . . . .Wayne Rogers

## Turtle Beach (1992; Australian)

### a.k.a. The Killing Beach

Joan Chen . . . . . . . . . . . . . . . . . . . . . . . . . . Minou

••• 0:07—Brief buns, dropping robe and leaving room while talking to Greta Scacchi.

Norman Kaye . . . . . . . . . . . . . . . . . .Sir Adrian Hobday

Greta Scacchi . . . . . . . . . . . . . . . . . . . . . . . . . Judith

• 0:44—Upper half of buns and almost breasts, making love.

Jack Thompson . . . . . . . . . . . . . . . . . . . . . . . . Ralph

## Tusks (1990)

Lucy Gutteridge . . . . . . . . . . . . . . . . . . . .Micah Hill

•• 0:23—Breasts in tub taking a bath.

## Twelfth Night (1988; Italian)

Carlo de Meijo . . . . . . . . . . . . . . . . . . . . . . . Orsino

• 0:00—Buns, while standing up after bath. Out of focus.

• 0:49—Half of buns, while sitting on rock, talking to Viola.

Viju Krim. . . . . . . . . . . . . . . . . . . . . . . . . . . . Maria

•• 1:09—Breasts, dancing in tavern in open top.

Ajita Wilson. . . . . . . . . . . . . . . . . . . . . . . . .Antonia

•• 0:50—Buns, taking off her dress and walking into stream with a guy.

• 0:51—Very brief breasts, making love with him in the stream.

•• 1:11—Right breast, hanging out of black dress, dancing in tavern.

## Twenty-One (1991)

Patsy Kensit. . . . . . . . . . . . . . . . . . . . . . . . . .Katie

••• 1:17—Breasts in reflection in bathroom mirror undressing, then dressing.

## Twice a Woman (1979)

Bibi Andersson . . . . . . . . . . . . . . . . . . . . . . . .Laura

• 0:05—Breasts taking off her bra and putting a blouse on.

• 0:06—Brief side view of left breast, getting into bed, brief left breast lying back in bed.

Sandrine Dumas. . . . . . . . . . . . . . . . . . . . . . .Sylvia

• 0:06—Breasts, kneeling on the bed, then more brief breasts in bed with Bibi Andersson.

••• 0:47—Brief right breast, then breasts in bed with Andersson. Long scene.

• 1:15—Left breast, lying in bed with Anthony Perkins. Long shot.

••• 1:23—Breasts with Andersson.

## Twice Dead (1989)

Charlie Spradling . . . . . . . . . . . . . . . . . . . . . . .Tina

•• 1:11—Breasts taking off jacket next to bed.

••• 1:14—Breasts making love with her boyfriend in bed.

• 1:18—Brief breasts dead in bed.

Jill Whitlow. . . . . . . . . . . . . . . . . . . . . .Robin/Myrna

0:27—In white slip, getting ready for bed, then walking around the house.

## Twin Peaks: Fire Walk With Me (1992)

Mädchen Amick. . . . . . . . . . . . . . . . . . .Shelly Johnson

David Bowie. . . . . . . . . . . . . . . . . . . . . .Phillip Jeffries

Miguel Ferrer . . . . . . . . . . . . . . . . . . Albert Rosenfield

Annie Gaybis . . . . . . . . . . . Uncredited Dancer on Stage

• 1:15—Breasts, dancing on stage. Lit with red light.

• 1:16—More breasts and very brief buns, while on stage.

• 1:18—More breasts while on stage.

Pamela Gidley . . . . . . . . . . . . . . . . . . Teresa Banks

Gary Hershberger. . . . . . . . . . . . . . . . . . Mike Nelson

Moira Kelly. . . . . . . . . . . . . . . . . . . . . Donna Hayward

•• 1:22—Breasts, while lying on table in cabin.

Sheryl Lee . . . . . . . . . . . . . . . . . . . . . . . Laura Palmer

• 0:37—Very brief breasts, letting her boyfriend feel her breast.

•• 1:18—Breasts when a guy takes off her dress in cabin.

••• 1:19—Breasts, while talking with Ronette at table.

••• 1:21—More breasts in cabin and while sitting at the table with Ronette. More breasts when getting up.

• 1:49—Side view of buns and upper half of right breast (wearing lingerie) while lying in bed and rolling over.

1:58—Brief upper half of left breast while dancing in lingerie in cabin.

•• 1:59—Breasts, while struggling on bed with big guy.

• 2:01—Brief breasts talking with her dad in the cabin.

Kyle MacLachlan . . . . . . . . . . . . . . . . . . Dale Cooper

James Marshall. . . . . . . . . . . . . . . . . . . . .James Hurley

Jürgen Prochnow . . . . . . . . . . . . . . . . . . . Woodsman

Harry Dean Stanton . . . . . . . . . . . . . . . . . Carl Rodd

Kiefer Sutherland . . . . . . . . . . . . . . . . . .Sam Stanley

## Twin Sisters (1992; Made for Cable Movie)
Susan Almgren . . . . . . . . . . . . . . . . . . . . . . . . . . . Sophie
•• 0:06—Breasts and buns, while making love in bed with a guy.
James Brolin . . . . . . . . . . . . . . . . . . . . . . . . . . Michael

## Twins of Evil (1971)
Madeleine Collinson . . . . . . . . . . . . . . . Freida Gelhorn
•• 1:07—Right breast, then brief breasts undoing dress, then full frontal nudity after turning into a vampire in bedroom.
Mary Collinson . . . . . . . . . . . . . . . . . . . . Maria Gelhorn
Luan Peters . . . . . . . . . . . . . . . . . . . . . . . . . . . . Gerta

## The Twist (1976)
Ann-Margret . . . . . . . . . . . . . . . . . . . . . Charlie Minerva
0:24—Left breast when Claire daydreams someone is sticking a pin into Ann-Margret's breast. A little bloody. Body double.
1:24—Very, very brief left breast during Bruce Dern's daydream. Seen from above, body double again.
Sybil Danning . . . . . . . . . . . . . . . . . . .Jacques' Secretary
•• 1:24—Brief breasts sitting next to Bruce Dern during his daydream.
Bruce Dern . . . . . . . . . . . . . . . . . . . . . . . . . . .William
•• 0:45—Buns, while taking off his clothes and walking onto stage during a play. Long shot.
Sydne Rome . . . . . . . . . . . . . . . . . . . . . . . . . . Nathalie

## Twisted Justice (1990)
Julie Austin . . . . . . . . . . . . . . . . . . . . . . . Andrea Leyton
Karen Black . . . . . . . . . . . . . . . . . . . . . . . . Mrs. Granger
Bonnie Paine . . . . . . . . . . . . . . . . . . . . . . . . . . Hooker
•• 0:11—Breasts, wearing black panties and stockings, while getting photographed.
Tanya Roberts . . . . . . . . . . . . . . . . . . . . . . . Secretary
Shannon Tweed . . . . . . . . . . . . . . . . . . . . . . . .Hinkle

## Twisted Obsession (1990)
Arielle Dombasle . . . . . . . . . . . . . . . . . . Marion Derain
Dexter Fletcher . . . . . . . . . . . . . . . . . . .Malcolm Greene
Jeff Goldblum . . . . . . . . . . . . . . . . . . . . . Daniel Gillis
Miranda Richardson . . . . . . . . . . . . . . . . . . . . .Marilyn
Liza Walker . . . . . . . . . . . . . . . . . . . . . . . Jenny Greene
1:12—Lower frontal nudity while lying down. (Don't see her face.)
• 1:35—Brief breasts in blue light when Jeff Goldblum sees her.

## Two Moon Junction (1988)
Sherilyn Fenn . . . . . . . . . . . . . . . . . . . . . . . . . . . April
••• 0:07—Breasts and brief buns, while taking a shower in the country club shower room.
•• 0:27—Brief breasts on the floor kissing Perry.
•• 0:42—Breasts in gas station restroom changing camisole tops with Kristy McNichol.
• 0:54—Brief breasts making love with Perry in a motel room.
••• 1:24—Nude at Two Moon Junction making love with Perry. Very hot!

• 1:40—Brief left breast, brief lower frontal nudity and buns in the shower with Perry.
Martin Hewitt. . . . . . . . . . . . . . . . . . . . . . . . . . .Chad
Milla Jovovich . . . . . . . . . . . . . . . . . . . . . . . . Samantha
Kristy McNichol . . . . . . . . . . . . . . . . . . . . . Patti Jean
•• 0:42—Breasts in gas station restroom changing camisole tops with Sherilyn Fenn.
Richard Tyson . . . . . . . . . . . . . . . . . . . . . . . . . Perry
• 0:58—Very, very brief buns while wrestling with April in a motel room. Dark, hard to see.

## Two to Tango (1988)
Adrianne Sachs. . . . . . . . . . . . . . . . . . . . . . . Cecilia Lorca
•• 0:29—Side of left breast and buns in bedroom with Lucky Lara. More left breast while Dan Stroud watches through camera.
•• 0:59—Breasts and buns in bed with Dan Stroud.
Alberto Segado . . . . . . . . . . . . . . . . . . . . . . .Lucky Lara
• 0:29—Buns while on top of Adrienne Sachs, making love with her in bed.

## Ultimate Desires (1991)
*a.k.a. Silhouette*
Sheri Able. . . . . . . . . . . . . . . . . . . . . . . Carlos' Girlfriend
Holly Chester . . . . . . . . . . . . . . . . . . . . . . . . . Streetgirl
Robyn Kelly . . . . . . . . . . . . . . . . . . . . . . . . . . Streetgirl
Tracy Scoggins. . . . . . . . . . . . . . . . Samantha Stewart
0:44—In white bra and panties, dancing sexily in her house, while two guys watch from outside.
0:53—Getting dressed in white bra and panties. Don't see her face.
• 0:59—Very brief buns and side of left breast taking off her dress and walking out of the room.
1:07—In black bra, panties, garter belt and stockings with Marc Singer.
••• 1:10—Breasts, several times, in bed with Singer.
Marc Singer . . . . . . . . . . . . . . . . . . . .Jonathan Sullivan

## Ultraviolet (1992)
Patricia Healy . . . . . . . . . . . . . . . . . . . . . . Kristen Halsey
0:04—In white bra, while changing into "something cooler" in motor home.
• 0:21—Brief breasts, after taking off blouse and posing for Esai Morales in motor home.
••• 0:50—In wet bra and panties, coming out of the pond. Side view of buns, then breasts while posing for Morales.
••• 0:52—More buns in panties and breasts in pond with Morales and struggling with him.
Stephen Meadows . . . . . . . . . . . . . . . . . . . . Sam Halsey

## The Unbearable Lightness of Being (1988)
Juliette Binoche . . . . . . . . . . . . . . . . . . . . . . . . . Tereza
0:22—In white bra in Tomas' apartment.
• 1:33—Brief breasts jumping onto couch.
1:36—Buns, sitting in front of fire being photographed, then running around, trying to hide.
• 2:18—Left breast in The Engineer's apartment.
Daniel Day-Lewis . . . . . . . . . . . . . . . . . . . . . . .Thomas
Derek De Lint . . . . . . . . . . . . . . . . . . . . . . . . . . . . Franz
Daniel Olbrychski . . . . . . . . . . .Interior Ministry Official

Lena Olin . . . . . . . . . . . . . . . . . . . . . . . . . . . . . Sabina
- •• 0:03—Breasts in bed with Tomas looking at themselves in a mirror.
  - 0:17—In black bra and panties looking at herself in a mirror on the floor.
  - 1:21—In black bra, panties, garter belt and stockings.
- •• 1:29—Breasts and buns while Tereza photographs her. Long shots, hard to see.
- • 1:43—Very brief left breast, in bed with Tomas.
  - 2:32—Brief breasts in B&W photo found in a drawer by Tomas.

Stellan Skarsgard . . . . . . . . . . . . . . . . . . The Engineer
- • 2:18—Buns, while making love with Tereza in his apartment.

### The Unborn (1991)
Brooke Adams . . . . . . . . . . . . . . . . . . . . Virginia Marshall
- • 1:12—Right breast, while breast feeding her baby creature.

Daryl Haney . . . . . . . . . . . . . . . . . . . . . . . . .Policeman

### Uncaged (1991)
*a.k.a. Angel in Red*
Sean'a Arthur . . . . . . . . . . . . . . . . . . . . . . . . . . Dancer
- •• 0:44—Buns in lingerie. Breasts dancing on stage.

Leslie Bega . . . . . . . . . . . . . . . . . . . . . . . . . . . . . Micki
- •• 0:02—Breasts on top of a customer, in bed.
- •• 0:16—Breasts in bed with Evan.
- • 0:42—Brief breasts with Evan on the floor.
  - 0:51—In white lingerie outfit with a customer and Ros.

Timothy Charles . . . . . . . . . . . . . . . . . . . . . . . Evan
- • 0:42—Brief buns, while on the floor with Micki.

Pamella D'Pella . . . . . . . . . . . . . . . . . . . . . . . . . . . . Ros
Monique Gabrielle . . . . . . . . . . . . . . . . Beautiful Hooker
Daryl Haney . . . . . . . . . . . . . . . . . . . . . John in Nova
Elena Sahagun . . . . . . . . . . . . . . . . . . . . . . . . . . Joey

### Under Cover (1987)
David Denney . . . . . . . . . . . . . . . . . . . . . . . .Hassie Pearl
- • 0:43—Brief buns while walking around boy's locker room wearing his jock strap.

Jennifer Jason Leigh . . . . . . . . . . . . . . . . Tanille Lareoux

### Under Seige (1992)
Bernie Casey . . . . . . . . . . . . . . . . . . Commander Harris
Erika Eleniak . . . . . . . . . . . . . . . . . . . . . . .Jordan Tate
- •• 0:43—Buns in T-back, then brief breasts in open coat, while popping out of cake.

Tommy Lee Jones . . . . . . . . . . . . . . . .William Stronnix

### Under Suspicion (1992)
Stephen Moore . . . . . . . . . . . . . . . . . . . . . . . . Roscoe
- • 1:01—Very, very brief frontal nudity when Frank pulls the sheet down after catching Roscoe in bed with a young boy.

Liam Neeson . . . . . . . . . . . . . . . . . . . . . . . . . . .Tony
- • 0:02—Buns, making love in bathroom with Hazel in bathroom while standing up. (Don't see his face.)

- • 0:03—Brief nude, running outside at night to get away from the husband. Long shot.
- • 0:04—Very brief frontal nudity, helping Frank over the fence.

Maggie O'Neill . . . . . . . . . . . . . . . . . . . . . . . . . . .Hazel
- • 0:02—Breasts and lower frontal nudity in shower with Liam Neeson.
- • 0:03—Very brief right breast, while ducking to avoid shotgun blast.

### Under the Gun (1989)
Nick Cassavetes . . . . . . . . . . . . . . . . . . . . .Tony Braxton
Sam Jones . . . . . . . . . . . . . . . . . . . . . . . . . . . . . Braxton
- • 0:41—Brief buns, while taking a shower at Vanessa Williams place. Don't see his face.

Karman Kruschke . . . . . . . . . . . . . . . . . . . . Girl at Pool
Vanessa Williams . . . . . . . . . . . . . . . Samantha Richards

### Under the Volcano (1984)
Anthony Andrews . . . . . . . . . . . . . . . . . . . Hugh Firmin
Jacqueline Bisset . . . . . . . . . . . . . . . . . . . Yvonne Firmin
Albert Finney . . . . . . . . . . . . . . . . . . . . Geoffrey Firmin
- ••• 0:49—Buns and brief frontal nudity in bathroom with Jacqueline Bisset and Anthony Andrews when they try to give him a shower.
- •• 0:52—Buns and very brief frontal nudity, putting on his underwear.

Hugo Stiglitz . . . . . . . . . . . . . . . . . . . . . . . .Sinarquista

### The Underachievers (1987)
Edward Albert . . . . . . . . . . . . . . . . . . . . . .Danny Warren
Barbara Carrera . . . . . . . . . . . . . . . . . . . . . . .Katherine
Carl Crew . . . . . . . . . . . . . . . . . . . . . . . . . . . Thug 2
Becky LeBeau . . . . . . . . . . . . . . . . . . . . . Ginger Bronsky
- ••• 0:40—Breasts in swimming pool playing with an inflatable alligator after her exercise class has left.

Jewel Shepard . . . . . . . . . . . . . . . . . . . . . Sci-Fi Teacher
- • 0:27—Breasts ripping off her Star Trek uniform when someone enters her classroom. Dark, hard to see.

Susan Tyrrell . . . . . . . . . . . . . . . . . . . . . . . . .Mrs. Grant

### Unexpected Encounters, Vol. 3 (1988)
Jasaé . . . . . . . . . . . . . . . . . . . . . . . . . . . . . . . .Neighbor
- ••• 0:32—Doing strip tease in front of guitar playing neighbor. Buns in G-string and breasts.

Charlie Spradling . . . . . . . . . . . . . . . . .Woman in House
- ••• 0:50—In lingerie, then breasts on sofa with the gardener.

### Unfaithfully Yours (1984)
Jane Hallaren . . . . . . . . . . . . . . . . . . . . . . . . . . . Janet
Nastassja Kinski . . . . . . . . . . . . . . . . . . Daniella Eastman
- • 0:37—Breasts and buns in the shower.

Dudley Moore . . . . . . . . . . . . . . . . . . . .Claude Eastman
Cassie Yates . . . . . . . . . . . . . . . . . . . . . Carla Robbins

### The Unholy (1988)
Jill Carroll . . . . . . . . . . . . . . . . . . . . . . . . . . . . . .Millie
- • 1:10—Very brief upper half of left breast, while talking in the courtyard with Ben Cross.

Hal Holbrook . . . . . . . . . . . . . . . . . . Archbishop Mosley

### Unholy Rollers (1972)
*a.k.a. Leader of the Pack*
Roberta Collins . . . . . . . . . . . . . . . . . . . . . . . .Jennifer
Claudia Jennings . . . . . . . . . . . . . . . . . . . Karen Walker
- ••• 0:32—Breasts on pool table, getting gang stripped by the other girls, then walking around and yelling at them.
- • 0:38—Buns on top of Nick, on table in the middle of the roller derby rink.
- •• 1:15—Breasts, twice, while changing clothes in locker room, then in bra and panties.

Charlene Jones . . . . . . . . . . . . . . . . . . . . . . . Beverly
Candice Roman. . . . . . . . . . . . . . . . . . . . . . . . Donna
- ••• 0:06—Breasts in bed with Greg when Karen comes home.
- •• 0:12—Breasts, dancing on stage in club next to a brunette dancer.
- • 0:13—More breasts in background.
- • 0:14—More breasts in background.

### Universal Soldier (1992)
Gene Davis . . . . . . . . . . . . . . . . . . . . . . . . . Lieutenant
Tom "Tiny" Lister, Jr. . . . . . . . . . . . . . . . . . . . . . . GR55
Dolph Lundgren . . . . . . . . . . . . . . . . . . . Andrew Scott
Joseph Malone . . . . . . . . . . . . . . . . . . . . . . . . .Huey
Ed O'Ross . . . . . . . . . . . . . . . . . . . . . . . Colonel Perry
Jean-Claude Van Damme . . . . . . . . . . . . . Luc Devreux
- ••• 0:34—Buns, while standing in front of air conditioner.
- ••• 0:35—Buns, while walking in motel parking lot after Ally Walker. Partial buns, while lying on ground.

### Unlawful Entry (1992)
Ray Liotta . . . . . . . . . . . . . . . . . . . Officer Pete Davis
- • 0:50—Brief, out of focus buns, while getting out of shower in locker room.

Sherrie Rose . . . . . . . . . . . . . . . . . . . . . . Girl in Jeep
- •• 0:42—Breasts, making love with Ray Liotta in police car, then getting thrown out.

Kurt Russell . . . . . . . . . . . . . . . . . . . . . . . .Michael Carr
Madeleine Stowe . . . . . . . . . . . . . . . . . . . Karen Carr
- ••• 0:56—Breasts and partial buns, while making love on top of Kurt Russell in bed.

### An Unmarried Woman (1978)
Alan Bates. . . . . . . . . . . . . . . . . . . . . . . . . . . . Saul
Jill Clayburgh . . . . . . . . . . . . . . . . . . . . . . . . . . Erica
- 0:05—Dancing around the apartment in white long sleeve T-shirt and white panties.
- •• 0:12—Brief breasts getting dressed for bed, kind of dark and hard to see.
- •• 1:10—In bra and panties in guy's apartment, then brief breasts lying on bed.

### The Unnameable (1988)
Laura Albert . . . . . . . . . . . . . . . . . . . . . . .Wendy Barnes
- •• 0:46—Left breast while lying on floor kissing John, then brief buns when he pulls her panties down.

### The Unnameable II (1992)
Maria Ford . . . . . . . . . . . . . . . . . . . . . . . Alyda Winthrop
- •• 0:52—Buns, when her long hair moves out of the way. Partial tip of right breast when looking at the telephone.
- • 0:53—Brief buns and side of right breast in bedroom.
- •• 0:54—Buns and breasts while checking out the bed.
- • 0:57—Brief buns, while getting out of bed.
- •• 0:58—Buns and brief breasts in bedroom with Mary.
- • 1:01—Right breast in gaping nightgown while kneeling on elevator floor.
- • 1:22—Brief glimpses of right breast in gaping nightgown.
- • 1:32—Very brief right breast in gaping nightgown while crawling on the floor.

Julie Strain . . . . . . . . . . . . . . . . . . . . . . . . . . Creature

### Until September (1984)
Karen Allen. . . . . . . . . . . . . . . . . . . . . . Mo Alexander
- •• 0:41—Breasts in bed making love with Thierry Lhermitte.
- •• 1:13—Breasts and buns walking from bed to Lhermitte.
- • 1:25—Brief breasts jumping out of bathtub.

Christopher Cazenove . . . . . . . . . . . . . . . . . . . .Philip
Maryam D'Abo. . . . . . . . . . . . . . . . . . . . . . .Nathalie
Marika Green . . . . . . . . . . . . . . . . . . . . . . . . . Banker
Thierry Lhermitte . . . . . . . . . . . . . .Xavier de la Pérouse
- •• 0:43—Buns, after making love with Karen Allen.
- 0:53—Almost frontal nudity getting out of bathtub.

### Until the End of the World (1991)
Lois Chiles . . . . . . . . . . . . . . . . . . . . . . . Elsa Farber
Solveig Dommartin . . . . . . . . . . . . . . . Claire Tourneur
- ••• 0:34—Left breast, then breasts, then full frontal nudity in bedroom with William Hurt and Winter.

Allen Garfield . . . . . . . . . . . . . . . . . . . . . . . Bernie
David Gulpilil . . . . . . . . . . . . . . . . . . . . . . . . . .David
William Hurt. . . . . . . . . . . . . Sam Farber/Trevor McPhee
Jeanne Moreau. . . . . . . . . . . . . . . . . . . . .Edith Farber
Sam Neill . . . . . . . . . . . . . . . . . . . . Eugene Fitzpatrick

### Unveiled (1993)
Peter Berg . . . . . . . . . . . . . . . . . . . . . . . . .Drug Dealer
Lisa Zane . . . . . . . . . . . . . . . . . .Stephania Montgomery
- • 1:06—Very, very brief left breast in gaping gown, while bending over to pick stuff up off the floor.

### Up 'n' Coming (1987)
(R-rated version reviewed, X-rated version available.)
Marilyn Chambers . . . . . . . . . . . . . . . . . . . . . . . Cassie
- ••• 0:01—Nude, getting out of bed and taking a shower.
- •• 0:08—Breasts making love in bed with the record producer.
- • 0:30—Brief breasts in bed with two guys.
- •• 0:47—Full frontal nudity getting suntan lotion rubbed on her by another woman.
- •• 0:55—Breasts taking off her top at radio station.

Lisa De Leeuw . . . . . . . . . . . . . . . . . .Altheah Anderson
- 0:33—Very brief breasts by the pool when her robe opens.
- 0:48—Brief breasts walking around the house when her robe open.
- • 0:49—Left breast talking with a guy, then breasts while walking into the bedroom.

Monique Gabrielle . . . . . . . . . . . . . . . . . . Boat Girl #1
- 0:39—Breasts wearing white shorts on boat. Long shot.
- 0:40—More brief nude shots on the boat.

Loni Saunders . . . . . . . . . . . . . . . . . . . . . . . . Dixanne
- 0:19—Breasts kissing a guy on the bus.

## Up in Smoke (1978)
Tommy Chong . . . . . . . . . . . . . . . . . . . . . Man Stoner
Madeleine Collinson . . . . . . . . . . . . . . . . . . . . . Pinup
- 0:44—Brief breasts in centerfold photo on inside of restroom stall door.

Mary Collinson . . . . . . . . . . . . . . . . . . . . . . . . Pinup
- 0:44—Brief breasts in centerfold photo on inside of restroom stall door.

June Fairchild . . . . . . . . . . . . . . . . . . . . . . Ajax Lady
Stacy Keach. . . . . . . . . . . . . . . . . . . . . . . . Sergeant
Richard "Cheech" Marin . . . . . . . . . . . . .Pedro De Pacas
Louisa Moritz . . . . . . . . . . . . . . . . . . Officer Gloria
Tom Skerritt . . . . . . . . . . . . . . . . . . . . . Strawberry
Cheryl Smith . . . . . . . . . . . . . . . . . . Laughing Lady
Wally Anne Wharton. . . . . . . . . . . . . . . . . . . . Debbie
1:03—Brief back side of left breast, while in back of van with Cheech Marin.

## Up the Creek (1984)
Jeff East . . . . . . . . . . . . . . . . . . . . . . . . . . . . . Max
Tim Matheson. . . . . . . . . . . . . . . . . . . . Bob McGraw
Dan Monahan. . . . . . . . . . . . . . . . . . . . . . . . . Max
Julie Montgomery . . . . . . . . . . . . . . . . . . . . . . .Lisa
Tom Nolan . . . . . . . . . . . . . . . . . . . . . . . . Whitney
Jennifer Runyon. . . . . . . . . . . . . .Heather Merriweather
Lori Sutton . . . . . . . . . . . . . . . . . . . . . . . .Cute Girl
- 0:40—Brief breasts, twice, after ripping open her blouse to get a crowd excited while cheerleading.

Jeana Tomasina. . . . . . . . . . . . . . . . . . . . . . Molly
Peggy Trentini. . . . . . . . . . . . . . . . . . . . . . . Co-Ed
Romy Windsor . . . . . . . . . . . . . . . . . . . . . . Corky

## Up Yours (Canadian)
Caleb Goodman . . . . . . . . . . . . . . . . . . . . . .Virgil
- 0:50—Buns, while dancing on roof of building with Mary Lou.

Cindy Morgan. . . . . . . . . . . . . . . . . . . . . . . Elaine

## Used Cars (1980)
Cheryl Rixon . . . . . . . . . . . . . . . . . . . . . . Margaret
- • 0:29—Breasts after getting her dress torn off during a used car commercial.

Kurt Russell . . . . . . . . . . . . . . . . . . . . Rudy Russo
- 1:04—Very brief buns while putting on red underwear.

Betty Thomas. . . . . . . . . . . . . . . . . . . . . . . . Bunny
0:37—Dancing on top of a car next to Kurt Russell wearing pasties to attract customers (wearing a brunette wig).

Jack Warden. . . . . . . . . . . . . . . Roy L. Fuchs/Luke Fuchs

## Vagabond (1985; French)
Sandrine Bonnaire . . . . . . . . . . . . . . . . . . . . . Mona
Macha Meril . . . . . . . . . . . . . . . . .Madame Landier
- • 0:45—Breasts, while sitting in the bathtub and talking on the phone.

## Valentino (1977; British)
Leslie Caron . . . . . . . . . . . . . . . . . . . . . . . . Nazimova
Carol Kane . . . . . . . . . . . . . . . . . . . . . . . .Fatty's Girl
Jennie Linden . . . . . . . . . . . . . . . . . . . . . .Agnes Ayres
Penelope Milford . . . . . . . . . . . . . . . . . . . .Lorna Sinclair
- • • 1:28—Nude, while making love with Rudolf Nureyev in bedroom. Long scene.

Rudolf Nureyev . . . . . . . . . . . . . . . .Rudolph Valentino
- • • 0:54—Nude, while on bed with Michelle Phillips.
- • • 0:55—Frontal nudity while getting up and out of bed.
- 0:58—Side view of buns while posing for photos.

Michelle Phillips . . . . . . . . . . . . . . . Natasha Rambova
- 0:53—Brief buns, enticing Rudolf Nureyev into tent.
- 0:54—Brief lower frontal nudity, when sitting up in bed.
- • • 0:55—Brief left breast when Nureyev moves her hair out of the way. Breasts, while getting up and out of bed.
- • 1:39—Brief right breast, after Nureyev rolls off her.

Dudley Sutton . . . . . . . . . . . . . . . . . . . . . . . . .Willie
Linda Thorson . . . . . . . . . . . . . . . . . . . Billie Streeter
- 0:14—Brief left breast, under a guy in bed.

## Valentino Returns (1988)
Veronica Cartwright. . . . . . . . . . . . . . . . . . .Pat Gibbs
- • • 0:33—Breasts sitting in bed with Frederic Forrest. Fairly long scene.

Miguel Ferrer . . . . . . . . . . . . . . . . . . . . . . . . . n.a.
Barry Tubb . . . . . . . . . . . . . . . . . . . . . .Wayne Gibbs
- • • 1:15—Buns, while fighting two other guys after skinny dipping with Jenny Wright at night. Very, very brief, blurry frontal nudity after getting hit and rolling into the water.

Jenny Wright . . . . . . . . . . . . . . . . . . . . . . Sylvia Fuller

## Valet Girls (1987)
Barbara Dare . . . . . . . . . . . . . . . . .Uncredited Party Girl
- 1:10—Brief breasts, getting photographed while sitting on railing.
- 1:14—Brief breasts, popping out of birthday cake and putting a pie in Dirk's face.

Kim Gillingham . . . . . . . . . . . . . . .Madonna Wannabe
Ron Jeremy. . . . . . . . . . . . . . . .Uncredited Party Goer
Mary Kohnert. . . . . . . . . . . . . . . . . . . . . . Carnation
Steve Lyon . . . . . . . . . . . . . . . . . . . . . . . . . . .Ike
- 1:17—Brief side view of buns, twice, when the girls make him and his two friends climb the "HOLLYWOOD" sign.

## Valley Girl (1983)

Michael Bowen . . . . . . . . . . . . . . . . . . . . . . . . .Tommy
Nicolas Cage. . . . . . . . . . . . . . . . . . . . . . . . . . .Randy
Colleen Camp. . . . . . . . . . . . . . . . . . . . Sarah Richman
Elizabeth Daily. . . . . . . . . . . . . . . . . . . . . . . . . Loryn
•• 0:16—In bra through open jumpsuit, then brief
    breasts on bed with Tommy.
Cameron Dye . . . . . . . . . . . . . . . . . . . . . . . . . . Fred
Deborah Foreman. . . . . . . . . . . . . . . . . . . . . . Julie
Joyce Hyser . . . . . . . . . . . . . . . . . . . . . . . . . . Joyce

## Valley of the Dolls (1967)

Patty Duke . . . . . . . . . . . . . . . . . . . . . . Neely O'Hara
Lee Grant . . . . . . . . . . . . . . . . . . . . . . . . . . . Miriam
Susan Hayward . . . . . . . . . . . . . . . . . . . .Helen Lawson
Barbara Parkins . . . . . . . . . . . . . . . . . . . . Anne Welles
• 0:28—Very brief silhouette of a breast, when taking
    off nightgown and getting into bed.
Sharon Tate. . . . . . . . . . . . . . . . . . . . .Jennifer North
• 1:21—In bra, acting in a movie. Very, very brief left
    breast in bed with a guy (curtain gets in the way).
• 1:23—Very brief side view of right breast, while sit-
    ting up in bed.
Corinna Tsopei . . . . . . . . . . . . . . . . . . . Telephone Girl

## The Vals (1982)

Tiffany Bolling. . . . . . . . . . . Valley Attorney and Parent
Gina Calabrese . . . . . . . . . . . . . . . . . . . . . . . Annie
• 0:04—Breasts changing clothes in bedroom with
    three of her friends. Long shot, hard to see.
• 0:15—Right breast, while making love with a guy at
    a party.
0:32—In black bra with her friends in a store dress-
    ing room.
Jill Carroll . . . . . . . . . . . . . . . . . . . . . . . . . . . Sam

## Vamp (1986)

Tricia Brown . . . . . . . . . . . . . . . . . . . . . . . . Candi
• 0:32—Brief breasts doing strip tease.
Grace Jones . . . . . . . . . . . . . . . . . . . . . . . . Katrina
0:23—Breasts under wire bra, dancing on stage.
    Body is painted, so it's difficult to see.
Lisa Lyon. . . . . . . . . . . . . . . . . . . . . . . . Cimmaron
Tanya Papanicolas. . . . . . . . . . . . . . . . . . Waitress
Dedee Pfeiffer . . . . . . . . . . . . . . . . . . . . . Amaretto
Robert Rusler. . . . . . . . . . . . . . . . . . . . . . . . .A.J.

## Vampire at Midnight (1988)

Esther Alise . . . . . . . . . . . . . . . . . . . . .Lucia Giannini
••• 1:01—In black lingerie, then breasts and buns while
    taking off clothes to wish Roger a happy birthday.
Barbara Hammond . . . . . . . . . . . . . . . . . . . . .Kelly
•• 0:07—Breasts and buns, getting out of the shower
    and drying herself off.
• 0:16—Left breast, dead, in Victor's car trunk. Blood
    on her.
Jeanie Moore. . . . . . . . . . . . . . . . . . . . . . . Amalia
•• 0:32—Breasts getting up to run an errand.
Christina Whitaker. . . . . . . . . . . . . . . . . . . . Ingrid
Jason Williams . . . . . . . . . . . . . Detective Roger Sutter

## Vampire Cop (1990)

Melissa Anne Moore. . . . . . . . . . . . . . .Melanie Roberts
••• 0:46—Breasts in bed with the Vampire Cop.
•• 0:51—Right breast, sitting in bed talking with Hans.
• 1:21—Right breast, in bed on the phone during end
    credits.

## Vampire Hookers (1979)

Lenka Novak . . . . . . . . . . . . . . . . . . . . . . . . Suzy
0:22—In sheer green dress getting into coffin.
0:33—In sheer green dress again.
0:45—In sheer green dress again.
•• 0:51—Breasts in bed during the orgy with the guy
    and the other two Vampire Hookers.

## Vampire Lovers (1970; British)

Ingrid Pitt. . . . . . . . . . . . . . . . . . . . . Marcilla/Carmilla
•• 0:32—Breasts and buns in the bathtub and reflec-
    tion in the mirror talking to Emma.
Madeline Smith . . . . . . . . . . . . . . . . . . . . . . Emma
•• 0:32—Breasts trying on a dress in the bedroom after
    Carmilla has taken a bath.
• 0:49—Breasts in bed, getting her top pulled down
    by Carmilla.
Pippa Steel. . . . . . . . . . . . . . . . . . . . . . . . . .Laura
• 0:24—Left breast in bed when the doctor pulls her
    top down to listen to her heart beat.

## Vampire's Kiss (1989)

Maria Conchita Alonso. . . . . . . . . . . . . . . . . . . .Alva
0:47—In white bra, ironing her clothes in her living
    room.
0:59—In white bra getting attacked by Nicolas
    Cage.
Elizabeth Ashley . . . . . . . . . . . . . . . . . . . . . Dr. Glaser
Jennifer Beals . . . . . . . . . . . . . . . . . . . . . . . Rachel
0:14—Almost breasts in bed with Nicolas Cage.
    Squished left breast against Cage while she bites
    him. In one shot, you can see the beige pastie she
    put over her left nipple.
0:27—In bed again with Cage.
0:41—In black lingerie taking her dress off for Cage.
Nicolas Cage . . . . . . . . . . . . . . . . . . . . . .Peter Loew
Kasi Lemmons . . . . . . . . . . . . . . . . . . . . . . .Jackie
•• 0:05—In black bra and panties, then breasts in living
    room with Nicolas Cage.

## Vampyres (1974; British)

Murray Brown . . . . . . . . . . . . . . . . . . . . . . . . Ted
•• 0:22—Buns, while making love in bed with Fran.
• 0:56—Buns, while falling into bed.
Brian Deacon . . . . . . . . . . . . . . . . . . . . . . . . John
Anulka Dziubinska . . . . . . . . . . . . . . . . . . . . .Miriam
• 0:00—Brief full frontal nudity in bed with Fran, kiss-
    ing each other before getting shot.
• 0:43—Breasts taking a shower with Fran.
••• 0:58—Breasts and buns in bed with Fran, drinking
    Ted's blood. Brief lower frontal nudity.
Sally Faulkner. . . . . . . . . . . . . . . . . . . . . . . .Harriet
• 1:14—Side of left breast, partial buns, then right
    breast while making love with John in the trailer.

•• 1:22—Full frontal nudity getting her clothes ripped off by Fran and Miriam in the wine cellar before being killed.

Marianne Morris . . . . . . . . . . . . . . . . . . . . . . . . . . Fran
- •• 0:00—Breasts, then full frontal nudity in bed with Miriam, kissing each other before getting shot.
- ••• 0:20—Side of right breast, then breasts in bed with Ted, drinking wine, then making love.
- • 0:23—Buns, lying in bed when Ted gets out.
- ••• 0:39—In black bra, panties, garter belt and stockings, then taking them off in front of Ted. Breasts and buns, then in bed.
- ••• 0:43—Breasts getting kissed by Miriam in the shower.
- •• 0:56—Breasts taking off dress in front of Ted and getting into bed. Partial lower frontal nudity getting into bed.
- ••• 0:58—Breasts and brief lower frontal nudity in bed with Miriam, drinking Ted's blood.
- • 1:00—Full frontal nudity getting dragged out of bed by Miriam.
- • 1:18—Brief left breast, getting fondled by the Playboy guy in the wine cellar.

## Van Nuys Blvd. (1979)
Bill Adler . . . . . . . . . . . . . . . . . . . . . . . . . . . . . . .Bobby
- • 0:21—Brief buns, while making out with Wanda in the back of his van.
- • 0:58—Brief buns, while making love on top of Moon.

Dennis Bowen. . . . . . . . . . . . . . . . . . . . . . . . . . . .Greg
- • 0:53—Brief buns, while putting his underwear on after getting caught in the wrong bedroom.

Melissa Prophet. . . . . . . . . . . . . . . . . . . . . . . . .Camille
Suzanne Severeid . . . . . . . . . . . . . . . . . . . . . . . . . . Jo
0:01—In white bra and panties in trailer with Bobby.
- ••• 0:02—Breasts and buns, bringing a beer to Bobby, then sitting and watching TV.

Tara Strohmeier . . . . . . . . . . . . . . . . . . . . . . Wanda
- •• 0:21—Breasts, while playing around with food with Bobby in the back of his van.
- • 0:51—Brief breasts, flashing while hitchhiking to get a ride.

Cyndi Wood . . . . . . . . . . . . . . . . . . . . . . . . . . . Moon
- •• 0:57—Left breast outside on boat with Bobby, then breasts, while making love in bed with him.

## Vanessa (1977)
Olivia Pascal . . . . . . . . . . . . . . . . . . . . . . . . . Vanessa
- ••• 0:08—Nude undressing, taking a bath and getting washed by Jackie. Long scene.
- ••• 0:16—Buns, then full frontal nudity getting a massage.
- • 0:26—Breasts, while getting fitted for new clothes.
- • 0:47—Full frontal nudity when Adrian rips her clothes off.
- ••• 0:56—Full frontal nudity on beach with Jackie.
- ••• 1:05—Nude making love with Jackie in bed. Nice close up of left breast.
- •• 1:19—Full frontal nudity lying on the table.

•• 1:27—Breasts, wearing white panties, garter belt and stockings shackled up by Kenneth.

## Vanishing Point (1971)
Gilda Texter . . . . . . . . . . . . . . . . . . . . . . . . Nude Rider
- • 1:17—Breasts while riding motorcycle outside.
- ••• 1:19—Breasts riding motorcycle and walking around without wearing any clothes. Long scene.

## Velvet Dreams (1991; Italian)
Alicia Moro. . . . . . . . . . . . . . . . . . . . . . . . . . . . . n.a.
Kathy Shower. . . . . . . . . . . . . . . . . . . . . . . . . . .Laura
- •• 0:15—Left breast, while making love with Paul in the dressing room.
- • 0:35—Brief buns, while getting a massage.
- •• 0:42—Breasts, tied to a tree during her writing fantasy.

## The Velvet Vampire (1971)
Michael Blodgett . . . . . . . . . . . . . . . . . . . . . .Lee Ritter
- •• 0:21—Buns, getting up out of bed during desert dream scene.
- ••• 0:42—Buns, in desert dream scene.
- •• 0:46—Buns, while on floor with Diane.

Sherry Miles . . . . . . . . . . . . . . . . . . . . . . . . Susan Ritter
- • 0:08—Brief breasts in bed with Lee.
- ••• 0:18—Breasts sitting up in bed, then making love with Lee.
- • 0:21—Breasts in bed in desert during dream scene.
- ••• 0:22—Breasts sitting up in bed and turning on the light.
- • 0:42—Breasts in bed during desert dream scene, long shot.
- • 0:55—Breasts in bed during desert dream scene.
- ••• 0:56—Breasts in bed in desert scene, closer shot with Diane.
- • 1:19—Brief breasts in desert scene during flashback.

Celeste Yarnall . . . . . . . . . . . . . . . . . . . . Diane Le Fanu
- • 0:32—Brief breasts, while zipping up her blouse after trying to seduce Lee.
- •• 0:42—Breasts in desert scene when Lee pulls her blouse down.
- ••• 0:45—Breasts, while on the floor, making love with Lee.
- •• 0:55—Breasts in desert scene with Lee.
- • 0:57—Side view of buns, lying on top of someone in a coffin.
- •• 1:02—Breasts, while in bed with Lee.

## Vendetta (1986)
Roberta Collins. . . . . . . . . . . . . . . . . . . . . . . .Miss Dice
Marta Kober. . . . . . . . . . . . . . . . . . . . . . . . . . . .Sylvia
- • 1:10—Very brief, dark, right breast in open blouse, in her prison cell with the guard.

Sandy Martin . . . . . . . . . . . . . . . . . . . . . . . Kay Butler
- • 0:34—Brief left breast, while making love with her boyfriend. Don't see her face.

Dirga McBroom . . . . . . . . . . . . . . . . . . . . . . . .Willow
Marianne Taylor. . . . . . . . . . . . . . . . . . . . . . . . . Star

## Vengeance... One by One

Romy Schneider . . . . . . . . . . . . . . . . . . . . . . . . .n.a.
   0:02—In black slip getting dressed.
- 0:28—Very brief left breast when a soldier rips her
   bra open during struggle.
   1:14—In black lingerie in her husband's flashback.

## Venus in Furs *(1970)*

Original version.
Klaus Kinski . . . . . . . . . . . . . . . . . . . . . . . . . . Ahmed
Margaret Lee. . . . . . . . . . . . . . . . . . . . . . . . . . .Olga
- 0:53—Buns, lying on floor with Maria.
- 0:54—Buns, while walking and holding candelabra.
Maria Rohm . . . . . . . . . . . . . . . . . . . . . .Wanda Reed
- 0:05—Breasts on beach, dead, after getting
   dragged from the ocean.
- 0:08—Breasts in stockings and panties, getting
   whipped by Olga.
- •• 0:10—Breasts before getting stabbed by Klaus Kinski.
- 0:11—More breasts on beach, dead.
- 0:17—Brief breasts.
- 0:21—Right breast several times, making love in bed
   with a guy.
- ••• 0:22—Breasts, lying in bed with the guy afterwards.
- 0:23—Brief breasts on beach again.
- 0:32—Breasts, dead on the beach with two cuts.
- 0:43—Breasts on couch when Olga opens her
   blouse.
- 0:45—Breasts in bed.
- •• 0:52—Breasts posing for Olga.
- 0:54—Breasts, dead.
- •• 0:56—Breasts walking down stairs, wearing panties.
- 0:59—Breasts in bed again.
- 1:02—Brief side view of right breast, hugging Jimmy.
- 1:05—Left breast while acting as a slave girl.
- 1:06—Brief breasts seen through sheer curtain.
   1:09—Very brief right breast, dead.
- •• 1:10—Left breast, with Klaus Kinski.
   1:12—Buns, lying on couch.

## Vice Academy *(1988)*

Ken Abraham . . . . . . . . . . . . . . . . . . . . . . . . . Dwayne
Ginger Lynn Allen . . . . . . . . . . . . . . . . . . . . . . . .Holly
   1:20—Buns, in white lingerie outfit when gradua-
   tion robe gets torn off.
Stephanie Bishop . . . . . . . . . . . . . . . . Desiree/Redhead
Linnea Quigley . . . . . . . . . . . . . . . . . . . . . . . . . . Didi
- ••• 0:45—Breasts making love with Chuck while he's
   handcuffed.
Karen Russell . . . . . . . . . . . . . . . . . . . . . . . . .Shawnee
- •• 0:09—Breasts exposing herself to Duane to disarm
   him.
- •• 1:13—Breasts pulling her top down to distract a bad
   guy.

## Vice Academy, Part 2 *(1990)*

Toni Alessandrini . . . . . . . . . . . . . . . . . . . . . Aphrodisia
- 0:33—Breasts in dressing room.
- ••• 0:34—Breasts and buns in G-string, dancing in club.
Ginger Lynn Allen . . . . . . . . . . . . . . . . . . . . . . Holly
- 0:44—Buns in black bra, panties, garter belt and
   stockings.
- •• 1:04—Buns in G-string, then breasts dancing with
   Linnea Quigley on stage at club.
Teagan Clive . . . . . . . . . . . . . . . . . . . . . Bimbo Cop
Scott Layne . . . . . . . . . . . . . . . . . . . . . . . Petrolino
- 0:49—Buns, twice, while in men's locker room when
   Linnea Quigley and Ginger Lynn Allen come in.
Melissa Anne Moore. . . . . . . . . . . . . . . . . . . . . .Glaze
Linnea Quigley. . . . . . . . . . . . . . . . . . . . . . . . . .Didi
- •• 1:04—Buns in G-string, then breasts dancing with
   Ginger Lynn Allen on stage at club.

## Vice Academy, Part 3 *(1991)*

Toni Alessandrini . . . . . . . . . . . . . . . . . . . . . . Stripper
- •• 0:26—Breasts taking off dress on stage.
- •• 0:27—More breasts on stage (about five times).
- 0:28—More breasts giving her money to the robbers.
- 0:34—Buns in G-string, while dancing on stage.
Ginger Lynn Allen . . . . . . . . . . . . . . . . . . . . . . Holly
Veronica Carothers. . . . . . . . . . . . . . . . . . . . .Loretta
Darcy De Moss. . . . . . . . . . . . . . Uncredited Samantha
Elizabeth Kaitan . . . . . . . . . . . . . . . . . . . . . . . . Candy
- ••• 0:12—Breasts in back of van with her boyfriend.
Steve Mateo. . . . . . . . . . . . . . .Professor Dirk Kaufinger
- •• 0:47—Buns, when Ginger Lynn Allen and Elizabeth
   Kaitan come into his lab.
Julia Parton. . . . . . . . . . . . . . . . . . Melanie/Malathion
- •• 0:44—Breasts, opening her blouse after seeing all
   the money.

## Vice Squad *(1982)*

Nina Blackwood. . . . . . . . . . . . . . . . . . . . . . . .Ginger
Wings Hauser. . . . . . . . . . . . . . . . . . . . . . . . . Ramrod
Season Hubley . . . . . . . . . . . . . . . . . . . . . . . Princess
   0:34—In black bra in Ramrod's apartment.
- •• 0:57—Brief left breast and buns, wearing garter belt
   and stockings, getting out of bed after making love
   with a John.
- 0:58—More buns, under sheer panties while fighting with the John.
   1:25—In black bra, panties and garter belt, while
   tied up by Ramrod.
Pepe Serna. . . . . . . . . . . . . . . . . . . . . . Pete Mendez
Cheryl Smith . . . . . . . . . . . . . . . . . . . . .White Prostitute

## Video Vixens *(1973)*

Angela Carnon. . . . . . . . . . . . . . . . . . . . . Mrs. Gordon
- •• 1:13—Full frontal nudity making love with Mr. Gordon in bed in various positions. Shot at fast speed.
Sandra Dempsey . . . . . . . . . . . . . . . . . . . . . . .Actress
- •• 0:05—Full frontal nudity, lying down getting make
   up put on.

Marva Farmer .............................. Girl
•• 0:59—Full frontal nudity in the swimming pool with three other women during commercial.
George "Buck" Flower.................. Rex Boorski
• 0:52—Frontal nudity taking off his pants, then buns in bed with actress during filming of a movie. In B&W.
Robyn Hilton............................. Inga
•• 1:18—Breasts, opening her top in a room full of reporters.
Kimberly Hyde ........................ Claudine
Terri Johnson.............................. Anita
•• 0:43—Full frontal nudity, talking with her mother in bedroom during commercial.
Marius Mazmanian .................... Psychiatrist
•• 0:42—Buns and balls from behind, while frolicking on couch with his patient. In B&W.
Bernie Scorpio...................... Turnip Twin
••• 1:05—Frontal nudity standing next to his identical twin brother after their trial.
Lennie Scorpio ..................... Turnip Twin
•• 1:03—Frontal nudity, then buns while on top of victim in bed.
••• 1:05—Frontal nudity standing next to his identical twin brother after their trial.
Cheryl Smith.................. Twinkle Twat Girl
••• 0:24—Full frontal nudity doing a commercial, sitting next to pool.
Robyn Whitting.............. Patient and Virginia
•• 0:40—Breasts, then nude on couch in psychiatrist's office. In B&W.
•• 0:52—Full frontal nudity acting in bed with Rex for a film. In B&W.
Linda York ..................... Dial-A-Snatch Girl
•• 0:34—Nude on a turntable during a commercial, getting felt by four blindfolded guys.

### *Videodrome* (1983; Canadian)
Deborah Harry ...................... Nicki Brand
•• 0:16—Breasts rolling over on the floor when James Woods is piercing her ear with a pin.
0:22—In black bra, sitting on couch with James Woods.
James Woods ......................... Max Renn

### *Vigilante* (1983)
Rutanya Alda............................ Vickie
Sandy Alexander ..................... Prisoner
Henry Judd Baker ...................... Quinn
Joseph Carberry ....................... Ramon
Robert Forster ......................... Eddie
•• 0:55—Buns, in the prison showers with other prisoners (he's on the right.)
Carol Lynley ..................... D.A. Fletcher
Fred Williamson ......................... Nick

### *Vindicator* (1986; Canadian)
*a.k.a. Frankenstein '88*
Caroline Arnold............................ Lisa
•• 0:40—Breasts in bed with a jerk, then putting her blouse on.

Teri Austin .................. Lauren Lehman
• 0:30—Very brief left breast and buns in mirror getting out of the bubble bath covered with bubbles. Long shot, hard to see anything.
Pam Grier.............................. Hunter

### *Violated* (1987)
Sharon Cain ..................... Party Guest
Samantha Fox ............................ Joan
• 0:52—Breasts, while in bed with Marilyn on video playback.
John Heard........................... Skipper
Elizabeth Kaitan ..................... Liz Grant
•• 0:03—Breasts and lower frontal nudity while Frank rapes her in bedroom.
• 0:53—Very brief right breast several times while getting raped by Frank. Seen on video playback.
••• 0:59—Breasts and buns, while in bed with a customer.
J. C. Quinn..................... Kevin McBane
April Daisy White ..................... Lisa Robb
••• 0:16—Breasts, while wearing panties while getting dressed in bedroom while talking to her little brother.
•• 0:22—Breasts, after taking off her dress and diving into pool.
•• 0:25—Full frontal nudity while getting raped in bedroom by Jack while Marilyn and Frank help.
• 0:28—Breasts and lower frontal nudity while washing herself off in bathtub.
•• 0:40—Breasts in flashback of rape scene.
• 0:53—Full frontal nudity in flashback of rape scene.
• 1:08—Breasts on video playback of taking her dress off by pool.

### *Violets Are Blue* (1986)
Bonnie Bedelia ..................... Ruth Squires
Kevin Kline......................... Henry Squires
• 1:02—Brief buns, while standing up and putting on his shorts, on island with Sissy Spacek.
Sissy Spacek ..................... Gussie Sawyer

### *Virgin High* (1990)
Michelle Bauer ....................... Miss Bush
Tracy Dali.............................. Christy
•• 0:04—Brief breasts several times when her blouse and bra pop open while talking to her parents.
Maureen La Vette.................. Mrs. Murphy
Linnea Quigley....................... Kathleen
•• 0:24—Breasts, nonchalantly making love on top of Derrick.
•• 0:55—Brief breasts several times on top of Derrick, then breasts.
• 1:21—Breasts in photo during party.

### *Virgin Witch* (1971; British)
Keith Buckley........................... Johnny
• 1:20—Brief buns, with Betty during ceremony.
Neil Hallett...................... Gerald Amberley
• 1:23—Buns, after ceremony.

Ann Michelle . . . . . . . . . . . . . . . . . . . . . . . . . Christine
- • 0:00—Brief right breast, during opening credits.
- ••• 0:06—Breasts and lower frontal nudity, after undressing and getting her body measured by Sybil.
- •• 0:17—Breasts, undressing and standing by doorway, then prancing around outside for Peter the photographer.
- ••• 0:23—Brief breasts, while lying on car, then more breasts while standing next to it and posing.
- ••• 0:27—Full frontal nudity, while posing for photographer outside. Buns while making love with him.
- •• 0:33—Nude, undressing and taking a shower.
- ••• 0:47—Nude, while standing, then lying on table during ceremony.
- •• 0:52—Breasts, while getting out of bed with Sybil.
- •• 1:20—Breasts, during ceremony.
- • 1:23—Breasts, while getting dressed.

Vicki Michelle . . . . . . . . . . . . . . . . . . . . . . . . . . Betty
- • 0:00—Brief breasts, while sitting up during opening credits.
- •• 0:31—Breasts, while sitting in bathtub. Nude, getting out. Seen through fish-eye lens.
- •• 1:17—Buns, during witches' ceremony. Left breast, then breasts while lying on table.
- • 1:23—Brief left breast, while on the ground with Johnny.
- • 1:25—Left breast, when Johnny gets up off her.

## Visionquest (1985)
Madonna . . . . . . . . . . . . . . . . . . . . Nightclub Singer
Linda Fiorentino . . . . . . . . . . . . . . . . . . . . . . . Carla
Matthew Modine . . . . . . . . . . . . . . . . . . . Louden Swain
- • 1:29—Very brief buns while taking off underwear to get weighed for wrestling match.

J. C. Quinn . . . . . . . . . . . . . . . . . . . . . . . . . . . . Elmo
Daphne Zuniga . . . . . . . . . . . . . . . . . . . . Margie Epstein

## Vital Signs (1989)
Diane Lane . . . . . . . . . . . . . . . . . . . . . . . Gina Wyler
- ••• 1:11—In white bra, then breasts making love with Michael in the basement.

Adrian Pasdar . . . . . . . . . . . . . . . . . . . Michael Chatham
1:11—Upper half of buns, with his pants partially down in basement with Diane Lane.

Jimmy Smits . . . . . . . . . . . . . . . . . . . Dr. David Redding
Gigi Vorgan . . . . . . . . . . . . . . . . . . . . . . . . . . . . Nell

## W. B., Blue and the Bean (1988)
a.k.a. Bail Out
Linda Blair . . . . . . . . . . . . . . . . . . . . . . . . . . . . Nettie
David Hasselhoff . . . . . . . . . . . . . . . . . . . White Bread
Debra Lamb . . . . . . . . . . . . . . . . . . . . . . . Motel Clerk
- • 0:42—Full frontal nudity opening door in motel to talk to David Hasselhoff.

## Wall Street (1987)
Michael Douglas . . . . . . . . . . . . . . . . . . Gordon Gekko
Daryl Hannah . . . . . . . . . . . . . . . . . . . . . Darian Taylor
Hal Holbrook . . . . . . . . . . . . . . . . . . . . Lou Mannheim
Annie McEnroe . . . . . . . . . . . . . . . . . Muffie Livingston
Sylvia Miles . . . . . . . . . . . . . . . . . . . . . . . . . Realtor

Suzen Murakoshi . . . . . . . . . . . . . . . . . . . Girl in Bed
- • 0:13—Brief full frontal nudity getting out of bed and walking past the camera in Charlie Sheen's bedroom (slightly out of focus).

Martin Sheen . . . . . . . . . . . . . . . . . . . . . . Carl Fox
Monique Van Vooren . . . . . . . . . . . . . . . . . . . . . . n.a.
Sean Young . . . . . . . . . . . . . . . . . . . . . Kate Gekko

## The War of the Roses (1989)
Sean Astin . . . . . . . . . . . . . . . . . . . . . . Josh, Age 17
Michael Douglas . . . . . . . . . . . . . . . . . . . . Oliver Rose
1:36—Almost buns, while cleaning himself in the bidet.

Susan Isaacs . . . . . . . . . . . . . . . . . Auctioneer's Assistant
Marianne Sägebrecht . . . . . . . . . . . . . . . . . . . . . Susan
Kathleen Turner . . . . . . . . . . . . . . . . . . . . Barbara Rose
0:04—In braless, wet white blouse.
0:06—In braless, wet white blouse walking around on the sidewalk with Michael Douglas.
- • 0:08—Very brief left breast, while lying in bed with Douglas and she moves the sheets.
- • 0:33—Very, very brief lower frontal nudity, after squeezing Douglas' waist with her legs in bed.

## Warlock: The Armageddon (1993)
Dawn Ann Billings . . . . . . . . . . . . . . . . . . Amanda Sloan
- • 0:10—Very brief side of left breast, walking through hallway while taking off robe. Brief breasts, while walking past doorway.

George "Buck" Flower . . . . . . . . . . . . . . Man in Crowd
Zach Galligan . . . . . . . . . . . . . . . . . . . . . . . . Douglas
Wendy Hamilton . . . . . . . . . . . . . . . . . . . . . . . Model
Paula Marshall . . . . . . . . . . . . . . . . . . . Samantha Ellison
Michelle Moffett . . . . . . . . . . . . . . . . . . . . . . . Celine
Elizabeth Nottoli . . . . . . . . . . . . . . . . . . . . . . . Model
- • 0:29—Very brief breasts under sheer black blouse, while backstage during fashion show. (She's blowing a bubble with bubble gum.)

Joanna Pacula . . . . . . . . . . . . . . . . . . . . . Paula Darc
Julian Sands . . . . . . . . . . . . . . . . . . . . . . . . Warlock
Rebecca Street . . . . . . . . . . . . . . . . . . . . . . . . . Kate

## Warlords (1988)
Michelle Bauer . . . . . . . . . . . . . . . . . . . . . Harem Girl
- ••• 0:14—Breasts, getting her top ripped off, then shot by a bad guy.

David Carradine . . . . . . . . . . . . . . . . . . . . . . . . Dow
Greta Gibson . . . . . . . . . . . . . . . . . . . . . Harem Girl
- •• 1:05—Breasts in tent with the other harem girls. Holding a snake.
- • 1:09—Breasts again.

Debra Lamb . . . . . . . . . . . . . . . . . . . . . . Harem Girl
- ••• 0:14—Breasts, getting her blouse ripped off by a bad guy, then kidnapped.
- ••• 0:17—Breasts in harem pants while shackled to another girl.

Victoria Sellers . . . . . . . . . . . . . . . . . . . . . Desert Girl
0:02—In back of car in sheer white harem girl top.
- • 0:06—Getting out of car and running into the desert while wearing the sheer white top.

Brinke Stevens . . . . . . . . . . . . . . . . . . . . . . Dow's Wife
Dawn Wildsmith . . . . . . . . . . . . . . . . . . . . . . . Danny

## Warlords 3000 (1992)

April Dawn Dollarhide . . . . . . . . . . . . . Terrified Girl
- • 0:11—Breasts, while struggling in room with bad guys who are trying to rape her.

Denice Duff . . . . . . . . . . . . . . . . . . . . . . . . . . Anani
- ••• 0:50—Breasts, after taking off blouse in front of Nova, then making love and sleeping after.

Ty Randolph . . . . . . . . . . . . . . . . . . . . . Bull Woman
Nicole Vasilopoulos . . . . . . . . . . . . . . . . . . . . Ox's Wife
- •• 0:23—Breasts, in open blouse in bedroom with Ox.

## Warm Summer Rain (1989)

Kelly Lynch . . . . . . . . . . . . . . . . . . . . . . . . . . . Kate
- • 0:03—Brief breasts and side view of buns in B&W lying on floor during suicide attempt. Quick cuts breasts getting shocked to start her heart.
- •• 0:23—Full frontal nudity when Guy gets off her in bed.
- •• 0:24—Side view of right breast in bed, then breasts.
- ••• 0:58—Buns then breasts, getting washed by Guy on the table.
- ••• 1:07—Brief buns making love. Quick cuts full frontal nudity spinning around. Side view of left breast with Guy.
- ••• 1:09—Nude picking up belongings and running out of burning house with Guy.

Barry Tubb . . . . . . . . . . . . . . . . . . . . . . . . . . Guy
- •• 0:23—Lower frontal nudity getting off Kelly Lynch in bed.
- 0:25—Side view of buns while dreaming in bed.
- •• 0:58—Frontal nudity kneeling on floor and behind the table while washing Lynch.
- • 1:00—Buns while getting washed by Lynch.
- • 1:07—Brief buns while making love with Lynch. Quick cuts.
- ••• 1:09—Nude picking up belongings and running out of burning house with Lynch.

## The Warrior and the Sorceress (1984)

David Carradine . . . . . . . . . . . . . . . . . . . . . . . Kain
Maria Socas . . . . . . . . . . . . . . . . . . . . . . . . . . Naja
- ••• 0:15—Breasts wearing robe and bikini bottoms in room with Zeg. Sort of brief buns, leaving the room.
- •• 0:22—Breasts standing by a wagon at night.
- •• 0:27—Breasts in room with David Carradine. Dark. Most of buns when leaving the room.
- •• 0:31—Breasts and buns climbing down wall.
- • 0:34—Brief breasts, then left breast with rope around her neck at the well.
- • 0:44—Breasts when Carradine rescues her.
- • 0:47—Breasts walking around outside.
- • 0:57—More breasts outside.
- • 1:00—Breasts watching a guy pound a sword.
- • 1:05—Breasts under a tent after Carradine uses the sword. Long shot.
- • 1:09—Breasts during big fight scene.
- • 1:14—Breasts next to well. Long shot.

## Warrior Queen (1987)

Tally Chanel . . . . . . . . . . . . . . . . . . . . . . . . . Vespa
- ••• 0:09—Breasts hanging on a rope, being auctioned.
- ••• 0:20—Breasts and buns with Chloe.
- •• 0:37—Nude, before attempted rape by Goliath.
- •• 0:58—Breasts during rape by Goliath.

Sybil Danning . . . . . . . . . . . . . . . . . . . . . . Berenice
Samantha Fox . . . . . . . . . . . . . . . . . Philomena/Augusta
- ••• 0:31—Nude, doing a dance with a snake during orgy scene.
- • 1:03—Brief right breast after unsuccessfully trying to seduce Marcus.

Josephine Jaqueline Jones . . . . . . . . . . . . . . . . . . . Chloe
- ••• 0:20—Breasts making love with Vespa.

## Watch It (1993)

Suzy Amis . . . . . . . . . . . . . . . . . . . . . . . . . . . Anne
Jordana Capra . . . . . . . . . . . . . . . . . . . . . . . Call Girl
- • 1:26—Brief partial buns, while making love with Michael in coat room during concert.

Peter Gallagher . . . . . . . . . . . . . . . . . . . . . . . . John
Cynthia Stevenson . . . . . . . . . . . . . . . . . . . . . . Ellen
Lili Taylor . . . . . . . . . . . . . . . . . . . . . . . . . . Brenda

## Watchers II (1990)

Irene Miracle . . . . . . . . . . . . . . . . . . . . Sarah Ferguson
    0:28—In pink leotard, going into aerobics studio.
- ••• 0:40—Side view in black bra, then breasts a few times in the bathtub.

Tracy Scoggins . . . . . . . . . . . . . . . . . . . . Barbara White
Marc Singer . . . . . . . . . . . . . . . . . . . . . Paul Ferguson
Mary Woronov . . . . . . . . . . . . . . . . . . . . Dr. Glatman

## The Waterdance (1991)

Helen Hunt . . . . . . . . . . . . . . . . . . . . . . . . . . Anna
- ••• 0:51—Breasts in bed, making love with Eric Stoltz.
- •• 0:52—Brief buns and brief right breast, coming back to the bed to clean up.

Elizabeth Peña . . . . . . . . . . . . . . . . . . . . . . . . Rosa
Eric Stoltz . . . . . . . . . . . . . . . . . . . . . . . . Joel Garcia
Barbara Alyn Woods . . . . . . . . . . . . . . . . Annabelle Lee
- • 1:24—Buns, in G-string, while on stage in a strip club.

## Waterland (1992; British/U.S.)

Cara Buono . . . . . . . . . . . . . . . . . . . . . . . Jody Dobson
- • 0:38—Brief breasts, while sitting in chair in classroom during Jeremy Irons' daydream.

Callum Dixon . . . . . . . . . . . . . . . . . . . . . . Freddie Parr
- • 0:05—Brief buns, pulling down his pants with his friends to show Mary (He's the second from the right).

Lena Headey . . . . . . . . . . . . . . . . . . . . . . Young Mary
- • 0:16—In braless white undershirt, then brief breasts while making love with Tom in train.
- ••• 0:20—Breasts, while talking with Tom.

John Heard . . . . . . . . . . . . . . . . . . . . . . . . Lewis Scott
Jeremy Irons . . . . . . . . . . . . . . . . . . . . . . . Tom Crick
David Morrissey . . . . . . . . . . . . . . . . . . . . . Dick Crick
- •• 1:04—Buns, after taking off his clothes on boat and diving into the water to commit suicide.

Siri Neal . . . . . . . . . . . . . . . . . . . . . . . Helen Atkinson
- 0:40—Brief side view of breast in mirror while rubbing her legs. Long shot at far left of TV screen.

Grant Warnock . . . . . . . . . . . . . . . . . . . . . . Young Tom
- 0:05—Brief buns, pulling down his pants with his friends to show Mary (He's on the far right).

## *Watermelon Man* (1970)
Godfrey Cambridge . . . . . . . . . . . . . . . . . . Jeff Gerber
- 0:01—Brief buns, twice, while lying in tanning bed during exercise session. He's made up to look like a white guy. Don't see his face very well.
- 0:20—Brief buns, after pulling down his pajamas after "turning" into a black guy. Don't see his face.

## *We're No Angels* (1989)
Robert De Niro . . . . . . . . . . . . . . . . . . . . . . . . . Ned
Bruno Kirby. . . . . . . . . . . . . . . . . . . . . . . . . Deputy
Demi Moore . . . . . . . . . . . . . . . . . . . . . . . . . Molly
- 0:18—One long shot, then two brief side views of left breast when Robert De Niro watches from outside. Reflections in the window make it hard to see.

Sean Penn. . . . . . . . . . . . . . . . . . . . . . . . . . . . Jim
James Russo . . . . . . . . . . . . . . . . . . . . . . . . .Bobby

## *A Wedding* (1978)
Geraldine Chaplin. . . . . . . . . . . . . . . .Rita Billingsley
Mia Farrow . . . . . . . . . . . . . . . . . . . . . Buffy Brenner
- •• 1:10—Breasts posing in front of a painting, while wearing a wedding veil.

Lauren Hutton. . . . . . . . . . . . . . . . . . . Florence Farmer

## *Weeds* (1987)
Kirsten Baker. . . . . . . . . . . . . . . . . . . . . . . . . Kirsten
Nick Nolte. . . . . . . . . . . . . . . . . . . . . .Lee Umstetter
- •• 0:51—Buns, while getting out of bed and putting his pants on.

## *Weekend Pass* (1984)
Sara Costa. . . . . . . . . . . . . . . . . . Tuesday Del Mundo
- ••• 0:07—Buns in G-string, then breasts during strip dance routine on stage.

Graem McGavin . . . . . . . . . . . . . . . . . Tawny Ryatt
Valerie McIntosh . . . . . . . . . . . . . . . . . . . . . . . .Etta
Hilary Shepard . . . . . . . . . . . . . . . . . . Cindy Hazard
- •• 1:05—In red bra, then breasts taking off bra.
- • 1:07—Buns and breasts getting into bathtub.

Annette Sinclair. . . . . . . . . . . . . . . . . . . . . . .Maxine
Cheryl Song . . . . . . . . . . . . . . . . . . . . . . . .Chop Suzi
- • 0:26—Breasts while giving a guy a massage.

Ashley St. Jon . . . . . . . . . . . . . . . . . . . . Xylene B-12
- •• 0:13—Breasts dancing on stage.

## *Weekend Warriors* (1986)
Monique Gabrielle . . . . . . . . . . . . . . Showgirl on plane
- •• 0:51—Brief breasts taking off top with other showgirls.

Daniel Greene. . . . . . . . . . . . . . . . . . .Phil McCracken
Brenda Strong. . . . . . . . . . . . . . . . . .Danny El Dubois
- • 0:44—Breasts, lit from the side, standing in the dark.

Tom Villard . . . . . . . . . . . . . . . . . . . . . . Mort Seblinsky

## *Weird Science* (1985)
Judie Aronson. . . . . . . . . . . . . . . . . . . . . . . . . . .Hilly
Kelly Le Brock. . . . . . . . . . . . . . . . . . . . . . . . . . . Lisa
- 0:12—In blue underwear and white top baring her midriff for the two boys when she is first created.
- 1:29—In blue leotard and grey tube top gym clothes to teach boy's gym class.

Kym Malin . . . . . . . . . . . . . . . . . Girl Playing Piano
- • 0:55—Brief breasts several times as her clothes get torn off by the strong wind and she gets sucked up and out of the chimney.

Bill Paxton . . . . . . . . . . . . . . . . . . . . . . . . . . . Chet
- •• 0:30—Buns, while taking off towel to give to his younger brother in the kitchen.

Renée Props. . . . . . . . . . . . . . . . . One of The Weenies
Robert Rusler . . . . . . . . . . . . . . . . . . . . . . . . . . .Max
Suzanne Snyder . . . . . . . . . . . . . . . . . . . . . . . . .Deb
Wally Ward . . . . . . . . . . . . . . . . . . . . . . . .A Weenie
Jill Whitlow. . . . . . . . . . . . . . . . . . . Perfume Salesgirl

## *Welcome Home Roxy Carmichael* (1990)
Jeff Daniels. . . . . . . . . . . . . . . . . . . . . . Denton Webb
Ava Fabian . . . . . . . . . . . . . . . . . Roxy Carmichael
- • 0:10—Buns in water in swimming pool, then more while getting out.

Frances Fisher. . . . . . . . . . . . . . . . . Rochelle Bossetti

## *Welcome to 18* (1986)
Mariska Hargitay . . . . . . . . . . . . . . . . . . . . . . .Joey
- • 0:26—Buns, taking a shower when video camera is taping her.
- 0:43—Watching herself on the videotape playback.

## *Welcome to Arrow Beach* (1973)
*a.k.a. Tender Flesh*
Meg Foster. . . . . . . . . . . . . . . . . . . . . . Robbin Stanley
- 0:12—Buns and brief side view of right breast getting undressed to skinny dip in the ocean. Don't see her face.
- •• 0:40—Breasts getting out of bed.

Joanna Pettet . . . . . . . . . . . . . . . . . . . . . Grace Henry

## *Welcome to L.A.* (1977)
Keith Carradine . . . . . . . . . . . . . . . . . Carroll Barber
Geraldine Chaplin . . . . . . . . . . . . . . . . . .Karen Hood
- •• 1:28—Full frontal nudity standing in Keith Carradine's living room.

Lauren Hutton . . . . . . . . . . . . . . . . . . . Nora Bruce
- • 0:56—Very brief, obscured glimpse of left breast under red light in photo darkroom.

Harvey Keitel . . . . . . . . . . . . . . . . . . . . . . . Ken Hood
Sally Kellerman . . . . . . . . . . . . . . . . . . Ann Goode
Sissy Spacek. . . . . . . . . . . . . . . . . . . .Linda Murray
- •• 0:51—Brief breasts after bringing presents into Keith Carradine's bedroom.

## *Wet and Wild Summer!* (1992; Australian)
Christopher Atkins . . . . . . . . . . . . . . . . .Bobby McCain
- ••• 0:22—Buns, taking off swimsuit at the beach.

Julian McMahon. . . . . . . . . . . . . . . . . . Mick Dooley
- •• 0:21—Buns, taking off his swimtrunks at the beach.

Vanessa Steele. . . . . . . . . . . . . . . . . . . . . . . .Charlene
•• 1:25—Breasts, opening her leather jacket to distract the other lifeguard boat.

### Wetherby (1985; British)
Suzanna Hamilton. . . . . . . . . . . . . . . . . . . Karen Creasy
   0:42—In white lingerie top and bottom.
   1:03—In white lingerie getting into bed and lying down.
   1:06—In white lingerie, fighting with John.
Richard Harris . . . . . . . . . . . . . . . . . . . . . . Sir Thomas
Vanessa Redgrave . . . . . . . . . . . . . . . . . Jean Travers
Joely Richardson . . . . . . . . . . . . . . . .Young Jean Travers
•• 1:10—Breasts in room with Jim when he takes off her coat.

### What the Peeper Saw (1971; British)
a.k.a. Night Hair Child
Britt Ekland . . . . . . . . . . . . . . . . . . . . . . . . . . . Elise
• 0:38—Sort of side view of left breast in bed. Don't really see anything.

### Wheels of Fire (1984)
a.k.a. Desert Warrior
Laura Banks. . . . . . . . . . . . . . . . . . . . . . . . . . Stinger
• 0:49—Brief breasts when Trace rips her top open outside.
Steve Parvin . . . . . . . . . . . . . . . . . . . . . . . . . . . Bo
• 0:07—Buns, mooning out the window of the car.
• 0:20—Buns, trying to get away from the bad guys "initiation."
Lynda Wiesmeier. . . . . . . . . . . . . . . . . . . . . . . . Arlie
••• 0:18—Breasts on the ground, being held down by two bad guys, then getting tied to hood of car.
•• 0:20—More breasts, long shot, tied to hood of car.
• 0:22—More breasts while tied to the hood of the car.
•• 0:23—Breasts, being brought into tent.
••• 0:34—Breasts, chained up in tent and trying to escape. Long scene.
•• 0:45—Left breast, while lying on cot.
•• 0:47—Breasts outside, fighting off crowd of guys.

### When a Stranger Calls (1979)
Rutanya Alda. . . . . . . . . . . . . . . . . . . . . .Mrs. Mandrakis
Tony Beckley. . . . . . . . . . . . . . . . . . . . . . . .Curt Duncan
• 1:07—Side view of buns, while kneeling in restroom.
Carol Kane . . . . . . . . . . . . . . . . . . . . . . . . . Jill Johnson

### When the Party's Over (1991)
Elizabeth Berridge . . . . . . . . . . . . . . . . . . . . . Frankie
   0:04—In white bra, while talking to Taylor.
Rae Dawn Chong . . . . . . . . . . . . . . . . . . . . . . . . MJ
• 0:03—Brief buns, while getting out of bed.
   0:27—In bra, while getting caught with Taylor by Will.
   0:45—In black bra, while getting dressed.
   1:23—Brief partial left breast, while taking off her dress and walking into closet.

Brian McNamara . . . . . . . . . . . . . . . . . . . . . . . Taylor
• 0:27—Brief buns, while pulling up his pants, after getting caught with Rae Dawn Chong by Will.
Stephen Meadows . . . . . . . . . . . . . . . . . . . . . . . n.a.
Fisher Stevens . . . . . . . . . . . . . . . .Alexander Midnight

### When Women Had Tails (1970; Italian)
Senta Berger . . . . . . . . . . . . . . . . . . . . . . . . . . . Felli
• 0:22—Buns, while lying in pit.
• 1:08—Buns, while getting carried around.
• 1:30—Buns, after her boyfriend gets caught in tree.
Frank Wolff. . . . . . . . . . . . . . . . . . . . . . . . . . . . n.a.

### When Women Lost Their Tails (1971; Italian)
Senta Berger . . . . . . . . . . . . . . . . . . . . . . . . . . . Felli
• 0:13—Very long shot of buns, while walking into pond.
Frank Wolff. . . . . . . . . . . . . . . . . . . . . . . . . . . . n.a.

### Where the Heart Is (1990)
Suzy Amis . . . . . . . . . . . . . . . . . . . . . . . Chloe McBain
• 0:08—Breasts during her art film. Artfully covered with paint, with a bird. Breasts again in the third segment.
• 0:09—Breasts during the film again. Hard to see because of the paint. Last segment while she narrates.
Joanna Cassidy. . . . . . . . . . . . . . . . . . . . . Jean McBain
Dabney Coleman . . . . . . . . . . . . . . . . . Stewart McBain
David Hewlett . . . . . . . . . . . . . . . . . . . . . . . . Jimmy
• 0:56—Buns, while walking around the hall in an angel costume.
Sheila Kelley. . . . . . . . . . . . . . . . . . . . . . . . . . Sheryl
Uma Thurman . . . . . . . . . . . . . . . . . . . .Daphne McBain
• 0:08—Breasts during art film, but her entire body is artfully painted to match the background paintings. The second segment.
   0:40—More breasts with body painted posing for her sister. Long shot.
   1:16—In slide of painting taken at 0:40.
   1:43—Same painting from 0:40 during the end credits.

### Where's Poppa? (1970)
Tom Atkins. . . . . . . . . . . . . . . Policeman in Apartment
Ron Liebman . . . . . . . . . . . . . . . . . . . . Sidney Hocheiser
• 0:45—Buns while running across the street, then in front of door in hall, then brief buns leaving George Segal's apartment.

### Whispers (1989)
Chris Sarandon. . . . . . . . . . . . . . . . . . . . Detective Tony
Linda Singer. . . . . . . . . . . . . . . . . . . . . . . . .Prostitute
Victoria Tennant. . . . . . . . . . . . . . . . . . . Hilary Thomas
• 0:43—Buns and side of right breast getting into bathtub. Long shot, looks like a body double (the ponytail in her hair changes position).
• 0:44—Buns and brief breasts running down the stairs. Looks like the same body double.

### Whispers in the Dark (1992)
Jill Clayburgh . . . . . . . . . . . . . . . . . . . . . .Sarah Green
Anthony LaPaglia . . . . . . . . . . . . . . . . . . . Morgenstern

John Leguizamo . . . . . . . . . . . . . . . . . . . . . . . Johnny C.
Annabella Sciorra . . . . . . . . . . . . . . . . . . . . . .Ann Hecker
  • 1:25—Buns in mirror in front of closet (don't see her face). Partial left breast.
Deborah Unger . . . . . . . . . . . . . . . . . . . . Eve Abergray
  • 0:14—Breasts during dream visualizations. Don't see her face.
    0:22—In black bra and panties, undressing in office in front of Annabella Sciorra.
  • 0:24—Brief breasts during visualization by Sciorra. Don't see her face.
  • 0:37—Brief breasts during Sciorra's dream.
  • 0:38—Buns and side view of left breast, dead, while hanging by her neck.

## *White Dog* (1982)
Kristy McNichol. . . . . . . . . . . . . . . . . . . . . Julie Sawyer
  • 1:25—Most of the inside of breasts in gaping tank top when bending over to help lift dog off Burl Ives.
Lynne Moody . . . . . . . . . . . . . . . . . . . . . . . . . . Molly
Jameson Parker . . . . . . . . . . . . . . . . . . . . . Roland Gray

## *White Fire* (1985)
Belinda Mayne . . . . . . . . . . . . . . . . . . . . . . . . .Ingrid
  •• 0:33—Nude, while swimming in pool.
  ••• 0:34—Nude, swimming in pool, then getting out and taking a shower.
  •• 0:35—Nude, after Robert Ginty steals her towel.
  •• 0:37—Nude, standing up in pool and getting out and going up stairs.
  •• 1:16—Breasts, while taking off her dress while on boat with Ginty.
Fred Williamson . . . . . . . . . . . . . . . . . . . . . . . . Noah

## *White Hot* (1988)
Robby Benson. . . . . . . . . . . . . . . . . . . . . . . . . .Scott
Sally Kirkland. . . . . . . . . . . . . . . . . . . . . . . . Harriet
Tawny Kitaen . . . . . . . . . . . . . . . . . . . . . . . . Vanessa
    1:04—Brief half of lower frontal nudity, while lying in bed.
Anna Levine Thomson. . . . . . . . . . . . . . . . . . Heather
  ••• 0:04—In bra, then breasts undressing for drug dealer in exchange for cocaine.

## *White Light* (1990)
Martin Kove . . . . . . . . . . . . . . . . . . . . . . . Sean Craig
    1:23—Upper half of buns, while on the floor with Rachel.
  • 1:24—Very brief buns, while getting out of bed.
James Purcell. . . . . . . . . . . . . . . . . . . . . . .Bill Dockerty
Raoul Trujillo. . . . . . . . . . . . . . . . . . . . . . . . . Hatchet
Heidi Von Palleske . . . . . . . . . . . . . Debra Halifax

## *White Men Can't Jump* (1992)
Woody Harrelson . . . . . . . . . . . . . . . . . . . .Billy Hoyle
  • 0:21—Very, very brief half of buns, while getting into shower.
  • 0:37—Very, very brief half of buns, while getting out of bed.

Rosie Perez. . . . . . . . . . . . . . . . . . . . . . Gloria Clemente
  •• 0:36—Breasts in shower and making love in bed with Woody Harrelson.
  • 0:39—Brief right breast, while sitting up in bed.
  • 0:40—Very brief side of right breast, three times, while getting out of bed quickly.

## *White Mischief* (1988)
Geraldine Chaplin . . . . . . . . . . . . . . . . . . . . . . . Nina
John Hurt. . . . . . . . . . . . . . . . . . . . . . . . . . . . Colville
Sarah Miles . . . . . . . . . . . . . . . . . . . . . . . . . . . Alice
Jacqueline Pearce . . . . . . . . . . . . . . . . . . . . . . . Idina
  •• 0:07—Buns, then breasts several times while standing up in the bathtub and talking with her male and female friends.
Greta Scacchi. . . . . . . . . . . . . . . . . . .Diana Broughton
  •• 0:16—Breasts taking a bath while an old man watches through a peephole in the wall.
  •• 0:24—Brief breasts in bedroom with her husband.
  •• 0:29—Brief breasts taking off bathing suit top in the ocean in front of Charles Dance.
  •• 0:30—Breasts while lying in bed, then talking to Dance.
  •• 0:49—Breasts while sitting in bed and talking to Dance.

## *White Palace* (1990)
Jason Alexander . . . . . . . . . . . . . . . . . . . . . Neil Horowitz
Kathy Bates . . . . . . . . . . . . . . . . . . . . .Rosemary Powers
Eileen Brennan . . . . . . . . . . . . . . . . . . . . . . . . . . . .Judy
Barbara Howard. . . . . . . . . . . . . . . . . . . . Sherri Klugman
Rachel Levin. . . . . . . . . . . . . . . . . . . . . . . . . . Rachel
Susan Sarandon . . . . . . . . . . . . . . . . . . . . . Nora Baker
  ••• 0:28—Breasts on top of James Spader. Great shots of right breast.
  • 0:38—Breasts on bed with Spader.
James Spader . . . . . . . . . . . . . . . . . . . . . . . .Max Baron
  •• 0:38—Buns, while taking off clothes and getting into bed with Susan Sarandon. Don't see his face.

## *White Sands* (1992)
Willem Dafoe . . . . . . . . . . . . . . . . . . . . . . . Ray Dolezal
Samuel L. Jackson. . . . . . . . . . . . . . . . . . . Greg Meeker
John Lafayette . . . . . . . . . . . . . . . . . . . . . . . Demott
Mary Elizabeth Mastrantonio . . . . . . . . . . .Lane Bodine
  • 1:11—Brief left breast in shower with Willem Dafoe. You see her face, so this shot is really her.
Mimi Rogers. . . . . . . . . . . . . . .Uncredited Molly Dolezal
Mickey Rourke . . . . . . . . . . . . . . . . . . . .German Lennox
Tera Tabrizi
    . . . . . . .Body Double for Mary Elizabeth Mastrontonio
  • 1:10—Left breast and upper half of buns in the shower undressing in the shower with Willem Dafoe. Don't see face, so it's probably Tera.
M. Emmet Walsh . . . . . . . . . . . . . . . . . . . . Bert Gibson

## *Who's That Knocking at My Door?* (1968)
Harvey Keitel . . . . . . . . . . . . . . . . . . . . . . . . . . . . . .J.R.
  • 0:42—Buns, several times, while in bed and standing up. Quick cuts.

### Whore *(1991)*
*a.k.a. If you're afraid to say it... Just see it*
Ginger Lynn Allen . . . . . . . . . . . . . . . . . . . .Wounded Girl
Stephanie Blake. . . . . . . . . . . . . . . . . . . . Stripper in Big T's
- 0:35—Buns, in G-string on stage.
- ••• 0:36—Breasts, dancing on stage in a club.
Dori Courtney . . . . . . . . . . . . . . . .Topless woman on TV
- 0:14—Brief breasts on TV in old folks home in a scene from *Mob Boss.*
John Diehl . . . . . . . . . . . . . . . . . . . . . . . . . . . . .Derelict
Theresa Russell . . . . . . . . . . . . . . . . . . . . . . . . . . . . Liz
- •• 0:13—Breasts and buns in G-string outfit, taking off her coat.
- ••• 0:25—In black bra, doing sit-ups. Breasts making love in spa with Blake.
- 1:18—Brief buns, in open skirt in back of car with a customer.
Tom Villard . . . . . . . . . . . . . . . . . . . . . . . . . . . . Hippy

### Whose Life Is It, Anyway? *(1981)*
Janet Eilber . . . . . . . . . . . . . . . . . . . . . . . . . . . . .Patty
- •• 0:30—Nude, ballet dancing during B&W dream sequence.
- 1:13—Very brief side of left breast when her back is turned while changing clothes.
Kaki Hunter . . . . . . . . . . . . . . . . . . . . . . . . . . . .Mary Jo
Lissa Layng . . . . . . . . . . . . . . . . . . . . . . . . . 1st Nurse

### The Wicked Lady *(1983; British)*
Glynnis Barber. . . . . . . . . . . . . . . . . . . . . . . . Caroline
- ••• 0:58—Breasts and buns making love with Kitt in the living room. Possible body double.
Alan Bates . . . . . . . . . . . . . . . . . . . . . . . . . Jerry Jackson
Faye Dunaway. . . . . . . . . . . . . . . . . . . Barbara Skelton
Marina Sirtis . . . . . . . . . . . . . . . . . . . . . . . Jackson's Girl
- ••• 1:06—Full frontal nudity in and getting out of bed when Faye Dunaway discovers her in bed with Alan Bates.
- ••• 1:20—Breasts getting whipped by Dunaway during their fight during Bates' hanging.
Oliver Tobias . . . . . . . . . . . . . . . . . . . . . . Kit Locksby
- 0:58—Buns, with Caroline in living room.

### Wicked Stepmother *(1989)*
Colleen Camp . . . . . . . . . . . . . . . . . . . . . . . . . . Jenny
Barbara Carrera . . . . . . . . . . . . . . . . . . . . . . . . Priscilla
- 1:14—Very, very brief upper half of right breast peeking out of the top of her dress when she flips her head back while seducing Steve.
Laurene Landon . . . . . . . . . . . . . . . . . . . . . . . Vanilla

### The Wicker Man *(1973; British)*
Britt Ekland . . . . . . . . . . . . . . . . . . . . . . . . . . . Willow
- ••• 0:58—Breasts in bed knocking on the wall, then more breasts and buns getting up and walking around the bedroom. Long scene. Body double used when you don't see her face when pounding on the wall. (Britt's hair is shorter than the body double's.)

Lorraine Peters . . . . . . . . . . . . . . . . . . . . . .Girl on Grave
- 0:22—Side view of right breast sitting on grave, crying. Dark, long shot, hard to see.
Ingrid Pitt . . . . . . . . . . . . . . . . . . . . . . . . . . . . Librarian
- •• 1:11—Brief breasts in bathtub seen by Edward Woodward.

### Wide Sargasso Sea *(1993)*
(Unrated version reviewed.)
Martine Beswicke . . . . . . . . . . . . . . . . . . . . . Aunt Cora
Rowena King . . . . . . . . . . . . . . . . . . . . . . . . . . .Amelie
- 0:54—Briefly nude in open window, while showing off for Rochester.
- ••• 1:16—Breasts, while making love standing up outside with Rochester.
- ••• 1:17—Full frontal nudity in bed, then getting out and getting dressed.
Karina Lombard . . . . . . . . . . . . . . . . . . . . . .Antoinette
- ••• 0:31—Buns and breasts, with her new husband, Rochester.
- •• 0:37—Breasts and partial frontal nudity while making love in bedroom with Rochester.
- •• 0:42—Buns and partial breasts, in wet white clothes. Left breast and buns while in bed with Rochester.
- ••• 0:52—Breasts while in bed before making love and after.
- 0:55—Right breast, while sitting in bed.
- 1:13—Breasts, while sitting in bed.
Nathaniel Parker. . . . . . . . . . . . . . . . . . . . . . .Rochester
- ••• 0:44—Buns while standing at the window, then frontal nudity while walking back to bed.
- 0:52—Buns, while making love making love in bed with Antoinette.
- •• 1:16—Buns, while making love standing up outside with Amelie.
Rachel Ward. . . . . . . . . . . . . . . . . . . . . Annette Cosway
Michael York . . . . . . . . . . . . . . . . . . . . . . . Paul Mason

### Wifemistress *(1977; Italian)*
Laura Antonelli. . . . . . . . . . . . . . . Antonia De Angelis
- 0:50—In lacy nightgown in her bedroom.
- 1:22—Brief upper half of left breast in bed with Clara and her husband.
- 1:25—In sheer lacy nightgown leaning out the window.
- 1:29—Almost right breast making love with a guy in bed.
Olga Karlatos . . . . . . . . . . . . . Miss Paula Pagano, M.D.
- •• 0:42—Breasts undressing in room with Laura Antonelli. Right breast and part of left breast lying in bed with Marcello Mastroianni.
- 0:46—Brief breasts in bed with Mastroianni and Clara.

### Wild at Heart *(1990)*
Lisa Ann Cabasa . . . . . . . . . . . . . . . . . Reindeer Dancer
- •• 0:30—Breasts standing while Mr. Reindeer talks on the phone. More breasts dancing in front of him.
Nicolas Cage . . . . . . . . . . . . . . . . . . . . . . . . . . . Sailor
Willem Dafoe . . . . . . . . . . . . . . . . . . . . . . . Bobby Peru

Laura Dern . . . . . . . . . . . . . . . . . . . . . . . . . . . Lula
- ••• 0:07—Breasts putting on black halter top.
- •• 0:26—Left breast, then breasts sitting on Nicolas Cage's lap in bed.
- •• 0:35—Breasts wriggling around in bed with Cage.
- • 0:41—Brief breasts several times making love with Cage. Hard to see because it keeps going overexposed. Great moaning, though.

Sherilyn Fenn . . . . . . . . . . . . . . . . . . . . .Girl in Accident
Sheryl Lee . . . . . . . . . . . . . . . . . . . . . . . . Good Witch
Isabella Rossellini. . . . . . . . . . . . . . . . . . . . . . Perdita
Mia M. Ruiz. . . . . . . . .Mr. Reindeer's Resident Valet #1
- •• 0:32—Breasts standing next to Mr. Reindeer on the right, holding a tray. Long scene.

Charlie Spradling. . . . . . . . . . . . . . . . . . . . . . . . Irma
- •• 0:40—Brief breasts in bed during flashback.

Harry Dean Stanton. . . . . . . . . . . . . . .Johnnie Farragut

## *Wild Cactus* (1992)
(Unrated version reviewed.)

India Allen. . . . . . . . . . . . . . . . . . . . . . . . . . . Alex
  0:02—In white body suit, in bedroom with David Naughton.
- ••• 0:21—Buns and breasts, making love in bed on top of Naughton.
- ••• 0:34—Breasts, while pouring maple syrup on herself and making love with Naughton in the kitchen. Yummy!
  1:07—In beige bra and panties, trying to escape.
- ••• 1:10—Nude, getting into and out of the shower.
- ••• 1:13—Nude, getting lotion rubbed on her by Maggie.
- •• 1:18—Breasts, while making love in bed with Randall.
- •• 1:20—Lower frontal nudity when Randall gets out of bed.
  1:21—In beige bra and panties.

Carrie Chambers . . . . . . . . . . . . . . . . . . . . . Waitress
Gary Hudson. . . . . . . . . . . . . . . . . . . . . . . . .Randall
- • 0:11—Buns, getting up out of bed and putting on his pants.
- ••• 1:18—Buns, while making love in bed on top of Alex.

Anna Karin . . . . . . . . . . . . . . . . . . . . . . . . . . . Inga
- ••• 0:09—In black lingerie, then breasts and buns after undressing and making love on bed with Randall.
- ••• 0:14—Breasts while tied by her wrists to the bed by Randall.

Wendy MacDonald . . . . . . . . . . . . . . . . . . . . . Abby
Michelle Moffett . . . . . . . . . . . . . . . . . . . . . . .Maggie
- •• 0:20—Breasts while making love with Randall on truck of car outside at night.
- ••• 0:58—Nude, taking a shower and getting out to talk to Alex.
- • 1:00—Brief buns, while walking into bedroom.
- ••• 1:14—Breasts, while sitting in bed with Alex, then buns in sheer black panties.

David Naughton . . . . . . . . . . . . . . . . . . . . . . Philip

Kathy Shower. . . . . . . . . . . . . . . . . . . . . . . . . Celeste
  0:50—In white bra in bed with Maggie.
- •• 0:52—Breasts, while lying in bed.
- •• 1:16—Breasts in bed with bullet through her head, when discovered by Philip.

## *The Wild Life* (1984)

Michael Bowen . . . . . . . . . . . . . . . . . . . . . . . . .Vince
Sherilyn Fenn . . . . . . . . . . . . . . . . . . . . . Penny Hallin
Tracey E. Hutchinson . . . . . . . . . . . . . . . . Poker Girl #2
- • 1:23—Brief breasts in a room full of guys and girls playing strip poker when Lea Thompson looks in.

Leigh Lombardi . . . . . . . . . . . . . . . . . . . . Stewardess
Francesca "Kitten" Natividad . . . . . . . . . . . Stripper #2
- ••• 0:50—Breasts doing strip routine in a bar just before a fight breaks out.

Christopher Penn . . . . . . . . . . . . . . . . . . . . Tom Drake
Randy Quaid . . . . . . . . . . . . . . . . . . . . . . . .Charlie
Ashley St. Jon. . . . . . . . . . . . . . . . . . . . . Stripper #1
- ••• 0:47—Breasts and brief buns doing strip tease routine in front of Christopher Penn and his friends.

Eric Stoltz. . . . . . . . . . . . . . . . . . . . . . . . .Bill Conrad
Lea Thompson . . . . . . . . . . . . . . . . . . . . . . . . Anita
  0:38—In bra and panties putting body stocking on.

Jenny Wright . . . . . . . . . . . . . . . . . . . . . . . . .Eileen
- •• 0:22—In bra and panties, then breasts changing in her bedroom while Christopher Penn watches from the window.

## *Wild Man* (1988)

Ginger Lynn Allen . . . . . . . . . . . . . . . . . . . . Dawn Hall
- •• 0:24—Breasts taking off her dress in front of Eric, then making love with him.

Michelle Bauer. . . . . . . . . . . . . . . . . . . .Trisha Collins
  1:02—In sheer white lingerie with Eric. Buns also.
- ••• 1:06—Breasts on couch making love with Eric. Brief lower frontal nudity.

Jeanie Moore . . . . . . . . . . . . . . . . . . . . . . .Lady at Pool

## *Wild Orchid* (1990)

Jacqueline Bisset. . . . . . . . . . . . . . . . . . . . . . Claudia
  1:21—Dancing in braless white tank top during carnival.

Daniel Blasco . . . . . . . . . . . . . . . . . . . . . .Man in Airport
Bruce Greenwood . . . . . . . . . . . . . Jermone McFarland
- •• 1:02—Buns, while in room with Carré Otis.

Carré Otis. . . . . . . . . . . . . . . . . . . . . . . .Emily Reed
- •• 0:51—Left breast in mirror looking at herself while getting dressed.
- ••• 1:01—Breasts when a guy takes off her dress while Mickey Rourke watches.
- ••• 1:02—Right breast, then breasts while on the floor with Jerome.
- • 1:31—Brief breasts in flashback with Jerome.
- • 1:42—Breasts while opening her blouse for Rourke.
- ••• 1:44—Nude while making love with Rourke. Nice and sweaty.

Jens Peter. . . . . . . . . . . . . . . . . . . . . . . Volleyball Player
- ••• 1:29—Buns, while in room with Jacqueline Bisset and Carré Otis.

Mickey Rourke . . . . . . . . . . . . . . . . . . . .James Wheeler

Assumpta Serna . . . . . . . . . . . . . . . . . . . . . . . . Hanna
••• 0:39—Breasts at the beach and in the limousine. Very erotic.

### Wild Orchid II: Two Shades of Blue (1992)
Lydie Denier . . . . . . . . . . . . . . . . . . . . . . . . . Dominique
••• 0:28—Breasts, undressing from lingerie while Blue and Elle watch.
Wendy Hughes . . . . . . . . . . . . . . . . . . . . . . . . . . . Elle
Nina Siemaszko. . . . . . . . . . . . . . . . . . . . . . . . . Blue
••• 0:27—Breasts and buns, getting undressed in front of Wendy Hughes.
•• 0:43—Breasts and buns in steam room with a customer.
•• 0:58—Breasts in panties, garter belt and stockings while undressing for Josh.
••• 1:06—Breasts while humiliating J. J. in front of everyone at a party.
Tom Skerritt . . . . . . . . . . . . . . . . . . . . . . . . . . . . Ham

### Wild Zone (1989)
Edward Albert. . . . . . . . . . . . . . . . . . . . Colonel Lavera
Cristobel D'Ortez . . . . . . . . . . . . . . . . . . . . . . . .Mary
•• 1:19—Breasts in the brush, getting molested by a bad guy.
Carla Herd. . . . . . . . . . . . . . . . . . . . . . . Nicole Laroche

### Wildcats (1986)
Woody Harrelson . . . . . . . . . . . . . . . . . . . . . Krushinski
Goldie Hawn. . . . . . . . . . . . . . . . . . . . . . . . . . Molly
• 0:30—Brief breasts in bathtub.
Bruce McGill . . . . . . . . . . . . . . . . . . . . . . Dan Darwill
M. Emmet Walsh. . . . . . . . . . . . . . . . . . . . . . . . .Coes

### Wildest Dreams (1987)
Deborah Blaisdell . . . . . . . . . . . . . . . . . Joan Peabody
• 1:10—Brief breasts during fight on floor with two other women.
Ruth Corrine Collins . . . . . . . . . . . . . . . . . . . . Stella
••• 0:22—Breasts wearing panties in bedroom on bed with Bobby.
• 1:10—Brief breasts fighting on floor with two other women.
Nicole Grey. . . . . . . . . . . . . . . . . . . . . Girl on Street
Jane Hamilton. . . . . . . . . . . . . . . . . . . . Ruth Delaney
Jill Johnson . . . . . . . . . . . . . . . . . . . . .Rachel Richards
•• 0:51—Breasts on bed underneath Bobby in a net.
• 1:10—Brief breasts during fight with two other women.
Jeanne Marie . . . . . . . . . . . . . . . . . . . . . . . .Isabelle
•• 0:35—Breasts in panties in bedroom with Bobby.
Susan Napoli. . . . . . . . . . . . . . . . . . . . . . . . Punk #4
• 0:21—Brief left breast, leaning backwards on couch with her boyfriend.
Angela Nicholas . . . . . . . . . . . . . . . . . . . .Claudia
•• 1:01—Breasts typing on computer doing Bobby's book keeping.
Karen Nielsen . . . . . . . . . . . . . . . . . . . . . . . . Punk #2
• 0:21—Left breast, while sitting on couch.

Heidi Paine. . . . . . . . . . . . . . . . . . . . . . . . . . Dancee
• 0:23—Breasts, while being held in the arms of a gladiator in Bobby's bedroom.
Miriam Zucker . . . . . . . . . . . . . . . . . . . . . . Customer

### Wilding, The Children of Violence (1990)
Catlyn Day. . . . . . . . . . . . . . . . . . . . .Officer Breedlove
Susan Jones . . . . . . . . . . . . . . . . . . . . .Alley Rape Victim
• 1:16—Breasts outside struggling with Jason and Bobby on the ground.
Jackie Moen . . . . . . . . . . . . . . . . . . . . . .Car Rape Victim
• 0:23—Very brief right breast in back of car with her boyfriend when the gang of kids terrorizes them.
Karen Russell . . . . . . . . . . . . . . . . . . . . . . . . . . Cathy
•• 0:20—Breasts in bedroom when Wings Hauser pulls her lingerie down.

### Willie and Phil (1980)
Kristine DeBell . . . . . . . . . . . . . . . . . . . . . . . . . Rena
• 1:36—Breasts on the beach (mostly silhouette). Brief side of left breast.
Jerry Hall . . . . . . . . . . . . . . . . . . . . . . . . . . . . .Karen
• 0:05—Brief breasts getting dressed in bedroom with Phil.
Kaki Hunter . . . . . . . . . . . . . . . . . . . .Patti Sutherland
Margot Kidder . . . . . . . . . . . . . . . .Jeanette Sutherland
• 0:36—Brief breasts in bed when Phil opens up her blouse. Long shot.
• 0:47—Brief breasts playing in a lake with Willie and Phil.
Michael Ontkean . . . . . . . . . . . . . . . . . . . . .Willie
•• 1:36—Buns, while taking off his swimsuit at the beach and jumping around.
•• 1:45—Buns, while getting into the hot tub. (He's on the left.)
Ray Sharkey . . . . . . . . . . . . . . . . . . . . . . . . . . Phil
•• 1:45—Buns, while getting into the hot tub. (He's on the right.)

### Wimps (1987)
Jim Abele . . . . . . . . . . . . . . . . . . . . . . . Charles Conrad
Deborah Blaisdell . . . . . . . . . . . . . . . Roxanne Chandless
• 1:22—Brief breasts and buns taking off clothes and getting into bed with Francis in bedroom.
Louis Bonanno. . . . . . . . . . . . . . . . . . . . . . . .Francis
• 1:13—Buns, while running into a restaurant kitchen.
Jane Hamilton . . . . . . . . . . . . . . . . . . . . . . . . .Tracy
• 0:40—Lifting up her sweater and shaking her breasts in the back of the car with Francis. Too dark to see anything.
•• 0:44—Breasts and buns taking off sweater in a restaurant.
Gretchen Kingsley . . . . . . . . . . . . . . . . . . . . . Debbie
Jeanne Marie . . . . . . . . . . . . . . . . . . . . . . . . . Janice
•• 0:20—Breasts in bed taking off top with Charles.
Derrick Roberts. . . . . . . . . . . . . . . . . . . . . . . . . n.a.
Annie Sprinkle . . . . . . . . . . . . . . . . . . . . Head Stripper
•• 1:12—Breasts on stage with two other strippers, teasing Francis.

### Windrider (1986; Australian)
Nicole Kidman . . . . . . . . . . . . . . . . . . . . . . . . . . Jade
- • 0:40—Brief breasts in the shower with Tom Burlinson.
- •• 0:42—Brief buns and breasts in bed with Burlinson.
- • 0:43—Brief left breast on top of Burlinson in bed. Dark.
- ••• 0:47—Buns and very brief back side of left and right breasts, getting out of bed and putting on robe.

### Wings (1927)
Clara Bow . . . . . . . . . . . . . . . . . . . . . . Mary Preston
- • 1:22—It looks like very, very brief left breast (blurry) when military guys walk in on her and she stands up straight while in front of a mirror.

### Wings of Desire (1987)
*a.k.a. Der Himmel Uber Berlin*
Solveig Dommartin . . . . . . . . . . . . . . . . . . . . . Marion
- • 0:34—Brief side of left breast, while putting robe on. (The film changes from B&W to color.)
Peter Falk . . . . . . . . . . . . . . . . . . . . . . . . . . . . Himself

### Winter Kills (1979)
Belinda Bauer . . . . . . . . . . . . . . . . . . . . Yvette Malone
- •• 0:46—Breasts making love in bed with Jeff Bridges, then getting out of bed.
- • 1:25—Breasts, dead as a corpse when sheet uncovers her body.
Jeff Bridges . . . . . . . . . . . . . . . . . . . . . . . Nick Kegan
- •• 0:50—Buns, while getting dressed after making love with Belinda Bauer.
Tisa Farrow . . . . . . . . . . . . . . . . . . . . . . . Nurse Two
Amanda Jones . . . . . . . . . . . . . . Beautiful Woman Seven
Candice Rialson . . . . . . . . . . . . . . . . Second Blonde Girl

### Winter of Our Dreams (1981)
Bryan Brown . . . . . . . . . . . . . . . . . . . . . . . . . . . . Reb
- • 0:48—Brief buns while falling into bed with Judy Davis.
Judy Davis . . . . . . . . . . . . . . . . . . . . . . . . . . . . Lou
- • 0:19—Brief left breast sticking out of yellow robe in bed with Pete.
- • 0:26—Very brief side view of left breast taking off top to change. Long shot.
- •• 0:48—Breasts taking off top and getting into bed with Bryan Brown, then brief right breast lying down with him.
Cathy Downes . . . . . . . . . . . . . . . . . . . . . . . . Gretel
- • 0:41—Brief right breast putting top on while talking to Judy Davis.
- •• 1:04—Breasts sitting up in bed at night.
- • 1:11—Breasts sitting up in bed while Bryan Brown and Davis talk.

### Wish You Were Here (1987)
Emily Lloyd . . . . . . . . . . . . . . . . . . . . . . . . . . Lynda
- • 0:43—Buns, while singing in the alley and lifting up her skirt to moon an older neighbor woman.

### Witchboard (1987)
Tawny Kitaen . . . . . . . . . . . . . . . . . . . . . . . . . Linda
- • 1:26—Nude, stuck in the shower and breaking the glass doors to get out.

### Witchboard 2: The Devil's Doorway (1993)
Julie Michaels . . . . . . . . . . . . . . . . . . . . . . . . Susan
- • 1:17—Brief breasts, in B&W photos that Russel looks at.

### Witchcraft 6: The Devil's Mistress (1993)
(Unrated version reviewed.)
Debra Beatty . . . . . . . . . . . . . . . . . . . . . . . . . . Keli
- ••• 0:50—Breasts, while sitting in bubble bath, then nude, while making love with Will in the tub.
- ••• 1:06—Full frontal nudity getting into the bathtub, then washing herself.
- • 1:11—Brief right breast, while washing herself.
Shannon McLeod . . . . . . . . . . . . . . . . . . . . . . Cat
- •• 0:17—In bra, then right breast, while making love with Jonathan in front seat of car.
- • 0:42—Brief lower frontal nudity, while cutting a string off her mini skirt.
- • 1:01—Left breast, while making love with Will in his office.
- ••• 1:13—Breasts, while making love with Jonathan on trunk of car.
Jerry Spicer . . . . . . . . . . . . . . . . . . . . . . . . . . . Will

### Witchcraft II: The Temptress (1989)
Mia M. Ruiz . . . . . . . . . . . . . . . . . . . . . . . . Michelle
- • 0:27—Brief breasts several times making love with a guy on the floor during William's hallucination.
Delia Sheppard . . . . . . . . . . . . . . . . . . . . . Dolores
- •• 1:20—Brief breasts several times with William.

### Witchcraft III: The Kiss of Death (1991)
Leana Hall . . . . . . . . . . . . . . . . . . . . . . . . . . . Roxy
- •• 1:08—Breasts on bed with William making love when Charlotte gets trapped in the room.
Lisa Toothman . . . . . . . . . . . . . . . . . . . . . . Charlotte
- •• 1:02—Buns and breasts in shower with Louis while William has a bad dream.
- •• 1:12—Left breast, while on bed with Louis, against her will.

### Witchcraft IV: Virgin Heart (1992)
Julie Strain . . . . . . . . . . . . . . . . . . . . . . Belladonna
- • 0:25—Buns, while dancing on stage in a red bra and red G-string.
- ••• 0:27—Breasts, dancing on stage.
- •• 0:46—Breasts on the floor with Santara.
- • 0:49—Brief breasts in open dress on couch with Will.
- • 1:15—Breasts, lying on couch in her dressing room while Will tries to talk to her.

### Witchcraft V: Dance with the Devil (1993)
Annastasia Alexander . . . . . . . . . . . . . . . . . . . Sacrifice
- ••• 1:15—Nude, undressing and getting sacrificed on table. Long scene.
Marklen Kennedy . . . . . . . . . . . . . . . . . . . . William
- • 1:03—Buns, while leaving the basement.

Nicole Sassaman . . . . . . . . . . . . . . . . . . . . . . . . Marta
　　0:02—In black bra, in hotel room with a customer.
　• 0:03—Brief breasts in open bra, just before the customer gets killed.
　••• 0:30—Breasts in bed, while making love with Bill while Keli is asleep.
　• 0:51—Breasts under sheer black blouse.
　••• 0:55—Breasts with Bill at the top of the stairs.
Carolyn Taye-Loren . . . . . . . . . . . . . . . . . . . . . . . Keli
　　0:18—In pink bra and panties in her bedroom.
　••• 1:01—Breasts while making love with Bill under leaky water pipes in the basement.

## *Witchfire* (1986)
Vanessa Blanchard . . . . . . . . . . . . . . . . . . . . . . . . Liz
　•• 0:52—Brief breasts in bed and then the shower.

## *The Witching* (1983)
*a.k.a. Necromancy*
(Originally filmed in 1971 as *Necromancy*, additional scenes were added and re-released in 1983.)
Sue Bernard . . . . . . . . . . . . . . . . . . . . . . . . . . . Nancy
　• 1:03—Brief breasts in bed with Michael Ontkean.
Pamela Franklin . . . . . . . . . . . . . . . . . . . . . . . . . . Lori
　•• 0:38—Breasts lying in bed during nightmare.
　　0:46—Partial right breast, tied to a stake. Flames from fire are in the way.
　• 1:07—Brief breasts putting on black robe.
　• 1:17—Brief breasts in several quick cuts.
Annie Gaybis . . . . . . . . . . . . . . . . . . . . . . . . . . . Spirit
Michael Ontkean . . . . . . . . . . . . . . . . . . . Frank Brandon
Barbara Peckinpaugh . . . . . . . . . . . . . . . . . . . . . Jennie
　••• 0:02—Breasts and buns in open gown during occult ceremony. Brief full frontal nudity holding a doll up.
Laurie Senit . . . . . . . . . . . . . . . . . . . . . Witches Coven
Brinke Stevens . . . . . . . . . . . . . . Black Sabbath Member

## *Witchtrap* (1989)
Linnea Quigley . . . . . . . . . . . . . . . . . . . Ginger Kowoski
　••• 0:34—Nude taking off robe and getting into the shower.
　•• 0:36—Breasts just before getting killed when the shower head goes into her neck.

## *With a Song in My Heart* (1952)
Susan Hayward . . . . . . . . . . . . . . . . . . . . . Jane Froman
　　0:48—Very brief upper half of left breast, when it pops out of the top of her strapless dress during song and dance number when she lifts her right arm over her dancing partner's head.

## *Without You I'm Nothing* (1990)
Steve Antin . . . . . . . . . . . . . . . . . . . . . . . . . Steve Antin
Sandra Bernhard . . . . . . . . . . Miscellaneous Characters
　••• 1:20—Dancing in very small pasties on stage. Buns in very small G-string. Long scene.
Carlton Wilborn . . . . . . . . . . . . . . . . . . . Ballet Dancer

## *Witness* (1985)
Kelly McGillis . . . . . . . . . . . . . . . . . . . . . . . . . Rachel
　••• 1:18—Breasts taking off her top to take a bath while Harrison Ford watches.

Viggo Mortensen . . . . . . . . . . . . . . . . Moses Hochleitner

## *Wolf Lake* (1978)
*a.k.a. Survive the Night at Wolf Lake*
Robin Mattson . . . . . . . . . . . . . . . . . . . . . . . . . . Linda
　• 0:54—Brief full frontal nudity during rape in cabin. Dark.
　• 0:55—Brief breasts afterwards.

## *Wolfen* (1981)
Max M. Brown . . . . . . . . . . . . Christopher Van der Veer
　• 0:21—Brief frontal nudity, lying dead as a corpse on the coroner's table. Don't see his face.
Albert Finney . . . . . . . . . . . . . . . . . . . . . . Dewey Wilson
Gregory Hines . . . . . . . . . . . . . . . . . . . . . . Whittington
　• 1:24—Buns, twice when he moons Albert Finney, who is looking through a green-tinted night vision scope.
Edward James Olmos . . . . . . . . . . . . . . . . . . Eddie Holt
　• 1:04—Buns, while lapping water, then nude, running around the beach. Dark.
　•• 1:05—Very brief frontal nudity, leaping off pier in front of Albert Finney.
　• 1:12—Very brief frontal nudity, running under pier during Finney's vision.
Diane Venora . . . . . . . . . . . . . . . . . . . . . Rebecca Neff

## *The Woman in Red* (1984)
Kelly Le Brock . . . . . . . . . . . . . . . . . . . . . . . Charlotte
　　0:02—Wearing the red dress, dancing over the air vent in the car garage while Gene Wilder watches.
　• 1:13—Brief right breast, getting into bed. Too far to see anything.
　　1:15—Brief lower frontal nudity getting out of bed when her husband comes home. Very brief left breast, but it's blurry and hard to see.
Gene Wilder . . . . . . . . . . . . . . . . . . . . . Theodore Pierce
　• 1:15—Side view of buns while getting back into bed with Kelly Le Brock after getting out to take his underwear off the lamp.

## *Woman of Desire* (1993)
Steven Bauer . . . . . . . . . . . . . . . . . Jonathan/Ted Ashby
Bo Derek . . . . . . . . . . . . . . . . . . . . . . . . Christina Ford
　• 0:07—Very brief right breast, while turning over in bed with Steven Bauer.
　• 0:14—Breasts, in photo that a detective finds on boat.
　••• 0:19—Breasts, while sunbathing on boat, then nude after taking off bikini bottoms and diving into the water.
　　0:33—Breasts, while getting out of bed. Seen in "flashback-vision."
　•• 0:40—Breasts, while taking off blouse and putting on leather jacket in front of Jeff Fahey.
　••• 0:41—Breasts and buns while making love with Fahey on a motorcycle inside. Great!
　•• 0:51—Breasts, in shower with Fahey.
　• 0:57—Breasts on floor, while making love.
　　1:07—Sort of breasts on boat while sunbathing. Seen in "flashback-vision."

Jeff Fahey . . . . . . . . . . . . . . . . . . . . . . . . . Jack Lynch
- 0:01—Buns, while lying face down on sand at beach.

Kimberleigh Stark . . . . . . . . . . . . . Nurse Vivian Donner

## A Woman, Her Men and Her Futon (1992)
Kathryn Atwood . . . . . . . . . . . . . . . . . . . . Waitress #2
Robert Lipton . . . . . . . . . . . . . . . . . . . . . . . . . . . Max
Jennifer Rubin . . . . . . . . . . . . . . . . . . . . . . . . . Helen
- •• 0:22—Breasts, making love in bed with Randy.
- ••• 0:31—Breasts, lying in bed with Donald.
- • 0:35—Brief breasts, while making love in bed with Randy.
- •• 1:04—Breasts, lying in bed and starting to make love with Donald.

## Women & Men: Stories of Seduction
### (1990; Made for Cable Movie)
Beau Bridges . . . . . . . . . . . . . . . . . . . . . Gerry Breen
Melanie Griffith . . . . . . . . . . . . . . . . . . . . . . . Hadley
Elizabeth McGovern . . . . . . . . . . . . . . . . . . . . Vicki
0:18—In white lingerie in train car with Beau Bridges.
- ••• 0:22—Breasts when Bridges takes her top off when she lies back in bed.

Peter Weller. . . . . . . . . . . . . . . . . . . . . . . . . . Hobie
James Woods . . . . . . . . . . . . . . . . . . . . . . . . Robert

## Women in Love (1971)
Alan Bates . . . . . . . . . . . . . . . . . . . . . . . . . . Rupert
- • 0:25—Buns and brief frontal nudity walking around the woods rubbing himself with everything.
- • 0:50—Buns, while making love with Ursula after a boy and girl drown in the river.
- ••• 0:54—Nude fighting with Oliver Reed in a room in front of a fireplace. Long scene.

Glenda Jackson . . . . . . . . . . . . . . . . . Gudrun Brangwen
- ••• 1:20—Breasts taking off her blouse on the bed with Oliver Reed watching her, then making love.
- •• 1:49—Brief left breast making love with Reed in bed again.

Jennie Linden . . . . . . . . . . . . . . . . . . Ursula Bragwen
- • 0:38—Brief breasts skinny dipping in the river with Glenda Jackson.
- • 1:11—Brief breasts in a field with Alan Bates. Scene is shown sideways.

Oliver Reed . . . . . . . . . . . . . . . . . . . . . . . Gerald Crich
- ••• 0:54—Nude, fighting with Alan Bates in a room in front of a fireplace. Long scene.

## The Women's Club (1987)
Maud Adams. . . . . . . . . . . . . . . . . . . . . . . Angie Blake
0:17—In black panties, garter belt and stockings making out with Michael Paré.

Michael Paré. . . . . . . . . . . . . . . . . . . . . . . . . Patrick
1:05—Brief buns, during nightmare. Hard to see because of fog.
- • 1:06—Buns, while standing in hallway during nightmare. Long shot.

Pamela Ward. . . . . . . . . . . . . . Fashion Show Woman

## Wonderland (1989; British)
Emile Charles . . . . . . . . . . . . . . . . . . . . . . . . . . Eddie
- ••• 1:27—Nude, taking off his clothes and swimming under water with the dolphins. Long scene.

Julie Graham . . . . . . . . . . . . . . . . . . . . . . . . . . Hazel
- •• 1:11—Nude, taking off her clothes at the beach while talking to Eddie.

Clare Higgins . . . . . . . . . . . . . . . . . . . . . . . . . . . Eve

## Working Girl (1989)
Alec Baldwin . . . . . . . . . . . . . . . . . . . . . . . Mick Dugan
Olympia Dukakis . . . . . . . . . . . . . . . . Personnel Director
Barbara Garrick . . . . . . . . . . . . . . . . . . Phyllis Trask
Melanie Griffith . . . . . . . . . . . . . . . . . . . . . Tess McGill
0:08—In bra, panties, garter belt and stockings in front of a mirror.
0:32—In black bra, garter belt and stockings trying on clothes.
0:43—In black bra, garter belt and stockings getting out of bed.
1:15—In white bra, taking off her blouse with Harrison Ford.
- • 1:18—Very, very brief right breast turning over in bed with Ford.
- • 1:20—Breasts, vacuuming. Long shot seen from the other end of the hall.

Jeffrey Nordling . . . . . . . . . . . . . . . . . . . . Tim Rourke
Sigourney Weaver . . . . . . . . . . . . . . . Katherine Parker
1:22—In white lingerie, sitting in bed, then talking to Harrison Ford.

Elizabeth Whitcraft. . . . . . . . . . . . . . Doreen DiMucci
- •• 0:29—Breasts on bed on Alec Baldwin when Melanie Griffith opens the door and discovers them.

## The Working Girls (1973)
Elvira . . . . . . . . . . . . . . . . . . . . . . . . . . . . . . Katya
0:18—Dancing in a G-string on stage in a club.
- ••• 0:20—Breasts, dancing on stage.

Lynne Guthrie . . . . . . . . . . . . . . . . . . . . . . . . . . Jill
- ••• 0:43—Breasts, dancing on stage at club.
- •• 0:48—Breasts in swimming pool with Nick.

Laurie Rose. . . . . . . . . . . . . . . . . . . . . . . . . Denise
Bob Schott. . . . . . . . . . . . . . . . . . . . . . . . . . Roger
- • 0:07—Buns, while getting out of bed to meet Honey.

## Working Girls (1987)
Roger Babb . . . . . . . . . . . . . . . . . . . . . . . . . . . Paul
- • 1:18—Frontal nudity with Molly.

## World According to Garp (1982)
Glenn Close . . . . . . . . . . . . . . . . . . . . . . Jenny Fields
John Lithgow . . . . . . . . . . . . . . . . . . . . . . . Roberta
Amanda Plummer . . . . . . . . . . . . . . . . . . Ellen James
Robin Williams . . . . . . . . . . . . . . . . . . . . . T.S. Garp
Jenny Wright . . . . . . . . . . . . . . . . . . . . . . . . Curbie
- •• 0:33—Brief breasts behind the bushes with Robin Williams giving him "something to write about."

### The World is Full of Married Men *(1979; British)*
Carroll Baker . . . . . . . . . . . . . . . . . . . . . Linda Cooper
• 0:19—Brief left breast, while sitting up in bathtub covered with bubbles.
Georgina Hale . . . . . . . . . . . . . . . . . . . . Lori Grossman

### The Wraith *(1986)*
Vickie Benson . . . . . . . . . . . . . . . . . . . . . . . Waitress
• 0:59—Breasts in bed with Packard when Loomis interrupts them.
Nick Cassavetes . . . . . . . . . . . . . . . . . . . . . .Packard
Sherilyn Fenn . . . . . . . . . . . . . . . . . . . . . . . . .Keri
• 0:13—Very brief breasts when Packard's gang catches her in bed with Jamie.
• 1:02—Brief breasts during flashback when caught in bed by Packard's gang.
• 1:03—Very brief right breast, pulling her swimsuit top off in pond with Charlie Sheen.
Clint Howard . . . . . . . . . . . . . . . . . . . . . . .Rughead
Randy Quaid . . . . . . . . . . . . . . . . . . . . . .Sheriff Loomis

### Write to Kill *(1990)*
Joan Severance . . . . . . . . . . . . . . . . . . .Belle Washburn
0:59—Wearing purple bra in house with Scott Valentine.
••• 1:01—Breasts, making love in bed with Valentine.
• 1:04—Very brief, blurry breasts when Valentine tosses her a blouse.
Scott Valentine . . . . . . . . . . . . . . . . . . . . Clark Sanford
• 1:03—Very brief partial frontal nudity, leaping out of bed.

### The Wrong Man *(1993; Made for Cable Movie)*
Kevin Anderson . . . . . . . . . . . . . . . . . . . . . . . . . Alex
••• 1:24—Buns, while getting out of bed and washing his face and getting back into bed.
Rosanna Arquette . . . . . . . . . . . . . . . . . . . . . . Missy
•• 0:34—Buns in black panties, then breasts, taking off her dress at the beach and going into the water. Medium long shot.
1:08—In red bra and panties in hotel room with John Lithgow and Kevin Anderson.
••• 1:15—Breasts after taking off bra and dancing on table in room, then putting on dress afterwards. Very nice, long scene.
• 1:23—Very, very brief part of right breast in open robe and very brief side view of buns while in bed on top of Anderson.
1:26—Brief squished left breast, while lying in bed.
John Lithgow . . . . . . . . . . . . . . . . . . . . . . Phillip Mills

### Xtro *(1982)*
Maryam D'Abo . . . . . . . . . . . . . . . . . . . . . . . Analise
••• 0:25—Breasts making love with her boyfriend on the floor in her bedroom.
•• 0:56—Brief breasts with her boyfriend again.

### Yanks *(1979)*
Lisa Eichhorn . . . . . . . . . . . . . . . . . . . . .Jean Moreton
• 1:48—Brief breasts in bed when Richard Gere rolls off her.
Richard Gere . . . . . . . . . . . . . . . . . . . . . . . . . . Matt
Vanessa Redgrave . . . . . . . . . . . . . . . . . . . . . .Helen
• 1:25—Brief side of left breast and buns, taking off robe and getting into bed.
Annie Ross . . . . . . . . . . . . . . . . . . . . . Red Cross Lady

### The Year of the Dragon *(1985)*
Ariane . . . . . . . . . . . . . . . . . . . . . . . . . .Tracy Tzu
• 0:59—Very brief breasts when Mickey Rourke rips her blouse off in her apartment.
•• 1:14—Nude, taking a shower in her apartment.
•• 1:18—Breasts straddling Rourke, while making love on the bed.
John Lone . . . . . . . . . . . . . . . . . . . . . . . . . . .Joey Tai
Mickey Rourke . . . . . . . . . . . . . . . . . . . . . Stanley White

### Year of the Gun *(1991)*
Luigi Amodeo . . . . . . . . . . . . . . . . . . . . . Piero Gagliani
Valeria Golino . . . . . . . . . . . . . . . . . . . . . . . Lia Spinelli
••• 0:17—Breasts, making love in bed with Andrew McCarthy.
• 0:25—Half of buns and side of right breast, lying in bed with McCarthy.
Andrew McCarthy . . . . . . . . . . . . . . . .David Raybourne
John Pankow . . . . . . . . . . . . . . . . . . . . . .Italo Bianchi
Sharon Stone . . . . . . . . . . . . . . . . . . . . . . . Alison King
• 1:00—Brief left breast, while standing against the door, with Andrew McCarthy. Long shot.
• 1:01—Side of left breast, while making love on bed.

### Yentl *(1983)*
Mandy Patinkin . . . . . . . . . . . . . . . . . . . . . . Avigdor
•• 0:49—Buns, after taking off his clothes to go skinny dipping.
• 0:51—Brief buns while sitting down next to Barbra Streisand, the brief buns, while standing up.
• 0:52—Buns, while walking around and sitting down. Long shot.

### You Can't Hurry Love *(1984)*
Bridget Fonda . . . . . . . . . . . . . . . . . . . . . . . . Peggy
Anthony Geary . . . . . . . . . . . . . . . . . . . . . . . . . Tony
Sally Kellerman . . . . . . . . . . . . . . . . . . . . . Kelly Bones
Danitza Kingsley . . . . . . . . . . . . . . . . . . . . . . . Tracey
Kristy McNichol . . . . . . . . . . . . . . . . . . . . . . . Rhonda
David Packer . . . . . . . . . . . . . . . . . . . . . . . .Eddie
• 0:59—Buns, in store taking his pants off while people watch him from the sidewalk.
Jean Poremba . . . . . . . . . . . . . . . . . . . . Model in Back
• 0:05—Breasts posing in the backyard getting photographed.
•• 0:48—Nude in backyard again getting photographed.
Kimber Sissons . . . . . . . . . . . . . . . . . . . . . . . .Brenda
0:48—Partial side of right breast in open shirt, bending over to pick up her bra off the coffee table.
Merete Van Kamp . . . . . . . . . . . . . . . . . . . . Monique

## You've Got to Have Heart (Italian)

*a.k.a. At Last, At Last*

Carroll Baker . . . . . . . . . . . . . . . . . . . . . . . . .Lucia
- •• 1:23—Left breast, while in cabin, consoling Giovanni.
- •• 1:24—More left breast, while with Giovanni.
- •• 1:25—Right breast while making love.

Edwige Fenech . . . . . . . . . . . . . . . . . . . . . . Valentina
- ••• 0:10—Breasts and buns, while taking off nightgown for Giovanni.
- • 0:11—Brief side view of left breast, while sitting up on the floor with Giovanni.
- ••• 0:20—Nude in bedroom with Giovanni.
- •• 0:26—Right breast, when Giovanni gets out of bed.
- •• 0:43—Left breast, while entertaining herself and fantasizing.
- ••• 0:47—Breasts, while on boat getting lotion rubbed on her by Brigitte.
- ••• 0:53—Breasts and buns in G-string when Giovanni takes off her body suit.
- • 0:58—Right breast, while getting molested by Uncle Frederico.
- •• 1:20—Breasts while getting out of her wet dress in tent.
- •• 1:24—Breasts in tent while making love with another man.
- •• 1:25—Right breast while making love.
- • 1:32—Brief full frontal nudity in bedroom during argument.

## Young Doctors in Love (1982)

Jaime Lyn Bauer . . . . . . . . . . . . . . . . . . . . . . Cameo
Ed Begley, Jr. . . . . . . . . . . . . . . . .Young Simon's Father
Dabney Coleman . . . . . . . . . . . . . . . .Dr. Joseph Prang
Kimberly McArthur . . . . . . . . . . . . . . . . . Jyll Omato
- •• 0:58—Breasts in front of Dabney Coleman after taking off her Santa Claus outfit in his study.

Ted McGinley . . . . . . . . . . . . . . . . . . . . . Dr. Bucky DeVol
Pamela Reed . . . . . . . . . . . . . . . . . . . . . Norine Sprockett
Tessa Richarde. . . . . . . . . . . . . . . . . . . . .Rocco's Wife
Harry Dean Stanton. . . . . . . . . . . . . . . Dr. Oliver Ludwig
Peggy Trentini. . . . . . . . . . . . . . . . . . . . . . .Christmas Elf
- •• 0:55—Brief breasts greeting visitors to the party.
- • 0:57—Breasts again sitting on couch.

Janine Turner . . . . . . . . . . . . . . . . . . . . . . . . . . Cameo
Sean Young. . . . . . . . . . . . . . . . . . Dr. Stephanie Brody
0:48—In white panties and camisole top in the surgery room with Michael McKean.

## Young Einstein (1989; Australian)

Glenn Butcher. . . . . . . . . . . . . . . . . . . Ernest Rutherford
- • 0:56—Buns, while standing in front of sink when Marie comes to rescue Einstein. (He's the one on the left.)

Warren Coleman. . . . . . . . . . . . . . . . .Lunatic Professor
- • 0:55—Buns while in Lunatic Asylum, taking a shower.
- • 0:56—More buns while standing in front of sink when Marie comes to rescue Einstein. (He's the one on the right.)

- • 0:58—Brief buns while crowding into the shower stall with the other Asylum people.

## Young Guns (1988)

Emilio Estevez. . . . . . . . William H. Bonney (Billy the Kid)
- • 1:19—Brief buns while standing up in the bathtub.

Pat Lee. . . . . . . . . . . . . . . . . . . . . . . . . . . . . . . . .Janey
Terry O'Quinn . . . . . . . . . . . . . . . . . .Alex McSween
Lou Diamond Phillips . . . . . . . . . . . . . .Chavez Y Chavez
Kiefer Sutherland . . . . . . . . . . . . . Josiah "Doc" Scurlock

## Young Guns II (1990)

Ginger Lynn Allen . . . . . . . . . . . . . . . . . . . . . . . Dove
Tom Byrd. . . . . . . . . . . . . . . . . . . . . . . . . . . Pit Inmate
Emilio Estevez. . . . . . . . William H. Bonney (Billy the Kid)
- •• 1:00—Buns, while getting up out of bed, putting his pants on.

Balthazar Getty . . . . . . . . . . . . . . . . . . . Tom O'Folliard
Viggo Mortensen . . . . . . . . . . . . . . . . . .John W. Poe
William L. Petersen. . . . . . . . . . . . . . . . . . . .Pat Garrett
Lou Diamond Phillips . . . . . . . . . Jose Chavez Y Chavez
Christian Slater. . . . . . . . . . . . .Arkansas Dave Rudbaugh
Kiefer Sutherland . . . . . . . . . . . . . . . . . Doc Scurlock
Tracey Walter. . . . . . . . . . . . . . . . . . . . Beever Smith
Jenny Wright . . . . . . . . . . . . . . . . . . Jane Greathouse
- • 1:07—Buns, taking off her clothes, getting on a horse and riding away. Hair covers breasts.
- • 1:38—Buns, while walking down stairs during epilogue.

## Young Lady Chatterley (1977)

Lindsay Freeman . . . . . . . . . . . . .Sybil (light-duty maid)
- • 1:35—Brief left breast, while on the floor, covered with cake.

Michael Hearne . . . . . . . . . . . . . . . . . . . . . . Hitchhiker
- ••• 0:52—Buns, several times in back of car with Harlee McBride.
- • 0:54—Brief buns when he's let out of the car.

Ray Martin . . . . . . . . . . . . . . . . . . . . Ronnie (stable boy)
- •• 1:35—Frontal nudity, covered with cake during cake orgy.

Harlee McBride . . . . . . . . . . . . . . . . .Cynthia Chatterley
- •• 0:19—Nude masturbating in front of mirror.
- • 0:28—Brief breasts with young boy.
- ••• 0:41—Nude in bathtub while maid washes her.
- ••• 0:52—Nude in back of car with the hitchhiker while the chauffeur is driving.
- ••• 1:03—Nude in the garden with the sprinklers on making love with the Gardener.
- ••• 1:31—Breasts and buns in bed with the gardener.

Ann Michelle . . . . . . . . . . . . . . . . . . . Gwen (roommate)
Peter Ratray . . . . . . . . . . . . . . . . . .Paul (young gardener)
- • 0:37—Very brief buns, while pulling his pants up after getting caught with Janette.
- • 1:03—Buns, while making love with Harlee McBride in the rain.
- •• 1:32—Buns, while in bed with McBride.

Patrick Wright . . . . . . . . . . . . . . . . Flash Back Gardener
- ••• 0:02—Nude, washing himself, outside while Lady Frances Chatterley watches.
- • 0:05—Buns, while in house with Lady Chatterley.

- 0:06—More buns, while on the floor.
- 0:33—Buns, with Lady Chatterley by the pond.

### Young Lady Chatterley II (1986)
Wendy Barry . . . . . . . . . . . . Sybil "Maid in Hot House"
- 0:12—Breasts in hot house with the Gardener.

Brett Clark. . . . . . . . . . . . . . . . . . Thomas "Gardener"
- •• 0:15—Brief buns, while pulling up his pants after getting caught with Monique Gabrielle in the woods by Adam West.
- 0:16—Very brief buns, when Monique pulls his pants down again.

Sybil Danning . . . . . . . . . . . . . . . . . . .Judith Grimmer
- ••• 1:02—Breasts in the hut on the table with the Gardener.

Alexandra Day. . . . . . . . . . . . . . . Jenny "Maid in Hut"
- ••• 0:06—Breasts and buns in hut on the bed with the Gardener.
- ••• 0:28—Breasts taking bath with Harlee McBride.

Monique Gabrielle . . . . . . . . . .Eunice "Maid in Woods"
- •• 0:15—Breasts in the woods with the Gardener.
- ••• 0:43—Breasts in bed with Virgil.

Stephen Kean Mathews. . . . . . . . . . . . .Robert Downing
- 0:59—Buns, while making love with Cynthia Chatterley outside on the grass.

Harlee McBride . . . . . . . . . . . . . . . Cynthia Chatterley
- •• 0:20—Breasts getting a massage with Elanor.
- •• 0:22—Full frontal nudity during flashback to the first time she made love with Robert.
- ••• 0:28—Breasts taking a bath with Jenny.
- ••• 0:35—Breasts in library seducing Virgil.
- ••• 0:50—Breasts in back of the car with the Count.
- ••• 0:58—Breasts in the garden with Robert.

Allene Simmons . . . . . . . . . . . . . Marta "Maid in Bed"

### Young Nurses in Love (1987)
John Altamura. . . . . . . . . . . . . . . . . . . . . . . . . .n.a.
Jennifer Delora . . . . . . . . . . . . . . . . . . . . . . .Bunny
Jamie Gillis . . . . . . . . . . . . . . . . . . . . . Dr. Spencer
Jane Hamilton . . . . . . . . . . . . . . . . . . . . . Franchesca
- •• 1:05—Breasts on top of a guy on a gurney.

Jeanne Marie. . . . . . . . . . . . . . . . . . .Nurse Ellis Smith
- 0:31—Brief side view of left breast in mirror with Dr. Riley.
- •• 1:09—Breasts in panties, getting into bed with Dr. Riley.

Sharon Moran. . . . . . . . . . . . . . . . . . . . . Bambi/Bibi
Annie Sprinkle. . . . . . . . . . . . . . . . . . . . . Twin Falls
- •• 0:23—Breasts getting measured by Dr. Spencer.

### The Young Warriors (1983; U.S./Canadian)
John Alden . . . . . . . . . . . . . . . . . . . . . . . . . Jorge
- 0:16—Dropping his pants in a room during pledge at fraternity.

Anne Lockhart. . . . . . . . . . . . . . . . . . . . . . . Lucy
- •• 0:42—Breasts and buns making love with Kevin on the bed. Looks like a body double.

Jimmy Patterson . . . . . . . . . . . . . . . . "Ice Test" Monty
- 0:14—Buns, while dropping pants and sitting on a block of ice during pledge at fraternity.

Linnea Quigley. . . . . . . . . . . . . . . . . . . . . . .Ginger
- 0:05—Nude in and getting out of bed in bedroom.

Richard Roundtree . . . . . . . . . . . . Sergeant John Austin
Nels Van Patten . . . . . . . . . . . . . . . . . . . . . Roger
Randy Woltz. . . . . . . . . . . . . . . . . . "Brick Test" Frank
- 0:16—Dropping his pants in a room during pledge at fraternity.

### Youngblood (1986)
Fionnula Flanagan . . . . . . . . . . . . . . . . . . . Miss McGill
Cynthia Gibb . . . . . . . . . . . . . . . . . . . Jessie Chadwick
- 0:50—Brief breasts and buns making love with Rob Lowe in his room.

Rob Lowe. . . . . . . . . . . . . . . . . . . Dean Youngblood
- ••• 0:16—Buns, standing in hallway in jockstrap and walking around while Cindy Gibb watches.

Keanu Reeves. . . . . . . . . . . . . . . . . . . . . . Hoover
Patrick Swayze . . . . . . . . . . . . . . . . . . . .Derek Sutton
Jim Youngs. . . . . . . . . . . . . . . . . . . Kelly Youngblood

### Your Ticket is No Longer Valid (1982)
Jennifer Dale . . . . . . . . . . . . . . . . . . . . . . . . .Laura
- •• 0:27—In black panties, then breasts when her husband fantasizes, then makes love with her.
  1:23—Left breast in bed with Montoya, then sitting, waiting for Richard Harris.

Richard Harris. . . . . . . . . . . . . . . . . . . . . . . . Jason
- 1:19—Buns, while taking off robe and sitting on the floor.

Winston Rekert. . . . . . . . . . . . . . . . Antonio Montoya
- 1:24—Buns, while in bed with Jennifer Dale.

### Zandalee (1991)
Erika Anderson . . . . . . . . . . . . . . . . . . . Zandalee Martin
- ••• 0:02—Nude, taking off robe and dancing around the room.
- ••• 0:21—Nude, undressing, then in bed with Judge Reinhold. Long scene.
- •• 0:30—Right breast, then breasts making love in bed with Nicolas Cage.
- •• 0:32—Breasts as Cage paints on her with his finger.
- ••• 0:45—Left breast, then breasts and lower frontal nudity on floor with Cage.
- •• 0:47—Nude, getting massaged by Cage with an oil and cocaine mixture.
- 0:48—Brief breasts getting into bed with Reinhold. Slightly out of focus.
- •• 1:09—Breasts opening her dress for Reinhold while lying on a river bank, then making love with him at night in bed.

Steve Buscemi . . . . . . . . . . . . . . . . . . . . . .Odd Man
Nicolas Cage . . . . . . . . . . . . . . . . . . . . Johnny Collins
- •• 0:30—Buns, while making love in bed with Zandalee.

Zach Galligan. . . . . . . . . . . . . . . . . . . . . . . . . . Rog
Judge Reinhold. . . . . . . . . . . . . . . . . . . Thierry Martin
- ••• 0:21—Buns while in bed with Zandalee.
- 0:23—Upper half of buns, while standing by the window.

## Zapped! (1982)

Willie Aames . . . . . . . . . . . . . . . . . . . . . . . . . . . . Peyton
Scott Baio . . . . . . . . . . . . . . . . . . . . . . . . . . . . Barney
Corinne Bohrer . . . . . . . . . . . . . . . . . . . . . . . . . Cindy
Rosanne Katon . . . . . . . . . . . . . . . . . . . . . . . . Donna
Jewel Shepard . . . . . . . . . . . . . . .Uncredited Girl in Car
- • 0:39—Brief breasts after red and white top pops off when Scott Baio uses his Telekinesis on her.

Marya Small . . . . . . . . . . . . . . . . . . . Mrs. Springboro
Heather Thomas . . . . . . . . . . . . . . . . . . . .Jane Mitchell
  0:20—Brief open sweater, wearing a bra when Scott Baio uses telekinesis to open it.
  1:28—Body double, very, very brief breasts in photo that Willie Aames gives to Robby.
  1:29—Body double brief breasts when Baio drops her dress during the dance.

## Zardoz (1974; British)

Sean Connery . . . . . . . . . . . . . . . . . . . . . . . . . . .Zed
Sara Kestelman . . . . . . . . . . . . . . . . . . . . . . . . . . May
- • 1:04—Left breast, in open blouse, under sheet with Sean Connery.
- • 1:05—Very brief breasts grabbing Connery from behind during struggle.

Charlotte Rampling . . . . . . . . . . . . . . . . . . . . . Consuella
  0:29—Breasts under yellow net blouse.
- • 1:05—Very brief left breast, when Sean Connery grabs her during struggle.
- • 1:26—Wearing yellow blouse, trying to kill Connery.
- • 1:44—Very brief right breast feeding her baby in time lapse scene at the end of the film.

## A Zed and Two Noughts (1985; British)

Frances Barber . . . . . . . . . . . . . . . . . . . . . .Venus de Milo
- ••• 0:22—Breasts, sitting in bed, talking to Oliver, then nude while getting thrown out of his place.

Brian Deacon . . . . . . . . . . . . . . . . . . . . . Oswald Deuce
- • 1:12—Buns (he's on the right), getting into bed with Alba and Oliver.
- •• 1:25—Nude (on the right), walking to chair and sitting down while Oliver does the same.
- ••• 1:27—Frontal nudity, standing up.
- ••• 1:50—Nude, injecting himself and lying down to time lapse photograph himself decay with Oliver.

Eric Deacon . . . . . . . . . . . . . . . . . . . . . . .Oliver Deuce
- •• 0:24—Buns in bed, then nude while throwing Venus out, then her clothes.
- ••• 0:30—Frontal nudity, sitting on bathroom floor.
- • 1:12—Buns (he's on the left), getting into bed with Alba and Oswald.
- •• 1:25—Nude (on the left), walking to chair and sitting down while Oswald does the same.
- ••• 1:27—Frontal nudity, standing up.
- ••• 1:50—Nude, injecting himself and lying down to time lapse photograph himself decay with Oswald.

Andrea Ferréol . . . . . . . . . . . . . . . . . . . . . Alba Bewick
Guusje Van Tilborgh . . . . . . . . . . . . . . .Caterina Bolnes
- • 0:42—Brief lower frontal nudity when Oliver lifts her skirt up in restroom to check to see what kind of panties she's wearing.

- • 0:51—Lower frontal nudity, then very brief breasts while posing for photo by Van Meegeren.

## Zombie (1980)

Tisa Farrow. . . . . . . . . . . . . . . . . . . . . . . . . Anne Bolles
Olga Karlatos . . . . . . . . . . . . . . . . . . . . . . . Mrs. Menard
- • 0:40—Breasts and buns taking a shower.

## Zombie Island Massacre (1984)

Rita Jenrette . . . . . . . . . . . . . . . . . . . . . . . . . . . . Sandy
- ••• 0:01—Breasts taking a shower while Joe sneaks up on her. Breasts in bed with Joe.
- •• 0:10—Brief right breast with open blouse, in boat with Joe. Left breast with him on the couch.

# OTHER SOURCES

Back issues of *Playboy* magazine can be purchased through *The Playboy Catalog*. Their catalog is free by calling 1-800-345-6066. They have a large assortment of *Playboy* magazine back issues from the 1960's to the present. They also sell *Playboy* Video Magazines, *Playboy* Video Centerfolds and other video tapes listed in this book such as *Nudity Required* and the *Mermaid* series.

If you can't find the video tapes listed in *The Bare Facts Video Guide* for rent at your local video tape rental stores, an excellent source for purchasing video tapes is *Movies Unlimited*. Their catalog costs $7.95 plus $3.00 shipping, but you get a $5.00 credit voucher to use on your order. The address is:

Movies Unlimited
6736 Castor Avenue
Philadelphia, PA 19149
(800) 4-MOVIES

Another source for locating hard to find video tapes is *Critics' Choice*. Their catalog is free by calling 1-800-544-9852. They have over 2,300 video tapes for sale. They also have a Video Search Line that operates Monday through Friday, from 9 a.m. to 5 p.m. EST. Their phone number is 1-900-370-6500. The cost is $1.95 for the first minute and $.95 for each additional minute. They will research your request and call you back within 1 to 2 weeks. The decision to buy—or not to buy—is yours.

An excellent magazine that you should definitely check out is *Celebrity Sleuth*. In it, you'll find photographs of many celebrities that don't or won't do nudity for video tapes. People like Jackie Onassis, Deidre Hall and Caroline Munro are featured in various issues of *Celebrity Sleuth*.

Celebrity Sleuth
P.O. Box 273
West Redding, CT 06896

If you are interested in writing to your favorite actor or actress to get an autograph or ask a question, you'll want to purchase *Celebrity Access—The Directory*. The book lists thousands of celebrity addresses. The cost is (Taxes, postage and handling are already included): For orders in the U.S. the cost is $24.45. California orders are $26.04, Orders outside of the U.S. are $30.00. Write or call:

Celebrity Access Publications
20 Sunnyside Avenue, Suite A241
Mill Valley, CA 94941
(415) 389-8133

Another source for celebrity addresses is the *V.I.P. Address Book* by James M. Wiggins. It costs $89.95 and is available from:

Associated Media Companies
P.O. Box 10190
Marina del Rey, CA 90295-8864
(213) 821-2011

Brinke Steven's *Private Collection* video tape can be purchased directly from her (she also has a fan club). Write to her at:

Brinke Stevens Fan Club
8033 Sunset Boulevard, Suite 557
Hollywood, CA 90046

Melissa Anne Moore has a fan club. You receive 4 issues of the Newsletter and an autographed photo. Send check or money order (payable to Melissa A. Moore) to her at:

Melissa Anne Moore Fan Club
11288 Ventura Boulevard, B-732
Studio City, CA 91604

Becky LeBeau's video tapes and still photos can be purchased directly from her (she also has a fan club). Call or write:

Soft Bodies
505 S. Beverly Drive, Suite 973
Beverly Hills, CA 90212
(800) 622-9920
(310) 652-3520 Outside the United States

The Vice Academy series of movies has a fan club. You can write to Linnea, Ginger, Liz and Julia. Write to (enclose a self-addressed, stamped envelope):

The Vice Academy Fan Club
P.O. Box 480593
Los Angeles, CA 90048

Video Oyster has a catalog of hard to find video tapes called *Pearls Magazine*. Issue #5 is $3.50 or an 11 issue subscription is $30.00. The issues come out about two per year. Video Oyster will also search for a video tape for free. Tell them The Bare Facts sent you.

Video Oyster
145 West 12th Street
New York, NY 10011
(212) 989-3300

Drive-in film critic, Joe Bob Briggs, publishes a weekly newsletter, *The Joe Bob Report*. He writes humorous columns and reviews movies in each edition. The movies he reviews are usually the type that are destined for inclusion in *The Bare Facts Video Guide*. It costs $35.00 for 52 issues. His address is:

The Joe Bob Report
P.O. Box 2002
Dallas, TX 75221

*VideoMania* is a good newspaper to place a classi-fied ad to reach other video enthusiasts who might be able to locate hard to find video tapes for trade or purchase. Published monthly, it costs $11.97 per year. Contact:

VideoMania
P.O. Box 47
Princeton, WI 54968

*Femme Fatales* is a great magazine with in-depth interviews and stories about B-movie beauties such as Brinke Stevens, Julie Strain, Robey, Debra Lamb and Patricia Tallman. *Femme Fatales* is a quarterly put out by the same people who do *Cinefantastique*. For information write to:

Femme Fatales
P.O. Box 270
Oak Park, IL 60303

Perfect 10 Video sells hundreds of video tapes, photos and calendars. Their selection includes video tapes with nudity such as *Dream Babies*, *Becky Bubbles* and *In Search of the Perfect 10* plus a large selection of bikini contests. Call or write for their catalog ($2.00). Tell them The Bare Facts sent you.

Perfect 10 Video
11684 Ventura Blvd., Suite 589
Studio City, CA 91604
(800) GIRL-USA

*Hot Body International* and *Hot Body Video Magazine* video tapes may be purchased from Hot Body International. Tell them The Bare Facts sent you. Call them at:

Hot Body International
401 Levering Avenue
Los Angeles, CA 90024
(800) 336-4321

Video Sports Ltd. carries a large selection of nude female wrestling and boxing video tapes featuring Jasaé, Venus de Light and others. Tell them The Bare Facts sent you. They can be reached at:

Video Sports Ltd.
1525 Aviation Blvd., Suite A199
Redondo Beach, CA 90278
(800) 926-2284

If you are interested in viewing the Rob Lowe video tape that he accidentally made in 1989, you can purchase it from Al Goldstein, publisher of *Screw* magazine. His New York cable TV show, *Midnight Blue*, showed some of the footage on show #672. The cost is $29.95, you need to specify VHS or Beta. Contact:

Media Ranch, Inc.
P.O. Box 432
Old Chelsea Station
New York, NY 10013

# REFERENCES

*Adam Film World Directory of Adult Films 1993*
Knight Publishing Corp.
8060 Melrose Avenue
Los Angeles, CA 90046-7082

*Bowker's Complete Video Directory 1990*
R. R. Bowker, 1990

*Microsoft Cinemania '94*
Interactive Movie Guide CD-ROM
Microsoft Corporation, 1994

*The Complete Directory to Prime Time Network TV Shows, 1946–Present*
Tim Brooks and Earle Marsh
Ballantine, 1992

*Halliwell's Film Guide, Seventh Edition*
Leslie Halliwell
HarperPerennial, 1990

*HBO's Guide to Movies on Videocassette and Cable TV 1991*
Daniel Eagan
Harper & Ross, 1990

*Leonard Maltin's TV Movies and Video Guide, 1993 Edition*
Leonard Maltin
Signet, 1992

*The Motion Picture Guide*
Baseline II, 1994
1984 through 1994 Editions

*Movies Unlimited* catalog
Movies Unlimited, 6736 Castor Avenue,
Philadelphia, PA 19149

*Roger Ebert's Movie Home Companion 1993 Edition*
Roger Ebert
Andrews and McMeel, 1992

*Russ Meyer—The Life and Films*
David K. Fraiser
McFarland & Company, Inc., 1990

*The TV Encyclopedia*
David Inman
The Putnam Publishing Group, 1991

*VideoHound's Golden Movie Retriever 1993*
Visible Ink Press, 1993

*Video Movie Guide 1995*
Mick Martin and Marsha Porter
Ballantine, 1994

*Adult Video News* magazine
8600 West Chester Pike, Suite 300
Upper Darby, PA 19082
Various issues from 1990–1994

*Entertainment Weekly* magazine
Entertainment Weekly Inc.
1675 Broadway, New York, NY 10019
Various issues from 1990–1994

*Playboy* magazine
919 North Michigan Avenue, Chicago, IL 60611
Various issues from 1972–1994

*Penthouse* magazine
1965 Broadway, New York, NY 10023-5965
Various issues from 1972–1994

*Premiere* magazine
Premiere Publishing
2 Park Avenue, New York, NY 10016
Various issues from 1987–1994

*The San Jose Mercury News* newspaper
750 Ridder Park Drive, San Jose, CA 95190
Various issues from 1987–1994

*Sight and Sound* magazine
21 Stephen Street
London W1P 1PL, England
Various issues from 1990–1994

*TV Guide* magazine
Triangle Publications Inc.
100 Matsonford Road, Radnor, PA 19088
Various issues from 1987–1994

*The Joe Bob Report* Newsletter
Joe Bob Briggs
P.O. Box 2002, Dallas, TX 75221
Various issues from 1990–1994

## ABOUT THE AUTHOR

Craig Hosoda is a Software Engineer. He grew up in Silicon Valley, California, then went to the University of California at Berkeley where he graduated with a B.S. degree in Electrical Engineering and Computer Science. After graduation, he worked at Hewlett-Packard for two years before getting a programming job at Industrial Light and Magic, George Lucas' special effects division of Lucasfilm Ltd. (Craig's film credits can be found in *The Golden Child, The Goonies* and *\*batteries not included*.)

While working at ILM, the seeds for *The Bare Facts Video Guide* were planted during a casual conversation one day with his friend, Marty Brenneis. While working on the film, *Howard the Duck*, Marty asked Craig about Lea Thompson's film credits. When Marty didn't know about her nude scene in *All the Right Moves*, Craig thought, "There should be a book that lists this type of important information in one place..."

After returning to Silicon Valley in 1987 to raise a family with his wife, he began research for the book during the evenings while working as a software engineer during the day. Unfortunately, it was difficult to balance a full-time job, work on *The Bare Facts* and have time for his family, so in July 1990, he quit his regular job to devote his life to uncovering the bare facts.

## HOW THIS BOOK WAS CREATED

This book was published using the latest in database publishing techniques on an Apple Macintosh IIci computer. A custom ACI *4th Dimension* database was created to keep track of the data. An export module was written in *4th Dimension* that outputs the information with *FrameMaker* format tags into a text file. The text file was read into Frame Technology's *FrameMaker* and cleaned up a bit. Camera-ready copy was printed on an Apple Personal LaserWriter, then sent to the book printer.